LINDLEY
&
BANKS
ON
PARTNERSHIP

LINDLEY

&

BANKS

ON

PARTNERSHIP

NINETEENTH EDITION

BY

RODERICK I'ANSON BANKS, LL.B.

of Lincoln's Inn, Barrister

SWEET & MAXWELL  THOMSON REUTERS

"A Treatise on the Law of Partnership, including its application to Companies,"
first edition (in two volumes) by Nathaniel Lindley, afterwards Lord Lindley,
M.R., and a Lord of Appeal   1860
Second Edition by the Author   1867
Third Edition by the Author   1873
Fourth Edition by the Author   1878
The work was divided in *Lindley on Companies* (one volume) and *Lindley on
Partnership* (one volume), each by the Author in   1888
Sixth Edition by the Hon. W. B. Lindley   1893
Seventh Edition by Judge the Hon. W. B. Lindley and T. J. C. Tomlin   1905
Eighth Edition by Judge the Hon. W. B. Lindley and A. Andrews Uthwatt   1912
Ninth Edition by Judge the Hon. W. B. Lindley   1924
Tenth Edition by Judge the Hon. W. B. Lindley   1935
Eleventh Edition by Henry Salt, K.C., and Hugh E. Frances   1950
Twelfth Edition by Ernest H. Scamell   1962
Thirteenth Edition by Ernest H. Scamell   1971
Fourteenth Edition by Ernest H. Scamell and R. C. I'Anson Banks   1979
Fifteenth Edition by Ernest H. Scamell and R. C. I'Anson Banks   1984
Sixteenth Edition by R. C. I'Anson Banks   1990
Seventeenth Edition by R. C. I'Anson Banks   1995
Eighteenth Edition by R. C. I'Anson Banks   2002
Nineteenth Edition by R. C. I'Anson Banks   2010

Published in 2010 by Thomson Reuters (Legal) Limited
(Registered in England & Wales, Company No 1679046.
Registered Office and address for service: 100 Avenue Road, London, NW3 3PF)
trading as Sweet & Maxwell

For further information on our products and services, visit www.sweetandmaxwell.co.uk

Typeset by Interactive Sciences Ltd, Gloucester
Printed in the UK by CPI William Clowes, Beccles NR34 7TL

No natural forests were destroyed to make this product; only farmed timber was used and
re-planted.

British Library Cataloguing in Publication Data

A CIP catalogue record for this book
is available from the British Library

ISBN 978 1 847 03748 0

PREFACE

"I love it when a plan comes together"

Col. John "Hannibal" Smith

This edition has been in gestation for an unconscionable period of time, despite the publication of supplements in 2005 and 2007. The twin problems have been the pressures of practice (during one notable period I "temporarily" broke off editorial work in March to deal with an urgent client matter and, in the event, was only able to resume in late November) and a flood of new cases and legislation, which caused passages long since completed to be re-written more than once. Even now late statutory changes which were or are not yet in force have, where possible, had to be accommodated by suitable footnote references. It was ever thus ...

The advent of the LLP, still something of a novelty at the time of the last edition, has proved an extremely popular development, particularly in the professions, but has not substantially impacted on the importance or widespread use of traditional partnerships. As in the case of the last edition, it is to the latter that this work is devoted. I simply do not accept that it is appropriate to address two fundamentally different legal vehicles which, ultimately, have little in common in the same volume. But that has not stopped the judiciary and others tending to treat the LLP as "just another form of partnership". A striking example is to be found in the judgment of Mrs Justice Proudman in *Re Kaupthing Capital Partners II Master LP Inc.* [2010] EWHC 836 (Ch) at [32], where she observed:

> "At the request of the court, counsel researched and explained the position with regard to the forms to be used by different types of partnership established in England. Thus a general partnership is required to use Form 1B. A limited partnership under the Limited Partnerships Act 1907 must do the same. However, a limited liability partnership established in Great Britain pursuant to the Limited Liability Partnerships Act 2000 is treated as a company for all the purposes of Schedule B1 so that Form 2.10B is to be used ... ".

A similar approach was adopted in the (then) BERR's 2008 Consultation Document on the reform of the Limited Partnerships Act 1907, when describing the LLP as "a third form of partnership". So much for my bemoaning in successive prefaces the way in which the expression "partner" was being misused outside the partnership field, long before the Civil Partnership Act 2004 was even thought of!

New cases of note since the last edition are, in reality, too numerous to mention but particularly significant are:

Goodchild v. Chadwick (2002), the only known case on garden leave provisions in partnership agreements;

Mullins v. Laughton (2003), adopting and approving Lord Millett's *obiter* views on the application of the doctrine of repudiation to partnerships (albeit that, as explained in Chapter 24, I, along with the courts of New South Wales, remain unconvinced as to the correctness of those views) and providing welcome guidance on the court's *Syers v. Syers* jurisdiction;

JJ Coughlan v. Ruparelia (2003), exemplifying the inexorable move towards something approaching a presumption that firms are vicariously liable for the actions of their partners;

Sandhu v. Gill (2005), clarifying the operation of section 42 of the 1890 Act;

Conlon v. Simms (2006), confirming when a duty of good faith arises between intending partners;

M. Young Legal Associates v. Zahid (2006) and *Hodson v. Hodson* (2010), finally laying to rest the idea that a division of profits is a necessary ingredient of partnership (although whether this message has yet got through to HMRC is more doubtful);

Revenue & Customs Commissioners v. Pal (2008), rejecting the view previously expressed in this work that it is possible for persons to be held out as partners to HMRC, at least for the purposes of VAT;

Hammonds v. Jones (2009), regarding the need to obtain the approval of outgoing partners to partnership accounts (and to be contrasted with the decision of the Scottish court in *Montgomery v. Cameron & Greig*, 2007); equally at first instance (sub nom *Hammonds v. Danilunas*, 2009), a more dubious issue was addressed (but not pursued on appeal), namely the application of section 5 of the 1890 Act to claims as between partners;

Tann v. Herrington (2009), on the duties owed by a partner undertaking prescribed management duties; and

Drake v. Harvey (2010), squeaking under the wire to confirm yet again what I have long regarded (despite the decision in *Re White*) as the court's predisposition to find that an outgoing partner is entitled to be paid out by reference to the market value of the partnership assets but, perhaps, in doing so sacrificing logic and predictability on the altar of fairness.

Regrettably, *Hopper v. Hopper* (2008) is notable more for the court's questionable decisions not only as to the relevance of a firm's profit sharing arrangements following a dissolution but also as to the applicability of limitation as between *continuing* partners. Other examples of unsatisfactory decisions are not hard to find.

On the statutory front, all restrictions on the size of partnerships were finally swept away by the Regulatory Reform (Reform of 20 Member Limit in Partnerships, etc.) Order 2002, a development that was long overdue. On a less positive note, the Business Names Act 1985 was repealed and replaced by Part 41 of the Companies Act 2006, although why subsuming a stand alone, conveniently sized and accessible Act into a statutory behemoth was thought to be an improvement is unclear. Moreover, the replacement of key provisions of the Mental Health Act 1983 with the less specific provisions of the Mental Capacity Act 2005 has, as will be seen in Chapter 24, served to create a doubt as to the Court of Protection's powers when none existed before. Meanwhile new rules in the CPR governing proceedings by and against firms have, regrettably, perpetuated the problems when dealing with dissolved firms that were created when RSC Order 81 was preserved in an amended form back in 1999.

Discrimination law is assuming increasing importance and can be an unexpected and effective weapon to be deployed when a partnership dispute develops. The current mish-mash of legislation in this area has finally been brought together in the consolidating and amending Equality Act 2010, but the main commencement order, the snappily named Equality Act 2010 (Commencement No. 4, Savings, Consequential, Transitional, Transitory and Incidental Provisions and Revocation) Order 2010 (SI 2010 No. 2317) (already itself amended in what is, for present purposes, an immaterial respect, by the Equality Act 2010 (Commencement No. 4, Savings, Consequential, Transitional, Transitory and Incidental Provisions and Revocation) Order 2010 (Amendment) Order 2010 (SI 2010/2337)) was only made as recently as September 2010, bringing most of the provisions of the Act into force on October 1, 2010. Although there have been a handful of partnership related cases in other areas, it is in the arena of age discrimination that partnership has taken centre stage, first with the Tribunal decision in *Bloxham v. Freshfields, Bruckhaus Deringer* in 2007 and then with the proceedings in *Seldon v. Clarkson Wright & Jakes*, culminating in the Court of Appeal judgment delivered in July 2010, just in time for inclusion in this edition. Whether firms will take comfort from the seemingly bullish approach adopted in the latter decision and continue to require the compulsory retirement of partners on age grounds remains to be seen. Equally, when considering the application of the discrimination legislation, the potential implications of the EAT's decision in *Dave v. Robinksa* (2003) merit careful attention. Whether the Employment Tribunal is the right place to decide issues between partners must be open to doubt but that is a battle which was lost before it even began.

Limited partnership law is currently in something of a state of flux. Although the main proposals for the reform of partnership law contained in the Law Commission's 2003 Report have been shelved, the reform of limited partnership law is technically still on the agenda. The declared intention was and is to reform the law piecemeal by putting in place a series of Legislative Reform Orders, but thus far there has been only one such order, namely the Legislative Reform (Limited Partnerships) Order 2009. This seemingly modest piece of legislation governing the formalities of registration of limited partnerships has, in fact, had the far reaching effect of removing the spectre of unlimited liability for most limited partners *but only if the partnership was registered on an application made on or after October 1, 2009.* For other limited partnerships, the potential application of section 5 of the Limited Partnerships Act 1907 in its original form remains a very real threat. New regulations clarifying the application of the Partnerships (Accounts) Regulations 2008 to limited partnerships are now only likely to be made and come into effect in 2011 and not, as was originally contemplated, in October 2010. As to further Legislative Reform Orders, it appears that these are yet another victim of Government cutbacks so that the further reforms which are so urgently needed are not expected any time soon. This at a time when there are the first signs of a resurgence on the limited partnership front now that the worst of the downturn is over.

Tax law has undergone several major upheavals, with the introduction of FRS 5 and UITF 40 on revenue recognition, the consolidation of the income and corporation tax legislation and the replacement of stamp duty with stamp duty land tax. Increasingly, the concentration seems to be on the charge to tax when assets are introduced *into* a partnership, with HMRC now for the first time having publicised their approach in the case of both capital gains tax and value added tax, although the new guidance on the VAT treatment of disposals of partnership shares (a subject Ernest Scamell and I first addressed in the 14th edition of this work) is also welcome.

In terms of other developments too late to be included in this work, these are blessedly few in number. Readers may however like to note that it has been held that interest earned on client account balances by a firm of solicitors is trading income (*Barnetts v. Revenue & Customs Commissioners* [2010] S.T.I. 2536) and a helpful summary of the nature and effect of set off is contained in *Fearns v. Anglo-Dutch Paint & Chemical Co. Ltd.* [2010] EWHC 2366 (Ch) (Lawtel 30/9/10). Finally, when considering the potential application of section 2 of the Law of Property (Miscellaneous Provisions) Act 1989 to partnerships, the decision of the Court of Appeal in *North Eastern Properties v. Coleman* [2010] 2 All E.R. (Comm) 494 to some extent chimes with the reasoning set out in paras. 7–09, 7–10, *infra*.

As regards the roll of honour for this edition, my heartfelt thanks go to:

1. The staff of Sweet & Maxwell who so patiently awaited the production of the manuscript despite the delivery date never seeming to get any closer. I am sure there were times when they doubted whether the end would ever come. They also very helpfully undertook the task of updating all the New Law Cases Online references which, since the last edition, had ceased to be maintained as a special section on Lawtel. This even enabled some transcripts which had been lost to be refound and reinstated.

2. My practice manager, Tyroon Win, who was unfailingly supportive throughout the long and painful writing process.

3. Simon Jelf who on so many occasions acted as a sounding board for various propositions.

4. Last, but by no means least, my wife Susie who again did the majority of the work on the index and, my sons now having flown the nest, somehow alone managed to keep my head above the water when it threatened to engulf me. She enabled me finally to pull "the plan" together and it is to her that this edition and the last few years are dedicated. Here's looking at you, kid.

Save where otherwise indicated, the law is, barring my own oversights, stated as at August 31, 2010.

Roderick I'Anson Banks   October 8, 2010
48 Bedford Row
London WC1

TABLE OF CONTENTS

Part Two

FORMATION OF A PARTNERSHIP BY FORMAL AGREEMENT

Part Three

THE RIGHTS AND OBLIGATIONS OF PARTNERS AS REGARDS
THIRD PARTIES

Part Seven

TAXATION

APPENDICES

TABLE OF CASES

TABLE OF STATUTES

TABLE OF STATUTORY INSTRUMENTS

Part One

THE NATURE OF PARTNERSHIP

CHAPTER 1

INTRODUCTION

1.   ORIGIN OF THE LAW OF PARTNERSHIP

UNTIL the Partnership Act of 1890, the law of partnership was to be found almost **1–01**
exclusively in legal decisions and in textbooks; few Acts of Parliament related
directly to partnerships as opposed to what were then styled "joint stock companies". The law of partnership was, on the whole, a good example of judge-
made law, developing slowly with the growth of trade and commerce and
representing generally perceived views of justice. On the other hand, it suffered
from the laws against usury, from what previous editors called "unsound views
of political economy" (culminating in *Waugh v. Carver*,[1] and not rectified until
reviewed by the House of Lords in *Cox v. Hickman*[2]) and from the parallel
systems of law and equity which prevailed until 1875, when the Judicature Acts
came into operation.

It was those Acts which, by merging the administration of law and equity,
greatly facilitated the legislative revision and improvement of various branches
of the law, including partnership which had begun as an off-shoot of the law of
contract but, by 1890, had become a virulent plant in its own right.

Limited partnerships

Prior to January 1, 1908, when the Limited Partnerships Act 1907 came into **1–02**
force, only one kind of partnership was known to English law, namely the
"general" partnership, in which the liability of every partner for the debts and
obligations of the firm was unlimited. The Limited Partnerships Act 1907
introduced a second kind of partnership, called limited partnership, in which the
liability of one or more (but not all) of its members could be limited.

Although limited partnerships are the creation of the 1907 Act and are subject
to its express provisions, they are otherwise governed by the Partnership Act
1890 and the general rules of equity and common law applicable to partnerships.
For this reason, the law applicable to such partnerships is considered separately,
after the treatment of general partnerships.[3]

Limited liability partnerships

Although an entity known as a limited liability partnership is now recognised **1–03**
under English law,[4] it does not represent a new form of partnership, but rather a
body corporate to which no part of the law of partnership is applicable, either

---

[1] (1793) 2 H.Bl. 235.
[2] (1860) 8 H.L.C. 268.
[3] See Pt. 6, *infra*, paras 28–01 *et seq.*
[4] Limited Liability Partnerships Act 2000, s.1(1). See further *infra*, para. 2–39.

expressly or by implication.[5] In this respect, the limited liability partnership differs markedly from its equivalents in other jurisdictions.[6]

2. THE PARTNERSHIP ACT 1890

Background to the Partnership Act 1890

1–04   In 1879, Sir Frederick Pollock drew a Bill for the consolidation and amendment of the law of partnership which was brought into the House of Commons in 1880 and again, with modifications, in 1882, 1883, 1884 and 1889. Ultimately, in its amended form, it was taken up by the Government of the day and, although altered in many respects, that bill was the foundation of the Act now known as the Partnership Act 1890.

Act not a complete codification

1–05   The Act is not (and does not purport to be) a complete code of partnership law[7]; thus, it contains no provisions relating to goodwill, to the administration of partnership assets in the event of a partner's death or bankruptcy[8] or, indeed, to the manner in which legal proceedings can be brought by and against a firm. Moreover, section 46 preserves the pre-existing rules of equity and common law, except in so far as they are inconsistent with the Act's express provisions. Although the Act did endeavour (for the most part successfully) to reduce an amorphous mass of largely uncorrelated case law into a series of authoritative propositions, it was, in the words of Lord Lindley, "not a perfect measure, nor even so good as Parliament might have made it."[9]

Alterations in the law

1–06   In real terms, the Partnership Act 1890 introduced no great change in the law. Apart from introducing a number of minor amendments and removing certain doubts, the only significant development lay in the new procedure for making a partner's share available for the payment of his separate judgment debts.[10]

---

[5] *ibid.* ss.1(2), (5). Nevertheless, the Limited Liability Partnerships Regulations 2001, regs. 7, 8 replicate certain provisions which are to be found in the Partnership Act 1890.

[6] See *infra*, para. 2–44.

[7] As expressly recognised by the Court of Appeal in *Hopper v. Hopper* [2008] EWCA Civ. 1417 (Lawtel 12/12/08) at [45].

[8] Or, for that matter, on the occurrence of any other event which will dissolve the firm: see ss.32–35, *infra*, paras A1–33 *et seq*. Note, however, the provisions of ss.38, 39 and 44, *infra*, paras A1–39, A1–40, A1–45. As to the position where one or more of the partners (or the firm itself) is insolvent, see *infra*, paras 27–01 *et seq*.

[9] Perhaps one of the Act's greatest failings lay in the provisions of s.42, which caused both Lord Lindley and the editor of the 6th edition of this work to question the value of a judgment for an account of profits thereunder: see *infra*, para. 25–30.

[10] See the Partnership Act 1890, s.23(2), *infra*, para. A1–24. Although no doubt welcome at the time, this procedure is now only rarely used by creditors.

Structure of the Act

The Act is divided into five parts, headed as follows: **1–07**

1. Nature of partnership, sections 1–4.

2. Relations of partners to persons dealing with them, sections 5–18.

3. Relations of partners to one another, sections 19–31.

4. Dissolution of partnership and its consequences, sections 32–44.

5. Supplemental, sections 45–50.

The first four parts correspond with the four books into which the pre-1890 editions of this work were subdivided. The division is a natural one which has, in the main, been adopted in all previous editions of this work and which is followed in the present edition.

Definitions of "partnership" and "firm": the conceptual problem

Partnership

The basic definition of the term "partnership" is contained in section 1 and at   **1–08** its very heart lie the words "carrying on a business with a view of profit"; however, the definition is further refined by section 2, which sets out those circumstances in which profits may be shared by persons who are *not* members of a partnership.

Pre-Act definitions: quasi-partnership

Before the Act, partnership was defined in various ways but there was no   **1–09** authoritative definition of the word. Persons might not be partners and yet incur liabilities as if they were: in pre-1890 editions of this work, the term "quasi-partner" was used when referring to such persons, in order to distinguish them from "true" partners. Although apt, this term did not find its way into section 14, which specifically provides for liability on the basis of "holding out", or indeed any other section of the Act and it was accordingly abandoned in subsequent editions.

The firm

The expression "firm" is defined in s.4(1). This definition highlights a feature   **1–10** which is peculiar to the English law of partnership and which, in turn, distinguishes it from the laws of Scotland[11] and of other EU countries,[12] *i.e.* a refusal to recognise the firm as an entity separate and distinct from the partners who compose it. Notwithstanding a number of inroads in recent years,[13] this feature

---

[11] See the Partnership Act 1890, s.4(2), *infra*, para. A1–05. Thus, a Scottish partnership may itself be a partner in another firm, something which would be impossible under English law: see *Major v. Brodie* [1998] S.T.C. 491, 510f *per* Park J.

[12] The general summary of the law of partnership in EU countries, which was previously included in Chap. 2 has not been retained in this edition. Readers are referred to the 18th ed. at paras 2–46 *et seq.*

[13] In particular, a firm may now be wound up as an unregistered company under the Insolvency Act 1986: see, *infra*, paras 27–04 *et seq.*

remains as central to the law of partnership as it was in Lord Lindley's day.[14] Thus, as no one can owe money to himself, it was held (and would still be held)[15] that no debt could exist between any member of a firm and the firm itself and, whilst the courts of equity would, in winding up the affairs of a firm, treat it as the debtor or creditor of its members (as the case might be), this was only for book-keeping purposes, so as to enable accounts to be settled between the partners.

This failure to accord recognition to "the firm" had for many years prior to 1890 been perceived as a defect in the law of partnership[16] and, in his supplement on the Partnership Act, Lord Lindley appears to have regretted that the Act did not, in this respect, seek to assimilate the English and Scots law. Had it done so, the procedural difficulties which can attend actions by and against firms, particularly where there has been a change in the partners[17] or where one or more of them are resident abroad, would have been greatly reduced.

Although in 2003 the Law Commission put forward a number of recommendations for a change in the law in this area,[18] it now seems unlikely that any of these will be adopted.

1–11   The term "firm" (as defined) seemingly does not include persons liable by reason of holding out (section 14),[19] but this is entirely consistent with the "pure" definition of partnership, which would exclude such persons on the ground that their liability is based on estoppel rather than on actual membership of the firm.

An obvious omission: goodwill

1–12   One aspect of great practical importance (and of no little difficulty) was unfortunately not dealt with in the Act, namely the treatment of goodwill on a general dissolution[20] and, in particular, the extent to which the firm name can continue to be used by the former partners. Sir Frederick Pollock's Bill dealt with this question, as did the Bill which passed through the House of Commons in 1889 and the Bill which was brought into the House of Lords in 1890. However, in the event, the clauses relating to this subject were struck out owing, so Lord Lindley believed, to "differences of opinion, and to the difficulty of arriving at a conclusion which would be acceptable to both Houses of Parliament". The relevant law is, therefore, to be found in the pre- and post-Act decisions (see section 46), so that a number of doubts and difficulties still inevitably persist.

Relevance of pre-1890 law

1–13   Cases decided prior to the Partnership Act 1890 must naturally be read subject to its provisions. Where those provisions are clear, they must be followed and

---

[14] Of course, a limited liability partnership is a separate legal entity but, as already noticed, *supra*, para. 1–03, it is not a partnership in law, so that the integrity of the current law remains unaffected.

[15] See *infra*, paras 3–04, 19–06.

[16] In his Supplement on the Act, Lord Lindley noted that, in 1855, the Mercantile Law Amendment Committee had expressed the opinion that it would be "very convenient and useful" to recognise firms as having separate legal personality under English law.

[17] See *infra*, paras 14–48 *et seq.*

[18] Law Commission report "Partnership Law" (CM 6015).

[19] See *Hudgell Yeates & Co. v. Watson* [1978] Q.B. 451, 467 *per* Waller L.J.; and note *Re C. & M. Ashberg, The Times*, July 17, 1990. But see also *infra*, para. 12–06.

[20] See, as to the meaning of this expression, *infra*, para. 24–03.

earlier decisions must not be regarded as binding authorities to be followed in preference thereto,[21] although they may be useful in order to explain the history of the Act and to show the state of the law up to that time.[22] There is now, of course, a more liberal and practical approach towards questions of construction and it is permissible to refer to some parliamentary and other materials as an aid to construction where that is necessary to overcome an ambiguity or to avoid an absurd result.[23] Thus, where the provisions of the Act are obscure or do not quite cover a particular case, reference to the previous case law may provide the only authoritative guidance.

[21] See the judgment of Lord Herschell in *Bank of England v. Vagliano* [1891] A.C. 107, 144–145; *Herdman v. Wheeler* [1902] 1 K.B. 361, 367 *per* Channell J.; *Hall v. Hayman* [1912] 2 K.B. 5, 12 *per* Bray J.; *Wimble, Sons & Co. v. Rosenberg & Sons* [1913] 3 K.B. 743, 747 *per* Vaughan Williams L.J.; *Despatie v. Tremblay* [1921] 1 A.C. 702, 709. See also *Grey v. I.R.C.* [1960] A.C. 1.

[22] See, for example, *Hopper v. Hopper* [2008] EWCA Civ. 1417 (Lawtel 12/12/08) at [45].

[23] *Pepper v. Hart* [1993] A.C. 593; also *Scher v. Policyholders Protection Board (No. 2)* [1994] 2 A.C. 57; *Wilson v. First County Trust Ltd. (No. 2)* [2004] 1 A.C. 816; *R (on the application of Age UK) v. Secretary of State for Business, Innovation & Skills* [2009] I.R.L.R. 1017 at [50], [53] *et seq.* *per* Blake J. This represented a substantial departure from the previous law: see, for example, *Black-Clawson International Ltd. v. Papierwerke Waldhof-Aschaffenburg A.G.* [1975] A.C. 591; *Davis v. Johnson* [1979] A.C. 264; *Fothergill v. Monarch Airlines Ltd.* [1981] A.C. 251; *Hadmore Productions Ltd. v. Hamilton* [1983] A.C. 191; *M/S Aswan Engineering Establishment Co. v. Lupdine Ltd.* [1987] 1 W.L.R. 1. *cf. Pickstone v. Freemans plc* [1989] A.C. 66; *Ex p. Factortame* [1990] 2 A.C. 85; *O'Rourke v. Binks* [1992] S.T.C. 703.

CHAPTER 2

DEFINITION OF PARTNERSHIP

1.   THE DEFINITION IN THE PARTNERSHIP ACT 1890

SECTION 1(1) of the Partnership Act 1890 provides as follows: **2–01**

> "Partnership is the relation which subsists between persons carrying on a business in common with a view of profit."

From this statutory definition it appears that, before a partnership can be said to exist, three conditions must be satisfied, *i.e.* there must be: (1) a business (2) which is carried on by two or more persons in common (3) with "a view of profit".[1] These conditions must also be satisfied when a new partner joins an existing firm pursuant to an assignment of another partner's share,[2] and cannot merely be assumed to be satisfied because they were met by the existing firm.[3] Historically, views differed as to whether a fourth condition was also to be imported, namely an agreement to *share* any profits realised but this issue has now been resolved by the Court of Appeal.[4]

Each of these conditions, actual or supposed, will now be considered in turn.[5]

A.   THE BUSINESS

By section 45 of the Act, "business" includes "every trade, occupation, or profession".[6] It follows that virtually any activity or venture of a commercial   **2–02**

---

[1] As to whether the profit motive is a question of fact or law or both, see *Morden Rigg & Co. & Eskrigge (R. B.) & Co. v. Monks* (1923) 8 T.C. 450, 464 *per* Sterndale M.R.

[2] See *infra*, para. 19–60.

[3] See *Backman v. R*, 3 I.T.L. Rep. 647, at [40]–[42] (Can. Sup Ct).

[4] It is now clear that there is no such fourth condition (see *infra*, paras 2–10, 2–11), even though Sir Frederick Pollock was the main proponent in favour of it: see *Pollock on the Law of Partnership* (15th ed.), pp. 9 *et seq.*

[5] This section was cited with apparent approval by Arnold J. in *Hodson v. Hodson* [2009] P.N.L.R. 23, at [10], his decision being affirmed at [2010] P.N.L.R. 8.

[6] See generally, *Smith v. Anderson* (1880) 15 Ch.D. 247, 258 *per* Jessel M.R.; *Newstead v. Frost* [1980] 1 W.L.R. 135 (HL). In his Supplement on the Act, Lord Lindley merely opined that "The meaning of the word [*business*] in this Act is very wide, but probably not wider than its ordinary meaning as given in dictionaries". *cf.* the definition of "business" in the Landlord and Tenant Act 1954, s.23(2); and see also the somewhat exceptional decision in *Three H. Aircraft Hire v. Customs and Excise Commissioners* [1982] S.T.C. 653, discussed *infra*, para. 37–01, n. 2. For the meaning of a bequest of a business, or of a partner's share or interest therein, see *Re Rhagg* [1938] Ch. 828, where the authorities are reviewed by Simonds J. In that case it was conceded (rather than held, as stated in the headnote) that the bequest was not adeemed by the supervening accession of the legatee to partnership with the testator in the interval between the date of the testator's will and the date of his death. But the headnote in [1938] 3 All E.R. 314, makes it clear that such concession was made.

nature, including a "one off" trading venture,[7] will be regarded as a business for this purpose. It obviously does not matter whether the business is a new or existing business, nor for how long it has been carried on.[8] On the other hand, the mere fact that a particular activity is profitable will not of itself turn it into a business: an example of such an activity is to be found in the management of a particular property, which may or may not qualify as a business, depending on the circumstances.[9] This is to an extent emphasised by section 2(1) of the Act which, embodying the effect of a number of earlier decisions, provides:

> "Joint tenancy, tenancy in common, joint property, common property, or part owner-ship does not of itself create a partnership as to anything so held or owned, whether the tenants or owners do or do not share any profits made by the use thereof."

Equally, an activity which might not ordinarily be classed as a business, *e.g.* buying, selling and holding investments, may qualify if it is carried on as a commercial venture; *a fortiori* if a partnership is formed to carry on such an activity.[10]

In the case of some activities, it may be necessary to demonstrate that there is a sufficient element of system, continuity and repetition before a business will be held to exist, even though there may be instances in which a single act will suffice.[11]

When a business is commenced

2–03   It should not be assumed that, for a business to exist, some actual trading activity must have taken place. In *Khan v. Miah*,[12] the parties had decided to open a restaurant together and, to that end, had acquired premises and were in the process of converting and fitting them out. They had also entered into a number of other contractual commitments and had advertised the restaurant in the local press. However, they fell out before the restaurant had actually opened. Never-theless, the House of Lords held that a business was being carried on and that

---

[7] *Re Abenheim* (1913) 109 L.T. 219; *Mann v. D'Arcy* [1968] 1 W.L.R. 893; and see also *ibid* s.32(b), *infra*, para. A1–33.

[8] See *Backman v. R*, 3 I.T.L. Rep. 647 at [40] (Can Sup. Ct.).

[9] In cases of this type, the subjective intentions of the participants *may* be determinative: see *Clarke v. British Telecom Pension Scheme Trustees* [2000] S.T.C. 222 (CA), albeit a decision concerning the existence of a trade for income tax purposes; also *Land Management Ltd. v. Fox* [2002] S.T.C. (S.C.D.) 152. And see *Revenue & Customs Commissioners v. Salaried Persons Postal Loans Ltd.* [2006] S.T.C. 1315, as to whether the receipt of rents would be treated as derived from a business for corporation tax purposes.

[10] See *Smith v. Anderson* (1880) 15 Ch.D. 247, 261 *per* Jessel M.R. On the facts, the Court of Appeal held that no association had been formed for the purpose of carrying on a business (within the meaning of the Companies Act 1862, s.4) but that the deed under consideration provided for the management of a trust fund. See also *Land Management Ltd. v. Fox*, *supra*, albeit a case concerning a company.

[11] See *Conroy v. Kenny* [1999] 1 W.L.R. 1340, 1344D–1346A (CA), concerning the business of moneylending.

[12] [2000] 1 W.L.R. 2123. A similar approach had previously been adopted by the Court of Appeal in *Medcalf v. Mardell*, Unreported, March 2, 2000 CA (Civ Div), where the business in question was the development and exploitation of the idea for the "Big Break" game show. A partnership was held to exist even though no monetary receipts were produced until several years later. See also *Chappell v. Revenue & Customs Commissioners* [2009] S.T.C. (S.C.D.) 11 at [7]. Similar principles apply in the case of a joint venture: *Chirnside v. Fay* [2007] P.N.L.R. 6 (Sup. Ct. of New Zealand). *cf.* the approach taken when considering whether a trade has been set up for the purposes of income tax: see *Mansell v. Revenue & Customs Commissioners* [2006] S.T.C. (S.C.D.) 605.

they were partners therein. Although it is difficult to question the correctness of the decision on the facts, the House of Lords' approach gives rise to great uncertainty. The ultimate test, as formulated by Lord Millett,[13] is "whether the parties [have] done enough to be found to have commenced the joint enterprise in which they had agreed to engage". Clearly not all preparatory acts will be sufficient for this purpose[14]; equally, a single act which involves long-term commercial consequences, *e.g.* the acquisition of premises, may in itself be enough. This should be contrasted with the situation considered by the Supreme Court of Victoria in *Goudberg v. Erniman Associates Pty. Ltd.*,[15] where the parties were not regarded as having done sufficient acts of preparation to constitute a business even though they had "embarked on a project".[16] Unaccountably, the decision in *Khan v. Miah* appears not to have been cited, although the editor doubts whether this would have led to a different decision on the particular facts.

Interruption to or changes in business

Equally, a business may still exist where, by reason of a temporary downturn in the market, no trading activities are being undertaken, provided that new work is still being sought and the parties have the capacity to do it.[17] It now seems clear that the sale of the *entire* partnership business to a company owned by the firm will not *per se* prevent the partnership continuing to exist, particularly if the partnership business can be regarded as extending to the business carried on through the medium of the company or other special circumstances exist.[18]   **2–04**

B.   TWO OR MORE PERSONS CARRYING ON A BUSINESS IN COMMON

If a partnership is to exist, it must be shown that two or more persons are carrying on the business. If a group of individuals carry on a business not on their own behalf but on behalf of a third party, they will not be regarded as partners[19]; on the other hand, if a business is run by one or more persons on behalf of themselves and others, a partnership may be held to exist.[20] Thus, a "sleeping   **2–05**

---

[13] [2000] 1 W.L.R. 2123, 2128E.

[14] *Semble*, in the case of a limited partnership, the application for registration under the Limited Partnerships Act 1907 may be such a preparatory act: see *infra*, para. 29–08. *cf.* the example of the licensed moneylender cited, albeit in a different context, in *Conroy v. Kenny* [1999] 1 W.L.R. 1340 at 1345H *per* Kennedy L.J.

[15] [2007] V.S.C.A. 12. See also *Curley v. Hollier* [2007] EWHC 3447 (Ch) (Lawtel 12/11/07), where some preparatory steps for a joint venture had been taken but were insufficient to prove that the venture had "proceeded" by a set date, as required by the agreement.

[16] [2007] V.S.C.A. 12 at [24].

[17] *Pamment v. Sutton, The Times*, December 15, 1998. This was not, however, a partnership case. Note that, where a partnership already exists, a permanent cessation of trade may result in a dissolution: see *infra*, para. 24–46.

[18] See *Chahal v. Mahal*, September 30, 2004 (Lawtel 5/10/04) at [90]–[94], affirmed at [2005] 2 B.C.L.C. 655; also *Reeves v. Sprecher* [2008] EWHC 583 (Ch) (Lawtel 3/4/08); *Train v. DTE Business Advisory Services Ltd.* (UKEAT/0201/08/LA) (Lawtel 10/3/09). And see further *infra*, para. 24–46.

[19] See *Holme v. Hammond* (1872) L.R. 7 Ex. 218; *Re Fisher & Sons* [1912] 2 K.B. 491.

[20] See *Cox v. Hickman* (1860) 8 H.L.Cas. 268.

partner" may be "carrying on a business" for the purposes of the Act.[21] It should, however, be noted that the business must actually be carried on for more than a scintilla of time: if it is disposed of almost as soon as the "partnership" is formed, this may not satisfy this requirement.[22] The fact that the business will, ultimately, be carried on through a company or other vehicle will seemingly not prevent the creation of a partnership.[23]

By virtue of the Interpretation Act 1978,[24] the word "person" includes "a body of persons corporate or unincorporate" and there is no doubt that a partnership can exist between an individual and a limited company or, indeed, between two or more such companies. In recent years, so called "corporate" partnerships have become popular as a vehicle for companies to pool their resources for a particular project, *e.g.* oil exploration, or for tax reasons. Further impetus has been given to this trend by the official recognition of the role which such partnerships have to play in the venture capital field (albeit in this case exploiting the advantages of the limited partnership).[25]

It is perhaps self evident, but nonetheless deserving of specific mention, that the definition of partnership requires the "carrying on" of a business. It naturally follows that a partnership cannot exist before the business is commenced.[26]

A business carried on "in common"

2–06   It is also a fundamental condition of the definition that the business is carried on by two or more persons "in common". In the first place, this necessarily means that there must be a single business, even if that business comprises a number of different and unrelated activities and/or is carried on in a number of separate divisions.[27] In the view of the current editor, this also presupposes that the parties are carrying on that business for their common benefit and that they have, as regards the business, expressly or impliedly accepted *some* level of mutual rights and obligations as between themselves.[28] However, it must be recognised that, whilst the absence of any such mutual rights and obligations is

---

[21] This passage was referred to with apparent approval in *Ward v. Newalls Insulation Co. Ltd.* [1998] 1 W.L.R. 1723, 1730A (CA). See also *Chahal v. Mahal*, September 30, 2004 (Lawtel 5/1/04) at [80] (this decision being affirmed [2005] 2 B.C.L.C. 655).

[22] See *Backman v. R*, 3 I.T.L. Rep. 647 at [28] (Can. Sup Ct).

[23] See *Dyment v. Boyden* [2004] B.C.L.C. 423, at [5]; *Rosenberg v. Nazarov* [2008] EWHC 812 (Ch) (Lawtel 10/4/08) at [6]. See also *infra*, para. 24–46.

[24] s.5, Sched. 1.

[25] See [1987] S.T.I. 783. See further, as to corporate partnerships, *infra*, paras 11–02 *et seq.*

[26] See, *infra*, paras 2–17 *et seq.* Note that, in his Supplement on the Act, Lord Lindley questioned whether the statutory definition "went too far . . . by making the actual carrying on business [*sic*] a test of partnership". See also *infra*, para. 2–15, n. 79. Equally, the decision in *Khan v. Miah* [2000] 1 W.L.R. 2123 (HL) has, in large measure, removed the anomalies created by this requirement, albeit at the cost of uncertainty, but *cf. Goudberg v. Erniman Associates Pty. Ltd.* [2007] V.S.C.A. 12: see further *supra*, para. 2–03.

[27] As in *C. Connelly & Co. v. Wilbey* [1992] S.T.C. 783, 790a.

[28] See *Backman v. R*, 3 I.T.L. Rep. 647 (Can. Sup. Ct.) at [21]; *Greville v. Venables* [2007] EWCA Civ. 878 (Lawtel 12/9/07). Note that, in *Whywait Pty Ltd. v. Davison* [1997] 1 Qd. R. 225, 231, the court expressed the view that partnership involved a "relation of mutual confidence". However, an agreement to share the profits derived from the business will not, in itself, be enough to constitute a partnership: see *infra*, paras 5–17 *et seq.*; also *Hibernia Management and Development Co. v. Newfoundland Steel* (1996) 140 Nfld. & P.E.I.R. 91, 107. Note also *Protectacoat Firthglow Ltd. v. Szilagyi* [2009] I.R.L.R. 365, where there was held to be no business in common and the partnership was a sham. A partnership is, in the current editor's view, unlikely to exist if any mutual rights and obligations relate not to the business but merely to the underlying assets.

likely to indicate that there is no partnership between the parties,[29] the mere acceptance of some such rights and obligations will clearly not, in itself, suffice. If, on a true analysis, each supposed partner is carrying on a separate business wholly independently of the other(s), as in the case of a mutual insurance society,[30] or a genuine share-farming agreement,[31] or one is actually supplying consultancy or other services to the other,[32] there can in law be no partnership between them.[33] Equally, joint venturers will not necessarily be partners.[34]

C.   "WITH A VIEW OF PROFIT"

In this element of the definition, by "profit" is meant the net amount remaining **2–07** after paying out of the receipts of a business all the expenses incurred in obtaining those receipts; this should be contrasted with "gross returns", *e.g.* the royalties received by an author.[35]

The intention to make a profit (even if a profit is not actually realised)[36] lies at the very heart of the partnership relation. As Lord Lindley put it:

> "An agreement that something shall be attempted with a view to gain, and that the gain shall be shared by the parties to the agreement, is the grand characteristic of every partnership, and is the leading feature of nearly every definition of the term."[37]

However, the *amount* of the profit to be realised by the venture does not matter, unless it is, on a true analysis, *de minimis*.[38]

It is where the profit motive can be identified as subsidiary to some other **2–08** purpose that difficult questions can arise: in such cases, it is necessary to ask whether there is in fact any genuine "view of profit" at all. Thus, if a partnership

---

[29] Note, however, the views expressed by Lord Coulsfield in *Dollar Land (Cumbernauld) Ltd. v. C.I.N. Properties Ltd.* 1996 S.L.T. 186, 195F, noted *infra*, para. 2–13.

[30] See *infra*, para. 2–46.

[31] See *infra*, para. 5–16.

[32] As in *Strathearn Gordon Associates Ltd. v. Customs & Excise Commissioners* (1985) V.A.T.T.R. 79. *cf. Walker West Developments Ltd. v. F.J. Emmett Ltd.* (1978) 252 E.G. 1171 (CA).

[33] This passage, in the truncated form set out in the 17th ed. of this work, was adopted by Dyson J. in *Brostoff v. Clarke Kenneth Leventhal*, March 11, 1996 (unreported). See also *Marsh v. Marsh* [2010] EWCA 1563 (Ch) (Lawtel 29/6/10) at 10 *per* Sir Edward Evans-Lombe (sitting as a Judge of the Chancery Division).

[34] See, *e.g.*, *Spree Engineering and Testing Ltd. v. O'Rourke Civil and Structural Engineering Ltd.*, Unreported, May 18, 1999 QBD, which involved what was styled a "non-integrated" joint venture. See further *infra*, para. 5–06.

[35] See the classic definition of the word "profit" by Fletcher Moulton L.J. in *Re Spanish Prospecting Co. Ltd.* [1911] 1 Ch. 92, 98. See also *Gresham Life Assurance Society v. Styles* [1892] A.C. 309, 322 *et seq. per* Lord Herschell; *Beauchamp v. J. W. Woolworth Plc* [1990] 1 A.C. 478, 489 *per* Lord Templeman. And note *Customs & Excise Commissioners v. Bell Concord Educational Trust Ltd.* [1990] 1 Q.B. 1040.

[36] See *Backman v. R*, 3 I.T.L. Rep. 647 (Can. Sup Ct). A court will only dissolve a partnership under the Partnership Act 1890, s.35(*e*) that if it is incapable of making a profit: see *infra*, para. 24–87. It follows that a partnership which makes a loss will only cease to satisfy the statutory definition if the partners have no *intention* of making a profit.

[37] *Mollwo, March & Co. v. Court of Wards* (1872) L.R. 4 P.C. 419; *R. v. Robson* (1885) 16 Q.B.D. 137. The quotation set out in the text was cited with apparent approval as an accurate statement of the pre-1890 law by Wilson L.J. in *M. Young Legal Associates v. Zahid* [2006] 1 W.L.R. 2562 at [24], but Hughes and Tuckey LJJ. left the point open. The Court nevertheless held that a sharing of profits between the partners is no longer a *necessary* characteristic of a partnership under the 1890 Act.

[38] *Backman v. R*, 3 I.T.L. Rep. 647 (Can. Sup Ct).

is formed with some other predominant motive, *e.g.* tax avoidance, but there is also a real, albeit ancillary, profit element, it may be permissible to infer that the business is being carried on "with a view of profit."[39] If, however, it could be shown that the sole reason for the creation of a partnership was to give a particular partner the "benefit" of, say, a tax loss, when there was no contemplation in the parties' minds that a profit (in the sense outlined above) would be derived from carrying on the relevant business, the partnership could not in any real sense be said to have been formed "with a view of profit".

Societies and clubs, the object of which is not to acquire profit, are clearly not partnerships,[40] nor are mutual insurance societies.[41]

2–09   Even where there is a genuine view of profit, a partnership will only exist if the profits are intended to be realised for the common benefit of the participants.[42] Thus, if a number of firms associate together with a view to promoting high standards in the professional services which they supply to their respective clients and, thereby, to improve the *individual* profitability of each firm's business, this will not be sufficient, as was made clear in *Brostoff v. Clark Kenneth Leventhal.*[43]

D.   A FOURTH CONDITION: DIVISION OF PROFITS?

2–10   Before the Partnership Act 1890 it was commonly said to be essential for a partnership to have as its object, not only the acquisition, but also the *division* of profit.[44] This approach derived no little support from the terms "partnership" and

---

[39] *Newstead v. Frost* [1980] 1 W.L.R. 135, 140; *Backman v. R, supra*; *cf. Overseas Containers (Finance) Ltd. v. Stoker* [1989] 1 W.L.R. 606. The judicial attitude to tax avoidance schemes underwent a fundamental change in the 1980s (see *W. T. Ramsey Ltd. v. I.R.C.* [1982] A.C. 300; *Furniss v. Dawson* [1984] A.C. 474), although subsequent decisions appear to have substantially restricted the scope of the "*Ramsay*" and "*Furniss*" principles: see, for example, *Craven v. White* [1989] A.C. 398; *Shepherd v. Lyntress Ltd.* [1989] S.T.C. 617; *Customs & Excise Commissioners v. Faith Construction Ltd.* [1990] 1 Q.B. 905; *I.R.C. v. Fitzwilliam* [1993] 1 W.L.R. 1189; *I.R.C. v. McGuckian* [1997] 1 W.L.R. 991, 1000F–H *per* Lord Steyn; *Griffin v. Citibank Investments Ltd.* [2000] S.T.C. 1010; *Macniven v. Westmoreland Investments Ltd.* [2001] 2 W.L.R. 377 (HL); *cf. Moodie v. I.R.C.* [1993] 1 W.L.R. 266. It is submitted that, in pursuance of such principles, a court could not ignore the existence of a genuine partnership brought into existence as part of a tax avoidance scheme: Millet J. was certainly not prepared to do so in *Ensign Tankers (Leasing) Ltd. v. Stokes* [1989] 1 W.L.R. 1222, 1242–1243 (this argument was not pursued in Court of Appeal at [1991] 1 W.L.R. 341 or in the House of Lords at [1992] 1 A.C. 655). But note the decision in *Gisborne v. Burton* [1989] Q.B. 390, where the Court of Appeal, in effect, sought to extend the application of the *Ramsay* principle outside the sphere of taxation. *cf. Belvedere Court Management Ltd. v. Frogmore Developments Ltd.* [1997] Q.B. 858 (CA); *MacFarlane v. Falfield Investments Ltd.* 1998 S.L.T. 145 (1st Div.), where it was attempted (unsuccessfully) to argue that the existence of a limited partnership could be ignored.

[40] See *infra*, para. 2–45.

[41] See *infra*, para. 2–46.

[42] It does not, however, follow that all the participants must necessarily share in that profit if a partnership is to exist: see *infra*, para. 2–10.

[43] March 11, 1996, an unreported decision of Dyson J.

[44] *Pooley v. Driver* (1876) 5 Ch.D. 458, 472 *per* Jessel M.R.: *Mollwo, March & Co. v. Court of Wards* (1872) L.R. 4 P.C. 419. Indeed, similar views were not unknown in more recent cases: in *Blackpool Marton Rotary Club v. Martin* [1988] S.T.C. 823, 830, Hoffmann J. observed that it is of the essence of the definition of partnership that a business is carried on "with a view to a profit to which the partners will be [*sic*] in some proportion or other each be individually entitled", whereas in *Davies v. Newman* 2000 W.L. 1841655, Pumfrey J. reportedly observed: "It is of the essence of a partnership that both profits and losses are shared."

"partner," which are self evidently derived from the verb "to part" in the sense of to divide amongst or share.[45] It must, on any footing, be accepted that division of profits amongst the partners has always been (and remains) the general, even if not the universal, object of partnership but this was not perceived as an essential element of the definition under the pre-1890 law. Thus, it is apprehended that persons who carried on a business in all other respects as partners, but with the object not of dividing the profits between themselves but of applying them towards some charitable purpose would have been regarded as partners.[46] In the same way, if two persons purported to carry on business as partners under a firm name, on terms that they were both to contribute capital and share losses equally, but that one of them was to be paid a fixed salary every year irrespective of the venture's profitability, whilst the other took the entirety of the profits (if any), they would, surely, have been treated as partners.[47]

If the above analysis is correct, then the omission of the supposed fourth **2–11** element from the definition of partnership was intentional and, indeed, accorded with the previous law,[48] so that it is not now permissible to import it.[49] The correctness of this view has been endorsed by the Court of Appeal in *M. Young Legal Associates v. Zahid*[50] and in *Hodson v. Hodson*.[51] In both cases one of the partners was entitled to remuneration irrespective of the profitability of the firm and it was held that this was not inconsistent with the existence of a partnership.[52]

In the circumstances, it is submitted that the division of profits must now be regarded as no more than a common incident of the partnership relation, rather than a precondition to its existence.[53] Thus, whilst the absence of this characteristic should, in any given case, never in itself be fatal, its presence may point strongly towards the existence of a partnership.

---

[45] Lord Lindley made the obvious point that there is more to partnership than merely sharing, since "persons may share almost anything imaginable, and may do so either by agreement amongst themselves or otherwise." It is the realisation and, in general, the sharing *of profits* which is at the heart of partnership.

[46] That this is not so far-fetched as might at first sight appear, see the trust in *R. v. Special Commissioners of Income Tax* [1922] 2 K.B. 729; also *The Abbey, Malvern Wells v. Minister of Local Government and Planning* [1951] Ch. 728. Moreover, the Value Added Tax Tribunal has accepted the correctness of this proposition: *Stephanie A. Manuel t/a Stage Coach Centre for the Performing Arts v. The Commissioners* (LON/90/807) [1992] S.T.I. 47. Note, however, the contrary (*obiter*) view seemingly expressed by Hoffmann J. in *Blackpool Marton Rotary Club v. Martin* [1988] S.T.C. 823, 830–831. The business in question may, of course, be a single adventure.

[47] In previous editions, reference was at this point made to *Watson v. Haggitt* [1928] A.C. 127, where Haggitt had for two years received a "salary" whilst Watson had drawn all the net profits of the business. However, it appears that there was in reality a sharing of profits in this case: see *ibid*. [1927] N.Z.L.R. 209, 212 *per* Alpers J. And see *Marsh v. Stacey* (1963) 107 S.J. 512, where the junior partner, who was to receive a fixed salary of £1,200 plus one-third of the profits of one branch of the firm, would undoubtedly have been liable as a partner; also *Stekel v. Ellice* [1973] 1 W.L.R. 191; and see *infra*, paras 5–20, 5–54, 5–55.

[48] Thus, a division of profits was not essential to a joint stock company: *Re Russell Institution* [1898] 2 Ch. 72; *Re Jones* [1898] 2 Ch. 83. Note that question arose in *Re Fisher & Sons* [1912] 2 K.B. 491, but it is unclear whether it was decided; see *infra*, para. 5–07.

[49] e.g. by arguing that, as an existing rule, it was saved by the Partnership Act 1890, s.46.

[50] [2006] 1 W.L.R. 2562.

[51] [2010] P.N.L.R. 8.

[52] Note that there were compelling reasons for the court to find the existence of a partnership in each case, in order to legitimise the arrangements which the intending partners had entered into.

[53] Note that Sir Frederick Pollock took a different view: see *Pollock on the Law of Partnership* (15th ed.), pp. 9 *et seq*.

At the same time, it must be recognised that section 44(a) of the Act does contemplate that if, on a general dissolution, there are sufficient funds available, there will be an ultimate division of the profits for the benefit of all the partners.[54]

E. THE NORMAL INCIDENTS OF PARTNERSHIP

2–12 Reference has already been made to the sharing of profits as one of the normal incidents of partnership.[55] Other attributes will be found similarly described in the authorities. Thus, in *Memec v. I.R.C.*,[56] Peter Gibson L.J. described the "characteristics of an ordinary English partnership" in these terms:

> "(1) the partnership is not a legal entity[57]; (2) the partners carry on the business of the partnership in common with a view of profit . . . [58]; (3) each does so both as principal and (see s.5 of the 1890 Act) as agent for each other, binding the firm and his partners in all matters within his authority; (4) every partner is liable jointly with the other partners for all the debts and other obligations of the firm (see s.9 of the 1890 Act); and (5) the partners own the business, having a beneficial interest in the form of an undivided share in the partnership assets . . . including any profits of the business."

In *Dollar Land (Cumbernauld) Ltd. v. C.I.N. Properties Ltd.*,[59] Lord Coulsfeld listed as potential key features: (1) mutual agency; (2) participation in profits; (3) sharing of losses; (4) common capital and (5) the basic non-assignability of the partnership relation,[60] whilst in *Dreyfus v. C.I.R.*[61] the existence of mutual agency was regarded as a "very common characteristic" of partnership. Various other formulations will be found in the authorities.

2–13 There is, however, a danger that what are, in truth, normal incidents or characteristics of partnership are wrongly perceived as *prerequisites* to the existence of that relationship, thus distorting the application of section 1(1) of the 1890 Act.[62] As Lord Coulsfied made clear in *Dollar Land (Cumbernauld) Ltd. v. C.I.N. Properties Ltd.*[63]:

> " . . . it is undoubtedly true that there is no one provision or feature which can be said to be absolutely necessary to the existence of a partnership, so that the absence of that feature inevitably negates the existence of a partnership . . . ".[64]

[54] See *infra*, paras 25–44 *et seq*. In earlier editions of this work reference was made at this point to s.39, rather than s.44; however the former section contains no reference to profits.

[55] See *supra*, para. 2–10.

[56] [1998] S.T.C. 754, 764e–f. See also *Swift v. Revenue & Customs Commissioners* [2010] S.F.T.D. 553.

[57] *per contra*, in Scotland: Partnership Act 1890, s.4(1).

[58] Peter Gibson L.J. naturally cross-referred to *ibid.* s.1(1) at this point.

[59] 1996 S.L.T. 186 (OH).

[60] This concept is referred to as *deluctus personae* in Scots law: see further *Miller's Partnership* (2nd ed.), pp. 16 *et seq.*, 204, 205.

[61] (1929) 14 T.C. 560, 574 *per* Lord Hanworth M.R. See also *ibid.* p. 579 *per* Lawrence J.

[62] This warning was cited with apparent approval by Arnold J. in *Hodson v. Hodson* [2009] P.N.L.R. 23, at [12], affirmed at [2010] P.N.L.R. 8.

[63] 1996 S.L.T. 186, 195F.

[64] It goes without saying that Lord Coulsfield should not be taken to have suggested that the express requirements set out in the Partnership Act 1890, s.1(1) do not need to be satisfied in all cases.

Thus, there must always be a *view* of profit for a partnership to exist[65] but, as was made abundantly clear in by the Court of Appeal in *M. Young Legal Associates v. Zahid*[66] and in *Hodson v. Hodson*,[67] a *sharing* of profits between the partners is not a necessary ingredient. The position is the same with the sharing of losses.[68] Again, whilst mutual agency may properly be regarded as a central feature of the law of partnership,[69] it is clearly something which flows from the partnership relation, not the other way around. In *Holme v. Hammond*,[70] Cleasby B. rightly rejected the notion that agency was the foundation of the idea of partnership,[71] and expressed the view that:

> "agency is deduced from partnership rather than partnership from agency. But neither does partnership always imply this mutual agency."[72]

Of course, if the position were otherwise, a limited partnership could not properly be regarded as a partnership within the meaning of the 1890 Act, since a limited partner in general has *no* authority to bind the firm.[73]

The proposition that a partnership cannot exist unless all the partners under- **2–14** take personal liability for the debts and obligations of the firm[74] is, in the current editor's view, equally fallacious, since not only can such personal liability be negated by express contract, but a limited partner will also, in the normal course, undertake no personal liability whatsoever,[75] yet will still be regarded as a partner in the eyes of the law.

Finally, in *Hodson v. Hodson*,[76] it was held that participation in management by all partners is not essential, given the recognition long accorded to so-called "sleeping" partners.[77]

---

[65] See *supra*, paras 2–07 *et seq.*

[66] [2006] 1 W.L.R. 2562. Both *Memec v. I.R.C., supra*, and *Dollar Land Cumbernauld Ltd. v. C.I.R. Properties Ltd., supra*, were cited without success in that case.

[67] [2010] P.N.L.R. 8. There a partner had a 1% profit entitlement but in practice chose to waive it.

[68] In contrast, a sharing of losses is inconsistent with a contract of service and points to some other contractual relationship, *e.g.* a partnership or other joint venture: see *Todd v. Adam* [2002] 2 All E.R. (Comm) 97 (CA), a decision concerning share fishermen.

[69] Partnership Act 1890, s.5: see *infra*, paras 12–01 *et seq.*

[70] (1872) L.R. 7 Ex. 218.

[71] *ibid.* p. 234. In this context, it is interesting to note that mutual agency appears not to have been an original feature of *societas* in Roman law, but was only introduced by Justinian.

[72] *ibid.* p. 233. Similarly, in *Dollar Land (Cumbernauld) Ltd. v. C.I.N. Properties Ltd., supra*, Lord Coulsfield, having listed the various features noted *supra*, para. 2–10, warned (at p. 195B) that it was "a mistake to put too much emphasis on the question of mutual agency" and went on to observe (at p. 195F–G) that "the absence of one or even more of these features might be reconcilable with the existence of a partnership." See also *Phillips v. Revenue & Customs Commissioners* [2010] S.F.T.D. 332 at [53]. The Partnership Act 1890 itself clearly contemplates that mutual agency may, to a greater or lesser extent, be excluded: *ibid.* ss.5, 8. See further, *infra*, paras 12–04, 12–138 *et seq.* For a different (and, in many ways, more extreme) perspective on the place of mutual agency in the law of partnership, see *Pooley v. Driver* (1876) 5 Ch. D. 458, 476 *per* Jessel M.R.

[73] See the Limited Partnerships Act 1907, s.6(1), considered *infra*, paras 30–03 *et seq.* In the current editor's view this cannot merely be explained away as a consequence of an express statutory provision, since a limited partnership is a "firm" (*ibid.* s.3) and the Partnership Act 1890 and partnership law generally is applicable to such partnerships (*ibid.* s.7).

[74] See the Partnership Act 1890, s.9, *infra*, paras 13–02 *et seq.*

[75] See the Limited Partnerships Act 1907, s.4(2), *infra*, paras 30–07 *et seq.*

[76] [2009] P.N.L.R. 23. This decision was affirmed at [2010] P.N.L.R. 8 (CA), albeit without specifically referring to this point.

[77] See *infra*, paras 13–53 *et seq.*

Partnership a contractual relationship

2–15   Partnership, although often called a contract, is more accurately described as a relationship *resulting from* a contract.[78] This was made clear in the original statutory definition introduced into the House of Lords[79] but not, ultimately, in the Act itself. Nevertheless, the origin of the relationship in an agreement, whether express or implied,[80] was clearly established before the Act and may legitimately be inferred from its provisions.[81] In *Hurst v. Bryk*,[82] Lord Millett enlarged on this analysis and expressed the following view:

> " . . . while partnership is a consensual arrangement based on agreement, it is more than a simple contract (to use the expression of Dixon J. in *McDonald v. Dennys Lacelles Ltd.*, 48 C.L.R. 457, 476); it is a continuing personal as well as commercial relationship."[83]

Like any other contract, the terms must be sufficiently certain, unless they fall to be implied by the Partnership Act 1890.[84]

Equally, where it is found that alleged partners have specifically agreed *not* to enter into a partnership, it comes as no surprise that the existence of a partnership is unlikely to be inferred from their subsequent conduct.[85]

Other definitions

2–16   The various comparative definitions of partnership, drawn from a number of different legal systems, which appeared in earlier editions of this work, are considered to be of more jurisprudential than practical interest and, given their accessibility in those editions, have not been retained in the present edition.[86]

---

[78] For a recent affirmation of this, see *Philips v. Symes* [2002] 1 W.L.R. 853, at [43] *per* Hart J.

[79] According to Lord Lindley's Supplement on the Partnership Act, the original definition was: "Partnership is the relation which subsists between persons who have agreed to carry on a business in common with a view of profit". Lord Lindley commented: "This definition was inaccurate, for, as pointed out by Parke J. in *Dickinson v. Valpy* [*(1829) 10 B. & C. 128, 141–142*] persons who have entered into an agreement that they will at some future time carry on business as partners, can *not* be considered as partners until the arrival of that time". This, of course, accords with the present position: see *infra*, paras 2–17 *et seq*.

[80] See *McPhail v. Bourne* [2008] EWHC 1235 (Ch) (Lawtel 13/6/08), where it was held that neither an express nor an implied agreement for partnership had come into existence between the original members of the group "Busted". To the same effect was the decision of the Royal Court of Jersey in *Bennett v. Lincoln* [2005] J.L.R. 125 at [22], although it should be noted that there the position was governed by the customary law, including the writings of *Pothier*.

[81] See especially *ibid*. ss.1, 2, 19, 24, 32, 33, 40 and 41; and *Davis v. Davis* [1894] 1 Ch. 393. This passage was cited with apparent approval by Arnold J. in *Hodson v. Hodson* [2009] P.N.L.R. 23, at [13]. His decision was affirmed at [2010] P.N.L.R. 8 (CA).

[82] [2002] 1 A.C. 185, 194. The remaining members of the House of Lords appear to have concurred in this view.

[83] This passage was cited in *Marsh v. Marsh* [2010] EWCA 1563 (Ch) (Lawtel 29/6/10) at [13] *per* Sir Edward Evans-Lombe (sitting as a Judge of the Chancery Division).

[84] See *Cayzer v. Beddow* [2007] EWCA Civ. 644 (Lawtel 29/6/07), where the terms for the particular venture were wholly *uncertain*.

[85] See *Greville v. Venables* [2007] EWCA Civ. 878 (Lawtel 12/9/07) (CA). Note also *Pine Energy Consultants Ltd., v. Talisman Energy (UK) Ltd.* [2008] CSOH 10 (OH), for another example of a case where the court was not prepared to *infer* the existence of a partnership.

[86] See the 15th ed., pp. 16–18; also the observations of Jessel M.R. thereon in *Pooley v. Driver* (1876) 5 Ch.D. 458, 471 *et seq*.

2. CONTEMPLATED PARTNERSHIPS

Business not yet commenced

An agreement between two or more persons to carry on business at a future **2–17** time cannot render them partners before they actually start to carry on that business. It is the carrying on of a business, not a mere agreement to carry it on, which is the test of partnership,[87] hence the importance of distinguishing between actual and contemplated partnerships. As Lord Lindley put it:

> "Persons who are only contemplating a future partnership, or who have only entered into an agreement that they will at some future time become partners, cannot be considered as partners before the arrival of the time agreed upon."[88]

He then went on to point out the difficulty of distinguishing between an agreement for an immediate partnership and an agreement for a future partnership. This difficulty may in practice be compounded where the parties depart from the strict terms of their agreement. If they opt for a future commencement date, but begin to carry on business together at an earlier date, they will be partners as from that earlier date; if they defer the date of commencement, no partnership will come into existence on the date originally chosen. Equally, if one intending partner carries on the business prior to the agreed commencement date without the approval or acquiescence of the others, no immediate partnership will come into existence.

Even if parties agree to form a partnership but fail to reach agreement on such fundamental issues as their capital contributions or profit shares, the court may be reluctant to infer that they intended to fall back on the default rules under the Partnership Act 1890.[89]

What amounts to a business

It has already been seen that a business may be treated as carried on even **2–18** though no trading activity has yet commenced.[90] It follows that a partnership may exist from an earlier stage than might at first sight be expected.

General principle

So long as an agreement to form a partnership remains executory, no partner- **2–19** ship will be created. Thus, save in the case previously noted,[91] intending partners will retain that status if the chosen commencement date has not yet arrived or if some act still remains to be done before the business can be commenced.

---

[87] See the statutory definition of partnership, *supra*, paras 2–01 *et seq*. And see *supra*, paras 2–05, n. 26, 2–15, n. 79. Note, however, the approach adopted by Lord Macfadyen in *Small v. Fleming* 2003 S.C.L.R. 647 (OH), when considering whether a joint venture (which he described as a "species of partnership") existed between the parties.

[88] See *Dickinson v. Valpy* (1829) 10 B. & C. 128, 141–142 *per* Parke J. And see, in addition to the cases cited below, *Osborne v. Jullion* (1856) 3 Drew. 596, where the partnership (?) depended on the result of experiments.

[89] *Pine Energy Consultants Ltd. v. Talisman Energy (UK) Ltd.* [2008] CSOH 10 (OH).

[90] See *Khan v. Miah* [2000] 1 W.L.R. 2123 (HL), noted *supra*, para. 2–03.

[91] See *supra*, para. 2–18.

Precisely the same principle applies as between the promoters of companies, as will be seen hereafter.

(a) Application of the Principle: Ordinary Partnerships

Share not yet taken

2–20   In *Howell v. Brodie*,[92] the defendant intended to become a partner in a market proposed to be erected and advanced considerable sums of money for that purpose; ultimately, on the completion of the market, he took a one-seventh share in it. The claimant builder sought to make him liable for the cost of work and materials employed in erecting the market, on the ground that he was a partner with the person by whom he (the claimant) had been employed; however, the court held that no partnership existed until the defendant took up his share, which he did not do until after the claimant's period of employment.

Share of profits expected in lieu of salary

2–21   In *Burnell v. Hunt*,[93] A and B agreed that A should take premises and purchase machinery and materials to carry on the business of a silk-lace maker, and that B should manage the business and receive half the profits as soon as any accrued. In the meantime, he was to be paid £2 a week. It was held that, so long as the £2 per week continued to be paid, no partnership existed.[94]

Option to become a partner

2–22   A person who is contemplating joining another in business may agree that the business is initially to be carried on upon terms which do not involve the creation of a partnership, but which confer upon him the right to become a partner, either at a specified time or at a time of his choosing. Such an agreement, if bona fide, and not a colourable device for disguising the existence of an immediate partnership,[95] will not constitute the parties as partners until the option has been exercised.[96] This is illustrated by *Ex p. Davis*,[97] where a creditor had a right to nominate himself as a partner with his debtor but had not exercised the right.

2–23   Similarly, in *Gabriel v. Evill*,[98] the defendant agreed to enter into partnership with two prospective partners and to bring in £1,000 in cash and £1,000 in goods.

---

[92] (1839) 6 Bing. N.C. 44.

[93] (1841) 5 Jur. 650, QB. The real point here was whether B had any interest in the goods, which he clearly had not, and would not have had even if there had been profits to divide.

[94] See also *Ex p. Hickin* (1850) 3 De G. & Sm. 662.

[95] See *Courtenay v. Wagstaff* (1864) 16 C.B.(N.S.) 110.

[96] In the opinion of the current editor, such an option will, in general, be personal to the prospective partner and, thus, not freely assignable, although much will naturally depend on the terms of the agreement. Note also that a mortgagor may give his mortgagee an option to become his partner and, thereupon, to acquire the mortgaged property: *Reeve v. Lisle* [1902] A.C. 461. However, if that arrangement forms part of the original mortgage transaction, it may be regarded as a clog on the equity of redemption: see *Lisle v. Reeve* [1902] 1 Ch. 53, 71 *et seq.*; also *Samuel v. Jarrah Timber and Wood Paving Co. Ltd.* [1904] A.C. 323, 329 *per* Lord Lindley; *Lewis v. Frank Love Ltd.* [1961] 1 W.L.R. 261.

[97] (1863) 4 De G.J. & S. 523.

[98] (1842) 9 M. & W. 297; also *Ex p. Turquand* (1841) 2 M.D. & D. 339; *Re Hall* (1864) 15 I.Ch.R. 287.

It was also agreed that the partnership would have a retrospective commencement date, but the defendant reserved to himself the option of determining at any time within 12 months from that date whether he would become a partner or not. He duly advanced the £2,000, and several other acts were done in pursuance of the agreement, but within the 12 months the defendant exercised his option and declared his intention not to become a partner. It was held that he never did in fact become one, and that he had not incurred any liability as if he had.[99]

In *Price v. Groom*,[100] a debtor carried on business under what was then styled **2–24** an inspectorship deed, which authorised the trustees to carry on the business themselves, and to take the profits, if they chose. Their interest in the profits, however, did not commence until the debtor's interest determined; and it was held that, whilst he carried on the business, there was no partnership between him and the trustees, they and he not being entitled to the profits at the same time.

In *Re Young, ex p. Jones*,[101] A lent B £500 for his business under a written **2–25** contract, by the terms of which A was to have sole control and management of the business, with the option of becoming a partner within a certain time; in the interim, for the use of his money, he was to be paid a weekly sum out of the profits of the business. B was to draw a similar weekly sum. Before the time for the exercise of the option had expired B became bankrupt. The court held that A, who had not exercised the option, was not a partner in the business.[102]

Equally, where a prospective partner makes a significant financial contribution to a business venture, the court may be reluctant to infer that he merely intended to become a partner at some future time.[103]

Partnership agreement to be drawn up

Persons who agree to become partners and who intend to sign a formal **2–26** partnership deed may become partners even though they never sign such a deed.[104] On the other hand, a deed may be prepared but never acted on, in which case no partnership will be created,[105] or it may purport to record the existence of a partnership as from an earlier date, when no such partnership can, on the facts, be shown to have existed at that date.[106] But if the parties agree that they are not to become partners until they have signed such a deed, the partnership will not commence until that condition has been performed, unless they can be shown to have waived the need for such performance. Thus, in *Battley v.*

---

[99] Compare this case with *Jefferys v. Smith* (1827) 3 Russ. 158. There A agreed to purchase B's share in a firm; A acted and was treated as a partner by the other members, but afterwards rescinded the contract with B: it was held that a partnership nevertheless subsisted between A and B's co-partners.

[100] (1848) 2 Ex. 542.

[101] [1896] 2 Q.B. 484.

[102] As to A's right to prove for the money lent, see *infra*, paras 5–33 *et seq.*, 27–82, 27–84, 27–106.

[103] As in *Nadeem v. Rafiq* [2007] EWHC 2959 (Ch) (Lawtel 2/1/08).

[104] See *Syers v. Syers* (1876) 1 App.Cas. 174; *Mavor v. Hill* [1952] C.P.L. 472; *Stekel v. Ellice* [1973] 1 W.L.R. 191; *Thakrar v. Vadera*, March 31, 1999 (unreported); *Gray v. Dickson* (A1116/05), August 10, 2007 (Sh. Ct.). Note also *Walters v. Bingham* [1988] 1 F.T.L.R. 260.

[105] This passage was approved in *Hodson v. Hodson* [2009] P.N.L.R. 23 at [14] to [16] *per* Arnold J. The decision was affirmed at [2010] P.N.L.R. 8 (CA).

[106] See *Alexander Bulloch & Co. v. I.R.C.* [1976] S.T.C. 514.

Lewis,[107] two persons had agreed to become partners as from a future date, on terms to be embodied in a deed to be executed on that date. In fact, the deed was executed, in an amended form, but on a later date. It was nevertheless held that the partnership began on the original date. Significantly, the parties had in fact commenced business as partners on that date, so that it was wholly immaterial (as regards the question before the court) what the *terms* of the partnership were.

Conditional agreement

2-27   If persons agree to become partners on certain terms and/or with a view to carrying on a particular business, they cannot be obliged to enter into partnership on some other terms or with a view to carrying on some other business; they will only be regarded as partners when they actually participate in the "new" partnership and thereby preclude themselves from objecting to the variation of their original agreement.[108]

(b) Application of the Principle: Promoters of Companies

2-28   Where two or more persons are preparing to set up a company and intend to become members of the company after its formation, they will not be regarded as partners if this is their only business association.[109] Admittedly, they may share a common object which is, ultimately, the acquisition of profit, but their immediate object is the formation of the company.[110] On the other hand, persons who together carry on the *business* of promoting companies with a view to making profits therefrom will unquestionably be partners.[111]

Early cases: statutory companies

2-29   Two old cases are technically at variance with the above propositions, namely *Holmes v. Higgins*[112] and *Lucas v. Beach*.[113] In the former, several persons, who had associated together in order to obtain the Act of Parliament necessary to form a railway company and subscribed money for that purpose, were held to be partners. Similarly, in *Lucas v. Beach*, the court held that persons associated together for the purpose of passing a turnpike Act, who had each subscribed for shares in the tolls from the proposed road, were partners. However, in both of these cases the real question was whether the claimant was, by virtue of an implied contract, entitled to recover from the defendants remuneration for services rendered by him for their joint benefit. It was held that he was not. As a

---

[107] (1840) 1 Man. & G. 155; and see *Wilson v. Lewis* (1840) 2 Man. & G. 197. *cf. Ellis v. Ward* (1872) 21 W.R. 100, where the intended partners quarrelled before they signed the deed.

[108] *Fox v. Clifton* (1830) 6 Bing. 776.

[109] *cf. supra*, para. 2–05.

[110] *Keith Spicer v. Mansell* [1970] 1 W.L.R. 333; also *Wood v. Argyll* (1844) 6 Man. & G. 928; *Hamilton v. Smith* (1859) 5 Jur. (N.S.) 32; *Hutton v. Thompson* (1846) 3 H.L.C. 161; *Bright v. Hutton* (1852) 3 H.L.C. 341; and see *Ness Training Ltd. v. Triage Central Ltd.* 2002 S.L.T. 675 (OH). *Cayzer v. Beddow* [2007] EWCA Civ. 644 (Lawtel 29/6/07) was a somewhat similar case, but ultimately turned on the uncertainty in the terms of the venture. *cf. Reeves v. Sprecher* [2008] EWHC 583 (Ch) (Lawtel 2/4/08), although this was only a decision rejecting a summary judgment application.

[111] See *Royal Victoria Palace Syndicate* (1873) 29 L.T. 668; affirmed (1874) 30 L.T. 3.

[112] (1822) 1 B. & C. 74.

[113] (1840) 1 Man. & G. 417; *Barnett v. Lambert* (1846) 15 M. & W. 489 was a similar case.

result, both cases were thought to be (and, on occasion, cited as) authorities for the proposition that persons engaged in setting up what is now known as a statutory company are partners. Indeed, in *Lucas v. Beach* it was asked in argument, "What is there to prevent a number of individuals from entering into a partnership with the limited object, in the first instance, of procuring an act of Parliament, and with an ulterior object in view when the act has passed?"[114] Lord Lindley had no hesitation in responding thus:

> "The answer is, that to call persons so associated partners is to ignore the difference between a contract of partnership and an agreement to enter into such a contract, to confound an agreement with its result, and to hold persons to be partners although they have not yet acquired any right to share profits. It cannot be contended that the right to share profits would, under such an agreement as is supposed, accrue before the passing of the act, and if not, how can the parties to such an agreement be *partners* at an earlier period?"[115]

It is accordingly submitted that Lord Lindley was justified in stating that **2–30** *Holmes v. Higgins* and *Lucas v. Beach* cannot be relied on as authorities on this issue.[116] They cannot even be reconciled with the later decisions in *Reynell v. Lewis*[117] and *Wyld v. Hopkins*[118] where, following detailed consideration, it was held that no partnership subsisted between persons who had subscribed for the purposes of forming a railway company and of procuring the necessary Act of Parliament. Lord Cranworth subsequently confirmed this to be the correct principle,[119] and there are numerous other decisions to the like effect.[120]

(c) Application of the Principle: Limited Liability Partnerships

One of the requirements for the incorporation of a limited liability partnership[121] **2–31** is that two or more persons "associated for carrying on a lawful business with a

---

[114] See also *per* Lord Brougham in *Hutton v. Upfill* (1850) 2 H.L.C. 674, 691–692.

[115] When considering the latter part of this passage, the terms of the statutory definition of partnership contained in the Partnership Act 1890, s.1(1) must be borne in mind, since there is now no express requirement that partners must actually *share* profits: see *supra*, para. 2–10.

[116] In editions of this work prior to the 16th the following footnote appeared at this point: "They are authorities for the point actually decided, *viz.* that a person doing work for the joint benefit of himself and others cannot recover compensation from them by virtue of any implied promise to pay him". However, it is submitted that this proposition ignores the finding of partnership in each case which was at the root of the decision. See also, as to the entitlement (or otherwise) of a partner to remuneration, *infra*, paras 20–39 *et seq*.

[117] (1846) 15 M. & W. 517.

[118] *ibid.*

[119] *Capper's Case* (1851) 1 Sim. N.S. 178.

[120] See *Batard v. Hawes* (1853) 2 E. & B. 287; *Walstab v. Spottiswoode* (1846) 15 M. & W. 501; *Forrester v. Bell* (1847) 10 I.L.R. 555; *Hutton v. Thompson* (1846) 3 H.L.C. 161; *Bright v. Hutton* (1852) 3 H.L.C. 341; *Hamilton v. Smith* (1859) 5 Jur. N.S. 32; *Norris v. Cottle* (1850) 2 H.L.C. 647; *Besley's Case* (1851) 3 Mac. & G. 287; *Tanner's Case* (1852) 5 De G. & Sm. 182. But see also the judgment of Lowry C.J. in *De Pol v. Cunningham* [1974] S.T.C. 487, where assets were jointly owned in equity pending the formation of a limited company. Lowry C.J. (but not the other Lords Justices) concluded that the parties were "bound to be in partnership" (see p. 500). It is thought that this conclusion was not in accordance with authority, or strictly justified on the facts of the case.

[121] Despite its name, a limited liability partnership is a body corporate and not a partnership: Limited Liability Partnerships Act 2000, s.1(2). See further *infra*, paras 2–39 *et seq*.

view of profit" should have subscribed their names to an incorporation document.[122] It is not necessary that they should actually be carrying on the business
pursuant to that association at or before the time the LLP is incorporated, and
there is no reason to suppose that they would be regarded as partners merely by
reason of such association, any more than would the promoters of a company.[123]
If, however, they are already carrying on the business pursuant to that association, it is almost inevitable that they will be regarded as doing so in partnership
until such time as the incorporation of the LLP is completed.[124]

3.   ASSOCIATIONS NOT GOVERNED BY
THE PARTNERSHIP ACT 1890

Statutory exceptions

2–32   The definition of "partnership" contained in section 1(1) of the Partnership
Act 1890,[125] if standing alone, would include not only partnerships in the
ordinary sense of the term, but also many companies and associations which
differ from ordinary partnerships in certain fundamental respects. The latter are,
however, expressly excluded from the ambit of the Act by section 1(2), which
provides as follows.

Partnership Act 1890, section 1(2)

2–33   "1.— . . . (2) But the relation between members of any company or association
which is—

(a) [registered under the Companies Act 2006[126]; or]
(b) Formed or incorporated by or in pursuance of any other Act of Parliament
or letters patent, or Royal Charter; [. . .][127]

is not a partnership within the meaning of this Act."

There are thus excluded from the Partnership Act 1890 registered companies
and incorporated and unincorporated companies which derive special privileges
from the Crown or the legislature.

---

[122] *ibid.* s.2(1)(a). A statement must also be delivered to the registrar confirming that this requirement is satisfied: *ibid.* s.2(1)(c).
[123] See *supra*, para. 2–28.
[124] Particularly given the similarity of the wording of *ibid.* s.2(1)(a) and the Partnership Act 1890,
s.1(1), *supra*, paras 2–01 *et seq.*
[125] See *supra*, para. 2–01.
[126] This paragraph was substituted by the Companies Act 2006 (Consequential Amendments,
Transitional Provisions and Savings) Order 2009 (SI 2009/1941), art. 2(1), Sched. 1, para. 2.
[127] The word "or" and the original para. (c), referring to companies working mines subject to the
Stannaries jurisdiction, were repealed by the Statute Law (Repeals) Act 1998 (c.43), Sched. 1, Pt X,
Group 1.

Distinction between corporations and partnerships

A corporation is an artificial person created by special authority[128] and **2–34** endowed with capacity to acquire rights and incur obligations.[129] Certainly a corporation is composed of a number of individuals, but the rights and obligations of those individuals are not the same as those of the corporation; nor are the rights and obligations of the corporation exercisable by or enforceable against those individuals, either jointly or separately, but only collectively, as an artificial entity, *i.e.* the corporation enjoys separate legal personality. Civilian lawyers put it in these terms: *Si quid universitati debetur singulis non debetur, nec quod debet universitas singuli debent.*[130] (If anything is owed to an entire body, it is not owed to the individual members, nor do the individual members owe what is owed by the entire body.)

With partnerships, it is the opposite: the firm is not an entity distinct from the   **2–35** individuals composing it[131] and the partners collectively cannot acquire rights or incur obligations. The rights and liabilities of a partnership are the rights and liabilities of the partners and are enforceable by and against them individually. The principle is stated by the civilian lawyers thus: *Si quid societati debetur singulis debetur et quod debet societas singuli debent.*[132] (If anything is owed to the partnership, it is owed to the individual members and the individual members owe what is owed by the partnership.) A limited exception to this principle is, however, to be found in the insolvency legislation as applied to partnerships.[133]

Companies

(1) *Unincorporated*

Unincorporated companies were once common and in many ways resembled   **2–36** partnerships. However, Lord Lindley identified the fundamental distinction in these terms:

> " . . . a partnership consists of a few individuals known to each other, bound together by the ties of friendship and mutual confidence, and who, therefore, are not at liberty without the consent of all to retire from the firm and substitute other persons in their places; whilst a company consists of a large number of individuals not necessarily nor indeed usually acquainted with each other at all, so that it is a matter of

---

[128] *i.e.* by the authority of the law of England, the Crown (*i.e.* royal charter) or Parliament or by prescription.

[129] Although a company may be formed for a specific purpose, its capacity cannot now be called into question by reference to the terms of its constitution: Companies Act 2006, s.39(1). A limited liability partnership is a body corporate which in any event enjoys unlimited capacity: Limited Liability Partnerships Act 2000, ss.1(2), (3).

[130] See also *Re Sheffield and South Yorkshire Permanent Building Soc.* (1889) 22 Q.B.D. 470, 476 *per* Cave J.; *Salomon v. Salomon & Co. Ltd.* [1897] A.C. 22.

[131] *cf.* the exceptional position of the International Tin Council as an unincorporated association with legal personality: *J.H. Rayner (Mincing Lane) Ltd. v. Department of Trade and Industry* [1990] 2 A.C. 418. And note also *Arab Monetary Fund v. Hashim (No. 3)* [1991] 2 A.C. 114.

[132] See *Lloyd v. Loaring* (1802) 6 Ves.Jr. 773; *Beaumont v. Meredith* (1814) 3 V. & B. 180; *Ryhope Coal Co. v. Foyer* (1881) 7 Q.B.D. 485.

[133] See *infra*, paras 27–04 *et seq.*

comparative indifference whether changes amongst them are effected or not.[134] Nearly all the differences which exist between ordinary partnerships and unincorporated companies, will be found traceable to the above distinction. Indeed it may be said that the law of unincorporated companies was composed of little else than the law of partnership modified and adapted to the wants of a large and fluctuating number of members."

2–37   Since the Companies Act 1862, unincorporated companies formed for the purpose of carrying on any business that has as its object the acquisition of gain had, with certain exceptions, required to be registered and this remained the position under the Companies Act 1985, until the remaining regulations on the size of partnerships, etc. were finally swept away in their entirety.[135] It follows that the unincorporated company is no longer a relevant concept.[136]

(2) *Incorporated*

2–38   Lord Lindley defined such companies in the following terms:

"Incorporated companies are societies consisting usually of many persons, having transferable shares in a common fund, but incorporated by Royal Charter or by Act of Parliament. They are not pure partnerships, for their members are recognised as an aggregate body; nor are they pure corporations, for their members are more or less liable to contribute to the debts of the collective whole. Incorporated companies are intermediate between corporations known to the common law and ordinary partnerships, and partake of the nature of both; and the law relating to these companies depends as well on the principles which govern ordinary partnerships, as on those which are applicable to corporations strictly so called."[137]

Now such companies are governed by the provisions of the Companies Act 2006 and the Insolvency Act 1986 and there is relatively little scope for the application of partnership principles.[138]

Limited liability partnerships

2–39   The limited liability partnership or LLP is an entirely new entity introduced by the Limited Liability Partnerships Act 2000.[139] Despite its name, an LLP is a body corporate which enjoys both separate legal personality and unlimited capacity[140] and, by definition, will not constitute a partnership within the mean-

---

[134] See *Smith v. Anderson* (1880) 15 Ch.D. 247, 273 *per* James L.J. and *Re Stanley* [1906] 1 Ch. 131, 134 *per* Buckley J.

[135] See the Regulatory Reform (Reform of 20 Member Limit in Partnerships etc.) Order 2002 (SI 2002/3203), which repealed the Companies Act 1985, ss.716, 717 and the various rules made or treated as made pursuant thereto with effect from December 21, 2002.

[136] But see, as to mutual insurance societies, *infra*, para. 2–46.

[137] See *Re Accidental and Marine Insurance Corp.* (1870) L.R. 5 Ch.App. 424, 431 *per* Giffard L.J.; also *Baird's Case*, *ibid*. 725, 734 *et seq. per* James L.J.

[138] Of course, there are still companies which are regarded as quasi-partnerships, to whom some partnership principles may be applied: see *Ebrahimi v. Westbourne Galleries* [1973] A.C. 360 and numerous other cases of that class.

[139] The Act came into force on April 6, 2001: the Limited Liability Partnerships Act 2000 (Commencement) Order 2000 (SI 2000/3316), art. 2.

[140] Limited Liability Partnerships Act 2000, s.1(2), (3).

ing of the Partnership Act 1890.[141] Its members[142] act as agents of the LLP and not of each other[143] and are not, in general, liable for its debts and obligations.[144] They may even be employed by the LLP,[145] although they will seemingly still continue to be treated as self employed in such a case.[146]

Formation of an LLP

Formation of an LLP involves two or more persons who are "associated for carrying on a lawful business with a view of profit",[147] subscribing their names to an incorporation document[148] which must then be registered.[149] The LLP must   **2–40**

---

[141] See the Partnership Act 1890, s.1(2), *supra*, para. 2–33. Nevertheless, it may be that, if the members of an LLP choose to carry on business as if they are partners, they will be liable as such: this possibility was canvassed by Lord Goldsmith in the House of Lords' debate on December 9, 1999 (*Hansard* 991209–10–Col. 1435).

[142] This, rather than "partners", is the expression used in the Act, although it is now not uncommon to find the latter expression used to describe both members of an LLP and senior employees who are, in effect, held out as "partners". In such cases, the LLP and its members should ensure that third parties are aware that use of the expression "partner" does not imply the existence of a partnership within the meaning of the Partnership Act 1890.

[143] *ibid.* s.6(1). *cf.* the Partnership Act 1890, s.5: see *infra*, paras 12–01 *et seq.*

[144] This is not, surprisingly, clearly stated in the Act. There is still scope for the court to find that an individual member of the LLP has assumed a personal duty of care to a client/customer and thus rendered himself personally liable. It is by no means clear whether the court will be disposed to make such a finding: it declined to do so, in the case of a director of a company, in *Williams v. Natural Life Health Foods Ltd.* [1998] 1 W.L.R. 830 (HL); also *Noel v. Poland* [2001] B.C.L.C. 645 (chairman of a company); *Bradford & Bingley Plc v. Martin Hayes, Dunphy & Hayes Ltd.*, 2001 WL 1560784 (an employee); *Devine v. McAteer* [2008] P.N.L.R. 31 (two directors, one of whom was potentially liable and the other not). However, an employee was held personally liable in *Merrett v. Babb* [2001] Q.B. 1174 (CA) (surveyors) and *Yazhou Travel Investment Company Ltd. v. Bateman Starr* [2005] P.N.L.R. 31 (Hong Kong High Court) (solicitors). And note also *Riyad Bank v. Ahli United Banks (UK) Plc* [2006] 2 All E.R. (Comm) 777 (CA). None of these decisions concerns an LLP. This diverging line of cases only raises issues in the case of negligence claims: in the case of other torts committed by a member, personal liability is almost inevitable: see, in particular, the Limited Liability Partnerships Act 2000, s.6(4). Whilst there may, in a normal case, be no liability to third parties, a member may, nevertheless, agree or be required to contribute to the LLP's assets on a winding up: see *ibid.* s.1(4); also the Insolvency Act 1986, ss.74, 214A as substituted/added by the Limited Liability Partnerships Regulations 2001 (SI 2001/1090), reg. 5, Sched. 3. Liability may also arise in the case of a sole member after 6 months: see *infra*, para. 2–40.

[145] Limited Liability Partnerships Act 2000, s.4(4). Note that the drafting of this subsection is wholly defective: a member is not to be regarded as employed "unless, if he and the other members were in a partnership, he would be regarded for that purpose as employed by the partnership". Partnership and employment are, of course, mutually exclusive concepts and there are *no* circumstances under English law where a partner could be regarded as employed by his own firm: see *infra*, paras 3–04, 5–54, 5–55. Nevertheless, the EAT found no difficulty in applying the subsection in *Kovats v. TFO Management LLP* [2009] I.C.R. 1140. Note that, in reaching its decision, the EAT took into account the tax treatment of the supposed employee (see *ibid.* at [36]), but this would seem to follow automatically from his status as a member and not be relevant to the issue of whether a member may be an employee.

[146] However illogical, this appears to be the effect of the Income Tax (Trading and Other Income) Act 2005, s.862 (as amended by the Income Tax Act 2007, Sched. 1, Pt. 2, para. 580) and is, at the time of writing, still acknowledged by HMRC in its Tax Bulletin dated December 2000. Whether this will remain the position indefinitely is, however, open to doubt: the current editor understands that HMRC are seeking to challenge the tax status of employed members of hedge fund LLPs, although on what precise basis is not known.

[147] Limited Liability Partnerships Act 2000, s.2(1)(a). See further *supra*, para. 2–31.

[148] *ibid.* s.2, as amended by the Limited Liability Partnerships (Application of Companies Act 2006) Regulations 2009 (SI 2009/1804), Sched. 1, para. 3. As to the form of the incorporation document, see *ibid.* s.2(2) (as amended) and Form LL IN01.

[149] *ibid.* s.3, as amended by *ibid.* Sched. 3, para. 2.

have a registered office,[150] its name must comply with the requirements of the Act[151] and the Companies Act 2006[152] and it must have two or more "designated members"[153] whose function it is to attend to various administrative matters.[154] Subsequent changes in composition of the LLP must be registered,[155] as must changes in the particulars entered in the register maintained by the LLP.[156] If the LLP carries on business with less than two members for more than 6 months, the sole member will be personally liable along with the LLP for its debts.[157]

Whilst many of the provisions of the Companies Act 2006 and the Insolvency Act 1986 will apply to the LLP, albeit in an amended form,[158] partnership law will, in general, be of no relevance.[159]

The LLP agreement and the internal regulation of the LLP

2–41   One area where the LLP does, in some ways, resemble a partnership is in the freedom of the members to agree terms for the internal running and regulation of the LLP by means of a "limited liability partnership agreement",[160] although it should not be assumed that such an agreement will simply replicate an ordinary

---

[150] Companies Act 2006, s.86(1), as substituted and applied by Limited Liability Partnerships (Application of Companies Act 2006) Regulations 2009, reg. 16.

[151] Limited Liability Partnerships Act 2000, Sched., Pt I (as amended by the Companies Act 2006, Sched. 16 and the Limited Liability Partnerships (Application of Companies Act 2006) Regulations 2009, Sched. 3, para. 10). The name must, *inter alia*, end with "limited liability partnership", "llp" or "LLP" or the Welsh equivalents (*ibid.* Sched. 1, para. 2,) and may not in general be the same as that under which a company or LLP is already registered (Companies Act 2006, s.66, as substituted and applied by the Limited Liability Partnerships (Application of Companies Act 2006) Regulations 2009, reg. 11 and in turn applying elements of the Company and Business Names (Miscellaneous Provisions) Regulations 2009 (SI 2009/1085)).

[152] See the restrictions on the use of names in *ibid.* ss.53–57, 65, as substituted and applied by *ibid.* regs. 8–10; also the Company and Business Names (Miscellaneous Provisions) Regulations 2009, elements of which are applied and amended by *ibid* ss.57, 65.

[153] *ibid.* ss.2(2)(f), 8 (the latter section having been amended by *ibid.* Sched. 3, para. 10). If no members of the LLP are specified as its designated members, all the members will assume that role: *ibid.* s.8(2). And note, as to the position of designated members, *Feetum v. Levy* [2006] Ch. 585 (CA).

[154] The functions are too numerous to list here. They will include signing the LLP's accounts once approved (Companies Act 2006, s.414(1), as amended and applied by the Limited Liability Partnerships (Accounts and Audit) (Application of Companies Act 2006) Regulations 2008 (SI 2008/1911), reg. 12), delivering a copy of those accounts and the auditor's report to the registrar, where applicable (*ibid.* ss.441, 444–446 as amended and applied by *ibid.* regs.17, 18), signing the LLP's annual return (*ibid.* ss.854, 858(1)(b) as amended and applied by the Limited Liability Partnerships (Application of Companies Act 2006) Regulations 2009, regs. 30, 31), the appointment of its first set of auditors and the filling of any casual vacancy in the auditors (*ibid.* s.485(3) as amended and applied by Limited Liability Partnerships (Accounts and Audit) Application of Companies Act 2006) Regulations 2008, reg. 36) and ensuring that notice of any change in the membership of the LLP is delivered under the Limited Liability Partnerships Act 2000, s.9(1), as amended (*ibid.* s.9(4)).

[155] *ibid.* s.9(1)(a).

[156] *ibid.* s.9(1)(b), as amended by the Limited Liability Partnerships (Application of Companies Act 2006) Regulations 2009, Sched.3, para. 5. As to the obligation to maintain the register, see the Companies Act 2006, ss.162 *et seq.*, as substituted and applied by *ibid.* reg. 18.

[157] *ibid.* s.4A(1), (2)(a), as added *ibid.* Sched. 3, para. 3. Any person who knew that the LLP was carrying on business with only one member will also be liable: *ibid.* s.4A(2)(b).

[158] See the Limited Liability Partnerships Regulations 2001, reg. 5, Sched. 3; the Limited Liability Partnerships (Accounts and Audit) (Application of Companies Act 2006) Regulations 2008; and the Limited Liability Partnerships (Application of Companies Act 2006) Regulations 2009.

[159] Limited Liability Partnerships Act 2000, s.1(5). Although there is a power to apply parts of partnership law by regulation (*ibid.* s.15(c)), this seems unlikely to be exercised.

[160] See *ibid.* s.5. Although the expression in the text does not appear in the Act, it is used in the Limited Liability Partnerships Regulations 2001: see the preamble to *ibid.* reg. 7.

partnership agreement.[161] In the absence of such an agreement, there are a number of default rules which apply as between the members, which cover much the same ground as certain sections of the Partnership Act 1890,[162] but which are by no means comprehensive.[163] It should be noted that, since an LLP is not a partnership, there is no implied duty of good faith as between the members,[164] although their relationship with the LLP itself will inevitably be of a fiduciary nature.[165]

Although management of the LLP is a matter for the members,[166] they unaccountably cannot permit a former member to participate therein.[167]

Capital, profits and "clawback"

There are no capital maintenance requirements applicable to an LLP[168] and the members can share profits in any way they see fit.[169] However, distributions of profit and any other withdrawal of money from the LLP[170] may be subject to "clawback" in the event of an insolvency of the LLP within two years.[171] Thus, a court may order that the sums withdrawn are to be restored to the LLP for the benefit of its creditors if the member in question knew or had reasonable grounds for believing that the LLP was, at the time of the withdrawal, unable to pay its debts or would become so unable by reason of that or some other contemporaneous or contemplated withdrawal.[172] However, such an order will not be made unless the member making the withdrawal knew or ought to have concluded at the time that there was no reasonable prospect of the LLP avoiding going into insolvent liquidation.[173] Clawback also applies to former members of the LLP.[174]

2–42

---

[161] See *infra*, paras 10–288, 10–289.

[162] Limited Liability Partnerships Regulations 2001, regs 7, 8.

[163] In the case of a partnership, there is the whole body of partnership law to fall back on if a particular issue is not addressed in the agreement, but as noted *supra*, para. 2–40, partnership law does not apply to an LLP.

[164] The importation of such a duty was extensively debated during the consultation process prior to the introduction of the 2000 Act, but was, ultimately, rejected by the Department of Trade and Industry: see the Summary of Responses issued in May 2000 (URN 00/865), page 8. In practice, many LLP agreements do include an express duty of good faith, albeit increasingly owed just to the LLP and not as between the members. Nevertheless, even in cases where such an express duty is not imposed, the current editor has encountered the argument that an implied duty between the members should still apply.

[165] See *ibid*.

[166] The default rules replicate the Partnership Act 1890, s.24(5), (8): see the Limited Liability Partnerships Regulations 2001, reg. 7(3), (6).

[167] Limited Liability Partnerships Act 2000, s.7(2). It appears that this prohibition cannot be overridden by agreement.

[168] Note, however, that the classification of capital as debt or equity will depend on the terms of the LLP Agreement: see the revised LLP SORP, issued on March 31, 2010, paras 38, 39.

[169] If the LLP agreement is silent on the point, both capital and profits will be shared by the members equally: Limited Liability Partnerships Regulations 2001, reg. 7(1).

[170] The types of withdrawal affected are framed very widely indeed, and include a share of profits, a salary, loan interest or capital repayments and "any other withdrawal of property".

[171] Insolvency Act 1986, s.214A, as inserted by the Limited Liability Partnerships Regulations 2001, Sched. 3.

[172] *ibid*. s.214A(2)(b).

[173] *ibid*. s.214A(5).

[174] Although this is clearly the legislative intention, the wording of *ibid*. s.214A(2)(a) is less than clear, *i.e.*: "This subsection applies in relation to a person if . . . (a) . . . he was a member of the limited liability partnership who withdrew property of the limited liability partnership . . . ". This at first sight presupposes that the person making the withdrawal was a member at the relevant time.

Winding up

2–43   An LLP may be wound up voluntarily[175] or by order of the court.[176] The winding up procedure broadly follows that applicable to a company[177] and there is no concept of dissolution in the sense encountered in partnership law.[178] Although the unfair prejudice provisions under section 994 of the Companies Act 2006 also apply to an LLP, they can be excluded by agreement between the members.[179]

Limited liability partnerships in other jurisdictions

2–44   Numerous jurisdictions, in the USA and elsewhere, have introduced limited liability partnership legislation but, save in the case of the USA and Jersey, have tended to follow the corporate rather than the partnership model.[180] Even where the latter model is favoured, most jurisdictions confer separate legal personality on the LLP. In the case of an LLP formed under Jersey law,[181] the Inland Revenue expressed its intention to treat the LLP as a company for tax purposes and an attempt to overturn this by means of a judicial review failed on procedural grounds.[182] Ironically, a similar attitude appears not to have been adopted towards Delaware LLPs which, though sharing many characteristics in common with a Jersey LLP, *have* been regarded as partnerships for tax purposes.

Clubs and societies

2–45   It follows from the terms in which partnership is defined by the Partnership Act 1890 that societies and clubs, which do not have as their object the acquisition of gain, are not partnerships; consistently with that conclusion, various cases show that their members are not as such liable for each other's acts.[183] Indeed, it has been recognised that an ordinary club is formed on the tacit understanding that its members do not become liable to pay any money beyond the subscription

---

[175] See the Insolvency Act 1986, s.84(1), as substituted by the Limited Liability Partnerships Regulations 2001, Sched. 3.

[176] See *ibid.* s.122(1), as substituted by *ibid.* and amended by the Limited Liability Partnerships (Amendment) Regulations 2005 (SI 2005/1989), Sched. 2, para. 6. One of the grounds for a winding up by the court is that the number of members of the LLP has reduced below 2: *ibid.* s.122(1)(c). As to claims for a winding up on the just and equitable ground, on the basis that the substratum of the LLP has gone, see *Tower Taxi Technology LLP v. Marsden* [2005] EWCA Civ. 1503 (Lawtel 14/101/05), a decision on a striking out application.

[177] Insolvency Act 1986, Pts. IV, VI and VII, as applied and amended by the Limited Liability Partnerships Regulations 2001, reg. 5, Sched. 3.

[178] See *infra*, paras 24–01 *et seq.*

[179] *ibid.* s.994(3), as amended and applied by the Limited Liability Partnerships (Application of Companies Act 2006) Regulations 2009, reg. 48.

[180] For a helpful review of the position in various other jurisdictions, see Whittaker & Machell, *The Law of Limited Liability Partnerships* (3rd ed.), Chap. 23.

[181] See the Limited Liability Partnerships (Jersey) Law 1996. It is understood that no Jersey LLPs were ever formed under this Law and its future is currently under review.

[182] See *R. v. I.R.C., ex p. Bishopp* [1999] S.T.C. 531. The court declined to express a view on the substantive issue.

[183] *Flemyng v. Hector* (1836) 2 M. & W. 172; *Caldicott v. Griffiths* (1853) 8 Ex. 898. See also *Todd v. Emly* (1841) 8 M. & W. 505; *The St. James's Club* (1852) 2 De G.M. & G. 383. And see, as to the nature of a club, *Fletcher v. Income Tax Commissioner* [1972] A.C. 414; *Kowloon Stock Exchange v. I.R.C.* [1985] 1 W.L.R. 133.

required by its rules.[184] Lord Lindley described it as "a mere misuse of words to call such associations partnerships".[185] If members *are* to be made liable, it will be by reason of their own acts[186] or the acts of their agents; in the latter case, the person who seeks to establish liability must prove the agency, since none will be implied by the mere fact of the association.[187] This principle is so clearly established that even the ordinary rule which entitles a trustee to be indemnified by his *cestui que trust*[188] does not apply as between the trustees of the club and individual members.[189]

Societies in which each member acts only for himself

It has been held that no partnership subsists between the members of a mutual insurance society, in which each member, in consideration of a payment made to him, underwrites a policy for a stipulated sum, on the ground that there is neither community of profit nor community of loss between them. A policy so underwritten in reality comprises a number of separate contracts, whereby each underwriter agrees, on a given event, to pay the whole or a proportionate part of the sum written against his name. In such a society there is no joint property nor do its members enter into any joint contract: each is alone liable to the insured, in accordance with the terms of the contract into which he has entered.[190]

2–46

---

[184] *Wise v. Perpetual Trustee Co.* [1903] A.C. 139; in the absence of an express power in the rules, the majority cannot even raise the subscriptions so as to bind existing members: *Harington v. Sendall* [1903] 1 Ch. 921. As to the effect of an express power to alter rules, see *Thellusson v. Valentia* [1906] 1 Ch. 480; [1907] 2 Ch. 1; *Doyle v. White City Stadium Ltd.* [1935] 1 K.B. 110.

[185] See *Blackpool Marton Rotary Club v. Martin* [1988] S.T.C. 823 (this aspect was not pursued in the Court of Appeal: see [1990] S.T.C. 1); also *Todd v. Emly*; *The St. James's Club*; *Wise v. Perpetual Trustee Co.*, *supra*; *R. v. Robson* (1885) 16 Q.B.D. 137. In *Lloyd v. Loaring* (1802) 6 Ves.Jr. 773, the Caledonian Lodge of Freemasons, and in *Silver v. Barnes* (1839) 6 Bing. N.C. 180 and *Beaumont v. Meredith* (1814) 3 V. & B. 180, friendly societies, were called partnerships, but this is incorrect: see *Re Lead Company's Workmen's Fund Soc.* [1904] 2 Ch. 196. In *Minnitt v. Lord Talbot* (1881) L.R.Ir. 1 Ch. 143, persons who had advanced money to add to and improve a club were held to have a lien on the property for their money. See further as to this case, (1881) L.R.Ir. 7 Ch. 407, and the comments thereon in *Wise v. Perpetual Trustee Co.* [1903] A.C. 139, 149, 150; *cf. Wylie v. Carlyon* [1922] 1 Ch. 51, where no lien or charge was created.

[186] As in *Cross v. Williams* (1862) 7 H. & N. 675, where the commandant of a rifle corps was held liable for all uniforms he had ordered; see also *Samuel Bros. Ltd. v. Whetherly* [1907] 1 K.B. 709; [1908] 1 K.B. 184. *cf. Lascelles v. Rathbun* (1919) 63 S.J. 410, where the commanding officer was not liable for goods supplied for the officers' mess.

[187] This sentence (in its original form) was cited with approval by Lord Parker in *London Association for Protection of Trade v. Greenlands Ltd.* [1916] 2 A.C. 15, 39, and by Fraser J. in *Hardie & Lane Ltd. v. Chiltern* [1928] 1 K.B. 663, 690; and see *Wise v. Perpetual Trustee Co.* [1903] A.C. 139. *cf. Flemyng v. Hector* (1836) 2 M. & W. 172 and *Wood v. Finch* (1861) 2 F. & F. 447 (where the agency was not established) with *Luckombe v. Ashton* (1862) 2 F. & F. 705; *Cockerell v. Aucompte* (1857) 2 C.B.(N.S.) 440; *Burls v. Smith* (1831) 7 Bing. 705; and *Delauney v. Strickland* (1818) 2 Stark. 416, (where it was). In *Luckombe v. Ashton* and *Burls v. Smith*, the defendant was a member of the managing committee. This was not the case in *Cockerell v. Aucompte* or *Delauney v. Strickland*. See also *Thomas v. Edwards* (1836) 2 M. & W. 215.

[188] *Hardoon v. Belilios* [1901] A.C. 118.

[189] *Wise v. Perpetual Trustee Co.* [1903] A.C. 139. As to subrogation, see *Wylie v. Carlyon* [1922] 1 Ch. 51.

[190] See *Strong v. Harvey* (1825) 3 Bing. 304; *Redway v. Sweeting* (1867) L.R. 2 Ex. 400; *Andrews' and Alexander's Case* (1869) 8 Eq. 176; *Gray v. Pearson* (1870) L.R. 5 C.P. 568. As to actions between the members of such societies, see *Bromley v. Williams* (1863) 32 Beav. 177; *Harvey v. Beckwith* (1864) 12 W.R. 819 and 896.

Although it was decided that such societies had for their object the acquisition of gain within the meaning of what, prior to its repeal,[191] became section 716 of the Companies Act 1985,[192] it is apprehended that, for the above reasons, they are still not partnerships within the meaning of the Partnership Act 1890.

Building Societies, Industrial and Provident Societies and Friendly Societies are all governed by specific statutes and do not require separate consideration.

European Economic Interest Groupings

2–47   The European Economic Interest Grouping or EEIG is a creation of EU law and was originally introduced in 1985 by means of an EC Council Regulation.[193] It consists of two or more individuals, companies or firms who carry on their principal activity or have their central administration in different Member States[194] and who combine together in order to develop their own respective businesses[195] rather than a joint business.[196] Consistently therewith, an EEIG cannot properly be formed with a view to making a profit for itself,[197] although there is obviously no objection to any incidental profits which may be realised being shared between its members.[198]

An EEIG must be registered in the Member State in which it has its official address[199] and its precise legal status will be determined by the law of the State where it is registered.[200] By virtue of the European Economic Interest Grouping

---

[191] See the Regulatory Reform (Reform of 20 Member Limit in Partnerships etc.) Order 2002 (SI 2002/3203), reg. 2.

[192] See the decisions under the corresponding section of the Companies Act 1862 (s.4): *Ex p. Hargrove* (1875) L.R. 10 Ch. 542; *Re Padstow Total Loss Association* (1882) 20 Ch.D. 137. As to mutual loan societies, see *Jennings v. Hammond* (1882) 9 Q.B.D. 225; *Shaw v. Benson* (1883) 11 Q.B.D. 563; *Ex p. Poppleton* (1884) 14 Q.B.D. 379; *Greenberg v. Cooperstein* [1926] Ch. 657. Freehold land societies did not require registration under that Act: *Re Siddall* (1885) 29 Ch.D. 1. See also as to carrying on business for gain, *England v. Webb* [1898] A.C. 758.

[193] Council Regulation 2137/85 of July 25, 1985. The text of this regulation is reproduced in the European Economic Interest Grouping Regulations 1989 (SI 1989/638), Sched. 1. For a more detailed consideration of the nature and regulation of an EEIG, see *Palmer's Company Law*, paras 16.201 *et seq.*

[194] It follows that an EEIG may not be formed between individuals, etc. based in the *same* Member State: Council Regulation 2137/85, Art. 4(2).

[195] The expression used in the Council Regulation 2137/85, Art. 3(1) is "economic activities" rather than "business".

[196] *ibid.* The activity of the EEIG must be related, but ancillary, to the economic activities of its members and it may not, *inter alia*, exercise any degree of control over its members' own activities or hold any shares in a member undertaking, employ more than 500 persons or be a member of another EEIG: *ibid.* Art. 3(1), (2). It should also be noted that, in the preamble to the Council Regulation, it is stated that "a grouping differs from a firm or company principally in its purpose, which is only to facilitate or develop the economic activities of its members to enable them to improve their own results" and that "by reason of that ancillary nature, grouping's activities must be related to the economic activities of its members but not replace them so that, for example, a grouping may not itself, with regard to third parties, practise a profession, the concept of economic activities being interpreted in its widest sense".

[197] *ibid.* Art. 3(1).

[198] *ibid.* Art. 21(1); see also *ibid.* Art. 40. As to the sharing of losses, see *ibid.* Art. 21(2).

[199] *ibid.* Art. 6. See also *ibid.* Arts 7, 10, 39(1).

[200] *ibid.* Art. 1(3). Note that *ibid.* Art. 1(2) provides that an EEIG will, once registered and irrespective of its legal status under the national law concerned, have the capacity to contract and to sue and be sued in its own name.

Regulations 1989,[201] an EEIG registered in the UK[202] will be a body corporate and will thus enjoy separate legal personality.[203] It naturally follows that it cannot exist as a partnership within the meaning of the Partnership Act 1890.[204] If an EEIG registered in some other Member State carries on any activities here,[205] it is considered that an English court would, on normal conflict principles, generally look to its status under the law of the State of registration.[206] However, whilst an EEIG displays many characteristics traditionally associated with partnership under English law,[207] it is doubted whether, given the express requirements of the Council Regulation, it could ever be said to involve "persons carrying on a business in common with a view of profit" in the sense contemplated by the Partnership Act 1890.[208]

4.   PARTNERSHIP IN EUROPE

Recognition and nationality of Member State partnerships

Partnership is recognised as a legal relationship throughout Europe and,   **2–48** provided that it has been formed in accordance with the laws of a Member State, and has its registered office or principal place of business within the EU, a firm will be treated for all purposes of EU law in the same way as a natural person who is a national of a Member State.[209]

Civil and commercial partnerships

All European jurisdictions recognise that partnership is a relationship founded   **2–49** on contract and thus accord partners considerable latitude in the terms which they

[201] SI 1989/638. These regulations were made pursuant to the powers conferred by the European Communities Act 1972, s.2(2) and were (*inter alia*) amended by the European Economic Interest Grouping (Amendment) Regulations 2009 (SI 2009/2399).

[202] European Economic Interest Grouping Regulations 1989, reg. 9, as amended by the European Economic Interest Grouping (Amendment) Regulations 2009, reg. 12.

[203] *ibid.* reg. 3 as amended by *ibid.* reg. 6.

[204] See the Partnership Act 1890, s.1(2), *supra*, para. 2–33.

[205] The 1989 Regulations do not require an EEIG which has its official address outside the United Kingdom to register under the Companies Act 2006, unless it maintains an establishment in the UK: European Economic Interest Grouping Regulations 1989, regs. 9(1), 12(1), as respectively amended by the European Economic Interest Grouping (Amendment) Regulations 2009, regs. 12(2), 15(2). See also Council Regulation 2137/85, Arts 6, 10.

[206] See Council Regulation 2137/85, Art. 2(1). And see, generally, Dicey & Morris, *The Conflict of Laws* (14th ed.), paras 30R–009 *et seq.*

[207] *e.g.* each member must have one vote on all issues (Council Regulation 2137/85, Art. 17(1)); major decisions affecting the EEIG must be taken unanimously (*ibid.* Art. 17(2)); members share profits equally in the absence of some other agreement (*ibid.* Art. 21(1)); members are subject to unlimited joint and several liability for debts, but only after the liquidation of the EEIG is completed (*ibid.* Art. 24(1)).

[208] s.1(1), *supra*, para. 2–01. Surely there is in reality no business in common?: see *supra*, n. 196. Moreover, the only legitimate "view of profit" is the profit to be realised by each member of the EEIG from carrying on his or its own business: see Council Regulation 2137/85, Art. 3(1). *Quaere*, could it be argued that there is a sufficient, albeit subsidiary, profit motive?: see further, *supra*, para. 2–08.

[209] Art. 54 of the Treaty on the Functioning of the European Union, as renumbered by the Treaty of Lisbon (formerly 48 EC, as renumbered by the Treaty of Amsterdam, Art. 12). As to the possibility of partnership involving a breach of *ibid.* Art. 101 (as renumbered by *ibid.*), see *infra*, para. 8–05.

may adopt, although a requirement for the registration of a commercial (as opposed to civil) partnership once formed is fairly widespread. This distinction between civil and commercial partnerships, which is still of importance in certain jurisdictions,[210] is not recognised by English or, for that matter, Irish law,[211] which is scarcely surprising given their common law origins. Although the distinction is now blurred in some States, and particularly in France, civil partnerships have traditionally been governed by the civil law as administered by the civil courts, whilst commercial partnerships have been governed by the commercial law as administered by the commercial courts.[212]

2–50   In some States, it is possible for prospective partners to opt for a commercial partnership irrespective of the nature of the business carried on,[213] but on the whole this is rare. In practice, in those States which recognise the civil partnership it is the object with which the partnership was formed which will determine its status. Thus, there are some activities which must be carried on through a civil partnership: these will include most land-based businesses, *e.g.* farming, building development, etc., the practice of various professions[214] and certain "one-off" ventures. On the other hand, where the business involves recognised commercial activities, particularly if they are performed continuously and repeatedly, the firm will almost certainly be treated as commercial, save in those States where the existence of such a partnership is dependent on the completion of certain formalities.

Most States also recognise the distinction between the general and limited partnership[215] and, in many instances, both types of partnership acquire separate legal personality on formation or, more commonly, as a result of registration.

It would be inappropriate in a work of this nature to engage in a more detailed analysis of the law of partnership in other jurisdictions, particularly given the expanding size of the EU.[216]

---

[210] *e.g.* France, Germany, Belgium and Spain.

[211] Partnerships in Ireland are still governed by the Partnership Act 1890 and the Limited Partnerships Act 1907. It should be noted that the distinction is also seemingly not recognised in a number of other States.

[212] Of course, there is inevitably a degree of overlap, so that in many cases parts of the civil law will apply to commercial partnerships; on the other hand, the commercial law is rarely, if ever, applied to civil partnerships. Equally, if a civil partnership carries out commercial activities, it may well become subject to the commercial law.

[213] France is the most obvious example, where prospective partners can choose the *société en nom collectif* instead of the *société civile*; Belgium and Spain appear to adopt a similar approach; similarly in the case of Austria. If there is any doubt as to which vehicle has been chosen, then it will be necessary to look at the objects of the partnership in order to identify whether they are civil or commercial. In some States, *e.g.* Germany, a partnership may start life as civil prior to the completion of the formalities requisite to qualify as a commercial partnership.

[214] Often referred to as the "liberal" professions, *e.g.* law, accountancy, medicine, dentistry, etc.

[215] In such States the law recognises that a limited partnership will, as here, comprise both general and limited partners, the latter being excluded from participation in the management of the firm.

[216] For a very helpful summary of the partnership law applicable in a number of Member States, see Andenas and Wooldridge, *European Comparative Company Law* (2009).

CHAPTER 3

GENERAL NATURE OF A PARTNERSHIP

1.   THE COMMERCIAL AND LEGAL VIEWS

The commercial view

PARTNERS are, in both commercial and legal terms, collectively referred to as "a   **3–01**
firm",[1] but with very different underlying perspectives.[2] Thus, the usual commercial view of partnership, as reflected in the approach of most accountants,
involves treating a firm in much the same way as a company, *i.e.* as an entity
distinct from its members and with independent rights and obligations.[3] As a
consequence, in drawing up partnership accounts, where money is due to or from
a partner he will normally be shown as a creditor or debtor of the *firm* and not
as a creditor or debtor of his co-partners.[4]

Consistently with its perceived status as a separate entity, there is a tendency   **3–02**
to regard a firm's rights and obligations as unaffected by any change in its
membership: in effect, the rights and obligations of the "old" firm prior to the
change are automatically deemed to have been assumed by the "new" firm. Lord
Lindley summarised the thinking which lies at the heart of the commercial view
in the following terms:

> "The partners are the agents and sureties of the firm: its agents for the transaction of
> its business; its sureties for the liquidation of its liabilities so far as the assets of the
> firm are insufficient to meet them. The liabilities of the firm are regarded as the
> liabilities of the partners only in case they cannot be met by the firm and discharged
> out of its assets."

This attitude is, if anything, encouraged by certain attributes displayed by a   **3–03**
majority of firms, ranging from the adoption of a distinctive name which is
unrelated to the names of the partners to the maintenance of a separate bank
account in the firm name. Because of these attributes, changes in a firm tend to

---

[1] Partnership Act 1890, s.4. See, as to the effect of this section under Scots law (where the firm has
separate legal personality), *Jardine-Paterson v. Fraser* 1974 S.L.T. 93, Ct. of Sess; also *Maillie v.
Swanney* 2000 S.L.T. 464, 468F *per* Lord Penrose. A single partner cannot constitute a firm in
anything other than a commercial sense: *Oswald Hickson Collier & Co. v. Carter-Ruck* [1984] A.C.
720 note, 721G *per* Denning M.R.; *Re C. & M. Ashberg, The Times*, July 17, 1990; *Re Rogers* [2006]
1 W.L.R. 1577, 1581B *per* Lightman J. See also *infra*, para. 3–08.
[2] In drawing a distinction between the two views, which he styled the mercantile and the legal,
Lord Lindley acknowledged his obligations to Cory's *Treatise on Accounts* (Pickering, 2nd ed., 1839)
and to a paper by J. M. Ludlow entitled "On the mercantile notion of the firm, and the need of its
legal recognition," in the 2nd vol. of the Papers read before the Juridical Society, p. 40.
[3] See *supra*, para. 2–34. For a recent summary of the commercial view, see *R v. L* [2009] 1 Cr. App.
R. 16 at [14].
[4] A relatively recent (albeit ultimately unsuccessful) example of this approach can be seen in
MacKinlay v. Arthur Young McClelland Moores & Co. [1990] 2 A.C. 239.

have no visible effect on its existence or on the continuity of its business; in short, partners may come and go but the firm *appears* to go on.

The legal view and its implications

3-04   The legal view of a firm is very different: in English law, the firm is not generally recognised as an entity distinct from the partners composing it.[5] Admittedly, in taking partnership accounts and in administering partnership assets, the courts have to some extent adopted the commercial view; moreover, actions may be brought by or against partners in the firm name.[6] There are also a number of statutory exceptions.[7] These apart, the general rule holds good, although there are occasional anomalies. Thus, whilst it has been held that a firm as such cannot be a tenant and claim protection under Part II of the Landlord and Tenant Act 1954,[8] in *Prudential Assurance Co. Ltd. v. Ayres*[9] a lease was purportedly assigned to a firm and no issue was taken as to the validity of that assignment.

Lord Lindley stated the orthodox legal view as follows:

> "The law, ignoring the firm, looks to the partners composing it; any change amongst them destroys the identity of the firm; what is called the property of the firm is their property, and what are called the debts and liabilities of the firm are their debts and their liabilities.[10] In point of law, a partner may be the debtor or the creditor of his co-partners, but he cannot be either debtor or creditor of a firm of which he is himself a member."[11]

---

[5] See *Meyer & Co. v. Faber (No. 2)* [1923] 2 Ch. 421; see also *Hoare v. Oriental Bank Corporation* (1877) 2 App.Cas. 589; *Ex p. Corbett* (1880) 14 Ch.D. 122, 126 *per* James L.J.; *Ex p. Gliddon* (1884) 13 Q.B.D. 43; *Sadler v. Whiteman* [1910] 1 K.B. 868, 889 *per* Farwell L.J. (affirmed [1910] A.C. 674); *R. v. Holden* [1912] 1 K.B. 483; *Malkinson v. Trim* [2003] 1 W.L.R. 463 at [23] *per* Chadwick L.J.; *Hammonds (A Firm) v. Danilunas* [2009] EWHC 216 (Ch) (Lawtel 18/2/09) at [8(b)], [106] *per* Warren J. (this aspect was not commented on in the Court of Appeal *sub nom Hammonds (A firm) v. Jones* [2009] EWCA Civ 1400 (Lawtel 21/12/09)). Note also, in this context, *BP Oil UK Ltd. v. Lloyds TSB Bank plc* [2005] 3 E.G. 116 (CS) (CA) (although this brief report does not disclose that the three companies were originally partners); *Kelly v. Northern Ireland Housing Executive* [1999] A.C. 428 (HL). As to Scotland, see the Partnership Act 1890, s.4(2); *Jardine-Paterson v. Fraser* 1974 S.L.T. 93, Ct. of Sess.; note also *Arif v. Levy & McRae* 1992 G.W.D. 3–156.

[6] As to actions, see CPR r. 7.2A, 7PDA, paras 5A.1, 5A.3, *infra*, paras A2–03, A2–04. And see also *infra*, paras 14–04 *et seq.*

[7] Thus, a firm may be registered in the firm name under the Value Added Tax Act 1994, s.45(1) (see *infra*, para. 37–08) and may be appointed as a statutory auditor under the Companies Act 2006, ss.1212, 1216(1), (2).

[8] *Kissane & Clarke v. Jones*, September 26, 1975, and March 1, 1976, unreported, discussed at (1976) 120 S.J. 827, 850. The position is more complex in Scotland: see *IRC v. Graham's Trustees* 1971 S.L.T. 46 (HL); *Jardine-Paterson v. Fraser* 1974 S.L.T. 93, Ct of Sess.; *Lujo Properties Ltd. v. Green* 1997 S.L.T. 225; *Moray Estates Development Co. v. Butler* 1999 S.C.L.R. 447 (OH); *Hiskett v. The Now Dissolved Firm of G & G Wilson* 2003 G.W.D. 38–1036 (OH).

[9] [2008] 1 All E.R. 1266 (CA). As to the effect in law, see *infra*, para. 18–63.

[10] This sentence was approved by the Supreme Court of Canada in *Backman v. R*, 3 I.T.L. Rep. 647 at [41]. See also *Byford v. Oliver* [2003] E.M.L.R. 20 at [26]; *Wan v. General Commissioners for Division of Doncaster*, 76 T.C. 211.

[11] *Green v. Hertzog* [1954] 1 W.L.R. 1309. See also Lord Cottenham's judgment in *Richardson v. The Bank of England* (1838) 4 My. & Cr. 165, 171, 172; *De Tastet v. Shaw* (1818) 1 B. & A. 664; *Lee v. Neuchatel Asphalte Co.* (1886) 41 Ch.D. 1. And see *Ellis v. Kerr* [1910] 1 Ch. 529; *Napier v. Williams* [1911] 1 Ch. 361, as to the invalidity of covenants entered into by a man with himself and others jointly before the alteration of the law by the Law of Property Act 1925, s.82. In *Rye v. Rye* [1961] Ch. 70, 78, Lord Evershed M.R. expressed the view that, whilst partners may be able to grant a lease to themselves, they cannot make any covenants therein which are enforceable. *cf.* Lord Ratcliffe's analysis in the House of Lords at [1962] A.C. 496, 512.

The following helpful statement of principle was made by Eichelbaum C.J. in   **3–05**
Hadlee v. Commissioner of Inland Revenue[12]:

> "In law the retirement of a partner or the admission of a new partner, constitutes the
> dissolution of the old partnership, and the formation of a new partnership.[13] Here
> upon the happening of such events there were no overt signs of dissolution; the
> partnership's financial structure and arrangements were such that none was required
> but that does not alter the underlying legal significance of any retirement or new
> admission."[14]

It is, of course, open to the partners to agree as between themselves that a
change in the firm will not affect the continuation of their partnership,[15] but this
only has effect as a matter of contract and does not alter the legal analysis set out
above. Although it has been held that Lord Lindley's proposition is not of general
application and is dependent on the precise terms of the partnership agreement,
it is submitted that this decision is unsupported by any authority and must be
regarded as *per incuriam*.[16]

It follows that any breach of a duty which one partner owes to his fellow   **3–06**
partners prior to a change in the firm will be actionable as between those partners
but the right of action will not pass automatically to the "new" firm which comes
into existence by virtue of the change.[17]

It should be added that a partner cannot be employed by his own firm, for no
man can employ himself.[18] Equally, it would seem that a partnership cannot itself
be an employee.[19] In the same way, as will be seen hereafter,[20] a partnership
cannot be a partner in another firm nor can it become a member of a limited

---

[12] [1989] N.Z.L.R. 447, 455. This case went to the New Zealand Court of Appeal and, ultimately,
to the Privy Council (see [1993] A.C. 524), but Eichelbaum C.J.'s original decision was upheld.

[13] To the same effect is the judgment of Judge Mackie Q.C. sitting as a judge of the Chancery
Division in *HLB Kidsons v. Lloyd's Underwriters* [2009] 1 All E.R. (Comm) 760 at [16].

[14] At this point Echelbaum C.J. cited *I.R.C. v. Gibbs* [1942] A.C. 402; *Brace v. Calder* [1895] 2
Q.B. 253 and an earlier edition of this work.

[15] See the remainder of the passage from the judgment in *Hadlee v. Commissioner of Inland
Revenue*, *supra*, reproduced *infra* para. 10–39; also *infra*, para. 24–02.

[16] *Cummings v. Stockdale*, November 11, 2008 , a decision of H.H. Judge Raynor, sitting as a judge
of the Chancery Division. See further as to this decision, *infra*, paras 9–13, 10–257.

[17] *Global Partners Fund Ltd. v. Babcock & Brown Ltd.* [2010] NSWSC 270. An argument that the
claim constituted partnership property failed. See further *infra*, paras 14–50, 18–22. This aspect was
not, ultimately, decisive on the appeal at [2010] NSWCA 196.

[18] On this basis, it was held in *Ellis v. Joseph Ellis & Co.* [1905] 1 K.B. 324 that a partner who
worked for the partnership at a weekly wage was not entitled to compensation under the Workman's
Compensation Act 1897; see also *Cowell v. Quilter Goodison Co. Ltd.* [1989] I.R.L.R. 393 (CA);
Train v. DTE Business Advisory Services Ltd. (UKEAT/0201/08/LA) (Lawtel 10/3/09); *Protectacoat
Firthglow Ltd. v. Szilagyi* [2009] I.R.L.R. 365 at [35] *per* Smith L.J. It follows that such a partner's
"salary" will inevitably be treated as part of his profit share for tax purposes: *MacKinlay v. Arthur
Young McClelland Moores & Co.* [1990] 2 A.C. 239, 249C. Note, however, that in *Rowley Holmes
& Co. v. Barber* [1977] 1 W.L.R. 371, it was held that a legal executive in his capacity as executor
of a deceased sole proprietor of a firm of solicitors *could* employ himself for redundancy payment
purposes. It should also be noted that a limited liability partnership *may*, in certain circumstances, be
regarded as the employer of one or more of its members: see the Limited Liability Partnerships Act
2000, s.4(4). The drafting of this provision leaves much to be desired (see *supra*, para. 2–39), but did
not appear to give the EAT much difficulty in *Kovats v. TFO Management LLP* [2009] I.C.R.
1140.

[19] See the *obiter* view expressed by Sedley L.J. in *Protectacoat Firthglow Ltd. v. Szilagyi*, *supra*,
at [74].

[20] See *infra*, para. 4–27.

liability partnership.[21] A Scottish partnership, which has separate legal personality,[22] will be in a different position.

Status and liability of a partner

3–07   Also central to an understanding of the law of partnership is the dual capacity in which a partner acts, *i.e.* both as a principal and an agent. Lord Lindley explained:

> "As a principal [a member of an ordinary partnership[23]] is bound by what he does himself and by what his co-partners do on behalf of the firm,[24] provided they keep within the limits of their authority; as an agent, he binds them by what he does for the firm, provided he keeps within the limits of his authority."

Thus, where a partner receives money belonging to the firm, he will do so both as principal (*i.e.* for himself) and as agent for his co-partners; in those circumstances, he cannot be treated as having received the money in a fiduciary capacity.[25]

However, as Lord Lindley took care to point out, it is wrong to regard a partner as a mere surety for the firm's debts[26]: as a principal, he is personally liable to meet those debts, whether or not they could be met out of the partnership assets.[27]

2.   STATUS OF FIRM IN SPECIFIC CONTEXTS

(a) Firm name

3–08   It is important to identify the precise significance of a firm name since, as previously noted,[28] it represents an attribute which tends to encourage the

---

[21] See the Companies Act 2006, s.164, as substituted by the Limited Liability Partnerships (Application of Companies Act 2006) Regulations 2009 (SI 2009/1804), reg. 18. *Per contra* if, under the law of its formation, the partnership has separate legal personality: *ibid.* This reflects the pre-existing view of the Registrar of Companies, even though it has been argued that the expression "person" in the Limited Liability Partnerships Act 2000, s.4 includes an unincorporated body (Interpretation Act 1978, s.5, Sched. 1): see Whittaker & Machell *The Law of Limited Liability Partnerships* (3rd ed.), para. 2.3. However, their view does not take account of the difficulty of applying the Limited Liability Partnerships Act 2000, ss.6 (members as agents), 7 (ex-members), 8 (designated members) or 9 (registration of membership changes). Thus, where the supposed member firm changes its composition, a new firm will, as a matter of law, come into existence and the old firm will be dissolved (see *supra*, paras 3–01 *et seq.*), but the firm name will remain the same. How could that change be registered under *ibid.* s.9(1) (as amended) in any meaningful way? How can notice be given to a person dealing with the LLP for the purposes of *ibid.* s.6(3)(a)? In the circumstances, it is submitted that the context in any event requires "person" to exclude a firm.

[22] Partnership Act 1890, s.4(2).

[23] It is presumed that by this expression, Lord Lindley referred to a partnership governed by the general law (rather than by some special contractual arrangement), since it is difficult to see what other form of partnership could have existed at that time. Now, of course, there exists the limited partnership, in which the limited partners have *no* authority to bind the firm: see the Limited Partnerships Act 1907, s.6(1) and *infra*, paras 30–01 *et seq.*

[24] Ironically, the use of the expression "the firm" in this context itself gives succour to the commercial view.

[25] *Piddocke v. Burt* [1894] 1 Ch. 343.

[26] See *supra*, para. 3–02.

[27] Until the law was altered by the Partnership Act 1890, s.23, the property of the firm was, of course, liable to be seized for the private debts of any of the partners composing it.

[28] See *supra*, para. 3–03.

commercial rather than the legal view of a firm. Lord Lindley put it in this way:

" . . . the name under which a firm carries on business is in point of law a conventional name applicable only to the persons who, on each particular occasion when the name is used, are members of the firm."[29]

Once this point is understood, the fallacy of the commercial view becomes apparent. The firm name is a convenient method of describing a group of persons associated together in business at a certain point of time: no more and no less.[30]

It follows that confusion will inevitably arise where an individual "A" trades under the name "A & Co." or continues to trade in the name of a former firm, either because he has become the sole continuing partner or because he is otherwise to be regarded as its successor, *e.g.* following a purchase of its goodwill. In such cases A is, and at all times remains, a sole proprietor and no question of partnership arises. When applied to such a person, the term "sole partner", although used in common parlance, is both inappropriate and misleading.[31]

When a firm is referred to by its name or trading style, evidence is admissible **3–09** to show who in fact was a member of the firm at the relevant time.[32] If a number of people carry on business under such a name or style, anything which they may do in that name or style will be just as effective as if their individual names had been used. An obvious example of this is the use of firm names on bills of exchange and promissory notes; indeed, more formal contracts *may* be valid, even though some of the executing parties are described as "A & Co."[33] It was formerly the case that partners might be registered as shareholders in the firm name,[34] but they could not insist on being so registered,[35] but it is now an express

[29] See the Partnership Act 1890, s.4(1). A firm should now be described in the claim form as "XYZ & Co. (a Firm)": see CPR 16PD, para. 2.6(c)(i), *infra*, para. A2–08. It would seem that the former alternatives, i.e. "XYZ & Co. (sued as a firm)" or "X, Y and Z trading as XYZ & Co." should no longer be used.

[30] See, for example, *Ernst & Young v. Butte Mining Plc (No. 2)* [1997] 1 W.L.R. 1485, 1491E–1492C *per* Lightman J.; *Hammonds (A Firm) v. Danilunas* [2009] EWHC 216 (Ch) (Lawtel 18/2/09) at [106] *per* Warren J. (this point was not discussed on the appeal). Of less interest in this context is the exceptional decision in *United Video Properties/Program Guide* (T482/02) [2005] E.P.O.R. 42, where a firm's opposition to a European patent failed because it was submitted in the firm name rather than in the names of the partners. However, the firm in question had been requested to provide proof of its legal status and had declined to do so and had, moreover, failed to provide details of the relevant partners' names and addresses. No principle of general application is established thereby.

[31] *Alexander Mountain & Co. v. Rumere* [1948] W.N. 243, reversed (on the facts) at [1948] 2 K.B. 436; *Oswald Hickson Collier & Co. v. Carter Ruck* [1984] A.C. 720 note, 721G *per* Denning M.R.; *Re C. & M. Ashberg, The Times*, July 17, 1990; *Re Rogers* [2006] 1 W.L.R. 1577, 1581B *per* Lightman J. See also *W. Hill & Son v. Tannerhill* [1944] K.B. 472 (CA), where Hill, trading without partners as W. Hill & Son, issued a writ in the supposed firm name contrary to what was then RSC Ord. 48A (see now CPR 7PDA, paras 5A.1, 5A.3). The relevant limitation period having expired, it was held that Hill might nevertheless amend the writ by substituting himself as plaintiff. Note also the decisions in *Harold Fielding Ltd. v. Mansi* [1974] I.C.R. 347; *Allen & Son v. Coventry* [1980] I.C.R. 9; *Jeetle v. Elster* [1985] I.C.R. 389.

[32] *Carruthers v. Sheddon* (1815) 6 Taunt. 15; *Bass v. Clive* (1815) 4 M. & S. 13; *Stubbs v. Sargon* (1838) 3 My. & Cr. 507; also *Latouche v. Waley* (1832) Hayes & Jones (Ir.Ex.) 43.

[33] See further *infra*, paras 12–151 *et seq.*

[34] *Weikersheim's Case* (1873) L.R. 8 Ch.App. 831.

[35] *Re Vagliano Anthracite Collieries Ltd.* [1910] W.N. 187, where the definition of "person" contained in the Interpretation Act 1889, s.19 (now the Interpretation Act 1978, Sched. 1), was not

requirement of the Companies Act 2006 that the register of members state the name of each joint holder separately, even if they are otherwise regarded as a single member.[36] Partners are just as much joint holders as others in that position.

Effect of change in the partners

3–10 Because the firm name represents no more than a convenient means of describing the partners who for the time being make up the firm, whenever the partners change that name must take on a new meaning. This can lead to a number of complications, as the following examples (which are, for convenience, arranged in alphabetical order) demonstrate.

Advances to a firm

3–11 An authority given to trustees to lend money to a firm would not, as a general rule, authorise a loan to the continuing partners after one partner has died or retired.[37]

Authority given to or on behalf of firm

3–12 An authority given to two partners to take out insurance in their names does not authorise them to insure in the names of themselves and a third party whom they have subsequently taken into partnership.[38] Similarly, if a firm, A, B and C, has an agent D, and C retires, D may continue to be the agent of the firm but he will in reality be the agent of A and B, but not of C.[39]

Companies Act 2006, Part 41

3–13 If there is a change of partners and the new firm continues to use the old name, this will often bring the firm within the scope of Part 41 of the Companies Act 2006. As a result it may no longer be permissible to retain the name[40] or it may be necessary to apply to the Secretary of State for written approval of the name,[41] and to ensure that the requisite information is included on all documents issued

adverted to. Note also that, in *Dunster's Case* [1894] 3 Ch. 473, the Registrar of Joint Stock Companies appears to have insisted that the company's memorandum of association could not properly be signed in a firm name; it is assumed that a similar attitude would be adopted in the case of a firm seeking to subscribe to a memorandum of association under the Companies Act 2006, s.8 in its firm name.

[36] *ibid.* s.113(5). *cf.* the approach adopted in the case of the register kept by an LLP: Companies Act 2006, s.164, as substituted and applied by the Limited Liability Partnerships (Application of Companies Act 2006) Regulations 2009 (SI 2009/1804), reg. 18.

[37] See *Fowler v. Reynal* (1851) 3 Mac. & G. 500; *Re Tucker* [1894] 1 Ch. 724, affirmed [1894] 3 Ch. 429; *Smith v. Patrick* [1901] A.C. 282.

[38] *Barron v. Fitzgerald* (1840) 6 Bing.N.C. 201. But of course a continuance of the authority may be inferred from subsequent dealings with the new firm. See *Pariente v. Lubbock* (1856) 8 De G. M. & G. 5.

[39] See *Jones v. Shears* (1836) 4 A. & E. 832.

[40] Companies Act 2006, ss.1197(1), 1198(1) and the Company and Business Names (Miscellaneous Provisions) Regulations 2009 (SI 2009/1085), Pt. 4 (as amended by the Company, Limited Liability Partnership and Business Names (Miscellaneous Provisions) (Amendment) Regulations 2009 (SI 2009/2404)).

[41] Companies Act 2006, ss.1193(1), 1194(1); also the Company, Limited Liability Partnership and Business Names (Sensitive Words and Expressions) Regulations 2009 (SI 2009/2615). It may, however be permissible to continue to use the name for 12 months under *ibid.* s.1199(3); *sed quaere.* See further, *infra*, para. 3–32.

by the firm and that a suitable notice is displayed in the partnership premises.[42]

Conveyance to a firm

In *Wray v. Wray*,[43] it was held that a conveyance of freeholds to "William **3–14** Wray in fee simple" passed the legal estate to the persons who were at the date of the conveyance the members of the firm which traded under that name.[44]

Employees of firm

A change in the firm will not generally affect the employees' continuity of **3–15** employment for the purposes of the Employment Rights Act 1996.[45] This is so even where the partnership is dissolved but the employment is continued by one of the former partners.[46]

Executorships and trusteeships

Where a testator appoints a firm—such as a firm of solicitors—to be the **3–16** executors and/or trustees of his will, only partners at the time the will was made can act[47]; partners admitted subsequently are only eligible if the testator has framed the appointment in such a way as to include them.[48]

Legacy to a firm

If a legacy is left to a firm, the legacy is, in the absence of a contrary intention, **3–17** payable to those partners who were members of the firm at the date of the will.[49]

[42] *ibid.* ss.1202–1204. See also *infra*, para. 3–33.
[43] [1905] 2 Ch. 349.
[44] See also *Maugham v. Sharpe* (1864) 17 C.B.(N.S.) 443 (a mortgage); *Brutton v. Burton* (1819) 1 Chit. 707 (a warrant of attorney); *Evans v. Curtis* (1826) 2 C. & P. 296 (an agreement for a lease); *Moller v. Lambert* (1810) 2 Camp. 548 (a bond); *Gorrie v. Woodley* (1864) 17 I.C.L.R. 221 (a guarantee); *Latouche v. Waley* (1832) Hayes & Jones (Ir.Ex.) 43; also *infra*, paras 14–29 *et seq.* For the current effect of a conveyance to partners see the Law of Property Act 1925, s.34(2) (as amended by the Trusts of Land and Appointment of Trustees Act 1996, Sched. 2, para. 3(2)); also *infra*, para. 18–32.
[45] See *ibid.* s.218(5) and the decision in *Stevens v. Bower* [2004] I.R.L.R. 957 (CA); see also *Harold Fielding Ltd. v. Mansi* [1974] I.C.R. 347; *Allen & Son v. Coventry* [1980] I.C.R. 9; *Jeetle v. Elster* [1985] I.C.R. 389; see also an article at 136 N.L.J. 353; *cf. Brace v. Calder* [1895] 2 Q.B. 253, considered *infra*, para. 3–41; *Briggs v. Oates* [1990] I.C.R. 473. The employees' rights would also be protected by the Transfer of Undertakings (Protection of Employment) Regulations 2006 (SI 2006/246). But see also, *infra*, para. 25–03.
[46] The *obiter* views expressed by Beldam J. in *Jeetle v. Elster supra*, were approved by the Court of Appeal in *Stevens v. Bower, supra*, where the partnership had been dissolved by reason of illegality and the business carried on by the sole remaining qualified "partner". Note that in *Jeetle v. Elster* the partner who continued Mrs Elster's employment had acquired premises and equipment from the firm; *cf.* the position in *S.I. (Systems and Instruments) v. Grist & Riley* [1983] I.C.R. 788 (which did not concern a firm). See also, as regards the effect of a general dissolution, *Tunstall v. Condon* [1980] I.C.R. 786; *Briggs v. Oates* [1990] I.C.R. 473; *Barnes v. Leavesley* [2001] I.C.R. 38; *Rose v. Dodd* [2005] I.C.R. 1776 (both of the latter cases concerning the effect of an intervention in a solicitors' partnership); and *infra*, paras 25–02, 25–03.
[47] However, if there are more than four of such partners, they cannot all accept the appointment: Trustee Act 1925, s.34(2) (as amended by the Trusts of Land and Appointment of Trustees Act 1996, Sched. 2, para. 3(2)); Senior Courts Act 1981, s.114(1) (formerly the Supreme Court Act 1981: Constitutional Reform Act 2005, Sched. 11, Pt.1 , para. 1(1)).
[48] See *Re Horgan* [1971] P. 50. As to the position where the firm has since transferred its business to an LLP, see *Re Rogers* [2006] 1 W.L.R. 1577.
[49] See *Stubbs v. Sargon* (1838) 3 My. & Cr. 507; *Re Smith* [1914] 1 Ch. 937. In *Mayberry v. Brooking* (1855) 7 De G. M. & G. 673, a legacy of a debt due to A was held to pass A's interest in a debt due to him and his co-partners. *cf. Ex p. Kirk* (1877) 5 Ch.D. 800.

Moreover, if a legacy is left to the "representatives" of an old firm, it will be payable to the personal representatives of the last survivor of the partners of that firm, and not to its successors in business.[50]

Offices and appointments held by firm

3–18   If a firm is by name appointed to a particular office, it is the partners at the time of such appointment who will, in law, fill that office, since the firm, as such, cannot, *unless* it enjoys separate legal personality.[51] Equally, the rights annexed to that office will only be exercisable by such partners and not, in the absence of some contrary intention, by partners admitted subsequently[52] or, for that matter, by a successor to the firm's business.[53] However, there are occasional exceptions to this principle: thus, the Companies Act 2006 now permits a firm *as such* to be appointed as the statutory auditor of a company[54] and, moreover, provides for such an appointment to devolve on a successor firm[55] or a sole continuing "partner",[56] provided that the eligibility conditions are satisfied.[57]

The mere fact that an office cannot be held by a firm will not, of itself, prevent it being held *on behalf* of the partners for the time being, so that it can, effectively, be treated as partnership property.[58]

Rights in and to firm name

3–19   Unless it forms part of the goodwill of the firm (as will usually be the case),[59] there is no proprietary right in a firm name[60]; nor, apart from certain statutory restraints[61] and questions of passing off,[62] is there any restriction on partners'

---

[50] *Leak v. M'Dowall* (1863) 3 N.R. 185; *Kerrison v. Reddington* (1847) 11 I.Eq.R. 451. And see *Greville v. Greville* (1859) 27 Beav. 594.

[51] *De Mazar v. Pybus* (1799) 4 Ves.Jr. 644; note also *Kelly v. Northern Ireland Housing Executive* [1999] A.C. 428 (HL). And see, as to Scotland, *Kirkintilloch Equitable Co-operative Society Ltd. v. Livingstone* 1972 S.L.T. 154, Ct. of Sess. In New Zealand it has been held that a firm cannot be appointed to act as director or secretary of a company: *Commercial Management Ltd. v. Registrar of Companies* [1987] N.Z.L.R. 744. The position is the same under the Companies Act 2006: *ibid.* ss.163, 164 (directors), 273, 277, 278 (secretaries).

[52] See *Barron v. Fitzgerald* (1840) 6 Bing.N.C. 201; *Stevens v. Benning* (1855) 1 K. & J. 168.

[53] *Hole v. Bradbury* (1879) 12 Ch.D. 886; *Robson v. Drummond* (1831) 2 B. & Ad. 303; see also *infra*, para. 3–39.

[54] Companies Act 2006, s.1216(1), (2).

[55] A firm will only be treated as a successor firm for this purpose if it has substantially the same members as the original firm and if it succeeded to the whole or substantially the whole of that firm's business: *ibid.* s.1216(3)(a), (4).

[56] *ibid.* s.1216(3)(b), (4)(b). The expression "sole partner" is, of course, something of a misnomer: see *supra*, para. 3–08.

[57] *ibid.* s.1212.

[58] See further, *infra*, para. 18–43.

[59] Lord Lindley observed "The name by which a firm is known is not of itself the property of the firm . . . ". Moreover, it does not necessarily follow that goodwill (and any associated name) will always be partnership property, see, for example, *Miles v. Clark* [1953] 1 W.L.R. 537, noted *infra*, para. 18–36.

[60] See, for example, *Benhams Ltd. v. Brown*, Unreported June 24, 1999 CA (Civ Div); also *HFC Bank Plc v. Midland Bank Plc* [2000] F.S.R. 176, 180 *per* Lloyd J.; *McPhail v. Bourne* [2008] EWHC 1235 (Ch) (Lawtel 13/6/08) at [287] *per* Morgan J.; and see *infra*, para. 3–23. Note, however, the decision in *Barr v. Lions* 1956 S.L.T. 250, where a Scots court appears to have accepted the propriety of a transfer of a business name independently of goodwill. And note also that in *Baker v. Benson*, August 3, 1988 (unreported), Hoffmann J. appears to have accepted that goodwill *can* exist in a firm name or part thereof; *sed quaere*.

[61] See *infra*, paras 8–26 *et seq.*

[62] See *infra*, para. 3–20.

freedom to adopt the name of their choice.[63] Indeed, they may adopt more than one name,[64] even though neither the Partnership Act 1890 nor Part 41 of the Companies Act 2006 directly seem to contemplate this possibility.[65] However, whether or not the firm name is a partnership asset,[66] it would seem that a partner may not make use of it in order to secure some private benefit for himself.[67]

Passing off

A firm may not adopt a name similar to that of another firm or comprising a **3–20** name or description of goods or services which has become identified with, and indicative of, goods produced or services supplied by another firm, in such a way as to pass itself off as being, or its goods or services as produced or supplied by, that other firm.[68] The position may be otherwise if the name is no longer capable of being used by the originator firm. Thus, in *Byford v. Oliver*[69] it was held that individual former members of the heavy metal band "Saxon", which was a partnership at will and had long since been dissolved, had no right to the name and, thus, could not claim that a subsequent band adopting that name was guilty of passing off. The position might have been otherwise if the claim had been made by or on behalf of the dissolved partnership, unless its right to the name could properly be regarded as having been abandoned. However, the fact that the name has not been in use is not, *per se*, fatal, provided that the right to the goodwill has been retained.[70]

Equally, there can be no objection to a person carrying on a business in his own name[71] or in a name which he, either alone or in partnership with others,[72] has

---

[63] See also *infra*, paras 5–45 *et seq.*

[64] Note that, in *Baker v. Benson, supra,* Hoffmann J. held that the firm had goodwill in its name *and* in a contraction of that name which had been used by a predecessor practice.

[65] See the Partnership Act 1890, s.4(1). As to the position under the Companies Act 2006, Pt. 41, see *infra*, para. 3–30.

[66] See *supra* n. 59.

[67] Partnership 1890, s.29; *Aas v. Benham* [1891] 2 Ch. 244; and see *infra*, paras 16–13 *et seq. Semble*, the application of this section is not dependent on establishing that the firm name is partnership property.

[68] As to the basic requirements for a passing-off action, see *Erven Warnink B.V. v. J. Townend & Sons (Hull) Ltd.* [1979] A.C. 731 and the earlier cases cited therein; also *Reckitt & Colman Products Ltd. v. Borden Inc.* [1990] 1 W.L.R. 491; *County Sound plc v. Ocean Sound Ltd.* [1991] F.S.R. 367; *Harrods Ltd. v. Harrodian School Ltd.* [1996] R.P.C. 697 (CA); *Dawnay Day Co. Ltd. v. Cantor Fitzgerald International* [2000] R.P.C. 669 (CA); *Sir Robert McAlpine Ltd. v. Alfred McAlpine Plc* [2004] R.P.C. 36; *Evans v. Focal Point Fires PLC* [2010] R.P.C. 15 and note also *Pontiac Marina Pte Ltd. v. CDL Hotels International Ltd.* [1997] F.S.R. 725. It should be noted that a passing-off action may be brought in England to protect the goodwill of a foreign business, where that goodwill prospectively extends to England: *Maxim's Ltd. v. Dye* [1977] 1 W.L.R. 1155; *cf. Anheuser-Busch Inc. v. Budejovicky Budvar N.P.* [1984] F.S.R. 413. See also *My Kinda Bones Ltd. (T/A Chicago Rib Shack) v. Dr. Pepper's Stove Co. Ltd. (T/A Dr. Pepper's Manhattan Rib Shack)* [1984] F.S.R. 289; *Hotel Cipriani SRL v. Cipriani (Grosvenor Street) Ltd.* [2010] R.P.C. 16 (CA).

[69] [2003] E.M.L.R. 20. And see also *Gill v Frankie Goes To Hollywood Ltd.* [2008] E.T.M.R. 4 (OHIM, Opposition Division).

[70] *Farmacia Chemists Ltd.'s Application v. Opposition of Pharmacia AB* [2005] E.T.M.R. 41.

[71] As to the fetters which may be imposed on the use of a person's own name following disposal of a business carried on by him, note the decision in *I. N. Newman Ltd. v. Adlem* [2006] F.S.R. 16 (CA). And see also *Asprey and Garrard Ltd. v. WRA (Guns) Ltd.* [2002] F.S.R. 30.

[72] *Fine Cotton Spinners and Doublers' Assoc. Ltd. v. Harwood Cash & Co. Ltd.* [1907] 2 Ch. 184, 188 *per* Joyce J.

acquired by reputation[73]; it follows that partners cannot be restrained from adopting a firm name which genuinely seeks to identify the membership of the firm, merely on the ground that it is so similar to the name of an established firm that mistakes are almost certain to arise.[74] Similarly, if the goodwill of a firm which originally carried on business under that name has been acquired by a successor firm.[75] *Per contra*, if the name is adopted dishonestly and with an intention to mislead members of the public,[76] when its use can be restrained.[77]

Firm name as a trade mark[78]

3-21   Although a monopoly in an ordinary English word cannot be acquired merely by assuming it as a trade name,[79] a firm name may be registered as a trade mark where it constitutes a "sign capable of being represented graphically which is capable of distinguishing goods or services of one undertaking from those of other undertakings".[80] A trade mark may be registered in the names of two or more partners jointly and held by them as a partnership asset,[81] but it will rarely be possible for two or more persons to be registered separately with the *same* trade mark.[82]

3-22   A registered trade mark is freely assignable and transmissible, whether or not in connection with the goodwill of a business.[83] An assignment may be partial and may, thus, relate to some, but not all, of the goods or services in respect of which the mark is registered or to its use in a particular manner or in a particular locality.[84] This might conceivably allow partners on a dissolution to divide up a

---

[73] *Jay's Ltd. v. Jacobi* [1933] Ch. 411; *Habib Bank Ltd. v. Habib Bank A.G. Zurich* [1981] 1 W.L.R. 1265. cf. *HFC Bank Plc v. Midland Bank Plc* [2000] F.S.R. 176, where the defendant could not demonstrate that it had any established goodwill under the disputed name. The claimant's action was, nevertheless, dismissed on other grounds.

[74] *Turton v. Turton* (1888) 42 Ch.D. 128; *Tussaud v. Tussaud* (1890) 44 Ch.D. 678; *Saunders v. Sun Life Assurance Co. of Canada* [1894] 1 Ch. 537; *Burgess v. Burgess* (1853) 3 De G.M. & G. 896. See also *Lee v. Popeck* (1967) 111 S.J. 114 (solicitor practising under the name of Tringhams and also under his own name, David Lee, held not entitled, in interlocutory proceedings, to an injunction restraining two solicitors from practising under the name of David Leigh & Co.). But see *Legal and General Assurance Society v. Daniel* [1968] R.P.C. 253.

[75] *Baker v. Benson*, August 3, 1988 (unreported), a decision of Hoffmann J.

[76] *Teofani & Co. Ltd. v. A. Teofani* [1913] 2 Ch. 545; *Holloway v. Holloway* (1800) 13 Beav. 209; *Croft v. Day* (1843) 7 Beav. 84; *Lewis's v. Lewis* (1890) 45 Ch.D. 281; *J. & J. Cash Ltd. v. Cash* [1902] W.N. 32.

[77] In editions of this work prior to the 15th, there appeared at this point extensive references to the right of a firm to prevent persons registering a company to carry on a rival business under a name identical or similar to the firm name. These have not been retained, but are to be found in the 15th ed. at pp. 40, 41.

[78] The Community trade mark regime under Council Regulation (EC) No. 49/94 on the Community trade mark is, in essence, the same as that introduced by the Trade Marks Act 1994 and is not considered separately here.

[79] *Areators Ltd. v. Tollitt* [1902] 2 Ch. 319.

[80] Trade Marks Act 1994, s.1(1). In *Byford v. Oliver* [2003] E.M.L.R. 20 (noted *supra*, para. 3–20) two former members of the band "Saxon" had sought to register the name, but it was, in the event, held that they were prohibited from doing so by *ibid.* ss.3(6) (bad faith) and 5(4) (use liable to be prevented by the law of passing off). Note that there is a limited "own name" defence in *ibid.* s.11(2): *Asprey and Garrard Ltd. v. WRA (Guns) Ltd.* [2002] F.S.R. 30; *Hotel Cipriani SRL v. Cipriani (Grosvenor Street) Ltd.* [2010] R.P.C. 16 (CA).

[81] *ibid.* s.23(1). As to the powers of a co-owner of a trade mark, see *ibid.* s.23(3)–(5).

[82] *ibid.* ss.5, 6. See also *Byford v. Oliver, supra.* As to cases of honest concurrent use, see *ibid.* s.7 and *Kerly's Law of Trade Marks and Trade Names* (14th ed.), paras 9–150 et seq.

[83] *ibid.* s.24(1).

[84] *ibid.* s.24(2). This is, however, a problem area: see *Kerly's Law of Trade Marks and Trade Names* (14th ed.), para. 13–016.

trade mark as between themselves on a geographical basis.[85] If, however, as a result of such an arrangement, the public would be likely to be misled, registration of the mark might be revoked.[86]

Unregistered trade marks are not governed by statute and will, in general, be assignable but may, as a matter of implication, be held to pass with an assignment of the firm's goodwill.[87]

Assignment of firm name

An assignment of the right to use a firm name in gross will not confer on the assignee any rights connected with the use of that name as against third parties; *per contra*, if it is assigned in conjunction with the business or part of the business.[88] A firm may, however, agree to confer on a third party the right to use the firm name in connection with his business and, if that agreement is not tainted by a fraudulent intention to deceive the public, it will be perfectly valid as between the parties.[89]

3–23

If, following the dissolution of a firm, its business is wholly discontinued, the old firm name may be adopted by another trader,[90] provided he does not thereby expose the members of the former firm to any risk of liability.[91] The position as between the partners following a dissolution will be noticed hereafter.[92]

Change in firm name

The rights and liabilities of a firm will not in general be affected by a change in its name, unless that change is also accompanied by a change in its members.

3–24

---

[85] *Semble*, they will not be able, even by agreement, to insist that they are each individually registered as proprietors of the same mark: see *Re Ehrmann's Application* [1897] 2 Ch. 495 (a decision under the Trade Marks Act 1883); also the Trade Marks Act 1994, ss.5, 46(1)(d); *sed quaere*. The position was formerly otherwise. Thus, in earlier editions of this work, the old law was summarised thus: "In any case where, by reason of a dissolution of partnership or otherwise, a person who was entitled to more than one registered trade mark ceased to carry on business, and the goodwill of the business did not pass to one successor but was divided, the registrar might, except in the case of associated trade marks, formerly have permitted an apportionment of his registered trade marks among the persons in fact continuing the business, subject to such conditions and modifications, if any, as he might think necessary in the public interest." This proposition rested on the Trade Marks Act 1905, s.23, as amended by the Trade Marks Act 1919, s.12, Sched. 2 (subsequently superseded and repealed by the Trade Marks (Amendment) Act 1937, s.7, and the Trade Marks Act 1938, s.70 and Sched. 4).

[86] Trade Marks Act 1994, s.46(1)(d). And see *Scandecor Development AB v Scandecor Marketing AB* [2002] F.S.R. 7 (HL).

[87] See *Kerly's Law of Trade Marks and Trade Names* (14th ed.), paras 13–059 *et seq.* Also the Trade Marks Act 1994, s.24(6).

[88] *Thorneloe v. Hill* [1894] 1 Ch. 569; *Kingston Miller & Co. Ltd. v. Thomas Kingston & Co. Ltd.* [1912] 1 Ch. 575, 581, 582 *per* Warrington J. But *cf. Barr v. Lions* 1956 S.L.T. 250; and see *infra*, para. 10–195.

[89] See *Coles (J. H.) Proprietary Ltd. v. Need* [1934] A.C. 82; *Benhams Ltd. v. Brown*, Unreported June 24, 1999 CA (Civ Div); also *Dawnay Day Co. Ltd. v. Cantor Fitzgerald International* [2000] R.P.C. 669 (CA). If the agreement amounts to a revocable licence and such licence is revoked, the firm can obtain an injunction against the licensee to restrain continued use of the firm name: *Coles (J. H.) Proprietary Ltd. v. Need, supra.*

[90] *Pink v. Sharwood (No. 2)* (1913) 109 L.T. 594.

[91] See *Townsend v. Jarman* [1900] 2 Ch. 698, and other cases of that class, noted *infra*, paras 10–201 *et seq.*; and see *infra*, paras 5–45 *et seq.*

[92] See *infra*, paras 10–200 *et seq.*

Admittedly, a change of name will be of significance to the partners where the old name is registered as a trade mark or where it effectively represents the firm's goodwill, but otherwise a mere change of name will mean no more than a change in the label by which they are collectively known. Equally, one partner does not have power to bind his co-partners by using a name under which they do not carry on business together, unless they have expressly or impliedly sanctioned its use.[93]

A change of name may, assuming that it does not involve the adoption of a prohibited name[94] (which would naturally not be permissible), necessitate an application to the Secretary of State for approval of the new name under Part 41 of the Companies Act 2006[95] and may also bring within the scope of the Act a firm to which its provisions formerly did not apply.[96]

Change in a partner's name

3–25   A change in the name of a partner will not normally have any impact on the firm name, unless it causes Part 41 of the Companies Act 2006 to apply and thus, conceivably, necessitates use of the name to be discontinued on the grounds that it is prohibited[97] or, alternatively, approval for the continued use of the name to be sought from the Secretary of State.[98] However, such approval would not in any event be required in relation to a name which was lawfully used by the firm immediately prior to October 1, 2009.[99]

Companies Act 2006, Part 41

3–26   Reference is made throughout this work to the application of Part 41 of the Companies Act 2006 to partnerships and, for convenience, a connected account of its main provisions will be given at this point. Part 41 replaced the Business

---

[93] See *Kirk v. Blurton* (1841) 9 M. & W. 284 and the other cases of that class noticed *infra*, paras 12–148 *et seq.*

[94] See the Companies Act 2006, ss.1197, 1198 and the Company and Business Names (Miscellaneous Provisions) Regulations 2009 (SI 2009/1085), Pt. 4 (as amended by the Company, Limited Liability Partnership and Business Names (Miscellaneous Provisions) (Amendment Regulations 2009 (SI 2009/2404)), noted *infra*, paras 3–27, 3–28.

[95] ss.1193(1), 1194(1); also the Company, Limited Liability Partnership and Business Names (Sensitive Words and Expressions) Regulations 2009 (SI 2009/2615), regs. 3, 5, 6, Scheds. 1, 2.

[96] As a result, the requisite information would have to be included on the firm's business letters and other documentation and displayed in the partnership premises: Companies Act 2006, ss.1202–1204.

[97] See the Companies Act 2006, ss.1197, 1198 and the Company and Business Names (Miscellaneous Provisions) Regulations 2009, Pt. 4 (as amended by the Company, Limited Liability Partnership and Business Names (Miscellaneous Provisions) (Amendment) Regulations 2009), noted *infra*, paras 3–27, 3–28.

[98] *ibid.* ss.1193(1), 1194(1); also the Company, Limited Liability Partnership and Business Names (Sensitive Words and Expressions) Regulations 2009: see *supra*, n. 95. In the case of a change of name by a woman in consequence of marriage, it is assumed that the position is effectively the same as it was under the Registration of Business Names Act 1916: see *Seymour v. Chernikeef* [1946] K.B. 434.

[99] *ibid.* ss.1191(2), (4). October 1, 2009 was the day appointed for the coming into force of the Companies Act 2006, Pt. 41, Chap. 1: see the Companies Act 2006 (Commencement No. 8, Transitional Provisions and Savings) Order 2008 (SI 2008/2860), art. 3(x).

Names Act 1985 with effect from October 1, 2009,[100] and forms part of the legislative framework controlling the use of (*inter alia*) firm names.[101]

There are two distinct regimes, one relating to the use of restricted or prohibited names[102] and the other to the disclosure requirements to be adopted.[103]

Persons affected by the restricted names regime

The approach of the Act is to apply restrictions on the use of restricted or prohibited names to *any* person[104] carrying on business in the UK,[105] and then to except from those restrictions the following: **3–27**

1. An individual carrying on business under a name consisting of his own surname, with the optional addition of his forename or initial[106] or an indication that the business is carried on in succession to a former owner.[107]

---

[100] The 1985 Act had in turn consolidated the provisions of the Companies Act 1981, Pt. II, which had repealed and replaced the Registration of Business Names Act 1916. The legislative approach since 1981 had been to abandon the registration requirements contained in the 1916 Act and, to that extent, it has been said to afford less protection. For an outline of the position under the 1916 Act, the reader is referred to the 14th ed. of this work, pp. 38–45.

[101] The provisions exclusively relating to company names, which are to be found in the Companies Act 2006, Pt. 5 and the Company and Business Names (Miscellaneous Provisions) Regulations 2009 (SI 2009/1085), fall outside the scope of the present work. It may, however, be noted that s.1099 of the 2006 Act requires the Registrar of Companies to keep an index of, *inter alia*, the names of all limited and limited liability partnerships.

[102] Companies Act 2006, Pt. 41, Chap. 1.

[103] *ibid.* Chap. 2.

[104] It is unclear whether, in the case of a partnership, it is the "person" referred to in the Act, or whether that expression is intended to denote each partner individually (a similar doubt as that which arose under the Business Names Act 1985). A partnership is certainly the relevant person under *ibid.* Chap. 2 (see s.1200(1)), but a similar provision is, for some reason, not replicated in *ibid.* Chap 1. There can be no doubt that a partnership is a "person" within the meaning of the Interpretation Act 1978, Sched. 1 and, more importantly, the Companies Act 2006, s.1207 clearly applies *ibid.* ss.1121 to 1123 as regards offences under Pt. 41, thus seemingly imposing liability on all the partners and any manager, secretary or similar officers of the partnership: *ibid.* s.1121(1) read with ss.1121(2), 1123(3). It should, however, be noted that *ibid.* s.1121(1) refers to "contravention of an enactment in relation to a *company*" (emphasis supplied), whereas the provisions of *ibid.* ss.1193(5), 1194(4), 1197(6) and 1198(3) without exception refer to an offence being committed "by a body corporate". Note that *ibid.* s.1123(2) deals with offences by bodies corporate separately, which would appear to conflict with the provisions noted in the previous sentence. *Semble* those sections should have referred to a "company" rather than a body corporate. See also *infra*, para. 3–33.

[105] Companies Act 2006, s.1192(1).

[106] This includes any "recognised abbreviation of a name": *ibid.* s.1208. This will include the obvious case of "Jim" or "Jimmy" for "James" (see the explanatory notes to the 2006 Act, para. 1543), but more modern usage may be more doubtful, e.g. Barry/Bazza.

[107] *ibid.* s.1192(2)(a), (3)(a), (c). It is tentatively submitted that, by virtue of the Interpretation Act 1978, s.6(c), the use of more than one forename or initial will not constitute an improper addition for the purposes of subs.(2)(a), but this should be compared with the more precise provisions of the Registration of Business Names Act 1916, s.1(6). Under the latter Act, if any Christian name or initial was added to the surname, *all* the Christian names or initials had to be added to escape the need for registration: *Brown v. Thomas and Burrows* (1922) 39 T.L.R. 132; *Limond v. Bernthal* 1953 S.L.T. (Sh.Ct.) 97. Whether there is a similar requirement under the 2006 Act is unclear, but it is tentatively thought not.

2. Individuals who carry on business[108] in partnership[109] under a name which consists of the surnames of all partners, with the optional addition of the forenames of individual partners or the initials thereof or, where there are two or more individual partners with the same surname, the addition of the letter "s" at the end of that surname,[110] and an indication that they carry on the business in succession to a former owner.[111]

If, following a change in the individual members of a partnership to which the restrictions originally did not apply, there is no longer the necessary correlation between the firm name and the surnames of the current partners, then the restrictions may become applicable and affect the continued use of that name.[112]

Under this part of the regime, no provision is made regarding the use of names by a corporate partnership,[113] and it thus follows that the restrictions will apply in all cases.

Restricted and prohibited names

3–28   Save where one of the limited exclusions set out in the preceding paragraph applies, no business can be carried on in the UK under a name which would be likely to give the impression that the business is connected with Her Majesty's Government, any part of the Scottish administration or Her Majesty's Government in Northern Ireland, any local authority or public authority specified in regulations,[114] or which includes any word or expression for the time being specified in regulations made under the Act,[115] without first obtaining the

---

[108] Business includes a profession: *ibid.* s.1208. As to the general meaning of the word, see *Smith v. Anderson* (1880) 15 Ch.D. 247, 258 *per* Jessel M.R.

[109] Partnership is expressed to include an 1890 Act partnership, a limited partnership formed under the Limited Partnerships Act 1907 (see *infra*, Pt.6) and "a firm or entity of similar character formed under the law of a country or territory outside the United Kingdon": Companies Act 2006, s.1208. Given that a Scottish partnership has separate legal personality (see the Partnership Act 1890, s.4(2)), such an attribute will clearly not be fatal to partnership status. It should be noted that a limited liability partnership formed under the Limited Liability Partnerships Act 2000 is *not* a species of partnership (see *supra*, paras 2–39 *et seq.*), but a limited liability partnership formed under a foreign system of law may well qualify.

[110] *ibid.* s.1192(2)(b), (3)(b). Surname in relation to a peer or person usually known by a British title different from his surname means the title by which he is known, and initial includes any recognised abbreviation of a name: *ibid.* s.8(1). The addition of the words "and Co." would clearly constitute an improper addition for these purposes: see *Evans v. Piauneau* [1927] 2 K.B. 374, 377 (a decision under the Aliens Restriction (Amendment) Act 1919—now repealed).

[111] *ibid.* s.1192(3)(c).

[112] See *infra*, paras 3–32 *et seq.*

[113] This is deliberate: see the explanatory notes to the 2006 Act, para. 1522. *cf.* the Business Names Act 1985, s.1(1)(a) and the Companies Act 2006, s.1200(2)(b), considered *infra*, para. 3–33.

[114] See the Company, Limited Liability Partnerships and Business Names (Public Authorities) Regulations (SI 2009/2982), reg. 3, Sched., col. (1).

[115] See the Company, Limited Liability Partnership and Business Names (Sensitive Words and Expressions) Regulations 2009 (SI 2009/2615), reg. 3, Sched. 1, Pt. 1. Note also the Company and Business Names (Chamber of Commerce, etc.) Act 1999, ss.1, 3, as respectively amended by the Companies Act 2006 (Consequential Amendments, Transitional Provisions and Savings) Order 2009 (SI 2009/1941), Sched. 1, para. 176(2), (4).

approval of the Secretary of State.[116] There is also a complete prohibition on the use of any name containing a word, expression or "other indication" associated with a particular type of company or form of organisation which is specified by regulation[117] or which is misleading as to the activities carried on.[118] Where, however, a business was carried on under a lawful business name[119] immediately before October 1, 2009,[120] and continues thereafter to be carried on under the same name, no approval is required and any applicable prohibition is disapplied.[121]

It should be noted that where the firm name comprises the surnames of some (but not all) of the individual partners, approval will have to be sought if any one or more of those surnames consist of a word specified in the regulations.[122] Similarly where the firm name comprises the name of a corporate partner which consists of such a word.[123]

3–29

Where it is necessary to obtain the approval of a name, the persons proposing to use it, *i.e.* in the case of a firm all the partners, must first approach any relevant body[124] specified for that purpose,[125] with a view to ascertaining whether and, if so, why that body has any objection to the proposed name.[126] There must then be submitted to the Secretary of State, apparently as part of the application for approval,[127] a statement that such a request has been made of the relevant body concerned, together with a copy of any response received.[128] Failure to comply with this requirement may result in the application being refused.[129] Such an

[116] Companies Act 2006, ss.1193, 1194. There is no provision as to the precise manner in which an application is to be made to the Secretary of State.

[117] Companies Act 2006, s.1197(1), (2) and the Company and Business Names (Miscellaneous Provisions) Regulations 2009, Pt. 4 (as amended, in the case of reg. 13, by the Company, Limited Liability Partnership and Business Names (Miscellaneous Provisions) (Amendment) Regulations 2009 (SI 2009/2404), reg. 2(2)), Sched. 1, para. 1(a), (b), Sched. 2, para. 3 (as amended by *ibid.* reg. 2(3)). As a result, a firm which is not a limited partnership could not use the word "limited" at the end of its name or "limited partnership" or "LP" as part of its name and a firm could only use the words "limited liability partnership" or "LLP" if it is such a partnership: *ibid.* regs. 13(2), 14(1). An LLP formed under the Limited Liability Partnerships Act 2000 is not, in any event, a partnership.

[118] Companies Act 2006, s.1198(1).

[119] A lawful business name is a name under which the business was carried on without contravening the Business Names Act 1985, s.2(1) or the Northern Ireland equivalent: Companies Act 2006, s.1199(4).

[120] This was the day appointed for the coming into force of the Companies Act 2006, Pt. 41, Chap. 1: see the Companies Act 2006 (Commencement No. 8, Transitional Provisions and Savings) Order 2008 (SI 2008/2860), art. 3(x).

[121] Companies Act 2006, s.1199(1), (2).

[122] *e.g.* Duke or King: see the Company, Limited Liability Partnership and Business Names (Sensitive Words and Expressions) Regulations 2009, Sched. 1, Pt. 1.

[123] See *supra*, para. 3–27. *cf.* the Business Names Act 1985, s.1(1)(a).

[124] This expression, although used in the heading to the Companies Act 2006, s.1195, is not used in the body of the section, which merely refers to the "other body".

[125] *ibid.* s.1195(1), (5). See also the Company, Limited Liability Partnership and Business Names (Sensitive Words and Expressions) Regulations 2009, regs. 5, 6, Sched. 2 (although in this case identification of the relevant body will depend on where the firm will carry on business: *ibid.*, reg. 6, Sched. 2, Pt. 2); the Company, Limited Liability Partnerships and Business Names (Public Authorities) Regulations, reg. 4, Sched., col. (2).

[126] Companies Act 2006, s.1195(2). The request must be in writing.

[127] This is by no means clear. It might be possible to supply the necessary statement after submitting the application to the Secretary of State without strictly contravening the provisions of the subsection.

[128] *ibid.* s.1195(3).

[129] *ibid.* s.1195(5).

approval, once obtained may be withdrawn by the Secretary of State where there are overriding considerations of public policy.[130]

Same firm using two or more names

3–30   In the case of a firm which carries on business under more than one name, approval may have to be sought in respect of each such name, but there would otherwise appear to be no restriction on the number of names which may be employed.

Two or more firms with the same name

3–31   There is no limit on the number of firms which can carry on business under the same name, and it is thought that more than one firm may, in theory at least, apply for, and obtain approval from the Secretary of State in respect of an identical name.[131]

Effect of changes in the firm

3–32   Unlike the position under the Business Names Act 1985,[132] it would seem possible that the "person" referred to in the relevant provisions of the Companies Act 2006 may be the firm itself.[133] If that is right, it would follow that, where approval of the firm name has been sought and obtained, and there is a subsequent change in the constitution of the firm, whether by the death, retirement or expulsion of an existing partner or the admission of a new partner, a new approval would have to be sought in all cases, which seems an odd result. If, on the other hand, the "person" is, in effect, each partner, then, as previously, the departure of an existing partner would not affect the validity of the approval previously obtained by all the partners and continued use of the firm name after the change would be permissible. However, the admission of a *new* partner would, in that event, unquestionably require a fresh approval to be sought, seemingly by the new partner alone.[134]

On the former hypothesis, the firm will have a 12 month period of grace to apply for a new approval, as a transferee of the "old" firm's business[135] but, on the latter, approval should prudently be obtained before the new partner is admitted to the firm, since it is doubtful whether he can properly be regarded as

---

[130] *ibid.* s.1196.

[131] It is by no means clear whether the Secretary of State will seek to refuse approval on the ground that some other partnership is carrying on business under the same name, but it is thought that any such refusal might be open to challenge.

[132] See the 18th ed. of this work, at para. 3–25.

[133] See Companies Act 2006, s.1207, applying *ibid.* ss.1121 to 1123 as regards offences under Pt. 41. s.1121(1) read with ss.1121(2) and 1123(3) would seem to impose liability on all the partners and any manager, secretary or similar officers of the partnership. Note, however, that s.1121(1) refers to "contravention of an enactment in relation to a company", whereas the provisions of ss.1193(5), 1194(4), 1197(6) and 1198(3) without exception refer to an offence being committed "by a body corporate". Note also that the point is addressed specifically in *ibid.* s.1200(1), which tends to support the alternative analysis in the text.

[134] On this analysis, the existing partners will, of course, already have obtained the requisite approval, and will not be obliged to make any further application.

[135] Companies Act 2006, s.1199(3), (4).

a transferee of the business.[136] The results of the former hypothesis would be more serious in the case of an existing firm which uses a prohibited name,[137] since a change in the firm would automatically render its continued use unlawful, subject to the application of the 12 month grace period.

In the case of a firm which carries on business under a name which initially does not attract the application of these provisions of the Act, a change of partners may well bring the firm within their scope and, moreover, require approval to be sought from the Secretary of State, if the existing firm name is to continue unchanged,[138] or even discontinuance of the use of the name if it falls within one of the prohibited classes.[139]

Information to appear on business letters, etc.

An entirely separate set of provisions applies to any partnership[140] which carries on business in the UK under a name which consists of the surnames of all the individual partners, together with any permitted additions, and the corporate names of all partners which are bodies corporate.[141] Such a partnership must state in legible characters on all its business documentation[142] the name of each partner and the address in the UK at which any document relating in any way to the business can be effectively served on him.[143] The only exception to this requirement consists of documents issued by a firm with more than 20 partners[144] which maintains at its principal place of business a list of all the partners' names, provided that none of their names appear in the document (otherwise than in the text or as a signatory) *and* the document states in legible characters the address of the firm's principal place of business and that the list of names is open to inspection there.[145] Any person is entitled to inspect that list during office hours.[146]

In addition to the above (and irrespective of the size of the firm), any person with whom anything is done or even discussed in the course of the partnership

3–33

---

[136] The new partner will, at most, be the transferee of a share or interest in the partnership business, although the point is eminently arguable.

[137] See *ibid.* ss.1197, 1198, noticed *supra*, para. 3–28.

[138] See *supra*, para. 3–28.

[139] See para. 3–28, n. 117.

[140] See *supra*, para. 3–27, n. 109.

[141] Companies Act 2006, s.1200. In the case of the individual partners, the permitted additions are identical to those set out in *ibid.* s.1192(3)(b), (c), noted *supra*, para. 3–26: *ibid.* s.1200(3)(b), (c). There are no permitted additions in the case of a corporate partner.

[142] *i.e.* all its business letters, written orders for goods or services to be supplied to the business, invoices and receipts issued in the course of the business and written demands for payment of debts arising in the course of the business: *ibid.* s.1202(1).

[143] *ibid.* ss.1201 (as substituted by the Companies Act 2006 (Substitution of Section 1201) Regulations 2009 (SI 2009/3182), reg. 2), 1202(1). If the partnership has a place of business in the UK, the address for service must be in the UK (*ibid.* s.1201(2)), but otherwise must be a place where service can be effected by physical delivery and a suitable acknowledgement of delivery can be obtained (*ibid.* s.1201(3)). It would seem that, as was the position under the Business Names Act 1985, the document, etc. does not need to state in terms that the address is an address for service: *Department of Trade and Industry v. Cedenio, The Times*, March 22, 2001 (DC).

[144] This was formerly the number of partners which attracted restrictions on the size of a partnership, but those restrictions have long since been swept away.

[145] Companies Act 2006, s.1203(1), (2).

[146] *ibid.* s.1203(3).

business is entitled to request, and must be supplied with, a written notice containing a list of the names and addresses of all the partners.[147]

A notice containing the names and addresses of all the partners must also be displayed in a prominent position, in any premises where the partnership business is carried on and to which the customers of, or suppliers of goods or services to, the business have access.[148]

Penalties

3–34   It is not entirely clear whether a firm's use of a prohibited name or its failure to obtain any requisite approval from the Secretary of State for the use of its name will result in the commission of an offence by the firm itself and/or by the individual partners.[149] On the other hand, where without reasonable excuse, a firm fails to include the necessary information on all its business documentation, to display the necessary notice in the partnership premises, to supply a list of the partners' names and addresses on request or to permit inspection of a list of those names and addresses maintained at the partnership premises, an offence will clearly be committed by the firm, although whether this will also involve the commission of an offence by the partners is less clear.[150]

Disability of firms in default

3–35   In addition to the penalties which may be imposed for breach of a firm's disclosure obligations under the Act,[151] the firm will be subject to a general disability as regards contracts entered into whilst the breach continues.[152] Thus, if at the time of the breach the firm entered into a contract in the course of its business, and the partners subsequently commence proceedings to enforce rights arising out of that contract, they may find those proceedings summarily dismissed if the defendant[153] can show that, by reason of the breach, he has been unable to pursue a claim against the firm arising out of the contract or that he has

---

[147] *ibid.* s.1202(2). The notice may need to be in a form specified in regulations made under the Act: *ibid.* s.1202(3). As yet, no such regulations have been made.

[148] *ibid.* s.1204(1). The notice may need to be in a form specified in regulations under the Act: *ibid.* s.1204(2). Again, no regulations have yet been made.

[149] *ibid.* ss.1197(5), 1198(2) (prohibited names), 1193(4), 1194(3) (unapproved names). As noted *supra*, para. 3–27, n. 104, it is not clear who is the relevant "person" for this purpose. If the partners are liable, the offence committed by a corporate partner will be attributed to its officers: *ibid.* s.1121.

[150] *ibid.* s.1205(1), read with *ibid.* s.1200(1), which makes it clear beyond argument that, in this case, the partnership is the relevant "person". Equally, *ibid.* s.1205(2) again refers to offences committed by a "body corporate", which might serve to engage *ibid.* ss.1121, 1123(3), thus rendering the partners liable: see further *supra*, para. 3–27, n. 104. If an offence is, as a result, committed by a corporate partner, its officers will again be liable: *ibid.* s.1121. Note, in this context, that the Divisional Court in *Department of Trade and Industry v. Cedenio*, The Times, March 22, 2001 declined to adopt a purposive interpretation when considering a potential breach of the Business Names Act 1985, s.4(1) by a sole trader.

[151] See *supra*, para. 3–34.

[152] *i.e.* a breach of the Companies Act 2006, s.1202(1), (2), 1204(1). Of course, if the partnership does not fall within the scope of *ibid.* s.1200(1), there can be no breach of these provisions.

[153] The vague expression "the defendant" is not expressly limited to the contracting parties. It is, however, doubtful whether a non-contracting party could ever be in a position to invoke the section.

suffered some financial loss in connection therewith.[154] This would appear to be the position even though the breach was the fault of only one partner and unknown to the other partners.[155] However, the court is given a residual discretion to permit the proceedings to continue, if it would be just and equitable so to do.[156]

The disability imposed by the Act is limited to the firm itself; it prima facie has no application to persons claiming under it, *e.g.* a trustee in bankruptcy or liquidator.[157]   **3–36**

Notwithstanding the above disability, where a contract appears to have been entered into by one partner, there is nothing to prevent the partners from seeking to demonstrate that the firm was, on a true analysis, the party to the contract, even if by so doing they are forced to admit a breach of their obligations under the Act.[158]

(b) Legal Proceedings

The complications which formerly resulted from the refusal of the law to recognise the firm as a separate entity are of largely historical interest.[159] Partners can now sue, and be sued, in the firm name,[160] although this has in no way affected their individual liability to satisfy judgments against the firm. Bankruptcy has, of course, always presented its own peculiar problems.[161]   **3–37**

Nevertheless, a graphic illustration of such refusal may be found in the old rule that, for taxation purposes, if London and country firms of solicitors shared a common partner, the former would not be entitled to agency fees when acting for the latter, but would rather be treated as acting on its own account.[162] It is

---

[154] *ibid.* s.1206(2). Ironically, in *Nigel Lowe & Associates v. John Mowlem Construction plc* 1999 S.L.T. 1298 (OH), a breach of the Business Names Act 1985, s.4 (the equivalent of the Companies Act 2006, ss.1202, 1204) was sought to be relied on by *the claimant firm* but the defendant did not, in the event, seek to rely on *ibid.* s.5 (the equivalent of s.1206).

[155] Unlike the position under the Business Names Act 1985, it is now clear that the "person" referred to in the Companies Act 2006, s.1206(1) is the firm: see *ibid.* s.1200(1). Given the agency which exists between partners, it is logical that all partners should suffer as a result of the actions of one of their number.

[156] *ibid.* s.1206(2). It is submitted that the court will be likely to approach the exercise of this discretion in a manner similar to that adopted in relation to the Registration of Business Names Act 1916, s.8. Relief under that section was granted where a foreign name had been wrongly spelt (*Hawkins v. Duché* [1921] 3 K.B. 226), and where the defaulter (the claimant) did not know of the Act or the need for registration thereunder, and the defendant knew he owned the business and was not misled (*Weller v. Denton* [1921] 3 K.B. 103). See also *Re Oxley* [1932] W.N. 271; *Lawrence Vanger & Co. v. Company Developments (Property Division) Ltd.* (1977) 244 E.G. 43. And see *Buckmaster and Moore v. Fado Investments* [1986] P.C.C. 95 (a decision under the equivalent Manx legislation, but concerning an English partnership).

[157] See *Hawkins v. Duché, supra* (a decision under the equivalent provision of the Registration of Business Names Act 1916).

[158] *Nigel Lowe & Associates v. John Mowlem Construction plc* 1999 S.L.T. 1298 (OH). As noted, *supra,* n. 154, the defendants did not seek to rely on the equivalent section in the Business Names Act 1985.

[159] In essence those complications were that: (1) a firm could not sue or be sued otherwise than in the names of the partners composing it, (2) an action could not be brought by the firm against a partner, or by a partner against the firm and (3) one firm could not bring an action against another if they both shared one or more partners in common.

[160] See CPR 7PDA, paras 5A.1, 5A.3, *infra,* para. A2–04. See also *infra,* paras 14–04 *et seq.*

[161] None more so than under the current insolvency legislation: see *infra,* paras 27–01 *et seq.*

[162] *Re Borough Commercial and Build. Soc.* [1894] 1 Ch. 289.

tentatively suggested that the same rule *may* still be applied on an assessment of costs under the Civil Procedure Rules.[163]

(c) Contractual Rights and Liabilities

Effect of change in the partners

3–38   Where there is a change in the partners, the members of the "new" firm may quite properly agree with the members of the "old" firm that the partnership should be treated as continuing and that all existing rights and obligations should be effectively taken over by the new firm.[164] However, so far as concerns third parties, such an agreement is *res inter alios acta*, unless they consent to be bound thereby.[165]

3–39   It naturally follows that any contract into which the firm has entered may be determined or breached by such a change. If, on its true construction, the contract is framed solely by reference to an existing firm, it will be determined by any change in its members. This is illustrated by the decision in *Tasker v. Shepherd*,[166] where two partners appointed an agent for four and a half years and one of them died before the expiration of that period. It was held that the surviving partner need no longer employ the agent's services, since the appointment was only by reference to the existing partnership, the contract being for a term of four and a half years but only if the parties should live that long. Similarly, if the contract is of a personal character, which is only to be performed by the individual partners who have entered into it or is otherwise dependent on their particular attributes, a change in the firm will determine the contract by rendering its performance impossible.[167]

3–40   If, on the other hand, it can be inferred that the contract is to be performed by the firm as from time to time constituted, then a change in the partners will not *per se* determine the contract or constitute a breach of it. However, this is a pure question of construction in relation to each individual contract, and no general principles can usefully be formulated.[168] However, as was made clear by Scott J.

---

[163] *i.e.* under CPR Pt 47.

[164] This is not a foregone conclusion: see *supra*, para. 3–06 and *infra*, para. 14–48.

[165] See *infra*, paras 13–22 *et seq.*

[166] (1861) 6 H. & N. 575; and see, generally, *IRC v. Graham's Trustees* 1971 S.L.T. 46; *Kirkintilloch Equitable Co-operative Society Ltd. v. Livingstone* 1972 S.L.T. 154 (both of which concerned Scottish partnerships which do, of course, enjoy separate legal personality).

[167] *Robson v. Drummond* (1831) 2 B. & Ad. 303. As a rule, contracts of agency are of such a character: see *Brace v. Calder* [1895] 2 Q.B. 253, *infra*, para. 3–41; *Friend v. Young* [1897] 2 Ch. 421, 429 *per* Stirling J. Similarly, in the case of contracts between an author and publisher: *Stevens v. Benning* (1855) 1 K. & J. 168; *Hole v. Bradbury* (1879) 12 Ch.D. 886; *Griffith v. Tower Publishing Co. Ltd.* [1897] 1 Ch. 21. And see also *Kemp v. Baerselman* [1906] 2 K.B. 604 (contract to supply goods); *Graves v. Cohen* (1929) 46 T.L.R. 121 (owner and jockey). As to contracts which are *not* of a personal character, see *Messager v. British Broadcasting Co.* [1929] A.C. 151; *Phillips v. Alhambra Palace Co.* [1901] 1 K.B. 59; *John Brothers Abergarw Brewery Co. v. Holmes* [1900] 1 Ch. 188; *Tolhurst v. Associated Portland Cement Manufacturers Ltd.* [1903] A.C. 414; *British Waggon Co. v. Lea* (1880) 5 Q.B.D. 149; *Re Worthington* [1914] 2 K.B. 300. Note that, even where the contract is personal and has been determined, an obligation to continue payments for services previously rendered may still remain: *Wilson v. Harper* [1908] 2 Ch. 370; *cf. Sales v. Crispi* (1913) 29 T.L.R. 491.

[168] See *Briggs v. Oates* [1990] I.C.R. 473, 481 *per* Scott J.; *Jardine-Paterson v. Fraser* 1974 S.L.T. 93. Of course, in Scotland a firm is a separate legal entity: Partnership Act 1890, s.4(2).

in *Briggs v. Oates*,[169] in approaching the question of construction the size of the firm will often be a material consideration.

Right to damages: Brace v. Calder

Where a change in the partners determines a contract which is not, in its terms, **3–41** conditional on the continued existence of the firm, the change may also constitute a breach of contract for which the partners will be liable in damages. Thus in *Brace v. Calder*,[170] a firm of four partners agreed to employ the claimant as a branch manager for two years, but before the two years had expired, two of the partners retired. The continuing partners were willing to employ the claimant on the same terms as before, but he declined and sued the four original partners for breach of contract. The court held that the engagement of the claimant was for a fixed term of two years[171] and that the retirement of the two partners determined the contract and constituted a breach of contract or wrongful dismissal, for which the four partners were liable in damages; however, as the continuing partners were willing to employ the claimant on the same terms as before, he was only entitled to nominal damages.[172]

Insurance policies

A contract of insurance is a personal contract and, unless it is assignable **3–42** without the consent of the insurers (as in the case of marine insurance) or, on its true construction, it is to continue notwithstanding a change in the firm, the admission of a new partner will, in the absence of such consent, terminate it.[173] Nevertheless, in the case of a third party motor insurance policy, it has been held that, where a new partner was admitted before an accident, the insurers were not

---

[169] *supra*, at 482.

[170] [1895] 2 Q.B. 253. *Quaere*, if the claimant would have been entitled to damages if the contract had been determined by the death of one of the partners: see *ibid.* p. 261 *per* Lopes L.J. *Brace v. Calder* was followed in *Briggs v. Oates* [1990] I.C.R. 473. As to the effect of a *general* dissolution, see *Tunstall v. Condon* [1981] I.C.R. 786 and *infra*, para. 25–02. Note also, in this context, that account must be taken of certain statutory provisions affecting employees' rights: see *supra*, para. 3–15 and *infra*, para. 25–03. Although it was held in *R. v. Leech* (1821) 3 Stark. 70 that an employee of a firm comprising two partners was properly to be treated as the individual employee of each partner and not as their joint employee, this cannot be right.

[171] As to when a discontinuance of a business will amount to a breach of contract entered into for a fixed term, *cf.* the cases in which an obligation to continue the business was implied (*Re R. S. Newman Ltd.* [1916] 2 Ch. 309; *Ogdens Ltd. v. Nelson* [1905] A.C. 109; *Turner v. Goldsmith* [1891] 1 Q.B. 544; *Telegraph Despatch Co. v. Maclean* (1873) L.R. 8 Ch. 658; *M'Intyre v. Belcher* (1863) 14 C.B. (N.S.) 654) with those in which it was not (*Hamlyn & Co. v. Wood & Co.* [1891] 2 Q.B. 488; *Re Railway and Electrical Appliances Co.* (1888) 38 Ch.D. 597; *Rhodes v. Forwood* (1876) 1 App.Cas. 256; *Catajee Nanabhoy v. Lallbhoy Vullubhoy* (1876) L.R. 3 Ind.App. 200, and *Bovine Ltd. v. Dent* (1905) 21 T.L.R. 82). And see *L. French & Co. Ltd. v. Leeston Shipping Co. Ltd.* [1922] 1 A.C. 451 (determination of a charter); also *cf. Turner v. Sawdon & Co.* [1901] 2 K.B. 653 and *Konski v. Peet* [1915] 1 Ch. 530 (where it was held there was no obligation to supply the claimant with work) with *Herbert Clayton, etc. Ltd. v. Oliver* [1930] A.C. 209; *Devonald v. Rosser* [1906] 2 K.B. 728; *Re Rubel Bronze & Metal Co. and Vos* [1918] 1 K.B. 315 (where it was held that there was such an obligation). As to the rules for determining what terms, if any, are to be implied, see generally *The Moorcock* (1889) 14 P.D. 64; *Liverpool City Council v. Irwin* [1977] A.C. 239; *Chitty on Contracts* (30th ed.), Chap. 13.

[172] As to the measure of damages where a subsequent offer is unreasonably refused, see also *Payzu Ltd. v. Saunders* [1919] 2 K.B. 581; as to whether a refusal is unreasonable, see *Yetton v. Eastwoods Froy* [1967] 1 W.L.R. 104. And see also *Re Foster Clark's Indenture Trusts* [1966] 1 W.L.R. 125 and *supra*, n. 170.

[173] See the Australian case of *Maxwell v. Price* [1959] 2 Lloyd's Rep. 352.

thereby relieved of their liability to indemnify the persons who were partners when the policy was effected, provided that they retained their undivided interest in the insured vehicle.[174]

(d) Partnership Disabilities

Disabilities of one partner affect the firm

3–43   The disability of one partner will affect the whole firm, so that the legal capacity of the firm will be no greater than that of the partner with the *least* legal capacity.[175] This proposition stems from the general rule that no person can by an agent do anything which he cannot do himself; it follows that, whilst each member of a firm may be a principal as regards his own conduct, he is also the agent of his co-partners and, therefore, he cannot do for the firm what they cannot do. However, this rule does not extend to *physical* capacity, since there can be no objection to an agent doing on his principal's behalf what that principal is himself physically unable to do. Thus, in *Newstead v. Frost*,[176] it was held that a partnership between Mr David Frost and a Bahamian company could validly carry on the business of exploiting Mr Frost's talent as a television personality with a view to sharing the profits therefrom, even though the company itself was incapable of appearing on television.

The corollary is that, in a case where *no* disability affects the partner in question, it is unlikely to be inferred that there is a disability affecting his firm.[177]

Conflicts of interest

3–44   Consistently with the above principle, where a partner is in possession of confidential information relating to the affairs of a former client which will give rise to a conflict of interests if his firm acts for another client,[178] the court will normally rule that the firm may not act/continue to act for the latter.[179] However,

---

[174] *Jenkins v. Deane* (1933) 150 L.T. 314; and see an article in 177 L.T. 415. *Semble*, the policy would be terminated by the death, retirement or expulsion of a partner on the principles discussed *infra*, paras 3–46 *et seq.*

[175] Illustrations of this doctrine will be found *infra*, paras 14–60 *et seq.* See also the following cases concerning solicitors: *Duke of Northumberland v. Todd* (1878) 7 Ch.D. TTI; *Re Borough Commercial and Building Society* [1894] 1 Ch. 289, noted *supra*, para. 3–37; *Re Scientific Investment Pension Plan, The Times*, December 10, 1992; and see the other cases cited *infra*, para. 3–44. Note also *Locobail (U.K.) Ltd. v. Bayfield Properties Ltd.* [2000] Q.B. 451 CA (Civ Div), where it was sought to be argued (unsuccessfully) that a partner, whilst sitting as a deputy judge, was disqualified from hearing a case by reason of his firm's involvement in a potentially related matter.

[176] [1980] 1 W.L.R. 135 (HL).

[177] *Malkinson v. Trim* [2003] 1 W.L.R. 463.

[178] The client may be an existing client, *e.g.* where the conflict arises by reason of a partner joining the firm or as a result of a merger. *cf. Winters v. Mishcon de Reya* (2008) 158 N.L.J. 1494, where the information was not confidential when imparted.

[179] *Rakusen v. Ellis, Munday & Clarke* [1912] 1 Ch. 831; *David Lee & Co. (Lincoln) Ltd. v. Coward Chance* [1991] Ch. 259; *Re a Firm of Solicitors* [1992] 1 Q.B. 959; *Re a Firm of Solicitors* [1997] Ch. 1; *Bolkiah v. K.P.M.G.* [1999] 2 A.C. 222, where the House of Lords disapproved the decision in *Rakusen v. Ellis, Munday & Clarke, supra*; *Koch Shipping Inc. v. Richards Butler* [2002] 2 All E.R. (Comm) 957; *Ball v. Druces & Attlee* [2002] P.N.L.R. 23 and [2004] P.N.L.R. 39; *Marks & Spencer Group plc v. Freshfields Bruckhaus Deringer* [2004] 1 W.L.R. 2331. Note also that in *Akai Holdings Ltd. v. RSM Robson Rhodes LLP* [2007] EWHC 1641 (Ch) (Lawtel 8/8/07), the court injuncted the defendant LLP from merging with another firm unless certain undertakings were provided.

there may be circumstances in which, exceptionally, the court will, having regard to the arrangements in place within the firm to preserve the confidentiality of that information,[180] supplemented where necessary with suitable undertakings,[181] be prepared to allow the firm to act.

That said, it will never be possible for the *same* firm to act for both sides in a dispute unless the parties give their informed consent[182]; however, such consent may conceivably be implied in a non-contentious matter.[183]

Statutory disabilities

There are a number of statutory disabilities which will affect not only the firm **3–45** but also each partner in his private capacity, *viz.*:

Auditors: By the Companies Act 2006, s.1214 a firm will be ineligible for appointment as the statutory auditor of a company if any partner is an officer or employee of that company.[184]

County Courts: By the County Courts Act 1984, s.13(1),[185] no officer of a county court may either by himself or his partner be directly or indirectly engaged as legal representative or agent for a party in proceedings in that court.[186]

Insolvency: The Insolvency Rules 1986[187] restrict (even if they do not in all cases actually prohibit) the partners of a liquidator or trustee in bankruptcy or of a member of a liquidation or creditors' committee from doing various acts which they would otherwise be free to do.

Solicitors Act 1974: By the Solicitors Act 1974, s.38(1),[188] it is unlawful for a solicitor who is a justice of the peace assigned to any local justice area, and for any partner of his, to act in connection with any proceedings before the justices acting in that area. As similar restriction applies to a solicitor who sits as a Deputy District Judge in the Magistrates' Court in that area.[189]

---

[180] *Bolkiah v. K.P.M.G., supra; Young v. Robson Rhodes* [1999] 3 All E.R. 524; *Halewood International Ltd. v. Addleshaw Booth & Co.* [2000] P.N.L.R. 788; *Gus Consulting GmbH v. Leboeuf, Lamb, Greene & MacRae* [2006] P.N.L.R. 32 (CA).

[181] *Young v. Robson Rhodes, supra; Gus Consulting GmbH v. Leboeuf, Lamb, Greene & MacRae, supra; Akai Holdings Ltd. v. RSM Robson Rhodes LLP, supra.*

[182] *Bolkiah v. K.P.M.G., supra*, pp. 234H–235B *per* Lord Millett; also *Hilton v. Barker Booth & Eastwood* [2005] 1 W.L.R. 567. And see also the Solicitors' Code of Conduct, r. 3.01(1), 3.02; also *ibid.* r.4 (confidentiality and disclosure) as amended by the Solicitors' Code of Conduct (Confidentiality and Disclosure) Amendment Rule 2010. Note that, in *Burkle Holdings v. Laing* [2005] EWHC 638 (QB), it was held that, where a solicitor acts for two parties to a transaction, professional privilege will only be available if there is a written retainer for *each* client: see L.S.Gaz. May 26, 2005, p. 6. This would seem to be at odds with the recognition in *Ball v. Druces & Attlee, supra*, that a retainer may be express or implied.

[183] *ibid.*; also *Kelly v. Cooper* [1993] A.C. 205. PC, a decision concerning estate agents.

[184] The appointment of a firm as a statutory auditor is authorised by *ibid.* 1216. See also *supra*, para. 3–18.

[185] As amended by the Courts and Legal Services Act 1990, Sched. 18, para. 49(2).

[186] See *R. v. Skierski* [1959] C.L.Y. 623.

[187] rr. 4.128(3), 4.149, 4.170, 6.139(3), 6.147, 6.165; Insolvency Act 1986, s.435.

[188] As amended by the Courts Act 2003, Sched. 8, para. 176(1), (2).

[189] *ibid.* s.38(3A), as added by the Access to Justice Act 1999, Sched. 11, para. 33 and amended by the Courts Act 2003, Sched. 8, para. 176(1), (4).

(e) Sureties and Securities

Sureties: effect of change in the firm

3–46   It is a fundamental principle of the law of suretyship, that any act on the part of the principal creditor which alters the risk of the surety without his consent, discharges him from future liability.[190]

Sureties to a firm

3–47   It follows that, where a person acts as surety *to* a firm, it is essential to ascertain whether or not in so doing he has agreed to act as surety to the firm as from time to time constituted. If he did, a subsequent change in its membership will obviously not discharge him from liability.[191] However, if there was no such agreement, his liability will continue only so long as the firm remains unchanged. This is recognised by section 18 of the Partnership Act 1890, which provides as follows:

> "18. A continuing guaranty or cautionary obligation given either to a firm or to a third person in respect of the transactions of a firm is, in the absence of agreement to the contrary, revoked as to future transactions by any change in the constitution of the firm to which, or of the firm in respect of the transactions of which, the guaranty or obligation was given."[192]

3–48   In such a case, whatever may be the cause of the change in the firm, *e.g.* the death,[193] retirement[194] or expulsion of an existing partner, or the introduction of a new partner,[195] it will immediately put an end to the surety's future liability, since his position and risk are thereby fundamentally altered; even though he may

---

[190] See as to sureties, *Holme v. Brunskill* (1877) 3 Q.B.D. 495; also *Bank of India v. Trans Continental Commodity Merchants Ltd.* [1982] 1 Lloyd's Rep. 506; *Beck Interiors Ltd. v. Russo* [2010] B.L.R. 37. As to the discharge of apprentices and their sureties by a change in the firm to which they are bound, see *Lloyd v. Blackburne* (1842) 9 M. & W. 363; *R. v. St. Martin's* (1835) 2 A. & E. 655.

[191] *Pease v. Hirst* (1829) 10 B. & C. 122; *Metcalfe v. Bruin* (1810) 12 East 400; and see *Barclay v. Lucas* (1783) 1 T.R. 291, note; *Kipling v. Turner* (1821) 5 B. & A. 261. In *Pariente v. Lubbock* (1856) 8 De G.M. & G. 5, an authority to a firm of consignees to recognise the consignor's son as his agent was held to continue, notwithstanding changes in the firm, as long as the consignor continued his business connections with the firm.

[192] This section replaced the Mercantile Law Amendment (Scotland) Act 1856, s.7 and the Mercantile Law Amendment Act 1856, s.4 (repealed by Partnership Act 1890, s.48). The latter section provided as follows: "No promise to answer for the debt, default or miscarriage of another made to a firm consisting of two or more persons, or to a single person trading under the name of a firm, and no promise to answer for the debt, default, or miscarriage of a firm consisting of two or more persons, or of a single person trading under the name of a firm, shall be binding on the person making such promise in respect of anything done or omitted to be done after a change shall have taken place in any one or more of the persons constituting the firm or in the persons trading under the name of a firm, unless the intention of the parties that such promise shall continue to be binding notwithstanding such change shall appear either by express stipulation or by necessary implication from the nature of the firm or otherwise." See, as to the position under that Act, *Backhouse v. Hall* (1865) 6 B. & S. 507. In his Supplement on the Partnership Act 1890, Lord Lindley commented "The wording of the present section [*i.e.* s.18] differs considerably from that of the previous acts, but so far at least as relates to England, it does not appear to have introduced any alteration in the law."

[193] *Holland v. Teed* (1848) 7 Hare 50; *Strange v. Lee* (1803) 3 East 484; *Weston v. Barton* (1812) 4 Taunt. 673; *Pemberton v. Oakes* (1827) 4 Russ. 154; *Simson v. Cooke* (1824) 1 Bing. 452; *Chapman v. Beckington* (1842) 3 Q.B. 703; *Backhouse v. Hall* (1865) 6 B. & S. 507.

[194] *Myers v. Edge* (1797) 7 T.R. 254; *Dry v. Davy* (1839) 10 A. & E. 30; and see *Solvency Mutual Guarantee Co. v. Freeman* (1861) 7 H. & N. 17.

[195] *Wright v. Russel* (1774) 2 Wm.Bl. 934.

not suffer as a result, he can quite properly say *non hoec in foedera veni* (*i.e.* this is not what I agreed). However, his liability in respect of a debt already accrued and ascertained is not affected, even by a transfer of the debt, whether by assignment or novation, from the old to the new firm.[196]

Sureties for a firm

The same principles apply in a case where a person acts as surety for the **3–49** conduct of a firm, as is demonstrated by section 18 of the 1890 Act.[197] However, the mere fact that a person has agreed to act as surety for another does not necessarily mean that he has agreed to act as surety for his conduct *as a partner*, still less for the conduct of him and his co-partners.[198]

Securities: effect of change in the firm

Analogous questions arise in relation to securities. Thus, if a banking firm is **3–50** given security for future advances and there is then a change in the members of the firm, the security will prima facie extend only to those advances which are made before the change.[199] Again, if a partner pledges his own property for future advances to be made to the firm and then dies, an advance made after his death to the surviving partners will not be chargeable against the property pledged.[200] Similarly, if a person deposits deeds as a security for advances to be made to him,[201] the security does not cover advances made to him and his partners.[202]

Equitable mortgages

Different principles applied in the case of equitable mortgages, but it has now **3–51** been held that a mortgage by deposit of title deeds can no longer be created in the face of the strict requirements of section 2 of the Law of Property (Miscellaneous Provisions) Act 1989.[203] Whilst the authorities cited in this paragraph can, as a result, no longer be relied on as such, they illustrate an interesting exception to the general rule and, for that reason, have been retained. Thus, it was held that an equitable mortgage by deposit of title deeds could be extended, even by parol, to cover advances made after a change in the firm with which the deeds had been

---

[196] *Bradford Old Bank v. Sutcliffe* [1918] 2 K.B. 833.

[197] As to the position before the Act, see *Bellairs v. Ebsworth* (1811) 3 Camp. 53; *University of Cambridge v. Baldwin* (1839) 5 M. & W. 580; *Simson v. Cooke* (1824) 1 Bing. 452. Also *Dance v. Girdler* (1804) 1 Bos. & Pull. N.R. 34. *cf. Universal Co. v. Yip*, June 18, 1986 (C.A.T. No. 581), [1987] C.L.Y. 1845, where, exceptionally, liability under the guarantee continued notwithstanding the fact that the firm had been taken over by a limited company. As to policies of insurance, see *supra*, para. 3–42.

[198] *London Assurance Co. v. Bold* (1844) 6 Q.B. 514; *Montefiore v. Lloyd* (1863) 15 C.B.(N.S.) 203, where the partnership was known to the surety.

[199] See *Ex p. Kensington* (1813) 2 V. & B. 79, 83 *per* Lord Eldon.

[200] *Bank of Scotland v. Christie* (1841) 8 Cl. & F. 214.

[201] Of course, such a deposit will only create a valid security if the requirements of the Law of Property (Miscellaneous Provisions) Act 1989, s.2 are satisfied: *United Bank of Kuwait plc v. Sahib* [1997] Ch. 107 (CA).

[202] *Ex p. M'Kenna* (1861) 3 De G.F. & J. 629; *Ex p. Freen* (1827) 2 Gl. & J. 246; also *Chuck v. Freen* (1828) 1 Moo. & M. 259. These cases turned on the terms of the memoranda of deposit, and on the circumstances under which the securities were given.

[203] *United Bank of Kuwait plc v. Sahib* [1997] Ch. 107 (CA).

deposited.[204] Moreover, although a legal mortgage could not be converted into an equitable mortgage by parol,[205] it might have been so converted by a written agreement; thereafter, it might, as an equitable mortgage, have become available as a security for advances made after a change in the firm to which the legal mortgage was originally given.[206] On this basis, Lord Lindley observed:

> "Owing to these doctrines a security given to a firm for advances to be made by it, is, upon a change in the firm, readily made a continuing security; and a slight manifestation of intention on the part of the borrower that it should so continue, will enable the new firm to hold the securities until the advances made by itself as well as those made by the old firm have been repaid."[207]

Lien of solicitors

3–52   The lien which a firm of solicitors has on the papers and deeds, etc., of its clients is not lost by a mere change in the firm.[208] However, that lien only attaches where such papers have come into the possession of the persons to whom the client is *legally* indebted; it follows that, if papers only come into the possession of a firm after the admission of a new partner[209] or the retirement or expulsion of an existing partner,[210] they cannot be retained on account of a debt due before the change. Lord Lindley went on to observe:

> "The death of a partner is not, however, it is conceived, equivalent to retirement, for the survivors become the legal creditors; and there is, therefore, no reason why they should not have a lien for a debt due to them and their deceased partner on papers coming into their possession after his death."

The dissolution and winding up of a solicitors' partnership discharges the partners from any obligation to act for a former client[211]; any lien they may have on his papers will naturally be subject to the client's right to insist on those papers being handed over to a fresh solicitor, albeit subject to the lien, to enable any pending business to be completed.[212]

The difficulties discussed above will not, of course, arise when the court exercises its statutory powers under section 73 of the Solicitors Act 1977.[213]

(f) Revenue Law

Effect of change in the firm

3–53   For income tax purposes, any change in the firm will no longer result in the cessation of the old firm and the creation of a new one, so that the need for the

---

[204] See *Ex p. Lloyd* (1824) 1 Gl. & J. 389; *Ex p. Lane* (1846) De G. 300; also *Ex p. Nettleship* (1841) 2 Mont.D. & De G. 124.

[205] *Ex p. Hooper* (1815) 2 Rose 328.

[206] *Ex p. Parr* (1835) 4 D. & C. 426.

[207] See *Ex p. Kensington* (1813) 2 Ves. & Bea. 79; *Ex p. Marsh* (1815) 2 Rose 240; *Ex p. Alexander* (1824) 1 Gl. & J. 409; *Ex p. Lloyd* (1838) 3 Desc. 305.

[208] *Pelly v. Wathen* (1849) 7 Hare 351. The point was left open on appeal: see (1851) 1 De G.M. & G. 16.

[209] *Re Forshaw* (1847) 16 Sim. 121; *Pelly v. Wathen, supra.*

[210] *Vaughan v. Vanderstegen* (1854) 2 Drew. 409.

[211] Subject to the application of the Partnership Act 1890, s.38, *infra*, paras 13–62 *et seq.*

[212] *Griffiths v. Griffiths* (1843) 2 Hare 587; *Rawlinson v. Moss* (1861) 7 Jur. (N.S.) 1053.

[213] See, generally, *Fairfold Properties Ltd. v. Exmouth Docks Co. Ltd. (No. 2)* [1993] Ch. 196.

service of a continuation election has now gone.[214] There may, however, be exceptional cases in which the departure of one or more partners *will* result in the notional trades of the continuing partners[215] being treated as having ceased.[216] For the purposes of value added tax, any change in the firm will, in general, be ignored for registration purposes, unless it will result in a complete identity of partners as between two formerly separate partnerships.[217]

---

[214] *cf.* the Income and Corporation Taxes Act 1988, s.113 in its original form and as amended by the Finance Act 1994, s.215(1). See further *infra*, paras 34–34 *et seq.*

[215] See the Income Tax (Trading and Other Income) Act 2005, s.852.

[216] *i.e.* if the outgoing partners are, in effect, perceived to have retained the firm's business and client base: see *infra*, para. 34–34.

[217] Value Added Tax Act 1994, s.45(1). See further, *infra*, paras 37–08 *et seq.* Note, however, that the change in the firm must be notified: see *infra*, para. 37–14.

CHAPTER 4

CAPACITY OF PARTNERS

1. CAPACITY

IN the normal course, there is nothing to prevent the creation of a valid partner-   **4–01**
ship between persons who are of full age and mental capacity. Admittedly there
are cases in which, by virtue of some statutory provision, one or more of the
partners are required to possess a specific qualification, particularly in the case of
certain trades and professions,[1] but otherwise, there is no class of persons, other
than alien enemies,[2] who are *per se* incapable of becoming partners.[3] This is so
even in the case of undischarged bankrupts, although they may suffer from
certain disabilities which will, ultimately, affect their ability to participate fully
in the firm's activities.[4] Whilst physical incapacity may affect the rights of the
partners *inter se*, it is irrelevant to the formation or continuance of a
partnership.[5]

Even where one or more of the partners is under 18 or suffering from mental   **4–02**
incapacity, the partnership will not be null and void, although the incapacity may
affect the partners' respective rights and duties[6] and, in some cases, lead to a
dissolution of the firm.[7]

Questions of incapacity can conveniently be considered under the following
headings: (a) aliens; (b) minors; (c) persons suffering from mental incapacity; (d)
husbands, wives and civil partners; (e) companies; (f) bankrupts and disqualified
persons; (g) trustees, personal representatives and nominees; and (h)
partnerships.

(a) Aliens[8]

An alien who is not an enemy has full capacity to enter into a partnership and will   **4–03**
be bound by its terms,[9] subject only to questions of diplomatic or sovereign
immunity.[10] However, an enemy alien is in a very different position.

---

[1] See *infra*, paras 8–30 *et seq.*

[2] See *infra*, paras 4–04 *et seq.*

[3] Formerly the clergy and convicts were subject to disabilities in terms of their capacity to contract,
but these have long since been swept away. It would seem that a disqualification order under the
Company Directors Disqualification Act 1986 will not prohibit entry into a partnership: see *infra*,
paras 4–24.

[4] See *infra*, paras 4–22, 4–23.

[5] See *Newstead v. Frost* [1980] 1 W.L.R. 135 (HL).

[6] See *infra*, paras 4–07 *et seq.*

[7] See *infra*, paras 4–11, 4–13, 4–14.

[8] This somewhat archaic expression is still in common usage and is, indeed, defined by the British
Nationality Act 1981, s.50(1), in the following terms: "a person who is neither a Commonwealth
citizen nor a British protected person not a citizen of the Republic of Ireland". See also the Status of
Aliens Act 1914, s.27(1).

[9] Co.Lit. 129b; Bac.Ab. Alien D.

[10] The diplomatic immunity accorded to a diplomatic agent by the Diplomatic Privileges Act 1964
does not extend to actions relating to professional or commercial activities exercised by the diplo-

Alien enemies

4–04   The expression "alien enemy" has a special meaning, namely a person who is either resident[11] or carrying on business in a country which is at war with the United Kingdom. Such a person's country of birth and personal attitude are wholly irrelevant[12]: either he is resident or carrying on business in such a country or he is not. Thus, a foreigner who resides in the United Kingdom and enters into partnership here will not become an alien enemy on the outbreak of war between the United Kingdom and his native country, unless he returns to reside or carry on business in that country.[13] His position will be the same if he is resident in an allied or neutral country.[14] Conversely, a United Kingdom citizen who resides or carries on business in a country with whom the United Kingdom is at war will be just as much an alien enemy as the nationals resident there.[15]

Effects of war

4–05   Where a state of war exists between the United Kingdom and another country,[16] all commercial and other dealings with alien enemies are, in the absence of a Crown licence, contrary to public policy and illegal.[17] It follows that, if such a

matic agent in the UK which are outside his official functions: *ibid.* Sched. 1, Art. 31. As to the definition of a diplomatic agent, see *ibid.* s.2(1) and Sched. 1, Art. 1(*e*). Even if the immunity conferred by the Act applies, it may be expressly waived by the sending state or by the initiation of proceedings by the diplomatic agent: *ibid.* Sched. 1, Arts 31(1), 32(2), (3). Waiver does not imply waiver of immunity in respect of the execution of the judgment, for which a separate waiver is necessary: *ibid.* Art. 32(4). It should also be noted that sovereign immunity, which was previously absolute, is now severely restricted, and is only available in respect of acts of a governmental, as opposed to commercial, nature: State Immunity Act 1978, s.3; *Amalgamated Metal Trading v. Department of Trade and Industry, Financial Times*, February 28, 1989. As to proceedings between partners where a state is a member of a UK partnership, see *ibid.* s.8.

[11] The word "residence" in the Trading with the Enemy Act 1939, s.2(1)(b) which defines "enemy" as "any individual resident in enemy territory," means *de facto* residence, irrespective of the circumstances: *Vamvakas v. Custodian of Enemy Property* [1952] 2 Q.B. 183.

[12] See *Johnstone v. Pedlar* [1921] 2 A.C. 262; also *Porter v. Freudenberg* [1915] 1 K.B. 857, and the cases cited therein; *Re Duchess of Sutherland, Bechoff & Co. v. Bubna* (1915) 31 T.L.R. 248 and 394 and (1921) 65 S.J. 513; *Janson v. Driefontein Consolidated Mines Ltd.* [1902] A.C. 510; *W. L. Ingle Ltd. v. Mannheim Insurance Co.* [1915] 1 K.B. 227.

[13] See the cases in n. 12, *supra*; also *Wells v. Williams* (1697) 1 Ld.Ray. 282, in which it was held that the defendant could not rely on his supposed status as an alien enemy by way of defence to an action brought by a foreigner resident here, even though a state of war did exist. An alien who is a subject of an enemy state and who resides in the UK may, however, be liable to seizure, imprisonment, and deportation, under statutory or common law powers.

[14] *Re Duchess of Sutherland, Bechoff & Co. v. Bubna* (1915) 31 T.L.R. 248 and 394 and (1921) 65 S.J. 513.

[15] As to residence in the enemy country, see *M'Connell v. Hector* (1802) 3 Bos. & Pul. 113; *O'Mealey v. Wilson* (1808) 1 Camp. 482; *cf. Roberts v. Hardy* (1815) 3 M. & S. 533 and *Ex p. Baglehole* (1812) 18 Ves.Jr. 525; as to carrying on business there, see *The Jonge Klassina* (1804) 5 Rob.Chr. 297; *The Indian Chief* (1801) 3 Rob.Chr. 12; *The Portland* (1800) 3 Rob.Chr. 41. Note also, as to the position of a partner who remains in the UK, *The Anglo-Mexican* [1918] A.C. 422; *The Lutzow* [1918] A.C. 435; *The Manningtry* [1916] P. 329. As to a partner who is an enemy subject in a neutral country, see *The Hypatia* [1917] P. 36.

[16] Note that, for this principle to apply, a state of war must exist in the *technical* sense: see *Amin v. Brown, The Times*, August 24, 2005.

[17] *Ertel Bieber & Co. v. Rio Tinto Co.* [1918] A.C. 260; *Re Badische Co. Ltd.* [1921] 2 Ch. 331; *Tingley v. Müller* [1917] 2 Ch. 144; *Halsey v. Lowenfeld* [1916] 2 K.B. 707; *Robson v. Premier Oil & Pipe Line* [1915] 2 Ch. 124; *R. v. Kupfer* [1915] 2 K.B. 321. The restrictions imposed by the common law are supplemented by statute: see for example the Trading with the Enemy Act 1939, s.1 (as amended), which provides that it is an offence to trade or attempt to trade with the enemy.

licence is not held, any contract entered into with an alien enemy will, save in very exceptional circumstances, be void *ab initio*.[18] Equally, any contract which remains executory on the outbreak of war will be automatically terminated if its further performance will require dealings with alien enemies[19]; this will be so even if the contract contains a provision suspending such performance for as long as the war continues.[20] However, in this case the illegality does not render the contract void *ab initio* but merely makes further performance impossible, so that the rights of the contracting parties are unaffected to the extent that they accrued *before* the war.[21]

An alien enemy may not, in the absence of a licence granted by the Crown, bring an action in the United Kingdom,[22] but there are no restrictions on proceedings brought *against* such a person. As a defendant, the alien enemy may appear in the proceedings and will be in the same position as any other defendant.[23]

The property of an alien enemy may be confiscated at the discretion of the Crown, and will generally be vested in a custodian during the war.[24] The disposition of such property will be provided for by the peace treaty.[25]   **4–06**

---

[18] In *Tingley v. Müller* [1917] 2 Ch. 441, a contract entered into after the outbreak of war by a British subject with a German (acting through another British subject pursuant to an irrevocable power of attorney granted before the war), was held to be valid since its performance did not necessitate any dealings with the enemy.

[19] *Re Coutinho, Caro & Co.* [1918] 2 Ch. 384; *Halsey v. Lowenfeld* [1916] 2 K.B. 707; *Duncan, Fox & Co. v. Schrempft & Bonke* [1915] 3 K.B. 355; see also the cases cited in n. 17, *supra*. If the contract only remains executory to the extent of a payment falling to be made by the enemy, such payment can be recovered during the war: *ibid.*; *Clapham S.S. Co. v. Naamlooze, etc. Rotterdam* [1917] 2 K.B. 639; *W. L. Ingle Ltd. v. Mannheim Insurance Co.* [1915] 1 K.B. 227. Leases and other contracts which confer rights of property are not terminated: *Halsey v. Lowenfeld, supra*; *London & Northern Estates Co. v. Schlessinger* [1916] 1 K.B. 20. As to arbitration clauses, see *Dalmia Dairy Industries Ltd. v. National Bank of Pakistan* [1978] 2 Lloyd's Rep. 223.

[20] *Ertel Bieber & Co. v. Rio Tinto Co.* [1918] A.C. 260; *Re Badische Co. Ltd.* [1921] 2 Ch. 331; *Naylor, Benzon & Co. v. Krainische Industrie Gesellschaft* [1918] 2 K.B. 486; *Clapham S.S. Co. v. Naamlooze, etc. Rotterdam* [1917] 2 K.B. 639; *Zinc Corpn. v. Hirsch* [1916] 1 K.B. 541; *Fried. Krupp Akt. v. Orconera Iron Ore Co.* (1919) 88 L.J.Ch. 304; *cf. Zinc Corpn. Ltd. v. Skipwith* (1914) 31 T.L.R. 106, as to a provision to resume trading operations after the war. *Quaere*, whether a clause of the type referred to in the text might operate if the suspension of the contract and the preservation of the parties' respective obligations thereunder would not be detrimental to this country or of advantage to the enemy.

[21] See *Ertel Bieber & Co. v. Rio Tinto Co.* [1918] A.C. 260, 268 *per* Lord Dunedin, as applied in *Helbert Wagg & Co.'s Claim* [1956] Ch. 323 and considered in *Arab Bank v. Barclays Bank (Dominion, Colonial and Overseas)* [1954] A.C. 495 (where it held that a right to be paid a credit balance on a current account is an accrued right which is suspended, but not abrogated, by the outbreak of war); see also *Naylor, Benzon & Co. v. Krainische Industrie Gesellschaft* [1918] 1 K.B. 331, 345 *per* McCardie J.; *Zinc Corpn. v. Hirsch* [1916] 1 K.B. 541, 556 *per* Swinfen Eady L.J.; *Chandler v. Webster* [1904] 1 K.B. 493; *Sovfracht (V/O) v. Van Udens Scheepvaart en Agentuur Maatschapp (N.V. Gebr.)* [1943] A.C. 203.

[22] *Porter v. Freudenberg* [1915] 1 K.B. 857; *Amin v. Brown, The Times*, August 24, 2005. Note, however, *The Mowe* [1915] P. 1.

[23] *Porter v. Freudenberg, supra*, at pp. 880 *et seq.*; *Robinson & Co. v. Continental Insurance Co. of Mannheim* [1915] 1 K.B. 155.

[24] *Re Ferdinand ex-Tsar of Bulgaria* [1921] 1 Ch. 107; *Porter v. Freudenberg, supra*, at p. 869. Unless the Crown's power of confiscation is exercised, the enemy holds his property subject to all its obligations which may be enforced against him during the war if their performance does not involve trade or other dealings with the enemy: *Halsey v. Lowenfeld* [1916] 2 K.B. 707; *London & Northern Estates Co. v. Schlesinger* [1916] 1 K.B. 20.

[25] *Daimler Co. v. Continental Tyre etc. Co.* [1916] 2 A.C. 307; *Hugh Stevenson & Sons v. Aktiengesellschaft etc.* [1918] A.C. 239; *Tingley v. Müller* [1917] 2 Ch. 144; *Ottoman Bank v. Jebara* [1928] A.C. 269.

It naturally follows from the foregoing that a partnership between a resident United Kingdom citizen or subject (or a resident alien) and an alien enemy is incapable of creation or, if validly created before the outbreak of war, of further continuation thereafter.[26] In the latter case, the dissolution of the firm will be automatic and is in no way dependent on the partners' knowledge of the illegality.[27] This, of course, assumes that the United Kingdom is one of the bellicose nations; under English law different principles apply to commercial disputes between members of warring nations if the United Kingdom is in the position of a neutral.[28]

(b) Minors

4–07 A minor, *i.e.* a person under the age of 18,[29] may enter into partnership[30] but will, as a general rule, incur no liability to his partners or to third parties whilst he remains under age. When he attains 18, or even before, he may, if he chooses, repudiate the agreement,[31] but his partners will now seemingly have two options. They may either seek a restitution order under the Minors' Contracts Act 1987[32] or proceed to apply the whole of the partnership property, which naturally includes the minor's share, in payment of the firm's debts and liabilities.[33] Equally, a creditor of the firm who has obtained judgment against the firm in the proper form[34] may levy execution against such property, but not against the separate property of the minor.[35]

4–08 Lord Lindley explained the rationale behind the minor partner's freedom from liability for partnership debts in these terms:

"The irresponsibility of an infant for the debts of a partnership of which he is a member is an obvious consequence of his general incapacity to bind himself by contract, and does not require to be supported by any special authority.[36] It might, perhaps, be thought that an infant who held himself out as a partner would be liable

---

[26] Partnership Act 1890, s.34; *R. v. Kupfer* [1915] 2 K.B. 321; *Hugh Stevenson & Sons v. Aktiengesellschaft etc., supra; Rodriguez v. Speyer Bros.* [1919] A.C. 59. The decision in *Feldt v. Chamberlain* (1914) 58 S.J. 788 cannot be regarded as good law. See also *infra*, para. 24–42.

[27] See *Hudgell Yeates & Co. v. Watson* [1978] Q.B. 451 (solicitor failing to renew his practising certificate).

[28] Thus, an award under an arbitration clause contained in a contract between two belligerent states (India and Pakistan) was held to be valid and enforceable in England: *Dalmia Dairy Industries Ltd. v. National Bank of Pakistan* [1978] 2 Lloyd's Rep. 223. Equally, there can be no objection to persons resident in a neutral country forming a partnership in order to trade with the belligerent nations: *Ex p. Chavasse* (1865) 4 De G.J. & S. 655; *The Helen* (1801) 3 Rob.Chr. 224.

[29] Family Law Reform Act 1969, s.1.

[30] In *Re A. and M.* [1926] Ch. 274, the only two partners were both minors. See also, *Alexander Bulloch & Co. v. I.R.C.* [1976] S.T.C. 514 (where two minors were held not to be partners on the particular facts of the case).

[31] See *infra*, paras 4–11, 4–12.

[32] s.3.

[33] See *Lovell v. Beauchamp* [1894] A.C. 607.

[34] *i.e.* on a judgment "against the defendant firm other than A B a minor" obtained in an action against the firm in the firm name. See the cases in the next note and *infra*, para. 14–20. If the action is not brought against the firm in the firm name, the minor partner ought not to be joined as a defendant, unless he is to be represented by a litigation friend appointed under the CPR Pt. 21: see the cases cited *infra*, n. 36; also *infra*, para. 14–44.

[35] *Lovell v. Beauchamp* [1894] A.C. 607; *Harris v. Beauchamp* [1893] 2 Q.B. 534.

[36] Lord Lindley nevertheless cited *Chandler v. Parkes* (1800) 3 Esp. 76; *Jaffray v. Frebain* (1803) 5 Esp. 47; *Gibbs v. Merrill* (1810) 3 Taunt. 307; and *Burgess v. Merrill* (1812) 4 Taunt. 468, which "show that an infant partner ought not to be joined as a defendant in an action against the firm".

to persons trusting to his representations if they did not know him to be under age; but this is not so[37] ... ".

It is thus clear that, in a case of holding out,[38] the third party would not, prior to the Partnership Act 1890, have been entitled to proceed against the minor partner, even if he did not appear to be under age. There is no reason to suppose that the Act altered the law in this respect.

Torts

Just as a minor is not responsible for the torts of his agent, a minor partner **4–09** cannot be held liable for the misconduct of his co-partners.[39] He is, however, liable for his own torts, including fraud and negligence, although the standard of care expected of him in relation to the latter will vary according to his age. It follows that, subject to the latter factor, there may be some scope for an action for negligent mis-statement[40] in respect of representations made by a minor partner, whether to his co-partners or to third parties dealing with the firm. Whether such an action will lie principally depends on whether the cause of action is in substance contractual, or is so directly connected with the contract as to amount to an indirect method of enforcement. In either of the above cases, *e.g.* where a minor's negligent mis-statement has induced a third party to enter into partnership with him as a result of which that third party suffers damage, no action would be allowed.[41] *Per contra*, if the minor's tortious act, although concerned with the subject-matter of the contract, is in truth independent of it.

Fraud

The liability of a minor who perpetrates a fraudulent act no longer varies solely **4–10** according to the relief sought, since a restitution order may now be made in all cases.[42] Nevertheless, equitable relief, *e.g.* rescission[43] or an injunction,[44] will seemingly be granted more readily than other forms of relief, although the limits are not clearly defined.[45]

An example of the type of attitude likely to be adopted by the courts is, perhaps, to be found in a number of cases decided under the old bankruptcy laws. The general principle was that a minor could not be made bankrupt, even on his own petition, in the absence of debts for necessaries supplied to him or other

---

[37] See *Price v. Hewitt* (1853) 8 Ex. 146; *Johnson v. Pye* (1665) 1 Sid. 258; Vin.Ab. Enfant, H.2, pl. 16; *Glossop v. Colman* (1815) 1 Stark 25; *Green v. Greenbank* [1816] 2 Marsh. 485.

[38] See *infra*, paras 5–35 *et seq.*

[39] Lord Lindley added "The irresponsibility of an infant as a partner, seems therefore to be complete, except in cases of fraud". There is now more than one such exception, as appears from the text.

[40] See generally, as to such actions, *Hedley Byrne & Co. Ltd. v. Heller & Partners* [1964] A.C. 465; *Mutual Life and Citizens Assurance Co. Ltd. v. Evatt* [1971] A.C. 793; *Esso Petroleum Co. Ltd. v. Mardon* [1976] Q.B. 801. But see also *Argy Trading Development Co. Ltd. v. Lapid Developments Ltd.* [1977] 1 W.L.R. 444.

[41] See *R. Leslie Ltd. v. Sheill* [1914] 3 K.B. 607, 620 *per* Kennedy L.J.

[42] Minors' Contracts Act 1987, s.3. And see *Wright v. Snowe* (1848) 2 De G. & Sm. 321.

[43] *Lemprière v. Lange* (1879) 12 Ch.D. 675.

[44] *Woolf v. Woolf* [1899] 1 Ch. 343, where a minor was restrained from carrying on his business in such a way as to represent it as the claimant's.

[45] See *R. Leslie Ltd. v. Sheill* [1914] 3 K.B. 607, where most of the earlier cases, including *Stocks v. Wilson* [1913] 2 K.B. 235, are considered. The minor may also be required to pay the costs of the action: *ibid.*; also the cases in the previous two notes. However, these older decisions must now be read subject to the court's overriding discretion when awarding costs under the CPR r. 44.3.

debts which were legally enforceable against him.[46] However, if a minor, having fraudulently represented himself as of full age and thereby obtained credit from third parties, were subsequently made bankrupt, the adjudication would not be annulled and his deceived creditors would be paid out of his estate.[47] It may be that the position remains the same under the Insolvency Act 1986.[48]

Repudiation by minor

4–11   Whilst a minor partner is, in general, free from liability in respect of partnership debts, he cannot insist, as against his co-partners, that in taking the partnership accounts he must be credited with his due share of any profits, but not be debited with his due share of any losses. He must either repudiate the whole agreement or abide by its terms, and it is only under the agreement that he can claim any share of the profits.[49]

A minor partner may repudiate the partnership contract either before or within a reasonable time after he has attained 18.[50] His right to recover any money paid (or property transferred) under that contract will depend on whether he has received any benefit out of the partnership, as Lord Lindley explained:

> "If [*the minor*] avoids the contract, and has derived no benefit from it, he is entitled to recover back any money paid by him in part performance of it[51]; but he cannot do this if he has already obtained advantages under the contract, and cannot restore the party contracting with him to the same position as if no contract had been entered into."[52]

Equally, the other partners may now seek a restitution order against the minor in respect of any property which he may have acquired under the contract.[53]

4–12   A minor partner who decides to exercise his right of repudiation on coming of age should do so promptly and unequivocally, since a person who retains a share

---

[46] *Re A. and M.* [1926] Ch. 274; *Lovell v. Beauchamp* [1894] A.C. 607; *Ex p. Jones* (1881) 18 Ch.D. 109; *Ex p. Henderson* (1798) 4 Ves.Jr. 163; *Ex p. Lees* (1836) 1 Deac. 705; *Belton v. Hodges* (1832) 9 Bing. 365; *Re a Debtor* [1950] Ch. 282.

[47] See *Ex p. Watson* (1809) 16 Ves.Jr. 265; *Ex p. Bates* (1841) 2 M.D. & D. 337; *Ex p. Unity Banking Association* (1858) 3 De G. & J. 63. A receiving order was set aside in *Stocks v. Wilson* [1913] 2 K.B. 235. Observations on the old bankruptcy cases are contained in that decision and in *R. Leslie Ltd. v. Sheill* [1914] 3 K.B. 607.

[48] This Act repealed and replaced the Insolvency Act 1985, which had itself replaced the Bankruptcy Act 1914 with a new regime of personal insolvency. The 1986 Act contains no provisions relating to minors but, by virtue of the Insolvency Rules 1986 (SI 1986/1925), r. 7.51A(2), as substituted by the Insolvency (Amendment) Rules 2010 (SI 2010/686), Sched., para. 469), CPR Pt 21 is applicable in the case of insolvency proceedings against a minor.

[49] See *Lovell v. Beauchamp* [1894] A.C. 607, 611; *London & N.W.Ry. v. McMichael* (1850) 5 Ex. 114.

[50] Co.Lit. 380b; *Newry and Enniskillen Railway v. Coombe* (1849) 3 Ex. 565; *Dublin and Wicklow Railway v. Black* (1852) 8 Ex. 181. It follows that no tort is committed if the minor is induced to breach the contract, etc.: *Proform Sports Management Ltd. v. Proactive Sports Management Ltd.* [2007] 1 All E.R. (Comm) 356. Note that, in some cases, a minor cannot repudiate a contract before he comes of age, unless it is to his benefit to do so: see *Waterman v. Fryer* [1922] 1 K.B. 499; *Roberts v. Gray* [1913] 1 K.B. 520. A contract of partnership is not one of such cases: see *Cowern v. Nield* [1912] 2 K.B. 419, 422 *per* Phillimore J.

[51] *Corpe v. Overton* (1833) 10 Bing. 253; *Steinberg v. Scala (Leeds) Ltd.* [1923] 2 Ch. 452.

[52] *Holmes v. Blogg* (1818) 8 Taunt. 5087; *Ex p. Taylor* (1856) 8 De G.M. & G. 254; *Valentini v. Canali* (1889) 24 Q.B.D. 166; *Steinberg v. Scala (Leeds) Ltd.* [1923] 2 Ch. 452; *Pearce v. Brain* [1929] 2 K.B. 310. *Hamilton v. Vaughan-Sherrin Electrical Engineering Co.* [1894] 3 Ch. 589 cannot be relied upon: see *Steinberg v. Scala (Leeds) Ltd., supra.*

[53] Minors' Contracts Act 1987, s.3.

in a partnership cannot rid himself of its incidental obligations[54] and will, moreover, risk liability for debts incurred after that date by reason of the doctrine of holding out.[55] This is well illustrated by the decision in *Goode v. Harrison*,[56] where the minor partner was known to be a member of the firm. After he had attained full age he did not expressly either affirm or disaffirm the partnership, and he was held liable for debts incurred subsequently by his co-partners. It follows that, if he is to avoid any risk of liability, a minor who has represented himself as a partner must, when he comes of age, ensure that he is not held out as a partner thereafter.

(c) Persons Suffering from Mental Incapacity

A contact entered into by a person suffering from a mental disorder[57] or mental incapacity[58] will be binding on him so long as the other contracting party acted bona fide and was unaware of his incapacity.[59] What is less clear is whether such a contract will also be binding where that condition is fulfilled if a declaration as to that person's mental capacity has been applied for or made[60] or, indeed, a deputy has already been appointed,[61] but it seems likely that it will not.[62] It necessarily follows that, subject to those two points, such a person may enter into a valid contract of partnership and, thereby, assume all the rights and liabilities which normally attend that relationship. However, it should be noted that, whether the contract is *per se* voidable or not, a judge of the Court of Protection[63] is empowered, in the course of administering the property and affairs of a person suffering from mental incapacity, *inter alia* to take decisions in relation to his property and affairs, including the carrying on of any profession, trade or business, the carrying out of any contract entered into by him and, indeed, the dissolution of any partnership of which he is a member.[64]

4–13

Similar principles apply in the case of a supervening mental disorder or incapacity affecting a member of an existing firm. Thus, it is clear that a partner's mental incapacity will not, of itself, dissolve the firm or, indeed, affect his continuing entitlement to a share of the partnership profits.[65] The corollary is, of

4–14

---

[54] See *London & North-Western Railway v. McMichael* (1850) 5 Ex. 855; *Cork and Bandon Railway v. Cazenove* (1847) 10 Q.B. 935; *Ebbett's Case* (1870) L.R. 5 Ch.App. 302. *cf. Baker's Case* (1870) L.R. 7 Ch.App. 115.

[55] Partnership Act 1890, s.14, *infra*, paras 5–35 *et seq*.

[56] (1821) 5 B. & A. 147.

[57] See the Mental Health Act 1983, s.1(2), as amended by the Mental Health Act 2007, s.1(1), (2).

[58] See the Mental Capacity Act 2005, s.2. And see, generally, *Masterman-Lister v. Jewell* [2003] 3 All E.R. 162 (CA), albeit a decision under the Mental Health Act 1983.

[59] See *Hart v. O'Connor* [1985] A.C. 1000 (PC), where the earlier cases (particularly *Imperial Loan Co. v. Stone* [1892] 1 Q.B. 599 and *Molton v. Camroux* (1849) 4 Ex. 17) are considered.

[60] See the Mental Capacity Act 2005, s.15.

[61] Pursuant to *ibid*. s.16. The role of deputy replaced that of a receiver appointed under the Mental Health Act 1983, s.99.

[62] See *Chitty on Contracts* (30th ed.) at para. 7–077. The position for formerly more certain: see *Re Marshall* [1920] 1 Ch. 284; also *Re Walker* [1905] 1 Ch. 160.

[63] As to the meaning of this expression, see the Mental Capacity Act 2005, s.46.

[64] See *ibid*. s.18(1)(d), (e), (f). *Quaere* can the court actually *order* a dissolution: it is thought not but a contrary view is adopted in *Heywood & Massey's Court of Protection Practice*, at para. 4–041: see further *infra*, paras 24–64 *et seq*. And see generally, as to the exercise of the Court of Protection's powers, *Re S (Protected Persons)* [2010] 1 W.L.R. 1082.

[65] *Jones v. Noy* (1833) 2 M. & K. 125.

course, his continuing responsibility for the debts and liabilities of the firm.[66] However, in such a case, account must again be taken of the overriding powers exercisable by the Court of Protection.[67]

(d) Husband, Wives and Civil Partners

4–15 Married women were formerly subject to wide ranging disabilities in terms of their legal capacity, but those disabilities have long since been removed.[68] Nevertheless, the involvement of a married woman in a business with her husband or of civil partners in a business together may still have certain specific consequences.

Loans

4–16 If a wife lends money to her husband, or vice versa, and a bankruptcy order is subsequently made against the borrower, the lender will be postponed to all the borrower's other creditors; similarly in the case of loans between civil partners.[69] As under the previous law,[70] if the borrower is a member of a firm and the money is lent for the purpose of its business, upon the firm being wound up as an unregistered company with concurrent petitions being presented against one or more of the partners,[71] or upon all the partners being bankrupted on the presentation of a joint bankruptcy petition,[72] the lender will be postponed to the borrower's separate creditors *and* to the joint creditors of the firm.[73] However, a loan to a firm of which the bankrupt spouse/civil partner was a member will be repayable out of its assets like any other partnership debt, even though his/her separate creditors may thereby be preferred.[74]

---

[66] *Sadler v. Lee* (1843) 6 Beav. 324. At this point Lord Lindley, referring to *Sadler v. Lee*, unaccountably mentioned only the continuing liability of the incapacitated partner for the "subsequent misconduct of the other members".

[67] See the Mental Capacity Act 2005, s.18(1).

[68] See as to these disabilities, the 14th ed. of this work, at pp. 60–63.

[69] Insolvency Act 1986, s.329, as amended by the Civil Partnership Act 2004, Sched. 27, para. 116. The predecessor of this section (the Bankruptcy Act 1914, s.36) treated a loan made by a husband differently from a loan made by a wife, but the distinction has, for obvious reasons, not been preserved. The current section also applies where the marriage/civil partnership registration takes place before the commencement of the bankruptcy.

[70] See *Ex p. Neilson and Craig v. The Trustee* [1929] 1 Ch. 534.

[71] See *infra*, paras 27–24 *et seq.*

[72] See *infra*, paras 27–44 *et seq.*

[73] See, in the former case, the Insolvency Act 1986, ss.175A(5), 175B(1) (as inserted by the Insolvent Partnerships Order 1994, Sched. 4, Pt II, para. 23 and applied, as regards the firm, by the Insolvency Act 1986, s.221(5) (as itself amended, in the case of a creditor's petition, by the Insolvent Partnerships Order 1994, art. 8(1), (2), Sched. 4, Pt I, para. 3 and, in the case of a member's petition, by *ibid.* art. 10(1)(a), Sched. 6, para. 4) and, as regards the individual partners, by the Insolvent Partnerships Order 1994, arts 8(6)–(8), 10(4)–(6)) and, in the latter, *ibid.* ss.328A(5), 328B(1) (as added by the Insolvent Partnerships Order 1994, art. 11(3), Sched. 7, para. 21). The expression "postponed debt" is defined in the Insolvent Partnerships Order 1994, art. 2(1) and that definition is added to the Insolvency Act 1986, s.436 by *ibid.* art. 2(2).

[74] *Semble*, in this case the debt will not be a postponed debt as regards *the firm* if the latter is wound up as an unregistered company with concurrent petitions being presented against the partners, since the Insolvency Act 1986, s.329 will not apply. *A fortiori* where no concurrent petitions are presented. It is submitted that the position will be the same where a joint bankruptcy petition is presented by the partners: see *Ex p. Nottingham* (1887) 19 Q.B.D. 88 (a decision under the Married Women's Property Act 1882, s.3), which is thought still to be good law; see also *Ex p. Neilson and Craig v. The Trustee, supra*.

Partnerships between spouses or civil partners

Husbands and wives frequently enter into partnership together although, as in **4–17**
the case of other contractual obligations, the court may be less ready to *infer* the
existence of that relationship.[75] A similar attitude is likely to be adopted in the
case of an alleged partnership between civil partners. Equally, where a partnership is found to exist, the court will not ignore the matrimonial/civil partnership
background. Thus, in *Bothe v. Amos*,[76] where the partnership was tied in closely
with the marital relationship, the break up of the marriage in effect put an end to
the partnership. In *Ward v. Newalls Insulation Co. Ltd.*[77] two partners, W and E,
had admitted their wives to the firm as sleeping partners. Although the existence
of the enlarged partnership was accepted as a matter of law,[78] the Court of
Appeal, in assessing W's economic loss in a claim against his former employer,
ignored his wife's entitlement to one-quarter of the partnership profits and treated
her as an effective nominee for W.[79]

It is now clear that, in an appropriate case, HMRC will seek to treat such a
partnership as involving a settlement for the purpose of income tax,[80] although
the same approach will not be maintainable outside the sphere of taxation, *e.g.* it
has been held that a partnership agreement is not a marriage settlement and, thus,
cannot not be varied under the Family Law (Scotland) Act 1985.[81]

It should also be noted that, on the termination of the marriage or civil **4–18**
partnership, the spouses'/civil partners' respective rights in and to the partnership
business may fall to be dealt with by the Family Division under the wide
jurisdiction exercised over their property rights.[82]

Contributions to spouse's/civil partner's business

Although not strictly relevant to the law of partnership, brief mention may also **4–19**
be made in this connection of the interest which a husband, wife or civil partner
may acquire as a result of contributions to the success of a business carried on by

[75] *Parrington v. Parrington* [1951] W.N. 534; *Nixon v. Nixon* [1969] 1 W.L.R. 1676; *Simon v. Simon* (1971) 115 S.J. 673; *Re Cummins* [1972] Ch. 62; *Britton v. The Commissioners* (1986) V.A.T.T.R. 209, also *cf.* the decisions in *Wilson v. C.&E. Commissioners* [2000] S.T.I. 552 and *Taste of Bangladesh v. C.&E. Commissioners* [2000] S.T.I. 554. It is submitted that the court's reluctance to infer the existence of a partnership will often stem from a failure specifically to raise the question for determination; in *Re John's Assignment Trusts* [1970] 1 W.L.R. 955, Goff J. found the conclusion that a partnership existed inescapable: see *ibid.* p. 960. See also *Burgess v. Florence Nightingale Hospital for Gentlewomen* [1955] 1 Q.B. 349; *Ward v. Newalls Insulation Co. Ltd.* [1998] 1 W.L.R. 1722, noted *infra.* *cf. Saywell v. Pope* [1979] S.T.C. 824, where the facts were almost identical to those in the latter case (save that, in this instance, the partners had purported to execute a partnership agreement *ex post facto*), but no partnership was held to exist.
[76] [1976] Fam. 46. *Quaere*, was the court fully seised of the partnership issue?
[77] [1998] 1 W.L.R. 1722.
[78] *cf. Saywell v. Pope*, noted *supra*, n. 75.
[79] [1998] 1 W.L.R. 1725C. The circumstances were, however, exceptional: much turned on the ability of W and E to terminate their wives' right to share in profits by dissolving the partnership or by ensuring that it had no income: see *ibid.* pp. 1730G–H, 1733E–G. The decision should not be regarded as establishing any general principle that the existence of a partnership can be ignored and was, in fact, distinguished in *Neal v. Jones* [2002] EWCA Civ 1731 (Lawtel 31/10/02).
[80] *i.e.* under the Income Tax (Trading and Other Income) Act 2005, ss.620, 624, 625: see, *infra*, para. 34–16.
[81] See *Robertson v. Robertson* 2003 S.L.T. 208 (OH).
[82] See further, *infra*, para. 24–54.

his or her spouse/civil partner. Thus, where a wife has worked for many years without wages and has thereby assisted her husband to build up a valuable business, the court will be likely to hold that she has acquired an interest therein, or in some asset purchased out of the profits thereof.[83] The position as between civil partners will, needless to say, be no different.

(e) Companies

General principle

4–20   Lord Lindley summarised the position in these terms:

> "There is no general principle of law which prevents a corporation from being a partner with another corporation or with ordinary individuals . . . ".[84]

This is still the position and partnerships involving companies are now common-place.[85] Any lack of capacity by reason of a provision of the company's constitution[86] can no longer affect the validity of its acts,[87] so that every last vestige of the *ultra vires* doctrine has now been swept away.[88] That does not, however, mean that, viewed from a purely internal perspective, the company's directors necessarily have authority under the constitution to act as they wish, irrespective of the terms of the constitution,[89] even though any limitation on their authority will be of no effect *vis-à-vis* a person dealing with the company in good faith.[90]

---

[83] See *Nixon v. Nixon* [1969] 1 W.L.R. 1676; *Muetzel v. Muetzel* [1970] 1 W.L.R. 188; *Simon v. Simon* (1971) 115 S.J. 673; *Re Cummins* [1972] Ch. 62. The principles enunciated in the above cases might conceivably be applied so as to confer on a wife an interest in a partnership business carried on by her husband and others, but surely that interest would be merely derivative (*i.e.* it would form part of the husband's share) and would not affect the other partners' entitlements. Such interest would, in any event, be subject to any provisions affecting the husband's share which may be contained in the partnership agreement, *e.g.* accruer on retirement or death.

[84] Lord Lindley went on to add "except the principle that a corporation cannot lawfully employ its funds for purposes not authorised by its constitution" but this is no longer in point. Lord Lindley referred to *Gill v. The Manchester, Sheffield etc., Railway Co.* (1873) L.R. 8 Q.B. 186 "as to one company being the agent of another, if not its partner". He went on "Having regard . . . to this principle [*i.e. the second principle set out at the beginning of this footnote*], it may be considered as prima facie *ultra vires* for an incorporated company to enter into partnership with other persons", citing in support two American cases, *Sharon Coal Corp. v. Fulton Bank*, 7 Wend. 412; *Catskill Bank v. Gray*, 14 Barb. 479. This cannot, on any footing, now be regarded as an accurate statement of the law: see *infra*.

[85] See, for example, *Hugh Stevenson & Son v. Aktiengesellschaft, etc., Industrie* [1918] A.C. 240; *Newstead v. Frost* [1980] 1 W.L.R. 135 (HL). And see *infra*, paras 11–02 *et seq.*

[86] See the Companies Act 2006, Pt 3. Note that a company's memorandum is now a largely formal document rquired merely for the purposes of its formation: *ibid.* ss.7(1)(a), 8 and the Companies (Registration) Regulations 2008 (SI 2008/3014). The key document is now a company's articles: *ibid.* s.17. In the case of a company formed under the old regime, the provisions of its memorandum now form part of its articles: *ibid.* s.28(1).

[87] *ibid.* s.39(1).

[88] This was a process started by the Companies Act 1985, s.35(1), as substituted by the Companies Act 1989, s.108(1).

[89] Note that a company's objects will now normally be unrestricted, absent a specific restriction being imposed: Companies Act 2006, s.31(1). In *Newstead v. Frost, supra*, it was held that the word "all kinds of financial . . . or other operations" in a company's memorandum did in fact authorise it to carry on a business in partnership.

[90] See *ibid.* ss.40, 41.

A company is a person within the meaning of that word in section 1(1) of the Partnership Act 1890.[91]

Enemy companies

In the event of war, whilst the question whether a company is to be regarded **4–21** as an enemy will prima facie be determined by reference to its country of incorporation, the ultimate test is one of control. In order to identify the seat of control, the "corporate veil" may be lifted in order to see whether the company's agents or the persons in *de facto* control of its affairs, whether authorised or not, are resident in an enemy country or, even if not so resident, are taking the side of, or are otherwise themselves controlled by, the enemy.[92] It is only on the latter question that it is necessary to enquire whether or not the shareholders themselves are enemies. However, if the country of incorporation is England, the company will remain English and control by the enemy will not exonerate it from the operation of English law.[93]

(f) Bankrupts and Disqualified Persons

The Partnership Act 1890 provides that the bankruptcy of a partner will dissolve **4–22** the firm, but this may be overridden by agreement.[94] There is, as such, no statutory or other prohibition on a bankrupt becoming or remaining a partner, although account must be taken of section 360(1) of the Insolvency Act 1986,[95] which is in the following terms:

"The bankrupt is guilty of an offence if—

(a) either alone or jointly with any other person, he obtains credit[96] to the extent of the prescribed amount[97] or more without giving the person from whom he obtains it the relevant information about his status; or

(b) he engages (whether directly or indirectly) in any business under a name other than that in which he was adjudged bankrupt without disclosing to all persons with whom he enters into any business transaction the name in which he was so adjudged."

---

[91] Interpretation Act 1978, s.5, Sched. 1. As to local authorities, see *Jones v. Sec. of State for Wales* (1974) 28 P. & C.R. 280. Note that the Limited Partnerships Act 1907, s.4(4) provides that a body corporate may be a *limited* partner, leaving it to be assumed that such a body may also be a general partner: see further *infra*, para. 29–06.

[92] See *Daimler Co. Ltd. v. Continental Tyre Co.* [1916] 2 A.C. 307, 345–346 *per* Lord Parker; *Kuenigl v. Donnersmarck* [1955] 1 Q.B. 515; *The Hamborn* [1919] A.C. 993; *Re Badische Co.* [1921] 2 Ch. 331, 338–342 and 365–372 *per* Russell J.; also *The Roumanian* [1915] P. 26. The question whether a company is to be regarded as an enemy is distinct from the question whether it is trading with the enemy: see *Re Hilckes* [1917] 1 K.B. 48.

[93] *Kuenigl v. Donnersmarck* [1955] 1 Q.B. 515.

[94] Partnership Act 1890, s.33(1). See further, *infra*, para. 24–32.

[95] Note that this subsection now also applies to a discharged bankrupt who is subject to a bankruptcy restriction order: *ibid.* subs.(5), as added by the Enterprise Act 2002, Sched. 21, para. 3.

[96] Two instances in which the bankrupt is treated as having obtained credit are set out in subs.(2). Note also *R. v. Smith* (1915) 11 Crim.App.R. 81; *R. v. Hartley* [1972] 2 Q.B. 1; *R. v. Miller* [1977] 1 W.L.R. 1129 (decisions under the Bankruptcy Act 1914, s.155).

[97] Currently £500: the Insolvency Proceedings (Monetary Limits) Order 1986 (SI 1986/1996), art. 3, Sched., Pt II, as amended by the Insolvency Proceedings (Monetary Limits) (Amendment) Order 2004 (SI 2004/547), art.2, Sched.

4–23   It is considered that, consistently with the position under the equivalent section of the Bankruptcy Act 1914,[98] no offence would be committed under limb (a) of the section if the bankrupt obtains credit for a third party, *e.g.* his partner[99]; if, however, he obtains credit on behalf of the *partnership* of which he is a member, it will be obtained jointly and an offence will be committed. As to limb (b), it is thought that a bankrupt could not properly enter into or join a partnership which carries on business in any name other than his own, unless the bankruptcy is disclosed to every person dealing with the firm.[100]

In addition to his liability to be prosecuted under the section, a bankrupt cannot enforce any agreement entered into in breach of its provisions.[101]

Disqualification orders

4–24   Where an insolvent partnership is wound up as an unregistered company, the court may in certain circumstances make an order against one or more of the partners under the Company Directors Disqualification Act 1986.[102] It would seem that such an order will not prohibit partners against whom it is made from entering into another partnership during the period of disqualification,[103] and the Department for Business, Innovation and Skills appears to share this view. If the position were otherwise, contravention of such an order would involve the commission of an offence[104] and might well render the firm illegal.[105]

(g) Trustees, Personal Representatives and Nominees

Trustees and personal representatives

4–25   A trustee or personal representative may clearly enter into partnership, although he will be personally liable for any debts and liabilities thereby incurred.[106] Whether he will be entitled to an indemnity out of the trust fund or estate will, in essence, depend on whether his activities constitute a breach of

---

[98] Bankruptcy Act 1914, s.155(a). Note, however, that in a number of cases, the courts have stressed that the Insolvency Act 1986 introduced a new insolvency regime, so that cases decided under the 1914 Act may have no or only limited relevance: see *infra*, para. 27–108, n. 494.

[99] *R. v. Godwin* (1980) 71 Cr.App.R. 97. *Per contra*, if credit is obtained for a company which is in reality the bankrupt's alter ego: *ibid.*

[100] It is submitted that a partnership formed with the intention of committing an offence under the above section would be illegal.

[101] *De Choisy v. Hynes* [1937] 4 All E.R. 54 (a decision under the Bankruptcy Act 1914, s.155).

[102] See *infra*, para. 27–64.

[103] This is on the basis that a partnership can only be wound up under the Insolvency Act 1986, Pt 5 where it is insolvent: see the Insolvent Partnerships Order 1994, arts 7–10. On that basis, a solvent partnership is not a company within the meaning of the Company Directors Disqualification Act 1986, s.22(2)(b), as substituted by the Companies Act 2006 (Consequential Amendments, Transitional Provisions and Savings) Order 2009 (SI 2009/1941), Sched. 1, para. 85(1), (11)(a). See also *Re Chartmore Ltd.* [1990] B.C.L.C. 673, 675e *per* Harman J.; *Re Probe Data Systems (No. 3)* [1991] B.C.C. 428, 434D *per* Harman J. *Sed quaere.*

[104] Company Directors Disqualification Act 1986, s.13, as amended by the Insolvency Act 2000, Sched. 4, Pt I, paras 1, 8(a) and the Insolvency Act 2000 (Company Directors Disqualification Undertakings) Order 2004 (SI 2004/1941), art.2(1), (3).

[105] See *infra*, paras 8–30 *et seq.*

[106] See *infra*, paras 26–22 *et seq.* Also *Muir v. City of Glasgow Bank* (1879) 4 App.Cas. 337.

trust.[107] It might be thought obvious that the trustee or personal representative will not thereby constitute his beneficiaries as partners,[108] but in 1987 the Department of Trade and Industry went so far as to confirm that, in the case of limited partnerships in the venture capital field,[109] "where one of the partners . . . is the trustee of an unauthorised unit trust for exempt funds the partner concerned will be regarded as a single partner for the purposes of the 20 partner limit". Why it was thought necessary to obtain such confirmation is unclear. Now, of course, the 20 partner limit has been abolished,[110] but the thinking behind the above statement still remains a matter of concern.

It should be noted that, in the case of a firm of solicitors, there is an express prohibition on partners creating any "third party interest" over their shares,[111] which would render the admission of a trustee partner in such a case improper and could lead to the firm's status as a recognised body being revoked.[112]

Nominees

The position of a nominee is more difficult. It is submitted that, in the case of   **4–26** a bare nominee whose status is known to and accepted by his co-partners, the true partner will be the nominee's principal.[113] Equally, if the other partners insist on contracting with the nominee as principal, albeit that he so contracts for the ultimate benefit of his own principal, it is difficult to see how the latter could be regarded as a partner.[114]

It goes without saying that a nominee partner of either type would not seem to be permissible in the case of a solicitors' partnership.[115]

(h) Partnerships

Since under English law a firm does not have separate legal personality,[116] it   **4–27** cannot, as such, be a member of another firm. Thus, where a firm purports to become a partner, this will, as a matter of law, constitute each of the members of

---

[107] See *infra*, paras 26–28 *et seq.*
[108] See *Smith v. Anderson* (1880) 15 Ch.D. 247; also the views expressed by Lewison J. in *Re Kilnoore Ltd.* [2006] Ch. 489 at [58], regarding the position of a bare trustee of shares in a company. And see, generally, *infra*, paras 26–30 *et seq.*
[109] See the Statement issued by the British Venture Capital Association on May 26, 1987.
[110] See the Regulatory Reform (Reform of 20 Member Limit in Partnerships etc.) Order 2002 (SI 2002/3203), reg. 2.
[111] Solicitors' Code of Conduct 2007, r. 14.04(11) (as amended by the Solicitors' Code of Conduct (LDPs and Firm Based Regulation) Amendment Rules 2009).
[112] SRA Recognised Bodies Regulations 2009, reg. 9.1(b). See also *infra*, paras 8–52 *et seq.*
[113] Note, however, that in *Ward v. Newall Insulation Co. Ltd.* [1998] 1 W.L.R. 1722, 1725C, the Court of Appeal appears to have held that one partner could be the nominee of another but still be a member of the firm. The circumstances were, however, exceptional (see further *supra*, para. 4–17) and it is doubtful whether the decision can be regarded as having established any principle of general application. *cf.* the position where a nominee holds shares in a company: see *Re Brightview Ltd.* [2004] 2 B.C.L.C. 191 at [31], [36]–[38].
[114] See, generally, the judgments of the Court of Appeal in *Smith v. Anderson* (1880) 15 Ch.D. 247. And see also, for an analogous situation, *infra*, para. 12–160.
[115] See the position of a trustee partner considered *supra*, para. 4–25.
[116] See *supra*, paras 3–01 *et seq. Per contra*, in the case of a limited liability partnership: see *supra*, para. 2–39.

that firm as a partner in his own right.[117] However, there is no reason in principle why, internally, the firm should not be treated as if it were a single partner.

The position is otherwise in Scotland, where the firm is a separate legal person[118] and its ability to enter into the partnership relation is well recognised.[119]

2.   NO RESTRICTIONS ON THE SIZE OF PARTNERSHIPS

4–28   There are now no statutory[120] or common law restrictions[121] on the number of persons who may be members of a partnership.

---

[117] This proposition was assumed to be correct in *Major v. Brodie* [1998] S.T.C. 491, 510h–j *per* Park J.; somewhat surprisingly, it was not even adverted to in *James Hay Pension Trustees Ltd. v. Hird* [2005] EWHC 1093 (Ch) (Lawtel 9/6/05), where a partnership was formed in order to become a special partner in a limited partnership. Such an arrangement may, from one point of view, be said to constitute a species of sub-partnership: see *infra*, para. 5–67.

[118] Partnership Act 1890, s.4(2). Note, however, that this separate personality automatically ceases on dissolution: *Balmer v. HM Advocate* 2008 S.L.T. 799 (HCJ).

[119] See *Major v. Brodie, supra*, p. 510f *per* Park J.

[120] The Regulatory Reform (Reform of 20 Member Limit in Partnerships etc.) Order 2002 (SI 2002/3203), reg. 2 abolished all the former restrictions which were to be found in the Companies Act 1985, ss.716, 717 and the regulations made or treated as made thereunder.

[121] The supposed illegality of partnerships so large as to be incapable of suing and being sued was, however, discussed in *Lindley on Companies* (6th ed.), Vol. I, pp. 180 *et seq.*

CHAPTER 5

RULES FOR ASCERTAINING THE EXISTENCE OF A PARTNERSHIP

1.   GENERAL OBSERVATIONS

THE ultimate test of the existence of a partnership is by reference to the statutory **5–01** definition set out in section 1 of the Partnership Act 1890,[1] as supplemented by the rules set out in section 2. Although the earlier cases, on which those sections were based, may be of relevance, they cannot take precedence over the provisions of the Act itself.

Partnership Act 1890, section 2

This section provides as follows: **5–02**

"2. In determining whether a partnership does or does not exist, regard shall be had to the following rules:

(1) Joint tenancy, tenancy in common, joint property, common property, or part ownership does not of itself create a partnership as to anything so held or owned, whether the tenants or owners do or do not share any profits made by the use thereof.

(2) The sharing of gross returns does not of itself create a partnership, whether the persons sharing such returns have or have not a joint or common right or interest in any property from which or from the use of which the returns are derived.[2]

(3) The receipt by a person of a share of the profits of a business is prima facie evidence that he is a partner in the business but the receipt of such a share, or of a payment contingent on or varying with the profits of a business, does not of itself make him a partner in the business; and in particular—

(a) The receipt by a person of a debt or other liquidated amount by instalments or otherwise out of the accruing profits of a business does not of itself make him a partner in the business or liable as such:

(b) A contract for the remuneration of a servant or agent of a person engaged in a business by a share of the profits of the business does not of itself make the servant or agent a partner in the business or liable as such[3]:

(c) A person being the widow[, widower, surviving civil partner][4] or child of a deceased partner, and receiving by way of annuity a

---

[1] See *supra*, paras 2–01 *et seq.*

[2] There may be an intermediate position between sharing (net) profits and sharing gross returns, *e.g.* where the expenses of only one of the parties are to be deducted in computing the profits: see the various decisions concerning arrangements between publishers and authors cited *infra*, para. 5–27, n. 118.

[3] Paragraphs (b) to (e) respectively re-enacted, with slight modifications, Bovill's Act (28 & 29 Vict. c.86), ss.2, 3, 1 and 4.

[4] These words were added by the Civil Partnership Act 2004, Sched. 27, para. 2.

portion of the profits made in the business in which the deceased person was a partner, is not by reason only of such receipt a partner in the business or liable as such:

(d) The advance of money by way of a loan to a person engaged or about to engage in any business on a contract with that person that the lender[5] shall receive a rate of interest varying with the profits, or shall receive a share of the profits arising from carrying on the business, does not of itself make the lender a partner with the person or persons carrying on the business or liable as such. Provided that the contract is in writing, and signed by or on behalf of all the parties thereto:

(e) A person receiving by way of annuity or otherwise a portion of the profits of a business in consideration of the sale by him of the goodwill of the business is not by reason only of such receipt a partner in the business or liable as such."

The three basic rules embodied in the section will be considered in detail in subsequent parts of this Chapter.

Application of section 2

5–03   With one exception (the receipt of a share of profits), the above rules are formulated as negative propositions and merely establish the evidential weight to be attached where the particular facts of a case precisely duplicate those set out in the section. However, it will rarely, if ever, be possible to divorce those facts from the surrounding circumstances so as to permit the statutory rules to be applied in their pure form, as Lord Lindley explained in his Supplement on the Partnership Act 1890:

"The rules contained in this section only state the weight which is to be attached to the facts mentioned, when such facts stand alone. Those facts, when taken in connection with the other facts of the case, may be of the greatest importance, but when there are other facts to be considered this section will be found to be of very little assistance."

In cases of the latter type, the statutory rules in effect give way to a principle so fundamental that it is not expressly stated in the Act itself,[6] namely that, in Lord Lindley's original formulation:

"in determining the existence of a partnership . . . regard must be paid to the true contract and intention of the parties as appearing from the whole facts of the case. Although this principle is no longer expressed it is still law."[7]

[5] *Not* a third party: *Re Pinto Leite and Nephews* [1929] 1 Ch. 221.

[6] In his Supplement on the Act, Lord Lindley pointed out that this principle was expressly stated when the Bill was first introduced into the House of Lords.

[7] See the Partnership Act 1890, s.46, and *Davis v. Davis* [1894] 1 Ch. 393; *Re Beard & Co.* [1915] Hansell Bank.Rep. 191; *Walker West Developments Ltd. v. F. J. Emmett Ltd.* (1978) 252 E.G. 1171; *Saywell v. Pope* [1979] S.T.C. 824. Lord Lindley observed that this principle had been recognised ever since *Cox v. Hickman* (1860) 8 H.C.L. 268; see also *Badeley v. Consolidated Bank* (1888) 38 Ch.D. 238, 258 *per* Lindley L.J.; *Hawksley v. Outram* [1892] 3 Ch. 359; *Mollwo, March & Co. v. Court of Wards* (1872) L.R. 4 P.C. 419; *Pooley v. Driver* (1876) 5 Ch.D. 458; *Walker v. Hirsch* (1884) 27 Ch.D. 460; *Ross v. Parkyns* (1875) 20 Eq. 331; *Trower & Sons v. Ripstein* [1944] A.C. 254. A recent example of the same principle, albeit applied in an employment context, is to be found in *Autoclenz Ltd. v. Belcher* [2010] I.R.L.R. 70 at [53] *per* Smith L.J.

Construction of agreement

Any agreement must be construed as a whole: the mere fact that the parties   **5–04**
describe themselves as partners is not conclusive,[8] nor does the use of the word
"syndicate" imply the existence of a partnership.[9] On the other hand, the parties
may agree to share profits and losses, but at the same time declare that they are
not to be partners: it will then be for the court to identify their real status.
Although a declaration against partnership will be ineffective when all the indicia
of partnership are present,[10] it may affect the interpretation of other clauses and,
thereby, rebut inferences which could otherwise be drawn from them if they
stood alone.[11] Thus, such a declaration may be of particular significance where
the nature of the relationship does not appear clearly from the remainder of the
agreement.[12] In *Adam v. Newbigging*,[13] Lord Halsbury summarised the position
as follows:

> "If a partnership in fact exists, a community of interest in the adventure being carried
> on in fact, no concealment of name, no verbal equivalent for the ordinary phrases of
> profit or loss, no indirect expedient for enforcing control over the adventure will
> prevent the substance and reality of the transaction being adjudged to be a partner-
> ship; and I think I should add, as applicable to this case, that the separation of
> different stipulations of one arrangement into different deeds[14] will not alter the real
> arrangement, whatever in fact that arrangement is proved to be, and no 'phrasing of
> it' by dexterous draftsmen, to quote one of the letters, will avail to avert the legal
> consequences of the contract."[15]

In *Weiner v. Harris*[16] Cozens-Hardy M.R. was more forceful: **5–05**

> "Two parties enter into a transaction and say 'It is hereby declared there is no
> partnership between us.' The Court pays no regard to that. The Court looks at the

---

[8] See *Goddard v. Mills, The Times*, February 16, 1929; *Newstead v. Frost* [1980] 1 W.L.R. 135
(HL); *H.E. the Minister of Public Works of the Government of Kuwait v. Sir Frederick Snow &
Partners* [1981] Com.L.R. 103; *Norton Warburg Holdings Ltd. v. Perera* (1982) 132 N.L.J. 296;
Cobbetts LLP v. Hodge (2009) 153(17) S.J.L.B. 29. In *Protectacoat Firthglow Ltd. v. Szilagyi* [2009]
I.R.L.R. 365, Smith L.J. at [61] summarised the position in these terms: "one cannot create a
partnership by signing a document which calls itself a partnership agreement". Equally, the use of
partnership terminology in documents, etc., was regarded as of considerable significance in *McLa-
chlan v. British Railways Board*, Unreported November 7, 1995 QBD, a decision of H.H. Judge
Rivlin sitting as a judge of the Queen's Bench Division.

[9] *Tyser v. The Shipowners Syndicate (Reassured)* [1896] 1 Q.B. 135.

[10] See *Adam v. Newbigging* (1888) 13 App.Cas. 308, 315 *per* Lord Halsbury; *Ex p. Delhasse* (1878)
7 Ch.D. 511; *Moore v. Davis* (1879) 11 Ch.D. 261 (where there was only a qualified declaration
against partnership; had it been unqualified, the outcome might have been different: see the observations of Wrottesley J. in *Fenston v. Johnstone (Inspector of Taxes)* (1940) 23 T.C. 29). See also *Weiner
v. Harris* [1910] 1 K.B. 285, 290 *per* Cozens-Hardy M.R.; *Pooley v. Driver* (1876) And see *Horne
v. Pollard and Anderson* [1935] N.Z.L.R. s.125.

[11] Such a declaration may be of greater significance in a borderline case: see, for example,
Dragonfly Consultancy Ltd. v. Revenue & Customs Commissioners [2008] S.T.C. 3030, at [55] *per*
Henderson J. This was not a case concerning a partnership.

[12] This sentence was cited with approval in *Spree Engineering and Testing Ltd. v. O'Rourke Civil
and Structural Engineering Ltd.*, Unreported May 18, 1999 (QBD).

[13] (1888) 13 App.Cas. 308, 315.

[14] cf. *Lewis v. Frank Love* [1961] 1 W.L.R. 261.

[15] This summary was cited with approval in *Dollar Land (Cumbernauld) Ltd. v. C.I.N. Properties
Ltd.* 1996 S.L.T. 186, 191K–192B; see also *McLachlan v. British Railways Board*, Unreported
November 7, 1995 (QBD).

[16] [1910] 1 K.B. 285, 290. This passage was cited by Smith L.J. in *Protectacoat Firthglow Ltd. v.
Szilagyi* [2009] I.R.L.R. 365 at [60]. There the supposed partnership was held to be a sham.

transaction and says 'Is this, in point of law, really a partnership?' It is not in the least conclusive that the parties have used a term or language intended to indicate that the transaction is not that which in law it is."[17]

If the agreement is not in writing the intention of the parties must naturally be ascertained from their words and conduct.[18] Moreover, in construing any agreement, account must be taken of any subsequent modifications which may have been introduced by the parties, whether intentionally or unintentionally.[19]

Equally, where no agreement at all has been concluded, the court may adopt a very different approach. Thus, in *Greville v. Venables*[20] the claimant wanted to be a partner but the defendant had refused. The Court of Appeal declined to infer a partnership by conduct and rejected an attempt to rely on the "labelling" principle.

Joint ventures

5–06   The courts tend to adopt a strangely inconsistent attitude towards joint ventures. Although partnerships and joint ventures obviously have a number of common characteristics, in some instances the two expressions appear to be used interchangeably,[21] whilst in others the joint venture is recognised as a relationship quite separate and distinct from partnership.[22] In the current editor's view, whilst it can properly be said that all partnerships involve a joint venture,[23] the

[17] *Quaere* whether it is a precondition that a party to the agreement should challenge the existence of a partnership. In *Launahurst Ltd. v. Larner* [2010] EWCA Civ 334 (Lawtel 30/3/10), the Court of Appeal was unwilling to uphold a finding that an entire agreement clause in a contract with a self-employed contractor was a sham when he had not himself taken the point.

[18] However, the evidence will frequently be insufficient to prove that a partnership exists: see, for example, *Swiss Air Transport Co. Ltd. v. Palmer* [1976] 2 Lloyd's Rep. 604; *McPhail v. Bourne* [2008] EWHC 1235 (Ch) (Lawtel 13/6/08); also note *Bennett v. Lincoln* [2005] J.L.R. 125 (where the position was governed by Jersey customary law. And see also *Eames v. Stepnell Properties Ltd.* [1967] 1 W.L.R. 593; *Scott v. Ricketts* [1967] 1 W.L.R. 828; *Johnston v. Heath* [1970] 1 W.L.R. 1567; *Vater v. Tarbuck* (1970) 214 E.G. 267.

[19] Partnership Act 1890, s.19. See also *infra*, paras 10–12 *et seq.*

[20] [2007] EWCA Civ. 878 (Lawtel 12/9/07) at [40] *per* Lloyd L.J.

[21] See, for example, *Dollar Land (Cumbernauld) Ltd. v. C.I.N. Properties Ltd.* 1996 S.L.T. 186, (OH); *Cayzer v. Beddow* [2007] EWCA Civ 644 (Lawtel 29/6/07); also *Mair v. Wood* 1948 S.C. 83, at pp. 86 *per* the Lord President, 89, 90 *per* Lord Keith. In *Small v. Fleming* 2003 S.C.L.R. 647 (OH), Lord Macfadyen described a joint venture as a "species of partnership" and went on to hold that a joint venture could not exist in the absence of agreement on all the terms. This seems odd, given the very general requirements of the Partnership Act 1890, s.1(1), to which he specifically referred. The decision in *Cayzer v. Beddow, supra*, is very much to the same effect: see *ibid.* at [56]. *cf. Chirnside v. Fay* [2007] P.N.L.R. 6 (Sup. Ct. of New Zealand), where a joint venture was held to exist even though not all the details had been contractually agreed: see [91] *per* Blanchard and Tipping JJ. They in fact treated the joint venture as analogous to a partnership (*ibid.* [71]), whilst Elias C.J. held that it was "indistinguishable from a single transaction partnership" (*ibid.* [14]). A joint venture unsuccessfully alleged in *Kilcarne Holdings Ltd. v. Targetfollow (Birmingham) Ltd.* [2005] P & C.R. 8 was "not simply a contract for a partnership": *ibid.* at [204] *per* Lewison J.

[22] *Hampton & Sons v. Garrard Smith* [1995] 1 E.G.L.R. 23 (CA); also *Ross River Ltd. v. Cambridge City Football Club Ltd.* [2007] EWHC 2115 (Ch) (Lawtel 1/10/07); *Rosenberg. v. Nazarov* [2008] EWHC 812 (Ch) (Lawtel 10/4/08) at [58] *per* Thomas Ivory Q.C., sitting as a deputy judge of the Chancery Division; *Daniels v. Deville* [2008] EWHC 1810 (Ch) (Lawtel 5/8/08) at [36] *per* Lindsay J.

[23] *Whywait Pty Ltd. v. Davison* [1997] 1 Qd. R. 225, 231.

converse proposition manifestly does not hold good.[24] This is demonstrated by the unreported decision in *Spree Engineering and Testing Ltd. v. O'Rourke Civil and Structural Engineering Ltd.*,[25] in which a distinction was drawn between a so-called non-integrated joint venture, which would not involve a partnership, and an integrated joint venture, which *would*, in general, constitute the joint venturers as partners. However, the use of such terminology should not be allowed to obscure the need in every case to scrutinise the parties' arrangements[26] in order to identify whether the requirements of section 1(1) of the Partnership Act 1890[27] are satisfied and whether their relationship displays any of the normal indicia of partnership.[28]

It naturally follows that it is not possible to avoid partnership merely by describing the participants as joint venturers; the label will be ignored and the court will look to the substance of the transaction rather than its outward form.[29] Equally, it cannot be assumed that the participants in a transaction described as a joint venture do not each intend to carry on their own separate businesses: such situations are by no means unknown, *e.g.* share farming and oil exploration ventures.[30]

2. CO-OWNERSHIP

Co-owners not necessarily partners

As is clearly established by section 2(1) of the Partnership Act 1890, a   **5–07** partnership will not necessarily subsist between the co-owners of property,

---

[24] Note, however, that Richards J. ultimately declined to express a view on this proposition in *Shanshal v. Al-Kishtaini* (Lawtel 16/6/99) although this does not appear from the report in *The Times*, June 16, 1999. A subsequent appeal was allowed on other grounds: see [2001] 2 All E.R. (Comm.) 601 (CA). *cf. Todd v. Adams* [2002] 2 All E.R. (Comm) 97 (CA) at [78] *per* Neuberger J. There the issue was whether share fishermen could be regarded as joint venturers, but the question of partnership was not even raised.

[25] Unreported May 18, 1999 (QBD).

[26] Such arrangements will include not only any agreement entered into between the parties, but also the way in which they have subsequently conducted their affairs: see, for example, *Hibernia Management and Development Co. v. Newfoundland Steel Inc.* (1996) 140 Nfld. & P.E.I.R. 90, 107.

[27] See *supra*, paras 2–01 *et seq.*

[28] Note, in this context, the views expressed by Lord Coulsfield in *Dollar Land (Cumbernauld) Ltd. v. C.I.N. Properties Ltd.*, *supra*, p. 195F; also *Ness Training Ltd. v. Triage Central Ltd.* 2002 S.L.T. 675 (OH). And see further, *supra*, paras 2–12, 2–13.

[29] See *Paterson v. McKenzie* [1921] G.L.R. 43; *Canny Gabriel Castle Jackson Advertising v. Volume Sales (Finance)* (1974) 131 C.L.R. 321; *Spree Engineering and Testing Ltd. v. O'Rourke Civil and Structural Engineering Ltd.*, *supra*; *Ness Training Ltd. v. Triage Central Ltd.*, *supra*.

[30] See further, as to share farming agreements, *infra*, para. 5–16. Another example cited in earlier editions of this work is that of underwriters assuming a fractional proportion of an insurance liability under the terms of a single policy (albeit dependent on the precise terms of that policy): *Tyser v. Shipowners Syndicate (Reassured)* [1896] 1 Q.B. 135. Similarly, the joint ownership and operation of a ship would not necessarily create a partnership. And note also *Hibernia Management and Development Co. v. Newfoundland Steel Inc.*, *supra*.

whatever the manner of their acquisition, unless that was their original inten-tion.[31] An early illustration of this principle may perhaps be found in *Re Fisher & Sons*,[32] albeit that the true basis for the decision is unclear. A more recent illustration is *Pratt v. Medwin*,[33] where the original two parties, Messrs. Pratt and Medwin, had over a period acquired three properties for renovation and use in their insurance broking business and/or for letting. Mr Medwin subsequently transferred his share in one property to his son. It was held that no partnership existed and this issue was not pursued on the appeal. On the other hand, if premises are purchased by, and vested in, co-owners who subsequently carry on a business from those premises, there may be a partnership in the business, even if there is none in the premises.[34]

Co-ownership and partnership compared

5–08   The principal differences between co-ownership and partnership[35] may be summarised as follows:

1. Co-ownership does not necessarily result from an agreement. Partner-ship is the result of an express or implied agreement, even in those cases where the creation of a partnership was not intended.[36]

2. Co-ownership does not necessarily involve a community of profit or of loss. Partnership, to a greater or lesser extent, does.[37]

---

[31] See the Partnership Act 1890, s.2(1); also *Kay v. Johnston* (1856) 21 Beav. 536. Whether the co-owners intend to become partners may, of course, be doubtful: see, for example, *Sharpe v. Cummings* (1844) 2 Dowl. & L. 504; *Wilson v. Holloway* [1893] 2 Ch. 340; *Davis v. Davis* [1894] 1 Ch. 393; *National Insurance Co. of New Zealand Ltd. v. Bray* [1934] N.Z.L.R. s.67. See also *George Hall & Son v. Platt* [1954] T.R. 331, and the judgment of Lowry C.J. in *De Pol v. Cunningham* [1974] S.T.C. 487 (where the issue was not clearly defined). And see *infra*, para. 5–09.

[32] [1912] 2 K.B. 491. In that case, a testator, who carried on business alone under the name E. W. Fisher & Sons, by his will appointed his wife and two other persons as his executors and trustees, and empowered them to carry on his business for the benefit of his wife for life. Following his death in 1903, the three executors continued to carry on the business in the old name and were still doing so in 1911, although the terms of the will and the manner in which the business was carried on are not apparent from the report. Phillimore J. held that the executors were clearly joint debtors, but were not partners, and did not elaborate further. The precise basis for the decision is thus unclear: the significant factor may have been the absence of any sharing of profits, the entirety being paid to the wife. Alternatively, it may have been that the executors were merely co-owners, there existing no other contractual relationship between them. Yet still they were held jointly liable, almost as if they were partners. Perhaps the explanation was that, by trading under a firm name, they had held themselves out as partners under the Partnership Act 1890, s.14.

[33] [2003] 2 P. & C.R. D22, a decision of Sonia Proudman Q.C., sitting as a deputy judge of the Chancery Division.

[34] *Re John's Assignment Trusts* [1970] 1 W.L.R. 955.

[35] A number of other differences once existed: see further, the 15th ed. of this work, at pp. 79–81.

[36] Lord Lindley put it more laconically: "Co-ownership is not necessarily the result of agreement. Partnership is". But see also, in this context, *supra*, para. 2–15.

[37] Again, Lord Lindley put this proposition shortly, *viz.*: "Co-ownership does not necessarily involve community of profit or of loss. Partnership does". This goes too far: it has already been seen that a division of profits is not a necessary incident of partnership: see *supra*, para. 2–09. Community of loss is not referred to in the statutory definition of partnership (Partnership Act 1890, s.1(1)) and, indeed, will not always be present: see *infra*, paras 5–13, 5–54, 5–55.

3. One co-owner can, without the consent of the others, transfer his interest[38] to a third party, who will thereafter stand in his shoes so far as concerns the other co-owners.[39] A partner will rarely, if ever, have such an extensive freedom.[40]

4. One co-owner is not as such the agent, real or implied, of the other co-owners.[41] A partner is the agent of his co-partners, at least so far as concerns activities falling within the scope of the partnership business.[42]

5. One co-owner has no lien on the jointly owned property for outlays or expenses or for the other co-owners' shares of a joint debt. A partner does enjoy such a lien.

6. One co-owner may in general compel a sale of jointly owned land pursuant to the provisions of the Trusts of Land and Appointment of Trustees Act 1996.[43] Although the same jurisdiction is now exercisable in the case of land owned by a partnership[44] and the discretion conferred on the Court is wider than that which existed under the Law of Property Act 1925,[45] it seems unlikely that a partner will be able to obtain an order for the sale of partnership land whilst the partnership is still subsisting.[46] Equally, on a dissolution a partner is usually entitled to have all the partnership property sold, whether land or not,[47] and the proceeds applied in the manner laid down in the Partnership Act 1890.[48]

7. Co-ownership does not necessarily have as its purpose the realisation of gain. Such a purpose is of the very essence of partnership. It follows

---

[38] In the case of land, this will consist of an interest under a trust of land: see the Trusts of Land and Appointment of Trustees Act 1996, s.1.

[39] It would seem, however, that an ordinary co-owner's freedom to dispose of his share could be restricted by agreement: see *Caldy Manor Estate v. Farrell* [1974] 1 W.L.R. 1303. It should be noted that, where such a transfer is made by a joint tenant, the joint tenancy will be severed and the third party will only become a tenant in common (or, in the case of land, a tenant in common in equity) with the other owners.

[40] See the Partnership Act 1890, s.31(1), considered *infra*, paras 19–51 *et seq*. This was regarded as a factor of some significance in *Pratt v. Medwin* [2003] 2 P. & C.R. D22, noticed *supra*, para. 5–07.

[41] *cf. Fairclough v. Berliner* [1931] 1 Ch. 60; *Gill v. Lewis* [1956] 2 Q.B. 1; *Jacobs v. Chaudhuri* [1968] 2 Q.B. 470. And see the Landlord and Tenant Act 1954, s.41A, as added by the Law of Property Act 1969, s.9 and amended by the Regulatory Reform (Business Tenancies) (England and Wales) Order (SI 2003/3096), Sched. 5, para 5.

[42] See the Partnership Act 1890, s.5, considered *infra*, paras 12–02 *et seq*.

[43] *ibid.* ss.14, 15. These sections replaced the Law of Property Act 1925, ss.26(3), 30.

[44] See *infra*, paras 19–13 *et seq*., 23–193.

[45] See *Mortgage Corporation v. Shaire* [2001] Ch. 743; *Bank of Ireland Home Mortgages Ltd. v. Bell* [2001] 2 All E.R. (Comm) 920 (CA). Note also, in this context, *Rodway v. Landy* [2001] Ch. 703, where the Court of Appeal upheld an order for the physical division of a property formerly occupied by partners for the purposes of the partnership business, albeit that the property itself was not a partnership asset.

[46] See, for example, *Re Buchanan-Wollaston's Conveyance* [1939] Ch. 738, albeit a decision under the Law of Property Act 1925, s.30. And see *Rodway v. Landy, supra*.

[47] It is doubtful whether a partition would be ordered in the case of partnership land unless all the partners were agreeable (albeit that the court *could*, in theory, dispense with their consents under the Trusts of Land and Appointment of Trustees Act 1996, s.7(3)); partition was discounted as an option in *Rodway v. Landy*, October 13, 2000 (Lawtel 4/4/01), although the physical division of the property ordered in that case was upheld by the Court of Appeal at [2001] Ch. 703. As to chattels, see the Law of Property Act 1925, s.188 (as amended). And see *infra*, paras 23–193, 23–194.

[48] See *infra*, paras 19–05 *et seq*., 23–183 *et seq*.

that the remedies by way of account and otherwise which one co-owner has against the others differ in many important respects from, and indeed are less extensive than, those which one partner has against his co-partners.[49]

Co-owners sharing profits, produce or gross returns

5-09   Where co-owners share the profits realised by the employment of their joint property, their relationship may appear to be almost indistinguishable from partnership. In such a case, the question will be whether, having regard to all the circumstances, an agreement for a partnership should be inferred, even if this is not susceptible of an easy answer.[50]

If each co-owner merely receives his due share of the produce or gross returns derived from the employment of the joint property, no partnership will be created.[51] Thus, if one co-owner of a house agrees to leave its general management to the other, on terms that the latter will lay out his own money on necessary repairs and then arrange for the house to be let, recouping himself out of the rent, the co-owners will not be partners even though they divide the net rent equally between them.[52] The same can be said of the co-owners of a racehorse, who share both winnings and expenses,[53] and, in general, of the co-owners of a ship.[54]

Equally, if the co-owners convert the produce or gross returns into money, use that fund in order to defray the cost of obtaining such produce or returns, and ultimately divide the net profits, a partnership may be created, albeit only in relation to those profits and *not* in relation to the property itself. However, the distinction between such cases and those considered in the preceding paragraph is obviously a fine one.

Joint purchase of goods for re-sale or division

5-10   If several persons together purchase goods intending to resell them and to divide the profits, a partnership will almost inevitably be created.[55] However, if their intention is to divide those goods between themselves, they will not be partners or liable as such. Thus, in *Coope v. Eyre*,[56] A agreed to purchase oil with

---

[49] Note that in *Roderick v. Mark*, December 14, 1981 (unreported), Mr Julian Jeffs Q.C., sitting as a deputy High Court judge in the Chancery Division, followed certain obiter remarks of Lord Denning M.R. in *A. E. Jones v. F. W. Jones* [1977] 1 W.L.R. 438, 442, and held that a partnership of doctors was liable to account to a co-owner (who was not a member of the partnership) for the notional rent received by the partnership in respect of the jointly owned premises pursuant to the then National Health Service (General Medical and Pharmaceutical Services) Regulations 1974. Since, however, both counsel conceded the principle of a co-owner's right to an account, it is thought that the point is still technically open to argument. Any reader interested in this issue should consider Lord Lindley's own analysis of the position, which is to be found in the 5th ed. of this work at pp. 57, 58.

[50] See, for example, *Fenston v. Johnstone (Inspector of Taxes)* (1940) 23 T.C. 29.

[51] Partnership Act 1890, s.2(3); also *infra*, paras 5–12 *et seq.*

[52] *French v. Styring* (1857) 2 C.B.(N.S.) 357, 366 *per* Willes J. See also *Lyon v. Knowles* (1864) 3 B. & Sm. 556; *London Financial Assoc. v. Kelk* (1884) 26 Ch.D. 107.

[53] *French v. Styring, supra; quaere*, whether in this case there was a partnership in the profits. It would seem not: the agreement was to divide the winnings as gross returns.

[54] *Helme v. Smith* (1831) 7 Bing. 709; *Ex p. Young* (1813) 2 V. & B. 242; *Ex p. Harrison* (1814) 2 Rose 76; *Green v. Briggs* (1848) 6 Hare 395; also *Att.-Gen. v. Borrodaile* (1814) 1 Price 148. Equally, the co-owners *may* be partners: *Campbell v. Mullett* (1819) 2 Swan. 551; *The James W. Elwell* [1921] P. 351, 368–369 *per* Hill J.

[55] *Reid v. Hollinshead* (1825) 4 B. & C. 867; *Oppenheimer v. Frazer and Wyatt* [1907] 2 K.B. 50.

[56] (1788) 1 H.Bl. 37.

a view to dividing it between himself and others, each of them paying him their due proportion of the purchase price. A purchased the oil and then went bankrupt. The vendor sought to make the other parties to the agreement liable for the purchase price, but he failed, it being held that A purchased as a principal and not as an agent and since there was no community of profit or loss, the persons among whom the oil was to be divided could not be made liable as partners or "quasi-partners" (*i.e.* partners by holding out). A similar result was achieved in *Hoare v. Dawes*,[57] notwithstanding Lord Mansfield's early doubts, and in *Gibson v. Lupton*.[58]

Co-owners of mines

Privately owned mines and quarries, although rarely encountered today,[59]   **5–11** represent a special class of jointly owned property; as such, they were accorded detailed consideration in earlier editions of this work. That account does not appear in the present edition.[60]

Although the co-owners of a mine or quarry may be partners and the mine or quarry may be partnership property, neither is a necessary incidence of co-ownership, for the reasons discussed above.[61] Nevertheless, it will be difficult, if not impossible, for those co-owners actually to work the mine or quarry without entering into partnership, at least as to the profits realised.[62]

3.   SHARING GROSS RETURNS

The distinction between sharing gross returns and sharing profits was well   **5–12** established before the Partnership Act 1890 and is, of course, preserved in section 2(2).

In order to appreciate the distinction, it is necessary to understand what is meant by the terms "profits", "losses" and "returns". Lord Lindley explained the distinction in this way:

> "Profits (or net profits) are the excess of returns over advances [*i.e. expenses*]; the excess of what is obtained over the cost of obtaining it.[63] Losses, on the other hand, are the excess of advances over returns; the excess of the cost of obtaining over what is obtained. Profits and net profits are for all legal purposes synonymous expressions; but the returns are often called gross profits; hence it becomes necessary to call profits net profits in order to avoid confusion."

[57] (1780) 1 Doug. 371.

[58] (1832) 9 Bing. 297.

[59] Most mines were nationalised by the Coal Industry Nationalisation Act 1946.

[60] For a detailed consideration of the position, see the 15th ed. of this work at pp. 82 *et seq.*

[61] See *supra*, paras 5–07 *et seq.*

[62] See *Jefferys v. Smith* (1820) 1 Jac. & W. 298; *Crawshay v. Maule* (1818) 1 Swan. 495; *Faraday v. Wightwick* (1829) 1 R. & M. 45.

[63] For a discussion of the meaning of "profits", see *Re Spanish Prospecting Co. Ltd.* [1911] 1 Ch. 91. See also *Gresham Life Assurance Society v. Styles* [1892] A.C. 309, 322 *et seq. per* Lord Herschell; *Beauchamp v. F. W. Woolworth PLC* [1990] 1 A.C. 478, 489 *per* Lord Templeman. And note *Customs and Excise Commissioners v. Bell Concord Educational Trust Ltd.* [1990] 1 Q.B. 1040.

Notwithstanding that admonition, the expression "profits", meaning net profits as opposed to gross returns, is conventionally used, in this work and elsewhere.

5-13   Persons who share gross returns and their attendant expenses or the difference between them (whether a positive or negative sum), necessarily share both profits and losses: profits, if the returns exceed the expenses; losses, if those expenses exceed the returns. But persons who merely share the profits, *i.e.* the excess of the returns over the expenses, do not necessarily share losses, at least as between themselves.[64] This is because those profits may be shared by persons who have made no contribution towards the expenses; indeed such persons may be entitled to an express indemnity against losses, as in the case of the so-called "salaried" or "fixed share" partner.[65]

Implications of sharing gross returns

5-14   Where the receipt of gross returns is dependent on incurring expenditure, those returns will obviously include a profit element (assuming that a profit has been made), but will not include losses. This is because a loss will result only if the expenses exceed the returns, and this will not occur because the expenses are borne by those incurring them and are not payable out of the returns. That is not to say that the recipient of a share of the returns may not himself make a loss, but it is not a *shared* loss.[66] It follows that, if gross returns are to be divided irrespective of a venture's profitability, the division will involve only an incidental sharing of profits rather than a sharing of profits in the true sense.

On the other hand, if the persons who share the gross returns also share the attendant expenses, a sharing of both profits and losses will necessarily be involved.[67]

Lord Lindley's view

5-15   Although this was the distinction which was seen to be of significance prior to, and consequently preserved in, the Partnership Act 1890,[68] and which accounts for the rule that the receipt of a share of profits is prima facie evidence of partnership whilst the sharing of gross returns is not,[69] Lord Lindley questioned its reasonableness "at least where there is any community of capital or common stock". He observed that:

> "the rule itself is probably attributable less to the difference which exists between net profits and gross returns than to the doctrine which so long confused the whole law of partnership in this country, and according to which all persons who shared profits incurred liability as if they were really partners. When this doctrine was rife, the distinction between sharing net profits and gross profits (*i.e.* returns) had considerable

---

[64] *Per contra*, perhaps, as regards third parties: see *infra*, paras 5–28 *et seq.*

[65] See further, *infra*, para. 5–54.

[66] As Sullivan J. put it in *Manufacturing Integration Ltd. v. Manufacturing Resource Planning Ltd.* 2000 WL 389471, in such a case "The element of shared risk is lacking".

[67] But *cf.* the position of co-owners discussed *supra*, para. 5–09.

[68] See Partnership Act 1890, s.2(2), (3), *supra*, para. 5–02.

[69] This rule appears clearly from the decisions in *Gibson v. Lupton* (1832) 9 Bing. 297 and *French v. Styring* (1857) 2 C.B.(N.S.) 357.

practical value; but ... the doctrine in question is now wholly exploded, and the distinction alluded to is of little importance."[70]

Share farming agreements

Notwithstanding Lord Lindley's doubts, a resurgence of interest in the sig- **5–16** nificance of the distinction was generated by the comparatively recent innovation of the share farming agreement, whereby a land owner and a working farmer combine their resources with a view to sharing the ultimate produce in agreed proportions.[71] In theory, each is carrying on a wholly separate business, so that there is no "business in common", let alone one carried on "with a view of profit".[72] Provided that the share farming agreement reflects this and the partici-pants adhere to its strict terms, no partnership should result, even though the superficial appearance may at times suggest otherwise.[73]

4.   SHARING PROFITS

Scope of section 2(3) of the Partnership Act 1890

In seeking to identify the consequences which may flow from the sharing of **5–17** profits, section 2(3) of the Partnership Act 1890[74] performs two interrelated, but nevertheless distinct, functions. First, it defines the extent to which profit sharing may be treated as evidence of a partnership as between actual or potential partners; secondly, it defines the extent to which the recipient of a profit share can, on that ground alone, be affixed with liability by a third party *as if* he were a partner. The formulation of the general rule at the beginning of the subsection appears to be confined in its application to the former function, whilst the specific rules contained in paragraphs (a) to (e) are, by the addition of the words "or liable as such", equally applicable to both.

---

[70] Further illustrations of the rule, to which reference was made in some detail in earlier editions of this work, are to a greater or lesser extent to be found in *Sutton & Co. v. Grey* [1894] 1 Q.B. 285; also *Lyon v. Knowles* (1864) 3 B. & S. 556; *Cox v. Coulson* [1916] 2 K.B. 177, 181 *per* Swinfen Eady L.J.; *Montagu Stanley & Co. v. J. C. Solomon Ltd.* [1932] 2 K.B. 287. Similarly in the old cases concerning whaling voyages: *Wilkinson v. Frasier* (1802) 4 Esp. 182; *Mair v. Glennie* (1815) 4 M. & S. 240; *Perrott v. Bryant* (1836) 2 Y. & C.Ex. 61; *Stavers v. Curling* (1836) 3 Bing.N.C. 355. And note also *Steel v. Lester* (1878) 3 C.P.D. 121, 128 *per* Lindley J.; *The Riverman* [1928] P. 33, 38 *per* Hill J. See further, the 15th ed. of this work at p. 88, n. 92.

[71] The land owner will usually supply both land and fixed equipment, whilst the farmer will physically carry out the farming operations, using his own labour and machinery. *cf.* the position in *George Hall & Son v. Platt* [1954] T.R. 331.

[72] See Partnership Act 1890, s.1(1), *supra*, paras 2–01 *et seq.*

[73] See *National Trust for Places of Historic Interest v. Birden* [2009] EWHC 2023 (Ch) (Lawtel 10/9/09); also the Australian case of *Cribb v. Korn* (1911) 12 C.L.R. 205, where it was held that no partnership resulted from such an agreement. This case demonstrates that share farming agreements have been familiar for many years in Australia. They have also been widely used in America and New Zealand.

[74] See *supra*, para. 5–02.

In the following consideration of the subsection and its history, the two functions will be treated separately under the headings: (a) sharing profits as evidence of partnership; and (b) sharing profits as a ground of liability.

(a) Sharing Profits as Evidence of Partnership

The statutory rule

5–18   The general rule, which is set out in the opening words of section 2(3) of the Partnership Act 1890, is in the following terms:

> "The receipt by a person of a share of the profits of a business is prima facie evidence that he is a partner in the business, but the receipt of such a share, or of a payment contingent on or varying with the profits of a business, does not of itself make him a partner in the business."

This rule predated the 1890 Act and had been the subject of detailed analysis by the Court of Appeal in *Badeley v. Consolidated Bank.*[75] In that case, Lord (then Lord Justice) Lindley himself summarised the position as follows[76]:

> "It is no longer right to infer either partnership or agency from the mere fact that one person shares the profits of another. It may be, and probably it is true, that if all that is known is that one person carries on a business and shares the profits of that business with another, prima facie those two are partners, or prima facie the person carrying on the business is carrying it on as the agent of the person with whom he shares his profits. That may be true, and I think is true even now; but when you have a great deal more to consider it appears to me to be a fallacy to say that you are to proceed upon the idea that sharing profits prima facie creates a partnership or an agency, and that prima facie presumption has to be rebutted by something else."

5–19   Lord Lindley was in fact critical of the terms of section 2(3) as an attempt to embody the existing rule in a statutory form and, in his Supplement on the Act, commented:

> "The first clause of this sub-section is not well expressed, and indeed appears to contain a contradiction in terms, for if the receipt of a share of the profits of a business is prima facie evidence of partnership, it necessarily follows that the receipt of such a share, if that is the only fact in the case, must of itself be sufficient to establish a partnership. The effect of the receipt of a share of profits in determining the existence or non-existence of a partnership was very carefully considered by the Court of Appeal in the recent case of *Badeley v. Consolidated Bank* (1888),[77] and it is conceived that this sub-section does not alter the law stated in that case."

---

[75] (1888) 38 Ch.D. 238; *cf. Pooley v. Driver* (1876) 5 Ch.D. 458. See also *Re Young* [1896] 2 Q.B. 484, noted *supra*, para. 2–25; and note the old building society cases: *Brownlie v. Russell* (1883) 8 App.Cas. 235; *Tosh v. North British Building Society* (1886) 11 App.Cas. 489; *Auld v. Glasgow, Working Men's Building Society* (1887) 12 App.Cas. 197.

[76] (1888) 38 Ch.D. 238, 258; also *ibid.* pp. 250 *per* Cotton L.J., 262 *per* Bowen L.J.

[77] See also *Mollwo March & Co. v. Court of Wards* (1872) L.R. 4 P.C. 419, 433. Lord Lindley also cited, in this context, the Irish case of *Barklie v. Scott* (1827) 1 Hud. & Br. 83. There a father paid a sum of money as his son's share of the capital of a partnership, it being agreed that during the son's minority the profits should be accounted for to the father; it was held that the father was not himself a partner since that was clearly not the parties' intention. *cf. Reid's Case* (1857) 24 Beav. 318, where the father who had transferred shares into his minor son's name was held to be a contributory. Equally, there were dicta the other way: see, for example, *Heyhoe v. Burgh* (1850) 9 C.B. 431; *Fox v. Clifton* (1832) 9 Bing. 115; *Ex p. Langdale* (1811) 18 Ves.Jr. 300.

Confirmation of the correctness of Lord Lindley's approach is to be found in the judgment of North J. in *Davis v. Davis*[78]:

"Adopting then the rule of law which was laid down before the Act, and which seems to me to be precisely what is intended by section 2, sub-section 3, of the Act, the receipt by a person of a share of the profits of a business is prima facie evidence that he is a partner in it, and, if the matter stops there, it is evidence upon which the Court must act. But, if there are other circumstances to be considered, they ought to be considered fairly together; not holding that a partnership is proved by the receipt of a share of profits, unless it is rebutted by something else; but taking all the circumstances together, not attaching undue weight to any of them, but drawing an inference from the whole."[79]

Illustrations of the statutory rule

There are obviously abundant examples of the application of the rule in cases decided both before and after the passing of the 1890 Act. **5–20**

Thus, ignoring for the present section 2(3)(b),[80] it was frequently held prior to the 1890 Act that employees who were remunerated by reference to the profits of a business were not partners therein, at least where it appeared from the agreement that no partnership was intended.[81] Indeed, the comparative popularity of this device may, in some measure, have contributed to the gradual introduction and recognition of the concept of "salaried" partnership, which in general involves an employee being held out as a partner[82] and remunerated by a fixed salary and/or a share of profits, but denied many of the rights and duties normally associated with partnership, *e.g.* an obligation to contribute capital and to share losses and a right to participate fully in the management of the firm.[83] A significant feature in such cases will often be that, on a true analysis, the salary is payable *irrespective* of the profitability of the firm, so that the element of risk participation is lacking, although this has recently been held not *per se* to be inconsistent with the existence of a partnership.[84] Equally, there are, inevitably, instances in which persons described as salaried partners are to be regarded as

---

[78] [1894] 1 Ch. 393, 399.

[79] See also *Walker West Developments Ltd. v. F. J. Emmett Ltd.* (1979) 252 E.G. 1171, 1173 *per* Goff L.J.; *Saywell v. Pope* [1979] S.T.C. 824.

[80] See *supra*, para. 5–02.

[81] *Ex p. Tennant* (1877) 6 Ch.D. 303; *Ross v. Parkyns* (1875) L.R. 20 Eq. 331; *Trower & Sons v. Ripstein* [1944] A.C. 254; *Rawlinson v. Clarke* (1846) 15 M. & W. 292; *Stocker v. Brockelbank* (1851) 3 Mac. & G. 250; *Shaw v. Galt* (1863) 16 I.C.L.R. 357; *Radcliffe v. Rushworth* (1864) 33 Beav. 484 (where there was a holding out and a deed executed by the alleged partners, in which they were described as carrying on business together). See also *Geddes v. Wallace* (1820) 2 Bli. 270; *R. v. Macdonald* (1861) 7 Jur.(N.S.) 1127, where an employee remunerated by a share of profits was convicted of embezzlement, which he could not then have been if he had been a partner (*cf.* the position now, as considered in *R. v. Bonner* [1970] 1 W.L.R. 838); *Withington v. Herring* (1829) 3 Moo. & Pay. 30. Moreover, the Employment Rights Act 1996 expressly contemplates the remuneration of certain employees in this way: see *ibid.* s.199(2) (as amended) and *Goodeve v. Gilsons* [1985] I.C.R. 401. See also *Thompson Brothers & Co. v. Amis* [1917] 2 Ch. 211, a decision on the former excess profits duty.

[82] Partnership Act 1890, s.14: see *infra*, paras 5–47 *et seq.*

[83] See generally, as to such partners, *Stekel v. Ellice* [1973] 1 W.L.R. 191; and note that in *Casson Beckman & Partners v. Papi* [1991] B.C.L.C. 299, the court was content, at the parties' invitation, not to draw any distinction between an employee and a salaried partner. See also *infra*, paras 5–54 *et seq.*

[84] *M. Young Legal Associates v. Zahid* [2006] 1 W.L.R. 2562 (CA); *Hodson v. Hodson* [2010] P.N.L.R. 8 (CA). See further *supra*, paras 2–10, 2–11.

partners in the true sense, particularly when their salary *is* dependent on the firm's profitability[85] *and* they have capital at risk in the firm.[86] Latterly, such persons have tended to be designated as "fixed share" partners to emphasise the difference in their status,[87] although the change of nomenclature is of no real significance.

5–21   Another illustration of the rule can be seen in the case of the vendor of a business who receives a share of profits as consideration for the sale, *i.e.* a case now falling within section 2(3)(a) of the 1890 Act.[88] Similarly, where a trader and his customers enter into an agreement under which the trader is to distribute a part of his profits to the customers in proportion to the purchases made by them, no partnership is created.[89] Share fishermen will also, seemingly, not be regarded as partners.[90]

Agreements to share profits and losses

5–22   An agreement to share profits and losses, in the sense of making good the losses if any are sustained, may be said to be characteristic—if not of the essence[91]—of a partnership contract. As Lord Lindley explained:

> "Whatever difference of opinion there may be as to other matters, persons engaged in any trade, business, or adventure upon the terms of sharing the profits *and* losses arising therefrom, are necessarily to some extent partners in that trade, business or adventure".[92]

However, there are, inevitably, instances in which no partnership has been held

---

[85] As in *Marsh v. Stacey* (1963) 107 S.J. 512, where a "junior" partner was entitled to "be paid a fixed salary of £1,200 as a first charge on the profits" but in one year the profits were not sufficient to pay that sum to him. The Court of Appeal held that he was not entitled to have the deficiency made good by the other parner.

[86] See *Reid v. Hollinshead* (1825) 4 B. & C. 867; *Ex p. Chuck* (1832) 8 Bing. 469; *Gilpin v. Enderby* (1824) 5 B. & A. 954. In such a case, an express term in the agreement negativing any implication of partnership may be ineffective *vis-à-vis* third parties, such as HMRC: see *Fenston v. Johnstone* (1940) 23 T.C. 29, where there was held to be a partnership and not merely remuneration for management services. The managing partner put up no capital and contributed no assets, but he was to share in profits and losses arising in the development or sale of certain land. See also *Tate v. Charlesworth* (1962) 106 S.J. 368. *cf. Walker v. Hirsch* (1884) 27 Ch.D. 460.

[87] Although not strictly necessary as a matter of law, there has, in recent years, been a tendency to provide that fixed share partners *should* contribute a small sum of capital and be entitled to a minimal share of residual profits and losses, in order to ensure that partnership status and, thus, the benefits of self-employed (formerly Schedule D) taxation are achieved. See also *infra*, para. 5–59.

[88] See *Hawksley v. Outram* [1892] 3 Ch. 359; also *Re Young* [1896] 2 Q.B. 484, noted *supra*, para. 2–25. And see *Pratt v. Strick* (1932) 17 T.C. 459.

[89] See *Ogdens Ltd. v. Nelson* [1905] A.C. 109 (where the existence of a partnership was not suggested).

[90] See *Todd v. Adams* [2001] Lloyd's Rep. 443, where the issue of partnership appears not even to have been raised.

[91] See *supra*, para. 2–10 and *infra*, paras 5–25 *et seq.*

[92] Lord Lindley went so far as to add "nor is the writer aware of any case in which the persons who have agreed to share profits and losses have been held *not* to be partners". He found no difficulty in reconciling the decisions in *Mair v. Glennie* (1815) 4 M. & S. 240 (on the basis that "the expression 'profit or loss' seems to have been used for gross returns") and *Geddes v. Wallace* (1820) 2 Bli. 270 (where "the arrangement as to profit and loss did not apply to the person as to whom the question of partnership or no partnership was raised").

to exist despite the presence of such an agreement. *Walker v. Hirsch*[93] was one such case; *Re Jane*[94] was another, albeit superficially less clear, example. Yet, even in such cases, the arrangements may, consistently with Lord Lindley's view, be said to partake of the nature of partnership, albeit only in the non-technical sense.[95]

Subject to those exceptional cases, persons who agree to share profits and losses will normally find themselves treated as partners, whether or not they have themselves used that word.[96] However, it is not the necessary corollary of such an agreement that each party will enjoy all the rights and privileges normally associated with partnership, *e.g.* a right to participate in the management of the business,[97] to dissolve the firm,[98] or to share in the value of goodwill on a dissolution. Rather, the partners' rights and duties will in each case be determined by the terms of their agreement or, in the absence of any such agreement, by the 1890 Act itself.[99]   **5–23**

At the same time, it may be inappropriate to describe as partners persons who have agreed to share profits and losses if there is no general obligation to *make good* the losses. For example, where a selling agent agrees to share the profits and losses realised on his sales, it may be intended that he should be paid by a share of profits, with the losses of one year merely being deducted from the gains of another. If this is the true intention, he will not be in partnership with the   **5–24**

---

[93] (1884) 27 Ch.D. 460. See, in particular, *ibid.* p. 464 *per* Bagallay L.J; also *Horner v. Hasted* [1995] S.T.C. 766; *Dollar Land (Cumbernauld) Ltd. v. C.I.N. Properties Ltd.* 1996 S.L.T. 186, 192E–H *per* Lord Coulsfield.

[94] (1914) 110 L.T. 556. In that case two partners, J. and W., agreed to dissolve partnership on September 20, 1909 and, on that date, W assigned his share and interest in the partnership to J. The deed of dissolution provided that an account should be taken on December 31, 1909, that W.'s share when ascertained was to be credited to him in the books of the firm and to remain as a loan to the firm for 10 years, bearing interest, and that if, on taking the account, there was found to be an insufficiency of assets to meet the liabilities, W. was to pay J. half the deficit. J. continued to carry on the business and was adjudicated bankrupt in January 1910. It was held by the Court of Appeal that the partnership terminated on September 20, 1909, though the final account was not to be taken until December 31. The precise point decided was that moneys standing to the credit of the current account of the firm on November 4 formed part of J.'s separate estate, and that the bank had no right to set this off in discharge of a debt due in respect of money advanced by them to the firm; it was not decided that W. was not liable for debts incurred between September 20 and December 31. See, in particular, the judgment of Eve J. at p. 558.

[95] Thus, in *Walker v. Hirsch, supra*, p. 466, Bagallay L.J. said of the arrangements under consideration: " . . . no doubt there is in a sense a kind of partnership created—a kind of joint interest or adventure provided for, namely, that during the time that [*the plaintiff*] is in this service as clerk, manager, or whatever else it may be, he is to have a certain fixed proportion of the profits and losses. Then it is suggested that to a certain extent there was an arrangement by virtue of which he is to have a share, and in that sense, and in that sense only, is there a partnership of a very limited or qualified character as between the Plaintiff and the Defendants. That is, however, very different from what has been urged of a general partnership existing here between the three."

[96] See *Green v. Beesley* (1835) 2 Bing. N.C. 108; *Brett v. Beckwith* (1856) 3 Jur.(N.S.) 31; also *Greenham v. Gray* (1855) 4 I.C.L.R. 501; *Fenston v. Johnstone* (1940) 23 T.C. 29. For a recent example, albeit inadequately reported, see *Rees v. Dartnall*, February 25, 2009 (Lawtel 25/2/09).

[97] See, *infra*, paras 5–54, 5–55, 10–32; note also *infra*, para. 10–105. *cf. Walker v. Hirsch, supra*, where the claimant had no right to participate in management and was held *not* to be a partner.

[98] See, as to this, *Moore v. Davis* (1879) 11 Ch.D. 261 and *Pawsey v. Armstrong* (1881) 18 Ch.D. 698, in both of which it was held that there *was* a right to dissolve. *Quaere* whether *Pawsey v. Armstrong* went too far: see *Walker v. Hirsch, supra*. Of course the court's jurisdiction to dissolve a firm under the Partnership Act 1890, s.35 will continue to be exercisable on the application of any partner, irrespective of the terms of the agreement.

[99] *Walker v. Hirsch, supra*; Partnership Act 1890, ss.24 *et seq.*

vendor.[100] Similarly, there may be an agreement involving some, but not all, losses being made good but disclosing an intention not to create a partnership. In such a case, unless there are other circumstances inconsistent with that avowed or apparent intention, there will be no partnership.[101] This is illustrated by the decision in *English Insurance Co. v. National Benefit Assurance Co. (Official Receiver)*[102] where two insurance companies ("English" and "National") entered into an agreement, styled a "participation" agreement, which in essence provided as follows: National was to be entitled to and had to accept a quota participation equal to a one-eighth share of all risks arranged by English through its marine department. The participation was to be equal to 50 per cent. of the share retained by English at its own risk of all marine insurance accepted on or after a certain date, but with a maximum limit on any one ship. The liability of the two companies was to commence automatically at the same time, the expressed intention being that they should participate *pari passu* in all the marine insurances accepted by English. National was to be entitled to a proportionate part of the net premiums and other benefits received by English and was to bear its proportionate share of all losses. English was alone to settle all claims which might arise under its policies, and National was to be bound thereby. English was to receive from National a commission on the net premiums paid to it in respect of its participation and on its profits under the agreement. The House of Lords decided that the agreement amounted to a contract of reinsurance[103] and did not create a partnership between the two companies. The true meaning of the agreement was that English was to carry on its business as principal and that National was, as between itself and English, to receive a proportion of the premiums paid to English less commission and was, in consideration of such receipt, to indemnify English against a proportion of the losses suffered by that company as principal.[104]

Loans and other agreements where no sharing of losses

5–25   Persons who agree to share the profits of a venture are prima facie partners, even though they may also have agreed between themselves that they will not be liable for losses beyond the amount of their respective contributions.[105] Indeed, so strong may be the inference of partnership where there is a sharing of profits that a provision expressly negating the sharing of losses as to one or more of the parties is insufficient to displace it. Thus, notwithstanding certain observations of Lord Loughborough in *Coope v. Eyre*,[106] there is nothing to prevent one or more partners from agreeing to indemnify the others against losses, or to

---

[100] See, for example, *Horner v. Hasted* [1995] S.T.C. 766. But see also *Fenston v. Johnstone* (1940) 23 T.C. 29, *supra*, para. 5–20, n. 86.

[101] See *Walker v. Hirsch* (1884) 27 Ch.D. 460; *Sutton & Co. v. Grey* [1894] 1 Q.B. 285.

[102] [1929] A.C. 114.

[103] The contract was invalid for non-compliance with the requirements of the Stamp Act 1891 and the Marine Insurance Act 1906. For similar cases, see *Re Home and Colonial Ins. Co.* [1930] 1 Ch. 102; *Re National Benefit Ass. Co.* [1931] 1 Ch. 46; *Motor Union Ins. Co. v. Mannheimer Versicherungsgesellschaft* [1933] 1 K.B. 812.

[104] [1929] A.C. 121 *per* Lord Hailsham L.C.

[105] *Brown v. Tapscott* (1840) 6 M. & W. 119; *cf. Assured Quality Construction Ltd. v. Thompson, The Times*, April 21, 2006. The sentence in the text was cited with apparent approval in *Todd v. Adam* [2002] 2 All E.R. (Comm) 97 (CA) at [78] *per* Neuberger J.

[106] (1788) 1 Bl.H. 48. Lord Loughborough is reported to have said: "In order to constitute a partnership, communion of profits and loss is essential."

prevent full effect from being given to a partnership agreement containing such an indemnity.[107]

It should be noted that, in this context, it will often be argued by one party that a transaction was, on a true analysis, one of loan not of partnership. Thus, in *Chahal v. Mahal*,[108] Mr Chahal had provided the sum of £30,000 towards a particular venture, which represented more than twice the value of his house and part of which was raised by means of a bank loan. It was held that it was unlikely that such a sum had been loaned on an unsecured and interest-free basis[109] and, ultimately, that a partnership existed. The existence of the partnership was not challenged on the subsequent appeal.[110] A different attitude may, however, be taken in the case of arrangements between members of the same family.[111]

However, if it were agreed that one or more of the parties should be indemni-   **5–26** fied not only in respect of losses beyond the amount of his or their contributions, but also in respect of the loss of those contributions themselves, there would, as to such parties, exist a contract of loan rather than partnership.[112] The mere fact that there may, in such circumstances, be a sharing of profits as between lender and borrower does not make them partners or liable as such,[113] and the old cases where the contrary was found, in order to avoid the consequences of the strict application of the usury laws, are no longer good law.[114]

Equally, a dormant partner, by which is meant a partner (in the true sense of that word) who is not known and does not appear to be a partner, cannot escape liability by seeking to masquerade as a mere lender of money.[115] In each case, his status will depend on a careful analysis of the purported "loan" agreement and the rights and duties which attach to him thereunder. All too often, the dividing line between loan and partnership will be a fine one. As Lord Lindley explained:

> "The right of a lender is to be repaid his money with such interest or share of profits as he may have stipulated for; and his right to a share of profits involves a right to an account and to see the books of the borrower, unless such right is expressly excluded by agreement. If however a lender stipulates for more than this (*e.g.* for a right to control the business or the employment of the assets or to wind up the

---

[107] See *Bond v. Pittard* (1838) 3 M. & W. 357 (two solicitors, one of whom was not to be liable for losses, were held to be partners for the purpose of suing for fees); also *Geddes v. Wallace* (1820) 2 Bli. 270; *Walker West Developments Ltd. v. F. J. Emmett Ltd.* (1979) 252 E.G. 1171.

[108] September 30, 2004 (Lawtel 5/10/04), a decision of Hazel Williamson Q.C., sitting as a deputy judge of the Chancery Division.

[109] *ibid.* at [67], [70]. *Nadeem v. Rafiq* [2007] EWHC 2959 (Ch) (Lawtel 2/1/08) was a somewhat similar case.

[110] See [2005] 2 B.C.L.C. 655.

[111] See *Mehra v. Shah*, August 1, 2003 (Lawtel 5/8/03), where a loan, again of £30,000, had been made by one sister to her brothers and, on the evidence fell to be treated as such: see *ibid.* [33] *per* Sonia Proudman Q.C., sitting as a deputy judge of the Chancery Division. The overall finding of no partnership was upheld on appeal at [2004] EWCA Civ 632 (Lawtel 20/5/04).

[112] See Pothier, *Contrat de Société*, ss.21 and 22. Compare *Pooley v. Driver* (1876) 5 Ch.D. 458 and *Badeley v. Consolidated Bank* (1888) 38 Ch.D. 238.

[113] Partnership Act 1890, s.2(3)(d); however, there must be a written agreement if that paragraph is to apply: see *infra*, paras 5–32, 5–33.

[114] See *Bloxham v. Pell* (1775) cited 2 Wm.Bl. 999; *Fereday v. Hordern* (1821) Jac. 144; *Gilpin v. Enderby* (1824) 5 B. & A. 954; see also *Ex p. Notley* (1833) 3 Dea. & Ch. 367.

[115] See *Pooley v. Driver* (1876) 5 Ch.D. 458.

business) or if his advance is risked in the business or forms part of his capital in it, he ceases to be a mere lender and becomes in effect a dormant partner."[116]

Agreements where no joint property

5-27   As is self evident from section 1(1) of the Partnership Act 1890,[117] partnership does not require the presence of any jointly owned or partnership property. Lord Lindley put it thus:

> "It is not . . . essential to the existence of a partnership, that there shall be any joint capital or stock. If several persons labour together for the sake of gain, and of dividing that gain, they will not be partners the less on account of their labouring with their own tools".[118]

Equally, where one person owns property and the other possesses a particular skill, they may agree that the latter should have control of the property for their mutual benefit and that they should divide the profits derived from its employ-ment between themselves. In such cases, it may be no easy task to identify whether or not a partnership has been created: everything will depend on the terms of the parties' agreement and on their underlying intentions.[119]

(b) Sharing Profits as a Ground of Liability

The original doctrine

5-28   The origins of the controversial and uncompromising doctrine that the recipi-ent of a share of the profits of a business is liable for its debts and obligations, just as if he were a full partner, may perhaps be traced to a decision of Lord Mansfield.[120] However its first formulation is traditionally ascribed to De Grey

---

[116] Compare *Mollwo March & Co. v. Court of Wards* (1872) L.R. 4 P.C. 419; *Re Young* [1896] 2 Q.B. 484; *Pooley v. Driver, supra.* See also *Re Beard & Co.* [1915] Hansell Bank. Rep. 191, where one person guaranteed another's business account in return for a share of profits.

[117] See *supra,* paras 2–01 *et seq.*

[118] See *Formont v. Coupland* (1824) 2 Bing. 170; *Lovegrove v. Nelson* (1834) 3 M. & K. 1; *French v. Styring* (1857) 2 C.B.(N.S.) 357; also *Meyer v. Sharpe* (1813) 5 Taunt. 74; *Smith v. Watson* (1824) 2 B. & C. 401; *Steel v. Lester* (1878) 3 C.P.D. 121; *Miles v. Clarke* [1953] 1 W.L.R. 537; *Memec Plc v. I.R.C.* [1996] S.T.C. 1336, 1353d; also the cases cited *supra,* para. 5–15, n. 70. The dictum of Lord Cairns L.C. in *Syers v. Syers* (1876) 1 App.Cas. 174, 181, to the effect that a partnership in profits is a partnership in the assets by which they are made is, in the words of Lord Lindley, "by no means universally true". Lord Lindley also referred in this context to the following cases concerning authors and publishers: *Gale v. Leckie* (1817) 2 Stark. 107; *Gardiner v. Childs* (1837) 8 C. & P. 345; *Venables v. Wood* (1839) 3 Ross L.C. on Com.Law. 529; *Reade v. Bentley* (1857) 3 K. & J. 271 and (1858) 4 K. & J. 656; *Wilson v. Whitehead* (1837) 10 M. & W. 503. Lord Lindley added that *Venables v. Wood, supra,* "is an authority for the proposition that authors and publishers are not partners at all, and *quaere* whether this is not the correct doctrine?" No partnership was created in *Kelly's Directories Ltd. v. Gavin and Lloyds* [1902] 1 Ch. 630; see also *Abrahams v. Herbert Reiach Ltd.* [1922] 1 K.B. 477, 482 *per* Atkin L.J.

[119] See *Stocker v. Brocklebank* (1851) 3 Mac. & G. 250, where it was clear that no partnership was intended; *Walker v. Hirsch* (1884) 27 Ch.D. 460; *Re Young* [1896] 2 Q.B. 484; also *Pawsey v. Armstrong* (1881) 18 Ch.D. 698. *cf.* the Irish case of *Greenham v. Gray* (1881) 4 L.R. Ir. 501, where a partnership was held to exist, even though the assets used to carry on the business belonged to one partner. It seems that in this instance the claimant intended to create a partnership, whilst the defendant did not. See also *Fenston v. Johnstone* (1940) 23 T.C. 29; *George Hall & Son v. Platt* [1954] T.R. 331. And see *supra,* paras 5–04 *et seq.*

[120] *Bloxham v. Pell* (1775), cited at 2 Wm.Bl. 999.

C.J. in the later case of *Grace v. Smith*,[121] where he sought to distinguish between the position of such a person and that of a mere lender thus:

> "Every man who has a share of the profits of a trade, ought also to bear his share of the loss. And if any one takes part of the profit, he takes a part of that fund on which the creditor of the trader relies for his payment. If any one advances or lends money to a trader, it is only lent on his general personal security. It is no specific lien upon the profits of the trade, and yet the lender is generally interested in those profits; he relies on them for repayment. And there is no difference whether that money be lent *de novo*, or left behind in trade by one of the partners who retires; and whether the terms of that loan be kind or harsh, makes also no manner of difference. I think the true criterion is to inquire whether Smith [*the defendant*] agreed to share the profits of the trade with Robinson [*the continuing partner*], or whether he only relied on those profits, as a fund of payment: a distinction, not more nice than usually occurs in questions of trade or usury. The jury have said this is not payable out of the profits, and I think there is no foundation for granting a new trial."[122]

Eighteen years later, the doctrine was emphatically approved in *Waugh v. Carver*[123] and, although criticised by Lord Lindley among others,[124] held sway until the decision of the House of Lords in *Cox v. Hickman*.[125]   **5–29**

In earlier editions of this work, the state of the law prior to *Cox v. Hickman* was analysed in some detail but, given its lack of current practical relevance, that analysis has not been retained.[126] Suffice it to say that the harshness of the doctrine led the courts to draw subtle distinctions between the sharing of profits on the one hand and the sharing of gross returns and the payment of sums computed by reference to profits on the other.[127]

The position following Cox v. Hickman

In *Cox v. Hickman*,[128] the House of Lords effectively decided that persons who   **5–30** share the profits of a business do not incur any liability as partners *unless* they personally carry on the business or it is carried on by others as their real or ostensible agents. Although *Waugh v. Carver*[129] and the other cases were technically distinguished, they were in effect overruled. Lord Lindley summarised the position thus:

> "In fact, although the House of Lords in deciding *Cox v. Hickman*, professed to overrule no previous authority, the effect of that decision has unquestionably been to put a great branch of partnership law on a substantially new footing."

---

[121] (1775) 2 Wm. Bl. 998.
[122] *ibid.* p. 1000. It was this judgment, rather than the decision in the case, that was regarded as the authority for the proposition referred to in the text.
[123] (1793) 2 H.Bl. 235.
[124] See the 15th ed. of this work at pp. 98, 99.
[125] (1860) 8 H.L.C. 268.
[126] See the 15th ed. of this work at pp. 99 *et seq.*
[127] See for example, *Benjamin v. Porteus* (1796) 2 H.Bl. 590; *Dry v. Boswell* (1808) 1 Camp. 330; *Ex p. Hamper* (1811) 17 Ves.Jr. 403, 412 *per* Lord Eldon L.C.; *Ex p. Rowlandson* (1811) 1 Rose 89; *Ex p. Langdale* (1811) 18 Ves.Jr. 300; *Ex p. Watson* (1815) 19 Ves.Jr. 459; *Mair v. Glennie* (1815) 4 M. & S. 240 (the expression "profits or loss" in this case being equivalent to gross returns); *Pott v. Eyton* (1846) 3 C.B. 32; *Heyhoe v. Burgh* (1850) 9 C.B. 431, 440, 444 *per* Coltman J.
[128] (1860) 8 H.L.C. 268. See also *Price v. Groom* (1848) 2 Ex. 542; *Re Stanton Iron Co.* (1855) 21 Beav. 164; *Gosling v. Gaskell* [1897] A.C. 575; and see *Owen v. Body* (1836) 5 A. & E. 28; *Janes v. Whitbread* (1851) 11 C.B. 406.
[129] (1793) 2 H.Bl. 235.

He then observed that the decisions in *Kilshaw v. Jukes*,[130] *Re English and Irish Church and University Insurance Society*,[131] *Bullen v. Sharp*,[132] *Holme v. Hammond*[133] and *Mollwo, March & Co. v. Court of Wards*[134] conclusively showed that analysis to be correct. Indeed, those cases went some way towards establishing a general principle that a person who does not hold himself out as a partner is not liable to third parties for the acts of persons whose profits he shares, unless he and they are really partners *inter se*, or unless they are his agents,[135] which is a doctrine that was firmly established by the House of Lords in *Gosling v. Gaskell*.[136]

It goes almost without saying that where parties *intentionally* enter into partnership, albeit for a limited purpose beneficial to themselves, they may find that they are treated as partners for more general purposes. This was the position before the Partnership Act 1890[137] and remains so thereafter.

Statutory modifications of the common law

5–31   Bovill's Act was passed in 1865 in order to remove any presumption of partnership or of liability as a partner in four specific cases, which were substantially re-enacted in the Partnership Act 1890, section 2(3)(b) to (e).[138] However, this subsection went further than Bovill's Act, first in establishing the general statutory principle that the receipt of a share of profits does not *of itself* constitute a partnership, even though it is prima facie evidence thereof[139] and, secondly, by providing that the repayment of a debt out of profits does not of itself make the recipient a partner or liable as such.[140]

Although the various cases referred to in paragraph (a) to (e) of section 2(3) to an extent illustrate the general statutory principle, they at the same time *expressly* negate the liability of persons entering into contracts or arrangements of the types described therein.[141] It follows that, should the conditions stated in any of those paragraphs not be entirely satisfied, there will be the normal prima facie inference of partnership resulting from the sharing of profits but it will still be necessary to consider all the circumstances in order to determine whether or not a partnership actually exists.[142] Equally, it is clear that a person who is in

[130] (1863) 3 B & S. 847.

[131] (1862) 1 Hem. & M. 85. *cf. Re Albion Life Assurance Society* (1880) 16 Ch.D. 83.

[132] (1865) L.R. 1 C.P. 86.

[133] (1872) L.R. 7 Ex. 218.

[134] (1872) L.R. 4 P.C. 419. *cf. Pooley v. Driver* (1876) 5 Ch.D. 458; *Pratt v. Strick* (1932) 17 T.C. 459.

[135] As in *Steel v. Lester* (1878) 3 C.P.D. 121. See also *Associated Portland Cement Manufacturers Ltd. v. Ashton* [1915] 2 K.B. 1.

[136] [1897] A.C. 575; followed in *Sowman v. David Samuel Trust Ltd. (In liquidation)* [1978] 1 W.L.R. 22. See also *Badeley v. Consolidated Bank* (1888) 38 Ch.D. 238; *Hawksley v. Outram* [1892] 3 Ch. 359; and see Baron Bramwell's judgment in *Bullen v. Sharp* (1865) L.R. 1 C.P. 86, 125 *et seq.*; *Holme v. Hammond* (1872) L.R. 7 Ex. 218; *Mollwo March & Co. v. Court of Wards* (1872) L.R. 4 P.C. 419; *Ex p. Tennant* (1877) 6 Ch.D. 303.

[137] See *Pooley v. Driver* (1876) 5 Ch.D. 458.

[138] These cases formed ss.1–4 of Bovill's Act (28 & 29 Vict. c. 86). However, that Act left various types of agreement wholly untouched, *e.g.* those considered in *Waugh v. Carver* (1793) 2 H.Bl. 235; *Cheap v. Cramond* (1821) 4 B. & A. 663; *Smith v. Watson* (1824) 2 B. & C. 401; *Cox v. Hickman* (1860) 8 H.L.C. 268.

[139] See *supra*, paras 5–18 *et seq.*

[140] Partnership Act 1890, s.2(3)(a). This is the type of agreement considered in *Cox v. Hickman* (1860) 8 H.L.C. 268.

[141] See *supra*, para. 5–03.

[142] *ibid.* See also *supra*, paras 5–18 *et seq.*

truth a partner, albeit dormant, cannot avoid liability merely by purporting to satisfy the letter of those conditions.[143]

In only one case, set out in paragraph (d), is there a requirement for a written **5–32** contract, signed by or on behalf of the parties. In some ways it is surprising that the same requirement was not applied throughout the subsection, although its value is, on a true analysis, doubtful, as Lord Lindley explained in his Supplement on the Act:

> "If it is law that a contract not within this sub-section is admissible as evidence to show the terms on which the loan is made,[144] and there appears to be nothing in this act to exclude such evidence, it is difficult to see the utility of the proviso to the present sub-section. Whether the contract is or is not within the sub-section, when its terms are once proved its real effect must be considered, and if on the construction of the contract the relation between the parties is that of debtor and creditor, there is nothing in this act or the general law to change this relation into the different relation of partners. If this be so, the only advantage of a signed contract appears to be that such a contract is more easily proved than a verbal or unsigned contract."[145]

Where a contract provides that a person will receive a fixed sum "out of the profits" of a business, that is equivalent to a contract that he will receive "a share of the profits" for the purposes of both this section and section 3.[146] However, where money is advanced on terms that a third party will receive a share of profits, neither section will apply.[147]

Partnership Act 1890, section 3

Section 3 of the Partnership Act 1890[148] must be read in conjunction with **5–33** section 2(3). It is framed in the following terms:

> "3. In the event of any person to whom money has been advanced by way of loan upon such a contract as is mentioned in the last foregoing section, or on any buyer of a goodwill in consideration of a share of the profits of the business, being adjudged a bankrupt, entering into an arrangement to pay his creditors less than [one hundred pence][149] in the pound, or dying in insolvent circumstances, the lender of the loan shall not be entitled to recover anything in respect of his loan, and the seller of the goodwill shall not be entitled to recover anything in respect of the share of profits contracted for, until the claims of the other creditors or the borrower or buyer for valuable consideration in money or money's worth[150] have been satisfied."

---

[143] See *Ex p. Delhasse* (1878) 7 Ch.D. 511; also *Syers v. Syers* (1876) 1 App.Cas. 174; *Pooley v. Driver* (1876) 5 Ch.D. 458. *cf. Mollwo, March & Co. v. Court of Wards* (1872) L.R. 4 P.C. 419; *Ex p. Tennant* (1877) 6 Ch.D. 303.

[144] Lord Lindley based this proposition on *Pooley v. Driver* (1876) 5 Ch.D. 458, a decision under Bovill's Act (which required the contract to be in writing but not signed).

[145] At that stage, it had not, of course, been decided that the Partnership Act 1890, s.3 was equally applicable to written and unwritten contracts (see *infra*, para. 5–34) and Lord Lindley perceived a possible advantage to the creditor whose agreement was *not* reduced to writing.

[146] *Re Young* [1896] 2 Q.B. 484. Note that the share of profits payable to a lender could not be deducted in estimating the profits of the firm for the purposes of the former excess profits duty: *Walker v. Commissioners of Inland Revenue* [1920] 3 K.B. 648.

[147] *Re Pinto Leite and Nephews, ex p. Visconde de Olivaes* [1929] 1 Ch. 221.

[148] This section was a substantial re-enactment of Bovill's Act (28 & 29 Vict. c. 86), s.5, which was probably the only section of that Act which introduced a change in the law; see the following decisions thereunder: *Ex p. Taylor* (1879) 12 Ch.D. 366; *Ex p. Corbridge* (1876) 4 Ch.D. 246.

[149] The words in square brackets were substituted by virtue of Decimal Currency Act 1969, s.10.

[150] As to the meaning of this expression, see *Midland Bank Trust Co. Ltd. v. Green* [1981] A.C. 513 (a decision under the Land Charges Act 1972, s.4(b)).

This section applies not only to loans to partners but extends also to loans to individuals and to companies.[151] It causes the lender to be treated as a deferred creditor but seemingly does not deprive him of the right to retain any security he may have taken for the advance,[152] nor of the right to foreclose on such security.[153]

Equally, if a loan is made to a trader pursuant to an agreement under which the interest is intended to vary according to the profits of his business, but which is drafted in such a way as to be unintelligible, that agreement will be treated as void and the lender will be allowed to prove in competition with the other creditors for the amount of his loan.[154]

However, if a loan is made to a firm on terms that the lender will share the profits of the business, and the partners subsequently dissolve the firm and one of their number continues to carry on the business and *de facto* takes over the loan (*i.e.* without any form of novation), but is then bankrupted, the section will apply and the lender will not be permitted to compete with his other creditors.[155]

5–34   It is clear from section 2(3)(d) that a loan on terms that the lender will be entitled to a share of profits does not *per se* constitute a partnership if the agreement is in writing and signed by both the borrower and the lender.[156] What, however, is the position if there is no writing,[157] or if the writing is not signed? Is the lender a partner with the borrower and, if not, can the lender compete with the borrower's other creditors in the event of his bankruptcy?[158] As already noted,[159] the answer to the first of these questions is dependent on an analysis of all the circumstances and upon the real intention of the parties. As to the second, the courts have, as might be expected, construed section 3 in such a way as to avoid placing a lender under an oral agreement in a better position than one under a written agreement and held that in neither case can he compete with the other creditors.[160]

It is not considered that the application of section 3 could be avoided by the device of splitting the loans, *e.g.* by lending the same person a small sum in consideration of a large share of profits, and a large sum at a low fixed rate of

---

[151] *Re Leng* [1895] Ch. 652; *Re Theo Garvin Ltd.* [1969] 1 Ch. 624; *cf. Re Rolls Royce Ltd.* [1974] 1 W.L.R. 1584. A debt to which s.3 applies will clearly be a postponed debt for the purposes of the Insolvency Act 1986, s.175A(2)(d) (as amended in the manner set out in the Insolvent Partnerships Order 1994, Sched. 4, Pt II, para. 23 and applied by the Insolvency Act 1986, s.221(5) (as itself amended by the Insolvent Partnerships Order 1994, art. 8(1) (as amended by the Insolvent Partnerships (Amendment) Order 2002 (SI 2002/1308), art. 4(1)), (2), Sched. 4, Pt I, para. 3 (creditor's petition *with* concurrent petitions) and *ibid.* art. 10(1)(a), Sched. 6, para. 4 (member's petition *with* concurrent petitions)) and s.328A(2)(d), (as inserted, where all the partners have presented a joint bankruptcy petition without winding up the firm, by *ibid.*, art. 11(3)). The expression "postponed debt" is defined in the Insolvent Partnerships Order 1994, art. 2(1) and that definition is added to the Insolvency Act 1986, s.436 by *ibid.* art. 2(2). See also *infra*, paras 27–82, 27–84, 27–106.
[152] *Ex p. Sheil* (1877) 4 Ch.D. 789.
[153] *Badeley v. Consolidated Bank* (1888) 38 Ch.D. 238. *Quaere* whether he has a right to present a petition for an insolvency order: see the arguments presented under the old bankruptcy law in *Re Miller* [1901] 1 K.B. 51.
[154] *Re Vince* [1892] 2 Q.B. 478. See also *Re Gieve* [1899] W.N. 41, 72.
[155] *Re Mason* [1899] 1 Q.B. 810.
[156] See *supra*, para. 5–02.
[157] See, as to this, *Pooley v. Driver* (1876) 5 Ch.D. 458.
[158] See s.3.
[159] See *supra*, paras 5–18, 5–19.
[160] *Re Fort* [1897] 2 Q.B. 495. *cf. Re Vince* [1892] 2 Q.B. 478.

interest. In such a case it is submitted that a court would either hold the lender liable as a partner or apply the section to both loans. Where, however, in the ordinary course of business dealings a person makes a loan falling within the section and then bona fide makes another loan to the same borrower upon different terms, he can prove for the second loan in competition with the other creditors, even though he cannot compete in respect of the original loan.[161] On the other hand, if a lender who is entitled to a share of profits agrees to the substitution of a fixed rate of interest, his loan will remain within the ambit of the section, so that he cannot prove in competition with the other creditors unless, on a true analysis, the old loan has been repaid and a new loan made on different terms.[162]

5. PARTNERSHIP BY ESTOPPEL

Doctrine of holding out

The doctrine that a person who holds himself out as a partner will be liable as   **5–35**
such to all persons who rely on his representation was well established long before the Partnership Act 1890 and was in truth no more than an illustration of the general principle of estoppel by conduct.[163] The Act now provides as follows:

> "14.—(1) Every one who by words spoken or written or by conduct represents himself, or who knowingly suffers himself to be represented, as a partner in a particular firm,[164] is liable as a partner[165] to any one who has on the faith of any such representation given credit to the firm, whether the representation has or has not been made or communicated to the person so giving credit by or with the knowledge of the apparent partner making the representation or suffering it to be made.
>
> (2) Provided that where after a partner's death the partnership business is continued in the old firm-name, the continued use of that name or of the deceased partner's name as part thereof shall not of itself make his executors or administrators estate or effects liable for any partnership debts contracted after his death."

---

[161] See *Ex p. Mills* (1873) 8 Ch.App. 569; *Re Mason* [1899] 1 Q.B. 810.

[162] *Ex p. Taylor* (1879) 12 Ch.D. 366; *Re Stone* (1886) 33 Ch.D. 541; *Re Hildesheim* [1893] 2 Q.B. 357; *Re Mason* [1899] 1 Q.B. 810. *cf. Re Abenheim* (1913) 109 L.T. 219, where there was a new agreement and the lender was entitled to prove in competition with other creditors; *Re Slade* [1921] 1 Ch. 160, decided under the Married Women's Property Act 1882, s.3.

[163] See in particular *Waugh v. Carver* (1793) 2 H.Bl. 235; *Dickinson v. Valpy* (1829) 10 B. & C. 128. *Scarf v. Jardine* (1882) 7 App.Cas. 345 was the last important case on this subject before the Act of 1890. See also *De Berkom v. Smith* (1793) 1 Esp. 29; *Ex p. Matthews* (1814) 3 V. & B. 125; *Ex p. Watson* (1815) 19 Ves.Jr. 459; *Ford v. Whitmarsh* (1840) Hurl. & Walm. 53. The proposition in the text was reaffirmed by the Court of Appeal in *Nationwide Building Society v. Lewis* [1998] Ch. 482, 487A. As to partnership by estoppel *inter partes*, see *Holiday Inns Inc. v. Broadhead* (1974) 232 E.G. 951.

[164] It does not matter that an actual firm does not, on a true analysis, exist: *Bunny (D. & H.) Pty Ltd. v. Atkins* [1961] V.R. 31.

[165] As to the nature of the liability so incurred, see *infra*, para. 13–04.

It should, however, be noted that, whilst the holding out doctrine can operate as regards third parties, it *cannot* operate as between the supposed partners themselves in order to give rise to a partnership.[166]

In order to establish liability under the section, the claimant must in essence prove: (a) a holding out, (b) reliance thereon and (c) the consequent giving of credit to the firm.[167] The detail of each of these statutory requirements will now be considered in turn, although it should be noted that, if they are not fulfilled, it may still be possible to establish the existence of a common law estoppel, which will be equally effective.[168]

(a) Holding Out

Question of fact or law?

5–36   The Court of Appeal has decided that the existence of a partnership raises a mixed question of both law and fact, requiring an inference to be drawn from the primary facts found by the trial judge.[169] By analogy, it is considered that holding out can no longer be regarded as a pure question of fact,[170] since in order to determine that a person has been held out as a partner it will be necessary to find the existence of an apparent (as opposed to a real) partnership.

Form and time of representation

5–37   The representation must be sufficiently clear and unambiguous[171] as to entitle a third party, acting reasonably, to infer that a partnership exists.[172] Subject thereto, and as is apparent from section 14(1), the holding out need not take any particular form: it may be express or implied, and made orally, in writing or by conduct or by any combination of the three.[173] Moreover, a person may hold himself out as a partner (or be so held out by others) without his name being revealed, so that if, with his authority, he is referred to as a person who does not wish to have his name disclosed, he will be liable to third parties who give credit to the firm in reliance on that representation.[174]

---

[166] See *Greville v. Venables* [2007] EWCA Civ. 878 (Lawtel 12/9/07) at [41] *per* Lloyd L.J.

[167] This formulation was accepted in *Nationwide Building Society v. Lewis* [1998] Ch. 482, 487A *per* Peter Gibson L.J.

[168] See *ibid.*; also *Wendover Developments Ltd. v. Fish*, Unreported November 23, 1999 QBD (TCC), a decision of H.H. Judge Thornton Q.C., sitting as a judge of the Technology and Construction Court. See also *infra*, para. 5–43.

[169] *Keith Spier Ltd. v. Mansell* [1970] 1 W.L.R. 333, 335 *per* Harman L.J. This accords with Lord Lindley's views: see *infra*, para. 7–11.

[170] Note, however, that Lord Lindley had observed "Whether a defendant has or has not held himself out to the plaintiff is in every case a question of fact, not a question of law . . . ". He then referred to *Wood v. Duke of Argyll* (1844) 6 Man. & G. 928; *Lake v. Duke of Argyll* (1844) 6 Q.B. 477.

[171] See *Hudgell Yeates & Co. v. Watson* [1978] Q.B. 451, 470C *per* Megaw L.J.

[172] See *Wendover Developments Ltd. v. Fish*, Unreported November 23, 1999 QBD (TCC), a decision of H.H. Judge Thornton Q.C. sitting as a judge of the Technology and Construction Court; also *Bunny Pty (D. & H.) Ltd. v. Atkins* [1961] V.R. 31. This will usually be the least problematic issue in a case of holding out. See, however, *Duke Group v. Pilmer* (1999) 73 S.A.S.R. 64. *cf. Bass Brewers Ltd. v. Appleby* (1996) 73 P.&.C.R. 165 (CA).

[173] Note that merely opening a bank account in a business name is unlikely to amount to a sufficient representation for this purpose: *Elite Business Systems UK Ltd. v. Price* [2005] EWCA Civ 920 (Lawtel 6/9/05).

[174] *Martyn v. Gray* (1863) 14 C.B.(N.S.) 824. See also *Maddick v. Marshall* (1864) 17 C.B.(N.S.) 829.

However, there can be no liability on the basis of holding out unless the relevant representation was made *before* the credit was given.[175]

Unauthorised holding out

Where a person has not held himself out but has been held out by others, their **5-38** authority to do so may be called into question. In such a case, express authority is not necessary since implied authority may be inferred.[176] Thus, if the person held out has signed or allowed his name to appear on documents or other materials prepared for public consumption,[177] or has made or authorised representations as to his position, albeit not intended for repetition,[178] that may be sufficient to affix him with liability.

Knowingly suffering a holding out

Liability can arise under section 14 of the Partnership Act 1890 where a person **5-39** "knowingly suffers" himself to be held out as a partner, although the precise scope of this limb remains unclear. It would appear that the knowledge on the part of the alleged partner must be judged objectively rather than subjectively, so that he can only claim that he did not knowingly suffer the holding out if it is reasonable so to do.[179] Consistently therewith, it has been held that a retiring partner cannot be said to have knowingly suffered himself to be represented as a partner merely because he did not take care at the time of his retirement to ensure that all notepaper bearing his name as a partner had been destroyed, where the firm subsequently, without his knowledge or authority, used that notepaper to place an order.[180] The position will be *a fortiori* where the representation was clearly unauthorised.[181] By way of contrast, where under the old law[182] a partner had failed to inform the Registrar of Business Names of the dissolution of his partnership, he was held liable (on the basis of holding out) to a subsequent creditor of his former partner, who had continued the business, on the ground that the creditor had seen the registration certificate in the name of the two partners.[183]

The dividing line is thus a fine one, as is illustrated by the following unresolved problem: Will a person who has not authorised others to hold him out as a partner but who, knowing that they are in fact holding him out, makes no

---

[175] *Baird v. Planque* (1858) 1 F. & F. 344.

[176] See *Wood v. Duke of Argyll* (1844) 6 Man. & G. 928; *Lake v. Duke of Argyll* (1844) 6 Q.B. 477; *Spooner v. Browning* [1898] 1 Q.B. 528. And see *Fox v. Clifton* (1830) 6 Bing. 776; *Edmundson v. Thompson* (1861) 2 F. & F. 564.

[177] *Collingwood v. Berkeley* (1863) 15 C.B.(N.S.) 145 (a decision relating to company prospectuses); also *Maddick v. Marshall* (1864) 17 C.B.(N.S.) 829. *cf. Fox v. Clifton* (1830) 6 Bing. 776.

[178] *Martyn v. Gray* (1863) 14 C.B.(N.S.) 824; *Spree Engineering and Testing Ltd. v. O'Rourke Civil and Structural Engineering Ltd.*, Unreported May 18, 1999 QBD.

[179] *Wendover Developments Ltd. v. Fish*, Unreported November 23, 1999 QBD (TCC), a decision of H.H. Judge Thornton Q.C. sitting as a judge of the Technology and Construction Court.

[180] *Tower Cabinet Co. v. Ingram* [1949] 2 K.B. 397. See also *Jackson v. White and Midland Bank* [1967] 2 Lloyd's Rep. 68.

[181] As in *Elite Business Systems UK Ltd. v. Price* [2005] EWCA Civ 920 (Lawtel 6/9/05), where the representation was made in a so-called registration form.

[182] The former Registration of Business Names Act 1916 was repealed by the Companies Act 1981. See now the Companies Act 2006, considered *supra*, paras 3-26 *et seq.*

[183] *Bishop v. Tudor Estates* [1952] C.P.L. 807.

attempt to stop them incur any liability under the section?[184] Will he knowingly suffer himself to be held out if he merely protests? Must he go further and advertise his true position or apply for an injunction?[185] In view of the imprecision inherent in the section, prudence would seem to dictate the immediate commencement of proceedings if the objections are ignored.[186]

Effect of fraud

5–40   If a person has been induced to hold himself out (or to allow himself to be held out) as a partner by fraud or by a promise of freedom from liability, he will remain fully liable under the section to third parties who have relied on the representation. So far as such third parties are concerned, the fraud or promise is strictly *res inter alios acta*.[187]

(b) Reliance

5–41   It need hardly be stated that, in order to establish liability under the section, a third party must show that he was aware of the holding out *and* that he relied on it[188]; if he was ignorant of it, he cannot have been misled or otherwise have acted "on the faith" of the representation.[189] There is no presumption of reliance, rebuttable or otherwise, as the Court of Appeal made clear in *Nationwide Building Society v. Lewis*.[190] There the name of an employee, Williams, was included on the letterhead of a solicitor's practice which, in reality, consisted of a sole principal, Lewis. Although the apparent firm had clearly been retained by the claimant building society, there was no evidence that it had actually relied on the fact that Williams had been held out as a partner, or even that anyone had noticed his name on the letterhead.[191] In those circumstances, Williams was held not to be liable.[192] This should be contrasted with the decision in *Sangster v. Biddulph*[193] where, on a somewhat similar set of facts, it was held that the claimant *had* relied on the presence of a second "partner" when instructing the firm.

---

[184] In *Bunny (D. & H.) Pty Ltd. v. Atkins* [1961] V.R. 31, the partner knew he was being held out but did nothing to prevent it or to ensure that the claimant was aware of the true position. He was predictably held liable.

[185] See *Barton v. Reed* [1932] 1 Ch. 362, 375 *et seq., per* Luxmoore J.; also *Atkin v. Rose* [1923] 1 Ch. 522; *Berton v. Alliance Economic Investment Co.* [1922] 1 K.B. 761; *Elders Pastoral Ltd. v. Rutherford*, noted at [1991] N.Z.L.J. 73; and note *Wilson v. Twamley* [1904] 2 K.B. 99; *Bryant v. Hancock & Co.* [1898] 1 Q.B. 716, affirmed at [1899] A.C. 442. Before the Act authority, express or implied, was necessary.

[186] As in *Walter v. Ashton* [1902] 2 Ch. 282. As to the right to an injunction when there is any risk of liability, see *ibid.*; also *Gray v. Smith* (1889) 43 Ch.D. 208; *Thynne v. Shove* (1890) 45 Ch.D. 577; *Burchell v. Wilde* [1900] 1 Ch. 551; *Townsend v. Jarman* [1900] 2 Ch. 698.

[187] See *Ex p. Broome* (1811) 1 Rose 69; *Ellis v. Schmoeck* (1829) 5 Bing. 521; *Collingwood v. Berkeley* (1863) 15 C.B.(N.S.) 145; *Maddick v. Marshall* (1864) 16 C.B.(N.S.) 387 and (1864) 17 C.B.(N.S.) 829.

[188] See *Nationwide Building Society v. Lewis* [1998] Ch. 482, 490F–H *per* Peter Gibson L.J.

[189] See *Vice v. Anson* (1827) 7 B. & C. 409; *Pott v. Eyton* (1846) 3 C.B. 32; *Hudgell Yeates & Co. v. Watson* [1978] Q.B. 451.

[190] [1998] Ch. 482.

[191] See *ibid.* p. 491G–H *per* Peter Gibson L.J.

[192] If there had been evidence that the claimant would not have instructed the firm if it had known that it comprised only one principal, *i.e.* if its established practice had been not to instruct sole practitioners, the result might well have been different.

[193] [2005] P.N.L.R. 33.

Accordingly, difficult questions may arise when a third party seeks to prove reliance at a time when he is in possession of information which indicates that the person held out is not in truth a partner.

A person held out as a partner will be liable whether or not he shares the profits or losses of the business,[194] and there would seem to be no logical reason why his liability should be negated or in any way affected merely because the third party knows that he shares neither and, indeed, (if such be the case) that he is entitled to a full indemnity from the persons who make use of his name. In the words of Lord Lindley:

> "His name does not induce credit the less on account of his right to be indemnified by others against any loss falling in the first instance on himself; and although, in the case supposed, he cannot be believed to be a *partner*, the lending of his name does justify the belief that he is willing to be responsible to those who may be induced to trust him for payment."[195]

On this basis, a "salaried" partner[196] could not reasonably expect to escape liability in the face of evidence of reliance merely by showing that the third party was aware that he enjoyed that status.[197]

However, there may be exceptional cases where the information available to **5–42** the third party is of such a nature that liability will be avoided, and the decision in *Alderson v. Pope*[198] may represent an example of just such a case. Lord Ellenborough is reported to have held:

> "that where there was a stipulation between A, B and C, who appeared to the world as co-partners, that C should not participate in the profit and loss, and should not be liable as a partner, C was not liable as such to those who had notice of this stipulation, and that notice to one member of a firm was notice to the whole partnership."

Since the above represents the entirety of the report, the precise significance of the words "should not be liable as a partner" is unclear. Lord Lindley's analysis was as follows:

> "If these words meant that C was to be indemnified by A and B . . . the decision was erroneous.[199] But if they meant that C could not be liable at all to third parties for the acts of A and B, then the question would arise whether this was not altogether inconsistent with C's conduct . . . ".

---

[194] *Ex p. Watson* (1815) 19 Ves.Jr. 459. See also *Kirkwood v. Cheetham* (1862) 2 F. & F. 798, where A was B's agent and held himself out as B's partner; both A and B were held to be liable for goods supplied to A for B. *cf. Hardman v. Booth* (1862) 1 Hurl. & Colt. 803.

[195] See *Brown v. Leonard* (1816) 2 Chitty 120, noted *infra*, para. 5–49.

[196] See further, *infra*, paras 5–54, 5–55.

[197] What, in any event, is a third party to assume on learning of the salaried partner's status? After all, some salaried partners may, for whatever reason, not be given a full indemnity against debts, etc. Equally, note the decision in *Nationwide Building Society v. Lewis* [1998] Ch. 482, *supra*, para. 3–41.

[198] (1808) 1 Camp. 404n. But note the terms of the Partnership Act 1890, s.8, considered *infra*, paras 12–143 *et seq*.

[199] Lord Lindley justified this conclusion by reference to his previous observations, which have already been set out *verbatim*.

In the latter case, the decision would be in accordance with section 8 of the Partnership Act 1890, and in no way inconsistent with the principle discussed in the preceding paragraph, since the creditors will have had notice not only that C should not participate in profits (which, it is submitted, would be strictly irrelevant) but also that he should *not be under any liability as a partner.*

(c) The Giving of Credit

5–43 This expression is not defined in section 14 of the Partnership Act 1890, and it is submitted that it should not be construed in a technical or restrictive sense but, in general, as describing any transaction with the firm, provided that it is of a private law nature arising directly or indirectly out of reliance on the representations made.[200] Thus, in *Lynch v. Stiff*[201] the High Court of Australia held, on the equivalent wording of the Partnership Act 1862 (New South Wales), that a client had given credit to a supposed firm of solicitors by entrusting the firm with his money for investment purposes. A similar approach appears to have been adopted by the Court of Appeal in *Bass Brewers Ltd. v. Appleby,*[202] although the point was not, in the event, argued in *Nationwide Building Society v. Lewis.*[203] Doubts as to the meaning of the expression have, however, been voiced in one case.[204]

Contrary to the views expressed in previous editions of this work, it was held in *Revenue & Customs Commissioners v. Pal*[205] that credit could *not* in any circumstances be given by HMRC when persons who were not in law partners were held out as such by allowing their names to be entered on the firm's VAT registration.

Inchoate partnerships, etc.

5–44 A person who holds himself out as willing to *become* a partner does not thereby incur any liability to third parties.[206] There is no justification for extending the liability of persons who have represented themselves as partners to those who merely indicate their intention to enter into partnership at some future

---

[200] *Revenue & Customs Commissioners v. Pal* [2008] S.T.C. 2442, at [33] *per* Patten J.

[201] [1943] 68 C.L.R. 428. The expression predated the Partnership Act 1890: see, for example, *Dickinson v. Valpy* (1829) 10 B. & C. 128, 141 *per* Parke J.

[202] (1996) 73 P.&C.R. 165, 168. There the giving of credit consisted of the claimants authorising their solicitors to pay the proceeds of sale of a property to a supposed firm of chartered accountants so that the costs associated with a receivership might be paid and the balance remitted to the claimants.

[203] [1998] Ch. 482, 487B–C, 488C *per* Peter Gibson L.J. It was unnecessary to pursue the point, since the claimant also relied on a common law estoppel. *cf. Sangster v. Biddulph* [2005] P.N.L.R. 33.

[204] Thus, in *Wendover Developments Ltd. v. Fish*, Unreported November 23, 1999 QBD (TCC), H.H. Judge Thornton Q.C., sitting as a judge of the Technology and Construction Court, acknowledged that it was arguable that credit was not given when a professional engagement to undertake designs for a client was undertaken. As in *Nationwide Building Society v. Lewis, supra*, the point was not critical, since the claimant had also raised a common law estoppel.

[205] [2008] S.T.C. 2442. Note, however, that in *Hussein v. Commissioners of Customs & Excise* [2003] V. & D.R. 439 at [50], it was held that HMRC was capable of being a person who "deals with a firm" under the Partnership Act 1890, s.36(2).

[206] See *Floydd v. Cheney* [1970] Ch. 602.

time.[207] This is implicit in the decisions in *Bourne v. Freeth*[208] and *Keith Spicer Ltd. v. Mansell.*[209]

Use of firm name after change in firm: outgoing partners

If often happens that, after the dissolution of a partnership, one or more of the **5–45** former partners continue to carry on the business under the old name; *a fortiori* in the case of a technical dissolution resulting from the retirement or expulsion of a partner. In applying the doctrine of holding out in such cases, it must be remembered that, until he has notice to the contrary, a person who deals with a firm after a change in its constitution is entitled to treat as partners all apparent members of the old firm and all persons whom he knows to have been members of the old firm.[210] Notice in the *Gazette* is sufficient notice in the case of persons who have had no dealings with the firm prior to the change but, in the case of those who have had such dealings, actual notice must be proved.[211] However, no notice of retirement is necessary in order to prevent a partner, who is not known to the person dealing with the firm to have been a partner, from becoming liable for debts contracted after his retirement.[212] This will be the position even if a person dealing with the firm discovers that he was a partner after the date of his retirement, because the date from which section 36(3) of the Partnership Act 1890 operates is the date of the retirement.[213]

A retiring partner may, nevertheless, remain liable for debts contracted in the course of completing a particular transaction commenced prior to the date of his retirement, irrespective of the above principles,[214] on the basis that, having authorised his co-partners to act as his agents, he is estopped from denying the agency as against persons who, without notice of the revocation of that authority, have acted on the footing that the agency continued.[215]

The current editor's view is that the position will be the same in the case of any other outgoing partner.[216]

---

[207] Lord Lindley put it thus: "Although a person who represents himself to be a partner is properly held liable as a partner to persons who have acted on the faith of his being so, it would be in the highest degree unjust to confound a representation by a person that he intended to become a partner with a representation that he was one in point of fact, and to hold him as much liable to third parties for the one representation as for the other." The argument that there was only an intended partnership was, however, advanced unsuccessfully in *Bunny (D. & H.) Pty Ltd. v. Atkins* [1961] V.R. 31. Equally, note that a partnership may now be held to exist even though no trading activities have actually commenced: see *supra*, para. 2–03.

[208] (1829) 9 B. & C. 632. See also *Reynell v. Lewis* and *Wyld v. Hopkins* (1846) 15 M. & W. 517. *cf. Martyn v. Gray* (1863) 14 C.B.(N.S.) 824.

[209] [1970] 1 W.L.R. 333.

[210] Partnership Act 1890, s.36; *Tower Cabinet Co. v. Ingram* [1949] 2 K.B. 397; also *Evans v. Drummond* (1801) 4 Esp. 89; *Farrar v. Deflinne* (1844) 1 Car. & K. 580; *Scarf v. Jardine* (1882) 7 App.Cas. 345, 349 *per* Lord Selborne L.C.; and see *infra*, paras 13–40 *et seq.*

[211] Partnership Act 1890, s.36(2): see the cases cited in the preceding note; also *Pillani v. Motilal* (1929) 45 T.L.R. 283.

[212] Partnership Act 1890, s.36(3); *Carter v. Whalley* (1830) 1 B. & Ad. 11; *Elders Pastoral Ltd. v. Rutherford*, noted at [1991] N.Z.L.J. 73.

[213] *Tower Cabinet Co. v. Ingram* [1949] 2 K.B. 397.

[214] *Court v. Berlin* [1897] 2 Q.B. 396.

[215] *Scarf v. Jardine* (1882) 7 App.Cas. 345, 349 *per* Lord Selborne, 357 (*per* Lord Blackburn). See also the Partnership Act 1890, s.5 and *infra*, paras 12–02 *et seq.*

[216] The Partnership Act 1890 s.36(3) refers only to death, bankruptcy and retirement, whilst *ibid.* subss. (1) and (2) are of general application. It is considered that retirement must for these purposes be construed widely, so as to include any form of departure, whether voluntary or compulsory.

Continued use of firm name

5–46   If the firm name does not disclose the fact that the retiring partner is a member of the firm, the continued use of that name after his retirement will not, as a matter of fact, involve any holding out, otherwise than to persons who knew of his former connection with the firm.[217] In the same way, if the firm name consists only of the surname of the retiring partner, followed by the words "and Co.", the continued use of that name will not, under ordinary circumstances, represent the retiring partner to be a continuing member of the firm and thereby expose him to liability.[218]

5–47   On the other hand, if the firm name indicates that the retiring partner *is* a member of the firm, the continued use of that name will inevitably represent him as still being such a member and, if he omits to give due notice of his retirement, his liability will continue.[219] If, however, he does give such notice, but authorises or "knowingly suffers"[220] his former partners to carry on business under the old name, it is doubtful whether or not he will thereby incur liability on the basis of holding out. Although the answer to this question depends on the true construction of sections 14 and 36 of the Partnership Act 1890,[221] the following pre-1890 cases may give some indication of the possible outcome.[222]

5–48   In *Williams v. Keats*,[223] after a partner had retired and notice thereof had been given by advertisement in the *Gazette*, a bill of exchange was accepted by his co-partner in the names of himself and his former partner. Both partners' names still remained painted up over their old business premises. Lord Ellenborough held that the retired partner was liable on the bill notwithstanding the advertisement, since there was no evidence to show that the claimants in fact knew of his retirement.[224] Significantly, the only evidence that the retired partner had authorised the continued use of his name was the fact that he had not prevented it.[225] *Dolman v. Orchard*[226] was a similar case, although it appears that there was no advertisement; nevertheless, the verdict favoured the retiring partner.

5–49   In *Brown v. Leonard*,[227] the claimant sued on a promissory note made in the name of Spring, Leonard and Bush. Before the note was made Bush had retired from the firm; moreover, he had informed the claimant of that fact before he accepted the note, but added that his name was to continue to be used for a certain time following the retirement. Bush was held liable on the note, notwithstanding his retirement, although he does seem to have undertaken that the note would be provided for.

5–50   In *Newsome v. Coles*,[228] a firm comprising a father, Thomas Coles, and his three sons carried on business under the name of Thomas Coles & Sons. Thomas Coles died, but the three sons carried on the partnership business under the old

[217] See the cases cited *supra*, para. 5–45, n. 210.
[218] *Burchell v. Wilde* [1900] 1 Ch. 551; *Townsend v. Jarman* [1900] 2 Ch. 698.
[219] Partnership Act 1890, s.36.
[220] As to the meaning of this expression, see *supra*, para. 5–39.
[221] In this connection, see the cases cited *supra*, para. 5–46, n. 218.
[222] As to how far they may be used for the purposes of construing the Act, see *Bank of England v. Vagliano* [1891] A.C. 107, 145 *per* Lord Herschell. See also *supra*, para. 1–13, n. 23.
[223] (1817) 2 Stark. 290.
[224] It appears from the arguments that the claimants were not old customers of the firm, so that notice in the *Gazette* would now be sufficient notice under the Partnership Act 1890, s.36.
[225] *cf. Newsome v. Coles* (1811) 2 Camp. 617, *infra*, para. 5–50.
[226] (1825) 2 Car. & P. 104.
[227] (1816) 2 Chitty 120.
[228] (1811) 2 Camp. 617.

name for several years. The firm was then dissolved. The business was thereafter carried on by one of the sons under the old name, the other sons having established a new business. The dissolution was advertised in the *Gazette* and notice was sent to all persons who had previously had dealings with the firm. The claimant did not know of the dissolution and had had no previous dealings with the firm, but he sought to make all three sons liable on a bill of exchange accepted after the dissolution by the one who had continued to trade under the old name and who had accepted the bill in that name. The other sons, however, had never held themselves out to the claimant as partners in any firm carrying on business under the name of Thomas Coles & Sons and they had done nothing to authorise the use of that name after the dissolution; equally, they did know that the old name was still being used and they had taken no steps to restrain such use. It was held that they were not bound to take such steps and the claimant's claim was rejected.[229]

In *Ex p. Central Bank of London*,[230] John Fraser and William Fraser were **5–51** partners in a business which was carried on under the name "W. and J. Fraser". John Fraser retired and notice of his retirement was sent to the firm's principal creditors. William, with the consent of John, thereafter continued to carry on the business under the old name and accepted a bill of exchange in that name. The Court of Appeal held that John was not liable to the holder of the bill. This case went further than *Newsome v. Coles*,[231] because John Fraser's name was part of the firm name, and he appears to have consented to, and not merely acquiesced in, the continued use of that name. Moreover the bank, who were holders of the bill, had had no previous dealings with the firm, and it does not appear from the report that notice of the dissolution had been advertised in the *Gazette* or otherwise given to them.

Incoming and outgoing partners: Scarf v. Jardine

The application of the holding out doctrine becomes more complicated when **5–52** a new partner is admitted to the firm on or immediately after a partner's retirement and the firm name continues unchanged. This may be illustrated by the following example. Assume that A and B carry on business under the name X & Co. Neither A nor B holds himself out as a member of that firm to anyone who does not know of his connection with it. Thus, if A retires from the firm but gives no notice thereof, he will remain liable to existing customers who know of that connection and continue to deal with the firm on the assumption that he is still a partner; but A will incur no liability to new customers of X & Co. who have never heard of him. If, on A's retirement, C enters into partnership with B, and B and C thereafter carry on business under the name X & Co., even an old customer of X & Co., who continues to deal with the firm and has no notice of A's retirement or C's admission, cannot truly say that A ever held himself out as a partner with C or with both B and C. Consequently, such an old customer cannot maintain an action against A, B and C jointly for a debt contracted by X

[229] cf. *Williams v. Keats, supra*, para. 5–48; and see the terms of the Partnership Act 1890, s.14(1), *supra*, para. 5–35.

[230] [1892] 2 Q.B. 633. The case was decided after the passing of the Partnership Act 1890 but was not a decision under that Act.

[231] Kay L.J. considered the case to be governed by *Newsome v. Coles, supra*: see [1892] 2 Q.B. 633, 639.

& Co. after A's retirement.[232] What he *may* do is either sue A and B, on the ground that he dealt with X & Co. relying on the fact that they were both still members of that firm, or sue B and C, on the ground that they are his real debtors. He must, however, elect between those two options: he may not sue A, B and C on the ground that B and C are in truth the partners of X & Co. and that A is estopped from denying that he is a member of that firm. This was decided in *Scarf v. Jardine*.[233]

On the other hand, if the old customer has no notice of A's retirement, but learns that C has become a partner of X & Co., it is submitted that he would be entitled to sue A, B and C jointly for a debt contracted by X & Co. after A's retirement and C's admission.[234]

The position would be different in the above example if A and B carried on business in their own names rather than in the name of X & Co. Thus, again assuming A to have retired but to have given no notice thereof and C to have entered into partnership with B, if the new firm, with A's consent, carries on business under the name A, B and C, A would necessarily hold himself out as being in partnership with B and C and would be estopped from denying it as against anyone dealing with the new firm in reliance thereon.

Position of estate of deceased partner

5–53   If a partner dies and the surviving partners carry on the business in the old name, they will not thereby impose any liability on the estate of the deceased partner (or on his personal representatives) on the basis of holding out, even when they deal with old customers of the firm who have no notice of the death. This is provided for in section 14(2) of the Partnership Act 1890, although even prior to that Act the holding out doctrine had never been extended to such a case.[235] Even if the deceased partner's personal representative is the surviving partner, the position will be the same: as a general rule a debt contracted by a personal representative in that capacity gives the creditor no right of recourse against the assets comprised in the estate.[236]

Salaried partners

5–54   Perhaps the most common case of a deliberate holding out which will be encountered today, particularly in the professions, is that of the so called "salaried partner". By this notoriously vague expression is usually meant a person who, though in reality an employee of the firm remunerated by a fixed or variable salary, is nevertheless held out to clients and to the world as a partner, as distinct

---

[232] In some editions of this work (*i.e.* prior to the 16th ed.) the following additional observations appeared at this point: "To allow him to do so would, indeed, be to give him the best of both worlds of partnership liability—apparent in the case of A and actual in the case of C—and it is appropriate that the customer should not be allowed to have it both ways when dealing with a firm whose name does not point to any specific members."

[233] (1882) 7 App.Cas. 345.

[234] Lord Lindley observed "*Scarf v. Jardine* is not an authority against this proposition, nor are Lord Selborne's observations in that case at 7 App.Cas. 350, as the author understands them." See also *infra*, para. 13–04.

[235] *Webster v. Webster* (1791) 3 Swan. 490; *Devaynes v. Noble* (*Houlton's Case*) (1816) 1 Mer. 616; *Vulliamy v. Noble* (1817) 3 Mer. 593.

[236] See *Farhall v. Farhall* (1871) 7 Ch.App. 123; *Owen v. Delamere* (1872) 15 Eq. 134; but see *Vulliamy v. Noble* (1817) 3 Mer. 593. And see further, *infra*, paras 26–21 *et seq.*

from a person who *is* a partner, but who does not enjoy all of the rights normally associated with that position.[237] However, that is not to say that a salaried partner may not be a partner in the true sense, as was made clear by Megarry J. in *Stekel v. Ellice*[238]:

> "Certain aspects of a salaried partnership are not disputed. The term 'salaried partner' is not a term of art, and to some extent it may be said to be a contradiction in terms. However, it is a convenient expression which is widely used to denote a person who is held out to the world as being a partner, with his name appearing as a partner on the notepaper of the firm and so on. At the same time, he receives a salary as remuneration, rather than a share of the profits, though he may, in addition to his salary, receive some bonus or other sum of money dependent upon the profits. *Quoad* the outside world it often will matter little whether a man is a full partner or a salaried partner; for a salaried partner is held out as being a partner, and the partners will be liable for his acts accordingly. But within the partnership it may be important to know whether a salaried partner is truly to be classified as a mere employee, or as a partner.
>
> " . . . It seems to me impossible to say that as a matter of law a salaried partner is or is not necessarily a partner in the true sense.[239] He may or may not be a partner, depending on the facts. What must be done, I think, is to look at the substance of the relationship between the parties; and there is ample authority for saying that the question whether or not there is a partnership depends on what the true relationship is, and not on any mere label attached to that relationship."[240]

Megarry J. rightly went on to opine that an entitlement to a share of profits on a dissolution was an indicator of partnership.[241]

An attempt to argue that *Stekel v. Ellice* was wrongly decided failed in *M. Young Legal Associates v. Zahid*.[242] There a partnership had been formed with a view to satisfying the (then) supervision requirements of the Solicitors' Practice Rules 1990, r. 13[243] and one of the partners agreed to be remunerated by a fixed sum payable irrespective of the profitability of the firm and was exempted from any obligation to contribute capital. It was nevertheless held that, looking at all the circumstances, he was in law a partner, even though the features described above did tend to point *against* the existence of a partnership.[244]

Partner or employee?

Consistently with the views expressed in *Stekel v. Ellice*, few identifiable **5–55** principles can be derived from the decided cases, save that the recognised

---

[237] Although such persons are also referred to as "salaried partners", it is now more common to find them described as "fixed share partners". See further *infra*, para. 5–59. Occasionally firms will be encountered which comprise both salaried *and* fixed share partners.

[238] [1973] 1 W.L.R. 191, 198D–F, 199G–H. See also *Finlayson v. Turnbull (No. 1)* 1997 S.L.T. 613, 614I–J (OH).

[239] See also *Cobbetts LLP v. Hodge* (2009) 153(17) S.J.L.B. 29.

[240] See further, as to the latter point, *supra*, paras 5–05 *et seq.*

[241] [1973] 1 W.L.R. 191, 200B. See also *Kovats v. TFO Management LLP* [2009] I.C.R. 1140 (EAT), at [28] *per* HH. Judge Birtles (albeit misquoting the page reference to *Stekel v. Ellice*), a decision concerning a member of an LLP.

[242] [2006] 1 W.L.R. 2562 (CA).

[243] See now the Solicitors' Code of Conduct 2007, r.5 (as amended).

[244] See *M. Young Legal Associates v. Zahid*, *supra*, at [33], [34] *per* Wilson L.J.; also *Hodson v. Hodson* [2010] P.N.L.R. 8 (CA). The former case appears not to have been cited in *Cobbetts LLP v. Hodge* (2009) 153(17) S.J.L.B. 29.

conditions for the existence of a contract of employment, must be satisfied if a salaried partner is to be treated as an employee.[245] In *Burgess v. O'Brien*,[246] the Industrial Tribunal took the view that Burgess was a partner, even though he was remunerated by a salary and commission and was not liable to meet any share of losses whereas, in *Briggs v. Oates*,[247] Scott J. appears to have regarded a similar remuneration package as indicative of employment rather than partnership.[248] In *Bower v. Hughes Hooker & Co.*,[249] the Employment Appeal Tribunal held that the salaried partner was a true partner, even though he did not contribute capital or bear a share of any losses: the determinative factor appears to have been the extent of his participation in the management of the firm.[250] Equally, in some instances, the courts appear to pay scant regard to a salaried partner's true status.[251] Thus, in *Farrell Matthews & Weir v. Hansen*,[252] the Employment Appeal Tribunal appears to have accepted without question that the salaried partner was merely an employee. In *Cobbetts LLP v. Hodge*,[253] Mr Hodge had been appointed as an "employed partner" and the partnership agreement (to which he was not a party but with certain provisions of which he was obliged to comply) made it clear that such a person was an employee of the firm "to be known, and held out, as a partner". Not surprisingly, he was held to be an employee rather than a partner. On the other hand, in *Dainty v. Ellerton Knight*[254] Mr Dainty had been engaged as an "associate partner" and was held to be self-employed.[255]

What is certain is that, if the salaried partner is held to be and treated as a partner in law, he cannot also be an employee of the firm.[256]

5–56   The tendency when dealing with a salaried partner is to have an agreement between the equity partners and each individual salaried partner which contains

---

[245] See *Ready Mixed Concrete (South East) Ltd. v. Minister of Pensions and National Insurance* [1968] 2 Q.B. 497 at 515C–D *per* MacKenna J.; *Montgomery v. Johnson Underwood Ltd.* [2001] I.R.L.R. 269 (CA); *Dragonfly Consultancy Ltd. v. Revenue & Customs Commissioners* [2008] S.T.C. 3030; also *Kovats v. TFO Management LLP* [2009] I.C.R. 1140 (EAT) at [18] *per* HH. Judge Birtles. And note, in this context, *Todd v. Adam* [2002] 2 All E.R. (Comm) 97 (CA) a decision concerning the status of share fishermen, who were held not to be employees. The issue of whether they were partners was not, however, decided.

[246] [1966] I.T.R. 164. The Tribunal also appears to have been influenced by the very act of holding out, but this cannot be right: see *Briggs v. Oates, infra.* And see an article at (1991) 135 S.J. 1058.

[247] [1990] I.C.R. 473. In this case, there was also evidence that Oates did not know that the partnership between Briggs and his existing partner was due to expire *before* the conclusion of Oates' contractual period of employment: *ibid.* p. 475E.

[248] *ibid.* p. 475D.

[249] March 27, 2003 (EAT).

[250] This aspect was not pursued on the appeal sub nom. *Stevens v. Bower* [2004] I.R.L.R. 957. But participation in management is not a requirement for partnership status: see *Hodson v. Hodson* [2009] P.N.L.R. 23, at [53] *per* Arnold J. (his decision being affirmed at [2010] P.N.L.R. 8 without referring specifically to this aspect).

[251] See, for example, *United Bank of Kuwait Ltd. v. Hammoud* [1988] 1 W.L.R. 1051; *Collie v. Donald* 1999 S.C.L.R. 127 (OH).

[252] [2005] I.C.R. 509.

[253] (2009) 153(17) S.J.L.B. 29.

[254] (UKEAT/0281/09/DM) (Lawtel 3/11/09).

[255] His status as a partner was not addressed by the EAT.

[256] See *Ellis v. Joseph Ellis & Co.* [1905] 1 K.B. 324; *Cowell v. Quilter Goodison Co. Ltd.* [1989] I.R.L.R. 393 (CA); *Train v. DTE Business Advisory Services Ltd.* (UKEAT/0201/08/LA) (Lawtel 10/3/09); *Protectacoat Firthglow Ltd. v. Szilagyi* [2009] I.R.L.R. 365 at [35] *per* Smith L.J. *cf.* the position under the Limited Liability Partnerships Act 2000, s.4(3), which ignores this fundamental proposition but was applied without difficulty in *Kovats v. TFO Management LLP* [2009] I.C.R. 1140.

partner like provisions of a somewhat one sided nature, *i.e.* the salaried partner owes duties to the equity partners but no correlative duties are owed by them to him. Frequently no mention at all is made of the existence of other salaried partners. It will be a question of construction whether such an agreement constitutes a partnership between: (a) all the partners, equity and salaried alike, or (b) only the equity partners and the particular salaried partner.[257] Whether there is scope, in such a situation, for the creation of more than one partnership is an open question, although it is difficult to see that there can be more than one business being carried on in common.[258] Equally, the one sided nature of the obligations may be a pointer to the fact that no partnership exists other than as between the equity partners.

Partner or worker?

What has not, as yet, been tested is whether a salaried partner might be classified as a "worker" within the meaning of section 230(3)(b) of the Employment Rights Act 1996,[259] which provides that: **5–57**

" ... 'worker' ... means an individual who has entered into or works under ...

    (b)   any other contract, whether express or implied and (if it is express) whether oral or in writing, whereby the individual undertakes to do or perform personally any work or services for another party to the contract whose status is not by virtue of the contract that of a client or customer of any profession or business undertaking carried on by the individual."[260]

Were the salaried partner to be classified as a worker, he would be entitled to the national minimum wage and certain other statutory rights, even if not to the full rights afforded to a true employee.

In a case where the salaried partner is engaged under a contract with the equity partners, rather than the firm itself, it would seem that this may be a significant risk, since there can be no doubt that the salaried partner is required to provide his services personally, and it is doubtful whether the equity partners can be regarded as his clients or customers for this purpose.[261] Equally, if, on a true analysis, that individual is a partner in the true sense, it is difficult to see that there is a contract with "another party" when that other party includes himself.

---

[257] The current editor has difficulty in seeing how the decision in *Clarke v. The Earl of Dunraven and Mount-Earl* [1897] A.C. 59 (HL), which concerned accession to a yacht club's sailing rules, could be applied in a case of this type, although much depends on the precise terms of the arrangement. Equally, the courts now adopt a more flexible approach: see also *General Accident Fire and Life Assurance Corp. Ltd. v. Tanter* [1984] 1 Lloyd's Rep. 58, 72 *per* Hobhouse J.; *Maple Leaf Macro Volatility Fund v. Rouvroy* [2009] 2 All E.R. (Comm) 287.

[258] See also *infra*, para. 5–68, n. 301.

[259] Note, in this context, the decision in *Autoclenz Ltd. v. Belcher* [2010] I.R.L.C. 70, where it was held that, on a true analysis of the arrangements, the individual in question was an employee and not what was styled a "limb (b) worker".

[260] The equivalent definition in the National Minimum Wage Act 1998, s.53(3) is in identical terms.

[261] *Quaere*, can it be said that he was engaged on a self-employed basis and therefore must be supplying his services to the equity partners on that basis. See, generally, on this issue, *Yorkshire Window Co Ltd. v. Parkes* (UKEAT/0484/09/SM) (Lawtel 28/5/10).

Salaried partners and VAT liability

5–58   It should be noted that only a salaried partner who is, on a true analysis, a partner in law could find himself liable to HMRC in respect of value added tax due from the firm, since it has now been held that there can be no liability merely by virtue of holding out.[262]

Fixed share partners

5–59   Given the overtones of employment which are so often associated with salaried partnership status, many firms now resort to the alternative status of "fixed share partner", denoting a partner who is principally remunerated by a fixed share of profits. Intrinsically, this is no different from the more traditional salaried partnership, but as a result of the *de facto* requirements which HMRC expect to be satisfied before partner status is accepted, the following attributes are now shared by most fixed share partners:

(a) entitlement to a small share of residual profits and losses (over and above their fixed profit shares);

(b) an obligation to contribute a small sum of capital; and

(c) a right to participate, to a greater or lesser extent, in the decision-making processes of the firm.

In the current editor's view, none of these attributes are truly determinative of partnership status, as is clear from the decisions in *M. Young Legal Associates v. Zahid*[263] and *Hodson v. Hodson*.[264] Whether these decisions have had a material effect on HMRC's approach is not clear.

Despite the clarity of the decision in *M. Young Legal Associates v. Zahid*, it is the current editor's recommendation that, when drafting a fixed share partner's terms, his fixed share should only be payable out of profits and not irrespective of the firm's profitability, because a "partner" who is remunerated even when the firm makes a loss is, in practice, more likely to be treated as an employee.[265]

Minors

5–60   A minor does not incur contractual liability by holding himself out as a partner.[266]

Torts

5–61   The doctrine of holding out only applies in favour of persons who have "given credit to the firm"[267] on the footing that the person whom they seek to make liable is a partner thereof.[268] The doctrine has no wider application, *e.g.* in

---

[262] *Revenue & Customs Commissioners v. Pal* [2008] S.T.C. 2442. See also *supra*, para. 5–43.
[263] [2006] 1 W.L.R. 2562 (CA).
[264] [2010] P.N.L.R. 8 (CA), affirming the decision at [2009] P.N.L.R. 23.
[265] See, for example, *Cobbetts LLP v. Hodge* (2009) 153(17) S.J.L.B. 29 at [87] *per* Floyd J. See also *infra*, para. 10–86.
[266] See *supra*, para. 4–08.
[267] See *supra*, para. 5–43.
[268] See *Scarf v. Jardine* (1882) 7 App.Cas. 357.

relation to pure torts which are in no way dependent upon the injured party having had any dealings with or placing trust in the firm. Admittedly, in *Stables v. Eley*,[269] a retired partner, whose name appeared on a cart, was held liable for the negligence of its driver, but the case did not establish any point of principle, as Lord Lindley explained:

" . . . although in that case there may have been evidence to go to the jury that the defendant was liable, proof by him that the driver was not his servant would have rendered him not liable."[270]

As observed in previous editions of this work, if the decision went further than this it is wrong, the Court of Appeal having disapproved it as reported.[271] Naturally, the position will be different in the case of professional negligence, negligent mis-statements and analogous forms of tortious liability, where there is ample scope for the application of the doctrine.

Judgment in firm name

As will be seen hereafter, a judgment obtained against a firm in the firm name may be enforced against a person who has rendered himself liable for the firm's debts by reason of the holding out doctrine and, on that basis, been held to be liable as a partner.[272]

5–62

Companies Act 2006, Part 41

Neither this Part of the 2006 Act nor its predecessors[273] made any direct alteration in the law on the subject under discussion. However, as has already been seen,[274] the Act does require the name and service address of each partner[275] in a firm having a place of business and carrying on business in the UK under a name which does not consist of the surnames of all the individual partners (together with any permitted additions) and the corporate names of all the corporate partners[276] to be shown on all business letters and other documents issued by the firm,[277] and in a notice prominently displayed in the partnership premises.[278] In this way it has had the incidental effect of reducing the risk of liability resulting from an inadvertent holding out.

5–63

---

[269] (1825) 1 C. & P. 614.

[270] As when A's servant was wearing B's livery: *Quarman v. Burnett* (1840) 6 M. & W. 499, 508–509 *per* Parke B.

[271] See *Smith v. Bailey* [1891] 2 Q.B. 403.

[272] See *infra*, paras 14–87 *et seq.*, and see *Davis v. Hyman & Co.* [1903] 1 K.B. 854.

[273] The use of business names was originally governed by the Registration of Business Names Act 1916 but that Act was repealed and replaced by a more liberal regime introduced by the Companies Act 1981, Pt II and subsequently replaced by the Business Names Act 1985. The 2006 Act replaced the 1985 with a broadly similar regime.

[274] See *supra*, paras 3–26 *et seq.*

[275] Companies Act 2006, s.1201, as substituted by the Companies Act 2006 (Substitution of Section 1201) Regulations 2009 (SI 2009/3182), reg. 2.

[276] Companies Act 2006, s.1200(2)(b), (3).

[277] *ibid.* s.1202(1). The other documentation referred to in the subsection comprises written orders for goods or services to be supplied to the business, invoices and receipts issued in the course of the business and written demands for payment of debts arising in the course of the business. The only exception to this requirement consists of documents issued by a firm of more than 20 partners, provided that certain conditions are met: *ibid.* s.1203.

[278] *ibid.* s.1204(1).

Outgoing partners

5–64   The presence of a partner's name on the firm's notepaper, etc.,[279] in compliance with the requirements of the 2006 Act, obviously provides a ready means whereby the continuing partners may, following his departure from the firm, hold him out as still remaining a member thereof. However, it has already been seen that an outgoing partner is not bound to secure the destruction of all such notepaper and other documentation in order to free himself from potential liability on that account,[280] although it would be otherwise if he authorised its use.[281]

6.   GENERAL AND PARTICULAR PARTNERSHIPS

5–65   It is now only rarely necessary to draw a formal distinction between general and particular partnerships, in the manner traditionally adopted by writers on partnership law.[282] Nevertheless, there are still many cases in which persons enter into a partnership limited to a particular trade, transaction or adventure where the distinction may be of relevance.[283]

Partnership for one transaction

5–66   If persons who are not partners in any other business share the profits and losses (or merely the profits) of a particular trade, transaction or adventure, they will become partners to that extent and to that extent only.[284] Thus, if two solicitors, who are not partners, are jointly retained to conduct litigation in a particular case, and they agree to share the profit costs arising therefrom, they will become partners only so far as concerns the conduct of that case.[285] In the same way, a partnership may be limited to the purchase and sale of a particular asset,[286] the working of a patent either at large[287] or confined to a particular area,[288] the development of a plot of land,[289] the exploitation of a contract of

---

[279] See generally, *ibid.* ss.1203, 1204; and see *supra*, para. 3–33.

[280] *Tower Cabinet Co. v. Ingram* [1949] 2 K.B. 397.

[281] *ibid.*

[282] This classification can be traced to the following passage in the Digest—"*Societates contrahuntur sive universorum bonorum, sive negotiationis alicujus, sive vectigalis, sive etiam rei unius*" (Partnerships are contracted either in the whole of the goods of the respective partners, or in some particular speculation, or in a state concession or even in a single piece of property): Dig. xvii, tit. 2 (*pro socio*), 1–5 pr. However, save for the purpose noted in the text, Lord Lindley considered such classification "not worth enlarging upon".

[283] These partnerships are referred to in the Partnership Act 1890, s.32(b). See *infra*, paras 24–15 *et seq.*

[284] See *Re Abenheim* (1913) 109 L.T. 219, 220 *per* Phillimore J.; *Mann v. D'Arcy* [1968] 1 W.L.R. 893; also *De Berkom v. Smith* (1793) 1 Esp. 29; *Smith v. Watson* (1824) 2 B. & C. 401; *Heyhoe v. Burgh* (1850) 9 C.B. 431. See, as to partnerships in profits only, *supra*, para. 5–27.

[285] *Robinson v. Anderson* (1855) 20 Beav. 98 and, on appeal, 7 De G.M. & G. 239; *McGregor v. Bainbrigge* (1848) 7 Hare 164.

[286] *Oppenheimer v. Frazer & Wyatt* [1907] 2 K.B. 50.

[287] *Lovell v. Hicks* (1837) 2 Y. & C.Ex. 472.

[288] *Ridgway v. Philip* (1834) 1 Cr.M. & R. 415.

[289] *Fenston v. Johnstone (Inspector of Taxes)* (1940) 23 T.C. 29; *Walker West Developments Ltd. v. F. J. Emmett* (1979) 252 E.G. 1171; *Whywait Pty Ltd. v. Davison* [1997] 1 Qd.R. 225.

service[290] or the sowing, cropping, harvesting and sale of a particular crop.[291] In all such cases, the rights and liabilities of the partners are governed by the same principles as apply to general partnerships,[292] albeit that they may be quantitatively (even if not qualitatively) less extensive.

The scope of any such partnership will naturally depend on the terms of the agreement into which the parties have entered as well as upon their subsequent conduct. This is illustrated by the decision in *J. & J. Cunningham v. Lucas*,[293] where the claimants had purchased potatoes from suppliers in Holland for resale in this country. Originally the potatoes were to be shipped in two vessels, but one vessel was damaged and a larger vessel was substituted. More potatoes were purchased in order to fill the substituted vessel. The claimants claimed that the defendants had agreed to enter into a joint venture whereby all the potatoes would be marketed in this country and the claimants and the defendants would share any loss or profit equally. The defendants claimed that only part of the cargo was agreed to be the subject of the joint venture. McNair J., after considering all the circumstances, held that the claimants had established their claim and directed an account to be taken accordingly.

7.   SUB-PARTNERSHIPS

Lord Lindley defined a sub-partnership as follows: **5–67**

> "A sub-partnership is as it were a partnership within a partnership; it presupposes the existence of a partnership to which it is itself subordinate. An agreement to share profits only constitutes a partnership between the parties to the agreement. If, therefore, several persons are partners and one of them agrees to share the profits derived by him with a stranger, this agreement does not make the stranger a partner in the original firm. The result of such an agreement is to constitute what is called a *sub-partnership*, that is to say, it makes the parties to it partners *inter se*; but it in no way affects the other members of the principal firm."[294]

Thus, a sub-partnership is, conventionally, a partnership in a share of another partnership and, whilst it is of a derivative nature, the sub-partnership normally operates outside the confines of the main partnership.[295] However, there is, in theory, no reason why a sub-partnership should not be formed between a group

---

[290] *E. Rennison & Son v. Minister of Social Security* (1970) 114 S.J. 952.

[291] *George Hall & Son v. Platt* (1954) 47 R. & I.T. 713.

[292] See *Reid v. Hollinshead* (1825) 4 B. & C. 867, and the cases cited *supra*, nn. 286 and 287.

[293] [1957] 1 Lloyd's Rep. 416.

[294] This principle was stated thus by civilian lawyers: "*Socius mei socii, socius meus non est*" (The partner of my partner is not my partner).

[295] In *Ex p. Barrow* (1815) 2 Rose 255, Lord Eldon stated the law thus: "I take it to have been long since established, that a man may become a partner with A where A and B are partners and yet not be a member of that partnership which existed between A and B. In the case of *Sir Chas. Raymond* [*(1734)*], a banker in the city, a Mr Fletcher agreed with Sir Chas. Raymond that he should be interested so far as to receive a share of his profits of the business, and which share he had a right to draw out from the firm of Raymond & Co. But it was held that he was no partner in that partnership; had no demand against it; had no account in it; and that he must be satisfied with a share of the profits arising and given to Sir Chas. Raymond." See also *Bray v. Fromont* (1821) 6 Madd. 5; *Ex p. Dodgson* (1830) Mont. & Mac. A. 445.

of partners within the head partnership, with or without the blessing of the other partners.[296]

In practice, most partnership agreements prohibit the creation of sub-partnerships without the consent of the other partners.[297]

Where a sub-partnership is created, the terms of the head partnership will not be incorporated as a matter of implication,[298] so that it cannot be assumed that the sub-partnership will endure for the same term as the head partnership.

It follows from the fact that a sub-partner will not become a partner in the head partnership that he will not be liable to the creditors of that firm; his indirect participation in the profits of the head partnership is naturally not sufficient to found any such liability.[299] Moreover, the sub-partnership and the head partnership will, in the current editor's view, be distinct entities for the purposes of the insolvency legislation.[300]

Arrangements analogous to sub-partnership

5–68   It is not unknown in some spheres for all the members of a partnership to enter into a series of partnerships with individual third parties regulating the terms on which the main firm's business will be carried on as between those members on the one hand and the third party on the other.[301] On one view this could be regarded as a true sub-partnership if it involves the creation of a partnership in the aggregate shares of the members of the main firm, although it is doubtful whether this will ever be the parties' intention. Equally, a member of Firm A may enter into a wholly separate partnership with third parties (Firm B), but in a representative capacity.[302] In such a case, that partner's share in Firm B will be an asset of Firm A and, to that extent, it could be said that there is a sub-partnership therein.[303]

So-called "group partnerships" will be adverted to hereafter.[304]

---

[296] This might be appropriate in the case of a national firm with an overall profit sharing structure, where individual offices are to be treated as separate "profit centres" with a greater or lesser degree of autonomy.

[297] See *infra*, para. 10–99.

[298] *Frost v. Moulton* (1856) 21 Beav. 596.

[299] See generally, *supra*, paras 5–28 *et seq.*

[300] See *infra*, paras 27–11, 27–29.

[301] Such a situation is occasionally encountered when a series of "salaried" partners are engaged. In an extreme case, the end result may even be a pyramidal structure, as each salaried partner is required to sanction the admission of subsequent salaried partners. The complications which can ensue are considerable and, accordingly, such an option is not to be commended. See further *supra*, para. 5–56.

[302] See, as to trustee and nominee partners, *supra*, paras 4–25, 4–26.

[303] Unusually, in this case the supposed sub-partnership is created *before* the main partnership.

[304] See *infra*, paras 11–17 *et seq.*

CHAPTER 6

CONSIDERATION FOR A CONTRACT OF PARTNERSHIP

AN agreement to enter into partnership, like any other contract, must be sup- **6–01** ported by consideration if it is to be enforceable. However, in a normal case such consideration can readily be found, whether in the form of a contribution of capital or a particular skill, or some act which may result in liability to third parties.[1]

Alternatively, it may (and, indeed, frequently will) be represented by the mutual obligations which the parties undertake by entering into partnership together.

A bona fide contract of partnership is not invalidated by the unequal size or value of the parties' contributions: each must be his own judge of the adequacy of the consideration which he will receive. Vice-Chancellor Wigram put it in this way:

> "If one man has skill and wants capital to make that skill available; and another has capital and wants skill; and the two agree that the one shall provide capital and the other skill, it is perfectly clear that there is a good consideration for the agreement on both sides; and it is impossible for the court to measure the quantum of value. The parties must decide that for themselves."[2]

Sharing of profits but not losses

It has already been seen that parties may enter into partnership on terms that **6–02** they will all share the profits, but that losses will be borne by only some of their number.[3] Such an agreement, which amounts to no more than an agreement that some parties will indemnify the others against losses, is not invalid as a *nudum pactum* even where the management of the firm is to be left in the hands of the parties offering the indemnity,[4] although there is one early expression of judicial opinion to the contrary.[5] Lord Lindley pointed out that the fact that the parties indemnified "become, or agree to become, partners is quite sufficient consideration to give validity to a contract that they shall be indemnified".

[1] See *The Herkimer* (1804) Stewart's Adm.Rep. 17, 23; *Andersons' Case* (1877) 7 Ch.D. 75.
[2] *Dale v. Hamilton* (1846) 5 Hare 369, 393 *per* Wigram V.-C.
[3] See *supra*, paras 5–25 *et seq*.
[4] *Geddes v. Wallace* (1820) 2 Bli. 270 is an example of such an agreement. Note also *Walker West Developments Ltd. v. F. J. Emmett Ltd.* (1979) 252 E.G. 1171.
[5] In *Brophy v. Holmes* (1828) 2 Moll. 5, Hart L.C. expressed the opinion that an agreement between A and B that A should advance capital, that B should be sole manager, and that they should divide the profits equally, but that all losses should fall on B was, as regards the last stipulation, void, as being a *nudum pactum*; his Lordship thought that under such an agreement the losses should be borne equally.

Premiums

6–03   At one time the payment of a premium as part of the consideration for entry into partnership was widespread, but such payments are now rarely encountered save, perhaps, in the case of certain "investment" partnerships. Nevertheless, where a premium is due but unpaid, it may be recovered by action, provided that the claimant has been ready and willing to take the defendant into partnership as agreed.[6] The return of premiums in the event of the premature termination of the partnership is now governed by section 40 of the Partnership Act 1890.[7]

Medical partnerships in the National Health Service

6–04   Under section 259 of and Schedule 21 to the National Health Service Act 2006,[8] it is an offence for any person who has at any time provided general medical services,[9] personal medical services[10] or, in prescribed circumstances, primary medical services[11] to sell the goodwill or any part of the goodwill of a medical practice unless he no longer provides or performs such services *and* has never carried on the practice in a relevant area.[12] It is also an offence for any person to buy such goodwill.[13] This prohibition applies equally to sales and purchases of shares of goodwill as between partners.[14]

6–05   However, the Act goes further by providing that where, in pursuance of a partnership agreement, any valuable consideration, other than the performance of services in the partnership business, is given as consideration for being taken into partnership, there is for the purposes of the section deemed to have been a sale of goodwill by the partner to whom the consideration is given.[15] It follows that the payment of a premium or the imposition on an incoming partner of some particularly onerous obligation unconnected with the practice will almost inevitably involve the commission of an offence. What is less clear is the extent to which the prohibition will affect any of the obligations normally imposed by a partnership agreement. It has been held to have no application in the case of restrictions on competition, whether they be mutual or unilateral.[16] As to other,

---

[6] *Walker v. Harris* (1793) 1 Anst. 245.

[7] See *infra*, para. 25–07 *et seq.*

[8] A further prohibition on the sale of goodwill by various types of contractors and certain medical practitioners providing "essential services" is also to be found in the Primary Medical Services (Sale of Goodwill and Restrictions on Sub-contracting) Regulations 2004 (SI 2004/906), reg. 3(1), which continues to have effect under the 2006 Act: National Health Service (Consequential Provisions) Act 2006, Sched. 2, para. 1(2).

[9] National Health Service Act 2006, s.259(2). In essence this refers to such services provided under the National Health Service Act 1977.

[10] National Health Service Act 2006, s.259(3). Again, such services will have been provided under the 1977 Act.

[11] National Health Service Act 2006, s.259(4). Such services may have been provided under the 1977 Act (as amended) or the 2006 Act, ss.83(2)(b) or 84. As yet, no regulations under this subsection have been made.

[12] *i.e.* an area in which he provided any such services: National Health Service Act 2006, s.259(5).

[13] *ibid.* Sched. 21, para. 1(1).

[14] See the definition of goodwill in *ibid.* s.259(5).

[15] *ibid.* Sched. 21, para. 2(4)(a).

[16] *Kerr v. Morris* [1987] Ch. 90, overruling *Hensman v. Traill, The Times,* October 22, 1980 (a decision under the National Health Service Act 1977, Sched. 10, para. 2(4)(a), (5), in their original form). Note that the Secretary of State is charged with the task of certifying whether particular transactions involve a sale of goodwill: see the National Health Service Act 2006, Sched. 21, para. 1(2).

less controversial provisions, the arguments have been canvassed before the Court of Appeal but, in the event, no judicial opinion has been formally expressed thereon.[17] It is submitted that it could only be argued that an offence has been committed in an exceptional case where the obligations assumed by one or more of the partners are grossly disproportionate to those assumed by the others.[18]

There will also be a deemed sale of goodwill if a partner, in pursuance of a **6–06** partnership agreement, performs services for a consideration which is substantially inadequate[19] or if an assistant agrees to perform services for a remuneration which is substantially less than might reasonably be expected, on the basis that he will subsequently be taken into partnership and succeed to that practice.[20]

Consideration and inheritance tax

The existence or adequacy of the consideration given by a partner on his **6–07** admission to the partnership may be material in determining whether the whole or any part of the share in the partnership assets to which he becomes entitled either immediately or on the death, retirement or expulsion of another partner, is to be treated as a chargeable transfer for the purposes of inheritance tax, albeit potentially exempt and, perhaps, qualifying for 100 per cent relief. This subject is more fully discussed in Part Seven of this work.[21]

---

[17] *Kerr v. Morris supra*, at pp. 109G, 115E.
[18] See further, as to the potential application of this prohibition, the *Encyclopedia of Professional Partnerships*, Pt 5.
[19] National Health Service Act 2006, Sched. 21, para. 2(4)(c).
[20] *ibid.* para. 2(7), (8).
[21] See *Att.-Gen. v. Boden* [1912] 1 K.B. 539; *Att.-Gen. v. Ralli* (1936) 15 A.T.C. 523; *Perpetual Executors and Trustees Association of Australia v. Taxes Commissioner of Australia* [1954] A.C. 114 (PC). Although these are all cases on estate duty, the principles embodied therein are equally applicable to inheritance tax: see further, *infra*, paras 36–02 *et seq.*

Chapter 7

EVIDENCE BY WHICH A PARTNERSHIP MAY BE PROVED

1.   INTRODUCTION

UNLIKE the position in most other European jurisdictions, no particular formal-   **7–01**
ities attend the creation of a partnership[1] and there is in general no need for a
written agreement, much less a deed. Nevertheless, reliance on an oral agreement
may, inter alia, present certain problems of proof.[2] There is now no requirement
for the registration of partnerships,[3] unless they choose to become limited
partnerships under the Limited Partnerships Act 1907.[4]

2.   PARTNERSHIPS INVOLVING LAND

Law of Property (Miscellaneous Provisions) Act 1989, section 2

Section 2 of the Law of Property (Miscellaneous Provisions) Act 1989 super-   **7–02**
seded the provisions of section 40 of the Law of Property Act 1925[5] and (so far
as material) provides as follows:

> "2.—(1) A contract for the sale or other disposition[6] of an interest in land[7] can only
> be made in writing and only by incorporating all the terms which the parties have
> expressly agreed in one document or, where contracts are exchanged, in each.
>   (2) The terms may be incorporated in a document either by being set out in it or
> by reference to some other document.
>   (3) The document incorporating the terms or, where contracts are exchanged, one
> of the documents incorporating them (but not necessarily the same one) must be
> signed by or on behalf of each party to the contract.
>   . . .
>   (5) This section does not apply in relation to—

---

[1] *Per contra* in the case of a limited liability partnership, which is a body corporate and *not* a
partnership: see *supra*, paras 2–39 *et seq.*

[2] See *Figes v. Cutler* (1822) 3 Stark. 139.

[3] The former restrictions on the size of partnerships under the Companies Act 1985 , ss.716, 717
and the regulations made or treated as made thereunder were swept away by the Regulatory Reform
(Reform of 20 Member Limit in Partnerships etc.) Order 2002 (SI 2002/3203), reg. 2.

[4] See *infra*, paras 29–16 *et seq.*

[5] Law of Property (Miscellaneous Provisions) Act 1989, ss.2(8), 4, 5(3), Sched. 2.

[6] This expression has the same meaning as in the Law of Property Act 1925: Law of Property
(Miscellaneous Provisions) Act 1989, s.2(6). Note that a contract for the disposition of an interest in
land is different from a disposition of an interest in land; *ibid.* s.2 only applies to the former:
McLaughlin v. Duffill [2010] Ch. 1.

[7] This expression means "any estate, interest or charge in or over land or in or over the proceeds
of sale of land": *ibid.*

> (a) a contract to grant such a lease as is mentioned in section 54(2) of the Law of Property Act 1925 (short leases);
>
> (b) a contract made in the course of a public auction; or
>
> [(c) a contract regulated under the Financial Services and Markets Act 2000, other than a regulated mortgage contract, a regulated home reversion plan, a regulated home purchase plan or a regulated sale and rent back agreement][8];

and nothing in this section affects the creation or operation of resulting, implied or constructive trusts."[9]

7–03   In contrast, section 40 of the Law of Property Act 1925 provided as follows:

> "40.—(1) No action may be brought upon any contract for the sale or other disposition of land or any interest in land, unless the agreement upon which such action is brought, or some memorandum or note thereof, is in writing, and signed by the party to be charged or by some other person thereunto by him lawfully authorised.
>
> (2) This section applies to contracts whether made before or after the commencement of this Act and does not affect the law relating to part performance, or sales by the court."

The potential application of the latter section (and its predecessor)[10] to agreements for partnership received close judicial attention over the years but, even prior to its repeal, a number of uncertainties still remained. Nevertheless, it is submitted that the cases decided thereunder and Lord Lindley's views thereon are indicative of the approach which the courts are likely to adopt in relation to section 2 of the 1989 Act.

Forster v. Hale

7–04   Lord Lindley observed in relation to that part of section 4 of the Statute of Frauds which related to land (which was itself the precursor of section 40 of the Law of Property Act 1925) that it had been held as follows:

> "1. that a partnership constituted without writing is as valid as one constituted by writing[11]; and 2. that if a partnership is proved to exist, then it may be shown by parol evidence that its property consists of land."[12]

He stated that these propositions had first been clearly laid down in *Forster v. Hale*,[13] where the claimant had attempted to obtain an account of the profits of a colliery on the ground that it was partnership property, to which a preliminary

---

[8] Para. (c) was substituted by the Financial Services and Markets Act 2000 (Consequential Amendments and Repeals) Regulations 2001 (SI 2001/3649), Pt 8, art. 317(2) and amended by the Financial Services and Markets Act 2000 (Regulated Activities) (Amendment) Order 2009 (SI 2009/1342), art. 24. The definitions in subs.(6) (as amended) are not reproduced.

[9] As to the scope and effect of the latter exception, see *Yaxley v. Gotts* [2000] Ch. 162 (CA). It does not apply in the case of a proprietary estoppel: *Cobbe v. Yeoman's Row Management Ltd.* [2008] 1 W.L.R. 1752 (HL); *Herbert v. Doyle* [2009] W.T.L.R. 589.

[10] Statute of Frauds, s.4.

[11] *Essex v. Essex* (1855) 20 Beav. 442.

[12] The Scottish case of *Munro v. Stein* 1961 S.C. 362, noted *infra*, para. 7–08, is a clear illustration of this second proposition. But see further, *infra*, para. 7–07.

[13] (1800) 5 Ves.Jr. 308.

objection was taken that there was no signed writing, such as was then required by the Statute of Frauds. The Lord Chancellor dealt with this submission as follows:

> "That was not the question: it was whether there was a partnership: the subject being an agreement for land, the question then is, whether there was a resulting trust for that partnership by operation of law. The question of partnership must be tried as a fact, and as if there was an issue upon it. If by facts and circumstances it is established as a fact, that these persons were partners in the colliery, in which land was necessary to carry on the trade, the lease goes as an incident. The partnership being established by evidence, upon which a partnership may be found, the premises necessary for the purposes of that partnership are by operation of law held for the purposes of that partnership."[14]

In the event, this ruling had no bearing on the ultimate decision, it being held that the agreement alleged was of such a nature as not to require a signed writing under the statute.[15] It should also be noted that the evidence clearly showed a partnership to have existed.[16]

Dale v. Hamilton

The principles canvassed in *Forster v. Hale* were subsequently applied,[17] but not without some hesitation, by Vice-Chancellor Wigram in *Dale v. Hamilton*.[18] In essence, he held that an agreement to form a partnership for the purpose of buying, improving and selling land might be proved by parol; that it might then be shown by parol that certain land had been bought for the purposes of the partnership and, consequently, that the claimant was entitled to a share of the profits obtained by its resale. The Vice-Chancellor directed an issue as to the fact of partnership, but Lord Lindley opined that: **7–05**

> "his decision is an authority for the proposition that the Statute of Frauds does not preclude a person from establishing by parol an agreement to form a partnership for the purpose of buying and selling land at a profit."[19]

Although an appeal was pursued by both parties, it went off on other grounds[20] and, notwithstanding a reference to a certain degree of "embarrassment" in the court below,[21] has not since been regarded as casting any doubt on the authority of the Vice-Chancellor's decision.[22]

Lord Lindley regarded the above decision as going a long way towards amending the Statute of Frauds and pointed out that in both of the cases discussed above there was in fact a signed writing showing a trust in the claimant's favour which, although relied on by Sir Richard Pepper Arden M.R. in *Forster v. Hale*[23]   **7–06**

---

[14] *ibid.* p. 309.

[15] *ibid.* p. 313. The Statute of Frauds, s.4, required written evidence to prove any agreement that was not to be performed within the space of a year.

[16] See also *Dale v. Hamilton* (1846) 5 Hare 369, 386; *Isaacs v. Evans* (1899) 16 T.L.R. 113.

[17] In earlier editions of this work the *Forster v. Hale* principle was described as "carried to its extreme limit"; *quaere* is this right: see *infra*, para. 7–09.

[18] (1846) 5 Hare 369.

[19] See also *Cowell v. Watts* (1850) 2 H. & Tw. 224.

[20] (1847) 2 Ph. 266.

[21] *ibid.* pp. 272, 273.

[22] See the cases cited *infra*, para. 7–08.

[23] (1798) 3 Ves.Jr. 696.

and by Lord Cottenham in *Dale v. Hamilton*,[24] was, curiously enough, not made the foundation of the decision of the Lord Chancellor in the former case nor considered sufficient by the Vice-Chancellor in the latter.

Caddick v. Skidmore

7–07   Lord Lindley observed that *Dale v. Hamilton* is difficult to reconcile with sound principle or with the later decision in *Caddick v. Skidmore*.[25] There the claimant alleged that it had been agreed between him and the defendant that they should become partners in a colliery and share the profits equally, and he sought to enforce that agreement. The defendant denied the alleged agreement and asserted that the true agreement was that the claimant and the defendant should share the royalties obtained from the colliery. The defendant also raised the Statute of Frauds as a defence to the claimant's claim. In this case no partnership in fact was proved[26] and there was no agreement for a partnership as distinguished from an agreement to share the profits of the colliery in question. The terms of that agreement were not in writing and were in dispute. Under these circumstances the Statute of Frauds was held to provide a good defence. Although both *Forster v. Hale* and *Dale v. Hamilton* were cited to the Court, no reference was made thereto in the Lord Chancellor's judgment.

The later decisions

7–08   Notwithstanding the above decision, it is fair to say that the authority of *Forster v. Hale* and *Dale v. Hamilton* has never seriously been challenged.[27] The principle was repeated (albeit without reference to either case) in *Essex v. Essex*,[28] and both decisions were approved (*obiter*) by Kekewich J. in *Gray v. Smith*[29] and applied by the same judge in *Re De Nicols*.[30] Moreover, the principle was not questioned by the Privy Council in *Abseculeratne v. Perera*[31] or by the Court of Appeal in *Steadman v. Steadman*,[32] and was accepted and applied in 1987 in an unreported decision of His Honour Judge Baker in *Froley v. Smith*.[33]

---

[24] (1847) 2 Ph. 266.

[25] (1857) 2 De G. & J. 52.

[26] This was Lord Lindley's view and, on that basis, it is considered that the decision is reconcilable with the other authorities: see *infra*, para. 7–09. However, it is submitted that the judgment of the Lord Chancellor is not wholly clear in this respect.

[27] Note that the proposition was set out without apparent qualification in Williams, *The Statute of Frauds*, s.4 (1932), p. 25, to which Edmund Davies L.J. referred in his dissenting judgment in *Steadman v. Steadman* [1974] Q.B. 161, 170.

[28] (1855) 20 Beav. 442.

[29] (1889) 43 Ch.D. 208. This case decided that the Statute of Frauds was applicable to an agreement for the retirement of a partner, where that agreement necessarily involved the assignment of his share in any land held by the partnership.

[30] [1900] 2 Ch. 410. This was not, however, a partnership case.

[31] [1928] A.C. 173. Again, this was not a partnership case.

[32] [1974] Q.B. 161. See in particular, *ibid.* p. 183 *per* Scarman L.J. The point was not referred to in the House of Lords: see [1976] A.C. 536.

[33] July 3, 1987. In this case, where H.H. Judge Baker was sitting as a judge of the Chancery Division, there was no dispute as to the existence of the partnership.

It is also interesting to note that a similar attitude appears to be adopted by the courts in Scotland, without reference to the English authorities. Thus in *Munro v. Stein*,[34] Lord Wheatley expressed the following view:

"In my opinion, in deciding the constitution of the partnership and what it comprehended, it is competent to prove by parole evidence what each party was bringing into the partnership estate. A different situation might have arisen if the situation had been that the [*deceased partner in question*] was alleged to have brought heritable property into the partnership agreement after the partnership had been constituted."[35]

It should, however, be noted that in *Isaacs v. Evans*,[36] where there was a disputed partnership in a gold mine in Wales, Farwell J. effectively distinguished *Forster v. Hale* on the basis that a partnership had clearly been established in that case and on that footing, following *Caddick v. Skidmore*, allowed a defence raising the Statute of Frauds.

The principle

Notwithstanding Lord Lindley's reservations regarding the decision in *Dale v. Hamilton*, it is submitted that there is a logical and consistent principle running through the authorities which, although originally formulated by reference to the Statute of Frauds, was (prior to its repeal) equally applicable to section 40 of the Law of Property Act 1925. That principle may be summarised in the following propositions (which are, for convenience, formulated on the supposition that section 40 remains in force):

7–09

1. The section is inapplicable when considering the pure issue of the existence of a partnership.[37]

2. Where an action is brought which is dependent on establishing the existence of a partnership and such existence is admitted, the section will not apply.[38]

3. Where the existence of an alleged partnership is disputed, the court must first determine that issue and may, in a suitable case, be asked to do so as a preliminary point.[39] If the existence of the partnership is proved, then the section will be inapplicable[40]; if its existence cannot be proved, the section will provide a good defence.

---

[34] 1961 S.C. 362.

[35] *ibid.* p. 368. In so holding, Lord Wheatley appears to have placed reliance on the provisions of the Partnership Act 1890, s.20(1).

[36] (1899) 16 T.L.R. 113. Decisions along similar lines appear to have been reached by the courts in Australia and New Zealand: see *Meyenberg v. Pattison* (1890) 3 Q.L.J. 184; *Imrie v. Nisbet* (1908) 27 N.Z.L.R. 783; *Douglas v. Hill* [1909] S.A.S.R. 28; *Cody v. Roth* (1909) 28 N.Z.L.R. 565. But see further, *infra*, para. 7–09, n. 42.

[37] *Forster v. Hale* (1800) 5 Ves.Jr. 308.

[38] *Forster v. Hale, Supra; Froley v. Smith*, unreported, July 3, 1987.

[39] *Forster v. Hale, supra; Dale v. Hamilton* (1846) 5 Hare 369; *Re De Nicols* [1900] 2 Ch. 410, 417. See also CPR, rr. 1.4(2)(d), 3.1(2)(i), (j).

[40] *ibid.*

It is considered that both *Caddick v. Skidmore* and *Isaacs v. Evans* were, on a true analysis, cases of the latter class.[41] This analysis is also, in fact, confirmed by a number of Australian and New Zealand authorities, albeit by reference to different legislation.[42]

The present position

7–10   The current editor submits that the propositions formulated above, which are fundamental to the law of partnership, are equally applicable in a case to which section 2 of the Law of Property (Miscellaneous Provisions) Act 1989 would otherwise apply. What is not clear is whether this should properly be regarded as a non-statutory exception to the section[43] or as an instance in which, the existence of a partnership having been proved, the court will, by virtue of the operation of section 20(1) of the Partnership Act 1890,[44] be prepared to impose a constructive trust.[45] The current editor favours the latter view.[46] However, doubts on this analysis were cast by Lewison J. in an *obiter* part of his judgment in *Kilcarne Holdings Ltd. v. Targetfollow (Birmingham) Ltd.*,[47] on the basis that section 2 prohibits the making of a contract, whereas the Statute of Frauds and section 40 of the Law of Property Act 1925 merely prohibited the *enforcement* of oral contracts relating to land. It should, however, be noted that the contract alleged to exist in that case was for a joint venture not a partnership.[48] Equally, if the property elements of the partnership agreement have already been implemented, section 2 will no longer apply in any event.[49] Clearly, until the position is finally clarified by judicial decision, the need for a written agreement cannot be over-emphasised.

---

[41] But see *supra*, para. 7–07, n. 26.

[42] See *Kilpatrick v. Mackay* (1878) 4 V.L.R. (E.) 28; *Ford v. Comber* (1890) 16 V.L.R. 540; *Griffith v. Graham* (1920) 15 M.C.R. 41; *Johnson v. Murray* (1951) 2 W.W.R. (N.S.) 447. *cf.* the cases cited *supra*, n. 36.

[43] *Quaere*, what is the scope for such exceptions, given the express terms of s.2(5)? It has been held that collateral contracts are outside the scope of the section: *Record v. Bell* [1991] 1 W.L.R. 853; also *Tootal Clothing Ltd. v. Guinea Properties Ltd.* (1992) 64 P. & C.R. 452. On the other hand, despite the views expressed in *Singh v. Beggs* (1995) 71 P. & C.R. 120, 122 (CA), it appears that the equitable doctrine of part performance can no longer be relied on: see *Firstpost Homes Ltd. v. Johnson* [1995] 1 W.L.R. 1567, 1571H (*per* Peter Gibson L.J.), cited with approval by Neill L.J. in *McAusland v. Duncan Lawrie Ltd.* [1997] 1 W.L.R. 38, 44 (CA). Similarly in the case of a proprietary estoppel: *Cobbe v. Yeoman's Row Management Ltd.* [2008] 1 W.L.R. 1752 (HL). Acts of part performance *may* be sufficient to give rise to a constructive trust for the purposes of *ibid.* s.2(5): *Yaxley v. Gotts* [2000] Ch. 162 (CA). Note also the approach adopted by Hoffmann J. in *Spiro v. Glencrown Properties Ltd.* [1991] Ch. 537.

[44] s.20(1) was relied on in *Munro v. Stein* 1961 S.C. 362, noted *supra*, para. 7–08. See generally, as to its operation, *infra*, paras 18–03 *et seq*. In *Nadeem v. Rafiq* [2007] EWHC 2959 (Ch) (Lawtel 2/1/08), a partnership was held to have been created, so that *ibid.* s.21 applied on the subsequent acquisition of business premises.

[45] And thus falling within the Law of Property (Miscellaneous Provisions) Act 1989, s.2(5), *supra*, para. 7–02. See, generally, in this context, *Yaxley v. Gotts*, *supra*.

[46] Note the view expressed Briggs J. in *North Eastern Properties Ltd. v. Coleman* (2010) 3 All E.R. 528, to the effect that it was no part of the intention behind section 2 to make it easier for people who have genuinely contracted to escape from their contractual commitments. Surely the position is *a fortiori* in the context of a partnership which, as Lord Millett pointed out in *Hurst v. Bryk* [2000] 1 A.C. 185, 194, is more than just a "simple contract".

[47] [2005] P & C.R. 8, at [200] to [205].

[48] *ibid.* at [204].

[49] See *Tootal Clothing Ltd. v. Guinea Properties Ltd.* (1992) 64 P & C R 452, 455 *per* Scott L.J.; *Kilcarne Holdings Ltd. v. Targetfollow (Birmingham) Ltd.*, *supra*, at [198]; *Mirza v. Mirza* [2009] F.S.R. 115.

3.   PARTNERSHIPS GENERALLY

A mixed question of law and fact

Lord Lindley pointed out that: **7–11**

"The question whether a partnership does or does not subsist between any particular persons is a mixed question of law and fact, and not a mere question of fact."[50]

This view was, many years later, endorsed by the Court of Appeal.[51] However, under the Civil Procedure Rules, it is no longer the case that an appeal on the partnership/no partnership issue can be brought without the permission of the court.[52]

Evidence

In considering the evidence which must be adduced in order to establish the   **7–12**
existence of a partnership, two distinct questions arise, *viz.*:

(a) What has to be proved?

(b) How it is to be proved?

(a) What has to be Proved

It has already been explained that persons who are not in fact in partnership   **7–13**
together may be held liable as if they were and, conversely, that those who are liable *as if* they were partners may not actually *be* partners.[53] It follows that proof of such liability will amount to no more than prima facie evidence that a real partnership exists[54]; if it is not even possible to prove such liability, there will necessarily be insufficient evidence to establish the existence of a partnership.[55]

On this footing, the crucial question is the *purpose* for which the existence of a supposed partnership must be proved: if a third party seeks to make persons liable as partners, then all that must be established is such liability, the existence or otherwise of a true partnership being largely irrelevant.[56] If, on the other hand, it is a question of liability as between the alleged partners, it will be necessary to prove the existence of a partnership in point of fact.[57] It may also be important

[50] This statement was in marked contrast to Lord Lindley's expressed view that holding out (or, in the terminology current at the time, *quasi-partnership*) involved a pure question of fact: see *supra*, para. 5–36, n. 170.

[51] See *Keith Spicer Ltd. v. Mansell* [1970] 1 W.L.R. 333. And see *supra*, para. 5–36.

[52] r. 52.3(1)(a); 52PD, para. 4.

[53] See *supra*, paras 5–35 *et seq.*

[54] See *Peacock v. Peacock* (1809) 2 Camp. 45; *Davis v. Davis* [1894] 1 Ch. 393, 400 *per* North J.

[55] Lord Lindley put it thus: "Proof of such a state of things as is sufficient to establish a *quasi*-partnership is prima facie evidence of a real partnership, but evidence which is insufficient to establish a *quasi*-partnership must, *a fortiori*, fail to establish a real partnership between the same persons."

[56] The position will, of course, be otherwise where it is sought to affix a party with liability on the basis of an act which can only be attributed to him under the Partnership Act 1890, s.5: see *infra*, para. 12–06.

[57] See generally, *supra*, paras 5–01 *et seq.*

to identify whether a supposed partnership actually exists or is merely in contemplation.[58]

(b) How is it to be Proved

7–14   Although it is outside the scope of this work to consider pure questions of evidence, attention can usefully be drawn to certain evidential points which may arise when attempting to establish the existence of a partnership.

Written agreements and other formal requirements

7–15   A person can obviously be made liable as a partner (or as if he were a partner) without the need to produce a copy, or otherwise to prove the existence, of any written partnership deed or agreement into which he may have entered.[59] Moreover, even though some formal step may be required for the creation of a valid partnership by the law of another country, failure to take that step will not prevent persons who in fact trade as partners from being so treated in this country, irrespective of whether the issue arises as between the alleged partners or as between them and a third party.[60]

If counterpart partnership deeds are executed, a partner can be compelled to produce his copy by way of disclosure[61] or pursuant to a witness summons.[62] Where there is only one deed, it has been held that a partner cannot be compelled to produce it unless all the other partners are parties to the action or otherwise consent to its production,[63] but it is questionable whether this approach would now be followed.[64]

No written agreement

7–16   It has already been seen that partnerships can be, and frequently are, created by parol.[65] It follows that the absence of direct documentary evidence of an agreement for partnership is not of itself fatal to the case of a claimant who seeks

---

[58] See *supra*, paras 2–17 *et seq.*

[59] See *Alderson v. Clay* (1816) 1 Stark. 405, where a person was proved to be a member of a company without the production of the company's deed. Note, however, the decision in *Figes v. Cutler* (1822) 3 Stark 139, noted *infra*, para. 23–207, n. 885.

[60] *Shaw v. Harvey* (1830) Moo. & M. 526; *Maudslay v. Le Blanc* (1827) 2 C. & P. 409n.; *Mavor v. Hill* [1952] C.P.L. 472; [1952] C.L.Y. 2497.

[61] CPR, Pt 31. Disclosure may be ordered against a person who is not a party to the action: Senior Courts Act 1981, s.34 (formerly the Supreme Court Act 1981: Constitutional Reform Act 2005, Sched. 11, Pt.1 , para. 1(1)); County Courts Act 1984, s.53; CPR, r. 31.17. See also, generally, *infra*, paras 23–96 *et seq.*

[62] CPR, r. 34.2. This procedure was formerly known as a *subpoena duces tecum.*

[63] *Forbes v. Samuel* [1913] 3 K.B. 706, 721–724 *per* Scrutton J. (although this was an action to recover a statutory penalty).

[64] See *Macmillan Inc. v. Bishopsgate Investments Trust plc* [1993] 1 W.L.R. 1372. And see *infra*, para. 23–97. *Quaere* whether, if a third party has entered into an agreement with the alleged partners, his solicitors can be compelled to produce that agreement: see *Harris v. Hill* (1822) 3 Stark. 140. However, the solicitor to the alleged partners may in any event be required to give evidence, subject to questions of professional privilege or confidence: see *Williams v. Mudie* (1824) 1 Car. & P. 158.

[65] See *supra*, paras 7–01 *et seq.* And note the decision in *Walters v. Bingham* [1988] 1 F.T.L.R. 260.

to establish a partnership between himself and the defendant.[66] In addition to the claimant's oral testimony,[67] the existence of such a partnership will have to be proved by reference to the parties' conduct and, in particular, to the way in which they have dealt with each other and with third parties. However, dealings of the latter type will only be of real evidential value if they were known to and, thus, conducted with the express or implied authority of the other alleged partner(s). Such knowledge may, *inter alia*, be proved by reference to books of account, letters, admissions and the oral evidence of employees, agents and other persons.[68]

Retrospective agreements

If partners agree that their partnership is deemed to have begun on a date earlier than its actual date of commencement, proof of that agreement would not enable a third party to render them liable as partners in respect of claims attributable to any period prior to the latter date. As regards the third party, such an agreement is strictly *res inter alios acta* and of no evidential or other value.[69] It is submitted that an admission as to the existence of a partnership which can be explained as referring to such a backdated commencement would be similarly regarded.[70] **7–17**

Partnership by holding out

When it is sought to make a person liable on the basis of holding out,[71] evidence must be adduced of: **7–18**

(1) his acts or of what has been done by others with his knowledge or consent;

(2) the claimant's reliance on the representation thereby made and

(3) the "credit" thereby given to the firm.[72]

---

[66] Equally, the absence of any writing to document the existence of an alleged partnership was regarded as significant and, indeed, extraordinary in *Patel v. Euro Investments (UK) Ltd.* [2005] EWHC 1075 (Ch) (Lawtel 6/6/2005) at [133] *per* Evans-Lombe J. If an action is brought by a third party, it is in any event unnecessary to prove the existence of an agreement: see *supra*, para. 7–13.

[67] See *infra*, para. 7–19.

[68] As to the presumption arising from the joint retainer of solicitors, see *McGregor v. Bainbrigge* (1848) 7 Hare 164; *Webster v. Bray* (1849) 7 Hare 159; *Robinson v. Anderson* (1855) 20 Beav. 98 and, on appeal, 7 De G.M. & G. 239. And for cases in which a partnership has been inferred from a number of circumstances, see *Jacobsen v. Hennekenius* (1714) 5 Bro.P.C. 482; *Peacock v. Peacock* (1809) 2 Camp. 45; *Nicholls v. Dowding* (1815) 1 Stark. 81; *Nerot v. Burnand* (1827) 4 Russ. 247, affirmed at (1828) 2 Bli.(N.S.) 215. For a more recent example, see *McLachlan v. British Railways Board*, Unreported November 7, 1995 QBD; note also *Hunter v. Customs & Excise Commissioners* [2000] S.T.I. 936 (VAT Trib.).

[69] *Wilsford v. Wood* (1794) 1 Esp. 182; *Vere v. Ashby* (1829) 10 B. & C. 288; *Waddington v. O'Callaghan* (1931) 16 T.C. 187; *Saywell v. Pope* [1979] S.T.C. 824. See further, *infra*, paras 13–17 *et seq.* and, as to the position *vis-à-vis* HMRC, *infra*, paras 34–10 *et seq.*

[70] Lord Lindley merely expressed the tentative view that such an admission "might be worth nothing".

[71] Partnership Act 1890, s.14.

[72] See further *supra*, paras 5–36 *et seq.*

However, the statements and acts of the defendant's alleged co-partners are not evidence against him until he and they are shown in some way to have been connected with each other.[73]

Acts and evidence of alleged co-partner

7–19   It goes almost without saying that the principle last described does not apply so as to exclude the testimony of a person deposing to the existence of a partnership between himself and another.[74] There are, however, a number of other exceptions, which apply even where a third party alleges the existence of a partnership.

Thus, if a partnership is alleged to exist between A and B, and A is called to prove it but denies its existence, then, although the person who called A cannot usually adduce evidence to discredit his testimony, he may adduce *other* evidence to show that the partnership does in fact exist.[75]

7–20   Moreover, once a prima facie case of partnership has been established, one alleged partner's acts will be admissible against the others, as Lord Lindley explained:

> " . . . after sufficient evidence has been given to raise a presumption that several persons are partners, then the acts of each of those persons are admissible as evidence against the others for the purpose of strengthening the prima facie case against them."

This is illustrated by the decision in *Norton v. Seymour*,[76] where, in order to prove a partnership between the defendants Seymour and Ayres, the claimant called a witness who gave evidence that Ayres had admitted the partnership in the course of a conversation. The claimant then adduced in evidence a circular and invoice issued by Seymour, headed Seymour and Ayres, stating that the business would in future be carried on in those names. Ayres disputed the admissibility of the document, contending that there was no evidence to connect her with it, but the court held it to be admissible on the footing that, before the document was introduced, evidence of a partnership had been given and the document tended to confirm that evidence. A similar approach was adopted in *Nicholas v. Dowding*.[77]

Presumption of continuance of partnership

7–21   If there is evidence that a partnership existed at some past date, it will be presumed to have continued unless the contrary is proved. Thus, in an action for the price of goods supplied to a firm between June 1893 and February 1894, a

---

[73] See *Grant v. Jackson* (1793) Peake 268; *Edmundson v. Thompson* (1861) 8 Jur.(N.S.) 235. Lord Lindley went on to observe at this point that "it is obviously reasoning in a circle to infer a partnership from acts of [*the alleged partners*], unless he and they can be connected by other evidence admissible against him". See further, *infra*, paras 7–19, 7–20.

[74] Such testimony was not excluded even before the alteration of the law relating to the competency of witnesses: *Blackett v. Weir* (1826) 5 B. & C. 385; *Hall v. Curzon* (1829) 9 B. & C. 646.

[75] *Ewer v. Ambrose* (1825) 3 B. & C. 746. Alternatively, application may be made for the witness to be ruled hostile and cross-examination allowed. Note also that previous inconsistent statements, once proved in relation to a hostile witness, are admissible as evidence of any fact stated therein of which direct oral evidence by him would be admissible: see the Civil Evidence Act 1995, s.6.

[76] (1847) 3 C.B. 792.

[77] (1815) 1 Stark. 81. See also *Alderson v. Clay* (1816) 1 Stark. 405.

letter written by one of the defendants in January 1893 stating that he had dissolved the partnership in April 1892 was held to be evidence that the partnership was still in existence when the goods were supplied, although the statement that the partnership had previously been dissolved was admissible in the defendant's favour.[78]

Companies Act 2006, Part 41

The provisions of this Part will often facilitate proof of the existence of a **7-22** partnership, given the obligation imposed on any firm carrying on business under a name which does not merely comprise the surnames of all the individual partners (together with any permitted additions) and the corporate names of all the corporate partners[79] to disclose their names[80] not only on all business letters and other documents issued by the firm,[81] but also in a notice prominently displayed in the partnership premises[82] and in a written notice made available to customers and others on request.[83]

Usual evidence of partnership

Certain types of evidence are frequently relied on in order to prove the **7-23** existence of an alleged partnership and might be termed the "usual" evidence thereof. They are, for convenience, presented in alphabetical order.

(i) *Accounts*, draft or final, whether prepared for internal use or for production to HMRC.[84] Approval of a set of accounts *may* be an indicator of the existence of a partnership, but much will depend on the capacity in which the alleged partner was acting: in *Hopper v. Hopper*[85] it was held that the fact that Mrs Hopper, who was a partner in her own right, had signed a set of accounts for a period following a dissolution brought about by the death of her husband was not evidence of the creation of a new partnership between her and the other surviving partners, since in so signing she was merely acting as *qua* executrix.

---

[78] *Brown v. Wren Bros.* [1895] 1 Q.B. 390. As the law then stood, it was left to the jury to decide what weight should be attached to the letter.

[79] *ibid.* ss.1200(2)(b), (3). *cf. ibid.* 1192(2), regarding the restrictions on the use of names. See further, *supra*, paras 3–27 *et seq.*

[80] *ibid.* s.1201(b), as substituted by the Companies Act 2006 (Substitution of Section 1201) Regulations 2009 (SI 2009/3182), reg. 2.

[81] *ibid.* s.1202(1). The other documentation referred to in the subsection comprises written orders for goods or services to be supplied to the business, invoices and receipts issued in the course of the business and written demands for payment of debts arising in the course of the business. The only exception to this requirement consists of documents issued by a firm of more than 20 partners, provided that certain conditions are met: *ibid.* s.1203.

[82] *ibid.* s.1204.

[83] *ibid.* s.1202(2).

[84] See *Ward v. Newalls Insulation Co. Ltd.* [1998] 1 W.L.R. 1722, 1725 (CA); also *Rees v. Dartnall*, February 25, 2009 (Lawtel 25/2/09); *Phillips v. Revenue & Customs Commissioners* [2010] S.F.T.D. 332. But see, as to the evidential value of accounts, *Barton v. Morris* [1985] 1 W.L.R. 1257, noted *infra*, para. 18–56, where, however, the existence of the partnership was not in dispute; *Mehra v. Shah*, August 1, 2003 (Lawtel 5/8/03) at [37], [38] *per* Sonia Proudman Q.C., sitting as a deputy judge of the Chancery Division. This evidence was, however, not pivotal on the appeal at [2004] EWCA Civ 632 at [27] (Lawtel 20/5/2004). Also *Amin v. Amin* [2009] EWHC 3356 (Ch) (Lawtel 5/1/10). And note *Abbott v. Price* [2003] EWHC 2760 (Ch) at [89] (Lawtel 26/11/03).

[85] [2008] EWHC 228 (Ch) (Lawtel 26/2/08) at [150] *per* Briggs J. This part of the decision was not the subject of the appeal at [2008] EWCA Civ. 1417 (Lawtel 12/12/08), but see *ibid.* at [53].

7-24   (ii) *Admissions*: A person's admission that he is a member of a particular partnership is evidence of that fact against him[86] and will normally make it unnecessary to prove the execution of a partnership agreement in order to affix him with liability.[87]

However, an admission is by no means conclusive evidence, as was clearly recognised by Parke B. in *Ridgway v. Philip*,[88] when he observed that:

> "An admission does not estop the party who makes it; he is still at liberty, as far as regards his own interest, to contradict it by evidence."

In that case, one defendant was allowed to explain an admission that he was in partnership with the other defendants.[89] Similarly, where defendants had in a letter referred to D as their "managing partner", they were permitted to adduce evidence showing that he was not in fact their partner.[90] Even the execution of a deed describing a person as a partner will not necessarily be conclusive, even though it will represent strong evidence against him.[91] Where an admission has been based on a false assumption, little weight ought to be attached to it: this seems to have been the true basis for the decision in *Vice v. Anson*.[92]

A clear admission of partnership may be explained as referable only to a partnership for a limited purpose.[93]

7-25   (iii) *Advertisements, etc.*: The names of the alleged partners may appear in advertisements,[94] on notices or nameplates inside or outside the partnership premises,[95] or on vehicles.[96]

Equally, advertisements directed at prospective participants in a business venture may be evidence of an intention that the venture should be carried on by those participants in partnership.[97]

---

[86] *Sangster v. Mazarredo* (1816) 1 Stark. 161; *Studdy v. Sanders* (1823) 2 D. & R. 347; *Clay v. Langslow* (1827) 1 Moo. & M. 45; *Brown v. Wren Bros.* [1895] 1 Q.B. 390, noted *supra*, para. 7–21. *cf. Grant v. Jackson* (1793) Peake 268. As to whether an admission may give rise to an issue estoppel, see *Hyatt v. Pitt*, Unreported December 18, 2000 ChD, noted *infra*, para. 7–30.

[87] *Harvey v. Kay* (1829) 9 B. & C. 356; *Ralph v. Harvey* (1841) 1 Q.B. 845; and see *Tredwen v. Bourne* (1840) 6 M. & W. 461.

[88] (1834) 1 Cromp., M. & R. 415, 417.

[89] See also *Newton v. Belcher* (1848) 12 Q.B. 921; *Newton v. Liddiard* (1848) 12 Q.B. 925 (both cases concerning admissions made by promoters of companies).

[90] *Brockbank v. Anderson* (1844) 7 Man. & G. 295. And see *Brown v. Brown* (1813) 4 Taunt. 752; *Mant v. Mainwaring and Hill* (1818) 8 Taunt. 139.

[91] See *Radcliffe v. Rushworth* (1864) 33 Beav. 484; *Empson's Case* (1870) L.R. 9 Eq. 597.

[92] (1827) 7 B. & C. 409; see also *Owen v. Van Uster* (1850) 10 C.B. 318. Lord Lindley questioned whether *Vice v. Anson* was good law, since although the defendant had no legal interest in the mine, she was entitled as a partner to share the profits obtained by working it. He asked rhetorically "And what more was necessary to make her liable to the supplier?"

[93] See *De Berkom v. Smith* (1793) 1 Esp. 29; *Ridgway v. Philip* (1834) 1 Cromp., M. & R. 415.

[94] See *Maudslay v. Le Blanc* (1827) 2 C. & P. 409, note; *Bourne v. Freeth* (1829) 9 B. & C. 632; *Reynell v. Lewis* (1846) 15 M. & W. 517; *Lake v. Argyll* (1844) 6 Q.B. 477; *Wood v. Argyll* (1844) 6 Man. & G. 928. In *Ex p. Matthews* (1814) 3 V. & B. 125, an advertisement of dissolution was relied on.

[95] *Williams v. Keats* (1817) 2 Stark. 290. See also *Pott v. Eyton* (1846) 3 C.B. 32. And note the terms of the Companies Act 2006, Pt. 41: see further, *supra*, paras 3–33, 7–22.

[96] *Stables v. Eley* (1825) 1 C. & P. 614: see further, *supra*, para. 5–61.

[97] See, for example, see *McLachlan v. British Railways Board*, Unreported November 7, 1995 QBD. In earlier editions of this work it was observed in the text that "A prospectus or advertisement issued by one person and assented to by another is abundant evidence of a contract upon the terms contained in the prospectus or advertisement": *Fox v. Clifton* (1830) 6 Bing. 776, 797 *per* Tindal C.J.

(iv) *Agreements and other documents*: A partnership may be proved by means of **7–26** a written agreement[98] or by other, less formal, documents, *e.g.* an unsigned memorandum or draft agreement acted on by the partners,[99] or a series of letters.[100] Moreover, an agreement between A and B may disclose a trust for C, and be evidence in his favour that he is a partner.[101] See also Admissions, *supra*.

If it is sought to rely on the terms of a partnership agreement as against a new partner who was not one of the original parties thereto, it will be necessary to prove conduct of such a nature as to show his unequivocal intention to be bound thereby.[102]

(v) *Bills, circulars and invoices* containing the names of the alleged **7–27** partners.[103]

(vi) *Bills of exchange*: The manner in which bills have been drawn, accepted, or endorsed has frequently been treated as providing evidence of partnership.[104]

(vii) *Brochures*: Where brochures are issued to attract participants in a venture, they may amount to evidence of an intention to form a partnership.[105]

(viii) *Conduct*: Although conduct will clearly be relevant, it will not be determinative, particularly if it can be demonstrated that there was actually no intention to create a partnership.[106]

(ix) *Draft agreements*: See Agreements, *supra*. **7–28**

(x) *Joint bank accounts*: The operation of such accounts in connection with a business may be some evidence of partnership, but is not conclusive, or even

---

[98] See generally, *supra*, paras 5–05 *et seq.*

[99] *Worts v. Pern* (1707) 3 Bro.P.C. 548; *Williams v. Williams* (1867) L.R. 2 Ch.App. 294; *Baxter v. West* (1858) 1 Dr. & Sm. 173; *Munro v. Stein*, 1961 S.C. 362. See also *Zamikoff v. Lundy* (1970) 9 D.L.R. (3d) 637 (CA, Ontario); *Walters v. Bingham* [1988] 1 F.T.L.R. 260; *Thakrar v. Vadera*, March 31, 1999 (unreported), a decision of Arden J.; *Gray v. Dickson* (A1116/05), August 10, 2007 (Sh. Ct); the point was, in the event, conceded in *Tann v. Herrington* [2009] P.N.L.R. 22. *cf. Firth v. Amslake* (1964) 108 S.J. 198, noticed *infra*, para. 9–14; *Abbott v. Price* [2003] EWHC 2760 (Ch), at [89] (Lawtel 26/11/03) at [75]. *Semble* the decision in *Cheverny Consulting Ltd. v. Whitehead Mann Ltd.* [2007] 1 All E.R. (Comm) 124 (CA), as to the unlikelihood of parties intending to enter into a complex agreement without a formal contract, will rarely be relevant in this context.

[100] See *McLachlan v. British Railways Board*, Unreported November 7, 1995 QBD. Note that, in *Phillips v. Revenue & Customs Commissioners* [2010] S.F.T.D. 332, reliance was placed on pleadings and a Tomlin order. However, the rules of evidence in a Tribunal differ from those in a court: *ibid.* at [24].

[101] As in *Dale v. Hamilton* (1847) 2 Ph. 266. See also *Page v. Cox* (1851) 10 Hare 163; *Murray v. Flavell* (1883) 25 Ch.D. 89; *Byrne v. Reid* [1902] 2 Ch. 735, 744 *per* Stirling L.J.

[102] *Zamikoff v. Lundy* (1970) 9 D.L.R. (3d) 637 (Ontario CA). *cf. Firth v. Amslake* (1964) 108 S.J. 198. See further, *infra*, paras 9–13, 9–14, 10–256. And note *Walters v. Bingham*, [1988] 1 F.T.L.R. 260.

[103] *Young v. Axtell* (1784) 2 H.Bl. 242; *Norton v. Seymour* (1847) 3 C.B. 792. Note also that, where the Companies Act 2006, Pt. 41 applies, the names of all the partners must in general appear on all documents issued by the firm: see *supra*, paras 3–33, 7–22.

[104] *Guidon v. Robson* (1809) 2 Camp. 302; *Spencer v. Billing* (1812) 3 Camp. 310; *Gurney v. Evans* (1858) 3 H. & N. 122; *Duncan v. Hill* (1873) 2 Brod. & B. 682.

[105] See *McLachlan v. British Railways Board*, Unreported November 7, 1995 QBD. *cf. Pine Energy Consultants Ltd. v. Talisman Energy (UK) Ltd.* [2008] CSOH 10 (OH).

[106] *Greville v. Venables* [2007] EWCA Civ. 878 (Lawtel 12/9/07).

prima facie evidence thereof.[107] Conversely, the absence of a joint bank account may be evidence *against* the existence of a partnership.[108]

(xi) *Judgments*: Apart from any question of issue estoppel[109] and the provisions of the Civil Evidence Act 1968,[110] a finding as to the existence of a partnership in one action will not generally be admissible as evidence in a subsequent action.[111]

7–29 (xii) *Letters and memoranda*: These may show an intention to admit a person to partnership or to give him a share of profits, but must be coupled with evidence that such intention was acted on.[112] See also Admissions, *supra*.

(xiii) *Meetings*: Evidence may be adduced to show that parties attended and took part in meetings[113] or required them to be called.[114]

(xiv) *Payment of money into court*: When, in an action against alleged partners, they make a payment into court, this does not amount to an admission of the partnership alleged to exist between them, but only of their joint liability to the extent of the payment.[115]

7–30 (xv) *Recitals in agreements*.[116]

(xvi) *Registers, etc.*: The entry of the name of a person in a particular register does not, in the absence of some specific statutory provision, affect him unless he can be proved to have authorised the use of his name.[117] Thus, an entry in

---

[107] See *Jackson v. White and Midland Bank* [1967] 2 Lloyd's Rep. 68; also *Engineer v. I.R.C.* [1997] S.T.C. (SCD) 189; *Hunter v. C.&E. Commissioners* [2000] S.T.I. 936 (VAT Trib.); *Neal v. Jones* [2002] EWCA Civ 1731 (Lawtel 31/10/02) at [37] *per* Rix L.J.; *Rees v. Dartnall*, February 25, 2009 (Lawtel 25/2/09); *cf. Spree Engineering and Testing Ltd. v. O'Rourke Civil and Structural Engineering Ltd.*, Unreported May 18, 1999 QBD.

[108] *Waddington v. O'Callaghan* (1931) 16 T.C. 187; *Saywell v. Pope* [1979] S.T.C. 824, 835 *per* Slade J.; *Kings v. King* [2004] S.T.C. (S.C.D.) 186, 198; *Pine Energy Consultants Ltd. v. Talisman Energy (UK) Ltd.* [2008] CSOH 10 (OH) at [28] *per* Lord Glennie; *Protectacoat Firthglow Ltd. v. Szilagyi* [2009] I.R.L.R. 365 at [63] *per* Smith L.J.

[109] The mere giving of evidence in one action will not give rise to an issue estoppel: see *Hyatt v. Pitt*, Unreported December 18, 2000 ChD, noted *infra*, para. 7–30.

[110] *ibid.* s.11 (as amended) provides that a conviction is admissible in civil proceedings for the purpose of proving that the offence was committed. This might be relevant where a conviction could only have been obtained on the basis that the defendant was a partner, *e.g.* as in *Clode v. Barnes* [1974] 1 W.L.R. 544 (a decision under the Trade Descriptions Act 1968).

[111] See generally, *Phipson on Evidence* (17th ed.), Chap. 43, and in particular paras 43–76 *et seq.*

[112] *Heyhoe v. Burgh* (1850) 9 C.B. 431; *Baxter v. West* (1858) 1 Dr. & Sm. 173, where a partnership for seven years was proved by an unsigned memorandum on which the parties had acted; also *McLachlan v. British Railways Board*, Unreported November 7, 1995 QBD. The terms of the letterhead in use from time to time may be relevant: *Phillips v. Revenue & Customs Commissioners* [2010] S.F.T.D. 332.

[113] *Lake v. Argyll* (1844) 6 Q.B. 477; *Wood v. Argyll* (1844) 6 Man. & G. 928. See also *Peel v. Thomas* (1855) 15 C.B. 714.

[114] *Tredwen v. Bourne* (1840) 6 M. & W. 461.

[115] *Charles v. Branker* (1844) 12 M. & W. 743.

[116] *Leiden v. Lawrence* (1863) 2 N.R. 283.

[117] *Fox v. Clifton* (1830) 6 Bing. 776; also note *Marsh v. Marsh* [2010] EWCA 1563 (Ch) (Lawtel 29/6/10). As to the registers of ships, see *Tinkler v. Walpole* (1811) 14 East 226; *Flower v. Young* (1812) 3 Camp. 240; and see *M'Iver v. Humble* (1812) 16 East 169. And as to the register of hackney carriage licences, see *Strother v. Willan* (1814) 4 Camp. 24; *Weaver v. Prentice* (1795) 1 Esp. 369.

custom-house books made by one of three alleged partners, to the effect that he and the other two were jointly interested in certain goods, though conclusive as between them and the Crown, was not so as between them and third parties.[118]

(xvii) *Releases* executed by all the alleged partners.[119]

(xviii) *Tax returns*: The fact that the alleged partners have submitted a partner-   **7–31**
ship return[120] will be an indication that they believed they were partners.[121]

(xix) *Use of property* by several persons jointly.[122]

(xx) *Witness*: A witness may be asked not only which persons compose a particular firm, but also whether named individuals do so.[123] If a witness admits that he is a partner in an action where the existence of the partnership is not in issue, this will naturally not give rise to any form of issue estoppel against him.[124]

---

[118] *Ellis v. Watson* (1818) 2 Stark. 453.

[119] *Gibbons v. Wilcox* (1817) 2 Stark. 43.

[120] Through the "nominated partner": see the Taxes Management Act 1970, s.12AA(11)(a), (12), considered *infra*, para. 34–17.

[121] As in *Phillips v. Revenue & Customs Commissioners* [2010] S.F.T.D. 332. Note, however, that the rules of evidence are different in a Tribunal: *ibid.* at [24].

[122] *Weaver v. Prentice* (1795) 1 Esp. 369; *Re John's Assignment Trusts* [1970] 1 W.L.R. 955. But see, as to co-owners who are not partners, *supra*, paras 5–07 *et seq.*

[123] *Acerro v. Petroni* (1915) 1 Stark. 100. Note that in *Burgue v. De Tastet* (1821) 3 Stark. 53, it was held that, to prove a partnership between A in England and B in Spain, it was not enough to show that A once dwelt in a town in Spain, that B resided and carried on business there under the name of A, B & Co., and that there was no one there of the name of A.

[124] *Hyatt v. Pitt*, Unreported December 18, 2000 ChD. Here in fact the questions had been put to the witness by the tribunal itself.

CHAPTER 8

ILLEGAL PARTNERSHIPS

1. WHICH PARTNERSHIPS ARE ILLEGAL

Illegality never presumed

A partnership cannot be created by, or be continued on the basis of, an illegal **8–01**
contract but such illegality is never presumed: if it is alleged by a party, he must
prove its existence.[1] However, if the illegality appears on the face of documents
comprised in the court file or otherwise becomes apparent during the course of
the hearing, the court will itself take the point, even though it is not relied upon
by any party to the proceedings.[2]

Lord Lindley summarised the evidence necessary to establish the illegality of **8–02**
a partnership in these terms:

" . . . in order to show that a partnership is illegal it is necessary to establish either
that the object of the partnership is one the attainment of which is contrary to law, or
that the object being legal, its attainment is sought in a manner which the law forbids.
But proof that a firm has been guilty of an illegal act is not sufficient to bring the firm
within the class of illegal partnerships; for if this were enough, every partnership
which does not pay its debts, or which commits any tort, or is guilty of culpable
negligence, would be illegal, which is obviously absurd.[3] Neither does it by any
means follow that because one or more clauses in a contract of partnership are illegal
the partnership is itself illegal."[4]

Illegality and *ultra vires*

A clear distinction must be drawn between a partnership which is carried on **8–03**
for illegal purposes and one which is merely void as being *ultra vires* one or more
of the partners. A partnership of the latter class, though not *per se* illegal, will
clearly be unenforceable. The most obvious example was formerly the company
whose memorandum did not permit it to enter into partnership, but the *ultra vires*

---

[1] See, for example, the attitude of the Court of Appeal when faced with a potential illegality
argument in *Ward v. Newalls Insulation Co. Ltd.* [1998] 1 W.L.R. 1722, 1729C–H.

[2] See further *infra*, para. 8–64.

[3] See *Thwaites v. Coulthwaite* [1896] 1 Ch. 496; also *Armstrong v. Armstrong* (1834) 3 M. & K.
45, 64–65 per Brougham L.C.; *Sharp v. Taylor* (1848) 2 Ph. 801; *Brett v. Beckwith* (1856) 3 Jur. (N.S.)
31; *Ex p. Longworth's Executors* (1859) 1 De G.F. & J. 17. The distinction in the text was clearly
drawn by the Court of Appeal in *Hall v. Woolston Hall Leisure Ltd.* [2001] 1 W.L.R. 225; see also
Dowling v. Abacus Frozen Foods Ltd. 2002 S.L.T. 491 (OH); *Colen v. Cebrian (UK) Ltd.* [2004]
I.C.R. 568 (CA).

[4] See *R. v. Stainer* (1870) L.R. 1 C.C.R. 230; *Re General Co. for the Promotion of Land Credit*
(1870) L.R. 5 Ch.App. 363; *Collins v. Locke* (1879) 4 App.Cas. 674; *Swaine v. Wilson* (1889) 24
Q.B.D. 252; *Gozney v. Bristol Trade and Provident Society* [1909] 1 K.B. 901; *Osborne v. Amalgamated Society of Railway Servants* [1911] 1 Ch. 540; *Russell v. Amalgamated Society of Carpenters
and Joiners* [1912] A.C. 421; *McEllistrim v. Ballymacelligott Co-op. Society* [1919] A.C. 548.

doctrine has now been swept away,[5] so that a better example is to be found in the case of local authorities and other statutory bodies who seek to enter into partnership in order to discharge their statutory functions.[6]

General grounds of illegality

8–04   Apart from those trades and professions the conduct of which is governed by specific statutory restrictions,[7] there are a number of grounds of general application on the basis of which a partnership or some term of a partnership agreement will or may be found to be illegal. For convenience, they will be considered in alphabetical order.

Competition

(A)   ARTICLE 101 TFEU

8–05   Article 101[8] renders null and void all agreements[9] between undertakings which may affect trade between Member States and which have as their object or effect the prevention, restriction or distortion of competition within the common market.[10] As will be seen hereafter,[11] a person who enters into partnership will generally accept an implied (even if not an express) obligation not to compete with the business of the firm; on this basis, could the partnership relationship *per se* involve an agreement in breach of Article 101? This is certainly the case with the relationship between joint venturers, as was demonstrated in *Re Wano Schwarzpulver GmbH*.[12] There, the Commission held that a joint venture between two corporations for the manufacture and sale of blackpowder involved a breach of the Article and observed:

> "Parties who hold significant stakes in a joint venture will not in general within the field of such a joint venture compete with each other's activities or with the activities of the joint venture, even if they are contractually free to do so."[13]

---

[5] See the Companies Act 2006, s.39(1) and, as regards the powers of directors, *ibid.* ss.40, 41. See also *supra*, para. 4–20 and *infra*, para. 11–03.

[6] See *Jones v. Secretary of State for Wales* (1974) 28 P. & C.R. 280, where the Court of Appeal considered whether it would be *intra vires* for a local planning authority to enter into a "partnership scheme" with a firm of developers for the redevelopment of a city centre. Whilst it was doubted that the Town and Country Planning Act 1971, s.52 (see now the Town and Country Planning Act 1990, s.106, as amended) would authorise such a scheme, the court held that it was probably *intra vires*. Note, however, that the expression "partnership" is used loosely in relation to arrangements of this type and may denote something more akin to co-operation rather than partnership in the true sense.

[7] See *infra*, paras 8–30 *et seq.*

[8] Originally Art. 85 of the EC Treaty, but subsequently renumbered as Art. 81 by the Treaty of Amsterdam, Art. 12 and then renumbered as Art. 101 of the Treaty on the Functioning of the European Union by the Treaty of Lisbon.

[9] This clearly includes conduct: *Volkswagen AG v. Commission of the European Communities* (C74/04 P) [2007] Bus. L.R. 35 (ECJ).

[10] The full text of Art. 101 is set out *infra*, paras A5–01, A5–02. See also *infra*, paras 10–238 *et seq.*

[11] See *infra*, paras 16–13 *et seq.*

[12] [1979] 1 C.M.L.R. 403 (78/921/EEC).

[13] [1979] 1 C.M.L.R. 403. p. 411, para. [29]. See also *Re De Laval-Stork VOF* [1977] 2 C.M.L.R. D.69 (77/543/EEC); *Re the Agreement between the General Electric Co. Ltd. and the Weir Group Ltd.* [1978] 1 C.M.L.R. D.42 (77/781/EEC); *Re the Joint Venture of Amersham Intl. and Buchler GmbH* [1983] 1 C.M.L.R. 619 (82/742/EEC); *Re Agreements between Rockwell Intl. Corp. and Iveco Industrial Vehicles Corp. BV* [1983] 3 C.M.L.R. 709 (83/390/EEC); *Re the Agreement between Volkswagenwerk A.G. and Maschinenfabrick Augsburg-Nurenberg (MAN)* [1984] 1 C.M.L.R. 621 (83/668/EEC), where the parties are referred to as partners, but appear in reality to have been joint venturers; *Carbon Gas Technologie GmbH* [1984] 2 C.M.L.R. 275 (83/669/EEC); *Volkswagen AG v. Commission of the European Communities* (T208/01) [2004] I.C.R. 1197 (ECJ).

Although the position is *a fortiori* in the case of a partnership, it is considered that a firm is likely to be regarded as a single "undertaking"[14] and, thus, outwith Article 101.[15] If, on the other hand, each of the partners were to be regarded as a *separate* "undertaking"[16] an attack based on Article 101 could not be ruled out.[17]

(B) COMPETITION ACT 1998

Similar reasoning to that outlined above might also be applied to the provisions **8-06** of the Competition Act 1998, which is framed in almost identical terms to Article 101 TFEU.[18] The expression "undertaking" is not defined, but appears to include all "companies, firms, businesses, partnerships [*and*] individuals operating as sole traders".[19] It follows that, if a partnership is, on the facts, regarded as a "single economic unit"[20] of which all partners are members, the Chapter 1 Prohibition[21] will not apply.[22]

(C) ENTERPRISE ACT 2002

A partnership formed in order to facilitate or commit a "cartel offence" under **8-07** section 188 of the Enterprise Act 2002 would clearly be illegal, since such an offence connotes positive dishonesty on the part of the participants in promoting the proscribed arrangement in relation to two or more undertakings.[23] For this purpose the expression "undertaking" has the same meaning as in Part I of the

---

[14] See, for example, *Royon v. Meilland* [1988] 4 C.M.L.R. 193. "Undertaking" is given a wide meaning: see, for example, *Gottfried Reuter v. BASF AG* [1976] 2 C.M.L.R. D.44 (76/743/EEC); *Re UNITEL* [1978] 3 C.M.L.R. 306; *Polypropylene* [1986] O.J.L. 230/1, para. 99; *Hofner & Elser v. Macrotron* [1993] 4 C.M.L.R. 306; *E.C. Commission v. Italy* [1998] 5 C.M.L.R. 889; *Hemat v. Medical Council* [2007] E.C.C. 12; *Federation Nationale de la Cooperation Betail et Viande (FNCBV) v. Commission of the European Communities* (T–217/03) [2008] 5 C.M.L.R. 5. Similarly under the Competition Act 1998: see *infra*, para. 8–06.

[15] On this analysis, there could, by definition, be no agreement between undertakings or associations of undertakings for the purposes of Art. 101.

[16] Each partner is certainly *capable* of being regarded as a separate undertaking: see *Gottfried Reuter v. BASF AG, supra,* at D.55, para. [35]. See also *infra*, para. 10–239.

[17] Note that, before Art. 101 can apply, it is not necessary to show that, in practice, the effect of the restriction is "appreciable" (*Federation Nationale de la Cooperation Betail et Viande (FNCBV) v. Commission of the European Communities* (T–217/03) [2008] 5 C.M.L.R. 5, at [68]), but the effect must not be insignificant (*Völk v. Vervaeke* [1969] C.M.L.R. 273, 282; *Raygems v. Attias* (1978) 75 L.S. Gaz. 224). And see also (1998) 95 L.S.Gaz., February 4, p. 27. The restraint of trade doctrine does not apply between continuing partners: *Esso Petroleum Co Ltd. v. Harper's Garage (Stourport) Ltd.* [1968] A.C. 269, 338 *per* Lord Pearce.

[18] See further *infra*, paras 10–241 *et seq.*

[19] See the Guidance in OFT 401, December 2004, para. 2.5. See also the various authorities under what is now Art. 101 TFEU cited *supra*, para. 8–05 n. 14.

[20] OFT 401, para. 2.6.

[21] As defined by the Competition Act 1998, s.2(8).

[22] *ibid.* s.2(1); OFT 401, para. 2.6.

[23] Enterprise Act 2002. s.188(1), (2).

Competition Act 1998.[24] However, it is difficult to conceive of circumstances in which such a partnership might be contemplated.

Criminal element

8–08   A partnership will be illegal if it is formed for the purpose of deriving profit from a criminal offence, *e.g.* from smuggling, robbery, theft, etc.[25] Perhaps the classic illustration of such a partnership is to be found in the curious (and, indeed, notorious) case of *Everet v. Williams.*[26]

Discrimination

8–09   The Equality Act 2010 was passed in April 2010 and the majority of its provisions are intended to come into force on October 2010 but, at the time of writing, the necessary commencement orders have not been made. The effect of the Act is to consolidate and, in some respects, to amend the diverse legislation in the discrimination field. Two amendments of note are that an additional "protected characteristic"[27] has been added to prevent discrimination on the grounds that a person is married or a civil partner[28] and a general exemption from

---

[24] *ibid.* s.188(7).

[25] See *Biggs v. Lawrence* (1789) 3 T.R. 454 and *Stewart v. Gibson* (1838) 7 Cl. & F. 707, as to smuggling. In the latter case, particular care had been taken to conceal the true nature of the illegal transactions. It does not matter that the crime is to be committed in a foreign, but friendly, country: *Foster v. Driscoll* [1929] 1 K.B. 470, where an agreement between co-adventurers for the export of whisky into the USA, when the prohibition laws were in force in that country, was held to be illegal, those laws not being mere revenue laws. See also the Scottish case *Lindsay v. Inland Revenue* 1933 S.C. 33. However, the courts will not, in general, enforce the penal, revenue or other public law of another country: see *Att.-Gen. of New Zealand v. Ortiz* [1982] Q.B. 349, and the cases referred to therein (this aspect not being considered by the House of Lords on appeal: see [1984] A.C. 1); *United States of America v. Inkley* [1989] Q.B. 255; *QRS 1 ApS v. Frandsen* [1999] 1 W.L.R. 2169 (CA). See also *Williams and Humbert Ltd. v. W. & H. Trade Marks (Jersey) Ltd.* [1986] A.C. 368.

[26] (1725), 2 *Pothier on Obligations*, by Evans, p. 3, note citing Europ. Mag., 1787, Vol. II, p. 360. Some interesting particulars relating to the case will also be found in 9 L.Q.R. 197. It was an action instituted by one highwayman against another for an account of their spoils. The bill stated that the claimant was skilled in dealing in several commodities, such as plate, rings, watches, etc.; that the defendant applied to him to become a partner; that they entered into partnership, and it was agreed that they should equally provide all sorts of necessaries, such as horses, saddles, bridles, and equally bear all expenses on the roads and at inns, taverns, alehouses, markets, and fairs; that the claimant and the defendant proceeded jointly in the said business with good success on Hounslow Heath, where they dealt with a gentleman for a gold watch; and afterwards the defendant told the claimant that Finchley, in the county of Middlesex, was a good and convenient place to deal in, and that commodities were very plentiful at Finchley, and it would be almost all clear gain to them; and they went accordingly, and dealt with several gentlemen for divers watches, rings, swords, canes, hats, cloaks, horses, bridles, saddles, and other things; that about a month afterwards the defendant informed the claimant that there was a gentleman at Blackheath, who had a good horse, saddle, bridle, watch, sword, cane, and other things to dispose of which he believed might be had for little or no money; that they accordingly went and met with the said gentleman, and after some small discourse they dealt for the said horse, etc.; that the claimant and the defendant continued their joint dealings together until Michaelmas, and dealt together at several places, *viz.* at Bagshot, Salisbury, Hampstead, and elsewhere to the amount of £2,000 and upwards. The rest of the bill was in the ordinary form for a partnership account. The bill is said to have been dismissed with costs to be paid by the counsel who signed it; and the solicitors for the claimant were attached and fined £50 apiece. The claimant and the defendant were, it is said, both hanged, and one of the solicitors for the claimant was afterwards transported. See *Ashhurst v. Mason* (1875) L.R. 20 Eq. 225, 230, note. The case was referred to by Jessel M.R. in *Sykes v. Beadon* (1879) 11 Ch.D. 170, 195. See also *Jeffrey & Co. v. Bamford* [1921] 2 K.B. 351, 355 *per* McCardie J.; *Foster v. Driscoll* [1929] 1 K.B. 470, 511 *per* Lawrence L.J.

[27] See, as to the meaning of this expression, the Equality Act 2010, s.4.

[28] *ibid.* ss.8, 13(4). *Semble*, this is unlikely to be of great relevance in the partnership field.

the provisions of the Act will be available where a firm takes positive action in relation to the recruitment of new partners to overcome or minimise any disadvantage suffered by candidates who share a protected characteristic or whose participation in the firm's area of business is disproportionately low, provided that such action can be justified as a proportionate means of achieving that aim.[29]

Due to the uncertainty over the timetable, alongside references to the existing legislation in the footnotes are included, in square brackets, the equivalent (or near equivalent) references to the 2010 Act[30] or, where relevant, a note that the legislative approach has been altered.

(1) *Sexual and gender discrimination*

It is unlawful[31] for a firm[32] to discriminate against a man or a woman[33] on the grounds of sex[34] in relation to a position as partner in the firm: **8–10**

(a) in the arrangements made for the purpose of determining who should be offered that position[35];

(b) in the terms on which that position is offered;

(c) by refusing or deliberately omitting to offer him/her that position[36]; or

(d) where he/she is already a partner, in the way access is afforded to any benefits, facilities or services, or by refusing or deliberately omitting to

---

[29] *ibid.* s.159(1)–(4), (5)(c). In essence this legitimises positive discrimination. As to the "proportionate means" test, see *infra*, paras 8–14, 8–24.

[30] Because of the approach adopted in the 2010 Act, it is often necessary to refer to a selection of provisions.

[31] Sex Discrimination Act 1975, s.11(1), as amended by the Sex Discrimination Act 1986, s.1(3); [Equality Act 2010, ss.11, 25(8), 44(1), (2)]. The subsection was formerly inapplicable to firms comprising five or less partners, but is now of general application; *cf.* the Race Relations Act 1976, s.10, albeit that the scope of the exemption in that section has now been dramatically reduced: see *infra*, para. 8–17. As to the consequences of a breach of the subsection, see the 1975 Act, Pt VII [Equality Act 2010, Pt. 9].

[32] See *infra*, paras 8–11, 8–12. Note that, in practice, a complaint of discrimination may also be made against the actual partner(s) responsible and the Tribunal will have power to award compensation on a joint and several basis: *Way v. Crouch* [2005] I.C.R. 1362 (EAT). This was not, however, a partnership case.

[33] Although *ibid.* s.11(1) refers only to a woman, discrimination against a man is equally unlawful: *ibid.* s.2(1) [Equality Act 2010, s.11].

[34] Discrimination on the grounds of a partner's pregnancy is now clearly unlawful: see the Sex Discrimination Act 1975, s.3A(1)(a), (3), as added by the Employment Equality (Sex Discrimination) Regulations 2005 (SI 2005/2467), reg. 4 and amended by the Sex Discrimination Act 1975 (Amendment) Regulations 2008 (SI 2008/656), reg. 2(2) [Equality Act 2010, s.18].

[35] There will be no unlawful discrimination in relation to a position as partner under this head where, if it were employment, being a man would be a genuine occupational qualification for the job: *ibid.* s.11(3), as amended by the Sex Discrimination (Gender Reassignment) Regulations 1999 (SI 1999/1102), reg. 4(4) [Equality Act 2010, Sched. 9, Pt. 1, para. 1(1), (2)(c)]. As to the meaning of "genuine occupational qualification", see *ibid.* s.7(2) [not replicated in the Equality Act].

[36] There will be no unlawful discrimination in relation to a position as partner under this head where, if it were employment, being a man would be a genuine occupational qualification for the job: *ibid.* s.11(3) (as amended) [Equality Act 2010, Sched. 9, Pt. 1, para. 1(1), (2)(c)]. And see the previous footnote.

afford him/her such access, by expelling[37] him/her from that position, or by subjecting him/her to any other detriment.[38]

Broadly the same provisions apply in the case of discrimination against a partner or prospective partner on the ground that he or she is intending to undergo, is undergoing or has undergone gender reassignment.[39]

8–11 *Meaning of "firm".* The discrimination legislation in this and other contexts is applied to "the firm", which has its normal meaning under section 4 of the 1890 Act.[40] At a simple level this will mean all the partners of an existing firm, as well as persons who are proposing to enter into partnership together.[41] Where the members of an existing firm discriminate against one of their number, the position becomes more complex, since that partner is, by definition, a member of "the firm" and would, thus, bear a share of any compensation which may be awarded. In these circumstances, it is likely that the Employment Tribunal will seek to ensure that the partner discriminated against will not bear a share of that compensation in one of two possible ways. First, it can recommend[42] that the other partners as respondents to the claim should:

"take ... action ... for the purpose of obviating or reducing the adverse effect on the complainant of any act of discrimination to which the complaint relates"

by absolving that partner from any obligation to contribute towards the compensation. However, it would seem that this power cannot be used to exonerate

---

[37] See, as to the meaning of this expression, *infra*, para. 8–13.

[38] As to what may amount to a detriment in a given context, see *Chief Constable of West Yorkshire v. Khan* [2001] 1 W.L.R. 1947 (HL); *Shamoon v. Chief Constable of the Royal Ulster Constabulary* [2003] I.C.R. 337 (HL); *St. Helens Metropolitan Borough Council v. J E Derbyshire* [2007] I.C.R. 841 (HL). Note that, formerly, a provision relating to death or retirement, as opposed to expulsion, could not be discriminatory (Sex Discrimination Act 1975, s.11(4), as amended by the Sex Discrimination Act 1986, s.2(2)), but this exemption was revoked by the Employment Equality (Sex Discrimination) Regulations 2005, reg. 14(3).

[39] *ibid.* ss.2A, 82(1), as added/amended by the Sex Discrimination (Gender Reassignment) Regulations 1999, reg. 2 [Equality Act 2010, s.7]. However, in this instance, the acts specified in *ibid.* s.11(1) (as amended) do not amount to discrimination where, if it were a case of employment, being a man/woman would be a genuine occupational qualification for the job *and* his/her treatment is otherwise reasonable. There is also a similar ability to require satisfaction of a *supplementary* genuine occupational qualification (see *ibid.* s.7B(2), as added by the Sex Discrimination (Gender Reassignment) Regulations 1999, reg. 4(1)) where existing or intending partners are deciding whether to admit a new partner or to expel a partner who ceases to satisfy that qualification: *ibid.* s.11(3C), as added by the Sex Discrimination (Gender Reassignment) Regulations 1999, reg. 4(5). However, *ibid.* ss.7B(2) and 11(3C) do not apply in the case of discrimination against a person who holds a full gender recognition certificate issued under the Gender Recognition Act 2004, s.9: *ibid.* ss.7A(4), 11(3D), as added by the Gender Recognition Act 2004, Sched. 6, paras 3, 5. [All combined in the Equality Act 2010, Sched. 1, para. 1(1), (2)(c)]

[40] *ibid.* s.82(1) [Equality Act 2010, s.46(2)]. See, as to the Partnership Act 1890, s.4, *supra*, paras 3–01 *et seq.* and *infra*, para. A1–05.

[41] Sex Discrimination Act 1975, s.11(2) [Equality Act 2010, s.46(3)]. It will also include a limited liability partnership: see *ibid.* s.11(6), as added by the Limited Liability Partnerships Regulations 2001 (SI 2001/1090), reg. 9(1), Sched. 5, para. 6 [LLPs are subject to a separate regime under the Equality Act 201, ss.45, 46(4)].

[42] Pursuant to *ibid.* s.65(1)(c) [Equality Act 2010, s.124(2), (3)].

a partner who has been discriminated against from contributing to the compensation awarded to *another* partner who has suffered similar acts of discrimination.[43] Alternatively, the Tribunal may, in any event, regard "the firm" as automatically excluding the complainant partner for this purpose, even if such an approach is scarcely justified by the legislation. Such an approach would be a logical extension of the decision of the Employment Appeal Tribunal in *Dave v. Robinska*,[44] where one or two partners had dissolved the partnership on the grounds of the other's pregnancy and sought to maintain that the Tribunal did not have jurisdiction to hear the applicant partner's claim because she alone, as the other partner, could not constitute "a firm". That argument was rejected, it being held that section 11(1) of the Sex Discrimination Act 1975[45] should be given a wide interpretation and that the reference to "the firm" could include not only the *other* members of a three-or more partner firm but also one member of a two-partner firm. The same result would be achieved even if one looked at the position following the dissolution.

Although the latter approach may be seen as a neat solution to the problem, in the view of the current editor, it leaves too many unanswered questions if applied in the context under consideration. The *obiter* assumption made by the Tribunal was that, where a majority of partners decide to commit an unlawful act of discrimination, the complainant partner can proceed against *all* the other partners. Precisely the same assumption was made by Warren J. in *Hammonds (A Firm) v. Danilunas*,[46] when considering liability for misrepresentations made by certain partners in management positions. As will be seen hereafter, the reasoning in that case is, in this respect, prima facie insupportable[47] and it is submitted that the position here is no different. Thus, if one of four partners dissolved the firm by reason of a partner's pregnancy, why should the remaining two innocent partners, who would be powerless to prevent the dissolution, be liable along with the partner guilty of the act of discrimination?[48] This scarcely seems a sensible or attractive result.

Inexplicably, the same result would not, in any event, be achievable in the case of discrimination by a limited liability partnership, since it is doubted that the reference to "the firm"[49] could be read as referring to the other members of the LLP; *sed quaere*. If that is correct, it follows that the only option open to the Tribunal would be to make an appropriate recommendation to the respondent LLP.

8–12

---

[43] See the provisional view expressed by the Employment Appeal Tribunal in *Sinclair Roche & Temperley v. Heard* [2004] I.R.L.R. 763 at [58]. Note that this decision seems not to have been cited to Warren J. when he was considering a similar example in *Hammonds (A Firm) v. Danilunas* [2009] EWHC 216 (Civ) (Ch) (Lawtel 18/2/09) at [152]. This issue was not pursued on the appeal *sub nom. Hammonds (A Firm) v. Jones The Times*, January 4, 2010. [The anomaly in question is catered for expressly in the Equality Act 2010, s.124(3)(b).]

[44] [2003] I.C.R. 1248. The decision in *Mair v. Wood* 1948 S.C. 83 (see, further, para. 20–12) appears not to have been cited to the Tribunal. Although permission to appeal was granted, it appears not to have proceeded beyond the EAT.

[45] See, for the equivalent provision, the Equality Act 2010, s.44(1), (2).

[46] [2009] EWHC 216 (Civ) (Ch) (Lawtel 18/2/09). In this instance, the assumption was, in terms, that the Partnership Act 1890, s.5 applies in such a case. This issue was not pursued on the appeal *sub nom. Hammonds (A Firm) v. Jones The Times*, January 4, 2010.

[47] See *infra*, para. 12–03.

[48] A similar example was considered in *Hammonds (A Firm) v. Danilunas, supra*, at [152], but Warren J. framed his tentative view by reference to the duty of good faith, which would have no relevance in the example considered in the text.

[49] No longer relevant under the Equality Act 2010: see s.45.

8–13 *Meaning of "expulsion".* For this purpose expulsion is defined[50] in such a way as to include any form of compulsory termination,[51] whether on notice or otherwise, and will even extend to a power to *dissolve* the firm.[52] It should, however, be noted that the statutory definition also includes:

> "the termination of that person's . . . partnership by any act of his (including the giving of notice) in circumstances such that he is entitled to terminate it without notice by reason of . . . the conduct of the other partners".[53]

This would, at first sight, seem to contemplate a case of repudiation and acceptance, but it is now clear that the doctrine of repudiation has no application to partnerships.[54] It is doubtful whether this is intended to be a reference to a partner's right to obtain a dissolution under the Partnership Act 1890,[55] and it is almost inconceivable that an agreement would entitle a partner to terminate his partnership *without* any form of notice whatsoever. This part of the definition accordingly remains something of a mystery.

8–14 *Forms and proof of unlawful discrimination.* Discrimination may be direct, i.e. less favourable treatment,[56] or indirect, i.e. the application of a provision, criterion or practice[57] which, though it applies or could apply equally to both sexes, not only puts or would put women (or men) at a particular disadvantage but also puts the complainant partner at that disadvantage and cannot be justified as a proportionate means of achieving a legitimate aim.[58] It is considered that the scope for satisfying this "legitimate aim" test will be narrow[59] and reference should be made to the consideration of the equivalent test in the age discrimination legislation, which has been the subject of pertinent judicial scrutiny.[60]

[50] Sex Discrimination Act 1975, s.82(1A), as added by the Sex Discrimination Act 1986, 2(3) [Equality Act 2010, s.46(6)].

[51] Note that in *Seldon v. Clarkson Wright & Jakes*, December 4, 2007 (Case 1100275/2007/EB), the Tribunal held that a failure to renew Mr Seldon's status as a partner when he reached the compulsory retirement age of 65 would amount to an expulsion for the purposes of the equivalent definition in the age discrimination legislation: see further *infra*, paras 8–22 *et seq*. This part of the decision was not the subject of an appeal.

[52] *Dave v. Robinska* [2003] I.C.R. 1248: see further *supra*, para. 8–11.

[53] *ibid.* s.82(1A)(b)'[Equality Act 2010, s.46(6)(b)].

[54] See *infra*, paras 24–05 *et seq.*

[55] See *infra*, paras 24–47 *et seq.*

[56] Sex Discrimination Act 1975, s.1(2)(a), as substituted by the Sex Discrimination (Indirect Discrimination and Burden of Proof) Regulations 2001 (SI 2001/2660), reg. 3 [Equality Act 2010, s.13]. As to the relevance of motivation in such a case, see *James v. Eastleigh Borough Council* [1990] 2 A.C. 751 (HL); *Ahmed v. Amnesty International* [2009] I.C.R. 1450 (EAT); *R.(E) v. Governing Body of JFS* [2010] 2 W.L.R. 153 (SC). The latter cases involved racial discrimination.

[57] As to the difference between these terms, note *ABN Amro Management Services Ltd. v. Hogben*, UKEAT/0266/09 DM (Lawtel 25/11/09) at [27] *per* Underhill J. (an age discrimination case).

[58] *ibid.* s.1(2)(b) (as substituted by the Employment Equality (Sex Discrimination) Regulations 2005 (SI 2005/2467), reg. 3(1)), (3)(a), read with *ibid.* s.2(1) [Equality Act 2010, s.19]. As to what is a "proportionate means" of achieving the aim, see *GMB v. Allen* [2008] I.R.L.R. 690 (CA).

[59] An attempted justification under an earlier formulation of this section failed in *Sinclair Roche & Temperley v. Heard* [2004] I.R.L.R. 763, but the Tribunal's decision was, in the event, set aside and remitted for a rehearing. Note, however, *Chief Constable of West Midlands Police v. Blackburn* [2009] I.R.L.R. 135 (CA), a decision under the Equal Pay Act 1970, s.1(3). The Court made clear that, if an aim is found to be legitimate (as it was there), the Tribunal must consider how that aim might otherwise be achieved, not how some *other* aim can be achieved.

[60] See *infra*, paras 8–23, 8–24. Although the EAT has stated that evidence, not mere assertion, will be required to back up a claim of justification (see *Seldon v. Clarkson Wright & Jakes* [2009] I.R.L.R. 267), the Court of Appeal appeared to water down that requirement on the appeal: see [2010] EWCA Civ 899 (Lawtel 28/7/10) at [38], [39].

Equally, it cannot simply be assumed that a decision adverse to the interests of a female/male partner which is *genuinely* taken in the best interests of the firm and not on the grounds of her/his sex will automatically be discriminatory.[61]

There can be unlawful discrimination by a firm against a partner even after she/he has left the firm, provided that the detriment "arises out of or is directly connected" to the partnership relationship.[62]

It is unlawful for a firm to harass a woman/man who holds or has applied for **8–15** the position of a partner in the firm in relation to that position,[63] or to harass him/her after ceasing to be a partner.[64] Moreover, once a *bona fide* allegation of discrimination has been made by a partner, any subsequent conduct *vis-à-vis* that partner, *e.g.* expulsion, *may* amount to victimisation.[65]

Where a complainant partner is able to prove facts which are capable of amounting to an act of discrimination, victimisation or harassment, the burden of proof shifts to the firm.[66] It should also be noted that, when considering whether there has been an act of discrimination, etc., the Tribunal may in certain circumstances be able to inquire into what has been said in "without prejudice" negotiations.[67]

Only an Employment Tribunal may entertain a claim for sex or gender discrimination.[68]

---

[61] *HM Prison Service v. Johnson* [2007] I.R.L.R. 951 (EAT) at [63], [64], a case of alleged disability discrimination. And note *Eagle Place Services Ltd. v. Rudd* [2010] I.R.L.R. 486 (EAT); also *Sahota v. Home Office* [2010] 2 C.M.L.R. 29 (EAT) at [48].

[62] Sex Discrimination Act 1975, s.20A, as added by the Sex Discrimination Act 1975 (Amendment) Regulations 2003 (SI 2003/1657), reg. 3 [Equality Act 2010, s.108(1), (3)]. There can be no doubt that partnership is a "relevant relationship" for the purposes of *ibid.* s.20A(2).

[63] *ibid.* s.11(2A), as added by the Employment Equality (Sex Discrimination) Regulations 2005, reg. 14(2) [Equality Act 2010, s.44(3), (4)]; see also *ibid.* s.4A, as added by *ibid.* reg. 5 and amended by the Sex Discrimination Act 1975 (Amendment of Legislation) Regulations 2008 (SI 2008/656), reg. 3 [Equality Act 2010, s.26]. There is no exemption for genuine occupational qualifications in such a case: *ibid.* s.11(3A), as added by the Sex Discrimination (Gender Reassignment) Regulations 1999, reg. 4(5) [not replicated in terms in the Equality Act 2010].

[64] *ibid.* s.20A(4), as added by the Employment Equality (Sex Discrimination) Regulations 2005, reg. 21 [Equality Act 2010, s.108(2)].

[65] *ibid.* s.4 as amended by the Pensions Act 1995, s.66(2) [Equality Act 2010, ss.27, 44(5), (6)]. A claim of victimisation failed in *Sinclair Roche & Temperley v. Heard*, *supra.* Note, however, that such a claim succeeded in *Seldon v. Clarkson Wright & Jakes*, December 4, 2007 (Case No. 1100275/2007/EB), where the continuing partners withdrew the offer of an *ex gratia* payment when Mr Seldon raised the issue of age discrimination (as to which see *infra*, paras 8–22 *et seq.*). This part of the Tribunal's decision was not the subject of the subsequent appeal. For an example of a case where the discrimination was not made in good faith so that there was no victimisation, see *HM Prison Service v. Ibimidun* [2009] I.R.L.R. 940 (EAT), a decision concerning an employee.

[66] *ibid.* s.63A, as added by the Sex Discrimination (Indirect Discrimination and Burden of Proof) Regulations 2001, reg. 5 and amended by the Employment Equality (Sex Discrimination) Regulations 2005, reg. 29 [Equality Act 2010, s.136]. See also *Wong v. Igen Ltd.* [2005] I.R.L.R. 258 (CA), refining the guidance originally given in *Barton v. Investec Securities Ltd.* [2003] I.C.R. 1205 (EAT); *Network Rail Infrastructure Ltd. v. Griffiths-Henry* [2006] I.R.L.R. 865 (EAT); *Madarassy v. Nomura International plc* [2007] I.C.R. 867 (CA); *Pothecary Witham Weld v. Bullimore* [2010] I.C.R. 1008 (EAT).

[67] *BNP Paribas v. Mezzotero* [2004] I.R.L.R. 508 (EAT); note also *Vaseghi v. Brunel University*, October 16, 2006 (EAT, Lawtel 20/11/06), although on the appeal (at [2007] I.R.L.R. 592) the court was not, in the event, prepared to decide this issue.

[68] *ibid.* s.63(1), as amended by the Employment Rights (Dispute Resolution) Act 1998, s.1(2) and the Employment Equality (Sex Discrimination) Regulations 2005, reg. 28(1), (2) [Equality Act 2010, s.120(1)]. The corollary is that no civil proceedings may be brought in respect of an unlawful act of discrimination: *ibid.* s.62(1), as substituted by the Race Relations Act 1976, Sched. 4, para. 3 [Equality Act 2010, s.113]. Note, however, that the court may, in certain circumstances, be prepared

8–16 *Consequences of unlawful discrimination.* Where an agreement contains a term which is unlawful by reason of any such discrimination, the consequences will depend upon whether or not the person discriminated against was a party thereto. If she/he was, the term will merely be unenforceable against her/him,[69] but if she/he was not, it will be void.[70] It follows that a discriminatory provision in a partnership agreement could not, of itself, render the partnership illegal.

(2) *Racial discrimination*

8–17 Discrimination by a firm against a partner or prospective partner on racial grounds is similarly unlawful.[71] Although there was formerly a wide ranging exemption for firms (or proposed firms) consisting of five or less partners, this has now been confined to discrimination *otherwise* than on the grounds of race or ethnic or national origins.[72]

The same issues discussed in relation to sex discrimination, regarding the meaning of "firm" and "expulsion", etc., will also arise in the present context and reference should be made thereto.[73]

(3) *Disability discrimination*

8–18 It is unlawful for a firm[74] to discriminate against a disabled partner or prospective partner[75] and the main provision is, to all intents and purposes, identical to that

---

to grant declaratory relief on what amounts to a pure issue of law: *Rolls-Royce Plc v. Unite the Union* [2010] 1 W.L.R. 318 (CA), a decision concerning age discrimination.

[69] *ibid.* s.77(2) [Equality Act 2010, ss.142(1), 144(1)].

[70] *ibid.* s.77(1). [Under the Equality Act 2010, such a term is merely unenforceable: see preceding footnote.]

[71] Race Relations Act 1976, s.10(1) [Equality Act 2010, ss.9, 44(1), (2)].

[72] *ibid.*, read subject to *ibid.* s.10(1A), as added by the Race Relations Act 1976 (Amendment) Regulations 2003 (SI 2003/1626), reg. 12(a) [not replicated in the Equality Act 2910]. Thus, it appears that it is still technically permissible in such a case to discriminate against a partner on the grounds of his *colour* but not his race, etc. Needless to say, this seems an unlikely scenario, particularly given the potential overlap between the various grounds: see, in this context, the decision in *Abbey National Plc v. Chagger* [2009] I.C.R. 624 (EAT), an employment case; *cf. Okonu v. G4S Security (UK) Ltd.* [2008] I.C.R. 589 (EAT). Note, as to when there is discrimination on the grounds of ethnic or national origins, *R.(E) v. JFS Governing Body* [2009] 2 W.L.R. 153 (SC).

[73] See *supra*, paras 8–11 *et seq.* For the equivalent references see the Race Relations Act 1976, ss.56(1)(c) (power for Tribunal to recommend exoneration from liability), 1(1A), as added by the Race Relations Act 1976 (Amendment) Regulations 2003, reg. 3 and amended by the Race Relations Act 1976 (Amendment) Regulations 2008 (SI 2008/3008), reg. 2 (direct/indirect discrimination), 27A, as added by *ibid.* reg. 29 (former partners), 3A, 10(1B), as respectively added by *ibid.* regs. 5, 12(a) (harassment), 2 (victimisation), 54A, as added by *ibid.* reg. 41 (burden of proof), 53(1), 54(1) (jurisdiction) and 72, as amended (consequences of unlawful discrimination on contracts) [the Equality Act 2010, ss.124(2)(c), (3) (power of Tribunal), 13, 19 (direct/indirect discrimination), 108(1) (former partners), 26, 44(3), (4) (harassment), 27, 44(5), (6) (victimisation), 136 (burden of proof), 120(1) (jurisdiction), 142(1), 144(1) (effect on contracts)]. Note, however, that the reverse burden of proof under *ibid.* s.54A does not apply in a case of discrimination on nationality or colour grounds (*Okonu v. G4S Security Services (UK) Ltd.*, *supra*) or victimisation (*Oyarce v. Cheshire County Council* [2008] I.R.L.R. 653 (CA)). [This approach is not replicated in the Equality Act 2010.]

[74] As to the meaning of "firm" in this context, see the Disability Discrimination Act 1995, s.6C, as added by the Disability Discrimination Act 1995 (Amendment) Regulations 2003 (SI 2003/1673), reg. 6 [Equality Act 2010, s.46(2)]. See, as to the implications, *supra*, paras 8–11, 8–12.

[75] If there is no disability, there can be no discrimination: *Aitken v. Commissioner of Police for the Metropolis* (UKEAT/0226/09/ZT) (Lawtel 13/7/10). Note that so called "associative discrimination" against a partner who cares for someone with a disability will also be unlawful: see *EBR Attridge Law LLP v. Coleman*, *The Times*, November 5, 2009 (EAT), where Underhill J. in effect sought to amend the 1995 Act by adding subsections in (inter alia) ss.3A (direct discrimination), 3B (harassment) and

contained in the Sex Discrimination Act 1975,[76] and the same issues arise in relation thereto.[77] However, in this instance, there are two distinct types of discrimination, namely:

(a) direct discrimination where, *on the grounds* of his disability, a firm treats a disabled partner less favourably than it treats or would treat a partner without that disability whose circumstances and abilities are otherwise the same or similar[78]; or

(b) indirect discrimination where, *for a reason which relates* to his disability, the firm treats a disabled partner less favourably than it treats or would treat a partner to whom that reason does not apply and the treatment cannot be justified.[79]

It follows that, as with most other cases of direct discrimination,[80] discrimination of the former type cannot be justified in any circumstances,[81] whereas the test for justification in relation to the latter is separate and distinct from the "legitimate aim" test encountered in other areas.[82] The potentially fine distinction between treatment on the grounds of a partner's disability and by reason of his disability[83] does not assist in this context. What is clear is that a firm must, when dealing with a disabled partner, make appropriate adjustments to alleviate any substantial disadvantage in which he would otherwise be placed.[84] Failure to do so will not

4 (discrimination by employers). As the case did not concern a partner he did not address the necessary amendment to cater for such a situation but it would be likely to follow his amendment to *ibid.* s.4. [This point is not addressed in the Equality Act 2010.]

[76] See *ibid.* s.6A, as added by *ibid.* The comparable provision is the Sex Discrimination Act 1975, s.11, considered *supra*, para. 8–08 [Equality Act 2010, s.44(1), (2)]. And see, as to the power of the Tribunal to recommend the exoneration of a complainant partner from any obligation to contribute towards his own compensation, *ibid.* reg. 17A(2)(c), as renumbered by the Disability Discrimination Act 1995 (Amendment) Regulations 2003, reg. 9(1) [Equality Act 2010, 124(2)(c), (3)]. Note also that, in assessing compensation, the tort measure is used: *ibid.* s.17A(2)(b), (3) [Equality Act 2010, ss.119(2)(a), 124(6), which are now of general application].

[77] See *supra*, paras 8–11 *et seq.*

[78] See *ibid.* s.3A(5), as added by the Disability Discrimination Act 1995 (Amendment) Regulations 2003, reg. 4(2) [Equality Act 2010, ss.13, 15, although the test is reformulated]: see *Stockton on Tees Borough Council v. Aylott* [2010] I.R.L.R. 994.

[79] See *ibid.* s.3A(1). as added by *ibid.* [Equality Act 2010, s.19]. The comparator in the case of both s.3A(1) and (5) will be a partner who has all the features of the complainant partner but who is not disabled: see *London Borough of Lewisham v. Malcolm* [2008] 1 A.C. 1399 (HL), which was held to apply to cases of employment (and thus, by inference, partnership) in *Child Support Agency v. Truman* [2009] I.R.L.R. 277 (EAT); *Carter v. London Underground Ltd.* (2009) 153(20) S.J.L.B. 38 EAT; *Stockton on Tees Borough Council v. Aylott, supra.*

[80] With the exception of age discrimination: see *infra*, para. 8–23.

[81] See *ibid.* s.3A(4), as added by *ibid.* [*cf.* the Equality Act 2010, ss.13(1), 15].

[82] In this case the justification must be material to the circumstances of the particular case *and* substantial: *ibid.* s.3A(3) [under the Equality Act 2010, the test is the same for all forms of indirect discrimination: *ibid.* s.19]. *cf. supra*, para. 8–14. Somewhat oddly, *ibid.* s.6B(1)(a), as added by the Disability Discrimination Act 1995 (Amendment) Regulations 2003, reg. 6, refers to a "provision, criterion or practice applied by or on behalf of the firm" (which precisely mirrors the language of the Sex Discrimination Act 1975, s.1(2)(b)), when *ibid.* s.3A does not contain similar wording.

[83] Thus, where a partner suffers a detriment because he is disabled, that will be direct discrimination, but where he suffers a detriment because he is constantly absent from the business by reason of his disability, that would seem to constitute indirect discrimination.

[84] *ibid.* ss.6B, 18B, (as added by the Disability Discrimination Act 1995 (Amendment) Regulations 2003, reg. 17(2) [Equality Act 2010, ss.20, 44(7), Sched. 8]. As to the likely scope of this duty, note *Archibald v. Fife Council* [2004] I.C.R. 954 (HL); also *Smiths Detection—Watford Ltd. v. Berriman*, August 9, 2005 (UKEAT/0712/04/CK & UKEAT/0144/05/CK) (Lawtel 27/9/05); *Romec Ltd. v. Rudham*, July 13, 2007 (UKEAT/0069/07/DA) 2007 WL 2041870. As to the potential exemption

only itself be an act of discrimination,[85] but may also prevent a claim of justification.[86] Whilst the cost of making such adjustments will be borne by the firm, including the disabled partner, his share of that cost must be reasonable.[87]

8–19   For the purposes of the legislation, a disability amounts to "a physical or mental impairment which has a substantial and long-term adverse effect on [a person's] ability to carry out normal day-to-day activities",[87a] although this must be read subject to certain detailed provisions set out in a schedule.[88]

It seems clear that action can be taken which adversely affects a partner suffering from a disability without committing an act of discrimination provided that his disability *genuinely* played no part in the other partners' decision.[89] Equally, the Court of Appeal has stated that the purpose of the legislation is not to treat the disabled as objects of charity, so that where a firm requires any partner who is absent by reason of incapacity for a prolonged period to forfeit all or part of his profit share, it is unlikely that the duty to make adjustments will require a disabled partner automatically to be exempted from the operation of such a provision.[90]

Similar considerations arise regarding the nature, proof and consequences of unlawful disability discrimination as were considered in relation to sex discrimination.[91]

---

where the existence of the disability is not known and could not reasonably be expected to be known to the firm, see *ibid.* s.6B(3)(b) [Equality Act 2010, Sched. 8, para. 20] and *Secretary of State for the Department of Work and Pensions v. Alam* [2010] I.C.R. 665, again a decision concerning the equivalent provision applicable to employees.

[85] *ibid.* s.3A(2), as added by the Disability Discrimination Act 1995 (Amendment) Regulations 2003, reg. 4(2) [Equality Act 2010, s.21(2)].

[86] *ibid.* s.3A(6), as added by *ibid.* [Equality Act 2010, s.21(2)]. Note that the defence may still succeed if the justification applies irrespective of any adjustments.

[87] *ibid.* s.6B(4) [*cf.* the Equality Act 2010, Sched. 8, Pt. 2, para. 7]. This is, of course, distinct from the power of the Tribunal to exempt a disabled partner who is the subject of discrimination from any obligation to contribute thereto under *ibid.* s.17A(2)(c), as renumbered by the Disability Discrimination Act 1995 (Amendment) Regulations 2003, reg. 9(1) [Equality Act 2010, 124(2)(c), (3)].

[87a] See *Patel v. Oldham Metropolitan Borough Council* [2010] I.C.R. 603 (EAT).

[88] *ibid.* s.1(1); Sched. 1, as amended by the Disability Discrimination Act 2005, s.18, Sched. 1, Pt 1, para. 36, Sched.2 [Equality Act 2010, s.6(1)]. Note also that official guidance as to what constitutes a disability was issued in 2006 pursuant to *ibid.* s.3, as amended [Equality Act 2010, s.6(5)]. As to past disabilities, see *ibid.* s.2, Sched. 2, as amended [Equality Act 2010, s.6(5), Sched. 1, Pt. 1, para. 9]. Where a condition no longer causes any impairment, the issue will be whether it is likely to recur, as to which see *ibid.* Sched. 1, para. 2(2) [Equality Act 2010, Sched. 1, Pt. 1, para. 2(2)] and *Richmond Adult Community College v. McDougall* [2008] I.R.L.R. 227 (CA). As regards the effect of sickness, note *Chacon Navas v. Eurest Colectividades SA* (C13/05) [2006] 3 C.M.L.R. 40 (ECJ). A tribunal can find that a claimant is disabled on the evidence before it, even if this is on a different basis from that argued by him: *Ministry of Defence v. Hay* [2008] I.C.R. 1247 (EAT).

[89] *HM Prison Service v. Johnson* [2007] I.R.L.R. 951 (EAT) at [63], [64].

[90] See *O'Hanlon v. Commissioners of HM Revenue & Customs* [2007] I.C.R. 1359 (CA), an employment case.

[91] See *supra*, paras 8–14 *et seq.* For the equivalent references see the Disability Discrimination Act 1995, s.16A, as added by the Disability Discrimination Act 1995 (Amendment) Regulations 2003, reg. 15(1) (former partners), 3B, 6A(2), as respectively added by *ibid.* regs. 4(2), 6 (harassment), 55 as amended (victimisation), 17A(1C), as renumbered and added by *ibid.* reg. 9 (burden of proof), 17A(1), as renumbered by *ibid.*, also *ibid.* Sched. 3, Pt. 1, para. 2(1), as substituted by *ibid.* reg. 29(2)(b) (jurisdiction) and 17C, Sched. 3A, paras 1(1), (2), as respectively added by *ibid.* reg. 16(1), (2), Sched. (consequences of unlawful discrimination on contracts) [the Equality Act 2010, ss.108(1) (former partners), 26, 44(3), (4) (harassment), 27, 44(5), (6) (victimisation), 136 (burden of proof), 120(1) (jurisdiction), 142(1), 144(1) (effect on contracts)].

(4) *Religious or belief-based discrimination*

It is unlawful for a firm[92] to discriminate against a partner or prospective partner **8–20** on the grounds of his or her religion or beliefs (or lack thereof)[93] and, in this case, the form of the legislation in all material respects closely follows that adopted in the Sex Discrimination Act 1975[94] and the issues which arise will be similar to those considered in relation thereto.[95]

(5) *Sexual orientation-based discrimination*

It is also unlawful for a firm[96] to discriminate against a partner or prospective **8–21** partner on the grounds of his or her sexual orientation[97] and, again, the legislation follows the same pattern as in the Sex Discrimination Act 1975[98] and gives rise to the same issues.[99]

(6) *Age discrimination*

It is unlawful for a firm[100] to discriminate against a partner or prospective partner **8–22**

[92] As to the meaning of "firm" in this context, see the Employment Equality (Religion or Belief) Regulations 2003 (SI 2003/1660), reg. 14(6), (7) [Equality Act 2010, s.46(2)]. See, as to the implications, *supra*, paras 8–11, 8–12.

[93] See *ibid*. regs. 2(1), 3(1), as substituted by the Equality Act 2006, s.77(1) [Equality Act 2010, ss.10, 13, 19]. Note that a philosophical or similar belief may qualify for protection: *Grainger plc v. Nicholson* [2010] 2 All E.R. 253.

[94] The provision equivalent to the Sex Discrimination Act 1975, s.11 is to be found in the Employment Equality (Religion or Belief) Regulations 2003, reg. 14 [Equality Act 2010, s.44]. See, as to the power of the Tribunal to recommend the exoneration of a complainant partner from any obligation to contribute towards his own compensation, *ibid*. reg. 30(1)(c) [Equality Act 2010, s.124(2)(c), (3)] and, as to direct and indirect discrimination and justification under the "legitimate aim" test, *ibid*. reg. 3(1), as amended by the Equality Act 2006, s.77(2) [Equality Act 2010, ss.13, 19]. Note the consideration of the legitimate aim test in *Islington LBC v. Ladele* [2009] I.C.R. 387 (EAT), affirmed at [2010] 1 W.L.R. 955 (CA), albeit not a partnership case.

[95] See *supra*, paras 8–14 *et seq*. For the equivalent references see *ibid*., regs. 21 (former partners), 5, 14(2) (harassment), 4 (victimisation), 29 (burden of proof), 27, 28 (jurisdiction) and 35, Sched. 4, para. 1(1), (2) (consequences of unlawful discrimination on contracts) [Equality Act 2010, ss.108(1) (former partners), 26, 44(3), (4) (harassment), 27, 44(5), (6) (victimisation), 136 (burden of proof), 120(1) (jurisdiction), 142(1), 144(1) (effect on contracts)].

[96] As to the meaning of "firm" in this context, see the Employment Equality (Sexual Orientation) Regulations 2003 (SI 2003/1661), reg. 14(6), (7) [Equality Act 2010, s.46(2)]. See, as to the implications, *supra*, paras 8–11, 8–12.

[97] See *ibid*. reg. 2(1), 3(1) [Equality Act 2010, ss.12, 12, 19]; note also *English v. Thomas Sanderson Blinds Ltd.*, *The Times*, January 5, 2009 (CA) (a case of harrassment).

[98] The provision equivalent to the Sex Discrimination Act 1975, s.11 is to be found in the Employment Equality (Sexual Orientation) Regulations 2003, reg. 14 [Equality Act 2010, s.44]. See, as to the power of the Tribunal to recommend the exoneration of a complainant partner from any obligation to contribute towards his own compensation, *ibid*. reg. 30(1)(c) [Equality Act 2010, 124(2)(c), (3)] and, as to direct and indirect discrimination and justification under the "legitimate aim" test, *ibid*. reg. 3(1) (Equality Act 2010, ss.13, 19].

[99] See *supra*, paras 8–14 *et seq*. For the equivalent references see *ibid*., regs. 21 (former partners), 5, 14(2) (harassment), 4 (victimisation), 29 (burden of proof), 27, 28 (jurisdiction) and 35, Sched. 4, para. 1(1), (2) (consequences of unlawful discrimination on contracts) [Equality Act 2010, ss.108(1) (former partners), 26, 44(3), (4) (harassment), 27, 44(5), (6) (victimisation), 136 (burden of proof), 120(1) (jurisdiction), 142(1), 144(1) (effect on contracts)].

[100] As to the meaning of "firm" in this context, see the Employment Equality (Age) Regulations 2006 (SI 2006/1031), reg. 17(6), (7) [Equality Act 2010, s.46(2)]. See, as to the implications, *supra*, paras 8–11, 8–12.

on the grounds of his or her age,[101] whatever age that may be.[102] Whilst the legislation again for the most part follows the same pattern as in the Sex Discrimination Act 1975 and subsequent discrimination legislation,[103] it differs in one fundamental respect, namely that it allows firms to justify *direct and indirect* discriminatory treatment[104] of partners on two separate bases.

8–23   *The "legitimate aim" test:* The first basis for justifying an act which would otherwise be discriminatory is of general application and mirrors the provisions which apply to indirect discrimination in other areas, i.e. that the treatment or the provision, criterion or practice in question represents "a proportionate means of achieving a legitimate aim".[105] It is now clear that the same standard is applied when considering justification of both direct and indirect discrimination, even though direct discrimination may in practice be more difficult to justify.[106] Negotiating this test will involve a number of stages,[107] as follows:

(a) Identification of the legitimate aim,[108] even though it is not necessarily fatal if the aim is only identified *ex post facto*.[109] Examples which have found favour with the Tribunal are the need to reform a firm's complex pension scheme,[110] a need to preserve and promote collegiality as

---

[101] See *ibid.* reg. 3(1) [Equality Act 2010, s.5]. It may, on a true analysis, be found that a requirement which *appears* to affect older partners adversely is in fact applicable to all partners equally and so is unobjectionable: see *Chief Constable of West Yorkshire v. Homer* [2010] I.C.R. 987 (CA). In the same way, a disadvantage which is the inevitable consequence of age and not a consequence of age discrimination is not *per se* discriminatory: *ibid.*

[102] It follows that the legislation protects young and old partners alike. Equally, it may be difficult to sustain a claim for age discrimination where the disparity in age is minimal: *ABN Amro Management Services Ltd. v. Hogben*, UKEAT/0266/09 DM (Lawtel 25/11/09) at [11], [15] *per* Underhill J.

[103] The provision equivalent to the Sex Discrimination Act 1975, s.11 is to be found in the Employment Equality (Age) Regulations 2006, reg. 17 [Equality Act 2010, s.44]. Note that in *Seldon v. Clarkson Wright & Jakes*, December 4, 2007 (Case 1100275/2007/EB), the Tribunal held that a failure to renew Mr Seldon's status as a partner when he reached the compulsory retirement age of 65 would amount to an expulsion for the purposes of *ibid.* reg. 17(1)(d)(ii) [Equality Act 2010, ss.44(2)(c), 46(6)]. This aspect of the decision was not the subject of an appeal. See also, as to the power of the Tribunal to recommend the exoneration of a complainant partner from any obligation to contribute towards his own compensation, *ibid.* reg. 38(1)(c) [Equality Act 2010, s.124(2)(c), (3)].

[104] See, as to the two forms of discrimination, *ibid.* reg. 3(1)(a) (direct discrimination) and (b) (indirect discrimination) [Equality Act 2010, ss.13(1), (2), 19]. *cf. supra*, para. 8–14.

[105] *ibid.* reg. 3(1) [Equality Act 2010, ss.13(2), 19(2)(d)].

[106] See *Seldon v. Clarkson Wright & Jakes* [2009] I.R.L.R. 267 (EAT) at [40], [41]. This point was not adverted to in the Court of Appeal.

[107] Note that, in *Tower Hamlets London Borough Council v. Wooster* [2009] I.R.L.R. 980 at [31], the EAT emphasised the need for the tribunal to adopt an analytical, step by step approach to discrimination cases.

[108] Examples given in the ACAS booklet "Age and the workplace" are encouraging loyalty and economic factors such as business needs and efficiency but not saving money *per se*. See also, in this context, *R. (on the application of Incorporated Trustees of the National Council on Ageing (Age Concern England)) v. Secretary of State for Business, Enterprise and Regulatory Reform* [2009] I.R.L.R. 373 (ECJ); *Rolls-Royce Plc v. Unite the Union* [2010] 1 W.L.R. 318 (CA), especially at [159] *per* Arden L.J. Note also that it would appear that a legitimate aim found to exist by the Tribunal will not be a pure issue of fact which cannot be reviewed by the EAT: *Ladele v. London Borough of Islington* [2010] 1 W.L.R. 955 (CA) at [45] (a decision under the Employment Equality (Religion or Belief) Regulations 2003).

[109] *Seldon v. Clarkson Wright & Jakes* [2010] EWCA Civ 899 (Lawtel 28/7/10) at [28], [29]. Note also *Pulham v. Barking and Dagenham L.B.C.* [2010] I.C.R. 333 (EAT) at [32] *per* Underhill J.

[110] *Bloxham v. Freshfields Bruckhaus Deringer* [2007] Pens L.R. 375 (ET).

between partners, facilitating succession planning and avoiding a purely performance driven culture.[111] In one instance the Tribunal preferred its own view of the legitimate aim over that identified by *both* of the parties.[112] The fact that the partners have all approved the aim as legitimate may be a factor to be taken into account but will not be determinative.[113]

(b) Identification of the way in which the treatment or provision, criterion or practice contributes to achieving the aim so identified and whether it can properly be justified in terms of that aim.[114] In this context, it is not appropriate to concentrate solely on the effect on the complainant partner but to look at the general effect, because general rules which achieve predictability and consistency are of the essence of the justification process.[115] Equally, providing for exceptions to the general rule may operate to undermine it but not in all cases.[116] However, it is clear that any justification must normally be based on actual evidence or, if appropriate, a reasoned and rational judgment.[117] It was on this basis that the firm failed in its justification defence before the Employment Appeal Tribunal in *Seldon v. Clarkson Wright & Jakes*[118] because, though the introduction of a compulsory retirement age was held to be justified in principle, there was no evidence before the Tribunal which actually justified the chosen retirement age of 65, although the Court of Appeal subsequently adopted a more relaxed view.[118a] Nevertheless, to rely on stereotyped assumptions or subjective impressions in this area is unlikely to be permissible,[119] although there is no reason in principle

8–24

---

[111] *Seldon v. Clarkson Wright & Jakes, supra*; see also the original Tribunal decision of December 4, 2007 (Case No. 1100275/2007/EB) and [2009] I.R.L.R. 267 (EAT). Note that, in the Tribunal, ensuring partner turnover and protecting the partnership model were held *not* to be legitimate aims. See also *Hampton v. Lord Chancellor* [2008] I.R.L.R. 258 (ET) at [48].

[112] *Bloxham v. Freshfields Bruckhaus Deringer, supra*, at [116].

[113] *Seldon v. Clarkson Wright & Jakes* [2010] EWCA Civ 899 (Lawtel 28/7/10) at [30]; also, in the EAT, [2009] I.R.L.R. 267 at [51] to [54].

[114] As to what constitutes "means" for this purpose, see *GMB v. Allen* [2008] I.R.L.R. 690 (CA), a case of indirect sex discrimination. Note that the aim and the means may not always be clearly separated: *Pulham v. Barking and Dagenham.*

[115] *Seldon v. Clarkson Wright & Jakes* [2009] I.R.L.R. 267 (EAT) at [58] to [61] and [2010] EWCA Civ 899 (Lawtel 28/7/10) at [31] to [37]. See also *Bloxham v. Freshfields Bruckhaus Deringer, supra*, at [118], where the Tribunal emphasised the need to look at treatment in context.

[116] Thus where some partners are exempted from compulsory retirement at a fixed age or, perhaps, where there is a power to allow individual partners to remain in the firm after attaining that age on an *ad hoc* basis there may be justifiable reasons for this: see *Seldon v. Clarkson Wright & Jakes* [2010] EWCA Civ 899 (Lawtel 28/7/10) at [35]; *cf.* the decision in the EAT: [2009] I.R.L.R. 267 at [59], [72].

[117] *Chief Constable of West Yorkshire v. Homer* [2009] I.C.R. 223 (EAT) at [48] *per* Elias J. This decision was subsequently affirmed (albeit without mentioning this point) at [2010] I.C.R. 987 (CA).

[118] [2009] I.R.L.R. 267. The Employment Appeal Tribunal remitted the case back to the Employment Tribunal in order to determine whether the provision could actually be justified by reference to one or both of the other legitimate aims which had been identified but, in the event, the case was not remitted and both of those other aims were upheld as legitimate by the Court of Appeal: see [2010] EWCA Civ 899 (Lawtel 28/7/10).

[118a] *ibid.* at [38], [39].

[119] See [2009] I.R.L.R. 267 at [74]. See also *Chief Constable of West Yorkshire v. Homer, supra*.

why a firm should not, in an appropriate case, rely on its own empirical experience.[120]

(c) Identification of any other means of achieving the aim which does *not* involve discriminatory treatment.[121] If such a means is available it should obviously be adopted but, on a true analysis, it may be concluded that, however the partners proceed, some of their number will still be adversely affected.[122]

(d) Establish that the treatment is "proportionate".[123] In this connection, it will be important to demonstrate that any available mitigation of the adverse effects of the treatment or provision, criterion or practice has been put in place and has not simply been ignored.[124]

Needless to say, these steps are cumulative: failure at any stage will mean that the justification defence will fail. What does seem clear is the fact that a particular provision has been accepted by partners of equal bargaining power and applies to all of them in the same way, *i.e.* where there is mutuality,[125] is likely to be a factor which carries considerable weight with the Tribunal.[126]

8–25   *The length of service test:* The second method of justification for an act which would otherwise be discriminatory is of more limited ambit, since it only applies to the award of a "benefit"[127] to a partner *otherwise* than on ceasing to hold that position.[128] Although such an award to one partner may place another at a disadvantage, this can be justified provided that it is *genuinely* awarded by reference to their respective lengths of service and not to their ages *per se*.[129] If the length of service of the partner who is disadvantaged is less than 5 years, there is automatically no unlawful discrimination[130] but, if it is more, the firm

---

[120] *Seldon v. Clarkson Wright & Jakes* [2009] I.R.L.R. 267 (EAT) at [76]. The same reasoning would seem to underpin the decision of the Court of Appeal: see [2010] EWCA Civ 899 (Lawtel 28/7/10) at [39].

[121] *ibid.* [2009] I.R.L.R. 267 (EAT) at [60], [62] and [2010] EWCA Civ 899 (Lawtel 28/7/10) at [31] *et seq.* Note also in this context, *Chief Constable of West Midlands Police v. Blackburn* [2009] I.R.L.R. 135 (CA), noted *supra*, para. 8–14, n. 59.

[122] This was, ultimately, the position in *Bloxham v. Freshfields Bruckhaus Deringer, supra.*

[123] See generally, as to the importance of this element of the test, *MacCulloch v. Imperial Chemical Industries plc* [2008] I.C.R. 1334 (EAT). See also *Hampton v. Lord Chancellor* [2008] I.R.L.R. 258 (ET); *R. (on the application of Age UK) v. Secretary of State for Business, Innovation & Skills* [2009] I.R.L.R. 1017 at [39]–[40] *per* Blake J.

[124] See the list of factors considered by the Tribunal to be significant in *Bloxham v. Freshfields Bruckhaus Deringer, supra*, at [128], [129]; note also *Seldon v. Clarkson Wright & Jakes*, December 4, 2007 (Case No. 1100275/2007/EB) at [60], albeit that the decision was not upheld in the EAT. See, however, the Court of Appeal's decision at [2010] EWCA Civ 899 (Lawtel 28/7/10). And see also *Rolls-Royce Plc v. Unite the Union* [2010] 1 W.L.R. 318 (CA).

[125] This is a concept which was developed by the Privy Council in *Bridge v. Deacons* [1984] A.C. 705, when considering the enforceability of restrictive covenants as between partners.

[126] See *Seldon v. Clarkson Wright & Jakes* [2009] I.R.L.R. 267 at [53] and, on appeal, [2010] EWCA Civ 899 (Lawtel 28/7/10) at [30]. A similar argument was advanced in *Bloxham v. Freshfields Bruckhaus Deringer, supra*, but, though referred to by the Tribunal (at [128]), was not ultimately ruled on.

[127] A benefit includes facilities and services: Employment Equality (Age) Regulations 2006, reg. 2(2) [Equality Act 2010, Sched. 9, Pt. 2, para. 10(1)]. See also, as to the meaning of this expression, *Rolls-Royce Plc v. Unite the Union* [2010] 1 W.L.R. 318 (CA).

[128] *ibid.* reg. 32(7) [Equality Act 2010, Sched. 9, Pt. 2, para. 10(7)].

[129] *ibid.* reg. 32(1) [Equality Act 2010, Sched. 9, Pt. 2, para. 10(1)].

[130] *ibid.*

must justify the use of length of service as a criterion which is, in its view, a reasonable (but not necessarily proportionate)[131] means of fulfilling a "business need" of the firm.[132] In this instance, the legislation unusually sets out specific examples of what may amount to a business need, namely "encouraging the loyalty or motivation, or rewarding the experience, of some or all of [the partners]".[133] In determining a partner's length of service for the purposes of this exemption it is permissible to take into account service in a different capacity in the same firm, *e.g.* as a salaried partner or employee,[134] but it is less clear whether service in a *predecessor* firm will be similarly regarded, but much will no doubt depend on the circumstances.[135] Periods of absence can also be discounted where appropriate.[136] Whilst there is, as yet, no reported case in which this exemption has been considered by the Tribunal in relation to a partnership, it is likely that, like the legitimate aim test, *ex post facto* justification of a particular approach to the award of benefits may be permissible.[136a]

Apart from the above tests, similar considerations arise regarding the nature, proof and consequences of unlawful age discrimination as were considered in relation to sex discrimination.[137]

If a firm discovers that a provision in its agreement does infringe the legislation and cannot be justified, no partner will be able to complain about its abandonment.[138]

Firm name

Part 41 of the Companies Act 2006 prohibits a firm from carrying on business   **8–26** under a name which does not consist of the surnames of all the individual partners (together with any permitted additions)[139] and which is likely to give the impression that the business is connected with Her Majesty's Government, any part of the Scottish administration or Her Majesty's Government in Northern Ireland, any local authority or any public authority specified in regulations,[140] or

---

[131] Note that in *Rolls-Royce Plc v. Unite the Union supra*, Wall L.J. regarded this reasonableness requirement as key: *ibid.* at [101].

[132] *ibid.* reg. 32(2) [Equality Act 2010, Sched. 9, Pt. 2, para. 10(2)]. Note that a current "business need" is not necessarily the same thing as a legitimate aim for the purposes of *ibid.* reg. 3(1) [Equality Act 2010, s.13(2)]: see *Rolls-Royce Plc v. Unite the Union supra*, at [159] *per* Arden L.J. But see also *supra*, para. 8–23.

[133] *ibid.* reg. 32(2), read with *ibid.* reg. 2(2) (definition of "worker") [not replicated in the Equality Act 2010]. A similar approach is not adopted in *ibid.* reg. 3.

[134] *ibid.* reg. 32(3) [Equality Act 2010, Sched. 9, Pt. 2, para. 10(3)].

[135] *Quaere* how will *ibid.* reg. 32(3)(b) [Equality Act 2010, Sched. 9, Pt. 2, para. 10(3)(b)] be applied in this context. The application of *ibid.* reg. 32(5) (as amended by the Employment Equality (Age) Regulations 2006 (Amendment) Regulations 2008 (SI 2008/573), reg. 3) [Equality Act 2010, Sched. 9, Pt. 2, para. 10(6)] is, by virtue of its content, strictly confined to employees. Even if service in a predecessor firm can be taken into account, it is difficult to see how service in a partnership prior to its "conversion" into an LLP could be similarly regarded, give that the LLP is a separate legal person.

[136] *ibid.* reg. 32(4) [Equality Act 2010, Sched. 9, Pt. 2, para. 10(5)].

[136a] See, *supra*, para. 8–23.

[137] See *supra*, paras 8–12 *et seq.* For the equivalent references see *ibid.* regs. 24 (former partners), 6, 17(2) (harassment), 4 (victimisation), 37 (burden of proof), 35, 36 (jurisdiction) and 43, Sched. 5, para. 1(1), (2) (consequences of unlawful discrimination on contracts) [the Equality Act 2010, ss.108(1) (former partners), 26, 44(3), (4) (harassment), 27, 44(5), (6) (victimisation), 136 (burden of proof), 120(1) (jurisdiction), 142(1), 144(1) (effect on contracts)].

[138] See, by way of analogy, *R. (British Medical Association) v. General Medical Council, The Times*, January 19, 2009.

[139] *ibid.*, s.1192. See generally, *supra*, paras 3–26 *et seq.*

[140] See the Company, Limited Liability Partnerships and Business Names (Public Authorities) Regulations (SI 2009/2982), reg. 3, Sched., col. (1).

which includes any word or expression for the time being specified in regulations made under the Act,[141] unless the prior approval of the Secretary of State has been obtained.[142] In addition to these restrictions there is now a complete prohibition on the use of any name containing a word, expression or "other indication" associated with a particular type of company or form of organisation which is specified by regulation[143] and a name which is misleading as to the activities carried on.[144] A breach of these prohibitions will result in the commission of an offence, in respect of which all the partners may be personally liable.[145] However, provided that the other provisions of the Act are complied with, use of such an unapproved name would not appear to impose any disability on the firm,[146] nor will the firm itself be illegal.

Breach of the other requirements of the Act[147] will attract criminal penalties,[148] and may impose certain disabilities on the firm,[149] but again does not appear to affect the legality of the firm.

8–27 Apart from the provisions of the 2006 Act and any question of fraud,[150] holding out[151] or passing off,[152] there is no general restriction on the use of business names by persons other than bankrupts.[153] Moreover, there may, depending on the circumstances, be no objection to the retention of a firm name by continuing or surviving partners.[154] Whilst there are numerous statutory

---

[141] See the Company, Limited Liability Partnership and Business Names (Sensitive Words and Expressions) Regulations 2009 (SI 2009/2615), reg. 3, Sched. 1, Pt. 1. Note also the Company and Business Names (Chamber of Commerce, etc.) Act 1999, ss.1, 3, as respectively amended by the Companies Act 2006 (Consequential Amendments, Transitional Provisions and Savings) Order 2009 (SI 2009/1941), Sched. 1, para. 176(2), (4).

[142] Companies Act 2006, ss.1193, 1194.

[143] *ibid.* s.1203 and the Company and Business Names (Miscellaneous Provisions) Regulations 2009, Pt. 4 (as amended, in the case of reg. 13, by the Company, Limited Liability Partnership and Business Names (Miscellaneous Provisions) (Amendment) Regulations 2009 (SI 2009/2404), reg. 2(2)), Sched. 1, para. 1(a), (b), Sched. 2, para. 3 (as amended by *ibid.*, reg. 2(3)). It follows from these provisions that a firm which is not a limited partnership cannot use the word "limited" at the end of its name or "limited partnership" or "LP" as part of its name and only a limited liability partnership can use the words "limited liability partnership" or "LLP": *ibid.* regs. 13(2), 14(1). An LLP formed under the Limited Liability Partnerships Act 2000 is not, in any event, a partnership. It should be noted that, in earlier editions of this work, consideration was given to the possibility of illegality resulting from the adoption by a firm of a business name implying incorporation, Lord Lindley having concluded that "even if assuming to act as a corporation is an offence at common law, which is very doubtful, the offence is not committed by trading under a name which is by usage as applicable to an unincorporated as to an incorporated body." For further details, the reader is referred to the 15th ed., at p. 147.

[144] Companies Act 2006, s.1198(1).

[145] Companies Act 2006, ss.1193(4), 1194(3), 1197(5), 1198(2). It is not clear who exactly is the "person" for this purpose nor whether the members are liable as the equivalent of officers of the firm: see *ibid.* ss.1121, 1123(3) and 1207 and *supra*, para. 3–34, n. 150.

[146] *ibid.* s.1206, which imposes disabilities in relation to certain proceedings, only applies in the event of a breach of *ibid.* ss.1202(1), (2), 1204(1).

[147] *i.e. ibid.* s.1202, 1204, as to which, see *supra*, para. 3–33.

[148] *ibid.* ss.1205(1). No offence is committed if a reasonable excuse can be shown: *ibid.*

[149] *ibid.* s.1206. In order to invoke the section, the defendant must satisfy certain requirements, and the court before which the proceedings are brought has a residual discretion to permit the proceedings to continue: see *supra*, para. 3–35.

[150] See *Gordon v. Street* [1899] 2 Q.B. 641.

[151] Partnership Act 1890, s.14: see *supra*, paras 5–35 *et seq.* See also *infra*, paras 10–201 *et seq.*

[152] See *supra*, para. 3–15.

[153] As to bankrupts, see *supra*, para. 4–22.

[154] See *infra*, paras 10–198 *et seq.* Lord Lindley wrote: "when a firm has an established reputation and one of its members dies, it is not deemed wrong for the survivors to continue the business under

restrictions on the adoption of names or titles which imply a professional qualification,[155] by reason of changing attitudes, there are now relatively few *professional* restrictions on the choice of firm names.[156]

Public policy, etc.

Lord Lindley observed that "a partnership may be illegal upon the general ground that it is formed for a purpose forbidden by the current notions of morality, religion, or public policy".[157] On that ground, he considered that a partnership formed for the purpose of deriving profit from the sale of obscene or blasphemous prints or books, or for the procurement of marriages[158] or of public offices of trust, would be "undoubtedly illegal".[159]   **8–28**

War

It has already been seen[160] that a partnership between a resident British citizen   **8–29** or a resident alien and an alien enemy is illegal and incapable of creation or continuation; on the same basis, a partnership formed in order to trade with an enemy nation would clearly be illegal.[161] However, since a neutral may lawfully trade with one of the belligerent nations, a partnership formed for that purpose would be unobjectionable.[162]

Statutory grounds of illegality

Lord Lindley stated that "a partnership is also illegal if formed for a purpose   **8–30** forbidden by statute, although independently of the statute there would be no illegality".[163] Of course, any question of illegality will depend on the construction of the particular statute concerned. Thus, in the case of the statutory

the old name, although, perhaps, the reputation of the firm may have been due mainly, if not entirely, to the ability and integrity of the deceased partner. The legal view of such conduct is in accordance with established usage, and it has been accordingly held not to be illegal for surviving partners to continue to carry on business under the old name", and referred to *Bunn v. Guy* (1833) 4 East 190; *Lewis v. Langdon* (1835) 7 Sim. 421; *Aubin v. Holt* (1855) 2 K. & J. 66; *cf. Thornbury v. Bevill* (1842) 1 Y. & C.Ch. 554. However, the current editor submits that this will only be the position where the business is not or cannot, for whatever reason, be sold; see *infra*, paras 10–203 *et seq.*

[155] *e.g.* Veterinary Surgeons Act 1966, s.20; Solicitors Act 1974, s.21; Medical Act 1983, s.49; Dentists Act 1984, s.39; Opticians Act 1989, s.28; Architects Act 1997, s.20 (all as amended).

[156] See generally, *infra*, paras 8–32 *et seq.*; also the *Encyclopedia of Professional Partnerships*.

[157] See *Bowman v. Secular Society* [1917] A.C. 406; *Rodriguez v. Speyer Bros.* [1919] A.C. 59; *Lemenda Trading Co. Ltd. v. African Middle East Petroleum Co. Ltd.* [1988] Q.B. 448 and the cases there cited.

[158] *Semble* this would not apply to an ordinary dating agency.

[159] See, generally, *Chitty on Contracts* (30th ed.), Chap. 16. As to the sale of offices, see *Sterry v. Clifton* (1850) 9 C.B. 110; as to associations formed with a view to disseminating irreligious views, see *Pare v. Clegg* (1861) 29 Beav. 589; *Thornton v. Howe* (1862) 8 Jur.(N.S.) 663. Note also the decision in *Herring v. Walround* (1682) 2 Ch.Ca. 110, where it seems to have been held that an agreement to share the profits derived from the public exhibition of a "human monster" (apparently Siamese twins) was illegal. On the basis that he was not aware of any similar case, Lord Lindley opined that "the decision . . . would not probably now be followed upon grounds of public policy."

[160] See *supra*, para. 4–06 and *infra*, para. 24–42.

[161] See *supra*, para. 4–05. Although the decision in *Feldt v. Chamberlain* (1914) 58 S.J. 788 would seem to support a contrary view, it cannot be regarded as good law.

[162] *Ex p. Chavasse* (1865) 4 De G.J. & S. 655; *The Helen* (1801) L.R. 1 Adm. & Ecc. 1.

[163] Lord Lindley then discoursed on the former distinction that was taken between *mala prohibita* and *mala in se*, pointing out that it had long ceased to be recognised as of any value for legal purposes: see *Aubert v. Maze* (1801) 2 Bos. & Pul. 371. This passage has not been retained.

prohibitions on the conduct of certain professions by unqualified persons, the mere entry into partnership of such a person may or may not result in an illegality, according to the terms of the relevant prohibition.[164] In this connection Lord Lindley observed:

> "With reference however to those statutes which prohibit unqualified persons from carrying on certain trades or businesses, it may be observed that such statutes are not infringed by an unqualified person who does nothing more than share the profits arising from those trades or businesses, if they are in fact carried on by persons who are duly qualified.[165] The unqualified person is not within the mischief of the statutes in question, and the partnership of which he is a member is not therefore illegal."[166]

The current editor considers that, as it stands, this statement is too widely drawn, since it takes no account of the agency which exists between partners, which will cause each partner's acts to be attributed to the other partners.[167]

8–31   Equally, although a statute may appear to prohibit certain activities and impose a penalty for failure to observe its provisions, it does not follow that conduct which would attract the penalty is necessarily illegal.[168] If the statute can genuinely be classed as prohibitory,[169] as will be the case if the penalty is imposed for the protection of the public,[170] then such conduct will be illegal. *Per contra* if, on a true construction of the statute, the penalty merely represents, as Lord Lindley put it, "the price of a licence for doing what the statute apparently forbids".[171] Thus, in *Brown v. Duncan*,[172] it was held that a partnership of distillers was not illegal, even though one partner carried on business as a retail dealer in spirits within two miles of the distillery (contrary to the Duties on Spirits Act 1823, ss.132, 133) and was not registered as a member of the firm in the excise books (as required by the Excise Licences Act 1825, s.7). Lord Lindley did, however, doubt whether the statutes in question were properly construed by the court.

---

[164] See *infra*, paras 8–43, 8–49, 8–52, 8–58.

[165] *cf.* the Dentists Act 1984, ss.40, 41 (as amended), noted *infra*, para. 8–42.

[166] *Raynard v. Chase* (1756) 1 Burr. 2.

[167] See, in particular, *Hudgell Yeates & Co. v. Watson* [1978] Q.B. 451, noticed *infra*, para. 8–52.

[168] *S.C.F. Finance Co. Ltd. v. Masri (No. 2)* [1987] Q.B. 1002; *Phoenix General Insurance Co. of Greece SA v. Halvanon Insurance Co. Ltd.* [1988] Q.B. 216; *Re Cavalier Insurance Co. Ltd.* [1989] 2 Lloyd's Rep. 430; *Estate of Dr. Anandh v. Barnet Primary Care Trust* [2004] EWCA Civ. 5 (Lawtel 19/2/04); also *R. v. Hall* [1891] 1 Q.B. 747; *R. v. Kakelo* [1923] W.N. 220; and the other cases in the next two notes.

[169] *Phoenix General Insurance Co. of Greece SA v. Halvanon Insurance Co. Ltd., supra*; *Re Cavalier Insurance Co. Ltd., supra*; also *Bartlett v. Vinor* (1692) Carth. 252; *Cope v. Rowlands* (1836) 2 M. & W. 149; *Taylor v. The Crowland Gas and Coke Co.* (1854) 10 Ex. 293; *Melliss v. Shirley Local Board* (1885) 16 Q.B.D. 446; *Whiteman v. Sadler* [1910] A.C. 514; *Cornelius v. Phillips* [1918] A.C. 199. Note that in *Estate of Dr. Anandh v. Barnet Primary Care Trust, supra*, it was held that, whilst it was illegal for an unqualified person to perform an eye test, a contract for such performance was *not* illegal.

[170] *Victorian Daylesford Syndicate v. Dott* [1905] 2 Ch. 624, 629 *per* Buckley J.; *Anderson Ltd. v. Daniel* [1924] 1 K.B. 138; also *Law v. Hodson* (1809) 11 East 300; *Little v. Poole* (1829) 9 B. & C. 192. The illegality may arise in connection with the performance of the contract: see *Anderson v. Daniel* [1924] 1 K.B. 138.

[171] *S.C.F. Finance Co. Ltd. v. Masri (No. 2)* [1987] Q.B. 1002; also *Johnson v. Hudson* (1809) 11 East 180; *Swan v. The Bank of Scotland* (1835) 2 Mont. & Ayr. 661; *Smith v. Mawhood* (1845) 14 M. & W. 452.

[172] (1829) 10 B. & C. 93; and see *Smith v. Mawhood* (1845) 14 M. & W. 452.

The following alphabetical list of businesses and professions contains the most important examples of partnerships whose legality is or may be affected by statute.

Accountants

Any person who acts as statutory auditor[173] to a company whilst ineligible for appointment to such an office[174] commits an offence.[175] Moreover, a statutory auditor who becomes ineligible during his term of office must forthwith vacate that position.[176] Eligibility is dependent on the prospective auditor maintaining membership of a recognised supervisory body[177] and satisfying that body's own eligibility test.[178] A firm may be appointed as an auditor[179] and changes in the firm will, in general, be ignored, provided that its eligibility is unaffected.[180]   **8–32**

Since audit work in general forms only one element of an accountancy practice, it is submitted that acceptance of an audit appointment by an ineligible firm could not of itself render the firm illegal unless, exceptionally, the firm was formed with the intention of committing such an offence.[181]

Bankers

A partnership which carries on the business of banking must hold a Part IV permission[182] under the Financial Services and Markets Act 2000 authorising it to carry on a regulated activity constituting the acceptance of deposits.[183] A summary of the procedure for obtaining such a permission and of the consequences of failure to comply with its provisions is set out later in this work.[184]   **8–33**

Bookmakers

Bookmaker's permits under the Betting, Gaming and Lotteries Act 1963 have been replaced by operating licences granted under Part 5 of the Gambling Act 2005.[185] A partnership may be a licensee thereunder, but at least one partner must also hold a personal licence[186] authorising him to act in relation to the licensed   **8–34**

---

[173] See, as to the meaning of this expression, the Companies Act 2006, s.1210.

[174] See generally, as to eligibility, *ibid.* s.1212.

[175] *ibid.* s.1213(1), (3). It is a defence for the appointee to prove that he "did not know and had no reason to believe that he was, or had become ineligible for appointment as a statutory auditor": *ibid.* s.1213(8).

[176] *ibid.* s.1213(2); but see also s.1213(8), noticed in the preceding note.

[177] See, as to the meaning of this expression, *ibid.* s.1217, Sched. 10. Recognition has been accorded to the Institute of Chartered Accountants in England and Wales, the Institute of Chartered Accountants of Scotland, the Institute of Chartered Accountants in Ireland and the Association of Chartered Certified Accountants.

[178] *ibid.* s.1212(1). As to individuals originally authorised pursuant to the Companies Act 1967, s.13(1), see *ibid.* ss.1212(2), 1222.

[179] *ibid.* ss.1212(1), 1216.

[180] *ibid.* s.1216(3)–(5). See also *supra*, para. 3–18.

[181] Even then the position is not entirely free from doubt: see *Dungate v. Lee* [1969] 1 Ch. 545, *infra*, para. 8–34, n. 190; *S.C.F. Finance Co. Ltd. v. Masri (No. 2)* [1987] Q.B. 1002.

[182] See, as to the meaning of this expression, the Financial Services and Markets Act 2000, s.40(4).

[183] Financial Services and Markets Act 2000, s.41(1), and Sched. 6, Pt 1, para. 1(2)(b).

[184] See *infra*, paras 8–44 *et seq.*

[185] See *ibid.* s.65(2)(c) (general betting operating licences). For examples of how the old law operated, see *infra*, para. 8–70.

[186] See, as to such licences, *ibid.* s.127, Sched. 6.

activities.[187] The holder of an operating licence may also apply for the grant of a premises licence.[188] Failure to hold a licence to carry on the relevant activity or to comply with the terms of that licence will result in the commission of an offence.[189] It would seem that a partnership formed to carry on such an activity without a licence would automatically be rendered illegal.[190]

Consumer credit businesses

8–35   By the Consumer Credit Act 1974[191] every person, firm or company carrying on a consumer credit business,[192] a consumer hire business,[193] or an ancillary credit business[194] is required to take out a licence issued by the Office of Fair Trading (OFT)[195] in respect of the activities proposed to be carried on.[196] There are no relevant exceptions to this requirement.[197]

---

[187] *ibid.* s.80(1), (5)(b).

[188] *ibid.* Pt. 8.

[189] *ibid.* s.33.

[190] The position under the old regime was different, since bookmakers' permits were held by the partners individually: see *Dungate v. Lee* [1969] 1 Ch. 545 (a decision under the Betting and Gaming Act 1960, s.2), where it was held to be sufficient if one of the partners held such a permit, unless there was from the outset a common intention that the other partners would also act as bookmakers. See also *Thwaites v. Coulthwaite* [1896] 1 Ch. 496; *Saffery v. Mayer* [1901] 1 K.B. 11; *Brookman v. Mather* (1913) 29 T.L.R. 276; *Keen v. Price* [1914] 2 Ch. 98; *Jeffrey & Co. v. Barnford* [1921] 2 K.B. 351. The cases to the contrary (*Thomas v. Dey* (1908) 24 T.L.R. 272; *O'Connor and Ould v. Ralston* [1920] 3 K.B. 451), and the dictum of Fletcher Moulton L.J. in *Hyams v. Stuart King* [1908] 2 K.B. 696, 718, cannot be relied on. See further *infra*, para. 8–70.

[191] This Act replaced the provisions of the Moneylenders Acts 1900 and 1927, and the Pawnbrokers Act 1872.

[192] Consumer credit business is defined in the Consumer Credit Act 1974, s.189(1) (as substituted by the Consumer Credit Act 2006, s.23(a)) as "any business being carried on by a person so far as it comprises or relates to (a) the provision of credit by him, or (b) otherwise his being a creditor, under regulated consumer credit agreements". Clearly some sort of "business" as opposed to an isolated series of transactions would need to be shown before a licence is required: see *ibid.* s.189(2); also *Edgelow v. MacElwee* [1918] 1 K.B. 205; *Wills v. Wood* (1984) 128 S.J. 222; *R. v. Marshall* [1990] Crim.App.R. 73; *Conroy v. Kenny* [1999] 1 W.L.R. 1340 (CA); *Khodari v. Tamimi* [2009] EWCA Civ 1109 (Lawtel 8/10/09). Note that, with the repeal of *ibid.* s.8(2) by the Consumer Credit Act 2006, s.2(1)(b), Sched.4, there are no longer any monetary limits attached to this regime. As to regulated agreements, see *ibid.* ss.8(3) (as amended by the Legislative Reform (Consumer Credit) Order 2008 (SI 2008/2826), art 3(2) and the Consumer Credit Act 2006, s.5(1)), 15(2), 82(3) (as amended) and 189(1).

[193] See as to the meaning of consumer hire business, *ibid.* ss.15, 189(1), as respectively amended/substituted by the Consumer Credit Act 2006, s.2(2), Sched. 4 and s.23(b). Again there are no longer any monetary limits here.

[194] An ancillary credit business is defined in *ibid.* s.145(1) (as amended by the Consumer Credit Act 2006, ss.24(1), 25(1)) as comprising credit brokerage, debt-adjusting, debt-counselling, debt-collecting, debt administration, the provision of credit information services and the operation of a credit reference agency. A number of exceptions are set out in *ibid.* s.146 (as amended).

[195] All functions originally required to be performed by the Director General of Fair Trading under the Act were transferred to the OFT (Enterprise Act 2002, s.2(1)) and all references to the Director General therein are amended accordingly (*ibid.* Sched. 25, para. 6). These amendments will not be noted hereafter.

[196] See *ibid.* s.21, as amended by the Consumer Credit Act 2006, s.33(1) (consumer credit business and consumer hire business), as applied by s.147, as amended by *ibid.* Sched. 4 (ancillary credit business). Obviously no licence will be required if there is no business: see *supra* n. 192.

[197] See generally, ss.16(1) (as amended), 21(2), (3); also the Consumer Credit (Exempt Agreements) Order 1989 (SI 1989/869), as amended and the exemptions for high net worth and business debtors and hirers in the Consumer Credit Act 1974, ss.16A, 16B, as added by the Consumer Credit Act 2006, ss.3, 4.

Licences. Two types of licence may be issued under the Act, namely a standard   **8–36** licence and a group licence.[198] In the case of a partnership, a standard licence will be issued in the firm name,[199] but will not cover any businesses carried on by the individual partners, for which each will need a separate licence. Once a licence to carry on a particular business has been obtained, all lawful activities done in the course of that business, whether by the licensee or other persons on his behalf, will be covered,[200] unless such activities have been limited by the licence itself.[201] The name specified in a standard licence will be the only name under which the business may be carried on and, when determining whether to grant such a licence, the OFT must be satisfied not only that the applicant is a fit person to engage in the activities which it will cover, but also that the name in which it is to be granted is not misleading or otherwise undesirable.[202]

Because a standard licence will be granted in the firm name, changes in the   **8–37** constitution of the firm (*e.g.* by death, retirement or otherwise) will not affect the validity of the licence, so long as the business continues to be carried on in that name. However, notice of any such change must be given to the OFT.[203] Only when the business ceases to be carried on in the firm name will the licence cease to have effect.[204] It would consequently appear that, if one partnership, A Co., which holds a licence to carry on, say, a consumer credit business under that name, amalgamates with another firm, B Co., which holds a licence to carry on, say, a consumer hire business under that name, the new firm, AB Co., may carry on the consumer credit business under the name A Co., or the consumer hire business under the name B Co., but may not carry on either business under any other name. In order to use the name AB Co., a new licence will be required.

An offence will be committed by each partner if the firm engages in any   **8–38** activity for which it does not hold a valid licence (including an activity falling outside the scope of its licence),[205] if it carries on business under a name not specified in the licence,[206] or if notice is not duly given of any change in the

---

[198] *ibid.* s.22(1), as amended by the Consumer Credit Act 2006, s.34(1). In the normal course of events, a standard licence will be applied for. A group licence may only be issued if it appears to the OFT that the public interest is better served by so doing than by obliging the persons concerned to apply separately for standard licences (*ibid.* s.22(5)) and may limit the activities which it covers (*ibid.* s.22(5A), as added by the Consumer Credit Act 2006, s.33(2)). A group licence will be particularly appropriate in the case of the professions: group licences have in fact been granted (*inter alios*) to the Law Society, the Institute of Chartered Accountants in England and Wales and the Association of Chartered Certified Accountants. Note also, as to the scope of a standard licence, *ibid.* s.24A(1), as added by the Consumer Credit Act 2006, s.28.

[199] *ibid.* s.22(4). *cf.* the Moneylenders Act 1927, s.2(3).

[200] Consumer Credit Act 1974, s.23(1) (as amended by the Consumer Credit Act 2006, s.33(3)). Thus the activities of employees and agents will be covered by the licence.

[201] *ibid.* s.24A(1), as added by the Consumer Credit Act 2006, s.28 (standard licence) and *ibid.* s.22(5A), as added by the Consumer Credit Act 2006, s.33(2) (group licence).

[202] *ibid.* ss.24, 25 (as amended by the Consumer Credit Act 2006, s.29). Note, as to applications by firms already holding a permission to accept deposits under Pt IV of the Financial Services and Markets Act 2000, the Consumer Credit Act 1974, s.25(1B), (1C), as added by the Financial Services and Markets Act 2000 (Consequential Amendments and Repeals) Order 2001 (SI 2001/3649), Pt 5, art. 167).

[203] Consumer Credit Act 1974, s.36(2)(c). Notice must also be given of any change in the registered particulars of the firm: *ibid.* s.36(1).

[204] *ibid.* s.36(5).

[205] *ibid.* ss.39(1), 167, Sched. 1 (as amended).

[206] *ibid.* s.39(2).

firm's constitution or in the particulars entered in the register.[207] However, the commission of any such offence will not render the partnership illegal.[208] *Quaere* whether there will be any question of illegality if the partnership was formed with the intention of carrying on unlicensed activities.[209]

8–39 *Renewal, variation, suspension and revocation of licences.* A standard licence, once granted, will remain valid indefinitely, save where it was originally granted for a limited period.[210] On the other hand, a group licence will be granted for a limited period[211] unless the OFT considers that there is good reason why it should have indefinite effect.[212] The duration of either type of licence can be varied at any time[213] and, in that event, must provide for the expiry of the licence.[214] Only licences of limited duration need to be renewed on the application of the licensee[215] or, in the case of a group licence only, of the OFT's own motion,[216] but indefinite licences will be subject to a periodic charge.[217]

Standard licences may at any time be varied upon application of the licensee.[218] Such an application may be made where the firm wishes to extend the scope of its business, *e.g.* where the licence covers a consumer credit business and it is also desired to carry on a credit brokerage business, or where it is desired to carry on the existing business under another name. In certain circumstances, the licence may be compulsorily varied at the insistence of the OFT.[219] Equivalent provisions apply in the case of group licences.[220]

8–40 If the OFT at any time forms the view that a current licence should be revoked or suspended, on the basis that, if the licence had expired at that time, it would have been minded not to renew it, it must give notice to the licensee (or in the case of a group licence give general notice)[221] that it is "minded to revoke the licence, or suspend it until a specified date or indefinitely", stating its reasons

---

[207] *ibid.* s.39(3).

[208] This would seem to be the effect of *ibid.* s.170(1).

[209] It is doubtful whether *ibid.* s.170(1) goes so far as to negate this argument: see *Dungate v. Lee* [1969] 1 Ch. 545, *supra*, para. 8–34, n. 190; *S.C.F. Finance Co. Ltd. v. Masri (No. 2)* [1987] Q.B. 1002.

[210] *ibid.* s.22(1A)–(1C), as added by the Consumer Credit Act 2006, s.34(2). A limited licence period may be imposed either at the applicant firm's request or if the OFT thinks there is good reason to do so (*ibid.* s.22(1C)), but may not exceed 5 years (*ibid.* s.22(1B) and the Consumer Credit (Information Requirements and Duration of Licences and Charges) Regulations 2007 (SI 2007/1167), reg. 42).

[211] Again, the period may not exceed 5 years: see the preceding footnote.

[212] *ibid.* s.22(1A), (1D), as added by the Consumer Credit Act 2006, s.34(2).

[213] See, as to variation at the request of the licensee, *ibid.* s.30(1)(e) and, as to variation by the OFT, *ibid.* s.31(1B) (as added by the Consumer Credit Act 2006, s.34(5)).

[214] *ibid.* s.22(1E), as added by the Consumer Credit Act 2006, s.34(2).

[215] *ibid.* s.29(1), as amended by the Consumer Credit Act 2006, s.34(3)(a). Note the power of the OFT under *ibid.* s.34A (as added by *ibid.* 32(1)), where renewal of a standard licence is refused.

[216] *ibid.* s.29(2).

[217] *ibid.* s.28A (as added by the Consumer Credit Act 2006, s.35) and the Consumer Credit (Information Requirements and Duration of Licences and Charges) Regulations 2007, reg. 43(2).

[218] Consumer Credit Act 1974, s.30(1)–(1B), as substituted by the Consumer Credit Act 2006, s.31(1).

[219] *ibid.* s.31, as amended by the Consumer Credit Act 2006, ss.31(2)–(4), 32(4). Note also the power of the OFT under *ibid.* s.34A (as added by *ibid.* 32(1)), where a standard licence is varied under *ibid.* s.31.

[220] *ibid.* ss.30(2)–(5) (variation on application), 31 as amended (compulsory variation).

[221] The OFT must also notify the original applicant: *ibid.* s.32(4).

therefore and inviting the licensee to make representations.[222] The OFT may thereafter proceed to revoke or suspend the licence.[223] If the licence is suspended, the firm can apply to the OFT for the suspension to be ended[224] or, if the period of suspension has not been specified, it may be ended by the OFT of its own motion.[225] During a period of suspension, the firm will be treated as if no licence had ever been granted.[226] As an alternative to the above options, the OFT now also has power, in an appropriate case, to impose requirements on an existing licence.[227]

In the case of a licence held by an individual, it will be terminated by his death, **8-41** bankruptcy or mental incapacity,[228] non-payment of the periodic charge[229] and on notice to the OFT.[230] As regards licences granted to, *inter alia*, partnerships, in addition to termination for non-payment of charges or by notice,[231] other terminating events may be specified by regulations made under the Act.[232] By the Consumer Credit (Termination of Licences) Regulations 1976[233] it is provided that, on the occurrence of any of the terminating events set out in the Schedule thereto,[234] the determination of the licence will in most cases[235] be deferred for a period of twelve months.[236] During the period of deferment, certain persons will be authorised to carry on the business.[237]

A standard licence will also cease to have effect whenever a change in a partnership has the result that the business ceases to be carried on under the name specified in the licence.[238]

---

[222] *ibid.* s.32(1)–(3), as respectively amended, in the case of subss.(1) and (2), by the Consumer Credit Act 2006, ss.34(6), 32(5).

[223] *ibid.* s.32(1) as amended. The revocation or suspension may not take effect before the expiry of the appeal period: *ibid.* s.32(7). Note also the limitation on the OFT's powers under *ibid.* s.32(9), as added by the Consumer Credit Act 2006, s.31(5). The OFT has power to authorise the licensee to carry on certain activities notwithstanding the suspension/revocation of the licence if they are required in order to transfer or wind up its business: *ibid.* s.34A, as added by *ibid.* s.32(1).

[224] *ibid.* s.33.

[225] *ibid.* s.32(8).

[226] *ibid.*

[227] See *ibid.* ss.33A, 33C, as respectively added by the Consumer Credit Act 2006, ss.38, 40. And see, as to the civil penalites which can be imposed on breach of those conditions, *ibid.* ss.39A–39C, as added by *ibid.* ss.52–54.

[228] *ibid.* s.37(1), as amended by the Mental Capacity Act 2005, Sched. 6, para. 21.

[229] *ibid.* s.28C(3), as added by the Consumer Credit Act 2006, s.37(1).

[230] *ibid.* s.37(1A), (1B), as added by the Consumer Credit Act 2006, s.34(8).

[231] *ibid.*

[232] *ibid.* s.37(2).

[233] SI 1976/1002. These Regulations have been amended by the Consumer Credit (Termination of Licences) (Amendment) Regulations 1981 (SI 1981/614) and the Consumer Credit Act 1974 (Electronic Communications) Order 2004 (SI 2004/3236), reg. 3(2).

[234] The additional "terminating events" specified in the Regulations are as follows: (a) the approval by the court of a composition or scheme of arrangement under the Bankruptcy Act 1914, s.16 (see now the Insolvency Act 1986, s.260) proposed by the licensee (whether the licensee is an individual or a partnership); (b) the registration under the Deeds of Arrangement Act 1914 of a deed of arrangement executed by the licensee (whether the licensee is an individual or a partnership); (c) in the case of a partnership where all the partners are adjudged bankrupt, the date of the last such adjudication; and (d) the relinquishment of the licence by the licensee by notice in writing served on the OFT: *ibid.* reg. 2, Sched., Pt I (as amended).

[235] Where the licence is voluntarily relinquished by the licensee, the period of deferment is one month: *ibid.* reg. 3(2), as substituted by the Consumer Credit (Termination of Licences) (Amendment) Regulations 1981.

[236] *ibid.* reg. 3(1) (as substituted by *ibid.*).

[237] *ibid.* reg. 5, Sched., Pt I (as amended).

[238] Consumer Credit Act 1974, s.36(5).

Dentists

8–42   Any person, other than a registered dentist or a registered dental care professional,[239] who carries on, or holds himself out as carrying on or prepared to carry on, the practice of dentistry[240] commits an offence.[241] Moreover, any individual, other than a registered dentist or a registered dental care professional, who carries on the *business* of dentistry[242] also commits an offence, unless he was carrying on such business on July 21, 1955.[243] The business of dentistry will be treated as carried on if that individual, or a partnership of which he is a member, receives a payment for services rendered in the course of the practice of dentistry by him or a partner of his.[244] It follows that a partnership between a registered dentist and an unqualified person is, almost by definition, illegal.[245] The position will be the same if the name of a qualified partner is for any reason erased from the dentists' register.[246]

It is also an offence for an unqualified person to take or use the title of dentist, dental surgeon or dental practitioner.[247]

Estate agents

8–43   Estate agents first became subject to statutory controls in 1982, with the coming into force of the greater part of the Estate Agents Act 1979.[248] However, in the event one of the main provisions of the Act, which would have enabled the Secretary of State to prescribe minimum standards of competence for persons engaging in estate agency work,[249] was never brought into force.[250]

---

[239] See, as to the meaning of these expressions, the Dentists Act 1984, s.53(1), as amended by the Dental Qualifications (Recognition) Regulations 1996 (SI 1996/1496), reg. 6(4) and the National Health Service (Primary Care) Act 1997, Sched. 2, Pt. 1, para. 62. As to the rights of visiting practitioners from other European states, see *ibid.* Sched. 4, as subsituted by the European Qualifications (Health and Social Care Professions) Regulations 2007 (SI 2007/3101), Pt. 7, reg. 132.

[240] This expression is defined in *ibid.* s.37, as amended by the Medical Act 1983 (Amendment) Order 2002 (SI 2002/3135), Sched. 1, Pt I, para. 11, the Dentists Act 1984 (Amendment) Order 2005 (SI 2005/2011), art.34 and the Health Care and Associated Professions (Miscellaneous Amendments) Order 2008 (SI 2008/1774), Sched. 5(1), para. 1.

[241] *ibid.* s.38, as amended by the Dentists Act 1984 (Amendment) Order 2005, art.35 and the European Qualifications (Health and Social Care Professions) Regulations 2007, reg. 127.

[242] This expression is defined in *ibid.* s.40(1).

[243] *ibid.* s.41, as amended by the Civil Partnership Act 2004, Sched. 27, para. 89, the Dentists Act 1984 (Amendment) Order 2005, art. 37 and the Health Care and Associated Professions (Miscellaneous Amendments and Practitioner Psychologists) Order 2009 (SI 2009/1182), Sched. 1, para. 9.

[244] *ibid.* s.40(1). Note, however the exceptions in *ibid.* s.40(2), as amended by the Dentists Act 1984 (Amendment) Order 1998 (SI 1998/1546), art. 2, the Health and Social Care (Community Health and Standards) Act 2003, Sched. 11, para. 50, Sched. 14, Pt. 4 and the National Health Service (Consequential Provisions) Act 2006, Sched. 1, para. 81.

[245] *Hill v. Clifford* [1907] 2 Ch. 236, 247 *per* Cozens Hardy M.R., 255 *per* Sir John Gorrell Barnes P. See also *infra*, para 24–45. A partnership formed with a view to providing *free* dentistry would not *per se* be illegal, but would it satisfy the test of partnership set out in the Partnership Act 1890, s.1, *i.e.* would there be the requisite "view of profit"? See further, the *Encyclopedia of Professional Partnerships*, Pt 4.

[246] See as to the circumstances in which a dentist's name may be so erased, *ibid.* ss.23, 24, 27, 27B, as respectively amended/substituted by the Dentists Act 1984 (Amendment) Order 2005, arts 11, 12 and 18.

[247] *ibid.* s.39, as amended by the Dentists Act 1984 (Amendment) Order 2005, art. 36 and the European Qualifications (Health and Social Care Professions) Regulations 2007, Pt 7, reg. 128.

[248] Most of the Act (excluding, *inter alia*, s.22) came into force on May 3, 1982: The Estate Agents Act 1979 (Commencement No. 1) Order 1981 (SI 1981/1517).

[249] *ibid.* s.22.

[250] See the Review of Estate Agency published by the Department of Trade and Industry in June 1989, para. 8.1.

An undischarged bankrupt is absolutely prohibited from engaging in any form of estate agency work, except as an employee.[251] Moreover, the Office of Fair Trading[252] is empowered to make orders prohibiting persons from carrying on estate agency work where they have committed certain offences[253] or discrimination in the course of estate agency work, failed to comply with an undertaking given or an enforcement order made in relation to estate agency work under the Enterprise Act 2002[254] or certain of their obligations under the Act, engaged in residential estate agency when in breach of a duty to maintain membership of a redress scheme[255] or engaged in any other undesirable practices which may be prescribed by the Secretary of State.[256] In the case of most of those grounds,[257] the act of one partner will automatically be imputed to his co-partners, unless they are able to show that it was done without their connivance or consent[258]; on that basis, the OFT may take the view that all the partners are unfit to carry on estate agency work and issue orders against each of them. Any person who fails without reasonable excuse to comply with such an order commits an offence,[259] but there would appear to be no reason why such a person should not remain as a partner, provided that he does not *personally* engage in estate agency work. The OFT may in certain circumstances make a warning order before making a full order under the Act,[260] and may revoke or vary an order once made on the application of the person to whom it was addressed.[261]

Financial services

By virtue of the Financial Services and Markets Act 2000,[262] no person may carry on, or purport to carry on, a regulated activity[263] in the United Kingdom   **8–44**

[251] Estate Agents Act 1979, s.23 (as amended by the Bankruptcy (Scotland) Act 1985, Sched. 7, para. 17 and the Insolvency Act 1985, Sched. 8, para. 33). An undischarged bankrupt may not, however, avoid the section by forming a company and employing himself: s.23(3). A breach of the section constitutes an offence, for which the penalty is a fine.

[252] All functions formerly required to be performed by the Director General of Fair Trading under the 1979 Act were transferred to the OFT (Enterprise Act 2002, s.2(1)) and all references to the Director General in the 1979 Act are amended accordingly (*ibid.* Sched. 25, para. 9). These amendments are not further referred to.

[253] See further, as to the type of offences taken into account, *Antonelli v. Secretary of State for Trade and Industry* [1998] Q.B. 948 (CA).

[254] See the Enterprise Act 2002, ss.217 (enforcement orders), 218 (interim enforcement orders) and 219 (undertakings).

[255] As to which see the Estate Agents (Redress Scheme) Order 2008 (SI 2008/1712), art.2.

[256] *ibid.* s.3, as amended by the Consumers, Estate Agents and Redress Act 2007, ss.53(2), 55(1)–(3), Sched. 7, para. 1; and see the Estate Agents (Undesirable Practices) (No. 2) Order 1991 (SI 1991/1032); the Estate Agents (Specified Offences) (No. 2) Order 1991 (SI 1991/1091), as amended by the Estate Agents (Specified Offences) (No. 2) (Amendment) Order 1992 (SI 1992/2833), art. 2. An order made under the section may prohibit the recipient from doing any estate agency work at all or merely any estate agency work of a particular description (s.3(2)) and may be limited to a particular area within the United Kingdom (s.3(5)). A register of orders made under the Act is to be kept by the OFT and is to be open to inspection on payment of the prescribed fee: *ibid.* s.8.

[257] *i.e.* excluding only criminal offences and acts of discrimination.

[258] Estate Agents Act 1979, ss.3(3)(c) (as amended), 31(3).

[259] *ibid.* s.3(8). The penalty is a fine.

[260] *ibid.* s.4, as amended by the Consumers, Estate Agents and Redress Act 2007, s.56. If the person to whom the warning order has been addressed fails to comply with its terms, that failure will be conclusive evidence that he is unfit to carry on estate agency work for the purposes of *ibid.* s.3: s.4(3).

[261] *ibid.* s.6, as amended by the Consumers, Estate Agents and Redress Act 2007, Sched. 8.

[262] s.19(1). This section establishes what is called "the general prohibition": *ibid.* s.19(2).

[263] As to what activities are regulated, see *ibid.* ss.22, 417(1) and the Financial Services and Markets Act 2000 (Regulated Activities) Order 2001 (SI 2001/544) (as amended).

unless he is duly authorised so to do[264] or is exempt from the provisions of the Act *in relation to that activity*.[265] Contravention of this general prohibition constitutes an offence[266] and any agreement made by a person whilst carrying on a regulated activity in breach of the prohibition will be unenforceable against the other party.[267]

Unlike the position under the Financial Services Act 1986,[268] authorisation can only be obtained in one way, namely by applying to the Financial Services Authority[269] (FSA) for a "Part IV permission" to carry on one or more regulated activities.[270] On the other hand, in addition to those persons and bodies which enjoy exemption as of right,[271] partial exemption will be enjoyed by firms controlled by the members of certain professions.[272] Such a firm will, in general, be able to carry on certain regulated activities[273] without seeking a Part IV permission, but must ensure that it carries on such activities as an incidental part of its professional practice[274] and that it does not receive and retain any pecuniary reward or other advantage from any person other than a client.[275] However, this freedom may be circumscribed either by a general direction made by the FSA[276] or by an order made against a specific firm.[277] Moreover, the firm must comply with any rules made by the relevant designated professional body[278] regulating the conduct of exempt regulated activities.[279] A firm which falsely claims to be exempted in this way will commit an offence.[280]

8–45   *FSA authorisation and powers.* An application for a Part IV permission[281] can

---

[264] See the Financial Services And Markets Act 2000, ss.31, 33 *et seq.*, Pt IV, Scheds 3, 4, 5, para. 1(1).

[265] *ibid.* ss.38, 39; also the Financial Services and Markets Act 2000 (Exemption) Order 2001 (SI 2001/1201), as amended.

[266] Financial Services and Markets Act 2000, s.23.

[267] *ibid.* ss.26 *et seq.* See, in this context, *In the Matter of Whiteley Insurance Consultants* [2009] Bus. L.R. 418, a decision concerning a partnership which had issued insurance policies both prior to and after obtaining authorisation. Note also *CR Sugar Trading Ltd. v. China National Sugar & Alcohol Group Corp* [2003] 1 Lloyd's Rep. 279 (a decision under *ibid.* s.5).

[268] Under the 1986 Act, authorisation could be obtained direct from the Securities and Investment Board (later the FSA), by means of membership of a Recognised Self-Regulating Organisation or by means of a certificate issued by a Recognised Professional Body. For a broad outline of these three options, see the 17th ed. of this work, at paras 8–45 *et seq.*

[269] See the Financial Services and Markets Act 2000, ss.1 *et seq.* Note, however, that it is currently proposed that the FSA will lose most of its regulatory powers.

[270] See *ibid.* Pt IV.

[271] See *supra*, n. 265.

[272] *ibid.* s.327(2)(b). Control is not defined.

[273] See *ibid.* ss.327(1), (6); also the Financial Services and Markets Act 2000 (Professions) (Non-Exempt Activities) Order 2001 (SI 2001/1227), as amended by the Financial Services and Markets Act 2000 (Miscellaneous Provisions) Order 2001 (SI 2001/3650), art. 3.

[274] *ibid.* s.327(4).

[275] *ibid.* s.327(3).

[276] *ibid.* s.328, as amended by the Insurance Mediation Directive (Miscellaneous Amendments) Regulations 2003 (SI 2003/1473), reg. 9.

[277] *ibid.* s.329.

[278] As to the meaning of this expression, see *ibid.* s.326 and the Financial Services and Markets Act 2000 (Designated Professional Bodies) Order 2001 (SI 2001/1226), as amended by the Financial Services and Markets Act 2000 (Designated Professional Bodies) (Amendment) Orders 2004 (SI 2004/3352) and 2006 (SI 2006/58).

[279] *ibid.* s.332(3)–(5); also *ibid.* s.325(1)(a). See, for example, the Solicitors' Financial Services (Scope) Rules 2001 and the Solicitors' Financial Services (Conduct of Business) Rules 2001.

[280] *ibid.* s.333(1).

[281] As to the form of the application, see *ibid.* s.51.

be made by a firm[282] and will be granted in the firm name, thereby permitting the firm to carry on the relevant regulated activities in that name.[283] It will, in appropriate circumstances, relate to those regulated activities in relation to which the firm is otherwise exempt from the general prohibition.[284] However, an application for permission will only be entertained if the firm satisfies, and will continue to satisfy, the "threshold conditions"[285] in relation to the relevant regulated activities.[286] Once a firm has obtained a permission to carry on one or more regulated activities, it may not make an application for an additional permission[287]; in such a case, a variation of the existing permission must be applied for[288] and it must, naturally, be demonstrated that the relevant threshold conditions are satisfied.[289]

A permission may be granted subject to various limitations[290] and to requirements which must be satisfied by the applicant firm on an ongoing basis.[291] Any such limitations or requirements may be removed or varied by the FSA, either on application[292] or on the FSA's own initiative.[293]

A permission, once obtained, will not be affected by any subsequent change in **8–46** the firm,[294] unless this causes the threshold conditions no longer to be satisfied,[295] and will, moreover, cover a successor firm in the event of the original firm's dissolution.[296] It should, however, be noted that any proposed change[297] which will alter voting control in the firm[298] to the requisite degree[299] will require to be notified to the FSA,[300] unless it falls within the relevant exemption.[301] Whilst the

---

[282] *ibid.* s.40(1)(c). Note, however, that a partnership constituted outside the UK which is a body corporate will *not* constitute a firm for this purpose.

[283] *ibid.* s.32(1)(a). The permission must specify the permitted regulated activities: *ibid.* s.42(6).

[284] *ibid.* s.42(3); *cf. ibid.* s.42(4), (5).

[285] *ibid.* s.41(1), Sched. 6 (as amended). The conditions *inter alia* include a requirement that the firm (a) should carry on business in the UK (*ibid.* Sched. 6, para. 2(2)), (b) has adequate resources to carry on the relevant regulated activities (*ibid.* para. 4) and (c) is "fit and proper" (*ibid.* para. 5). Note, however, that a firm will never be eligible to effect or carry out contracts of insurance: *ibid.* para. 1(1).

[286] *ibid.* s.41(2).

[287] *ibid.* s.40(2).

[288] *ibid.* s.44.

[289] *ibid.* s.41(2), Sched. 6 (as amended). See further, *supra*, n. 285.

[290] *ibid.* s.42(7).

[291] *ibid.* s.43.

[292] *ibid.* s.44(1).

[293] *ibid.* ss.45, 53.

[294] *ibid.* s.32(1)(b).

[295] *ibid.* s.45(1).

[296] *ibid.* s.32(2), as amended by the Regulatory Reform (Financial Services and Markets Act 2000) Order 2007 (SI 2007/1973), art. 3(a). In the case of a dissolved firm, the successor firm must have succeeded to the whole or substantially the whole of its business, but the composition of the successor firm no longer matters: *ibid.* s.32(3), as substituted by *ibid.* art. 3(b).

[297] This may include a new or existing partner acquiring control within the meaning of *ibid.* s.181, increasing his control within the meaning of *ibid.* s.182 or reducing or ceasing to have control within the meaning of *ibid.* s.183, as respectively substituted by the Financial Services and Markets Act 2000 (Controllers) Regulations 2009 (SI 2009/534), art. 3, Sched. 1.

[298] As a UK authorised person within the meaning of *ibid.* s.191G(1), as substituted by *ibid.*

[299] See *ibid.* ss.181(2)(b), (c), 182(1)(b), (2), 183(1)(b), (2), (3)(b), as substituted by *ibid.*

[300] *ibid.* ss.178(1), 191D(1), as respectively substituted by *ibid.* Failure to notify is an offence: *ibid* s.191F(1), as substituted by *ibid.*

[301] See the Financial Services and Markets Act 2000 (Controllers) (Exemption) Order 2009 (SI 2009/774), art. 4, which increases the relevant thresholds for notification in the case of most "relevant UK authorised persons" as defined in *ibid.* art. 2. Note also that there are certain holdings which are disregarded for this purpose: see the Financial Services and Market Act 2000, s.184, as substituted by the Financial Services and Markets Act 2000 (Controllers) Regulations 2009, art. 3, Sched. 1.

FSA will then have power to approve the proposed change involving an acquisition or increase of voting control, with or without conditions,[302] or to object,[303] there is no such power where notice is given of a decrease or cessation of control. The FSA also has power to object to a partner holding voting control of the firm[304] and may, in an appropriate case, serve a notice restricting exercise of that control[305] or seek an order from the court that the partner do shed all or part of his voting power.[306]

A Part IV permission may be cancelled at the request of the firm[307] or at the instance of the FSA.[308] In the latter case, the firm must first be given a warning notice.[309] The FSA may also suspend or impose limitations on a Part IV permission in appropriate cases.[309a]

It would be possible for the FSA, if it felt that one or more partners were not fit and proper persons to be involved in carrying on a regulated activity, to issue a prohibition order against those partners[310] and thereby prevent them from performing specified functions.[311] However, it is, perhaps, doubtful whether the firm's Part IV permission would be allowed to continue in such a case.

8–47   An authorised firm which carries on a regulated activity outside the scope of its Part IV permission does not commit an offence,[312] so that questions of illegality will not arise. If an *unauthorised* firm carries on such an activity, an offence will be committed; similarly where an exempt firm carries on such an activity outside the scope of the relevant exemption.[313] However, in either of these cases, it is considered that there would again be no illegality, save where there was at the outset an intention to commit such an offence; even then, the position is far from clear.[314]

8–48   *Winding up.* A firm which holds or has at any time held a Part IV permission[315] or which is or was an appointed representative[316] or carrying on a regulated activity when neither exempt nor authorised to do so may be wound up as an

---

[302] *ibid.* ss.185(1)(a), (b)(i), 187, 191, as substituted by *ibid.* A warning notice must be served if conditions are to be imposed: *ibid.* s.189(4)(b)(i), (5), as substituted by *ibid.*

[303] *ibid.* s.185(b)(ii), (3), as substituted by *ibid.* Again a warning notice must be served in that event: *ibid.* s.189(4)(b), as substituted by *ibid.* The objection may then be referred to the Tribunal: *ibid.* s.189(8), as substituted by *ibid.*

[304] *ibid.* s.191A, as substituted by *ibid.*

[305] *ibid.* s.191B, as substituted by *ibid.*

[306] *ibid.* s.191C, as substituted by *ibid.*

[307] *ibid.* s.44(2). It does not necessarily follow that an application for cancellation with be granted by the FSA: see *ibid.* s.44(3).

[308] *ibid.* ss.45(2), (2A), (3), as added, in the case of subs.(2A), by the Financial Services and Markets Act 2000 (Markets in Financial Instruments) Regulations 2007 (SI 2007/126), Sched. 5, para. 4. Note also *ibid.* s.44(4).

[309] *ibid.* s.54(1).

[309a] *ibid.* s.206A, as added by the Financial Services Act 2010, s.9.

[310] *ibid.* s.56(1), (2).

[311] *ibid.* s.56(2), (3).

[312] *ibid.* s.20. Needless to say, in such a case, the firm will be liable to be disciplined by the FSA, pursuant to *ibid.* Pts IV, XIII, XIV, XXV.

[313] See *supra*, para. 8–44.

[314] See *Dungate v. Lee* [1969] 1 Ch. 545, *supra*, para. 8–34, n. 190; *S.C.F. Finance Co. Ltd. v. Masri (No. 2)* [1987] Q.B. 1002.

[315] See *supra*, para. 8–44.

[316] See, as to appointed representatives, *ibid.* s.39.

unregistered company on a petition presented by the FSA on the "just and equitable ground".[317]

Medical practitioners

The Medical Act 1983[318] prohibits the recovery in a court of law of any charge **8–49** for medical advice, attendances, operations, or medicines prescribed or supplied by a person who is not fully registered and licensed to practise under the Act.[319] However, whilst this provision might prevent a firm comprising one or more unregistered/unlicensed partners from recovering such charges, it would not make the firm itself illegal.[320] Indeed, the National Health Service Act 2006 expressly contemplates the creation of partnerships between qualified and unqualified persons, provided that there is at least one medical practitioner and the other partners fall within one of four categories.[321]

It is an offence for an unqualified person to take or use certain names or titles which denote or imply a medical qualification[322] or registration under the Act[323] or for a person to hold himself out as having a licence to practise[324] or to engage in conduct suggesting that he has such a licence.[325]

---

[317] *ibid.* s.367(1)–(3), (6)(a), (7); see also the Insolvent Partnerships Order 1994, art. 19(4)(b), as amended by the Financial Services and Markets Act 2000 (Consequential Amendments and Repeals) Order 2001 (SI 2001/3649), art. 467 and the Insolvent Partnerships (Amendment) (No.2) Order 2002 (SI 2002/2708), art.5. For an example of a case in which this power was exercised, see *In the Matter of Whiteley Insurance Consultants* [2009] Bus. L.R. 418. See also *infra*, paras 24–50 and 27–04.

[318] s.46(1), as amended by the Medical Act 1983 (Amendment) Order 2002 (SI 2002/3135), art.12(4) and the European Qualifications (Health and Social Care Professions) Regulations 2007 (SI 2007/3101), reg. 26. The section does not apply to fees in respect of medical services lawfully provided under the National Health Service or by a person who has an enforceable Community right to provide them: *ibid.* s.46(2A) as added by the Medical Act 1983 (Amendment) and Miscellaneous Amendments Order (SI 2006/1914), Pt 12, art.73(b) and amended by the General and Specialist Medical Practice (Education, Training and Qualifications) Order 2010 (SI 2010/234), Sched. 1, para. 14. Note also that certain medical appointments may also only be held by fully registered practitioners: *ibid.* s.47(1).

[319] As to the meaning of the expression "fully registered," see *ibid.* s.55(1) (as amended).

[320] *Turner v. Reynall* (1863) 14 C.B.(N.S.) 328, 333, 334 *per* Erle C.J. However, the decision itself, to the effect that the disability imposed by a predecessor of *ibid.* s.46(1) is cured by registration prior to the hearing of the proceedings, was subsequently disapproved: see *Leman v. Houselay* (1874) L.R. 10 Q.B. 66; *Howarth v. Brearley* (1887) 19 Q.B.D. 303; also *De la Rosa v. Prieto* (1864) 16 C.B.(N.S.) 578. And see generally, the *Encyclopedia of Professional Partnerships*, Pt 5.

[321] *ibid.* s.86(1)(b), (2). See also the National Health Service (General Medical Services Contracts) Regulations 2004 (SI 2004/291), regs. 4(2), 11(b), 13, which continue to have effect under the 2006 Act: National Health Service (Consequential Provisions) Act 2006, Sched. 2, para. 1(2). *cf.* the position under the National Health Service (Personal Medical Services Agreements) Regulations 2004 (SI 2004/627), as amended (which also continue to have effect under the 2006 Act: *ibid.*), where no provision is made for such agreements to be concluded with a partnership.

[322] *i.e.* physician, doctor of medicine, licentiate in medicine and surgery, bachelor of medicine, surgeon, general practitioner or apothecary.

[323] Medical Act 1983, s.49(1) (as amended).

[324] See, as to the grant and withdrawal of such licences, *ibid.* ss.29A, 29B, as added by the Medical Act 1983 (Amendment) Order 2002, art. 10 and as respectively amended by the Medical Act 1983 (Amendment) and Miscellaneous Amendments Order 2006, arts. 3(2), 7 and, as from a date to be appointed, the Medical Profession (Miscellaneous Amendments) Order 2008 (SI 2008/3131), Sched. 1, Pt. 2, paras 8, 9 and the General and Specialist Medical Practice (Education, Training and Qualifications) Order 2010 (SI 2010/234), Sched. 1, paras 1, 2; also the General Medical Council (Licence to Practise) Regulations 2009 (SI 2009/2739).

[325] *ibid.* s.49A(1), as added by the Medical Act 1983 (Amendment) Order 2002, art. 12(7).

8–50   Although, in the case of practices carried on within the National Health Service, there is an absolute prohibition on actual or deemed sales of goodwill,[326] there is nothing in the relevant legislation which would *per se* render a partnership illegal. The former power which existed for a Health Authority to decline to recognise a firm's existence[327] has not been replicated in the current regulations dealing with contracts for the provision of general medical services.[328]

Patent and trade mark agents

8–51   Although it is no longer an offence under the Copyright, Designs and Patents Act 1988 for unregistered persons to practise as patent agents,[329] a firm may not in general carry on business under any name or description which contains the words "patent agent" or "patent attorney" or otherwise in the course of its business describe itself (or permit itself to be described) as such, unless it is registered in the register of patent agents.[330] Contravention of this restriction will involve the commission of an offence.[331]

Similarly, a firm can only use a name or description which includes the words "registered trade mark agent" or "registered trade mark attorney" or in the course of its business describe itself (or permit itself to be described) as such if it is itself registered in the register of trade mark attorneys.[332]

Solicitors

8–52   Although the main statutory provision which prevented the formation of a partnership between a solicitor and an unqualified person[333] was repealed by the Courts and Legal Services Act 1990,[334] until March 31, 2009 strict professional rules continued to prohibit a solicitor from entering into partnership with anyone other than an appropriately qualified lawyer from another jurisdiction.[335] As from

---

[326] National Health Service Act 2006, s.259, Sched. 21. See in particular, *Kerr v. Morris* [1987] Ch. 90; also the *Encyclopedia of Professional Partnerships*, paras 5–023 *et seq*. A further prohibition on the sale of goodwill by various types of contractors and certain medical practitioners providing "essential services" is also to be found in the Primary Medical Services (Sale of Goodwill and Restrictions on Sub-contracting) Regulations 2004 (SI 2004/906), reg. 3(1). These regulations continue to have effect under the 2006 Act: National Health Service (Consequential Provisions) Act 2006, Sched. 2, para. 1(2).

[327] See the former National Health Service (General Medical Services) Regulations 1992 (SI 1992/635), reg. 24(4).

[328] *i.e.* the National Health Service (General Medical Services Contracts) Regulations 2004, noticed *supra*.

[329] s.274, as amended by the Legal Services Act 2007, s.185(2). *cf.* the Patents Act 1977, s.114 (repealed by the 1988 Act).

[330] Copyright, Designs and Patents Act 1988, s.276(2), as amended by the Legal Services Act 2007, s.185(4)(a). Note, however, the exceptions set out in *ibid.* ss.277, 278. As to what does *not* amount to describing oneself as a patent agent, see *Graham v. Tanner* [1913] 1 K.B. 17 and *Hans v. Graham* [1914] 3 K.B. 400 (both decisions under the former Patents and Designs Act 1907). As to the register of patent attorneys, see the Copyright, Designs and Patents Act 1988, ss.275, 275A, as substituted by the Legal Services Act 2007, s.185(3).

[331] *ibid.* s.276(6).

[332] Trade Marks Act 1994, s.84(2), as amended by the Legal Services Act 2007, Sched. 21, para. 111(2). As to the register of trade mark attorneys, see *ibid.* ss.83, 83A, as substituted by the Legal Services Act 2007 s.184(3). Again, contravention of this restriction will involve the commission of an offence: *ibid.* s.84(4).

[333] *i.e.* the Solicitors Act 1974, s.39, which prohibited a solicitor from acting as agent for an unqualified person in any action or bankruptcy matter.

[334] s.66(1).

[335] See the Solicitors' Code of Conduct 2007, r. 12.01(1)(b), replacing the Solicitors' Practice Rules 1990, r.7(6) (as amended) and related regulations. It should, in this context, be noted that it still

that date, under the new regime introduced by the Legal Services Act 2007,[336] all partnerships must be or become recognised bodies[337] and can, in addition to registered European lawyers,[338] registered foreign lawyers,[339] exempt European lawyers[340] and legally qualified bodies corporate,[341] admit up to 25% of partners (for this purpose styled "managers")[342] who are unqualified but who have obtained approval from the Solicitors Regulation Authority.[343] It is, however a precondition that unqualified partners do not control more than 25% of the voting rights[344] within the firm or have an ultimate beneficial interest of more than 25%.[345]

remains an offence for any person to act as a solicitor unless he has been admitted as such, his name is on the roll and he holds a current practising certificate: see the Solicitors Act 1974, ss.1, 20 (although the latter section will as from a day to be appointed, be substituted by the Legal Services Act 2007, Sched. 16, para. 25, the new section is to the same effect). Given that each partner unquestionably acts as the agent of his co-partners (Partnership Act 1890, s.5; see in particular *Hudgell Yeates & Co. v. Watson* [1978] Q.B. 451, at pp. 461 D–G *per* Bridge L.J., 467F *per* Waller L.J., 471B *per* Megaw L.J.), it is difficult to see how a partnership between a solicitor and an unqualified person could be created *without* such an offence being committed. It is assumed that the rationale for the conclusion that there is no illegality is that agency has no relevance in this context, but the editor remains unconvinced by this. This issue is discussed in greater detail in the Encyclopedia of Professional Partnerships, Pt 8 and in an article by the current editor at (1991) 135 S.J. 696. But see also *Raynard v. Chase* (1756) 1 Burr. 2 and Lord Lindley's view set out *supra*, para. 8–30. As to what may amount to acting as a solicitor in this context, see *Piper Double Glazing Ltd. v. D.C. Contracts* [1994] 1 W.L.R. 777, 783 *per* Potter J.

[336] See the Administration of Justice Act 1985, ss.9, 9A, as respectively amended and added by the Legal Services Act 2007, Sched. 16, Pt. 2, paras 81, 82 and amended, in the case of *ibid.* s.9A, by the Legal Services Act 2007 (Functions of a Designated Regulator) Order 2008 (SI 2008/3074), art. 2.

[337] This expression denotes a partnership, company or LLP recognised under the Administration of Justice Act 1985, s.9 (as amended) and the SRA Recognised Bodies Regulations 2009: Solicitors' Code of Conduct 2007, r. 24 (as amended by the Solicitors' Code of Conduct (LDPs and Firm Based Regulation) Amendment Rules 2009). See also *ibid.* r. 14 (as amended by *ibid.*). All partnerships in existence on March 31, 2009 with an office in England and Wales automatically became recognised bodies, provided that the requirements of *ibid.* r.14.01 were satisfied on that date: see the SRA Recognised Bodies Regulations 2009, reg. 8.4. The fact that the partners will themselves constitute the recognised body is expressly recognised by *ibid.* r. 14.02(5) (as amended). It should be noted that all recognised bodies will not also be legal disciplinary practices or LDPs, which denote the presence of unqualified members: the latter expression is used in the commentary to the Code but not in the substantive rules.

[338] See, generally, as to registration of European lawyers, the European Communities (Lawyer's Practice) Regulations 2000 (SI 2000/1119), as amended by the European Communities (Lawyer's Practice) (Amendment) Regulations 2001 (SI 2001/644) and the European Communities (Lawyer's Practice) (Amendment) Regulations 2004 (SI 2004/1628).

[339] See, as to the registration of foreign lawyers, the Courts and Legal Services Act 1990, s.89, Sched. 14. And note the decision in *R v. The Master of the Rolls* [2005] 2 All E.R. 640.

[340] *i.e.* a member of a profession listed in the Establishment of Lawyers Directive 98/5/EC, art. 1.2(a) who is either registered with the Bar Standards Board or based entirely at an office outside England and Wales and who is not a practising or non-practising lawyer of England and Wales: see the definition in the Solicitors' Code of Conduct 2007, r. 24 (as amended).

[341] *i.e.* a company, an LLP or a partnership with separate legal personality: see the definitions of "body corporate" and "legally qualified body" in *ibid.*

[342] See the definition in *ibid.*

[343] *ibid.* rr. 14.01(3)(a), 14.04(1) (as amended); also the SRA Recognised Bodies Regulations 2009, reg. 3. Needless to say, lawyers may not be approved: see *ibid.* reg. 3.2.

[344] This expression is merely defined as *including* the right to vote in a partners' meeting: *ibid.* r. 24 (as amended). Whether it also includes rights to manage conferred on a managing partner or committee or a chief executive officer is open to doubt.

[345] *ibid.* r. 14.01(3)(b)–(e) (as amended). Note that voting rights can, seemingly, be conferred on a non-partner who is qualified as a lawyer of England and Wales, a lawyer of an Establishment Directive profession or a registered foreign lawyer: *ibid.* r. 14.01(3)(d)(i).

Recognition of a firm, once obtained, can be revoked by the Solicitors Regulation Authority if (inter alia) the firm ceases to be eligible or if its recognition is not renewed at the due time.[346] Where, due to unforeseen circumstances, a firm ceases to comprise at least one solicitor with a practising certificate, registered European lawyer or legally qualified body corporate[347] or to satisfy the conditions mentioned at the end of the preceding paragraph, it will have 28 days to remedy the problem and, if it does so, its recognition cannot be revoked.[348] A change in the firm will be ignored, provided that the conditions for existence of a recognised body continue to be fulfilled after the change[349] and there is not a complete change in the membership.[350] Where there is a demerger or other split, *e.g.* on a dissolution, the Solicitors' Regulation Authority will determine whether the recognised body can be regarded as continuing,[351] otherwise both new firms will have to seek fresh recognition, if necessary on an emergency basis.[352]

8–53   The emphasis on formal revocation of recognition would seem to indicate that a partnership which, once it has achieved recognised body status, contravenes the structural requirements of the Code of Conduct will, even if strictly illegal,[353] not be automatically dissolved under the Partnership Act 1890.[354] If the position were otherwise, the period of grace provided under the Code would be redundant.[355] The position will be otherwise in the case of a new firm which is purportedly set up *without* seeking recognition. In this instance, the dissolution will occur irrespective of the partners' knowledge or state of mind.[356] There are a number of examples of dissolutions being brought about in an equivalent way in the case of solicitors' partnerships, the most notable of which is *Hudgell Yeates & Co. v. Watson*,[357] where one partner had accidentally failed to renew his practising certificate and thereby rendered himself unqualified. Although in that

---

[346] SRA Recognised Bodies Regulations 2009, reg. 9.1.

[347] In this case the body corporate must have a member or director who is a solicitor with a practising certificate or a registered European lawyer: Solicitors' Code of Conduct 2007, r. 14.01(2)(iii) (as amended).

[348] *ibid.* r. 14.01(2)(a), (b), (3)(f) (as amended). Note, however, *ibid.* r. 14.01(2)(c), as to the position where the last remaining solicitor, registered European lawyer or body corporate ceases to or to be able to participate in the firm's practice.

[349] *ibid.* r. 14.04(2) (as amended).

[350] *ibid.* r. 14.04 (3) (as amended). There is no 28 day grace period in this case: *ibid.*

[351] *ibid.* reg. 14.04(7) (as amended).

[352] *ibid.* reg. 14.04(6), (8), (9) (as amended); also the Solicitors Regulated Bodies Regulations 2009, reg. 5.

[353] Note that the Code of Conduct constitutes subordinate legislation: see *Mohamed v. Alaga & Co.* [2000] 1 W.L.R. 1815 (CA), applying *Swain v. The Law Society* [1983] 1 A.C. 588, (HL); the arrangement in that case involved (*inter alia*) the purported sharing of professional fees, as to which see *infra*, para. 8–54. See also *Hughes v. Kingston upon Hull City Council* [1999] Q.B. 1193 (DC); *Wells v. Barnsley Metropolitan Borough Council, The Times*, November 12, 1999 (CA); *Awwad v. Geraghty & Co.* [2001] Q.B. 570 (CA); *Westlaw Services Ltd. v. Boddy* [2010] EWCA Civ 929 (Lawtel 30/7/10). *cf. Garbutt v. Edwards* [2006] 1 W.L.R. 2907 (CA), where a breach of the then Solicitors' Information and Client Care Code 1999 was held not to have the effect of making a retainer unlawful and unenforceable.

[354] s.34: see *infra*, paras 24–42 *et seq.*

[355] See *ibid.* r. 14.01(2)(b), (3)(f) (as amended), which provides for *deemed* compliance with the relevant requirements during the period of grace, notwithstanding the potential illegality.

[356] *Hudgell Yeates & Co. v. Watson* [1978] Q.B. 451 (CA).

[357] *ibid.* See also *Bower v. Hughes Hooker & Co*, March 27, 2003 (EAT), where a partner had been struck off the roll of solicitors (this issue was not pursued further on appeal: see *Stevens v. Bower* [2004] I.R.L.R. 957 (CA)); *Rose v. Dodd* [2005] I.C.R. 1776 (CA), where the court observed (albeit on an *obiter* basis) that there would be an automatic dissolution in the event of an intervention by the Law Society in a firm's practice; and see *Williams v. Jones* (1826) 5 B. & C. 108; *Scott v. Miller* (1859) Johns. 220. Where parties had entered into a written agreement which contemplated their

case the court was able to infer that the partnership had been reconstituted without the unqualified partner,[358] such an inference will, by definition, not be possible in the case under consideration, since the firm, however constituted, will remain unrecognised.

Solicitors may also enter into an authorised non-SRA firm, *i.e.* a partnership **8–54** authorised by another regulator, but there will be limits to the work such a firm may do.[359] Moreover, as from 2011, solicitors will be permitted to enter into partnerships which are licensed "alternative business structures",[360] in which non-authorised persons may be partners or have ownership rights.[361] Such firms will have to appoint both a Head of Legal Practice and a Head of Finance and Administration[362] and will be subject to detailed rules set by the relevant licensing authority.[363] Pending the coming into force of that legislation, the creation of such a partnership would clearly be illegal and, again, an automatic dissolution would result.

Professional rules limit the extent to which a solicitor can share his professional fees with an unqualified person under arrangements falling short of partnership.[364] Any arrangement which contravenes the above restrictions will be illegal.[365]

A solicitor's firm which carries on one of the specified types of ancillary credit **8–55** business[366] may be covered by the Law Society's group licence,[367] but otherwise will require a licence under the Consumer Credit Act 1974.[368] Moreover, if the firm is to carry on investment business, it may be able to do so without obtaining authorisation from the Financial Services Authority,[369] provided that the activities it proposes to carry on are not proscribed by the Solicitors' Financial Services (Scope) Rules 2001.[370] The firm will, however, have to ensure com-

---

immediate entry into partnership, parol evidence was not admissible to show that the agreement was only intended to take effect when they had both qualified: *Williams v. Jones, supra*. As to illegality by reason of holding out an unqualified person under the old law, see *Edmondson v. Davis* (1801) 4 Esp. 14.

[358] See [1978] Q.B. 451, at p. 462 *per* Bridge L.J.

[359] Solicitors' Code of Conduct 2007, r. 12.01(1)(d) (as amended by the Solicitors' Code of Conduct (LDPs and Firm Based Regulation) Amendment Rules 2009).

[360] See the Legal Services Act 2007, Pt. 5.

[361] *ibid.* s.89, Sched. 13.

[362] *ibid.* ss.91, 92.

[363] *ibid.* s.83.

[364] Solicitors' Code of Conduct 2007, r. 8 (as amended by the Solicitors' Code of Conduct (LDPs and Firm Based Regulation) Amendment Rules 2009).

[365] *Mohamed v. Alaga & Co.* [2000] 1 W.L.R. 1815 (CA); *Westlaw Services Ltd. v. Boddy* [2010] EWCA Civ 929 (Lawtel 30/7/10). See also *supra*, para. 8–53, n. 353.

[366] *i.e.* credit brokerage, debt-adjusting, debt-counselling, debt-collecting, debt administration, the provision of credit information services and the operation of a credit reference agency: see the definition in the Consumer Credit Act 1974, s.145(1), as amended by the Consumer Credit Act 2006, ss.24(1), 25(1). There must however be a "business" of the relevant type: see *Edgelow v. MacElwee* [1918] 1 K.B. 205; *Wills v. Wood* (1984) 128 S.J. 222; *R. v. Marshall* [1990] Crim.App.R. 73; *Conroy v. Kenny* [1999] 1 W.L.R. 1340 (CA); *Khodari v. Tamimi* [2009] EWCA Civ 1109 (Lawtel 8/10/09).

[367] It is understood that the Law Society's group licence has technically expired but remains in force whilst its renewal is negotiated with the OFT.

[368] See further, *supra*, paras 8–36 *et seq.*

[369] See *supra*, paras 8–44 *et seq.*

[370] As amended by the Solicitors' Financial Services (Scope) Amendment Rules 2009. There are certain activities which cannot, in any event, be carried on without obtaining authorisation from the FSA: see *ibid.* rr. 3, 5. All other activities *must, inter alia*, be provided in a manner which is incidental to the firm's provision of professional services: *ibid.* r. 4(b).

pliance with the applicable rules made by the Solicitors' Regulation Authority.[371]

Stockbrokers

8–56   A stockbroking firm must obtain authorisation under the Financial Services and Markets Act 2000[372] before it can lawfully carry on any activities regulated thereby,[373] and such authorisation will, in the absence of an exemption from that requirement, be a prerequisite to membership of the London Stock Exchange.[374] There is accordingly no real scope for questions of illegality to arise.[375]

Unregistered partnerships, etc.

8–57   It is no longer possible for a a firm comprising 20 or more partners to become illegal by reason of its failure to register as a company, since all restrictions on the size of partnerships were swept away in 2002.[376]

Veterinary surgeons

8–58   With a few minor exceptions,[377] veterinary surgery may only be practised by persons who are registered either as veterinary surgeons[378] or veterinary practitioners.[379] An unregistered person who practises or holds himself out as practising or prepared to practise veterinary surgery[380] or who uses any name or title

---

[371] See the Solicitors' Financial Services (Scope) Rules 2001, r. 4; the Solicitors' Financial Services (Conduct of Business) Rules 2001.

[372] Such authorisation can now only be obtained from the Financial Services Authority: see *supra*, paras 8–44 *et seq.*

[373] See the Financial Services and Markets Act 2000, ss.22, 417(1) and the Financial Services and Markets Act 2000 (Regulated Activities) Order 2001 (SI 2001/544), as amended.

[374] Rules of the London Stock Exchange, r. 1010. This Exchange has obtained recognition as an investment exchange pursuant to the Financial Services and Markets Act 2000, s.286 and so is itself exempt from the provisions of the Act by virtue of *ibid.* s.285(2).

[375] See *supra*, para. 8–47.

[376] See the Regulatory Reform (Reform of 20 Member Limit in Partnerships etc.) Order 2002 (SI 2002/3203), reg. 2.

[377] Veterinary Surgeons Act 1966, s.19(4), Sched. 3 (as amended); the Veterinary Surgery (Exemptions) Order 1962 (SI 1962/2557), as amended; the Veterinary Surgery (Exemptions) Order 1973 (SI 1973/308); the Veterinary Surgery (Blood Sampling Order) 1983 (SI 1983/6), as amended; the Veterinary Surgery (Artificial Insemination of Mares) Order 2004 (SI 2004/1504); the Veterinary Surgery (Vaccination against Foot-And-Mouth Disease) Order 2004 (SI 2004/2780); the Veterinary Surgery (Testing for Tuberculosis in Bovines) Order 2005 (SI 2005/2015); the Veterinary Surgery (Wing and Web Tagging) Order 2009 (SI 2009/1217); the Veterinary Surgery (Vaccination of Badgers Against Tuberculosis) Order 2010 (SI 2010/580); the Veterinary Surgery (Rectal Ultrasound Scanning of Bovines) Order 2010 (SI 2010/2056); the Veterinary Surgery (Epidural Anaesthesia of Bovines) Order 2010 (SI 2010/2058); and the Veterinary Surgery (Artificial Insemination) Order 2010 (SI 2010/2059).

[378] *i.e.* a person who is duly registered in the register of veterinary surgeons maintained pursuant to the Veterinary Surgeons Act 1966, s.2 (as amended). As to the registration of eligible European veterinary surgeons, see the Veterinary Surgeons Act 1966, ss.5A (as originally added by the Veterinary Surgeons Qualifications (EEC Recognition) Order 1980 (SI 1980/1951), art.3(2), but most recently substituted in its entirety by the Veterinary Surgeons' Qualifications (European Recognition) Regulations 2008 (SI 2008/1824), Sched., para. 6), 5B (as added by the Veterinary Surgeons' Qualifications (European Recognition) Regulations 2008, Sched., para. 7). Note also that a visiting European veterinary surgeon may qualify for registration in the visiting European list in connection with veterinary services provided on a temporary and occasional basis: *ibid.* s.7A, Sched. 1B (as added by *ibid.* Sched., paras 11, 17).

[379] *i.e.* a person who is duly registered in the supplementary veterinary register maintained pursuant to *ibid.* s.8(1). The number of persons who are so registered is, in fact, negligible.

[380] *ibid.* s.19(1).

which implies that he is registered or that he is a practitioner of or qualified to practise veterinary surgery commits an offence.[381]

It is submitted that a partnership between qualified and unqualified persons formed solely with a view to permitting the latter to practise veterinary surgery would clearly be illegal[382]; what is more doubtful is whether an unqualified partner could in any event be regarded as practising veterinary surgery through the agency of his co-partners.[383] If he were, any partnership involving an unqualified person would be *per se* illegal.[384]

2.   CONSEQUENCES OF ILLEGALITY

Any event which makes it unlawful for the business of a firm to be carried on or for the members of the firm to carry on that business in partnership will cause an immediate dissolution, even if the partners are unaware of the illegality.[385] This is graphically illustrated by the decision in *Hudgell Yeates & Co. v. Watson*,[386] where a partner in a firm of solicitors had accidentally omitted to renew his practising certificate and thus rendered himself unqualified for a period of some seven months.[387] It follows that a partnership which is illegal *ab initio* is strictly incapable of existing, since its dissolution will occur at the very moment of its creation.

8–59

Agreements for partnership

If a partnership would, once formed, be illegal, any agreement for its formation must necessarily itself be illegal.[388] On this ground it has been held that no action lies for the recovery of a premium agreed to be paid by a prospective partner on being taken into an illegal partnership.[389] Similarly, no action to

8–60

---

[381] *ibid.* s.20(1), (2), (4). It is also unlawful to apply to any business a description which implies that any person involved therein possesses veterinary qualifications which he does not in fact possess: *ibid.* s.20(3).

[382] See *Dungate v. Lee* [1969] 1 Ch. 545, *supra*, para. 8–34, n. 190; *S.C.F. Finance Co. Ltd. v. Masri (No. 2)* [1987] Q.B. 1002.

[383] Partnership Act 1890, s.5. See further, *supra*, para. 8–52, n. 335. *cf.* the view expressed by Lord Lindley, *supra*, para. 8–30.

[384] It should be noted that, in its Guide to Professional Conduct, the Royal College of Veterinary Surgeons does not recognise this risk and now accepts the propriety of partnerships between qualified and unqualified persons, provided that all clinical decisions are reserved to the former: *ibid.* Part 2, Section E. See further the *Encyclopedia of Professional Partnerships*, Pt 10.

[385] Partnership Act 1890, s.34. See further, *infra*, paras 24–42 *et seq*. But note the situation considered *supra*, para. 8–53.

[386] [1978] Q.B. 451. See also *Bower v. Hughes Hooker & Co*, March 27, 2003, EAT (this issue not being pursued on appeal: see *Stevens v. Bower* [2004] I.R.L.R. 957); *Rose v. Dodd* [2005] I.C.R. 1776 (all cases concerning solicitors).

[387] See further, *supra*, para. 8–53.

[388] For a recent statement of the principle (albeit not in a partnership context), see *Stone & Rolls Ltd. v. Moore Stephens* [2009] 1 A.C. 1391 (HL) at [26] *per* Lord Phillips (citing *Holman v. Johnson* (1775) 1 Cowp, 341, 343).

[389] *Williams v. Jones* (1826) 5 B. & C. 108. And see *Harse v. Pearl Life Assurance Co.* [1904] 1 K.B. 558; also *Duvergier v. Fellows* (1832) 1 Cl. & F. 39. As to whether the illegality of a partnership can be determined by arbitration pursuant to the terms of the agreement by which it was constituted, see *Harbour Assurance Co. (U.K.) v. Kansa General International Insurance Co. Ltd.* [1993] Q.B. 701; *Westacre Investments Inc. v. Jugoimport-SPDR Ltd.* [1999] Q.B. 740 (the point not being pursued on the appeal reported at [2000] 1 Q.B. 288); *Soleimany v. Soleimany* [1999] Q.B. 785 (CA).

enforce such an agreement will be entertained, irrespective of part performance, as illustrated by the decision in *Ewing v. Osbaldiston*.[390] In that case, the claimant and the defendant agreed to become partners in a theatre and the claimant advanced certain monies which were, together with other monies provided by the defendant, applied by the latter in acquiring the lease of the theatre. However, the defendant procured an assignment of the lease into his sole name and failed to perform his obligations under the agreement. The claimant commenced proceedings seeking a declaration that he and the defendant were partners in the theatre and in the lease thereof, an order that the agreement between them should be performed and, if necessary, dissolution of the partnership and the taking of the usual accounts. However, the agreement was illegal, by virtue of the Plays Act 1736, and the action was dismissed. On appeal it was held that, due to the illegality of the agreement, the court could not decree its specific performance. The court also held that, if the claimant sought to recover the amount of his advance, he could not do so in the same proceedings since, even assuming him to have had a lien on the property acquired (which the court did not accept), he had not claimed to enforce it therein.

There may, however, be instances where there was an intention to commit an illegal act in the background but this is, on a true analysis, too remote to taint the partnership contract itself.[391]

Actions by an illegal partnership

8-61   If a partnership is illegal, its members cannot in general maintain an action in respect of any transaction tainted with the illegality.[392] For example, if a partnership is formed in order to sell smuggled goods, it cannot recover the price of any such goods which it may have sold.[393] In an exceptional case, the court *may* be prepared to circumvent the consequences of illegality, as in *Hudgell Yeates & Co. v. Watson*,[394] where it was held the illegal firm had been dissolved and automatically reconstituted without the partner whose lack of qualifications gave rise to the illegality but there was, of course, no intent to commit an illegal act in this instance. Where, however, the members of an illegal partnership can establish title to any property *without* having to rely on their illegal contract, they are at liberty to take proceedings to recover that property.[395] By the same token, the members of an illegal partnership can seemingly prosecute a person for stealing

---

[390] (1837) 2 M. & Cr. 53.

[391] See *21st Century Logistic Solutions Ltd. v. Madysen Ltd.* [2004] 2 Lloyd's Rep. 92. This was not a partnership case.

[392] But *cf. S.C.F. Finance Co. Ltd. v. Masri (No. 2)* [1987] Q.B. 1002 and *Phoenix General Insurance Co. of Greece SA v. Halvanon Insurance Co. Ltd.* [1988] Q.B. 216. See also *Re Cavalier Insurance Co. Ltd.* [1989] 2 Lloyd's Rep. 430; *Tinsley v. Milligan* [1994] 1 A.C. 340 (HL); *Dowling v. Abacus Frozen Foods Ltd., The Times,* April 26, 2000 (OH); *Macdonald v. Myerson* [2001] E.G.C.S. 15, (CA); *Awwad v. Geraghty & Co.* [2001] Q.B. 570 (CA); *Stone & Rolls Ltd. v. Moore Stephens* [2009] 1 A.C. 1391 (HL); *K/S Lincoln v. CB Richard Ellis Hotels Ltd.* [2009] B.L.R. 591.

[393] See *Biggs v. Lawrence* (1789) 3 T.R. 454. And see also *Jennings v. Hammond* (1882) 9 Q.B.D. 225; *Shaw v. Benson* (1883) 11 Q.B.D. 563.

[394] [1978] Q.B. 451 (CA).

[395] *Bowmakers Ltd. v. Barnet Instruments Ltd.* [1945] K.B. 65; *Singh v. Ali* [1960] A.C. 167; *Belvoir Finance Co. Ltd. v. Stapleton* [1971] Q.B. 210; *Tinsley v. Milligan, supra*; *Macdonald v. Myerson, supra*; *Stone & Rolls Ltd. v. Moore Stephens, supra*. Note, however, that none of these cases concerned the rights of an illegal partnership. *cf. Chettiar v. Arunsalam Chettiar* [1962] A.C. 294.

its property[396] and, moreover, enforce a bequest in its favour, provided that it is of a beneficial nature and not impressed with any trust.[397]

Actions against an illegal partnership

The illegality of a partnership affords no ground of defence where an action is   **8–62** brought against it by a third party, unless that third party was aware of all the facts and is seeking to enforce a transaction which is itself tainted by the illegality.[398] In the latter case, his claim must necessarily be defeated by the operation of the rule *ex turpi causa non oritur actio*.[399] Thus, where partners have been fraudulently induced to join a firm, that fraud is no defence to an action brought by a creditor of the firm,[400] unless the creditor was himself party thereto.[401] Similarly, where a third party has, in good faith, contracted with a partnership which is illegal.

Actions between members of illegal partnership

So far as concerns a member of an illegal partnership, the most serious   **8–63** consequence of the illegality is undoubtedly his inability to maintain an action against his co-partners in relation to matters affecting the firm and his interest therein.

Lord Lindley summarised the position thus:

> "However ungracious and morally reprehensible it may be for a person who has been
> engaged with another in various dealings and transactions to set up their illegality as
> a defence to a claim by that other, for an account and payment of his share of the
> profits made thereby, such a defence must be allowed to prevail in a court of justice.
> Were it not so, those who—*ex hypothesi*—have been guilty of a breach of the law,
> would obtain the aid of the law in enforcing demands arising out of that very breach;
> and not only would all laws be infringed with impunity, but, what is worse, their very
> infringement would become a ground for obtaining relief from those whose business
> it is to enforce them. For these reasons, therefore, and not from any greater favour to
> one party to an illegal transaction than to his companions, if proceedings are
> instituted by one member of an illegal partnership against another in respect of the

---

[396] See *R. v. Frankland* (1883) L. & C. 276. This would still appear to be the position under the Theft Act 1968: see generally, as to thefts of partnership property, *R. v. Bonner* [1970] 1 W.L.R. 838. Formerly, a person could be prosecuted for embezzling the funds of an illegal partnership (*R. v. Tankard* [1894] 1 Q.B. 548), but the offence no longer exists.

[397] See *Bowman v. Secular Society* [1917] A.C. 406, 436–438 *per* Lord Parker. Since the firm is not a legal person, the individual partners are in fact the legatees: see *supra*, para. 3–17.

[398] *Re South Wales Atlantic Steamship Co.* (1876) 2 Ch.D. 763. See also *Newland v. Simons & Willer (Hairdressers) Ltd.* [1981] I.C.R. 521. And note *Phoenix General Insurance Co. of Greece SA v. Halvanon Insurance Co. Ltd.* [1988] Q.B. 216; *Re Cavalier Insurance Co. Ltd.* [1989] 2 Lloyd's Rep. 430 and the other cases cited supra, para. 8–61, n. 392.

[399] Lord Lindley put it thus: " . . . the illegality of the firm does not *per se* afford any answer to a demand against it, arising out of a transaction to which it is a party, and which transaction is legal in itself. Unless the person dealing with the firm is *particeps criminis*, there can be no *turpis causa* to bring him within the operation of the rule *ex turpi causa non oritur actio*; and he, not being implicated in any illegal act himself, cannot be prejudiced by the fact that the persons with whom he has been dealing are illegally associated in partnership." In support he cited the judgment of Mellish L.J. in *Re South Wales Atlantic Steamship Co.*, *supra*, and *Brett v. Beckwith* (1856) 3 Jur.(N.S.) 31.

[400] *Henderson v. The Royal British Bank* (1857) 7 E. & B. 356.

[401] See *Batty v. M'Cundie* (1828) 3 C. & P. 203.

partnership transactions, it is competent to the defendant to resist the proceedings on the ground of illegality."[402]

8-64 Illegality will be raised by the court of its own motion if it is clear on the face of the pleadings or documents, or otherwise becomes apparent during the course of the trial.[403] It does not matter that the parties do not themselves seek to rely on the illegality: if all the relevant facts have been adduced and the court is satisfied that no further evidence can cure the illegality, it will decline to interfere.[404] However, the doctrine does not extend so far as to prevent the court from exercising jurisdiction over its own officers.[405]

Examples of illegality between partners

8-65 When partnerships between marine insurers were illegal, it was held that a partner in such a firm, who had personally met all its liabilities, could not recover any contribution from his co-partners.[406] Equally, if one partner received premiums payable under a policy, his partners could not recover their shares from him,[407] even pursuant to an express covenant.[408] An arbitrator's award in favour of one partner was even held to be unenforceable by reason of the illegality.[409] Lord Lindley observed that "[*the foregoing*] cases are of undoubted authority, and are always referred to as such, although the particular ground of illegality on which they rested no longer exists".

8-66 Although it had been held in two very old cases that one partner might maintain an action for a contribution where he had met the liabilities of an illegal partnership at the express request of the other partner, the latter promising to pay his share at a later stage,[410] Lord Lindley was in no doubt that these decisions had subsequently been overruled. He cited *De Begnis v. Armistead*,[411] where the claimant and the defendant had entered into an illegal agreement to produce an opera and to divide the resulting profits. By the agreement, the claimant was

---

[402] See *Holman v. Johnson* (1775) 1 Cowp. 341; *Thomson v. Thomson* (1802) 7 Ves.Jr. 470; *Cousins v. Smith* (1807) 13 Ves.Jr. 544; *Sykes v. Beadon* (1879) 11 Ch.D. 170; *Foster v. Driscoll* [1929] 1 K.B. 470. Lord Lindley did in fact go on to observe that "there are indeed some old cases in which this defence was not allowed to prevail; but they have long been overruled". Those old cases were in fact *Dover v. Opey* (1733) 2 Eq.Ca.Abr. 7 and *Watts v. Brooks* (1798) 3 Ves.Jr. 611. It should, however, be noted that a right of contribution which arises under the Civil Liability (Contribution) Act 1978, s.1(1) (as to which see further, *infra*, para. 20–23) where there is no such right under the general law will *not* be affected by the *ex turpi causa non oritur actio* rule: see *K v. P* [1993] Ch. 140. Illegality must always be specifically pleaded: see CPR Pt 16PD, para. 8.2(2).

[403] *Re Mahmoud and Isphahani* [1921] 2 K.B. 716, 729 (*per* Scrutton L.J.); *Bank of India v. Trans Continental Commodity Merchants* [1982] 1 Lloyd's Rep. 427, 429 (*per* Bingham J.), 434 (CA); also *Birkett v. Acorn Business Machines Ltd.* [1999] 2 All E.R. (Comm) 429 (CA); *Pickering v. Deacon*, *The Times*, April 19, 2003 (CA).

[404] *Evans v. Richardson* (1817) 3 Mer. 469. *Scott v. Brown Doering & Co.* [1892] 2 Q.B. 724; *Gedge v. Royal Exchange, etc. Corp.* [1900] 2 Q.B. 214; *North-Western Salt Co. v. Electrolytic Alkali Co.* [1914] A.C. 461; *Lipton v. Powell* [1921] 2 K.B. 51; *Rawlings v. General Trading Co.* [1921] 1 K.B. 635; *Chettiar v. Arunsalam Chettiar* [1962] A.C. 294.

[405] *Re Thomas* [1894] 1 Q.B. 747.

[406] *Mitchell v. Cockburn* (1794) 2 H.Bl. 380. See also *Thwaites v. Coulthwaite* [1896] 1 Ch. 496, 501–502 *per* Chitty J.

[407] *Booth v. Hodgson* (1795) 6 T.R. 405. In this case the premiums had been received by two of the partners *qua* brokers.

[408] *Lees v. Smith* (1797) 7 T.R. 338. Such a covenant will itself be tainted by the illegality.

[409] *Aubert v. Maze* (1801) 2 Bos. & Pul. 371.

[410] See *Faikney v. Reynous* (1767) 4 Burr. 20; *Petrie v. Hannay* (1789) 3 T.R. 418.

[411] (1833) 10 Bing. 107. And see *Fisher v. Bridges* (1854) 3 E. & B. 642.

required to pay the singers and the defendant to provide a theatre and to pay the dancers. All the requisite payments were made in accordance with the agreement, but the concern proved to be loss-making. When an account was prepared in the course of winding up its affairs, a balance was found to be due to the claimant. When the claimant brought proceedings on a bill of exchange given by the defendant in respect of that balance, he successfully proved that it was made up of sums which he had paid at the defendant's request. It was nevertheless held that, by reason of the illegality, the claimant could not recover the balance in question, either on the bill of exchange or as a simple debt.[412]

In the same way, an action for an account in respect of the dealings and transactions of an illegal partnership cannot be sustained by one partner against another[413] nor will an action lie on a settled account in respect of such dealings and transactions.[414]

Fraud

If a person is induced to enter into an illegal contract by fraudulent mis-representations, which do not relate to its legality, he can make no claim under the contract; however, if he is himself unaware of the illegality, he may recover damages from the person who deceived him.[415] The position would appear to be the same where he is induced by the misrepresentations to believe that the contract is legal, when in fact it is not.[416]   **8–67**

Concealed illegality

It is perhaps self evident that the consequences of illegality cannot be avoided by concealing the true purpose for which a partnership was formed.[417] In such a case, whether or not the partnership agreement has been reduced to writing, the illegality may be proved by parol evidence.[418]   **8–68**

Where illegality is not a defence

Illegality will, in general, only constitute a defence to an action brought by one partner against another if it taints the partnership itself, since that is the contract upon which the claimant must rely in order to maintain his claim.[419] There is no general rule that, where money has been illegally obtained, the person in posses-sion must necessarily be permitted to retain it.[420]   **8–69**

---

[412] In fact, the claimant did recover £30 which he had loaned to the defendant in order to meet hotel expenses.

[413] *Knowles v. Haughton* (1805) 11 Ves.Jr. 168; *Armstrong v. Armstrong* (1834) 3 M. & K. 45; *Harvey v. Collett* (1846) 15 Sim. 332; also *Farmers' Mart Ltd. v. Milne* [1915] A.C. 106. But see *Greenberg v. Cooperstein* [1926] Ch. 657.

[414] *Re Home & Colonial Insurance Co. Ltd.* [1930] 1 Ch. 102; *Law v. Dearnley* [1950] 1 K.B. 400. And see *Joseph Evans & Co. v. Heathcote* [1918] 1 K.B. 418.

[415] *Shelley v. Paddock* [1980] Q.B. 348; *Saunders v. Edwards* [1987] 1 W.L.R. 1116.

[416] *Re Mahmoud and Ispahant* [1921] 2 K.B. 716; *Burrows v. Rhodes* [1899] 1 Q.B. 816; see also *Haseldine v. Hosken* [1933] 1 K.B. 822. As to the position where the claimant can rely on a proprietary right, see *supra*, para. 8–61.

[417] *Armstrong v. Armstrong* (1834) 3 M. & K. 45, 53; *Stewart v. Gibson* (1838) 7 Cl. & F. 707.

[418] See *Collins v. Blantern* (1767) 2 Wils. 341; *Foster v. Driscoll* [1929] 1 K.B. 470.

[419] See *Farmers' Mart Ltd. v. Milne* [1915] A.C. 106, 113 *per* Lord Dunedin; *Euro-Diam Ltd. v. Bathurst* [1990] 1 Q.B. 1; *Re Cavalier Insurance Co. Ltd.* [1989] 2 Lloyd's Rep. 430; *Tinsley v. Milligan* [1994] 1 A.C. 340 (HL); *Skilton v. Sullivan, The Times*, March 25, 1994; *cf. Whiteman v. Sadler* [1910] A.C. 514. See also *infra*, para. 20–20.

[420] See, for example, *Re Cavalier Insurance Co. Ltd., supra*; *Tinsley v. Milligan, supra*; *cf. Gordon v. Commissioner of Police* [1910] 2 K.B. 1080.

Thus, if A and B are parties to an illegal contract and, in pursuance thereof, B pays money to C for A's benefit, A can recover such money from C.[421] It follows that if two partners, A and B, enter into an illegal agreement with C and, pursuant thereto, C pays money to D for the benefit of A and B, not only can A and B recover this money from D but, if he pays it over to A or B, the recipient must account to the other for his share. This must also be the case if C, instead of paying the money to D, pays it directly to A or B. The principle was summarised by Lord Lindley in these terms:

> " . . . if an illegal act has been performed in carrying on the business of a legal partnership, and gain has accrued to the partnership from such act, and the money representing that gain has been actually paid to one of the partners for the use of himself and co-partners, he cannot set up the illegality of the act from which the gain accrued as an answer to a demand by them for their shares of what he has received."[422]

On this basis, it was held that a partner was entitled to an account of moneys which had actually come into the hands of his co-partner as a result of the employment of a ship in a manner prohibited by the navigation laws.[423]

Equally, if money is paid by A to B to be applied for an illegal purpose, A may require B to return the money if B has not already parted with it[424] and the illegal purpose has not been carried out,[425] either wholly or in part.[426]

Other former examples: bookmaking partnerships

8–70   A number of other examples of cases in which illegality is not a defence are to be found in the field of bookmaking partnerships, prior to the introduction of

---

[421] *Tenant v. Elliott* (1797) 1 Bos. & Pul. 3; *Farmer v. Russell* (1798) 1 Bos. & Pul. 296; *Bousfield v. Wilson* (1846) 16 M. & W. 185; *Nicholson v. Gooch* (1856) 5 E. & B. 999.

[422] Lord Lindley stated that this proposition followed from the decisions in *Tenant v. Elliott, supra,* and other cases of that class.

[423] *Sharp v. Taylor* (1848) 2 Ph. 801; see also *Sheppard v. Oxenford* (1855) 1 K. & J. 491. *cf. Sykes v. Beadon* (1879) 11 Ch.D. 170.

[424] See *Taylor v. Lendey* (1807) 9 East 49; *Barclay v. Pearson* [1893] 2 Ch. 154 (a decision under the Lottery Acts; also the following cases under the old Gaming Acts (which made gaming contracts void though not illegal): *Varney v. Hickman* (1847) 5 C.B. 271; *Hampden v. Walsh* (1847) 1 Q.B.D. 189; *Taylor v. Bowers* (1876) 1 Q.B.D. 291; *Diggle v. Higgs* (1877) L.R. 2 Ex. 422; *O'Sullivan v. Thomas* [1895] 1 Q.B. 698; *Burge v. Ashley & Smith Ltd.* [1900] 1 Q.B. 744; *Shoolbred v. Roberts* [1900] 2 Q.B. 497; and see *Re Futures Index* [1985] F.L.R. 147. Note also, as to the operation of resulting trusts, *Rowan v. Dann* (1991) 64 P & C.R. 202.

[425] See *Herman v. Jeuchner* (1884) 15 Q.B.D. 561; *Strachan v. Universal Stock Exchange (No. 2)* [1895] Q.B. 697; *Re Futures Index* [1985] F.L.R. 147.

[426] *Kearley v. Thomson* (1890) 24 Q.B.D. 742; *Bigos v. Bousted* [1951] 1 All E.R. 92; also *Ouston v. Zurowski* [1985] 5 W.W.R. 169. *cf. Hermann v. Charlesworth* [1905] 2 K.B. 123 and *Parkinson v. College of Ambulance* [1925] 2 K.B. 1, where the money was given to a charity. At this point, Lord Lindley also briefly discoursed on the rights of the subscribers to an illegal company in the following terms: "Although, therefore, the subscribers to an illegal company have not a right to an account of the dealings and transactions of the company and of the profits made thereby, they have a right to have their subscriptions returned [*Harvey v. Collett (1846) 15 Sim. 332*]; and even though the moneys subscribed have been laid out in the purchase of land and other things for the purpose of the company, the subscribers are entitled to have that land and those things reconverted into money, and to have it applied as far as it will go in payment of the debts and liabilities of the concern, and then in repayment of the subscriptions. In such cases no illegal contract is sought to be enforced; on the contrary the continuance of what is illegal is sought to be prevented [*Sheppard v. Oxenford (1855) 1 K. & J. 491*; *Butt v. Monteaur (1854) 1 K. & J. 98*. See also *Symes v. Hughes (1870) L.R. 9 Eq. 475*; *Taylor v. Bowers (1876) 1 Q.B.D. 291*]." See also, as to the taking of accounts in such a case, *Greenberg v. Cooperstein* [1926] Ch. 657.

the new regime in 2007.[427] Thus, under the old law, such a partnership would not have been illegal if it was to be carried on in a lawful manner, even though one of the partners might have been guilty of some illegal acts in the conduct of the business.[428] The court would not have hesitated to direct an account between partners in such a business, save perhaps in relation to any particular transactions which had been carried out in an illegal manner; moreover, the claimant would have been entitled to recover any balance of his capital which had not been applied in payment of bets[429] and, it was thought, his share of profits (if any).[430] Money lent to a firm of bookmakers to be used as capital in their business was recoverable and a charge on the firm's assets to secure the loan was enforceable: *per contra* if it could be shown that the money was, in fact, knowingly lent for betting purposes.[431]

Illegality set up by personal representatives

The liability of a deceased partner's personal representative to account to creditors and beneficiaries for the assets comprised in the estate is not affected by the illegality of any transactions in which the deceased may himself have been involved.[432] In such a case, the maxim *ex turpi causa non oritur actio* clearly cannot defeat the claims of such persons, since the illegality has no bearing thereon. Even if the personal representative was one of the deceased's partners and was himself involved in the illegal transactions, he must account for the deceased's share of the resulting profits, provided that such share has actually been placed to the deceased's credit in the partnership books and has come (or might have come) into the personal representative's hands.[433] On the other hand, if no account has been settled as between the partners in respect of such profits, the personal representative could seemingly rely on the illegality *qua* partner by way of defence to a claim for an account.[434]

8–71

---

[427] See *supra*, para. 8–34.

[428] *Dungate v. Lee* [1969] 1 Ch. 545.

[429] See *Thwaites v. Coulthwaite* [1896] 1 Ch. 496; *Keen v. Price* [1914] 2 Ch. 98. As to the illegal transactions in the former case, see [1896] 1 Ch. 501, 502 *per* Chitty J.; but see also *supra*, para. 8–69.

[430] See *Harvey v. Hart* [1894] W.N. 72. A share of profits was not sought in *Keen v. Price, supra*, but the right to recovery of such a share was ultimately left open by Sargant J.; though it was said in the latter case that the Gaming Act 1892 was overlooked in *Thwaites v. Coulthwaite, supra*, that Act was considered in *Harvey v. Hart*. See also *Bookman v. Mather* (1913) 29 L.T. 276, where the claimant recovered on an IOU given to him by the defendant for the balance due to him on an account taken on the dissolution of their betting partnership; *cf. Joseph Evans & Co. v. Heathcote* [1918] 1 K.B. 418, where it was said that an action on an account stated under a contract void as in restraint of trade would not lie.

[431] *Humphery v. Wilson* (1929) 45 T.L.R. 535.

[432] See *Joy v. Campbell* (1804) 1 Sch. & Lef. 328; *Hale v. Hale* (1841) 4 Beav. 369.

[433] See *Joy v. Campbell, supra*.

[434] See *Ottley v. Browne* (1810) 1 Ball & B. 360; *cf. Sharp v. Taylor* (1848) 2 Ph. 801.

Criminal liability

8–72   The final, and perhaps the most obvious, consequence of partners engaging in an illegal enterprise is, of course, the risk of criminal prosecution.[435] The sanctions available to the court may include an order for the forfeiture of the partners' interests in assets owned by the firm,[436] although such an order will, perhaps, only rarely be made if an innocent partner also has an interest in those assets.[437]

---

[435] See further *infra*, para. 14–01.

[436] See the Misuse of Drugs Act 1971, s.27 (as amended); Powers of Criminal Courts (Sentencing) Act 2000, s.143 (as amended); Proceeds of Crime Act 2002, Pts. 2 (confiscation), 5 (civil recovery). *Quaere*, does a partner hold an interest in property owned by the firm for the purposes of the Proceeds of Crime Act 1994, s.84(2)(a)? The current editor tentatively submits that he does not, although his share in the partnership is undoubtedly property for this purpose. *Semble*, the court to adopt the same approach in relation to partnership property as it would in the case of jointly owned property, as to which see *R. v. Modjiri, The Times*, June 1, 2010 (CA). Equally. if the partnership has been dissolved, the assets will ultimately have to be sold in order to wind up its affairs.

[437] *R. v. Troth* [1980] Crim.L.R. 249, where an order for the forfeiture of a partner's interest in a tipper lorry owned by a firm, pursuant to the then Powers of Criminal Courts Act 1973, s.43, was quashed since the order would be likely to lead to difficulties and might prove so onerous as to be not worth making.

CHAPTER 9

DURATION OF PARTNERSHIP

The normal rule: partnership at will

IN a statement of principle formulated prior to the Act but which has since   **9–01**
received judicial approval,[1] Lord Lindley summarised the position thus:

> " . . . the result of a contract of partnership is a partnership at will, unless some
> agreement to the contrary can be proved."[2]

However, there are two, seemingly overlapping, sections of the Partnership Act
1890 in which the status of a partnership at will is addressed.

First, under the somewhat misleading rubric "Retirement from partnership at   **9–02**
will", the Partnership Act 1890, section 26(1) provides that:

> "(1) Where no fixed term has been agreed upon for the duration of a partnership, any
> partner may determine the partnership at any time on giving notice of his intention
> so to do to all the other partners."[3]

In a similar vein is section 32, which states:

> "32. Subject to any agreement between the partners, a partnership is dissolved—
>
> . . .
>
>   (c)   If entered into for an undefined time, by the partner giving notice to the
>   other or others of his intention to dissolve the partnership."

Both sections thus appear to cover the same ground, albeit that only section 32   **9–03**
expressly takes account of any contrary agreement which may have been reached
between the partners. The nature and extent of the potential overlap was considered in *Moss v. Elphick*,[4] but ultimately the Court of Appeal reached no
concluded view on the point. However, Fletcher Moulton L.J. did opine that
section 26(1) "refers only to cases where the partnership agreement is silent as
to the duration of the partnership",[5] which may, perhaps, be contrasted with those
cases in which there is an agreed, but inherently uncertain, duration, to which
section 32(c) might be said to apply. It was the latter distinction which seems to

---

[1] See *Moss v. Elphick* [1910] 1 K.B. 846, 849 *per* Farwell L.J.; *Abbott v. Abbott* [1936] 3 All E.R.
823, 826 *per* Clauson J.
[2] The burden of proof will fall on the party seeking to allege such an agreement: see *Burdon v.
Barkus* (1862) 4 De G.F. & J. 42.
[3] This was also the position prior to the Act: see *Heath v. Sansom* (1831) 4 B. & Ad. 172, 175 *per*
Parke J.; *Frost v. Moulton* (1856) 21 Beav. 596; *Syers v. Syers* (1876) 1 App.Cas. 174.
[4] [1910] 1 K.B. 846, affirming the decision at [1910] 1 K.B. 465. See also *Thakrar v. Vadera*,
March 31, 1999 (unreported), a decision of Arden J.
[5] *ibid.* p. 849. Farwell L.J. appears to have been in agreement: *ibid.*

have been adopted by the Court of Session in *Maillie v. Swanney*,[6] although, again, no concluded view as to the effect of section 26(1) was expressed.[7] The court in that case appeared to place considerable significance on the words "*entered into* for an undefined time" in section 32(c), as indicative of something which forms part of the original or current partnership agreement.[8] In the current editor's view, this emphasis is unwarranted: not only does it ignore the express reference to "*any* [not 'the'] agreement between the partners" at the beginning of the section, but surely all partners can properly be said to "enter into" partnership together, whether they realise that they have taken that step or not.

Whatever may be the true extent of the overlap, both sections will inevitably take effect subject to any contrary agreement between the partners, whether express or implied.[9]

Continuation partnership

9–04   As will be seen hereafter,[10] where a partnership is continued after the expiry of a fixed term, it will, in the absence of some contrary agreement, become a partnership at will, although the partners' rights and duties under the original agreement will be unaffected, unless they are inconsistent with the incidents of a partnership at will. Although the court in *Maillie v. Swanney*[11] reportedly decided that section 32(c) of the Partnership Act 1890 cannot apply to such a continuation partnership,[12] that decision is, in the current editor's view, insupportable. A partnership at will which is incapable of being determined is a contradiction in terms.[13] On a true analysis, the court appears to have decided that, by reason of the inclusion of certain provisions in the agreement, the partnership was *not* at will; in those circumstances, its reliance on section 27 of the 1890 Act is inexplicable.[14]

Express and implied agreements negating partnership at will

9–05   In order to negate the implication of a partnership at will, there must be some express or implied agreement that is inconsistent with the right which a partner would otherwise have to determine the partnership by notice. Thus, an express term that "This agreement shall be terminated by mutual arrangement only" will

---

[6] 2000 S.L.T. 464 (OH). The court did *not* decide that *Moss v. Elphick, supra*, was good law in Scotland, but regarded its decision as consistent therewith.

[7] It should be noted that the court did appear to view with some sympathy the proposition that s.26(1) does not provide for the *general* dissolution of a partnership but only a determination as regards the "retiring" partner: *ibid.* p. 469B *per* Lord Penrose. Such an interpretation is, in the current editor's view, wholly unwarranted, whether in terms of the 1890 Act or the preceding law.

[8] The court also highlighted the difference in terminology used in ss.26(1) and 32(a) ("fixed term") and s.32(c) ("undefined time"), and concluded that there was a "deliberate selection of a different criterion for dissolution" in the latter section: see *ibid.* p. 468L.

[9] *Moss v. Elphick, supra.* See also the Partnership Act 1890, s.19, considered *supra*, paras 10–12 *et seq.*

[10] See *infra*, paras 9–10, 10–18 *et seq.*

[11] 2000 S.L.T. 464, OH. See further *supra*, para. 9–03.

[12] *ibid.* 469D–E *per* Lord Penrose.

[13] The court did not, ultimately, address the issue of whether the Partnership Act 1890, s.26(1) would apply to such a partnership and, if so, with what effect.

[14] On this basis, the views expressed by the court must be regarded as strictly *obiter.*

clearly amount to such an agreement[15] and will constitute a partnership for joint lives,[16] unless all the partners agree to dissolve the partnership at some earlier date.[17] Similarly, where the agreement specifically restricts the partners' ability to terminate the partnership after an initial fixed term.[18] Equally, where a fixed term partnership has come to an end and the partners have, in the course of negotiating a new agreement, expressly agreed to be bound by the terms of a draft "pending the adoption of a new deed", the creation of a new fixed term partnership may be implied.[19] It should also be noted that, where a new agreement remains in draft, the partners may have adopted some or all of its terms by conduct,[20] particularly if they have subsequently agreed to amend those terms,[21] or the draft may accurately record some or all of the terms which they have agreed verbally or by conduct.[22]

Cases where a contrary agreement is sought to be drawn from the conduct of the partners inevitably give rise to difficulty, and Lord Lindley was forced to observe that:

> "it is not possible to lay down any rule by means of which the intention of the partners on this head can be certainly ascertained, where no express agreement has been come to."

Partners have sought to rely on a number of external and internal factors as indicative of their intentions, with varying degrees of success. These will now be considered.

(a) External Factors

Debts

The mere fact that a firm has incurred debts and, indeed, secured them on its assets, does not imply an agreement that the firm will continue until those debts

9-06

9-07

---

[15] *Moss v. Elphick* [1910] 1 K.B. 465 and (on appeal) *ibid.* 846; *Thakrar v. Vadera*, March 31, 1999 (unreported), a decision of Arden J. And see *Abbott v. Abbott* [1936] 3 All E.R. 823, where the agreement declared that the death or retirement of any partner should not terminate the partnership and contained various other provisions relating to retirement; also *Wilson v. Kircaldie* (1895) 13 N.Z.L.R. 286, where the partnership was to continue so long as it was profitable; *cf. Arcus v. Richardson* [1933] N.Z.L.R. 348, which seems exceptional. However, it is not considered that, just because certain provisions in an agreement deal specifically with a future period (*e.g.* staged increases in certain partners' profit shares), there is sufficient evidence of an intention that the partnership will endure for that period. Note also *Wheeler v. Van Wart* (1838) 2 Jur. 252.

[16] Note that, in his Supplement on the Partnership Act 1890, Lord Lindley observed: "It is presumed, although there appears to be no decision on the point, that a partnership for the joint lives of the partners is a partnership for a fixed term, which would expire on the death of the partner who first died."

[17] Needless to say, there will be no prospect of implying a term which permits the partners to terminate the partnership on reasonable notice in such a case: see, for an analogous example, *Jani-King v. Pula Enterprises Ltd.* [2008] 1 All E.R. Comm. 451 (concerning a franchise agreement)

[18] *Maillie v. Swanney* 2000 S.L.T. 464, OH. See further, as to this decision, *supra*, paras 9–03, 9–04.

[19] *Walters v. Bingham* [1988] 1 F.T.L.R. 260. See further, as to this case, *infra*, paras 10–24, 10–25.

[20] Pursuant to the Partnership Act 1890, s.19: see *infra*, para. 10–12.

[21] See *Thakrar v. Vadera, supra*.

[22] As in *Gray v. Dickson* 2007 GWD 31–540 (Sh. Ct).

have been paid, for they can equally well be paid after the dissolution of the firm.[23]

Employees

9–08 The current editor considers that the offer of fixed term contracts to employees will not *per se* affect the existence of a partnership at will.[24]

Leases

9–09 Similarly, where partners have taken a lease of premises from which to carry on the partnership business, there can be no implication that the partnership must necessarily subsist during the term of the lease,[25] indeed such a proposition would in most cases be absurd. The argument was analysed by Lord Eldon in *Crawshay v. Maule*[26] in the following terms:

> "Without doubt, in the absence of express there may be an implied contract as to the duration of a partnership, but I must contradict all authority if I say that wherever there is a partnership, the purchase of a leasehold interest of longer or shorter duration, is a circumstance from which it is to be inferred that the partnership shall continue as long as the lease. On that argument the court, holding that a lease for seven years is proof of partnership for seven years, and a lease of fourteen of a partnership for fourteen years, must hold that if the partners purchase a fee simple, there shall be a partnership for ever. It has been repeatedly decided that interests in land purchased for the purpose of carrying on trade are no more than stock in trade."

(b) Internal Factors

Continuation after fixed term

9–10 Where a partnership, which was originally entered into for a fixed term, is continued after its expiry and there is no evidence as to the intended duration of that continuation partnership,[27] it will be treated as a partnership at will rather than as having been renewed for a further fixed term.[28] This emphasises a danger of the fixed term partnership, which is all too often overlooked.

Joint adventure

9–11 If a partnership is entered into for a single adventure or undertaking, it will usually be possible to infer an agreement that the partnership is to endure until

---

[23] See *King v. The Accumulative Assurance Co.* (1857) 3 C.B. (N.S.) 151. *Quaere* whether, if the firm agrees to pay a profit-based annuity to an outgoing partner, it can be implied that the partnership must continue for so long as the annuity is payable: see further, *infra*, para. 10–184.

[24] See, for example, *Briggs v. Oates* [1990] I.C.R. 473, where the fixed term offered to a salaried "partner" extended beyond the term of the partnership. See, in particular, *ibid.* p. 475 *per* Scott J. Equally, it would seem that this point may not have been addressed directly.

[25] See *Featherstonhaugh v. Fenwick* (1810) 17 Ves.Jr. 298; *Jefferys v. Smith* (1820) 1 Jac. & W. 301; *Alcock v. Taylor* (1830) Tam. 506; *Burdon v. Barkus* (1862) 4 De G.F. & J. 42.

[26] (1818) 1 Swan. 495, 508. See also *Syers v. Syers* (1876) 1 App.Cas. 174, 189 *per* Lord Hatherley; *Popat v. Shonchhatra* [1995] 1 W.L.R. 908, 912D (*per* David Neuberger Q.C.).

[27] *e.g.* as in *Walters v. Bingham* [1988] 1 F.T.L.R. 260. *cf. Maillie v. Swanney* 2000 S.L.T. 464, OH, noted *supra*, paras 9–03 *et seq.*

[28] Partnership Act 1890, s.27; and see also *Featherstonhaugh v. Fenwick* (1810) 17 Ves.Jr. 307; *Booth v. Parks* (1828) 1 Moll. 465; *Neilson v. Mossend Iron Co.* (1886) 11 App.Cas. 298. And note *Cuffe v. Murtagh* (1881) 7 Ir.L.R. 411; *Daw v. Herring* [1892] 1 Ch. 284. But note also the views reportedly voiced as to the inapplicability of *ibid.* s.32(c) to such a continuation partnership in *Maillie v. Swanney, supra*: see *supra*, para. 9–04.

its completion.[29] In *Reade v. Bentley*,[30] an agreement between a publisher and an author, which required the publisher to defray the expenses of a work written by the author and entitled him to receive a percentage on the gross sales, and which provided that the net profits of each edition should be divided equally between the parties, was held to create an agreement for a joint adventure between the author and the publisher lasting for as long as might be necessary to dispose of a complete edition. The publication of each new edition prolonged the adventure until the completion of that edition; thereafter, either party was free to withdraw.

Sub-partnerships and group partnerships

In *Frost v. Moulton*,[31] it was held that an agreement by one of two partners to **9–12** enter into a sub-partnership with a third party did not incorporate any of the terms of the head partnership and, in particular, did not warrant the implication of a term that the sub-partnership should have the same duration as the head partnership.

In contrast, where a number of existing partnerships agree to form a group partnership[32] which is to endure for a fixed period, the current editor submits that a term must necessarily be implied that each of those existing partnerships will not be determined during that period.[33]

Change in partners

Where a new partner is admitted to a fixed term partnership, as a matter of law **9–13** that partnership will determine and a new partnership will be created between the enlarged number of partners.[34] However, whether that new partnership is at will depends on the terms of the original agreement, *i.e.* whether it contemplates the admission of additional partners, and, more importantly, whether the new partner has expressly or impliedly agreed to be bound either by that or some other agreement.[35] Although it was held in *Cummings v. Stockdale*[36] that this proposition is not correct[37] and that, in all cases, a person who has been validly admitted as a partner must, absent a clear agreement to abandon the existing partnership terms, have been admitted on those terms, it is submitted that this decision cannot be correct, as it is based on the fundamental misconception that the enlarged partnership is the same firm and that a new partner can *only* be admitted on those terms.

[29] Partnership Act 1890, s.32(b); *Reade v. Bentley* (1858) 4 K. & J. 656; see also *McClean v. Kennard* (1874) L.R. 9 Ch.App. 336.

[30] (1858) 4 K. & J. 656. As to whether such an agreement constitutes a partnership, see *supra*, para. 5–27, n. 118.

[31] (1856) 21 Beav. 596. See generally, at to such partnerships, *supra*, paras 5–67 *et seq.*

[32] See further, as to these partnerships, *infra*, paras 11–17 *et seq.*

[33] This would, in turn, require a term to be implied into each existing partnership pursuant to the Partnership Act 1890, s.19.

[34] See *supra*, paras 3–01 *et seq.* Note that this proposition was not accepted in the unreported decision of *Cummings v. Stockdale*, November 11, 2008, a decision of H.H. Judge Raynor sitting as a judge of the Chancery Division.

[35] *e.g.* there might be some temporary agreement, pending the execution of a formal deed, as in *Walters v. Bingham* [1988] 1 F.T.L.R. 260 (albeit not a case involving the admission of a new partner). See also *Zamikoff v. Lundy* (1970) 9 D.L.R. (3d) 637; and see *infra*, para. 10–256.

[36] See *supra*, n. 34.

[37] In fact, the judgment was framed by reference to the formulation of the same proposition which appears, *infra*, at para. 10–256.

9–14   In a leading case in this area, *Firth v. Amslake*,[38] two doctors had, prior to 1958, carried on practice in partnership under the terms of a deed which provided for the partnership to continue during their joint lives. In 1958, they agreed in principle with a third doctor that all three would enter into partnership and share profits and losses equally. From May 1959, the three doctors practised together and a draft deed was drawn up but, in the event, never signed because one of the doctors objected to certain of its provisions. In October 1959, the two original partners wrote to the third partner saying that, since agreement could not be reached, the partnership ought to be dissolved as from November 30, 1959. Plowman J. held that, when the third doctor joined the firm in May 1959, the new partnership thereby created, which had superseded the old partnership, was a partnership at will, since no agreement had been reached as to its duration. As a result, that partnership could be (and in fact had been) validly determined by notice.

Firth v. Amslake is, accordingly, a very clear example of a case where the existing agreement had been abandoned. In the vast majority of cases the existing partners' intentions will be a matter of inference from the agreement and from their conduct, but instances in which the requirements of the agreement have been wholly ignored with little or no thought as to the implications are by no means unusual. In those circumstances, the outcome is by no means as predictable as the decision in *Cummings v. Stockdale* appeared to suggest.

Dissolution

9–15   Whether a partnership has been entered into for a fixed term or is merely at will, the right to rescind the agreement for fraud or misrepresentation[39] (but not to accept a repudiatory breach of the agreement)[40] will, in an appropriate case, remain. Similarly, the power of the court (or an arbitrator) to dissolve a firm pursuant to the provisions of the Partnership Act 1890[41] will override any agreement as to duration into which the partners may have reached.[42]

---

[38] (1964) 108 S.J. 198. Note also *Hensman v. Traill*, *The Times*, October 22, 1980, where the agreement expressly provided for a dissolution on the retirement of a partner.

[39] See *infra*, paras 23–49, 23–52 *et seq*.

[40] It is now clear that the doctrine of repudiation has no application to partnerships: see further *infra*, paras 24–05 *et seq*. Equally, the doctrine of frustration does *not* apply either: see *infra*, para. 24–13.

[41] *ibid*. s.35: see further, *infra*, paras 24–47 *et seq*.

[42] See *Syers v. Syers* (1876) 1 App.Cas. 174.

Part Two

FORMATION OF A PARTNERSHIP BY FORMAL AGREEMENT

CHAPTER 10

PARTNERSHIP AGREEMENTS

ALTHOUGH the formation of a partnership *may* be unintentional,[1] in the majority **10–01** of cases the relationship will be entered into by design. Yet, it is surprising that so many firms, particularly in the professions, are not governed by a written agreement, whether because the partners thought it unnecessary or "never got around to it", or because they allowed their existing agreement to lapse following the admission of a new partner.[2] In truth, a well-drawn agreement represents the most elementary form of protection for partners and should, given the fragility of the partnership at will as a business medium,[3] and the increasingly complex financial and management structures adopted in modern-day firms, now be regarded as indispensable.

In earlier editions of this work, the present chapter was entitled "Partnership Articles", reflecting the common usage of that expression in Lord Lindley's day. Although references to partnership articles are still encountered,[4] the correct generic term is now more properly partnership *agreements*, thus including all forms of documentation, whether under hand or seal.[5]

Before considering the usual clauses found in partnership agreements, it will be useful to set out a number of general principles governing the construction and application of such agreements.

1.   CONSTRUCTION AND APPLICATION OF PARTNERSHIP AGREEMENTS

A partnership agreement, like any other agreement, must be construed according **10–02** to the normal rules of construction,[6] although these have not remained static over the years. Formerly, greater reliance was, perhaps, placed on a number of so-called "canons of construction",[7] but the courts increasingly proved unwilling to develop unnecessarily rigid rules or to apply those canons in a wholly mechanical way. Thus, as long ago as 1928, it was held that there was *no* general principle that the same meaning had to be assigned to a particular expression wherever it occurred in a partnership agreement, and that resort to such a device

---

[1] See *supra*, paras 5–01 *et seq.*

[2] See, for example, *Firth v. Amslake* (1964) 108 S.J. 198, *supra*, para. 9–14.

[3] See *infra*, paras 24–18 *et seq.*

[4] In fact, the current editor has adopted this style for one of the precedents in the *Encyclopedia of Professional Partnerships*: see *ibid.* Precedent 2.

[5] Note, as to the execution of deeds, the provisions of the Law of Property (Miscellaneous Provisions) Act 1989, s.1, as amended by the Regulatory Reform (Execution of Deeds and Documents) Order 2005 (SI 2005/1906), art.8.

[6] Lord Lindley referred in this context to *Story on Partnership*, Chap. 10; *Collyer on Partnership* (2nd ed.), pp. 137 *et seq.*

[7] See, generally, Lewison, *The Interpretation of Contracts* (4th ed.), paras 7.01 *et seq.*

was only justifiable in cases of particular difficulty or ambiguity.[8] Use of the *contra proferentem* rule has been similarly restricted.[9]

The modern approach, which has, inevitably, seen a steady move away from mechanical rules in favour of a more purposive interpretation of documents,[10] has now culminated in what might be styled the "commonsense" rule of construction.[11] Although this new liberal attitude has swept away much of the baggage of the past,[12] there are still limits to the court's power to look at the parties' intentions[13] and, more importantly, to use a point of construction to circumvent the need for rectification of an agreement.[14]

In this section an attempt will be made to outline some of the main principles which should be adopted when construing a partnership agreement, although there is, in practice, an inevitable degree of overlap between them.[15]

A.   AGREEMENT CONSTRUED IN THE FACTUAL MATRIX

10–03   In construing a partnership agreement, regard must always be had to the factual matrix in which it was executed, as Lord Wilberforce explained in *Reardon Smith Line Ltd. v. Hansen-Tangen*[16]:

> " . . . what the court must do must be to place itself in thought in the same factual matrix as that in which the parties were. All of these opinions seem to me implicitly to recognise that, in the search for the relevant background, there may be facts which form part of the circumstances in which the parties contract in which one, or both, may take no particular interest, their minds being addressed to or concentrated on other facts so that if asked they would assert that they did not have these facts in the forefront of their mind, but that will not prevent those facts from forming part of an objective setting in which the contract is to be construed."

A relatively recent example of the application of this principle is to be found in *Re White*,[17] where the Court of Appeal had regard to the tax planning considerations likely to have been in view at the time the partnership agreement was drafted.

---

[8] *Watson v. Haggitt* [1928] A.C. 127, 131 *per* Warrington L.J. But, for a different approach, see *Smith v. Gale* [1974] 1 W.L.R. 9.

[9] *Macey v. Quazi, The Times*, January 13, 1987 (CA).

[10] See, for example, *Re Marr* [1990] Ch. 773, 784 *per* Nicholls L.J.; *Bank of Scotland v. Wright* [1991] B.C.L.C. 244.

[11] See *infra*, para. 10–06.

[12] See *Investors Compensation Scheme Ltd. v. West Bromwich Building Society* [1998] 1 W.L.R. 896, 912G–H *per* Lord Hoffmann.

[13] See *infra*, para. 10–04.

[14] *Tucker v. Tucker*, Unreported March 19, 1999 Ch D, noted *infra*, para. 10–07.

[15] This is particularly so as regards the first three principles considered hereafter.

[16] [1976] 1 W.L.R. 989, 997. See also *Prenn v. Simmonds* [1971] 1 W.L.R. 1381; *Bunge SA v. Kruse* [1977] 1 Lloyd's Rep. 492; *Staffordshire Area Health Authority v. South Staffordshire Waterworks Co.* [1978] 1 W.L.R. 1387; *Clarke v. Newland* [1991] 1 All E.R. 397 (CA), noted *infra*, para. 10–226, n. 1094. The importance of this principle was re-emphasised in *Investors Compensation Scheme Ltd. v. West Bromwich Building Society* [1998] 1 W.L.R. 896, 912 *per* Lord Hoffmann.

[17] [2001] Ch. 393 at [67] *per* Chadwick L.J., [75] *per* Peter Gibson L.J. The Court also took into account a course of dealing which predated the agreement: *ibid.* at [50] (*per* Chadwick L.J.). For another example, see *Prudential Assurance Co. Ltd. v. Ayres* [2008] 1 All E.R. 1266 (CA).

This principle does not, however, enable the court to enquire into the negotia-tions which preceded the agreement[18] or the subjective intentions of the parties.[19] It naturally follows that an earlier draft of the agreement will not be admitted into evidence as an aid to construction,[20] even though regard may be had to the partners' conduct under a *previous* agreement,[21] and no regard will be had to "without prejudice" exchanges prior to the agreement in question.[22] The deletion of words or clauses in the course of negotiations are unlikely to be relevant to the construction of the agreement as executed.[23]

10–04

Although it has been suggested that, subject to the above limitations, this principle will allow the admission of evidence as to *anything* which was reason-ably available to the parties,[24] it seems unlikely that this will find favour with the courts on the grounds of cost[25] or proportionality.[26]

B.   AGREEMENT CONSTRUED BY REFERENCE TO THE PARTNERS' OBJECTIVES

Lord Lindley stated this important principle in the following terms:

10–05

> "The attainment of the objects which the partners have declared they had in view is always regarded as of the first importance. All the provisions of the articles[27] are to be construed so as to advance and not to defeat those objects; and however general the language of partnership articles may be, they will be construed with reference to

[18] *Prenn v. Simmonds*, *supra*, the continued relevance of which was forcibly underlined (albeit on an *obiter* basis) by the House of Lords in *Chartbrook Ltd. v. Persimmon Homes Ltd.* [2009] 1 A.C. 1101 (HL); also *Absalom v. TCRU Ltd.* [2006] 1 All E.R. (Comm) 375 at [7] *per* Longmore L.J.; *Khan v. Khan* [2008] Bus. L.R. D73 at [38] *per* Arden L.J. A limited exception is represented by the "private dictionary" principle, but this falls within a very narrow compass: *Chartbrook Ltd. v. Persimmon Homes Ltd.*, *supra*, at [45] to [47] *per* Lord Hoffmann (holding that the decision in *Partenreederei MS Karen Oltmann v. Scarsdale Shipping Co. Ltd.* [1976] 2 Lloyd's Rep. 708 represented an "illegimitate extension" of the principle). Clearly, the principle cannot be used where the agreement itself defines the relevant term: *Harper v. Interchange Group Ltd.* [2007] EWHC 1834 (Comm) (Lawtel 3/9/07) at [89] *per* Aikens J. As to the procedure to be followed when a party seeks to rely on such evidence, note *Anglo Continental Educational Group (GB) Ltd. v. Capital Homes (Southern) Ltd.* [2009] C.P.Rep. 30 (CA) at [24].

[19] *Plumb Bros. v. Dolmac (Agriculture)* (1984) 271 E.G. 373; *Re Fleet Disposal Services Ltd.* [1995] 1 B.C.L.C. 345; *Scottish Power plc v. Britoil (Exploration) Ltd.*, *The Times*, December 2, 1997 CA; *Investors Compensation Scheme Ltd. v. West Bromwich Building Society* [1998] 1 W.L.R. 896, 913 *per* Lord Hoffmann; *Hurst-Bannister v. New Cap Reinsurance Co. Ltd.* [2000] Lloyd's Rep. I.R. 166; *Zoan v. Rouamba* [2000] 1 W.L.R. 1509 (CA); *Khan v. Khan*, *supra*; *Chartbrook Ltd. v. Persimmon Homes Ltd.*, *supra*.

[20] *National Bank of Australasia v. Falkingham* [1902] A.C. 585, 591 *per* Lord Lindley; *Mercantile Bank of Sydney v. Taylor* [1893] A.C. 317. *cf.* the exceptional circumstances in *KPMG v. Network Rail Infrastructure Ltd.* [2007] Bus. L.R. 1336 (CA).

[21] *Re White* [2001] Ch. 393, at [50] *per* Chadwick L.J.

[22] *Oceanbulk Shipping and Trading SA v. TMT Asia Ltd.* [2010] 1 W.L.R. 1803 (CA).

[23] See *Punjab National Bank v. de Boinville* [1992] 1 W.L.R. 1138 (CA); *Berkeley Community Villages Ltd. v. Pullen* [2007] E.G.L.R. 101 at [50]–[55] *per* Morgan J.; *Mopani Copper Mines plc v. Millenium Underwriting Ltd.* [2008] 1 C.L.C. 992.

[24] *Mannai Investment Co. Ltd. v. Eagle Star Life Assurance Co. Ltd.* [1997] A.C. 749, 779F–G *per* Lord Hoffmann; *Investors Compensation Scheme Ltd. v. West Bromwich Building Society* [1998] 1 W.L.R. 896, 912H–913A *per* Lord Hoffmann.

[25] See *Scottish Power plc v. Britoil (Exploration) Ltd.*, *supra*. And see also the CPR, r.1.1(2)(b).

[26] CPR, r.1.1(2)(c).

[27] *i.e.* the agreement: see *supra*, para. 10–01.

the end designed and, if necessary, receive a restrictive interpretation[28] accordingly."[29]

Thakrar v. Vadera[30] exemplifies this principle. There Arden J. had to construe an agreement which included provision that:

"The termination of the Partnership with regard to a Partner shall terminate the Partnership with regard to the remaining Partners".

She nevertheless held that the partnership was not a partnership at will.

The current editor considers that this principle also lay behind the older decision in *Mann v. D'Arcy*,[31] where Megarry J. held, on purely commercial grounds, that a managing partner had authority to enter into a subsidiary partnership venture with a third party in the course of carrying on the partnership business. Similarly, in *Hitchman v. Crouch Butler Savage Associates Services*,[32] the court refused to construe a provision requiring the signature of a particular senior partner to all expulsion notices as applicable to an expulsion notice served on him by the other partners.[33]

It must be emphasised that this principle presupposes that the partner's objectives are apparent on the face of the agreement or that they can be determined from the factual matrix. As previously explained, what the court cannot properly do is enquire into the *intentions* of the partners.[34]

C.   WORDS AND DOCUMENTS GIVEN THEIR NATURAL AND ORDINARY MEANING

10–06   In *Mannai Investment Co. Ltd. v. Eagle Star Life Assurance Co. Ltd.*[35] and, subsequently, in *Investors Compensation Scheme Ltd. v. West Bromwich Building Society*,[36] the House of Lords attempted to identify and summarise the principles to be adopted when construing contractual documents.[37] Central to these is the

---

[28] Or, where appropriate, a generous interpretation: see *Hitchman v. Crouch Butler Savage Associates* (1983) 127 S.J. 441, *infra*, para. 10–123.

[29] In this context, Lord Lindley referred to *Collyer on Partnership* (2nd ed.), p. 137 and cited the decision in *Chapple v. Cadell* (1822) Jac. 537. See also *Equitable Life Assurance Society v. Hyman* [2002] 1 A.C. 408 (HL); *Att.-Gen. of Belize v. Belize Telecom Ltd.* [2009] 1 W.L.R. 1988 (PC) at [22] (both decisions concerning implied terms).

[30] March 31, 1999, unreported.

[31] [1968] 1 W.L.R. 893. And see *infra*, para. 12–18.

[32] (1983) 127 S.J. 441. And see, for further examples, *Sykes v. Land* (1984) 271 E.G. 1265; *Clarke v. Newland* [1991] 1 All E.R. 397 (CA), noted *infra*, para. 10–226, n. 1094.

[33] cf. *Re A Solicitors' Arbitration* [1962] 1 W.L.R. 353 and *Bond v. Hale* (1969) 72 S.R. (N.S.W.) 201, noted, *infra*, para. 10–123.

[34] See *supra*, para. 10–04.

[35] [1997] A.C. 749 and, in particular, pp. 774, 775 *per* Lord Hoffmann.

[36] [1998] 1 W.L.R. 896.

[37] For a concise summary of the applicable principles, see *Absalom v. TCRU Ltd.* [2006] 1 All E.R. (Comm) 375 at [7] *per* Longmore L.J., citing the judgment of Aikens J. And see also *Prudential Assurance Co. Ltd. v. Ayres* [2008] 1 All E.R. 1266 (CA).

need for a commonsense approach when attempting to identify what the document would mean to a reasonable man.[38] As Lord Hoffmann put it in the latter decision[39]:

> "The meaning which a document (or any other utterance) would convey to a reasonable man is not the same thing as the meaning of its words. The meaning of words is a matter of dictionaries and grammars; the meaning of the document is what the parties using those words against the relevant background would reasonably have been understood to mean. The background may not merely enable the reasonable man to choose between the possible meanings of words which are ambiguous but even (as occasionally happens in ordinary life) to conclude that the parties must, for whatever reason, have used the wrong words or syntax: see *Mannai Investments Co. Ltd. v. Eagle Star Life Assurance Co. Ltd.* [1997] A.C. 749. . . . The 'rule' that words should be given their 'natural and ordinary meaning' reflects the common sense proposition that we do not easily accept that people have made linguistic mistakes, particularly in formal documents. On the other hand, if one would nevertheless conclude from the background that something must have gone wrong with the language, the law does not require judges to attribute to the parties an intention which they plainly could not have had. Lord Diplock made this point more vigorously when he said in *Antaios Compania Naviera S.A. v. Salen Rederierna A.B.* [1985] A.C. 191, 201:
>
>> 'if detailed semantic and syntactical analysis of words in a commercial contract is going to lead to a conclusion that flouts business commonsense, it must be made to yield to business commonsense.' "[40]

Application of this principle may enable a court to conclude that the parties have used the wrong words or syntax in their agreement and to correct the error as a matter of construction, thus securing the objectives which they must be taken to have sought to achieve.[41] However, this presupposes that those objectives are clear on the face of the document and do not require the court to speculate on or investigate the parties' intentions.[42] Examples of this principle in action are to be

---

[38] Equally, this approach must not be taken too far: the court will start from the assumption that the words used by the parties *do* effect a sensible commercial purpose and a party who relies on those words is not obliged to establish this, at least in the first instance: see *City Alliance Ltd. v. Oxford Forecasting Services Ltd.* [2001] 1 All E.R. (Comm.) 233 at [13] *per* Chadwick L.J.; *Nearfield Ltd. v. Lincoln Nominees Ltd.* [2007] 1 All E.R. (Comm) 441 (concerning a procurement obligation in a joint venture agreement); *Hammonds (A Firm) v. Danilunas* [2009] EWHC 216 (Ch) (Lawtel 18/2/09) at [44] *per* Warren J. (but compare the approach adopted on appeal, *sub nom. Hammonds (A Firm) v. Jones* [2009] EWCA Civ. 1400, *The Times*, January 4, 2010. *cf. Folkes Group Plc v. Alexander* [2002] 2 B.C.L.C. 254.

[39] [1998] 1 W.L.R. 896, 912, 913.

[40] These paragraphs were cited by Lightman J. in *Don King Productions Inc. v. Warren* [2000] Ch. 291, 311. See also *Zelouf v. Republic National Bank of New York* [1999] 2 All E.R. (Comm.) 215; *Egan v Static Control Components (Europe) Ltd.* [2004] 2 Lloyd's Rep. 429 (CA); *Sirius International Insurance Co (Publ) v. FAI General Insurance Ltd.* [2004] 1 W.L.R. 3251 (HL). *cf. HSBC Bank plc v. Liberty Mutual Insurance Company (UK) Ltd., The Times*, June 11, 2001.

[41] See, for example, *Folkes Group Plc v. Alexander, supra*; and see further, *supra*, para. 10–05. Note that there is no requirement, when construing a document, to produce an alternative formulation of the drafting but merely to decide what a reasonable person would understand the parties to have meant by the wording they have used: *Chartbrook Ltd. v. Persimmon Homes Ltd.* [2009] 1 A.C. 1101 (HL) at [21] *per* Lord Hoffmann. There is no limit on the court's freedom to construe a document in this way: *ibid.* at [25]. *cf. William Hare Ltd. v. Shepherd Construction Ltd.* [2010] B.L.R. 358 (CA).

[42] The court cannot hear evidence as to the parties' subjective intentions: see, *supra*, para. 10–04.

found in *Ellis v. Coleman*,[43] where Lawrence Collins J. had no hesitation in holding that an arbitration clause was equally applicable to continuing and outgoing partners, even though on its face it appeared to be limited merely to "partners", and in *Purewall v. Purewall*,[44] where it was held that the expressions "determination" and "dissolution" were used synonymously in the agreement, so that interest on sums due to an outgoing partner began to run as from the date of dissolution, not when the quantum of his entitlement was finally determined by arbitration.

10–07   What "business commonsense" cannot justify and the court cannot do is to invoke this principle with a view to ordering the effective rectification of an agreement. This important limitation appears clearly from the unreported decision of Park J. in *Tucker v. Tucker*.[45] There, a partnership agreement between a husband and wife permitted either partner to give the other a notice of termination but, surprisingly,[46] gave the party *serving* the notice the right to purchase the recipient's share. It was held that the agreement was clear and workable as drafted and, accordingly, could not be corrected as a matter of construction so as to confer the right of acquisition on the recipient of the notice, even though this might have been a more logical result. Whether the decision would have been different if the clause had, by reason of defective drafting, been rendered meaningless or wholly unworkable is, however, more questionable.[47] A similar approach was adopted by Carswell L.C.J. in *Finnegan v. McAreavey*,[48] when declining to adapt machinery designed to value the goodwill of the firm so as to render it workable.

Equally, where, as will often be the case, the agreement makes use of defined terms or expressions "unless the context otherwise requires",[49] the expectation should be that those terms/expressions will have the specified meanings *throughout* the agreement and a court may be reluctant to depart from those meanings in the absence of convincing evidence that it is appropriate so to do.[50]

D.   AGREEMENT CONSTRUED SO AS TO DEFEAT FRAUD

10–08   Lord Lindley observed that:

> "Any provision, however worded, will, if possible, be construed so as to defeat any attempt by one partner to avail himself of it for the purpose of defrauding his co-partner."

[43] [2004] EWHC 3407 (Ch) (Lawtel 10/12/04).

[44] [2009] CSIH 74.

[45] Unreported March 19, 1999 ChD. *cf. Folkes Group Plc v. Alexander, supra.* Note also *Bruce v. Kordula* 2001 S.L.T. 983 (OH).

[46] Park J. did describe the formulation of the clause as "surprising".

[47] The inference is that Park J. would have been influenced by this factor, but he did not consider it in any detail.

[48] [2002] N.I. Q.B. 24. See also *infra*, para. 10–216.

[49] Variations on this form of words will be encountered, *e.g.* "where the context so admits", etc.

[50] See *Hammonds (A Firm) v. Danilunas* [2009] EWHC 216 (Ch) (Lawtel 18/2/09) at [44] *per* Warren J., following *City Alliance Ltd. v. Oxford Forecasting Services Ltd.* [2001] 1 All E.R. (Comm.) 233 at [13] *per* Chadwick L.J. On the appeal *sub nom. Hammonds (A Firm) v. Jones* [2009] EWCA Civ 1400 (Lawtel 21/12/09), the court upheld the decision and observed that the words quoted in the text permitted a departure from the ascribed meaning only where it is "necessary", not merely where it is "sensible or reasonable": see *ibid.* at [32].

Thus, where the agreement provides for the preparation of accounts which are to be signed by the partners and thereafter to be binding on them, a false account knowingly drawn up by one partner will not bind his co-partners if they signed it believing its contents to be correct.[51] In the same way, it would seem that the exercise of a power conferred on a partner will be treated as invalid if it was intended to cover up or avoid the consequences of his own fraud.[52]

E.   AGREEMENT CONSTRUED SO AS TO AVOID UNFAIRNESS AND EXPLOITATION

Lord Lindley's formulation of this principle,[53] which is closely related to that considered in the previous paragraph, was as follows: **10–09**

> "Every power conferred by the articles[54] on any individual partner, or on any number of partners, is deemed to be conferred with a view to the benefit of the whole concern; and an abuse of such power, by an exercise of it, warranted perhaps by the words conferring it, but not by the truth and honour of the articles, will not be countenanced."

Thus, a power of expulsion or compulsory retirement may not be exercised with a view to securing a financial or other benefit at the cost of the expelled or retiring partner.[55]

F.   AGREEMENT NOT EXHAUSTIVE

It would be virtually impossible to draft an agreement which regulates every aspect of the partnership relation,[56] and this was clearly recognised by Lord Lindley when he observed that partnership agreements: **10–10**

> "are not intended to define, and are not construed as defining, all the rights and obligations of the partners *inter se*. A great deal is left to be understood."

---

[51] See *Oldaker v. Lavender* (1833) 6 Sim. 239. See also the various cases cited *infra*, paras 10–163 *et seq.* And see *infra*, para. 10–75.

[52] *Walters v. Bingham* [1988] 1 F.T.L.R. 260, 267–268 *per* Browne-Wilkinson V.-C. However, this part of his decision was clearly *obiter*.

[53] He actually headed this section "Articles to be construed so as to defeat the taking of unfair advantages".

[54] *i.e.* the agreement: see *supra*, para. 10–01.

[55] See *Blisset v. Daniel* (1853) 10 Hare 493, *infra*, para. 10–124.

[56] Ironically, an assumption that it is a possible to draft a comprehensive agreement which covers all possible eventualities underpins the Limited Liability Partnerships Act 2000: see *infra*, para, 10–288.

Thus, although the maxim *expressum facit cessare tacitum*[57] naturally applies to such agreements, it will not as a general rule exclude those rights and obligations which are implied by the Partnership Act 1890 or by the general law. In this context, Lord Lindley quoted from the judgment in *Smith v. Jeyes*,[58] where Lord Langdale reportedly said:

> "The transactions of partners with each other cannot be considered merely with reference to the express contract between them. The duties and obligations arising from the relation between the parties are regulated by the express contract between them, so far as the express contract extends and continues in force; but if the express contract, or so much of it as continues in force, does not reach to all those duties and obligations, they are implied and enforced by the law ... When it is insisted that the conduct of one partner entitles the other to a dissolution, we must consider not merely the specific terms of the express contract, but also the duties and obligations which are implied in every partnership contract."[59]

Equally, where an agreement contains a detailed and seemingly comprehensive set of provisions governing some particular aspect of the firm's affairs, it is still necessary to ensure that the partners have not, by their conduct, inadvertently confined or altogether excluded the application of those provisions.[60]

G.   TERMS IMPLIED TO GIVE THE AGREEMENT BUSINESS EFFICACY

10–11   Where necessary, the court will be prepared to imply a term to give business efficacy to the agreement into which the partners have entered.[61] In *Miles v. Clarke*,[62] Harman J. employed this principle to identify which assets had become the property of the partnership and which had remained in the separate ownership

---

[57] *i.e.* the express mention of one thing implies the exclusion of the other: see *Broom's Legal Maxims* (10th ed.), pp. 443 *et seq.*

[58] (1841) 4 Beav. 503, 505. See also, as to the inapplicability of the maxim *expressio unius est exclusio alterius*, *Nelson v. Bealby* (1862) 4 De G.F. & J. 321; *Browning v. Browning* (1862) 31 Beav. 316.

[59] And see *Blisset v. Daniel* (1853) 10 Hare 493, 533 *per* Page Wood V.-C.

[60] Partnership Act 1890, s.19: see *infra*, paras 10–10 *et seq.*

[61] For a helpful summary of the requirements which must be satisfied before a term can be implied into a contract, see *Att.-Gen. of Belize v. Belize Telecom Ltd.* [2009] 2 All E.R. (Comm) 1 at [16] to [28]. The Privy Council emphasised that the issue is, ultimately, one of construction, however it is described: *ibid.* at [21]. Needless to say, the implication of a term which will produce an uncommercial or unreasonable result is unlikely to commend itself to the court: *Temple Legal Protection Ltd. v. QBE Insurance (Europe) Ltd.* [2010] 1 All E.R. (Comm) 703 or is inconsistent with an express term (*Lancore Services Ltd. v. Barclays Bank plc* [2010] 1 All E.R. 763 (CA)). Similarly, if the implied term in question might be formulated in a number of different ways (*Port of Tilbury (London) Ltd. v. Stora Enso Transport and Distributions Ltd.* [2009] 1 Lloyd's Rep. 391 (CA) at [25]) or itself lacks precision (*Durham Tees Valley Airport Ltd. v. BMI Baby Ltd.* [2009] 2 All E.R. (Comm) 1083); *Rutherford v. Seymour Pierce Ltd.* [2010] I.R.L.R. 606.

[62] [1953] 1 W.L.R. 537, *infra*, para. 18–36; see also *Times Newspapers Ltd. v. George Weidenfeld & Nicolson Ltd.* [2002] F.S.R. 29; *Northern and Shell Plc v. John Laing Construction Ltd.*, 90 Con. L.R. 26, noted *infra*, para. 10–37; *Townends Group Ltd. v. Cobb, The Times*, December 1, 2004. *cf. Lane v. Bushby* [2000] N.S.W.S.C. 1029. And see, generally, *Chitty on Contracts* (30th ed.), Chap. 13.

of the partners. Equally, the more complex and detailed the partnership agreement, the less inclined the court may be to imply a term.[63] Needless to say, reasonableness alone does not justify the implication of a term.[64]

Partnership agreements increasing contain "entire agreement" clauses, but these may not be effective to exclude implied terms,[65] nor will they be determinative of the true bargain between the parties.[66]

H.   TERMS VARIED BY EXPRESS OR IMPLIED AGREEMENT

Prior to the Partnership Act 1890, it was well established that any term of a **10–12** partnership agreement (in Lord Lindley's words, "however express") could be abandoned with the consent of all the partners, and that such consent might be given expressly or impliedly, *i.e.* by conduct.[67]

This principle, which applies equally to written and oral agreements,[68] was given statutory force by section 19 of the Partnership Act 1890, which provides as follows:

"19. The mutual rights and duties of partners, whether ascertained by agreement or defined by this Act, may be varied by the consent of all the partners, and such consent may be either express or inferred from a course of dealing."

It goes without saying that no variation will be effective if the consent of *all* the partners is not forthcoming.

What is less clear is whether, to be valid, a variation must be supported by consideration. It is certainly not an *express* requirement under the section. In *Joyce v. Morrisey*[69] it was held that, save in the case of a variation pursuant to an express power, consideration *was* required on normal contractual principles.[70] In

---

[63] *Jani-King (GB) Ltd. v. Pula Enterprises Ltd.* [2008] 1 All E.R. (Comm) 451 (a decision concerning a franchise agreement). Note also *Aymard v. SISU Capital Ltd.* [2009] EWHC 3214 (QB) (Lawtel 21/12/09) at [33] *per* Hamblen J., where it was held that a term which would involve "substantial and difficult drafting" could not properly be implied.

[64] *Friends Provident v. Sirius* [2005] 1 All E.R. (Comm) 145 (CA) at [32] *per* Waller L.J.

[65] See *Exxonmobil Sales and Supply Corp v. Texaco Ltd.* [2004] 1 All E.R. (Comm) 435; *cf. North Sea Ventilation Ltd. v. Consafe Engineering (UK) Ltd.*, July 20, 2004 (Lawtel 4/10/04) noted *infra*, para. 10–15.

[66] See *Royal National Lifeboat Institution v. Bushaway* [2005] I.R.L.R. 675 (EAT). See also *infra*, paras 10–12 *et seq.*

[67] See, generally, *Const. v. Harris* (1824) T. & R. 496; *England v. Curling* (1844) 8 Beav. 129; *Somes v. Currie* (1855) 1 K. & J. 605; *Coventry v. Barclay* (1863) 3 De G.J. & S. 320; *Pilling v. Pilling* (1887) 3 De G.J. & S. 162. The rule appears to have been of nineteenth-century origin, since it was not applied in *Smith v. The Duke of Chandos* (1740) Barn. 412.

[68] Previous editors have described this as an exception to the parol evidence rule in the case of written agreements, but this is not correct since the rule does not apply to *subsequent* variations: see *Berry v. Berry* [1929] 2 K.B. 316; *McCauseland v. Duncan Lawrie Ltd.* [1997] 1 W.L.R. 38, 49B *per* Morritt L.J.

[69] [1999] E.M.L.R. 233, (CA).

[70] It was made clear that the court would normally be ready to find such consideration in the partners' agreement not to terminate the relationship: *ibid.* p. 244 *per* Waller L.J.

the current editor's view, the point is, in practice, academic: an ongoing partnership relation inevitably involves mutual consideration passing between the partners,[71] so that the supposed requirement for consideration, if it exists, will be satisfied as a matter of course.

Express agreement

10–13   Where the agreement confers power on a majority of partners to vary its terms[72] but does not otherwise specify how such decision is to be taken, notice of the proposed variation and of the meeting at which it is to be considered must be given to all the partners.[73] If the minority are not given an opportunity to be heard, they will, on normal principles, not be bound by the variation.[74] Although Lord Lindley appeared to suggest that the majority have power to alter the agreement in *all* cases,[75] he qualified that suggestion in his Supplement on the Partnership Act 1890.[76]

Equally, where such a power is exercised in accordance with its terms, it does not matter that some partners will suffer an incidental disadvantage, unless that was the sole purpose of the exercise (when the majority would, almost by definition, not be acting in good faith).[77]

A more difficult question is whether there is any implied limitation on the type of amendment which can be introduced pursuant to such a power. Much will, of course, depend on the terms of the power itself and the parties' reasonable contemplation at the time the agreement was entered into.[78] Whilst it may well be that the power cannot be used to alter the *nature* of the partnership and, thus, to increase the potential liability of partners,[79] it may be easier to justify a variation which brings about the premature determination of the firm. Thus, a court might look more sympathetically on an attempt to introduce a power to dissolve the firm on notice or, indeed, to commit the firm to a merger against the

---

[71] This is, in a sense, the inevitable corollary of the consideration which the court expected to find in *Joyce v. Morrisey, supra.*

[72] See the *Encyclopedia of Professional Partnerships*, Precedent 2, Art. 8.00.

[73] See *Const v. Harris* (1824) T. & R. 496.

[74] *ibid.* pp. 518, 525 *per* Lord Eldon. See further, *infra*, para. 15–08.

[75] The passage originally read: "If it is proposed to make an alteration in the articles by an agreement which shall be binding on all parties, notice of the proposed change and of the time and place at which it is to be taken into consideration, ought to be given to all the partners. For, even if the change is one which it is competent for a majority to make against the assent of the minority, all are entitled to be heard upon the subject; and unless all have an opportunity of opposing the change, those who object to it will not be bound by the others."

[76] Lord Lindley observed: "The mutual rights and duties of partners cannot be varied except by the consent of all the partners, and the passage in Lord Eldon's judgment in *Const v. Harris*, in which he says that 'that is the act of all which is the act of the majority, provided all are consulted and the majority are acting bona fide', is only true of cases in which the majority has the power of binding the minority." See also *Const v. Harris* (1824) T. & R. 496, 517 *per* Lord Eldon.

[77] See, generally, *Redwood Master Fund Ltd. v. TD Bank Europe Ltd.*, The Times, January 30, 2003 (relating to decisions taken under a syndicated loan agreement).

[78] See, generally, *Morgan v. Driscoll* (1922) 38 T.L.R. 251 (which concerned a voluntary association); *Hole v. Garnsey* [1930] A.C. 472, 496 *per* Lord Atkin (a decision relating to an industrial and provident society); *Lord Napier and Ettrick v. R.F. Kershaw Ltd.* [1999] 1 W.L.R. 756, 766 (which concerned a trust in the nature of security for Lloyd's policyholders). Note also *Capital Cranfield Trustees Ltd. v. Beck* [2009] Pens. L.R. 71, where a power to vary a pension deed "in any particular case" was held not to authorise a variation of a more general nature, applying to a class of members or, indeed, all members.

[79] The prospect of additional liability was a factor which clearly concerned the House of Lords in *Hole v. Garnsey, supra.*

wishes of a minority.[80] It must, however, be emphasised that strict adherence to the procedures established by the agreement will, in all cases, be essential; if those procedures are ignored, any decision to vary the agreement, however reasonable, will clearly be rendered invalid.

Implied agreement

For the partnership terms to be varied by an implied agreement, there must be evidence of a course of conduct adopted by all the partners which is inconsistent with the continued application of those terms.[81] Thus, in *Jackson v. Sedgwick*,[82] Lord Eldon held that the executors of a deceased partner were not entitled to enforce a provision in the agreement entitling them to the payment of an allowance in lieu of profits for the period from the last annual account to the date of death, because the partners had for some years failed to draw up annual accounts and had, moreover, engaged in a business different from that originally contemplated: in those circumstances, adherence to the strict terms of the agreement would clearly have worked an injustice.[83]   **10–14**

Equally, if the agreement provides for the entitlement of a deceased partner to be determined by reference to an account similar in form to the firm's annual accounts, any accounting practice habitually adopted by the partners in drawing up such accounts will be applied, even if this will result in a payment to the outgoing partner of more than he would otherwise have been entitled to.[84]

Again, if all the partners agree to contribute towards losses but one is never called on to do so, this may be sufficient to warrant an inference that the original agreement has been varied *vis-à-vis* that partner.[85]

It is, of course, essential to demonstrate that all partners have impliedly accepted the variation. This may be more difficult in a large firm or where there is a dormant partner.[86] It goes without saying that if none of the partners have actually turned their minds to the significance of what they are doing, a variation is unlikely to be inferred.[87] In *Hodson v. Hodson*,[88] Arnold J. expressed the view that a variation which resulted in the cessation of the partnership itself would be "difficult to conceive". This is surely correct.   **10–15**

---

[80] Note, however, the observations of the Court of Appeal in *Chahal v. Mahal* [2005] 2 B.C.L.C. 655 at [40]; to a similar effect were views expressed by Etherton J. in *Ashborder BV v. Green Gas Power Ltd.* [2005] B.C.C. 634 at [227] (albeit a decision relating to the construction and application of a company debenture). In a case of this type, the current editor would recommend that the variation incorporates a mechanism whereby dissentient partners can leave the firm rather than join the merged firm, but again much depends on the terms of the power itself.

[81] As to the difficulties which may be experienced in establishing the adoption of a term by virtue of an implied agreement, see *Summers v. Smith*, March 27, 2002 (Lawtel 2/4/02).

[82] (1818) 1 Swan. 460; also *Simmons v. Leonard* (1844) 3 Hare 581. *cf. Cruickshank v. Sutherland* (1922) 92 L.J. Ch. 136 and the other cases noted *infra*, paras 10–165 *et seq.*

[83] (1818) 1 Swan. 470.

[84] *Ex p. Barber* (1870) L.R. 5 Ch.App. 687. In this case, the partners had adopted the practice of debiting bad debts to the profit and loss account in the year in which they were discovered to be bad.

[85] *Geddes v. Wallace* (1820) 2 Bli. 270.

[86] See *Re Frank Mills Mining Co.* (1883) 23 Ch.D. 52, 56 *per* Jessell M.R.

[87] *Tann v. Herrington* [2009] P.N.L.R. 22, at [25] to [28] *per* Bernard Livesey Q.C. sitting as a deputy judge of the Chancery Division. There the issue was whether the partners had agreed on a retirement or a dissolution.

[88] [2009] EWCA 430 (Ch) (Lawtel 16/3/09) at [58]. This aspect was not adverted to on the appeal at [2010] P.N.L.R. 8 (CA).

Equally, it may also be difficult to infer an implied agreement to vary the existing terms where the agreement contains an "entire agreement" clause,[89] or where the agreement requires all variations to be in writing, although the partners may be shown to have dispensed with this requirement.

Admission of new partner

10–16   When a new partner is admitted to a firm on the terms of an existing written agreement,[90] he may in practice not be informed that those terms have subsequently been varied by an implied agreement for the simple reason that the partners themselves are unaware of that fact. Moreover, in the current editor's experience, partners frequently omit to draw an incoming partner's attention to *express* variations which may, for example, be fully documented in partnership minutes, etc. In either case, it is submitted that there can be only one result: the variation will fall and the original terms will apply, until such time that the variation can be re-established by conduct or otherwise.[91] It would be legally and commercially unacceptable to produce a result which condemns the incoming partner to partnership on terms of which he has been kept in ignorance.

Derivative partner

10–17   If, exceptionally, a partner is brought into the firm derivatively, *i.e.* by taking over the share of an existing partner *in specie*,[92] he will be bound by an amendment to the partnership agreement previously acquiesced in by that partner.[93]

I.   AGREEMENT PRESUMED TO APPLY AFTER EXPIRATION OF FIXED TERM

10–18   Consistently with the pre-existing law,[94] section 27 of the Partnership Act 1890 provides as follows:

> "**27.**—(1) Where a partnership entered into for a fixed term is continued after the term has expired, and without any express new agreement, the rights and duties of the partners remain the same as they were at the expiration of the term, so far as is consistent with the incidents of a partnership at will.

[89] See *North Sea Ventilation Ltd. v. Consafe Engineering (UK) Ltd.*, July 20, 2004 (Lawtel 4/10/04) at [27] *per* H.H. Judge Cockcroft sitting as a deputy judge of the High Court, citing *Inntrepreneur Pub Co (GL) v. East Crown Ltd.* [2000] 2 Lloyd's Rep. 611 at [7] *per* Lightman J.; but *cf.* the cases cited *supra*, para. 10–11.

[90] See further, *supra*, paras 9–12, 9–13.

[91] Note, however, that a practice adopted by the partners over an extended period may *not* have the effect of varying the agreement: see, for example, *Noble v. Noble* 1965 S.L.T. 415 (Ct of Sess.), noted *infra*, para. 10–168.

[92] *cf.* the position under the Partnership Act 1890, s.31, *infra*, paras 19–51 *et seq.*

[93] See *Const v. Harris* (1824) T. & R. 496, 521 *per* Lord Eldon. Lord Lindley's original formulation of this somewhat obscure proposition was as follows: "It seems that a person who comes into a firm through another who has acquiesced in a variation of the terms of the partnership articles, is bound by that acquiescence, and cannot revert to the original articles." Note also *Zamikoff v. Lundy* (1970) 9 D.L.R. (3d) 637 and *infra*, paras 10–256, 10–257.

[94] See *Crawshay v. Collins* (1808) 15 Ves.Jr. 218; *Featherstonhaugh v. Fenwick* (1810) 17 Ves.Jr. 298; *Booth v. Parks* (1828) 1 Moll. 465; *Neilson v. Mossend Iron Co.* (1886) 11 App.Cas. 298.

(2) A continuance of the business by the partners or such of them as habitually acted therein during the term, without any settlement or liquidation of the partnership affairs, is presumed to be a continuance of the partnership."

Effect of new agreement

The application of the section is naturally displaced by a new agreement, but **10–19** not by the existence of an unexecuted draft,[95] unless the partners have agreed to be bound by that draft pending the execution of a formal deed[96] or have otherwise acted on the footing that it governs the continuing partnership.[97]

Clauses framed by reference to fixed term partnership

The rule embodied in section 27 will, in an appropriate case, enable a **10–20** provision of the agreement framed solely by reference to the original fixed term to apply after its expiration. Thus, in *Essex v. Essex*,[98] the partners had entered into a fixed-term partnership for 14 years and agreed that, if either should die "during the said co-partnership term", the other should be entitled to acquire his share at a certain price. The fixed term expired but the partnership was continued on the old terms. One partner then died. It was held that the survivor was entitled to acquire his share as originally agreed: the court in effect regarded the reference to "the partnership term" as equivalent to "the continuation of the partnership".[99]

This principle will be of considerable importance in the case of any reference in an agreement to an event occurring "during the term" or "during the partnership".[100]

Clauses consistent with partnership at will

In order to ascertain whether a particular clause is capable of being carried **10–21** over into a partnership at will, account must naturally be taken of its precise terms,[101] so that generalisation is difficult. Nevertheless, it has already been seen that a right to acquire an outgoing partner's share can survive the expiration of the fixed term[102]; a similar attitude has been adopted towards a right to acquire

---

[95] *Neilson v. Mossend Iron Co., supra.* See also *Stekel v. Ellice* [1973] 1 W.L.R. 191.

[96] *Walters v. Bingham* [1988] 1 F.T.L.R. 260.

[97] In such a case, the draft will have effect by virtue of the Partnership Act 1890, s.19, *supra*, para. 10–10.

[98] (1855) 20 Beav. 442; see also *Cox v. Willoughby* (1880) 13 Ch.D. 863; *McLeod v. Dowling* (1927) 43 T.L.R. 655; *Hammond v. Brearley*, December 10, 1992 (CA, unreported), noted *infra*, para. 10–21.

[99] Lord Lindley observed that "The expression 'the partnership term' was held equivalent to the time during which the partners continue in partnership without coming to any fresh agreement." However, this is not borne out by the report at (1855) 20 Beav. 442.

[100] But see *Neilson v. Mossend Iron Co.* (1886) 11 App.Cas. 298.

[101] *Essex v. Essex* (1855) 20 Beav. 442, *supra*, para. 10–18; also *King v. Chuck* (1853) 17 Beav. 325; *Cox v. Willoughby* (1880) 13 Ch.D. 863; *McLeod v. Dowling* (1927) 43 T.L.R. 655; *Hammond v. Brearley*, December 10, 1992 (CA, unreported). *cf. Cookson v. Cookson* (1837) 8 Sim. 529, which has not been followed.

[102] *Daw v. Herring, supra*, explaining *Yates v. Finn* (1875) referred to at 13 Ch.D. 839, 840; *Brooks v. Brooks* (1901) 85 L.T. 453; *M'Gown v. Henderson* 1914 S.C. 839. See also *Neilson v. Mossend Iron Co.* (1886) 11 App.Cas. 298.

a partner's share "after the determination of the partnership"[103] and a provision vesting the firm's goodwill in a particular partner "upon any partner ceasing to be a partner otherwise than on death or upon the determination of the partnership on the 26th August 1986", that date being the expiration of the fixed term of the partnership.[104]

An arbitration clause drawn in wide terms has been held to apply,[105] but it is submitted that such a clause, like any other common form provision, will normally be carried over even if it is in more restricted terms.[106]

Clauses inconsistent with partnership at will

10–22   Although a number of provisions governing the position *following* a dissolution have, with one exception, been held to survive, a different attitude is adopted towards those clauses which relate to the manner in which the partnership is to be terminated. Thus, a clause declaring that the partnership should stand dissolved if one partner assigned, mortgaged or disposed of his share without the consent of the other has been held not to survive[107]; similarly in the case of a clause which in effect required each partner to decide whether to carry on the business or to retire and be paid out the value of his share within the "three months before the termination of [the] contract".[108]

The exception to which reference was made in the previous paragraph is a covenant restraining competition, which has been held not to be carried forward into a partnership at will.[109]

Although it was held in *Maillie v. Swanney*[110] that section 32(c) of the Partnership Act 1890[111] does not apply to a continuation partnership at will, the decision must, in the current editor's view, be regarded as erroneous.[112]

Expulsion: the doubtful case

10–23   It was held in *Clark v. Leach*[113] that a power to dissolve a partnership if a partner should "neglect or refuse to attend to the business of the . . . partnership" which, if exercised, would entitle the other partners to acquire his share, did not survive the expiration of the initial fixed term. On this basis, it might legitimately be expected that any power of expulsion or compulsory retirement[114] should be similarly regarded; indeed, in his Supplement on the Partnership Act 1890, Lord Lindley pointed out that:

---

[103] See *Yates v. Finn, supra* (as explained in *Daw v. Herring* [1892] 1 Ch. 284); also *Cookson v. Cookson* (1837) 8 Sim. 529 (which has not been followed); *Murphy v. Power* [1923] 1 I.R. 68.

[104] *Hammond v. Brearley*, December 10, 1992 (CA, unreported).

[105] *Gillett v. Thornton* (1875) L.R. 19 Eq. 599. See also *Morgan v. William Harrison Ltd.* [1907] 2 Ch. 137.

[106] See *Essex v. Essex* (1855) 20 Beav. 442, 450 *per* Sir John Romilly M.R.

[107] *Campbell v. Campbell* (1893) 6 R. 137, (HL).

[108] *Neilson v. Mossend Iron Co.* (1886) 11 App.Cas. 298.

[109] *Hensman v. Traill, The Times*, October 22, 1980. This part of the decision was not overruled in *Kerr v. Morris* [1987] Ch. 90, but its authority is now, perhaps, reduced.

[110] 2000 S.L.T. 464 (OH).

[111] See, as to this section, *supra*, paras 9–01 *et seq.* and *infra*, paras 24–18 *et seq.*

[112] See *supra*, para. 9–04.

[113] (1863) 1 De G.J. & S. 409. This decision was seemingly approved in an *obiter* part of the judgment of Stirling J. in *Daw v. Herring* [1892] 1 Ch. 284, 290.

[114] See further, as to such powers, *infra*, paras 10–114 *et seq.*

"It has . . . been decided that a right of expulsion cannot be exercised after the expiration of the original term[115]; and it is clear that any clause which prevents a partner from determining the partnership at his will would be inapplicable."[116]

However, in an *obiter* part of his judgment in *Walters v. Bingham*,[117] Browne-Wilkinson V.-C., after referring to Lord Westbury's decision in *Clark v. Leach*, reportedly observed: **10–24**

"Lord Westbury said that whether or not the power of expulsion continued to apply depended on the intention of the parties. He held that a 'stipulation so special and extraordinary' and one 'not ordinarily found in contracts of partnership' could not be held to survive. He also relied on the fact that, being a partnership at will, there was no longer any need for a power of expulsion and that the power was in the nature of a power to forfeit.

I do not regard that case as providing binding authority as to the law applicable in a case occurring 120 years later in wholly different circumstances, after the passing of the Partnership Act 1890. In modern professional partnerships with very numerous partners a power of expulsion, far from being 'special and extraordinary,' is commonplace and normal.[118] Indeed, such a power is essential if a total dissolution as between all the partners is to be avoided when it is necessary to get rid of one unsatisfactory partner. Where there is a large number of continuing partners, the power of expulsion is not inconsistent with a partnership at will. Expulsion and dissolution by notice are two different concepts producing different results. In *Clark v. Leach* there were only two partners: therefore whether there were expulsion or dissolution, the whole partnership was at an end. But in large modern partnerships there is a fundamental difference between expulsion (leaving the partnership continuing between the remainder) and dissolution (which puts an end to the whole partnership as between all partners). In large, modern professional partnerships there is no inconsistency between a power of expulsion and a partnership at will."

The following points should be noted in relation to the Vice-Chancellor's   **10–25**
decision:

1. The Partnership Act 1890 expressly preserved the pre-existing law, save in so far as it was inconsistent with the express provisions of the Act.[119]

2. Although it is correct that a power of expulsion is now commonplace, there is still a clear and fundamental inconsistency between the existence of such an express power and the inherent power of each partner (including a partner proposed to be expelled)[120] to bring about a general dissolution of the partnership at a moment's notice.[121]

[115] In support of this proposition, Lord Lindley cited *Clark v. Leach* (1863) 1 De G.J. & S. 409 and *Neilson v. Mossend Iron Co.* (1886) 11 App.Cas. 298.

[116] At this point, Lord Lindley referred to the Partnership Act 1890, s.26 and the decision in *Neilson v. Mossend Iron Co., supra.*

[117] [1988] 1 F.T.L.R. 260, 268. The Vice Chancellor had, in fact, already held that the partnership was not at will (see *supra*, para. 10–16), so that this point strictly did not require to be decided.

[118] Note that, in the 5th edition of this work, Lord Lindley clearly regarded a power of expulsion as falling within the category "Usual Clauses in Articles of Partnership": see *ibid.* pp. 426 *et seq.*

[119] See *ibid.* s.46.

[120] Unless such a partner is in all cases prohibited from exercising the power because of his duty of good faith: see *Walters v. Bingham* [1988] 1 F.L.T.R. 260, 267. And see *infra*, paras 10–143, 24–21.

[121] See the Partnership Act 1890, s.26(1), 32(c), *infra*, paras 24–18 *et seq.*; also *ibid.* s.25, *infra*, para. 24–99. And see *Clark v. Leach* (1863) 1 De G.J. & S. 409, 415 *per* Lord Westbury.

3. If there is such an inconsistency, it is difficult to see how it can be removed by the sheer size of the partnership or by the fact that it carries on a professional practice.

4. A power of expulsion is clearly of an expropriatory nature and, on that account, will always be construed strictly.[122] By analogy, the court should be cautious in seeking to extend the scope of such a power beyond the term originally contemplated.

Although the Vice-Chancellor's decision naturally commands great respect, the current editor believes that its basis in law is questionable and should be approached with a degree of caution.[123]

2.   STATUTORY INTERFERENCE WITH CONTRACTUAL RIGHTS

10–26   It has already been seen that certain types of provision in a partnership agreement which seek to discriminate against a partner or prospective partner on any of the prescribed grounds[124] of his or her are, in general, unlawful and will, to that extent, be either unenforceable or void,[125] although discrimination on the grounds of a partner's colour or nationality is not (for the present at least)[126] unlawful in the case of small firms comprising five partners or less.[127]

10–27   The potential impact which the provisions of the Human Rights Act 1998[128] will have on the application and enforcement of partnership agreements remains unclear.[129] Under that Act, a court[130] must ensure that it does not act in a way which is incompatible with a Convention right,[131] which will include each partner's individual right to the "peaceful enjoyment of his possessions".[132] It

[122] See *infra*, para. 10–123.

[123] Note that in *Re White* [2001] Ch. 393 at [11] and [22], Chadwick L.J. appears to have assumed that a power of expulsion was carried over, although it is doubtful whether the point was argued.

[124] i.e. sex, gender reassignment, colour, race, nationality, ethnic or national origins, disability, religion or belief, sexual orientation or age. Under the Equality Act 2010, s.8, discrimination on the grounds of a partner's marriage or civil partnership will be added to the list.

[125] See, *supra*, paras 8–09 *et seq.*

[126] This exception will not exist when the Equality Act 2010 comes into force.

[127] Race Relations Act 1976, ss.3(1), 10(1), (1A) (the latter subsection having been added by the Race Relations Act 1976 (Amendment) Regulations 2003 (SI 2003/1626), reg. 12(a)). This approach will not, however, be replicated in the equivalent provisions of the Equality Act 2010, when they comes into force.

[128] This Act came fully into force on October 2, 2000: see *ibid.* s.22(2); the Human Rights Act 1998 (Commencement No. 1) Order 1998 (SI 1998/2882); the Human Rights Act 1998 (Commencement No. 2) Order 1999 (SI 1999/1851).

[129] The horizontal effect of the Human Rights Act 1998 is the subject of some debate: see *X v. Y (Employment: Sex Offender)* [2004] I.C.R. 1634 (CA). In that case, it was held that the Act *may* in certain circumstances be engaged in disputes between private employers and employees under the statutory regime established by the Employment Rights Act 1996. Might a similar argument be deployed in the case of, say, an application for a dissolution under the Partnership Act 1890, s.35? Although the scope for involving the 1998 Act is naturally limited, the current editor believes that this possibility cannot be entirely ruled out.

[130] For this purpose a court is clearly a "public authority": see the Human Rights Act 1998, s.6(3)(a).

[131] *ibid.* s.6(1). See, as to the definition of "the Convention rights", *ibid.* s.1(1).

[132] See *ibid.* Sched. 1, Pt II, First Protocol, Art. 1, which (*inter alia*) provides that "No one shall be deprived of his possessions except in the public interest and subject to the conditions provided by law and by the general principles of international law."

might, on a superficial view, be assumed that this would prevent the court from enforcing *any* provision of an expropriatory nature, *e.g.* forfeiture of a partner's share on expulsion,[133] but such an assumption would be mistaken. It is submitted that, where a partner has, as a matter of contract, voluntarily relinquished rights to his own partnership share in certain defined circumstances, enforcement of that agreement as against him should not involve any incompatibility with his Convention rights.[134] The position may, however, be different where a court is exercising a discretion which falls outwith the agreement[135]: in such a case it will seemingly have to have direct regard to questions of incompatibility, even though it may ultimately conclude that interference is proportionate and justified in the public interest.[136] In approaching an issue of this type, the court must take care to avoid acting in a way which would amount to discrimination against any partner.[137] How inclined the court will be to adopt an interventionist approach in this respect remains to be seen, but it is thought unlikely that the 1998 Act will have a significant impact in the partnership field, and especially not in terms of the drafting of partnership agreements.

It should also be noted in passing that sections 2 to 4 of the Unfair Contract Terms Act 1977 will *not* apply to a contract for the formation of a partnership,[138] although it is, perhaps, difficult to imagine the type of provision which might otherwise have attracted their application. In addition, it was, predictably, held in *Robertson v. Robertson*[139] that a partnership agreement was not a marriage settlement and, thus, could not be varied under the Family Law (Scotland) Act 1985.   **10–28**

3.   USUAL CLAUSES FOUND IN A PARTNERSHIP AGREEMENT

Drafting the agreement

This section is devoted to a consideration of those clauses which are commonly encountered in partnership agreements. In terms of subject matter, as opposed to content, these have changed little since Lord Lindley's day[140];   **10–29**

[133] Such provisions are in practice rare, and may give rise to other difficulties: see *infra*, paras 10–152, 10–153. *Semble*, the same considerations would apply to provisions authorising the expulsion or compulsory retirement of partners, as to which see *infra*, paras 10–113 *et seq.*

[134] See *The Holy Monasteries Case* [1995] 66 B.Y.B.I.L. 525, ECHR, judgment of December 9, 1994, Series A, No. 301A. *Per contra*, where an expropriatory provision is imposed by an outside authority on the partnership or some of its members: see *Van Marle v. The Netherlands* [1986] 8 E.H.R.R. 483, ECHR, Series A, No. 101. But note also the views canvassed in an article entitled "Human rights and trusts" by Dirik Jackson in *Trusts and Estates Law Journal*, June 2000, p. 12.

[135] *e.g.* a *Syers v. Syers* order, as to which see *infra*, paras 23–187 *et seq.* Similarly, where a court declines to enforce a contractual right to buy out one or more partners' shares following a dissolution: see *infra*, para. 10–266. *Semble*, interference with any partner's Convention rights in such a case would be unlikely. See also *supra*, n. 129.

[136] *i.e.* under the Human Rights Act 1998, Sched. 1, Pt II, First Protocol, Art. 1, noted *supra*.

[137] See *ibid.* Sched. 1, Pt I, Art. 14, which provides that "The enjoyment of the rights and freedoms set forth in this Convention shall be secured without discrimination on any ground such as sex, race, colour, language, religion, political or other opinion, national or social origin, association with a national minority, property, birth or other status."

[138] *ibid.* Sched. 1, para. 1.

[139] 2003 S.L.T. 208 (OH).

[140] Although a few of Lord Lindley's original headings can no longer be regarded as "usual", they have been retained in the interests of completeness.

however, there is no such thing as a standard partnership agreement, and it should not be assumed either that each of these "usual" clauses will be required in every case or that their inclusion guarantees the suitability of the agreement.[141]

The potential draftsman should also bear in mind that the majority of the provisions of the Partnership Act 1890 apply unless they are expressly or impliedly excluded by the agreement.[142] In some cases, he may be content with those provisions; in others he may not. Yet he must at the same time have regard to the position of the partners themselves, who may be unfamiliar with the workings of the Act. Lord Lindley made this point in the following passage written prior to the Act (thereby incidentally seeming to ignore the use of partnerships in the solicitors' profession):

> "In framing articles of partnership, it should always be remembered, that they are intended for the guidance of persons who are not lawyers; and that it is therefore unwise to insert only such provisions as are necessary to exclude the application of rules which apply where nothing to the contrary is said. The articles should be so drawn as to be a code of directions to which the partners may refer as a guide in all their transactions, and upon which they may settle among themselves differences which may arise, without having recourse to Courts of Justice."

10–30   The practice of resorting to short form "Heads of Agreement", although occasionally required on grounds of expediency, should never be regarded as a long-term substitute for a comprehensive agreement. Regrettably, once such heads of agreement are in place, there is an understandable tendency to regard the proliferation of documentation as an unnecessary evil, but this is frequently an economy that partners live to regret.

As in previous editions of this work, the current editor has not sought to reproduce typical precedents of the "usual" clauses in an attempt to place them in context. The basic content of this chapter is directed towards identifying the purpose and effect of each clause: this is not a drafting work, and any standardised form which does not encompass all the variations considered in the text and which is not accompanied by a commentary specifically directed towards the particular form of words used might inadvertently mislead the prospective draftsman.[143]

Form of agreement

10–31   Partnership agreements traditionally take the form of a deed,[144] although this is not strictly necessary save where the agreement will operate to convey land or an interest in land from one partner to another[145] or where it purports to grant a

---

[141] See, further, the checklist in the *Encyclopedia of Professional Partnerships*, paras 1–050 *et seq.*

[142] See, in particular, *ibid.* ss.19, 24, 25, 29 and 30.

[143] However, for the assistance of the reader, footnote references to the *Encyclopedia of Professional Partnerships*, which is a companion to this volume, have been incorporated.

[144] See, as to the formalities for the execution of a deed, the Law of Property (Miscellaneous) Provisions) Act 1989, s.1, as amended by the Regulatory Reform (Execution of Deeds and Documents) Order 2005 (SI 2005/1906), art.8.

[145] Law of Property Act 1925, s.52(2), as amended by the Insolvency Act 1986, Sched. 14 and the Law of Property (Miscellaneous) Provisions) Act 1989, Sched. 1, para. 2. The proposition in the text is not absolute: it is still seemingly possible to prove the existence and terms of a partnership solely on the basis of oral evidence, even where the partnership property consists of land: see *supra*, paras 7–02 *et seq.*

power of attorney.[146] Since consideration will clearly flow from each partner to the other(s),[147] an agreement under hand will normally suffice.[148] It should be noted that use of a deed is no longer necessary in order to confer rights of enforcement on a third party.[149]

A. PARTIES

It is always necessary to identify the parties to the agreement and to state whether they will be partners in the true sense (normally styled "equity" partners), partners with only limited rights to participate in profits and in the management of the firm (normally styled "non-equity" or, where appropriate, "salaried" or "fixed share" partners), or mere employees who are to be held out as partners (also misleadingly styled "salaried" partners).[150] In fact, persons falling within the latter class should not be made parties to the agreement at all.   **10–32**

Where the parties are numerous, the modern practice is to schedule their names and addresses, often in such a way as to permit the schedule to be added to or altered in order to accommodate future changes in the firm.[151]

Senior and managing partners, etc.

If one partner is to hold a particular position in the firm, *e.g.* "senior partner", "managing partner" or "administration partner", that should be stated in the agreement and provision made for: **10–33**

(a) the manner in which partners are to be appointed or elected to that position[152];

(b) the term during which that position is to be held; and

(c) the manner in which a partner can be removed from or relinquish that position.

---

[146] *e.g.* to sign *Gazette* notices and other notifications: see the Powers of Attorney Act 1971, s.1, as amended by the Law of Property (Miscellaneous) Provisions) Act 1989, Sched. 1, para. 6(a). Equally, such a power of attorney may be created by a separate document executed pursuant to an express obligation contained in the agreement: see *infra*, paras 10–97, 10–252.

[147] See *supra*, paras 6–01 *et seq.*

[148] *Quaere*, could there be a partnership under which one or more partners accept no obligations whatsoever? It is thought not, given the definition in the Partnership Act 1890, s.1(1), *supra*, paras 2–01 *et seq.*

[149] Nevertheless, note the decision in *Moody v. Condor Insurance Ltd.* [2006] 1 W.L.R. 1847 regarding the enforceability of a guarantee document executed as an *inter partes* deed. Given the provisions of the Contracts (Rights of Third Parties) Act 1999 (see *infra*, paras 10–188, 10–259), reliance will rarely have to be placed on the Law of Property Act 1925, s.56(1): see *infra*, para. 10–190. Somewhat surprisingly, the provisions of the former Act have no application in the case of an LLP agreement: Limited Liability Partnerships Regulations 2001 (SI 2001/1090), Sched. 5, para. 20. Note also the inheritance tax implications of conferring a gratuitous benefit on a third party: see *infra*, para. 36–28.

[150] See further *supra*, paras 5–54 *et seq.*

[151] See the *Encyclopedia of Professional Partnerships*, Precedent 2, Art. 1.00.14, Sched. 1.

[152] It may also be desirable to record whether a partner is eligible to stand for re-election and, if so, on how many occasions. It is, in practice, quite rare to find partners being permitted to hold the same office more than twice in succession.

The latter will be particularly important, since it can be embarrassing if a partner continues to hold office as, say, senior partner after he has given notice of his intention to retire from the firm and to take up a partnership elsewhere. It cannot be assumed that, in all cases, his removal can be effected pursuant to the normal decision-making powers in the agreement[153] or, in default of any such provision, pursuant to section 24(8) of the Partnership Act 1890.[154]

B.   NATURE OF THE BUSINESS[155]

10–34   Lord Lindley emphasised the need for the agreement to establish the nature of the business to be carried on, explaining:

> "Upon it depends the extent to which each partner is to be regarded as the implied agent of the firm in his dealings with strangers[156]; and upon it also in a great measure depends the power of a majority of partners to act in opposition to the wishes of the minority."[157]

However, as demonstrated by the arguments advanced in *Nixon v. Wood*,[158] disputes can still arise even where the nature of the business *is* clearly established in the agreement.

C.   COMMENCEMENT DATE[159]

10–35   It is essential that the commencement date of the partnership is established with certainty, since it is only from that date that each partner will be liable for the acts of his co-partners and, thus, for the debts and obligations of the firm.[160]

No commencement date specified

10–36   Lord Lindley observed:

> "Prima facie, articles of partnership, like other instruments, take effect from their date; and if they are executed on the day of their date, and contain no expression indicating when the partnership is to begin, it must be taken to commence on the day

---

[153] See *infra*, paras 10–102 *et seq.*
[154] See *infra*, paras 15–04 *et seq.*
[155] *Encyclopedia of Professional Partnerships* Precedent 1, cl. 2.
[156] See the Partnership Act 1890, s.5, *infra*, paras 12–02 *et seq.*
[157] See *ibid.* s.24(8), *infra*, paras 15–04 *et seq.*
[158] (1987) 284 E.G. 1055.
[159] See the *Encyclopedia of Professional Partnerships*, Precedent 1, cl. 2.
[160] See *infra*, paras 13–17 *et seq.*

of the date of the articles, and parol evidence to show that this was not intended is not admissible."[161]

A deed takes effect at the moment of its execution, irrespective of the date which appears on its face[162]; thus, if it can be demonstrated by extrinsic evidence that the deed was executed on some other date, the partnership will be regarded as commencing on that date,[163] unless the partners were in fact carrying on the business with effect from some earlier date.[164]

Retrospective and future commencement dates

Agreements frequently provide that the partnership is to be deemed to have commenced on some past date. If, as will usually be the case, the partners were in fact carrying on business together at that date, the agreement will have retrospective effect as regards them, but not as regards third parties, *e.g.* HMRC. If, on the other hand, no business was carried on at that date, the agreement cannot regulate a non-existent relationship[165] and will, therefore, only have full effect when business is actually commenced.[166] However, it might, depending on its terms, have a limited effect as regards the interim period, *e.g.* so as to deem debts incurred during that period to be liabilities of the partnership.[167] The retrospectivity of an agreement naturally depends on the parties' intentions which may be apparent from the terms of the agreement itself or may be implied as a matter of business efficacy, having regard to the factual matrix.[168]

10–37

Similarly, an agreement providing for a *future* commencement date will not prevent the partnership coming into existence at an earlier date, if the partners in fact carry on business together with effect from that date.[169]

Formal agreement to be drawn up

If prospective partners enter into an interim agreement,[170] intending that a more formal agreement will be prepared and executed in due course, it does not mean that the commencement of the partnership will necessarily be delayed until the formal agreement is in place. Everything will depend on the terms of the

10–38

---

[161] *Williams v. Jones* (1826) 5 B. & C. 108. If the agreement is not dated, parol evidence is admissible to show that it was not intended to take effect from the time of execution: *Davis v. Jones* (1856) 17 C.B. 625.

[162] *Morell v. Studd & Millington* [1913] 2 Ch. 648.

[163] See *Browne v. Burton* (1847) 17 L.J. Q.B. 49.

[164] In such a case, the actual date of commencement will be provable as a fact independently of the date on which the agreement was executed. See also *supra*, para. 2–17 and *infra*, para. 13–18.

[165] It is clear that until such time as a business is actually carried on, no partnership can, as a matter of law exist: see the Partnership Act 1890, s.1(1). However, a business may be carried on even if no trading activity has commenced: see *Khan v. Miah* [2000] 1 W.L.R. 2123, (HL); *cf. Goudberg v. Erniman Associates Pty. Ltd.* [2007] V.S.C.A. 12, noted, *supra*, para. 2–03. See further, *supra*, paras 2–03, 2–17 *et seq.* and *infra*, para. 13–18.

[166] *Vere v. Ashby* (1829) 10 B. & C. 288; *Waddington v. O'Callaghan* (1931) 16 T.C. 187; *Saywell v. Pope* [1979] S.T.C. 824. See also *infra*, paras 34–13 *et seq.*

[167] No rights against the intended firm would be conferred on third party creditors in such a case.

[168] See *Northern and Shell Plc v. John Laing Construction Ltd.*, 90 Con. L.R. 26 (CA) at [51] to [54], [58].

[169] *Battley v. Lewis* (1840) 1 Man. & G. 155.

[170] *e.g.* heads of agreement, see *supra*, para. 10–25.

interim agreement, assuming it to be binding on the partners,[171] and on the partners' conduct.[172]

D.   DURATION[173]

10–39   The duration of the partnership must always be stated in the agreement, if the creation of a partnership at will is to be avoided.[174] This usually takes the form of a fixed term of years, or a term for the "joint lives" of the partners.[175] On occasion, an unlimited duration is adopted, but the right of each partner to dissolve the firm is expressly excluded.[176] In any such case, it would rarely, if ever, be appropriate to infer an implied term allowing a partner to bring the partnership to an end at an earlier date.[177] Adoption of a "rolling" term may also give rise to difficulties of construction in terms of when, if at all, it can be brought to an end.[178]

Since a partnership will normally be dissolved by the death or bankruptcy of a partner,[179] it is essential that this consequence is expressly negated.[180] At the same time, it should also be confirmed, *ex abundanti cautela*, that the retirement or expulsion of a partner under any power contained in the agreement will not determine the partnership as regards the continuing partners.[181] However, whilst such express provisions may avoid the worst effects of a dissolution, they cannot as a matter of law prevent there being a *technical* dissolution on any change in the composition of the firm.[182] As Eichelbaum C.J. put it in *Hadlee v. Commissioner of Inland Revenue*[183]:

---

[171] See *England v. Curling* (1844) 8 Beav. 129; also *Branca v. Cobarro* [1947] K.B. 854.

[172] The existence of a formal agreement is not, of course, a prerequisite to the existence of a partnership: see *supra*, paras 2–01 *et seq.*

[173] See the *Encyclopedia of Professional Partnerships*, Precedent 1, cl. 3.

[174] Partnership Act 1890, ss.26(1), 32(c), *supra*, paras 9–01 *et seq.* and *infra*, paras 24–18 *et seq.*

[175] Where the term is referable to the joint lives of the partners, care must be taken to ensure that the relevant lives are those of the *current* partners.

[176] This may be appropriate where one or more of the partners is a company: see further, as to corporate partnerships, *infra*, paras 11–02 *et seq.*

[177] *Jani-King (GB) Ltd. v. Pula Enterprises Ltd.* [2008] 1 All E.R. 451 (albeit a decision concerning a fixed term franchise agreement).

[178] Note, in this context, *G & A Ltd. v. HN Jewelry (Asia) Ltd.* (2004)148 S.J.L.B. 695, albeit that this did not concern a partnership agreement.

[179] Partnership Act 1890, s.33(1), *infra*, paras 24–29 *et seq.*

[180] In the case of bankruptcy, the current editor considers that the effects of *ibid.* s.33(1) will be impliedly excluded if there is power under the agreement to expel a bankrupt partner. And see, generally, *William S. Gordon & Co. Ltd. v. Mrs Mary Thomson Partnership*, 1985 S.L.T. 122 (but note that the actual decision in this case appears to be out of line with the other authorities, as seemingly accepted by Lord Kingarth *sub silentio* in *Knapdale (Nominees) Ltd. v. Donald (O.H.)*, 2000 S.C.L.R. 1013, 1033D). *Semble*, an *ad hoc* agreement will not be sufficient to avoid a dissolution resulting from a partner's bankruptcy: *Quarantelli v. Forbes* 2000 G.W.D. 2–67.

[181] The agreement should also, of course, provide for the acquisition of the outgoing partner's share, so that the point is largely academic. Note the decision in *William S. Gordon & Co. Ltd. v. Mrs Mary Thomson Partnership*, *supra*.

[182] See *supra*, paras 3–01 *et seq.* and *infra*, para. 24–02. Note, however, that the court in *Cummings v. Stockdale*, November 11, 2008 (noted *supra*, para. 3–05) took a different view.

[183] [1989] 2 N.Z.L.R. 447, 445. This issue was not canvassed before the Privy Council: see [1993] A.C. 524.

" . . . no doubt it is competent for partners to agree in advance that in the event of a retirement the remaining partners will continue to practise in partnership but that does not overcome the consequence that the partnership practising the day after the retirement is a different one from that in business the previous day."

Where such a provision is sought to be applied as between two partners or on the retirement, etc., of all the partners bar one,[184] clearly there can be no question of the partnership continuing when only one "partner" remains,[185] but there is no reason in principle why such a contractual provision, if properly drafted, should not have effect as if it did.   **10–40**

The inclusion of such a provision will not guarantee that rights of action in favour of the existing firm will automatically vest in the new firm which comes into existence on the change.[186]

If the chosen term expires, but the partnership continues without a new agreement, it will do so as a partnership at will.[187] This will also be the position if a new partner is admitted during the term, unless the existing agreement contemplates the possibility of such admission and the incoming partner agrees to be bound by its terms.[188]

E.   FIRM NAME[189]

It is desirable, but not essential,[190] that the firm name should be stated in the agreement, together with the procedure for altering that name.[191] It is also not unusual to include a reference to the need to comply with the provisions of Part 41 of the Companies Act 2006,[192] by way of an *aide-mémoire* to the partners.   **10–41**

Use of firm name

Lord Lindley said: **10–42**

" . . . it should be declared that no partner shall enter into an engagement on behalf of the firm except in its name. Such an agreement is capable of being enforced[193]; and

---

[184] It will be a question of construction as to whether it does apply in such a case: the Court of Appeal was unwilling to construe the agreement in that way in *Hurst v. Bryk* [1999] Ch. 1, and there was no appeal on this point.

[185] See *Oswald Hickson Collier & Co. v. Carter-Ruck* [1984] A.C. 720 note, 721G *per* Denning M.R.; *Re C. & M. Ashberg, The Times*, July 17, 1990; *Re Rogers* [2006] 1 W.L.R. 1577, 1581B *per* Lightman J.; *Tann v. Herrington* [2009] P.N.L.R. 22 at [24] *per* Bernard Livesey Q.C. sitting as a deputy judge of the Chancery Division. See also *supra*, para. 3–08.

[186] *Global Partners Fund Ltd. v. Babcock & Brown Ltd.* [2010] NSWSC 270 at [90] *per* Hammerschlag J. The appeal went off on other grounds: see [2010] NSWCA 96. Much will, of course, depend on the precise terms of the agreement.

[187] Partnership Act 1980, s.27, *supra*, paras 10–18 *et seq.*

[188] See *supra*, paras 9–12, 9–13 and *infra*, paras 10–256, 10–257.

[189] See the *Encyclopedia of Professional Partnerships*, Precedent 1, cl. 5.

[190] The name may, of course, give some indication of the type of business carried on by the firm and, thereby, assist in identifying the extent of each partner's implied authority pursuant to the Partnership Act 1890, s.5, *infra*, paras 12–01 *et seq.*

[191] This will usually be dealt with, if at all, in the clauses governing decision making: see *infra*, paras 10–102 *et seq.*

[192] See *supra*, paras 3–26 *et seq.* It is not necessary to be too specific as to the requirements of the Act.

[193] See *Marshall v. Colman* (1820) 2 J. & W. 266.

it may be of use in determining, as between the partners, whether a given transaction is to be regarded as a partnership transaction or not."

In practice, such declarations tend not to be included in modern agreements, save in relation to cheques.[194]

F.   THE PREMIUM

10–43   Although a reference to premiums[195] has been retained, they are now rarely, if ever, encountered and most certainly could not be considered "usual". If a premium is to be paid, the agreement should identify both the time and manner of payment[196] and the circumstances in which it is to be returned, whether on dissolution or otherwise.[197]

G.   PARTNERSHIP PREMISES[198]

10–44   It is desirable, but not in all cases essential, to identify the premises from which the firm will carry on business and the manner in which decisions in relation to those and any other premises will in the future be taken.[199]

Premises owned by one or more partners

10–45   What is of greater importance is to ensure that the occupation rights of the firm are clearly established where the premises are to remain in the sole ownership of one or more of the partners.[200]

If a lease in favour of the firm is to be granted, then it must be in writing.[201] The termination of such a lease may, however, not be without difficulty[202] and its existence may conceivably have adverse inheritance tax consequences.[203]

If the agreement omits any reference to such occupation rights then, in the absence of any other evidence, it will not be assumed, merely because the

---

[194] See the *Encyclopedia of Professional Partnerships*, Precedent 1, cl. 6(3).

[195] This expression is not defined in the Partnership Act 1890: see further, as to its meaning, *infra*, para. 25–07.

[196] *e.g.* if it is payable in instalments, will they continue even if the partnership is dissolved? See also *infra*, para. 25–15.

[197] See the Partnership Act 1890, s.40 and *Handyside v. Campbell* (1901) 17 T.L.R. 623, 6234 *per* Farwell J. See also *infra*, para. 25–11.

[198] See the *Encyclopedia of Professional Partnerships*, Precedent 1, cl. 4.

[199] See *Clements v. Norris* (1878) 8 Ch.D. 129.

[200] The importance of this is underlined by the decision in *Latchman v. Pickard* [2005] EWHC 1011 (Ch) (Lawtel 12/5/05).

[201] *Rye v. Rye* [1962] A.C. 496.

[202] See *Sykes v. Land* (1984) 271 E.G. 1265; *Featherstone v. Staples* [1986] 1 W.L.R. 861; *cf. Brenner v. Rose* [1973] 1 W.L.R. 443. An agreement that such a lease will be surrendered in the event of a dissolution may well not be effective: see *Joseph v. Joseph* [1967] Ch. 78 and *infra*, para. 18–48. Note, however, that the termination of a tenancy by notice to quit given on a *consensual* basis as between landlord and head tenant will not be treated as an effective surrender and will, therefore, also terminate the sub-tenant's rights: *Barrett v. Morgan* [2000] 2 A.C. 264 (HL).

[203] See *infra*, paras 36–31 *et seq.*

premises are indispensable to the partnership business, that they belong to the firm[204] or are subject to the firm's right to: (i) a lease or tenancy[205] or, where that is still relevant,[206] (ii) an exclusive licence to occupy within the meaning of the Agricultural Holdings Act 1986.[207] It will rather be inferred that each individual partner who is not beneficially interested in the premises has been granted a non-exclusive licence to enter them in order to carry on the partnership business.[208] Such licences would seem to be contractual in nature and might, as a matter of implication, not be terminable during the currency of the partnership, particularly if it can be shown that the partnership business can only be carried on from those premises and that the termination of the licences would strike at the substratum of the partnership agreement.[209] In such circumstances the only effective way of determining the licences would be to dissolve the partnership but, even then, they would prima facie continue until the winding up is complete,[210] although this will not always be the case.[211]

It should also be noted that premises owned in this way may now in some cases be deemed to be partnership property for the purposes of stamp duty land tax and a charge to the tax may be incurred when they "become" partnership property.[212]

Covenant against assignment, etc.

Where leasehold premises owned by a partner are occupied by the firm, there will be no breach of a covenant against assignment, underletting, parting with or sharing possession if that partner merely permits his co-partners to go into occupation for the purposes of carrying on the partnership business.[213] The position may be otherwise if an assignment of the tenancy to the firm can be   **10–46**

---

[204] *Eardley v. Broad, The Times,* April 28, 1970 and (1970) 215 E.G. 823. See also *infra, para.* 18–34.

[205] *Rye v. Rye, supra.* A tenancy was inferred in *Pocock v. Carter* [1912] 1 Ch. 663, but this can no longer be considered good law.

[206] Where the licence was granted after September 1, 1995, it cannot attract the protection of the Agricultural Holdings Act 1986: Agricultural Tenancies Act 1995, s.4(1), as amended by the Regulatory Reform (Agricultural Tenancies) (England and Wales) Order 2006 (SI 2006/2805), art. 12(2)–(5). By definition, an implied tenancy under the latter Act could not be created, since as well as fulfilling the "business conditions" (*ibid.* s.1(2)), a tenancy thereunder must either fulfil the "agricultural condition" (*ibid.* s.1(3)) or the "notice conditions" (*ibid.* s.1(4)): *ibid.* s.1(1). It would be impossible to fulfil either of the latter conditions unintentionally.

[207] *Harrison-Broadley v. Smith* [1964] 1 W.L.R. 456. A contrary view was advanced in *Harrison v. Wing* [1988] 29 E.G. 101, 103, but the point appears not to have been fully argued, since their Lordships make no reference to the decision in *Harrison-Broadley v. Smith.* See also *Bahamas International Trust Co. Ltd. v. Threadgold* [1974] 1 W.L.R. 1514. It is considered that occupation pursuant to such a licence would properly fall to be disregarded for the purposes of the eligibility test under the Agricultural Holdings Act 1986, s.36(3)(b) in relation to other land: see *ibid.* Sched. 6, para. 6(1)(e). *Per contra,* perhaps, if the licence cannot be terminated whilst the partnership continues: see an article by Michele Slatter in [1986] Conv. 320.

[208] *Harrison-Broadley v. Smith, supra.*

[209] *cf.* the position where the firm has a tenancy: *Brenner v. Rose* [1973] 1 W.L.R. 443; *Sykes v. Land* (1984) 271 E.G. 1265; *Featherstone v. Staples* [1986] 1 W.L.R. 861.

[210] See *infra,* para. 25–04.

[211] See *Latchman v. Pickard* [2005] EWHC 1011 (Ch) (Lawtel 12/5/05), albeit a decision made on an interim application.

[212] See *infra,* paras 38–04, 38–10.

[213] *Gian Singh & Co. v. Nahar* [1965] 1 W.L.R. 412 (PC), where, however, there appears to have been merely a covenant against assignment and subletting; also *Knapdale (Nominees) Ltd. v. Donald,* 2000 S.C.L.R. 1013 (OH). See also *infra,* para. 18–60.

inferred or if the covenant prohibits the sharing of occupation but, even then, no breach of covenant may be involved.[214]

H.   PARTNERSHIP PROPERTY[215]

10–47   The agreement should, so far as possible,[216] identify:

(a)   those assets which are to constitute partnership property,[217]

(b)   those assets which are to be retained in the ownership of a partner but to be used by the firm and, if so, on what basis[218]; and

(c)   if partnership money is to be spent on an asset belonging to a partner, whether the firm will be entitled to a lien for its return.[219]

In earlier editions of this work, the view was advanced that the agreement should also record the partners' respective beneficial interests in the partnership property. In the current editor's opinion, such a provision is neither usual nor necessary, provided that the partners' capital contributions and shares in asset surpluses or capital profits[220] are clearly stated.[221] However, if a partner is to have *no* interest whatsoever in such property, a declaration to this effect should be included, if only for the avoidance of doubt.[222]

Incoming partners

10–48   It is equally important to consider the above issues when a new partner is admitted to an existing firm, since it does not necessarily follow that he is

---

[214] Note that in *Wallace v. C. Brian Barratt & Son Ltd.* [1997] 31 E.G. 97 it was held that there was no breach of a covenant against sharing occupation where a partnership farmed land as agent for the tenant company. In this case much depended on the nature of the land, *i.e.* an arable farm. *Quaere* would the position have been different had the company been a member of the partnership? Morritt J. hinted that it might (see *ibid.* p. 100), but could it not be argued that the partners were in occupation as the tenant partner's agents under the Partnership Act 1890, s.5?

[215] *Encyclopedia of Professional Partnerships*, Precedent 1, cl. 8(1).

[216] It is not, of course, feasible to list every item and certain generic descriptions may have to be resorted to.

[217] See, as to the possible tax implications, *infra,* paras 35–04, 35–05 (capital gains tax), 36–20, 36–21 (inheritance tax), 37–17 (value added tax) and 38–09, 38–10 (stamp duty land tax). Note that, whilst milk quota is technically incapable of existing as an asset independently of the land to which it relates (*Faulks v. Faulks* [1992] 1 E.G.L.R. 9; *Davies v. H. & R. Ecroyd* [1996] 2 E.G.L.R. 5, noted *infra*, para. 18–19), this does not mean that it is incapable of being held on trust for the firm and, thereby, constituting a partnership asset: see *Swift v. Dairywise Farms Ltd.* [2000] 1 W.L.R. 1177. The subsequent appeal ([2003] 1 W.L.R. 1606) ultimately went off on other grounds. But see also, as to transfers of milk quota without the land to which it relates, the Dairy Produce Quotas Regulations 2005 (SI 2005/465), reg. 13, as amended by the Dairy Produce Quotas (Amendment) Regulations 2008 (SI 2008/439), reg. 2, Sched., para. 4. And note *Harries v. Barclays Bank* [1997] 2 E.G.L.R. 15 (CA).

[218] See, in the case of land, *supra*, para. 10–45.

[219] See *infra*, paras 18–38 *et seq.*, 20–31, 20–32.

[220] See, as to these expressions, *infra*, paras 10–158, 17–04.

[221] See *infra*, para. 10–79. Note, however, that complications may arise where preferential "salaries" are payable to partners as a first charge on profits: see *infra*, para. 10–85 (where the same problem is considered in relation to the sharing of losses).

[222] *e.g.* in the case of a so-called "salaried" partner.

intended to acquire a full share of the existing partnership assets.[223] This can be achieved either by withdrawing those assets from the firm simultaneously with his admission, or by adjusting the capital profit shares accordingly.[224]

Goodwill

The agreement should establish whether or not goodwill is a partnership asset: **10–49**
although there is something akin to a presumption that it belongs to the firm, this will not always be the case.[225] If the goodwill is to be retained by a particular partner or partners, it should be decided whether any *increase* in its value will also belong to those partners or to the firm and, if the latter, how the firm's entitlement is to be ascertained and realised on a dissolution.

Land[226]

If one partner is entitled to land which is to be brought into the partnership, it   **10–50**
is certainly advisable to ensure that the legal estate is conveyed into the names of at least two of the partners.[227] However, as between the partners themselves, all that is required is a simple declaration in the agreement that the land will constitute partnership property. Such a declaration will take effect under section 53(1)(b) or (c) of the Law of Property Act 1925[228]; the position where there is no written agreement has already been noted earlier in this work.[229] It should be noted that such a declaration may also attract a charge to stamp duty land tax.[230]

Offices and appointments[231]

Although a particular office or appointment cannot normally itself be regarded   **10–51**
as a partnership asset, it may be (and often is) treated as held on the firm's behalf, so that the partner concerned is obliged to account to the firm for any fees or other remuneration received.[232] Where partners hold such positions, or are likely to do so, their duty to account or their right to retain any fees, etc., should be clearly stated in the agreement.[233]

---

[223] See, for example, *Bennett v. Wallace*, 1998 S.C. 457, discussed *infra*, para. 10–173.

[224] See *infra*, para. 10–79.

[225] See *Miles v. Clarke* [1953] 1 W.L.R. 537; *Stekel v. Ellice* [1973] 1 W.L.R. 191; see also *infra*, paras 10–197 *et seq.*, 18–17, 18–36.

[226] See also *supra*, paras 10–44 *et seq.*

[227] See *infra*, paras 18–61 *et seq.*

[228] *Quaere*, is there any advantage in giving the trustee partners an *express* indemnity? The decision in *Hurst v. Bennett* [2001] EWCA Civ 182 (briefly reported (*sub nom. Re a Debtor (No. 303 of 1997)*) in *The Times*, October 3, 2000) might suggest that there is. However, the decision is not entirely satisfactory: see *infra*, paras 14–76 n. 293, 23–76.

[229] See *supra*, paras 7–02 *et seq.* Otherwise, it will be necessary to prove that the other partners have acted to their detriment, if the effects of the Law of Property Act 1925, s.53(1)(b) are to be avoided: see *Midland Bank v. Dobson* (1986) 1 F.L.R. 171. And see *Rye v. Rye* [1962] A.C. 496.

[230] See *infra*, para. 38–09. As to the other tax implications, see *supra*, n. 217.

[231] See the *Encyclopedia of Professional Partnerships*, Precedent 11, cl. 12(1).

[232] See *Smith v. Mules* (1852) 9 Hare 556; *Collins v. Jackson* (1862) 31 Beav. 645; *Casson Beckman & Partners v. Papi* [1991] B.C.L.C. 299, 309 *per* Balcombe L.J. and *infra*, para. 18–18. See also *Carlyon Britton v. Lumb* (1922) 38 T.L.R. 298. *cf. Osborne & Hunter Ltd. v. Hardie Caldwell (No. 2)*, 2001 G.W.D. 4–174 (OH).

[233] See, for example, the *Encyclopedia of Professional Partnerships*, Precedent 11, cl. 12(1).

Outgoing partners

10–52   In some cases, it may be appropriate to require an outgoing partner to relinquish any offices he may hold, with a view to one of the continuing partners seeking to be appointed in his place, but this is not common.[234] Whether it is more practical merely to require the outgoing partner to employ the services of the firm when carrying out his official duties[235] will ultimately depend on the nature of the office and the propriety of the holder fettering his discretion in this way,[236] but the current editor ventures to suggest that this will rarely provide a satisfactory solution.

In the case of an insolvency appointment, it may be possible for the continuing partners to apply to the court for the removal of the outgoing partner from that appointment,[237] and the agreement might usefully oblige him to concur and co-operate in making such an application.[238]

Dissolution

10–53   Consideration should also be given to the treatment of the office in the event of a general dissolution: it would be possible to legislate in advance for the payment of an agreed sum in consideration of its retention by the then incumbent, thus reflecting the approach likely to be adopted by a court, which was summarised by Lord Lindley as follows:

> "If the profits of the office are partnership assets, and the firm is dissolved whilst the office is held by one of its members, the Court, in winding up the partnership, will leave him in the enjoyment of the office, but charge him with its value in his account with the firm."[239]

However, this will not be possible in all cases.[240]

---

[234] This is confirmed by the expert evidence (in relation to liquidation appointments) adduced in *Casson Beckman & Partners v. Papi*, *supra*, at pp. 302b–d, 307b. In the case of an executorship, such a provision would in any event be unworkable and, in the case of a trusteeship, would prima facie place the trustee partner in breach of the obligations which he owes to his beneficiaries, which are paramount: see *Don King Productions Inc. v. Warren* [2000] Ch. 291, 320G–H *per* Lightman J. This point was not adverted to in the Court of Appeal judgments.

[235] This appears to be a fairly common practice in the accountancy profession, so far as concerns liquidation appointments: see *Casson Beckman & Partners v. Papi*, *supra*, at p. 302b–d.

[236] The current editor submits that this would be wholly inappropriate in the case of an executorship or trusteeship, where the primary duty is owed to the relevant estate or trust: see n. 2, *supra*.

[237] *Re A & C Supplies Ltd.* [1998] 1 B.C.L.C. 603, where Blackburne J. declined to follow the more restrictive approach adopted in *Re Sankey Furniture Ltd.* [1995] 2 B.C.L.C. 594; *Clements v. Udal* [2001] B.C.C. 658; *Cork v. Rolph, The Times*, December 21, 2000; *Customs & Excise Commissioners v. Allen* [2003] B.P.I.R. 830; *Donaldson v. O'Sullivan* [2009] 1 W.L.R. 924 (CA) (regarding the appointment of a replacement trustee in bankruptcy); see also *Re Bullard & Taplin Ltd.* [1996] B.C.C. 973; *Re Equity Nominees Ltd.* [1999] 2 B.C.L.C. 19; *Re Alt Landscapes* [1999] B.P.I.R. 459. Note that such an order cannot, however, be retrospective: *Darrell v. Miller* [2004] B.P.I.R. 470. As to the powers exercisable by the court, see the Insolvency Act 1986, ss.7(5), (6), 108, 171(2), 172(2), 263(5), (6), 298(1), 302(2), 363(1) (as amended, in the case of ss.7(5) and 263(5), by the Insolvency Act 2000); the Insolvency Rules 1986 (SI 1986/1925), rr. 4.119, 4.120, 6.132, as respectively amended, in the case of the former rules only, by the Insolvency (Amendment) Rules 2008 (SI 2008/737) r. 7(1) and, in each case, by the Insolvency (Amendment) Rules 2010 (SI 2010/686), Sched. 1.

[238] See the *Encyclopedia of Professional Partnerships*, Precedent 5, cl. 24(2)(n). See, as to the attitude of the court where the outgoing partner makes the application, *Re Equity Nominees*, *supra*.

[239] See *Smith v. Mules* (1852) 9 Hare 556. *cf. Ambler v. Bolton* (1871) L.R. 14 Eq. 427.

[240] *e.g.* a payment in consideration of the retention of the office of under-sheriff would appear to contravene the Sheriffs Act 1887, s.27(1) (as amended): see further, *infra*, para. 23–199.

The benefit of unassignable contracts

There is no reason in principle why the benefit of an unassignable contract held   **10–54**
by one or more of the partners should not become a partnership asset, as was
clearly established in *Don King Productions Inc. v. Warren.*[241] It follows that,
where the partnership business involves the exploitation of such contracts, it
should be made clear whether or not they are to form part of the partnership
assets and how they are to be treated on the retirement, etc. of a partner or in the
event of a general dissolution.[242] The same treatment should be applied to any
renewals of such contracts whilst the partnership subsists and during the period
of any winding up.[243]

Trade secrets, etc.

If a partnership is formed with a view to exploiting a new and unpatented   **10–55**
invention, the agreement should identify whether the invention will belong to the
firm or to the partner who discovered it and, if the former, how it is to be treated
in the event of a dissolution. Lord Lindley explained the position following a
dissolution in these terms:

> " . . . if there be no agreement on the subject, all the parties will have a right to work
> it, in opposition to each other, there being no ground upon which any of them can be
> prevented from so doing. If, however, it can be proved by the inventor that his secret
> was to be kept from his co-partners, or that they, if they discovered it, were not to
> make use of their discovery, they will not be allowed to violate the agreement into
> which they have entered, or the trust reposed in them; and the circumstance that the
> invention has not been patented will not be material."[244]

To this should be added the qualification that, if the invention is a partnership
asset, it may effectively form part of the goodwill of the business and fall to be

---

[241] [2000] Ch. 291 (CA).

[242] The approach will broadly follow that advocated in relation to offices and appointments, *supra*,
paras 10–51, 10–52.

[243] See *Don King Productions Inc. v. Warren, supra.*

[244] See *Morison v. Moat* (1851) 9 Hare 241; also *Deacons v. White & Case LLP* (HCA 2433/2002),
October 24, 2003 (Hong Kong High Court); and, generally, *Terrapin v. Builders Supply Co.* [1960]
R.P.C. 128; *Seager v. Copydex* [1967] 1 W.L.R. 923; *Coco v. A. N. Clark, Engineers* [1968] F.S.R.
415; *Schering Chemicals Ltd. v. Falkman Ltd.* [1982] Q.B. 1; *Fraser v. Thames Television Ltd.* [1984]
Q.B. 44. The employment cases may also be relevant in the present context: see *Faccenda Chicken
Ltd. v. Fowler* [1987] Ch. 117 and the cases there cited; *cf. Lansing Linde Ltd. v. Kerr* [1991] 1
W.L.R. 251; also *FSS Travel and Leisure Systems Ltd. v. Johnson* [1998] I.R.L.R. 382. As to the status
of lists of customers and addresses, see *PennWell Publishing (UK) Ltd. v. Ornstien* [2007] I.R.L.R.
700; *Crowson Fabrics Ltd. v. Rider* [2008] I.R.L.R. 288 (both employee cases). Note also that the
constructive trust argument (of the type contemplated in the last sentence in the text) failed in
Kilcarne Holdings Ltd. v. Targetfollow (Birmingham) Ltd. [2005] P & C.R. 8 and *Cayzer v. Beddow*
[2007] EWCA Civ 644 (Lawtel 29/6/07). As to the possible remedies where confidential information
is shared with an intending partner, see *LAC Minerals Ltd. v. International Corona Resources Ltd.*
[1990] F.S.R. 441 (Sup. Ct of Canada); also *Shanshal v. Al-Kishtaini* (Lawtel 16/6/99), where it was
held that fiduciary obligations were owed by the parties to an abortive joint venture (although this
aspect is not referred to in the report in *The Times*, June 16, 1999 and an appeal was subsequently
allowed on other grounds: [2001] 2 All E.R. (Comm.) 601 (CA)); *cf. Arklow Investments Ltd. v.
Maclean* [2000] 1 W.L.R. 594 (PC), where there was no such underlying relationship between the
parties. And note, as to the scope for imposing a constructive trust in such circumstances, *Banner
Homes Group Plc v. Luff Developments Ltd.* [2000] Ch. 372 (CA).

sold on dissolution, thereby precluding the partners from its further exploitation.[245]

I.   INCOME AND LIABILITIES DERIVED FROM PREVIOUS BUSINESS[246]

10–56 Where a new partner is admitted to an existing firm, the agreement should properly establish, on the one hand, his entitlement (if any) to share in profits derived from: (i) bills delivered prior to the date of his admission and (ii) work in progress as at that date[247] and, on the other, his obligation to contribute towards debts or liabilities incurred prior to but outstanding at that date.[248] If the finances of the old and new firms are to be kept separate, that fact should be clearly stated. Nevertheless, in the case of a partner admitted to a solicitors' firm, the "new" firm created by the admission will, almost inevitably, be a successor practice within the meaning of Appendix 1 to the current Solicitors' Indemnity Insurance Rules.[249]

A clause of the type under consideration will not, of itself, confer any additional rights on or against third parties,[250] and is unlikely to be of any relevance when considering the application of stamp duty land tax on the acquisition of an incoming partner's share.[251]

---

[245] See *Re Keene* [1922] 2 Ch. 475; *Floydd v. Cheney* [1970] Ch. 602, 608 *per* Megarry J.; also *Trego v. Hunt* [1896] A.C. 7; *Murray v. King* [1986] F.S.R. 116 (concerning a copyright). As to the partners' rights to enforce a sale of the goodwill, see *infra*, paras 10–200 *et seq.*

[246] See the *Encyclopedia of Professional Partnerships*, Precedent 1, cl. 8.

[247] See *supra*, para. 10–48 and *infra*, para. 10–173.

[248] See generally, as to the significance of such a provision, *infra*, paras 13–26 *et seq.*, 14–48 *et seq.* *Semble*, there is no presumption, either internally or externally, that, merely because the whole business or assets of the existing firm become assets of the new firm, the former's liabilities are assumed by the latter: see *Creasey v. Breachwood Motors Ltd.* [1992] B.C.C. 638 (albeit overruled, as to the main part of the decision, by *Ord v. Belhaven Pubs Ltd.* [1998] 2 B.C.L.C. 447); also *HF Pension Trustees Ltd. v. Ellison* [1999] Lloyd's Rep. PN 489; *cf. Carter v. Freeman Group Plc* [2008] EWHC 3576 (QB) (Lawtel 26/8/08), where a partnership business had been transferred to a company. Note that in *Hammonds (A Firm) v. Danilunas* [2009] EWHC 216 (Ch) (Lawtel 18/2/09), Warren J. expressly declined to decide this issue: see *ibid.* at [117]. In the course of his judgment in *Creasey v. Breachwood Motors Ltd.*, *supra*, Richard Southwell Q.C. (sitting as a deputy judge of the Queen's Bench Division) reviewed a number of Scots authorities and held that the principles established thereby were not applicable under English law: see further, as to the position in Scotland, *Miller v. MacLeod*, 1973 S.C. 172; *Ocra (Isle of Man) Ltd. v. Anite Scotland Ltd.* 2003 S.L.T. 1232 (OH). Note, however, that, as between the partners, there *is* a presumption that liabilities are taken over on a partner's *retirement*: see *infra*, para. 10–248. It should also be noted in this context that it was held in *Robertson v. Brent* [1972] N.Z.L.R. 406 that work in progress does not exist as an asset of a continuing firm, at least in the case of a solicitor's practice, although the current editor doubts the correctness of the decision (these doubts being shared by the court in *Bennett v. Wallace* 1998 S.C. 457, 462D and *Browell v. Goodyear, The Times*, October 24, 2000). There is no doubt that work in progress exists as an asset on a *dissolution: Browell v. Goodyear*, *supra*. See further, *infra*, para. 10–158, n. 739.

[249] See the article "Lateral Thinking" at (2005) 102 L.S.Gaz., March 24, p. 19.

[250] See, in particular, the Partnership Act 1890, s.17(1), *infra*, para. 13–23. In practice, an express assignment of book debts under the Law of Property Act 1925, s.136 is rare: see *infra*, para. 10–245.

[251] See *infra*, paras 38–12 *et seq.*

Warranty regarding existing debts

Where an incoming partner agrees to undertake liability for existing debts, he should prudently require the other partners to warrant that they have made full disclosure of the nature and amount of those debts.   **10–57**

In *Walker v. Broadhurst*[252] the incoming partner secured an effective *guarantee* from the father of one of the other partners that the debts did not exceed a stated sum, but this is most unusual.

J.   CAPITAL[253]

It is obviously important that the agreement records the amount of capital which each partner is required to contribute and the manner in which such capital, once contributed, is to be owned.[254] If the agreement is unclear, the partners might conceivably find that their shares in capital are treated as equal, notwithstanding the fact that their contributions were unequal.[255] In some instances, it may be appropriate for partners to make a *joint* capital contribution, e.g. in the case of spouses, etc.,[256] or trustees, in which case it will be credited to a joint capital account maintained in their names.[257]   **10–58**

Capital should be stated as a sum of money

Lord Lindley observed: **10–59**

> "The capital should be expressed to be so much money; and if one of the partners is
> to contribute lands or goods instead of money, such lands or goods should have a
> value set upon them, and their value in money should be considered as his
> contribution."[258]

This elementary step will ensure that the firm's capital structure is readily identifiable from the outset.[259] Whether it remains readily identifiable depends on

---

[252] (1853) 8 Ex. 889. Lord Lindley unaccountably referred to this case when dealing with capital.

[253] See the *Encyclopedia of Professional Partnerships*, Precedent 1, cl. 7.

[254] Lord Lindley commented at this point: "It by no means follows that the partners are to be entitled to the assets in the proportions in which they contribute to the capital. Indeed, if no express declaration upon the subject is made, the prima facie inference is that all the partners are entitled to share the assets (minus the capital) equally, although they may have contributed to the capital unequally." This, in a sense, begs the real question as to how the capital itself is to be owned. The surplus assets will normally be shared in the same manner as profits: see *infra*, paras 10–79, 17–04, 19–15 *et seq*. As to the possible tax implications, see *supra*, para. 10–47, n. 217.

[255] See the Partnership Act 1890, ss.24(1) and the decision in *Popat v. Shonchhatra* [1997] 1 W.L.R. 1367, 1373, (CA). See further, *infra*, paras 17–07 *et seq*.

[256] See *Hopper v. Hopper* [2008] EWHC 228 (Ch) (Lawtel 26/2/08), noticed, *infra*, para. 17–06. Note, however, that this will not be possible in the case of a limited partnership, at least for registration purposes: see *infra*, para. 29–04.

[257] The maintenance of a joint capital account as between *all* the partners (save as between two spouses, etc., as sought to be maintained in *Hopper v. Hopper*, *supra*) would be most unusual.

[258] Lord Lindley went on, somewhat delphically, "If this be not done, the articles and accounts and the proportions in which profits and losses are to be shared will be less perspicuous and free from doubt than will otherwise be the case". It is unclear whether the profits and losses to which he refers are of an income or capital nature. If the former, the respective size of each partner's capital contribution would normally be irrelevant. See also *infra*, para. 17–01.

[259] See further, *infra*, paras 17–02 *et seq*.

the manner in which the partners subsequently conduct their affairs and, more importantly, the way in which they draw up their accounts.[260]

Capital expressed in terms of assets

10–60   Nevertheless, agreements will be encountered in which capital is treated as synonymous with the partnership assets,[261] so that the value of the firm's capital base, and thus of each partner's contribution, will constantly fluctuate. It follows that, unless the assets are revalued annually,[262] the firm's accounts will never show the true capital position as between the partners.[263] Lord Lindley also pointed out that, where this practice is adopted:

> " . . . the partner who contributes land will generally be inclined to look upon such land as his, and not as part of the common stock."

It is, however, doubted whether many partners would be swayed towards such a view.

Capital contribution in form of debts

10–61   A capital contribution may take the form of good debts owed to a partner, either to a stated value or generally. An example of the former is to be found in *Toulmin v. Copland*,[264] where a partner had agreed to contribute £40,000 of good debts owing by customers of his former firm. Those customers thereafter dealt with the new firm and, in due course, an aggregate sum in excess of £40,000 was received from them. The partner was held to have satisfied his obligation to bring in capital, even though the customers had incurred further debts due to the new firm, since a single continuous account had been maintained in respect of each customer and those payments which were not specifically appropriated to an item in the relevant account were applied to the earliest item therein, *i.e.* the debts originally brought in.

10–62   If, on the other hand, a partner merely agrees to contribute capital in the form of book debts, but not to a stated value, the size of his contribution will, in the absence of some other agreement, depend on the amount which they actually realise. This is illustrated by *Cooke v. Benbow*,[265] where a father had taken his sons into partnership and agreed to contribute all the capital, plant, and stock in trade then and usually employed by him in the business. For the purposes of an account drawn up at the commencement of the partnership, the father's book debts were discounted by 20 per cent but, in the event, almost the full value was realised. The surplus was held to form part of the father's capital and was, therefore, not distributable as profit.

Capital contribution as a condition precedent

10–63   In some cases, a partner's right to participate in profits and his other entitlements under the agreement may be made conditional on the introduction of his

---

[260] See, in particular, *infra*, para. 17–06.

[261] See, for example, *Sykes v. Land* (1984) 271 E.G. 1264. See also *infra*, para. 17–03.

[262] Quite apart from the expense, this would have adverse capital gains tax consequences: see *infra*, para. 35–14.

[263] Thus, calculation of interest on capital will be impossible: see *infra*, para. 10–67.

[264] (1834) 2 Cl. & F. 681 and (1838) 7 Cl. & F. 349.

[265] (1865) 3 De G.J. & S. 1. See also *Binney v. Mutrie* (1886) 12 App.Cas. 160.

capital contribution, *i.e.* that contribution will be treated as a condition precedent.[266] However, in practice this is rare. Thus, in *Kemble v. Mills*,[267] A and B had agreed to become partners, on terms that A would bring in £2,000 and do certain things, and B would bring in £5,000. It was held that A could bring an action in respect of B's failure to bring in the £5,000, even though he did not prove that he had brought in the £2,000 or that those things had been done.

Additional capital

A partner cannot normally be required to contribute additional capital, even if the continued existence of the firm depends upon it.[268] Accordingly, it may in some cases be necessary to provide a mechanism whereby a binding decision to increase the partnership capital can be taken, thus forcing each partner to bring in additional sums. In the case of larger firms, clauses providing for such a decision to be taken on a majority vote are now becoming fairly commonplace.   **10–64**

Variable and graduated contributions

It is not uncommon to encounter agreements under which the size of each partner's capital contribution is directly related to the size of his profit share so that, as the latter varies, so does his contribution. Such an arrangement will frequently form part of any "points" or "lockstep" system for profit-sharing,[269] designed to enable incoming partners to fund their contributions out of profits over a set period. Under such a scheme, a partner whose profit share is reduced will naturally receive a partial return of his capital, even though the firm's capital base will remain unchanged.   **10–65**

Borrowed capital

It is common for partners to borrow from outside sources in order to fund their capital contributions. Whilst this will normally involve personal borrowing by each partner and will have no direct implications for the firm or any of the other   **10–66**

---

[266] In this connection, Lord Lindley referred to the rules laid down in the "well-known" note to *Pordage v. Cole* (1669) 1 Wms.Saund. 320a. Those rules are by no means easy to understand, but are set out in full for the convenience of the reader: "1. If a day be appointed for payment of money, or part of it, or for doing any other act, and the day is to happen, or may happen, before the thing which is the consideration of the money, or other act, is to be performed, an action may be brought for the money, or for not doing such other act before performance; for it appears that the party relied upon his remedy, and did not intend to make the performance a condition precedent; and so it is where no time is fixed for performance of that which is the consideration of the money or other act. 2. When a day is appointed for the payment of money, etc., and the day is to happen after the thing which is the consideration of the money, etc., is to be performed, no action can be maintained for the money, etc., before performance. 3. Where a covenant goes only to part of the consideration on both sides, and a breach of such covenant may be paid for in damages it is an independent covenant, and an action may be maintained for a breach of the covenant on the part of the defendant, without averring performance in the declaration. 4. But where the mutual covenants go to the whole consideration on both sides, they are mutual conditions, and the performance must be averred. 5. Where two acts are to be done at the same time, as where A covenants to convey an estate to B on such a day, and in consideration thereof B covenants to pay a sum of money on the same day, neither can maintain an action without showing performance of, or an offer to perform, his part, thought it is not certain which of them is obliged to do the first act; and this particularly applies to all cases of sale."

[267] (1841) 9 Dow. 446. *cf. Marsden v. Moore* (1859) 4 H. & N. 500. See also *Stavers v. Curling* (1836) 3 Bing. N.C. 355.

[268] See *infra*, para. 17–10.

[269] See *infra*, para. 10–80.

partners,[270] the lender will, in practice, often require an undertaking from the firm[271] that any repayment of capital[272] will be made directly to the lender, at least up to the amount of the loan then outstanding. The undertaking may also, depending on its terms, extend to other sums due to a partner on his retirement, etc. The existence of such undertakings will, in some cases, be reflected in the partnership agreement, by way of a qualification to the outgoing partner's financial entitlement.[273]

Interest on capital

10–67   If interest on capital is to be paid, this must be provided for in the agreement.[274] In general, such interest amounts to no more than an allocation of profits and, for that reason, should in the current editor's view properly be included in the clause dealing with profit-sharing,[275] although it is rare to see this in practice. A provision for interest to be paid *irrespective* of the profitability of the firm is unusual.

The importance of ensuring that each partner's capital contribution is stated in cash terms has already been noted.[276] It goes without saying that interest cannot be computed by reference to an indeterminate sum of capital.[277]

Interest on capital should normally be made payable *after* interest on advances.[278]

K.   BANKERS OF THE PARTNERSHIP[279]

10–68   It is usual for the agreement to name the bank[280] (and, where relevant, the particular branch) at which the firm will maintain its account(s), even though that decision could quite properly be taken at a subsequent date.[281] In the case of a large partnership with branch offices nationwide, a number of different banks or branches may be involved; these may conveniently be incorporated in a schedule. Some professions require members to maintain separate client accounts, and this fact will usually be reflected in the agreement.[282]

---

[270] See *infra*, paras 12–49, 13–19.

[271] *i.e.* all the partners at the time the undertaking is given. It is not unusual to find that the undertaking has not been updated to reflect subsequent changes in the firm, but this tends not to cause any difficulties in practice.

[272] This may include a repayment capital whilst the partnership continues, *e.g.* on a capital restructuring, as well as on a partner's departure from the firm.

[273] See *infra*, para. 10–179.

[274] See the Partnership Act 1890, s.24(4), *infra*, para. 17–12.

[275] See the *Encyclopedia of Professional Partnerships*, Precedent 1, cl. 11(3).

[276] See *supra*, para. 10–59.

[277] Thus, undrawn profits left in the firm and used as a form of circulating capital should not be credited to the partners' capital accounts (a practice which has become increasingly common) unless it is intended thereby to increase the capital base of the firm: see further, *infra*, paras 17–05, 17–06.

[278] *i.e.* effectively reflecting the precedence accorded to interest on advances by the Partnership Act 1890, s.24(3).

[279] See the *Encyclopedia of Professional Partnerships*, Precedent 1, cl. 6.

[280] Or building society.

[281] *e.g.* pursuant to an express power in the agreement or by a majority decision under the Partnership Act 1890, s.24(8), *infra*, paras 15–04 *et seq*.

[282] *e.g.* accountants, architects, solicitors, and surveyors. See, further, the *Encyclopedia of Professional Partnerships*.

A clause requiring all partnership moneys not required for current expenses to be paid into the appropriate bank account is traditionally included.[283]

Cheque signing

It is important to establish each partner's *express* authority to draw cheques on the partnership account[284]: thus, the agreement should state whether cheques drawn in the firm name require the signatures of one, two or more partners or, where appropriate, the signatures of one partner and a designated employee.[285] The bank mandate should naturally reflect the terms so agreed. If the mandate permits any one partner to sign cheques and there is no restriction in the agreement, each partner will have authority to issue cheques *vis-à-vis* both the bank and his co-partners.[286]   **10–69**

If the agreement declares that the signature of one partner is sufficient, this will amount to a binding agreement between the partners to arrange and thereafter maintain a continuing mandate in those terms.[287]

Other forms of transfer

Whilst most agreements scrupulously provide for the signing of cheques by partners, it is rare to find any clause restricting their authority to initiate transfers between accounts and other similar transactions. This does, however, merit consideration in some cases.[288]   **10–70**

L.   BOOKS AND ACCOUNTS[289]

It is usual to include in the agreement provisions governing both the maintenance of the partnership books and the preparation of accounts, either annually or on a   **10–71**

---

[283] Where client accounts are maintained, a similar clause relating to clients' money is also generally included.

[284] See *infra*, para. 12–51.

[285] Where the firm maintains both an office and clients' account, different cheque signing arrangements may be made for each. Moreover, account may have to be taken of the relevant professional rules: see, for example, the Solicitors' Accounts Rules 1998, r. 23(1) as amended. For an illustration of the dangers which can be presented by allowing a single partner to sign cheques on a client account, see *Lipkin Gorman v. Karpnale Ltd.* [1991] 2 A.C. 548.

[286] Since this is, as regards the bank, a case of *express* authority, the firm will be bound even if the cheque is issued otherwise than in the ordinary course of business. However, the position will prima facie be different as between the partners.

[287] Thus, absent an express power to amend the agreement (see *supra*, para. 10–13), it may not technically be possible to revoke a partner's authority to sign cheques, despite clear evidence of abuse. If the other partners change the mandate unilaterally, a court would be unlikely to assist the miscreant partner, either by the grant of injunctive relief or by ordering a dissolution under the Partnership Act 1890, s.35, *infra*, para. A1–36. The problem is, in any event, likely to be a short-term one: abuse of a partner's cheque-signing authority is likely to lead to his expulsion under an express power in the agreement or, failing that, an application for dissolution on the part of the other partners.

[288] See the *Encyclopedia of Professional Partnerships*, Precedent 8, cl. 6(6). Also *infra*, para. 12–51.

[289] See *ibid.* Precedent 1, cll. 9, 10.

more frequent basis.[290] Lord Lindley explained the purpose lying behind such clauses in this way:

> "The object of taking partnership accounts is twofold, viz. (1) To show how the firm stands as regards strangers; and (2) To show how each partner stands towards the firm.[291] The accounts, therefore, which the articles should require to be taken, should be such as will accomplish this twofold object. The articles should consequently provide, not only for the keeping of proper books of account, and for the due entry therein of all receipts and payments, but also for the making up yearly of a general account, showing the then assets and liabilities of the firm, and what is due to each partner in respect of his capital[292] and share of profits, or what is due from him to the firm, as the case may be."

It should be noted that, in the case of certain corporate partnerships, there is now a *statutory* obligation to prepare annual accounts just as if the firm were a company.[293]

Maintenance and custody of books

10-72   As well as requiring the partners to maintain the partnership books, the agreement should also provide where those books are to be kept and record any limitations on the partners' rights of access thereto. The position will otherwise be governed by the Partnership Act 1890.[294] Any unauthorised attempt by a partner to remove the books from the place where they are required to be kept will be restrained by the court.[295] It follows that if a partner is to be permitted to have temporary custody of the books, this must be clearly stated.[296]

Preparation of annual (or other) accounts

10-73   The normal form of clause governing the preparation of partnership accounts will specify: (a) the date (or dates) up to which such accounts are to be prepared[297]; (b) by whom[298]; and (c) on what accounting basis, *e.g.* whether goodwill is to be valued, whether losses of capital are to be recouped, etc. Work in progress is now of less importance since it is now a mandatory requirement that a firm's accounts should recognise income as it arises,[299] even if its internal

---

[290] The advent of computerisation has greatly facilitated the preparation of so-called "interim" and "management" accounts, which may be prepared on a quarterly, or even monthly, basis.

[291] To this list should now, perhaps, be added a third object, namely for the purposes of enabling the partners to prepare the partnership return: see *infra*, paras 34–17, 34–18.

[292] See *supra*, paras 10–58 *et seq.* and *infra*, paras 17–02 *et seq.*

[293] See the Partnerships (Accounts) Regulations 2008 (SI 2008/569), regs 3(1), 4(1)(a). See further, *infra*, para. 22–08.

[294] *ibid.* s.24(9), *infra*, para. 22–10.

[295] See *Taylor v. Davis* (1842) 3 Beav. 388, note; *Greatrex v. Greatrex* (1847) 1 De G. & Sm. 692.

[296] See *infra*, para. 22–15.

[297] The agreement usually establishes the date up to which the firm will prepare its annual accounts and the manner in which a decision to alter that date can be taken. The date(s) up to which interim accounts are to be prepared are of less significance.

[298] Annual accounts will generally be prepared by the partnership accountants and, where necessary, audited by them. On the other hand, interim accounts will in all probability be prepared internally.

[299] Both in order to ensure compliance with FRS5/UITF 40 (see *infra*, para. 21–04) and when computing the firm's profits for income tax purposes (see *infra*, para. 34–22).

accounts do not.[300] However it is treated internally, the status of work in progress as an asset of the partnership is unlikely to be affected.[301] It may also be desirable to record any unusual expenses which are to be borne by the firm, whether or not these will be deductible against profits.[302]

The agreement should also record the manner in which the annual accounts are to be approved, whether by a majority vote or otherwise,[303] and oblige the partners to sign the accounts once approved.[303a] In the case of a large firm, the senior or managing partner (or some other partner(s) designated for the purpose) may be authorised to sign the accounts on the other partners' behalf.[304] Where there is a procedure enabling partners to object to the contents of the accounts, it would seem that a general objection may be sufficient, although much will depend on the precise terms of the agreement.[305]

It must be remembered that the accounts may cover a period during which an **10–74** outgoing partner was a member of the firm. For such a partner to be bound by accounts approved by the continuing partners, this should be expressly stated in the agreement. If, as is often the case, the agreement is unclear on the point, it will be necessary to determine whether, on its true construction, this is the effect, since there will be little or no scope for implying a term to resolve the issue.[306] In *Hammonds (A Firm) v. Jones*[307] it was held that, whilst the agreement in question gave an outgoing partner the ability to object to items in the relevant set of accounts, those objections would, in the first instance, be referred to the partnership board and, if its determination was not accepted by the outgoing partner, would be referred to a meeting of the *continuing* partners for final determination. It followed that the outgoing partners in dispute with the continuing partners did not have the right to refer their objections to the court for final determination. It is submitted that a court would be reluctant to find, as a matter of implication, that an outgoing partner has been deprived of his right to make

---

[300] Thus, is perfectly permissible to draw up management accounts which ignore the value of work in progress and to use these when deciding the manner of division of the profits or the entitlement of an outgoing partner.

[301] See *Bennett v. Wallace* 1998 S.C. 457; *Browell v. Goodyear, The Times*, October 24, 2000. Note also, in this context, *Montgomery v. Cameron & Greig* [2007] CSOH 63 (OH), considered *infra*, para. 10–174.

[302] Lord Lindley gave the following examples of unusual allowances: "an allowance for treating customers, for management, for rent, maintenance of servants, etc." It would seem that he must have been contemplating the payment of such allowances to partners, rather than to third parties. With the exception of rent, such allowances are unlikely to be deductible by the firm: see *MacKinlay v. Arthur Young McClelland Moores & Co.* [1990] 2 A.C. 239 and *infra*, para. 34–25. In such a case, they are better expressed as a preferential profit share: see *infra*, para. 10–80.

[303] See further, *infra*, para. 10–102.

[303a] If the argument provides that only partners who sign are bound and some do not, the accounts will not bind anyone: *Drake v. Harvey* [2010] EWHC 1446 (Ch) (Lawtel 17/6/10) at [30] *per* Mann J.

[304] Note that, historically, HMRC did not, as a general rule, insist on all partners signing the firm's annual accounts, although practice varied as between inspectors of taxes. This point is of reduced importance since the introduction of self assessment, since accounts are not generally submitted, save where the firm's turnover exceeds £15m.

[305] See *Purewall v. Purewall* [2006] CSOH 182 (OH). The argument that the objections should be formulated in much the same way as would apply on the Scottish equivalent of taking of an account was rejected by the court.

[306] *Hammonds (A Firm) v. Danilunas* [2009] EWHC 216 (Ch) (Lawtel 18/2/08) at [73] *per* Warren J. This term was not pursued on the appeal: see the next footnote.

[307] *The Times*, January 4, 2010, on appeal from *Hammonds v. Danilunas, supra*.

any objection to the contents of the accounts,[308] although the position would clearly be otherwise if the accounts will not affect his entitlement.[309]

Reopening agreed accounts

10–75   It is obviously desirable that, once the annual accounts have been approved and signed by the partners, they should be regarded as conclusive: this is normally provided for in the agreement, subject to the proviso that each partner is entitled to have obvious or "manifest" errors corrected within a set period. However, such provisions do not provide absolute finality, as Lord Lindley explained:

> "A provision to this effect is extremely useful, and should never be omitted[310]; but, however stringently it may be drawn, no account will be binding on any partner who may have been induced to sign it by false and fraudulent representations, or in ignorance of material circumstances dishonourably concealed from him by his co-partners.[311] Where, however, all parties act *bona fide*, such clauses are operative; but the usual provision as to manifest errors applies only to errors in figures and obvious blunders, not to errors in judgment, *e.g.* in treating as good debts which ultimately turn out to be bad, or in omitting losses not known to have occurred.[312] All errors are manifest when discovered; but such clauses as those referred to here are intended to be confined to oversights and blunders so obvious as to admit of no difference of opinion."[313]

This explanation was cited with approval by Lord Reed in *Montgomery v. Cameron & Greig*,[314] when considering certain revised accounts in circumstances where it was unclear to what extent they had been prepared in accordance with the agreement and/or approved.

The circumstances in which a settled account can be re-opened in the absence of such a provision are considered in greater detail hereafter.[315]

Agreed accounts not binding for all purposes

10–76   Although an account, once signed and approved, may be binding on the partners, it does not follow that it will be binding for all purposes. Thus, unless the agreement provides otherwise,[316] annual accounts prepared for the purposes of calculating the firm's divisible profits may be of no relevance when calculating

---

[308] In the previous edition, the current editor cited the decision in *Wylie v. Corrigan* 1999 S.C. 97 (2nd Div.) in support of this proposition (see, in particular, *ibid.* p. 103C), but Warren J. in *Hammonds (A Firm) v. Danilunas*, *supra*, at [70] found it if no assistance on the point. See also, in this context, *ibid.* at [45] and, on the appeal (*sub nom. Hammonds (A Firm) v. Jones*) [2009] EWCA Civ 1400 (Lawtel 21/12/09) at [26].

[309] See further, *infra*, paras 10–76, 10–162 *et seq.*

[310] See *London Financial Ass. v. Kelk* (1834) 26 Ch.D. 107, 151 *per* Bacon V.-C.

[311] See *Oldaker v. Lavender* (1833) 6 Sim. 239; *Blisset v. Daniel* (1853) 10 Hare 493.

[312] See *Ex p. Barber* (1870) L.R. 5 Ch.App. 687; also *Laing v. Campbell* (1865) 36 Beav. 3 (where there was no agreement).

[313] The last sentence of this passage was cited with approval, albeit in a different context, by Potter J. in *Healds Foods Ltd. v. Hyde Dairies Ltd.*, December 1, 1994 (unreported but affirmed on December 6, 1996); see also *Dixons Group plc v. Murrey-Oboynski*, 86 B.L.R. 16; *Conoco U.K. Ltd. v. Phillips Petroleum Co. (U.K.) Ltd.* [1996] C.I.L.L. 1204.

[314] [2007] CSOH 63 (OH) at [28].

[315] See *infra*, paras 23–111 *et seq.*

[316] See *Coventry v. Barclay* (1864) 3 De G.J. & S. 320; *Ex p. Barber* (1870) L.R. 5 Ch.App. 687; also *infra*, para. 10–164.

the financial entitlement of an outgoing partner.[317] In particular, the fact that goodwill[318] or work in progress[319] has been treated as valueless in such accounts or that other assets have consistently appeared therein at their original or depreciated book value[320] will not, of itself, necessarily justify the adoption of those accounting practices on the death, retirement or expulsion of a partner; *a fortiori* in the case of a general dissolution.[321] The recent decisions in *Gadd v. Gadd*,[322] *Champion and Workman*[323] and *Drake v. Harvey*[323a] illustrate the differing approaches which may be adopted in this area.

Equally, the fact that an asset is included in the firm's accounts is not necessarily conclusive of its status as a partnership asset.[324]

Failure to sign accounts

Bona fide accounts drawn up on the usual basis may be binding on a partner   **10–77** even if he has not signed them,[325] provided that he has seen a copy and has not suggested that they are erroneous.[326]

M.   PROFITS AND LOSSES[327]

The agreement should always record the manner in which profits and losses are   **10–78** to be shared[328]: if it fails to do so, and no other agreement or understanding can be proved, the Partnership Act 1890 will ensure that all profits and losses are

---

[317] *Blisset v. Daniel* (1853) 10 Hare 493. *cf. Coventry v. Barclay, supra; Montgomery v. Cameron & Greig* [2007] CSOH 63.

[318] *Wade v. Jenkins* (1860) 2 Giff. 509. *cf. Steuart v. Gladstone* (1878) 10 Ch.D. 626; *Hunter v. Dowling* [1895] 2 Ch. 223, *infra*, para. 10–166.

[319] *Bennett v. Wallace*, 1998 S.C. 457 (2nd Div.), *infra*, para. 10–173. But note that a firm's annual accounts should now properly *include* income attributable to work in progress as it arises: see *supra*, para. 10–73.

[320] *Cruickshank v. Sutherland* (1922) 92 L.J.Ch. 136; *Noble v. Noble* 1965 S.L.T. 415, Ct of Sess. and 1983 S.L.T. 339 (IH); *Shaw v. Shaw*, 1968 S.L.T. (Notes) 94; *Clark v. Watson* 1982 S.L.T. 450 (OH); *Bennett v. Wallace, supra; Wilson v. Dunbar* 1988 S.L.T. 93 (OH); *cf. Thom's Executrix v. Russel & Aitken* 1983 S.L.T. 335 (OH); *Re White* [2001] Ch. 393 (CA). See further, *infra*, paras 10–162 *et seq*.

[321] Any adjustments which have to be made in the event of a dissolution will inevitably distort the position as it appears in the accounts: see *infra*, paras 25–44 *et seq*.

[322] [2002] 08 E.G. 160, noticed *infra*, paras 10–162, 10–167.

[323] June 20, 2001 (Lawtel 22/8/01), noticed *infra*, para. 10–162.

[323a] [2010] EWHC 1446 (Ch) (Lawtel 17/6/10).

[324] *Barton v. Morris* [1985] 1 W.L.R. 1257; also *Mehra v. Shah*, August 1, 2003 (Lawtel 5/8/03) at [37], [38] *per* Sonia Proudman Q.C., sitting as a deputy judge of the Chancery Division (albeit that this evidence was not pivotal on the appeal at [2004] EWCA Civ 632 at [27] (Lawtel 20/5/2004)); *Amin v. Amin* [2009] EWHC 3356 (Ch) (Lawtel 5/1/10). And note *Abbott v. Price* [2003] EWHC 2760 (Ch) at [89] (Lawtel 26/11/03); See further, *infra*, paras 18–56 *et seq*.

[325] Assuming, that is, that he is required to sign them: see *supra*, para. 10–73.

[326] *Coventry v. Barclay* (1864) 3 De G.J. & S. 320, 328 *per* Lord Westbury. See also *Ex p. Barber* (1870) L.R. 5 Ch.App. 687; *Hunter v. Dowling* [1893] 1 Ch. 391 (affirmed [1893] 3 Ch. 212). See also *infra*, para. 10–164.

[327] See the *Encyclopedia of Professional Partnerships*, Precedent 1, cl. 11.

[328] Unaccountably, Lord Lindley did not include this among the "usual" clauses to be found in a partnership agreement.

shared equally.[329] Even where the partners are content with the position under the Act, it is usual to declare that the sharing ratios are equal.

Capital and income profits and losses

10–79   Profits and losses may be of a capital or income nature.[330] Most firms do not seek to apply different sharing ratios to each class, although it is prudent to establish the general application of the agreed shares by referring *specifically* to capital profits and losses. However, in some cases the partners may wish to ensure that the greater part, if not the whole, of any capital profit or loss will accrue to a particular partner or group of partners.[331] In such a case, the chosen capital profit sharing ratios will be applied when dividing the surplus assets on a dissolution[332] or, where relevant, on a partner leaving the firm.[333]

Profit sharing arrangements

10–80   Whilst a partner might, typically, expect to be allocated an initial share of profits which will remain unchanged as long as the partnership continues,[334] more complex arrangements are now commonplace, particularly in the professional sphere. A combination of two or more of the following sharing arrangements are, in practice, frequently encountered:

    (a)   preferential "salaries" expressed as a first charge on profits[335];

    (b)   sharing ratios varying according to the level of the firm's profits, *i.e.* where differing ratios are applied to each tranche of profits[336];

    (c)   sharing ratios varying according to each partner's seniority within the firm[337];

    (d)   sharing ratios directly related to capital contributions[338];

---

[329] *ibid.* s.24(1); *Popat v. Shonchhatra* [1997] 1 W.L.R. 1367 (CA). See further, *infra*, paras 19–15 *et seq.*, 20–03 *et seq.*

[330] Capital profits or losses represent the amount by which the value (or net sale proceeds) of the partnership assets exceed or fall short of their book value: see *infra*, para. 17–04. This is not necessarily the same thing as a loss of part of the firm's *fixed* capital, which may have to be made good before any profits are divided: see *infra*, para. 21–03.

[331] See *infra*, paras 35–05, 35–06 n. 24, 36–20 *et seq.*

[332] Partnership Act 1890, s.44(b) *infra*, paras 25–45 *et seq.*

[333] See *infra*, paras 10–157 *et seq.*

[334] Barring, of course any change in the composition of the firm, which will, in any event, technically result in the creation of a new partnership: see *supra*, paras 3–01 *et seq.*

[335] Such a salary may be paid for a number of reasons, *e.g.* where the firm occupies premises owned by a partner, it may represent a payment in lieu of rent. *cf.* the position of a salaried partner *infra*, para. 10–86. See further, as to the true status of a partner's salary as a share of profits, *MacKinlay v. Arthur Young McClelland Moores & Co.* [1990] 2 A.C. 239, 249A–C (HL). Note that in *Chartered Accountants' Firm v. Braisby* [2005] S.T.C. (SCD) 389, an agreed adjustment to an outgoing partner's profit share unusually caused the continuing partners' "salaries" to be of a negative amount. It was held that this did not matter, since such salaries only represent a method of arriving at the allocation of profits.

[336] In such cases, there may well be a residual sharing ratio applied to all profits over a certain figure. This may indicate the manner in which losses are to be shared: but see *infra*, para. 10–85.

[337] See *infra*, para. 10–81.

[338] The ownership of capital may itself be tied to a "points" or "lockstep" system (see *infra*, para. 10–81), so that alterations in the partners' profits shares will follow automatically.

(e) incentive or "merit" profit pools, consisting of a set proportion of the firm's profits distributable at the discretion of a particular partner or committee of partners[339];

(f) "target" based sharing ratios, which are subject to reduction if the target is not met; and

(g) *ad hoc* sharing ratios agreed shortly after the year end.[340]

The above arrangements will naturally require specific adjustment if the firm is to comprise one or more "part-time" partners.[341]

The payment of interest on capital[342] and special allowances to partners[343] may also form part of the overall profit sharing structure, along with the allocation of a particular source of income received by the firm.[344]

There is no objection in principle to a partner being allocated a nominal profit share or to a partner waiving his entitlement on an occasional or more permanent basis.[345]

Lockstep and similar arrangements

The traditional "lockstep" consisted of a fairly rigid "points" or "ladder" **10–81** system under which each partner acquired an ever increasing share year on year until he reached a "plateau", on which he would remain until he neared retirement age, when his share would start to decrease. Two factors have now impacted on this traditional approach. The first is a recognition that this approach is too rigid and rewards seniority and not performance. As a result, a modified form of lockstep has developed which enables partners to be moved up and down according to their performance and which, moreover, halts partners at particular stages of the lockstep (often referred to as "gateways") through which they cannot pass until their performance is judged to have reached a particular level. There may also be a discretion to award additional points (often styled "super-points") on a temporary basis to recognise conspicuous performance, which may even take partners above the plateau. As a result, few pure lockstep arrangements now remain.

The second factor is the advent of Employment Equality (Age) Regulations 2006,[346] which renders unlawful any direct or indirect attempt to discriminate against partners on the grounds of their age.[347] It will be immediately apparent

---

[339] See *infra*, para. 10–82.

[340] It must be appreciated that, if no agreement is reached, the profits will prima facie be shared equally: Partnership Act 1890, s.24(1). This may constitute an incentive to some partners so to conduct themselves that agreement is impossible. *Quaere*, would this involve a breach of the duty of good faith? Even if it would, surely the court could not dispense with those partners' agreement.

[341] See further, *infra*, para. 10–93.

[342] See *supra*, para. 10–67.

[343] See *infra*, paras 20–43, 34–25.

[344] In medical partnerships, it may be provided that certain payments received under the National Health Service will be allocated to a particular partner; alternatively, it may be agreed that a particular source of income will not be accounted for by the recipient partners: see the *Encyclopedia of Professional Partnerships*, Precedent 8, cll. 12, 13.

[345] In *Hodson v. Hodson* [2010] P.N.L.R. 8 (CA), one partner was allocated a 1% share but consistently chose not to take it. She was still held to be a partner.

[346] SI 2006/1031. See further *supra*, para. 8–22 *et seq.* As from October 2010, it is expected that these regulations will be replaced by the consolidating and amending Equality Act 2010.

[347] *ibid.* regs. 3, 17, noticed *supra*, para. 8–22 *et seq.* As to the equivalent provisions in the Equality Act 2010, see ss.5, 13, 19, 44.

that the traditional form of lockstep will tend to favour those partners with longer service who will, inevitably, be older, thus indirectly discriminating against younger partners.[348] Nevertheless, the Regulations permit the retention of any arrangement under which benefits are awarded to partners based on the length of their service with the firm,[349] provided that the length of service requirement is less than 5 years[350] or, if it is longer, that it can reasonably be said to fulfil a business need *vis-à-vis* the firm.[351] This exemption should enable the retention of a lockstep in most cases, but it should not simply be assumed that such retention can be justified as a matter of routine. Certainly it will be difficult, if not impossible, to justify any automatic decrease in a partner's lockstep position as he nears retirement age, particularly given that the retention of a compulsory retirement age must itself be justified under a more stringent test.[352]

It is because of these twin factors that many firms have moved onto a basis for profit sharing that is wholly performance or merit based.

Discretionary profit sharing

10–82   This device is particularly in vogue in mid- to large-sized firms and is often administered by a committee elected for the purpose.[353] The process will involve judging each partner's performance against a number of set criteria and will usually (but not always) go hand in hand with a structured appraisal process. The ultimate decision as to each partner's discretionary share may fall to be decided by a partner vote or there may be some form of appeal system, either to a different committee or to the partners. Although potentially divisive, the current editor has encountered relatively few problems in practice, save where outgoing partners are allocated a minimal share to reflect their decision to leave rather than their performance during the relevant period.[354] It will be a matter of construction whether a partner can properly be allocated a nil performance share.

Where the decision is to be taken at the discretion or absolute discretion of the nominated partner(s)/committee, it may in practice be difficult to challenge the exercise of that discretion, absent bad faith[355] and, perhaps, provided that the discretion is exercised rationally and not arbitrarily.[356]

---

[348] *ibid.* reg. 3(1)(b). As to the equivalent provisions in the Equality Act 2010, see s.19.

[349] Such service may also encompass service *qua* employee or, more doubtfully, as a partner in a predecessor firm: *ibid.* reg. 32(3), (4). *Semble ibid.* reg. 32(5) does not apply to partners who were not formerly employees. As to the equivalent provisions in the Equality Act 2010, see Sched. 9, Pt 2, para. 10(3), (6).

[350] *ibid.* reg. 32(1), (2). Thus, a lockstep which runs over a 5-year period will be permissible without more. As to the equivalent provisions in the Equality Act 2010, see Sched. 9, Pt 2, para. 10(1), (2).

[351] *ibid.* reg. 32(2). As to the equivalent provision in the Equality Act 2010, see Sched. 9, Pt 2, para. 10(2). See further *supra*, para. 8–25.

[352] *i.e.* as a proportionate means of achieving a legitimate aim, under *ibid.* reg. 3(1): see *infra*, para. 10–112. As to the equivalent provision in the Equality Act 2010, see s.13(2).

[353] Formerly often known as "the three wise men": this terminology is appears to have fallen into disuse.

[354] If such a partner's decision is to be taken into account, this should be made clear in the performance criteria.

[355] See, generally, *Keen v. Commerzbank AG* [2007] I.C.R. 623; *McCarthy v. McCarthy & Stone plc* [2008] 1 All E.R. 221, both cases concerning employees.

[356] See, analogous examples in the case of contracts of employment, *Horkulak v. Cantor Fitzgerald International* [2005] I.C.R. 402 (CA); *Rutherford v. Seymour Pierce Ltd.* [2010] I.R.L.R. 606; note also *Lymington Marina Ltd. v. Macnamara* [2007] 2 All E.R. (Comm) 825 (CA), albeit concerning a licence agreement. It is not considered that the cases regarding incidental benefits or disadvantages noted *infra*, para. 16–09 are likely to be of relevance in this context.

Power to reduce profit share

Some agreements provide for a notional deduction to be made from the profit **10–83** share of a partner who is incapacitated for more than a certain period, that deduction being shared between the other partners as a recompense for the additional workload which they are forced to shoulder. It would seem that a disabled partner will not, in general, have to be exempted from the effect of such provisions by way of an adjustment under the Disability Discrimination Act 1995.[357] More common, at least in the professions, is a provision entitling the other partners to employ a locum, initially at the firm's expense but, if the partner's incapacity is prolonged, subsequently at his expense.[358] Equally, where the agreement contains a power to place partners on "garden leave", it may also authorise a reduction in the suspended partner's profit share, although this is relatively unusual.[359]

Applicability of profit sharing arrangements following a dissolution

As will be seen hereafter, the Court of Appeal in *Hopper v. Hopper*[360] assumed **10–84** that the profit sharing arrangements applicable whilst the partnership was continuing also apply following a dissolution, at least where all the partners have agreed to carry on the business pursuant to section 38 of the Partnership Act 1890,[361] and held that, in such a case, section 42[362] will not apply, but the current editor has some concerns as to the correctness of this decision.[363] What is undeniable is that the agreed profit shares will be relevant when determining the ultimate division of the surplus assets under section 44,[364] provided that, as a matter of construction, they are capable of being applied in such circumstances.[365]

Losses

The agreement may provide that losses (whether of an income or capital **10–85** nature) are to be shared in a different way to profits. On the other hand, if the agreement merely establishes the proportions in which profits are to be shared but does not mention losses, it will be inferred, in the absence of any evidence indicating a contrary intention, that losses are to be borne in the same proportions.[366] This can lead to unforeseen difficulties where the profit shares are not fixed but vary according to the level of profits or where some partners enjoy a preferential or discretionary profit entitlement; if the court is not prepared to infer

---

[357] *O'Hanlon v. Commissioners of HM Revenue & Customs* [2007] I.C.R. 1359 (CA), an employment case. As to adjustments under the 1995 Act, see *ibid.* s.6B, as added by the Disability Discrimination Act 1995 (Amendment) Regulations 2003 (SI 2003/1673), reg. 6. The position should be the same under the equivalent provisions of the Equality Act 2010 (i.e. ss.20, 44(7)), when they come into force. See further, *supra*, para. 8–19.

[358] See the *Encyclopedia of Professional Partnerships*, Precedent 8, cl. 19.

[359] See *infra*, para. 10–146.

[360] [2008] EWCA Civ. 1417 (Lawtel 12/12/08) at [47]. See also *Popat v. Shonchhatra* [1997] 1 W.L.R. 1367, 1374 (CA), as regards the size of the partners' profit shares prior to and following a dissolution.

[361] See *infra*, paras 13–62 *et seq.*

[362] See *infra*, paras 25–24 *et seq.*

[363] See *infra*, paras 13–70, 25–22, 25–25.

[364] See *infra*, para. 25–45 *et seq.*

[365] See *infra*, para. 25–48.

[366] See *Re Albion Life Assurance Society* (1880) 16 Ch.D. 83.

that losses should be borne in the same way, it may have no alternative but to hold the partners liable in equal shares.[367] Accordingly, it is, in such cases, essential that the agreement deals specifically with the treatment of losses.

"Salaried" and "fixed share" partners

10–86   The remuneration of a salaried or fixed share partner[368] will normally be expressed as a fixed share of profits or merely as a "salary". The agreement should, in either case, clearly establish whether such remuneration is payable irrespective of the firm's profitability and whether such a partner will be liable for losses and, if so, to what extent. It is usual to deal with the latter point by means of an express indemnity.[369]

Provided that the salaried or fixed share partner's remuneration is stated to be payable out of profits, the court will usually be prepared to infer that it will abate if those profits are insufficient. Thus, in *Marsh v. Stacey*,[370] a partnership deed provided for the payment to a junior partner of a "fixed salary of £1,200 as a first charge on the profits and in addition thereto one-third share of the net profits arising from the Reigate branch" of the firm. For two consecutive years the firm's profits were less than £1,200. The court held that, on a true construction of the deed, the junior partner's salary was only payable out of profits, but would have priority over any payments due to the other partners. Equally, in an appropriate case, the agreement may be construed as providing for a guaranteed salary as well as an indemnity against losses,[371] but it is clear from the decision in *M. Young Legal Associates v. Zahid*[372] that this will not necessarily result in the recipient being denied the status of partner[373] and being treated as a mere employee of the firm.[374]

Medical partnerships within the National Health Service

10–87   The National Health Service Act 2006 contains stringent prohibitions on the actual or deemed sale of what may conveniently be styled National Health Service goodwill.[375] Whilst partners are free to divide their profits in any way they may choose, the Secretary of State, who is now charged with the task of

---

[367] Partnership Act 1890, s.24(1), *infra*, paras 20–03 *et seq.*

[368] See as to the status of such partners *Stekel v. Ellice* [1973] 1 W.L.R. 191 and *supra*, paras 5–54 *et seq.*

[369] Note that an indemnity against losses may not be the same thing as an indemnity against *liabilities*: *James & George Collie v. Donald*, 1999 S.C.L.R. 420 (OH). See also *infra*, para. 20–06.

[370] (1963) 107 S.J. 512. Note that in the Bar Library transcript ([1963] No. 169 at p. 4), the partner in question is not referred to as the "junior" partner.

[371] See *Geddes v. Wallace* (1820) 2 Bli. 270.

[372] [2006] 1 W.L.R. 2562 (CA), noted *supra*, para. 5–54; also *Hodson v. Hodson* [2010] P.N.L.R. 8 (CA).

[373] But note, in this context, the *de facto* requirements imposed by HMRC as a condition of recognition of a fixed share partner, considered *supra*, para. 5–59.

[374] He will, nevertheless, be held out as a partner: Partnership Act 1890, s.14.

[375] See the National Health Service Act 2006, s.259, Sched. 21; also *Kerr v. Morris* [1987] Ch. 90 (a decision under the forerunner to these provisions). A further prohibition on the sale of goodwill by various types of contractors and certain medical practitioners providing "essential services" is also to be found in the Primary Medical Services (Sale of Goodwill and Restrictions on Sub-contracting) Regulations 2004 (SI 2004/906), reg. 3(1) which continues to have effect under the 2006 Act: National Health Service (Consequential Provisions) Act 2006, Sched. 2, para. 1(2). The effect of these restrictions is to remove all economic value from the goodwill: *R v. Waltham Forest NHS Primary Care Trust* [2007] 1 W.L.R. 2092 (CA).

policing the statutory prohibitions, may conceivably treat as evidence of a deemed sale of goodwill the fact that an incoming partner has been substantially underpaid in the early years following his admission.[376]

Drawings in anticipation of profits

Since the precise quantum of a partner's share of profits will not be known   **10–88** until the partnership accounts have been prepared and approved,[377] the agreement should generally provide for each partner to draw on account of his *anticipated* profit share, whether monthly or otherwise.[378] The precise amount of such drawings may be stated in the agreement, but will almost inevitably require adjustment if the partnership is to endure for anything other than a short period. Where appropriate, drawings may be directly related to the size of a partner's preferential "salary".[379]

Although it is always desirable to pitch drawings at a level which will ensure that no partner receives more than his ultimate profit entitlement, an unforeseen downturn in profits can undermine even the most conservative of estimates. The agreement should accordingly require any overdrawings to be repaid to the firm within a set period, usually without interest. The current editor is aware of cases in which firms have in mid-year been forced to limit, or even to suspend, partners' drawings in order to avoid an imminent financial crisis, and this has prompted some firms to address this issue directly in the agreement.[380]

Division of profits

The agreement will normally provide for the ultimate division of profits after   **10–89** the approval of the annual accounts, although this is arguably unnecessary.[381] The decision to divide profits (in contradistinction to the manner in which they are to be shared between the partners once divided) is likely to be regarded as a routine management decision unless the agreement provides otherwise.[382]

Tax and other provisions

Tax provisions: Although tax is no longer assessable on all the partners jointly,[383]   **10–90** many firms are continuing to insist that an income tax retention is made out of each partner's profit share and taken to a reserve or tax account, thus ensuring

[376] National Health Service Act 2006, Sched. 12, para. 2(4)(c). Note also that in a Guidance Note on the Prohibition on the Sale of Goodwill of NHS Medical Practice in England and Wales, reissued by the former Medical Practices Committee in May 1992, it was suggested that there might be a sale of goodwill if an incoming partner did not reach parity within three years of admission.

[377] See *supra*, paras 10–73 *et seq.*

[378] This will not always be appropriate, *e.g.* where profits will only be realised at the conclusion of a particular venture.

[379] See *supra*, para. 10–80.

[380] It may well be that the agreement will provide that the level of partners' drawings is to be set by a majority vote of the partners. Depending on the precise terms of the agreement, this may enable a majority to vary the level of drawings mid-year as required. More doubtful is whether such a power could properly be used to limit the drawings of some but not all of the partners. *Semble*, this might be possible where limitations are introduced in respect of partners whose current accounts are overdrawn.

[381] See also *infra*, paras 21–06, 21–07.

[382] See *Stevens v. South Devon Railway Co* (1851) 9 Hare 313, 326 *per* Sir G.J. Turner V.-C.; also *Burland v. Earle* [1902] A.C. 83, 95.

[383] See the Income Tax (Trading and Other Income) Act 2005, ss.848 *et seq.*; also *infra*, paras 34–04 *et seq.*

that funds are available as and when individual partners are bound to pay instalments of tax under the self assessment regime.[384] Such a practice instils a level of financial discipline in all partners and avoids potential embarrassment for the firm in the event that a partner finds himself unable to fund his own tax liabilities. Where such retentions are to be made, this should be reflected in the agreement[385] and provision should also be made for the return of each partner's unused tax reserve when he leaves the firm.[386]

10–91   *Other provisions*: It is not uncommon for a firm also to make provisions on account of bad debts, uninsured losses and other contingent or apprehended liabilities, whether on a yearly or "one-off" basis. Such provisions will reduce the firm's profits and thus, in effect, be contributed by the partners in their profit shares, but will rarely appear in the firm's balance sheet. Where an excess provision has been made, the surplus will, in the absence of some other express or implied agreement,[387] be returnable to the partners who contributed to it, even if some of them have since left the firm.[388] It is obviously desirable that the partners consider, when authorising a provision, whether it should rather be regarded as an asset of the ongoing firm, so that any unused surplus is divisible merely between the *current* partners, to the exclusion of former partners. Although it would be unusual for the agreement to legislate in advance on the ownership of all provisions, it might usefully highlight the need for a positive decision on the issue of ownership, if only as an *aide-mémoire* to the partners. It might also record the manner in which that decision is to be taken.[389]

Champion v. Workman[390] is one of the rare cases where the propriety of making a provision as against a retiring partner has been considered by the court. There the provision was allowed, even though there was evidence that the claim in question had been settled for a lesser amount.[391]

N.   POWERS AND DUTIES OF PARTNERS[392]

Just and faithful clause

10–92   Lord Lindley observed:

> "It is the practice to insert in partnership articles an express covenant by each partner to be true and just in all his dealings with the others. This, however, is always

---

[384] See also *infra*, para. 22–04.

[385] See the *Encyclopedia of Professional Partnerships*, Precedent 1, cl. 11(8). It will be a matter for decision as to whether each partner is to have an individual tax reserve or whether there is to be combined reserve. Clearly, each partner's share of a combined reserve must be readily identifiable.

[386] See *infra*, paras 10–157, 10–179.

[387] There may be a contrary implied agreement where a general provision is made on account of, say, bad debts, which is topped up year by year and in which the unused element of the contributions made by partners in any given year cannot readily be ascertained. Much will, of course, depend on the particular circumstances.

[388] *Coventry v. Barclay* (1850) 3 De G.J. & S. 320, noted *infra*, para. 10–164. For an analogous case concerning entitlement to overpaid value added tax, see *Hawthorn v. Smallcorn* [1998] S.T.C. 591 (although the decision largely turned on the construction of a retirement deed).

[389] See generally, *infra*, para. 10–102.

[390] June 20, 2001 (Lawtel 22/8/01).

[391] *ibid.* at [43], [44] *per* Lawrence Collins J.

[392] See the *Encyclopedia of Professional Partnerships*, Precedent 1, cll. 12 *et seq.*

implied[393]; and the clause in question therefore adds little from a legal point of view, although it may serve to remind the partners of their mutual obligations to good faith."

Although no longer framed as covenants, such clauses are still found in most agreements,[394] and will frequently replicate the duty to provide information regarding the partnership affairs which is otherwise implied by section 28 of the Partnership Act 1890.[395]

Attention to partnership affairs

A clause specifying how much time each partner is required to devote to the   **10–93** partnership business is vital, even though Lord Lindley put it in less emphatic terms:

> "The time and attention which the partners are to give to the affairs of the firm should be expressly mentioned; especially if one of them is to be at liberty to give less of his time and attention than the others."

This will be particularly in point where the firm is to comprise a number of "part-time" partners.[396]

The mere fact that some partners are devoting all their time and efforts to the success of the partnership business is no guarantee that other partners will do likewise. If an *express* obligation has not been imposed, it may be difficult, if not impossible, to show that a partner's lack of commitment or outside interests involve a breach of some other clause of the agreement,[397] much less that such a partner has in some way impliedly ceased to be a member of the firm.[398] A dissolution under the Partnership Act 1890,[399] even if obtainable, will scarcely represent an attractive remedy.

It perhaps goes without saying that an allegation of a breach of this type of provision must be backed up by evidence: it will not be inferred merely from an absence of timesheets or the equivalent.[400]

An obligation on a partner to devote his whole time to the business should be   **10–94** accompanied by a prohibition on engaging in other forms of business.[401] Equally, if one partner holds a particular office or appointment to which he is required to devote time during normal working hours, this should be specifically mentioned

---

[393] See *infra*, paras 16–01 *et seq*.

[394] A covenant in such terms will not cause any sum due from one partner to another on taking the partnership accounts to be treated as a specialty debt: see *Powdrell v. Jones* (1854) 2 Sm. & G. 305. *Semble*, breach of such a clause gives rise to a claim in damages: see *infra*, para. 16–10.

[395] See *infra*, para. 16–03. The inclusion of such a provision may be particularly helpful when seeking information as to the activities of an outgoing partner in the run up to his retirement (e.g. solicitation of clients and staff, etc.).

[396] The concept of the part-time partner is relatively new, although it has been recognised for some time in the medical profession). Where such partners are to be admitted to the firm, the application of a number of provisions will require consideration, *e.g.* profit-sharing, holiday entitlement, etc.

[397] *Quaere*, can the other partners complain of a breach of that partner's express or implied duty of good faith in such circumstances? As to the possible remedies where wilful inattention to the business can be proved, see *infra*, para. 20–45.

[398] See *Hodson v. Hodson* [2010] P.N.L.R. 8 (CA) at [40].

[399] See *infra*, paras 24–47 *et seq*.

[400] In *Kao Lee & Yip v. Hoi-Yan* [2003] H.K.C. 113, evidence was not even led as to the firm's practice on the filling out of timesheets. Predictably, the claim was rejected: see *ibid*. at [101] to [104].

[401] See *infra*, para. 10–95.

and, if appropriate, he should be required to account to the firm for any fees or other remuneration derived therefrom.[402]

Lord Lindley also drew attention to the fact that:

> "Inattention to business by reason of illness is . . . no breach of an agreement to attend to it."[403]

The current editor considers that the same principle should, in general, be applied whenever a partner is prevented from fulfilling his obligations by any other circumstances beyond his control. However, it may be appropriate, depending on the duration of a partner's incapacity, to impose some form of financial penalty, whether by way of a reduction in his profit share or by forcing him to bear the cost of employing a locum.[404]

Agreement not to carry on other businesses, etc.

10–95   Each partner will normally agree not only that he will devote his whole time to the partnership business but also that he will not engage in any other business, whether or not competing with the firm's business.[405] Such an agreement can be enforced by injunction,[406] but it does not follow that a partner who acts in breach of it will *necessarily* be bound to account to the firm for any profits which he may realise in the course of his outside activities.[407] Thus, a duty to account will in general arise only where the business is of the same nature as the firm's business and is carried on in competition with it[408] or where an express provision is included in the agreement. It will, of course, be a question of fact whether a partner who is making preparations to set up a new business which is to be run in competition with the firm is in breach of such an obligation.[409]

A similar prohibition will often be imposed in the case of offices and appointments, although it may be necessary to exempt any position held by a partner when the partnership commenced.[410]

Other miscellaneous duties

10–96   The majority of agreements contain a variety of other duties, ranging from a partner's obligation to the partnership property and the other partners indemni-

---

[402] See the *Encyclopedia of Professional Partnerships*, Precedent 11, cl. 12(1).

[403] Lord Lindley referred to *Boast v. Firth* (1868) L.R. 4 C.P. 1; *Robinson v. Davison* (1871) L.R. 6 Ex. 269. Neither concerned a partnership.

[404] See *supra*, para. 10–83.

[405] As to the position in the absence of such a clause, see the Partnership Act 1890, s.30, *infra*, paras 16–14 *et seq.*

[406] See the first part of the injunction in *England v. Curling* (1878) 8 Beav. 129; also *Whitwood Chemical Co. v. Hardman* [1891] 2 Ch. 416; *Grimston v. Cuningham* [1894] 1 Q.B. 125. *cf. Davis v. Foreman* [1894] 3 Ch. 654; *Kirchner & Co. v. Gruban* [1909] 1 Ch. 413 (where seemingly negative obligations were held to be of a positive nature); also *Metropolitan Electric Supply Co. Ltd. v. Ginder* [1901] 2 Ch. 799 (the reverse case). See also *infra*, para. 16–35.

[407] *Aas v. Benham* [1891] 2 Ch. 244; also *Dean v. Macdowell* (1878) 8 Ch.D. 345; *Trimble v. Goldberg* [1906] A.C. 494, 500.

[408] See the Partnership Act 1890, s.30 and *infra*, para. 16–35.

[409] See *infra*, para. 16–08; also *Lancashire Fires Ltd. v. S A Lyons & Co. Ltd.* [1997] I.R.L.R. 113; *Helmet Integrated Systems Ltd. v. Tunnard* [2007] I.R.L.R. 126 (CA); *PennWell Publishing (UK) Ltd. v. Ornstien* [2008] 2 B.C.L.C. 246, all cases concerning employees.

[410] See also *supra*, paras 10–51 *et seq.*

fied against liability for his private debts,[411] to an obligation to ensure compliance with any relevant professional or regulatory rules.[412]

Powers of attorney

Some larger firms wish to streamline their administration processes by ensuring that deeds and other documents can be executed on behalf of the firm without having to circulate a copy for each partner's signature.[413] For this purpose a wide-ranging power of attorney can be useful, in addition to the attorney rights often sought to be conferred on continuing partners.[414] It is not possible to create such a power if the partnership agreement itself is not in the form of a deed.[415] Accordingly, it may in such cases be necessary to resort to the device of requiring each partner to execute a power of attorney in a form annexed to the agreement. This will ensure that incoming partners are obliged to execute such a power as and when they become members of the firm.

10–97

Holidays, leave, etc.

The agreement should state each partner's entitlement to holidays and, where relevant, maternity, sabbatical or other periods of leave.[416] It goes without saying that any obligation to devote time to the partnership business must be read subject thereto.

10–98

Restrictions on the authority of partners

Any restriction on the implied authority of a partner should be specifically mentioned in the agreement.[417] This will usually take the form of a clause prohibiting any partner from doing certain acts without the prior consent of the other partners, *e.g.* engaging and dismissing employees,[418] giving guarantees, assigning or charging his share in the partnership, entering into any form of sub-partnership as regards that share[419] and drawing, accepting, or endorsing bills of exchange (other than cheques).[420] Certain of the restrictions may be qualified in such a way that they do not apply to acts done in the usual or ordinary course of

10–99

---

[411] See the *Encyclopedia of Professional Partnerships*, Precedent 1, cl. 13(5).

[412] See *ibid.* Precedent 11, cl. 17(5).

[413] See, as to the execution of deeds by and on behalf of partners, *infra*, paras 12–62 *et seq.*, 12–157 *et seq.*

[414] See *infra*, para. 10–252.

[415] Powers of Attorney Act 1971, s.1(1), as amended by the Law of Property (Miscellanous Provisions) Act 1989, Sched. 1, para. 6(a).

[416] Regrettably, experience shows that disagreements over the timing of holidays can be extremely divisive. Accordingly, it is in some cases necessary to provide for a particular "pecking" order as between the partners: see, generally, the *Encyclopedia of Professional Partnerships*, Precedent 1, cl. 12, Precedent 2, Art. 7.05. Needless to say, any such pecking order should not use age or seniority as a criterion unless this can be justified under the Employment Equality (Age) Regulations 2006 (see *ibid.* regs 3(1), 17(1)(d)(i), 32) or the equivalent provisions of the Equality Act 2010, when it come sinto force. See further *supra*, paras 8–22 *et seq.*, 10–78.

[417] As to the effect of such a restriction, see the Partnership Act 1890, s.8, *infra*, paras 12–138 *et seq.*

[418] This can be contentious: see *infra*, para. 12–66.

[419] See *supra*, para. 5–67. As to a partner's implied authority to enter into a partnership with a third party in order to further the interests of the main partnership business, see *infra*, paras 12–18, 12–78.

[420] The agreement should, as a separate matter, establish how and by whom cheques are to be drawn: see *supra*, para. 10–69. And see *infra*, paras 12–42 *et seq.*, 12–51, 12–161.

business, etc.[421] A partner acting in breach of such a restriction is generally required to indemnify his co-partners against resulting losses,[422] but this will of no avail as regards third parties dealing with him, unless they are actually aware of the restriction.[423]

In giving or withholding their consent to a particular act, the general body of partners must act bona fide in the interests of the partnership but, in the view of the current editor, they will not normally be subject to an implied duty to act reasonably.[424]

Managing and senior partners, etc.

10–100   If one partner is to be given special or exclusive authority to carry out certain functions in the firm, the limits of that authority should be clearly stated.[425] Contrary to popular belief amongst partners and others, a "senior" partner has no special rights or authority merely because he is the first named in the agreement.[426] Again, it will not follow from the fact that a partner is designated as the "managing partner" and given power to conduct litigation on behalf of the firm that he automatically has power to initiate proceedings on behalf of *retired* partners, unless the agreement specifically authorises him to do so.[427]

Exercise of powers and discretions conferred on partners

10–101   Where a discretion is conferred on one or more partners, it hardly needs to be said that the discretion must be exercised honestly, in good faith and for a proper purpose.[428] The ultimate benchmark against which such an exercise must be measured is what is in the best interests of the partnership as a whole and the fact that one or more partners may be disadvantaged thereby is not, in itself, objectionable.[429] It would seem to follow from this that, as a normal rule, such a power cannot be exercised capriciously or arbitrarily,[430] but this will not always be the

---

[421] See the Partnership Act 1890, ss.5, 7 *infra*, paras 12–02 *et seq.*, 12–138.

[422] See the *Encyclopedia of Professional Partnerships*, Precedent 1, cl. 15.

[423] See, for example, *Goldberg v. Miltiadous* [2010] EWHC 450 (QB) (Lawtel 19/3/10). And see *infra*, paras 12–04, 12–09, 12–11 *et seq.*

[424] See *Price v. Bouch* (1987) 53 P. & C.R. 257 (a decision concerning restrictive covenants); *Imperial Group Pension Trust Ltd. v. Imperial Tobacco Ltd.* [1991] 1 W.L.R. 589, 596F *et seq. per* Browne-Wilkinson V.-C. (a pension fund case). This will, however, be a matter of construction of the particular agreement: see *Mahon v. Sims* (2005) 39 E.G. 138, a restrictive covenant case; *Lymington Marina Ltd. v. Macnamara* [2007] 2 All E.R. (Comm) 825 (CA), which concerned a licence agreement.

[425] See also *supra*, para. 10–33 and *infra*, para. 10–106.

[426] Indeed, the senior partner is no longer *per se* responsible for ensuring that the firm delivers its partnership return under the Taxes Management Act 1970, s.12AA(2) (as added by the Finance Act 1994, s.184 and amended by the Finance Act 1995, s.115(4) and the Finance Act 1996, s.123(1)). *cf. ibid.* s.9(1) in its original form. See also *infra*, para. 34–17.

[427] *HLB Kidsons v. Lloyd's Underwriters* [2009] 1 All E.R. (Comm) 760.

[428] See *infra*, paras 10–124, 10–125, 10–135, 16–01 *et seq.*

[429] See *infra*, paras 15–07, 16–09.

[430] See, for example, *Ludgate Insurance Co. Ltd. v. Citibank NA* [1998] 1 Lloyd's Rep. 397 (CA) at [35] *per* Brooke L.J. (this was not a partnership case); *Greck v. Henderson Asia Pacific Equity Partners (FP) LP* [2008] CSOH 2 at [76] *per* Lord Glennie. *Semble*, the partner exercising the power must not take into account an extraneous consideration which has no bearing on the partnership's interests: *ibid.* at [82].

case.[431] It is not, however, the function of the court to take over the discretion with a view to exercising it on the relevant partner's behalf.[432]

Whether reasons for the decision must always be volunteered is more questionable: if the discretion is required to be exercised by reference to specific factors, it is more likely that reasons should be given.[433] In one recent partnership case it was held that reasons "ought usually to be given, not necessarily in any formal way but in some manner sufficient to indicate to interested parties what decision has been taken and why".[434] Of course, in most cases a partner will, quite legitimately, be entitled to demand details of the reasons by invoking section 28 of the Partnership Act 1890.[435]

O.   DECISION-MAKING[436]

Although it is no longer strictly necessary, where there are more than two **10–102** partners, to confer power on the majority to decide ordinary matters connected with the partnership business,[437] it is still highly desirable that the agreement establishes how decisions on both large and small issues affecting the firm are to be taken. Differing majorities or complete unanimity may be required, depending on the precise nature of the decision.[438] Particular attention should be paid to those decisions which relate to the nature of the firm's business,[439] the approval of its accounts,[440] the amendment of the agreement,[441] the admission of new

---

[431] See *Russell v. Russell* (1880) 14 Ch.D. 471, 480 *per* Jessell M.R. This case concerned an express power to dissolve conferred upon one member of a two partner firm, so should not be taken to have established a principle of general application.

[432] See *Keen v. Commerzbank AG* [2007] I.C.R. 623 (CA) at [39]. The decision concerned the discretionary award of bonuses to a bank employee, but the circumstances were unusual in that it was unclear not only on what basis the decision has been made but also by whom. In the event, Mr Keen did not plead his case on the basis of breach of an implied term of trust and confidence as between employer and employee and the court held that he had failed to show that the exercise of the bank's admittedly wide discretion was irrational or perverse and thus he could not challenge the result: see *ibid.* at [56] to [61].

[433] *ibid.* at [44]. See also *Greck v. Henderson Asia Pacific Equity Partners (FP) LP, supra*, at [81] *per* Lord Glennie.

[434] *Greck v. Henderson Asia Pacific Equity Partners (FP) LP, supra*, at [76] *per* Lord Glennie. This case concerned a power for a general partner in a limited partnership formed under the Limited Partnerships Act 1907 to designate an outgoing carried interest partner as a good or bad leaver under the agreement. In the event it was held that the discretion had not been exercised nor even requested to be exercised, so no complaint about the general partner's actions was maintainable.

[435] See *infra*, para. 16–03. That section may, however, be excluded by agreement.

[436] See the *Encyclopedia of Professional Partnerships*, Precedent 1, cl. 17, Precedent 2, cl. 7.11.

[437] See the Partnership Act 1890, s.24(8), *infra*, paras 15–04 *et seq.*; note also *Falkland v. Cheney* (1704) 5 Bro.P.C. 476.

[438] See, for example, the approach adopted in the *Encyclopedia of Professional Partnerships*, Precedent 2.

[439] See the Partnership Act 1890, s.24(8), *infra*, paras 15–04, 15–08. And see also *Nixon v. Wood* (1987) 284 E.G. 1055.

[440] See *supra*, para. 10–73.

[441] See *supra*, para. 10–13.

partners,[442] the expulsion or compulsory retirement of a partner,[443] the dissolution of the firm[444] and now, increasingly, a merger with another firm or firms,[445] incorporation and conversion to limited liability partnership status.[446] It is no longer usual to provide how the option of dissolving the firm is to be exercised in the event of a partner suffering his share in the partnership property to be charged for his separate debts,[447] since this will usually be made a ground for expulsion. Some firms may be content for all decisions to be taken on a simple majority vote, particularly where the number of partners is small.

It is common to find that all decisions relating to the "management and control" of the business are required to be taken on a simple majority vote,[448] even though this expression is notoriously vague.[449] If this device is resorted to, it would be wise to ensure that the more contentious classes of decision are *specifically* referred to and, if necessary, excepted from the scope of the provision.

No majority possible

10–103   Lord Lindley observed:

> "It is difficult to lay down a general rule for the determination of what is to be done if the partners are equally divided. Articles of partnership, as usually drawn, are silent upon this question, but if it were declared that in such a case matters should be left in *statu quo*, probably some little assistance would be given to the preservation of peace and goodwill."

This view is perhaps optimistic in the face of today's commercial pressures, so that it is now sometimes provided that the senior partner or chairman of the partners' meeting will have a second or casting vote.[450]

In the case of a two man partnership, unanimity will always be required for any decision.[451]

Weighted voting

10–104   Where a majority vote is to be taken on a particular issue, it does not follow that each partner must have a single vote of equal weight: voting weighted

---

[442] See *infra*, paras 10–255 *et seq.*

[443] See *infra*, paras 10–114 *et seq.*

[444] See *infra*, paras 10–137 *et seq.*

[445] If (as will normally be the case in a small firm), a unanimous vote in favour of merger is required, one partner will be able to frustrate its implementation, however necessary it may be for the survival of the firm. Equally, whilst a partner may be content that decisions to admit additional partners can be taken on a majority vote, should he really be forced into a wholly different partnership, with, perhaps, a different name and business ethic, against his will?

[446] Either course will inevitably involve the dissolution of the firm, and the transfer of all or part of its assets to an effective third party, *i.e.* the new company or LLP. See further *infra*, para. 15–09.

[447] See the Partnership Act 1890, s.33(2), *infra*, paras 24–38 *et seq.*

[448] In the case of a large firm, management and control may be vested in a designated managing partner or management/executive committee rather than the general body of partners: see *infra*, para. 10–107.

[449] *cf. ibid.* s.24(8), *infra*, paras 15–04 *et seq.*

[450] Such a vote should, in general, be expressed to be exercisable only where a simple majority of votes is required. To authorise a senior partner/chairman to push through a vote requiring a higher specified majority would prima facie be inappropriate.

[451] But see the decision in *Donaldson v. Williams* (1833) 1 Cromp. & M. 342, considered *infra*, para. 12–66.

according to seniority or capital contribution/profit share is by no means uncommon, thus permitting a particular cadre of partners to maintain overall control. Equally, if voting is weighted according to seniority, it is likely to be necessary to justify this approach, if potential age discrimination is to be avoided.[452]

Disenfranchised partners

It is becoming increasingly common to find that a partner who has given or,   **10–105**
perhaps, been given notice to retire from the firm[453] is deprived of the right to vote on some or all issues,[454] and this may even be coupled with a right for the other partners to exclude him from partners' meetings. Such provisions are obviously designed to avoid unnecessary disruption to the decision-making process during what may be a tense and difficult period and to free the continuing partners to take what may be sensitive decisions affecting the firm's future without involving the outgoing partner.[455] It need hardly be said that, to authorise such a major inroad into the normal right of a partner to participate in the firm's management,[456] a very clear provision in the agreement will be required. As a *quid pro quo*, consideration might be given to limiting the rights of the continuing partners to take decisions which will have an adverse financial impact on the outgoing partner but, in balancing the interests of the outgoing and continuing partners, care must be taken to ensure that this does not impose an unduly rigid financial straightjacket on the latter.[457]

Meetings

In medium to large sized firms, it is usual for the agreement to contain detailed   **10–106**
provisions governing the calling of meetings, quorums, agendas and, where appropriate, proxy voting. It may also be declared that a written resolution signed by the requisite number of partners should be binding on all without the need for a formal meeting to be convened.[458]

---

[452] See the Employment Equality (Age) Regulations 2006, regs 3(1), 17(1)(d)(i), 32, noticed *supra*, paras 8–22 *et seq.*, 10–81. The position will be the same under the Equality Act 2010, when its provisions are brought into force.

[453] See, as to voluntary and compulsory retirement, *infra*, paras 10–108, 10–134.

[454] One of the most obvious issues falling within this class will be the decision to dissolve the firm and thus, perhaps, to override the disenfranchised partner's notice of retirement. See generally, as powers to dissolve a firm by resolution, *infra*, para. 10–137.

[455] Note that it is the current editor's view that, if the decision will not be implemented until after he has left the firm and will not involve any expenditure in the meantime, there is no reason why the continuing partners should not take it without reference to the outgoing partner, even in the absence of a provision of the type discussed in the text.

[456] See *infra*, paras 15–01 *et seq*. Although it is theoretically possible that the inclusion of such a provision might result in the firm being regarded as a collective investment scheme within the meaning of the Financial Services and Markets Act 2000, s.235 (see *infra*, paras 29–30 *et seq*., in practice this will only rarely be the case for a professional or trading firm.

[457] The firm will obviously need to incur expenditure during the notice period and there is no reason why the outgoing partner should be wholly insulated therefrom. What needs to be discouraged is expenditure of an unusual nature which is, perhaps, accelerated so as to make the outgoing partner bear a share thereof. Although the outgoing partner might be able to allege a breach of the duty of good faith in such a case (see *supra*, para. 10–92 and *infra*, paras 16–01 *et seq*.), proving it may be difficult.

[458] This runs counter to the normal principles of partnership law: see *infra*, para. 15–07.

Management structures in large firms

10–107   In larger professional firms it is now common to find that the agreement establishes a complex management structure, usually based around a managing or executive partner/committee and a series of committees/sub-committees charged with diverse responsibilities.[459] Some decisions will be capable of being taken in committee, whilst others will be referred to a full partners' meeting. The managing or executive partner will normally fulfil a co-ordinating role, although he may be responsible for *implementing* decisions once taken.

It is a matter for debate whether such a structure is better implemented on an *ad hoc* basis rather than being the subject of detailed provision in the agreement. In practice, the answer is likely to be dictated by the size of the firm: in a mid-sized firm based around a small number of offices, where the partners are in more or less regular contact, undue formality in the agreement may stultify flexibility in the approach to management. On the other hand, a large firm, with, perhaps, a national or multi-national practice, must have clearly established procedures from the outset, because it will only be feasible to convene partners' meetings on an infrequent basis.

P.   RETIREMENT[460]

(a) Voluntary retirement

10–108   Since there is, as such, no inherent right to "retire" from a partnership under the Partnership Act 1890 or under the general law,[461] otherwise than by agreement, it is usually desirable to provide for the voluntary retirement of partners from the outset. Otherwise, the only course open to a partner who wishes to leave the firm may be to bring about a general dissolution.

Retirement will normally be dependent on the service of a written notice which may only be permitted to take effect on a particular date, *e.g.* the end of an accounting period.[462] The minimum period of notice will usually be specified, and will vary according to the trade or profession concerned. Although such a notice requirement can be waived by the other partners,[463] care should be taken to ensure that the retirement is still treated as having occurred under the agreement.[464]

---

[459] In professional firms, the position of "head of department" is also gaining in importance and will usually confer on the holder a degree of day to day control over the running of the relevant department, as well as an automatic seat on the firm's management committee. Needless to say, despite the theoretical danger referred to *supra*, para. 10–105, n. 456, none of these devices will in the normal course result in the firm being regarded as a collective investment scheme.

[460] See the *Encyclopedia of Professional Partnerships*, Precedent 1, cll. 18 *et seq.*

[461] See *infra*, paras 24–93 *et seq.*

[462] This may well facilitate the calculation of the retiring partner's financial entitlement, by obviating the need for special "retirement" accounts: see *infra*, paras 10–161 *et seq.*

[463] Unless the agreement gives a particular partner or committee or a majority of the partners power to waive the requirement, it will prima facie involve a variation of the agreement and may require unanimity: see *supra*, paras 10–13, 10–102. This is often overlooked.

[464] If the position is in doubt, the outgoing partner might be in a position to seek the payment of the value of his share ascertained in the manner explored in *Sobell v. Boston* [1975] 1 W.L.R. 1587. See further *infra*, paras 19–11, 23–184.

The concept of "retirement" connotes a continuation of the firm. Since a court will be reluctant to construe an agreement as permitting retirement if only one partner will remain,[465] where such a possibility is contemplated, this should be clearly stated.[466]

With a view to limiting the disruption caused by the retirement of a partner, some firms restrict the number of partners who may give notice of retirement at any one time or within a given period.[467] This is not without risk, since a partner who truly does not wish to remain with the firm, but who is unable to give notice to retire may vent his frustrations to the detriment of all the partners.[468]

A retirement notice, once given, cannot be unilaterally withdrawn,[469] although it may be superseded by a general dissolution.[470]

Acquisition of retiring partner's share

The agreement should provide for the continuing partners to acquire the retiring partner's share at a valuation or in some other manner,[471] although a failure to do so will not always result in a general dissolution.[472]   **10–109**

If the continuing partners' rights are framed in terms of an option to acquire the retiring partner's share, and the option is exercisable *before* the chosen retirement date, the retiring partner's room for manoeuvre may be severely limited, as Lord Lindley explained:

"If such a clause is acted on, and a partner notifies his desire to retire to his co-partner, and the latter declares his option to purchase the share of the retiring partner, a contract is thereby concluded between them, from which neither can depart without the consent of the other. Consequently, the retiring partner cannot withdraw his notice and dissolve the partnership under some other clause in the deed.[473] Even if the co-partner who is to purchase the other's share infringes the partnership articles, the Court will not willingly interfere and dissolve the partnership; although, if the partner who is to retire conducts himself so as to prejudice the business and

---

[465] *Hurst v. Bryk* [1999] Ch. 1 (CA). This aspect was not pursued on appeal to the House of Lords: see [2002] 1 A.C. 185.

[466] See the *Encyclopedia of Professional Partnerships*, Precedent 1, cl.18(1).

[467] Despite contrary views aired in some quarters, the current editor has no doubt that such restrictions are valid and effectual. Proponents of the contrary view tend to forget that, as stated *supra*, para. 10–108, there is no *right* to retire under partnership law. See also: *Esso Petroleum Co Ltd. v. Harper's Garage (Stourport) Ltd.* [1968] A.C. 269, 338 *per* Lord Pearce, as cited in *Proactive Sports Management Ltd v. Rooney* [2010] EWHC 1807 (QB) (Lawtel 21/7/10).

[468] *e.g.* by seeking a dissolution under the Partnership Act 1890, s.35.

[469] See *Warder v. Stilwell* (1856) 3 Jur. (N.S.) 9; *Toogood v. Farrell* [1988] 2 E.G.L.R. 233 (CA). *Quaere*, could a partner argue that the retirement was tantamount to an expulsion. It is thought not: see *infra*, para. 24–93.

[470] See *infra*, para. 24–24, where the position is considered in relation to dissolution notices. See also, *supra*, para. 10–105.

[471] See *infra*, paras 10–150 *et seq.*

[472] See *Sobell v. Boston* [1975] 1 W.L.R. 1587. As noted *supra*, para. 10–108, the concept of "retirement" itself connotes the continuation of the firm, which will be impossible if it is placed in *general* dissolution. See also *infra*, para. 10–204.

[473] See *Warder v. Stilwell* (1856) 3 Jur.(N.S.) 9; *Homfray v. Fothergill* (1866) L.R. 1 Eq. 567; also *Jones v. Lloyd* (1874) L.R. 18 Eq. 265. It is, however, submitted that the notice could not be withdrawn even *prior* to the service of the option notice: *Warder v. Stilwell, supra*; *Toogood v. Farrell* [1988] 2 E.G.L.R. 233 (CA).

exclude the other, the Court will interpose for the protection of the latter; for otherwise the business to which he is shortly to be solely entitled may be entirely ruined."[474]

Power to sell or assign share

10–110   Subject to any restriction contained in the agreement,[475] a partner is free to sell or otherwise assign his share to a third party, but he will still remain a member of the partnership.[476] In Lord Lindley's day, an express provision permitting such a sale, as a species of retirement, appears to have been common, since he went on to explain:

> "If it is provided that a partner may sell his share, and no restrictions are mentioned, he may sell to anyone he likes, even to a pauper[477]; and, on giving his co-partners notice of his withdrawal from the firm, he will cease to be a member thereof as between himself and them; even although the purchaser from him does not come forward to take his place as a partner in the firm.[478]
>
> It is sometimes declared that a partner who is desirous of retiring shall offer his share to his co-partners before selling it to anyone else."

10–111   A clause of this type would now be wholly exceptional, but might, perhaps, be encountered in a corporate or investment partnership. Nevertheless, the following principles may be drawn from the older cases:

1. Subject to the precise terms of the clause, if the offer is duly made to all the other partners, one or more of them may accept it and acquire the share.[479]

2. A written notice of a partner's wish to dispose of his share may be treated as sufficient even though it is not seen by all the other partners, *e.g.* where it is written in a book which is produced at partners' meetings and which each partner has at all times been at liberty to inspect.[480] However, notice should in general be given to each partner individually.

3. If the other partners decline to purchase the share but seek to frustrate attempts to sell it to a third party by refusing to take that third party into

---

[474] See *Warder v. Stilwell, supra.* See further, as to the court's willingness to grant injunctive relief, *infra*, paras 23–15 *et seq.*, 23–135 *et seq.*

[475] It is, in practice, rare to see an agreement which does *not* contain such a restriction: see *supra*, para. 10–99.

[476] Partnership Act 1890, s.31, *infra*, paras 19–51 *et seq.* See also *infra*, para. 24–92.

[477] See *infra*, para. 19–62. Alternatively, the sale may be to one of the other partners: see *Cassels v. Stewart* (1881) 6 App.Cas. 64.

[478] *Jefferys v. Smith* (1827) 3 Russ. 158. As to the vendor partner's right to an indemnity from the purchaser, see *Dodson v. Downey* [1901] 2 Ch. 620. Previous editors have questioned whether the headnote in this case is supported by the facts or the judgment. The current editor does not share those doubts. See also *infra*, para. 19–57.

[479] *Homfray v. Fothergill* (1866) L.R. 1 Eq. 567.

[480] *Glassington v. Thwaites* (1833) Coop., temp. Brough. 115. *cf. Moffat v Longmuir*, 2001 S.C. 137 (Ex. Div.), noted *infra*, para. 10–156, n. 726.

the partnership, they may ultimately be compelled to acquire it at a valuation.[481]

4. The time limit for acceptance of the offer cannot in general be enlarged, otherwise than by agreement.[482]

(b) Compulsory retirement on grounds of age[483]

In professional firms it has until recently been common to see partners being   **10–112** required to retire on or shortly after attaining a specified age, unless the operation of that provision is waived by agreement prior to the relevant retirement date. However, since such a provision is blatantly discriminatory against partners on the grounds of their age, it can now only be retained if it can be justified as a "proportionate means of achieving a legitimate aim" under the Employment Equality (Age) Regulations 2006.[484] Although it has been held by the Court of Appeal that such a provision is capable of being justified in an appropriate case, whether retirement is required at age 65 or even at some lower age,[485] this may need to be backed up by suitably cogent evidence.[486] Whilst most firms are still currently retaining such a provision in the hopes that they can justify it if the need arises, it may be that this will gradually be replaced by a move over to a power of compulsory retirement of the type considered hereafter.[487]

If a particular partner is to be exempted from such a requirement, or is to retire at a different age, this fact should obviously be recorded in the agreement, but the presence of such exceptions may conceivably make justification of the provision itself more difficult for age discrimination purposes.[488] Whether the inclusion of a discretionary power to permit partners to remain even after the set age, though

---

[481] *Featherstonhaugh v. Turner* (1858) 25 Beav. 382.

[482] See *Holland v. King* (1848) 6 C.B. 727; *Brooke v. Garrod* (1857) 2 De G. & J. 62; *Lord Ranelagh v. Melton* (1864) 2 Dr. & Sm. 278; also *infra*, para. 10–156. And see as to the position when the recipient of the offer is mentally incapacitated, *Rowlands v. Evans* (1861) 30 Beav. 302.

[483] See the *Encyclopedia of Professional Partnerships*, Precedent 1, cl. 20.

[484] SI 2006/1031, regs. 3(1)(a), 17(1)(d), (8)(a), which are due to be replaced by the Equality Act 2010, ss.13(2), 44(2)(c), 46(6). Note that in *Seldon v. Clarkson Wright & Jakes*, December 4, 2007 (Case 1100275/2007/EB), the Employment Tribunal held that a failure to renew Mr Seldon's status as a partner when he reached the compulsory retirement age of 65 would amount to an expulsion for the purposes of *ibid.* reg. 17(1)(d). This part of the decision was not the subject of any appeal. The various stages which must be satisfied in order to meet the "legitimate aim" test are outlined *supra*, paras 8–23, 8–24.

[485] See *Seldon v. Clarkson Wright & Jakes* [2010] EWCA Civ 899 (Lawtel 28/7/10) at [38], [39]; also *ibid.* [2009] I.R.L.R. 267 (EAT) at [71]. It should be noted that 65 is currently the statutory retirement age for employees (see the Employment Equality (Age) Regulations 2006, reg. 30(2), as replicated in the Equality Act 2010, Sched. 9, Pt 2, para. 8(1)), but it has recently been announced, following the decision in *R. (on the application of Age UK) v. Secretary of State for Business, Innovation & Skills* [2009] I.R.L.R. 1017, that this will be dispensed with. There is no equivalent age prescribed for partners. Ironically, both the Court of Appeal and the EAT in *Seldon*, acknowledged that the statutory retirement age for employees might be of some limited significance when considering such a provison in the partnership context: see [2010] EWCA Civ 899 at [39] and [2009] I.R.L.R. 267 at [78], [83].

[486] See *Seldon v. Clarkson Wright & Jakes*, *supra*. Note that the Court of Appeal adopted a more relaxed view than the EAT on this point. See further *supra*, para. 8–24.

[487] See *infra*, para. 10–134.

[488] Note the views of the EAT in *Seldon v. Clarkson Wright & Jakes* [2009] I.R.L.R. 267 at [59], [72]. The Court of Appeal appeared less concerned: see [2010] EWCA Civ 899 at [35].

eminently desirable, will give rise to similar difficulties is more questionable.[489]

Provision should be made for the acquisition of the retiring partner's share, as in the case of voluntary retirement.[490]

Q.   EXPULSION, ETC.[491]

10–113   In the absence of an express power in the agreement, no partner can be expelled from, or otherwise forced to leave, a partnership.[492] It follows that, if one partner is so misconducting himself that the other partners are unable to carry on in partnership with him,[493] their only options may be to pay the recalcitrant partner off or to seek a dissolution from the court. Lord Lindley observed:

> "In order, therefore, that an objectionable partner may be summarily got rid of, clauses are sometimes inserted providing for expulsion in certain events."

This is now something of an understatement: draconian though the power of expulsion is, it will be found in most well drawn agreements,[494] although its true value may only be appreciated by the partners when circumstances have arisen for its exercise. On occasion, such a power may be coupled with (or replaced by) a power of compulsory "retirement".[495]

(a) Powers of Expulsion

Grounds for expulsion

10–114   A traditional power of expulsion will set out a detailed list of grounds on which the power will be exercisable, ranging from breach of the agreement and actual or impending bankruptcy[496] to mental or physical incapacity and conduct which is likely to have an adverse effect on the business or practice concerned.[497]

---

[489] The EAT appeared to imply that this might cause difficulties in *Seldon v. Clarkson Wright & Jakes* [2009] I.R.L.R. 267 at [59], [72] but, again, the Court of Appeal was unconcerned: *ibid.*

[490] See *infra*, paras 10–150 *et seq.*

[491] See the *Encyclopedia of Professional Partnerships*, Precedent 1, cll. 20, 21.

[492] Partnership Act 1890, s.25, *infra*, paras 24–99 *et seq.*

[493] In such cases, the right to injunctive relief against the recalcitrant partner may be more theoretical than real: see *infra*, paras 23–141, 24–85, 24–100.

[494] See, for example, *Walters v. Bingham* [1988] 1 F.T.L.R. 260, 268 *per* Browne-Wilkinson V.-C. See further, *supra*, para. 10–24.

[495] See *infra*, paras 10–134 *et seq.*

[496] It is desirable to ensure that a partner can be expelled *before* he is made bankrupt, so that insolvency and/or an application for an interim order under the Insolvency Act 1986, s.253 and/or the presentation of a bankruptcy (or insolvency) petition should normally be made a ground for expulsion. The inclusion of actual bankruptcy as a ground will, by implication, exclude the operation of the Partnership Act 1890, s.33(1), so far as it concerns bankruptcy. But see also *infra*, paras 10–152, 10–153.

[497] This will be of particular importance in the case of a professional practice: see for example, *Goodman v. Sinclair, The Times*, January 24, 1951, *infra*, para. 10–117. In *Thakrar v. Vadera*, March 31, 1999, an unreported decision of Arden J., a ground was framed by reference to a partner committing "a serious breach of any of the provisions of this deed resulting in the partnership's suffering a material disadvantage". It was held that the acts complained of were not sufficient.

Although it is usual for the last ground to refer to "conduct which would be a ground for dissolving the partnership under the Partnership Act 1890",[498] in practice reliance will rarely be placed thereon.[499]

Insolvency: If a ground is framed by reference to a partner's "insolvency", the power will normally be exercisable before the initiation of insolvency proceedings,[500] as Lord Lindley explained: **10–115**

> "The word *insolvent*, unless controlled by the context, means unable to pay debts, in the ordinary acceptation of that phrase. A person may therefore be insolvent, although his assets, if all turned into money, might enable him to pay his debts in full,[501] and although he has not been adjudicated bankrupt or compounded with his creditors.[502] But a person is not deemed insolvent merely because he keeps renewing a bill which he cannot conveniently meet."[503]

Misconduct: Lord Lindley pointed out that: **10–116**

> "When a power of expulsion is given in the event of a partner omitting to do certain things, *e.g.* entering in the partnership books all monies he may receive on account of the partnership, the power will not, as a rule, be exercisable, unless the omission was a studied omission."[504]

However, this must be read subject to the precise terms of the agreement. If the adjective "wilful" is appended to "misconduct", this might connote either deliberate or reckless misconduct.[505]

Dishonesty, etc.: Honesty, integrity and restraint are vital in a partner. Thus, in *Carmichael v. Evans*,[506] a member of a trading partnership was held to be guilty of a flagrant breach of his duties as a partner, having been convicted of travelling on the railway without a ticket with intent to avoid payment; again, in *Goodman*   **10–117**

---

[498] *ibid.* s.35, *infra*, paras 24–47 *et seq.*

[499] An unsuccessful attempt to rely on a ground of this type was made in *Thakrar v. Vadera*, *supra*. It is almost inconceivable that a successful expulsion could be founded on *ibid.* s.35(e) (partnership carried on at a loss) or (f) (the just and equitable ground). Note that reliance may only be placed on s.35(b) to (d) where the other partners are themselves blameless (which should in any event be the position if they are considering the exercise of a power of expulsion). *Semble* a similar approach is likely to be adopted in a case falling within s.35(f): see *infra*, para. 24–92.

[500] See *infra*, paras 27–43 *et seq.*

[501] See *Bayly v. Schofield* (1813) 1 M. & S. 338, 353 *per* Le Blanc J.

[502] See *Parker v. Gossage* (1835) 2 C.M. & R. 617; *Biddlecombe v. Bond* (1835) 4 A. & E. 332; also *London & Counties Assets Co. v. Brighton Grand Concert Hall and Picture Palace Ltd.* [1915] 2 K.B. 493 and the cases there cited.

[503] *Cutten v. Sanger* (1828) 2 Y. & J. 459; and see *Anon.* (1808) 1 Camp. 492.

[504] See *Smith v. Mules* (1852) 9 Hare. 556. Note, however, that, in this case, the power was exercisable only in the case of omissions made "knowingly and wilfully". It would equally be dangerous to expel a partner on the basis of breaches of duty which are of a trivial nature: see *Rice v. Great Yarmouth Borough Council, The Times*, July 26, 2000 (CA), which did *not*, however, concern a partnership agreement.

[505] *Ronson International Ltd. v. Patrick* [2006] 2 All E.R. (Comm) 344 (CA), albeit a decision on the construction of an insurance contract.

[506] [1904] 1 Ch. 486.

v. Sinclair,[507] a doctor was held to be guilty of flagrantly immoral behaviour by having an affair with a woman patient. It is clear that a physical assault by one partner on another will be regarded unsympathetically, even if it was provoked.[508]

In *Kelly v. Denman*[509] it was, not surprisingly, held that a partner's admitted dishonesty in underdeclaring and underpaying PAYE and national insurance contributions on behalf of the firm would justify his expulsion.[510] Where, however, a partner genuinely (but wrongly) suspects that there has been an underdeclaration of tax and reports the matter to the appropriate authorities without informing his fellow partners, they may be unable to expel him, despite any embarrassment or inconvenience which his actions may have caused.[511]

10–118   Equally, notions as to the seriousness of some forms of criminal, unprofessional and anti-social behaviour have changed markedly in recent years and it should not be supposed that attitudes displayed by the courts in cases decided in the early parts of the twentieth century would necessarily be followed today. By the same token, conduct which once would have been regarded as less than serious, even if reported,[512] could now be regarded as sufficiently serious to justify immediate expulsion, especially where such conduct might expose the firm to claims for damages.

Where the exercise of the power requires actual dishonesty on the part of a partner, there are seemingly three possible standards of dishonesty which may be applied, namely a purely subjective test, a purely objective test or a hybrid combination of the two.[513] Clearly the subjective test will not be apposite in the present context. Although the current editor favours the objective test, an argument might, perhaps, be mounted in favour of the combined test.[514] On any

---

[507] *The Times*, January 24, 1951. *cf. Snow v. Milford* (1868) 16 W.R. 554 (which concerned a banking firm).

[508] *Greenaway v. Greenaway* (1940) 84 S.J. 43.

[509] An unreported decision of Rimer J. in May 1996. The case is discussed in [1996] 11 Comm. Lawyer 74.

[510] To sustain the expulsion the defendants had to show that the claimant was "guilty of conduct which would be likely to have a serious adverse effect upon the Partnership business". It should be noted that the claimant did concede that his conduct would, prima facie, justify his expulsion. It was also alleged that the claimant was guilty of a VAT fraud, but the judge found that whilst, in this regard, the claimant was thoroughly careless and negligent in his duties to the partnership, he was not actually dishonest. As a result, because of the way in which the defendants' case was pleaded, they could not place reliance on this as an additional ground for expulsion. *Semble*, the position would have been different if the case had been pleaded differently.

[511] *DB Rare Books Ltd. v. Antiqbooks* [1995] 2 B.C.L.C. 306 (CA). Here the expulsion clause required the respondents to show a material breach of the partnership agreement: in that regard they relied on a breach of an express duty of good faith and a duty to act in the best interests of the partnership so as to promote its business. Note, however, that the relationship of trust and confidence between the partners appears already to have been destroyed: *ibid.* p. 332a–d *per* Stuart-Smith J. See also, as to this case, *infra*, para. 10–119.

[512] Particularly sexual harassment and conduct involving discrimination of any sort. See, for example, the approach of the court in *Proceedings Commissioner v. Ali Hatem* [1999] 1 N.Z.L.R. 305.

[513] *Royal Brunei Airlines v. Tan* [1995] 2 A.C. 378 (PC); *Twinsectra Ltd. v. Yardley* [2002] 2 A.C. 164 (see expecially at [27] *per* Lord Hutton), as interpreted in *Barlow Clowes International Ltd. v. Eurotrust International Ltd.* [2006] 1 W.L.R. 1476 (PC); also *Abou-Rahmah v. Abacha* [2007] 1 Lloyd's Rep 115 (CA); *Dolley v. Ogunseitan* [2009] EWHC 1601 (Ch) (Lawtel 9/7/09); *Aerostar Maintenance International Ltd. v. Wilson* [2010] EWHC 2032 (Ch) (Lawtel 4/8/10).

[514] By analogy with *Bryant v. Law Society* [2009] 1 W.L.R. 163, which concerned an appeal from a finding of the Solicitors' Disciplinary Tribunal. Yet surely the combined test, which would seemingly admit evidence of good character, cannot be relevant here. *cf. infra*, para. 16–07.

footing, mere carelessness will not constitute dishonesty and there will nearly always need to be a degree of conscious impropriety.[515]

Depending on the precise terms of the expulsion clause, it may be possible to rely on an act of dishonesty, etc., which *pre-dates* the agreement,[516] if the other partners were unaware of the relevant facts at the time the agreement was executed.

Material breach of agreement: It is sometimes provided that a partner can be expelled if he is guilty of a "material breach" of the partnership agreement. This expression connotes a serious breach but does not require the conduct complained of to be of a repudiatory nature.[517] As Dillon L.J. put it in his dissenting judgment[518]:   **10–119**

> "It is enough if a breach goes to the root of the confidence and good faith which should exist between partners."[519]

Discretionary grounds: It is theoretically possible to frame a ground of expulsion which requires a degree of subjective judgment by the other partners,[520] but this is not generally to be commended.[521]   **10–120**

Discrimination: The chosen grounds should not be discriminatory on the grounds of partner's sex,[522] gender reassignment,[523] colour, race, nationality or

---

[515] See *Royal Brunei Airlines v. Tan*, *supra*, at p. 389.

[516] See *Bland v. Sparkes*, *The Times*, December 17, 1999 (CA). This was not a partnership case. And note also *Re Casey's Film and Video Ltd.* [2002] 1 B.C.L.C. 454, a decision under the Companies Act 1985, s.459. *cf.* the decision in *Andrewes v. Garstin* (1861) 10 C.B. 444, where the evidence of dishonesty was vague and uncertain: see *infra*, para. 16–06, n. 26. This was *not* an expulsion case.

[517] *DB Rare Books Ltd. v. Antiqbooks* [1995] 2 B.C.L.C. 306 (CA). Although Dillon L.J. delivered a dissenting judgment, he concurred in this view: see *ibid.* p. 322b. Of course, the doctrine of repudiation *per se* has no application to partnerships: see *infra*, paras 24–05 *et seq.*

[518] *ibid.* p. 322c.

[519] See also, generally, *infra*, paras 24–82 *et seq.*, where a similar issue is discussed in the context of the Partnership Act 1890, s.35(d).

[520] See, for example, *Fairman v. Scully* 1997 G.W.D. 29–1492. Here it was provided that the partner to be expelled should be "considered" to have been guilty of professional misconduct, etc. In the absence of such a requirement, the test will be a wholly objective one: see, for example, *DB Rare Books Ltd. v. Antiqbooks* [1995] 2 B.C.L.C. 306 (CA).

[521] The courts will, almost inevitably, scrutinise the ground relied on and may conclude that the partners are obliged to take a "reasonable" view of the expelled partner's conduct: see *Kerr v. Morris* [1987] Ch. 90, 111D *per* Dillon L.J., although this part of his judgment was clearly *obiter*. But see *Wood v. Woad* (1874) L.R. 9 Ex. 190; *Russell v. Russell* (1880) 14 Ch.D. 471 (which concerned a power to dissolve).

[522] Sex Discrimination Act 1975, ss.11(1)(b)(ii), 82(1A) (as added, in the case of the latter subsection, by the Sex Discrimination Act 1986, s.2(3)). These provisions will be replaced by the consolidating and amending Equality Act 2010 as from a day to be appointed: see *supra*, paras 8–09 *et seq.*

[523] *ibid.* There will, however, be no discrimination where, if the partner were an employee, being a man/woman would be a genuine occupational qualification for the job and the provision can be shown to be reasonable or where there would be a supplementary genuine occupational qualification for the job: *ibid.* s.11(3B), (3C) (as added by the Sex Discrimination (Gender Reassignment) Regulations 1999 (SI 1999/1102), reg. 4(5)). As to the meaning of the expression "supplementary genuine occupational qualification", see *ibid.* s.7B(2) (as added by *ibid.* reg. 4(1)). As to the Equality Act 2010, see the preceding footnote.

ethnic or national origins,[524] disability,[525] religion or belief,[526] sexual orientation,[527] age[528] or, as from the day to be appointed, married or civil partner
status.[529]

Time limits

10–121   Some agreements seek to impose time constraints on the power of expulsion
by requiring the other partners to exercise the power within a set period after
becoming aware of the relevant facts.[530] Whilst this approach has some attractions in terms of certainty for the partner to be expelled, it is not generally to be
commended, since it will often deter a proper investigation of those facts and can
ultimately result in over hasty decisions to expel being taken, to the detriment of
all the partners. This may be particularly so where the partners would otherwise
wish to defer their decision until after the conclusion of criminal or disciplinary
proceedings.

Expulsion procedure

10–122   The agreement should provide the manner in which a partner can be expelled.
This will usually involve the service of an expulsion notice with the approval of
all, or a specified majority, of the other partners.[531] It is prima facie undesirable
to provide that the notice will specify the precise matters of complaint which
have led to its service, although reference should in practice be made to the
relevant ground(s) set out in the agreement.[532] It may, of course, be that the full
extent of the expelled partner's misdeeds will only come to light *after* the
expulsion; in such a case, it should be possible for the other partners to place
reliance thereon in the event of the expulsion being challenged,[533] although much

---

[524] Race Relations Act 1976, s.10(1)(d)(ii), (1A), (6), as added in the case of subs. (1A) by the Race
Relations Act 1976 (Amendment) Regulations 2003 (SI 2003/1626), reg. 12(a). In this case, however,
it will seemingly be permissible to discriminate on the grounds of a partner's colour or nationality if
the firm comprises less than six partners: see *ibid.* s.3(1), 10(1), (1A). This exception, the application
of which is severely limited (see *supra*, para. 8–17, n. 72), will, however, no longer apply under the
Equality Act 2010.
[525] Disability Discrimination Act 1995, s.6A(1)(d)(ii), (4), (as added by the Disability Discrimination Act 1995 (Amendment) Regulations 2003 (SI 2003/1673), reg. 6. As to the Equality Act 2010,
see *supra*, n. 522.
[526] Employment Equality (Religion or Belief) Regulations 2003 (SI 2003/1660), reg. 14(1)(d)(ii),
(8). As to the Equality Act 2010, see *supra*, n. 522.
[527] Employment Equality (Sexual Orientation) Regulations 2003 (SI 2003/1661), reg. 14(1)(d)(ii),
(8). As to the Equality Act 2010, see *supra*, n. 522.
[528] Employment Equality (Age) Regulations 2006 (SI 2006/1031), reg. 17(1)(d)(ii), (8). As to the
Equality Act 2010, see *supra*, n. 522.
[529] See the Equality Act 2010, ss.8, 13(4).
[530] As in *Kelly v. Denman*, an unreported decision of Rimer J. in May 1996, discussed at [1996]
11 Comm. Lawyer 74. See also, *supra*, para. 10–117.
[531] Provided that all partners have concurred in (or are otherwise bound by) the decision to serve
the notice, there is no need for them all to sign it, unless the agreement so requires. Some agreements
provide that a preliminary "warning notice" should be served, thus giving the recipient an opportunity to mend his ways but, in the view of the current editor, such provisions are of questionable value,
since the initial misconduct will usually be symptomatic of a serious underlying problem which can
only be resolved by expulsion.
[532] But see *Kerr v. Morris* [1987] Ch. 90, 111D *per* Dillon L.J. It is submitted that this *obiter* view
is not justified in law: see *Green v. Howell* [1910] 1 Ch. 493 and *infra*, paras 10–127, 10–128.
[533] See *Boston Deep Sea Fishing and Ice Company v. Ansell* (1888) 39 Ch.D. 339 (CA) (an
employment case). The point was canvassed in *Kelly v. Denman* (an unreported decision of Rimer J.
in May 1996, discussed at [1996] 11 Comm. Lawyer 74), but was not, in the event, ruled on, because
of the way the case had been pleaded: see further, *supra*, para. 10–117, n. 510. Given the tenor of the

will depend on the precise terms of the power.[534] Whether reliance can be placed on a ground which the partners have considered and rejected is more doubtful.[535]

If more than one partner is to be capable of being expelled at the same time, that fact should be clearly stated.[536]

It has become increasingly common to include a power to suspend a partner for a short period pending the decision to expel, in order to avoid unnecessary embarrassment, particularly where potentially criminal conduct is involved.[537] If this course is adopted, the suspended partner will normally continue to receive his full profit share and other benefits until such time as he is either fully reinstated or expelled. Alternatively, where the agreement contains a suitably wide power to place a partner on "garden leave",[538] a separate power of suspension prior to expulsion may be unnecessary.

Construction of expulsion clauses

Since a true power of expulsion is expropriatory in nature,[539] it will always be construed strictly, notwithstanding the modern approach to construction noticed earlier in this chapter.[540] Thus in *Re A Solicitors' Arbitration*,[541] a power which permitted "any partner" to be expelled by "the other partners" was held not to authorise a single partner to expel either or both of his co-partners.[542] Moreover, in *Bond v. Hale*,[543] the Court of Appeal of New South Wales followed *Re A Solicitors' Arbitration* and held that, on a true construction of the power in question, three members of a five man firm could not expel the other two, even though grounds justifying an exercise of the power seemingly could be proved.[544]

10–123

In earlier editions of this work a distinction was sought to be drawn between the approach to construction in the case of firms comprising two partners and those comprising more than two partners, on the footing that, in the former case, the power is in truth a power to determine the partnership (albeit with different consequences than a normal dissolution), whereas in the latter it is a power of expulsion properly so called. Yet the fact remains that, if the sole continuing "partner" is entitled to acquire the partnership business following the expulsion,

---

judgment, it would appear likely that Rimer J. would have allowed reliance on the additional ground had the case been pleaded differently.

[534] It might, in any event, be possible to serve a second expulsion notice in such a case.

[535] Some support for the proposition that they may not is to be found in the observations of Arden J. in *Thakrar v. Vadera*, March 31, 1999 (unreported). *Sed quaere.*

[536] See, *Re A Solicitors' Arbitration* [1962] 1 W.L.R. 353; *Bond v. Hale* (1969) 72 S.R. (N.S.W.) 201, noted *infra*, para. 10–123.

[537] See the *Encyclopedia of Professional Partnerships*, Precedent 1, cl. 21(1), proviso (i). See further, as to the exercise of such a power, *infra*, para. 10–146.

[538] See *infra*, paras 10–146, 10–147.

[539] Even if the expelled partner receives the full value of his share, he will still be deprived of his share of *future* profits: *Blisset v. Daniel* (1853) 10 Hare 493, 518 *per* Page Wood V.-C.

[540] See *supra*, paras 10–06, 10–07.

[541] [1962] 1 W.L.R. 353.

[542] Note, however, that in *Thakrar v. Vadera*, March 31, 1999 (an unreported decision of Arden J.), the decision in *Re A Solicitors' Arbitration* was held to be of no relevance to the construction of a power of expulsion exercisable in a two partner firm.

[543] (1969) 72 S.R. (N.S.W.) 201. This decision was followed in *Russell v. Clarke* [1995] 2 Qd. R. 310 and *Hanlon v. Brookes* (1996) A.T.P.R. 41–523.

[544] *ibid.* p. 204F *per* Wallace P.

an exercise of the power is in commercial terms no different from the position where one partner is expelled from a multi-partner firm. The current editor accordingly considers this distinction to be of doubtful validity.[545]

The courts will not, however, permit the strict rule of construction to be taken to extreme or absurd limits. Thus, in *Hitchman v. Crouch Butler Savage Associates*[546] a clause requiring a particular senior partner to sign all expulsion notices was construed in such a way as to avoid the need for him to sign his own expulsion notice.

Exercise of the power

10–124   A power of expulsion must not be exercised with an ulterior motive, financial or otherwise.[547] Lord Lindley put it in this way:

> "The Court cannot control the exercise of a power to expel if it is exercised *bona fide*.[548] But all clauses conferring such a power are construed strictly, on account of the abuse which may be made of them, and of the hardship of expulsion[549]; and the Court will never allow a partner to be expelled if he can show that his co-partners, though justified by the wording of the expulsion clause, have, in fact, taken advantage of it for base and unworthy purposes of their own, and contrary to that truth and honour which every partner has a right to demand on the part of his co-partners."

Equally, an expulsion will not be struck down merely because it happens to fit in with the continuing partners' wish to be rid of the expelled partner: the fact that they have previously been actively looking for a means to remove him from the partnership does not call their bona fides into question if grounds for the exercise of the power exist.[550] The decision in *Blisset v. Daniel*[551] illustrates the type of conduct which *will* invoke this principle. There a majority of partners were given a wide power of expulsion which did not require a reason to be given for its exercise nor any prior meeting of the partners to be convened. The power was exercised against one partner, Blisset, and the appropriate notice was served on him. At the trial of the action it appeared that the other partners wished to get rid of Blisset, not because this would in any way benefit the firm but because he had objected to a proposal that the firm should appoint one of the other partners, Vaughan, and his son co-managers of the business.[552] Unknown to Blisset,

---

[545] Note, however, the decision in *Thakrar v. Vadera*, noted *supra*, n. 542.

[546] (1983) 127 S.J. 441. *Thakrar v. Vadera*, *supra*, is another example, albeit less compelling as there were only two partners.

[547] For example, the motive for the purported expulsion was addressed directly by Arden J. in *Thakrar v. Vadera*, *supra*.

[548] *Russell v. Russell* (1880) 14 Ch.D. 471 (which was not a case of expulsion but of dissolution); also *Steuart v. Gladstone* (1878) 10 Ch.D. 626.

[549] The extent of such hardship will, of course, depend on the quantum of the expelled partner's financial entitlement and the manner in which it falls to be paid: see *infra*, paras 10–150 *et seq.*

[550] *Kelly v. Denman*, an unreported decision of Rimer J. in May 1996, discussed at [1996] 11 Comm. Lawyer 74; *Mullins v. Laughton* [2003] Ch. 250 at [95] *per* Neuberger J. The position is the same in the case of a power to dissolve the firm: see *Sobell v. Hooberman*, an unreported decision of Mummery J. on April 1, 1993.

[551] (1853) 10 Hare 493. See also *Wood v. Woad* (1874) L.R. 9 Ex. 190; *Ebrahimi v. Westbourne Galleries* [1973] A.C. 360.

[552] Vaughan was already acting as sole manager.

Vaughan then delivered an ultimatum to the other partners, threatening to leave the partnership if Blisset remained, and thereby prevailed on them to sign the expulsion notice. However, before that notice was served on Blisset or any intimation of its existence given to him, the other partners induced him to sign certain accounts, with a view to acquiring his share at a favourable value following the expulsion. In these circumstances, the notice was declared void and Blisset was restored as a partner.

The editor of the 6th edition of this work expressed the view that the court would be unable to control the exercise of a power of expulsion which is exercisable "at the mere will and pleasure of one partner". However, since the authority which he cited concerned a power of dissolution in a two partner firm,[553] the proposition is highly questionable if it is taken as legitimising capricious expulsions.[554]   **10–125**

A more difficult question is whether, if two partners are guilty of conduct which amounts to grounds for expulsion, one can be expelled whilst the other is not. Previous misconduct may conceivably be a relevant factor,[555] but the ultimate test must be the best interests of the partnership. In principle, there is no reason why differing treatment of partners could not be justified on objective grounds.

Quite apart from issues of good faith, an expulsion which involves discrimination against a partner on any of the prescribed grounds will, in general, be unlawful,[556] although it would seem that there will only be unlawful discrimination on the grounds of a partner's colour or nationality (as opposed to his race or ethnic or national origins) where the firm comprises six or more partners.[557]

---

[553] See *Russell v. Russell* (1880) 14 Ch.D. 471.

[554] Note the arguments canvassed in *Walters v. Bingham* [1988] 1 F.T.L.R. 260: see *infra*, paras 10–143, 24–21. And see *infra*, para. 10–134.

[555] *i.e.* this might render the current misconduct more serious in the case of one partner than another. It is not an excuse for bringing in non-expulsion grounds as a relevant factor. Provided that the wholly different context is borne in mind, the decision in *Airbus UK Ltd. v. Webb* [2008] I.C.R. 561 (CA) is quite interesting as to the type of reasoning which might be employed.

[556] i.e. sex or gender reassignment (Sex Discrimination Act 1975, ss.11(1)(d)(ii), 82(1A), as added, in the case of the latter subsection, by the Sex Discrimination Act 1986, s.2(3)), colour, race, nationality, ethnic or national origins (Race Relations Act 1976, s.10(1)(d)(ii), (1A), (6) as added, in the case of the latter two subsections, by the Race Relations Act 1976 (Amendment) Regulations 2003 (SI 2003/1626), reg. 12), disability (Disability Discrimination Act 1995, s.6A(1)(d(ii), (4), as added by the Disability Discrimination Act 1995 (Amendment) Regulations 2003 (SI 2003/1673), reg. 6), religion or belief (Employment Equality (Religion or Belief) Regulations 2003 (SI 2003/1660), reg. 14(1)(d)(ii), (8)), sexual orientation (Employment Equality (Sexual Orientation) Regulations 2003 (SI 2003/1661), reg. 14(1)(d)(ii), (8))) or age (Employment Equality (Age) Regulations 2006 (SI 2006/1031), reg. 17(1)(d)(ii), (8)). An additional ground of discrimination, namely married or civil partner status, will, as from a date to be appointed, be added by the Equality Act 2010, ss.8, 13(4). Note, however, that, in the case of gender reassignment, there will be no discrimination where, if the partner were an employee, being a man/woman would be a genuine occupational qualification for the job and the provision can be shown to be reasonable or where there would be a supplementary genuine occupational qualification for the job: *ibid.* s.11(3B), (3C) (as added by the Sex Discrimination (Gender Reassignment) Regulations 1999 (SI 1999/1102), reg. 4(5)). As to the meaning of the expression "supplementary genuine occupational qualification", see *ibid.* s.7B(2) (as added by *ibid.* reg. 4(1)). All of the above provisions will be consolidated and amended in the Equality Act 2010, the majority of which is expected to come into force in October 2010: see, in particular, *ibid.* ss.44(2)(c), (6)(c), 46(6) and *supra*, paras 8–09 *et seq.*

[557] See the Race Relations Act 1976, ss.3(1), 10(1), (1A). This exception will not, however, be replicated in the Equality Act 2010.

Care should also be taken in expelling a partner once a complaint of discrimination has been made, since this may be classed as an act of victimisation.[558]

Compliance with strict terms of expulsion clause

10–126   In his Supplement on the Partnership Act 1890, Lord Lindley explained that:

> "Powers of expulsion are '*strictissimi juris*,' and parties who seek to enforce them must exactly pursue all that is necessary in order to enable them to exercise this strong power."[559]

Thus, if the agreement requires all the other partners to concur in the expulsion, the power cannot normally be exercised if the concurrence of one or more partners has not been obtained.[560] Similarly, if the agreement obliges the partners to take the decision to expel at a meeting, that requirement cannot be circumvented, even in the case of a two partner firm.[561]

Opportunity for explanation

10–127   Where a power of expulsion is exercisable on certain specified grounds,[562] it is a vexed question whether, before it can be invoked against a partner, he must *invariably* be given an opportunity to explain his conduct. Lord Lindley originally observed:

> " . . . it is conceived that a power to expel for misconduct cannot safely be acted upon until the delinquent partner has had an opportunity of explaining his conduct."

This proposition was, somewhat surprisingly, supported by a reference to *Blisset v. Daniel*.[563] Yet, whilst it was held, on the facts of that case, that Vaughan should not have proceeded behind Blisset's back, it seems tolerably clear that, if there had been no breach of the duty of good faith, the result would have been otherwise.[564] In his Supplement on the Partnership Act 1890, Lord Lindley made the same point, if anything, more forcefully:

---

[558] Sex Discrimination Act 1975, s.4, as amended by the Pensions Act 1995, s.66(2); Race Relations Act 1976, s.3; Disability Discrimination Act 1995, s.55; Employment Equality (Religion or Belief) Regulations 2003, reg. 4; Employment Equality (Sexual Orientation) Regulations 2003, reg. 4; Employment Equality (Age) Regulations 2006, reg. 4. As to equivalent provisions under the Equality Act 2010, see ss.27, 44(6)(c), 46(6).

[559] See *Clarke v. Hart* (1858) 6 H.L.C. 633, 650 *per* Lord Chelmsford. See also *Blisset v. Daniel* (1853) 10 Hare 493.

[560] See *Smith v. Mules* (1852) 9 Hare 556; *Steuart v. Gladstone* (1878) 10 Ch.D. 626; *Re A Solicitors' Arbitration* [1962] 1 W.L.R. 353; *Bond v. Hale* (1969) 72 S.R. (N.S.W.) 201; *Russell v. Clarke* [1995] 2 Qd. R. 310; *Hanlon v. Brookes* (1996) A.T.P.R. 41–523; *Fairman v. Scully*, 1997 G.W.D. 29–1492. *cf. Hitchman v. Crouch Butler Savage Associates* (1983) 127 S.J. 441. See further, *supra*, para. 10–123.

[561] *Thakrar v. Vadera*, March 31, 1999 (an unreported decision of Arden J.).

[562] See *supra*, paras 10–114 *et seq*.

[563] (1853) 10 Hare 493, *supra*, para. 10–125. Lord Lindley also referred to *Cooper v. Wandsworth Board of Works* (1863) 14 C.B.(N.S.) 180, but *not* to *Russell v. Russell* (1880) 14 Ch.D. 471.

[564] See (1853) 10 Hare 504 *per* Turner V.-C.; also the arguments advanced in *Kerr v. Morris* [1987] Ch. 90, 95.

" . . . the partner, whom his co-partners seek to expel, must have a full opportunity of explaining his conduct."[565]

However, in *Green v. Howell*,[566] which admittedly concerned a two partner firm, the Court of Appeal held that there is *no* general obligation to give a fair hearing (a view which was subsequently endorsed in *Mullins v. Laughton*[567]), even though in *Kerr v. Morris*[568] that court had declined to express a final view. The courts in New Zealand originally appear to have followed the *Green v. Howell* line,[569] but more recently there appears to have been a move towards recognising a general right to a fair hearing in all cases.[570] That trend does not appear to have been replicated in Australia.[571]

The position on the authorities thus appears to be somewhat confused. It must, however, be borne in mind that, in situations of the type under consideration, any dispute as to whether a case for expulsion has arisen will in general be referred to the court or to an arbitrator, who will naturally afford each side a fair hearing.[572] In those circumstances, it is, in the current editor's view, inappropriate to try to import into the law of partnership the principle *"audi alteram partem"*, as applied in trade union cases and the like.[573] On a true analysis, the position would seem to be as follows:

10–128

1. In general, and subject to the terms of the agreement, a partner need *not* be given an opportunity to explain his conduct before the expulsion notice is served[574]; *a fortiori* where all the partners entitled to exercise the power[575] independently form the view that grounds for an expulsion exist.[576]

2. Where one or more partners seek to persuade the others that grounds for expulsion exist, prudence dictates that the partner to be expelled should

---

[565] On this occasion, Lord Lindley referred to *Wood v. Woad* (1874) L.R. 9 Ex. 190; *Steuart v. Gladstone* (1878) 10 Ch.D. 626; *Labouchere v. Wharncliffe* (1879) 13 Ch.D. 346.

[566] [1910] 1 Ch. 495 (CA).

[567] [2003] Ch. 250 at [95] *per* Neuberger J.

[568] [1987] Ch. 90, 111 *per* Dillon L.J.

[569] *Wilkie v. Wilkie (No. 2)* (1900) 18 N.Z.L.R. 734. But note that, in this case, the court decided that an opportunity to explain in general had to be offered where no set grounds for an expulsion had to be established; *per contra*, where a prior warning had been given and ignored.

[570] *Jackson v. Moss* [1978] N.Z. Recent Law 20; *Re Northwestern Autoservices Ltd.* [1980] 2 N.Z.L.R. 302, 308–309 *per* Cooke J.; see also *Malborough Harbour Board v. Goulden* [1985] 2 N.Z.L.R. 378, 383 *per* Cooke J.

[571] *Hanlon v. Brookes* (1996) A.T.P.R. 41–523. The point went *sub silentio* in *Russell v. Clarke* [1995] 2 Qd. R. 310.

[572] See also, *supra*, para. 10–120.

[573] See the arguments in *Kerr v. Morris* [1987] Ch. 90, 98, noticed by Dillon L.J. at *ibid.* p. 111. *cf. McLory v. Post Office* [1992] I.C.R. 758 (an employment case). A similar view to that expressed in the text was advanced in an article by Bernard J. Davies in The Conveyancer and Property Lawyer (N.S.), Vol. 33, 1969, pp. 32–42.

[574] *Green v. Howell* [1910] 1 Ch. 495 (overruling, on this point, *Barnes v. Youngs* [1898] 1 Ch. 414).

[575] This may not be *all* the other partners, *e.g.* where the power is exercisable by a specified majority, as in *Blisset v. Daniel* (1853) 10 Hare 493, *supra*, para. 10–125; *Carmichael v. Evans* [1904] 1 Ch. 486.

[576] *Green v. Howell* [1910] 1 Ch. 495; also *Peyton v. Mindham* [1972] 1 W.L.R. 8, which concerned a power to dissolve.

in all cases be given an opportunity to state his case, even if this is not always strictly required as a matter of law.[577] This will be particularly in point in a large firm, perhaps with numerous outlying offices, where the partners may have little or no knowledge of each other's circumstances, much less of the grounds for a proposed expulsion, and a case in favour of the expulsion resolution will have to be made out, either in writing or at a meeting called for the purpose.[578] This should be contrasted with the position where one partner draws another's conduct to the attention of his co-partners, merely with a view to their considering the implications and the courses of action open to them.

3. If, exceptionally, the partners serving the notice are themselves charged with the task of determining their *entitlement* to exercise the power,[579] then an opportunity for explanation should always be given.[580] It would seem that a similar approach should be adopted where the relevant ground(s) for expulsion are framed in purely *subjective* terms.[581]

4. Where a fair hearing is to be afforded to a partner, it is obviously desirable that he should be informed of the grounds and facts relied on in advance of any meeting, so that he has a proper opportunity to prepare his defence.

Despite the strict position as set out above, it would in practice be most unusual for a partner to be expelled without some intimation being given to him of his partners' intentions and the grounds upon which they propose to rely.

Waiver of right to expel

10–129   Once partners have notice that a ground for expulsion exists, they should not unduly delay their exercise of the power[582] or otherwise do anything which might

---

[577] *Blisset v. Daniel* (1853) 10 Hare 493, *supra*, para. 10–124; *Wood v. Woad* (1874) L.R. 9 Ex. 190. In both cases there seems to have been collusion between the partners exercising the power.

[578] If there is a written resolution procedure (see *supra*, para. 10–106), a paper explaining the reasons for the resolution will almost invariably be circulated to all partners. Alternatively, such a paper may well be circulated in advance of the relevant meeting. In the current editor's view, the partner to be expelled should, if possible, be afforded the opportunity of circulating a written response with the paper itself, which will necessitate a copy being supplied to him before the other partners. However, this will not always be practicable.

[579] This presupposes that, under the agreement, the other partners (or a committee appointed for the purpose) not only decide whether to serve an expulsion notice but also whether they are *entitled* so to do: such a provision would be unusual.

[580] *Wood v. Woad* (1874) L.R. 9 Ex. 190; *Green v. Howell* [1910] 1 Ch. 495; *Peyton v. Mindham* [1972] 1 W.L.R. 8 (which concerned a power to dissolve). *cf. Blisset v. Daniel* (1853) 10 Hare 493.

[581] *Fairman v. Scully*, 1997 G.W.D. 29–1492 was such a case: the agreement provided for the expulsion of any partner "considered to have been guilty of professional misconduct or considered to have brought himself or the business into disrepute . . . ". However, in the event, the application of the rules of natural justice was conceded. *Quaere*, if the conduct is proved and the other partners have acted bona fide but, on any reasonable analysis, misguidedly, could the court properly interfere? See also, in this context, the approach adopted in *Wilkie v. Wilkie (No. 2)* (1900) 18 N.Z.L.R. 734.

[582] See Lord Lindley's statement of principle in relation to the exercise of powers to dissolve, *infra*, para. 10–144.

be construed as a waiver of their right to expel, *e.g.* by admitting a new partner[583] or agreeing to a variation of the agreement.

Effect of invalid expulsion notice

Lord Lindley explained that: **10–130**

> "A notice of expulsion under one clause cannot, if invalid, operate as a notice of dissolution under some other clause."[584]

Such a notice will thus be ineffective for all purposes and the recipient partner will remain a member of the firm and will retain all his rights under the agreement.[585] Nevertheless, service of the purported notice may be relied on as evidence of a breakdown in the relationship between the partners, thus justifying an application to the court for a dissolution under the Partnership Act 1890.[586]

Remedies for wrongful expulsion

It has been held that, since the service of an invalid notice of expulsion does   **10–131** not affect the recipient's status as a partner, he cannot claim damages against his co-partners for wrongful expulsion.[587] However, the editors of the 7th edition of this work[588] pointed out that:

> " . . . if a partner has been in fact wrongfully expelled and damnified, it is not easy to see why an action for damages should not lie."[589]

Although the current editor wholeheartedly agrees with this view, cases in which a recoverable loss can be proved are likely to be rare.[590] There would, however,

---

[583] The admission of a new partner would in law constitute a new partnership and the current editor submits that, quite apart from waiver, a partner could not, in general, be expelled on grounds relating to his conduct in a *previous* partnership; much will, however, depend on the precise terms of the power. But see also *supra*, para. 10–118.

[584] Lord Lindley cited *Smith v. Mules* (1852) 9 Hare 556 and *Clarke v. Hart* (1858) 6 H.L.C. 633. However, the current editor is of the view that the former decision is *not* authority for the proposition in the text, since it turned on one partner's inability to exercise a power which, under the terms of the agreement, was conferred on him and one of his co-partners.

[585] *Wood v. Woad* (1874) L.R. 9 Ex. 190; similarly in the case of an office holder who is invalidly removed: see *McLaughlin v. Governor of the Cayman Islands* [2007] 1 W.L.R. 2839 (PC); see also *Concord Trust v. The Law Debenture Trust Corporation Plc* [2004] 2 All E.R. (Comm) 737 (CA), which concerned a notice given under a trust deed. The recipient may, of course, choose to treat the notice as valid, but it is considered that he could not later seek to argue that the partnership was thereby dissolved, otherwise than as regards himself: *cf. Smith v. Mules, supra*. At most, he would be entitled to be paid the value of his share at the date of his "expulsion": see *Sobell v. Boston* [1975] 1 W.L.R. 1587. If this is different from his entitlement under the agreement as an expelled partner, questions of estoppel may also arise.

[586] See *infra*, para. 10–131.

[587] *Wood v. Woad* (1874) L.R. 9 Ex. 190.

[588] Unlike the 6th edition, Lord Lindley was not involved in the preparation of this edition, which was published in 1905.

[589] The editors referred to *Catchpole v. Ambergate Ry. Co.* (1852) 1 E. & B. 111 (which did not concern a partnership) and to *Wood v. Woad* (1874) L.R. 9 Ex. 190, 199 *per* Cleasby B., 201 *per* Pollock B. And see also *infra*, para. 10–132. Note, however, that there will be no tortious remedy merely because the partners were acting *ultra vires* when they served the notice: see generally, *Abbott v. Sullivan* [1952] 1 K.B. 189. See also, as to claims for damages as between partners, *infra*, paras 23–208 *et seq.*

[590] Such a loss might, perhaps, be provable if, by reason of his purported expulsion, the partner was not eligible to share in an incentive profit "pool": see *supra*, para. 10–80.

seem to be no reason in principle why a partner who is wrongfully expelled should not recover damages for loss of reputation.[591]

Even if a remedy in damages is not available, the circumstances in which the notice was served, even if not its service *per se*, may provide grounds for the wronged partner either to serve a cross-expulsion notice on his co-partner(s)[592] or, more usually, to seek a dissolution.[593]

No repudiation by wrongful expulsion

10–132   As will be seen hereafter, it has now been held that the doctrine of repudiation has no application to partnerships.[594] It follows that the service of an invalid expulsion notice can *never* amount to a repudiatory breach of a partnership agreement.[595]

Expulsion and partnerships at will

10–133   Although it had long been regarded as settled law that a power of expulsion would not be carried over into a partnership at will constituted following the expiration of an initial fixed term,[596] it has already been seen that this proposition has been called into question.[597]

---

[591] See *Mullins v. Laughton* [2003] Ch. 250 at [128] to [131] *per* Neuberger J.

[592] In the case of a firm comprising three or more partners, this presupposes that the power is exercisable by one partner against *all* his co-partners: see *supra*, paras 10–123; 10–124.

[593] See the Partnership Act 1890, s.35(d), (f), *infra*, paras 24–80 *et seq.*, 24–89, 24–90. Interestingly, in *Thakrar v. Vadera*, March 31, 1999 (unreported), the service of an invalid expulsion notice was seemingly not regarded as material by Arden J. when ordering a dissolution under the Partnership Act 1890, s.35(f). It should be noted that, in the case of *ibid.* s.35(d), it is an express requirement that the partner seeking a dissolution must be blameless. The position may, in practice, be the same under *ibid.* s.35(f): see *infra*, para. 24–90. Where cross-expulsion notices are served but none of them is upheld, a dissolution will be almost inevitable: in *DB Rare Books Ltd. v. Antiqbooks* [1995] 2 B.C.L.C. 306, the point was conceded: see *ibid.* p. 322i.

[594] See *infra*, paras 24–05 *et seq.*

[595] Prior to this change in the law, it was the current editor's view that service of an invalid notice could not, in general, have amounted to a repudiatory breach in any event, given the decision in *Woodar Investment Development Ltd. v. Wimpey Construction U.K. Ltd.* [1980] 1 W.L.R. 277; also *Quest Advisors Ltd. v. McFeely* [2009] EWHC 2651 (Ch) (Lawtel 28/10/09); but *cf. Gulf Agri Trade FZCO v. Aston Agrop Industrial AG* [2009] 1 All E.R. (Comm) 991. It may, however, be noted that the contrary appeared to have been accepted by the court in *Fulwell v. Bragg* (1983) 127 S.J. 171 (albeit that the issue was not fully argued, as the claimant was merely seeking an interlocutory injunction compelling his former partners to circularise all the firm's clients, which application failed) and *Hitchman v. Crouch Butler Savage Associates* (1983) 80 L.S.Gaz. 550 (this aspect was not adverted to in the report of the decision of the Court of Appeal at (1983) 127 S.J. 441). It was the current editor's ultimate conclusion that if, on a true analysis, a notice was served in conformity with the terms of the power but on grounds which were ultimately held not to justify its exercise, this would not constitute a repudiatory breach; similarly, where the partners exercising the power *genuinely* believed that they were acting in accordance with its terms: see *Hanlon v. Brooks* (1996) A.T.P.R. 41–523. Where, on the other hand, those terms were, in effect, wilfully ignored and a notice was served which was clearly defective on its face, *e.g.* because it was not signed by the requisite number of partners (as in *Re A Solicitors' Arbitration* [1962] 1 W.L.R. 353, noted *supra*, para. 10–123), such conduct *might* have been regarded as of a repudiatory nature. *A fortiori* where there was no power of expulsion in the agreement.

[596] *Clark v. Leach* (1863) 1 De G.J. & S. 409; *Neilson v. Mossend Iron Co.* (1886) 11 App.Cas. 298.

[597] *Walters v. Bingham* [1988] 1 F.T.L.R. 260, considered *supra*, paras 10–24, 10–25.

(b) Powers of Compulsory Retirement, etc.[598]

As an alternative (or, more frequently, as an adjunct) to a traditional power of **10–134**
expulsion, many agreements now contain a power for a majority of partners to
require one of their number to retire without the need to give or substantiate any
grounds for its exercise. Needless to say, such a power is of an exceptional nature
and will not be appropriate in all cases.

It should be noted that, in his Supplement on the Partnership Act 1890, Lord
Lindley observed:

> "It may be a question how far an express power to expel a partner without giving any
> reasons for such expulsion and without hearing him would be upheld by the
> Court."[599]

Yet, no such doubts were expressed in *Blisset v. Daniel*,[600] where the power was
a forerunner of the modern provision.[601] This issue is considered further
below.

Since a power of this type is, in substance, a power of expulsion, similar
principles will generally apply to its construction and exercise.[602]

Exercise of the power

The primary value of a power of compulsory retirement lies in the fact that no **10–135**
overt ground or reason for its exercise need be relied on, thus substantially
reducing the scope for the validity of that exercise to be challenged by the
"retired" partner. Subject as mentioned in the next paragraph, it is the current
editor's opinion that, if the partners refuse to disclose their reasons, they cannot

---

[598] See the *Encyclopedia of Professional Partnerships*, Precedent 1, cl. 20.

[599] In a footnote reference, Lord Lindley referred to Pollock's *Digest of the Law of Partnership* (5th ed.), p. 76. It should be noted that a different view was espoused in later editions of that Digest: see the 15th ed. at p. 79.

[600] (1853) 10 Hare 493. See *supra*, para. 10–125. See also *Hanlon v. Brooks* (1996) A.T.P.R. 41–523.

[601] For a hybrid power, see *Kerr v. Morris* [1987] Ch. 90.

[602] See *supra*, paras 10–123 *et seq*. Such clauses are subject to the same laws on discrimination as ordinary powers of expulsion: see *supra*, para. 8–13; also the Sex Discrimination Act 1975, ss.11(1)(b), (d)(ii), 82(1A) (as added, in the case of the latter subsection, by the Sex Discrimination Act 1986, s.2(3)); Race Relations Act 1976, s.10(1)(b), (d)(ii), (6) (as added, in the case of the latter subsection, by the Race Relations Act 1976 (Amendment) Regulations 2003 (SI 2003/1626), reg. 12(d)); Disability Discrimination Act 1995, s.6A(1)(b), (d)(ii), (4) (as added by the Disability Discrimination Act 1995 (Amendment) Regulations 2003 (SI 2003/1673), reg. 6)); Employment Equality (Religion or Belief) Regulations 2003 (SI 2003/1660), reg. 14(1)(b), (d)(ii), (8); Employment Equality (Sexual Orientation) Regulations 2003 (SI 2003/1661), reg. 14(1)(b), (d)(ii), (8); Employment Equality (Age) Regulations 2006 (SI 2006/1031), reg. 17(1)(b), (d)(ii), (8). There are, however, certain limited exceptions in the case of discrimination on the grounds of gender reassignment: see the Sex Discrimination Act 1975, s.11(3B), (3C) (as added by the Sex Discrimination (Gender Reassignment) Regulations 1999 (SI 1999/1102), reg. 4(5)). The former general exception for firms comprising 5 partners or less under the Race Relations Act 1976, s.10(1) no longer applies in the case of discrimination on the grounds of race or ethnic or national origins: *ibid.* s.10(1A), as added by the Race Relations Act 1976 (Amendment) Regulations 2003, reg. 12. All these provisions (apart from the latter exception, which is not replicated) will be consolidated and amended in the Equality Act 2010, the majority of which is expected to come into force in October 2010: see *ibid.* ss.44(2(c), 46(6) and *supra*, paras 8–09 *et seq*. Note also that, under *ibid.* ss.8, 13(4), an additional ground of discrimination will be introduced, namely married or civil partner status.

be forced to do so.[603] If, however, a reason is *volunteered*, it will almost inevitably be scrutinised by the court and its "reasonableness" may thereupon be called into question.[604] Needless to say, a compulsory retirement should not involve unlawful discrimination on any of the prescribed grounds[605] and it should be noted that invoking the power following a complaint of discrimination could, depending on the circumstances,[606] amount to an act of victimisation.[607]

As in the case of a power of expulsion, the power must be exercised in perfect good faith and, thus, for the benefit of the partnership as a whole.[608] In a normal case, it would be wholly inappropriate to afford the partner on whom the notice is to be served an opportunity to meet any criticisms which are levelled against him, since this would run counter to the whole purpose of the provision,[609] particularly in the case of a small firm where the other partners had individually come to the view that the power should be exercised.[610] However, the position is more complex in the case of a large firm, where the firm's management or other responsible partner(s) are likely to have to make a case for the exercise of the power to the other partners. In such a case, the current editor considers that, consistently with the decision in *Blisset v. Daniel*[611] and the principles considered above,[612] a fair hearing should usually be afforded to the subject partner. This will in turn mean that reasons for the exercise of the power will, ultimately, have to be formulated with considerable care.

An invalid exercise of such a power will not affect the subject partner's status

---

[603] See *Price v. Bouch* (1987) 53 P. & C.R. 257 (a case concerning restrictive covenants); also *Re Gresham Life Assurance Society* (1872) L.R. 8 Ch.App. 446; *Berry and Stewart v. Tottenham Hotspur Football & Athletic Co. Ltd.* [1935] Ch. 718; *Tett v. Phoenix Property and Investment Co. Ltd.* [1984] B.C.L.C. 599, 621 *per* Vinelott J.; and note *Wong v. Benn* [1992] C.L.Y. 528. But see *Kerr v. Morris* [1987] Ch. 90, 111 *per* Dillon L.J.

[604] See the (*obiter*) views expressed by Dillon L.J. in *Kerr v. Morris, supra*, at p. 111; and for an analogous situation concerning trustees, see *Breakspear v. Ackland* [2009] Ch. 32. Equally, the duty of good faith is not synonymous with a duty of reasonableness: *Imperial Group Pension Trust Ltd. v. Imperial Tobacco Ltd.* [1991] 1 W.L.R. 589, 597–598 *per* Browne-Wilkinson V.-C. And see also *Mahon v. Sims* (2005) 39 E.G. 138, concerning a restrictive covenant; *Lymington Marina Ltd. v. Macnamara* [2007] 2 All E.R. (Comm) 825 (CA), concerning a licence agreement.

[605] See *supra*, paras 8–09 *et seq.* and 10–134, n. 602.

[606] There may, of course, be no link between the complaint and the compulsory retirement but it may be difficult for the other partners to prove this to an Employment Tribunal's satisfaction. For an example of a case where withdrawal of an *ex gratia* payment was regarded as victimsation, see *Seldon v. Clarkson Wright & Jakes*, December 4, 2007 2007 (Case 1100275/2007/EB). This point was not pursued in the EAT: see further, *supra*, para. 8–15.

[607] Sex Discrimination Act 1975, s.4, as amended by the Pensions Act 1995, s.66(2); Race Relations Act 1976, s.3; Disability Discrimination Act 1995, s.55; Employment Equality (Religion or Belief) Regulations 2003, reg. 4; Employment Equality (Sexual Orientation) Regulations 2003, reg. 4; Employment Equality (Age) Regulations 2006, reg. 4. These provisions will, as from a date to be appointed (expected to be in October 2010) be replaced the Equality Act 2010, ss.27, 44(6)(c), 46(6).

[608] *Blisset v. Daniel* (1853) 10 Hare 493. See *supra*, para. 10–124. Note also *Kovats v. TFO Management LLP* [2009] I.C.R. 1140 at [33] *per* HH. Judge Birtles (a decision concerning an LLP).

[609] See, generally, *Green v. Howell* [1910] 1 Ch. 495 and *supra*, paras 10–127, 10–128, 10–134. But note *Steuart v. Gladstone* (1879) 10 Ch.D. 626.

[610] This certainly seems to be the view adopted by the Australian courts: see *Hanlon v. Brooks* (1996) A.T.P.R. 41–523. However, it appears that the New Zealand Courts take a different view: see *Wilkie v. Wilkie (No. 2)* (1900) 18 N.Z.L.R. 734; *Jackson v. Moss* [1978] N.Z. Recent Law 20; also *supra*, para. 10–127, n. 570.

[611] (1853) 10 Hare 493.

[612] See *supra*, paras 10–127, 10–128.

but may, as in the case of an invalid expulsion, give him grounds to seek a dissolution of the partnership.[613]

(c) Acquisition of Expelled/Retired Partner's Share

The agreement should always contain provision for the acquisition of the share   **10–136**
of an expelled or compulsorily retired partner.[614] However, in some cases, the financial entitlement of an expelled partner may be less generous than that applicable to any other outgoing partner.[615] Where, as is often the case, an additional entitlement is conferred on a compulsorily retired partner, this will usually be taxed either as a profit share in his hands[616] or as a goodwill payment.[617]

It should be noted that it does not follow that the court will, in all cases, be prepared to give effect to such a provision: it may instead think it appropriate that the firm should be dissolved and its affairs wound up.[618]

R.   POWER TO DISSOLVE FIRM[619]

(a) General Power

A power for any partner to bring about a general dissolution by notice, which is   **10–137**
of the essence of a partnership at will,[620] will rarely be encountered in a fixed term partnership, for obvious reasons.[621] However, with the advent of increased partner mobility and the possibility of large-scale "team moves", such powers have become popular as an effective means of overriding retirement notices and affixing prospective outgoing partners with a full share of the firm's liabilities.[622] In such cases, it is usual to find that any partners under notice will be disenfranchised so far as concerns the dissolution vote.[623] A power to dissolve the firm may also be a necessary adjunct to a provision which permits a specified majority of partners to bring about the merger or incorporation of the firm or its adoption of limited liability partnership status.[624] It should, however, be noted that the

---

[613] See *supra*, para. 10–130.

[614] See *infra*, para. 10–150 *et seq.*

[615] Thus, an expelled partner may not be entitled to a payment for goodwill: see *infra*, para. 10–157, n. 736. *Quaere* whether this is permissible in the case of expulsion on bankruptcy: see *infra*, paras 10–152, 10–153. Compulsorily retired partners should not, in general, be treated in the same way, since such retirement does not necessarily connote any form of misconduct.

[616] See *Morgan v. Revenue & Customs Commissioners* [2009] S.F.T.D. 160 and *infra*, para. 34–25.

[617] See *infra*, para. 35–15.

[618] See *DB Rare Books Ltd. v. Antiqbooks* [1995] 2 B.C.L.C. 306, 323c *per* Dillon J. in a dissenting judgment. *Quaere*, would the exercise of the court's discretion in such a case be incompatible with the other partners' Convention rights under the Human Rights Act 1998? See further *supra*, para. 10–27.

[619] See the *Encyclopedia of Professional Partnerships*, Precedent 1, cl. 23.

[620] See *supra*, paras 9–01 *et seq.* and *infra*, paras 24–18 *et seq.*

[621] See *infra*, paras 24–02, 24–03, 25–01 *et seq.*

[622] This presupposes that the power is exercised so as to dissolve the firm *before* the retirement notice(s) have had effect. It is obviously not possible to dissolve a firm *ex post facto*. Needless to say, a partner cannot retire from a dissolved firm.

[623] See further, *supra*, para. 10–105.

[624] In such a case, the agreement will often authorise a majority of partners to pass a resolution for the merger, etc., of the firm, but may not mention dissolution specifically, even though this will be an inevitable result.

exercise of such a power may be regarded as an expulsion for the purposes of the discrimination legislation,[625] but this will not *per se* invalidate the notice.

It is also necessary to address the consequences of a dissolution pursuant to such a power. In many cases, the agreement will provide that the majority of the "continuing" partners[626] may take over the dissolved firm's name and goodwill for no or only a nominal consideration, thus facilitating the creation of a "phoenix" firm.[627] It cannot, however, be guaranteed that a court will necessary give effect to such a provision.[628]

Exercise of the power

10–138   Subject to the precise terms of the agreement, the exercise of such a power will be governed by the same principles as apply to the dissolution of a partnership at will.[629] If the notice must expire on a certain date, *e.g.* at the end of an accounting period, a notice expiring on any other date will be invalid.[630]

Effect of invalid dissolution notice

10–139   If the recipients of an invalid dissolution notice choose to treat it as effective, the partnership will obviously be at an end, but it does not follow that any

---

[625] See *Dave v. Robinska* [2003] I.C.R. 1248, noted *supra*, para. 8–11, in the context of sex discrimination; also the Sex Discrimination Act 1975, ss.11(1)(d)(ii), 82(1A) (as added, in the case of the latter subsection, by the Sex Discrimination Act 1986, s.2(3)); Race Relations Act 1976, s.10(1)(d)(ii), (6) (as added, in the case of the latter subsection, by the Race Relations Act 1976 (Amendment) Regulations 2003 (SI 2003/1626), reg. 12(d)); Disability Discrimination Act 1995, s.6A(1)(d)(ii), (4) (as added by the Disability Discrimination Act 1995 (Amendment) Regulations 2003 (SI 2003/1673), reg. 6)); Employment Equality (Religion or Belief) Regulations 2003 (SI 2003/1660), reg. 14(1)(d)(ii), (8); Employment Equality (Sexual Orientation) Regulations 2003 (SI 2003/1661), reg. 14(1)(d)(ii), (8); Employment Equality (Age) Regulations 2006 (SI 2006/1031), reg. 17(1)(d)(ii), (8). There are, however, certain limited exceptions in the case of discrimination on the grounds of gender reassignment: see the Sex Discrimination Act 1975, s.11(3B), (3C) (as added by the Sex Discrimination (Gender Reassignment) Regulations 1999 (SI 1999/1102), reg. 4(5)). The former general exception for firms comprising 5 partners or less under the Race Relations Act 1976, s.10(1) no longer applies in the case of discrimination on the grounds of race or ethnic or national origins: *ibid.* s.10(1A), as added by the Race Relations Act 1976 (Amendment) Regulations 2003, reg. 12. With the exception of the latter provision (which is not carried forward), the various elements of the discrimination legislation will be consolidated and amended in the Equality Act 2010, the majority of which is expected to come into force in October 2010: see *ibid.* ss.44(2(c), 46(6) and *supra*, paras 8–09 *et seq.* Note also that, under *ibid.* ss.8, 13(4), an additional ground of discrimination will be introduced, namely married or civil partner status.

[626] *i.e.* partners who have not previously given/been given notice to retire from the firm.

[627] In some cases a right to acquire the whole of the minority partners' shares in the firm may be conferred on the majority: this will be tantamount to a power of compulsory retirement and should be approached on that basis: see *supra*, paras 10–134 *et seq.*

[628] See, for example, *DB Rare Books Ltd. v. Antiqbooks* [1995] 2 B.C.L.C. 306, 323c *per* Dillon J. in a dissenting judgment. This case concerned a power of *expulsion*; and see *infra*, para. 10–266. Note also that in *PWA Corp v. Gemini Group Automated Distribution Systems Inc.* [1993] 103 D.L.R. (4th) 609, 629, Dublin C.J.O., in his dissenting judgment, held that certain unspecified provisions in the agreement relating to dissolution were of no application on a *court ordered* dissolution. *Quaere*, would the exercise of the court's discretion in such a way as to override the terms of an agreement freely entered into by the partners be incompatible with their Convention rights under the Human Rights Act 1998? See further *supra*, para. 10–27.

[629] See *infra*, paras 24–18 *et seq.*

[630] See *Watson v. Eales* (1857) 23 Beav. 294; also *Hunter v. Wylie* 1993 G.W.D. 1–60; also reported (but less clearly on this point) at 1993 S.L.P. 1091. *Per contra* if the recipient partners ought reasonably to have appreciated that the notice merely specified the wrong date: see *Carradine Properties v. Aston* [1976] 1 W.L.R. 442; *Mannai Investment Co. Ltd. v. Eagle Star Life Assurance Co. Ltd.* [1997] A.C. 749 (HL); *Garston v. Scottish Widows' Fund and Life Assurance Society* [1998] 1 W.L.R. 1583 (CA). These were all landlord and tenant cases.

provisions of the agreement governing the position following the service of a valid notice will necessarily apply.[631]

Equally, if one partner serves a potentially invalid notice and is subsequently expelled by his co-partners pursuant to an express power in the agreement,[632] the expelling partners could not later seek to contend either that his original notice was valid and effectual[633] or that it constituted a repudiatory breach of the agreement.[634]

(b) Power to Dissolve for Cause

It was formerly common for agreements, particularly in the case of two partner **10–140** firms, to include a power to dissolve on specified grounds as an *alternative* to a power of expulsion,[635] but this is now relatively unusual.[636] In practice, the inclusion of such a provision should only be considered where the continuation of the business will be impossible without the participation of all the original partners.[637]

Where the partners serving a "dissolution" notice are in fact entitled to acquire the recipient's share[638] or otherwise to prevent him from carrying on business in competition with them,[639] the power will be tantamount to a power of expulsion and should be construed accordingly.[640]

Grounds for dissolution

These will, in general, follow the same format as in a power of expulsion, **10–141** although purely subjective grounds are, perhaps, more susceptible of inclusion since there are no pejorative or expropriatory overtones.[641]

---

[631] See *Smith v. Mules* (1852) 9 Hare 556 (which concerned an effective power to expel).

[632] See generally *supra*, paras 10–114 *et seq.*

[633] Although it at first sight appears unlikely that the expelling partners would ever wish to adopt such an argument, one need only suppose the case where an outgoing partner is entitled to a notional goodwill payment which far exceeds his entitlement on a general dissolution (when the goodwill may be valueless).

[634] Not only is the doctrine of repudiation clearly inapplicable in such a situation (see *infra*, paras 24–05 *et seq.*) but, even if that were not the case, the expulsion would represent a clear affirmation of the contract. See also *supra*, para. 10–132.

[635] See for example, *Russell v. Russell* (1880) 14 Ch.D. 471; *Barnes v. Youngs* [1898] 1 Ch. 414; *Clifford v. Timms* [1908] A.C. 12; *Bellerby v. Heyworth* [1910] A.C. 377; *Tattersall v. Sladen* [1928] Ch. 318.

[636] But see *Peyton v. Mindham* [1973] 1 W.L.R. 8 (which was, however a quasi-expulsion case, since a restriction on competition was imposed on the recipient of the dissolution notice). Such powers are, perhaps, more common in corporate partnership agreements: see *infra*, para. 11–11. *cf.* the observations of Browne-Wilkinson V.-C. in *Walters v. Bingham* [1988] 1 F.T.L.R. 260, 268, *supra*, para. 10–24.

[637] The partners must appreciate that such a power will effectively penalise all the partners for the misconduct of one.

[638] See for example, *Smith v. Mules* (1852) 9 Hare 556; *Steuart v. Gladstone* (1879) 10 Ch.D. 626; *Green v. Howell* [1910] 1 Ch. 495. *Quaere*, might the court nevertheless decline to enforce such a provision in an appropriate case? See *DB Rare Books Ltd. v. Antiqbooks* [1995] 2 B.C.L.C. 306, 323c *per* Dillon J. in a dissenting judgment concerning a power of expulsion. If so, would such interference be incompatible with the other partners' Convention rights under the Human Rights Act 1998? See further *supra*, para. 10–27.

[639] See *Peyton v. Mindham* [1973] 1 W.L.R. 8.

[640] See *supra*, para. 10–123.

[641] See *Russell v. Russell* (1880) 14 Ch.D. 471. See further *supra*, paras 10–114 *et seq.*

Dissolution procedure

10–142   This will usually involve the service of a written notice, which may be expressed to take effect forthwith or to be of a certain minimum duration.[642] It is generally unnecessary to require the notice to specify the actual complaint which has caused it to be served, although it should in practice contain a reference to the relevant ground set out in the agreement.[643]

Construction and exercise of powers to dissolve

10–143   Since a true power to dissolve is not of an expropriatory nature,[644] it should not be construed in the same strict manner as a power of expulsion[645]; however, this does not mean that exact compliance with the procedure laid down in the agreement is unnecessary.[646]

Although *Russell v. Russell*[647] is sometimes cited as authority for the proposition that all powers of dissolution can be exercised capriciously, the actual decision turned on the particular nature of the power and on the fact that there were only two partners. It is submitted that, in cases of the type under consideration, the normal duty of good faith will apply so that a notice served for an improper purpose would not be upheld.[648] However, the fact that a dissolution will be beneficial to the partners exercising the power will not, in the absence of such an improper purpose, be a justification for impugning that exercise.[649]

The current editor is of the view that there is, in general, no obligation to give the recipient of a dissolution notice an opportunity for explanation prior to its service.[650]

A valid notice, once given, cannot be withdrawn otherwise than with the consent of *all* the partners.[651] However, it might, perhaps, be superseded by a subsequent notice which specifies an earlier dissolution date.[652]

Waiver of right to dissolve

10–144   Lord Lindley observed that the power conferred by a clause of this type:

> " . . . may be waived by mutual consent; and even if not waived, advantage cannot be taken of it to dissolve the partnership on the ground of the commission of any

---

[642] If the grounds include misconduct, it is usually desirable to ensure that a dissolution can be brought about as quickly as possible.

[643] See *supra*, para. 10–122.

[644] *i.e.* the partner upon whom the notice is served is entitled to precisely the same rights in the winding up as each of his co-partners.

[645] Conversely, where the power *is* of an expropriatory nature, it should be strictly construed: see *supra*, para. 10–140.

[646] See, nevertheless, *supra*, para. 10–126.

[647] (1880) 14 Ch.D. 471. The power was exercisable by one of the two partners if "the business . . . shall not be conducted or managed, or the results thereof shall not be to the satisfaction" of that partner.

[648] It was so assumed by Mummery J. in *Sobell v. Hooberman*, April 1, 1993 (unreported). Note also the exceptional decision in *Aymard v. SISU Capital Ltd.* [2009] EWHC 3214 (QB) (Lawtel 21/12/09), where the power was exercisable not by a partner but by the limited partnership's investment manager. See also *infra*, para. 24–21.

[649] *Sobell v. Hooberman*, *supra*.

[650] See *Green v. Howell* [1910] 1 Ch. 495; but see also, *supra*, paras 10–127, 10–128.

[651] *Jones v. Lloyd* (1874) L.R. 18 Eq. 265. *cf. Finch v. Oake* [1896] 1 Ch. 409; *Glossop v. Glossop* [1907] 2 Ch. 370.

[652] See *infra*, para. 24–24.

forbidden act, after the lapse of any considerable time since such act came to the knowledge of the partner seeking to avail himself of it."[653]

Invalid dissolution notice

The current editor considers that the position will, in principle, be no different **10–145** from that where there is a general power to dissolve,[654] although a right to damages might conceivably be available.[655]

S.   GARDEN LEAVE AND RELATED MATTERS[656]

It is now becoming standard practice in professional firms to include in the **10–146** agreement a power to place a partner under notice on "garden leave", *i.e.* to suspend him from acting as a partner for a certain period, which may comprise the whole or only part of his notice period. This is entirely separate from any power to suspend a partner whilst his expulsion is under consideration,[657] although the two types of provision will sometimes be combined within a single clause. It is a matter for consideration whether the power should be exercisable only in the case of voluntary retirement,[658] or whether it should also extend to cases of compulsory retirement.[659] Some agreements go so far as to permit *any* partner to be suspended at any time, although this is rare.[660]

Where such a power is to be created, the agreement should specify how the decision to suspend is to be taken[661] and, more importantly, what is meant by suspension. A popular format gives the partners exercising the power a range of options which can be tailored to suit the circumstances and subsequently varied as required.[662] These options can range from exclusion from the partnership premises and a prohibition against contacting clients and others,[663] to exclusion from partners' meetings and the normal free flow of information which a partner

---

[653] Lord Lindley cited *Anderson v. Anderson* (1857) 25 Beav. 190 and went on to point out that this decision "must not be considered as an authority for the doctrine that the Court will not hold partners to their articles. The notice to dissolve in that case was given six months after the commission of the act complained of, and not on account of such act, but in consequence of other disputes." It is, however, doubtful whether the judgment of Sir John Romilly M.R. supports the proposition in the text.

[654] See *supra*, para. 10–139.

[655] See *supra*, para. 10–131.

[656] See the *Encyclopedia of Professional Partnerships*, Precedent 1, cl. 18(2).

[657] See *supra*, para. 10–122. But note the decision in *Standard Life Health Care Ltd. v. Gorman* [2010] I.R.L.R. 233 (CA), an employment case.

[658] See *supra*, paras 10–108 *et seq.*

[659] See *supra*, paras 10–134 *et seq.*

[660] Although there is nothing intrinsically wrong with such a power in partnership law terms, instances of abuse tend to be more common, *e.g.* where an attempt is made to use the power to "persuade" a partner to accept a particular retirement package or a variation of the agreement which cannot be achieved without his consent.

[661] Save in the case of a large firm, a fairly significant majority vote in favour would normally be required. In some instances, the senior/managing partner may be authorised to exercise it in the first instance, but subject to a requirement that he seeks ratification from the partners within a set period.

[662] *e.g.* see the *Encyclopedia of Professional Partnerships*, Precedent 1, cl. 18(2)(ii).

[663] It will often be important to restrict the outgoing partner's access to the firm's staff, as well as other professional contacts/referrers of work. Whether access to other partners should be restricted is more questionable.

would expect. Some agreements provide that the suspended partner will not be entitled to his full profit share, although this is not to be commended.[664]

If such a power is threatened to be exercised on an improper basis, *i.e.* in bad faith or otherwise than in accordance with its terms, there is no reason in principle why injunctive relief should not be granted.[665]

Validity of garden leave clauses

10–147   The concept of garden leave is well recognised in the case of employment contracts, even in the absence of an express power.[666] Instances in which a court has been unwilling to uphold attempts to place an employee on garden leave tend to be confined to those cases in which the employee has a positive right to work,[667] although considerations similar to those raised by the restraint of trade doctrine may also be of relevance.[668] Given a power which is of universal application and which is not obviously unreasonable in its scope,[669] there is, in the current editor's view, no reason why an express garden leave clause should not be upheld in a partnership context. Indeed, there appears to be no reported instance in which such a provision has been struck down. Although in *Goodchild v. Chadwick*[670] the court ultimately declined to grant an interim injunction enforcing a garden leave clause on the grounds that the claimants were unlikely to suffer any loss of business, the validity of the clause was not called into question. Faced with an argument that principles drawn from the employment cases should be applied, the judge observed:

> "These and other cases cited . . . are all employment cases. Great care needs to be taken before applying the same kind of considerations to a partnership agreement which is a different animal. In the case of a partnership agreement, different considerations apply, not least from the fact that the obligations of the partners to one another are mutual. Covenants and provisions in a partnership agreement are

---

[664] The right to continuing receipt of remuneration underpins the courts' willingness to enforce garden leave provisions in the employment field: see *Provident Financial Group Plc v. Hayward* [1989] I.C.R. 160 (CA). *Quaere*, might a court adopt a similar view in a partnership context? It is tentatively thought not, but the point is arguable. *Per contra*, if the suspended partner's profit share is merely reduced and not eliminated in its entirety.

[665] *Mezey v. South West London and St. George's Mental Health Trust* [2007] I.R.L.R. 244 (CA); *Watson v. Durham University* [2008] EWCA Civ 1266 (Lawtel 24/10/08), both decisions concerning employees. Note that the court in the former case recognised that suspension "inevitably casts a shadow over the employee's competence" (*ibid.* at [12]); that may be but placing employees or partners on garden leave surely does not have the same connotation. This may be more a matter of terminology than anything else.

[666] *Provident Financial Group Plc v. Hayward, supra*; *Credit Suisse Asset Management Ltd. v. Armstrong* [1996] I.C.R. 882, 892B–893E, (CA); *SG&R Valuation Service LLC v. Boudrais* [2008] I.R.L.R. 770. These cases demonstrate the courts' flexible attitude towards the enforcement of such clauses, but see also the views expressed in *William Hill Organisation Ltd. v. Tucker* [1998] I.R.L.R. 313, 318, (CA); and note *TFS Derivatives Ltd. v. Morgan* [2005] I.R.L.R. 246. However, the courts' willingness to enforce a garden leave clause will not extend to preventing an employee's involvement in a business which does not compete with that of his employer: *Provident Financial Group Plc v. Hayward, supra*. *Semble*, different considerations might, in any event, arise in a partnership context, given the terms of the Partnership Act 1890, ss.29, 30, *infra*, paras 16–14 *et seq.*

[667] *William Hill Organisation Ltd. v. Tucker, supra*.

[668] *ibid.* p. 318.

[669] Note that any issue as to enforceability will, seemingly, be determined at the time of its exercise and not when the agreement was originally entered into: see *Tullett Prebon plc v. BGC Brokers LP* [2010] I.R.L.R. 648 at [222] *per* Jack J.

[670] September 18, 2002 (unreported), a decision of Kevin Garnett Q.C. (sitting as a deputy judge of the Chancery Division).

obtained not for the benefit of an employer, but for the benefit of each partner, including of course those giving the covenant."

An argument frequently deployed is that a partner's skills will atrophy during a period of extended garden leave[671] but it is doubted whether this is, in itself, a basis for attacking the power.[672]

Whether the use of such clauses will have any effect on the court's attitude towards the enforceability of the more traditional restrictions on competition remains to be seen.[673]

Options available in the absence of a garden leave clause

An attempt to place a partner on garden leave without his consent when there **10–148** is no express power in the agreement would almost certainly involve conduct which, even if not of a repudiatory nature,[674] would justify an order for the dissolution of the partnership by the court.[675] However, it does not follow that the remaining partners are powerless to restrict an outgoing partner's activities during his notice period. In an *obiter* part of his judgment in *Voaden v. Voaden*,[676] Lindsay J., when considering the powers of a board of partners charged with the management of the partnership, observed:

" . . . given the size and diversity of the plaintiffs' practice, the term 'management' must, in my view, include the ability in the board, within broad limits, to assign particular types of work and places of work to particular partners in the best interests of the firm, as the board reasonably and honestly perceives those interests to be. I say 'within broad limits' as there could, no doubt, be cases where, for example, the assignment by the board infringed a partner's rights as such or where the assignment was such that no reasonable board truly acting in the best interests of the firm could bona fide have assigned as it did.

However, where an equity partner retires from the firm but without intending to retire from work altogether, one can readily see that it may very well be in the firm's best interests that he should in the year of his notice be required fully to co-operate with his continuing partners to ensure a smooth transition to the continuing partners of the clients with whom he has been dealing and to ensure that the outgoing partner should not in that year serve his own future interests but rather the present and future interests of the firm.

There has been discussion during the course of argument of the so-called "garden" or "gardening leave" cases under which an employer requires an employee during the period of his notice not to attend the employer's premises and excludes him from access to the employer's business and affairs, although still on full pay. I can see that to seek fully to impose such conditions on an equity partner under this Partnership Deed could offend the provisions of the Deed. But I do not take [*the defendant's counsel*] to deny that it could have been open to the Partnership Board closely to regulate the defendant's activities during the period of his notice. I see no problem in the board requiring him, for example, not to mention his intending retirement to

---

[671] Note, in this context, the observations of Cranston J. in *SG&R Valuation Service LLC v. Boudrais, supra*, at [21], in the context of an employee.

[672] *Quaere*, if this were a good argument, why is sabbatical leave not objectionable on the same basis?

[673] See *infra*, para. 10–228.

[674] It is now clear that the doctrine of repudiation has no application to partnerships: see *infra*, paras 24–05 *et seq*.

[675] *i.e.* under the Partnership Act 1890, s.35(d) and/or (f): see *infra*, paras 24–80 *et seq.*, 24–89 *et seq*.

[676] February 21, 1997 (unreported).

any clients other than in the terms and in cases agreed with the board and not to mention to clients his intention to practice (sic) on his own account and to work out his notice under the supervision of some delegated partner so as to introduce continuing partners to the clients with whom he had been dealing and so as to ensure as smooth a transition as practicable without there being any poaching for his next practice."[677]

10–149   It follows that, in a case where the power to manage the partnership business is expressly conferred on a majority of the partners by the agreement[678] or where the partners are exercising their right to take decisions by a majority vote under section 24(8) of the Partnership Act 1890,[679] they may, within reason, take and implement decisions designed to protect the firm's ongoing business and its relationships with its clients but clearly cannot go so far as to impose what one might style "full" garden leave type terms. What they must, however, ensure is that they afford to the partner under notice his full rights to participate in the decision-making process, whether express or implied.[680] If they seek to take decisions in his absence when there is no power to do so, he will not be obliged to comply therewith.[681]

A partner who declines to act in compliance with a decision properly taken by the majority could, in theory, be expelled from the firm,[682] although this may be precisely what he is seeking to achieve.[683]

T.   THE OUTGOING PARTNER'S FINANCIAL ENTITLEMENT[684]

10–150   If it is intended that the partnership should continue notwithstanding the death, bankruptcy,[685] retirement[686] or expulsion[687] of a partner, the agreement must contain provision for the continuing or surviving partners to acquire the outgoing partner's share. If the agreement is silent on the point, the outgoing partner (or his personal representatives) will be in a position to argue that the affairs of the partnership should be wound up, its assets sold and the proceeds applied in the

---

[677] It should be noted that, in argument, Lindsay J. suggested that a retiring partner might be required to do photocopying duties during his period of notice, but surely this goes too far.

[678] See *supra*, paras 10–102 *et seq.*

[679] See *infra*, paras 15–01 *et seq.*

[680] Note, however, that these powers may themselves be restricted by the agreement: see *supra*, para. 10–105. As to the general principle which applies in the absence of any express provision, see *infra*, para. 15–07.

[681] It would no longer be possible for such a partner to argue that the majority's actions amount to a repudiation of the partnership (see *infra*, paras 24–05 *et seq.*), even though this is an argument which is still frequently advanced. A threat of an application for a dissolution under the Partnership Act 1890, s.35 would be more potent in this context.

[682] *i.e.* under a power of the type considered *supra*, paras 10–113 *et seq.* It must be ensured that the right to exercise the power is, on its true construction, still exercisable against the partner under notice.

[683] In such a case, injunctive relief may be more appropriate, as to which see *infra*, paras 23–135 *et seq.*

[684] See the *Encyclopedia of Professional Partnerships*, Precedent 1, cl. 22, Precedent 2, Arts. 6.00 *et seq.*

[685] See *supra*, para. 10–39.

[686] See *supra*, paras 10–39, 10–108 *et seq.*

[687] See *supra*, paras 10–39, 10–114 *et seq.*

manner specified in the Partnership Act 1890.[688] Although it might be possible to defeat such an argument, thus forcing the outgoing partner to accept the assessed value of his share,[689] this could not be guaranteed; moreover, an immediate obligation to pay out that assessed value might be financially ruinous to the remaining partners if, as will often be the case, assets such as goodwill are valued at a high figure but no liquid funds or readily realisable assets are available.[690]

(a) Manner of Acquisition

There are, in essence, two ways in which continuing or surviving partners can acquire an outgoing partner's share, *i.e.* pursuant to an option or a so-called "automatic accruer". By the latter expression is meant a provision which states that the share of an outgoing partner will automatically vest in the remaining partners on the date that he ceases to be a member of the partnership, whether by reason of his death or otherwise.[691] In either case, the agreement will, of course, establish the financial entitlement of the outgoing partner in respect of his share, whether expressed in terms of an option price or the sum payable on or in consideration of the accruer.[692] A further variation on this theme is the so-called "poison pill" provision, *i.e.* a right for one or more partners to insist that the other(s) buy out their shares in the firm.[693] Needless to say, such provisions are unusual.

10–151

It will, perhaps, be self evident that an option will permit the remaining partners to assess the viability of the partnership business, having regard to the price which they must pay to the outgoing partner, *before* deciding whether to acquire his share, whilst an accruer will deprive them of that right. Regrettably, in some cases, as where a high notional value has been placed on goodwill,[694] the effect of an accruer can be financially devastating, particularly if more than one partner chooses to retire at the same time[695]; on the other hand, an inadvertent failure to exercise an option may be equally damaging to the remaining partners' interests given that it will normally lead to a general dissolution.[696]

---

[688] See *infra*, paras 19–10 *et seq.*, 19–24 *et seq.*, 23–175 *et seq.*, 25–44 *et seq.* It follows that the outgoing partner will be entitled to share in any increase in the capital value of the partnership assets prior to the date of sale: *Barclays Bank Trust Co. Ltd. v. Bluff* [1982] Ch. 172, approved in *Chandroutie v. Gajadhar* [1987] A.C. 147 (PC); *Popat v. Shonchhatra* [1997] 1 W.L.R. 1367, 1374G (CA).

[689] See *Sobell v. Boston* [1985] 1 W.L.R. 1587. Note also that the court has jurisdiction to order one partner to sell his share to his co-partners (*Syers v. Syers* (1876) 1 App.Cas. 174), but the court has in the past been reluctant to exercise this jurisdiction. Although this attitude appears to be changing, there is no certainty in this area, especially in the case of a small firm: see further *infra*, paras 23–187 *et seq.* The effect of the Partnership Act 1890, s.43 is, to say the least obscure: see *infra*, paras 19–10 *et seq.*, 23–34, 26–03.

[690] If realisable assets are available, any capital gains could be rolled over into the acquisition of the outgoing partner's share: see *infra*, para. 35–07.

[691] Note that, in drafting such a provision, care should be taken not to phrase it in terms of a purchase of the share, so as to minimise (even if not to eliminate) the risk that it will be construed as a "buy and sell agreement" for the purposes of inheritance tax: see *infra*, para. 36–16.

[692] This may include a right to an annuity: see further, *infra*, paras 10–180 *et seq.*

[693] As considered in *Criterion Properties Plc v. Stratford UK Properties LLC* [2004] 1 W.L.R. 1846 (HL).

[694] See *infra*, paras 10–160, 10–214 *et seq.*

[695] See also *supra*, para. 10–108.

[696] See *infra*, paras 10–154, 10–263. It is, of course, open to the partners to negotiate terms to avoid this result, but this will usually involve the outgoing partner seeking some form of financial "sweetener".

It will be for consideration in each case whether to follow the option or accruer route: in practice, the decision will often be dictated by the nature of the partnership business[697] and the basis on which the outgoing partner is to be paid out.[698]

The mere fact that one or more of the surviving partners are the sole or only executors and trustees of a deceased partner's will does not in any way preclude them from exercising their right to acquire his share in the manner contemplated by the agreement.[699]

10–152 *Bankruptcy of partner*: It was held in *Wilson v. Greenwood*[700] that an option to acquire an outgoing partner's share in the event of his bankruptcy, which was introduced by means of a deed entered into some years after the commencement of the partnership but only a few months before one partner actually went bankrupt, was, as against that partner's creditors,[701] void as a fraud on the then bankruptcy laws.[702] This prompted Lord Lindley to write:

> "*Wilson v. Greenwood* throws considerable doubt on the validity, in the event of bankruptcy, of an agreement that the share of a bankrupt partner shall be taken at a valuation by his co-partners."

However, this cautious view was seemingly not borne out by subsequent case law,[703] so that, in the 15th edition of this work, it was observed:

> "Notwithstanding the case of *Wilson v. Greenwood* it would appear that a clause in the articles of partnership that the share of a bankrupt partner shall be taken at a valuation by his co-partners is valid if entered into bona fide."

10–153 A detailed analysis of what now appears to be styled the general "anti-deprivation principle" has recently been undertaken by the Court of Appeal in *Perpetual Trustee Co. Ltd. v. BNY Corporate Trustee Services Ltd.*[704] and, based on that analysis, the current editor believes that the current position is as follows:

1. A bona fide agreement providing for the acquisition of a bankrupt partner's share, whether pursuant to an option or an automatic accruer, will *per se* be valid provided that the continuing partners are required to

---

[697] Most professional firms adopt automatic accruer provisions, although the current editor has encountered a number of instances where this has caused severe financial hardship to the continuing partners. Note, however, the possible inheritance tax implications: see *supra*, para. 10–151, n. 691 and *infra* para. 36–16.

[698] See *infra*, paras 10–157 *et seq.*

[699] *Vyse v. Foster* (1874) L.R. 7 H.L. 318; *Hordern v. Hordern* [1910] A.C. 465.

[700] (1818) 1 Swan. 471.

[701] Such a provision is, of course, valid as between the partners, but this is, in the circumstances supposed, academic.

[702] See also *Whitmore v. Mason* (1861) 2 J. & H. 204; *Re Williams* (1872) 21 W.R. 51, where the continuing partners had acquired the expelled partner's share at a value agreed between them prior to his bankruptcy (albeit that this was expressly permitted by the agreement).

[703] See *Borland's Trustee v. Steel Bros. & Co. Ltd.* [1901] 1 Ch. 279 (a decision involving a company); *cf. Collins v. Barker* [1893] 1 Ch. 578, where the agreement purported to authorise the continuing partners to retain the bankrupt partner's share as loan for the remainder of the partnership term.

[704] [2010] 3 W.L.R. 87. All the authorities, including *Wilson v. Greenwood, supra*, were reviewed by the court.

pay the full value of the share.[705] It would, however, seem that such an agreement might be not upheld where the full value of the share is payable, but only by instalments.[706]

2. A bona fide agreement which provides for the acquisition of a bankrupt partner's share at *less* than its full value *would* appear to involve a fraud on the insolvency laws,[707] save perhaps in the exceptional case where the acquisition of the share was originally funded by the other partners.[708] Although it might also amount to a preference,[709] it will not involve a transaction at an undervalue.[710]

3. If the agreement cannot be attacked in the above ways, *e.g.* where the share passes to the other partners *prior* to a partner's bankruptcy, it will prima facie be binding on the bankrupt partner's trustee.[711]

4. Since the exercise of an option involves a disposition of the bankrupt partner's share, the consent of the court will seemingly be required if the date of exercise falls between the presentation of the bankruptcy petition and the date on which his estate vests in his trustee.[712] On the other hand, it is submitted that the operation of an automatic accruer will not, on a true analysis, involve any such disposition.[713]

The position will, in essence, be the same in the case of the insolvency of a corporate partner.[714]

---

[705] *Borland's Trustee v. Steel Bros. & Co. Ltd., supra.* The correctness of the decision in *Borland* does not appear to have been doubted by the Court of Appeal in *Perpetual Trustee Co. Ltd. v. BNY Corporate Trustee Services Ltd., supra.*

[706] See *Wilson v. Greenwood* (1818) 1 Swan. 471, 481 (albeit that the conclusion is expressed in very tentative terms); *Collins v. Barker* [1893] 1 Ch. 578.

[707] *Perpetual Trustee Co. Ltd. v. BNY Corporate Trustee Services Ltd., supra;* also *Borland's Trustee v. Steel Bros & Co. Ltd., supra,* at 292; *Mosaic Oil NL v. Anagir Pty Ltd. [No. 2]* (1990) N.S.W.L.R. 280.

[708] *Perpetual Trustee Co. Ltd. v. BNY Corporate Trustee Services Ltd., supra,* at [64] *per* Neuberger L.J., citing the decision in *Whitmore v. Mason, supra.*

[709] Insolvency Act 1986, s.340; also *Goel v. Pick* [2007] 1 All E.R. 982. It would seem that prospective partners who are unrelated to each other will not fall to be treated as "associates", so that the agreement can only be treated as a preference if a partner is adjudicated bankrupt within six months, rather than two years: *ibid.* ss.341(1)(b), (c), 435(3). *Sed quaere.*

[710] On the assumption that the agreement is bona fide and, thus, not tainted with any improper motive, each partner will, almost by definition, provide consideration of broadly equal value on entering into the partnership: see *ibid.,* s.339(3)(c); also *ibid.* s.423(1)(c). Note that it is not enough to prove that a transaction is commercially sensible in order to escape it being treated as at an undervalue: *Arbuthnot Leasing International Ltd. v. Havelet Leasing Ltd. (No. 2)* [1990] B.C.C. 636; also *Chohan v. Saggar* [1992] B.C.C. 306; *Re Brabon* [2001] 1 B.C.L.C. 11; *Money Markets International Stockbrokers Ltd. v. London Stock Exchange Ltd.* [2001] 4 All E.R. 223. See generally, as to the requirements to invoke the section, *I.R.C. v. Hashmi* [2002] 2 B.C.L.C. 489 (CA); *Hill v. Spread Trustee Co. Ltd.* [2007] 1 W.L.R. 2404 (CA); *Department for the Environment, Food and Rural Affairs v. Feakins* [2007] B.C.C. 54 (CA); *Barnett v. Semenyuk* [2008] B.P.I.R. 1427; *4Eng Ltd. v. Harper, The Times,* November 6, 2009.

[711] *Borland's Trustee v. Steel Bros. & Co. Ltd.* [1901] 1 Ch. 279; *Perpetual Trustee Co. Ltd.. v. BNY Corporate Trustee Services Ltd.* [2010] 3 W.L.R. 87 at [92] *per* Neuberger L.J., [162] *per* Patten L.J.

[712] Insolvency Act 1986, s.284. See also *infra,* para. 27–37.

[713] See further *infra,* paras 27–71, 35–16.

[714] See the Insolvency Act 1986, ss.127 (avoidance of dispositions), 238–240 (transactions at an undervalue and preferences), 423.

The above principles are not, however, applicable outside the bankruptcy/insolvency field.[715]

(b) Option to Acquire Outgoing Partner's Share

Mechanics

10–154   An option to acquire a partnership share does not differ intrinsically from any other option, and will require the remaining partners to exercise their rights within a certain period prior to or following the date on which the outgoing partner ceases to be a member of the firm. In the case of expulsion or compulsory retirement, it is sometimes provided that the option must be exercised (if at all) in the expulsion or retirement notice, which is not unreasonable. For the avoidance of doubt, the agreement should also record the fact that, if the option is *not* exercised, the partnership will be placed in general dissolution.[716]

The agreement should in general require the option notice to be in writing for evidential purposes, even if this is not otherwise necessary.[717]

10–155 *Perpetuity*: It is now clear that such an option will not be subject to the rule against perpetuities, even where the partnership assets comprise land.[718]

Exercise

10–156   If the continuing or surviving partners' rights under the option are to be exercised within a given period, a purported exercise after the expiration of that period will not be valid, unless, on a true construction of the agreement, time is not of the essence as to the time of such exercise[719] or the parties have themselves agreed to its extension.[720] As Lord Lindley put it when dealing with rights of pre-emption[721]:

> "Courts will not extend the time on the ground that it was accidentally allowed to slip by."[722]

[715] See *Perpetual Trustee Co. Ltd. v. BNY Corporate Trustee Services Ltd.*, *supra*, at [124], where Patten L.J. disapproved the decision in *Fraser v. Oystertec Plc* [2004] B.C.C. 233. It would seem that Neuberger L.J. was of a similar view: see, for example, *ibid.* at [92], but *cf.* what he said at [56].

[716] See the *Encyclopedia of Professional Partnerships*, Precedent 1, cl. 24.

[717] The option notice need not be in writing even where the partnership assets include land, notwithstanding the requirements of the Law of Property (Miscellaneous Provisions) Act 1989, s.2 (*supra*, para. 7–02): see *Spiro v. Glencrown Properties Ltd.* [1991] Ch. 537. Equally, there is little to be said in favour of stipulating for an oral notice. Note that, unless it formed part of the original partnership terms (as to which see, *supra*, paras 7–02 *et seq.*), the *grant* of the option would have to satisfy the s.2 requirements in so far as it relates to an interest in land.

[718] See the Perpetuities and Accumulation Act 2009, s.1. The position was prima facie the same prior to that Act: see *Borland's Trustee v. Steel Bros & Co. Ltd.* [1901] 1 Ch. 279 (which concerned rights under a company's articles of association).

[719] Time will normally be of the essence in the case of an option: see *United Scientific Holdings Ltd. v. Burnley Borough Council* [1978] A.C. 904, 928–929 *per* Lord Diplock, 945 *per* Lord Simon. The point was canvassed in *Kelly v. Denman*, an unreported decision of Rimer J. in May 1996 but, in the event, was not ruled on.

[720] The period may be extended by express agreement (see *Hill v. Hill* [1947] Ch. 231) or by conduct (see *Bruner v. Moore* [1904] 1 Ch. 305; *Morrell v. Studd and Millington* [1913] 2 Ch. 648). However, it may be necessary for the agreement to be reduced to writing in order to satisfy the requirements of the Law of Property (Miscellaneous Provisions) Act 1989, s.2: *Hill v. Hill, supra* (a decision under the Law of Property Act 1925, s.40).

[721] Such rights were once common but are not now encountered: see *supra*, paras 10–110, 10–111.

[722] Lord Lindley cited *Holland v. King* (1848) 6 C.B. 727; *Brooke v. Garrod* (1857) 2 De G. & J. 62; *Lord Ranelagh v. Melton* (1864) 2 Dr. & Sm. 278.

The fact that the sole surviving partner was unable to serve the notice in due time by reason of mental disorder will not affect the position.[723]

If no time for the exercise of the option is specified in the agreement, it must be exercised within a reasonable time.[724]

A notice required to be given to the personal representatives of a deceased partner within a certain period after his death will be valid if served on his executors before they have obtained a grant of probate.[725] Where an option notice was required to be served on "the representative" of a deceased partner, service on one of the persons who was entitled to seek a grant of representation in respect of his estate (and who also happened to be the surviving partner) was held not to be sufficient.[726]

(c) Quantifying the Amount due to the Outgoing Partner

There are numerous bases on which the financial entitlement of an outgoing partner can be quantified, but that entitlement will normally be made up of the following components: **10–157**

    (a) his profit share up to the date he ceased to be a partner, adjusted by reference to his drawings[727];

    (b) the balance on his capital account[728];

    (c) the balance on his current account[729];

    (d) his entitlement in respect of surplus assets[730];

    (e) any tax provision held in his name[731]; and

---

[723] See *Dibbins v. Dibbins* [1896] 2 Ch. 348; also *Rowlands v. Evans* (1861) 30 Beav. 302.

[724] See the decisions of the Australian courts in *Ballas v. Theophilos (No. 2)* (1957) 31 A.L.J.R. 917 and *Oliver v. Oliver* (1958) 32 A.L.J.R. 198. *cf. Re Longlands Farm* [1968] 3 All E.R. 552.

[725] *Kelsey v. Kelsey* (1922) 91 L.J.Ch. 382. And note also *Biles v. Caesar* [1957] 1 W.L.R. 156.

[726] *Moffat v. Longmuir*, 2001 S.C. 137 (Ct. of Sess.). In fact, the deceased partner had died intestate and the surviving partner was merely one of several persons entitled to be appointed as her personal representatives. The particular "notice" relied on was no more than an entry in the surviving partner's diary. The court left open the position which would have resulted if the surviving partner had alone been entitled to a grant. Surely service on oneself is not effective in such a case.

[727] See generally, *supra*, paras 10–78 *et seq*. It appears once to have been common for agreements to provide for the payment of interest in lieu of a share of profits from the date of the last signed annual accounts down to the date on which the outgoing partner left the partnership: see *Pettyt v. Janeson* (1819) 6 Madd. 146 and other cases of that class, *infra*, paras 10–165 *et seq*. This would now be unusual: an outgoing partner should expect to receive either his *actual* profit entitlement up to the relevant date or an apportioned part of his notional profit entitlement for the then current accounting year (assuming that he does not leave at a year end).

[728] See *supra*, paras 10–58 *et seq*. It should be noted that all or part of the outgoing partner's capital may, in fact, be payable to a third party lender, pursuant to an undertaking given by the firm on that partner's admission: see *supra*, para. 10–66 and *infra*, para. 10–179.

[729] This balance will represent profits undrawn in previous accounting periods: see *infra*, para. 17–06. It would be unusual to find that the outgoing partner has agreed to forego his share of profits in respect of those periods, when their quantum has not been asertained at the date of his retirement, etc.: see *Hammonds (A Firm) v. Danilunas* [2009] EWHC 216 (Ch) (Lawtel 18/2/09) at [30] *per* Warren J. This aspect was not pursued on the appeal *sub nom. Hammonds (A Firm) v. Jones* [2009] EWCA Civ. 1400 (Lawtel 21/12/09).

[730] See *infra*, paras 10–158 *et seq*.

[731] See *supra*, para. 10–90. Since income tax is no longer a joint liability (see *infra*, para. 34–19), there is no real justification for the continuing partners to retain the outgoing partner's tax reserve. Notwithstanding this, the current editor has encountered a number of cases in which such reserves are routinely retained, albeit that this tends to be for cash flow reasons rather than a desire to assist the outgoing partner with the management of his tax affairs.

(f) his share of any unused or excess reserves.[732]

Subject to any adjustments in respect of sums due from the outgoing partner to the firm, *e.g.* in respect of overdrawings, there will usually be little question of his entitlement to components (a) to (c) and (e). Component (f) is unlikely to be problematic if the partners have addressed the issue of the ownership of reserves as and when they are made.[733] It follows that the real question will generally centre on component (d).

It will also be for consideration whether his entitlement is to be computed by reference to the ordinary partnership accounts or to a special set of accounts prepared as at the date of his departure,[734] which may itself depend on whether that date coincides with the firm's normal accounting date[735] and whether all outgoing partners are to be treated in the same way.[736] The agreement may also specify whether those accounts are to be approved by all the partners (including the outgoing partner) or merely by the continuing partners and how disputes over those accounts are to be resolved.[737]

Outgoing partner's share of surplus assets

10–158   For this purpose, the surplus assets comprise those assets which do not appear in the firm's balance sheet, *e.g.* goodwill, and the amount by which the true value of those assets which *do* appear therein exceed their balance sheet value.[738] In some firms, the partners will at the outset decide that the surplus assets should

---

[732] See *supra*, para. 10–91.

[733] If the partners have *not* addressed the issue, it is unlikely that anyone will consider it as a component of the outgoing partner's entitlement until such time as the excess reserve falls to be released. Cases where an excess has been identified as at the date of a partner's retirement, etc., are rare.

[734] See *infra*, paras 10–162 *et seq.*

[735] See *supra*, paras 10–73, 10–108. For obvious reasons, this will not usually be the case where a partner dies or is expelled.

[736] Thus, it is not uncommon to find that an expelled partner is treated less generously than, say, a retiring partner, *e.g.* by being deprived of any payment for goodwill. This will not, in general, be regarded as a penalty: see *C.R.A. Ltd v. N.Z. Goldfields Investments* [1989] V.R. 873 (an analogous Australian decision concerning joint venturers). Care must, however, be taken to avoid any form of unlawful discrimination: see the Sex Discrimination Act 1975, ss.11(1)(b), 82(1A) (as inserted, in the case of the latter two subsections, by the Sex Discrimination Act 1986, ss.2(2), (3)); Race Relations Act 1976, s.10(1)(b), (d)(ii); Disability Discrimination Act 1995, s.6A(1)(b), (d)(ii) (as added by the Disability Discrimination Act 1995 (Amendment) Regulations 2003 (SI 2003/1673), reg. 6)); Employment Equality (Religion or Belief) Regulations 2003 (SI 2003/1660), reg. 14(1)(b), (d)(ii); Employment Equality (Sexual Orientation) Regulations 2003 (SI 2003/1661), reg. 14(1)(b), (d)(ii); Employment Equality (Age) Regulations 2006 (SI 2006/1031), reg. 17(1)(b), (d)(ii). There are, however, certain limited exceptions in the case of discrimination on the grounds of gender reassignment: see the Sex Discrimination Act 1975, s.11(3B) (as added by the Sex Discrimination (Gender Reassignment) Regulations 1999 (SI 1999/1102), reg. 4(5)). The former general exception for firms comprising 5 partners or less under the Race Relations Act 1976, s.10(1) no longer applies in the case of discrimination on the grounds of race or ethnic or national origins: *ibid.* s.10(1A), as added by the Race Relations Act 1976 (Amendment) Regulations 2003 (2003/1626), reg. 12. Apart from the latter exception (which will not be retained), the foregoing provisions will, as from a date to be appointed (expected to be in October 2010) be consolidated and amended by the Equality Act 2010: see *ibid.* ss.44(1)(b), (2)(c), (d) and, *supra*, paras 8–09 *et seq.* Note also that, under *ibid.* ss.8, 13(4), discrimination on the grounds of a partner's marital or civil partner status will also become unlawful. As to the possible insolvency implications: see *supra*, paras 10–153, 10–154.

[737] See further *supra*, para. 10–74 and *infra*, para. 10–177.

[738] Surplus assets are, in this context, synonymous with capital profits: see *supra*, para. 10–79 and *infra*, para. 17–04. Note also that assets appearing in the firm's balance sheet may well appear at a written down value rather than their original acquisition cost.

benefit the partners for the time being, so that an outgoing partner will receive no payment on giving up his share of those assets,[739] but in others this will be wholly inappropriate.

There are, in fact, four basic approaches to this problem, which may, depending on the nature of the assets, be combined in a single agreement.

(1) *Fixed Value*

Perhaps the simplest way of tackling the problem of surplus assets is for the outgoing partner's entitlement to be determined by reference to a predetermined notional value,[740] but this is not to be commended since no account can be taken of the numerous variable factors which may affect the true value of those assets.   **10–159**

(2) *Profit Related Value*

Goodwill

The valuation of goodwill is extremely problematic and is frequently based on a multiple of the average net profits of the firm over a given period of between three and five years.[741] There is no reason in principle why the calculation should not be based on a single year's net profit, but this is unlikely to produce a reliable figure.   **10–160**

Less common is a payment for goodwill which takes the form of an income provision funded out of the profits of the continuing firm since, quite apart from the tax implications,[742] this would place an undue burden on the continuing partners, both in terms of a reduction in their profit shares and an overall loss of flexibility.[743] Were this course, nevertheless, to be adopted, the agreement should

---

[739] This is frequently the case in professional firms, at least so far as concerns goodwill and work in progress, albeit now less so in the case of the latter, since the introduction of FRS5/UITF40: see *infra*, para. 22–07. Equally, in *Robertson v. Brent* [1972] N.Z.L.R. 406, it was held that work in progress does not exist as an asset on a partner's retirement from a solicitors' firm and cannot be treated as such in the absence of an *express* agreement. This decision turned on the technical nature of a solicitors' retainer as an "entire contract" and the result would, in the current editor's view, have been different if the relevant retainers had, expressly or by implication, provided for delivery of interim bills. As to whether such a term should be implied: see *Re Romer & Haslam* (1893) 2 Q.B. 286 (CA); *Davidsons v. Jones-Fenleigh* [1980] 124 S.J. 204, (CA); *Penningtons v. Abedi* (2000) 150 N.L.J. 465 (CA). Note also, in this context, the so-called "natural break" principle, as established in *Re Hall and Barker* (1878) 9 Ch.D. 538 and *Re Romer & Haslam*, *supra* and explored by the Court of Appeal in *Penningtons v. Abedi*, *supra*. The doubts expressed as to the correctness of the decision in *Roberston v. Brent* in a previous edition of this work were shared by the court in *Bennett v. Wallace*, 1998 S.C. 457, 462 and *Browell v. Goodyear, The Times*, October 24, 2000. And see, as to valuing work in progress on a dissolution, *Browell v. Goodyear*, *supra*. And note *R.A. Logan, Solicitors v. Maxwell* [2007] CSOH 163 (OH), where an expert valuer proved unable to value the firm's work in progress thus preventing the financial position between the partners being determined: see *infra*, paras 23–132, 23–201.

[740] See for example, *Essex v. Essex* (1855) 20 Beav. 442; *Wade v. Jenkins* (1860) 2 Giff. 509. See also *infra*, para. 10–216, n. 1015.

[741] There are obviously a number of variables here. The net profits to be taken may be confined to the *sustainable* or recurring net profits, and an allowance may have to be made for basic notional salaries payable to each partner so as to identify the "super profit" element. See further, as to the valuation of goodwill, *infra*, paras 10–216 *et seq.*, 36–58.

[742] Thus, the payments would be taxable as income in the outgoing partner's hands, whilst the capital value of the right to those payments would also be subject to a charge to capital gains tax. See further, *infra*, paras 34–66, 34–67, 35–20, 35–21 (where the position is considered in relation to partnership annuities paid in consideration of goodwill).

[743] See *infra*, paras 10–182 *et seq.*

establish whether the outgoing partner's entitlement is to abate in the event of the profits proving insufficient[744] and, if the outgoing partner's entitlement is computed by reference to the amount of those profits, it should specify how they are to be determined, *e.g.* what deductions may properly be made.[745]

Other assets

10–161   A profit based valuation or payment would be wholly inappropriate in the case of assets other than goodwill, unless they are of such insignificant value that the partners are prepared to agree some notional addition to the average profit figure and/or multiplier or to the continuing profit share (as the case may be).

(3) *Book or Balance Sheet Value*

10–162   It is most usual to find that the entitlement of an outgoing partner is determined by reference to a set of partnership accounts drawn up to a certain date, which may fall prior to, on or after the date on which he ceases to be a partner.[746] In all such cases, it is essential that the agreement identifies:

(a)   whether the accounts referred to are the firm's normal annual accounts[747] or a special set of accounts prepared solely for the purpose of quantifying the outgoing partner's entitlement[748];

(b)   the basis on which such accounts are to be drawn up[749]; and

(c)   which partnership assets are to be taken into account and at what value.

If the agreement is unclear in its terms, it may be that *all* assets will have to be taken into account[750] and that they will have to be taken at their fair or market values as at the relevant accounting date,[751] so that the outgoing partner will ultimately receive his full share of the surplus assets. In *Re White*[752] Park J. endeavoured to formulate a default rule in these terms[753]:

> "Where a partner dies or retires[754] and his interest in the partnership assets accrues to the continuing partners, the amount payable to him is determined by reference to the partnership agreement. However the court leans to the conclusion that the agreement requires the amount payable to be ascertained by reference to the true current values of the assets, not by reference to their historic costs. That conclusion

---

[744] Equally, if an abatement is applied, it must be determined whether the outgoing partner is to be entitled to recover the shortfall in subsequent year(s).

[745] *e.g.* it might be provided that the continuing partners are to have a minimum "salary" entitlement before any payment is made to the outgoing partner: *Watson v. Haggitt* [1928] A.C. 127.

[746] As noted *supra*, para. 10–157, it is unlikely that all departures will coincide with the firm's normal annual accounting date.

[747] See *supra*, paras 10–73 *et seq.* and *infra*, paras 10–164 *et seq.*, 10–168.

[748] See *supra*, para. 10–157 and, *infra*, para. 10–174.

[749] See *supra*, para. 10–73 and *infra*, paras 10–172, 10–174, 10–175.

[750] See *Bennett v. Wallace*, 1998 S.C. 457, 462 and *infra*, para. 10–169.

[751] *Drake v. Harvey* [2010] EWHC 1446 (Ch) (Lawtel 17/6/10) is a very recent example. See also *infra*, para. 10–172. *Quaere*, must account also be taken of the values of the assets when the outgoing partner joined the firm? See *infra*, para. 10–173.

[752] [1999] 1 W.L.R. 2079.

[753] *ibid.* p. 2083E–G.

[754] The position will be no different when a partner is expelled.

can be displaced by contrary provisions in the partnership agreement, but the provisions need to be clear. If the wording is broadly neutral as between taking current values or taking historic costs, it is very likely that the court will take current values. Further, a decision to take historic costs is unlikely to be justified merely on the ground that in earlier balance sheets which have not been relevant to the death or retirement of a partner the book values of assets have been their historic costs, without revaluations to current values."[755]

However, his judgment was subsequently overturned by the Court of Appeal,[756] who were at pains to emphasise that it is inappropriate to formulate a general rule on an issue which, ultimately, comes down to the construction of a specific partnership agreement.[757] Equally, the ultimate formulation of principle by Chadwick L.J. was in more limited terms[758]:

"There is, as it seems to me, no room for a presumption (*at least in the context of a family partnership*) that the partners do or do not intend that a retiring or deceased partner should receive full value for his share. Each case must depend on its own facts" [emphasis supplied].[759]

Gadd v. Gadd[760] and *Drake v. Harvey*[760a] are recent instances in which the court favoured a market value approach, albeit emphasising, consistently with the decision of the Court of Appeal in *Re White*, that the construction of the partnership deed is paramount. Equally, in *Champion v. Workman*,[761] Lawrence Collins J. held that, on the true construction of a deed effecting the retirement of a partner, where accounts had to be prepared as at a certain date, they should be prepared on the same basis as previous accounts of the firm and should *not* adopt a different approach in valuing work in progress.

Even assuming that the agreement is clear in its terms, account must also be taken of the conduct of the partners, which may have operated to vary those terms.[762]

Notwithstanding the decision in *Re White*, a general reluctance on the part of **10–163** the court to tie an outgoing partner to the book value of assets may be traced through the decided cases, many of them of Scottish origin,[763] which can conveniently be broken down into three categories, namely:

(i) those which involved reliance on the last signed annual accounts[764];

---

[755] See also *Cruickshank v. Sutherland* (1922) 92 L.J.Ch. 136, 137; *Shaw v. Shaw* 1968 S.L.T. 94 *per* Lord Hunter; *Clark v. Watson* 1982 S.L.T. 450, 452 *per* Lord Dunpark; *Thom's Executrix v. Russel & Aitken* 1983 S.L.T. 335, 337 *per* Lord Jauncey; *Wilson v. Dunbar* 1988 S.L.T. 93, 94 *per* Lord Mayfield.

[756] [2001] Ch. 393. See further *infra*, para. 10–169.

[757] *ibid.* at [67] *per* Chadwick L.J., [73] *per* Peter Gibson L.J. Mance L.J. concurred with Chadwick L.J.

[758] *ibid.* at [67].

[759] Peter Gibson L.J. did not attempt a similar formulation, but did agree with the reasons given by Chadwick L.J.: *ibid.* at [77].

[760] [2002] 08 E.G. 160 (a decision of Jules Sher Q.C., sitting as a deputy judge of the Chancery Division).

[760a] [2010] EWHC 1446 (Ch) (Lawtel 17/6/10).

[761] June 20, 2001 (Lawtel 22/8/01).

[762] See *infra*, paras 10–167, 10–170.

[763] Note that the Scottish authorities were reviewed by Chadwick l.J. in *Re White*, *supra*, at [53] *et seq*.

[764] See *infra*, paras 10–164 *et seq*.

(ii) those which involved reliance on the annual accounts for the current accounting year[765]; and

(iii) those where the agreement was not specific in its terms.[766]

(i) *Reliance on the last signed annual accounts*

10–164 Some agreements provide for the entitlement of an outgoing partner to be determined by reference to the last annual accounts approved and signed by the partners prior to the date on which he ceased to be a member of the firm.[766a] If the agreement establishes the date to which and the basis on which such accounts are to be prepared,[767] and the partners adhere to such terms, significant problems are unlikely to arise, as Lord Lindley explained:

> "If . . . the accounts have been regularly taken and signed, or regularly taken but not signed,[768] so that the shares of the partners appear from the accounts as intended, all parties must abide by the stipulation,[769] although difficulties may arise as to the true construction of the articles."[770]

The decision in *Coventry v. Barclay*[771] illustrates the latter point. There the partners had, in preparing their accounts, habitually placed a nominal value on its capital assets and carried part of their profits to a reserve fund to meet contingent losses. Accounts were made up on this basis shortly before the death of a partner and their contents were duly approved (albeit not signed) by him. It was held that the manner in which the partners had valued the capital assets was consistent with the terms of the agreement, so that the deceased partner's executors were bound thereby. On the other hand, whilst the executors were not in a position to question the practice of taking profits to the reserve fund, there was nothing in the agreement which operated to deprive them of the deceased's share of any ultimate balance remaining once the relevant losses had been met.[772]

The position naturally becomes more complex where the partners have not drawn up annual accounts on a regular basis or have drawn them up otherwise than in accordance with the agreement.

10–165 *Accounts not drawn up*: If accounts are not drawn up as contemplated by the agreement, the court will ensure that neither the outgoing partner nor the continuing partners are unfairly prejudiced, as Lord Lindley explained:

> "But if, as frequently happens,[773] the accounts intended to be taken and signed have not been taken, or have been taken irregularly, so that the last-signed account is not

---

[765] See *infra*, para. 10–168.

[766] See *infra*, paras 10–169, 10–170.

[766a] In *Drake v. Harvey* [2010] EWHC 1446 (Ch) (Lawtel 17/6/10), Mann J. was at pains to avoid construing the agreement in this way: see *ibid.* at [26].

[767] See *supra*, paras 10–73 *et seq.*

[768] See *Coventry v. Barclay* (1863) 3 De G.J. & S. 320; *Ex p. Barber* (1870) L.R. 5 Ch.App. 687.

[769] *Gainsborough v. Stork* (1740) Barn. 312; *King v. Chuck* (1853) 17 Beav. 325.

[770] *e.g.* see *Blisset v. Daniel* (1853) 10 Hare 493, where a provision that a share should be valued "as it stood" on a certain date meant as it stood in the partnership books: *ibid.* p. 511. See also *Browning v. Browning* (1862) 31 Beav. 316; *Ex p. Barber* (1870) L.R. 5 Ch.App. 687; *Steuart v. Gladstone* (1878) 10 Ch.D. 626; *Ewing v. Ewing* (1882) 8 App.Cas. 822. *cf. infra*, para. 25–44.

[771] (1863) 3 De G.J. & S. 320.

[772] See further, as to the ownership of reserves, *supra*, para. 10–91.

[773] Instances of firms failing to draw up accounts are, perhaps, now less frequent than in Lord Lindley's day, although it is by no means uncommon.

so late a one as is contemplated by the articles, in such a case the account must be made up to the latest date at which it ought to have been made up, regard being had to the articles and the practice of the partners[774]; and the share of the outgoing or deceased partner must be taken at its value, as the same appears by the account so taken."

Thus, in *Pettyt v. Janeson*,[775] the agreement provided that accounts should be settled on March 25 in each year and that the entitlement of a deceased partner's estate should be determined by reference to the last account so settled. For an initial period, accounts were duly settled on March 25 but subsequently came to be settled on a very irregular basis. A partner died in February 1813 but the last account had been settled on November 5, 1811. The court accepted that the partners had agreed to change their accounting date but, in effect, ordered that an account should be settled as at November 5, 1812 (*i.e.* the accounting date prior to the deceased's death) and the executors' entitlement determined accordingly.[776]

The same principle was applied in *Simmons v. Leonard*,[777] where no accounts had ever been drawn up by the partners. However, in the particular circumstances, Wigram V.-C. treated the accounting date specified in the agreement as of little significance[778] and directed the account to be prepared not as at that date but as at the date of the partner's death.

Again, in *Lawes v. Lawes*[779] the agreement contained provision for the preparation of half-yearly accounts and for the share of a deceased partner to be taken at the value shown in the last such account. In fact, accounts were prepared on an annual basis. It was held, following a partner's death, that a half-yearly account would have to be prepared and that his share could not be taken at the value shown in the last *annual* account.

10–166

In *Hunter v. Dowling*[780] the agreement provided for accounts to be prepared on March 31 in each year but, in practice, this was usually delayed until the end of April (although the March 31 accounting date was adhered to). The accounts for the year ended March 31, 1890 were duly agreed and signed, but did not ascribe any value to certain leasehold premises which had recently been acquired by the firm, although other premises were valued. A partner died on April 10, 1891, before the accounts for the year ended March 31, 1891 had been prepared. It was held that the deceased partner's share should be determined by reference to those accounts when completed and that the leaseholds omitted from the previous account should be shown therein at their 1891 values.[781]

---

[774] See further, *infra*, para. 10–167.

[775] (1819) 6 Madd. 146.

[776] See the analysis of this decision in *Hunter v. Dowling* [1893] 3 Ch. 212, 216–217 *per* Bowen L.J.

[777] (1844) 3 Hare 581.

[778] The relevant clause of the agreement required accounts to be drawn up on a certain date in each year "or on such other day in any partnership year as should be most convenient, and agreed upon by all the partners".

[779] (1881) 9 Ch.D. 98.

[780] [1893] 1 Ch. 391, affirmed [1893] 3 Ch. 212. The defendant's argument that there was no time to prepare the March 1891 account before April 10 was rejected: but *cf.* [1893] 3 Ch. 214–215 *per* Bowen L.J. and *ibid.* 219–220 *per* Kay L.J. As to the subsequent proceedings, see [1895] 2 Ch. 223.

[781] This emphasises the need for the agreement to establish whether the contents of the last signed balance sheet are to be adjusted to take account of subsequent acquisitions or disposals of assets.

The principle was most recently applied by the Court of Appeal in *Re White*[782] and by Mann J. in *Drake v. Harvey*.[782a]

Lord Lindley remarked of the earlier decisions:

> "These cases not only afford good illustrations of the rule that in construing partnership articles regard must be had to the conduct of the partners,[783] even where a circumstance has arisen of which the partners had no previous experience,[784] but they also show that this rule will not be applied unfairly . . . ".

10–167   *Relevance of past conduct*: Notwithstanding Lord Lindley's emphasis on the need to have regard to the partners' conduct, it should not be assumed that all accounting practices adopted in previous annual accounts will *necessarily* be applied when drawing up the balance sheet which governs an outgoing partner's entitlement. In reality, a variation of the agreement by conduct is only likely to be inferred when those practices have also been applied on an earlier death or retirement, etc.[785]

Thus, in *Shaw v. Shaw*[786] the agreement provided that a deceased partner should be paid the sum standing to his credit in the balance sheet of the immediately preceding year. In all previous balance sheets of the firm, its properties had been carried forward at the values ascribed to them in the original balance sheet annexed to the agreement. When a partner died, the balance sheet for the immediately preceding year had not yet been prepared and agreed. It was held that, in the absence of any express provision in the agreement as to how those properties were to be valued in the accounts, they were to be shown in that balance sheet at their fair values.[787] Similarly, in *Wilson v. Dunbar*,[788] where only one previous balance sheet had ever been prepared which showed the partnership assets at their book values.

Gadd v. Gadd[789] is another case of this class. There accounts had been drawn up for some time prior to the date of death showing the property in question at its historic cost. It was held that, in drawing up those accounts, the partners had not concentrated on the difference between historic costs and market value. *Drake v. Harvey*[789a] is a more perplexing example. There Mann J. discounted earlier conduct, preferring to concentrate on the issue of "fairness".[789b]

Conduct which *pre-dates* the partnership agreement may be more relevant to the construction of its terms than to establishing the existence of a particular course of conduct.[790]

---

[782] [2001] Ch. 393.

[782a] [2010] EWHC 1446 (Ch) (Lawtel 17/6/10).

[783] See now the Partnership Act 1890, s.19, *supra*, paras 10–12 *et seq.*

[784] See also *Jackson v. Sedgwick* (1818) 1 Swan. 460; *Coventry v. Barclay* (1863) 3 De G.J. & S. 320, *supra*, para. 10–164; *Ex p. Barber* (1870) L.R. 5 Ch.App. 687.

[785] See *infra*, paras 10–168, 10–169.

[786] 1968 S.L.T. 94.

[787] In the event this was equated with market value: see *ibid.* p. 95. See also *infra*, para. 10–172.

[788] 1988 S.L.T. 93.

[789] [2002] 08 E.G. 160 (a decision of Jules Sher Q.C. sitting as a deputy judge of the Chancery Division). *cf. Champion v. Workman*, June 20, 2001 (Lawtel 23/8/01), noticed *supra*, para. 10–163. Note also *Beaver v. Cohen* [2006] EWHC 199 (Ch) (Lawtel 17/2/06).

[789a] [2010] EWHC 1446 (Ch) (Lawtel 17/6/10).

[789b] See *ibid.* at [42], [49]. Equally, Mann J. accepted that his approach introduced an element of chance into the valuation equation: *ibid.* at [51]. If so, can this be the correct construction?

[790] *Re White* [2001] Ch. 393, at [49], [50] *per* Chadwick L.J.; also *Thom's Executrix v. Russel & Aitken*, 1983 S.L.T. 335, noted *infra*, para. 10–170.

(ii) *Reliance on the annual accounts for the current accounting period*

This is, perhaps, the type of provision most frequently encountered in modern **10–168** partnership agreements. Difficulties tend to arise either because the agreement does not specify with sufficient particularity the basis on which the accounts are to be prepared[791] or, more commonly, because previous annual accounts have been prepared on a different basis. In such cases, it will again be necessary to ascertain whether the terms of the agreement have been varied by a course of conduct,[792] but it should be noted that the courts have shown a marked reluctance to infer such a variation in the absence of compelling evidence.

Thus, in *Cruickshank v. Sutherland*[793] the agreement provided that, on April 30 in each year, a full and general account was to be made of the partnership dealings for the preceding year, and of its property, credits and liabilities, and that the share of a deceased partner was to be determined by reference to the accounts prepared up to April 30 next after the date of his death. One partner died. Whilst the partnership was continuing, the accounts had, with his approval, consistently shown its assets at book value. However, it was clear that this did not accord with the requirements of the agreement and, on that basis, it was held that the executors of the deceased partner were not bound to accept the book values of the assets, but were entitled to have them properly valued. An argument that the agreement had been varied by the partners' previous course of conduct failed because, during the years when the assets were shown at book value in the accounts, no partner had died or retired.[794]

Although it did not strictly involve consideration of an outgoing partner's entitlement, the decision is *Noble v. Noble*[795] clearly illustrates the difficulties of establishing a variation by conduct in this area. There the value of the partnership farm had, from 1947 to 1963, consistently been entered in the balance sheet at £8,000. The Court of Session held that, notwithstanding this practice, one partner was entitled to insist on the farm being entered in the balance sheet at its real value, even though the partnership was continuing.

(iii) *Where the agreement is not specific in its terms*

It will often be the case that the agreement purports to record the general nature **10–169** of the outgoing partner's entitlement, *e.g.* to his capital and current account balances, but does not state *how* the precise amount due to him is to be quantified, *i.e.* whether by reference to the firm's normal annual accounts, the partnership books or a special account prepared for the purpose.

In such a case, the first question will be whether, on a true construction of the agreement, it is right to say that no basis for the valuation is established: an agreement which appears to be silent on this issue may, ultimately, be held to be clear in its intent. Thus, in *Re White*,[796] the Court of Appeal was required to construe an agreement which merely provided that a deceased partner was entitled to be paid "his share of the capital of the partnership". A particular freehold property had always been shown in the firm's accounts at its historic

---

[791] See *supra*, para. 10–73.

[792] See the Partnership Act 1890, s.19, *infra*, para. A1–20 and *supra*, paras 10–12 *et seq*.

[793] (1922) 92 L.J.Ch. 136. The partnership had, in fact, only lasted from 1914 to 1917, and for two years the deceased had been too ill to attend to the business. Note also *Wade v. Jenkins* (1860) 2 Giff. 509. See the analysis of this decision by Chadwick L.J. in *Re White* [2001] Ch. 393, [44] *et seq*.

[794] (1922) 92 L.J.Ch. 138.

[795] 1965 S.L.T. 415 (Ct of Sess.), affirmed by the 1 Div. at 1983 S.L.T. 339 (note).

[796] [2001] Ch. 393. See further *supra*, para. 10–163.

acquisition cost, but was worth significantly more than that at the date of death. The court held that the value of the deceased's capital could only be determined by reference to an account between the partners, but that it was clearly not intended that a general account should be taken at the date of death.[797] On that basis, the only conclusion which could be reached was that the relevant account was the last general account prepared (or which should have been prepared)[798] before that date. In those circumstances, it was inevitable that only the historic cost of the property would be taken into account.[799]

It is only where the agreement is wholly silent on the issue that the court may be impelled to infer that, in computing the sum due to the outgoing partner, all the assets of the partnership must be taken into account at their fair or market values.[800] *Cruickshank v. Sutherland*[801] was clearly a case of this class.

The decision in *Clark v. Watson*,[802] whilst similar on the facts to *Re White*, produced a startlingly different result. There, it was provided that the representatives of a deceased partner should be entitled to "the Capital standing to [*his*] credit . . . in the Accounts of the Partnership".[803] The evidence showed that in previous annual accounts the partnership assets had been shown at their original cost price and only adjusted to reflect renovations and improvements (in the case of land) and depreciation (in the case of equipment). The court held that a balance sheet would have to be drawn up as at the date of death and all assets shown therein at their fair values. The fact that the partners had previously made up their accounts on a different basis did not affect the position.

10–170   The decision in *Clark v. Watson* should be contrasted with that in *Thom's Executrix v. Russel & Aiken*.[804] There the agreement expressly provided that, on the death of a partner, no accounts should be drawn up, but that his representatives should be entitled to receive "the share standing at his credit in the capital of the firm as the amount thereof [*might*] be determined by the partnership's auditors". Whilst accepting the general principle that, in cases of this type, the fair value of the partnership assets should be taken into account,[805] Lord Jauncey held that the deceased partner's entitlement to his capital was not the same thing as his share of the surplus assets[806] and that, in any event, the partners had varied the agreement by a course of conduct which could be traced back through the currency of two previous agreements, during which period a number of new partners had been admitted to the firm and had been required to contribute capital

---

[797] *ibid.* at [23]–[25] *per* Chadwick L.J.

[798] *ibid.* at [26]–[30], following *Hunter v. Dowling* [1893] 3 Ch. 212, noted *supra*, para. 10–166.

[799] There was, in fact ample other evidence to support this conclusion, including a specific clause in the partnership agreement which provided that "In the case of death . . . for the purpose of ascertaining any partner's interest in the freehold property . . . the figure appearing in the partnership accounts shall be deemed to be the value of the whole . . . ". Moreover, there appears to have been some cogent evidence of the partners' intentions from a witness: *ibid.* at [76] *per* Peter Gibson L.J.

[800] See, as to these expressions, *infra*, para. 10–171.

[801] (1922) 92 L.J. Ch. 136, noted *supra*, para. 10–168. See also *Re White*, *supra* at [47] *per* Chadwick L.J.; *Drake v. Harvey* [2010] EWHC 1446 (Ch) (Lawtel 17/6/10).

[802] 1982 S.L.T. 450 (OH). See the observations of Chadwick L.J. on this decision in *Re White*, *supra*, at [59], [60].

[803] The court declined to construe these words as referring to the last annual accounts prior to the date of death: see 1982 S.L.T. 451.

[804] 1983 S.L.T. 335 (OH).

[805] *ibid.* p. 337.

[806] *ibid.* pp. 337–338. This is, of course, a valid distinction: see *supra*, paras 10–59, 10–60 and *infra*, paras 17–02 *et seq.*

on the basis of the firm's annual accounts. At least one incoming partner clearly understood that he would not be entitled to insist on a revaluation of the partnership assets on leaving the firm.[807] There was also other evidence as to an understanding to that effect between the partners in the firm.[808] It is clear that the Court of Appeal in *Re White*[809] regarded this decision as a more useful illustration of the applicable principles than *Clark v. Watson*.

It is interesting to note that the distinction between capital and surplus assets was not drawn in *Clark v. Watson* or, seemingly, in *Re White*, although at first instance in the latter case, Park J. was clear that, on a true construction of the agreement, the deceased's capital account was not frozen at its original value.[810] Whilst such a construction might be entirely justifiable in the case of a firm which maintains combined capital/current accounts,[811] as appears to have been the case in *Re White*,[812] it is, in the current editor's view, more questionable in a case where there are separate capital and current accounts. Of course, even if the outgoing partner's share of surplus assets does not fall to be treated as part of his capital entitlement, it may fall to be added to his current account as an additional share of profits, depending on the terms of the agreement.[812a]

Effect of a direction that a specific asset should be/should not be revalued

If the agreement directs that a specific asset, such as a freehold property, should be revalued when determining the outgoing partner's entitlement, this may be indicative of an intention that the remaining assets should *not* be revalued. By the same token, a direction that the value of a particular asset, such as goodwill, should be ignored may suggest that the value of all the other assets should be taken into account.[813]   **10–171**

The basis of valuation: fair or market value?

The decided cases tend to use the expressions "fair value" and "market value" interchangeably, although the former is more frequently encountered.[814] It would, however, be dangerous to assume that market value will be the appropriate measure in *all* cases where book value is rejected, even if a court may, in an appropriate case, lean towards that result.[815] It is, in the current editor's view, questionable whether a "fair value" of assets could ever equate to their *book*   **10–172**

---

[807] *ibid.* p. 338.

[808] *ibid.* pp. 338–339.

[809] See [2001] Ch. 393 at [61]–[63].

[810] See [1999] 1 W.L.R. 2079, 2087. Note that it was clear from the provisions of the agreement that the expression "capital" included the freehold property.

[811] See *infra*, para. 17–06.

[812] See [2001] Ch. 393 at [26] *per* Chadwick L.J.

[812a] Note, in this connection, the unsuccessful argument advanced in *Drake v. Harvey* [2010] EWHC 1446 (Ch) (Lawtel 17/6/10) at [66], [67].

[813] See *Re White* [1999] 1 W.L.R. 2089E–H. This judgment was, however reversed on appeal at [2001] Ch. 393, but the point referred to in the text was not adverted to in the Court of Appeal.

[814] *Cruickshank v. Sutherland* (1922) 92 L.J. Ch. 136, 137; *Noble v. Noble* 1965 S.L.T. 415, 417 and 1983 S.L.T. 339 (note), 340 ("fair market value"); *Shaw v. Shaw* 1968 S.L.T. 94; *Clark v. Watson* 1982 S.L.T. 450, 452; *Thom's Executrix v. Russel & Aitken* 1983 S.L.T. 335, 337 ("fair market value"); *Wilson v. Dunbar* 1988 S.L.T. 93; *Drake v. Harvey, supra.* The expression "market value" was used in *Gadd v. Gadd* [2002] 08 E.G. 160.

[815] The helpful statement of principle formulated by Park J. in *Re White* [1999] 1 W.L.R. 2079, 2083E–G was subsequently overturned by the Court of Appeal at [2001] Ch. 393, but on a strictly limited basis: see *supra*, para. 10–163.

value, unless that conclusion is warranted by the true construction of the agreement or by the surrounding circumstances; similarly in the case of the expression "true value".[816]

The anomalous decision in Bennett v. Wallace

10–173   The decision in *Bennett v. Wallace*[817] concerned the treatment of work in progress on the dissolution of a firm of solicitors. Under the partnership agreement, the capital contribution of one partner (W) was to be the amount shown in the accounts of his previous practice, in which the assets would, at W's option, be shown at market value or book value. In the event, no value was attributed to work in progress in those accounts, but the partners were nevertheless in agreement that it should be taken into account on the dissolution and had, in fact, agreed the value to be ascribed to it. The dispute centred on the question whether an allowance should be made for the *opening* value of work in progress. The court conventionally held that, in an accounting between partners, all assets had to be taken into account,[818] but then went on[819]:

" . . . it would appear to us to be inherent in the nature of a partnership that all assets brought into the partnership should be included in the accounting between the partners both at the start and at the end of their relationship unless there is some agreement to the contrary."

Although superficially attractive, this proposition is, in the current editor's view, highly questionable. It seems to presuppose that movements in the value of off balance sheet assets over the life of the partnership should be ignored. Thus, if A and B were to admit C to their partnership in 2000 at a time when the work in progress of the AB partnership was worth £100,000 and C were to retire in the year 2010 when the value had increased to £200,000, he would, according to *Bennett v. Wallace*, be entitled to a share of the increase in value in the sum of £100,000. A and B would retain their right to the original opening value of £100,000. Yet, the reality might be that, during the life of the ABC partnership, its fortunes waned and the value of its work in progress fell to, say, £50,000. It was due to the efforts of all the partners that the value had then increased from £50,000 to £200,000. On what basis should C properly be excluded from sharing in the £150,000 of work in progress that he has helped to built up? Why should the value of A and B's original "investment" be artificially protected?

The only alternative would be to trace the movements in the value of the relevant asset over the life of the partnership and to divide the notional increase/decrease in value year by year. Not only would this be prohibitively expensive in terms of valuer's fees but in many instances it would be impossible to reconstruct the history of the firm in this way, particularly if there have been a number of admissions and retirements in the meantime.

---

[816] *Re White* [2001] Ch. 393 (CA).

[817] 1998 S.C. 457 (2nd Div.). See also, as to this case, *infra*, para. 17–04.

[818] Given the agreement between the partners, such a finding was strictly unnecessary. It should be noted that the court also referred to the decision in *Roberston v. Brent* [1972] N.Z.L.R. 406, in which it was held that work in progress in a solicitors' firm cannot exist as an asset on a partner's retirement. The court shared the current editor's views as to whether this decision was correct in principle and whether it, in any event, would be followed today: see 1998 S.C. 462D–E. See further, *supra*, para. 10–158 n. 739.

[819] 1998 S.C. 462F–G.

A principle of law which is potentially arbitrary in its operation or which is dependent on evidence which is inherently unlikely to be available cannot, in the current editor's view, be justified.[819a] The partnership owns an asset. All partners are, in right of their shares, interested in that asset[820] and entitled to share in any value which may be ascribed to it. That, it is submitted, has always been the position[821] and should remain so.

Special balance sheet to be drawn up

It will, perhaps, be apparent from the foregoing that, in cases where the entitlement of an outgoing partner is expressly directed to be determined by reference to a special set of accounts drawn up as at the date of his departure,[822] all the assets should properly be included therein at their fair or market value,[823] unless that would be inconsistent with the true construction of the agreement[824] or with an established course of conduct adopted by the partners on previous retirements, etc.[825] The fact that goodwill and work in progress have been omitted from the firm's annual accounts will, of itself, be irrelevant.[826]

10–174

Where this is not the partners' intention, the agreement should clearly state the basis on which the accounts are to be prepared, even if this merely takes the form of a requirement that the partners should adhere to the same accounting principles and practices as are adopted when drawing up normal annual accounts.[827]

In *Montgomery v. Cameron & Greig*,[828] it was held, on a true construction of the agreement, that so-called "termination accounts" would be binding on the outgoing and continuing partners if they were prepared in accordance with the agreement and in good faith, *even if the partners had not approved them*. One key factor was that the agreement expressly required the firm's annual accounts to be approved but was silent in relation to the termination accounts. The editor has some doubts as to the correctness of this decision.

(4) *Revaluation of Assets*

It has already been seen that, when construing partnership agreements, there is a tendency for the court to lean in favour of assets being revalued when a partner dies or otherwise leaves the firm,[829] even if there is no presumption to that effect. In recognition of this, partners may decide to include an express revaluation provision in their agreement, with a view to ensuring that the outgoing partner is

10–175

[819a] But see *Drake v. Harvey, supra.*

[820] See *infra*, paras 19–01 *et seq.*

[821] See *infra*, para. 17–04.

[822] A variation on this theme allows the outgoing partner or the continuing partners to insist on the preparation of a special account within a specified period, failing which the former's entitlement will be determined by reference to the firm's normal annual accounts.

[823] See *supra*, para. 10–172.

[824] See *Re White* [2001] Ch. 393, *supra*, para. 10–169; *Drake v. Harvey* [2010] EWHC 1446 (Ch) (Lawtel 17/6/10).

[825] See *supra*, para. 10–167.

[826] Following the introduction of FRS5/UITF40 (see *infra*, para. 22–07), cases in which income attributable to work in progress is omitted will be a rarity. Note also the decision in *Robertson v. Brent* [1972] N.Z.L.R. 406: see *supra*, para. 10–158 n. 739.

[827] Such a formula was adopted in *Smith v. Gale* [1974] 1 W.L.R. 9. A similar view of the agreement was taken in *Champion v. Workman*, June 20, 2001 (Lawtel 22/8/01), noticed *supra*, para. 10–163.

[828] [2007] CSOH 63 (OH). See also *supra*, paras 10–73, 10–74 and *infra*, para. 10–77.

[829] See *supra*, paras 10–162 *et seq.*

credited with his full share of the asset surpluses or, if the assets have decreased in value, debited with his share of any deficit. Such provisions, which have much to commend them in terms of fairness, were common form in years past but are now encountered less frequently, particularly in the professional sphere. This perhaps reflects a concern to limit the financial burden undertaken by the remaining partners, which can become insupportable in the event of a succession of voluntary retirements.[830] Equally, in times of recession, firms with overrented leasehold premises might welcome the opportunity to debit an outgoing partner with his share of their negative value and regret having tied themselves to the contents of the firm's normal annual accounts.

The mechanics of the revaluation

10–176   Where this approach is adopted, the agreement should identify which assets are to be revalued,[831] the basis of valuation[832] and the manner in which it is to be carried out.[833] It is clear from the landmark decision in *Sudbrook Trading Estate Ltd. v. Eggleton*[834] that, if no valuation machinery is specified or the chosen machinery breaks down, the court will normally itself supply the valuation unless, in the latter case, the particular machinery adopted can be regarded as an essential term of the agreement, *e.g.* valuation by a named individual.[835] Indeed, this was always the position in the case of partnership agreements, as Lord Lindley made clear:

> " . . . where persons enter into partnership upon certain terms, one of which is, that on a dissolution one partner shall take the share of another at a valuation,[836] the Court will, on a dissolution under the articles, enforce such a stipulation, and if necessary itself ascertain the value of the share."[837]

A valuation of the assets carried out by an agreed expert valuer must, if honestly made, be accepted and cannot subsequently be attacked on the grounds that

[830] See *supra*, para. 10–137.

[831] See for example, *Hordern v. Hordern* [1910] A.C. 465. Particular attention should be directed to the treatment of goodwill (as in that case) and work in progress, which are notoriously contentious items. See further, as to the valuation of goodwill, *infra*, paras 10–214 *et seq.* and, as to work in progress, *supra*, para. 10–172.

[832] Market value will usually be the most appropriate, although this may on occasion be discounted to take account of factors such as the costs of realisation, taxation, etc. The expression "just valuation" is not to be commended but is likely to be equated with market value: see *Hunter v. Dowling* [1893] 1 Ch. 391; *cf. Re White* [2001] Ch. 393 (CA), where a just valuation was held to equate to the historic cost of the asset in question: see *supra*, para. 10–169. It is clear that additional factors will be taken into account on a just valuation: *ibid.* at [75] *per* Peter Gibson L.J. As to the valuation of work in progress, see *infra*, para. 34–22, but see also *supra*, para. 10–158, n. 739.

[833] *i.e.* by a single valuer acting as an expert or an arbitrator, by two valuers (one representing each side) with or without an umpire, by arbitration, etc. Note that, in the case of expert determination, it will be difficult to argue in favour of an implied term that the principles of natural justice should apply: *Owen Pell Ltd. v. Bindi (London) Ltd.* [2008] B.L.R. 436.

[834] [1983] A.C. 444. See also *Re Malpass* [1985] Ch. 42 (which concerned a testamentary option); *Macro v. Thompson (No. 3)* [1997] 2 B.C.L.C. 36. The court will have no jurisdiction if the agreed machinery has not broken down: *Northern Regional Health Authority v. Crouch Construction Co. Ltd.* [1984] Q.B. 644; *Gillatt v. Sky Television Ltd.* [2000] 1 All E.R. (Comm.) 461 (CA). Note also *Miller v. Lakefield Estates Ltd.* [1989] 19 E.G. 67.

[835] [1983] A.C. 483–484 *per* Lord Fraser.

[836] The expression "taking a share at a valuation" is commonly encountered in the older cases, but is not much used today. The transaction is, of course, the same as that currently under consideration.

[837] *Dinham v. Bradford* (1869) L.R. 5 Ch.App. 519; also *Smith v. Gale* [1974] 1 W.L.R. 9.

higher or lower valuations have been obtained elsewhere.[838] In one recent Scottish case, the valuer was unable to value the asset on the evidence available to him and the court declined to overturn this conclusion.[839] The remedy of a dissatisfied partner (or former partner) in such a case is solely against the valuer, assuming that negligence can be proved.[840] This naturally presupposes that the appointment of the agreed expert is valid: the fact that the parties have agreed on his identity but not on his terms of engagement will not normally be enough.[841]

A variation in the agreed valuation procedure may, where appropriate, be agreed to by a deceased partner's executors even before probate is obtained.[842]

Approval of the relevant accounts

Whichever of the above options are pursued, if the outgoing partner's entitle- **10–177** ment is to be determined by reference to a set of accounts which have not been

---

[838] See *Campbell v. Edwards* [1976] 1 W.L.R. 403; *Baber v. Kenwood Manufacturing Co. Ltd.* [1978] 1 Lloyd's Rep. 175; *Jones v. Sherwood Computer Services Plc* [1992] 1 W.L.R. 277; *Nikko Hotels (U.K.) Ltd. v. M.E.P.C. Plc* [1991] 28 E.G. 86; *Macro v. Thompson* [1996] B.C.C. 707; *British Shipbuilders v. VSEL Consortium Plc* [1997] 1 Lloyd's Rep. 106, 109 per Lightman J.; *Shell U.K. Ltd. v. Enterprise Oil plc* [1999] 2 Lloyd's Rep. 456; *Morgan Sindall plc v Sawston Farms (Cambs) Ltd.* [1999] 1 EGLR 90 (CA); *Bouygues (U.K.) Ltd. v. Dahl-Jensen (U.K.) Ltd.* [2001] 1 All E.R. (Comm.) 1041 (CA); also *Montgomery v. Cameron & Greig* [2007] CSOH 63, at [32], [33] per Lord Reed. A valuation can clearly be upset if fraud or collusion is proved or if it is not made in accordance with the terms of the agreement, *e.g.* where the wrong property is valued: see, as to the latter possibility, *Jones v. Sherwood Computer Services Plc, supra*; *Macro v. Thompson, supra; Veba Oil Supply & Trading GmbH v. Petrotrade Inc.* [2002] 1 All E.R. 703 (CA). The departure from the expert's instructions must be material, but whether or not it would materially affect the result is seemingly not relevant: *Jones v. Sherwood Computer Services Plc, supra*, p. 287B; *Shell U.K. Ltd. v. Enterprise Oil plc, supra; Veba Oil Supply & Trading GmbH v. Petrotrade Inc., supra; cf. Pilon Ltd. v. Breyer Group Plc* [2010] C.I.L.L. 2865. Note that, in *Burgess v. Purchase & Sons (Farms) Ltd.* [1983] Ch. 216, Nourse J. took the view that a speaking valuation (*i.e.* a valuation supported by reasons or calculations) could be upset when it is made on a wholly erroneous basis, but the Court of Appeal has since refused to draw any distinction between speaking and non-speaking valuations: see *Jones v. Sherwood Computer Services Plc, supra*; also *Nikko Hotels (U.K.) Ltd. v. M.E.P.C. Plc, supra*; *Morgan Sindall plc v Sawston Farms (Cambs) Ltd., supra; Doughty Hanson & Co. Ltd. v. Roe* [2008] 1 B.C.L.C. 404. Note, however, that, where the expert has agreed to provide his reasons, the court may order him to provide them if he fails to do so or to provide further reasons if they are inadequate: *Halifax Life Ltd. v. Equitable Life Assurance Society* [2007] 2 All E.R. (Comm) 672. See also, in this context, *Re Imperial Foods Ltd. Pension Scheme* [1986] 1 W.L.R. 717. Reference should also be made to the earlier cases: *Collier v. Mason* (1858) 25 Beav. 200; *Dean v. Prince* [1953] 1 Ch. 590 and [1954] 1 Ch. 409; *Frank H. Wright (Constructions) Ltd. v. Frodoor Ltd.* [1967] 1 W.L.R. 506; *Smith v. Gale* [1974] 1 W.L.R. 9. It will be for consideration whether the agreement should positively *require* a speaking valuation, although this is in practice somewhat rare. *cf.* the Arbitration Act 1996, s.70(4).

[839] *R.A. Logan, Solicitors v. Maxwell* [2007] CSOH 163. The result had serious consequences: see further *infra*, paras 23–132, 23–201.

[840] *Sutcliffe v. Thackrah* [1974] A.C. 727; *Arenson v. Casson Beckman Rutley & Co.* [1977] A.C. 405. The effect of these cases would appear to be that a "mutual" valuer chosen by the parties may be held liable for negligence unless he is, on a true analysis, acting as an arbitrator, *i.e.* in a judicial or quasi-judicial capacity; however, even the immunity of an arbitrator cannot be assured: see *Arenson v. Casson Beckman Rutley & Co. supra*, pp. 431–432 per Lord Kilbrandon, 440 per Lord Salmon and 442 per Lord Fraser. As to determining the capacity in which a valuer is acting, see also *Palacath Ltd. v. Flanagan* [1985] 2 All E.R. 161; *North Eastern Co-operative Society Ltd. v. Newcastle upon Tyne City Council* (1987) 282 E.G. 1409.

[841] See *Cream Holdings Ltd. v. Davenport* [2009] B.C.C. 183 (CA), a decision concerning a provision in a company's articles. Much naturally depends on the true construction of the agreement.

[842] *Kelsey v. Kelsey* (1922) 91 L.J.Ch. 382; and see *Biles v. Caesar* [1957] 1 W.L.R. 156.

approved or agreed prior to his retirement, etc., the agreement should establish how those accounts are to be approved. Unless the agreement is clear on the point, the court may be reluctant to infer that the outgoing partner does not have a right to object to items in the account.[843] There is no reason in principle why the accounts should not be deemed to become binding in the absence of some objection from the outgoing partner within a set time limit, but the court is unlikely to regard such a provision as requiring him to set his objections out with a high degree of particularity.[844] If the agreement specifies how any dispute as to the contents of the accounts is to be resolved, *e.g.* by arbitration or expert determination, that term must be adhered to. However, that method of determination will usually be final and it is not open to the partners to add additional items into the account or to raise further queries on existing items, once the disputed items have been resolved in the agreed manner.[845]

Whether the continuing partners are able to defer payment of sums due to an outgoing partner until the relevant accounts have been approved by them will depend on the terms of the agreement. In one case, it was held to be an "absurd" result that payment might be deferred in this way.[846]

Failure to comply with agreed valuation procedure

10–178   The mere fact that the continuing or surviving partners have not complied with the strict terms of the valuation procedure will not deprive them of their right to acquire the outgoing partner's share.[847]

(d) Payment of Outgoing Partner's Entitlement

10–179   The agreement should record the manner in which the outgoing partner's entitlement is to be paid out. Any proposed payment schedule must necessarily take account of any undertakings which the firm may have given to third parties regarding the repayment of borrowed capital[848] and, in general, the need to return to the outgoing partner any tax reserves which may have been made out of his profit share.[849] Subject thereto, it is, in practice, not uncommon to find that part, if not the whole amount,[850] is made payable by instalments, thus easing the financial burden on the continuing partners.[851] In such a case, provision for interest on the outstanding balance and for such balance to become immediately due in the event of default is generally included.[852] If the quantification of the

---

[843] See *Hammonds (A Firm) v. Jones The Times*, January 4, 2010, noticed *supra*, para. 10–74. *cf. Montgomery v. Cameron & Greig* [2007] CSOH 63, noticed *supra*, 10–174.

[844] See *Purewall v. Purewall* [2006] CSOH 182.

[845] See *Reid v. Crabbe* [2009] CSIH 81, which concerned a retirement agreement, Much will naturally depend on the terms of the agreement.

[846] *Reid v. Crabbe*, *supra*, at [21] *per* Lord Carloway.

[847] *Hordern v. Hordern* [1910] A.C. 465.

[848] See *supra*, para. 10–66.

[849] It has already been seen that there is no longer any justification for retaining an outgoing partner's tax reserve: see *supra*, para. 10–157, n. 731. See also, as to such reserves, *supra*, para. 10–90.

[850] It would be unusual for payment of the outgoing partner's share of profits up to the date of his departure to be delayed much beyond the preparation and approval of the relevant accounts. On the other hand, capital and/or current account balances are more suitable for deferred payment.

[851] This may represent an alternative solution to the problem of multiple retirements: see *supra*, para. 10–108. Equally, it may be a way of penalising an expelled partner.

[852] The agreement should establish at what rate interest is to be paid (usually tied to the base rate of the partnership bankers) and from what date, *i.e.* the date of outgoing or some later date.

outgoing partner's entitlement is delayed for any reason, it naturally does not follow that the provision for instalment payments and interest will be suspended, although much will depend on the precise terms of the agreement.[853] If any retentions are to be made out of the amount due to the outgoing partner, e.g. in respect of contingent liabilities,[854] this should be provided for since such a right will not normally be implied.

The fact that the outgoing partner has committed a serious breach of the partnership agrement or of the fiduciary duties which he owes to the other members is not *per se* a justification for refusing to pay him sums due under the agreement,[855] although a claim based thereon may justify the exercise of a right of set off in an appropriate case.

(e) Annuities to Outgoing Partners, Widows, etc.[856]

Another constituent element of an outgoing partner's entitlement may be the payment of a fixed or profit related annuity to him[857] or, if he is dead, to his widow[858] and/or dependants. This device, which was once common, particularly in the professions, has now become something of a rarity, in large measure due to the popularity of the more tax-efficient registered pension scheme and its predecessors.[859] An annuity payable only to partners retiring over a certain age would be discriminatory and would, if it is to be retained, have to be justified as a proportionate means of achieving a legimate aim.[860]   **10–180**

Where such an entitlement is to be included in the agreement, care should be taken to ensure that events in which it will not arise, e.g. following an expulsion, are clearly identified. Just because a partner has behaved improperly and leaves voluntarily or is expelled will not *per se* deprive him of his rights under the agreement,[861] although the other partners may be able to exercise a right of set off in respect of any losses which they may suffer as a result of his actions.

---

[853] *Reid v. Crabbe* [2009] CSOH 182, noticed *supra*, 10–177.

[854] It has long since been standard practice to fix an outgoing partner with liability for his own negligent or wrongful acts (to the extent that they are not covered by insurance) and to require a sufficient retention to be made on that account. A more modern trend is to impose liability on the outgoing partners for *all* uninsured acts of negligence whilst he is a partner, whether he or some other partner or employee is at fault. See further *infra*, para. 10–249.

[855] See *Forster v. Ferguson & Forster* 2008 S.L.T. (Sh. Ct.) 52. Similarly, the fact that the outgoing partner has been expelled does not affect his entitlement, unless the agreement provides for this specifically: see *ibid.* at [9].

[856] *Encyclopedia of Professional Partnerships*, Precedent 2, art. 6.06.

[857] It will usually be considered appropriate to provide that an annuity will not be payable to an *expelled* partner.

[858] Naturally, the same considerations apply in the case of widowers and surviving civil partners.

[859] See the Finance Act 2004, Pt. 4. Equally, it is fair to say that the current regime is by no means as favourable as the arrangements which preceded it, namely the personal pension scheme or its forerunner, the retirement annuity contract, particularly given the restriction on the availability of relief introduced by the Finance Act 2009, Sched. 35 and the Finance Act 2010, Sched. 2.

[860] See the Employment Equality (Age) Regulations 2006 (SI 2006/1031), reg. 3(1), considered *supra*, paras 8–22 *et seq.* As from a date to be appointed, this provision will be replaced by the consolidating and amending Equality Act 2010, ss.5, 13(2).

[861] See *Forster v. Ferguson & Forster* 2008 S.L.T. (Sh. Ct.) 52, which admittedly turned on principles of Scottish law. There the partner in question had committed a number of frauds and retired on short notice rather than be expelled. His entitlement to his pension was held to be unaffected. The underlying assumption was that his retirement was treated as effected in accordance with the agreement, albeit that the required period of notice had not been given.

Although HMRC appear to regard most annuities as disguised goodwill payments, at least for the purposes of capital gains tax,[862] in reality this is not always the case.[863]

Term of the annuity

10–181   It is important that the agreement specifies the term of the annuity. Although once common, lifetime annuities are now only rarely encountered. In those cases where annuities are still payable, partners tend to restrict their duration to a fixed period of between 5 and 10 years, or the earlier death of the annuitant. In some instances, an annuity of a similar or a reduced amount is stated to be payable to the annuitant's widow or dependants for the balance of the period or, again, until death.[864]

Profit-related annuities

10–182   It is clear that the receipt of a profit share in the form of an annuity will not, of itself, cause the recipient to be treated as a partner,[865] although an outgoing partner is more at risk than his widow or dependants.[866]

A true profit-based annuity will only be payable if profits are actually realised by the continuing business; indeed, Lord Lindley illustrated this proposition with the following (now largely historical) example:

> " . . . if the surviving partner has an option to pay either an annuity or a share of the profits, and there should be no profits, he will not be bound to pay anything; for, *ex hypothesi*, it is competent for him to elect to pay out of the profits, and his right to make this election in no way depends on their amount."[867]

10–183   *Calculation of profits*: The relevant profits for the purposes of the annuity will in large measure depend on the terms of the agreement which should identify not only those sources of income or expenditure which are to be left out of account, but also the extent to which the continuing partners can introduce changes, whether to the nature of the business or to the management structure of the firm, which may have an adverse effect on its profitability.[868] It does not follow that, because the partners have habitually been paid salaries as a first charge on profits,[869] those salaries should necessarily be deducted when computing the profits for the purposes of an annuity.[870] Equally, the recipient of the annuity cannot properly argue that the continuing partners are carrying on a new business, so that no account should be taken of the liabilities of the old firm.[871]

It is generally prudent to impose a maximum ceiling on the percentage of the continuing firm's profits which can be taken up by annuitants, since their

---

[862] See *infra*, paras 35–20, 35–21.

[863] For an unusual example of an annuity conditional on the continuing partner enjoying continued occupation of certain premises, see *Holyland v. De Mendez* (1817) 3 Mer. 184.

[864] Note that the widow/dependants may now have a right to enforce payment of such an annuity under the Contracts (Rights of Third Parties) Act 1999: see *infra*, para. 10–188.

[865] See the Partnership Act 1890, s.2(3), *supra*, paras 5–02, 5–28 *et seq.*

[866] See *ibid.* s.2(3)(c).

[867] *Ex p. Harper* (1857) 1 De G. & J. 180.

[868] Thus, if the firm acquires new premises and takes on additional staff, this will inevitably affect its profits, at least in the short term.

[869] See *supra*, para. 10–80.

[870] See *Watson v. Haggitt* [1928] A.C. 127.

[871] *Ex p. Harper* (1857) 1 De G. & J. 180.

aggregate entitlement may otherwise threaten the financial viability of the firm.

Discontinuance of business: Since a discontinuance of the business would defeat   **10–184**
the annuitant's rights, the continuing partners are subject to certain implied constraints whilst an annuity is payable, as Lord Lindley explained:

> "An agreement to pay an annuity out of profits for a certain period usually involves an obligation not wilfully to prevent the earning of profits during that period; if in such a case, therefore, the person who has to pay the annuity wilfully ceases to carry on business before the expiration of that period, he becomes liable to an action for damages."[872]

It is in this area that annuity provisions are at their most contentious. On the one hand, the continuing partners will wish to preserve their freedom to develop the business as they see fit, *e.g.* by mergers, hiving off, etc., without the need to consult the annuitants. On the other hand, the annuitants will be seeking some form of entrenched protection for their rights, along the following lines suggested by Lord Lindley:

> " . . . it is desirable that the partner continuing the business should covenant not only that he will carry on the business and pay the annuity,[873] but that he will not transfer the business, or take in any fresh partner, without procuring from the transferee or new partner a similar covenant on his part."[874]

Mergers: It is prima facie impossible to legislate in advance for a merger   **10–185**
scenario, unless the annuitants' rights are to attach solely to the continuing partners' profit shares in the merged firm, and it is commercially undesirable for annuitants to be involved in potentially sensitive merger negotiations.

Commutation of annuity rights

Some agreements attempt to anticipate the effect of a dissolution or merger by   **10–186**
providing that any annuity then in payment will be commuted by the payment of its actuarial value as at that date. What partners frequently fail to appreciate at the outset is that the actuarial value of even a single annuity may, in the event, amount to a substantial sum[875]; *a fortiori* where there are several annuitants. In

---

[872] See *M'Intyre v. Belcher* (1863) 14 C.B.(N.S.) 654; *Telegraph Dispatch & Intelligence Co. v. McLean* (1873) L.R. 8 Ch.App. 658; and see, generally, *Turner v. Goldsmith* [1891] 1 Q.B. 544; *Ogdens Ltd. v. Nelson* [1905] A.C. 109; *Devonald v. Rosser* [1906] 2 K.B. 728; *Re R. S. Newman Ltd.* [1916] 2 Ch. 309; *Re Rubel Bronze & Metal Co. and Vos* [1918] 1 K.B. 315; *Collier v. Sunday Referee Publishing Co. Ltd.* [1940] 2 K.B. 647. *cf. Rhodes v. Forwood* (1876) L.R. 1 App.Cas. 256; *Cowasjee Nanabhoy v. Lallbhoy Vullubhoy* (1876) L.R. 3 Ind.App. 200; *Re Railway and Electric Appliances Co.* (1888) 38 Ch.D. 597; *Hamlyn & Co. v. Wood & Co.* [1891] 2 Q.B. 488; *Turner v. Sawdon & Co.* [1901] 2 K.B. 653. For a recent illustration of a similar principle being applied in the case of a commercial contract, see *CEL Group Ltd. v. Nedlloyd Lines UK Ltd.* [2004] 1 All E.R. (Comm) 689 (CA).

[873] It is in practice rare to see such an obligation framed as a covenant.

[874] It seems clear that a purchaser of the business, with or without notice of such a covenant, would not be bound by it unless the annuity constituted a charge thereon: see *Werderman v. Société Générale d'Electricité* (1881) 19 Ch.D. 246; *British Mutoscope Co. Ltd. v. Homer* [1901] 1 Ch. 671; *Dansk Rekylriffel Syndikat Aktieselskab v. Snell* [1908] 2 Ch. 127; also the criticism on these cases in *Barker v. Stickney* [1919] 1 K.B. 121 and *Bagot Pneumatic Tyre Co. v. Clipper Pneumatic Tyre Co.* [1902] 1 Ch. 146; and see *Law Debenture Trust Group v. Ural Caspian Oil Corp.* [1993] 1 W.L.R. 138.

[875] This will be particularly so where there is a lifetime annuity (see *supra*, para. 10–181) or where the annuitant is young and/or in good health. As to the tax effects of commutation, see *infra*, para. 34–68.

such cases, the continuing partners may find that the commutation rights represent a substantial deterrent to any form of merger or other restructuring. There can, of course, be no guarantee that the annuitants will be prepared to negotiate a variation of their rights so as to facilitate the merger, etc.

Enforcement of annuity provisions

10–187   It goes without saying that an outgoing partner will be entitled to enforce his right to an annuity under the terms of the agreement, but it obviously does not follow that his widow and/or dependants necessarily have the same right. On the assumption that the annuitant was not a party to the original agreement[876] and is not in a position to enforce the relevant term *qua* the deceased partner's personal representative,[877] it will be necessary to show that the Contracts (Rights of Third Parties) Act 1999 applies, that there is a trust of the benefit of the annuity or that its payment is charged on the partnership assets. Neither of the latter courses is straightforward.

10–188   *Contracts (Rights of Third Parties) Act 1999*:   This Act applies to all contracts[878] made after May 11, 2000[879] and confers on a third party the right to enforce a contractual term if: (a) the contract so provides or (b) it confers a benefit on him[880] and there is nothing in the contract which expressly or impliedly negates such a right of enforcement.[881] It is not necessary that the third party is actually named in the contract, provided that he is identifiable as a member of a class or as answering a particular description.[882] Where the Act applies, the third party will have the same rights of enforcement as a party to the contract[883] and, moreover, his consent *may* be required before the contract can be varied in such a way as to affect his entitlement thereunder.[884] The Act takes care to ensure that there is no right to double recovery by the third party and another party to the contract on his behalf.[885]

---

[876] Although annuitants are, on occasion, made parties to a partnership agreement, this is not to be commended in the interests of long-term flexibility.

[877] *Re Flavell* (1883) 25 Ch.D. 89, 99 *per* North J.; *Beswick v. Beswick* [1968] A.C. 58.

[878] Certain types of contract are, however, excluded: Contracts (Rights of Third Parties) Act 1999, s.6. The exceptions do *not* include a partnership agreement. Note, however, that the same cannot be said of a limited liability partnership agreement: *ibid.* s.6(2), as added by the Limited Liability Partnerships Regulations 2001 (SI 2001/1090), Sched. 5, para. 20.

[879] *ibid.* s.10(2). The Act also applies to contracts made after the date on which the Act was passed but which expressly provide for its application: *ibid.* s.10(3).

[880] A mere improvement in the third party's position on the contract being performed is not, *per se*, such a benefit: *Dolphin Maritime & Aviation Services Ltd. v. Sveriges Angartygs Assurans Forening* [2010] 1 All E.R. (Comm) 473.

[881] *ibid.* s.1(1), (2). Note, as to whether the Act has been disapplied by a contrary intention, *Nisshin Shipping Co. Ltd. v. Cleaves & Co. Ltd.* [2004] 1 Lloyd's Rep. 38. See also, *infra*, para. 10–259, n. 1283.

[882] *ibid.* s.1(3). It does not matter that the person is not in existence at the time the contract is entered into: *ibid.* See further, as to this subsection, *Avraamides v. Colwill* [2007] B.L.R. 76 (CA).

[883] *ibid.* s.1(5). The subsection specifically mentions the right to damages, an injunction or specific performance. Equally, the right of the person against whom the term is enforceable by the third party, who is styled "the promisor" (see *ibid.* s.1(7)), to raise all defences open to him is expressly recognised: *ibid.* s.3.

[884] *ibid.* s.2(1). Consent will only be required where: (i) the third party has by words or conduct communicated his assent to the relevant term to the promisor, (ii) the promisor is aware that the third party has relied on the term or (iii) there is such reliance and the promisor ought reasonably to have foreseen it: *ibid.* s.2(1), (2). It is, however, possible contractually to exclude the need for such consent (*ibid.* s.2(3)) and, in certain cases, that consent may be dispensed with (*ibid.* s.2(4)–(6)).

[885] *ibid.* s.5.

It follows that, in most cases, it will no longer be necessary for a widow and/or dependants of a deceased partner to establish a right to enforce the annuity in one or other of the ways described below, which are, of course, not in any way affected by the Act.[886] Obviously in the case of agreements entered into before May 11, 2000 those will be the *only* possible means of enforcement available.

Trust of annuity: A trust of an annuity will not readily be inferred and must be   **10–189** clearly warranted by the terms of the agreement. Admittedly, the court had little hesitation in drawing the necessary inference in *Re Flavell*,[887] where the agreement, in essence, provided for the surviving partner to pay an annuity to his deceased co-partner's executors or administrators to be applied for the benefit of his widow,[888] but this was an exceptional case. In practice, the strict approach which found voice in *Re Schebsman*[889] will now be followed.

Charge on partnership assets: If the annuity is charged on the partnership assets   **10–190** (or on the shares of the continuing partners) and it is clear that the annuitant is intended to have a direct right of enforcement, he may be able to rely on section 56(1) of the Law of Property Act 1925.[890] It was a failure to satisfy the latter condition that caused the annuities to be treated as unenforceable in *Re Miller's Agreement*.[891] As an alternative, the annuitant might seek to show that he is entitled to the benefit of the charge by virtue of an express assignment or the combined operation of the partnership agreement and the deceased's will.[892]

It follows that Lord Lindley may have been somewhat optimistic when remarking that:

"... after her husband's death [*the widow*] can enforce payment of the provision intended for her."[893]

Taxation of annuities

The payment of annuities can give rise to a number of complications from the   **10–191** point of view of both income and capital taxation: these are considered later in this work.[894]

---

[886] *ibid.* s.7(1). Equally, it is almost unimaginable that, in a case where the Act does not apply because of the terms of the contract itself (*ibid.* s.1(2)), a widow/dependant could then go on to establish the existence of a trust or that the annuity is charged on the partnership assets.

[887] (1833) 25 Ch.D. 89. See also *Page v. Cox* (1851) 10 Hare 163.

[888] The relevant clause was in fact redolent of the language of trusts, *viz.* "any yearly sum which may ... become payable to the executors or administrators of a deceased partner to be applied in such manner as such partner shall by deed or will direct for the benefit of his widow and children or child (if any) or any of them, and in default of such direction to be paid to such widow, if living, for her own benefit ... ".

[889] [1944] Ch. 83; also *Green v. Russell* [1959] 2 Q.B. 226.

[890] This subsection provides "A person may take an immediate or other interest in land or other property, or the benefit of any condition, right of entry, covenant or agreement over or respecting land or other property, although he may not be named as a party to the conveyance or other instrument." *Quaere* the extent of its application outside the sphere of real property: see *Beswick v. Beswick* [1968] A.C. 58; *Southern Water Authority v. Carey* [1985] 2 All E.R. 1077.

[891] [1947] Ch. 615.

[892] See *Att.-Gen. v. Gosling* [1892] 1 Q.B. 545.

[893] Lord Lindley cited *Page v. Cox* (1851) 10 Hare 163 and *Re Flavell* (1883) 25 Ch.D. 89, *supra*, para. 10–189.

[894] See *infra*, paras 34–66, 34–67 (income tax), 35–20, 35–21 (capital gains tax), 36–28, 36–44, 36–51 (inheritance tax).

U.   GOODWILL AND RESTRICTIONS ON COMPETITION[895]

10–192   The goodwill of a firm will frequently be one of its most valuable assets, even though it may not feature as such in its annual accounts. It is accordingly essential that the agreement deals with its ownership and, where necessary, its protection in the event of one or more partners leaving the firm.

(a) Meaning of "Goodwill"

10–193   Given its intangible nature, it is difficult to produce a precise definition of "goodwill",[896] as Lord Lindley explained:

> "The term goodwill can hardly be said to have any precise signification. It is generally used to denote the benefit arising from connection and reputation; and its value is what can be got for the chance of being able to keep that connection and improve it. Upon the sale of an established business its goodwill may have a marketable value, whether the business is that of a professional man or of any other person.[897] But it is plain that goodwill has no meaning except in connection with a continuing business[898]; it may have no value except in connection with a particular house,[899] and may be so inseparably connected with it as to pass with it under a will or deed without being specially mentioned.[900] In such a case the goodwill increases the value of the house; but the value of the goodwill of any business to a purchaser depends, in some cases entirely, and in all very much, on the absence of competition on the part of those by whom the business has been previously carried on."

10–194   It is apparent from the above passage that the existence (in terms of marketability) of goodwill is dependent on a number of variable factors, including the nature of the business and the availability of identifiable premises.[901] However, it is possible to go further, particularly in the case of a trading concern, and to analyse goodwill into its component elements. In this connection, reference must

---

[895] See the *Encyclopedia of Professional Partnerships*, Precedent 1, cl. 22(2)(a), (l).

[896] See, generally, *Trego v. Hunt* [1896] A.C. 7, 16–18 *per* Lord Herschell; *Commissioners of Inland Revenue v. Muller & Co.'s Margarine Ltd.* [1901] A.C. 217; *Hill v. Fearis* [1905] 1 Ch. 466, 471 *per* Warrington J.; also *Whiteman Smith Motor Co. v. Chaplin* [1934] 2 K.B. 35; *Simpson v. Charrington & Co.* [1935] A.C. 325; *Clift v. Taylor* [1948] 2 K.B. 394 (all decisions under the Landlord and Tenant Act 1927); *Govt. of Malaysia v. Selangor Pilot Association* [1978] A.C. 337, 357–358 *per* Lord Salmon.

[897] See *Davidson v. Wayman* [1984] 2 N.Z.L.R. 115. Note that goodwill was regarded as property for stamp duty purposes: see *Potter v. Commissioners of Inland Revenue* (1854) 10 Ex. 147; *Benjamin Brooke & Co. Ltd. v. Commissioners of Inland Revenue* [1896] 2 Q.B. 356; *West London Syndicate v. Commissioners of Inland Revenue* [1898] 2 Q.B. 507; *Eastern National Omnibus Co. Ltd. v. Commissioners of Inland Revenue* [1939] 1 K.B. 161; and see also *Commissioners of Inland Revenue v. Muller & Co.'s Margarine Ltd.* [1901] A.C. 217. As to inheritance tax, see *infra*, paras 36–03 *et seq.*, 36–22, 36–58.

[898] See *Kingston, Miller & Co. v. Thomas Kingston & Co.* [1912] 1 Ch. 575. See also *Robertson v. Quiddington* (1860) 28 Beav. 529 (which concerned a legacy of goodwill).

[899] This word, in the present context, merely denotes the partnership premises. However, in Scots cases it is used to describe a *partnership* as constituted from time to time.

[900] See *Chissum v. Dewes* (1828) 5 Russ. 29; *Pile v. Pile* (1876) 3 Ch.D. 36; *Ex p. Punnett* (1880) 16 Ch.D. 266; also *Cooper v. Metropolitan Board of Works* (1883) 25 Ch.D. 472, 479 *per* Cotton L.J. In *Blake v. Shaw* (1860) Johns. 732 and *Re Rhagg* [1938] Ch. 828, a bequest of goodwill carried the premises in which the business was carried on, but such a construction will not readily be adopted: see *Re Betts* [1949] 1 All E.R. 568. Note also, as to the former severance of goodwill and premises for the purposes of stamp duty, *West London Syndicate Ltd. v. Commissioners of Inland Revenue* [1898] 2 Q.B. 507.

[901] See, for example, *Hill v. Fearis* [1905] 1 Ch. 466; also *infra*, para. 10–197.

inevitably be made to the following classic statement by Scrutton L.J. in *White-man Smith Motor Co. v. Chaplin*[902]:

> "A division of the elements of goodwill was referred to during the argument and appears in Mr. Merlin's book[903] as 'cat, rat and dog' basis. The cat prefers the old home though the person who has kept the house leaves. The cat represents that part of the customers who continue to go to the old shop, though the old shopkeeper has gone; the probability of their custom may be regarded as an additional value given to the premises by the tenant's trading. The dog represents that part of the customers who follow the person rather than the place; these the tenant may take away with him if he does not go too far. There remains a class of customer who may neither follow the place nor the person, but drift away elsewhere. They are neither a benefit to the landlord nor the tenant, and have been called 'the rat' for no particular reason except to keep the epigram in the animal kingdom. I believe my brother Maugham has introduced the rabbit, but I will leave him to explain the position of the rabbit.[904] It is obvious that the division of customers, into 'cat, rat and dog' must vary enormously in different cases and different circumstances."

Firm name

An important element of a firm's goodwill may lie in its name[905] or even in part of its name.[906] Accordingly, the right to use that name may itself have a substantial value, although it is doubtful whether it can be acquired independently of any other component of the goodwill.[907] Complications may, however, arise where the name comprises the names of one or more of the partners.[908]   **10–195**

Trade marks[909]

The partnership trade marks[910] may constitute yet another element of a firm's goodwill and, like any other asset, will fall to be sold in the event of a dissolution.[911] Under the Trade Marks Act 1994, a firm's registered trade   **10–196**

---

[902] [1934] 2 K.B. 35, 42. But see *ibid.* p. 49 *per* Maugham L.J.; also *Mullins v. Wessex Motors Ltd.* [1947] W.N. 316.

[903] *i.e.* Merlin on the Landlord and Tenant Act 1927.

[904] In fact, Maugham L.J. introduced both the rabbit and the mouse, the rabbit being the customers who come simply from propinquity to the premises, and the mouse being the somewhat strange result of a shrinking in the "cat"!

[905] See generally, as to existence of goodwill in a name, *Maxim's Ltd. v. Dye* [1977] 1 W.L.R. 1155; *My Kinda Bones Ltd. (T/A Chicago Rib Shack) v. Dr. Pepper's Stove Co. Ltd. (T/A Dr. Pepper's Manhattan Rib Shack)* [1984] F.S.R. 289; *County Sound plc v. Ocean Sound plc* [1991] F.S.R. 367; *Byford v. Oliver* [2003] E.M.L.R. 20, noticed *infra,* para. 10–202. *cf. McPhail v. Bourne* [2008] EWHC 1235 (Ch) (Lawtel 13/6/08) at [287], where Morgan J. held that, as there was no goodwill attached to the band name "Busted", it could not be an asset of the supposed partnership contended for.

[906] This possibility was accepted by Hoffmann J. in *Baker v. Benson*, August 3, 1998, unreported.

[907] The propriety of such a transfer was clearly accepted in the Scottish case of *Barr v. Lions*, 1956 S.L.T. 250, but it seems unlikely that the point was fully argued: see further *supra,* para. 3–23.

[908] See *infra,* paras 10–201, 10–202, 10–205 *et seq.*

[909] The Community trade mark regime under Council Regulation (EC) No. 49/94 on the Community trade mark is, in essence, replicated in the Trade Marks Act 1994 and is not considered separately here.

[910] This expression is defined in the Trade Marks Act 1994, s.1(1) and includes what used to be known as service marks.

[911] See *Hall v. Barrows* (1863) 4 De G.J. & S. 150; *Bury v. Bedford* (1864) 4 De G.J. & S. 352.

marks[912] are freely assignable,[913] either in whole or in part[914] and, as under the previous law, with or without a simultaneous assignment of its goodwill.[915] The Act does not, however, govern the assignment of *unregistered* trade marks[916] and it is, accordingly, no longer necessary that the latter should be assigned along with any registered trade marks.[917] However, unlike registered trade marks, it will not in general be possible to assign such marks independently of an assignment of the firm's goodwill.[918]

The firm name may be registrable as a trade mark,[919] but registration will not, of itself, prevent a partner from making honest use[920] of his own name or, seemingly, a firm name.[921]

(b) Ownership of Goodwill

Goodwill technically valueless

10–197   It will be seen hereafter that relatively few *implied* restrictions are imposed on a vendor of goodwill,[922] so that a valuable partnership business may, in practical terms, be unsaleable[923] and, thus, worthless to anyone but a former partner who wishes to acquire it.[924] Equally, goodwill may have no value independently of the partnership premises[925] or the firm name.[926]

Lord Lindley pointed out that:

---

[912] As defined in the Trade Marks Act 1994, s.2(1).

[913] *ibid.* s.24(1). Note that where two or more persons hold a registered trade mark jointly, one may not assign his share in it without the consent of the other(s): *ibid.* s.23(1), (4)(a).

[914] *ibid.* s.24(2). A partial assignment may relate to some but not all of the goods or services for which the mark is registered or to the use of the mark in a particular manner/locality: *ibid.* The application of this section is problematic: see *supra*, para. 3–21.

[915] *ibid.* s.24(1).

[916] *ibid.* s.24(6).

[917] *cf.* the position under the Trade Marks Act 1938 s.22(3) (as amended).

[918] See *Kerly's Law of Trade Marks and Trade Names* (14th ed), paras 13–059 *et seq.*

[919] Trade Marks Act 1994, s.1(1). Under that subsection, the name must be "capable of distinguishing goods or services of one undertaking from those of another undertaking". See *Byford v. Oliver* [2003] E.M.L.R. 20; also *supra*, para. 3–21.

[920] *i.e.* "use in accordance with honest practices in industrial or commercial matters": *ibid.* s.11(2).

[921] *ibid.* s.11(2)(a); see also *Asprey and Garrard Ltd. v. WRA (Guns) Ltd.* [2002] F.S.R. 30. The application of this paragraph to firm names is not, however, free from doubt. It should be noted that, unlike the provisions of the Trade Marks Act 1938, s.8 (as amended), this paragraph does not give a partner the right to make honest use of a *former* partner's name.

[922] See *infra*, paras 10–206 *et seq.*

[923] This was, for example, the view reached in *Gray v. Dickson* (A1116/05), August 10, 2007 (Sh. Ct.) in relation to a garage business which had traded for only a short time.

[924] See *Davies v. Hodgson* (1858) 25 Beav. 177; *Browell v. Goodyear*, March 14, 2000 (unreported), which concerned a solicitors' practice: see further *infra*, para. 10–200, n. 942. *cf. Davidson v. Wayman* [1984] 2 N.Z.L.R. 115.

[925] See for example, *Blake v. Shaw* (1860) Johns. 732; *Re Rhagg* [1938] Ch. 828. *cf. Condliffe v. Sheingold* [2007] EWCA Civ 1043 (Lawtel 31/10/07) at [15], where it was held that the goodwill of a company carrying on a restaurant business could be owned separately from the premises from which it operated.

[926] As an example of such a case, Lord Lindley referred to the goodwill of a newspaper, which "attaches to its name, and is scarcely, if at all, dependent on the place of publication". A sale of goodwill will normally carry the right to use the firm name: (see *Levy v. Walker* (1879) 10 Ch.D. 436, (CA)), but the position may conceivably be otherwise on a partner's retirement: see *Gray v. Smith* (1889) 43 Ch.D. 208. *Semble*, this will rarely be the case: see *infra*, para. 10–205.

"It is only so far as the goodwill has a saleable value, that it can be regarded as an asset of any partnership . . . "[927]

However, the current editor submits that, as a statement of principle, this goes too far, since goodwill, even though unmarketable, clearly exists as an asset and is capable of protection.[928]

Goodwill as a partnership asset

It has already been seen that a well drawn agreement should establish whether **10–198** or not goodwill is a partnership asset[929] and should, moreover, provide for the acquisition of an outgoing partner's share (including his share of goodwill) by the continuing partners.[930] Although this may not, in itself, afford adequate protection to the continuing partners, their position will inevitably be less secure if the agreement is silent on the latter point. This can best be illustrated by considering the consequences of:

   (i) the dissolution of the partnership;

   (ii) the death of a partner;

   (iii) the retirement or expulsion of a partner.

In each case, it will be assumed that the goodwill is an asset of the firm.

(i) *Dissolution of firm*

In the event of a *general* dissolution,[931] the goodwill must normally be sold,[932] **10–199** unless the partners agree otherwise.[933] It follows that, whilst the winding up is continuing, a partner will normally be prevented from attempting to appropriate the goodwill for himself, at least where it has a saleable value.[934] However, as

---

[927] What Lord Lindley perhaps meant was that unsaleable goodwill must be ignored for accounting purposes: see *Wilson v. Williams* (1892) 29 L.R.Ir. 176, where the goodwill of a stockbroker's business was excluded from the accounts for this reason; *cf. Hill v. Fearis* [1905] 1 Ch. 466, where the goodwill of such a business was held to have a saleable value. Although it was once suggested that the goodwill of a solicitor's practice has no value (see *Arundell v. Bell* (1883) 52 L.J.Ch. 537), this is clearly not the present position: see *Sobell v. Boston* [1975] 1 W.L.R. 1587; *Bridge v. Deacons* [1984] A.C. 705; also *Burchell v. Wilde* [1900] 1 Ch. 551; *Fitch v. Dewes* [1921] 2 A.C. 158, 168 *per* Lord Cave. The goodwill of a medical partnership practising within the National Health Service (the sale of which is prohibited by the National Health Service Act 2006, s.259, Sched. 21), clearly exists as an asset of the firm: *Whitehill v. Bradford* [1952] Ch. 236; *Lyne-Pirkis v. Jones* [1969] 1 W.L.R. 1293; *Kerr v. Morris* [1987] Ch. 90. And see, generally, *Allied Dunbar (Frank Weisinger) Ltd. v. Weisinger* [1988] I.R.L.R. 60, 65 *per* Millett J.; also *Davidson v. Wayman* [1984] 2 N.Z.L.R. 115.
[928] See in particular, *Kerr v. Morris, supra.*
[929] See *supra*, para. 10–49; also *infra*, para. 18–17. It does not follow that, merely because goodwill is an asset of the firm, all the partners are interested therein: see *Stekel v. Ellice* [1973] 1 W.L.R. 191.
[930] See *supra*, paras 10–150 *et seq.*
[931] See, as to the meaning of this expression, *infra*, para. 24–03.
[932] *Per contra*, of course, if the goodwill is valueless or otherwise inherently unsaleable: see *supra*, para. 10–197.
[933] *Bradbury v. Dickens* (1859) 27 Beav. 53; *Pawsey v. Armstrong* (1881) 18 Ch.D. 698; *Re David and Matthews* [1899] 1 Ch. 378; *Hill v. Fearis* [1950] 1 Ch. 466. It is, of course, open to the partners not to insist on a sale. *Quaere* whether, if one partner gives his co-partners a power of attorney for the purposes of effecting the sale, this will authorise them to sell with the benefit of an *express* restriction on competition: see *Hawksley v. Outram* [1892] 3 Ch. 359. And, as to the treatment of the sale proceeds, note *McClelland v. Hyde* [1942] N.I. 1.
[934] See *Turner v. Major* (1862) 3 Giff. 442 (where there was an express agreement for the sale of goodwill). Lord Lindley commented "In *Lewis v. Langdon* (1835) 7 Sim. 421, 425, the V.-C.

Lord Lindley explained, the position on the older authorities is not entirely free from doubt:

> "If . . . the goodwill of the partnership business has any saleable value at all, it seems impossible to hold that on a dissolution of a partnership, whether by death or otherwise, any partner can continue the old business in the old name for his own benefit, unless there is some agreement to that effect, or at least to the effect that the assets are not to be sold. Such a right on his part is inconsistent with the right of the other partners to have the goodwill sold for the common benefit of all.[935] There are, however, authorities tending to show that, in the case of death, the surviving partners are entitled to continue to carry on business in the old name,[936] and to restrain the executors of the deceased partner from doing the like.[937] But if these cases are carefully examined, they will be found not to warrant so general a proposition."[938]

It goes without saying that, if the firm's business and its associated goodwill ceases to exist on dissolution, there will be nothing to realise. In *Ryder v. Frohlich*[939] the business consisted of the provision to a company of the services of the two partners. Since one partner had abandoned the partnership,[940] the business had, by definition, ceased to exist. It was not possible to go back to the position which existed *prior* to the dissolution for valuation purposes.

10–200   However, it must at the same time be appreciated that section 38 of the Partnership Act 1890 contemplates that the members of a dissolved firm will complete any unfinished business,[941] but that they will not take on any *new* work.[942] Yet, it is self apparent that, if no new work can be taken on, the value

---

Shadwell seemed to think that a surviving partner was under no obligation to preserve the goodwill. But his opinion was probably influenced by *Hammond v. Douglas* (1800) 5 Ves.Jr. 539, which was not then overruled." See also *Re David and Matthews* [1899] 1 Ch. 378, 382 *per* Romer J.

[935] See *Hill v. Fearis* [1905] 1 Ch. 466.

[936] *Webster v. Webster* (1791) 3 Swan. 490; *Lewis v. Langdon* (1835) 7 Sim. 421; *Robertson v. Quiddington* (1860) 28 Beav. 529; *Banks v. Gibson* (1865) 34 Beav. 566.

[937] *Lewis v. Langdon* (1835) 7 Sim. 421.

[938] Lord Lindley analysed the cases thus: "In *Webster v. Webster* [*(1791) 3 Swan. 490*], the executors of a deceased partner sought to restrain the surviving partners from carrying on business in the name of the old firm; but the application was based upon the untenable ground that by so doing the surviving partners exposed the estate of the deceased partner to continued liability. No question of goodwill appears to have been in dispute. In *Lewis v. Langdon* [*(1835) 7 Sim. 421*], V.-C. Shadwell certainly intimated his opinion to be, that surviving partners had a right to continue to carry on business in the old name [*See, too, per Lord Romilly in Robertson v. Quiddington (1860) 28 Beav. 529, 536*]; but the real question there was, whether the executors of a deceased partner were entitled to continue the use of that name; and it was held that they were not, which is quite consistent with the absence of the same right on the part of the surviving partner. There seems, moreover, to have been some agreement not set out in the report [*See the last line in (1835) 7 Sim. 425*], which influenced the judge's decision; and at the time it was pronounced the doctrine that goodwill is, if saleable, a partnership asset, was not so well established as it is at present." See also *Re David and Matthews* [1899] 1 Ch. 378, 382–383 *per* Romer J.

[939] [2006] NSWSC 833.

[940] See further [2004] NSWCA 472.

[941] See *infra*, paras 13–64 *et seq.*; also *infra*, para. 16–30.

[942] A suggestion that a dissolved solicitors' firm should be forced to take on new business was rejected as "wholly unrealistic" and "inappropriate" in *Browell v. Goodyear*, March 14, 2000 (unreported). Equally, in *Don King Productions Inc. v. Warren* [2000] Ch. 291, at [42], the Court of Appeal held that it was the duty of a partner to renew a contract *after* a dissolution if that was required "to facilitate the beneficial winding up of [*the partnership*] affairs". This is, conceptually, not without difficulty: see *infra*, para. 13–65.

of the firm's goodwill will be swiftly dissipated unless, exceptionally, a forced sale can be secured on or shortly following the dissolution date.[943] The tension between these two opposing principles is most apparent in the case of a professional practice, yet appears not to have received detailed attention from the courts, which can, perhaps, be attributed to the infrequency with which judicial assistance in the winding up process is actually sought.[944]

Whatever limitations are imposed by section 38, a partner must still take care to ensure that he does nothing to damage the *existing* goodwill of the dissolved firm, *e.g.* by unilaterally removing client files. Such action may involve a breach of duty on his part, which will ultimately sound in damages.[945]

If one partner in fact manages to secure the benefit of the firm's goodwill for himself, he can be compelled to account for its value, but such value will naturally reflect the fact that he and the other partners would be entitled to set up business in competition with the notional purchaser.[946]

Where a partner purchases an interest in goodwill on his admission to the firm, his entitlement in the event of a dissolution will be as set out above; the price originally paid to acquire that interest will be irrelevant.[947]

The implied restrictions imposed following a sale of goodwill are considered in relation to the retirement and expulsion of a partner.[948]

Use of firm name following dissolution

If the goodwill is sold in the course of winding up the firm's affairs, the **10–201** purchaser will be entitled to use the old firm name, even if it consists of the names of one or more of the former partners, but not in such a way as to expose them to an appreciable risk of continuing liability[949]; *per contra* if the name is

---

[943] As to obtaining such an order, see *infra*, paras 23–183 *et seq.*

[944] Nevertheless, the current editor is aware of one instance in which the court declined to interfere to protect the goodwill of a solicitors' partnership which was about to be dissolved, on the basis that: (1) a forced sale of the goodwill would not, in the particular circumstances, have been practicable; (2) the former partners could not be forced to take on new work for the benefit of the dissolved firm, having regard to the provisions of the Partnership Act 1890, s.38; and (3) they could not be prevented from setting up new practices as from the dissolution date. Equally, there would on the facts have been no difficulty in debiting each of the former partners with the value of the goodwill appropriated in taking the accounts of the dissolved firm. Exactly the same approach was adopted in *Browell v. Goodyear, supra.*

[945] *Finlayson v. Turnbull (No. 1)* 1997 S.L.T. 613 (OH). In that case, on the dissolution of their partnership, three salaried partners had carried out a pre-planned operation which involved, *inter alia*, taking away a large number of client files with a view to facilitating the establishment of their new practice. A claim for an account was also pursued subsequently: see *Finlayson v. Turnbull (No. 3)* [2001] G.W.D. 37–1412 (OH); and see, as to the taking of the account, *Finlayson v. Turnbull (No.4)* 2003 G.W.D. 12–374 (OH). *Deacons v. White & Case LLP* (HCA 2433/2002), October 24, 2003 (Hong Kong High Court) was a similar case.

[946] *Smith v. Everett* (1859) 27 Beav. 446; *Mellersh v. Keen* (1860) 28 Beav. 453; *Re David and Matthews* [1899] 1 Ch. 378.

[947] See *Bond v. Milbourn* (1871) 20 W.R. 197, where an incoming partner failed in his attempt to obtain a return of the purchase price.

[948] See *infra*, paras 10–206 *et seq.*

[949] *Thynne v. Shove* (1890) 45 Ch.D. 577; *Burchell v. Wilde* [1900] 1 Ch. 551; *Townsend v. Jarman* [1900] 2 Ch. 698. Note also *Banks v. Gibson* (1865) 34 Beav. 566 (an extreme case, which goes further than *Thynne v. Shove, supra*). In *Gray v. Smith* (1889) 43 Ch.D. 208, there was no agreement for the sale of goodwill; but note that the Court of Appeal authorised the sale of certain stock bearing the firm name: see *ibid.* p. 221.

expressly assigned to the purchaser without qualification.[950] If, on the other hand, the goodwill has no saleable value, each partner will seemingly have an equal right to use the firm name, subject to two important qualifications. First, it may be impossible for any partner to demonstrate that the goodwill has no saleable value until the partnership affairs have been fully wound up. If that is the case, a partner could be restrained from appropriating the name in the interim, even if he is within his rights to carry on a competing business.[951] Secondly, it may not, in general, be exercised by one of the former partners if this would involve holding out another as a partner in his *new* business.[952] Lord Lindley summarised the position in this way:

" . . . where [*a partner's*] name is part of the name of the firm, *e.g.* if his name is A B, and the name of the firm is A B & Co., so long as he lives he would, it is apprehended, in the absence of an agreement to the contrary, be entitled to restrain his late co-partners and their representatives from carrying on business under the old name, and so continually exposing him to risk . . . The right of a late partner to prevent the continued use of his own name on the ground of exposing him to risk is a purely personal right, and does not devolve either on his executors or on his trustee in bankruptcy, for they would not be exposed to risk.[953] Their right, and indeed the right of any partner whose name does not appear in the name of the firm, to prevent the continuance of the use of the name of the firm, can only be maintained upon the ground that such right is involved in the more general right of having the partnership assets, including the goodwill, sold for the common benefit. And if upon a dissolution this right is waived, or if the terms of dissolution are such as to preclude its exercise, then each partner can not only carry on business in competition with the others, but each can represent himself as late of, or as successor to, the old firm: and each may use the old name without qualification[954]; at all events if he does not hold out the other partners as still in partnership with himself."[955]

10–202   Whether the use of the firm name does expose a former partner to any appreciable risk of liability will involve a mixed question of law and fact.[956]

---

[950] *Townsend v. Jarman* [1900] 2 Ch. 698; also *Levy v. Walker* (1879) 10 Ch.D. 436. Although the latter decision was subsequently said not to apply in the case of a partner's retirement (see *Gray v. Smith* (1889) 43 Ch.D. 208), as a statement of general principle, this should be viewed with caution: see *infra*, para. 10–205.

[951] From one perspective it could be said that to commence such a business prior to the conclusion of the winding up would involve a prima facie breach of the duty not to compete imposed by the Partnership Act 1890, s.30 (as seemingly applied by *ibid.* s.38) and, perhaps, a breach of the duty of good faith; see also *ibid.* s.29(2). However, this would be to ignore the prohibition on taking on new work to be found in *ibid.* s.38: see further, *supra*, para. 10–200. It follows that the new business carried on by the former partner would, by definition, not be competing with the old "run-off" business being carried on by the dissolved firm. Perhaps this explains why no such difficulties appear to have been perceived by Romer J. in *Re David and Matthews* [1899] 1 Ch. 378, when considering the position of a surviving partner. And see *supra*, para. 10–200, n. 944.

[952] See *Routh v. Webster* (1847) 10 Beav. 561; *Bullock v. Chapman* (1848) 2 De G. & Sm. 211; *Troughton v. Hunter* (1854) 18 Beav. 470. And see also *supra*, paras 5–45 *et seq.*

[953] See the Partnership Act 1890, ss.14(2), 36(3); also *supra*, para. 5–53 and *infra*, paras 13–53 *et seq.*

[954] See *Banks v. Gibson* (1865) 34 Beav. 566; *Burchell v. Wilde* [1900] 1 Ch. 551. And note *Glenny v. Smith* (1865) 2 Dr. & Sm. 476.

[955] See the cases cited *supra*, nn. 949, 950 and 952.

[956] See *supra*, para. 5–36. Note also the provisions of the Companies Act 2006, Pt. 41, noticed *supra*, paras 3–26 *et seq.*, 5–63.

However, it is apprehended that, if the name merely consists of a partner's surname with the addition of the words "and Co." and he has not used that name otherwise than in connection with the firm, its continued use by his former partners will not expose him to risk.[957]

The decision in *Byford v. Oliver*[958] is interesting in this context. There it was held that individual former members of the heavy metal band "Saxon" had no right to the firm name following a dissolution of their partnership at will, but that the dissolved firm itself might be in a position to assert rights thereto, subject to questions of abandonment, etc. Laddie J. distinguished the decision in *Burchell v. Wilde*,[959] holding that it laid down no rule of general application. The key factor was, ultimately, that the former partners had not actually used the name following the dissolution and, accordingly, had not acquired any proprietary interest of their own in that name. Had they done so, the position might well have been different.

(ii) *Death of a partner*

Where death results in the dissolution of the partnership,[960] the position will generally be as described in the preceding paragraphs. There is no question of the goodwill accruing to the surviving partners beneficially, even though there is an old authority to that effect.[961] However, that is not to say that the surviving partners may not ultimately be in the same position *as if* they had acquired the goodwill by survivorship. Thus, their ability to carry on a competing business in the same locality[962] may, for all practical purposes, represent a sufficient deterrent to prospective purchasers to render the goodwill unsaleable[963] and, in those circumstances, the surviving partners might ultimately be in a position to carry on using the old firm name.[964] Lord Lindley observed:

10–203

> "[*The surviving partner*] will therefore acquire all the benefit of the goodwill; but he does not acquire it by survivorship, as something belonging to him exclusively, and with which the executors of the deceased partner have no concern; for if he did, he might sell the goodwill for his own benefit whenever it had a saleable value, and this

---

[957] *Burchell v. Wilde* [1900] 1 Ch. 551; *Townsend v. Jarman* [1900] 2 Ch. 698.

[958] [2003] E.M.L.R. 20. And see also *Gill v Frankie Goes To Hollywood Ltd.* [2008] E.T.M.R. 4 (OHIM, Opposition Division).

[959] *supra.*

[960] Partnership Act 1890, s.33(1), *infra*, paras 24–29 *et seq.* See also *supra*, para. 10–39.

[961] *Hammond v. Douglas* (1800) 5 Ves.Jr. 539. This decision is wholly inconsistent with the later authorities: see *Wedderburn v. Wedderburn* (1856) 22 Beav. 84; *Smith v. Everett* (1859) 27 Beav. 446; *Mellersh v. Keen* (1860) 28 Beav. 453. And see, in particular, *Re David and Matthews* [1899] 1 Ch. 378, 382 *per* Romer J.

[962] See *Farr v. Pearce* (1818) 3 Madd. 74; *Davies v. Hodgson* (1858) 25 Beav. 177; *Trego v. Hunt* [1896] A.C. 7. The surviving partners may not, of course, use the old firm name: *Re David and Matthews* [1899] 1 Ch. 378; *Manley v. Sartori* [1927] 1 Ch. 157. Lord Lindley also referred to the possibility of them using the old place of business, but this must be dependent on whether the premises are in fact owned by them or by the firm. *Quaere*, are the rights of the surviving partners unrestricted whilst the winding up is continuing? See *supra*, para. 10–201, n. 951.

[963] Note that the sale particulars should refer to the rights of the surviving partners: see *Johnson v. Helleley* (1864) 34 Beav. 63; *Jennings v. Jennings* [1898] 1 Ch. 378, 389 *per* Stirling J.; *Re David and Matthews* [1899] 1 Ch. 378, 385 *per* Romer J.

[964] See *supra*, para. 10–201. Note also the arguments canvassed (unsuccessfully) in *Hill v. Fearis* [1905] 1 Ch. 466, 472, 473.

he cannot do.[965] When, therefore, it is said that on the death of one partner the goodwill of the firm survives to the other, what is meant is, that the survivor is entitled to the advantages incidental to his former connection with the firm, and that he is under no obligation, in order to render those advantages saleable, to retire from business himself."[966]

If the personal representatives of the deceased partner do not seek to force a sale of the partnership assets and are content to receive the value of his share as at the date of death,[967] a payment will only fall to be made in respect of goodwill if it has a marketable value.

It has already been seen that the personal representatives cannot restrain the surviving partners from continuing to use the old firm name on the grounds that it would expose the deceased partner's estate to continuing liability.[968]

(iii) *Retirement or expulsion of partner*

10–204   Although a partner's retirement or expulsion technically dissolves the firm, it would seem that, if the agreement contains no provision specifically governing his entitlement in respect of goodwill[969] and the other assets of the partnership, the court would normally be reluctant to order anything but a payment out of the value of his share *as at the date he ceased to be a partner*.[970] To order a sale or a valuation as at some later date would be inconsistent with the concept of retirement or expulsion and would prima facie confer an unjustified "windfall" benefit on the outgoing partner.[971] This does not, however, mean that, in the absence of some clear contrary provision in the agreement, an outgoing partner will necessarily be deprived of his right to be paid out by reference to the market value of the firm's goodwill and other assets as at that date[972] or to the profits

---

[965] See *Wedderburn v. Wedderburn* (1856) 22 Beav. 84; *Smith v. Everett* (1859) 27 Beav. 446; *Mellersh v. Keen* (1860) 28 Beav. 458. But see *Farr v. Pearce* (1818) 3 Madd. 74; *Hammond v. Douglas* (1800) 5 Ves.Jr. 539. Lord Lindley commented that the latter case "cannot be regarded as now law"; see also *Re David and Matthews* [1899] 1 Ch. 378, 382 *per* Romer J.

[966] See *Farr v. Pearce* (1818) 3 Madd. 74; *Davies v. Hodgson* (1858) 25 Beav. 177; *Mellersh v. Keen* (1860) 28 Beav. 453.

[967] *i.e.* relying on their strict rights under the Partnership Act 1890, s.43. The application of this section in the case of a *general* dissolution is, however, not without difficulty: see *infra*, paras 19–09 *et seq.*, 23–34, 26–03.

[968] See *supra*, para. 10–201.

[969] The agreement may, of course, declare that goodwill should be treated as valueless, *e.g.* where the outgoing partner's entitlement is determined by reference to the firm's annual accounts, which ignore the existence of goodwill: see *supra*, paras 10–162 *et seq.*

[970] *i.e.* his strict entitlement pursuant to the Partnership Act 1890, ss.43, 44. Lord Lindley observed that "when a partner retires not only from the firm, but from the business carried on by it, the continuing partners will acquire the benefit arising out of the goodwill for nothing, unless it has been agreed that they shall pay for it; for they retain possession of the old place of business, and they continue to carry on that business under the old name. This, in fact, secures the goodwill to them, and they cannot be compelled to pay separately for it, unless some agreement to that effect has been entered into." As a statement of principle, this cannot be right and, indeed, does not bear comparison with Lord Lindley's analysis of the position following the death of a partner: see *supra*, para. 10–203. It is only correct if: (a) the goodwill has no value and (b) the continued use of the firm name would not expose the retired partner to the risk of continuing liability.

[971] See *Sobell v. Boston* [1975] 1 W.L.R. 1587, 1591 *per* Goff J. Although this case concerned the *retirement* of a partner, the current editor considers that the same principles will apply in the event of an expulsion. *cf. Barclays Bank Trust Co. Ltd. v. Bluff* [1982] Ch. 172, *infra*, para. 25–32.

[972] See *supra*, paras 10–162 *et seq.* But note, in particular, the decision in *Re White* [2001] Ch. 393, *supra*, paras 10–163, 10–169.

attributable to the use of his share of goodwill, etc., up to the time that his entitlement is paid out.[973]

Continued use of outgoing partner's name

The agreement will normally provide, either expressly or by necessary impli-   **10–205**
cation, for the continued use of the firm name following a retirement or expulsion, irrespective of the risk to the outgoing partner. Where, exceptionally, the
agreement contains no such provision or, more commonly, where the retirement
is the result of an *ad hoc* agreement, the retiring partner cannot necessarily be
taken to have authorised his former partners to continue to use the old firm name,
if by so doing they would expose him to the risk of liability on the basis of
holding out[974]; *per contra*, if he seeks to be paid out the full value of his share
in goodwill and attributes part of that value to the firm name.[975] The current
editor submits that an expelled partner will, in the absence of any clear provision
in the agreement, be in no different position.[976]

Implied restrictions on sale of goodwill by outgoing partner

If a partner retires and is paid out the value of his share, including his interest   **10–206**
in the firm's goodwill,[977] but the agreement does not contain any express
restriction on competition by outgoing partners, he, like any other vendor of
goodwill, will be immediately entitled to set up a similar business in the same
locality,[978] to advertise that fact[979] and to deal with any customer of the firm who
chooses to do business with him.[980] What he may *not* do is: (1) solicit such

---

[973] Partnership Act 1890, s.42, *infra*, paras 25–24 *et seq.*; *Manley v. Sartori* [1927] 1 Ch. 157.

[974] See *Gray v. Smith* (1889) 43 Ch.D. 208, where an exception was made in the case of certain
stock bearing the firm name: see *ibid.* p. 221 *per* Cotton L.J. See also, as to this decision, *Jennings
v. Jennings* [1898] 1 Ch. 378, 384, 388–389 *per* Stirling J. And see *Churton v. Douglas* (1859) Johns.
174, 190 *per* Page Wood V.-C. It is, nevertheless, the current editor's view that, in this respect, the
decision in *Gray v. Smith* should be approached with caution: the fact that an outgoing partner does
not actually receive a payment for goodwill does not mean that he is not giving up his share therein:
see *infra*, para. 10–206, n. 977. Why should the firm name and its associated goodwill be artificially
separated in this way?

[975] See *supra*, para. 10–201. But *quaere* whether, if the outgoing partner merely receives his
entitlement as a debt pursuant to the Partnership Act 1890, s.43, he can properly be regarded as a
vendor of goodwill. The point will not arise if, as is usually the case, the agreement makes it clear
that the partnership is not dissolved by the retirement of a partner (see *supra*, para. 10–39) and
establishes the name under which it will carry on business (see *supra*, para. 10–41).

[976] Note, however, the approach adopted in *Dawson v. Beeson* (1882) 12 Ch.D. 504, *infra*, para.
10–210.

[977] For this purpose, it would not seem to matter whether any sum is actually paid in respect of the
goodwill itself: see *Churton v. Douglas* (1859) Johns. 174, 186 *per* Page Wood V.-C.; *Trego v. Hunt*
[1896] A.C. 7; also *Bridge v. Deacons* [1984] A.C. 705, 718. But see also *supra*, para. 10–205, n.
975.

[978] *Shackle v. Baker* (1808) 14 Ves.Jr. 468; *Cruttwell v. Lye* (1810) 17 Ves.Jr. 335; *Harrison v.
Gardner* (1817) 2 Madd. 198; *Kennedy v. Lee* (1817) 3 Mer. 441; *Davies v. Hodgson* (1858) 25 Beav.
177; *Bradbury v. Dickens* (1859) 27 Beav. 53; *Mellersh v. Keen* (1859) 27 Beav. 236; *Smith v. Everett*
(1859) 27 Beav. 446; *Churton v. Douglas* (1859) Johns. 174, *infra*, para. 10–207. Where goodwill is
sold in the open market, the particulars should refer to this right: see *Johnson v. Helleley* (1864) 34
Beav. 63; *Re David and Matthews* [1899] 1 Ch. 378 at 385 *per* Romer J.

[979] *Hookham v. Pottage* (1872) L.R. 8 Ch.App. 91; *Labouchere v. Dawson* (1872) 13 Eq. 322; also
Cruttwell v. Lye (1810) 17 Ves.Jr. 335.

[980] *Leggott v. Barrett* (1880) 15 Ch.D. 306; *Trego v. Hunt* [1896] A.C. 7.

customers as long as they remain customers of the firm,[981] even if they have had dealings with him since the date of his retirement[982] and his right to carry on a competing business is expressly recognised by the agreement,[983] or (2) represent himself as continuing the firm's business.[984] It follows that he may not carry on business under the firm name or under a name which is so similar to the firm name as to lead members of the public to believe that it is the same business. Equally, if the firm name happens to be the same as his own, he cannot be restrained from carrying on business in that name, unless he seeks to make dishonest use of it.[985]

10–207   Thus, in *Churton v. Douglas*,[986] two of the claimants and the defendant, whose name was John Douglas, carried on a partnership business under the name "John Douglas & Co.". The defendant retired and assigned his share, including his share of goodwill, to his co-partners and a new partner (the third claimant) who was admitted in his place. The claimants thereafter continued to carry on the old business under a new name, but with the addition "late John Douglas & Co.". The defendant entered into a new partnership with three employees of the old firm whom he had (on his own admission) enticed to join him: that partnership acquired premises next door to those occupied by the old firm and carried on an identical business under the name "John Douglas & Co.". That name was prominently displayed outside the new premises and customers of the old firm were circularised in terms that would have lead them to suppose that the business of the old firm was being carried on by the defendant and his new partners. In proceedings brought by the claimants against the defendant, his right to carry on business, either alone or in partnership with others, in direct competition with the business carried on by the claimants was accepted,[987] but the court went on to hold that:

(i) the claimants alone had the right to carry on the business previously carried on by John Douglas & Co.;

(ii) they alone had the right to represent themselves as the successors of that firm and the defendant had no such right;

---

[981] *Trego v. Hunt* [1896] A.C. 7 and the cases there cited; *Derby v. Meehan, The Times*, November 25, 1998; also *Jennings v. Jennings* [1898] 1 Ch. 378; *Re David and Matthews* [1899] 1 Ch. 378; *Gargan v. Ruttle* [1931] I.R. 152; and see *Davidson v. Wayman* [1984] 2 N.Z.L.R. 115. It appears that this restriction may not apply where the share of a bankrupt partner is sold by his trustee: see *Cruttwell v. Lye* (1810) 17 Ves.Jr. 335; *Walker v. Mottram* (1881) 19 Ch.D. 355; and note also *Farey v. Cooper* [1927] 2 K.B. 384; *Green & Sons v. Morris* [1914] 1 Ch. 562. The position of an expelled partner is less clear: see *infra*, para. 10–210. On the other hand, the restriction does apply in the case of the sale of a deceased partner's share by his personal representatives (*Boorne v. Wicker* [1927] 1 Ch. 667) and a sale pursuant to a court order in dissolution proceedings (*Johnson v. Helleley* (1864) 34 Beav. 63; *Jennings v. Jennings, supra; Re David and Matthews, supra*, p. 385 *per* Romer J.); see also *infra*, paras 23–186 *et seq.*

[982] *Curl Bros. v. Webster* [1904] 1 Ch. 685.

[983] *Gillingham v. Beddow* [1900] 2 Ch. 242.

[984] *Churton v. Douglas* (1859) Johns. 174; *Hookham v. Pottage* (1872) L.R. 8 Ch.App. 91: *Mogford v. Courtenay* (1881) 45 L.T. 303.

[985] *ibid.*; also *supra*, para. 3–20. For a recent analysis of the relevant principles, see *I. N. Newman Ltd. v. Adlem* [2006] F.S.R. 16 (CA). And see *Vernon v. Hallam* (1886) 34 Ch.D. 748 (where there was a covenant not to carry on business under a particular name which happened to be that of the defendant); *Pomeroy Ltd. v. Scalé* (1907) 23 T.L.R. 170.

[986] (1859) Johns. 174.

[987] *ibid.* p. 187 *per* Page Wood V.-C.

(iii) the defendant could not acquire such a right by taking other persons into partnership with him; and

(iv) although his name was John Douglas, the defendant had no right, either alone or in partnership with others, to carry on the same kind of business in the same neighbourhood *under the name of "John Douglas & Co."*.

The defendant was accordingly restrained from carrying on such a business, either alone or in partnership, under that name or in any other manner which involved holding out that he was carrying on the business in continuation of, or in succession to, the business carried on by the old firm of John Douglas & Co.

Express restriction invalid: If an *express* restriction on competition sought to be imposed on the outgoing partner is unenforceable as an unlawful restraint of trade,[988] there may be no scope for implying any restriction on solicitation, etc., at least to the extent that the two terms would be mutually inconsistent.[989] However, the point is certainly not free from doubt.[990]   **10–208**

Post-dissolution agreements: The position will be the same where one or more partners agree to sell their shares of goodwill to their former co-partners following a dissolution.[991]   **10–209**

Expelled partners: Although there is authority for the proposition that an expelled partner will not be restrained from soliciting the customers of the firm,[992] the current editor submits that he will only enjoy such a freedom where the continuing partners are *not* obliged to purchase his share under the terms of the agreement.[993] Similarly, in the case of a partner compulsorily retired from the firm pursuant to an express power in the agreement.[994]   **10–210**

---

[988] See *infra*, paras 10–219 *et seq*.

[989] *Townends Group Ltd. v. Cobb, The Times,* December 1, 2004; also *Malden Timber v. McLeish* 1992 S.L.T. 727 (OH). *cf. Davey Offshore v. Emerald Field Contractors Ltd.* (1991) 55 B.L.R. 1.

[990] The contrary view is espoused in Kamerling and Goodwill, *Restrictive Covenants under Common and Competition Law* (6th ed. 2010), para. 10.1 p. 235, citing *Wessex Dairies Ltd. v. Smith* [1935] 2 K.B. 80 and *Triplex Safety Glass Co. Ltd. v. Scorah* [1938] Ch. 211. Both cases concerned the imposition of duties on an employee during the continuance of his employment and may therefore be distinguishable.

[991] This, of course, presupposes that any goodwill exists following the dissolution: see *supra*, paras 10–199 *et seq*.

[992] *Dawson v. Beeson* (1882) 22 Ch.D. 504. Although this decision was cited in *Trego v. Hunt* [1896] A.C. 7, it is not referred to in their Lordships' speeches.

[993] It is significant that in *Dawson v. Beeson, supra*, the expelled partner was to be paid out the amount of his capital as if he were dead (although it is not clear from the report whether this meant a mere return of capital contribution): see *ibid.* p. 511. It seems implicit in the judgment that, if he had not suffered financially as a result of the expulsion, the outcome would have been different. Where an outgoing partner's entire share is acquired by the continuing partners, it is immaterial that nothing is actually paid in respect of his share of goodwill: see *supra*, para. 10–206, n. 977. Equally, note the views expressed by the court regarding the difference between voluntary and involuntary sales in *Walker v. Mottram* (1881) 19 Ch.D. 355.

[994] *i.e.* pursuant to the type of power considered *supra*, para. 10–134 *et seq*.

10–211   *The nature of solicitation*

It was stated in *Taylor Stuart & Co. v. Croft*[995] that it was not solicitation for an employee merely to inform a client that he had left his former employment, even if he also gave his current address and acted in the hope that the client would transfer his custom.[996] Although parallel reasoning could be applied in the case of an outgoing partner, the current editor considers that, as a statement of general principle, this decision should be viewed with caution. It will, in practice, be extremely difficult to devise a form of announcement which does not have solicitatory overtones. In *Deacons v. White & Case LLP*[997] there appears to have been no direct evidence of the solicitation of clients, but there was sufficient evidence of what was intended to infer that it had taken place.

Other implied restrictions

10–212   Equally, even in the absence of an express restriction on competition, the partnership agreement or some subsequent agreement may justify an inference that an outgoing partner is not permitted to set up a competing business. Thus, where a power to retire was framed in terms of relinquishing involvement in a particular line of business carried on by the firm, it was held that a partner could not retire and still continue his involvement in that line of business.[998] Similarly, where the amount to be paid to a retiring partner in respect of goodwill was left to be ascertained by arbitrators, who acted on the understanding that the retiring partner would not commence a new business in the same neighbourhood, the partner concerned was later restrained from carrying on business in that neighbourhood, even though the award was silent on the point.[999]

Court imposed restrictions

10–213   A more difficult question is whether a court or an arbitrator could, when ordering the sale of the firm's goodwill, either to one or more of the partners or to a third party, impose more stringent restrictions on competition than those normally implied on such a sale. It is certainly right that the realisable value of goodwill would be much increased if such a jurisdiction were exercisable, but there is scant authority to support it. Certainly, such an order *appears* to have been made by the arbitrator in *Morley v. Newman*,[1000] but the report of the decision is brief and it is difficult to discern any statement of principle therein. Although the Court of Appeal did, with some reservations, accept the existence

---

[995] (Lawtel 14/10/97), an unreported decision of Stanley Burnton Q.C. sitting as a deputy judge of the Chancery Division. See also *infra*, para. 10–225, n. 1069.

[996] The decision in *Kao Lee & Yip v Hoi-Yan* [2003] 2 H.K.C. 113 is to the same effect: see *ibid.* at [59] *per* Ma J. Note also *Associated Foreign Exchange Ltd. v. International Foreign Exchange (UK) Ltd.* [2010] EWHC 1178 (Ch) (Lawtel 22/5/10) at [101].

[997] HCA 2433/2002, October 24, 2003 (Hong Kong High Court) at [155] to [168] *per* Deputy High Court Judge Gill.

[998] See *Cooper v. Watson* (1784) 3 Doug. 413, where a partnership agreement between two brewers provided that either partner might, on giving six months' notice to the other, "quit the trade and mystery of a brewer", and that the other would thereafter be at liberty to continue the trade on his own account. Such a provision might, of course, be regarded as an unlawful restraint of trade but this is a separate issue: see *infra*, paras 10–219 *et seq.*

[999] *Harrison v. Gardner* (1817) 2 Madd. 198. The likelihood of competition will normally be taken into account in valuing the goodwill: see *Re David and Matthews* [1899] 1 Ch. 378 and *infra*, paras 10–218 *et seq.*

[1000] (1824) 5 D. & R. 317.

of an analogous jurisdiction in *Crittenden v. Crittenden*,[1001] this was pursuant to the wide powers conferred on the court by the Matrimonial Causes Act 1973. It thus remains to be seen whether this is an area in which judicial creativity is likely to be deployed.

In one unreported case,[1002] the court circumvented the above difficulty by, in effect, imposing a restriction as a condition of giving the partners liberty to bid,[1003] but the current editor questions the propriety of this solution.

Finally, it should in this connection be noted that it may be possible to obtain a so-called "springboard" injunction, to prevent advantage being taken of breaches of duty committed whilst an outgoing partner still remained a member of the firm, independently of any express contractual restrictions,[1004] but the court will need to be satisfied that the unfair advantage still exists and that the injunction can counter it. In *Deacons v. White & Case LLP*[1005] relief was refused because too much time had already passed since the partner's retirement date.[1006]

(c) Valuation of Goodwill

It has already been seen that a well drawn agreement should provide for the acquisition of an outgoing partner's share by the continuing or surviving partners.[1007] Lord Lindley warned that: **10–214**

" . . . too great care cannot be taken to express as clearly as possible what is intended to be done with respect to goodwill; and in order to avoid all ambiguity, the word goodwill itself should be made use of."

This still holds true as regards the *valuation* of goodwill, which would otherwise prima facie be comprehended within the expressions "assets", "property", "effects", "stock"[1008] or, perhaps, "premises"[1009] of the partnership and paid for accordingly.

[1001] [1990] 2 F.S.R. 361.
[1002] *Clements v. Pope* (October 10, 1999), a decision of H.H. Judge Weeks Q.C. sitting as a judge of the Chancery Division.
[1003] In fact, this condition was introduced by way of a variation of an order previously made, and the condition was that the partners should sign a contract of sale in whatever terms the solicitor having the conduct of the sale should deem reasonable.
[1004] See *Roger Bullivant Ltd. v. Ellis* [1987] I.C.R. 464; *UBS Wealth Management (UK) Ltd. v. Vestra Wealth LLP* [2008] I.R.L.R. 965; *Dass Solicitors v. Southcott*, April 2, 2009 (Lawtel 14/12/09) (all cases concerning employees).
[1005] HCA 2433/2002, October 24, 2003 (Hong Kong High Court).
[1006] It should be noted that, even if the court had been minded to grant an injunction for a longer period, too little of that period would still have remained to be any more than "upsetting": *ibid.* at [241].
[1007] See *supra*, paras 10–150 *et seq.*
[1008] See *Hall v. Barrows* (1863) 4 De G.J. & S. 150; *Page v. Ratcliffe* (1897) 75 L.T. 371; *Jennings v. Jennings* [1898] 1 Ch. 378; *Re David and Matthews* [1899] 1 Ch. 378; *Manley v. Sartori* [1927] 1 Ch. 157; *McClelland v. Hyde* [1942] N.I. 1. And see also *Salter v. Leas Hotel Co.* [1902] 1 Ch. 332. The decisions in *Kennedy v. Lee* (1817) 3 Mer. 452 and *Hall v. Hall* (1855) 20 Beav. 139 are no longer in point.
[1009] See *Blake v. Shaw* (1860) Johns. 732; *Re Rhagg* [1938] Ch. 828. But *cf. Burfield v. Rouch* (1862) 31 Beav. 241; *Re Betts* [1949] W.N. 91. And see also *supra*, para. 10–193, n. 900.

Goodwill treated as valueless

10–215   If goodwill is to be treated as valueless,[1010] this fact should be stated in the agreement.[1011] The mere fact that goodwill has been written out of the partnership accounts or that it appears therein at a nominal value may be irrelevant when determining the entitlement of an outgoing partner,[1012] *unless* such entitlement is to be determined by reference to the contents of the last signed balance sheet which has, indeed, been prepared on that basis.[1013]

Agreed basis for valuation

10–216   If goodwill is to be valued, the agreement should state on what basis and by whom the valuation is to be made.

Fixed value: Although the agreement could establish a fixed notional value for goodwill,[1014] it would be dangerous to adopt anything other than a nominal figure, since its true value will fluctuate with the fortunes of the firm.[1015]

Profit related value: The simplest method is essentially profit based and will usually involve applying an agreed number of years' purchase to the average profits of the firm over a set period, usually of between three and five years.[1016] Equally, in some businesses, the same approach will be adopted but with the substitution of average gross receipts for profits.[1017] In all such cases, the valuation exercise will be a simple one and can be carried out by the partnership accountants. However, the result may be arbitrary, particularly if the profits of the

---

[1010] Note, in this context, *Ryder v. Frohlich* [2006] NSWC 833, noted *supra*, para. 10–199.

[1011] This is, however, strictly unnecessary in the case of a medical partnership practising within the National Health Service, since an outgoing partner could not in any event receive any consideration for his share of goodwill without committing an offence: see the National Health Service Act 2006, s.259, Sched. 21. Note that a further prohibition on the sale of goodwill by various types of contractors and certain medical practitioners providing "essential services" is also to be found in the Primary Medical Services (Sale of Goodwill and Restrictions on Sub-contracting) Regulations 2004 (SI 2004/906), reg. 3(1), which continues to have effect under the 2006 Act: National Health Service (Consequential Provisions) Act 2006, Sched. 2, para. 1(2).

[1012] See the review of the authorities, culminating in *Re White* [2001] Ch. 393 (CA), *supra*, paras 10–163 *et seq*.

[1013] See *supra*, paras 10–164 *et seq*.

[1014] See, for example, *Wade v. Jenkins* (1860) 2 Giff. 509.

[1015] If a substantive value were to be placed on goodwill at the outset, this could impose a severe (and possibly unsupportable) financial burden on the continuing or surviving partners in the event of an unexpected downturn in the profitability of the business. *A fortiori* if that sum was negotiated on the footing that outgoing partners would be restrained from competing with the partnership business but the chosen restriction proves to be wholly or partially invalid. Although the agreement might permit account to be taken of such imponderable factors by means of an adjustment to the fixed value, this is unlikely to produce a satisfactory result.

[1016] This presupposes that the partnership has subsisted for that length of time. If it has not, eccentric results may be produced if account is taken of the profits of a predecessor firm or if the calculation is based on (say) a single year's profits (even assuming this to be permitted under the agreement). There is, perhaps, something to be said for adopting a fixed notional value for goodwill to cover the initial period.

[1017] *e.g.* the goodwill of an accountancy practice is normally valued by reference to its gross annual recurring fees: see, for example, the evidence adduced in *Stekel v. Ellice* [1973] 1 W.L.R. 191, 195. Note, however, that there may, depending on the circumstances, be a dispute as to whether particular fees are recurring or non-recurring.

firm are subject to severe fluctuations.[1018] Equally, in *Finnegan v. McAreavey*[1019] the agreement provided for a profit related value to be determined but, in the event, this was held not to be applicable since the required number of complete financial years had not been achieved when the valuation fell to be made. Carswell L.C.J. held that, in those circumstances, the clause did not apply and goodwill would have to be valued as on a dissolution. This amounted to a rewriting of the agreement in a way *neither* partner expected.

As an alternative, it is sometimes provided that a partner's interest in goodwill should be valued by applying the relevant number of year's purchase to *his* average profit share over the designated period. Such a formula should be approached with caution if: (a) the profit shares are variable[1020] or (b) those shares do not accord with the partners' shares in surplus assets[1021] since, in either case, the figure produced may bear no relation to the outgoing partner's interest in goodwill as at the date he ceases to be a member of the firm.

Market value: Some agreements require the market value of the goodwill to be ascertained, although this is increasingly rare. There are, in fact, two recognised methods of valuing goodwill, *i.e.* "total capitalisation"[1022] and "super profits",[1023] but these are appropriate only in the case of large firms and, even then, are not of universal application.[1024] Moreover, account must always be taken of the particular circumstances of the firm and business under consideration.[1025] Thus, if the partnership was originally constituted for a fixed term which has almost expired, the goodwill may have only a nominal value.[1026] Again, if the continued existence of the goodwill is dependent on the active participation of a "key" partner, this will affect its value, as will the ability of outgoing partners to set up competing businesses.[1027]

It follows that the valuation process involves a high degree of professional judgment on the part of the chosen valuer(s) and, if the partners opt for an "expert" valuation, they will normally be bound thereby.[1028]

10–217

[1018] *A fortiori* if the partnership is dissolved shortly after the death or retirement of a partner: see *Austen v. Boys* (1858) 2 De G. & J. 626.

[1019] [2002] N.I. Q.B. 24.

[1020] See, for example, *supra*, para. 10–80.

[1021] See *supra*, paras 10–79, 10–158.

[1022] This basis requires the valuer to ascertain the average maintainable profits of the firm over a given period, to multiply that figure by the appropriate number of years purchase and then to deduct the net value of the firm's tangible assets: see *Findlays' Trustees v. I.R.C.* (1938) 22 A.T.C. 437.

[1023] This basis requires the valuer to deduct from the average maintainable profits of the firm over a given period the average assumed yield attributable to the firm's tangible assets together with a sum representing a reasonable level of remuneration for the partners, and then to multiply the balance (the "super profit") by an appropriate number of years' purchase. Note that the expert witnesses in *Findlays' Trustees v. I.R.C.*, *supra*, did not consider this basis to be appropriate when valuing the goodwill of a partnership owning a newspaper.

[1024] See, for example, *Page v. Ratcliffe* (1897) 75 L.T. 371 (where the goodwill of a brewery business fell to be valued); also *Findlays' Trustees v. I.R.C.*, *supra*, p. 440 *per* Lord Fraser. And see the Law Society's former paper on Goodwill issued on July 16, 1981.

[1025] Relevant factors will include the size of the firm, the location of its premises, profit trends, etc.

[1026] *Austen v. Boys* (1858) 2 De G. & J. 626. This was an extreme case, where notice to retire was given two days before the expiration of a fixed term of seven years. This decision must, however, be approached with caution, since it does not follow that goodwill is necessarily unsaleable and, therefore, valueless in the event of a dissolution: see *supra*, paras 10–200 *et seq.*

[1027] See *supra*, paras 10–204 *et seq.* This may be of particular relevance for the purposes of inheritance tax: see *infra*, paras 36–22, 36–58.

[1028] See *supra*, para. 10–176.

(d) Restrictions on Competition[1029]

Need for express restriction

10–218   It has already been seen that an outgoing partner is subject to few implied restrictions on his ability to set up business in competition with his former partners, even where he has sold them his share of the firm's goodwill.[1030] As Lord Lindley put it:

> "In the absence of any agreement upon the subject, a retiring partner is as much at liberty to set up for himself, in opposition to the firm he has quitted, as he would be if he had never belonged to it."

An expelled partner may, if anything, be in an even stronger position.[1031]

It follows that effective protection from the possible depredations of an outgoing partner can only be secured if the agreement contains an *express* restriction on competition.[1032]

Enforceability of restrictions

10–219   It has long been settled that the courts take a stricter and less favourable view of restrictions on competition as between employer and employee than of similar restrictions as between vendor and purchaser.[1033] Partnership in the true sense does not create the relationship of employer and employee and may or may not involve the relationship of vendor and purchaser. It is, therefore, strictly *sui generis*. Although this was confirmed in *Bridge v. Deacons*,[1034] the Privy Council emphasised that categorisation serves little purpose, since the true test of enforceability lies in the legitimate interests of the parties seeking to enforce the restraint.[1035] Nevertheless, it is still true to say that an outgoing partner who disposes of his share in exchange for a payment will, at least to an extent, partake of the character of a vendor.[1036]

Where a restraint has been entered into between partners who are on broadly equal terms at the inception of the partnership, this will represent a powerful

---

[1029] See the *Encyclopedia of Professional Partnerships*, Precedent 1, cl. 22(2)(1).

[1030] See *supra*, paras 10–206 *et seq.*

[1031] See *Dawson v. Beeson* (1882) 22 Ch.D. 504 and *supra*, para. 10–210.

[1032] Note, however, that the existence of an express restriction will increase the value of the firm's goodwill for inheritance tax purposes: see *supra*, paras 36–22, 36–58.

[1033] See *Ronbar Enterprises v. Green* [1954] 1 W.L.R. 815 and the cases there cited. As to restraints of trade generally, see *Nordenfelt v. Maxim Nordenfelt Guns & Ammunition Co. Ltd.* [1894] A.C. 535; *Mason v. Provident Clothing & Supply Co. Ltd.* [1913] A.C. 724; *Att.-Gen. of Australia v. Adelaide Steamship Co. Ltd.* [1913] A.C. 781; *Herbert Morris v. Saxelby* [1916] 1 A.C. 689; *Attwood v. Lamont* [1920] 3 K.B. 571; *Esso Petroleum Co. Ltd. v. Harper's Garage (Stourport) Ltd.* [1968] A.C. 269; *Greig v. Insole* [1978] 1 W.L.R. 302; *Bridge v. Deacons* [1984] A.C. 705. It should be noted that a freedom to trade does not constitute property in its own right: *SmithKline Beecham plc v. Apotex Europe Ltd.* [2007] Ch. 71 at [71] *per* Jacob L.J. Note also the potential application of Art. 101 TFEU and the Competition Act 1998, *infra*, paras 10–238 *et seq.*

[1034] [1984] A.C. 705.

[1035] *ibid.* p. 714, endorsing the approach adopted by Lord Reid in *Esso Petroleum Co. Ltd. v. Harper's Garage (Stourport) Ltd.* [1968] A.C. 269, 301; see also *Dawnay, Day & Co. v. D'Alphen* [1998] I.C.R. 1068, 1105B–1107A (CA). The concept of proportionality has no place in this sphere: *Allied Dunbar (Frank Weisinger) Ltd. v. Weisinger* [1988] I.R.L.R. 60, 65 *per* Millett J.

[1036] See *Re Jenkins' Deed of Partnership* [1948] W.N. 98 (which, however, was a case of a non-partner, who was a party to the partnership deed, seeking to enforce a restriction against a former partner); *Whitehill v. Bradford* [1952] Ch. 236; *Lyne-Pirkis v. Jones* [1969] 1 W.L.R. 1293; *Ronbar Enterprises v. Green* [1954] 1 W.L.R. 815.

argument in favour of enforceability.[1037] Equally, where the partnership terms are of a one-sided nature and effectively permit some partners to dictate to the others on a wide variety of matters, the court may be less sympathetic when considering the validity of a restriction applicable to the subordinate partners.[1038]

It is an open question whether a restriction on competition could be invalidated because it breaches an outgoing partner's right of freedom of establishment in another Member State under Article 49 TFEU.[1038a] The current editor considers that there might be some scope for such an argument since Article 49 does appear to have horizontal effect as between private parties,[1039] although the instances in which it could be invoked will be rare.

Salaried partners

Where, on a true construction of his contract, a "salaried partner" is nothing   **10–220**
more than a mere employee,[1040] the validity of any restriction sought to be imposed on him will be judged according to the harsher employment test.[1041] As demonstrated by the decision in *Kao Lee & Yip v. Edwards*,[1042] critical factors pointing to employment are likely to include a fixed remuneration payable irrespective of the firm's profitability[1043] coupled with an express (or implied) indemnity against debts and liabilities, the absence of a capital contribution or any entitlement to share in the firm's surplus assets[1044] and the exclusion of any right to participate in the firm's management. Any attempt to impose on a salaried partner a more rigorous restriction than that imposed on the equity partners is unlikely to succeed.[1045]

Test of reasonableness

In accordance with the general doctrine that restraint of trade is against public   **10–221**
policy, any restriction on a person's freedom to carry on his trade or profession

---

[1037] See *Lyne-Pirkis v. Jones* [1969] 1 W.L.R. 1293, 1301 *per* Edmund Davies L.J.; *Esso Petroleum Co. Ltd. v. Harper's Garage (Stourport) Ltd.* [1968] A.C. 269, 300 *per* Lord Reid. *A fortiori*, in the case of a solicitors' partnership: see *Bridge v. Deacons* [1984] A.C. 705, 716–717.

[1038] See *Kao, Lee & Yip v. Hoi-Yan* [1995] 1 H.K.L.R. 248 (CA, Hong Kong). In this case there were two classes of partners, namely the "founding partners" and the "equity partners". Despite that nomenclature the latter did not contribute capital and had no interest in the firm's goodwill. Numerous powers were reserved to the former, including the right to oust equity partners with or without cause. This subordination of the equity partners was regarded by the court as fatal to the attempt to enforce the restriction. For previous litigation relating to salaried partners in the same firm, see *infra*, para. 10–220.

[1038a] Formerly Art. 43 EC, but renumbered by the Treaty of Lisbon.

[1039] See *Viking Line ABP v. International Transport Workers' Federation* [2008] I.C.R. 741 (ECJ).

[1040] See *supra*, paras 5–54 *et seq.*

[1041] In considering the validity of covenants as between employer and employee, emphasis has tended to be placed on their inequality of bargaining power (see, for example, *Schroeder Music Publishing Co. v. Macaulay* [1974] 1 W.L.R. 1308; *Clifford Davis Management Ltd. v. W.E.A. Records Ltd.* [1975] 1 W.L.R. 61) but this is, in reality, only one factor to be taken into account, albeit an important one: *Dawnay, Day & Co. v. D'Alphen* [1998] I.C.R. 1068, 1081 *per* Robert Walker J. See also *Texaco Ltd. v. Mulberry Filling Station Ltd.* [1972] 1 W.L.R. 814.

[1042] [1993] 1 H.K.C. 314 (CA, Hong Kong).

[1043] Note, however, that it is now clear that such an entitlement is not *per se* inconsistent with partnership status: see *supra*, paras 2–10, 2–11, 5–54.

[1044] Note that this was an attribute which the salaried partners shared with the "equity partners" in that firm: see *Kao, Lee & Yip v. Hoi-Yan, supra.*

[1045] As in *Taylor Stuart & Co. v. Croft*, (Lawtel 14/10/97), a decision of Stanley Burnton Q.C. sitting as a deputy judge of the Chancery Division. The contents of the partnership agreement are likely to be regarded as a conclusive indicator of what is reasonable in such a case.

is prima facie void, but may be valid if it is shown to be reasonable: (1) in the interests of the parties, and (2) in the interests of the public.

(1) *Reasonableness in the Interests of the Parties*

10–222 The onus of proving that a particular restriction is reasonable in the interests of the parties, and thus valid, is on the party seeking to enforce it.[1046] Thus the burden will generally fall upon the continuing partners, although in certain circumstances an outgoing partner might himself seek to rely on the restriction, *e.g.* where there is some dependent obligation on the part of the continuing partners.[1047]

Legitimate interest capable of protection

10–223 In order to show that the restriction is reasonable, the continuing partners must above all else demonstrate that they have a legitimate interest capable of being protected.[1048] That interest will, inevitably, lie in the firm's business and good-will, a share of which will usually have been acquired from the outgoing partner,[1049] but may also extend to the firm's confidential information.[1050] Whilst it is, within reason, permissible to seek protection for any anticipated expansion in the firm's business,[1051] an attempt to impose a restriction in gross, with a view to protecting a wholly different business in which the firm has never been involved, will inevitably fail.[1052] If the partnership agreement seeks to define the interest to be protected, it is unlikely to be possible to justify the restraint by reference to some other interest.[1053]

[1046] See the cases cited *supra*, para. 10–219, n. 1033.

[1047] See, for example, *Wyatt v. Kreglinger & Furneau* [1933] 1 K.B. 793; *Macfarlane v. Kent* [1965] 1 W.L.R. 1019; *Bull v. Pitney-Bowes Ltd.* [1967] 1 W.L.R. 273.

[1048] See in particular, *Bridge v. Deacons* [1984] A.C. 705, 714; also *Allied Dunbar (Frank Weisinger) Ltd. v. Weisinger* [1988] I.R.L.R. 60; *Office Angels Ltd. v. Rainer-Thomas* [1991] I.R.L.R. 214; *Dawnay, Day & Co. Ltd. v. D'Alphen* [1998] I.C.R. 1068. And note *Prontaprint plc v. London Litho Ltd.* [1987] F.S.R. 315 (which concerned a franchising agreement). In an appropriate case, the restriction may extend to potential clients/customers with whom the firm is in negotiations at the date of a partner's departure: *International Consulting Services (U.K.) Ltd. v. Hart* [2000] I.R.L.R. 227. Note also that, in *Beckett Investment Management Group Ltd. v. Hall* [2007] I.C.R. 1539, the Court of Appeal did not hesitate to construe an employee's non-dealing restriction as extending to clients of the employer's subsidiary, when the employer did not carry on any client business itself. However, there the employees were clearly well aware of the overall business structure: *ibid.* at [16]. *cf. Dunwoody Sports Marketing v. Prescott* [2007] 1 W.L.R. 2343, notes, noted *infra*, para. 10–231.

[1049] It does not matter whether or not the outgoing partner has received a cash consideration for his share of goodwill: *Bridge v. Deacons* [1984] A.C. 705, 718.

[1050] Confidential information can be protected, even if it may be difficult to draw the line between such information and other information which is not confidential: see *Littlewoods Organisation Ltd. v. Harris* [1977] 1 W.L.R. 1472, 1479 *per* Lord Denning M.R.; *Turner v. Commonwealth and Minerals Ltd.* [2000] I.R.L.R. 114 at [18] *per* Waller L.J.; *Thomas v. Farr PLC* [2007] I.C.R. 932 at [42], all employee cases. See also *infra*, para. 10–225.

[1051] *Lyne-Pirkis v. Jones* [1969] 1 W.L.R. 1293; also *Texaco v. Mulberry Filling Station* [1972] 1 W.L.R. 814; *Dawnay, Day & Co. Ltd. v. D'Alphen* [1998] I.C.R. 1068. And see *Maxim's Ltd. v. Dye* [1977] 1 W.L.R. 1155; *My Kinda Bones Ltd. (T/A Chicago Rib Shack) v. Dr. Pepper's Stove Co. Ltd. (T/A Dr. Pepper's Manhattan Rib Shack)* [1984] F.S.R. 289.

[1052] See *Horner v. Graves* (1831) 7 Bing. 735; *Townsend v. Jarman* [1900] 2 Ch. 698, 702–703 *per* Farwell J.; *Henry Leetham & Sons Ltd. v. Johnston-White* [1907] 1 Ch. 322; *Morris & Co. v. Ryle* [1910] 103 L.T. 545; *British Reinforced Concrete Co. Ltd. v. Schelff* [1921] 2 Ch. 563; *Vancouver Malt & Sake Brewing Co. Ltd. v. Vancouver Breweries Ltd.* [1934] A.C. 181; *Anscombe & Ringland v. Butchoff* (1984) 134 N.L.J. 37; *Scully U.K. Ltd. v. Lee* [1998] I.R.L.R. 259.

[1053] See *Office Angels Ltd. v. Rainer-Thomas* [1991] I.R.L.R. 214 at [39] *per* Slade L.J.; *Country-wide Assured Financial Services Ltd. v. Smart* [2004] EWHC 1214 (Ch) (Lawtel 7/5/04).

The fact that the firm's goodwill is inherently unsaleable in no way affects the continuing partners' interest in its protection.[1054]

In *Bridge v. Deacons*,[1055] which concerned a solicitors' partnership, the goodwill was of an unusually departmentalised nature. On that basis, it was argued that the continuing partners were only entitled to protection as regards the goodwill of the particular department in which the outgoing partner had worked. This argument was rejected by the Privy Council, who pointed out that the outgoing partner was, prior to his retirement, interested in the totality of the firm's goodwill.[1056]

Restriction not excessive

On the assumption that the continuing partners have a legitimate interest   **10–224**
capable of protection, they must then go on to show that the particular restriction is no more than adequate to protect that interest, *i.e.* that it is not excessive as regards area,[1057] duration,[1058] or prohibited activities.[1059] As a broad rule of thumb, it can be said that any restriction on competition by outgoing partners which is genuinely designed to protect the value of the firm's business and goodwill is likely to be upheld, provided that it is mutual[1060] and does not exceed the geographical area and scope of the firm's business (allowing for any reasonable anticipated expansion)[1061] or the duration of the partnership itself.[1062] A *unilateral* restraint may be treated less sympathetically,[1063] but the circumstances in which the outgoing partner leaves (or is forced to leave) the firm are unlikely

---

[1054] This is clearly illustrated in the case of medical partnerships practising within the National Health Service: see *Whitehill v. Bradford* [1952] Ch. 236; *Macfarlane v. Kent* [1965] 1 W.L.R. 1019; *Anthony v. Rennie* 1981 S.L.T. (Notes) 11; *Kerr v. Morris* [1987] Ch. 90.

[1055] [1984] A.C. 705.

[1056] *ibid.* pp. 718–719.

[1057] See *British Reinforced Concrete Co. Ltd. v. Schelff* [1921] 2 Ch. 563; *Butt v. Long* (1953) A.L.J. 576; *Ronbar Enterprises v. Green* [1954] 1 W.L.R. 815; *Scorer v. Seymour Jones* [1966] 1 W.L.R. 1419; *Lyne-Pirkis v. Jones* [1969] 1 W.L.R. 1293; *Marley Tile Co. Ltd. v. Johnson* [1982] I.R.L.R. 75; *Office Angels Ltd. v. Rainer-Thomas* [1991] I.R.L.R. 214; *Kao Lee & Yip v. Edwards* [1993] 1 H.K.C. 314, noted *supra*, para. 10–220; *Kao, Lee & Yip v. Hoi-Yan* [1995] 1 H.K.L.R. 248, noted *supra*, para. 10–219; *Kall-Kwik Printing (U.K.) Ltd. v. Frank Clarence Rush* [1996] F.S.R. 114; *Espley v. Williams* [1997] 1 E.G.L.R. 9; *Scully U.K. Ltd. v. Lee* [1998] I.R.L.R. 259. See also *infra*, para. 10–225. In the case of area covenants, distances are measured as the crow flies: see *Duignan v. Walker* (1859) Johns. 446; *Mouflet v. Cole* (1872) L.R. 8 Ex. 32. As to the approach which might be adopted when the proscribed area includes land falling on the far side of a significant stretch of water (*e.g.* an estuary or the sea), see *Kall-Kwik Printing (U.K.) Ltd. v. Frank Clarence Rush, supra*, at p. 122 *per* H.H. Judge Cooke (sitting as a judge of the Chancery Division).

[1058] See *Fitch v. Dewes* [1921] 2 A.C. 158; *Re Jenkins' Deed of Partnership* [1948] W.N. 98; *Whitehill v. Bradford* [1952] Ch. 236; *Lyne-Pirkis v. Jones* [1969] 1 W.L.R. 1293. But see also *infra*, para. 10–225. As to the current relevance of *Fitch v. Dewes*, see *ibid.* n. 1081.

[1059] See *Nordenfelt v. Maxim Nordenfelt Guns & Ammunition Co.* [1894] A.C. 535; *Goldsoll v. Goldman* [1915] 1 Ch. 292; *Konski v. Peet* [1915] 1 Ch. 530; *British Reinforced Concrete Co. v. Schelff* [1921] 2 Ch. 563; *Routh v. Jones* [1947] 1 All E.R. 758; *Re Jenkins' Deed of Partnership* [1948] W.N. 98; *Ronbar Enterprises v. Green* [1954] 1 W.L.R. 815; *Lyne-Pirkis v. Jones* [1969] 1 W.L.R. 1293; *Peyton v. Mindham* [1972] 1 W.L.R. 8.

[1060] *i.e.* it applies to all partners, irrespective of their age or seniority in the firm: see *Bridge v. Deacons* [1984] A.C. 705, 716. *cf. Kao, Lee & Yip v. Hoi-Yan* [1995] 1 H.K.L.R. 248 (CA, Hong Kong), where the mutuality of the restriction was held to be "illusory", given the one-sided nature of the agreement: see further, *supra*, para. 10–219.

[1061] See *supra*, para. 10–223.

[1062] See *Morris v. Colman* (1812) 18 Ves.Jr. 437; *Wilkinson v. Pettit* (1889) 7 N.Z.L.R. 342; *Ronbar Enterprises Ltd. v. Green* [1954] 1 W.L.R. 815.

[1063] But note that the Court of Appeal, without any apparent hesitation, enforced a unilateral restriction in *Clarke v. Newland* [1991] 1 All E.R. 397.

to affect the validity of a restriction.[1064] The restriction may (and, indeed, frequently will) be taken for the benefit of both present and future partners.[1065]

It will, as a general rule, be possible to justify a relatively wide restriction with a view to protecting trade secrets and confidential information, since they may be capable of use in more than one type of business.[1066] Similarly, where the business is highly specialised and, thus, appeals only to a limited market.[1067] The fact that it may be difficult to draw the line between confidential and non-confidential information may actually justify the imposition of a suitable restriction.[1068]

10–225   Although non-solicitation[1069] and non-dealing restrictions are, in practice, more likely to be held upheld than area or "brass plate" restrictions,[1070] the

[1064] In *Hensman v. Traill, The Times*, October 22, 1980, Bristow J. held that a unilateral restriction was invalid because it was capable of applying when Dr Traill was "banish[ed] for no reason". However, in *Lawrence v. Farndon*, January 23, 1998 (unreported), H.H. Judge Rich Q.C. (sitting as a judge of the Chancery Division) held that this proposition had been "implicitly" overruled by the judgment of Dillon L.J. in *Kerr v. Morris* [1987] Ch. 90, 106F–G. *Quaere*, is this correct? In any event, whilst at first instance in *Kerr v. Morris*, Falconer J. regarded himself as bound to follow *Hensman v. Traill*, this part of the decision appears to have been *obiter*. Micklem J. certainly took that view in *Agarwal v. Jayaratnam*, May 6, 1986 (unreported).

[1065] *Hitchcock v. Coker* (1837) 6 A. & E. 438, cited with approval in *Eastes v. Russ* [1914] 1 Ch. 468, 482 *per* Swinfen Eady L.J. and *Fitch v. Dewes* [1921] 2 A.C. 158, 168–169 *per* Viscount Cave.

[1066] See generally *Hagg v. Darley* (1878) 38 L.T. 312; *Littlewoods Organisation Ltd. v. Harris* [1977] 1 W.L.R. 1472. As to what is confidential information, see *Thomas Marshall (Exporters) Ltd. v. Guinle* [1979] Ch. 227; *Faccenda Chicken Ltd. v. Fowler* [1987] Ch. 117; *Lansing Linde Ltd. v. Kerr* [1991] 1 W.L.R. 251; *FSS Travel and Leisure Systems Ltd. v. Johnson* [1998] I.R.L.R. 382 (all cases concerning employees). See also *supra*, para. 10–55.

[1067] *e.g.* see *Nordenfelt v. Maxim Nordenfelt Guns & Ammunition Co. Ltd.* [1894] A.C. 535. Account must be taken of whether the business sought to be protected is conducted impersonally by, say, correspondence (which will merit a wide restraint) or is primarily dependent on personal contact (which will only warrant a more limited restraint). *cf. Calvert, Hunt & Barden v. Elton* (1974) 233 E.G. 391 (where a three-year restraint on an employee of an estate agent was upheld) and *Marion White Ltd. v. Francis* [1972] 1 W.L.R. 1423 (where a 12-month restraint on an employee of a hairdresser was upheld). Note also *Office Angels Ltd. v. Rainer-Thomas* [1991] I.R.L.R. 214. Another relevant factor will be whether the clientele is of a casual or recurring character.

[1068] See *Littlewoods Organisation Ltd. v. Harris* [1977] 1 W.L.R. 1472, 1479 *per* Lord Denning M.R.; *Turner v. Commonwealth and Minerals Ltd.* [2000] I.R.L.R. 114 at [18] *per* Waller L.J.; *Thomas v. Farr PLC* [2007] I.C.R. 932 at [42], all employee cases.

[1069] *Semble* it is not general necessary to impose a geographcial limitation on a non-solicitation restriction: *G.W. Lowman & Son Ltd. v. Ash* [1964] 1 W.L.R. 568, 572 *per* Harman L.J.; *First People Solutions Group Ltd. v. Jack* [2007] CSOH 80 at [70] *per* Lord Kinclaven. As to what will constitute solicitation, note the decision in *Taylor Stuart & Co. v. Croft*, (Lawtel 14/10/97). Stanley Burnton Q.C., sitting as a deputy judge of the Chancery Division observed: "It is of the essence of solicitation and of canvassing . . . that the client should be requested to transfer his custom. A communication which does no more than inform a client that an employee has left his employer is not a solicitation, even if it contains the address of the former employee, and even if it is sent in the hope that the client will transfer his custom." In the view of the current editor, as a statement of general principle, this should be viewed with some caution: much will depend on the particular circumstances. See also *Deacons v. White & Case LLP* (HCA 2433/2002), October 24, 2003 (Hong Kong High Court) and *supra*, para. 10–211.

[1070] See *Baines v. Geary* (1887) 35 Ch.D. 154; *East Essex Farmers Ltd. v. Holder* (1926) 70 S.J. 1001; *Express Dairy Co. v. Jackson* (1929) 99 L.J.K.B. 181; *Gilford Motor Co. v. Horn* [1933] 1 Ch. 935; *Konski v. Peet* [1915] 1 Ch. 530; *Spafax (1965) Ltd. v. Dommett* (1972) 116 S.J. 711 (where a covenant not to solicit "customers" was held to be invalid as being too uncertain); *Marley Tile Co. Ltd. v. Johnson* [1982] I.R.L.R. 75; *Office Angels Ltd. v. Rainer-Thomas* [1991] I.R.L.R. 214; *Dentmaster (U.K.) Ltd. v. Kent* [1997] I.R.L.R. 636. Needless to say, a geographical limit on a client-based restriction may, in an appropriate case, have to be imposed in order to ensure its validity. The world-wide nature of the restriction proved fatal in *Kao Lee & Yip v. Edwards* [1993] 1 H.K.C. 314,

courts are by no means unsympathetic towards the latter, particularly in professional partnerships.[1071] Notable examples of wide area covenants being upheld are to be found in two unreported decisions, once concerning a firm of solicitors[1072] and the other a firm of veterinary surgeons.[1073] Much will depend, ultimately, on whether a client-based restriction would be perceived as adequate to protect the firm's goodwill.[1074] Whether activities carried on predominatly outside the proscribed area will, nevertheless, result in a breach will naturally depend on the precise wording of the restriction. Thus, where a taxi driver was prohibited from carrying on business within a particular area, he was held not to be in breach merely by entering the area in order to ply for hire, but he could not regularly use a taxi rank in that area.[1075] Similarly, a solicitor may write letters to and receive letters from clients or opposing parties who live in the proscribed area because he will not thereby be carrying on business there.[1076] Whether regular appearances in the courts within the area will amount to a breach in such a case is, perhaps, a more difficult issue.[1077] If the covenant prohibits carrying on business in a particular area or market "in competition with" the firm, it may only be enforceable if the firm has a legitimate interest capable of protection in that area or market.[1078]

---

noted *supra*, para. 10–220 and *Kao, Lee & Yip v. Hoi-Yan* [1995] 1 H.K.L.R. 248, noted *supra*, para. 10–219. *cf. Plowman v. Ash* [1964] 1 W.L.R. 568; *Business Seating (Renovations) Ltd. v. Broad* [1989] I.C.R. 729; *Dentmaster (U.K.) Ltd. v. Kent*, *supra*; *Scully U.K. Ltd. v. Lee* [1998] I.R.L.R. 259 (all employment cases).

[1071] See for example, *Whitehill v. Bradford* [1952] Ch. 236; *Lyne-Pirkis v. Jones* [1969] 1 W.L.R. 1293; *Clarke v. Newland* [1991] 1 All E.R. 397; *Espley v. Williams* [1997] 1 E.G.L.R. 9. *Cf. Allan Janes LLP v. Johal* [2006] I.C.R. 742, which concerned an employee of a solicitors' LLP.

[1072] *Lawrence v. Farndon*, January 23, 1998, a decision of H.H. Judge Rich Q.C. sitting as a judge of the Chancery Division. In this case the restriction had a duration of two years and a radius of five miles, which extended to the whole of the conurbation of Leeds. It should be noted that the decision turned on the nature of the solicitors' practice in question, which comprised a large number of small, low value cases and relatively little repeat work. See also *Hollis & Co. v. Stocks* [2000] I.R.L.R. 712, in which the Court of Appeal upheld a 12 month/10 mile area restriction in an *employee's* contract.

[1073] *Naish v. Thorp Wright & Puxon*, May 21, 1998, a decision of H.H. Judge Taylor, sitting as a judge of the Queen's Bench Division. In this case the restriction had a duration of 8 years and covered a radius of 15 miles (albeit in a sparsely populated rural area), but the question of enforceability arose in the context of a claim in negligence against the outgoing partner's legal advisers. The judge held that, whilst the arguments were finely balanced, the restriction "would probably have been upheld", although one crucial factor which led him to this conclusion was a provision in the agreement entitling the outgoing partner to be paid a substantial sum in respect of his share of the firm's goodwill.

[1074] See *Espley v. Williams*, *supra* (non-solicitation restriction held inadequate to protect an estate agency business: two year/two mile area covenant upheld); note also *Exchange Communications Ltd. v. Masheder* 2009 S.L.T. 1141 (OH), where the court did not regard a 1 year area covenant relating to the "Greater Glasgow area" in an employee's contract as *per se* invalid. And see, generally, *Bridge v. Deacons* [1984] A.C. 705; *Allied Dunbar (Frank Weisinger) Ltd.* [1988] I.R.L.R. 60; *Kall-Kwik Printing (U.K.) Ltd. v. Frank Clarence Rush* [1996] F.S.R. 114.

[1075] *William Fraser & Son v. Renwick* 1906 S.L.T. 443 (OH).

[1076] See *Woodbridge & Sons v. Bellamy* [1911] 1 Ch. 326 (CA), a decision concerning an employee.

[1077] In *Llewellyn v. Simpson* (1891) 91 L.T. 9, the employee was held to be in breach but the report is very brief. *cf* the discussion of the effect of isolated incidents in *Edwards v. Warboys* [1984] A.C. 724 (note) at p. 727 *per* Dillon L.J.

[1078] See *Dawnay, Day & Co. Ltd. v. D'Alphen* [1998] I.C.R. 1068 (CA), which concerned a joint venture; *TFS Derivatives Ltd. v. Morgan* [2005] I.R.L.R. 246, an employee case; *ChipsAway International Ltd. v. Kerr* [2009] EWCA Civ 320 (Lawtel 11/3/09), a decision concerning a franchise agreement; *Phoenix Partners Group LLP v. Asoyag* [2010] I.R.L.R. 594, another employee case.

Questions of *duration* have not been extensively considered by the courts; indeed, in *Bridge v. Deacons*,[1079] the Privy Council observed that "there appears to be no reported case where a restriction which was otherwise reasonable has been held unreasonable solely because of its duration".[1080] Although the House of Lords in *Fitch v. Dewes*[1081] *did* uphold an area restriction as between a solicitor and his managing clerk which was unlimited in point of time, the current editor considers that exceptional circumstances would now be required to justify such an extreme approach.[1082] *Per contra*, in the case of restrictions on the solicitation of existing (as opposed to potential) customers or clients.[1083] There is no necessary assumption that a non-dealing restriction should be shorter in duration than a non-solicitation restriction,[1084] but the duration must be certain.[1085]

10–226   It is, of course, for the partners to specify the precise terms of the restriction, since it is not possible to prevent competition "so far as the law allows".[1086] Subject to any question of severance,[1087] such terms are specified at the continuing partners' peril, *i.e.* the risk of invalidity falls solely on them. Moreover, the court will not be prepared to declare in advance what activities are likely to

---

[1079] [1984] A.C. 705, 717.

[1080] Note that in one unreported case (*Pandit v. Shah*, November 6, 1987), Whitford J. held that a 10 year restriction in the case of a doctors' partnership would be "impossible, in any circumstances, to support" at trial. However, consistently with the Privy Council's observation, the validity of the area restriction was also in doubt. Equally, in another unreported case (*Taylor Stuart & Co. v. Croft*, (Lawtel 14/10/97)). Stanley Burnton Q.C., sitting as a deputy judge of the Chancery Division, appears to have regarded the duration of the covenant (three years in the case of a salaried "partner" in a firm of accountants) as decisive, although he does also seem to have had doubts about its scope. When considering duration, he was clearly influenced by the fact that only a two year restriction was imposed on an outgoing *equity* partner. See also *Kao Lee & Yip v. Edwards* [1993] 1 H.K.C. 314. Note that, in *Beckett Investment Management Group Ltd. v. Hall* [2007] I.C.R. 1539 (CA), it was held that an employee's 12 month non-dealing covenant was valid (contrary to the view of the judge at first instance), but the court expressed the *obiter* view that a longer period would have been unreasonable. As to 2 year covenants in the case of employees, see *Duarte v. Black & Decker Ltd.* [2008] 1 All E.R. (Comm) 401 at [109] *per* Field J.

[1081] [1921] 2 A.C. 158. As to the current relevance of this decision, *cf. Allan Janes LLP v. Johal* [2005] EWHC 2864 (Ch) (Lawtel 25/10/05) at [26] *per* H.H. Judge Rich Q.C. sitting as a judge of the Chancery Divison on an interim application and *ibid.* [2006] I.C.R. 742, at [46] *per* Bernard Livesey Q.C. sitting as a deputy judge of the Chancery Division.

[1082] Note also that unlimited restrictions on the use of confidential information by employees did not find favour in *International Computers Ltd. v. Eccleson* [2000] ScotCS 245 (OH) or *First People Solutions Group Ltd. v. Jack* [2007] CSOH 80.

[1083] *cf. Konski v. Peet* [1915] 1 Ch. 530, where the restriction extended to *future* customers. This does not mean that questions of duration are wholly irrelevant in the case of non-solicitation restrictions: see *D v. M* [1996] I.R.L.R. 192, 197 *per* Laws J.; *Scully U.K. Ltd. v. Lee* [1998] I.R.L.R. 259, 264 *per* Aldous L.J.

[1084] *Thomas v. Farr PLC* [2007] I.C.R. 932 at [50], a decision concerning an employee.

[1085] See *Seabrokers Ltd. v. Riddell* 2007 G.W.D. 26–451 (OH), where an employer had power to specify the duration but failed to do so in a meaningful way.

[1086] *Davies v. Davies* (1887) 36 Ch.D. 359, where the covenant was held to be too uncertain to be enforced; also *Days Medical Aids Ltd. v. Pihsiang Machinery Manufacturing Co. Ltd.* [2004] 1 All E.R. (Comm) 991, which concerned the construction of a renewable distribution agreement alleged to be in restraint of trade. Note also that the court will not be disposed to cut down the scope of an otherwise invalid restriction in order to render it valid: *J.A. Mont (U.K.) v. Mills* [1993] I.R.L.R. 172; *Credit Suisse Asset Management Ltd. v. Armstrong* [1996] I.C.R. 882, 892 *per* Neill L.J.; note that a more flexible approach is adopted in the case of garden leave: *ibid.*; also *Provident Financial Group Plc v. Hayward* [1989] I.C.R. 160 (CA). And see, as to purporting to confer on the court power to modify an invalid restriction, *Living Design (Home Improvments) Ltd. v. Davidson* [1994] I.R.L.R. 69.

[1087] See *infra*, para. 10–232.

contravene the chosen restriction,[1088] nor will it in general[1089] be possible to supplement an express (and arguably invalid) restriction with an implied term.[1090]

In order to determine whether a particular restriction is reasonable, the court will first construe it according to its natural meaning,[1091] having regard to the object sought to be achieved[1092] and to the factual matrix in which the agreement was prepared,[1093] and only *then* apply the rule of reasonableness.[1094] Developments after the date of the agreement are not relevant for this purpose[1095] and unduly hypothetical or extravagant possibilities should be ignored.[1096] Opinion evidence of reasonableness is generally inadmissible since it involves a question of law and is, indeed, the primary issue to be decided by the court.[1097] Evidence will, however, be admissible as to the usual practice in any particular business[1098]

[1088] *Mellstrom v. Garner* [1970] 1 W.L.R. 603.

[1089] Save, perhaps, in the specific circumstances discussed, *supra*, paras 10–206 *et seq*. But see *supra*, para. 10–208.

[1090] See *Townends Group Ltd. v. Cobb, The Times*, December 1, 2004 and the other cases noted *supra*, para. 10–208, n. 989.

[1091] In *Scully U.K. Ltd. v. Lee* [1998] I.R.L.R. 259, 262, Aldous L.J. observed: "The Court's task is to ascertain the intention of the parties from the words of the contract. In so doing it should not indulge in too formal an analysis of the words, an approach often adopted by lawyers, but should look at the purpose of the contract and give it an appropriate meaning." See also *Hollis & Co. v. Stocks* [2000] I.R.L.R. 712, (CA); *Arbuthnot Fund Managers v. Rawlings* [2003] EWCA Civ 518 (Lawtel 13/3/03); *TFS Derivatives Ltd. v. Morgan* [2005] I.R.L.R. 246; *Exchange Communications Ltd. v. Masheder* 2009 S.L.T. 1141 (OH) at [42]. And see further, as to the modern approach to construction, *supra*, paras 10–06, 10–07.

[1092] *Haynes v. Doman* [1899] 2 Ch. 13, 25 *per* Lindley M.R.; *Littlewoods Organisation Ltd. v. Harris* [1977] 1 W.L.R. 1472; *Clarke v. Newland* [1991] 1 All E.R. 397; *J.A. Mont (U.K.) v. Mills* [1993] I.R.L.R. 172; *Scully U.K. Ltd. v. Lee, supra*; *Greck v. Henderson Asia Pacific Equity Partners (FP) LP* [2008] CSOH 2 at [86] *per* Lord Glennie in an *obiter* part of his judgment. Note also *Office Angels Ltd. v. Rainer-Thomas* [1991] I.R.L.R. 214. For a striking example of the pragmatic way in which a court might approach issues of construction, see *Kall-Kwik Printing (U.K.) Ltd. v. Frank Clarence Rush* [1996] F.S.R. 114, 122 *per* H.H. Judge Cooke (sitting as a judge of the Chancery Division).

[1093] See *supra*, paras 10–03, 10–04. An example of this approach is to be found in the unreported decision of Stanley Burnton Q.C. (sitting as a deputy judge of the Chancery Division) in *Taylor Stuart & Co. v. Croft*, (Lawtel 14/10/97), noted *supra*, para. 10–226; see also *TFS Derivatives Ltd. v. Morgan* [2005] I.R.L.R. 246; *Exchange Communications Ltd. v. Masheder* 2009 S.L.T. 1141 (OH) at [42]. Note that in *Greck v. Henderson Asia Pacific Equity Partners (FP) LP, supra*, at [88], Lord Glennie expressed the *obiter* view that if, on a consideration of the circumstances of the partners, it was concluded that the restriction would impact differently on partners within the same class, it could be held enforceable against some but not others, which would not "make much commercial sense". *Quaere* whether such a result is possible.

[1094] See *Moenich v. Fenestre* (1892) 67 L.T. 602; *Haynes v. Doman* [1899] 2 Ch. 13, 24–27 *per* Lindley M.R.; *Littlewoods Organisation Ltd. v. Harris* [1977] 1 W.L.R. 1472; *Clarke v. Newland* [1991] 1 All E.R. 397. The latter decision was a striking example of this approach, since the court was able to construe a restriction in a doctors' partnership agreement prohibiting practice in a certain area as confined to practice *as a general medical practitioner*, thus enabling the decisions in *Routh v. Jones* [1947] 1 All E.R. 758 and *Lyne-Pirkis v. Jones* [1969] 1 W.L.R. 1293 to be distinguished and the restriction upheld.

[1095] *Chipsaway International Ltd. v. Kerr* [2009] EWCA Civ. 320 (Lawtel 11/3/09) at [24] *per* Dyson L.J. Note, however, that the restriction may itself refer to a state of affairs current as at the date of *enforcement*: *Phoenix Partners Group LLP v. Asoyag* [2010] I.R.L.R. 594 at [22] *per* Sir Charles Gray sitting as a judge of the Queen's Bench Division.

[1096] *Scully U.K. Ltd. v. Lee* [1998] I.R.L.R. 259, 262 *per* Aldous L.J.; also *Kao Lee & Yip v. Edwards* [1993] 1 H.K.C. 314, 325.

[1097] *Haynes v. Doman, supra; Dowden & Pook Ltd. v. Pook* [1904] 1 K.B. 45; see also *Mason v. Provident Clothing and Supply Co. Ltd.* [1913] A.C. 724, 732–733 *per* Lord Haldane L.C.

[1098] *Haynes v. Doman, supra*, at p. 20 *per* Lindley M.R.

and if it is established that the restriction is an unusual one in that business, there is a greater likelihood of invalidity.[1099] The fact that the partners have taken the trouble to declare that the restriction is reasonable *may* be a relevant factor.[1100]

It should be noted that the application of the above principles may, however, be called into question if Article 101 TFEU would apply but for the availability of some exclusion or exemption thereunder.[1101]

10–227   *Medical partnerships*: There has, over the years, been a relatively high proportion of decided cases relating to restrictions in medical partnerships[1102] which, because of the unique (albeit changing) characteristics of practice within the National Health Service, tend to be regarded as a separate sub-culture. However, in *Kerr v. Morris*,[1103] the Court of Appeal in effect confirmed that normal principles apply, so that a special treatment of those cases is no longer appropriate in a work of this nature.[1104]

10–228   *Interaction with garden leave*: The advent of garden leave provisions in partnership agreements has already been noted.[1105] What is not clear is whether, in assessing the reasonableness of a restrictive covenant, a court might take into account any additional period of restriction to be imposed by way of garden leave. Although this possibility cannot be ruled out,[1106] the current editor takes the view that this would, in principle, be unsound: in most cases garden leave will be an option open to the prospective continuing partners and will not be imposed automatically. Since the validity of a covenant must be determined as at the time the agreement is entered into, it is difficult to see how the prospect of an indeterminate period of garden leave could properly affect the court's attitude.[1107]

(2) *Reasonableness in the Interests of the Public*

10–229   Once the continuing partners have shown that the restriction is reasonable in the interests of the parties, the burden of proving that the restriction is unreasonable

---

[1099] *Leng v. Andrews* [1909] 1 Ch. 763, 770 *per* Fletcher Moulton L.J.

[1100] *SAB Miller Africa BV v. East African Breweries Ltd.* [2010] 1 Lloyd's Rep. 392 at [139] *per* Christopher Clarke J. Equally, the current editor is sceptical of such declarations, which tend to be included as a matter of routine and may actually indicate little in the way of serious consideration.

[1101] *Days Medical Aids Ltd. v. Pihsiang Machinery Manufacturing Co Ltd.* [2004] 1 All E.R. (Comm) 991.

[1102] *Routh v. Jones* [1947] 1 All E.R. 758; *Jenkins v. Reid* [1948] 1 All E.R. 471; *Re Jenkins' Deed of Partnership* [1948] W.N. 98; *Whitehill v. Bradford* [1952] Ch. 236; *Macfarlane v. Kent* [1965] 1 W.L.R. 1019; *Lyne-Pirkis v. Jones* [1969] 1 W.L.R. 1293; *Peyton v. Mindham* [1972] 1 W.L.R. 8; *Hensman v. Traill, The Times*, October 22, 1980; *Anthony v. Rennie* 1981 S.L.T. (Notes) 11; *Kerr v. Morris* [1987] Ch. 90; *Pandit v. Shah*, unreported, November 6, 1987, noted *supra*, para. 10–226, n. 1080; *Clarke v. Newland* [1991] 1 All E.R. 397, noted *supra*, para. 10–226, n. 1094. See also *Blakeley and Anderson v. de Lambert* [1959] N.Z.L.R. 356.

[1103] [1987] Ch. 90.

[1104] But see, further, the *Encyclopedia of Professional Partnerships*, Pt 5.

[1105] See generally, *supra*, paras 10–146 *et seq.*

[1106] See *Credit Suisse Asset Management Ltd. v. Armstrong* [1996] I.C.R. 882, 894. Note also the (ultimately inconclusive) analysis of the interaction between garden leave and restrictive covenants by Cox J. in *TFS Derivatives Ltd. v. Morgan* [2005] I.R.L.R. 246.

[1107] It should be noted that the enforcement of garden leave provisions tends to be approached more flexibly than restrictive covenants: *Credit Suisse Asset Management Ltd. v. Armstrong, supra*, p. 892; also *Provident Financial Group Plc v. Hayward* [1989] I.C.R. 160 (CA). However, this must not be taken too far: *William Hill Organisation Ltd. v. Tucker* [1998] I.R.L.R. 313, 318 (CA).

in the interests of the public will fall on the outgoing partner.[1108] In such circumstances the burden of proof is extremely heavy,[1109] and the current editor considers that the public interest alone would rarely invalidate a restriction, save where it affects the right of an outgoing partner to engage (but not necessarily to solicit)[1110] employees of the firm.[1111]

The apparent movement in the early 1980s towards striking down restrictions in professional partnerships on public policy grounds, merely because they deprived the client of his right to consult the adviser of his choice,[1112] was summarily halted, first in the case of solicitors[1113] and, subsequently, in the case of doctors practising within the National Health Service.[1114]

Consideration

Lord Lindley wrote: **10–230**

> "An agreement entered into when a partnership is formed, to the effect that a retiring partner[1115] shall not carry on the business carried on by the firm, cannot be invalid for want of consideration."[1116]

It has long been held unnecessary to enquire into the *adequacy* of the consideration,[1117] but the Privy Council did just that in *Bridge v. Deacons*[1118];

[1108] Note that the public interest featured prominently in the decisions in *Dranez Anstalt v. Hayek* [2003] 1 B.C.L.C. 278 (CA), where a restriction was sought to be imposed on a pioneer in the field of medical science, and *Leah Health Care Services v. Deluca* 2003 G.W.D. 32–892 (Sh. Ct), concerning an area restriction imposed on an employee of a chiropractors' business.

[1109] See *Att.-Gen. Australia v. Adelaide Steamship Co. Ltd.* [1913] A.C. 781 at 797 *per* Lord Parker.

[1110] Although there were, at one time, conflicting Court of Appeal authorities on the point (see *Ingham v. ABC Contract Services Ltd.*, November 12, 1993 (unreported); *Hanover Insurance Brokers Ltd. v. Schapiro* [1994] I.R.L.R. 82), it is now clear that a non-solicit covenant is not *per se* unenforceable: *Alliance Paper Group plc v. Prestwich* [1996] I.R.L.R. 25; *Dawnay, Day & Co. Ltd. v. D'Alphen* [1998] I.C.R. 1068 (CA); see also *Office Angels Ltd. v. Rainer-Thomas* [1991] I.R.L.R. 214, 219 *per* Slade L.J. Whilst the restriction should not generally be extended to *all* employees irrespective of their position in the firm, if invalidity is to be avoided (*Alliance Paper Group Plc v. Prestwich*, *supra*; *Dawnay, Day & Co. Ltd. v. D'Alphen*, *supra*), there may be exceptional cases where this is justified, *e.g.* in the case of a small firm with few employees: see *Hydra Plc v. Anastasi* (2005) 102 L.S.Gaz., September 1, p. 23.

[1111] See *Kores Manufacturing Co. v. Kolok Manufacturing Co.* [1959] Ch. 108; *Esso Petroleum Co. Ltd. v. Harper's Garage (Stourport) Ltd.* [1968] A.C. 269, 300 *per* Lord Reid, 319 *per* Lord Hodson; *Kao, Lee & Yip v. Hoi-Yan* [1995] 1 H.K.L.R. 248 (CA, Hong Kong); *Dawnay, Day & Co. Ltd. v. D'Alphen*, *supra*, at p. 1096 *per* Robert Walker J. (this point not being the subject of any appeal); *cf. SBJ Stephenson Ltd. v. Mandy* [2000] I.R.L.R. 233, where a covenant by an employee against soliciting *or employing* fellow employees was upheld.

[1112] See *Hensman v. Traill*, *The Times*, October 22, 1980 (doctors practising within the National Health Service); *Oswald Hickson Collier & Co. v. Carter-Ruck* [1984] A.C. 720, note (solicitors); *cf. Edwards v. Warboys* [1984] A.C. 724, note.

[1113] *Bridge v. Deacons* [1984] A.C. 705, 719–720.

[1114] *Kerr v. Morris* [1987] Ch. 90. The Court of Appeal also held that restrictions on competition are not invalidated by the National Health Service Act 1977, Sched. 10, para. 2(2)(a) (see now the National Health Service Act 2006, Sched. 21, para. 2(4)(a)). See further the *Encyclopedia of Professional Partnerships*, Pt 5.

[1115] An expelled partner is, of course, in the same position.

[1116] See *Austen v. Boys* (1858) 2 De G. & J. 626, 637 *per* Lord Cranworth. Note also *Clarkson v. Edge* (1863) 33 Beav. 227, where the consideration took the form of an agreement with a bankrupt to take his son into partnership and to employ the bankrupt. As to whether any consideration for accepting the imposition of a restriction would be taxable in the outgoing partner's hands, see *Kirby v. Thorn E.M.I. Plc* [1988] 1 W.L.R. 445.

[1117] *Hitchcock v. Coker* (1837) 6 A. & E. 438.

[1118] [1984] A.C. 705, 718.

nevertheless, their Lordships appear not to have been much troubled thereby. However, when looking at the severability of a restriction,[1119] the court will also have regard to the severability of the consideration given for it.[1120]

Assignability

10–231   The benefit of a restriction will normally be incidental to the goodwill of the business and, thus, pass with an assignment of it.[1121] However, much may depend on the precise terms of the restriction. Thus, in *Dunwoody Sports Marketing v. Prescott*,[1122] it was held that, on a true construction of the partnership agreement, a restriction on interference with the relationship between *the partnership* and its customers could not be enforced by an assignee company. No such problem affected a restriction on soliciting, etc., employees and partners in the same case.

Severance

10–232   An excessive restriction will be void and unenforceable as to its entirety unless, as a matter of construction, any element which is confined within reasonable limits can be severed from the remainder. Such severance is only available if it is possible to apply the so-called "blue pencil" test, *i.e.* can the offending part(s) be excised without altering the sense or requiring the amendment of what remains?[1123] It follows that, in drafting a restriction, it is desirable to ensure that each element of the restriction in effect stands alone[1124] and is, thus, readily severable. In the case of vendor and purchaser restrictions, the court will, in applying the blue pencil test, generally be prepared to excise parts of a restriction even if they are not of a merely trivial nature[1125]; it is likely that the approach to severance in the case of restrictions between partners will be the same.

Although agreements often seek to anticipate the possibility of severance by

---

[1119] See *infra*, para. 10–232.

[1120] See *Putsman v. Taylor* [1927] 1 K.B. 741; *Sadler v. Imperial Life Assurance Co. of Canada Ltd.* [1988] I.R.L.R. 388; *Marshall v. N.M. Financial Management Ltd.* [1997] 1 W.L.R. 1527.

[1121] *Jacoby v. Whitmore* (1883) 49 L.T. 335; *Showell v. Winkup* (1889) 60 L.T. 389; *Townsend v. Jarman* [1900] 2 Ch. 698; also *John Bros. Abergarw Brewery v. Holmes* [1900] 1 Ch. 188. For an example of a restriction of a personal nature (albeit too uncertain to be enforced), see *Davies v. Davies* (1887) 36 Ch.D. 359.

[1122] [2007] 1 W.L.R. 2343, note.

[1123] See *T. Lucas & Co. v. Mitchell* [1974] Ch. 129; also *Goldsoll v. Goldman* [1915] 1 Ch. 292; *Putsman v. Taylor* [1927] 1 K.B. 637, affirmed at [1927] 1 K.B. 741 without considering the question of severance; *Macfarlane v. Kent* [1965] 1 W.L.R. 1019; *Scorer v. Seymour Jones* [1966] 1 W.L.R. 1419; *Sadler v. Imperial Life Assurance Co. of Canada Ltd.* [1988] I.R.L.R. 388; *Living Design (Home Improvements) Ltd. v. Davidson* [1994] I.R.L.R. 69; *Kall-Kwik Printing (U.K.) Ltd. v. Frank Clarence Rush* [1996] F.S.R. 114; *D v. M* [1996] I.R.L.R. 192; *Scully U.K. Ltd. v. Lee* [1998] I.R.L.R. 259. For recent examples of cases in which severance has been permitted, see *TFS Derivatives Ltd. v. Morgan* [2005] I.R.L.R. 246; *First Global Locums Ltd. v. Andrew* [2005] I.R.L.R. 873 at [63]; *Allan Janes LLP v. Johal* [2006] I.C.R. 742 at [17]; *Beckett Investment Management Group Ltd. v. Hall* [2007] I.C.R. 1539 (CA); *Norbrook Laboratories (GB) Ltd. v. Adair* [2008] I.R.L.R. 878.

[1124] Thus, one element should not be dependent on another: see *Amoco Australia Pty. Ltd. v. Rocca Bros. Motor Engineering Co. Pty. Ltd.* [1975] A.C. 561; *Sadler v. Imperial Life Assurance Co. of Canada Ltd.*, *supra*. *cf. Alec Lobb Ltd. v. Total Oil* [1985] 1 W.L.R. 173; *Scully U.K. Ltd. v. Lee*, *supra*. As to clauses purporting to confer power on the court to modify a restriction, see *Living Design (Home Improvements) Ltd. v. Davidson* [1994] I.R.L.R. 69.

[1125] See *Goldsoll v. Goldman* [1915] 1 Ch. 292.

expressly declaring that each limb of the restriction is separate and distinct, this does not represent a substitute for careful drafting.[1126]

Effect of dissolution

Subject to the precise terms of the agreement,[1127] a *general* dissolution will effectively prevent any partner from seeking to enforce a restriction against his co-partners[1128] but will not necessarily affect the enforceability of a restriction imposed on a partner who retired *before* the date of the dissolution.   **10–233**

Injunctive relief

A threatened breach of a valid restriction will normally be restrained by injunction, unless the order would, in substance, involve the specific performance of a contract for personal services. Such relief will be granted on normal principles,[1129] although it is in practice rare for proceedings to continue beyond the interlocutory stage.[1130]   **10–234**

An injunction may be obtained even though other provisions of the agreement are unenforceable, provided that the restriction sought to be enforced is not dependent on those provisions.[1131]

It does not follow from the fact that the restriction is judged to be reasonable that the court will necessarily enforce it to its fullest extent.[1132]

This remedy is, of course, separate and distinct from any right to a so called "springboard" injunction, which will be dependent on showing a prior breach of duty committed by a prospective outgoing partner rather than a breach of a contractual restriction applicable on his retirement, etc.[1133]

[1126] Note also the approach adopted by the court in *J.A. Mont (U.K.) Ltd. v. Mills* [1993] I.R.L.R. 172; also *Credit Suisse Asset Management Ltd. v. Armstrong* [1996] I.C.R. 882, 892. *cf. Hanover Insurance Brokers Ltd. v. Schapiro* [1994] I.R.L.R. 82, 87 *per* Nolan L.J.

[1127] It is, of course, possible to provide that a restriction will apply in the event of a dissolution, as in *Peyton v. Mindham* [1972] 1 W.L.R. 8.

[1128] See, generally, *Brace v. Calder* [1895] 2 Q.B. 253. Since it is now clear that the doctrine of repudiation has no application to partnerships (see *infra*, paras 24–05 *et seq.*), no useful analogy can be drawn with the case of repudiation of a contract of employment, as considered in *Rock Refrigeration Ltd. v. Jones* [1997] I.C.R. 938 (CA).

[1129] See *Doherty v. Allman* (1878) 3 App.Cas. 709, 720 *per* Lord Cairns; *Snell's Principles of Equity* (31st ed.), paras 16–06 *et seq.*; also *infra*, paras 23–135 *et seq.* Interim relief was refused in *Bell & Scott LLP v. Kaye* [2009] CSOH 51 because damages would be an adequate remedy (and on the final hearing it was held that there was, in any event, no breach: [2009] CSOH 111).

[1130] See as to the principles on which interim injunctions are granted, *Fellowes & Son v. Fisher* [1976] Q.B. 122; *Kerr v. Morris* [1987] Ch. 90; *Prontaprint plc v. London Litho Ltd.* [1987] F.S.R. 315; *Lawrence David Ltd. v. Ashton* [1989] I.C.R. 123; also, generally, *National Commercial Bank Jamaica Ltd. v. Olint Corpn Ltd.* [2009] 1 W.L.R. 1405 (HL). The fact that customers have indicated that they do not wish to deal with the continuing partners will be an irrelevant consideration: see *John Michael Design v. Cooke* [1987] 2 All E.R. 232. In *Centre for Maritime & Industrial Safety Technology Ltd. v. Crute* 2003 G.W.D. 8–194 (OH), an injunction against an employee was refused, in part on the basis that the client he was joining already had a subsisting contractual relationship with his former employer which still had two years to run. And note also, as to the *status quo* sought to be preserved, the decision in *Unigate Dairies Ltd. v. Bruce, The Times*, March 2, 1988.

[1131] As to interdependent provisions and conditions, see *Amoco Australia Pty. Ltd. v. Rocca Bros. Motor Engineering Co. Pty. Ltd.* [1975] A.C. 561; *Sadler v. Imperial Life Assurance Co. of Canada Ltd.* [1988] I.R.L.R. 388.

[1132] See, for example, *Symbian Ltd. v. Christensen* [2001] I.R.L.R. 77 (CA); also *Provident Financial Group Plc v. Hayward* [1989] I.C.R. 160, 170D *per* Taylor L.J. However, this principle cannot be employed to justify partial enforcement of a restriction which is otherwise in restraint of trade: *J.A. Mont (U.K.) Ltd. v. Mills* [1993] I.R.L.R. 172 (CA).

[1133] See further *supra*, para. 10–213.

Availability of an account/damages

10–235   It would seem that, in an appropriate case, an account of profits may be available, as an alternative to damages,[1134] where a former partner breaches a valid restriction on competition. Although Jacob J. had, notwithstanding the decision in *Att.-Gen. v. Blake*,[1135] held in *WWF-World Wide Fund for Nature v. World Wrestling Federation Entertainment Inc*[1136] that an account was not available in such a case, the possibility was certainly left open by the Court of Appeal in *Experience Hendrix LLC v. PPX Enterprises Inc*.[1137] Since then the availablity of the remedy has been acknowledged in *WWF-World Wide Fund for Nature v. World Wrestling Federation Entertainment Inc*[1138] and in *Devenish Nutrition Ltd. v. Sanofi-Aventis SA*.[1139] It should, however, be recognised that that such a remedy will be granted sparingly, where the justice of the case demands it; after all a former partner is no longer in a fiduciary relationship with the continuing partners,[1140] so there would be no automatic entitlement to this relief.

It is also now clear that, in addition to an injunction, the court can award damages on the *Wrotham Park* basis[1141] in a case where the firm cannot establish any financial loss arising out of past breaches, i.e. the damages will represent the amount which it would be reasonable for the departing partner to pay for a hypothetical release of the restriction.[1142]

Penalties and liquidated damages

10–236   It was formerly common to find agreements which provided for the payment of a fixed sum by way of liquidated damages on breach of a restriction,[1143] thus in general forcing the continuing partners to decide between injunctive relief and

[1134] Note, as to exemplary damages in such a case, *Deacons v. White & Case LLP* (HCA 2433/2002), October 24, 2003 (Hong Kong High Court).

[1135] [2001] 1 A.C. 268 (HL).

[1136] [2002] F.S.R. 504 at [63],

[1137] [2003] 1 All E.R. (Comm) 830 (CA) at [32]. See also *ibid.* at [55] *per* Peter Gibson L.J.

[1138] [2008] 1 W.L.R. 445 (CA).

[1139] [2009] Ch. 390 (CA), albeit a decision concerning non-proprietory torts. Arden L.J. analysed the various cases, including *Att.-Gen. v. Blake, supra*, in considerable detail.

[1140] But see *infra*, para. 16–06.

[1141] See *Wrotham Park Estate Co. Ltd. v. Parkside Homes Ltd.* [1974] 1 W.L.R. 798. But note, as to the nature of such damages, the review of the authorities in *Pell Frischmann Engineering Ltd. v Bow Valley Iran Ltd.* [2010] B.L.R. 73 (PC).

[1142] *Experience Hendrix LLC v. PPX Enterprises Inc., supra*; *WWF-World Wide Fund for Nature v. World Wrestling Federation Entertainment Inc, supra*; *Vercoe v. Rutland Fund Management Ltd.* [2010] EWHC 424 (Ch) (Lawtel 11/3/10).

[1143] See generally, as to the difference between penalties and liquidated damages, *Chitty on Contracts* (30th ed.), paras 26–125 *et seq.*; also for a useful step by step guide on the question of enforceability, see *Murray v. Leisureplay Plc* [2005] I.R.L.R. 946 at [54] *per* Arden L.J. Self evidently, a true penalty will involve payment of a sum which is extravagant and unconscionable in amount as compared with the prospective loss: *Jeancharm Ltd. v. Barnet Football Club Ltd.* (2003) 92 Con L.R. 26; *Office of Fair Trading v. Abbey National Plc* [2008] 2 All E.R. (Comm) 625. A payment which is to be made on the occurrence of a specified event is *not* a penalty: see *Export Credits Guarantee Dept. v. Universal Oil Products Co.* [1983] 1 W.L.R. 399; *E.F.T. Commercial Ltd. v. Security Change Ltd. (No. 1)* 1993 S.L.T. 128 (1st Div.), where both the English and Scots authorities are reviewed; also *Office of Fair Trading v. Abbey National Plc, supra*. Moreover, a term which is commercially justifiable will not be struck down where it was freely negotiated between parties of equal bargaining power and there is no oppression, unless its dominant purpose is to deter a party from breaching the agreement: see *M & J Polymers Ltd. v. Imerys Minerals Ltd.* [2008] 1 All E.R. (Comm) 893; *Tullett Prebon Group Ltd. v. El-Hajjali* [2008] I.R.L.R. 760. See also *infra*, para. 10–287.

the recovery of such damages.[1144] Provisions of this type are now rare, although they appear to have enjoyed something of a resurgence in the accountancy profession.

The decision in *Taylor Stuart & Co. v. Croft*[1145] demonstrates the difficulty of drafting an effective liquidated damages clause. There the agreement sought to charge an outgoing salaried partner[1146] who might be in breach of the applicable restriction[1147] with damages equal to twice the aggregate fees derived by the firm in the year prior to his departure from any client whose work should be taken away from the firm. Since this took no account of the reasons why a client would disinstruct the firm[1148] nor of the amount of work which might, as a result, be given to the outgoing salaried partner,[1149] the clause was, almost inevitably, held to be a penalty and therefore unenforceable. Similar considerations may apply where the clause obliges the outgoing partner to account for a percentage of the actual fees earned from work carried out by him or his new firm on behalf of former clients of his old firm during a specified period following his retirement, particularly if the percentage significantly exceeds the profit costs likely to be derived from such work. However, it is submitted that it can, in such a case, properly be argued that account must also be taken of the overhead burden assumed by the continuing partners, *e.g.* where existing staff are retained but are, in the event, underemployed.

Claims against third parties

Where a former partner breaches a restriction at the behest of his new firm, it may be possible to maintain a claim for the tort of inducing or facilitating a breach of contract.[1150] It is, however, now clear that an *intention* to bring about such a breach is a necessary ingredient of the tort.[1151] Needless to say, absent any breach, no tort is committed.[1152]

10–237

[1144] *General Accident Assurance Corp. v. Noel* [1902] 1 K.B. 377. *cf. Stiles v. Ecclestone* [1903] 1 K.B. 544, 546 *per* Lord Alverstone; *Imperial Tobacco Co. v. Parslay* [1936] 2 All E.R. 515; *Elsley v. Collins Insurance Agencies* (1978) 83 D.L.R.(3d) 1 (Can.Sup. Ct.). Note also that it may be possible to demonstrate that the liquidated damages were only intended to cover damage sustained *before* the grant of an injunction: see *Braid v. Lawes*, an unreported decision of a Divisional Court (Acton and Talbot JJ.) on May 18, 1933, affirming a decision of a former editor of this work sitting as a judge of the Exeter county court.

[1145] May 7, 1997 (Lawtel 14/10/97), a decision of Stanley Burnton Q.C. sitting as a deputy judge of the Chancery Division.

[1146] It is clear that the "partner" in question was, in reality, an employee. See further, as to salaried partners, *supra*, paras 5–54 *et seq.*

[1147] A three year non-solicitation/non-acting covenant which was, in the event, held to be in restraint of trade: see *supra*, para. 10–225, n. 1080.

[1148] Instances cited by the judge included cessation of business, emigration, liquidation and dissatisfaction with the services provided by the firm.

[1149] This will be a particular problem for the draftsman. It is almost impossible to legislate in advance for all the possible scenarios (*e.g.* the outgoing partner being given a single "one-off" piece of work, when the majority of the work stays with the firm), otherwise than by simply forcing the outgoing partner to account for the sums which he earns from acting for the client(s) in question.

[1150] As in *Deacons v. White & Case LLP* (HCA 2433/2002), October 24, 2003 (Hong Kong High Court). In *Norbrook Laboratories (GB) Ltd. v. Adair* [2008] I.R.L.R. 878 (an employee case), an injunction was granted to prevent continuing inducement by a prospective employer.

[1151] *OBG Ltd. v. Allan* [2008] 1 A.C. 1 (HL); *Meretz Investments NV v. ACP Ltd.* [2008] Ch. 244 (CA); *Tullett Prebon plc v. BGC Brokers L.P.* [2010] I.R.L.R. 648, at [146] to [152] *per* Jack J.; also note *Aerostar Maintenance International Ltd. v. Wilson* [2010] EWHC 2032 (Ch) (Lawtel 4/8/10). The turning of a "blind eye" will suffice: *ibid.* at [151]; also *Global Respources Group Ltd. v. Mackay* 2009 S.L.T. 104 (OH) *per* Lord Hodge in an *obiter* passage at [11].

[1152] *ibid.*

Article 101 TFEU

10–238   Article 101 TFEU[1153] renders null and void certain practices considered to be incompatible with the Common Market. The prohibited practices are summarised as:

> "all agreements[1154] between undertakings,[1155] decisions by associations of undertakings and concerted practices, which may affect trade between Member States and which have as their object or effect the prevention, restriction or distortion of competition within the Common Market."[1156]

The prohibited practices need not have an "appreciable" effect on trade between Member States, etc., in order to attract the application of Article 101.[1157] It should be noted, where Article 101 does not apply, *e.g.* because of the application of an available exemption,[1158] the restriction cannot then be invalidated under the normal restraint of trade doctrine.[1159]

Where an agreement breaches Article 101, it is self evident that its terms cannot be enforced as between the parties. However, it now appears that one party can pursue a claim for damages against another arising out of that breach, even though the agreement itself will be illegal,[1160] although an account of profits will *not* be available in such a case.[1161]

[1153] The former Art. 85 of the EC Treaty was renumbered Art. 81 by the Treaty of Amsterdam, Art. 12 and then renumbered Art. 101 of the Treaty on the Functioning of the European Union by the Treaty of Lisbon. It is reproduced *infra*, paras A5–01, A5–02. Older cases cited in this and the following paragraphs will, inevitably, use the old numbering.

[1154] An "agreement" for this purpose may consist of a formal agreement *and* the conduct of the parties: *Volkswagen AG v. Commission of the European Communities* (C74/04 P) [2007] Bus. L.R. 35 (ECJ); see also *Bayer AG v. Commission of the European Communities* (Case T–41/96) [2001] I.C.R. 735 (ECJ).

[1155] As to what constitutes an "undertaking", see *Federation Nationale de la Cooperation Betail et Viande (FNCBV) v. Commission of the European Communities* (T–217/03) [2008] 5 C.M.L.R. 5; also *supra*, para. 8–05 and *infra*, paras 10–239, 10–241.

[1156] Art. 101(1), *infra*, para. A5–01. As to the territorial scope of Art. 101, see *Åhlström Osakeyhtiö v. E.C. Commission* [1988] 4 C.M.L.R. 901. *Quaere* whether the relationship of partnership can itself lead to a breach of Art. 101: see *supra*, para. 8–05. And see, generally, the Notice on Co-operation between National Courts and the Commission in applying Articles 81 and 82 of the European Community Treaty [*subsequently renumbered Arts. 101 and 102 TFEU*] (1993) O.J. C39/6. Note also the terms of the Competition Act 1998, which imposes a similar regime in the case of anti-competitive agreements within the UK: see *infra*, paras 10–241, 10–242.

[1157] See *Federation Nationale de la Cooperation Betail et Viande (FNCBV) v. Commission of the European Communities* (T–217/03) [2008] 5 C.M.L.R. 5 at [68]. *cf. Pirtek (UK) Ltd. v. Joinplan Ltd.* [2010] EWHC 1641 (Ch) (Lawtel 8/7/10) at [61] *per* Briggs J. Equally, the effect must not be insignificant: *Völk v. Vervaeke* [1969] C.M.L.R. 273, 282; *Raygems v. Attias* (1978) 75 L.S. Gaz. 224. See also (1998) 95 L.S.Gaz., February 4, p. 27 and *infra*, para. 10–241, n. 1190.

[1158] See, as to exemptions, *infra*, para. 10–240.

[1159] See *Days Medical Aids Ltd. v. Pihsiang Machinery Manufacturing Co Ltd.* [2004] 1 All E.R. (Comm) 991.

[1160] *Courage Ltd. v. Crehan* [2002] Q.B. 207 (ECJ); *Crehan v. Inntrepreneur Pub Co (CPC)* [2004] 3 E.G.L.R. 128 (CA); also *Provimi Ltd. v. Roche Products Ltd.* [2003] 2 All E.R. (Comm) 683. The position may be otherwise where the Commission has already imposed a fine, especially if exemplary damages were claimed: *Devenish Nutrition Ltd. v. Sanifi-Aventis SA* [2008] Bus. L.R. 600. This aspect was not pursued on the appeal, but see the comments of Arden L.J. at [2009] Ch. 390 at [102]. Note also *Safeway Stores Ltd. v. Twigger* [2010] Bus. L.R. 974.

[1161] *Devenish Nutrition Ltd. v. Sanifi-Aventis SA* [2009] Ch. 390 (CA), where it was held that the court was bound to follow the decision in *Stoke-on-Trent City Council v. W & J Wass Ltd.* [1988] 1 W L.R. 1406 (CA) in the case of a non-proprietary tort. *cf. supra*, para. 10–235.

The application of Article 101 to restrictions imposed for the protection of **10–239** goodwill was considered in *Gottfried Reuter v. BASF A.G.*,[1162] from which the following propositions may be drawn:

(1) An outgoing partner would be regarded as an outgoing "undertaking" for the purposes of Article 101 and, thus, any restriction imposed on him which might interfere with trade between Member States would prima facie be void under Article 101(2).[1163]

(2) A restriction imposed on an outgoing partner will be regarded as infringing Article 101 if it affects goods and services which could be offered by that partner and which could be the subject of trade between Member States.[1164]

(3) It is, however, permissible to impose a restriction on an outgoing partner if that is "necessary" to protect the goodwill or know-how acquired by the continuing partners,[1165] *e.g.* to prevent solicitation of customers.[1166]

(4) The Commission's approach to potential infringements of Article 101 is broadly similar to that adopted by the English courts when applying the restraint of trade doctrine, *i.e.* in determining whether the restriction is wider than necessary to protect the value of the goodwill, account must be taken of the nature of the business carried on and of any know-how forming part of that business. It is permissible to protect reasonable developments of the business but, in normal circumstances, the restriction should not extend beyond the area and scope of the existing business.[1167]

(5) Where a particular restriction is only partially invalid, severance will generally be possible.[1168]

(6) The protection afforded by the restriction must be limited to a reasonable period, during which the continuing partners would be expected to have consolidated and safeguarded their position from competition by the outgoing partner.[1169]

[1162] [1976] 2 C.M.L.R. D.44 (76/743/EEC). Note that all references in this case are to Art. 85, now renumbered Art. 101 TFEU.

[1163] *ibid.* D.55, para. [35]; see also *Re Unitel* [1978] 3 C.M.L.R. 306. *cf.* the position of a *continuing* partner: see *supra*, para. 8–05.

[1164] *Gottfried Reuter v. BASF A.G., supra*, D.61, para. [71]. The effect on trade need not be appreciable, but there will be no infringement where trade would only be affected to an insignificant extent: see; *supra*, para. 10–238, n. 1157.

[1165] See also *Kall-Kwik Printing (U.K.) Ltd. v. Bell* [1994] F.S.R. 674 (a case concerning a franchise agreement).

[1166] Note that an outgoing partner who disposes of his share in goodwill is, in any event, subject to certain implied obligations, including an obligation not to solicit: see *supra*, paras 10–206 *et seq.*

[1167] *Gottfried Reuter v. BASF A.G., supra*, D.55–57, paras [41]–[47]; and see generally *Technique Minière S.A. v. Maschinenbau Ulm GmbH* [1966] C.M.L.R. 357; *Consten S.A. and Grundig-Verkaufs GmbH v. EEC Commission* [1966] C.M.L.R. 418.

[1168] See the cases referred to in the preceding footnote; also *Inntrepreneur Estalis (G.L.) Ltd. v. Boyes* [1993] 47 E.G. 140. And see an interesting article by Valentine Korah at (1984) 134 N.L.J. 134.

[1169] See *Gottfried Reuter v. BASF A.G., supra*, D.56, para. [43].

10–240   In addition to the Commission,[1170] a competition authority or national court of a Member State may now apply both its national competition law *and* Article 101,[1171] and will have the powers required for that purpose.[1172] However, the burden of proving an infringement of Article 101 will lie on the party or authority alleging infringement.[1173] Where such an infringement has been found, the Commission or a competition authority of a Member State can require the undertakings concerned to put an end to it,[1174] can accept commitments in relation to that infringement[1175] or impose a fine or periodic penalty payment.[1176] As part of the investigative process, a partner of an undertaking which is a partnership may be required to supply information to the Commission on request.[1177]

Even where a particular restriction does prima facie contravene Article 101(1), it may be possible to obtain exemption for the agreement under Article 101(3),[1178] on the basis that it "contributes to improving the production or distribution of goods or to promoting technical or economic progress, while allowing consumers a fair share of the resulting benefit", provided that it neither imposes on the undertakings concerned[1179] restrictions which are not indispensable to the achievement of the above objectives nor affords such undertakings the possibility of eliminating competition in respect of a substantial part of the products in question. However, whilst individual and block exemptions are available, the old notification procedure under Council Regulation 17[1180] has now ceased to apply, as has the negative clearance procedure.[1181] An exemption, even if obtained, can be withdrawn at any time, either by the Commission or, in relation to a particular territory, by the competition authority of the relevant Member State in the event of incompatibility with Article 101(3).[1182]

Competition Act 1998[1183]

10–241   Consistently with the drive to harmonise European and domestic competition law,[1184] the provisions of Article 101 TFEU[1185] are now, in effect, replicated in

[1170] Council Reg. (EC) No.1/2003 of 16 December 2003 on the implementation of the rules laid down in Articles 81 and 82 of the Treaty [*subsequently renumbered Arts. 101 and 102 TFEU*] Art. 4, *infra*, para. A5–06.

[1171] *ibid.* Art. 3, para. 1, *infra*, para. A5–05. Note also the requirement for co-operation in *ibid.* Art. 11, *infra*, para. A5–13.

[1172] *ibid.* Arts. 5, 6, *infra*, paras A5–07, A5–08

[1173] *ibid.* Art. 3, *infra*, para. A5–04. A complaint of infringement may be made by a natural or legal person who can show a legitimate interest or by a Member State: *ibid.* Art. 7, para. 2, *infra*, para. A5–09.

[1174] *ibid.* Art. 7, para. 1, *infra*, para. A5–09 (Commission), Art.5, *infra*, para. A5–07 (competition authority).

[1175] *ibid.* Art. 9, para. 1, *infra*, para. A5–11 (Commission), Art.5, *infra*, para. A5–07 (competition authority).

[1176] *ibid.* Arts. 16, 24, *infra*, paras A5–16 *et seq.* (Commission), Art.5, *infra*, para. A5–07 (competition authority).

[1177] *ibid.* Art. 18, para. 4, *infra*, para. A5–15.

[1178] *ibid.* Art.1, para. 2, Art. 10, *infra*, paras A5–03, A5–12.

[1179] *i.e.* the outgoing partner: see *supra*, para. 10–239.

[1180] *i.e.* Council Regulation 17 of February 6, 1962 First Regulation implementing Articles 85 and 86 [*subsequently renumbered 81 and 82*] of the Treaty, Art. 4. This regulation ceased to apply when Council Reg. (EC) No.1/2003 came into effect on May 1, 2004.

[1181] Council Reg. 17, Art. 2.

[1182] Council Reg. (EC) No.1/2003, Art. 19, *infra*, para. A5–21.

[1183] This Act replaced the Restrictive Trade Practices Acts and the Competition Act 1980, ss.2–10: *ibid.* ss.1, 74(3), Sched. 4.

[1184] See the Enterprise Act 2002, s.209; also Council Reg. (EC) No.1/2003, Arts. 3, 11 (*infra*, paras A5–05, A5–13), as noted *supra*, para. 10–240.

[1185] Formerly Art. 81 EC: see *supra*, paras 10–238 *et seq.*

domestic law by section 2(1) of the Competition Act 1998, which establishes "the Chapter 1 prohibition"[1186] in the following terms:

> "Subject to section 3,[1187] agreements between undertakings,[1188] decisions by associations of undertakings or concerted practices which—
>
> (a) may affect trade within the United Kingdom,[1189] and
> (b) have as their object or effect the prevention, restriction or distortion of competition with the United Kingdom,[1190]
>
> are prohibited unless they are exempt in accordance with the provisions of this Part."[1191]

Any agreement which breaches the Chapter 1 prohibition is automatically rendered void[1192] and may attract penalties.[1193] As in the case of Article 101,[1194] it will also give rise to an independent right to damages on the part of one of the contracting parties,[1195] but not an account of profits.[1196]

[1186] As defined by the Competition Act 1998, s.2(8).

[1187] This section sets out a number of agreements which are expressly excluded from the Act (*ibid.* s.3(1)) and provides for the Secretary of State, by regulation, to add to or restrict the classes of excluded agreements (*ibid.* s.3(2)–(6), as amended in the case of subs.(4) by the Enterprise Act 2002, Sched. 25, para. 38(2)).

[1188] As to what will amount to an agreement for this purpose, see *Bayer AG v. Commission of the European Communities* (Case T–41/96) [2001] I.C.R. 735 (ECJ); *Volkswagen AG v. Commission of the European Communities* (C74/04 P) [2007] Bus. L.R. 35 (ECJ), both decisions under what is now Art. 101 TFEU (formerly Art. 81 EC).

[1189] Where an agreement operates or is intended to operate only in a part of the United Kingdom, this expression denotes that part: *ibid.* s.2(7).

[1190] In either case, it is not clear whether it is necessary to show that, in practice, the effect of the restriction is "appreciable" (*Federation Nationale de la Cooperation Betail et Viande (FNCBV) v. Commission of the European Communities* (T–217/03) [2008] 5 C.M.L.R. 5, at [68]) a decision under EC Art. 81; *cf. Pirtek (UK) Ltd. v. Joinplan Ltd.* [2010] EWHC 1641 (Ch) (Lawtel 8/7/10) at [57], [58] *per* Briggs J., provided that it is not actually "insignificant" (*Völk v. Vervaeke* [1969] C.M.L.R. 273, 282; *Raygems v. Attias* (1978) 75 L.S. Gaz. 224). *cf.* the terms of the Guidance in OFT 401, December 2004, paras 2.15 *et seq.*, from which it is clear that the Office of Fair Trading will, in general, regard an agreement as having have no appreciable (sic) effect on competition if the parties' combined share of the relevant market does not exceed 10% if the parties are in competition or 15% if they are not (*ibid.* para. 2.16). However, the fact that either of those thresholds is exceeded is not *per se* fatal: *ibid.* para. 2.20.

[1191] Competition Act 1998, s.2(3) sets out a number of specific instances in which s.2(1) will apply, but none are of particular significance in the present context.

[1192] *ibid.* s.2(4). Obviously, in such a case it will normally be possible to sever those parts of the agreement which are actually rendered void under this subsection.

[1193] See *ibid.* ss.36 *et seq.* (as amended).

[1194] See *supra*, para. 10–238.

[1195] See *Courage Ltd. v. Crehan* [2002] Q.B. 207 (ECJ); *Crehan v. Inntrepreneur Pub Co (CPC)* [2004] 3 E.G.L.R. 128 (CA); also *Provimi Ltd. v. Roche Products Ltd.* [2003] 2 All E.R. (Comm) 683 (ECJ), all decisions under what is now Art. 101 TFEU; also *supra*, para. 10–238, n. 1160. Monetary claims may be brought in the Competition Appeal Tribunal: see the Competition Act 1998, s.47A, as added by the Enterprise Act 2002, s.18(1) and amended by the Constitutional Reform Act 2005, Sched. 9(1), para. 65(3) and the EC Competition Law (Articles 84 and 85) Enforcement (Revocation) Regulations 2007 (SI 2007/1846), Sched.; also the decisions in *BCL Old Co. Ltd. v. BASF SE* [2009] Bus. L.R.1516 (CA) and *Enron Coal Services Ltd. v. English Welsh and Scottish Railway Ltd.* [2010] Bus. L.R. 28 (CA). Note, however, that there is a strict two year time limit applicable to such claims: see the Competition Appeal Tribunal Rules 2003 (SI 2003/1372), r. 31; *BCL Old Co. Ltd. v. BASF SE, supra*.

[1196] See *Devenish Nutrition Ltd. v. Sanifi-Aventis SA* [2009] Ch. 390 (CA), following *Stoke-on-Trent City Council v. W & J Wass Ltd.* [1988] 1 W L.R. 1406 (CA). See also *supra*, para. 10–235.

The expression "undertaking" is not defined in the Act, but appears to include all "companies, firms, businesses, partnerships [*and*] individuals operating as sole traders".[1197] Whilst a partnership constitutes a "single economic unit"[1198] of which all partners are members, it is assumed that, when an outgoing partner leaves the firm, he will cease to be part of that unit, so that the Act is capable of applying to a restriction then sought to be imposed on him.[1199]

10–242   The treatment of anti-competitive practices under the Act will, so far as possible, follow the treatment of such practices under Article 101 TFEU.[1200] It follows that the earlier analysis of the potential application of that Article to restrictions on competition[1201] will be equally applicable to domestic restrictions, save that the relevant factor will, of course, be whether the restriction will have an impact *within* the United Kingdom or any part thereof. Severance of the invalid part of a restriction may be available on normal principles.[1202]

Provision is made both for individual[1203] and block exemptions[1204] from the Chapter 1 prohibition by reference to criteria framed in terms which are almost identical to Article 101(3) TFEU.[1205] A restriction which is exempted under Article 101 will, inevitably, not infringe the Chapter 1 prohibition.[1206]

Where the Office of Fair Trading has reasonable grounds to suspect that an agreement may infringe the Chapter 1 prohibition, it may conduct an investigation[1207] and decide whether there has been such an infringement[1208] and, if there has, it may give appropriate directions to bring that infringement to an end[1209] and, in the case of an intentional or negligent infringement, impose a penalty on a party to the agreement.[1210]

[1197] See the Guidance in OFT 401, December 2004, para. 2.5. See also the authorities under Art. 101 TFEU noted *supra*, para. 8–05, n. 14.

[1198] OFT 401, para. 2.6.

[1199] See, for example, *Gottfried Reuter v. BASF AG, supra*, at D55, para. [35], noted *supra*, para. 10–239. *Semble* no objection could be taken to a restriction applicable as between the continuing members of a firm: *ibid*. See also *supra*, para. 8–06.

[1200] Competition Act 1998, s.60, as amended by the Enterprise Act 2002, Sched. 25, para. 45. See also *supra*, para. 10–240 and Council Reg. (EC) No.1/2003, Arts. 3, 11, *infra*, paras A5–05, A5–13.

[1201] See *supra*, para. 10–239.

[1202] See *supra*, paras 10–232, 10–239.

[1203] See the Competition Act 1998, s.9(1), as renumbered and amended by the Competition Act 1998 and Other Enactments (Amendment) Regulations 2004 (SI 2004/1261), Sched. 1, para. 6. With the repeal of the notification procedure under *ibid*. ss.4, 5 by *ibid*. para. 2, parties are now required themselves to assess whether the requirements of *ibid*. s.9(1) are satisfied.

[1204] See *ibid*. s.6, as amended by the Enterprise Act 2002, Sched. 25, para. 38(5) and the Competition Act 1998 and Other Enactments (Amendment) Regulations 2004, Sched. 1, para. 4. To justify a block exemption, the OFT must be satisifed that *ibid*. s.9 is likely to apply thereto.

[1205] Note that *ibid*. s.9 refers to "improving production or distribution" whereas Art. 101(3) TFEU refers to "improving production or distribution *of goods*" (emphasis supplied).

[1206] *ibid*. s.10, as amended by the Competition Act 1998 and Other Enactments (Amendment) Regulations 2004, Sched. 1, para. 7.

[1207] *ibid*. s.25, as substituted by *ibid*. Sched. 1, para. 10.

[1208] *ibid*. s.31, as substituted by *ibid*. Sched. 1, para. 17.

[1209] *ibid*. s.32(1), as amended by the Enterprise Act 2002, Sched. 1, para. 38(24) and the Competition Act 1998 and Other Enactments (Amendment) Regulations 2004, Sched. 1, para. 19(2).

[1210] *ibid*. s.36, as amended by the Enterprise Act 2002, Sched. 1, para. 38(28) and the Competition Act 1998 and Other Enactments (Amendment) Regulations 2004, Sched. 1, para. 22.

Enterprise Act 2002: cartel offences

Although this Act introduced the concept of a "cartel offence" in relation to **10–243** arrangements affecting one or more undertakings,[1211] the offence can only be committed by individuals and a primary ingredient is actual dishonesty. In the circumstances, it is doubted whether this will have any direct impact on partnership arrangements.

V.   PROVISIONS CONSEQUENTIAL ON THE DEATH, RETIREMENT OR EXPULSION OF A PARTNER[1212]

(a) Assignment of Outgoing Partner's Share, etc.[1213]

Assignment of share

Lord Lindley observed: **10–244**

> "When a partner retires[1214] or dies, and he or his executors[1215] are paid what is due in respect of his share, it is customary for him or them formally to assign and release his interest in the partnership, and for the continuing or surviving partners to take upon themselves the payment of the outstanding debts of the firm, and to indemnify their late partner or his estate from all such debts."[1216]

In practice, a formal assignment of an outgoing partner's share is unusual, even though it will no longer attract a charge to *ad valorem* stamp duty.[1217] As a result, modern agreements generally contain a standard "further assurance" obligation, so that an assignment can be called for if it should prove necessary. Such a provision will also facilitate the retirement of the outgoing partner from the trusteeship of any partnership assets which he may have undertaken.

An assignment of a partnership share will be construed in the same way as any other document and will not necessarily comprehend all of the outgoing partner's rights. Thus, in *Hawthorn v. Smallcorn*,[1218] it was held that a payment made to an outgoing partner in respect of his share of the current assets of the firm did not prevent him from claiming a share of a repayment of value added tax overpaid whilst he was a partner.

Assignment of debts

Although an express assignment of partnership debts will, if the requirements **10–245** of section 136 of the Law of Property Act 1925 are satisfied, entitle the continuing partners to recover such debts without reference to the outgoing partner, this option is rarely adopted in practice.[1219]

[1211] Enterprise Act 2002, s.188.
[1212] See the *Encyclopedia of Professional Partnerships*, Precedent 1, cl. 22(2)(g)–(k).
[1213] See *ibid.* Precedent 1, cl. 22(2)(g), (k).
[1214] An expelled partner will be in the same position.
[1215] Similarly, in the case of an administrator.
[1216] See *infra*, paras 10–248 *et seq.*
[1217] As to the potential for a charge to stamp duty land tax, see *infra*, para. 10–247.
[1218] [1998] S.T.C. 591.
[1219] This is largely because commercial considerations militate against giving express written notice of the assignment to all customers, etc. See also *infra*, para. 14–84. As to the effect on such an assignment of the bankruptcy of the assignor, see the Insolvency Act 1986, s.344.

Where the agreement obliges the continuing partners to get in the old firm's debts and requires such debts, when paid, to be taken into account in ascertaining the outgoing partner's entitlement, the continuing partners will be chargeable with the value of any debts that they, for whatever reason, choose not to get in.[1220] Equally, an outgoing partner who, after assigning his interest in such debts, does anything to prejudice the continuing partners' rights, e.g. by releasing a creditor, will be guilty of a derogation from grant for which he can be held liable.[1221]

Where a debt is owed by the outgoing partner to the firm and is intended to be recoverable by the continuing partners notwithstanding any financial settlement reached with him, this fact should be specifically mentioned.[1222]

Assignment of share in partnership land

10–246   If the partnership assets consist of land, a written assignment of the outgoing partner's interest therein will seemingly be required.[1223]

Stamp duty land tax

10–247   In general, an assignment of a partnership share will now only be chargeable to stamp duty land tax[1224] if the partnership's sole or main activity is investing or dealing in chargeable interests (i.e. land or an interest in land).[1225] It seems clear that the old stamp duty regime will no longer have any application in such circumstances, where the partnership property consists of assets other than land.[1226]

(b) Indemnity to Outgoing Partner[1227]

10–248   As already noticed,[1228] it is usual for the continuing or surviving partners to indemnify the outgoing partner or his estate against the partnership debts and obligations,[1229] although such an indemnity is, in practice, usually implied. Lord Lindley observed:

> " ... in the absence of any agreement to that effect, a retiring partner[1230] or the executor of a deceased partner[1231] has no right to an indemnity from the other partners, except so far as he may be entitled to have assets of the firm applied in

---

[1220] *Lees v. Laforest* (1851) 14 Beav. 262.

[1221] *Aulton v. Atkins* (1856) 18 C.B. 249. Such a situation is unlikely to arise if the requirements of the Law of Property Act 1925, s.136 are satisfied.

[1222] *ibid.* See also *infra*, para. 19–06.

[1223] See further *infra*, para. 19–65.

[1224] i.e. under the Finance Act 2003, Sched. 15 (as amended).

[1225] See *infra*, paras 38–03, 38–13.

[1226] See *infra*, paras 38–01, 38–20. See as to the former position, the 17th ed. of this work at para. 10–246.

[1227] See the *Encyclopedia of Professional Partnerships*, Precedent 1, cl. 22(2)(h).

[1228] See *supra*, para. 10–244.

[1229] Lord Lindley pointed out that the indemnity "is ordinarily given by a bond or covenant entered into by the continuing or surviving partners, in consideration of the assignment to them of all the share and interest of the retiring or deceased partner". This is now rarely done. However, if the agreement is executed under seal, the outgoing partner will be a specialty creditor of the continuing partners if he is called on to pay a partnership debt: *Musson v. May* (1814) 3 V. & B. 194.

[1230] An expelled partner will be in the same position.

[1231] Similarly, in the case of an administrator.

payment of its debts, and to enforce contribution in case he has to pay more than his share of those debts.[1232] But if all the assets of the firm are assigned to the continuing or the surviving partners, it is only fair that they should undertake to pay its debts: and if it appears that it was the intention of all parties that they should do so, effect will be given to such intention, although the undertaking on their part is not explicit in its terms."[1233]

Consistently with this statement of principle, the Court of Appeal had no hesitation in recognising the existence of an implied right to indemnity in *Gray v. Smith*.[1234] It is, of course, rare to encounter a case in which an outgoing partner does not, either expressly or by necessary implication, relinquish his share in the partnership assets.[1235]

In its usual form the indemnity will not entitle the outgoing partner or his personal representatives to call on the continuing or surviving partners to pay the debts until a demand has been made for their payment.[1236]

Debts, etc., excluded from ambit of indemnity

The implied indemnity will cover all debts and liabilities of the firm, of whatever nature,[1237] but not any claims which any other partner may have against the outgoing partner for breach of duty or otherwise.[1238] In the case of express indemnities it has become common to exclude debts or liabilities attributable to the outgoing partner's own acts or omissions[1239] and even, in recent years, debts or liabilities attributable to *any* partner's acts or omissions. To the extent that adequate provisions have already been made[1240] (or will be made out of the outgoing partner's entitlement[1241]) under an express power in the agreement, such specific exclusion may be regarded as unnecessary, but it cannot safely be assumed that all debts will be known and quantified at or shortly after the retirement date.

10–249

Effect of indemnity

Whilst the outgoing partner remains directly liable for the partnership debts and obligations,[1242] such an indemnity places him in the position of surety *vis-*

10–250

[1232] See the Partnership Act 1890, s.39, *infra*, paras 19–25 *et seq.*; also *infra*, paras 20–04 *et seq.*

[1233] See *Saltoun v. Houston* (1824) 1 Bing. 433; *Gray v. Smith* (1889) 43 Ch.D. 208, 220. See also, as to the position of a purchaser of a partnership share, *Dodson v. Downey* [1901] 2 Ch. 620; also *infra*, para. 19–57.

[1234] (1889) 43 Ch.D. 208, 220, 221. See also the judgment of Kekewich J. at first instance: *ibid.* p. 213, 214.

[1235] *ibid.*; see also *Sobell v. Boston* [1975] 1 W.L.R. 1587.

[1236] *Bradford v. Gammon* [1925] Ch. 132. See further *infra*, para. 20–25.

[1237] Under the old regime of partnership taxation, this would have included income tax which, when assessed, was a joint debt: see *Stevens v. Britten* [1954] 1 W.L.R. 1340.

[1238] It follows that this would prima facie not include a liability falling within the principle enunciated in *Bury v. Allen* (1845) 1 Colly. 589, noted *infra*, paras 20–11 *et seq. Sed quaere.*

[1239] Such an exclusion would obviously catch liabilities of the *Bury v. Allen* type.

[1240] *i.e.* under the type of provision discussed, *supra*, para. 10–91.

[1241] See *supra*, para. 10–179.

[1242] See *infra*, paras 13–78 *et seq.*

à-vis the continuing partners.[1243] It follows that he may be discharged if a creditor, with notice of that arrangement, deals with the continuing partners in such a way as to prejudice the outgoing partner's rights against them.[1244]

Equally, it would seem that, by taking such an indemnity, the outgoing partner will forfeit his partner's lien, as Lord Lindley explained:

> "When a retiring partner[1245] assigns his interest in the partnership assets, and obtains from the continuing partners a covenant of indemnity,[1246] his lien on the partnership assets seems to be at an end."

Thus, in *Re Langmead's Trusts*,[1247] the retiring partners were held to have no lien on the assets of the old firm, even though the assignment of their interest therein was expressed to be subject to the payment of their share of the partnership debts, and they were accordingly left to pursue their remedy on the covenant for indemnity given by the continuing partner, who was by then bankrupt.

(c) Gazette Notices, etc.[1248]

10–251   Prior to the Partnership Act 1890, Lord Lindley wrote:

> "When power is given to retire or dissolve the firm, or to expel a partner from it, power should also be given to any partner to sign, in the name of himself and co-partners, a notice of dissolution for insertion in the '*Gazette*.' "

Although the 1890 Act does confer on each partner the right to notify the dissolution of the partnership or the retirement of a partner,[1249] an express right to sign a *Gazette* notice on an unco-operative outgoing partner's behalf will be essential in order to streamline the notification process.[1250] Equally, a specific provision dealing with *Gazette* notices will be required if the outgoing partner's rights in this respect are to be in any way restricted.[1251]

[1243] *Oakeley v. Pasheller* (1836) 4 Cl. & F. 207, *infra*, para. 13–99; *Rodgers v. Maw* (1846) 4 Dow. & L. 66. If the indemnity is given by deed, the outgoing partner will be specialty creditor in respect of any debt which he is called on to pay: *Musson v. May* (1814) 3 V. & B. 194.

[1244] See *Oakeley v. Pasheller, supra; Overend, Gurney & Co. v. Oriental Financial Corpn.* (1874) L.R. 7 H.L. 348; *Rouse v. Bradford Banking Co.* [1894] A.C. 586; also *infra*, paras 13–98 *et seq.* Equally, a part payment by one of the continuing partners will clearly restart the limitation period running as against the outgoing partner *qua* surety: *UCB Corporate Services Ltd. v. Kohli* [2004] 2 All E.R. (Comm) 422. And see as to the position once a judgment has been obtained, *Re a Debtor (No. 14 of 1913)* [1913] 3 K.B. 11.

[1245] Or an expelled partner.

[1246] As noted *supra*, para. 10–248, n. 1229, a *covenant* of indemnity is, as such, no longer given.

[1247] (1855) 7 De G.M. & G. 353. See also *Lingen v. Simpson* (1824) 1 Sim. & St. 600 and *infra*, para. 19–37.

[1248] See the *Encyclopedia of Professional Partnerships*, Precedent 1, cl. 22(2)(i).

[1249] s.37: see *infra*, para. 13–40.

[1250] The continuing partners will, of course have the right to require the outgoing partner to concur in giving a *Gazette* notice under *ibid.*, but enforcing this right through proceedings/an arbitration would be impractical in most cases.

[1251] The continuing partners may, understandably, wish to retain control over the form of the advertisement, etc. However, so far as concerns the outgoing partner, he will continue to be exposed to risk until such time as the advertisement appears: see the Partnership Act 1890, s.36(1), (2), *infra*, paras 13–40 *et seq.*

The agreement may also record the manner in which existing customers are to be notified, whether by circular letter or otherwise.[1252]

(d) Power of attorney

It used to be common form for the continuing partners to be appointed as the **10–252** outgoing partner's attorney for the purposes of executing any necessary documents, notices, etc., consequent on his retirement.[1253] In recent years such attorney provisions have become something of a rarity but, as previously noticed,[1254] are now enjoying something of a revival in large firms, albeit that their application is not confined to outgoing partners.

Where attorney rights are to be granted, the agreement will have to be executed as a deed[1255] unless resort is to be had to stand alone powers of attorney.[1256]

(e) Books and Papers[1257]

It is usual to include in the agreement an express obligation on the part of an **10–253** outgoing partner to deliver up to the continuing partners all books and papers, etc., in his possession which relate to the partnership business, although a limited right of access may be afforded to the outgoing partner for, say, a period of 12 months after he ceases to be a member of the firm. This will normally reflect an attempt to balance the competing interests of the outgoing partner, who will be concerned to ensure that he has received his full financial entitlement, and the continuing partners, who will be concerned to ensure that the outgoing partner does not have access to confidential information regarding the affairs of the ongoing firm.[1258]

Clients' documents

It is also desirable, in the case of a firm which holds clients' documents in the **10–254** course of its business, that the agreement addresses their disposition in the event of a change in the firm or a general dissolution.[1259] However, subject to the availability of any lien, the partners obviously cannot thereby prejudice a client's

---

[1252] See *ibid.* s.36(1) and *infra*, paras 13–74 *et seq*. Note also that, in the case of a professional practice, there may be a rule of conduct which requires certain clients or classes of clients to be notified of a change in the firm: see, for example, the Solicitors' Code of Conduct 2007, r. 2, commentary, para. 20 (which is less specific than the former *Law Society's Guide to the Professional Conduct of Solicitors* (8th ed.), principle 3.11). Such letters *may* represent a covert form of solicitation, but not in all cases: see the views expressed in *Taylor Stuart & Co. v. Croft*, May 7, 1997 (Lawtel 14/10/97), noted *supra*, para. 10–211.

[1253] See *supra*, paras 10–244, 10–251.

[1254] See *supra*, para. 10–97.

[1255] Powers of Attorney Act 1971, s.1(1), as amended by the Law of Property (Miscellaneous Provisions) Act 1989, Sched. 1, para. 6(a).

[1256] See *supra*, para. 10–97.

[1257] See the *Encyclopedia of Professional Partnerships*, Precedent 1, cl. 22(2)(j).

[1258] In the case of a professional firm, access by the outgoing partner to information relating to any period *after* his departure may have serious implications in terms of client confidentiality.

[1259] This avoids any doubt as to whether the custody of the papers passes with the goodwill: see *James v. James* (1889) 22 Q.B.D. 669, 675, note.

right to his own papers,[1260] nor can one partner, absent instructions from the client, claim them as his own.[1261]

(f) Procurement of release from personal obligations

10–255 Where the partners have personally guaranteed the firm's overdraft or assumed some other similar obligation, it is often agreed that the continuing partners will procure an outgoing partner's release from that obligation on or following his retirement, etc. It goes without saying that a breach of this term will not avail the outgoing partner in his dealings with the third party to whom the obligation is owed.[1262] A claim for specific performance or damages will, however, be maintainable.

W.   ADMISSION OF NEW PARTNERS[1263]

10–256 In the absence of an express provision in the agreement, a new partner can only be admitted with the consent of all the existing partners.[1264] An attempt to ignore this requirement will only result in the proposed new partner actually being admitted to the firm if the existing partners expressly or impliedly accept the position.[1265]

It is now usual, particularly in the professions, to encounter agreements which expressly provide not only for the manner in which the decision to admit a new partner is to be taken[1266] but also how that admission is to be effected, whether by requiring him to execute a separate deed of accession or suchlike or to append his signature to a special "signing schedule." In this way, the new partner will indicate his unequivocal acceptance of the existing partnership terms.[1267] If he fails to do so, uncertainty will inevitably be created, as Lord Lindley explained:

> "When a person has been admitted into an existing firm, and no express agreement has been made as to his rights and liabilities, the inference is that as between themselves his position is the same as that of the other partners. If they are bound by existing articles he will be bound by the same articles, if his conduct justifies the conclusion that he has assented to them; and if any special agreement is made with him, it will be regarded as incorporated with any previous agreement between the other partners, although so far as the two agreements may be inconsistent, the latest

---

[1260] *Ex p. Horsfall* (1827) 7 B. & C. 528; also *Casson Beckman & Partners v. Papi* [1991] B.C.L.C. 299. And see *supra*, para. 3–52.

[1261] See *Ingram v. Keeling* [2006] EWHC 2725 (Ch) (Lawtel 27/10/06), where one partner had removed client files without authority following a dissolution. See also *Finlayson v. Turnbull (No.1)* 1997 S.L.T. 613 (OH), noted *infra*, para. 16–07.

[1262] *Williamson v. Governor of the Bank of Scotland* [2006] B.P.I.R. 1085.

[1263] See the *Encyclopedia of Professional Partnerships*, Precedent 2, Art. 2.02, Precedent 9, cl. 21.

[1264] Partnership Act 1890, s.24(7).

[1265] See, for example, *Hodson v. Hodson* [2010] P.N.L.R. 8 (CA), affirming the decision at [2009] P.N.L.R. 23.

[1266] See also *supra*, para. 10–102.

[1267] See the *Encyclopedia of Professional Partnerships*, Precedent 2, Art. 2.02.00.

will prevail.[1268] If, indeed, the incoming partner has no knowledge of any prior agreement between the others, he cannot be bound thereby[1269] for nothing that he can have done can be regarded, under these circumstances, as evidence of any assent thereto on his part; and it is upon such presumed assent that the rule in question is founded."[1270]

In a case where the incoming partner is not, for whatever reason, bound by the agreement, the normal inference will be that it has ceased to apply as regards *all* the partners, not merely that it is inapplicable to him. The result may well be the creation of a partnership at will.[1271] It should, however be noted that this statement of principle was disapproved in the unreported decision of *Cummings v. Stockdale*,[1272] where it was, in effect, held that, if the existing agreement specifies how a partner is to be admitted to a firm and the manner of admission does not accord therewith, either the prospective partner has not been validly admitted or, if he has been admitted, he must necessarily be regarded as bound by the agreement. This decision is conceptually unsound since, not only did the judge ignore the effects of section 4 of the Partnership Act 1890,[1273] but he also conflated what is, in fact, a two stage process. First it must be determined whether a prospective partner has, as a matter of law, actually become a partner. The provisions of the agreement, though relevant, cannot ultimately be determinative on this issue. If, as a matter or law, the partnership relationship has been created, the next issue is what terms govern the partnership. Whilst there may be a *likelihood* that the existing agreement applies, this is by no means a necessary conclusion. It is, in any event, a surprising proposition that existing partners can ignore the express requirements of their agreement with impunity in all cases, especially where, as in *Cummings v. Stockdale*, at least one partner was unaware of the departure from those requirements.[1274]

Even where the agreement is shown to the incoming partner, it will frequently be the case that minor variations to its terms have been agreed at a partners' meeting and minuted accordingly, but it is rare to find such minutes being disclosed to an incoming partner; *a fortiori* in the case of variations by conduct.[1275] In such circumstances, the presumption must be that the incoming

10–257

[1268] See *Austen v. Boys* (1857) 24 Beav. 598. It should be noted that Sir John Romilly M.R. analysed the position in more dogmatic terms (i.e. without Lord Lindley's reference to conduct) at *ibid*. p. 606: "There is no doubt that if two partners take a third partner without specifying the terms on which he becomes such partner, he has the same rights and is subject to the same liabilities as the two original partners; the terms and conditions of the partnership which bind them bind him, unless a new contract is made between them. So also if the conditions of his becoming partner are partially set forth to the extent that they are not specified and involved by necessary inference therein, he will be bound by the terms of the partnership contract affecting the two original partners with whom he associates himself." It is submitted that these views were strictly *obiter* and went too far. There is no similar statement of principle on the appeal at (1858) 2 De G. & J. 626. Note, however, the unreported decision in *Cummings v. Stockdale*, noted *infra*, para. 10–257.

[1269] *Austin v. Boys, supra.*

[1270] *cf.* the Partnership Act 1890, s.27, *supra*, paras 10–18 *et seq.*

[1271] See *Firth v. Amslake* (1964) 108 S.J. 198, noted *supra*, para. 9–13.

[1272] November 11, 2008, a decision of H.H. Judge Raynor sitting as a judge of the Chancery Division, on an application under CPR r. 24(2).

[1273] See *supra*, para. 2–07.

[1274] Of course, they may be held to have varied their agreement by conduct, pursuant to the Partnership Act 1890, s.19 (see *supra*, para. 10–12), but that is a separate issue.

[1275] See *supra*, para. 10–16.

partner is not bound thereby.[1276] This was not an issue in *Cummings v. Stockdale, supra.*

The right to nominate a successor partner[1277]

10–258   A provision entitling an outgoing partner or his executors to nominate a successor to be admitted to the partnership in his place, which was once commonplace,[1278] is now rarely, if ever, encountered in practice.[1279] Nevertheless, it is useful to summarise the rules applicable to such provisions, as originally formulated by Lord Lindley.

Rule 1:

10–259   " . . . clauses of this kind, although they bind the surviving partners[1280] to let in the person nominated,[1281] do not bind him to come in, but give him an option whether he will do so or not."[1282]

If the agreement contemplates that possibility, the nominee may have an enforceable right to be admitted to the firm by virtue of the Contracts (Rights of Third Parties) Act 1999.[1283] In any other case, unless the nominee was a party to the agreement or is the deceased's personal representative,[1284] he will seemingly only have an enforceable right if he is able to establish the existence of an immediate trust in his favour,[1285] as the widow was able to do in *Page v. Cox.*[1286]

[1276] It follows that such terms must then be *re-established* by conduct under the Partnership Act 1890, s.19.

[1277] See the *Encyclopedia of Professional Partnerships*, Precedent 9, cl. 21.

[1278] Lord Lindley went as far as to say: "It is a common provision in partnership articles that on the death of a partner his executors, or his son, or some other person, shall be entitled to take his place." In some cases, succession to the share was not even dependent on any form of nomination: see *Balmain v. Shore* (1804) 9 Ves.Jr. 500; *Ponton v. Dunn* (1830) 1 R. & M. 402.

[1279] Note, however, that the current editor has explored the use of this device as a means of preserving the right to pay inheritance tax by instalments: see the *Encyclopedia of Professional Partnerships*, Pt 6.

[1280] Similarly, in the case of continuing partners, where the nomination is by a retiring partner.

[1281] See *Byrne v. Reid* [1902] 2 Ch. 735; also *Wainwright v. Waterman* (1791) 1 Ves.Jr. 311, where a declaration was granted. *cf. Milliken v. Milliken* (1845) 8 I.Eq.R. 16, where the nominee was held to be remediless. As to the position once the nominee has been admitted, see *infra*, para. 19–61. Subject to the terms of the agreement, a mere bequest of residue will not amount to a sufficient nomination: see *Beamish v. Beamish* (1869) 4 Eq. I.R. 120; *Thomson v. Thomson*, 1962 S.L.T. 109 (HL).

[1282] *Pigott v. Bagley* (1825) McCle. & Yo. 569; *Madgwick v. Wimble* (1843) 6 Beav. 495; *Page v. Cox* (1851) 10 Hare 163; *Thomson v. Thomson, supra,* at p. 111 *per* Lord Reid. See also *Pearce v. Chamberlain* (1750) 2 Ves.Sen. 33.

[1283] *ibid.* s.1(1), (2). Note that this Act only applies where the agreement was made after May 11, 2000. The nominee must be identified by name, as a member of a class or as answering a particular description, even if he is not in existence when the agreement is signed: *ibid.* s.1(3); and see *Avraamides v. Colwill, The Times,* December 8, 2006 (CA). As to whether the application of the Act is excluded by a contrary intention, see *Nisshin Shipping Co Ltd. v. Cleaves & Co Ltd.* [2004] 1 Lloyd's Rep. 38. See further *supra*, para. 10–188.

[1284] See *Beswick v. Beswick* [1968] A.C. 58.

[1285] *Ehrmann v. Ehrmann* (1894) 72 L.T. 17. Note, however, that in *Byrne v. Reid* [1902] 2 Ch. 735, only Stirling L.J. referred to the existence of a trust: see *ibid.* pp. 744–745. This decision was distinguished in *Re Franklin and Swathling's Arbitration* [1929] 1 Ch. 238, although Maugham J. appears to have assumed that a trust was established: see *ibid.* p. 242. *Quaere* whether (independently of the Contracts (Rights of Third Parties) Act 1999) there is a residual class of cases in which *no* trust exists but an effective nomination confers all the rights of a partner on the nominee.

[1286] (1851) 10 Hare 163. See also *Drimmie v. Davies* [1899] 1 I.R. 176; *Byrne v. Reid, supra; Re Franklin and Swathling's Arbitration, supra.* And see further, as to establishing the existence of a trust, *supra*, para. 10–189.

Where, however, the nominee's right to be admitted is conditional on the consent of the continuing or surviving partners being obtained and such consent is, in the event, withheld, any rights which he may have under the 1999 Act will be of no avail[1287] nor can any trust in his favour be held to exist.[1288]

Even where the agreement clearly states that the nominee will join the firm, specific performance will not be ordered as against him, although the outgoing partner or his estate may be liable in damages.[1289]

Rule 2:

"... before making up his mind [*the nominee*] is entitled to make himself acquainted with the state of the partnership affairs, although he is not entitled to have its accounts formally taken."[1290]   **10–260**

It follows that the share of the outgoing partner may fall to be treated as a debt due to him or to his estate during the interim period.[1291]

Rule 3:

"... if [*the nominee*] is desirous of coming in, he must comply strictly with the terms upon which alone he is entitled to do so."[1292]   **10–261**

By so doing, he will, of course, indicate his acceptance of the partnership terms.[1293]

Rule 4:

"... if [*the nominee*] declines to come in, and there is no provision as to what is then to be done, the partnership must be dissolved and wound up in the usual way."[1294]   **10–262**

X.   WINDING UP[1295]

Agreements frequently make special provision for the winding up of the partnership affairs in the event of a *general* dissolution, whether resulting from the continuing partners' failure to exercise an option to acquire an outgoing partner's share,[1296] the exercise of an express power to dissolve[1297] or even an order of the   **10–263**

[1287] *Semble*, it is unlikely that the existing partners' right to withhold consent will, as a matter of implication, be held to be subject to a requirement of reasonableness.

[1288] *Re Franklin and Swathling's Arbitration, supra*. Note also *Ehrmann v. Ehrmann* (1894) 72 L.T. 17.

[1289] See *Downs v. Collins* (1848) 6 Hare 418; also *Lisle v. Reeve* [1902] 1 Ch. 53 (affirmed *sub nom. Reeve v. Lisle* [1902] A.C. 461), where an inquiry as to damages was directed: see *ibid.* p. 70. The latter case concerned an option to become a partner, as to which see *supra*, paras 2–22 *et seq. cf. Byrne v. Reid* [1902] 2 Ch. 735, 745 *per* Stirling L.J.

[1290] *Pigott v. Bagley* (1825) McCle. & Yo. 569.

[1291] See the Partnership Act 1890, s.43; also *Thomson v. Thomson*, 1962 S.L.T. 109, 110–111 *per* Lord Reid.

[1292] *Holland v. King* (1848) 6 C.B. 727; *Brooke v. Garrod* (1857) 3 K. & J. 608; also *Milliken v. Milliken* (1845) 8 I.Eq.R. 16. *cf. Ex p. Marks* (1832) 1 D. & Ch. 499.

[1293] See *supra*, para. 10–256.

[1294] *Kershaw v. Matthews* (1826) 2 Russ. 62; *Downs v. Collins* (1848) 6 Hare 418; *Madgwick v. Wimble* (1843) 6 Beav. 495.

[1295] See the *Encyclopedia of Professional Partnerships*, Precedent 1, cl. 24.

[1296] See *supra*, para. 10–154.

[1297] See *supra*, paras 10–137 *et seq.*

court (or an arbitrator).[1298] Such a provision is, of course, strictly unnecessary if the partnership affairs are to be wound up in accordance with the provisions of the Partnership Act 1890,[1299] although it may be useful to record the fact that each partner is to have liberty to purchase any partnership assets which fall to be sold.[1300]

Division of assets in specie

10-264   Where it is intended that the partnership assets will be divided between the partners *in specie*, this fact should be clearly stated. Lord Lindley explained:

> "An agreement that on a dissolution the partnership property shall be fairly and equally divided, after payment of its debts, has been held to mean that the property shall be sold, and that the money produced by the sale shall be divided after the debts have been paid."[1301]

Even if such a construction is avoided, it would seem that a court might still, in an appropriate case, order a sale.[1302]

Where the partnership assets include land, such a division of assets *in specie* following a dissolution is likely to lead to the imposition of a charge to stamp duty land tax, even where the division directly reflects the former partners' shares in the partnership.[1303]

10-265   Some assets are obviously more susceptible of division than others. Goodwill, expressed in terms of client connection, is a case in point, as Lord Lindley observed in a passage written in relation to solicitors' partnerships, but which is equally applicable to firms carrying on business in other spheres:

> " . . . as between the solicitors themselves, it is competent for them to agree that, if they dissolve partnership, the clients of the old firm, and all their deeds and papers, shall be divided amongst the partners, or belong solely to the partner who continues to carry on the business of the firm; and such an agreement will be enforced."[1304]

[1298] See the Partnership Act 1890, s.35, *infra*, paras 24–47 *et seq.*; see also *infra*, para. 10–272. Note, however, that in *PWA Corp v. Gemini Group Automated Distribution Systems Inc.* [1993] 103 D.L.R. (4th) 609, 629, Dublin C.J.O., in his dissenting judgment, held that certain unspecified provisions in the agreement relating to dissolution were of no application on a court ordered dissolution.

[1299] See *ibid.* ss.37–39, 42, 44; also *infra*, paras 25–22 *et seq.*

[1300] Otherwise see *infra*, para. 23–194.

[1301] *Rigden v. Pierce* (1822) 6 Madd. 353; *Cook v. Collingridge* (1822) Jac. 607.

[1302] *Taylor v. Neate* (1888) 39 Ch.D. 538. However, it appears that the parties agreed to a sale in this case: see *ibid.* p. 542. See also *infra*, para. 10–266.

[1303] See *infra*, paras 38–21, 38–22. And see *infra*, para. 37–26, regarding value added tax.

[1304] *Whittaker v. Howe* (1841) 3 Beav. 383. But see *Davidson v. Napier* (1827) 1 Sim. 297. In the case of solicitors, it is considered that such an arrangement would not contravene the Solicitors' Code of Conduct 2007, r. 1.04 (best interests of client), provided that undue pressure is not applied in order to persuade the client to remain with the partner(s) in question. As to the right of a solicitor to act against a former client of his firm, see *Cholmondeley v. Clinton* (1815) 19 Ves.Jr. 261; *Rakusen v. Ellis, Munday & Clarke* [1912] 1 Ch. 831; *David Lee & Co. (Lincoln) Ltd. v. Coward Chance* [1991] Ch. 229; *Re A Firm of Solicitors* [1992] Q.B. 959; *Re a Firm of Solicitors* [1997] Ch. 1; *Halewood International Ltd. v. Addleshaw Booth & Co.* [2000] P.N.L.R. 788; *Koch Shipping Inc v. Richards Butler* [2002] 2 All E.R. (Comm) 957; *Ball v. Druces & Attlee* [2002] P.N.L.R. 23 and [2004] P.N.L.R. 39; *Marks & Spencer Group plc v. Freshfields Bruckhaus Deringer* [2004] 1 W.L.R. 2331; *Gus Consulting GmbH v. Leboeuf, Lamb, Greene & MacRae* [2006] P.N.L.R. 32 (CA); *cf. Winters v. Mishcon de Reya* (2008) 158 N.L.J. 1494; note also *Bolkiah v. KPMG* [1999] 2 A.C. 222; *Young v. Robson Rhodes* [1999] 3 All E.R. 524; *Akai Holdings Ltd. v. RSM Robson Rhodes LLP* [2007] EWHC 1641 (Ch) (Lawtel 8/8/07) (as to the protection of a former client's confidential information). See also the Solicitors' Code of Conduct 2007, r. 4 as amended by the Solicitors' Code of Conduct

However, where such an arrangement is implemented, a client or customer cannot be forced to deal with the partner to whom he is allocated[1305] and, subject to any questions of lien, he may legitimately seek the delivery up of any papers, etc., which belong to him.[1306] It will generally be desirable to prevent any partner attempting to frustrate such an arrangement by coupling it with a suitable *express* restriction on competition.[1307]

Provisions facilitating the formation of a "phoenix" firm

A more modern variation on the above theme is an agreement which, in the event of a dissolution, entitles a majority of partners[1308] to retain the old firm's name and goodwill, with a view to their forming a new firm as an effective continuation of the old, *i.e.* a so-called "phoenix" firm. The agreement may provide that the majority must account for the assessed value of the name and goodwill[1309] or, more commonly, it may expressly relieve them of any such obligation. It is, in practice, rare to see this approach extended to other assets, which will therefore fall to be realised in the course of the winding up in the usual way.

10–266

Whilst such a provision would normally be upheld as between the partners,[1310] the editor apprehends that a court might be unwilling to do so in a case where a dissolution is brought about by the misconduct of the majority.[1311]

Getting in debts

Lord Lindley observed:

10–267

"When a firm is dissolved, it is usual to appoint one of the partners, or some third person, to collect and get in the debts of the firm. But notwithstanding any such arrangement and notice thereof, a debtor to the firm will be discharged if he pays to any one of the partners.[1312] Effect, however, will be given by the Court to an agreement of the nature in question, by appointing a receiver, and if necessary, granting an injunction."[1313]

(Confidentiality and Disclosure) Amendment Rule 2010 and *supra*, para. 3–44. As to the position in the absence of such an agreement, see *supra*, paras 10–199 *et seq.*

[1305] *Cook v. Rhodes* (1815) 19 Ves.Jr. 273, note.

[1306] *Colegrave v. Manley* (1823) T. & R. 400; *Griffiths v. Griffiths* (1843) 2 Hare 587. See also *supra*, para. 3–52.

[1307] See, as to the position in the absence of such a restriction, *supra*, paras 10–206 *et seq.* And see generally, *supra*, paras 10–218 *et seq.*

[1308] The size of the majority will be for consideration: the right may be conferred on partners holding a majority of equity shares, rather than on a straight *per capita* basis.

[1309] See generally, as to methods of valuing goodwill, *supra*, paras 10–160, 10–216 *et seq.* and *infra*, para. 36–58. It does not, however, follow that, in all cases, goodwill has a significant value on a dissolution: see *supra*, paras 10–197, 10–200 *et seq.*

[1310] The position would be otherwise if the firm is insolvent: see generally, *infra*, paras 27–65, 27–78 *et seq.*

[1311] See for example, *DB Rare Books Ltd. v. Antiqbooks* [1995] 2 B.C.L.C. 306, 323c *per* Dillon L.J. in a dissenting judgment concerning a power of expulsion. And note also that in *PWA Corp v. Gemini Group Automated Distribution Systems Inc.* [1993] 103 D.L.R. (4th) 609, 629, Dublin C.J.O., in his dissenting judgment, held that certain unspecified provisions in the agreement relating to dissolution were of no application on a court ordered dissolution. In such a case, would an exercise of judicial discretion in this way be incompatible with the other partners' Convention rights under the Human Rights Act 1998? See further *supra*, para. 10–27.

[1312] See *infra*, para. 12–53.

[1313] *Davis v. Amer* (1854) 3 Drew. 64.

In practice, an arrangement of this type is usually made on an *ad hoc* basis and will not be legislated for in the agreement itself.

A right to damages for breach of such an arrangement will, if the agreement establishing it is not under seal,[1314] be dependent on showing that it is supported by consideration. This may in fact take the form of the other partners' acceptance that they will take no steps to collect in the debts.[1315]

Gazette notices

10–268 It is, in general, unnecessary to include any specific provision governing notification of the dissolution by means of a *Gazette* notice, since this is provided for in the Partnership Act 1890.[1316]

Dissolution committees

10–269 Some modern agreements provide machinery for the appointment of what may be styled a "dissolution committee", which is charged with the task of super-intending the winding up and taking any decisions which are required during the course thereof.[1317] This would involve an effective delegation to the committee of the whole or part of each partner's continuing authority under section 38 of the Partnership Act 1890,[1318] which would be perfectly effective as a matter of partnership law. Although such a provision could not oust the jurisdiction of the court to wind up the firm's affairs, it is apprehended that the court might be reluctant to interfere in the absence of misconduct on the part of members of the committee.[1319]

Y. ARBITRATION AND ALTERNATIVE DISPUTE RESOLUTION[1320]

(a) Arbitration

10–270 An arbitration clause will be found in the majority of modern partnership agreements, even though it may not necessarily be of the "all disputes" variety,[1321] and will, in general, be carried over when a partnership is continued beyond an initial fixed term.[1322]

The conduct of arbitrations is now governed by Part I of the Arbitration Act 1996,[1323] which replaced the provisions of the Arbitration Acts 1950 to 1979.[1324]

[1314] *cf. Belcher v. Sikes* (1827) 6 B. & C. 185.

[1315] See *Lewis v. Edwards* (1840) 7 M. & W. 300.

[1316] *ibid.* s.37, *infra*, paras 13–40 *et seq.*

[1317] In the alternative, the relevant functions could be conferred on a named partner or an office holder, such as the managing partner.

[1318] See *infra*, paras 13–62 *et seq.*

[1319] See, for example, *infra*, para. 23–18.

[1320] See the *Encyclopedia of Professional Partnerships*, Precedent 1, cl. 26.

[1321] Thus, it may deal only with accountancy or valuation matters, leaving questions of construction, etc., to be dealt with by the courts.

[1322] *Gillett v. Thornton* (1875) L.R. 19 Eq. 599. See also *supra*, para. 10–21.

[1323] This Part of the Act applies to all arbitrations, both domestic and non-domestic. Although *ibid.* Pt II, ss.85–87 contains provisions applicable to domestic arbitration agreements (as defined in *ibid.* s.85(2)), those sections have not, in the event, been (and will not in the future be) brought into force.

[1324] For an outline of the relevant provisions of those Acts, see the 17th ed. of this work at paras 10–226 *et seq.*

A prerequisite to the application of that Part is the existence of an arbitration agreement, *i.e.* an agreement to submit present or future disputes[1325] to arbitration,[1326] which must be made[1327] or evidenced[1328] in writing,[1329] but need not actually be signed by the parties.[1330] Incorporation of an arbitration clause in an agreement by reference is sufficient.[1331]

An arbitration agreement will not be invalidated because an agreement of which it forms part is or has become invalid or ineffective.[1332] Equally, since the doctrine of repudiation does not apply to partnership agreements, at least whilst the partnership subsists,[1333] this issue will perhaps only rarely arise.[1334] Even the illegality of the main agreement will not be fatal.[1335]

Where the seat of the arbitration[1336] is in England and Wales,[1337] certain mandatory provisions of the Act will apply and any attempt to exclude them will be ineffective.[1338] Subject thereto, the parties are free to agree how the arbitration

[1325] This expression includes differences: Arbitration Act 1996, s.82(1).

[1326] *ibid.* s.6(1). An agreement which provides for the determination of disputes may, on its true construction, amount to an arbitration agreement even if there is, as such, no reference to "arbitration": *David Wilson Homes Ltd. v. Survey Services Ltd.* [2001] 1 All E.R. (Comm.) 449. An option in favour of one party to insist on disputes being referred to arbitration may, if exercised, amount to an arbitration agreement: see *NB Three Shipping Ltd. v. Harebell Shipping Ltd.* [2005] 1 All E.R. (Comm) 200. *cf.* the position where one party has the option to litigate the matter in court and, thus, to override the arbitration agreement: *Law Debenture Trust Corp v. Elektrim Finance BV* [2005] 2 All E.R. (Comm) 476. Note also, in this context, the exceptional decision in *Flight Training International Inc. v. International Fire Training Equipment Ltd.* [2004] 2 All E.R. (Comm) 568. It goes without saying that an arbitration clause which is held to be void for uncertainty will *not* constitute an arbitration agreement: *E.J.R. Lovelock Ltd. v. Exportles* [1968] 1 Lloyd's Rep. 163; *Bruce v. Kordula* 2001 S.L.T. 983.

[1327] *ibid.* s.5(2)(a), (b). An oral agreement "by reference to" terms in writing will, for this purpose, constitute an agreement in writing: *ibid.* s.5(3).

[1328] *ibid.* s.5(2)(c). An agreement is evidenced in writing is there is a written record of it prepared by one of the parties or by a third party with their authority: *ibid.* s.5(4).

[1329] This will include any means of recording: *ibid.* s.5(6).

[1330] *ibid.* s.5(1)(a).

[1331] *ibid.* s.6(2). However, general words of incorporation may not suffice: *Excess Insurance Co Ltd. v. Mander* [1995] I.R.L.R. 358; *Trygg Hansa Insurance Co Ltd. v. Equitas and Butcher* [1998] 2 Lloyd's Rep. 439. Note also *Axa Re v. Ace Global Markets Ltd.* [2006] Lloyd's Rep I.R. 683, where it was held that an English law jurisdiction clause was not inconsistent with the arbitration clause which had been incorporated.

[1332] *ibid.* s.7, as interpreted in *Fiona Trust & Holding Corp. v. Privalov* [2007] Bus. L.R. 686 (CA). This represents the doctrine of separability. The position will, of course, be otherwise if the arbitration agreement is avoided, *e.g.* by reason of economic duress: *Capital Structures plc v. Time & Tide Construction Ltd.* [2006] B.L.R. 226 at [28] *per* HH. Judge Wilcox; *El Nasharty v. J. Sainsbury plc* [2008] 1 Lloyd's Rep. 360. Similarly if the agreement containing an arbitration clause is a forgery: *Albon v. Naza Motor Trading Sdn Bhd (No 4)* [2008] 1 All E.R. (Comm) 351 (CA). As to severance of a partially invalid arbitration agreement, see *Jivray v. Hashwari* [2010] I.R.L.R. 797 (CA).

[1333] See *infra*, paras 24–05 *et seq.*

[1334] An arbitration clause in a partnership agreement could, in theory. be repudiated and, in such a case, will no longer be enforceable: see *Downing v. Al Tameer Establishment* [2002] 2 All E.R. (Comm) 545 (CA). Note that a repudiation argument failed in *Indescon Ltd. v. Ogden* [2005] B.L.R. 152. See also, *infra*, para. 10–273.

[1335] See *Vee Networks Ltd. v. Econet Wireless International Ltd.* [2005] 1 All E.R. (Comm) 303.

[1336] *i.e.*, in general, the juridical seat of the arbitration designated by the parties: Arbitration Act 1996, s.3(a). See also *Braes of Doune Wind Farm (Scotland) Ltd. v. Alfred McAlpine Business Services Ltd.* [2008] 2 All E.R. (Comm) 493; *Shashoua v. Sharma* [2009] 2 All E.R. (Comm) 477.

[1337] *ibid.* s.2(1).

[1338] *ibid.* s.4(1), Sched. 1. Thus, the choice of another system of law to govern the partnership agreement will not, without more, mean that any award can be challenged in a way not sanctioned by the Act: *C v. D* [2008] 1 All E.R. (Comm) 1001 (CA).

is to be conducted and it is only in the absence of agreement that the default provisions set out in the Act will apply.[1339]

Persons bound by the arbitration agreement

10–271   An arbitration agreement will be binding on the partners and, as a general rule, on their personal representatives,[1340] as well as any person entitled to enforce rights under the partnership agreement by virtue of the Contracts (Rights of Third Parties) Act 1999,[1341] *e.g.* an annuitant.[1342] An incoming partner will be bound as soon as he comes a signatory to or bound by a partnership agreement containing an arbitration clause, even if the dispute arose prior to his admission.[1343]

However, it was formerly the position that the assignee or mortgagee of a partnership share was not bound by an arbitration clause in the partnership agreement as regards his statutory right to an account on a dissolution[1344] save, perhaps, where the clause in terms extended to persons claiming under a partner.[1345] Now that such an extension is applicable in all cases,[1346] it would appear that an assignee or mortgagee should be bound to have the account taken by an arbitrator.[1347]

Construction and scope of arbitration agreement

10–272   An arbitration agreement will fall to be construed in the same way as any other contract,[1348] but the House of Lords in *Fiona Trust & Holding Corp. v. Privalov*[1349] made clear that there will be an assumption that all disputes will fall within the ambit of such an agreement. Accordingly, whilst the expression "dispute or difference" is likely to be construed more widely than the word "dispute" appearing alone,[1350] little may in practice turn on this.

Arbitration clauses in partnership agreements tend to be drawn in a wide form and are likely to cover any dispute arising between partners or between them and a former partner.[1351] In most instances, the clause will, either expressly or by necessary implication, authorise the arbitrator to order a dissolution of the firm

---

[1339] *ibid.* s.4(2).

[1340] *ibid.* s.8(1).

[1341] Contracts (Rights of Third Parties) Act 1999, s.8. And see *Nisshin Shipping Co Ltd. v. Cleaves & Co Ltd.* [2004] 1 Lloyd's Rep. 38.

[1342] See further *supra*, paras 10–188, 10–259.

[1343] See *CMA CGM SA v. Hyundai Mipo Dockyard Co. Ltd.* [2009] 1 All E.R. (Comm) 568, which concern a novated shipbuilding contract.

[1344] Partnership Act 1890, s.31(2). See further, *infra*, para. 19–56.

[1345] As to the position prior to the 1996 Act, see *Bonnin v. Neame* [1910] 1 Ch. 732 (a decision under the Arbitration Act 1889, s.4, when the grant of a stay was discretionary).

[1346] See the Arbitration Act 1996, s.82(2);. also *Schiffahrtsgesellschaft Detlev Von Appen GmbH v. Voest Alpine Intertrading GmbH* [1997] 2 Lloyd's Rep. 279 (CA); *Through Transport Mutual Insurance Association (Eurasia) Ltd. v. New India Assurance Co Ltd.* [2005] 1 C.L.C. 376.

[1347] See also *infra*, para. 19–50.

[1348] See *supra*, paras 10–03 *et seq.* In particular, the expression "dispute" will be given its ordinary and common-sense meaning: *Halki Shipping Corp. v. Sopex Oils Ltd.* [1998] 1 W.L.R. 727 (CA).

[1349] [2007] Bus. L.R. 686. Note, however, that these comments were made in the context of international commercial arbitrations. See also *Norscot Rig Management Pvt Ltd. v. Essar Oilfields Services Ltd.* [2010] 2 Lloyd's Rep. 209.

[1350] See *Amec Civil Engineering Ltd. v. Secretary of State for Transport* [2005] 1 W.L.R. 2339 (CA). And see also *Jagger v. Decca Music Group Ltd.* [2005] F.S.R. 26; *Tjong Very Sumito v. Antig Investments Pte Ltd.* [2010] 2 All E.R. (Comm) 366 (CA).

[1351] *Wedlake Bell v. Jones* [2007] EWHC 1143 (Ch) is an example of such a case.

under section 35 of the Partnership Act 1890.[1352] By way of illustration, in *Phoenix v. Pope*[1353] the clause was in this form:

"All disputes which shall arise between the partners or between any one or more of them and the personal representatives of any other or others of them or between their respective personal representatives and whether during or after the determination of the partnership so far as concerns any one or more or all of them and whether in relation to the interpretation of these presents or to any act or omission of any of the parties to the dispute or as to any act which ought to be done by the parties in dispute or any of them or in relation to any other matter whatsoever touching the partnership affairs shall be referred to a single arbitrator to be appointed by the partners or other parties to the dispute or if they cannot agree then to a single arbitrator to be nominated by the President of the Law Society for the time being at the request of any partner or other party to the dispute. And the provisions of the Arbitration Act 1950 or any statutory modification thereof shall apply and the partners shall be bound by any decision of the said arbitrator."

Goff J. was satisfied that the clause was apt to cover a dissolution claim and, after reviewing the authorities, concluded that there was no basis on which it could be said that questions of dissolution automatically fell outwith an arbitrator's jurisdiction.[1354] The old cases in which the court declined to allow questions of dissolution to be the subject of a reference[1355] can no longer be relied on, since they were decided under a wholly different regime in which the grant of a stay of proceedings was discretionary.[1356]

Other points of construction arise less frequently in partnership cases but, in *Ellis v. Coleman*,[1357] Lawrence Collins J. had no hesitation in holding that the expression "partners" in an arbitration clause extended not only to current but also to *former* partners in the firm.

It should also be noted that a transaction set off may not fall within the scope of an arbitration clause if it arises out of a different contract.[1358]

Arbitration agreement generally no defence

Lord Lindley wrote that an arbitration agreement: **10–273**

" . . . is one which (independently of the Common Law Procedure Act of 1854[1359]) cannot be effectually set up as a defence to any action relative to a matter agreed to

[1352] See *infra*, paras 24–47 *et seq.*
[1353] [1974] 1 W.L.R. 719.
[1354] He held that the principle had been established in the following cases: *Russell v. Russell* (1880) 14 Ch.D. 471; *Walmsley v. White* (1892) 40 W.R. 675; *Vawdrey v. Simpson* [1896] 1 Ch. 166; *Olver v. Hillier* [1959] 1 W.L.R. 551. Note that, in *Hutchinson v. Whitfield* (1830) Hayes 78, where there was a provision that the partnership could only be dissolved by deed, it was held that a reference by deed and a subsequent award under seal dissolving the partnership did bring about a dissolution, even though the reference did not mention dissolution. The decision is an extraordinary one and is unlikely to be of any general application.
[1355] *Cooker v. Catchpole* (1864) 10 Jr.(N.S.) 1068; *Joplin v. Postelthwaite* (1889) 61 L.T.(N.S.) 629; *Turnell v. Sanderson* (1891) 64 L.T.(N.S.) 654 (disapproved by Goff J. in *Phoenix v. Pope, supra*); *Barnes v. Youngs* [1898] 1 Ch. 414; note also the Scottish decision *Roxburgh v. Dinardo*, 1981 S.L.T. 291.
[1356] See the Arbitration Act 1996, s.9, *infra*, para. 10–274.
[1357] [2004] EWHC 3407 (Ch) (Lawtel 10/12/04).
[1358] See *Econet Satellite Services Ltd. v. Vee Networks Ltd.* [2006] 2 All E.R. (Comm) 1000, although this decision turned on the terms of the UNCITRAL rules. A more liberal approach was adopted *Norscot Rig Management Pvt Ltd. v. Essar Oilfields Services Ltd., supra*. Inevitably, the ultimate decision will turn on the terms of the arbitration clause.
[1359] The forerunner of the Arbitration Acts 1889 and 1950 and, now, the Arbitration Act 1996.

be referred[1360]; unless, indeed, the reference has been . . . made[1361] a condition precedent to the right to sue."[1362]

Although this is still, in essence, the position under the Arbitration Act 1996, a party to an arbitration agreement who is made a defendant to proceedings falling within the ambit of that agreement is now, in most instances, entitled to a mandatory stay.[1363] Moreover, if such a stay is, for whatever reason, refused, any condition precedent of the type referred to above will be of no effect.[1364]

Even where the reference has been made a condition precedent and that condition continues to have effect, a party to the agreement may be precluded from setting up the absence of an award as a defence, either by his conduct before the proceedings were commenced[1365] or by seeking to resist the claim on a ground which, in effect, amounts to a repudiation of that agreement.[1366]

Power of court to order stay of proceedings

10–274   Under the Arbitration Act 1950,[1367] the court had a discretion as to whether to order a stay of proceedings commenced by a party to an arbitration agreement in respect of any dispute falling within its ambit. Although it was originally intended that a similar discretion should be exercisable in the case of domestic arbitration agreements[1368] under the Arbitration Act 1996,[1369] in the event those provisions have not been, and now are not intended to be, brought into force. As a result, the applicable power in the case of *all* arbitration agreements is set out section 9(1) to (4) of the 1996 Act, which provides as follows:

[1360] See *Doleman & Sons v. Ossett Corporation* [1912] 3 K.B. 257 and the cases there cited; also *Cooke v. Cooke* (1867) L.R. 4 Eq. 77; *Dawson v. Fitzgerald* (1876) 1 Ex.D. 257; *Edwards v. Aberayron Mutual Ship Insurance Soc.* (1876) 1 Q.B.D. 563.

[1361] The word "expressly" originally appeared at this point, but this is no longer a requirement: see *Cipriani v. Burnett* [1933] A.C. 83.

[1362] See *Scott v. Avery* (1856) 5 H.L.C. 811; *Caledonian Ins. Co. v. Gilmour* [1893] A.C. 85; *Spurrier v. La Cloche* [1902] A.C. 446; *Smith, Coney & Barrett v. Becker, Gray & Co.* [1916] 2 Ch. 86; *Woodall v. Pearl Ass. Co.* [1919] 1 K.B. 593; *Hallen v. Spaeth* [1923] A.C. 684; *Jagger v. Decca Music Group Ltd.* [2005] F.S.R. 26. Lord Lindley observed of the decision in *Halfhide v. Fenning* (1788) 2 Bro.C.C. 336: "[*This*] case is generally regarded as overruled, but *quaere* whether it is not capable of being supported on the principle recognised in *Scott v. Avery*. See the observations of Lord St. Leonards in *Dimsdale v. Robertson* (1844) 2 Jo. & LaT. 91, and of V.-C. Wood in *Cooke v. Cooke* (1867) 4 Eq. 77."

[1363] See *infra*, para. 10–274.

[1364] Arbitration Act 1996, s.9(5). The court no longer has power to order that such a condition shall cease to have effect: the provisions of the Arbitration Act 1950, s.25(4) are not replicated in the 1996 Act.

[1365] *e.g.* by improperly interfering with the arbitrator in the discharge of his duties (*Hickman & Co. v. Roberts* [1913] A.C. 229; *Eaglesham v. MacMaster* [1920] 2 K.B. 169) or by waiver (*Toronto Railway v. National British and Irish Millers Ins. Co.* (1914) 111 L.T. 555).

[1366] *Jureidini v. National British and Irish Millers Ins. Co. Ltd.* [1915] A.C. 499. *cf. Stebbing v. Liverpool & London Ins. Co.* [1917] 2 K.B. 433; *Woodall v. Pearl Ass. Co.* [1919] 1 K.B. 593; *Freshwater v. Western Australian Ass. Co. Ltd.* [1933] 1 K.B. 515.

[1367] s.4(1). See further the 17th ed. of this work at paras 10–229 *et seq.*

[1368] *i.e.* an arbitration agreement to which none of the parties is an individual who is a national of or habitually resident in a state other than the UK or a body corporate incorporated in or whose central control and management is exercised in such a state but under which the seat of the arbitration is in the UK: Arbitration Act 1996, s.85(2).

[1369] *ibid.* s.86.

"9.—(1) A party to an arbitration agreement[1370] against whom legal proceedings are brought (whether by way of claim or counterclaim) in respect of a matter which under the agreement is to be referred to arbitration may (upon notice to the other parties to the proceedings) apply to the court in which the proceedings have been brought to stay the proceedings so far as they concern that matter.

(2) An application may be made notwithstanding that the matter is to be referred to arbitration only after the exhaustion of other dispute resolution procedures.[1371]

(3) An application may not be made by a person before taking the appropriate procedural step (if any) to acknowledge the legal proceedings against him or after he has taken any step in those proceedings to answer the substantive claim.

(4) On an application under this section the court shall grant a stay unless satisfied that the arbitration agreement is null and void, inoperative or incapable of being performed."[1372]

It has already been seen that an arbitration agreement will not cease to apply by reason of the invalidity of the agreement of which it forms part.[1373] It follows that cases in which the condition specified in subsection (4) can be satisfied will be rare,[1374] particularly given the court's power to appoint an arbitrator if there is no machinery in the arbitration agreement or if the prescribed machinery for whatever reason does not result in an appointment.[1375]

If there is a genuine doubt as to whether an arbitration agreement has been concluded, a stay cannot be ordered under the section but only under the court's inherent jurisdiction[1376]

10–275

It follows that, where the proceedings relate to a genuine dispute within the ambit of the agreement,[1377] the court *must* order that they are stayed on the

---

[1370] It goes almost without saying that a stay cannot be ordered against a person who is not a party to the arbitration agreement (or a person claiming through or under such a party: see the Arbitration Act 1996, s.82(2)): *Mayor and Commonalty & Citizens of London v. Sancheti* [2009] 1 Lloyd's Rep 117 (CA).

[1371] As to this subsection, see *Holloway v. Chancery Mead Ltd.* [2008] 1 All E.R. (Comm) 653 at [30] *per* Ramsey J.

[1372] The remaining subsection deals with the effect of conditions precedent to the issue of proceedings and is noted *supra*, para. 10–273.

[1373] See *supra*, para. 10–270.

[1374] See, for example, *Star Shipping A.S. v. China National Foreign Trade Transportation Corp.* [1993] 2 Lloyd's Rep. 445 (CA), a decision under the Arbitration Act 1975, s.1. *cf. E.J.R. Lovelock Ltd. v. Exportles* [1968] 1 Lloyd's Rep. 163 (CA); *Bruce v. Kordula*, 2001 S.L.T. 983 (OH). As to the options open to the court when faced with an argument as to the existence of an arbitration agreement, see *Birse Construction Ltd. v. St David Ltd.* [1999] B.L.R. 194, 196 *per* H.H. Judge Humphrey Lloyd (albeit that his actual decision was reversed on appeal). This decision was considered in *Al-Naimi v. Islamic Press Agency Inc* [2000] 1 Lloyd's Rep 522 (CA); see also *Law Debenture Trust Corp v. Elektrim Finance BV* [2005] 2 All E.R. (Comm.) 476.

[1375] Arbitration Act 1996. s.18. This power takes effect subject to any agreement between the parties. Note also the terms of *ibid.* s.17, in the case of default on the part of one party to appoint an arbitrator. And note, in this context, *Mylcrist Builders Ltd. v. Buck* [2009] 2 All E.R. (Comm) 259, where *ibid.* s.17 was held not to apply.

[1376] *Albon v. Naza Motor Trading Sdn Bhd (No.3)* [2007] 2 All E.R. (Comm) 513. See also *infra*, para. 10–276.

[1377] *i.e.*, in effect, any claim which is not admitted or discharged, irrespective of the validity or otherwise of any defence sought to be raised: *Halki Shipping Corp. v. Sopex Oils Ltd.* [1998] 1 W.L.R. 726 (CA); also *Collins (Contractors) Ltd. v. Baltic Quay Management (1994) Ltd.* [2005] B.L.R. 63 (CA); *Exfin Shipping (India) Ltd. Mumbai v. Tolani Shipping Co. Ltd. Mumbai* [2006] 2 Lloyd's Rep 389 (where an admitted sum was due but had not been paid). And note the exceptional decision in *Law Debenture Trust Corp v. Elektrim Finance BV* [2005] 2 All E.R. (Comm) 476. This will include the issue of whether the arbitration agreement is time barred, but this must not be allowed prejudice a party's right to seek an order of the court extending time under the Arbitration Act 1996, s.12: *Grimaldi Compagnia di Navigazione SpA v. Sekihyo Lines Ltd.* [1999] 1 W.L.R. 708.

application of any defendant who is a party to the agreement,[1378] unless he has already taken a step in the proceedings.[1379] Cases decided under the former Arbitration Acts as to the type of dispute more suited to be determined by the court[1380] can no longer be regarded as good law and should be ignored. If court proceedings are already on foot and one party seeks to introduce an *additional* claim by amendment, it will be necessary to scrutinise the nature of the original claims to see whether that additional claim ought properly to be referred to arbitration at the insistence of that party. Thus, where the issue of a partner's misconduct and its implications was already raised in and central to the proceedings, it was held that a subsequent purported expulsion or dissolution arising out of the same facts ought properly to be heard by the court seised of those original issues.[1381] Equally, if, once the arbitration is under way, a party issues court proceedings but excludes from their ambit claims which must be determined by arbitration, that will, predictably, not in itself amount to a repudiation of the arbitration agreement.[1382]

Where an action is stayed under section 9, an order for indemnity costs should now follow, almost as a matter of course, subject to the applicant demonstrating that the breach of the arbitration agreement caused him to incur those costs,[1383] although the court naturally retains an overriding discretion in the matter. Equally, the court may penalise a party in costs if he fails to raise the need to arbitrate the dispute at an early stage.[1384]

10–276   In addition to the statutory power, the court has an *inherent* power to stay proceedings brought in breach of an agreement to resolve disputes in a particular way, whether by arbitration or otherwise.[1385] In some instances, this jurisdiction will be exercised in a common sense manner in order to facilitate the resolution of all issues between the parties, *e.g.* where there is some doubt as to the

[1378] It is clear from the terms of s.9(1) that the application may not be made by a person who is *not* a party to the arbitration agreement; *cf.* the position under the Arbitration Act 1950. The proceedings will, of course, only be stayed as between the parties to the agreement. As to who are to be regarded as such parties, see *supra*, para. 10–271.

[1379] Arbitration Act 1996, s.9(3), *supra*, para. 10–274. In *Patel v. Patel* [2000] Q.B. 551 (CA), it was held that a defendant who had applied for a default judgment to be set aside, for leave to defend and counterclaim and consequential directions, had not taken a step in the proceedings and a stay was consequently ordered. An application for summary judgment will be similarly regarded: *Capital Trust Investments Ltd. v. Radio Design TJ AB* [2001] 3 All E.R. 756 (an appeal being dismissed at [2002] 2 All E.R. 159). Note also *Delta Reclamation Ltd. v. Premier Waste Management Ltd.* [2008] EWHC 2579 (QB) (Lawtel 13/11/08); *Bilta (UK) Ltd. v. Nazir* [2010] 2 Lloyd's Rep. 29.

[1380] *e.g.* in cases involving fraud or dishonesty (*Russell v. Russell* (1880) 14 Ch.D. 471; *Radford v. Hair* [1971] Ch. 758); professional incompetence (*Turner v. Fenton* [1982] 1 W.L.R. 52); or pure questions of law (*Barnes v. Youngs* [1898] 1 Ch. 414; *Turner v. Fenton, supra*). See further the 17th ed. of this work at para. 10–231. As to questions involving a dissolution under the Partnership Act 1890, s.35, see *supra*, para. 10–272. Note that there is no longer any power for the court to revoke an arbitrator's authority in cases involving fraud: *cf.* the Arbitration Act 1950, s.24(2), (3).

[1381] *Ahad v. Uddin, The Times,* June 30, 2005 (CA).

[1382] *BEA Hotels NV v. Bellway LLC* [2007] 1 C.L.C. 920.

[1383] *A v. B (No.2)* [2007] 1 All E.R. (Comm) 633; also *National Westminster Bank plc v. Radobank Nederland (No. 3)* [2008] 1 All E.R. (Comm) 266 at [31] *et seq. per* Sir Anthony Colman.

[1384] *Bovis Homes Ltd. v. Kendrick Construction Ltd.* [2009] T.C.L.R. 8 (a decision in relation to the pre-action protocol for construction and engineering disputes).

[1385] See *Channel Tunnel Group Ltd. v. Balfour Beatty Construction Ltd.* [1993] A.C. 334 (HL); *Cott (U.K.) Ltd. v. F.E. Barber Ltd.* [1997] 3 All E.R. 540. Note, however, that the alternative method of dispute resolution must be specified and, seemingly, be of a determinative nature: *Halifax Financial Services Ltd. v. Intuitive Systems Ltd.* [1999] 1 All E.R. (Comm.) 303. *cf.* the position under the CPR, r. 26.4. If the applicant *could* have sought a stay under the Arbitration Act 1996, s.9 but has chosen not to do so, it seems that the court will decline to exercise its inherent jurisdiction: *British Telecommunications plc v. SAE Group Inc.* [2009] B.L.R. 231.

existence of a valid arbitration agreement or where an arbitration is inevitable on some issues and a stay will ensure that the arbitrator can decide all the real issues between the parties.[1386] Alternatively, the court will, in an appropriate case, order that part of the claim be stayed and continue to deal with the remainder.[1387]

If the proceedings are not stayed, any award made after their commencement will be invalid, unless the parties have subsequently agreed to proceed with the arbitration.[1388] Conversely, the power of an arbitrator, once appointed, generally cannot be revoked otherwise than with the agreement of the parties[1389] or, in certain circumstances, by an order of the court.[1390]

If arbitration proceedings prove abortive, the court will in any event entertain an action and decide the question in dispute.[1391]

Injunction to restrain or in aid of arbitration

The court will, in an appropriate case, grant an injunction to restrain a party **10–277** from referring a dispute to arbitration.[1392] Thus, in *Albon v. Naza Motor Trading Sdn Bhd (No. 4)*[1393] the court granted an interim injunction in circumstances where the agreement containing the arbitration clause was said to be a forgery.

An anti-suit injunction against proceedings being commenced or continued in another country may be granted in aid of an arbitration,[1394] but will not be

---

[1386] *Al-Naimi v. Islamic Press Agency Inc.* [2000] 1 Lloyds' Rep. 522 (CA); see also *Reichold Norway ASA v. Goldman Sachs International* [2000] 1 W.L.R. 173; *T and N Ltd. v. Royal and Sun Alliance Plc* [2002] C.L.C. 1342; *El Nasharty v. J Sainsbury Plc* [2004] 1 Lloyd's Rep. 309; *Law Debenture Trust Corp v. Elektrim Finance BV* [2005] 2 All E.R. (Comm) 476. *cf. X Ltd. v. Y Ltd.* [2005] B.L.R. 341.

[1387] *Phoenix v. Pope* [1974] 1 W.L.R. 719, 727 *per* Goff J.; also *Belfield v. Bourne* [1894] 1 Ch. 521, 524 *per* Stirling J. (both decisions concerning claims for the appointment of a receiver). There is, of course, no doubt as to the court's power to grant such relief in support of an arbitration under the Arbitration Act 1996, s.44(2)(e).

[1388] *Doleman & Sons v. Ossett Corp.* [1912] 3 K.B. 257. However, the commencement of an action will seemingly not *per se* extinguish the arbitration proceedings: *Lloyd v. Wright* [1983] Q.B. 1065.

[1389] Arbitration Act 1996, s.23.

[1390] *ibid.* ss.23(5), 18, 24.

[1391] *Hamlyn & Co. v. Talisker Distillery* [1894] A.C. 202, 211 *per* Lord Watson; *Cameron v. Cuddy* [1914] A.C. 651. Note that, in the absence of a contrary agreement, the arbitrator has power to dismiss an arbitration for want of prosecution: Arbitration Act 1996, s.41(2), (3). As to repudiation of an arbitration agreement, see *Bremer Vulkan Schiffbau und Maschinenfabrik v. South India Shipping Corporation Ltd.* [1981] A.C. 909; *Rederi Kommanditselskaabet Merc-Scandia IV v. Couniniotis S.A. (The "Merchanaut")* [1980] 2 Lloyd's Rep. 183. *Semble*, an arbitration agreement can never be frustrated merely by reason of delay or inactivity, unless one party has acted to his detriment: see *Paal Wilson & Co. A/S v. Partenreederei Hannah Blumenhal* [1983] A.C. 854; also *Andre et Compagnie SA v. Marine Transocean Ltd.* [1981] Q.B. 694; *Allied Marine Transport Ltd. v. Vale Do Rio Doce Navegacao SA* [1985] 1 W.L.R. 925.

[1392] See, generally, *Russell on Arbitration* (23rd ed.), para. 7–058 *et seq. Quaere*, is the decision in *Farrar v. Cooper* (1890) 44 Ch.D. 323 (injunction to restrain futile arbitration) still good law in the face of the provisions of the Arbitration Act 1996? It is thought not.

[1393] [2008] 1 All E.R. (Comm) 351 (CA).

[1394] See *Russell on Arbitration* (23rd ed.), para. 7–011. Note, however, that the court's power is circumscribed by the provisions of the Arbitration Act 1996, s.44: see, for example, *Starlight Shipping Co. v. Tai Ping Insurance Co. Ltd.* [2008] 1 All E.R. (Comm) 593; *Sheffield United Football Club Ltd. v. West Ham United Football Club plc* [2009] 1 Lloyd's Rep. 167. Damages are not an adequate remedy in such a case: *ibid.* It is unlikely that a stay application will be entertained at the suit of a party facing an application for such an injunction: see *Sheffield United Football Club Ltd. v. West Ham United Football Club plc, supra,* at [40] *per* Teare J.

permissible where that would oust the foreign court's ability to rule on its own jurisdiction under EC Council Regulation 44/2001.[1395]

Interim remedies

10–278 Unless otherwise agreed by the parties, the court has power to make various interim orders in relation to an arbitration,[1396] but only so far as the arbitrator himself does not have or cannot exercise the relevant power.[1397] It should, however, be noted that, save in a case of urgency, these powers will only be exercisable with the permission of the arbitrator or of all the other parties to the arbitration,[1398] and this represents a substantive and very real fetter on the court's power to intervene.[1399]

In *Vertex Data Science Ltd. v. Powergen Retail Ltd.*,[1400] the parties had excluded the arbitrator's power to grant injunctive relief but it was held that this did not exclude the court's power to grant such relief, even though this attributed to the parties an intention which was, in the words of Tomlinson J.,[1401] not "entirely sensible".

Powers of arbitrator

10–279 The extent of the arbitrator's powers will primarily depend on the terms of the arbitration clause.[1402] Provided that it is in a wide form covering all disputes and differences between the partners, the arbitrator will in general be able to deal with the following matters (which are, for convenience, arranged in alphabetical order).

Accounts: The arbitrator can take an account as between the partners.[1403]

[1395] *West Tankers Inc. v. Riunione Adriatica di Sicurtà SpA* [2009] A.C. 1138 (ECJ). *cf. Shashoua v. Sharma* [2009] 2 All E.R. (Comm) 477, where Regulation 44/2001 did not apply.

[1396] Arbitration Act 1996, s.44(1), (2). Such orders may, *inter alia*, relate to the preservation of evidence or property, the grant of an interim injunction or the appointment of a receiver. As to ordering the attendance of witnesses, see *ibid.* s.43 and *BNP Paribas v. Deloitte & Touche LLP* [2004] 1 Lloyd's Rep. 233. See also, as to orders for disclosure of documents, *Assimina Maritime Ltd. v. Pakistan Shipping Corporation* [2005] 1 All E.R. (Comm) 460. Note that, where the agreement records the ability of the court to grant an interim injunction and to determine all relevant issues for that purpose, it does not follow that the court can grant any relief it wishes, final or otherwise: *Argentia Ltd. v. British Telecommunications plc*, 119 Con L.R. 50. The court does not have jurisdiction to order pre-action disclosure prior to the commencement of an arbitration: *Edo Corp v. Ultra Electronics Ltd.* [2009] Bus. L.R. 1306.

[1397] *ibid.* s.44(5). See also the cases cited *infra*, n. 1402.

[1398] *ibid.* s.44(3), (4).

[1399] See *Cetelem SA v. Roust Holdings Ltd.* [2005] 2 All E.R. (Comm) 203 (CA); *Starlight Shipping Co and Another v Tai Ping Insurance Co Ltd.* [2008] 1 All E.R. (Comm) 593. And note also *Econet Wireless Ltd. v. Vee Networks Ltd.* [2006] 2 Lloyd's Rep. 428.

[1400] [2006] 2 Lloyd's Rep. 591.

[1401] *ibid.* at [35].

[1402] *ibid.* s.48(1); also *Vertex Data Science Ltd. v. Powergen Retail Ltd.* [2006] 2 Lloyd's Rep. 591. There are, however, some limits on the powers and discretions which may be conferred on an arbitrator: see *Home and Overseas Insurance Co. Ltd. v. Mentor Insurance Co. (U.K.) Ltd.* [1990] 1 W.L.R. 153.

[1403] See *Bonnin v. Neame* [1910] 1 Ch. 732 (where it was held that a mortgagee of a partner's share would not be bound by an account taken in the arbitration: see *supra*, para. 10–271); *Wylie v. Corrigan* 1999 S.C. 97.

Actions: The arbitrator can direct one partner to sue in the name of himself and his co-partners, subject to indemnifying them against costs.[1404]

Competition: In certain circumstances, the arbitrator may, in settling the terms on which a partnership is to be dissolved, direct that one partner should not carry on a business in competition with another who has taken over the former partnership business.[1405] However, in the view of the current editor, the ambit of such a power, even if it is exercisable, will be confined within a very narrow compass.[1406]

Conveyances: The arbitrator can order conveyances to be made.[1407]

Declarations: The arbitrator can make a declaration as to any matter raised in the arbitration.[1408]

Dissolution: It has already been seen that an arbitrator may be empowered to dissolve a partnership.[1409]

Injunctions: Although it is now clear that an arbitrator has power to grant injunctive relief,[1410] his ability to grant an interim injunction is more questionable.[1411] In any case, enforcement of an injunction ordered by an arbitrator will ultimately be a matter for the courts.[1412] **10–280**

Payments: The arbitrator can order one partner to pay a sum of money to the other(s).[1413] However, he may seemingly not direct one partner to pay money to himself (*i.e.* the arbitrator), in order that he may apply it in payment of certain specified debts.[1414] However, it should be noted that an arbitrator only has power to make a *provisional* order for the payment of money with the agreement of the parties.[1415]

Premiums: An arbitrator may clearly award the return of a portion of any premium as one of the terms of a dissolution awarded by him.[1416] It is submitted

---

[1404] *Burton v. Wigley* (1835) 1 Bing.N.C. 665; also *Philips v. Knightley* (1731) 2 Str. 902; *Goddard v. Mansfield* (1850) 19 L.J.Q.B. 305.

[1405] *Morley v. Newman* (1824) 5 D. & R. 317. Note also *Burton v. Wigley* (1835) 1 Bing.N.C. 665, where the award permitted a partner to carry on the business, despite a contrary provision in the partnership agreement.

[1406] See *supra*, para. 10–213.

[1407] *Wood v. Wilson* (1835) 2 Cromp., M. & R. 241.

[1408] Arbitration Act 1996, s.48(3).

[1409] See *supra*, para. 10–272.

[1410] Arbitration Act 1996, s.48(5)(a). That power may, however, be excluded by agreement: *Vertex Data Science Ltd. v. Powergen Retail Ltd.* [2006] 2 Lloyd's Rep. 591, but it does not follow that the court's power is similarly limited: see *supra*, para. 10–278.

[1411] See *Russell on Arbitration* (23rd ed.), para. 5–077. The concern stems from the fact that, save where provisional awards are permitted (Arbitration Act 1996, s.39), an award must be made on a final, and not merely interim, basis. The editors of that work speculate that an appropriate order may, nevertheless, be made under *ibid.* s.38.

[1412] See the Arbitration Act 1996, s.66.

[1413] *ibid.* s.48(4).

[1414] *Re Mackay* (1834) 2 A. & E. 356.

[1415] Arbitration Act 1996, s.39(4).

[1416] *Bellfield v. Bourne* [1894] 1 Ch. 521. And see generally, as to the return of premiums, *infra*, paras 25–06 *et seq.*

that such an award may also, in a proper case, be made where the dissolution *precedes* the arbitration.[1417]

Procedural orders: Subject to his overriding duty under section 33 of the Arbitration Act 1996[1418] and to any agreement between the parties, the arbitrator has full discretion as to the manner in which the arbitration will be conducted and the evidence to be adduced before him.[1419] This will include the use of pleadings,[1420] the manner and extent of any disclosure of documents,[1421] the application of the strict rules of evidence[1422] and the need for an attended hearing.[1423] If a party fails to comply with an order of the arbitrator, he may make a peremptory order[1424] which can, ultimately, be enforced by the court.[1425]

10–281 *Rectification*: The arbitrator can order the rectification of the partnership agreement.[1426]

Releases: The arbitrator can direct the partners to execute mutual releases.[1427]

Rights and duties of partners: The arbitrator can determine the existence of a custom affecting the rights and/or duties of the partners which would have effect under section 19 of the Partnership Act 1890.[1428]

Specific performance: The arbitrator can, in an appropriate case, order the specific performance of any contract, other than a contract relating to land.[1429]

Winding up: The arbitrator can apportion the assets between the partners,[1430] place a value on goodwill[1431] and make other consequential orders.[1432] What an

---

[1417] But see *Tattersall v. Groote* (1800) 2 Bos. & Pul. 131, as explained in *Belfield v. Bourne, supra*. The editors of the 7th edition of this work observed that " . . . it is doubtful how far this decision would be followed at the present day."

[1418] *i.e.* to act fairly and impartially between the parties so as to afford each of them the opportunity of putting his case and meeting that of the other party and to adopt suitable procedures to avoid unnecessary delay and expense and a fair means of resolving the issues in the arbitration. Note also the parties' obligations under *ibid*. s.40.

[1419] *ibid*. s.34.

[1420] *ibid*. s.34(2)(c).

[1421] *ibid*. s.34(2)(d).

[1422] *ibid*. s.34(2)(f).

[1423] *ibid*. s.34(2)(e), (g), (h). See, in this context, *O'Donoghue v. Enterprise Inns Plc* [2009] 1 P. & C.R. 14.

[1424] *ibid*. s.41(5).

[1425] *ibid*. s.42. See, as to this power, *Emmott v. Michael Wilson & Partners Ltd.* [2009] 1 Lloyd's Rep. 233.

[1426] *ibid*. s.48(5)(c).

[1427] See *Lingood v. Eade* (1747) 2 Atk. 501, 506 (where the arbitrator directed the form of the releases to be settled by a Chancery Master).

[1428] *Produce Brokers Co. v. Olympia Oil Co.* [1916] 1 A.C. 314 (not a partnership case). As to the operation of s.19, see *supra*, paras 10–12 *et seq*.

[1429] Arbitration Act 1996, s.48(5)(b).

[1430] *Lingood v. Eade* (1747) 2 Atk. 501; *Wood v. Wilson* (1835) 2 Cromp., M. & R. 241; *Wilkinson v. Page* (1842) 1 Hare 276.

[1431] *Re David and Matthews* [1899] 1 Ch. 378. See also *supra*, para. 10–212.

[1432] See Competition, *supra*, para. 10–279.

arbitrator seemingly *cannot* do is appoint a receiver to collect and get in the partnership assets and debts.[1433]

Limitation

The Limitation Act 1980 applies to arbitrations just as it applies to legal proceedings.[1434] For this purpose, any provision in an arbitration agreement that an award is a condition precedent to the bringing of legal proceedings[1435] will be ignored.[1436]   **10–282**

In the case of *contractual* time limits, the court has discretion to extend time in an appropriate case,[1437] but this jurisdiction will be exercised sparingly.[1438]

Costs

Although the general principle under the Arbitration Act 1996 is that costs should follow the event, it is clear that, subject to the terms of the arbitration agreement,[1439] the arbitrator will have a wide discretion in relation to the costs of the reference and award[1440] and it should not be assumed that such discretion will necessarily be exercised according to the principles set out in the Civil Procedure Rules.[1441] Although submissions on costs are normally made *before* the award is published,[1442] it is not uncommon for an interim award to be delivered on the factual/legal issues in the arbitration, thus leaving the question of costs to be dealt with thereafter.[1443] This is, in fact, the usual practice in partnership cases.   **10–283**

Interest on awards

Subject to any agreement between the parties, the arbitrator has discretion as to whether and, if so, on what terms to make an award of interest.[1444] If that   **10–284**

[1433] *Lingood v. Eade* (1747) 2 Atk. 501; *Re Mackay* (1834) 2 A. & E. 356; *Cook v. Catchpole* (1864) 10 Jur.(N.S.) 1068. But a receiver was appointed in *Routh v. Peach* (1795) 2 Anst. 519 and 3 Anst. 637. See also the obscure observation in Roxburgh J. in *Olver v. Hillier* [1959] 1 W.L.R. 551, 554. Of course, the court can appoint a receiver under the Arbitration Act 1996, s.44(2)(e): see *supra*, para. 10–278.

[1434] Arbitration Act 1996, s.13(1).

[1435] See *supra*, para. 10–273.

[1436] Arbitration Act 1996, s.13(3).

[1437] *ibid.* s.12(1), (3).

[1438] See, for example, *Harbour and General Works Ltd. v. Environment Agency* [1999] All E.R. (Comm) 953 (albeit a case under a standard form contract).

[1439] *Mansfield v. Robinson* [1928] 2 K.B. 353.

[1440] Arbitration Act 1996, s.61(2). It is by no means clear that the discretion must be exercised judicially: see *Russell on Arbitration* (23rd ed.) at para. 6–137. *cf.* the position prior to the 1996 Act: *Smeaton Hanscomb & Co. v. Sassoon I. Setty, Son & Co. (No. 2)* [1953] 1 W.L.R. 1481; *Stotesbury v. Turner* [1943] K.B. 370; *Everglade Maritime Inc. v. Schiffahrtsgesellschaft Detlef Von Appel m.b.H.* [1993] 1 W.L.R. 33.

[1441] See, in particular, CPR, Part 44.3(4), (5).

[1442] *Harrison v. Thompson* [1989] 1 W.L.R. 1325.

[1443] Note that in *King v. Thomas McKenna Ltd.* [1991] Q.B. 480, the failure of one party's counsel to request the arbitrator to defer consideration of costs was treated as a sufficient "procedural mishap" to warrant remission of the award on costs pursuant to the (then) Arbitration Act 1950, s.22(1) (see now the Arbitration Act 1996, ss.68(3)(a), 69(7)(c)).

[1444] Arbitration Act 1996, s.49. Interest may be awarded on any sum claimed in the arbitration which is paid *before* the date of the award: *ibid.* s.49(3)(b). When the arbitrator awards interest at a particular rate, he must normally explain why he has adopted that rate, in fairness to the parties: *Van der Giessen-de-Noord Shipbuilding Division BV v. Imtech Marine & Offshore BV* [2009] 1 Lloyd's Rep. 273. Note that, under the Arbitration Act 1950, s.20, an award *automatically* carried interest at the judgment rate.

discretion is not exercised, the court cannot itself order the payment of interest under its statutory powers.[1445]

Appeals

10–285   An appeal against an arbitration award may only be brought on a question of law[1446]; no appeal lies on a pure question of fact.[1447] Even that limited right of appeal may be excluded by agreement.[1448] Before an appeal will be entertained the consent of all parties[1449] or the leave of the court must be obtained[1450] and leave will only be forthcoming if the court is satisfied that the appeal will substantially affect the rights of one or more of the parties, that the question of law was one which the arbitrator was asked to determine[1451] and that the award was, on the basis of the facts as found, obviously wrong[1452] or open to serious doubt and (in the latter case only) the question is of general public importance *and* if it would otherwise be just and proper for that question to be determined.[1453] Appeals to the Court of Appeal are generally prohibited, save in exceptional cases.[1454]

(b) Alternative Dispute Resolution[1455]

10–286   The introduction of so-called "alternative dispute resolution" techniques[1456] has provided a realistic and, in the current editor's view, valuable alternative to the traditional arbitration route in the case of partnership disputes.[1457] Although some agreements now provide for the parties to a dispute to attempt to resolve it by ADR *before* embarking on an arbitration, such clauses have not yet obtained general acceptance and may, in practice, be used as a device to delay an arbitration in cases which have little or no prospect of a satisfactory mediated

---

[1445] *Walker v. Rowe* [2000] 1 Lloyd's Rep. 116.

[1446] Arbitration Act 1996, s.69(1).

[1447] See *Geogas SA v. Trammo Gas Ltd.* [1993] 1 Lloyd's Rep. 215, 228 (CA); also *Demco Investments & Commercial SA v. SE Banken Forsakring Holding Aktiebolag* [2005] Lloyd's Rep. 650; *Surefire Systems Ltd. v. Guardian ECL Ltd.* [2005] B.L.R. 534. Note that, where the arbitrator has failed to deal with all the issues before him, it may be possible to challenge the award for serious irregularity: Arbitration Act 1996, s.68(2)(d).

[1448] *ibid.* s.69(1). The agreement excluding the right of appeal may, in appropriate circumstances, merely be incorporated by reference: *Arab African Energy Corp. Ltd. v. Olie Produkten Nederland B.V.* [1983] 2 Lloyd's Rep. 419; *Sukuman Ltd. v. Commonwealth Secretariat* [2006] 1 All E.R. (Comm) 621. Note also *Essex County Council v. Premier Recycling Ltd.* [2007] B.L.R. 2333, where the alleged agreement was ambiguous.

[1449] As to what will amount to prospective consent, see *Royal & Sun Alliance Insurance plc v. BAE Systems (Operations) Ltd.* [2008] 1 Lloyd's Rep. 712.

[1450] *ibid.* s.69(2). Note that there are limited circumstances in which a refusal of permission to appeal by the court may itself be appealed: *CGU International Insurance plc v. Astrazenica Insurance Co. Ltd.* [2007] 1 All E.R. 501 (CA).

[1451] If the position is otherwise, an application should be made under *ibid.* s.67.

[1452] This may be difficult when a question of construction is involved: see, for example, *Stern Settlement Trustees v. Levy*, 113 Con. L.R. 92.

[1453] *ibid.* s.69(3). See generally, as to these requirements, *CMA CGM SA v. Beteiligungs-KG MS "Northern Pioneer" Schiffahrtsgesellschaft mbH & Co* [2003] 1 W.L.R. 1015 (CA); *London Underground Ltd. v. Citylink Telecommunications Ltd. (Note)* [2007] 2 All E.R. (Comm) 694.

[1454] *ibid.* s.69(8).

[1455] See the *Encyclopedia of Professional Partnerships*, Precedent 1, cl. 26 (second variation).

[1456] *i.e.* conciliation, mediation and the "mini-trial" or "executive tribunal".

[1457] The value of ADR in a partnership context was analysed by the current editor in an article entitled "Dispute, what dispute" at (1991) 135 S.J. 768.

settlement. In any event, even in the absence of such a clause, ADR can be set up on an *ad hoc* basis prior to or alongside a reference to arbitration.

The court now has power to grant a temporary stay of proceedings with a view to the parties engaging in ADR,[1458] and may even, in an appropriate case, order the parties to mediate their dispute.[1459] In the case of an agreement which provides for ADR, the court could exercise its inherent jurisdiction to order a stay,[1460] but would only be likely to do so if the ADR process will be of a determinative nature.[1461] It would seem that no such difficulty will arise if the agreement provides for an ADR process and, in default of a successful outcome, arbitration.

Z.   PENALTIES AND LIQUIDATED DAMAGES

Lord Lindley wrote: **10–287**

> "The last clause in a partnership deed is often one by which each partner binds himself to pay, either by way of penalty or by way of liquidated damages, a certain sum in case of the infringement by him of any agreement contained in the previous clauses."[1462]

As already noted,[1463] such clauses are now relatively rare. Since they do not involve any considerations peculiar to the law of partnership, they are not further considered in this work.[1464]

[1458] CPR, r. 26.4. A party's refusal to mediate may, ultimately, be penalised in costs, but this is now something of a rarity: see *Halsey v. Milton Keynes General NHS Trust* [2004] 1 W.L.R. 3002 (CA); *Hickman v. Blake Lapthorn* [2006] 3 Costs L.R. 452; *Wethered Estate Ltd. v. Davis* [2006] B.L.R. 86; *cf. P4 Ltd. v. Unite Integrated Solutions plc* [2007] B.L.R. 1. And see, as to a party adopting an unreasonable stance in a mediation, *Earl of Malmesbury v. Strutt & Parker*, 118 Con. L.R. 68.

[1459] See *Shirayama Shokusan Co Ltd. v. Danovo Ltd.* [2004] B.L.R. 207.

[1460] See *Channel Tunnel Group Ltd. v. Balfour Beatty Construction Ltd.* [1993] A.C. 334 (HL); *Cable & Wireless Plc v. IBM United Kingdom Ltd.* [2002] 2 All E.R. (Comm) 1041.

[1461] *Halifax Financial Services Ltd. v. Intuitive Systems Ltd.* [1999] 1 All E.R. (Comm.) 303. In *Balfour Beatty Construction Northern Ltd. v. Modus Corovest (Blackpool) Ltd.* [2008] EWHC 3029 (TCC), a stay was refused on the basis that the mediation clause was a mere agreement to agree.

[1462] The hallmark of a true penalty is the payment of a sum which is extravagant and unconscionable in amount as compared with the prospective loss: *Jeancharm Ltd. v. Barnet Football Club Ltd.* (2003) 92 Con L.R. 26; *Office of Fair Trading v. Abbey National Plc* [2008] 2 All E.R. (Comm) 625. Note that an agreement which provides for a payment to be made *otherwise* than on a breach of its provisions cannot amount to a penalty: see *Export Credits Guarantee Dept. v. Universal Oil Products Co.* [1983] 1 W.L.R. 399; *E.F.T. Commercial Ltd. v. Security Change Ltd. (No. 1)*, 1993 S.L.T. 129 (1st Div.), where the English and Scots authorities are reviewed; also *Office of Fair Trading v. Abbey National Plc, supra*. Moreover, a term which is commercially justifiable is unlikely to be struck down if it was freely negotiated between parties of equal bargaining power and in the absence of oppression, unless its dominant purpose is to deter a party from breaching the agreement: see *M & J Polymers Ltd. v. Imerys Minerals Ltd.* [2008] 1 All E.R. (Comm) 893.

[1463] See *supra*, para. 10–236.

[1464] It would, however, seem that the use of hypothetical situations to invalidate a liquidated damages clause as a penalty will be resisted in commercial contracts: see *Philips Hong Kong Ltd. v. Att.-Gen. of Hong Kong* (1993) 61 B.L.R. 41. And see generally, *Chitty on Contracts* (30th ed.), paras 26–125 *et seq.* And see *supra*, para. 10–236, n. 1143.

4.   LIMITED LIABILITY PARTNERSHIP AGREEMENTS

10–288   Since a limited liability partnership (LLP) is not a partnership but a body corporate,[1465] detailed consideration of the terms properly to be included in an LLP agreement (or members' agreement) is outside the scope of this work. Nevertheless, such an agreement will have much in common with the traditional partnership agreement, although care must be taken to reflect the fact that:

(a)   the business will be carried on by the LLP itself[1466];

(b)   the members will act as agents of the LLP and not of each other[1467];

(c)   the members will not, in general, undertake any personal liability for the debts and obligations of the LLP[1468];

(d)   the members will primarily owe duties to the LLP, even though they may also, as a matter of contract, owe duties to the other members;

(e)   there will be no implied duty of good faith as between the members[1469];

(f)   the Contracts (Rights of Third Parties) Act 1999 does not apply.[1470]

In order to preserve the full benefits of limited liability,[1471] it should be ensured that provisions which contemplate the existence of any form of mutual agency as between the members[1472] or their undertaking personal liability for the LLP's debts or obligations[1473] are eliminated. Although it might be thought that describing members as "partners" should, so far as possible, be avoided, the practice is

---

[1465] Limited Liability Partnerships Act 2000, s.1(2).

[1466] Although the LLP is a separate legal person (*ibid.*) and will, as such, carry on the business, one of the requirements for incorporation is that "two or more persons [*are*] associated for carrying on a lawful business with a view of profit . . . ": *ibid.* s.2(1)(a).

[1467] *ibid.* s.6.

[1468] A member may be liable to contribute towards its assets on a winding up: see *ibid.* s.1(4); the Insolvency Act 1986, s.214A, as added by the Limited Liability Partnerships Regulations 2001 (SI 2001/1090), reg. 5(2)(f), Sched. 3. It is not clear to what extent, if at all, a member responsible for a wrongful act will be personally liable along with the LLP: see the Limited Liability Partnerships Act 2000, s.6(4). *Quaere,* will the court treat a member of the LLP in the same way as a director and, thus, apply the decision in *Williams v. Natural Life Health Foods Ltd.* [1998] 1 W.L.R. 830 (HL) and other cases of that class? See further *supra,* para. 2–39, n. 147.

[1469] The imposition of such an implied duty was expressly rejected by the Department of Trade and Industry during consultations prior to the introduction of LLPs: see the Summary of Responses on the Regulatory Default Provisions Governing Relationship between Members (URN)/865 dated May 2000. The extent of any fiduciary duties owed as between a member and the LLP itself is intended to be governed by the general law. Nevertheless, many LLP agreements do, in practice, include an express duty of good faith, albeit increasingly owed just to the LLP and not as between the members. Nevertheless, even in cases where such an express duty is not imposed, the current editor has encountered the argument that an implied duty between the members should still apply.

[1470] See the Limited Liability Partnerships Regulations 2001, Sched. 5, para. 20.

[1471] The dangers for members of an LLP who continue to act as if they are partners were highlighted by Lord Goldsmith in the House of Lords' debate on December 9, 1999 (*Hansard* 991209-10—Col. 1435).

[1472] *i.e.* thereby replicating the Partnership Act 1890, s.5: see *infra,* paras 12–02 *et seq.*

[1473] This should be distinguished from the case where members agree to contribute to the assets of the LLP on its liquidation: Insolvency Act 1986, s.74 (as substituted by the Limited Liability Partnerships Regulations 2001, reg. 5(2)(f), Sched. 3). See also, as to personal liability, *supra,* n. 1468.

now widespread, with senior employees also often being similary designated.[1474] Such use is, however, usually (and prudently) accompanied by an explanation that such designation does not signify the existence of a partnership in law, since there remains some danger that confusion as to the capacity in which such a "partner" is acting will arise, particularly where a partnership which has transferred part of its business to the LLP is allowed to continue to trade alongside the LLP.[1475] Wholesale importation of partnership principles by reference would involve an unacceptable level of risk.[1476]

It has already been seen that it is difficult to draft a partnership agreement **10–289** which is fully comprehensive and that much is, inevitably, left to be understood.[1477] The same approach cannot properly be taken in the case of an LLP agreement, since there is little in the way of a default body of LLP law to fall back on.[1478] There can be no certainty that the court will apply partnership law by analogy.[1479] Accordingly, the draftsman must ensure that the LLP agreement covers as many eventualities as possible and, if necessary, that it recreates elements of the "partnership ethos"[1480] contractually as between the members. In the interests of long term flexibility, a power to amend the agreement by a majority vote of the members[1481] is to be commended, as is the contractual exclusion of section 994 of the Companies Act 2006.[1482]

Although inclusion of an arbitration clause in an LLP agreement is desirable to cover disputes between members or between members and the LLP, it should not be assumed that such a clause will also cover disputes regarding the winding up of the LLP[1483] or, where it applies, a claim for relief under section 994.[1484] Although certain issues arising in relation to the winding up of an LLP *were*

[1474] See, for example, the guidance issued by the Law Society at (2005) 102 L.S.Gaz., June 16, p.39.

[1475] In such a case, unless great care is taken, it may be difficult to ascertain in which capacity the member/partner is acting and the risk of incurring personal liability will be significant.

[1476] Since much of partnership law is (perhaps erroneously: see *supra*, paras 2–12 *et seq.*) based on an assumption of mutual agency and unlimited personal liability in all cases, it would be difficult to apply particular elements of that law without automatically importing those assumptions.

[1477] See *supra*, para. 10–10.

[1478] See the Limited Liability Partnerships Regulations 2001, regs 7, 8, which contain most of the default regime. Those regulations are based on the Partnership Act 1890, ss.24, 25, 28–30.

[1479] Particularly in the face of the Limited Liability Partnerships Act 1890, s.1(5) which states " . . . except as otherwise provided by this Act or any other enactment, the law relating to partnerships does not apply to a limited liability partnership." There is, however, power to apply elements of partnership law by regulation (*ibid.* s.15(c)), but this power has not been exercised.

[1480] This will often take the form of an express duty of good faith owed as between the members and as between them and the LLP, although the former element is increasingly omitted. Where such a duty is created contractually between the members, it does not follow that a more extensive duty (*e.g.* a fiduciary duty) will easily be implied, unless such a duty would exist in any event (*i.e.* as between the member *qua* agent and the LLP): see *Ross River Ltd. v. Cambridge City Football Club Ltd.* [2008] 1 All E.R. 1004 at [197] *per* Briggs J. (a decision concerning joint venturers).

[1481] See, by way of analogy, *supra*, para. 10–13.

[1482] This section, which deals with unfair prejudice, is applied in an amended form by the Limited Liability Partnerships (Application of Companies Act 2006) Regulations 2009 (SI 2009/1804), reg. 48, but may be excluded by *unanimous* agreement of the members "either indefinitely or for such period as is specified in the agreement", which must be recorded in writing: s.994(3).

[1483] *A Best Floor Sanding Party Ltd. v Skyer Australia Party Ltd.* [1999] V.S.C. 170, followed (albeit on an *obiter* basis) in *Exeter City AFC Ltd. v. Football Conference Ltd.* [2004] 1 W.L.R. 2910 (both decisions concering companies). And note also *Best Beat Ltd. v. Rossall* [2006] B.P.I.R. 1357.

[1484] *Exeter City AFC Ltd. v. Football Conference Ltd.*, *supra*, in which H.H. Judge Weeks Q.C. (sitting as a judge of the Chancery Division) declined to follow *Re Vocam Europe Ltd.* [1998] B.C.C. 396 (again a decision concerning a company).

referred to arbitration in *Re Magi Capital Partners LLP*,[1485] this was a matter of case management of the proceedings and is not authority for any wider proposition.[1486]

5.   OTHER PARTNERSHIP DOCUMENTATION

10–290   Of the other forms of partnership documentation likely to be encountered, the most important are:

    (a) deeds of accession;

    (b) retirement deeds;

    (c) merger agreements; and

    (d) dissolution agreements.

Deeds of accession

10–291   Deeds of accession have become less popular with the advent of the signing schedule,[1487] but are still common. They amount to no more than an affirmation of the application of the main partnership agreement as between the existing partners and an incoming partner,[1488] although they may also be used to record changes in the firm since the last such deed. All partners should be parties to (and execute) the deed if it is to take effect as such[1489]; if an agreement under hand will suffice, then one partner may sign it as agent for the other partners, provided that he has their authority so to do.[1490] Even if he does not, by signing up to the deed of accession rights may have been conferred on the other partners without the need for them to rely on the Contracts (Rights of Third Parties) Act 1999.[1491]

Retirement deeds

10–292   Where the partnership agreement contains detailed provisions governing the consequences of a partner's retirement,[1492] a retirement deed[1493] will be unnecessary unless those terms are to be varied. The deed may contain a complete set of

---

[1485] [2003] EWHC 2790 (Ch), also a decision of H.H. Judge Weeks Q.C. sitting as a judge of the Chancery Division.

[1486] See *Exeter City AFC Ltd. v. Football Conference Ltd.*, *supra*, at [24]. The reference to a limited partnership is clearly erroneous: see *ibid.* at [22].

[1487] See *supra*, paras 10–32, 10–256.

[1488] In the absence of such an affirmation, a partnership at will may be created: *ibid.*

[1489] See *supra*, para. 10–31. As to the execution of deeds on behalf of partners, see *infra*, paras 12–62, 12–157 *et seq.* In such cases, a suitable power of attorney of the type discussed *supra*, para. 10–97 may be of assistance.

[1490] Such authority may again be conferred by a suitable power of attorney.

[1491] See *Clarke v. The Earl of Dunraven and Mount-Earl* [1897] A.C. 59 (HL), which concerned accession to a yacht club's sailing rules; also *General Accident Fire and Life Assurance Corp. Ltd. v. Tanter* [1984] 1 Lloyd's Rep. 58 at p. 72 *per* Hobhouse J.; *Maple Leaf Macro Volatility Fund v. Rouvroy* [2009] 2 All E.R. (Comm) 287.

[1492] See *supra*, paras 10–150 *et seq.* Identical considerations arise in relation to a partner's compulsory retirement or expulsion.

[1493] Although conventionally executed as a deed, it may be that an agreement under hand will suffice: see generally *supra*, para. 10–31.

retirement provisions which will have effect in substitution for the provisions in the agreement or it may merely vary certain of those provisions, leaving the balance of the agreement to apply in the normal way.

Where there is no partnership agreement, the retirement deed should provide for the retirement of the outgoing partner and the continuation of the partnership as between the remaining partners,[1494] and deal with the various consequential provisions discussed earlier in this chapter.[1495]

Merger agreements

These are of such a diverse nature that little can usefully be said about their content. The primary focus of the draftsman will normally be: (a) to identify the property which each firm will introduce into the merged firm, whether in terms of tangible assets (leases, equipment, etc.) or intangible assets (goodwill, work in progress) and at what values; (b) the harmonisation of the former firms' accounting practices and (c) the treatment of existing and future liabilities.[1496] Extensive warranties will usually be exchanged, notwithstanding the inevitable "due diligence" exercise which each firm will have undertaken. **10–293**

One of the other principal ingredients will be to establish the terms of the partnership agreement which will govern the merged firm, whether it be the agreement currently applying to one of the constituent firms or a wholly new agreement. The form of the agreement may well be annexed to the merger agreement itself.

Dissolution agreements

As in the case of a retirement agreement, a dissolution agreement[1497] will tend to be entered into on an *ad hoc* basis and the terms will reflect whatever agreement has been reached between the partners. Such an agreement may still be useful where the partnership is dissolved under an express power,[1498] although much will depend on the terms of the partnership agreement.[1499] **10–294**

First and foremost the agreement will establish, or recite, the date of the dissolution and will then deal with various aspects of the winding up of its affairs. These may include the division of assets *in specie*, the authority of the former partners and, perhaps, the constitution of a dissolution committee.[1500]

[1494] This mirrors the normal provision to be found in a partnership agreement: see *supra*, para. 10–39.

[1495] *i.e.* the outgoing partner's financial entitlement (see *supra*, paras 10–150 *et seq.*), restrictions on competition (see *supra*, paras 10–218 *et seq.*) and other consequential provisions (see *supra*, paras 10–244 *et seq.*).

[1496] See *infra*, paras 13–22 *et seq.*

[1497] In an appropriate case, the agreement should be executed under seal: see *supra*, para. 10–31.

[1498] See *supra*, paras 10–137 *et seq.*

[1499] See *supra*, paras 10–264 *et seq.*

[1500] See *supra*, para. 10–269.

Chapter 11

CORPORATE AND GROUP PARTNERSHIPS

Although not conceptually different from any other form of partnership, the **11–01** corporate and the group partnership are two distinct sub-species which are encountered in the commercial field.[1]

1.   THE CORPORATE PARTNERSHIP

Nature and formation

The expression "corporate partnership" usually denotes a partnership all the **11–02** members of which are companies, whether limited or unlimited, but is occasionally used loosely to refer to any partnership which has one or more corporate members. The existence of both types of corporate partnership is clearly recognised by statute[2] and by the courts.[3] It remains to be seen whether, with the advent of the limited liability partnership (which, despite its name, is itself a body corporate),[4] the expression will also be applied to partnerships comprising one or more LLPs.[5]

No special statutory provisions govern such partnerships and the Partnership **11–03** Act 1890 will apply in the normal way, save to the extent that its provisions are excluded by agreement.[6] The company's constitution will no longer represent a limiting factor, now that the *ultra vires* doctrine has been swept away.[7]

---

[1] Note that the incorporation of solicitors' practices is now permitted: see the Administration of Justice Act 1985, s.9 (as amended by the Legal Services Act 2007, Sched. 16, Pt. 2, para. 81), the Solicitors' Code of Conduct 2007, rr. 12, 14 (as amended) and the SRA Recognised Bodies Regulations 2009. However, whilst the Solicitors' Code of Conduct, r. 14.04(1)(f) clearly contemplates that a firm might consist of one or more "recognised bodies", such partnerships are, in practice, likely to be a rarity (although the current editor has seen a solicitors' partnership consisting only of companies, each controlled by an individual "partner"). The position in the accountancy profession is no different.

[2] See, for example, the Insolvent Partnerships Order 1994 (SI 1994/2421), arts 8(4), (8), 10(2), (6) (as amended), considered *infra*, paras 27–24 *et seq.*; the Partnerships (Accounts) Regulations 2008 (SI 2008/569), considered *infra*, para. 11–13; the Corporation Tax Act 2009, ss.80(2), 162(3), 1259(1), considered *infra*, paras 34–55 *et seq.*

[3] See, for example, *Re Rudd & Son Ltd.* [1984] Ch. 237; *Pinkney v. Sandpiper Drilling Ltd.* [1989] I.C.R. 389 (partnerships between companies); *Newstead v. Frost* [1980] 1 W.L.R. 135; *Scher v. Policyholders Protection Board* [1994] 2 A.C. 57 (partnerships between companies and individuals).

[4] Limited Liability Partnerships Act 2000, s.1(2). See, generally, *supra*, paras 2–39 *et seq.*

[5] As a body corporate there is, of course, nothing to prevent an LLP from becoming a member of a partnership.

[6] Partnership Act 1890, s.19, *supra*, para. 10–12.

[7] See *supra*, para. 4–20.

Partnerships between "one man companies"

11–04   There is no reason why a valid partnership should not exist between two companies owned and controlled by a single person,[8] since each will enjoy a distinct legal personality.[9] Indeed, the formation of partnerships between members of the same group of companies is by no means unusual. Although it might be thought possible to constitute such a partnership on terms that, if a winding up petition is presented or order made against one corporate partner, the partnership can be terminated, whereupon the insolvent partner's share will automatically accrue to the continuing partner(s), this would risk invalidity as a fraud on the insolvency laws, unless full value were paid on the accruer.[10] Such an approach might also be subject to attack under various sections of the Insolvency Act 1986.[11]

Partnership between a "one man company" and its owner

11–05   Equally, there is, in principle, no reason why a valid partnership should not be created between a "one man" company and its sole or controlling shareholder/director, although the court may, inevitably, be less willing to *infer* the existence of a partnership from their dealings.[12]

Advantages

11–06   In its full form, the corporate partnership, as well as providing a vehicle for two or more companies to pursue a particular business objective,[13] can offer

[8] See, as to single member companies, the Companies Act 2006, s.123.

[9] See *Salomon v. Salomon & Co.* [1897] A.C. 22; *Lee v. Lees Air Farming* [1961] A.C. 12; *Woolfson v. Strathclyde Regional Council* (1978) 38 P. & C.R. 521; *Adams v. Cape Industries Plc* [1990] Ch. 433; *Ord v. Bellhaven Pubs Ltd.* [1998] B.C.C. 607; *Trustor AB v. Smallbone (No. 2)* [2001] 1 W.L.R. 1177; *Ben Hashem v. Ali Shayif* [2009] 1 F.L.R. 115; *Secretary of State for Business, Enterprise and Regulatory Reform v. Neufeld* [2009] I.R.L.R. 475 (CA).

[10] See *Perpetual Trustee Co. Ltd. v. BNY Corporate Trustee Services Ltd.* [2010] 3 W.L.R. 87 (CA), where all the authorities were reviewed by the court. See also *supra*, paras 10–152, 10–153.

[11] See the Insolvency Act 1986, s.423, which entitles the court to set aside transactions intended to defraud the company's creditors. Note that a commercial justification alone is not sufficient to avoid the application of this section: *Arbuthnot Leasing International Ltd. v. Havelet Leasing Ltd. (No. 2)* [1990] B.C.C. 636; also *Chohman v. Saggar* [1992] B.C.C. 306; *Re Brabon* [2001] 1 B.C.L.C. 11; *I.R.C. v. Hashmi* [2002] 2 B.C.L.C. 489 (CA); *Hill v. Spread Trustee Co. Ltd.* [2007] 1 W.L.R. 2404 (CA); *Department for the Environment, Food and Rural Affairs v. Feakins* [2007] B.C.C. 54 (CA); *Barnett v. Semenyuk* [2008] B.P.I.R. 1427. See also *ibid.* s.238 (as amended by the Enterprise Act 2002, Sched. 17, paras 9, 25), under which the court may set aside (*inter alia*) any transaction "on terms that provide for the company to receive no consideration" (see *ibid.* s.238(4)(a)) or "for a consideration the value of which, in money or money's worth, is significantly less than the value, in money or money's worth, of the consideration provided by the company" (*ibid.* s.238(4)(b)) unless: (i) the company entered into the transaction in good faith and for the purposes of carrying on its business and (ii) there were at the time reasonable grounds for believing that the transaction would benefit the company (see *ibid.* s.238(5)). However, unlike the position under *ibid.* s.423, this power is only exercisable in respect of transactions entered into within two years of the commencement of the winding up: *ibid.* s.240 (as amended by the Enterprise Act 2002, Sched. 17, paras 9, 26, Sched. 26). *Semble, ibid.* s.127 would not apply in such case: see *infra*, para. 27–71.

[12] See *Secretary of State for Business, Enterprise and Regulatory Reform v Neufeld* [2009] I.R.L.R. 475, where the Court of Appeal reviewed the authorities and held that a controlling director and sole shareholder of a company may, on a true analysis, be its employee.

[13] In such a case, the possible application of Art. 101 TFEU (the former Art. 85 of the EC Treaty, as renumbered by the Treaty of Amsterdam, Art. 12 and, subsequently, by the Treaty of Lisbon), must not be overlooked: see *supra*, para. 8–05.

investors the twin attractions of flexibility and limited liability, without the need to comply with the cumbrous provisions of the Limited Partnerships Act 1907.[14] It will, however, be necessary for the partnership to comply with the requirements of the Partnerships (Accounts) Regulations 2008.[15] Equally, the ability to "collapse" an unsuccessful corporate partner, with a view to gaining the full benefit of its limited liability, will not always be commercially acceptable to the directors and shareholders.[16]

On the other hand, the corporate partnership in its restricted form, *i.e.* a partnership comprising both companies and individuals, offers no special advantage (otherwise than in the field of taxation),[17] although it will permit some investors to participate in the venture indirectly, through the medium of a corporate partner. However, there is at least the potential for the formation of a limited partnership[18] in which the general partner[19] is a limited company, thus minimising the exposure which is normally attendant on that position,[20] although the tendency now may be to prefer the formation of a limited liability partnership in such a case. **11–07**

Contents of corporate partnership agreement

Relatively few alterations need to be made to a traditional partnership agreement in order to accommodate the requirements of a corporate partnership.[21] It will naturally be essential to adapt any clause which refers to an event peculiar to an individual partner, *e.g.* death or incapacity,[22] but the draftsman's primary concern must be to legislate against the possibility of the corporate partner's actual or apprehended insolvency. This will, in particular, require him to identify the potential impact on the firm of: **11–08**

    (a) an administrative or other receiver being appointed in respect of the whole or any part of a corporate partner's assets[23];

    (b) a corporate partner's directors making a proposal for a voluntary arrangement[24];

    (c) an administration order being made against a corporate partner[25];

---

[14] See *infra*, paras 29–01 *et seq*. A limited liability partnership is, of course, another option.

[15] SI 2008/569. See further *infra*, paras 11–13, 22–08.

[16] Note also the provisions of the Insolvency Act 1986, ss.213, 214 (fraudulent and wrongful trading).

[17] *i.e.* by "sheltering" profits in the corporate partner's hands, thus avoiding the higher rate charge to income tax imposed on individual partners.

[18] See the Limited Partnerships Act 1907, s.4 and *infra*, paras 29–02 *et seq*.

[19] *ibid.* s.4(2): see *infra*, para. 29–03. In such a case, there is no reason why some or all of the investors should not have a seat on the corporate general partner's board.

[20] Note, however, that the individual (limited) partners must not control the management decisions taken by a general partner, unless they wish to risk forfeiture of their limited liability under *ibid.* s.6(1): see *infra*, paras 31–02 *et seq*.

[21] Various management structures are adopted: see for example, *Pinkney v. Sandpiper Drilling Ltd.* [1989] I.C.R. 389.

[22] But note that a corporate partner need not be *physically* capable of carrying on the firm's business: see *Newstead v. Frost* [1980] 1 W.L.R. 125, *supra*, para. 3–43.

[23] See, generally, the Insolvency Act 1986, ss.33 *et seq*. The expression "administrative receiver" is defined in *ibid.* s.29(2).

[24] *ibid.* ss.1 *et seq*.

[25] *ibid.* s.8, Sched. B1, as substituted/added by the Enterprise Act 2002, s.248(1), (2).

    (d)   the passing of a resolution for the voluntary winding up of an insolvent corporate partner[26];

    (e)   a winding up petition being presented against a corporate partner, no concurrent petition being presented against the firm[27]; and

    (f)   a winding up order being made against a corporate partner.[28]

Each such event should, at the very least, be regarded as a potential ground either for expelling the corporate partner or for dissolving the partnership. Similar considerations will apply where the firm comprises one or more limited liability partnerships.[29]

In the case of an unusual term, such as a so-called "poison pill" provision,[30] it may be necessary to consider whether the directors have authority under the corporate partner's constitution[31] to authorise it to enter into an agreement containing such a term, particularly in the case of a public company.[32]

Expulsion

11–09   Consistently with the approach normally adopted in the case of individual partners,[33] the current editor suggests that most, if not all, of the foregoing events should give rise to a right to *expel* the relevant corporate partner.[34] A power of expulsion is, after all, a remedy of last resort and need not be invoked by the other partners.

If the presentation of a winding up petition is *not* made a ground for expulsion (or if the power is not, for whatever reason, exercised), there will inevitably be a degree of uncertainty for the firm during the period leading up to the hearing of the petition. If an order is made on the petition, the winding up will be deemed to have commenced at the time when the petition was presented[35] and any disposition of the corporate partner's property thereafter will be void unless the court orders otherwise.[36] It follows that, in the interim period, the corporate

---

[26] *ibid.* ss.84 *et seq.* As to the position where a *solvent* partner is voluntarily wound up, see *infra*, para. 11–10.

[27] As to the circumstances in which concurrent petitions may be presented against the firm and against two or more of the partners, see *infra*, paras 27–24 *et seq.*

[28] See the Insolvency Act 1986, s.125. And see *infra*, paras 24–35 *et seq.*

[29] As a body corporate, the LLP is subject to a corporate insolvency regime, albeit adapted by the Limited Liability Partnerships Regulations 2001 (SI 2001/1090), reg. 5, Sched. 3. See further *supra*, para. 2–43.

[30] *i.e.* a provision whereby one partner is forced to buy the other out in certain eventualities, such as on a change in the former's management.

[31] See further *supra*, para. 4–20.

[32] See *Criterion Properties Plc v. Stratford UK Properties LLC* [2004] 1 W.L.R. 1846 (HL).

[33] See *supra*, paras 10–113 *et seq.*

[34] Similarly in the case of a limited liability partnership which is a member of a firm: see *supra*, para. 11–08, n. 29.

[35] Insolvency Act 1986, s.129(2). Where, however, a winding up by the court supersedes a voluntary winding up, the relevant date is that on which the original resolution was passed (*ibid.* s.129(1)) but it will be the date of the order where a winding up is ordered on the hearing of an administration application (*ibid.* s.129(1A), as added by the Enterprise Act 2002, Sched. 17, paras 9, 16). These subsections apply to the winding up of a limited liability partnership: Limited Liability Partnerships Regulations 2001, reg. 5, Sched. 3.

[36] Insolvency Act 1986, s.127, as amended by the Enterprise Act 2002, Sched. 17, paras 9, 15. As to the principles applied by the court under this section, see *Denney v. John Hudson & Co. Ltd.* [1992] B.C.L.C. 901 (CA). The section also applies where a limited liability partnership is wound up, albeit in an amended form: Limited Liability Partnerships Regulations 2001, reg. 5, Sched. 3. See also *infra*, para. 27–16.

partner is unlikely to be able to function as a fully active partner. The appointment of a provisional liquidator[37] may exacerbate the difficulties. Whether the other partners will be prepared to countenance the potential disruption which this may cause must be open to doubt.

Even if a more benign approach is adopted, it will still prima facie be desirable   **11–10**
to ensure that expulsion is possible in the event that a winding up order is actually made. If such a limited power is not included, the other partners may have to accept the continued presence of the insolvent partner until such time as it is finally dissolved on the completion of the winding up,[38] unless they apply to the court for an earlier dissolution of the partnership under the Partnership Act 1890.[39]

Similar considerations will in fact arise in the case of a voluntary winding up, even where the corporate partner is *solvent*.[40] Cases of winding up with a view to reconstruction or amalgamation require special consideration: the other partners may well not be prepared to countenance the substitution of the reconstructed, etc., company for the company with which they originally entered into partnership.[41]

As already noted,[42] it may not be possible to provide that the share of an expelled corporate partner should accrue to the other partners without payment in all cases. Where such a term *is* sought to be applied, the grounds for expulsion will inevitably be less extensive.

Alternative to expulsion: dissolution

If the continuation of the partnership business is dependent on the involvement   **11–11**
of a particular corporate partner, the expulsion of that partner in the event of its insolvency is unlikely to be an acceptable solution to the other partners. In such a case, a power to dissolve the partnership should be substituted.[43] Again, it will be a matter for consideration whether the power should be exercisable on the presentation of a petition or merely on the making of a winding up order. However, in the case supposed, it is difficult to see how the partnership could effectively function until the latter date.[44]

---

[37] *ibid.* s.135(1), (2). This section also applies to a limited liability partnership.

[38] Unlike the position under some other statutes, *e.g.* the Law of Property Act 1925, s.205(1)(i), "bankruptcy" for the purposes of the Partnership Act 1890, s.33(1) does not include the winding up of a company, so that a winding up order will not, of itself, work a dissolution; however, it is submitted that the actual dissolution of a company (see the Insolvency Act 1986, ss.202, 205) would do so: see further, *infra*, paras 24–35 *et seq.* The position is the same in the case of a limited liability partnership, to which the Insolvency Act 1986, ss.202, 205 are applied by the Limited Liability Partnerships Regulations 2001, reg. 5.

[39] The existence of the winding up order might justify an application on the "just and equitable" ground: see the Partnership Act 1890, s.35(f), *infra*, paras 24–89, 24–90.

[40] See the Insolvency Act 1986, s.87(1), which provides that "the company shall from the commencement of the winding up cease to carry on its business, except so far as may be required for its beneficial winding up". See also *ibid.* s.87(2). This section also applies (in an amended form) to a limited liability partnership: see the Limited Liability Partnerships Regulations 2001, reg. 5, Sched. 3.

[41] *i.e.* drawing an analogy with the Partnership Act 1890, s.24(7), *infra*, paras 15–09, 19–49.

[42] See *supra*, para. 11–04; see also *supra*, paras 10–152, 10–153 and *infra*, 27–71.

[43] See *supra*, paras 10–137 *et seq.*

[44] *A fortiori* once the petition has been advertised: see the Insolvency Rules 1986, r. 4.11, as substituted by the Insolvency (Amendment) Rules 2009 (SI 2009/642), r. 18 and amended by the Insolvency (Amendment) Rules 2010 (SI 2010/686), Sched. 1, paras 1, 145.

Management structure of corporate partner

11–12   An individual partner will generally be admitted to a partnership on the strength of the personal qualities which he possesses; in the case of a corporate partner, those qualities may be possessed by its board of directors or by some other management team whose services it is able to offer to the firm.[45] The other partners must decide whether, given the qualities of the relevant individuals, they should reserve the right to expel the corporate partner or to dissolve the partnership if, for whatever reason, those services can no longer be made available.[46]

A similar right may also, in appropriate cases, be reserved in the case of changes in the ownership and/or voting control of a corporate partner.[47]

Annual accounts

11–13   The Partnerships (Accounts) Regulations 2008[48] now require a qualifying partnership[49] to prepare annual accounts, a directors' report, and an auditor's report in the same way as any other company and each corporate partner must append those accounts to its own accounts for filing purposes.[50] The other requirements of the regulations are noted elsewhere in this work.[51]

Charge on partnership assets

11–14   It is submitted that a charge over the assets of a corporate partnership need not be registered under the Companies Act 2006,[52] but a charge over a corporate partner's *share* would unquestionably require registration.

---

[45] In the case of a limited liability partnership, it is likely to be the qualities possessed by one or more key members or, perhaps, employees, which will be critical.

[46] The introduction of a new management team (or, in the case of a limited liability partnership, a significant change in its membership) might, in such a case, be regarded as equivalent to the admission of a new partner: see the Partnership Act 1890, s.24(7), *infra*, paras 15–09, 19–49.

[47] For an analogous provision in a licensing agreement, see *Philip Morris Products Inc. v. Rothmans International Enterprises Ltd.* [2001] E.T.M.R. 108 (CA). Similar considerations will arise in the case of a change in the voting control/membership of a limited liability partnership.

[48] SI 2008/569.

[49] *i.e.* a partnership formed under the law of any part of the UK where each of the members is: (i) a limited company; (ii) an unlimited company or a Scottish partnership, each of whose members is a limited company; or (iii) a comparable undertaking incorporated in or formed under the laws of another country or territory: *ibid.* reg. 3(1), (4). The definition will be amended in the case of limited partnerships (as from October 2011) to ensure that the presence of individual limited partners does not prevent the regulations from applying. It should also be noted that the regulations will *not* apply merely because one of the partners is a limited liability partnership.

[50] *ibid.* regs. 4(1), 5(1). As regards the contents of such accounts, *ibid.* Sched., Pt 1 makes certain modifications to the application of the Small Companies and Groups (Accounts and Directors' Report) Regulations 2008 (SI 2008/409) and the Large and Medium-sized Companies and Groups (Accounts and Reports) Regulations 2008 (SI 2008/410).

[51] See *infra*, para. 22–05.

[52] *ibid.* ss.860 *et seq. Per contra*, perhaps, if each partner were, for the purposes of these sections, regarded as entitled to a direct interest in each partnership asset (see, for example, *Burdett-Coutts v. IRC* [1960] 1 W.L.R. 1027; *Gray v. IRC* [1994] S.T.C. 360, 377) and the charged assets comprise land or an interest in land and/or a ship or aircraft: *ibid.* s.860(7)(a), (h). *cf.* the descriptions of the other registrable charges. Note in any event that *ibid.* s.874(1) only renders a charge void "so far as any security on the company's property or undertaking is conferred by it", so that, even if that subsection applies, the supposedly unregistered charge would, as regards the other partners, unquestionably be valid. The same statutory regime also applies, in an amended form, to limited liability partnerships: see the Limited Liability Partnerships (Application of Companies Act 2006) Regulations 2009 (SI 2009/1804), Pt. 9, Chap. 1.

Insolvency

Where concurrent insolvency petitions are presented against the firm and **11–15**
against one or more partners, any of whom are corporate partners, the Insolvency
Act 1986 is specially adapted in its application to such corporate partner(s).[53]

Otherwise, insolvency proceedings against a corporate partner will follow the
normal procedure laid down in the Act and the Insolvency Rules 1986.[54]

Taxation

The tax treatment of corporate partnerships is considered later in this **11–16**
work.[55]

2.   THE GROUP PARTNERSHIP

Nature and formation

Less common than the corporate partnership is the entity known as the group **11–17**
partnership which, in essence, consists of a partnership between two or more
partnerships. It may in many ways be likened to a series of sub-partnerships,[56]
save that each member of a constituent firm will himself be a member of the
group partnership.[57] With the demise of any restrictions on the size of partnerships,[58] there are now no special statutory or other provisions governing the
formation of such a partnership. Moreover, there is no reason why one or more
members of a group partnership should not themselves be corporate
partnerships.

Advantages

The group partnership obviously provides a means whereby a number of **11–18**
separate partnerships carrying on business in a certain field of activity can pool
their respective skills and resources, whilst retaining their individual identities
and, to a greater or lesser extent, their autonomy.[59] In this way, small firms may
be able to compete on more equal terms with their larger counterparts.

However, it must at the same time be appreciated that the partial integration
which is the hallmark of the group partnership may itself present certain practical
dangers: once common facilities are set up within the confines of the group, it
may be difficult, if not impossible, for any of the constituent firms to withdraw

---

[53] See the Insolvent Partnerships Order 1994, arts 8(4), (5), (8), (9) (creditor's petitions), 10(2), (3),
(6) (as substituted by the Insolvent Partnerships (Amendment) Order 2005 (SI 2005/1516), art. 5(b)),
(members' petitions), Sched. 4, Pt. II. See further *infra*, paras 27–24 *et seq.*

[54] See *ibid.* art. 19(5) and *infra*, paras 27–48, 27–75.

[55] See *infra*, paras 34–55 *et seq.*

[56] See *supra*, para. 5–67.

[57] This, in essence, seems to have been the arrangement in *Nixon v. Wood* (1987) 284 E.G. 1055.
See also *Bass Brewers Ltd. v. Appleby* (1996) 73 P. & C.R. 165, 170 *per* Millett L.J.

[58] See the Regulatory Reform (Reform of 20 Member Limit in Partnerships etc.) Order 2002 (SI
2002/3203), reg. 2.

[59] Much will, of course, depend on the scope of the group partnership business and the terms of the
agreement: see *infra*, paras 11–20 *et seq.*

in anything approaching a viable state; *a fortiori* if clients have developed an allegiance to the group, rather than to those firms.[60]

Firm name

11–19   Each constituent firm may either continue to function under its own name or under a single "flagship" name common to the group. In either case, it must be ensured that the use of the name is not prohibited[61] or that any prior approval required under Part 41 of the Companies Act 2006 is obtained.[62] It is considered that the Secretary of State would not object to approval being sought for a number of different names in respect of the same partnership; *sed quaere*.

Contents of group partnership agreement

Decision-making

11–20   The management structure of a group partnership will be critical to its survival. That structure will largely depend on the scope of the partnership business and the independence which is to be retained by each of the constituent firms. It must be remembered that, if the group partnership is to function as such, some decisions will require to be taken at group level and others at constituent firm level: the agreement must clearly state which decisions fall in each class.[63] Where the group partnership business will incorporate only some of the activities carried on by the constituent firms, the overall control exercised at group level will inevitably be reduced.

11–21   However, the agreement should normally seek only to establish the manner in which *group* level decisions will be taken, leaving other decisions to be taken in accordance with the established procedures in the constituent firms. There are a number of management structures which may be adopted for group level decisions, namely:

1. A majority vote of all the partners.[64] This is only likely to be workable if the group is relatively small.

2. A "block" vote system, treating each constituent firm as a single partner, with weighted voting where appropriate.

---

[60] This may occur notwithstanding the fact that each constituent firm retains the ownership of its own goodwill under the terms of the agreement.

[61] Companies Act 2006, ss.1197, 1198 and the Company and Business Names (Miscellaneous Provisions) Regulations 2009 (SI 2009/1085), Pt. 4 (as amended, in the case of reg. 13, by the Company, Limited Liability Partnership and Business Names (Miscellaneous Provisions) (Amendment) Regulations 2009 (SI 2009/2404), reg. 2(2)), Sched. 1, para. 1(a), (b), Sched. 2, para. 3 (as amended by *ibid.*, reg. 2(3)). See also *supra*, para. 3–28.

[62] *ibid.* ss.1193–1195; the Company, Limited Liability Partnership and Business Names (Sensitive Words and Expressions) Regulations 2009 (SI 2009/2615), regs. 3, 5, 6, Scheds. 1, 2; the Company, Limited Liability Partnerships and Business Names (Public Authorities) Regulations (SI 2009/2982), reg. 3, Sched. See further *supra*, paras 3–28 *et seq.*

[63] As to the type of difficulties which can arise, see *Nixon v. Wood* (1987) 284 E.G. 1055.

[64] This does not mean that all decisions must be decided by a simple majority, in the same way as "ordinary matters connected with the partnership business" under the Partnership Act 1890, s.24(8): see *infra*, para. 15–04. If necessary, different majorities may be required according to the nature of the decision required to be taken, following the example of the Companies Act 2006, ss.282, 283. If this approach is adopted, consideration should also be given to the quorum requirements at partners' meetings.

3. A management committee system. If, in fact, each constituent firm is represented on the committee, this may in practice not differ significantly from the previous alternative.

Consistently with the approach currently adopted by a number of the larger professional firms, a combination of the first and third options, with the procedure varying according to the nature of the decision to be taken, may in practice provide the most acceptable solution.

Property

The agreement must specify whether the property of the constituent firms will remain in their ownership or will become assets of the group partnership.[65] If they are to be retained by the constituent firms but made available for the use of the group, the terms upon which such user is to be permitted should be expressly stated.[66]   **11–22**

The ownership of goodwill, whether as an asset of the group or of the constituent firms, should also be clearly established.

Retirement and dissolution

Suitable provisions should normally be included in the agreement dealing with: **11–23**

(a) the automatic retirement or expulsion of any partner who ceases to be a member of a constituent firm[67];

(b) the voluntary retirement of a constituent firm;

(c) the expulsion of a constituent firm on set grounds, including insolvency[68] and failure to expel a member of a constituent firm whose conduct might affect the reputation of the group; and

(d) the dissolution of the group partnership and the distribution of its assets.

Insolvency

If a group partnership is insolvent, concurrent petitions may be presented against the group and against one or more of the constituent firms which will, for   **11–24**

---

[65] Once, however, assets are held at group level, it may be more difficult for a constituent firm to disentangle itself with a view to regaining its independence: according to the circumstances, this may be seen as an advantage or a disadvantage.

[66] See, generally, *supra*, para. 10–45 and *infra*, paras 18–33 *et seq.*

[67] It is obviously undesirable for there to be a "floating" partner who is a member of the group partnership but who is not also a member of one of the constituent firms.

[68] Note that insolvency proceedings may be commenced against some or all of the members of a constituent firm and/or against the constituent firm itself: see *infra*, paras 27–24 *et seq.*

this purpose, be treated as corporate partners.[69] Insolvency proceedings against the group or against one or more of the constituent firms will proceed in the normal way.[70]

Taxation

11–25   There are no special provisions governing the taxation of group partnerships. However, it should be noted that a separate value added tax registration will be available to the group.[71]

---

[69] Insolvent Partnerships Order 1994, art. 12: see *infra*, para. 27–29. In such a case, the creditors of a constituent firm will be deemed to be separate creditors when determining the priority of debts in the joint estate of the group partnership and in the separate estate of that constituent firm: see the Insolvency Act 1986, s.175C(6) (as inserted by the Insolvent Partnerships Order 1994, Sched. 4, Pt II, para. 23 and applied, as regards the group partnership, by the Insolvency Act 1986, s.221(5) (as itself amended, in the case of a creditor's petition, by the Insolvent Partnerships Order 1994, art. 8(1), as amended by the Insolvent Partnerships (Amendment) Order 2002 (SI 2002/1308), art. 4(2)), (2), Sched. 4, Pt I, para. 3 and, in the case of a member's petition, by *ibid*. art. 10(1)(a), Sched. 6, para. 4) and, as regards the constituent firms, by the Insolvent Partnership Order 1994, arts. 8(4), (5), (8), 10(2), (3), (6)), as substituted by the Insolvent Partnerships (Amendment) Order 2005 (SI 2005/1516), art. 5(b)). See further *infra*, para. 27–84. The position will be the same where the members of a group partnership are bankrupted on a joint bankruptcy petition: *ibid.* s.328C(6) (as added by the Insolvent Partnerships Order 1994, Art. 11, Sched. 7, para. 21). See further *infra*, para. 27–107.

[70] See *infra*, paras 27–08 *et seq.*

[71] See *Customs & Excise Commissioners v. Glassborow* [1975] Q.B. 465, *infra*, paras 37–09 *et seq.*

Part Three

THE RIGHTS AND OBLIGATIONS OF PARTNERS AS REGARDS THIRD PARTIES

CHAPTER 12

THE LIABILITY OF A PARTNER FOR THE ACTS OF HIS CO-PARTNERS

1.   PARTNERS AS AGENTS

The general principle of agency as between partners

WRITING prior to the Partnership Act 1890, Lord Lindley stated the general **12–01**
principle in these terms:

> "Every member of an ordinary partnership is its general agent for the transaction of
> its business in the ordinary way; and the firm is responsible for whatever is done by
> any of the partners when acting for the firm within the limits of the authority
> conferred by the nature of the business it carries on.[1] Whatever, as between the
> partners themselves, may be the limits set to each other's authority, every person not
> acquainted with those limits is entitled to assume that each partner is empowered to
> do for the firm whatever is necessary for the transaction of its business, in the way
> in which that business is ordinarily carried on by other people.[2] But no person is
> entitled to assume that any partner has a more extensive authority than that above
> described."

As is clear from the above passage, mutual agency as between partners is no
more than a normal incident of the partnership relation[3]; the fact that it is absent
in a given case does not, of itself, mean that no partnership exists.[4]

Partnership Act 1890, section 5

The above general principle was enacted by section 5 of the Partnership Act **12–02**
1890, which provides as follows:

> "5. Every partner is an agent of the firm and his other partners for the purpose of the
> business of the partnership; and the acts of every partner who does any act for
> carrying on in the usual way business of the kind carried on by the firm of which he
> is a member bind the firm and his partners, unless the partner so acting has in fact no
> authority to act for the firm in the particular matter, and the person with whom he is

---

[1] Lord Lindley observed in a footnote that "The case is different with mere part-ownerships,
Barton v. Williams (1822) 5 B. & A. 395; *Helme v. Smith* (1831) 7 Bing. 709."

[2] See *Hawken v. Bourne* (1841) 8 M. & W. 703, 710 *per* Parke B.; *Baird's Case* (1870) L.R. 5
Ch.App. 725, 733 *per* James L.J.

[3] See, for example, *Holme v. Hammond* (1872) L.R. 7 Ex. 218, 233, 234 *per* Cleasby B. And see
also *supra*, paras 2–12, 2–13.

[4] *ibid.* Significantly, Lord Lindley referred to members of "an ordinary partnership". In the case of
a limited partnership formed under the Limited Partnerships Act 1907, the limited partners will have
no implied authority to bind the firm (*ibid.* s.6(1)), but the relationship will still be one of partnership:
see further *infra*, paras 30–03 *et seq.*

dealing either knows that he has no authority,[5] or does not know or believe him to be a partner."[6]

Analysis and application of the section

12–03   There are in fact two distinct but overlapping limbs in the section. The first, and most important, is contained in the opening words "Every partner is an agent of the firm and his other partners for the purpose of the business of the partnership": this governs the position both as between the partners themselves and as between them and third parties and may conveniently be styled the "general limb".[7] The remainder of the section deals only with the rights of third parties and may therefore be styled the "third party limb".[8]

Whilst the section clearly establishes an agency relationship between the partners, it does not, in the current editor's view, follow from this that the existence of that relationship can be relied on by one partner when making a claim *against* his co-partners, otherwise than for a contribution towards a third party liability. It is submitted that it was an incorrect assumption that the section does apply in such a case which led Warren J. to approach the decision in *Hammonds (A Firm) v. Danilunas*[9] in the way that he did. There the defendant outgoing partners were seeking to bring a counterclaim against the continuing partners in respect of certain misrepresentations alleged to have been made to them by two partners holding management positions. On the hearing of an interim application,[10] it was from the outset assumed that the alleged misrepresentations were made "in the course of the management . . . of the partnership business"[11] and that, as a result, the section was immediately in play.[12] This predictably led Warren J. to express the tentative view that the defendant partners would, ultimately, have to bear a share of any damages resulting from that claim, if successful.[13] It is accepted that this might arguably be the case where the firm purports to act for a partner *qua* client,[14] but it is wrong in principle to regard internal partnership dealings between partners as "for the purpose of the business of the partnership",[15] whatever their nature. It is, moreover, important to note that section 5 appears in the group of sections[16] headed "Relations of Partners to

---

[5] See also Partnership Act 1890, s.8, *infra*, paras 12–138 *et seq.*

[6] The concluding words of the section echo the judgments of Cockburn C.J. in *Nicholson v. Ricketts* (1860) 2 E. & E. 497, 524, and of Cleasby B. in *Holme v. Hammond* (1872) L.R. 7 Ex 218, 233. See *infra*, para. 12–11, n. 38.

[7] Note that the existence of the general limb was not sufficient to save the firm's opposition to a European patent in *United Video Properties/Program Guide* (T482/02) [2005] E.P.O.R. 42. See further as to this case *supra*, para. 3–08.

[8] A similar analysis is to be found of the Australian counterpart of s.5 in *Construction Engineering (Aust.) Pty Ltd. v. Hexyl Pty Ltd.* (1985) 155 C.L.R. 541, 547. See also *Proceedings Commissioner v. Ali Hatem* [1999] 1 N.Z.L.R. 305, 309. See further, as to the two limbs, *Bank of Scotland v. Henry Butcher & Co* [2003] 2 All E.R. (Comm) 557, noted *infra*, para. 12–04.

[9] [2009] EWHC 216 (Ch) (Lawtel 18/2/09). This aspect was not pursued on the appeal, *sub nom.* *Hammonds (A firm) v. Jones* [2009] EWCA Civ 1400 (Lawtel 21/12/09).

[10] For summary judgment or to strike out that part of the counterclaim.

[11] See *ibid.* at [128]. At *ibid.* [164], Warren J. stated that "There will be tasks of internal administration of the firm which can also properly be described as carrying on in the usual way the business of the partnership"; see also *ibid.* [165].

[12] See *ibid.* at [166].

[13] *ibid.* at [161].

[14] The example given by Warren J. at *ibid.* [161], [162], albeit without deciding the point.

[15] This is the wording in first limb of s.5: see *supra*, para. 12–02.

[16] ss.5–18.

Persons dealing with them", as opposed to the later group of sections[17] headed "Relations of Partners to one another" and, consistently therewith, it was clearly decided by the Court of Session in *Mair v. Wood*[18] that the agency relationship which exists between partners only has effect as regards third parties. It would seem that this decision was not cited to Warren J. and, in those circumstances, his *obiter* analysis of the position should be approached with caution.

Where a partner acts as agent of the firm within the scope of his *actual* **12–04** authority, *i.e.* a case falling within the general limb, liability will attach to the firm irrespective of the provisions of the third party limb; this will be the usual case. However, it should not be imagined that the third party limb is thereby rendered otiose, since it is permissible for partners to agree that one or more of their number will have only limited, or possibly no, authority to bind the firm.[19] In such a case, the general limb would be effectively excluded, but liability would still be imposed by the third party limb unless the conditions set out at the end of the section are fulfilled. The distinction between the two limbs was analysed in a similar way by Chadwick L.J. in *Bank of Scotland v. Henry Butcher & Co.*,[20] as follows:

> "The inquiry under the first limb of s 5 of the 1890 Act is whether the act of one partner, say partner A, is done for the purpose of the business of the partnership. If it is, then, in doing that act, A is the agent of the firm and the other partners are bound by A's act. There is no need, in such a case, for the persons seeking to rely on the act to invoke the second limb.
>
> The hypothesis which underlies the second limb of s 5 is that A's act is not, in fact, done for the purpose of the partnership business—so that the first limb is not in point. The inquiry under the second limb—in a case where it is necessary to invoke that limb—is whether A's act is an 'act for carrying on in the usual way business of the kind carried on by the firm'. That requires consideration of two elements: (i) what business is 'business of the kind carried on by the firm'; and (ii) is A's act 'an act for carrying on in the usual way' that business. Where those two elements are present, the person with whom A is dealing is entitled to treat the act as done for the purpose of the business of the partnership unless he knows that A has in fact no authority, or does not know or believe A to be a partner."

It goes without saying that an express restriction on a partner's authority which has been included in the partnership agreement will be of little or no relevance under the second limb unless it is actually brought to the attention of third parties dealing with him.[21]

---

[17] ss.19–31, which includes s.24(5), governing partners' default rights to participate in the management of the firm.

[18] 1948 S.C. 83 (noted *infra*, para. 20–12, n. 47) at pp. 88 *per* the Lord President, 90 *per* Lord Keith. This case concerned a tort committed by one partner against another. The court did not regard the specific exception in the Partnership Act 1890, s.10 ("loss or injury is caused to any person not being a partner in the firm") as determinative on this issue. The fact that a Scottish partnership has separate legal personality (see *ibid.* s.4(2), *infra*, para. A1–05) means that the reasoning is *a fortiori* in the case of a partnership without such personality.

[19] See the Partnership Act 1890, s.8, *infra*, paras 12–138 *et seq.*

[20] [2003] 2 All E.R. (Comm) 557 (CA), at [88] to [89].

[21] Compare the position of the fraudulent partner under the two agreements considered in *Goldberg v. Miltiadous* [2010] EWHC 450 (QB) (Lawtel 19/3/10). Under the first, there was no restriction on his authority but such a restriction was introduced in the second: *ibid.* at [132], [133]. Both of the other partners had differing levels of knowledge as to his activities but neither did anything to prevent his contravention of the restriction: *ibid.* at [134] to [137].

12–05   *The dual agency concept*: The reference to each partner being "the agent of the firm and his other partners" requires explanation. At first sight the reference to the firm appears to be mere surplusage, since that expression is merely shorthand for all the partners[22]; such, indeed, appears to have been the view of Park J. in *Major v. Brodie*.[23] However, in the current editor's view, these words may serve a function and establish what might be styled the pure form of mutual agency, under which each partner acts in a dual capacity, *i.e.* as agent for the partners collectively[24] and as agent for each of the other partners in their individual or separate capacities. This is consistent with the dual nature of a partner's liability under the Partnership Act 1890[25] and, to an extent, the treatment of a partnership debt under the insolvency laws,[26] but it is fair to say that the concept does not appear to have been recognised by Lord Lindley himself.[27]

Situations where the section does not apply

Partner by holding out

12–06   The section seems to presuppose the existence of a partnership in the true sense and will therefore not apply in a case of holding out[28]; this was so decided in *Hudgell Yeates & Co. v. Watson*.[29] Although the decision in *United Bank of Kuwait Ltd. v. Hammoud*[30] would appear to be an authority to the contrary, in that case the status of the salaried partner appears not to have been considered.

Intending partners

12–07   The section will only apply as between intending partners when the partnership commences.[31] Their liability prior to that date must be determined on normal agency principles.

Dormant partner

12–08   In the case of a true dormant partner, *i.e.* an undisclosed partner[32] who carries on business through his fellow partners, the section will apply in the normal way.

---

[22] Partnership Act 1890, s.4(1), *supra*, paras 3–01 *et seq.*

[23] [1998] S.T.C. 491, 504c–e.

[24] It is, at the same time, recognised that this necessarily entails the partner also acting as his own agent, which is a something of a contradiction in terms. This point was not adverted to in *Major v. Brodie, supra*.

[25] See *ibid.* ss.9, 12, *infra*, paras 13–02 *et seq.*, 13–12. The position is more complex under Scots law, where the firm is a separate legal person (Partnership Act 1890, s.4(2)) and is primarily liable for the firm's debts, whereas the individual partners are only *secondarily* liable.

[26] Thus, joint or partnership debts are primarily payable out of the partnership assets although they may, in certain circumstances, be proved against the individual partners' separate estates in competition with their respective separate debts: see *infra*, paras 26–19, 27–78 *et seq.*

[27] See the passage set out *supra*, para. 5–01. Note, however, that in his Supplement on the 1890 Act, Lord Lindley did observe: "This section is in accordance with the existing law", both as regards English *and* Scots law.

[28] See, as to holding out, *ibid.* s.14, *supra*, paras 5–35 *et seq.* Note that the section merely renders the person held out "liable as a partner"; it does not purport to make him a partner.

[29] [1978] Q.B. 451, 467B–F *per* Waller L.J. and, *semble*, 471B *per* Megaw L.J. *cf.* the judgment of Bridge L.J. at *ibid.* 462H–463A.

[30] [1988] 1 W.L.R. 1051.

[31] See, for example, *Blythe Limited Partnership v. C. & E. Commissioners* [1999] S.T.I. 1178 (VAT Trib.). As to when a partnership is regarding as commencing, see *supra*, paras 2–17 *et seq.*

[32] Note, in this context, the implications of the Companies Act 2006, Pt. 41: see *supra*, paras 3–26 *et seq.*, 5–63.

However, a person who simply enjoys a share in the profits of a business carried on by others on their own account[33] cannot properly be regarded as a partner nor can the persons who carry on the business properly be treated as his agents, real or apparent; in such a case, no liability will attach to him either under the section or under the general law relating to undisclosed principals.

Partner not purporting to act on firm's behalf

The application of the section is also dependent on a partner having acted, or **12–09** purported to act, on the firm's behalf; if he at all times acted on his own behalf and this was recognised by the third party, the firm will not be bound.[34] The fact that there was an obvious conflict of interest between the firm and the partner in question is not *per se* sufficient to give rise to an inference that he was acting otherwise than on the firm's behalf or in the ordinary course of its business.[35]

Professional misconduct

It should not be assumed that the mutual agency between partners will apply **12–10** for all purposes. Thus, in *Akodu v. Solicitors Regulation Authority*,[36] the Divisional Court held that a solicitor could not be found guilty of conduct unbefitting his profession solely on the basis that he was a partner at the relevant time.

Practical effects of the section

The operation of section 5 of the Partnership Act 1890 may be summarised[37] **12–11** in this way:

(1) An act done by a partner on behalf of the firm and within the scope of his *actual* authority will bind the firm, whether or not the act was done in carrying on the partnership business in the usual way.

(2) An act done by a partner on behalf of the firm in the course of carrying on the partnership business in the usual way will prima facie bind the firm, even if the partner acted without authority, unless the third party with whom he dealt knew of that lack of authority or did not know or believe him to be a partner.[38]

---

[33] See the Partnership Act 1890, s.2(3), *supra*, paras 5–02 *et seq.*

[34] *British Homes Assurance Corporation Ltd. v. Paterson* [1902] 2 Ch. 404; also *Polkinghorne v. Holland* (1934) 51 C.L.R. 143, 157; *Construction Engineering (Aust.) Pty Ltd. v. Hexyl Pty Ltd.* (1985) 155 C.L.R. 541, where the partner appears to have contracted as principal but also as trustee for the firm. *cf. Goldberg v. Miltiadous* [2010] EWHC 450 (QB) (Lawtel 19/3/10), where the other partners failed to demonstrate that the claimants were aware that a fraudulent partner was acting on his own behalf.

[35] *Goldberg v. Miltiadous*, *supra*, at [147].

[36] [2009] EWHC 3588 (Admin) (Lawtel 13/11/09).

[37] This summary was cited with approval by Turner J. in his dissenting judgment in *Dubai Aluminium Co. Ltd. v. Salaam* [2001] Q.B. 113, 145H. As to the final decision in the House of Lords, see [2003] 2 A.C. 366.

[38] In the latter case, there is neither real nor apparent authority to bind the firm: see, generally, the cases cited *supra*, para. 12–02, n. 6; also *Farquharson Bros. & Co. v. King & Co.* [1902] A.C. 325, 341 *per* Lord Lindley. *Watteau v. Fenwick* [1893] 1 Q.B. 346 and *Kinahan & Co. Ltd. v. Parry* [1910] 2 K.B. 389 (which was reversed on a question of fact: see [1911] 1 K.B. 459) are, however, inconsistent with this view; *sed quaere*: see 9 L.Q.R. 3, 111 (Sir Frederick Pollock); *Bowstead & Reynolds on Agency* (19th ed.), para. 8–079; also *infra*, paras 12–143 *et seq.*

(3) An act done by a partner on behalf of the firm *otherwise* than in the course of carrying on the partnership business in the usual way will prima facie not bind the firm, in the absence of express authority or subsequent ratification by the other partners.[39]

Usual course of business sets limit on authority

12–12   It is submitted that, just as was the position prior to the Partnership Act 1890,[40] the limit of a partner's *implied* authority to bind the firm is in all cases set by the usual course of the particular business carried on. However, it should be noted that, in earlier editions of this work, the same proposition was advanced more timidly, namely:

> "It will be observed that the extent of a partner's authority to bind the firm is related to things done in 'the usual way' of the 'business of the kind carried on,' where no actual authority or ratification can be proved. This probably means the same thing as saying that what is necessary to carry on the partnership business in the usual way is the test of a partner's implied authority to bind the firm. It is apprehended that the Act has not extended the power of a partner to bind the firm."[41]

It is the usual course of the business, not the nature of the particular partner's involvement therein, which is generally material, hence Lord Lindley's footnote in these terms:

> "The fact that one partner ordinarily attends to one branch of the business does not prevent his binding the firm when acting out of his own department."[42]

Nature and ordinary course of business

12–13   Whether a given act will fall to be treated as done in the usual course of carrying on a particular business is essentially a mixed question of fact and law[43] and will naturally depend on the nature of that business and on the practices normally adopted by persons engaged in carrying on businesses of that type. Evidence will necessarily be admissible on both points and expert evidence on the latter may prove to be crucial,[44] given the diversity of business enterprises and the fact that what is normally done on a day to day basis in one type of

---

[39] See *Dickinson v. Valpy* (1829) 10 B. & C. 128; *Crellin v. Brook* (1845) 14 M. & W. 11.

[40] See *supra*, para. 12–01.

[41] This quotation is taken from the 15th ed. (p. 287), but substantially the same view was expressed in the 6th ed. (1893) at p. 134. As appears from the preface to that edition, Lord Lindley did approve its content.

[42] *Morans v. Armstrong* (1840) Arm. M. & O. 25.

[43] i.e. it involves a factual conclusion based on an assessment of the primary facts so is not a question of primary fact: see *Dubai Aluminium Co Ltd. v. Salaam* [2003] 2 A.C. 366 at [18], [24] *per* Lord Nicholls and [112] *per* Lord Millett. Although this was a decision under the Partnership Act 1890, s.10 (*infra*, para. 12–88), it has been held that the expressions "acting in the ordinary course of the business of the firm" in that section and "carrying on in the usual way business of the kind carried on by the firm" in s.5 in substance amount to the same thing: see *J.J. Coughlan Ltd. v. Ruparelia* [2004] P.N.L.R. 4, at (CA) [2]. It follows that decided cases are unlikely to be of great assistance: see *Dubai Aluminium Co. Ltd. v. Salaam* [2001] Q.B. 113, 142B–E *per* Aldous L.J. (albeit that the main part of the decision was reversed on appeal: see *supra*); also *McDonic v. Hetherington* (1997) 142 D.L.R. (4th) 648, 656b. However, Panckhurst J. had no hesitation in referring to earlier authorities in *Clasper v. Duns* [2007] NZHC 1000.

[44] See *United Bank of Kuwait Ltd. v. Hammoud* [1988] 1 W.L.R. 1051, *infra*, para. 12–17.

business may be exceptional in another. It follows that general rules are difficult, if not impossible, to formulate,[45] as Lord Lindley recognised:

" . . . no answer of any value can be given to the abstract question—Can one partner bind his firm by such and such an act? unless, having regard to what is usual in business, it can be predicated of the act in question either that it is one without which no business can be carried on, or that it is one which is not necessary for carrying on any business whatever.[46] There are obviously very few acts of which any such assertions can be truly made. The great majority of acts, and practically all which give rise to doubt, are those which are usual in one business and not in another."[47]

Thus, whilst it may not be in the ordinary course of business for a partner in a firm of solicitors to accept the role of trustee,[48] the position may conceivably be different in the case of a partner in a firm of accountants.[49] Equally, in *McHugh v. Kerr*,[50] it was conceded that it was part of the ordinary business of "many firms of accountants" to buy and sell shares and the fact that the firm in question had, on occasion, done so put the matter beyond doubt.[51] Again, in *Goldberg v. Miliadous*[52] it was without more held that it was part of the ordinary business of an accountant to express a view on the risks associated with an investment.

It must, nevertheless, be accepted that, where a firm enters into a contract for the purposes of its business, any act required to be done pursuant to that contract will automatically be treated as done for such purposes and, thus, be within the usual course of that business, even if the same act, if done independently of the contract, may be treated differently.[53] Equally, an act which actually brings the

---

[45] See *Dubai Aluminium Co. Ltd. v. Salaam* [2001] Q.B. 113, 142B–E *per* Aldous L.J. (the main decision being reversed on appeal: see *supra*); *McDonic v. Hetherington* (1997) 142 D.L.R. (4th) 648, 656 *et seq.*

[46] Note that a partner in a solicitors' firm, who assaulted his opponent within the precincts of the court, was held to be acting outside the ordinary course of business in *Flynn v. Robin Thompson & Partners, The Times*, March 14, 2000 (CA). *Per contra*, perhaps, in the case of an assault in court during the course of a hearing: *ibid.* In *Petrou v. Hatzigeorgiou* [1991] Aust. Torts Rep. 81–071 (CA, NSW), when considering an act of horseplay by a partner which resulted in injury to an employee, the court decided that the act had to be viewed in an industrial context and compared to the type of conduct to be expected of employees.

[47] Lord Lindley went on: "Take, for example, negotiable instruments: it may be necessary for one member of a firm of bankers to draw, accept, or indorse a bill of exchange on behalf of the firm, and to require that each member should put his name to it would be ridiculous; but it by no means follows, nor is it in fact true, that it is usual for one of several solicitors to possess a similar power, for it is no part of the ordinary business of a solicitor to draw, accept, or indorse bills of exchange. The question, therefore, Can one partner bind the firm by accepting bills in its name? admits of no general answer; the nature of the business and the practice of those who carry it on (usage or custom of the trade) must be known before any answer can be given: see *Hogarth v. Latham* (1878) 3 Q.B.D. 643; *Taunton v. Royal Ins. Co.* (1864) 2 H. & M. 135." The current editor is of the opinion that it is now at the very least "usual" for a solicitor to draw cheques on behalf of the firm so that Lord Lindley's example is no longer accurate. See also *infra*, para. 12–51.

[48] See *infra*, para. 12–15.

[49] *Clasper v. Duns* [2007] NZHC 1000 at [52] *per* Panckhurst J. This observation was, however, *obiter*.

[50] [2003] EWHC 2985 (Ch) (Lawtel 22/12/03).

[51] *ibid.* at [42] *per* Lawrence Collins J.

[52] [2010] EWHC 450 (QB) (Lawtel 19/3/10) at [138] *per* Tugendhat J.

[53] *Bank of Scotland v. Henry Butcher & Co* [2003] 2 All E.R. (Comm) 557 (CA).

firm's business to an end (or which is clearly intended to have that effect) will *not* be regarded as done in the usual or ordinary course of its business.[54]

12–14   It should be noticed that the courts are now more ready than they once were to find that a partner was acting in the usual or ordinary course of the firm's business[55] and the fact that vicarious liability is involved tends to bring overt policy considerations into play.[56] This trend led Lord Nicholls in *Dubai Aluminium Co. Ltd. v. Salaam* to formulate the test for liability under section 10 of the 1890 Act[57] in these terms[58]:

> " . . . the wrongful conduct must be so closely connected with acts the partner . . . was authorised to do that, for the purpose of the liability of the firm . . . to third parties, the wrongful conduct may *fairly and properly* be regarded as done by the partner while acting in the ordinary course of the firm's business . . . ".[59]

There is an obvious risk that this liberal approach will in future colour the court's approach in cases falling within sections 5 and 10, as illustrated by Dyson L.J.'s observation in *J.J. Coughlan Ltd. v. Ruparelia*,[60] that:

> " . . . the court should not be too ready to find that the ordinary business requirement is not satisfied."

Equally, it is fair to say that he went on to recognise that the test formulated in *Dubai Aluminium* in relation to section 10 is "broader"[61] but, on the facts, the court held that the fraud in question perpetrated by a solicitor in the course of promoting a "preposterous" and "abnormal" investment scheme did *not* satisfy the requirements of either section.[62]

Solicitors' firms

12–15   Although it is dangerous to place too great a reliance on the decided cases,[63] the general approach of the court can usefully be illustrated by the attitude which has, over the years, been adopted when considering the authority of a member of a firm of solicitors. Thus, it is clearly within the usual course of a solicitor's

---

[54] See *Chahal v. Mahal* [2005] 2 B.C.L.C. 655 at [40] (albeit not a decision under s.5 or 10 of the 1890 Act); also *Ashborder BV v. Green Gas Power Ltd.* [2005] B.C.C. 634 at [227] *per* Etherton J. (a decision relating to the construction and application of a company debenture).

[55] See, for example, *Dubai Aluminium Co Ltd. v. Salaam* [2003] 2 A.C. 366 (HL); *McHugh v. Kerr* [2003] EWHC 2985 (Ch) (Lawtel 22/12/03); *Goldberg v. Miltiadous* [2010] EWHC 450 (QB) (Lawtel 19/3/10), all decisions under s.10.

[56] See *Dubai Aluminium Co Ltd. v. Salaam, supra*, at [21], [22] *per* Lord Nicholls and [107] *per* Lord Millett. Note also *Strother v. 3464920 Canada Inc.* [2007] 2 S.C.R. 177 (Can. Sup. Ct.) at [103].

[57] The test is, in effect, the same under this section: see *supra*, para. 12–13, n.43.

[58] [2003] 2 A.C. 366 at [23].

[59] See also *ibid.* at [124] *per* Lord Millett.

[60] [2004] P.N.L.R. 4 at [30].

[61] *ibid.* at [37].

[62] Note also *Sweetman v. Nathan* [2004] P.N.L.R. 7, where the Court of Appeal allowed a negligence action brought against a solicitor's partners to proceed even though he had seemingly participated in a fraud jointly with the claimant. The court observed (at [66]) that " . . . the plight of the innocent partners arouses sympathy but becoming a partner with a negligent or fraudulent person has as a consequence that you may be liable for his negligence or fraud."

[63] This view was expressed by Aldous L.J. in *Dubai Aluminium Co. Ltd. v. Salaam* [2001] Q.B. 113, 142B–E, although the main decision was reversed on appeal; see also *McDonic v. Hetherington* (1997) 142 D.L.R. (4th) 648, 656b. cf. *Clasper v. Duns* [2007] NZHC 1000, where Panckhurst J. did appear to derive assistance from the decided cases.

business to receive a client's money in the course of handling a transaction on his behalf[64] or to receive trust money as agent of the trustees,[65] but not necessarily to receive money in other circumstances.[66] Again it is normal for solicitors to give undertakings,[67] but the terms of a particular undertaking or the true nature of the underlying transaction may be of such a nature that its propriety is called into question: the fact that an undertaking is given by a solicitor is not, *per se*, sufficient to affix the firm with liability.[68] *A fortiori*, in the case of a solicitor guaranteeing a client's debt.[69] When considering issues of this kind, it is unlikely to be relevant that the firm does little or no work in the area in question.[70]

It is perfectly possible for a solicitor to commit a fraud or other wrong in the usual course of his firm's practice,[71] but it is again the nature of the underlying transaction and the activities carried out which are of critical importance. If the partner is clearly acting in some capacity other than that of a solicitor or is involved in a transaction which is not normal for a solicitor to engage in, *e.g.* promoting a "preposterous" investment scheme, the firm will not be liable, even if he has carried out work which would otherwise be normal for a solicitor to do.[72] Equally, where, as will usually be the case, the underlying transaction is not clearly divorced from his capacity and is not obviously of an unusual nature, the result is likely to be very different.[73] Thus, where a partner knowingly colluded with his clients and others in structuring and implementing a dishonest scheme involving the preparation of sham documents, the firm was held liable because the drafting of those documents was closely associated with the work he would normally be expected to carry out in the ordinary course of business.[74] Similarly where a partner carried out routine conveyancing work *qua* solicitor in pursuance of an unlawful conspiracy.[75] By way of contrast, where a partner and his client collude in a fraudulent act, the client may still be entitled to proceed against the

12–16

[64] *Hirst v. Etherington* [1999] Lloyd's Rep. P.N. 938, 941 (CA); *Ruparel v. Awan* [2001] Lloyd's Rep. P.N. 258; *cf. Langley Holdings v. Seakins* 2000 WL 1675192, where there was held to be no *genuine* client transaction in contemplation when money was received from a third party. As to the receipt of money for investment, see *Doobey v. Watson* (1888) 39 Ch.D. 178, 183 *per* Kekewich J.; *McDonic v. Hetherington, supra. cf. Polkinghorn v. Holland* [1934] 51 C.L.R. 143.

[65] *Mara v. Browne* [1896] 1 Ch. 199 (CA); *Re Bell's Indenture* [1980] 1 W.L.R. 1217, *infra*, paras 12–30, 12–112.

[66] *Hirst v. Etherington, supra*; *Langley Holdings v. Seakins, supra*; *Antonelli v. Allen* [2001] Lloyd's Rep. PN 487, where money was received in circumstances where there was no underlying transaction, actual or contemplated. See further, *infra*, paras 12–106 *et seq.*

[67] *United Bank of Kuwait Ltd. v. Hammoud* [1988] 1 W.L.R. 1051 (CA).

[68] *Hirst v. Etherington, supra*; *Ruparel v. Awan, supra.*

[69] *Hirst v. Etherington, supra*, citing *Silver v. Baines* [1971] 1 Q.B. 396; *Ruparel v. Awan, supra.*

[70] *McHugh v. Kerr* [2003] EWHC 2985 (Ch) (Lawtel 22/12/03) at [43] *per* Lawrence Collins J.

[71] See *infra*, paras 12–87 *et seq.*

[72] *J.J. Coughlan Ltd. v. Ruparelia* [2004] P.N.L.R. 4; also *Polkinghorn v. Holland* [1934] 51 C.L.R. 143, where the partner had entered into a business engagement with a client: *ibid.* p. 157. Equally, in other respects he had clearly acted as solicitor and the firm was held liable. Note also *Rowntree v. Roach Pittis* 2000 WL 1421213, where a partner had approached clients of the firm with a particular investment opportunity.

[73] The decision in *Korz v. St. Pierre* [1987] 43 D.L.R. (4th) 528 (CA Ontario) would seem to be a case of this type. There a partner had personally entered into a business arrangement with clients of the firm but had failed to inform them that he had previously divested himself of his assets. It was held that he had also acted as their solicitor and should have disclosed that fact, so that his partner was liable.

[74] *Dubai Aluminium Co. Ltd. v. Salaam* [2003] 2 A.C. 366 (HL).

[75] *Scarborough Building Society v. Howes Percival* (1998) 76 P. & C.R. D4 (CA). This case was seemingly not cited in *Dubai Aluminium Co. Ltd. v. Salaam, supra.*

firm in respect of a breach of the duty which that partner owed to him, provided that the act and the breach were independent of each other.[76]

Whilst it may not be within the usual course of business for a solicitor to accept the office of trustee[77] or to act as a trustee *de son tort*,[78] it does not necessarily follow that, whilst acting within the scope of his implied authority, a partner may not render himself liable as a *constructive* trustee.[79]

Finally, a physical assault by a partner on his opponent will not entail liability on the part of his firm, unless, exceptionally, it takes place during the course of a court hearing.[80]

The impact of changing business practices

12–17   What is "usual" in a particular business will vary from time to time[81] and, accordingly, the older authorities should, in any event, be approached critically. This was emphasised in *United Bank of Kuwait Ltd. v. Hammoud*,[82] where Staughton L.J., having been referred to a number of "elderly cases" relating to the ordinary authority of a solicitor, observed:

> "That material should today be treated with caution, in my judgment; the work that solicitors do can be expected to have changed since 1888; it has changed in recent times and is changing now. So I prefer to have regard to the expert evidence of today in deciding what is the ordinary authority of a solicitor."

The opportunities for the diversification of solicitors' practices into the realm of financial services are a case in point.[83] Equally, it may be that changing business practices serve to *reinforce* decisions in earlier cases.[84]

---

[76] *Sweetman v. Nathan* [2004] P.N.L.R. 7 (CA), noted *supra*, para. 12–14, n.62.

[77] *Re Fryer* (1857) 3 K. & J. 317; *Tendring Hundred Waterworks v. Jones* [1903] 2 Ch. 615, *infra*, para. 12–125. The decision in *Re Bell's Indenture* [1980] 1 W.L.R. 1217 can no longer be relied on this context: see *Dubai Aluminium Co Ltd. v. Salaam, supra*, at [42] *per* Lord Nicholls, and [143] *per* Lord Millett. *Quaere*, could it be argued that the usual course of a solicitors' business has changed in this respect? The Court of Appeal in *Walker v. Stones* [2001] Q.B. 902, 950F–G certainly appeared to think so but Lord Millett in *Dubai Aluminium* did not agree: see *ibid.* at [134]. Lord Nichols expressed no view on this issue: *ibid.* at [42]. See also *Hansen v. Young* [2004] 1 N.Z.L.R. 37 at [35] (CA). *cf. Public Trustee v. Mortimer* (1985) 16 D.L.R (4th) 404.

[78] *Mara v. Browne* [1896] 1 Ch. 199, as explained in *Dubai Aluminium Co Ltd. v. Salaam, supra*, at [132] to [143] *per* Lord Millett, who in fact preferred the expression "*de facto* trustee". Again, Lord Nicholls preferred to leave the whole point open at *ibid.* [40] to [42].

[79] *Dubai Aluminium Co. Ltd. v. Salaam, supra*. Equally, Lord Millett appeared to deprecate the use of the expression "constructive trustee" in this sense: *ibid.* at [142], [143]. *cf. Estate Realities Ltd. v. Wignall* [1992] 2 N.Z.L.R. 615. See further, *infra*, paras 12–30, 12–102.

[80] *Flynn v. Robin Thompson & Partners, The Times*, March 14, 2000 (CA).

[81] See for example, *Mann v. D'Arcy* [1968] 1 W.L.R. 893, where Megarry J. seems to have been swayed by considerations of commercial expediency without reference to evidence of what was "usual" in the particular business.

[82] [1988] 1 W.L.R. 1051, 1063F. See also *Dubai Aluminium Co. Ltd. v. Salaam* [2001] Q.B. 113, 142B–E *per* Aldous L.J. (although the main decision was overturned on appeal); *Walker v. Stones* [2001] Q.B. 902, 950F–G (CA); *Bank of Scotland v. Henry Butcher & Co* [2003] 2 All E.R. (Comm) 557 (CA) at [20] to [23] *per* Munby J.

[83] See *infra*, para. 12–114. See also *Doobey v. Watson* (1888) 39 Ch.D. 178, 183 *per* Kekewich J.; *McDonic v. Hetherington* (1997) 142 D.L.R. (4th) 648. *cf. Polkinghorn v. Holland* [1934] 51 C.L.R. 143.

[84] See *Dubai Aluminium Co Ltd. v. Salaam* [2003] 2 A.C. 366 at [134] where Lord Millett was considering the decisions in *Re Fryer* (1857) 3 K. & J. 317 and *Mara v. Browne* [1896] 1 Ch. 199.

Commercial requirements of business

Commercial considerations will also be of relevance in this context. Thus, **12–18** whilst one partner does not, in general, have implied authority to enter into partnership with a third party in order to carry on a business wholly different to that carried on by the main firm,[85] he may have such authority if the subsidiary partnership will, in effect, carry on the *same* business, *i.e.* where the arrangement represents a means of carrying on the main firm's business. This was the position in *Mann v. D'Arcy*.[86] However, it is doubtful whether the decision established any principle of more general application, given the exceptional circumstances, *i.e.* a subsidiary partnership formed for a single venture which at all times remained under the direct control of the main firm.

The current editor does not consider that the above argument could be deployed with a view to overriding the specific provisions of section 24(7) of the Partnership Act 1890, thus forcing an unwilling minority of partners to take on a new partner or partners, either for a particular venture or generally.[87]

Scope of business

What is usual in relation to a particular business may also depend on what can **12–19** properly be regarded as within its scope. Thus, in *Lindern Trawler Managers v. W. H. J. Trawlers*,[88] a member of a firm formed for the purpose of promoting a trawler company was held to have ostensible (albeit not actual) authority to employ agents to manage a trawler. Similarly, in *Mercantile Credit Co. v. Garrod*,[89] the scope of a garage business concerned mainly with letting lock-up garages and car repairs was treated as including the buying and selling of cars, even though this was expressly prohibited by the partnership agreement.[90]

The scope of a particular business will, of course, vary according to the circumstances[91] and is, essentially, a question of fact.[92] It may even be defined by the terms of a contract into which the firm has entered and, thus, authorise all acts required in connection with the implementation of that contract, even if they would otherwise be outside the scope of that business.[93]

Authority in cases of urgency or necessity

Urgency or necessity does not alter the extent of a partner's implied author- **12–20** ity.[94] Thus, even if the firm's future or the safety of its assets depend on a partner

---

[85] *Singleton v. Knight* (1888) 13 App.Cas. 788; *Hawksley v. Outram* [1892] 3 Ch. 359; also *Ex p. British Nation Life Assurance Association* (1878) 8 Ch.D. 679, 704. But see the review of these authorities by Megarry J. in *Mann v. D'Arcy* [1968] 1 W.L.R. 893.

[86] [1968] 1 W.L.R. 893.

[87] See the Partnership Act 1890, s.24(8), *infra*, paras 15–04 *et seq.*

[88] (1949) 83 Ll.L.Rep. 131.

[89] [1962] 3 All E.R. 1103.

[90] The claimant finance company, which had purchased a car from one of the partners, did not know of the restriction contained in the agreement and believed it was dealing with the partnership.

[91] See *Re Bell's Indenture* [1980] 1 W.L.R. 1217 (albeit that the major part of the decision was overruled in *Dubai Aluminium Co. Ltd. v. Salaam* [2003] 2 A.C. 366 (HL)). Note also *Nixon v. Wood* (1987) 284 E.G. 1055.

[92] See *supra*, para. 12–13.

[93] *Bank of Scotland v. Henry Butcher & Co* [2003] 2 All E.R. (Comm) 557 (CA).

[94] The current editor believes that the doctrine of agency of necessity will not apply, since it is confined to a number of recognised exceptional cases: see *Gwilliam v. Twist* [1895] 2 Q.B. 84, 87 *per* Lord Esher M.R.; *Jebara v. Ottoman Bank* [1927] 2 K.B. 254, 270; *Sachs v. Miklos* [1948] 2 K.B. 23, 35–36; *cf. Prager v. Blatspiel, Stamp & Heacock* [1924] 1 K.B. 566. And see generally, *Bowstead & Reynolds on Agency* (19th ed.), Art. 33, paras 4–001 *et seq.*

doing a particular act, the firm will not be bound unless that act is done within the usual course of its business. Lord Lindley explained:

> "Nor it seems will necessity itself be sufficient if it be an extraordinary necessity . . . therefore, in a case where the nature of the business was one in which there was no necessity to borrow money to carry it on under ordinary circumstances and in the ordinary manner, the Court held the firm not liable for money borrowed by its agent under extraordinary circumstances, although money was absolutely requisite to save the property of the firm from ruin.[95] This case is an authority for saying that a power to do what is usual does not include a power to do what is unusual, however urgent[96]; and although in the case referred to the money was not borrowed by a partner, but by a person who was only an agent of the firm, the decision would, it is apprehended, have been the same if he had been a partner. For notwithstanding the fact that every partner is to a certain extent a principal as well as an agent, the liability of his co-partners for his acts can only be established on the ground of agency. As their agent he has no discretion except within the limits set by them to his authority, and the fact that he is himself, as one of the firm, a principal, does not warrant him in extending those limits, save on his own responsibility."[97]

Admissions and representations

Partnership Act 1890, section 15

12–21   The Partnership Act 1890 contains the following section:

> "15. An admission or representation made by any partner concerning the partnership affairs, and in the ordinary course of its business, is evidence against the firm."[98]

Although an admission may, in this way, be evidence against the firm,[99] it is not necessarily conclusive,[100] unless it gives rise to an estoppel.[101] Similarly, in the case of a representation.

Where the section does not apply

12–22   The section will only apply where the admission or representation is made in the "ordinary" course of the firm's business.[102] This will not only exclude the obvious case of admissions made in an action brought by or against the firm, *e.g.*

---

[95] See *Hawtayne v. Bourne* (1841) 7 M. & W. 595; also *Ex p. Chippendale* (1854) 4 De G.M. & G. 19; *Simpson's Claim* (1887) 36 Ch.D. 532. See also *infra*, para. 12–47.

[96] And see *Cox v. Midland Counties Ry.* (1849) 3 Ex. 268; *Houghton v. Pilkington* [1912] 3 K.B. 308.

[97] See *Dickinson v. Valpy* (1829) 10 B. & C. 128; *Ricketts v. Bennett* (1847) 4 C.B. 686.

[98] This accords with the previous law: *Thwaites v. Richardson* (1790) Peake 23; *Grant v. Jackson* (1793) Peake 268; *Wood v. Braddick* (1808) 1 Taunt. 104; *Pritchard v. Draper* (1834) 2 Cl. & F. 379; *Nicholls v. Dowding* (1815) 1 Stark. 81; *Sangster v. Mazarredo* (1816) 1 Stark. 161; *Wright v. Court* (1825) 2 Car. & P. 232. As to representations, see *Rapp v. Latham* (1819) 2 B. & A. 795; *Blair v. Bromley* (1847) 2 Ph. 354. It should be noted that most out of court statements, whether written or oral, are now generally admissible in evidence, subject to compliance with the requirements of the Civil Evidence Act 1995.

[99] *Quaere* does the section apply in criminal cases?

[100] See *Newton v. Belcher* (1848) 12 Q.B. 921; *Newton v. Liddiard* (1848) 12 Q.B. 925; *Wickham v. Wickham* (1855) 2 K. & J. 478; *Hollis v. Burton* [1892] 3 Ch. 226; also *supra*, para. 7–24.

[101] See *Re Coasters Ltd.* [1911] 1 Ch. 86, where the estoppel was relied on by the firm.

[102] Note that the expression "usual" is not used in this section: *cf.* s.5, *supra*, para. 12–02. The current editor is of the opinion that the words "ordinary" and "usual" are to all intents and purposes synonymous.

in pleadings,[103] but also representations as to a partner's authority to bind the firm.[104] As Lord Donaldson M.R. put it in *United Bank of Kuwait Ltd. v. Hammoud*[105]:

" . . . it is trite law that an agent cannot ordinarily confer ostensible authority on himself. He cannot pull himself up by his own shoe laces."

The position is likely to be the same where a partner makes representations as to the nature and extent of the firm's business and, thus, only indirectly to his authority to bind the firm.[106]

An admission made by an *intending* partner does not fall within the section since, by definition, he cannot have made it in the ordinary course of the firm's business.[107] The mere fact that he has become a partner when the admission is sought to be used against the firm is irrelevant. Equally, a representation made by an existing proprietor of a business does not bind persons with whom he subsequently enters into partnership, even if they relate to that proposed partnership.[108]

Notice to partners

Lord Lindley summarised the application of the doctrine of notice as between **12–23**
partners in this way:

" . . . as a general rule, notice to one partner of any matter relating to the business of the firm is notice to all the other members."[109]

Partnership Act 1890, section 16

This approach is now reflected in section 16 of the Partnership Act 1890, **12–24**
which provides:

"16. Notice to any partner who habitually acts in the partnership business of any matter relating to partnership affairs operates as notice to the firm, except in the case of a fraud on the firm committed by or with the consent of that partner."

Effect of the section

The section has the following two consequences: **12–25**

 (1) If a firm claims the benefit of a transaction entered into by a partner or
     is otherwise bound by his acts, it cannot use its own ignorance of what

---

[103] *Hollis v. Burton* [1892] 3 Ch. 226. Similarly in the case of answers to interrogatories under the old rules of procedure: see *Dale v. Hamilton* (1846) 5 Hare 369; *Parker v. Morrell* (1848) 2 Ph. 453; also *Hollis v. Burton* [1892] 3 Ch. 226. Equally, if the other partners do not choose to challenge or contradict an admission so made, they may be taken to have adopted it, quite apart from the provisions of s.15: *ibid.*

[104] *Ex p. Agace* (1792) 2 Cox 312, *infra*, para. 12–99; *United Bank of Kuwait v. Hammoud* [1988] 1 W.L.R. 1051; *Hirst v. Etherington* [1999] Lloyd's Rep. P.N. 938, 942–943 (CA). See also *Armagas Ltd. v. Mundogas S.A.* [1986] A.C. 717 and the cases there cited.

[105] [1988] 1 W.L.R. 1051, 1066H, as cited in *Hirst v. Etherington, supra.*

[106] *Ex p. Agace, supra.* See further *infra*, para. 12–100.

[107] *Tunley v. Evans* (1845) 2 Dow. & L. 747; *Catt v. Howard* (1820) 3 Stark. 3.

[108] *In the matter of Burton Marsden Douglas* [2004] 3 All E.R. 222 at [30]. There it was sought to be argued, unsuccessfully, that there had been a representation by silence *after* the partnership had been formed.

[109] *Porthouse v. Parker* (1807) 1 Camp. 82; *Alderson v. Pope* (1808) 1 Camp. 404; *Bignold v. Waterhouse* (1813) 1 M. & S. 255; also *Salomons v. Nissen* (1788) 2 T.R. 674.

that partner knew[110] to place itself in a more favourable position than could have been achieved by that partner if he had been acting on his own account.[111]

(2) When it is necessary to prove that a firm has notice of some fact, all that is required is to show that notice was given to one of the partners who habitually acts in the partnership business.[112]

It should be emphasised that the firm does not have notice of everything done by each of its members, but only of those matters which relate to the partnership. Any other result would be absurd.[113] Moreover, the section does not result in the other partners having *actual* knowledge of something known to one of their number but merely imputed knowledge of it.[114]

Firms with a common partner

12–26   If two firms have a common partner, notice which is imputable to one firm is also imputable to the other, so long as it relates to the latter's business.[115] Where, however, a partner's knowledge relates to the affairs of a client or customer of one firm, that knowledge will not be imputed to the other firm.[116] This will be of particular relevance in the case of firms of solicitors and accountants who may act for clients with opposing interests, although the court will, in any such case, always be concerned to ensure that the clients' rights to confidentiality are fully protected.[117]

---

[110] This connotes actual knowledge: *Zurich GSG Ltd. v. Gray & Kellas* 2007 S.L.T. 917 (OH) at [19] *per* Lord Brodie. Note that the existence of a duty of confidentiality as regards the clients of a solicitor's firm was held insufficient to displace the application of the section: *ibid.*

[111] See, generally, *Collinson v. Lister* (1855) 7 De G.M. & G. 634; *Oppenheimer v. Frazer & Wyatt* [1907] 2 K.B. 50.

[112] This formulation was approved in *Zurich GSG Ltd. v. Gray & Kellas supra Financial Services Authority v. Fox Hayes* [2009] 1 B.C.L.C. 603 would appear to be a case of this class, albeit that the Partnership Act 1890, s.16 was not referred to: see *ibid.* at [34] *per* Longmore L.J. *Quaere*, must the partner be acting in the partnership business when notice if given to him?

[113] This was the word used by Lord Lindley.

[114] See *Zurich GSG Ltd. v. Gray & Kellas, supra.*

[115] See *Steele v. Stuart* (1866) L.R. 2 Eq. 84; also *Porthouse v. Parker* (1807) 1 Camp. 82; *Jacaud v. French* (1810) 12 East 317; *Powles v. Page* (1846) 3 C.B. 16; *Re Worcester Corn Exchange Co.* (1853) 3 De G.M. & G. 180.

[116] *Campbell v. McCreath*, 1975 S.L.T. (Notes) 5, distinguishing *Steele v. Stuart, supra. cf. Zurich GSG Ltd. v. Gray & Kellas* 2007 S.L.T. 917 (OH), noted *infra*, para. 12–27.

[117] If leakage of confidential information were apprehended, the court could, in theory, injunct either or both of the firms from acting. See the following cases concerning solicitors' firms: *Rakusen v. Ellis, Munday & Clarke* [1912] 1 Ch. 831; *David Lee & Co. (Lincoln) Ltd. v. Coward Chance* [1991] Ch. 229; *Re A Firm of Solicitors* [1992] Q.B. 959; *Re A Firm of Solicitors* [1997] Ch. 1; *Halewood International Ltd. v. Addleshaw Booth & Co.* [2000] P.N.L.R. 788; *Koch Shipping Inc. v. Richards Butler* [2002] 2 All E.R. (Comm) 957; *Ball v. Druces & Attlee* [2002] P.N.L.R. 23 and [2004] P.N.L.R. 39; *Marks & Spencer Group Plc v. Freshfields Bruckhaus Deringer* [2004] 1 W.L.R. 2331; *Gus Consulting GmbH v. Leboeuf, Lamb, Greene & MacRae* [2006] P.N.L.R. 32 (CA); *cf. Winters v. Mishcon de Reya* (2008) 158 N.L.J. 1494. Similarly in the case of accountants: *Bolkiah v. K.P.M.G.* [1999] 2 A.C. 222 (HL); *Young v. Robson Rhodes* [1999] 3 All E.R. 524; *Akai Holdings Ltd. v. RSM Robson Rhodes LLP* [2007] EWHC 1641 (Ch) (Lawtel 8/8/07). It will never be possible for the *same* firm to act for both sides in a dispute unless the parties give their informed consent: *Bolkiah v. K.P.M.G., supra*, pp. 234H–235B *per* Lord Millett. *Semble*, it will not be possible to imply consent in such a case; *per contra* in a non-contentious matter: *ibid.*; also *Kelly v. Cooper* [1993] A.C. 205 (PC), a decision concerning estate agents. See also the Solicitors' Code of Conduct 2007, r. 4 as amended by the Solicitors' Code of Conduct (Confidentiality and Disclosure) Amendment Rule 2010.

Knowledge of solicitors

In addition to the case last supposed, it would seem that knowledge acquired   **12–27**
by a partner in a firm of solicitors whilst transacting business on behalf of a client
would not be imputed to the firm on a subsequent purchase of property by the
firm itself.[118] However, apart from this statutory exception, there is no general
justification for excluding the application of section 16 to a firm merely because
a partner is in receipt of confidential information from a client.[119]

Constructive notice

The equitable doctrine of constructive notice[120] is not, as a general rule,   **12–28**
imported into commercial transactions[121] and, accordingly, has no place in the
law of partnership.[122]

Frauds

Lord Lindley stated that: **12–29**

> "Where one member is acting beyond his powers, or is committing a fraud on his
> co-partners, or is the person whose duty it is to give his firm notice of what he himself
> has done, in all such cases notice on his part is not equivalent to notice to
> them."[123]

It is the view of the current editor that, as a statement of general principle, this
must be approached with caution, since section 16 of the Partnership Act 1890
only excepts cases which amount to "a fraud on the firm committed by or with
the consent of [*the partner who has notice of the matter in question*]." A partner
who merely acts beyond his powers or who is otherwise in breach of a duty of
disclosure will not *necessarily* be acting in fraud of his co-partners, even if fraud
is construed in its widest sense.

An illustration of the fraud exception is to be found in *Bignold v. Waterhouse*.[124] There a partner in a firm of carriers had entered into an agreement to
carry valuable parcels free of charge in fraud of his co-partners, so that they were
not bound thereby. A particular parcel, which only the partner who had made the
agreement knew to be valuable, was sent and lost. The other partners were held

---

[118] See the Law of Property Act 1925, s.199(1)(ii)(b). The same principle applies where the firm
takes a lease or mortgage of property: *ibid.* s.205(1)(xxi).

[119] *Zurich GSG Ltd. v. Gray & Kellas* 2007 S.L.T. 917 (OH) at [19] *per* Lord Brodie.

[120] *i.e.* that a person is deemed to know what he might have discovered on inquiry.

[121] *Greer v. Downs Supply Co.* [1927] 2 K.B. 28; *Nelson v. Larholt* [1948] 1 K.B. 339; *Feuer
Leather Corp. v. Frank Johnstone & Sons* [1981] Com.L.R. 251; also *Manchester Trust v. Furness*
[1895] 2 Q.B. 539, 545 *per* Lindley L.J.; *Newsholme Bros. v. Road Transport and General Insurance
Co.* [1929] 2 K.B. 356. Note that in *Re Montagu's Settlement* [1987] Ch. 264, 285, Megarry V.-C.
doubted whether there is any general doctrine of imputed *knowledge* as opposed to imputed notice.
See also the review of that and other authorities in *Bank of Credit and Commerce International
(Overseas) Ltd. v. Akindele* [2001] Ch. 437 (CA).

[122] See for example, *Lacey v. Hill* (1876) 4 Ch.D. 537, 547 *per* Jessel M.R.

[123] See the judgment of Jessel M.R. in *Williamson v. Barbour* (1877) 9 Ch.D. 529, 535 *et seq.*; also
Lacey v. Hill (1876) 4 Ch.D. 537 (affirmed *sub nom. Read v. Bailey* (1877) 3 App.Cas. 94). See further
Re Hampshire Land Co. [1896] 2 Ch. 743; *Houghton & Co. v. Nothard, Lowe & Wills Ltd.* [1928]
A.C. 1, 14, 15 *per* Viscount Dunedin, 19 *per* Viscount Sumner; *Newsholme Bros. v. Road Transport
and General Insurance Co.* [1929] 2 K.B. 356.

[124] (1813) 1 M. & S. 255.

not to have had notice of the parcel's true nature and were not liable for its loss.

It should be noted that if, in a case of this class, an employee of the firm has notice of what the fraudulent partner is doing, such notice will not be imputed to the other partners.[125]

Breaches of trust

12–30   If one partner, who is a trustee, improperly employs trust money in the partnership business, his knowledge will not be imputed to the firm and the other partners will not, without more, be liable for the breach of trust.[126] In any other case, whether one partner's knowledge that money in the firm's hands belongs to a trust will be so imputed must be determined, according to the principles previously discussed,[127] by reference to the nature of the partnership business and the purpose for which the money was received by the firm.

A member of a firm of solicitors has implied authority to receive trust money as agent for the trustees[128] but, whilst he may also be acting within his implied authority by rendering himself liable as a *constructive* trustee,[129] the same cannot be said for acting as a trustee *de son tort* or *de facto* trustee.[130] If, in the latter type of case, such authority cannot be established,[131] the innocent partners will not themselves be liable if they have no knowledge of the circumstances in which their partner constituted himself as such a trustee.[132]

The liability of a firm for breaches of trust committed by a partner will be considered in greater detail later in this work.[133]

Incoming and outgoing partners

12–31   An incoming partner is not affected with notice of what occurred before he joined the firm[134] and an outgoing partner is not in general affected with notice of what has occurred since he left the firm, provided that there is no continuing agency between him and the remaining partners.[135] However, where notice of dishonour is given to a continuing partner in respect of a partnership bill, that is, exceptionally, treated as sufficient notice to the outgoing partner.[136]

---

[125] See *Lacey v. Hill* (1876) 4 Ch.D. 537, affirmed *sub nom. Read v. Bailey* (1877) 3 App.Cas. 94; *Williamson v. Barbour* (1877) 9 Ch.D. 529, 536 *per* Jessell M.R.

[126] See the Partnership Act 1890, s.13, *infra*, paras 12–127 *et seq.*; also *Ex p. Heaton* (1819) Buck 386. Note, however, that the employment of the trust money in the business must have been improper; in any other case in which a partner holds a trusteeship, liability seemingly cannot arise under any other section: *Walker v. Stones* [2001] Q.B. 902 (CA), noted *infra*, para. 12–130. See also *infra*, paras 12–126 *et seq.*

[127] See *supra*, paras 12–13 *et seq.*

[128] *Mara v. Browne* [1896] 1 Ch. 199 (CA); *Re Bell's Indenture* [1980] 1 W.L.R. 1217.

[129] *Dubai Aluminium Co. Ltd. v. Salaam* [2003] 2 A.C. 366 (HL), noted *supra*, para. 12–16, overruling *Re Bell's Indenture, supra*, in this respect. *cf. Estate Realties v. Wignall* [1992] N.Z.L.R. 615.

[130] *Mara v. Browne, supra*, as explained in *Dubai Aluminium Co. Ltd. v. Salaam, supra*, at [132] to [143] *per* Lord Millett.

[131] This will, obviously, be a question of fact.

[132] *Mara v. Browne, supra*; also *Estate Realties v. Wignall, supra*.

[133] See *infra*, paras 12–126 *et seq.*

[134] See *Williamson v. Barbour* (1877) 9 Ch.D. 529, 535 *per* Jessel M.R.

[135] *Adams v. Bingley* (1836) 1 M. & W. 192. Note, however, the terms of the Partnership Act 1890, s.38, *infra*, paras 13–62 *et seq.*

[136] *Goldfarb v. Bartlett and Kremer* [1920] 1 K.B. 639.

Ratification

It is perhaps self evident that section 16 of the Partnership Act 1890 cannot be **12–32** used to circumvent the provisions of section 5, *i.e.* so as to show that the other partners have ratified an act which falls outside the scope of a partner's implied authority. Lord Lindley, writing prior to the Act, put it thus:

> " . . . if a partner exceeds his authority, and it is contended that the firm is bound by what he has done, on the ground that it has ratified his acts, evidence must be given to prove that at the time of the alleged ratification his co-partners knew of those acts. It would be absurd, if in such a case, knowledge by him was equivalent to knowledge by them."[137]

It should also, in this context, be noted that if one partner defrauds another, *e.g.* by improperly withdrawing moneys from the partnership bank account and crediting the amount withdrawn to his own account at another bank, and his co-partner is minded to ratify his actions, the ratification must relate to the whole transaction: he cannot ratify only part, merely because that would best serve his interests.[138]

2.   LIABILITY FOR ACTS WHICH ARE NOT IN THEMSELVES WRONGFUL

Although the difficulty of formulating general rules has already been noted,[139] it **12–33** is possible to demonstrate how the general principles embodied in the Partnership Act 1890 have been (and are, in the future, likely to be)[140] applied in a number of practical contexts. For ease of reference, these are arranged in alphabetical order.

For present purposes, the incidence of torts, frauds and other wrongs is ignored.[141]

Accounts

An account rendered by one partner in respect of a partnership transaction is **12–34** equivalent to an account rendered by the firm and will bind it.[142]

The authority of a partner to settle an account in relation to a partnership debt is less clear and will be considered hereafter.[143]

---

[137] See *Lacey v. Hill* (1876) 4 Ch.D. 537, affirmed *sub nom. Read v. Bailey* (1877) 3 App.Cas. 94; *Williamson v. Barbour* (1877) 9 Ch.D. 529. See also *Marsh v. Joseph* [1897] 1 Ch. 213, 246; *Hambro v. Burnand* [1903] 2 K.B. 399, 414 *per* Bigham J. (the actual decision being reversed at [1904] 2 K.B. 10).

[138] *Commercial Banking Co. of Sydney v. Mann* [1961] A.C. 1. But see also *Lipkin Gorman v. Karpnale Ltd.* [1989] 1 W.L.R. 1340, 1371 *per* Parker L.J. and [1991] 2 A.C. 548, 573, 584 *per* Lord Goff of Chievely.

[139] See *supra*, para. 12–13.

[140] Equally, account must always be taken of current business practices, which are by no means immutable: see *supra*, para. 12–17.

[141] See, as to liability for torts, frauds and other wrongs, *infra*, paras 12–87 *et seq.*

[142] *Fergusson v. Fyffe* (1841) 8 Cl. & F. 121. As to false accounts so rendered, see *infra*, para. 12–97.

[143] See *infra*, para. 12–57.

Actions

12–35   A partner will in general have the implied authority of his co-partners to bring or defend legal proceedings in their joint names or in the firm name, subject to indemnifying them against costs where he does so without their consent,[144] although this authority will normally cease once a partner has retired.[145] He may also enter, but not necessarily prosecute (otherwise than on his own behalf), an appeal against a joint assessment to value added tax.[146] What a partner seemingly cannot do is bring proceedings in his own name but on behalf of the firm[147] or, perhaps, bring proceedings in the firm name where the other party knows that he is doing so against the opposition of his co-partners.[148]

The right of a partner to submit a dispute to *arbitration* is considered later in this chapter.[149]

Insolvency proceedings

12–36   Prior to the introduction of the current insolvency legislation,[150] the power of a partner to act for the firm was, by statute,[151] extended to bankruptcy proceedings, including the proof of debts and voting at creditors' meetings.[152] Moreover, it was held that, notwithstanding the general rule prohibiting a partner from binding his firm by deed,[153] one partner might execute a power of attorney authorising a third party to represent the firm in such proceedings.[154] Since the current legislation does not confer any express authority on partners in relation to insolvency proceedings, it would seem that the limits of their implied authority will be the same as in any other legal proceedings.[155]

---

[144] See *infra*, paras 14–66 *et seq*. Note, however, as to the ability of one partner to represent the firm in proceedings in Scotland, *Clark Advertising Ltd. v. Scottish Enterprise Dunbartonshire* 2004 S.L.T. 85 (Sh Ct.).

[145] See *HLB Kidsons v. Lloyd's Underwriters* [2009] 1 All E.R. (Comm) 760. The position may be otherwise if the Partnership Act 1890, s.38 applies (see *infra*, paras 13–61 *et seq*.) or if the partnership agreement provides for the authority to continue: *ibid.* Authority as between the continuing partners will, of course, be unaffected. Note also that an incoming partner will not automatically acquire such authority: see *infra*, para. 14–50.

[146] See the *obiter* views of Glidewell J. in *Customs and Excise Commissioners v. Evans* [1982] S.T.C. 342, 349. Although Glidewell J. intimated that one partner *can* also prosecute the appeal, this would seem to be inconsistent with *Sutherland v. Gustar* [1994] Ch. 304, where the Court of Appeal held that a partner did not have authority to prosecute an appeal against a joint assessment to income tax. Tax is now assessed on the partners individually: see *infra*, para. 34–19. Note also, in this connection, *Phillips v. Revenue & Customs Commissioners* [2010] S.F.T.D. 332.

[147] *Re Sutherland & Partners' Appeal* [1993] S.T.C. 399, 406 *per* Lindsay J. This issue was not addressed in the Court of Appeal, *sub nom. Sutherland v. Gustar, supra*.

[148] This point was ultimately left open by Lindsay J.: *ibid.* See also [1994] Ch. 304, 310C–313B.

[149] See *infra*, para. 12–40.

[150] See the Insolvency Act 1986, the Insolvency Rules 1986 (as amended) and the Insolvent Partnerships Order 1994, considered *infra*, paras 27–01 *et seq*.

[151] Bankruptcy Act 1914, s.149; Bankruptcy Rules 1952, rr. 279 *et seq*.

[152] *Ex p. Mitchell* (1808) 14 Ves. Jr. 597.

[153] See Deeds, *infra*, para. 12–62.

[154] *Ex p. Mitchell* (1808) 14 Ves. Jr. 597; *Ex p. Hodgkinson* (1815) 19 Ves. Jr. 291, 298 *per* Lord Eldon.

[155] See the Insolvency Rules 1986, r. 7.51A, as substituted by the Insolvency (Amendment) Rules 2010 (SI 2010/686), Sched., para. 469) which applies specified parts of the CPR to insolvency proceedings, albeit "with any necessary modifications". Note also *ibid.* rr. 8.1 *et seq*. (as amended), relating to proxies.

Admissions

This subject has already been considered earlier in this chapter.[156]   **12–37**

Advice

It is submitted that a partner will normally have implied authority to seek   **12–38**
advice from solicitors or other professional advisers on behalf of his firm and, in
such cases, no obligation will be imposed on the adviser to communicate his
advice to all the partners individually, even where the transaction is of a risky
nature.[157]

Agents

It is submitted that a partner has implied authority to employ or to dispense   **12–39**
with the services of an agent.[158]

Arbitration

Lord Lindley wrote: **12–40**

> "One partner cannot, without special authority, bind the firm by a submission to
> arbitration.[159] The power to refer disputes, even although they relate to dealings with
> the firm, cannot be said to be an act done for carrying on its business in the ordinary
> way."[160]

Thus, if, following a dissolution, one partner undertakes to get in the partnership
debts and commences an action in the firm name in respect of one such debt, he
cannot then agree to refer all matters in dispute in the action to an arbitrator.[161]
The current editor is of the view that this is, in general, still the position. It
should, however, be noted that a partner may properly enter into a contract in the
usual way of business, *e.g.* for the supply of goods or services, under which all
disputes are to be resolved by arbitration. In such a case, the firm will be bound.
A distinction must thus be drawn between contractual and *ad hoc* references.

It goes almost without saying that the partner who actually agrees to the
reference will be bound by the award[162] and the other partners may subsequently
become bound by ratification.[163]

Bank accounts

Although it is considered that a partner will in general have implied authority   **12–41**
to open a bank account in the firm name, the same cannot be said of an account
in his own name.[164]

---

[156] See *supra*, paras 12–21 *et seq.*
[157] See *Berlevy v. Blyth Dutton* [1997] E.G.C.S. 133 (CA), which appears to have been a case of
express authority. See also *infra*, para. 14–69, n. 271.
[158] See the cases cited *infra*, para. 12–66, in relation to employees.
[159] See *Antram v. Chace* (1812) 15 East 209; *Stead v. Salt* (1825) 3 Bing. 101; *Adams v. Bankart*
(1835) 1 Cr. M. & R. 681; *Thomas v. Atherton* (1878) 10 Ch.D. 185, 190 *per* Bacon V.-C.
[160] *Stead v. Salt* (1825) 3 Bing. 101; *Adams v. Bankart* (1835) 1 Cr. M. & R. 681; and see *Boyd v.
Emmerson* (1834) 2 A. & E. 184.
[161] *Hatton v. Royle* (1858) 3 H. & N. 500.
[162] *Strangford v. Green* (1677) 2 Mod. 228.
[163] As in *Thomas v. Atherton* (1878) 10 Ch.D. 185.
[164] *Alliance Bank Ltd. v. Kearsley* (1871) L.R. 6 C.P. 433.

Bills of exchange and promissory notes

Trading partnerships

12–42   Lord Lindley observed that:

> "Every member of an ordinary trading partnership[165] has implied power to bind the firm by drawing, accepting, or indorsing bills of exchange, or by making and indorsing promissory notes in its name and for the purposes of the firm."

Even prior to the Partnership Act 1890, this general proposition had to be read subject to the requirement that the member should be acting in the ordinary course of business[166]; if it were otherwise, the firm would clearly not be bound.[167] This is still the position.

12–43   *Acceptances in blank.* A partner does not have implied power to accept bills in blank or to bind his co-partners, otherwise than jointly with himself. A bill accepted in blank by one partner in the firm name does not bind the firm, otherwise than in favour of a bona fide holder for value without notice of the manner of acceptance.[168]

Joint and several notes. A joint and several promissory note signed by one partner on behalf of himself and his co-partners, binds them jointly[169] but not severally.[170] However, the partner concerned is both jointly and severally liable.[171]

Two bills for same demand. If two partners, unknown to each other, give two bills in the firm name in payment of the same debt, the firm will be liable on both, provided that they are held by bona fide holders for value without notice of the mistake.[172]

Non-trading partnerships

12–44   Of such partnerships, Lord Lindley said this:

> "With respect to partnerships which are not trading partnerships, the question whether one partner has any implied authority to bind his co-partners by putting the name of the firm to a negotiable instrument, depends upon the nature of the business

---

[165] There is no authoritative definition of the expression "trading partnership", although it has been said that its business must consist in buying and selling goods: see *Wheatley v. Smithers* [1906] 2 K.B. 321; *Higgins v. Beauchamp* [1914] 3 K.B. 1192.

[166] See *Pinckney v. Hall* (1696) 1 Salk. 126; *Smith v. Baily* (1727) 11 Mod. 401; *Sutton v. Gregory* (1797) 2 Peake 150; *Dickinson v. Valpy* (1829) 10 B. & C. 128; *Lewis v. Reilly* (1841) 1 Q.B. 349; *Stephens v. Reynolds* (1860) 5 H. & N. 513; *Re Riches* (1865) 4 De G.J. & S. 581. See also the Bills of Exchange Act 1882, s.23(2) and *Ringham v. Hackett, The Times,* February 9, 1980 and (1980) 124 S.J. 201.

[167] See *Simpson's Claim* (1887) 36 Ch.D. 532.

[168] *Hogarth v. Latham* (1878) 3 Q.B.D. 643.

[169] *Maclae v. Sutherland* (1854) 3 E. & B. 1.

[170] See *Perring v. Hone* (1826) 4 Bing. 28, 32 *per* Best C.J.

[171] *Elliot v. Davis* (1800) 2 Bos. & Pul. 338; *Gillow v. Lillie* (1835) 1 Bing.N.C. 695; *Maclae v. Sutherland* (1854) 3 E. & B. 1.

[172] *Davison v. Robertson* (1815) 3 Dow. 218.

of the partnership.[173] In the absence of evidence showing . . . usage,[174] the power has been denied to one of several mining adventurers,[175] quarry workers,[176] farmers,[177] solicitors."[178]

To this list were subsequently added auctioneers.[179] Save in relation to cheques,[180] this statement of principle would still seem to hold good.

Implied authority to endorse bill. If a partner in such a firm concurs in drawing, or authorises his partner to draw, a bill in the firm name, he thereby impliedly authorises its endorsement in the same name for the purpose for which it was drawn.[181]

Authority to transfer bill

Even though a partner may have no authority to use the firm name so as to render his co-partners liable on a bill or note, he may nevertheless have sufficient authority to transfer the property in the firm's bills or notes.[182]   **12–45**

Bills not drawn in proper form

This subject will be considered later in this chapter.[183]

Promise to provide for bill

If one partner, in consideration of a person accepting a partnership bill, promises that the firm will put him in funds to meet it when it is due, the firm will be bound.[184]

Borrowing money

Trading partnerships

Lord Lindley was in no doubt as to the existence of the implied authority of the members of a trading partnership to borrow money: **12–46**

"One of the most important of the implied powers of a partner is that of borrowing money on the credit of the firm. The sudden exigencies of commerce render it

---

[173] See *Dickinson v. Valpy* (1829) 10 B. & C. 128.

[174] Lord Lindley in fact referred to "necessity or usage" at this point, having previously rejected necessity as a ground for extending a partner's implied authority: see *supra*, para. 12–20. The reference thereto was deleted in subsequent editions.

[175] *Brown v. Byers* (1847) 16 M. & W. 252; *Dickinson v. Valpy* (1829) 10 B. & C. 128; *cf. Brown v. Kidger* (1858) 3 H. & N. 853.

[176] *Thicknesse v. Bromilow* (1832) 2 Cr. & J. 425.

[177] *Greenslade v. Dower* (1828) 7 B. & C. 635.

[178] *Hedley v. Bainbridge* (1842) 3 Q.B. 316; *Levy v. Pyne* (1842) Car. & M. 453; *Harman v. Johnson* (1853) 2 E. & B. 61. And see *supra*, para. 12–13, n. 47.

[179] *Wheatley v. Smithers* [1906] 2 K.B. 321. This decision was in fact reversed on the construction of the partnership deed and on the facts, the Court of Appeal declining to express any opinion on the point of law: [1907] 2 K.B. 684.

[180] See *infra*, para. 12–51.

[181] See *Lewis v. Reilly* (1841) 1 Q.B. 349; *Garland v. Jacomb* (1873) L.R. 8 Ex. 216. And see also *Ringham v. Hackett, The Times*, February 9, 1980 and (1980) 124 S.J. 201.

[182] See *Smith v. Johnson* (1897) 3 H. & N. 222; also *Heilbut v. Nevill* (1870) L.R. 5 C.P. 478 (where the property was held not to have passed).

[183] See *infra*, paras 12–161 *et seq.*

[184] *Johnson v. Peck* (1821) 3 Stark. 66.

absolutely necessary that such power should exist in the members of a trading partnership, and accordingly in a comparatively early case this power was clearly recognised."[185]

This principle is clearly demonstrated by the unquestioned authority of partners to draw, accept or indorse bills of exchange[186] and to pledge partnership goods.[187]

It is, of course, still necessary to show that the money was borrowed in the usual way of the partnership business, if the firm is to be bound.[188] Thus if money is borrowed by a partner for the declared purpose of raising the whole or part of his capital contribution,[189] the borrowing will demonstrably be outside the scope of his implied authority. On the other hand, if money is actually required by the firm but can only be obtained on unusual terms, it is considered that acceptance of such terms will be within a partner's implied authority and the lender need not inquire whether such acceptance was justified.[190]

Non-trading partnerships

12–47   The implied power of a partner to borrow money will only exist where the firm's business is of such a kind that it cannot be carried on in the usual way without such a power.[191] In the case of a pure cash business[192] or a business where borrowing is not strictly necessary[193] the firm will not be bound unless some actual authority or ratification can be proved. It is the current editor's view that the older cases in this area are deserving of particularly critical consideration, given that a significant number, if not the majority, of businesses, both trading and non-trading, are now, to some extent, financed by borrowed money.

Borrowing prohibited

12–48   It goes almost without saying that, where authority to borrow would otherwise be implied, the firm will not be bound if borrowing is prohibited by the partnership agreement and the lender is aware of that fact.[194]

---

[185] See *Lane v. Williams* (1692) 2 Vern. 277, 292; *Rothwell v. Humphreys* (1795) 1 Esp. 406; *Ex p. Bonbonus* (1803) 8 Ves. Jr. 540; *Denton v. Rodie* (1813) 3 Camp. 493; *Loyd v. Freshfield* (1826) 2 Car. & P. 325; see also *Gordon v. Ellis* (1844) 7 Man. & G. 607; *De Ribeyre v. Barclay* (1857) 23 Beav. 125; *Brown v. Kidger* (1858) 3 H. & N. 853.

[186] See *supra*, para. 12–42.

[187] See *infra*, para. 12–75.

[188] Partnership Act 1890, s.5, *supra*, para. 12–02.

[189] *Greenslade v. Dower* (1828) 7 B. & C. 635; *Fisher v. Tayler* (1843) 2 Hare 218. See *infra*, para. 12–49.

[190] See *Montaignac v. Shitta* (1890) 15 App.Cas. 357, which concerned the general agent of a firm.

[191] See *supra*, paras 12–12 *et seq.*

[192] Lord Lindley cited the case of mining on the cost-book principle as a "ready money" business: see *Hawtayne v. Bourne* (1841) 7 M. & W. 595; *Ricketts v. Bennett* (1847) 4 C.B. 686; *Burmester v. Norris* (1851) 6 Ex. 796.

[193] Lord Lindley cited a solicitor as the example in this case: *Plumer v. Gregory* (1874) L.R. 18 Eq. 621. A subsequent editor added the "cinematograph theatre proprietor" as a further example: *Higgins v. Beauchamp* [1914] 3 K.B. 1192.

[194] Partnership Act 1890, ss.5, 8: see *supra*, para. 12–02 and *infra*, para. 12–138; *Re Worcester Corn Exchange Co.* (1853) 3 De G.M. & G. 180. See also the cases cited in the next note.

What amounts to borrowing on behalf of firm

Overdrawing a bank account. As is to be expected, this clearly amounts to   **12–49**
borrowing money.[195]

Increasing firm's capital. Care must be taken when considering loans taken out
by a partner with the express purpose of increasing the firm's capital, since use
of such an expression may be indicative of a confusion of terms. Lord Lindley
explained the position in this way:

> "A sole trader who borrows money for the purpose of his trade cannot with propriety
> be said to increase his capital; but if two or more persons are in partnership, and each
> borrows money on his own separate credit, and the money is then thrown into the
> common stock, the capital of the firm, as distinguished from the separate capitals of
> the persons composing it, may with propriety be said to be increased. But, in this
> case, the firm is not the borrower, nor is it debtor to the lender for the money
> borrowed. If a firm borrows money so as to be itself liable for it to the lender, the
> capital of the firm is no more increased than is the capital of an ordinary individual
> increased by his getting into debt. When, therefore, it is said that one partner has no
> implied power to borrow on the credit of the firm for the purpose of increasing its
> capital, what is meant is that one partner, as such, has no power to borrow, on the
> credit of himself and co-partners, money, which each was to obtain on his individual
> credit, and then to bring into the common stock.[196] Unless the expression means this,
> it means nothing."[197]

It follows that a loan taken out for such a purpose cannot ordinarily bind the firm
in the absence of subsequent ratification.

Obtaining goods, etc., on credit. The mere fact that a partner has implied   **12–50**
authority to obtain goods or services on credit does not, of itself, authorise him
to borrow money, since the two acts are quite different. Lord Lindley summarised
the distinction in these terms:

> "The difference consists in this, that he who possesses power to borrow on the credit
> of another, has a much more extensive, and therefore more easily abused, trust
> reposed in him than one who is empowered only to pledge the credit of another for
> value received, when the pledge is given. A power, therefore, to incur debt, which is
> necessarily incidental to almost every partnership, by no means involves a power to
> borrow money."

This proposition is supported by a number of older cases concerning mines run
on the cost-book principle,[198] and would still appear to be good law.[199]
  See also *Mortgages and Pledges, infra*, paragraphs 12–74 *et seq.*

---

[195] *Looker v. Wrigley* (1882) 9 Q.B.D. 397; *Blackburn Building Society v. Cunliffe, Brooks & Co.*
(1884) 9 App.Cas. 857; *Re Wrexham, Mold & Connah's Quay Ry. Co.* [1899] 1 Ch. 440; *Re Pyle
Works (No. 2)* [1891] 1 Ch. 173. Lord Lindley observed that the contrary decisions in *Waterlow v.
Sharp* (1869) L.R. 8 Eq. 501 and *Re Cefn Cilcen Mining Co.* (1868) L.R. 7 Eq. 88 must be considered
as overruled.
[196] See *Greenslade v. Dower* (1828) 7 B. & C. 635; *Fisher v. Tayler* (1843) 2 Hare 218.
[197] See *Bryon v. Metropolitan Saloon Omnibus Co.* (1858) 3 De G. & J. 123.
[198] As to liability for supplies, see *Tredwen v. Bourne* (1840) 6 M. & W. 461; *Hawken v. Bourne*
(1841) 8 M. & W. 703; as to borrowings, see *Hawtayne v. Bourne* (1841) 7 M. & W. 595; *Ricketts
v. Bennett* (1847) 4 C.B. 686; *Brown v. Byers* (1847) 16 M. & W. 252; *Burmester v. Norris* (1851)
6 Ex. 796; also *Beldon v. Campbell* (1851) 6 Ex. 886.
[199] See also *Re Pyle Works (No. 2)* [1891] 1 Ch. 173, 185 *per* Stirling J.; *Jacobs v. Morris* [1901]
1 Ch. 261, 267–268 *per* Farwell J. and [1902] 1 Ch. 816, 828–829 *per* Vaughan Williams L.J.

Firm enjoying benefit of improperly borrowed money

This subject will be considered later in this chapter.[200]

Cheques and transfers between accounts

12–51   A partner unquestionably has implied power to bind the firm by drawing a cheque in the firm name[201] and, seemingly, to stop payment on such a cheque.[202] There is, however, authority for the proposition that he may not properly draw a post-dated cheque.[203] There would seem to be no reason why a partner should not draw a cheque in his own favour, *e.g.* in the case of drawings on account of his profit share, unless this is prohibited by the bank mandate or professional rules.[204]

There is also implied authority to transfer funds from one bank account to another.[205] Again, this would appear to include transfers from the firm's account to a partner's private account; *sed quaere*.[206]

Contracts

12–52   There can be little doubt that partners will have a general power to bind the firm by contract, although the extent of the authority will inevitably depend on the nature of the business concerned.[207] In an appropriate case, this may include signing a contract satisfying the requirements of the Law of Property (Miscellaneous Provisions) Act 1989.[208] Equally, once a contract binding the firm has been entered into, any action to *implement* that contract will automatically be authorised, even if it would otherwise fall outside the normal scope of a partner's authority.[209]

---

[200] See *infra*, paras 12–175 *et seq.*

[201] *Laws v. Rand* (1857) 3 C.B.(N.S.) 442; *Backhouse v. Charlton* (1878) 8 Ch.D. 444; also *Ringham v. Hackett, The Times*, February 9, 1980 and (1980) 124 S.J. 201. But see also, *supra*, para. 12–13, n. 47.

[202] Lord Lindley observed in a footnote at this point: "Before the Judicature Acts, an action for dishonouring the cheque must have been brought in the names of all the partners, and in the case supposed such an action could not have been sustained ... It is conceived that the statement in the text is correct, notwithstanding the modern rules as to parties."

[203] See *Forster v. Mackreth* (1867) L.R. 2 Ex. 163. *Quaere* whether this will now always be the position.

[204] Note that the Solicitors' Accounts Rules 1998, r. 23(3) provides that a withdrawal authorised under *ibid.* r. 23(1) must be made "by way of a cheque to the solicitor or practice or by way of a transfer to the office account or to the solicitor's personal account". The expression "solicitor" is defined so as to include the firm, as a recognised body: *ibid.* r. 2(1)(x), as amended. *Quaere*, does this authorise a partner to draw a client account cheque in his own favour rather than in favour of the firm? It is tentatively submitted that it does, given the later reference to the solicitor's *personal* account.

[205] See *Backhouse v. Charlton* (1878) 8 Ch.D. 444.

[206] Note the terms of the Solicitors' Accounts Rules 1998, r. 23(3): see *supra*, n. 204.

[207] See *Employees, Purchases* and *Sales, infra*, paras 12–66, 12–79, 12–80, 12–82.

[208] *ibid.* s.2(3), as amended by the Regulatory Reform (Execution of Deeds and Documents) Order 2005 (SI 2005/1906), Sched. 2. *Quaere* can the contract be signed by the partner as an undisclosed agent, and thereby bind the firm? This was the position under the Law of Property Act 1925, s.40: see *Davies v. Sweet* [1962] 2 Q.B. 300; *Basma v. Weeks* [1950] A.C. 441, but the position is less certain under the 1989 Act: see *Bowstead & Reynolds on Agency* (19th ed.), para. 8–004.

[209] *Bank of Scotland v. Henry Butcher & Co* [2003] 2 All E.R. (Comm) 557 (CA).

A partner may also vary a contract entered into by all the partners in the ordinary course of business.[210]

Debts

Payment to one partner

A partner has implied authority to accept the payment of partnership debts; **12–53** hence the general rule that, if payment is received by any partner in respect of such a debt, the claims of all the partners are extinguished.[211]

The position is the same following a dissolution,[212] even where a third party has been appointed to collect the debts and the debtor is aware of that fact.[213] Where, however, a debt has been assigned to one of the partners and the debtor has notice of the assignment, he will only be discharged if he pays the assignee partner.[214]

Debt not due to firm. The above rule will not apply if the debt was owed not to **12–54** the firm but to one of the partners. In such a case, payment must be made to that partner.[215] This may be of particular relevance where there is a partnership or other agreement to share the profits derived from the sale of certain goods. As Lord Lindley pointed out:

> " ... if an owner of goods sells them the purchase-money must be paid to him or his agent; and payment to a person interested with him in the profits accruing from the sale will not do: for though the two may be liable as if they were partners by reason of their community of interest in the profits,[216] it does not therefore follow that he who is to share the profits is entitled to receive the proceeds of the sale of the goods themselves which belong exclusively to the other."[217]

If the court (exceptionally) orders payment to be made to one partner by name, that order must be complied with; payment to any other partner will not suffice.[218]

---

[210] *Leiden v. Lawrence* (1863) 2 N.R. 283.

[211] *Anon.*, 12 Mod. 446 (Case 777); see also *Powell v. Brodhurst* [1901] 2 Ch. 160. And see *Jacaud v. French* (1810) 12 East 198, where there were two firms with a common partner and a bill of exchange was given to one and indorsed by it to the other. Payment to the first firm was held to be an answer to an action brought on the bill by the second. Note that a partner who receives money as agent for the firm will not necessarily be regarded as doing so in a fiduciary capacity: see *infra*, para. 16–04.

[212] Partnership Act 1890, s.38, *infra*, para. 13–62; *Powell v. Brodhurst* [1901] 2 Ch. 160; and see *Duff v. East India Co.* (1808) 15 Ves. Jr. 198; *Brazier v. Hudson* (1836) 9 Sim. 1. The *obiter* observations to the contrary in *Gopala Chetty v. Vayaraghavachariar* [1922] 1 A.C. 488, 495 do not accord with the position under English law: see the Partnership Act 1890, s.38.

[213] *Bristow v. Taylor* (1817) 2 Stark. 50; *Porter v. Taylor* (1817) 6 M. & S. 156; *King v. Smith* (1829) 4 Car. & P. 108.

[214] See *Duff v. East India Co.* (1808) 15 Ves. Jr. 198; also *Powell v. Brodhurst* [1901] 2 Ch. 160.

[215] Payment to the firm will not be sufficient unless the firm was authorised to receive the money: *Powell v. Brodhurst* [1901] 2 Ch. 160.

[216] This part of the passage (which was omitted in later editions) was, of course, written prior to the Partnership Act 1890: see now *ibid.* s.2(3) and *supra*, paras 5–18 *et seq.*

[217] See *Smith v. Watson* (1824) 2 B. & C. 401.

[218] See *Showler v. Stoakes* (1844) 2 Dow. & L. 3.

12–55 *Acceptance of bill of exchange.* A partner's implied authority to accept payment will normally extend to receipt of a bill of exchange by way of payment[219]; *per contra*, if the bill is drawn in the partner's own name and payable to his order, unless he had express authority to receive a bill in this form or the money is actually paid over to the firm.[220]

Releases and receipts

12–56   In the same way that he can accept payment, a partner may give a valid release[221] or receipt in respect of a partnership debt.[222] However, a receipt is not conclusive so that, if the partner giving it was acting in fraud of his co-partners, they will not be bound by it[223]; similarly, if that partner colluded with the debtor in giving the release.[224]

Power to settle debts

12–57   A partner does not have authority to compromise a debt owing to the firm, without receiving payment. Lord Lindley put it in this way:

> "As a general proposition, an authority to receive payment of a debt does not include an authority to settle it in some other way[225]; and a partner has no implied authority to discharge a separate debt of his own by agreeing that it shall be set off against a debt due to his firm."[226]

Deeds of arrangement, IVAs, CVAs and PVAs

12–58   It would seem that one partner has authority to assent to a deed of arrangement executed by a debtor[227]; this represents an exception to the normal rule that a partner cannot bind the firm by deed.[228] On the same principle, it is submitted that a partner would have authority to vote in favour of an individual, company or partnership voluntary arrangement proposed by a debtor of the firm.[229]

---

[219] See *Tomlins v. Lawrence* (1830) 3 Moo. & Pay. 555.

[220] See *Hogarth v. Wherley* (1875) L.R. 10 C.P. 630.

[221] See *Hawkshaw v. Parkins* (1819) 2 Swan. 539; see also *Deeds* and *Releases, infra*, paras 12–62, 12–81.

[222] *Henderson v. Wild* (1811) 2 Camp. 561.

[223] *Henderson v. Wild* (1811) 2 Camp. 561; *Farrar v. Hutchinson* (1839) 9 A. & E. 641.

[224] *Aspinall v. London & N.W. Ry.* (1853) 11 Hare 325; see also *Releases, infra*, para. 12–81.

[225] See *Hogarth v. Wherley* (1875) L.R. 10 C.P. 630; *Pearson v. Scott* (1878) 9 Ch.D. 198; *Niemann v. Niemann* (1889) 43 Ch.D. 198; *cf. Weikersheim's Case* (1873) L.R. 8 Ch.App. 831. And see *Young v. White* (1844) 7 Beav. 506; *Underwood v. Nicholls* (1855) 17 C.B. 239.

[226] *Piercy v. Fynney* (1871) L.R. 12 Eq. 69. See also *Kendal v. Wood* (1870) L.R. 6 Ex. 243. *cf. Wallace v. Kelsall* (1840) 7 M. & W. 264.

[227] See *Morans v. Armstrong* (1840) Arm. M. & O. 25; *Dudgeon v. O'Connell* (1849) 12 Ir.Eq. 566. And see generally, the Deeds of Arrangement Act 1914 (as amended) and *Muir Hunter on Personal Insolvency*, Pt II.

[228] *Dudgeon v. O'Connell* (1849) 12 Ir.Eq. 566. See further *infra*, para. 12–62.

[229] See, as to the approval of an IVA, the Insolvency Act 1986, ss.258, 260 (as amended by the Insolvency Act 2000, Sched. 3, para. 10) and the Insolvency Rules 1986, rr. 5.21 *et seq.* (as substituted by the Insolvency (Amendment) (No. 2) Rules 2002 (SI 2002/2712), Sched. 1, Pt. 3, para. 24) and, as to the approval of a CVA, the Insolvency Act 1986, ss.4, 4A, 5 (as respectively amended/ added by the Insolvency Act 2000, Sched. 2, paras 4–6, Sched. 5 and, in the case of s.5, further amended by the Enterprise Act 2002, Sched. 17, para. 11(a) and the Energy Act 2004, Sched. 20, Pt. 4, para. 43) and the Insolvency Rules 1986, rr. 1.17 *et seq.* (as substituted/amended). As to the approval of PVAs, see *infra*, paras 27–151 *et seq.*

Transfer or assignment of debt

If a creditor of the firm transfers the debt due to him to a third party, one **12–59** partner may properly assent to the transfer.[230] Similarly, where the debt is assigned by the debtor, *e.g.* to his successor in business.[231]

It follows that one partner also has authority to assign a debt due to the firm.[232] Where two partners purport to assign the same debt, a question of priority as between the assignees will inevitably arise: this will be determined on the normal principles of notice.[233]

Promise to pay debt of firm

A promise by one partner to pay a debt owing by the firm undoubtedly binds **12–60** the firm[234] and will prima facie constitute an acknowledgment of the debt for limitation purposes.[235]

Tender

Lord Lindley summarised the position in this way: **12–61**

"If a debt is owing to a firm, tender to one partner is tender to all; and if a debt is owing by a firm, tender by one partner is tender by all[236]; and if, after tender by a firm, the creditor demands the sum tendered, a refusal to pay made by the partner on whom the demand is made is a refusal by the firm."[237]

Deeds

Express authority to execute a deed must itself be given by deed.[238] It follows **12–62** that such authority cannot be conferred by a partnership agreement which is under hand.[239] It therefore comes as no surprise that the general rule is that a partner has no implied authority to bind his co-partners by deed, however the partnership was originally constituted.[240] The only true exceptions are a deed of release executed by one partner[241] and an assent by one partner to a debtor's deed of arrangement,[242] which *will* in each case bind the firm.[243]

---

[230] *Lacy v. McNeile* (1824) 4 Dow. & Ry. 7.
[231] *Beale v. Caddick* (1857) 2 H. & N. 326. See also *Backhouse v. Charlton* (1878) 8 Ch.D. 444.
[232] *Ex p. Wright* [1906] 2 K.B. 209.
[233] *Marchant v. Morton, Down & Co.* [1901] 2 K.B. 829.
[234] *Anon. v. Layfield*, Holt K.B. 434; *Lacy v. McNeile* (1824) 4 Dow. & Ry. 7.
[235] Limitation Act 1980, ss.29(5), 30(2). See further, *infra*, paras 13–133 *et seq.*
[236] *Douglas v. Patrick* (1790) 3 T.R. 683.
[237] *Peirse v. Bowles* (1816) 1 Stark. 323.
[238] *Steiglitz v. Egginton* (1815) Holt N.P. 141; *Berkeley v. Hardy* (1826) 5 B. & C. 355. See also the Powers of Attorney Act 1971, s.1(1) (as amended by the Law of Property (Miscellaneous Provisions) Act 1989, Sched. 1, para. 6(a)), 7(1).
[239] See *supra*, para. 10–252. Even where there is express authority, the firm will only be bound if the deed is in the correct form: see *infra*, paras 12–157 *et seq.*
[240] *Harrison v. Jackson* (1797) 7 T.R. 207; *Steiglitz v. Egginton, supra*; *Marchant v. Morton, Down & Co.* [1901] 2 K.B. 829.
[241] See *Hawkshaw v. Parkins* (1819) 2 Swan. 539; also *Releases, infra*, para. 12–81.
[242] See *supra*, para. 12–58.
[243] For another (historic) exception, see *supra*, para. 12–36.

It should be noted that a deed may be validly executed by one partner on behalf of all his partners where he does so at their direction *and in their presence*[244]; this does not represent a substantive exception to the above principles.

Deed not necessary

12–63   If a deed is unnecessary for the validity of a particular transaction which is otherwise within the scope of a partner's implied authority, but he nevertheless executes a document in the form of a deed, the firm may still be bound by that transaction, even if not by the deed.[245] Thus, where a partner had executed such a deed in the name of his firm, purporting to assign a debt due to it, it was held that the deed did not bind his co-partner but that there was nevertheless a good assignment of the debt, no deed being required.[246] The position may be the same where the inoperative deed is executed in pursuance of a contract, which is not required to be made by deed and therefore binds the firm.[247]

Executing partner bound

12–64   Although a deed may be inoperative against the other partners, the partner who executed it will generally be bound.[248]

Partnership Act 1890

The foregoing principles are unaffected by the Partnership Act 1890.[249]

Distress

Distress by partner

12–65   If the firm is a landlord of premises,[250] any partner has authority to distrain, or to appoint a bailiff to distrain, for arrears of rent due to the firm.[251]

Distress against firm

In certain cases, the Law of Distress Amendment Act 1908 protects goods which are not the property of the immediate tenant against distress for rent. If the goods distrained on belong to a firm, the declaration required to obtain the protection of the Act may be made on behalf of the firm and signed by one partner.[252]

---

[244] See the Law of Property (Miscellaneous Provisions) Act 1989, s.1(3)(a)(ii).

[245] See further, as to the circumstances in which a firm will be bound by a deed executed by one partner, *infra*, paras 12–157 *et seq*. This point appears not to have been addressed by the court in *Bank of Scotland v. Henry Butcher & Co.* [2001] 2 All E.R. (Comm.) 691 at [51] or, subsequently, by the Court of Appeal: see [2003] 2 All E.R. (Comm) 557.

[246] *Marchant v. Morton, Down & Co.* [1901] 2 K.B. 829; see also *Ex p. Wright* [1906] 2 K.B. 209 (where one partner had forged the name of his co-partner).

[247] See *Davis v. Martin* [1894] 3 Ch. 181.

[248] *Elliot v. Davis* (1800) 2 Bos. & Pul. 338 (joint and several bond). See also *Bowker v. Burdekin* (1843) 11 M. & W. 128; *Cumberlege v. Lawson* (1857) 1 C.B.(N.S.) 709. *cf. Latch v. Wedlake* (1840) 11 A. & E. 959; *Lascaridi v. Gurney* (1862) 9 Jur.(N.S.) 302; *Bank of Scotland v. Henry Butcher & Co.* [2003] 2 All E.R. (Comm) 557 (CA).

[249] *ibid*. s.6: see *infra*, paras 12–149, 12–157 *et seq*.

[250] Itself a slightly unusual scenario: see *supra*, para. 3–04.

[251] See *Robinson v. Hofman* (1828) 4 Bing. 562.

[252] *ibid*. s.1 (as amended); *Rogers, Eungblut & Co. v. Martin* [1911] 1 K.B. 19, explained in *Lawrence Chemical Co. Ltd. v. Rubinstein* [1982] 1 W.L.R. 284. Note, however, that the goods of a partner of the tenant are not protected: *ibid*. s.4(2)(a).

Employees

Lord Lindley observed: **12–66**

> "One partner has implied authority to hire servants to perform the business of the partnership[253]; and the writer presumes that one partner has also implied authority to discharge them, although he cannot do so against the will of his co-partners."[254]

The current editor considers that Lord Lindley's reference to the will of the other partners (which is equally applicable to the engagement of employees) must be approached with a degree of caution. In the case which he cited, *Donaldson v. Williams*,[255] the claimant was an employee of two partners, Williams and Whyte, and resided in their jointly owned premises. His employment was terminated by Williams, who required him to vacate the premises, but Whyte authorised him to remain. Lord Lyndhurst held that such authority, given by one joint tenant, made the claimant's continued occupation of the premises lawful and observed "As the partners are jointly interested in the house, has not either of them a right to retain a servant in the house?" It would accordingly seem that this was, if anything, a case of re-engagement,[256] not a case where the original dismissal was invalid as being contrary to the wishes of the other partner.[257] In the result, there might be an endless succession of dismissals and re-engagements, so that it may properly be said that, at least in the case of a two partner firm, the *status quo ante* must ultimately prevail.[258]

Although the position may technically be the same in the case of a larger firm, the majority might properly restrict the partners' express authority to engage or dismiss staff with a view to resolving the position.[259]

Guarantees, etc.

A partner will not, in general, have power to give a guarantee binding on the   **12–67**
firm. Lord Lindley summarised the position in these terms:

> "How far one partner can bind the firm by a guarantee, obliging the firm to pay, if some other person does not, has been much disputed. The later cases, however, decide that unless it can be shown that the giving of guarantees is necessary for carrying on the business of the firm in the ordinary way,[260] one of the members will be held to have no implied authority to bind the firm by them; for, generally speaking,

---

[253] *Beckham v. Drake* (1841) 9 M. & W. 79, affirmed (on this point) at (1843) 11 M. & W. 315.

[254] *Donaldson v. Williams* (1833) 1 Cromp. & M. 345; also the unreported decision in *Williams v. Williams*, January 30, 1979 (1980 C.L.Y. p. 134). But see *Dixon on Partnership*, p. 139, where a contrary view is expressed. As to dismissal resulting from a change in the firm, see *supra*, para. 3–15.

[255] (1833) 1 Cromp. & M. 345.

[256] But re-engagement by whom: the firm or Whyte alone? The report is not clear on this point.

[257] Indeed, the headnote refers to the fact that Williams had "regularly given [*the claimant*] a week's notice to leave". Note that in *R. v. Leech* (1821) 3 Stark. 70, it was held that an employee of a firm comprising two partners is properly to be treated as the individual employee of each partner and not as their joint employee. *Semble*, this cannot be right.

[258] See *infra*, para. 15–06.

[259] See *infra*, para. 15–05.

[260] As was the position in *Bank of Scotland v. Henry Butcher & Co.* [2003] 2 All E.R. (Comm.) 557 (CA).

it is not usual for persons in business to make themselves answerable for the conduct of other people. The subject was much considered in *Brettel v. Williams*."[261]

The position under the Partnership Act 1890 is, of course, the same.[262]

A guarantee given without authority may become binding on the firm by ratification[263] or estoppel[264] and will, in any event, bind any partner who signs it.[265]

Statute of Frauds 1677

12–68   A guarantee must be in writing in order to satisfy the requirements of section 4 of the Statute of Frauds,[266] but will be sufficient if signed by one partner in the name of the firm, provided that his authority can be proved.[267]

Promise to provide for bill

Such a promise, to which reference has already been made,[268] is not regarded in the same way as a guarantee.[269]

Representations as to credit

12–69   It has been held that a partner is not liable for a false and fraudulent representation as to the character or solvency of another person, unless the representation is in writing and signed by that partner; accordingly, if he signs in the name of the firm, only he will be liable.[270] It is apprehended that this is still the position.[271]

---

[261] (1849) 4 Ex. 623. See also *Crawford v. Stirling* (1802) 4 Esp. 207; *Duncan v. Lowndes* (1813) 3 Camp. 478; *Hasleham v. Young* (1844) 5 Q.B. 833; *Simpson's Claim* (1887) 36 Ch.D. 532. Lord Lindley also pointed out that "The dictum of Lord Mansfield in *Hope v. Cust* (1774) 1 East 53, and the decision of Lord Eldon in *Ex p. Gardom* (1808) 15 Ves. Jr. 286, are opposed to these authorities, but cannot be relied on after the decision in *Brettel v. Williams*."

[262] *ibid.* s.5, *supra*, para. 12–02.

[263] See *Sandilands v. Marsh* (1819) 2 B. & A. 673 and *Bank of Scotland v. Henry Butcher & Co.*, *supra*, where there was evidence of ratification by the firm of the contract of which the guarantee formed part.

[264] See for example, *Amalgamated Investment & Property Co. Ltd. (In Liquidation) v. Texas Commerce International Bank Ltd.* [1982] Q.B. 84 (parent company guaranteeing the indebtedness of subsidiary).

[265] *Ex p. Harding* (1879) 12 Ch.D. 557 (joint and several guarantee). Lord Lindley observed that this case and the case first cited *supra*, n. 263 "cannot . . . be considered as opposed to those in which it has been held that one partner has no implied power to bind the firm by guarantees in its name". See also *Bank of Scotland v. Henry Butcher & Co.*, *supra*.

[266] *Actionstrength Ltd. v. International Glass Engineering IN.GL.EN SpA* [2003] 2 A.C. 541 (HL). Note that an offer made in writing (including by e-mail) and accepted orally will satisfy the requirements of s.4: *J Pereira Fernandes SA v. Mehta* [2006] 1 W.L.R. 1543. As to the difference between a contract of guarantee and an indemnity, see *Pitts v. Jones* [2008] Q.B. 706 (CA); *Associated British Ports v. Ferryways NV* [2009] 1 Lloyd's Rep. 595 (CA).

[267] See *Duncan v. Lowndes* (1813) 3 Camp. 478. This part of the Statute of Frauds, s.4, was unaffected by the provisions of the Law Reform (Enforcement of Contracts) Act 1954 (itself now repealed).

[268] See *supra*, para. 12–45.

[269] *Guild & Co. v. Conrad* [1894] 2 Q.B. 885.

[270] Statute of Frauds Amendment Act 1828, s.6; *Williams v. Mason* (1873) 28 L.T.(N.S.) 232; *Swift v. Jewsbury* (1874) L.R. 9 Q.B. 301; *Hirst v. West Riding Union Banking Co.* [1901] 2 K.B. 560. See also *infra*, para. 12–98.

[271] But see the Partnership Act 1890, ss.6, 10, *infra*, paras 12–88, 12–149.

Insurance

A partner has implied authority to insure partnership property[272] and a partner   **12–70**
in a firm of solicitors has authority to enter into a professional indemnity
insurance policy, which is required pursuant to the applicable Solicitors' Indemnity Insurance Rules.[273]

Interest

An admission by one partner that a partnership debt bears interest at a given   **12–71**
rate will prima facie bind the firm.[274]

See also *Debts, supra*, paragraphs 12–53 *et seq*.

Leases

Lord Lindley stated that: **12–72**

"One partner, as such, has no authority to contract on behalf of the firm for a lease
of a house for partnership purposes."

This proposition was supported by reference to *Sharp v. Milligan*,[275] in which, as
Lord Lindley noted, specific performance was decreed against the firm, the
contract having been ratified by the other partners. However, the following *obiter*
views of Sir John Romilly M.R. are instructive in this context:

"I do not think it necessary to decide this point, but I am disposed to concur in the
argument that where partners simply enter into an agreement to carry on a partnership
of which the term is not fixed, one of those partners would not have authority, within
the scope of the partnership contract, to take a lease for twenty-one years, and to bind
the other partners."[276]

Accordingly, the current editor's view is that there is no *general* principle with
regard to leases, such as Lord Lindley implied, but that in order to determine the
extent of a partner's implied authority account must not only be taken of the
nature of the business but also of the duration of the partnership.

Notice to quit, etc.

Where a lease is granted by a number of partners jointly, a notice to quit may   **12–73**
be given by one on behalf of them all.[277]

---

[272] *Hooper v. Lusby* (1814) 4 Camp. 66; also *Armitage v. Winterbottom* (1840) 1 Man. & G. 130.
As to notice of abandonment in the case of a marine insurance policy, see *Hunt v. Royal Exchange
Assurance Co.* (1816) 5 M. & S. 47.

[273] *Jones v. St Pauls International Insurance Co Ltd.* [2004] EWHC 2209 (Ch) (Lawtel 23/4/04)
at [12] *per* Hart J.

[274] See *Fergusson v. Fyffe* (1841) 8 Cl. & F. 121. See also *supra*, para. 12–60.

[275] (1856) 22 Beav. 606.

[276] *ibid.* p. 609.

[277] *Doe d. Aslin v. Summersett* (1830) 1 B. & Ad. 135; also *Goodtitle v. Woodward* (1820) 3 B. &
A. 689; *Doe v. Hulme* (1825) 2 Man. & Ry. 433; and see the review of the later authorities in
Featherstone v. Staples [1986] 1 W.L.R. 861, 868 *et seq.* and *Hammersmith and Fulham LBC v. Monk*
[1992] A.C. 478.

In the case of a lease granted *to* partners, it would seem that a notice to quit given by one would only be valid in the case of a periodic tenancy.[278] If the lease is a partnership asset, the giving of such a notice might, as against the other partners (whether co-lessees or not), amount to a breach of trust[279] or fiduciary duty.[280]

In the case of a tenancy protected by the Agricultural Holdings Act 1986,[281] the concurrence of one partner in the service of a counter notice under section 26(1)(b) may, in certain circumstances, be dispensed with, if the operation of that Act would otherwise be frustrated. This was graphically demonstrated in *Featherstone v. Staples*,[282] where the partner withholding its concurrence was, in fact, a company controlled by the landlord which played no active part in the business.[283] Equally, where one of the tenants is a *former* partner and has no continuing interest in the tenancy, he may be ordered to concur in the service of such a counter notice.[284]

Mortgages and pledges

Mortgages of partnership land

12-74   Although, under the common law, a legal mortgage of partnership land requires the concurrence of all the partners,[285] two or more partners who hold such land on a trust of land[286] can now create a valid mortgage without such

---

[278] *Doe d. Aslin v. Summersett, supra*, as approved in *Hammersmith and Fulham LBC v. Monk, supra; Cork v. Cork* [1997] 1 E.G.L.R. 5; *per contra*, in the case of a *contractual* break clause: *Hounslow LBC v. Pilling* [1993] 1 W.L.R. 1242. A notice under the Law of Property Act 1925, s.146(1) should seemingly be served on each lessee partner: *Blewett v. Blewett* [1936] 2 All E.R. 188; *Wilson v. Hagon* (1958) 109 L.J. 204 (Cty.Ct.); *cf. Fairclough v. Berliner* [1931] 1 Ch. 60 (where the joint lessees were not partners). As to the service of notices under the Landlord and Tenant Act 1954, Pt II, note the terms of *ibid.* s.41A, as added by the Law of Property Act 1969, s.9 and amended by the Regulatory Reform (Business Tenancies) (England and Wales) Order 2003 (SI 2003/3096), Sched. 5, para. 5.

[279] But note the doubts expressed by Lord Browne-Wilkinson in *Hammersmith and Fulham LBC v. Monk, supra*, at p. 493D; *Crawley Borough Council v. Ure* [1996] Q.B. 13 (CA) (both decisions under the Law of Property Act 1925, s.26(3)); *Notting Hill Housing Trust v. Brackley* [2001] 35 E.G. 106 (CA) (a decision under the Trusts of Land and Appointment of Trustees Act 1996, s.11(1)).

[280] See *Ward v. Brunt* [2000] W.T.L.R. 731, 750A–B; *cf. Sykes v. Land* (1984) 271 E.G. 1264.

[281] The incidence of such tenancies is, of course, much reduced since the coming into force of the Agricultural Tenancies Act 1995.

[282] [1986] 1 W.L.R. 861; see also *Sykes v. Land* (1984) 271 E.G. 1264. *cf. Dickson v. MacGregor* 1992 S.L.T. 83 (Land Ct.); *MacFarlane v. Falfield Investments Ltd.* 1998 S.L.T. 145 (1st Div.).

[283] The decision did not ultimately turn on the provisions of the Partnership Act 1890, s.5 (see [1986] 1 W.L.R. 878), but on the principles enunciated in *Johnson v. Moreton* [1980] A.C. 37: see further *infra* para. 23–202.

[284] See *Cork v. Cork* [1997] 1 E.G.L.R. 5. There the claimant and the defendant were brothers and joint tenants of the agricultural holding, but had seemingly *never* been partners. It nevertheless appeared to the court that there may have been a family agreement that the claimant should alone enjoy the benefit of the tenancy. In ordering that the defendant should concur in the service of the counter notice at an interim hearing, Knox J. was at pains to ensure that his position was protected in the event that it should transpire that he was still beneficially interested in the tenancy and, thus, strictly entitled to withhold his consent to such service: *ibid.* p. 8.

[285] See Deeds, *supra*, para. 12–62. Note, however, that in *Juggeewundas Keeka Shah v. Ramdas Brjbooken Das* (1841) 2 Moo.Ind.App. 487, a mortgage by one partner was, in special circumstances, held to bind the firm.

[286] See the Trusts of Land and Appointment of Trustees Act 1996, s.1(1).

concurrence.[287] However, the creation of such a mortgage might, as against partners whose consent is not sought, constitute a breach of trust.[288]

On the footing that a member of an ordinary trading partnership has implied authority to borrow money on behalf of the firm,[289] it almost necessarily follows that he will also have power to pledge partnership property as security for such borrowing.[290] It would also seem that, before the demise of the equitable mortgage by deposit of title deeds,[291] a member of a trading partnership would have had power to create such a mortgage in respect of land held by the firm.[292]

Pledges of partnership chattels

The implied authority of partners to pledge chattels is clear and was stated by Lord Lindley in this way: **12–75**

"The implied authority of a partner who has power to borrow, to pledge the personal property of the firm for money borrowed, is beyond dispute[293]; and the power is not confined to cases in which there is a general partnership; for if several join in a purchase of goods to be sold for their common profit, a pledge of those goods by one of the persons interested is binding on them all.[294] The implied power to pledge, moreover, extends to pledges for antecedent debts."[295]

Lord Lindley also considered the potential application of the then Factors Acts[296] in this context, concluding:

"The writer is not aware of any authority upon this subject, but he conceives that those acts neither extend nor abridge the power in question. The Factors Acts do not

---

[287] *ibid.* s.6(1).

[288] See also *supra*, para. 12–73, n. 279.

[289] See *supra*, para. 12–46.

[290] See further *infra*, para. 12–75.

[291] By virtue of the Law of Property (Miscellaneous Provisions) Act 1989, s.2: see *United Bank of Kuwait plc v. Sahib* [1997] Ch. 107 (CA).

[292] Lord Lindley put it more tentatively: "The writer is not aware of any decision in which an equitable mortgage made by one partner by a deposit of deeds relating to partnership real estate, has been upheld, or the contrary; he can therefore only venture to submit, that such a mortgage ought to be held valid in all cases in which it is made by a partner having an implied power to borrow on the credit of the firm." He then referred, in a footnote, to the following cases: *Re Clough* (1885) 31 Ch.D. 324 (equitable mortgage by surviving partner for existing partnership debt held valid); *Ex p. Lloyd* (1834) 1 Mont. & Ayr. 494; *Re Patent File Co.* (1870) L.R. 6 Ch. 83; *Ex p. National Bank* (1872) L.R. 14 Eq. 507. See also, as to security for advances, *Re Bourne* [1906] 2 Ch. 427.

[293] See *Ex p. Bonbonus* (1803) 8 Ves. Jr. 540; *Gordon v. Ellis* (1844) 7 Man. & G. 607; *Brownrigg v. Rae* (1850) 5 Ex. 489; *Butchart v. Dresser* (1853) 4 De G.M. & G. 542; see also *Re Langmead's Trust* (1855) 20 Beav. 20, affirmed at 7 De G.M. & G. 353; *Ex p. Howden* (1842) 2 M.D. & D. 574. See also *supra*, para. 12–74.

[294] *Re Gellar* (1812) 1 Rose 297; *Tupper v. Haythorne* (1815) Gow 135; *Raba v. Ryland* (1819) Gow 133; *Reid v. Hollinshead* (1825) 4 B. & C. 867; but see *Barton v. Williams* (1822) 5 B. & A. 395, 405 *per* Best J. (where the goods pledged were not at the time partnership property). Lord Lindley pointed out that "In *Ex p. Copeland* (1833) 2 Mont. & Ayr. 177, it was questioned whether a pledge by one partner was valid if the pledgee had notice that the pledgor was not the only owner, but this it is conceived could only be material where the pledge is not made for ostensible partnership purposes."

[295] *Re Patent File Co.* (1870) L.R. 6 Ch.App. 83; *Re Clough* (1885) 31 Ch.D. 324; and see *Story on Partnership*, s.101.

[296] See now the Factors Act 1889. That Act is wider in scope than its predecessors: see *ibid.* s.9 (as amended by the Consumer Credit Act 1974, Sched. 4).

apparently render valid any sale or pledge by one partner of partnership goods which is not valid independently of the acts upon the principles of the common law."

The current editor believes that Lord Lindley's observations are still pertinent in relation to the Factors Act 1889.

Redemption of pledge

12–76   It is the view of the current editor that, just as he may pledge the firm's goods in the first instance, so one partner may redeem such a pledge.[297]

Mortgages and pledges to partners

12–77   It is clear that one partner will normally have implied authority to accept security for a debt due to the firm. The exceptional example previously given in this work was of acceptance of a security in the form of shares registered in the name of the firm, thus rendering all the partners liable as contributories.[298] However, the Companies Act 2006 now requires the register of members to state the name of each joint holder separately, even if they are otherwise regarded as a single member,[299] so that for such a scenario to arise is even less likely.

Partnerships

12–78   Although a partner will in general have no implied authority to enter into a subsidiary partnership with a third party,[300] he may, in certain circumstances, have the requisite authority if the business to be carried on represents no more than an extension of the firm's existing business.[301]

Payments

See *Debts, supra*, paragraphs 12–53 *et seq.*

Purchases

12–79   As might be expected, the implied authority of a partner to purchase goods on the firm's behalf is not open to question, even in the case of a non-trading partnership. Lord Lindley observed:

"It has been long decided that every member of an ordinary trading partnership has implied power to purchase on the credit of the firm such goods as are or may be

---

[297] Lord Lindley said, of redemption, "Any partner may, on behalf of the firm, redeem a pledge of the firm; but he alone is not the proper person to bring an action to recover the thing pledged." He then cited *Harper v. Godsell* (1870) L.R. 5 Q.B. 422, which was a case of an action in trover brought by an assignee of certain partners' shares in goods pledged to the defendant. In fact, the action was held not to be maintainable because the defendant had sold the pledged goods under an authority given by one of the other partners and scarcely seems to support Lord Lindley's proposition.

[298] *Weikersheim's Case* (1873) L.R. 8 Ch.App. 831; *cf. Niemann v. Niemann* (1889) 43 Ch.D. 198.

[299] *ibid.* s.113(5). *cf.* the approach adopted in the case of the register kept by an LLP: Companies Act 2006, s.164, as substituted and applied by the Limited Liability Partnerships (Application of Companies Act 2006) Regulations 2009 (SI 2009/1804) , reg. 18.

[300] *Singleton v. Knight* (1888) 13 App.Cas. 788; *Hawksley v. Outram* [1892] 3 Ch. 359; also *Ex p. British Nation Life Assurance Association* (1878) 8 Ch.D. 679, 704. These authorities were reviewed critically by Megarry J. in *Mann v. D'Arcy* [1968] 1 W.L.R. 893.

[301] *Mann v. D'Arcy* [1968] 1 W.L.R. 893: see further, *supra*, para. 12–18.

necessary for carrying on its business in the usual way.[302] This cannot be more strongly exemplified than by the case of *Bond v. Gibson*[303] ... The power of one partner to bind the firm by a purchase of goods on its credit is not confined to trading partnerships.[304] ... It is of no consequence what the partnership business may be, if the goods supplied are necessary for its transaction in the ordinary way."

In such cases, the firm's liability is dependent on a partner ordering the goods on its behalf in the usual way of business; it does not matter that the supplier did not know that he was a member of the firm, unless he appeared to be acting as a principal and not as an agent.[305] Equally, if a partner purchases goods which are to be introduced into the firm as his capital contribution, the firm will not be bound if that purpose was known to the supplier, in the absence of subsequent ratification.[306]

Return of goods sold on credit

If goods are sold to the firm on credit but the firm is unable to pay for them, one partner may properly return them to the supplier,[307] provided that this is not held to be a transaction defrauding the firm's creditors.[308]   **12–80**

Receipts

See *Debts, supra*, para. 12–56.

Releases, etc.

In this context, it is necessary to distinguish between a true release and a mere covenant not to sue, since the former will in general bind the firm whilst the latter will not. Lord Lindley put it in this way: **12–81**

"A covenant by one partner not to sue for a partnership debt does not amount to a release of that debt by the firm,[309] although a covenant by all the partners not to sue would be equivalent to a release,[310] and a release by one partner operates as a release by the firm."[311]

---

[302] *Hyat v. Hare* (1696) Comb. 383.

[303] (1808) 1 Camp. 185. In that case, the partner had acquired goods on the credit of the firm and then pawned them for his own benefit; both partners were nevertheless held liable for the purchase price of the goods.

[304] In this context, Lord Lindley cited *Gardiner v. Childs* (1837) 8 Car. & P. 345; *cf. Wilson v. Whitehead* (1842) 10 M. & W. 503.

[305] *Ruppell v. Roberts* (1834) 4 Nev. & Man. 31; *Gardiner v. Childs* (1837) 8 Car. & P. 345; *City of London Gas Co. v. Nicholls* (1862) 2 Car. & P. 365. See also *infra*, paras 12–151 *et seq.*

[306] See *supra*, para. 12–49 and *infra*, paras 13–19 *et seq.*; also *Heap v. Dobson* (1863) 15 C.B.(N.S.) 460.

[307] *De Tastet v. Carroll* (1815) 1 Stark. 88.

[308] See the Insolvency Act 1986, ss.238, 239, 339, 340, 423, as applied (where relevant) pursuant to various provisions of the Insolvent Partnerships Order 1994.

[309] *Walmesley v. Cooper* (1839) 11 A. & E. 216.

[310] *Deux v. Jefferies* (1594) Cro.Eliz. 352. It should be noted that a covenant not to sue will not be the equivalent of a release if given in favour of one joint debtor: see *Duck v. Mayeu* [1892] 2 Q.B. 511; *Re E. W. A.* [1901] 2 K.B. 642. See further, *infra*, para. 13–94.

[311] 2 Ro.Ab.Release, 410 D.; *Hawkshaw v. Parkins* (1819) 2 Swan. 539.

Thus, a bona fide release by one partner will not normally be set aside at the instance of the other partners,[312] unless there is evidence of fraud and collusion.[313]

Sales

Goods

12–82   A partner will, as a general rule, have implied authority to sell any goods belonging to his firm.[314] This goes beyond mere sales of stock in trade and even, in one old case, was held to extend to a sale of the partnership books.[315] It is considered that the Factors Act 1889 does not apply to such sales.[316]

Land

12–83   Where land is held beneficially by a firm, the legal estate will inevitably be vested in not more than four partners as trustees of a trust of land.[317] Those trustees, if they are more than two in number,[318] will be able to effect a sale without the concurrence of the other partners, even though this may involve the commission of a breach of trust[319] or fiduciary duty.[320]

Ships

12–84   It appears that a partner will, in an appropriate case, have authority to charter a ship or to mortgage a ship belonging to the firm.[321]

---

[312] *Arton v. Booth* (1820) 4 Moore 192; *Furnival v. Weston* (1822) 7 Moore 356; *Phillips v. Clagett* (1843) 11 M. & W. 84. See also *Jones v. Herbert* (1817) 7 Taunt. 421.

[313] See *Barker v. Richardson* (1827) 1 Y. & J. 362, where one partner had, following a dissolution, deliberately given a release to a partnership debtor as part of a scheme for discharging a private debt which he, in turn, owed to that debtor. The debtor knew it had been agreed that the other partner would get in the debts and clearly colluded in the fraud. See also *Phillips v. Clagett* (1843) 11 M. & W. 84; *Aspinall v. London and N.W. Ry.* (1853) 11 Hare 325.

[314] *Lambert's Case* (1690) Godb. 244. Lord Lindley then discoursed on what would be the position if the partners had become "mere" tenants in common of the partnership goods, referring to Litt. s.323; *Fox v. Hanbury* (1776) Cowp. 445; also *Buckley v. Barber* (1851) 6 Ex. 164, as to which see further *infra*, para. 18–65. However, since such a situation can only arise following a dissolution, in which case the authority of any partner to sell partnership goods is now clearly established by the Partnership Act 1890, s.38, *infra*, para. 13–62, the passage has not been retained. It is to be found in the 15th ed. of this work at p. 314.

[315] *Dore v. Wilkinson* (1817) 2 Stark. 287. The opinion of the current editor is that this decision was wholly exceptional and should not be regarded as a general authority in relation to partnership books.

[316] See *supra*, para. 12–75.

[317] See Law of Property Act 1925, ss.34(2) (as amended by the Trusts of Land and Appointment of Trustees Act 1996, Sched. 2, para. 3(2)); and see *infra*, para. 18–61.

[318] *ibid.* s.27 (as amended by the Law of Property (Amendment) Act 1926, Sched. and the Trusts of Land and Appointment of Trustees Act 1996, Sched. 3, para. 4(8)). As to whether a purchaser from a *sole* partner will take free of the other partners' interests, see *infra*, para. 18–62, n. 202.

[319] See the Trusts of Land and Appointment of Trustees Act 1996, ss.6(1), 11(1). *cf. Notting Hill Housing Trust v. Brackley* [2001] 35 E.G. 106 (CA).

[320] See *Ward v. Brunt* [2000] W.T.L.R. 731, 750A–B; *cf. Sykes v. Land* (1984) 271 E.G. 1264.

[321] See, as to charters, *Thomas v. Clarke* (1818) 2 Stark. 450 and, as to mortgages, *Ex p. Howden* (1842) 2 M.D. & D. 574.

Solicitors

It has already been seen that a partner will prima facie have implied authority **12–85**
to seek advice from a firm of solicitors on behalf of his firm.[322]

Trusts

A partner in a firm of solicitors still does not appear to have authority in the **12–86**
ordinary course of his practice to accept office as a trustee of a trust[323] or as a
trustee de son tort,[324] but may conceivably render himself liable as a *constructive*
trustee whilst acting within the scope of his implied authority.[325] Whether an
accountant is in the same position as regards formal trusteeships has, however,
been called into question.[326]

3.   LIABILITY OF PARTNERS IN RESPECT OF TORTS, FRAUDS AND OTHER WRONGS

In his introduction to this subject, Lord Lindley said: **12–87**

> "If it were necessary, in order that one person should be liable for the fraud or tort
> of another, that the former should have authorised the commission of such tort or
> fraud, it would be a comparatively easy matter to determine in any particular case
> whether a tort or fraud committed by an agent could or could not be imputed to his
> principal. But as a principal is liable, not only for the authorised acts of his agent, but
> also for such unauthorised acts as fall within the scope of the authority apparently
> conferred upon him,[327] the question whether a tort or fraud committed by an agent
> is or is not imputable to his principal becomes one of considerable difficulty; for it
> is obvious that it does not follow from the circumstance that such tort or fraud was
> not authorised, that therefore the principal is not legally responsible for it."[328]

---

[322] See *supra*, para. 12–38.

[323] *Re Fryer* (1857) 3 K. & J. 317; *Tendring Hundred Waterworks v. Jones* [1903] 2 Ch. 615, *infra*,
para. 12–125. *Re Bell's Indenture* [1980] 1 W.L.R. 1217 can no longer be regarded as good law: see
Dubai Aluminium Co. Ltd. v. Salaam [2003] 2 A.C. 366 (HL) at [42] *per* Lord Nicholls and [143] *per*
Lord Millett. *Quaere*, is the position still as set out in the text? See the views expressed by the Court
of Appeal in *Walker v. Stones* [2001] Q.B. 902, 950F–G. Lord Millett took a different view in *Dubai
Aluminium* (*ibid.* at [134]), but Lord Nichols expressed no view on this issue (*ibid.* at [42]). See also
Hansen v. Young [2004] 1 N.Z.L.R. 37 (CA) at [35]. *cf. Public Trustee v. Mortimer* (1985) 16 D.L.R
(4th) 404. And see further *supra*, para. 12–16 and *infra*, para. 12–112.

[324] *Mara v. Browne* [1896] 1 Ch. 199, as explained in *Dubai Aluminium Co Ltd. v. Salaam*, *supra*,
at [132] to [143] *per* Lord Millett, who in fact preferred the expression "*de facto* trustee". Again,
Lord Nicholls left the whole point open at *ibid.* [40] to [42].

[325] *Dubai Aluminium Co. Ltd. v. Salaam*, *supra*. However, Lord Millett appeared to deprecate the
use of the expression "constructive trustee" in this sense: *ibid.* at [142], [143]. See further, *supra*,
para. 12–30 and *infra*, para. 12–112.

[326] *Clasper v. Duns* [2007] NZHC 1000 at [52] *per* Panckhurst J. This observation was, however,
obiter.

[327] These words were, in fact, cited with approval by Evans L.J. in *Dubai Aluminium Co. Ltd. v.
Salaam* [2001] Q.B. 113 at 133A. This part of the decision was affirmed at [2003] 2 A.C. 366
(HL).

[328] Lord Lindley then went on to explore the conditions which are required to be fulfilled before
a principal will be held liable for the torts and frauds of his agent. The passage has not been retained,
but is to be found in the 15th ed. of this work at pp. 315–318.

Partnership Act 1890, section 10

12–88   These principles are clearly reflected in section 10 of the Partnership Act 1890, which provides:

> "10. Where, by any wrongful act or omission of any partner acting in the ordinary course of the business of the firm, or with the authority of his co-partners, loss or injury is caused to any person not being a partner in the firm, or any penalty is incurred, the firm is liable therefor to the same extent as the partner so acting or omitting to act."[329]

Scope of the section

12–89   Although Lord Lindley's statement of principle was formulated solely by reference to torts and frauds, it now seems clear that the section extends to *all* wrongful acts and omissions committed by a partner in the course of carrying on the partnership business, including equitable wrongdoing[330] and a breach of statute resulting in the imposition of a penalty.[331] Although the view has been expressed that the section does not apply in the case of a breach of trust committed by a partner who is a trustee, where liability is determined by reference to the principles set out in section 13 of the Partnership Act 1890,[332] this view has not been accepted in New Zealand.[333] It follows that the extent of any overlap as between sections 10, 11 and 13 is doubtful.[334]

The section contains two limbs, *i.e.* direct liability for an act which is specifically authorised by the other partners and vicarious liability where a partner acts in the ordinary course of business.[335] It is, however, only directed to establishing the liability of the firm, and the words "to the same extent" do not artificially restrict that liability. Thus, it does not follow that, merely because the partner who commits a wrongful act with the express or implied authority of his co-partners is not personally liable, such liability cannot, on normal principles, attach to some *other* partner.[336] In such a case, the liability of the firm will be determined by the extent of the latter partner's liability, not that of the former.[337]

---

[329] As to the nature of the liability under this section see *ibid.* s.12, *infra*, para. 13–12.

[330] *e.g.* dishonest participation in a breach of trust.

[331] *Dubai Aluminium Co. Ltd. v. Salaam* [2003] 2 A.C. 366 (HL); *Strother v. 3464920 Canada Inc.* [2007] 2 S.C.R. 177 (Can. Sup.Ct). See also *Scarborough Building Society v. Howes Percival* (1998) 76 P. & C.R. D4 (CA); *Flynn v. Robin Thompson & Partners, The Times*, March 14, 2000 (CA).

[332] See *Walker v. Stones* [2001] Q.B. 902 (CA) and *supra*, para. 12–30 and *infra*, para. 12–130. See further, as to s.13, *infra*, paras 12–127 *et seq.*

[333] *Clasper v. Duns* [2007] NZHC 1000. See also *infra*, para. 12–130.

[334] In *Dubai Aluminium Co. Ltd. v. Salaam, supra*, at [110], Lord Millett appeared to reject any perceived overlap between the sections (but note that the report of that paragraph at [2002] 3 W.L.R. 1913, 1939 is inaccurate). *cf.* the views expressed in the Court of Appeal at [2001] Q.B.113, 140F–G *per* Aldous L.J.; also *Walker v. Stones, supra*. For an instance in which liability was imposed on a firm under the equivalent of *both* sections 10 and 11(a), see *McDonic v. Hetherington* (1997) 142 D.L.R. (4th) 648. See further *infra*, para. 12–105.

[335] See *Zurich GSG Ltd. v. Gray & Kellas* 2007 S.L.T. 917 (OH) at [31] *per* Lord Brodie.

[336] In *Meekins v. Henson* [1964] 1 Q.B. 472, one partner, with the authority of his co-partners, had defamed the claimant on a privileged occasion and without malice and was accordingly held not to have committed any tort. Malice was, however, proved against one of the other two partners and he alone was held liable to the claimant in damages. Winn J. held the Partnership Act 1890, s.10 to be irrelevant in this context.

[337] In *Meekins v. Henson, supra*, the action was brought against the three partners individually and no attempt was therefore made to argue in favour of the liability of the firm. Ironically, an argument framed by reference to the Partnership Act 1890, s.10 was advanced not by the claimant but by the partners themselves.

It should also be noted that the section has no application where one partner commits a wrongful act against another.[338]

Although the terminology used in the section is different to that appearing in section 5,[339] the current editor takes the view that the test for identifying whether a partner was acting in the "ordinary course of the business of the firm" will be the same.[340] Indeed, Lord Lindley used the expression "carrying on the business in the usual way" in this context.

12–90

The practical operation of section 10 can best be illustrated by considering torts, frauds and other wrongs separately and by referring to a number of cases decided prior to the Partnership Act 1890.

(a) Torts

Examples of cases in which a firm had been held liable for torts committed by partners in the ordinary course of business are many and varied. They range from liability for the negligent driving of a coach,[341] injuring an employee during horseplay,[342] failure to keep a mineshaft in a proper condition,[343] breach of the old revenue laws,[344] and participation in a conspiracy to defraud[345] to liability for negligent advice or the negligent conduct of a claim by a partner in a firm of solicitors.[346] In cases of this type, whilst the firm may be vicariously liable for the partner's act of negligence, it does not follow that the firm *itself* has been negligent, should that be relevant.[347]

12–91

It does not matter that the firm itself is incapable of committing the tortious act. Thus, where a partner, with the express authority of his co-partners or in the ordinary course of business, holds a particular office or appointment which the firm is ineligible to hold, the firm will be liable for his negligent acts and omissions in carrying out the duties attached to that position.[348] Similarly, a firm may be liable if a partner assaults a third party in the course of carrying on the

---

[338] See *Mair v. Wood* 1948 S.C. 83, which concerned a Scots partnership enjoying separate legal personality. It is considered that the position is *a fortiori* in England, where the firm has no such personality. See, however, as to claims for breach of duty as between partners, *infra*, paras 20–10 *et seq.*

[339] See *supra*, para. 12–02.

[340] See *supra*, paras 12–12 *et seq.*

[341] *Moreton v. Hardern* (1825) 4 B. & C. 223. As to ships, see *Steel v. Lester* (1878) 3 C.P.D. 121.

[342] *Petrou v. Hatzigeorgiou* (1991) Aust. Torts Rep. 81–071 (NSW). Similarly in the case of sexual harassment of employees: *Proceedings Commissioner v. Ali Hatem* [1999] 1 N.Z.L.R. 305.

[343] *Mellors v. Shaw* (1861) 1 B. & S. 437; *Ashworth v. Stanwix* (1861) 3 E. & E. 701. See also *Duke of Brunswick v. Slowman* (1849) 8 C.B. 317.

[344] *R. v. Stranyforth* (1721) Bunb. 97; *Att.-Gen. v. Burges* (1726) Bunb. 223; *Att.-Gen. v. Weeks* (1726) Bunb. 223; *R. v. Manning* (1739) 2 Com. 616. See also *Att.-Gen. v. Siddon* (1830) 1 C. & J. 220.

[345] *Scarborough Building Society v. Howes Percival* (1998) 76 P. & C.R. D4 (CA).

[346] *Blyth v. Fladgate* [1891] 1 Ch. 337; *Midland Bank Trust Co. Ltd. v. Hett, Stubbs & Kemp* [1979] Ch. 384; *Sweetman v. Nathan* [2004] P.N.L.R. 7 (CA), noted *supra*, para. 12–14; and other cases of that class. See also *Sawyer v. Goodwin* (1867) 36 L.J.Ch. 578. It perhaps goes without saying that where a firm acts for the spouse of a partner and allows that partner to conduct the matter, the firm will be liable for his actions: *Dayman v. Lawrence Graham* [2008] EWHC 2036 (Ch) (Lawtel 3/9/08) at [73] *per* Judge Hodge Q.C. sitting as a judge of the Chancery Division. *Per contra* if he was solely acting *qua* spouse: see *ibid.*

[347] See *Duncan v. Beattie* 2003 S.L.T. 1243 (OH). See also *Zurich GSG Ltd. v. Gray & Kellas* 2007 S.L.T. 917 (OH) at [31] *per* Lord Brodie.

[348] *Kirkintilloch Equitable Co-operative Society Ltd. v. Livingstone* 1972 S.L.T. 154.

partnership business, even though the firm itself could not commit an assault.[349]

Wilful torts

12–92   Lord Lindley observed:

> "As a rule . . . the wilful tort of one partner is not imputable to the firm.[350] . . . But a wilful tort committed by a partner in the course and for the purpose of transacting the business of the firm may make the firm responsible."[351]

Thus, if part of the normal business of a firm involves obtaining details of contracts entered into by its business competitors, albeit by legitimate means, the firm will be responsible if one partner obtains such information by the use of a bribe.[352] Similarly in the case of an assault.[353]

Right to indemnity

12–93   It would seem that, in cases where section 10 of the Partnership Act 1890 applies, the innocent partners may be entitled to seek an indemnity from the partner who committed the tort, unless they expressly or impliedly authorised it.[354]

(b) Frauds and Fraudulent Representations

12–94   Section 10 of the Partnership Act 1890 introduced no change in the law as regards the liability of the firm for frauds committed by its members, as is demonstrated by the following passage which, though written by Lord Lindley prior to the Act, clearly explains its operation in this context:

> " . . . [a] firm is liable for frauds committed by one of its members whilst acting for the firm, and in transacting its business[355] and the innocent partners cannot divest themselves of responsibility on the ground that they never authorised the commission of the fraud. On the other hand, the firm is not liable for the other frauds of its members, unless it has in fact sanctioned such frauds, or the transactions of which they form part."[356]

---

[349] See *Flynn v. Robin Thompson & Partners*, *The Times*, March 14, 2000 (CA). In that case, there were two separate assaults by a partner in a firm of solicitors on his opponent: one was held to be plainly outside the scope of s.10, whilst the other (which had actually occurred in court during the course of a hearing) was not.

[350] Lord Lindley cited *Arbuckle v. Taylor* (1815) 3 Dow. 160 (malicious prosecution for theft of partnership property).

[351] See *Limpus v. London General Omnibus Co.* (1861) 1 H. & C. 526; also *Citizens' Life Assurance Co. v. Brown* [1904] A.C. 423. Various other instances are noted *supra*, para. 12–91.

[352] *Hamlyn v. John Houston & Co.* [1903] 1 K.B. 81; *Janvier v. Sweeney* [1919] 2 K.B. 316; *Petrograde Inc. v. Smith* [2000] 1 Lloyd's Rep. 486. Note also, in this context, the Bribery Act 2010, ss.7(1), (5)(c), 8, which are not yet in force.

[353] *Flynn v. Robin Thompson & Partners*, *The Times*, March 14, 2000 (CA). See further *supra*, para. 12–91.

[354] See *infra*, paras 20–10 *et seq.*

[355] Of course, the formulation of the rule in s.10 now refers to the "ordinary course of the business," but this is not a change of substance.

[356] See further, *infra*, paras 12–122 *et seq.*

It should be noted that, as under the general law,[357] liability under the section is not dependent on showing that the firm has benefited from the fraud, although acceptance of such a benefit may justify an inference that the firm has adopted the fraud.[358] A relatively recent illustration of a case in which the firm was held liable for a fraud perpetrated by a partner in a firm of accountants is to be found in *McHugh v. Kerr.*[359]

Prior to the decision in *Hedley Byrne & Co. Ltd. v. Heller & Partners Ltd.*[360] and the passing of the Misrepresentation Act 1967, there was in general no right to damages in respect of misrepresentations which were made otherwise than fraudulently.[361] Now damages are, in general, available for negligent mis-state-ments[362] and for negligent and careless (but not wholly innocent) misrepresenta-tions.[363] It is accordingly no longer as vital to distinguish, as Lord Lindley did, between those cases in which there is a right to damages and those in which there is some other remedy. Nevertheless, the distinction is useful as a means of illustrating the potential application of section 10 of the Partnership Act 1890.

[357] See *Lloyd v. Grace Smith & Co.* [1912] A.C. 716.

[358] See [1912] A.C. 716, 738 *per* Lord Macnaghten.

[359] [2003] EWHC 2985 (Ch) (Lawtel 22/12/03). See also the cases concerning solicitors noticed *supra*, para. 12–16.

[360] [1964] A.C. 465.

[361] A fraudulent statement must, in essence, be false and either known to the maker to be false or made by him recklessly and without any belief as to its truth: see *Derry v. Peek* (1889) 14 App.Cas. 337; *Glasier v. Rolls* (1889) 42 Ch.D. 436; *Angus v. Clifford* [1891] 2 Ch. 449; *Low v. Bouverie* [1891] 3 Ch. 82; *Le Lievre v. Gould* [1893] 1 Q.B. 491; *Thomas Witter Ltd. v. TBP Industries Ltd.* [1996] 2 All E.R. 573. It is sufficient to show that the fraudulent misrepresentation was actively present in the claimant's mind, even if he might still have entered into the contract: *Edgington v. Fitzmaurice* (1885) 29 Ch.D. 459; *Ross River Ltd. v. Cambridge City Football Club Ltd.* [2008] 1 All E.R. (Comm) 1028. As to damages for breach of an implied warranty of authority, see *Collen v. Wright* (1857) 8 E. & B. 647; *Starkey v. Bank of England* [1903] A.C. 114; *Bowstead & Reynolds on Agency* (19th ed.), Art. 105, paras 9–060 *et seq.* And see also, as to the position where there is a breach of a special or fiduciary duty arising from the relationship of the parties, *Nocton v. Lord Ashburton* [1914] A.C. 932 (solicitor and client).

[362] *Hedley Byrne & Co. Ltd. v. Heller & Partners Ltd.* [1964] A.C. 465; *Mutual Life and Citizens' Assurance Co. Ltd. v. Evatt* [1971] A.C. 793; *Esso Petroleum Ltd. v. Mardon* [1976] Q.B. 801; *ADT Ltd. v. BDO Binder Hamlyn* [1996] B.C.C. 808. But see as to the possible limitations on such an action, *Argy Trading Development Co. Ltd. v. Lapid Developments Ltd.* [1977] 1 W.L.R. 444.

[363] See the Misrepresentation Act 1967, s.2(1). To escape liability the person making the repre-sentation must prove that "he had reasonable grounds to believe and did believe up to the time the contract was made that the facts represented were true". See generally, as to this subsection, *Gosling v. Anderson* [1972] E.G.D. 709; *Watts v. Spence* [1976] Ch. 165; *Howard Marine and Dredging Co. Ltd. v. A. Ogden & Sons (Excavations) Ltd.* [1978] Q.B. 574; *Chesneau v. Interhome Ltd.* (1983) 134 N.L.J. 341 (CA); *Sharneyford Supplies Ltd. v. Edge* [1986] Ch. 128; *Cemp Properties (U.K.) Ltd. v. Dentsply Research & Development Corp.* [1991] 34 E.G. 62 (CA); *Royscot Trust Ltd. v. Rogerson* [1991] 2 Q.B. 297 (CA); *MCI Worldcom International Inc v. Primus Telecommunications Inc* [2004] 1 All E.R. (Comm) 138; also *Garden Neptune Shipping Ltd. v. Occidental Worldwide Investment Corp.* [1990] 1 Lloyd's Rep. 330. Although it has for some years been clear that the measure of damages under the subsection is tortious (indemnity for loss) rather than contractual (loss of expectation), the Court of Appeal in *Royscot Trust Ltd. v. Rogerson, supra,* decided that the true measure is that for *fraudulent* misrepresentation rather than mere negligence at common law, so that, where appropriate, unforeseen losses flowing from the fraud will be recoverable; see also *Smith New Court Securities v. Citibank NA* [1997] A.C. 254; *Avon Insurance plc v. Swire Fraser Ltd.* [2000] 1 All E.R. (Comm.) 573. Somewhat confusingly, the subsection is often spoken of as having estab-lished liability for *innocent* misrepresentation (*e.g.* see *Howard Marine and Dredging Co. Ltd. v. A. Ogden & Sons (Excavations) Ltd., supra,* p. 592 *per* Denning M.R.), but in such cases the word "innocent" is used in a special sense. See also *infra*, para. 23–51. Note that *ibid.* s.3 does not apply to provisions which seek to restrict the ostensible authority of an agent: *Overbrooke Estates Ltd. v. Glencombe Properties Ltd.* [1974] 1 W.L.R. 1335 (a decision under s.3 in its original form, and not as substituted by the Unfair Contract Terms Act 1977, s.8(1)).

Actions for damages

12–95   Whilst section 10 of the Partnership Act 1890 clearly establishes the liability of the firm for damages in respect of a fraud committed by a partner in the ordinary course of its business,[364] it is still necessary to prove an *actionable* fraud.[365] Constructive fraud, *i.e.* a combination of a false statement made innocently by one partner and knowledge of the true facts on the part of another partner, is not sufficient[366]; moreover, it would seem that damages on the basis of innocent misrepresentation would not be recoverable in such a case.[367] Where, however, one partner, who knows the true facts, expressly authorises another partner, who has no such knowledge, to make a false statement,[368] or deliberately stands by in the knowledge, expectation or hope that he will make such a statement, that statement, although made innocently, would be treated as a fraudulent misrepresentation made by the firm.[369] Similarly, where the partner who makes the statement is reckless in not consulting his co-partners before doing so.[370]

Other remedies

12–96   Lord Lindley observed that:

> " . . . there is no doubt that a firm can be compelled to restore property, or refund money, obtained by it by the misrepresentation of one of its members. Nor in such a case is it necessary to prove that the misrepresentation was fraudulent as well as false."[371]

Thus, in *Rapp v. Latham*,[372] Parry, who was the active partner in a firm of wine and spirit merchants, had received a substantial sum of money from a customer

---

[364] In such a case, the firm will be liable to the same extent as the partner responsible for the fraud: see *supra*, para. 12–89. It should be noted that, whilst Lord Lindley, writing in the Supplement to the 5th ed. of this work, said of the section: " . . . it removes the doubt as to whether a firm is or is not liable in an action of damages for the fraud of one of its members, if committed by him in the ordinary course of the business of the firm, by making the firm liable in every case in which the partner himself is liable", in subsequent editions the same view was expressed more tentatively, namely, that the section "seems clearly to make a firm liable . . . ".

[365] In *Scarborough Building Society v. Howes Percival* (1998) 76 P.& C.R D4 (CA), a partner in a firm of solicitors had participated in a conspiracy to defraud, but this was treated as a case of tort rather than fraud. It is interesting to note that Roch L.J. cited *National Commercial Banking Corporation of Australia Ltd. v. Batty* (1986) 65 A.L.R. 385 as "authority for the proposition that the mere fact that an act of a partner is fraudulent will not of itself take that act out of the normal course of his firm's business". Were the position otherwise, there would be little scope for liability under s.10.

[366] See *Armstrong v. Strain* [1952] 1 K.B. 232, where an unsuccessful attempt was made to prove fraud by linking an innocent misrepresentation as to the state of a property made by an agent on behalf of the owner (but without his knowledge) with the owner's awareness of the true state of the property. And see also *supra*, para. 12–28.

[367] The Misrepresentation Act 1967, s.2(1) gives a remedy only where damages would have been recoverable if the misrepresentation had been made fraudulently, which for the above reasons they would not. *Quaere*, could the firm in any event rely on the reasonable belief of the partner who made the statement? Having regard to the terms of the Partnership Act 1890, s.10, the current editor tentatively submits that it could.

[368] See *London County Freehold Properties Ltd. v. Berkeley Property Investment Co. Ltd.* [1936] 2 All E.R. 1039.

[369] See *Ludgater v. Love* (1881) 44 L.T. 694.

[370] See *Armstrong v. Strain* [1952] 1 K.B. 232, 244 *per* Singleton L.J. See also *supra*, n. 366.

[371] See *Arkwright v. Newbold* (1880) 17 Ch.D. 301; *Redgrave v. Hurd* (1881) 20 Ch.D. 1.

[372] (1819) 2 B. & A. 795.

to be applied in the purchase and sale of wine. He falsely and fraudulently represented that he was carrying out various transactions on the customer's behalf and accounted to him for the supposed proceeds. There was, however, a considerable sum unaccounted for, which Parry alleged had been invested in the purchase of wine. The customer sought to recover this amount against Parry and his partner, Latham. Notwithstanding an attempt by Latham to argue that he was not affected by Parry's fraud, on the basis that the fictitious purchases and sales were not made in the ordinary course of trade and were, therefore, not partnership transactions, it was held that Latham was liable to the customer. The decisions in *Lovell v. Hicks*[373] and *Blair v. Bromley*[374] are to the same effect.

False accounts rendered by partner

The cases cited in the previous paragraph would appear to demonstrate that a   **12–97** false and fraudulent account rendered by a partner, in the name of the firm and within the scope of its business, would have bound all the partners even prior to the Partnership Act 1890[375] and there is no reason to suppose that the current position is any different, having regard to the provisions of sections 10 and 15 of that Act.[376]

Cases where the firm is not liable

Statute of Frauds Amendment Act 1828, section 6

By section 6 of the Statute of Frauds Amendment Act 1828, a firm is not liable   **12–98** for a false and fraudulent representation as to the character or solvency of any person unless the representation is in writing and signed by all the partners.[377] It has been decided that the signature of one partner in the firm name will not bind any partner other than himself[378] and it is submitted that the same decision would still be reached today, notwithstanding the terms of section 10 of the Partnership Act 1890.[379]

---

[373] (1837) 2 Y. & C.Ex. 472.

[374] (1847) 2 Ph. 354. Lord Lindley pointed out that the case "was in fact decided by the Lord Chancellor [*Lord Cottenham*] expressly upon the ground that persons who, having a duty to perform, represent to those who are interested in the performance of it that it has been performed, make themselves responsible for all the consequences of non-performance; and as one partner may bind another as to any matter within the limits of their joint business, so he may by an act which, though not constituting a contract by itself, is on equitable principles considered as having all the consequences of one". See also, as to this case *infra*, para. 12–119. And see *Moore v. Knight* [1891] 1 Ch. 547.

[375] Lord Lindley put it very tentatively: "Whether accounts, rendered by one partner in the name of the firm and showing that money is in the hands of the firm when in truth he has misapplied it, are to be treated as representations of the firm, is a question which has given rise to much discussion and upon which the cases are not uniform. But on the whole it is conceived that if the accounts relate to matters within the scope of the partnership business the firm is bound by them." He also referred to *Devaynes v. Noble, Baring's Case* (1816) 1 Mer. 611; *Marsh v. Keating* (1834) 2 Cl. & F. 250; *De Ribeyre v. Barclay* (1857) 23 Beav. 107, contrasting those decisions with *Hume v. Bolland* (1832) 1 Cromp. & M. 130 and *Sims v. Brutton* (1850) 5 Ex. 802, noted *infra*, para. 12–111.

[376] See *supra*, paras 12–21, 12–88.

[377] See as to the scope of the section, *Banbury v. Bank of Montreal* [1918] A.C. 626; also *Diamond v. Bank of London and Montreal Ltd.* [1979] Q.B. 333.

[378] See *Williams v. Mason* (1873) 28 L.T.(N.S.) 232; *Swift v. Jewsbury* (1874) L.R. 9 Q.B. 301; *Hirst v. West Riding Union Banking Co.* [1901] 2 K.B. 560.

[379] See *Keen v. Mear* [1920] 2 Ch. 574, a decision which turned on the application of the Partnership Act 1890, s.5 and the Statute of Frauds 1677, s.4 (it being held that the former section did not override the provisions of the latter).

It should be noted that the 1828 Act provides no defence in the case of a *negligent* misrepresentation as to character or solvency made by a partner in the ordinary course of the firm's business.[380]

Representations as to authority

12–99   Consistently with the views expressed earlier in this work,[381] Lord Lindley wrote:

> "If a partner, acting apparently beyond the limits of his authority, untruly represents that he is acting with his co-partners' consent, they are not bound by this representation, nor are they liable for what may be done on the faith of it."

He illustrated this proposition by reference to the decision in *Ex p. Agace*,[382] where one partner had given partnership bills in payment of a personal debt and represented to the creditor that his partner was agreeable to this being done. The other partner had done nothing to justify an inference that he consented to that arrangement or that he authorised the representation. On the bankruptcy of the firm, those bills were held not to be provable against the joint estate. Although the creditor was genuinely misled, he must be taken to have known that the partner who made the representation was not acting in the ordinary course of the firm's business and had thus exceeded the scope of his implied authority.[383]

Representations as to nature of business

12–100   It is submitted that the position is no different where the false representation relates, not directly to the extent of the partner's authority, but to the nature of the partnership business and, thus, indirectly to the extent of that authority. Lord Lindley analysed the position in this way:

> "A question of more difficulty arises when a partner alleges that the business of the firm is more extensive than it really is, or that it is different from what it is. But even in this case the firm would probably be held not liable[384] for such a misrepresentation. *Ex hypothesi* the representation is not referable to anything falling within the scope of the partnership business; and it would probably be contended in vain that each partner was impliedly authorised by his co-partners to answer questions as to what business they really carried on in partnership. If the person seeking to make the firm liable knew anything of the firm and of its business as ordinarily carried on, then *Ex p. Agace* is an authority to show that he could not succeed. If he knew nothing of the firm, he would be in the position of a person dealing with an agent whose authority is wholly unknown. Now an agent whose authority is wholly unknown cannot bind his principal by misrepresenting the authority conferred,[385] and it is difficult, therefore, to see upon what principle a partner could, in the case now

---

[380] See *W. B. Anderson & Sons v. Rhodes (Liverpool)* [1967] 2 All E.R. 850; also *Banbury v. Bank of Montreal* [1918] A.C. 626.

[381] See *supra*, para. 12–22.

[382] (1792) 2 Cox 312.

[383] See also *Kendal v. Wood* (1870) L.R. 6 Ex. 243; *Mahony v. East Holyford Mining Co.* (1875) L.R. 7 H.L. 869, 879–880 *per* Kelly C.B; *United Bank of Kuwait v. Hammoud* [1988] 1 W.L.R. 1051, 1066H *per* Lord Donaldson M.R., *supra*, para. 12–22; *Hirst v. Etherington* [1999] Lloyd's Rep. P.N. 938, 942–943 (CA). And see, generally, *Armagas Ltd. v. Mundogas S.A.* [1986] A.C. 717, where numerous authorities are reviewed in the context of employer and employee.

[384] In later editions, the words "can hardly be held liable" were substituted.

[385] See *United Bank of Kuwait v. Hammoud* [1988] 1 W.L.R. 1051 (CA); *Hirst v. Etherington* [1999] Lloyd's Rep. P.N. 938 (CA); also *Armagas Ltd. v. Mundogas S.A.* [1986] A.C. 717 and the cases there cited.

supposed, bind the firm by misrepresenting his authority, or by misrepresenting the nature of the business of the firm which, as to strangers, determines that authority."[386]

Representations to incoming partner

It is doubtful whether a false or fraudulent representation designed to induce **12–101** a person to become a partner could ever be given in the ordinary course of carrying on the firm's business,[387] although Lord Lindley put it more categorically:

> "It is not necessary, in order to carry on the business of a firm in the ordinary way, that any of the partners should have power to induce other persons to join the firm."

It follows that, in the absence of express authority or subsequent ratification by the other partners, such a representation will not be imputed to the firm. Ratification will, however, be inferred if the firm, with knowledge of the false or fraudulent nature of the representation, seeks to retain money or property introduced by the incoming partner; in such circumstances, the firm will clearly be liable for its return.[388]

(c) Other Wrongs

As already noticed, the House of Lords in *Dubai Aluminium Co. Ltd. v. Salaam*[389] **12–102** held that the application of section 10 of the Partnership Act 1890 is not confined to torts and frauds and could extend to a partner's knowing and dishonest assistance in a breach of trust or fiduciary duty, such as would render that partner liable as a constructive trustee.[390] Thus, even though it was, on the facts, clear that the partner in question had actively colluded with his client and third parties in developing a dishonest scheme and the other partners had not authorised him to act as he did, the firm was held liable.[391]

4.   LIABILITY OF PARTNERS FOR MISAPPLICATION OF MONEY AND PROPERTY

Although cases in this class are closely allied to those in the previous section, **12–103** they are governed by a different section of the Partnership Act 1890[392] and, for that reason, are considered separately.

---

[386] Lord Lindley then put forward the following example, which is scarcely of relevance today: "A member of a banking firm could hardly bind it by underwriting a policy in the name of the firm, and by untruly representing that he and his partners were insurers as well as bankers."

[387] *Quaere*, might such an argument perhaps be sustainable in the case of an investment partnership?

[388] See the cases cited *supra*, para. 12–96.

[389] [2003] 2 A.C. 366. See also *supra*, para. 12–89.

[390] See, as to the use of this expression, *Dubai Aluminium Co. Ltd. v. Salaam, supra*, at [140] to [143] *per* Lord Millett.

[391] The House of Lords reversed the Court of Appeal's decision on the facts. For another example of a case in which the firm was held liable, see *Agip (Africa) Ltd. v. Jackson*[1990] Ch. 265 (Millett J.), affirmed at [1991] Ch. 547. There, however, the potential application of s.10 received scant attention from the court.

[392] *Quaere* whether there may be a degree of overlap with the Partnership Act 1890, ss.10, 13: see *supra*, para. 12–89 and *infra*, para. 12–105.

Lord Lindley's formulation

Lord Lindley explained the position prior to the Partnership Act 1890, in terms of four basic principles:

> "In order that a firm may be liable for the misapplication of money by one of its members, some obligation on the part of the firm to take care of the money must be shown. A receipt of the money by the firm prima facie imposes this obligation; but where there is no receipt by the firm, there is prima facie no obligation on its part with respect to the money in question. It becomes important, therefore, to determine accurately when money is to be considered as received by the firm. Upon this point the following observations suggest themselves:
>
> 1.   The firm must be treated as receiving what any partner receives as its real or ostensible agent, *i.e.* in the course of transacting the business of the firm.
> 2.   In a case of this sort it is immaterial whether the other partners know anything about the money or not; for *ex hypothesi*, it is in the custody of one who must be regarded as their agent.[393]
> 3.   The firm cannot be treated as receiving what one partner receives otherwise than as its real or ostensible agent, unless the money actually comes into the possession or under the control of the other partners.[394]
> 4.   Agency being excluded in such a case as the last, the money cannot be considered as in the possession or under the control of the innocent partners, unless they know that it is so, or unless they are culpably ignorant of the fact."[395]

Partnership Act 1890, section 11

12–104   The foregoing principles are all encapsulated in the Partnership Act 1890, which provides:

> "11. In the following cases; namely:
>
> (a)   Where one partner acting within the scope of his apparent authority receives the money or property of a third person and misapplies it; and
> (b)   Where a firm in the course of its business receives money or property of a third person, and the money or property so received is misapplied[396] by one or more of the partners while it is in the custody of the firm;
>
> the firm is liable to make good the loss."[397]

12–105   It will be apparent that the section seeks to impose liability in two distinct cases, *i.e.* where money or property has been received and misapplied by a partner (section 11(a)) and where money or property has been received by the firm and subsequently misapplied by a partner (section 11(b)). Both require an application of the same fundamental principle which underlies sections 5 and 10, *i.e.* the firm will only be liable where money is received within the scope of a

---

[393] See *infra*, paras 12–106 *et seq.*

[394] See *infra*, paras 12–115 *et seq.*

[395] See *infra*, paras 12–109 *et seq*, 12–129. As to culpable ignorance, *cf. Marsh v. Keating* (1834) 2 Cl. & Fin. 289; *Sims v. Brutton* (1850) 5 Ex. 802; *Ex p. Greaves* (1856) 8 De G.M. & G. 291; *Cleather v. Twisden* (1884) 28 Ch.D. 340; *National Commercial Banking Corp. of Australia Ltd. v. Batty* (1986) 65 A.L.R. 385.

[396] Note, as to the meaning of this expression, *Clasper v. Duns* [2007] NZHC 1000.

[397] As to the nature of the liability under this section, see *ibid.* s.12, *infra*, para. 13–12.

partner's express or implied authority, the latter being determined by reference to the manner in which the partnership business is carried on in the usual or ordinary way.[398] However, as Lord Lindley pointed out, in all cases liability presupposes the receipt of money by or on behalf of the firm: if there is no receipt, there will be no liability.[399]

Although the scope of section 11 and its interaction with sections 10 and 13 has received recent judicial scrutiny,[400] there are still a relative dearth of decisions under the section. It follows that the operation of its two limbs must in part be illustrated by reference to a number of pre-1890 authorities. The cases will be grouped according to result, *i.e.* those in which the firm was held liable and those in which it was not, each group being preceded by a general proposition or rule originally formulated by Lord Lindley.

Section 11(a): Receipt of money or property by partner

Group 1: Firm held liable

> *Where one partner, acting within the scope of his authority, as evidenced by the business of the firm, obtains money and misapplies it, the firm is answerable for it.*[401]

12–106

In *Willett v. Chambers*,[402] a partner in a firm of solicitors and conveyancers received money from a client to invest on mortgage and misapplied it. A bill for the supposed transaction was rendered to the client in the firm name and was in fact paid to the other partner: it was therefore clearly a partnership transaction[403] and the other partner, whilst himself innocent of any wrongdoing, was held liable to the client for the return of the money. *McDonic v. Hetherington*[404] was a very similar case, in which two sisters had entrusted money to a partner in a law firm for investment.

A more unusual case was *Rhodes v. Moules*.[405] There R, again a partner in a firm of solicitors, was instructed by a client to arrange a loan secured by a

12–107

---

[398] See *supra*, paras 12–12 *et seq.*

[399] See *British Homes Assurance Corporation Ltd. v. Paterson* [1902] 2 Ch. 404, *infra*, para. 13–24; *Bass Brewers Ltd. v. Appleby* (1997) 73 P. & C.R. 165 (CA); *Dubai Aluminium Co. Ltd. v. Salaam* [2003] 2 A.C. 366 at [110] *per* Lord Millett. As the House of Lords made clear in *Dubai Aluminium*, it does not follow that, in the absence of receipt by or on behalf of the firm, this precludes liability under s.10.

[400] See *Bass Brewers Ltd. v. Appleby*, *supra*; *Walker v. Stones* [2001] Q.B. 902 (CA); *Dubai Aluminium Co. Ltd. v. Salaam*, *supra*; *Clasper v. Duns* [2007] NZHC 1000. *McDonic v. Hetherington* (1997) 142 D.L.R. (4th) 648 is an example of a case in which liability was imposed under the equivalent of *both* sections 10 and 11(a): see further *infra*, para. 12–106. See also *supra*, para. 12–89.

[401] This was Lord Lindley's first rule.

[402] (1778) Cowp. 814. See also *Atkinson v. Mackreth* (1866) L.R. 2 Eq. 570; *St Aubyn v. Smart* (1868) L.R. 3 Ch.App. 646; *Earl of Dundonald v. Masterman* (1869) L.R. 7 Eq. 504 (as discussed in *Clasper v. Duns* [2007] NZHC 1000). *cf. Bourdillon v. Roche* (1858) 27 L.J.Ch. 681; *Viney v. Chaplin* (1858) 2 De G. & J. 483; *Harman v. Johnson* (1853) 2 E. & B. 61; *Plumer v. Gregory* (1874) L.R. 18 Eq. 621; *Cleather v. Twisden* (1884) 28 Ch.D. 340: see further, *infra*, paras 12–109 *et seq.* In *Mann v. Hulme* [1962] A.L.R. 75, the partner receiving the money gave his own promissory note as additional security, but this was held not to affect the firm's primary liability.

[403] Lord Mansfield relied upon the fact that the bill for the fictitious mortgage was made out in the name of the firm, and was paid to the innocent partner.

[404] (1997) 142 D.L.R. (4th) 648 (CA, Ontario). Liability was held to arise under the equivalent of the Partnership Act 1890, ss.10 *and* 11.

[405] [1895] 1 Ch. 236. *cf. Cleather v. Twisden* (1884) 28 Ch.D. 340, *infra*, para. 12–110.

mortgage on his freehold property. R duly arranged the loan, but informed the client that the mortgagees required collateral security, which was untrue. The client gave R some bearer share warrants to be used as such security, but these were misappropriated by R, who then absconded. The other partners did not know that the share warrants had been received and were innocent of any fraud. Significantly, R had on two previous occasions received the same share warrants from this client with a view to raising loans; moreover, the firm were in the habit of receiving and holding bearer bonds belonging to clients. In those circumstances, it was held that the share warrants were received in the course of a normal partnership transaction and that R's partners were liable for their value.

12–108   In *Brydges v. Branfill*,[406] a solicitor had connived at a fraud committed by a client of his firm with a view to obtaining the payment out of certain funds in court. He received those funds under a power of attorney and handed them over to the client. The other partners knew nothing of the transaction, but were nevertheless held liable to make good the loss.

In each of the above cases, receipt by a partner was treated as receipt by the firm, so that liability attached even though the other partners knew nothing of the transaction.[407] Where, however, money or property is received by a partner pursuant to a contract entered into by him *qua* individual and not *qua* partner, the firm will not be liable even if the contract was of a nature that would fall within the scope of the firm's business.[408] Equally, the fact that a partner holds an office which is personal to him does not mean that, whilst fulfilling his duties as office holder, he is not acting *qua* partner.[409]

Group 2: Firm not liable

12–109   *If a partner in the course of some transaction unconnected with the business of the firm, or not within the scope of such business, obtains money and then misapplies it, the firm is not without more*[410] *liable to make good the loss.*[411]

In *Harman v. Johnson*,[412] a partner in a firm of solicitors was entrusted with money for the purpose of investing it on mortgage when a good opportunity arose, but misapplied it. His partner was not held liable for the misapplication because there was no evidence to show that it was part of the business either of the particular firm or of solicitors in general to act as scriveners, *i.e.* to receive

---

[406] (1842) 12 Sim. 369. See also *Todd v. Studholme* (1857) 3 K. & J. 324. *cf. Marsh v. Joseph* [1897] 1 Ch. 213.

[407] See *St. Aubyn v. Smart* [1868] L.R. 3 Ch.App. 646. There was no such receipt in *Agip (Africa) Ltd. v. Jackson* [1991] Ch. 547.

[408] *British Homes Assurance Corporation v. Paterson* [1902] 2 Ch. 404, *infra*, para. 13–24; and see also *New Mining & Exploring Syndicate Ltd. v. Chalmers & Hunter* 1912 S.C. 126.

[409] *Bass Brewers Ltd. v. Appleby* (1997) 73 P. & C.R. 165, 173 (CA). Note that this case was decided on the basis of receipt by the firm, rather than the partner in question: see *infra*, para. 12–120.

[410] As to the effect of knowledge on the part of the other partners, see *Cleather v. Twisden* (1884) 28 Ch.D. 340, *infra*, para. 12–110. And see also the Partnership Act 1890, s.13, *infra*, para. 12–127.

[411] This was in fact Lord Lindley's third rule, being the corollary of the first. See also *infra*, para. 12–122.

[412] (1853) 2 E. & B. 61.

and hold money pending investment.[413] Consistently with the decision in *Willett v. Chambers*,[414] the court intimated that if it had been shown that the money was received with a view to investment on a specific mortgage, the co-partner would have been liable for its misapplication.

Similarly, in *Plumer v. Gregory*,[415] where the solicitor had borrowed money   **12–110** from a client without the knowledge of his co-partners, saying that the firm wanted to lend it to another client on mortgage. The other partners were held not to be liable, even though two of them had in fact previously borrowed money from that client.

In *Cleather v. Twisden*,[416] trustees had placed certain bearer bonds in the hands of a solicitor for safe custody but he misappropriated them. His partners, who did not know of the transaction, were held not to be responsible for the loss, since it was not part of their business to accept such securities for safe custody. The decision would, however, have been otherwise if it had been proved that those partners had known the bonds to be in the custody of their co-partner on behalf of the firm; in such circumstances, the bonds would have been treated as in their own custody.[417]

It would seem that the decision in *Sims v. Brutton*[418] also falls within this   **12–111** group, although the decision is an exceptional one and requires explanation. It again concerned a firm of solicitors comprising two partners, B and C. B received £500 from a client, S, to invest on a mortgage, and the money was duly invested. The mortgage deed was retained by the firm. The mortgage debt was ultimately repaid to C, who delivered up the deed to the mortgagor. Shortly thereafter, C re-lent part of the money to the mortgagor and the mortgage deed was returned to him as security. The new mortgage debt was then repaid and the deed again delivered up. C had no authority to receive payment of the original mortgage debt, to re-lend any part of it or to receive payment of the subsequent mortgage debt. Neither B nor S knew anything about these transactions, although full details were contained in the partnership books. Moreover, S was at all times credited with the receipt of interest on the whole amount of the original payment, such interest being regularly paid to his agent. C having misapplied the original payment, B was held not to be liable to make it good. It was found that B and C had discharged their duty to S by laying out the money as directed and that they had no authority to receive it back. Therefore, whilst C may have treated the repayment of the original mortgage debt as a partnership transaction, in point of law it did not have that character and did not bind the firm. The entries in the partnership books were only evidence of knowledge on B's part and the case stated for the opinion of the court expressly declared that he had no knowledge of the true facts.

---

[413] Note that a scrivener would have been entitled, pending the investment of the money, to use it for his own purposes and to retain any profits made thereby; see also *Doobey v. Watson* (1888) 39 Ch.D. 178, 182–183 *per* Kekewich J.; *cf. McDonic v. Hetherington* (1997) 142 D.L.R. (4th) 648, 656. Such a person would now be subject to the strict requirements of the Financial Services and Markets Act 2000: see *infra*, para. 12–114. And see the Solicitors' Accounts Rules 1998, noted *infra*, para. 12–131.

[414] (1778) Cowp. 814, *supra*, para. 12–106.

[415] (1874) L.R. 18 Eq. 621.

[416] (1884) 28 Ch.D. 340; also *National Commercial Banking Corp. of Australia Ltd. v. Batty* (1986) 65 A.L.R. 385. *cf. Rhodes v. Moules* [1895] 1 Ch. 236, *supra*, para. 12–107. See in particular, *ibid.* pp. 244–245 *per* Lord Herschell.

[417] See *infra*, paras 12–115 *et seq.*

[418] (1850) 5 Ex. 802. See also *Coomer v. Bromley* (1852) 5 De G. & Sm. 532, *infra*, para. 12–124.

Lord Lindley observed:

" . . . if, as appears to have been the case, the [*original payment*] when paid off was placed to the credit of the firm with its bankers, the decision is difficult to reconcile with *Stone v. Marsh*[419] and *Marsh v. Keating.*"[420]

Furthermore, having regard to the representations made to the client by the regular payment of interest to him, it is also difficult to reconcile the decision with *Blair v. Bromley*[421] and other cases of that class.

12–112   In *Re Bell's Indenture*[422] a solicitor acting for the trustees of a marriage settlement had actively assisted them to dissipate the entire trust fund, and thereby rendered himself liable to the beneficiaries as a constructive trustee. His partner had no knowledge of these activities, but moneys received and paid out in breach of trust clearly passed through the firm's client account. It was held that the other partner was not liable for the misapplication of the trust fund, since the moneys had not been received by the firm as trustees but by the partner concerned as a constructive trustee and he had no authority in the ordinary course of his practice either to constitute himself a constructive trustee or to accept office as a trustee of the trust.[423] However, this part of the decision has now been overruled by the House of Lords in *Dubai Aluminium Co. Ltd. v. Salaam*,[424] on the basis that it confused acceptance of the role of trustee *de son tort*, which may be outwith the normal course of a solicitor's business,[425] with a case in which a person is liable to account *as if* he was a constructive trustee, where no such assumption can be made.[426]

12–113   Finally, in *Antonelli v. Allen*,[427] money was received by a partner, A, in a firm of solicitors on terms that he should await the instructions of the owner, who was not a client. There was no evidence of any underlying transaction, actual or contemplated. The money was paid into the firm's client account but part of it was subsequently drawn out by A on the instructions of a third party. In the circumstances, A was held not to have been acting within the scope of his apparent authority or in the ordinary course of the firm's business when receiving the money[428] and the firm was not liable.

---

[419] (1827) 6 B. & C. 551, *infra*, para. 12–117.

[420] (1834) 2 Cl. & F. 250, *infra*, para. 12–117. Lord Lindley also pointed out that "The Statute of Limitations afforded a good defence to the action in *Sims v. Brutton*. The propriety of the decision in that respect is untouched by the observations in the text."

[421] (1847) 2 Ph. 354, *infra*, para. 12–119.

[422] [1980] 1 W.L.R. 1217, distinguishing *Blyth v. Fladgate* [1891] 1 Ch. 337. *cf. Agip (Africa) Ltd. v. Jackson* [1991] Ch. 547.

[423] [1980] 1 W.L.R. 1230. And see *Re Fryer* (1857) 3 K. & J. 317. Also *Tendring Hundred Waterworks v. Jones* [1903] 2 Ch. 615, *infra*, para. 12–125.

[424] [2003] 2 A.C. 366; also *Walker v. Stones* [2001] Q.B. 902 (CA). See further *supra*, paras 12–16, 23–30.

[425] See *Mara v.Browne* [1896] 1 Ch. 199. Lord Millett *in fact* preferred the expression *de facto* trustee: see [2003] 2 A.C. 366 at [138].

[426] See [2003] 2 A.C. 366 at [140] to [143] *per* Lord Millett; also *ibid.* at [42] *per* Lord Nicholls.

[427] [2001] Lloyd's Rep. P.N. 487. See also *Langley Holdings v. Seakens* 2000 WL 1675192, where there *appeared* to be a prospective underlying transaction but, on analysis, this was found not to be genuine.

[428] Thus the receipt fell outside both limbs of the Partnership Act 1890, s.11.

Solicitors and the Financial Services and Markets Act 2000

All of the cases cited in the above groups concerned solicitors and their ability **12–114** to receive money and property in the normal course of practice. As illustrations of instances in which section 11(a) of the Partnership Act 1890 may apply, they are of considerable value. However, they should not be taken as establishing principles of general application as regards the implied authority of solicitors, for two reasons. In the first place, as was emphasised by the Court of Appeal in *United Bank of Kuwait Ltd. v. Hammoud*,[429] old authorities are inherently unreliable, given that the scope of a solicitor's implied authority is constantly changing.[430] Secondly, most firms will now be authorised to conduct at least some regulated activities within the meaning of the Financial Services and Markets Act 2000,[431] either as exempt professional firms[432] or by virtue of a permission obtained from the Financial Services Authority.[433] Accordingly, it can no longer be stated, as a general proposition, that a partner in a firm of solicitors does not have implied authority to accept money for investment at large[434]; equally, the detailed regulatory requirements[435] would seem to minimise, even if not entirely to eradicate, the possibility of an unauthorised receipt of funds which does not come to the attention of the other partners.

Section 11(b): Money or property in custody of firm

Group 1: Firm held liable

> Where a firm in the course of its business[436] receives money belonging to other **12–115** people, and one of the partners misapplies that money whilst it is in the custody of the firm, the firm must make it good.[437]

Having formulated the above rule, Lord Lindley explained the principle which underlies the cases in this group, as follows:

[429] [1988] 1 W.L.R. 1051, 1063F: see *supra*, para. 12–17. See also *Dubai Aluminium Co. Ltd. v. Salaam* [2003] Q.B. 113, 143B–E *per* Aldous L.J. (the main part of the decision itself was reversed on appeal at [2003] 2 A.C. 366); also *McDonic v. Hetherington* (1997) 142 D.L.R. (4th) 648, 656b; *Walker v. Stones* [2001] Q.B. 902 (CA). *cf. Clasper v. Duns* [2007] NZHC 1000, where Panckhurst J. did appear to derive assistance from the decided cases.

[430] Of course, the authority may in some cases be derived from statute: *e.g.* see the Law of Property Act 1925, s.69; *cf. Re Bellamy and Metropolitan Board of Works* (1883) 24 Ch.D. 387 (a decision under the Conveyancing Act 1881, s.56).

[431] The expression "regulated activity" is defined in *ibid.* s.22, Sched. 2. As to what are "exempt regulated activities", see *ibid.* ss.325(2), 327. See further *supra*, paras 8–44 *et seq.* and, generally, the *Encyclopedia of Financial Services Law*, Pt. IIA.

[432] See *ibid.* s.327. Such firms must only carry on exempt regulated activities as an *incidental* part of their professional practices: *ibid.* s.327(4). They will, for the most part, be regulated by the Law Society as a designated professional body under *ibid.* s.326: see the Solicitors' Financial Services (Scope) Rules 2001 and the Solicitors' Financial Services (Conduct of Business) Rules 2001 (as amended). See also *supra*, para. 8–44.

[433] As to the procedure for obtaining permission from the FSA, see *ibid.* Pt IV. See further *supra*, para. 8–45.

[434] Note that such authority was, in any event, implied on the facts in *McDonic v. Hetherington* (1997) 142 D.L.R. (4th) 648, noted *supra*, para. 12–106.

[435] See, for example, in the case of firms regulated by the Law Society, the Solicitors' Financial Services (Conduct of Business) Rules 2001, rr. 5–7. It is not feasible, in a work of this nature, to describe these and other requirements in any detail. Reference should accordingly be made to the standard works on the subject, *e.g.* the *Encyclopedia of Financial Services Law*.

[436] See *supra*, para. 12–109, and Partnership Act 1890, s.13, *infra*, para. 12–127, as to the importance of this qualification.

[437] This was in fact Lord Lindley's second rule.

"The principle . . . is that the firm has, in the ordinary course of its business, obtained possession of the property of other people, and has then parted with it without their authority. Under such circumstances the firm is responsible[438]: and the fact that the property has been improperly procured and placed in the custody of the firm by one of the partners does not lessen the liability of the firm; for whether the firm is or is not liable for the original fraud by which the property got into his hands, it is responsible for the subsequent misapplication thereof by one of its members."

12–116   In *Devaynes v. Noble, Clayton's Case*,[439] the owner of some exchequer bills had deposited them with a firm of bankers. The bills were sold by one of the partners without the owner's knowledge and the proceeds applied by the firm for its own benefit. It being clear that such proceeds had been received by the firm, all the partners were held liable to the owner of the bills, irrespective of whether they were privy to the sale.

In *Devaynes v. Noble, Baring's Case*,[440] certain stock belonging to customers was, according to the firm's normal practice, held in the sole name of one of the partners. He improperly sold it and the proceeds were received by the firm which, in the accounts rendered to its customers, had falsely represented the stock as still standing in the name of that partner and had given credit for the dividends as if the stock was still so held. The firm was liable for the misapplication of the proceeds.

12–117   In the so-called *Fauntleroy Forgery* cases,[441] F, a partner in a firm of bankers, M & Co., had forged powers of attorney for the sale of certain stock belonging to the firm's clients. The stock was sold by the firm's broker, who remitted the proceeds to its account with another banking firm, MS & Co. F later withdrew those proceeds, using a cheque drawn in the firm name, and misapplied them. M & Co. was held liable for the loss even though the other partners knew nothing of the fraud. Liability was imposed because the sale of the stock and receipt of the resultant proceeds fell within the scope of the firm's business and the transactions initiated by F were conducted in the usual way of that business. F's fraudulent misappropriation of the proceeds of sale was no defence once they had been received by the firm; even though the other partners were not aware of such receipt, if they had used ordinary diligence and not placed such implicit confidence in their co-partners, they could have learned of it and, thus, discovered their true source.[442]

12–118   In *Ex p. Biddulph*,[443] trust money in the hands of a firm of bankers was drawn out and misapplied by one partner and all the partners were held liable for the loss.

Similarly, in *Sadler v. Lee*,[444] a partner in a firm of bankers sold stock in the name of a customer, as he was authorised to do, and the proceeds were credited

---

[438] See the Partnership Act 1890, s.11(b), *supra*, para. 12–104.

[439] (1816) 1 Mer. 572. See also *Rhodes v. Moules* [1895] 1 Ch. 236, *supra*, para. 12–107.

[440] (1816) 1 Mer. 611; see also *Warde's Case* (1816) 1 Mer. 624; *Vulliamy v. Noble* (1817) 3 Mer. 593.

[441] *Stone v. Marsh* (1827) 6 B. & C. 551; *Ex p. Bolland* (1828) 1 M. & A. 570; *Hume v. Bolland* (1832) 1 Cromp. & M. 130; *Keating v. Marsh* (1834) 1 M. & A. 582; *Marsh v. Keating* (1834) 2 Cl. & F. 250. Lord Lindley noted that *Hume v. Bolland* is "hardly consistent with *Stone v. Marsh*, *Marsh v. Keating*, or *Ex p. Bolland*".

[442] In *Stone v. Marsh* and *Ex p. Bolland*, *supra*, F's partners knew that the stock had been sold by the broker, but did not know that the powers of attorney were forged. In *Marsh v. Keating*, *supra*, they appear not to have known either of the sale or of the receipt of the proceeds. *cf.* the cases cited *supra*, paras 12–109 *et seq.* and *infra*, paras 12–122 *et seq.*

[443] (1849) 3 De G. & Sm. 587.

[444] (1843) 6 Beav. 324.

to the firm. Those proceeds were subsequently misapplied by a partner and again the firm was held liable.

The decision in *Blair v. Bromley*[445] clearly illustrates the principle under **12–119** consideration. There a client of a firm of solicitors entrusted certain money to one partner to be invested on mortgage; he was told that the money had been so invested, but in fact the partner had misapplied it. For many years the client was regularly paid interest by that partner, and the fraud was not discovered until the latter went bankrupt. The other partner, who knew nothing about the fraud, was held liable to make good the money, which had originally been credited to the firm's bank account. The representation that the money had been duly invested was held to have been made in the normal course of business and the other partner's attempts to avoid liability, by showing that he had no control over the bank account and was not involved in the financial side of the business, failed.

Finally, in *Bass Brewers Ltd. v. Appleby*,[446] the first defendant, A, by agree- **12–120** ment practised as a chartered accountant and insolvency practitioner under the name "Latham Crossley & Davies", which was, in fact, the name of the second defendant firm. The claimants appointed A to act as a receiver of certain premises under the Law of Property Act 1925 and, whilst he was so acting, A received a cheque from the claimants (made out in the name *Latham Crossley & Davies*) in respect of the proceeds of sale of those premises. The cheque was paid into a client account maintained in the above name but was then transferred to A's overdrawn office account, which was also maintained in that name.[447] A never accounted for the money so received. The partners in the second defendant firm were held liable to the claimants on the basis of holding out[448] and on the basis that the cheque drawn by the claimants had been received by the apparent firm in the ordinary course of its business.

Partner becoming trustee: De Ribeyre v. Barclay

In cases where the firm has accepted custody of money or property, it would **12–121** not seem to matter if the partner responsible for its subsequent misapplication has in the interim been appointed a trustee thereof, provided that he continues to act *qua* partner. Thus, in *De Ribeyre v. Barclay*[449] the defendants were in partnership as stockbrokers, and regularly received money from friends, etc., for investment. They also seem to have made a practice of retaining the investments so made on their customers' behalf. The claimant had some Portuguese bonds held by a partner in this way; when she married, the bonds were assigned to trustees, of whom the partner was one. The bonds remained in his custody as before, and were in fact deposited with the partnership bankers (seemingly along with a number of securities held on behalf of other customers). That partner later converted the bonds into other bonds, which were deposited with the partnership bankers as before. He at all times acted *qua* stockbroker in the ordinary course of the firm's business, periodically advising the claimant, in the name of the firm,

---

[445] (1847) 2 Ph. 354. See also *Eager v. Barnes* (1862) 31 Beav. 579; *Moore v. Knight* [1891] 1 Ch. 547. And see *supra*, paras 12–94 *et seq.*

[446] (1997) 73 P. & C.R. 165 (CA).

[447] It appears only to have been an inference that the accounts were maintained in this way: see *ibid.* p. 166.

[448] *i.e.* under the Partnership Act 1890, s.14: see *supra*, paras 5–35 *et seq.*

[449] (1857) 23 Beav. 107; *cf. Ex p. Eyre* (1842) 1 Ph. 227; *Coomer v. Bromley* (1852) 5 De G & Sm. 532; *Bishop v. The Countess of Jersey* (1854) 2 Drew. 143. See *infra*, paras 12–122 *et seq.*

of what had been done on her behalf. He later misapplied the bonds. It was held that the bonds were originally in the firm's custody and not in the custody of one partner *qua* trustee and that their assignment into the trust did not take them out of such custody. Accordingly, the firm was liable for the loss resulting from their unauthorised removal.

It should be noted that, in this case, the firm was also held liable for the loss of other bonds and securities purchased on the claimant's behalf and left in its custody in the manner described above, as well as for money borrowed from her in the name of the firm, but from which the firm derived no benefit. The fact that the claimant had dealt only with one partner was held to be immaterial, since the business was transacted in the normal way and so appeared in the firm's books and accounts.

Group 2: Firm not liable

12–122   *A fraud committed by a partner whilst acting on his own separate account is not imputable to the firm, although had he not been connected with the firm he might not have been in a position to commit the fraud.*[450]

This rule is, to an extent, little more than a re-statement of the rule which appears at paragraph 12–109; accordingly, reference should also be made to the cases cited in the succeeding paragraphs.

In *Ex p. Eyre*,[451] a customer deposited a box containing certain securities with a firm of bankers and, subsequently, agreed to lend some of them to one of the partners, authorising him to withdraw them from the box but to replace them with others. That partner did so, but then secretly withdrew the substituted securities and misapplied them. The firm was held not to be responsible for the loss, since it appeared that the firm as such did not have authority to open the box or to examine its contents: the removal of the securities was a tortious act committed by one partner, who had such authority but who was not acting on behalf of the firm but in an individual capacity and for his own purposes.[452]

12–123   In *Bishop v. The Countess of Jersey*,[453] a partner in a firm of bankers advised a customer to sell certain stock and informed her that a secured loan of £5,000 could be made on advantageous terms to his own son. The customer duly authorised the sale and the proceeds were credited to her account. She then drew a cheque for the £5,000 and handed it to the partner concerned. He misapplied it and then absconded, no proper security ever having been given. It appears that interest on the £5,000 was for some time credited to the customer's account at the bank, but by whom was not clear. The other partners only learned of the fraud subsequently and were held not to be liable for the customer's loss. The transaction had nothing to do with the firm's business and, as Lord Lindley observed: "if [*the transaction*] had not taken place at the bank, there would have been no pretence for saying that the one partner was acting otherwise than in a separate affair of his own."

12–124   The decision in *Coomer v. Bromley*[454] is more difficult to account for, but would appear to rest on the same principle. There WB, a partner in a firm of

---

[450] This was Lord Lindley's fourth rule, being the corollary of rule stated at para. 12–115.

[451] (1842) 1 Ph. 227.

[452] It should be noted that the firm had, in a separate transaction, itself borrowed other securities in the box from the customer: see *ibid.* pp. 229, 236.

[453] (1854) 2 Drew. 143.

[454] (1852) 5 De G. & Sm. 532. See also *Sims v. Brutton* (1850) 5 Ex. 802, *supra*, para. 12–111. *cf. St. Aubyn v. Smart* (1868) L.R. 3 Ch.App. 646.

solicitors, was a trustee of certain annuities, his co-trustees being three clients who were also life tenants under the trust. With a view to increasing the trust income, it was arranged that the annuities would be sold and the proceeds invested on a mortgage to be taken in WB's sole name. The sale was completed and the proceeds were paid into the firm's bank account. However, they were not in fact invested on mortgage as arranged, but apparently used as partnership money; WB nevertheless pretended that he had invested them and paid interest accordingly. With the clients' knowledge, a mortgage, under which WB was the sole mortgagee and with a value marginally less than the requisite amount, was later appropriated as security for the annuity proceeds, the excess being divided between the clients. This security was then realised by WB and the money misappropriated by him. Unlike the original sale proceeds, this money was not credited to the firm's bank account and the other partner, JB, knew nothing of its receipt or misapplication. In the circumstances, JB was held not to be responsible for the loss, since his duties were at an end once the moneys had, as originally contemplated, been invested on a mortgage in WB's sole name. The clients could not hold him liable for the loss of the mortgage money arising from WB's subsequent fraud.

Lord Lindley identified the distinguishing feature common to *Bishop v. The*   **12–125** *Countess of Jersey* and *Coomer v. Bromley*, in these terms:

" . . . it will be observed that although the money in question had at one time been in the custody of the firm, such was not the case when the money was misapplied. This circumstance distinguishes the cases last referred to from *De Ribeyre v. Barclay*[455] and other cases of that class . . . ".

This same feature is displayed in a later decision, *Tendring Hundred Waterworks Co. v. Jones.*[456] In that case, G, a partner in a firm of solicitors, held office as a company secretary in the course of the firm's business. The company purchased some property which, for its own convenience, was conveyed to G alone, without any declaration of trust. The firm acted on the transaction and settled the relevant conveyance. The conveyance was retained by G, who subsequently mortgaged the property to secure a personal debt. The company sought, unsuccessfully, to make G's partner liable for the loss: he had no knowledge of the transaction, save in so far as notice was imputed to him by reason of the firm having acted therein. So far as the firm was concerned, the transaction was completed and its duties were at an end when the executed conveyance was received by G, who was legally entitled to receive it; it was therefore not responsible for his subsequent acts. Significantly, it was neither a part of G's duties as company secretary nor within the scope of the firm's business for him to constitute himself a trustee for a client.[457]

The decision in *Antonelli v. Allen*[458] has already been noted.

---

[455] (1857) 23 Beav. 107, *supra*, para. 12–115.

[456] [1903] 2 Ch. 615. See also *Terrill v. Parker and Thomas* (1915) 32 T.L.R. 48.

[457] See [1903] 2 Ch. 621, 623 *per* Farwell J.; also *Walker v. Stones* [2001] Q.B. 902 (CA); *Dubai Aluminium Co. Ltd. v. Salaam* [2003] 2 A.C. 366 at [40] to [42] *per* Lord Nicholls and [132] to [143] *per* Lord Millett. *Re Bell's Indenture* [1980] 1 W.L.R. 1217, *supra*, para. 12–112, is no longer an authority for this proposition. *cf. Clasper v. Duns* [2007] NZHC 1000. See further *supra*, paras 12–16, 23–33.

[458] [2001] Lloyd's Rep. P.N. 487: see *supra*, para. 12–113.

5.   LIABILITY OF PARTNERS FOR BREACHES OF TRUST

12–126   The liability of a firm for the improper employment of trust property in the partnership business is based on similar principles to those considered in the previous section; indeed, Lord Lindley's fifth rule[459] was as follows:

> "If a partner, being a trustee, improperly employs the money of his *cestui que trust* in the partnership business, or in payment of the partnership debts, this alone is not sufficient to entitle the *cestui que trust* to obtain repayment of his money from the firm."[460]

Partnership Act 1890, section 13

12–127   The above rule is now incorporated in section 13 of the Partnership Act 1890, which provides:

> "13. If a partner, being a trustee, improperly employs trust property in the business or on the account of the partnership, no other partner is liable for the trust property to the persons beneficially interested therein:
>   Provided as follows:
>
> (1) This section shall not affect any liability incurred by any partner by reason of his having notice of a breach of trust[461]; and
> (2) Nothing in this section shall prevent trust money from being followed and recovered from the firm if still in its possession or under its control."

It naturally follows that, unless a partner has previously accepted the role of trustee, the main part of the section will be of no application[462] and the liability of the firm will be determined on normal principles.[463]

Relevance of pre-1890 cases

12–128   Given the similarity between the opening words of the section and Lord Lindley's own formulation of the rule, it will be readily apparent that no change in the law was sought to be introduced thereby. Accordingly, the pre-1890 authorities are again of relevance.
    Thus, in *Ex p. Apsey*,[464] what would now be styled a trustee in bankruptcy[465] applied part of the bankrupt's estate towards his own firm's debts. On that firm's bankruptcy, the amount misapplied was held not to be provable against the joint estate. Similarly, in *Ex p. Heaton*,[466] where trust money had been misapplied by

---

[459] Lord Lindley's other rules, albeit not in their original order, are set out *supra*, paras 12–106, 12–109, 12–115, 12–122.

[460] *Quaere* whether the receipt of trust monies considered in *Earl of Dundonald v. Masterman* (1869) L.R. 7 Eq. 504, 517 was a case of this class. See also *Clasper v. Duns* [2007] NZHC 1000.

[461] See *supra*, para. 12–30.

[462] See *Bass Brewers Ltd. v. Appleby* (1997) 73 P. & C.R. 165, 175 *per* Millett L.J.; *Walker v. Stones* [2001] Q.B. 902; *Dubai Aluminium Co. Ltd. v. Salaam* [2003] 2 A.C. 366 at [110] *per* Lord Millett.

[463] See, however, as to the interaction of this section with s.10, *infra*, para. 12–130.

[464] (1791) 3 Bro.C.C. 265. See also *Ex p. White* (1871) L.R. 6 Ch.App. 397.

[465] In fact, the partner concerned was one of two "assignees in bankruptcy".

[466] (1819) Buck 386.

the trustees of a will, an inquiry was directed in order to determine whether the non-trustee partner knew that the money had been applied for partnership purposes.[467]

Since, in each of the above cases, the trust money came into the hands of the   **12–129** firm *otherwise* than in the ordinary course of its business, it is submitted that they cannot be regarded as inconsistent with the provisions of section 11 of the Partnership Act 1890[468] or, for that matter, with *Marsh v. Keating*[469] and the other decisions which preceded the enactment of that section.[470] Lord Lindley explained the distinction in this way:

> " . . . in [*Marsh v. Keating and the other cases*], the money came to the hands of the firm in the ordinary course of its business[471]; whilst in the cases now under consideration it is supposed to come otherwise. Liability must therefore attach to the firm, if at all, on wholly different principles, and the fact that the firm has had the benefit of the trust monies is not sufficient to render it responsible for them. To be liable, the firm must be implicated in the breach of trust, and this it cannot be unless all the partners either knew whence the money came, or knew that it did not belong to the partner making use of it. Knowledge on the part of one partner will not affect the others, for the fact to be known has nothing to do with the business of the firm[472]; and the case of *Ex p. Heaton* . . . shows that in cases of this kind the liability as for a breach of trust does not extend to those who are ignorant of the matters before mentioned."[473]

Interaction between sections 10 and 13

It was held in *Walker v. Stones*[474] that sections 10 and 13 of the Partnership Act   **12–130** 1890 are mutually exclusive: in a case where a partner holds the office of trustee, the liability of the other partners will be determined solely by reference to section 13 and there is no scope for liability in the alternative under section 10. The court accepted that there is an assumption underlying section 13 that a breach of trust by a trustee partner must, necessarily, fall outside the scope of the ordinary course of the firm's business. This decision appeared to the current editor to have been endorsed by Lord Millett's analysis of the scope of sections 10 and 13 in *Dubai Aluminium Co Ltd. v. Salaam*,[475] where he stated that:

> "Section 13 deals with money which is misappropriated by a trustee who happens to be a partner and who in breach of trust or fiduciary duty afterwards pays it to his firm

[467] Lord Lindley considered that "*Ex p. Clowes* (1789) 2 Bro.C.C. 595 is not opposed to the case in the text, for there the joint and separate estates were consolidated."

[468] See *supra*, para. 12–104.

[469] (1834) 2 Cl. & F. 250: see *supra*, para. 12–117.

[470] See *supra*, paras 12–106 *et seq*.

[471] In a footnote at this point, Lord Lindley explained that, in *Marsh v. Keating*, the stock was sold in the ordinary course of the firm's business, albeit under a forged power of attorney: see *supra*, para. 12–117. Moreover, whilst F's partners did not know that the money had been received by the firm, their ignorance was considered culpable.

[472] See the Partnership Act 1890, s.16, *supra*, paras 12–24 *et seq*.

[473] This passage (apart from the reference to *Ex p. Heaton*) was cited with apparent approval in *Bass Brewers Ltd. v. Appleby* (1997) 73 P. & C.R. 165, 175.

[474] [2001] Q.B. 902 (CA). The court cited with approval the analysis of Rix J. in *Dubai Aluminium Co. Ltd. v. Salaam* [1999] 1 Lloyd's Rep. 415, 470, as approved in *ibid.* [2001] Q.B. 113, 132E *per* Evans L.J., 141 *per* Aldous L.J., 144 *per* Turner J. The majority of the Court of Appeal's decision in *Dubai Aluminium* was, of course, overturned by the House of Lords: [2003] 2 A.C. 366. See also *Hansen v. Youmg* [2004] N.Z.L.R. 37 (CA).

[475] [2003] 2 A.C. 366 at [110].

or otherwise improperly employs it in the partnership business. The innocent partners are not vicariously liable for the misappropriation, which will have occurred outside the ordinary course of business. But they are liable to restore the money if the requirements of the general law of knowing receipt are satisfied."

However, in New Zealand a very different approach was espoused on a striking out application in *Clasper v. Duns*.[476] There Panckhurst J. held[477] that the distinction drawn in *Walker v. Stones* was unjustified and that, in an appropriate case, a trustee partner *could* be held liable under the equivalent of section 10 and/ or 11 of the 1890 Act, provided that the relevant act is performed in the ordinary course of the firm's business or with the actual or apparent authority of the other partners.

Be that as it may, even if section 13 does have the effect suggested in *Walker v. Stones*, it does not follow that innocent partners cannot be held liable if a partner so conducts himself as to attract liability as a *constructive* trustee.[478]

Application of section to solicitors and other professions

12–131   Solicitors are subject to stringent professional rules regarding the receipt of clients' money.[479] Thus, where one or more of the partners is a trustee[480] and his firm receives money belonging to the trust, it must normally be paid into a client account.[481] Withdrawals from such accounts may only be made for a number of specific purposes[482] and their operation will be scrutinised by an independent accountant each year.[483] Notwithstanding these safeguards, instances of the misapplication of money in such accounts do occur and, in such cases, section 13 of the Partnership Act 1890 will apply in the normal way.[484] The same observations are equally pertinent in the case of other professions or businesses which are subject to rules governing the treatment of clients' money.[485]

Where the section does not apply

12–132   The provisos to section 13 of the Partnership Act 1890[486] preserve the liability of the firm in those cases where all the partners have notice of the breach of trust or where a tracing remedy is available.

---

[476] [2007] NZHC 1000.

[477] See *ibid.* at [41]–[51]. Panckhurst J. referred in particular to Millett L.J.'s analysis in *Bass Brewers Ltd. v. Appleby* (1997) 73 P. & C.R. 165, 175.

[478] *Dubai Aluminium Co. Ltd. v. Salaam, supra.* Note that the expression "constructive trustee" must be approached with caution: see further, *supra*, paras 12–16, 12–30, 12–112.

[479] See the Solicitors Act 1974, ss.32–34 (as amended); the Solicitors Accounts Rules 1998 (as amended).

[480] Note that no special rule now covers the position where a partner is a sole trustee or all the trustees are either partners or employees of the firm. Formerly, such a trust was designated "a controlled trust" under the Solicitors Accounts Rules 1998.

[481] *ibid.* rr. 13 (definition of "client money"), 14–17 (as amended).

[482] *ibid.* rr. 22, 23 (as amended).

[483] *ibid.* Pt F.

[484] Note, however, the existence of the Compensation Fund, administered under the Solicitors Act 1974, s.36, which may be used to relieve hardship suffered by a defaulting solicitor's partner. It is doubted whether a grant would ever be made in a case where the Partnership Act 1890, s.13, proviso (1) applies, since this connotes a degree of complicity; *sed quaere.*

[485] *e.g.* accountants, architects and surveyors. Note that separate rules will govern the receipt of moneys by a firm which is authorised to carry on regulated activities within the meaning of the Financial Services and Markets Act 2000, s.22, Sched. 2 by virtue of a permission granted by the Financial Services Authority under *ibid.* Pt. IV: see *ibid.* s.139.

[486] See *supra*, para. 12–127.

Proviso (1): Notice of breach of trust

This proviso ensures that section 13 does not relieve the firm of liability where all the partners are implicated in a breach of trust. Lord Lindley, writing prior to the Act, explained the position thus:

> "But if knowledge . . . can be imputed to the other partners, if they know, or ought to be treated as knowing, that trust monies are being employed in the partnership business, they will be held bound to see that the trust to which the money is subject authorises the use made of it, and will be answerable for a breach of trust in case of its misapplication or loss."[487]

By way of qualification to the above passage, it should be noted that it is strictly immaterial whether the trust money has been applied in the partnership business or otherwise.[488]

Instances in which it has been inferred that partners have knowledge of or are **12–133** implicated in a breach of trust are rare.[489] However, despite the court's previous reluctance to impose liability on the basis that a partner has rendered himself liable as a constructive trustee,[490] and even, on occasion, to hold the partner directly involved in the wrongdoing liable on that basis,[491] it would seem that this will change following the decision of the House of Lords in *Dubai Aluminium Co. Ltd. v. Salaam*,[492] where some of the earlier authorities were reviewed and explained.[493] Thus, whilst there may still be a reluctance to find that a partner has constituted himself a trustee *de son tort*[494] and thereby rendered his partners liable for his acts, in other cases of wrongdoing which give rise to a duty on a partner to account as a constructive trustee the result will almost inevitably be different. It should, however, be emphasised that these were *not* decisions under section 13.

It has already been seen that section 16 of the Partnership Act 1890 does not **12–134** generally apply in the case of a breach of trust.[495] However, particular note must be taken of the position following the death of a partner. Lord Lindley observed that:

---

[487] See *Keble v. Thompson* (1790) 3 Bro.C.C. 112; *Smith v. Jameson* (1794) 5 T.R. 601; *Ex p. Watson* (1814) 2 V. & B. 414; *Ex p. Woodin* (1843) 3 M.D. & D. 399; *Ex p. Poulson* (1844) De Gex. 79. *cf. Ex p. Burton* (1843) 3 M.D. & D. 364; *Ex p. Barnewall* (1855) 6 De G.M. & G. 795; *Ex p. Greaves* (1856) 8 De G.M. & G. 291.

[488] *Blyth v. Fladgate* [1891] 1 Ch. 337, 354 *per* Stirling J.

[489] *Blyth v. Fladgate, supra*, was one such instance. Although "vicarious" liability was imposed on an innocent partner in a firm of accountants in *Agip (Africa) Ltd. v. Jackson* [1990] Ch. 265 (Millett J.) and [1991] Ch. 547 (CA), the report does not disclose what arguments were addressed to the court on this issue. Perhaps significantly, the defendants elected not to call any evidence.

[490] See *Mara v. Browne* [1896] 1 Ch. 199; *Re Bell's Indenture* [1980] 1 W.L.R. 1217; *Walker v. Stones* [2001] Q.B. 902 (CA). See also *Estate Realities Ltd. v. Wignall* [1992] 2 N.Z.L.R. 615.

[491] See *Brinsden v. Williams* [1894] 3 Ch. 185; *Mara v. Browne* [1896] 1 Ch. 199 (where the firm might, in fact, have been liable for negligence in the performance of its duties as solicitor had such an action not been statute barred); also *Rae v. Meek* (1889) 14 App.Cas. 558.

[492] [2003] 2 A.C. 366.

[493] *ibid.* at [40] to [42] *per* Lord Nicholls, and [132] to [143] *per* Lord Millett. Thus, on a true analysis, *Mara v. Browne, supra*, was only authority for the proposition that a solicitor does not have authority to accept the role of trustee *de son tort* or, as Lord Millett preferred to put it, a *de facto* trustee. On this point *Re Bell's Indenture, supra*, was overruled. See also *supra*, paras 12–16, 12–30.

[494] In *Dubai Aluminium Co Ltd. v. Salaam, supra*, at [138]. Lord Millett preferred the expression *de facto* trustee.

[495] See *supra*, para. 12–30.

" . . . if the surviving partners deal with his property, knowing that it belongs to his estate, knowledge of the trust on which the property is held will be imputed to them, and they may be thus involved in all the consequences of a breach of trust. But this doctrine can hardly extend to the case of incoming partners, who do nothing except leave matters as they find them when they enter the firm."[496]

The current editor's opinion is that, as a statement of general principle, this is no longer correct and that, if the deceased partner's personal representatives choose to leave his share outstanding in the surviving partners' hands, it can normally be assumed that they are acting within their powers[497]; *per contra*, if the surviving partners knew (or ought to have known) that a breach of trust was being committed.

As will be noted hereafter, where partners are implicated in a breach of trust, their liability will be joint and several.[498] It was formerly held that a trustee sued by his beneficiaries could not enforce a claim to indemnity against a firm in respect of the breach by means of third party proceedings,[499] and it may be that a similar approach would be adopted in relation to a Part 20 claim under the Civil Procedure Rules.[500]

Proviso (2): Tracing remedy

12–135   The second proviso to section 13 confirms what should in any event be obvious, namely that, even if the firm is not implicated in the breach of trust, a *cestui que trust* should not be deprived of the right to trace his own money, if it is still in the firm's hands.[501] Lord Lindley explained the rationale behind this rule, which existed prior to the 1890 Act, as follows:

"The true owner of money traced to the possession of another has a right to have it restored, not because it is a debt but because it is his money. His right is incidental to his ownership; and whether the money is traced to the hands of a single individual or to the hands of a firm is wholly immaterial."

Secret profits where partner holds directorship

12–136   Although not strictly within the class of cases currently under consideration, it should be noted that the firm will be liable to account for any profit which it may receive under a contract between a partner and a company of which he is a director, if the contract was made with the knowledge of the other partners and there was no full disclosure.[502]

---

[496] See *Twyford v. Trail* (1834) 7 Sim. 92.

[497] See *infra*, para. 26–42.

[498] See *infra*, para. 13–13.

[499] *Wynne v. Tempest* [1897] 1 Ch. 110. Note that the claim in question appears to have been brought under the Partnership Act 1890, s.11 and not *ibid.* s.13.

[500] See the CPR, rr. 20.7, 20.9.

[501] See generally, as to the tracing remedy, *Snell's Equity* (30th ed.), paras 13–26 *et seq.*; *Goff & Jones' The Law of Restitution* (7th ed.), Chap. 2. Also *Agip (Africa) Ltd. v. Jackson* [1991] Ch. 547 (CA). And note *Foskett v. McKeown* [2001] 1 A.C. 102 (HL).

[502] *Imperial Mercantile Credit Association v. Coleman* (1871) L.R. 6 (HL) 189. And see also, generally, *Boardman v. Phipps* [1967] 2 A.C. 46; *Industrial Development Consultants Ltd. v. Cooley* [1972] 1 W.L.R. 443.

6.   LIABILITY OF PARTNERS FOR ACTS KNOWN TO BE UNAUTHORISED

It has already been seen that the extent of a partner's implied authority is set by **12–137** what is required to carry on the partnership business in the usual way.[503] It follows that a third party who knowingly deals with a partner[504] may in general assume that the firm will be bound by anything which that partner does within the scope of his implied authority but not by anything done outside that scope. However, the position will be different if the third party knows that wider or narrower limits have in fact been set on that partner's authority, as Lord Lindley explained[505]:

"So long as one partner does nothing beyond the scope of his apparent authority . . . so long is the firm responsible for his conduct, although he may have acted beyond or in direct violation of the authority within which his co-partners may have attempted to confine him. Restrictions placed by the partners upon the powers which each shall exercise do not affect non-partners, who act bona fide and without notice of the restriction.[506]

But when it is sought to make the firm liable for some act not prima facie authorised by it, an actual authority by it must be shown; and if this cannot be done, no case is made out against the firm, however ignorant the person seeking to charge it may have been of what was authorised and what was not. In the case now supposed the firm did not mislead him; and if he was mislead by the representations of the partner with whom he dealt, his remedy is against that partner."[507]

Partnership Act 1890, section 7 and 8

These principles are expressly recognised by two sections of the Partnership **12–138** Act 1890, namely:

"7. Where one partner pledges the credit of the firm for a purpose apparently not connected with the firm's ordinary course of business, the firm is not bound, unless he is in fact specially authorised by the other partners; but this section does not affect any personal liability incurred by an individual partner.

8. If it has been agreed between the partners that any restriction shall be placed on the power of any one or more of them to bind the firm, no act done in contravention of the agreement is binding on the firm with respect to persons having notice of the agreement."

[503] See the Partnership Act 1890, s.5, *supra*, paras 12–02 *et seq*.

[504] See the concluding words of *ibid*. s.5.

[505] This passage is composed of extracts from two separate paragraphs written by Lord Lindley, which were in fact transposed in the 5th ed. of this work. However, it is submitted that, presented in this manner, they more clearly state the relevant principles.

[506] See for example, *Morans v. Armstrong* (1840) Arm.M. & O. 25 (where the partnership business had been organised into separate departments and one partner had acted outside his department). In cases of this type, it is clearly not enough for one partner merely to tell his co-partners that he will not be bound by their acts: see *Gleadon v. Tinkler* (1817) Holt, N.P. 586. *Per contra*, if a third party has actual notice: see *infra*, paras 12–143 *et seq*.

[507] See *supra*, paras 12–94 *et seq*. And see, as to the circumstances in which an individual partner may be estopped from denying his authority, *Kendal v. Wood* (1870) L.R. 6 Ex. 243, 251 *per* Blackburn J., 253–254 *per* Montague Smith J.

Operation of section 7

12–139   An example of the practical application of section 7[508] is to be found in *Kennedy v. Malcolm Bros.*[509] There, two brothers carried on a farming business in partnership and had identified certain adjoining farmland for potential acquisition. They both inspected the land and made an offer to the owner, which was declined. Shortly thereafter one of the brothers (D) purported to enter into a contract to purchase the land in the firm name. Although D did not have actual authority to enter into the contract and the purchase of land would not have been regarded as within the scope of the ordinary business of a farming partnership, it was nevertheless held that the brothers' conduct when inspecting the land had led the owner to believe that they were treating it as an acquisition for a purpose connected with their ordinary course of business. Accordingly, the section did not apply and the firm was bound.

Apparent purpose of section 8

12–140   It appears that section 8 was intended to settle a doubtful question raised by *dicta* of Lord Ellenborough in *Gallway v. Mathew and Smithson*[510] and *Alderson v. Pope*,[511] to the effect that, if partners have agreed between themselves that none of them shall do a certain act, a third party with notice of that stipulation will be bound thereby, although Lord Lindley himself had already rejected such a proposition as "too wide".[512]

The current editor's view is that, in its terms, the section only partially resolved this issue, since it is still technically unclear whether the third party must have notice that the partner is prohibited from doing a certain act *and*

---

[508] In fact this was a decision under the New Zealand equivalent of s.7, *i.e.* the Partnership Act 1908, s.10.

[509] [1909] 28 N.Z.L.R. 461.

[510] (1808) 10 East 264. Lord Ellenborough is reported to have said (at p. 266): "It is not essential to a partnership that one partner should have power to draw bills and notes in the partnership firm to charge the other: they may stipulate between themselves that it shall not be done: and if a third person, having notice of this, will take such a security from one of the partners, he shall not sue the others upon it in breach of such stipulation, nor in defiance of a notice previously given to him by one of them, that he will not be liable for any bill or note signed by the others."

[511] (1808) 1 Camp. 404n. Lord Ellenborough reportedly held that "where there was a stipulation between A, B and C, who appeared to the world as co-partners, that C should not participate in the profit and loss, and should not be liable as a partner, C was not liable as such to those who had notice of this stipulation."

[512] Lord Lindley explained, "A stranger dealing with a partner is entitled to hold the firm liable for whatever that partner may do on its behalf within certain limits. To deprive the stranger of this right, he ought to have distinct notice that the firm will not be answerable for the acts of one member, even within these limits. Now notice of an agreement between the members that one of them shall not do certain things is by no means necessarily equivalent to notice that the firm will not be answerable for them if he does. For there is nothing inconsistent in an agreement between the members of a firm that certain things shall not be done by one of them, and a readiness on the part of all the members to be responsible to strangers for the acts of each other, as if no such an agreement had been entered into. It is immaterial to a stranger what stipulations partners may make amongst themselves, so long as they do not seek to restrict their responsibility as to him; and it is only when knowledge of an agreement between partners necessarily involves knowledge that they decline to be responsible for the acts of each other within the ordinary limits, that a stranger's rights against a firm may be prejudiced by what he may know of the private stipulations between its members." In this context, Lord Lindley referred to the decisions in *Brown v. Leonard* (1816) 2 Chitty 120, *supra*, para. 5–49; *Hawken v. Bourne* (1841) 8 M. & W. 703; *Greenwood's Case* (1854) 3 De G.M. & G. 459. See also *Pollock on Partnership* (15th ed.), pp. 40–41.

thereby binding the firm or whether mere notice of the prohibition is sufficient. It is, nevertheless, submitted that a restriction or prohibition on a partner's ability to do an act must necessarily carry with it the implication that he is not authorised to do that act and, thus, that the firm will not be bound if he exceeds his authority; *sed quaere*.[513]

Operation of section 8

It will be apparent from the terms of the section that questions of notice will only arise where the firm is seeking to avoid liability in respect of an act which falls within the scope of a partner's implied authority but outside the scope of his actual authority; it is therefore not surprising to find that the authorities which illustrate the principles underlying the section[514] primarily concern frauds practised by one partner on the firm.   **12–141**

Cases where no notice

Lord Lindley observed that: **12–142**

> "if one partner acts in fraud of his co-partners, still they will be bound, if he has not exceeded his apparent authority, and if the person dealing with him had no notice of the fraud."[515]

Thus, in *Bond v. Gibson*,[516] one partner purchased goods on the credit of the firm and immediately pawned them for his own benefit; the firm was nevertheless held liable to pay for the goods. Similarly, if a partner, who has implied authority to draw, accept or indorse bills of exchange in the firm name,[517] does so, but for a private purpose of his own, still the firm will be liable on any such bill *vis-à-vis* a holder for value who does not have notice of the fraud.[518] It has already been seen that the position will be no different where a partner fraudulently misapplies money received by or in the custody of the firm in the ordinary course of its business.[519] In all of these cases, the fact that the *partners* have no notice of the fraud is wholly irrelevant.

Cases where express notice

The most effective method of invoking the protection of section 8 is, of course, to give express notice of any restriction on a partner's implied authority to bind   **12–143**

---

[513] It is interesting to note that, in his Supplement on the Partnership Act 1890, Lord Lindley wrote of s.8: "This section adopts the dicta of Lord Ellenborough in *Galway v. Mathew* and *Alderson v. Pope*, and is probably an extension of the law."

[514] In fact, all the relevant authorities pre-date the Partnership Act 1890.

[515] *Hambro v. Burnand* [1904] 2 K.B. 10; also *Bank of Bengal v. Fagan* (1849) 7 Moo.P.C. 61, 74; *Bryant, Powis, and Bryant Ltd. v. Quebec Bank* [1893] A.C. 170.

[516] (1808) 1 Camp. 185.

[517] See *supra*, paras 12–42 *et seq.*

[518] *Ex p. Bushell* (1844) 3 M.D. & D. 615; *Ex p. Meyer* (1848) De Gex. 632. See also *Lane v. Williams* (1692) 2 Vern. 277; *Sutton v. Gregory* (1797) 2 Peake 150; *Swan v. Steele* (1806) 7 East 210; *Ridley v. Taylor* (1810) 13 East 175; *Sanderson v. Brooksbank* (1830) 4 Car. & P. 286; *Wintle v. Crowther* (1831) 1 C. & J. 316; *Thicknesse v. Bromilow* (1832) 2 C. & J. 425; *Lewis v. Reilly* (1841) 1 Q.B. 349. Note, in particular, the terms of the Bills of Exchange Act 1882, s.30(2) and, as to the meaning of "fraud" in that subsection, the decision in *Österreichische Landerbank v. S'Elite Ltd.* [1981] Q.B. 565. And see *Hogg v. Skeen* (1865) 18 C.B.(N.S.) 426.

[519] See *supra*, paras 12–104 *et seq.*

the firm. Therefore, if one partner sends a circular to a supplier, instructing him not to supply goods to the firm without his written order, he will not be liable if the supplier chooses to ignore that instruction and supplies goods to his partner.[520] Equally, the extent of a partner's authority to accept bills of exchange in the firm name may, in an appropriate case, be publicly notified.[521]

In *Gallway v. Mathew and Smithson*[522] one partner, S, published an advertisement warning all persons not to give credit to his partner, M, on his, S's, account, and stating that he would not be liable for any bills or notes issued by M in the firm name. A third party, who had seen the advertisement, was nevertheless prevailed upon by M to accept a bill of exchange in respect of money required to pay partnership debts and to take a promissory note drawn by M in the firm name. M then discounted the bill and applied most (but not all) of the proceeds towards the firm's debts. It was held that the firm was not bound by the promissory note.

However, it should be noted that, notwithstanding the decisions in *Galway v. Mathew* and other cases, there is at least some doubt whether one partner can *unilaterally* restrict the implied authority of a co-partner, at least while the partnership continues.[523]

Cases where implied notice

12–144   In some cases, the circumstances of the transaction will be sufficient to put a third party on notice that the partner with whom he is dealing is acting outside the scope of his implied authority, *i.e.* where the partner is clearly attempting to secure some purely personal benefit for himself. If this is the position, the firm will, on normal principles, be liable only if *express* authority can be proved. The decision in *Bignold v. Waterhouse*[524] would seem to fall within this class.

12–145   Three other obvious examples were cited by Lord Lindley, namely where a partner:

(a) accepts a bill of exchange in the firm name for his own personal debts[525];

(b) pledges partnership goods for such debts[526]; or

(c) otherwise uses partnership funds to pay such debts.[527]

---

[520] *Minnit v. Whinery* (1721) 5 Bro.P.C. 489; *Willis v. Dyson* (1816) 1 Stark. 164. See also *Vice v. Fleming* (1827) 1 Y. & J. 227; *Ex p. Holdsworth* (1841) 1 M.D. & D. 475.

[521] *Rooth v. Quin* (1819) 7 Price 193. Such notice will affect those who see or hear of it, save that an indorsee with notice may avail himself of the ignorance of his indorser.

[522] (1808) 10 East 264. See also *Ex p. Holdsworth* (1841) 1 M.D. & D. 475.

[523] See *infra*, paras 13–31 *et seq.*

[524] (1813) 1 M. & S. 255. See *supra*, para. 12–29.

[525] *Leverson v. Lane* (1862) 13 C.B.(N.S.) 278; *Re Riches* (1865) 4 De G.J. & S. 581. See also *Ellston v. Deacon* (1866) L.R. 2 C.P. 20. There are even older cases to the same effect: *Ex p. Agace* (1792) 2 Cox 312; *Arden v. Sharpe* (1797) 2 Esp. 524; *Wells v. Masterman* (1799) 2 Esp. 731; *Ex p. Bonbonus* (1803) 8 Ves. Jr. 540; *Green v. Deakin* (1818) 2 Stark. 347; *Frankland v. M'Gusty* (1830) 1 Knapp. 274; *Ex p. Thorpe* (1836) 3 M. & A. 716; *Ex p. Austen* (1840) 1 M.D. & D. 247; *Miller v. Douglas* (1840) 3 Ross L.C. 500. Lord Lindley also cited the following, more obscure, example: "And if a bill is drawn by one partner in the name of the firm in fraud of his co-partners, and is accepted by the drawee, and is afterwards indorsed by the drawer in the name of the firm, the acceptor may successfully deny the indorsement, although he cannot deny the drawing." See *Garland v. Jacomb* (1873) L.R. 8 Ex. 216.

[526] *Snaith v. Burridge* (1812) 4 Taunt. 684.

[527] *Kendal v. Wood* (1870) L.R. 6 Ex. 243; *Heilbut v. Nevill* (1870) L.R. 5 C.P. 478.

All of these examples may be explained by reference to the following principle, as originally formulated by Lord Lindley:

" . . . a person who knows that a partner is using the name and assets of the firm for a private purpose of his own, knows that he is prima facie committing a fraud on his co-partners."[528]

Position of incoming partners

If, following the admission of a new partner, a bill of exchange is drawn and accepted in the names of all the partners (both old and new) in settlement of a debt of the former firm, the new partner will not, by an extension of the same principle, be liable thereon. This was decided in *Shirreff v. Wilks*,[529] which Lord Lindley described as "clear law".[530] However, the position will be otherwise if the new partner has agreed to take on the liabilities of the existing firm.[531]   **12–146**

Position of outgoing partners

In addition to the more usual instances of restricted authority noticed in the preceding paragraphs, specific attention should also be drawn to the position of an outgoing partner, since the continuing partners' implied authority to bind him will continue for as long as he remains an apparent member of the firm.[532] Accordingly, due notice that he has ceased to be a partner must be given to all persons who have dealings with the firm, which effectively amounts to notice that the continuing partners' authority is, to this extent, now restricted.[533]   **12–147**

7.   LIABILITY OF PARTNERS IN RESPECT OF CONTRACTS IN IMPROPER FORM

Before it can be said whether a contract made by a partner is binding on the firm, it must first be ascertained whether, in making the contract, that partner was purporting to act as the agent of the firm or as a principal in his own right, as Lord Lindley explained: **12–148**

"The general proposition that a partnership is bound by those acts of its agents which are within the scope of their authority[534] . . . must be taken with the qualification that

---

[528] In later editions, the wording was changed to " . . . a person who knows that a partner is using the credit of the firm for a private purpose of his own, knows that *he is using it for a purpose prima facie outside the limits of his authority*" (emphasis supplied).

[529] (1800) 1 East 48. There was no evidence to show that the incoming partner knew of the acceptance. Lord Lindley went on to observe that "Lord Kenyon went so far as to say that the transaction was fraudulent on the face of it; but that is going rather far, as it is not uncommon for in-coming partners to agree to take upon themselves the existing liabilities of the firm. When such an agreement is entered into, the in-coming partner can hardly say he has been defrauded, if a bill in the name of the new firm is accepted for a debt of the old firm without any specific authority on his part."

[530] See also *Ex p. Goulding* (1829) 2 Gl. & J. 118; *Wilson v. Lewis* (1840) 2 Man. & G. 197.

[531] See *supra*, n. 535; also *supra*, para. 10–56.

[532] See the Partnership Act 1890, ss.36(1), 38. See further, *infra*, paras 13–36 *et seq.*

[533] *ibid.* s.36(2).

[534] See *supra*, paras 12–01 *et seq.*

the agent whose acts are sought to be imputed to the firm, was acting in his character of agent, and not as a principal. If he did not act in his character of agent, but as a private individual on his own account, his acts cannot be imputed to the firm, and he alone is liable for them, even though the firm may have benefited by them."[535]

Partnership Act 1890, section 6

12–149   The same qualification is reflected in section 6 of the Partnership Act 1890, which provides:

> "6. An act or instrument relating to the business of the firm done or executed in the firm-name, or in any other manner showing an intention to bind the firm, by any person thereto authorised, whether a partner or not, is binding on the firm and all the partners.
>
> Provided that this section shall not affect any general rule of law relating to the execution of deeds or negotiable instruments."[536]

Form of contract

12–150   Section 6 presupposes that it is apparent from the form of the contract whether the partner is contracting as principal or agent, whereas in practice this will often be unclear. Given the terms of the proviso to the section, it is both necessary and convenient to consider this subject under three separate headings, namely:

(a) Written and oral contracts.

(b) Contracts under seal.

(c) Bills of exchange and promissory notes.

(a) Written and Oral Contracts

The general principle

12–151   The liability of the firm in the case of what Lord Lindley called "ordinary contracts" is dependent on the application of normal agency principles, which may be summarised as follows:

1. If the agency is disclosed, liability under the contract will generally attach to the principal and not to the agent, even if the identity of the principal was not revealed.[537]

2. If the agency is undisclosed, liability under the contract will attach to the agent.[538]

3. If, in the latter case, the other contracting party discovers the existence of the undisclosed principal, he may hold him, as well as the agent, liable under the contract.[539]

---

[535] See *British Homes Assurance Corporation Ltd. v. Paterson* [1902] 2 Ch. 404.

[536] For an example of the practical effects of the proviso, see *Littlejohn v. Mackay*, 1974 S.L.T. 82, Sh.Ct. (a Scottish case concerning holograph execution on behalf of a firm). And see also *Marchant v. Morton Down Co.* [1901] 2 K.B. 829, *infra*, para. 12–158.

[537] See *Bowstead & Reynolds on Agency* (19th ed.), Art. 71, paras 8–001 *et seq.*; also Art. 97, paras 9–001 *et seq.*

[538] See *ibid.* Art. 98, paras 9–012 *et seq.*

[539] See *ibid.* Art. 76, paras 8–070 *et seq.* And see, generally, *Siu Yin Kwan v. Eastern Insurance Co. Ltd.* [1994] 2 A.C. 199 (PC).

4. In the case of an apparent agency, *i.e.* where the agent is in fact the principal, he will seemingly be liable under the contract once the true facts are known.[540]

Partner acting as a principal

Equally, if a partner enters into a contract in circumstances where he is **12–152** demonstrably acting on his own account, *i.e.* as a principal and not as agent of the firm, he alone will be liable,[541] even if the contract has some connection with the partnership business. Lord Lindley illustrated this (largely self evident) class of cases by the following two examples:

> "Thus, where persons work a coach in partnership, each having his own horses, and one of them orders fodder on his own account, he alone is liable for it.[542] So, in the ordinary case of an agreement between an author and a publisher, to the effect that the publisher shall pay for the paper, printing, and other expenses of publication, and that after reimbursing himself and deducting a commission, the profits shall be divided equally, the author is not liable for the paper or printing which may have been supplied and executed by the publisher."[543]

Written contracts

Having regard to the principles summarised in the preceding paragraphs, it is **12–153** clear that, if one partner enters into a written contract, it cannot be determined whether the firm is bound simply by considering its terms, unless those terms expressly negate, or are otherwise inconsistent with, the status of the firm as a contracting party.[544] Lord Lindley gave the following example:

> " . . . supposing a contract to be entered into by one partner in his own name only, still if in fact he was acting as the agent of the firm, his co-partners will be in the position of undisclosed principals; and they may therefore be liable to be sued on the contract, although no allusion is made to them in it."

This proposition is clearly supported by the decision in *Beckham v. Drake*.[545] In that case, there were three partners, A, B and C, but A's existence was undisclosed.[546] In the course of carrying on the firm's business, B and C entered into a written contract with a third party, who later sued for breach of its terms.

[540] See the discussion of this difficult question in *Bowstead & Reynolds on Agency* (19th ed.), Art. 108, paras 9–088 *et seq.*

[541] See for example, *Ex p. Eyre* (1842) 1 Ph. 227, noted *supra*, para. 12–122; *British Homes Assurance Corporation v. Paterson* [1902] 2 Ch. 404; also *Greer v. Downs Supply Co.* [1927] 2 K.B. 28 (which did not concern a partnership).

[542] *Barton v. Hanson* (1809) 2 Taunt. 49. Lord Lindley observed that "Mr. Collyer treats this as an exception depending on particular custom, but this view is not correct."

[543] See the Scottish case of *Venables v. Wood* (1839) 3 Ross L.C. on Com. Law, 529; *Wilson v. Whitehead* (1842) 10 M. & W. 503; and see *supra*, para. 5–27, n. 118. But note also the decision in *Gardiner v. Childs* (1837) 8 C. & P. 345.

[544] But see *Humble v. Hunter* (1848) 12 Q.B. 310; *O/Y Wasa S.S. Co. v. Newspaper Pulp and Wood Exports* (1949) 82 Ll.L.Rep. 936; *Formby Bros. v. Formby* (1910) 102 L.T. 116; *Drughorn Ltd. v. Rederiaktiebolaget Transatlantic* [1919] A.C. 203. These cases are considered in *Bowstead & Reynolds on Agency* (19th ed.), para. 8–080.

[545] (1843) 11 M. & W. 315.

[546] He was therefore what is commonly styled a "secret" or "dormant" partner: see *supra*, para. 12–08.

A neither signed nor was named in the contract and was not known to the third party to be a partner. Nevertheless, A, B and C were held jointly liable for the breach, since the contract was clearly entered into by the firm and A, like any other undisclosed principal, was liable to be sued as soon as his position was discovered.[547]

Form of contract

12–154   Two additional observations should be made in this context. First, if the contract is required by statute to be in writing and signed by the party to be charged, then, notwithstanding the foregoing principles, only those partners who actually sign it will be bound[548]; *per contra*, if signature by an agent is permissible.[549]

Secondly, when construing a contract entered into by a partner, care must be taken to identify whether he acted as agent for the firm and/or as a principal, whether on his own account or for the benefit of the firm[550]; it is only in the former case that the firm will be rendered liable. This aspect is considered in greater detail later in this chapter.[551]

Oral contracts

12–155   Precisely the same principles apply in the case of an oral contract. Thus, if one partner, whilst acting on the firm's behalf, places an order for goods and they are supplied to him, the firm will be liable to pay for them, even if no mention was made of the other partners[552] and they were unknown to the supplier.[553]

Position of dormant partners

12–156   It follows that a dormant partner cannot escape liability merely because his existence was unknown when a contract was entered into,[554] although the

---

[547] Lord Lindley cited the following additional example, which is of little current relevance: "So, if A in his own name only underwrites a policy of insurance, but the profit or loss arising from the transaction is to be divided between him and B, both A and B will be liable to the insured: *Brett v. Beckwith* (1856) 3 Jur.(N.S.) 31."

[548] See *Swift v. Jewsbury* (1874) L.R. 9 Q.B. 301.

[549] See, for example, the Law of Property (Miscellaneous Provisions) Act 1989, s.2(3). In cases of this class, the contract must be signed in the name or on behalf of the firm: see *Duncan v. Lowndes* (1813) 3 Camp. 478. In *Ex p. Harding* (1879) 12 Ch.D. 557, a letter of guarantee was framed in such a way as to bind both the firm *and* the actual signatories. *cf. Keen v. Mear* [1920] 2 Ch. 574, where it was held that the Partnership Act 1890, s.5 did not override the (then) requirements of the Statute of Frauds, s.4. See also *Davies v. Sweet* [1962] 2 Q.B. 300.

[550] See, generally, *Paice v. Walker* (1870) L.R. 5 Ex. 173; *Southwell v. Bowditch* (1876) 1 C.P.D. 374; *Gadd v. Houghton* (1876) 1 Ex.D. 357; *Hough v. Manzanos* (1879) 4 Ex.D. 104; *H. O. Brandt & Co. v. H. N. Morris & Co. Ltd.* [1917] 2 K.B. 784.

[551] See *infra*, paras 12–175 *et seq.*

[552] *Whitwell v. Perrin* (1858) 4 C.B.(N.S.) 412; *City of London Gas Light and Coke Co. v. Nicholls* (1862) 2 Car. & P. 365.

[553] *Robinson v. Wilkinson* (1817) 3 Price 538; *Ruppell v. Roberts* (1834) 4 Nev. & Man. 31; *Bottomley v. Nuttall* (1858) 5 C.B.(N.S.) 122. *cf.* the position where the firm merely enjoys the benefit of a contract entered into by a partner, whilst acting beyond the scope both of his actual and implied authority: see *infra*, paras 12–175 *et seq.*

[554] *Beckham v. Drake* (1843) 11 M. & W. 315, *supra*, para. 12–153; see also *Court v. Berlin* [1897] 2 Q.B. 396.

incidence of such partners is in any event much reduced by the requirements of Part 41 of the Companies Act 2006 and its predecessors.[555]

(b) Contracts under Seal

The general rule

Reference has already been made to the fact that a partner will have no implied **12–157** authority to bind his firm by deed.[556] However, even in a case where a partner has the *express* authority of his co-partners to enter into a deed on the firm's behalf,[557] the form of the deed will ultimately determine whether or not the firm is bound. Somewhat surprisingly, Lord Lindley dealt with this important limitation in a terse way, as follows:

> "If a deed is executed by an agent in his own name, he and he only can sue or be sued thereon, although the deed may disclose the fact that he is acting for another.[558] Therefore, where a partner covenants that anything shall be done, he and he only is liable on the covenant, and the firm is not bound thereby to the covenantee.[559] A person who has to execute a deed as an agent, should take care that the deed and the covenants in it are expressed to be made not by him, but by the person intended to be bound. Thus, if A is the principal and B his agent, the deed and covenants should not be expressed to be made by B for A, but by A; and the execution in like manner should be expressed to be made by A by his agent B."[560]

This long standing rule is expressly preserved by the Partnership Act 1890[561] **12–158** and was applied in *Marchant v. Morton Down Co.*[562] There, two partners, T. J. Woolls and J. Allen, carried on business under the name "T. J. Woolls & Co." Allen purported to execute an indenture made between "T. J. Woolls and J. Allen, trading in co-partnership as T. J. Woolls & Co. of the one part, and T. B. Marchant of the other part" by signing it "T. J. Woolls & Co., by J. Allen, a partner in the said firm". Channell J. held that the indenture could not be treated as a deed made by Woolls, even though it was held to be binding on him on other grounds.[563] Although the decision in *Bank of Scotland v. Henry Butcher & Co.*[564] appears inconsistent with the rule, there the Court of Appeal focused solely on the issue of authority and did not address the implications of section 6 of the 1890 Act.[565] Perhaps this was because, as a part of the transaction which had clearly been authorised by the partners, the guarantee would have been binding on them in any event,[566] as in *Marchant v. Morton Down & Co.*

[555] See *supra*, paras 3–26 *et seq.*

[556] See *supra*, para. 12–62.

[557] Such authority must itself be given by deed: *Steiglitz v. Egginton* (1815) Holt N.P. 141; *Berkeley v. Hardy* (1826) 5 B. & C. 355. See also the Powers of Attorney Act 1971, s.1(1) (as amended by the Law of Property (Miscellaneous Provisions) Act 1989, Sched. 1, paras 6(a)), 7(1)).

[558] *Appleton v. Binks* (1804) 5 East 148; *Pickering's Case* (1871) L.R. 6 Ch.App. 525; see also *infra*, n. 559 and *Bowstead & Reynolds on Agency* (19th ed.), Art. 102, paras 9–047 *et seq.*

[559] *Hall v. Bainbridge* (1840) 1 Man. & G. 42. And note the decision in *John Brothers v. Holmes* [1900] 1 Ch. 188.

[560] *Combe's Case* (1613) 9 Co. 76b; *Wilks v. Back* (1802) 2 East 141.

[561] *ibid.* s.6, proviso, *supra*, para. 12–149.

[562] [1901] 2 K.B. 829.

[563] [1901] 2 K.B. 832, 833.

[564] [2003] 2 All E.R. (Comm) 557.

[565] Inexplicably, the point was raised at first instance but not pursued on the appeal: see [2001] 2 All E.R. (Comm) 691 at [51].

[566] Note also that the partnership deed did expressly contemplate that a partner could enter into guarantees on behalf of the firm provided that he had the consent of the other partners.

The rule is not affected by the relaxations in the formalities for the execution of deeds introduced by the Law of Property (Miscellaneous Provisions) Act 1989.[567]

Exception to the general rule

12–159   It should be noted that if a partner executes a deed as trustee for the firm, the firm *may* be entitled to enforce its provisions in the name of the trustee partner.[568]

All partners as parties to deed

12–160   The existence of this inflexible rule caused lessors of property to a tenant firm to insist that each partner was made a party to the lease, so as to ensure that he had a direct right to enforce the covenants against each of them,[569] although a more recent trend has been for leases to be granted on terms which limit the liability of the tenant partners to the assets of the firm, thus avoiding personal liability on their part.[570]

(c) Bills of Exchange and Promissory Notes

12–161   Bills of exchange and promissory notes are not governed by the same rules as ordinary contracts not under seal.[571] The position was summarised by Lord Lindley in these terms:

> " . . . subject to the qualification that the name of a firm is equivalent to the name of all the persons liable as partners in it,[572] no person whose name is not on a bill or note is liable to be sued upon it.[573] In order, therefore, that a bill or note may be binding on a firm, the name of the firm or the names of all its members must be upon it; and if the names of one or more of the partners only are upon it, the others will not be liable to be sued upon the instrument, whatever may be their liability as regards the consideration for which it may have been given."[574]

These rules are expressly preserved by the Partnership Act 1890.[575]

The decided cases in this area are numerous and may usefully be grouped as follows:

(1) Bills drawn, etc., in the firm name.

(2) Bills drawn, etc., in improper form.

(3) Promissory notes.

---

[567] s.1, as amended by the Regulatory Reform (Execution of Deeds and Documents) Order 2005 (SI 2005/1906), art.8. See also *supra*, para. 12–62.

[568] *Harmer v. Armstrong* [1934] 1 Ch. 65. But note *Re Kay's Settlement* [1939] Ch. 329; *Re Cook's Settlement Trusts* [1965] Ch. 902.

[569] See further *infra*, para. 18–61.

[570] See, as to the effect of one such provision (albeit badly drafted), *Prudential Assurance Co. Ltd. v. Ayres* [2008] 1 All E.R. 1266 (CA).

[571] See *supra*, paras 12–151 *et seq.*

[572] Bills of Exchange Act 1882, s.23(2); see further, *infra*, para. 12–162.

[573] *ibid.* s.23; and see *Ducarry v. Gill* (1830) 4 C. & P. 121; *Lloyd v. Ashby* (1831) 2 C. & P. 138; *Eastwood v. Bain* (1858) 3 H. & N. 738.

[574] *Bottomley v. Nuttall* (1858) 5 C.B.(N.S.) 122; *Miles' Claim* (1874) L.R. 9 Ch.App. 635.

[575] *ibid.* s.6, proviso, *supra*, para. 12–149.

(1) *Bills of Exchange Drawn, etc., in the Firm Name*

As might be expected, a bill in the firm name will normally bind all the partners, **12–162** as Lord Lindley explained:

> "A bill drawn, indorsed or accepted in the name of the firm is considered as bearing the names of all the persons who actually or ostensibly compose the firm at the time its name is put to the bill; and consequently all those persons, including as well dormant partners[576] and *quasi-partners*,[577] may be sued upon the bill."[578]

Thus, where a cheque bearing the firm name is signed by a partner, his co-partner will be liable even though there is no connection on the face of the cheque between the firm name and the manuscript signature.[579]

The fact that the person drawing, indorsing or accepting the bill is not a true partner, but is merely held out as such,[580] is immaterial provided that he was acting within the scope of his implied authority.[581] However, it should be emphasised that such a person only has *apparent* authority to bind his co-partners, since section 5 of the Partnership Act 1890 is prima facie inapplicable in cases of holding out.[582]

More difficult questions arise where a firm carries on business under the name of one of the partners or where two firms carry on business under the same name.

Business carried on in name of partner

In cases of this type, the normal rule is that the firm will be bound, whether the **12–163** bill is drawn, etc., by the partner in whose name the business is carried on or by one of his co-partners.[583] Indeed, in one case,[584] a firm was held liable under a bill accepted by one partner, B, in the name of his co-partner, A, even though it was addressed to A at a place where he carried on a wholly separate business.[585]

However, if it is possible to prove that a bill drawn, etc., by the partner whose name the firm bears is in fact his own, and not the firm's, bill, the firm will not

---

[576] See *Swan v. Steele* (1806) 7 East 210; *Wintle v. Crowther* (1831) 1 C. & J. 316.

[577] See *Gurney v. Evans* (1858) 3 H. & N. 122. The expression "quasi-partner" is no longer in common usage; its modern equivalent is a partner by holding out or estoppel: see the Partnership Act 1890, s.14, *supra*, paras 5–35 *et seq*. See also *supra*, para. 1–09.

[578] Bills of Exchange Act 1882, s.23(2).

[579] *Ringham v. Hackett*, *The Times*, February 9, 1980 and (1980) 124 S.J. 201; *Central Motors (Birmingham) v. P.A. & S.N.P. Wadsworth (Trading as Pensgain)*, May 28, 1982 (C.A.T. No. 231), [1983] C.L.Y., p. 80.

[580] Partnership Act 1890, s.14: see *supra*, paras 5–35 *et seq*.

[581] *Edmonds v. Bushell* (1865) L.R. 1 Q.B. 97; also *Gurney v. Evans* (1858) 3 H. & N. 122. And see *Watteau v. Fenwick* [1893] 1 Q.B. 346; *Kinahan & Co. v. Parry* [1910] 2 K.B. 389 (reversed on a question of fact at [1911] 1 K.B. 459); and *supra*, para. 12–11, n. 38. *cf. Odell v. Cormack* (1887) 19 Q.B.D. 223, where there was no holding out.

[582] See *Hudgell Yeates & Co. v. Watson* [1978] Q.B. 451, 467 *per* Waller L.J.

[583] Lord Lindley quite naturally perceived the dangers solely in terms of bills drawn, etc., by the partner in whose name the business is carried on: " . . . persons may carry on business in partnership in the name of one of themselves, and if they do, they expose themselves to serious liability. Prima facie his acceptances will bind them, even although dishonestly given": see *Yorkshire Banking Co. v. Beatson* (1880) 5 C.P.D. 109, 123–124.

[584] *Stephens v. Reynolds* (1860) 5 H. & N. 513. The proceedings at *Nisi Prius* are reported at (1860) 1 Fost. & Fin. 739 and (1860) 2 Fost. & Fin. 147.

[585] It should be noted that the bill was drawn on Reynolds at Woolwich, not at Walworth, as stated in (1860) 1 Fost. & Fin. 740.

be liable, even to a bona fide holder for value. This was decided in *Yorkshire Banking Co. v. Beatson*,[586] where bills were accepted and indorsed by the partner in the course of a private transaction which was neither intended to bind the other (dormant) partner nor entered in the partnership books. Since the holders of the bills did not know of that other partner's existence, they could not be treated as having given credit to him merely because they gave credit to the partner whose name was on the bills.[587]

12–164   Similarly, where one partner accepts a bill drawn on him by a co-partner, the firm will not be bound even if the partnership business is carried on in his name. Lord Lindley summarised the position in this way:

> "If A, B and C are partners, and A draws a bill of exchange on B, and he accepts the bill, A, B and C cannot be sued upon it; and this is so whether A, B and C have a business name or not; and even although the bill may have been used for the joint benefit of the three partners.[588] Even if it is agreed that the business of the three shall be carried on in the name of one of them, it will not follow that all bills accepted by him will bind all the three partners. The question remains, whose bill is it?"

12–165   This is clear from the decision commonly known as *Miles' Claim*,[589] where four separate firms, A & Co., B & Co., C & Co. and D & Co. became partners in a certain venture and carried on business under the name of D & Co.[590] They agreed that finance for the venture should be raised by means of bills drawn by any one of the individual firms on the others. A & Co. thereupon drew bills on B & Co., C & Co. and D & Co., which were duly accepted. It was held that none of these bills bound all four firms jointly. The bills drawn on B & Co. and C & Co. respectively were clearly not bills of the partnership venture, since they were neither drawn nor accepted in the firm name of D & Co. Although the remaining bills were drawn and accepted in the firm name, the court found that there was no evidence of any intention to bind all four firms, as opposed to the individual firm which carried on business under that name.

12–166   Lord Lindley then referred to the unreported decision in *Hall v. West*,[591] in which there were *dicta* to the same effect. This case is therefore of only limited value; nevertheless, since details of it were apparently taken from the shorthand writer's notes, the original passage has been retained in its entirety:

> "Again, in *Hall v. West*, three brothers of the name of Dawson carried on in partnership under the name of Dawson & Sons, the business of millers, farmers, coal and corn dealers, and bone crushers. The defendant was a dormant partner in the bone-crushing business only. Dawson & Sons overdrew their account with their bankers, who knew nothing of West, nor of his connection with the bone business. Having, however, discovered this, they sued him for the amount of the overdrawn

---

[586] (1880) 5 C.P.D. 109. See also *South Carolina Bank v. Case* (1828) 8 B. & C. 427; *Ex p. Law* (1839) 3 Deac. 541.

[587] Lord Lindley put it in this way: "The fact that the plaintiffs took the bill as the bill of the persons, whoever they were, who might be associated with the partner whose name was on the bill was held immaterial. The plaintiffs never knew of or gave credit to anyone else."

[588] See *Nicholson v. Ricketts* (1860) 2 E. & E. 497; *Miles' Claim* (1874) L.R. 9 Ch.App. 635, *infra*, para. 12–165.

[589] *Re Adansonia Fibre Co., Miles' Claim* (1874) L.R. 9 Ch.App. 635. This appears to have been an early example of a group partnership: see *supra*, paras 11–17 *et seq*.

[590] It appears, significantly, that the name adopted for the partnership venture was not intended to be used publicly: see *ibid*. pp. 636, 647.

[591] The case went first to the Court of Exchequer and then to the Court of Exchequer Chamber in June 1875.

account. He was held not liable; for in point of fact the balance due to the bankers was not in respect of any debt contracted by Dawson & Sons in connection with the bone-crushing business; it was not, therefore, as between the partners themselves a debt of the firm of which the defendant was a member; and there was no apparent as distinguished from real authority on which the bankers could rely as against West.

In the same case bills were drawn by West on and accepted by Dawson & Sons. With one exception these bills were drawn for purposes unconnected with the bone business. On the facts stated (but which it is unnecessary here to detail) the court held that all these bills had in fact been paid: it became unnecessary, therefore, to consider whether West could have been sued as an acceptor. It was contended, on the authority of *Baker v. Charlton*,[592] that he was liable; but the Court of Exchequer[593] dissented from that case and expressed a clear opinion that West could not have been liable as an acceptor of the bills, with the exception of the one which had been given for the purposes of the bone business in which he was a partner. The Court of Exchequer Chamber expressed no opinion on this point, it being unnecessary to do so."

Two firms with same name

As Lord Lindley made clear, a factor of critical importance in this class of case will be whether the partner sought to be made liable is a member of one or both of the firms concerned: **12–167**

"If there are two firms with one name, a person who is a member of both firms is liable to be sued on all bills bearing that name, and binding on either firm. But if a member of only one of the two firms is sued on the bill, his liability will depend first on the authority of the person giving the bill to use the name of the firm of which the defendant is a member[594] and, secondly, on whether the name of that firm has in fact been used. If both these questions are answered in the affirmative, he will be liable, but not otherwise."[595]

In *Swan v. Steele*[596] such affirmative answers could clearly be given. There, two firms, one comprising A, B and C (the ABC Partnership) and the other comprising only B and C (the BC Partnership), carried on wholly separate businesses under the name "B & C". A was a dormant partner. A bill of exchange, payable to the order of the ABC Partnership, was received by that firm in respect of a debt due to it, but was indorsed over by B and C, in the name "B & C", for a debt owed to a third party, X, by the BC Partnership. A was held liable on the bill, X being a bona fide holder for value, without notice of the fraud on A committed by his co-partners. It was clear that the bill was properly indorsed "B & C": the only real question was whether that indorsement referred to the ABC Partnership or the BC Partnership. Since the bill could only have been indorsed by the ABC Partnership, A's liability was inevitable; indeed, Lord Ellenborough held it to be too clear for argument.   **12–168**

---

[592] (1791) Peake 111 (a case where two firms carried on business under the same name). After a footnote reference to *Davison v. Robertson* (1815) 3 Dow. 218 and *McNair v. Fleming* (1812) 1 Mont. Part. 37, Lord Lindley observed: "But *Baker v. Charlton* cannot now be relied on."

[593] Kelly C.B. and Amphlett B.

[594] See the Partnership Act 1890, s.5, *supra*, para. 12–02; also *supra*, paras 12–42 *et seq.*

[595] cf. *Baker v. Charlton* (1791) Peake 111, which is no longer good law: see *supra*, para. 12–166, n. 592.

[596] (1806) 7 East 210.

The position is not affected by the restrictions on the use of names imposed by Part 41 of the Companies Act 2006 since, even where that Part applies,[597] there is no restriction on the number of firms which can carry on business under the same name.[598] Certainly, the decision in *Swan v. Steele* would have been no different had there been equivalent provisions in force at the time.[599]

(2) Bills Drawn, etc., in Improper Form

12–169   Lord Lindley observed:

> "In the absence of evidence to the contrary, a partner has no authority to use for partnership purposes any other name than the name of the firm[600]; and if he does, and there is any substantial variation which cannot be shown to be authorised by his co-partners, the firm will not be liable. If, however, there is no substantial variation, the firm will be bound."

Consistently with this principle, in *Faith v. Richmond*,[601] partners in a firm carrying on business under the name of "The Newcastle and Sunderland Wallsend Coal Company" were held not to be liable on a promissory note issued in the name of "the Newcastle Coal Company". Similarly, in *Kirk v. Blurton*,[602] where the business was carried on under the name of "John Blurton", one partner was held not to be liable on a bill of exchange drawn and indorsed by the other in the name of "John Blurton & Co."

However, the rule is not absolute: in *Norton v. Seymour*,[603] where the firm name consisted of the partners' surnames, *i.e.* "Seymour and Ayres," both partners were held to be bound by a promissory note signed by one in the names "Thomas Seymour, Sarah Ayres". This signature obviously consisted of the partners' surnames, with the addition of their respective Christian names; it is considered that the decision would have been otherwise if the wrong Christian names had been used.

---

[597] Pt. 41 will not apply if each firm's name consists only of the surnames of its individual members, even if this results in two firms, who do not share identical partners, adopting the same name: Companies Act 2006, s.1192(2)(b). See further, *supra*, para. 3–27.

[598] In certain circumstances, the approval of a firm name must be obtained from the Secretary of State: *ibid.* ss.1193, 1194; also the Company, Limited Liability Partnership and Business Names (Sensitive Words and Expressions) Regulations 2009 (SI 2009/2615), regs. 3, 5, 6, Scheds. 1, 2; the Company, Limited Liability Partnerships and Business Names (Public Authorities) Regulations (SI 2009/2982), reg. 3, Sched., col. (1); see also *supra*, para. 3–29. There would, in theory, appear to be no reason why such approval should not be given for the use of an identical name by two or more wholly separate firms; *sed quaere*.

[599] Since, even if the holder of the bill had seen both firms' notepaper, etc., (see Companies Act 2006, ss.1202(1)) and the statutory notices at their premises (see *ibid.* s.1204(1)), the indorsement on the bill would still have been ambiguous and the indorsing partners would still have been acting within the scope of their implied authority. See further, as to these requirements, *supra*, para. 3–34.

[600] *Kirk v. Blurton* (1841) 9 M. & W. 284; *Hambro v. Hull and London Fire Insurance Co.* (1858) 3 H. & N. 789.

[601] (1840) 11 A. & E. 339.

[602] (1841) 9 M. & W. 284. Lord Lindley observed: "This case was decided on the right principle; but most persons will probably agree with Martin B., in thinking that the principle was not properly applied, and that it should have been left to the jury to say whether John Blurton and John Blurton & Co. did not in fact mean the same thing." See *Stephens v. Reynolds* (1860) 5 H. & N. 513, 517 *per* Martin B. See also *Odell v. Cormack* (1887) 19 Q.B.D. 223, 226 *per* Hawkins J.

[603] (1847) 3 C.B. 792.

Acceptance in firm name

An acceptance in the firm name of a bill drawn on the firm in the wrong name   **12–170**
will bind the firm.[604]

Habitual use of different name

However, notwithstanding the general principle described above, if it can be   **12–171**
proved that the name on the bill, though not the firm name, is a name which the
firm habitually *uses*, the firm will be bound.[605] As Lord Lindley put it:

> " . . . for whatever the name used may be, if it is that ordinarily employed by a
> partner whose business it is to attend to the bills and notes of the firm, the other
> partners will not be heard to say that such name is not the name of the firm for the
> purpose for which he has habitually used it."

Thus, where a firm carried on business under the name "Hapgood & Co.", but
the managing partner was in the habit of indorsing partnership bills in the name
"Hapgood & Fowler" (which had formerly been the firm name), the indorse-
ments were held to be binding on the firm, even though there was no proof that
the other partners had authorised the use of that name.[606]

Such a situation is now, perhaps, less likely to arise, having regard to the
requirements of Part 41 of the Companies Act 1996, which the partners could not
lightly ignore.[607]

Personal liability of persons using wrong name

Even if the firm is not bound, because its name (or a name which it habitually   **12–172**
uses) does not appear on the bill, the partners who actually drew, etc., the bill in
the wrong name will be treated as having adopted that name for the purposes of
the bill and will, therefore, be personally liable thereon.[608]

On the same principle, where a firm draws and indorses blank bills in the firm
name but, before they can be negotiated, one partner dies and the surviving
partners change the firm name and then negotiate the bills, the new firm will be
liable on the bills, even though its name does not appear thereon.[609]

Bill drawn, etc., in name of partner

A firm will not be liable on a bill drawn, etc., in the name of a partner,[610] unless   **12–173**
it in fact carries on business under his name.[611] This will be the position even if

---

[604] *Lloyd v. Ashby* (1831) 2 B. & Ad. 23.

[605] There was, of course, no such evidence in *Faith v. Richmond* (1840) 11 A. & E. 339 or *Kirk
v. Blurton* (1841) 9 M. & W. 284, *supra*, para. 12–169.

[606] *Williamson v. Johnson* (1823) 1 B. & C. 146.

[607] See in particular, *ibid.* ss.1202–1204 and, generally, *supra*, paras 3–34 *et seq.*

[608] *Faith v. Richmond* (1840) 11 A. & E. 339; *Kirk v. Blurton* (1841) 9 M. & W. 284: see *supra*,
para. 12–169. See also *Wilde v. Keep* (1833) 6 C. & P. 235; *Odell v. Cormack* (1887) 19 Q.B.D. 223,
226 *per* Hawkins J.

[609] *Usher v. Dauncey* (1814) 4 Camp. 97. And note also *Mitchell v. Lapage* (1816) Holt, N.P. 253;
cf. Boulton v. Jones (1857) 2 H. & N. 564.

[610] *Williams v. Thomas* (1806) 6 Esp. 18; *Emly v. Lye* (1812) 15 East 7; *Ex p. Bolitho* (1817) Buck
100; *Lloyd v. Ashby* (1831) 2 C. & P. 138. The cases of *Mason v. Rumsey* (1808) 1 Camp. 384 and
Jenkins v. Morris (1847) 16 M. & W. 877, which decided that a firm might be bound by the
acceptance of one partner in his own name of a bill drawn on the firm, are no longer good law: see
the Bills of Exchange Act 1882, ss.17, 23.

[611] See *supra*, paras 12–163 *et seq.*

the partner in whose name the bill is drawn accepts it on behalf of the firm, since the other partners will not be drawees.[612]

A bill drawn on a firm and accepted by one partner in the firm name and in his own name does not bind him separately if the firm is bound by his acceptance.[613] However, if he did not have authority to bind the firm, he will be liable on the bill. Thus, in *Owen v. Van Uster*,[614] Van Ulster was held to be personally liable on a bill drawn on "The Allty-Crib Mining Company", which had been accepted "per proc. The Allty-Crib Mining Company, W. T. Van Uster, London Manager".

(3) Promissory Notes

12–174 Lord Lindley formulated the following five rules[615] in relation to promissory notes, by reference to the decided cases:

(1) If a partner promises for himself and co-partner, this amounts to a promise by the firm.[616]

(2) If a partner promises for himself, and not for himself and co-partners, he only is liable on the note, though he may promise to pay a partnership debt.[617]

(3) If one partner promises in the name of the firm to pay that for which he and not the firm is liable, the promise binds him at all events.[618]

(4) If several partners sign a note in this form, "I promise to pay", all who sign the note are liable on it, jointly and severally.[619]

(5) One partner has no authority, as such, to bind himself and co-partners jointly and severally.[620] But if some members of a firm make a joint and *several* promissory note they will be personally liable, although they may have signed only on behalf of themselves and co-partners.[621]

---

[612] *Nicholls v. Diamond* (1853) 9 Ex. 154; *Mare v. Charles* (1856) 5 E. & B. 978.

[613] *Re Barnard* (1886) 32 Ch.D. 447; also *Malcolmson v. Malcolmson* (1851) L.R.Ir. 1 Ch.D. 228.

[614] (1850) 10 C.B. 318. Van Ulster was a partner in the Allty-Crib Mining Company and, therefore, both a drawee and an acceptor of the bill.

[615] The order in which the rules appear in the text is not that originally adopted by Lord Lindley. Moreover, his detailed illustrations of certain of the rules (involving the reproduction of various promissory notes culled from the decided cases) have not been retained.

[616] Bills of Exchange Act 1882, s.91; *Lane v. Williams* (1693) 2 Vern. 292; *Smith v. Baily* (1727) 11 Mod. 401; *Smith v. Jarves* (1727) 2 Ld. Ray. 1484. This was Lord Lindley's fifth rule. He specifically illustrated it by reference to *Galway v. Matthew and Smithson* (1808) 1 Camp. 403; *Ex p. Buckley* (1845) 14 M. & W. 469; *Ex p. Clarke* (1845) De Gex. 153 (the latter two decisions being contrary to the "older decision" in *Hall v. Smith* (1823) 1 B. & C. 407).

[617] *Siffkin v. Walker* (1809) 2 Camp. 308; *Murray v. Somerville* (1889) 2 Camp. 99n.; also *Ex p. Harris* (1816) 1 Madd. 583. This was Lord Lindley's first rule.

[618] *Shipton v. Thornton* (1838) 9 A. & E. 314; also *Hudson v. Robinson* (1816) 4 M. & S. 475. This was Lord Lindley's third rule.

[619] Bills of Exchange Act 1882, s.85; *Clerk v. Blackstock* (1816) Holt, N.P. 474; *March v. Ward* (1792) 1 Peake 177. This was Lord Lindley's second rule.

[620] *Maclae v. Sutherland* (1854) 3 E. & B. 1, which shows that a joint and several promissory note is valid as a joint note, even though it is not binding, as a several note, on any person who does not sign it.

[621] This was Lord Lindley's fourth rule. He specifically illustrated it by reference to *Healey v. Story* (1848) 3 Ex. 3; *Penkivil v. Connell* (1850) 5 Ex. 381; *Bottomley v. Fisher* (1862) 1 H. & C. 211.

8.   LIABILITY OF PARTNERS IN RESPECT OF CONTRACTS BENEFITING FIRM

When considering liability in respect of a contract entered into by a partner **12–175** *otherwise* than on behalf of the firm, it is wholly irrelevant that the firm may have received some direct or indirect benefit under or by virtue of the contract, as Lord Lindley explained in this passage:

> "It is an erroneous but popular notion that if a firm obtains the benefit of a contract made with one of its partners, it must needs be bound by that contract. Now, although the circumstance that the firm obtains the benefit of a contract entered into by one of its members tends to show that he entered into the contract as the agent of the firm,[622] such circumstance is no more than evidence that this was the case, and the question upon which the liability or non-liability of the firm upon a contract depends is not—Has the firm obtained the benefit of the contract? but—Did the firm, by one of its partners or otherwise, enter into the contract?"[623]

Numerous cases have been decided on this principle, but Lord Lindley drew particular attention to *Emly v. Lye*[624] and *Bevan v. Lewis*.[625]

The most common cases in which the principle will fall to be applied are where partners borrow money or obtain the supply of goods or services.

Money borrowed by a partner

If a partner borrows money without the actual or implied authority of his **12–176** co-partners,[626] he and not the firm will enter into the contract of loan and the nature of that contract will not be altered or affected by the manner in which he chooses to apply the money borrowed. Accordingly, the lender cannot seek repayment from the firm merely because the money has been applied for its benefit[627]; however, he may enjoy an equivalent right by way of an equitable form of subrogation.[628]

Goods supplied to a partner

The position will be no different where goods or services are supplied at the **12–177** request of a partner who is acting either on his own account or (which amounts to the same thing) outside the scope of his actual or implied authority.[629] Thus,

---

[622] *Beckham v. Drake* (1841) 9 M. & W. 79, 100 *per* Rolfe B.

[623] *ibid.* See also *Kingsbridge Flour Mill Co. v. The Plymouth Grinding Co.* (1848) 2 Ex. 718; *Ernest v. Nicholls* (1857) 6 H.L.Cas. 423. The position is analogous to that under the Partnership Act 1890, s.13: see *supra*, paras 12–127 *et seq.* The corollary is also true, *i.e.* the fact that one partner has obtained the benefit of a contract does not conclusively prove that the firm is *not* liable thereunder: see *Ex p. Bonbonus* (1803) 8 Ves. Jr. 540.

[624] (1812) 15 East 7, where a partner had drawn bills in his own name, had them discounted and then applied the money for the benefit of the firm.

[625] (1827) 1 Sim. 376, where the partner had borrowed money and applied it for the firm's benefit. Interestingly, it appears that his partner had some knowledge of the borrowing.

[626] See *supra*, paras 12–46 *et seq.*

[627] See *Smith v. Craven* (1831) 1 C. & J. 500; *Hawtayne v. Bourne* (1841) 7 M. & W. 595; *Fisher v. Tayler* (1843) 2 Hare 218; *Ricketts v. Bennett* (1847) 4 C.B. 686; *Burmester v. Norris* (1851) 6 Ex. 796; *Re Worcester Corn Exchange Co.* (1853) 3 De G.M. & G. 180.

[628] See *infra*, para. 12–178.

[629] See *supra*, para. 12–79.

the firm does not enter into any contract nor does it incur any liability merely because its receives the benefit of the goods or services supplied.[630] However, again a right against the firm may arise by way of subrogation.

The creditor's right of subrogation

12–178   Where the firm is not liable on a contract entered into by a partner, the other contracting party may not be entirely remediless, at least to the extent that the firm has been benefited thereby. Lord Lindley stated the equitable principle applied in such cases in these terms:

> "Where, however, money borrowed by one partner in the name of the firm but without the authority of his co-partners has been applied in paying off debts of the firm, the lender is entitled in equity to repayment by the firm of the amount which he can show to have been so applied[631]: and the same rule extends to money *bona fide* borrowed and applied for any other legitimate purpose of the firm.[632] This doctrine is founded partly on the right of the lender to stand in equity in the place of those creditors of the firm whose claims have been paid off by his money; and partly on the right of the borrowing partner to be indemnified by the firm against liabilities *bona fide* incurred by him for the legitimate purpose of relieving the firm from its debts or of carrying on its business.[633] The equitable doctrine in question is limited in its application to cases falling under one or other of the principles above indicated."[634]

It is clear from the qualification at the end of the passage that a right of subrogation will *not* arise in all cases. Thus, if money is borrowed by a partner and applied for the firm's benefit in a manner which does not increase or preserve its assets, that partner will not be entitled to reimbursement from his co-partners.[635] The lender can be in no better position.

---

[630] See in addition to the cases previously cited, *Ball v. Lanesborough* (1713) 5 Bro.P.C. 480; *Kilgour v. Finlyson* (1789) 1 H.Bl. 155, *Ex p. Wheatly* (1797) *Cooke's Bank. Law,* (8th ed.) 534; *Ex p. Peele* (1802) 6 Ves. Jr. 602, 604 *per* Lord Eldon; *Ex p. Hartop* (1806) 12 Ves. Jr. 349; *Gallway v. Mathew* (1808) 10 East 264; *Loyd v. Freshfield* (1826) 2 Car. & P. 325; *Kingsbridge Flour Mill Co. v. Plymouth Grinding Co.* (1848) 2 Ex. 718.

[631] At this point a later editor added the words "even though he knew that the money was borrowed without authority": see *Reversion Fund and Insurance Co. v. Maison Cosway Ltd.* [1913] 1 K.B. 364; also the cases cited in the next note.

[632] See, in particular, *Ex p. Chippendale (The German Mining Co.'s Case)* (1854) 4 De G.M. & G. 19; *Re Cork and Youghal Ry.* (1866) L.R. 4 Ch.App. 748; *Blackburn Building Society v. Cunliffe, Brooks & Co.* (1884) 9 App.Cas. 857 and (1885) 29 Ch.D. 902; *Baroness Wenlock v. River Dee Co.* (1883) 36 Ch.D. 675n. and (1887) 19 Q.B.D. 155; *Bannatyne v. McIver* [1906] 1 K.B. 103. See also *Reid v. Rigby & Co.* [1894] 2 Q.B. 40; *cf. Wylie v. Carlyon* [1922] 1 Ch. 51.

[633] See *infra*, paras 20–26 *et seq.*

[634] See in addition to the cases cited in n. 632, *Athenaeum Life Assurance Society v. Pooley* (1858) 3 De G. & J. 294; *Magdalena Steam Navigation Co.* (1860) Johns. 690; *Re National Permanent Benefit Building Society* (1870) L.R. 5 Ch.App. 309. And see also the general review of the doctrine of subrogation in *Orakpo v. Manson Investments Ltd.* [1978] A.C. 95.

[635] See *infra*, para. 20–27.

CHAPTER 13

THE NATURE AND DURATION OF A PARTNER'S LIABILITY TO THIRD PARTIES

1. NATURE AND EXTENT OF THE LIABILITY

IT has already been seen[1] that the liability of a firm for the acts of a partner will **13–01** vary according to the nature of those acts. In cases where such liability is established, the nature of the acts in question will also determine whether that liability will be merely joint or both joint and several. For convenience, this subject will be considered under the same general classifications as were adopted in the previous Chapter.

A. LIABILITY FOR ACTS WHICH ARE NOT IN THEMSELVES WRONGFUL

This section is effectively confined to liability arising out of contract, of which **13–02** Lord Lindley said:

"An agent who contracts for a known principal is not liable to be himself sued on the contract into which he has avowedly entered only as agent. Consequently, a partner who enters into a contract on behalf of his firm is not liable on that contract except as one of the firm: in other words, the contract is not binding on him separately, but only on him and his co-partners jointly.[2] One partner may render himself separately liable by holding himself out as the only member of the firm[3]; or by so framing the contract, as to bind himself separately from his co-partners as well as jointly with them[4]; but unless there are some special circumstances of this sort, a contract which is binding on the firm is binding on all[5] the partners jointly and on none of them severally."[6]

[1] See *supra*, paras 12–02 *et seq.*
[2] See *Ex p. Wilson* (1842) 3 M.D. & D. 57; *Ex p. Buckley* (1845) 14 M. & W. 469; *Re Clarke* (1845) De G. 153.
[3] *De Mautort v. Saunders* (1830) 1 B. & Ad. 398; *Bonfield v. Smith* (1844) 12 M. & W. 405.
[4] See *supra*, paras 12–151 *et seq.*; also *Higgins v. Senior* (1841) 8 M. & W. 834; *Ex p. Wilson* (1842) 3 M.D. & D. 57; *Ex p. Harding* (1879) 12 Ch.D. 557; *Bank of Scotland v. Henry Butcher & Co.* [2003] 2 All E.R. (Comm) 557 (CA). Note also that a contract framed in terms which leave it doubtful whether it is joint or joint and several will be construed as joint and several if it appears from the face of the contract that each partner has both a joint and a separate interest in its performance: see *Sorsbie v. Park* (1843) 12 M. & W. 146, 158 *per* Parke B; *Bradburne v. Botfield* (1845) 14 M. & W. 559; *Palmer v. Mallet* (1887) 36 Ch.D. 411. And note *AIB Group (UK) Ltd. v. Martin, The Times,* December 17, 2001 (HL). See also *infra,* para. 13–10.
[5] This will include a dormant partner: *Beckham v. Drake* (1843) 11 M. & W. 315; *Brett v. Beckwith* (1856) 3 Jur.(N.S.) 31; *Court v. Berlin* [1897] 2 Q.B. 396. See also *supra,* para. 12–08.
[6] In fact this was the position both at law and in equity: see *Kendall v. Hamilton* (1879) 4 App.Cas. 504.

Partnership Act 1890, section 9

13–03   This long established principle is incorporated directly into section 9 of the Partnership Act 1890, which provides:

> "9. Every partner in a firm is liable jointly with the other partners, and in Scotland severally also, for all debts and obligations[7] of the firm incurred while he is a partner; and after his death his estate is also severally liable in a due course of administration for such debts and obligations, so far as they remain unsatisfied, but subject in England or Ireland[8] to the prior payment of his separate debts."

It should be noted that, in *Dubai Aluminium Co Ltd. v. Salaam,*[9] Lord Millett observed that this section "is not concerned with the liability of the firm at all but with the liability of the individual partners."

Holding out

13–04   A person who is merely held out as a partner is liable "as a partner"[10] and will therefore be jointly liable along with the actual partners. Indeed, it is the current editor's view that there will be such joint liability even if no partnership in fact exists.[11] Lord Lindley certainly considered this to be the position prior to the Partnership Act 1890:

> "A creditor who alleges that A, B, and C are his debtors, can, it is apprehended, prove his case by showing that one of them contracted on behalf of all three and that the other two are estopped from denying his authority to do so. Cases in which persons have been held jointly liable on this principle are to be found in the books.[12] The case of *Scarf v. Jardine,*[13] which seems at first sight to throw some doubt on this doctrine, is really not opposed to it."[14]

He went on to explain that, in *Scarf v. Jardine,* the retired partner was at no time held out as a partner in the new firm.[15]

---

[7] Given the terms of *ibid.* s.12, *infra*, para. 13–12, the debts and obligations referred to must arise by way of contract; see also *Friend v. Young* [1897] 2 Ch. 421; *Bagel v. Miller* [1903] 2 K.B. 212. But note the anomalous position of a firm's liability for breach of trust under *ibid.* s.13: see *infra*, para. 13–13.

[8] This should be construed as including a reference to Northern Ireland: Irish Free State (Consequential Adaptation of Enactments) Order 1923 (S.R. & O. 1923 No. 405), Art. 2.

[9] [2003] 2 A.C. 366 at [110]. Note that the report of this paragraph at [2003] 3 W.L.R. 1913, 1939 is inaccurate.

[10] Partnership Act 1890, s.14, *supra*, paras 5–35 *et seq.*

[11] *Quaere* whether, in such a case, the apparent partners are partners "in a firm": see *ibid.* s.9. It is nevertheless thought that the firm need not actually exist: see also the terms of *ibid.* s.14(1). Note also that *ibid.* s.5 apparently does not apply in the case of holding out: see *Hudgell Yeates & Co. v. Watson* [1978] Q.B. 451, 467 *per* Waller L.J. See also *infra*, para. 13–17, n. 56.

[12] *Waugh v. Carver* (1793) 1 H.Bl.235; see also *supra*, paras 5–35 *et seq.*

[13] (1882) 7 App.Cas. 345.

[14] See further, as to this case, *supra*, para. 5–52.

[15] Lord Lindley observed: "The importance of this case turns on the grounds on which it was held that J. [*the creditor*] could not have sued S. [*the retired partner*] jointly with the members of the new firm. The reason why he could not have done so was that J. did not in fact contract with the new firm upon the faith that S. was a member of it. If it had been proved that J. had so contracted he could, it is apprehended, have sued S. and the other members of the new firm, and have proved S. to have been a partner by estoppel." He referred in particular to the speeches of Lords Selborne and Blackburn at (1882) 7 App.Cas. 350, 357–358. See also *S. Kaprow & Co. v. MacLelland & Co.* [1948] 1 K.B. 618.

Judgment against one partner

It was formerly held that, because partners are only jointly liable, judgment **13–05** against one partner in respect of a partnership debt would discharge the others,[16] but the bar on subsequent proceedings has now been completely removed by section 3 of the Civil Liability (Contribution) Act 1978.[17] Equally, where proceedings between a claimant and one partner are compromised and the terms are incorporated into a consent order, that section will not prevent the release of the other partners by virtue of the doctrine of accord and satisfaction.[18]

Liability of deceased partner's estate

The several liability attaching to a deceased partner's estate is of an excep- **13–06** tional nature and was recognised as such long before the Partnership Act 1890.[19] Indeed, judgment against one or more of the surviving partners would *never* have been a bar to subsequent proceedings against a deceased partner's estate.[20]

Discretion of creditor

The traditional view of the effect of section 9 has always been[21] that it creates **13–07** concurrent rights against the surviving partners and against the deceased partner's estate, so that a creditor may, if he wishes, proceed first against the estate, without the need to show that the surviving partners are insolvent or that the partnership assets are insufficient to meet the partnership debts.[22] Indeed, this view never appears to have been questioned, despite the qualification that the estate is liable "so far as [*the debts*] remain unsatisfied". It would therefore seem

---

[16] *Kendall v. Hamilton* (1879) 4 App.Cas. 504; and see *infra*, paras 13–130, 13–131. Note also *Wilson, Sons & Co. v. Balcarres Brook Steam Co.* [1893] 1 Q.B. 422.

[17] This section also extends to actions for damages, whether tortious, contractual or otherwise: see *ibid.* s.6(1). However, in the case of actions for damages, the plaintiff may be deprived of his costs in any action subsequent to that in which judgment was first given: *ibid.* s.4. See also *infra*, para. 20–23.

[18] *Morris v. Wentworth-Stanley* [1999] Q.B. 1004 (CA).

[19] Lord Lindley wrote: "It has often been said that in equity partnership debts are separate as well as joint; but this proposition is inaccurate and misleading. It is true that a creditor of a partnership can obtain payment of his debt out of the estate of a deceased partner; but the judgment which such a creditor obtains is quite different from that which a separate creditor is entitled to; and it is a mistake to say that the joint creditor of the firm is also in equity a separate creditor of the deceased partner. In Bankruptcy the joint debts of a firm are never treated as joint and several; and yet in Bankruptcy equitable as well as legal principles are always recognised." As to the form of the judgment to which Lord Lindley referred, see *Hills v. M'Rae* (1851) 9 Hare 297; *Re McRae* (1883) 25 Ch.D. 16; *Re Hodgson* (1885) 31 Ch.D. 177; *Re Barnard* (1886) 32 Ch.D. 447; *Moore v. Knight* [1891] 1 Ch. 547, 557; also *infra*, para. 26–16.

[20] *Jacomb v. Harwood* (1751) 2 Ves.Sen. 265; *Liverpool Borough Bank v. Walker* (1859) 4 De.G. & J. 24.

[21] Lord Lindley wrote of s.9, in his Supplement on the Partnership Act 1890: "In the event of the death of a partner, a creditor of the firm has concurrent remedies against the surviving partners and the estate of the deceased partner, and it is immaterial which remedy he pursues first . . . ".

[22] *Wilkinson v. Henderson* (1833) 1 Myl. & K. 582. This is a rule of procedure: it was accordingly held to apply to an action against the executors of a partner in a Spanish firm, who had died in England and left property here, even though such an action would not have been allowed in Spain: see *Re Doetsch, Matheson v. Ludwig* [1896] 2 Ch. 836. See also *infra*, paras 26–14 *et seq*. The necessary corollary is, of course, that the surviving partners (or their separate creditors) cannot force the partnership creditors to proceed first against the deceased partner's estate: *Ex p. Kendall* (1811) 17 Ves.Jr. 514.

that these words must be construed merely as a reference to the *fact* of non-payment; *sed quaere*.[23]

13–08   The position will apparently be no different even where the creditor has taken a joint bond or covenant by way of security for the debt.[24] This was clearly established in *Bishop v. Church*,[25] where two partners had borrowed £2,000, in respect of which they later gave a joint bond. One died and the other went bankrupt. The creditors sought payment out of the deceased partner's estate, which was held to be liable.[26] Similarly, in *Beresford v. Browning*,[27] four partners agreed that, on the death of any of them, the survivors should pay out his share in instalments. Although the agreement did not purport to bind the surviving partners jointly and severally, it was held that the estate of one of them was liable for the instalments due to a partner who had predeceased him.

13–09   Contrary to the position prior to the Partnership Act 1890,[28] the doctrine applied in the above cases cannot now be applied so as to benefit joint creditors at the expense of a deceased partner's *separate* creditors. Section 9 is specific in its effect of postponing all partnership debts and obligations to the deceased's separate debts.[29]

It is clear that, by first seeking payment from the deceased partner's estate, the creditor in no way prejudices his rights against the surviving partners.[30]

Cases where joint liability is express

13–10   Notwithstanding the terms of section 9, it must not be assumed that a deceased partner's estate will be severally liable in all cases, since the terms of the contract may expressly negate such liability, as Lord Lindley explained:

> "If . . . partners enter into a contract binding themselves jointly and not severally, and if such contract is not a mere security for the payment of a debt, or for the performance of a joint and several obligation, and if it has not been made joint in

---

[23] Note that a contrary view appears to be adopted by the editors of *Chitty on Contracts* (30th ed.), para. 17–005.

[24] See, in addition to the other cases cited in this paragraph, *Lane v. Williams* (1692) 2 Vern. 292; *Primrose v. Bromley* (1739) 1 Atk. 90; *Darwent v. Walton* (1742) 2 Atk. 510; and see *Sleech's Case* (1816) 1 Mer. 539; *Devaynes v. Noble* (1839) 2 R. & M. 495; *Smith v. Smith* (1861) 3 Giff. 263. *cf. Turner v. Turner* [1911] 1 Ch. 716.

[25] (1751) 2 Ves.Sen. It was also held that the bond ought to be treated as joint and several, so as to make the estate of the deceased partner liable for a specialty debt, and not merely a simple contract debt.

[26] See also *Simpson v. Vaughan* (1739) 2 Atk. 31; *Thomas v. Frazer* (1797) 3 Ves. Jr. 399; *Burn v. Burn* (1798) 3 Ves. Jr. 573; *Orr v. Chase* (1812) 1 Mer. 729, Appendix.

[27] (1875) 1 Ch.D. 30.

[28] See *Burn v. Burn* (1798) 3 Ves. Jr. 573.

[29] This is expressly recognised in the application of the Insolvency Act 1986 to insolvent partnerships: see *ibid.* ss.175A(1) (as inserted by the Insolvent Partnerships Order 1994, Sched. 4, Pt II, para. 23 and applied, as regards the firm, by the Insolvency Act 1986, s.221(5) (as itself amended by the Insolvent Partnerships Order 1994, art. 8(1) (as amended by the Insolvent Partnerships (Amendment) Order 2002 (SI 2002/1308), art. 4(1)), (2), Sched. 4, Pt I, para. 3 (creditor's petition with concurrent petitions) and *ibid.* art. 10(1)(a), Sched. 6, para. 4 (member's petition with concurrent petitions)) and, as regards insolvent corporate and individual partners, by the Insolvent Partnerships Order 1994, arts 8(4)–(8), 10(2)–(6), as amended by the Insolvent Partnerships (Amendment) Order 2005 (SI 2005/1516), art. 5(b), s.328A(1) (as inserted, where all the partners have presented a joint bankruptcy petition without winding up the firm, by *ibid.*, art. 11(3), Sched. 7, para. 21). *Semble*, the position will be the same in any case not falling within the Insolvent Partnerships Order 1994, arts 8, 10 or 11. See further *infra*, paras 27–78 *et seq.*

[30] *Re Hodgson* (1885) 31 Ch.D. 177.

form by mistake, the effect of the contract will be in equity as in law to impose a joint obligation and no other."[31]

This was the basis for the decision in *Sumner v. Powell*,[32] where a joint indemnity against partnership debts and liabilities was given to the executors of a deceased partner by the surviving partners and by a new partner. The new partner died and the executor sought to rely on the indemnity as against his estate. It was held that the estate was not liable, since the new partner's obligation existed solely by virtue of the indemnity, which was clearly joint in form.

Similarly, in *Clarke v. Bickers*,[33] where two partners had taken a lease of   **13–11**
property and given the tenant's covenants jointly. One partner having died, proceedings were commenced against his estate for breach of the covenants, but it was held[34] that, the covenants being joint, the estate was not liable.

This principle was carried to extreme lengths in *Wilmer v. Currey*,[35] where, on the retirement of a partner, the continuing partners jointly covenanted to pay and indemnify him against the partnership debts and to pay him certain sums of money. One of the continuing partners died and the retired partner sought to enforce the covenant against his estate and against the surviving partner. It was held[36] that the estate was not liable under the covenant, even though it was bound to contribute towards payment of the partnership debts. Lord Lindley observed that "It is . . . difficult to reconcile this case with *Beresford v. Browning*."[37]

B.   LIABILITY IN RESPECT OF TORTS, FRAUDS AND OTHER WRONGS AND MISAPPLICATION OF MONEY AND PROPERTY

Partnership Act 1890, section 12

The joint and several liability of partners for torts, frauds and other wrongs and   **13–12**
the misapplication of money and property received by or in the custody of the firm is clearly established by section 12 of the Partnership Act 1890, which provides:

"12. Every partner is liable jointly with his co-partners and also severally for everything for which the firm while he is a partner therein becomes liable under either of the two last preceding sections."[38]

---

[31] See, in addition to the cases cited in the text, *Rawstone v. Parr* (1827) 3 Russ. 424, 539; *Richardson v. Horton* (1843) 6 Beav. 185; *Jones v. Beach* (1852) 2 De G.M. & G. 886; *Other v. Iveson* (1855) 3 Drew. 177; and see, generally, as to construing a contract to be joint, several or joint and several: *White v. Tyndall* (1888) 13 App.Cas. 263; *Tyser v. Shipowners' Syndicate (Reassured)* [1896] 1 Q.B. 135; *National Society for the Distribution of Electricity, etc. v. Gibbs* [1900] 2 Ch. 280; also *supra*, para. 13–02, n. 4.

[32] (1816) 2 Mer. 30, affirmed at (1823) T. & R. 423.

[33] (1845) 14 Sim. 639. Now, by virtue of the Law of Property Act 1925 and the Trusts of Land and Appointment of Trustees Act 1996, the lease would in any event be held by the partners as joint tenants on a trust of land: see *infra*, para. 18–61. There is, however, no reason why a landlord should not require joint and several covenants from the tenants and, in practice, this is often done.

[34] On demurrer.

[35] (1848) 2 De G. & Sm. 347.

[36] On demurrer.

[37] (1875) 1 Ch.D. 30. The Court of Appeal, however, thought that they were distinguishable: *ibid*.

[38] See ss.10, 11, *supra*, paras 12–88 *et seq.*, 12–104 *et seq.*

This section introduced a partial alteration to the previous law.[39] Thus, it does not now matter whether a misapplication of money involves a breach of contract or a tort: the partners' liability will remain joint and several.[40] The current editor apprehends that the position will be the same in the case of a negligent misrepresentation which gives rise to a claim in damages under section 2(1) of the Misrepresentation Act 1967.[41]

As Lord Millett explained in *Dubai Aluminium Co Ltd. v. Salaam*,[42] notwithstanding that both sections 10 and 11 are compendiously referred to in this section, section 10 renders the firm vicariously liable for the wrongful acts of its partners, whereas section 11 addresses the firm's original liability for the receipt of money by a partner or the firm, *i.e.* they perform very different functions, albeit with the same result in terms of liability.

C.   LIABILITY IN RESPECT OF BREACH OF TRUST

13–13   It is clear that section 12 of the Partnership Act 1890[43] does not apply to breaches of trust for which the firm is liable.[44] Since section 9 of the Act applies only to *contractual* debts and obligations,[45] liability for breach of trust remains as it was prior to the Act, *i.e.* joint and several.[46]

D.   EXTENT OF LIABILITY IN ALL CASES

13–14   A distinct feature of the law of partnership has always been the unlimited liability accepted by partners for the debts and obligations of the firm, as Lord Lindley explained:

> "By the common law of this country, every member of an ordinary partnership is liable to the utmost farthing of his property for the debts and engagements of the firm. The law, ignoring the firm as anything distinct from the persons composing it, treats

---

[39] See generally, as to torts and frauds, *Mitchell v. Tarbutt* (1794) 5 T.R. 649; *Ex p. Adamson* (1878) 8 Ch.D. 807; 1 Wms.Saund. 291 f and g; Com.Dig. Abatement, F.8. The old exception in the case of the wrongful use of land (see 1 Wms.Saund. 291 f and g) was not preserved.

[40] See the discussion in the 5th ed. of this work at pp. 198–200.

[41] See *supra*, para. 12–94 and, *infra*, para. 23–51.

[42] [2003] 2 A.C. 366 at [110]. The report of this paragraph at [2003] 3 W.L.R. 1913, 1939 is inaccurate.

[43] See *supra*, para. 13–12.

[44] Partnership Act 1890, s.13, *supra*, paras 12–127 *et seq.* See also *Dubai Aluminium Co. Ltd. v. Salaam* [2003] 2 A.C. 366, at [110], per Lord Millett. Note, however, that the report of this paragraph at [2003] 3 W.L.R. 1913, 1939 is inaccurate.

[45] See *supra*, para. 13–03. Interestingly, the reference in that section to the "debts and obligations of the firm" is unqualified.

[46] *Blyth v. Fladgate* [1891] 1 Ch. 337, 353 *per* Stirling J. (a decision which in fact predates the coming into force of the Partnership Act 1890); see also *Re National Funds Assurance Co.* (1878) 10 Ch.D. 118; *Re Oxford Benefit Building Society* (1886) 35 Ch.D. 502; *Ex p. Shepherd* (1887) 19 Q.B.D. 84. And see the older cases: *Sleech's Case* (1816) 1 Mer. 539; *Clayton's Case* (1816) 1 Mer. 572; *Baring's Case* (1816) 1 Mer. 611; *Warde's Case* (1816) 1 Mer. 624; *Vulliamy v. Noble* (1817) 3 Mer. 593; *Wilson v. Moore* (1832) 1 Myl. & K. 126 and (1834) *ibid.* 337; *Brydges v. Branfill* (1842) 12 Sim. 369. *cf. Parker v. McKenna* (1874) L.R. 10 Ch.App. 96; *Vyse v. Foster* (1874) L.R. 7 H.L. 318.

the debts and engagements of the firm as the debts and engagements of the partners, and holds each partner liable for them accordingly. Moreover, if judgment is obtained against the firm for a debt owing by it, the judgment creditor is under no obligation to levy execution against the property of the firm before having recourse to the separate property of the partners; nor is he under any obligation to levy execution against all the partners rateably; but he may select any one or more of them and levy execution upon him or them until the judgment is satisfied, leaving all questions of contribution to be settled afterwards between the partners themselves."[47]

Attempts to limit liability

Attempts to avoid such unlimited liability by contract are unlikely to succeed, short of an express stipulation that a creditor of the firm is only entitled to payment out of the partnership assets, with no right of recourse against the partners personally. Although historically such a term has rarely proved commercially acceptable,[48] there are now more frequent instances of such agreements being reached, particularly in the case of leases, as demonstrated by the decision in *Prudential Assurance Co. Ltd. v. Ayres.*[49]   **13–15**

In practice, there are only two real options which offer prospective partners the benefits of limited liability in all cases. First, there is the limited partnership formed under the Limited Partnerships Act 1907[50]; however, this vehicle has proved unpopular in practice, due in large measure to the need to recruit at least one partner who is prepared to accept unlimited liability[51] and to the inability of the limited partners to participate in the management of the firm.[52] The second alternative is the corporate partnership,[53] which naturally precludes the prospective partner from *direct* participation in the venture and thus, to an extent, negates the essentially personal nature of the partnership relation. Although there appears to be a third option, namely the formation of a limited liability partnership, this involves a relationship which does not amount to a partnership in anything but name.[54]

2.   DURATION OF LIABILITY

It has already been seen that a partner is regarded as the agent of the firm for the purposes of carrying on its business in the usual or ordinary way.[55] This section   **13–16**

---

[47] See *Abbott v. Smith* (1760) 2 Wm.Blacks. 947, 949 *per* De Grey C.J.; also Com.Dig. Execution H. See further, as to execution against partners, *infra*, paras 14–87 *et seq.*

[48] In fact, Lord Lindley himself observed that "in modern times [*such stipulations*] are practically confined to Insurance and other companies formed before the passing of the Companies Act 1862."

[49] [2008] 1 All E.R. 1266 (CA). An attempt to argue that the term also benefited the guarantors failed on the construction of the documents. The court appeared to accept that the term would be effective in the event of the firm being wound up as an unregistered company (see *infra*, paras 27–04 *et seq.*), albeit that the other contracting party could then prove for his whole debt: see *ibid.* at [27], [28], [35]. This does, however, raise some difficult issues: see *infra*, para. 27–61 *et seq.*

[50] See *infra*, paras 29–01 *et seq.*

[51] Limited Partnerships Act 1907, s.4(1). Note, however, that the general partner may be a limited company: see *supra*, para. 11–07 and *infra*, para. 29–06.

[52] *ibid.* s.6(1), *infra*, paras 31–02 *et seq.*

[53] See *supra*, paras 11–02 *et seq.*

[54] An LLP is a body corporate, not a partnership: see the Limited Liability Partnerships Act 2000, s.1(2). See also *supra*, paras 2–39 *et seq.*

[55] See the Partnership Act 1890, s.5, *supra*, paras 12–02 *et seq.*

addresses three distinct questions. First, when does a partner's agency (and, thus, his co-partners' liability for his acts) commence? Secondly, when and in what circumstances does such agency terminate? Finally, how can a partner rid himself of a liability once it has accrued?

A.   COMMENCEMENT OF AGENCY

13–17   It is a largely self evident proposition that the agency of a partner presupposes the existence of a partnership; indeed, it has been held that section 5 of the Partnership Act 1890 does not apply in a case of holding out.[56] Lord Lindley put it in these terms:

> "The doctrine that each partner has implied authority to do whatever is necessary to carry on the partnership in the usual way, is based upon the ground that the ordinary business of a firm cannot be carried on either to the advantage of its members or with safety to the public unless such a doctrine is recognised. The existence of a partnership is, therefore, evidently presupposed; and although persons negotiating for a partnership, or about to become partners, *may* be the agents of each other before the partnership commences, such agency, if relied on, must be established in the ordinary way, and is not to be inferred from the mere fact that the persons in question were engaged in the attainment of some common end, or that they have subsequently become partners."[57]

Intended partnership

13–18   It does not follow from the fact that prospective partners have agreed to enter into partnership with effect from a certain date, on terms to be embodied in a formal agreement to be executed on that date, that no partnership will come into existence if execution of the agreement is, in the event, deferred. In such a case, the only relevant question will be: when, as a matter of fact, did the partners begin to carry on business together?[58] If they did so on the agreed date, then the partnership and, thus, the agency of each partner will be treated as commencing on that date.[59] Indeed, it may even be possible to prove an effective commencement of the partnership *prior* to the agreed date.

On the other hand, if the agreement is executed on the correct date, but the business is not in fact commenced for some time thereafter, there can be no implied agency in the interim period.[60] Equally, if in such a case the facts are equivocal or there is nothing to suggest that the partnership commenced at a later

---

[56] See *Hudgell Yeates & Co. v. Watson* [1978] Q.B. 451, 467 *per* Waller L.J. and, *semble*, 471B *per* Megaw L.J. *cf.* the judgment of Bridge L.J. at *ibid.* 462H–463A.

[57] See the authorities cited *supra*, paras 2–17 *et seq.*; also *Gabriel v. Evill* (1842) 9 M. & W. 297; *Edmundson v. Thompson* (1861) 2 F. & F. 564. Lord Lindley observed that "each of those cases in which the [*claimant*] failed is an authority for the proposition that so long as there is no partnership there is no implied authority similar to that which exists after a partnership is formed." And see *Keith Spicer v. Mansell* [1970] 1 W.L.R. 333.

[58] This concept should not be viewed too narrowly: partners may be regarded as carrying on business together even if they have not actually commenced trading: see *Khan v. Miah* [2000] 1 W.L.R. 2123 (HL).

[59] *Battley v. Lewis* (1840) 1 Man. & G. 155: see *supra*, para. 2–26. And see *Floydd v. Cheney* [1970] Ch. 602.

[60] In such a case, no partnership will exist during the interim period: see *supra*, para. 12–06.

or earlier date, each partner's agency will be treated as commencing on the date of the agreement.[61]

Acts preparatory to partnership

Where a person agrees to do some preparatory act prior to entering into partnership, his prospective partners will obviously not be bound thereby. *A fortiori* if the act in question is the acquisition of an asset which is to be brought into the partnership by way of capital contribution or otherwise, as Lord Lindley explained:

13–19

> " . . . if several persons agree to become partners, and contribute each a certain quantity of money or goods for the joint benefit of all, each one is solely responsible to those who may have supplied him with the money or goods agreed to be contributed by him[62]; and the fact that the money or goods so supplied have been brought in by him as agreed will not render the firm liable."[63]

He then referred to *Wilson v. Whitehead*,[64] which was apparently decided on this principle. There, an author and a publisher, who had agreed with a printer to share the profits derived from the publication of a certain work, were held not to be liable for quantities of paper ordered by the printer.[65] However, it would seem that, even assuming the decision to have been correct,[66] it should more properly be regarded as a case of restricted authority.[67]

It must not be assumed that an act which appears to be merely preparatory will always be regarded as such. Thus, in *Khan v. Miah*,[68] where the parties intended to carry on a restaurant business together, the House of Lords readily recognised that the ambit of such a business would extend to the acquisition, conversion and fitting out of suitable premises, so that it could not properly be said that a partnership would only come into existence when the restaurant actually opened for business. Equally, in *Goudberg v. Erniman Associates Pty. Ltd.*[69] it was held that the parties had not done sufficient acts of preparation to constitute a business even though they had "embarked on a project".

13–20

Reference should also be made in this context to two older cases which involved similar facts but strikingly different results. In the first, *Saville v.*

---

[61] See *Williams v. Jones* (1826) 5 B. & C. 108.

[62] See *Greenslade v. Dower* (1828) 7 B. & C. 636; *Dickinson v. Valpy* (1829) 10 B. & C. 128; *Fisher v. Tayler* (1843) 2 Hare 218; also the cases in the next note.

[63] *Smith v. Craven* (1831) 1 C. & J. 500; *Heap v. Dobson* (1863) 15 C.B.(N.S.) 460.

[64] (1842) 10 M. & W. 503. See the observations of Wightman J. on this case in *Kilshaw v. Jukes* (1863) 3 B. & S. 847, 871.

[65] The case was likened to that of coach proprietors, as to which see *Barton v. Hanson* (1809) 2 Taunt. 49. And see *supra*, para. 12–152.

[66] The propriety of the decision was doubted by Wightman J. in *Kilshaw v. Jukes* (1863) 3 B. & S. 847, 871. Moreover, it is difficult to reconcile with *Gardiner v. Childs* (1837) 8 Car. & P. 345.

[67] Lord Lindley submitted that "upon principle *Wilson v. Whitehead* is perfectly correct; for the publisher had no real authority to buy the paper on the author's credit, and no authority so to do ought to be implied in favour of a person who knew nothing of the author or of any partnership or quasi-partnership existing between him and the publisher: see *Kilshaw v. Jukes* (1863) 3 B. & S. 847." And see now the concluding words of the Partnership Act 1890, s.5, *supra*, para. 12–02.

[68] [2000] 1 W.L.R. 2123.

[69] [2007] V.S.C.A. 12 (Sup.Ct. of Victoria) at [24]. Unaccountably, the decision in *Khan v. Miah* appears not to have been cited to the court, although the current editor doubts whether this would have led to a different decision on the particular facts.

Robertson,[70] several persons agreed to embark on a venture involving the shipment of certain goods. It was provided that each participant's share in the venture should be proportionate to the quantity of goods which he ordered and shipped and that no participant should be responsible for goods ordered or shipped by another. One ordered goods but did not pay for them and the supplier sought payment from the others on the basis that they were liable as his partners. The court held that the partnership did not commence until the goods were on board ship, that each partner was only to bring in his share of the cargo and that the other partners were not liable to the supplier of the goods which made up the defaulting partner's share.[71]

13–21   The venture in *Gouthwaite v. Duckworth*[72] was of a similar nature, but two of the participants, Browne and Powell, were already in partnership together and were indebted to the third, Duckworth. It was agreed that the goods should be bought, paid for, and shipped by Browne and Powell and the proceeds of sale remitted to Duckworth, who would apply them in settlement of his debt, any remaining profit (or loss) being shared between the three. In pursuance of this agreement, Browne bought certain goods on credit, for which all three partners were ultimately held liable, on the basis that, even though it was never intended that Duckworth should pay for the goods, the partnership commenced at and from the moment of their purchase. Of this case, Lord Lindley said:

> "There is considerable difficulty in supporting this decision if rested on the ground of partnership and implied agency resulting therefrom; for it is not easy to see how any partnership existed prior to the purchase of the goods. But if rested on the ground of agency independently of partnership, there is not the same difficulty. For although the goods were to be paid for by Browne and Powell, that might be regarded as nothing more than a stipulation to take effect as between them and Duckworth; it did not necessarily exclude the inference that as Browne and Powell were to buy for the adventure, they were at liberty to procure the goods on the credit of all concerned."[73]

Incoming partners

13–22   It follows from the foregoing that the members of an existing firm will not be liable for the acts of an incoming partner prior to the date of his admission; the corollary is also true, *i.e.* that the incoming partner will not be liable for their acts prior to that date. Lord Lindley put it in this way:

> " . . . the firm is not distinguishable from the persons from time to time composing it; and when a new member is admitted he becomes one of the firm for the future, but not as from the past, and his present connection with the firm is no evidence that he ever expressly or impliedly authorised what may have been done prior to his

---

[70] (1792) 4 T.R. 720. See also *Kilshaw v. Jukes* (1863) 3 B. & S. 847; *Hutton v. Bullock* (1874) L.R. 9 Q.B. 572.

[71] See also *supra*, para. 12–79.

[72] (1811) 12 East 421. *Kilshaw v. Jukes* (1863) 3 B. & S. 847 was a similar case, but the decision accorded with that in *Saville v. Robertson, supra*.

[73] See the judgment of Gibbs J. in *Young v. Hunter* (1812) 4 Taunt. 582, 583. *Gouthwaite v. Duckworth* was, in fact, followed and Lord Lindley's criticisms considered in *Karmali Abdullah Allarakhia v. Vora Karimji Jiwanji* (1914) L.R. 42 Ind.App. 48.

admission.[74] It may perhaps be said that the entry of the new partner amounts to a ratification by him of what his now partners may have done before he joined them.[75] But it must be borne in mind that no person can be rendered liable for the act of another on the ground that he has ratified, confirmed, or adopted it, unless, at the time the act was done, it was done professedly on his behalf."[76]

To this might be appended the observation that the admission of an additional partner will, as a matter of law, constitute a new partnership[77] and it should therefore come as no surprise that special circumstances must be shown before that new firm will be treated as having taken over the debts and obligations of the old firm.[78]

Partnership Act 1890, section 17(1)

This principle is expressly recognised by section 17 of the Partnership Act 1890, which provides: **13–23**

> "17.—(1) A person who is admitted as a partner into an existing firm does not thereby become liable to the creditors of the firm for anything done before he became a partner."

Scope of section 17(1)

Because section 17(1) of the Partnership Act 1890 is expressed in purely   **13–24** negative terms, it does not in itself render an incoming partner liable for debts contracted *after* he became a partner, and the extent of his liability will ultimately depend on the application of normal agency principles.[79] Thus, if a customer refuses to recognise the existence of the new firm and insists on dealing with a member of the old firm, the incoming partner will not in general incur any liability *vis-à-vis* that customer. This was the position in *British Homes Assurance Corporation Ltd. v. Paterson*.[80] There, the claimants, who habitually employed the services of a solicitor, Atkinson (who practised under the name "Atkinson and Atkinson"), instructed him to act on their behalf in a mortgage transaction. Shortly after receiving these instructions, Atkinson took Paterson into partnership, informing the claimants that he had done so and that the business would in future be carried on under the name "Atkinson and Paterson". The claimants ignored this communication and continued to correspond with Atkinson under the old name. The claimants then sent Atkinson a cheque, made payable to "Atkinson and Atkinson or order", to complete the mortgage transaction. Atkinson indorsed the cheque and signed the receipt in that name, the

---

[74] See, for example, *Ex p. Jackson* (1790) 1 Ves. Jr. 131; *Young v. Hunter* (1812) 4 Taunt. 582. Lord Lindley also referred to *Beale v. Mouls* (1843) 10 Q.B. 976 and a number of other cases demonstrating that the same principle applies as between the promoters of a company: see *Kerridge v. Hesse* (1839) 9 Car. & P. 200; *Whitehead v. Barron* (1839) 2 Moo. & Rob. 248; *Bremner v. Chamberlayne* (1848) 2 Car. & K. 569; *Newton v. Belcher* (1848) 12 Q.B. 921; *cf. Beech v. Eyre* (1843) 5 Man. & G. 415.

[75] See *Horsley v. Bell* (1778) 1 Bro.C.C. 101n. *per* Gould J.

[76] *Wilson v. Tumman* (1843) 6 Man. & G. 236; *Keighley Maxsted & Co. v. Durant* [1901] A.C. 240.

[77] See *supra*, paras 3–04 *et seq.*

[78] This sentence was cited with apparent approval by Lloyd J. in *In the matter of Burton Marsden Douglas* [2004] 3 All E.R. 222 at [28]. See also *ibid.* at [33].

[79] See *supra*, paras 12–01 *et seq.*

[80] [1902] 2 Ch. 404.

receipt then being sent to and accepted by the claimants. Atkinson paid the cheque into his personal account, misapplied the proceeds and absconded. Paterson knew nothing of the transaction. It was held that the claimants, by their conduct after receiving notice that Paterson had joined the firm, had elected to abide by the original contract with Atkinson alone and, therefore, declined to accept the joint liability of the two partners; they were, accordingly, bound by that election and could not thereafter pursue Paterson.[81]

New contract

13–25   Equally, the nature of the contractual arrangement with the existing firm may be such that the existence of a fresh contract entered into after the admission of the new partner can be inferred, thus rendering him liable on normal principles.[82] In *Dyke v. Brewer*,[83] the claimant had agreed to supply A with bricks at a price quoted per thousand. After supplies began, A took B into partnership. The claimant continued to supply bricks as before. A and B were both held liable to pay for the bricks supplied after the commencement of the partnership, at the rate originally quoted to A. The basis for the decision was that A had not ordered a specific number of bricks, so that each separate delivery and acceptance involved a new implied promise to pay on the terms previously agreed; had all the bricks delivered been ordered by A in the first instance, B would not have been liable.[84] Obviously, situations in which this principle can be invoked will be relatively rare, as is clear from *In the matter of Burton Mardsen*.[85]

Agreement to take on existing debts

13–26   It is, of course, open to an incoming partner voluntarily to take on liability for the existing firm's debts; indeed, the offer of partnership will often be made conditional on him so doing. Whilst such an agreement may be inferred, there is no presumption that, merely because the whole business and assets of the existing firm are taken over, so are its liabilities.[86] However, different principles apply in Scotland.[87]

---

[81] The court held also that the money had never come into the custody of the firm: see the Partnership Act 1890, s.11, *supra*, paras 12–98 *et seq.*

[82] See *supra*, paras 12–11 *et seq.* It should be noted that this is *not* a case of novation.

[83] (1849) 2 Car. & K. 828.

[84] *Helsby v. Mears* (1826) 5 B. & C. 504 was decided on the same basis: see *Beale v. Mouls* (1843) 10 Q.B. 976, 984 *per* Lord Denman.

[85] See [2004] 3 All E.R. 222 at [31], [32] *per* Lloyd J.

[86] See *Creasey v. Breachwood Motors Ltd.* [1992] B.C.C. 638 (albeit overruled, as to the main part of the decision by *Ord v. Belhaven Pubs Ltd.* [1998] 2 B.C.L.C. 447); also *HF Pension Trustees Ltd. v. Ellison* [1999] Lloyd's Rep. PN 489, 492 *per* Parker J.; *cf. Carter v. Freeman Group Plc* [2008] EWHC 3576 (QB) (Lawtel 26/8/08), where the partnership business had been transferred to a company. Note that in *Hammonds (A Firm) v. Danilunas* [2009] EWHC 216 (Ch) (Lawtel 18/2/09), Warren J. expressly declined to decide this issue: see *ibid.* at [117] (this issue was not pursued on the appeal). See also *supra*, para. 10–56. It should, nevertheless, be noted that, in the case of a solicitors' partnership, a "new" firm will be required to take on responsibility for insuring the "old" firm's liabilities, if (as will often be the case) it is regarded as a successor practice within the meaning of Appendix 1 to the current Solicitors' Indemnity Insurance Rules: see, for example, the article "Lateral Thinking" at (2005) 102 L.S.Gaz., March 24, p. 19.

[87] See, for example, *Miller v. MacLeod* 1973 S.C. 172; also *Ocra (Isle of Man) Ltd. v. Anite Scotland Ltd.* 2003 S.L.T. 1232 (OH). In the course of his judgment in *Creasey v. Breachwood Motors Ltd., supra*, Richard Southwell Q.C. (sitting as a deputy judge of the Queen's Bench Division) reviewed a number of Scots authorities and held that the principles established thereby were not applicable under English law.

Where an incoming partner agrees to the debts of the existing firm being discharged out of profits received after the date of his admission, he will be accepting liability for those debts, *vis-à-vis* his co-partners, if his profit share is thereby reduced. It must be emphasised that entry into such an agreement will not render the incoming partner directly liable to creditors of the firm, as Lord Lindley explained:

" . . . if an incoming partner agrees with his co-partners that the debts of the old shall be taken by the new firm, this, although valid and binding between the partners, is, as regards strangers, *res inter alios acta*, and does not confer upon them any right to fix the old debts on the new partner.[88] In order to render an incoming partner liable to the creditors of the old firm, there must be some agreement, express or tacit, to that effect entered into between him and the creditors, and founded on some sufficient consideration. If there be any such agreement, the incoming partner will be bound by it, but his liabilities in respect of the old debts will attach by virtue of the new agreement, and not by reason of his having become a partner."[89]

Evidence of agreement

An incoming partner's agreement to take on *direct* liability for the existing debts of the firm will usually be a matter of inference.[90] Lord Lindley observed:

13–27

"The Courts, it has been said, lean in favour of such an agreement, and are ready to infer it from slight circumstances[91]; and they seem formerly to have inferred it whenever the incoming partner agreed with the other partners to treat such debts as those of the new firm.[92] But this certainly is not enough, for the agreement to be proved is an agreement with the creditor; and of such an agreement an agreement between the partners is of itself no evidence."[93]

Although the courts would not now be ready to draw the necessary inference,[94] as regards the incoming partner, the question is likely to be of only academic interest since the *quantum* of his potential liability will be unaffected.[95]

---

[88] See *Vere v. Ashby* (1829) 10 B & C. 288, 298 *per* Parke J.; also *Ex p. Peele* (1802) 6 Ves. Jr. 602; *Ex p. Williams* (1817) Buck 13. And note the decision in *Carter v. Freeman Group Plc, supra.*

[89] This passage was cited with approval in *HF Pension Trustees Ltd. v. Ellison, supra*, p. 492; see also *In the matter of Burton Marsden Douglas* [2004] 3 All E.R. 222 at [31].

[90] In practice, the partners may not wish to draw attention to the change in the firm or, for that matter, to offer a creditor *additional* rights. Nevertheless, in the case of leases, landlords now sometimes require incoming partners to enter into express surety covenants: see *supra*, para. 12–160 and, *infra*, para. 18–61.

[91] *Ex p. Jackson* (1790) 1 Ves. Jr. 131; *Ex p. Peele* (1802) 6 Ves. Jr. 602. See also *Rolfe v. Flower* (1865) L.R. 1 P.C. 27.

[92] See *Cooke's Bankruptcy Law* (8th ed.), p. 534, citing *Ex p. Bingham* and *Ex p. Clowes* (1789) 2 Bro.C.C. 595.

[93] *Ex p. Peele* (1802) 6 Ves. Jr. 602; *Ex p. Parker* (1842) 2 M.D. & D. 511. See also *Ex p. Williams* (1817) Buck 13; *Ex p. Freeman* (1819) Buck 471; *Ex p. Fry* (1821) 1 Gl. & J. 96.

[94] As in *HF Pension Trustees Ltd. v. Ellison* [1999] Lloyd's Rep. PN 489, which concerned pre-merger liabilities.

[95] If the partnership is solvent, the incoming partner will be bound to contribute his due share of the liability, either by way of a reduction in his profit share or by way of contribution. If the other partners are insolvent, have absconded or are otherwise beyond the jurisdiction of the court, the creditor can in any event present a petition to wind up the firm, in which case the incoming partner, *qua* contributory, will be unable to evade the liability which he originally agreed to undertake. See further, *infra*, paras 27–61 *et seq.*

13–28   An example of the type of evidence required to establish such an agreement is to be found in *Ex p. Whitmore*.[96] In that case Warwick, having taken Clagett into partnership, duly informed persons with whom he had previously had business dealings in America of this fact, requesting them to make up their accounts and to transfer any balance due to or from him to the new firm. These instructions were subsequently repeated and confirmed by both Warwick and Clagett and acted on. A debt owing from Warwick was treated as a debt of the new firm and a bill of exchange was drawn on the firm for the amount of the debt. This bill was accepted but later dishonoured. On the bankruptcy of the firm, it was held that the debt had become the joint debt of Warwick and Clagett and that their joint liability had been accepted in substitution for the sole liability of Warwick.

Fraud on new partner

13–29   If the incoming partner has *not* agreed to undertake liability for the debts of the existing firm, but the other partners nevertheless settle such a debt by means of a bill of exchange drawn and accepted in his and their names, this will prima facie amount to a fraud on the incoming partner and he will not be liable on the bill.[97] On the same principle, it is considered that an incoming partner will not be bound if one of his co-partners states an account, admitting that such a debt is due from the new firm.[98]

The position in the case of an open running account maintained both before and after the date of the incoming partner's admission is more complex, as will been seen hereafter.[99]

B.   TERMINATION OF AGENCY

13–30 It is a self evident proposition that each partner's express or implied authority to bind the firm will, on normal agency principles, continue until such time as it is revoked and notice of the revocation is given to any third party with whom he deals.[100] Of a partner's *implied* authority, Lord Lindley said:

> "The same reason which leads to the imputation of the power to act for the firm at all, demands that such power shall be imputed so long as it can be exercised and is not known to have been determined."[101]

It is the latter question, *i.e.* notice of the revocation of a partner's authority, that gives rise to difficulty in practice.

---

[96] (1838) 3 Deac. 365. See also *Rolfe v. Flower* (1865) L.R. 1 P.C. 27.

[97] See *Shirreff v. Wilks* (1800) 1 East 48. See also *supra*, para. 12–146.

[98] See *French v. French* (1841) 2 Man. & G. 644; *Lemere v. Elliott* (1861) 6 H. & N. 656. This sentence was cited with apparent approval by Lloyd J. in *In the matter of Burton Marsden Douglas* [2004] 3 All E.R. 222 at [31].

[99] See *infra*, paras 13–85 *et seq.*

[100] See *supra*, paras 12–137 *et seq.*

[101] See *Lindern Trawler Managers. v. W. H. J. Trawlers* (1949) 83 Ll.L.Rep. 131. And see also *Scarf v. Jardine* (1882) 7 App.Cas. 345, *supra*, paras 5–52, 13–04.

Express revocation

Implied authority

There is very little authority on the ability of a partner unilaterally to revoke **13–31** the authority of his co-partner whilst the partnership continues; the Partnership Act 1890 is itself silent on the point. Writing prior to that Act, Lord Lindley put forward the following view:

"The agency of each partner in an ordinary firm, and his consequent power to bind the firm, *i.e.* himself and his co-partners, may be determined by notice at any time during the continuance of the partnership[102]; for his power to act for the firm is not a right attaching to him as partner independently of the will of his co-partners, and although any stipulations amongst the partners themselves will not affect non-partners who have not notice of them, yet if any person has notice that one member of the firm is not authorised to act for it, that person cannot hold the firm liable for anything done in the teeth of such notice."[103]

On the other hand, in the 6th[104] and subsequent editions of this work, the following view was espoused:

"On general principles it would seem that unless he is in a position to dissolve the firm a notice that he will no longer be bound by their acts will be inoperative."[105]

The inconclusive discussion of revocation in *Bourne v. Davis*[106] does not amount to authority for or against the proposition that one partner can unilaterally revoke another's authority under section 5 of the 1890 Act.

Faced with these conflicting opinions, it is submitted that, in the absence of **13–32** some contrary agreement,[107] the true position as between the partners is as follows:

1. A revocation which purports to exclude one or more partners from their rightful participation in the management of the partnership business cannot be effective.[108]

2. Subject thereto, a majority of the partners may properly decide to introduce an express or implied limitation on the authority of each and every partner, if that can be justified as an ordinary matter connected

[102] Lord Lindley referred specifically to *Gallway v. Matthew* (1808) 10 East 264; *Willis v. Dyson* (1816) 1 Stark. 164; *Rooth v. Quin* (1819) 7 Price 193; *Vice v. Fleming* (1827) 1 Y. & J. 227. See also *Ex p. Holdsworth* (1841) 1 M.D. & D. 475.

[103] See *supra*, paras 12–137 *et seq.* But note the precise terms of the Partnership Act 1890, s.8, *supra*, para. 12–138.

[104] Lord Lindley apparently approved the contents of this edition.

[105] A dissolution will not itself terminate the other partners' authority: see the Partnership Act 1890, s.38, *infra*, paras 13–62 *et seq.*

[106] [2006] EWHC 1567 (Ch) (Lawtel 22/6/07) at [30] *per* Mark Herbert Q.C. (sitting as a deputy judge of the Chancery Division).

[107] See, in particular, *supra*, paras 10–146 *et seq.*

[108] Partnership Act 1890, ss.19, 24(5), 25: see *supra*, paras 10–12 *et seq.* and *infra*, paras 15–01 *et seq.*, 24–99. Note that there was a purported revocation of a partner's implied authority (limited to the service of a counter notice under the agricultural holdings legislation) in *Sykes v. Land* (1984) 271 E.G. 1264, but its effectiveness was not commented on by the court; a similar point was left open in *Re Sutherland & Partners' Appeal* [1993] S.T.C. 399 and was not commented on in the Court of Appeal *sub nom. Sutherland v. Gustar* [1994] Ch. 304.

with the partnership business.[109] This may take the form of a resolution that certain acts will, in the future, require the concurrence of two partners, *e.g.* cheque signing, or an alteration in the way in which the partnership business is carried on which incidentally alters the scope of each partner's implied authority.[110]

3. An attempt to place limitations on the implied authority of a single partner or group of partners would be unlikely to qualify as an ordinary matter and would, therefore, appear to be improper.[111] However, it *may* still be permissible to introduce such a restriction if it can genuinely be said to be required for the protection of the firms interests, *e.g.* in the run up to a partner's retirement.[112]

13–33 A purported, but invalid, revocation of a partner's authority would not take effect as a notice of dissolution,[113] nor could it amount to an act of repudiation,[114] but it would prima facie give grounds for seeking an order dissolving the partnership.[115]

Of course, until such time as an *effective* revocation has been communicated to third parties, it can only have effect as between the partners *inter se*.[116]

Express authority

13–34 If express authority has been conferred on a partner under the terms of the partnership agreement, any attempt to revoke that authority would obviously involve varying those terms. On that basis, it is submitted that a purported revocation would only be valid if it is expressly or impliedly accepted by the relevant partner,[117] if the agreement permits such a variation to be introduced against his wishes[118] or, perhaps, where this can be justified as required for the protection of the firm.[119] In any other circumstances, there would be a clear, albeit not repudiatory,[120] breach of the agreement, as well as grounds for seeking a dissolution.[121]

On the other hand, if authority is only conferred on an *ad hoc* basis, it can prima facie be revoked at any time.[122]

Notice of purported revocation

13–35 If the express or implied authority of a partner is purportedly revoked and a third party is notified of such revocation, he can thereafter safely deal with that partner only *qua* principal.[123] However, there would seem to be no reason why

---

[109] See *ibid.* s.24(8), *infra*, paras 15–04 *et seq.*
[110] *ibid.* s.19, *supra*, paras 10–12 *et seq.*
[111] But see *supra*, n. 108.
[112] See *supra*, para. 10–148.
[113] See *infra*, para. 24–22.
[114] See *infra*, paras 24–05 *et seq.*
[115] Partnership Act 1890, s.35(d), (f): see *infra*, paras 24–80 *et seq.*, 24–89.
[116] See *Gleadon v. Tinkler* (1817) Holt, N.P. 586; also, *supra*, para. 12–137.
[117] Partnership Act 1890, s.19, *supra*, para. 10–12.
[118] See *supra*, para. 10–13.
[119] See *supra*, paras 10–146, 13–32.
[120] See *infra*, paras 24–05 *et seq.*
[121] See the Partnership Act 1890, s.35(d), (f), *infra*, paras 24–80 *et seq.*, 24–89.
[122] See *Tomlinson v. Broadsmith* [1896] 1 Q.B. 386 (managing partner).
[123] See *supra*, paras 12–143 *et seq.*

he should not hold the firm liable as an undisclosed principal[124] if the partner's authority did in fact continue; *sed quaere.*

It is submitted that the act of giving notice of a wrongful revocation, whilst not involving a repudiatory breach of the partnership agreement,[125] could found a claim for a dissolution.[126]

Mental incapacity

If a partner becomes subject to a mental disorder or incapacity but this is neither apparent nor made known,[127] his power to bind the firm and his liability for the acts of his co-partners[128] will seemingly be unaffected.   **13–36**

Outgoing partners

It is obvious that when a person ceases to be a partner, he will no longer be the agent of his co-partners nor they his agents, save for the purpose of winding up the firm's affairs (should that be required).[129] However, as regards third parties, effective termination of each partner's ostensible agency will normally depend on notice having been given of the change in or the dissolution of the firm (as the case may be). It is here that difficulties frequently arise.   **13–37**

Position prior to the Partnership Act 1890

Lord Lindley summarised the position in these terms: **13–38**

" . . . when a dormant (*i.e.* non-apparent) partner retires, he need give no notice of his retirement in order to free himself from liability in respect of acts done after his retirement.[130] The reason is that, as he was never known to be a partner, no one can have relied on his connection with the firm, or truly allege that, when dealing with the firm, he continued to rely on the fact that the dormant partner was still connected therewith.

But when an ostensible partner retires, or when a partnership between several known partners is dissolved, the case is very different; for then those who dealt with the firm before a change took place are entitled to assume that no change has occurred until they have notice to the contrary.[131] And even those who never had dealings with the firm, and who only knew of its existence by repute, are entitled to assume that it still exists until something is done to notify publicly that it exists no longer.[132] An old customer, however, is entitled to a more specific notice than a person who never dealt with the firm at all[133]; and in considering whether notice of

---

[124] See *supra*, para. 12–151.

[125] See *infra*, paras 24–05 *et seq.*

[126] See the Partnership Act 1890, s.35(d), (f), *infra*, paras 24–80 *et seq.*, 24–89.

[127] The position may be otherwise if Court of Protection proceedings have been initiated or a deputy has been appointed: see *supra*, para. 4–13.

[128] See *Imperial Loan Co. v. Stone* [1892] 1 Q.B. 599; also *Baxter v. The Earl of Portsmouth* (1826) 5 B. & C. 170; *Molton v. Camroux* (1849) 4 Ex. 17; *Drew v. Nunn* (1879) 4 Q.B.D. 661. And see *infra*, paras 24–64 *et seq.*

[129] See the Partnership Act 1890, s.38, *infra*, paras 13–62 *et seq.*

[130] See now the Partnership Act 1890, s.36(3), *infra*, para. 13–40.

[131] *Scarf v. Jardine* (1882) 7 App.Cas. 345, 349 *per* Lord Selborne. See now the Partnership Act 1890, s.36(1), *infra*, para. 13–40.

[132] *Parkin v. Carruthers* (1800) 3 Esp. 248. See now the Partnership Act 1890, s.36(1), *infra*, para. 13–40.

[133] *Graham v. Hope* (1792) Peake 208. See now the Partnership Act 1890, s.36(1), (2), *infra*, para. 13–40.

dissolution or retirement is or is not sufficient, a distinction must be made according as the person sought to be affected by notice was or was not a customer of the old firm."

Position under the Partnership Act 1890

13–39   The Partnership Act 1890 embodies precisely the same principles. The relevant sections will be set out in full and then considered under three natural headings, namely: (a) when such notice requires to be given and when it may be dispensed with; (b) the effect of such notice, once given; and (c) the form of such notice.

Partnership Act 1890, sections 36 and 37

13–40   The Partnership Act 1890 provides as follows:

> "36.—(1) Where a person deals with a firm[134] after a change in its constitution he is entitled to treat all apparent members[135] of the old firm as still being members of the firm until he has notice of the change.
>
> (2) An advertisement in the *London Gazette* as to a firm whose principal place of business is in England or Wales, in the *Edinburgh Gazette* as to a firm whose principal place of business is in Scotland, and in the [*Belfast*][136] *Gazette* as to a firm whose principal place of business is in Ireland, shall be notice as to persons who had no dealings with the firm before the date of the dissolution or change so advertised.
>
> (3) The estate of a partner who dies, or who becomes bankrupt, or of a partner who, not having been known to the person dealing with the firm to be a partner, retires from the firm, is not liable for partnership debts contracted after the date of the death, bankruptcy, or retirement[137] respectively.[138]
>
> 37. On the dissolution of a partnership or retirement[139] of a partner any partner may publicly notify the same, and may require the other partner or partners to concur for that purpose in all necessary or proper acts, if any, which cannot be done without his or their concurrence."

(a) Need for Notice

Position in absence of notice

13–41   Section 36(1) of the Partnership Act 1890 merely applies the normal rules of agency to an outgoing partner, *i.e.* the implied authority of his co-partners will

---

[134] Note that in *Hussein v. Commissioners of Customs & Excise* [2003] V. & D.R. 439 at [50], the VAT Tribunal held that the then Commissioners of Customs & Excise were capable of being a person who "deals with a firm" within the meaning of s.36(1); *cf. Revenue & Customs Commissioners v. Pal* [2008] S.T.C. 2442 (a decision under *ibid.* s.14). Equally, it should be noted that the Value Added Tax Act 1994, s.45(2) (*infra*, para. 37–08) is expressly stated to have effect without prejudice to s.36.

[135] In his Supplement on the Partnership Act 1890, Lord Lindley queried whether these words were intended to refer only to those partners whose names are included in the firm name, but concluded that the question was of no practical importance, since persons who are otherwise known to be partners would, under the pre-existing law, have been liable in any event. And see *Tower Cabinet Co. Ltd. v. Ingram* [1949] 2 K.B. 397; *Bishop v. Tudor Estates* [1952] C.L.Y. 2493; *Hamerhaven Pty Ltd. v. Ogge* [1996] 2 V.R. 488; *Wood v. Fresher Foods Ltd.* [2008] 2 N.Z.L.R. 248.

[136] A reference to the Belfast *Gazette* is substituted for the Dublin *Gazette* by virtue of the General Adaptation of Enactments (Northern Ireland) Order 1921 (S.R. & O. 1921 No. 1804), art. 7(a).

[137] Of course, in the case of a partnership at will, the retirement of a partner may result in a dissolution: see the Partnership Act 1890, s.26(1), 32(c), *infra*, paras 24–18 *et seq.* As to what falls to be treated as a retirement, see *infra*, para. 13–43.

[138] See *Court v. Berlin* [1897] 2 Q.B. 396, *infra*, para. 13–54.

[139] See *supra*, n. 137.

continue until notice of its revocation is given.[140] Thus, if no notice is given, an outgoing partner may be liable on a promissory note given by his former partners after the date of his departure.[141]

Liability under the subsection is independent of (and strictly distinguishable from) that imposed in cases of pure holding out,[142] since a prospective claimant does not have to prove any form of reliance other than the fact that he dealt with the firm. His previous dealings with the firm (or lack of them) are prima facie irrelevant.

Partially dormant partner

A truly dormant partner will, by definition, not be an apparent member of the firm, so that section 36(1) will not apply to him.[143] If, however, his existence has been disclosed to any third party with whom the firm has had dealings, notice must be given to that third party if continuing liability is to be avoided.[144]   **13–42**

Expelled partner

Although sections 36 and 37 refer only to the "retirement" of a partner, it is submitted that they will equally apply where a partner is expelled under an express power in the agreement.[145]   **13–43**

Torts

Whilst section 36(1) will not in its terms apply,[146] an outgoing partner who fails to give notice of his retirement may also expose himself to the risk of liability in respect of torts committed by his co-partners.[147]   **13–44**

Unilateral power to notify retirement or dissolution

Each partner is given an express statutory power to give notice of the dissolution of the partnership or of the retirement (or expulsion)[148] of a partner.[149] However, that right may be excluded by agreement.[150] If, in the absence of any such agreement, a partner is prevented from exercising that right, his co-partners   **13–45**

---

[140] See *Mulford v. Griffin* (1858) 1 F. & F. 145; *Faldo v. Griffin* (1858) 1 F. & F. 147. And see *supra*, paras 5–45 *et seq.*, 12–31.

[141] See *Parkin v. Carruthers* (1800) 3 Esp. 248; *Brown v. Leonard* (1816) 2 Chitty 120; *Williams v. Keats* (1817) 2 Stark. 290; *Dolman v. Orchard* (1825) 2 C. & P. 104. See further, *supra*, paras 5–48, 5–49.

[142] Partnership Act 1890, s.14, *supra*, paras 5–35 *et seq.*

[143] See *infra*, paras 13–53 *et seq.*

[144] See the Partnership Act 1890, s.36(3). This was also the position before the Act: see *Farrar v. Deflinne* (1844) 1 Car. & K. 580; also *Evans v. Drummond* (1801) 4 Esp. 89; *Carter v. Whalley* (1830) 1 B. & Ad. 11.

[145] But note that the Partnership Act 1890 does contain *one* reference to expulsion: see *ibid.* s.25, *infra*, para. 24–99. And see generally, as to powers of expulsion, *supra*, paras 10–113 *et seq.*

[146] The section only applies in favour of a person who "deals with a firm"; and see also s.36(3).

[147] See *Stables v. Eley* (1825) 1 Car. & P. 614, where the true circumstances were proved but liability was based on holding out. However, it is doubtful whether this decision was correct: see *supra*, para. 5–61.

[148] See *supra*, para. 13–43.

[149] Partnership Act 1890, s.37, *supra*, para. 13–40.

[150] See *supra*, para. 10–251.

can be compelled to do whatever may be necessary to ensure that the requisite notice is given, *e.g.* to sign advertisements for publication in the *Gazette*.[151]

Circumstances where no notice required

13–46   Section 36(3) of the Partnership Act 1890 provides for three obvious exceptions to the general rule, in which freedom from continuing liability is not dependent on notice.

(1) *Death*

13–47   It is settled law that the authority of an agent is determined by the death of his principal, so that, even before the Partnership Act 1890, Lord Lindley could write:

> "Notice of death is not requisite to prevent liability from attaching to the estate of a deceased partner, in respect of what may be done by his co-partners after his decease."[152]

Authority given on behalf of firm

13–48   However, if a partner authorises a person to do an act, but the authority in fact derives from the firm, it will be unaffected by that partner's death and any subsequent exercise will bind the surviving partners. Thus, in *Usher v. Dauncey*,[153] a partner drew and indorsed a number of bills of exchange in blank and gave them to a clerk to be completed and negotiated as and when required. The partner died and the firm name was altered. The clerk then completed and negotiated one of the bills. Lord Ellenborough held that the bill was binding on the surviving partners, on the footing that the clerk's authority derived from the firm and not from the deceased partner.

Contribution due from deceased partner

13–49   Even though a deceased partner's estate may not be *directly* liable for the acts of the surviving partners after the date of death, it may nevertheless be liable to contribute towards debts and liabilities incurred after that date. This will, however, depend on the precise terms agreed.[154]

(2) *Insolvency*

13–50   Again, the effect of a partner's bankruptcy is just as it was prior to the Partnership Act 1890, as is clear from the following observation made by Lord Lindley:

---

[151] *Troughton v. Hunter* (1854) 18 Beav. 470; *Hendry v. Turner* (1886) 32 Ch.D. 355.

[152] See now the Partnership Act 1890, s.14(2), s.36(3), *supra*, paras 5–35, 13–40; *Friend v. Young* [1897] 2 Ch. 421. Lord Lindley referred to *Webster v. Webster* (1791) 3 Swan. 490; *Devaynes v. Noble, Houlton's Case* (1816) 1 Mer. 616; *Johnes' Case* (1816) 1 Mer. 619; *Brice's Case* (1816) 1 Mer. 620. Also *Vulliamy v. Noble* (1817) 3 Mer. 593; *Brown v. Gordon* (1852) 16 Beav. 302, as to the position of surviving partners who are the executors of a deceased partner's will.

[153] (1814) 4 Camp. 97.

[154] See *Blakeley's Executor's Case* (1851) 3 Mac. & G. 726; *Hamer's Devisees' Case* (1852) 2 De G.M. & G. 366; *Baird's Case* (1870) L.R. 5 Ch. App. 725; also *McClean v. Kennard* (1874) L.R. 9 Ch. App. 356.

"If one partner only becomes bankrupt, his authority is at an end,[155] and his estate cannot be made liable for the subsequent acts of his solvent co-partners."[156]

Equally, if the solvent partners continue to hold the bankrupt partner out as a member of the firm, they will be liable for *his* acts.[157] If the partnership is dissolved by reason of the bankruptcy,[158] the solvent partners will, of course, have authority to wind up the firm's affairs.[159] On the other hand, if *all* the partners are bankrupt, no-one will have authority to wind up the firm's affairs, not even a bankrupt partner's trustee.[160]

Insolvency of corporate partner

Since neither the presentation of a winding up petition nor the making of a winding up order against a corporate partner constitute "bankruptcy",[161] section 36(3) of the 1890 Act will not apply. **13–51**

Insolvency of firm

If, on the other hand, the firm is wound up as an unregistered company,[162] there will be no possibility of subsequent dealings with the firm, otherwise than through the liquidator, so that section 36 of the 1890 Act will be of no relevance. **13–52**

(3) Dormant Partner

Section 36(3) of the Partnership Act 1890 exempts persons who are not known to be partners, *i.e.* truly dormant partners,[163] from the need to give notice of their retirement. Since such persons would not in any event be exposed to continuing liability under section 36(1),[164] such an express exemption was scarcely required. The position was the same prior to the Act, as Lord Lindley explained: **13–53**

"Another apparent but not real exception to the rule is that if a dormant partner (*i.e.* one not known to be a partner) retires, the authority of his late partners to bind him ceases on his retirement, although no notice of it be given.[165] But this is because he never was known to be a partner at all, and the reason for the general rule has therefore no application to his case."

---

[155] See the Partnership Act 1890, ss.33(1), 38, proviso. But note that s.33(1) may be excluded by agreement: see *supra*, para. 10–40 and *infra*, para. 24–32.

[156] Partnership Act 1890, s.36(3), *supra*, para. 13–40.

[157] *ibid.* s.38, proviso, *infra*, para. 13–62. As to the position before the Act, see *Lacy v. Woolcott* (1823) 2 Dow. & Ry. 458.

[158] *ibid.* s.33(1) and, *infra*, paras 24–32 *et seq.*

[159] *ibid.* s.38, *infra*, para. 13–62. See also *infra*, paras 27–67 *et seq.*

[160] *Official Receiver v. Hollens* [2007] Bus. L.R. 1402 at [7] *per* Blackburne J.

[161] See *Andersen Group Pty Ltd. (in liquidation) v. Davies* [2001] N.S.W.S.C. 1482 (a decision on the equivalent of the Partnership Act 1890, s.33(1)); note also *Fryer v. Ewart* [1902] A.C. 187 (HL) (a decision on the Conveyancing and Law of Property Act 1881, s.14(6)). See further *infra*, paras 24–35 *et seq. cf.* the Law of Property Act 1925, s.205(1)(i).

[162] See *infra*, paras 27–59 *et seq.*

[163] As to the position of partners who are only *partially* dormant, see *supra*, para. 13–42.

[164] As dormant partners, they will not at any stage be "apparent members" of the old firm within the meaning of s.36(1). See, generally, *Elders Pastoral Ltd. v. Rutherford* noted at [1991] N.Z.L.J. 73 (a decision under the equivalent provision of the New Zealand Partnership Act 1908); *Hamerhaven Pty Ltd. v. Ogge* [1996] 2 V.R. 488, 451 *per* Callaway J.A.; *Wood v. Fresher Foods Ltd.* [2008] 2 N.Z.L.R. 248.

[165] See the Partnership Act 1890, s.36(3).

Thus, in *Carter v. Whalley*,[166] Saunders was a partner in the "Plas Madoc Colliery Co." but there was no evidence that his involvement in the business was known either to the claimant or to the public at large. Saunders retired but no notice was given of that fact. The firm later became indebted to the claimant. Saunders was held not to be liable for the debt, since the firm name did not indicate the identity of the partners and he was not known to be a partner, either to the claimant or generally, prior to his retirement. *Heath v. Sansom*[167] was a similar case.

13–54   The decision in *Court v. Berlin*[168] requires explanation as an apparent (but not real) exception to this principle. There an active partner in a firm, which comprised himself and two dormant partners, retained a solicitor to conduct an action for the recovery of a partnership debt. The dormant partners retired while the proceedings were still pending, but were nevertheless held liable for the solicitor's costs incurred *after* the date of their retirement, even though the solicitor never knew of their existence. However, the true basis for the decision lay in the nature of the solicitor's retainer, which authorised him to conduct the action until its conclusion[169]; that retainer having been given whilst the dormant partners were still members of the firm, their liability continued on normal principles. Although the retainer could have been terminated by the dormant partners, that would have required notice to the solicitor, which was never given. Accordingly, there was no scope for the application of section 36(3).

Technically dormant partner

13–55   It should be noted that the application of section 36(3) is not confined merely to dormant partners in the true sense: it may equally well apply in the case of a outgoing *active* partner, provided that the conditions are fulfilled at the relevant time. Thus, in *Tower Cabinet Co. v. Ingram*[170] one partner, the defendant, retired, leaving the other to carry on the business in the firm name. Thereafter, the claimant company, which had not previously dealt with or had any knowledge of the firm, received an order from it which, by mistake, was written on its old notepaper and showed the defendant as a partner. The defendant was held to be relieved of liability because, at the date of his retirement, the requirements of section 36(3) were satisfied.

Companies Act 2006, Part 41

13–56   Although the applicable provisions of Part 41 of the Companies Act 2006[171] have reduced the scope for partners to maintain dormant status, section 36(3) of

---

[166] (1830) 1 B. & Ad. 11.

[167] (1831) 4 B. & Ad. 172. Note that, in this case, the firm name comprised the name of the active partner. See also *Evans v. Drummond* (1801) 4 Esp. 89. Lord Lindley pointed out in a footnote that "The case of the *Western Bank of Scotland v. Needell* (1859) 1 F. & F. 461, seems at first sight opposed to the authorities in the text, but it is conceived that in that case there must have been evidence to show that the defendant was known to the [*claimants*] to have been a partner before he retired."

[168] [1897] 2 Q.B. 396.

[169] See *Elders Pastoral Ltd. v. Rutherford* noted at [1991] N.Z.L.J. 73. See generally, as to the duration of a solicitor's retainer, *Cordery on Solicitors*, paras H301, 302.

[170] [1949] 2 K.B. 397.

[171] Companies Act 2006, ss.1201–1204 (replacing the Business Names Act 1985, s.4): see *supra*, para. 3–34. Note that *ibid.* s.1201 was substituted by the Companies Act 2006 (Substitution of Section 1201) Regulations 2009 (SI 2009/3182), reg. 2.

the Partnership Act 1890 will still apply in cases where such provisions are not, for whatever reason, complied with. Thus, there are no truly effective safeguards against mistakes of the type exemplified in *Tower Cabinet Co. v. Ingram.*[172]

(b) Effect of Notice

The general principle

The effect of giving notice either of the dissolution of a firm or of the **13–57** retirement of a partner[173] was summarised by Lord Lindley prior to the Partnership Act 1890 in this way:

"Subject to two exceptions, . . . notice of dissolution of a firm or of the retirement of a partner duly given, determines the power previously possessed by each partner to bind the others. Hence, after the dissolution of a firm or the retirement of a member and notification of the fact, no member of the previously existing firm is, by virtue of his connection therewith, liable for goods supplied to any of his partners subsequently to the notification[174]; nor is he liable on bills or notes subsequently drawn, accepted, or indorsed by any of them in the name of the late firm[175]; even although they may have been dated before the dissolution[176]; or have been given for a debt previously owing from the firm[177] by the partner expressly authorised to get in and discharge its debts."[178]

Although Lord Lindley only referred specifically to two exceptions to the general principle, he in fact went on to consider three, namely: (1) bills or notes binding on outgoing partners in special cases; (2) continued holding out; and (3) continuing authority for the purposes of winding up the affairs of a dissolved firm. Each of these exceptions will now be considered in turn.

Exceptional cases in which liability continues

(1) *Bills of Exchange and Promissory Notes—Special Cases*

All of the cases in this supposed class had distinct features which justified a **13–58** departure from the normal rule. Thus, in *Burton v. Issitt,*[179] the continuing partner had authority to use the name of the retired partner in any proceedings for the recovery of partnership property; this authority was held to extend to giving a promissory note for the sum of sixpence payable to the defendant under what was known as the Lord's Act.[180] Similarly, in *Smith v. Winter,*[181] the continuing partner had express permission to use the former partner's name and his liability on a bill of exchange given in the old firm name after the date of his retirement was not seriously in doubt.

---

[172] [1949] 2 K.B. 397. See *supra*, para. 13–55.
[173] This will include cases of expulsion: see *supra*, para. 13–43.
[174] *Minnit v. Whinery* (1721) 5 Bro.P.C. 489.
[175] *Ex p. Central Bank of London* [1892] 2 Q.B. 633; also *Abel v. Sutton* (1800) 3 Esp. 108; *Paterson v. Zachariah* (1815) 1 Stark. 71; *Spenceley v. Greenwood* (1858) 1 F. & F. 297.
[176] *Wrightson v. Pullan* (1816) 1 Stark.
[177] *Kilgour v. Finlyson* (1789) 1 H.Bl. 155; *Dolman v. Orchard* (1825) 2 Car. & P. 104.
[178] *Kilgour v. Finlyson, supra.* But see also *infra*, para. 13–59.
[179] (1821) 5 B. & A. 267.
[180] The Debtors Imprisonment Act 1758.
[181] (1838) 4 M. & W. 454.

13–59   A more perplexing decision was that in *Lewis v. Reilly*.[182] There two partners, A and B, had previously drawn a bill of exchange payable to their own order. They then dissolved their partnership and A indorsed the bill to the claimant in the firm name. Although the claimant appears to have known of the dissolution, it was held that this was immaterial and that he was entitled to recover on the bill against both of the former partners. Lord Lindley observed:

> "The precise ground of this decision does not distinctly appear. The Court seems to have proceeded on the supposition that an indorsement by one of several payees in the name of all is sufficient; but the writer has been unable to find any previous authority for such a doctrine, save where the indorsers are partners, which in the case in question they were not, as the [*claimant*] was found by the jury to have known. The case is certainly anomalous and requires reconsideration."[183]

It is the opinion of the current editor that, *Lewis v. Reilly* apart, this class (if, indeed, such an appellation is justified) represents little more than examples of liability imposed by reason of express authority or holding out.

(2) *Continued Holding Out*

13–60   If, notwithstanding notification of his retirement,[184] an outgoing partner permits himself to be represented as a continuing member of the firm, he will, on normal principles, be liable to any third party who gives credit to the firm in reliance on that representation.[185] Whether merely authorising his former partners to continue using the old firm name will have that result has already been considered earlier in this work.[186]

(3) *Continuing Authority for Purposes of Winding Up*

13–61   Prior to the Partnership Act 1890, the extent of each partner's authority to bind his co-partners following a dissolution was in doubt, although Lord Lindley submitted that the true position was as follows:

> " . . . notwithstanding dissolution, a partner has implied authority to bind the firm so far as may be necessary to settle and liquidate existing demands, and to complete transactions begun, but unfinished, at the time of the dissolution."[187]

Partnership Act 1890, section 38

13–62   Lord Lindley's summary presaged the content of section 38 of the Partnership Act 1890, which provides as follows:

---

[182] (1841) 1 Q.B. 349.

[183] See *Abel v. Sutton* (1800) 3 Esp. 108. Lord Lindley added in a footnote "The cases go further than is suggested in *Garland v. Jacomb* (1873) L.R. 8 Ex. 216, for the notice of dissolution is what creates the difficulty."

[184] Or expulsion: see *supra*, para. 13–43.

[185] Partnership Act 1890, s.14, *supra*, paras 5–35 *et seq.* And see *Brown v. Leonard* (1816) 2 Chitty 120; also *Bishop v. Tudor Estates* [1952] C.L.Y. 2493.

[186] See *supra*, paras 5–45 *et seq.*, 10–202. Note also the implications of the Companies Act 2006, Pt. 41, *supra*, paras 5–63, 5–64.

[187] See *Lyon v. Haynes* (1843) 5 Man. & G. 541; also *Smith v. Winter* (1838) 4 M. & W. 454, 462 *per* Parke B. For cases supporting the less restrictive view, see *Ex p. Williams* (1805) 11 Ves. Jr. 3; *Crawshay v. Collins* (1808) 15 Ves. Jr. 218 and (1826) 2 Russ. 325; *Peacock v. Peacock* (1809) 16 Ves. Jr. 49; *Wilson v. Greenwood* (1818) 1 Swan. 471; *Crawshay v. Maule* (1818) 1 Swan. 495; *Butchart v. Dresser* (1853) 4 De G.M. & G. 542. But note that Lord Eldon's observations were all *obiter*, since in none of the cases did any question concerning the authority of a partner following a dissolution strictly arise for decision.

"38. After the dissolution of a partnership the authority of each partner to bind the firm, and the other rights and obligations of the partners continue notwithstanding the dissolution so far as may be necessary to wind up the affairs of the partnership, and to complete transactions begun but unfinished at the time of the dissolution, but not otherwise.

Provided that the firm is in no case bound by the acts of a partner who has become bankrupt; but this proviso does not affect the liability of any person who has after the bankruptcy represented himself or knowingly suffered himself to be represented as a partner of the bankrupt."[188]

The section only applies on a general dissolution and has no application on a technical dissolution brought about by the retirement or expulsion of a partner.[189]

Duty of partners under section

The scope and practical consequences of section 38 were considered by the House of Lords in *I.R.C. v. Graham's Trustees*,[190] where Lord Reid observed: **13–63**

"What is meant by transactions begun but unfinished when the partnership was dissolved? If the common law had been clearly settled before 1890, I would interpret this section in light of the earlier law. But it appears that there was then little authority on this matter. So this section should if possible be construed so as to reach a reasonable result. It was argued that 'transactions' meant bargains. But that would deprive this provision of all content, for it is clear that surviving partners have no right to bind the assets of the dissolved firm by making new bargains and contracts. Their right and duty is to wind up its affairs. In my view this must mean that the surviving partners have the right and duty to complete all unfinished operations necessary to fulfil contracts of the firm which were still in force when the firm was dissolved.

Otherwise the position would be intolerable. Suppose the firm was employed to build a bridge and the bridge was half finished when the firm was dissolved. The surviving partners must be bound to finish the work, for otherwise they could hold the employer to ransom by refusing to proceed unless he made a new contract more favourable to them, and conversely the employer could refuse to allow the work to proceed unless the surviving partners made a new contract more favourable to him. That could not be right."[191]

The various authorities on this section were reviewed by the court in *Duncan v. The MFV Marigold PD145*.[192]

New bargains and contracts

It has been suggested that Lord Reid's reference to the partners' inability to make new bargains and contracts should not be applied "too widely"[193] and that   **13–64**

---

[188] See, as to this proviso, *Official Receiver v. Hollens* [2007] Bus. L.R. 1402, noticed *supra*, para. 13–50.

[189] *HLB Kidsons v. Lloyd's Underwriters* [2009] 1 All E.R. (Comm) 760.

[190] 1971 S.L.T. 46.

[191] *ibid.* p. 48; see also *Hillerns and Fowler v. Murray* (1932) 17 T.C. 77; *Welsh v. Knarston* 1972 S.L.T. 96, 97 *per* Lord Stott (albeit that the decision was ultimately recalled on the basis that the facts had not been found: see 1973 S.L.T. 66 (2nd Div.); also *Lujo Properties Ltd. v. Green* 1997 S.L.T. 225, 236 *et seq.* (OH) *per* Lord Penrose.

[192] 2006 S.L.T. 975 (OH) at [41] *et seq.*

[193] See Blackett-Ord, *Partnership Law* (3rd ed.), para. 18.2.

the partners must be entitled to carry on the partnership business in order to facilitate its eventual realisation.[194] Whilst, on a practical level, there is much to be said for this view, particularly when considering a trading concern, such as a restaurant or shop where stock is turned over swiftly, the position is more complex in the case of a professional practice: there taking on new work may involve long term commitments to clients.[195] Equally, to extend Lord Reid's own example, whilst the firm is obliged to complete the construction of the half-finished bridge, can it be right that, in order to facilitate the sale of its business, a contract to construct *another* bridge should be taken on? In this connection, it should be borne in mind that the dissolved firm is technically likely to have no employees.[196] It cannot be right that section 38 differs in its application according to the nature of the business carried on by the firm, since there is no warrant for such an approach in the terms of the section.

Consistently with the views expressed in the preceding paragraph, in *Duncan v. The MFV Marigold PD145*,[197] Lord Reed observed that:

> "On any view . . . section 38 cannot warrant the continuation of the business for more than a temporary period".

In *Friends Provident Management Services Ltd. v. Evans*[198] a liability was held to have arisen by reason of new business undertaken by one of the former partners after the dissolution. As the claimant was aware of the dissolution, the other partner was not liable. It appears that, had it been necessary to decide the point, a similar inference would have been drawn in *Duncan v. The MFV Marigold PD145*.[199]

13–65   Equally, some support for the view expressed above may be derived from the decision in *Don King Productions Inc. v. Warren*.[200] There, it was held that the benefit of certain boxing promotion and management contracts in the name of individual partners formed part of the partnership assets and that the firm's right to the benefit of those contracts did not determine on dissolution. Thus far, the decision was entirely consistent with Lord Reid's view. Certain of the contracts had been renewed following the dissolution but before the completion of the winding up. The Court of Appeal held that the benefit of such renewed contracts belonged to the dissolved firm and went on to recognise the "duty of a partner to renew a management or promotion agreement for the benefit of the partnership so as to facilitate the beneficial winding up of its affairs".[201] This, however, would seem to beg the question of when the winding up could ever properly be said to be complete: if there is an obligation to renew the initial contract, why should a further renewal not be similarly treated? For how long is this renewal

---

[194] This is, of course, one of the prime objectives on a dissolution: see *supra*, paras 10–199 *et seq.* and *infra*, 23–183 *et seq.*

[195] In one unreported case (*Browell v. Goodyear*, March 14, 2000), Jonathan Parker J. rejected as "wholly unrealistic" and "inappropriate" that the former members of a firm of solicitors should be compelled to continue to carry on business in partnership together following a dissolution. On the evidence, he regarded a sale of the practice as a going concern to a third party as more theoretical than real.

[196] See, *infra*, para. 25–02.

[197] 2006 S.L.T. 975 (OH) at [43].

[198] [2006] EWCA Civ 581 (Lawtel 27/3/06).

[199] See 2006 S.L.T. 975 at [66].

[200] [2000] Ch. 291 (CA). See further *infra*, para. 18–16.

[201] *ibid.* p. 341 at [42]. Inexplicably the judgment of the court continued "*cf.* section 38 of the Partnership Act 1890". *cf. Sew Hoy v. Sew Hoy* [2001] N.Z.L.R. 391 (CA, New Zealand) at [33].

process to be allowed to continue? Although the issue was not addressed by the court, it is assumed that this was regarded as a temporary expedient pending the completion of the winding up and that an infinite number of renewals was not contemplated.[202] Whilst the decision itself accords with recognised partnership principles,[203] the current editor questions the above formulation of a partner's duty, which appears to be quite inconsistent with section 38 of the 1890 Act.[204]

It is submitted that there is, in any event, no scope for the application of the above principles if the firm's supposed rights amount, on a true analysis, to no more than a mere expectancy.[205]

New partnership

Whilst a continuation of the business following a dissolution *may* be evidence of the creation of a new partnership *between* the surviving or continuing partners, this will rarely be the case where the continuation can be explained by reference to section 38.[206]

13–66

Nature of the continuing duty

Naturally, whilst attending to unfinished business, the partners must show a proper degree of care and skill if they are to avoid liability in negligence to third parties; such claims will naturally be unaffected by the dissolution.[207]

13–67

Scope of a partner's implied authority

Notwithstanding Lord Reid's strictures about the state of the law prior to the Partnership Act 1890[208] and the doubts which exist as to the extent of a partner's ability to enter into *new* contractual commitments,[209] the current editor's view is that a partner will clearly have authority to do any of the following acts in the course of winding up the firm's affairs:

13–68

Bills and notes: A partner may draw, accept or indorse a bill of exchange or promissory note in settlement of (or as security for) partnership debts.[210] Moreover, notice of dishonour may be given to a single partner.[211]

---

[202] Although the point was only briefly adverted to in the Court of Appeal, it appears that one partner was obliged to purchase the assets of the firm on dissolution: see [2000] Ch. 323E-G. It follows that the winding up process was unlikely to be unduly prolonged: this may well account for the Court of Appeal's approach.

[203] See *infra*, para. 16–30.

[204] See further, as to the difficulties raised by s.38, *supra*, para. 10–200. And see *Browell v. Goodyear, supra*.

[205] As in *Sew Hoy v. Sew Hoy* [2001] 1 N.Z.L.R. 391 (CA, New Zealand). The expectancy in question arose out of the fact that, under a particular Act, the Crown might, in certain circumstances, be obliged to offer to sell land back to the dissolved firm.

[206] See *Hopper v. Hopper* [2008] EWHC 228 (Ch) (Lawtel 26/2/08) at [150], [151] *per* Briggs J. This part of the decision was not the subject of the appeal at [2008] EWCA Civ. 1417 (Lawtel 12/12/08), but see *ibid.* at [47], [53].

[207] See *Welsh v. Knarston* 1972 S.L.T. 96.

[208] See *supra*, para. 13–63.

[209] See *supra*, paras 13–64, 13–65.

[210] *Ex p. Robinson* (1833) 3 D. & C. 376. But note the decision in *Re McGae* (1816) 19 Ves. Jr. 606, as to the position where bills are accepted and notes issued in the name of a firm after the bankruptcy of one or more partners; see also *Jombart v. Woolett* (1837) 2 Myl. & Cr. 389.

[211] *Goldfarb v. Bartlett and Kremer* [1920] 1 K.B. 639. *Quaere* can a partner waive notice of dishonour? See *ibid.* p. 650 *per* McCardle J.

Contracts: A partner may complete a current contract, whether involving the supply of goods or services.[212]

Debts: A partner may pay a debt owing by or receive payment of a debt owing to the firm.[213]

Deposits: A partner may withdraw money deposited with the firm's bankers.[214]

Partnership assets: A partner may sell the partnership assets[215]; he may also pledge them for the purpose of: (i) completing a transaction already commenced[216]; (ii) securing a debt already incurred[217]; or (iii) securing an overdraft on the firm's bank account. Thus, in *Re Bourne*[218] the survivor of two partners was held to have created a valid mortgage by deposit in respect of certain partnership land as security for the overdraft on the firm's bank account, that account having been overdrawn at the date of dissolution.[219]

The anomalous decision in Ault v. Goodrich

13–69   Finally, brief reference should be made to the curious decision in *Ault v. Goodrich*.[220] In that case, Wilcox the elder (W1) and Wilcox the younger (W2), who carried on the business of timber merchants in partnership, agreed with the claimant and another party to engage in a joint speculation involving the purchase and sale of certain trees. W2 was seemingly engaged to manage this venture but, before it was completed, the partnership between W1 and W2 was dissolved. W2 then appears to have misapplied certain money derived from the venture. Sir John Leach M.R. considered that W1 was clearly responsible for the actions of W2 whilst their partnership was continuing and went on to hold that, in the absence of any evidence of a new agreement between the parties to the venture following the dissolution of W1 and W2's partnership, the other parties should be treated as having continued to rely on the joint responsibility of W1 and W2 for the actions of W2. On that basis, W1 was declared to be responsible for the conduct of W2 after the date of dissolution.

---

[212] *I.R.C. v. Graham's Trustees* 1971 S.L.T. 46, 48, *supra*, para. 13–63; also *Hillerns and Fowler v. Murray* (1932) 17 T.C. 77.

[213] See *supra*, para. 12–53.

[214] *Dickson v. National Bank of Scotland* 1917 S.C. 50 (HL). In this case, the money was deposited by one of the firm's clients, on terms that it could be withdrawn by the firm. Note that the receipt and withdrawal of clients' money in other circumstances may now, in the case of certain professions and businesses, be governed by strict accounts rules: see *supra*, para. 12–131.

[215] See *Fox v. Hanbury* (1776) Cowp. 445; *Smith v. Stokes* (1801) 1 East 363; *Smith v. Oriell* (1801) 1 East 368; *Harvey v. Crickett* (1816) 5 M. & S. 336; *Morgan v. Marquis* (1853) 9 Ex. 145; *Fraser v. Kershaw* (1856) 2 K. & J. 496; *Lewis v. White* (1863) 2 N.R. 81. But see also, *infra*, paras 18–62 *et seq.*

[216] *Butchart v. Dresser* (1853) 4 De G.M. & G. 542.

[217] *Re Clough* (1885) 31 Ch.D. 324.

[218] [1906] 2 Ch. 427. See also *supra*, paras 12–74 *et seq.*

[219] In fact, the executors also made an unsuccessful attempt to invoke the rule in *Clayton's Case* in order to show that the original overdraft at the date of dissolution had been paid off before the title deeds were deposited. Note, however, that the creation of an equitable mortgage by the deposit of title deeds is no longer possible, having regard to the requirements of the Law of Property (Miscellaneous Provisions) Act 1989, s.2 (as amended): *United Bank Kuwait plc v. Sahib* [1997] Ch. 107 (CA).

[220] (1828) 4 Russ. 430.

Lord Lindley explained the unsatisfactory nature of this decision in this **13–70**
way:

> "Upon this case it may be observed: first, that the facts are not satisfactorily stated;
> and, secondly, that the judgment leads to the inference that the responsibility of
> Wilcox the elder for the conduct of Wilcox the younger did not turn upon the
> circumstance that they were partners,[221] but upon the circumstance that they were
> jointly entrusted with the management of the tree speculation. In this view of the case
> it was obviously immaterial whether the Wilcoxes had dissolved partnership or
> not."

The current editor submits that, consistently with Lord Lindley's views, the
decision could equally well be explained as a case of the completion of unfinished business following the dissolution.

Restrictions on implied authority

Any restrictions placed upon the implied authority of a partner following a **13–71**
dissolution will, on normal principles, bind a third party with notice.[222]

Profit sharing following dissolution

The assumption made by the Court of Appeal in *Hopper v. Hopper*[223] was that, **13–72**
where partners agree to carry on the business following a dissolution pursuant to
section 38, the profit sharing arrangements which applied during the continuation
of the partnership will automatically apply. Only in a case where one or more of
the partners are effectively excluded will section 42 of the 1890 Act apply.[224] The
current editor questions the correctness of this assumption. Granted the partners
may agree to proceed in this way or the court may authorise it but, absent such
an agreement or ruling, surely the profits form part of the assets of the dissolved
firm to be applied in the manner set out in section 44 of the 1890 Act?[225] It cannot
be right that the partners can withdraw all the profits when there are third party
debts to be paid which have a first claim on the partnership assets.[226] This is,
surely, confirmed by the fact that interest on a partner's capital (which, on a true
analysis normally constitutes an appropriation of profits)[227] will, as a general
rule, automatically cease to be payable on a dissolution[228] and by the priority
given to the payment of losses under section 44a. Equally, it is accepted that such

[221] Yet at *ibid.* pp. 432–433, Sir John Leach M.R. observed that "Prima facie it must be intended,
that, the partnership being interested in one third of this joint speculation, all sales and all receipts of
money by Wilcox the younger, during the continuance of the partnership, were partnership
transactions."

[222] See the Partnership Act 1890, s.8, *supra*, paras 12–138 *et seq. Quaere* to what extent such a
restriction may properly be imposed: see *supra*, paras 13–31 *et seq.*

[223] [2008] EWCA Civ. 1417 (Lawtel 12/12/08) at [47]. See also *Popat v. Shonchhatra* [1997] 1
W.L.R. 1367, 1374, as to the size of the partners' shares (albeit not in the context of s.38).

[224] [2008] EWCA Civ. 1417 at [48]. See further *infra*, paras 25–22 *et seq.*

[225] See *infra*, paras 25–44 *et seq.* Also *supra*, para. 10–84.

[226] See the Partnership Act 1890, s.44(b)(1), *infra*, para. 25–45.

[227] See *supra*, paras 10–67, 10–80.

[228] See *Barfield v. Loughborough* (1862) L.R. 8 Ch. App. 1; *Watney v. Wells* (1861) L.R. 2 Ch. App
250; also *infra*, para. 20–35. Note that, in *Watney v. Wells*, at p. 252, Lord Chelmsford L.C. observed
"No doubt profits might have resulted, and apparently did result, from the sale of the partnership
stock and property, but they cannot be regarded as the 'gains and profits of the joint trade' in the terms
of the articles of partnership."

an approach may leave a fixed share partner[229] in a difficult position if he has no share in the surplus assets and a distinction may have to be drawn between the entitlement of such partners and true equity partners.

Of course, the profit shares originally agreed between the partners will usually be relevant when it comes to determining how the ultimate surplus is divided between them under section 44.[230]

(c) Form of Notice

13–73 It has already been seen that no notice is required in the case of a truly dormant partner,[231] so that the precise form in which notice is to be given to actual and potential customers of the firm will only be of concern to someone who has at some stage been an *apparent* partner.[232] As was the position prior to the Partnership Act 1890,[233] a general notice will normally be given by advertisement but, in the case of persons with whom the firm has previously had dealings, a more specific notice will also be required.

Notice by advertisement

13–74 Since section 36(2) of the Partnership Act 1890 introduced no change in the law and since the only authorities pre-date that Act, it is convenient to set out Lord Lindley's summary of the law in full:

> "Public notice given by advertisement in the *Gazette* is sufficient, not only against all who can be shown to have seen it, but also as against all who had no dealings with the old firm, whether they saw it or not.[234] But an advertisement in any other paper is no evidence against anyone who cannot be shown to have seen it.[235] If, however, it can be shown that he was in the habit of taking the paper,[236] that is evidence ... of his having seen not only the particular paper containing the advertisement, but also the advertisement itself[237]; and if the [*court is satisfied*][238] that he saw the advertisement, that will be sufficient, although no advertisement was inserted in the *Gazette*.[239] An advertisement, moreover, is not indispensable; its place may be supplied by something else. Thus a change in the name of a firm painted on its counting-house, accompanied by a removal of the business of the old firm (for the purpose of winding up), and coupled with announcements of the change by circulars sent to the old customers, was held to be sufficient without any advertisement as

---

[229] See, as to such partners, *supra*, paras 5–54 *et seq.*, 10–32, 10–86.

[230] See *infra*, para. 25–48.

[231] See *supra*, paras 13–53 *et seq.*

[232] Note that it is not a requirement for liability under s.36(1) that the retired partner is *still* an apparent member of the firm: *Tower Cabinet Co, Ltd. v. Ingram* [1949] 2 K.B. 397; *Hamerhaven Pty Ltd. v. Ogge* [1996] 2 V.R. 488; *Wood v. Fresher Foods Ltd.* [2008] 2 N.Z.L.R. 248.

[233] See *supra*, para. 13–38.

[234] *Godfrey v. Turnbull* (1795) 1 Esp. 371; *Godfrey v. Macaulay* (1795) Peake 290n.; *Newsome v. Coles* (1811) 2 Camp. 617; *Wrightson v. Pullan* (1816) 1 Stark. 375. See now the Partnership Act 1890, s.36(2), *supra*, para. 13–40.

[235] *Boydell v. Drummond* (1808) 2 Camp. 157; *Leeson v. Holt* (1816) 1 Stark. 186.

[236] It is not enough to show that the paper is available in the relevant neighbourhood: *Norwich and Lowestoft Co. v. Theobald* (1828) M. & M. 153.

[237] See *Jenkins v. Blizard* (1816) 1 Stark. 418 (where, however, the claimant succeeded before the jury); *Rowley v. Horne* (1825) 3 Bing. 2.

[238] The original words were "the jury are satisfied".

[239] *Rooth v. Quin* (1819) 7 Price 193.

against a person who had not been an old customer, and who was not proved to have had any distinct notice."[240]

It follows that a *Gazette* notice is a desirable precaution in all cases; indeed, most partnership agreements contain a specific provision relating thereto.[241]

Notice to existing customers

As regards the firm's existing customers, a *Gazette* notice or other public advertisement will, in Lord Lindley's words, be "of little or no value".[242] If, however, *actual* notice can be proved, that will be sufficient. **13–75**

No particular form of notice to existing customers is prescribed by the Partnership Act 1890[243] nor was it required under the pre-existing law. It will obviously be sufficient to prove that the customer saw an advertisement, whether in the *Gazette* or elsewhere; proof that he took a certain paper is some evidence that he saw an advertisement placed in it.[244] A change in the firm name and general publicity may be sufficient, depending on the circumstances.[245] Thus where, following a change in a firm of bankers, the new firm name appeared on the face of its cheques, that was held to be sufficient notice to those customers who had used such cheques.[246]

Notice must be unambiguous

Equally, the court may not be prepared to assume that clients or customers appreciate the subtlety of a partner's apparent change of status if it is not properly drawn to their attention. In *Hamerhaven Pty Ltd. v. Ogge*[247] a partner in a firm of solicitors (O) had retired and thereafter the claimant company and its alter ego, an elderly farmer, received communications from the firm over an extended period, first on a letterhead which showed O as a consultant and later on a letterhead which omitted his name altogether. The Court held that this was insufficient notice of O's retirement, Ormiston J.A. remarking that "a retiring partner must make it unambiguously clear to the recipient of the notice that he or she is no longer a partner of the firm."[248] To the same effect was *Wood v. Fresher Foods Ltd.*,[249] where representatives of the defendant company had merely been informed that one of the partners in question was "ceasing to work" in the firm. **13–76**

Companies Act 2006, Part 41

The Companies Act 2006 will in practice often ensure that notice of a change in the firm is given to its customers. Thus, if the firm name does not itself disclose **13–77**

---

[240] *M'Iver v. Humble* (1812) 16 East 169; but see also *Gorham v. Thompson* (1791) Peake 60.
[241] See *supra*, para. 10–251. See also the Partnership Act 1890, s.37, *supra*, para. 13–40.
[242] See *Graham v. Hope* (1792) Peake 208.
[243] See the Partnership Act 1890, s.36(1), *supra*, para. 13–40.
[244] See *supra*, para. 13–74, n. 237.
[245] See, for example, *Hart v. Alexander* (1837) 2 M. & W. 484.
[246] *Barfoot v. Goodall* (1811) 3 Camp. 147.
[247] [1996] 2 V.R. 488 (CA). This was a decision under the Partnership Act 1958, s.40(1), being the equivalent of the Partnership Act 1890, s.36(1).
[248] *ibid.* p. 489.
[249] [2008] 2 N.Z.L.R. 248.

the names of the present partners[250] their names must normally appear on all documents issued by the firm, as well as in a notice prominently displayed in any partnership premises to which customers have access.[251]

C.   TERMINATION OF ACCRUED LIABILITY

13–78   Writing prior to the Partnership Act 1890, Lord Lindley observed:

> "When once it can be shown that liability has attached to any partner, the onus of proving that such liability has ceased is upon that partner or those representing him."[252]

Consistently with this principle, where partners take a lease of premises, they will normally remain liable on the covenants in that lease notwithstanding the dissolution of their partnership.[253]

Partnership Act 1890, section 17(2)

13–79   The same principle is reflected in section 17(2) of the Partnership Act 1890, which provides as follows:

> "17.—(2) A partner who retires[254] from a firm does not thereby cease to be liable for partnership debts or obligations incurred before his retirement."[255]

It is accordingly necessary to identify the circumstances in which an outgoing partner *will* cease to be liable for accrued debts and liabilities.

Events terminating accrued liability

13–80   Following Lord Lindley's own classification, there are four classes of event which are capable of affecting a partner's accrued liability to a creditor of the firm, namely:

(a)   Events over which neither he nor the creditor has any effective control, *i.e.* the partner's death or insolvency. These will be considered later in this work.[256]

(b)   Dealings and transactions between the partner and the creditor. Since this does not raise any question peculiar to the law of partnership, it does not justify further consideration in this work.

---

[250] Companies Act 2006, s.1200. See further, *supra*, para. 3–27.

[251] Companies Act 2006, ss.1202–1204. See *supra*, para. 3–34.

[252] See *Vulliamy v. Noble* (1817) 3 Mer. 593, 619; also *Wood v. Braddick* (1808) 1 Taunt. 104; *Blundell v. Winsor* (1837) 8 Sim. 613.

[253] See *Hoby v. Roebuck* (1816) 7 Taunt. 157; *Graham v. Whichelo* (1832) 1 C. & M. 188. Note also *Court v. Berlin* [1897] 2 Q.B. 396, *supra*, para. 13–54.

[254] This subsection will also apply in the case of an expulsion: see *supra*, para. 13–43.

[255] See, as to this subsection, *Friends Provident Management Services Ltd. v. Evans* [2006] EWCA Civ 581 (Lawtel 27/3/06), noted *supra*, para. 13–64.

[256] See, as regards the position following the death of a partner, *infra*, paras 26–11 *et seq.* As to insolvency, see *infra*, paras 27–43 *et seq.*

(c) Dealings and transactions between the creditor and the *other* partners.[257]

(d) Limitation.

The remainder of this chapter is devoted to the third and fourth classes.

(a) Dealings and Transactions Terminating Accrued Liability

General principles applicable to joint obligations

It has already been seen that the liability imposed on partners for the debts and **13–81** obligations of the firm may, according to the circumstances, be either joint or joint and several.[258] Once its precise nature has been established, the termination of a partner's liability will be governed by the same principles as apply in the case of any other joint/joint and several obligation. Although Lord Lindley summarised these principles in general terms,[259] they can more usefully be reformulated in terms of partnership, as follows:

(i) Performance by one partner of a joint (or joint and several) obligation will discharge the other partners.[260]

(ii) Anything which extinguishes the joint (or joint and several) obligation of one partner will also discharge the other partners.[261]

(iii) Anything which merely prevents one partner being sued on a joint (or joint and several) obligation will not necessarily discharge the other partners.[262]

(iv) If partners agree, as between themselves, that one of their number will only be surety for the performance of a joint (or joint and several) obligation, any person who, with notice of that agreement, seeks to enforce the obligation must not do anything to prejudice that partner's rights against his co-partners; if he does so without that partner's consent, the latter will be discharged.[263]

The practical application of these principles in the case of outgoing partners can most usefully be illustrated under three heads namely: (1) payment and appropriation of payments; (2) release and discharge; and (3) substitution of debtors and securities.

---

[257] See the Partnership Act 1890, s.17(3), *infra*, paras 13–102 *et seq.*
[258] See *supra*, paras 13–02 *et seq.*
[259] This summary is to be found, in its original form, in the 15th ed. of this work at pp. 393, 394.
[260] See *infra*, paras 13–82 *et seq.*
[261] See *infra*, paras 13–94 *et seq.* And see, generally, *Jenkins v. Jenkins* [1928] 2 K.B. 501; *Re E. W. A.* [1901] 2 K.B. 642; *Deanplan Ltd. v. Mahmoud* [1993] Ch. 151 and the cases there cited; also *Cheetham v. Ward* (1797) 1 Bos. & Pul. 630; *Ex p. Slater* (1801) 6 Ves. Jr. 146; *Ballam v. Price* (1818) 2 Moo. 235; *Cocks v. Nash* (1832) 9 Bing. 341; *Nicholson v. Revill* (1836) 4 A. & E. 675; *Wallace v. Kelsall* (1840) 7 M. & W. 264.
[262] See *infra*, para. 13–94. And see, generally, *Duck v. Mayeu* [1892] 2 Q.B. 511; *Re E. W. A.*, *supra*; *Deanplan Ltd. v. Mahmoud, supra*; also *Lacy v. Kinnaston* (1701) 1 Ld.Ray. 688; *Dean v. Newhall* (1799) 8 T.R. 168; *Walmesley v. Cooper* (1839) 11 A. & E. 216. And note *Watters v. Smith* (1831) 2 B. & Ad. 889.
[263] See *infra*, para. 13–98.

(1) *Payment and Appropriation of Payments*

Payment of partnership debt by one partner

13–82   Whether payment of a partnership debt made by one partner will discharge his co-partners from liability in respect of that debt will depend on his intentions and on the derivation of the funds so applied, as Lord Lindley made clear:

> "Payment of a partnership debt by any one partner discharges all the others, if the object of the partner paying was to extinguish the whole debt, or if he made the payment out of the partnership funds.[264] But if a firm is unable to pay a debt, and one partner out of his moneys pays it, but in such a way as to show an intention to keep the debt alive against the firm for his own benefit, this payment by him will be no answer to an action brought against the firm by the creditor suing on behalf of the partner who made the payment."[265]

The application of this principle was considered by the Court of Appeal in *Zaman v. Zoha*[266] but, on the facts it was clear that the debt, which had been paid following a dissolution of the firm, had not been kept alive.

Position where partner and firm have common creditor

13–83   If a partner and his firm are both indebted to the same creditor, any payment made by that partner out of partnership funds must be applied towards the partnership debt, even though not specifically paid on that account.[267]

Payment by new firm

13–84   Similar principles will be applied following a change in a firm, if the new firm pays the debts of the old, as Lord Lindley explained:

> " . . . a payment by the new firm expressly or impliedly on behalf of the old firm, of the debts contracted by the old firm, will extinguish its debts as between that firm and its creditor.[268] But if there are circumstances showing that the money was paid, not on behalf of the old firm, and in discharge of its liability, but as the consideration for a transfer to the new firm of the creditor's right against the old firm, the right of the creditor to sue the old firm will not be extinguished, but can still be exercised for the benefit of the new firm."[269]

Appropriation of payments: the rule in *Clayton's Case*

13–85   The general principle governing the appropriation of payments will be well known and may be summarised as follows: if a debtor owes several debts to the

---

[264] See *Watters v. Smith* (1831) 2 B. & Ad. 889; *Beaumont v. Greathead* (1846) 2 C.B. 494; *Thorne v. Smith* (1851) 10 C.B. 659.

[265] *M'Intyre v. Miller* (1845) 13 M. & W. 725.

[266] [2006] EWCA Civ. 770 (Lawtel 24/3/06).

[267] *Thompson v. Brown* (1827) Moo. & M. 40. See also *Nottidge v. Prichard* (1834) 2 Cl. & F. 379.

[268] Lord Lindley had earlier referred, in support of a proposition framed in more general terms, to Co.Litt. 207a; also *Jones v. Broadhurst* (1850) 9 C.B. 193; *Belshaw v. Bush* (1851) 11 C.B. 191; *Kemp v. Balls* (1854) 10 Ex. 607; *Lucas v. Wilkinson* (1856) 1 H. & N. 420. See also *Hirachand Punamchand v. Temple* [1911] 2 K.B. 330.

[269] See *M'Intyre v. Miller* (1845) 13 M. & W. 725; *Lucas v. Wilkinson* (1856) 1 H. & N. 420.

same creditor, he is entitled to appropriate any payment to the debt of his choice; but if he does not exercise that right, either expressly or by implication, at the time of making the payment, it will become exercisable by the creditor, who may even appropriate the payment to a debt the recovery of which is barred by the Limitation Act 1980.[270] Further consideration of this principle is outside the scope of the present work.

However, the rule in *Clayton's Case*,[271] which may displace the normal right of appropriation, is of particular importance in the present context. Lord Lindley stated the rule as follows:

> " . . . where there is one single open current account between two parties, every payment which cannot be shown to have been made in discharge of some particular item, is imputed to the earliest item standing to the debit of the payer at the time of payment."

It will perhaps be self evident that the operation of this rule may, in an appropriate case, result in the discharge of an outgoing partner, whether active[272] or dormant,[273] or of the estate of a deceased partner.[274]

Application of the rule in Clayton's Case

In his consideration of the rule in *Clayton's Case*, Lord Lindley formulated a number of general propositions by way of illustration of its scope. Those propositions are retained in their original form.   **13–86**

Proposition 1:

> "The rule . . . applies to all accounts of the nature of one entire debit and credit account[275] without reference to any question of partnership, and is available not only by a firm against an old creditor, but also against a firm for the benefit of its debtors."

Thus, if a person guarantees a debt owing to a firm by a third party and the debt, being an item in a single running account between the third party and the firm, is liquidated by the operation of the rule, the guaranteed debt will be extinguished and the guarantor discharged, even though there may at all times

---

[270] Lord Lindley formulated eight general rules regarding the appropriation of payments, with copious references to the older authorities, but these are not reproduced in the present edition. They will, however, be found in the 15th ed. of this work at pp. 395 *et seq.* And see, generally, *Chitty on Contracts* (30th ed.), paras 21–059 *et seq.*

[271] (1816) 1 Mer. 572. See generally, as to this rule, *Ex p. Randleson* (1833) 2 D. & Ch. 534; *Copland v. Toulmin* (1840) 7 Cl. & F. 349; *Brown v. Adams* (1869) L.R. 4 Ch. App. 764; *Laing v. Campbell* (1865) 36 Beav. 3; *Re Yeovil Glove Co.* [1965] Ch. 148; *Re James R. Rutherford & Sons* [1964] 1 W.L.R. 1211.

[272] *Hooper v. Keay* (1875) 1 Q.B.D. 178.

[273] *Newmarch v. Clay* (1811) 14 East 239; *Brooke v. Enderby* (1820) 2 Brod. & B. 70.

[274] As in *Clayton's Case* (1816) 1 Mer. 572.

[275] *e.g.* current accounts for the supply of goods which have been treated as one account: see *Hooper v. Keay* (1875) 1 Q.B.D. 178; *Albemarle Supply Co. Ltd. v. Hind & Co.* [1928] 1 K.B. 307. See also the cases cited *infra*, para. 13–87, n. 278.

have been an overall balance due from the third party to the firm.[276] *Per contra* if the guaranteed debt is not wholly extinguished.[277]

Proposition 2:

13–87   "The rule . . . applies only to an entire unbroken account,[278] and to items in that account.[279] It has no application to cases where one person is indebted to another in respect of several matters, each of which forms the subject of a distinct account."[280]

Accordingly, where there are such distinct accounts and the debtor does not himself make the appropriation, the creditor can apply the payment to whichever account he sees fit.[281]

This is of particular relevance following a change in a firm, since a creditor of the old firm is not bound to agree that his debt should be carried over to a fresh account with the new firm; if he prefers to keep the two accounts separate and distinct, general payments made by the new firm will not *necessarily* liquidate the debt owed by the old firm. Thus, in *Simson v. Ingham*,[282] where a bank to whom two partners were indebted had, following the death of one, sent in two separate accounts of receipts and payments, one relating to the period prior to the death and the other to the subsequent period, it was held that the rule in *Clayton's Case* did not apply, even though in the bank's own books the original account had been continued.

13–88   The same principle is applicable in the case of a debt owed *to* a firm, as demonstrated by the decision in *Jones v. Maund*.[283] There being no evidence in that case that the debt had been made an item in the account between the debtor and the new firm,[284] it was held that he could not insist on payments made by him generally to the new firm being applied to a balance due from him in respect of that debt.[285]

---

[276] See *Kinnaird v. Webster* (1878) 10 Ch.D. 139; also *Bodenham v. Purchas* (1818) 2 B. & A. 39; *Field v. Carr* (1828) 5 Bing. 13; *Pemberton v. Oakes* (1827) 4 Russ. 154; *Toulmin v. Copland* (1836) 3 Y. & C.Ex. 625; *Copland v. Toulmin* (1840) 7 Cl. & F. 349; *Bank of Scotland v. Christie* (1841) 8 Cl. & F. 214; *Re Medewe's Trust* (1859) 26 Beav. 588. *cf. Ex p. Whitworth* (1841) 2 M.D. & D. 164; *City Discount Co. v. Maclean* (1874) L.R. 9 C.P. 692.

[277] *Re Sherry* (1884) 25 Ch.D. 692; also *Williams v. Rawlinson* (1825) 3 Bing. 71; *Bradford Old Bank v. Sutcliffe* [1918] 2 K.B. 833, where there were two separate accounts, only one of which had been satisfied. The latter decision was applied by Buckley J. in *Re E. J. Morel (1934)* [1962] Ch. 21.

[278] *Cory Brothers & Co. v. Owners of The Mecca* [1897] A.C. 286; also *Re Sherry* (1884) 25 Ch.D. 692, 702; *A.M.K.M.K. v. Chettiar* [1955] A.C. 230. See also *supra*, para. 13–86, n. 275.

[279] See *Smith v. Betty* [1903] 2 K.B. 317, 323 *per* Stirling L.J.

[280] See *Bradford Old Bank v. Sutcliffe* [1918] 2 K.B. 833, *supra*, n. 277.

[281] *i.e.* in accordance with the general principle summarised *supra*, para. 13–85.

[282] (1823) 2 B. & C. 65.

[283] (1839) 3 Y. & C.Ex. 347.

[284] In fact there was no identity between the partners in the new firm and those in the old; however, it is considered that the decision would have been the same even if this had not been the case.

[285] This case was decided on demurrer. It was reportedly held that the balance due to the old firm could not be considered as liquidated, unless it could be shown that it had, with the consent of one of the partners of that firm (who had, in fact, assigned her share to one of the partners of the new firm), been made an item in the account between the debtor and the new firm. Lord Lindley observed in a footnote: "But *quaere* what [*that partner*] had to do with it, she having assigned all her interest in the debt to the new firm? Did she not thereby authorise the new firm to deal with the debt as it liked? See *Pemberton v. Oakes* (1827) 4 Russ. 154."

It should, however, be noted in this connection that one partner will normally have implied authority to assent to the transfer of a debt owed by or to the firm from one account to another.[286]

Proposition 3:

" . . . the rule applies even as between persons who do not know that they are being affected by it, and who, if they did, might take care to exclude its operation."[287]   **13–89**

It follows that a deceased or outgoing partner may be discharged by the operation of the rule, even if the creditor does not know that there has been a change in the firm. The fact that the creditor might, if he had known of the change, have refused to deal with the new firm unless the old and new accounts were kept distinct, is strictly irrelevant if he has dealt with both firms on the footing that there is only one continuous account.[288]

Proposition 4:

" . . . a debtor, after making general payments in respect of one entire account, is not   **13–90**
at liberty to have those payments applied in liquidation of the subsequent rather than of the earlier items."[289]

This proposition is of particular relevance to an incoming partner. It has already been seen that he will not normally be liable for debts contracted prior to the date of his admission[290]; yet if he permits those debts to form a single running account with other debts incurred *since* that date, general payments made by the new firm in respect of that account will be applied first in the liquidation of the old debts and may accordingly leave a balance due in respect of new debts, for which the incoming partner is clearly liable.[291]

However, such a result can only be achieved with the express or implied consent of the incoming partner: a creditor of the old firm who continues to deal with the new firm has no inherent right to appropriate a payment made by a new partner to a debt owing by his co-partners, nor to run two otherwise distinct accounts together in order to bring the rule into play.[292]

---

[286] *Beale v. Caddick* (1857) 2 H. & N. 326. See further, *supra*, para. 12–59.

[287] *Newmarch v. Clay* (1811) 14 East 239; *Brooke v. Enderby* (1820) 2 Brod. & B. 70; *Scott v. Beale* (1859) 6 Jur.(N.S.) 559; *Merriman v. Ward* (1860) 1 J. & H. 371. Note, however, that the rule may, in certain circumstances, be held not to apply where it would be impractical or where injustice would be caused: *Barlow Clowes International v. Vaughan* [1992] 4 All E.R. 22 (CA). See also *Re Registered Securities* [1991] 1 N.Z.L.R. 545.

[288] *ibid.*

[289] *Beale v. Caddick* (1857) 2 H. & N. 326.

[290] Partnership Act 1890, s.17(1): see *supra*, paras 13–23 *et seq.*

[291] See *Beale v. Caddick* (1857) 2 H. & N. 326; also *Scott v. Beale* (1859) 6 Jur.(N.S.) 559. Of the latter decision, Lord Lindley observed "This case is badly reported, but it is tolerably plain that the incoming partner was held liable to pay, not the debt due to the [*claimant*] when the partnership commenced, but the balance of monies due to him on his whole account, and which balance consisted of monies received by the defendants after the partnership between them was created."

[292] *Burland v. Nash* (1861) 2 F. & F. 687. In a footnote, Lord Lindley queried "whether the evidence did not warrant the inference that the two accounts had been run into one with the consent of the defendant."

Proposition 5:

13–91   "The rule . . . is . . . based on the presumed intention of the parties.[293] It is not, as is sometimes represented, a rule of law obtaining independently of their will; and consequently, if it can be shown that some other appropriation was intended, the rule ceases to be applicable."

There is, in fact, no inconsistency between this and proposition 3. In cases where the parties are not aware that the rule is applicable, there is obviously no scope for an express or implied agreement to exclude or modify its operation; accordingly, their *presumed* intention will not be displaced. Where, on the other hand, some other intention can be inferred from the parties' conduct, *e.g.* to appropriate a payment to a later rather than an earlier item in the account, the rule will not apply.[294] Among the circumstances which may give rise to such an inference are the usual course of business between the parties[295] and the source of the funds applied in making the relevant payment.[296] In *Wickham v. Wickham*,[297] the rule was held to be displaced as between two firms by representations made to a third party[298] by a partner common to both firms that the relevant debts were still owing.

Proposition 6:

13–92   " . . . the rule . . . cannot be applied as against a person who is a creditor in respect of a fraud committed on him of which he is ignorant."

This is founded on the same principle as the previous proposition and was, in fact, determined in *Clayton's Case*[299] itself, where the liability of a firm in respect of the fraudulent sale of certain exchequer bills was held not to be extinguished by payments which the surviving partners had subsequently made.[300]

Similarly, if one partner fraudulently overdraws his account with the firm and keeps paying money in and drawing money out, so that his fraudulent over-drawing is never discovered, it will not be treated as having been made good so long as there is a balance due from him.[301]

---

[293] *Re Hodgson's Trusts* [1919] 2 Ch. 189, 195–196 *per* Peterson J.; *Re Registered Securities* [1991] 1 N.Z.L.R. 545; *Barlow Clowes International v. Vaughan* [1992] 4 All E.R. 22 (CA); also *Wilson v. Hurst* (1833) 4 B. & Ad. 760, 767 *per* Denman C.J.; *Re Hallett's Estate* (1880) 13 Ch.D. 696; *Cory Brothers & Co. v. Owners of The Mecca* [1897] A.C. 286; *Deeley v. Lloyds Bank* [1912] A.C. 756. In *Copland v. Toulmin* (1840) 7 Cl. & F. 349, there was evidence of an agreement for a different appropriation, but it was not regarded as sufficient to exclude the rule.

[294] For a relatively recent example of a case in which the rule was held to be inconsistent with the presumed intention of the parties, see *Barlow Clowes International v. Vaughan, supra*; and see also *Re Registered Securities, supra.*

[295] *Lysaght v. Walker* (1831) 5 Bli.(N.S.) 1; *Taylor v. Kymer* (1832) 3 B. & Ad. 320.

[296] *Stoveld v. Eade* (1827) 4 Bing. 154; *Thompson v. Brown* (1827) Moo. & M. 40. For examples of other relevant circumstances, see *Newmarch v. Clay* (1811) 14 East 240 (nature of security); *City Discount Co. v. Maclean* (1874) L.R. 9 C.P. 692 (earlier item secured and intended to be kept separate); also, generally, *Hancock v. Smith* (1889) 41 Ch.D. 456; *Cory Brothers & Co. v. Owners of The Mecca* [1897] A.C. 286; *Re Hodgson's Trusts* [1919] 2 Ch. 189; and the cases cited *supra*, n. 293. *cf. Henniker v. Wigg* (1843) 4 Q.B. 792 and *Re Boys* (1870) L.R. 10 Eq. 467.

[297] (1855) 2 K. & J. 478; *Merriman v. Ward* (1860) 1 J. & H. 371; see also *Firestone Tyre & Rubber Co. Ltd. v. Evans* [1977] S.T.C. 104.

[298] The third party was in fact the claimant, for whom one of the firms acted as agent in the supply of goods to the other.

[299] (1816) 1 Mer. 572.

[300] See further, as to frauds committed by a partner, *supra*, paras 12–87 *et seq.*

[301] *Lacey v. Hill* (1876) 4 Ch.D. 537, affirmed *sub nom. Read v. Bailey* at (1877) 3 App.Cas. 94.

It should also in this context be noted in passing that application of the rule is doubtful where where monies are traced into a single account.[302]

Partner and firm sharing common debtor/creditor

The position where a partner makes a payment out of partnership funds to a **13–93** person who is both his own and the firm's creditor has already been noted.[303] Greater difficulties are encountered in the converse situation, *i.e.* where a debtor who owes money both to a partner and to the firm makes a payment to that partner without specifying to which debt the payment is to be applied. Lord Lindley observed:

> "Pothier[304] says that good faith requires that the partner receiving the money, should apply it proportionately to both demands. The writer is not aware of any decision on this subject, but he apprehends that, as between the partner and the debtor, the payment might be applied to either debt at the option of the partner, whilst, as between the partner and his co-partners, good faith would require that the payment should be applied wholly to the partnership debt."[305]

The position is no clearer now, but the opinion of the current editor is that Lord Lindley's view is the correct one.

(2) *Release and Discharge*

Releases and covenants not to sue

The traditional view has always been that a creditor may discharge a partner **13–94** from a partnership debt or obligation by means of a release or a covenant not to sue, with differing consequences for the other partners, as Lord Lindley explained:

> "A release of one partner from a partnership debt discharges all the others[306]; for where several persons are bound jointly, or jointly and severally, a release of one is a release of them all.[307] But in this respect a covenant not to sue differs from a release; for, although where there is only one debtor and one creditor, a covenant by the latter never to sue the former is equivalent to a release, it has been decided on several occasions that a covenant not to sue does not operate as a release of a debt owing to or by other persons besides those who are parties to the covenant."[308]

---

[302] See *Commerzbank Aktiengesellschaft v. IMB Morgan Plc* [2005] 1 Lloyd's Rep. 298.

[303] See *supra*, para. 13–83.

[304] Pothier, *Société*, s.121.

[305] See *Thompson v. Brown* (1827) Moo. & M. 40; *Nottidge v. Prichard* (1834) 2 Cl. & F. 379.

[306] *Bower v. Swadlin* (1738) 1 Atk. 294; *Cheetham v. Ward* (1797) 1 Bos. & Pul. 630; *Ex p. Slater* (1801) 6 Ves. Jr. 146; *Cocks v. Nash* (1832) 9 Bing. 341.

[307] The authorities for this proposition were reviewed in *Deanplan Ltd. v. Mahmoud* [1993] Ch. 151. See also, generally, Co.Lit. 232a; *Kiffin v. Evans* (1694) 4 Mod. 379; *Lacy v. Kinnaston* (1701) 1 Ld.Ray 688; *Jenkins v. Jenkins* [1928] 2 K.B. 501. The same rule applies to judgment debts: *Re E.W.A.* [1901] 2 K.B. 642.

[308] *Clayton v. Kynaston* (1699) 2 Salk. 573; *Lacy v. Kinnaston* (1701) 1 Ld.Ray 688; *Dean v. Newhall* (1799) 8 T.R. 168; *Hutton v. Eyre* (1815) 6 Taunt. 289; *Walmesley v. Cooper* (1839) 11 A. & E. 216; *Commercial Bank of Tasmania v. Jones* [1893] A.C. 313, 316 *per* Lord Morris; *Deanplan Ltd. v. Mahmoud* [1993] Ch. 151, 170B *per* Judge Paul Baker Q.C. See also *Price v. Barker* (1855) 4 E. & B. 760. As to the position of a creditor who assents to a deed of arrangement or approves a voluntary arrangement under the Insolvency Act 1986, see the review of the law in *Johnson v. Davies* [1999] Ch. 117, 129 *et seq.*

It should, however, be noted that the rigid distinction between releases and covenants not to sue has not found favour in the Court of Appeal.[309]

Contractual and tortious liabilities stand on the same footing for this purpose.[310]

13–95   A relatively recent example of discharge by means of a release is to be found in *Morris v. Wentworth-Stanley*.[311] There, the claimant had issued proceedings against a partnership which had originally comprised three partners, namely O, his brother C (who had died before the proceedings were issued) and the defendant (who was C's wife and only a sleeping partner).[312] Having been informed of C's death and the dissolution of the partnership, the claimant opted to proceed solely against O and amended the proceedings accordingly. At trial, the proceedings were settled on terms which were ultimately incorporated into a consent order. When O proved unable to comply with the consent order, the claimant sought to issue fresh proceedings against the defendant. The Court of Appeal held that the settlement of the original proceedings against O amounted to an accord and satisfaction and, thereby, released the defendant from liability.[313]

True nature of a purported release

13–96   It should not, however, be assumed that a purported release will *necessarily* discharge the other partners: if, on a true construction,[314] it does not preclude a subsequent action against all the partners, including the partner to whom it is given, it will not in fact operate as a release and the continuing liability of the other partners will be unaffected.[315] Indeed, it seems clear that the courts will now be more ready to adopt such an approach.[316]

Thus, in *Solly v. Forbes*,[317] two partners, A and B, were indebted to a third party, C. B paid a certain sum to C, in consideration of which he was released

---

[309] *Watts v. Aldington, The Times*, December 23, 1993; *Johnson v. Davies, supra*; *Heaton v. Axa Equity & Law Life Assurance Society Plc* [2001] Ch. 173 (CA). As to the manner in which a release should be construed, see *B.C.C.I. SA v. Ali* [2002] 1 A.C. 251 (HL); also *Satyam Computer Services Ltd. v. Upaid Systems Ltd.* [2008] 2 All E.R. (Comm) 465 (CA), which concerned the construction of a settlement agreement.

[310] *Duck v. Mayeu* [1892] 2 Q.B. 511; *Gardiner v. Moore* [1969] 1 Q.B. 55; *Watts v. Aldington, supra*; *Jameson v. Central Electricity Generating Board* [2000] 1 A.C. 455; *Heaton v. Axa Equity & Law Life Assurance Society Plc, supra*; but see also *Minton v. Kenbrugh Investments (Northern) Ltd.* [2000] Lloyd's Rep. P.N. 736 (CA); *Cape & Dalgleish v. Fitzgerald* [2001] Lloyd's Rep. P.N. 110 CA (Civ Div).

[311] [1999] Q.B. 1004.

[312] In fact, the claimant had previously issued proceedings against O "trading as [*the*] partnership" and these were consolidated with the proceedings referred to in the text.

[313] An attempt to circumvent this result by relying on the Civil Liability (Contribution) Act 1978, s.3 failed: see *supra*, para. 13–05.

[314] Note that the true purpose and scope of a release may be apparent from its recitals and, thus, require a restrictive interpretation to be placed on its operative clauses: see, generally, *Payler v. Homersham* (1815) 4 M. & S. 423; *Lampon v. Corke* (1822) 5 B. & A. 606; *Simons v. Johnson* (1832) 3 B. & Ad. 175; *Lindo v. Lindo* (1839) 1 Beav. 496; *Boyes v. Bluck* (1853) 13 C.B. 652.

[315] *Gardiner v. Moore* [1969] 1 Q.B. 55.

[316] *Watts v. Aldington, The Times*, December 16, 1993 (CA); *Johnson v. Davies* [1999] Ch. 117 (CA).

[317] (1820) 2 Brod. & B. 38. See also *Thompson v. Lack* (1846) 3 C.B. 540; *Price v. Barker* (1855) 4 E. & B. 760; *Willis v. De Castro* (1858) 4 C.B.(N.S.) 216; *Bateson v. Gosling* (1871) L.R. 7 C.P. 9; *Duck v. Mayeu* [1892] 2 Q.B. 511; *Re E.W.A.* [1901] 2 K.B. 642; *Watts v. Aldington, supra*; *Finley v. Connell Associates* [1999] Lloyd's Rep P.N. 895; *Morris v. Wentworth-Stanley* [1999] Q.B. 1004, 1012.

from all further demands in respect of the debt. However, under the terms of the release, C expressly reserved all his rights not only against A but also against A and B jointly, so that he could obtain repayment either from the partnership or from A. As might be anticipated, that release was held not to be a bar to C's subsequent proceedings against A and B. *Hartley v. Manton*[318] was decided on the same principle.

Receipt in full

Similarly, a receipt given to one partner in satisfaction of all demands against him will discharge his co-partners unless its operation is qualified, either by its terms or by the surrounding circumstances.[319]   **13–97**

Outgoing partner entitled to indemnity against debts, etc.

Continuing or surviving partners who, either expressly or impliedly,[320] agree to indemnify an outgoing partner (or the estate of a deceased partner) against the accrued debts and liabilities of the firm thereby constitute themselves as principal debtors and the outgoing partner (or his estate) as surety for the payment of those debts and liabilities.[321] Where a creditor of the firm has notice of such an agreement and subsequently deals with the remaining partners in a way which will or may prejudice the outgoing partner's rights *qua* surety, *e.g.* by giving additional time to pay, this will on normal principles[322] discharge the outgoing partner, unless the creditor expressly or impliedly[323] reserved his rights or the outgoing partner consented. The fact that the creditor neither knew of nor consented to the agreement prior to its conclusion is immaterial.   **13–98**

This is clearly demonstrated by the decision in *Oakeley v. Pasheller.*[324] There two partners, A and B, had given a number of joint and several bonds to the claimant. A died. B carried on the partnership business for a time and then took in C as a partner. B and C agreed to indemnify A's executors against the debts of the old firm, including the liability under the bonds, and the claimant seemingly had notice of this agreement.[325] The new firm accordingly adopted the debt due under the bonds and paid the claimant interest thereon. It appears that the   **13–99**

---

[318] (1843) 5 Q.B. 247.

[319] *Ex p. Good* (1877) 5 Ch.D. 46; *Re E.W.A.* [1901] 2 K.B. 642; *Deanplan Ltd. v. Mahmoud* [1993] Ch. 151.

[320] See further, *supra*, para. 10–248.

[321] *Oakeley v. Pasheller* (1836) 10 Bli.(N.S.) 548; *Rodgers v. Maw* (1846) 4 Dow. & L. 66; also *Overend, Gurney & Co. v. Oriental Financial Corporation* (1874) L.R. 7 H.L. 348; *Rouse v. Bradford Banking Co.* [1894] A.C. 586; *Goldfarb v. Bartlett & Kremer* [1920] 1 K.B. 639. And see *supra*, para. 10–250.

[322] See, generally, *Chitty on Contracts* (30th ed.), paras 44–091 *et seq.*

[323] See, as to the extent to which rights can be *impliedly* reserved, *Finley v. Connell Associates* [1999] Lloyd's Rep P.N. 895, adopting the reasoning in *Watts v. Aldington, The Times*, December 16, 1993. It should be noted that this case concerned a covenant not to sue the principal debtor, although the distinction between releases and such covenants has been criticised by the Court of Appeal: see *supra*, para. 13–94.

[324] (1836) 10 Bli.(N.S.) 548 and 4 Cl. & F. 207. This decision was followed in *Wilson v. Lloyd* (1873) L.R. 16 Eq. 60, even though no new partners had been admitted. However, Lord Lindley observed that "*Wilson v. Lloyd* cannot be relied upon"; see also *Simpson v. Henning* (1875) L.R. 10 Q.B. 406, 413 *per* Amphlett B. Although *Oakeley v. Pasheller* was distinguished in *Swire v. Redman* (1876) 1 Q.B.D. 536, its authority was reaffirmed in *Rouse v. Bradford Banking Co.* [1894] 2 Ch. 32 and, on appeal, [1894] A.C. 586.

[325] See (1836) 4 Cl. & F. 212. The marginal note seems to be misleading: but see also *ibid.* p. 211. This point is not mentioned in the report at 10 Bli.(N.S.) 548.

claimant later agreed with B and C to defer payment under the bonds for three years, but A's executors were not informed of this arrangement. It was held that, by so doing, the claimant had discharged A's executors from liability.[326]

It should, however, be noted that the giving of time will not discharge the outgoing partner once judgment has been obtained both against him and the remaining partners.[327]

It also follows from the outgoing partner's status as surety that a part payment (but not an acknowledgment) by one of the continuing partners will be effective as against him.[328]

(3) *Substitution of debtors and securities*

13–100 An outgoing partner may be discharged from liability in respect of an accrued debt or obligation if the creditor acquires new and different rights against other persons *in place* of that liability. This may either occur with the creditor's agreement[329] or by operation of the doctrine of merger.

(A)   SUBSTITUTION BY AGREEMENT

General principle

13–101   It is perhaps self evident that a creditor's rights will not normally be prejudiced by an agreement transferring an accrued liability from one partner to another unless the creditor is made a party to the agreement or assents to its operation. Otherwise the agreement will, as regards him, be strictly *res inter alios acta*.[330] Lord Lindley illustrated this proposition by the following example:

> " . . . let it be supposed that a firm of three members, A, B, and C, is indebted to D; that A retires, and B and C either alone, or together with a new partner, E, take upon themselves the liabilities of the old firm. D's right to obtain payment from A, B and C is not affected by the above arrangement, and A does not cease to be liable to him for the debt in question.[331] But if, after A's retirement, D accepts as his sole debtors

---

[326] It appears that the claimant had subsequently taken an assignment of some policies from B and C by way of collateral security for payment of sums due under the bonds, at that point expressly reserving his rights against A's estate. However, by this time, the estate had already been released from liability, for the reasons mentioned in the text. Lord Lindley originally observed of this case "The true *ratio decidendi*, however, was that the [*claimant*] had accepted B and C as his sole debtors." This view was shared by Kekewich J. (see *Rouse v. Bradford Banking Co.* [1894] 2 Ch. 32, 45–46), but Lord Lindley later resiled therefrom (see *ibid.* pp. 57 *et seq.*).

[327] *Jenkins v. Robertson* (1854) 2 Drew. 351; *Re A Debtor* [1913] 3 K.B. 11.

[328] See *UCB Corporate Services Ltd. v. Kohli* [2004] 2 All E.R. (Comm) 422, applying the Limitation Act 1980, s.31(7), albeit not in the case of a partnership.

[329] Lord Lindley observed that this is "[s]ometimes called novation but nothing is really gained by using this word." However, the word is commonly used: see, for example, *Re Head* [1893] 3 Ch. 426; *Head v. Head (No. 2)* [1894] 2 Ch. 236.

[330] See *In the matter of Burton Marsden Douglas* [2004] 3 All E.R. 222 at [31], [32]. But note that such an agreement may result in an outgoing partner becoming a surety for the continuing partners' obligations and thereby indirectly prejudice the creditor's rights once he has notice of the agreement: see *supra*, para. 13–98.

[331] *Smith v. Jameson* (1794) 5 T.R. 601; *Dickenson v. Lockyer* (1798) 4 Ves. Jr. 36; *Cummins v. Cummins* (1845) 8 I. Eq. R. 723; *Rodgers v. Maw* (1846) 4 Dow. & L. 66. But see also the previous footnote.

B and C, or B, C, and E (if E enters the firm), then A's liability will have ceased, and D must look for payment to B and C, or to B, C and E, as the case may be."

Partnership Act 1890, section 17(3)

This approach is directly reflected in the Partnership Act 1890, which provides: **13–102**

"17.—(3) A retiring partner may be discharged from any existing liabilities, by an agreement to that effect between himself and the members of the firm as newly constituted and the creditors, and this agreement may be either express or inferred as a fact from the course of dealing between the creditors and the firm as newly constituted."

Lord Lindley's rules on substitution

Before turning to the numerous authorities on this topic, it may be convenient to set out nine rules, which were originally formulated by Lord Lindley prior to the Partnership Act 1890 but which still retain current relevance.[332]   **13–103**

General rules

Rule 1: "There is no *a priori* presumption to the effect that the creditors of a firm do, on the retirement of a partner, enter into any agreement to discharge him from liability."[333]

Rule 2: "An express agreement by the creditor to discharge a retired partner, and to look only to a continuing partner, is not [*necessarily*][334] inoperative for want of consideration. . . . "[335]

Introduction of new partners

Rule 3: "The introduction of a new partner has no effect on the liability of a retired partner, unless the liability of the former is substituted for that of the latter, which cannot be the case unless the creditor can, as of right, hold the new partner liable for the old debt."[336]   **13–104**

---

[332] In fact, the rules set out in the text represent a combination of (1) three rules set out in the 5th ed. of this work at p. 241, (2) three propositions incorporated in Lord Lindley's discussion of the decided cases and (3) six propositions set out in his review of the effect of those cases at *ibid*. pp. 253, 254. The latter were also in fact reproduced in his commentary on the Partnership Act 1890, s.17(3) (Supplement, p. 45).

[333] Such an agreement must be proved: see *Benson v. Hadfield* (1844) 4 Hare 32.

[334] The current editor believes it is appropriate to include this additional word since Lord Lindley's general formulation of the rule (see the 5th ed. of this work at p. 241) was in these terms: "An agreement by a creditor of several persons, liable to him jointly, to discharge one or more of them, and look only to the others, is not necessarily invalid for want of consideration." The version in the text has been retained, since it was stated in terms of partnership and was, moreover, reproduced by Lord Lindley in his Supplement on the Partnership Act 1890: see *supra*, n. 332.

[335] *Lyth v. Ault* (1852) 7 Ex. 669; *Smith v. Patrick* [1901] A.C. 282. *cf. Collier v. P & M J Wright (Holdings) Ltd.* [2008] 1 W.L.R. 643 (CA), albeit not a case involving an outgoing partner; also the earlier decisions to the contrary: see *infra*, paras 13–109 *et seq*.

[336] *Gough v. Davies* (1817) 4 Price 200; *Blew v. Wyatt* (1832) 5 Car. & P. 397; *Kirwan v. Kirwan* (1836) 2 C. & M. 617: see *infra*, para. 13–115.

Rule 4: "The inference that a retired partner has been discharged is greatly facilitated by the circumstance that a new partner has joined the firm and become liable to the creditor in respect of the debt in question.[337] But this is not necessarily conclusive; for there may be circumstances showing that such was not the intention of the parties."[338]

Adoption of new firm as debtor

13–105 *Rule 5*: "An adoption by the creditor of the new firm as his debtor does not by any means necessarily deprive him of his rights against the old firm. . . . [339] And it will certainly not do so if, by expressly reserving his rights against the old firm, he shows that by adopting the new firm he did not intend to discharge the old firm."[340]

Rule 6: " . . . by adopting a new firm as his debtor, a creditor cannot be regarded as having intentionally discharged a person who was a member of the old firm, but was not known to the creditor so to be."[341]

13–106 *Rule 7*: " . . . the fact that a creditor has taken from a continuing partner a new security for a debt due from him and a retired partner jointly is strong evidence of an intention to look only to the continuing partner for payment."[342]

Rule 8: " . . . a creditor who assents to a transfer of his debt from an old firm to a new firm, and goes on dealing with the latter for many years, making no demand for payment against the old firm, may not unfairly be inferred to have discharged the old firm[343] . . . [*although*] the leaning of the Court is strongly in favour of the creditor."[344]

Rule 9: "In whatever way a creditor may have dealt with the surviving partners, he cannot be held to have adopted them as his sole debtors, in respect of a

---

[337] See, as to the acceptance of liability for existing debts by an incoming partner, *supra*, paras 13–26 *et seq.*

[338] See *Thompson v. Percival* (1834) 5 B. & Ad. 925, *infra*, para. 13–110; *Hart v. Alexander* (1837) 2 M. & W. 484, *infra*, para. 13–120; also *Keay v. Fenwick* (1876) 1 C.P.D. 745. And see *infra*, paras 13–115 *et seq.*

[339] Lord Lindley noted that the rule was the same at law and in equity. As to the position at law, he referred to *David v. Ellice* (1826) 5 B. & C. 196; *Thompson v. Percival* (1834) 5 B. & Ad. 925; also *Heath v. Percival* (1720) 1 P.W. 682; *Gough v. Davies* (1817) 4 Price 200; *Blew v. Wyatt* (1832) 5 C. & P. 397; *Kirwan v. Kirwan* (1836) 2 C. & M. 617. As to the position in equity, see *Oakford v. European and American Steam Shipping Co.* (1863) 1 Hem. & M. 182; also *Sleech's Case* (1816) 1 Mer. 539; *Clayton's Case* (1816) 1 Mer. 572; *Palmer's Case* (1816) 1 Mer. 623; *Braithwaite v. Britain* (1836) 1 Keen 206; *Winter v. Innes* (1838) 4 M. & C. 101; *Re Head* [1893] 3 Ch. 426; *Rouse v. Bradford Banking Co.* [1894] A.C. 586. And see *Matthews v. Ruggles Brise* [1911] 1 Ch. 194.

[340] *Jacomb v. Harwood* (1751) 2 Ves.Sen. 265; *Bedford v. Deakin* (1818) 2 B. & A. 210.

[341] *Robinson v. Wilkinson* (1817) 3 Price 538.

[342] *Evans v. Drummond* (1801) 4 Esp. 89; *Reed v. White* (1804) 5 Esp. 122. *cf. Re Head* [1893] 3 Ch. 426 and *Head v. Head (No. 2)* [1894] 2 Ch. 236.

[343] Lord Lindley pointed out that, in such a case, the court will consider all the circumstances and infer a discharge if "upon the whole, justice to all parties so requires": see *Ex p. Executors of James Douglas* [1930] 1 Ch. 342, 350 *per* Luxmoore J.; also *Ex p. Kendall* (1811) 17 Ves. Jr. 514; *Oakeley v. Pasheller* (1836) 10 Bli.(N.S.) 548; *Brown v. Gordon* (1852) 16 Beav. 302; *Wilson v. Lloyd* (1873) L.R. 16 Eq. 60.

[344] This view was based on the relative paucity of cases in which a discharge had been inferred, as compared to the number of cases in which it had not.

demand arising out of a fraudulent transaction, of which he has been constantly kept in ignorance."[345]

One additional point should be noted in this context. It has already been seen **13–107** that a release of one partner will release all his co-partners.[346] It follows that if a creditor discharges an outgoing partner but does not acquire any new rights against the continuing or new partners, he is likely to be remediless.[347] However, the position may be otherwise where the outgoing partner was, to the creditor's knowledge, merely a surety for the continuing partners' obligations.[348]

The decided cases

Virtually all the cases which illustrate Lord Lindley's rules pre-date the **13–108** Partnership Act 1890 and may conveniently be grouped under the following headings:

Group 1: Cases in which the outgoing partner was not discharged and either:

    (a) no new partner was introduced; or

    (b) one or more new partners were introduced.

Group 2: Cases in which the outgoing partner was discharged.

Group 3: Analogous cases concerning the discharge of the estate of a deceased partner.

GROUP 1(a): *Outgoing partner not discharged; no new partner introduced*

Agreement to look only to continuing partners for payment

This group of cases reflects Rules 1, 2 and 5.[349] The most extreme examples **13–109** are *Lodge v. Dicas*[350] and *David v. Ellice*.[351] Both involved a similar set of facts, *i.e.* one partner retiring and the other(s) continuing the business and agreeing to pay the debts of the old firm. The claimant creditor in each case appears to have known of the arrangement and to have assented to the transfer of his debt to the books of the new firm; moreover, there was strong evidence indicating that he had agreed to discharge the retired partner and to look only to the other(s) for payment. In both cases, the retired partner was nevertheless held not to have been discharged, the court relying on the fact that no additional person had become liable to the claimant as evidence that the supposed agreement was not supported by consideration.[352]

---

[345] See *Clayton's Case* (1816) 1 Mer. 572: see further, *supra*, para. 13–92.

[346] See *supra*, paras 13–94 *et seq.*

[347] On this basis, Lord Lindley observed "One test, therefore, by which to determine whether a retired partner has been discharged is to see whether the creditor has obtained a new right to demand payment; for if he has not, no discharge can possibly be made out by any evidence which fails to establish an extinguishment of the creditor's demand altogether."

[348] See *supra*, para. 13–98.

[349] See *supra*, paras 13–103, 13–105.

[350] (1820) 3 B. & A. 611.

[351] (1826) 5 B. & C. 196.

[352] See also *Thomas v. Shillibeer* (1836) 1 M. & W. 124.

13–110   On the other hand, this approach was not followed in *Thompson v. Percival*,[353] where the facts were almost identical, save that the creditor, C, having applied to the remaining partner, A, for payment and been informed that he ought thereafter to look to A alone, had drawn a bill of exchange on A, which he subsequently accepted. This bill was dishonoured and proceedings were commenced against A and the retired partner, B. The jury gave a verdict in C's favour, whereupon A and B moved for a nonsuit on the grounds that B had been discharged. Although the court did not finally decide the point, it ordered a new trial, holding that there was a question of fact for the jury whether C had agreed to accept A as his sole debtor and to take the bill accepted by him in satisfaction of A and B's joint debt. It was clearly recognised that such an agreement, if proved, would have discharged B, on the basis of accord and satisfaction.[354]

13–111   Lord Lindley explained the true legal position as follows:

> "[*Lodge v. Dicas*[355] and *David v. Ellice*[356]] have been much criticised[357] and they certainly went too far: for the proposition that a creditor of a firm cannot, for want of consideration, abandon his right against a retiring partner, and retain it against the others, unless they give some fresh security, has been shown to be erroneous, and is now exploded[358] ...
>
> It is not unusual to represent [*both cases*] as altogether overruled by *Thompson v. Percival*[359] and other cases. This, however, is not quite correct. The three cases together establish (1) that a creditor who treats the continuing partners as his debtors, does not necessarily abandon his right to resort to a retired partner for payment; (2) that whether he does or does not is a mixed question of law and fact ... and (3) that [*a decision*][360] will not be disturbed by the court upon the grounds acted on in *Lodge v. Dicas* and *David v. Ellice*."

Treating continuing partners as debtors

13–112   As noted in the preceding paragraphs, if a creditor merely treats the continuing partners as his debtors, this will not in itself be enough to discharge an outgoing partner.[361] In addition to the cases cited therein, the old case of *Heath v. Percival*[362] clearly illustrates this principle. There two partners, A and B, were liable to the claimant under a bond, in respect of which interest was payable at the rate of 5 per cent. The partnership was dissolved and one partner, A, agreed to carry on the business and to take over the partnership debts. Creditors were publicly notified that they should either seek immediate payment of their debts or

---

[353] (1834) 5 B. & Ad. 925.

[354] Retired partners were held to be discharged on this basis in *Evans v. Drummond* (1801) 4 Esp. 89 and *Reed v. White* (1804) 5 Esp. 122: see *infra*, para. 13–119.

[355] (1820) 3 B. & A. 611.

[356] (1826) 5 B. & C. 196.

[357] See *Thompson v. Percival* (1834) 5 B. & Ad. 925, 933 *per* Denman C.J.; *Kirwan v. Kirwan* (1834) 2 C. & M. 617, 624; *Hart v. Alexander* (1837) 2 M. & W. 484, 493 *per* Parke B.

[358] See *Lyth v. Ault* (1852) 7 Ex. 669 and Rule 2, *supra*, para. 13–103. Lord Lindley in fact went on "and there can be little doubt that if similar cases were to arise again, and the jury found for the defendant, the verdict would not be disturbed."

[359] (1834) 5 B. & Ad. 925.

[360] The original reference was to the verdict of a jury.

[361] See Rules 1 and 5, *supra*, paras 13–103, 13–105. An estoppel may conceivably arise in such a case: see *Collier v. P & M J Wright (Holdings) Ltd.* [2008] 1 W.L.R. 643 (CA); also *infra*, para. 13–121.

[362] (1720) 1 P.Wms. 682. See also *Harris v. Farwell* (1846) 15 Beav. 31, *infra*, para. 13–123; *Rouse v. Bradford Banking Co.* [1894] A.C. 586; *Smith v. Patrick* [1901] A.C. 282.

in future look for payment from A alone. The claimant called in the money due to him but, instead of being paid off, he kept the bond and was paid interest at an increased rate. It was held that he did not thereby discharge the retired partner, B, from his liability under the bond.

New security taken from continuing partners

An outgoing partner will not necessarily be discharged even if the continuing partners give the creditor a new security for his debt.[363] In *Bedford v. Deakin*,[364] three partners were indebted to the claimant on certain bills of exchange. The partnership was dissolved and it was agreed that one of the partners, A, should pay the claimant. The claimant was so informed and accepted three promissory notes from A for the amount of the debt; however, he expressly reserved his right to look to all three partners for payment and retained the bills already in his possession. Two of the notes were renewed several times, but the third was not. The claimant successfully sued all three partners on the original bills, never having discharged any of them, either intentionally or otherwise.[365]

13–113

Dormant partners

The position is in many ways *a fortiori* in the case of a dormant partner, since the creditor, being unaware of his existence, cannot intentionally discharge him.[366] Lord Lindley gave the following simple example:

13–114

" . . . if A and B are partners, and the two become indebted to a creditor who knows only of A, and then B, the dormant partner, retires, no dealings between the creditor and A will discharge B from his liability to be sued when discovered, unless those dealings extinguished the original debt not only as against B, but also as against A."

This was clearly decided in *Robinson v. Wilkinson*.[367]

GROUP 1(b): *Outgoing partner not discharged; one or more partners introduced*

Effect of introducing new partner

If an outgoing partner is to be discharged following the admission of a new partner, it is not sufficient merely to show that the new firm has adopted an old debt pursuant to some express or implied agreement between the partners.[368]

13–115

---

[363] See Rule 7, *supra*, para. 13–106.

[364] (1818) 2 B. & A. 210. See also *Swire v. Redman* (1876) 1 Q.B.D. 536 (but note the observations of the Court of Appeal in *Rouse v. Bradford Banking Co.* [1894] 2 Ch. 32, 59–60, 69 *et seq.*). And see *Featherstone v. Hunt* (1822) 1 B. & C. 113; *Spenceley v. Greenwood* (1858) 1 F. & F. 297. *cf. Evans v. Drummond* (1801) 4 Esp. 89, *infra*, para. 13–119.

[365] See also *Re Head* [1893] 3 Ch. 426; *cf. Head v. Head (No. 2)* [1894] 2 Ch. 236, *infra*, para. 13–122.

[366] See Rule 6, *supra*, para. 13–105.

[367] (1817) 3 Price 538.

[368] See Rules 3 and 4, *supra*, para. 13–104; also *supra*, paras 13–22 *et seq.* Lord Lindley pointed out that " . . . even if the new firm adopts the old debt and pays interest on it, this is *prima facie* only in pursuance of some agreement between the partners themselves: and a creditor who does no more than allow the partners to carry out that agreement does not debar himself of his right to look for payment to those originally indebted to him." See *supra*, para. 13–26.

Thus, in *Kirwan v. Kirwan*,[369] three partners, C, M and N, were indebted to the claimant. On C's retirement, M and N continued in partnership together and agreed to discharge the debts of the old firm. M then retired and N took in a new partner. The claimant's account was, on each change, transferred to the books of the new firm; interest was paid and accounts rendered to him as before. The claimant, having been informed of the dissolution of the old firm, had apparently stated in a letter written to C that he was aware he had no further claim on him. It was nevertheless held that C, M and N remained liable, as there was nothing to show that the liability of either new firm had been substituted for that of the old; moreover, the claimant's letter to C did not amount to an agreement to discharge him.

13–116   In *Gough v. Davies*,[370] which concerned a banking partnership, it is not entirely clear whether the claimant had assented to the transfer of his debt to the books of the new firm,[371] nevertheless he continued to deposit money with that firm, which paid him interest on both the old debt and the new deposits, as if they formed a single debt. It was again held that this did not prove an agreement by the claimant to discharge the retired partner, who was consequently held liable for the old debt. *Blew v. Wyatt*[372] was a similar case, save that the creditor was at all times an employee of the firm and thus had first hand knowledge of the changes in its membership.

13–117   Lord Lindley observed:

> "Whether in these cases . . . the creditor could have sued the new firm, may perhaps be open to doubt.[373] If he could not, it would be absurd to contend that the liability of the new firm was substituted for that of the old; whilst if he could, the evidence was not sufficient to show an intention on his part to deprive himself of the security afforded by the undoubted liability of the original firm before any change in it took place. It by no means follows that a creditor who assents to an arrangement by which a new person becomes liable to him consents to abandon his hold on another person clearly liable to him already; and unless a substitution of liability can be established, the old liability remains."[374]

GROUP 2: *Outgoing partner discharged*

13–118   In each of the cases in this group, the court (or a jury) concluded that the creditor had, either expressly or by implication, treated the members of the new firm as his sole debtors, thereby discharging the outgoing partner.[375]

---

[369] (1836) 2 C. & M. 617.

[370] (1817) 4 Price 200.

[371] Lord Lindley stated that he did so assent, but this does not appear to be borne out by the judgments of Graham B. (*ibid.* p. 212) or Wood B. (*ibid.* p. 214).

[372] (1832) 5 Car. & P. 397.

[373] See *Kirwan v. Kirwan* (1836) 2 C. & M. 617, 628 *per* Bolland B.; also *Daniel v. Cross* (1796) 3 Ves. Jr. 277; *Fergusson v. Fyffe* (1841) 8 Cl. & F. 121.

[374] See *Harris v. Farwell* (1846) 15 Beav. 31, *infra*, para. 13–123; *Rouse v. Bradford Banking Co.* [1894] 2 Ch. 32, 54 *per* Lindley L.J. (the decision being affirmed at [1894] A.C. 586); *Matthews v. Ruggles Brise* [1911] 1 Ch. 194.

[375] Lord Lindley commented (by way of footnote) "[*Sir Frederick*] Pollock says truly that there is nothing to prevent a firm from stipulating with any creditor that he shall look only to the members of the firm for the time being": see *Pollock on the Law of Partnership* (15th ed., 1952), p. 61. Also *Hort's Case* and *Grain's Case* (1875) 1 Ch.D. 307.

No new partner introduced

An obvious example of a case in this class[376] is *Thompson v. Percival*,[377] the **13–119** facts of which have already been outlined.

In *Evans v. Drummond*,[378] two partners, A and B, gave a bill of exchange to the creditor in respect of certain goods which he had supplied to them. A retired and B continued the business. The bill fell due but was not paid; it was renewed by another bill given by B. The creditor took this bill knowing of the change in the firm. It was held that, by so doing, the creditor had relied on the sole liability of B, and had thereby discharged A. *Reed v. White*[379] is a decision to the same effect.

One or more new partners introduced

Consistently with Rule 4,[380] *Hart v. Alexander*[381] demonstrates the relative **13–120** ease with which the discharge of an outgoing partner may be inferred from a creditor's acceptance of direct rights against a new partner. In that case, the claimant had opened an account with a firm of bankers. The defendant retired from the firm some years later, when a new partner was introduced; his retirement was duly advertised and there was evidence to show that the claimant was aware of it. The new firm thereafter rendered accounts to the claimant and paid him interest, at rates which varied from time to time. After a number of other changes in the membership of the new firm, it was bankrupted and the claimant proceeded to prove his debt against the joint estate. He then sued the defendant. Lord Abinger's summing up to the jury was in forceful terms[382] and the verdict was given to the defendant. The claimant sought a new trial on the ground that there was no evidence to show that he had agreed to discharge the defendant from his liability, but this application was refused. A majority of the court[383] con-

---

[376] See Rules 1, 2, 5 *et seq., supra*, paras 13–103, 13–105 *et seq.*

[377] (1834) 5 B. & Ad. 925; see *supra*, para. 13–110.

[378] (1801) 4 Esp. 89. *cf. Bedford v. Deakin* (1818) 2 B. & A. 210, *supra*, para. 13–113. Note, however, the possible implications of renewing a bill where an outgoing partner is, to the knowledge of the creditor, merely a surety for the continuing partners: see *Goldfarb v. Bartlett and Kremer* [1920] 1 K.B. 639 and *supra*, para. 13–98.

[379] (1804) 5 Esp. 122.

[380] See *supra*, para. 13–104.

[381] (1837) 2 M. & W. 484. See also *Oakeley v. Pasheller* (1836) 10 Bli.(N.S.) 548, *supra*, para. 13–99; *Wilson v. Lloyd* (1873) L.R. 16 Eq. 60 (this decision is unsatisfactory: see *supra*, para. 13–99, n. 324). *cf. Re Commercial Bank Corporation of India and the East* (1869) 16 W.R. 958 and *Ex p. Gibson* (1869) L.R. 4 Ch.App. 662.

[382] (1837) 7 C. & P. 746. The summing up reportedly contained the following passage: "I take the law to be this: Where a debtor who is a partner in a firm, leaves that firm, and any person trading with the firm has notice of it, and he goes on dealing with the firm and making fresh contracts, that discharges the retiring partner, though no new partner comes in. So it is if the creditor draws for part of his balance, and sends in more goods; so, if the creditor strikes a fresh balance with the new partners for a different rate of interest; so, if a new partner comes in, and the creditor accept an account in which the new partner is made liable for the balance—that discharges the old firm, as both firms cannot be liable at once for the same debt. This is the law as laid down in several cases, in which indeed, there is some contradiction: however, I believe that what I have stated is the result of them.": see *ibid.* p. 754. However, Lord Lindley observed that "the learned judge was scarcely warranted by those cases in going so far as he did."

[383] Lord Abinger C.B. and Parke B (Bolland B. dissenting).

sidered that there was abundant evidence to show that the claimant knew of the defendant's retirement.

Ex p. Whitmore[384] was a similar case.

Estoppel

13–121   In certain circumstances, a creditor may so conduct himself that he will be estopped from proceeding against an outgoing partner.[385] However, such cases will be rare, as Lord Lindley explained:

> "A settlement by partners of their accounts on the footing that one of them only is liable to a creditor will not affect him[386] unless he has been guilty of some fraud, or has done some act or made some statement in order to induce the partners, or one of them, to settle their accounts on the faith that one of them is no longer liable."[387]

GROUP 3: *Discharge of estate of deceased partner*

13–122   The principles illustrated in the previous paragraphs are also applicable following the death of a partner.[388]

No new partner introduced

Consistently with Rules 1 and 5 *et seq.*,[389] if a creditor of a firm, knowing that one partner has died, continues to deal with the surviving partners, he will not lose his rights against the deceased partner's estate, unless there is evidence of his intention to abandon those rights.[390] Such an intention will not, without more, be inferred from an attempt to obtain payment from the surviving partners, *e.g.* by suing them to judgment[391] or proving against the joint estate of the new firm in the event of its insolvency.[392]

---

[384] (1838) 3 Deac. 365, *supra*, para. 13–28. See also *Rolfe v. Flower* (1865) L.R. 1 P.C. 27.

[385] See, for an analogous case, *Collier v. P & M J Wright (Holdings) Ltd.* [2008] 1 W.L.R. 643 (CA), where one partner in a firm (since dissolved) had agreed with the firm's creditor to bear only his pro rata share of a joint liability. The agreement was held not to be binding in the absence of consideration, but nevertheless a triable issue as to the existence of a promissory estoppel did arise.

[386] So far as the creditor is concerned, such a settlement will normally be *res inter alios acta*.

[387] See *Davison v. Donaldson* (1882) 9 Q.B.D. 623; also *Featherstone v. Hunt* (1822) 1 B. & C. 113 (a case of alleged fraud). And see *The Huntsman* [1894] P. 214, 219 *per* Gorell Barnes J.

[388] Noting the similarities between the position of a retired partner and the estate of the deceased partner, Lord Lindley observed: "The parallel between the two would be complete were it not that before the Judicature Acts the estate of a partner who died in the lifetime of his co-partners was liable for the joint debts of the firm in equity only; and there might have been circumstances to induce a Court of equity to hold that estate discharged, although the same circumstances would not, in the case of a retiring partner, have operated as a discharge at law, and *vice versa*." He then referred to *Ex p. Kendall* (1811) 17 Ves. Jr. 514 and *Jacomb v. Harwood* (1751) 2 Ves.Sen. 265. The position is now, of course, governed by the Partnership Act 1890, s.9, *supra*, paras 13–03 *et seq.*

[389] See *supra*, paras 13–103, 13–105 *et seq.*

[390] *Winter v. Innes* (1838) 4 M. & Cr. 101; also *Devaynes v. Noble, Sleech's Case* (1816) 1 Mer. 539; *Clayton's Case* (1816) 1 Mer. 579; *Palmer's Case* (1816) 1 Mer. 623; *Braithwaite v. Britain* (1836) 1 Keen 206. These were cases decided in equity: see *supra*, para. 13–122, n. 388. See also *supra*, paras 13–109 *et seq.*

[391] *Jacomb v. Harwood* (1751) 2 Ves. Sen. 265. See also *supra*, para. 13–06 and *infra*, para. 13–130.

[392] *Sleech's Case* (1816) 1 Mer. 570; *Harris v. Farwell* (1846) 15 Beav. 31, *infra*, para. 13–123. See also *Rouse v. Bradford Banking Co.* [1894] 2 Ch. 32 (affirmed at [1894] A.C. 586). *cf. Brown v. Gordon* (1852) 16 Beav. 302, *infra*, para. 13–125; *Bilborough v. Holmes* (1876) 5 Ch.D. 255, *infra*, para. 13–123, n. 398; *Ex p. Executors of James Douglas* [1930] 1 Ch. 342, 350 *per* Luxmoore J.

Thus, in *Re Head*[393] a customer of a banking partnership, knowing of the death of one of the partners, had accepted a fresh deposit note from the surviving partner for the balance of a debt due from the firm. The deceased partner's estate was held not to have been discharged thereby. On the other hand, in *Head v. Head (No. 2)*[394] the customer, who wished to withdraw the balance on his current account, was persuaded by the surviving partner to transfer that balance to an interest bearing deposit account and accepted a deposit note for that balance. By so doing he was held to have discharged the estate of the deceased partner.

It is perhaps self evident that a creditor will not be prejudiced by any dealings with the surviving partner which are induced by fraud.[395]

One or more new partners introduced

Again, consistently with Rules 3 and 4,[396] a creditor of the old firm who, **13–123** following the admission of a new partner, continues to deal with the new firm and is paid interest by that firm as if the debt was its own, will not thereby deprive himself of his rights against the estate of a deceased member of the old firm.[397]

Thus, in *Harris v. Farwell*,[398] the three partners of a banking firm were indebted to a customer on a deposit note. One partner died and his son was admitted to the partnership. The new firm paid interest on the note for some time and then became bankrupt. The claimant proved for the amount of his debt and received a dividend out of the new firm's joint estate. By so doing, he was held not to have precluded himself from subsequently proceeding against the deceased partner's estate.

Where creditor allows estate to be administered

However, once he has learned of a partner's death, a creditor should prudently **13–124** take steps to obtain payment out of his estate: if he fails to do so and allows the administration to proceed on the footing that there is no liability, his rights may be prejudiced, as Lord Lindley explained:

> " . . . if, after the death of a partner, a creditor of the old firm knows of the death, and . . . lies by and allows [*the*] estate to be administered as if he had no claim upon it, and if he continues to deal with the surviving partners as if they and they alone were his debtors, in that case the creditor will not be allowed to resort to the assets of the deceased."[399]

[393] [1893] 3 Ch. 426.
[394] [1894] 2 Ch. 236.
[395] As in *Plumer v. Gregory* (1874) L.R. 18 Eq. 621.
[396] See *supra*, para. 13–104.
[397] *Daniel v. Cross* (1796) 3 Ves. Jr. 277.
[398] (1851) 15 Beav. 31. The report does not indicate when the customer first learned of the change in the firm. *cf. Bilborough v. Holmes* (1876) 5 Ch.D. 255, which was a somewhat similar case. There the deceased partner's estate was held to be discharged, although the proof was for money lent (or deemed to have been lent) to the new firm.
[399] *Oakeley v. Pasheller* (1836) 10 Bli.(N.S.) 548: see *supra*, para. 13–99 and, in particular, nn. 324, 326. *Quaere*, would a similar approach have been adopted if proceedings against the deceased partner's estate had been commenced in *Morris v. Wentworth-Stanley* [1999] Q.B. 1004, noted *supra*, para. 13–95?

13–125   This doctrine is illustrated by *Brown v. Gordon.*[400] There the claimant had deposited money with a banking partnership comprising three partners, A, B and C. D subsequently became a partner. A died, having made a will containing a trust for the payment of his debts. E (who was A's son and the executor and residuary beneficiary under his will) was admitted as a partner. B and C then died. Each successive firm paid interest to the claimant on his debt. D and E were eventually made bankrupt and the claimant proved for the amount of his debt. He then sought payment out of A's estate, but it was held that, by neglecting to make any claim against that estate for some 16 years and by treating the successive firms as his debtors, he had discharged the estate from liability; accordingly, he could not be regarded as a creditor of the deceased, so as to benefit under the express trust for the payment of his debts.

(B)   MERGER AND JUDGMENT RECOVERED

Merger of securities

13–126   Reference must also be made in this context to the doctrine of merger, which may operate to discharge a partnership debt or obligation where a creditor obtains a security of a *higher* nature than that which he previously possessed,[401] provided that he does not accept it as a collateral security.[402]

Nature of obligation

13–127   The application of the doctrine to joint and joint and several obligations is not entirely clear. Lord Lindley wrote:

> " . . . there is no mean authority for saying that if two parties are jointly indebted by simple contract, and one of them gives his bond for payment of the debt, the joint debt is at an end[403]; but there are more recent decisions to the contrary,[404] and the question cannot be considered as yet settled."

Although subsequent editors have expressed the view that the "more recent decisions will probably prevail,"[405] it is submitted in the latest edition of *Chitty on Contracts*[406] that, in the situation supposed, there will be a merger in the case of a joint debt but not in the case of a joint and several debt. On that basis, a security given by continuing partners in respect of a joint debt of the old firm will

---

[400] (1852) 16 Beav. 302; *Bilborough v. Holmes* (1876) 5 Ch.D. 255 is a somewhat similar case: see *supra*, para. 13–123, n. 398.

[401] *Higgen's Case* (1605) 6 Co. 44b; *Owen v. Homan* (1851) 3 Mac. & G. 378; *Price v. Moulton* (1851) 10 C.B. 561; *Kidd v. Boone* (1871) 40 L.J. Ch. 531; *Ex p. Oriental Financial Corporation* (1876) 4 Ch.D. 33.

[402] *Twopenny v. Young* (1824) 3 B. & C. 208; *Ex p. Hughes* (1872) 4 Ch.D. 34, note; *Barclays Bank v. Beck* [1952] 2 Q.B. 47.

[403] *Owen v. Homan* (1851) 3 Mac. & G. 378; *Ex p. Hernaman* (1848) 12 Jur. 642 (*quaere* was this not a case of satisfaction rather than merger?).

[404] *Ansell v. Baker* (1850) 15 Q.B. 20; *Sharpe v. Gibbs* (1864) 16 C.B.(N.S.) 527.

[405] This change in fact dates from the 6th ed., in the preparation of which Lord Lindley was involved.

[406] 30th ed., para. 25–001.

be capable of discharging an outgoing partner; *per contra*, perhaps, if the security is given by the continuing partners and other persons subsequently admitted to the partnership.[407]

Security for future advances

The operation of the doctrine is dependent on the existence of a present debt: it cannot apply where security is given in respect of a present *and* future debt, *e.g.* the fluctuating balance due on a running account.[408] **13–128**

Nature of security

To effect a merger, the security must clearly be of a higher nature that the existing security. A bill of exchange or promissory note does not enjoy such a character, as Lord Lindley recognised: **13–129**

> "If a person solely indebted enters into partnership with another, and the two give a joint note or bill for the debt of the first, and the note or bill is not paid, the creditor is not precluded from demanding payment from his original debtor,[409] unless it can be shown that the bill or note was taken in satisfaction of the original demand.[410] So, if two partners are indebted on the partnership account, and one of them gives a bill or note for the debt, and that bill or note is dishonoured, the creditor who took it will not be precluded from having recourse to both partners for payment,[411] unless it can be shown that he intended to substitute the liability of the one for the joint liability of the two."[412]

Judgment recovered

Joint obligations

Although judgment recovered does technically effect a merger,[413] a judgment against one partner in respect of a partnership debt or obligation will not be a bar to a subsequent action against other partners who are jointly liable with him[414] unless, on a true analysis, there is an underlying accord and satisfaction.[415] **13–130**

---

[407] Surely, in such a case the security will not be co-extensive with the existing security, since it will be made between different parties: see, for example, *Bell v. Banks* (1841) 3 Man. & G. 258. But see *Ex p. Hernaman* (1848) 12 Jur. 642, *supra*, n. 403.

[408] *Holmes v. Bell* (1840) 3 Man. & G. 213; *Barclays Bank v. Beck* [1952] 2 Q.B. 47.

[409] *Ex p. Seddon* (1788) 2 Cox. 49; *Ex p. Lobb* (1802) 7 Ves. Jr. 592; *Ex p. Hay* (1808) 15 Ves. Jr. 4; *Ex p. Kedie* (1832) 2 D. & C. 321; *Ex p. Meinertzhagen* (1838) 3 Deac. 101.

[410] *Ex p. Kirby* (1819) Buck 511; *Ex p. Whitmore* (1838) 3 Deac. 365; *Ex p. Jackson* (1841) 2 M.D. & D. 146.

[411] *Ex p. Hodgkinson* (1815) 19 Ves.Jr. 291; *Whitwell v. Perrin* (1858) 4 C.B.(N.S.) 412; *Bottomley v. Nuttall* (1858) 5 C.B.(N.S.) 122; *Keay v. Fenwick* (1876) 1 C.P.D. 745. See also *Bedford v. Deakin* (1818) 2 B. & A. 210, *supra*, para. 13–113; *Ex p. Raleigh* (1838) 3 M. & A. 670.

[412] See, for example, *Evans v. Drummond* (1801) 4 Esp. 89, *supra*, para. 13–119; *Reed v. White* (1804) 4 Esp. 122. *cf.* the cases in the previous note.

[413] *Ex p. Oriental Financial Corporation* (1876) 4 Ch.D. 33; *Kendall v. Hamilton* (1879) 4 App.Cas. 504; *Fraser v. Hlmad Ltd.* [2006] I.C.R. 1395 (CA); but see also *Messer Griesheim GmbH v. Goyal MG Gases PVT Ltd.* [2006] 1 C.L.C. 283. And see *supra*, para. 13–05.

[414] Civil Liability (Contribution) Act 1978, s.3; see also *infra*, para. 20–23. For a summary of the law prior to that Act, see the 15th ed. of this work at pp. 422, 423.

[415] See *Morris v. Wentworth-Stanley* [1999] Q.B. 1004 (CA), noted *supra*, paras 13–05, 13–95.

Joint and several obligations

13–131   As in the case of joint liability, judgment recovered against a partner in respect of a joint and several partnership debt or obligation will not prevent a subsequent action against other partners jointly liable with him[416]; nor will it affect the *several* liability of any partner,[417] unless there is an underlying accord and satisfaction[418] or the judgment is satisfied.[419] It follows that judgment against the surviving partners of a firm will not normally discharge the estate of a deceased partner.[420]

Proof against insolvent partner's estate

13–132   It should be noted that proof against an insolvent partner's estate[421] will not prevent a partnership creditor from subsequently proceeding against the solvent partners for the balance of the debt.[422]

(C)   LIMITATION

13–133   A consideration of the general law governing the limitation of actions is obviously outside the scope of the present work.[423] What is, however, of importance is to identify the extent to which an acknowledgment or part payment[424] may be made by a single partner and, thus, extend the limitation period against the firm.

Continuing partnership

13–134   It is submitted that both an acknowledgment and a part payment made by a partner within the scope of his express or implied authority[425] will bind his

---

[416] Civil Liability (Contribution) Act 1978, s.3. If, however, judgment is obtained against all the partners jointly, their several liability will be extinguished, by operation of the principle *nemo debet bis vexari pro una et eadem causa* (it is a rule of law that man shall not be twice vexed for one and the same cause).

[417] *Ex p. Christie* (1832) Mont. & Bl. 352; *Lechmere v. Fletcher* (1833) 1 C. & M. 623, 635 *per* Bayley B.; *Re Davison* (1884) 13 Q.B.D. 50; *Blyth v. Fladgate* [1891] 1 Ch. 337, 353 *per* Stirling J. See also *Ansell v. Baker* (1850) 15 Q.B. 20.

[418] See *Morris v. Wentworth-Stanley* [1999] Q.B. 1004 (CA), noted *supra*, paras 13–05, 13–95.

[419] *Higgen's Case* (1605) 6 Co.44b; *Lechmere v. Fletcher, supra*; *Field v. Robins* (1838) 8 A. & E. 90; *King v. Hoare* (1844) 13 M. & W. 494; also *Drake v. Mitchell* (1803) 3 East 251.

[420] Partnership Act 1890, s.9, *supra*, paras 13–03 *et seq.*; *Jacomb v. Harwood* (1751) 2 Ves.Sen. 265; *Rawlins v. Wickham* (1858) 3 De G. & J. 304; *Liverpool Borough Bank v. Walker* (1859) 4 De G. & J. 24.

[421] See generally, *infra*, paras 27–78 *et seq.*

[422] *Whitwell v. Perrin* (1858) 4 C.B.(N.S.) 412; *Bottomley v. Nuttall* (1858) 5 C.B.(N.S.) 122; *Keay v. Fenwick* (1876) 1 C.P.D. 745.

[423] See, generally, *McGee, Limitation Periods* (5th ed.); *Preston and Newsom's Limitation of Actions* (4th ed.).

[424] Limitation Act 1980, ss.29–31. The two concepts are free standing: *Ashcroft v. Bradford & Bingley Plc* [2010] 2 P. & C.R. 13 (CA). Note that in *Winning v. Cunningham* 2009 GWD 01–19 (Sh. Ct.), it was held that producing a set of dissolution accounts amounted to an acknowledgment of a duty to account to a former partner under Scots law.

[425] See generally, *supra*, para. 12–02 *et seq.*

co-partners, since it will be given by him in his capacity as agent of the firm.[426] If, however, in giving an acknowledgment, the partner has exceeded such authority, his co-partners will not be affected thereby[427]; *per contra* in the case of a part payment.[428]

An acknowledgment of a partnership liability given by a partner in some other capacity will naturally bind him in his capacity as a partner, as well as his co-partners.[429]

Dissolved partnership

The position will be the same following the dissolution of a partnership, since **13–135** each partner's authority will continue for the purposes of winding up its affairs.[430] It should, however, be noted that a part payment (but not an acknowledgment) will be effective as against an outgoing partner who has become a surety for the firm's obligations.[431]

Notwithstanding the views expressed in previous editions of this work,[432] the current editor considers that neither an outgoing partner nor the estate of a deceased partner can escape the consequences of an acknowledgment or part payment given by the continuing or surviving partners, save only in the case of an acknowledgment given without authority. The fact that a deceased partner's estate is only *severally* liable for the debts and obligations of the firm is immaterial.[433]

---

[426] Partnership Act 1890, s.5; Limitation Act 1980, s.30(2). See, for example, *Winning v. Cunningham, supra,* at [69], where the acknowledgment of a duty to account was given to a former partner.

[427] Limitation Act 1980, s.31(6).

[428] *ibid.* s.31(7). See also, under the old law, *Watson v. Woodman* (1875) L.R. 20 Eq. 721: *Goodwin v. Parton* (1880) 42 L.T. 568.

[429] *Harper v. John C Harper & Co (No.2)* 2003 S.L.T. 102 (Sh Ct.).

[430] Partnership Act 1890, s.38, *supra,* paras 13–62 *et seq.*

[431] See *supra*, para. 13–98.

[432] See the 15th ed. of this work at p. 427 and the decisions in *Watson v. Woodman* (1875) L.R 20 Eq. 721 (retired partner) and *Thompson v. Waithman* (1856) 3 Drew. 628 (executors of deceased partner). *cf. Re Tucker* [1894] 3 Ch. 429 (where the retirement was not advertised).

[433] See the Partnership Act 1890, s.9, *supra*, para. 13–03; and see, in particular, the terms of the Limitation Act 1980, s.31(7).

CHAPTER 14

ACTIONS BY AND AGAINST PARTNERS

CIVIL actions brought by partners against a third party or vice versa are governed **14–01**
by the same rules of procedure as other actions, save that the partners must now,
in general, sue or be sued in the firm name.[1] However, this procedural nicety
should not be permitted to obscure the importance of identifying the *correct*
parties to such an action, particularly where the composition of the firm has not
remained static. This aspect will be considered in the first section of this chapter.
Subsequent sections are devoted to the authority of a partner to act for the firm
in legal proceedings, set off and the execution of money and other judgments
obtained against partners.

Criminal proceedings

As regards criminal proceedings, the existence of a partnership is of little **14–02**
general significance,[2] since in the case of common law offences a partnership
has no existence separate from the partners of which it is composed and therefore seemingly cannot *itself* commit an offence.[3] In the case of a statutory
offence, everything will depend on the terms of the statute in question.[4] In
Clode v. Barnes[5] it was held that section 1 of the Trade Descriptions Act 1968
created an offence of strict liability, so that where one partner had committed
an offence under the section in the course of carrying on the partnership
business, his partner was automatically guilty of the same offence. The position would, it appears, have been different if *mens rea* was an ingredient of
the offence.[6] More recently, specific statutes have made clear that a partnership may commit an offence in its own right and that individual partners may
also commit an offence alongside their firm.[7] In *W. Stevenson & Sons v.*

---

[1] CPR 7APD, para. 5A, *infra*, para. A2–04. See further, *infra*, paras 14–04 *et seq*.

[2] See *R. v. Bonner* [1970] 1 W.L.R. 838 (theft of partnership property); *Garrett v. Hooper* [1973]
Crim.L.R. 61; *Bennett v. Richardson* [1980] R.T.R. 358 (both road traffic cases).

[3] This proposition would, by implication, seem to have been accepted by the Court of Appeal in
W. Stevenson & Sons v. R [2008] Bus. L.R. 1200 at paras [25], [26].

[4] See generally *R v. L* [2009] 1 Cr. App. R. 16, where the court was considering the position of an
unincorporated association under the Water Resources Act 1991, s.85. It was held that a prosecution
could be brought against the unincorporated association (in that case a club) or its members.

[5] [1974] 1 W.L.R. 544

[6] As appears to be the position under *ibid*. s.14(1): see *Clode v. Barnes, supra*, at p. 546. In *Parsons
v. Barnes* [1973] Crim.L.R. 537, the Divisional Court had declined to lay down a general proposition
that one partner will *necessarily* be responsible for the acts of his co-partner in relation to an offence
under *ibid*. s.14(1). See also *W. Stevenson & Sons v. R, supra*, at para. [28]; *R v. L, supra*, at [30].

[7] See, for example, the Copyright, Designs and Patents Act 1988, s.285(1), (3); Trade Marks Act
1994, s.101(1), (4); Financial Services and Markets Act 2000, s.403; Political Parties, Elections and
Referendums Act 2000, s.153; Education Act 2002, s.168C (as added by the Education and
Inspections Act 2006, s.172); the Health Act 2006, ss.76(4), 77(1), (5); the Companies Act 2006,
ss.1121, 1123(3), 1207; the Safeguarding Vulnerable Groups Act 2006, s.18(2); the Legal Services
Act 2007, s.197(7) (not yet in force); Money Laundering Regulations 2007 (SI 2007/2157), regs. 45,
47; Bribery Act 2010, ss.7(1), (5), 8 (not yet in force).

R,[8] it was held that the conviction of a partnership for an offence under the Sea Fishing (Enforcement of Community Control Measures) Order 2000[9] did not also automatically involve the conviction of each of the partners. In cases of this kind, the partnership will usually be indicted in the firm name[10] and any financial penalty must normally be met out of the partnership assets and *not* by the individual partners.[11] Where the partnership commits an offence and is then dissolved, it would seem that it can no longer be prosecuted, but the partners may be.[12]

1.   PARTIES TO ACTIONS AND RELATED MATTERS

14–03   In earlier editions of this work there were set out, by way of introduction to this section, a number of general propositions regarding the joinder and misjoinder of parties, based on Lord Lindley's original formulation, but these have not been retained in the present edition.[13]

A.   ACTIONS IN FIRM NAME

The general rule

14–04   Proceedings by or against two or more partners who carry on business within the jurisdiction must, unless it is inappropriate so to do, be commenced in the name under which they carried on business when the cause of action accrued.[14] For this purpose, partners include persons claiming or alleged to be partners.[15] However, as Lord Lindley observed in relation to a forerunner of the modern rule[16]:

> " . . . the firm's name, when used in any action, is merely a convenient method of expressing the names of those who constituted the firm when the cause of action accrued. The rule does not incorporate the firm[17]; so that if A is a creditor of a firm, B, C and D, and D retires and E takes his place and the name of the firm continues unchanged, A cannot maintain an action against B, C and E in the name of the firm,

---

[8] [2008] Bus. L.R. 1200 (CA).

[9] (SI 2000/51), arts. 3, 11(3).

[10] Although there was no statutory requirement to this effect in *W Stevenson & Sons, v. R, supra,* the court held that this made no difference in practice: see *ibid.* at para. [32].

[11] See the various statutory provisions listed *supra,* n. 7. There was no such provision in the regulations considered in *W Stevenson & Sons, v. R, supra,* but this was thought by the court to be "by accident rather than by design": *ibid.* para. [35].

[12] See *R v. Wakefield* 2004 WL 1959718, a decision under the Trade Marks Act 1994, s.101; also *Balmer v. HM Advocate* 2008 S.L.T. 799 (HCJ), where it was held that a dissolved Scottish partnership had ceased to have any legal personality and could not be indicted for an offence.

[13] The propositions are to be found in the 15th ed. of this work, at pp. 430 *et seq.*

[14] CPR 7APD, paras 5A.1, 5A.3, *infra,* para. A2–04.

[15] *ibid.* para. 5A.2, *infra,* para. A2–04.

[16] *i.e.* the (then) RSC Ord. xvi, r. 9.

[17] Lord Lindley referred at this point to the judgment of James L.J. in *Ex p. Blain* (1879) 12 Ch.D. 522, which scarcely seems in point. See, as to the derivation of this rule, *Bullock v. Caird* (1875) L.R. 10 Q.B. 276.

unless B, C and E have become or are content to be treated as his debtors.[18] In the case supposed, an action against the firm would mean an action against B, C and D, *i.e.* A's real debtors".

Thus, the composition of the firm at the date the proceedings are *issued* will normally be irrelevant.

It should be noted that this is a mere rule of procedure, which will neither affect the rights of the parties nor give rise to any new or independent cause of action.[19]

The claim form should be headed with the full name of the firm, where that is known, followed by the words "(A Firm)".[20]

Carrying on business within the jurisdiction

The firm name may only be used where the partners were carrying on business   **14–05** within the jurisdiction when the cause of action accrued.[21] It does not matter that the business has since ceased to be carried on or that the partnership has been dissolved.[22] Provided that this test is satisfied, the nationality, domicile or residence of the partners will be immaterial.[23]

Where, on the other hand, the partners cannot be shown to be (or to have been) carrying on business within the jurisdiction at the relevant time, the proceedings must be issued in their individual names,[24] unless it can be proved that the firm has separate legal personality under the law by which it was constituted.[25]

---

[18] See further, as to agreements to take on existing debts, *supra*, paras 13–26 *et seq.* and *infra*, paras 14–48 *et seq.*

[19] *Meyer & Co. v. Faber (No. 2)* [1923] 2 Ch. 421, 441 *per* Warrington L.J.; *Mephistopheles Debt Collection Service v. Lotay* [1994] 1 W.L.R. 1064 (CA).

[20] CPR 16PD, para. 2.6(c)(i), *infra*, para. A2–08.

[21] *ibid.* 7APD, para. 5A.3, *infra*, para. A2–04. As to what will amount to carrying on business within the jurisdiction, see *Baillie v. Goodwin* (1886) 33 Ch.D. 604; *Grant v. Anderson & Co.* [1892] 1 Q.B. 108; *Singleton v. Roberts & Co.* (1894) 70 L.T. 687; *The Lalandia* [1933] P. 56; *Okura v. Forsbacka Jernverks Aktiebolag* [1914] 1 K.B. 715; *Thames and Mersey Marine Insurance Co. v. Societa di Navigazione a Vapore del Lloyd Austriaco* (1914) 111 L.T. 97; *Adams v. Cape Industries Plc* [1990] Ch. 433; and see also *Re Brauch* [1978] Ch. 316 (a decision under the former Bankruptcy Act 1914, s.4).

[22] See *Re Wenham* [1900] 2 Q.B. 698; *Ernst & Young v. Butte Mining Plc* [1997] 1 W.L.R. 1485, 1491F *per* Lightman J. Note also the decision in *Willmott v. Berry Brothers* (1982) 126 S.J. 209 (writ served in accordance with RSC Ord. 81 held valid even though the partnership business had by then been transferred to a company). *cf.* the decision of the Sheriff's Court in *D. Forbes Smith & Johnston v. Kaye* 1975 S.L.T. 33, in relation to the Sheriff Courts (Scotland) Act 1907, Sched. 1, r. 11, which provides that "any individual or individuals, or any corporation or association carrying on business under a firm or trading or descriptive name, may sue or be sued in such name without the addition of the name or names of such individual or individuals or any of them, or of any member or official of such corporation or association . . . ". It should, of course, be remembered that, in Scotland, the firm has separate legal personality: see the Partnership Act 1890, s.4(2).

[23] See *Hobbs v. Australian Press Association* [1933] 1 K.B. 1; *Worcester City and County Banking Co. v. Firbank, Pauling & Co.* [1894] 1 Q.B. 784. Although this proposition was doubted in *Grant v. Anderson & Co.* [1892] 1 Q.B. 108, the effect of the then RSC Ord. 48A, r. 8 (see now CPR 70PD, paras 6A.2 to 6A.4, *infra*, para. A2–09) appears to have been overlooked.

[24] *Bullock v. Caird* (1875) L.R. 10 Q.B. 276 (DC); *Indigo Co. v. Ogilvy* [1891] 2 Ch. 31; *Western National Bank of the City of New York v. Perez Triana & Co.* [1891] 1 Q.B. 304; *Dobson v. Festi Rasini & Co.* [1891] 2 Q.B. 92; *Von Hellfeld v. Rechnitzer and Mayer Frères & Co.* [1914] 1 Ch. 748 (CA); *Oxnard Financing SA v. Rahn* [1998] 1 W.L.R. 1465 (CA). And note also *Rowan Companies Inc. v. Lambert Egglink Offshore Transport Consultants VOF* [1997] 2 Lloyd's Rep. 218 (action against a Dutch VOF partnership); and, on appeal [1998] C.L.C. 1574 (CA).

[25] *ibid.* A Scots partnership is, of course, a case in point: see the Partnership Act 1890, s.4(2). Equally, note the decision in *Bullock v. Caird*, *supra*. And see also *Dreyfus v. I.R.C.* (1929) 14 T.C. 560.

It is, perhaps, questionable whether the members of a dissolved partnership can still be said to be carrying on business when they are merely engaged in winding up its affairs.[26] Since much is likely to turn on the precise stage reached in the winding up, prudence would seem to dictate that proceedings in respect of any cause of action accruing *after* the date of dissolution should, where possible, not be commenced in the firm name.[27]

Change in the firm name

14–06   Proceedings can only be issued in a firm name which was in use when the cause of action accrued: if the name has changed since then, *e.g.* by reason of a merger, it is not permissible to issue proceedings in the *new* firm name.[28]

Use of firm name in specific instances

Apparent partnership

14–07   Proceedings in a supposed firm name may properly be commenced by or against the members of an apparent partnership.[29] If it transpires that a true partnership does not exist, the court will ensure that the action proceeds against the correct parties.[30]

Change in firm

14–08   The use of the firm name following a change in the firm is permissible,[31] although no special provision is made for service of the claim form in such a case.[32] It should, however, be noted that a change in the firm *after* proceedings have been issued in the firm name will not automatically result in a change in the parties to the action.[33]

Dissolved firm

14–09   There can be no objection to proceedings being commenced against a dissolved partnership in the firm name,[34] save perhaps where the cause of action accrued after the date of dissolution and no business was being carried on at that time.[35] However, again service of the claim form must be effected in precisely

---

[26] See the Partnership Act 1890, s.38, *supra*, paras 13–62 *et seq.*

[27] See *D. Forbes Smith & Johnston v. Kaye* 1975 S.L.T. 33, noted *supra*, para. 14–05, n. 22.

[28] *Ernst & Young v. Butte Mining PLC* [1997] 1 W.L.R. 1485; *HF Pension Trustees v. Ellison* [1999] Lloyd's Rep. PN 489.

[29] CPR 7APD, para. 5A.2, *infra*, para. A2–04 applies in the case of "persons *claiming* to be entitled as partners and persons *alleged* to be partners . . . " (emphasis supplied). This is a slightly different formulation to RSC Ord. 81, r.1 but to the same effect.

[30] See *Noble Lowndes and Partners (a firm) v. Hadfields Ltd.* [1939] Ch. 569. *Semble* the position would be no different under the CPR: see, generally, *ibid.* r. 19.2.

[31] *Re Wenham* [1900] 2 Q.B. 698.

[32] The only provision governing service in the case of actions brought against a firm in its name is CPR r. 6.9(2), para. 3, *infra*, para. A2–02: see *infra*, para. 14–14. Although RSC Ord. 81, r. 3(3) formerly provided that, in the case of an action against a firm which the plaintiff knew to have been dissolved, the writ ought to be served on all the alleged partners, this provision was not carried forward into the CPR: see *infra*, para. 14–16.

[33] *Dean & Dean (a firm) v. Angel Airlines SA* [2009] B.P.I.R. 409 at [46] *per* Patten J.

[34] *Re Wenham* [1900] 2 Q.B. 698.

[35] See *supra*, para. 14–05.

the same way as in the case of a continuing firm, whether the claimant knows of the dissolution or not.[36]

Firm not liable

If a claim lies against one or more partners personally, *e.g.* as office holders **14–10** and not as partners, it is clearly inappropriate to issue proceedings in the firm name.[37] Needless to say, where one firm's business is acquired by another firm but none of its partners join the acquiring firm, an action cannot be brought against the latter firm, whether in its name or otherwise. In *Kesslar v. Moore & Tibbits*,[38] the claimant had mistakenly issued proceedings against the acquiring firm but was, ultimately, permitted to substitute the partner in the acquired firm as defendant.[39]

Merged firm

Proceedings against a firm which has merged may only be issued in the **14–11** merged firm's name if the latter has assumed the same name as the former. However, it goes without saying that use of that name will not enable a claim to be maintained against the members of the merged firm.[40]

Two firms with common partner

Proceedings between two firms with a common partner may be brought in their **14–12** respective names, even though, by so doing, that partner will technically be constituted both a claimant and a defendant.[41] It is not considered that this eventuality would *per se* render use of the names as "inappropriate".[42]

Partnership membership statements

Where proceedings are commenced by or against a firm in the firm name, the **14–13** claimant or defendant (as the case may be) may require the production of a written statement setting out the full names and last known places of residence of those partners who were members of the firm when the cause of action

---

[36] See *infra*, paras 14–14 *et seq.*; *cf.* the former RSC Ord. 81, r. 3(3). And see also *infra*, paras 14–21, 14–91.

[37] *Ramsay & Maclain v. Leonard Curtis* [2001] B.P.I.R. 389 (CA). Here a claim was sought to be made in respect of the actions of two individual partners who had acted as administrative receivers. It was clear that the firm could not have acted as such. In a case of this kind, CPR 16PD, para. 2.6(c)(ii), *infra*, para. A2–08 will apply as regards the heading to the claim form.

[38] [2005] P.N.L.R. 17 (CA).

[39] Under CPR r. 19.5(3)(a).

[40] *Ernst & Young v. Butte Mining PLC* [1997] 1 W.L.R. 1485; *HF Pension Trustees v. Ellison* [1999] Lloyd's Rep. PN 489; this is in many ways analogous to the situation in *Kesslar v. Moore & Tibbits, supra*. See also *supra*, para. 14–06.

[41] Although the CPR do not expressly provide for this eventuality, there is no reason to suppose that the old practice does not continue to apply: see, in particular, CPR 7APD, para. 5A.3, *infra*, para. A2–04.

[42] See *ibid.*

accrued.[43] In all cases, the statement must be provided within 14 days of the request.[44]

It is no longer provided that the contents of this statement will thereafter identify the true parties to the proceedings[45] and, unlike the position under the old rules, there is no longer any jurisdiction under which the court may direct such a statement to be verified on oath or in some other manner.[46] Nevertheless, given the wide case management powers under the Civil Procedure Rules,[47] it would, in an appropriate case, be possible for the court to order the trial of an issue designed to determine whether the persons named in a partnership membership statement were, in fact, partners at the relevant date.[48]

Service of claim form on firm

14–14   Where proceedings are commenced against partners in a firm name, service of the claim form[49] may be effected in one of six ways, namely:

(1) by effecting personal service on a partner[50];

(2) by effecting personal service on any person who, at the time, has control or management of the partnership business at its principal place of business[51];

(3) by effecting service on a solicitor instructed to accept service on behalf of the partners/the firm[52];

(4) by effecting service at an address within the jurisdiction which the partners/the firm have given for the purpose[53];

(5) by effecting service by a contractually agreed method[54]; or

---

[43] See CPR 7APD, para. 5B.1, *infra*, para. A2–05. The request must specify the date on which the cause of action accrued: *ibid.* para. 5B.3.

[44] CPR 7APD, para. 5B.2, *infra*, para. A2–05.

[45] *Cf.* the former RSC Ord. 81, r. 2(2); CCR Ord. 5, r. 9(4).

[46] See the former RSC Ord. 81, r. 2(1).

[47] CPR rr. 1.4, 3.1.

[48] Note that, under the pre-CPR rules, it was held that there was no jurisdiction to order cross-examination of the person verifying the statement or, indeed, the trial of an issue of the type indicated in the text: *Abrahams & Co. v. Dunlop Pneumatic Tyre Co.* [1905] 1 K.B. 46. This can no longer, as such, be regarded as good law.

[49] As to the meaning of this expression, see CPR r. 6.2(c).

[50] *ibid.* r. 6.5(3)(c)(i), *infra*, para. A2–01. See further, as to what constitutes personal service in the case of a partner, *Kenneth Allison Ltd. v. A.E. Limehouse & Co.* [1992] 2 A.C. 105 (HL); *Nottingham Building Society v. Peter Bennett & Co., The Times,* February 26, 1997 (CA) (both decisions under the old rules of procedure).

[51] CPR r. 6.5(3)(c)(ii), *infra*, para. A2–01. The principal place of business must be within the jurisdiction: *ibid.* r. 6.6(1). Note the exceptional decision in *Willmott v. Berry Brothers* (1982) 126 S.J. 209, where proceedings were held to have been validly served on the person having control of the former partnership business (which, unknown to the claimant, was then being carried on by a limited company) notwithstanding the fact that he had *never* been an employee of the firm. And see also *Meyer v. Louis Drefus et Cie* [1940] 4 All E.R. 157. *Quaere,* will these decisions be followed under the CPR?

[52] *ibid.* r. 6.7. This is the usual method of service. See further *Nanglegan v. Royal Free Hampstead NHS Trust* [2001] 3 All E.R. 793 (CA). And see also, as service of documents other than a claim form, *ibid.* r. 6.23(2)(a).

[53] *ibid.* r. 6.8(a).

[54] *ibid.* r. 6.11(1).

(6) by sending or transmitting[55] a copy to, or leaving a copy at, a partner's usual or last known residence or the principal or last known place of business of the firm.[56]

In case (6), if the claimant has reason to believe that the partner in question no longer lives at the address in question or that the firm no longer carries on business there, he must take reasonable steps to identify the partner's/firm's current address and, if he cannot identify it, he may only effect service at his/its last known address if he is unable to apply to the court to effect service at an alternative address or by an alternative method.[57]

Despite the revision of the rules on service, it is not clear whether, in case (1) or (6) above, good service can be effected on a person who is not a partner but who is merely liable as such by reason of holding out under section 14 of the Partnership Act 1890.[58] It should, however, be noted that it is no longer a requirement that the person on whom the claim form is served in case (2) must also be served with a notice stating the capacity in which he is so served.[59]

14–15

Where the claim form is to be served by the court, it is for the court to decide which method of service to use.[60]

If the claim form is sent to the wrong address, but is, ultimately, forwarded to the correct address within due time, that will be good service,[61] but it would seem unlikely that this principle could be applied where it results in service at a partner's/firm's former address since, by definition, the new requirements of the Civil Procedure Rules would not have been met.

Provided that service is successfully effected in one of the above ways, it will not matter that some or all of the partners are outside the jurisdiction.[62] However, it may not be possible to levy execution on such partners in respect of a judgment obtained against the firm.[63]

---

[55] See, as to the authorised means of sending and transmitting a claim form, *ibid.* r. 6.3(1); also *ibid.* 6PD, paras 2.1 *et seq.* This includes leaving a copy of the proceedings at one of the places mentioned in the text: *ibid.* r. 6.3(1)(c).

[56] *ibid.* r. 6.9(2), para. 3, *infra*, para. A2–02. The last known place of business of the firm denotes the last place known to the claimant: *Mersey Docks Property Holdings Ltd. v. Kilgour* [2004] B.L.R. 412 (a decision under the former version of this rule).

[57] *ibid.* r. 6.9(3)–(6), *infra*, para. A2–02. As to applying for an order for service by an alternative method or at an alternative address, see *ibid.* 6PD, paras 9.1–9.3. This marks a change of approach: under the previous version of r. 6, service at a partner's usual or last known place of residence was normally regarded as good service on the firm, save in one exceptional case where the partner in question was known to the claimant to be serving a substantial term of imprisonment: see *Lexi Holdings PLC v. Luqman, The Times*, February 19, 2008, Service on a dissolved firm at its former premises was also held to be good service under those old rules in *Cameron v. Lee Crowder*, May 1, 2008 (unreported).

[58] See, generally, *supra*, paras 5–35 *et seq.* A person liable by reason of holding out is not *per se* the agent of the true partners: see *supra*, para. 12–06.

[59] This was formerly provided for in CPR 6PD, para. 4.2 and is a somewhat surprising omission.

[60] CPR rr. 6.4(1), (2). The court will usually serve by first class post: see *ibid.* 6PD, para. 8.1.

[61] *Austin Rover Group Ltd. v. Crouch Butler Savage Associates* [1986] 1 W.L.R. 1102, a decision under the RSC which would seem to be equally applicable under the CPR.

[62] CPR rr. 6.5(3)(c), 6.9(2), para. 3, *infra*, paras A2–01, A2–02. See the following decisions under the old rules of procedure: *Shepherd v. Hirsch, Pritchard & Co.* (1890) 45 Ch.D. 231; *Lysaght Ltd. v. Clark & Co.* [1891] 1 Q.B. 552; *Meyer v. Louis Dreyfus et Cie* [1940] 4 All E.R. 157.

[63] CPR 70PD, paras 6A.3, 6A.4, *infra*, para. A2–10. There will, however, be no problem enforcing the judgment against partnership assets in the jurisdiction: *ibid.* para. 6A.1.See further, *infra*, para. 14–21.

Dissolved firm

14-16   Under the Rules of the Supreme Court, it was an express requirement that proceedings against a firm which was known to have been dissolved should be served on all the partners within the jurisdiction.[64] This requirement was not replicated in the Civil Procedure Rules, nor has the omission been corrected in any subsequent amendment of those rules.[65] It follows that good service can be effected in any authorised manner,[66] even if that may, ultimately, result in the existence of the proceedings failing to come to the attention of all the former partners.[67] This is, however, now less likely given that service at the dissolved firm's last known address will no longer be possible as a matter of course.[68]

Alternative methods of service

14-17   In an appropriate case, the court will order that the proceedings be served on the firm by an alternative method[69] and may even, in exceptional circumstances, dispense with service altogether.[70] However, it is seemingly not open to the parties to agree some alternative method of service as between themselves on an *ad hoc* basis,[71] even if they can provide for this in the contract which is the subject matter of the proceedings.[72]

Service out of jurisdiction

14-18   Where it is required,[73] permission to effect service of the proceedings on a partner who is outside the jurisdiction must be obtained in the normal way.[74] Where the proceedings have been properly issued in the firm name,[75] it would seem that service effected with such permission will be good service on the firm, even if it transpires that service could have been effected here.[76] However, it may be that, as under the old rules of procedure, if there is some special reason for

---

[64] RSC Ord. 81, r. 3(3); similarly in the county court: CCR Ord. 7, r. 13(2). See also *Shepherd v. Hirsch, Pritchard & Co.* (1890) 45 Ch.D. 231; *Wigram v. Cox, Buckley & Co.* [1894] 1 Q.B. 792; *Chohan Clothing v. Fox Brooks Marshall, The Times*, December 9, 1997.

[65] Unaccountably, when the CPR were first introduced, an equivalent provision to RSC Ord 81, r. 3(3) relating to the enforcement of traffic penalties in the county court (*i.e.* CCR Ord. 48B, r. 2(6C)) was retained and applied by CPR r. 51.1, Sched. 2, but was not carried forward into CPR Pt. 75.

[66] See *supra*, para. 14–14. Note that this was conceded to be the position in *R. v. Financial Ombudsman Services* [2007] Pens. L.R. 287 at [21], [22].

[67] This was the position in *Cameron v. Lee Crowder*, May 1, 2008 (unreported), albeit decided before the most recent change in the rules. There the solicitor for the claimant had gone to some effort to obtain another address for service and there was, in any event, no doubt that the existence of the proceedings had come to the attention of most if not all of the partners in the dissolved firm and their solicitors.

[68] See CPR r. 6.9(2)–(6), *infra*, para. A2–02, noted *supra*, para. 14–14.

[69] CPR r. 6.15. Such an application may be required where the firm no longer carries on business at the address specified in *ibid*. r. 6.9(2), para. 3: see *ibid*. r. 6.9(4)(b)(ii) and (3).

[70] *ibid*. r. 6.16. Service will not be dispensed with lightly: *Cranfield v. Bridgegrove* [2003] 1 W.L.R. 3206 (CA).

[71] *cf.* the position under the RSC: *Kenneth Allison Ltd. v. A.E. Limehouse & Co.* [1992] 2 A.C. 105 (service on the senior partner's personal assistant authorised for the purpose).

[72] CPR r. 6.11(1).

[73] As to the circumstances in which permission is not required, see CPR r. 6.33.

[74] *ibid*. rr. 6.30 *et seq*.

[75] See *supra*, paras 14–04 *et seq*.

[76] See *Hobbs v. Australian Press Association* [1933] 1 K.B. 1. In that case, the claimant did not know that the firm was carrying on business within the jurisdiction. *Semble*, this is still good law under the CPR.

effecting service on a partner outside the jurisdiction, *e.g.* with a view to executing any judgment in the proceedings against him,[77] the proceedings should either be commenced both against him *and* the firm or against all the partners in their individual names "trading as . . . "[78]; permission to serve such proceedings on that partner should then be obtained.[79]

Acknowledgment of service

The service of proceedings commenced against a firm in the firm name must in all cases be acknowledged in the firm name on behalf of all the partners when the cause of action accrued.[80] Somewhat surprisingly, it would seem that the same rule applies even in the case of proceedings which are *not* commenced in the firm name.[81] The acknowledgment may in either case be signed by any of the partners or by a person authorised by one of them.[82] Signature by a person with control or management of the partnership business will not suffice unless, in that capacity, he has the necessary authority from the partners.[83] It would seem that someone who is alleged to be a partner but who denies that he holds that status may not acknowledge service *qua* partner unless he actually is a partner.[84] Provision is no longer made for a person served as a partner to acknowledge service subject to a denial that he was a partner at the relevant time (or at all)[85] and a purported acknowledgment in that form could seemingly not stand as an acknowledgment by the firm. However, where a genuine partner does acknowledge service on behalf of the firm, there is nothing to prevent an alleged partner contesting his status in his defence.[86]

14–19

Judgment

Where proceedings are commenced against a firm in the firm name, judgment must normally be entered against the firm in that name, as under the old rules.[87]

14–20

---

[77] See CPR 70PD, para. 6A.3(3), *infra*, para. A2–09. See also *infra*, para. 14–21.

[78] Thus, in such a case, it may conceivably be "inappropriate" merely to bring the proceedings against the firm in its name: see CPR 7APD, para. 5A.3, *infra*, para. A2–04.

[79] See *West of England Steamship Owners' Protection and Indemnity Association v. John Holman & Sons* [1957] 1 W.L.R. 1164.

[80] CPR 10PD, para. 4.4(1), *infra*, para. A2–07.

[81] *ibid.* para. 4.4 applies "Where a claim is brought against a partnership . . . ", no mention being made of the firm name.

[82] *ibid.* para. 4.4(2), *infra*, para. A2–07. Provided that they were partners when the cause of action accrued, it would seem that this authority will not be affected by the subsequent cessation of their partnership, by retirement or otherwise; *cf. HLB Kidsons v. Lloyd's Underwriters* [2009] 1 All E.R. (Comm) 760.

[83] *cf.* CPR 10PD, para. 4.4 in its original form

[84] *cf.* CPR 7APD, para. 5A.2, *infra*, para. A2–04, which only applies for the purposes of *ibid.* para. 5A. Note that in *Blackett-Ord's Partnership Law* (3rd ed.) at para. 21–30, it is argued that an acknowledgment by a person who maintains that he is a partner but who is not accepted as such will be valid, by reference to *Robinson v. Ward & Son* (1892) 36 S.J. 415, but this is to ignore the express terms of CPR 10PD, para. 4.4(1). Situations of this kind will, fortunately, be rare.

[85] *cf.* RSC Ord. 81, r. 4(2).

[86] This was formerly provided for in terms: see RSC Ord. 81, r. 4(3)(b). As under that rule, the alleged partner might, by his defence, deny either or both: (i) his liability as a partner and (ii) the liability of the firm. *Semble* it would not be in the alleged partner's interests to argue that a valid acknowledgment of service had not been given on his behalf.

[87] *Jackson v. Litchfield* (1882) 8 Q.B.D. 474. *cf. Munster v. Cox* (1885) 10 App.Cas. 680.

Where, however, it appears that one of the partners is a minor, judgment should be entered against the firm "other than" the minor partner.[88]

Where a partner has acknowledged service on behalf of the firm,[89] it will clearly not be possible for a default judgment to be entered against the firm or against any partner separately.[90] *Semble* the position will be the same if one partner subsequently files a defence.[91]

Persons against whom judgment may not be executed

14–21   A judgment against a firm cannot, without the permission of the court,[92] be executed against any person who has not: (i) acknowledged service of the claim form as a partner[93]; (ii) been served as a partner and failed to acknowledge service[94]; (iii) pleaded that he is or was at the material time a partner; or (iv) been held to be a partner.[95] There is, moreover, an absolute bar on execution against a limited partner[96] or a partner who is ordinarily resident out of the jurisdiction when the claim form was issued, unless in either case he has acknowledged service as a partner or was served as a partner within or (if permission was obtained)[97] outside the jurisdiction.[98] What is less clear is the position of such a partner who was served as a partner outside the jurisdiction in a case where no permission was required,[99] but it would seem that permission to execute is required in such a case.[100] It follows that a claimant who has obtained judgment against a firm, not realising that it comprises foreign or (less likely) limited partners, may find that, at best, its effective enforcement requires the initiation of further proceedings,[101] although nothing will prevent execution of the judgment against partnership assets which are within the jurisdiction.[102]

---

[88] *Lovell & Christmas v. Beauchamp* [1894] A.C. 607.

[89] See *supra*, para. 14–19.

[90] i.e. under CPR r.12.1(a). And see, as to the position under the old rules of procedure, *Jackson v. Litchfield, supra; Adam v. Townend* (1884) 14 Q.B.D. 103; also *Alden v. Beckley & Co.* (1890) 25 Q.B.D. 543.

[91] This was, perhaps, clearer under the old rules: see the cases cited in the preceding note.

[92] CPR 70PD, para. 6A.4, *infra*, para. A2–09. An application for permission will be made in accordance with *ibid.* Pt 23.

[93] Note that, in the case of an action against a firm in its name, one partner can acknowledge service in the firm name on behalf of all the partners: see *supra*, para. 14–19. *Semble* this will suffice for the purpose of this requirement.

[94] This presupposes that no partner has acknowledged service in the type of case contemplated in the preceding note.

[95] CPR 70PD, para. 6A.2, *infra*, para. A2–09.

[96] See the Limited Partnerships Act 1907, s.4(2), *infra*, para. A3–04; see also *infra*, Pt. 6.

[97] See *supra*, para. 14–18.

[98] CPR 70PD, para. 6A.3, *infra*, para. A2–09. Only under the recent changes to the Practice Direction has it become clear that the conditions also apply to a limited partner.

[99] See CPR r. 6.33 (as amended by the Civil Jurisdiction and Judgments Regulations 2009 (SI 2009/3131), regs. 30, 31).

[100] Since the requirements of CPR 70PD, paras 6A.2 and 6A.3 are, by definition, not satisfied in such a case, *ibid.* para. 6A.4 would appear to apply.

[101] See *Munster v. Cox* (1885) 10 App.Cas. 680. And see also *infra*, paras 14–92 *et seq*. In previous editions of this work, reference was also made to cases in which the composition of the firm had changed since the cause of action had accrued in this context, but assuming an acknowledgment of service to have been served on the firm's behalf, this would no longer seem to present a problem, save as regards limited partners or partners resident out of the jurisdiction.

[102] CPR 70PD, para. 6A.1, *infra*, para. A2–09.

B.   PARTIES WHERE FIRM UNCHANGED

(1) Actions by the Firm

The Civil Procedure Rules provide that: **14–22**

> "Where a claimant claims a remedy to which some other person is jointly entitled with him, all persons jointly entitled to the remedy must be parties unless the court orders otherwise."[103]

It follows that, whilst additional parties can be added at a later stage,[104] it would normally be inappropriate for proceedings on behalf of a firm to be commenced by some only of the partners, unless the others are joined as defendants.[105] Equally, since proceedings on behalf of a firm can normally be issued in the firm name,[106] this rule should have little impact in practice.[107]

ACTIONS IN CONTRACT

Just as the liability of a firm depends on the precise nature and form of any   **14–23** contract entered into by a partner on its behalf,[108] so does identification of the correct parties to an action by the firm in respect of such a contract. It is, accordingly, necessary to distinguish between:

  (a)   Written and oral contracts.[109]

  (b)   Contracts under seal.[110]

  (c)   Bills of exchange and promissory notes.[111]

(a) Written and Oral Contracts

Rights of firm as principal

If a partner, acting within the scope of his express or implied authority,[112]   **14–24** enters into a written or oral contract with a third party, the firm will, as principal, be entitled to sue on that contract, whether or not its existence was disclosed to the third party.[113] As Lord Lindley put it:

---

[103] CPR r. 19.3(1).

[104] CPR r. 19.2. Note also the court's case management powers under *ibid.* rr. 1.4, 3.1. And see *Noble Lowndes and Partners (a firm) v. Hadfields Ltd.* [1939] Ch. 569, noted *supra*, para. 14–07.

[105] This principle was clearly affirmed in *HLB Kidsons v. Lloyd's Underwriters* [2009] 1 All E.R. (Comm) 760, at [19]. Note also Lord Lindley's observations on the consequences of the misjoinder/non-joinder of parties: " . . . mistakes create delay and expense . . . and if all the members of a firm sue when one only ought to do so, or one only sues when all ought to do so, and the defendant can show that he is thereby prejudiced, he can apply to have the improper parties struck out or the proper parties joined, as the case may be." The position is, if anything, *a fortiori*, under the CPR.

[106] See CPR 7APD, para. 5A, *infra*, para. A2–04. See also, *supra*, para. 14–04.

[107] Note, however, that the defendant may request a partnership membership statement under CPR 7APD, para. 5B, *infra*, para. A2–05: see *supra*, para. 14–13.

[108] See *supra*, paras 12–148 *et seq.*

[109] See further, *supra*, paras 12–151 *et seq.*

[110] See further, *supra*, paras 12–157 *et seq.*

[111] See further, *supra*, paras 12–161 *et seq.*

[112] Partnership Act 1890, s.5, *supra*, paras 12–02 *et seq.*

[113] See *supra*, para. 12–151.

" . . . it happens every day that a firm sues on a contract entered into on its behalf by one of its members, and it is not by any means necessary that the person dealing with him should have been aware that the one partner was acting on behalf of himself and other people. The question is, With whom was the contract made in point of law? And the true answer to this question does not by any means entirely depend on the answer to be given to the more simple question, With whom was the contract made in point of fact?"

Thus in *Garrett v. Handley*[114] all the members of a firm were held to be entitled to sue on a written guarantee given to one of them, there being evidence to show that it was intended to benefit the firm. Similarly, where one partner in a firm of bankers had made a loan out of partnership funds, it was held that an action for the recovery of that loan was properly brought by all the partners, even though the borrower had not sought a loan from the firm.[115] Numerous other examples can be imagined.[116]

All partners should join as parties

14–25   Where a firm sues as principal, it has already been seen that *all* the partners should normally be made parties to the proceedings, unless the court orders otherwise.[117]

Dormant and apparent partners

14–26   It used to be the rule that the joinder of a dormant partner was optional,[118] as Lord Lindley pointed out:

" . . . a dormant partner never *need* be joined as a co-plaintiff in an action on a contract entered into with the firm or with one of its members."[119]

However, since it is not yet clear whether this exception to the general rule has survived the introduction of the Civil Procedure Rules, it may now prudent to join such a partner as a party.[120] The same cannot be said of a person who is merely held out as a partner, unless he is *actually* a contracting party.[121]

---

[114] (1825) 4 B. & C. 664; and see, as to the previous proceedings (where an action by the one partner failed), (1824) 3 B. & C. 462. See also *Hopkinson v. Smith* (1822) 1 Bing. 13, as to an action by an attorney not retained by the defendant.

[115] *Alexander v. Barker* (1831) 2 C. & J. 133. *cf. Sims v. Britain* (1832) 4 B. & Ad. 375; *Sims v. Bond* (1833) 5 B. & Ad. 389.

[116] *e.g.* the supply of goods and services: see *Townsend v. Neale* (1809) 2 Camp. 189; *Skinner v. Stocks* (1821) 4 B. & A. 437; *Arden v. Tucker* (1832) 4 B. & Ad. 815. See also *Cooke v. Seeley* (1848) 2 Ex. 746, where a bank account maintained in a partner's name was held to be a partnership account, thus entitling all the partners to sue the bank for dishonouring a cheque drawn by that partner for partnership purposes.

[117] See *supra*, para. 14–22. And see also, as to position under the old rules of procedure, *Cabell v. Vaughan* (1669) 1 Wms.Saund. 291k.

[118] *Cothay v. Fennell* (1830) 10 B. & C. 671; also *Robson v. Drummond* (1831) 2 B. & Ad. 303, 307 *per* Littledale J. This proposition was originally doubted: see *Mawman v. Gillett* (1809) 2 Taunt. 235; *Lloyd v. Archbowle* (1810) 2 Taunt. 324.

[119] *Leveck v. Shafto* (1796) 2 Esp. 468.

[120] CPR r. 19.3 (which is, admittedly, framed in terms similar to the former RSC Ord. 15, r. 4(2)) would appear to admit of no exceptions.

[121] *Kell v. Nainby* (1829) 10 B. & C. 20. See also *Cox v. Hubbard* (1847) 4 C.B. 317; *Spurr v. Cass* (1870) L.R. 5 Q.B. 656. Lord Lindley used the expression "nominal" partners in this context. See generally, as to holding out, the Partnership Act 1890, s.14, *supra*, paras 5–35 *et seq.*

Rights of contracting partner

In certain circumstances, it may be either unnecessary or inappropriate for the **14–27** firm to commence proceedings, as Lord Lindley explained:

"One partner may sue alone on a written contract made with himself if it does not appear from the contract itself that he was acting as agent of the firm[122]; and one partner ought to sue alone on a contract entered into with himself, if such contract is in fact made with him as a principal, and not on behalf of himself and others."

Thus, if a number of partners make loans out of their respective personal funds, each ought to sue individually for repayment of his loan, even if it was made pursuant to some arrangement between the partners.[123] Similarly, if one partner is the holder of an office or appointment, he alone ought to sue for payment in respect of work done in that capacity.[124]

A partner who sues on a contract made in his own name but for the benefit of the firm may recover liquidated or unliquidated damages on the firm's behalf.[125]

Partner as apparent principal

Where a contract is entered into by a partner who represents himself as a **14–28** principal but is in fact acting on the firm's behalf, he alone should sue on it since it was ostensibly entered into on his own account.[126]

(b) Contracts under Seal

The old rule was strict in the case of a contract under seal, *i.e.* that only the **14–29** parties to that contract might sue on it.[127] Lord Lindley summarised the position in this way:

" . . . if such a contract was entered into with one partner only, he alone could sue upon it; . . . if it was entered into with more than one partner, all those with whom it was expressly entered into must sue upon it, and no others could, whatever their interest in its performance might be."[128]

Although this rule no longer applies, the court will still be concerned to ensure that the correct parties are joined.[129]

---

[122] See *Skinner v. Stocks* (1821) 4 B. & A. 437; *Cothay v. Fennell* (1830) 10 B. & C. 671. See also *Agacio v. Forbes* (1861) 14 Moo.P.C. 160, where the Privy Council held that one partner might sue on a written agreement made by him alone, even though the agreement related to the partnership business and was entered into for its benefit, and the consideration was a release of a debt due to the firm.

[123] *Thacker v. Shepherd* (1773) 2 Chitty 652; *Brand v. Boulcott* (1802) 3 Bos. & Pul. 253.

[124] *Brandon v. Hubbard* (1820) 2 Brod. & B. 11. See further, as to the status of an office or appointment held by a partner, *supra*, paras 10–51 *et seq.* and *infra*, para. 18–18.

[125] *Roberts v. Ward*, unreported, February 8, 1985 (C.A.T. No. 71); [1985] C.L.Y. p. 137.

[126] *Lucas v. De la Cour* (1813) 1 M. & S. 249.

[127] The law relating to such contracts is unaffected by the Partnership Act 1890: see *ibid.* s.6, *supra*, paras 12–149, 12–157 *et seq.*

[128] See *Cabell v. Vaughan* (1669) 1 Wms.Saund. 291; *Scott v. Godwin* (1797) 1 Bos. & Pul. 67; *Vernon v. Jefferys* (1740) 2 Str. 1146; *Metcalf v. Rycroft* (1817) 6 M. & S. 75.

[129] See CPR rr. 19.2, 19.3. See also *supra*, para. 14–22.

It follows that, whilst it is proper to join a person who is merely held out as a partner if he was a party to the contract,[130] in practice such joinder may not be essential.[131]

Covenant with firm

14-30   Lord Lindley summarised the position in these terms:

"It is apprehended that a covenant entered into with A, B & Co. may be sued upon by the persons who, when the covenant was made, constituted that firm."[132]

Recovery of partnership moneys

14-31   If one partner enters into a contract under seal and, pursuant thereto, a payment is made out of partnership funds, that partner may sue for the return of the money if it ultimately transpires that the contract was invalidated by some fraud.[133]

(c) Bills of Exchange and Promissory Notes

14-32   Unless the only or last indorsement is in blank, the proper parties to an action on a bill or note are those named in it as drawers, payees, or indorsees, as the case may be.[134] The fact that they are partners or that the bill or note relates to partnership matters is strictly irrelevant: thus, if a debtor of the firm makes his promissory note payable to one partner, that partner should himself sue on the note.[135] If, on the other hand, the only or last indorsement is in blank, any person holding the bill or note may sue on it.[136]

It the name of a person who is merely held out as a partner appears on the bill or note, he may be joined as a party to the proceedings,[137] although failure to join him may not be fatal.[138]

Bills in firm name

14-33   Lord Lindley observed:

"If a bill is drawn by or in favour of a firm in its commercial name, the persons who composed the firm when the bill was drawn, ought to be plaintiffs."[139]

---

[130] *Guidon v. Robson* (1809) 2 Camp. 302 (a case of a bill of exchange).

[131] It remains to be seen how strictly the court applies CPR r. 19.3. Its predecessor (RSC Ord. 15, r. 4(2)) was regarded as subject to certain exceptions: see, for example, *supra*, para. 14–26.

[132] See generally, *supra*, paras 3–08 *et seq.*

[133] *Lefevre v. Boyle* (1832) 3 B. & Ad. 877.

[134] See *Pease v. Hirst* (1829) 10 B. & C. 122; also *Guidon v. Robson* (1809) 2 Camp. 302. But see now CPR rr. 19.2, 19.3.

[135] *Bawden v. Howell* (1841) 3 Man. & G. 638.

[136] See the Bills of Exchange Act 1882, ss.8(3), 89. And see the old cases: *Ord v. Portal* (1812) 3 Camp. 239; *Attwood v. Rattenbury* (1822) 6 Moore 579; *Lowe v. Copestake* (1828) 3 Car. & P. 300.

[137] *Guidon v. Robson* (1809) 2 Camp. 302. But *cf.* the Bills of Exchange Act 1882, s.23(2).

[138] See CPR rr. 19.2(2), 19.3(1); also *supra*, paras 14–22, 14–26.

[139] At this point, Lord Lindley cited *McBirney v. Harran* (1843) 5 I.L.R. 428 and *Phelps v. Lyle* (1839) 10 A. & E. 113; yet the former case, if anything, appears to be contrary to the proposition in the text, whilst the latter hardly seems relevant. A later editor added a reference to the Bills of Exchange Act 1882, s.23(2), which deals with the *liability* of a firm.

Those partners ought normally to sue in the firm name, unless such a course would be "inappropriate" (which would seem unlikely).[140]

Bills accepted for honour

If one partner in his own name accepts a bill drawn on a third party for honour and, with his co-partners' consent, pays that bill when it falls due out of partnership funds, he should sue the drawee for indemnity.[141]   **14–34**

ACTIONS IN TORT

In the case of tortious claims, the general rule, as formulated by Lord Lindley, is that: **14–35**

> " . . . where a joint damage accrues to several persons from a tort, they ought all to join in an action founded upon it[142]; whilst on the other hand several persons ought not to join in an action *ex delicto*, unless they can show a joint damage".[143]

Thus, if a firm is libelled, all the partners may maintain an action for damages[144] and ought properly to bring the action in the firm name[145]; and if the libel directly affects one partner and, through him, the firm, two independent causes of action will arise, one in favour of the libelled partner and the other in favour of him and his co-partners.[146] Where, however, the firm suffers no damage, only the libelled partner should sue.[147]

Wrongful interference with goods

A claim relating to the detention of goods belonging to a firm[148] should now be brought in the firm name[149]; however, one partner may be given written authority to make such a claim on the firm's behalf.[150] If he does not have such authority and the claim is not based on a right to possession of the goods, he will prima facie only be entitled to recover damages in respect of *his* interest in the goods.[151] This will not prevent one of his co-partners bringing a subsequent action, unless this would involve "double liability".[152]   **14–36**

---

[140] See CPR 7APD, paras 5A.1, 5A.3, *infra*, para. A2–04. And see *supra*, paras 14–04 *et seq.*

[141] *Driver v. Burton* (1852) 17 Q.B. 989.

[142] See *Cabell v. Vaughan* (1669) 1 Wms.Saund. 291m; *Addison v. Overend* (1796) 6 T.R. 766; *Sedgworth v. Overend* (1797) 7 T.R. 279. And note the terms of CPR r. 19.3(1).

[143] 2 Wms.Saund. 116a.

[144] See *Cook v. Batchellor* (1802) 3 Bos. & Pul. 150; *Forster v. Lawson* (1826) 3 Bing. 452; *Williams v. Beaumont* (1833) 10 Bing. 260; *Le Fanu v. Malcolmson* (1848) 1 H.L.C. 637; *Metropolitan Saloon Omnibus Co. v. Hawkins* (1859) 4 H. & N. 87; and see generally, *South Hetton Coal Co. v. North-Eastern News Association* [1894] 1 Q.B. 133.

[145] See CPR 7APD, paras 5A.1, 5A.3, *infra*, para. A2–04. See also *supra*, para. 14–04.

[146] The two claims can now be combined in one claim form: see CPR rr. 7.3, 19.1. And see, as to the damage recoverable under each claim, *Forster v. Lawson* (1826) 3 Bing. 452; *Haythorn v. Lawson* (1827) 3 Car. & P. 196; *Harrison v. Bevington* (1838) 8 Car. & P. 708.

[147] *Solomons v. Medex* (1816) 1 Stark. 191; also *Pullman v. Hill & Co.* [1891] 1 Q.B. 524. It is immaterial that the libel affects him in his business capacity: see *Harrison v. Bevington* (1838) 8 Car. & P. 708; *Robinson v. Marchant* (1845) 7 Q.B. 918.

[148] See the Torts (Interference with Goods) Act 1977, s.3.

[149] CPR 7APD, paras 5A.1, 5A.3, *infra*, para. A2–04. And see *supra*, para. 14–04.

[150] See CPR r. 40.14(2).

[151] *ibid.*; the Torts (Interference with Goods) Act 1977, ss.5, 7; also *Addison v. Overend* (1796) 6 T.R. 766; *Bleadon v. Hancock* (1829) 4 Car. & P. 152. *Quaere*, what is the nature of a partner's interest in goods owned by the firm for this purpose? See *infra*, paras 19–01 *et seq.*

[152] *ibid.* s.5(4); see also *Sedgworth v. Overend* (1797) 7 T.R. 279.

Fraud and collusion between partner and third party

14–37   If one partner and a third party collude together with a view to perpetrating a fraud on the firm, the innocent partners may clearly maintain an action against the third party. Thus, where one partner was, to the knowledge of the firm's bankers, in the habit of drawing bills in the firm name for his own private purposes and the bankers colluded with him, keeping the true facts from the other partners and paying the bills when they fell due out of funds standing to the firm's credit, it was held that the other partners could bring an action against the bankers.[153] In such cases, the fraudulent partner will normally be joined as a defendant, if he refuses to be a claimant.[154]

ACTIONS IN RESPECT OF LAND

14–38   Where a firm seeks possession of land, the action should be brought in the names of those partners (or other persons)[155] in whom the legal estate is vested.[156] However, Lord Lindley went on to point out:

> "[*if*] one partner only has made a lease of the partnership property, then, as his title cannot be disputed by the lessee, notice to quit may be given and ejectment maintained by the lessor alone; and if he alone has the legal estate, the circumstances that rent has been paid to the firm, and receipts for it have been given by all the partners, will not affect his right to give the notice and bring the action in his own name."[157]

(2) Actions against the Firm

14–39   When considering actions against a firm, it should be remembered that not only is failure to join all partners as parties when the claim form is issued not likely to be fatal,[158] but the recovery of judgment against one partner in respect of any debt or damage is no longer a bar to subsequent proceedings against another partner jointly liable with him.[159] Nevertheless, it will still be desirable to ensure that the correct parties are joined so as to avoid unnecessary argument[160] and, more importantly, adverse consequences in costs.[161]

---

[153] *Longman v. Pole* (1828) Moo. & M. 223.

[154] CPR r. 19.3(2); *Johnson v. Stephens & Carter Ltd. and Golding* [1923] 2 K.B. 857. See also *Williamson v. Barbour* (1877) 9 Ch.D. 529, 536 *per* Jessel M.R.

[155] *e.g.* one or more former partners or the estate of a deceased partner.

[156] In this connection, Lord Lindley referred to *Chitty on Pleading* (7th ed., 1844), Vol. 1, p. 74.

[157] See *Doe v. Baker* (1818) 8 Taunt. 241.

[158] See CPR rr. 19.2(2), 19.4. However, there may be instances where failure to join a party *will* preclude subsequent proceedings against him: see *Morris v. Wentworth-Stanley* [1999] Q.B. 1004 (CA) at [42].

[159] Civil Liability (Contribution) Act 1978, s.3. See further *supra*, para. 13–05 and *infra*, para. 20–23.

[160] *i.e.* under CPR r. 19.4. See, for example, the following decisions under the old rules of procedure: *Pilley v. Robinson* (1887) 20 Q.B.D. 155; *Wilson, Sons & Co. Ltd. v. Balcarres Brook Steamship Co. Ltd.* [1893] 1 Q.B. 422; *Robinson v. Geisel* [1894] 2 Q.B. 685; *Norbury, Natzio & Co. v. Griffiths* [1918] 2 K.B. 369.

[161] Civil Liability (Contribution) Act 1978, s.4.

Equally, once a partner has been joined, it may be dangerous to allow him to be *removed* as a party,[162] unless the claimant ensures that his right to issue separate proceedings against that partner is reserved.[163]

ACTIONS IN CONTRACT

The general rule

The circumstances in which partners may become bound in contract, and thus **14–40** liable to be sued by a third party, have been considered in some detail in the preceding chapters. It follows that, if the firm is liable on a contract, all the partners ought normally to be sued jointly[164] and in the firm name[165]; if, on the other hand, a contract entered into by a partner does *not* bind the firm,[166] that partner alone should be sued.[167] Where, as will usually be the case, the liability of the firm is in doubt, prudence dictates that all the partners should in the first instance be joined and the claim formulated in the alternative, so that judgment can be obtained against the correct parties at trial.[168] If one of the original contracting partners is dead, his personal representatives may (and, in some cases, should) be joined along with the surviving partners.[169]

Where all the partners are joined, failure to serve one partner should not prevent the action from proceeding against the others.[170]

Dormant partners

Since a dormant partner will be liable in the same way as any other partner,[171] **14–41** he ought normally to be joined as a party to any action brought on a contract which binds the firm.[172] However, it may be that the other partners will not themselves be able to apply to have the dormant partner joined as a party, as Lord Lindley explained:

---

[162] On an application under CPR r. 19.4(1).

[163] See *Morris v. Wentworth-Stanley* [1999] Q.B. 1004 (CA).

[164] This is no longer mandatory: see *supra*, para. 14–39. See also *Cabell v. Vaughan* (1669) 1 Wms.Saund. 291b, note; *Byers v. Dobey* (1789) 1 H.Blacks. 236; *Bonfield v. Smith* (1844) 12 M. & W. 405; *Robinson v. Geisel* [1894] 2 Q.B. 685. And note the Carriers Act 1830, ss.5, 6.

[165] See CPR 7APD, paras 5A.1, 5A.3, *infra*, para. A2–04. See also *supra*, para. 14–04.

[166] See, generally, *supra*, paras 12–01 *et seq.*

[167] If the partner contracted as a principal, he can be sued on the contract; if he contracted as an agent, he can be sued for damages for breach of an implied warranty of authority: see *Lewis v. Nicholson* (1852) 18 Q.B. 503; *Collen v. Wright* (1857) 8 E. & B. 647. See also *Hudson v. Robinson* (1816) 4 M. & S. 475, as to the recovery of money paid under a contract which does not bind the firm.

[168] CPR rr. 7.3, 19.1. *Semble* in such a case it may be "inappropriate" to bring the action in the firm name: see CPR 7APD, para. 5A.3, *infra*, para. A2–04; also *supra*, para. 14–04. Equally, note in this context the ability to obtain a partnership membership statement, listing the partners in the firm at the date the cause of action accrued (as specified in the request): *ibid.* para. 5B, *infra*, para. A2–05; also *supra* para. 14–13.

[169] See *infra*, para. 26–18.

[170] *Robinson v. Geisel* [1894] 2 Q.B. 685.

[171] *Robinson v. Wilkinson* (1817) 3 Price 538; *Beckham v. Drake* (1843) 11 M. & W. 315, *supra*, para. 12–153; *Court v. Berlin* [1897] 2 Q.B. 396, *supra*, para. 13–54. And see also *supra*, paras 12–156, 13–53 *et seq.*

[172] See *Bonfield v. Smith* (1844) 12 M. & W. 405; also *Dubois v. Lubert* (1814) 5 Taunt. 609 (but see the next note). If a person is sued as a dormant partner, his membership of the firm must be proved if liability is to be established: see *Hall v. Bainbridge* (1840) 8 Dow. 583.

" . . . a person who holds himself out to another, as the only person with whom that other is dealing, cannot be allowed afterwards to say that such other was also dealing with somebody else."[173]

It is by no means certain that this approach will continue to be adopted under the Civil Procedure Rules, particularly given the need to take into account the overriding objective[174]; if it does, it will clearly apply whenever a partner enters into a written contract without making it clear that he is acting on behalf of the firm.[175] Equally, if the partners are asked for a partnership membership statement,[176] they will be obliged to name the dormant partner if he was a member of the firm at the date specified in the request.

No distinction now requires to be drawn between actions in respect of joint and joint and several contracts.[177]

Partners out of the jurisdiction

14–42   A partner who is out of the jurisdiction need not be joined.[178] If, however, he is to be made a party, permission to serve the proceedings on him may be required,[179] unless the proceedings are issued in the firm name.[180] However, as has already been noted,[181] execution of a judgment against a partner who is ordinarily resident out of the jurisdiction and who has not been served with the proceedings is heavily circumscribed.

Limited partners

14–43   By the same token, it may be that a limited partner[182] need not be joined if, as will usually be the case, he is not personally liable and there is no wish to execute any judgment against him.[183] This issue will, however be academic if the claim form is issued in the firm name.[184] Equally, there is much to be said for ensuring that he is bound by any judgment against the firm, which will be executed against its assets.[185]

---

[173] See *Stansfield v. Levy* (1820) 3 Stark 8; *De Mautort v. Saunders* (1830) 1 B. & Ad. 398. Whether a defendant has held himself out in such way is, for the most part, a question of fact: *cf.* the cases in the preceding note. See also *Colson v. Selby* (1796) 1 Esp. 452; *Baldney v. Ritchie* (1816) 1 Stark. 338; *Mullett v. Hook* (1827) Moo. & M. 88. Lord Lindley observed that the contrary decision in *Dubois v. Ludert* (1814) 5 Taunt. 609 "cannot, it is conceived, be supported".

[174] CPR r. 1.1.

[175] See *Higgins v. Senior* (1841) 8 M. & W. 834.

[176] CPR 7APD, para. 5B, *infra*, para. A2–05; also *supra*, para. 14–13.

[177] See, as to the old law, *Cabell v. Vaughan* (1669) 1 Wms.Saund. 291g, note.

[178] See, under the old rules of procedure, *Wilson, Sons & Co. Ltd. v. Balcarres Brook Steamship Co. Ltd.* [1893] 1 Q.B. 422. But *cf. West of England Steamship Owners' Protection and Indemnity Association v. John Holman & Sons* [1957] 1 W.L.R. 1164, *supra*, para. 14–18.

[179] See CPR rr. 6.30 *et seq.* In certain circumstances permission to serve the proceedings out of the jurisdiction will not be required: see *ibid.* r. 6.33 (as amended by the Civil Jurisdiction and Judgments Regulations 2009 (SI 2009/3131), regs. 30, 31).

[180] See *supra*, para. 14–05.

[181] See *supra*, para. 14–21; also *infra*, para. 14–91.

[182] See *infra*, Part 6, as to limited partnerships formed under the Limited Partnerships Act 1907.

[183] See *supra*, para. 14–21; also *infra*, para. 14–89.

[184] See *supra*, para. 14–04.

[185] CPR 70PD, para. 6A.1, *infra*, para. A2–09.

Minor partners

Since a minor partner will not be bound by any contract entered into by or on **14–44** behalf of the firm, he ought not, in general, to be joined[186]; however, there is nothing improper in issuing proceedings in the firm name.[187]

ACTIONS IN TORT

It has already been seen that partners are jointly and severally liable for torts **14–45** committed by a partner in the ordinary course of carrying on the firm's business,[188] so that proceedings may properly be issued against any one or more of them.[189] It seems that, under the old law, if some of the partners were sued, they could not insist on the others being joined,[190] even where the tort was committed by an employee,[191] but it is doubted that the court would still adopt such a rigid approach.[192]

(3) Equitable Remedies

Lord Lindley dealt with equitable remedies as a separate subject, observing **14–46** that:

> "As a general rule an action in the Chancery Division by or against an ordinary partnership will be defective for want of parties, unless all the partners are before the Court."[193]

Since, however, the same rules as to parties currently apply to all actions, whether in any Division of the High Court or in the county court,[194] no such general rule now exists. Nevertheless, since the court might conceivably, in the exercise of its discretion, have regard to the older cases,[195] the following passage from Lord Lindley's original text has been retained:

> "All the members of a firm ought to be parties to an action for a general account[196]; and in an action for payment of a partnership debt out of the assets of a deceased

---

[186] See 1 Wms.Saund. 207a; *Chandler v. Danks* (1800) 3 Esp. 76; *Jaffray v. Frebain* (1803) 5 Esp. 47; *Burgess v. Merrill* (1812) 4 Taunt. 468. *cf.* the views expressed in *Ex p. Henderson* (1798) 4 Ves.Jr. 164; *Gibbs v. Merrill* (1810) 3 Taunt. 307. If a minor is to be a party to proceedings, he must be represented by a litigation friend appointed under CPR Pt. 21.

[187] See *Harris v. Beauchamp Bros* [1893] 2 Q.B. 534; *Lovell & Christmas v. Beauchamp* [1894] A.C. 607; also *supra*, para. 14–20. *Quaere* whether, if the claimant knows of the minor partner's existence, he should issue the proceedings against the firm "other than" the minor partner.

[188] See the Partnership Act 1890, ss.10, 12, *supra*, paras 12–88 *et seq.*, 13–12.

[189] This will prima facie extend to tortious claims in respect of land held by the firm and to actions for the recovery of penalties imposed by statute. This represented a change in the law: see, as to claims relating to land, 1 Wms.Saund. 298f and g; *Mitchell v. Tarbutt* (1794) 5 T.R. 649; and, as to penalties, *Bristow v. James* (1797) 7 T.R. 257.

[190] *Sutton v. Clarke* (1815) 6 Taunt. 29.

[191] *Mitchell v. Tarbutt* (1794) 5 T.R. 649; *Ansell v. Waterhouse* (1817) 6 M. & S. 385.

[192] This is particularly so, given the wide discretions now conferred on the court under the CPR r. 19.2(a) and the overriding objective under *ibid.* r. 1.1.

[193] There were exceptions to this rule: see *Cowslad v. Cely* (1698) Pr. Ch. 83; *Darwent v. Walton* (1742) 2 Atk. 510; also *Orr v. Chase* (1812) 1 Mer. 729.

[194] See CPR Pt. 19. See also *supra*, para. 14–22.

[195] This is much less likely under the CPR.

[196] *Coppard v. Allen* (1864) 2 De G.J. & S. 173.

partner the surviving partners ought to be parties.[197] But if the ground of action is fraud it is not necessary to join a partner not implicated in it and not sought to be made liable."[198]

Actions for account against agents

14–47   Where the services of an agent are employed by one partner in the course of carrying on the partnership business, the firm may, on normal principles, sue the agent for an account even though he did not know of its existence.[199] *Per contra* if the partner concerned was himself acting as a principal or if the agent was induced by the other partners to *believe* that he was so acting.[200] Equally, in such a case, whilst under the old rules of procedure the agent prima facie could not insist on the other partners being joined as parties to the action,[201] it is questionable whether the same approach would now be adopted.[202]

A surviving partner may clearly sue an agent of the firm for an account, since he alone has authority to wind up the firm's affairs.[203]

C.   PARTIES WHERE CHANGE IN FIRM HAS OCCURRED

Incoming and outgoing partners

14–48   It has already been seen that, as a general rule, an outgoing partner will not be freed from liability in respect of the debts and obligations of the firm incurred prior to the date on which he ceased to be a partner, but that his liability for *future* debts and obligations will cease once his retirement (or expulsion) has been duly notified.[204] Similarly, an incoming partner will not normally undertake liability for debts and obligations incurred prior to the date of his admission to the firm.[205] Although an application of these principles may (and, indeed, frequently will) determine who should properly be made a party to an action by or against a firm following a change in its composition, further guidance is to be found in a number of propositions originally formulated by Lord Lindley.[206] These propositions must, however, be read subject to the overriding discretion of the Court under the Civil Procedure Rules.[207]

---

[197] *Hills v. M'Rae* (1851) 9 Hare 297; *Re Hodgson* (1885) 31 Ch.D. 177. See also *infra*, para. 26–14.

[198] See *Atkinson v. Mackreth* (1866) L.R. 2 Eq. 570; *Plumer v. Gregory* (1874) L.R. 18 Eq. 621.

[199] See *Killock v. Greg* (1828) 4 Russ. 285; *Anon.* (1653) Godb. 90.

[200] See *Killock v. Greg, supra*; *Maxwell v. Greig* (1828) 1 Coop. P.C. 491.

[201] *Benson v. Hadfield* (1844) 4 Hare 32; see also *Aspinall v. The London and North-Western Ry.* (1853) 11 Hare 325.

[202] Given the wide discretion conferred on the court under the CPR r. 19.2(a), as well as the requirements of the overriding objective under *ibid.* r. 1.1.

[203] Partnership Act 1890, s.38, *supra*, paras 13–62 *et seq.*; and see *Dixon v. Hammond* (1819) 2 B. & A. 310; *Philips v. Philips* (1828) 3 Hare 281; also *Haig v. Gray* (1850) 3 De G. & Sm. 741.

[204] See the Partnership Act 1890, ss.17(2), (3), 36, *supra*, paras 13–40 *et seq.*

[205] *ibid.* s.17(1), *supra*, paras 13–23 *et seq.* See also *supra*, para. 10–56.

[206] These propositions, which do not appear in their original order, are drawn from various statements which appeared in the 5th ed. of this work at pp. 284–287.

[207] See the CPR r. 19.2. *Semble*, it will rarely be fatal to an action if a partner has not been joined or if an unnecessary party has been joined, even though this may, ultimately, have adverse consequences in costs. But see also *supra*, para. 14–22.

Proposition 1: Joinder of outgoing partners

"... a retired partner[208] ought to join as a [*claimant*], and be joined as a defendant, **14–49** in every action to which, had he not retired, he would have been a necessary party.[209] This rule holds good even where a contract is entered into before, and the breach of it occurs after the retirement of a partner."[210]

It is, however, prima facie neither necessary nor appropriate to join an outgoing partner as a claimant if he has no beneficial interest in the outcome of the proceedings and the defendant has no claim against him.[211]

Proposition 2: Joinder of incoming partners

"... an incoming partner can neither sue nor be sued in respect of a liability of the **14–50** old firm, unless there is some agreement express or implied between himself and the person suing him or being sued by him."[212]

In any event, it will be a question of fact whether any right of action vested in the old firm became an asset of the new firm: this will not happen automatically, just because the agreement states that the partnership is unaffected by the change in its composition.[213] In the case of a claim *between* the partners of the old firm such a result may be at best unlikely[214] or at worst legally impossible.[215]

Proposition 3: Incoming partner undertaking debts, etc.

"... if an incoming partner has agreed with his co-partners to take upon himself the **14–51** debts and liabilities of the old firm,[216] they can require him to be made a defendant for their own partial indemnity."

What is contemplated here is, in practice, the joinder of the incoming partner pursuant to a Part 20 claim for contribution.[217]

---

[208] An expelled partner will be in precisely the same position.

[209] Lord Lindley did, however, refer to the fact that, in *Atkinson v. Laing* (1822) Dowl. & Ry.N.P. 16, "it was held at Nisi Prius that where two partners sold goods, and they afterwards dissolved partnership, an action for the price of those goods was sustainable by the one partner who continued to carry on the business of the late firm; but the propriety of this decision is more than questionable." Note also *Queensland Southern Barramundi v. Ough Properties Pty Ltd.* [2000] 2 Qd.R. 172. *cf. HLB Kidsons v. Lloyd's Underwriters* [2009] 1 All E.R. (Comm) 760, where there had been a technical dissolution due to the retirement of several partners.

[210] See *Dobbin v. Foster* (1844) 1 Car. & K. 323.

[211] See *William Brandt's Sons & Co. v. Dunlop Rubber Co. Ltd.* [1905] A.C. 454, 462, where Lord Macnaghten considered the position of the trustees in bankruptcy of the members of a bankrupt firm who were the assignors of the debt sought to be recovered by the claimants. Lord Lindley's original proposition was more tentative: "Whether, however, it is now necessary to joint as a plaintiff a retired partner against whom the defendant has no claim, and who has no beneficial interest in what is sought to be recovered admits of some doubt."

[212] See *Wilsford v. Wood* (1794) 1 Esp. 182; *Ord v. Portal* (1812) 3 Camp. 239, note; *Young v. Hunter* (1812) 4 Taunt. 582; *Waters v. Paynter* (1826) Chitty on Bills (10th ed.), p. 406, note 5; *Vere v. Ashby* (1829) 10 B. & C. 288. And see further *supra*, paras 10–56, 13–22 *et seq.*

[213] *Global Partners Fund Ltd. v. Babcock & Brown Ltd.* [2010] NSWSC 270 at [90]–[92] *per* Hammerschlag J. An appeal went off on other grounds: [2010] NSWCA 196. *cf.* the somewhat cavalier approach adopted in *Carter v. Freeman Group Plc* [2008] EWHC 3576 (QB) (Lawtel 26/8/08), where a partnership business had been transferred to a company

[214] *Patel v. Patel* [2008] EWCA Civ 1520 (Lawtel 7/4/08) at [7] *per* May L.J.

[215] *Global Partners Fund Ltd. v. Babcock & Brown Ltd.*, *supra*, at [87].

[216] See *supra*, paras 10–56, 13–26 *et seq.*

[217] CPR r. 20.2(1)(b).

Proposition 4: Incoming partner with interest in action

14–52   " . . . a new partner may, it is apprehended, always be joined in an action to recover a debt or enforce a demand in which he has an interest,[218] provided his joinder does not prejudice the rights of the defendants."[219]

Proposition 5: Express assignment of debts

14–53   " . . . if on the introduction of a new partner or the retirement of an old partner the debts due to the old firm are . . . assigned to the new firm, the new firm can sue in respect of them, either in its mercantile name or in the names of its members."

The rights of the new firm are dependent on an express assignment of the debts pursuant to section 136 of the Law of Property Act 1925,[220] but such assignments are, in practice, rare. It would seem that, in such a case, the action should be brought in the firm name.[221]

Proposition 6: Contract made by agent in ignorance of change

14–54   "[If] one partner retires, and a new partner comes in, and an agent of the firm, in ignorance of the change which has occurred, enters into a contract on behalf of the firm . . . the members of the new firm may sue on the contract, unless the defendant is prejudiced by their so doing.[222] The liability of the retired partner on such a contract will, however, cease if the creditor sues the new firm and recovers judgment against it."[223]

Proposition 7: Bills of exchange and promissory notes

14–55   "As regards negotiable instruments, . . . any persons who can agree to sue jointly upon them may do so, provided the instrument is in such a state as to pass by delivery; therefore, if a bill or note, indorsed in blank, is given to a firm consisting of certain individuals, who afterwards take in a new partner, they and he, or some or one of them, may sue on that bill or note."[224]

Proposition 8: Fresh contract

14–56   "A new firm may sue or be sued in respect of a fresh contract entered into by or with it to pay a debt owing to or by an old firm."

Thus, if a debtor of the old firm contracts a further debt with the new firm and then settles an account with the latter in respect of the debts due to it and to the old firm, the new firm may sue on an account stated for the entire amount due.[225]

---

[218] Such an interest may be acquired by means of an equitable assignment of the debt or other chose in action: see *Holt v. Heatherfield Trust* [1942] 2 K.B. 1. *cf.* Proposition 2, *supra*, para. 14–50.

[219] See now CPR rr. 1.1, 3.1(2)(m), 19.2(3).

[220] This section replaced the Judicature Act 1873, s.25(6).

[221] CPR 7APD, paras 5A.1, 5A.3, *infra*, para. A2–04. See also *supra*, para. 14–04.

[222] *Mitchell v. Lapage* (1816) Holt, N.P. 253; but see also *Boulton v. Jones* (1857) 2 H. & N. 564.

[223] See *Scarf v. Jardine* (1882) 7 App. Cas. 345, *supra*, paras 5–52, 13–04.

[224] See *Ord v. Portal* (1812) 3 Camp. 239; also *supra*, para. 14–32.

[225] *Moor v. Hill* (1795) Peake Add. Cases 10.

Proposition 9: Where firm cannot sue

"Although a change in a firm, whether by the introduction of a new partner or the **14–57** retirement of an old one, cannot, except as already mentioned, confer upon the partners any new right of action against strangers, or *vice versa*, as regards what may have occurred before the change took place, it may, nevertheless, operate so as to discharge a person from a contract previously entered into by him."

The potential consequences of a change in the firm as regards contracts of a personal nature and sureties have already been noticed earlier in this work.[226]

Deceased partners

The personal representatives of a deceased partner may be joined as co-clai- **14–58** mants or co-defendants with the surviving partners,[227] although this would be inappropriate where the obligation sought to be enforced by or against the firm is solely of a joint nature.[228] Nevertheless, it is considered that the surviving partners will usually be the only *necessary* parties to proceedings brought by the firm.[229]

Bankrupt or insolvent partners

A bankrupt partner need not be joined as a party to any proceedings brought **14–59** by or against the firm,[230] and the position would seem to be the same in the case of an insolvent corporate partner.[231] However, in an appropriate case, the trustee in bankruptcy or liquidator should, perhaps, be joined as a claimant.[232] If a bankrupt partner is joined as a co-defendant with the solvent partners, the court may order a stay as against him[233]; in contrast, proceedings may only be *commenced* against an insolvent corporate partner with the leave of the court.[234]

---

[226] See *supra*, paras 3–38 *et seq.*, 3–46 *et seq.*
[227] CPR rr. 7.3, 19.1.
[228] This will be relatively rare: see the Partnership Act 1890, ss.9, 12; also *supra*, paras 13–06 *et seq.* Note also CPR r. 19.3.
[229] See *Chandroutie v. Gajadhar* [1987] A.C. 147; as to the position in Scotland, see *Nicoll v. Reid* 1877 S.C. 137. And see, as to the devolution of the title to debts and other partnership assets, *infra*, paras 18–63 *et seq.*; also, generally, the following cases decided prior to the Judicature Acts: *Martin v. Crompe* (1698) 1 Ld. Ray. 340; *Richards v. Heather* (1817) 1 B. & A. 29; *Dixon v. Hammond* (1819) 2 B. & A. 310; *Calder v. Rutherford* (1822) 3 Brod. & B. 302; *Philips v. Philips* (1828) 3 Hare 281; *Haig v. Gray* (1850) 3 De G. & Sm. 741.
[230] Insolvency Act 1986, s.345(4). A similar provision was contained in the Bankruptcy Act 1914, s.118, as to which see *Josselson v. Borst* [1938] 1 K.B. 723, 736 *per* Greer L.J.; and see *Hawkins v. Ramsbottom* (1814) 6 Taunt. 179.
[231] See generally, the Insolvency Act 1986, ss.126(1), 128(1), 130(2). No provision corresponding to *ibid.* s.345(4) applies to insolvent companies. See also the Insolvent Partnerships Order 1994, art. 19(5).
[232] See, for example, the views formerly expressed in *Williams and Muir Hunter on Bankruptcy* (19th ed.), p. 471. If the success of the action is dependent on impeaching an act of the bankrupt or insolvent partner and this can only be done by the trustee or liquidator, the latter will be a *necessary* party: see *Heibut v. Nevill* (1870) L.R. 5 C.P. 478, *infra*, para. 14–63. There is no provision in the Insolvency Act 1986 equivalent to that contained in the Bankruptcy Act 1914, s.117, which enabled the court to authorise the trustee to commence proceedings on the firm's behalf.
[233] Insolvency Act 1986, s.285(1). And see *Ex p. Mills* (1871) L.R. 6 Ch. App. 594; also the notes to *ibid.* s.285 in *Muir Hunter on Personal Insolvency*.
[234] *ibid.* s.130(2).

Once a firm has been ordered to be wound up as an unregistered company,[235] no action may be commenced against it or against any partner, solvent or insolvent, without the leave of the court.[236]

D.   CONDUCT OF ONE PARTNER AFFECTING FIRM'S RIGHTS

Actions by firm: disability affecting one partner

14–60   The general principle that a disability affecting one partner will also affect the firm has already been noticed,[237] and it is nowhere more pertinent than in the present context. Summarising the apparent effect of the decided cases, Lord Lindley observed:

> " . . . the conduct of one partner affords a defence to an action by him and his co-partners, or by them without him, where they are bound by his act, either by adopting and seeking the benefit of it,[238] or upon the ground that it is on ordinary principles of agency the act of the firm; and binding upon him and his co-partners accordingly."[239]

14–61   Thus, it has repeatedly been held that if a solicitor accepts the office of trustee but has no power under the trust instrument to charge for his services, that disability will prevent his firm from recovering any profit costs for acting as solicitors to the trust.[240] Similarly, if a partner committed some fraud when entering into a contract on behalf of the firm[241] or is involved in some illegal act in the course of a partnership transaction,[242] he and his co-partners may be unable to sue because, as Lord Lindley put it, "their innocence does not purge his guilt". A civil proceedings or all proceedings order[243] against one partner will necessarily prevent the firm from instituting proceedings without the permission of the court.[244]

The same principle will prevent a partner, who has drawn a bill of exchange in his own name and secured its acceptance by a third party subject to conditions,

---

[235] See *infra*, paras 27–04 *et seq*.

[236] Insolvency Act 1986, ss.130(2), 228, as applied pursuant to various provisions of the Insolvent Partnerships Order 1994: see *infra*, paras 27–20, 27–40.

[237] See *supra*, paras 3–43 *et seq*. And see also *Salomons v. Nissen* (1788) 2 T.R. 674.

[238] As in *Ex p. Bell* (1813) 1 M. & S. 751, *infra*, para. 14–62; *Broughton v. Broughton* (1854) 5 De G.M. & G. 160.

[239] Lord Lindley then went on to point out that " . . . the cases at law which go further than this cannot, it is submitted, be now relied upon."

[240] See *Collins v. Carey* (1839) 2 Beav. 128; *Christophers v. White* (1847) 10 Beav. 523; *Broughton v. Broughton* (1854) 5 De G.M. & G. 160; *Matthison v. Clarke* (1854) 3 Drew. 3; also *Re Boyle* [1947] I.R. 61. An exception is made in the case of litigation: see *Craddock v. Piper* (1850) 1 Mac. & G. 664; *Re Corsellis* (1883) 34 Ch.D. 675; and see *Re Doody* [1893] 1 Ch. 129, 141–142 *per* Lindley L.J. The worst effects of such disability may be avoided by suitable arrangements between the solicitor trustee and the other partners: see *Clack v. Carlon* (1861) 30 L.J. Ch. 639; *Re Gates* [1933] 1 Ch. 913.

[241] See *Kilby v. Wilson* (1825) Ry. & M. 178.

[242] See *Biggs v. Lawrence* (1789) 3 T.R. 454.

[243] See, as to such orders, the Senior Courts Act 1981, s.42 (as amended by the Prosecution of Offences Act 1985, s.24). The Supreme Court Act 1981 was so renamed by the Constitutional Reform Act 2005, Sched. 11, Pt.1, para. 1(1).

[244] *Mephistopheles Debt Collection Service v. Lotay* [1994] 1 W.L.R. 1064 (CA). The partner in question was a *limited* partner.

from seeking to avoid those conditions merely by indorsing the bill to his firm.[245] His partners will be in no better position even if they alone sue on the bill.[246]

Death of partner affected by disability

It is, perhaps, self evident that a disability which affects one partner and, through him, the firm may persist even after the date of his death.[247] Thus, in *Ex p. Bell*,[248] where one partner had loaned partnership money to a third party for an illegal purpose and then died, the surviving partners were not able to recover that loan from the third party.

14–62

Insolvency of partner affected by disability

In the same way, the trustee in bankruptcy or liquidator of an insolvent partner or firm will in general be in no better position than the partners,[249] unless he can set aside the transaction entered into by the insolvent partner which gives rise to the disability.[250] Thus, in *Heilbut v. Nevill*,[251] which was decided under the old bankruptcy laws, a solvent partner and the assignees of a bankrupt partner were able to maintain an action on a bill of exchange belonging to the firm, which the bankrupt partner had indorsed to his own creditor in circumstances which constituted a fraudulent preference.

14–63

Frauds on firm and other exceptional cases

Although the position was formerly otherwise,[252] the principle under consideration does not apply in cases where one partner has, with the connivance of the defendant, committed a fraud on the firm.[253]

Moreover, if a partner colludes with a partnership debtor and gives him a receipt for his debt, even though it remains unpaid, the firm may bring proceedings to recover the debt,[254] since a receipt does not preclude the person giving it from demonstrating that the money has not in fact been received[255] nor does it discharge the debt.

Similarly, if a partner covenants not to sue for a partnership debt he may join with his co-partners in an action brought to recover that debt.[256] Again a right of

14–64

---

[245] *Sparrow v. Chisman* (1829) 9 B. & C. 241; see also *Richmond v. Heapy* (1816) 1 Stark. 202.

[246] *Astley v. Johnson* (1860) 5 H. & N. 137.

[247] Although the disability will persist as to *past* transactions, it may be removed for the future, *e.g.* where, in the example given *supra*, para. 14–61, the solicitor trustee dies.

[248] (1813) 1 M. & S. 751. See also *Brandon v. Scott* (1857) 7 E. & B. 234; *cf. Innes v. Stephenson* (1831) 1 Moo. & Rob. 147.

[249] See *Jones v. Yates* (1829) 9 B. & C. 532.

[250] See the Insolvency Act 1986, ss.238, 239 (winding up), 339, 340 (bankruptcy), 423, as applied (where relevant) pursuant to various provisions of the Insolvent Partnerships Order 1994. See also *supra*, paras 10–152, 10–153 and *infra*, para. 27–101.

[251] (1870) L.R. 5 C.P. 478.

[252] As to the position at law, see *Jones v. Yates* (1829) 9 B. & C. 532; *Wallace v. Kelsall* (1840) 7 M. & W. 264; *Gordon v. Ellis* (1844) 7 Man. & G. 607; *Brownrigg v. Rae* (1850) 5 Ex. 489; *Brandon v. Scott* (1857) 7 E. & B. 234. The position was otherwise in equity: see *Midland Ry. v. Taylor* (1862) 8 H.L.C. 751; *Piercy v. Fynney* (1871) L.R. 12 Eq. 69. Lord Lindley apprehended that "the cases at law above referred to can no longer be relied upon; the Judicature Acts having removed the technical difficulties which led to their decision."

[253] See further, as to such cases, *supra*, para. 12–29. Note also *Heilbut v. Nevill, supra*.

[254] *Henderson v. Wilde* (1811) 2 Camp. 561; *Farrar v. Hutchinson* (1839) 9 A. & E. 641.

[255] *Skaife v. Jackson* (1824) 5 Dow. & Ry. 290.

[256] See *Walmesley v. Cooper* (1839) 11 A. & E. 216.

set-off which might be raised against one partner cannot be raised against him and his co-partners.[257] As Lord Lindley explained:

"In each of these cases there is only a right of cross-action[258] against the one partner; and although such right might be relied on as a defence to an action by him alone, it is held not to affect the firm to which he belongs."

Actions against firm

14–65   If all the partners are sued in respect of a joint debt or obligation and each puts in a separate defence, any ground of defence pleaded and established by one partner which is fatal to the claimant's entire claim will benefit both him and his co-partners.[259] Equally, where proceedings are commenced against the partners of an insolvent firm and one partner successfully defends the claim through or in the name of his *current* firm, costs incurred by that firm will be recoverable from the other party, even though the defendant partner has no liability for such costs *vis-à-vis* the other members of that firm.[260]

2.   AUTHORITY OF PARTNERS IN LEGAL PROCEEDINGS

Actions by firm

14–66   Any partner may, without the consent of his co-partners, commence proceedings in his and their names or (which amounts to the same thing) in the firm name.[261] However, if his co-partners' consent is not forthcoming, such a partner must normally[262] offer them an indemnity against costs.[263] Where, on the other hand, a partner purports to commence proceedings in his own name and against the express wishes of his co-partners, it would seem that the proceedings cannot

---

[257] See *infra*, paras 14–75 *et seq.*

[258] Or counterclaim: see CPR r. 20.2(1)(a).

[259] *Pirie v. Richardson* [1927] 1 K.B. 448.

[260] *Malkinson v. Trim* [2003] 1 W.L.R. 463 (CA). There the costs were, in fact, payable following a discontinuance of the proceedings against the defendant partner.

[261] *Whitehead v. Hughes* (1834) 2 C. & M. 318; *Tomlinson v. Broadsmith* [1896] 1 Q.B. 386; *Seal v. Kingston* [1908] 2 K.B. 579; see also *Harwood v. Edwards* (1739); *Gow on Partnership*, p. 65, note; *Court v. Berlin* [1897] 2 Q.B. 396. *Quaere*, does the Partnership Act 1890, s.24(8) enable a majority of partners to prevent an action being brought? It has been so held in Scotland: see *Hutcheon & Partners v. Hutcheon* 1979 S.L.T. (Sh. Ct.) 62. This point was left open in *Sutherland v. Gustar* [1994] Ch. 304, 312H–313A. Note also *Mephistopheles Debt Collection Service v. Lotay* [1994] 1 W.L.R. 1064 (CA).

[262] Such an offer need not be made in certain circumstances, *e.g.* where the partner refusing his consent is acting in collusion with the defendant: *Johnson v. Stephens & Carter Ltd.* [1923] 2 K.B. 857.

[263] *Whitehead v. Hughes* (1834) 2 C. & M. 318; *Tomlinson v. Broadsmith* [1896] 1 Q.B. 386; *Seal v. Kingston* [1908] 2 K.B. 579. See also *Cullen v. Knowles and Birks* [1898] 2 Q.B. 380; *Sutherland v. Gustar* [1994] Ch. 304, 310F. Note that in one unreported case, *Davey & Co. v. Alby United Carbide Factories Ltd.*, March 19, 1914 (referred to in the *Supreme Court Practice 1999* at para. 81/1/12, but inexplicably omitted from subsequent editions of *Civil Procedure*), the indemnity appears to have been coupled with an order for security. *Quaere* whether such an order was justified.

be treated as brought on their behalf.[264] However, once a partner has left the firm this principle ceases to apply *vis-à-vis* him, unless continuing authority is conferred by the partnership agreement or that partner's departure caused a general dissolution of the firm.[265]

If an interim remedy is granted *against* the partners, the partner who initiated the proceedings may seemingly enforce that order against his co-partners if their non-compliance will prejudice the firm's claim.[266]

Stay of proceedings, etc.

Lord Lindley observed: 14–67

" ... if it is competent for one partner to sue for the firm, it is as competent to any other partner to stay proceedings, or to put an end to the action altogether by means of a release; and, although the Court will not allow this to be done by collusion with the defendant, for the purpose of defrauding the other partners of their rights,[267] a release will be effectual where there is no fraud in the case."

Thus, in *Harwood v. Edwards*,[268] one partner, without the knowledge or consent of his co-partners, brought an action in their joint names for the recovery of a debt due to the firm. The other partners later agreed with the defendant that the proceedings should be stayed and this agreement was held to be binding on all the partners, even though the partner who had commenced the action disputed its validity and could point to a provision in the partnership agreement which prohibited any partner from giving a release without the consent of the others.

Reference to arbitration

On the other hand, once proceedings have been commenced, one partner may   14–68
seemingly not consent to all matters in dispute being referred to arbitration, unless he has specific authority so to do.[269]

Actions against firm

A managing partner may, subject to the terms of the partnership agreement,[270]   14–69
have implied authority to instruct a solicitor to defend proceedings brought against the firm[271] and can clearly sign an acknowledgment of service on behalf

---

[264] *Re Sutherland & Partners' Appeal* [1993] S.T.C. 399; this point was not addressed in the Court of Appeal: see [1994] Ch. 304 (*sub nom. Sutherland v. Gustar*). What would have been the position if the proceedings had been brought in the firm name or the names of all the partners was left open by Lindsay J.: [1993] S.T.C. 406f. But see, on this point, *Harwood v. Edwards* (1739) *Gow on Partnership*, p. 65, note, noted *infra*, para. 14–67. See also *supra*, para. 12–35. The position is *a fortiori* in Scotland, where the firm has separate legal personality: see *Arif v. Levy & McRae* 1992 G.W.D. 3–156.

[265] *i.e.* so that the Partnership Act 1890, s.38 applies: see *HLB Kidsons v. Lloyd's Underwriters* [2009] 1 All E.R. (Comm) 760. In that case there had merely been a technical dissolution so that s.38 had no application.

[266] *Seal v. Kingston* [1908] 2 K.B. 579 (where the partnership had been dissolved).

[267] See *supra*, paras 14–64 *et seq.*

[268] (1739) *Gow on Partnership*, p. 65, note.

[269] *Hatton v. Royle* (1858) 3 H. & N. 500. And also *supra*, para. 12–40.

[270] See, for example, *HLB Kidsons v. Lloyd's Underwriters* [2009] 1 All E.R. (Comm) 760, which concerned a managing partner's authority to *initiate* proceedings on behalf of retired partners.

[271] *Tomlinson v. Broadsmith* [1896] 1 Q.B. 386. In such a case, the solicitor must keep the managing partner informed as to the progress of the action, but need not report to all the partners. See also *supra*, para. 12–38.

of all the partners.[272] Equally, *any* partner can sign such an acknowledgment[273] but must, absent their authority, offer his co-partners an indemnity against costs should they not consent to him defending the proceedings.[274] It may be that even a managing partner must, ultimately, offer such an indemnity.[275]

Service

14–70   It has already been seen that proceedings commenced in the firm name may be personally served on any partner.[276] This option is, however, not available where the proceedings are commenced in the names of the individual partners nor, obviously, where they do not concern partnership matters unless proceedings in the firm name can be justified.[277]

Lord Lindley pointed out that:

> " ... even in proceedings relating to partnership matters, although service on one partner is sometimes held equivalent to service on all, this is not the case where the service is relied on as the foundation of process of contempt, or of any proceedings of a penal nature."[278]

This would still seem to be the position.[279]

Death of partner

14–71   If the proceedings against a firm have been commenced in the firm name and one partner dies after service has been acknowledged, the surviving partners must put in a defence in the firm name.[280]

Consenting to judgment

14–72   One partner seemingly has no authority to bind the firm by consenting to a judgment against it.[281]

---

[272] CPR 10PD, para. 4.4, *infra*, para. A2–07. See also *supra*, para. 14–19. It would not seem to matter that some of the partners have, at the time of signing the acknowledgment, left the firm; *cf. HLB Kidsons v. Lloyd's Underwriters, supra.*

[273] *ibid.*

[274] See the cases cited *supra*, para. 14–66, n. 263.

[275] This would seem to have been the view of Rigby L.J. in *Tomlinson v. Broadsmith, supra,* at p. 392.

[276] See *supra*, para. 14–14.

[277] See *Petty v. Smith* (1828) 2 Y. & J. 111; *Fairlie v. Quin* (1839) Smythe 189. Also *supra*, para. 14–10.

[278] See *Young v. Goodson* (1826) 2 Russ. 255; also *Moulston v. Wire* (1843) 1 Dow. & L. 527; *Re Holiday* (1841) 9 Dow. 1020. The following additional cases were referred to by Lord Lindley in this context: *Carrington v. Cantillon* (1722) Bunb. 107; *Coles v. Gurney* (1815) 1 Madd. 187; *Grant v. Prosser* (1824) Sm. & Bat. 95; *Carter v. Southall* (1831) 3 M. & W. 128; *Figgins v. Ward* (1834) 2 C. & M. 242; *Murray v. Moore* (1835) 1 Jo. 129; *Doe d. Overton v. Roe* (1841) 9 Dow. 1039; *Nolan v. Fitzgerald* (1851) 2 I.C.L.R. 79; *Kitchen v. Wilson* (1858) 4 C.B.(N.S.) 483; *Leese v. Martin* (1871) L.R. 13 Eq. 77.

[279] See RSC Ord. 46, r. 5(2) (sequestration), Ord. 52, rr. 3(3), 4(2) (committal) and CCR Ord. 29, r. 1(2)(a) (as respectively applied by CPR Pt. 50, Scheds 1, 2).

[280] *Ellis v. Wadeson* [1899] 1 Q.B. 714.

[281] *Hambidge v. De La Crouée* (1846) 3 C.B. 742; also *Munster v. Cox* (1885) 10 App.Cas. 680. And see *Rathbone v. Drakeford* (1830) 4 M. & P. 57.

Costs

If costs are ordered to be paid to one partner, payment to another partner is not **14–73** sufficient.[282]

Payment out of court

Before money can be paid out of court to a partner, the Accountant General **14–74** may require to be satisfied as to his identity and entitlement.[283] Such a partner may thus be required to demonstrate his authority to receive the payment out.[284]

3. SET-OFF

Lord Lindley's rules on set-off

Where proceedings are brought against a defendant in respect of a money **14–75** claim,[285] he may pursue a monetary cross-claim against the claimant by means of a set-off[286] or counterclaim.[287] Although the right to raise a set-off is more

---

[282] *Showler v. Stoakes* (1844) 2 Dow. & L. 3.

[283] Court Funds Rules 1987 (SI 1987/821), r. 40(9)(i) (as substituted by the Courts Funds (Amendment) Rules 1997 (SI 1997/177), r. 4 and amended by the Court Funds (Amendment) Rules 2010 (SI 2010/172), r. 5).

[284] See generally, as to the authority of a partner to receive payments on behalf of the firm, *supra*, paras 12–53 *et seq.*

[285] This will, seemingly, include a claim for an account: see *Secret Hotels Ltd. v. E.A. Traveller Ltd.* [2010] I.L. Pr. 33.

[286] CPR r. 16.6. The scope and availability of equitable set off has, *inter alia*, been explored in the following cases: *Aries Tanker Corp. v. Total Transport Ltd.* [1977] 1 W.L.R. 185 (set-off against freight not allowed); *Federal Commerce & Navigation Co. Ltd. v. Molena Alpha Inc.* [1978] Q.B. 927 (set-off against hire under a charterparty allowed, although this question was left open by the House of Lords on appeal: see [1979] A.C. 757); *British Anzani (Felixstowe) Ltd. v. International Marine Management (U.K.) Ltd.* [1980] Q.B. 137 (set-off against rent under lease allowed); *Sim v. Rotherham Metropolitan Borough Council* [1987] Ch. 216 (set-off against salary due under a contract of employment allowed); *Colonial Bank v. European Grain and Shipping Ltd.* [1989] A.C. 1056 (set-off against freight not allowed); *Esso Petroleum Co. Ltd. v. Milton* [1997] 1 W.L.R. 938 (set-off not allowed where payment for goods or services effected by direct debit); *Benford Ltd. v. Lopecan SL (No.2)* [2004] 2 Lloyd's Rep. 618 (distinction between transaction and independent set off); *Geldof Metaalconstructie NV v. Simon Carves Ltd., The Times*, June 21, 2010 (CA) (set-off of counter-claim allowed). And note CPR r. 66.4 (set-off against Crown not permitted in certain instances). A right of set-off may also be excluded by agreement: *Hong Kong and Shanghai Banking Corp v. Kloeckner & Co. A.G.* [1990] 2 Q.B. 514 and the other cases noted *infra*, para. 14–81, n. 304. However, such a term may, in an appropriate case, fail to satisfy the test of reasonableness under the Unfair Contract Terms Act 1977, s.13: *Stewart Gill Ltd. v. Horatio Myer & Co. Ltd.* [1992] 2 All E.R. 257. Similarly in the case of the Misrepresentation Act 1967, s.3: *Skipskredittforeningen v. Emperor Navigation* [1998] 1 Lloyd's Rep. 66. Any such term will in any event be ineffective on the insolvency of one of the parties: see *infra*, para. 27–77.

[287] CPR r. 20.2(1)(a). And note that a counterclaim may be dismissed or ordered to be dealt with separately if it cannot conveniently be disposed of in the same action: *ibid.* rr. 3.1(2)(e), (j), 20.9.

extensive that it once was,[288] it is still governed by the principles originally developed by the courts of equity which, so far as concerns partnerships, were encapsulated by Lord Lindley in four rules,[289] *viz.*:

Rule 1:

> "Joint debts owing to and by the same persons in the same right can be set off."

Rule 2:

> "Separate debts owing to and by the same person in the same right can also be set off."

Rule 3:

> "Debts not owing to and by the same persons in the same rights cannot be set off."

It is this third rule which prevents a debt owed to or by a sole surviving partner on his own account from being set off against a debt owed by or to the former firm.[290] Where, however, the debt owed by the surviving partner is, in substance, a partnership debt, a set-off may be permitted.[291]

14–76   On the same basis, a partnership creditor may not, when seeking payment out of a deceased partner's estate, set off a debt which he owes to that estate on his own account, at least where this would place him in competition with the deceased's separate creditors.[292]

Again, where certain partners in a dissolved firm sought an indemnity from another partner in respect of liabilities which they had incurred as trustees on behalf of the firm, he could not set off a claim for money which he believed to be due to him *qua* partner on the dissolution.[293]

---

[288] Note, in particular, the wide terms of CPR r. 16.6. See also the observations of the House of Lords as to the general nature of set off in *Burton v. Mellham Ltd.* [2006] 1 W.L.R. 2820.

[289] In Lord Lindley's original formulation, the words "both at law and in equity" appeared at the end of Rules 1–3; the same point was also made in relation to Rule 4, albeit in a separate sentence.

[290] *cf.* the position at law: *Golding v. Vaughan* (1782) 2 Chitty 436; *Slipper v. Stidstone* (1794) 5 T.R. 493; *French v. Andrade* (1796) 6 T.R. 582.

[291] *Smith v. Parkes* (1852) 16 Beav. 115. See also *Government of Newfoundland v. Newfoundland Ry.* (1888) 13 App.Cas. 199.

[292] *Addis v. Knight* (1817) 2 Mer. 117. Lord Lindley explained the rationale behind this application of the rule as follows: " . . . the creditor must pay [*the debt due from himself to the deceased*] in full, and then, as regards the debt in respect of which he sues, rank as any other creditor of the firm against the assets of the deceased. It is obvious that if in such a case the two debts were set against each other, the separate creditors of the deceased would be paying a joint creditor of the firm, unless the assets of the deceased were sufficient to pay both classes of creditors in full." *Quaere*, would a set-off not be allowed if there were such a sufficiency? See also the Partnership Act 1890, s.9, which establishes the *several* liability of a deceased partner for the debts and obligations of the firm. And see *supra*, paras 13–06 *et seq.*

[293] *Hurst v. Bennett* [2001] B.P.I.R. 287 (CA). This was, in fact, an application to set aside a statutory demand under the Insolvency Rules 1986, r. 6.5(4)(a), so that it did not raise a pure question of set-off. Note also that it, in any event, appeared unlikely that any sums would be due to Mr Hurst, even if the dissolution accounts were taken. Although the full implications of the indemnity having been given by the *firm* (*i.e.* including the trustees themselves) seem not to have been extensively considered, it is clear that the court was of the view that no sums would, in any event, have been due from the trustees: *ibid. at* [49] *per* Sir Christopher Staughton.

Rule 4:

"Except under special circumstances, a debt due to or from several persons jointly **14–77**
cannot be set off against a debt due from or to one of such persons separately."[294]

It follows that a debt owed by a firm may not be set off against a debt owed
to a partner in his personal capacity or vice versa,[295] because to allow a set-off
in either case would, in Lord Lindley's words, "enable a creditor to obtain
payment of what is due to him from persons in no way indebted to him".[296]
Equally, it appears that the rationale for this rule may lie in the absence of
authority from all the partners to permit the set off. On that basis, in *Anselm v.
Anselm*,[297] Hart J. held that, where a debt was owed to a firm comprising two
partners, A and B, and A joined the debtor as a co-claimant when bringing
proceedings against B, A should be taken to have authorised the set-off.

Single partner dealt with

The fourth rule applies even where the third party has only had dealings with **14–78**
a single partner, so long as he was acting on the firm's behalf. Thus, in *Gordon
v. Ellis*,[298] three partners, A, B and C, sued the defendant to recover money
received by him in respect of goods sold on the firm's behalf. The defendant in
effect sought to plead that A had employed him to sell the goods as if they were
A's own, that they had accordingly been sold as A's goods and that A was
indebted to him in an amount greater than that sought to be recovered in the
action. It was admitted that, if B and C had, by their conduct, induced the
defendant to believe that A was the sole owner of the goods and to deal with him
on that basis, the defendant would have had a good defence but, since that was
not alleged, a set-off was not permissible.[299]

Where, however, the debt apparently owed by the partner is in fact shown to **14–79**
be a partnership debt, a set-off will be allowed. In this connection, Lord Lindley
referred to the earlier proceedings in *Gordon v. Ellis*,[300] observing:

" . . . the defendant . . . was held entitled to set off a debt due to him for an advance
made by him to one of the partners on account of those goods. The Court thought that
although the money was advanced to one partner only, the defendant had a right to

---

[294] See *Bowyear v. Pawson* (1881) 6 Q.B.D. 540; *Re Pennington and Owen* [1925] Ch. 825; also
the Senior Courts Act 1981, s.49(2) (formerly the Supreme Court Act 1981: Constitutional Reform
Act 2005, Sched. 11, Pt.1, para. 1(1)). And see *Kinnerley v. Hossack* (1809) 2 Taunt. 170; *Vulliamy
v. Noble* (1817) 3 Mer. 593; *Jebsen v. East and West India Dock Co.* (1875) L.R. 10 C.P. 300. Lord
Lindley pointed out that, in *Manchester, Sheffield, and Lincolnshire Ry. v. Brooks* (1877) 2 Ex.D. 243,
a defendant was permitted to plead a separate debt by way of set-off in an action on a joint debt but
concluded "This can hardly have been right." Indeed, equity did not permit such a set-off even in a
case of fraud: see *Middleton v. Pollock* (1875) L.R. 20 Eq. 515.

[295] *MacGillivray v. Simson* (1826) 2 Car. & P. 320; *Boswell v. Smith* (1833) 6 Car. & P. 60; *France
v. White* (1839) 8 Scott 257; *Gordon v. Ellis* (1844) 2 C.B. 821; *Arnold v. Bainbrigge* (1853) 9 Ex.
153.

[296] *Powell v. Brodhurst* [1901] 2 Ch. 160, 165 *per* Farwell J.

[297] June 29, 1999 (Lawtel 2/7/99).

[298] (1844) 2 C.B. 821.

[299] Lord Lindley pointed out that, in this case, "an attempt was made to extend the principle on
which Lord Kenyon decided *Stracey v. Deey* [*(1789) 7 T.R. 261, note*], to all cases in which one
partner only transacts the business of the firm, and becomes himself indebted to the person with
whom he deals." See, as to the latter decision, *infra*, para. 14–83. And see *Bonfield v. Smith* (1844)
12 M. & W. 405; also *Baring v. Corrie* (1818) 2 B. & A. 137; *Ramazotti v. Bowring* (1859) 7
C.B.(N.S.) 851.

[300] (1844) 7 Man. & G. 607.

treat it as an advance to the firm made on that partner's requisition, whilst acting within the scope of his apparent authority as agent of the firm. In point of fact, the defendant, instead of waiting until he had sold the goods, and then handing over the money produced by their sale, made a payment on account; and he sought nothing more than to have the amount so prepaid deducted from the sum for which he sold the goods."

It should, however, be observed that no plea of set-off had been raised at this stage.[301]

Bank accounts

14–80 The fourth rule is also applied, by analogy, where a firm shares the same bankers as one or more of the partners. Thus, any sum due from the firm on the partnership account may not be set off against sums due to those partners on their personal accounts.[302]

Although set-off *is* available as between two current accounts maintained by a firm, it will not be permitted as between a current account and a loan account, unless the firm consents.[303] The position will naturally be the same as between accounts maintained by a single partner.

Exceptions to rule 4

14–81 The general rule which precludes a debt due to a firm being set off against a debt owing by a partner, and vice versa, is subject to the following exceptions.

Agreement: It is almost too obvious to require comment that effect will be given to any express or implied agreement authorising (or prohibiting)[304] a set-off, and that such an agreement may be inferred from the conduct of the parties.[305]

However, if one partner agrees that a personal debt which he owes to a third party will be set off against a debt owed by that third party to the firm, he will prima facie be acting in fraud of his co-partners; Lord Lindley pointed out that:

---

[301] See *ibid.* p. 620 *per* Tindal C.J.

[302] See *Watts v. Christie* (1849) 11 Beav. 546; *Cavendish v. Geaves* (1857) 24 Beav. 163. Lord Lindley stated the principle in these terms: "In strict analogy to the above rule, it has been decided in equity that if the members of a firm have separate private accounts with the bankers of the firm, and a balance is due to the bankers from the firm on the partnership account, the bankers have no lien for such balance on what may be due from themselves to the members of the firm on their respective separate accounts; and that the debt due to the bankers from the partners jointly cannot be set off against the debts due from the bankers to the partners separately." *Per contra*, perhaps, if the partners hold their personal accounts as nominees for the firm: see *Ex p. Morier* (1879) 12 Ch.D. 491; *Re Hett, Maylor & Co. Ltd.* (1894) 10 T.L.R. 412; *Bhogal v. Punjab National Bank* [1988] 2 All E.R. 296; *Uttamchandani v. Central Bank of India* (1989) 139 N.L.J. 222.

[303] *Bradford Old Bank Ltd. v. Sutcliffe* [1918] 2 K.B. 833, 844 *per* Scrutton L.J., approved in *National Westminster Bank Ltd. v. Halesowen Presswork & Assemblies Ltd.* [1972] A.C. 785, 819 *per* Lord Kilbrandon.

[304] *Hong Kong and Shanghai Banking Corp. v. Kloechner & Co. A.G.* [1990] 2 Q.B. 514; *Coca-Cola Financial Corp. v. Finsat International Ltd.* [1998] Q.B. 43 (CA); *Re Kaupthing Singer and Friedlander Ltd.* [2009] 2 Lloyd's Rep. 154; also *BOC Group v. Centeon* [1999] 1 All E.R. (Comm.) 53. But see also *supra*, para. 14–75, n. 286, as to the reasonableness of such an agreement.

[305] See *Downam v. Matthews* (1721) Pr. Ch. 580; *Kinnerley v. Hossack* (1809) 2 Taunt. 170; *Vulliamy v. Noble* (1817) 3 Mer. 593; *Cheetham v. Crook* (1825) McCle. & Y. 307.

" . . . a set-off founded on such an agreement cannot, it is apprehended, be maintained in the absence of special circumstances, rendering such an agreement binding on the other parties."[306]

Joint and several obligation: If a debt is owed by partners jointly and severally, it may be set off against a separate debt due to one of them alone.[307]   **14–82**

Dormant partners, etc.: Where one partner has been permitted to act as if he were a principal, and not merely the agent of his firm, a set-off of what are technically joint and separate debts may be allowed. Thus, whilst dormant partners may clearly be joined as co-claimants in an action on a contract entered into on the firm's behalf,[308] Lord Lindley observed that: **14–83**

" . . . dormant partners cannot, by coming forward and suing on such contracts, deprive the defendant of any right of set-off of which he might have availed himself if the non-dormant partners only had been [*claimants*]."

This principle was established in *Stracey v. Deey*.[309] There the defendant had dealt with the one active member of the firm, R, who in fact appeared to be the only person concerned in the business, and had become indebted in respect of certain goods supplied by him. At the same time, the defendant had incurred expenditure on R's behalf, assuming that a set off would take place. The claimants (R and his two dormant partners) contended that a set-off should not be permitted but this argument was rejected by Lord Kenyon, who effectively held that the defendant should be able to take advantage of all the defences which would have been available to him if the action had been brought by R alone.[310] Of course, the position would have been otherwise if R had not led the defendant to believe that he alone was being dealt with.[311]

Change in firm: express assignments of debts

It is, perhaps, obvious that there may be difficulties raising a set-off defence following a change in a firm, *e.g.* where a debt owing to the old firm is sought to be set off against a debt incurred by the new firm.[312] In such a case, the set-off can, however, usually be preserved by the members of the new firm taking an   **14–84**

---

[306] *Nottidge v. Pritchard* (1834) 2 Cl. & F. 379; *Piercy v. Fynney* (1871) L.R. 12 Eq. 69; see also *supra*, paras 14–64 *et seq*. Lord Lindley noted that "*Wallace v. Kelsall* (1840) 7 M. & W. 264, is the other way, but is to be explained by the old technical rules of pleading, which are now abolished."

[307] See *Owen v. Wilkinson* (1858) 5 C.B.(N.S.) 526.

[308] See *supra*, para. 14–26.

[309] (1789) 7 T.R. 361, note. See also *Teed v. Elworthy* (1811) 14 East 213; *De Mautort v. Saunders* (1830) 1 B. & Ad. 398. *cf. Gordon v. Ellis* (1844) 2 C.B. 821, *supra*, para. 14–78, where the court refused to extend the *Stracey v. Deey* principle.

[310] See *George v. Clagett* (1797) 7 T.R. 359; *Borries v. Imperial Ottoman Bank* (1873) L.R. 9 C.P. 38; *Cooke v. Eshelby* (1887) 12 App.Cas. 271.

[311] Commenting on the decision in *Gordon v. Ellis* (1844) 2 C.B. 821, *supra*, para. 14–78, Lord Lindley observed " . . . it was held, and rightly, that a person liable to be sued by a firm cannot set off a debt due from one only of its members, on the ground that he only was dealt with by the defendant, unless it can be shown that the other members of the firm induced the defendant by their conduct to treat their co-partner as the only partner with whom the defendant had to do" [*sic*]. See *Bonfield v. Smith* (1844) 12 M. & W. 405; also *Baring v. Corrie* (1818) 2 B. & A. 137; *Ramazotti v. Bowring* (1859) 7 C.B.(N.S.) 851.

[312] See Rule 3, *supra*, para. 14–75; also *supra*, paras 14–48 *et seq*.

express assignment of the debt owed to the old firm and giving the debtor notice thereof.[313]

Attempts to avoid set-off

14–85   It is no longer possible to prevent a defence of set-off being raised by a firm merely by suing one of the partners: in such a case, the defendant may, if necessary, require his co-partners to be joined as parties,[314] unless they are out of the jurisdiction.[315]

Other devices designed to achieve such a procedural advantage are also likely to be unsuccessful. Thus, a firm which holds a promissory note made by a third party cannot indorse it over to one of the partners with a view to him suing on it and thereby depriving that third party of a right of set-off which he would otherwise have enjoyed against the firm.[316] A similar attitude might, in the current editor's view, be adopted if the firm were to assign a debt to a partner for that purpose.

Insolvency

14–86   Set-off in the case of bankruptcy or insolvency is considered later in this work.[317]

4.   EXECUTION AGAINST PARTNERS

(a) Judgment In Firm Name

Execution without permission

14–87   A judgment obtained against a firm[318] may be freely enforced against any partnership property within the jurisdiction[319] and, with certain exceptions, against any partner who: (i) acknowledged service of the claim form as a partner; (ii) though served as a partner, failed to acknowledge service; (iii) pleaded that

---

[313] Law of Property Act 1925, s.136. See, in particular, *Cavendish v. Geaves* (1857) 24 Beav. 163 (from the judgment in which Lord Lindley quoted extensively); also *Bennett v. White* [1910] 2 K.B. 643. Note that the assignee takes subject to all equities having priority over his rights: *ibid.* s.136(1). See, in this context, *Jeffrys v. Agra and Masterman's Bank* (1866) L.R. 2 Eq. 674; *Watson v. Mid Wales Ry.* (1867) L.R. 2 C.P. 593; *Young v. Kitchin* (1878) 3 Ex.D. 127; *Government of Newfoundland v. Newfoundland Ry.* (1888) 13 App.Cas. 199; *Christie v. Taunton, Delmard, Lane & Co.* [1893] 2 Ch. 175; *Stoddard v. Union Trust Ltd.* [1912] 1 K.B. 181; *Re Pinto Leite and Nephews* [1929] 1 Ch. 221. Notice of the assignment must be clear and distinct to prevent a set-off: see, generally, *Lloyd v. Banks* (1868) L.R. 3 Ch.App. 488, 490 *per* Lord Cairns; *Bence v. Shearman* [1898] 2 Ch. 582, 587 *per* Chitty L.J.; also *W. F. Harrison & Co. v. Burke* [1956] 1 W.L.R. 419.

[314] CPR r. 19.2(2). And see, under the old rules of procedure, *Stackwood v. Dunn* (1842) 2 Q.B. 823; *Bonfield v. Smith* (1844) 12 M. & W. 405; *Pilley v. Robinson* (1887) 20 Q.B.D. 155; also *Norbury, Natzio & Co. v. Griffiths* [1918] 2 K.B. 369.

[315] See *Wilson, Sons & Co. Ltd. v. Balcarres Brook Steam Co. Ltd.* [1893] 1 Q.B. 422. It is thought likely that the court will adopt a similar approach under the CPR.

[316] See *Puller v. Roe* (1793) 1 Peake N.P. 260.

[317] See *infra*, paras 27–73 *et seq.*

[318] See *supra*, para. 14–20.

[319] CPR 70PD, para. 6A.1, *infra*, para. A2–09.

he was a partner; or (iv) was held to be a partner.[320] This rule applies whether or not the proceedings against the firm are brought in its name.[321] It follows that the judgment creditor does not need to levy execution against the partnership property before proceeding against such partners' separate estates.

The judgment debt may obviously found an insolvency petition against the firm.[322]

No execution allowed

Former partner: A claimant could not properly seek to execute such a judgment against a *former* partner who, to his knowledge, had left the firm before the cause of action accrued.[323] The position will, however be otherwise if the partner in question left the firm after the cause of action accrued.[324]   **14–88**

Limited partner: A judgment against a limited partnership formed under the Limited Partnerships Act 1907[325] may not be executed against a limited partner[326] unless he acknowledged service of the claim form as a partner, was served with it as a partner within or, with permission,[327] outside the jurisdiction.[328] Where the claim form was served on such a partner outside the jurisdiction in a case where permission was *not* required,[329] permission to execute the judgment against him will seemingly be required.[330] It will, of course, rarely be the case that a limited partner will have any personal liability over and above his capital contribution.[331]   **14–89**

Minor partner: It has already been seen that judgment may not be entered against a minor partner,[332] so that execution against such a partner is not possible. Where the judgment has been obtained against the firm other than the minor, execution may clearly issue against the partnership property without leave.[333]   **14–90**

Partner resident out of the jurisdiction: A judgment may not be executed against a partner who was ordinarily resident out of the jurisdiction when the claim form   **14–91**

---

[320] *ibid.* para. 6A.2, *infra*, para. A2–09. See also *supra*, para. 14–21.

[321] See, as to when proceedings must be brought in the firm name, *supra*, para. 14–04.

[322] *Re a Debtor (No. 72 of 1982)* [1984] 1 W.L.R. 1143 (a decision under the Bankruptcy Act 1914). See generally, as to petitions against a firm, *infra*, paras 27–06 *et seq.*

[323] In such a case, he will, by definition, not be a partner nor liable as such, subject to any question of continuing holding out.

[324] Under the former rules of procedure, service had to be effected on all the partners of a dissolved firm, but this rule has not been retained under the CPR: see *supra*, para. 14–16. The decision in *Wigram v. Cox, Sons, Buckley & Co.* [1894] 1 Q.B. 793 is clearly not in point in a case where the conditions of CPR 70PD, para. 6A.2 are satisfied, but may be of some relevance in a case where permission is required under *ibid.* para. 6A.4: see *infra*, para. 14–92.

[325] See, as to such partnerships, *infra*, Part. 6.

[326] See the Limited Partnerships Act 1907, s.4(2), *infra*, para. A3–04.

[327] Given under CPR Pt. 6, Section III: see *supra*, para. 14–18.

[328] *ibid.* 70PD, para. 6A.3, *infra*, para. A2–09.

[329] *i.e.* under *ibid.* r. 6.33 (as amended by the Civil Jurisdiction and Judgments Regulations 2009 (SI 2009/3131), regs. 30, 31).

[330] As noted *supra*, para. 14–21, it would seem that the requirements of *ibid.* 70PD, paras 6A.2 and 6A.3 are, by definition, not satisfied so that *ibid.* para. 6A.4 would apply

[331] See the Limited Partnerships Act 1907, ss.4(2), 5, 6(1), *infra*, paras A3–04 *et seq.*; see also *infra*, paras 30–07 *et seq.*

[332] See *supra*, para. 14–20.

[333] See CPR 70PD, para. 6A.1, *infra*, para. A2–09; *Lovell & Christmas v. Beauchamp* [1894] A.C. 607; also *Harris v. Beauchamp Bros.* [1893] 2 Q.B. 534.

was issued, unless he acknowledged service as a partner or was served with the proceedings as a partner within or, with permission,[334] outside the jurisdiction.[335] What is, however, unclear is whether the judgment can be executed against a non-resident on whom the claim form was served outside the jurisdiction in a case where permission was *not* required,[336] although the better view must be that the permission of the court is required in such a case.[337]

Execution with permission, etc.

14–92   Subject to the exceptions noted above, execution can only issue against the separate estate of any other partner with the permission of the court.[338] If, on the hearing of the judgment creditor's application for such permission, a dispute as to liability arises, *e.g.* in a case of alleged holding out,[339] the court can, as under the old rules, direct a trial of that issue.[340] The above procedure is, however, optional: the judgment creditor may, if he wishes, bring a separate action against an alleged partner founded on the judgment in the previous action and, in due course, execute any judgment obtained therein.[341]

It is no longer necessary to obtain permission to execute a judgment obtained by one firm against another, if they share one or more members in common, provided that one of the conditions set out in the preceding paragraph is satisfied.[342]

Receiver already appointed

14–93   Where the court has already appointed a receiver in respect of the partnership assets,[343] permission to issue execution must be obtained in that action.[344] In an appropriate case, the receiver will be directed to pay the judgment creditor out of moneys coming into his hands[345] or the judgment creditor will be given a charge on such moneys for his debt and costs.[346]

---

[334] See *supra*, para. 14–18.

[335] CPR 70PD, para. 6A.3, *infra*, para. A2–09.

[336] *i.e.* under *ibid.* r. 6.33 (as amended by the Civil Jurisdiction and Judgments Regulations 2009, regs. 30, 31).

[337] As noted *supra*, para. 14–21, it would seem that the requirements of *ibid.* 70PD, paras 6A.2 and 6A.3 are, by definition, not satisfied so that *ibid.* para. 6A.4 would apply.

[338] CPR 70PD, para. 6A.4, *infra*, para. A2–09. The application for permission will be made under CPR Pt 23. See also *Davis v. Morris* (1883) 10 Q.B.D. 436.

[339] See, generally, the Partnership Act 1890, s.14, *supra*, paras 5–35 *et seq.*

[340] See *Davis v. Hyman & Co.* [1903] 1 K.B. 854. This is, however, no longer specifically provided for in the CPR; *cf.* RSC Ord. 81, r. 5(5).

[341] *Clark v. Cullen* (1882) 9 Q.B.D. 355.

[342] RSC Ord. 81, r. 6(1)(b) has not been replicated in the current rules on enforcement.

[343] See *infra*, paras 23–153 *et seq.*

[344] The current editor does not believe that this requirement has altered under the CPR.

[345] *Mitchell v. Weise* [1892] W.N. 139.

[346] *Kewney v. Attrill* (1886) 34 Ch.D. 345. Such a charging order gives the judgment creditor priority over the general body of creditors in the application of the partnership assets: *Newport v. Pougher* [1937] 1 Ch. 214. *Quaere,* would such an order be set aside as a transaction at an undervalue (within the meaning of the Insolvency Act 1986, ss.239, 339) on the application of the trustee in bankruptcy or liquidator of an insolvent partner? It is tentatively thought not: see *Re Gershon & Levy* [1915] 2 K.B. 527 (a decision under the Bankruptcy Act 1914, s.45).

Amending judgment with a view to execution

If proceedings have been commenced against a firm in the firm name but have **14–94** at all times been treated as brought against an individual defendant trading under that name,[347] the court will not, once judgment by consent has been obtained in the latter form and execution levied against the defendant, amend that judgment into a judgment against the firm, with a view to enabling the claimant to issue execution against someone whom he has since discovered to be a partner.[348]

Third party debt orders

An interim or final third party debt order[349] may be made against a firm **14–95** carrying on business within the jurisdiction, even if one or more of the partners are resident outside the jurisdiction.[350] However, the interim order must be served on a partner within the jurisdiction, a person authorised by a partner to accept service or on some other person who has control or management of the partnership business.[351] Where the firm is required to appear on a hearing fixed to consider whether a final order should be made, it can appear by any partner.[352]

Charging orders

A charging order can be made against any partnership property within the **14–96** jurisdiction.[353] The interim charging order must again be served on a partner within the jurisdiction, a person authorised by a partner to accept service or on some other person who has control or management of the partnership business.[354] Where an order requires the firm to appear before the court, it can appear by any partner.[355]

(b) Manner of Execution

Where a judgment has been obtained against two or more partners jointly, a writ **14–97** of execution should be issued against all of those partners,[356] even though it may be levied on any one or more of them.[357] Lord Lindley pointed out:

---

[347] *i.e.* as if brought under CPR 7APD, para. 5C.2, *infra*, para. A2–06.

[348] *Munster v. Cox* (1885) 10 App.Cas. 680. Although this was a decision under the old rules of procedure, the current editor sees no reason why a court should adopt a different approach under the CPR.

[349] CPR rr.72.4, 72.8. This procedure replaced the former garnishee order. See, as to applications for an interim order, *ibid.* r. 72.4.

[350] This is no longer specifically stated in *ibid.* Pt. 72 but must follow from *ibid.* 72PD, para. 3A.2(1), *infra*, para. A2–10; *cf.* RSC Ord. 81, r. 7(1).

[351] *ibid.* 72PD, para. 3A.2, *infra*, para. A2–10. *Semble* service on a person who was merely held out as a partner and has not been found to be a partner will not suffice. Note that service under *ibid.* para. 3A.2(3) need not be at the firm's *principal* place of business, unlike the position under *ibid.* r. 6.5(3)(c)(ii), *infra*, para. A2–01 and noticed *supra*, para. 14–14.

[352] *ibid.* 72PD, para. 3A.3 *infra*, para. A2–10.

[353] *ibid.* 73PD, para. 4A.1, *infra*, para. A2–12.

[354] *ibid.* para. 4A.2, *infra*, para. A2–12. And note also *supra*, para. 14–95, n. 351.

[355] *ibid.* para. 4A.3, *infra*, para. A2–12.

[356] See *Penoyer v. Brace* (1698) 1 Lord Ray. 244; *Clarke v. Clement* (1796) 6 T.R. 526; 2 Wms.Saund. 72, 1; Bac.Ab.Exec.G. 1.

[357] See *Abbot v. Smith* (1760) Wm.Blacks 974, 949 *per* De Gray C.J.; also *Herries v. Jamieson* (1794) 5 T.R. 553, 556 *per* Lord Kenyon.

"The consequence of this is that the sheriff may execute a writ issued against several partners jointly, either on their joint property, *or* on the separate property of any one or more of them, *or* both on their joint and on their respective separate properties[358] ... Of course, if the judgment creditor has had execution and satisfaction against one of the partners, he cannot afterwards go against any of the others[359]; but ... the sheriff is not bound to levy on the goods of the firm before having recourse to the separate properties of its members, and ... they cannot require the sheriff to execute the writ in one way rather than another."[360]

Whilst execution can in all cases be levied against the partnership property within the jurisdiction,[361] there are, of course, certain partners against whom execution cannot be levied, either at all[362] or only with the permission of the court.[363]

In former editions of this work it was observed that a similar rule applies to garnishee proceedings.[364] This is, perhaps, still correct to the extent that third party debt orders are obtained against the firm and one or more of the partners.[365]

Insolvency

14–98 The inhibitions on the right of a judgment creditor to issue execution against an insolvent firm or partner will be noticed later in this work.[366]

(c) Execution in Respect of Separate Debts

Execution against partnership share

14–99 The manner in which a partner's share can be made liable for his separate debts will be examined in a subsequent chapter.[367]

Interpleader by sheriff

14–100 Since execution may not be levied against partnership property in respect of a partner's separate debts,[368] if the sheriff seizes goods under a judgment against one partner but the other partners claim that they are partnership property, the sheriff should either withdraw, if he is satisfied that their claim is valid, or interplead.[369] If a partner of the judgment debtor claims that the goods are his

---

[358] Lord Lindley went on "and so long as there is, within the sheriff's bailiwick, any property of the partners, or any of them, a return of *nulla bona* is improper: see *Jones v. Clayton* (1815) 4 M. & S. 349." See as to the present procedure in the High Court, RSC Ord. 46, r. 9, as applied by CPR Pt. 50, Sched. 1. There are, of course, certain restrictions on execution against a partner's separate estate where judgment has been obtained in the firm name: see *supra*, paras 14–92 *et seq.*

[359] See Com.Dig. Execution, H.

[360] This must, of course be read subject to the provisions of RSC Ord. 81, r. 5 and CCR, Ord. 25, r. 9, as respectively applied by CPR Pt. 50, Scheds 1, 2.

[361] CPR 70PD, para. 6A.1, *infra*, para. A2–09.

[362] See *supra*, paras 14–21, 14–88 *et seq.*

[363] See *supra*, para. 14–92.

[364] By reference to *Miller v. Mynn* (1859) 1 E. & E. 1075.

[365] See, as to obtaining such an order against a firm., *supra*, para. 14–95.

[366] See *infra*, paras 27–20, 27–40.

[367] See the Partnership Act 1890, s.23, *infra*, paras 19–37 *et seq.*

[368] *ibid.* s.23(1).

[369] *Peake v. Carter* [1916] 1 K.B. 652.

own property but, on the trial of the interpleader issue, it appears that they are in fact partnership property, that partner will be entitled to succeed, unless this would result in injustice to the execution creditor, *e.g.* if he has been misled.[370]

(d) Order for Possession of Land

An order for possession is normally obtained against the persons in whom the legal estate is vested.[371] The order is enforced in the High Court by means of a writ of possession,[372] which may not be issued without the permission of the court unless the order was made in a mortgage action.[373] Permission to issue will not be granted unless it can be shown that every person in actual possession of the whole or any part of the land has received such notice of the proceedings as appears to the court sufficient to enable him to apply for any relief to which he may be entitled and, if the operation of the judgment or order is suspended under the Landlord and Tenant Act 1954,[374] that the applicant has not received notice in writing from the tenant that he desires certain provisions of that Act[375] to have effect.[376] In the county court, an order for the recovery of land or for the delivery of possession is enforced by a warrant of possession,[377] which may be issued at any time after the order for possession is made or, if later, the date on which the defendant is ordered to give possession.[378]

14–101

Once a writ of possession has been obtained, the claimant goes on the premises with the sheriff so as to identify the property in respect of which the order has been made. Thereafter the sheriff is obliged to deliver complete and vacant possession of those premises to the claimant and the writ is not fully executed until all persons and goods have been removed therefrom. Thus, where an order for possession is made in respect of partnership premises, the sheriff is entitled to remove all partners and partnership property which he finds there.[379] On the other hand, in executing a warrant of possession issued in the county court, the bailiff is only required to remove *persons* from the premises, and not any goods or chattels.[380]

14–102

In either case, it would seem that any person on the premises can be evicted, irrespective of whether he was made a party to the proceedings.[381]

---

[370] *Peake v. Carter, supra; cf. Flude Ltd. v. Goldberg* [1916] 1 K.B. 662, note.

[371] See *supra*, para. 14–38.

[372] RSC Ord. 45, r. 3(1)(a), as applied by CPR Pt. 50, Sched. 1.

[373] *ibid.* Ord. 45, r. 3(2).

[374] See the Landlord and Tenant Act 1954, s.16(2), which affords relief to long leaseholders in respect of the performance of certain covenants.

[375] *ibid.* s.16(2)(a), (b).

[376] RSC Ord. 45, r. 3(3)(b).

[377] CCR, Ord. 26, r. 17, as applied by CPR Pt. 50, Sched. 2.

[378] See also *ibid.* Ord. 24, r. 6(1), as applied by *ibid.*

[379] See *Upton & Wells Case* (1589) 1 Leo. 145.

[380] County Courts Act 1984, s.111(1).

[381] See *Re Wykeham Terrace* [1971] Ch. 204; *McPhail v. Persons, Names Unknown* [1973] Ch. 447; *R. v. Wandsworth County Court* [1975] 1 W.L.R. 1314.

Part Four

THE RIGHTS AND OBLIGATIONS OF PARTNERS BETWEEN THEMSELVES

CHAPTER 15

MANAGEMENT AND DECISION-MAKING

Management of firm

IT is inherent in the contract of partnership that each partner will be permitted **15–01**
and, indeed, have the right to participate in the management and administration
of the firm. Lord Lindley put it thus:

> "In partnerships, the good faith of the partners is pledged mutually to each other that
> the business shall be conducted with their actual personal interposition, so that each
> may see that the other is carrying it on for their mutual advantage."[1]

That right is enshrined in the Partnership Act 1890, section 24(5), which
provides:

> "Every partner may take part in the management of the partnership business"

although this takes effect subject to any express or implied agreement between
the partners.[2]

So fundamental is this right that, if one of two partners mortgages his share to **15–02**
the other, the latter cannot, during the continuance of the partnership, exercise his
rights as mortgagee with a view to excluding his co-partner from the management of the firm.[3] Indeed, Lord Lindley went so far as to remark that:

> " ... speaking generally ... nothing is considered as so loudly calling for the
> interference of the Court between partners, as the improper exclusion of one of them
> by the others from taking part in the management of the partnership business."[4]

Exclusion from management by agreement

Notwithstanding the general rule, partners may, of course, agree that the right **15–03**
to manage the whole or some part of the firm's affairs is to be conferred on one
or more of their number to the exclusion of the others.[5] Such agreements are now
common as many large firms move towards a more corporate style of management at the cost of what may conveniently be styled "partner power," and may

---

[1] See *Peacock v. Peacock* (1809) 16 Ves.Jr. 49, 51 *per* Lord Eldon. For a modern statement of the
same principle, see *Sankey v. The Helping Hands Group Plc* [2000] C.P. Rep. 11, where Robert
Walker L.J. observed: "Nor do [*parties*] go into partnership or quasi partnership on the basis that they
expect to have no say in the management of its affairs."
[2] See the opening words of *ibid.* s.24. As to the position before the Act, see *Rowe v. Wood* (1795)
2 J. & W. 558; also *Lloyd v. Loaring* (1802) 6 Ves. Jr. 773.
[3] *Rowe v. Wood* (1795) 2 J. & W. 553; see also the Partnership Act 1890, s.31, considered *infra*,
paras 19–51 *et seq.*
[4] See, in addition to the cases cited above, *Goodman v. Whitcomb* (1820) 1 J. & W. 589; *Marshall
v. Colman* (1820) 2 J. & W. 266.
[5] See *Hodson v. Hodson* [2009] P.N.L.R. 23 at [53] *per* Arnold J. This decision was affirmed at
[2010] P.N.L.R. 8; also *supra*, paras 10–105, 10–107.

confer on the designated partner(s) the right to take all or merely a certain class of management decisions without reference to the general body of partners. Although Lord Lindley observed that "it is not competent for those who have agreed to take no part in the management, to transact the partnership business without the consent of all the other partners", the current editor submits that this confuses the management function with the conduct of the partnership business[6]: the extent of each partner's actual authority will inevitably depend on the terms of the agreement. Even where that authority is limited in the manner described by Lord Lindley, the partners who are excluded from the management may still retain *apparent* authority to bind the firm *vis-à-vis* third parties,[7] unless those third parties have actual notice of the true position.[8]

It should, however, be noted that any term purporting to exclude a partner from taking part in the management of the partnership business might in theory be unenforceable as against a particular partner if it constitutes unlawful discrimination.[9]

Disputes between partners

15–04   Questions frequently arise as to the manner in which decisions affecting the partnership are to be taken in the absence of unanimous agreement between the partners. It might be supposed that the majority of partners can always prevail over the minority, but that is only true within strictly defined limits. The starting point when considering such a question will inevitably be the partnership agreement itself. If it contains an express provision dealing with decision-making, as will often be the case, then the prescribed procedure must be followed.[10] If the agreement is silent on the point, then it is necessary to identify the precise subject matter of the decision, since the Partnership Act 1890 distinguishes between those differences which relate to "ordinary matters" and those which relate to other matters, in the following way:

> "24.—(8) Any difference arising as to ordinary matters connected with the partnership business may be decided by a majority of the partners, but no change may be

---

[6] This distinction is clearly drawn by the Limited Partnerships Act 1907, s.6(1).

[7] Partnership Act 1890, s.5, *supra*, paras 12–02 *et seq.*

[8] *ibid.* s.8, *supra*, para. 12–138.

[9] Sex Discrimination Act 1975, s.11(1)(b), (d)(ii); Race Relations Act 1976, s.10(1)(b), (d)(ii); Disability Discrimination Act 1995, s.6A(1)(b), (d)(ii), (as added by the Disability Discrimination Act 1995 (Amendment) Regulations 2003 (SI 2003/1673), reg. 6)); Employment Equality (Religion or Belief) Regulations 2003 (SI 2003/1660), reg. 14(1)(b), (d)(ii); Employment Equality (Sexual Orientation) Regulations 2003 (SI 2003/1661), reg. 14(1)(b), (d)(ii); Employment Equality (Age) Regulations 2006 (SI 2006/1031), reg. 17(1)(b), (d)(ii). There is, however, a limited exception in the case of discrimination on the grounds of gender reassignment: see the Sex Discrimination Act 1975, s.11(3B) (as added by the Sex Discrimination (Gender Reassignment) Regulations 1999 (SI 1999/1102), reg. 4(5)). The former general exception for firms comprising 5 partners or less under the Race Relations Act 1976, s.10(1) no longer applies in the case of discrimination on the grounds of race or ethnic or national origins: *ibid.* s.10(1A), as added by the Race Relations Act 1976 (Amendment) Regulations 2003 (SI 2003/1626), reg. 12. Apart from the latter exception (which will not be carried forward), these provisions will, as from a date to be appointed, be replaced by the consolidating and amending Equality Act 2010 (see, in particular, *ibid.* ss.44(1)(b), (2)(a), (d)) which also, by ss.8, 13(4), add an additional class of discrimination, *i.e.* marital or civil partner status. See further, *supra*, paras 8–09 *et seq.*

[10] See generally, *supra*, paras 10–102 *et seq.* Note *Clements v. Norris* (1878) 8 Ch.D. 129, which might be regarded as a case of this class; see also *infra*, paras 15–06, 16–23, 23–140.

made in the nature of the partnership business without the consent of all existing partners."[11]

This subsection, which naturally takes effect subject to any express or implied agreement between the partners,[12] was largely declaratory of the existing law.[13]

Disputes on ordinary matters

If it is sought to argue that a particular decision relates to "ordinary matters connected with the partnership business" and thus can properly be taken by a majority, but the court is not prepared to take judicial notice of the usual practice in the relevant trade or profession, evidence of that practice must be adduced, since a question of fact is seemingly involved. It is the connection with the business which is emphasised in section 24(8), rather than what is required to carry on the business "in the usual way",[14] although the current editor submits that any decision which satisfies the latter test must also necessarily satisfy the "connection" test. In *Highley v. Walker*,[15] the decision whether a partner's son should be brought in to learn the business was held to fall within this category. It is submitted that most decisions involving the manner in which the business is to be conducted on a day to day basis, including the enlargement of a partner's authority to bind the firm,[16] the engagement and dismissal of staff, the choice of the firm's bankers and accountants and the renewal of a lease of partnership premises, should normally be regarded in the same way[17]; *sed quaere*, in the case of bringing or defending actions.[18]

It will be be seen hereafter that decisions as to whether expenses are to be treated as ordinary or extraordinary,[19] as to the quantum of the firm's divisible profits and as to the timing of their division[20] will usually be capable of being

[11] *cf. ibid.* s.19, *supra*, para. 10–12.

[12] See the opening words of *ibid.* s.24(1).

[13] Lord Lindley's summary of the pre-1890 law in relation to differences "which relate to matters incidental to carrying on the legitimate business of a partnership" was as follows: "If . . . in a case of this description, unprovided for by previous agreement, the partners are unequally divided, the minority must, the author apprehends, give way to the majority. . . . The only alternative is to hold that if the partners disagree, even as to trifling matters of detail, the minority can forbid all change, and perhaps bring the business of the firm to a dead-lock, for which the only remedy is a dissolution. At the same time the author is not aware of any clear and distinct authority in support of the proposition that even in such matters a dissentient partner must give way to his co-partners." See *Robinson v. Thompson* (1687) 1 Vern. 465; *Const v. Harris* (1824) T. & R. 496; *Gregory v. Patchett* (1864) 33 Beav. 595; also *Morgan's Case* (1849) 1 Mac. & G. 225. *cf. Beveridge v. Beveridge* (1872) L.R. 2 Sc.App. 183; *Clements v. Norris* (1878) 8 Ch.D. 129.

[14] See the Partnership Act 1890, s.5, considered *supra*, paras 12–02 *et seq*.

[15] (1910) 26 T.L.R. 685.

[16] *Per contra* in the case of a restriction sought to be imposed on only one partner, if that would be inconsistent with his right to participate in the management of the business: see the Partnership Act 1890, ss.19, 24(5), 25. See also *supra*, paras 13–31, 13–32.

[17] In *Donaldson v. Williams* (1833) Cr. & M. 345 and *Clements v. Norris* (1878) 8 Ch.D. 129, the partners were *equally* divided. See further, as to these decisions, *supra*, para. 12–25 and *infra*, paras 16–23, 23–140.

[18] In Scotland it has been held that a majority of partners can prevent an action being brought against their wishes: *Hutcheon & Partners v. Hutcheon* 1979 S.L.T. (Sh. Ct.) 62. This decision appears to be out of line with the English authorities: see *supra*, paras 12–35, 14–66. The point was argued, but not decided, in *Sutherland v. Gustar* [1994] Ch. 304.

[19] See *infra*, para. 21–02.

[20] See *infra*, para. 21–07.

taken on a majority basis. Also falling within this class may be decisions affecting the type of work to be done by a partner who is serving out his notice period.[21]

Power of the majority: deadlock

15–06   Although the Act clearly empowers a numerical majority of the partners to take decisions on ordinary matters, notwithstanding the other partners' objections,[22] it is of no assistance where the partners are equally divided. In such circumstances, the general rule is in favour of maintaining the *status quo ante*, as Lord Lindley explained:

> "With respect to [*this*] class of differences, regard must be had to the state of things actually existing; for, as a rule, if the partners are equally divided, those who forbid a change must have their way: *in re communi potior est conditio prohibentis.*"[23]

On this basis, one of two partners cannot unilaterally insist on engaging or dismissing an employee[24] or renewing an expired lease of the partnership premises with a view to the firm continuing to carry on business there.[25]

Rights of the minority

15–07   If a majority of partners is to outvote a minority, the former must ensure that they act with complete good faith and, in particular, that the views of the latter are fully canvassed, since it is a fundamental right of every partner to be heard and to have his views duly considered before any decision is taken. Lord Eldon stated the law thus:

> " ... I call that the act of all, which is the act of the majority, provided all are consulted, and the majority are acting *bona fide*, meeting, not for the purpose of negativing, what any one may have to offer, but for the purpose of negativing, what, when they are met together, they may, after due consideration, think proper to negative: For a majority of partners to say; We do not care what one partner may say, we, being the majority, will do what we please, is, I apprehend, what this Court will not allow."[26]

---

[21] See *supra*, para. 10–149.

[22] Partnership Act 1890, s.24(8). This was probably the law even before the Act, but the point was not settled: see *supra*, para. 15–04, n. 13.

[23] The original footnote to this passage read: "But see as to the employment of a ship, *Abbott on Shipping*, p. 82, ed. 9 and p. 58 ed. 12; and as to completing contracts already entered into, *Butchart v. Dresser* (1853) 4 De G.M. & G. 545." See also *supra*, para. 10–103.

[24] *Donaldson v. Williams* (1833) 1 Cr. & M. 345. However, this decision does not go as far as is commonly supposed: see *supra*, para. 12–66.

[25] *Clements v. Norris* (1878) 8 Ch.D. 129. But note that the terms of the partnership had not expired and that a specific clause in the agreement governed decisions as to the premises from which the business was to be carried on. *Quaere* would the trust of land which would now be implied have affected the decision? It is thought not: see *Harris v. Black* (1983) 46 P. & C.R. 366, where one trustee beneficiary sought (unsuccessfully) to compel another, who was his ex-partner, to renew a lease; and see *infra*, paras 16–20 *et seq.* As to the extent of a partner's implied authority to take a lease of premises, see *supra*, para. 12–72.

[26] *Const v. Harris* (1824) T. & R. 496, 525 (as applied in *Abbatt v. Treasury Solicitor & Others* [1969] 1 W.L.R. 1575); see also Lord Eldon's observations in the course of argument, at *ibid.* p. 518; *G.W. Ry. v. Rushout* (1852) 5 De G. & Sm. 310; *Blisset v. Daniel* (1853) 10 Hare 493; *Wall v. London and Northern Assets Corp.* [1898] 2 Ch. 469.

Where a majority have a power under the partnership agreement and exercise that power in good faith,[27] the fact that a minority of partners may be disadvantaged is not *per se* a ground for attacking the exercise of the power. However, the position will be otherwise if the majority exercise the power *in order* to victimise or otherwise to disadvantage the minority.[28]

Majorities at meetings

It is perhaps self evident that if a majority of partners are empowered to take decisions at a quorate partners' meeting, that power may only be exercised at a duly convened meeting at which the requisite number of partners is present. Although it may be correct that all the partners have been requested to attend and that, even if they had attended, the result would have been the same, failure to adhere to the agreed procedure will clearly invalidate any decision taken at an inquorate meeting.[29]

15–08

What is more questionable is whether a partner can, by absenting himself from a meeting, exercise an effective power of veto. Although this might not be permitted in the case of a company,[30] the current editor considers that the court cannot properly override a partner's rights in this way. In the absence of an appropriate power in the agreement,[31] the only course open to the other partners in such a case may be to seek a dissolution of the firm.[32]

Disputes on other matters

So far as concerns decisions which do *not* relate to ordinary matters connected with the partnership business, it has long been settled law that, in the words of Lord Lindley:

15–09

> "no majority, however large, can lawfully engage the partnership in such matters against the will of even one dissentient partner. Each partner is entitled to say to the others, 'I became a partner in a concern formed for a definite purpose, and upon terms which were agreed upon by all of us, and you have no right, without my consent, to engage me in any other concern,[33] nor to hold me to any other terms, nor to get rid of me, if I decline to assent to a variation in the agreement by which you are bound to me and I to you.' Nor is it at all material that the new business is extremely profitable."[34]

---

[27] See further *supra*, para. 10–101.

[28] See, generally, *Redwood Master Fund Ltd. v. TD Bank Europe Ltd.* [2006] 1 B.C.L.C. 149 (albeit a case relating to decisions taken under a syndicated loan agreement). See also *infra*, para. 16–07.

[29] See *Ex p. Morrison* (1847) De Gex 539; *Howbeach Coal Co. v. Teague* (1860) 5 H. & N. 151; *Re London and Southern Counties Freehold Land Co.* (1885) 31 Ch.D. 223; *Young v. Ladies' Imperial Club Ltd.* [1920] 2 K.B. 523; *Knowles v. Zoological Society of London* [1959] 1 W.L.R. 823.

[30] See the court's power under the Companies Act 2006, s.306; and see *Re H.R. Paul & Co. Ltd.* (1974) 118 S.J. 166; *Re Opera Photographic* [1989] 1 W.L.R. 634; *Re Sticky Fingers Restaurant Ltd.* [1992] B.C.L.C. 84 (all decisions under a predecessor section). However, there are clearly limits to the circumstances in which this statutory power can be used: *Harman v. BML Group Ltd.* [1994] 1 W.L.R. 893 (CA); *Ross v. Telford* [1998] 1 B.C.L.C. 82 (CA).

[31] *e.g.* a power of expulsion or a contractual power to dissolve the firm: see *supra*, paras 10–113 *et seq.*, 10–137 *et seq.*

[32] *i.e.* under the Partnership Act 1890, s.35: see *infra*, paras 24–47 *et seq.*

[33] For a relatively recent example of this principle, see *Bissell v. Cole*, December 12, 1997 (unreported), noted at [1998] C.L.Y. 4071. However, in some cases, it may be unclear whether the business proposed to be carried on is a new business or a mere extension of the existing business: see *Nixon v. Wood* (1987) 284 E.G. 1055.

[34] *Att.-Gen. v. Great Northern Ry.* (1860) 1 Dr. & Sm. 154.

This principle, which is embodied in section 24(8) of the Partnership Act 1890 itself,[35] will, in the absence of some other agreement, apply to all firms, large and small, and scarcely requires specific authority, although Lord Lindley particularly commended the reader to two decisions of Lord Eldon.[36] The position will be precisely the same where the decision concerns the admission of a new partner,[37] the expulsion of an existing partner[38] or, indeed, the dissolution of the firm itself.[39] Most notable in this context is, perhaps, the decision to "convert" a partnership into a limited liability partnership.[40] It is inconceivable that such a far reaching decision, involving as it does committing the partners to a relationship which is fundamentally different to that of partnership, stripping out all or virtually all of the firm's assets and, ultimately, bringing about its dissolution could ever be regarded as an ordinary matter connected with the partnership business. Similarly in the case of incorporation properly so called.

[35] See *supra*, para. 15–04.

[36] *Natusch v. Irving* (1824); *Gow on Partnership* (3rd. ed.), p. 398 and the 5th ed. of this work at p. 316; *Const v. Harris* (1824) T. & R. 496. See also *Hole v. Garnsey* [1930] A.C. 472, 494 *per* Lord Atkin; *Abbatt v. Treasury Solicitor & Others* [1969] 1 W.L.R. 1575. The following cases also illustrate the principle: *Fennings v. Grenville* (1808) 1 Taunt. 241; *Davies v. Hawkins* (1815) 3 M. & S. 488; *Glassington v. Thwaites* (1823) 1 Sim. & St. 124; *Re Phoenix Life Insurance Co.* (1862) 2 J. & H. 441; *Auld v. Glasgow Working Men's Society* (1887) 12 App.Cas. 197; *The Hereward* [1895] p. 284. See also *Bissell v. Cole*, December 12, 1997 (unreported), noted at [1998] C.L.Y. 4071 (substantial change in the nature of the partnership business); *cf. Nixon v. Wood* (1987) 284 E.G. 1055.

[37] Partnership Act 1890, s.24(7).

[38] A majority of partners cannot expel a partner otherwise than pursuant to an express power (*ibid.* s.25, *infra*, para. 24–99) and such a power will generally be strictly construed: see *Re A Solicitors' Arbitration* [1962] 1 W.L.R. 353; also *supra*, paras 10–123 *et seq*. Equally, a majority has no power to sell the shares of a dissentient minority: see *Chapple v. Cadell* (1822) Jac. 537.

[39] See, for example, the Partnership Act 1890, s.33(2), considered *infra*, para. 24–38.

[40] The expression "conversion" is commonly used in this context but is a misnomer. The LLP is not a species of partnership (see *supra*, para. 2–39) and the process of conversion will, as noted in the text, involve the existing firm's demise.

CHAPTER 16

THE DUTY OF GOOD FAITH

1.   THE NATURE OF THE DUTY

The general duty

PERHAPS the most fundamental obligation which the law imposes on a partner **16–01** is the duty to display complete good faith towards his co-partners in all partnership dealings and transactions. Lord Lindley summarised that duty in the following terms:

> "The utmost good faith is due from every member of a partnership towards every other member[1]; and if any dispute arise between partners touching any transaction by which one seeks to benefit himself at the expense of the firm, he will be required to show, not only that he has the law on his side, but that his conduct will bear to be tried by the highest standard of honour."[2]

Thus, if one partner enters into an agreement with another, at a time when he possesses relevant information regarding the state of the partnership accounts which is not known to that other partner and which he fails to disclose, the agreement will not be allowed to stand.[3] However, if the innocent partner subsequently learns that material facts have been concealed from him by his co-partner, but deliberately elects to stand by the agreement without insisting on full disclosure, the existence of the duty of good faith will not prevent his co-partner from relying on that election and treating the agreement as binding.[4] Thus, in *Lindsley v. Woodfull*,[5] an agreement for a partner's retirement was affirmed by the continuing partners when they already had knowledge of a breach of duty on his part. As a result they forfeited their right to an account going

---

[1] This principle may be traced back to Roman law, where it was stated thus "*In societatis contractibus fides exuberet*": Cod. iv, tit. 37, 1, 3.

[2] See *Blisset v. Daniel* (1853) 10 Hare 493. And see *Kao Lee & Yip v. Hoi-Yan* [2003] 2 H.K.C. 113, at [40] *per* Ma J.; *Deacons v. White & Case LLP* (HCA 2433/2002), October 24, 2003 (Hong Kong High Court) at [108] *per* Deputy High Court Judge Gill. The application of the principle will, however, not always be straightforward: *cf. Cassels v. Stewart* (1881) 6 App.Cas. 64 and *Trimble v. Goldberg* [1906] A.C. 494, noted *infra*, para. 16–36. As to limited partnerships, see *infra*, para. 31–01.

[3] See *Maddeford v. Austwick* (1826) 1 Sim. 89; *Law v. Law* [1905] 1 Ch. 140. *cf. Hale v. Waldock* [2007] 1 B.C.L.C. 520, where an agreement had already been reached and was in the course of implementation. Note, however, that this was a situation in which partners had agreed to sell assets to a company not to each other.

[4] *Law v. Law, supra*. But see generally, as to the requirements for a valid election, *Peyman v. Lanjani* [1985] Ch. 457.

[5] [2004] 2 B.C.L.C. 131 (CA). See further *infra*, para. 16–29.

forward, although their accrued rights as to past breaches of duty had, in the circumstances, been preserved.

16–02 The duty carries with it a so-called "duty to speak",[6] which will usually require a partner to disclose not only his own misconduct but that of any other partner or employee of the firm.[7]

Needless to say, it is of particular importance that good faith should be shown where one partner is attempting to get rid of another or to buy out his interest in the firm[8] and, indeed, where a majority of partners are proposing to outvote a minority on some issue affecting the firm.[9] Moreover, whilst the point is not entirely free from doubt, the current editor takes the view that a partner must display good faith when he seeks to dissolve the firm by notice, whether pursuant to an express power in the agreement or the provisions of the Partnership Act 1890.[10]

Partnership Act 1890, section 28

16–03 This general obligation is to a large extent reflected in the terms of section 28 of the Partnership Act 1890, which provides as follows:

> "28. Partners are bound to render true accounts[11] and full information of all things affecting the partnership to any partner or his legal representatives."

It is this section which also allows any partner to *require* one or more of his fellow partners to answer questions or to provide information which relate to the firm or its business, something which can often prove to be a potent weapon in partnership disputes.[12] The court or an arbitrator can, if necessary, require a partner to respond to such a request.[13]

---

[6] *Law v. Law, supra; Conlon v. Simms* [2008] 1 W.L.R. 484 (CA). This will be the position even in the case of a joint venture agreement: see *Huyton SA v. Distribuidora Internacional de Productos Agricolas SA* [2004] 1 All E.R. (Comm) 402 (CA). *cf. Andrewes v. Garstin* (1861) 10 C.B.(N.S.) 444, noted *infra*, para. 16–06, n. 26.

[7] The existence of this duty was recognised in *Deacons v. White & Case LLP* (HCA 2433/2002), October 24, 2003 (Hong Kong High Court). See also as to disclosure of a person's own misconduct, *Sanders v. Parry* [1967] 1 W.L.R. 753 (employee); *Sybron Corp. v. Rochem Ltd.* [1984] 1 Ch. 112 (employee); *Kao Lee & Yip v. Hoi-Yan* [2003] H.K.C. 113 (employee); *Tesco Stores Ltd. v. Pook* [2004] I.R.L.R. 618 (senior employee); *Item Software (UK) Ltd. v. Fassihi* [2005] I.C.R. 450 (CA) (director).

[8] See *Chandler v. Dorsett* (1679) Finch 431; *Maddeford v. Austwick* (1826) 1 Sim. 89; *Blisset v. Daniel* (1853) 10 Hare 493; *Perens v. Johnson* (1857) 3 Sm. & G. 419; *Law v. Law* [1905] 1 Ch. 140; also *Ferguson v. Mackay* 1985 S.L.T. (OH) 94. And see the South African case of *Purdon v. Muller* 1961 (2) S.A. 211 and the Canadian case of *Hogar Estates Ltd. In Trust v. Shebron Holdings Ltd.* (1979) 23 O.R. (2d) 543. As to withholding information, see *McLure v. Ripley* (1850) 2 Mac. & G. 274.

[9] See *supra*, para. 15–07.

[10] See *infra*, para. 24–20.

[11] See, as to the obligation under this limb of the section, *Winning v. Cunningham* 2009 GWD 01–19 (Sh.Ct.).

[12] *e.g.* when dealing with an outgoing partner who is thought to have solicited clients or staff whilst still a member of the firm.

[13] The position is, in many ways, analogous to that in *Intelsec Systems Ltd. v. Grech-Cini* [2000] 1 W.L.R. 1190, where the court ordered former employees to disclose the names and addresses of certain business contacts. *cf. Aon Ltd. v. JCT Reinsurance Brokers Ltd.* [2010] I.R.L.R. 600, where an order was sought by way of pre-action disclosure.

The nature of the duty

It hardly needs to be stated that the duty of good faith is of general applica- **16–04**
tion[14] and that the relationship between partners is of a fiduciary nature,[15] as
Vice-Chancellor Bacon made clear in *Helmore v. Smith*[16]:

> "If fiduciary relation means anything I cannot conceive a stronger case of fiduciary
> relation than that which exists between partners. Their mutual confidence is the life
> blood of the concern. It is because they trust one another that they are partners in the
> first instance; it is because they continue to trust each other that the business goes
> on."

However, notwithstanding the existence of the fiduciary relationship, it does not
follow that a partner who, as the agent of the firm,[17] receives partnership money
from a third party will necessarily be treated as acting in a fiduciary
capacity.[18]

The duty is a reciprocal one: thus, if one partner chooses, in the words of Lord **16–05**
Lindley, to "repudiate"[19] the contract of partnership and refuses to perform his
duty towards his co-partners, he cannot complain if they adopt a similar attitude
towards him.[20] As observed by Lord Eldon in *Const v. Harris*[21]:

> "A partner who complains that the other partners do not do their duty towards him,
> must be ready at all times and offer himself to do his duty towards them."

Accordingly, if a partner, faced with his co-partner's breach of duty, chooses
to commit a breach of his own, by way of retaliation or otherwise, he may find

---

[14] See, for example, *Moser v. Cotton* (1990) 140 N.L.J. 1313, where a partner in a firm of solicitors
sought (unsuccessfully) to argue that his duty to his partners was overridden by a solicitor/client
relationship between himself and the firm which was created *after* the date of his retirement. *Quaere*,
can the duty be excluded in whole or in part? See *infra*, para. 16–11.

[15] The fiduciary relationship is derived from the existence of obligations of a fiduciary nature, not
the other way around: see *Bristol and West Building Society v. Mothew* [1978] Ch. 1, 18. In the case
of a partnership, it is, self-evidently, the duty of good faith which gives rise to that relationship:
Thompson's Trustee in Bankruptcy v. Heaton [1974] 1 W.L.R. 605, 613 *per* Pennycuick V.-C. Note
that when partners choose to carry on their business through a corporate vehicle, they will no longer
be able to resurrect their former fiduciary relationship as such: see *Ness Training Ltd. v. Triage
Central Ltd.* 2002 S.L.T. 675 (OH). And note also that a duty of good faith created *contractually* will
not necessarily give rise to a fiduciary duty: see *Ross River Ltd. v. Cambridge City Football Club Ltd.*
[2008] 1 All E.R. 1004 at [197] *per* Briggs J. (a decision concerning joint venturers).

[16] (1886) 35 Ch.D. 436, 444; see also *Cassels v. Stewart* (1881) 6 App.Cas. 64, 79 *per* Lord
Blackburn; *Roxburgh Dinardo & Partners' Judicial Factor v. Dinardo* 1993 S.L.T. 16 (2nd Div.);
Hogar Estates Ltd. In Trust v. Shebron Holdings Ltd. (1979) 23 O.R. (2d.) 543; *Kao Lee & Yip v Hoi-
Yan* [2003] 2 H.K.C. 113 at [41]; *Deacons v. White & Case LLP* (HCA 2433/2002), October 24, 2003
(Hong Kong High Court) at [109].

[17] See *supra*, paras 12–53 *et seq.*

[18] See *Piddocke v. Burt* [1894] 1 Ch. 343 (a decision under the Debtors Act 1869, s.4(3)). *cf.* the
observation of Lord Blackburn in *Cassels v. Stewart, supra.*

[19] This was the word used in the 5th ed. of this work. He used it in the non-technical sense, since,
at that time, the application of the doctrine of repudiation to partnerships had not been addressed. It
is now clear that the doctrine has no application in the case of a continuing partnership: see *infra*,
paras 24–05 *et seq.*

[20] See *McLure v. Ripley* (1850) 2 Mac. & G 274; *Reilly v. Walsh* (1848) 11 I.Eq. R. 22. *Quaere*:
could the partners invoke this principle if one of their number *deliberately* neglects the affairs of the
partnership? See *supra*, para. 10–93.

[21] (1824) T. & R. 496, 524. See also *Abbatt v. Treasury Solicitor* [1969] 1 W.L.R. 1575.

that he has substantially prejudiced his position.[22] There are, however, limits to this principle: partners obviously cannot complain of a co-partner's failure to perform his duties towards them if they have previously sought to deny that he was a partner and rejected his right to participate in the firm's affairs.[23]

Although a partner is under a duty not to expose his firm to avoidable risks,[24] it is doubtful whether this constitutes an integral part of his wider duty of good faith.[25]

Inchoate and dissolved partnerships

16–06   The duty of good faith exists not only as between persons who are actually in partnership together, but also as between persons who are merely negotiating their entry into partnership.[26] Thus, if an intending partner receives a bonus or commission when acquiring property for the use of the firm, he must account for it once the firm has come into existence.[27] The position will, however, be otherwise where the proposed partners abandon their intention to form a partnership and decide to form a company instead.[28] In the case of existing partners, the duty will even extend to a situation in which the partners are agreeing to sell an asset to a company in which they are both interested,[29] but will prima facie not

---

[22] Although such a scenario may seem fanciful, the current editor's experience is that "tit-for-tat" breaches are by no means uncommon. Note also, in this context, *Forster v. Ferguson & Forster* 2008 S.L.T. (Sh. Ct.) 52, which ultimately turned on the principle of mutuality under Scots law. A partner who had committed a number of frauds and retired from the firm was held not thereby to have deprived himself of his pension entitlement.

[23] See *Dale v. Hamilton* (1847) 2 Ph. 266. A partner who finds himself in such a situation should not, however, delay in asserting his rights: see further, *infra*, paras 23–19 *et seq*.

[24] See *infra*, paras 20–11 *et seq*.

[25] See *infra*, para. 20–12.

[26] *Conlon v. Simms* [2008] 1 W.L.R. 484 (CA), applying views expressed by Lord Atkin in *Bell v. Lever Brothers Ltd.* [1932] A.C. 161, 227. At first instance (see [2006] 2 All E.R. 1024), Lawrence Collins J. did not regard the cases previously cited in this work as authority for this proposition, *i.e.* *Hichens v. Congreve* (1828) 1 Russ. & M. 150 (cited by Lord Lindley in the 18th ed. at this point); also *New Brunswick Ry. v. Muggeridge* (1860) 1 Dr. & Sm. 363; *Central Ry. of Venezuela v. Kisch* (1867) L.R. 2 H.L. 99. Note that in *Andrewes v. Garstin* (1861) 10 C.B.(N.S.) 444, it was held that a prospective partner was not obliged, when negotiating a partnership, to disclose that he had allegedly committed acts of fraud and dishonesty in *another* partnership, but it should be noted that the allegations in this respect were, in any event, too "vague and uncertain" (*ibid.* 412 *per* Erle C.J.).

[27] *Fawcett v. Whitehouse* (1829) 1 Russ. & M. 132. *Quaere*: would the other intending partners have any rights if, in the event, the firm never came into existence? The answer will depend on the circumstances, *e.g.* the derivation of the funds applied in acquiring the property or the misuse of confidential information. A breach of duty in relation to the latter was established in *LAC Minerals Ltd. v. International Corona Resources Ltd.* [1990] F.S.R. 441 (Sup. Ct. of Canada). And see *Shanshal v. Al-Kishtaini* (Lawtel 16/6/99), where it was held that fiduciary obligations were owed by the parties to an abortive joint venture (this aspect is not referred to in the report in *The Times*, June 16, 1999); an appeal was, ultimately, allowed on other grounds: see [2001] 2 All E.R. (Comm.) 601. *cf. Arklow Investments Ltd. v. Maclean* [2000] 1 W.L.R. 594 9PC), where there was no such underlying relationship. There may also be scope for imposing a constructive trust in cases of this type: see *Banner Homes Group Plc v. Luff Developments Ltd.* [2000] Ch. 372 (CA). Note, however, that the constructive trust argument failed in *Kilcarne Holdings Ltd. v. Targetfollow (Birmingham) Ltd.* [2005] P & C.R. 8 and *Cayzer v. Beddow* [2007] EWCA Civ 644 (Lawtel 29/6/07) (CA).

[28] *Ness Training Ltd. v. Triage Central Ltd.* 2002 S.L.T. 675 (OH).

[29] See *Hale v. Waldock* [2007] 1 B.C.L.C. 520 at [62] *per* Mann J. In this case the partners' shares in the company reflected the size of their partnership shares, but the views expressed were clearly *obiter*.

apply where they have already reached agreement and are merely engaged in implementing that agreement.[30]

Equally, the duty will continue to be owed to and by an outgoing partner[31] and will also apply as between the partners of a dissolved firm, until such time as its affairs are finally wound up and settled.[32]

Ingredients of a breach of the duty

In other contexts, the courts have recognised that breach of a duty of good faith **16–07** connotes an intentional act, borne out of dishonesty[33] or some other improper motive and that, whilst recklessness may be the equivalent of intent, mere negligence is not sufficient.[34] The current editor considers that this approach is equally applicable to partnerships and is, indeed, consistent with the scope of a partner's implied duty not to expose his firm to avoidable risks.[35]

Examples of conduct which will involve a breach of the duty of good faith are too numerous to list.[36] Suffice it to say that any conduct which is motivated by a desire to damage the firm or the other partners' interests therein must necessarily involve such a breach, as exemplified by the decision in *Finlayson v. Turnbull (No. 1)*.[37] Equally, it is no part of the duty of a partner to avoid falling out with a fellow partner or to continue to place trust and confidence in him when his conduct does not justify it.[38]

It goes without saying that if one partner asks another for information relating to partnership matters, the recipient of the request should either provide the

---

[30] *ibid.* at [64]. Much will naturally depend on the precise circumstances.

[31] See *Moser v. Cotton* (1990) 140 N.L.J. 1313, noted *supra*, para. 16–04, n. 14; *Hammonds (A Firm) v. Jones* [2009] EWCA Civ 1400 (Lawtel 21/12/09) at [37].

[32] Partnership Act 1890, ss.29(2) (*infra*, para. 16–14), 38 (*supra*, para. 13–62); *Don King Promotions Inc. v. Warren* [2000] Ch. 291 (CA). And see *Clegg v. Fishwick* (1849) 1 Mac. & G. 294; *Lees v. Laforest* (1851) 14 Beav. 250; *Perens v. Johnson* (1857) 3 Sm. & G. 419; *Clements v. Hall* (1858) 2 De G. & J. 173. See also *Chirnside v. Fay* [2007] P.N.L.R. 6 (Sup. Ct. of New Zealand); *Disctronic Ltd. v. Kingston Links Country Club Pty Ltd.* [2005] V.R. 513 (Victoria CA), albeit both decisions concerning joint venturers.

[33] As noted *supra*, para. 10–118, there are three possible tests for dishonesty but, in this context, it is submitted that the combined subjective/objective test propounded in *Twinsectra Ltd. v. Yardley* [2002] 2 A.C. 164 and explained in *Barlow Clowes International Ltd. v. Eurotrust International Ltd.* [2006] 1 W.L.R. 1476 (PC) will almost inevitably be applied; see also *Abou-Rahmah v. Abacha* [2007] 1 Lloyd's Rep 115 (CA); *Dolley v. Ogunseitan* [2009] EWHC 1601 (Ch) (Lawtel 9/7/09); *Aerostar Maintenance International Ltd. v. Wilson* [2010] EWHC 2032 (Ch) (Lawtel 4/8/10). *cf. Bryant v. Law Society* [2009] 1 W.L.R. 163.

[34] *Medforth v. Blake* [2000] Ch. 86, 103B–C (CA); *Starling v. Lloyds Bank plc* [2000] Lloyd's Rep. Bank. 8 (CA). See also *Kao Lee & Yip v. Hoi-Yan* [2003] H.K.C. 113 at [45], where Ma J. stated " . . . not every breach of duty by a person in a fiduciary position amounts to a breach of fiduciary duty".

[35] See *supra*, para. 16–05 and *infra*, paras 20–11 *et seq.*

[36] Various examples are, however, explored in the second part of this chapter, *infra*, paras 16–13 *et seq.*

[37] 1997 S.L.T. 613 (OH). There three salaried partners, who were not interested in the firm's goodwill, had embarked on a plan to leave the firm without prior warning and to take away a large number of client files. It was held that their actions had damaged the firm's goodwill and damages were awarded on that basis. A claim for an account was also pursued subsequently: see *Finlayson v. Turnbull (No. 3)* 2001 G.W.D. 37–1412 (OH); see also, as to the taking of the account, *Finlayson v. Turnbull (No. 4)* 2003 G.W.D. 12–374 (OH). *Deacons v. White & Case LLP* (HCA 2433/2002), October 24, 2003 (Hong Kong High Court) was a similar case. See also *Sanders v. Parry* [1967] 1 W.L.R. 753 (which concerned a breach of duty by an employee).

[38] See *Johnson v. Snaddon* [2001] V.S.C.A. 91 (CA, Victoria).

information or unequivocally refuse to provide it.[39] To provide a partial and potentially misleading response will be a clear breach of the duty.[40]

Preparatory acts

16–08   It is doubted whether merely making preparations to set up a competing business, *e.g.* acquiring premises or setting up a company which remains dormant, will without more involve a breach of the duty, but much will, inevitably, depend on the precise facts.[41] The more overt the preparatory acts that are carried out, the greater the chance of a breach, particularly where clients and staff of the existing firm are involved in the arrangements, as in two Hong Kong cases, *Kao Lee & Yip v. Hoi-Yan*[42] and *Deacons v. White & Case LLP.*[43] Equally, the position may also be affected by the terms of the partnership agreement. Thus, in *Ward Evans Financial Services Ltd. v. Fox*[44] the employees' contracts specifically prohibited them from holding an interest in a company which would impair their duties to act in the best interests of their employer, even if it remained dormant.

The exercise of a discretion and collateral benefits

16–09   Where a discretion is conferred on the management of the firm or on a majority of partners,[45] a partner will normally be entitled to expect that it will be exercised rationally and in good faith and not arbitrarily or capriciously.[46] Equally, if the discretion is *genuinely* exercised in good faith and in the best interests of the firm, the fact that it may disadvantage a minority of the partners is not *per se*

---

[39] Equally, that refusal may itself be a breach of duty: see the Partnership Act 1890, s.28, *supra*, para. 16–03; also *supra*, para. 10–92.

[40] See *Ross River Ltd. v. Cambridge City Football Club Ltd.* [2008] 1 All E.R. (Comm) 1028, a case concerning a quasi joint venture.

[41] See the principles summarised by Ma J. in *Kao Lee & Yip v. Hoi-Yan* [2003] H.K.C. 113 at [57]. And see *British Midland Tool Ltd. v. Midland International Tooling Ltd.* [2003] 2 B.C.L.C. 523, where the directors of a company were ultimately held to have been part of an unlawful means conspiracy; *Shepherds Investments Ltd. v. Walters* [2007] I.R.L.R. 110 (again a case concerning directors); *cf. Foster Bryant Surveying Ltd. v. Bryant* [2007] Bus. L.R. 1565 (CA), an exceptional case. As to employees, see *Helmet Integrated Systems Ltd. v. Tunnard* [2007] I.R.L.R. 126 (CA) and the other cases cited *supra*, para. 10–95, n. 409; also note *Cobbetts LLP v. Hodge* (2009) 153(17) S.J.L.B. 29 at [94] *per* Floyd J.

[42] [2003] H.K.C. 113. Interestingly, in this instance the proposed new firm's premises were leased and credit facilities were obtained from a client, which converted what might otherwise have been unobjectionable acts into a clear breach of duty.

[43] HCA 2433/2002, October 24, 2003 (Hong Kong High Court). Here the outgoing partner had gone far beyond the realm of preparation in a number of respects, *e.g.* providing confidential information to his new firm and approaching clients and staff of his existing firm.

[44] [2002] I.R.L.R. 120 (CA).

[45] An obvious example is a performance-related profit sharing scheme, as noted *supra*, para. 10–82.

[46] See the following cases concering employees: *Horkulak v. Cantor Fitzgerald International* [2005] I.C.R. 402 (CA); *Keen v. Commerzbank AG* [2007] I.C.R. 623; *McCarthy v. McCarthy & Stone plc* [2008] 1 All E.R. 221; also *Lymington Marina Ltd. v. Macnamara* [2007] 2 All E.R. (Comm) 825 (CA), a decision concerning consent under a licence. Note, however, *Russsell v. Russell* (1880) 14 Ch.D. 471, where it was held that a power to dissolve a firm conferred on one member of a two partner firm *could* be exercised capriciously. It is not considered that this decision establishes any principle of general application.

objectionable.[47] Similarly, if the exercise of the discretion results in an incidental benefit to one or more of the other partners,[48] although in such a case the court is likely to scrutinise the circumstances with care.[49] The position will, naturally, be otherwise where the decision is proved to be motivated by a collateral and improper purpose.[50]

Remedies for breach of duty

There can be no doubt that a breach of the duty will give rise to a claim for **16–10** damages or equitable compensation in an appropriate case.[51] However, such a claim may not be sustainable where the breach involves a mere non-disclosure.[52] An account may, in some circumstances, represent an alternative remedy to damages,[53] and will exist in any event in any case falling within section 29 or 30 of the Partnership Act 1890.[54] Where an account is ordered, the court will tailor the period of the account and the allowances and deductions to be made in favour of the accounting party to the precise circumstances.[55]

---

[47] *Redwood Master Fund Ltd. v. TD Bank Europe Ltd.*, *The Times*, January 30, 2003 (a decision relating to a syndicated loan agreement).

[48] See *Colin Gwyer & Associates Ltd. v. London Wharf (Limehouse) Ltd.* [2003] 2 B.C.L.C. 153 at [76] *per* Leslie Kosmin Q.C. sitting as a deputy judge of the Chancery Division, concerning a decision by the directors of a company.

[49] *ibid.*

[50] *ibid.* at [75], citing *Re Smith & Fawcett Ltd.* [1942] Ch 304 at 306 *per* Lord Greene M.R. and *Howard Smith Ltd. v. Ampol Petroleum Ltd.* [1974] A.C. 821; *Redwood Master Fund Ltd. v. TD Bank Europe Ltd.*, *supra*. In *Re Smith & Fawcett Ltd.*, Lord Greene actually drew the analogy between private companies and partnerships.

[51] *Trimble v. Goldberg* [1906] A.C. 494, 500; *Rama v. Miller* [1996] 1 N.Z.L.R. 257 (PC); *Finlayson v. Turnbull (No. 1)* 1997 S.L.R. 613 (OH); also *Ferguson v. Mackay* 1985 S.L.T. 94 (OH); *Disctronic Ltd. v. Kingston Links Country Club Pty Ltd.* [2005] V.R. 513 (Victoria CA), a decision regarding a joint venture. And see *Sanders v. Parry* [1967] 1 W.L.R. 753; *Downsview Nominees Ltd. v. First City Corporation Ltd.* [1993] A.C. 295 (duty owed by mortgagee/receiver); *Imperial Group Pension Trust Ltd. v. Imperial Tobacco Ltd.* [1991] 1 W.L.R. 589, 597 *per* Browne-Wilkinson V.-C. (a pension fund case). Note that a finding of bad faith can, in an appropriate case, be made on an application for summary judgment: *Wrexham Associated Football Club Ltd. (In Administration) v. Crucialmove Ltd.* [2007] B.C.C. 139 (CA). See further, as to claims for damages as between partners, *infra*, paras 23–208 *et seq.*

[52] In *Uphoff v. International Energy Trading*, *The Times*, February 4, 1989, it was held that no claim for damages lay as between co-venturers, even though the duty of disclosure was of a fiduciary nature. The position is *a fortiori* where the duty is not fiduciary: see *Banque Keyser Ullman SA v. Skandia Life (U.K.) Insurance Co. Ltd.* [1990] 1 Q.B. 665; *Bank of Nova Scotia v. Hellenic Mutual War Risks Assoc. (Bermuda) Ltd.* [1990] 1 Q.B. 818 (both decisions relating to insurance contracts). This issue was, in the event, not considered by the House of Lords when the latter case went to appeal: see [1992] 1 A.C. 233. The propositions in the text were referred to with apparent approval in *Conlon v. Simms* [2006] 2 All E.R. 1024 at [201] *per* Lawrence Collins J.; see also *ibid.* [2008] 1 W.L.R. 484 at [129] *per* Jonathan Parker L.J. And see also *supra*, para. 16–07.

[53] See *Murad v. Al-Saraj* [2005] W.T.L.R. 1573, an extreme case, and *Chirnside v. Fay* [2007] P.N.L.R. 6 (Sup. Ct. of New Zealand), both decisions concerning joint venturers; also *Imageview Management Ltd. v. Jack* [2009] 1 Lloyd's Rep 436 (CA), a decision concerning an agent. *cf. Disctronic Ltd. v. Kingston Links Country Club Pty Ltd.*, *supra*, where an account was refused in the case of a joint venture, on the ground of the claimant's delay. The existence of this right was acknowledged in *Kao Lee & Yip v. Hoi-Yan* [2003] H.K.C. 113 and *Deacons v. White & Case LLP* (HCA 2433/2002), October 24, 2003 (Hong Kong High Court).

[54] See *infra*, paras 16–14 *et seq.*

[55] *Kao Lee & Yip v. Hoi-Yan*, *supra*, is an example of the flexibility open to the court. There the account was limited to a period of one year (*ibid.* at [158]) and an allowance was made for expenses and overheads (*ibid.* at [159]).

Excluding the duty

16–11   There is little authority on the ability of partners expressly to exclude the duty of good faith as between themselves. In *Moser v. Cotton*,[56] the Court of Appeal acknowledged that partners' rights and obligations under sections 24(9) and 28 of the Partnership Act 1890 can be excluded by agreement.[57] What is more questionable is whether *all* elements of the duty of good faith could be so excluded.[58] Although the current editor is tentatively of the view that they can, since the duty is clearly not a part of the statutory definition of partnership[59] or, indeed, expressly recognised by the 1890 Act,[60] it is difficult to imagine circumstances where parties would think this appropriate, *i.e.* one "partner" condoning in advance all potential breaches of duty by another.[61] Indeed, questions might arise in such a case as to whether the parties could truly be said to be carrying on a business "in common".[62]

The duty of honesty

16–12   In *Carmichael v. Evans*,[63] Byrne J. stated that:

> "I conceive it to be one of the first duties of a partner to be an honest man, and that not merely in his accounts as between himself and his partners, but in relation to third persons, at least to the extent of abstaining from being guilty of a fraud bringing him within the penalties of the criminal law."

The duty of honesty[64] in partnership dealings, whether as between partners[65] or as between the firm and third parties,[66] cannot seriously be doubted. However, in previous editions of this work, the view has been advanced that there is also a

---

[56] (1990) 140 N.L.J. 1313. A similar view appears to have been adopted in *Williams v. Harris* [1980] I.L.R.M. 237 (Ir. Sup. Ct). A contrary view was, however, voiced in *Rosenberg. v. Nazarov* [2008] EWHC 812 (Ch) (Lawtel 10/4/08) at [64]] *per* Thomas Ivory Q.C., sitting as a deputy judge of the Chancery Division. Note also that, in *Kao Lee & Yip v. Hoi-Yan* [2003] H.K.C. 113 at [48], Ma J. expressed the view that an agreement can qualify "the extent or rigour with which the fiduciary duties will be applied".

[57] *ibid.* s.24(9) (*infra*, paras 22–10 *et seq.*) expressly contemplates this possibility, whilst s.28 (*supra*, para. 16–03) does not. However, a variation of *any* of the rights and duties defined in the Act is contemplated by *ibid.* s.19: see *supra*, paras 10–12 *et seq.* Interestingly, *ibid.* ss.29, 30 (*infra*, para. 16–14) do admit of the possibility that partners may agree to exclude their application, either generally or on a case-by-case basis. Note also the decision in *PWA Corp v. Gemini Group Automated Distribution Systems Inc.* [1993] 103 D.L.R. (4th) 609, where, in the particular circumstances, the partners' disclosure obligations had to be modified and they were not obliged to put the partnership's interests ahead of their own. See also the review of the authorities in *CPC Group Ltd. v. Qatari Diar Real Estate Investment Co.* [2010] N.P.C. 74, albeit not in the context of a partnership.

[58] The assumption made in *Rosenberg. v. Nazarov, supra*, was, however, that this is impossible.

[59] *ibid.* s.1(1), *supra*, paras 2–01 *et seq.*

[60] Only certain basic ingredients of the duty are recognised: see *ibid.* ss.24(9), 28–30. See further *supra*, n. 57. Somewhat surprisingly, a breach of the duty of good faith is not even recognised as a ground for dissolution *per se*, under *ibid.* s.35: see *infra*, paras 24–62 *et seq.*

[61] For an analogous consideration of the ability of parties to exclude the duty in the case of a contract of insurance, see *HIH Casualty and General Insurance Ltd. v. Chase Manhattan Bank* [2001] 1 Lloyd's Rep. 30 and, in particular, at [26] *per* Aikens J.

[62] *ibid.* s.1(1): see *supra*, para. 2–03.

[63] [1904] 1 Ch. 486, 492. See further, as to this case, *supra*, para. 10–117.

[64] See, as to what may amount to dishonesty in this context, *supra*, para. 16–07, n. 33.

[65] See *supra*, para. 16–01.

[66] Such conduct would, in any event, almost certainly involve a breach the duty discussed *infra*, paras 20–11 *et seq.*

general duty of honesty in all dealings with third parties *outside* the partnership business, as an effective adjunct to the normal duty of good faith. However, the current editor is now more doubtful of this proposition, giving changing contemporary views as to what conduct should properly be regarded as dishonest. If the duty is framed in the limited terms adopted by Byrne J., *i.e.* a duty not to engage in criminal frauds, it surely must exist, but a duty framed in wider terms is more questionable. However, this issue may, in practice, be academic, since any "dishonest", criminal or other anti-social behaviour on which a partner may embark outside the partnership business is likely to be raised not as a breach of duty *per se*, but as a ground for dissolving the firm under the Partnership Act 1890.[67]

2. THE OBLIGATION OF PARTNERS NOT TO BENEFIT THEMSELVES AT THE EXPENSE OF THEIR CO-PARTNERS

Although this obligation is, for present purposes, formulated separately from the general duty of good faith, it in truth represents no more than a particular branch of that duty. Lord Lindley explained it thus: **16–13**

> "Good faith requires that a partner shall not obtain a private advantage at the expense of the firm. He is bound in all transactions affecting the partnership, to do his best for the common body, and to share with his co-partners any benefit which he may have been able to obtain from other people, and in which the firm is in honour and conscience entitled to participate; *Semper enim non id quod privatim interest unius ex sociis servari solet, sed quod societati expedit.*"[68]

The passage from the Digest which Lord Lindley quoted may be translated as follows: "The invariable practice being not to have regard to the private interest of one of the partners but to the advantage of the firm."[69]

Accountability of partners for private profits

In accordance with this principle, it was established by numerous decisions prior to the Partnership Act 1890, that one partner was not at liberty to make a profit at the expense of his co-partners without their full knowledge and consent, whether that profit was made directly or indirectly, *e.g.* by appropriating some benefit to himself which he ought to have acquired, if at all, on behalf of all the partners.[70] The obligation established by those decisions was placed on a statutory footing in the Partnership Act 1890:   **16–14**

> "29.—(1) Every partner must account to the firm for any benefit derived by him without the consent of the other partners from any transaction concerning the

---

[67] See *ibid.* s.35(c), (f), discussed *infra*, paras 24–73 *et seq.*, 24–89, 24–90.
[68] Dig. xvii, tit. 2, pro socio, 1. 65, para. 5.
[69] Trans. by C.H. Munro, 1902.
[70] This passage, in an earlier formulation, was cited with approval in *Thompson's Trustees v. Heaton* [1974] 1 W.L.R. 605.

partnership, or from any use by him of the partnership property name[71] or business connexion.[72]

(2) This section applies also to transactions undertaken after a partnership has been dissolved by the death of a partner, and before the affairs thereof have been completely wound up, either by any surviving partner or by the representatives of the deceased partner.

30. If a partner, without the consent of the other partners, carries on any business of the same nature as and competing with that of the firm, he must account for and pay over to the firm all profits made by him in that business."

Neither section can be avoided by sheltering the benefit or profits in a company or other third party.[73]

16–15 It should be emphasised that, where either section applies, the obligation is to account to *the firm*, not merely to the other partners. It follows that a partner will, in the normal way, be entitled to share in the profits, etc., in respect of which the duty to account arises.[74]

These sections illustrate the distinction between the fiduciary duties owed by a partner and those owed by others in a fiduciary position[75] as analysed by the Court of Appeal in *O'Donnell v. Shanahan*,[76] since a partner's duties are, in general,[77] circumscribed by the terms of the partnership agreement and the ambit of the partnership business.[78] This distinction must always be borne in mind when considering authorities outside the partnership field.

Although all questions of accountability must now be determined by reference to the above sections, the pre-1890 cases still afford a valuable illustration of the principles on which the sections were based and will frequently indicate the way in which they are likely to be applied by the courts.

---

[71] Even apart from this section, a partner might be liable to account for profits made whilst representing himself as an agent of the firm, when he in fact has no express authority: see *English v. Dedham Vale Properties Ltd.* [1978] 1 W.L.R. 93.

[72] It should be noted that this section may overlap with *ibid.* s.42 (considered *infra*, paras 25–24 *et seq.*): see *John Taylors v. Masons* [2005] W.T.L.R. 1519 at [38] *per* Arden L.J. In *Kao Lee & Yip v. Hoi-Yan* [2003] H.K.C. 113 at [148], Ma J. observed that the section did not add much to the common law position.

[73] See *Lindsley v. Woodfull* [2004] 2 B.C.L.C. 131 (CA) at [27] *per* Arden L.J.; also *Trustor AB v. Smallbone (No. 2)* [2001] 1 W.L.R. 1177; *CMS Dolphin Ltd. v. Simonet* [2001] 2 B.C.L.C. 704. *cf. Aerostar Maintenance International Ltd. v. Wilson* [2010] EWHC 2032 (Ch) (Lawtel 4/8/10).

[74] *Olson v. Gullo* (1994) 113 D.L.R. (4th) 42. Whilst Morden A.C.J.O. accepted that the equivalent of the Partnership Act 1890, s.29(1) does not, as such, preclude the possibility that the accounting partner may be deprived of his share of the profits, he emphatically rejected the argument that such share should be forfeited on the grounds that the accounting partner would otherwise profit from his own wrong.

[75] *Semble* a member of a limited liability partnership will be in a similar position to a partner: see the Limited Liability Partnerships Regulations 2001 (SI 2001/1090), reg. 7(9), (10), which replicates the Partnership Act 1890, ss.29, 30.

[76] [2009] 2 B.C.L.C. 666 (CA), explaining the decision in *Aas v. Benham* [1891] 2 Ch. 244, noted *infra*, para. 16–31. The actual decision concerned the duties owed by the director of a company.

[77] *Quaere* does this apply only in the case of a *commercial* partnership, as in *Aas v. Benham, supra*. It is thought not.

[78] And, possibly, the potential scope of that business: see *infra*, para. 16–35.

Sale by or to the firm

A partner may not make a secret profit in the course of buying property from,   **16–16**
or selling property to, his own firm.[79] Thus, in *Bentley v. Craven*,[80] a partner, who
had been employed to purchase sugar on the firm's behalf, unbeknown to his
co-partners supplied the firm with sugar which he had previously purchased on
his own account at a favourable price and for which he charged the firm full
market value. He was held accountable to the firm for the profit so realised.

Similarly in *Dunne v. English*,[81] the claimant and the defendant had agreed to
buy a mine for £50,000, with a view to reselling it at a profit. It was ultimately
arranged that the defendant would sell the mine to a third party for £60,000 and
that the claimant and the defendant would divide the resulting profit of £10,000.[82]
In fact the defendant sold the mine for a sum far in excess of £60,000 to a
company in which he himself had a substantial interest. The claimant was held
entitled to one-half of the actual profit made on the resale.[83]

Full disclosure

If the duty to account is to be avoided in such a case, it is essential that the   **16–17**
partner concerned makes full disclosure of his interest to his co-partners. However, nothing short of such full disclosure will suffice. It appears that, in *Dunne
v. English*, the claimant knew that the defendant had some interest in the purchase
beyond his share of the known profit of £10,000 but he did not know what that
interest was and the real position was concealed from him. It was held that the
defendant, being the claimant's partner and expressly entrusted with the conduct
of the sale, was bound to make full disclosure of the true facts; having failed to
do so, he could not exclude the claimant from his due share of the profits realised
on the sale.[84]

Authority to sell at a fixed price

Dunne v. English is also authority for the (largely self evident) proposition   **16–18**
that, if one partner authorises another to sell partnership property at a certain
price, he does not thereby deprive himself of his right to a full share of the sale
proceeds if a higher price is in fact realised.[85]

---

[79] See in addition to the cases cited in the text, *Gordon v. Holland* (1913) 108 L.T. 385, where a
partner improperly sold partnership property to a purchaser for value without notice and subsequently
repurchased it for his own benefit; also the Canadian case of *Denison v. Fawcett* (1958) 12 D.L.R.
(2d) 537, where a partner secretly procured a third party to buy the partnership business, ostensibly
as a principal but in fact as his agent.

[80] (1853) 18 Beav. 75. See also *Kuhlirz v. Lambert* (1913) 108 L.T. 560.

[81] (1874) 18 Eq. 524.

[82] It was in fact part of the arrangement ultimately agreed that the defendant would acquire the
mine so as to be able to sell it on to the third party without involving the claimant.

[83] It would not have been permissible to deprive the defendant of his share of the profit: *Olson v.
Gullo* (1994) 113 D.L.R. (4th) 42, noted *supra*, para. 16–15.

[84] See also *Imperial Mercantile Credit Association v. Coleman* (1871) L.R. 6 H.L. 189; *Gwembe
Valley Development Co Ltd. v. Koshy* [2004] 1 B.C.L.C. 131 (CA); *Murad v. Al-Saraj* [2005]
W.T.L.R. 1573; *Foreman v. King* [2008] EWHC 592 (Ch) (Lawtel 24/6/08), noted *infra*, para. 16–25;
O'Donnell v. Shanahan [2009] 2 B.C.L.C. 666 (CA); also the other cases cited *infra*, para. 16–19,
n. 87.

[85] See also *Parker v. McKenna* (1874) 10 Ch.App. 96; *De Bussche v. Alt* (1878) 8 Ch.D. 286 and,
in particular, *ibid.* p. 317, as to the illegality of a custom authorising such a practice.

Other benefits due to the firm

16–19   The same principles apply where a partner attempts to secure a personal benefit for himself which should, consistently with his duties to his co-partners, only be obtained for the benefit the firm as a whole.[86]

Thus, in *Carter v. Horne*[87] the claimant and the defendant agreed to purchase an estate subject to certain incumbrances, which fell to discharged out of the purchase price. Some of the incumbrancers were, for personal reasons, prepared to allow the defendant to enjoy the benefit of a reduction in certain sums due in respect of interest and otherwise. However, in proceedings brought against him by the claimant for an account of rents and profits, the defendant was held liable to account for these reductions, since the purchase had been made for their joint benefit and on the basis of mutual trust. Similarly, in *Broadhurst v. Broadhurst*,[88] the defendant was held to be accountable for a range of secret benefits which he had enjoyed as a partner in a car importation business.

Leases: renewal

16–20   It is settled law that, in Lord Lindley's own words:

> " . . . if one partner obtains in his own name, either during the partnership or before its assets have been sold,[89] a renewal of a lease of the partnership property, he will not be allowed to treat this renewed lease as his own and as one in which his co-partners have no interest."

This principle was established by Sir William Grant in *Featherstonhaugh v. Fenwick*,[90] where two partners had obtained a renewal of the lease of the partnership premises in their own names and immediately dissolved the partnership. They sought to exclude the claimant (their co-partner) from all interest in the new lease but, in taking the accounts of the partnership, it was held that the lease was an asset of the firm.

---

[86] Lord Lindley remarked in a footnote that the decision in *Parker v. Hills* (1861) 7 Jur. (N.S.) 833 "is not opposed to these cases, for there the money was paid for a lease which was held to belong to one partner only".

[87] (1728) Eq.Ab. 7. See also *Olson v. Gullo* (1994) 113 D.L.R. (4th) 42; *Cobbetts LLP v. Hodge* (2009) 153(17) S.J.L.B. 29, although there the defendant was held not to be a partner. And see *Morison v. Thompson* (1874) L.R. 9 Q.B. 480; *De Bussche v. Alt* (1878) 8 Ch.D. 286; *Powell and Thomas v. Evan Jones & Co.* [1905] 1 K.B. 11; *Nitedals Taendstikfabrik v. Bruster* [1906] 2 Ch. 408; *Hurstanger Ltd. v. Wilson* [2007] 1 W.L.R. 2351; *Imageview Management Ltd. v. Jack* [2009] 1 Lloyd's Rep 436 (CA), as to the right of a principal to profits made by his agent or sub-agent (although note that special rules apply to partners as agents: see *supra*, para. 16–15). In earlier editions of this work, this footnote contained extensive references to decided cases establishing the extent of a principal's right to recover commissions, bribes, etc., from his agent; however, given the wide nature of the statutory duty to account which the law imposes on partners, such references have not been retained. The full footnote is to be found in the 15th ed., at p. 485, n. 26.

[88] [2006] EWHC 2727 Ch (Lawtel 23/10/06).

[89] *i.e.* following a dissolution.

[90] (1810) 17 Ves.Jr. 298. See also *Keech v. Sandford* (1726) Sel.Cas. Ch. 61; *Re Biss* [1903] 2 Ch. 40, 56 *per* Collins M.R., 60, 62 *per* Romer L.J.; *Griffith v. Owen* [1907] 1 Ch. 195; *Re Knowles' Will Trusts* [1948] 1 All E.R. 866 (where a trustee had renewed a lease of trust property in his own name); *Chelsea Estates Investment Trust Co. v. Marche* [1955] Ch. 328 (where a mortgagee of a lease had renewed the mortgaged lease under an option contained therein); *Gordon v. Gonda* [1955] 1 W.L.R. 885 (tracing partnership asset into other property following a dissolution); *Chan (Kak Loui) v. Zacharia* (1984) 154 C.L.R. 178; *Don King Promotions Inc. v. Warren* [2000] Ch. 291 (CA).

Clegg v. Fishwick[91] was a similar case. There the claimant, who was the **16–21** administratrix of a partner in a coal-mine, commenced proceedings against the surviving partners some years after the date of death, by which she sought an account and a dissolution, and a declaration that a renewed lease, which had been obtained by the defendants, was held in trust for the benefit of the former firm. Two defences were set up: first, it was said that the former firm had come to an end at the same time as the old lease and the claimant could not therefore claim any interest in the new lease. Secondly, it was said that, before the proceedings were commenced, the claimant had assigned the deceased's partnership share to his children, so that she, at least, had no right to institute proceedings in respect thereof. On the first defence, it was held that the old lease was the "foundation" for the new lease and that, where parties are jointly interested in a lease, some of them cannot take the benefit of a renewal to the exclusion of the others; on the second, it was held that what had been assigned by the claimant was the deceased's share, which had never been ascertained, and that the assignment constituted her as a trustee of the share for the assignees but did not deprive her of her right to call for the partnership property to be realised.

In cases of this type, the other partners cannot restrain the landlord from granting the new lease to their co-partner: their remedy is rather to treat the lessee as holding the lease for the benefit of the firm.[92]

Open renewal

In both *Featherstonhaugh v. Fenwick* and *Clegg v. Fishwick*, the lease was **16–22** renewed in a clandestine way, but this is by no means an essential ingredient. This is illustrated by the decision in *Clegg v. Edmondson*[93] where a partnership at will was dissolved by the managing partners, who gave notice to the other partners of their intention to renew the old lease for their own benefit. They in fact did so, despite those other partners' objections, and evidence was adduced to the effect that the landlord would have opposed the grant of a renewed lease to anyone other than the managing partners.[94] It was nevertheless held that the managing partners could not acquire the benefit of the renewed lease for their own exclusive benefit.[95] A similar decision was reached by the Privy Council in *Pathirana v. Pathirana*,[96] when considering the renewal of certain petrol supply agreements by one of two partners for his own benefit, by the Court of Appeal in *Don King Promotions Inc. v. Warren*,[97] when considering the renewal of certain boxing promotion contracts, and in *John Taylors v. Masons*,[98] when considering the open renewal of a *licence*.

[91] (1849) 1 Mac. & G. 294. See also *Clements v. Hall* (1858) 2 De G. & J. 173.
[92] *Alder v. Fouracre* (1818) 3 Swans. 489. Where the lease is the sole property of one partner, see *Burdon v. Barkus* (1862) 4 De G.F. & J. 42; *Bevan v. Webb* [1905] 1 Ch. 620, 631 *per* Warrington J; also *infra*, para. 18–13. And see *Re Thomson* [1930] 1 Ch. 203, 210 *per* Clauson J., where one of three executors took a new lease for his own benefit.
[93] (1856) 8 De G.M. & G. 787. See also *Re Biss* [1903] 2 Ch. 40, 61, 62 *per* Romer L.J.
[94] See *Fitzgibbon v. Scanlan* (1813) 1 Dow. 269.
[95] However, the other partners were in fact denied any relief by reason of laches and delay: see further, *infra*, paras 23–24 *et seq.*
[96] [1967] 1 A.C. 233. See further, *infra* para. 16–27.
[97] [2000] Ch. 291. See further *infra*, para. 16–27.
[98] [2005] W.T.L.R. 1519, noticed *infra*, para. 16–28.

Right to reject renewed lease

16–23   Although one partner cannot exclude his co-partners from the benefit of the renewed lease, he cannot force them to treat it as acquired on behalf of the firm, unless he acted with their authority or they have otherwise bound themselves to accept such treatment.[99]

Laches

16–24   It goes almost without saying that a claim of the above type must be brought promptly, if a successful plea of laches is to be avoided.[100]

Leases: purchase of reversion

16–25   A partner who purchases the reversion to the firm's lease may enjoy a more secure position, but only if the purchase is entirely independent of any interest in the lease.[101] Thus, in *Bevan v. Webb*,[102] a partner who had purchased such a reversion out of his own moneys was held to be entitled to retain it, there being no evidence that the purchase had been obtained by virtue of his interest in the lease and the lease not being renewable by custom or by contract.[103] Similarly in *Ward v. Brunt*.[104] On the other hand, in *Thompson's Trustee v. Heaton*,[105] where a lease remained as an undistributed asset after the dissolution of a firm, it was held that each of the former partners was precluded from acquiring the reversion for his own benefit without giving the other the opportunity of coming in on the acquisition. As a result, the partner who had acquired the reversion was under a fiduciary duty to account to the other for the benefit derived therefrom. The decisions in *Popat v. Shonchhatra*[106] and *Foreman v. King*[107] were to a similar effect. In the latter case, the possibility of acquiring the freehold reversion had been raised with one of the claimant partners, but they were not informed that the defendants proposed to proceed with the purchase or that they had done so until some time later. As a result there was no informed consent.[108]

---

[99] *Clements v. Norris* (1878) 8 Ch.D. 129. But see also *supra*, paras 15–04, 15–06.

[100] *Clegg v. Edmondson* (1856) 8 De G.M. & G. 787; *Re Jarvis* [1958] 1 W.L.R. 815; see also, generally, *infra*, paras 23–19 *et seq.*

[101] See *Griffith v. Owen* [1907] 1 Ch. 195.

[102] [1905] 1 Ch. 620. *Brenner v. Rose* [1973] 1 W.L.R. 443 appears to have been another case of this class.

[103] See as to such leases, *Phillips v. Phillips* (1884) 29 Ch.D. 673; *Griffith v. Owen* [1907] 1 Ch. 195, 204–205 *per* Parker J. In view of the provisions of the Landlord and Tenant Act 1954, Part II (as amended), these cases may now be of more general application.

[104] [2000] W.T.L.R. 731. There the opportunity to acquire the reversion arose under a personal option contained in the freeholder's will.

[105] [1974] 1 W.L.R. 605. See also *Wicks v. Bennett* (1921) 30 C.L.R. 80 (albeit that relief was refused because a specific claim therefor was not included in the prayer) and, generally, *Boardman v. Phipps* [1967] 2 A.C. 46. For the position as between husband and wife, see *Protheroe v. Protheroe* [1968] 1 W.L.R. 519.

[106] [1995] 1 W.L.R. 908, 916–917. The appeal concerned only the *proportions* in which the freehold reversion was held in trust for the former partners: see [1997] 1 W.L.R. 1267, 1375.

[107] [2008] EWHC 592 (Ch) (Lawtel 24/6/08). Note that Mr Mark Cawson Q.C. (sitting as a deputy judge of the Chancery Division) expressed the view that he could not place undue reliance on any case predating *Protheroe v. Protheroe*, *supra*: *ibid.* at [45].

[108] There was evidence of other unsatisfactory behaviour on the part of the first defendant in relation to the acquisition, *e.g.* after he and his wife had acquired the reversion, he caused the firm to pay an increased rent without telling the other partners. Only some months later did he purport to pursue an outstanding review of the rent.

Use of partnership property

The principle which precludes a partner from retaining benefits which he ought   **16–26**
properly to share with his co-partners is equally applicable where those benefits
result from the use of partnership property, as is made clear in the Partnership Act
1890 itself.[109] Thus, in *Burton v. Wookey*,[110] the claimant and the defendant (who
was a shopkeeper) were partners as dealers in *lapis calaminaris*. The defendant
lived near the mines and purchased the ore from the miners, paying them not in
money but in goods from his shop. In his account with the claimant, the
defendant treated the ore as having been purchased for an amount equal to the
sale price of those goods; the claimant contended that, as between himself and
the defendant, the purchase price should be treated as the *cost* price of the goods,
and that the defendant should account to the firm for the profit on the transaction.
That argument was upheld, the court holding that it was the defendant's duty to
buy the ore at the lowest possible price and to charge the firm with no more than
the cost price of the goods given in exchange therefor.

Similarly, in *Gardner v. McCutcheon*,[111] the defendant, who was both the
master and a part owner of a ship, was held liable to account for profits which he
had obtained by trading on his own account whilst the ship was employed for the
joint benefit of himself and his co-owners, the claimants. Although he contended
that the profits were made solely by the employment of his own private funds and
that, by custom, masters of ships were allowed to trade for their own benefit, the
court declined to recognise such a custom and held the profits to have been made
by the use of jointly owned property. *Broadhurst v. Broadhurst*[112] is another case
of this class.

Post-dissolution profits

If a partner continues in business following the dissolution of his firm and   **16–27**
makes use of the firm's assets or a business connection derived therefrom, he will
be accountable to his former partners for any profits which he may make thereby.
Thus, in *Pathirana v. Pathirana*,[113] the claimant and the defendant were partners
in a petrol service station business in Ceylon. A dispute arose and the defendant
gave notice terminating the partnership; before that notice had expired, he
obtained the renewal of certain petrol supply agreements in his sole name and,
after the determination of the partnership, carried on trading from the same
premises in his own name. The Privy Council held that he was accountable to the
claimant for a share of the profits attributable to those new petrol supply
agreements. Similarly, in *Don King Promotions Inc. v. Warren*,[114] the claimant
and Warren had formed a partnership to promote and manage boxers, under the
terms of which certain promotion and management contracts with individual
boxers held in Warren's sole name fell to be treated as partnership assets.[115] The

---

[109] s.29, *supra*, para. 16–14.
[110] (1882) 6 Madd. 367.
[111] (1842) 4 Beav. 534. See also *Benson v. Heathorn* (1842) 1 Y. & C. Ch. 326; *Shallcross v. Oldham* (1862) 2 J. & H. 609; *Miller v. Mackay* (1865) 31 Beav. 77; *Williamson v. Hine* [1891] 1 Ch. 390. *cf. Miller v. Mackay* (1865) 34 Beav. 295; also *Moffat v. Farquharson* (1788) 2 Bro.C.C. 338 (but see the note on this case in Belt's edition of Brown's Reports). And see *infra*, para. 18–14.
[112] [2006] EWHC 2727 Ch (Lawtel 23/10/06), noticed *supra*, para. 16–19.
[113] [1967] 1 A.C. 233.
[114] [2000] Ch. 291.
[115] See further, *infra*, paras 18–16, 23–198.

partnership was dissolved before those contracts had run their full terms. The Court of Appeal held not only that the benefit of those contracts continued to be partnership property until their expiry or earlier disposal, but also that renewals of those contracts prior to the conclusion of the winding up were to be treated in the same way.[116] It was, however, accepted that new promotion and management contracts concluded by Warren after the date of the dissolution with boxers who had not previously been in contract with him were not to be so treated.

16–28   The decision in *John Taylors v. Masons*[117] is another example of a case in this class. There two of five partners brought about a dissolution of the firm on the precise date on which its licence from the District Council to conduct a market at certain premises expired. Prior to the date of dissolution, those partners obtained the grant of a provisional licence to run the market in place of the firm and some months later, pursuant to an open tender process, acquired a new 3-year licence. The Court of Appeal held that the opportunity to renew the licence was a partnership asset and that, in obtaining both the provisional and 3-year licences, the two partners had made use of the firm's business connection with the District Council. Accordingly, they were liable to account for the benefit of the goodwill which they had appropriated to themselves by engineering the grant of the new licences in their own favour and for any resulting profits. Arden L.J. also held that an overlapping claim might also be maintainable under section 42 of the Partnership Act 1890.[118]

16–29   Again, in *Lindsley v. Woodfull*,[119] whilst an outgoing partner's continuing liability to account for profits under a contract (including all renewals thereof) was held to have been terminated as to the future by affirmation of a retirement agreement by the continuing partners, he was nevertheless held to be accountable for the value of the contract, including the prospective right of renewal, as at the date of his retirement. In *Gorne v. Scales*,[120] the claim for use of confidential information (in the form of a card index system) was framed in damages rather than under section 29, which affected the basis on which recovery could be sought. Interestingly, the inability of the dissolved firm to exploit that information was seemingly regarded as a relevant factor in assessing the damages.[121]

Equally, if all that the partnership has is a mere expectancy, no duty to account will arise.[122]

16–30   It should be noted that, following a dissolution, each partner's authority to bind the firm only continues "as far as may be necessary to wind up the affairs of the

---

[116] *Quaere*, why should any further renewals not be treated in the same way? Equally, the prospect of the winding up being prolonged by reason an unlimited series of renewals seems unattractive. This is an issue which was not addressed by the Court of Appeal, perhaps because of the terms of the partnership agreement, which obliged Warren to purchase all the partnership assets in the event of a dissolution: see *supra*, para. 13–65 and *infra*, para. 23–198.

[117] [2005] W.T.L.R. 1519.

[118] *ibid.* at [38]. See also *supra*, para. 16–14.

[119] [2004] 2 B.C.L.C. 131 (CA).

[120] [2006] EWCA Civ. 311 (Lawtel 29/3/06).

[121] See *ibid.* at [17] *per* Moore-Bick L.J.

[122] *Sew Hoy v. Sew Hoy* [2001] 1 N.Z.L.R. 391 (CA, New Zealand). There the trustees of a deceased partner's estate had purchased certain land which had originally been acquired by the Crown from the firm and which, under the provisions of a particular statute, had to be offered back to the firm when it was no longer needed. The court distinguished *Thompson's Trustee v. Heaton* [1974] 1 W.L.R. 605, noted *supra*, para. 16–25 and held that, at the date of the dissolution (some 10 years before), the right to buy the land back was no more than an expectancy. Accordingly, no fiduciary duties were owed to the other partners.

partnership, and to complete transactions begun but unfinished at the time of the dissolution, *but not otherwise*"[123] (emphasis supplied). Accordingly, a partner who exploits the firm's business connection in order to take on *new* business for his own benefit may be accountable for any profits realised, even though such business could not properly have been transacted by the firm without the agreement of all the other partners.[124]

Information gained as a partner

If a partner comes into possession of information in the course of carrying on the partnership business or otherwise as a result of his connection with the firm, and uses it to secure some personal benefit from a transaction *which is within the scope of the partnership business*,[125] he will be accountable therefor.[126] However, no such duty to account will in general arise if the transaction does not involve competition with the partnership business and falls outside its scope, as illustrated by the decision in *Aas v. Benham*.[127] There the defendant, a partner in a firm of shipbrokers, used information which he had acquired in transacting the firm's business when setting up a shipbuilding company, for which he received both remuneration and a salaried directorship. His co-partners sought an account of both remuneration and salary, but failed because the company's business was held to be entirely beyond the scope of the firm's business. Nevertheless, an injunction was granted to restrain the defendant from making use of the firm name for his own purposes.

16–31

Similarly, in *Re Coffey's Registered Design*,[128] it was held that a partner in a firm trading in home brewing materials, who had himself developed a design for a container for brewing beer, was beneficially entitled to the design and innocent of any breach of the duty of good faith owed to his co-partners, since the firm was involved solely in the business of buying and selling products manufactured by others, and not in manufacturing such products itself.

---

[123] Partnership Act 1890, s.38. See further, *supra*, paras 10–199, 13–61 *et seq*.

[124] Conceptually this must be correct, because the partner in the example has, in effect, appropriated part of the firm's goodwill (*i.e.* customer connection) for his own benefit. See also, *infra*, para. 16–32. And note the decision in *Castle v. Castle* [1951] G.L.R. 541. Interestingly, the Court of Appeal in *Don King Promotions Inc. v. Warren*, *supra*, appeared unconcerned at the prospect of boxing promotion contracts being renewed for the benefit of the dissolved firm, even though this would technically involve taking on new business: see further, *supra*, para. 13–65 and *infra*, para. 23–198.

[125] This qualification is unique to partners as fiduciaries and does not apply in other contexts: see *O'Donnell v. Shanahan* [2009] 2 B.C.L.C. 666 (CA), noted *supra*, para. 16–15.

[126] See *Regal (Hastings) Ltd. v. Gulliver* [1942] 1 All E.R. 378; *Boardman v. Phipps* [1967] 2 A.C. 46; *Industrial Development Consultants Ltd. v. Cooley* [1972] 1 W.L.R. 443; *Re Bhullar Bros Ltd.* [2003] B.C.L.C. 241 (CA). But note, when considering these decisions, what is said in the previous footnote. As to the assessment of damages, see *Seager v. Copydex (No. 2)* [1969] 1 W.L.R. 809.

[127] [1891] 2 Ch. 244, explaining *Dean v. Macdowell* (1878) 8 Ch.D. 345. *Aas v. Benham* was considered by the House of Lords in *Boardman v. Phipps*, *supra* and by the Court of Appeal in *O'Donnell v. Shanahan*, *supra*. The various employment cases cited *supra*, para. 10–55 (*e.g.* *Faccenda Chicken Ltd. v. Fowler* [1987] Ch. 117) are of less relevance in this area. When applying such decisions to partners, it must be remembered that they are, at one and the same time, both principals *and* agents: see *Trego v. Hunt* [1895] 1 Ch. 462, 467 *per* Stirling J. and [1896] A.C. 7, 26 *per* Lord Davey.

[128] [1982] F.S.R. 227. In fact, the firm had been incorporated prior to registration of the design, and the company (unsuccessfully) claimed rectification of the register.

Other benefits derived from connection with the firm

16–32   However, the scope of the partnership business will not always be the deter-mining factor. There may also be circumstances in which a duty to account will arise in respect of a transaction unconnected with the partnership business, where a partner exploits an opportunity which comes to him only as a result of his membership of the firm. As Lord Lindley explained:

> "A partner . . . is not allowed in transacting the partnership affairs, to carry on for his own sole benefit any separate trade or business which, were it not for his connection with the partnership, he would not have been in a position to carry on. Bound to do his best for the firm, he is not at liberty to labour for himself to their detriment; and if his connection with the firm enables him to acquire gain, he cannot appropriate that gain to himself on the pretence that it arose from a separate transaction with which the firm had nothing to do."

The underlying rationale is, perhaps, that such gains fall within the *potential* scope of the partnership business so that it is logical that a duty to account should arise. The operation of this principle has already been seen when considering the renewal of leases[129] and the use of partnership property,[130] and is further illus-trated by the decisions in *Russell v. Austwick* and *Lock v. Lynham.*[131]

Russell v. Austwick[132]

16–33   In this case, several persons agreed to carry on business as carriers between London and Falmouth, on terms that they would each carry on such business along the route between the towns assigned to them and that no partnership would exist between them. In pursuance of this business, Austwick, who appears to have been the London agent of the carriers, entered into a contract for the carriage of a new silver coinage to towns on the road between London and Falmouth. Shortly afterwards, he entered into a second contract for the carriage of such coinage to towns in Middlesex and the adjoining counties, none of which lay on the London to Falmouth route and many of which were only accessible by cross-country roads, thus involving increased risks. As a result, the mint author-ities agreed to increase all payments for the carriage of the coinage, so that the consideration payable under the first contract was increased by a sizeable amount. No dispute arose in relation thereto, but Austwick, on behalf of himself and Maddeford (another party to the original agreement), sought to retain the benefit of the second contract, on the basis that it had nothing to do with the London to Falmouth business. However, the court held that he was accountable for the profits made thereunder, seemingly accepting the claimant's argument that the second contract represented a continuation of the first and resulted from the confidence reposed in Austwick by the mint authorities resulting from his participation therein.

---

[129] See *supra*, paras 16–20 *et seq.*

[130] See *supra*, para. 16–30.

[131] See also the following New Zealand authorities: *Gibson v. Tyree* (1901) 18 N.Z.L.R. 701; *Gibson v. Tyree (No. 2)* (1901) 20 N.Z.L.R. 278.

[132] (1826) 1 Sim. 52. This decision demonstrates that the same principles apply whenever there is an agreement to share profits, whether or not a partnership is created. See also *Clegg v. Clegg* (1861) 3 Giff. 322. *cf. Trimble v. Goldberg* [1906] A.C. 494, noticed *infra*, para. 16–36. And see, generally, the Partnership Act 1890, s.29, *supra*, para. 16–14.

Lock v. Lynham[133]

Here the claimant and the defendant had agreed to share the profits and losses **16–34** arising from contracts entered into by the defendant for the supply of foodstuffs to the armed forces in Ireland. Whilst this agreement was operating, the defendant secretly agreed to share the profits and losses arising from similar contracts entered into by third parties. The claimant sought a share of such profits, but the defendant contended that he was entitled to retain them for his own exclusive benefit. The Lord Chancellor observed that, even though the partners were not under any obligation to refrain from entering into another partnership of the same kind, it never could have been in their contemplation that one of them could, in his own name or in that of a third party, enter into contracts prejudicial to the other's interests.[134] However, on the second day of the hearing and after considering the authorities, the Lord Chancellor modified his opinion and emphasised that the true issue in cases of this type is whether there is "an express or implied contract against other dealings of like character".[135] In the event, he made no finding on this issue and directed an inquiry with a view to ascertaining whether, whilst the partnership was subsisting, the defendant had either alone or jointly with some other person or persons entered into, or been beneficially interested in, any other contract or dealing of the like nature to those in which the claimant and the defendant were engaged as partners.

One partner competing with firm

A partner must not, without the consent of his co-partners, carry on any **16–35** business in competition with the firm; if he does so, he will be accountable for any profits he may realise, even if he has acted in an entirely open manner.[136] Where, however, the business is not carried on in competition with the firm and has no connection with its business, no duty to account will arise, even if the partner concerned has agreed not to carry on any other business whilst he remains a member of the firm.[137] For this reason, it may in some cases be appropriate to include an express duty to account for profits derived from non-competing businesses in the partnership agreement.[138]

Exceptional cases: purchase of co-partner's share, etc.

One notable exception to the principles discussed in the preceding paragraphs **16–36** is recognised in the freedom of one partner, in the absence of any contrary

[133] (1854) 4 Ir.Ch.R. 188. *cf. Miller v. Mackay* (1865) 34 Beav. 295; and see *Somerville v. Mackay* (1810) 16 Ves.Jr. 382.

[134] See the Partnership Act 1890, s.30, *supra*, para. 16–14.

[135] (1854) 4 Ir.Ch.R. 190, 191.

[136] Partnership Act 1890, s.30; and see *Glassington v. Thwaites* (1823) 1 Sim. & St. 124; *England v. Curling* (1844) 8 Beav. 129 (in which there was more than mere business rivalry). See also *Re Thomson* [1930] 1 Ch. 203, 210 *et seq. per* Clauson J. (an executor competing with his testator's business). Reference may also usefully be made to the following New Zealand authorities: *Gibson v. Tyree* (1901) 18 N.Z.L.R. 701; *Gibson v. Tyree (No. 2)* (1901) 20 N.Z.L.R. 278.

[137] *Aas v. Benham* [1891] 2 Ch. 244, *supra*, para. 16–31; *Dean v. Macdowell* (1878) 8 Ch.D. 345. In the former case the defendant was not bound to give his whole time to the partnership business; in the latter he was so bound, and damages for breach of covenant might, perhaps, have been obtained, even though the covenant probably could not have been enforced by injunction. And see, as to claims in damages, *supra*, para. 16–10; also *Grimston v. Cuningham* [1894] 1 Q.B. 125; *Davis v. Foreman* [1894] 3 Ch. 655; *Kirchner & Co. v. Gruban* [1909] 1 Ch. 413. But see *Hill v. C. A. Parsons & Co. Ltd.* [1972] Ch. 305.

[138] See also *supra*, para. 10–95.

provision in the agreement, to acquire another's partnership share for his own benefit, without informing the other partners or giving them an opportunity to join in such acquisition.[139]

An analogous principle was applied in *Trimble v. Goldberg*,[140] where three partners had purchased certain building plots and shares in a company with a view to resale. Most, if not all, of the company's assets consisted of other building plots in the same locality as those purchased. Two of the partners bought such other plots from the company without the knowledge of the third. The latter's claim to share in the benefit of this purchase was rejected, since it was not within the scope of the partnership business, nor made in competition with it, nor forbidden by the partnership agreement. It was further held that, even if the purchase had been forbidden by the agreement, it did not necessarily follow that the third partner could claim a share of the profits made by his co-partners.[141]

---

[139] *Cassels v. Stewart* (1881) 6 App.Cas. 64. In this case, the partnership agreement did not forbid such a purchase and it was not part of the firm's business to buy the shares of its members.
[140] [1906] A.C. 494.
[141] *ibid.* p. 500.

CHAPTER 17

PARTNERSHIP CAPITAL

The nature of capital

LORD Lindley defined partnership capital in these terms: **17–01**

> "By the capital of a partnership is meant the aggregate of the sums contributed by its members for the purpose of commencing or carrying on the partnership business, and intended to be risked by them in that business. The capital of a partnership is not therefore the same as its property: the capital is a sum fixed by the agreement of the partners; whilst the actual assets of the firm vary from day to day, and include everything belonging to the firm and having any money value . . . The amount of each partner's capital ought . . . always to be accurately stated, in order to avoid disputes on a final adjustment of account; and this is more important where the capitals of the partners are unequal, for if there is no evidence as to the amounts contributed by them, the shares of the whole assets will be treated as equal".[1]

Distinction between capital and assets

As Lord Lindley pointed out there is a fundamental distinction between a   **17–02**
firm's capital on the one hand and its assets (sometimes confusingly called its capital assets) on the other. That distinction is critical to an understanding of the true nature of capital and is, moreover, frequently overlooked by partners and their advisers.[2] It has already been pointed out that a partner's capital should be expressed in cash terms, whether the contribution from which it was derived took the form of cash or a specific asset, e.g. land or goodwill.[3] Although a value must be placed upon any asset so contributed, there is in principle no reason why partners should not agree, as between themselves, to ascribe a notional value thereto, whether higher or lower than the true value.[4] Once a partner has brought in the asset and been credited with its agreed "capital" value in the firm's books, the asset as such will cease to be his property and will thereafter belong to the firm. Equally, that partner's capital will be unaffected by fluctuations in the value of the asset, which will represent capital profits or losses potentially divisible between the partners in their capital profit/loss sharing ratios.[5] It is, of course, at any time open to the partners to revalue the asset and to credit any increase in

---

[1] See the Partnership Act 1890, s.24(1) and *infra*, paras 17–08, 17–09, 19–15 *et seq.*

[2] The importance of the distinction was recognised by the House of Lords in *Reed v. Young* [1986] 1 W.L.R. 649, 654 and by the Court of Appeal in *Popat v. Shonchhatra* [1997] 1 W.L.R. 1367, 1371G–H.

[3] See *supra*, para. 10–59.

[4] Note, however, that the adoption of an artificially low value may have inheritance tax implications, depending on the partners' respective capital profit shares: see *infra*, para. 36–20.

[5] *Robinson v. Ashton* (1875) L.R. 20 Eq. 25; *McClelland v. Hyde* [1942] N.I. 1, 7 *per* Andrews L.C.J. *cf. Sykes v. Land* (1984) 271 E.G. 1265 (which turned on the construction of the agreement).

value to their capital accounts, thus increasing the firm's capital, or to debit any reduction in value against those accounts, thus writing off part of its capital.

17–03   Provided that the foregoing procedure is strictly adhered to, there should be no difficulty in identifying the amount of the firm's capital and the size of each partner's interest therein. Where, however, an attempt is made to treat the underlying assets of the firm as its capital, such identification will become impossible, in the absence of a full scale valuation of all the partnership assets. This (*inter alia*) means that the partners cannot agree any sensible basis either for the payment of interest on capital[6] or for the acquisition of an outgoing partner's share following his retirement, expulsion, etc.,[7] without incurring the costs attendant on such a valuation, which must in any event be carried out in the certain knowledge that, once completed, it will be virtually obsolete. Equally, such an approach causes less difficulty in the case of a full scale dissolution, since a realisation of the partnership assets is inevitable, thus enabling each partner's capital entitlement (in the form of his due share of the proceeds of sale) to be readily identified.

A further variation on the above theme is occasionally encountered: this involves each partner who contributes capital in the form of an asset being treated as entitled to that asset.[8] In such a case, it is doubtful whether there is any contribution of capital by such a partner; rather he is merely permitting his firm to have the use of the asset for so long as he remains a partner.

Distinction between capital and capital profits

17–04   The failure properly to distinguish between a firm's capital and its assets can also lead to confusion with regard to the partners' ownership of capital profits, particularly following the admission of a new partner. If (as will usually be the case) the assets appear in the partnership accounts at their written down book value, there will be a hidden fund of capital profits, commonly referred to as an "asset surplus", which is not reflected in the partners' capital accounts. That fund when realised, *e.g.* on a dissolution, ought, in the current editor's view, properly to be shared between the partners in their normal profit sharing ratios, in the absence of some contrary agreement.[9] An incoming partner will be just as much entitled to a share of that fund as an existing partner, even though it may have been made clear to him when he joined the firm that he would be required to contribute a sum of capital and that he would not be interested in the old firm's "capital", *i.e.* the aggregate of the existing partners' contributions.[10] However, that conclusion did not find favour with a Scottish court in *Bennett v. Wallace*.[11] There W was carrying on a solicitors' practice in partnership with P. That partnership came to an end and W agreed to enter into partnership with B. The agreement between W and B provided that W's capital should be as shown in the final accounts of the W/P partnership and, seemingly, that the assets of that firm should be shown in those accounts at market value or book value at W's option. B agreed to contribute a sum of capital when required by W so to do. The final

---

[6] See *supra*, para. 10–67 and *infra*, para. 17–12.

[7] See *supra*, paras 10–157 *et seq*. But see *Sykes v. Land* (1984) 271 E.G. 1265.

[8] This was, in substance, the position in *Faulks v. Faulks* [1992] 1 E.G.L.R. 9, *infra*, para. 18–19.

[9] See the Partnership Act 1890, ss.24(1), 44; *Robinson v. Ashton* (1875) L.R. 20 Eq. 25. See also *supra*, para. 10–79 and *infra*, para. 25–48.

[10] This may, of course, have inheritance tax implications: see *infra*, paras 36–20 *et seq*.

[11] 1998 S.C. 457 (2nd Div.).

W/P accounts were, in the event, prepared on a cash basis and, accordingly, did not attribute any value to work in progress. The partnership between W and B was dissolved within a short period. Both partners acknowledged that, on the dissolution, account had to be taken of the value of work in progress,[12] but W argued that he should receive a credit for the opening value of the work in progress which he had brought into the firm. It was held that he was entitled to such a credit as a matter of proper accounting principle as between partners.[13] Nevertheless, the current editor remains unconvinced by the court's reasoning, given the potential arbitrariness which would result from the application of the principle supposed.[14]

Given the uncertainties created by the above decision, it is obviously desirable that the agreement addresses the partners' entitlement to existing unrealised capital profits directly. To ensure that an incoming partner does not share therein, it would either be necessary to revalue the assets and credit the existing partners' capital accounts with the increase in value,[15] or to provide that all capital profits up to the date of admission will belong to the existing partners.[16] Although an attempt to treat the underlying assets as the firm's capital might avoid this difficulty, such an approach is wrong in principle and, moreover, may create as many problems as its solves.[17]

Distinction between capital and advances

When ascertaining the amount due to a partner from the firm, there are, of course, numerous items to be taken into account and it will only be the net balance which is ultimately due. If the partner concerned owes money to the firm, he will not be entitled to the return of his full capital contribution. Equally, the firm may owe him sums in addition to his capital entitlement, *e.g.* in respect of advances to the firm by way of loan, which were not intended to be wholly risked in the business, or in respect of undrawn profits. It is always necessary to distinguish between such sums and a partner's capital. As Lord Lindley observed: **17–05**

> "The distinction between a partner's capital and what is due to him for advances by way of loan to the firm is frequently very material: *e.g.* with reference to interest[18]; with reference to clauses in partnership articles fixing the amount of capital to be advanced and risked, and prohibiting the withdrawal of capital; and above all with reference to priority of payment in the event of dissolution and a deficiency of assets."[19]

Joint capital and current accounts—the accounting heresy

Particular difficulty in identifying a partner's capital will often be encountered in the case of firms which adopt the increasingly common accounting practice of   **17–06**

---

[12] Indeed, the partners had agreed its value: see *ibid.* p. 459D.

[13] *ibid.* p. 462: see further *supra*, para. 10–173.

[14] The anomalies are explored, *supra*, para. 10–173.

[15] But note the capital gains tax consequences which may flow from such a revaluation: see *infra*, para. 35–14.

[16] See *supra*, para. 10–79 and *infra*, paras 36–20, 36–39.

[17] See *supra*, para. 17–03.

[18] See the Partnership Act 1890, s.24(3), (4) and *infra*, paras 17–12, 20–34.

[19] *ibid.* s.44. See further, *infra*, paras 25–44 *et seq.*

maintaining a single account for each partner (almost invariably styled a "capital" account) to which are credited his undrawn profits and against which he is permitted to draw at will in subsequent years. In such circumstances, it may be almost impossible to ascertain whether the partners have intended to capitalise those undrawn profits[20] or to treat them as what is often loosely styled "circulating capital",[21] even though the latter will, in the current editor's view, usually represent the correct analysis in law.[22] It should, however, be noted that in *Hopper v. Hopper*,[23] the Court of Appeal readily upheld a finding on the facts that undrawn profits had been capitalised, principally on the basis that the partners had year on year approved annual accounts recontaining joint capital accounts. It is doubtful wheher this should be regarded as having established any principle of general application.

It is to avoid this uncertainty that separate capital and current accounts should be maintained in the firm's books, so that transfers from current to capital account (or vice versa) are only effected when the partners have positively decided to increase (or decrease) the firm's "fixed capital".[24]

Shares of capital

17–07   The Partnership Act 1890, section 24 provides as follows:

> "24. The interests of partners in the partnership property and their rights and duties in relation to the partnership shall be determined, subject to any agreement express or implied between the partners by the following rules;
> (1) All the partners are entitled to share equally in the capital and profits of the business, and must contribute equally towards the losses whether of capital or otherwise sustained by the firm."[25]

In his Supplement on the 1890 Act Lord Lindley said of the subsection:

> "If it be proved that the partners contributed the capital of the partnership in unequal shares it is presumed that, in the absence of an agreement to the contrary, on a final settlement of accounts, the capital of the business remaining after the payment of outside debts and liabilities, and of what is due to each partner for advances, will, subject to all proper deductions, be divided amongst the partners in the proportions in which they contributed it and not equally."[26]

---

[20] *cf. Binney v. Mutrie* (1886) 12 App.Cas. 160, JC, where the partners had clearly intended to capitalise their shares of the declared or estimated profits in each year. See also *Bouche v. Sproule* (1887) 12 App.Cas 385, 402 *per* Lord Bramwell, cited in *Hopper v.* Hopper [2008] EWCA Civ 1417 (Lawtel 12/12/08), *infra*.

[21] This expression will often be encountered in practice together with the expression "fixed capital", *i.e.* capital properly so called. Whilst in strict partnership law both expressions are misnomers, they represent a useful shorthand method of distinguishing between two types of funding which may at any one time be available to a firm.

[22] See generally, as to the capitalisation of undrawn profits, *Re Bridgewater Navigation Co.* [1891] 2 Ch. 317, 327 *per* Lindley L.J.

[23] [2008] EWCA Civ 1417 (Lawtel 12/12/08). Etherton L.J. rightly stated, at [16], "None of the [annual] accounts show undrawn profits being allocated to a current account", but surely this begs the whole question and indicates a potentially skewed view of the assumed underlying intention behind the maintenance of a joint capital/current account.

[24] For the desirability of this, see *Smith v. Gale* [1974] 1 W.L.R. 9.

[25] The subsection must also be read in the light of *ibid.* s.44(b), which deals with the distribution of the proceeds of partnership property on dissolution: see *infra*, paras 25–45 *et seq.* As to losses, see *infra*, paras 20–04 *et seq.*

[26] See also *infra*, para. 19–17.

In earlier editions of this work, Lord Lindley's original interpretation was **17–08** sought to be justified in this way:

> "Despite the ambiguous reference in subsection (1) to 'capital,' it is conceived that the opening words of the section which refer to 'partnership property' make it clear that 'capital' in this context means such property—though generally this is not so."[27]

Although this approach has its attractions, it is difficult to see how the second reference to "capital" in section 24(1) can be to anything other than capital properly so called, since it would be a misuse of language to speak of partners contributing towards losses of partnership property.[28] Moreover, despite the opening words of the section, it is clear beyond argument that when the expression "capital" is used in sections 24(3) and (4),[29] it cannot refer to partnership property. This analysis forms the basis for the current editor's view, as now endorsed by the Court of Appeal in *Popat v. Shonchhatra*,[30] that "capital" should be given its normal meaning throughout the section so that, if the partners contribute capital in unequal proportions but do not agree to share it in those proportions, they will each be entitled to an equal share of the firm's capital.

Equally, an agreement displacing the provisions of section 24(1) need not be express and may well be implied from the circumstances, *e.g.* where the capital contributions precisely reflect the partners' agreed (unequal) profit sharing ratios.[31] Indeed, it is clear that the court will readily infer such an implied agreement.[32]

Joint capital accounts

There is, in principle, nothing wrong with two or more partners maintaining a **17–09** joint capital account,[33] although this may make it difficult to ascertain ownership of the balance as between those partners, save in cases where they share equally in the partnership profits.[34]

Increase, reduction and return of capital

It is a fundamental principle of partnership law that, in the absence of some **17–10** contrary agreement, the capital of a firm cannot be increased or reduced without

[27] The original footnote stated "The distinction is clearly made by s.44 of the Partnership Act 1890." This is so: *cf.* the references to "capital" in para. (a) and sub-para. 2 of para. (b) and the reference to "the assets of the firm" at the beginning of para. (b).

[28] In view of the contents of the previous footnote, it should be noted that *ibid.* s.44(a) and (b) both refer to "losses . . . of capital" *not* of partnership property.

[29] See *infra*, paras 17–12, 20–33 *et seq.*

[30] [1997] 1 W.L.R. 1367, 1373B.

[31] However, it might, in such a case, be argued that there is no *necessary* correlation between the partners' capital contributions and their profit shares: see further, *infra*, para. 19–18.

[32] In *Popat v. Shonchhatra*, *supra*, at p. 1373, Nourse L.J. remarked: " . . . I am in no doubt that the slightest indication of an implied agreement between the partners that their shares of capital should correspond with their contributions to it will suffice to displace the provisions that they are entitled to share equally."

[33] This is not uncommon in partnerships involving spouses, etc. (see, for example, *Hopper v. Hopper* [2008] EWCA Civ 1417 (Lawtel 12/12/08)) and trustees. The current editor has never encountered an instance in which, as unsuccessfully alleged in *Hopper*, such an account has been maintained as between *all* the partners, save in the case of husband and wife partnerships.

[34] Equally, depending on the state of the accounts, it may not be difficult to analyse how the capital was contributed as between them. *Semble,* if this is not possible, the Partnership Act 1890, s.24(1), *supra*, para. 17–07, may apply.

the consent of all the partners.[35] Thus, where the original capital has been exhausted, the partners cannot be compelled to replace it; indeed, if the business can no longer be carried on profitably, a dissolution may be ordered at the instance of any one of the partners.[36] Similarly, if the firm is offered a lucrative deal which can only be taken up if additional capital is raised,[37] no partner can be forced to make a contribution against his will, whatever may be the consequences for the firm.

The corollary of the foregoing is, of course, that a partner who agrees to contribute a sum of capital is not only bound to bring that sum into the firm but he will be prevented from withdrawing any part of it for so long as he remains a partner. Whether he will be entitled to the return of his capital once he has ceased to be a partner will depend on the terms of the agreement[38] and/or the proper application of section 44 of the Partnership Act 1890[39] and the rule in *Garner v. Murray*.[40]

Borrowing money to fund capital contribution

17–11   It has already been seen[41] that if the firm borrows money, there cannot properly be said to have been an increase in its capital; *per contra* if individual partners borrow money on their own account and bring it into the firm *qua* capital.[42] Equally, whilst the members of a trading partnership will normally have implied authority to borrow money on behalf of the firm, that authority will not extend to loans taken out in order to fund their capital contributions.[43]

Interest on capital

17–12   Section 24(4) of the Partnership Act 1890 is quite explicit:

> "(4) A partner is not entitled, before the ascertainment of profits,[44] to interest on the capital subscribed by him."

This accorded with the previous law.[45]

---

[35] See *Heslin v. Hay* (1884) 15 L.R. Ir. 431, where an attempt was made to violate this principle; see also *Bouche v. Sproule* (1887) 12 App.Cas. 385, 405 *per* Lord Bramwell; *Re Bridgewater Navigation Co.* [1891] 2 Ch. 317, 327 *per* Lindley L.J.; *McClelland v. Hyde* [1942] N.Ir. 1, 6 *per* Andrews L.C.J. For an example of a case (not involving a partnership) in which damages were awarded for breach of an agreement not to withdraw capital from a business, see *Teacher v. Calder* [1899] A.C. 451, 467. *Quaere* would such a claim lie against a partner? See, as to such claims, *infra*, paras 23–208 *et seq*. See also, as to the tax implications of a contribution or reduction in capital, *infra*, paras 35–04, 35–05 (capital gains tax), 36–20, 36–21 (inheritance tax), 37–17 (value added tax), 38–09, 38–16, 38–17, 38–19 (stamp duty land tax).

[36] See *infra*, para. 24–87.

[37] Such instances are becoming increasingly rare, with many firms now relying more on bank financing than partners' capital.

[38] See *supra*, paras 10–157 *et seq*.

[39] See *infra*, para. 25–45.

[40] [1904] 1 Ch. 57. See further, *infra*, paras 25–50 *et seq*.

[41] See *supra*, para. 12–49.

[42] See *supra*, para. 10–66.

[43] See *supra*, paras 12–46, 13–19.

[44] These somewhat enigmatic words do not, by inference, suggest that interest on capital is normally payable *after* the ascertainment of profits. Note, however, that where such interest is payable, it is treated as an allocation of profits for income tax purposes: see *supra*, para. 10–67 and *infra*, para. 34–25.

[45] See *infra*, para. 20–34.

Accordingly, in those cases in which partners are to be entitled to interest on their respective capitals, *e.g.* where their contributions are disproportionate, it is essential that this is expressly provided for in the agreement.[46]

---

[46] See *supra*, para. 10–67.

CHAPTER 18

PARTNERSHIP PROPERTY

IN earlier editions of this work, this chapter was, somewhat inelegantly, entitled **18–01** "Joint and separate property", thereby reflecting the fundamental distinction between the joint estate of the firm and the respective separate estates of the partners, which is still of such importance in the event of the insolvency of the firm or of any one or more of the partners.[1] However, since the Partnership Act 1890 itself contains a section headed "Partnership property",[2] that is surely the more appropriate title, even though the expression "separate property" will still, for convenience, be used to denote property belonging to a partner.

Lord Lindley's definition

Lord Lindley defined partnership property in this way: **18–02**

"The expressions partnership property, partnership stock, partnership assets, joint stock, and joint estate,[3] are used indiscriminately to denote everything to which the firm, or in other words *all* the partners composing it, can be considered to be entitled as such. The qualification *as such* is important; for persons may be entitled jointly or in common to property, and the same persons may be partners, and yet that property may not be partnership property; *e.g.* if several persons are partners in trade, and land is devised or a legacy is bequeathed to them jointly or in common, it will not necessarily become partnership property and form part of the common stock in which they are interested as partners."[4]

In fact, with the development of the so-called "salaried" or "fixed share" partner, Lord Lindley's pure definition must now be qualified to take account of those cases in which assets are treated as partnership property even though one or more partners have no beneficial interest therein.[5] Although it might once have been argued that such assets cannot truly constitute partnership property, the current editor submits that any theoretical definition must ultimately give way to the clear intention and agreement of the parties[6] and the relevant assets be treated accordingly.

---

[1] See *infra*, paras 27–78 *et seq.*

[2] *ibid.* s.20, *infra*, para. 18–03.

[3] Lord Lindley observed in a footnote that "The expression joint estate sometimes has a wider signification, including all property which, on the bankruptcy of the firm, is distributable amongst its creditors." However, this comment was framed by reference to the (then) doctrine of reputed ownership, which has not been preserved under the Insolvency Act 1986: see *infra*, para. 27–98.

[4] *Morris v. Barrett* (1829) 3 Y. & J. 384; see also *Ex p. Fife Banking Co.* (1843) 6 Ir.Eq. 197 and, on appeal, *sub nom. Re Littles* (1847) 10 Ir.Eq. 275.

[5] In such cases, those partners who are interested in the assets are frequently styled "equity" partners.

[6] See the Partnership Act 1890, s.19, *supra*, paras 10–12 *et seq.* But *cf. supra*, para. 17–03.

Importance of agreement

18–03   As intimated in the previous paragraph, it is up to the partners to agree between themselves what assets are to be treated as partnership property.[7] In the absence of an express agreement, the relevant factors will generally be: (1) the circumstances of the acquisition, with particular reference to the source from which it was financed, (2) the purpose of the acquisition, and (3) the manner in which the asset has subsequently been dealt with. The importance of these factors, which are illustrated in many of the earlier cases, is firmly established by sections 20 and 21 of the Partnership Act 1890, which provide as follows:

> "20.—(1) All property and rights and interests in property originally brought into the partnership stock or acquired, whether by purchase or otherwise, on account of the firm, or for the purposes and in the course of the partnership business, are called in this Act partnership property, and must be held and applied by the partners exclusively for the purposes of the partnership and in accordance with the partnership agreement.[8]
>
> (2) Provided that the legal estate or interest in any land, or in Scotland the title to and interest in any heritable estate, which belongs to the partnership shall devolve according to the nature and tenure thereof, and the general rules of law thereto applicable, but in trust, so far as necessary, for the persons beneficially interested in the land under this section.[9]
>
> (3) Where co-owners of an estate or interest in any land, or in Scotland of any heritable estate, not being itself partnership property, are partners as to profits made by the use of that land or estate, and purchase other land or estate out of the profits to be used in like manner, the land or estate so purchased belongs to them, in the absence of an agreement to the contrary, not as partners, but as co-owners for the same respective estates and interests as are held by them in the land or estate first mentioned at the date of the purchase.
>
> 21. Unless the contrary intention appears, property bought with money belonging to the firm is deemed to have been bought on account of the firm."

18–04   Although these statutory rules will assist in determining what is and what is not partnership property when the intentions of the partners are not readily apparent, they cannot be applied in the face of a contrary agreement, whether express or implied.[10] Moreover, the status of a particular asset, once determined in accordance with the statutory rules, may subsequently be altered by agreement of the partners, so that what was partnership property may be converted into the separate property of one or more of the partners or vice versa.

18–05   It follows from the foregoing that any attempt to analyse what is and what is not partnership property requires a consideration of three separate (albeit inter-related) topics, *viz.*:

1. partnership property;

2. separate property;

3. agreements transferring assets from one class to the other.

---

[7] Note, however, the potential application of the Law of Property (Miscellaneous Provisions) Act 1989, s.2 (as amended): see *supra*, paras 7–02 *et seq*.

[8] Note, as to the operation of this sub-section, the exceptional decision in *Bourne v. Davis* [2006] EWHC 1567 (Ch) (Lawtel 22/6/07), noticed *infra*, para. 18–21.

[9] See, as to the effect of this proviso, *infra*, para. 18–63.

[10] Partnership Act 1890, s.19, *supra*, para. 10–12.

Attention will then be drawn to a number of points relating to the *legal* title to partnership property.

1.   PARTNERSHIP PROPERTY

Lord Lindley posited the following general rule: **18–06**

> "Whatever at the commencement of a partnership is thrown into the common stock, and whatever has from time to time during the continuance of the partnership been added thereto or obtained by means thereof, whether directly, by purchase or circuitously by employment in trade, belongs to the firm, unless the contrary can be shown."[11]

This is in fact the principle which is incorporated in section 20(1) of the Partnership Act 1890.[12] In appropriate circumstances, partnership property may comprise the shares in a company which, in commercial terms at least, carries on part (or even the whole) of the partnership business.[13]

It has already been seen that, where the terms of the partnership expressly or by necessary implication require one or more partners to introduce land as an asset of the firm, there may be no need to comply with the requirements of section 2 of the Law of Property (Miscellaneous Provisions) Act 1989.[14]

Property paid for by the firm

Lord Lindley said of such acquisitions: **18–07**

> "The mere fact that the property in question was purchased by one partner in his own name is immaterial, if it was paid for out of the partnership monies; for in such a case he will be deemed to hold the property in trust for the firm, unless he can show that

---

[11] See *Crawshay v. Collins* (1826) 15 Ves.Jr. 218; *Nerot v. Burnand* (1827) 4 Russ. 247, affirmed at (1828) 2 Bli. (N.S.) 215; *Bone v. Pollard* (1857) 24 Beav. 283. As to outlays of partnership money on the separate property of a partner, see *infra*, paras 20–31, 20–32.

[12] Note that, in *Dolley v. Ogunseitan* [2009] EWHC 1601 (Ch) (Lawtel 9/7/09), Alan Steinfeld Q.C., sitting as a deputy judge of the Chancery Division, held that so-called "seed money" contributed by one partner (A) amounted to part of the working capital of the partnership but did *not* constitute a partnership asset in the hands of the other partner (B): see *ibid.* at [39]. This finding should not be taken at face value: it was held that, on a true construction of the partnership agreement, A and B intended that B would have the use of the money for the purposes of its own business so was free to do with it what it wished. In that sense it had ceased to be partnership property impressed with the obligations set out in section 20(1).

[13] See *National Westminster Bank plc v. Jones* [2001] 1 B.C.L.C. 98; *Dyment v. Boyden* [2004] B.C.L.C. 423 at [5]; *Chahal v. Mahal*, September 30, 2004 (Lawtel 5/10/04), and, on appeal, at [2005] 2 B.C.L.C. 655. In the latter case, the *entire* partnership business had been transferred to and thereafter operated by the company. And note also *Reeves v. Sprecher* [2008] EWHC 583 (Ch) (Lawtel 2/4/08), albeit only a decision rejecting a summary judgment application.

[14] See *supra*, paras 7–02 *et seq.*

he holds it for himself alone.[15] Upon this principle it has been held that land purchased in the name of one partner, but paid for by the firm, is the property of the firm, although there may be no declaration or memorandum in writing disclosing the trust, and signed by the partner to whom the land has been conveyed.[16] So, if shares in a company are bought with partnership money, they will be partnership property, although they may be standing in the books of the company in the name of one partner only, and although it may be contrary to the company's deed of settlement[17] for more than one person to hold shares in it."[18]

This principle is given statutory force by the Partnership Act 1890.[19] Both in *Hardie's Executors v. Wales*[20] and *Simmons Gainsford LLP v. Shah*[21] it was held that policies taken out on the life of a partner and paid for by the firm were partnership property. The position would have been otherwise if the premiums had been treated as a drawing by the partner in question, even if the other partners were not aware of this.[22] Similarly in *Nadeem v. Rafiq*[23] business premises acquired using partnership funds were held to be partnership assets even though they had been purchased in the names of one partner and the wife of another partner.

Rebutting the statutory presumption

18–08   The statutory presumption that assets purchased with partnership money constitute partnership property may, of course, be rebutted. An obvious example is where the asset is vested in some or all of the partners upon express trusts which are inconsistent with it being partnership property.[24] The mere fact that the property is vested in the name of one partner is clearly not sufficient to rebut the presumption, especially where it is shown as a partnership asset in the firm's accounts.[25] Equally, if it can be shown that what appeared to be the firm's money

[15] See *per* Lord Eldon in *Smith v. Smith* (1880) 5 Ves.Jr. 189, 193; also *Robley v. Brooke* (1833) 7 Bli. (N.S.) 90; *Morris v. Barrett* (1829) 3 Y. & J. 384. And see *Helmore v. Smith* (1887) 35 Ch.D. 436. For a more recent example of the principle in action, see *Longmuir v. Moffat* [2009] S.C. 329.

[16] *Forster v. Hale* (1800) 5 Ves.Jr. 308; *Bathurst v. Scarborow* [2005] 1 P. & C.R. 58 (CA), noticed *infra*, para. 19–13, is another example, notwithstanding the fact that the partners had agreed to purchase the land in question as joint tenants; also *Mehra v. Shah*, August 1, 2003 (Lawtel 5/8/03) at [68], affirmed on appeal at [2004] EWCA Civ 632 (Lawtel 20/5/04). *cf.* the Law of Property Act 1925, s.53. If, however, the payment made by the firm is insignificant, *e.g.* the payment of a small amount of stamp duty, a trust in favour of the partnership would not necessarily arise: see *Hodson v. Cashmore* (1972) 226 E.G. 1203 (where, on the facts, a trust was established).

[17] Now the articles of association.

[18] *Ex p. Connell* (1838) 3 Deac. 201; *Ex p. Hinds* (1850) 3 De G. & Sm. 613. Lord Lindley then went on to consider a difficulty formerly presented, in the case of ships, by the ship registration Acts, but concluded that this difficulty would no longer arise: see generally, the 15th ed. of this work at p. 499.

[19] *ibid.* ss.20(1), 21, *supra*, para. 18–03.

[20] 2003 G.W.D. 13–448 (OH).

[21] [2008] EWHC 2554 (Ch) (Lawtel 24/10.08). Here the partnership business and assets had subsequently been transferred to an LLP. A similar result was achieved in the case of the second policy subject to the counterclaim in *Strover v. Strover, The Times,* May 30, 2005.

[22] *Pratt v. Medwin* [2003] 2 P. & C.R. D22 at [13]; *Strover v. Strover, supra* (the first policy in issue).

[23] [2007] EWHC 2959 (Ch) (Lawtel 2/1/08).

[24] It may, nevertheless, still be possible to show that the asset has subsequently *become* partnership property. Thus, in *Clark v. Kessell* (June 30, 1998, unreported), land subject to an express trust fell to be treated as a partnership asset by reason of an estoppel. See further, as to the transfer of property into and out of partnerships, *infra*, paras 18–44 *et seq.*

[25] *Longmuir v. Moffat* [2009] S.C. 329. See also *Marshall v. Marshall* 2007 Fam. L.R. 48 (OH).

was in fact lent by the firm to one of the partners and thus became *his* money prior to the acquisition, no trust in favour of the firm will arise.[26]

Land purchased by co-owners out of profits

Where co-owners of land[27] are partners in the profits produced by its use but **18–09** the land itself is not a partnership asset,[28] the general rule will not apply where *additional* land is purchased out of such profits. The statutory presumption in such a case is that the co-owners intended to acquire and hold the additional land in the same way as the original land.[29] In earlier editions of this work the operation of the presumption was illustrated (*inter alia*) by reference to the decision in *Davis v. Davis*[30]; however, no land was in fact acquired by the partners in that case.

The earlier decision in *Phillips v. Phillips*,[31] which was cited by Lord Lindley in this context, is something of an enigma. There, certain public houses had been devised to two persons who carried on a brewery business in partnership; it was (conventionally) held that those public houses were not assets of the firm, even though they were used for the purposes of its business. Moreover, it appears that certain mortgage debts secured on public houses were also bequeathed to the two partners and they later purchased the equities of redemption out of partnership funds: it was held that the equities followed the mortgage debts and thus again did not become partnership property. However, it was also held that other public houses, which had been purchased out of partnership funds and used for the purposes of its business, *did* belong to the firm.[32]

Rebutting the statutory presumption

The statutory presumption may be rebutted. An example of such case, decided **18–10** long before the Partnership Act 1890, is *Morris v. Barrett*,[33] where land had been devised to two persons as joint tenants and farmed by them for many years. Profits derived from the farming enterprise were paid into a joint fund to which they each had access, but no account was ever taken. Further land was purchased in the name of one partner out of the joint fund and farmed with the original land. It was held that, although the original land was not partnership property, the further land was.

---

[26] See *Smith v. Smith* (1880) 5 Ves.Jr. 189; also *Ex p. Emly* (1811) 1 Rose 61; *Walton v. Butler* (1861) 29 Beav. 428.

[27] This will include any interest in land.

[28] See further, *infra*, para. 18–26.

[29] Partnership Act 1890, s.20(3), *supra*, para. 18–03; see also *Steward v. Blakeway* (1869) L.R. 4 Ch.App. 603.

[30] [1894] 1 Ch. 393: see *infra*, para. 18–11.

[31] Details of this case are derived from a passage in *Bisset on Partnership* (1847), p. 50, which was based on the notes of one of the counsel appearing in the case. The report at (1832) 1 M. & K. 649 does not refer to the property devised. Lord Lindley observed: "Mr. Bisset considers the decision as an authority on the point of conversion. But if, as he represents, the Court came to the conclusion that the devised property was not in fact partnership property, the question of conversion would not have arisen. Compare *Waterer v. Waterer* (1873) L.R. 15 Eq. 402."

[32] See (1832) 1 M. & K. 649, 663. Lord Lindley considered that these public houses were "partnership property to all intents and purposes"; yet surely the decision of Sir John Leach M.R. is clear upon the point.

[33] (1829) 3 Y. & J. 384; also *Christie v. Christie* [1917] 1 I.R. 17. And see *infra*, paras 18–29, 18–30.

Scope of the statutory presumption

18–11   The statutory presumption is confined to the *purchase* of land and strictly does not apply to the improvement of land or to the acquisition of chattels and other assets. However, the court may, in certain circumstances, be prepared to apply the presumption by analogy, as in *Davis v. Davis.*[34] There a testator had devised his residuary estate, comprising his business, the freehold premises on which it was carried on, and some adjoining freehold premises, to his two sons as tenants in common. The sons carried on the business without any express agreement. On one occasion they mortgaged the adjoining premises and used the money raised to extend their workshops onto those premises; on another, they mortgaged the business premises and used the money in the business, mainly in the purchase of new plant and machinery. The premises on which the business was carried on were not particularly suitable for that purpose. It was held that the sons were partners in the business, but that none of the premises constituted partnership property. North J. recognised that, because no land was acquired, section 20(3) of the Partnership Act 1890 was strictly inapplicable, but observed that "the same law applies".[35]

It would also seem that the presumption may not apply where part of the original land is held by the co-owners as joint tenants and part as tenants in common.[36]

Circumstances of acquisition

18–12   In order to determine whether an asset acquired by a partner has in truth been acquired "on account of the firm, or for the purposes and in the course of its business",[37] all the surrounding circumstances must inevitably be taken into account.[38] Thus, where a partner had applied for the grant of a new tenancy under Part II of the Landlord and Tenant Act 1954 in respect of premises at which the firm carried on its business and it could be shown that all the partners (including the applicant) regarded the application as having been made by and for the benefit of the firm, just as had happened on a previous occasion, it was held that the tenancy, when acquired, was a partnership asset and that, on the death of the tenant partner, it vested in his personal representatives on trust for the benefit of the surviving partners.[39]

On the other hand, even though property was acquired in connection with the partnership business, it does not follow that it will necessarily belong to the firm. Thus, in *Kelly v. Kelly,*[40] a partner (A) held a fishing licence and abalone permit which was, on the facts, held not to have been introduced as a partnership asset. Abalone permits were then replaced by abalone authorities, which had to be attached to a particular boat. A applied for such an authority in respect of the boat used for the partnership business, which *was* a partnership asset. The annual

---

[34] [1894] 1 Ch. 393. *cf. Jackson v. Jackson* (1804) 9 Ves.Jr. 591; *Waterer v. Waterer* (1873) 15 Eq. 402: see further, *infra,* paras 18–29, 18–30.

[35] [1894] 1 Ch. 405.

[36] *Christie v. Christie* [1917] 1 I.R. 17, 36 *per* O'Connor M.R.

[37] Partnership Act 1890, s.20(1), *supra,* para. 18–03.

[38] See, for example, *Harwood v. Harwood* [1991] 2 F.L.R. 274.

[39] See *Hodson v. Cashmore* (1972) 226 E.G. 1203.

[40] (1990) 64 A.L.J.R. 234. See also *Lukin v. Lovrinov* [1998] S.A.S.C. 6614, which was a similar decision regarding the ownership of fishing quota.

renewal fees for the authority were treated as a partnership expense.[41] It was nevertheless held that the authority, like the licence which preceded it, remained the sole property of A.[42]

Property used by the firm

More difficult questions arise when an asset paid for by a partner has been used **18–13** by the firm and treated as its property. There is no presumption that it remains the property of the partner concerned, simply because he paid for it; in fact, the presumption is the reverse, *i.e.* that he has brought the asset in question "into the common stock".[43] In such a case, the crucial question is always: was the asset both used *and treated* as partnership property? Mere use in itself is usually insufficient to bring about a change in the status of such an asset.[44] This principle has, in particular, been applied in the case of goodwill[45] and a lease of premises from which a firm carried on business.[46]

Secret and other benefits obtained by a partner

It has been already seen that property acquired by a partner in breach of the **18–14** duty of good faith which he owes to his co-partners will be treated as acquired for the benefit of all the partners and must be accounted for to the firm[47]; it is, however, questionable whether such property constitutes a partnership asset in the acquiring partner's hands on acquisition[48] or only when accounted for to the

---

[41] The court rejected the argument that payment of such fees should be regarded as the purchase price for the authority.

[42] Equally, a rock lobster licence in respect of another boat owned by the partnership, which had been applied for and held in the name of the other partner, *was* held to be a partnership asset. It appears that the value of this licence was reflected in the partnership accounts, whilst the value of the abalone authority was not.

[43] See *Ex p. Hare* (1835) 1 Deac. 16, 25 *per* Sir J. Cross; also the Partnership Act 1890, s.20(1) *supra*, para. 18–03. And see, in this context, the unusual decision in *Faulks v. Faulks* [1992] 1 E.G.L.R. 9, noted *infra*, para. 18–19.

[44] Note, however, that the partners may acquire limited *rights* in respect of such an asset: see *supra*, para. 10–45 and *infra*, para. 18–34. As to the position where the asset is improved by expenditure financed by the firm or by one or more of the non-owning partners, see *infra*, paras 18–38 *et seq.*

[45] *Miles v. Clarke* [1953] 1 W.L.R. 537: see *infra*, para. 18–36.

[46] *Gian Singh v. Devraj Nahar* [1965] 1 W.L.R. 412; *Eardley v. Broad*, The Times, April 28, 1970 and (1970) 215 E.G. 823, *infra*, para. 18–34. See also *Barton v. Morris* [1985] 1 W.L.R. 1257 (where both partners were in any event co-owners).

[47] See *supra*, paras 16–13 *et seq.*

[48] Lord Lindley put it thus: "Whatever property has been so acquired, will be treated as obtained for the benefit of all the partners, and as being part of the assets of the firm." If it is such an asset, the acquiring partner will be bound to deliver it up to the liquidator in the event of the firm being wound up as an unregistered company: Insolvency Act 1986, s.234(2), as amended, where there are no concurrent petitions, by the Insolvent Partnerships Order 1994, Sched. 3, Pt II, para. 9 and applied by the Insolvency Act 1986, s.221(5) (as itself amended by the Insolvent Partnerships Order 1994, art. 7(1), (2), Sched. 3, Pt I, para. 3 (creditor's petition) and *ibid.* art. 9(a), Sched. 5, para. 2 (member's petition)) and as amended, where there *are* concurrent petitions, by *ibid.* Sched. 4, Pt II, para. 27 and applied by the Insolvency Act 1986, s.221(5) (as itself amended by the Insolvent Partnerships Order 1994, art. 8(1) (as amended by the Insolvent Partnerships (Amendment) Order 2002 (SI 2002/1308), art. 4(1)), (2), Sched. 4, Pt I, para. 3 (creditor's petition), and *ibid.* art. 10(1)(a), Sched. 6, para. 4 (member's petition)). See also, *infra*, para. 27–65. Moreover, no period of limitation will normally apply as regards such an asset, at least while the partnership continues: see *infra*, paras 23–32 *et seq.* As to the position where a partner holds an asset on trust for the firm, see *infra*, para. 23–43.

firm.[49] Precisely the same rule applies to property acquired by a continuing or surviving partner in breach of the duty owed to a former partner or to the representatives of a deceased partner, so long as he or they retain an interest in the partnership assets.[50]

The position will be otherwise if there is no breach of duty and the benefit is unconnected with the partnership or, though connected, is conferred on the partner *personally*. Thus, if one partner holds a lease of property to which the firm is entitled only for so long as the partnership continues[51] and that lease is sold or renewed following a dissolution, the proceeds of sale or the renewed lease (as the case may be) will belong not to the firm but to the partner in whom the lease is, by reason of such dissolution, exclusively vested.[52] Similarly, in the case of compensation payable to two out of three partners following the capture of their ship during a time of war, where the third partner, as an alien enemy, was expressly excluded from sharing therein.[53]

Property acquired after dissolution

18–15   Assets acquired by a partner whilst the affairs of a dissolved firm are still in the course of being wound up will not necessarily be regarded as partnership property, even though that partner has continued to carry on the firm's business without the consent of his former partners. In any such case, it will prima facie be necessary for the court to order an inquiry, with a view to identifying those assets which were, or which can properly be said to represent,[54] partnership property as at the date of dissolution and those which have subsequently been acquired by the partner concerned out of his own moneys. This is demonstrated by the decision in *Nerot v. Burnand*.[55] There Lord Chancellor Lyndhurst affirmed

[49] In earlier editions of this work, it was submitted that such property only becomes a partnership asset *when recovered* and that, until then, the relationship is arguably that of debtor and creditor. Reference was made to the decision in *Gordon v. Scott* (1858) 12 Moo. P.C. 1 (which concerned a partnership, but which does not otherwise appear to support the proposition) and to the following non-partnership cases: *Lister & Co. v. Stubbs* (1890) 45 Ch.D. 1; *Re Thorpe* [1891] 2 Ch. 360; *Archer's Case* [1892] 1 Ch. 322; *Powell and Thomas v. Evan Jones & Co.* [1905] 1 K.B. 11. Now, of course, *Lister & Co. v. Stubbs* has been disapproved by the Privy Council in *Att.-Gen. for Hong Kong v. Reid* [1994] 1 A.C. 324, which would seem to suggest that Lord Lindley's view (see *supra*, n. 48) was correct; see also *Daraydan Holdings Ltd. v. Solland International Ltd.* [2005] Ch. 119. In any event, it should be noted that the other partners' interest in the property may be defeated by laches so that, even if it *does* constitute a partnership asset from the outset, that status is by no means absolute: see *supra*, para. 16–24 and *infra*, paras 23–19 *et seq.*

[50] See, as to outgoing partners, the decision in *Pathirana v. Pathirana* [1967] 1 A.C. 233, noted *supra*, para. 16–27; as to deceased partners, see the Partnership Act 1890, s.29(2), *supra*, para. 16–14.

[51] See *Rye v. Rye* [1962] A.C. 496; *Gian Singh & Co. v. Devraj Nahar* [1965] 1 W.L.R. 412; *Eardley v. Broad*, The Times, April 28, 1970 and (1970) 215 E.G. 823; *Faulks v. Faulks* [1992] 1 E.G.L.R. 9.

[52] See *Burdon v. Barkus* (1861) 3 Giff. 412, affirmed at (1862) 4 De G.F. & J. 42; *Bevan v. Webb* [1905] 1 Ch. 620, 631 *per* Warrington J. See also *supra*, paras 16–20 *et seq.*

[53] *Campbell v. Mullett* (1819) 2 Swan. 551. In that case, the captured ship was a partnership asset. See also *Thompson v. Ryan* (1817) 2 Swan. 565n.; *Moffat v. Farquharson* (1788) 2 Bro.C.C. 338; *Burnand v. Rodocanachi* (1882) 7 App.Cas. 333.

[54] *Quaere* whether, where a partner sells partnership property and reinvests the proceeds in the purchase of other property, he can properly claim the latter as his own. It is tentatively thought not, but see the decisions referred in the next two footnotes. However, the current editor doubts whether this argument could be sustained where a partner has used both his own and partnership money to acquire an asset.

[55] (1827) 4 Russ. 247, affirmed at (1828) 2 Bli. (N.S.) 215; see also *Payne v. Hornby* (1858) 25 Beav. 280.

an order for the sale of a freehold hotel property (which was, on the facts, held to be partnership property), but declined to uphold an order requiring a sale of all the stock in trade and other effects on the premises at the time of the order appealed from, without inquiring whether they did in fact belong to the partnership at the dissolution date.[56]

Similarly, whilst certain boxing promotion and management contracts held on trust for the firm which had been renewed in the course of winding up its affairs were held to be partnership property in *Don King Productions Inc. v. Warren*,[57] contracts entered into with *new* boxers were not. No such distinction was, however, required to be drawn in *John Taylors v. Masons*,[58] where two partners had brought about the dissolution of their firm with a view to securing the grant of a *new* licence to occupy the existing partnership premises in connection with their proposed business as livestock auctioneers. They first obtained a provisional licence, then a full three-year licence following an open tender process in which the other former partners participated. Despite this, they were held accountable to the dissolved firm, *inter alia*, for the value of the goodwill which existed in the opportunity to secure the new licences.

Intangible assets

It might be thought that assets of an intangible nature would give rise to   **18–16** particular difficulties in terms of their ownership. However, as the Court of Appeal made clear in *Don King Productions Inc. v. Warren*,[59] use of the trust concept will enable the benefit of almost any asset to be held as partnership property, even if it is incapable of being held by or transferred to the firm. In that case, it was held that the benefit of certain boxing promotion and management contracts into which the defendant had entered were, notwithstanding their personal nature, to be treated as partnership property. Other examples will be found in the following paragraphs.

Goodwill

In so far as the goodwill and name of a firm has a pecuniary value, it is capable   **18–17** of constituting and, in most cases, will constitute partnership property.[60] This will

---

[56] See also *Ex p. Morley* (1873) L.R. 8 Ch.App. 1026, where a surviving partner had continued the business and sold the stock in trade: it was held that the new stock in trade formed part of his separate estate; *Sobell v. Boston* [1975] 1 W.L.R. 1587. *cf. Pathirana v. Pathirana* [1967] 1 A.C. 233, *supra*, para. 16–27.

[57] [2000] Ch. 291 (CA). See further, *supra*, paras 13–65, 16–27 and *infra*, paras 18–16, 23–198.

[58] [2001] EWCA Civ 2106 (CA).

[59] [2000] Ch. 291. See also *Pathirana v. Pathirana* [1967] 1 A.C. 233 (PC); *Swift v. Dairywise Farms Ltd.* [2000] 1 W.L.R. 1177, noted *infra*, para. 18–19. *cf. Sew Hoy v. Sew Hoy* [2001] 1 N.Z.L.R. 391 (CA, New Zealand), where the asset was a mere expectancy.

[60] The firm name may be an asset along with its associated goodwill, as in the case of the "heavy metal" band Saxon: *Byford v. Oliver* [2003] E.M.L.R. 20; also *Gill v Frankie Goes To Hollywood Ltd.* [2008] E.T.M.R. 4 (OHIM, Opposition Division). *cf. McPhail v. Bourne* [2008] EWHC 1235 (Ch) (Lawtel 13/6/08) at [287], where Morgan J. held that there was no or only *de minimis* goodwill attached to the name, so that it could not constitute partnership property. Note, however, that no partnership was actually found to exist in this case, so that observation was strictly *obiter*.

be so even if, as in the case of National Health Service goodwill,[61] such
pecuniary value is incapable of being realised.

Where a firm establishes a new business and thereby generates its own
goodwill, such goodwill will almost inevitably be a partnership asset.[62] Whilst
the position may be the same where a partnership is formed in order to carry on
an *existing* business,[63] there is no such inevitability about the result: in such a
case it will be necessary to consider all the circumstances, including the conduct
of the partners and, where relevant, the anticipated duration of the
partnership.[64]

Offices and appointments

18–18   Offices and appointments held by partners frequently give rise to difficulty.
Although it may be wrong to speak of a particular office or appointment as a
partnership asset,[64a] especially if, as will often be the case, it is not in the
disposition of the firm,[65] nevertheless it may properly be regarded as held on
behalf and for the benefit of the firm, which in real terms amounts to the same
thing.[66] Thus, in *Collins v. Jackson*,[67] various appointments were held by a
partner in a firm of solicitors[68] and the question arose whether the fees, etc.,
derived therefrom belonged to the partnership. No written agreement covered the
point, but there was a memorandum relating to a number of other appointments
retained by the father of one of the partners when he retired from practice. In the
circumstances, it was held that all the appointments in question were to be treated
as held on behalf of both partners, and not for the exclusive benefit of the
holder.[69]

There will be less doubt if the fees, etc., derived from the office or appointment
are paid to the firm rather than to the office holder: in such a case, the office in
question will be treated as held for the benefit of the firm and any duties

[61] See the National Health Service Act 2006, s.259, Sched. 21 and the decisions in *Whitehill v.
Bradford* [1952] Ch. 236; *Macfarlane v. Kent* [1965] 1 W.L.R. 1019; *Anthony v. Rennie* 1981, S.L.T
(Notes) 11; *Hensman v. Traill, The Times*, October 22, 1980; *Kerr v. Morris* [1987] Ch. 90. See also
infra, para. 23–200.

[62] See *Steuart v. Gladstone* (1879) 10 Ch.D. 626; *Hunter v. Dowling* [1895] 2 Ch. 223; *Jennings
v. Jennings* [1898] 1 Ch. 378. See also *supra*, paras 10–49, 10–192 *et seq.*

[63] This may, depending on the circumstances, also include any case where a new firm is constituted
by the admission of one or more additional partners to an *existing* firm.

[64] See *Miles v. Clarke* [1953] 1 W.L.R. 537, *infra*, para. 18–36; *Stekel v. Ellice* [1973] 1 W.L.R.
191.

[64a] This, nevertheless, appears to have been the terminology used in *Uppal v. Revenue & Customs
Commissioners* [2010] UKFTT 215 (TC) [2010] S.T.I. 2382.

[65] Note, however, that, in the case of insolvency appointments held by partners, the court may
recognise that the firm has an effective proprietary interest therein: see *Re A & C Supplies Ltd.* [1998]
1 B.C.L.C. 603; *Clements v. Udal* [2001] B.C.C. 658; *Cork v. Rolph, The Times*, December 21, 2000.
And see also *supra*, para. 10–52.

[66] See, generally, *Don King Productions Inc. v. Warren* [2000] Ch. 291 (CA), noted *supra*, para.
18–16.

[67] (1862) 31 Beav. 645.

[68] The particular positions held were: clerk to Poor Law guardians, superintendent registrar of
births, marriages and deaths, treasurer of a turnpike trust, steward of a manor, treasurer of a charity,
and receiver of tithes.

[69] See also *Smith v. Mules* (1852) 9 Hare 556; *Ambler v. Bolton* (1871) L.R. 14 Eq. 427; *Casson
Beckman & Partners v. Papi* [1991] B.C.L.C. 299, 310f–h *per* Balcombe L.J. See also *infra*, para.
23–198, as to the position on a dissolution.

associated therewith performed in the course of its business, notwithstanding the fact that the firm, as such, could not hold such an office.[70]

The tax treatment of fees received by partners in respect of offices and appointments held on behalf of the firm will be noticed later in this work.[71]

Milk quota

The decision in *Faulks v. Faulks*[72] raised doubts as to whether milk quota was an asset which could be owned by a partnership independently of the land to which it related. There two brothers, John and Harry Faulks, were farming certain land in partnership. The agreement provided that the tenancy of that land, which was held by John Faulks and in respect of which quota was allocated to the firm, should only be held on trust for the firm during the continuance of the partnership. Harry Faulks died and the partnership was duly determined. It was held that the firm's equitable interest in the tenancy ceased on Harry's death and that the quota thereupon passed to John. As a result, the value of the quota fell to be ignored when calculating the price to be paid for Harry's share under the terms of an option contained in the agreement. However, the doubts so raised were, seemingly, resolved by *Swift v. Dairywise Farms Ltd.*,[73] where it was held that *Faulks v. Faulks* turned on its own particular facts[74] and that there was no reason why milk quota should not be held on trust for a third party, in the same way as any other asset.[75] Equally it is now provided by regulation that quota may be transferred independently of the land to which it relates.[76]

18–19

Other forms of quota

There is no reason why the same principles should not be applied in the case of other forms of quota, although courts appear to be unaccountably reluctant to infer that quota is to be treated as a partnership asset.[77]

18–20

Copyright and performer's property rights

Even if a copyright developed by a partner is regarded as partnership property, legal title may still be vested in that partner, barring an assignment to the firm.[78]

In *Bourne v. Davis*,[79] it was held that performer's property rights under the Copyright, Designs and Patents Act 1988, Pt II were *capable* of constituting

18–21

[70] See *Kirkintilloch Equitable Co-operative Society Ltd. v. Livingstone* 1972 S.L.T. 154; *Casson Beckman & Partners v. Papi* [1991] B.C.L.C. 299 (which concerned the office of liquidator held by a *salaried* partner); note, in particular, the nature of the expert evidence given in the latter case: see *ibid.* p. 302b–d. *cf. Osborne & Hunter Ltd. v. Hardie Caldwell (No. 2)* 2001 G.W.D. 4–174 (OH).

[71] See *infra*, paras 34–23, 37–18, 37–19.

[72] [1992] 1 E.G.L.R. 9; see also *Davies v. H.&R. Eckroyd Ltd.* [1996] 2 E.G.L.R. 5. It does not follow that milk quota is not transferable: see *Harries v. Barclays Bank plc* [1997] 2 E.G.L.R. 15 (CA).

[73] [2000] 1 W.L.R. 1177. An appeal ultimately went off on other grounds: [2003] 1 W.L.R. 1606.

[74] See also *Don King Productions Inc. v. Warren* [2000] Ch. 291, at [24] *per* Morritt L.J.

[75] See further *supra*, para. 18–16.

[76] See the Dairy Produce Quotas Regulations 2005 (SI 2005/465), reg. 13 (as amended by the Dairy Produce Quotas (Amendment) Regulations 2008 (SI 2008/439), reg. 2, Sched., para. 4).

[77] See *Kelly v. Kelly* (1990) 64 A.L.J.R. 234, noted *supra*, para. 18–12; *Lukin v. Lovrinov* [1998] S.A.S.C. 6614.

[78] See *Tayplan Ltd. v. D&A Contracts* [2005] CSOH 17 (OH) at [26].

[79] [2006] EWHC 1567 (Ch) (Lawtel 22/6/07).

partnership property but that section 20(1) of the Partnership Act 1890, if applicable, would only confer a right on the other members of the partnership to have the property applied for its benefit and would "not create a beneficial interest for the partnership in respect of partnership property".[80] This result is conceptually perplexing and can only be explained (if at all) by reference to the statutory rights which the 1988 Act confers on each individual performer.

Successive partnerships

18–22   Where one partnership succeeds another,[81] it will obviously be a question of fact whether the assets of the first partnership have become assets of the second. However, a claim by one partner against another in relation to the first partnership is unlikely to be regarded as having become an asset of the second and, as a matter of law, cannot be so regarded if both partners are members of the second partnership.[82] Similarly in the case of a debt due from one partner to another.[83]

Outgoing partners

18–23   It goes without saying that, where a partner holds an asset which belongs to the firm, its status will not change when he ceases to be a member of the firm, absent some agreement which entitles him to the asset beneficially. Indeed, it has been observed that, in such a case, the fiduciary duties of the outgoing partner if anything intensify when he leaves the firm.[84]

2.   SEPARATE PROPERTY

18–24   It was noted at the outset that this and the previous section are interrelated: accordingly, certain rules for identifying what constitutes the separate property of the individual partners have already been noticed in that section. Any agreement between the partners is, of course, paramount[85] but in most cases where the status of a particular asset is in dispute there will be little tangible evidence of such an agreement, as illustrated by the various cases referred to in subsequent paragraphs.

Property producing partnership profits

18–25   The mere fact that there is a partnership in the profits produced by a certain asset does not, in itself, indicate that the asset is partnership property. Numerous

[80] *ibid.* at [28] *per* Mark Herbert Q.C. sitting as a deputy judge of the Chancery Division.

[81] For this purpose, it is assumed that the two partnerships are not, as a matter of contract, treated as one and the same: see *supra*, paras 10–39, 10–40.

[82] *Global Partners Fund Ltd. v. Babcock & Brown Ltd.* [2010] NSWSC 270, especially at [88] *per* Hammerschlag J. The appeal went off on other grounds: see [2010] NSWCA 196. Clearly the partnership cannot have a claim against one of the partners, since that partner would be forced to proceed against himself.

[83] *Patel v. Patel* [2008] EWCA Civ 1520 (Lawtel 7/4/08) (CA) at [7] *per* May L.J.

[84] *Simmons Gainsford LLP v. Shah* [2008] EWHC 2554 (Ch) (Lawtel 24/10/08) at [31] *per* Sales J. Note that this remark was *obiter* and made in the context of retirement from an LLP.

[85] See *supra*, para. 18–03.

cases on one or other side of the line may be imagined, but Lord Lindley cited the following examples:

> "To take an old example, coach-proprietors who horse a coach and divide the profits, may each make use of horses which belong to himself alone and not to the firm of proprietors.[86] So, where a merchant employs a broker to buy goods for him and to sell them again on his account, although it may be agreed that the profits are to be divided, the goods themselves, and the money arising from their sale, are the property of the merchant, and not the joint property of himself and the broker[87]; and it not infrequently happens that dormant partners have no interest in anything except the profits accruing to the firm to which they belong."[88]

A more recent illustration is perhaps to be found in the case of a landowner and a builder who agree to develop and sell land and to share the resulting profit.[89]

Co-owners sharing profits

The position may be less clear in those cases where co-owners become partners in respect of the profits produced by their jointly owned property,[90] in view of the complete identity between the partners and the co-owners. However, the current editor submits that the same general principle applies, *i.e.* the mere fact that profits and expenses are shared is not, of itself, sufficient to change the status of an asset. Lord Lindley recognised this: **18–26**

> "Suppose, for example, that two or more joint tenants, or tenants in common of a farm or a mine, work their common property together as partners, contributing to the expenses and sharing all profits and losses equally, there will certainly be a partnership; and yet, unless there is something more in the case, it seems that the land will not be partnership property, but will belong to the partners as co-owners, just as if they were not partners at all."[91]

This would also seem to be an incidental effect of section 2(1) of the Partnership Act 1890, which provides: **18–27**

> "Joint tenancy, tenancy in common, joint property, common property or part ownership does not of itself create a partnership as to anything so held or owned, whether the tenants or owners do or do not share any profits made by the use thereof."[92]

A case cited by Lord Lindley as falling within this class was *Brown v. Oakshot*[93] where, in essence, two sons used certain land, the reversion to which had been

---

[86] As in *Barton v. Hanson* (1809) 2 Taunt. 49; *Fromont v. Coupland* (1824) 2 Bing. 170.

[87] *Meyer v. Sharpe* (1813) 5 Taunt. 74; *Smith v. Watson* (1824) 2 B. & C. 401; *Burnell v. Hunt* (1841) 5 Jur. 650.

[88] See *Ex p. Hamper* (1811) 17 Ves.Jr. 403; *Ex p. Chuck* (1831) Mont. 373. The position is the same in the case of "salaried" and "fixed share" partners: see *supra*, para. 18–02.

[89] This seems to be implicit in the decision in *Walker West Developments Ltd. v. F.J. Emmett Ltd.* (1979) 252 E.G. 1171.

[90] See further, as to such cases, *supra*, paras 5–07 *et seq.*

[91] See *Crawshay v. Maule* (1818) 1 Swan. 495; *Roberts v. Eberhardt* (1853) Kay 148; also *Williams v. Williams* (1867) L.R. 2 Ch.App. 294.

[92] The principal purpose of this subsection is, of course, to avoid any prima facie implication of partnership as between co-owners: see *supra*, paras 5–03 *et seq.*

[93] (1857) 24 Beav. 254; see also *Morris v. Barrett* (1829) 3 Y & J. 384, *supra*, para. 18–10; *Phillips v. Phillips* (1832) 1 M. & K. 649, *supra*, para. 18–09.

devised to them jointly by their father, in carrying on his brewing business in partnership. In an *obiter* part of the decision, it was held that the reversion continued to belong to the sons as joint tenants and not as tenants in common (in which capacity they would necessarily have held the reversion if it had become partnership property).[94]

The "accessory" principle

18–28   Land may nevertheless, in certain circumstances, fall to be treated as partnership property where it is acquired solely for the purposes of the partnership business and there is some indication of the co-owners' intention to treat it as partnership property, or, as it was put in earlier editions of this work:

> "the land is merely accessory to the trade and is treated as part of the common stock."[95]

Land devised to co-owners for purposes of trade

18–29   The "accessory" principle is well illustrated by and, in fact, originates from a number of cases involving the devise of a business and land to be used for the purpose of carrying it on. In *Jackson v. Jackson*[96] a testator had, in effect, devised his business and land to his two sons jointly, with a view to them carrying on that business after his death.[97] They did so as partners. Lord Eldon held that the land had become partnership property, so that the joint tenancy was severed.[98] There was some evidence to show that the sons regarded the land as partnership property; moreover, as Lord Lindley pointed out:

> " . . . there was also this peculiarity, that a trading business was left to them, and that the land was accessory to that trade; so that it was very difficult, as observed by the Lord Chancellor, to sever the profits from the land and to hold the devisees to be partners as to the former, but not as to the latter."

A similar case was *Crawshay v. Maule*,[99] where certain mines were devised for the express purpose of being worked by the beneficiaries in partnership. The mines were worked in that way and were accordingly held to be partnership property.

18–30   In *Waterer v. Waterer*,[100] a nurseryman who carried on business with his sons, although not in partnership, left his residuary estate, including the goodwill of his business and the nursery ground, to his sons as tenants in common. After his death, the sons carried on the business in partnership and completed the purchase of additional land which the father had previously contracted to buy for the purposes of the business, paying for it out of moneys in the estate. One son then died and the others bought out his share, partly with money raised by a mortgage of the nursery ground and again partly out of moneys in the estate. On the death of one of the surviving sons, it was held that all the land, including the nursery ground, had become partnership property.

[94] See *infra*, para. 19–13.
[95] See *Steward v. Blakeway* (1869) L.R. 4 Ch.App. 603.
[96] (1804) 9 Ves.Jr. 591. *cf.* the cases cited *supra*, para. 18–27, n. 93.
[97] Details of the devise are set out at (1802) 7 Ves.Jr. 535.
[98] See further, as to implied severance, *infra*, para. 19–13.
[99] (1818) 1 Swan. 495.
[100] (1873) L.R. 15 Eq. 402. See also *Davies v. Games* (1879) 12 Ch.D. 813.

Land acquired for purposes of trade

As is demonstrated by the case last cited, the "accessory" principle may also **18–31** be applied in the case of land acquired for the purposes of a trade *otherwise* than pursuant to a devise. Lord Lindley stated the position in this way:

> "By a slight extension of the same principle, if several persons take a lease of a colliery, in order to work the colliery as partners, and they do so work it, the lease will be partnership property.[101] So, if co-owners of land form a partnership, and the land is merely accessory to their trade, and is treated as part of the common stock of the firm, the land will be partnership property."[102]

To this statement should be added one important qualification, namely that there must be no indication that what is treated as forming part of the common stock is an interest in the land *less* than the co-owners' full interest.

As will be seen hereafter,[103] if the land is acquired by one partner, to the exclusion of the others, the position will be very different, in the absence of evidence indicating that partner's intention to treat the land as partnership property.[104]

Land purchased by co-owners out of profits

It has already been seen that, if the land is not partnership property but profits **18–32** derived from its use are applied in purchasing additional land, there is a statutory presumption that such additional land does *not* constitute partnership property.[105]

Property used for partnership purposes

Lord Lindley observed that: **18–33**

> " . . . it by no means follows that property used by all the partners for partnership purposes is partnership property. For example, the house and land in and upon which the partnership business is carried on often belongs to one of the partners only, either subject to a lease to the firm, or without any lease at all."[106]

---

[101] *Faraday v. Wightwick* (1829) 1 R. & M. 45. See also *Bentley v. Bates* (1840) 4 Y. & C. Ex. 182.

[102] *Essex v. Essex* (1855) 20 Beav. 442. *cf. Steward v. Blakeway* (1869) L.R. 4 Ch.App. 603. See also *Rye v. Rye* [1962] A.C. 496; *Barton v. Morris* [1985] 1 W.L.R. 1257. If the beneficial interests in the land do not change when it becomes partnership property, no question can arise as to the need for a written disposition under the Law of Property Act 1925, s.53(1)(c). See also, *infra*, para. 18–44.

[103] See *infra*, paras 18–33 *et seq.*

[104] Merely showing the land as an asset in the partnership balance sheet may not, in itself, be enough: see *Barton v. Morris* [1985] 1 W.L.R. 1257; *Amin v. Amin* [2009] EWHC 3356 (Ch) (Lawtel 5/1/10). See further, *infra*, para. 18–56.

[105] Partnership Act 1890, s.20(3), *supra*, paras 18–03, 18–09.

[106] This passage was quoted with approval by Lord Pearce and applied by the Privy Council in *Gian Singh & Co. v. Devraj Nahar* [1965] 1 W.L.R. 412; see also *Eardley v. Broad, The Times*, April 28, 1970 and (1970) 215 E.G. 823, *infra*, para. 18–34; *Harrison-Broadley v. Smith* [1964] 1 W.L.R. 456; *Harvey v. Harvey* [1970] 120 C.L.R. 529; *Barton v. Morris* [1985] 1 W.L.R. 1257; *Latchman v. Pickard* [2005] EWHC 1011 (Ch) (Lawtel 12/5/05). See further, as to the rights which may be implied in favour of the firm, in a case where land is held not to have become partnership property, *supra*, para. 10–45 and, *infra*, para. 18–34.

Land

18–34   It has already been seen that, in some cases, land may belong to *all* the partners, but solely in the capacity of co-owners.[107] Indeed, the land may even be owned in shares different to those in which the co-owners share profits or, indeed, surplus assets within the firm.[108] The mere fact that the land forms the substratum of the partnership business and that the firm is debited with the outgoings is not, of itself, sufficient to make it partnership property.[109] This is clearly demonstrated by *Eardley v. Broad*,[110] where the deed governing a farming partnership between a father and son stated that the partnership "capital" was to consist of the stock, machinery and other "assets" of the farming business carried on by the father at certain premises, but did not specifically refer to the lease of those premises. Nield J. held that, even though the rent had been paid by the firm and the premises were indispensable to its business, there was no ground for inferring an assignment of the lease to the firm.

   If the land itself does not become partnership property, it would seem that no tenancy in favour of the firm can, as a matter of law, be inferred.[111] However, each partner will normally be regarded as entitled to a non-exclusive licence to enter the land for the purposes of carrying on the partnership business,[112] although that licence will be a personal right and will not as such belong to the firm.[113]

Assets other than land

18–35   Cases in which assets other than land, *e.g.* office furniture and equipment, are used by the firm but remain the separate property of a partner, are occasionally encountered. Thus, in *Ex p. Owen*,[114] Bowers carried on business as a grocer, provision dealer, and wine merchant and had certain stock in trade and household furniture at his business premises. He took in two partners, who were entitled to share in profits but who neither contributed capital nor paid a premium. No formal agreement was entered into. Bowers purchased new stock in the name of the firm and for the purposes of its business, but paid for it out of his own moneys. The firm then went bankrupt and questions arose as to the ownership of both the stock and the furniture. It was held, on

---

[107] See *supra*, paras 18–26, 18–27.

[108] As in *Rye v. Rye* [1962] A.C. 496. See also *Brown v. Oakshot* (1857) 24 Beav. 254, *supra*, para. 18–27. See further, as to the significance of the partners' asset surplus sharing ratios, *supra*, para. 17–04 and *infra*, paras 19–05 *et seq*.

[109] This sentence was cited with approval by Lord Kingarth in *Knapdale (Nominees) Ltd. v. Donald* 2000 S.C.L.R. 1013, 1021C (OH).

[110] *The Times*, April 28, 1970 and (1970) 215 E.G. 823. See also *Gian Singh & Co. v. Devraj Nahar* [1965] 1 W.L.R. 412; *Re John's Assignment Trusts* [1970] 1 W.L.R. 955; *Barton v. Morris* [1985] 1 W.L.R. 1257. And note also *Parker v. Hills* (1861) 7 Jur.(N.S.) 833 (lease of saltworks).

[111] *Rye v. Rye* [1962] A.C. 496. It is submitted that *Pocock v. Carter* [1912] 1 Ch. 663 (where a tenancy was inferred) is no longer good law. It is equally impermissible to infer an exclusive licence under the Agricultural Holdings Act 1986, s.2 (where that is still of relevance): *Harrison-Broadley v. Smith* [1964] 1 W.L.R. 456; *cf. Harrison v. Wing* [1988] 29 E.G. 101, 103, where a contrary view appears to be expressed. However, it seems that the point may not have been fully argued, since their Lordships made no reference to the decision in *Harrison-Broadley v. Smith*. See also *Bahamas International Trust Co. Ltd. v. Threadgold* [1974] 1 W.L.R. 1514.

[112] *Harrison-Broadley v. Smith, supra. cf. Latchman v. Pickard* [2005] EWHC 1011 (Ch) (Lawtel 12/5/05). See further *supra*, para. 10–45.

[113] Note, however, that each partner's licence will only subsist as long as he remains a member of the firm. And see *infra*, para. 25–04.

[114] (1851) 4 De G. & Sm. 351. See also *Pilling v. Pilling* (1887) 3 De G.J. & S. 162.

the available evidence, that there was an express or implied agreement that all the stock should belong to the firm, but that Bowers would be credited with the value of any items which belonged to him or for which he had paid. However, there were no grounds for making a similar inference in the case of the furniture, which was held to have remained in the ownership of Bowers alone and thus formed part of his separate estate.

A similar case was *Miles v. Clarke*.[115] There the claimant and the defendant **18–36** carried on a photography business as partners at will. The claimant, who was well-known in the field, brought his goodwill into the partnership; the leasehold premises, furniture and studio equipment belonged to the defendant. Both partners contributed to the stock in trade. They had originally intended to enter into a formal partnership agreement under which all such property would be brought into the partnership but no terms, other than as to the sharing of profits, were ever finally agreed. On the dissolution of the partnership, it was held that no terms ought to be implied except those required to give business efficacy to the arrangement; accordingly, only the consumable items of stock in trade actually used in the business were to be regarded as partnership assets.

A more recent example is to be found in *Broadhurst v. Broadhurst*,[116] where it was held that certain cars, which were to be sold by the partnership and the profits of which were to be shared by the partners, had not become partnership assets and remained in the ownership of a company established by one of them.

It appears from these cases that, as a general rule, stock in trade is more likely to be treated as partnership property than other chattels used in the business.[117] Reference should also be made in this context to the decision in *Kelly v. Kelly*,[118] although the circumstances there were, perhaps, exceptional.

Capital contribution in form of assets

It should be noted in this context that, once a partner has brought an asset into **18–37** the firm by way of capital contribution, it will become partnership property and he will cease to enjoy any beneficial interest therein which is qualitatively different to that of his co-partners.[119]

Outlays and improvements

Difficult questions may arise where there is an outlay of partnership money on **18–38** an asset belonging to one of the partners or, conversely, an outlay of a partner's own money on an asset belonging to the firm. In either case, it must be

---

[115] [1953] 1 W.L.R. 537.

[116] [2006] EWHC 2727 (Ch) (Lawtel 23/10/06) at [20].

[117] See, in addition to the cases previously cited, *Ex p. Smith* (1818) 3 Madd. 63; *Ex p. Hare* (1835) 1 Deac. 16; *Ex p. Murton* (1840) 1 M.D. & D. 252.

[118] (1990) 64 A.L.J.R. 234: see further *supra*, para. 18–12. *Lukin v. Lovrinov* [1998] S.A.S.C. 6614 was a similar case.

[119] Partnership Act 1890, s.20(1), *supra*, para. 18–03. See also *supra*, para. 17–02 and *infra*, paras 19–04 *et seq*. Naturally, any increase in the value of the asset will also constitute partnership property and, when realised, be distributable to the partners as a capital profit: see *Robinson v. Ashton* (1875) 20 Eq. 25; also *supra*, paras 17–02 *et seq*.

determined whether such an outlay will confer any rights in respect of the asset benefited. Of the possibility that it might give rise to a charge over the asset, Lord Lindley observed:

> "The agreement of the partners, if it can be ascertained, determines the rights in such cases. But where, as often happens, it is extremely difficult, if not impossible, to ascertain what was agreed, the only guide is that afforded by the burden of proof. It is for those claiming an allowance in respect of the outlay to establish their claim.[120] On the other hand, an intention to make a present of a permanent improvement is not to be presumed."

He then referred to the somewhat perplexing decision known as the *Bank of England Case*.[121] There two partners had used partnership money to purchase a property known as the Trotsworth Estate, which was conveyed to them in undivided moieties. A Trotsworth Estate account was opened in the partnership books and debited with the purchase price and all other sums expended on the Estate and credited with the rent received from a tenant and other receipts derived from the Estate. Having regained possession of certain parts of the Estate from the tenant, each partner built a dwelling house thereon. At least one partner[122] used partnership money for this purpose, debiting the amount drawn to his private account in the partnership books. Although there was apparently an understanding that the Estate would be divided between the partners, they were bankrupted before the arrangements could be finalised. In the circumstances, it was held that both the Estate and the dwelling houses were partnership property. Yet, if it is right that the construction of one of the houses was financed by a partner out of his own resources, it is somewhat surprising that his separate estate was not given any allowance in respect of that expenditure.

18–39   The same theme was developed further (and in many ways more forcibly) when Lord Lindley considered the subject of outlays and advances: he expressed the view that, in the case of an outlay of partnership money on an asset belonging to one partner, justice would require the improved value to be treated as a partnership asset.[123] The general principle was endorsed (albeit in an *obiter* part of his judgment) by Chadwick J. in *Faulks v. Faulks*[124] and, subsequently, by Blackburne J. in *Davies v. H.&R. Eckroyd Ltd.*[125]

---

[120] A later editor added a footnote reference to *Pawsey v. Armstrong* (1881) 18 Ch.D. 698 at this point. But note also the decision in *Harvey v. Harvey* (1970) 120 C.L.R. 529.

[121] (1861) 3 De G.F. & J. 645.

[122] Lord Lindley stated that both partners used partnership money, which was the assumption made by Turner L.J. at (1861) 3 De G.F. & J. 657; however, in the statement of the facts at *ibid.* p. 648, it is clearly stated that one partner, Laurence, drew "upon an account which he kept with his own private bankers." The headnote is equivocal.

[123] See *infra*, para. 20–31. Note also that, in certain circumstances, a spouse/civil partner may be able to claim an interest in the other spouse's/civil partner's business as a result of his/her contributions to its success: see *Nixon v. Nixon* [1969] 1 W.L.R. 1676; also *supra*, para. 4–19.

[124] [1992] 1 E.G.L.R. 9, 17.

[125] [1996] 2 E.G.L.R. 5, 8–9. It should be noted that these decisions preceded the recognition in *Swift v. Dairywise Farms Ltd.* [2000] 1 W.L.R. 1177 that milk quota could be the subject of a trust, just like any other asset. This part of Jacob J.'s judgment was not overturned on the appeal, which went off on other grounds: see [2003] 1 W.L.R. 1606. See further *supra*, para. 18–19.

Purpose of outlay

The purpose of the outlay will in all cases be highly material and may go a   **18–40**
long way towards discharging the burden of proof.[126]

Need for an inquiry

Where the court is satisfied that the outlay justifies some form of charge or   **18–41**
allowance, an inquiry will be directed in order to ascertain the precise amount
thereof.[127]

Proprietary estoppel

When Lord Lindley considered this subject, the so-called doctrine of "proprie-   **18–42**
tary estoppel"[128] was in its relative infancy. That doctrine, in its developed state,
may operate in a case where a partner is induced to make an outlay of his own
money on a partnership asset[129] or to authorise an outlay of partnership money
on an asset belonging to one of his co-partners. However, the current editor
submits that, in the latter case, no substantive proprietary interest could be
conferred on the firm as such, since the partner who owns the improved asset
cannot raise an estoppel against himself.

Offices and appointments

The questions which can arise where offices and appointments are held by   **18–43**
members of a firm have already been noted.[130]

3.   ASSETS TRANSFERRED INTO OR OUT OF PARTNERSHIP

Whilst all the partners remain solvent,[131] they may at any time agree, both as   **18–44**
between themselves and as against their creditors, either to remove assets from
or to introduce assets into the common pool of partnership property. Lord
Lindley wrote of such agreements:

---

[126] See *Miles v. Clarke* [1953] 1 W.L.R. 537, where Harman J. directed an inquiry whether any, and
if so what, sum should be allowed to the partnership in respect of an outlay on the leasehold property
of one of the partners, having regard to the terms of the partnership and the purpose for which the
outlay was made. In this respect, the headnote at [1953] 1 W.L.R. 537 is inaccurate. Note also
Harwood v. Harwood [1991] 2 F.S.R. 274.

[127] See *Burdon v. Barkus* (1862) 4 De G.F. & J. 42, *infra*, para. 20–32; *Pawsey v. Armstrong* (1881)
18 Ch.D. 698 (buildings erected on the separate property of a partner but paid for by firm); *Miles v.
Clark, supra.*

[128] See generally, *Dillwyn v. Llewellyn* (1862) 4 De G.F. & J. 517; *Inwards v. Baker* [1965] 2 Q.B.
29; *Hopgood v. Brown* [1955] 1 W.L.R. 213; *Crabb v. Arun District Council* [1976] Ch. 179; *Gillett
v. Holt* [2001] Ch. 210 (CA); *Cobbe v. Yeoman's Row Management Ltd.* [2008] 1 W.L.R. 1752 (HL);
Thorner v. Major [2009] 1 W.L.R. 776 (HL); *Fisher v. Brooker* [2009] 1 W.L.R. 1764 (HL); and see
generally *Snell's Equity* (31st ed.), paras 10–15 *et seq.* Note that it has now been held that there may,
in some cases, be no real difference between a constructive trust and a proprietary estoppel: *Oxley v.
Hiscock* [2005] Q.B. 211.

[129] As in *Strover v. Strover, The Times*, May 30, 2005, noted *infra*, para. 18–60.

[130] See *supra*, para. 18–18.

[131] But see *supra*, paras 10–152, 10–153 and *infra*, paras 27–100 *et seq.*

"It is competent for partners by agreement amongst themselves to convert that which was partnership property into the separate property of an individual, or vice versa.[132] And the nature of the property may be thus altered by any agreement to that effect; for neither a deed nor even a writing is absolutely necessary[133]; but so long as the agreement is dependent on an unperformed condition, so long will the ownership of the property remain unchanged."[134]

To this must, of course, be added one important qualification, to which Lord Lindley briefly referred in a footnote,[135] namely that a written disposition will normally be necessary in order to effect a transfer of an interest in land.[136] Where, however, no such interest is transferred, *e.g.* where co-owners, who are partners only as to the profits produced by their jointly owned land,[137] agree to treat the land as a partnership asset, there being no change in the quantum of their beneficial interests, writing will be unnecessary.[138] It should also be noted that an agreement taking land into or out of a partnership is now likely to attract a charge to stamp duty land tax.[139]

Agreement binding on creditors

18–45   The general rule is that, in the absence of fraud, the joint creditors of the firm and the separate creditors of each partner have no right to prevent the implementation of a bona fide agreement converting partnership property into the separate property of one or more of the partners or vice versa, even though they may be prejudiced thereby. Lord Lindley's formulation of the rule was as follows:

" . . . as the ordinary creditors of an individual have no lien on his property, and cannot prevent him from disposing of it as he pleases, so the ordinary creditors of a firm have no lien on the property of the firm so as to be able to prevent it from parting with that property to whomsoever it chooses. Accordingly it has frequently been held, that agreements come to between partners converting the property of the firm into the separate estate of one or more of its members, and *vice versa*, are, unless fraudulent, binding not only as between the partners themselves, but also on their

---

[132] *Ex p. Ruffin* (1801) 6 Ves.Jr. 119; *Ex p. Fell* (1805) 10 Ves.Jr. 348; *Ex p. Williams* (1805) 11 Ves.Jr. 3; *Ex p. Rowlandson* (1811) 1 Rose 416. Note also, in this context, the somewhat exceptional decision in *Dolley v. Ogunseitan* [2009] EWHC 1601 (Ch) (Lawtel 9/7/09), noticed *supra*, para. 18–06, n. 12, where part of the working capital of the firm was held to have ceased to have the status of partnership property in one of the partner's hands.

[133] Lord Lindley referred at this point to *Pilling v. Pilling* (1887) 3 De G.J. & Sm. 162; *Ex p. Williams* (1805) 11 Ves.Jr. 3; *Ex p. Clarkson* (1834) 4 D. & Ch. 56, 67 *per* Sir G. Rose; *Ex p. Owen* (1851) 4 De G. & Sm. 351; he then observed "None of these cases, however, turned on the effect of an unwritten agreement relating to land." See now the Partnership Act 1890, s.19, *supra*, para. 10–12.

[134] *Ex p. Wheeler* (1817) Buck. 25; *Ex p. Cooper* (1840) 1 M.D. & D. 358; *Hawkins v. Hawkins* (1858) 4 Jur.(N.S.) 1044. See further, *infra*, para. 18–47.

[135] See *supra*, n. 133.

[136] Law of Property Act 1925, s.53(1)(a), (c); also the Law of Property (Miscellaneous Provisions) Act 1989, s.2 (as amended). However, no writing will be necessary in the case of an implied or constructive trust: Law of Property Act 1925, s.53(2); Law of Property (Miscellaneous Provisions) Act 1989, s.2(5). See further, *infra*, para. 19–65. *cf.* the position when a partnership is created: see *supra*, paras 7–02 *et seq.*

[137] See *supra*, paras 5–07 *et seq.*, 18–26, 18–27.

[138] The point was not even argued in *Barton v. Morris* [1985] 1 W.L.R. 1257, *infra*, para. 18–56.

[139] See *infra*, paras 38–09, 38–21, 38–22.

joint and on their respective several creditors; and that, in the event of bankruptcy, the trustees must give effect to such agreements."[140]

There are in fact two further conditions implicit in the foregoing, which assume particular importance where insolvency orders are made against the firm or against one or more partners[141]: these are that the agreement must not remain executory and that, in any case where partnership property is converted into the separate property of a partner, it must not remain subject to the liens of the other partners.

Fraudulent agreements

It is a self evident proposition that an agreement tainted by fraud will not be **18–46** capable of altering the status or ownership of an asset. However, Lord Lindley took care to point out that a distinction must sometimes be drawn between a fraud practised by one partner on his co-partners and a fraud practised by all the partners on their creditors:

" . . . an agreement which can be successfully impeached for fraud will not affect the property to which it may relate[142]; and it must not be forgotten, that in the event of bankruptcy, the trustee, as representing the creditors, may be able to impeach as fraudulent against them, agreements by which the bankrupt himself would have been bound.[143] In a case where both the partnership and the individual partners were insolvent, an agreement by one of them transferring his interest to the others, and thereby converting what was joint estate into the separate estate of the transferee, was held invalid; for, although no fraud may have been intended, the necessary effect of the arrangement was to delay and defeat the joint creditors.[144] The firm became bankrupt shortly after the assignment was made."

The current editor submits that this still represents the position under the Insolvency Act 1986, although it should be noted that such an agreement might now equally well be impeached by the liquidator of the insolvent firm.[145] Moreover, the court will, within certain limits, have power to set aside such an agreement if it is unsupported by consideration or is otherwise at an undervalue, if it is intended to prefer one set of creditors over another or otherwise represents a fraud on the insolvency laws.[146]

Executory agreements

An agreement of the type under consideration will only be effective if it is **18–47** executed, not if it still remains executory.[147] Although this may, in some cases,

---

[140] See *Re Jane* (1914) 110 L.T. 556; also *Ex p. Peake* (1816) 1 Madd. 346; *Campbell v. Mullett* (1819) 2 Swan. 551; *Ex p. Clarkson* (1834) 4 D. & Ch. 56. And see the cases cited in subsequent paragraphs.

[141] See, as to the circumstances in which such orders can be made against a firm and/or against one or more of the partners, *infra*, paras 27–04 *et seq.*

[142] *Ex p. Rowlandson* (1813) 1 Rose 416.

[143] See *Anderson v. Maltby* (1793) 2 Ves.Jr. 244; *Ex p. Rowlandson* (1813) 1 Rose 416; *Billiter v. Young* (1856) 6 E. & B. 1, 40 *per* Jervis C.J.; *Re Kemptner* (1869) L.R. 8 Eq. 286.

[144] *Ex p. Walker* (1862) 4 De G.F. & J. 509; *Ex p. Mayou* (1865) De G.J. & S. 664; see also *Luff v. Horner* (1862) 3 Fos. & Fin. 480. *cf. Pearce v. Bulteel* [1916] 2 Ch. 544, where there was no intention to defeat the creditors: *ibid.* p. 555.

[145] See generally, *infra*, paras 27–100 *et seq.*

[146] See *supra*, paras 10–152, 10–153 and *infra*, para. 27–101.

[147] But note that, in the case of an insolvency, the court may have power to set aside even an *executed* agreement: see *infra*, para. 27–101.

be difficult to determine and reference should always be made to the precise terms agreed, an agreement will, as a general rule, be treated as executory if the transfer of the relevant asset into or out of the partnership can properly be regarded as dependent on the completion of some further act.[148] Thus, in *Ex p. Wheeler*,[149] a retiring partner had agreed to assign partnership property to the continuing partner on terms that the latter would make certain payments to or for his benefit, with the continuing partner's father acting as a surety therefor. On the bankruptcy of the continuing partner, the agreement was held to be executory because his father, who was not a party to the agreement (but who was, apparently, a witness to it), had declined to stand as surety. On the other hand, in *Ex p. Clarkson*,[150] the retiring partner had, in consideration of the assignment, agreed to accept a certain sum of money, partly in cash and partly in bills; that sum was duly paid, but the bills were subsequently dishonoured. It was, nevertheless, held that the assignment was effective.[151]

18–48   Although not strictly within this class of case, reference should perhaps be made to the special position of tenancies protected by the Landlord and Tenant Act 1954, Part II or by the Agricultural Holdings Act 1986, since agreements to contract out of the protection of either Act are in general void and unenforceable.[152] It follows that, in a case where the firm holds such a tenancy from one or more of the partners, any agreement which provides for its surrender or assignment to those partners[153] cannot affect the status of the tenancy as a partnership asset,[154] unless the surrender or assignment is actually completed.[155]

---

[148] It would seem that, if nothing remains to be done to make the agreement operative, it does not matter that it has not been entirely completed: see *Pearce v. Bulteel* [1916] 2 Ch. 544, 556 *per* Neville J.; see also *Re Jane* (1914) 110 L.T. 556; *Re Fox* (1915) 49 I.L.T. 224; *Re Owen* [1949] W.N. 201; *Re Rose* [1952] Ch. 499; *Re Wale* [1956] 1 W.L.R. 1346.

[149] (1817) Buck 25. See also *Ex p. Wood* (1879) 10 Ch.D. 554; *Ex p. Cooper* (1840) 1 M.D. & D. 358; and see the *Bank of England case* (1861) 3 De G.F. & J. 645, noticed *supra*, para. 18–36. *cf. Ex p. Gibson* (1834) 2 Mont. & Ayr. 4; *Ex p. Sprague* (1853) 4 De G.M. & G. 866; *Hawkins v. Hawkins* (1858) 4 Jur.(N.S.) 1044.

[150] (1834) 4 D. & Ch. 56.

[151] *cf. Ex p. Cooper* (1840) 1 M.D. & D. 358 and *Ex p. Gurney* (1842) 2 M.D. & D. 541; *Re Kemptner* (1869) L.R. 8 Eq. 286.

[152] As to business tenancies, see *Joseph v. Joseph* [1967] Ch. 78; also the Landlord and Tenant Act 1954, s.38 (as amended by the Law of Property Act 1969, s.5 and the Regulatory Reform (Business Tenancies) (England and Wales) Order 2003 (SI 2003/3096), art.21, Sched. 5, para. 4, Sched. 6). As to agricultural tenancies, see *Johnson v. Moreton* [1980] A.C. 37; *Featherstone v. Staples* [1986] 1 W.L.R. 861; also *Gisborne v. Burton* [1989] Q.B. 390; but *cf. Elsden v. Pick* [1980] 1 W.L.R. 898 (tenant agreeing to accept short notice to quit); *Dickson v. MacGregor* 1992 S.L.T. (Land Ct.) 83 (landlord attempting unsuccessfully to argue that his own scheme to evade security of tenure was void and unenforceable); also *MacFarlane v. Falfield Investments Ltd.* 1998 S.L.T. 145 (1st Div.); *Knapdale (Nominees) Ltd. v. Donald* 2000 S.C.L.R. 1013 (OH). Of course, most tenancies of agricultural land created after September 1, 1995 will not be protected by the 1986 Act but will be farm business tenancies within the meaning of the Agricultural Tenancies Act 1995: *ibid.* ss.1, 4.

[153] See *Re Hennessey's Agreement* [1975] Ch. 60.

[154] *Quaere*, would the position be the same if the landlord partners were not parties to the agreement? It is tentatively thought not, provided that the agreement is bona fide.

[155] See as to business tenancies, the Landlord and Tenant Act 1954, s.24(2) as amended by the Law of Property Act 1969, s.4(1) and the Regulatory Reform (Business Tenancies) (England and Wales) Order 2003, Sched. 6) and *Joseph v. Joseph* [1967] Ch. 78. There is no equivalent provision in the Agricultural Holdings Act 1986. It should be noted that a surrender will have not bring any subtenancies to an end. Where a notice to quit is allowed to take effect by agreement between a landlord and a tenant, this will be regarded as an effective surrender and the subtenants' rights will be preserved: *Sparkes v. Smart* [1990] 2 E.G.L.R. 245 (CA); *Barrett v. Morgan* [1999] 1 W.L.R. 1109 (CA).

Property still subject to liens of other partners

Even if the partners have agreed that, in the event of a dissolution, the **18–49** continuing or surviving partners will be entitled to all the firm's assets, such assets will still technically constitute partnership property, at least for insolvency purposes, as long as they remain subject to the liens of the outgoing partners.[156] Accordingly, such an agreement will only be effective if it is inconsistent with the continued existence of those liens[157] or they are otherwise lost or discharged.[158]

Agreements where intention clear

An express agreement is often encountered in cases where there has been a **18–50** change in the firm or where one or more partners are carrying on a trade distinct from that carried on by the firm.

Change in firm

Although most partnership agreements now provide that, in the event of a **18–51** partner's death, retirement or expulsion, the other partners will, as against him, become entitled to all the partnership assets,[159] similar terms are often negotiated on an *ad hoc* basis, prior to or following a dissolution.[160] Equally, partners occasionally agree to a division of the partnership assets *in specie*, with a view to carrying on a number of separate businesses, *e.g.* following an unsuccessful merger. In each of these cases, assets which were partnership property will, on a true analysis, become the separate property of one or more of the partners, even though, as between the acquiring partners, the assets may become the property of a new firm. Conversely, where a new partnership is formed, which includes the case of a new partner admitted to an existing firm[161] and the merger of two or more existing firms, assets which were the separate property of one or more of the partners[162] may become the property of the new, enlarged or merged firm.

Lord Lindley observed: **18–52**

> "All such agreements, if bona fide, and not fraudulent against creditors, are valid, and have the effect of altering the equitable ownership in the property affected by them."[163]

---

[156] As to partners' liens, see the Partnership Act 1890, s.39 and *infra*, paras 19–24 *et seq.*

[157] See *Ex p. Morley* (1873) L.R. 8 Ch.App. 1026; *Ex p. Dear* (1876) 1 Ch.D. 514; *Ex p. Butcher* (1880) 13 Ch.D. 465. *cf. Re Simpson* (1874) L.R. Ch.App. 572.

[158] See *infra*, para. 19–34.

[159] See *supra*, paras 10–150 *et seq.*

[160] The terms agreed will normally be incorporated in a formal retirement or dissolution deed, although this is not strictly necessary: see *Ex p. Williams* (1805) 11 Ves.Jr. 3, *infra*, para. 18–52. See also *supra*, para. 10–266.

[161] As a matter of law, the admission of a new partner will technically result in the dissolution of the old firm and the creation of a new firm, whether or not such admission is contemplated by the partnership agreement: see *supra*, paras 3–01 *et seq.*

[162] Of course, in the case of an existing firm, the assets will, as between such partners, constitute partnership property.

[163] This will certainly be so in the case of land (subject to the requirements of the Law of Property Act 1925 and/or the Law of Property (Miscellaneous Provisions) Act 1989, s.2), since the partner's respective interests will subsist behind a trust of land; however, in the case of chattels, the agreement may well also be effective to transfer the *legal* title. See further, *infra*, paras 18–61 *et seq.*, 19–65.

This proposition was clearly established in *Ex p. Ruffin*,[164] which Lord Lindley described as "the leading case on this subject." There, two partners agreed to dissolve their partnership, one retiring from the business and the other taking an assignment of the former firm's buildings, premises, stock in trade, debts and effects. The partner who continued the business was then bankrupted and some of the former firm's debts remained unpaid. It was argued that the partnership assets which had been assigned to the bankrupt partner should be applied towards meeting those debts, but it was held that such assets no longer constituted the joint property of the two former partners, but had been converted into the separate property of the bankrupt partner.

The position in *Ex p. Williams*[165] was similar, save that there was neither a written agreement nor an assignment of the relevant assets. However, it was possible to show that the partner who continued the business was intended to take over all the stock and effects of the former firm and, on that basis, they were held to have become his separate property.

18–53   The authority of these cases is unquestioned, as Lord Lindley explained:

> "These decisions have always been regarded as settling the law upon the subject of conversion of partnership property, and have been constantly followed. They were not, it will be observed, decided with reference to the doctrine of reputed owner-ship,[166] but with reference only to the real agreement come to between the partners. They apply as much to cases of a change of interest on death as on retirement."[167]

The decision in *Ex p. Owen*[168] demonstrates that the same principles are applicable in the converse situation, *i.e.* on the formation of a partnership.[169]

Distinct trades

18–54   If one or more of the partners, in the normal course of carrying on a business which is separate and distinct from that carried on by the firm, acquire assets from or dispose of assets to the firm, such transactions will be binding on their respective joint and separate creditors. Lord Lindley stated the principle thus:

> "When a firm and one of its members carry on distinct trades, property passing in the

---

[164] (1801) 6 Ves.Jr. 119. See also *Ex p. Fell* (1805) 10 Ves.Jr. 348; *Ex p. Peake* (1816) 1 Madd. 346; *Ex p. Clarkson* (1834) 4 D. & Ch. 56; *Ex p. Gurney* (1842) 2 M.D. & D. 541; *Ex p. Sprague* (1853) 4 De G.M. & G. 866; *Ex p. Walker* (1862) 4 De G.F. & J. 509; *Re Jane* (1914) 110 L.T. 556.

[165] (1805) 11 Ves.Jr. 3. *cf. Ex p. Cooper* (1840) 1 M.D. & D. 358.

[166] It should be noted that this doctrine has not been preserved under the Insolvency Act 1986 and now has no place in insolvency law. As to the position under the Bankruptcy Act 1914, see *ibid.* s.38(c) and the 15th ed. of this work at pp. 844 *et seq.*

[167] See *Re Simpson* (1874) L.R. 9 Ch.App. 572; *cf. Ex p. Morley* (1873) L.R. 8 Ch.App. 1026; *Ex p. Butcher* (1880) 13 Ch.D. 465, affirming (1879) 12 Ch.D. 917. All three cases turned on the construction of the partnership agreement and (in the second and third cases only) the wills of the deceased partners; in both of those cases the combined effect of the agreement and the will prevented a conversion.

[168] (1851) 4 De G. & Sm. 351, *supra*, para. 18–35.

[169] See also *Ex p. Barrow* (1815) 2 Rose 255. In *Belcher v. Sikes* (1828) 8 B. & C. 185, certain contracts, which constituted the separate property of one partner, were (unusually) converted into partnership property by a deed of dissolution. And see *Gian Singh & Co. v. Devraj Nahar* [1965] 1 W.L.R. 412.

ordinary way of business from the partner to the firm ceases to be his and becomes the property of the partnership, and vice versa, just as if he were a stranger to the firm. This was settled in the great case of *Bolton v. Puller.*"[170]

In *Bolton v. Puller* the entitlement to certain bills of exchange was in issue as **18–55** between two insolvent banking firms, in circumstances where all the members of one firm were also members of the other. In the course of his judgment, Lord Chief Justice Eyre said:

> "There can be no doubt, that, as between themselves, a partnership may have transactions with an individual partner, or with two or more of the partners having their separate estate engaged in some joint concern in which the general partnership is not interested; and that they may by their acts convert the joint property of the general partnership into the separate property of an individual partner, or into the joint property of two or more partners or *è converso*. And their transactions in this respect will, generally speaking, bind third persons, and third persons may take advantage of them in the same manner as if the partnership were transacting business with strangers; for instance, suppose the general partnership to have sold a bale of goods to the particular partnership, a creditor of the particular partnership might take those goods in execution for the separate debt of that particular partnership. In some respects therefore an individual partner, or a particular partnership consisting of two or more of those persons, who are partners in some larger partnership, may be considered as third persons in transactions, in which the general partnership may happen to be engaged with their correspondent."[171]

Agreements where intention unclear

Difficult questions may arise where an *implied* agreement to transfer an asset **18–56** into or out of the partnership is sought to be proved merely by reference to the partners' conduct. Thus, in *Barton v. Morris*,[172] two partners had purchased a farmhouse/guest house which was conveyed to them as beneficial joint tenants. One of the partners, Miss Barton, who had contributed the greater part of the purchase price, prepared partnership accounts which showed the property as a partnership asset for tax purposes. She later died and her administratrix sought to argue that the joint tenancy had been severed when the property became a partnership asset.[173] Nicholls J. rejected that argument, holding that the mere inclusion of the property in the accounts was not in itself sufficient evidence of an agreement or course of dealing which would alter the status of the property.

---

[170] (1796) 1 Bos. & Pul. 539.

[171] *ibid.* pp. 546, 547. Lord Chief Justice Eyre then continued: "On the other hand it will be difficult, if not impossible, for individual partners, or for particular partnerships composed of individual partners, to shake off privity in all transactions of the general partnership, or to avoid all the consequences of privity. Each partner is a party, as well as privy, to the transactions of the general partnership, though the general partnership is not party to the separate transactions of the individual partners."

[172] [1985] 1 W.L.R. 1257; also *Mehra v. Shah,* August 1, 2003 (Lawtel 5/8/03), affirmed on appeal at [2004] EWCA Civ 632 (Lawtel 20/5/04). There the fact that the Barking Road property was *omitted* from the firm's accounts was clearly not material. Inclusion of properties in the accounts was not regarded as significant in *Amin v. Amin* [2009] EWHC 3356 (Ch) (Lawtel 5/1/10). And note *Helm v. Facey* (1981) 131 N.L.J. 291.

[173] See *infra*, para. 19–13.

However, it is submitted that the circumstances were exceptional[174] and the decision should not be regarded as establishing a general principle that the implications of including an asset in the partnership balance sheet can, in this context, be effectively ignored.[175]

18–57   On the other hand, the *exclusion* of an asset from the balance sheet is more equivocal: it is in practice common to find that certain assets, such as goodwill and rack rent tenancies, are omitted from the partnership balance sheet, even though no partner would seek to question their status as partnership property. The position may, however, be otherwise if an asset is deliberately excluded from the balance sheet.[176]

In cases of this type it is obviously necessary to consider *all* the circumstances: it may be that, where certain assets appear to have been removed from the partnership in an identical way, on a true analysis some remain as partnership property whilst others do not.[177]

Leases and covenants against assignment

18–58   If the agreement alters the status and, where relevant, quantum of the partners' beneficial interests in a leasehold property but does not affect the *legal* title thereto,[178] there may be no breach of a covenant against assignment or parting with possession contained in the lease, until such time as a formal assignment is completed[179]; *per contra*, perhaps, where there is a covenant against parting with or sharing the *occupation* of the demised premises.[180]

---

[174] Thus, Miss Barton appears to have been motivated to include the property in the accounts "for the sake of completeness" and by a desire to disclose everything to the Inland Revenue (as it then was): see [1985] 1 W.L.R. 1260D.

[175] Equally, in *Clark v. Kessell* (June 30, 1998, unreported) a property had been purchased out of partnership funds but was vested in four partners as beneficial tenants in common. Although the property was subsequently shown as an asset in the partnership accounts, it was held that this did not *per se* override the declaration of trust. *cf. Longmuir v. Moffat* 2009 S.C. 329 at [17]. But see also *supra*, para. 18–08, n. 24.

[176] See *Mehra v. Shah, supra*; and note, in this context, *Robertson v. Brent* [1972] N.Z.L.R. 406 regarding the status of work in progress on the retirement of a partner. This decision is not, however, without difficulty: see *supra*, para. 10–158, n. 739.

[177] This is illustrated by *Anand v. I.R.C.* [1997] S.T.C. (S.C.D.) 58. There, certain moneys representing partnership profits were placed in various bank accounts in the sole name of one of the partners. It was held that the majority of the money was held in this way for convenience only and that it continued to be held for the benefit of the partners. However, moneys held in one particular account, which had been specifically earmarked to meet that partner's medical bills, fell to be treated as his property.

[178] The Law of Property Act 1925, s.52(1) requires any assignment of a lease to be made by deed, even where the lease was originally granted by parol pursuant to *ibid.* s.54(2): *Crago v. Julian* [1992] 1 W.L.R. 372. However, such a deed may not be necessary where the lease is already vested in the partners concerned *qua* trustees for the firm.

[179] See *Corporation of Bristol v. Westcott* (1879) 12 Ch.D. 461; *Harrison v. Povey* (1956) 168 E.G. 613; *Gian Singh & Co. v. Devraj Nahar* [1965] 1 W.L.R. 412; also *Pincott v. Moorstons Ltd.* (1937) 156 L.T. 139; *Gentle v. Faulkner* [1900] 2 Q.B. 267; *Knapdale (Nominees) Ltd. v. Donald* 2000 S.C.L.R. 1013 (OH); *Clarence House Ltd. v. National Westminster Bank Plc* [2010] 2 All E.R. 201 (CA), where the status of a so called "virtual assignment" was considered. *cf. Varley v. Coppard* (1872) L.R. 7 C.P. 505; *Langton v. Henson* (1905) 92 L.T. 805. Each case will naturally depend on the precise terms of the covenant under consideration.

[180] This, of course, presupposes that the relevant partners have taken up exclusive occupation (otherwise see *Gian Singh & Co. v. Devraj Nahar* [1965] 1 W.L.R. 412 (PC)). Even then, could there properly be said to be an impermissible *sharing* of occupation in such a case? Much will depend on the nature of the covenant, which might well be framed in terms of occupation by the firm. Note that, in *Clarence House Ltd. v. National Westminster Bank Plc, supra*, the defendant who had made the "virtual assignment" had already sublet the premises so was not in physical occupation of them.

Milk quota

Whilst milk quota strictly cannot exist as an asset independently of the land to **18–59**
which it relates,[181] it has already been seen that this does not, as such, prevent it
from being treated as a partnership asset.[182] Where the agreement provides that
a particular tenancy is to be held as a partnership asset but will automatically
revert to a named partner in the event of a dissolution or other change in the firm,
any quota enjoyed in relation to that land may also cease to be a partnership asset
at the same time as the tenancy.[183] Equally, the court may be prepared to infer
that the quota remains as a partnership asset in that partner's hands, so that he can
be forced to account for its value.[184] In the alternative, an allowance for the value
of the "lost" quota may, conceivably, be given in taking accounts between the
partners.[185]

Estoppel

A change in the status of an asset may be brought about by virtue of the **18–60**
doctrine of estoppel.[186] A recent example of such a case is *Strover v. Strover*,[187]
where an outgoing partner had, after his retirement, undertaken responsibility for
payment of the premiums on a life insurance policy originally taken out for the
benefit of the surviving partners in the event of his death. In holding that a
proprietary estoppel arose in favour of the outgoing partner's estate, Hart J. held
that this would affect entitlement to only 80 per cent of the policy monies,
reflecting the relatively small probability that, if they had addressed the issue, the
partners might have proceeded differently.

4.   LEGAL TITLE TO PARTNERSHIP PROPERTY

Land

Land held by a firm can be vested in no more than four partners[188]; accordingly **18–61**
in any case in which the firm comprises five or more partners, the legal estate in
partnership land will inevitably be held by some of the partners on trust for
themselves and their fellow partners, according to their respective beneficial
interests.[189] It should be noted that, in an appropriate case, the partners may hold

---

[181] *Faulks v. Faulks* [1992] 1 E.G.L.R. 9; *Davies v. H.&R. Eckroyd Ltd.* [1996] 2 E.G.L.R. 5. Note,
however, that it may, nevertheless, be possible to transfer quota: *Harries v. Barclays Bank plc* [1997]
2 E.G.L.R. 15 (CA). Moreover, see also the procedure for transfer under the Dairy Produce Quotas
Regulations 2005 (SI 2005/465), reg. 13 (as amended by the Dairy Produce Quotas (Amendment)
Regulations 2008 (SI 2008/439), reg. 2, Sched., para. 4).
[182] See *supra*, para. 18–19.
[183] As in *Faulks v. Faulks, supra*.
[184] This was not an option perceived to be open to Chadwick J. in *Faulks v. Faulks, supra*, but
necessarily follows from the decision in *Swift v. Dairywise Farms Ltd.* [2000] 1 W.L.R. 1177. That
decision would still seem to be good law, since the appeal ultimately went off on other grounds:
[2003] 1 W.L.R. 1606.
[185] See *Faulks v. Faulks, supra*, p. 15 *per* Chadwick J.; *Davies v. H.&R. Eckroyd Ltd., supra*, pp.
8–9 *per* Blackburne J. See also *infra*, paras 20–31, 20–32.
[186] As in *Clark v. Kessell* (June 30, 1998, unreported), noted *supra*, para. 18–08 n. 24.
[187] *The Times*, May 30, 2005.
[188] Trustee Act 1925, s.34(2) (as amended by the Trusts of Land and Appointment of Trustees Act
1996, Sched. 3, para. 3(9)); Law of Property Act 1925, s.34(2) (as amended by *ibid.* Sched. 2, para.
3(2))
[189] See *infra*, paras 19–02 *et seq.*

the land as joint tenants, both legally *and* beneficially.[190] Where a lease is to be granted to a firm comprising more than four partners, as a matter of strict conveyancing practice only the trustee partners need be made parties thereto. It should, however, be noted that some landlords are now in fact insisting that all the partners be joined, either as contractual tenants[191] or, more usually, as sureties for the trustee partners' obligations. In this way the landlord secures direct rights of action against all the partners, albeit that complications inevitably arise when an additional partner joins the firm or when a partner retires.[192] Equally, there has been at least one reported instance in which, despite this, the landlord had agreed to limit his claims to the partnership assets so that he was unable to proceed against the partners personally.[193]

Orders in relation to trusts of land

18–62   Land held for the benefit of a firm will now be held on a trust of land under the Trusts of Land and Appointment of Trustees Act 1996[194] and the court will enjoy a wide discretion to make orders relating to the exercise of the trustees' functions thereunder,[195] including dispensing with any consents which would otherwise be required.[196] In the exercise of that discretion, the court will have

---

[190] See *Bathurst v. Scarborow* [2005] 1 P. & C.R. 58 (CA). See *infra*, para. 19–13.

[191] Although the Trustee Act 1925, s.34(2) and the Law of Property Act 1925, s.34(2) (as amended) restrict the number of trustees to four, they do not appear to affect the *contractual* liability of the parties to the relevant disposition. This surely must have been the legal effect of the assignment in *Prudential Assurance Co. Ltd. v. Ayres* [2008] 1 All E.R. 1266 (CA), albeit that the partners' personal liability was excluded. *Quaere* whether the non-tenant partners will, in the event of a subsequent assignment of the lease, obtain an automatic release from liability under the Landlord and Tenant (Covenants) Act 1995, s.5. The definition of "tenant" in *ibid.* s.28(1) would certainly not be apt to apply to them. Whilst the landlord might, in an appropriate case, be entitled to require the tenant partners to guarantee the assignee's observance of the covenants in the lease under *ibid.* s.16, it cannot have been contemplated that he would also be able to hold the non-tenant partners liable on those covenants during its whole term. This is an eventuality which should, obviously, be covered in the lease itself. If it is not, it might still be possible to argue that the joinder of the non-tenant partners is void by virtue of *ibid.* s.25(1)(a), as an agreement which "frustrate[*s*] the operation of any provision of [*the*] Act".

[192] Thus, new surety covenants will have to be taken from an incoming partner and (ideally) a release given to an outgoing partner. However, the landlord may insist that an outgoing partner's release is conditional on his place being taken by a new partner. Ironically, arrangements of the type considered in the text may provide incidental benefits for the firm, by ensuring that all partners are treated alike; otherwise, the partners whose names are on the lease may find themselves at a disadvantage when compared to their colleagues who have not undertaken direct liability to the landlord and who can, by the simple expedient of retiring from the firm, even free themselves from any liability to indemnify the former in respect of rent, etc., due under the lease.

[193] See *Prudential Assurance Co. Ltd. v. Ayres, supra*. The Court of Appeal did not question the validity of such an arrangement.

[194] See *ibid.* s.1(1). A trust of land may, but will not *necessarily* involve an immediate trust for sale: see the Law of Property Act 1925, s.205(1)(xxix) (as amended by the Trusts of Land and Appointment of Trustees Act 1996, Sched. 4).

[195] Trusts of Land and Appointment of Trustees Act 1996, s.14(1), (2)(a). This discretion is wider than that conferred on the court by the Law of Property Act 1925, s.30: *Mortgage Corp. v. Shaire* [2001] Ch. 743; *Bank of Ireland Home Mortgages Ltd. v. Bell* [2001] 2 All E.R. (Comm.) 920 (CA). Thus, in *Rodway v. Landy* [2001] Ch. 703, the Court of Appeal upheld an order refusing a sale of certain surgery premises (which were *not* partnership property) and directing them to be physically divided (but not partitioned) between the former partners with a view to their continuing in occupation, pursuant to the Trusts of Land and Appointment of Trustees Act 1996, s.13. Note, in this context, that trustees of land generally have all the powers of an absolute owner: *ibid.* s.6(1).

[196] See *Page v. West* [2010] EWHC 504 (Ch) (Lawtel 18/3/10), an exceptional case. See also generally, as to consents, *ibid.* s.10. This should be distinguished from the obligation to consult with the beneficiaries of the trust: *ibid.* s.11.

regard to all the circumstances,[197] and an order can be sought by a trustee or any other person interested in the land in question.[198] As was the position under the Law of Property Act 1925,[199] it is almost inconceivable that a partner would succeed in obtaining an order for the sale of partnership land as long as the partnership is continuing[200]; *per contra*, after the partnership has been dissolved.[201] However, it would seem that the trustee partners, if they are more than two in number,[202] may properly sell the land without the concurrence of the other partners, even if by so doing they commit a breach of trust[203] or fiduciary duty.[204]

Devolution of title

Devolution of the legal estate in land will in all cases be governed by the normal law affecting real property[205]; thus, on the death of a partner, any land vested in him and his co-partners will devolve on the latter in their capacity as surviving trustees of a trust of land.[206] Those partners will accordingly be entitled to charge or sell the land for the purpose of paying partnership debts or otherwise winding up its affairs.[207] As regards the *beneficial* entitlement of the deceased

18–63

[197] See the specific factors listed in *ibid.* s.15. However, these are not exhaustive, as is made clear by the opening words of *ibid.* subs.(1). Numerous factors were taken into account by the court in *Rodway v. Landy, supra.* For a consideration of the manner in which the parties' intentions and purposes under *ibid.* s.15(1)(a) and (b) can affect the position and whether they can change over time, see *W v. W* [2004] 2 F.L.R. 321 (CA). Where an application under *ibid.* s.14 is made by one of the co-owners' trustee in bankruptcy, *ibid.* s.15 does not apply (*ibid.* s.15(4)) and the position is instead governed by the Insolvency Act 1986, s.335A, as added by *ibid.* Sched. 3, para. 23. In such a case, the creditors' interests will normally prevail, in the absence of exceptional circumstances: *Avis v. Turner* [2008] Ch. 218 (CA) at [36] *per* Chadwick L.J.

[198] *ibid.* s.14(1). See further, as to the procedure, CPR r.40.16, 40 DPD, Pt 1, paras 2 *et seq.*

[199] See *Re Buchanan-Wollaston's Conveyance* [1939] Ch. 738. *cf. Re John's Assignment Trusts* [1970] 1 W.L.R. 955.

[200] In such a case, surely the trustee partners' acceptance of the land as partnership property carries with it the general implication that, whilst the partnership is continuing, they will postpone sale under the power conferred upon them by the Trusts of Land and Appointment of Trustees Act 1996, s.4. See also *ibid.* s.11(1) and the Partnership Act 1890, s.24(8), *supra,* para. 15–04.

[201] Equally, in the event of a dissolution, the court might permit one or more partners to purchase the land: see further *infra,* para. 23–193. But see also *Rodway v. Landy, supra.*

[202] Law of Property Act 1925, s.27 (as amended by the Law of Property (Amendment) Act 1926, Sched. and the Trusts of Land and Appointment of Trustees Act 1996, Sched. 3, para. 4(8)). If title to the land is vested in only one partner, he should ensure that the sale proceeds are paid to two partners as trustees. If he fails to do so, the purchaser will still take free of the other partners' equitable interests if, in the case of unregistered land, he is a bona fide purchaser without notice of the trust (see *Williams & Glyn's Bank Ltd. v. Boland* [1979] Ch. 312, 330 *per* Denning M.R.), or, in the case of registered land, unless there is a restriction on the register or the other partners' interests are overriding interests by reason of their being in actual occupation (see the Land Registration Act 2002, ss.28, 29).

[203] See the Trusts of Land and Appointment of Trustees Act 1996, s.11(1); *cf. Notting Hill Housing Trust v. Brackley* [2001] 35 E.G. 106 (CA).

[204] See *Ward v. Brunt* [2000] W.T.L.R. 731 at 750A–B; *cf. Sykes v. Land* (1984) 271 E.G. 1264.

[205] Partnership Act 1890, s.20(2), *supra,* para. 18–03.

[206] Note, however, that partners may hold the land as joint tenants, both legally *and* beneficially: *Bathurst v. Scarborow* [2005] 1 P. & C.R. 58 (CA). See *infra,* para. 19–13.

[207] See the Trusts of Land and Appointment of Trustees Act 1996, s.6(1); also the Partnership Act 1890, s.38, *supra,* paras 13–62 *et seq.* And see the following old cases (decided prior to the imposition of the now defunct statutory trust for sale under the Law of Property Act 1925): *Re Clough* (1885) 31 Ch.D. 324, *Re Bourne* [1906] 2 Ch. 427 (charges); *West of England and South Wales Bank v. Murch* (1883) 23 Ch.D. 138 (sale).

partner in respect of the land (if any),[208] the surviving partners on whom the legal estate devolves are naturally bound to account to his estate therefor.[209]

If an insolvency order is made against one of the partners in whom the land is vested,[210] the trustee or liquidator will seemingly not become a joint tenant with the solvent partners.[211]

Choses in action

18–64   On the death of a partner, the right to recover a debt owed to the firm will devolve on the surviving partners,[212] although the debt must be brought into account in determining the entitlement of the deceased partner's estate.[213] The position will be the same in the case of any other chose in action belonging to the firm.

Chattels

18–65   Although it was formerly held otherwise,[214] it is clear that the surviving partners may give a good title to chattels owned by the firm, without the co-operation of the personal representative(s) of a deceased partner.[215] Nevertheless, it is seemingly arguable that, in strict law, the legal title devolves to the surviving partners *and* such personal representative(s).[216]

---

[208] See *infra*, para 19–02 *et seq*.

[209] Partnership Act 1890, s.20(2), *supra*, para. 18–03; see also *Jefferys v. Small* (1683) 1 Vern. 217; *Lake v. Gibson* (1729) 1 Eq.Ca.Abr. 290; *Lake v. Craddock* (1732) 3 P.W. 158; *Elliot v. Brown* (1791) 3 Swan. 489n; *Lyster v. Dolland* (1792) 1 Ves.Jr. 435; *Jackson v. Jackson* (1804) 9 Ves.Jr. 591. See also *Re Ryan* (1868) L.R.Ir. 3 Eq. 222, where the title of persons claiming under a deceased partner prevailed against a mortgagee of the surviving partner. Note that the mortgage was taken to secure a separate debt of the surviving partner and the mortgagee had notice of the equitable interest; as to part of the property there was no such notice and the mortgagee's title prevailed. The position will, of course, be otherwise if the land was not partnership property: see *Morris v. Barrett* (1829) 3 Y. & J. 384; *Reilly v. Walsh* (1848) 11 Ir.Eq. 22 (lease acquired for the purposes of a partnership which was never formed).

[210] See, as to the circumstances in which such an order may be made against a partner, *infra*, paras 27–24 *et seq.*, 27–43 *et seq*.

[211] See *infra*, para. 27–69.

[212] This was the position at law prior to the Judicature Acts: see *Kemp v. Andrews* (1691) Carth. 170; *Martin v. Crompe* (1698) 1 Ld. Raymd. 340; *Dixon v. Hammond* (1819) 2 B. & A. 310; *Knox v. Gye* (1872) L.R. 5 H.L. 656; *McLean v. Kennard* (1874) L.R. 9 Ch.App. 336; also *Slipper v. Stidstone* (1794) 5 T.R. 493; *French v. Andrade* (1796) 6 T.R. 582. Lord Lindley observed: "There is indeed an old case in which an action of *assumpsit* for a partnership debt was held to be properly brought by the executors of a deceased partner and the surviving partners jointly: *Hall v. Huffam*, alias *Hall v. Rougham* (1677) 2 Lev. 188 and 228, and 3 Keble 798; but this case is in direct opposition to those last cited, and is contrary to what was clearly settled before the Judicature Acts." As to receipts by the surviving partners, see *Brazier v. Hudson* (1836) 9 Sim. 1; *Philips v. Philips* (1828) 3 Hare 281.

[213] See *infra*, paras 19–05 *et seq*.

[214] *Buckley v. Barber* (1851) 6 Ex. 164; also *R. v. Collector of Customs* (1813) 2 M. & S. 223; *Fox v. Hanbury* (1776) Cowp. 445. Note that *Buckley v. Barber* (which Lord Lindley described as "perplexing") was disapproved by James L.J. (sitting for Wickens V.-C.) in *Taylor v. Taylor*, March 7, 1873.

[215] Partnership Act 1890, s.38, *supra*, paras 13–62 *et seq*. See also *Chandroutie v. Gajadhar* [1987] A.C. 147.

[216] See for example, Williams, *Law of Personal Property* (18th ed., 1926), p. 521 (seemingly endorsing *Buckley v. Barber, supra*); *Crossley Vaines on Personal Property* (11th ed., 1973), p. 56; *Halsbury's Laws of England* (4th ed. reissue), Vol. 35, para. 1246. Note, however, that the Privy Council appears to have taken a different view in *Chandroutie v. Gajadhar* [1987] A.C. 147, 153. In

Goodwill

On the death of a partner, legal (but not beneficial) title to the firm's goodwill **18–66**
vests in the surviving partners.[217]

Partnership property held by trustees

Any actual or theoretical doubt as to the devolution of the legal title to **18–67**
partnership property may be avoided if the partners expressly declare that all
partnership assets will be held by two or more of them[218] as joint tenants upon
trust for the partners as partnership property. There will clearly be survivorship
as between such trustees, so that the surviving partners will always be in a
position to make title to all such assets. However, such a course is rarely, if ever,
adopted.

---

earlier editions of this work, it was submitted that "the principle underlying *Buckley v. Barber* (if it
exists) is of great importance in relation to other matters, *e.g.* s.43 of the Partnership Act 1890". The
point sought to be made is obscure: why should such a question arise in relation to a chattel, but not
in relation to land? Arguably s.43 imposes a limited form of survivorship in these cases.

[217] See *supra*, para. 10–203.

[218] In the case of land, there must, of course, be no more than four trustees: Trustee Act 1925,
s.34(2) (as amended by the Trusts of Land and Appointment of Trustees Act 1996, Sched. 3, para.
3(9)); Law of Property Act 1925, s.34(2) (as amended by *ibid.* Sched. 2, para. 3(2)).

CHAPTER 19

PARTNERSHIP SHARES

1.   THE NATURE OF A PARTNERSHIP SHARE

Precise definition impossible

ALTHOUGH it is convenient to refer to a partner's interest in the firm as his **19–01** "share," that expression is notoriously difficult to define, not least because its meaning differs according to the context in which it is used. In common parlance, a share is usually seen merely in terms of an interest in the profits of a business and of a capital or "equity" stake therein; indeed, this may well be the partners' own perception. However, in legal terms, such an approach is too simplistic, since the constituent elements which go to make up a share are not only infinitely variable but subject to alteration during the continuance of the partnership and thereafter. Thus, whilst the "share" of an outgoing partner may quite properly be viewed solely in financial terms,[1] reference to the "share" of a *continuing* partner must include the totality of the rights which he enjoys under the partnership agreement and under the general law.[2] It follows that no single meaningful definition is possible and, if the expression is used without regard to the context, confusion and potential disputes are inevitable.

Proprietary nature of a share

It has already been seen that partnership is a relationship which results from a **19–02** contract,[3] although the House of Lords has been at pains to point out that the relationship involves far more than a simple contract.[4] Although generalisation is dangerous in this (as in any other) area, it might be said that one particular feature which distinguishes a partnership from an ordinary contract[5] is that, in addition to creating contractual rights and obligations between the partners, it will usually (but by no means necessarily)[6] confer on each partner certain proprietary rights in respect of the partnership assets.[7] Certainly, it is difficult to imagine a partnership which involves no proprietary rights whatsoever, even though the

---

[1] See for example, the Partnership Act 1890, s.43, considered *infra*, paras 23–34, 26–04. And see *infra*, para. 19–10.

[2] As a result, a share is often conveniently referred to as a "bundle of rights": see, for example, *infra*, para. 35–16.

[3] See *supra*, para. 2–15.

[4] See *Hurst v. Bryk* [2002] 1 A.C. 185, 194 *per* Lord Millett. See further, as to this decision, *infra*, paras 24–05 *et seq.*

[5] Certain other distinguishing features are identified in *ibid.* p. 194.

[6] Note, however, that one of the primary attributes of a so-called "salaried" or "fixed share" partner may be the absence of any interest in partnership property: see *Stekel v. Ellice* [1973] 1 W.L.R. 191 and, generally, *supra*, paras 5–54, 10–86, 18–02.

[7] With the proliferation of contractual arrangements (other than partnership) which involve the creation of proprietary rights, this feature is, perhaps, less distinctive than it once was.

only partnership property may be of an intangible nature, *e.g.* goodwill, or of negligible value.

The internal and external perspectives

19–03   When analysing the proprietary nature of a partnership share, it is necessary to distinguish between the internal and external perspectives, since they are very different. The distinction was clearly drawn by Lord Justice Hoffmann in *I.R.C. v. Gray*[8] in these terms:

> "As between themselves, partners are not entitled individually to exercise proprietary rights over any of the partnership assets. This is because they have subjected their proprietary interests to the terms of the partnership deed which provides that the assets shall be employed in the partnership business, and on dissolution realised for the purposes of paying debts and distributing any surplus. As regards the outside world, however, the partnership deed is irrelevant. The partners are collectively entitled to each and every asset of the partnership, in which each of them therefore has an undivided share."[9]

This chapter is concerned principally with the *internal* perspective. However, the external perspective *may* still be of relevance in certain circumstances, *e.g.* when determining the manner in which a partnership share should be transferred[10] and, perhaps, where a firm holds shares subject to a right of pre-emption, if one partner were to assign his partnership share.[11]

Essential nature of a partner's proprietary interest

19–04   It is clear that, in the absence of some other agreement (express or implied), all the members of an ordinary partnership have identical and equal interests in its assets[12] and that no partner is entitled, without the concurrence of all his co-partners, to insist that a particular asset (or an interest therein) is vested in him, either during the continuance of the partnership or following its dissolution.[13] Although these propositions are simply stated, an analysis of the precise legal and beneficial nature of a partner's interest in the firm's assets raises a number of difficult issues.[14]

---

[8] [1994] S.T.C. 360, 377c–e.

[9] See also *Re Fuller's Contract* [1933] Ch. 652, 656 *per* Luxmoore J.

[10] See *infra*, para. 19–65.

[11] See the (ultimately inconclusive) discussion of the position of nominee shareholdings in *Rose v. Lynx Express Ltd.* [2004] 1 B.C.L.C. 455.

[12] This results from the combined effect of the Partnership Act 1890, ss.24(1), 44(b)(4): see further *supra*, paras 17–07, 17–08 and *infra*, paras 19–16 *et seq.* As to what assets may properly be treated as belonging to the firm, see *supra*, paras 18–01 *et seq.*

[13] *Lingen v. Simpson* (1824) 1 Sim. & St. 600; *Cockle v. Whiting* (1829) Tam. 55; *Popat v. Shonchhatra* [1997] 1 W.L.R. 1367, 1372C (CA); also *Gopala Chetty v. Vijayaraghavachariar* [1922] 1 A.C. 488; *Marshall v. Bullock*, March 27, 1998 (unreported), noted *infra*, para. 23–36. And see the cases cited *infra*, paras 19–05, n. 15 and 19–08, n. 30. *cf.* the unusual terms of the agreement in *Faulks v. Faulks* [1992] 1 E.G.L.R. 9, noted *supra*, para. 18–19.

[14] See for example, *Brown v. Oakshot* (1857) 24 Beav. 254; *Re Fuller's Contract* [1933] Ch. 652; *Green v. Whitehead* [1930] 1 Ch. 38. See further *supra*, paras 18–61 *et seq.* and, *infra*, paras 19–05 *et seq.* Note also that a partner's beneficial share has been described as an equitable interest and not a "mere" equity: see *Canny Gabriel Castle Jackson Advertising Pty Ltd. v. Volume Sales (Finance) Pty Ltd.* (1974) 131 C.L.R. 321; also *Connell v. Bond Corp. Pty Ltd.* (1992) 8 W.A.R. 352.

The classic definition

Lord Lindley observed: **19–05**

"What is meant by the *share* of a partner is his proportion of the partnership assets after they have been all realised and converted into money, and all the debts and liabilities have been paid and discharged.[15] This it is, and this only, which on the death of a partner passes to his representatives, or to a legatee of his share[16]; which under the old law was considered as *bona notabilia*[17]; which on his bankruptcy passes to his trustee[18] . . . ".

Although it would be more accurate to speak of a partner's entitlement to a proportion of the *net proceeds of sale* of the assets, the correctness of the statement of principle embodied in the above passage cannot seriously be questioned, reflecting as it does the proper application of sections 39 and 44 of the Partnership Act 1890.[19]

Accordingly, a partner's entitlement will reflect not only his capital and current   **19–06**
account balances[20] and the size of his capital profit (or asset surplus) share,[21] but also any amounts which he may owe to the firm, *e.g.* in respect of over-drawings.[22] It is submitted that any attempt to demonstrate that a particular element of a partner's share, *e.g.* his entitlement to capital, has an existence independent of the remainder must, in the absence of an express agreement,

---

[15] See *Rodriguez v. Speyer Bros.* [1919] A.C. 59, 68 *per* Finlay L.C.; *Re Ritson* [1899] 1 Ch. 128; *Burdett-Coutts v. I.R.C.* [1960] 1 W.L.R. 1027; *Livingstone v. Commissioner of Stamp Duties* [1961] A.L.R. 534; *Popat v. Shonchhatra* [1997] 1 W.L.R. 1367, 1372C–E; also *Dimov v. Dimov* [1971] W.A.R. 113; *Re Ward* [1985] 2 N.Z.L.R. 352. Lord Lindley in fact referred to the following pre-1890 cases: *Croft v. Pyke* (1733) 3 P.W. 180; *West v. Skip* (1749) 1 Ves.Sen. 239; *Doddington v. Hallet* (1750) 1 Ves.Sen. 497; *Taylor v. Fields* (1799) 4 Ves.Jr. 396; *Crawshay v. Collins* (1808) 15 Ves.Jr. 218; *Featherstonhaugh v. Fenwick* (1810) 17 Ves.Jr. 298; *Darby v. Darby* (1856) 3 Drew. 495; see also *Richardson v. Bank of England* (1838) 4 Myl. & Cr. 165. Note the decisions in *Re Rhagg* [1938] Ch. 828; *Re Betts* [1949] W.N. 91; *Re White* [1958] Ch. 762. And see *supra*, paras 10–157 *et seq.*

[16] *Re Ritson* [1899] 1 Ch. 128. And see *Farquar v. Hadden* (1871) L.R. 7 Ch.App. 1, noticed *infra*, paras 19–06 n. 23, 26–54; *Re Holland* [1907] 2 Ch. 88; see also *Re Rhagg, Re Betts* and *Re White*, *supra*. The situs of a share for tax and other purposes will in general be determined by reference to the firm's principal place of business: *Re Ewing* (1881) 6 P.D. 19; *Laidlay v. Lord Advocate* (1890) 15 App.Cas. 468; *Beaver v. Master in Equity of Supreme Court of Victoria* [1895] A.C. 251; *Commissioners of Stamp Duties v. Salting* [1907] A.C. 449. See also *infra*, para. 36–55.

[17] *Ekins v. Brown* (1854) 1 Spinks, Ecc. & Adm.Rep. 400; *Att.-Gen. v. Higgins* (1857) 2 H. & N. 339.

[18] See *infra*, para. 27–70; also *Smith v. Stokes* (1801) 1 East 363.

[19] See *infra*, paras 19–25 *et seq.*, 25–45 *et seq.* See also, as to the nature of a partner's interest in the partnership assets, *Byford v. Oliver* [2003] E.M.L.R. 20 at [19] (and cited in *Gill v Frankie Goes To Hollywood Ltd.* [2008] E.T.M.R. 4 (OHIM, Opposition Division)); *Taylor v. Grier (No. 3)*, May 12, 2003 (Lawtel 20/5/2003); *Sandhu v. Gill* [2006] Ch. 456 (CA) at [18] *et seq. per* Neuberger L.J.

[20] See generally, as to the need to distinguish between such balances, *supra*, para. 17–06 and *infra*, paras 22–02, 22–03.

[21] See *supra*, paras 10–79, 17–04 and *infra*, para. 19–17.

[22] *Richardson v. Bank of England* (1838) 4 Myl. & Cr. 165; *Rodriguez v. Speyer Bros.* [1919] A.C. 59, 68; *Dewan v. Hiranandani* (unreported), February 23, 1989. See also *Aulton v. Atkins* (1856) 18 C.B. 249; *Meyer & Co. v. Faber (No. 2)* [1923] 2 Ch. 421; *Brown v. Rivlin*, unreported, February 1, 1983 (C.A.T. No. 56), [1984] C.L.Y., p. 138; *Marshall v. Bullock*, March 27, 1998 (CA, unreported), noted *infra*, para. 23–36; *Hurst v. Bennett* [2001] B.P.I.R. 287 (CA); also *Re Ward* [1985] 2 N.Z.L.R. 352.

fail.[23] Thus, in *Green v. Moran*,[24] an outgoing partner's action to recover a fixed sum representing his perceived value of his share on retirement without taking an account was dismissed, *inter alia* on the basis that he had sought to "cherry pick" certain assets and ignored the firm's liabilities. Moreover, to speak of a share in financial terms *otherwise* than by reference to a partner's net entitlement (whether calculated in the above way or in some other manner prescribed by the partnership agreement) is both misleading and legally incorrect.

Nevertheless, it is considered that Lord Lindley's definition is, as such, incomplete and that a full understanding of the nature of a share (viewed solely in terms of the financial and proprietary entitlement which it confers upon its owner) is only possible if that entitlement is analysed at three stages in the life of a firm, namely: (1) whilst the partnership is continuing; (2) on a general dissolution and (3) on the death, retirement or expulsion of a partner.

The nature of a share—an analysis

(1) *Continuing partnership*

19–07   Whilst the partnership continues, each partner interested in the capital and assets of the firm[25] will unquestionably be entitled to a beneficial interest in respect of those assets and *may* also hold the legal title thereto, either alone or in conjunction with one or more of the other partners. If the legal title is vested in *all* the partners, it might be described as an incident of each partner's share, even if not part of the share itself[26]; if, on the other hand, title is vested in only some of the partners,[27] they will hold the relevant assets as trustees for the firm and the title therefore cannot properly be regarded even as an incident of their shares.

19–08   So far as concerns each partner's *beneficial* interest in the partnership assets, its precise nature will to an extent depend on the contents of the agreement, which may, for example, direct that, as between the partners, no account is to be taken of goodwill, thus purportedly negating their interests therein,[28] or declare that an outgoing partner is only to be entitled to the return of his capital. Nevertheless, it is submitted that, irrespective of the terms of the agreement, each partner's share will display two characteristics which may be regarded as constants. First, each partner's beneficial interest, expressed in terms of its realisability, is in the nature of a *future* interest taking effect in possession on (and not before) the determination of the partnership, whether brought about by his departure or by a general dissolution. This limitation on his entitlement may be

---

[23] Such an attempt was made (unsuccessfully) in *Dewan v. Hiranandani, supra*, albeit that the decision ultimately turned on the construction of a deed of retirement. See also *Green v. Hertzog* [1954] 1 W.L.R. 1309. Note that a bequest by a testator of his share in particular partnership assets may be valid as between the beneficiaries under his will, so that, if the partnership is solvent, the legatee will take free from liability to contribute to the partnership debts: *Re Holland* [1907] 2 Ch. 88. *Per contra*, if the partnership is insolvent: *Farquhar v. Hadden* (1871) L.R. 7 Ch.App. 1. See also, as to the latter cases, *infra*, para. 26–50. And see, as to agreements permitting effective dissection of a partner's share, *infra*, para. 19–50.

[24] 2002 S.L.T. 1404 (OH).

[25] There may, of course, be partners who do not enjoy such an interest: see *supra*, para. 18–02.

[26] See for example, *Re Bourne* [1906] 2 Ch. 427, 432, 433 *per* Romer L.J.

[27] *e.g.* where land is vested in four of the partners pursuant to the Trustee Act 1925, s.34(2) (as amended by the Trusts of Land and Appointment of Trustees Act 1996, Sched. 3, para. 3(9)) or the Law of Property Act 1925, s.34(2) (as amended by *ibid*. Sched. 2, para. 3(2)).

[28] This does not, of course, mean that the goodwill ceases to be an asset of the firm, merely that, in the events contemplated by the agreement, its value is to be ignored. The position will, however, be different on a general dissolution: see further, *supra*, para. 10–76 and *infra*, para. 25–44.

explained by reference to the fact that, as long as the partnership continues,[29] each partner is entitled to require the partnership assets to be applied for partnership purposes and no partner is entitled to use or enjoy his share of those assets to the exclusion of his co-partners.[30] Secondly, when the partnership is determined and the partner's beneficial interest in the partnership assets notionally falls into possession, it will take effect subject to the right of the other partners to have those assets applied towards payment of the firm's debts and liabilities and any surplus divided between the partners in the manner prescribed by the Partnership Act 1890.[31] This will normally entail a sale of such property.[32] Thus, in the absence of any agreement to the contrary,[33] the share of a partner will represent (and should always be stated in terms of) his proportionate share in the net proceeds of sale of the partnership assets, after all the firm's debts and liabilities have been paid or provided for.[34]

The foregoing analysis appears to have been accepted by the Privy Council in *Hadlee v. Commissioner of Inland Revenue*[35] and, in substance, by the Court of Appeal in *Popat v. Shonchhatra*.[36]

(2) *General dissolution*

In the event of a general dissolution,[37] each partner will again be entitled to insist on the partnership assets being applied towards payment of the firm's debts and liabilities and a division of any surplus proceeds.[38] Until such time as those assets are either sold or divided *in specie*,[39] it is submitted that each partner's share will

19–09

---

[29] For this purpose a partnership must be regarded as continuing notwithstanding the death, retirement or expulsion of a partner, unless that event causes a general dissolution: see further, *supra*, paras 10–39, 10–40.

[30] See *Lingen v. Simpson* (1824) 1 Sim. & St. 600; *Cockle v. Whiting* (1829) Tam. 55; *Marshall v. Maclure* (1885) 10 App.Cas. 325; *Gray v. I.R.C.* [1994] S.T.C. 360, 377c–e, noted *supra*, para. 19–03; *Popat v. Shonchhatra* [1997] 1 W.L.R. 1367, 1372C (CA); also *Re Bainbridge* (1878) 8 Ch.D. 218 (where a mortgage of a partnership share in chattels was held not to be subject to the Bills of Sale Acts). And see *supra*, para. 19–04.

[31] See *ibid.* ss.39, 44, *infra*, paras 19–25 *et seq.*, 25–45 *et seq.*

[32] See *infra*, paras 23–183 *et seq.*

[33] It is, of course, possible for the partnership agreement to provide that, subject to payment of the firm's debts and liabilities, its assets will be distributed between the partners *in specie*: see *supra*, paras 10–264, 10–265.

[34] See *supra*, paras 19–05, 19–06.

[35] [1993] A.C. 524, 532G. In this case, a partner in a firm of accountants sought (unsuccessfully) to argue that, by assigning part of his share to trustees for his wife and child, he had divested himself of liability for income tax under the relevant New Zealand legislation in respect of the income profits attributable to that part. See also *infra*, para. 19–57.

[36] [1997] 1 W.L.R. 1367, 1372C–E. The major part of the passage in the text was also cited and applied by Evans-Lombe J. in *Fengate Developments v. Customs & Excise Commissioners* [2004] S.T.C. 772 at [14], [15]. Note also the discussion of an earlier formulation of the analysis in *Connell v. Bond Corp. Pty Ltd.* (1992) 8 W.A.R. 352, 364–365. There, the court held that a partner's interest in land owned by the firm is sufficient to support a *caveat*. However, an entirely contrary conclusion was reached in *Chettle v. Brown* (1993) 2 Qd. R. 604. See further, on the issue of protecting a partner's lien over the firm's land, *infra*, para. 19–25, n. 102.

[37] Such a dissolution may be brought about in any of the ways discussed *infra*, paras 24–04 *et seq.*

[38] Partnership Act 1890, ss.39, 44, *infra*, paras 19–25 *et seq.*, 25–45 *et seq.* And see *Re Ward* [1985] 2 N.Z.L.R. 352.

[39] Such a division must be made with the agreement of the partners or, conceivably, by an order of the court or an arbitrator.

have the same proprietary character as it had prior to the dissolution.[40] Nevertheless, in terms of value, the share must still be expressed as a net entitlement since, in the absence of some specific agreement between the partners, it cannot properly be viewed in any other light.[41] This analysis was, in effect, confirmed by the Court of Appeal in *Popat v. Shonchhatra*.[42] The fact that a partner's share may have been ascribed a certain value as at the date of dissolution, *e.g.* in a dissolution account, is neither here nor there, since it does not represent his ultimate entitlement.[43]

(3) *Death, retirement or expulsion of a partner*

19–10   If any of the above events cause a general dissolution, the position will be as described in the preceding paragraph.[44] Where, however, it is expressly or impliedly agreed that the partnership will continue notwithstanding the change in the firm,[45] the precise nature and value of the deceased or outgoing partner's share will depend on the terms of the partnership agreement.

If, as will usually be the case, the agreement establishes the manner in which the deceased or outgoing partner's financial entitlement in respect of his share is to be ascertained and paid[46] and provides for the devolution of the legal title to any partnership assets which may be vested in him,[47] his share may properly be regarded as a pure debt with effect from the date on which he ceased to be a partner.[48] It is only where such terms are omitted that difficulties may arise.

19–11   In the absence of any *express* provision in the agreement, the entitlement of the deceased or outgoing partner in respect of his share will, in the normal way, strictly be represented by his proportionate share in the net proceeds remaining after all the partnership assets have been sold and the partnership debts and liabilities paid and discharged.[49] However, where there is an implied recognition on the part of the outgoing partner that the other partners will continue the business, those other partners will be treated as entitled to acquire his share at a valuation and the court will direct the necessary accounts and inquiries for that purpose.[50] If, on the other hand, there is no such implied recognition but the other partners wish to carry on the business and are prepared to pay the outgoing

---

[40] See *supra*, para. 19–08. Note also, in this context, the partners' continuing obligations *inter se* pursuant to the Partnership Act 1890, s.38: see *supra*, paras 13–62 *et seq*.

[41] This is quite apart from the provisions of *ibid*. s.43, which is strictly inapplicable in the case of a general dissolution: see *infra*, paras 23–34, 26–03. Note that the potential application of that section was not considered by the court in *Barclays Bank Trust Co. Ltd. v. Bluff* [1982] Ch. 172, *infra*, para. 25–32.

[42] [1997] 1 W.L.R. 1367, 1372D–E. See also *Hurst v. Bennett* [2001] B.P.I.R. 287 (CA).

[43] *Winning v. Cunningham* 2009 GWD 01–19 (Sh. Ct.).

[44] In the case of a partnership at will, the death or bankruptcy of a partner will cause such a dissolution: Partnership Act 1890, s.33(1). See further, *infra*, paras 24–29 *et seq*.

[45] See *supra*, para. 10–39 and *infra*, para. 23–184.

[46] See *supra*, para. 10–150.

[47] See *supra*, paras 10–244 *et seq*.

[48] In such a case, it is submitted that the Partnership Act 1890, s.43 will clearly apply: see *infra*, paras 23–34, 26–04. This was the conclusion reached in *Beckman v. I.R.C.* [2000] S.T.C. (S.C.D.) 59. Equally, an agreement could in theory provide that the share will be retained by the outgoing partner *in specie* until its value has been ascertained. In such a case, the operation of s.43 will be deferred.

[49] See *supra*, para. 19–05.

[50] See *Sobell v. Boston* [1975] 1 W.L.R. 1587; also *Green v. Moran* 2002 S.L.T. 1404 (OH); *Summers v. Smith*, March 27, 2002 (Lawtel 2/4/2002) at [64] *per* Kevin Garnett Q.C. (sitting as a deputy judge of the Chancery Division). Although the report is wholly inadequate, it would seem that *Small v. Cohen, The Times*, September 7, 1992, was also a case of this class.

partner the market value of his share, the court may, in its discretion, refuse a sale of the partnership assets and order an inquiry as to the market value of the share and the payment of that value by the continuing partners.[51] However, the latter discretion has tended to be exercised sparingly and, as a general rule, only when the outgoing partner's share is of modest size or when, as in the case of a professional firm, a sale of all its assets, including goodwill, is regarded as impracticable.[52]

In any case in which a share falls to be valued in the above way, it will be **19–12** important to determine the date on which such value is to be taken. Where there is an implied agreement for the acquisition of the deceased or outgoing partner's share, the relevant date will be the date on which he ceased to be a partner[53]; where, however, a valuation is directed by the court in the exercise of its discretion, some other date may be regarded as more appropriate, *e.g.* the date of the application.[54] In the former case, the outgoing partner can, seemingly, only be "compensated" for any delay in the payment of his financial entitlement by a claim under section 42 of the Partnership Act 1890,[55] unless a claim for interest at a more realistic rate is allowed under the Senior Courts Act 1981.[56] What such a partner cannot on any footing claim is a share of any capital profits attributable to increases in the value of the partnership assets since the date on which he ceased to be a partner.[57] On the other hand, in the latter case, if the share is valued at a date later than the outgoing partner's retirement, etc., he will necessarily be entitled to share in any capital profits accruing up to that date, but otherwise must necessarily be limited to his rights under section 42 of the 1890 Act.[58]

The doctrine of non-survivorship between partners

It has long been recognised that partnership is not a species of joint tenancy **19–13** and that, in the absence of some contrary agreement,[59] there is no survivorship

---

[51] *Syers v. Syers* (1876) 1 App.Cas. 174. And see *Rivett v. Rivett* (1966) 200 E.G. 858. See also *infra*, paras 23–187 *et seq.*

[52] It would appear that the court is now more receptive to applications for such orders, although they are never made as a matter of course: see *infra*, para. 23–189. The conviction that values can only be accurately assessed by an actual realisation in the open market still tends to persist, although this may, perhaps, be overcome by the court directing the employment of a joint expert valuer pursuant to the CPR r. 35.7.

[53] Partnership Act 1890, s.43; *Sobell v. Boston* [1975] 1 W.L.R. 1587.

[54] See *infra*, para. 23–191.

[55] *i.e.* a claim for interest at 5% or, at the outgoing partner's (or his estate's) option, the share of profits attributable to the use of his share. See further, as to the nature of the entitlement under the section, *infra*, paras 25–22 *et seq.*

[56] Note that the former Supreme Court Act 1981 was renamed by the Constitutional Reform Act 2005, Sched. 11, Pt.1, para. 1(1). Pursuing a claim under the Senior Courts Act 1981, s.35A (or the County Courts Act s.69) may well, however, be problematic: see further *infra*, para. 20–41. So far as the current editor is aware, there is no reported case in which payment of interest has been awarded under the 1981 Act in such circumstances. Moreover, it must be recognised that the claim in *Sobell v. Boston*, *supra*, was, in the orthodox manner, formulated under s.42 of the 1890 Act.

[57] Consistently with the earlier decisions (and with the provisions of the Partnership Act 1890, s.43), it is considered that the decision in *Barclays Bank Trust Co. Ltd. v. Bluff* [1982] Ch. 172 is confined to cases where there is a *general* dissolution.

[58] It could, of course, be argued that the Partnership Act 1890, s.43 in any event applies in such a case so as to ground a claim under the 1981 Act, but this would be difficult to sustain: see *infra*, para. 23–34.

[59] *e.g.* for the automatic accruer of an outgoing partner's share without payment: see *infra*, paras 35–16, 36–24. But see also *supra*, para. 10–153.

as between partners, at least so far as concerns their *beneficial* interests in the partnership assets. Lord Lindley put it thus:

"It is an old and well-established maxim, that *Jus accrescendi inter mercatores locum non habet.*[60] This is a common law, and not only an equitable maxim; but whilst its application in equity was subject to few, if any, exceptions,[61] it was not at law so universally applicable as the generality of its terms might lead one to suppose."

He then concluded:

"Before quitting the present subject, it may be observed that the doctrine of non-survivorship amongst partners is not confined to merchants nor even to traders, but extends to partners generally."[62]

It, was, however, held in *Bathurst v. Scarborow*[63] that, in an appropriate case, partners *may* agree to hold partnership property as joint tenants and that agreement will be respected by the courts and the doctrine of non-survivorship will be displaced. As was pointed out by Rix L.J.,[64] this may be easier to demonstrate in the case of a partnership between a husband and wife or the like.

The devolution of the *legal* title to land and other assets owned by a firm was considered in the previous chapter.[65]

Conversion of shares in partnership land

19–14 Writing prior to the Partnership Act 1890, Lord Lindley said:

"From the principle that a share of a partner is nothing more than his proportion of the partnership assets after they have been turned into money and applied in liquidation of the partnership debts, it necessarily follows that, in equity, a share in a partnership, whether its property consists of land or not, must, as between the real and personal representatives of a deceased partner, be deemed to be his personal and not real estate, unless indeed such conversion is inconsistent with the agreement between the parties."[66]

[60] Co. Lit. 182a.

[61] In *Nelson v. Bealby* (1862) 4 De G.F. & J. 321, a partnership agreement between A and B provided that, on A's death, his executors should receive one-half of the assets from B, but did not specify what was to happen on B's death. It was, nevertheless, held that B's executors were entitled to one-half of the assets from A.

[62] See *Buckley v. Barber* (1851) 6 Ex. 164; also *Aunand v. Honiwood* (1682) 2 Ch.Ca. 129; *Jefferys v. Small* (1683) 1 Vern. 217; *Lake v. Gibson* (1729) 1 Eq.Ca.Abr. 290; *Lake v. Craddock* (1732) 3 P.W. 158. *cf. Barton v. Morris* [1985] 1 W.L.R. 1257, 1262 *per* Nicholls J.

[63] [2005] 1 P. & C.R. 58 (CA).

[64] *ibid.* at [52].

[65] See *supra*, paras 18–61 *et seq.*

[66] See *Steward v. Blakeway* (1869) L.R. 4 Ch.App. 603; *Re Wilson* [1893] 2 Ch. 340; also *Re Kent County Gas, Light and Coke Co. Ltd.* [1909] 2 Ch. 195. Although there were conflicting authorities on this point, those favouring Lord Lindley's view were preponderant: in favour were *Ripley v. Waterworth* (1802) 7 Ves.Jr. 425; *Townshend v. Devaynes* (1808) 1 Mont.Part., note 2, App., p. 96; and see also 11 Sim. 498n.; *Phillips v. Phillips* (1832) 1 M. & K. 649, noted *supra*, para. 18–09; *Broom v. Broom* (1834) 3 M. & K. 443; *Morris v. Kearsley* (1836) 2 Y. & C.Ex. 139; *Houghton v. Houghton* (1841) 11 Sim. 491; *Essex v. Essex* (1855) 20 Beav. 442; *Darby v. Darby* (1856) 3 Drew. 495; *Holroyd v. Holroyd* (1859) 7 W.R. 426; *Waterer v. Waterer* (1873) 15 Eq. 403, noted *supra*, para. 18–30; *Murtagh v. Costello* (1881) 7 L.R.Ir. 428. Opposing authorities were *Thornton v. Dixon* (1791) 3 Bro.C.C. 199; *Bell v. Phyn* (1802) 7 Ves.Jr. 453; *Randall v. Randall* (1835) 7 Sim. 271; *Cookson v. Cookson* (1837) 8 Sim. 529.

Although this principle was duly reflected in section 22 of the Partnership Act 1890,[67] that section has now been repealed.[68] In addition the general doctrine of conversion has been abolished, but *only* in the case of land held on trust for sale.[69] It has already been seen[70] that partnership land will in all cases be held on a trust of land and instances in which the potential application (or non-application) of the doctrine of conversion, in so far as it still survives, will be of any relevance to partners are likely to be extremely rare.[71] However, the logic behind the doctrine as applied to partnership property and analysed by Lord Lindley in the above passage, is still compelling when viewed in terms of the true nature of a partnership share.

It should also be noted that, even in those rare cases in which the doctrine of conversion applies, the court might still, in exceptional circumstances, be prepared to treat a partner's share in land as identified with the land itself.[72]

2.   THE SIZE OF EACH PARTNER'S SHARE

The size of each partner's share, expressed in terms of his interest in the **19–15** partnership assets, is primarily dependent on the terms agreed by the partners.[73] It is only in the absence of such terms that it is necessary to resort to the provisions of section 24(1) of the Partnership Act 1890.[74]

The normal rule: equality

Lord Lindley, writing before the Partnership Act 1890, said: **19–16**

> "In the event of a dispute between the partners as to the amount of their shares, such dispute, if it does not turn on the construction of written documents, must be decided

---

[67] The section provided as follows: "22. Where land or any heritable interest therein has become partnership property, it shall, unless the contrary intention appears, be treated as between the partners (including the representatives of a deceased partner), and also as between the heirs of a deceased partner and his executors or administrators, as personal or moveable and not real or heritable estate."

[68] Trusts of Land and Appointment of Trustees Act 1996, Sched. 4. It should be noted that s.22 had, in any event, largely been overtaken by the mandatory provisions of the Law of Property Act 1925, s.34, which imposed a trust for sale in most cases, so that all partners' beneficial interests were, as the law then stood, automatically converted into personal property. This is no longer the case: see *infra*.

[69] Trusts of Land and Appointment of Trustees Act 1996, s.3(1). The rubric to this section ("Abolition of doctrine of conversion") is misleading. *Semble*, the section does not apply in the case of a constructive or resulting trust.

[70] See *supra*, paras 18–62 *et seq.*

[71] Since there is no longer any distinction between real and personal representatives, it seems that such a question would only arise where a partner makes a specific devise or bequest of his realty/personalty without more. Equally, this is likely to be of little real concern to the other partners.

[72] See for example, the decision in *Burdett-Coutts v. I.R.C.* [1960] 1 W.L.R. 1027 (estate duty); *Gray v. I.R.C.* [1994] S.T.C. 360, 377 (inheritance tax); also *Cooper v. Critchley* [1955] Ch. 431 and the authorities cited therein.

[73] See *supra*, paras 10–78 *et seq.*

[74] This and the following two paragraphs were considered in *Sandhu v. Gill* [2006] Ch. 456 (CA) at [52], [55]–[58] *per* Neuberger L.J. And see also *Neal v. Jones* [2002] EWCA Civ 1731 (Lawtel 31/10/02) at [44] *per* Rix L.J.

like any other pure question of fact[75]; and if there is no evidence from which any satisfactory conclusion as to what was agreed can be drawn,[76] the shares of all the partners will be adjudged equal."[77]

This still remains true, as is made clear by section 24 of the Partnership Act 1890, which provides that:

> "24. The interests of partners in partnership property and their rights and duties in relation to the partnership shall be determined, subject to any agreement express or implied between the partners by the following rules:
>
> > (1) All the partners are entitled to share equally in the capital and profits of the business, and must contribute equally towards the losses whether of capital or otherwise sustained by the firm."

Scope of the rule

19–17   The rule of equality embodied in the above section will, in the absence of any contrary agreement, always be applied when determining partners' shares in the firm's fixed capital,[78] income or trading profits and capital profits or asset surpluses, *i.e.* the amount by which the market value of the partnership assets exceeds their acquisition or book value.[79]

The same rule is applied to losses, whatever their nature.[80] Thus, even where it is clear that capital has been contributed *and is thereafter to be owned* in unequal proportions, the rule will still apply in the case of a loss of that capital, as Lord Lindley explained:

> "When it is said that the shares of partners are prima facie equal, although their capitals are unequal, what is meant is that losses of capital like other losses must be shared equally but it is not meant that, on a final settlement of accounts, capitals contributed unequally are to be treated as one aggregate fund which ought to be divided between the partners in equal shares."

The latter part of the above passage should not, however, be taken as indicating that the rule can *never* apply to the firm's fixed capital.[81]

Justification for the rule

19–18   Lord Lindley explained the basis for the pre-1890 Act rule of equality in the following terms:

[75] *Binford v. Dommett* (1799) 4 Ves.Jr. 756; *Peacock v. Peacock* (1809) 16 Ves.Jr. 49; *McGregor v. Bainbrigge* (1848) 7 Hare 164.

[76] *Copland v. Toulmin* (1840) 7 Cl. & F. 349; *Stewart v. Forbes* (1849) 1 Mac. & G. 137; *Webster v. Bray* (1849) 7 Hare 159.

[77] *Robinson v. Anderson* (1855) 20 Beav. 98 and, on appeal, (1855) 7 De G.M. & G. 239 (noted *infra*, para. 19–22); also *Peacock v. Peacock* (1809) 16 Ves.Jr. 49; *Farrar v. Beswick* (1836) 1 Moo. & Rob. 527; *Webster v. Bray* (1849) 7 Hare 159.

[78] *Popat v. Shonchhatra* [1997] 1 W.L.R. 1367, 1372H–1373C (CA). However, it will take little evidence of an implied agreement to displace the rule in the case of fixed capital: *ibid.* See further *supra*, paras 17–07, 17–08.

[79] See *supra*, para. 17–04. This may be of critical importance for the purposes of any charge to capital gains or inheritance tax: see *infra*, paras 35–06, 36–20 *et seq.*, 36–39. Note, however, the anomalous decision in *Bennett v. Wallace* 1998 S.C. 457, discussed *supra*, para. 10–173.

[80] See further, as to losses, *infra*, paras 20–04 *et seq.*

[81] See *Popat v. Shonchattra, supra.*

"This rule no doubt occasionally leads to apparent injustice; but it is not easy to lay down any other rule which, under the circumstances supposed, could be fairly applied. It is sometimes suggested that the shares of partners ought to be proportionate to their contributions; but without in any way denying this, it may be asked, how is the value of each partner's contribution to be measured? Certainly not merely by the capital he may have brought into the firm. His skill, his connection, his command of the confidence and respect of others, must all be taken into account; and if it is impossible to set a money value on each partner's contribution in this respect, it is impossible to determine in the manner suggested the shares of the partners in the partnership. Nor is it unreasonable to infer, in the absence of all evidence to the contrary, that the partners themselves have agreed to consider their contributions as of equal value, although they may have brought in unequal sums of money, or be themselves unequal as regards skill, connection, or character. Whether, therefore, partners have contributed money equally or unequally, whether they are or are not on a par as regards skill, connection, or character, whether they have or have not laboured equally for the benefit of the firm, their shares will be considered as equal, unless some agreement to the contrary can be shown to have been entered into."[82]

The last sentence of the above passage was quoted with approval in *Joyce v. Morrisey*.[83]

Evidence of an agreement displacing the rule

An agreement displacing the normal rule of equality may be inferred from a **19–19** course of conduct or from the contents of the partnership books.[84] Thus, if the proceeds of the sale of a particular partnership asset have been shared between the partners in proportion to their capital contributions, this will represent strong evidence in favour of an inference that all capital profits are to be shared in those proportions. This may be so, even though the partners have shared income profits equally or in some other way.[85]

Subsequent changes in sharing ratios

In *Joyce v. Morrisey*,[86] it was held that, where a partnership operates on the **19–20** basis of equal sharing ratios, an agreement to vary them must be supported by consideration, which will normally be found in "the agreement not to terminate the partnership if the new terms are agreed".[87] In the current editor's view, consideration, if it is indeed required for such a variation,[88] will more properly be found in the partners' ongoing partnership relation.[89]

By the same token, where unequal sharing ratios have been established, the partners will not be presumed to have abandoned them merely because one or more of their number have retired from the firm. As Lord Lindley said "in the absence of evidence to the contrary, the inference is that the shares of the retiring members have been taken by the continuing parties in the proportions in which

---

[82] See the cases cited in the footnotes to para. 19–16, *supra*. Lord Lindley pointed out that the decisions in *Peacock v. Peacock* (1809) 2 Camp. 45 and *Sharpe v. Cummings* (1844) 2 Dow. & L. 504 cannot be supported.

[83] [1999] E.M.L.R. 233, 243 *per* Waller L.J.

[84] As in *Stewart v. Forbes* (1849) 1 Mac. & G. 137.

[85] But see *infra*, para. 19–21.

[86] [1999] E.M.L.R. 233 (CA).

[87] *ibid.* p. 244 *per* Waller L.J.

[88] There is no such requirement imposed by the Partnership Act 1890, s.19, *supra*, para. 10–12.

[89] See *supra*, para. 10–12.

these last were originally interested in the concern."[90] Where, however, a new partner has been admitted to the firm, such an inference will be more difficult to draw.

Relation between income and capital profit shares

19–21   If the partners agree to share income profits in unequal shares, the inference must be, in the absence of evidence indicating a contrary intent, that they will share capital profits, and thus be interested in the partnership assets, in the same proportions. Any other approach would result in absurdity, *i.e.* an application of the presumption of equality under section 24(1) whilst the partnership continues, but its rejection in the event of a dissolution, when the agreed (unequal) profit sharing ratios are applied by virtue of section 44 of the Partnership Act 1890.[91]

Application of the rule to single adventure

19–22   The fact that the partnership has been formed in order to carry out a single business transaction or venture in itself provides no justification for departing from the normal rule of equality. This is illustrated by the decision in *Robinson v. Anderson*,[92] where two solicitors, who were not in partnership together, were jointly retained to defend certain actions. In the absence of any satisfactory evidence as to the proportions in which they were to divide their remuneration, the rule was applied, even though the amount of work they had done was not equal and they had received separate payments therefor. Sir John Romilly M.R.,[93] after stressing the importance of the burden of proof in such cases, said:

> "Now I should entertain no doubt, even if I had not been confirmed by the two cases of *Webster v. Bray*[94] and *McGregor v. Bainbrigge*,[95] that where two solicitors undertake a matter of business on behalf of a client, the same rule would follow in that, as in any other undertaking where two persons carry on a business jointly on behalf of themselves, or as agents of other persons. It is, in point of fact, a limited partnership[96] for a particular sort of business. Assuming nothing to have been said as

---

[90] *Robley v. Brooke* (1833) 7 Bli.(N.S.) 90; and see *Copland v. Toulmin* (1840) 7 Cl. & F. 349. A similar observation was made in Lord Lindley's commentary on s.24(1) in his Supplement on the Partnership Act 1890.

[91] *ibid.* para. 4: see *infra*, paras 25–45 *et seq*. This argument would also ignore the true nature of a partner's interest in the partnership assets, as discussed *supra*, paras 19–02 *et seq*. And note, in this context, the decision in *Popat v. Shonchhatra* [1997] 1 W.L.R. 1367, 1374 in which the Court of Appeal held that, where s.24(1) applies, it determines the partners' profit shares both before *and after* a dissolution; also *Hopper v. Hopper* [2008] EWCA Civ. 1417 (Lawtel 12/12/08) (CA) at [47]. But see further on this point, *supra*, paras 10–84, 13–72 and *infra*, para. 25–22.

[92] (1855) 20 Beav. 98 and, on appeal, (1855) 7 De G.M. & G. 239. See also *Hanslip v. Kitton* (1862) 8 Jur.(N.S.) 835.

[93] See (1853) 20 Beav. 102.

[94] (1848) 7 Hare 159.

[95] (1848) 7 Hare 164, note.

[96] This expression referred to the restricted nature of the venture; at the time of the judgment, the concept of limited partnership (as it is now formulated under the Limited Partnerships Act 1907) had been under consideration but had not been introduced into English law: see *infra*, paras 28–03 *et seq*.

to the manner in which the profits were to be divided, it appears to me to follow as a necessary consequence of law that they are to be divided equally between them. . . . It was the duty of the party who intended that this should not be a partnership transaction, and that he should be paid for the amount of business which he did, without participating in that of the other, so to express himself."

Position where a firm enters into partnership

Where a firm (AB) comprising two partners (A and B) purports to enter into **19–23** partnership with a third party (C), the question arises whether, in applying the rule of equality, the partnership should be treated as having two partners (*i.e.* the firm AB and the third party C) or three (*i.e.* A, B and C). The answer must depend on the terms of the agreement and the capacity in which A and B entered into the partnership venture: if they purported to do so as a firm, *e.g.* in the name AB, they will prima facie be treated as a single partner, internally at least,[97] and the size of their joint share determined accordingly; if they contracted as individuals, they will each be treated as partners and their joint entitlement correspondingly increased.[98] Such difficulties will obviously be avoided if the profit shares are clearly specified in the agreement.[99]

3.   THE PARTNER'S LIEN AND ITS CONSEQUENCES

Reference has already been made to the right of a partner to insist on the **19–24** partnership property being applied in payment of the partnership debts and any surplus divided between the partners according to their respective entitlements.[100] It is this right which is conventionally styled "the partner's lien", even though that expression will not be found in the Partnership Act 1890 itself. Prior to that Act, Lord Lindley defined the lien thus:

"In order to discharge himself from the liabilities to which a person may be subject as partner, every partner has a right to have the property of the partnership applied in payment of the debts and liabilities of the firm. And in order to secure a proper division of the surplus assets, he has a right to have whatever may be due to the firm from his co-partners, as members thereof, deducted from what would otherwise be payable to them in respect of their shares in the partnership. In other words, each partner may be said to have an equitable lien on the partnership property for the purpose of having it applied in discharge of the debts of the firm; and to have a similar lien on the surplus assets for the purpose of having them applied in payment

---

[97] It hardly needs to be said that a firm will not *in law* constitute a single partner, since it has no separate personality: see *supra*, para. 4–27. *Per contra* in the case of a Scottish firm: see *Major v. Brodie* [1998] S.T.C. 491.

[98] See *Warner v. Smith* (1863) 1 De G.J. & S. 337, where the firm contracted as such and the profits were held to be divisible into two and not three parts.

[99] As in *Mann v. D'Arcy* [1968] 1 W.L.R. 893, where the agreement was for an equal division of profits between the firm and the individual.

[100] See *supra*, paras 19–08 *et seq.*

of what may be due to the partners respectively, after deducting what may be due from them, as partners, to the firm."[101]

Partnership Act 1890, section 39

19-25   Lord Lindley was at pains to point out that, irrespective of the title which it may be given, the foregoing right normally has little practical application prior to the dissolution of a partnership, when its affairs fall to be wound up or the share of a partner ascertained. This is now expressly recognised by section 39 of the Partnership Act 1890, which provides as follows:

> "39. On the dissolution of partnership every partner is entitled, as against the other partners in the firm, and all persons claiming through them in respect of their interests as partners, to have the property of the partnership applied in payment of the debts and liabilities of the firm, and to have the surplus assets after such payment applied in payment of what may be due to the partners respectively after deducting what may be due from them as partners to the firm; and for that purpose any partner or his representatives may on the termination of the partnership apply to the court to wind up the business and affairs of the firm."

It is submitted that the above section does no more than give statutory recognition to the partner's lien on dissolution and does not purport to exclude its operation at other times. Thus, the possibility of its enforcement could conceivably arise during the continuance of the partnership, *e.g.* if a partner in whom is vested the legal title to a partnership asset were to dispose of it to a third party who had notice of its status. In such a case, the existence of the lien could well be material in the event of the third party's insolvency.[102]

Property subject to the lien

19-26   Whilst the partnership continues, the lien attaches to *every* item of partnership property, including stock in trade. Of the latter, Lord Lindley pointed out that the lien "is not . . . lost by the substitution of new stock in trade for old", thus

---

[101] *Skipp v. Harwood* (1747) 2 Swan. 586; *West v. Skip* (1749) 1 Ves.Sen. 239; *Doddington v. Hallet* (1750) 1 Ves.Sen. 497, 498–499 *per* Hardwicke L.C.; *Ex p. Ruffin* (1801) 6 Ves.Jr. 119; *Ex p. Williams* (1805) 11 Ves.Jr. 3; *Holderness v. Shackels* (1828) 8 B. & C. 612. Lord Lindley pointed out that "*Smith v. De Silva* (1776) Cowp. 469 can hardly be reconciled with the other cases, but see upon it the observations of Lord Tenterden in *Holderness v. Shackels* (1828) 8 B. & C. 618." See also *Re Ward* [1985] 2 N.Z.L.R. 352, 354. As to the right of a minority of partners to insist on the payment of a partnership debt out of the partnership assets, see the observations of Turner V.-C. in *Stevens v. The South Devon Ry.* (1851) 9 Hare 313, 326. A member of a firm is normally entitled to pay any of its debts and to charge that sum to the firm; see *infra*, paras 20–04 *et seq.*

[102] In the case of a purchaser acquiring the legal estate in partnership land (other than trading stock), it would appear that enforcement would, in the case of unregistered land, depend on the prior registration of the lien as a general equitable charge under the Land Charges Act 1972. The position in the case of registered land is more complex: the lien can only be protected by registration of a unilateral notice or a restriction: see the Land Registration Act 2002, ss.32, 34(2)(b) (unilateral notice), 40, 42(1) (restriction). The current editor is aware of one instance in which a unilateral notice was accepted by the Land Registry, albeit reluctantly. If a notice *can* be registered, no restriction will be permissible on the basis that it will protect the right to the lien under *ibid.* s.42(1)(c); see *ibid.* s.42(2). It should be noted that, in *Connell v. Bond Corp. Pty Ltd.* (1992) 8 W.A.R. 352, it was held that a partner's interest in partnership land *was* sufficient to support a *caveat*, although the opposite conclusion was subsequently reached in *Chettle v. Brown* (1993) 2 Qd. R. 604. The basis for the caveats entered in *Bush v. Hanlon* [1998] N.S.W.S.C. 326 is unclear. Note also, in this context, *London & Cheshire Insurance Co. Ltd. v. Laplagrene Property Co.* [1971] Ch. 499, regarding the registrability of an unpaid vendor's lien under what is now the Companies Act 2006, s.860.

recognising that, to this extent at least, the lien has a "floating" character, *i.e.* it attaches to the stock for the time being.[103] This aspect of the lien will be considered in greater detail hereafter.[104]

The corollary of the foregoing is, naturally, that the lien does not attach to anything other than partnership property. Thus, if there is in truth no such property because the partnership is confined to the profits produced by property belonging to one or more of the partners, there will be nothing to which the lien can attach.[105]

Position on dissolution

On a dissolution, the lien will only be exercisable in respect of the partnership **19–27** property at that time and will not extend to assets acquired subsequently, unless they can properly be said to be partnership assets.[106] It follows that, if surviving or continuing partners carry on the business and, in the course of so doing, acquire property, it will prima facie be free of the lien. Lord Lindley observed that "in this respect the lien in question differs from the lien of a mortgagee on a varying stock in trade assigned to him as a security for his loan."[107] Subject to the foregoing, on the death or insolvency of a partner, his lien continues in favour of his personal representatives or trustee, and does not terminate until his share has either been ascertained and paid by the other partners[108] or, seemingly, extinguished by effluxion of time under the Limitation Act 1980.[109]

Enforceability of lien against persons claiming through partner

The Partnership Act 1890[110] confirms that the lien may not only be enforced **19–28** as between the partners, but also as against persons claiming through them, *e.g.* personal representatives, trustees in bankruptcy, liquidators, assignees and execution creditors.[111]

In *Re Ritson*[112] one of two partners charged his own land as security for a debt owed by his firm to its bankers. He died, having devised the land to his son and

---

[103] See *Skipp v. Harwood* (1747) 2 Swan. 586; *West v. Skip* (1749) 1 Ves.Sen. 239; *Stocken v. Dawson* (1845) 9 Beav. 239, affirmed (1848) 17 L.J.Ch. 282. *cf.* the cases cited *infra*, para. 19–27, n. 107.

[104] See *infra*, paras 19–29 *et seq.*

[105] See *Stekel v. Ellice* [1973] 1 W.L.R. 191. Lord Lindley also cited the following example, which is of more limited relevance: "Moreover, if two persons engage in a joint adventure, each consigning goods for sale upon the terms that each is to have the produce of his own goods, neither of them will have a lien on the goods of the other, nor on the produce of such goods, although each may have raised the money to pay for his own goods by a bill drawn on himself by the other, and ultimately dishonoured": *Ex p. Gemmel* (1843) 3 M.D. & D. 198. It is clear from the report that no partnership existed between the consignors.

[106] *Quaere*, could the lien attach to an asset acquired after the date of dissolution which in effect *represents* a partnership asset, *e.g.* where a particular asset is sold and the proceeds reinvested in some other asset? A similar issue is canvassed, *supra*, para. 18–15, n. 54.

[107] *Payne v. Hornby* (1858) 25 Beav. 280. See also *Nerot v. Burnand* (1827) 4 Russ. 247, affirmed (1828) 2 Bli.(N.S.) 215, *supra*, para. 18–15; *Ex p. Morley* (1873) L.R. 8 Ch.App. 1026. *cf.* the cases cited *supra*, para. 19–26, n. 103.

[108] See *Stocken v. Dawson* (1845) 9 Beav. 239, affirmed (1848) 17 L.J.Ch. 282; also *Re Fox* (1915) 49 Ir.L.T. 224 and the cases cited *supra*, para. 19–26, n. 103.

[109] It is submitted that, where the Partnership Act 1890, s.43 applies, a partner's lien will normally become statute-barred, along with his entitlement under that section, six years after the date on which he ceases to be a partner: see *infra*, paras 19–35, 23–34 *et seq.*

[110] See the opening words of *ibid.* s.39, *supra*, para. 19–25.

[111] See *West v. Skip* (1749) 1 Ves.Sen. 239 and the other cases cited *supra*, para. 19–26, n. 103.

[112] [1899] 1 Ch. 128.

the residue of his property, including his partnership share, to all his children.[113] The partnership assets were sufficient to pay all the partnership debts, including the secured debt. It was argued on behalf of the children (other than the son) that the testator's share of that debt should be borne by the land charged with its payment but they were ultimately unsuccessful. The court held that: (1) the share bequeathed to the children was only the testator's share in the surplus partnership assets remaining after payment of *all* the partnership debts, including the secured debt, (2) as the assets were sufficient to pay all the debts, Locke King's Act[114] did not apply and (3) the surviving partner being entitled to insist on the partnership assets being applied in payment of its debts, the devisee of the land should have the same right as against the testator's executors and children.

Enforceability of lien against purchasers

19–29   In relation to purchasers of partnership property, a distinction must, on the one hand, be drawn between trading stock and fixed assets and, on the other, between a continuing and a dissolved partnership.

Trading stock: Brief reference has already been made to the operation of the lien as regards trading stock.[115] It has long been recognised that trading stock disposed of in the normal course of business ceases to be subject to the lien[116]; to hold otherwise would effectively prevent any sale of that stock without the consent of all the partners and make the transaction of business impossible. The position will be the same where the disposal merely *appears* to be effected in the normal course of business, but the purchaser is unaware of the irregularity. On the other hand, a purchaser of a partner's share inevitably acquires his interest in the partnership assets subject to the liens of the other partners, even as regards trading stock.[117]

19–30   *Fixed Assets*: It is, however, considered that the same arguments cannot *necessarily* be applied to the fixed assets of a firm, at least while the partnership is continuing. In such a case, a purchaser with notice of the asset's true status would prima facie be bound by a partner's lien, unless the partner(s) purporting to effect the sale are clothed with the necessary authority.[118]

19–31   *Sales following dissolution*: Be that as it may, once the partnership has been dissolved, a partner's authority to sell the partnership assets (whether trading stock or fixed assets) will derive from the Partnership Act 1890[119] and any sale pursuant thereto will clearly be free from the other partners' liens.[120]

---

[113] The testator had in fact given his wife a prior life interest both in the land and the residue, but this is not material.

[114] See now the Administration of Estates Act 1925, s.35, which substantially re-enacted the Real Estate Charges Acts. Note also *Re Turner* [1938] Ch. 593 (bequest of shares in a company subject to a lien).

[115] See *supra*, para. 19–26.

[116] See *Re Langmead's Trusts* (1855) 20 Beav. 20, affirmed at 7 De G.M. & G. 353. Interestingly, Lord Lindley referred only to a sale of chattels at this point, having earlier referred to trading stock.

[117] *Cavander v. Bulteel* (1873) L.R. 9 Ch.App. 79.

[118] See generally, the Partnership Act 1890, s.5 and *supra*, paras 12–01 *et seq.*

[119] *ibid.* s.38: see *supra*, paras 13–62 *et seq.*

[120] *Re Langmead's Trusts* (1855) 20 Beav. 20, affirmed at 7 De G.M. & G. 353; *Re Bourne* [1906] 2 Ch. 427.

Limits of lien

Ordinary debts, etc., due from partner to firm

The partner's lien is exercisable only in respect of sums due as between the **19–32** firm and a partner *in that capacity*. It therefore clearly applies in the case of a partner who has failed to introduce his agreed capital contribution[121] or who has borrowed money from the firm[122]; however, any attempt to extend that application to non-partnership debts owed by one partner to another will fail, as Lord Lindley explained:

> "The lien of partners on the partnership property extends ... to whatever is due to or from the firm by or to the members thereof, as such. It does not, however, extend to debts incurred between a partner and the other members of the firm, otherwise than in their character of members. It has therefore been held that where a partner borrowed money (not partnership money) from his co-partners for some private purpose of his own, and then became bankrupt, his assignees were entitled to his share in the partnership, ascertained without taking into account the sum due from him to his co-partners in respect of this loan; and that the solvent partners were driven to prove against his estate in order to obtain payment of the money lent."[123]

Illegality

No lien will exist if the partnership is illegal.[124] Its members have no lien upon **19–33** the common property, or upon each other's shares therein, otherwise than by virtue of some agreement which is not tainted by the illegality.

Loss of lien

Once partnership property is converted into the separate property of a partner, **19–34** the other partners' liens thereover will inevitably be lost. Thus, if the partners agree, following a dissolution, that the partnership assets will be divided between them *in specie* and that some other provision will be made for the partnership debts, once that agreement has been implemented and the assets divided, each partner's lien will have been forfeited, even though the debts are not ultimately paid in the manner contemplated. In such a case, there will be no direct right of recourse to the former partnership assets in order to meet those debts.[125] The position will be the same where, under the terms of the agreement, an outgoing

---

[121] *Re Ward* [1985] 2 N.Z.L.R. 352.

[122] See *Meliorucchi v. Royal Exchange Assurance Co.* (1728) 1 Eq.Ca.Abr. 8; *Croft v. Pyke* (1733) 3 P.W. 180.

[123] See *Croft v. Pyke, supra*; *Ryall v. Rowles* (1749) 1 Ves.Sen. 348. Lord Lindley questioned whether *Smith v. De Silva* (1776) Cowp. 469 was perhaps decided on this principle, as suggested by Lord Tenterden in *Holderness v. Shackels* (1828) 8 B. & C. 618. See also *Re Ward* [1985] 2 N.Z.L.R. 352, 354.

[124] See *Ewing v. Osbaldiston* (1837) 2 Myl. & Cr. 53.

[125] *Lingen v. Simpson* (1824) 1 Sim. & St. 600; and see the judgment of Turner L.J. in *Re Langmead's Trusts* (1855) 7 De G.M. & G. 353, 360 *et seq.* Lord Lindley also cited the following example, on the authority of *Holroyd v. Griffiths* (1856) 3 Drew. 428: " ... if two partners consign goods for sale, and direct the consignee to carry the proceeds of the sale equally to their separate accounts without any reserve, and this is done, neither partner has any lien on the share of the other in those proceeds; although it would have been otherwise if they had remained part of the common property of the two." In *Holderness v. Shackels* (1828) 8 B. & C. 612, the lien was not lost because the transfer to each partner was expressed to be subject thereto.

partner's share is acquired by the continuing partners[126] and he becomes entitled to an express or implied indemnity against the partnership debts.[127] It is not clear whether, in such a case, the outgoing partner could seek to argue that, in the event of non-payment of the sums due to him under the agreement, he enjoys an unpaid vendor's lien over his partnership share.[128] Much will depend on the terms of the agreement: if, on a true analysis, the outgoing partner is merely withdrawing his capital and current account balances, it is difficult to see how this could properly be characterised as a sale.[129] Where, on the other hand, there is an option to acquire the outgoing partner's share[130] or an automatic accruer thereof,[131] it may be easier to show that, in substance, a sale is taking place.

Alternatively, a partner's lien may be lost if he impliedly abandons it in favour of some other security, *e.g.* by taking a specific charge over certain assets.[132]

Limitation

19–35   The right of an outgoing partner or the estate of a deceased partner in respect of his share is, by virtue of section 43 of the Partnership Act 1890, stated to be a debt accruing at the date of dissolution or death,[133] although it must, in the current editor's view, be open to question whether this section applies in the case of a *general* dissolution.[134] Where the section does apply, the outgoing/deceased partner's entitlement will prima facie become statute-barred after six years[135]; it would seem unlikely that a lien in support of that debt would survive its extinguishment.

Insolvency

19–36   If a partnership is wound up as an unregistered company,[136] whether or not concurrent petitions are presented against one or more of the partners,[137] the

---

[126] See *supra*, paras 10–150 *et seq.*

[127] See *supra*, paras 10–248 *et seq.*

[128] See, as to the nature of an unpaid vendor's lien, *Re Birmingham* [1959] Ch. 523.

[129] Reference should, in this context, be made to the following statement of principle by Lord Lindley (which was formerly included in Chapter 10, when considering the incidence of stamp duty on the retirement of a partner): " . . . if the retiring partner, instead of assigning his interest, takes the amount due to him from the firm, gives a receipt for the money, and acknowledges that he has no more claims on his co-partners, they will practically obtain all they want; but such a transaction, even if carried out by deed, could hardly be held to amount to a sale . . . ". This statement was approved by Darling J. in *Garnett v. I.R.C.* (1899) 81 L.T. 633, 637. It was for this reason that such a transaction did not attract a charge to *ad valorem* stamp duty: see *Fleetwood-Hesketh v. Commissioners of Inland Revenue* [1936] 1 K.B. 351. *cf. Grey v. I.R.C.* [1960] A.C. 1. Equally, the retiring partner will inevitably relinquish his share in the partnership on his retirement so that, on one view, there will be an assignment in favour of the continuing partners: see *Gray v. Smith* (1880) 43 Ch.D. 208.

[130] See *supra*, paras 10–154 *et seq.*

[131] See *supra*, para. 10–151. HMRC may, depending on the precise terms of the accruer, seek to treat the transaction as one of sale for inheritance tax purposes: see *infra*, para. 36–16.

[132] See *Burston Finance Ltd. v. Speirway* [1974] 1 W.L.R. 1648 (a case concerning the loss of an unpaid vendor's lien).

[133] See *infra*, para. 23–34; also *supra*, para. 19–10.

[134] See *infra*, paras 23–34, 26–03. *cf. HLB Kidsons v. Lloyd's Underwriters* [2009] 1 All E.R. (Comm) 760 at [16] *per* Judge Mackie Q.C. (sitting as a judge of the Chancery Division). It seems unlikely that the point was properly argued.

[135] See, for example, *Patel v. Patel* [2008] EWCA Civ 1520 (Lawtel 7/4/08). It is not clear whether the debt under s.43 is a sum recoverable by statute (to which the Limitation Act 1980, s.9 would apply) or a simple contract debt (to which *ibid.* s.5 would apply) but, in either case, the limitation period is the same. As to the limitation period where an account is sought, see *infra*, para. 23–36.

[136] See *infra*, paras 27–04 *et seq.*

[137] See *infra*, paras 27–24 *et seq.*

solvent partners' liens will not be enforceable against the liquidator; however, this is largely irrelevant, since the partnership property will in any event be applied towards payment of the partnership debts and any surplus returned to the partners according to their respective entitlements.[138]

4.   EXECUTION AGAINST SHARE FOR PARTNER'S SEPARATE DEBTS

The Partnership Act 1890 introduced a new procedure whereby a judgment **19-37** obtained against a partner could be executed against his share rather than, as under the previous law,[139] against the property of the partnership itself. That procedure is set out in section 23 of the Act which provides as follows:

"23.—(1) [. . .][140] a writ of execution[141] shall not issue against any partnership property except on a judgment against the firm.

(2) The High Court, or a judge thereof, [. . .][142] or a county court, may, on the application by summons[143] of any judgment creditor of a partner, make an order charging that partner's interest in the partnership property and profits with payment of the amount of the judgment debt and interest thereon, and may by the same or a subsequent order appoint a receiver of that partner's share of profits (whether already declared or accruing), and of any other money which may be coming to him in respect of the partnership, and direct all accounts and inquiries, and give all other orders and directions which might have been directed or given if the charge had been made in favour of the judgment creditor by the partner, or which the circumstances of the case may require.

(3) The other partner or partners shall be at liberty at any time to redeem the interest charged, or in case of a sale being directed, to purchase the same.

(4) [. . .][144]

(5) This section shall not apply to Scotland."

It should be noted that charging orders under this section are distinct from charging orders made under the Charging Orders Act 1979.

Foreign firms

It is clear that the section applies to a foreign firm with a branch office in **19-38** England.[145]

Applications under the Civil Procedure Rules

The procedure for obtaining an order under the section, both in the High Court **19-39** and county court, is now governed by paragraph 6 of the Practice Direction to

---

[138] See *infra*, paras 27–78 *et seq.*

[139] See generally, as to the difficulties under the old procedure, the 5th ed. of this work at pp. 356 *et seq.* and the 4th ed. (Vol. 1) at pp. 687 *et seq.*

[140] The words "After the commencement of this Act", which appeared at this point, were repealed by the Statute Law Revision Act 1908.

[141] See RSC Ord. 46, r. 1, as applied by the CPR Pt. 50, Sched. 1.

[142] The words omitted were repealed by the Courts Act 1971, Sched. 11, Pt II.

[143] Now an application notice under the CPR Pt 23.

[144] Subs. (4) was repealed by the Statute Law Repeals Act 1998, Sched. 1, Pt X, Group 1.

[145] *Brown, Janson & Co. v. A. Hutchinson & Co.* [1895] 1 Q.B. 737.

Part 73 of the Civil Procedure Rules.[146] The application will be made under the CPR Part 23, whether it is by the judgment creditor for an order under section 23(2) or by another partner for an order in consequence thereof.[147] The judgment creditor must serve his application notice and any order on the debtor partner and all his co-partners who are within the jurisdiction,[148] whereas any of the other partners must serve his application notice and any order on the judgment creditor, the debtor partner and any other partners within the jurisdiction who are not already parties to the application.[149] In either case service on one partner within the jurisdiction is treated as service on them all.[150]

It was formerly pointed out in the *Supreme Court Practice*[151] that a summons under the predecessor rule[152] would usually also seek the appointment of a named receiver,[153] and it is apprehended that the procedure may well be the same under the Civil Procedure Rules. In any event, such applications are, in practice, likely to continue to be a rarity.

Mentally incapacitated and deceased partners

19–40   A charging order under section 23 of the Partnership Act 1890 may be obtained in respect of the share of a partner suffering from mental incapacity,[154] but seemingly not in respect of a share held by the executors of a deceased judgment debtor.[155]

Rights of creditor under charging order

19–41   Although a charging order under section 23 of the Partnership Act 1890 will charge the whole of the debtor's share, it will not give the judgment creditor any rights more extensive than those enjoyed by the debtor (*qua* partner) when the order was obtained.[156] Thus, the judgment creditor will have no priority over an assignee of the share, where the assignment was effected between the date of judgment and the date of the order.[157] Equally, it would seem that the partners (including the debtor) will subsequently be free to implement an arrangement

---

[146] See *infra*, para. A2–13. An order under the section may be made by a Master, the Admiralty Registrar or a district judge: CPR 73PD, para. 6.3, *infra*, para. A2–13.

[147] *ibid.* para. 6.2, *infra*, para. A2–13.

[148] *ibid.* para. 6.4, *infra*, para. A2–13.

[149] *ibid.* para. 6.5, *infra*, para. A2–13.

[150] *ibid.* para. 6.6, *infra*, para. A2–13. Note that this paragraph does not actually refer to the partners being within the jurisdiction.

[151] *Supreme Court Practice 1999*, para. 81/10/3.

[152] RSC Ord. 81, r.10.

[153] Such an application can be made irrespective of the size of the judgment debt: *Summers v. Simpson*, May 1, 1902 (Bucknell J., unreported).

[154] *Re Sir F. Seager Hunt* [1900] 2 Ch. 54, note; also *Horne v. Pountain* (1889) 23 Q.B.D. 264; *Re Leavesley* [1891] 2 Ch. 1 (cases decided under the Judgments Act 1838).

[155] See *Stewart v. Rhodes* [1900] 1 Ch. 386 (also a decision under the Judgments Act 1838), and the observations therein on *Haly v. Barry* (1868) L.R. 3 Ch.App. 452 and *Finney v. Hinde* (1899) 4 Q.B.D. 102. See also *supra*, paras 19–10 *et seq.*, as to the nature of a partnership share on the death of a partner.

[156] *Gill v. Continental Gas Co.* (1872) L.R. 7 Ex. 332; *Re Onslow's Trusts* (1875) L.R. 20 Eq. 677; *Cooper v. Griffin* [1892] 1 Q.B. 740; *Howard v. Sadler* [1893] 1 Q.B. 1; *Sutton v. English and Colonial Produce Co.* [1902] 2 Ch. 502 (cases decided under Judgments Act 1838).

[157] *Brearcliff v. Dorrington* (1850) 4 De G. & Sm. 122; *Scott v. Lord Hastings* (1858) 4 K. & J. 633 (again, cases decided under the Judgments Act 1838).

detrimental to the judgment creditor's interests, *e.g.* reducing the profits distributable in the normal profit sharing ratios by paying preferential "salaries"[158] to partners, provided that they can demonstrate that the arrangement is bona fide and introduced pursuant to a specific provision in the partnership agreement or otherwise pursuant to their normal management powers.[159]

If the debtor seeks to dispose of his share before a charging order can be obtained, an interim injunction may be obtained pending the hearing of the application under the section.[160]

Accounts and inquiries

Consistently with the foregoing, a charging order gives the judgment creditor **19–42** no greater rights than would be enjoyed by a mortgagee or assignee of a share,[161] so that he will normally have no right to insist on an account of the partnership dealings being taken whilst the partnership subsists. However, the court might direct such an account in special circumstances, *e.g.* with a view to a dissolution.[162]

Sale or foreclosure

A judgment creditor who has obtained a charging order will be entitled to an **19–43** order for the sale of the debtor's share[163] and, seemingly, to an order for foreclosure against him.[164] Either of such orders may be obtained by means of a Part 23 application, without commencing a separate action.[165] The rights and duties of the other partners in the event that a sale is ordered will be considered hereafter.[166]

Insolvency of judgment debtor

A final charging order against an individual partner's share under section 23 of **19–44** the Partnership Act 1890 will, if made prior to his bankruptcy order,[167] seemingly be regarded as completed execution for the purposes of section 346 of the

---

[158] See, as to such salaries, *supra*, para. 10–80 and *infra*, para. 20–43.

[159] See *Watts v. Driscoll* [1901] 1 Ch. 294 (and particularly at p. 311 *per* Vaughan Williams L.J., citing *Kelly v. Hutton* (1868) L.R. 3 Ch.App. 703); *Re Garwood* [1903] 1 Ch. 236; and see also an article entitled "Partnership: Equitable Execution" by Mr H. E. Markson in (1981) 125 S.J. 109. Both of the above cases were, of course, decided under the Partnership Act 1890, s.31 (see further *infra*, para. 19–55), but it is thought that the same principles apply. Of course, if the partners can be shown to have acted mala fide or fraudulently, any arrangement of the type supposed will be ineffective as regards the judgment creditor.

[160] Such an injunction bears a marked resemblance to a freezing injunction and might properly be regarded as one of its precursors. See further *infra*, para. 23–150.

[161] Partnership Act 1890, s.31: see *infra*, paras 19–51 *et seq*.

[162] See *Brown, Janson & Co. v. A. Hutchinson & Co.* [1895] 1 Q.B. 737.

[163] Partnership Act 1890, s.23(3), *supra*, para. 19–37.

[164] See the following cases decided under the Judgments Act 1838, s.13: *Ford v. Wastell* (1847) 6 Hare 229 and 2 Ph. 591; *Jones v. Bailey* (1853) 17 Beav. 582; *Messer v. Boyle* (1856) 21 Beav. 559; *Beckett v. Buckley* (1874) L.R. 17 Eq. 435. See also *Redmayne v. Forster* (1866) L.R. 2 Eq. 467 and the comments of Lord Cozens-Hardy M.R. on *D'Auvergne v. Cooper* [1899] W.N. 256 in *Hosack v. Robins* [1917] 1 Ch. 332, 336. *cf. Footner v. Sturgis* (1852) 5 De G. & Sm. 736. And see generally, as to when foreclosure is an appropriate remedy, *Re Owen* [1894] 3 Ch. 220; *Harrold v. Plenty* [1901] 2 Ch. 314. See also *infra*, para. 19–45.

[165] See CPR 73PD, para. 6.2, *infra*, para. A2–13; also *supra*, para. 19–39. *cf. Legott v. Western* (1884) 12 Q.B.D. 287.

[166] See *infra*, para. 19–45.

[167] The bankruptcy only commences from this date: Insolvency Act 1986, s.278(a).

Insolvency Act 1986.[168] However, in the case of the winding up of a corporate partner, the final order must in general be made prior to the presentation of the petition,[169] if it is to have the same status for the purposes of section 183 of the 1986 Act.[170] An order *nisi* will not have the same effect and is, in the former case, unlikely to be made absolute if the court has notice that a bankruptcy petition has been presented.[171]

If a final charging order were not regarded as a completed execution and the other partners had paid a sum of money into court with a view to redeeming or purchasing the debtor's share,[172] his trustee (or liquidator) would be entitled to that sum, unless the money has already been paid out to the creditor before the commencement of the bankruptcy or winding up; similarly if the purchase or redemption moneys had been paid directly to the judgment creditor prior to that date.[173]

Rights and duties of judgment debtor's partners

19–45   The partners of a judgment debtor against whom a charging order has been obtained may at any time redeem his share.[174] It would, however, seem that this right will be exercisable only whilst the charge subsists, so that its existence would not preclude a foreclosure or entitle a partner to reopen a foreclosure once it had become absolute.

If a sale of the debtor's share is ordered on the application of the judgment creditor, the other partners are entitled to purchase it.[175] However, in so doing they must act with absolute fairness. If they do anything to conceal the true value of the share, thus enabling themselves to purchase it at less than its market value,

---

[168] See *Nationwide Building Society v. Wright* [2010] 2 W.L.R. 1097 (CA), a decision relating to charging orders under the Charging Orders Act 1979. Note, however, that unlike charging orders of the latter type, charging orders under s.23 are not specified in the Insolvency Act 1986, s.346(5). The proposition in the text is not, however, inconsistent with the old decision in *Wild v. Southwood* [1897] 1 Q.B. 317, since there the order was made after the commencement of the bankruptcy which, as the law then stood, related back to the commission of the original act of bankruptcy.

[169] Where a winding up order is made, the insolvency will commence as from the date of presentation of the winding up petition, save where the order is made on the hearing of an administration application: see the Insolvency Act 1986, s.129(1A), (2) (as added, in the case of subs.(1A) by the Enterprise Act 2002, Sched. 17, para. 16).

[170] Note, as to the meaning of "execution" in *ibid.* s.183, *Re Modern Jet Support Centre Ltd.* [2005] 1 W.L.R. 3880. *Semble* the legislative policy which the court found to underlie *ibid.* s.346(1) in *Nationwide Building Society v. Wright, supra,* at [18] also underlies *ibid.* s.183(1), albeit that (as the court noted at [17]) the approach to charging orders is different in the case of individual bankruptcy as against corporate insolvency. Note, however, that again charging orders under s.23 are not mentioned in the Insolvency Act 1986, s.183(3).

[171] See *Roberts Petroleum Ltd. v. Bernard Kennedy Ltd.* [1983] 2 A.C. 192 (a decision concerning a charging order against a company); *Industrial Diseases Compensation Ltd. v. Marrons* [2001] B.P.I.R. 600 (a decision concerning a garnishee order).

[172] Partnership Act 1890, s.23(3), *supra,* para. 19–37.

[173] See, under the old law, *Wild v. Southwood, supra.* In the case of a bankrupt partner, either payment would arguably amount to a sum paid to avoid the execution, within the meaning of the Insolvency Act 1986, s.346(1); *sed quaere.* The same words do not appear in *ibid.* s.183(1). *Semble* such a purchase or redemption would not involve a disposition by a bankrupt partner for the purposes of *ibid.* s.284. The position might in any event be otherwise in the case of an insolvent corporate partner: *ibid.* s.127.

[174] Partnership Act 1890, s.23(3), *supra,* para. 19–37.

[175] *ibid.*

the sale will be overturned. Such a case was *Perens v. Johnson*,[176] where the partners in a colliery had by various underhand means concealed the fact that a valuable seam of coal would soon be uncovered. The seam was in fact reached with a single day's work after the partners had purchased the debtor's share at auction. The sale was subsequently set aside at the instance of the debtor, on the basis of his partners' breach of good faith.[177]

Management decisions

The right of all the partners (including the judgment debtor) to agree bona fide **19–46** changes in the partnership terms, even if they may have the effect of devaluing the share in respect of which the charging order was obtained, has already been noticed.[178]

Share purchased with partnership moneys

If the other partners buy the judgment debtor's share with partnership moneys, **19–47** it will be partnership property and they cannot claim it as exclusively theirs.[179]

Right to dissolve

If a judgment creditor obtains a charging order on a partner's share, this will **19–48** entitle the other partners, if they so wish, to dissolve the partnership.[180]

5.   THE TRANSFER OF A SHARE

A hallmark of the partnership relation has always been its essentially *personal* **19–49** character, as Lord Lindley recognised in this passage:

> "When persons enter into a contract of partnership, their intention ordinarily is that a partnership shall exist between themselves and themselves alone. The mutual confidence reposed by each in the other is one of the main elements in the contract, and it is obvious that persons may be willing enough to trust each other, and yet be unwilling to place the same trust in any one else. Hence it is one of the fundamental principles of partnership law that no person can be introduced as a partner without the consent of all those who for the time being are members of the firm. If, therefore, a partner dies, his executors or devisees have no right to insist on being admitted into partnership with the surviving partners, unless some agreement to that effect has been entered into by them.[181]

---

[176] (1857) 3 Sm. & G. 419. See also *Smith v. Harrison* (1857) 26 L.J. Ch. 412; *Helmore v. Smith* (1887) 35 Ch.D. 436. It should, however, be noted that the partners might already have properly agreed some amendment to the partnership terms which adversely affects the value of the debtor's share: see *supra*, para. 19–41. If their motives cannot be impugned (*e.g.* by showing that the amendment was introduced with a view to depressing the sale price), there would seem to be no basis on which the sale could be attacked.

[177] See further, as to the duty of good faith, *supra*, paras 16–01 *et seq.*

[178] See *supra*, para. 19–41.

[179] See *Helmore v. Smith* (1887) 35 Ch.D. 436.

[180] Partnership Act 1890, s.33(2): see *infra*, paras 24–38 *et seq.*

[181] *Pearce v. Chamberlain* (1750) 2 Ves.Sen. 33; *Tatam v. Williams* (1844) 3 Hare 347; *Gillespie v. Hamilton* (1818) 3 Madd. 251; *Crawshay v. Maule* (1818) 1 Swan. 495; *Bray v. Fromont* (1821) 6 Madd. 5. See also *supra*, paras 10–258 *et seq.*

> Still less can a partner by assigning his share entitle his assignee to take his place
> in the partnership against the will of the other members.[182] The assignment, however,
> is by no means inoperative; on the contrary, it involves several important conse-
> quences, more especially as regards the dissolution of the firm and the right of the
> assignee to an account."[183]

The fundamental principle to which Lord Lindley referred is naturally recognised in the Partnership Act 1890,[184] which also contains an express provision
governing the rights of an assignee of a partnership share.[185] However, as will be
seen hereafter,[186] the assignment of a partner's share does not now, of itself, give
the other partners grounds to dissolve the firm.

Partner's right to transfer share

19–50   The ability of a partner to transfer his share to a third party (or to one of his
co-partners), though expressly recognised by the Partnership Act 1890, does not
derive therefrom: a share is no different from any other asset and may, subject to
the terms of the partnership agreement,[187] be transferred in any manner authorised by law.[188]

It follows that, whatever may be the scope of section 31 of the 1890 Act,[189] a
transfer of part of a share will be valid and effectual. The part assigned may be
a fraction of the assigning partner's entire share or, if that is permissible under the
agreement, all or part of any specific entitlements which go to make up that share,
e.g. his right to share in prospective income or capital profits.[190] The validity of
an assignment of the latter type was not in any way questioned by the Privy
Council in *Hadlee v. Commissioner of Inland Revenue*,[191] even though it was, in
the event, held to be ineffective for tax purposes.

Partnership Act 1890, section 31

19–51   The rights of the assignee of a share are set out in section 31 of the Partnership
Act 1890, which is in the following terms:

> "31.—(1) An assignment by any partner of his share in the partnership, either
> absolute or by way of mortgage or redeemable charge, does not, as against the other
> partners, entitle the assignee, during the continuance of the partnership, to interfere

---

[182] See *Jefferys v. Smith* (1827) 3 Russ. 158.

[183] Lord Lindley's footnote at this point read: "In *Marshall v. Maclure* (1885) 10 App.Cas. 325, a
surrender of a partner's share in property mortgaged was held, under special circumstances, to include
the firm's share." In fact, the firm's share appears to have been held by the partner concerned as
trustee; he sought (unsuccessfully) to argue that the "share" surrendered was limited to the proportionate part of the firm's share to which he was entitled *qua* partner.

[184] *ibid.* s.24(7); see also *supra*, para. 15–09. As to the position in a limited partnership, see *infra*,
paras 31–12, 31–13.

[185] *ibid.* s.31, *infra*, para. 19–51.

[186] See *infra*, para. 24–92.

[187] See *supra*, paras 10–258 *et seq.* and *infra*, para. 19–60.

[188] Note that the Bills of Sale Acts 1878 and 1882 do not apply to the assignment of a partner's
share: *Re Bainbridge* (1878) 8 Ch.D. 218 (a decision under the Bills of Sale Act 1854).

[189] See *infra*, para. 19–52.

[190] Such assignments are commonly encountered in limited partnerships governed by the Limited
Partnerships Act 1907, where a founder or general partner will assign all or part of its so-called
"carried interest" to relevant third parties: see further *infra*, para. 31–12.

[191] [1993] A.C. 524 (PC). *cf.* the general principle analysed *supra*, para. 19–06.

in the management or administration of the partnership business or affairs, or to require any accounts of the partnership transactions, or to inspect the partnership books, but entitles the assignee only to receive the share of profits to which the assigning partner would otherwise be entitled, and the assignee must accept the account of profits agreed to by the partners.

(2) In case of a dissolution of the partnership, whether as respects all the partners or as respects the assigning partner, the assignee is entitled to receive the share of the partnership assets[192] to which the assigning partner is entitled as between himself and the other partners, and for the purpose of ascertaining that share, to an account as from the date of the dissolution."

Scope of section

There is at least some doubt as to whether the section applies in the case of an   **19–52** assignment of a share in a *dissolved* partnership, particularly given the terms of subsection (2). However, in *Public Trustee v. Elder*,[193] Sargant L.J expressed the *obiter* view that, even if the section does not apply, its provisions should be applied to such an assignment by analogy.[194]

The section also appears to be framed in terms of an assignment of an entire share and, thus, might be thought to have no application where only part of a share is assigned.[195] However, this did not appear to trouble the Privy Council when considering the New Zealand equivalent in *Hadlee v. Commissioner of Inland Revenue*.[196] In any event, the assignability of a share does not depend on the section,[197] which merely seeks to preclude the assignee from interfering in management, etc. and from demanding the taking of an account whilst the partnership continues. Since it is self evident that an assignee of part of a share can have no greater rights than an assignee of the whole, the point may well be largely academic.[198]

Position as between the assignee and the other partners

Section 31 settled the doubts which had arisen prior to the Act,[199] as to   **19–53** whether an assignee of a share had a right to an account *vis-à-vis* the other partners, by emphatically rejecting the existence of any such right, otherwise than following a dissolution. In other respects, the section did not alter the law, as is demonstrated by the following passage written by Lord Lindley prior to the 1890 Act:

" . . . if a partner does assign or mortgage his share, he thereby confers upon the assignee or mortgagee a right to payment of what, upon the taking the accounts of the

---

[192] See, as to the meaning of this expression, *Sandhu v. Gill* [2006] Ch. 456, CA at [44] *per* Neuberger L.J. and [98] *per* Black J.

[193] [1926] Ch. 776.

[194] *ibid.* p. 790. See also *ibid.* p. 785 *per* Lord Hanworth M.R. Warrington L.J. appears to have had no doubts: see *ibid.* p. 786. Although the contrary appears not to have been argued, the Court of Appeal in *Harwood v. Harwood* [1991] 2 F.L.R. 274 treated s.31(2) as *authorising* the assignment of a share following a dissolution.

[195] *Quaere,* can the application of the section in such a case not be justified on the principle that "*omne majus continet in se minus*" (the greater includes the less)?

[196] [1993] A.C. 524.

[197] See *supra*, para. 19–50.

[198] In such a case, the section might again be applied by analogy: see, *supra*, para. 19–52.

[199] See the decisions in favour of such a right (*Glyn v. Hood* (1859) 1 Giff. 328, affirmed at (1859) 1 De G.F. & J. 334; *Kelly v. Hutton* (1868) L.R. 3 Ch.App. 703; *Whetham v. Davey* (1885) 30 Ch.D. 574) and against (*Brown v. De Tastet* (1819) Jac. 284).

partnership, may be due to the assignor or mortgagor.[200] But the assignee or mortgagee acquires no other right than this[201]; and he takes subject to the rights of the other partners; and will be affected by equities arising between the assignor and his co-partners subsequently to the assignment.[202] Even if the assignee gives notice of the assignment, he cannot (if the partnership is for a term) acquire a right to the assignor's share as it stands at the time of the assignment or notice, discharged from subsequently arising claims of the other partners."[203]

19-54   The 1890 Act clearly establishes that, whilst the partnership continues, an assignee of a partner's share cannot, as against the other partners, interfere in the management or administration of the partnership, require the taking of accounts or inspect the partnership books and that he is, moreover, bound to accept an account of profits agreed[204] by the partners. However, once the partnership has been dissolved,[205] the assignee will be entitled to insist on an account being taken in order to ascertain the amount due to him in respect of the assigned share.

Arrangements affecting the assignee's rights

19-55   Subject to the point made in the next paragraph, the partners (including the assignor) will, so long as their actions are bona fide, be free to manage the partnership in any way they see fit, even if this prejudices the position of the assignee. Thus, where partners had, following a mortgage of one partner's share, implemented a bona fide arrangement under which partners were to receive "salaries" in consideration of additional services undertaken, it was held that the payment of such salaries formed part of the management and administration of the partnership business and bound the mortgagee, even though he thereby suffered a financial detriment.[206] The current editor is of the opinion that the position would be the same in the case of a bona fide arrangement which does *not* fall under the "management and administration" umbrella, provided that it is introduced pursuant to a specific provision in the partnership agreement and not on a purely *ad hoc* basis.[207]

Account following a dissolution

19-56   The assignee's right to an account following a dissolution is a statutory right which exists independently of the partnership agreement and it is questionable to

---

[200] *Glyn v. Hood* (1859) 1 Giff. 328, affirmed at (1859) 1 De G.F. & J. 334; *Whetham v. Davey* (1885) 30 Ch.D. 574. See also *Cassels v. Stewart* (1881) 6 App.Cas. 64.

[201] *Smith v. Parkes* (1852) 16 Beav. 115.

[202] See *Lindsay v. Gibbs* (1856) 3 De G. & J. 690; *Guion v. Trask* (1860) 1 De G.F. & J. 373, 379 *per* Turner L.J.; *Cavander v. Bulteel* (1873) L.R. 9 Ch.App. 78. See also *Morris v. Livie* (1842) 1 Y. & C.C. 380; *Bergmann v. McMillan* (1881) 17 Ch.D. 423; *Re Knapman* (1881) 18 Ch.D. 300.

[203] See *Redmayne v. Forster* (1866) L.R. 2 Eq. 467; *Kelly v. Hutton* (1868) L.R. 3 Ch.App. 703; *Cavander v. Bulteel* (1873) L.R. 9 Ch.App. 78; *Bergmann v. McMillan* (1881) 17 Ch.D. 423.

[204] It is implicit that such agreement must be bona fide: see *infra*, para. 19–55.

[205] The dissolution may be either general or limited, *e.g.* a technical dissolution resulting from the death, retirement or expulsion of the assignor partner: Partnership Act 1890, s.31(2), *supra*, para. 19–51. But see also *infra*, para. 19–56.

[206] *Re Garwood's Trusts* [1903] 1 Ch. 236. No attempt was made to analyse whether the "salaries" concerned should more properly be treated as an allocation of profit: see further, *infra*, paras 20–43, 34–25. See also an article entitled "Partnership: Equitable Execution" by Mr H. E. Markson in (1981) 125 S.J. 109.

[207] See *Watts v. Driscoll* [1901] 1 Ch. 294, 311 *per* Vaughan Williams L.J., citing *Kelly v. Hutton* (1868) L.R. 3 Ch.App. 703.

what extent (if at all) it may be affected or excluded thereby.[208] It is clear that, once the partners have notice of the assignment, they cannot agree to adopt new terms which will adversely affect that right.[209] What is, perhaps, more doubtful is whether they could extend the duration of a fixed term partnership,[210] thereby deferring the exercise of the assignee's right to an account. It is tentatively submitted that they could not.[211]

If the partnership agreement contains an arbitration clause limited to differences arising between the partners, their executors or administrators, it was formerly the position that the assignee could not be forced to have the account taken by an arbitrator and would, moreover, not be bound by any account taken in an arbitration to which he was not made a party. The position was, seemingly, otherwise if the arbitration clause was also applicable to persons claiming through or under the partners.[212] Now, however, under the Arbitration Act 1996 references to a party to an arbitration agreement in all cases include any person claiming under or through such a party,[213] so that the position would seem to have changed, despite the independent statutory right conferred on the assignee. This would certainly be consistent with the general approach adopted by the 1996 Act.[214]

Position as between the assignor and the assignee

Although the assignee does not become a partner in place of the assignor, he **19–57** effectively stands in his shoes and is accordingly bound to indemnify the assignor against any liability for the partnership debts.[215] In this way, the assignee will be indirectly liable for the assignor's share of any losses.[216] It is, however, doubtful whether the assignor could properly seek an indemnity in respect of liabilities attributable to his own wrongful acts whilst conducting the partnership business.[217]

---

[208] It is submitted that if the agreement clearly establishes the financial entitlement of the assignor partner in respect of his share, *e.g.* by reference to his capital and current account balances, there will be little or no scope for the taking of an account. In such a case, notwithstanding the assignee's statutory right, it seems likely that a court would refuse to order an account: see further, *infra*, para. 23–76. Equally, an attempt to exclude the assignee's right by a specific provision would seem to be ineffective.

[209] *Watts v. Driscoll* [1901] 1 Ch. 294.

[210] See the Partnership Act 1890, s.27.

[211] This was an issue raised by Lord Lindley in his Supplement on the Partnership Act 1890, although he did not go so far as to express a view thereon.

[212] *Bonnin v. Neame* [1910] 1 Ch. 732. Equally, the fact that the arbitration clause does not mention assignees is not *per se* sufficient to give rise to an implication that the share is unassignable: see *Shayler v. Woolf* [1946] Ch. 320.

[213] s.81(2). See also *Schiffahrtsgesellschaft Detlev Von Appen GmbH v. Voest Alpine Intertrading GmbH* [1997] 2 Lloyd's Rep. 279 (CA); *Through Transport Mutual Insurance Association (Eurasia) Ltd. v. New India Assurance Co Ltd.* [2005] 1 C.L.C. 376.

[214] See *supra*, paras 10–271, 10–272.

[215] *Dodson v. Downey* [1901] 2 Ch. 620. See in particular the judgment of Farwell J. at p. 623. Note, however, that previous editors of this work have questioned whether the headnote is supported by the facts or the judgment. The current editor does not share these doubts.

[216] There is no *direct* liability for losses: the Partnership Act 1890, s.31(1) refers only to the receipt of a share of profits.

[217] In such a case, the assignor partner's claim might, in an appropriate case, be defeated by the principle "*ex turpi causa non oritur actio*".

As was made clear in *Hadlee v. Commissioner of Inland Revenue*,[218] when a partner assigns his share to a third party, he is not normally to be taken thereby to have disposed of an income producing asset. The assignee's right to the assignor's profit share may in reality be attributable not to the share itself but to the assignor continuing to fulfil his obligations under the agreement.[219]

Charge by deed

19–58   If one partner charges his share in favour of another by deed, the latter will, as against the former, prima facie be entitled either to sell the share or to appoint a receiver under the powers conferred by the Law of Property Act 1925.[220]

Insolvency of assignor

19–59   The bankruptcy of a partner will normally dissolve the partnership,[221] thus entitling the assignee to exercise his rights under section 31(2) of the Partnership Act 1890.[222]

In one exceptional case decided under the old bankruptcy law, it was held that the trustee in bankruptcy of a partner in a firm of dentists, who had previously mortgaged his share, was entitled to the profits which that partner derived from the practice carried on after the commencement of the bankruptcy, even though the mortgagees had previously obtained the appointment of a receiver in an action to enforce their security.[223] However, it should be noted that the decision appears to have turned on the nature of the "new" arrangement under which the practice was continued, which was not subject to the mortgage.

Transfer allowed by agreement

19–60   A partnership agreement may, exceptionally, give a partner the right to transfer his share to a third party and, thereby, to constitute that third party a partner in his place.[224] Lord Lindley observed:

> "If partners choose to agree that any of them shall be at liberty to introduce any other person into the partnership, there is no reason why they should not; nor why, having so agreed, they should not be bound by the agreement.[225] Persons who enter into such an agreement consent prospectively and once for all to admit into partnership any person who is willing to take advantage of their agreement, and to observe those stipulations, if any, which may be made conditions of his admission. Such an

---

[218] [1993] A.C. 524 (PC). In this case, which concerned a professional firm, the partner concerned had assigned part of his share to a trust for his wife and child and sought (unsuccessfully) to argue that, under the relevant New Zealand income tax legislation, he thereby ceased to be liable for tax on an equivalent part of his profit share.

[219] See [1993] A.C. 533D. This does not, however, mean that the assignment is ineffective: see *supra*, paras 19–50, 19–52. *Quaere*, would this analysis in any event hold up in the case of an investment partnership where profits are *not* dependent on the partners' efforts?

[220] See *ibid.* ss.101, 205(xvi), (xx). The definition of "property" would seem to be wide enough to cover a share in a partnership; but see *Blaker v. Herts and Essex Waterworks Co.* (1889) 41 Ch.D. 399 (a decision under the Conveyancing Act 1881).

[221] Partnership Act 1890, s.33(1): see *infra*, paras 24–29, 24–32 *et seq.*

[222] See *supra*, para. 19–51.

[223] *Ex p. Collins* [1894] 1 Q.B. 425; also *Re Collins* [1925] Ch. 556.

[224] See *supra*, paras 10–258 *et seq.*

[225] *Lovegrove v. Nelson* (1834) 3 M. & K. 1.

agreement as this is the basis of every partnership, the shares in which are transferable from one person to the other. Those who form such partnerships, and those who join them after they are formed, assent to become partners with anyone who is willing to comply with certain conditions."[226]

However, the fact that such a transfer is permitted does not mean that the fundamental conditions for the existence of a partnership set out in section 1(1) of the Partnership Act 1890[227] do not require to be satisfied as between the incoming partner and the continuing partners.[228]

19–61

It follows that if, having entered into such an agreement, the other partners refuse to admit the new partner or to complete the consequential steps required to confer the rights of a partner on him, he may be in a position to seek relief from the court in the same way as any other partner,[229] whether in the form of specific performance,[230] an injunction,[231] an account[232] or even an order for the dissolution of the partnership. However, he will only be entitled to such relief if he has himself complied with any conditions which must be satisfied by him under the terms of the agreement.[233]

Transfer to a man of straw

A partner under such an agreement might seek to free himself from continuing liability by transferring his share to a man of straw or to a company which is subsequently wound up.[234] This possibility was recognised by Lord Lindley, who observed:

19–62

"Where a partner has an unconditional right to transfer his share, he may transfer it to a pauper, and thus get rid of all liability as between himself and his co-partners in respect of transactions subsequent to the transfer and notice thereof given to them.[235] But even in this case the transfer alone does not render the transferee a member of the partnership, and liable as between himself and the other members to any of the

---

[226] See *Fox v. Clifton* (1832) 9 Bing. 120. Lord Lindley also cited the following passage taken from the judgment Lord Brougham L.C. in *Lovegrove v. Nelson* (1834) 3 M. & K. 1 (at p. 20): "To make a person a partner with two others their consent must clearly be had, but there is no particular mode or time required for giving that consent; and if three enter into partnership by a contract which provides that on one retiring, one of the remaining two, or even a fourth person who is no partner at all, shall name the successor to take the share of the one retiring, it is clear that this would be a valid contract which the Court must perform, and that the new partner would come in as entirely by the consent of the other two as if they had adopted him by name."

[227] See *supra*, para. 2–01.

[228] *Backman v. R*, 3 I.T.L. Rep. 647 at [40]–[43] (Sup Ct (Can)).

[229] See *supra*, para. 10–259.

[230] See *infra*, paras 23–45 *et seq.*

[231] See *infra*, paras 23–135 *et seq.*

[232] See *infra*, paras 23–74 *et seq.*

[233] *Byrne v. Reid* [1902] 2 Ch. 735; also *Ehrmann v. Ehrmann* (1894) 72 L.T. 17. And see *supra*, para. 10–259.

[234] *i.e.* an approach similar to that adopted in the 1950s with a view to getting rid of onerous leases: see *Morelle v. Waterworth* [1955] 1 Q.B. 1; *Morelle v. Wakeling* [1955] 2 Q.B. 379; *Att.-Gen. v. Parsons* [1956] A.C. 421.

[235] The assumption underlying this sentence is, of course, that the transfer of the share is capable of constituting the transferee as a partner: *cf.* the Partnership Act 1890, s.24(7). See also *supra*, para. 10–110.

debts of the firm. In order to render him a partner with the other members, they must acknowledge him to be a partner, or permit him to act as such."[236]

Such a course should be adopted with circumspection, since the other partners might seek to argue that the transfer amounts to a breach of the transferor partner's express or implied duty of good faith or, perhaps, of some other provision of the agreement.[237]

Effect of transfer on firm and firm name

19–63   A transfer of a share which constitutes the transferee a partner in the place of the transferor will, on normal principles, result in a dissolution of the old firm and the creation of a new firm.[238] It may also result in continued use of the firm name requiring approval to be sought from the Secretary of State under Part 41 of the Companies Act 2006 or becoming entirely prohibited.[239]

Mining partnerships

19–64   Lord Lindley observed:

> "An apparent exception to the rule that a share in a partnership cannot be transferred without the consent of all the partners exists in the case of mining partnerships.[240] Mines are a peculiar species of property, and are in some respects governed by the doctrines of real property law, and in others by the doctrines which regulate trading concerns. Regarding them as real property, and their owners as joint tenants or tenants in common, each partner is held to be at liberty to dispose of his interest in the land without consulting his co-owners[241]; and a transfer of this interest confers upon the transferee all the rights of a part-owner, including a right to an account against the other owners.[242] But even here, if the persons originally interested in the mine are not only part-owners but also partners, a transferee of the share of one of them, although he would become a part-owner with the others, would not become a partner with them in the proper sense of the word, unless by agreement, express or tacit."[243]

It is perhaps questionable to what extent mining partnerships can be as treated as strictly *sui generis* since the Partnership Act 1890[244] but, in any event, it would seem that, on a true analysis, the position in relation to such partnerships does not differ significantly from that discussed in the preceding paragraphs.

---

[236] *Jefferys v. Smith* (1827) 3 Russ. 158.

[237] As to whether a breach of the implied duty of good faith would sound in damages, see *supra*, para. 16–10 and *infra*, paras 23–208 *et seq.*

[238] See *supra*, paras 3–01 *et seq.*

[239] *ibid.* ss.1193, 1194, 1197, 1198 and the Company and Business Names (Miscellaneous Provisions) Regulations 2009 (SI 2009/1085), as amended. See further *supra*, paras 3–28, 3–29.

[240] Lord Lindley appears to have had in mind a transfer which would confer on the assignee all the rights of a partner, thus regarding mining partnerships as within the class "Transfer allowed by agreement".

[241] All partnership land will now be subject to a trust of land: Trusts of Land and Appointment of Trustees Act 1996, s.1(1). It has already been seen that the doctrine of conversion has, for the most part, been abolished: see *supra*, para. 19–14.

[242] See *Bentley v. Bates* (1840) 4 Y. & C.Ex. 182; *Redmayne v. Foster* (1866) L.R. 2 Eq. 467.

[243] As in *Crawshay v. Maule* (1818) 1 Swan. 495; *Jefferys v. Smith* (1827) 3 Russ. 158. Lord Lindley added that the same principles apply in the case of transfers of shares in ships.

[244] See *ibid.* s.46.

Form of transfer

It has already been seen that a share in a continuing partnership will comprise **19–65** a beneficial interest in each of the partnership assets.[245] The orthodox view[246] is that a transfer of a share will involve a transfer of those beneficial interests and must be in a form appropriate to the asset concerned. Thus, if the assets consist of chattels and legal (as opposed to equitable) choses in action, in respect of which there is no prescribed form of transfer, the transfer could be effected informally by word of mouth,[247] even though this might be undesirable from an evidential standpoint. Where, however, such assets include land[248] or an equitable interest[249] in land or personalty,[250] it would follow that section 53(1)(a) or (c) of the Law of Property Act 1925[251] would require a written transfer to be signed by or on behalf of the assigning partner. This would be the position irrespective of whether the share is transferred to a third party or to one or more of the other partners. Moreover, where the partnership assets comprise land or an interest in land, a contract for the transfer of a partner's share therein would inevitably have to be reduced to writing and otherwise satisfy the strict requirements of section 2 of the Law of Property (Miscellaneous Provisions) Act 1989.[252] That said, however, the fact remains that, otherwise than under the external perspective,[253] a partner cannot properly be said to have a direct interest in any of the partnership assets, whatever their nature.[254] The position in the case of co-owners is, inevitably, very different.[255] It would seem a very odd result that the enforceability or otherwise of a contract for the transfer of a partnership share ultimately depends on whether the partnership assets consist of land at a given point in time, *e.g.* where land is acquired after the contract is concluded or where it is disposed of between contract and completion. Perhaps the ultimate rationale is that the

---

[245] See *supra*, paras 19–02 *et seq.*

[246] See the decision of Kekewich J. in *Gray v. Smith* (1889) 43 Ch. D. 208, 212, to the effect that an agreement by a partner to retire and assign his share to the continuing partners would have to comply with the Statute of Frauds if the partnership assets comprise land (this issue was not, in the event, argued on appeal). See also *Ashworth v. Munn* (1878) 15 Ch. D. 367, albeit a decision under the Mortmain Act.

[247] See *Brandt's Sons and Co. v. Dunlop Rubber Co. Ltd.* [1905] A.C. 454. Note that, for a *legal* assignment of a *legal* chose in action, writing is required by virtue of the Law of Property Act 1925, s.136.

[248] The beneficial interest of a partner in land held as a partnership asset will in all cases consist of an interest under a trust of land, to which the doctrine of conversion will not, in general, apply: see *supra*, para. 19–14.

[249] See the Law of Property Act 1925, ss.1(8), 205(1)(x) (as amended by the Trusts of Land and Appointment of Trustees Act 1996, Sched. 4).

[250] See *Grey v. I.R.C.* [1960] A.C. 1; *Oughtred v. I.R.C.* [1960] A.C. 206.

[251] *Quaere* whether a partner's interest in land held as a partnership asset constitutes an interest in land for the purposes of *ibid.* s.53(1)(a) or an equitable interest for the purposes of *ibid.* s.53(1)(c). Given the similarity between the requirements of the two paragraphs, the distinction may be of little importance in practice. Reference to cases decided prior to the Trusts of Land and Appointment of Trustees Act 1996 (and thus prior to the abolition of the doctrine of conversion) are unlikely to be of assistance on this issue.

[252] *ibid.* s.2(6) (as amended by the Trusts of Land and Appointment of Trustees Act 1996, Sched. 4) provides that "'interest in land' means any estate, interest or charge in or over land". This is clearly apt to include a share in land held by a partnership. Note, however, that this section may have only a limited application to agreements for the *creation* of a partnership: see *supra*, paras 7–02 *et seq.*

[253] See *supra*, para. 19–03.

[254] See *supra*, paras 19–05 *et seq.*

[255] See *Cooper v. Critchley* [1955] Ch. 431.

court will have regard only to the external perspective and will not concern itself with the internal financial arrangements between the partners; *sed quaere.*

19–66   Be that as it may, there is no doubt that the doctrine of constructive trusts remains unaffected by the statutory provisions referred to in the preceding paragraph.[256] Thus, if the assignment were effected verbally and the assignee were then admitted to the partnership and treated as entitled to the assignor's share, it is difficult to see why a constructive trust should not arise in the former's favour.[257]

The application of stamp duty land tax to various partnership transactions has, of course, reduced the importance of the issues canvassed above, since the existence or otherwise of a document evidencing an assignment is no longer determinative of whether a charge to tax can be imposed.[258] Equally, there is now little scope for SDLT to be charged on the transfer of a partnership share.[259]

Since a transfer of a share does not normally affect the assigning partner's continued membership of the firm,[260] there will be no impact on the *legal* title to any partnership assets which may be vested in him on trust for the firm. The position may, however, be different where the transfer is linked to the partner's retirement from the firm, when it may be necessary, *as a wholly separate matter,* to ensure that he also gives up his trusteeship and vests the relevant assets in one or more of the continuing partners.[261]

---

[256] Law of Property Act 1925, s.53(2); Law of Property (Miscellaneous Provisions) Act 1989, s.2(5)

[257] For an analogous situation which did not involve a partnership, see *Hameed v. Qyyum* [2009] B.P.I.R. 35.

[258] See further, *infra*, paras 38–02 *et seq.*

[259] See *infra*, paras 38–12 *et seq.* Note also, as to the treatment of such a transfer for value added tax purposes, *infra*, paras 37–27, 37–28.

[260] See *supra*, paras 10–110, 19–57.

[261] This will usually be secured pursuant to the so called "further assurance" obligation: see *supra*, para. 10–244.

CHAPTER 20

THE FINANCIAL RIGHTS AND DUTIES OF A PARTNER

IN taking partnership accounts it is necessary to differentiate between those **20–01** expenses and losses which, as between the partners, are chargeable to the firm and those which are properly chargeable to one or more of the partners on an individual basis. Once the expenses and losses of the former class have been identified, it must be determined in what shares they are to be borne by the partners. This chapter is devoted to a consideration of these and other related issues which must be addressed when ascertaining a partner's financial rights and duties *vis-à-vis* his co-partners.

The fundamental principles

Writing prior to the Act, Lord Lindley observed that the following principles **20–02** form the basis for this branch of partnership law:

" . . . it must always be borne in mind that every member of an ordinary firm is, to a certain extent, both a principal and an agent. He is liable as a principal to the debts and engagements of the firm, and in respect of them he is entitled to contribution from his co-partners; for they have no right to throw on him alone the burden of obligations which, *ex hypothesi*, are theirs as much as his.[1] Again, each member as an agent of the firm is entitled to be indemnified by the firm against losses and expenses bona fide incurred by him for the benefit of the firm, whilst pursuing the authority conferred upon him by the agreement entered into between himself and his co-partners.[2] On the other hand, a partner has no right to charge the firm with losses or expenses incurred by his own negligence or want of skill, or in disregard of the authority reposed in him."[3]

Partnership Act 1890, section 24

The above principles are clearly reflected in section 24 of the Partnership Act **20–03** 1890 which, so far as material, provides as follows:

"24. The interests of partners in the partnership property and their rights and duties in relation to the partnership shall be determined, subject to any agreement express or implied between the partners, by the following rules:

   (1) All the partners are entitled to share equally in the capital and profits of the business, and must contribute equally towards the losses whether of capital or otherwise sustained by the firm.

---

[1] See *Lefroy v. Gore* (1844) 1 Jo. La T. 571; *Spottiswoode's Case* (1855) 6 De G.M. & G. 345; *Robinson's Case* (1856) 6 De G.M. & G. 572.

[2] See further, as to such agency, *supra*, paras 12–01 *et seq.*

[3] *Bury v. Allen* (1845) 1 Colly. 589; *Thomas v. Atherton* (1878) 10 Ch.D. 185. See further *infra*, paras 20–10 *et seq.*

(2) The firm must indemnify every partner in respect of payments made and personal liabilities incurred by him

   (a) In the ordinary and proper conduct of the business of the firm; or

   (b) In or about anything necessarily done for the preservation of the business or property of the firm.

(3) A partner making, for the purpose of the partnership, any actual payment or advance beyond the amount of capital which he has agreed to subscribe, is entitled to interest at the rate of five per cent. per annum from the date of the payment or advance.

(4) A partner is not entitled, before the ascertainment of profits, to interest on the capital subscribed by him.

   . . .

(6) No partner shall be entitled to remuneration for acting in the partnership business."

The practical application of these statutory rules can best be illustrated by considering the rights and duties of partners with respect to: (1) debts, liabilities and losses; (2) outlays and advances; (3) interest; and (4) remuneration for services rendered to the firm.[4]

1.   DEBTS, LIABILITIES AND LOSSES

General obligation of partners to contribute to losses

20–04   Section 24(1) and (2) of the Partnership Act 1890 clearly establishes the rule that, in the absence of some other agreement, losses are to be borne by all the members of a firm in equal shares, thereby giving statutory recognition to principles which had long been recognised as fundamental to the law of partnership. Lord Lindley summarised the previous law in these terms:

"The general principle . . . that partners must contribute rateably to their shares towards the losses and debts of the firm, is not open to question. Their obligation to contribute is not necessarily founded upon, although it may be modified and even excluded altogether by, agreement.[5] For example, where there is no agreement to the

---

[4] In earlier editions of this work, there appeared at this point an analysis of the general right of agents and trustees to a contribution or indemnity, both before and after the Judicature Acts. Save to the extent that points of principle of direct relevance to the law of partnership are concerned, the relevant passage has not been retained. For reference purposes, the original passage appeared in the 15th ed. at pp. 546 *et seq.*

[5] At this point Lord Lindley cross referred to an earlier passage, in which he had observed: "Whether a person who has suffered loss is entitled to be indemnified wholly or partly by others is a question which cannot be decided in the negative merely upon the ground that no agreement for contribution or indemnity has been entered into. An agreement may undoubtedly give rise to a right to indemnity or contribution; but the absence of an agreement giving rise to such a right, is by no means fatal to its existence. The general principle which prescribes equality of burden and of benefit, is amply sufficient to create a right of contribution in many cases in which it is impossible to found it upon any genuine contract, express or tacit. The common feature of such cases is, that one person has sustained some loss which would have fallen upon others as well as upon himself, but which has been averted from them at his expense . . . In all these cases a right of contribution arises; not by virtue of any contract, but because the safety of some cannot justly be purchased at the expense of others; and all must therefore contribute to the loss sustained . . . But although a right to contribution may exist where there is no contract upon which it can be founded, it cannot exist if excluded by agreement; and it is so excluded whenever those who would otherwise be contributories have entered into any contract, express or tacit, amongst themselves, which is inconsistent with a right on the part

contrary, it is clear that if execution for a partnership debt contracted by all the partners, or by some of them when acting within the limits of their authority, is levied on any one partner, who is compelled to pay the whole debt, he is entitled to contribution from his co-partners.[6] So, if one partner enters into a contract on behalf of the firm, but in such a manner as to render himself alone liable to be sued, he is entitled to be indemnified by the firm, provided he has not, as between himself and his co-partners, exceeded his authority in entering into the contract[7]; and if, in such a case, he with their knowledge and consent defend an action brought against him, he is entitled to be indemnified by the firm against the damages, costs, and expenses which he may be compelled to pay."[8]

Sharing of losses: the general presumption

It is self evident from the terms of section 24(1) that, in the absence of any   **20–05** agreement to the contrary, each partner is entitled to an equal share of the firm's profits and must bear an equal share of the firm's losses.[9] However, where profits are divisible in some other proportions, the normal inference is that losses are to be divided in those proportions, unless there is some express or implied agreement which requires them to be divided in some other way.[10] Accordingly, where one partner is compelled to pay more than his share of a partnership debt or incurs a personal liability in the course of carrying on the firm's business, he will in general be entitled to a contribution from his co-partners to the extent necessary to reflect those express or implied loss-sharing ratios.[11]

Presumption rebutted by evidence: "fixed share" and "salaried" partners

However, the mere fact that a person is liable to third parties as a partner does   **20–06** not necessarily render him liable, as between himself and his co-partners, to bear a share of the firm's losses: his co-partners may have agreed to indemnify him against such losses, in which case they cannot require him to contribute thereto.[12] This will usually be the case with a "fixed share" partner,[13] who is entitled to a

---

of one to demand contribution from the others. This is too obvious to require comment, but it must be borne in mind as qualifying the common saying, that the right to contribution is independent of agreement." See generally, *Gillan v. Morrison* (1847) 1 De G. & S. 421; *Re Worcester Corn Exchange Co.* (1853) 3 De G.M. & G. 180; also *Mowatt and Elliott's Case* (1853) 3 De G.M. & G. 254; *Carew's Case* (1855) 7 De G.M. & G. 43. But note the terms of the Civil Liability (Contribution) Act 1978, s.7(3)(b); *quaere*, can the right to contribution under that Act be excluded by an *implied* as opposed to an express agreement?

[6] *Evans v. Yeatherd* (1824) 2 Bing. 132; *McOwen v. Hunter* (1838) 1 Dr. & Wal. 347; *Robinson's Executor's Case* (1856) 6 De G.M. & G. 572. See also *Lefroy v. Gore* (1844) 1 Jo. & La T. 571.

[7] *Gleadow v. Hull Glass Co.* (1849) 13 Jur. 1020; *Sedgwick's Case* (1856) 2 Jur. (N.S.) 949.

[8] *Browne v. Gibbins* (1725) 5 Bro P.C. 491; *Croxton's Case* (1852) 5 De G. & Sm. 432.

[9] Partnership Act 1890, s.24(1), *supra*, para. 20–03. See also *supra*, paras 19–15 *et seq.*; and *Walker West Developments Ltd. v. F.J. Emmett Ltd.* (1979) 252 E.G. 1171.

[10] See *Re Albion Life Assurance Society* (1880) 16 Ch.D. 83, where this rule was recognised, but was held not to apply to policy-holders participating in profits. The inference referred to in the text is also supported by the terms of the Partnership Act 1890, s.44(a), *infra*, para. 25–45. See also *supra*, para. 10–85.

[11] Partnership Act 1890, s.24(2), *supra*, para. 20–03; *Wright v. Hunter* (1801) 5 Ves.Jr. 792. See also *Lefroy v. Gore* (1844) 1 Jo. & La T. 571; *Robinson's Executor's Case* (1856) 6 De G.M. & G. 572; *Hamilton v. Smith* (1859) 7 W.R. 173, as to promoters of companies.

[12] See *Geddes v. Wallace* (1820) 2 Bli. 270; also *Gillan v. Morrison* (1847) 1 De G. & Sm. 421; *Re Worcester Corn Exchange Co.* (1853) 3 De G.M. & G. 180; *Mowatt and Elliott's Case* (1853) 3 De G.M. & G. 254; *Carew's Case* (1855) 7 De G.M. & G. 43.

[13] See *supra*, paras 5–52, 10–86.

pre-determined fixed share of the firm's profits, but who is, either expressly or by necessary implication,[14] not required to bear a commensurate share of its losses, save, perhaps, for any losses attributable to his own acts or defaults.[15] If such a partner is forced to meet a partnership debt or liability, he will be entitled to a *full* indemnity from his co-partners in respect thereof.[16] The analysis may, however, be different in the case of a so-called "salaried" partner: if he is, on a true analysis, a partner,[17] it is likely that, as with a fixed share partner, there will be no room for an implication that he is intended to share losses.[18] Where, on the other hand, such a "partner" is in truth an employee of the firm whose liability to third parties is solely based on holding out,[19] section 24(1) of the 1890 will, in any event, be inapplicable and no question of sharing losses will arise. Such an employee will unquestionably be entitled to an indemnity in respect of any liability from *the firm*.[20]

One partner unable to contribute his due share

20-07   As was the position in equity prior to the Judicature Acts, if one partner is unable to contribute his due share of a loss, *e.g.* by reason of insolvency, the other partners must, in the absence of some other agreement, make good the defaulting partner's share in the relevant proportions.[21] Thus, in *Wadeson v. Richardson*,[22] one of four partners assigned property to trustees upon trust *inter alia* to pay his proportion or share of all such debts as were or should be owing by him and the other three partners. On the subsequent bankruptcy of all four partners, it was held that the trustees were bound to pay not merely the share and proportion of the firm's debts which, as between the assignor and his co-partners, he was bound to contribute to the funds of the firm, but the share and proportion which, as

---

[14] Where, for example, such a partner is entitled to a preferential profit share expressed as a first charge on the firm's profits, but no loss-sharing ratios are prescribed, it is prima facie unlikely that the agreement will be construed as requiring him to bear a similar preferential share of any losses. Equally, it is not unknown to find that such partners *are* required to bear a small share of any overall loss (*e.g.* in excess of a set figure), in order to underline their status as partners.

[15] As in *James & George Collie v. Donald* 1999 S.C.L.R. 420 (OH).

[16] It should be noted that an indemnity against losses is not the same as an indemnity against *liabilities*: before the former can be invoked, it is technically necessary to identify whether an overall trading loss has been made in any given year: see *James & George Collie v. Donald, supra.* However, in practice the distinction is unlikely to be of significance, given the terms of the Partnership Act 1890, s.24(2), *supra*, para. 20–03.

[17] See *supra*, para. 5–54.

[18] See *Marsh v. Stacey* (1963) 107 S.J. 512; *Stekel v. Ellice* [1973] 1 W.L.R. 191; also the cases cited in n. 12 *supra*. The salaried partner's right to remuneration is prima facie inconsistent with such remuneration being of a negative amount; however, if there are no profits, such a partner may (but need not necessarily) forego his salary. See further, *supra*, para. 10–86.

[19] Partnership Act 1890, s.14: see *supra*, paras 5–35 *et seq.*

[20] *Sed quaere*, if the liability is the result of the employee's own acts or defaults. A *fortiori*, if the holding out was not authorised by the firm.

[21] Lord Lindley illustrated the general proposition thus: "if A, B, C, and D are liable to a debt, A can compel B and C to contribute one-third each, if D can contribute nothing; and this, as between A, B, and C, is evidently only fair and just: *Dering v. Winchelsea* (1787) 1 Cox 318; *Hole v. Harrison* (1673) 1 Ch.Ca. 246; *Peter v. Rich* (1629) 1 Rep. Ch. 34." See also *Lowe v. Dixon* (1886) 16 Q.B.D. 455. cf. the position at law: *Cowell v. Edwards* (1800) 2 Bos. & Pul. 268; *Batard v. Hawes* (1853) 2 E. & B. 287. As to agreements negating the equitable rule, see *McKewan's Case* (1877) 6 Ch.D. 447. Note also the terms of the Civil Liability (Contribution) Act 1978, *infra*, para. 20–23. And see, as to the manner in which losses of capital will be shared when one or more of the partners are insolvent, *infra*, paras 25–50 *et seq.* As to the position where an insolvent firm is wound up as an unregistered company, see *infra*, paras 27–61 *et seq.*

[22] (1812) 1 V. & B. 103.

between him and the firm's creditors, was required to ensure that those creditors received payment in full. The creditors were therefore entitled to come in under the deed for any balance which could not be recovered out of partnership funds or from the estates of the other partners.

The position will be the same where a loss is properly chargeable against only one partner, if he personally is unable to meet the liability.[23]

Losses for which one partner is primarily responsible

The general principle is that any loss or liability suffered by a firm should be borne by *all* the partners, even where responsibility therefor can be attributed to a particular partner. Some element of culpability on the part of the partner responsible must be shown in order to justify a departure from that principle, as Lord Lindley explained: **20–08**

> "Even if a loss sustained by a firm is imputable to the conduct of one partner more than to that of another, still, if the former acted bona fide with a view to the benefit of the firm, and without any culpable negligence,[24] the loss must be borne equally by all."[25]

Thus, where A had represented to his co-partner B that a holding of shares in a certain company entailed only limited liability and B had thereupon, at A's request, authorised him to take shares on account of the firm, it was held that, as between A and B, B could not throw the loss on A alone when it transpired that the liability of the shareholders was not limited and A and B were both made contributories.[26] Similarly in *Cragg v. Ford*,[27] where the partnership between the claimant and the defendant had been dissolved and the winding up of its affairs had devolved on the defendant, who had formerly acted as managing partner. Part of the partnership assets consisted of bales of cotton, and the claimant requested their immediate sale. The defendant, however, delayed the sale, as a result of which a much lower price was achieved. The claimant contended that the loss sustained by the postponement of the sale ought to be borne by the defendant alone, but the court held that the claimant could himself have sold the cotton, if he had so chosen, and that the defendant had acted bona fide and in the exercise of his discretion in delaying the sale. As a result, the loss fell to be borne by both of the former partners. The position might, however, have been otherwise if the claimant been able to establish culpable negligence on the defendant's part.[28]

It should, however, be noted that, in *AMP General v. Macalister Todd*,[29] the Supreme Court of New Zealand accepted that the absence of personal liability may, to a large extent, depend on the contractual position, whether that be explicit (*e.g.* contained in the partnership agreement) or implicit (*e.g.* to be inferred from **20–09**

---

[23] See *Oldaker v. Lavender* (1833) 6 Sim. 239; *Cruikshank v. McVicar* (1844) 8 Beav. 106, 118 *per* Lord Langdale M.R. See further, as to such cases, *infra*, para. 20–10 *et seq.*

[24] *i.e. vis-à-vis* his co-partners. See *infra*, para. 20–12.

[25] The application of this principle was accepted without argument in *Tann v. Herrington* [2009] P.N.L.R. 22 at [47], [48] *per* Bernard Livesey Q.C. sitting as a deputy judge of the Chancery Division. However, notwithstanding what Lord Lindley said in this passage, losses are not necessarily shared equally: see *supra*, paras 20–04, 20–05.

[26] *Ex p. Letts and Steer* (1857) 26 L.J.Ch. 455. See also *Lingard v. Bromley* (1812) 1 V. & B. 114.

[27] (1842) 1 Y. & C.Ch. 280.

[28] See *Winsor v. Schroeder* (1979) 129 N.L.J. 1266, noted *infra*, para. 20–11.

[29] [2007] 1 N.Z.L.R 485 at [15] *et seq.*

the partnership's insurance or other arrangements).[30] In the current editor's view, this approach is likely to be relevant only where there is a clear indicator that liability is to be imposed on the partner responsible for the loss; if there are no indicators one way or the other, whether in the partnership agreement or elsewhere, the default position will be as set out above, *i.e.* the liability will be shared by all the partners.

Cases of the above type must, however, be distinguished from those in which the loss arises out of a breach of the duty which one partner owes to his co-partners: these are considered in the following paragraphs.

Exceptions to the normal rights of contribution

Losses attributable to one partner's misconduct, negligence or breach of duty

20–10   Prior to the Partnership Act 1890, if a partner was guilty of a breach of his duty to the firm and loss resulted therefrom, he was in effect required to bear the entirety of that loss. As Knight Bruce V.-C. observed in *Bury v. Allen*[31]:

> " . . . it is, I apprehend, plain that one of two partners may have a demand against the other for compensation, substantially in the nature of liquidated damages, enforceable in equity, and in equity only. Suppose the case of an act of fraud, or culpable negligence, or wilful default, by a partner during the partnership, to the damage of its property or interests, in breach of his duty to the partnership: whether at law compellable, or not compellable, he is certainly in equity compellable to compensate or indemnify the partnership in this respect."[32]

However, the nature and extent of this duty was not much explored by the courts.[33]

20–11   Despite a relative dearth of authority of English origin,[34] there is no reason to suppose that the Partnership Act 1890 altered the law and negated the existence of the implied duty recognised in *Bury v. Allen*. Confirmation of this is now to be found in a number of decisions. In *Winsor v. Schroeder*[35] two partners, S and W, had agreed to develop a property with a view to sale. Whilst the property was being marketed, there was a property slump. Although a substantial offer was made by a prospective purchaser, W rejected it and withdrew the property from sale, seemingly without consulting S. It was held that his actions amounted to more than an error of judgment and fell below the standards to be expected of him.[36] As a result, the majority of the resulting losses fell to be borne by him

---

[30] Note that, in *Tann v. Herrington* [2009] P.N.L.R. 22, at [64], it was held (*per* Bernard Livesey Q.C. sitting as a deputy judge of the Chancery Division) that the corollary of this must be the imposition of a duty to exercise skill and care on the partner responsible for dealing with such arrangements. See further, as to this decision, *infra*, para. 20–11.

[31] (1845) 1 Colly. 589, 604.

[32] See also *Thomas v. Atherton* (1878) 10 Ch.D. 185 (a case of gross negligence on the part of the managing partner of a mine).

[33] See, for example, *McIlreath v. Margetson* (1785) 4 Doug. 278, 279, where Lord Mansfield merely observed that the defendant had been "guilty of negligence".

[34] But see *AMP General v. Macalister Todd* [2007] 1 N.Z.L.R 485, noted *supra*, para. 20–09.

[35] (1979) 129 N.L.J. 1266. And note *Lane v. Bushby* [2000] N.S.W.S.C. 1029.

[36] It should be noted that Woolf J. distinguished between W's duty as a trustee and his duties as a partner, but nevertheless held that they were, in any event, "very much the same". A similar view of the duties owed by a partner with experience in property matters is to be seen in *Gallagher v. Schulz* (1988) 2 N.Z.B.L.C. 103, 196, where one partner with particular skills had encouraged the other to leave the organisation of a development project to him, with financially disastrous results.

alone.[37] *Broadhurst v. Broadhurst*[38] appears to be a decision falling within this principle, even though the point was not the subject of extensive argument. There the defendant partner, who appeared to have attempted to evade payment of VAT on the importation of certain cars, was held liable for the resulting additional tax, interest and penalties payable. A clearer example is seen in *Tann v. Herrington,*[39] where Mr Herrington was the partner responsible for looking after the firm's professional indemnity insurance[40] but failed to pass on details of a claim in due time, which resulted in the firm not being covered. He was held liable to bear the entirety of the cost of an out of court settlement and could not treat it as a partnership debt.

The existence of a similar duty has also been recognised in Scotland,[41] although the courts there have tended to devote more attention to analysing its precise nature and extent,[42] culminating in the landmark (but not necessarily authoritative) decision in *Ross Harper & Murphy v. Scott Banks.*[43]

Nature of the duty

The duty of a partner not to expose his firm and his co-partners to an avoidable liability is clearly one which is implied into the partnership relation in the absence of some contrary agreement.[44] Although it might, perhaps, be regarded as an aspect or extension of the duty of good faith,[45] this is not widely accepted.[46] It is distinct from any duty which may be owed between one partner and another *qua* individuals[47] and, inevitably, from any duty owed as between the firm and a third party, whether a client or otherwise. It follows that, whatever the precise

20–12

---

[37] W in fact recovered a small contribution of £274, as against a sum claimed in excess of £10,000.

[38] [2006] EWHC 2727 Ch (Lawtel 23/10/06) at [32] *per* Edward Bartley Jones Q.C. sitting as a deputy judge of the Chancery Division.

[39] [2009] P.N.L.R. 22. In the course of his judgment, Bernard Livesey Q.C. (sitting as a deputy judge of the Chancery Division) reviewed all the authorities.

[40] Note that there was no provision in the partnership agreement to this effect, merely a duty of diligence and good faith: see *ibid.* at [46].

[41] Of course, in Scotland, the firm is a separate legal person to whom such a duty can be owed (Partnership Act 1890, s.4(1)), even if there is a secondary duty owed to the other partners.

[42] See *Mair v. Wood* 1948 S.C. 83; *Blackwood v. Robertson* 1984 S.L.T. 68 (Sh.Ct.).

[43] 2000 S.L.T. 699 (OH).

[44] The existence of such a duty was advanced in *Tann v. Herrington, supra,* but in the event the judgment was not framed in those terms. Although the existence of the duty was also referred to in *AMP General v. Macalister Todd* [2007] 1 N.Z.L.R. 485 at [16], the Supreme Court of New Zealand did not seek to analyse its nature. Note that in *Ross Harper & Murphy v. Scott Banks, supra,* Lord Hamilton approached the duty as an implied term *and,* seemingly, as an independent duty of care: *ibid.* at [30]–[32]. *cf. Blackwood v. Robertson* 1984 S.L.T. 68, 70. There is, in the current editor's view, no reason to suppose that either type of duty cannot be excluded by an express or implied agreement, even if there are some doubts as to the ability of partners to exclude the duty of good faith in its entirety: see *supra*, para. 16–11.

[45] This was the assumption made in *Gallagher v. Schulz* (1988) 2 N.Z.B.L.C. 103 and also, seemingly, in *Tann v. Herrington* [2009] P.N.L.R. 22.

[46] Significantly, there was no linkage between the two duties in *Ross Harper & Murphy v. Scott Banks, supra.*

[47] In *Mair v. Wood, supra,* a partner was injured as a result of the negligent act of another. It was clear that the former had a cause of action against the latter personally (see 1948 S.C. 93 *per* Lord Keith), but not as a partner. Accordingly no liability could attach to the firm itself. The position would be no different in English law, save that the firm does not exist as a separate entity: the claimant in such a case would be attempting to sue himself along with the other partners. Note, however, that there was an assumption to the contrary in *Hammonds (A Firm) v. Danilunas* [2009] EWHC 216 (Ch) (Lawtel 18/2/09), noted *supra*, para. 12–03.

extent of the duty, there can be no *automatic* assumption that, merely because the firm has been rendered liable by a partner's breach of duty *vis-à-vis* a third party, he will necessarily have to indemnify his co-partners against any resultant losses. Equally, a liability incurred *without* any breach of duty *vis-à-vis* a third party, *e.g.* under a contract or involving a business transaction, may involve a breach of the duty which he owes to his partners. In each such case it will be necessary to analyse the circumstances in which the liability was incurred in order to establish whether there is an actionable breach. To these two classes of case must now be added a third, namely where a partner has *de facto* undertaken the responsibility of managing all or only certain aspects of the partnership business and fails to show the requisite degree of skill and care when doing so, causing loss to the firm.[48]

Extent of the duty

20–13   The fundamental question is whether the standard of care required by the duty is of a subjective or objective nature. In *Winsor v. Schroeder*,[49] Woolf J. appears to have adopted an objective test, applying the standards of the reasonable businessman[50] and the same approach was adopted in *Tann v. Herrington*[51] although, in this instance, the court was at pains to point out that the standard of skill and care might differ as between the three different classes of case noted in the preceding paragraph.[52] Although the subjective approach, *i.e.* requiring a partner to exercise the standard of care which he adopts in his own affairs, is more consistent with the normal attitude of the English courts, which is to recognise that partners must be taken as they are, with all their inherent failings,[53] that was expressly rejected in *Tann v. Herrington*.

Historically, something more than "mere" negligence has tended to be been required in the first and second classes of case noted above, hence the references in the older cases to "culpable" negligence[54] or recklessness,[55] personal misconduct[56] and wilful default.[57] Whether the expression "gross negligence" is a

---

[48] *Tann v. Herrington* [2009] P.N.L.R. 22, noted *supra*, para. 20–11. Note, however, that a similar argument did not appear to find favour with Carnwath J. in *Hurst v. Bryk*, April 11, 1995 (unreported). This part of the decision was not the subject of any appeal.

[49] (1979) 129 N.L.J. 1266, noted *supra*, para. 20–11.

[50] Note that Woolf J. reportedly did qualify this by the words "in the situation in which he found himself". See also *Gallagher v. Schulz* (1988) 2 N.Z.B.L.C. 103, 196. And note the reference to the claimant's "want of reasonable care" in *Thomas v. Atherton* (1878) 10 Ch.D. 185, 202.

[51] [2009] P.N.L.R. 22, noted *supra*, para. 20–11.

[52] *i.e.* (1) where a liability is incurred to a third party, (2) where there is "incompetent performance of business transactions involving partnership property", and (3) where the loss arises out of the administration of the firm's own internal affairs (the situation then under consideration): see *ibid.* at [60] *per* Bernard Livesey Q.C. (sitting as a deputy judge of the Chancery Division).

[53] It is this approach which underlies Lord Lindley's statement of principle, *supra*, para. 20–08 and, indeed, the Partnership Act 1890, s.35, *infra*, paras 24–47 *et seq.*

[54] This was an expression used in *Bury v. Allen* (1845) 1 Colly. 589, 604, noted *supra*, para. 20–10; also *Thomas v. Atherton* (1878) 10 Ch.D. 185, 199; *Winsor v. Schroeder, supra*; *Lane v. Bushby* [2000] N.S.W.S.C. 1029; and see Lord Lindley's statement of principle, *supra*, para. 20–08. Equally, in *McIlreath v. Margetson* (1785) 4 Doug. 278, 279, Lord Mansfield merely referred to the defendant's "negligence", without more. In *Wilson v. Brett* (1843) 11 M.&W. 113, the expressions "gross negligence" and "negligence" were used interchangeably: though not a partnership case the decision was regarded as relevant in *Tann v. Herrington* [2009] P.N.L.R. 22 at [53] to [56].

[55] This was an expression used in *Thomas v. Atherton, supra*, at p. 200. Elsewhere the epithet "culpable" was omitted: *ibid.* p. 199.

[56] This was, again, an expression used in *Thomas v. Atherton, supra*, at p. 199.

[57] This was an expression used in *Bury v. Allen, supra* and *Lane v. Bushby* [2000] N.S.W.S.C. 1029.

helpful one to use in this context is, perhaps, more questionable.[58] Equally, where a partner professes to have a particular skill, he may well be expected to exercise that skill to an objective standard.[59]

In Scotland, the courts also tended to favour the subjective standard,[60] until the **20–14** decision in *Ross Harper & Murphy v. Scott Banks.*[61] There, the court rejected both a wholly subjective standard and a wholly objective standard, in favour of what might be styled a modified or quasi-objective standard. In the words of Lord Hamilton[62]:

> "In the absence of clear and binding authority I favour a standard which requires the exercise of reasonable care in all the relevant circumstances. Those circumstances will include recognition that the relationship is one of partnership (which may import some mutual tolerance of error), the nature of the particular business conducted by that partnership (including any risks or hazards attendant on it) and any practices adopted by that partnership in the conduct of that business. The adjective 'gross', as used in some of the authorities, appears to me to be essentially a word of emphasis rather than one indicative of a category distinction."

This hybrid standard, whilst superficially attractive, leaves many unanswered questions. For example, will the mutual tolerance of error apply in all partnerships and what precise level of tolerance is to be expected in any given case? One minor mistake can safely be overlooked, but what if such mistakes are repeated on a regular basis? Will the size of the loss affect the level of tolerance? Are the same errors to be tolerated more in some businesses than others?

Since *Tann v. Herrington* has only provided clear guidance in the new (third) class of case, it is submitted that a subjective standard should continue to be applied,[63] so that sole liability for a loss will only attach to the partner responsible in the more extreme cases. However, it must be recognised that cases involving a partner with a special skill may well attract a higher and *objective* standard.[64]

Examples of acts involving a breach of duty

There are a number of obvious examples which scarcely require explanation. **20–15** Thus, where a partner has done an act which, though imputable to the firm on normal agency principles, is in fact a fraud on his co-partners, the latter will clearly be entitled, as between themselves and such partner (but *not* as between themselves and a third party), to throw any resultant losses onto him alone.[65]

---

[58] See the observations of Lord Hamilton in *Ross Harper & Murphy v. Scott Banks* 2000 S.L.T. 699 at [30]F, reproduced *infra*, para. 20–14. No such qualifications were voiced in *Lane v. Bushby, supra.*

[59] *Winsor v. Schroeder* (1979) 129 N.L.J. 1266; *Gallagher v. Schulz* (1988) 2 N.Z.B.L.C. 103; *Tann v. Herrington, supra,* at [65].

[60] *Mair v. Wood* 1948 S.C. 83, 90, 91 *per* Lord Keith; *Blackwood v. Robertson* 1984 S.L.T. 68, 71.

[61] 2000 S.L.T. 699 (OH). It is understood that, on appeal, the court did not appear to endorse Lord Hamilton's approach, but in the event expressed no concluded view thereon. Nevertheless, in *Duncan v. The MFV Marigold PD145* 2006 S.L.T. 975 (OH), Lord Reed referred to the decision without questioning its authority: see *ibid.* para. [66]. *cf. Tann v. Herrington, supra,* at [62].

[62] 2000 S.L.T. 699 at [30]E–F.

[63] Inevitably, the subjective standard will not be the same for all partners, irrespective of the business carried on.

[64] See the cases cited *supra*, n. 59.

[65] See *Robertson v. Southgate* (1848) 6 Hare 536.

Again where one partner, without the authority of his co-partners, wilfully commits an illegal act, he will be required to indemnify them against the consequences.[66] Similarly, where a claim is made for payment of a debt allegedly (but not in fact) due from a firm, and one partner carelessly chooses to pay it, he will not be permitted to charge such payment to the account of the firm.[67] Anything other than a minor failure on the part of a partner charged with a particular responsibility for dealing with any aspects of the firm's management and administration may attract liability,[68] as may a wanton failure to sign a document, e.g. a tax election, required by the firm in due time, provided that the need for such signature is backed up by a decision of the partners which is valid *and binding on the partner in question.*[69]

It is in the sphere of professional negligence that the greatest difficulties arise. It is submitted that a partner who engages in a persistently careless or reckless approach to his professional engagements must potentially be in breach of the implied duty owed his co-partners.[70] Similarly, perhaps, in the case of a single, but obvious and catastrophic blunder. Other evidence of such a breach may lie in a partner's studied unwillingness to comply with the firm's internal procedures or his failure to heed his partners' warnings about his approach towards the conduct of the partnership practice. What is clear is that it is not possible to lay down rules of general application, and that much will inevitably depend on the precise nature of the firm's practice.

Remedies for breach

20–16   As was made clear in *Bury v. Allen*,[71] the remedy for a breach of the duty under consideration is a claim for damages which will, normally, be pursued by way of an account.[72]

Effect of ratification

20–17   There will, however, be no actionable breach of duty if the relevant partner's conduct has been ratified by his co-partners and the loss accepted by them as a partnership loss which is to be shared by them all. However, in order to establish such ratification, the other partners must be shown to have *knowingly* allowed a loss properly chargeable to the account of one partner to be charged to the account of the firm and thus to have assumed liability therefor. This is clearly

---

[66] See *Campbell v. Campbell* (1839) 7 Cl. & F. 166. See also, as to losses arising from illegal acts, the observations of Lord Eldon in *Aubert v. Maze* (1801) 2 Bos. & Pul. 371, 374, regarding the decision in *Watts v. Brooks* (1798) 3 Ves.Jr. 611. And see *infra*, paras 20–20, 20–21.

[67] *Re Webb* (1818) 8 Taunt. 443; also *McIlreath v. Margetson*, *supra*, where a payment was made bona fide and on the faith of false and fraudulent representations. *Quaere*, would the same rule apply if a partner paid a time-barred debt of the firm? See *Stahlschmidt v. Lett* (1853) 1 Sm. & G. 415.

[68] As in *Tann v. Herrington* [2009] P.N.L.R. 22, noticed *supra*, para. 20–11. Of course, in such a case, there may be an express *contractual* duty associated with that responsibility, which may override the implied duty, and/or there may be a provision exonerating the responsible partner from personal liability save in the case of fraud, etc.

[69] Thus, where one group of partners regards the completion of such a document as beneficial, they are unlikely to be able to complain if one or more of the other partners disagree and refuse to sign it.

[70] *A fortiori*, if the other partners have remonstrated with him regarding that approach. *cf. Lane v. Bushby* [2000] N.S.W.S.C. 1029, where the act was an isolated one.

[71] (1845) 1 Colly. 589, 604: see *supra*, para. 20–10.

[72] See *infra*, para. 23–210. And see generally, as to actions for an account between partners, *supra*, paras 23–74 *et seq.*

illustrated by the decision in *Cragg v. Ford*,[73] where the defendant had engaged in adventures not authorised by the partnership agreement. The claimant (his partner) protested but did not at the time object to the fact that losses attributable to those adventures were charged against the firm in the partnership books nor, indeed, did he insist that they should be borne by the defendant alone. However, when the partnership was later dissolved and its accounts taken, the claimant refused to allow the losses in question to be charged against the firm. The court held that, under the circumstances, the Master had not acted incorrectly in charging the losses against the firm and the claimant's objections were overruled.

As might be expected, questions of the above type will usually be raised in the course of taking accounts between the partners.[74]

Partnership induced by fraud or misrepresentation

Where a person is induced to join a partnership by the fraud or misrepresenta-   **20–18** tion of one or more of the other partners, he is entitled to rescind the partnership contract and, as between himself and his co-partners, to throw all losses upon the guilty partner(s).[75]

Repudiation of partnership

It is now clear that the doctrine of repudiation has no application whilst a   **20–19** partnership is continuing.[76] Even if the doctrine did apply, an innocent partner accepting a repudiatory breach of a partnership agreement would not thereby be entitled to an automatic indemnity against the debts and liabilities of the dissolved firm,[77] but he might be able to recover certain losses thrown up on the resulting dissolution by way of damages.[78]

Illegal partnerships

It has already been pointed out that one member of an illegal partnership   **20–20** cannot maintain an action for a contribution against another[79]; however, the mere fact that an illegal act has been committed will not of itself constitute a defence to such an action, unless the illegality taints the partnership itself.[80] As Lord Lindley pointed out:

" . . . there is no authority for saying that if one of the members of a firm sustains a loss owing to some illegal act not attributable to him, but nevertheless imputable to

---

[73] (1842) 1 Y. & C.Ch. 280 (noted, on another point, *supra*, para. 20–08).

[74] See *Bury v. Allen* (1845) 1 Colly. 589, 604 *per* Knight Bruce V.-C. As to the circumstances in which accounts will be ordered between partners, see *infra*, paras 23–75 *et seq*.

[75] See the Partnership Act 1890, s.41, *infra*, paras 23–53 *et seq*.; also *Pillans v. Harkness* (1713) Colles P.C. 442; *Rawlins v. Wickham* (1858) 1 Giff. 355 and, on appeal, 3 De G. & J. 304; *Adam v. Newbigging* (1888) 13 App.Cas. 308. And see *Carew's Case* (1855) 7 De G.M. & G. 43.

[76] *Mullins v. Laughton* [2003] Ch. 250, adopting the *obiter* views voiced by Lord Millett in *Hurst v. Bryk* [2002] 1 A.C. 185, 193 *et seq*. See further *infra*, para. 24–06.

[77] This was decided by the House of Lords in *Hurst v. Bryk, supra*.

[78] See *infra*, para. 24–12.

[79] See *supra*, paras 8–63 *et seq*.

[80] See *supra*, paras 8–69 *et seq*.

the firm, such loss must be borne entirely by him, and that he is not entitled to contribution in respect thereof from the other partners."[81]

Equally, if the illegal act was committed by the partner seeking a contribution and he knew or ought to have known of its illegality, his claim must necessarily fail, leaving him alone to face the consequences of that act.[82]

20–21   The more difficult case is where an unlawful act has been knowingly committed by all the partners, so that they all are *in pari delicto*. Although there is a dictum of Lord Cottenham which might be cited in support of the proposition that, in such a case, each partner must bear any loss which he may happen to sustain without any contribution from his co-partners,[83] there is, in Lord Lindley's words:

> "a decision which goes far to show that the loss ought to be apportioned between all the partners,[84] unless the illegal act in question is a pure tort,[85] or a direct violation of some statute, or unless the contract of partnership is itself void on the ground of illegality."

Breach of trust

20–22   On the basis of the above principle, Lord Lindley apprehended that, in the case of a breach of trust committed by all the members of a firm, if one partner were to make good the breach out of his own moneys, he would be allowed, in taking the partnership accounts, to charge his co-partners, rateably with himself, with the amount so paid.[86] This must be right.

Civil Liability (Contribution) Act 1978

20–23   This Act places the right to contribution in respect of damages,[87] both as between partners or other wrongdoers, on a clear statutory footing.[88]

Having established that judgment recovered against any person liable in respect of damage suffered as a result of a tort, breach of contract, breach of trust

---

[81] See (at law) *Adamson v. Jarvis* (1827) 4 Bing. 66; *Betts v. Gibbins* (1834) 2 A. & E. 57; and (in equity) *Lingard v. Bromley* (1812) 1 V. & B. 114; *Baynard v. Woolley* (1855) 20 Beav. 583; *Ashhurst v. Mason* (1875) L.R. 20 Eq. 225; *Ramskill v. Edwards* (1885) 31 Ch.D. 100; also *Jackson v. Dickinson* [1903] 1 Ch. 947, in which the principle of *Ashhurst v. Mason* was explained and applied to the case of a breach of trust and contribution between trustees. As to criminal acts, see *R. Leslie Ltd. v. Reliable Advertising, etc. Agency* [1915] 1 K.B. 652; also *Weld Blundell v. Stephens* [1919] 1 K.B. 520, 529, 539 *per* Scrutton L.J. *Quaere*, can the decision in *Campbell v. Campbell* (1839) 7 Cl. & F. 166 be reconciled with the former decision, where it was not cited? See also *Wooley v. Batte* (1826) 2 Car. & P. 417; *Pearson v. Skelton* (1836) 1 M. & W. 504; *Thomas v. Atherton* (1878) 10 Ch.D. 185.

[82] See *Adamson v. Jarvis* (1827) 4 Bing. 66; *Betts v. Gibbins* (1834) 2 A. & E. 57; *Thomas v. Atherton* (1878) 10 Ch.D. 185. See also *Burrows v. Rhodes* [1899] 1 Q.B. 816; *Haseldine v. Hosken* [1933] 1 K.B. 822.

[83] See *Att.-Gen. v. Wilson* (1840) Cr. & Ph. 1, 28 *per* Lord Cottenham L.C.

[84] See *Baynard v. Woolley* (1855) 20 Beav. 583. But see also *supra*, paras 20–10 *et seq.*

[85] This exception must now be read subject to the wide provisions of the Civil Liability (Contribution) Act 1978: see *infra*, para. 20–23. And note also the decision in *K. v. P.* [1993] Ch. 140.

[86] See *Ashhurst v. Mason* (1875) L.R. 20 Eq. 225; *Jackson v. Dickinson* [1903] 1 Ch. 947; also *Baynard v. Woolley* (1855) 20 Beav. 583. And see the Civil Liability (Contribution) Act 1978, ss.1, 2, 6(1), noted *infra*.

[87] It has no application to claims in debt: *Hampton v Minns* [2002] 1 W.L.R. 1; *HM Revenue & Customs v. Yousef* [2008] B.C.C. 805.

[88] See *K. v. P.* [1993] Ch. 140.

or otherwise is no longer a bar to an action against another person jointly liable in respect of the same damage,[89] the Act provides that any person liable or bona fide compromising a claim in respect of such damage[90] may recover a contribution from any person liable in respect of the same damage, *whether jointly with him or otherwise*.[91] A contribution may be obtained notwithstanding that the person claiming it, or the person from whom it is claimed, has subsequently ceased to be liable in respect of such damage,[92] unless (in the latter case) he has ceased to be liable by reason of a limitation defence[93] and, moreover, cannot be defeated by a defence of *ex turpi causa non oritur actio*.[94] The amount of the contribution is in the court's discretion, regard being had to responsibility for the damage.[95] The court also has power to exempt any person from liability to make a contribution, or to direct that the contribution to be recovered from any person will amount to a complete indemnity.[96]

The Act does not affect any express or implied contractual or other right to indemnity, but it would seem that the statutory right to *contribution* may only be excluded by means of an express contractual provision.[97]   **20–24**

The right to contribution will be lost two years after the date on which it accrued, *i.e.* the date on which the quantum, and not merely the existence, of the liability is established or, where some form of compensation payment is to be made independently of any proceedings, the earliest date on which its amount is agreed.[98]

[89] Civil Liability (Contribution) Act 1978, ss.3, 6(1). The former section also applies to debts. However, in the case of an action for damages (but not debt), a successful claimant may be deprived of his costs in any action other than that in which judgment is first given: *ibid.* s.4.

[90] See *ibid.* s.1(4).

[91] *ibid.* s.1(1). As to the meaning of the words "the same damage", see *Birse Construction Ltd. v. Hastie Ltd.* [1996] 1 W.L.R. 675 (CA); *Howkins & Harrison v. Tyler* [2001] Lloyd's Rep. P.N. 1 (CA); *Eastgate Group Ltd. v. Lindsey Morden Group Inc* [2001] 2 All E.R. (Comm.) 1050 (CA); *Royal Brompton Hospital NHS Trust v. Hammond* [2002] 1 W.L.R. 1397 (HL); *Hurstwood Developments Ltd. v. Motor & General & Aldersley & Co Insurance Services Ltd.* [2002] P.N.L.R. 10 (CA); *Charter Plc v. City Index Ltd.* [2008] Ch. 313 (CA); *Greene Wood & McClean v. Templeton Insurance Ltd.* [2009] 1 C.L.C. 123 (CA). A claim for debt is *not* a claim for damages for this purpose, see *Hampton v. Minns, The Times,* March 27, 2001; *cf. Friends' Provident Life Office v. Hillier Parker May & Rowden* [1997] Q.B. 85, 103H (CA); also *Jameson v. Central Electricity Generating Board* [1998] Q.B. 323, 353C–E. As to the position where a different measure of loss is recoverable from two different parties liable in respect of the same damage, see *Nationwide Building Society v. Dunlop Haywards (DHL) Ltd.* [2010] 1 W.L.R. 258.

[92] *e.g.* by reason of a compromise: see *Heaton v. Axa Equity and Law Life Assurance Society Plc* [2001] Ch. 173 (CA).

[93] *ibid.* s.1(2), (3). Judgment given in any action brought by the person suffering the damage is conclusive evidence in the contribution proceedings as to any issue determined thereby in favour of the person from whom contribution is sought: *ibid.* s.1(5).

[94] See *K. v. P.* [1993] Ch. 140. Note, however, that Ferris J. contemplated that, in cases affected by illegality, the court *might* set the contribution at zero: *ibid.* p. 149B.

[95] Civil Liability (Contribution) Act 1978, s.2(1). The discretion conferred by this section is a wide one: *City Index Ltd. v. Gawler* [2008] Ch. 313 (CA). Note that the damage referred to is the "same damage" as specified in *ibid.* s.1(1): see *Nationwide Building Society v. Dunlop Haywards (DHL) Ltd., supra.* And see the preceding note.

[96] *ibid.* s.2(2). See also *Semtex v. Gladstone* [1954] 1 W.L.R. 945; *Lister v. Romford Ice and Cold Storage Co.* [1957] A.C. 555 (decisions under the former Law Reform (Married Women and Tortfeasors) Act 1935).

[97] *ibid.* s.7(3). The Act does not, however, render enforceable any agreement for indemnity or contribution which would not be enforceable apart from the Act: *ibid.*

[98] Limitation Act 1980, s.10; *Aer Lingus plc v. Gildacroft Ltd.* [2006] 1 W.L.R. 1173 (CA).

Time for claiming contribution or indemnity

20–25   As was the position in equity prior to the passing of the Judicature Acts, any person entitled to a contribution or indemnity from another can, even in the absence of any special agreement, enforce his right before sustaining an actual loss,[99] provided that a loss is imminent.[100] Thus, where continuing partners have agreed to indemnify an outgoing partner or the estate of a deceased partner against partnership liabilities, the creditor must have made a demand for payment before the right to indemnity can be pursued.[101] Similarly, where partners are individually liable to be sued on a bond or promissory note, which as between them and their co-partners is to be regarded as the bond or note of the firm, they are entitled to call for contribution before it is actually paid.[102] Nevertheless, such a claim as between partners may (and, indeed, usually will) entail the taking of an account[103] and may become barred by reason of limitation or laches.[104]

2.   OUTLAYS AND ADVANCES

Outlays and advances made by one partner

20–26   Even before that right was expressly recognised by the Partnership Act 1890,[105] a partner was entitled to charge the partnership with sums bona fide expended by him in conducting its business.[106] This was made clear by Lord Hardwicke in *West v. Skip*,[107] when he observed that:

> "when an account is to be taken, each [*partner*] is intitled to be allowed against the other everything he has advanced or brought in as a partnership transaction, and to charge the other in the account with what that other has not brought in, or has taken out more than he ought; and nothing is to be considered as his share, but his proportion of the residue on balance of the account."[108]

On this principle, a partner is clearly entitled to charge the firm with any sums he may have been compelled to pay in respect of its debts[109] or in respect of an

---

[99] See *Lacey v. Hill* (1874) L.R. 18 Eq. 182; *Hobbs v. Wayet* (1887) 36 Ch.D. 256; *Ex p. Governors of St. Thomas's Hospital* [1911] 2 K.B. 705.

[100] *ibid.; Hughes-Hallett v. Indian Mammoth Gold Mines Co.* (1882) 22 Ch.D. 561.

[101] *Bradford v. Gammon* [1925] 1 Ch. 132.

[102] See, for example, *Norwich Yarn Co.'s Case* (1850) 22 Beav. 143. Lord Lindley appended the following comment: "the money borrowed by the directors in that case was secured by their own notes, but these notes had not been actually paid when the call on the shareholders was made. This does not appear very clearly from the report referred to, but the writer was informed by persons conversant with the case that the above statement is correct."

[103] See further, as to the taking of partnership accounts, *infra*, paras 23–74 *et seq.*

[104] See *infra*, paras 23–20, 23–32 *et seq.*

[105] *ibid.* s.24(2), *supra*, para. 20–03.

[106] See *Burden v. Burden* (1813) 1 V. & B. 172, where a surviving partner (who was also an executor) was allowed to charge expenses actually incurred, but not an allowance for his time and trouble. *cf. Hutcheson v. Smith* (1842) 5 I.Eq.R. 117. See also *infra*, paras 20–43 *et seq.* And note *Ex p. Chippendale* (1854) 4 De G.M. & G. 19; *Ex p. Sedgwick* (1856) 2 Jur. (N.S.) 949 (both of which concerned mining companies).

[107] (1749) 1 Ves.Sen. 239, 241.

[108] See also *supra*, paras 19–05 *et seq.*

[109] *Prole v. Masterman* (1855) 21 Beav. 61. As to the position where a partner negligently pays a debt claimed but not due, see *Re Webb* (1818) 8 Taunt. 443; *McIlreath v. Margetson* (1785) 4 Doug. 278, noted *supra*, para. 20–15, n. 67.

obligation which he has personally incurred at the request of the firm,[110] or indeed where he sacrifices a debt due to himself in order to enable the firm to recover its own debt.[111] However, determining whether particular expenses incurred by a partner fall to be reimbursed will, almost inevitably, give rise to difficult factual issues.[112]

Authorised but useless outlays

It need hardly be pointed out that moneys laid out by a partner for the benefit of the firm with the consent of his co-partners must be made good by the firm, however useless such outlay may have been. Thus, if a partner personally finances the purchase by his firm of a particular patent, the purchase price will be chargeable to the firm, even if the patent proves wholly worthless.[113] On the other hand, if such an outlay is not authorised in advance, it cannot be charged to the firm unless it is subsequently ratified by the other partners or the firm's assets have been increased or preserved thereby.[114]

20–27

Unauthorised but useful outlays

An outlay made by a partner, which is otherwise proper and even necessary for the conduct of the partnership business, cannot be charged to the firm, if that would be inconsistent with (or, more obviously, a breach of) the partnership agreement. In *Thornton v. Proctor*,[115] the claimant and the defendant were in partnership as wine merchants and the claimant, who had for some time been primarily responsible for running the business, had spent considerable sums entertaining customers, which was found to be a necessary incident of the trade. In keeping the accounts of the partnership, which he had done for several years, the claimant neither made any charge for such entertainment nor sought any allowance therefor. He nevertheless subsequently contended that an entertainment allowance of £50 a year ought to be made in taking the accounts of the partnership and proved this to be a reasonable sum. However, it was demonstrated that, in such cases, a specific provision authorising the payment of such an allowance would usually be included in the partnership agreement, whereas the agreement under consideration contained no such provision, but merely a general stipulation that all losses and expenses should be borne by the partners equally. It was accordingly held that the claimant was not entitled to the allowance sought; although he might have treated the sums laid out as a direct partnership expense, he was precluded from doing so by omitting them from the annual accounts.

20–28

---

[110] *Gleadow v. Hull Glass Co.* (1849) 13 Jur. 1020; *Croxton's Case* (1852) 5 De G. & Sm. 432; *Sedgwick's Case* (1856) 2 Jur. (N.S.) 949.

[111] *Lefroy v. Gore* (1844) 1 Jo. & La T. 571, where one partner released a witness whose evidence was essential to the firm.

[112] See, for example, *Medcalf v. Mardell*, Unreported March 31, 1999 Ch D, where Lloyd J. declined to decide whether certain travel and administrative expenses were properly incurred on the evidence before him and referred the matter back to the Master. This aspect was not pursued on the appeal, Unreported March 2, 2000 CA (Civ Div).

[113] *Gleadow v. Hull Glass Co.* (1849) 13 Jur. 1020.

[114] The latter qualification is rendered necessary by *Ex p. Chippendale* (1854) 4 De G M. & G. 19. See further *supra*, paras 12–175 *et seq*.

[115] (1792) 1 Anst. 94. See also *East India Co. v. Blake* (1673) Finch 117; *Hutcheson v. Smith* (1842) 5 I.Eq.R. 117.

Particulars of outlays

20–29   A partner may not charge the firm with moneys allegedly laid out by him for its benefit if he declines to give particulars thereof. Thus, he cannot charge for expenditure incurred in securing or rewarding the services of third parties, the nature of which he refuses to disclose,[116] nor for general expenses.[117] Moreover, he obviously cannot charge the firm with travelling expenses, unless they were bona fide and properly incurred by him when travelling on partnership business.[118]

Transactions between partners

20–30   Where a partner pays for a valuation required in connection with a transaction between himself and his co-partners which is subsequently set aside on the application of those other partners, they cannot be charged with any part of the valuation costs.[119]

Outlays by the firm on a partner's own property

20–31   Where a firm expends money for the benefit of a partner, the outlay will in general amount to a loan by the firm in his favour and must be treated as such in taking the partnership accounts. However, more difficult cases inevitably arise, such as where a firm expends money on property which is owned by one of the partners but used by the firm for the purposes of its business. In the absence of a specific agreement or circumstances giving rise to a "proprietary estoppel",[120] Lord Lindley took the view that:

> " . . . justice seems to require that in taking the partnership accounts the owner of the property in question should not be allowed exclusively to gain the benefit of the outlay, but that the improved value of his property should be treated as a partnership asset, and be shared between him and his co-partners accordingly".[121]

20–32   Thus, in *Burdon v. Barkus*,[122] a managing partner had, with the knowledge of his co-partner, expended partnership moneys in sinking a pit on the latter's land for partnership purposes. The managing partner had erroneously supposed that the partnership was for a term of years, but it was suddenly and unexpectedly dissolved and the pit thereby became the sole property of the landowning partner. An inquiry was directed as to whether any allowances should be made in respect of the outlay in sinking the pit. A similar inquiry was directed in *Pawsey v. Armstrong*,[123] in respect of buildings erected by a firm on the property of one of the partners.

---

[116] See *York and North Midland Ry. v. Hudson* (1845) 16 Beav. 485.

[117] *East India Co. v. Blake* (1673) Finch 117.

[118] *Stainton v. The Carron Co.* (1857) 24 Beav. 346.

[119] *Stocken v. Dawson* (1843) 6 Beav. 375.

[120] See *supra*, para. 18–42.

[121] See *supra*, paras 18–38 *et seq*. But note the decision in *Harvey v. Harvey* (1970) 120 C.L.R. 529; also *Harwood v. Harwood* [1991] 2 F.L.R. 274.

[122] (1862) 4 De G. F. & J. 42.

[123] (1881) 18 Ch.D. 698. See also *Miles v. Clarke* [1953] 1 W.L.R. 537; *cf. the Bank of England Case* (1861) 3 De G.F. & J. 645; and see *supra*, para. 18–38.

Although it has been recognised that, in appropriate circumstances, an allowance might be made in respect of the expenditure of partnership moneys in acquiring or increasing milk quota which attaches to a partner's land,[124] there is no reported case in which such an argument has succeeded.

3. INTEREST

Interest not generally payable

As a matter of general law, a loan does not bear interest in the absence of some contrary custom or agreement.[125] Mercantile custom has, however, long recognised the commercial realities which justify a demand for interest in cases where it would not otherwise have been payable.[126] Furthermore, the court has a wide statutory power to award interest in any proceedings brought for the recovery of a debt.[127]

20–33

It is accordingly necessary, when applying what appears to be a general rule *against* the allowance of interest in the taking of partnership accounts,[128] to have regard not only to any express agreement between the partners, but also to the firm's accounting practices and (where relevant) to the customs of the trade which it seeks to carry on.

Interest on capital

The Partnership Act 1890[129] confirms the pre-existing rule that partners are not, in the absence of some contrary agreement, entitled to interest on their respective capital contributions; however, an agreement for the payment of interest may be inferred if the partners have themselves been in the habit of charging such interest in their accounts.[130] The rule applies even where one partner has brought in his agreed sum of capital but his co-partner has not[131] and as against a person remunerated for his services by a share of profits.[132]

20–34

---

[124] *Faulks v. Faulks* [1992] 1 E.G.L.R. 9, 17 *per* Chadwick J. (albeit that his views were strictly *obiter*); *Davies v. H.&R. Ecroyd Ltd.* [1996] 2 E.G.L.R. 5, 8–9 *per* Blackburne J.

[125] This rule prevailed both at common law and in equity and was doubtless attributable to the old laws against usury. See (for the position at law) *Calton v. Bragg* (1812) 15 East 223; *Gwyn v. Godby* (1812) 4 Taunt. 346; *Higgins v. Sargent* (1823) 2 B. & C. 349; *Shaw v. Picton* (1825) 4 B. & C. 723; *Page v. Newman* (1829) 9 B. & C. 378; and (in equity) *Tew v. Earl of Winterton* (1792) 1 Ves.Jr. 451; *Creuze v. Hunter* (1793) 2 Ves.Jr. 157; *Booth v. Leycester* (1838) 3 Myl. & Cr. 459.

[126] See *Ex p. Chippendale* (1854) 4 De G.M. & G. 19.

[127] Senior Courts Act 1981, s.35A (formerly the Supreme Court Act 1981: Constitutional Reform Act 2005, Sched. 11, Pt. 1, para. 1(1)); County Courts Act 1984, s.69: see *infra*, para. 20–41.

[128] Although Lord Lindley recognised the existence of this general rule, he had previously observed "The principles on which, in taking partnership accounts, interest is allowed or disallowed, do not appear to be well settled. The state of the authorities is, in fact, not such as to justify the deduction from them of any general principle upon this important subject."

[129] *ibid.* s.24(3): see *supra*, para. 20–03. And see *supra*, para. 17–12, n. 44.

[130] See *Millar v. Craig* (1843) 6 Beav. 433; *Cooke v. Benbow* (1865) 3 De G.J. & S. 1 (where interest was allowed); also *Pim v. Harris* (1876) Ir.Rep. 10 Eq. 442, where the decision was based on the terms of the contract.

[131] *Hill v. King* (1863) 3 De G.J. & Sm. 418.

[132] *Rishton v. Grissell* (1870) L.R. 10 Eq. 393, where the capital had been borrowed at interest.

The mere fact that interest is payable on capital does not necessarily mean that such interest is also payable on undrawn profits,[133] unless they can be treated as an advance.[134]

Position following a general dissolution

20–35 It scarcely needs to be stated that, if interest on capital is not payable whilst the partnership is continuing, it will not be payable following a general dissolution.[135] Indeed, where interest on capital *is* payable under an agreement, the partners' continuing entitlement thereto will automatically cease in the event of a dissolution, unless there is an express provision to the contrary.[136]

However, in either case the partners may still retain a residual entitlement in lieu of any right to interest.[137] As will be seen hereafter, on a general dissolution the assets of the partnership will normally be converted into cash and the fund thereby produced applied in the manner set out in section 44 of the Partnership Act 1890.[138] If, after the payment of the firm's debts and liabilities and the repayment of any advances, that fund is more than sufficient to repay the partners' capital contributions,[139] each such contribution will carry its proportionate share of the income of the fund, which must be accounted for *before* the ultimate residue (if any) is divided between the partners.[140]

Interest on advances

20–36 Where a partner advances money to the firm over and above his capital contribution, the advance is, as might be expected, treated not as an increase in his capital but as a loan on which interest ought to be paid,[141] and this is expressly recognised in the Partnership Act 1890.[142] Accordingly, provided that the advance was made for partnership purposes, simple interest will be payable

---

[133] *Dinham v. Bradford* (1869) L.R. 5 Ch.App. 519. See also *Rishton v. Grissell* (1870) 10 Eq. 393, as to interest on arrears of a share of profits. *Quaere* whether such undrawn profits are to be treated as advances attracting interest under the Partnership Act 1890, s.24(3): see *infra*, para. 20–36. In many firms, undrawn profits are indiscriminately credited to the partners' capital accounts, and it may be extremely difficult to ascertain their true status: see *supra*, para. 17–06.

[134] See the Partnership Act 1890, s.24(3) and *infra*, para. 20–36.

[135] But see *ibid.* s.42, *infra*, paras 25–22 *et seq.*

[136] *Barfield v. Loughborough* (1872) L.R. 8 Ch.App. 1; *Watney v. Wells* (1861) L.R. 2 Ch.App. 250; Lord Lindley observed that the contrary decision in *Pilling v. Pilling* (1887) 3 De G.J. & S. 162 is, on this point, "practically overruled." As to the calculation of interest where the capital is payable by instalments with interest, see *Ewing v. Ewing* (1882) 8 App.Cas. 822. *cf.* the views of the court in *Hopper v. Hopper* [2008] EWCA Civ. 1417 (Lawtel 12/12/08) at [47], regarding the continued application of the normal profit sharing arrangements following a dissolution; also *Popat v. Shonchhatra* [1997] 1 W.L.R. 1367, 1374. See further on this issue *supra*, paras 10–84, 13–72 and *infra*, para. 25–25.

[137] *Quaere*, whether such an entitlement is inconsistent with the express provisions of the Partnership Act 1890, s.44(b): see *ibid.* s.46, *infra*, para. A1–47. It is tentatively thought not, although there is no post-1890 authority on the point.

[138] See *infra*, paras 23–183 *et seq.*, 25–44 *et seq.*

[139] Partnership Act 1890, s.44(b), paras 1–3.

[140] *Watney v. Wells* (1861) L.R. 2 Ch.App. 250. *Quaere*, could this principle be extended to a case where the partners' capital contributions are, in effect, represented by an income producing asset of the former firm which has not yet been realised? But see *Barfield v. Loughborough* (1872) L.R. 8 Ch.App. 1, 3, 4 *per* Lord Selborne L.C.

[141] See *Ex p. Chippendale* (1854) 4 De G.M. & G. 19; also *Omychund v. Barker* (1744); *Collyer on Partnership* (2nd ed.), p. 231, note; *Denton v. Rodie* (1813) 3 Camp. 493. *Per contra, Stevens v. Cook* (1859) 5 Jur.(N.S.) 1415.

[142] *ibid.* s.24(3): see *supra*, para. 20–03.

thereon at the rate of 5 per cent.[143] However, an agreement to pay a different rate may be inferred if interest at that rate has been charged and allowed in the books of the firm[144] or, perhaps, where it is payable by the custom of the particular trade.[145]

Interest on overdrawings and balances in hand

Of the converse situation, *i.e.* a partner owing money to the firm, Lord Lindley observed: **20–37**

> "Inasmuch as what is fair for one partner is so for another, and the firm when debtor is charged with interest, it seems to follow that if one partner is indebted to the firm either in respect of money borrowed, or in respect of balances in his hands, he ought to be charged with interest on the amount so owing, even though on the balance of the whole account, a sum might be due to him.[146] Except, however, where there has been a fraudulent retention,[147] or an improper application[148] of money of the firm, it is not the practice of the Court to charge a partner with interest on money of the firm in his hands[149]; for example, under ordinary circumstances a partner is not charged with interest on sums drawn out by him or advanced to him."[150]

Although Lord Lindley cited the decision in *Rhodes v. Rhodes*[151] in this context, the current editor submits it is not directly in point. There A and B were partners; A died and his son and executor, C, succeeded him in partnership with B. B then retired in favour of his own son, D. At the time of his retirement, a considerable sum was due to B from A's estate in respect of moneys drawn out by A. This sum was treated as a debt of the new firm of C and D, and was not paid. B died and his executors claimed interest but only from the date of B's retirement: the claim was rejected on the ground that there was no agreement for the payment of interest and that such a claim was in any event inconsistent with the course of dealing between the partners themselves. It should be noted that, in a case of this

---

[143] *ibid.* And see, as to the position prior to the Act, *Ex p. Bignold* (1856) 22 Beav. 143; *Troup's Case* (1860) 29 Beav. 353. See also *Hart v. Clarke* (1854) 6 De G.M. & G. 232, 254 *per* Turner L.J. (affirmed *sub nom. Clarke v. Hart* (1858) 6 H.L.C. 633).

[144] As in *Re Magdalena Steam Navigation Co.* (1860) Johns. 690, where interest at 6% was allowed.

[145] As to compound interest in the case of bankers, see *National Bank of Greece S.A. v. Pinios Shipping Co. No. 1* [1990] 1 A.C. 637, where the authorities are reviewed. *Sed quaere*, would such a custom necessarily justify the implication of an agreement for the payment of interest at such a rate, in the face of the statutory rate under the Act? Note also the exceptional decision in *Roxburgh Dinardo & Partners' Judicial Factor v. Dinardo* 1993 S.L.T. 16 (2nd Div.), noted *infra*, para. 20–39.

[146] See *Beecher v. Guilburn* (1726) Moseley 3.

[147] As in *Hutcheson v. Smith* (1842) 5 I.Eq.R. 117, where, however, the partner retaining the money was also a receiver appointed by the court.

[148] As in *Evans v. Coventry* (1857) 8 De G.M. & G. 835; see also *Daniels v. Angus* [1947] N.Z.L.R. 329.

[149] See *Webster v. Bray* (1849) 7 Hare 159, where interest on balances in the hands of the defendants was sought but not obtained. See also *Stevens v. Cook* (1859) 5 Jur.(N.S.) 1415; *Turner v. Burkinshaw* (1867) L.R. 2 Ch.App. 488.

[150] *Meymott v. Meymott* (1862) 31 Beav. 445; *Cooke v. Benbow* (1865) 3 De G.J. & S. 1; *Barfield v. Loughborough* (1872) L.R. 8 Ch.App. 1, 7 *per* Lord Selborne L.C.

[151] (1860) 6 Jur.(N.S.) 600. See also *Barfield v. Loughborough* (1872) L.R. 8 Ch.App. 1, 7 *per* Lord Selborne.

type, interest might now be awarded by the court under its statutory jurisdiction.[152]

Interest on benefits obtained by one partner

20–38   Where one partner successfully claims to share a benefit obtained by his co-partner, he must, as the price of obtaining such relief, give credit for all expenditure bona fide incurred in obtaining that benefit together with interest on his (the claimant's) due share thereof at the rate of 5 per cent.[153] On the other hand, where a partner has, in breach of the duty of good faith, obtained money for which he is bound to account to the firm, he will be charged with interest thereon at the rate of 4 per cent,[154] unless the court is prepared to award interest at a higher rate.[155]

Interest following a dissolution

20–39   Where a partnership has been dissolved by the death of one partner and the surviving partner keeps the accounts in such a way that the balances due to himself and to the deceased partner's estate cannot be ascertained for a considerable time, neither the surviving partner nor his representatives can claim interest on the sum ultimately found due to him or his estate.[156]

This may be contrasted with the exceptional decision in *Roxburgh Dinardo & Partners' Judicial Factor v. Dinardo*,[157] where a Scottish firm had been dissolved and a judicial factor (X) had *de facto* distributed its assets between the partners in such a way that one partner (A) took the net assets whilst the other (B) took the net liabilities.[158] When X sought the court's approval for a scheme of division of those assets, he sought to charge A with compound interest in respect of the assets in his hands. The court held that such interest was, on the facts, properly chargeable, since B had had to finance the liabilities which he had taken over on overdraft, in respect of which compound interest was obviously payable. It was also held that compound interest could in any event be charged against A on the grounds that he was accountable for the assets in his hands as a result of his fiduciary relationship with B.

---

[152] Senior Courts Act 1981 s.35A (formerly the Supreme Court Act 1981: Constitutional Reform Act 2005, Sched. 11, Pt.1, para. 1(1)); County Courts Act 1984, s.69: see *infra*, para. 20–41.

[153] See *Hart v. Clarke* (1854) 6 De G.M. & G. 232, 254 *per* Turner L.J. The order was subsequently affirmed at (1858) 6 H.L.C. 633. See also *Perens v. Johnson* (1857) 3 Sm. & G. 419.

[154] See *Fawcett v. Whitehouse* (1829) 1 Russ. & M. 132.

[155] See *Wallersteiner v. Moir (No. 2)* [1975] Q.B. 373 (compound interest at 1% above bank base rate/minimum lending rate with yearly rests awarded where a party had improperly profited from a fiduciary position); *O'Sullivan v. Management Agency and Music Ltd.* [1985] Q.B. 428; *cf. Westdeutsche Landesbank Girozentrale v. Islington London Borough Council* [1996] A.C. 669 (HL). In *Roxburgh Dinardo & Partners' Judicial Factor v. Dinardo* 1993 S.L.T. 16 (2nd Div.) (noted *infra*, para. 20–39), compound interest at an unspecified rate was awarded as between partners, albeit in unusual circumstances. The older cases should be approached with caution: *e.g.* interest at only 3% was awarded in *Re Olympia Ltd.* [1898] 2 Ch. 153 and *Barclay v. Andrews* [1899] 1 Ch. 674; *cf.* the remarks of Lord Macnaghten in *Gluckstein v. Barnes* [1900] A.C. 240, 255.

[156] *Boddam v. Ryley* (1787) 4 Bro.P.C. 561. But see also *supra*, para. 20–37.

[157] 1993 S.L.T. 16 (2nd Div.).

[158] It appears that such a distribution was not agreed by A and B.

A partner may also be entitled to interest at the rate of 5 per cent pursuant to section 42 of the Partnership Act 1890 where, following a dissolution, the remaining partners continue to carry on the business without any settlement of accounts as regards him.[159]

Alien enemy

It is apprehended that any entitlement which a partner may have to interest will not cease if he becomes an alien enemy,[160] so that interest will continue to accrue during the relevant hostilities even though it cannot be recovered until they are concluded.[161]

20–40

Interest awarded by the court

The High Court[162] and the county court[163] have power to order the inclusion, in the judgment given in any proceedings for the recovery of a debt or damages, of simple interest at such rate as they think fit, or as rules of court may provide, on all or part of the debt or damages for all or any part of the period between the date when the cause of action arose and the date of judgment.[164] Such interest is payable without deduction of tax.[165] It is questionable whether and, if so, to what extent the statutory power has altered the rights of partners to interest as between themselves: certainly, where a balance can be shown to be due to a partner following the taking of a partnership account, there is in principle no reason why the court should not order the payment of interest under its statutory power.[166] In an earlier edition of this work, the current editor questioned whether such an order could be made in a case where section 42 of the Partnership Act 1890[167] would otherwise apply and advanced the tentative view that the two jurisdictions

20–41

---

[159] *Quaere*, does this section apply on a *general* dissolution? See, *infra*, paras 25–24 *et seq.*

[160] See, as to the meaning of this expression, *supra*, para. 4–04.

[161] *Hugh Stevenson & Sons v. Aktiengesellschaft für Cartonnagen Industrie* [1918] A.C. 239, 245 *per* Finlay L.C.

[162] Senior Courts Act 1981, s.35A (as inserted by the Administration of Justice Act 1982, s.15, Sched. 1). This Act was renamed by the Constitutional Reform Act 2005, Sched. 11, Pt. 1, para. 1(1). The power superseded the provisions of the Law Reform (Miscellaneous Provisions) Act 1934, s.3. Note also that an arbitrator may award interest: Arbitration Act 1996, s.49. And see, generally, *R. v. Denbighshire Local Health Board* [2006] 3 All E.R. 141; *Maher v. Groupama Grand Est* [2010] 1 W.L.R. 1564 (CA).

[163] County Courts Act 1984, s.69.

[164] Where a sum is paid before judgment, interest may be ordered down to the date of payment: Senior Courts Act 1981, s.35A(1)(a); County Courts Act 1984, s.69(1)(a). Where interest already runs on a debt, no interest may be ordered under either section: s.35A(4) of the 1981 Act or s.69(4) of the 1984 Act. As to the position where a debt is paid *before* the commencement of proceedings, see *Wadsworth v. Lydall* [1981] 1 W.L.R. 598; *President of India v. La Pintada Compania* [1985] A.C. 104 (HL).

[165] The only cases in which tax may now be deducted at source from interest payments are those set out in the Income Tax Act 2007, Pt. 15, Chap. 6; interest of the kind considered in the text does not fall within these provisions.

[166] Although a partner was awarded interest (pursuant to the Law Reform (Miscellaneous Provisions) Act 1934) in respect of sums due under a dissolution agreement in *Wadsworth v. Lydall* [1981] C.L.Y. 2015 (this point not being referred to in the report at [1981] 1 W.L.R. 598), his entitlement thereto could not have been seriously questioned even by reference to the older cases.

[167] See *infra*, paras 25–24 *et seq.*

were co-extensive.[168] It has now been decided[169] that interest under the Senior Courts Act 1981 *cannot* be claimed in such a case, since that Act specifically provides that interest shall not be awarded in respect of a period "during which, for whatever reason, interest on the debt already runs".[170] This does, however, ignore the fact that a claim for interest under section 42 of the 1890 Act is only claimable at the option of the outgoing partner.[171]

Pleading a claim for interest

20–42   Where a claim for interest is to be made, it must be specifically pleaded in the relevant party's statement of case.[172] Since most claims between partners or former partners will be dependent on the taking of an account,[173] it will usually be unnecessary to quantify the interest sought.[174]

4.   REMUNERATION FOR SERVICES RENDERED TO FIRM

The general rule

20–43   Writing prior to the Partnership Act 1890, Lord Lindley stated the general rule as follows:

> "Under ordinary circumstances the contract of partnership excludes any implied contract for payment for services rendered for the firm by any of its members.[175] Consequently, under ordinary circumstances and in the absence of an agreement to that effect, one partner cannot charge his co-partners with any sum for compensation, whether in the shape of salary, commission, or otherwise, on account of his own trouble in conducting the partnership business."

This rule was given statutory force by section 24(6) of the Partnership Act 1890.[176]

On this basis it was held that, in taking the accounts of three successive firms, comprising: (1) A and B, (2) A, B and C, and (3) B and C, the latter firm was not entitled to charge a commission for collecting the debts due to the two preceding

---

[168] It was, at that time, the current editor's experience that claims for interest under what was then the Supreme Court Act 1981 or the County Courts Act 1984 were routinely pleaded in such cases and that the jurisdiction under those Acts tended not to be questioned by the parties or by the court. Obviously, where a share of profits was sought, the claim *had* to be formulated under the 1890 Act.

[169] *William v. Williams* [1999] C.L.Y. 4095. Note also, in this context, *Sobell v. Boston* [1975] 1 W.L.R. 1587, 1593, where Goff J. criticised the fact that the rate of interest under s.42 of the 1890 Act had never been amended.

[170] Senior Courts Act 1981, s.35A(4). The County Courts Act 1984, s.69(4) is in similar terms.

[171] See *infra*, paras 25–26 *et seq.*

[172] CPR r. 16.4(1)(b), (2). This rule does not apply in the case of Pt 8 claims: *ibid.* r. 8.9(a)(i).

[173] See *infra*, para. 23–76.

[174] CPR r. 16.4(2)(b).

[175] *Holmes v. Higgins* (1822) 1 B. & C. 74. *cf. Thompson v. Williamson* (1831) 7 Bli.(N.S.) 432 *per* Lord Wynford.

[176] See *supra*, para. 20–03.

firms.[177] Similarly, a partner employed to buy or sell goods for his firm was not permitted to charge commission for so doing.[178]

The fact that it might, in the circumstances, have been *reasonable* for partners   **20–44** to agree that one of their number should be remunerated for his efforts over and above his profit share is not enough to displace section 24(6), as the Court of Appeal made clear in *Medcalf v. Mardell*.[179] Thus, performance by a partner of services of particular value to the firm[180] or his acceptance of additional and, perhaps, onerous duties, *e.g.* as managing partner,[181] will confer no special rights in this respect. Moreover, it is not possible for a partner to circumvent the subsection by providing his services through a company which he controls.[182]

Where (exceptionally) it is agreed that a partner *will* be remunerated in respect of services provided to the firm in his capacity as a partner, any remuneration paid to him will not be deductible by the firm for income tax purposes.[183]

Exceptions to the general rule

Wilful inattention to business

The general rule will be applied no matter how unequal the effort which each   **20–45** partner may put into promoting the success and prosperity of the firm.[184] Where, however, the partnership agreement imposes an express (or, perhaps, an implied) obligation on the partners to attend to the firm's affairs,[185] the position may be different, as Lord Lindley pointed out:

" ... where, as is usually the case, it is the duty of each partner to attend to the partnership business, and one partner in breach of his duty wilfully leaves the others to carry on the partnership business unaided, they are, it would seem, entitled to compensation for their services."

Thus, in *Airey v. Borham*[186] two partners had agreed to devote their whole time to the partnership business but later quarrelled, with the result that one of them

---

[177] *Whittle v. McFarlane* (1830) 1 Knapp 311.

[178] See *Bentley v. Craven* (1853) 18 Beav. 75.

[179] Unreported March 2, 2000 CA (Civ Div).

[180] See further, *infra*, para. 20–45.

[181] *Hutcheson v. Smith* (1842) 5 I.Eq.R. 117. And see *Thornton v. Proctor* (1792) 1 Anst. 94, noted *supra*, para. 20–28; also *East India Co. v. Blake* (1673) Finch 117.

[182] *Medcalf v. Mardell, supra*. The court rejected an argument seeking to import equitable principles, based on the decision in *O'Sullivan v. Management Agency and Music Ltd.* [1985] Q.B. 428 (CA).

[183] *MacKinlay v. Arthur Young McClelland Moores & Co.* [1990] 2 A.C. 239, 249A–C; also *Heastie v. Veitch & Co.* (1934) 18 T.C. 305; *Watson and Everitt v. Blunden* (1933) 18 T.C. 402. *A fortiori* where, by the payment of such remuneration, an attempt is made to create or inflate a loss: *PDC Copyprint (South) v. George* [1997] S.T.C. (S.C.D.) 326. See also, *infra*, para. 34–25.

[184] Lord Lindley put it thus: "Even where the amount of the services rendered by the partners is exceedingly unequal, still, if there is no agreement that their services shall be remunerated, no charge in respect of them can be allowed in taking the partnership accounts. In such a case the remuneration to be paid to either for personal labour exceeding that contributed by the other, is considered as left to the honour of the other; and where that principle is wanting, a court of justice cannot supply it." See *Webster v. Bray* (1849) 7 Hare 159, 179 *per* Wigram V.-C. In that case an allowance was given to the defendant, pursuant to an offer made by the claimant. In a similar case, *Robinson v. Anderson* (1855) 20 Beav. 98, no such offer was made so that the court could not award any allowance. This is, in a sense, the corollary of the principle now embodied in the Partnership Act 1890, s.24(1): see *supra*, para. 19–18.

[185] See *supra*, paras 10–93 *et seq*.

[186] (1861) 29 Beav. 620.

was left to carry the business on alone. The partnership was ultimately dissolved and an inquiry was directed in order to ascertain what allowance ought to be made to him for so doing. It is the opinion of the current editor that such a claim is still maintainable in an appropriate case.

Services rendered after dissolution

20-46   Before the Partnership Act 1890, the general rule was not applied in the case of services rendered by a partner in carrying on the firm's business following a dissolution. On that basis, a surviving partner who had carried on the business to its ultimate benefit was held to be entitled to remuneration for his trouble in so doing,[187] unless no profits were realised[188] or there was some special reason for denying his entitlement.[189] Both Lord Lindley and the editor of the 6th edition of this work apprehended that, in this respect, the Act had not altered the law, a view which proved to be amply justified when it was subsequently held that a partner appointed as a receiver and manager without remuneration in a dissolution action was entitled to wages for work done by him which proved beneficial to the business, even though such work formed no part of his duties as receiver and manager.[190] Equally, where a partner has breached his fiduciary duties to his former partners, he is less likely to be remunerated for his efforts, but much will depend on the circumstances.[191]

In the same way, where a claim for a share of profits is made by a former partner under section 42 of the Partnership Act 1890,[192] an allowance is normally made to the partners who have carried on the business by way of remuneration for their services.[193] Indeed, in *Emerson v. Estate of Emerson,*[194] the surviving partner was held to be entitled to an allowance, even though the business had been making trading *losses*. The quantum of the allowance ultimately equalled the losses he had incurred.

---

[187] *Brown v. De Tastet* (1819) Jac. 284; *Crawshay v. Collins* (1826) 2 Russ. 325; *Featherstonhaugh v. Turner* (1858) 25 Beav. 382; *Page v. Ratcliffe* (1897) 75 L.T.(N.S.) 371. See also *Mellersh v. Keen* (1859) 27 Beav. 236, where one partner became of unsound mind and the business was continued by the others. *cf. Tibbits v. Phillips* (1853) 10 Hare 355, where there was a *contractual* right to a salary which, on a true construction of the agreement, ceased on the dissolution.

[188] *Re Aldridge* [1894] 2 Ch. 97.

[189] *e.g.* where he was the personal representative of the deceased partner: see *Burden v. Burden* (1813) 1 V. & B. 170; *Stocken v. Dawson* (1843) 6 Beav. 371. *cf. Forster v. Ridley* (1864) 4 De G.J. & S. 452.

[190] *Harris v. Sleep* [1897] 2 Ch. 80. See also *Meyer & Co. v. Faber (No. 2)* [1923] 2 Ch. 421, 450–451 *per* Younger L.J.

[191] See, by way of analogy, *O'Sullivan v. Management Agency Ltd.* [1985] 1 Q.B. 428 (CA), which concerned a void joint venture agreement; *Guinness v. Saunders* [1990] 2 A.C. 663 at pp. 700, 701 *per* Lord Goff of Chieveley, which concerned a director; *Cobbetts LLP v. Hodge* (2009) 153(17) S.J.L.B. 29 at [115] *per* Floyd J., which concerned an "employed partner" who was not a partner in law.

[192] See *infra*, paras 25–24 *et seq.*

[193] See *infra*, para. 25–33.

[194] [2004] 1 B.C.L.C. 575 (CA).

CHAPTER 21

ASCERTAINMENT AND DIVISION OF PROFITS

DESPITE the apparently strict terms of the statutory definition,[1] the ultimate object   **21-01**
of a normal partnership will be the realisation *and division* of profits.[2] Thus, Lord
Lindley justifiably observed that:

" . . . the right of every partner to a share of the profits made by the firm to which he
belongs is too obvious to require comment."

It has already been seen that, whilst the division of profits may be a normal
incident of partnership, it is not a pre-requisite for its creation, so that a person
in receipt of "remuneration" rather than a share of profits (or even no share of
profits) may, depending on the precise circumstances, still fall to be treated as a
partner properly so called.[3]

What is divisible as profit

It has already been seen that profit is the excess of receipts over expenses[4]: in   **21-02**
winding up a partnership, nothing is properly divisible as profits which does not
answer this description.[5] However, such a counsel of perfection is in practice
modified in the case of a continuing firm, so as to facilitate the annual division
of profits. Thus, a distinction is usually drawn between ordinary and extraordinary receipts and expenses: ordinary expenses will be treated as defrayed out of
the normal trading income of the firm and extraordinary expenses out of capital
or borrowings. Accordingly, the divisible profits in a given year will in general
be ascertained merely by comparing ordinary receipts with ordinary expenses. As
Lord Lindley pointed out:

" . . . unless some such principle as this were had recourse to, there could be no
division of profits, even of the most flourishing business, whilst any of its debts were
unpaid, and any of its capital sunk."

When asked, partners' views may genuinely differ as to whether a particular   **21-03**
expense ought to be treated as ordinary or extraordinary; it was this scope for an
"honest diversity of opinion" which led Lord Lindley to express the view that
such a decision could be taken by a majority vote.[6] In terms of the Partnership

---

[1] Partnership Act 1890, s.1(1): see *supra*, para. 2–01.

[2] See *supra*, para. 2–10.

[3] See *M. Young Legal Associates v. Zahid* [2006] 1 W.L.R. 2562 (CA), noticed *supra*, para. 5–54;
Hodson v. Hodson [2010] P.N.L.R. 8 (CA), where a 1% partner had consistently waived her right to
profits. And see *supra*, paras 2–10, 10–86.

[4] See *supra*, paras 2–07, 5–12; also *Re Spanish Prospecting Co. Ltd.* [1911] 1 Ch. 92. As to profits
for the purposes of income tax, see *infra*, paras 21–04 *et seq.*, 34–20 *et seq.*

[5] Profits may be of an income or capital nature: see *supra*, paras 10–79, 17–04.

[6] In this context, Lord Lindley cited *Gregory v. Patchett* (1864) 33 Beav. 595 (a company case);
see also *Re Bridgewater Navigation Co.* [1891] 1 Ch. 155; *Re National Bank of Wales Ltd.* [1899] 2
Ch. 629, affirmed *sub nom. Dovey v. Cory* [1901] A.C. 477.

Act 1890, such a decision can now, perhaps, properly be classed as an "ordinary [*matter*] connected with the partnership business."[7]

There is, in general, no obligation to replace lost capital prior to the division of profits,[8] although this may be provided for in the agreement.[9]

Method of accounting

21–04   There was some early authority for the proposition that, under ordinary circumstances and in the absence of any agreement to the contrary, moneys earned ought to be treated as profits of the year in which they are *received* and not as profits of the year in which they are earned,[10] which was in turn allied to the general and overriding principle that neither profit nor loss should be anticipated,[11] as exemplified in decisions such as *Willingale v. International Commercial Bank*,[12] and *Symons v. Weeks*.[13] However, such an approach is no longer generally maintainable in the face of the Accounting Standards Board's Application Note G[14] to Financial Reporting Standard 5,[15] under which all firms engaged in the supply of goods and services are, in general, required to produce accounts which recognise income as and when they can properly be regarded as entitled thereto, even in the case of a contract which is ongoing. Only where the right to consideration can truly be said not to have arisen, *e.g.* in the case of a fee payable only on a contingency, will it be possible to ignore this principle. Although strong representations were made against the introduction of this approach as regards

---

[7] And thus falling within *ibid.* s.24(8): see further *supra*, paras 15–04 *et seq.* and *infra*, para. 21–07.

[8] Lord Lindley put it thus: " . . . if the current receipts exceed the current expenses, the writer apprehends that the difference can be divided as profit, although the capital may be spent and not represented by saleable assets." See, as to the construction of clauses relating to the payment of dividends out of profits, *Davison v. Gillies* (1879) 16 Ch.D. 347n; *Dent v. London Tramways Co.* (1880) 16 Ch.D. 344; *Birch v. Cropper* (1889) 14 App. Cas. 525; *Re Bridgewater Navigation Co.* [1891] 1 Ch. 155 (varied at [1891] 2 Ch. 317); *Fisher v. Black and White Publishing Co.* [1901] 1 Ch. 174; *Bagot Pneumatic Tyre Co. v. Clipper Pneumatic Tyre Co.* [1902] 1 Ch. 146, 158, 159 *per* Romer L.J. As to paying dividends after a loss of capital under the old company law rules, see *Flitcroft's case* (1855) 21 Ch.D. 519; *Bloxam v. Metropolitan Ry.* (1868) L.R. 3 Ch. App. 337; *Lee v. Neuchatel Asphalte Co.* (1886) 41 Ch.D. 1; *Bolton v. Natal Land, etc., Co.* [1892] 2 Ch. 124; *Lubbock v. British Bank of South America* [1892] 2 Ch. 198; *Verner v. General & Commercial Investment Trust* [1894] 2 Ch. 239; *Dovey v. Cory* [1901] A.C. 477, and the other cases referred to in *Buckley on the Companies Acts* (14th ed.), pp. 1031 *et seq.* These were not retained in the 15th ed. of that work.

[9] See *supra*, para. 10–73.

[10] See *Hall & Co. v. Inland Revenue Commissioners* [1921] 3 K.B. 152; *Elson v. Prices Tailors Ltd.* [1963] 1 W.L.R. 287; also *Maclaren v. Stainton* (1852) 3 De G.F. & J. 202, 214 *per* Turner L.J.; *Badham v. Williams* (1902) 86 L.T.(N.S.) 191. *cf. Browne v. Collins* (1871) 12 Eq. 586.

[11] See *B.S.C. Footwear Ltd. v. Ridgway* [1972] A.C. 544 (HL), 552 *per* Lord Reid; *Beauchamp v. Woolworth plc* [1990] 1 A.C. 478 (HL), 489 *per* Lord Templeman; *R. v. I.R.C., ex p. S.G. Warburg & Co. Ltd.* [1994] S.T.C. 518.

[12] [1978] A.C. 834. There it was held that the taxpayer bank was not chargeable to tax upon any annual increase in the value of discounted bills of exchange as the maturity date approached (even though such increase was included in the bank's accounts on normal accountancy principles), but should only be chargeable when the bills were disposed of or reached maturity and any profit was actually realised. The position would, however, have been different if the bills of exchange had been stock in trade (*per* Sir John Pennycuick in the Court of Appeal, reported at [1977] Ch. 78, 99).

[13] [1983] S.T.C. 195. There it was held that progress payments received by a firm of architects under standard R.I.B.A. long-term contracts did not need to be brought into account when computing the firm's profits for tax purposes, at least until the contracts were sufficiently far advanced that the profit thereon could be ascertained with some degree of certainty.

[14] Entitled "Revenue Recognition" and issued in November 2003.

[15] Entitled "Reporting the Substance of Transactions".

contracts for services, on March 10, 2005 the Urgent Issues Taskforce issued Abstract 40,[16] confirming its application and giving further guidance in the case of firms working under such contracts.[17]

In addition, partners must ultimately prepare a set of accounts or computations complying with Application Note G and, where relevant, UITF 40 for income tax purposes, since the profits of a trade, profession or business must now, in general, be computed "in accordance with generally accepted accounting practice"[18]; it is no longer possible simply to ignore those accounting standards. As a result, the so-called "earnings" basis must be applied in all cases and work in progress (including partners' work in progress) must in effect be taken into account.[19]

Divisible profits ascertained for different purposes

Since it is the tax-adjusted profit which is relevant for income tax purposes,[20] there is, in general,[21] no reason why accounts produced for internal purposes should not compute profits on a wholly different basis. Thus, partners may, as between themselves, properly decide to treat as divisible profit some source of income which is not taxable at the time of receipt or, indeed, at all or to exclude from the divisible profits a particular source of income, *e.g.* with a view to it being taken to a reserve in which no partner will have a direct interest.[22]

21–05

Time and manner of division

The partnership agreement will in general prescribe:

21–06

(a) the ratios in which the profits are to be shared between the partners, which may involve the payment of preferential "salaries", interest on capital and the like;

(b) the time or times at which division is to take place.[23]

In the absence of such a provision, the time of division, but not the manner in which the profits are to be *shared* between the partners, will ultimately be a matter of internal management and can, in general, be taken on a majority vote under section 24(8) of the Partnership Act 1890.[24]

However, once a division of the profits has taken place, each partner will not necessarily be entitled to withdraw his share: under the terms of the agreement,

---

[16] Entitled "Revenue recognition and service contracts" and generally referred to as UITF 40.

[17] It was confirmed that accounts complying with this requirement should be produced in respect of any accounting period ending on or after June 22, 2005: *ibid.* para. 30.

[18] Income Tax (Trading and Other Income) Act 2005, s.25(1).

[19] See further *infra*, para. 34–22.

[20] See *supra*, para. 21–04 and *infra*, para. 34–22.

[21] Note, however, the special requirements applicable to the accounts of a qualifying corporate partnership under the Partnerships (Accounts) Regulations 2008 (SI 2008/569), noted *infra*, para. 22–08.

[22] This is a device which some firms are using to avoid shares in work in progress being credited to partners' current accounts. As to the tax treatment of sums taken to such a reserve, see *infra*, para. 34–21.

[23] See generally, *supra*, paras 10–78 *et seq.* And see, as to the income tax treatment of payments made to partners out of profits, *infra*, para. 34–25.

[24] See *infra*, para. 21–07.

a set or variable proportion may be taken to a taxation or other reserve.[25] Only where there is no express or implied agreement between the partners will the rules contained in the Partnership Act 1890 apply.[26]

The agreement will also normally provide a framework authorising each partner to draw sums on account of his anticipated share of profits as it accrues.[27] In the absence of such a provision, no partner will be entitled to anything until the profit is ascertained and divided at the year end.

Power of the majority

21–07   Lord Lindley observed that:

> "With respect to the times of division and quantum to be divided at any given time, it is conceived that the majority must govern the minority where no agreement upon the subject has been come to[28]; for these are matters of purely internal regulation, and with respect to such matters a dissentient minority have only one alternative, *viz.*, either to give way to the majority, or, if in a position so to do, to dissolve the partnership."

The current editor ventures to suggest that, as a statement of general principle, this goes too far, since what is an "ordinary" matter connected with the partnership business may vary from firm to firm.[29]

Exclusion from share of profits

21–08   Just as partners have no inherent right to expel one of their number or to forfeit his share,[30] they cannot properly exclude him from the enjoyment of his share of profits,[31] unless this is expressly authorised by the partnership agreement.[32] If they attempt to do so, they can be compelled to restore the excluded partner to his rightful share and to account to him accordingly.[33]

---

[25] See, as to tax reserves, *supra*, para. 10–90. However, most other types of reserve will be made *before* the divisible profits are ascertained: see *supra*, para. 10–91. The type of reserve noted, *supra*, para. 21–05 is, of course, exceptional.

[26] Partnership Act 1890, s.24(1): see *supra*, para. 19–16. As to the mode of ascertaining profits where a third party is entitled to a share thereof, see *Geddes v. Wallace* (1820) 2 Bli. 270; *Rishton v. Grissell* (1870) L.R. 10 Eq. 393.

[27] See *supra*, para. 10–88.

[28] See the Partnership Act 1890, s.24(8), *supra*, para. 15–04. *Stevens v. South Devon Railway Co* (1851) 9 Hare 313, 326 *per* Sir G.J. Turner V.-C.; see also *Burland v. Earle* [1902] A.C. 83, 95. Lord Lindley also referred to the following cases in this context: *Corry v. Londonderry and Eniskillen Railway Co.* (1860) 29 Beav. 263, as to declaring dividends before paying debts; *Browne v. Monmouthshire Railway and Canal Co.* (1851) 13 Beav. 32, as to paying dividends before works are finished.

[29] See *supra*, para. 15–05; also *supra*, para. 20–02.

[30] Partnership Act 1890, s.25; see also *infra*, paras 24–99 *et seq.*

[31] *Adley v. Whitstable Co.* (1815) 19 Ves.Jr. 304; *Griffith v. Paget* (1877) 5 Ch.D. 894.

[32] Thus, the agreement may provide for a partner's profit share to be abated in the event of his illness or incapacity: see *supra*, para. 10–83. More unusually, it may provide that a partner's share can be reduced if he is placed on "garden leave": see *supra*, para. 10–146.

[33] *Adley v. Whitstable Co., supra; Griffith v. Paget, supra.* See also *infra*, paras 23–85 *et seq.*, 23–138.

Waiver of a share of profits

A partner is free to waive the entirety of his profit share, either year on year **21–09** or indefinitely, and this will not result in him ceasing to be a partner.[34]

---

[34] See *Hodson v. Hodson* [2009] EWCA 430 (Ch) (Lawtel 16/3/09) at [53] *per* Arnold J. The decision was affirmed at [2010] P.N.L.R. 8 (CA).

Chapter 22

PARTNERSHIP ACCOUNTS

By partnership accounts are meant, for present purposes, those accounts main- **22–01**
tained within a firm in order to show the financial standing of each partner *vis-
à-vis* the firm and his co-partners and, by inference, the financial standing of the
firm *vis-à-vis* third parties.[1] Partnership accounts as taken by the court are
considered elsewhere in this work.[2]

1. MANNER IN WHICH ACCOUNTS SHOULD BE KEPT

Capital and current accounts

It has already been observed[3] that, in keeping partnership accounts, it is **22–02**
desirable that a capital account and a current or "drawings" account be opened
for each partner in the books of the firm. This will enable the capital of the firm
to be kept separate from any temporary retentions of undrawn profits, thus
minimising the risks of confusion between the two. Nevertheless, the maintenance of combined capital/current accounts is commonplace.[4]

A partner's capital and current accounts will show his personal position as
regards the firm. The value of any cash or property brought into the firm by way
of capital contribution will be credited to his capital account and the value of any
such cash or property which is subsequently withdrawn will be debited
thereto.

On the other hand, when a partnership profit or loss is divided, each partner's **22–03**
share thereof will normally be credited or debited to his current account, as will
any drawings which he may have made in anticipation of such share. A share of
profits attributable to the sale or revaluation of a partnership asset will be
similarly treated, unless the partners have agreed to take such profits to capital
account, thus increasing the firm's fixed capital.[5] Balances may be transferred
between the partners' capital and current accounts in order to accommodate
changes in the firm's capital structure, *e.g.* funding a new partner's capital
contribution pursuant to a "lockstep" or other system or, indeed, restoring an
existing partner's capital contribution to the agreed level following a proper or
improper reduction therein.

---

[1] The contents of these internal accounts will ultimately be reflected in the balance sheet, which
inevitably shows the firm's overall financial standing.

[2] See *infra*, paras 23–75 *et seq.*

[3] See *supra*, para. 17–06.

[4] Note in this context, the decision in *Hopper v. Hopper* [2008] EWCA Civ 1417 (Lawtel
12/12/08), noticed *supra*, para. 17–06.

[5] See, as to the possible tax consequences attendant on a revaluation of assets, *infra*, para.
35–14.

Where a combined capital and current account is maintained, the operation is that much simpler, since all debits and credits will appear in a single account.[6]

Other funds held by the firm

22–04 Although a partner's capital and current account balances will, for present purposes, represent his main financial entitlement *vis-à-vis* the firm and his co-partners, there may be other funds recorded in the firm's books in which he has an actual or potential interest.[7] The most obvious example will be a reserve made in respect of a partner's prospective income tax liability which, whilst unexpended, may technically remain his property and which should properly be returnable to him on leaving the firm.[8] Equally, in some firms, capital or income profits "realised" on a revaluation of assets may, instead of being credited to the partners' current accounts, be taken to a special reserve account, in which no individual partner has a specific interest, save on leaving the firm or, perhaps, only on a dissolution.[9] In addition, any number of other reserves or provisions may have been made in respect of actual or apprehended liabilities or other eventualities, in which individual partners may remain interested to the extent that they are not applied for the designated purpose.[10]

Partners treated as debtors or creditors of firm

22–05 As previously noted,[11] a partner's financial entitlement in respect of his share can only be viewed in the context of his net position, once account is taken of all sums due to or from him in his capacity as a partner. Subject thereto, it is often said that a partner is a creditor of the firm, to the extent that there is a net credit balance due to him, or a debtor of the firm, to the extent that there is a net debit balance due from him. It is only on the ultimate payment of that credit/debit balance that it can be said that his account with the firm is closed and settled.

However, such an analysis is strictly inaccurate, as was made clear by Lord Cottenham,[12] when he observed:

" . . . though these terms 'debtor' and 'creditor' are so used, and sufficiently explain what is meant by the use of them, nothing can be more inconsistent with the known

---

[6] It may still be necessary to analyse the true status of the balance in that account, as in *Hopper v. Hopper* [2008] EWCA Civ 1417 (Lawtel 12/12/08), noticed *supra*, para. 17–06.

[7] He will, of course, also enjoy other prospective financial entitlements which are *not* recorded in the firm's books, *e.g.* a share of any surplus over and above the book value of the partnership assets.

[8] Tax retentions may be held in a joint reserve or, alternatively, in a separate reserve for each partner. The latter is more logical, now that liability for partnership tax is no longer joint: see *infra*, para. 34–19. See further, as to such reserves, *supra*, para. 10–90.

[9] This was the way in which the value attributed to work in progress originally brought into account by virtue of the Finance Act 1998, s.42(1) (see now the Income Tax (Trading and Other Income) Act 2005, s.25(1)) was dealt with. Similarly with the one off uplift resulting from the accounting adjustments required as a result of the application of FRS5 and UITF 40: see *supra*, para. 21–04. As to the tax treatment of profits taken to a reserve, see further *infra*, paras 34–21 (income tax) and 35–06 (capital gains tax).

[10] See *supra*, paras 10–91, 10–157.

[11] See *supra*, paras 19–05 *et seq.*

[12] *Richardson v. Bank of England* (1838) 4 Myl. & Cr. 165, 171–172.

law of partnership, than to consider the situation of either party as in any degree resembling the situation of those whose appellation has been so borrowed. The supposed creditor has no means of compelling payment of his debt; and the supposed debtor is liable to no proceedings either at law or in equity—assuming always that no separate security has been taken or given. The supposed creditor's debt is due from the firm of which he is partner; and the supposed debtor owes the money to himself in common with his partners."[13]

Ultimate adjustment of accounts

The final adjustment of the accounts as between the partners following a dissolution inevitably gives rise to questions of difficulty and is considered later in this work.[14]

22–06

Annual accounts

Save in the case of corporate partnerships,[15] there is no general statutory requirement that firms must produce annual accounts[16] in a certain form (or at all), although this will normally be the subject of an express provision in the agreement.[17] Whilst the profits of a trade must, for income tax purposes, be computed "in accordance with generally accepted accounting practice",[18] this need not necessarily affect the form or presentation of the partnership accounts.[19] Equally, whilst a firm may choose to prepare one set of accounts for income tax purposes and another for internal use, this may be unduly burdensome in terms of cost.[20] That said, the requirements of Application Note G[21] to Financial Reporting Standard 5,[22] as issued by the Accounting Standards Board in November 2003, and the Urgent Issues Taskforce Abstract 40[23] issued on March 10, 2005 (commonly referred to as UITF 40), which require firms to recognise income in their accounts as and when a right to it arises,[24] are an accounting and not a tax driven requirement and, should, logically, be complied with in whatever form the firm's accounts are prepared.

22–07

---

[13] See also *Lee v. Neuchatel Asphalte Co.* (1889) 41 Ch.D. 1, 23 *per* Lindley L.J.; *Green v. Hertzog* [1954] 1 W.L.R. 1309. And see *supra*, paras 3–04, 19–05, 19–06.

[14] Partnership Act 1890, s.44: see *infra*, paras 25–45 *et seq.*

[15] See *infra*, para. 22–08.

[16] *i.e.* a balance sheet and profit and loss account.

[17] See *supra*, paras 10–73, 10–157 *et seq.*

[18] Income Tax (Trading and Other Income) Act 2005, s.25(1). This replaced the former requirement that a "true and fair" basis be used: see the Finance Act 1998, s.42(1) prior to the amendment introduced by the Finance Act 2002, s.103(5). See further *supra*, para. 21–04 and *infra*, para. 34–22.

[19] Thus, it is perfectly permissible to compute the firm's profits on the basis required by HMRC *independently* of the partnership accounts.

[20] It has for some years been common practice for firms to prepare so-called "management" accounts for internal purposes, as well as for production to interested third parties, *e.g.* the firm's bankers. Such accounts, which tend to be of a fairly informal nature, are likely to be prepared *without* the assistance of the firm's accountants.

[21] Entitled "Revenue Recognition".

[22] Entitled "Reporting the Substance of Transactions".

[23] Entitled "Revenue recognition and service contracts".

[24] See further, *supra*, para. 21–04.

22–08 *Corporate partnerships*: In the case of a qualifying partnership,[25] it is now provided by the Partnerships (Accounts) Regulations 2008[26] that annual accounts and a directors' report, together with an auditors' report,[27] should be prepared just as if the firm were a company governed by the Companies Act 2006 and the relevant accounts regulations made thereunder.[28] Changes in the firm are ignored, save where it ceases to exist as a partnership.[29] Each corporate partner is required to append a copy of those accounts to its own annual accounts and reports prior to their delivery to the Registrar of Companies[30] and must, in effect, supply the names of the partners to any person who requests them.[31] It should be noted that, in the case of a limited partnership formed under the Limited Partnerships Act 1907,[32] the limited partners are, in effect, deemed not to be partners, so have no obligations under the regulations.[33] Where the firm's head office is situate in the UK and each of the partners[34] is an undertaking comparable to either a limited company incorporated outside the UK or an unlimited company or partnership incorporated or formed outside the UK all the members of which are undertakings comparable to a limited company so incorporated, those accounts must in general be held available for inspection by any person at that office.[35] These provisions do not, however, apply where the partnership is dealt with on a consolidated basis in group accounts prepared by a member of the partnership or its parent undertaking, provided that certain conditions are satisfied.[36]

It should be noted that whilst these Regulations require the like annual accounts as "would be required, if the partnership were a company, under Part 15

---

[25] *i.e.* a partnership formed under the law of any part of the UK where each of the members is: (i) a limited company; (ii) an unlimited company or a Scottish partnership, each of whose members is a limited company; or (iii) a comparable undertaking incorporated in or formed under the laws of another country or territory. It should be noted that the regulations will not apply if one of the partners is a limited liability partnership. Although there is currently some doubt as to their status (see *infra*, para. 31–18), it will as from 2011 be made clear (by amending regulations) that a limited partnership with one or more individual *limited* (but not general) partners constitutes a qualifying partnership.

[26] SI 2008/569, replacing the Partnerships and Unlimited Companies (Accounts) Regulations 1993 as from April 6, 2008.

[27] The members of the qualifying partnership must appoint the auditor: *ibid.* reg. 8. In certain circumstances, the court can override the partnership's decision to remove an auditor, once appointed: *ibid.* reg. 11.

[28] *ibid.* reg. 3(1), 4(1). Note that *ibid.* reg. 3 is likely to be amended in 2011 so as clarify its application in the case of limited partnerships. As regards the contents of such accounts, *ibid.* Sched., Pt. 1 makes certain modifications to the application of the Small Companies and Groups (Accounts and Directors' Report) Regulations 2008 (SI 2008/409) and the Large and Medium-sized Companies and Groups (Accounts and Reports) Regulations 2008 (SI 2008/410). See also, as to the penalties for non-compliance: *ibid.* reg. 15(1), (2).

[29] *ibid.* reg. 3(3).

[30] *ibid.* reg. 5(1). See also *ibid.* reg. 15(3), as to the penalty for non-compliance.

[31] *ibid.* reg. 5(2). And see the preceding note.

[32] See *infra*, paras 29–01 *et seq.*

[33] *ibid.* reg. 2(2), treating all references to "the members of a qualifying partnership" as referring only to the general partner(s). See further *infra*, para. 31–18.

[34] Other than limited partners: see the preceding footnote.

[35] *ibid.* reg. 6(1), (3)(a). This requirement does not, however, apply where the relevant undertaking is, if comparable to a limited company, incorporated in another Member State of the EC or, if comparable to an unlimited company or partnership incorporated in or formed under the laws of such a State and comprising partners which are undertakings comparable to limited companies so incorporated, provided that the firm's accounts are appended to the accounts of any such partner and duly published under the laws of that State: *ibid.* reg. 6(2). The penalties for non-compliance are set out in *ibid.* reg. 15(3).

[36] *ibid.* reg. 7. As to the meaning of the expression "dealt with on a consolidated basis", see *ibid.* reg. 2(1).

(accounts and reports) and Chapter 1 of Part 16 (requirement for audited accounts) of the Companies Act 1986",[37] not all of UK GAAP needs to be complied with, since the requirements of the applicable regulations are specially modified for this purpose.[38] The Regulations also do not apply the other provisions of the 2006 Act.[39]

Limited liability partnerships: Although the limited liability partnership is, as previously noted,[40] not a species of partnership, it should be noted that the provisions of the Companies Act 2006 regarding the preparation, audit and filing of its annual accounts[41] will be applied, albeit in a modified form according to the size of the LLP.[42]

22–09

2. THE PARTNERS' RIGHTS AND OBLIGATIONS

The primary duty

Lord Lindley pointed out that: **22–10**

> "it is one of the clearest rights of every partner to have accurate accounts kept of all money transactions relating to the business of the partnership, and to have free access to all its books and accounts."[43]

These rights are, of course, expressly recognised by the Partnership Act 1890 which provides:

> "24.—(9) The partnership books are to be kept at the place of business of the partnership (or the principal place, if there is more than one), and every partner may, when he thinks fit, have access to and inspect and copy any of them.[44]
> 28. Partners are bound to render true accounts[45] and full information of all things affecting the partnership to any partner or his legal representatives."[46]

---

[37] *ibid.* reg. 4(1).

[38] *ibid.* reg.4(3), Sched., Pt. 1, para. 2, which modifies the Small Companies and Groups (Accounts and Directors' Report) Regulations 2008 and the Large and Medium-sized Companies and Groups (Accounts and Reports) Regulations 2008 respectively.

[39] *e.g.* the prohibition on distributions contained in *ibid.* s.830.

[40] See *supra*, para. 2–39.

[41] Companies Act 2006, Pts 15, 16.

[42] See the Limited Liability Partnerships (Accounts and Audit) (Application of Companies Act 2006) Regulations 2008 (SI 2008/1911); the Small Limited Liability Partnerships (Accounts) Regulations 2008 (SI 2008/1912); and the Large and Medium Sized Limited Liability Partnerships (Accounts) Regulations 2008 (SI 2008/1913).

[43] See *per* Lord Eldon in *Rowe v. Wood* (1822) 2 Jac. & W. 553, 558–559 and *Goodman v. Whitcomb* (1820) 1 Jac. & W. 589, 593; also *Trego v. Hunt* [1896] A.C. 7, 26 *per* Lord Davey.

[44] This is subject to any agreement between the partners: see the words at the beginning of s.24 *supra*, para. 20–03; and see *supra*, paras 10–71 *et seq.* For the position prior to the Act, see (as to custody of books) *Charlton v. Poulter* (1753) 19 Ves.Jr. 148, note; *Taylor v. Davis* (1842) 3 Beav. 388, note; *Greatrex v. Greatrex* (1847) 1 De G. & Sm. 692; and (as to the right to inspect and copy) *Stuart v. Lord Bute* (1841) 11 Sim. 442 and (1842) 12 Sim. 460; *Taylor v. Rundell* (1843) 1 Ph. 222. This right was not enforceable at law even in an action by one partner against another: *Ward v. Apprice* (1704) 6 Mod. 264.

[45] See, as to the obligation under this limb of the section, *Winning v. Cunningham* 2009 GWD 01–19 (Sh.Ct.).

[46] Although the expression "legal representatives" is not defined, it will prima facie extend to a partner's trustee in bankruptcy or liquidator: see *Wilson v. Greenwood* (1818) 1 Swan. 471. See also, as to this section *supra*, para. 16–03.

The right of access afforded under s.24(9) would appear to be an absolute one[47] and was the foundation for the decision in *Wan v. General Commissioners for Division of Doncaster*,[48] where a penalty was held to have been properly imposed on each partner for failure to provide information to the Inspector of Taxes which *any* of them could have obtained by exercising that right.

Duty of continuing or surviving partners

22–11   It is the duty of continuing or surviving partners to keep the accounts of the firm in such a way as to show the financial position when the composition of the firm changed.[49]

Presumptions where books not kept or destroyed

22–12   If no books of account whatsoever are kept, or if such books as are kept are unintelligible or are destroyed or otherwise wrongfully withheld, on an account being directed by the court all necessary presumptions will be made against those partners responsible for the non-production of proper accounts.[50] However, where all the partners are *in pari delicto*, this rule cannot be applied.

The right of inspection

22–13   A partner cannot deprive his co-partners of their right of inspection by keeping records in a private book containing other material which is said to be of no concern to them.[51] However, it would seem that a partner could in theory bind himself not to investigate the partnership books or accounts and to accept balance sheets prepared by his co-partners.[52]

An assignee or mortgagee of a partner's share has no right of inspection whilst the partnership is continuing.[53]

Inspection by agent

22–14   A partner is in general entitled to examine the firm's books and accounts through the medium of an agent appointed for the purpose, provided that the agent is a person to whom no reasonable objection can be taken by the other partners.[54] However, this right, unlike the right to personal inspection, is not absolute: it may be denied if the court is satisfied that the assistance of an agent

---

[47] See *infra*, paras 22–14, 22–16.

[48] 76 T.C. 211.

[49] See *Ex p. Toulmin* (1815) 1 Mer. 598, note; *Toulmin v. Copland* (1836) 3 Y. & C.Ex. 625.

[50] See *Walmsley v. Walmsley* (1846) 3 Jo. & La T. 556; *Gray v. Haig* (1855) 20 Beav. 219; also *Armorie v. Delamirie* (1722) 1 Str. 505; *Malhotra v. Dhawan* [2001] Med. L.R. 319 (CA); and note *Finlayson v. Turnbull (No. 3)* 2001 G.W.D. 37–1412 (OH). And see, as to the loss of a right to interest, *Boddam v. Ryley* (1787) 4 Bro.P.C. 561, noted *supra*, para. 20–39.

[51] See *Freeman v. Fairlie* (1812) 3 Mer. 43; *Toulmin v. Copland* (1836) 3 Y. & C.Ex. 625.

[52] See *Turner v. Bayley* (1864) 4 De G.J. & S. 332. Note, however, that this case involved a profit sharing arrangement falling short of true partnership.

[53] Partnership Act 1890, s.31: see *supra*, paras 19–51 *et seq.*

[54] *Bevan v. Webb* [1901] 2 Ch. 59; also *Dadswell v. Jacobs* (1887) 34 Ch.D. 278. And see *Re Credit Co.* (1879) 11 Ch.D. 256; *Nelson v. Anglo-American Land Mortgage Agency Co.* [1897] 1 Ch. 130 (decisions as to the right of inspection of a company's register under the Companies Act 1862, s.43); also *Mutter v. East & Midlands Ry.* (1888) 38 Ch.D. 92. See, as to the remedy for enforcing these rights *Davies v. Gas Light & Coke Co.* [1909] 1 Ch. 248, affirmed at [1909] 1 Ch. 708 (CA).

is not reasonably required or that the inspection is sought for an improper purpose.[55] It is, perhaps, self evident that, having obtained information as a result of such an inspection, neither the partner nor his agent is entitled to make use of it for such an improper purpose[56]; indeed, an agent may be required to give an undertaking to this effect.[57]

Removal of books for inspection

Whilst the Partnership Act 1890 secures the right of each partner to have **22–15** access to and to inspect and copy the partnership books, it does not entitle any partner to remove those books from the place where they are kept unless the other partners are agreeable. This may give rise to difficulty in practice, where, for example, a partner wishes to obtain a photographic or other reproduction of the books or to have them scrutinised by his financial advisers, neither of which can conveniently be done on the partnership premises. As a result, it may be desirable for the agreement expressly to authorise temporary removal, provided that free access to the books by the other partners is not inhibited.[58] Such a provision may be particularly valuable in the case of a non-active or dormant partner who is not kept fully informed as to the day to day running of the partnership business.

Good faith and the purpose of the inspection

Because the statutory right of inspection is an absolute one, it would appear **22–16** that the motives and bona fides of the partner seeking to exercise it will be irrelevant and the court will have no discretion to refuse appropriate relief.[59] The position is otherwise where a director seeks to exercise his right to inspect the company's books, but the analogy is is not a good one since the right of inspection in that case is merely a common law right.[60] Even if bad faith did affect the court's approach, it would never be permissible to presume its existence.[61]

---

[55] See *Duché v. Duché* (1920) 149 L.T. 300; *Dodd v. Amalgamated Marine Workers' Union* [1924] 1 Ch. 116; cf. *Davies v. Gas Light and Coke Co.*, *supra*. See also *infra*, para. 22–16.

[56] *Bevan v. Webb* [1901] 2 Ch. 59. See also *infra*, para. 23–100.

[57] *Bevan v. Webb*, *supra*. See also *Norey v. Keep* [1909] 1 Ch. 561; *Dodd v. Amalgamated Marine Workers' Union* [1924] 1 Ch. 116 (decisions under the Trade Union Act 1871).

[58] See the *Encyclopaedia of Professional Partnerships*, Precedent 1, cl. 9(3).

[59] See *Davies v. Gas Light & Coke Co.* [1909] 1 Ch. 248, affirmed at [1909] 1 Ch. 708 (CA), a decision in relation to a shareholder's rights under the Companies Clauses Consolidation Act 1845, s.10. cf. the position where inspection is sought though an agent, noted *supra*, para. 22–14.

[60] See *Oxford Legal Group Ltd. v. Sibbasbridge Services plc* [2008] Bus. L.R. 1244 (CA), where a number of earlier authorities are reviewed.

[61] *ibid.*

CHAPTER 23

ACTIONS BETWEEN PARTNERS

1.   INTRODUCTION

Effect of Judicature Acts

PRIOR to the Judicature Acts, proceedings could not be brought as between a **23–01**
firm and one or more of its members.[1] At the heart of this rule lay the fundamental objection, which still persists,[2] to any party to proceedings being at the
same time both a claimant and a defendant. Moreover, because the old action for
an account had become obsolete, it was also a rule that no action at law could be
maintained by one partner against another if it in any way involved taking a
partnership account.[3]

In their strict application, these rules were effectively swept away by the
Judicature Acts, causing Lord Lindley to observe:

> " . . . there appears to be no reason why an action should not now be maintained for
> the recovery of a debt due from one partner to the firm[4]; nor why, if two firms have
> a common partner, an action should not be maintainable by one firm against
> another."[5]

In the former respect, Lord Lindley perhaps went too far, since a debt owed by   **23–02**
a partner to his firm (*i.e.* to himself and his co-partners) cannot normally be
recovered *otherwise* than by means of a partnership account.[6] Elsewhere, he went
on to explain:

---

[1] Lord Lindley explained that, as a consequence, "All proceedings, . . . which had for their object
the enforcement of the mutual rights and obligations of partners, had to be taken by some or one of
the members of a firm individually against some others or other of them also individually. The
consequences of this rule were important, for it followed from it—
1. That no action at law could be brought by one partner against another for the recovery of money
or property payable to the firm as distinguished from the partner suing;
2. That no suit in equity was maintainable by one partner against another in respect of a matter in
which the firm was interested, without bringing all the members thereof before the court." The pre-
Judicature Act law was summarised in greater detail in the 11th ed. of this work, at pp. 665–672. And
see also *infra*, para. 23–209.
[2] See *Ellis v. Kerr* [1910] 1 Ch. 529; *Meyer & Co. v. Faber (No. 2)* [1923] 2 Ch. 421. But see also,
supra, para. 14–12.
[3] See the summary of the pre-Judicature Act law in the 11th ed. of this work, at pp. 665–672.
[4] The footnote at this point read "*Piercy v. Fynney* (1871) L.R. 12 Eq. 69; *Taylor v. Midland Rail.
Co.* (1860) 28 Beav. 287 and (1862) 8 H.L.C. 751, show that suits in equity would lie in these cases
in aid of legal rights. See also *Luke v. South Kensington Hotel Co.* (1879) 11 Ch.D. 121; *Williamson
v. Barbour* (1877) 9 Ch.D. 536 *per* Jessel M.R.". Reference might also, perhaps, be made to *Palmer
v. Mallet* (1887) 36 Ch.D.
[5] See *supra*, para. 14–12.
[6] See *Meyer & Co. v. Faber (No. 2)* [1923] 2 Ch. 421, although the headnote of this case is framed
in misleadingly wide terms; *Green v. Hertzog* [1954] 1 W.L.R. 1309. See also *supra*, paras 19–05 *et
seq.* and *infra*, para. 23–76.

" . . . the fact that an account has to be taken in order to ascertain what is due from one party to another is no longer any reason why an action by one against the other should fail; at most, such a circumstance may render it expedient to transfer the action from one division of the High Court to another at some stage of the action."[7]

This is still the position under the Senior Courts Act 1981[8] and the County Courts Act 1984,[9] although account must also now be taken of the wide powers of transfer under the Civil Procedure Rules.[10]

Actions in firm name

23–03   It has already been seen that proceedings may be commenced by or against a firm in the firm name, but that this is merely a rule of procedure which does not affect the rights of the parties or give rise to any new or independent cause of action.[11] Although use of the firm name is permissible in the case of an action between two firms with a common partner,[12] it is questionable whether this is appropriate under the Civil Procedure Rules where one partner is suing his co-partners or vice versa.[13] If the firm name is used in the latter case, it will amount to no more than a compendious expression denoting the partners other than the claimant or defendant (as the case may be).[14]

2.   PARTIES

23–04   The Civil Procedure Rules introduced a completely new regime governing the conduct of proceedings and the courts have been at pains to point out that the old

---

[7] Notwithstanding the terms of the Senior Courts Act 1981 (as renamed by the Constitutional Reform Act 2005, Sched. 11, Pt 1, para. 1(1)), Sched. 1, para. 1(f) (which assigns to the Chancery Division all causes and matters relating to the taking of partnership accounts), the mere fact that a claim will involve the taking of an account may, in practice, not be regarded as a sufficient ground for seeking a transfer to that Division. But note the views expressed by the Court of Appeal in *Elvee Ltd. v. Taylor, The Times*, December 18, 2001 (CA), relating to copyright proceedings; also *Cayzer v. Beddow* [2007] EWCA Civ 644 (Lawtel 26/6/07) at [16], in relation to joint ventures/partnerships; and see further, *infra*, para. 23–70.

[8] See *ibid.* s.49. See also the preceding note.

[9] ss.40(2) (as substituted by the Courts and Legal Services Act 1990, s.2(1)), 41(1), 42(2) (as substituted by *ibid.* s.2(3)).

[10] CPR Pt 30. This Part applies not only to transfers between Divisions of the High Court (*ibid.* r. 30.5(1)), but also to transfers between county courts (*ibid.* r. 30.2(1), (2)) and to, from and between district registries (*ibid.* r. 30.2(4), (5)). Save in the case of a transfer between Divisions, the factors to be taken into account are, in general, as set out in *ibid.* r. 30.3(2). The fact that the county court would not otherwise have jurisdiction is irrelevant: *National Westminster Bank plc v. King* [2008] Ch. 385. *ibid.* r. 26.2 (automatic transfer) will not be in point since it only applies in the case a claim for a specified sum of money. See also *infra*, para. 23–70.

[11] See *supra*, para. 14–04.

[12] This is no longer specifically provided for: see *supra*, para. 14–12.

[13] As to whether the use of the firm name is inappropriate, see CPR 7APD, para. 5A.3, *infra*, para. A2–04; also *supra*, paras 14–04 *et seq*. Does *ibid.* para. 5A.1, *infra*, para. A2–04 in fact contemplate that all the partners are suing/being sued? It is thought not, since the wording is similar to that adopted in the former RSC Ord. 81, r. 1, but note that *ibid.* r. 6(1) (dealing with execution in such a case, thus putting the matter beyond doubt) has not been replicated in the CPR.

[14] *Meyer & Co. v. Faber (No. 2)* [1923] 2 Ch. 421, 435 *per* Sterndale M.R., 441 *per* Warrington L.J. Younger L.J. left the point open: see *ibid.* p. 450. The headnote of this case is misleading.

rules of procedure developed under the Rules of the Supreme Court are now of little, if any, assistance.[15] In all cases, regard must now be had to the overriding objective set out in the Rules[16] and the court in any event has a wide discretion with regard to the addition, substitution and removal of parties.[17] Nevertheless, there is retained in the following paragraphs a summary of the traditional approach towards the joinder of parties in partnership actions, since, in many instances, it is hard to see how a court could now reach a fundamentally different conclusion as to the parties who ought properly to be before it.

The general rule

In those, relatively rare, cases in which the proceedings do *not* involve the taking of a partnership account or some other form of relief which materially affects all the partners, *e.g.* an injunction or the appointment of a receiver, the choice of parties should be determined on normal principles.[18] Otherwise, it will generally be desirable that all the partners are joined, as Lord Lindley explained:

23–05

> " . . . it has been a long standing rule in Chancery that where the number of partners is not great they must all be parties to a suit for an account if within the jurisdiction of the court[19]; and subject to the question how far the firm can be treated as representing them all,[20] this rule is still in force."

It seems unlikely that a failure to join one or more of the partners will, in such circumstances, be fatal,[21] even if the need for such joinder is not picked up as a matter of case management.[22] It should, however, be noted that, if two or more partners (or former partners) are *jointly* entitled to an account or other relief,[23] they must all be made parties to the proceedings, either as co-claimants or, if any of them refuses, as defendant(s).[24]

Parties following change in the firm

Where there is a claim for an account against an outgoing partner the correct claimants will normally be the continuing partners. The fact that an incoming partner may, ultimately, be entitled to a share in the amount recovered will not, of itself, be a sufficient reason to join him as a party. Nevertheless, in *Hammonds*

23–06

---

[15] Equally, the introduction of the new regime has not involved a wholesale rejection of established principles: see, for example, *Hamblin v. Field* [2000] B.P.I.R. 621 (CA), a decision on striking out for want of prosecution. Note also that, as an interim measure, certain of the old rules were applied (with minor modifications) by the CPR, although these are now few in number: see *ibid.* Pt 50 Scheds 1, 2.

[16] *ibid.* Pt 1.

[17] *ibid.* Pt 19.

[18] See *supra*, paras 14–22 *et seq.*

[19] See *Hills v. Nash* (1845) 1 Ph. 594. *cf. Weymouth v. Boyer* (1792) 1 Ves.Jr. 416; *Smith v. Snow* (1818) 3 Madd. 10.

[20] See *infra*, paras 23–09, 23–10, 23–13.

[21] Although this was expressly so provided in the RSC (Ord. 15, r. 6(1)), the provision is not replicated in the CPR, but see *ibid.* r. 19.2(2)(a). Note also the terms of *ibid.* r. 3.10 (power to remedy an error of procedure).

[22] See CPR rr. 1.4, 3.1, 26.

[23] *Semble*, this would depend on the terms of the relevant agreement (if any).

[24] CPR r. 19.3.

(A Firm) v. Danilunas[25] Warren J. appeared to accept that the right to recover an overpayment of profits to such a partner was vested in the partners from time to time,[26] but surely as regards the outgoing partner this is *res inter alios acta* and should not confer any right of action on the incoming partner in the absence of an express assignment and notification thereof. Of course, in practice little may turn on the presence of an additonal partner as a party to the proceedings.

Sub-partners, assignees, etc.

23–07   It is perhaps self evident that, where an account is sought as between a third party and a partner which does not, as such, concern the partnership, the other partners would neither be necessary nor proper parties. Lord Lindley cited the following example:

> "If . . . a partner has agreed to share his profits with a stranger, and the latter seeks an account of those profits, he should bring his action against that one partner alone, and not make the others parties."[27]

The same rule would apply in the case of an account sought by an assignee of a partner's share whilst the partnership is continuing, but not following a dissolution.[28]

Action for account against surviving partners

23–08   Where surviving partners, who are also the personal representatives of a deceased partner, render themselves liable to account for profits made by the wrongful employment of his share in the partnership business,[29] it is unclear whether the other partners would also be *necessary* parties to the proceedings. Lord Lindley observed:

> "The rule appears to be that they are necessary parties if the account sought is an account of all the profits made by the use of the capital of the deceased; but not if the account is confined to so much of those profits as the executors have themselves received."[30]

Relief other than account

23–09   A party who would not otherwise be a proper party to an action for an account as between partners may be joined if some other form of relief, *e.g.* an injunction, is sought against him in the same proceedings.[31]

---

[25] [2009] EWHC 216 (Ch) (Lawtel 18/2/09). This aspect was not pursued on the appeal *sub nom. Hammonds (A Firm) v Jones, The Times*, January 4, 2010.

[26] *ibid.* at [113]–[115], [118]. Note that Warren J. also had some doubts as to the propriety of using the firm name in such circumstances: *ibid.* at [115]. See further *supra*, para. 14–04.

[27] *Raymond's case*, cited in *Ex p. Barrow* (1815) 2 Rose 252, 255 *per* Lord Eldon; *Brown v. De Tastet* (1819) Jac. 284; *Bray v. Fromont* (1821) 6 Madd. 5. See also *Killock v. Greg* (1828) 4 Russ. 285.

[28] See the Partnership Act 1890, s.31, *supra*, paras 19–51, 19–54, 19–56; also *Public Trustee v. Elder* [1926] Ch. 776. The decision in *Redmayne v. Forster* (1866) L.R. 2 Eq. 467 (all partners to be joined as parties to a foreclosure action brought by an equitable mortgagee of a share in a mining partnership by reason of their pre-emption rights) is now of limited relevance.

[29] See *infra*, paras 25–40 *et seq.*, 26–40 *et seq.*

[30] *Simpson v. Chapman* (1853) 4 De G.M. & G. 154; *Vyse v. Foster* (1874) L.R. 7 H.L. 318. *cf. Macdonald v. Richardson* (1858) 1 Giff. 81.

[31] See, for example, *Vulliamy v. Noble* (1817) 3 Mer. 593; *Bevan v. Lewis* (1827) 1 Sim. 376.

Representative parties

The stringent statutory restrictions on the size of partnerships have now been **23–10**
swept away in their entirety.[32] Accordingly, when dealing with proposed proceedings between members of a large firm,[33] it may be appropriate to consider
the joinder of representative claimants and/or defendants.[34] The use of this device
was well established in Lord Lindley's day, as the following passage makes
clear:

> "It was held in *Wallworth v. Holt*,[35] that where partners are too numerous to be
> brought before the Court, and they are divisible into classes, and all the individuals
> in one class have a common interest, a suit instituted by a few individuals of that
> class on behalf of themselves and all the other individuals of the same class against
> the other members of the company is sustainable. Since this decision, there have been
> many suits by some shareholders on behalf of themselves and others, praying for
> very general accounts (but studiously avoiding a prayer for a dissolution),[36] and such
> suits have been successful whenever the interest of the absent partners has been the
> same as that of the plaintiffs on the record."[37]

Whether the use of representative parties will be appropriate in any given case **23–11**
will naturally depend on the nature of the relief sought. Thus, where an account
is required, a decision on representation can only be made once the interest of
each partner has been identified: if each partner's interest is distinct from and in
conflict with that of *all* his co-partners, then representative proceedings will be
inappropriate and all the partners should properly be joined, however numerous
they may be.[38] Where, on the other hand, no such conflict arises and two or more
partners share the same interest,[39] it will be sufficient if one partner is joined to
represent each distinct interest.[40] Representative proceedings may be particularly
useful where one or more partners are outside the jurisdiction.[41] Equally, if the
proceedings merely concern the construction of the partnership agreement or

---

[32] See the Regulatory Reform (Reform of 20 Member Limit in Partnerships etc.) Order 2002 (SI
2002/3203), reg. 2.

[33] As to what is likely to be regarded as a large firm, see *Re Braybrook* [1916] W.N. 74.

[34] See, generally, CPR r. 19.6. For old examples of actions brought by representative claimants on
behalf of a firm, see *Chancey v. May* (1722) Pr. Ch. 592; *Hichens v. Congreve* (1828) 4 Russ. 562;
Attwood v. Small (1838) 6 Cl. & F. 232; *Taylor v. Salmon* (1838) 4 Myl. & Cr. 134; *Beck v.
Kantorowicz* (1857) 3 K. & J. 230. There are no modern examples of which the current editor is
aware.

[35] (1841) 4 Myl. & Cr. 619. See also *Cockburn v. Thompson* (1809) 16 Ves.Jr. 321.

[36] As to the position where a dissolution is sought, see *infra*, para. 23–14.

[37] See *Apperley v. Page* (1847) 1 Ph. 779; also *Wilson v. Stanhope* (1846) 2 Colly. 629; *Harvey v.
Collett* (1846) 15 Sim. 332; *Cooper v. Webb* (1847) 15 Sim. 454; *Richardson v. Hastings* (1847) 7
Beav. 323; *Sibson v. Edgeworth* (1848) 2 De G. & Sm. 73; *Clements v. Bowes* (1852) 17 Sim. 167
and (1853) 1 Drew 684; *Butt v. Monteaux* (1854) 1 K. & J. 98; *Sheppard v. Oxenford* (1855) 1 K. &
J. 491; *Cramer v. Bird* (1868) L.R. 6 Eq. 143. *cf. Williams v. Salmond* (1855) 2 K. & J. 463.

[38] See *Van Sandau v. Moore* (1826) 1 Russ. 441; *McMahon v. Upton* (1829) 2 Sim. 473; *Seddon
v. Connell* (1840) 10 Sim. 58; *Abraham v. Hannay* (1843) 13 Sim. 581; *Sibley v. Minton* (1857) 27
L.J.Ch. 53.

[39] As to the meaning of the expression "the same interest" as used in the predecessor to CPR r.
19.6(1) (*i.e.* RSC Ord. 15, r. 12(1)), see *Prudential Assurance Co. Ltd. v. Newman Industries Ltd.*
[1981] Ch. 229; *Roche v. Sherrington* [1982] 1 W.L.R. 599; also *Irish Shipping Ltd. v. Commercial
Union Assurance Co. Plc* [1991] 2 Q.B. 206, where numerous authorities were reviewed by the Court
of Appeal.

[40] *cf. Harrison v. Brown* (1852) 5 De.G. & Sm. 728.

[41] See *Irish Shipping Ltd. v. Commercial Union Assurance Co. Plc* [1991] 2 Q.B. 206. *cf. Public
Trustee v. Elder* [1926] Ch. 776.

some other document, it will be possible to seek a representation order in respect of a partner/former partner whose whereabouts are not known.[42]

A partner can, where appropriate, be appointed to represent the interests of himself and his co-partners against his will.[43]

Whilst a judgment or order will bind all partners represented in the proceedings, it cannot be enforced against a partner who was not made a party without the permission of the court.[44]

Dissolution and winding up

23–12   All the partners should normally be joined as parties to a dissolution action.[45] This long standing rule was originally of an absolute nature[46] and, in Lord Lindley's words, its justification lay in the fact that:

> " . . . the affairs of a partnership cannot be finally wound up and settled without deciding all questions arising between all the partners, which cannot be done in the absence of any one of them."[47]

On the same principle, the personal representatives of a deceased partner should also be joined as parties, if they will be interested in the accounts taken in winding up the firm's affairs.[48] However, it is unnecessary to join any person who, though nominated as a partner, is not legally in a position to assert his rights as such.[49]

Action for account by assignee

23–13   It has already been seen that an assignee of a partnership share has a statutory right to an account following a dissolution.[50] If that right is exercised, *all* the partners, including the assignor, should properly be joined as parties to the proceedings, since the assignment does not affect their rights and obligations *inter se*.[51] Indeed, it would seem that the assignor will be regarded as a necessary party even if he is out of the jurisdiction: the assignee's personal undertaking to pay whatever may be found due to the other partners will not, in such a case, be sufficient.[52]

---

[42] CPR r. 19.7(1)(c), (2)(b).

[43] *ibid.* r. 19.6(1)(b). And see *Wood v. McCarthy* [1893] 1 Q.B. 775.

[44] *ibid.* r. 19.6(4).

[45] *Ireton v. Lewes* (1673) Finch 96; *Moffat v. Farquharson* (1788) 2 Bro.C.C. 338; *Long v. Yonge* (1830) 2 Sim. 369; *Evans v. Stokes* (1836) 1 Keen 24; *Wheeler v. Van Wart* (1838) 9 Sim. 193; *Deeks v. Stanhope* (1844) 14 Sim. 57; *Richardson v. Hastings* (1844) 7 Beav. 301; *Harvey v. Bignold* (1845) 8 Beav. 343.

[46] Lord Lindley observed: "This rule is supposed to admit of no exception, and it has, though with expressions of regret, been held to apply to unincorporated companies as well as to ordinary partnerships." See, in addition to the cases cited in the last note, *Van Sandau v. Moore* (1826) 1 Russ. 441; *Davis v. Fisk*, cited in *Small v. Attwood* (1832) Younge 407, 425; *Seddon v. Connell* (1840) 10 Sim. 58; *Abraham v. Hannay* (1843) 13 Sim. 581.

[47] See *Richardson v. Hastings* (1847) 7 Beav. 301.

[48] See *Cox v. Stephens* (1863) 9 Jur.(N.S.) 1144; also *Baboo Janokey Doss v. Bindabun Doss* (1843) 3 Moo.Ind.App. 175. As to the position where there is no personal representative, see *Cawthorn v. Chalie* (1824) 2 Sim. & St. 127 and *infra*, para. 26–08.

[49] *Ehrmann v. Ehrmann* (1894) 72 L.T. 17. *cf. Page v. Cox* (1851) 10 Hare 163. See also *supra*, para. 10–259.

[50] Partnership Act 1890, s.31(2), *supra*, paras 19–51, 19–56.

[51] See *supra*, para. 19–53.

[52] *Public Trustee v. Elder* [1926] Ch. 776.

Representative parties

Although the use of representative parties in dissolution actions was once **23–14** effectively proscribed,[53] such an approach could not be sustained in the face of the Civil Procedure Rules: the considerations applicable to such actions are, in principle, no different to any other.[54] Lord Lindley put it more tentatively, but in a statement of principle which cannot realistically be bettered:

> " . . . it may be permitted to doubt whether it can be considered as a rule admitting of no exception whatsoever, that to every action for a dissolution, all the partners must individually be parties. All that can on principle be requisite, is that every conflicting interest shall be substantially represented by some person before the court. If, which is possible, the interest of each partner conflicts with that of all the others, then all must undoubtedly be parties. But if the partners are numerous,[55] and it can be shown that they are divisible into classes, and that all the individuals in each class have a common interest, then although the interest in each class conflicts with that of every other class, there seems to be no reason why, if each class is represented by one or two of the individuals composing it, a decree for a dissolution should not be made.[56] There is not, however, so far as the writer is aware, any case in which a decree for a dissolution has actually been made in the absence of any of the partners."[57]

3.   CASES IN WHICH THE COURT WILL NOT INTERFERE BETWEEN PARTNERS

Courts of equity would, in general, decline to grant relief to a partner in **23–15** proceedings brought against his co-partners in three distinct cases, namely:

(1) where a dissolution was not sought;

(2) where a matter of internal regulation was involved; or

(3) where the partner concerned was guilty of laches or acquiescence.

This is still technically the position where the relief sought by a partner is of an equitable nature,[58] although, as will be seen hereafter, the first rule is no longer applied with its original strictness.

---

[53] See the cases cited *supra*, para. 23–12, nn. 45, 46.

[54] Even before the advent of the CPR, the courts adopted a pragmatic approach: see *Irish Shipping Ltd. v. Commercial Union Assurance Co. Plc* [1991] 2 Q.B. 206; also *Bank of America National Trust & Savings Assoc. v. Taylor* [1992] 1 Lloyd's Rep. 484. As to the current position, see the review of the authorities in *Emerald Supplies Ltd. v. British Airways plc* [2010] Ch. 48.

[55] Five partners are not "numerous": *Re Braybrook* [1916] W.N. 74.

[56] See *Richardson v. Larpent* (1843) 2 Y. & C.Ch. 514; also the observations of Lord Cottenham in *Wallworth v. Holt* (1841) 4 Myl. & Cr. 619, 637 *et seq.* As to the decision in *Cockburn v. Thompson* (1809) 16 Ves.Jnr. 321, Lord Lindley referred to the observations of Shadwell V.-C. in *Long v. Yonge* (1830) 2 Sim. 369, 380, and cautioned the reader to "observe that the real object was to make the defendants account for the money they had received, and that the question as to want of parties was not raised with reference to that part of the prayer of the bill which sought a dissolution."

[57] Note that an order was made in a representative action for the winding-up of an unregistered friendly society: *Re Lead Company's Workmen's Fund Society* [1904] 2 Ch. 196.

[58] *i.e.* specific performance, rescission, accounts, a receiver or an injunction. These subjects are considered in successive sections of this chapter. See, generally, the Senior Courts Act 1981, s.49. This Act was formerly known as the Supreme Court Act 1981: Constitutional Reform Act 2005, Sched. 11, Pt 1, para. 1(1).

Rule 1: The court will not interfere otherwise than with a view to dissolution.

23–16   The courts of equity normally displayed a marked reluctance to interfere as between partners otherwise than with a view to dissolving the firm or, if it had already been dissolved, winding up its affairs. Accordingly, instances in which an account or injunctive relief was refused solely on the ground that a dissolution was not sought can be found in the older reported cases. It is not surprising that this rule, which Lord Lindley described as "at no time perhaps very inflexible," was gradually relaxed. Yet, while the courts more readily granted relief as between the members of a continuing partnership, traces of the original strict rule remained,[59] as Lord Lindley explained:

> " . . . one of the first points for consideration, even now, when one partner sues another for equitable relief, is, can relief be had without dissolving the partnership? Undoubtedly it may, much more certainly than formerly, but not always when perhaps it ought.[60] . . . [*It*] may be stated as a general proposition, that courts will not, if they can avoid it, allow a partner to derive advantage from his own misconduct by compelling his co-partner to submit either to continued wrong, or to a dissolution[61]; and that rather than permit an improper advantage to be taken of a rule designed to operate for the benefit of all parties, the court will interfere . . . where formerly it would have declined to do so. At the same time courts will not take the management of a going concern into their own hands, and, if they cannot usefully interfere in any other manner, they will not interfere at all unless for the purpose of winding up the partnership."

Although the courts are now likely to adopt a more flexible and constructive approach than in Lord Lindley's day, it is submitted that the general proposition formulated in the above passage still, in essence, holds good.

Rule 2: The court will not interfere in matters of internal regulation.

Trivial disputes

23–17   The court will inevitably take a view on any matters of complaint raised by one partner against another and, if they are of an essentially trivial nature, will usually decline to give relief. Lord Lindley summarised the position in these terms:

> "A court of justice will not interfere between partners merely because they do not agree. It is no part of the duty of the Court to settle all partnership squabbles: it expects from every partner a certain amount of forbearance and good feeling towards his co-partner; and it does not regard mere passing improprieties, arising from infirmities of temper, as sufficient to warrant a decree for dissolution, or an order for an injunction, or a receiver."[62]

Interference with managing partner

23–18   If partners have agreed to entrust the management of the firm to a particular partner, the court will not readily deprive him of his responsibilities, by the

---

[59] This is particularly evident in the decisions relating to the specific performance of partnership agreements and to the appointment of receivers and managers: see *infra*, paras 23–45 *et seq.*, 23–153 *et seq.* As to accounts and inquiries, see *infra*, paras 23–82 *et seq.*

[60] See *infra*, paras 23–69 *et seq.*

[61] See *Fairthorne v. Weston* (1844) 3 Hare. 392; also *infra*, paras 23–85, 23–141, 24–82.

[62] See *Lawson v. Morgan* (1815) 1 Price 303; *Cofton v. Horner* (1818) 5 Price 537; *Marshall v. Colman* (1820) 2 J. & W. 266; *Smith v. Jeyes* (1841) 4 Beav. 503; *Warder v. Stilwell* (1856) 3 Jur.(N.S.) 9; *Anderson v. Anderson* (1857) 25 Beav. 190. See also *infra*, para. 24–81.

appointment of a receiver or otherwise, unless he can clearly be shown to have acted improperly.[63]

Rule 3: The court will not interfere at the instance of partner guilty of laches or acquiescence.

A partner may, on normal principles, be precluded from obtaining equitable relief by reason of laches or acquiescence. Laches is, of course, quite independent of the Limitation Act 1980,[64] and presupposes not only the passage of time, but also the existence of circumstances which render it inequitable to afford a claimant the relief which he seeks.[65] Similarly in the case of acquiescence.[66]

Where, however, a partner has himself acted in an underhand fashion, the court may be unwilling to give credence to any plea of laches or acquiescence which he may seek to raise against his co-partners.[67]

23–19

Action for account precluded by laches or acquiescence

It has long been recognised that proceedings for an account may be defeated by laches or acquiescence,[68] although it was held in *Hopper v. Hopper*[69] that a laches defence cannot apply where there is an applicable statutory limitation period.[70] What the court seemingly ignored in that case is the fact that time does not normally run between partners in an ongoing partnership.[71] Be that as it may, the court will not, in the absence of fraud, re-open an erroneous account which has been rendered and thereafter acquiesced in, even if it has not been finally settled.[72]

The same principle is applied in taking accounts as between partners, so that if one partner has improperly sought to charge an item to the firm and this has been acquiesced in by his co-partners or, conversely, if he has knowingly omitted

23–20

---

[63] See *Waters v. Taylor* (1808) 15 Ves.Jr. 10; *Lawson v. Morgan* (1851) 1 Price 303. *cf.* the position following a dissolution: *Tibbits v. Phillips* (1853) 10 Hare 355.

[64] See, however, as to the interaction between a potential laches defence and an applicable statutory period of limitation, *infra*, para. 23–20. Equally, the court may apply a statutory limitation period by analogy: see *P & O Nedlloyd BV v. Arab Metals Co.* [2007] 1 W.L.R. 2288 (CA), considering the application of the Limitation Act 1980, s.36(1). See further, as to limitation as between partners, *infra*, paras 23–32 *et seq*.

[65] See *Nelson v. Rye* [1996] 1 W.L.R. 1378; *Frawley v. Neill, The Times*, April 5, 1999 (CA); *Fisher v. Brooker* [2009] 1 W.L.R. 1764 (HL); also *Jones v. Stones* [1999] 1 W.L.R. 1739 (CA); *Patel v. Shah, The Times*, March 2, 2005. It follows from the flexibility of the doctrine that laches may preclude relief, even though actual assent or conscious acquiescence on the part of the claimant is not proved: see *Lindsay Petroleum Co. v. Hurd* (1874) L.R. 5 P.C. 221; *Erlanger v. New Sombrero Phosphate Co.* (1878) 3 App.Cas. 1218, 1230 *per* Lord Penzance, 1279 *per* Lord Blackburn. However, mere delay is rarely sufficient: *Ridgway v. Newstead* (1861) 3 D.F. & J. 474; *Blake v. Gale* (1886) 32 Ch.D. 571; *Re Eustace* [1912] 1 Ch. 561; *Nelson v. Rye, supra; Lynch v. James Lynch & Sons (Transport) Ltd.*, March 8, 2000 (Lawtel 8/3/00) (CA). Note that a laches argument failed in *Hopper v. Hopper, infra*.

[66] See, generally, *Jones v. Stones, supra*, where the earlier authorities are reviewed. See also the cases cited in the previous footnote.

[67] *Blundon v. Storm* (1971) 20 D.L.R. (3d) 413, noted *infra*, para. 23–23.

[68] *Sherman v. Sherman* (1692) 2 Vern. 276; *Sturt v. Mellish* (1743) 2 Atk. 610. For a more recent reaffirmation of this principle, see *John v. James* [1991] F.S.R. 397.

[69] [2008] EWHC 228 (Ch) (Lawtel 26/2/08) at [146] *per* Briggs J., approved at [2008] EWCA Civ. 1417 (Lawtel 12/12/08) at [32], [33].

[70] Limitation Act 1980, s.23: see *infra*, para. 23–36.

[71] See *infra*, para. 23–32.

[72] *Scott v. Milne* (1843) 7 Jur. 709. See also *Stupart v. Arrowsmith* (1856) 3 Sm. & G. 176; *Williams v. Page* (1858) 24 Beav. 654.

to charge a legitimate item to the firm, the court may, in the absence of fraud, infer that this was done by agreement and is not open to challenge on the grounds of mistake.[73]

Agreements for partnership and laches/acquiescence

23–21   Questions of laches and/or acquiescence frequently arise where a person has agreed to enter into partnership but has, in effect, hung back in order to see whether participation in the venture is worthwhile. Lord Lindley explained:

> "The doctrine of laches is of great importance where persons have agreed to become partners, and one of them has unfairly left the other to do all the work, and then, there being a profit, comes forward and claims a share of it. In such cases as these, the plaintiff's conduct lays him open to the remark that nothing would have been heard of him had the joint adventure ended in loss instead of gain; and a court will not aid those who can be shown to have remained quiet in the hope of being able to evade responsibility in case of loss, but of being able to claim a share of gain in case of ultimate success".[74]

23–22   Thus, in *Cowell v. Watts*[75] the claimant and the defendant agreed to acquire and improve certain leasehold land with a view to sub-letting it for building purposes. However, the lease was taken in the sole name of the defendant, who declined to enter into a written agreement recording the terms of the venture. He thereafter treated the land as his own, mortgaging it and applying the funds raised in erecting buildings, and even removing the claimant's cattle which were grazing there. The claimant, though aware of the defendant's activities, did nothing for some 18 months. He then called on the defendant to perform the original agreement and, when the defendant refused, sought specific performance. That claim was dismissed, on the ground that the claimant had, by his conduct, induced the defendant to believe that he had abandoned the venture and that the defendant was solely entitled to the land.

23–23   On the other hand, a plea of laches failed in *Blundon v. Storm*,[76] because the partner who sought to raise it had himself acted in an unscrupulous manner. Here, a partnership had been formed to search for sunken treasure "for an indefinite period of time . . . [*or until*] all parties agree in writing that the purposes of the partnership have been completed . . . ". One partner served a notice purporting to terminate the partnership, which under Canadian law was of no legal effect, and at the same time informed the other partners of his intention to continue the search on his own account. The other partners took no further part in the search and made no objection until 14 months later, after treasure had been found. It was held by the Canadian Supreme Court (reversing the decision of the Nova Scotia Supreme Court) that, as the partner who had purported to terminate the partnership had, before serving the notice, secretly obtained a renewal of his licence under the Treasure Trove Act and the approval of the Receiver of Wrecks, the other partners were in no way barred from relief by a plea of laches or acquiescence, notwithstanding their delay.

---

[73] *Thornton v. Proctor* (1792) 1 Anst. 94, noticed *supra*, para. 20–28.
[74] *cf. Clarke v. Hart* (1858) 6 H.L.C. 633, *infra*, para. 23–28. Note that the passage in the text was approved and applied in *Patel v. Shah*, *The Times*, March 2, 2005.
[75] (1850) 2 H. & Tw. 224.
[76] (1971) 20 D.L.R. (3d) 413.

Mining partnerships and other speculative ventures

A plea of laches or acquiescence is most likely to succeed where the partner- **23–24**
ship business is of a highly speculative nature.[77] Lord Lindley took mining
partnerships as the most obvious example, observing that:

> "Mining operations are so extremely doubtful as to their ultimate success that it is of
> the highest importance that those engaged in them should know on whom they can
> confidently rely for aid."

A significant factor in cases of this type will usually be the expenditure
required to carry on the mining or other operations. Thus, in *Senhouse v.
Christian*,[78] the defendant, one of five joint lessees of a colliery, had obtained a
renewal of the lease in his own name. The other lessees, though aware of all the
facts, did nothing for four years, during which time the defendant worked the
colliery single handed and at great expense.[79] Lord Rosslyn dismissed their claim
to the benefit of the renewed lease. This decision was subsequently cited with
approval by Lord Eldon in *Norway v. Rowe*.[80]

A laches defence may still succeed even where the mining or other operation
is self financing, as demonstrated by the decision in *Clegg v. Edmondson*,[81]
where the facts were otherwise broadly similar to those in *Senhouse v.
Christian*.

Evidence of abandonment, etc.

In order to sustain a plea of laches or acquiescence, it is not necessary to **23–25**
provide positive evidence that the claimant has abandoned his rights.[82] Indeed, in
Clegg v. Edmondson,[83] the claimants had repeatedly insisted on their right to
participate in the profits obtained by the defendants under the renewed lease, but
this was held, on the facts, not to be sufficient to preserve that right.[84] However,
this case should not be taken as establishing a principle of general application, as
Lord Lindley explained:

---

[77] See, for example, *Blundon v. Storm* (1971) 20 D.L.R. (3d) 413, *supra*, para. 23–23 (where,
however, the plea did not succeed).

[78] (1795), reported in a note to *Hart v. Clarke* (1854) 19 Beav. 349, 356. See also *Norway v. Rowe*
(1812) 19 Ves.Jr. 144, 157.

[79] This fact does not appear from the brief report at (1854) 19 Beav. 356.

[80] (1812) 19 Ves.Jr. 144. Lord Lindley commented: "There were more grounds than one for this
decision, but the case is always regarded as an authority in support of the doctrine acted on by Lord
Rosslyn in *Senhouse v. Christian*."

[81] (1856) 8 De G.M. & G. 787.

[82] It is now clear that the doctrines of laches and acquiescence will be applied flexibly and are not
tied to any rigid rules: see *Jones v. Stones* [1999] 1 W.L.R. 1739 (CA); *Frawley v. Neill, The Times*,
April 5, 1999 (CA); also *Patel v. Shah, The Times*, March 2, 2005. Equally, positive evidence of
abandonment was *never* necessary: see, for example, *Davis v. Johnston* (1831) 4 Sim. 539; *Reilly v.
Walsh* (1848) 11 I.Eq.R. 22 (speculative development of leasehold land). Lord Lindley also cited the
decision in *Jekyl v. Gilbert*, which appeared in McNaghten's *Select Cases in Chancery*, p. 29. There,
in his own words, "two artificers agreed to do work for their joint benefit; after the work was done,
the person for whom it was done refused to pay; the defendant requested the plaintiff to join in legal
proceedings to compel payment, but the plaintiff declined. Thereupon the defendant brought an action
for payment of the work done by him, and obtained a verdict. The plaintiff then claimed half the
amount recovered, but the Court held that he was not entitled to any share of it."

[83] (1856) 8 De G.M. & G. 787.

[84] See the apparently wide statement of principle formulated by Turner L.J. at *ibid*. p. 810.

"It cannot be laid down as universally true that protests are useless. They exclude inferences which, in their absence, might fairly be drawn from the conduct of the party protesting, and are conclusive to show that no abandonment of right was intended."[85]

What the court must do in each case is to consider the whole conduct of the parties in order to see whether it would be unconscionable for the claimant to rely on his strict rights.[86]

It goes almost without saying that, whilst mere protests may be insufficient, a plea of laches will be defeated if there is positive evidence of the defendant continuing to recognise the claimant's rights.[87]

23–26   Where abandonment *can* be proved, it may in practice be unnecessary to rely on laches or acquiescence. Lord Lindley observed:

" . . . if a partner formally withdraws from an adventure when its prospects are bad [*he will*] be unable to claim a share of the profits resulting from it if it ultimately proves to be profitable[88]; such cases, however, are not so much cases of laches as of estoppel or agreements to release."

It would seem that *Prendergast v. Turton*,[89] falls within this class, although it has often been cited as a simple case of laches.[90] There the partnership capital was exhausted and the claimant partners refused to contribute additional funds. The other partners did, however, provide such funds and, several years later, succeeded in running the mine at a profit. Only then did the claimants seek to assert their interest in the concern, but their claim was rejected.

23–27   Similarly, in *Rule v. Jewell*,[91] where a member of a cost-book mining company, which was seriously in debt, had his shares forfeited for non-payment of calls. After five years he disputed the validity of the forfeiture and claimed to be reinstated as a partner. That claim was duly rejected on the basis of estoppel and, if necessary, abandonment.[92]

In *Palmer v. Moore*,[93] a joint lessee of a gold mine had given written notice to his co-lessees that he was unable to contribute to the joint expenses and that they could do as they liked with the lease; this was held to be an abandonment of his

---

[85] See *Clarke v. Hart* (1858) 6 H.L.C. 633, *infra*, para. 23–28. *cf. Blundon v. Storm* (1971) 20 D.L.R. (3d) 413, *supra*, para. 23–23.

[86] See *Jones v. Stones* and *Frawley v. Neill, supra.*

[87] See *Penny v. Pickwick* (1852) 16 Beav. 246; also *Clements v. Hall* (1858) 2 De G. & J. 173, *infra*, para. 23–30.

[88] *Maclure v. Ripley* (1850) 2 Mac. & G. 274; also *Lukin v. Lovrinov* [1998] S.A.S.C. 6614. *cf. Blundon v. Storm* (1971) 20 D.L.R. (3d) 413, *supra*, para. 23–23. See also *Ryder v. Frohlich* [2004] NSWCA 472, where the issue of repudiation and acceptance was also under consideration: see *infra*, para. 24–07.

[89] (1841) 1 Y. & C.Ch. 98 and, on appeal, (1843) 13 L.J.Ch. 268.

[90] Indeed, Lord Lindley treated it in this way. But see *Clarke v. Hart* (1858) 6 H.L.C. 633, 657–659 *per* Lord Chelmsford; *Rule v. Jewell* (1880) 18 Ch.D. 660, 666 *per* Kay J.; *Garden Gully United Quartz Mining Co. v. McLister* (1875) 1 App.Cas. 39, 57.

[91] (1880) 18 Ch.D. 660. *cf. Clarke v. Hart* (1858) 6 H.L.C. 633, *infra*, para. 23–28.

[92] (1880) 18 Ch.D. 667–668 *per* Kay J. Although the Statute of Limitations was pleaded, it was held not to be a defence, even though the action was commenced more than six years after the purported forfeiture: see *ibid.* p. 662. *Quaere* is this correct? See *infra*, para. 23–35.

[93] [1900] A.C. 293.

beneficial interest therein, which was accepted by one of his co-lessees subsequently working the mine at his own expense.

Exceptional cases: *Clarke v. Hart* and *Clements v. Hall*

Leaving aside the decision in *Lake v. Craddock*,[94] which turned on another   **23–28**
point,[95] there are two notable cases which appear to be inconsistent with the
principles described in the preceding paragraphs, *i.e. Clarke v. Hart* and *Clements v. Hall*.

Clarke v. Hart[96]

In this case, A, B and C were shareholders in a mining company run on the
cost-book principle and lessees of the mine worked by the company. Finance was
required for mining operations but C failed to provide his due proportion when
called on so to do. C was on more than one occasion warned by A and B that,
if this failure continued, they would forfeit his shares in the company (even
though they did not, in fact, have power to do so under the agreement). Ultimately, A and B did purport to forfeit C's shares. C, who had at all times denied
that there was any such right and who had also suggested other methods of
raising the necessary finance, gave A and B notice that, if the mining operation
proved successful, he would expect his share of the profits and, if necessary, take
legal proceedings to enforce his claim. Some 18 months passed and C then
asserted his claim. A and B rejected it and proceedings were commenced. The
House of Lords held that the purported notice of forfeiture did not cause a
dissolution[97] and that, in the particular circumstances, C could not be held to
have indicated an intention to abandon his interest in the concern.

Lord Lindley explained the rationale underlying this decision as follows: **23–29**

> "The ground of the decision . . . and that which distinguishes it from *Senhouse v.
> Christian*[98] and other cases alluded to above,[99] is this, *viz.* that the plaintiff in *Hart
> v. Clarke*[100] had, as one of the lessees of the mine, a legal interest therein, which
> nothing had displaced. The Court, therefore, was in this position: it was compelled
> either to make a decree in favour of the plaintiff, or to declare him a trustee of his

---

[94] (1732) 3 P.W. 158. This case concerned an action for an account brought by one partner against
his co-partners, one of whom had long ceased to take any part in the partnership affairs.

[95] Lord Lindley observed that "this case, in truth, only decided that if one of several partners
chooses to claim the benefit of partnership dealings, after having for some time ceased to take any
part in the affairs of the partnership, he must contribute his share of the outlays made by the other
partners, with interest. It was not decided . . . that a partner could, on the above terms, claim the
benefit of what had been done by the others; and although the decree gave a partner who had long
abandoned the concern the option of either claiming a share on proper terms or of being excluded
altogether, the other partners do not appear to have raised any objection to this option being
given."

[96] (1858) 6 H.L.C. 633, affirming *Hart v. Clarke* (1854) 6 De G.M. & G. 232. See also *Garden
Gully United Quartz Mining Co. v. McLister* (1875) 1 App.Cas. 39. *cf. Rule v. Jewell* (1881) 18 Ch.D.
660, *supra*, para. 23–27.

[97] See further, *infra*, para. 24–22.

[98] (1795), reported in a note to *Hart v. Clarke* (1854) 19 Beav. 349, 356.

[99] See *supra*, para. 23–24.

[100] Lord Lindley used the title of the action at first instance.

share in the mine for the defendants; and there not being sufficient grounds for justifying the latter alternative, the former was necessarily adopted.[101] Upon no other ground can the case, it is submitted, be distinguished from *Clegg v. Edmondson*[102] and the other cases alluded to above; for, although reliance was placed, in the judgment in *Hart v. Clarke*, on the distinct notice given by the plaintiff that he did not acquiesce in the defendant's conduct, and should insist on his rights, it was decided in *Clegg v. Edmondson* that a protest did not enlarge the time within which redress must be sought in a court of equity."[103]

Equally, it would seem that the House of Lords may have treated *Clarke v. Hart* more as a case of potential abandonment[104] than laches, unlike the position in *Clegg v. Edmondson*.

Clements v. Hall[105]

23–30   The facts of this case were most unusual. A and B were lessees of a mine which they worked as partners. The lease expired but A and B continued in possession as tenants from year to year, working the mine as before. In 1847 A died, leaving a will in which he appointed C as his executor and bequeathed an interest in the mine to D. B thereafter treated the mine as his own and, despite constant pressure from C, refused to render any accounts. In 1850 B, without C's knowledge, negotiated a new lease from the landlord, but on more onerous terms than before. Prior to the grant of the new lease, B had merely kept the mining operation "ticking over" so that no profits were produced; now he began to work the mine in earnest and at a profit. In 1851 D commenced an action against B and C in order to establish his interest in the mine. C admitted D's title, but B put in no defence, because the action was stayed pending security for costs being given. In the event, D did not proceed further with the action. B died in 1853 and C became his personal representative. In 1854 the claimant, who was the assignee of D's interest in the mine, sought to have that interest secured for his own benefit.[106] C, who had (as A's executor) admitted D's right, now (as B's personal representative) opposed the claimant's claim. Although the decision was not unanimous, it was held: (1) that on A's death, his interest in the mine did not determine; (2) that his estate was entitled to share the benefit of the renewed lease; (3) that C, as A's executor, was not precluded in 1853 from asserting this right against B, since B had kept C in ignorance of the real state of the concern; and (4) that there had been no laches on the part of the claimant or D, through whom he claimed, because there had, since 1851, been proceedings on foot to secure their interest.[107]

---

[101] See *Rule v. Jewell* (1881) 18 Ch.D. 660; *Palmer v. Moore* [1900] A.C. 293, *supra*, para. 23–27.

[102] (1856) 8 De G.M. & G. 787.

[103] But see *supra*, para. 23–25.

[104] See (1858) 6 H.L.C. 633, 655–660 *per* Lord Chelmsford, 670 *per* Lord Wensleydale; *cf. ibid.* pp. 662 *per* Lord Brougham, 666 *per* Lord Cranworth.

[105] (1858) 2 De G. & J. 173. See also (1857) 24 Beav. 333.

[106] In fact, procedurally, this claim was raised by the claimant in a bill supplemental to the bill originally filed by D.

[107] *Semble* the position would have been different if D's action had been struck out for want of prosecution. Now the procedural position is different: see the CPR r. 3.4(2)(c); *Biguzzi v. Rank Leisure PLC* [1999] 1 W.L.R. 1926 (CA); *cf. Hamblin v. Field* [2000] B.P.I.R. 621 (CA).

Lord Lindley's final summary

The exceptional nature of the decisions in *Clarke v. Hart*[108] and *Clements v.*   **23–31**
Hall[109] will be self evident and they do not in fact call into question the general
principles which may be drawn from the other cases, as Lord Lindley
confirmed:

> " . . . it is submitted that the doctrine laid down and acted upon in *Norway v. Rowe*,[110]
> *Senhouse v. Christian*,[111] *Prendergast v. Turton*,[112] *Clegg v. Edmondson*,[113] and *Rule
> v. Jewell*[114] may still be safely relied on in all cases except those in which the court
> can be driven, as it was in *Hart v. Clarke*,[115] to the alternative of holding either that
> the plaintiff is entitled to relief, or that he has abandoned and lost his former *legal*
> status."[116]

4.   LIMITATION AS BETWEEN PARTNERS

Application of the Limitation Act 1980

It appears that time will only run under the Limitation Act 1980 once the   **23–32**
partnership has terminated. Lord Lindley stated the general principle thus:

> "So long . . . as a partnership is subsisting, and each partner is exercising his rights
> and enjoying his own property, the statute of limitations has, it is conceived, no
> application at all[117]; but as soon as a partnership is dissolved, or there is any
> exclusion of one partner by the others, the case is very different, and the statute
> begins to run."[118]

Somewhat surprisingly, in *Hopper v. Hopper*,[119] the Court of Appeal, in
upholding the decision of Briggs J. that Mrs Hopper's entitlement to her and her
deceased husband's joint capital account balance was not barred by limitation or
laches,[120] appears to have assumed that this principle is not of general application
and would not automatically apply in a case where a partner seeks to reopen

---

[108] (1858) 6 H.L.C. 633.
[109] (1858) 2 De G. & J. 173.
[110] (1812) 19 Ves.Jr. 144.
[111] (1795), reported in a note to *Hart v. Clarke* (1854) 19 Beav. 349, 356. See *supra*, para.
23–24.
[112] (1841) 1 Y. & C.Ch. 98 and, on appeal, (1843) 13 L.J.Ch. 268. See *supra*, para. 23–26.
[113] (1856) 8 De G.M. & G. 787.
[114] (1881) 18 Ch.D. 660, *supra*, para. 23–27.
[115] Again, Lord Lindley used the title of the case at first instance.
[116] See also *Garden Gully United Quartz Mining Co. v. McLister* (1875) 1 App.Cas. 39; *Palmer v.
Moore* [1900] A.C. 293, *supra*, para. 23–27. In *Beningfield v. Baxter* (1886) 12 App.Cas. 167, the
defendant was an executor.
[117] *Miller v. Miller* (1869) L.R. 8 Eq. 499. But see *infra*, para. 23–34, n. 126.
[118] *Noyes v. Crawley* (1878) 10 Ch.D. 31; also *Barton v. North Staffs Ry.* (1887) 38 Ch.D. 458; *The
Pongola* (1895) 73 L.T. 512.
[119] [2008] EWCA Civ. 1412 (Lawtel 12/12/08).
[120] See [2008] EWHC 228 (Ch) (Lawtel 26/2/08).

settled accounts whilst the partnership is still continuing.[121] The current editor doubts the correctness of this approach.

Continuing partnership

23–33   It follows that a claim for an account by one or more partners against the other or others should properly never become time barred whilst the partnership is continuing.[122] The position will be the same as between continuing or surviving partners if, notwithstanding a dissolution, they carry on the old firm's business without any break in or settlement of its accounts. Thus, in *Betjemann v. Betjemann*[123] A, B and C carried on business as partners from 1856 to 1886; following A's death in 1886, B and C continued the business until 1893, when B died. C obtained an order for accounts to be taken as against B's executors with effect from 1856, on the footing that the accounts of the original firm had been carried on into the new firm without interruption or settlement.

There is authority for the proposition that time will not run where there has been a purported (but ineffective) forfeiture of a partner's share by his co-partners, but this is obviously dependent on showing that the partnership still continues.[124] Of course, defences other than limitation may be available to the forfeiting partners in such a case.[125]

Dissolved partnership

23–34   That a limitation defence will be effective as between the continuing or surviving partners on the one hand and the outgoing partner or his estate on the other was clearly decided in *Knox v. Gye*.[126] This proposition might at first sight appear to be reinforced by the terms of section 43 of the Partnership Act 1890, which provides:

> "43. Subject to any agreement between the partners,[127] the amount due from surviving or continuing partners to an outgoing partner or the representatives of a deceased

---

[121] Briggs J., having referred to the principle at *ibid.* [142], went on to found his decision on re-opening the accounts on the Limitation Act 1980, s.32(1)(c): see *ibid.* at [145]. The Court of Appeal merely endorsed his view: see [2008] EWCA Civ. 1412 at [32]. Of course, a settled account will not normally be reopened: see *infra*, paras 23–110 *et seq.*

[122] This would seem to be the position even in respect of secret profits made by a partner, for which he is bound to account to the firm under the Partnership Act 1890, s.29 (*supra*, paras 16–14 *et seq.*): *The Pongola, supra. Sed quaere.* But note the decision in *Hopper v. Hopper, supra.*

[123] [1895] 2 Ch. 474. See also *The Pongola, supra.*

[124] See *Rule v. Jewell* (1881) 18 Ch.D. 660, 662 *per* Kay J.

[125] See *Rule v. Jewell, supra*; also *supra*, para. 23–27.

[126] (1872) L.R. 5 H.L. 656. In a footnote, Lord Lindley observed: "*Miller v. Miller* (1869) L.R. 8 Eq. 499, is hardly consistent with this, unless it be upon the ground that there was no dissolution, or that there was a trust deed excluding the statute". See *Noyes v. Crawley* (1878) 10 Ch.D. 31, 37 *per* Malins V.-C.; *Gopala Chetty v. Vayaraghavachariar* [1922] 1 A.C. 488; *Mehra v. Shah*, August 1, 2003 (Lawtel 5/8/03) at [74] *per* Sonia Proudman Q.C. (sitting as a deputy judge of the Chancery Division), this aspect not being pursued on the appeal at [2004] EWCA Civ 632 (Lawtel 20/5/04)) *Hopper v. Hopper* [2008] EWCA Civ. 1417 (Lawtel 12/12/08) (CA), noted *supra*, para. 23–32; also *Wheatley v. Bower* [2001] W.A.S.C.A. 293. It should be noted that, prior to 1876, equitable suits for an account were not caught by any Statutes of Limitation and, whilst the Court of Chancery frequently applied them by analogy if pleaded (see *Knox v. Gye, supra*, at p. 674), it even more frequently ignored them. See also *infra*, n. 131.

[127] Needless to say, any such agreement must be reached *prior* to the date of dissolution or death: *Patel v. Patel* [2008] EWCA Civ 1520 (Lawtel 7/4/08) (CA).

partner in respect of the outgoing or deceased partner's share is a debt accruing at the date of the dissolution or death."

It is, however, difficult to see how this section can apply in the case of a *general* dissolution[128]: if the outgoing/deceased partner's share is indeed converted into a debt, it is of a most unusual nature, since it is clear that he or his estate is entitled to a full share of any increase in the value of the partnership assets accruing in the period between the date of dissolution and the date of realisation[129] and, conversely, must bear a full share of any diminution in value during that period. Interestingly, in the commentary on the above section in his Supplement on the Partnership Act 1890, Lord Lindley observed, as regards the position under *Scots* law:

> "This section proceeds on the footing that there is no winding up, but that by contract, the value of the deceased or retiring partner's share is to be ascertained and paid out. Accordingly, the date, unless otherwise stipulated, at which the value falls to be ascertained will be the date of dissolution. The amount thus becomes a debt bearing interest from that date."

Why the same point was not made in relation to English law is by no means clear, and the current editor remains of the view that the above analysis should be treated as of general application.[130]

Where section 43 *does* apply, the debt will become time barred six years after **23–35** the date of dissolution[131] or death on normal principles.[132] Where, however, the partnership was originally constituted by deed, the sum due to the outgoing partner thereunder will be recoverable as a specialty, to which a 12 year limitation period will apply.[133]

---

[128] These doubts appear to have been shared by Nourse L.J. in *Popat v. Shonchhatra* [1997] 1 W.L.R. 1367, 1372D. However, in *Duncan v. The MFV Marigold PD145* 2006 S.L.T. 975 (OH), Lord Reed held that the section applies in the case of *all* dissolutions: see *ibid.* at [48] *et seq.* In *Purewall v. Purewall* 2009 S.C.L.R. 50 (OH), Lord Drummond Young regarded s.43 as a default provision which applies in the absence of agreement but did not address the issue further: see *ibid.* at [15]; see also, on the reclaiming motion, 2010 S.L.T. 120 (Ex Div.) at [29] *per* Lord Osborne. In *HLB Kidsons v. Lloyd's Underwriters* [2009] 1 All E.R. (Comm) 760 at [16], Judge Mackie Q.C. (sitting as a judge of the Chancery Division) observed that ss.32–44 were "concerned with a more 'general' dissolution" (as opposed to a technical dissolution). It seems unlikely he was addressed on the intricacies of s.43, although *Duncan v. The MFV Marigold PD145, supra,* was referred to in his judgment.

[129] See *Barclays Bank Trust Co. Ltd. v. Bluff* [1982] Ch. 172; *Chandroutie v. Gajadhar* [1987] A.C. 147. See also *infra,* paras 25–32, 26–03.

[130] The above analysis would appear to have been approved by Lightman J. in *Sandhu v Gill* [2005] 1 W.L.R. 1979 at [12], but his decision was overturned on appeal: see [2006] Ch. 456. Only Black J. commented on the effect of s.43 in passing: *ibid.* at [98]. *cf. Duncan v. The MFV Marigold PD145* 2006 S.L.T. 975, noted *supra,* n. 128.

[131] Time will, of course, only start running as from the *actual* date of dissolution, rather than from some earlier deemed dissolution date adopted by the parties: see *Coull v. Maclean* 1991 G.W.D. 21–1249.

[132] See, for example, *Patel v. Patel* [2008] EWCA Civ 1520 (Lawtel 7/4/08) (CA). It is, however, unclear whether this will be by virtue of the Limitation Act 1980, s.5 (simple contract debt) or s.9 (sum recoverable by statute). The point is, in any event, largely academic. *Semble,* this will *not* constitute an action on a specialty within the meaning of *ibid.* s.8(1); *cf. Rahman v. Sterling Credit Ltd.* [2001] 1 W.L.R. 496 (CA) (a decision in relation to the Consumer Credit Act 1974, s.139(1)). *Sed quaere.*

[133] *ibid.* s.8(1). See, generally, *Global Financial Recoveries Ltd. v. Jones* [2000] B.P.I.R. 1029. And note that, in *Harper v. John C. Harper & Co* 2003 S.L.T. (Sh Ct) 102, it appears to have been held that the right to an account did not arise under the agreement, so that the general law applied for limitation purposes under Scots law. *Quaere,* could a similar argument be raised under s.8(1)?

23–36   In practice, claims between the members of a dissolved firm will normally be framed as actions for an account, in respect of which the relevant limitation period is that applicable to the claim on which the duty to account is based.[134] Accordingly, an account will not normally be ordered in respect of the dealings and transactions of a partnership which has been dissolved more than six years before the proceedings were issued,[135] unless the original agreement was under seal.[136]

A graphic illustration of this principle is to be found in the unreported decision in *Marshall v. Bullock*.[137] There, one partner sought a contribution from his former partner in respect of certain liabilities of the dissolved firm which he had personally discharged. More than six years had elapsed since the date of the dissolution, but less than six since the date on which the relevant liabilities were discharged. It was held that the claim was, in substance, an action for an account and that such an action was clearly time barred.[138] The court reportedly observed:

> "There are good policy reasons why this should be so. When a partnership comes to an end, there is an obligation on the partners to agree, or to have determined by the court, their respective liabilities and their respective entitlements. Once partners have dissolved the partnership, each should after six years be free of risk of any claims being made by another partner."

This decision was followed in *Manning v. English*.[138a]

Right to an account

23–37   Nevertheless, a number of factors may affect an outgoing or other partner's right to an account and these are, for convenience, arranged in alphabetical order.

Acknowledgment: An acknowledgment will only result in the accrual of a fresh cause of action for limitation purposes if it is in writing and signed by the person making it,[139] but it may not matter in what *capacity* that acknowledgment is made.[140] In one old case, where no account had been taken for six years, it was held that a signed acknowledgment of a liability to account in respect of matters more than six years old was sufficient to justify an account being ordered in respect of those matters, even though the acknowledgment did not contain an

---

[134] *ibid.* s.23.

[135] See *Noyes v. Crawley* (1878) 10 Ch.D. 31. *cf. Betjemann v. Betjemann* [1895] 2 Ch. 474, *supra*, para. 23–33.

[136] Limitation Act 1980, ss.8(1), 23.

[137] March 27, 1998 (CA).

[138] The court rejected an argument that a claim for a contribution towards liabilities discharged was in some way different from a claim in respect of money or property in the hands of a member of the dissolved firm. Both ultimately depend on the taking of an account, save in exceptional cases, as to which see *infra*, paras 23–39, 23–76.

[138a] [2010] Bus. L.R. D89.

[139] Limitation Act 1980, ss.29(5), 30(1). Note that a signed balance sheet can constitute an acknowledgment: see *Re Compania De Electricidad, etc.* [1980] Ch. 146, applying *Jones v. Bellgrove Properties Ltd.* [1949] 2 K.B. 700; *cf. Re Overmark Smith Warden Ltd.* [1982] 1 W.L.R. 1195. And see also, generally, as *Bradford & Bingley plc v. Rashid* [2006] 1 W.L.R. 2066 (HL).

[140] See *Harper v. John C. Harper & Co* 2003 S.L.T. (Sh Ct) 102, where a partner had acknowledged a former partner's right to an account in his personal capacity and this was held also to be binding in his capacity as a partner. The two partners in question were former spouses.

admission that any debt was actually due.[141] The current editor considers that a similar approach might properly be adopted under the Limitation Act 1980,[142] but recognises that, in *Manning v. English*,[142a] it was held that merely agreeing to an account being taken did *not* amount to an acknowledgment to pay any amount found to be due.

Agreed accounts: If the partners have agreed that the firm's annual accounts, once approved, should not be reopened,[143] that agreement will normally be given effect to, unless fraud,[144] misrepresentation or serious errors can be proved.[145]   **23–38**

Assets received after accounts settled: If, after the affairs of the partnership have been wound up and its accounts settled, an asset is received by one of the former partners which was not included in those accounts, time will only start to run as regards the other partners' entitlement in respect of that asset with effect from the date of its receipt: the fact that those other partners have lost their general right to an account will, in such circumstances, be irrelevant.[146] *Per contra*, if the dissolution accounts have not been settled and the right to a general account is time barred.[147]   **23–39**

Fraud and concealment: Time will not run in the case of a partner's fraud or concealment, unless the other partners could with reasonable diligence have discovered the true position.[148] As a general rule, partners will be regarded as having shown reasonable diligence even where they have had ample means of discovering the concealment or fraud, but have not in fact done so nor had their   **23–40**

---

[141] See *Prance v. Sympson* (1854) Kay 678, where one partner had written: "You and I must go into it and settle the account." See also *Skeet v. Lindsay* (1877) 2 Ex.D. 314; *Banner v. Berridge* (1881) 18 Ch.D. 254; *Friend v. Young* [1897] 2 Ch. 421; *Kamouh v. Associated Electrical Industries International Ltd.* [1980] Q.B. 199. *cf. Mitchell's Claim* (1871) L.R. 6 Ch.App. 822. Note that the pre-1940 cases contain references to the need for an express or implied promise to pay, but this requirement has no place in the modern law. Moreover, the decided cases provide only limited guidance in this area: see *Spencer v. Hemmerde* [1922] 2 A.C. 507, 519 *per* Lord Sumner.

[142] On the basis that an acknowledgement of a right to an account must relate to the claim which is the basis for the duty to account under the Limitation Act 1980, s.23. Note, however, the terms of *ibid.* s.29(5)(a); and see also *Re Flynn (No. 2)* [1969] 2 Ch. 403, 412 *per* Buckley J.

[142a] [2010] Bus. L.R. D89 at [47] *per* Judge Kirkham sitting as a judge of the Chancery Division. This part of the decision was clearly *obiter*.

[143] See *supra*, para. 10–75.

[144] See the Limitation Act 1980, s.32(1)(a), as amended.

[145] See *infra*, paras 23–111 *et seq.*

[146] *Gopala Chetty v. Vayaraghavachariar* [1922] 1 A.C. 488, 494 *et seq.*

[147] *ibid.* p. 496. See further *Marshall v. Bullock*, March 27, 1998 (unreported), noted *supra*, para. 23–36.

[148] Limitation Act 1980, s.32(1), as amended by the Consumer Protection Act 1987, Sched. 1, para. 5(a). The deliberate commission of a breach of duty in circumstances in which it is unlikely to be discovered for some time amounts to deliberate concealment for this purpose: *ibid.* s.32(2). For this purpose "breach of duty" will be given a wide meaning and will not only include any breach of duty in a contractual or tortious sense, but also any act involving wrongdoing, *e.g.* entering into a transaction at an undervalue within the meaning of the Insolvency Act 1986, s.423: *Giles v. Rhind (No. 2)* [2009] Ch. 191 (CA). An intentional act, such as the giving of negligent advice, will be regarded as deliberate: *Brocklesby v. Armitage & Guest* [2001] 1 All E.R. 172 (CA); *Liverpool Roman Catholic Archdiocese Trustees Inc v. Goldberg* [2001] 1 All E.R. 182; *Cave v. Robinson Jarvis & Rolf* [2001] Lloyd's Rep. P.N. 290.

suspicions aroused.[149] In such cases, the court will demonstrate a willingness to interfere many years after the event, as demonstrated by *Betjemann v. Betjemann*[150] and *Stainton v. The Carron Co.*,[151] where accounts were directed over a 25 year period.

23-41 *Liabilities arising after accounts settled:* As in the case of receipt of an asset by a partner after accounts have been finally settled following a dissolution,[152] time will only start to run as regards a claim for a contribution in respect of an unanticipated liability which was not reflected in those accounts as from the date on which it arises.[153] However, where there has been no settlement of the accounts, the right to a contribution will fall as soon as the right to an account becomes time barred.[154]

23-42 *Part payment:* A part payment will result in the accrual of a fresh cause of action, but only if it is made in respect of the relevant debt or liquidated pecuniary claim by the partner or his agent.[155] Thus, in *Whitley v. Lowe*,[156] a payment was made by a receiver to the personal representatives of a deceased partner, A, with the approval of the surviving partner and the personal representatives of the other deceased partner, B. Although it was estimated that B's estate was then indebted to A's estate, the payment was held not to have been made in recognition of that indebtedness, so that time continued to run.[157] Given that most claims as between partners *will* require the taking of an account,[158] the scope for a part payment to avoid a limitation defence arising will be minimal.[159]

23-43 *Trusts and fiduciary relationships:* It has been held that there is limited scope for a limitation defence in the case of a claim for an account based on a true fiduciary relationship,[160] but this does not in any way affect the authority of the decision

---

[149] See *Rawlins v. Wickham* (1858) 3 De G. & J. 304; *Betjemann v. Betjemann* [1895] 2 Ch. 474.

[150] [1895] 2 Ch. 474. See *supra*, para. 23–33.

[151] (1857) 24 Beav. 346. See also *Wedderburn v. Wedderburn* (1838) 4 Myl. & Cr. 41; *Allfrey v. Allfrey* (1849) 1 Mac. & G. 87. And see *infra*, para. 26–36.

[152] See *supra*, para. 23–39.

[153] This proposition was accepted by the Court of Appeal in *Marshall v. Bullock*, March 27, 1998 (unreported), noted *supra*, para. 23–36.

[154] *Marshall v. Bullock, supra*.

[155] Limitation Act 1980, s.29(5).

[156] (1858) 2 De. G. & J. 704.

[157] Sir John Romilly M.R. in fact based his decision on the fact that the receiver could not have been acting as the agent of B's personal representatives: see (1858) 25 Beav. 421, 431. This aspect was not highlighted in the Court of Appeal.

[158] See *infra*, para. 23–76.

[159] Examples of the exceptional cases in which an account is *not* required as between partners are noted *supra*, paras 23–39, 23–41 and *infra*, para. 23–76.

[160] See *Att.-Gen. v. Cocke* [1988] Ch. 414, 421 *per* Harman J. See also *Pearse v. Green* (1819) 1 J. & W. 135; *Re Landi* [1939] Ch. 828; *Tito v. Waddell (No. 2)* [1977] Ch. 106, 250–251 *per* Megarry V.-C.; however, the decision in *Nelson v. Rye* [1996] 1 W.L.R. 1378 went too far: see *Paragon Finance plc v. Thakerar & Co.* [1999] 1 All E.R. 400 (CA); *Coulthard v. Disco Mix Club Ltd.* [2000] 1 W.L.R. 707; *Cia de Seguras Imperio v. Heath (REBX) Ltd.* [2001] 1 W.L.R. 112 (CA); *Clarke v. Malborough Fine Art (London) Ltd.*, The Times, July 5, 2001; *DEG-Deutsche Investitions und Entwicklungsgesellschaft mbH v. Koshy* [2004] 1 B.C.L.C. 131 (CA); *Gwembe Valley Development Co Ltd. v. Koshy (No.3)* [2004] 1 B.C.L.C. 131 (CA); *Halton International Inc (Holdings) SARL v. Guernroy Ltd.* [2006] W.T.L.R. 1241 (CA); *Cattley v. Pollard* [2007] Ch. 353. *cf. John v. James* [1991] F.S.R. 397, 439 *per* Nicholls J.; *Patel v. Shah*, The Times, March 2, 2005.

in *Knox v. Gye*.[161] Be that as it may, where freehold or leasehold land is held on trust for the benefit of a firm,[162] it must follow that an outgoing partner's rights in relation thereto will not be prejudiced as long as he retains an interest under that trust.[163] In addition, no limitation period will apply where the claim against the trustees involves fraud or a fraudulent breach of trust.[164]

Arbitrations

The Limitation Act 1980 applies to arbitrations in the same way as it applies **23–44** to legal proceedings.[165]

5.   ACTIONS FOR SPECIFIC PERFORMANCE

Agreements for partnership: the general rule

It has long been an established rule that the court will not order the specific **23–45** performance of an agreement for partnership. Lord Lindley explained the basis for this rule as follows:

> "If two persons have agreed to enter into partnership, and one of them refuses to abide by the agreement, the remedy for the other is an action for damages, and not, excepting in the cases to be presently noticed, for specific performance. To compel an unwilling person to become a partner with another would not be conducive to the welfare of the latter, any more than to compel a man to marry a woman he did not like would be for the benefit of the lady. Moreover, to decree specific performance of an agreement for a partnership at will would be nugatory, inasmuch as it might be dissolved the moment after the decree was made[166]; and to decree specific perform- ance of an agreement for a partnership for a term of years would involve the court in the superintendence of the partnership throughout the whole continuance of the

---

[161] (1872) L.R. 5 H.L. 656 (noted *supra*, para. 23–34): see *Coulthard v. Disco Mix Club Ltd., supra.*; *Cia de Seguras Imperio v. Heath (REBX) Ltd., supra*; also *Paragon Finance plc v. Thakerar & Co., supra.* Although partnership clearly *does* involve a fiduciary relationship (see *supra*, para. 16–04), in *Coulthard v. Disco Mix Club Ltd., supra,* the partnership claim was regarded as wholly separate from the claim based on fiduciary duty: see *ibid.* p. 725H *per* Jules Sher Q.C. sitting as a deputy judge of the Chancery Division.

[162] This will include any type of trust of land within the meaning of the Trusts of Land and Appointment of Trustees Act 1996, s.1. Also *supra*, paras 18–61 *et seq.*, 19–14 *et seq.*

[163] *Quaere*, could this principle be extended to *any* case involving an asset held by a former partner in respect of which he is bound to account to the firm, *e.g.* under the Partnership Act 1890, s.29? It is tentatively thought not: see *supra*, para. 23–33, n. 122.

[164] Limitation Act 1980, s.21(1). Note also *ibid.* s.21(2). And see *Cattley v. Pollard* [2007] Ch. 353.

[165] Arbitration Act 1996, s.13(1).

[166] Note that in *Cuffe v. Murtagh* (1881) 7 Ir. L.R. 411, a deceased partner had the right to nominate a successor to take his place in the partnership. It was held that this right continued to subsist when the partnership became at will and that it did not necessarily follow that an order of specific performance in such a case would be futile: *ibid.* p. 422 *per* Chatterton V.-C. The views expressed were, however, strictly *obiter.*

term.[167] As a rule, therefore, courts will not decree specific performance of an agreement for a partnership.[168] Nor will specific performance be decreed of an agreement to become a partner and bring in a certain amount of capital, or in default to lend a sum of money to the plaintiff."[169]

This is still the position.[170] Although it might be thought that this principle would preclude the grant of injunctive relief in the case of the wrongful exclusion of a partner, it is clear from the authorities that it does not.[171]

Exceptions to the general rule

23–46 There are two recognised exceptions to the general rule, although these are, on a true analysis, more apparent than real.

(1) Execution of formal agreement

Whilst the court will not be prepared to force a person into partnership against his will, once he has become a partner, it will readily order him to execute a formal agreement setting out the terms of the partnership, if that was what the parties intended. In such a case, it does not matter that the execution of the agreement will, in effect, alter the partners' rights. Lord Lindley put it in this way:

" . . . if the parties have agreed to execute some formal instrument which would have the effect of conferring rights which do not exist so long as the agreement is not carried out, in such a case, and for the purpose of putting the parties into the position agreed upon, the execution of that formal instrument may be decreed, although the

[167] *Quaere* to what extent this particular objection to a decree of specific performance still holds good. See *Shiloh Spinners Ltd. v. Harding* [1973] A.C. 691, 724 *per* Lord Wilberforce; *Tito v. Waddell (No. 2)* [1977] Ch. 106, 321–323 *per* Megarry V.-C.; *Gravesham Borough Council v. British Railways Board* [1978] Ch. 379, 404 *per* Slade J.; *Co-operative Insurance Society Ltd. v. Argyll Stores (Holdings) Ltd.* [1998] A.C. 1, 11–16; *Rainbow Estates Ltd. v. Tokenhold Ltd.* [1999] Ch. 64. *cf.* the position in Scotland: *Highland and Universal Properties Ltd. v. Safeway Properties Ltd.* 2000 S.C. 297. See also *infra*, n. 170.

[168] *Hercy v. Birch* (1804) 9 Ves.Jr. 357; *Downs v. Collins* (1848) 6 Hare 418; *Sheffield Gas Consumers' Co. v. Harrison* (1853) 17 Beav. 294; *Scott v. Rayment* (1868) L.R. 7 Eq. 112. Note also *Vivers v. Tuck* (1863) 1 Moo.(N.S.) 516 (an exceptional case, in which the claimant had drawn up the agreement but the defendant did not understand its contents).

[169] *Sichel v. Mosenthal* (1862) 30 Beav. 371.

[170] One of the more "recent" reaffirmations of this principle is to be found in *Byrne v. Reid* [1902] 2 Ch. 735, 743 *per* Stirling L.J., although it was seemingly acknowledged in passing by Lindsay J. in *Voaden v. Voaden*, February 21, 1997 (unreported), noted, *infra*, paras 23–68, 23–139; also *Blundon v. Storm* (1971) 20 D.L.R. (3d) 413, 421; *Lauritzencool AB v. Lady Navigation Inc* [2005] 1 W.L.R. 3686 (CA), which concerned the grant of negative injunctive relief. Note also *Akai Holdings Ltd. v. RSM Robson Rhodes LLP* [2007] EWHC 1641 (Ch) (Lawtel 8/8/07), where the court injuncted a merger otherwise than on certain undertakings, thereby potentially forcing the defendant LLP to continue in practice; *Ferrara Quay Ltd. v. Carillion Construction Ltd.* [2009] B.L.R. 367; *Lauffer v. Barking, Havering and Redbridge University Hospitals NHS Trust* [2010] Med. L.R. 68; *SAB Miller Africa v. East African Breweries* [2010] 1 Lloyd's Rep. 392; *cf. Data Science Ltd. v. Powergen Retail Ltd.* [2006] 2 Lloyd's Rep. 591; *Ericsson AB v. EADS Defence and Security Systems Ltd.* [2010] B.L.R. 131. And see *Fry on Specific Performance* (6th ed.), pp. 699–700; *Snell's Equity* (31st ed.) paras 15–20 *et seq.* Note also the observations of Megarry J. in *C.H. Giles & Co. v. Morris* [1972] 1 W.L.R. 307, regarding the enforcement of contracts involving the performance of personal services; *cf. Provident Financial Group Plc v. Hayward* [1989] I.C.R. 160 (CA); *Warren v. Mendy* [1989] 1 W.L.R. 853 (CA). And see *supra*, n. 167.

[171] See *infra*, para. 23–138.

partnership thereby formed might be immediately dissolved.[172] The principle upon which the Court proceeds in a case of this description, is the same as that which induces it to decree execution of a lease under seal, notwithstanding the term for which the lease was to continue has already expired."[173]

Such an order was made in *England v. Curling*,[174] after the partners had carried on business for some 12 years under what were, in effect, initialled heads of agreement and after one partner (the defendant) had purported to given a notice of dissolution.[175] The value of such an order was also clearly recognised in *Byrne v. Reid*,[176] where one partner had nominated his son to take over a part of his share pursuant to an express power in the agreement but, despite his acceptance of the nomination, the other partner had refused to recognise the son as a partner.[177]

(2) *Account following dissolution*

The court may also, in effect, order the specific performance of an agreement for **23–47** partnership where two or more persons have agreed to share the profits derived from a particular venture and one seeks the payment of his share after the venture has come to an end. Lord Lindley observed:

> "Although the decree giving him the relief he asks may be prefaced by a declaration that the agreement relied upon ought to be specifically performed, this has not the effect of creating a partnership to be carried on by the litigants, but merely serves as a foundation for the decree for an account, which is the substantial part of what is sought and given."

Cases of this type will almost inevitably involve an outright denial of partnership by the defendant(s), as in *Dale v. Hamilton*[178] and *Webster v. Bray*.[179]

Other instances where specific performance granted

A partner may, in an appropriate case, seek an order for specific performance **23–48** or, more usually, an injunction to compel his co-partners to adhere to the terms

---

[172] *Buxton v. Lister* (1746) 3 Atk. 385; and see *Crawshay v. Maule* (1813) 1 Swanst. 495, 513, note; *Stocker v. Wedderburn* (1857) 3 K. & J. 403.

[173] See *Wilkinson v. Torkington* (1837) 2 Y. & C.Ex. 726.

[174] (1844) 8 Beav. 129. See further, as to this case, *Sichel v. Mosenthal* (1862) 30 Beav. 371, 376 *per* Lord Romilly.

[175] The following was the minute of the decree: "The Court doth declare that the agreement for a co-partnership dated, etc., is a binding agreement between the parties thereto, and ought to be specifically performed and carried into execution, and doth order and decree the same accordingly. Refer it to the Master to inquire whether any and what variations have been made in the said agreement, by and with the assent of the several parties thereto since the date thereof. Let the Master settle and approve of a proper deed of co-partnership between the said parties in pursuance of the said agreement, having regard to any variations which he may find to have been made in the said agreement as herein before directed, and let the parties execute it. Continue the injunction against the defendant Curling. Liberty to apply." For the form of the injunction see (1844) 8 Beav. 130.

[176] [1902] 2 Ch. 735. See also *supra*, paras 10–259, 19–61.

[177] In such a case, account would now also have to be taken of the son's rights of enforcement under the Contracts (Rights of Third Parties) Act 1999: see *supra*, paras 10–188, 10–259.

[178] (1846) 5 Hare 369 and (1847) 2 Ph. 266. See further, *supra*, paras 7–05 *et seq.*

[179] (1849) 7 Hare 159. See also *Robinson v. Anderson* (1855) 20 Beav. 98 and 7 De G.M. & G. 239.

of their agreement whilst the partnership is continuing. The principles on which the court will act in such cases is considered later in this chapter.[180]

The enforcement of obligations arising on and following the dissolution of a partnership does not give rise to any questions peculiar to the law of partnership and is not further considered in this work. However, it should be noted that the courts have, by way of specific performance or injunction, enforced (*inter alia*) the following agreements, which are for convenience arranged in alphabetical order.

Annuities: Agreements to pay an annuity to an outgoing partner or his widow.[181]

Books: Agreements as to the custody of partnership books and the provision of copies thereof.[182]

Getting in debts: Agreements that a particular person will get in the partnership debts.[183]

Outgoing partner's share: Agreements that the value of an outgoing or deceased partner's share will be ascertained and/or acquired in a certain way.[184]

Retirement: Agreements by one partner to retire from a firm and to assign his share to his co-partners.[185]

6.   ACTIONS FOR FRAUD AND MISREPRESENTATION

23–49   When considering the remedies available to a partner who has been induced to enter into partnership by fraud or misrepresentation, it is necessary to identify whether the fraud or misrepresentation has been perpetrated by one of the other partners or by a third party. As Lord Lindley explained, in a passage dealing solely with the consequences of fraud:

> "Speaking generally and subject to certain qualifications . . . if the fraud complained of has been committed by the other partner, the person defrauded has the option of affirming or of rescinding the contract into which he has been induced to enter; and whether he affirms it or disaffirms it he is entitled to damages for any loss which he

---

[180] See *infra*, paras 23–135 *et seq.*

[181] *Aubin v. Holt* (1855) 2 K. & J. 66; *Re Flavell* (1833) 25 Ch.D. 89. *cf. Bonville v. Bonville* (1860) 6 Jur. (N.S.) 414, where the terms of the agreement were unclear. See also *supra*, paras 10–187 *et seq.*

[182] *Lingen v. Simpson* (1824) 1 Sim. & St. 600; also *Whittaker v. Howe* (1841) 3 Beav. 383. And see, generally, *supra*, paras 10–72, 22–07 *et seq.*

[183] See *Davis v. Amer* (1854) 3 Drew. 64; *Turner v. Major* (1862) 3 Giff. 442. See also *supra*, para. 10–267.

[184] *Morris v. Kearsley* (1836) 3 Y. & C.Ex. 139; *King v. Chuck* (1853) 17 Beav. 325; *Gibson v. Goldsmid* (1854) 5 De G.M. & G. 757; *Essex v. Essex* (1855) 20 Beav. 442; *Featherstonhaugh v. Turner* (1858) 25 Beav. 382; *Homfray v. Fothergill* (1866) L.R. 1 Eq. 567; *Daw v. Herring* [1892] 1 Ch. 284. *cf. Downs v. Collins* (1848) 6 Hare 418, where enforcement would have been tantamount to specific performance of a contract for a partnership; also *Cooper v. Hood* (1858) 7 W.R. 83, where the agreement was too vague. And see, generally, *supra*, paras 10–150 *et seq.*

[185] *Gray v. Smith* (1889) 43 Ch.D. 208.

may have sustained by reason of the fraud.[186] But if the fraud has been committed by some third person and is not in point of law imputable to the other partner, then the person defrauded has no such option; he cannot rescind the contract: he can only sue those who defrauded him for damages."

The position is, in essence, the same in the case of a negligent or careless (but not wholly innocent) misrepresentation, although damages are not in any event recoverable under the Misrepresentation Act 1967 against a non-contracting party.[187]

This section is, of course, concerned solely with claims as between partners and not as between one partner and a third party.

A.   DAMAGES

Fraud

On the assumption that a partner has in fact been induced to enter into partnership by a false and fraudulent representation made by one of his co-partners,[188] an action in damages will clearly lie in respect of any loss which he may thereby suffer.[189]

23–50

Misrepresentation

Prior to the Misrepresentation Act 1967, damages could in certain circumstances be recovered by a person induced to enter into a contract as a result of a negligent misrepresentation[190] but not, in general, if the misrepresentation was innocent.[191] That Act, in effect, extended the right to damages to *any* case in which a negligent misrepresentation is made by one contracting party to another,

23–51

---

[186] *Archer v. Brown* [1985] Q.B. 401; also *Attwood v. Small* (1838) 6 Cl. & F. 232; *Cruikshank v. McVicar* (1844) 8 Beav. 106; *Pulsford v. Richards* (1853) 17 Beav. 87; *Redgrave v. Hurd* (1881) 20 Ch.D. 1. And see *Beck v. Kantorowicz* (1857) 3 K. & J. 230, and cases of that class. As to the measure of damages, see *Doyle v. Olby (Ironmongers) Ltd.* [1969] 2 Q.B. 158; *Archer v. Brown, supra.*

[187] See *ibid.* s.2(1), (2). See also *supra,* para. 12–94. Note, however, that damages for negligent mis-statement can be obtained against a third party: see *Hedley Byrne & Co. Ltd. v. Heller & Partners* [1964] A.C. 465; *Mutual Life and Citizens' Assurance Co. Ltd. v. Evatt* [1971] A.C. 793; *Esso Petroleum Ltd. v. Mardon* [1976] Q.B. 801. As to the limitations on such a claim, see *Argy Trading Development Co. Ltd. v. Lapid Developments Ltd.* [1977] 1 W.L.R. 444, 459 *et seq. per* Croom-Johnson J.

[188] Lord Lindley summarised the requirements which must be satisfied to sustain an allegation of fraud under the headings: (1) Untruth necessary; (2) Untruth must be material and have been relied upon; and (3) Whether untruth must have been known at the time. This passage has not been retained in the present edition as it raises no considerations peculiar to the law of partnership. The reader is referred to the treatment of this subject in *Chitty on Contracts* (30th ed.), paras 6–042 *et seq.* It should, however, be noted that there may be a (rebuttable) presumption of reliance on a fraudulent misrepresentation: see *County NatWest Bank Ltd. v. Barton* [1999] Lloyd's Rep. Bank. 408.

[189] See *Derry v. Peek* (1889) 14 App.Cas. 337; *Doyle v. Olby (Ironmongers) Ltd.* [1969] 2 Q.B. 158; *Archer v. Brown* [1985] Q.B. 401. *cf. Redgrave v. Hurd* (1881) 20 Ch.D. 1. There is no requirement that the loss should be foreseeable in this case: *Nationwide Building Society v. Dunlop Haywards (DHL) Ltd.* [2009] 2 All E.R. (Comm) 715.

[190] See *Hedley Byrne & Co. Ltd. v. Heller & Partners Ltd.* [1964] A.C. 465; also the cases cited *supra,* para. 23–49, n. 187. And see, generally, *Chitty on Contracts* (30th ed.), paras 6–067 *et seq.*

[191] *Heilbut, Symonds & Co. v. Buckleton* [1913] A.C. 30; *Gilchester Properties Ltd. v. Gomm* [1948] W.N. 71.

provided that damages would have been recoverable if the misrepresentation been made fraudulently.[192] To avoid liability, the party making the misrepresentation must prove that he had reasonable grounds to believe and *did* believe up to the time the contract was made that the facts represented were true. Thus, mere belief in the truth of a representation is not, in itself, sufficient.[193] Where damages are recoverable, they are assessed according to the tortious measure, but on the basis of fraud rather than negligence.[194]

The 1967 Act also empowered the court, in any case where it would be equitable to do so, to award damages in lieu of rescission where a person has been induced to enter into a contract as a result of a negligent *or a wholly innocent* misrepresentation.[195] It is not yet clear whether the tortious, contractual or some other measure of damages applies in such a case.[196]

B.   RESCISSION

Agreements for partnership

23–52   A fraudulent, negligent or innocent misrepresentation made by one prospective partner to another which induces the latter to enter into partnership will give rise to a right of rescission, on normal principles.[197] However, rescission of a partnership contract has long been attended by a number of specific and well recognised consequences, as Lord Lindley made clear, when writing prior to the Partnership Act 1890:

---

[192] Misrepresentation Act 1967, s.2(1). See, generally, *Gosling v. Anderson* [1972] E.G.D. 701; *Watts v. Spence* [1976] Ch. 165; *Howard Marine and Dredging Co. Ltd. v. A. Ogden & Sons (Excavations) Ltd.* [1978] Q.B. 574; *Chesnau v. Interhome Ltd.* (1983) 134 N.L.J. 341; *Sharneyford Supplies Ltd. v. Edge* [1986] Ch. 128; *Naughton v. O'Callaghan* [1990] 3 All E.R. 191; *Cemp Properties (U.K.) Ltd. v. Dentsply Research & Development Corp.* [1991] 34 E.G. 62; *Royscot Trust Ltd. v. Rogerson* [1991] 2 Q.B. 297; also *Garden Neptune Shipping Ltd. v. Occidental Worldwide Investment Corp.* [1990] 1 Lloyd's Rep. 330. Note that the expression "innocent" misrepresentation is used in these cases in a special sense: the 1967 Act did *not* introduce a general right of action in the case of all forms of innocent misrepresentation.

[193] See *Howard Marine and Dredging Co. Ltd. v. A. Ogden & Sons (Excavations) Ltd., supra.*

[194] See *Royscot Trust Ltd. v. Rogerson* [1991] 2 Q.B. 297 (CA); *Smith New Court Securities v. Citibank NA* [1997] A.C. 254; *Avon Insurance plc v. Swire Fraser Ltd.* [2000] 1 All E.R. (Comm.) 573; also the other cases cited *supra*, n. 192.

[195] Misrepresentation Act 1967, s.2(2). As to the meaning of the word "loss" in this subsection, see *UCB Corporate Services Ltd. v. Thomason* [2005] 1 All E.R. (Comm) 601 (CA). Note that it may be the position that damages under this subsection can only be awarded where the right to rescission continues to exist: *Zanzibar v. British Aerospace (Lancaster House) Ltd.* [2000] 1 W.L.R. 2333, declining to follow *Thomas Witter Ltd. v. TBP Industries Ltd.* [1996] 2 All E.R. 573 and the analysis in *Chitty on Contracts* (30th ed.), para. 6–098.

[196] See *Chitty on Contracts* (30th ed.), para. 6–099. Note that, in *Thomas Witter Ltd. v. TBP Industries Ltd., supra*, it was held that the damages recoverable under *ibid.* s.2(2) are likely to be *lower* than those recoverable under *ibid.* s.2(1), because the court must have regard to the nature of the representation.

[197] See *Adam v. Newbigging* (1888) 13 App.Cas. 308; *Redgrave v. Hurd* (1881) 20 Ch.D. 1; and, generally, *Chitty on Contracts* (30th ed.), paras 6–98 *et seq.* There may be a (rebuttable) presumption of reliance in the case of a *fraudulent* misrepresentation: see *County NatWest Bank Ltd. v. Barton* [1999] Lloyd's Rep. Bank. 408. Note also, as to reliance, *Museprime Properties Ltd. v. Adhill Properties Ltd.* [1990] 61 P. & C.R. 111.

"Where a person is induced by the false representations of others to become a partner with them, the Court will rescind the contract of partnership at his instance; and will compel them to repay him whatever he may have paid them, with interest, and to indemnify him against all the debts and liabilities of the partnership, and if the defendants have been guilty of fraud[198] against all claims and demands to which he may have become subject by reason of his having entered into partnership with them, he on the other hand accounting to them for what he may have received since his entry into the concern."[199]

This was the position even where the partner to whom the misrepresentation was made had the means of ascertaining the true facts but did not do so.[200]

Partnership Act 1890, section 41

The same principles are, for the most part, reflected in section 41 of the **23–53** Partnership Act 1890, which provides as follows:

"41. Where a partnership contract is rescinded on the ground of the fraud or misrepresentation of one of the parties thereto, the party entitled to rescind is, without prejudice to any other right, entitled—

(*a*) to a lien on, or right of retention of, the surplus of the partnership assets, after satisfying the partnership liabilities, for any sum of money paid by him for the purchase of a share in the partnership and for any capital contributed by him, and is

(*b*) to stand in the place of the creditors of the firm for any payments made by him in respect of the partnership liabilities, and

(*c*) to be indemnified by the person guilty of the fraud or making the representation against all the debts and liabilities of the firm."[201]

An express indemnity against the partnership debts and obligations is, of course, required because rescission in no way affects a partner's accrued liability to third parties.[202]

Additional rights preserved by the Act

It will be noted that the rights conferred by the section are expressed to be **23–54** "without prejudice to any other right", thus obviously preserving any right to damages which may exist.[203] Indeed, that right may prove more valuable than the

---

[198] The words "if the defendants have been guilty of fraud" were, in the current editor's view inappropriately, omitted in later editions. *cf.* the Partnership Act 1890, s.41(c), *infra*, and the judgments of the Court of Appeal in *Newbigging v. Adam* (1886) 34 Ch.D. 582.

[199] See *Pillans v. Harkness* (1713) Colles. P.C. 442; *Ex p. Broome* (1811) 1 Rose 69; *Hamil v. Stokes* (1817) 4 Price 161; *Stainbank v. Fernley* (1839) 9 Sim. 556; *Rawlins v. Wickham* (1858) 1 Giff. 355 and, on appeal, 3 De G. & J. 304; *Jauncey v. Knowles* (1859) 8 W.R. 69; *Senanayake v. Cheng* [1966] A.C. 63. *Clifford v. Brooke* (1806) 13 Ves.Jr. 131 was not a case of this class.

[200] *Rawlins v. Wickham, supra.*

[201] This paragraph accords with the views expressed regarding the extent of the indemnity in the case of a contract induced by misrepresentation in *Newbigging v. Adam* (1886) 34 Ch.D. 582. This point was, in fact, left open by the House of Lords in *Adam v. Newbigging* (1888) 13 App.Cas. 308.

[202] See *Ex p. Broome* (1811) 1 Rose 69; *Jefferys v. Smith* (1827) 3 Russ 158; *Macbride v. Lindsay* (1852) 9 Hare 574. Also *Howard v. Shaw* (1846) 9 I.L.R. 335; *Henderson v. Royal British Bank* (1857) 7 E. & B. 356; *Daniell v. Royal British Bank* (1857) 1 H. & N. 681; *Powis v. Harding* (1857) 1 C.B. (N.S.) 533; *Reese River Mining Co. v. Smith* (1869) L.R. 4 H.L. 64, 70 *per* Lord Cairns.

[203] See *supra*, paras 23–50, 23–51. And see *Archer v. Brown* [1985] Q.B. 401.

statutory indemnity.[204] However, it would seem that certain other rights, which were established prior to the Act, have also been preserved. Thus, the partner concerned may, in addition to an order for the repayment of the purchase price originally paid for his share and any capital contributed, be entitled to interest on those sums[205] and to a lien on the surplus assets both for such interest and for the costs of the action.[206] Furthermore, he may also be entitled to interest on all payments made by him in respect of partnership debts and liabilities, although he must give credit with interest for any share of profits received whilst he remained a partner.[207]

Dissolution agreements, etc.

23–55   Although not governed by a specific statutory provision in the same way as agreements for partnership, questions of rescission also arise in relation to agreements reached in and about the *termination* of a partnership. This will not only include dissolution agreements properly so called, but also agreements for the voluntary retirement of a partner, agreements entered into prior to a partner's expulsion and agreements with a deceased partner's personal representatives.

No rescission for bad bargain

23–56   It is, perhaps, self evident that the rescission of a dissolution or other agreement cannot be obtained merely because it turns out to be disadvantageous to one or more of the partners. As Lord Lindley explained:

> "Supposing every member of a firm to be *sui juris*, any one may retire upon any terms to which he and his co-partners may choose to assent; and if there is no fraud, misrepresentation, or concealment on either side, all will be bound by any agreement into which he and they may enter, although it may ultimately turn out that a bad bargain has been made."

Thus, in *Knight v. Marjoribanks*,[208] a partner unsuccessfully sought to set aside an agreement, under which he had, in effect, sold his share in the firm to his co-partners in exchange for a modest payment and the release of his indebtedness to the firm, on the grounds of fraud, collusion and inadequacy of consideration. The partnership venture was at the time unprofitable and his partners had stated that a sum in excess of £5,000 was due from him. He never sought to question this statement or to examine the partnership books in order to establish its accuracy, nor did he seek independent advice before concluding the agreement, even though he was then in a financially distressed state. In the absence of any evidence that his co-partners had practised a fraud or otherwise taken unfair advantage of his financial position, the agreement was held to be binding on him.[209]

---

[204] See the judgments in *Newbigging v. Adam* (1886) 34 Ch.D. 582.

[205] *Adam v. Newbigging* (1888) 13 App.Cas. 308, affirming *Newbigging v. Adam, supra.* In this case the claimant had withdrawn part of his capital and the defendants were held jointly and severally liable for the balance with interest at 4%. See also *Pillans v. Harkness* (1713) Colles, P.C. 442; *Rawlins v. Wickham* (1858) 1 Giff. 355 and, on appeal, 3 De G. & J. 304.

[206] *Mycock v. Beatson* (1879) 13 Ch.D. 384. Interest was allowed at 5%.

[207] *Rawlins v. Wickham, supra.*

[208] (1848) 11 Beav. 322 and, on appeal, (1849) 2 Mac. & G. 10.

[209] See also *Ex p. Peake* (1816) 1 Madd. 346; *Ramsbottom v. Parker* (1821) 6 Madd. 5; *Cockle v. Whiting* (1829) Taml. 55; *McLure v. Ripley* (1850) 2 Mac. & G. 274.

Blay v. Pollard and Morris[210] was a somewhat similar case, although rescis- **23–57** sion was not actually sought. There, two partners, P and M, orally agreed to dissolve their partnership on terms that M should take over all the liabilities of the firm incurred after a certain date. Subsequently a written agreement was drawn up by P's father, who was a solicitor, under which M was required to indemnify P against all rent due *before* that date. The agreement was handed to M, who looked through it and signed it, but said he did not understand it. The landlord then brought an action against P and M for such rent. P sought to rely on the indemnity as against M, who in turn argued that he had signed the agreement in the belief that it embodied the terms of the previous oral agreement and that it was drawn up under a mutual mistake of fact. In the absence of any allegation of fraud or misrepresentation, it was held that M was bound by the agreement, since he knew its nature when he signed it and there was no evidence of mutual mistake.

In cases of this type, the dissolution agreement will not only bind the partners but also their respective personal representatives, trustees in bankruptcy or liquidators,[211] save to the extent that it can be set aside under the insolvency legislation or the general law.[212]

Agreements based on false accounts

A dissolution or retirement agreement may, and often will, be rescinded if **23–58** there has been fraud or misrepresentation with regard to the state of the partnership accounts, as Lord Lindley explained:

"Notwithstanding the inability of a retiring partner, and of those claiming under him, to avoid an agreement fairly come to between him and his co-partners,[213] the good faith and open dealing which one partner has a right to expect from another never require to be more scrupulously observed than when one of them is retiring upon terms agreed to upon the strength of representations as to the state of the partnership accounts; and an agreement entered into on a dissolution will be set aside if it can be shown to have been based upon error[214] or to have been tainted by fraud, whether in the shape of positive misrepresentation or of concealment of the truth."

In *Chandler v. Dorsett*,[215] the claimant and the defendant had dissolved their partnership and the defendant drew up an account in a form which made it appear that a balance was due to him from the claimant. The claimant gave the defendant a promissory note for this sum, but later discovered mistakes in the account and commenced proceedings for a fresh account to be taken. The defendant's plea of account stated[216] was not upheld and a new account was ordered.

---

[210] [1930] 1 K.B. 628. See also *Saunders v. Anglia Building Society* [1971] A.C. 1004.

[211] *Ex p. Peake* (1816) 1 Madd. 346; *Ramsbottom v. Parker* (1821) 6 Madd. 5; *Luckie v. Forsyth* (1846) 3 Jo. & LaT. 388.

[212] See *supra*, paras 10–152, 10–153 and *infra*, paras 27–16, 27–37, 27–100 *et seq.* And see the following decisions under the old bankruptcy laws: *Anderson v. Maltby* (1793) 2 Ves.Jr. 244, 254 *per* Lord Loughborough; *Billiter v. Young* (1856) 6 E. & B. 1, 40 *per* Jervis C.J.; *Warden v. Jones* (1857) 23 Beav. 497; *Heilbut v. Nevill* (1870) L.R. 5 C.P. 478.

[213] See *supra*, para. 23–56.

[214] This expression seemingly comprehends any non-fraudulent misrepresentation, as well as a mutual mistake of fact.

[215] (1679) Finch 431. See also *Maddeford v. Austwick* (1826) 1 Sim. 89; *Spittal v. Smith* (1829) Taml. 45; *Law v. Law* [1905] 1 Ch. 140.

[216] Or, more properly, a settled account: see *infra*, paras 23–109, 23–110.

Accounts agreed prior to expulsion

23–59   On the same basis, where a partner is induced to sign accounts in ignorance of his impending expulsion, he will not subsequently be bound by those accounts if they affect the nature or quantum of his entitlement as an outgoing partner.[217]

Agreements made with personal representatives of deceased partner

23–60   Special considerations apply where an agreement is reached between the surviving partners and the personal representatives of a deceased partner.

(a) Where Personal Representatives are not Partners

In the simple case, where the personal representatives are not themselves partners, it is clear that any agreement that the deceased's share will be ascertained in a certain way or taken at a certain value cannot be impeached, unless there has been fraud or collusion between them and the surviving partners.[218] Naturally, if such fraud or collusion can be proved, the agreement will be set aside at the instance of any person interested in the deceased partner's estate.[219]

However, it should be noted that, even if the agreement is binding, the personal representatives may still be liable for any loss suffered by the estate, as Lord Lindley pointed out in the following passage:

> " . . . even although there be no fraud or collusion, still if the executor[220] has obtained less than the true value of the deceased's share in the partnership estate, the executor may be liable as for a *devastavit*, although the surviving partner may be protected against all demands. But if, in a case of difficulty, the executor has acted with a bona fide view to do his best for the estate he represents, the Court will not be willing to make him account for what, without his wilful default, he might have received from the surviving partners."[221]

(b) Where Personal Representatives are Partners

23–61   Where the personal representatives are also surviving partners, there will be such a conflict of interest and duty that, in Lord Lindley's words, it will be "almost

---

[217] See *Blisset v. Daniel* (1853) 10 Hare 493. The expulsion was, of course, held to be wrongful in this case: see further, *supra*, para. 10–124.

[218] See the Trustee Act 1925, s.15 (as amended by the Trustee Act 2000, Sched. 2, para. 20). At this point, Lord Lindley explained that "although it has been said that the creditors, or other persons interested in the estate of the deceased, may impeach such an agreement by instituting proceedings against the surviving partners and the executors of the deceased, [*See Bowsher v. Watkins (1830) 1 R. & M. 277; Gedge v. Traill (1823) 1 R. & M. 281*] still agreements of the kind in question cannot be successfully impeached, unless there has been some fraud or collusion between them and the executors". He then quoted from the judgment of Lord Langdale in *Davies v. Davies* (1837) 2 Keen 534, 539. See also *Chambers v. Howell* (1847) 11 Beav. 6; *Stainton v. The Carron Co.* (1853) 18 Beav. 146; *Smith v. Everett* (1859) 27 Beav. 446.

[219] See *Cook v. Collingridge* (1823) Jac. 607; *Rice v. Gordon* (1848) 11 Beav. 265; also *Beningfield v. Baxter* (1886) 12 App.Cas. 167. Lord Lindley added in a somewhat elliptical footnote at this point: "Less than fraud or collusion will justify an action against an executor of a deceased partner and the surviving partners, *Travis v. Milne* (1851) 9 Hare 141, but will not, it is apprehended, invalidate arrangements into which they may have entered for payment of the share of the deceased." *Quaere*, is this correct? If the agreement amounts to a breach of trust in which the surviving partners are implicated, it seems unlikely that it would be upheld by the court. And see also, as to bringing actions against surviving partners, *infra*, para. 26–42.

[220] An administrator will be in the same position.

[221] See *Rowley v. Adams* (1844) 7 Beav. 395 and (1849) 2 H.L.C. 725. And note also the Trustee Act 1925, s.61.

impossible for [*them*] to enter into any arrangement with respect to the share of the deceased in the partnership estate which those interested in that share may not afterwards succeed in setting aside".[222] This is a principle of general application,[223] although in the decided cases some other ground for setting aside the arrangement has usually been found.

Thus, in *Wedderburn v. Wedderburn*,[224] where an account of a deceased partner's estate was directed 30 years after the date of his death, despite a number of changes in the firm and the execution of partial releases by the beneficiaries, it appears that the releases were executed in ignorance of the true state of the partnership accounts. In *Stocken v. Dawson*,[225] the surviving partner was one of the deceased's executors and purported to purchase his share at a valuation pursuant to an express power in the will. It appears that the valuation was not a proper one and the sale was set aside seven years later on the application of the deceased's son.

Acquisition of share pursuant to partnership agreement

These difficulties will not, however, arise where surviving partners who are **23–62** also the deceased partner's personal representatives acquire his share pursuant to an express term of the partnership agreement.[226] In such a case, it will not be possible to impugn the acquisition, unless any impropriety on the part of those partners can be proved.[227] If the agreement requires the deceased partner's share to be valued, but some error is made in the valuation, this will not, in general, affect the surviving partners' right to acquire the share, although the error will, in an appropriate case, be corrected by the court.[228] Equally, an honest and fair valuation prepared substantially in accordance with the terms of the agreement, which has stood unimpeached for many years, will not be upset save, perhaps, where it is clearly proved to be erroneous.[229] It has already been seen that a valuation carried out by an agreed expert valuer cannot normally be challenged.[230]

Position where one executor is not a partner

If at least one of the deceased partner's executors is not himself a member of **23–63** the firm, he will have power to settle any claim which the other executor(s) may have against the estate.[231] This will obviously facilitate any arrangement in relation to the deceased's share.

Right of retainer out of assets

It should be noted that, despite the conflict of interest previously referred to, **23–64** a surviving partner who was the executor of his deceased co-partner was formerly entitled to retain out of the estate any sum found to be due from the

---

[222] See *Cook v. Collingridge* (1822) Jac. 607.
[223] See *ibid.* at p. 621 *per* Lord Eldon.
[224] (1838) 2 Myl. & Cr. 41. See also *infra*, para. 26–36. *Millar v. Craig* (1843) 6 Beav. 433 was a somewhat similar case, although no question was raised as against the partners who were not executors.
[225] (1848) 17 L.J.Ch. 282. Note also *Rice v. Gordon* (1848) 11 Beav. 265.
[226] See generally, as to such provisions, *supra*, paras 10–150 *et seq.*
[227] As in *Stocken v. Dawson, supra*, para. 23–61.
[228] *Vyse v. Foster* (1874) L.R. 7 H.L. 318; *Hordern v. Hordern* [1910] A.C. 465.
[229] *Hordern v. Hordern, supra*, at pp. 475–476.
[230] See *supra*, para. 10–175.
[231] *Re Houghton* [1904] 1 Ch. 622. *Semble* an administrator has the same power.

deceased to the firm or to himself on taking the partnership accounts,[232] but this right was later abolished.[233]

Loss of right to rescind

23–65   Where a right to rescind exists, it can, on normal principles, be lost: (1) by laches, acquiescence or affirmation or (2) if *restitutio in integrum* is impossible. Moreover, in the case of an innocent or negligent misrepresentation, the court may, if it considers it equitable to do so, refuse to rescind the contract and award damages in lieu.[234]

Laches, acquiescence and affirmation

23–66   A partner entitled to rescind a contract for fraud or misrepresentation will lose that right if he does not exercise that right within a reasonable time after discovering the true facts[235]; *a fortiori*, if he then affirms the contract or otherwise does anything which is inconsistent with his right to rescind.[236]

Thus, in *Law v. Law*,[237] a partner sold his share to his co-partner and later discovered that material information had been withheld from him. Notwithstanding his belief that further material facts had been concealed, he agreed to a modification of the terms on which the share had been sold without insisting on a full disclosure. It was held that he could not, on discovering the full extent of the concealment, repudiate the sale. Similarly, in *Lindsley v. Woodfull*[238] two partners affirmed the retirement of a third at a time when they were aware of his previous misrepresentation, and thereby lost their right to an account of *future* profits resulting from his breaches of fiduciary duty prior to his retirement. Their right to an account of past profits had, however, been expressly reserved and was not affected.

Restitution impossible

23–67   A partner who seeks rescission must, in general, be in a position to ensure that *restitutio in integrum* is possible, unless his inability to do so can be attributed to the partner(s) responsible for the fraud or misrepresentation.[239] The fact that the

---

[232] *Morris v. Morris* (1874) L.R. 10 Ch.App. 68. In this case, the accounts were still unsettled.

[233] Administration of Estates Act 1971, s.10(1).

[234] Misrepresentation Act 1967, s.2(2). See also *supra*, para. 23–51.

[235] See, generally, *Clough v. L. & N.W. Ry.* (1871) L.R. 7 Ex. 26, 35 *per* Mellor J. Note, however, that it is not enough to prove that the partner seeking rescission has for some time had the *means* to discover the true facts: *Rawlins v. Wickham* (1858) 3 De. G. & J. 304; *Betjemann v. Betjemann* [1895] 2 Ch. 474. And see, for examples of cases in which the right was purportedly exercised too late, *Ashley's case* (1870) L.R. 9 Eq. 263; *Scholey v. Central Ry. of Venezuela* (1868) L.R. 9 Eq. 266, note. *cf. Campbell v. Fleming* (1834) 1 A. & E. 40; *Macneill's case* (1868) L.R. 10 Eq. 503. See also *supra*, paras 23–19 *et seq.*

[236] See *Senanayake v. Cheng* [1966] A.C. 63; also *Ex p. Briggs* (1866) L.R. 1 Eq. 483; *Sharpley v. Louth and East Coast Ry.* (1876) 2 Ch.D. 663; *Abram Steamship Co. v. Westville Shipping Co.* [1923] A.C. 773, 779 per Lord Dunedin, 787 *et seq.* per Lord Atkinson. And see *Chitty on Contracts* (30th ed.), paras 6–123 *et seq.*

[237] [1905] 1 Ch. 140.

[238] [2004] 2 B.C.L.C. 131 (CA).

[239] See *Urquhart v. McPherson* (1878) 3 App.Cas. 831, which concerned a deed of dissolution and release. Also *Maturin v. Tredinnick* (1863) 2 N.R. 514 and (1864) 4 N.R. 15; *Laing v. Campbell* (1865) 36 Beav. 3; *Phosphate Sewage Co. v. Hartmont* (1876) 5 Ch.D. 394; *Erlanger v. New Sombrero Phosphate Co.* (1878) 3 App.Cas. 1218; *Lagunas Nitrate Co. v. Lagunas Syndicate* [1899] 2 Ch. 392; *Armstrong v. Jackson* [1917] 2 K.B. 822, 828 *et seq. per* McCardie J; *Abram Steamship Co. v. Westville Shipping Co.* [1923] A.C. 773.

share acquired has become worthless will not prevent rescission,[240] but the incorporation of the partnership will.[241]

Reconstituting a partnership by rescission

A more debatable question is whether an order for rescission could ever have **23–68** the effect of *reconstituting* the partnership relation between former partners, *e.g.* following the rescission of a retirement or dissolution agreement. In the current editor's view, rescission in such circumstances would be tantamount to an order for specific performance of a contract of partnership, something which the court will, as a general rule, not entertain.[242] Lindsay J. went some way towards recognising this difficulty in *Voaden v. Voaden*,[243] where the retirement agreement provided for an abridgement of the notice period required under the partnership deed. In the event, injunctive relief was granted in terms which, to an extent, replicated the effects of the defendant being reinstated as a partner, but which at the same time left him free to accept paid employment elsewhere.[244] It should also be noted that an attempt to reconstitute a joint venture agreement by rescission failed in *Huyton SA v. Distribuidora Internacional de Productos Agricolas SA*.[245]

7.   RELIEF COMMONLY SOUGHT BETWEEN PARTNERS

In this section there will be considered those forms of relief most commonly **23–69** sought between partners, namely:

A. Accounts, inquiries and production of documents etc.

B. Injunctions.

C. Receivers.

D. Orders for the sale of partnership property.

E. Declarations and ancillary relief.

---

[240] *Adam v. Newbigging* (1888) 13 App.Cas. 308.
[241] *Clarke v. Dickson* (1858) E.B. & E. 148.
[242] See *supra*, paras 23–45 *et seq.*
[243] February 21, 1997 (unreported). Equally, Lindsay J. did not appear to be deterred by the fact that there had been minor changes in the firm since the date of the defendant's early retirement.
[244] The corollary of the injunction granted was that the claimants were required to undertake to pay the defendant an amount equal to what he would have been entitled to draw as a partner over the original notice period, after giving credit for his earnings derived from employment during that period. See further, as to this case, *infra*, para. 23–139.
[245] [2004] 1 All E.R. (Comm) 402 (CA) at [5]. Note, however, that in *Roberts v. West Coast Trains Ltd.* [2004] I.R.L.R. 788 (CA), it was held that an employment contract could be reconstituted following a dismissal, albeit pursuant to an internal appeals procedure. *cf. Crystal Palace FC (2000) Ltd. v. Dowie* [2007] I.R.L.R. 682, where reconstitution of the employment contract was, on the facts, held to be impossible.

As will be seen hereafter, cases in which such relief is sought whilst the partnership is continuing are comparatively rare, but nevertheless require special consideration, given the traditional reluctance of the courts to interfere between partners otherwise than with a view to dissolution.[246] It follows that, in the case of a dissolution action, such relief will tend to be more routinely awarded.

Jurisdiction in partnership actions

23–70   A dissolution action should, in general, be commenced in the Chancery Division of the High Court[247] or in a county court.[248] Although the county court technically has jurisdiction only in cases in which in the value of the partnership assets does not exceed £30,000,[249] the High Court can order a transfer to the county court[250] or to a district registry[251] in an appropriate case. It was formerly the practice that a transfer to a county court would only be regarded as appropriate if the partnership assets were worth less than £50,000, unless the issues raised were of such complexity that a continuation of the case in the High Court was warranted,[252] but the court's discretion is now unrestricted in this respect, so that a transfer may be appropriate where the value of the assets exceeds £50,000.[253] In such a case, the transfer will generally be to the Central London County Court (Chancery List), unless the parties express a preference for some other county court.[254] Equally, where the value of the partnership assets is significant, or if the action raises complex factual or legal issues, the proceedings should properly be started in the Chancery Division.[255] Proceedings commenced in the county court can be transferred to the High Court as required.[256]

In the case of a husband and wife partnership, if the dissolution coincides with the breakdown of the marriage, it may be appropriate that the proceedings should

---

[246] See *supra*, para. 23–16.

[247] See, as to the jurisdiction of the Chancery Division, the Senior Courts Act 1981, s.61(1), Sched. 1, para. 1(f) (formerly the Supreme Court Act 1981: Constitutional Reform Act 2005, Sched. 11, Pt 1, para. 1(1)). It should be noted that the assignment of partnership actions to the Chancery Division is not a mere matter of administrative convenience: see *Cayzer v. Beddow* [2007] EWCA Civ. 644 (Lawtel 29/6/07) at [16].

[248] See, generally, CPR 7APD, para. 2. In the county court the claim form should be marked "Chancery Business": *ibid*. para. 2.5. See further *infra*, paras 24–53 *et seq*.

[249] County Courts Act 1984, s.23(f); County Courts Jurisdiction Order 1981 (SI 1981/1123); and see *Cowan v. Wakeling* [2008] EWCA Civ 229 (Lawtel 25/2/08) at [25]. Note, however, that the county court's jurisdiction can, in any event, be enlarged by agreement between the parties: County Courts Act 1984, s.24 (as amended). Although the Lord Chancellor has a wide power to make orders under the Courts and Legal Services Act 1990, s.1 (as amended), the position set out in the text is unaffected by the High Court and County Courts Jurisdiction Order 1991 (SI 1991/724) made pursuant thereto.

[250] County Courts Act 1984, s.40(2) (as substituted by the Courts and Legal Services Act 1990, s.2(1)); CPR r. 30.3(1)(a), (2). The fact that the claim technically falls outside the jurisdiction of the county court does not matter: *National Westminster Bank plc v. King* [2008] Ch. 385.

[251] CPR r. 30.2(4)(a). Equally, an action may be transferred between district registries or from a district registry to the High Court: *ibid*. r. 30.2(4)(b).

[252] *ibid*. r. 30.3(1)(a), (2) and the former Chancery Guide, para. 13.8. This paragraph has, however, been removed from the current version.

[253] Chancery Guide, para. 13.10. See also *National Westminster Bank plc v. King, supra*.

[254] Chancery Guide, para. 13.6.

[255] CPR 7APD, para. 2.4.

[256] County Courts Act 1984, s.41(1), 42(1) (as substituted by the Courts and Legal Services Act 1990, s.2(3)); also CPR r. 30.3(1)(a), (2). And note the decision in *Cayzer v. Beddow, supra*.

be commenced (or continue)[257] in the Family Division rather than in the Chancery Division.[258] Similarly in the case of a partnership between civil partners.

Proceedings for an account or other relief as between partners should also be brought in the Chancery Division or the county court as appropriate,[259] although it is by no means uncommon to find injunctive relief being sought in the Queen's Bench Division.[260] Where the proceedings are brought in the county court, they may be transferred to another county court with Chancery expertise.[261]

Dissolution actions

In practice, the majority of proceedings between partners will involve the dissolution of their firm, so that it is desirable to outline the nature of a dissolution action as a prelude to what follows.   **23–71**

Form and content of proceedings

A dissolution action will normally be commenced by a Part 7 claim form,[262] although a Part 8 claim form may be used if there is unlikely to be any real dispute of fact.[263]

If the partnership is still subsisting when the proceedings are commenced, the relief sought will invariably comprise an order for dissolution of the partnership, an order that its affairs be wound up and all necessary consequential accounts, directions and inquiries. Where necessary, there may be added a claim for the appointment of a receiver/manager[264] and an injunction to restrain the defendants

---

[257] See CPR r. 30.5(1). But note that a transfer was refused in *Matz v. Matz* (1984) 14 Fam. Law 178. *Quaere*, would a similar approach be adopted under the CPR? Much is likely to depend on the court's view of the case, having regard to the overriding objectives in *ibid.* r. 1.1. See also *infra*, para. 24–54.

[258] See *Williams v. Williams* [1976] Ch. 278; also *Bothe v. Amos* [1976] Fam. 46; *Bernard v. Josephs* [1982] Ch. 391; *White v. White* [1999] Fam. 304.

[259] Note that the taking of partnership accounts is expressly referred to in the Senior Courts Act 1981, Sched. 1, para. 1(f) (formerly the Supreme Court Act 1981: Constitutional Reform Act 2005, Sched. 11, Pt 1, para. 1(1)), but *not* in the County Courts Act 1984, s.23(f). It follows that the county court's jurisdiction will, in other cases, be dependent on establishing a claim within the county court's jurisdiction upon which the right to an account is based: County Courts Act 1984, ss.15, 65(1)(b). Ultimately, however, the choice of court is likely to be governed by the same criteria as discussed in relation to dissolution actions. It will, of course, be rare for a pure money claim to be brought as between partners: see *infra*, para. 23–76.

[260] As to transfers between the Divisions of the High Court, see the Senior Courts Act 1981, ss.61(6), 65; CPR r. 30.5(1). The discretion is a wide one and will be exercised pragmatically: *NATL Amusements (UK) Ltd. v. White City (Shepherds Bush) Limited Partnership* [2010] 1 W.L.R. 1181 (CA), where various authorities are reviewed. Note, however, that the strict approach adopted by Harman J. in *Apac Rowena Ltd. v. Norpol Packaging Ltd.* [1991] 4 All E.R. 516, 518 (a copyright case) was, to an extent, endorsed by the Court of Appeal in *Elvee Ltd. v. Taylor, The Times,* December 18, 2001 (CA) (another copyright case). It may also be of some significance that Lord Millett observed in *Hurst v. Bryk* [2002] 1 A.C.185, 194 that "[o]nly the Court of Chancery was equipped with the machinery necessary to enable [*an*] account to be taken . . . ".

[261] CPR rr. 30.2(1), 30.3(1)(b). See also (2004) 101 L.S.Gaz., October 14, p. 37.

[262] See the CPR rr. 7.2, 7.4; *ibid.* 7APD, paras 3 *et seq.*; Practice Form N1.

[263] See CPR rr. 8.1, 8.2; *ibid.* 8PD para. 3.1; Practice Form N208; see also *ibid.* 7APD, paras 3.1, 3.3. As to the evidence in support a Part 8 claim form, see *ibid.* 8PD, para. 7.

[264] It should not be assumed that the appointment of a receiver will always be appropriate: see *infra*, para. 23–153.

from dealing with the partnership assets.[265] In the case of a partnership at will, the service of the claim form will itself work a dissolution.[266]

23–72   If, on the other hand, the partnership has already been dissolved before the commencement of proceedings, the claimant should seek a declaration to that effect in lieu of an order for dissolution.[267]

There is no objection to proceedings in which rescission of the partnership contract and dissolution are sought as alternative remedies.[268]

If neither the existence of the partnership nor the claimant's right to dissolve is contested, summary judgment may be obtained[269] or, more usually, an application can be made for an order by consent.[270]

The grounds on which a dissolution order may be made if the action is defended are outlined later in this work.[271]

Insolvent partnerships

23–73   The procedure for winding up an insolvent partnership as an unregistered company, with or without concurrent petitions being presented against one or more of the partners, is considered later in this work.[272]

A.   ACCOUNTS, INQUIRIES AND PRODUCTION OF DOCUMENTS

23–74   This subject can most conveniently be considered under three headings, namely:

(a) The right to an account, inquiries and production of documents.

(b) The defences to an action for an account, inquiries and production of documents.

(c) The order for a partnership account.

(a) The right to an account, inquiries and production of documents

(1) Accounts and inquiries

23–75   Lord Lindley wrote:

> "The right of every partner to have an account from his co-partners of their dealings and transactions is too obvious to require comment."

---

[265] Lord Lindley also referred to the need for an injunction to restrain the partners from issuing bills of exchange or promissory notes in the name of the firm, but such an order is, in practice, rarely sought.

[266] See *infra*, para. 24–28. And see *Master v. Kirton* (1796) 3 Ves.Jr. 74.

[267] The precise date on which the partnership was dissolved will, of course, depend on the circumstances: see generally, *infra*, paras 24–15 *et seq.*

[268] *Bagot v. Easton* (1877) 7 Ch.D. 1.

[269] CPR Pt 24. Equally, where a claim is admitted in writing, judgment may be obtained under *ibid.* r. 14.3. In either case, the fact that the *terms* of the partnership are in dispute will not necessarily prevent an immediate order for dissolution (see *Thorp v. Holdsworth* (1876) 3 Ch.D. 637), particularly given the overriding objective in CPR r. 1.1.

[270] *ibid.* r. 40.6(1), (5). Note that all the parties need not apply (*ibid.* r. 40.6(5)) and the application *may* be dealt with without a hearing (*ibid.* r. 40.6(6)).

[271] See *infra*, paras 24–62 *et seq.*

[272] See *infra*, paras 24–49, 24–50, 27–04 *et seq.*

That right is now enshrined in the Partnership Act 1890.[273] It follows that an action for an account will in almost all cases be maintainable by a partner,[274] even where he has himself destroyed some of the firm's books of account, made false entries in the accounts, and otherwise misconducted himself in relation to the partnership business.[275] The court may, in practice, be reluctant to infer that a partner has been deprived of his right to an account when he has had no opportunity to object to a set of accounts produced by, or on the instructions of, another partner.[276] Where, on the other hand, he has had an opportunity to object to such a set of accounts but has, for whatever reason, raised no substantial objections thereto, the court is unlikely to order the whole account to be taken again.[277] It is simply not possible to "cherry pick" one or more elements of a partner's entitlement with a view to avoiding the need for an account.[278]

Account normally required between partners

It is a well recognised rule[279] that, whenever money allegedly belonging or owing to the firm in respect of a partnership transaction is sought to be recovered from a partner, an action for an account is required,[280] unless an account has already been taken between the partners[281] or, exceptionally, taking an account

23–76

---

[273] See *ibid.* s.28, *infra*, para. A1–29 and *Winning v. Cunningham* 2009 GWD 01–19 (Sh.Ct.). And see *supra*, paras 16–01 *et seq.*, 22–10.

[274] Lord Lindley pointed out that "an action for an account may be maintained by partners although the partnership accounts are not complicated [*Cruikshank v. McVicar (1844) 8 Beav. 106; also Frietas v. Dos Santos (1827) 1 Y. & J. 574*]; and although an action for damages may be sustainable [*Wright v. Hunter (1801) 5 Ves.Jr. 792; Blain v. Agar (1826) 1 Sim. 37 and (1828) 2 Sim. 289; also Townsend v. Ash (1745) 3 Atk. 336*]; and although the defendant may have stolen or embezzled the money of the firm [*Roope v. D'Avigdor (1883) 10 Q.B.D. 412*]." In the latter case, no prosecution had been brought against the partner concerned. It is immaterial that the defendant and the books and documents relied on are abroad: *International Corporation v. Besser Manufacturing Co.* [1950] 1 K.B. 488. Equally, there will be no such right to an account where the partnership relationship has been superseded by some other relationship: see *Ness Training Ltd. v. Triage Central Ltd.* 2002 S.L.T. 675 (OH).

[275] *Ram Singh v. Ram Chand* (1923) L.R. 51 Ind.App. 154.

[276] See, for example, *Wylie v. Corrigan* 1999 S.C. 97; *Hammonds (A Firm) v. Jones*, The Times, January 4, 2010. See also *supra*, paras 10–75, 10–76 and *infra*, paras 23–111 *et seq.*, as to reopening settled accounts.

[277] See *Hurst v. Bryk* [1999] Ch. 1, 15–16. This point did not arise on the appeal: see [2002] 1 A.C. 185 (HL).

[278] See *Green v. Moran* 2002 S.L.T. 1404 (OH) and the other cases noticed *supra*, para. 19–06.

[279] This sentence was cited with approval by the Court of Appeal in *Marshall v. Bullock*, March 27, 1998 (CA, unreported), noted *supra*, para. 23–36.

[280] *Meyer & Co. v. Faber (No. 2)* [1923] 2 Ch. 421, 439 *per* Warrington L.J.; *Gopala Chetty v. Vayaraghavachariar* [1922] 1 A.C. 488; *Green v. Hertzog* [1954] 1 W.L.R. 1309; *Marshall v. Bullock, supra; Hurst v. Bryk* [2002] 1 A.C. 185, 194 (HL); *Cowan v. Wakeling* [2008] EWCA Civ 229 (Lawtel 25/2/08) at [24], [25]. Note that acceptance by a partner of an obligation to account as a contractual term does not convert it into a debt: *Lyons Laing v. Land* 2001 S.L.T. 1246 (Note) (Ex. Div.).

[281] In *Carter v. Harold Simpson Associates (Architects) Ltd.* [2005] 1 W.L.R. 919 (PC) the financial position between the partners had been determined by an arbitration award which was then remitted to the arbitrator for amendment. Since the award continued to have legal effect, the need for an account was not resurrected. And see *Duncan v. The MFV Marigold PD145* 2006 S.L.T. 975 (OH) at [60] *per* Lord Reed. It should also be noted that, where accounts have been settled as between the partners following a dissolution, there may be no need to take an account if an asset or liability not reflected in those accounts is subsequently identified. In such a case, a direct right of action for a share of the asset/contribution towards the liability may lie, unless the claim is barred by limitation etc., as recognised by the Court of Appeal in *Marshall v. Bullock, supra*.

would serve no useful purpose.[282] In such an action, it will, of course, be open to the defendant partner to show that the money is his or even that a larger sum is due to him. In one case, the court even short circuited the normal procedure and proceeded straight to the identification of objections, rather than starting the accounting process *ab initio*.[283] An area where there is, however, considerably more doubt is the availability of an account in the case of a breach of a restraint covenant by a *former* partner, although the better view appears to be that such a remedy will, in an appropriate case, be available.[284]

Where, on the other hand, a claim is made by one partner against another in some other capacity, *e.g.* as trustee, this principle may not apply. Such was the position in *Hurst v. Bennett*.[285] There, following a dissolution,[286] four partners who were trustees of the firm's lease sought to enforce an express indemnity against one of the other partners (H) by means of a statutory demand. An attempt to have the statutory demand set aside[287] on the basis that money might be due to H on the taking of dissolution accounts was rejected.[288]

Other persons entitled to an account

23–77   *Assignee/mortgagee of share:* An assignee or mortgagee of a partnership share will, so long as the partnership continues, have no right to seek an account of partnership transactions.[289] However, once the partnership has been dissolved, he will be entitled to an account as from the date of dissolution.[290] Where, unusually, a partner has an express right to assign his share and thereby to constitute the

---

[282] See *Brown v. Rivlin*, unreported, February 1, 1983 (C.A.T. No. 56); [1984] C.L.Y., p. 138; *Marshall v. Bullock, supra. Hurst v. Bryk, supra*, is another example: there, at first instance, Carnwath J. refused to order accounts *inter alia* on the basis that detailed accounts had been prepared by the partnership accountants and the claimant had failed to take any substantial objection thereto: see *supra*, para. 23–75. See also the observations of the Court of Appeal in the subsequent proceedings: *Hurst v. Bennett* [2001] B.P.I.R. 287 at [45], [49], [56].

[283] *Montgomery v. Cameron & Greig* [2007] CSOH 63 (OH) at [35], [36] *per* Lord Reed.

[284] See *supra*, para. 10–235.

[285] [2001] B.P.I.R. 287 (CA).

[286] As to the circumstances in which the partnership came to be dissolved, see *Hurst v. Bryk* [2002] 1 A.C. 185 (HL).

[287] Under the Insolvency Rules 1986, r. 6.5(4)(a).

[288] In terms of the establishment of a general principle, the decision is not entirely satisfactory. The trustee partners relied on an express indemnity given in their favour by the firm, *i.e.* all the partners including themselves: see also *Hurst v. Bryk* [2002] 1 A.C. 185, 196–197 *per* Lord Millett. Three special factors were in operation, namely: (1) in earlier proceedings, Carnwath J. had, in fact, determined H's percentage share of the firm's debts and liabilities, including, in particular, the rent under the lease, although this appears not to have been a final determination (see [2001] B.P.I.R. 287 at [22], [31] *per* Arden L.J.); (2) there was at least some doubt whether dissolution accounts could still be taken (*ibid.* at [17] *per* Arden L.J., [50] *per* Sir Christopher Staughton, [56] *per* Peter Gibson L.J.); and (3) the court appears to have thought it unlikely that any sums would ultimately be due to H, even if dissolution accounts *were* taken (*ibid.* at [41], [42] *per* Arden L.J., [49] *per* Sir Christopher Staughton), [56] *per* Peter Gibson L.J.). Had the position been otherwise, the decision might have resulted in a grave injustice to H. It is not possible simply to ignore the trustee partners' own obligation to bear a share of the rent. If, on the taking of the accounts, it had been found that, in net terms, they owed money to H, but H had nevertheless been forced to pay them his share of the rent *qua* trustees, the result would have been insupportable. *A fortiori*, if the trustees were made bankrupt in the meantime, as was alleged to be a possibility: *ibid.* [29].

[289] Partnership Act 1890, s.31(1), *supra*, paras 19–51 *et seq*. And see also, as to the rights of a creditor who has obtained a charging order over a partner's share, *ibid.* s.23, *supra*, paras 19–37 *et seq*.

[290] *ibid.* s.31(2); and see *supra*, para. 19–56.

assignee as a partner in his place,[291] the assignee will be entitled to an account from the other partners.[292]

Creditors, legatees, etc. of deceased partner: Although a partnership creditor can, in effect, seek an account of a deceased partner's share as against his personal representatives and the surviving partners, with a view to obtaining payment out of the estate,[293] the deceased's separate creditors, legatees and next-of-kin do not enjoy an equivalent right. Their only remedy lies against the personal representatives, unless the latter have colluded with the surviving partners or are otherwise unable or unwilling to seek an account from them.[294]

Employee: An employee who is remunerated by means of a share of profits, e.g. a salaried "partner",[295] has a right to an account.[296]   **23–78**

Personal representatives: An account may be sought by or against the personal representatives of a deceased partner.[297]

Sub-partner: A sub-partner will have no right to an account against the head partnership or any member of it, other than the person with whom he is in partnership.[298]

Trustee in bankruptcy/liquidator: An account may be sought by or against the trustee or liquidator of an insolvent partner.[299]

Scope of account

The scope of the account will naturally vary according to the subject matter of the dispute. Lord Lindley explained: **23–79**

> "The account which a partner may seek to have taken, may be either a general account of the dealings and transactions of the firm, with a view to a winding up of the partnership; or a more limited account, directed to some particular transaction as to which a dispute has arisen."

[291] See *supra*, paras 19–60 *et seq.*; also, *supra*, paras 10–258 *et seq.*
[292] See *Fawcett v. Whitehouse* (1829) 1 R. & M. 132, 148 *per* Lord Lyndhurst L.C.; *Redmayne v. Forster* (1866) L.R. 2 Eq. 467.
[293] *Wilkinson v. Henderson* (1833) 1 M. & K. 582. See also *infra*, paras 26–32 *et seq.*
[294] See *infra*, para. 26–34.
[295] See further, as to the status of such "partners", *supra*, para. 5–54.
[296] See *Harrington v. Churchward* (1860) 6 Jur.(N.S.) 576; *Turner v. Bayley* (1864) 4 De G.J. & S. 332; *Rishton v. Grissell* (1870) L.R. 10 Eq. 393. Although Lord Lindley expressed an unqualified view in favour of such a person's right (*qua* employee) to an account, the terms of Bovill's Act left some room for doubt; no such doubt persists under the Partnership Act 1890, s.2(3)(b), *supra*, para. 5–02. *Semble*, there will be no right to an account if the salaried partner's entitlement is to a fixed sum payable out of profits.
[297] *Heyne v. Middlemore* (1665) 1 Rep. Ch. 138; *Hackwell v. Eustman* (1616) Cro.Jac. 410; *Beaumont v. Grover* (1701) 1 Eq.Ab. 8, pl. 7; *Addis v. Knight* (1817) 2 Mer. 117.
[298] *Raymond's case*, cited in *Ex p. Barrow* (1815) 2 Rose 252, 255; *Brown v. De Tastet* (1819) Jac. 284; *Bray v. Fromont* (1821) 6 Madd. 5. See also *Killock v. Greg* (1828) 4 Russ. 285.
[299] See *Addis v. Knight* (1817) 2 Mer. 117; *Wilson v. Greenwood* (1818) 1 Swan. 471.

The court will, in general,[300] deal with every claim and cross-claim which must be investigated in order to adjust and finally settle the account,[301] although any dispute which does not affect the account or which is outside its ambit[302] will naturally be excluded.

Several partnerships

23–80   The account sought may relate to the dealings of a number of firms which have carried on the same business in succession,[303] but is likely to be objectionable if it relates to the dealings of two or more co-existing firms.[304]

Summary judgment for accounts and inquiries

23–81   Where the relief sought in a claim form in a partnership action[305] includes, or necessarily involves, the taking of an account or the making of an inquiry[306] it may be possible for *any* party to obtain a summary judgment for that account or inquiry under Part 24 of the Civil Procedure Rules.[307] Similarly where the relief is sought by way of counterclaim.[308] However, such a judgment is only likely to be obtained where the existence of the partnership is admitted or is not open to serious doubt,[309] and either there is nothing in dispute between the parties except the accounts or the defendant is unable to satisfy the court that there is some other reason why the action should proceed to trial.[310] Prior to the advent of the Civil Procedure Rules, the practice of the court was not to order accounts and inquiries if there was a substantive factual issue to be resolved between the parties, particularly if this would have an impact on the contents of the accounts. It is thought likely that, subject to the impact of the overriding objective,[311] a similar approach will continue to be adopted,[312] although the parties may agree that the

---

[300] This must, of course, be read subject to the overriding objective set out in the CPR r. 1.1.

[301] See, for example, *Green v. Hertzog* [1954] 1 W.L.R. 1309. This was also the position in the old Court of Chancery: see *Bury v. Allen* (1845) 1 Colly. 589; *Mackenna v. Parkes* (1866) 36 L.J.Ch. 366. *cf. Great Western Insurance Co. v. Cunliffe* (1879) 9 Ch.D. 525. It should not be assumed that the account will necessarily be limited to sums actually received: *Finlayson v. Turnbull (No. 3)* [2001] G.W.D. 37–1412 (OH).

[302] For an example of such a case, see *Dickinson T/A John Dickinson Equipment Finance v. Rushmer T/A FJ Associates*, February 14, 2000 (Lawtel 14/2/00) (CA), where a substantive counterclaim was, unsuccessfully, sought to be introduced into the account as a just allowance; also *Welsh v. Dyce* [2009] CSOH 102, where Lord Drummond Young observed (at [7]) that " . . . it should be recalled that accounts are designed to represent a pre-existing financial situation. They are a record rather than a document that gives rise to new rights and obligations. Objections to accounts should in my view relate to the pre-existing financial situation, rather than to any new matters that may have arisen during the course of the action." This inevitably raises an issue as to how a claim for damages as between partners should properly be pursued: see *infra*, para. 23–210.

[303] See *Jefferys v. Smith* (1827) 3 Russ. 158.

[304] See *Rheam v. Smith* (1848) 2 Ph. 726. Again regard must inevitably be had to the overriding objective set out in the CPR r. 1.1.

[305] See, as to manner in which such an action should be commenced, *supra*, paras 23–71, 23–72. The same procedure now applies in the High Court and the county court.

[306] As already noticed, this will usually be the case: see *supra*, para. 23–76.

[307] CPR 24PD, para. 6.

[308] *ibid.* r. 20.3(1), effectively applying *ibid.* Pt 24.

[309] *ibid.* r. 24.2(a); Chancery Guide, para. 22.2.

[310] *ibid.* r. 24.2(b); Chancery Guide, paras 22.1, 22.2. For an early example of a summary order for accounts being made where there was no real dispute save as to the state of the account, see *Turquand v. Wilson* (1875) 1 Ch.D. 85.

[311] *ibid.* r. 1.1.

[312] This would seem to be implicit in the Chancery Guide, para. 22.2.

factual issues should be determined by the Master as a preliminary to taking the account.[313] There would seem to be no reason why such a summary order should not be made even where fraud is alleged.[314]

The application will be made by means of an application notice[315] to the court in which the claim was started.[316] It must be verified by a statement of truth[317] unless the evidence in support is contained in a separate witness statement[318] or affidavit.[319]

When giving judgment, the court will usually give directions as to the manner in which the account is to be taken or inquiry made.[320]

Account without a dissolution

Although it was formerly considered that an account could only be taken **23–82** between partners with a view to a dissolution,[321] it has long been recognised that a strict application of this rule would lead to injustice.[322] Lord Lindley observed:

> "The old rule . . . that a decree for an account between partners will not be made save with a view to the final determination of all questions and cross-claims between them, and to a dissolution of the partnership, must be regarded as considerably relaxed, although it is still applicable where there is no sufficient reason for departing from it."

In the light of this, Lord Millett perhaps overstated the position in this respect in *Hurst v. Bryk*,[323] when observing:

> "Neither during the continuance of the relationship nor after its determination has any partner any cause of action at law to recover moneys due to him from his fellow partners. The amount owing to a partner by his fellow partners is recoverable only by the taking of an account in equity after the partnership has been dissolved: see

---

[313] See *ibid.* para. 22.3. Note that the Chancery Guide no longer suggests that factual isses might be determined by way of an inquiry at the same time as the account is taken. The course suggested in the text is unlikely to be appropriate if the existence of the partnership is in dispute and there will, no doubt, be other instances in which such an approach would not be practical or result in a saving of costs. In any case, the court will not be bound by what the parties have agreed: *Re Debtors (No. 13-MISC-2000 and No. 14-MISC-2000), The Times,* April 10, 2000.

[314] See *Newton Chemical Ltd. v. Arsenis* [1989] 1 W.L.R. 1297, 1303 *per* Nicholls L.J. Stocker and O'Connor L.JJ. concurred with this view: see *ibid.* p. 1307. This was a decision under RSC Ord. 43.

[315] CPR r. 23.1. As to the content of the application notice, see *ibid.* r. 23.6.

[316] *ibid.* r. 23.2(1).

[317] *ibid.* r. 22.1(3).

[318] Such a statement must itself be verified by a statement of truth: *ibid.* r. 22.1(1)(c).

[319] See generally, as to the evidence in support of such application, *ibid.* 23APD, para. 9. Affidavit evidence will not ordinarily be appropriate: see *ibid.* r. 32.15(2).

[320] *ibid.* 40APD, para. 1; Chancery Guide, paras 9.17, 9.18. See further, *infra* para. 23–119.

[321] *Forman v. Homfray* (1813) 2 V. & B. 329; *Loscombe v. Russell* (1830) 4 Sim. 8; *Knebell v. White* (1836) 2 Y. & C.Ex. 15.

[322] Lord Lindley explained: " . . . it has been felt that more injustice frequently arose from the refusal of the Court to do less than complete justice, than could have arisen from interfering to no greater extent than was desired by the suitor aggrieved." See further *supra,* para. 23–16. And see, generally, *Prole v. Masterman* (1855) 21 Beav. 61 (a decision concerning the promoters of a company); also *Wright v. Hunter* (1801) 5 Ves.Jr. 792; *cf. Munnings v. Bury* (1829) Tam. 147. Also the following cases relating to mutual insurance societies: *Taylor v. Dean* (1856) 22 Beav. 429; *Hutchinson v. Wright* (1858) 25 Beav. 444; *Bromley v. Williams* (1863) 32 Beav. 177.

[323] [2002] 1 A.C. 185, 194.

Richardson v Bank of England (1838) 4 My & Cr 165; *Green v Hertzog* [1954] 1 WLR 1309."

This in turn led the Court of Appeal into a similar (albeit more tentative) overstatement in *Cowan v. Wakeling*.[324]

23–83   Lord Lindley then went on to summarise the three classes of case in which an action for an account *without* a dissolution is most commonly encountered, although these should, in the current editor's view, more properly be divided into four classes, *viz*.:

1. Where one partner seeks to withhold some private profits in which his co-partners are interested.

2. Where the partnership is for a fixed term and one partner has sought to exclude or expel his co-partner or otherwise to drive him into a dissolution.

3. Where the existence of the partnership is denied.[325]

4. Where, exceptionally, the partnership venture has failed and the partners are too numerous to be made parties to the action, but a limited account will do justice between them.

Class 1: Partner withholding private profits

23–84   Of this class, Lord Lindley wrote:

"Where one partner has obtained a secret benefit, from which he seeks to exclude his co-partners, but to which they are entitled, they can obtain their share of such benefit by an action for an account, and such action is sustainable, although no dissolution is sought."

The principles on which a partner will be held liable to account to his co-partners for private profits made at their expense have already been noticed[326] and it is sufficient in the present context to note that there are four decided cases, all of which pre-date the Partnership Act 1890, in which an account was directed, even though the claimant did not seek to have the partnership dissolved or its affairs wound up.[327] In most of the other cases, it is unclear whether or not a general winding up was sought.[328]

Where the agreement under which a benefit will be obtained by a partner has not been performed by the other contracting party, his co-partners will, in

---

[324] [2008] EWCA Civ 229 (Lawtel 25/2/08) at [25]. Note that, by the time of the appeal, proceedings for a dissolution and the taking of an account had been launched: *ibid.* at [26].

[325] Lord Lindley in fact treated this head as part of Class 2.

[326] See *supra*, paras 16–13 *et seq.*

[327] *Hichens v. Congreve* (1828) 1 R. & M. 150; *Fawcett v. Whitehouse* (1829) 1 R. & M. 132; *The Society of Practical Knowledge v. Abbott* (1840) 2 Beav. 559; *Beck v. Kantorowicz* (1857) 3 K. & J. 230.

[328] A dissolution was, in fact, sought in *Clegg v. Fishwick* (1849) 1 Mac. & G. 294. In *Aas v. Benham* [1891] 2 Ch. 244 and *Dean v. MacDowell* (1878) 8 Ch.D. 345 (where the partnership had expired) an account was in any event refused on the merits.

general, have no *locus standi* as against that party to restrain further perform-ance.[329] In such a case, they should proceed against the partner concerned and claim the benefit of the agreement from him.[330]

Class 2: Exclusion, etc.

The general proposition that an account will be ordered without a dissolution where a fixed term partnership is continuing and one partner seeks improperly to exclude or expel his co-partner or to drive him into a dissolution was originally laid down by Sir John Leach V.-C. in *Harrison v. Armitage*.[331] Lord Lindley cited *Chapple v. Cadell*[332] in this context, but the facts there were wholly exceptional and scarcely afford a convincing example. The decision in *Fairthorne v. Weston*[333] is more in point. This case concerned a fixed term solicitors' partner-ship, in which the defendant was trying to force the claimant into a dissolution by conducting himself in such a way that no business could be carried on. However, instead of seeking a dissolution, the claimant commenced proceedings for an account and for the appointment of a receiver. The defendant's objection to this tactic failed.[334]

Richards v. Davies[335] appears to be a more extreme case. There a fixed term partnership had been entered into but the defendants would not account to the claimant in respect of the partnership dealings and transactions. Although an account of those dealings and transactions was ordered by Sir John Leach (by then the Master of the Rolls), on the grounds that the claimant would otherwise be remediless, it would seem that an effective case of exclusion may have been made out.[336]

The fact that new proceedings will be required as and when further profits are received is, seemingly, an irrelevant consideration.[337]

23–85

Expulsion

Lord Lindley expressed the view that:

23–86

" . . . if a partner is wrongfully expelled, and he is restored to his status as partner by the judgment of the Court, an account will be directed, but the partnership will not necessarily be dissolved."[338]

---

[329] *Per contra*, in the case of a bribe: see, generally, *Bowstead and Reynolds on Agency* (19th ed.), Art. 49, paras 6–084 *et seq.*

[330] *cf. Powell and Thomas v. Evan Jones & Co.* [1905] 1 K.B. 11; and see *Alder v. Fouracre* (1818) 3 Swan. 489, where an injunction was granted restraining the executors of a deceased partner, who had, prior to his death, agreed to take a lease of premises to be used for partnership purposes, from disposing of the lease when granted, except for the benefit of the partnership.

[331] (1819) 4 Madd. 143.

[332] (1822) Jac. 537.

[333] (1844) 3 Hare 387.

[334] It is no longer possible for a partner, faced with such conduct, to treat the partnership as dissolved by reason of the defendant's repudiatory conduct but he can pursue his right to damages: see further *infra*, paras 23–210 and 24–05 *et seq.*

[335] (1831) 2 R. & M. 347.

[336] Such an allegation was made: see the statement of facts at *ibid.* p. 347.

[337] See *Richards v. Davies, supra*, at pp. 351–352. *cf. Forman v. Homfray* (1813) 2 V. & B. 329 *per* Lord Eldon; *Loscombe v. Russell* (1830) 4 Sim. 8 *per* Shadwell V.-C.; *Knebell v. White* (1836) 2 Y. & C.Ex. 15 *per* Baron Alderson.

[338] See *Blisset v. Daniel* (1853) 10 Hare 493, where a dissolution was sought but not, in the event, ordered. Lord Lindley regarded the underlying principle as similar to that which applies in a case where the existence of a partnership is denied: see *infra*, para. 23–88.

The current editor would, however, observe that a failed expulsion will *usually* result in a dissolution.[339]

Mining partnerships

23–87   Although Lord Lindley also referred to the position in the case of mining partnerships in this context,[340] he concluded that:

> " . . . as each co-owner of a mine can sell his share[341] without the consent of the other owners, there is no occasion for him to ask for a dissolution, and the case of a mine is therefore, perhaps, not an apt illustration of the doctrine in question."

Class 3: Existence of partnership denied

23–88   Although he did not treat this class as in any way distinct from the previous class, Lord Lindley observed:

> " . . . where a person seeks to establish a partnership with another who denies the plaintiff's title to be considered a partner, if the former is successful upon the main point in dispute, an account of the past dealings and transactions will be decreed, although the plaintiff does not seek for a dissolution of the partnership which he has proved to exist."[342]

Class 4: Failure of large concern

23–89   Lord Lindley formulated the following general proposition, by reference to the celebrated judgment of Lord Cottenham in *Wallworth v. Holt*[343]:

> "Where the partnership has proved a failure, and the partners are too numerous to be made parties to the action, and a limited account will result in justice to them all, such an account will be directed, although a dissolution is not asked for."

In *Wallworth v. Holt*, certain shareholders of an insolvent joint-stock banking company, acting on behalf of themselves and others, sought an account against the officers of the company and a number of other shareholders who had not paid up their calls, for the sole purpose of having the assets of the company applied in payment of its debts. An objection to the proceedings by way of demurrer was overruled.

23–90   Although Lord Lindley doubted whether the result would have been the same if an account had been sought in order to obtain a division of profits,[344] subsequent decisions had demonstrated that proceedings seeking a division of surplus assets might be maintained even where a dissolution was not expressly

---

[339] See *supra*, para. 10–132 and *infra*, para. 24–84.

[340] See *Bentley v. Bates* (1840) 4 Y. & C.Ex. 182; also *Redmayne v. Forster* (1866) L.R. 2 Eq. 467.

[341] *Quaere*, in any event, whether this is still the position: see *supra*, para. 19–64.

[342] *Knowles v. Haughton* (1805) 11 Ves.Jr. 168, as reported in *Collyer on Partnership*, p. 198, note. The defendant did not, however, resist the account after the question of partnership was decided against him. See also the judgment of Stirling L.J. in *Byrne v. Reid* [1902] 2 Ch. 735, 741 *et seq.*

[343] (1841) 4 Myl. & Cr. 619.

[344] Either on the basis that a dissolution ought to have been sought or that all the shareholders were not parties to the proceedings: see *Richardson v. Hastings* (1844) 7 Beav. 301, 323 and (1847) 11 Beav. 17; *Deeks v. Stanhope* (1844) 14 Sim. 57.

claimed.[345] In the light of these and other cases,[346] he then went on to express the following view:

> " . . . it is conceived that the doctrine established in *Wallworth v. Holt* may be considered as extending not only to cases where an account is sought for the purpose of having joint assets applied in discharge of the joint liabilities, but also to cases where an account is sought for the additional purpose of obtaining a division of the surplus assets and profits amongst the persons entitled thereto. If this be so, the last remnant of the doctrine that, in partnership cases, there can be no account without a dissolution, must be considered as swept away, at least as regards partnerships the members of which are too numerous to be made parties to the action."

Since all of the former restrictions on the size of partnerships have been swept away,[347] Lord Lindley's observations are, perhaps, even more apposite now than they once were.

The possible use of representative proceedings in cases of this class should not be forgotten.[348]

Interim orders: payment into court

Payment in pending trial

It is clear that, in an appropriate case, a party can be ordered to pay a sum into court[349] and, moreover, where entitlement to a specified fund is in dispute, a payment in of that fund may be ordered.[350] Under the old procedure, the general rule was stated by Lord Lindley in the following terms: **23–91**

> " . . . a partner having partnership monies in his hands, cannot be made to pay those monies into court before trial, if he insists that, on taking the accounts, a balance will be found due to him."[351]

Nevertheless, where proceedings for an account were pending and the defendant admitted that he had or had had money in his hands which belonged to the firm and, in the latter case, he also admitted, or it otherwise plainly appeared,[352]

---

[345] See *Wilson v. Stanhope* (1846) 2 Colly. 629; *Apperly v. Page* (1847) 1 Ph. 779; *Cooper v. Webb* (1847) 15 Sim. 454; *Clements v. Bowes* (1852) 17 Sim. 167; also *Sheppard v. Oxenford* (1855) 1 K. & J. 491, 493, where all forms of relief normally associated with a dissolution were sought, but not dissolution itself.

[346] See, in particular, *Apperly v. Page, supra*; *Clements v. Bowes, supra*.

[347] See the Regulatory Reform (Reform of 20 Member Limit in Partnerships etc.) Order 2002 (SI 2002/3203), reg. 2.

[348] See *supra*, paras 23–10, 23–11, 23–14.

[349] See CPR r. 3.1(2)(m), which is drawn in very wide terms. There are also specific, but more limited, powers under *ibid.* r. 3.1(3)(a), (5). See, generally, *Training in Compliance Ltd. v. Drewse* [2001] C.P. Rep. 46 (CA).

[350] CPR r. 25.1(1)(l). See, generally, as to the circumstances in which a payment in may be ordered under *ibid*, r. 25.1(1), *Myers v. Design Inc (International) Ltd.* [2003] 1 W.L.R. 1642.

[351] *Richardson v. Bank of England* (1838) 4 Myl. & Cr. 165. *cf. Birley v. Kennedy* (1865) 6 N.R. 395, where a partner who admitted that he had drawn more out of the partnership than he ought to have done was ordered to pay the excess into court.

[352] See, generally, *Freeman v. Cox* (1878) 8 Ch.D. 148; *Dunn v. Campbell* (1879) 27 Ch.D. 254, note; *Hampden v. Wallis* (1884) 27 Ch.D. 251; *Porrett v. White* (1885) 31 Ch.D. 52; *Wanklyn v. Wilson* (1887) 35 Ch.D. 180; *Re Benson* [1899] 1 Ch. 39.

that he ought still to have that money,[353] a payment in could be ordered.[354] *A fortiori* if it appeared from that partner's own statements that the money came into his hands improperly[355] or in breach of the duty of good faith which he owed to his co-partners.[356] It is to be expected that, in such cases, the court would continue to adopt the same approach under the Civil Procedure Rules, although there is clearly a wide discretion to order a payment in in other circumstances, whether in pursuance of the overriding objective[357] or as a matter of case management.

It is unlikely that a partner will be compelled to pay any partnership moneys into court if the other partners are not prepared to do likewise.[358]

23–92   The following principles, established prior to the advent of the Civil Procedure Rules, would also still seem to have current relevance:

Debt owed to firm: A partner will not be ordered to pay in any sum in respect of a debt owed to the firm, where the amount is not admitted and cannot be readily ascertained.[359] Where, however, the amount of the debt is ascertained and the partner concerned does not insist that an overall balance is due to him from the firm, he may be ordered to make a payment in.[360]

Admissions: A verbal admission may be sufficient for these purposes,[361] but a payment in is unlikely to be ordered on the strength of an admission made by another partner.[362] The court may permit a partner to withdraw an inadvertent admission.[363]

23–93   *Debtors Act 1869:* An order for the payment of partnership moneys into court cannot be enforced by attachment or committal under the Debtors Act 1869 since, for this purpose at least, a partner does not act in a fiduciary capacity.[364]

Partnership debts unpaid: If the partnership debts are unpaid and the defendant is liable to be sued for them, the order directing payment in should give him

---

[353] See the cases cited in the previous note; also *Neville v. Matthewman* [1894] 3 Ch. 345; *Crompton and Evans' Union Bank v. Burton* [1895] 2 Ch. 711.

[354] In *White v. Barton* (1854) 18 Beav. 192, an admission by one partner that he and his co-partner (who was not a party) had money in their hands was held to be sufficient. *cf.* the cases cited *infra*, para. 23–92, n. 362.

[355] *Jervis v. White* (1802) 6 Ves.Jr. 737; *Costeker v. Horrox* (1839) 3 Y. & C.Ex. 530.

[356] *Foster v. Donald* (1820) 1 J. & W. 252. See also *Hichens v. Congreve* (1828) 1 R. & M. 150, note; *Gaskell v. Chambers* (1858) 26 Beav. 360; *cf. Hagell v. Currie* (1867) L.R. 2 Ch.App. 449.

[357] CPR r. 1.1.

[358] See *Foster v. Donald, supra.*

[359] See *Mills v. Hanson* (1802) 8 Ves.Jr. 68; *Wanklyn v. Wilson* (1887) 35 Ch.D. 180.

[360] *Toulmin v. Copland* (1836) 3 Y. & C.Ex. 625, affirmed at (1840) 7 Cl. & F. 349; *Costeker v. Horrox* (1839) 3 Y. & C.Ex. 530. See also *Domville v. Solly* (1826) 2 Russ. 372, where an order was made even though the defendants insisted that the claimant was entitled to nothing.

[361] *Re Beeny* [1894] 1 Ch. 499.

[362] *Hollis v. Burton* [1892] 3 Ch. 226; also *Boschetti v. Power* (1844) 8 Beav. 98. *cf. White v. Barton* (1854) 18 Beav. 192, *supra*, para. 23–91, n. 354.

[363] CPR r. 14.1(5); and see also *Hollis v. Burton, supra.* Conditions may, in an appropriate case, be imposed as a condition of such withdrawal: *ibid.* r. 3.1(3)(a). As to the withdrawal of pre-action admissions, see *ibid.* r. 14.1A(3).

[364] *ibid.* s.4(3); *Piddocke v. Burt* [1894] 1 Ch. 343. See also *supra*, para. 16–04.

liberty to apply for a payment out of the amount of any such debts which he may be compelled or pressed to pay.[365]

Freezing injunction[366]: Where, for any of the reasons discussed above, the court is unable to compel a partner to pay money into court, it may be possible to obtain a freezing injunction to prevent dissipation of his assets pending the trial of the action.[367]

Payment in after trial

An order for payment in of a sum plainly due from a partner can also be made after judgment has been given in an appropriate case,[368] *e.g.* when the right to an account has been established but the relevant account has not yet been taken.[369] **23–94**

Interim payments

As an alternative to an order for payment into court, a partner could, once he has obtained an order for an account,[370] apply for an interim payment on account of his prospective entitlement on the taking of accounts as between him and the other partner(s).[371] However, it would seem that such an order is only likely to be made where, on the taking of the account, a sum is *bound* to be due to the applicant.[372] Cases in which this test can be satisfied will be rare. **23–95**

(2) *Production of documents, etc.*

Right to production of documents

Lord Lindley observed: **23–96**

"The right of every partner to a discovery[373] from his co-partner of all matters relating to the partnership dealings and transactions is as incontestable as his right to an account; and such right, like the right to an account, devolves upon and is enforceable against a partner's legal personal representatives and trustees in bankruptcy."

This right, which is enshrined in the Partnership Act 1890,[374] is separate and distinct from any right to disclosure and inspection of documents under the Civil

---

[365] *Toulmin v. Copland* (1836) 3 Y. & C.Ex. 625, 643 *et seq. cf. Toulmin v. Copeland* (1819) 6 Price 405.

[366] Formerly known as a *Mareva* injunction.

[367] See *infra*, para. 23–150.

[368] CPR r. 25.2(1)(b).

[369] *Creak v. Capell* (1821) 6 Madd. 114; *London Syndicate v. Lord* (1878) 8 Ch.D. 84.

[370] CPR 25BPD, para. 2A.1.

[371] *i.e.* pursuant to CPR rr. 25.1(1)(k), 25.6, 25.7(1)(c). As to the manner in which such an application is made, see *ibid.* r. 25.3; also *ibid.* Pt 23.

[372] *ibid.* 25BPD, para. 2A.2 provides that if, on the evidence, a sum is bound to be payable to the applicant once the account has been taken, the court will make an order that he be paid "the amount shown by the account to be due" *before* ordering an interim payment. Although the Practice Direction appears to assume that an order could be made in other cases, it is difficult to imagine circumstances in which this would be justified.

[373] This expression, which mirrors the terminology adopted in the RSC, is of no particular significance.

[374] Partnership Act 1890, ss.24(9), 28. See *supra*, paras 22–10 *et seq.*

Procedure Rules[375] and, indeed, data subject access applications under the Data Protection Act 1998,[376] which partners are now using to supplement their more traditional rights to production of documents.

If a partner chooses to keep his own personal records in the same book as the partnership records, he will normally be compelled to produce the entire book, unless the former can be physically severed from the latter.[377] Moreover, a former partner in a firm of solicitors cannot refuse to produce his ledger, if it is relevant, on the ground of professional privilege.[378]

Court orders in aid of production of documents, etc.

Books belonging to defendant and another

23–97   Although a person technically cannot be forced to produce books which belong to himself and other persons who are not before the court,[379] it is clear that disclosure of documents can now, in an appropriate case, be ordered against a third party.[380] Accordingly, it can no longer be said to be a *general* rule that, where the existence of a partnership is in dispute, it is not possible to compel the production of any books unless all the alleged partners are joined as parties.[381] Yet even whilst such a general rule did exist, it was not without exceptions, as Lord Lindley made clear:

> " . . . the doctrine[382] . . . does not apply to cases in which the absent parties interested in the books are in fact represented by the defendants on the record, and have no interest in conflict with theirs[383]; nor, it is said, to an action by a *cestui que trust* against a trustee who is charged with trading with trust monies in partnership with other persons not before the Court."[384]

Where a third party is in possession of a document, production of which is required for the purposes of deciding an issue in the proceedings, the alternative

---

[375] CPR Pt 31. But see *Bevan v. Webb* [1901] 2 Ch. 59, 76, 77 *per* Collins L.J.

[376] See *ibid*. s.7 (as amended). Whether such requests actually add anything useful, other than a further tier of complexity is, in the current editor's view, doubtful: note, in this connection, *Durant v. Financial Services Authority* [2004] F.S.R. 28 (CA); *Johnson v. Medical Defence Union Ltd.* [2005] 1 W.L.R. 750.

[377] See *Re Pickering* (1883) 25 Ch.D. 247; *BBGP Managing General Partner Ltd. v. Babcock & Brown Global Partners* [2010] EWHC 2176 (Ch) *cf. Mansell v. Feeney* (1861) 2 J. & H. 313, *infra*, para. 23–112. See also *supra*, para. 22–13.

[378] *Brown v. Perkins* (1843) 2 Hare 540; *Lewthwaite v. Stimson* (1966) 110 S.J. 188.

[379] *Stuart v. Lord Bute* (1841) 11 Sim. 442 and (1842) 12 Sim. 460; *Reid v. Langlois* (1849) 1 Mac. & G. 627; *Burbidge v. Robinson* (1850) 2 Mac. & G. 244; *Penney v. Goode* (1853) 1 Drew. 474; *Hadley v. McDougall* (1872) L.R. 7 Ch.App. 312. *cf. Vyse v. Foster* (1872) L.R. 13 Eq. 602.

[380] Senior Courts Act 1981, s.34, as amended by the Civil Procedure (Modification of Enactments) Order 1998 (SI 1998/2940), art. 5(b) (formerly the Supreme Court Act 1981: Constitutional Reform Act 2005, Sched. 11, Pt 1, para. 1(1)); County Courts Act 1984, s.53, as amended by the Courts and Legal Services Act 1990, Sched. 18, para. 44 and by the Civil Procedure (Modification of Enactments) Order 1998, art. 6(b); CPR r. 31.17. But see *Re Howglen Ltd.* [2001] 1 All E.R. 376. Note also *ibid*. r. 31.18.

[381] See *Murray v. Walter* (1839) Cr. & Ph. 114. Note that it is not permissible to join a party solely with a view to obtaining inspection of a document: *Douihech v. Findlay* [1990] 1 W.L.R. 269; also *Unilever v. Chefaro, The Times*, March 29, 1993.

[382] *i.e.* the doctrine laid down in *Murray v. Walter, supra*.

[383] *Glyn v. Caulfield* (1851) 3 Mac. & G. 463.

[384] See *Vyse v. Foster* (1872) L.R. 13 Eq. 602; also *Freeman v. Fairlie* (1812) 3 Mer. 24, 43 *per* Lord Eldon.

remedy may, of course, be the issue of a witness summons.[385] However, this may give rise to difficulty where the document is the joint property of a number of persons. Thus, in *Forbes v. Samuel*,[386] Scrutton J. upheld an order for the production of a counterpart partnership deed when all the partners were not before the court,[387] but made it clear that the position would be otherwise if he were concerned with the only signed copy of that deed.[388]

Disputed partnership

In addition to the points noted in the previous paragraph, the extent to which production of documents can be obtained from a person who denies the existence of an alleged partnership will be considered later in this work.[389]

23–98

Agreement precluding inspection

If one partner agrees to accept his co-partner's computation of the partnership profits and, moreover, agrees not to examine or investigate the partnership books and accounts, the court will not order the production of those books and accounts until his right to an account has been established and, even then, may still decline to do so.[390]

23–99

Inspection by agent

Where a partner obtains an order for the production and inspection of documents, he may, if he wishes, have them inspected by his solicitors or some other agent,[391] but not by an agent to whom his co-partners reasonably object.[392]

Information obtained on such an inspection may not be made public[393] and an injunction will, if necessary, be granted to restrain its communication to third parties.[394]

23–100

---

[385] CPR r. 34.2(1)(b). This procedure was formerly known as a *subpoena duces tecum*. See, as to the requirements which must be satisfied in the case of a witness summons, *Tajik Aluminium Plant v. Hydro Aluminium AS* [2006] 1 W.L.R. 767 (CA).

[386] [1913] 3 K.B. 706.

[387] *ibid.* at 721–724. It should be noted that this was an action to recover a statutory penalty.

[388] *ibid.* at 722, citing, *inter alia*, *Crowther v. Appleby* (1873) L.R. 9 C.P. 23. *Quaere*, would the same approach be adopted today: see *Macmillan Inc. v. Bishopsgate Investment Trust Plc* [1993] 1 W.L.R. 837; also *supra*, para. 7–15.

[389] See *infra*, paras 23–107 *et seq.*

[390] *Turner v. Bayley* (1864) 4 De G.J. & S. 332. See also, as to such agreements, *supra*, para. 22–13; and generally, *supra*, paras 10–71 *et seq.*

[391] *Williams v. Prince of Wales', etc., Co.* (1857) 23 Beav. 338; *Bevan v. Webb* [1901] 2 Ch. 59; *McIvor v. Southern Health and Social Services Board* [1978] 1 W.L.R. 757. As to production to an accountant or other expert appointed for the purpose, see *Bonnardet v. Taylor* (1861) 1 J. & H. 383; *Swansea Co. v. Budd* (1866) L.R. 2 Eq. 274; *Lindsay v. Gladstone* (1869) L.R. 9 Eq. 132. And see *supra*, para. 22–14.

[392] *Draper v. Manchester & Sheffield Ry.* (1861) 7 Jur.(N.S.) 86; *Dadswell v. Jacobs* (1887) 34 Ch.D. 278; *Bevan v. Webb, supra; Davies v. Eli Lilly & Co.* [1987] 1 W.L.R. 428. And see *supra*, para. 22–14.

[393] *Per contra*, perhaps, where the order is obtained pursuant to a partner's statutory rights under the Partnership Act 1890, ss.24(9), 28. But see also *supra*, paras 22–14, 22–16.

[394] *Williams v. Prince of Wales' Life, etc., Co.* (1857) 23 Beav. 338; *Distillers Co. (Biochemicals) Ltd. v. Times Newspapers Ltd.* [1975] Q.B. 613; *Riddick v. Thames Board Mills Ltd.* [1977] Q.B. 881; *Church of Scientology of California v. Department of Health and Social Security* [1979] 1 W.L.R. 723; *I.T.C. Film Distributors Ltd. v. Video Exchange Ltd.* [1982] Ch. 431. But note *Crest Homes Plc v. Marks* [1987] A.C. 829; *Levi Strauss & Co. v. Barclays Trading Corp. Inc.* [1993] F.S.R. 179. And see, generally, *Phipson on Evidence* (15th ed.) Chap. 23.

Books in constant use

23–101   Production of partnership books which are in constant use will normally be ordered to take place at the firm's premises, although the court ultimately has complete discretion in the matter.[395] A special reason must be shown before they will be ordered to be deposited in court.[396]

Inspection for an improper purpose

23–102   Given that the statutory rights conferred on him by the Partnership Act 1890 are of an absolute nature,[397] it is doubtful whether a court can deny a partner access to the partnership books, etc., even if there is credible evidence that the right is being exercised for an improper purpose, *e.g.* in order to damage the partnership's interests or otherwise than for its benefit.[398]

Search order

23–103   There is no reason why, in an appropriate case, a search order[399] should not be obtained with a view to protecting any documents which, even though not the subject matter of the proceedings, will constitute vital evidence therein, *e.g.* the sole copy of the partnership agreement or books of account.[400] However, this jurisdiction is exercised sparingly,[401] and it would be necessary to show that there is a *probability* that the relevant documents would disappear if an order is not made.[402]

Requests for information

23–104   Although it is no longer possible to administer interrogatories under the Civil Procedure Rules, Part 18 requests for information will, in effect, perform the same function. It is clear that, if such a request would put the recipient to disproportionate expense, an order will not be made under that Part.[403] Although the attitude of the court under the new Rules will inevitably be different,[404] still the old cases which addressed the duties of a partner faced with wide ranging and potentially oppressive interrogatories in an action for an account may give *some* indication of the relevant considerations. As Lord Lindley put it, the obligation of the interrogated partner was as follows:

> " . . . all that he is bound to do is to furnish the interrogator with every means of information possessed or obtainable by himself, leaving the interrogator to make

---

[395] See CPR rr. 31.3, 31.15.

[396] *Mertens v. Haigh* (1860) Johns. 735.

[397] *ibid.* ss.24(9), 28. See *supra*, para. 22–10.

[398] See further *supra*, para. 22–16.

[399] Formerly known as an *Anton Piller* Order: see *Anton Piller K.G. v. Manufacturing Processes Ltd.* [1976] Ch. 55. See now the Civil Procedure Act 1997, s.7 (as amended); CPR r. 25.1(1)(h); 25APD, para. 7.

[400] See, for example, *Yousif v. Salama* [1980] 1 W.L.R. 1540; *Emanuel v. Emanuel* [1982] 1 W.L.R. 669; *Distributori Automatici Italia SpA v. Holford General Trading Co. Ltd.* [1985] 1 W.L.R. 1066.

[401] Note that, in *Lock International Plc v. Beswick* [1989] 1 W.L.R. 1268, 1281, Hoffman J. emphasised that there must be proportionality between the perceived threat and the remedy granted and thereby, in effect, anticipated the considerations which must be taken into account under the overriding objective in the CPR r. 1.1.

[402] See *ibid.* 25APD, para. 7.3(2).

[403] See *ibid.* 18PD, paras 1.2, 4.2(2).

[404] In particular, the court must now have regard to the overriding objective in *ibid.* r. 1.1.

what he can of the materials thus furnished to him. The party interrogated is not bound to digest accounts, nor to set out voluminous accounts existing already in another shape which he offers to produce."

Thus, in *Christian v. Taylor*,[405] where an account was sought by the executor of one deceased partner against the executors of another deceased partner, it was held that the defendants were under no obligation to go through the books in their possession in order to supply the claimant with the information requested: all that they were required to do was to refer to those books in such a way as to entitle him to have them produced for his inspection.[406]

The position was, however, different where the interrogatories were of a more specific nature. In such a case it would not have been sufficient merely to refer to the partnership books, etc., in general terms and to say that, save as appeared therein, no answer could be given. The partner interrogated had to go further, and point out where the particular information required by each interrogatory was to be found.[407] This might have entailed him making inquiries and obtaining documents of which he was entitled to possession.[408]

It is submitted that similar considerations will apply where information regarding the firm's accounts is requested under section 28 of the Partnership Act 1890.[409]

Arbitrations

In the case of an arbitration, the arbitrator now has the same powers to order the production of documents, etc., as the court.[410] The court no longer has jurisdiction over such matters, save in a case of urgency or with the consent of the arbitrator or the agreement of parties.[411]   **23–105**

(b) Defences to an action for an account

A number of defences to an action for an account have already been considered earlier in this work, *i.e.* illegality,[412] fraud,[413] laches[414] and limitation.[415] Moreover, an equitable set off may be raised against a claim for an account.[416] It has   **23–106**

---

[405] (1841) 11 Sim. 401.

[406] See also *Seeley v. Boehm* (1817) 2 Madd. 176; *White v. Barker* (1852) 5 De G. & Sm. 746; *Lockett v. Lockett* (1869) L.R. 4 Ch.App. 336.

[407] *Drake v. Symes* (1859) Johns. 647, 651 *per* Page Wood V.-C.; also *Telford v. Ruskin* (1860) 1 Dr. & Sm. 148.

[408] See *Taylor v. Rundell (No. 1)* (1841) Cr. & Ph. 104; *Stuart v. Lord Bute* (1841) 11 Sim. 442 and (1842) 12 Sim. 460; *Earl of Glengall v. Frazer* (1842) 2 Hare 99; *Taylor v. Rundell (No. 2)* (1843) 1 Ph. 222; *Att.-Gen. v. Rees* (1849) 12 Beav. 50; *Bolckow v. Fisher* (1882) 10 Q.B.D. 161; *Alliott v. Smith* [1895] 2 Ch. 111. *cf. Martineau v. Cox* (1837) 2 Y. & C.Ex. 638, where a partner in a firm carrying on business in another country was held not to be bound to set out a list of documents in the possession of the partners abroad. As to setting out a list of the firm' debtors, see *Telford v. Ruskin* (1860) 1 Dr. & Sm. 148. *cf.* the observation of Page Wood V.-C. in *Drake v. Symes* (1859) Johns. 647, 651.

[409] See *supra*, paras 16–03, 22–10.

[410] Arbitration Act 1996, ss.38(4)(a), (6), 48(5)(a). See also *supra*, paras 10–278 *et seq.*

[411] *ibid.* s.44(2)(b), (c), (3), (4). *cf.* the former Arbitration Act 1950, s.12(6)(b), which was repealed by the Courts and Legal Services Act 1990, s.103.

[412] See *supra*, paras 8–63 *et seq.*

[413] See *supra*, paras 23–49 *et seq.*

[414] See *supra*, paras 23–19 *et seq.*

[415] See *supra*, paras 23–32 *et seq.*

[416] See *Secret Hotels Ltd. v. E.A. Traveller Ltd.* [2010] I.L.Pr. 33.

also been seen that the non-joinder of any necessary parties is no longer fatal.[417]

There are, however, a number of additional defences which merit specific attention, namely:

> (i) Denial of partnership.
>
> (ii) Settled account.
>
> (iii) Arbitration award.
>
> (iv) Accord and satisfaction.
>
> (v) Waiver.
>
> (vi) Release.

(i) *Denial of alleged partnership*

23–107   It is self evident that an action for an account of the dealings and transactions of an alleged partnership may be met by a denial that any such partnership exists.[418] Such a defence may have certain implications so far as concerns disclosure and orders under Part 18 of the Civil Procedure Rules.[419] Lord Lindley explained the position by reference to the old procedure as follows:

> "This defence if relied upon as a reason for not answering interrogatories[420] or making a discovery of documents,[421] must be accompanied by statements on oath[422] denying those allegations which, if true, would establish the partnership, and denying the possession of documents relevant to the question of partnership or no partnership."[423]

23–108   In *Mansell v. Feeney*,[424] it was held that the claimant was entitled to inspect all documents admitted by the defendant to be in his possession which were relevant to the dispute, even though the defendant denied the alleged partnership and, moreover, denied that those documents tended to prove its existence. The defendant was, however, permitted to seal up parts of certain books which he swore had no bearing on the issues in the action.[425] On the same principle, the

---

[417] See *supra*, para. 23–05.

[418] Notwithstanding the obviousness of the proposition in the text, Lord Lindley referred to *Drew v. Drew* (1813) 2 V. & B. 159; *Hare v. London and North-Western Ry.* (1860) John. 722. Note, however, that the position was more complicated prior to the Judicature Acts: see the 15th ed. of this work at p. 635.

[419] See *ibid.* r. 18.1. The response to an order under this rule must be verified by a statement of truth: *ibid.* r. 22.1(1)(b). See generally, as to such orders, *Lexi Holdings (In Administration) v. Pannone & Partners* [2010] EWHC 1416 (Ch) (Lawtel 21/6/10).

[420] The CPR does not permit the administration of interrogatories. The modern equivalent is an order under *ibid.* r. 18.1.

[421] Now styled disclosure of documents: *ibid.* Pt 31.

[422] The modern equivalent would be a witness statement filed in opposition to a Pt 23 application (see *ibid.* 23APD, para. 9), which must be verified by a statement of truth: *ibid.* r. 22.3.

[423] *Sanders v. King* (1821) 6 Madd. 61; *Harris v. Harris* (1844) 3 Hare 450; *Mansell v. Feeney* (1861) 2 J. & H. 313.

[424] (1861) 2 J. & H. 313. See also *Saull v. Browne* (1874) L.R. 9 Ch.App. 364. *cf. Re Pickering* (1883) 25 Ch.D. 247, *supra*, para. 23–96.

[425] See the hearing reported at (1861) 9 W.R. 610.

claimant in *Kennedy v. Dodson*,[426] who was seeking to establish the existence of a partnership in the acquisition of certain land, was not permitted to administer interrogatories directed towards proving that the defendant and he had been partners in various other purchases, both before and after the acquisition in question.

In practice, unnecessary disputes as to disclosure, etc., can be avoided by having the existence of the partnership determined as a preliminary issue.[427] If that course is adopted, then in Lord Lindley's words:

"Whilst on the one hand [*the defendant*] must give all such discovery as bears upon the question of partnership or no partnership, he will not be compelled to set out accounts or produce documents which he swears throw no light on that question and can only be material after it has been decided in favour of the plaintiff."[428]

(ii) *Settled account*

Nature of settled account

An account which has been agreed between the partners,[429] conventionally referred to as a "settled account" or, more inaccurately, as an "account stated,"[430] naturally constitutes a good defence to an action seeking a further account of any transactions or dealings covered thereby.[431] Lord Lindley summarised the requirements for a settled account as follows:

23–109

"No precise form is necessary to constitute a stated and settled account; but an account stated,[432] unless it be in writing, is no defence to an action for a further account. It is not, however, necessary that the account should be signed by the parties, if it can be shown to have been acquiesced in by them[433]; and an account may be stated and settled, although a few doubtful items are omitted."[434]

However, merely *rendering* an account is clearly not sufficient to deprive the claimant of his right to have the same account taken under the direction of the

23–110

---

[426] [1895] 1 Ch. 334.

[427] CPR rr. 1.4(2)(d), 3.1(2)(i), (j).

[428] See *Re Leigh* (1876) 6 Ch.D. 256; *Parker v. Wells* (1881) 18 Ch.D. 477; *Whyte v. Ahrens* (1884) 26 Ch.D. 717.

[429] If the account has not been settled as between all the partners, it will be *res inter alios acta* as regards those partners who are not bound by it: see *Carmichael v. Carmichael* (1846) 2 Ph. 101. An account settled by a majority of partners might, in certain circumstances, bind the minority: see *Robinson v. Thompson* (1687) 1 Vern. 465; *Kent v. Jackson* (1852) 2 De G.M. & G. 49; *Stupart v. Arrowsmith* (1856) 3 Sm. & G. 176 (non-partnership cases). Much will, of course, depend on the terms of the agreement, as to which see *supra*, paras 10–73, 10–74.

[430] A true "account stated" is wholly distinct from a settled account and, in fact, gives rise to a cause of action: see *Chitty on Contracts* (30th ed.), para. 29–191.

[431] *Taylor v. Shaw* (1824) 2 Sim. & St. 12; *Endo v. Caleham* (1831) Younge 306. Note also *Pelosi v. Luca* 2004 G.W.D. 23–513 (OH) at [21]; *Montgomery v. Cameron & Greig* [2007] CSOH 63 (OH).

[432] This is strictly a misuse of the term: see *supra*, n. 430.

[433] See *Morris v. Harrison* (1701) Colles 157; *Willes v. Jernegan* (1741) 2 Atk. 252; *Hunter v. Belcher* (1864) 2 De G.J. & S. 194. A verbal account and a receipt in full is not equivalent to a settled account: *Walker v. Consett* (1801) Forest 157.

[434] *Sim v. Sim* (1861) 11 I.Ch.R. 310.

court[435]: he must be shown both to have received and acquiesced in the account.[436] Moreover, such acquiescence must relate not only to the principles on which the account was prepared, but also to the items included in it.[437]

Equally, where an account has been settled up to the date of dissolution, it does not mean that the partners have foregone their right to have full dissolution accounts taken thereafter, without re-opening the settled account.[438] The corollary is that it cannot be assumed that an amount shown as due to a partner in a settled account is necessarily payable to that partner since it may be affected by subsequent accounts which have not yet been taken.

Settled accounts not normally reopened

23–111   In taking accounts under an ordinary judgment, a settled account will not be disturbed in the absence of a specific direction to that effect.[439] Such a direction may, however, be obtained if fraud, misrepresentation or errors can be proved.

Fraud and misrepresentation

If any part of a settled account is affected by fraud[440] or misrepresentation,[441] a new account will be directed, even after a considerable lapse of time.

Errors

23–112   Where errors affect the whole of a settled account, a new account will be directed,[442] unless the account has stood unimpeached for many years. Lord Lindley explained:

> " . . . if no fraud be proved, an account which has been long settled will not be reopened *in toto*; the utmost which the Court will then do will be to give leave to surcharge and falsify[443]; and there are cases in which, in consequence of lapse of

---

[435] See *Clements v. Bowes* (1853) 1 Drew. 684, 692 *per* Kindersley V.-C. *Quaere*, should this proposition in any way be qualified in the light of the overriding objective in the CPR r. 1.1? Would a partner's insistence on having accounts taken in court when an account rendered to him is demonstrably correct constitute a waste of the court's resources? Note, in this context, *Hurst v. Bennett* [2001] B.P.I.R. 287, *supra*, para. 23–76.

[436] *Irvine v. Young* (1823) 1 Sim. & St. 333.

[437] See *Clancarty v. Latouche* (1810) 1 Ball & Beatty 420; *Mosse v. Salt* (1863) 32 Beav. 269. *cf. Hunter v. Belcher* (1864) 2 De. G.J. & S. 194.

[438] *Winning v. Cunningham* 2009 GWD 01–19 (Sh.Ct.). Obviously the partners may have reached an agreement which obviates the need for such accounts, but that is a different matter.

[439] See *Newen v. Wetten* (1862) 31 Beav. 315; *Holgate v. Shutt* (1884) 27 Ch.D. 111 and 28 Ch.D. 111. But see also *Milford v. Milford* (1868) McCle. & Yo. 150. Note that this rule will only apply where the account is mutual.

[440] *Vernon v. Vawdry* (1740) 2 Atk. 119; *Wharton v. May* (1799) 5 Ves.Jr. 26, 68 *per* Lord Loughborough; *Beaumont v. Boultbee* (1800) 5 Ves.Jr. 484a and (1802) 7 Ves.Jr. 599; *Clarke v. Tipping* (1846) 9 Beav. 284; *Allfrey v. Allfrey* (1849) 1 Mac. & G. 87; *Coleman v. Mellersh* (1850) 2 Mac. & G. 309; *Stainton v. The Carron Co.* (1857) 24 Beav. 346; *Williamson v. Barbour* (1877) 9 Ch.D. 529; *Gething v. Keighley* (1878) 9 Ch.D. 547.

[441] See *supra*, para. 23–58.

[442] *Williamson v. Barbour* (1877) 9 Ch.D. 529; *Gething v. Keighley* (1878) 9 Ch.D. 547.

[443] *i.e.* permission to challenge specific items in the account: see *Brownell v. Brownell* (1786) 2 Bro.C.C. 61; *Millar v. Craig* (1843) 6 Beav. 433; *Gething v. Keighley, supra; Wheatley v. Bower* [2001] W.A.S.C.A. 293. *cf. Williamson v. Barbour, supra.* The expression "leave to surcharge and falsify" does not appear in the CPR and it seems unlikely that, given the general rejection of "outdated" terminology therein, it will continue to survive. Note, however, that the expression *was* used in Lord Millett's speech in *Hurst v. Bryk* [2002] 1 A.C. 185, 192.

time, the Court will do no more than itself rectify particular items, instead of giving leave to surcharge or falsify generally."[444]

In any other case, permission to serve notice of objection to specific items in the account will be the only available remedy.[445] An item omitted by mutual mistake will normally be put right.[446] However, the mere fact that items are treated in an improper way, or are improperly omitted, is not in itself sufficient to induce the court to reopen a settled account; if the partners knew about those items and no fraud or undue influence can be proved, it will be inferred that they were dealt with in an agreed manner.[447]

In order to impeach a settled account, any errors must be positively identified and proved[448]; similarly, where the account is settled on an "errors excepted" basis.[449]

If permission to serve notice of objections is obtained, errors both of fact and law can be corrected.[450] All parties to the action will normally be given such permission.[451]

Limitation

Although in *Hopper v. Hopper*[452] it appears to have been assumed that **23–113** limitation might, despite serious errors, bar the reopening of settled accounts as between continuing partners, the current editor doubts that this assumption was justified.[453]

Settled account accompanied by release

If, following the death, retirement or expulsion of a partner, an account is **23–114** settled between the surviving or continuing partners and the outgoing partner or his personal representatives and mutual releases are given, that account can only be impeached once the relevant release has been set aside.[454] The circumstances in which rescission may be obtained have already been considered earlier in this chapter.[455]

---

[444] See *Twogood v. Swanston* (1801) 6 Ves.Jr. 485; *Maund v. Allies* (1840) 5 Jur. 860.

[445] CPR 40APD, paras 1.1, 1.2, 3. See further *Vernon v. Vawdry* (1740) 2 Atk. 119; *Pit v. Cholmondeley* (1754) 2 Ves.Sen. 565; *Gething v. Keighley* (1878) 9 Ch.D. 547; *Holgate v. Shutt* (1884) 27 Ch.D. 111 and 28 Ch.D. 111; *Montgomery v. Cameron & Greig* [2007] CSOH 63 (OH).

[446] *Pritt v. Clay* (1843) 6 Beav. 503.

[447] See *Maund v. Allies* (1840) 5 Jur. 860; *Laing v. Campbell* (1865) 36 Beav. 3 (where bad debts were treated as good). And see *supra*, paras 10–76, 23–20.

[448] *Dawson v. Dawson* (1737) 1 Atk. 1; *Taylor v. Haylin* (1788) 2 Bro.C.C. 309; *Kinsman v. Barker* (1808) 14 Ves.Jr. 579; *Parkinson v. Hanbury* (1867) L.R. 2 H.L. 1.

[449] *Johnston v. Curtis* (1791) 2 Bro.C.C. 311, note.

[450] *Roberts v. Kuffin* (1741) 2 Atk. 112; also *Daniell v. Sinclair* (1881) 6 App.Cas. 181.

[451] See 1 Madd.Ch.Pr., 3rd ed., 144, where it is said to have been so held by Leach V.-C. in *Anon.*, March 6, 1821.

[452] [2008] EWCA Civ. 1412 (Lawtel 12/12/08) (CA), affirming the decision of Briggs J. at [2008] EWHC 228 (Ch) (Lawtel 19/2/08). Note that Briggs J. held, on the facts, that the Limitation Act 1980, s.32(1)(c) applied so as to preclude the son's reliance on a limitation defence.

[453] See *supra*, para. 23–32.

[454] See *Millar v. Craig* (1843) 6 Beav. 433; *Fowler v. Wyatt* (1857) 24 Beav. 232; *Parker v. Bloxham* (1855) 20 Beav. 295.

[455] See *supra*, para. 23–58.

(iii) *Arbitration award*

23–115   It is a good defence to an action for an account that the matters in dispute between the partners have previously been settled by arbitration, provided that the award is binding on the claimant.[456] However, a mere agreement to refer such matters to arbitration is not sufficient,[457] although a stay of the action may be obtained in such a case.[458]

Where the award relates to matters other than those which are the subject matter of the action, it will obviously not represent a ground of defence.[459] Lord Lindley gave the following example:

> " . . . an award on a reference of all matters in difference is no defence to an action for an account of moneys received after the making of the award, and not dealt with by it, owing to a mistake on the part of the arbitrator."[460]

Thus, in *Spencer v. Spencer*[461] all matters in dispute between the partners on a dissolution had been referred to arbitration and the arbitrator's award directed one partner to get in the outstanding debts, which were estimated at a certain amount. The award was acted on, but it appeared that the debts, when collected, exceeded the estimate put on them by the arbitrator. A partner claimed a share of that excess and an account was duly ordered by the court, it being evident that the award was founded on a mistake.[462]

(iv) *Accord and satisfaction*

23–116   Payment, as such, is not a defence to an action for an account, since the purpose of the action is to ascertain how much is or was payable. However, where a sum of money is paid by one partner to another and is accepted in lieu of all demands, that will amount to an accord and satisfaction, which *is* a good defence.[463]

Although the agreement representing the accord must be certain, it is not, in general, necessary to show that it has been performed in order to show satisfaction. The satisfaction lies in the consideration which makes the agreement operative and may take the form of an executory promise.[464]

---

[456] *Tittenson v. Peat* (1747) 3 Atk. 529; *Routh v. Peach* (1795) 2 Anst. 519 and 3 Anst. 637. The decision in *Reid v. Crabbe* [2009] CSIH 81 (IH) is a case of this class. There a retirement agreement required disputes as to a set of accounts to be determined by arbitration. The arbitrator ruled on the disputed issues and one of the partners then sought to raise additional issues on the accounts: it was held that she was not entitled to do so.

[457] *Michell v. Harris* (1793) 4 Bro.C.C. 312; *Thompson v. Charnock* (1799) 8 T.R. 139. See also *supra*, para. 10–273.

[458] Arbitration Act 1996, s.9: see *supra*, paras 10–274 *et seq.*

[459] As in *Farrington v. Chute* (1682) 1 Vern. 72.

[460] Note, however, the arbitrator's power to correct clerical errors in the award and, if necessary, to make an additional award: Arbitration Act 1996, s.57(3).

[461] (1827) 2 Y. & J. 249. An analogous principle was applied in *Teacher v. Calder* [1899] A.C. 451, where an accountant was required to certify the profits of a particular business, but did so without knowing that his certificate was intended to bind a person interested in such profits. In the circumstances, his certificates were held not to be binding.

[462] *Semble,* under the Arbitration Act 1996, in such a case the new account ought to be taken by an arbitrator since the arbitration clause will still apply.

[463] See, generally, *Chitty on Contracts* (30th ed.), paras 22–012 *et seq.* Lord Lindley's footnote at this point read "Bac.Ab.Accompt.E.; Vin.Ab.Account N.; *Brown v. Perkins* (1842) 1 Hare 564. But see Com.Dig.Accompt.E. 6, pl. 8."

[464] See *British Russian Gazette and Trade Outlook Ltd. v. Associated Newspapers Ltd.* [1933] 2 K.B. 616, 643 *et seq. per* Scrutton L.J. Also *Chitty on Contracts* (30th ed.), para. 22–015.

(v) *Waiver*

Lord Lindley observed: **23–117**

" . . . if an agreement to waive all accounts is entered into, and is founded on a sufficient consideration,[465] and is free of all taint of fraud or undue influence, the parties to it will be precluded from suing each other in respect of the accounts so agreed to be waived."[466]

(vi) *Release*

A release is obviously a good defence to an action for an account,[467] unless it was   **23–118** executed on the faith that certain accounts were correct which are later shown to be erroneous. In such a case, the release will be set aside and an fresh account ordered,[468] unless the parties clearly intended to abide by those accounts, irrespective of their content. A release can also be set aside on the grounds of fraud or misrepresentation.[469]

An effectual release must be by deed; if it is not, it will be regarded as a settled account.[470]

(c) Judgments for a partnership account

Form of judgment

Lord Lindley stated that a judgment for a partnership account would, in its   **23–119** simplest form, be as follows:

"Let an account be taken of all partnership dealings and transactions between the [*claimant*][471] and the defendant as co-partners from—. And let what upon taking the said account shall be certified to be due from either of the said parties to the other of them, be paid by the party from whom to the party to whom the same shall be certified to be due. Liberty to apply."[472]

---

[465] Such an agreement might, alternatively, be supported by a promissory estoppel.

[466] Lord Lindley referred, in this context, to the decision in *Sewell v. Bridge* (1749) 1 Ves.Sen. 297. This, however, would seem to be more a case of a settled account; *sed quaere*.

[467] See, generally, *Chitty on Contracts* (30th ed.), paras 22–003 *et seq.* Lord Lindley referred to Mitford, *Pleas* (5th ed.), p. 304 and the decision in *Brooks v. Sutton* (1868) L.R. 5 Eq. 361.

[468] See, for example, *Phelps v. Sproule* (1833) 1 M. & K. 231; *Wedderburn v. Wedderburn* (1838) 4 Myl. & Cr. 41; *Millar v. Craig* (1843) 6 Beav. 433; *Pritt v. Clay* (1843) 6 Beav. 503. See also *supra*, paras 23–109 *et seq.*

[469] See *supra*, paras 23–56 *et seq.*

[470] See *Chitty on Contracts* (30th ed.), paras 22–003, 22–004. Lord Lindley referred to Mitford, *Pleas* (5th ed.), p. 307. As to agreements to waive accounts, see *supra*, para. 23–117.

[471] The new terminology has been substituted.

[472] This form was derived from *Seton on Decrees* (4th ed.), p. 1197. A number of the older decided cases may usefully be referred to for the form of order adopted; for convenience, these are arranged alphabetically, according to the circumstances in which the account was sought (all references being to the relevant page of the report at which the order is to be found): (i) application of surplus assets (*Binney v. Mutrie* (1886) 12 App.Cas. 165; *Beningfield v. Baxter* (1886) 12 App.Cas. 181); (ii) executors trading with deceased partner's assets (*Travis v. Milne* (1851) 9 Hare 157); (iii) fraudulent representations (*Pillans v. Harkness* (1713) Colles, P.C. 448; *Rawlins v. Wickham* (1858) 1 Giff. 362); (iv) mortgagee of a partner's share (*Whetham v. Davey* (1885) 30 Ch.D. 580); (v) post-dissolution profits (*Crawshay v. Collins* (1808) 15 Ves.Jr. 230; (1826) 2 Russ. 347; *Manley v. Sartori* [1927] 1 Ch. 166); (vi) property acquired by one partner (*Fereday v. Wightwick* (1829) Tam. 262); (vii) release set aside and accounts reopened (*Millar v. Craig* (1843) 6 Beav. 442); (viii) sale, receiver and account (*Wilson v. Greenwood* (1818) 1 Swan. 483); (ix) sale of share set aside (*Cook v. Collingridge* (1822) Jac. 624 and, more fully, at 27 Beav. 456, note); (x) specific performance of agreement for partnership (*England v. Curling* (1844) 8 Beav. 140); (xi) successor firm (*Wedderburn v. Wedderburn* (1836) 2 Keen 752); (xii) wrongful expulsion (*Blisset v. Daniel* (1853) 10 Hare 538).

This is, in essence, the form of order which is still in use, although the consequential order for payment is commonly omitted.[473] When giving judgment, the court may, in addition, give directions as to the manner in which the account is to be conducted[474] and may further direct that the relevant books of account shall be taken as evidence of their contents, subject to any objections that may be taken to such contents.[475] Alternatively, such directions may be sought by an application at a later stage.[476] It should, however, be noted that where an account has already been produced by or on behalf of one party, the court *may* adopt a more streamlined approach and merely require the other party to identify what parts of the account he objects to.[477]

If the order does not provide otherwise:

(a) an account produced must be verified by an affidavit or witness statement and filed in court, with notice being given to the other parties to that effect[478];

(b) any item in the account which is disputed by another party must be identified in a written notice of objection verified in the same way.[479]

Self evidently, a party to the proceedings cannot, under the guise of an objection, raise an issue that has nothing to do with the entries in the account.[480]

Costs

Initial order

23–120   Prior to the advent of the Civil Procedure Rules, it had long been an established rule that all the costs of proceedings consequent on a dissolution should be

---

[473] See *Heward's Chancery Orders*, p. 62; *Atkin's Court Forms* (2nd ed.), Vol. 30(2) (2006 Issue), paras [224], [325] *et seq*. But see *ibid.* para. [332], as to the final order once the account has been taken.

[474] CPR 40APD, para. 1.1; Chancery Guide, para. 9.17.

[475] CPR 40APD, para. 1.2.

[476] *ibid.* paras 1.1, 1.3. Such an application will be made under CPR Pt 23 and should be made as soon as possible. The terms of the directions sought must be canvassed between the parties in correspondence *before* the application is made: Chancery Guide, para. 9.18.

[477] See *Montgomery v. Cameron & Greig* [2007] CSOH 63 (OH) at [36] *per* Lord Reed.

[478] CPR 40APD, para. 2. As to what is required where the order also directs all vouching documents to be produced, see *Sahota v. Sohi* [2004] EWHC 1469 (Ch) (Lawtel 8/7/04).

[479] *ibid.* para. 3.1, 3.3. Where possible, the notice should state the grounds of the objection and the correct amount(s) which should appear in the account: *ibid.* para. 3.2. It goes without saying that a generalised objection to the conents of the account will not suffice: see, under the equivalent Scottish procedure, *Gupta v. Ross* 2005 S.L.T. 548 (IH). Note that the absence of vouchers for an item in the account will not inevitably result in that item being disallowed: see *Sinclair v. Sinclair* [2009] 2 P. & C.R. DG15, at [41] *per* Proudman J.

[480] See *Welsh v. Dyce* [2009] CSOH 102 (OH). There an issue was purportedly raised as to whether a compromise agreement was binding but was held to be extraneous to the accounting process: *ibid.* at [7] *per* Lord Drummond Young. *cf.* the other issues raised at [11]. See further *supra*, para. 23–79.

paid out of the partnership assets, unless there was a good reason for making some other order.[481] Although the court now has a wide discretion on costs,[482] and must have regard to a number of factors in exercising that discretion,[483] the old rule will continue to be applied in most cases,[484] as confirmed both in *Sahota v. Sohi*[485] and *Stocking v. Montila*.[486] Where, however, proceedings are, in reality, commenced in order to obtain an adjudication on some disputed claim between the partners, the unsuccessful litigant will, as before, normally be ordered to pay the costs[487] unless his conduct justifies some other order.[488]

Where an account is sought without a dissolution,[489] the costs are likely to follow the event, in the usual way.[490]

There may, of course, be scope for a party to make an effective Part 36 offer, in relation to the whole claim or one or more issues arising therein, which will affect the incidence of costs.[491]

Taking the account

In the same way, the costs of taking any accounts, etc., which may be directed are, subject to the court's overriding discretion, likely to be ordered to be paid out **23–121**

---

[481] *Hamer v. Giles* (1879) 11 Ch.D. 942. However, this was not always the case: see *Hawkins v. Parsons* (1862) 8 Jur. (N.S.) 452; *Parsons v. Hayward* (1862) 4 De G.F. & J. 474. In the case of proceedings seeking a dissolution under the Partnership Act 1890, s.35, costs will, as a general rule, follow the event: see *infra*, para. 24–61.

[482] CPR r. 44.3. Although the general rule is that costs will follow the event (*ibid.* r. 44.3(2)(a)), it is clear that the courts will not slavishly adhere thereto: see, for example, *A.E.I. Rediffusion Music Ltd. v. Phonographic Performance Ltd.* [1999] 1 W.L.R. 1507, 1522 *et seq. per* Lord Woolf M.R.; *Bank of Credit & Commerce International SA v. Ali (No. 4), The Times*, March 2, 2000. The principles set out in *Re Elgindata Ltd. (No. 2)* [1992] 1 W.L.R. 1207 still, in general, hold good: *A.E.I. Rediffusion Music Ltd. v. Phonographic Performance Ltd., supra*; however, Lightman J. took a somewhat different view in *BCCI v. Ali (No. 4), supra*. Note that, when there is a split trial, the court may reserve the costs of the liability issue until after the account has been taken: *Shepherds Investments Ltd. v. Walters* [2007] C.P. Rep. 31 (CA).

[483] *ibid.* r. 44.3(4), (5). These factors include the conduct of the parties both before and during the proceedings.

[484] In cases of the type under consideration, *e.g.* which involve orders relating to the winding up of the partnership affairs, etc., it may be impossible to say that there has been a winner or a loser for the purposes of the "costs follow the event" principle. The position is, thus, analogous to that in *A.E.I. Rediffusion Music Ltd. v. Phonographic Performance Ltd., supra* (which concerned a decision of the Copyright Tribunal).

[485] [2006] EWHC 344 (Ch) (Lawtel 8/3/06). The principle justified no order for costs, but Park J. confined this to only 40% of the overall costs. As to the remainder, he determined the parties' liability by reference to the outcome of the various disputed points, in the usual way.

[486] [2007] EWHC 56 (Ch) (Lawtel 2/2/07). In this instance, this resulted in no costs order being made.

[487] *Warner v. Smith* (1863) 9 Jur.(N.S.) 169; *Hamer v. Giles, supra*; also *Norton v. Russell* (1875) L.R. 19 Eq. 343 (where a surviving partner refused to account to the executor of his deceased co-partner).

[488] See the CPR r. 44.3(4)(a), (5). The court may also take account of any offer to settle, whether under *ibid.* Pt 36 or otherwise: *ibid.* r. 44.3(4)(c).

[489] See *supra*, paras 23–82 *et seq.*

[490] Again this must be read subject to the court's overriding discretion under *ibid.* r. 44.3.

[491] It would, perhaps, be difficult to formulate such an offer until the issues arising on the taking of the account have been identified. See generally, as to the form of a Part 36 offer, *ibid.* r. 36.2, 36APD, para. 1.1 and Form N242A. Note that offers to settle do not *have* to be in a Part 36 form: *ibid.* r. 36.1(2); and see *Sahota v. Sohi, supra*; *Stocking v. Montila, supra*. It is clear that a *Calderbank* offer can be made in an action for an account: *Malhotra v. Dhawan* [1997] 8 Med.L.R. 319 (CA).

of the partnership assets and, if necessary, by a contribution between the partners.[492]

Priority of costs

23-122   Costs payable out of the partnership assets rank after the partnership debts and liabilities, including any sums due to the partners in respect of advances and the like.[493] Moreover, a partner will only be permitted to take his costs out of the partnership assets if he has made good any sums due from him to the firm, either by means of an actual payment or by an appropriate adjustment in the account. Thus, in *Ross v. White*,[494] where the claimant and defendant were equal partners, it appeared that £649 was due to the claimant in respect of an advance to the firm and that the defendant had withdrawn £601 more capital than the claimant. The funds in court being insufficient to defray these two sums as well as the costs of the action, it was held that the rights of the partners ought first to be adjusted by paying to the claimant the sums of £649 and £601 out of such funds, with the balance being applied towards payment of the costs of the action. The remainder of the costs fell to be borne by the partners in equal shares. This approach naturally accords with the requirements of the Partnership Act 1890.[495]

Solicitor's lien and charge for costs

23-123   If, after obtaining an order for dissolution and the appointment of a receiver, the claimant changes his solicitors, his former solicitors are not entitled to assert their lien for costs by retaining papers which have come into their hands in the course of the action, but must deliver them up to the new solicitors in return for the usual undertaking to preserve the lien.[496] This limitation on their rights is imposed in order to avoid embarrassment to the other partners and to the partnership creditors.

   If a partner's solicitor obtains a charge over the partnership assets for his taxed costs,[497] that charge may take priority over the rights of the partnership creditors,[498] even where the latter have previously obtained orders, in the usual form,[499] giving them a charge for their respective debts and costs on any moneys in the receiver's hands.[500] However, since the power is discretionary, where assets are "recovered" by one partner from his co-partners, the charge will only

---

[492] See *Austin v. Jackson* (1878) 11 Ch.D. 942, note; *Hamer v. Giles* (1879) 11 Ch.D. 942; *Potter v. Jackson* (1880) 13 Ch.D. 845; *Butcher v. Pooler* (1883) 24 Ch.D. 273; *Sahota v. Sohi* [2006] EWHC 344 (Ch) (Lawtel 8.3.06); *Stocking v. Montila* [2007] EWHC 56 (Ch) (Lawtel 2/2/07).

[493] *Austin v. Jackson, supra; Hamer v. Giles, supra; Potter v. Jackson, supra.*

[494] [1894] 3 Ch. 326.

[495] *ibid.* s.44, *infra*, paras 25–45 *et seq.*

[496] *Dessau v. Peters, Rushton & Co.* [1922] 1 Ch. 1.

[497] See the Solicitors Act 1974, s.73, as amended by the Legal Services Act 2007, Sched. 18, Pt 1, para. 68(b). As to the operation of this section, see *Harris v. Yarm* [1960] Ch. 256 (a decision under the equivalent provision in the Solicitors Act 1957); *Fairfold Properties Ltd. v. Exmouth Docks Co. Ltd. (No. 2)* [1993] Ch. 196. And see, as to waiver of the lien, *Clifford Harris & Co v. Solland International Ltd. (No.2)* [2005] 2 All E.R. 334.

[498] *Jackson v. Smith* (1884) 53 L.J.Ch. 972; *Ridd v. Thorne* [1902] 2 Ch. 344; *Newport v. Pougher* [1937] Ch. 214.

[499] *Kewney v. Attrill* (1886) 34 Ch.D. 345. See further, *supra*, para. 14–93.

[500] *Ridd v. Thorne* [1902] 2 Ch. 344.

extend to that partner's interest in such assets and will, thus, be subject to the prior claims of the partnership creditors.[501]

Taking the account

Lord Lindley summarised the method of taking a partnership account under a judgment in the usual form as follows:

23–124

> "(1) Ascertain how the firm stands as regards non-partners.
>
> (2) Ascertain what each partner is entitled to charge in account with his co-partners; remembering, in the words of Lord Hardwicke, that 'each is entitled to be allowed as against the other, everything he has advanced or brought in as a partnership transaction, and to charge the other in the account with what that other has not brought in, or has taken out more than he ought.'[502]
>
> (3) Apportion between the partners all profits to be divided or losses to be made good; and ascertain what, if anything, each partner must pay to the others, in order that all cross-claims may be settled."

This still holds true. It is accordingly necessary, when taking a partnership account, to identify and distinguish between:

23–125

(a) partnership property and the separate property of the partners[503];

(b) joints debts and separate debts[504];

(c) those profits and losses which are to be credited or debited to all the partners and those which are only to be credited or debited to one or more of them to the exclusion of the others.[505]

Obviously, much will depend on the terms of the original partnership agreement[506] and the subsequent conduct of the partners.[507]

Just allowances

Just allowances will be made in taking the account even where the order is silent on the point.[508] Lord Lindley pointed out that:

23–126

---

[501] *Wimbourne v. Fine* [1952] Ch. 869. In this case, the solicitor's charge did, however, rank in priority to a mortgage of the partner's interest in the assets.

[502] *West v. Skip* (1749) 1 Ves.Sen. 239, 242. Note that the rule in *Clayton's case*, relating to the appropriation of payments (*supra*, paras 13–85 *et seq.*), applies as between partners: see *Toulmin v. Copland* (1840) 7 Cl. & F. 349. Lord Lindley also observed, by way of footnote, that "It is said a partner is not to be charged as such with what he might have received, without his wilful default, *Rowe v. Wood* (1795) 2 J. & W. 553, but *quaere* whether a surviving partner could not be made so to account, as he alone can get in the assets of the firm. See, also, *Bury v. Allen* (1845) 1 Colly. 589." See further, *infra*, paras 26–31 *et seq.*

[503] See *supra*, paras 18–01 *et seq.*

[504] See *supra*, paras 12–01 *et seq.*

[505] See *supra*, paras 10–78 *et seq.*, 16–13 *et seq.* (profits), 20–04 *et seq.* (losses).

[506] See *supra*, paras 10–75 *et seq.*, 10–162 *et seq.* But see also *Watney v. Wells* (1867) L.R. 2 Ch.App. 250.

[507] See *supra*, paras 10–12 *et seq.*, 10–162, 10–165 *et seq.*

[508] CPR 40APD, para. 4.

" . . . when a partnership account is ordered, it is not usual for the Court to determine beforehand what are, and what are not, just allowances.[509] That is determined on taking the account; and, if necessary, the order will direct the [*Master*][510] to state the facts and reasons upon which he shall adjudge any allowances to be just allowances."[511]

In order to identify what allowances ought to be made, regard must be had to the terms of the partnership agreement and the principles noticed earlier in this work.[512] Thus, the court cannot, under the guise of a just allowance, award remuneration to a partner, when he has no right thereto under the Partnership Act 1890.[513] Nor can a party bring in a substantive claim which falls outside the parameters of the account which has been ordered, merely by seeking to treat it as a just allowance.[514] Interestingly, in *Emerson v. Estate of Emerson*,[515] an allowance was made in respect of a loss incurred by the surviving partner in carrying on the business following the death of his partner.

The court's attitude towards the availability and/or the amount of the allowance may, however, change if the partner seeking it has acted in breach of his fiduciary duties.[516]

Period to which account will relate

23–127 *Commencement:* A general account of partnership dealings and transactions will normally be taken as from the date on which the partnership commenced, unless some account has been settled between the partners in the meantime.[517] Since a settled account will not normally be reopened,[518] the general account will, in such a case, be taken as from the date of the last settled account.[519]

---

[509] For an example of the court's reluctance to prejudge any question of just allowances, see *Popat v. Shonchhatra* [1995] 1 W.L.R. 908, 917H–918A *per* David Neuberger Q.C. sitting as a judge of the Chancery Division. The allowance claimed was in respect of the defendant's occupation of a flat above the shop from which the partnership business had been carried on since the date of dissolution. See further, as to this case, *infra*, para. 25–28.

[510] In the original passage, the words "chief clerk" appeared at this point.

[511] See *Brown v. De Tastet* (1819) Jac. 284; *Cook v. Collingridge* (1823) Jac. 607; *Crawshay v. Collins* (1826) 2 Russ. 325; *Wedderburn v. Wedderburn* (1836) 2 Keen 753.

[512] See *supra*, paras 20–45 *et seq.*

[513] *Medcalf v. Mardell*, Unreported March 31, 1999 Ch D *per* Lloyd J. This point was not adverted to in the judgment of the Court of Appeal, Unreported March 2, 2000 CA (Civ Div). See generally, as to the right of a partner to remuneration, the Partnership Act 1890, s.24(6) and, *supra*, paras 20–43 *et seq.*

[514] See *Dickinson T/A John Dickinson Equipment Finance v. Rushmer T/A FJ Associates*, Unreported February 14, 2000 CA (Civ Div).

[515] [2004] 1 B.C.L.C. 575 (CA). Note also *Stocking v. Montila* [2005] EWHC 2210 (Ch) (Lawtel 24/10/05).

[516] See *Chirnside v. Fay* [2007] P.N.L.R. 6 (Sup. Ct. of New Zealand), albeit a decision concerning joint venturers.

[517] *Beak v. Beak* (1675) Finch 190; *Cook v. Collingridge* (1822) Jac. 607, 624. An incoming partner has no right to profits made before he became a partner, unless there is an agreement to that effect: *Gordon v. Rutherford* (1823) T. & R. 373. See, as to laches and limitation, *supra*, paras 23–19 *et seq.*, 23–32 *et seq.*

[518] See *supra*, paras 23–109 *et seq.*

[519] This used to be expressly provided for by inserting the following words in the order: "And in case it shall appear that any account has been settled and agreed upon between the parties up to any given time, the same is not to be disturbed". However, this is not necessary: see *Newen v. Wetten* (1862) 31 Beav. 315; *Holgate v. Shutt* (1884) 27 Ch.D. 111 and 28 Ch.D. 111; *cf. Milford v. Milford* (1868) McCle. & Yo. 150. See, nevertheless, as to the current recommended form, *Atkin's Court Forms* (2nd ed.), Vol. 30(2) (2006 issue), para. [325]. *cf. Heward's Chancery Orders*, p. 62.

Notwithstanding the normal rule, account may also be taken of the partners' dealings whilst the partnership was being set up, as Lord Lindley made clear:

> "Where the partners have had dealings together preparatory to the commencement of their partnership, these dealings cannot be excluded from consideration in taking the partnership accounts."[520]

Termination: Although it might be thought that a general account of partnership **23–128** dealings and transactions should not extend beyond the date of dissolution,[521] it cannot be assumed that such dealings and transactions will automatically come to a halt on that date.[522] Indeed, the Partnership Act 1890 provides that each partner's authority to bind to firm will continue for the purposes of winding up the partnership affairs.[523] Thus, in practice, the account will be taken up to the conclusion of the winding up, as Lord Lindley explained:

> " . . . some time or other must elapse between the dissolution and the final winding up of the affairs of the concern, and such time cannot in fairness to anyone be excluded from consideration.[524] . . . [A]n account of partnership dealings and transactions, although in one sense it stops at the date at which the partnership is dissolved, must still be kept open for the purpose of debiting and crediting the proper parties with the monies payable by or to them in respect of fresh transactions incidental to the winding up, as well as in respect of old transactions engaged in prior to the dissolution."[525]

Where a deceased or outgoing partner's share is retained in the partnership business in circumstances which attract the application of section 42(1) of the Partnership Act 1890,[526] any account of profits will, of course, extend from the date of death, retirement, etc., until the share is actually paid out.

Evidence on which accounts are taken

Where any item is challenged in the course of taking the account,[527] the **23–129** validity of that challenge will, ultimately, have to be determined by the court if it cannot be agreed between the parties.[528] The mere fact that certain figures produced by each side are similar is in itself unlikely to be determinative.[529] For this purpose, the contents of the partnership books will be of considerable importance. The court can direct that such books will stand as evidence of their contents, but this will not prevent a partner from objecting to such contents.[530]

---

[520] See *Cruikshank v. McVicar* (1844) 8 Beav. 106, 116 *per* Lord Langdale. Note also, in this context, the decision in *Khan v. Miah* [2000] 1 W.L.R. 2123 (HL), noted *supra*, para. 2–03; *cf. Goudberg v. Erniman Associates Pty. Ltd.* [2007] V.S.C.A. 12.

[521] See *Beak v. Beak* (1675) Finch 191 (dissolution by death); *Jones v. Noy* (1833) 2 M. & K. 125 (dissolution on grounds of mental disorder).

[522] See *infra*, paras 24–01 *et seq.*, 25–01.

[523] *ibid.* s.38. See *supra*, paras 13–62 *et seq.*

[524] See *Crawshay v. Collins* (1826) 2 Russ. 325, 345 *per* Lord Eldon; *Hale v. Hale* (1841) 4 Beav. 369, 375 *per* Lord Lansdale.

[525] See *Willett v. Blanford* (1842) 1 Hare 253, 270 *per* Wigram V.-C. However, the rights of the partners may be different after the date of dissolution: see *Watney v. Wells* (1867) L.R. 2 Ch.App. 250, noticed *supra*, para. 20–35; also *Booth v. Parks* (1828) 1 Moll. 465.

[526] See *infra*, paras 25–24 *et seq.*

[527] CPR 40APD, para. 3.1.

[528] Pursuant to *ibid.* para. 5. The service of points of claim and defence may be ordered: *ibid.*

[529] See *Gharavi-Nakhjavani v. Pelagias* [2005] EWCA Civ 908 (Lawtel 20/6/05).

[530] CPR 40APD, para. 1.2.

This largely replicates the position in Lord Lindley's day, when he pointed out that the partnership books:

" . . . being accessible to all the partners,[531] and being kept more or less under the surveillance of them all, are *prima facie* evidence against each of them, and, therefore, also, for any of them against the others.[532] But entries made by one partner without the knowledge of the other do not prejudice the latter as between himself and his co-partners[533] . . . ".

In *Morehouse v. Newton*,[534] a surviving partner drew up an account which he furnished to the executors of his late partner. It was held that the account was admissible against the surviving partner, but that the executors were not bound, merely because they had used it against him, to accept the accuracy of its contents.

If any books, etc., have been lost, so that the account cannot be proved in the normal way, special directions can be obtained from the court as to the manner in which the accounts are to be taken and verified.[535] Thus, where clients' files had been improperly removed from the partnership premises and subsequently lost, certain presumptions were made against the accounting party.[536]

23–130   *Production of books, etc.:* It was once the practice that a judgment for an account would direct all parties to produce on oath all books and papers in their custody relating to the taking of the accounts, but this is no longer the case.[537] Nevertheless, production of such books and papers will inevitably be required by way of disclosure.[538]

It has already been seen that a partner who chooses to keep partnership records in a private book of his own will be compelled to produce it and that professional privilege cannot be used to avoid such production.[539] The same obviously goes for any new books opened following a dissolution, if they relate to the subject matter of the account.[540] Where, however, the relevant books belong to the partner and a third party, the latter may be entitled to object to their production if he is not joined as a party to the proceedings, unless an order for disclosure of those books is obtained against him.[541]

---

[531] But see *supra*, para. 22–13.

[532] See *Lodge v. Prichard* (1853) 3 De G.M. & G. 906; *Gething v. Keighley* (1878) 9 Ch.D. 551; also *Smith v. Duke of Chandos* (1740) Barnard.Ch. 412 and (1741) 2 Atk. 158. But see *Stewart's Case* (1866) L.R. 1 Ch.App. 574, 587 *per* Turner L.J.

[533] *Hutcheson v. Smith* (1842) 5 I.Eq. R. 117.

[534] (1849) 3 De G. & Sm. 307. See also *Reeve v. Whitmore* (1865) 2 Dr. & Sm. 446.

[535] CPR 40APD, para. 1.1. Note, as to the old practice, *Adley v. Whitstable Co.* (1810) 17 Ves.Jr. 315; *Turner v. Corney* (1841) 5 Beav. 515; *Millar v. Craig* (1843) 6 Beav. 444; *Rowley v. Adams* (1844) 7 Beav. 391; *Lodge v. Prichard* (1853) 3 De G. M. & G. 906; *Stainton v. The Carron Co.* (1857) 24 Beav. 346; *Ewart v. Williams* (1855) 7 De G.M. & G. 68. And see, as to the provisions of the Bankers' Books Evidence Act 1879 (as amended), *Phipson on Evidence* (17th ed.), paras 32–108 *et seq.*

[536] See *Finlayson v. Turnbull (No.4)* 2003 G.W.D. 12–374 (OH).

[537] See *Heward's Chancery Orders*, p. 62; *Atkin's Court Forms* (2nd ed.), Vol. 30(2) (2006 issue), paras [224], [325] *et seq.*

[538] See also *supra*, paras 23–96 *et seq.*

[539] See *supra*, paras 22–13, 23–96; also *supra*, paras 23–107 *et seq.* Of the partner who has intermingled partnership records with his own, Lord Lindley commented: " . . . he should have kept his private accounts elsewhere, if he did not want them to be seen".

[540] *Hue v. Richards* (1839) 2 Beav. 305.

[541] See *supra*, para. 23–97.

If a partner has destroyed any books or accounts in his possession or otherwise improperly refuses to produce them, all necessary presumptions will be made against him when the account is taken.[542] This may even involve estimating the profits of the firm.[543] On the other hand, if there are simply no records at all, it may be impossible to proceed with that part of the account.[544]

Use of expert evidence: Prior to the Civil Procedure Rules, the commissioning   **23–131**
of an expert's report by each party to an action for an account was not uncommon. Now it would seem likely that, if expert evidence is required,[545] the court will insist on the employment of a joint expert, with a view to the saving of costs.[546]

Accountants employed by court: The court has power to employ a professional accountant as an assessor to assist it in taking the accounts and may act on his report.[547]

Result of taking the account

In the usual way the account will result in an order that one or more of the   **23–132**
partners will pay whatever is due from them to the other partner(s).[548] Unusually, in *R.A. Logan, Solicitors v. Maxwell*[549] the expert appointed to value the firm's work in progress proved unable to place a value on it, as a result of which the state of the account between the partners could not be ascertained and no sum could be shown as due from the defendant partner.[550]

Alternatives to an action for an account

The court has power to stay an action with a view to the parties attempting to   **23–133**
settle their differences by means of alternative dispute resolution.[551] As is made clear in the Chancery Guide,[552] parties are encouraged to look at this option or some other form of expert determination[553] as an alternative to the cumbersome accounts procedure.

---

[542] See *supra*, para. 22–12. And see *Finlayson v. Turnbull (No.4)* 2003 G.W.D. 12–374 (OH), noticed *supra*, para. 23–129.

[543] *Walmsley v. Walmsley* (1846) 3 Jo. & LaT. 556; see also *Gray v. Haig* (1855) 20 Beav. 219.

[544] See *R.A. Logan, Solicitors v. Maxwell* [2007] CSOH 163 (OH), noted *infra*, para. 23–132.

[545] Parties no longer have the *right* to put an expert's report into evidence: CPR r. 35.4(1). Note that the need for restraint in the use of expert evidence in commercial disputes was emphasised by Aikens J. in *JP Morgan Chase Bank v. Springwell Navigation Corp* [2006] 1 All E.R. (Comm) 549.

[546] *ibid.* r. 35.8.

[547] *ibid.* r. 35.15. *R.A. Logan, Solicitors v. Maxwell* [2007] CSOH 163 (OH) was a case of this type, albeit under the jurisdiction of the Scottish courts. Reference may also be made to the following older cases: *Re London, Birmingham & Bucks Ry.* (1855) 6 W.R. 141; *Hill v. King* (1863) 1 N.R. 341; *Meymott v. Meymott (No. 2)* (1864) 33 Beav. 590.

[548] See *supra*, paras 23–119, 23–124.

[549] [2007] CSOH 163 (OH).

[550] Lord Drummond Young observed that the result was not "obviously unfair" as the inability to value the work in progress resulted from the inadequacy of the partnership records, for which the other partners were largely responsible: *ibid.* at [27].

[551] CPR rr. 1.4(2)(e), 3.1(2)(f), 26.4. See further, as to the use of ADR, *supra*, para. 10–286.

[552] Chancery Guide, para. 22.4.

[553] See, as to the effect of an expert determination, *supra*, para. 10–175.

Stay of proceedings

23–134   In *Phillips v. Symes*,[554] the court in very exceptional circumstances, where the partnership was insolvent and there had already been extensive litigation between the parties, ordered that the accounts and inquiries be stayed for 2 years, after which the parties would be debarred from bringing any further claims against each other.

B.   INJUNCTIONS

Distinction between injunction and receiver

23–135   Where one or more partners are intent on ignoring the terms of the partnership agreement or otherwise acting in breach of the implied duty of good faith which they owe to their co-partners,[555] the court will, in an appropriate case, intervene either by granting an injunction against the miscreant partner(s) or by appointing a receiver or a receiver and manager.[556] These two remedies are very different in their effect, not least because the appointment of a receiver will affect all the partners, both claimant(s) and defendant(s) alike.[557] Lord Lindley summarised the position as follows:

> "These two modes of interference require to be considered separately; for they are not had recourse to indiscriminately. The appointment of a receiver, it is true, always operates as an injunction, for the Court will not suffer its officer to be interfered with by anyone[558]; but it by no means follows that because the Court will not take the affairs of a partnership into its own hands, it will not restrain some one or more of the partners from doing what may be complained of."[559]

Injunction without a dissolution

23–136   It has already been seen that courts were once reluctant to interfere between partners, save with a view to dissolution.[560] However, as Lord Lindley explained:

---

[554] [2008] B.P.I.R. 212.

[555] See *supra*, paras 16–01 *et seq.*

[556] In practice, the court may grant an injunction as well as a receiver, in Lord Lindley's words "to mark its sense of the impropriety of the conduct of those it specially restrains". See *Evans v. Coventry* (1854) 3 Drew. 75, 82 *per* Kindersley V.-C. See further, as to receivers, *infra*, paras 23–153 *et seq.*

[557] See *Dixon v. Dixon* [1904] 1 Ch. 164 and, *infra*, para. 23–153.

[558] See *Helmore v. Smith (No. 2)* (1887) 35 Ch.D. 449. As to restraining interference with a receiver, see *infra*, para. 23–181.

[559] See *Hall v. Hall* (1850) 12 Beav. 414; but see also, as to the injunctions that were granted, *ibid.* (1850) 3 Mac. & G. 79, 84 *per* Truro L.C. And see *Tate v. Charlesworth* (1962) 106 S.J. 368 (where partnership principles were applied by analogy).

[560] See *supra*, para. 23–16; also *Hall v. Hall* (1850) 3 Mac. & G. 79.

"Whatever doubt there may formerly have been upon the subject, it is clear that an injunction will not be refused simply because no dissolution of partnership is sought."[561]

Degree of misconduct required

Even though the court is prepared to grant injunctive relief as between partners, it will not do so lightly. In a passage which was echoed in his consideration of the grounds on which a court will dissolve a partnership,[562] Lord Lindley observed: **23–137**

"Mere squabbles and improprieties, arising from infirmities of temper, are not considered sufficient ground for an injunction[563]; but if one partner excludes his co-partner from his rightful interference in the management of the partnership affairs, or if he persists in acting in violation of the partnership articles on any point of importance, or so grossly misconducts himself as to render it impossible for the business to be carried on in a proper manner, the Court will interfere for the protection of the other partners.[564] Where, however, the partner complained of has by agreement been constituted the active managing partner, the Court will not interfere unless a strong case be made out against him[565]; nor will the Court restrain a partner from acting as such, merely because if he is known so to do, the confidence placed in the firm by the public will be shaken."[566]

By way of illustration, an injunction has been granted in the following circumstances, which are, for convenience, arranged in alphabetical order:

Exclusion: Where a partner, who had recovered from a temporary mental dis-   **23–138** order, was excluded from the management of the partnership affairs, he was granted an injunction restraining the other partners from seeking to prevent him transacting the business of the partnership.[567] In another case,[568] an excluded partner was granted an injunction restraining the defendant from applying any of the moneys and effects of the partnership otherwise than in the ordinary course of business, and from obstructing or interfering with the claimant in the exercise or enjoyment of his rights under the partnership agreement. A similar attitude

---

[561] This is, if anything, underlined by the terms of the Senior Courts Act 1981, s.37(1)–(3) (formerly the Supreme Court Act 1981: Constitutional Reform Act 2005, Sched. 11, Pt 1, para. 1(1)) and its predecessors. See also the County Courts Act 1984, s.38(1), as substituted by the Courts and Legal Services Act 1990, s.3.

[562] See *infra*, paras 24–81, 24–82.

[563] See *Lawson v. Morgan* (1815) 1 Price 303; *Cofton v. Horner* (1818) 5 Price 537; *Marshall v. Colman* (1820) 2 J. & W. 266; *Smith v. Jeyes* (1841) 4 Beav. 503; *Warder v. Stilwell* (1856) 3 Jur.(N.S.) 9.

[564] See generally, *infra*, paras 24–85, 24–100. And note the decision in *Anderson v. Wallace* (1835) 2 Moll. 540.

[565] See *Waters v. Taylor* (1808) 15 Ves.Jr. 10; *Lawson v. Morgan* (1815) 1 Price 303; *Automatic Self-Cleaning Filter Syndicate Co. Ltd. v. Cuninghame* [1906] 2 Ch. 34, 44 *per* Cozens Hardy L.J. See also *Walker v. Hirsch* (1884) 27 Ch.D. 460.

[566] *Anon.* (1856) 2 K. & J. 441.

[567] *ibid.*

[568] *Hall v. Hall* (1855) 20 Beav. 139; but see also *ibid.* (1850) 3 Mac. & G. 79, 84 *per* Truro L.C. And see *Blisset v. Daniel* (1853) 10 Hare 493; *Carmichael v. Evans* [1904] 1 Ch. 486 (where an injunction was refused on the merits); *Barnes v. Youngs* [1898] 1 Ch. 414.

will be adopted where any partner seeks to exclude his co-partners from possession of any partnership chattels[569] or land, even if he is the sole trustee thereof.[570] The position will be no different after the firm has been dissolved.[571]

23-139   *Purported retirement:* Where a partner in a fixed term partnership purported to retire and entered into a new partnership with third parties, which assumed the name of the old firm, opened letters addressed to it, and circulated notices of its dissolution, an injunction was granted restraining the "retired" partner from carrying on any business otherwise than with his original partners and from publishing or circulating any notice of the old firm's dissolution, before the expiration of the fixed term.[572] Moreover, his new partners were restrained from carrying on business with him, or otherwise, in the name of the old firm, from receiving or opening letters addressed to it, and from interfering with its property.[573]

A somewhat similar situation arose in *Voaden v. Voaden.*[574] There, the defendant had served notice to retire from the firm and subsequently secured his partners' agreement to the abridgement of his notice period, on the footing that he would immediately enter the full-time employment of a client company. In the event he did not enter such employment full-time,[575] but sought to practise on his own account in competition with the firm. Having concluded on the evidence that there was a serious question to be tried as to whether the abridgement of the notice period was effective,[576] Lindsay J. granted an interlocutory injunction to prevent the defendant from practising otherwise than as an employee during the

---

[569] Lord Lindley wrote: "Partners are tenants in common or joint tenants of the goods and chattels belonging to the firm; but one partner has no right to take possession of them and to exclude his co-partners from them; and he can, it is apprehended, be restrained from doing so." See also *supra,* paras 19–03 *et seq.*

[570] Lord Lindley observed: "The equitable as well as the legal ownership must be considered; no partner can eject or expel his co-partners from land in which he may have the legal estate, but of which he is a trustee for the firm; nor can he maintain an action against his co-partners for coming on such land. On the other hand, they can restrain him from excluding them therefrom. [*See Peaceable v. Read (1801) 1 East 568; Doe v. Horn (1838) 3 M. & W. 333*]. Whether the relation of trustee and *cestuis que trustent* exists depends upon whether the property is partnership property or not, upon whether the partnership is dissolved or not, and upon whether, if dissolved, the property is a partnership asset in which all the partners are still interested." See also *Hawkins v. Hawkins* (1858) 4 Jur.(N.S.) 1044. Now rights of occupation under a trust of land are, in general, governed by the Trusts of Land and Appointment of Trustees Act 1996, ss.12, 13. A partner who is excluded from occupation of the land may well be entitled to an occupation rent under *ibid.* s.13(6) or, in certain circumstances, under the general law: see *French v. Barcham* [2009] 1 W.L.R. 1124, where the earlier authorities are reviewed; also *Amin v. Amin* [2009] EWHC 3356 (Ch) (Lawtel 5/1/10). And see *Stocking v. Montila* [2005] EWHC 2210 (Ch) (Lawtel 24/10/05), where there was, as such, no ouster following the dissolution of a partnership. However, it is doubtful whether such a rent could be recovered otherwise than by an action for an account: see *supra,* para. 23–76.

[571] Since all the partners' rights and obligations continue for the purposes of the winding up: Partnership Act 1890, s.38: see *supra,* paras 13–62 *et seq.* See further, *infra,* paras 23–145 *et seq.*

[572] Note that it would, in such a case, not be open to the remaining partners to treat the "retired" partner's conduct as repudiatory and thereby to bring about the dissolution of the firm: see *infra,* paras 24–05 *et seq.*

[573] *England v. Curling* (1844) 8 Beav. 129. See also *Warder v. Stilwell* (1856) 3 Jur.(N.S.) 9; *Tate v. Charlesworth* (1962) 106 S.J. 368.

[574] February 27, 1997 (unreported).

[575] The circumstances in which he came not to be employed full-time by the client company were, however, in dispute.

[576] *Quaere,* if the agreement abridging the notice period were rescinded or otherwise avoided, would this recreate the partnership relationship? See further *supra,* para. 23–68.

balance of the original notice period, but did not go so far as to force him back into the partnership.[577] Nevertheless, the effect of the injunction was to replicate the restrictions which would have been applicable to the defendant if he had remained a partner for the balance of that notice period.[578]

Unauthorised business: Where the lease of a particular branch office had expired **23–140** and the claimant was unwilling to concur in taking a new lease, the defendant was restrained from carrying on the partnership business at that office against the claimant's wishes.[579]

Use of firm name: An injunction has been granted restraining a partner from using the firm name in a business carried on by him on his own account.[580]

Misconduct with a view to dissolution

It is clear that the courts will, where appropriate, interfere by way of injunction **23–141** with a view to preventing one partner from misconducting himself in such a way that his co-partners are forced either to condone his misconduct or agree to a dissolution.[581]

Attempts to frustrate the decision making process

On the same basis, it may be that injunctive relief could be obtained against a **23–142** partner who seeks to obstruct a particular course of action which will benefit the partnership at no detriment to himself, if his actions involve a deliberate breach of the duty of good faith, *e.g.* where he is attempting to secure an alteration to the partnership agreement in his own favour as the price of his co-operation.[582] However, the current editor considers that such an order would only be entertained by the court in exceptional circumstances.[583]

Injunction where partnership is at will

Although the view was advanced, in some earlier cases,[584] that it is more **23–143** difficult for the court to interfere by way of injunctive relief in the case of a partnership at will, on the grounds that the court's order can be rendered nugatory

---

[577] Lindsay J. appeared to recognise that so to do would infringe the principle that the court will not specifically enforce a partnership agreement: see further *supra*, paras 23–45 *et seq.*

[578] The corollary was that he was entitled to the drawings he would have received during this period, subject to his obligation to give credit for any earnings derived from his employment.

[579] *Clements v. Norris* (1878) 8 Ch.D. 129. See also *Nixon v. Wood* (1987) 284 E.G. 1055, where an interim injunction was in fact refused, following an application of the principles enunciated in *American Cyanamid Co. v. Ethicon Ltd.* [1975] A.C. 396.

[580] *Aas v. Benham* [1891] 2 Ch. 244.

[581] See *supra*, paras 23–16, 23–85 and *infra*, paras 24–85, 24–100.

[582] For an analogous case involving consent to the amendment of a pension scheme, see *Imperial Group Pension Trust Ltd. v. Imperial Tobacco Ltd.* [1991] 1 W.L.R. 589. There, however, injunctive relief was not sought.

[583] *e.g.* where a freezing injunction would be justified: see *infra*, paras 23–150, 23–151. There are, of course, no such powers as exist under the Companies Act 2006, s.306 in the case of a partnership: cf. *Re Woven Rugs Ltd.* [2002] 1 B.C.L.C. 324.

[584] See *Peacock v. Peacock* (1809) 16 Ves.Jr. 49; *Miles v. Thomas* (1839) 9 Sim. 606.

by the simple expedient of giving notice of dissolution,[585] such caution was not in truth justified. As Lord Lindley put it, if the partnership is dissolved:

" . . . an injunction will not necessarily be futile, inasmuch as so long as it continues in force, the defendant is rendered powerless for evil,[586] and a notice by him to dissolve the partnership cannot, *per se*, operate as a dissolution of the injunction."

Surprisingly, there appear to be no direct authorities on this point: Lord Lindley referred to the decisions in *Glassington v. Thwaites*,[587] *Morris v. Colman*[588] and *Homfray v. Fothergill*,[589] but conceded that, according to the reports, none of them actually involved a partnership at will.[590]

23–144 However, in *Floydd v. Cheney*,[591] where an interim injunction restraining the defendant, who was an assistant in the claimant's architectural practice, from making improper use of certain papers, Megarry J. held that there was no evidence of a partnership at will as the defendant contended, but that the same relief would have been ordered even if the existence of such a partnership had been proved.[592]

It should also be noted in this context that a notice of dissolution served with the sole purpose of evading the effects of the injunction might be held *mala fide* and, thus, invalid.[593]

Injunction in dissolution actions

23–145 There has never been any doubt that the court will, in appropriate circumstances, grant injunctive relief where dissolution proceedings are pending or, in the case of a dissolved partnership, where it is sought, in Lord Lindley's words, "to restrain one of the partners from doing any act which will impede the winding up of the concern".[594] Examples in the reports are numerous, and may be classified as follows:

Assets: A partner will be restrained from appropriating assets for his own benefit[595] or disposing of or getting in the partnership assets if he is likely to

---

[585] See generally, *infra*, paras 24–18 *et seq*. And note the implications of the decision in *Walters v. Bingham* [1988] 1 F.T.L.R. 260: see *infra*, para. 24–21.

[586] *i.e.* he cannot damage or otherwise act against the interests of the partnership.

[587] (1823) 1 Sim. & St. 124.

[588] (1812) 18 Ves.Jr. 437.

[589] (1866) L.R. 1 Eq. 567.

[590] Lord Lindley observed: "It does not appear from the reports of these cases whether the partnerships were partnerships at will or not; but supposing them to have been merely partnerships at will, it is clear that the injunctions were far from valueless." Note, however, the decision in *Cuffe v. Murtagh* (1881) 7 Ir. L.R. 411, noted *supra*, para. 23–45, n. 166.

[591] [1970] Ch. 602.

[592] *ibid.* p. 608. This part of the judgment is clearly *obiter*.

[593] See *infra*, para. 24–21.

[594] A person who merely shares the profits of the business will normally have no such right: see *Walker v. Hirsch* (1884) 27 Ch.D. 460.

[595] *Ingram v. Keeling* [2006] EWHC 2725 (Ch) (Lawtel 27/10/06) is, in effect, a case of this class. There a partner who had removed client files without authority following a dissolution was ordered to deliver them up to to the dissolved firm.

misapply them.[596] Moreover, the personal representatives of a deceased partner will be restrained from making any improper use of partnership property, if the legal estate happens to devolve on them.[597] Equally, in *Latchman v. Pickard*,[598] an interim injunction permitting one partner to have access to the former partnership premises was refused, ultimately because of the practical difficulties which this was likely to cause.[599]

Bills of exchange: A partner will be restrained from drawing, accepting or indorsing bills of exchange in the firm name otherwise than for partnership purposes.[600]

Books: A partner will be restrained from withholding the partnership books.[601]

Business: A partner will be restrained from carrying on the partnership business **23–146** for any purpose other than winding up[602] or from improperly interfering with, obstructing or otherwise damaging such business.[603] Such an order can, if necessary, be made against a partner suffering from mental incapacity.[604]

Debts: A partner will, in an appropriate case, be restrained from getting in debts owing to the firm[605] and any debtor who, with knowledge of the order, makes a payment to that partner will not be discharged from liability to the firm.[606]

Dissolution agreements: The court will naturally grant relief in order to restrain any breach of the partnership agreement or any other agreement governing the dissolution. Thus, it will readily enforce an express[607] or implied[608] restriction on

---

[596] *Hartz v. Schrader* (1803) 8 Ves.Jr. 317 (surviving partner); *O'Brien v. Cooke* (1871) I.R. 5 Eq. 51 (where the claimant was allowed to get in the debts, on indemnifying the defendant against costs, etc.). See also *Garrett v. Moore* (1891), Seton (6th ed.), p. 696, where an interim injunction was granted to restrain a partner from drawing out partnership moneys which he had paid into his private account. The case was not, however, referred to in the 7th edition of Seton.

[597] *Alder v. Fouracre* (1818) 3 Swan. 489.

[598] [2005] EWHC 1011 (Ch) (Lawtel 12/5/05).

[599] *ibid.* at [25]. Note that Warren J. expressed a strong preference for the appointment of a receiver in all the circumstances, although no application for such an appointment was before him.

[600] *Williams v. Bingley* (1692) 2 Vern. 278, note, and Coll.Prt. (2nd. ed.) 233; *Jervis v. White* (1802) 6 Ves.Jr. 738; *Hood v. Aston* (1826) 1 Russ. 412.

[601] *Charlton v. Poulter* (1753) 19 Ves.Jr. 148, note; *Taylor v. Davis* (1842) 3 Beav. 388, note; *Greatrex v. Greatrex* (1847) 1 De G. & Sm. 692.

[602] See *De Tastet v. Bordenave* (1822) Jac. 516 (where, on the evidence, an injunction was refused). The report is, however, less than clear on the point. See also the Partnership Act 1890, s.38, considered *supra*, paras 13–62 *et seq.*

[603] *Charlton v. Poulter* (1753) 19 Ves.Jr. 148, note; *Smith v. Jeyes* (1841) 4 Beav. 503; also *Hermann Loog v. Bean* (1884) 26 Ch.D. 306, (an agency case which is, by analogy, applicable to partnerships). Note that in *Marshall v. Watson* (1858) 25 Beav. 501, an injunction to restrain a partner from publishing the accounts of the firm was, under special circumstances, refused.

[604] *J. v. S.* [1894] 3 Ch. 72.

[605] *Read v. Bowers* (1793) 4 Bro.C.C. 441.

[606] *Eastern Trust Co. v. McKenzie, Mann & Co. Ltd.* [1915] A.C. 750.

[607] See *supra*, paras 10–218 *et seq.*

[608] *Churton v. Douglas* (1859) Johns. 174; *Hookham v. Pottage* (1872) L.R. 8 Ch.App. 91. See further, *supra*, paras 10–206 *et seq.*

competition or a term relating to the collection of debts[609] or the treatment of trade secrets.[610]

23–147   *Goodwill:* A partner will be restrained from damaging the value of the goodwill if it ought to be sold for the benefit of all the partners,[611] or if it belongs solely to his co-partners.[612] However, a surviving partner will not be restrained from continuing to carry on business in the name of himself and his deceased co-partner, unless this would involve a breach of the partnership agreement or the goodwill ought to be sold.[613]

Representatives of deceased or insolvent partner: The personal representatives of a deceased partner or the trustee in bankruptcy or liquidator of an insolvent partner will be restrained from interfering in the business, at the instance of the surviving partners.[614] Equally, a surviving partner will, where necessary, be restrained from improperly ejecting such personal representatives, etc.[615]

Springboard relief: Where a partner has committed a breach of duty prior to the dissolution, it may be possible to obtain a so-called "springboard" injunction to prevent him taking unfair advantage of that breach after the dissolution, provided that the advantage still exists and can be effectively reversed.[616] Relief was refused in *Deacons v. White & Case LLP*[617] because of the passage of time.

Misconduct by partner seeking injunction

23–148   It is self evident that injunctive relief cannot, in general, be obtained by a partner who is himself in breach of any obligation owed to his co-partners, whether arising by agreement or pursuant to the provisions of the Partnership Act 1890. As Lord Lindley put it:

"... a partner who seeks an injunction against his co-partner must himself be able and willing to perform his own part of any agreement which he seeks to restrain his co-partner from breaking[618]; and the plaintiff's own misconduct may be a complete bar to his application, however wrong the defendant's conduct may have been.[619] As

---

[609] *Davis v. Amer* (1854) 3 Drew. 64. See also *supra*, para. 10–267.

[610] *Morison v. Moat* (1851) 9 Hare 241. See also *supra*, para. 10–55.

[611] *Bradbury v. Dickens* (1859) 27 Beav. 53; *Turner v. Major* (1862) 3 Giff. 442; *Dixon v. Dixon* [1904] 1 Ch. 161; also *Davis v. Smaggasgale* (1890), Seton (7th ed.), pp. 680, 681; *Re David and Matthews* [1899] 1 Ch. 378.

[612] *Trego v. Hunt* [1896] A.C. 7; *Boorne v. Wicker* [1927] 1 Ch. 667; *Gargan v. Ruttle* [1931] I.R. 152.

[613] See *supra*, paras 10–198 *et seq.*, 10–218 *et seq.*

[614] See *Allen v. Kilbre* (1819) 4 Madd. 464; *Davidson v. Napier* (1827) 1 Sim. 297; *Ex p. Finch* (1832) 1 D. & Ch. 174; *Freeland v. Stansfeld* (1854) 2 Sm. & G. 479; *Fraser v. Kershaw* (1856) 2 K. & J. 496. *cf.* the position where all the partners are dead: *Philips v. Atkinson* (1787) 2 Bro.C.C. 272.

[615] *Hawkins v. Hawkins* (1858) 4 Jur.(N.S.) 1044. Note also *Elliot v. Brown* (1791) 3 Swan. 489, note.

[616] See *Roger Bullivant Ltd. v. Ellis* [1987] I.C.R. 464; *UBS Wealth Managment (UK) Ltd. v. Vestra Wealth LLP* [2008] EWCA 1974 (Ch) (Lawtel 18/9/08); *Dass Solicitors v. Southcott*, April 2, 2009 (Lawtel 14/12/09) (all cases concerning employees).

[617] HCA 2433/2002, October 24, 2003 (Hong Kong High Court). See also *supra*, para. 10–213.

[618] *Smith v. Fromont* (1818) 2 Swan. 330.

[619] See *Littlewood v. Caldwell* (1822) 11 Price 97, where an injunction was refused because the claimant had taken away the partnership books.

stated by Lord Eldon in *Const v. Harris*,[620] a partner who complains that his co-partners do not do their duty to him must be ready at all times, and offer to do his duty to them."

This principle does, however, have limits.[621]

Injunction to restrain holding out

The liability undertaken by a person who is held out as a partner has already been noticed.[622] Unauthorised holding out will, not unnaturally, be restrained by the court.[623] **23–149**

Freezing injunction

A freezing injunction[624] seeks to prevent a defendant frustrating a judgment by removing money or assets out of the jurisdiction of the court or otherwise dissipating money or assets in his hands.[625] Examples of such injunctions as between partners are few, but there can be no doubt that the court will grant the relief in an appropriate case.[626] Where it is sought to safeguard moneys due to the firm[627] or an asset in a partner's hands,[628] the application will be relatively straightforward.[629] If, however, the underlying claim is dependent on the taking of an account as between the partners,[630] it will, at the very least, be necessary for the claimant to demonstrate that he has a right to an account[631] *and* that a net **23–150**

---

[620] (1824) T. & R. 496, 526.

[621] See *supra*, para. 16–05.

[622] See *supra*, paras 5–35 *et seq.*

[623] See *Dixon v. Holden* (1869) L.R. 7 Eq. 488; *Thynne v. Shove* (1890) 45 Ch.D. 577; *Gray v. Smith* (1889) 43 Ch.D. 208. See also *supra*, paras 10–201, 10–202.

[624] Formerly known as a *Mareva* injunction, after the order made in *Mareva Compania Naviera S.A. v. International Bulk Carriers S.A.* [1975] 2 Lloyd's Rep. 509.

[625] See the Senior Courts Act 1981, s.37(1), (3) (formerly the Supreme Court Act 1981: Constitutional Reform Act 2005, Sched. 11, Pt 1, para. 1(1)); CPR r. 25.1(1)(f). Such an order can be made at any time and may thus be used in aid of execution: CPR r. 25.2(1)(b); see also *Orwell Steel (Erection and Fabrication) Ltd. v. Asphalt and Tarmac (U.K.) Ltd.* [1984] 1 W.L.R. 1097; *Babanaft International Co. S.A. v. Bassatne* [1990] Ch. 13.

[626] See *Don King Productions Inc. v. Warren (No. 2)*, *The Times*, June 18, 1998; also *Don King Productions Inc. v. Warren* [1999] 2 Lloyd's Rep. 392. And note *Investment and Pensions Advisory Service Ltd. v. Gray* [1990] B.C.L.C. 38, where the injunction was obtained by the liquidator of an insolvent firm against a member of that firm.

[627] This appears to have been the basis of the injunction granted in *Don King Productions Inc. v. Warren (No. 2)*, *supra*, in respect of assets up to a value of £1,750,000, representing the amount of certain consultancy fees payable to Mr Warren under an agreement with a third party. Another example would be monies for which the defendant is accountable under the Partnership Act 1890, ss.29, 30, as to which see *supra*, paras 16–14 *et seq.*

[628] Such an order was made in *Phillips v. Symes* (where the existence of the partnership was in dispute), but the history of the action is not set out in the report in *The Times*, October 2, 2001. See, as to the type of assets which may be made subject to a *Mareva* injunction, *Darashah v. U.F.A.C. (U.K.) Ltd.*, *The Times*, March 30, 1982 (goodwill); *C.B.S. United Kingdom Limited v. Lambert* [1983] Ch. 37.

[629] Of course, a freezing injunction will not be granted lightly and a strong case must *always* be made out. The application will be made under CPR Pt 23 see also *ibid.* 25APD, Annex.

[630] As to the need for a general account to be taken before the respective entitlements of the partners can be ascertained, see *supra*, para. 23–76.

[631] See *Ali & Fahd Shobokshi Group Ltd. v. Moneim* [1989] 1 W.L.R. 710, 714 *per* Mervyn Davies J. (although a continuation of the injunction was refused in this case on the grounds of non-disclosure).

sum is likely to be due to him once the account has been taken.[632] No such difficulties will, of course, arise if the account has already been taken and a balance found to be due from the defendant.

23–151   Although it would, in theory, be possible for a court to grant a freezing-type injunction preventing a partner from voting against a particular resolution on the ground that he is actuated by an ulterior and improper motive, it would seemingly be necessary to demonstrate that his withholding of consent would have such catastrophic effects for the firm that it is akin to a wilful dissipation of assets.[633] Cases of this type will obviously be extremely rare.

The court will not grant a freezing injunction if, by so doing, it would interfere with the business rights of third parties.[634] It is accordingly desirable to ensure that all the partners are before the court, either as claimants or defendants.

In an appropriate case, the court will appoint a receiver in aid of a freezing injunction.[635]

Arbitrations

23–152   The court has the same powers of granting interim injunctions where a dispute has been referred to arbitration as it has in relation to legal proceedings.[636] Although an arbitrator clearly has power to grant a final injunction,[637] it is more doubtful whether he can grant similar relief on an interim basis.[638]

C.   RECEIVERS

Purpose and desirability of appointing a receiver and manager

23–153   Lord Lindley summarised the position in these terms:

"The object of having a receiver appointed by the Court[639] is to place the partnership

---

[632] In *Hardick v. Morgan*, December 22, 1997 (unreported), a freezing injunction confined to assets in England and Wales was granted to a retired partner in respect of sums apprehended to be due to her in respect of her partnership share, which could only be quantified in fairly broad terms. On January 13, 1998 this was extended to a worldwide injunction. Although, in Z *Ltd. v. A-Z and AA-LL* [1982] Q.B. 558, 585, Kerr L.J. said that the claimant would have to satisfy the court that he was likely to recover judgment "for a certain or approximate sum", it is clear from cases such as *Hardick v. Morgan* that the court will not, in practice, approach the issue of quantum in an overly restrictive way. See also *Wanklyn v. Wilson* (1887) 35 Ch.D. 180, where a payment into court was sought against a defendant who had already rendered an account. *Semble*, a freezing order will often be more appropriate than an order for the payment of money into court (see *supra*, paras 23–91 *et seq.*) or for an interim payment (see *supra*, para. 23–95).

[633] See *Standard Chartered Bank v. Walker* [1992] 1 W.L.R. 561, where the injunction was granted against a shareholder in a company.

[634] *Galaxia Maritime S.A. v. Mineralimportexport* [1982] 1 W.L.R. 539. Note also the obligations which may be imposed upon the claimant in respect of expenses and liabilities incurred by third parties when a freezing injunction is granted: see Z *Ltd. v. A-Z and AA-LL* [1982] Q.B. 558.

[635] *Don King Productions Inc. v. Warren* [1999] 2 Lloyd's Rep. 392. There the court, in the face of certain undertakings, etc., offered by the defendant, declined to make the appointment.

[636] Arbitration Act 1996, s.44(1), (2)(e). But note, in non-urgent cases, *ibid.* s.44(3), (4) and the decision in *Cetelem SA v. Rous Holdings Ltd.* [2005] 2 All E.R. (Comm) 203 (CA).

[637] *ibid.* s.48(5)(a).

[638] See *supra*, para. 10–280.

[639] See generally, as to the court's jurisdiction to appoint a receiver, the Senior Courts Act 1981, s.37(1) (formerly the Supreme Court Act 1981: Constitutional Reform Act 2005, Sched. 11, Pt 1, para. 1(1)); CPR Pt 69, 69PD.

assets under the protection of the Court, and to prevent everybody, except the officer of the Court, from in any way intermeddling with them. The object of having a manager is to have the partnership business carried on under the direction of the Court[640]; a receiver, unless he is also appointed manager, has no power to carry on the business."

In practice, claims for the appointment of a receiver or receiver and manager have tended to be included in partnership actions as a matter of course, with scant regard to the suitability of that form of relief or the consequences for the partners, either in terms of disruption or expense.[641] It is essential to appreciate that the appointment of a receiver operates in a very different way from an injunction, in that it affects the rights of *all* the partners[642] and will be granted according to different principles. As Lord Lindley put it:

"It ... does not follow that because the Court will grant an injunction it will also appoint a receiver; nor that because it refuses to appoint a receiver it will also decline to interfere by injunction."[643]

Even before the advent of the Civil Procedure Rules, the courts had regard to the potentially disproportionate expense of appointing a receiver[644] and it would now seem likely that an application for such relief will be subjected to particularly careful scrutiny in terms of the overriding objective.[645] In addition, it would seem that the court will not, in general, favour a receivership which will have an extended duration.[646] For this reason, the current editor is fortified in his view that the appointment of a receiver (or a receiver and manager) should normally be regarded as a remedy of last resort.[647]

Nature of partnership business

In all cases in which the appointment of a receiver (or receiver and manager) is sought, the court will have regard to the nature of the business carried on and the probable effects which such an appointment would have on the reputation of the firm and the partners. This will be of particular relevance in the case of a

23–154

---

[640] Note that the manager's powers may be limited: see *Taylor v. Neate* (1888) 39 Ch.D. 538. And see, generally, as to the appointment of managers, *Gardner v. London, Chatham and Dover Ry.* (1867) L.R. 2 Ch.App. 201; *Re Manchester and Milford Ry.* (1881) 14 Ch.D. 645, 653 *per* Jessell M.R.; *Re Newdigate Colliery* [1912] 1 Ch. 468.

[641] See, as to the remuneration of a receiver, *infra*, para. 23–177.

[642] *Dixon v. Dixon* [1904] 1 Ch. 161; see also *supra*, para. 23–135.

[643] See *Read v. Bowers* (1793) 4 Bro.C.C. 441; *Hartz v. Schrader* (1803) 8 Ves.Jr. 317; *Hall v. Hall* (1850) 3 Mac. & G. 79.

[644] See *Toker v. Akgul*, CHANI 94/0943/b, November 2, 1995 (CA). *cf. Wilton-Davies v. Kirk* [1997] B.C.C. 770, 775F–G *per* H.H. Judge Weeks sitting as a judge of the Chancery Division, in relation to an application brought in proceedings under what is now the Companies Act 2006, s.994 (unfair prejudice).

[645] CPR r. 1.1. Note also the terms of the Chancery Guide, para. 22.4.

[646] See *Walbrook Trustees (Jersey) Ltd. v. Fattal* [2010] 1 All E.R. (Comm) 526 at [77] *per* Blackburne J.

[647] See, for example, *Don King Productions Inc. v. Warren* [1999] 2 Lloyd's Rep. 392, 400 *per* Neuberger J. In this instance, the appointment was sought in aid of what is now styled a freezing injunction: see further *supra*, para. 23–150.

professional practice.[648] Equally, in *Latchman v. Pickard*,[649] Warren J. expressed the *obiter* view that the appointment of a receiver might be appropriate following the dissolution of a medical partnership.

Size of partnership

23-155   The other relevant factor when considering the appointment of a receiver (or receiver and manager) will be the size of the firm. In essence, the larger the firm, the more reluctant the court will be to interfere otherwise than by way of injunctive relief, particularly where complaints are levelled at the conduct of some but not all of the other partners. Lord Lindley explained why:

> "In those cases in which special grounds for the appointment of a receiver must be shown,[650] it follows that in a firm of several members there is more difficulty in obtaining a receiver than in a firm of two. For the appointment of a receiver, operating in fact as an injunction against all the members, there must be some ground for excluding all who oppose the application. If the object is to exclude some or one only from intermeddling, the appropriate remedy is rather by an injunction than by a receiver."[651]

Receiver and manager without a dissolution

23-156   The general reluctance of the courts to interfere between partners otherwise than with a view to dissolution has already been noticed,[652] and is nowhere more apparent than in the present context. Indeed, Lord Lindley wrote:

> "Courts of justice are by no means anxious to take upon themselves the management of a partnership business, and they will, it is said, never do so, save with a view to a dissolution or final winding up of the affairs of the concern."

This rule still appears to hold good in the case of applications for the appointment of a receiver *and manager*, since there is no reported instance in which such an appointment has been made in the case of an ongoing partnership. Indeed, in such cases as have come before the courts, relief has always been refused.[653] However, it would seem that if the relief sought is confined to the

---

[648] See *Floydd v. Cheney* [1970] Ch. 602, 610 *per* Megarry J.; *Sobell v. Boston* [1975] 1 W.L.R. 1587, 1593 *per* Goff J.; also *Don King Productions Inc. v. Warren, supra. cf. Wilton-Davies v. Kirk, supra*, at p. 775G *per* H.H. Judge Weeks sitting as a judge of the Chancery Division. The current editor doubts whether clients' misapprehensions as to the implications of a receivership can easily be dispelled by "diplomacy and discretion" as Judge Weeks suggested. It should be remembered that this was a case concerning a quasi-partnership company: the position may be very different where the receivership concerns the business of a firm.

[649] [2005] EWHC 1011 (Ch) (Lawtel 12/5/05) at [21], [22]. There was no application before him for such an appointment.

[650] Lord Lindley in effect used the phrase "special grounds" to denote those cases in which a receiver was not appointed as a matter of course: see *infra*, paras 23–160, 23–161.

[651] See *Hall v. Hall* (1850) 3 Mac. & G. 79.

[652] See *supra*, para. 23–16.

[653] *Hall v. Hall, supra*; *Roberts v. Eberhart* (1853) Kay 148. See also *Oliver v. Hamilton* (1794) 2 Anstr. 453; *Waters v. Taylor* (1808) 15 Ves.Jr. 10; *Harrison v. Armitage* (1819) 4 Madd. 143; *Goodman v. Whitcomb* (1820) 1 Jac. & W. 589; *Smith v. Jeyes* (1841) 4 Beav. 503; *Rowlands v. Evans* (1862) 30 Beav. 302. Lord Lindley noted that, in *Morris v. Colman* (1812) 18 Ves.Jr. 438, "there was a reference for the appointment of a manager"; however, whilst a perusal of the report demonstrates that such relief was sought, it does not appear to have been granted.

appointment of a receiver *simpliciter*, the rule will not apply, as Lord Lindley explained:

"If the appointment of a receiver does not involve the appointment of a manager, *Const v. Harris*[654] is a clear authority to show that a receiver may be obtained in an action not seeking a dissolution of the partnership; the later cases are not opposed to this."

It is considered that the wide discretions conferred on the courts by the Senior Courts Act 1981[655] and its predecessors[656] are unlikely to have materially altered the position.[657]

Receiver and manager in dissolution action

Where an action is brought seeking the dissolution of a partnership and/or the winding up of its affairs, a receiver and, in particular, a receiver and manager will more readily be appointed, but it is clear from the Court of Appeal's judgments in *Toker v. Akgul*[658] that such an application will not be granted as a matter of routine. In every case, it will be necessary to show sufficient grounds for the appointment[659] and that the expenses associated therewith will not be disproportionate to the nature and value of the partnership business.[660] The court will be particularly concerned to ensure that there is no other way of resolving the dispute between the partners, *e.g.* by suitable undertakings,[661] an order for accounts and inquiries[662] or the making of a *Syers v. Syers* order.[663]

23–157

Dissolution not sought in terms

It goes without saying that the court will not refuse relief on the ground that no dissolution is sought, if it can be demonstrated that the purpose of the action is to wind up the firm's affairs and the appointment of a receiver and manager is sought to that end.[664]

23–158

---

[654] (1824) T. & R. 496.

[655] *ibid.* s.37 (formerly the Supreme Court Act 1981: Constitutional Reform Act 2005, Sched. 11, Pt 1, para. 1(1)); County Courts Act 1984, s.38(1) (as substituted by the Courts and Legal Services Act 1990, s.3).

[656] See the Supreme Court of Judicature Act 1873, s.25(8); the Supreme Court of Judicature (Consolidation) Act 1925, s.45.

[657] Thus, in *Anselm v. Anselm*, June 26, 1999 (NLD 2990610701), Hart J. seemingly appointed a receiver of the rents and profits of certain partnership properties and other moneys as between two partners on the assumption that their partnership was still subsisting.

[658] CHANI 94/0943/b, November 2, 1995. See also *Wilton-Davies v. Kirk* [1997] B.C.C. 770, 773F *per* H.H. Judge Weeks sitting as a judge of the Chancery Division. *cf. Latchman v. Pickard* [2005] EWHC 1011 (Lawtel 12/5/05) at [21], [22] (albeit that the views expressed there by Warren J. were *obiter*).

[659] See *infra*, paras 23–162 *et seq.*

[660] *Toker v. Akgul, supra*; CPR r. 1.1(2)(c). Note also *Lancefield v. Lancefield* [2002] B.P.I.R. 1108, where, following the appointment of a receiver, it appeared that the business was unsaleable because of the size of its debts and there appeared to be insufficient assets even to remunerate the receiver. In the event, the firm was wound up: see *infra*, para. 27–03.

[661] As in *Don King Productions Inc. v. Warren* [1999] 2 Lloyd's Rep. 392.

[662] See *supra*, paras 23–74 *et seq.* Equally, the court in *Toker v. Akgul, supra*, recognised that accounts and inquiries can involve significant expense.

[663] See *infra*, paras 23–187, 23–188.

[664] *Shepherd v. Oxenford* (1855) 1 K. & J. 491. In this case, various forms of relief normally associated with dissolution were sought, but not dissolution itself. See also *Evans v. Coventry* (1854) 5 De G.M. & G. 911. Of this case, Lord Lindley commented: "It does not appear very distinctly what the manager, as distinguished from the receiver, was expected to do."

Right to a receiver

23–159   The considerations which apply where the appointment of a receiver (or receiver and manager) is sought by one partner against his co-partners differ from those which apply where such appointment is sought by or against the representatives of a deceased or bankrupt partner.

(a) As between partners

23–160   Lord Lindley wrote:

> "Where one partner seeks to have a receiver appointed against his co-partners, the first thing to ascertain is, whether the partnership between them is still subsisting, or has already been dissolved; for if it is still subsisting no receiver will be appointed unless some special grounds for the appointment can be shown,[665] or unless it is plain that an order for a dissolution will be made[666]; whilst if the partnership is already dissolved, the Court usually appoints a receiver, almost as a matter of course."[667]

Consistently with the views which he had previously expressed,[668] the current editor takes the view that Lord Lindley's strictures concerning the position whilst the partnership is subsisting apply only where the appointment of a receiver *and manager* is sought. Furthermore, Lord Lindley's use of the expression "almost as a matter of course" in relation to appointments following a general dissolution[669] should not be taken too literally: there is nothing approaching a presumption that a receiver will be appointed in such a case and sufficient grounds will always have to be shown, as the Court of Appeal made clear in *Toker v. Akgul*.[670] Where a partner has retired by mutual agreement, on the understanding that the other partners can continue to carry on the business without him, relief by way of a receiver will almost inevitably be refused.[671] *A fortiori* if a partner retires or is expelled pursuant to an express provision in the partnership agreement.

A receiver (or receiver and manager) may be appointed even though all other matters in dispute between the partners are referred to arbitration.[672]

[665] See *supra*, para. 23–155 and *infra*, paras 23–162 *et seq.*

[666] *Goodman v. Whitcomb* (1820) 1 Jac. & W. 589.

[667] See *Goodman v. Whitcomb, supra; Tibbits v. Phillips* (1853) 10 Hare 355; *Thomson v. Anderson* (1870) L.R. 9 Eq. 533; *Sargant v. Read* (1876) 1 Ch.D. 600; *Taylor v. Neate* (1888) 39 Ch.D. 538; *Pini v. Roncoroni* [1892] 1 Ch. 633; *Tottey v. Kemp* (1970) 215 E.G. 1021; *Sobell v. Boston* [1975] 1 W.L.R. 1587, 1591 *per* Goff J.; *Re a Company (No. 00596 of 1986)* [1987] BCLC 133 (where partnership principles were applied by analogy in the case of a company constituting a "quasi-partnership"). *cf. Harding v. Glover* (1810) 18 Ves.Jr. 281, where Lord Eldon rightly disavowed any principle that a dissolution is, in itself, a sufficient ground for appointing a receiver. Lord Lindley also, somewhat elliptically, added at this point in the text: "In the case supposed, the common property has to be applied in paying the partnership debts, and has to be divided amongst the partners; and each partner has as much right as the others to wind up the partnership affairs. Their position is, therefore, essentially different from that of mere co-owners, between whom courts decline to interfere by appointing a receiver, except under special circumstances." The effect of appointing a receiver and manager is, of course, to *deprive* all the partners of their right to wind up the partnership affairs.

[668] See *supra*, para. 23–156.

[669] See, as to the meaning of this expression, *infra*, para. 24–03.

[670] CHANI 94/0943/b, November 2, 1995. The court read the quote in the text in conjunction with the views expressed by Lord Lindley with regard to orders for sale, as set out, *infra*, para. 23–185.

[671] See *Sobell v. Boston* [1975] 1 W.L.R. 1587, 1591 *per* Goff J. See also *Tottey v. Kemp* (1970) 215 E.G. 1021, where one partner had exercised a contractual option to acquire the other's share following the dissolution.

[672] Arbitration Act 1996, s.44(2)(e); *Pini v. Roncoroni* [1892] 1 Ch. 633; also *Phoenix v. Pope* [1974] 1 W.L.R. 719. But note, in non-urgent cases, *ibid.* s.44(4).

(b) As between partners and non-partners

The outcome of any application for the appointment of a receiver and manager **23–161** in this type of case will, for the most part, depend on whether the person principally[673] sought to be excluded from interference in the business is a partner. If he is, special grounds justifying the court's interference must be made out.[674] Lord Lindley explained the underlying rationale as follows:

> " . . . whilst the Court is reluctant to exclude a partner from the management of the partnership affairs, it will readily interfere to prevent other persons from intermeddling therewith. The reason given for this is, that each partner is at the outset trusted by his co-partners, and has confidence reposed by them in him; and until it can be shown that he ought not to be allowed to take part any longer in the management of the partnership affairs, the court will not interfere with him. But this reasoning has no application to persons who acquire an interest in the partnership assets by events over which the partners have no control, *e.g.* the death or bankruptcy of one of the members of the firm."

It follows that a receiver may more readily[675] be appointed where all the partners are dead and an action is pending between their representatives[676]; similarly, where the appointment is sought by a partner against a deceased partner's personal representatives or the trustee in bankruptcy or liquidator of an insolvent partner.[677]

The assignee or mortgagee of a partnership share will, if anything, be in an even weaker position.[678]

Grounds for appointment of receiver and manager

Reference has previously been made to the need to show grounds for the **23–162** appointment of a receiver (or a receiver and manager).[679] In practice, there are four recognised grounds, namely:

(1) Breach of a dissolution agreement under which the partners have given up their personal right to wind up the firm's affairs.

(2) Misconduct plus jeopardy to the partnership assets.

(3) Fraud.

---

[673] A successful application will, of course, exclude both claimant and defendant from interfering in the business.

[674] *Collins v. Young* (1853) 1 Macq. 385; see also *Harding v. Glover* (1810) 18 Ves.Jr. 281; *Lawson v. Morgan* (1815) 1 Price 303; *Kennedy v. Lee* (1817) 3 Mer. 441; *Kershaw v. Matthews* (1826) 2 Russ. 62; *Horrell v. Witts* (1866) L.R. 1 P. & D. 103. And see, as to showing special grounds, *supra*, para. 23–155 and *infra*, paras 23–162 *et seq.*

[675] But not as a matter of course: see *Toker v. Akgul*, CHANI 94/0943/b, November 2, 1995 (CA), noted *supra*, paras 23–157, 23–160.

[676] *Philips v. Atkinson* (1787) 2 Bro.C.C. 272.

[677] *Freeland v. Stansfeld* (1854) 2 Sm. & G. 479.

[678] See *Fraser v. Kershaw* (1856) 2 K. & J. 496, where the assignees of a bankrupt partner (*i.e.* what would now be the trustee in bankruptcy) obtained the appointment of a receiver against a creditor of the solvent partner, who (under the then law) had taken an assignment of his share from the sheriff, following execution under a *fi. fa.* And see *Candler v. Candler* (1821) Jac. 225. See further, as to the rights of an assignee or mortgagee of a partnership share, *supra*, paras 19–49 *et seq.*

[679] See *supra*, paras 23–155 *et seq.*, 23–160, 23–161.

(4) Wrongful exclusion.

(1) *Breach of dissolution agreement*

23–163   A receiver will be appointed, even at the instance of the representatives of a deceased or insolvent partner,[680] where one or more partners act in breach of the terms of an agreement under which, in Lord Lindley's words:

> " . . . the partners have divested themselves more or less of their right to wind up the affairs of the concern."

Thus, in *Davis v. Amer*,[681] the claimant and the defendant, on dissolving their partnership, agreed to appoint a third party to get in the firm's assets. They also agreed not to interfere with the third party while he was so engaged. The agreement was partially implemented, prior to the death of one of the partners. Thereafter, disputes arose between that partner's executors and the surviving partner, whereupon the latter proceeded to get in the partnership debts, contrary to the terms of the agreement. The court appointed a receiver at the instance of the executors, but declined to grant an injunction on the ground that no sufficient impropriety had been shown to warrant such an order being made.[682]

It need hardly be said that agreements of this type are rarely encountered in practice.[683]

(2) *Misconduct plus jeopardy to assets*

23–164   Lord Lindley described this ground as where:

> " . . . by misconduct, the right of personal intervention has been forfeited, and the partnership assets are in danger of being lost . . . "

and then went on to elaborate:

> "If the partnership is not yet dissolved,[684] there must be something more than a partnership squabble[685]; the due winding up of the affairs of the concern must be endangered to induce the Court to appoint a receiver of its assets; and non-co-operation of one partner, whereby the whole responsibility of management is thrown on his co-partner, is not sufficient."[686]

---

[680] See *supra*, para. 23–161.

[681] (1854) 3 Drew. 64. See also *Turner v. Major* (1862) 3 Giff. 442 (where an injunction was held to be sufficient).

[682] See *Evans v. Coventry* (1854) 3 Drew. 75, 82 *per* Kindersley V.-C. See also *supra*, para. 23–135, n. 556.

[683] It will usually be one of the partners who is appointed to get in the debts, etc.: see *supra*, para. 10–267.

[684] Where the partnership has already been dissolved, the court may be more ready to appoint a receiver, but will not make the appointment as a matter of course: see *supra*, para. 23–157.

[685] Note that evidence of past disagreements or misconduct will seemingly not, of itself, suffice: see *Walbrook Trustees (Jersey) Ltd. v. Fattal* [2010] 1 All E.R. (Comm) 526 at [98] *per* Blackburne J. This was not a partnership case.

[686] See *Rowe v. Wood* (1795) 2 J. & W. 553; *Roberts v. Eberhardt* (1853) Kay 148.

The position will be *a fortiori* where the appointment of a receiver and manager is sought.

Degree of misconduct required

The degree of misconduct necessary to induce a court to interfere between partners by way of injunction has already been noticed,[687] and the principles applicable in the case of the appointment of a receiver (or receiver and manager) are broadly the same, *i.e.* it must, in essence be demonstrated that the misconduct is of such a nature that the partner concerned can no longer be trusted. By way of illustration, the following forms of misconduct, which are, for ease of reference, arranged alphabetically, have been held sufficient[688]:   **23–165**

Misappropriation of assets: Where a partner in control of partnership assets has already made off with some of them,[689] or where partnership property is abroad and a partner has absconded, as Lord Lindley put it, "in order to do what he likes with it there".[690]   **23–166**

Collusion with debtors: Where one partner has colluded with the partnership debtors and permitted them to delay payment of their debts.[691]

Improper use of partnership assets: Where a partner is carrying on a business on his own account using partnership property,[692] or where a surviving partner insists on carrying on the partnership business, utilising the share of his deceased partner.[693]

Mismanagement: Where a partner is guilty of such mismanagement as to endanger the whole concern.[694]

Jeopardy to assets

Misconduct alone is never sufficient: it is also necessary to demonstrate that the safety of the partnership assets is in jeopardy.[695] In some cases, the danger will be obvious from the very nature of the misconduct, whilst, in others, positive evidence will have to be adduced.   **23–167**

---

[687] See *supra*, paras 23–137 *et seq.*

[688] And see, generally, *Smith v. Jeyes* (1841) 4 Beav. 503.

[689] *Evans v. Coventry* (1854) 5 De G.M. & G. 911.

[690] *Sheppard v. Oxenford* (1855) 1 K. & J. 491. Note that there was no evidence of impropriety in this case, other than the clandestine manner in which the partner had left the country.

[691] *Estwick v. Conningsby* (1682) 1 Vern. 118.

[692] *Harding v. Glover* (1810) 18 Ves.Jr. 281.

[693] *Madgwick v. Wimble* (1843) 6 Beav. 495. Note also, in this context, the provisions of the Partnership Act 1890, s.42(1), *infra*, paras 25–24 *et seq.*

[694] See *De Tastet v. Bordieu* (1805), cited in a note in 2 Bro.C.C. 272. The expression used in the report is "mutual" mismanagement, but its import is not explained. But see also *Const v. Harris* (1824) T. & R. 496.

[695] The absence of any jeopardy to the assets was mentioned specifically by the Court of Appeal in *Toker v. Akgul*, CHANI 94/0943/b, November 2, 1995, noted *supra*, para. 23–157.

(3) *Fraud*

23–168   Although fraud was not, in earlier editions of this work, treated as a separate ground for the appointment of a receiver,[696] it does not partake of the same characteristics as the other grounds, as Lord Lindley made clear in the following passage:

> " . . . the reluctance of the Court in appointing a receiver against a partner, being based on the confidence originally reposed in him, . . . disappears if it can be shown that such confidence was originally misplaced. Therefore, where a defendant, by false and fraudulent representations, induced the plaintiff to enter into partnership with him, and the plaintiff soon afterwards filed a bill, praying that the partnership might be declared void, and for a receiver, the Court on motion ordered that a receiver should be appointed."[697]

(4) *Exclusion*

23–169   Lord Lindley observed:

> " . . . even although there be no misconduct jeopardising the partnership assets, the Court will appoint a receiver if the defendant wrongfully excludes his co-partner from the management of the partnership affairs.[698] This doctrine is acted on where the defendant unsuccessfully contends that the plaintiff is not a partner,[699] or that he has no interest in the partnership assets."[700]

Cases of exclusion should not, however, be confused with those in which the partnership has been dissolved by a partner leaving the firm, following which his co-partner(s) carry on the partnership business without winding up its affairs.[701]

Interim application where partnership disputed

23–170   Where the existence of the partnership is disputed and the appointment of a receiver (or receiver and manager) is sought by way of an interim remedy,[702] the court will, in an appropriate case, have jurisdiction to make the order sought, but will be reluctant to do so if such an order would inflict irreparable injury on the defendant (who might, of course, succeed at trial) or adequate protection can be

---

[696] Lord Lindley appears to have treated this ground as an offshoot of "misconduct plus jeopardy to assets", even though jeopardy seemingly need not be shown.

[697] See *Ex p. Broome* (1811) 1 Rose 69.

[698] See the judgment of Long Innes J. in *Tate v. Barry* (1928) 28 S.R. (N.S.W.) 380, 387, with which Megarry J. concurred in *Floydd v. Cheney* [1970] Ch. 602, 610. And see *Wilson v. Greenwood* (1818) 1 Swan. 481; *Goodman v. Whitcomb* (1820) 1 J. & W. 589. H.H. Judge Weeks (sitting as a judge of the Chancery Division) adopted the same approach in *Wilton-Davies v. Kirk* [1997] B.C.C. 770, 775B–C, when considering an application relating to a quasi-partnership company.

[699] *Peacock v. Peacock* (1809) 16 Ves.Jr. 49; *Blakeney v. Dufaur* (1851) 15 Beav. 40.

[700] See *Wilson v. Greenwood* (1818) 1 Swan. 471, where the claimants were the assignees (*i.e.* what would now be the trustee in bankruptcy) of a bankrupt partner; *Clegg v. Fishwick* (1849) 1 Mac. & G. 294, where the claimant was a deceased partner's administratrix.

[701] *Toker v. Akgul, supra,* was such a case. The application for the appointment of a receiver was refused. The position might, however, have been otherwise if there had been a suggestion of impropriety in the conduct of the business by the defendant. Note also, in this context, the provisions of the Partnership Act 1890, s.42(1), *infra*, paras 25–24 *et seq.*

[702] CPR r. 69.2(1)(a), (b); 69PD, para. 2.1; also CPR r. 25.1(3). The application will be made under *ibid.* Pt 23; see also *ibid.* r. 69.3.

otherwise afforded to the claimant.[703] The court is likely to be especially sensitive to the potential implications of the publicity attendant on appointing a receiver in the case of a professional practice.[704]

Illegal partnerships

It has already been seen that illegality will, in general, constitute a defence to an action concerning the affairs of an illegal partnership.[705] On that footing, Lord Lindley went so far as to say: **23–171**

> "If the illegality is established, the Court cannot, it is conceived, interfere."

Where, however, a receiver is sought by way of an interim remedy before the illegal nature of the partnership has been proved, the court may be prepared to intervene, unless it is satisfied that, such is the obvious nature of the illegality, no relief will ultimately be awarded. Indeed, Lord Lindley pointed out that:

> " . . . the character of the defence will go far to remove any scruples the Court might otherwise have in interfering."

Thus, in *Hale v. Hale*,[706] a receiver and manager was appointed in the case of a brewing business claimed by the defendant to be illegal, notwithstanding the fact that the claimant was only a dormant partner and that no complaint was made as regards the manner in which the defendant had managed the business.

Partnerships comprising alien enemies

There are a number of cases, dating from the 1914–18 War, in which an application was made for the appointment of a receiver in respect of a firm comprising alien enemies,[707] but such questions are usually covered by specific wartime legislation.[708]   **23–172**

Mining partnerships

Prior to the Partnership Act 1890, mining partnerships constituted a distinct sub-species, governed by different rules to those applicable to ordinary trading partnerships, but it is questionable to what extent, if at all, such treatment is now   **23–173**

---

[703] *Peacock v. Peacock* (1809) 16 Ves.Jr. 49; *Chapman v. Beach* (1820) 1 J. & W. 594; *Fairburn v. Pearson* (1850) 2 Mac. & G. 144; *Hardy v. Hardy* (1917) 62 S.J. 142. A receiver was clearly appointed at an early stage in *Phillips v. Symes*, but the history of the action is not set out in the report in *The Times*, October 2, 2001. Note also *Wilton-Davies v. Kirk* [1997] B.C.C. 770, where H.H. Judge Weeks (sitting as a judge of the Chancery Division) ordered the appointment of a receiver in the case of a quasi-partnership company.

[704] See *Floydd v. Cheney* [1970] Ch. 602; *Sobell v. Boston* [1975] 1 W.L.R. 1587. And see *supra*, para. 23–154.

[705] See *supra*, paras 8–63 *et seq.*

[706] (1841) 4 Beav. 369. See also *Sheppard v. Oxenford* (1855) 1 K. & J. 491.

[707] A receiver was appointed in *Rombach v. Rombach* [1914] W.N. 423; *Armitage v. Borgmann* (1914) 84 L.J.Ch. 784; *Re Bechstein* (1914) 58 S.J. 863; *Kupfer v. Kupfer* [1915] W.N. 397. However, such an appointment was refused in *Maxwell v. Grunhut* (1914) 31 T.L.R. 79; *Re Gaudig and Blum* (1915) 31 T.L.R. 153. See, further, the 9th ed. of this work, at pp. 655–656.

[708] No equivalent cases were reported in respect of the 1939–45 War, doubtless because the position was governed by the Trading with the Enemy Acts. See generally, as to alien enemies and the effects of war, *supra*, paras 4–04 *et seq.*

justified.[709] Nevertheless, it is clear that the appointment of a receiver (or receiver and manager) of a mining partnership will be governed by normal principles.[710] There are, admittedly, two cases in which a receiver was refused following the exclusion of a partner,[711] but in each the facts were exceptional.[712]

Defendant may apply for receiver

23–174   A defendant may seek the appointment of a receiver (or receiver and manager) by an application notice in the claimant's proceedings,[713] a counterclaim or, if appropriate, some other Part 20 claim.[714] It was formerly the rule that, where the claimant did not found his action on the existence of a partnership, a defendant would have to file a counterclaim[715] or issue his own proceedings[716] before he could seek the appointment of a receiver, since otherwise his application would not arise out of the claimant's cause of action. Although the old rules have been swept away by the Civil Procedure Rules, it is, in the current editor's view, unlikely that the court would appoint a receiver on the application of a defendant without being convinced that he has a bona fide Part 20 claim based on the existence of a partnership. Equally, the reluctance of the court to appoint a receiver where the existence of the partnership is in dispute has already been noted.[717]

Identity and remuneration of receiver

23–175   The usual practice is to seek the appointment of a named receiver (or receiver and manager),[718] although it was once common to deal with the actual appointment at a subsequent hearing. This can still be done,[719] but is obviously not appropriate where the appointment is sought on an application without notice.[720] In such cases, leave may be given to each partner to propose himself as receiver.[721] Although a period of delay may provide a useful stimulus to the

---

[709] See *supra*, paras 5–11, 19–64, 23–87.

[710] See, as to the position whilst the partnership is continuing, *Roberts v. Eberhardt* (1853) Kay 148; *Rowlands v. Evans* (1861) 30 Beav. 302; and, as to the appointment of a receiver and manager with a view to a dissolution or winding up, *Clegg v. Fishwick* (1849) 1 Mac. & G. 294; *Sheppard v. Oxenford* (1855) 1 K. & J. 491 (where, however, a dissolution was not sought). And see, as to cases in which the partners cannot agree on the proper method of working the mine until a sale can be arranged, *Jefferys v. Smith* (1820) 1 J. & W. 298; *Lees v. Jones* (1857) 3 Jur.(N.S.) 954.

[711] *Rowe v. Wood* (1795) 2 J. & W. 553; *Norway v. Rowe* (1812) 19 Ves.Jr. 144.

[712] Lord Lindley explained: " . . . *Rowe v. Wood* . . . was a peculiar case, for the partner complained of was not only a partner, but also a mortgagee in possession, and his mortgage debt was still unsatisfied. Again, in *Norway v. Rowe*, although the plaintiff was excluded, a receiver was refused on the ground of his laches, he having been excluded for some time, and having taken no steps to assert his rights until the mine proved profitable."

[713] CPR r. 69.2(1)(b); also *ibid.* Pt 23. Note also *Sargant v. Read* (1876) 1 Ch.D. 600.

[714] CPR rr. 20.2(1)(a), (b), 20.4, 20.7(3). As to the position where the court's permission to issue a Part 20 claim is required, see *ibid.* r. 20.9.

[715] *Hardy v. Hardy* (1917) 62 S.J. 142; *Carter v. Fey* [1894] 2 Ch. 541; also *Collison v. Warren* [1901] 1 Ch. 812.

[716] As is *Floydd v. Cheney* [1970] Ch. 602; also *Carter v. Fey, supra*.

[717] See *supra*, para. 23–170.

[718] CPR r. 69.3(b), 69PD, para. 4.2.

[719] *ibid.* 69PD, paras 4.3, 4.4. Note, as to the pre-CPR practice, *Heward's Chancery Practice* (2nd ed.), p. 102; also *Heward's Chancery Orders*, p. 259.

[720] In such a case, the appointment will necessarily be for a limited period: Chancery Guide, para. 5.26. An application without notice would, in any event, be exceptional: *ibid.* para. 5.4.

[721] See *Sargant v. Read* (1876) 1 Ch.D. 600.

partners to agree terms in the interim,[722] it should be appreciated that the court may question the motives of a partner who puts forward a case for the appointment of a receiver but, at the same time, appears to wish to defer that appointment.

Partner appointed as receiver

In an appropriate case one of the partners may be appointed receiver (or receiver and manager), as Lord Lindley explained:

23–176

> "If the Court, on being applied to for the appointment of a receiver, thinks that a proper case for such appointment is made, and the partner actually carrying on the business has not been guilty of such misconduct as to have rendered it unsafe to trust him, the Court generally appoints him receiver and manager without salary.[723] It is usual, however, to require him to give security duly to manage the partnership affairs, and to account for money received by him.[724] . . . A partner who is appointed receiver becomes the officer of the court, and must act and be respected accordingly."

Although the above passage appears to be framed in terms of a single partner carrying on the partnership business, the court's discretion will also be exercisable where there are two or more partners competing for appointment; however, in such a case, care will obviously be taken to ensure that no partner thereby obtains an unfair advantage.[725]

Where the receiver is not a partner, he may be given liberty to employ a partner as manager, thus securing a degree of continuity in the partnership business.[726]

Remuneration, etc.

A receiver (or receiver and manager) will be allowed such remuneration as is authorised by the court,[727] which is likely to be assessed on a *quantum meruit* basis, even where he is a partner.[728] Where a partner is appointed without

23–177

---

[722] See the CPR rr. 1.4(2)(f), 3.1(2)(f). In *Wilton-Davies v. Kirk* [1997] B.C.C. 770, 777C–D (a case concerning a quasi-partnership company) H.H. Judge Weeks (sitting as a judge of the Chancery Division) suspended the appointment for a short period for this purpose.

[723] See *Wilson v. Greenwood* (1818) 1 Swan. 471; *Blakeney v. Dufaur* (1851) 15 Beav. 40; *Collins v. Barker* [1893] 1 Ch. 578; *Harris v. Sleep* [1897] 2 Ch. 80. It is, however, no longer the general practice to deprive a partner of remuneration for acting as receiver: see *infra*, para. 23–177.

[724] See *Collins v. Barker, supra*; also the form of order in *Heward's Chancery Orders*, at p. 257. As to the giving of security, see CPR r. 69.5, 69PD, paras 7.1–7.3; also the Chancery Guide, Appendix 10 (Guide for Receivers in the Chancery Division), paras 6 *et seq.*

[725] See *Sargant v. Read* (1876) 1 Ch.D. 600.

[726] This was the course adopted in *Anselm v. Anselm*, Unreported June 29, 1999 ChD.

[727] CPR r. 69.7, 69PD, paras 9.1–9.3. In deciding a receiver's remuneration, the court will take into account the nature of the receivership, the value of the partnership assets and the other factors listed in *ibid.* r. 69.7(4); also *ibid.* 69PD, para. 9.2; Chancery Guide, Appendix 10 (Guide for Receivers in the Chancery Division), para. 10. The receiver's remuneration does not constitute costs: *Mirror Group Newspapers Plc v. Maxwell* [2001] B.C.C. 488. Note that, in *Lancefield v. Lancefield* [2002] B.P.I.R. 1108, Neuberger J. declined to give directions on the receiver's costs application, due to the parlous state of the firm's finances and claims that money in its bank account was impressed with a trust.

[728] *i.e.* pursuant to *ibid.* r. 69.7(3); and see *Davy v. Scarth* [1906] 1 Ch. 55. Note, however the wide discretion conferred on the court under *ibid.* r. 69.7(1).

salary,[729] he may, nevertheless, be allowed remuneration for services performed beyond the scope of his duties, if they prove beneficial.[730] However a receiver will not be entitled to remuneration for preparing partnership accounts.[731]

A partner's remuneration and receivership costs[732] will normally be payable out of any funds in his hands *qua* receiver,[733] even if he owes money to the firm and is unable to discharge that indebtedness,[734] but may now be ordered to be paid by one or more of the partners in an appropriate case.[735]

Order appointing receiver

23–178   Lord Lindley wrote:

> "The order appointing a receiver usually directs the partners to deliver up to him all the effects of the partnership, and all securities in their hands, for the outstanding personal estate, together with all books and papers relating thereto. The receiver is directed to get in the debts of the firm, and he is, if necessary, empowered to bring actions with the approbation of the judge; he is directed to pay the partnership debts, and to pass his accounts and to pay balances in his hands into court."[736]

This is still, in essence, the form of order used today.[737] However, an order for the delivery up of the partnership books, etc., will not be made if that would either be unnecessary or unduly inconvenient.[738]

Powers of receiver

23–179   The functions of a receiver are limited and will not, without the permission of the court, extend to a sale of the partnership assets.[739] The court cannot confer power on a receiver to do anything which a partner would not have authority to do, whether pursuant to the terms of the partnership agreement or, where

---

[729] This was formerly a common practice: see *supra*, para. 23–176, n. 723.

[730] *Harris v. Sleep* [1897] 2 Ch. 80. See also *supra*, para. 20–46.

[731] Chancery Guide, Appendix 10 (Guide for Receivers in the Chancery Division), Appendix C, para. 6.

[732] Such costs are not part of the receiver's remuneration but are accounted for in the receivership accounts: CPR 69PD, para. 9.6.

[733] CPR r. 69.7(2)(b). Note that the discretion which exists under this rule has seemingly not altered the basic right of a receiver to be paid his remuneration and costs out of the funds in his hands: *Capewell v. Revenue and Customs Commissioners (No.2)* [2007] 1 W.L.R. 386 (HL); also *Dayman v. Aziz* [2008] EWHC 2244 (Ch) (Lawtel 30/9/09). The receiver's right to remuneration cannot, however, be made to rank before a prior charge on the partnership assets: *Chandhri v. Palta* [1992] B.C.C. 787.

[734] *Davy v. Scarth* [1906] 1 Ch. 55.

[735] See the CPR r. 69.7(2)(a). There was no such power in RSC Ord. 30, r. 3.

[736] See the forms of order in *Wilson v. Greenwood* (1818) 1 Swan. 471, 484; *Whitley v. Lowe* (1858) 4 Jur.(N.S.) 815 (where the application was not opposed: see *ibid.* p. 197); *Taylor v. Neate* (1888) 39 Ch.D. 538; *Collins v. Barker* [1893] 1 Ch. 578; also Seton (7th ed.), p. 728.

[737] See *Heward's Chancery Orders*, pp. 257 *et seq.* And see, generally, as to the receiver's accounts and payments into court, CPR r. 69.8, 69PD, para. 6.3(2), (3); Chancery Guide, Appendix 10 (Guide for Receivers in the Chancery Division), para. 11–13.

[738] See *Dacie v. John* (1824) McCle. 206.

[739] See *Kerr & Hunter on Receivers and Administrators* (19th ed.), paras 7–48 *et seq.*; Chancery Guide, Appendix 10 (Guide for Receivers in the Chancery Division), Appendix C, para. 2(d).

relevant, under the general law.[740] A receiver may, as and when required, apply to the court for directions as to the exercise of his powers or on any issues where there is doubt.[741]

Conversely, the court will not restrict the activities of a receiver *after* he has ceased to hold that position. Thus, a person who has acted as receiver and manager of a partnership business up to the time of its sale will not be restrained from soliciting orders from or doing business with the customers of the firm on his own account after he has ceased so to act[742]; *per contra* if he is one of the partners.[743]

Liability of receiver

A receiver appointed by the court is neither the agent of the parties to the **23–180** action nor of the party on whose application he was appointed.[744] Thus, he is prima facie personally liable on all contracts entered into *qua* receiver,[745] unless such liability is excluded by express or implied agreement.[746] He is, however, entitled to be indemnified out of the partnership assets in his hands in priority to the claims of the creditors of the business,[747] but he does not enjoy a similar right to indemnity from the partners, even if he was appointed with their consent.[748] To the extent that the receiver is entitled to be indemnified out of the partnership assets, any creditors to whom he is personally liable will enjoy subrogated rights against those assets.[749] It does, however, appear that a receiver will not be personally liable for tax in respect of his realisations of partnership property, etc.[750]

Where it is alleged that a receiver has mismanaged the partnership business, the only recoverable loss will be that suffered by the partners *as such*.[751]

---

[740] *Niemann v. Niemann* (1889) 43 Ch.D. 198, 201–202 *per* Cotton L.J. This sentence is framed solely by reference to the partnership contract, but the current editor takes the view that the same considerations apply to any act authorised by the Partnership Act 1890, save to the extent that its provisions are excluded by the agreement. Note also *Murray v. King* [1986] F.S.R. 116, a decision of the Federal Court of Australia.

[741] CPR r. 69.6(1), 69PD, paras 6.1, 6.3, 8.1 *et seq.*; Chancery Guide, Appendix 10 (Guide for Receivers in the Chancery Division), Appendix C, paras 2, 5.

[742] *Re Irish* (1880) 40 Ch.D. 49.

[743] See *supra*, paras 10–200 *et seq.*

[744] *Burt, Boulton and Hayward v. Bull* [1895] 1 Q.B. 276; *Re Flowers* [1897] 1 Q.B. 14; *Re Glasdir Copper Mines Ltd.* [1906] 1 Ch. 365; *Boehm v. Goodall* [1911] 1 Ch. 155; *Moss S.S. Co. v. Whinney* [1912] A.C. 254; *Evans v. Clayhope Properties Ltd.* [1988] 1 W.L.R. 358.

[745] *Burt, Boulton and Hayward v. Bull, supra. cf.* the absence of liability of a judicial factor in Scotland: *Scottish Brewers Ltd. v. J. Douglas Pearson & Co.* 1996 S.C.L.R. 197.

[746] *Re Boynton Ltd.* [1910] 1 Ch. 519. See also *Burt, Boulton and Hayward v. Bull, supra; Moss S.S. Co. v. Whinney* [1912] A.C. 254.

[747] *Batten v. Wedgwood Coal Co.* (1884) 28 Ch.D. 317; *Strapp v. Bull, Sons & Co.* [1895] 2 Ch. 1; *Re Glasdir Copper Mines* [1906] 1 Ch. 365; *Re British Power Traction and Lighting Co. Ltd.* [1906] 1 Ch. 497 and [1907] 1 Ch. 528; *Re Boynton Ltd.* [1910] 1 Ch. 519. *cf.* the position of a *secured* creditor: *Choudhri v. Palta* [1992] BCC 787. As to the costs of actions brought against the receiver, see *Walters v. Woodbridge* (1878) 7 Ch.D. 504; *Re Dunn, Brinklow v. Singleton* [1904] 1 Ch. 648.

[748] *Boehm v. Goodall* [1911] 1 Ch. 155; *Evans v. Clayhope Properties Ltd.* [1988] 1 W.L.R. 358; also *Choudhri v. Palta, supra. Quaere* whether an order for costs can be made covering the receiver's remuneration and expenses after final judgment in the action: *ibid.*

[749] *Re British Power Traction and Lighting Co. Ltd.* [1910] 2 Ch. 470. *cf. Re Boynton Ltd.* [1910] 1 Ch. 519.

[750] *Re Piacentini* [2003] Q.B. 1497 (a decision concerning a receiver appointed under the Criminal Justice Act, s.77).

[751] *McGowan v. Chadwick* [2003] B.P.I.R. 647 (CA).

Interference with receiver

23–181   A receiver is an officer of the court and, accordingly, any interference with him, or with property under his control,[752] constitutes a contempt of court[753] and will, if necessary, be restrained by injunction.[754] It has already been seen that a judgment creditor who wishes to levy execution against property in the receiver's hands should apply to the court in the action in which he was appointed, thus enabling that court to make a suitable order, whether for payment of the judgment debt or otherwise.[755]

Arbitrations

23–182   The court has the same powers of appointing a receiver where a dispute has been referred to arbitration as it has in relation to legal proceedings,[756] but an arbitrator cannot make such an appointment.[757]

D.   ORDERS FOR THE SALE OF PARTNERSHIP PROPERTY

The normal rule

23–183   It has already been seen that, in the event of a general dissolution,[758] each partner[759] is normally entitled to insist that all the partnership property is sold,[760] even if the firm's debts and liabilities could be discharged without such a sale.[761] Indeed, Lord Lindley observed:

> "This mode of ascertaining the value of the partnership effects is adopted by the Courts, unless some other course can be followed consistently with the agreement

---

[752] As to the position where the property is out of the jurisdiction, see *Re Maudslay Sons and Field* [1900] 1 Ch. 602.

[753] See *Lane v. Sterne* (1862) 3 Giff. 629; *Helmore v. Smith (No. 2)* (1887) 35 Ch.D. 449; *Re Bechstein (No. 2)* (1914) 58 S.J. 864; *Dixon v. Dixon* [1904] 1 Ch. 161. *cf.* the position before the receiver's appointment has been perfected: see *Defries v. Creed* (1865) 6 N.R. 17.

[754] *Dixon v. Dixon, supra.*

[755] See *supra*, para. 14–93.

[756] Arbitration Act 1996, s.44(2)(e). But note, as to non-urgent cases, the requirements of *ibid.* s.44(3), (4) and the decision in *Cetelem SA v. Rous Holdings Ltd.* [2005] 2 All E.R. (Comm) 203 (CA).

[757] See *supra*, para. 10–281.

[758] As to the meaning of this expression, see *infra*, para. 24–03.

[759] But not a person who is merely remunerated by a share of profits: see *Walker v. Hirsch* (1884) 27 Ch.D. 460; *Stekel v. Ellice* [1973] 1 W.L.R. 191. Lord Lindley observed: "*Pawsey v. Armstrong* (1881) 18 Ch.D. 698, went too far. See [*Walker v. Hirsch*]."

[760] See *supra*, paras 19–05 *et seq.* And see *Rowlands v. Evans* (1861) 30 Beav. 302; *Burdon v. Barkus* (1862) 4 De G.F. & J. 42; *Hugh Stevenson & Sons v. Aktiengesellschaft für Cartonnagen Industrie* [1917] 1 K.B. 842, affirmed [1918] A.C. 239; also *Crawshay v. Collins* (1808) 15 Ves.Jr. 218, 227 *per* Lord Eldon; *Featherstonhaugh v. Fenwick* (1810) 17 Ves.Jr. 298; *Crawshay v. Maule* (1818) 1 Swan. 495; *Hale v. Hale* (1841) 4 Beav. 369, 375 *per* Lord Langdale. *cf.* the position where a partnership business is transferred to a company: *Re A Company (No. 002567 of 1982)* [1983] 1 W.L.R. 927. There must, of course, be something in the nature of property, and not a mere expectancy: see *Sew Hoy v. Sew Hoy* [2001] 1 N.Z.L.R. 391 (CA, New Zealand) noted *supra*, paras 16–27 n. 122. As to valuable, but unsaleable, assets, etc., see *infra*, paras 23–198 *et seq.*

[761] See *Wild v. Milne* (1859) 26 Beav. 504.

between the partners. And even where the partners have provided that their shares shall be ascertained in some other way, still, if owing to any circumstances their agreement in this respect cannot be carried out, or if their agreement does not extend to the event which has in fact arisen, realisation of the property by a sale is the only alternative which a Court can adopt."[762]

Thus, in *Cook v. Collingridge*,[763] where the partners had agreed that, on the expiration of their partnership, the stock in trade would be divided between them, it was held that, since a physical division of the stock was impossible, it would have to be sold and the proceeds divided. A sale will, similarly, be directed where continuing partners have an option to acquire an outgoing partner's share[764] but fail to exercise it,[765] or where any other provision for such acquisition cannot, for whatever reason, be implemented.[766]

It should, however, be noted that the application of the normal rule presupposes that the partnership property still exists: no sale or valuation of a business will be possible if it ceased to exist on or prior to the date of dissolution.[767]

Agreements excluding the normal rule

It goes without saying that a sale will not normally be ordered where that would be inconsistent with the terms or spirit of the agreement between the partners.[768] Thus, where a partner agrees to retire from the partnership and thereby recognises the continuing partners' right to continue the business, he will normally be taken to have forgone his right to insist on a sale.[769]

23–184

The court's discretion

The effective presumption in favour of a sale is not, however, by any means absolute, as Lord Lindley explained:

23–185

"The rule as to selling partnership property is merely adopted in order that justice may be done to all parties, when no other course has been or can be agreed upon. It is not an arbitrary rule, inflexibly applied in all cases whether it is necessary or not; and although, if one partner or his representatives insist on a sale, the Court may not be able to refuse to enforce that right,[770] still the Court is always inclined to accede to any other mode of settlement which may be fair and just between the partners."

This flexible approach has been endorsed in two important but unreported Court of Appeal decisions. In *Hammond v. Brearley*[771] the court allowed an

23–186

---

[762] But see *Syers v. Syers* (1876) 1 App.Cas. 174, *infra*, paras 23–187, 23–188; also *Taylor v. Neate* (1888) 39 Ch.D. 538, where the parties appear to have agreed to a sale: see *ibid.* p. 542.

[763] (1822) Jac. 607. See also *Rigden v. Pierce* (1822) 6 Madd. 353.

[764] See generally, as to such options, *supra*, paras 10–151 *et seq.*

[765] See *Kershaw v. Matthews* (1826) 2 Russ. 62; *Madgwick v. Wimble* (1843) 6 Beav. 495; *Downs v. Collins* (1848) 6 Hare 418. The agreement may itself specify what is to happen in the event of the option not being exercised: see *supra*, para. 10–263.

[766] See, for example, *Wilson v. Greenwood* (1818) 1 Swan. 471.

[767] See *Ryder v. Frohlich* [2006] NSWSC 833, noted *supra*, para. 10–200.

[768] See *supra*, para. 10–150.

[769] *Sobell v. Boston* [1975] 1 W.L.R. 1587, 1591 *per* Goff J.; also *Bothe v. Amos* [1976] Fam. 46; *Green v. Moran* 2002 S.L.T. 1404 (OH), albeit that a sale of assets was not sought. *Small v. Cohen, The Times*, September 7, 1992 appears to be a case of this class. And see *supra*, para. 19–11.

[770] *Wild v. Milne* (1859) 26 Beav. 504; *Rowlands v. Evans* (1861) 30 Beav. 302.

[771] December 10, 1992.

appeal against a peremptory order for the sale of the partnership assets, thus reserving to the trial judge the decision as to how best to wind up the partnership affairs.[772] However, it is clear that the court's thinking was influenced by the fact that the claimant had no interest in the firm's goodwill,[773] so that a sale of the business as a going concern was out of the question. In *Toker v. Akgul*[774] the defendant was appealing against the appointment of a receiver with an express power of sale. In allowing the appeal, the court cited Lord Lindley's statement of principle set out above[775] and intimated that, in the absence of agreement between the parties for determination of the value of the partnership assets by an arbitrator or valuer, it was minded to order accounts and inquiries and to defer further consideration of sale until that procedure was completed.[776]

The decision in *Latchan v. Martin*[777] is another, but less clear, example of this approach. There, the court declined to order a sale where the business had been carried on by one of the partners for some years after the date of dissolution.

Syers v. Syers orders

23–187   It was the width of the court's discretion which ultimately led to the development of the so-called "*Syers v. Syers* order", *i.e.* an order permitting a majority of partners to buy out a minority's share(s) in the partnership on a dissolution. In *Syers v. Syers*,[778] two brothers, Daniel and Morris, were carrying on the business of running a music hall and tavern in partnership,[779] with Daniel holding a one-eighth share and Morris the remaining seven-eighths. That partnership was found to have been dissolved.[780] The House of Lords declined to make an order for the sale of the business as a going concern and, in effect, ordered that Daniel's share should be valued at the date of dissolution *as if* the business had been sold as a going concern and that Morris should have the right to acquire his share at that value.[781] Only in the event of Morris failing to pay that sum was a sale of the business to take place. It is clear that, in making this order, the House of Lords

---

[772] Note that there was also some doubt as to the date on which and the circumstances in which the partnership was dissolved. A similar approach was adopted by Hart J. in *Anselm v. Anselm*, Unreported June 29, 1999 ChD, when deferring an order for the sale of certain partnership properties.

[773] The partnership agreement originally provided that, on the determination of the partnership, the goodwill would accrue to the defendant and this term was carried over into the partnership at will which came into existence at the expiry of the original fixed term by virtue of the Partnership Act 1890, s.27(1): see further *supra*, paras 10–18 *et seq.*

[774] CHANI 94/0943/b, November 2, 1995.

[775] See *supra*, para. 23–185.

[776] Note also the views expressed by Neuberger J. as to the feasibility of selling a professional insolvency practice in *Mullins v. Laughton* [2003] Ch. 250 at [118].

[777] (1984) 134 N.L.J. 745. The report is, however, very brief and gives little indication of the true basis for the decision.

[778] (1876) 1 App.Cas. 174.

[779] The existence of the partnership was disputed by Morris, but this issue was resolved in Daniel's favour. It should be noted that Lord Lindley commented: "The agreement between the partners was probably not intended to create a partnership but a loan . . . ".

[780] The partnership was held to be at will and had been dissolved by a pleading filed by Morris.

[781] See the order at (1876) 1 App.Cas. 192. In fact the order was also dependent on Morris paying Daniel the sums found to be due to him on the taking of an account of the partnership dealings during the subsistence of the partnership. The order was otherwise rather elliptical: rather than providing that Morris should acquire Daniel's share, it merely stated that, having paid the assessed value of that share, "no further accounts [*should*] be taken".

was influenced by the relatively small size of Daniel's share, by the nature of the business and by the effect which a forced sale would have.[782]

There is no limit on the considerations which can be taken be taken into **23–188** account in the exercise of the court's discretion. Thus an order may be made where one partner is a minor[783] and a sale of his share to his co-partners would demonstrably be for his benefit. However, the other partners cannot be forced to purchase a minority partner's share, as Lord Lindley pointed out in this passage:

> " . . . although it may[784] be for the benefit of an infant[785] . . . partner that his share should be sold, yet if the other partners insist on the sale of the whole property they are entitled to such a sale."[786]

Although the court did appear to make such an order of its own motion in *Mullins v. Laughton*,[787] this is out of line with the authorities.

There is no doubt that the court still retains the power to make a *Syers v. Syers* **23–189** order in an appropriate case,[788] although apart from *Mullins v. Laughton* there are no recent reported examples of such orders being made. Indeed, in *Hammond v. Brearley*,[789] Hoffmann L.J. is reported to have observed:

> "It is I think notorious in the Chancery Division that *Syers v. Syers* is an authority which is far more frequently cited by counsel than applied. But the discretion which it gives seems to me to be a valuable one which I think judges should not hesitate to use when it suits the justice of the case."[790]

He went on to point out that the claimant might actually, on the facts of the case before him,[791] have been worse off if a sale of the partnership assets were ordered but, in the event, the final decision was left to the trial judge. The availability of

---

[782] See (1876) 1 App.Cas. 174, 183 *per* Lord Cairns, 191 *per* Lord Hatherley. See also *supra*, para. 19–11.

[783] See *Crawshay v. Maule* (1818) 1 Swan. 495, 530. Here the minors were, in fact, beneficially interested in the share of a deceased partner. In the case of a partner suffering from mental incapacity, the decision to accept the other partners' offer to purchase his share ought properly to be referred to his deputy or to the Court of Protection: see the Mental Capacity Act 2005, ss.16, 18. See, as to the position under the old lunacy laws, *Leaf v. Coles* (1851) 1 De G.M. & G. 171; *Prentice v. Prentice* (1853) 10 Hare (App.) 22.

[784] Unaccountably, Appendix II to Lord Lindley's Supplement on the Partnership Act 1890 introduced the word "not" at this point. Surely, the distinction between a sale of the minor partner's share and the sale of all the partnership assets is the correct one? If the other partners insist on the latter, there will, as such, be no sale of the minor's share.

[785] The words "or lunatic" formerly appeared at this point.

[786] See *Rowlands v. Evans* (1861) 30 Beav. 302; also *Burdon v. Barkus* (1862) 4 De G.F. & J. 42.

[787] [2003] Ch. 250. It is, however, understood that the majority may at some stage have indicated their willingness that such an order be made.

[788] It should be noted that Lord Lindley put it in more tentative terms: " . . . *quaere* whether the discretion alluded to [*in Syers v. Syers*] exists in all cases. But why should it not? Its exercise would often be most beneficial." This was, in retrospect, overcautious.

[789] December 10, 1992 (unreported). Hoffmann L.J. also cited passages from *Hugh Stevenson & Sons Ltd. v. Aktiengesellschaft für Cartonnagen Industrie* [1918] A.C. 239, 255 *per* Lord Atkinson.

[790] This view was cited by Neuberger J. in *Mullins v. Laughton* [2003] Ch. 250, at [110].

[791] The claimant had no interest in the goodwill of the firm, which rendered a sale as going concern impossible: see further *supra*, para. 23–186.

the jurisdiction was also highlighted by the Court of Appeal in *Toker v. Akgul*.[792]

23–190   The following points should be borne in mind when considering an application for a *Syers v. Syers* order:

    (a)   The jurisdiction is only exercisable once the partnership has been dissolved: such an order cannot be obtained whilst the partnership is continuing.[793] It may, however, be that the court would be prepared to entertain an application for an order which will only have effect as from the dissolution date, if the justice of the case so requires.[794]

    (b)   The order may relate to a partner's entire share or may, in an appropriate case, be confined to specific assets.[795]

    (c)   There is no reason in principle why the order should not relate to the shares of more than one partner, provided that they together represent a sufficiently small minority. As their proportionate share of the firm increases, so will the court's reluctance to make an order. Interestingly, in *Anselm v. Anselm*,[796] Hart J. appeared to contemplate that the equities might justify an order that one equal partner should buy out the share of the other in certain partnership properties. In the current editor's view, cases in which such an order might be warranted, particularly in the case of a two partner firm, will be extremely rare.[797]

23–191   (d)   The order may be in mandatory terms and need not give the purchasing partners the option of not proceeding with the purchase once the value of the share is known, unlike the approach adopted in *Syers v. Syers* itself.[798] In *Mullins v. Laughton*,[799] Neuberger J. was prepared to make a mandatory order but threatened to revisit the question of an order for

---

[792] CHANI 94/0943/b, November 2, 1995, noted *supra*, para. 23–157.

[793] The position is, thus, very different to that under the Companies Act 2006, s.994 (unfair prejudice).

[794] Such an order would only be possible where neither the fact of the dissolution nor its date are in dispute between the parties. Equally, there is no reason why, when a dissolution order is sought under the Partnership Act 1890 s.35 (see *infra*, paras 24–47 *et seq.*), the claim form should not include a claim for a *Syers v. Syers* order by way of consequential relief.

[795] The current editor was involved in one case in which the order was confined to the goodwill, firm name and lease of the partnership premises. Such an approach may, in fact, involve a mandatory purchase from the dissolved firm (rather than a purchase of the minority partner's share therein), so that the whole value has to be paid by the acquiring partners, leaving them to be repaid such part of the net proceeds as is actually due to them after the affairs have been wound up in the manner contemplated by the Partnership Act 1890, s.44, considered *infra*, paras 25–44 *et seq.*

[796] Unreported June 29, 1999 ChD.

[797] It is interesting to note that in *Wilton-Davies v. Kirk* [1997] B.C.C. 770, H.H. Judge Weeks (sitting as a judge of the Chancery Division) accepted the possibility that, where the shareholdings in a quasi-partnership company were equally divided between two camps, one might be ordered to buy out the other under what is now the Companies Act 2006, s.994. Although the discretion under consideration was statutory (see now, in particular, *ibid.* s.996(1), (2)(e)), in essence it does not differ fundamentally from that exercisable by a court in a partnership case, as noted *supra*, para. 23–185. *Quaere*, might a court, where the circumstances warrant it, adopt the same approach in the case of a two-man firm? Equally, the exercise of the discretion in such a case might be susceptible to a challenge under the Human Rights Act 1998, as to which see *infra*, para. 23–192.

[798] See the order at (1876) 1 App.Cas. 193, para. 3. *cf.* the approach adopted under the Companies Act 2006, s.994: *Re Cumana* [1986] B.C.L.C. 430.

[799] [2003] Ch. 250 at [112], [134].

sale if the valuation process consequent on the proposed *Syers v. Syers* order was unnecessarily drawn out.

(e) The appropriate valuation date will usually be the date of the dissolution, as in *Syers v. Syers*, although this will not necessarily be the case, *e.g.* where the application is made some time after that date.[800]

(f) It will not always be appropriate to value a share on the basis of a sale of the partnership business as a going concern.[801]

(g) In valuing a minority partner's share, all assets and liabilities will fall to be taken into account.[802] This may include the negative value of an unfavourable lease. Consistently therewith, in *Mullins v. Laughton*,[803] Neuberger J. regarded it as conceivable that the partner bought out might end up as a net debtor to the partnership, although the current editor doubts whether the court's discretion should properly be exercised in such a case. Be that as it may, it would seem to be a necessary corollary of the order that the partner bought out should be indemnified against those liabilities, in the same way as an outgoing partner,[804] and the principle of this was accepted in *Mullins v. Laughton*,[805] albeit based on a concession by the defendants.

(h) Such an order is unlikely to be made if the majority have brought about **23–192** the dissolution by their own misconduct,[806] although *Mullins v. Laughton*[807] was a case in which an order was made that the defendants buy out the claimant, despite their misconduct, in order to do justice between the parties.

(i) Active case management will be required at an early stage, in order to ensure that the application and any valuation exercise are progressed

---

[800] In *Amin v. Amin* [2009] EWHC 3356 (Ch) (Lawtel 5/1/10) at [407], Warren J. left the point open for further argument. Equally, the current editor is aware of a case in which the value was taken as at the dissolution date even though the transaction was not completed until more than a year later, during which time the firm name had not been used and all the former partners had occupied the partnership premises. Note also, by way of comparison, the decisions in *Re Cumana, supra*; *Profinance Trust SA v. Gladstone* [2002] 1 B.C.L.C. 141 (CA), especially at *ibid.* p. 160; *Re Clearsprings (Management) Ltd.* [2003] EWHC 2516 (Ch) (Lawtel 21/11/03) at [32], [33]; *Croly v. Good* [2010] EWHC 1 (Ch) (Lawtel 25/1/10).

[801] *Hammond v. Brearley,* December 10, 1992 (unreported), was such a case. Equally, the assumption that a sale as a going concern would have been possible if all the partners had been interested in the goodwill seems unwarranted. The sale of a professional practice as a going concern following a dissolution will often not be feasible: see *supra*, para. 10–200.

[802] This is similar to the position on an *ad hoc* retirement, as analysed in *Sobell v. Boston* [1975] 1 W.L.R. 1587.

[803] [2003] Ch. 250 at [123].

[804] See *Gray v. Smith* (1889) 43 Ch.D. 208, considered *supra*, para. 10–248. If the position were otherwise, it is doubtful whether the court would be prepared to make an order which left the selling partner, in effect, exposed to the risk of double jeopardy, *i.e.* to his co-partners and to the landlord, etc.

[805] [2003] Ch. 250 at [132].

[806] *e.g.* in the case of a dissolution ordered following a failed expulsion (as appears to have happened in *Clements v. Pope*, October 7, 1999, an unreported decision of H.H. Judge Weeks Q.C. sitting as a judge of the Chancery Division: see also *supra*, para. 10–213) or if the minority partner obtains an order under the Partnership Act 1890, s.35(c) or (d) (see *infra*, paras 24–73 *et seq.*). Equally, in the case of a large firm, the wider interests of clients and employees may counterbalance this factor.

[807] *supra* at [112] *et seq.*

swiftly and cost effectively.[808] As regards the latter, the use of a single joint expert is likely to be encouraged.[809]

(j) There may be some scope for a challenge to such an order under the Human Rights Act 1998.[810]

Land

23–193   It has already been seen[811] that land owned by a firm will no longer be treated as personal property and it would seem that a sale or other order relating to property which is subject to a trust of land[812] will, technically, be made pursuant to the powers conferred on the court by the Trusts of Land and Appointment of Trustees Act 1996,[813] rather that pursuant to the general jurisdiction to order a sale of partnership assets. Be that as it may, the approach adopted by the court is likely to be the same irrespective of the nature of the asset.[814] Indeed, the view has been expressed that the general approach will not differ even where the land acquired for the firm's use is held *otherwise* than as a partnership asset.[815] Certainly, an order for the sale of such land would not be expected whilst the partnership is continuing[816] and, in the event of a dissolution, an opportunity to purchase the land might be given to one or more of the former partners.[817]

In *Rodway v. Landy*,[818] the court ordered the physical division of the land as between the former partners, since a forced sale would have had disadvantageous

---

[808] This proposition was cited by Neuberger J. with apparent approval in *Mullins v. Laughton, supra*, at [111]. Such an application is, in this respect, clearly analogous to an application under the Companies Act 2006, s.994: see *North Holdings Ltd. v. Southern Tropics Ltd.* [1999] B.C.C. 746 (CA).

[809] *ibid.* As to the use of single joint experts, see CPR r. 35.7, 35PD, para. 7; also the Chancery Guide, paras 4.11 *et seq.*

[810] See generally, *supra*, para. 10–27. Equally, given the fact that a partner against whom such an order is made will, ultimately, receive the full value of his share and, absent such an order, a sale of the partnership business/assets will be unavoidable, can it properly be said that he has been "deprived of his possessions" for the purposes of *ibid.* Sched. 1, Pt II, First Protocol, Art. 1?

[811] See *supra*, paras 19–14 *et seq.*

[812] See, as to the meaning of this expression, the Trusts of Land and Appointment of Trustees Act 1996, s.1(1)(a), (2).

[813] *ibid.* ss.14, 15. These sections replaced the Law of Property Act 1925, s.30 and clearly confer a wider discretion on the court: *Mortgage Corp. v. Shaire* [2001] Ch. 743; *Bank of Ireland Home Mortgages Ltd. v. Bell* [2001] 2 All E.R. (Comm) 920 (CA). Note that *ibid.* s.15 does not apply where the application under *ibid.* s.14 is made by a partner's trustee in bankruptcy (*ibid.* s.15(4)) and the position is instead governed by the Insolvency Act 1986, s.335A, as added by *ibid.* Sched. 3, para. 23. In such a case, the creditors' interests will normally prevail, absent exceptional circumstances: *Avis v. Turner* [2008] Ch. 218 (CA) at [36] *per* Chaldwick L.J. See further, as to the procedure, CPR r. 40.16, 40DPD, Pt 1, paras 2 *et seq.*

[814] See, for example, *Anselm v. Anselm*, June 29, 1999 (Lawtel 2/7/99), noted *supra*, para. 23–190.

[815] *Hammond v. Brearley*, December 10, 1992 (CA, unreported), a decision under the Law of Property Act 1925, s.30.

[816] See *Re John's Assignment Trusts* [1970] 1 W.L.R. 955 where, following the parties' divorce, Goff J. ordered the sale of the matrimonial home, from which they had carried on a business in partnership. *cf. Bothe v. Amos* [1976] Fam. 46. And see *supra*, para. 18–64.

[817] *Hammond v. Brearley, supra*, citing *Jones v. Challenger* [1961] 1 Q.B. 176, 183 and *Ali v. Hussain* (1974) 231 E.G. 372.

[818] Unreported October 13, 2000 ChD, affirmed on appeal at [2001] Ch. 703. The land was not, in fact, partnership property.

consequences.[819] It is, however, doubtful whether a partition will ever be ordered against the opposition of the partners.[820]

Chattels

The Law of Property Act 1925 authorises the court to direct a division of **23–194** chattels held in undivided shares,[821] but it is doubted whether this jurisdiction would be exercised in the case of chattels which constitute partnership property, save in an exceptional case.

Manner of sale

The court has a discretion as to the manner in which any sale of the partnership **23–195** assets will be conducted. As Lord Lindley observed:

> "The sale to which each partner has a right is a sale to the highest bidder.[822] But with a view to doing as little injustice as possible, when the Court orders a sale, it will, if necessary, direct an inquiry as to the proper mode of selling[823]; and whether it will be for the benefit of all parties that there should be an immediate sale, or that the concern should be carried on for the purpose only of winding up its affairs: and if the latter is the case, the Court will give any of the parties liberty to propose himself as manager until a sale."[824]

Thus, in *Rowlands v. Evans*,[825] partnership property was ordered to be sold as a going concern by a disinterested third party, each partner being given liberty to bid, and an interim receiver and manager was appointed.[826]

Conduct of sale and leave to bid

Conduct of the sale is normally given to the claimant. However, since the court **23–196** is, in Lord Lindley's words, "extremely reluctant" to give liberty to bid to the party who has the conduct of a sale, if the claimant wishes to bid it will usually be necessary to entrust such conduct to a third party.[827] Other interested parties, apart from a receiver,[828] are unlikely to have any difficulty in obtaining liberty to bid.[829]

---

[819] In particular, there was a potential breach of the then National Health Service Act 1977, s.54, Sched. 10, para. 2(1) (as amended): see further, as to this, *infra*, para. 23–200.

[820] Partition appears to have been discounted as an option in *Rodway v. Landy, supra*. However, the court could, in theory, dispense with any consents required under the Trusts of Land and Appointment of Trustees Act 1996, s.7(3) by an order under s.14(2)(a). *Quaere*, could such an order be challenged under the Human Rights Act 1998? See further *supra*, paras 10–27, 23–192.

[821] s.188 (as amended).

[822] See *Burdon v. Barkus* (1862) 4 De G.F. & J. 42 and the other cases cited *supra*, para. 23–183, n. 760.

[823] See *Wilson v. Greenwood* (1818) 1 Swan. 471, 484; *Cook v. Collingridge* (1822) Jac. 607. And see *Syers v. Syers* (1876) 1 App.Cas. 174, considered *supra*, paras 23–187 *et seq.*

[824] *Waters v. Taylor* (1813) 2 V. & B. 299; *Crawshay v. Maule* (1818) 1 Swan. 495, 529 *per* Lord Eldon; *Wild v. Milne* (1859) 26 Beav. 504. As to the position where a sale is delayed and the partnership assets increase in value in the meantime, see *Barclays Bank Trust Co. Ltd. v. Bluff* [1982] Ch. 172, noted *infra*, para. 25–32.

[825] (1861) 30 Beav. 302.

[826] See also *Pawsey v. Armstrong* (1881) 18 Ch.D. 698; *Taylor v. Neate* (1888) 39 Ch.D. 538.

[827] As in *Rowlands v. Evans, supra*.

[828] A receiver requires special sanction from the court before he may purchase any asset of which he is receiver: *Nugent v. Nugent* [1908] 1 Ch. 546.

[829] See Seton (7th ed.), p. 330. Note that the partnership agreement may itself provide for such liberty: see *supra*, para. 10–263.

Where the court has given the conduct of a sale to any person, it will not allow him to be interfered with.[830]

Goodwill

23-197   Lord Lindley wrote:

> "In selling the goodwill of a going concern, the book debts and business ought to be sold in one lot, and the purchaser ought to be informed, if the facts be so, that the sellers are entitled to carry on business in competition with him."[831]

Equally, it should not be assumed that a sale of a business as a going concern will always be possible.[832]

Unsaleable but valuable assets

23-198   Complications inevitably arise where the firm owns assets[833] which, although valuable to the partners, have no *realisable* value. In Lord Lindley's day, the only assets giving rise to difficulty were offices and appointments held by partners on behalf of the firm,[834] in relation to which he observed:

> "If one of the partners holds an appointment which is not saleable, but the profits of which are by agreement to be accounted for by him to the partnership, the partner holding the appointment will be debited with its value; for that is the only mode in which, upon a dissolution, such a source of gain can be dealt with.[835] The same principle applies to other unsaleable but valuable assets, to which one partner has no exclusive right."[836]

It should not, however, be assumed that, because a contract is (or is expressed to be) unassignable, it will *necessarily* be impossible to realise its value by sale, as is made clear by the decision in *Don King Productions Inc. v. Warren*.[837] There the benefit of certain unassignable boxing management and promotion contracts entered into by individual partners were held to be partnership assets[838] and the relevant partnership agreement in effect required one partner (Mr Warren) to purchase all the partnership assets in the event of a dissolution. It was held that this term was workable (and enforceable) even in the case of contracts entered into by another partner[839] and that, if Mr Warren did not, for whatever reason,

---

[830] *Dean v. Wilson* (1878) 10 Ch.D. 136.

[831] See *Johnson v. Helleley* (1864) 34 Beav. 63 and 2 De G.J. & S. 446; *Jennings v. Jennings* [1898] 1 Ch. 378; *Re David and Matthews* [1899] 1 Ch. 378, 385 *per* Romer J. See further, as to the respective rights of a vendor and purchaser of goodwill, *supra*, paras 10–199 *et seq*.

[832] See *supra*, para. 10–199.

[833] Contrast the position where a once valuable partnership asset, such as the partnership business itself, has ceased to exist on or prior to the date of dissolution: see *supra*, para. 23–183.

[834] See generally, *supra*, para. 18–18.

[835] See *Smith v. Mules* (1852) 9 Hare 556; *Ambler v. Bolton* (1871) L.R. 14 Eq. 427. See also *supra*, paras 10–51, 10–52.

[836] *ibid.* And see *Lees v. Jones* (1857) 3 Jur.(N.S.) 954.

[837] [2000] Ch. 291 (CA).

[838] The court reached this view on the basis that the benefit of the contracts was held in trust for the partnership: see *ibid.* at [30]–[35]. See further *supra*, para. 18–17.

[839] See *ibid.* p. 324B–C *per* Lightman J. This was only addressed in passing by the Court of Appeal: *ibid.* p. 339 at [34].

purchase the benefit of the contracts, their sale to a third party would be feasible.[840] Passing reference might also be made in this context to the somewhat anomalous status of performer's property rights under Part II of the Copyright, Designs and Patents Act 1988.[841]

Equally, there are certain assets which, by virtue of a statutory prohibition or by reason of their nature, cannot be dealt with in accordance with the apparently straightforward general principle outlined above.

Statutory prohibitions

Shrievalty offices: It is provided by the Sheriffs Act 1887[842] that "A person shall **23–199** not directly or indirectly by himself or by any person in trust for him or for his use buy, sell, . . . the office of under-sheriff, deputy-sheriff, bailiff, or any other office or place appertaining to the office of sheriff . . . nor give, promise, or receive any valuable consideration whatever for such office or place". Whilst such an office may, on normal principles, be regarded as held by a partner on behalf of the firm,[843] it would seem that to debit the holder with the value of the office on a dissolution would prima facie involve the commission of an offence under that Act, as an effective sale of the office to him.[844]

National Health Service goodwill: The goodwill of a medical practice carried on **23–200** within the National Health Service unquestionably has a value, but any direct or indirect attempt to realise that value will involve an offence under the National Health Service Act 2006.[845] It follows that it would not be permissible to debit a partner with the value of the goodwill in the way that Lord Lindley suggested. Unlike the former position,[846] a general medical services contract will now be entered into between a Primary Care Trust (PCT) and the *partnership*[847] and, consistently therewith, the partnership will have its own list of patients.[848] Such a contract will subsist until it is terminated in accordance with its terms or the

---

[840] *ibid.* p. 324B *per* Lightman J. This point was not directly adverted to by the Court of Appeal, but see *ibid.* p. 339 at [34].

[841] See *Bourne v. Davis* [2006] EWHC 1567 (Ch) (Lawtel 22/6/07), noticed *supra,* para. 18–21.

[842] s.27(1), as amended by the Statute Law Repeals Act 1998, Sched. 1, Pt 1.

[843] See *supra,* paras 18–18, 18–19.

[844] An offence will not only be committed by the office holder, but also by the other partners: Sheriffs Act 1887, s.27(3). The position is, in many ways, analogous to the sale of National Health Service goodwill, as considered in the next paragraph.

[845] *ibid.* s.259, Sched. 21. And see, generally, as to the application of these provisions to partnership agreements, *Kerr v. Morris* [1987] Ch. 90; also the *Encyclopedia of Professional Partnerships,* Pt 5. A further prohibition on the sale of goodwill by various types of contractors and certain medical practitioners providing "essential services" is also to be found in the Primary Medical Services (Sale of Goodwill and Restrictions on Sub-contracting) Regulations 2004 (SI 2004/906), reg. 3(1). These regulations continue to have effect under the 2006 Act: National Health Service (Consequential Provisions) Act 2006, Sched. 2, para. 1(2). The effect of these restrictions is to remove all economic value from the goodwill: *R v. Waltham Forest NHS Primary Care Trust* [2007] 1 W.L.R. 2092 (CA).

[846] See the 18th ed. of this work, at para. 23–198.

[847] See the National Health Service (General Medical Services Contracts) Regulations 2004 (SI 2004/291), reg. 11. These regulations continue to have effect under the National Health Service Act 2006: National Health Service (Consequential Provisions) Act 2006, Sched. 2, para. 1(2).

[848] *ibid.* Sched. 6, Pt 2, paras 14, 15.

general law[849] and should contain arrangements applicable on such termination.[850] It would seem that a dissolution will not necessarily bring about a termination, although much will depend on the terms of the contract.[851] It is possible for the contract to be continued with *one* of the former partners pursuant to the variation procedure,[852] but the notice nominating the former partner must be signed by all the partners,[853] so that competing notices would seem to be an impossibility. The regulations do not lay down a procedure under which a *group* of former partners can apply to continue the contract. In such a case, each group can apply for the new contract and it will be for the PCT to decide how to deal with the matter.[854] The PCT may permit only one new contract.[855] In the case of a two partner firm, on the death of one partner the contract will continue with the surviving partner if he is suitably qualified.[856]

Other potentially anomalous assets

23–201   *Work in progress:* Following the decision in *Browell v. Goodyear*,[857] it can no longer properly be suggested that work in progress does not exist as an asset on the dissolution of a firm. The doubts raised by the decision in *Robertson v. Brent*[858] as to the existence of work in progress in a solicitors' practice have now effectively been laid to rest. The position will be the same in the case of other professional firms. However, the fact that work in progress exists as an asset does not mean that it has a significant or any value or that such value can necessarily be ascertained. In *R.A. Logan & Co., Solicitors v. Maxwell*[859] an expert had been directed to value the work in progress of a firm of solicitors but, on the evidence available to him, was unable to assess its value. The court was not prepared to override that conclusion or to force the valuer to guess that value.

---

[849] *ibid.* reg. 14(1).

[850] *ibid.* reg. 25.

[851] See *Latchman v. Pickard* [2005] EWHC 1011 (Ch) (Lawtel 12/5/05) at [2].

[852] Under *ibid.* Sched. 6, Pt 8, para. 106(1).

[853] *ibid.* para. 106(3)(c).

[854] See *Latchman v. Pickard, supra,* at [3].

[855] *ibid.*

[856] *ibid.* para. 106(4), (4A), as amended/added by the National Health Service (Primary Medical Services) (Miscellaneous Amendments) Regulations 2005 (SI 2005/893), reg. 4(20).

[857] *The Times*, October 24, 2000. Note also *Champion v. Workman*, June 20, 2001 (Lawtel 22/8/01), noted *supra*, para. 10–162; *Finlayson v. Turnbull (No.4)* 2003 G.W.D. 12–374 (OH); *Beaver v. Cohen* [2006] EWHC 199 (Ch) (Lawtel 17/2/06). Equally, account must also now be taken of the manner in which partnership accounts are required to be drawn up: see *supra*, para. 21–04.

[858] [1972] N.Z.L.R. 406. This was, however, a case of retirement, *not* a general dissolution. The authority of the decision was, in any event, doubtful: it turned on the entire nature of a solicitor's contract of retainer and the inability of the firm as originally constituted to complete the work which was the subject thereof. Given that most retainers will now expressly or impliedly authorise interim billing (see *supra*, para. 10–158, n. 739) and the obligations imposed on the partners under the Partnership Act 1890, s.38, taken together with the professional requirements of the Solicitors' Regulation Authority (see the *Solicitors' Code of Conduct 2007*, rule 2, commentary, paragraph 20, which represents a truncated version of the former *Guide to the Professional Conduct of Solicitors* (8th ed.), principle 3.11), a scenario in which the firm is unable to recover any fee for work done prior to the dissolution is unlikely. The doubts as to the correctness of the decision in *Robertson v. Brent* expressed by the current editor in the 17th ed. of this work were shared by the court in *Bennett v. Wallace* 1998 S.C. 457, 462 and *Browell v. Goodyear, supra.*

[859] [2007] CSOH 163 (OH).

Unassignable tenancies[860]: Where a rack rent is payable, such tenancies may **23–202** have a significant, albeit hypothetical, value to the partners whilst the partnership is continuing, but little, if any, real market value.[861] To attempt to bring that hypothetical value into account would be unrealistic and would, moreover, distort the dissolution accounts. It is accordingly suggested that, unless an agreed value can be placed on the tenancy[862] or the court is prepared to sanction an arrangement whereby one or more of the partners (or, perhaps, a third party) will purchase the benefit of the tenancy under some form of trust arrangement,[863] a surrender should be negotiated with the landlord and any sums received on the surrender brought into account.[864] The position will, of course, be different if the tenancy is at less than a rack rent[865] or if it is assignable.[866]

Where the landlord is one of the partners, he will usually have been concerned to ensure that the partnership agreement contains a specific provision dealing with the tenancy in the event of a dissolution.[867]

---

[860] *e.g.* tenancies protected by the Agricultural Holdings Act 1986. Although such tenancies are not inherently unassignable, they will usually contain a specific covenant against assignment, either at the insistence of the landlord or on the terms of the tenancy being referred to arbitration pursuant to *ibid.* s.6. In the latter case, the covenant will not be absolute but will prohibit assignment, etc., without the written consent of the landlord: *ibid.* Sched. 1, para. 9. The landlord does, however, have an unfettered right to withhold his consent, since the Landlord and Tenant Act 1927, s.19, is inapplicable to agricultural tenancies: see *ibid.* s.19(4) (as amended). It should be noted that, in the case of a tenancy or licence of agricultural land granted *after* September 1, 1995, the Agricultural Holdings Act 1986 will, in general, not apply: Agricultural Tenancies Act 1995, s.4(1). If a farm business tenancy (within the meaning of *ibid.* s.1(1)) is expressed to be unassignable, similar considerations to those described in the text will, of course, arise.

[861] HMRC have been known to argue that, for tax purposes, an unassignable, rack-rent tenancy has a substantial value: see, for example, *Baird's Executors v. I.R.C.* 1991 S.L.T. 9 (Lands Tr.). It is submitted that this approach is incorrect and should be resisted. See further *infra*, para. 36–59. *cf.* the position where the rent payable is *less* than a rack rent: *Walton v. I.R.C.* [1996] S.T.C. 68 (CA).

[862] In *Greenbank v. Pickles* [2001] 09 E.G. 230 (CA) the parties had agreed that the tenancy should be valued. However, it appears that the rent payable was *less* than a rack rent.

[863] Somewhat surprisingly, such an arrangement would not necessarily constitute a breach of a covenant against assignment contained in the lease: see *Pincott v. Moorstons Ltd.* (1936) 156 L.T. 139; *Gentle v. Faulkner* [1900] 2 Q.B. 267); see also the "virtual assignment" in *Clarence House Ltd. v. National Westminster Bank plc* [2010] 2 All E.R. 201 (CA), which was, on the facts, held to have been based on contract and agency not a trust. The willingness of the court to use the trust concept in a creative way is demonstrated by the decision in *Don King Productions Inc. v. Warren* [2000] Ch. 291 (CA): see, in particular, *ibid.* at [26]. It must, however, be recognised that the court might not be prepared to sanction such an arrangement, particularly if this would leave the tenant partner's exposed to the risk of continuing liability: see also *supra*, para. 23–191.

[864] See *Re Martin Coulter Enterprises Ltd.* [1988] B.C.L.C. 12 (concerning a company winding up).

[865] *Greenbank v. Pickles, supra.* The court followed the same approach as adopted in *Walton v. I.R.C., supra.*

[866] Either by virtue of an express provision of the lease or where the landlord is prepared to consent to an assignment on an *ad hoc* basis.

[867] It would, however, appear to be impossible to provide that a tenancy protected by the Agricultural Holdings Act 1986 *must* be surrendered in the event of a dissolution: see the decision of the House of Lords in *Johnson v. Moreton* [1980] A.C. 37; *cf. Elsden v. Pick* [1980] 1 W.L.R. 898; also *Knapdale (Nominees) Ltd. v. Donald* 2000 S.C.L.R. 1013 (OH). However, the same result may, in practice, be achieved by providing either that the tenancy will belong solely to the landlord partner on a dissolution (*i.e.* the converse of the situation in *Sykes v. Land* (1984) 271 E.G. 1264; see also *Faulks v. Faulks* [1992] 1 E.G.L.R. 9) or, perhaps, that no partner will be entitled to claim or to acquire the tenancy beneficially. With the latter provision, there would, at least theoretically, be no real alternative to a surrender, but *quaere* would the court strike such a provision down on the *Johnson v. Moreton* principle? Irrespective of any such provision, it would seem that the non-landlord partners could prima facie serve a valid counter notice under the Agricultural Holdings Act 1986: see *Featherstone v. Staples* [1986] 1 W.L.R. 861; *cf. Dickson v. MacGregor* 1992 S.L.T. (Land Ct.) 83.

23–203   *Milk quota:* Although milk quota clearly exists as an asset, it has no existence independently of the land to which it relates.[868] It follows that, if the partners have agreed that, on a dissolution, the land in question will cease to be a partnership asset and will vest in one of the partners beneficially, the firm may not be able to lay claim to the quota unless an independent trust of the quota can be implied.[869] Equally, absent such a trust, an express agreement to the contrary or some other exceptional circumstances,[870] the firm will not even be entitled to credit for any part of the assumed value of the quota. The position will, if anything, be *a fortiori* if the land was never a partnership asset.

Pending contracts

23–204   It has already been seen that it is, in general, the duty of the partners to complete all unfinished contracts as at the dissolution date.[871] Consistently therewith, Lord Lindley wrote:

> " . . . if the object of the partnership is to carry out a certain contract which is unfinished when the partnership is dissolved, the Court will not necessarily order the benefit of it to be sold; nor order the share of a partner in it at the time of dissolution to be ascertained by valuation; but will leave the partners to complete the contract, and will postpone the ultimate account until its completion."[872]

Thus, in *Don King Productions Inc. v. Warren*,[873] it was clear that the partnership would have to fulfil any obligations under certain boxing management and promotion contracts until such time as the defendant acquired the benefit of those contracts under an express provision of the agreement or until the completion of the winding up.[874]

Interim order for sale

23–205   An interim order for the sale of any asset[875] or, if appropriate, of the entire business can be obtained, although a strong case would need to be made out. As Lord Lindley explained:

Semble, similar considerations will arise in the case of a farm business tenancy, given that it is not possible to override the notice requirements under the Agricultural Tenancies Act 1995, s.5 by agreement: *ibid.* s.5(4).

[868] *Faulks v. Faulks, supra*; *Davies v. H. & R. Ecroyd* [1996] 2 E.G.L.R. 5, noted *supra*, para. 18–19. *cf. Harries v. Barclays Bank* [1997] 2 E.G.L.R. 15 (CA). Note, however, that provision is made in the Dairy Produce Quotas Regulations 2005 (SI 2005/465), reg. 13 (as amended by the Dairy Produce Quotas (Amendment) Regulations 2008 (SI 2008/439), reg. 2, Sched., para. 4) for the transfer of quota without the land to which it relates.

[869] See *Swift v. Dairywise Farms Ltd.* [2000] 1 W.L.R. 1177, applying the principles enunciated in *Don King Productions Inc. v. Warren* [2000] Ch. 291 (CA); although the former decision went to appeal, this issue was not, ultimately, addressed by the Court: see [2003] 1 W.L.R. 1606 (CA). *Semble*, the implication of a trust in circumstances similar to those in *Faulks v. Faulks, supra*, is unlikely.

[870] See *Faulks v. Faulks, supra*, at p. 16 *per* Chadwick J.

[871] Partnership Act 1890, s.38, *supra*, paras 13–62 *et seq.*

[872] See *McClean v. Kennard* (1874) L.R. 9 Ch.App. 336. See also *infra*, para. 26–02.

[873] [2000] Ch. 291.

[874] See *ibid.* p. 323B–D *per* Lightman J. This aspect was not adverted to in the Court of Appeal. At this stage of his judgment, Lightman J. ignored the possibility of a sale of the benefit of the contracts to a third party, which he returned to at *ibid.* p. 324B.

[875] Under the CPR r. 25.1(1)(c)(v). As to the circumstances in which a court will order a sale of assets on an interim basis (albeit under the pre-CPR regime), see *On Demand Information Plc v. Michael Grierson (Finance) Plc* [2003] 1 A.C. 368 (HL).

"Although it is not usual for the Court to direct a sale before the trial of the action, still, if circumstances require it, an order for a sale will be made on motion,[876] even although the partnership has not been previously dissolved."[877]

The tendency of a court when faced with such an application will be to defer its decision to cater for the probability that some other relief, such as a *Syers v. Syers* order,[878] will be more appropriate when the matter comes to trial.[879]

E.   DECLARATIONS AND ANCILLARY RELIEF

The court will, in an appropriate case, grant declaratory relief as to the rights and   **23–206** duties of a partner under a partnership or dissolution agreement, or, in the view of the current editor, under the general law,[880] and may even be prepared to do so on a summary basis.[881] Thus, in *Smith v. Gale*,[882] it was declared that an auditor's certificate, on which the entitlement of a retiring partner was to be based, was founded on an erroneous interpretation of the dissolution agreement and was, therefore, not binding on that partner. However, what the court will not do is to grant a declaration "in the air", *i.e.* where there is only a theoretical dispute between the partners, of the "what if . . . " variety.[883]

The court will also be prepared, where necessary, to give directions (whether by way of final or interim relief) in an action between partners, *e.g.* as to the manner in which clients should be circularised following the purported expulsion of a partner.[884]

8.   ACTIONS FOR DAMAGES

Agreements for partnership

There is no doubt that an action for damages may be maintained for breach of   **23–207** an agreement for partnership, whether involving a person's admission to an

---

[876] This terminology is obsolete: an application for an interim order will now be brought under CPR Pt 23.

[877] See *per* Lord Eldon in *Wilson v. Greenwood* (1818) 1 Swan. 471, 483; *Crawshay v. Maule* (1818) 1 Swan. 495, 506, 523 *et seq.* And see also *Bailey v. Ford* (1843) 13 Sim. 495; *Hargreaves v. Hall* (1871) L.R. 11 Eq. 415 (the order made on July 22, 1869).

[878] See *supra*, paras 23–187 *et seq.*

[879] See, for example, *Hammond v. Brearley*, December 10, 1992 (CA, unreported) and *Toker v. Akgul* CHANI 94/0943/b, November 2, 1995 (CA), noted *supra*, para. 23–186; also *Anselm v. Anselm*, Unreported June 29, 1999 ChD.

[880] Note *Rosenberg v. Nazarov* [2008] EWHC 812 (Ch) (Lawtel 10/4/08) at [53] *per* Thomas Ivory Q.C., sitting as a deputy judge of the Chancery Division, referring to Lord Lindley's inconclusive statement of principle reproduced *infra*, para. 23–208.

[881] *BBC Worldwide Ltd. v. Bee Load Ltd.*, *The Times*, March 15, 2007. Note also that, in an appropriate case, an interim declaration can be made: CPR r. 25.1(1)(b).

[882] [1974] 1 W.L.R. 9. The main part of this decision must be read subject to the later authorities: see *supra*, para. 10–176, n. 838.

[883] *Mellstrom v. Garner* [1970] 1 W.L.R. 603.

[884] See *Fulwell v. Bragg* (1983) 127 S.J. 171 (interlocutory proceedings relating to a firm of solicitors).

existing firm or the establishment of a wholly new business venture. Lord Lindley explained:

"If a person agrees to become a partner, and he breaks his agreement, an action for damages will lie against him; and any premium he may have agreed to pay may be recovered[885]; and it is no defence that the defendant has discovered that the plaintiff is a person with whom a partnership is undesirable.[886] So, if a member of a firm agrees to introduce a stranger, an action lies at the suit of the stranger against the partner for a breach of this agreement, although it may have been made without the knowledge of the other members of the firm, and they may decline to recognise it."[887]

Similarly, if a partner agrees with his co-partners that his executors will become partners in the event of his death but the executors refuse to do so, the surviving partners will have a right of action in damages for the breach of that agreement.[888] Moreover, a third party who is nominated to join the partnership under an express power in the agreement will now, in general, have a right to damages if the existing partners then decline to admit him.[889]

The right to damages as between partners

23–208   The extent to which one partner can recover damages for breach of the partnership agreement from his co-partners is, in many ways, one of the most difficult and unresolved areas of partnership law. Lord Lindley's analysis of the position was of such an unspecific nature that little real guidance is to be found therein, but it is appropriate to set the passage out in full, as a prelude to the current editor's own conclusions:

"The three following rules may be taken as guides:

1. An action for damages may be maintained by one partner against another in all those cases in which such an action might have been maintained before the Judicature Acts; provided the action would not have been restrained by a court of equity.
2. Any action which would have been so restrained cannot be supported.
3. An action may be maintained by one partner against another for any money demand which before the Judicature Acts could have been made the subject of a suit for an account.

Practically, the important questions which will arise under the new procedure[890] are reduced to the following:

---

[885] *Walker v. Harris* (1793) 1 Anst. 245; *Gale v. Leckie* (1817) 2 Stark. 107. In *Figes v. Cutler* (1822) 3 Stark. 139, it was held that an action for breach of an agreement for partnership could not be sustained without proof of the terms of such partnership; and note *Morrow v. Saunders* (1819) 1 Brod. & B. 318. *cf. M'Neill v. Reid* (1832) 9 Bing. 68. See also, as to premiums, *infra*, paras 25–07 *et seq.*

[886] *Andrewes v. Garstin* (1861) 10 C.B.(N.S.) 444. See further, as to this decision, *supra*, para. 16–06, n. 26.

[887] *M'Neill v. Reid* (1832) 9 Bing. 68.

[888] See *Downs v. Collins* (1848) 6 Hare 418 and, in particular, the decree at *ibid.* p. 441. See also *supra*, para. 10–259.

[889] *i.e.* under the Contracts (Rights of Third Parties) Act 1999, s.1(1), (2): see further *supra*, para. 10–259.

[890] *i.e.* the post Judicature Acts procedure.

1. When can an action be maintained between partners without taking a general account of all the partnership dealings and transactions?
2. When will such an account be ordered without a dissolution of the firm?

The second of these questions has been already considered.[891] The first, which has already been alluded to,[892] can only be answered generally by saying that each case must depend upon its own circumstances, and upon whether justice can really be done without taking such an account.[893] But there appears to be no reason why an action should not be brought to have some disputed item in an account settled, and why a declaratory judgment should not be pronounced settling that dispute without going further, unless it should become necessary to do so."[894]

Pre-Judicature Act law

It seems clear that, prior to the Judicature Acts, a breach of the express terms **23–209** of a partnership agreement would have sounded in damages: in a summary of the earlier law which was eliminated in more recent editions of this work, Lord Lindley wrote:

"An action for damages for the breach of an express agreement entered into by one partner with another would lie, if the damages when recovered would have belonged to the plaintiff alone. Thus where a partner retired, and he covenanted with his co-partners not to carry on business within certain limits, or they covenanted to indemnify him against the debts of the firm, actions for damages occasioned by breaches of these covenants would clearly lie.[895] So, if a partnership was entered into for a definite time, and one partner was turned out by his co-partners before that time had expired, he could sue them for this breach by them of their agreement, and recover damages for the injury he had sustained[896]; so an action might be maintained for not rendering accounts and dividing profits[897]; for a penalty stipulated to be paid in case of a breach of agreement[898]; for rent covenanted to be paid[899]; for not

---

[891] See *supra*, paras 23–82 *et seq.*

[892] See *supra*, para. 23–76.

[893] In this context Lord Lindley cross-referred to the old cases where an action at law was brought "in respect of a matter which, though relating to the partnership business, was separate and distinct from all other matters in question between the partners." The cases may be classified as follows: (a) action on agreement to take partnership property at a valuation: *Jackson v. Stopherd* (1834) 2 Cromp. & M. 361; (b) action after final balance struck between partners: *Wells v. Wells* (1669) 1 Vent. 40; *Moravia v. Levy* (1786) 2 T.R. 483, note; *Foster v. Allanson* (1788) 2 T.R. 479; *Preston v. Strutton* (1792) 1 Anst. 50; *Rackstraw v. Imber* (1816) Holt 368; *Henley v. Soper* (1828) 8 B. & C. 16; *Brierly v. Cripps* (1836) 7 C. & P. 709; *Wray v. Milestone* (1839) 5 M. & W. 21; *Morley v. Baker* (1862) 3 Fost. & Fin. 146; *cf. Fromont v. Coupland* (1824) 2 Bing. 170; (c) action on bill or note given by partner personally: *Preston v. Strutton, supra; Neale v. Turton* (1827) 4 Bing. 151; *Heywood v. Watson* (1828) 4 Bing. 496; *Fox v. Frith* (1842) 10 M. & W. 131; *Graves v. Cook* (1856) 2 Jur.(N.S.) 475; *Beecham v. Smith* (1858) E.B. & E. 442; (d) action for rent against partners holding as trustees for firm: *Bedford v. Brutton* (1834) 1 Bing.(N.S.) 399; (e) action in respect of money which ought to be divided without reference to other matters: *Graham v. Robertson* (1788) 2 T.R. 282; (f) action in respect of money placed in one partner's hands by another for a particular purpose: *Wright v. Hunter* (1800) 1 East 20 and (1801) 5 Ves. Jr. 792; (g) action for money overpaid by purchaser of share: *Townsend v. Crowdy* (1860) 8 C.B.(N.S.) 477; (h) action on express and independent indemnity: *Coffee v. Brian* (1825) 3 Bing. 54; (i) action for contribution in respect of a particular loss: *Sedgwick v. Daniel* (1857) 2 H. & N. 319; *cf. Sadler v. Nixon* (1834) 5 B. & Ad. 936.

[894] See *supra*, para. 23–206. And note also *Rosenberg v. Nazarov* [2008] EWHC 812 (Ch) (Lawtel 10/4/08) at [53] *per* Thomas Ivory Q.C., sitting as a deputy judge of the Chancery Division.

[895] *White v. Ansdell* (1836) T. & G. 785; *Leighton v. Wales* (1838) 3 M. & W. 545. See also *Haddon v. Ayers* (1858) 1 E. & E. 118; *Barker v. Allan* (1859) 5 H. & N. 61.

[896] See *Greenham v. Gray* (1855) 4 I.C.L.R. 501.

[897] *Owston v. Ogle* (1811) 13 East 538; also *Stavers v. Curling* (1836) 3 Bing.(N.C.) 355.

[898] *Radenhurst v. Bates* (1826) 3 Bing. 463.

[899] *Bedford v. Brutton* (1834) 1 Bing.(N.C.) 399.

indemnifying the plaintiff against a debt[900]; for not putting the plaintiff in funds to enable him to defray expenses as agreed."[901]

To the above list might also be added the right of a partner to compensation in the nature of damages in respect of a loss resulting from the misconduct or culpable negligence of his co-partner.[902] It should also be noted that, in *Dean v. Macdowell*,[903] the Court of Appeal had no compunction in observing that an action for damages would lie for breach of a covenant not to "engage, directly or indirectly, in any business except upon the account and for the benefit of the partnership" although, in the instant case, not only could no loss be proved, but no claim for damages had been put forward.

The modern law

23–210   It is clear that a partnership agreement is a species of contract, but it is a contract of a special nature, as Lord Millett made clear in *Hurst v. Bryk*.[904] Whilst it cannot necessarily be said that *all* the normal remedies for breach of contract are available to a partner,[905] there is, in the current editor's view, no doubt as to his right to recover damages for breach of the partnership terms,[906] including any duty implied by law.[907] In *Mullins v. Laughton*,[908] Neuberger J. accepted the principle that an action for damages for loss of reputation would lie as between partners, whilst in *Gorne v. Scales*[909] damages were successfully claimed for use of confidential information following a dissolution.

---

[900] *Want v. Reece* (1822) 1 Bing. 18.

[901] *Brown v. Tapscott* (1840) 6 M. & W. 119.

[902] See *supra*, para. 20–10.

[903] (1876) 8 Ch.D. 345, 352 *per* James L.J., 355 *per* Thesiger L.J.

[904] [2002] 1 A.C. 185 (HL), 194. These observations were, in fact, *obiter* but were followed and applied in *Cowan v. Wakeling* [2008] EWCA Civ 229 (Lawtel 25/2/08) at [24], [25]. No such distinction had been drawn by Harman J. in *Hitchman v. Crouch Butler Savage Associates* (1983) 80 L.S. Gaz. 554.

[905] Thus, the doctrine of repudiation has little or no application as between the members of an ongoing firm: see *infra*, paras 24–05 *et seq*. The doctrine of frustration is also, in the current editor's view, inapplicable: see *infra*, para. 24–13. Equally, it is now clear that the court will approach the remedies for breach of contract flexibly and will not *necessarily* confine a claimant merely to a right to damages: see *Att.-Gen. v. Blake* [2001] 1 A.C. 268 (HL).

[906] See *Trimble v. Goldberg* [1906] A.C. 494, 500; *Hurst v. Bryk* [1999] Ch. 1, 9F *per* Peter Gibson L.J., 29F *per* Simon Brown L.J.; *ibid.* [2002] 1 A.C. 185, at 199, 200 *per* Lord Millett; *Broadhurst v. Broadhurst* [2006] EWHC 2727 Ch (Lawtel 23/10/06). *Winsor v. Schroeder* (1979) N.L.J. 1266 appears to be case where damages were recovered in accordance with the principles discussed *supra*, paras 20–10 *et seq.*, although the report is very sketchy. Note also, in this context, *Mair v. Wood* 1948 S.C. 83; *Blackwood v. Robertson* 1984 S.L.T. 68 (Sh. Ct.); *Ross Harper & Murphy v. Banks* 2000 S.L.T. 699 (OH). Damages are clearly recoverable by a partner in New Zealand: see *Gallagher v. Schulz* (1988) 2 N.Z.B.L.C. 103, 196.

[907] Although the appeal on liability was ultimately allowed in *Rama v. Miller* [1996] 1 N.Z.L.R. 257, the Privy Council expressed no doubts as to a partner's right to damages for breach of a partner's fiduciary duty. The position is the same in Scotland: see *Finlayson v. Turnbull (No. 1)* 1997 S.L.T. 613 (OH), where damages were awarded against three salaried partners in respect of a breach of their fiduciary obligations prior to the dissolution of a partnership at will. See further *supra*, para. 16–10.

[908] [2003] Ch. 250 at [128] to [131]. Note that this example was cited without apparent disapproval by Warren J. in *Hammonds (A Firm) v. Danilunas* [2009] EWHC 216 (Civ) (Ch) (Lawtel 18/2/09) at [146] to [149], although his attempt to explain the rationale of the decision by reference to the agency which exists as between partners is doubtful. This issue was not referrred to on the appeal *sub nom. Hammonds (A Firm) v. Jones, The Times*, January 4, 2010.

[909] [2006] EWCA Civ. 311 (Lawtel 29/3/06).

In fact, the only question is, as Lord Lindley pointed out, whether, in order to establish a right to such damages, a partnership account *must* be taken: on the basis of the pre-Judicature Act cases,[910] it is submitted that this is not an invariable rule,[911] although the observations of Lord Millett in *Hurst v. Bryk*[912] and the decision of the Court of Appeal in *Cowan v. Wakeling*[913] appear to be authority for the proposition that such a claim must proceed by way of an action for an account[914] and will only be maintainable on or following a dissolution. The latter proposition is, as has already been seen,[915] strictly unsustainable but, in any event, a breach serious enough to warrant one partner seeking damages against his co-partners will almost inevitably lead to a dissolution, thus enabling that claim to be pursued in taking the final accounts between the partners.[916] In such a case, the breach of the agreement and resulting loss should, in general, be particularised in the claim form, rather than being left over to be raised only when the accounts are taken.[917]

Although a secondary issue was canvassed in *Hammonds (A Firm) v. Danilunas*,[918] to the effect that a partner with a claim against his co-partners may find that, in taking the accounts, he ultimately has to bear a share of any damages, it is the current editor's view that there will, in practice, be little scope for such an argument, since section 5 of the Partnership Act 1890 will rarely, if ever, be applicable to such a claim.[919] The sole exception may be in cases of discrimination where, in any event, different principles are likely to apply.[920]   **23–211**

9.   EXECUTION BETWEEN PARTNERS

Where a partner sues or is sued by his own firm in the firm name,[921] any judgment or order made in the proceedings may be enforced in the same way as   **23–212**

[910] See *supra*, para. 23–209, nn. 895 *et seq.*

[911] *Per contra* in the case of a loss suffered by *the firm* as opposed to one or more individual partners. And note also the decision in *Brown v. Rivlin*, unreported, February 1, 1983 (C.A.T. No. 56); [1984] C.L.Y., p. 138, noted *supra*, para. 23–76.

[912] [2002] 1 A.C. 185, 194.

[913] [2008] EWCA Civ 229 (Lawtel 25/2/08) at [25]. It should be noted that, at the time of the appeal, proceedings for a dissolution and the taking of an account had already been launched: *ibid.* at [26].

[914] Note that, even if this is strictly correct, it is still a claim for damages within the account. In a case of this type, the order for the account should make it clear that the claim for damages is within its ambit: see *supra*, paras 23–79, 23–119.

[915] See *supra*, para. 23–82.

[916] This sentence was approved and adopted in *Gray v. Dickson* 2007 GWD 31–540 (Sh. Ct). Note that, unusually, an order for the taking of a fresh account was refused by the Court of Appeal in *Hurst v. Bryk* [1991] Ch. 1 (see *supra*, para. 23–75) in the context of a dissolution brought about by virtue of repudiation and acceptance (as the law then stood). In any event, an equitable set off of any damages claim might can be raised in the account proceedings: *Secret Hotels Ltd. v. E.A. Traveller Ltd.* [2010] I.L.Pr. 33.

[917] See *Dickinson T/A John Dickinson Equipment Finance v. Rushmer T/A FJ Associates*, Unreported February 14, 2000 CA (Civ Div), where a substantive counterclaim was, unsuccessfully, sought to be introduced on the taking of an account, under the guise of a just allowance. As was made clear in that case, much will depend on the parameters of the account ordered to be taken, as to which see *supra*, para. 23–79.

[918] [2009] EWHC 216 (Ch) (Lawtel 18/2/09). This issue was not pursued on the appeal *sub nom. Hammonds (A Firm) v. Jones*, *The Times*, January 4, 2010.

[919] See further, *supra*, para. 12–03.

[920] See *supra*, paras 8–11, 8–12.

[921] Assuming this to be appropriate: see *supra*, para. 23–03.

any other judgment, save where there are restrictions on the execution of a judgment or order made *against* a partnership.[922] No special rules now govern execution as between a partner and his own firm[923] or as between two firms with a partner in common.[924] *Semble*, in those cases where permission to execute is required,[925] the court may direct the taking of suitable accounts and inquiries.[926]

---

[922] CPR 70PD, paras 6A.1 *et seq.*, *infra*, para. A2–09: see further *supra*, paras 14–22, 14–92 *et seq.*

[923] *cf.* RSC Ord. 81, r. 6(1)(a).

[924] *cf.* RSC Ord. 81, r. 6(1)(b).

[925] CPR 70PD, para. 6A.4, *infra*, para. A2–09.

[926] This was formerly provided for specifically in RSC Ord. 81, r. 6(2), but not in other cases. See generally, as to taking accounts between partners, *supra*, paras 23–74 *et seq.*

Part Five

DISSOLUTION AND WINDING-UP

CHAPTER 24

DISSOLUTION AND ITS CAUSES

1.   INTRODUCTION

Meaning of dissolution

WHAT is meant by the "dissolution" of a partnership is often misunderstood,   **24–01**
not only because that word is used in two distinct senses but also because it has
a very different meaning when applied to a company or limited liability partnership.[1] In the case of a partnership, it invariably refers to the moment of time when
the ongoing nature of the partnership relation terminates, even though the
partners may continue to be associated together in a new partnership or merely
for the purposes of winding up the firm's affairs.[2] Indeed, the outward appearance of a partnership immediately prior to and immediately following a dissolution will frequently be unchanged. For a company or LLP, on the other hand,
dissolution marks not the commencement of the winding up but its conclusion,
i.e. the moment of extinction.[3]

Distinction between technical and general dissolution

It does not necessarily follow from the fact that a partnership has been   **24–02**
dissolved that its affairs will fall to be wound up in the manner prescribed by the
Partnership Act 1890.[4] It has already been seen that, as a matter of law, a change
in the composition of a partnership results in a dissolution of the existing firm and
the creation of a new firm[5]; in such a case, the new firm will usually take on the
assets and liabilities of the old, without any break in the continuity of the
business.[6] This is often referred to as a "technical" dissolution and is usually, but
not always,[7] the result of agreement.

---

[1] The words "dissolved" and "dissolution" are not defined by the Partnership Act 1890.

[2] *ibid.* s.38, *supra*, paras 13–62 *et seq.*

[3] Insolvency Act 1986, ss.202(5), 205(2), as applied to LLPs (with modifications) by the Limited
Liability Partnerships Regulations 2001 (SI 2001/1090), art. 5. See also *infra*, para. 24–36.

[4] *ibid.* ss.39, 44: see further, *supra*, paras 19–08 *et seq.*, 19–25 *et seq.*, 23–183 *et seq.* and *infra*,
paras 25–44 *et seq.*

[5] See *supra*, paras 3–01 *et seq.* And see, in particular, *Jardine-Paterson v. Fraser* 1974 S.L.T. 93,
97 *per* Lord Maxwell (albeit a decision relating to a Scots partnership with a separate legal identity);
also *Hadlee v. Commissioner of Inland Revenue* [1989] 2 N.Z.L.R. 447, 455 *per* Eichelbaum J. This
aspect was not pursued on appeal: see [1993] A.C. 524. The only authority to the contrary is
Cummings v. Stockdale (unreported, November 11, 2008) which is, for the reasons noted *supra*, para.
3–05, in the current editor's view clearly *per incuriam*.

[6] Note, however, that a creditor of the old firm is unlikely to acquire rights against the new firm,
even where the liabilities are taken over: see *supra*, paras 13–22 *et seq.* See also *supra*, para.
10–56.

[7] See, for example, *Hudgell Yeates & Co. v. Watson* [1978] Q.B. 451, where the partnership was
dissolved under the Partnership Act 1890, s.34. See *infra*, para. 24–45.

24-03   In contrast, the expression "general" dissolution is used to denote a dissolution involving a full scale winding up, which may well have been brought about at the instance of one partner, against the wishes of the others. When a firm is referred to as "in dissolution", this usually indicates that a general dissolution has taken place, but that the winding up of its affairs is still continuing. Once the winding up is complete and the accounts are finally settled as between the partners,[8] there will be nothing left which could properly be referred to as a partnership, whether in dissolution or otherwise.

The above distinction between a technical and a general dissolution was accepted without demur in *HLB Kidsons v. Lloyd's Underwriters*,[9] when considering the potential application of section 38 of the Partnership Act 1890[10] on a change in a firm.

This and subsequent chapters are primarily concerned with dissolution in the second sense.

Causes of dissolution

24-04   The general dissolution of a partnership may be brought about in a number of well recognised ways, which can be classified into the following groups:

1. By mutual agreement of the partners. Thus, whatever duration may have been agreed at the outset, the partners can, if they so wish, bring the partnership to an end at an earlier date.[11] However, unanimity is a prerequisite.[12]

2. By the exercise of an express power to dissolve reserved by the agreement.[13]

3. By rescission for fraud or misrepresentation.[14]

4. By the service of notice or the occurrence of some other determining event prescribed by the Partnership Act 1890.[15] It should, however, be appreciated that the relevant provisions of the Act can, for the most part, be excluded by agreement.[16]

5. By order of a court of competent jurisdiction or, where relevant, by an arbitration award.[17]

---

[8] See *supra*, paras 23–74 *et seq.* and *infra*, paras 25–44 *et seq.*

[9] [2009] 1 All E.R. (Comm) 760 at [16] *per* Judge Mackie Q.C. sitting as a judge of the Chancery Division. Note that the distinction also appears not to have been challenged in *Summers v. Smith*, March 27, 2002 (Lawtel 2/4/02) at para. [65].

[10] See, as to this section *supra*, paras 13–61 *et seq.*

[11] If authority were required for this self evident proposition, reference should be made to the Partnership Act 1890, s.19, *supra*, para. 10–12. See also *infra*, para. 24–93.

[12] It is not possible for a majority to vary the terms of the partnership unless they have an express power so to do: see *supra*, para. 10–12. *cf.* the terms of the Partnership Act 1890, s.24(8), *supra*, paras 15–04 *et seq.*

[13] Such a power may be explicit in its terms (see *supra*, paras 10–137 *et seq.*) or may merely authorise a majority to take *any* decision in relation to the partnership's affairs, including the decision to dissolve (see *supra*, paras 10–102 *et seq.*).

[14] See *supra*, paras 23–52 *et seq.*

[15] *ibid.* ss.26(1), 32–34, *infra*, paras 24–15 *et seq.*

[16] Partnership Act 1890, s.19, *supra*, para. 10–12; see also *infra*, paras 24–15, 24–19, 24–30, 24–32. It is, however, impossible to exclude *ibid.* s.34, even though the practical effects of that section may be avoided: see *infra*, paras 24–44, 24–45.

[17] Partnership Act 1890, s.35, *infra*, paras 24–47 *et seq.* As to the power of an arbitrator to order a dissolution, see *supra*, para. 10–272.

Subsequent sections of this chapter principally concentrate on dissolutions brought about in the fifth and sixth ways.

The doctrine of repudiation

Application of the doctrine

Whether a partnership could be dissolved by an innocent partner's acceptance **24–05** of his partners' repudiatory breach of the partnership terms had been a vexed issue for many years and has only relatively recently been resolved in favour of the proposition that the doctrine does *not* apply,[18] even though some doubts and difficulties remain.[19]

Although it is clear that partnership is a relationship which arises out of an agreement (express or implied),[20] it is fair to say that the editors of this work had, over the years, expressed doubts as to whether the normal contractual doctrine of repudiation would have any application in a partnership context.[21] Such doubts were, however, emphatically rejected by Harman J. in *Hitchman v. Crouch Butler Savage Associates*,[22] where he held that the doctrine applied to partnership agreements in the same way as to other contracts, and the application of the doctrine also appeared to have been recognised by Nourse J. in *Fulwell v. Bragg*.[23]

It therefore came as no particular surprise that, when *Hurst v. Bryk*[24] came before Carnwath J. and the Court of Appeal, it was common ground between the partners that the doctrine *was* applicable[25] and, moreover, that acceptance of a repudiatory breach would bring about a dissolution of the firm.[26] In that case, all the partners bar one[27] had served notice to retire from the firm with effect from May 31, 1991. It was held that, as a matter of construction, the partnership would have been dissolved at the expiration of those notices.[28] The defendants nevertheless decided to bring the partnership to an end at an earlier date and, without the claimant's consent, they all executed an agreement which provided for the dissolution of the firm as at October 31, 1990 and then purported to carry that agreement into effect. These actions were held to be a repudiation of the partnership agreement which the claimant was entitled to, and did, accept and this part of the decision was not challenged in the House of Lords.[29] The more contentious question was whether the claimant was, by virtue of his acceptance

---

[18] *Hurst v. Bryk* [2002] 1 A.C. 185 (HL); *Mullins v. Laughton* [2003] Ch. 250, noted *infra*.

[19] See *infra*, paras 24–07, 24–08.

[20] *Hurst v. Bryk, supra*, p. 194 *per* Lord Millett. Although he rightly pointed out that the Partnership Act 1890, s.1 makes no reference to contract (see *ibid.*), this does, perhaps, ignore Lord Lindley's analysis of what lies at the heart of the relationship: see *supra*, paras 2–07, 2–15.

[21] Indeed, Lord Millett in *Hurst v. Bryk, supra*, referred to this fact at p. 194.

[22] (1983) L.S. Gaz. 550 (judgment being delivered on November 19, 1982). It should be noted that an appeal from this decision was, ultimately, allowed on other grounds: see (1983) 127 S.J. 441 and *supra*, para. 10–123.

[23] (1983) 127 S.J. 171 (judgment being delivered on December 23, 1982).

[24] [1999] Ch. 1 (CA). The decision of Carnwath J. is not reported.

[25] See [1999] Ch. 9 *per* Peter Gibson L.J.

[26] It is clear that this point was not argued: see *ibid.* pp. 3, 4.

[27] Not, ironically, the claimant.

[28] See [1999] Ch. 9–10 *per* Peter Gibson L.J.

[29] See [2002] 1 A.C. 196.

of the repudiatory breach, released from any obligation to contribute to the liabilities of the dissolved firm. In this respect, Carnwath J. and the majority of the Court of Appeal[30] found in the defendants' favour and it was this issue which was the subject of the appeal to the House of Lords.

24–06   Although the decision of the Court of Appeal was unanimously upheld and their Lordships appear to have acknowledged the application of the doctrine to agreements for partnership and to dissolution agreements,[31] grave doubts were expressed as to whether the doctrine could ever, of itself, bring about the dissolution of a partnership. In his speech, with which all of their Lordships appear to have agreed, Lord Millett pointed out that partnership is "more than a simple contract . . . it is a continuing personal as well as commercial relationship"[32] and, as such, it had always been regulated by rules developed by the Court of Chancery. He then went on to draw a crucial distinction between the partnership *contract* and the partnership *relationship*: whilst he appeared to accept that the doctrine was applicable to the former, he questioned whether it could ever operate to bring about an automatic dissolution of the latter.[33] On that basis, repudiation could only operate at a time when no partnership relationship exists, *i.e.* before the partnership has commenced or after it has terminated.[34] Lord Millett's rejection of the full application of the doctrine was founded on the absence of any reference to repudiatory breach as a cause of dissolution in the Partnership Act 1890[35] and the potential overlap between automatic dissolution resulting from repudiation and acceptance and the discretionary power conferred on the court to order a dissolution under section 35(d) of the Partnership Act 1890, which would inevitably give rise to anomalies.[36] He concluded:

---

[30] Hobhouse J. dissented.

[31] *ibid.* 193.

[32] *ibid.* 194.

[33] *ibid.* 195.

[34] Thus, on Lord Millett's view, the doctrine may apply to an agreement for partnership, provided that no business is actually being carried on by the prospective partners: see *supra*, paras 2–17 *et seq.* Again, it may apply as between former partners, *e.g.* where continuing partners repudiate an agreement which sets out the rights and duties of an outgoing partner. Lord Millett should, however, not be taken to have suggested that a repudiation of the partnership contract whilst the partnership relationship subsists would terminate the former but leave the latter in existence: were that to be the position, the partnership would, in any event, be transformed into a partnership at will and could be terminated at any time, without the need for any application under the Partnership Act 1890, s.35: see *supra*, paras 9–01 *et seq.* and *infra*, paras 24–18 *et seq.* See also *infra*, para. 24–11, n. 79. Needless to say, it would be a very exceptional case in which it could be argued that, notwithstanding a repudiatory breach, an express right to terminate the contract would have to be exercised: see further, as to such cases, *Chitty on Contracts* (30th ed.), para. 22–049; also *infra*, para. 24–08. It should be noted that, in reaching his conclusion in *Mullins v. Laughton* [2003] Ch. 250, noted *infra*, Neuberger J. contrasted the views expressed in the text and in this footnote with those set out in para. 6.29 of the Law Commission's Consultation Paper No.159 (2000) on Partnership Law: see *ibid.* at [91]. Unknown to his Lordship, much of the reasoning set out in that paragraph of the Consultation Paper was derived from an earlier draft of this chapter, representing the current editor's then preliminary view, whilst absorbing the full implications of Lord Millett's speech.

[35] [2002] 1 A.C. 195. Equally, as Harman J. pointed out in *Hitchman v. Crouch Butler Savage Associates* (1983) 80 L.S. Gaz. 550, 555, the 1890 Act is not a complete code: see further *ibid.* s.46, *infra*, para. A1–47 and *supra*, para. 1–05.

[36] [2002] 1 A.C. 196. It is interesting to note that Lord Millett himself admitted that, if the doctrine were to apply to the partnership relationship, there might still be circumstances in which section 35(d) of the 1890 would operate. However, the current editor is somewhat sceptical as to these: see *infra*, para. 24–11.

"By entering into the relationship of partnership, the parties submit themselves to the jurisdiction of the court of equity and the general principles developed by that court in the exercise of its equitable jurisdiction in respect of partnerships. There is much to be said for the view that they thereby renounce their right of unilateral action to bring about the automatic dissolution of their relationship by acceptance of a repudiatory breach of the partnership contract, and instead submit the question to the discretion of the court."[37]

In the event this issue did not fall to be decided and the views expressed were strictly *obiter*. However, these views were subsequently endorsed and adopted by Neuberger J. in *Mullins v. Laughton*,[38] who held that the doctrine of repudiation has no application to partnerships, albeit only after brief oral argument.[39] In that case the defendants had, in the face of the claimant's refusal to resign, sought to treat him as if he were no longer a partner without going through the correct expulsion procedure under the partnership agreement, which would, under the pre-*Hurst v. Bryk* law, clearly have amounted to an act of repudiation.[40]

Interestingly, the Court of Appeal of New South Wales in *Ryder v. Frohlich*[41] has since accepted without hesitation that the doctrine of repudiation *does* apply to continuing partnerships and declined to adopt the reasoning deployed in *Hurst v. Bryk* and *Mullins v. Laughton*.[42]

In the previous edition of this work it was submitted that, when rejecting the **24–07** application of the doctrine, Lord Millett failed to take proper account of the position in which the innocent partner is placed. Whilst acknowledging that the point made was "not negligible", Neuberger J in *Mullins v. Laughton*[43] rejected it as not having sufficient force to overturn Lord Millett's conclusion. The current editor remains unconvinced. If one takes the classic scenario exemplified in *Mullins v. Laughton* itself, *i.e.* where a partner's continuing membership of the firm is denied by the other partners and he is, as a result, excluded from further participation therein, on Lord Millett's and Neuberger J.'s approach, the partnership and the excluded partner's liability as a member thereof[44] will necessarily continue until such time as an order has been made under section 35 of the 1890

---

[37] [2002] 1 A.C. 196.

[38] [2003] Ch. 250. Note that 3 months prior to this decision, in the unreported decision of *Goodchild v. Chadwick* (September 18, 2002), Kevin Garnett Q.C. sitting as a deputy judge of the Chancery Division, when faced with a repudiation argument observed that "The reasoning in [*Hurst v. Bryk*] is extremely powerful, and in any event I would feel bound to accept it." This comment was made in the context of an application for an interim injunction to enforce a garden leave provision.

[39] See [2003] Ch. 250 at [93]. In the circumstances, it is somewhat perplexing that the Court of Appeal in *Cowan v. Wakeling* [2008] EWCA Civ 229 (Lawtel 25/2/08) at [24] referred to the fact that Mr Cowan did not suggest that Mr Wakeling's conduct "amounted to a repudiation of the partnership agreement that he had accepted so as to dissolve the partnership".

[40] See [2003] Ch. 250 at [103]. Although repudiation was not mentioned in *Hodson v. Hodson* [2009] P.N.L.R. 8 (CA), the reasoning of Rimer L.J. at [40] reflects a similar approach to that adopted in *Hurst v. Bryk* and *Mullins v. Laughton*.

[41] [2004] NSWCA 472. This consideration seems to have stemmed from the court's own researches and not from submissions of the parties: *ibid.* at [133].

[42] It should also be noted in this context that the reasoning in these cases is *not* applicable in the case of LLP agreements, where no possibility of a dissolution of the LLP arises: see *infra*, para. 24–08.

[43] [2003] Ch. 250 at [92].

[44] See, generally, the Partnership Act 1890, ss.9–13. Note that such liability follows automatically from the status of partner: see further *infra*, n. 53.

Act.[45] The court has no power to backdate the dissolution[46] and the excluded partner will, if held liable to a third party,[47] have to seek an indemnity from his co-partners, either on the basis of their unauthorised conduct[48] or by way of damages.[49] The efficacy of such a right of indemnity will necessarily be dependent on the financial status of the other partners. Granted that the court has power to make a summary order for dissolution in such a case,[50] but the reality is that this will take time to obtain. There is, of course, the counter argument that, even if the doctrine *does* apply, there will still be scope for liability to be imposed on the innocent partner as a result of holding out[51] or, perhaps, by virtue of section 38 of the 1890 Act,[52] but his exposure is by no means as extensive as it would be under section 5 of that Act.[53] The determinative factor in Neuberger J.'s view was, ultimately, that there will in any event be a period of uncertainty as to the effectiveness of the repudiation and acceptance until the court has ruled on the matter, so that there is equal detriment either way. Yet surely, uncertainty with a probable absence of continuing liability is preferable to uncertainty with a *guarantee* of continuing liability. It should be noted that the current editor's analysis was cited without apparent disapproval in *Ryder v. Frohlich*.[54]

Be that as it may, the issue in the case of continuing partnerships must be taken as resolved[55] unless and until the matter again comes before a higher court. It is, in those circumstances, surprising that repudiation arguments are still, in practice, continuing to be advanced on a regular basis.

Agreements to which the doctrine can still apply

24–08   The objections to the application of the doctrine voiced in *Hurst v. Bryk* and *Mullins v. Laughton* do not apply in the case of an agreement between partners which does not regulate their ongoing relationship as partners.[56] Thus, an agreement documenting the terms of a partner's *retirement* could be repudiated, as could a dissolution agreement. Although such an argument seemingly failed in

---

[45] See, as to such applications, *infra*, paras 24–47 *et seq.*

[46] See *infra*, para. 24–91.

[47] The fact that the other partners may have excluded the innocent partner will not affect his exposure to third parties: this is not an instance in which the Partnership Act 1890, s.36 will apply.

[48] This will be in point only as regards decisions which, under the agreement, require the innocent partner's consent or in respect of which he was excluded from his right to participate.

[49] See further, as to the right to damages, *supra*, paras 23–208 *et seq.* and *infra*, para. 24–12.

[50] CPR Pt 24; see also *ibid.* Pt 25 (interim remedies).

[51] See the Partnership Act 1890, s.14, *supra*, paras 5–35 *et seq.*; also *ibid.* s.36, *infra*, paras 13–41 *et seq.*

[52] See *infra*, paras 13–62 *et seq.*

[53] See *infra*, paras 12–02 *et seq.* Thus, liability is imposed on all the partners even their existence is not disclosed to third parties: see *infra*, para. 12–11. By way of contrast, there is no automatic liability based on holding out under the Partnership Act 1890, s.14, even if there may be in a case falling within *ibid.* s.36(1).

[54] [2004] NSWCA 472 at [130].

[55] Note, for example, the views expressed in Blackett-Ord's *Partnership Law* (3rd ed.) at para. 14.13. The current editor finds his example of a two man partnership hard to follow: surely if one treats the other as no longer a partner and the latter accepts the position this is a case of a consensual dissolution (even if the terms may be in dispute). The alternative example of all the partners being in repudiatory breach is simply not understood, unless it again refers to a consensual dissolution. The decision in *Gray v. Dickson* 2007 GWD 31–540 (Sh. Ct.), noted *infra*, para. 24–26 appears not to be a case of repudiation and is, in many way, similar to the first case considered by Blackett-Ord.

[56] See *supra*, para. 24–06.

the case of a retirement agreement in *Jenkins v. Holy*,[57] it is not clear from the brief report on what basis.

Notwithstanding its similarity to a partnership,[58] a joint venture agreement can clearly be repudiated,[59] as can an LLP members' agreement since, unlike a partnership agreement, its continued application is not inextricably bound up with the continued existence of the LLP itself.

One other unresolved issue is whether, if a partner exercises a *contractual* right to dissolve the partnership by reason of conduct on the part of the other partners which would, but for the non-application of the doctrine, amount to a repudiation, he can still recover the same measure of damages as he would if repudiation were available.[60] Give that the considerations which drove the decisions in *Hurst v. Bryk* and *Mullins v. Laughton* will not be applicable in such a case, it is considered that the point is at least arguable, provided that this is not inconsistent with the terms of the partnership agreement. It is not considered that a similar argument would be maintainable in a case where a partnership at will is dissolved by notice[61] or where the partnership is dissolved by an order of the court.[62]

Factors which would be relevant if the doctrine applied

Despite the apparent demise of the repudiation doctrine in the present context, **24–09** the following consideration of the pre-*Mullins v. Laughton* position is retained against the possibility that that decision may at some future stage be overruled or held not to apply in a given set of circumstances.[63]

Nature of the breach: It goes without saying that, in order to sustain a repudiation argument, the breach of the partnership terms must be of a fairly extreme nature, amounting to a denial of the partnership agreement or of the partnership itself.[64] Examples would include an attempt to bring the partnership to an end prematurely and without the court's involvement,[65] the purported exclusion of a partner where no power of expulsion exists or where the requirements of an express power are ignored,[66] and other conduct which involves an effective denial of a partner's status as such. It has already been seen that, in the editor's view, the purported (but wrongful) exercise of a power of expulsion in strict

---

[57] June 25, 2004 (Lawtel 25/6/04), a decision of D. Donaldson Q.C. sitting as a deputy judge of the Chancery Division.

[58] See *supra*, para. 5–06.

[59] *Dymocks Franchise Systems (NSW) Pty Ltd. v. Todd* [2002] 2 All E.R. (Comm) 849 (PC); *Donnelly v. Weybridge Construction Ltd. (No. 2)* [2007] 111 Con. L.R. 112 (TCC).

[60] See *Stocznia Gdynia SA v. Gearbulk Holdings Ltd.* [2010] Q.B. 27 (CA); also *Shell Egypt West Manzala GmbH v. Dana Gas Egypt Ltd.* [2010] EWHC 465 (Comm) (Lawtel 16/3/10). Needless to say, neither case involved a partnership.

[61] See *infra*, para. 24–12.

[62] See *infra*, paras 24–47 *et seq.*

[63] See *supra*, para. 24–07.

[64] See *Hitchman v. Crouch Butler Savage Associates* (1983) 80 L.S.Gaz. 550, 555 *per* Harman J. A cumulation of breaches might conceivably suffice, especially if coupled with the likelihood of future breaches: *Alan Auld Associates Ltd. v. Rick Pollard Associates* [2008] B.L.R. 419 (CA). Note also that the conduct relied on must, on an objective test, be of a repudiatory nature and must be believed to be so by the person accepting it: *SK Shipping (S) PTE Ltd. v. Petroexport Ltd.* [2010] 2 Lloyd's Rep. 158.

[65] As in *Hurst v. Bryk* [2002] 1 A.C. 185: see *supra*, para. 24–05.

[66] As in *Mullins v. Laughton* [2003] Ch. 250 at [94] *et seq.*

conformity with its terms would rarely involve a repudiatory breach.[67] Despite the potential overlap identified by Lord Millett in *Hurst v. Bryk*,[68] it cannot be assumed that conduct of the type which might otherwise induce a court to order a dissolution under section 35 of the Partnership Act 1890[69] will automatically be sufficient: the current tendency to allege repudiatory breach almost as a matter of course is misguided.

It should be noted that, once a repudiatory act has been committed, it cannot subsequently be cured at the instance of the party guilty of the repudiation.[70]

24–10 *Acceptance by two or more partners:* In *Hurst v. Bryk*[71] the House of Lords appeared to accept that, where there are two or more innocent partners, it is not open to any one of them unilaterally to accept the repudiatory breach. In the current editor's view, it is axiomatic that the decision to accept a repudiation requires a unanimous decision of the innocent partners and cannot be taken on a majority basis.[72] Equally, such a unanimous decision might, in an appropriate case, be inferred from their conduct.[73]

24–11 *Consequences of repudiation and acceptance:* If repudiation and acceptance *did* result in an automatic dissolution of the partnership,[74] it is clear that the normal consequences would flow therefrom.[75] It is doubtful whether the partners guilty of the repudiatory breach could prevail on the court to grant a *Syers v. Syers* order[76] in their favour, although such an order was made in *Mullins v. Laughton*[77] in the face of just such conduct. In the *obiter* part of Lord Millett's speech in *Hurst v. Bryk*,[78] he suggested that, if the doctrine applies, the acceptance would, at most, discharge the innocent partners from their obligations under the partnership contract to the partners guilty of the breach and *vice versa*, but would not operate to discharge the two groups from those obligations *inter se*. This not only ignores the fact that, on a true analysis, a full-scale dissolution is inevitable,[79] but

---

[67] See *supra*, para. 10–132, n. 595.

[68] See *supra*, para. 24–06.

[69] See *infra*, paras 24–47 *et seq.*

[70] This proposition was recently affirmed in *Buckland v. Bournemouth University Higher Education Corporation* [2010] I.R.L.R. 445 (CA).

[71] [2002] 1 A.C. 185, 195 *per* Lord Millett.

[72] It goes without saying that such a decision could never fall within the Partnership Act 1890, s.24(8), since it is not an "ordinary matter connected with the partnership business". It is not even a partnership decision since it is, by definition, one to be taken by some only of the partners. See also, for an analogous case, *infra*, para. 24–39.

[73] *e.g.* where all the innocent partners accept offers of partnership/employment with other firm(s). That such conduct may amount to acceptance of a repudiation was accepted by the Court of Appeal in *Hurst v. Bryk*: see [1999] Ch. 9G *per* Peter Gibson L.J.

[74] As the law stands it does not: see *supra*, paras 24–05 *et seq.*

[75] *Hurst v. Bryk* [2002] 1 A.C. 185 (HL). Note that in *Goodchild v. Chadwick* (September 18, 2002, unreported) it was, on an application for an interim injunction, sought to be argued that repudiation results in merely a technical dissolution but neither this argument nor the main repudiation argument was accepted.

[76] See, as to such orders, *supra*, paras 23–187 *et seq.*

[77] [2003] Ch. 250. See also *supra*, para. 23–192.

[78] [2002] 1 A.C. 195. As to why this part of the speech was *obiter*, see *supra*, para. 24–06.

[79] If the result of the acceptance *were* merely to create a partnership at will (as to which see *supra*, para. 24–06, n. 34), surely that acceptance would normally demonstrate the innocent partner's unwillingness to remain in the partnership, which would itself be capable of amounting to a notice of dissolution under the Partnership Act 1890, s.26(1) and/or s.32(c).

would also produce a potential absurdity, *i.e.* the automatic creation of two separate partnerships[80] which are not within the contemplation of the partnership agreement[81] and which will have no business and no assets.[82] This should be contrasted with the position where a group of the former partners, expressly or by implication, agree to continue in partnership together on the old terms, as is their right.

The innocent partner's right to damages: There can be no doubt that the innocent partner's right to damages in respect of the repudiatory breach is not affected by his acceptance of the repudiation and the consequent dissolution of the firm, as the Court of Appeal and House of Lords recognised in *Hurst v. Bryk*.[83] What was not much canvassed in that case was the *measure* of damages, in part because of the unusual facts, *i.e.* the repudiation at most precipitated a premature dissolution,[84] and in part because of the absence of a substantive claim for damages.[85] However, in an *obiter* part of his judgment, Simon Brown L.J. did advert to the fact that any additional winding up expenses would have been recoverable, as would damages in respect of the acceleration of such expenses.[86] In the current editor's view, subject to any question of mitigation, there must be set against any losses suffered by the innocent partner, whether resulting directly from the breach or from the dissolution,[87] any benefits accruing to him by reason of the dissolution, *e.g.* the realisation of his share of goodwill and work in progress, etc., which would not have been receivable if the partnership had continued in existence. What loss could be said to have been suffered by a partner who is deprived of his theoretical right to remain a partner for life[88] or until normal retirement age,[89] will be a matter for argument.[90]

24–12

---

[80] These partnerships would, as a matter of law, each constitute new firms: see *supra*, para. 3–02.

[81] It by no means follows that a partnership agreement will survive a change in its membership: everything depends on its terms. The normal type of provision discussed *supra*, para. 10–39 would not be likely to apply in the scenario under consideration.

[82] There must, inevitably, be a dissolution of the partnership as between the two groups and the affairs of *that* partnership would clearly fall to be wound up. It is that partnership which owns the business and assets. All that the members of each group have is their individual shares in that partnership: as to the nature of a partner's share, see *supra*, paras 19–01 *et seq.*

[83] See [1999] Ch. 1, 9 *per* Peter Gibson L.J., 29 *per* Simon Brown L.J.; [2002] 1 A.C. 185, 199, 200 *per* Lord Millett (HL). See further, as to claims to damages as between partners, *supra*, paras 23–208 *et seq.*

[84] See *supra*, para. 24–05.

[85] See [1999] Ch. 29 *per* Simon Brown L.J.

[86] See [1999] Ch. 32.

[87] *e.g.* an adverse tax charge that would not otherwise have been incurred. Contrast ongoing liability under a lease of the partnership premises, which would have existed even if the partnership had continued: *Hurst v. Bryk* [2002] 1 A.C. 199 (HL).

[88] The concept of a partnership for life is now somewhat outmoded, but term partnerships with no right to retire are still encountered. Obviously, account would have to be taken of the possibility that the partnership might be dissolved by an order under the Partnership Act 1890, s.35 or in one of the other ways considered *infra*, paras 24–15 *et seq.*

[89] This presupposes that a requirement for retirement on age grounds is included in the agreement (see *supra*, para. 10–112) *and* is capable of justification under the Employment Equality (Age) Regulations 2006 (SI 2006/1031), reg. 3(1), but due to be replaced by the Equality Act 2010, ss.5, 13(2), as from a date to be appointed (see *supra*, paras 8–23, 8–24). Satisfying the latter condition may be difficult.

[90] This was a possibility contemplated by Lord Millett in *Hurst v. Bryk* [2002] 1 A.C. 185, 199.

The doctrine of frustration

24–13   The application of the doctrine of frustration to partnerships has never been directly considered by the courts,[91] although it is interesting to note that in *Hurst v. Bryk*,[92] Peter Gibson L.J. noted, without further comment, that no submissions had been made on the basis of frustration. In this context, the *obiter* reasoning of Lord Millett in *Hurst v. Bryk*,[93] when considering the application of the doctrine of repudiation to partnerships,[94] as subsequently endorsed and applied by Neuberger J. in *Mullins v. Laughton*,[95] admittedly becomes more convincing, since a number of potentially frustrating events *are* specifically catered for by the Partnership Act 1890.[96] It is on this basis that the current editor, along with the previous editor of this work, remains of the view that a partnership cannot be dissolved by virtue of frustration,[97] although a contrary view has been expressed.[98]

Even if the doctrine were capable of applying, much would, inevitably, depend on the terms of the partnership agreement.[99] The inclusion of a contractual power of dissolution by majority vote[100] would, almost certainly, be fatal.

Retirement and expulsion

24–14   The retirement and expulsion of partners will normally be regulated by the partnership agreement[101] and will not involve anything other than a technical dissolution.[102] However, more serious dissolution-related questions will on occasion arise: these are considered in the last two sections of this chapter.

---

[91] Equally, in *Hitchman v. Crouch Butler Savage Associates* (1983) 80 L.S. Gaz. 550, 555, Harman J. reportedly held that "the doctrine of repudiation *and other contractual provisions* applied to a partnership . . . in the same way as it did to all other contracts" (emphasis supplied), thus providing some (strictly inferential) support for an argument that the frustration doctrine does apply. This aspect was not raised on the appeal: see (1983) 127 S.J. 441. It has already been seen that the simplicity of Harman J.'s analysis was disapproved by the House of Lords in *Hurst v. Bryk*, *supra*, albeit on an *obiter* basis: see *supra*, para. 24–06.

[92] [1999] Ch. 1, 9F.

[93] [2002] 1 A.C. 185 (HL).

[94] *ibid.* pp. 193–196: see further *supra*, paras 24–06, 24–07.

[95] [2003] Ch. 250.

[96] See *ibid.* ss.33(1), 34, 35(b), (e), considered *infra*, paras 24–29 *et seq.*, 24–43 *et seq.*, 24–69 *et seq.* and 24–87, 24–77. *cf. ibid.* s.40. The dissolution of a partnership of which a mental patient is a partner under the Mental Health Act 1983, s.96(1)(g) no longer represents an additional example, since the repeal of that section by the Mental Capacity Act 2005, Sched. 7. The powers of the court under the 2005 Act appear to be much less extensive: see *infra*, para. 24–48. Equally, it should be noted that the Law Reform (Frustrated Contracts) Act 1943, s.1(1) does not exclude partnership contracts.

[97] An analogy might formerly have been drawn with leases (see, for example, *Total Oil Great Britain v. Thompson Garages (Biggin Hill)* [1972] 1 Q.B. 318), but it has been held by the House of Lords that a lease can, in principle, be frustrated: see *National Carriers Ltd. v. Panalpina (Northern) Ltd* [1981] A.C. 675.

[98] See an article in the *Conveyancer and Property Lawyer* (N.S.), Vol. 11, p. 43. And see also *F. C. Shepherd & Co. Ltd. v. Jerrom* [1987] Q.B. 301, 328–329 *per* Mustill L.J. (a decision concerning a contract of apprenticeship).

[99] See *Chitty on Contracts* (30th ed.), para. 23–014.

[100] See *supra*, paras 10–137 *et seq.*

[101] See *supra*, paras 10–108 *et seq.*, 10–113 *et seq.* But see *infra*, para. 24–25.

[102] See *supra*, para. 24–02.

2.   DISSOLUTION OTHERWISE THAN BY THE COURT

A.   EXPIRATION OF TERM, ETC.

If a partnership is entered into for a fixed term,[103] it must necessarily be dissolved **24–15** once that term has expired, unless the partners agree to extend its duration. Similarly, if a partnership is formed solely with a view to carrying out a particular transaction, it will be dissolved once the transaction is complete,[104] again subject to any contrary agreement. These somewhat obvious propositions are clearly established by section 32(a) and (b) of the Partnership Act 1890, which provides:

"32. Subject to any agreement between the partners, a partnership is dissolved—

(a)   If entered into for a fixed term, by the expiration of that term:
(b)   If entered into for a single adventure or undertaking, by the termination of that adventure or undertaking."

Continuation after fixed term: the statutory presumptions

If, however, the partnership is continued *after* the expiration of the fixed term, **24–16** then, in the absence of any evidence as to its intended further duration, it will be regarded as a partnership at will and, thus, determinable at any time on notice.[105] Such a consequence was only avoided in *Walters v. Bingham*[106] because the partners had agreed to be bound by the terms of a draft agreement "pending the adoption of a new deed".

If the partners, or those of them who were actively involved in the firm's business, continue that business after the expiration of the term without attempting to wind up its affairs, a continuation of the partnership will be presumed.[107]

Continuation after transaction complete

No statutory presumption applies where a partnership formed to carry out a **24–17** particular transaction is continued beyond the completion of that transaction.[108]

---

[103] See generally, *supra*, para. 10–39.
[104] See *Lindern Trawler Managers v. W.H.J. Trawlers* (1949) 83 Ll.L.R. 131; also *J. & J. Cunningham v. Lucas* [1957] 1 Lloyd's Rep. 416; *Mann v. D'Arcy* [1968] 1 W.L.R. 893; *Landford Greens Ltd. v. 746370 Ontario Inc* (1994) 12 B.L.R. (2d) 196.
[105] Partnership Act 1890, s.27(1): see *supra*, paras 10–18 *et seq*. The position was the same prior to the Act: see *Neilson v. Mossend Iron Co.* (1886) 11 App.Cas. 298; also *Featherstonhaugh v. Fenwick* (1810) 17 Ves.Jr. 298; *Booth v. Parks* (1828) 1 Moll. 465.
[106] [1988] 1 F.T.L.R. 260. For another example of a case in which partners were treated as having adopted a draft agreement, albeit otherwise than following the expiration of a fixed term, see *Thakrar v. Vadera*, March 31, 1999 (unreported).
[107] Partnership Act 1890, s.27(2).
[108] Unaccountably, *ibid.* s.27(1) applies only to "a partnership entered into for a fixed term".

However, the current editor submits that, in practice, the same presumptions as are made in the case of fixed term partnerships will be applied by analogy.[109]

B.   NOTICE

Partnership Act 1890, sections 26(1) and 32

24–18   The Partnership Act 1890 contains two separate provisions dealing with the termination of partnerships by notice. Under the rubric, "Retirement from partnership at will", section 26(1) provides:

> "(1) Where no fixed term has been agreed upon for the duration of a partnership, any partner may determine the partnership at any time on giving notice of his intention so to do to all the other partners."

Section 32 then provides as follows:

> "32. Subject to any agreement between the partners, a partnership is dissolved—
>
>   . . .
>
>   (c)   If entered into for an undefined time, by any partner giving notice to the other or others of his intention to dissolve the partnership.
>
> In the last-mentioned case the partnership is dissolved as from the date mentioned in the notice as the date of dissolution, or, if no date is so mentioned, as from the date of the communication of the notice."

The difference in wording between these two sections is discussed in an earlier part of this work.[110]

Exclusion of right to dissolve

24–19   Notwithstanding that difference in wording, it is clear that the right to dissolve may be excluded by an express or implied agreement.[111] In such a case, the partnership will neither be "at will" nor for an undefined time.[112] This accords with the position prior to the Partnership Act 1890.[113]

---

[109] However, where the partnership is continued for the purposes of carrying out a second transaction identical to the first, there may be an almost irresistible implication that the partners intend the partnership to subsist until the completion of that second transaction. See also *supra*, para. 9–11.

[110] See *supra*, paras 9–02 *et seq.*

[111] See *Moss v. Elphick* [1910] 1 K.B. 465 (this decision being affirmed at [1910] 1 K.B. 846); *Abbott v. Abbott* [1936] 3 All E.R. 823; *Walters v. Bingham* [1988] 1 F.T.L.R. 260; also *Maillie v. Swanney* 2000 S.L.T. 464 (OH). And see *supra*, paras 9–05, 9–06.

[112] The usual implication, if a partnership cannot be determined otherwise than by agreement, is that it will subsist during the joint lives of the partners: see *supra*, para. 9–05. See also *Walters v. Bingham* [1988] 1 F.T.L.R. 260, 266–267 *per* Browne-Wilkinson V.-C. A court will clearly not be ready to imply a term which permits the partners to terminate the partnership in such a case: see, for an analogous example, *Jani-King v. Pula Enterprises Ltd.* [2008] 1 All E.R. Comm. 451 (concerning a franchise agreement)

[113] See *Heath v. Sansom* (1831) 4 B. & Ad. 172, 175 *per* Parke J.; *Frost v. Moulton* (1856) 21 Beav. 596; *Syers v. Syers* (1876) 1 App.Cas. 174. See also *supra*, para. 9–01.

When notice will dissolve

In the case of a true partnership at will, notice of dissolution may be given by **24–20** any partner at any time.[114] It is a commonly held misconception that a "reasonable" period of notice is required but, in fact, the notice can be instantaneous.[115]

A dissolution notice may be served even though one of the recipient partners is suffering from mental incapacity.[116]

Fraud and mala fides

Although there is no duty on a partner to act reasonably in deciding whether **24–21** to serve a dissolution notice,[117] a notice served with fraudulent intent[118] or, in the current editor's view, *mala fide* and for an improper purpose[119] will not be upheld. Indeed, Lord Lindley, writing prior to the Partnership Act 1890, observed:

> " . . . it is apprehended that the court can restrain an immediate dissolution and sale of the partnership property, if it appears that irreparable mischief will ensue from such a proceeding."[120]

In *Sobell v. Hooberman*,[121] which concerned a *contractual* power to dissolve,[122] Mummery J. was, for the purposes of the interlocutory hearing before him, prepared to assume that there was a duty not to exercise the power for an

---

[114] See *Firth v. Amslake* (1964) 108 S.J. 198; also *Connell v. Slack* (1909) 28 N.Z.L.R. 560, 561 *per* Edwards J. As to the position prior to the Act (which was the same), see *Peacock v. Peacock* (1809) 16 Ves.Jr. 49; *Featherstonhaugh v. Fenwick* (1810) 17 Ves.Jr. 298; *Crawshay v. Maule* (1818) 1 Swan. 495, 508 *per* Lord Eldon; *Ex p. Nokes* (1801) cited 1 Mont.Part. 108, note.

[115] The contrary argument was taken without success several times prior to the Partnership Act 1890: see the cases cited in the previous footnote. Note, however, that the notice can only have effect once communicated to all the partners: see *infra*, para. 24–22. *cf.* the Limited Liability Partnerships Act 2000, s.4(3).

[116] *Mellersh v. Keen* (1859) 27 Beav. 236.

[117] *Russell v. Russell* (1880) 14 Ch.D. 471 (which concerned an *express* power to dissolve).

[118] *Walters v. Bingham* [1988] 1 F.T.L.R. 260, applying *Lazarus Estates Ltd. v. Beasley* [1956] 1 Q.B. 702. This part of the decision was, however, strictly *obiter*.

[119] *Neilson v. Mossend Iron Co.* (1886) 11 App.Cas. 298, 309 *per* Lord Watson; *Daw v. Herring* [1892] 1 Ch. 284, 291 *per* Stirling J.; *Peyton v. Mindham* [1972] 1 W.L.R. 8. The point was left open in *Walters v. Bingham* [1988] 1 F.T.L.R. 260 (on the basis that the law may be different in England than in Scotland, although it is not clear from the report what authorities were cited to Browne-Wilkinson V.-C.), but the ability to set aside a dissolution notice given in bad faith was conceded in *Thakrar v. Vadera*, March 31, 1999 (unreported). It should be noted that Lord Lindley was at pains to point out that *Neilson v. Mossend Iron Co., supra*, was a Scottish case (even though this did not later deter Stirling J.). He then went on, "By the civil law a dissolution made *mala fide*, and at an unreasonable time, is not allowed": see Pothier, *Partnership*, 150. Note also, in this context, *Hunter v. Wylie* 1993 S.L.T. 1091 (OH), where it was held that two partners, who were in material breach of the partnership terms by withdrawing capital without their co-partners' consent, were not entitled to serve a notice of dissolution under an *express* power in the agreement. In the current editor's view, this case cannot properly be regarded as having established a principle of general application. *cf. Aymard v. Sisu Capital Ltd.* [2009] EWHC 3214 (QB) (Lawtel 21/12/09), where a power to dissolve a limited partnership was exercisable by its investment manager.

[120] See *Chavany v. Van Sommer* (1771) 3 Woodd.Lect. 416 and 1 Swan. 512n. Lord Lindley also referred to *Blisset v. Daniel* (1853) 10 Hare 493 (which was a case of compulsory retirement).

[121] March 31, April 1, 1993 (unreported).

[122] See further, as to such powers, *supra*, paras 10–137 *et seq.*

improper purpose, but he went on to hold that it was no evidence of bad faith to show that the dissolution would be more beneficial to the partners exercising the power than a continuation of the partnership.[123]

Even if the notice cannot be attacked on the grounds of fraud or *mala fides*, it does not follow that the partner giving it can necessarily retain any personal benefit he may secure as a result of the dissolution.[124]

No damages are recoverable where a wrongful act, *e.g.* the exclusion of a partner, causes the dissolution of a partnership at will.[125]

Form of notice

24–22   A dissolution notice must be clear and unambiguous[126] but it is not necessary that the partner giving it appreciates its legal effect.[127] It follows that a proposal to dissolve on terms which are not accepted will not be effective[128]; neither will a notice that a partner's share has been forfeited, since that is indicative of an intention to dissolve only as regards that partner.[129] References to "retirement" or "resignation" should, for the same reason, be avoided.[130] The notice may take effect immediately[131] or on a future date,[132] but will only be effective once it has been communicated to all the partners.[133]

If a dissolution action is commenced by a partner, service of the claim form will be treated as an immediate notice to dissolve.[134]

Whether written notice required

24–23   Section 26(2) of the Partnership Act 1890 provides:

> "(2) Where the partnership has originally been constituted by deed, a notice in writing, signed by the partner giving it, shall be sufficient for this purpose."

---

[123] Notwithstanding the fact that the matter was raised on an interlocutory motion, Mummery J. regarded the proposition set out in the text as so clear that he was justified in making a declaration in a final form as to the dissolution of the partnership under the former RSC Ord. 14A. For the modern procedure, see the CPR Pt 24.

[124] See, for example, *Clegg v. Edmondson* (1856) 8 De G.M. & G. 787; also *supra*, paras 16–13 *et seq.* As to the return of premiums, see *infra*, paras 25–07 *et seq.*

[125] *Connell v. Slack* (1909) 28 N.Z.L.R. 560.

[126] But see *Syers v. Syers* (1876) 1 App.Cas. 174, 183 *per* Lord Cairns; *Walters v. Bingham* [1988] 1 F.T.L.R. 260, 267 *per* Browne-Wilkinson V.-C. As to the problems which can arise where an ambiguous notice is given, see *Toogood v. Farrell* [1988] 2 E.G.L.R. 233 (which concerned a notice of *retirement* given pursuant to a contractual provision); also *Lukin v. Lovrinov* [1998] S.A.S.C. 6614 (which again concerned the exercise of contractual powers).

[127] *Toogood v. Farrell, supra.*

[128] *Hall v. Hall* (1855) 20 Beav. 139.

[129] See *Clarke v. Hart* (1858) 6 H.L.C. 633.

[130] See, for example, *Sobell v. Boston* [1975] 1 W.L.R. 1587. But note that the Partnership Act 1890, s.26 is headed "Retirement from partnership at will", even though there is no reference to retirement in the body of the section.

[131] See *supra*, para. 24–20.

[132] *Mellersh v. Keen* (1859) 27 Beav. 236.

[133] Partnership Act 1890, ss.26(1), 32; *Walters v. Bingham* [1988] 1 F.T.L.R. 260; also *Van Sandau v. Moore* (1826) 1 Russ. 441; *Wheeler v. Van Wart* (1838) 9 Sim. 193; *Parsons v. Hayward* (1862) 4 De G.F. & G. 474.

[134] *Unsworth v. Jordan* [1896] W.N. 2(5). See also *infra*, para. 24–28.

Surprisingly, no similar qualification is attached to section 32(c).[135] Nevertheless, it would seem that, since the former subsection establishes that a notice in writing is merely *sufficient*, not necessary, to work a dissolution, an oral notice will be effective in all cases, even where the partnership was originally constituted by deed.[136] This accords with the law prior to the Act.[137] However, since a written notice will usually be desirable for evidential purposes, it is perhaps sensible to heed the admonition which has appeared in all editions of this work since the Act:

> " ... it would be imprudent not to give a notice in accordance with this provision, in cases to which it applies."[138]

On the same principle, it should perhaps be ensured that the partner signs the notice personally; where, however the partnership was not constituted by deed, no such precautions are necessary and it is, indeed, not unusual to find notices being given in the course of inter-solicitor correspondence.

Withdrawal of notice

A dissolution notice, once given, cannot be withdrawn without the consent of all the partners.[139]   **24–24**

However, it would seem that a *prospective* notice may, at any time up to the moment of its expiration, be superseded by the occurrence of an event which dissolves the partnership at an earlier date.[140] Such an event may be the service of a subsequent dissolution notice, requiring an immediate dissolution, as Lord Lindley explained in his Supplement on the Partnership Act 1890:

> "If one partner gave notice, specifying a date more or less distant, it would still be in the power of another partner to expedite the dissolution by a notice with a shorter date, or without specified date.[141] The first notice would not of itself make an agreement for a fixed term. But (*quaere*) might not the actings of parties on such a first notice rear up an agreement?"[142]

---

[135] See *supra*, para. 24–18. This is particularly odd, if the words "entered into" are given the significance attributed to them in *Maillie v. Swanney* 2000 S.L.T. 464, 469E (OH) *per* Lord Penrose: see further *supra*, para. 9–03.

[136] See, for example, *Walters v. Bingham* [1988] 1 F.T.L.R. 260, 267 *per* Browne-Wilkinson V.-C. (albeit that this part of the decision was *obiter* and it is not clear to what extent the point was argued). *Quaere*, is s.32(c) merely declaratory of the effects of a notice under section 26(1)? This has, so far as the current editor is aware, never been argued (but would certainly be inconsistent with the decision in *Maillie v. Swanney, supra*). Alternatively, should effect be given to section 26 in preference to s.32(c), on the grounds that the former section contains a qualification? See *Moss v. Elphick* [1910] 1 K.B. 465, 468 *per* Pickford J. Although interesting, the point is largely academic given the terms of s.26(2).

[137] Lord Lindley put it thus: "It has never been determined that a partnership constituted by deed can only be dissolved either by deed or by operation of law; and it is apprehended that no deed is requisite." He then referred to *Doe v. Miles* (1816) 1 Stark 181 and 4 Camp. 373. Note also *Hutchinson v. Whitfield* (1830) Hayes 78.

[138] As to the problems which may arise when reliance is placed on an oral notice, see *Toogood v. Farrell* [1988] 2 E.G.L.R. 233.

[139] *Jones v. Lloyd* (1874) L.R. 18 Eq. 265; also *Finch v. Oake* [1896] 1 Ch. 409; *Glossop v. Glossop* [1907] 2 Ch. 370; *Toogood v. Farrell, supra*; and see *supra*, para. 10–109.

[140] *McLeod v. Dowling* (1927) 43 T.L.R. 655 (dissolution resulting from the death of a partner).

[141] Account must, of course, be taken of the terms of the partnership agreement, if any.

[142] Alternatively, an estoppel might arise in such a case.

Express dissolution clauses

24–25   The considerations applicable to the exercise of an *express* power to dissolve a partnership for a fixed term[143] will be no different, subject to the precise terms of the agreement.[144]

It should, in this context, be noted that notices of *retirement* given by all but one of the partners under an express power in the agreement[145] may take effect as a notice of dissolution, unless the agreement clearly confers on the sole remaining "partner"[146] the right to acquire their shares and to continue the former partnership business.[147] Equally, where continuing partners have an option to acquire a retiring partner's share but, for whatever reason, decline to exercise it, his retirement notice will have the effect of dissolving the firm.[148]

Dissolution inferred although no notice

24–26   Lord Lindley observed that:

> "A dissolution of a partnership at will may be inferred from circumstances, *e.g.* a quarrel, although no notice to dissolve may have been given."[149]

This is still the position,[150] notwithstanding the views expressed in *Hurst v. Bryk*[151] and *Mullins v. Laughton*,[152] which were clearly not made in the context of a partnership at will. The correctness of this proposition (and the potential application of the principle to partnerships for a term) is confirmed by the decision of the Court of Appeal in *Chahal v. Mahal*,[153] where it was held that the incorporation of a partnership business will usually (but not invariably) result in a dissolution being inferred. Equally, it should be noted that the court will not be too ready to infer a dissolution, as illustrated by *Hodson v. Hodson*,[154] where it was held that a partnership would continue notwithstanding the fact that one partner might have ceased to participate actively in the partnership business, either wilfully or due to circumstances beyond his control. In such a case, even

---

[143] See *supra*, paras 10–137 *et seq.*

[144] Thus, it would seem that, if there are sufficient grounds (and the other partners' motives cannot be impugned), a partner who has served a prospective dissolution notice might, at least in theory, be expelled before his notice has expired.

[145] See *supra*, paras 10–108 *et seq.*

[146] This is, strictly, a misnomer: the concept of a sole partner does not exist.

[147] See *Hurst v. Bryk* [1999] Ch. 1, 10 *per* Peter Gibson L.J. This point was not the subject of the appeal to the House of Lords: see [2002] 1 A.C. 185.

[148] See *supra*, para. 10–154.

[149] *Pearce v. Lindsay* (1860) 3 De G.J. & S. 139.

[150] See *Bothe v. Amos* [1976] Fam. 46 (husband and wife partnership); also *Primary Health Care Centres (Broadford) Ltd. v. Ravangave* [2008] Hous. L.R. 24 (OH), where the partners had all become salaried employees (note, however, that the cessation of the partnership was also recorded in a partnership tax return signed by all the partners). Equally, it appears to have been assumed that a dissolution by conduct was not possible in *Millar v. Strathclyde Regional Council* 1988 S.L.T. 9 (Lands Trib.): see also *infra*, para. 24–46.

[151] [2002] 1 A.C. 185 (HL).

[152] [2003] Ch. 250.

[153] [2005] 2 B.C.L.C. 655. This decision did not concern a partnership at will. See further *infra*, para. 24–46. Another example (albeit in the VAT and Duties Tribunal) is to be found in *Hussein v. Commissioners of Customs & Excise* [2003] V. & D.R. 439 at [38].

[154] [2009] P.N.L.R. 8 (CA) at [40]. Again this decision is not directly in point as it did not concern a partnership at will.

nominal continuing participation will be sufficient to keep the partnership in existence.

The decision of the Scottish court in *Gray v. Dickson*[155] is, however, something of an anomaly in this area. It was held that the two partners were carrying on business on terms embodied in a draft agreement which required a specified period of notice before the partnership could be dissolved. Mr Dickson purported to terminate the partnership at a meeting without giving the required notice and was held to have acted in breach of contract by so doing. However, it also appears to have been accepted that the partnership came to an end at or around the time of the meeting and *before* the required notice period had elapsed, even though there was clearly no agreement to waive the notice requirement. Absent any reference to repudiation and acceptance,[156] it is submitted that this must be an example of dissolution by conduct.

Dissolution notice as an act of discrimination

Service of a notice of dissolution, whether under an express power or under the Partnership Act 1890, may, of itself, amount to an act of discrimination,[157] but this will seemingly not *per se* invalidate the notice.

24–27

Date of dissolution

The partnership will be dissolved as soon as the notice is communicated to *all* the partners or, if that is later, on the date specified in the notice.[158] However, it has already been seen that a prospective notice may be superseded by a subsequent determining event, *e.g.* the death of a partner.[159]

24–28

If the notice takes the form of a claim form in a dissolution action, the partnership will be dissolved on the date of its service.[160]

C.   DEATH AND BANKRUPTCY, ETC.

Partnership Act 1890, section 33(1)

This subsection provides as follows:

24–29

> "33.—(1) Subject to any agreement between the partners, every partnership is dissolved as regards all the partners by the death or bankruptcy of any partner."

---

[155] 2007 GWD 31–540 (Sh. Ct).

[156] Of course, the doctrine of repudiation does not apply to partnerships, at least under English law: see *supra*, paras 24–05 *et seq.*

[157] See *Dave v. Robinska* [2003] I.C.R. 1248, noticed *supra*, paras 8–11, 8–13, in the context of sex discrimination. The same principle applies to all other forms of discrimination: see *supra*, paras 8–17 *et seq.*

[158] Partnership Act 1890, s.32, *supra*, para. 24–18. And see also *Robertson v. Lockie* (1846) 15 Sim. 285; *Bagshaw v. Parker* (1847) 10 Beav. 532; *Mellersh v. Keen* (1859) 27 Beav. 236; *Jones v. Lloyd* (1874) L.R. 18 Eq. 265.

[159] See *supra*, para. 24–24.

[160] *Unsworth v. Jordan* [1896] W.N. 2(5); see also *Kirby v. Carr* (1838) 3 Y. & C.Ex. *Shepherd v. Allen* (1864) 33 Beav. 577. And note *Phillips v. Melville* [1921] N.Z.L.R. 571, noted *infra*, para. 24–91.

Death

24–30   The inclusion of the death of a partner as an event which will, in the absence of some contrary agreement,[161] dissolve the firm[162] accorded with the law prior to the Partnership Act 1890.[163] Lord Lindley explained this rule as:

> " . . . obviously reasonable, for by the death of one of the members it is no longer possible to adhere to the original contract, the essence of which is (in the case supposed), that all the parties to it shall be alive."

It is important to note that this rule is applied strictly: the mere fact that the partnership was originally entered into for a fixed term which has not expired will not, of itself, be sufficient to prevent a dissolution caused by the untimely death of a partner.[164]

The position is even the same in Scotland, where a firm is accorded separate legal personality.[165]

It goes without saying that, irrespective of the terms of the agreement, a partnership cannot continue where there is a sole surviving partner,[166] but this does not mean that such a partner may not have a contractual right to acquire all the former partnership assets.[167]

Date of dissolution

24–31   It hardly needs to be observed that the partnership will be dissolved as from the date of the partner's death.[168]

Bankruptcy

24–32   As was the position prior to the Partnership Act 1890,[169] the bankruptcy of an individual partner will clearly dissolve the firm, unless the partners have agreed otherwise.[170] Although mining partnerships were once treated as an apparent exception to the general rule,[171] this is no longer permissible under the Act.

---

[161] See, as to such agreements, *supra*, para. 10–39. *Quaere*, must the contrary agreement be contained in the partnership agreement itself: see *Quarantelli v. Forbes* 2000 G.W.D. 2–66 (Sh. Ct.), citing *Miller's Partnership* (2nd ed.) at p. 461. The current editor does not consider that such a conclusion is warranted by the words of the subsection.

[162] See *McLeod v. Dowling* (1927) 43 T.L.R. 655; *I.R.C. v. Graham's Trustees* 1971 S.L.T. 46 (HL); *Jardine-Paterson v. Fraser* 1974 S.L.T. 93 (Ct. of Session).

[163] See *Pearce v. Chamberlain* (1750) 2 Ves.Sen. 33; *Vulliamy v. Noble* (1817) 3 Mer. 593; *Gillespie v. Hamilton* (1818) 3 Madd. 251; *Crawshay v. Maule* (1818) 1 Swan. 495; *Crosbie v. Guion* (1857) 23 Beav. 518.

[164] *Crawford v. Hamilton* (1818) 3 Madd. 251; *Downs v. Collins* (1848) 6 Hare 418; *Lancaster v. Allsup* (1887) 57 L.T.(N.S.) 53.

[165] *I.R.C. v. Graham's Trustees*, *supra*; *Jardine-Paterson v. Fraser*, *supra*.

[166] *Hurst v. Bryk* [1999] Ch. 1, 10 *per* Peter Gibson L.J. This point was not pursued in the House of Lords at [2002] 1 A.C. 185.

[167] In *Hurst v. Bryk*, *supra*, the terms of the agreement did not admit this possibility. See, generally, as to such provisions *supra*, paras 10–108, 10–150 *et seq.*

[168] Partnership Act 1890, s.33(1), *supra*, para. 24–29.

[169] See *Fox v. Hanbury* (1776) Cowp. 445; also *Hague v. Rolleston* (1768) 4 Burr. 2175; *Ex p. Smith* (1800) 5 Ves.Jr. 295; *Crawshay v. Collins* (1808) 15 Ves.Jr. 218, 228 *per* Lord Eldon.

[170] Partnership Act 1890, s.33(1), *supra*, para. 24–29; *Re Ward* [1985] N.Z.L.R. 352. Note, however, the decision *Quarantelli v. Forbes* 2000 G.W.D. 2–66 (Sh. Ct.), noted *supra*, para. 24–30, n. 161. As to the circumstances in which a partner can be made the subject of a bankruptcy order, see *infra*, paras 27–43 *et seq. cf.* the position of a corporate partner, *infra*, paras 24–35 *et seq.* The current editor considers that an express power to expel a bankrupt partner will be sufficient evidence of an agreement to exclude s.33(1): see *supra*, para. 10–114, n. 496.

[171] *Ex p. Broadbent* (1834) 1 Mont. & Ayr. 635; *Bentley v. Bates* (1840) 4 Y. & C.Ex. 182.

It would seem that the bankruptcy of *all* the partners will necessarily dissolve the firm, irrespective of any terms in the agreement.[172]

Foreign bankruptcy

It is not clear whether the equivalent of a bankruptcy order made against a **24–33** partner in a foreign country will cause a dissolution. Although there are no reported decisions on the point, the current editor tentatively submits that it will in a case where Council Regulation (EC) 1346/2000 on insolvency proceedings applies[173] or where the partner is domiciled in that country or, if he is not, where he submits to the jurisdiction of its court. In any other case, it is doubtful whether an English court would recognise the title of the creditors' representative appointed under the relevant foreign law[174] and he might therefore be unable to lay claim to the bankrupt partner's share. In such circumstances, it is prima facie unlikely that the partnership would be treated as dissolved.

Date of dissolution

The Partnership Act 1890 does not state when the partnership is to be treated **24–34** as dissolved but, under the current insolvency legislation, the dissolution will clearly date from the making of the bankruptcy order.[175]

Where, however, the partnership is ordered to be wound up as an unregistered company, whether on a concurrent petition or otherwise,[176] the date of dissolution may precede any bankruptcy order made against an individual partner.[177]

Winding up and dissolution of corporate partner

Winding up order

An order for the winding up of a corporate partner is the nearest equivalent to **24–35** the bankruptcy of an individual.[178] On the other hand, a resolution for a *voluntary*

---

[172] See *Official Receiver v. Hollens* [2007] Bus. L.R. 1402, noted *infra*, para. 27–22, where both partners had been made bankrupt on their own petitions. There was, however, no contrary provision in this case.

[173] See *ibid.* arts. 1, 3, 16, Annex A.

[174] See, generally, *Dicey & Morris on the Conflict of Laws* (14th ed.), paras 31R–59 *et seq.*, 31R–72 *et seq.* and *Re Blithman* (1866) L.R. 2 Eq. 23; *Ex p. André Châle* (1890) 24 Q.B.D. 640; *Re Hayward* [1897] 1 Ch. 905; *cf. Emanuel v. Symon* [1908] 1 K.B. 302. But see also *Re Davidson's Settlement Trusts* (1873) L.R. 15 Eq. 383; *Re Lawson's Trusts* [1896] 1 Ch. 175; *Re Anderson* [1911] 1 K.B. 896 (although the reasoning in this case is open to criticism). Note that Council Regulation (EC) No. 44/2001 of December 22, 2000 on jurisdiction and the recognition and enforcement of judgments in civil and commercial matters does not apply in the case of bankruptcy: art. 1, para. 2(b). See also the Civil Jurisdiction and Judgments Act 1982, s.18(3)(ba) (as added by the Insolvency Act 1985, Sched. 8, para. 36), Sched. 1, art. 1(2) (as substituted by the Civil Jurisdiction and Judgments Act 1982 (Amendment) Order 2000 (SI 2000/1824), art. 8(1), Sched. 1). And see Briggs and Rees, *Civil Jurisdiction and Judgments* (5th ed) at para. 2–37.

[175] Insolvency Act 1986, s.278(a). *cf.* the position under the Bankruptcy Act 1914, s.37(1), (2).

[176] See *infra*, paras 27–07 *et seq.*

[177] Where there are concurrent petitions, the petition against the firm will be heard first: Insolvency Act 1986, s.124(6) (as amended by the Insolvent Partnerships Order 1994, Sched. 4, Pt II, para. 8 and applied, as regards the firm, by the Insolvency Act 1986, s.221(5) (as itself amended by the Insolvent Partnerships Order 1994, art. 8(1) (as amended by the Insolvent Partnerships (Amendment) Order 2002 (SI 2002/1308), art. 4(1)), (2), Sched. 4, Pt I, para. 3) and, as regards the corporate partners, by the Insolvent Partnerships Order 1994, art. 8(4), (5), (9) (creditor's petition) and as amended and applied, as regards the firm, by the Insolvent Partnerships Order 1994, art. 10(1)(a), Sched. 6, para. 2 and, as regards the corporate partners, by *ibid.* art. 10(2), (3), (6) (as amended by the Insolvent Partnerships (Amendment) Order 2005 (SI 2005/1516), art. 5(b)) (member's petition)). See further, *infra*, paras 27–38, 27–39.

[178] *cf.* the Law of Property Act 1925, s.205(1)(i).

winding up may be passed for many reasons other than insolvency.[179] Given that the relationship between partners will inevitably be of a less personal nature where a corporate partner is involved,[180] it is submitted that neither an order nor a resolution to wind up such a partner would *per se* dissolve the firm, although there is, admittedly, no decision of an English court on the point.[181]

Nevertheless, given that the ability of a corporate partner to function effectively would be severely impaired by the presentation of a winding up petition,[182] the current editor is of the opinion that there would in that event be grounds for an application to the court for a dissolution on the just and equitable ground.[183] In practice, this option is more theoretical than real, since it is doubtful whether the application could be brought on for hearing *before* the petition. This underlines the desirability of including a specific provision in the agreement to cater for such an eventuality.[184]

Where concurrent petitions are presented against the firm and against one or more partners,[185] the petition against the firm will be heard and determined first,[186] so that it may not in any event be necessary to enquire into the effect of a subsequent winding up order made against a corporate partner.

Dissolution

24–36   The dissolution of a corporate partner by the law of the country of its incorporation terminates its existence and is equivalent to the death of an individual.[187] On that footing, it is considered that such an event will, in the absence of an agreement to the contrary,[188] dissolve the firm. *A fortiori* where there are only two partners.[189] Even if this conclusion were wrong, there would clearly be grounds for the court to order a dissolution.[190]

Foreign corporate partner

24–37   Leaving aside cases to which Council Regulation (EC) 1346/2000 on insolvency proceedings applies,[191] a winding up order made in accordance with the law of a company's place of incorporation will normally be recognised under

---

[179] See the Insolvency Act 1986, s.84 (as amended).

[180] But see *supra*, para. 11–12.

[181] However, in *Anderson Group Pty Ltd. v. Davies* [2001] N.S.W.S.C. 356, Barrett J. reached the same conclusion as advanced in the text. *cf.* the views advanced in Twomey, *Partnership Law*, para. 23–40. Blackett-Ord's *Partnership Law*, (3rd ed.) at para. 16.30 adopts a neutral position, but cites *Fryer v. Ewart* [1902] A.C. 187 (HL), a decision which turned on the extended definition of "bankruptcy" in the Conveyancing and Law of Property Act 1881, s.2(xv) and therefore scarcely seems in point.

[182] See *supra*, para. 11–09.

[183] See *infra*, paras 24–89 *et seq.*

[184] See *supra*, paras 11–08 *et seq.*

[185] See *infra*, paras 27–24 *et seq.*

[186] Insolvency Act 1986, s.124(6) (as amended and applied in the manner set out *supra*, para. 24–35, n. 177). See further, *infra*, paras 27–38, 27–39.

[187] See *Salton v. New Beeston Cycle Co.* [1900] 1 Ch. 43. As to when a company will be dissolved, see the Insolvency Act 1986, ss.201(2), 205(2). The same sections apply with modifications in the case of an LLP: see the Limited Liability Partnerships Regulations 2001 (SI 2001/1090), reg. 5.

[188] *Quaere* whether a provision that the "death" of a partner will not dissolve the partnership, would amount to such an agreement.

[189] The concept of a partnership with only one partner is, of course, impossible: see *supra*, para. 24–25.

[190] Partnership Act 1890, s.35(b), (f), *infra*, paras 24–69 *et seq.*, 24–89 *et seq.*

[191] See *ibid.* arts. 1, 3, 16, Annex A.

English law.[192] Equally, a corporate partner might, exceptionally, be regarded as *dissolved* in one country but not in another.[193] The attitude of the English courts will obviously determine whether or not the continued existence of the partnership is affected.

D.   CHARGING ORDER ON A PARTNER'S SHARE

Partnership Act 1890, section 33(2)

This subsection provides as follows: **24–38**

> "33.—(2) A partnership may, at the option of the other partners, be dissolved[194] if any partner suffers his share of the partnership property to be charged under this Act for his separate debt."

The circumstances in which a charging order may be obtained in respect of a partner's share have already been noted.[195]

Nature of the option

It is not entirely clear whether each of the other partners has an independent   **24–39**
option to dissolve the partnership, as Lord Lindley explained in his Supplement on the Act:

> "As a general rule, if several persons have an election the first election made by any one of them would seem to determine the election for all,[196] but this rule can hardly apply to the case referred to in this section. The majority would not, it is conceived, have the power to dissolve the partnership against the wishes of the minority.[197] The meaning apparently is either that all the other partners must be unanimous, or that a separate option is given to each of the other partners, so that any one of them can

---

[192] See, generally, *Dicey & Morris on the Conflict of Laws* (14th ed.), paras 30R–097 *et seq.* Equally, an English court may itself have jurisdiction to wind up a corporate partner formed in accordance with the laws of another country: *ibid.* paras 30R–033 *et seq.* Note, however, the position under Council Regulation (EC) No. 44/2001 of December 22, 2000 on jurisdiction and the recognition and enforcement of judgments in civil and commercial matters, art. 1, para. 2(b); also the Civil Jurisdiction and Judgments Act 1982, s.18(3)(ba) (as added by the Insolvency Act 1985, Sched. 8, para. 36), Sched. 1, art. 1(2) (as substituted by the Civil Jurisdiction and Judgments Act 1982 (Amendment) Order 2000 (SI 2000/1824), art. 8(1), Sched. 1). See also Briggs and Rees, *Civil Jurisdiction and Judgments* (5th ed.), para. 2–37.

[193] *Dicey & Morris on the Conflict of Laws* (14th ed.), paras 30R–009 *et seq.* And see *Russian Commercial and Industrial Bank v. Comptoir D'Escompte de Mulhouse* [1923] 2 K.B. 630; *Banque Internationale de Commerce de Petrograd v. Goukassow* [1923] 2 K.B. 682. Note, however, that both decisions were reversed on the facts: see [1925] A.C. 112 and 150. See also *Lazard Bros. & Co. v. Midland Bank Ltd.* [1933] A.C. 289; *Re Russian Commercial and Industrial Bank* [1955] Ch. 148.

[194] It should be noted that the word "dissolved" is not followed by the words "as regards all the partners", as in s.33(1), *supra*, para. 24–29. However, this omission is not thought to be significant. As Lord Lindley pointed out, the additional words do not appear in ss.26, 32, 34 or 35 either.

[195] Partnership Act 1890, s.23, *supra*, para. 19–37 *et seq.*

[196] Co.Litt. 145a.

[197] This would not on any footing constitute an ordinary matter connected with the partnership business: see the Partnership Act 1890, s.24(8), *supra*, paras 15–04 *et seq.* Note also the views set out *supra*, para. 24–10, even though the situation under consideration there is, as the law stands, largely theoretical.

dissolve the partnership, whether the others have or have not expressed their intention of not doing so."

The current editor considers that the former view is correct and that, notwithstanding the provisions of the Interpretation Act 1978,[198] the reference to "the other partners" should not be construed as "the other partners or any of them".[199] The position is, of course, wholly different under sections 26(1) and 32(c),[200] where the right to dissolve the firm is clearly expressed to be exercisable by a single partner. Accordingly, the other partners must be unanimous in their decision to exercise the option.

Exercise of option

24–40   The Act gives no guidance as to when and how the option is to be exercised. However, Lord Lindley observed:

> "Any unequivocal act done to the knowledge of the partner whose share is charged will be an exercise of the option which cannot be withdrawn.[201] The option must be exercised within a reasonable time."[202]

Date of dissolution

24–41   Although the Act does not state when the partnership is to be dissolved, it would seem beyond argument that the relevant date will be that on which the option is exercised. As already noted, an effective exercise presupposes knowledge on the part of every partner.

E.   ILLEGALITY

24–42   Prior to the Partnership Act 1890, Lord Lindley wrote:

> " . . . if, by any change in the law, it becomes illegal to carry on a business, every partnership formed before the making [of] the law for the purpose of carrying on that business, must be taken to have been dissolved by the law in question. So if, the law remaining unchanged, some event happens which renders it illegal for the members of a firm to continue to carry on their business in partnership, such event dissolves the firm. For example, if a partnership exists between two persons residing and

---

[198] s.6(c).

[199] It would obviously not be sufficient merely to construe the reference as "the other partners or partner". See further *Re A Solicitors' Arbitration* [1962] 1 W.L.R. 353 and *Bond v. Hale* (1960) 72 S.R. (N.S.W.) 201 (noted *supra*, para. 10–123), in relation to the construction of powers of expulsion.

[200] See *supra*, para. 24–18.

[201] Lord Lindley treated this as a case of election, referring to *Scarf v. Jardine* (1882) 7 App.Cas. 345, 361 *per* Lord Blackburn; *Clough v. L.N.W. Ry.* (1871) L.R. 7 Ex. 26, 34 *per* Mellor J. And see *Jones v. Carter* (1846) 15 M. & W. 718, cited therein.

[202] *Scarf v. Jardine* (1882) 7 App.Cas. 345, 360 *per* Lord Blackburn. Lord Lindley also referred to *Anderson v. Anderson* (1857) 25 Beav. 190, which scarcely seems to support the proposition. And see *Re Longlands Farm* [1968] 3 All E.R. 552.

carrying on trade in different countries, and war between those countries is pro-claimed, a stop is thereby put to further intercourse between the partners, and the partnership subsisting between them is consequently dissolved."[203]

Partnership Act 1890, section 34

This principle is now clearly embodied in section 34 of the Partnership Act 1890, which provides: **24–43**

"34. A partnership is in every case dissolved by the happening of any event which makes it unlawful for the business of the firm to be carried on, or for the members of the firm to carry it on in partnership."

Scope of section

The section refers to *the* business of the firm and thus does not appear to   **24–44** contemplate the possibility of more than one business being carried on. The current editor's view is that if only one of the businesses is illegal, there will be no dissolution.[204] *Per contra*, if the illegality of the one business taints the others or if the legal business(es) will not remain viable independently of the illegal business.

The application of the section is not dependent on the partners' knowledge of the illegality: indeed, a partnership may be treated as dissolved even though the partners continue to carry on their business just as if nothing had happened.[205] The duration of the illegality will also be irrelevant.[206]

It is clear from the inclusion of the words "in every case" that the section cannot be excluded by agreement.[207]

Illegality caused by one partner

In *Hudgell Yeates & Co. v. Watson*[208] a partner in a firm of solicitors acciden-   **24–45** tally failed to renew his practising certificate, thus rendering himself unquali-fied.[209] Since a partnership between a solicitor and an unqualified person was, as the law then stood, prohibited by statute,[210] the partnership became illegal and

---

[203] See generally, *supra*, paras 4–05, 8–29. *Feldt v. Chamberlain* (1914) 58 S.J. 788 is not good law.

[204] *Quaere* whether this will still be the case where the firm's *main* business is illegal. Clearly this will be a matter of degree.

[205] *Hudgell Yeates & Co. v. Watson* [1978] Q.B. 451: see *infra*, para. 24–45. And see also *supra*, para. 8–53.

[206] *ibid. cf. Denny, Mott and Dickson Ltd. v. James B. Fraser & Co. Ltd.* [1944] A.C. 265.

[207] It may, however, be that the worst *effects* of the illegality can, to some extent, be circumvented in the manner set out in the next paragraph.

[208] [1978] Q.B. 451. *Bower v. Hughes Hooker & Co.*, March 27, 2003 (EAT) was a similar case, but there the partner had been struck off. The dissolution issue was not pursued on appeal: see *Stevens v. Bower* [2004] I.R.L.R. 957. As to the effects of an intervention in a solicitors' practice, see the *obiter* views expressed in *Rose v. Dodd* [2005] I.C.R. 1776 (CA) at [40].

[209] Such a failure will no longer *per se* have this effect: see the SRA Practising Certificate Regulations 2009, reg. 9.1(a).

[210] Solicitors Act 1974, s.39 (repealed by the Courts and Legal Services Act 1990, ss.66(1), 125(7), Sched. 20). Note that an unqualified person may now be a "manager" (*i.e.* partner) in a legal disciplinary practice provided that he has been approved by the Solicitors Regulation Authority: see *supra*, para. 8–52. As noted, *supra*, para. 8–53, it is doubtful whether there will be an automatic dissolution if a partner ceases to be appropriately qualified so long as the firm retains its recognised body status, but the position will be otherwise where the firm is not recognised in the first place, since it will be illegal however it is made up.

was automatically dissolved. In the same way, a partnership between dentists would clearly be dissolved if one partner should cease to be registered.[211]

In cases of this type, it may be possible to avoid the worst effects of a dissolution by including a suitable provision in the agreement, *e.g.* to the effect that the unqualified partner should be deemed to have retired from the partnership on the date of dissolution.[212]

F.   CESSATION OF BUSINESS

24–46   A temporary cessation of the partnership business[213] will not cause a dissolution.[214] However, the current editor has always taken the view that, if the partners agree a *permanent* cessation of all forms of business, this must take effect as an agreement to dissolve since, in the absence of a business, no partnership can exist within the meaning of the Partnership Act 1890.[215] Although in *National Westminster Bank plc v. Jones*[216] Neuberger J. expressed the view that a cessation of trading activities would not, *per se*, put an end to a partnership, in the event he was not required to decide the point.[217] His view was, nevertheless, echoed in *Chahal v. Mahal*[218] at first instance where the entire partnership business had been transferred to a company but this was held not to have brought about an automatic dissolution. Although this decision was upheld on appeal,[219] the Court of Appeal expressed the view that where a partnership business is incorporated and shares are issued to the partners in proportion to their partnership interests, it *will* usually be appropriate to infer that a dissolution has occurred,[220] but the position is likely to be otherwise if the shares become partnership property or if one partner has been kept in ignorance of the incorporation.[221] There are other reported instances in which the business of a partnership has been carried on

---

[211] Dentists Act 1984, ss.40, 41, as amended (see *supra*, para. 8–42); *Hill v. Clifford* [1907] 2 Ch. 236, 247 *per* Cozens Hardy M.R., 255 *per* Sir John Gorrell Barnes P., affirmed on other grounds *sub nom. Clifford v. Timms* [1908] A.C. 12. See also the *Encyclopedia of Professional Partnerships*, Pt 4.

[212] See further the *Encyclopedia of Professional Partnerships*, Precedent 7, cl. 3(3).

[213] This presupposes a conscious decision by the partners: if, on a true analysis, the firm's workload has, for whatever reason, dried up but the partners are actively seeking (and are able to carry out) further work, the business will be regarded as continuing: see *Pamment v. Sutton, The Times,* December 15, 1998 (which was not a partnership case).

[214] See *Millar v. Strathclyde Regional Council* 1988 S.L.T. 9 (Lands Trib.). However, the assumption made by the Lands Tribunal that a notice to dissolve is required in all cases is not correct: see *supra*, para. 24–26. Note also that in Scotland the firm has separate legal personality: Partnership Act 1890, s.4(2).

[215] *ibid.* s.1: see *supra*, paras 2–01 *et seq. cf. Millar v. Strathclyde Regional Council, supra.* Note also the Insolvency Act 1986, s.221(7)(a) (as amended and applied to partnerships): see *infra*, para. 27–08.

[216] [2001] B.C.L.C. 98, at [113].

[217] In this context, Neuberger J. adverted to the implications of the decision of the House of Lords in *Hurst v. Bryk* [2002] 1 A.C. 185, considered *supra*, paras 24–05 *et seq.*: [2001] B.C.L.C. 98, at [114]. The issue referred to in the text was not addressed by the Court of Appeal: see *The Times*, November 19, 2001.

[218] September 30, 2004 (Lawtel 5/10/04).

[219] [2005] 2 B.C.L.C. 655. The leading judgment was given by Neuberger L.J.

[220] See *ibid.* at [17], [29], [36].

[221] *ibid.* at [36], [38], [39].

through a company without the existence of the partnership being called into question.[222]

It follows that it cannot be stated for certain whether or not a cessation of business will bring about a dissolution: much will depend on the precise circumstances.

3.   DISSOLUTION BY THE COURT

A.   STATUTES UNDER WHICH A PARTNERSHIP MAY BE DISSOLVED

Partnership Act 1890, section 35

Section 35 of the Partnership Act contains the five grounds on which a court **24–47** may order the dissolution of a partnership. It provides as follows:

> "35. On application by a partner the Court may decree a dissolution of the partnership in any of the following cases:
>
> (a)   [...][223]
> (b)   When a partner, other than the partner suing, becomes in any other way permanently incapable of performing his part of the partnership contract:
> (c)   When a partner, other than the partner suing, has been guilty of such conduct as, in the opinion of the Court, regard being had to the nature of the business, is calculated to prejudicially affect the carrying on of the business:
> (d)   When a partner, other than the partner suing, wilfully or persistently commits a breach of the partnership agreement, or otherwise so conducts himself in matters relating to the partnership business that it is not reasonably practicable for the other partner or partners to carry on the business in partnership with him:
> (e)   When the business of the partnership can only be carried on at a loss:
> (f)   Whenever in any case circumstances have arisen which, in the opinion of the Court, render it just and equitable that the partnership be dissolved."

Mental Capacity Act 2005

Unlike the position under sections 95 and 96 of the Mental Health Act 1983,[224] **24–48** there is now no express statutory power to dissolve a partnership where a partner lack capacity.[225] Rather section 18(1) of the 2005 Act now provides:

> "The powers under section 16[226] as respects P's[227] property and affairs extend in particular to—

---

[222] See *Dyment v. Boyden* [2004] B.C.L.C. 423 at [5]; *Rosenberg v. Nazarov* [2008] EWHC 812 (Ch) (Lawtel 10/4/08) at [6].

[223] This paragraph was repealed by the Mental Health Act 1959, Sched. 8.

[224] Now repealed by the Mental Capacity Act 2005, Sched. 7.

[225] See, as to the meaning of this expression, *ibid.* s.2.

[226] This section gives the Court of Protection wide powers to make orders or take decisions concerning an individual's personal welfare, property and affairs, including the appointment of a deputy to take any decisions on his behalf. These powers are subject to the general principles set out in *ibid.* s.1 and the best interest of an individual must be determined in accordance with *ibid.* s.4: *ibid.* s.16(3).

[227] This expression, as defined in *ibid.* s.16(1), means the person who lacks capacity.

(a) the control and management of P's property;

. . .

(d) the carrying on, on P's behalf, of any profession, trade or business; .

(e) the taking of a decision which will have the effect of dissolving a partnership of which P is a member;

. . .

(k) the conduct of legal proceedings in P's name or on P's behalf."

This would clearly include service of a notice of retirement or dissolution under the agreement or a notice dissolving a partnership at will under the Partnership Act 1890[228] and the initiation or defence of proceedings seeking a dissolution under section 35 of the 1890 Act,[229] but it is doubted that the Court of Protection is thereby given jurisdiction to *order* a dissolution, whether under the latter section or otherwise.[230] It should, however, be noted that a contrary view is advanced in *Heywood & Massey's Court of Protection Practice.*[231]

If the Court of Protection does not have the necessary power, then resort will have to be had to an application under the 1890 Act in the normal way.

Insolvency Act 1986

24-49   An insolvent partnership which carries on (or has carried on) business in England and Wales[232] may, as a general rule, be wound up as an unregistered company.[233] A petition may, if there are no concurrent petitions against one or more of the partners, be presented by a creditor, liquidator[234] or temporary administrator,[235] a responsible insolvency practitioner,[236] the Secretary of State

---

[228] See *ibid.* ss.26(1), 32(c): see *supra*, paras 24–15 *et seq.*

[229] As in *Re W (EEM)* [1971] Ch. 123, where the court authorised divorce proceedings to be commenced on a patient's behalf under the powers conferred on it by the Mental Health Act 1959.

[230] Note that, under the Mental Capacity Act 2005, s.47(1), the court only has the same powers, etc., as the High Court "in connection with its jurisdiction". The current editor regards the move from an express power to dissolve to a new provision which no longer even refers to such a possibility obliquely as significant.

[231] *ibid.* para. 4–041. This jurisdiction is said to be exercisable only where there are no disputes over the accounts or other matters in dispute. A similar view is also advanced in Blackett-Ord's *Partnership Law* (3rd ed.) at para. 17.11. See also *infra*, para. 24–64.

[232] A firm can, broadly, only be wound up in this way if it has (or had) a principal place of business in England and Wales or (where appropriate) if the debt on which the petition is based arose in the course of a business carried on by the firm at a place of business in England and Wales *and*, in either case, the firm carried on business in England and Wales within three years of the date of presentation of the petition: Insolvency Act 1986, s.221(1), (2), as amended and applied by the Insolvent Partnerships Order 1994, art. 7(1) (as amended by the Insolvent Partnerships (Amendment) Order 2002 (SI 2002/1308), art. 3), (2), Sched. 3, Pt I, para. 3 (petition of creditor, etc., with no concurrent petitions), art. 8(1) (as amended by the Insolvent Partnerships (Amendment) Order 2002, art. 4(2)), (2), Sched. 4, Pt I, para. 3 (petition of creditor, etc., with concurrent petitions), art. 9(a), Sched. 5, para. 2 (member's petition with no concurrent petitions), art. 10(1)(a), Sched. 6, para. 4 (member's petition with concurrent petitions). See further *infra*, paras 27–07, 27–25.

[233] See the Insolvent Partnerships Order 1994, arts 7–10 (as amended). See, *infra*, paras 27–04 *et seq*. Note also the exceptional decision in *Lancefield v. Lancefield* [2002] B.P.I.R. 1108, where Neuberger J. ordered the winding up of a firm even though no petition had been presented: see further *infra*, para. 27–03.

[234] Appointed in proceedings by virtue of Council Regulation (EC) No. 1346/2000 of May 29, 2000 on insolvency proceedings, art. 3(1).

[235] Within the meaning of *ibid.* art. 38.

[236] See the Insolvent Partnerships Order 1994, art. 2(1); also the Insolvency Act s.221A, as added by *ibid.* art. 7(2), Sched. 3, Pt I, para. 3.

or any other person who is not a member of the partnership.[237] A partner can only present a petition if the firm has eight or more members or with the leave of the court.[238] Although a petition presented by a creditor, liquidator[239] or temporary administrator[240] may be accompanied by concurrent petitions against one or more of the partners,[241] a member's petition may only be accompanied by concurrent petitions against *all* the partners, including the petitioner himself.[242] Where concurrent petitions are presented, the only grounds for the petition against the firm are that it is unable to pay its debts[243] or that, when a moratorium under the Insolvency Act 1986[244] ends, no voluntary arrangement approved under Part 1 of that Act has effect.[245] The latter ground may also be relied on where a petition against the firm is presented by one or more creditors.[246] Otherwise, the petition must be based on the fact that the firm has already been dissolved or ceased to carry on business or is only carrying on business for the purposes of winding up its affairs[247] or on the "just and equitable" ground.[248]

An order for the winding up of an insolvent partnership will, obviously, bring about an immediate dissolution, assuming the firm not already to have been dissolved, as will the making of bankruptcy orders against all the partners.[249]

Administration orders

Where an administration order has been applied for or is in effect in respect of an insolvent firm[250] or where notice is given of an intention to appoint an administrator outside court,[251] the court will no longer have jurisdiction to make

24–50

---

[237] Insolvent Partnerships Order 1994, art. 7(1), as amended by the Insolvent Partnerships (Amendment) Order 1996 (SI 1996/1308), art. 2 and the Insolvent Partnerships (Amendment) Order 2002, art. 3, read with the Insolvency Act 1986, s.221A(1), as added by *ibid.* art. 7(2), Sched. 3, para. 3.

[238] Insolvency Act 1986, s.221A(1), (2), as amended and applied by the Insolvent Partnerships Order 1994, Art. 9(a), Sched. 5, para. 2.

[239] See *supra*, n. 234.

[240] See *supra*, n. 235.

[241] *ibid.* art. 8(1), as amended by the Insolvent Partnerships (Amendment) Order 2002, art. 4(2). See further *infra*, paras 27–24 *et seq.*

[242] *ibid.* art. 10(1).

[243] Insolvency Act 1986, s.221(8), as amended and applied by the Insolvent Partnerships Order 1994, art. 8(1) (as amended: see *supra*, n. 241), (2), Sched. 4, Pt I, para. 3 (creditor's petition), art. 10(1)(a), Sched. 6, para. 4 (member's petition). See further *infra*, para. 27–26.

[244] See the Insolvency Act 1986, s.1A, as amended and applied by the Insolvent Partnerships Order 1994, art. 4(1), Sched. 1, as themselves respectively substituted by the Insolvent Partnerships (Amendment) (No. 2) Order 2002 (SI 2002/2708), arts. 4, 6, Sched. 1.

[245] See *ibid.* s.221(8)(b), as amended and applied by the Insolvent Partnerships Order 1994, Sched. 4, Pt I, para. 3 and the Insolvent Partnerships (Amendment) (No. 2) Order 2002, art. 9(2).

[246] See *ibid.* s.227(7)(d), (7A) as added by the Insolvent Partnerships Order 1994, Sched. 3, para. 3, as itself amended by the Insolvent Partnerships (Amendment) (No. 2) Order 2002, art. 8.

[247] *ibid.* s.221(7)(a), as amended and applied by the Insolvent Partnerships Order 1994, art. 7(1) (as amended: see *supra*, n. 237), (2), Sched. 3 Pt I, para. 3 (creditor's, etc., petition), art. 9(a), Sched. 5, para. 2 (member's petition). See further *infra*, paras 27–08 *et seq.*

[248] *ibid.* s.221(7)(c), as amended and applied by *ibid.* See further *infra*, paras 24–89 *et seq.*, 27–10.

[249] See *Official Receiver v. Hollens* [2007] Bus. L.R. 1402, noticed *infra*, para. 27–21, where both partners had been made bankrupt on their own petitions.

[250] See generally, as to administration orders, *infra*, paras 27–160 *et seq.*

[251] This will only be possible at the instance of the holder of a qualifying agricultural floating charge: see the Insolvency Act 1986, Sched. B1, para. 14, as amended and applied by the Insolvent Partnerships Order 1994, art. 6(1), Sched. 2, para. 7, as itself substituted by the Insolvent Partnerships (Amendment) Order 2005 (SI 2005/1516), art. 7, Sched. 1 and amended by the Insolvent Partnerships (Amendment) Order 2006 (SI 2006/622), art. 5(2)(a).

an order for the dissolution of the firm under section 35 of the Partnership Act 1890.[252]

Moratorium under the Insolvency Act 1986, Sched. A1

24–51   Similarly, a court will not have jurisdiction to make an order under section 35 of the 1890 Act whilst a moratorium is in place to facilitate the proposal of a partnership voluntary arrangement.[253]

Firms providing financial services

24–52   A partnership which is or was an authorised person[254] or an appointed representative[255] under the Financial Services and Markets Act 2000 or which is or was carrying on a regulated activity[256] when neither exempt[257] nor authorised so to do may be wound up as an unregistered company on a petition presented by the Financial Services Authority[258] on the "just and equitable" ground.[259] Although such a partnership may also be wound up on the ground that it is unable to pay its debts, in this case it will *not* be treated as an unregistered company.[260]

B.   JURISDICTION TO DISSOLVE A PARTNERSHIP

24–53 Proceedings for the dissolution of a partnership will normally be brought in the Chancery Division of the High Court,[261] unless the value of the partnership assets does not exceed £30,000, when the county court will have jurisdiction.[262] It

---

[252] Insolvency Act 1986, Sched. B1, paras 42(1), (4), 44(1), (2), (5), as amended and applied by the Insolvent Partnerships Order 1994, art. 6(1), Sched. 2, para. 17, as themselves respectively substituted by the Insolvent Partnerships (Amendment) Order 2005, arts.3, 7, Sched. 2.

[253] *ibid.* Sched. A1, para. 12(1)(j), as substituted and applied by the Insolvent Partnerships Order 1994, art. 4(1), Sched.1, as respectively substituted by the Insolvent Partnerships (Amendment) (No. 2) Order 2002 (SI 2002/2708), arts 4, 6, Sched. 1. See further *infra*, para. 27–153.

[254] See, as to the authorisation of firms, the Financial Services and Markets Act 2000, ss.31 *et seq.* And see *supra*, para. 8–45 *et seq.*

[255] See *ibid.* s.39.

[256] This expression is defined in *ibid.* s.22.

[257] See, as to the circumstances in which a firm will be exempt, *ibid.* ss.38, 39, 327.

[258] *ibid.* s.367(1), (2). *In the Matter of Whiteley Insurance Consultants* [2009] Bus. L.R. 418 was a case in which this power was exercised. See also the Insolvent Partnerships Order 1994, art. 19(4), as substituted by the Financial Services and Markets Act 2000 (Consequential Amendments and Repeals) Order 2001 (SI 2001/3649), Pt 9, art. 467 and amended by the Insolvent Partnerships (Amendment) (No. 2) Order 2002, art. 5.

[259] *ibid.* s.367(3)(b), (6)(a), (7).

[260] *ibid.* s.367(3)(a).

[261] Senior Courts Act 1981, s.61(1), Sched. 1, para. 1(f) (formerly the Supreme Court Act 1981: Constitutional Reform Act 2005, Sched. 11, Pt.1, para. 1(1)). Note than in *Cayzer v. Beddow* [2007] EWCA Civ. 644 (Lawtel 29/6/07) (CA) at [16], the court emphasised the importance of litigation regarding partnerships being brought in the Chancery Division and that this is not a mere matter of administrative convenience.

[262] County Courts Act 1984, s.23(f); County Courts Jurisdiction Order 1981 (SI 1981/1123). And note also *Cowan v. Wakeling* [2008] EWCA Civ 229 (Lawtel 25/2/08) (CA) at [25]. Although the Lord Chancellor has a wide power to make orders under the Courts and Legal Services Act 1990, s.1, the jurisdiction of the county court in the case of equity proceedings is unaffected by the High Court and County Courts Jurisdiction Order 1991 (SI 1991/724) made pursuant thereto. See also *supra*, para. 23–70 and *infra*, para. 24–55.

follows that questions of jurisdiction may ultimately depend on which assets can properly be regarded as partnership property.[263] The value of the alleged partnership assets will be the determinative factor even where the existence of the partnership is in dispute.[264] It is, however, possible to extend the jurisdiction of the county court by an agreement in writing between the parties or their legal advisers.[265] Moreover, a case which involves a dissolution claim may be transferred from one county court to another with Chancery expertise.[266]

Transfer between divisions of the High Court and to or from district registries

Where proceedings are commenced in another Division of the High Court, a transfer to the Chancery Division *may* be ordered, but this is by no means obligatory.[267] Equally, in the case of a partnership between a husband and wife or between civil partners, it may on occasion be appropriate to transfer dissolution proceedings out of the Chancery Division, if matrimonial or equivalent proceedings are pending in the Family Division; such an order was, however, refused in *Matz v. Matz*.[268]

24–54

The High Court may order the transfer of an action to a district registry in an appropriate case.[269] Equally, an action may be transferred between district registries or from a district registry to the High Court.[270]

Transfer of proceedings between High Court and county court

If proceedings are commenced in the county court which are in fact outside its jurisdiction, they will either be struck out or transferred to the High Court,[271] unless the parties agree to extend the county court's jurisdiction.[272] Such a

24–55

---

[263] See *supra*, paras 18–02 *et seq*.

[264] County Courts Act 1984, s.23(f). This had, in any event, been decided in *R. v. Lailey* [1932] 1 K.B. 568.

[265] *ibid*. s.24(1) (as amended by the Courts and Legal Services Act 1990, Sched. 18, para. 49(3)), (2)(g).

[266] CPR rr. 30.2(1), 30.3(1)(b). See also (2004) 101 L.S.Gaz., October 14, p. 37.

[267] Senior Courts Act 1981, ss.61(6), 65 (formerly the Supreme Court Act 1981: Constitutional Reform Act 2005, Sched. 11, Pt.1, para. 1(1)); CPR r. 30.5(1). The discretion is a wide one and will be exercised in a pragmatic way: *NATL Amusements (UK) Ltd. v. White City (Shepherds Bush) Limited Partnership* [2010] 1 W.L.R. 1181, where a number of authorities are reviewed. Note also *Bothe v. Amos* [1976] Fam. 46; *White v. White* [1999] Fam 304. When considering the question of jurisdiction in a copyright matter, Harman J. adopted a very strict approach in *Apac Rowena Ltd. v. Norpol Packaging Ltd.* [1991] 4 All E.R. 516, 518 and this has, since the advent of the CPR, to an extent been endorsed by the Court of Appeal in *Elvee Ltd. v. Taylor, The Times*, December 18, 2001 (CA) (another copyright case). It should also be noted that, in *Hurst v. Bryk* [2002] 1 A.C. 185, Lord Millett emphasised the primacy of equitable principles in the partnership context and, moreover, observed that "[o]nly the Court of Chancery was equipped with the machinery necessary to enable [*an*] account to be taken . . . ": *ibid*. p. 194.

[268] (1984) 14 Fam.Law. 178. *cf. Williams v. Williams* [1976] Ch. 278.

[269] CPR r. 30.2(4)(a). As to the criteria to be applied, see *ibid*. r. 30.3(1)(c), (2).

[270] *ibid*. r. 30.2(4)(b). See, for example, the approach of the court in *Neath Talbot CBC v. Currie & Brown Project Management Ltd.* (2008) B.L.R. 464 (transfer from the Bristol TCC to the High Court refused); *Tai Ping Carpets UK Ltd. v. Arora Heathrow T5 Ltd.* (2009) B.L.R. 601 (transfer from the Birmingham District Registry to the TCC in London rather than the Birmingham TCC refused).

[271] County Courts Act 1984, s.42(1), (7), as substituted by the Courts and Legal Services Act 1990, s.2(3).

[272] *ibid*. s.24(1) (as amended by the Courts and Legal Services Act 1990, Sched. 18, para. 49(3)), (2)(g).

transfer may also be ordered in other appropriate cases,[273] *e.g.* where some important question of law or fact is likely to arise. The order may be made by the court of its own motion or on the application of any party to the proceedings.[274] Such an order may also be made by the High Court itself.[275]

Proceedings commenced in the High Court may be transferred to the county court if the High Court is satisfied that such an order is appropriate.[276] In exercising its discretion, the court must have regard to a variety of factors,[277] including the value of the partnership assets,[278] whether the issues of fact or law which will arise are simple or complex and whether they are of any public importance. It was formerly the case that a transfer would usually be ordered where the value of the assets was less than £50,000, unless the other criteria warranted the retention of the action in the High Court,[279] but now there is no such general practice and the discretion to transfer is unfettered.[280] The transfer will, in general, be to the Central London County Court (Chancery List), unless the parties express a preference for some other county court.[281] Again, the requisite order may be made by the court of its own motion or on the application of any party.[282]

Court of Protection

24–56   It has already been noted that it is the current editor's view that the Court of Protection does not itself have jurisdiction to dissolve a partnership of which a person who lacks capacity is a member, although it can authorise a deputy to commence (or defend) dissolution proceedings on such a person's behalf.[283] However, it is recognised that views differ on this point.[284]

Foreign court

24–57   An order for the dissolution of a partnership made by a foreign court will not normally be recognised under English law unless that court had jurisdiction over the defendant(s) according to the rules of private international law. Jurisdiction will not be established merely by showing that the partnership was entered into in the country concerned or that its assets included land situated there.[285]

---

[273] *ibid.* s.42(2), as substituted by the Courts and Legal Services Act 1990, s.2(3); also CPR r. 30.3(1)(a), (2). See generally *Collins v. Drumgold* [2008] T.C.L.R. 5 (which concerned a transfer to the TCC).

[274] *ibid.* s.42(3), as substituted by the Courts and Legal Services Act 1990, s.2(3).

[275] *ibid.* s.41(1), (3), as added by the Courts and Legal Services Act 1990, s.2(2).

[276] *ibid.* s.40(2), as substituted by the Courts and Legal Services Act 1990, s.2(1).

[277] CPR r. 30.3(1)(a), (2).

[278] See further *supra*, para. 24–53.

[279] The former Chancery Guide, para. 13.8. Now, however, this paragraph no longer appears. As noted *supra*, para. 24–53, the jurisdiction of the county court in partnership matters is technically £30,000.

[280] *National Westminster Bank plc v. King* [2008] Ch. 385; Chancery Guide, para. 13.5. See also *supra*, para. 23–70.

[281] Chancery Guide, para. 13.6.

[282] County Courts Act 1984, s.40(3), as substituted by the Courts and Legal Services Act 1990, s.2(1).

[283] See the Mental Capacity Act 2005, s.18(1)(e), noticed *supra*, para. 24–48.

[284] See *supra*, para. 24–48

[285] *Emanuel v. Symon* [1908] 1 K.B. 302; *cf. Blohn v. Desser* [1962] 2 Q.B. 116. See further, as to these cases, *Dicey & Morris on the Conflict of Laws* (14th ed.), para. 14–69. And see also the Foreign Judgments (Reciprocal Enforcement) Act 1933 and the Administration of Justice Act 1956, s.51 (as amended).

However, in the case of a decree made by a court of a Member State of the EU,[286] the position is now governed by Council Regulation (EC) No. 44/2001 of December 22, 2000[287] and, in the case of certain EFTA States, by the 2007 Lugano Convention[288] on jurisdiction and the recognition and enforcement of judgments in civil and commercial matters. Article 22 of Regulation 44/2001 provides:

> "The following courts shall have exclusive jurisdiction regardless of domicile[289]:
>
> . . .
>
> 2. in proceedings[290] which have as their object the validity of the constitution, the nullity or the dissolution of . . . associations of natural or legal persons,[291] or of the validity of their organs, the courts of the Member State in which the . . . association has its seat. In order to determine that seat, the courts shall apply its rules of private international law."[292]

A similarly worded rule applies under the 2007 Lugano Convention.[293] The position as between courts in the United Kingdom is governed by the Civil Jurisdiction and Judgments Act 1982.[294]

Arbitrator

An arbitrator may be given jurisdiction to order the dissolution of a partnership.[295]

24–58

---

[286] Denmark was formerly an exception but is now also subject to this regime: Civil Jurisdiction and Judgments Order 2001 (SI 2001/3929), art. 3A, as added by the Civil Jurisdiction and Judgments Regulations 2007 (SI 2007/1655), reg. 3(3)

[287] It has already been seen that this Regulation does not apply in the case of bankruptcy/insolvency proceedings: see *supra*, para. 24–33, n. 174, 24–37, n. 192.

[288] OJ No. L339. See also the Civil Jurisdiction and Judgments Act 1981, s.1(1), as amended by the Civil Jurisdiction and Judgments Regulations 2009 (SI 2009/3131), reg. 3(2). The Convention applies in the case of Norway but the 1988 Lugano Convention continues to apply as regards Switzerland and Iceland until they ratify the 2007 Convention.

[289] See, as to the domicile of an association of natural or legal persons, *ibid.* Art. 60(1) which provides that it is its statutory seat (*i.e.* its place of formation (see *ibid.* Art. 60(2)), its place of central administration or its principal place of business. Note also that the list in Art. 22 is mandatory and exhaustive as between Member States: *Orams v. Apostolides* [2010] 1 All E.R. (Comm) 950 (ECJ).

[290] See, as to the scope of this word, *JP Morgan Chase Bank NA v. Berliner Verkehrsbetriebe (BVG) Anstalt des Öffentlichen Rechts* [2009] 2 All E.R. (Comm) 1167.

[291] This will clearly include a partnership: see *Phillips v. Symes* [2002] 1 W.L.R. 853, where Hart J. held that the English court had exclusive jurisdiction in a dispute concerning an alleged partnership, by virtue of the then 1968 Brussels Convention, Art. 16(2) (a predecessor of Council Regulation 44/2001). This article does not merely cover internal disputes but can also extend to disputes with third parties: see *JP Morgan Chase Bank NA v. Berliner Verkehrsbetriebe etc.*, *supra*.

[292] See further, as to the location of the seat under English law, the Civil Jurisdiction and Judgments Order 2001, reg. 3, Sched. 1, para. 10, applying the Civil Jurisdiction and Judgments Act 1981, s.43 with modifications. In essence the seat of a partnership will be determined by reference to the place of its central management and control: *ibid.* Sched. 10, paras 2(b), 3(b).

[293] *ibid.* Art. 22. See also the Civil Jurisdiction and Judgments Act 1981, s.43A (as added by the Civil Jurisdiction and Judgments Regulations 2009, reg. 20(2)), as to the location of a firm's seat.

[294] See *ibid.* s.16(1) (as amended by the Civil Jurisdiction and Judgments Order 2001, Sched. 2(II), para. 3(a)), Sched. 4, para. 11(b) (as amended by *ibid.* para. 4).

[295] See *supra*, para. 10–272.

C.   PROCEDURE

Form of proceedings

24–59   Dissolution proceedings in the High Court or county court should be commenced by means of a Part 7 claim form,[296] unless the partnership is clearly at will and the service of the proceedings will itself bring about the dissolution,[297] when a Part 8 claim form may be used.[298] In the county court the claim form should be marked "Chancery Business".[299] A Part 7 claim form or, if served separately, the particulars of claim[300] should obviously identify under which of the grounds in section 35 of the Partnership Act 1890[301] the order is sought and must, in the usual way, be verified by a statement of truth.[302] It hardly needs to be said that matters of accounting as between the partners which arise in consequence of the dissolution will be dealt with at a later stage of the proceedings,[303] unless they form part of the grounds on which the dissolution is sought, *e.g.* a failure to account for moneys properly due to the firm. Even in the latter case, the issue of quantum might be left over until after trial of the dissolution claim.

Summary judgment

24–60   There is no reason why, in a clear case, a summary order for dissolution should not be obtained under Part 24 of the Civil Procedure Rules.[304]

Costs

24–61   Although costs will normally follow the event in the usual way,[305] the court has a wide discretion and must take into account the various factors listed in the Civil Procedure Rules.[306] This should be compared with the approach historically adopted by the courts in the case of proceedings relating to the *winding up* of partnerships, when there has been a tendency to order costs to be paid out of the

---

[296] See the CPR rr. 7.2, 7.4; 7APD, paras 3 *et seq.*; Practice Form N1.

[297] See *Unsworth v. Jordan* [1896] W.N. 2(5); also *supra*, paras 24–22, 24–28.

[298] See CPR rr. 8.1, 8.2; 8PD, para. 4; Practice Form N208; see also *ibid.* 7APD, paras 3.1, 3.3. As to the evidence in support of a Part 8 claim form, see *ibid.* 8PD, para. 7.

[299] *ibid.* 7APD, para. 2.5.

[300] *ibid.* r. 7.4, 7APD, para. 6.

[301] See *supra*, para. 24–47 and *infra*, paras 24–69 *et seq.*

[302] CPR r. 22.1(1)(a); also 7APD, para. 7.

[303] See the Chancery Guide, para. 22.2. As to taking accounts as between partners, see *supra*, paras 23–74 *et seq.*

[304] *i.e.* under CPR r. 24.2(a)(i) or (b). As to the form and content of an application for summary judgment, see *ibid.* Pt 23.

[305] *ibid.* r. 44.3(2)(a). It is clear that the courts will not apply this rule automatically: see *A.E.I. Rediffusion Music Ltd. v. Phonographic Performance Ltd.* [1999] 1 W.L.R. 1507, 1522 *et seq.* per Lord Woolf M.R.; *Bank of Credit & Commerce International SA v. Ali (No. 4)*, The Times, March 2, 2000. The principles set out in *Re Elginlata Ltd. (No. 2)* [1992] 1 W.L.R. 1207 are still, in general, applicable: *A.E.I. Rediffusion Music Ltd. v. Phonographic Performance Ltd., supra*; see, however, the approach of Lightman J. in *B.C.C.I. v. Ali (No. 4), supra*. Note that the court might conceivably reserve the costs of the dissolution claim until after any necessary accounts have been taken: *Shepherds Investments Ltd. v. Walters* [2007] C.P. Rep. 31 (CA).

[306] *ibid.* r. 44.3(4), (5). These factors include the conduct of the parties both before and during the proceedings.

partnership assets.[307] A similar order is, in fact, likely to be made where the partnership is wound up by reason of a partner's mental incapacity.[308]

D. GROUNDS FOR DISSOLUTION

Overriding discretion of court

In his Supplement on the Partnership Act 1890, Lord Lindley stressed the **24–62** discretionary nature of the Court's power to order a dissolution under the Act:

> "The Court has a wide discretion given to it, and though in exercising that discretion it will no doubt follow the principle of previous decisions, it must not be forgotten that the Court has a discretion and will not be bound to dissolve a partnership *ex debito justitiae* in any of the cases mentioned in [*section 35 of the Act*]."

The same sentiments were more recently expressed by Neuberger J. in *Mullins v. Laughton*[309] in these terms:

> "In this connection, it appears to me that the way in which section 35 of the 1890 Act is worded, namely 'the court may decree a dissolution of the partnership' in the cases therein set out, makes it clear that the court has a discretion whether or not to dissolve the partnership, and that, even where a dissolution would otherwise be appropriate, the court may refuse to order a dissolution if another course would achieve a more just result."

Availability of another remedy

In exercising its discretion, the court will inevitably take into account whether **24–63** there is some other remedy open to the partner(s) seeking a dissolution. Thus, where the agreement contains a power of expulsion[310] which could be, but has not been, exercised against the partner(s) whose conduct is complained of,[311] a dissolution might conceivably be refused, unless there is some compelling reason why the contractual power was not exercised.[312] Equally, if an overwhelming majority of partners seek a dissolution and are able to prove that they have sufficient grounds under the 1890 Act, it is difficult to see why the court should deny them relief. Where, on the other hand, a *minority* of innocent partners seek a dissolution, the fact that they could otherwise choose to retire from the firm voluntarily, subject to serving a period of notice and, perhaps, on unfavourable financial terms, should not, in the current editor's view, weigh against them in the exercise of the court's discretion; *per contra*, perhaps, if their rights on retirement broadly replicate their entitlement on dissolution.[313] In *Ruut v. Head*,[314] Santow

---

[307] See *supra*, para. 23–120.

[308] See *infra*, para. 24–68.

[309] [2003] Ch. 250 at [108].

[310] See *supra*, paras 10–113 *et seq.*

[311] This would, therefore, not include a case in which a multi-partner expulsion is prohibited as a matter of construction: see *Re A Solicitors' Arbitration* [1962] 1 W.L.R. 353, noted *supra*, para. 10–123.

[312] The fact that the expelled partner would otherwise receive an unrealistically generous payment under the terms of the agreement might be such a reason.

[313] See, generally, as to the financial entitlement of outgoing partners, *supra*, paras 10–157 *et seq.*

[314] (1996) 20 A.C.S.R. 160, 161, 163.

J. was clearly influenced by the fact that an alternative contractual remedy was available to the claimant, but this case concerned a two-man partnership and it was the *claimant* who had, on his wrongful exclusion of the defendant, brought about the breakdown of the relationship.[315]

(a) Mental incapacity

Effect of Mental CapacityAct 2005

24–64   Prior to the Mental Health Act 1959, the Chancery Division of the High Court had concurrent jurisdiction with the Judge in Lunacy to order the dissolution of a partnership where one or more of its members became of unsound mind.[316] However, the 1959 Act removed that jurisdiction from the Chancery Division, and the jurisdiction to dissolve a partnership was, by the Mental Health Act 1983[317] conferred exclusively on the "judge", which expression included all the Chancery judges as "nominated judges".[318] However, with the advent of the Mental Capacity Act 2005, it seems that the jurisdiction to dissolve a partnership may have moved back to the Chancery Division, since the powers under section 16 of that Act[319] extend only to taking decisions on the incapacitated partner's behalf and the consequential powers in section 18 refer only to the taking of a decision which will have the effect of dissolving a partnership of which he is a member.[320] Equally, it has already been noticed that a different view is espoused in *Heywood & Massey's Court of Protection Practice*.[321] It the latter view is correct then, as was the position under the Mental Health Act 1983,[322] it would seem that the Court of Protection will give primary consideration to the incapacitated partner's interests[323] and will only order a dissolution where there are no disputes under the partnership agreement, whether as to accounts or otherwise.[324] If that condition is not satisfied, an order will have to be sought under section 35 of the Partnership Act 1890 in any event.

Relevance of old law

24–65   It is questionable whether the principles adopted by the Chancery Court prior to the Mental Health Act 1959 are of any continuing relevance, although the apparent shift of jurisdiction back to the Chancery Division may mean that they are now of more interest.[325] Thus, under the old lunacy laws a dissolution would be ordered both for the protection of the lunatic[326] and to relieve his co-partners

---

[315] And see *Re American Pioneer Leather Co. Ltd.* [1918] 1 Ch. 556 (a company case); also, *infra*, para. 24–89.

[316] Partnership Act 1890, s.35(a); Lunacy Act 1890, s.119. It may be noted that the concurrent jurisdiction was somewhat theoretical, since in practice all the Chancery judges were also the Judges in Lunacy.

[317] *ibid.* s.96(1)(g).

[318] *ibid.* ss.93(1), 94(1) (as amended by the Public Trustee and Administration of Funds Act 1986, s.2(2)).

[319] See especially *ibid.* s.16(2)

[320] See *ibid.*s.18(1)(e), reproduced *supra*, para. 24–48.

[321] See *ibid.* para. 4–041: see *supra*, para. 24–48.

[322] *ibid.* s.96(1)(g).

[323] The interests of his creditors will be only secondary. Note also *Re 5* [2010] 1 W.L.R. 1082.

[324] See *Heywood & Massey's Court of Protection Practice, supra.*

[325] It is perhaps significant that no reference is made to the old cases in *Heywood & Massey's Court of Protection Practice.*

[326] *Jones v. Lloyd* (1874) L.R. 18 Eq. 265.

from the difficult position in which they were placed.[327] In one case,[328] the court ordered a dissolution on the application of one partner, even though the incapacitated partner's representatives had made a cross application for the appointment of a manager on the ground that the affairs of the partnership could be carried on to the advantage of all parties, notwithstanding such incapacity.[329] Equally, the other partners did not have to apply for a dissolution: if they preferred to wait and see whether the incapacity was temporary or permanent, the partnership would continue.[330]

In the absence of any authority, the current editor submits that a broadly similar approach may be adopted under the present law, although it is inevitable that the court will have particular regard to the incapacitated partner's position and requirements.[331]

Dormant partner

If a dormant partner suffers from a lack of capacity, this is unlikely to have any appreciable effect on his status within the firm.[332] In those circumstances, it is thought that a dissolution will not normally be ordered.   **24–66**

Date of dissolution

Where a judge orders a dissolution under section 35 of the 1890 Act, he will declare the partnership dissolved as from the date judgment is delivered and not from some earlier date.[333] If, however, an order of the Court of Protection authorises a partner's deputy to take some formal step to terminate the partnership, the dissolution will inevitably occur on a subsequent date.   **24–67**

Costs

Formerly, when the court dissolved a partnership on the ground of a partner's mental disorder, it would normally direct the costs to be paid out of the partnership assets[334] and it is considered that the position will be no different in the case of a lack of capacity.   **24–68**

---

[327] See *Wrexham v. Hudleston* (1734) 1 Swan. 514, note; *Sayer v. Bennet* (1784) 1 Cox 107; *Jones v. Noy* (1833) 2 M. & K. 125; *Sadler v. Lee* (1843) 6 Beav. 324; *Leaf v. Coles* (1851) 1 De G.M. & G. 171; *Anon.* (1856) 2 K. & J. 441; also *Waters v. Taylor* (1813) 2 V. & B. 299, 303 *per* Lord Eldon.

[328] *Rowlands v. Evans* (1861) 30 Beav. 302.

[329] The partnership property was ordered to be sold as a going concern, with liberty to all parties to bid, and a receiver and manager was appointed pending sale.

[330] *Jones v. Noy* (1833) 2 M. & K. 125.

[331] Mental Incapacity Act 2005, ss.16, 18: see further *supra*, para. 24–48.

[332] See *supra*, para. 13–36.

[333] *Besch v. Frolich* (1842) 1 Ph. 172. See also *Sander v. Sander* (1845) 2 Coll. 276; *Jones v. Welch* (1855) 1 K. & J. 765 (although it is not clear from the reports whether these cases involved partnerships at will). Of course, the dissolution may have occurred at some earlier date, *e.g.* by the service of notice under the partnership agreement or under the Partnership Act 1890, s.26(1) and/or 32(c): see *Robertson v. Lockie* (1846) 15 Sim. 285; *Bagshaw v. Parker* (1847) 10 Beav. 532: *Mellersh v. Keen* (1859) 27 Beav. 236; also *supra*, paras 10–137, 24–28. Lord Lindley observed: "It was probably on the ground that a partnership at will is determinable on notice, that in *Kirby v. Carr* (1838) 3 Y. & C.Ex. 184 the dissolution was decreed as from the filing of the bill, no previous notice having been given." See also *Shepherd v. Allen* (1864) 33 Beav. 577 and *infra*, para. 24–91.

[334] *Jones v. Welch* (1855) 1 K. & J. 765.

(b) Permanent Incapacity

Mental incapacity

24–69   Prior to the Partnership Act 1890, a dissolution could be ordered where a partner was of unsound mind, on the grounds that he had become permanently incapable of performing his duties as a partner. Thus, in *Jones v. Noy*,[335] Sir John Leach M.R. observed:

> "It is clear upon principle that the complete incapacity of a party to an agreement to perform that which was a condition of the agreement is a ground for determining the contract. The insanity of a partner is a ground for the dissolution of the partnership, because it is immediate incapacity; but it may not in the result prove to be a ground of dissolution, for the partner may recover from his malady."

This is still the position under the Partnership Act 1890.[336] Alternatively, the court might order a dissolution on the "just and equitable" ground.[337]

Other forms of incapacity

24–70   Although a lack of mental capacity is the most obvious illustration of this ground, it is clear that any other form of incapacity will suffice, provided that it appears to the court to be permanent at the date of trial.[338] In the case of a physical incapacity, medical evidence will almost invariably be required. In *Whitwell v. Arthur*[339] one of two partners was unable to perform his duties as a partner following an attack of paralysis, but the medical evidence showed that his health was improving and a probability that the incapacity was only of a temporary nature. On that basis a dissolution was refused. Although this would seem to militate in favour of an early application to the court, unseemly haste would be counter-productive; the current editor suggests that, save in the clearest of cases, time should normally be allowed for the relevant condition to stabilise.

Partial incapacity

24–71   A dissolution can only be obtained if the partner is "incapable of performing his part of the partnership contract".[340] Whilst this will not generally be in doubt in the case of *total* mental or physical incapacity, the position may be less clear where a partner is only able to perform some, but not all, of his duties.[341] It is, nevertheless, submitted that a partial incapacity of this type should suffice, subject to an application of the normal *de minimis* principle.[342]

---

[335] (1833) 2 M. & K. 125, 129–130.

[336] *ibid.* s.35(b), *supra*, para. 24–47.

[337] *ibid.* s.35(f), *supra*, para. 24–47 and *infra*, paras 24–89, 24–90.

[338] This presupposes that the incapacity does not take the form of a disability the effects of which could be alleviated by appropriate adjustments under the Disability Discrimination Act 1995, ss.6B, 18B: see *supra*, para. 8–18. Were the position otherwise, a dissolution would not be ordered.

[339] (1865) 35 Beav. 140.

[340] See Partnership Act 1890, s.35(b), *supra*, para. 24–47.

[341] But see *supra*, n. 338.

[342] Although there is no authority for the view put forward in the text, any other result would hold the partners to a bargain different from the one that they originally made; *cf. Peyton v. Mindham* [1972] 1 W.L.R. 8. However, in practice the point is largely academic, given that a dissolution could be sought on the "just and equitable" ground: see the Partnership Act 1890, s.35(f), *supra*, para. 24–47 and *infra*, paras 24–89, 24–90.

On the other hand, it is not enough to prove an overall reduction in a partner's capacity, which merely causes him to perform his duties in a way that his co-partners consider unsatisfactory.[343]

Who may seek dissolution

The incapacitated partner may not himself apply for a dissolution on this ground, so that any proceedings must be brought by one or more of his co-partners.[344]

24–72

(c) Conduct Injurious to the Partnership Business

In deciding whether a partner's conduct is "calculated to prejudicially affect the carrying on the [*partnership*] business" within the meaning of section 35(c) of the Partnership Act 1890,[345] the court is required to form an essentially subjective view,[346] having regard to the precise nature of the business concerned.[347] This, coupled with the absence of any reported cases and changing attitudes towards certain types of criminal, sexual and anti-social behaviour,[348] makes the formulation of general propositions somewhat difficult.

24–73

Criminal conduct

The current editor submits that the commission of a criminal act of a violent or dishonest nature would prima facie have an adverse effect on most types of business, given the risk of prosecution and its attendant publicity. Thus it was held, prior to the Partnership Act 1890, that a partnership should stand dissolved where one partner had rendered himself liable to prosecution by committing a fraudulent breach of trust.[349] On the other hand, the commission of a minor road traffic offence would clearly not suffice.

24–74

Immoral behaviour

The effect of sexual promiscuity and other forms of perceived immoral conduct will vary according to the nature of the business carried on. Although it may be of little or no concern in the case of a trading partnership,[350] the same cannot be said of partnerships in the medical and allied professions, where the

24–75

[343] *Sadler v. Lee* (1843) 6 Beav. 324.

[344] Partnership Act 1890, s.35(b), *supra*, para. 24–47.

[345] See *supra*, para. 24–47.

[346] This is emphasised by the words "in the opinion of the court": see also *supra*, para. 24–62.

[347] Given the formulation of s.35(c), it goes without saying that it would not be possible to rely on conduct *before* a partner's admission to the partnership. *cf.* the position under an express power of expulsion, discussed *supra*, para. 10–117.

[348] There can be no doubt that behaviour involving any form of discrimination or sexual harassment would now be regarded unfavourably (see, for example *Proceedings Commissioner v. Ali Hatem* [1999] 1 N.Z.L.R. 305, albeit not a dissolution case), whilst conduct which would once have been classed as unacceptable (including some forms of criminal behaviour) may now be treated as of little significance.

[349] *Essel v. Hayward* (1860) 30 Beav. 158 (where, in fact, a notice to dissolve had been given, even though the partnership was not at will). See also *Carmichael v. Evans* [1904] 1 Ch. 486, noted *supra*, para. 10–117.

[350] See *Snow v. Milford* (1868) 16 W.R. 554, which concerned a banking firm.

integrity of the practitioner/patient relationship is still paramount.[351] In one old
case, which was not fully reported but mentioned in argument before Page Wood
V.-C., a partnership between *accoucheurs* (male midwives) appears to have been
dissolved on the ground of one partner's immoral conduct.[352] An affair between
a doctor and his (or her) patient would unquestionably have an adverse effect on
the partnership practice, since it would involve professional misconduct.[353] On
the other hand, it is submitted that sexual conduct *outside* the practice would
have to be of a well publicised or exaggerated nature before a dissolution could
be obtained.

Professional misconduct

24–76   In the case of a professional firm, anything which amounts to professional
misconduct must *ipso facto* be capable of having a prejudicial effect on the
partnership business.[354]

Conduct unconnected with the business

24–77   It will already be apparent that the conduct complained of need not, as such,
be connected with the partnership business, provided that it is capable of injuring
it.[355]

Guilt and intent

24–78   It must be shown that the partner is "guilty" of the conduct complained of: this
obviously does not connote criminal guilt, but may imply an element of intent,
as Lord Lindley explained in his Supplement on the Partnership Act 1890:

> "This expression implies voluntary action, and an attempt by one partner to commit
> suicide while suffering from temporary insanity[356] would not justify a dissolution
> under this clause, even if such conduct would otherwise be within it."[357]

A more difficult question is whether the use of the word "calculated" implies
the existence of a positive *intention* to injure the business or merely a likelihood

---

[351] See the General Medical Council's guidance "Good Medical Practice", paras 20 to 40, and
"Maintaining Boundaries" (both produced in November 2006); also the General Dental Council's
guidance "Standards for Dental Professionals" (2005), para. 2.

[352] *Anon.* (1856) 2 K. & J. 441, 446. The Vice-Chancellor reportedly observed: "In such a case,
immoral conduct would materially affect the particular business of the firm." However, in his
Supplement on the Partnership Act 1890, Lord Lindley questioned whether the Vice-Chancellor
would have granted a dissolution on this ground, referring to *ibid.* pp. 452, 453.

[353] See *Goodman v. Sinclair, The Times*, January 24, 1951, where Vaisey J. held the partner to be
guilty of flagrantly immoral conduct, thus entitling his co-partner to dissolve under an express power
in the agreement.

[354] See for example, *Clifford v. Timms* [1908] A.C. 12; also *supra*, para. 24–45.

[355] *Pearce v. Foster* (1886) 17 Q.B.D. 536 (a case concerning an employee speculating in
"differences" on the Stock Exchange). See also *Carmichael v. Evans* [1904] 1 Ch. 486, noted *supra*,
para. 10–117.

[356] *Anon* (1856) 2 K. & J. 441; see also *supra*, para. 24–75, n. 352.

[357] See also *Anderson v. Kydd* 1991 G.W.D. 11–670. *cf.* the decision in *Bland v. Sparkes, The Times*,
December 17, 1999 CA (Civ Div), where the concept of "guilt" in a consultancy contract was
construed as involving either an independent finding or an *admission* of guilt.

of injury. The current editor submits that the latter interpretation is to be preferred.[358]

Who may seek dissolution

A partner seeking a dissolution on this ground must be innocent of any **24-79** misconduct of the type discussed above.[359]

(d) Breach of Agreement and Destruction of Mutual Confidence

This ground[360] in fact comprises two wholly separate limbs, *i.e.*: **24-80**

(i) a wilful[361] or persistent breach of the partnership agreement; and

(ii) conduct in relation to the partnership business which makes the continuation of that business impracticable.[362]

In his Supplement on the Partnership Act 1890, Lord Lindley noted that this accorded with the previous law, although it is submitted that the two limbs were then less distinct.[363]

Reluctance of court to interfere

Writing prior to the 1890 Act, Lord Lindley explained that the court will not **24-81** readily become embroiled in trivial differences between partners:

" . . . it is not considered to be the duty of the Court to enter into partnership squabbles, and it will not dissolve a partnership on the ground of the ill-temper or misconduct of one or more of the partners, unless the others are in effect excluded from the concern[364]; or unless the misconduct is of such a nature as . . . to destroy[365]

---

[358] Such an interpretation has been adopted in a number of statutory contexts: see, for example, *North Cheshire & Manchester Brewery Co. Ltd. v. Manchester Brewery Co. Ltd.* [1899] A.C. 83, 86 *per* Lord Halsbury L.C.; *British Vacuum Cleaner Co. Ltd. v. New Vacuum Cleaner Co. Ltd.* [1907] 2 Ch. 313, 320 *per* Parker J. (both decisions under the Companies Act 1862, s.20); *R. v. Davison* [1972] 1 W.L.R. 1540 (a decision under the House to House Collections Act 1939, s.5); *Turner v. Shearer* [1973] 1 W.L.R. 1387 (a decision under the Police Act 1964, s.52). *cf. Re Registered Trade-Marks of Bass, Ratcliffe & Gretton Ltd.* [1902] 2 Ch. 579; *Re Maeder's Trade Mark Application* [1916] 1 Ch. 304 (a decision under the Trade Marks Act 1905, ss.11, 19). Alternatively, the word might be construed in such a way as to require merely an element of wilfulness or recklessness, *i.e.* a realisation or conscious disregard of the potential injury to the business.

[359] Partnership Act. s.35(*c*), *supra*, para. 24-47.

[360] *ibid.* s.35(d), *supra*, para. 24-47.

[361] See, generally, as to when conduct will be regarded as "wilful", *Ronson International Ltd. v. Patrick* [2006] 2 All E.R. (Comm) 344 (CA), albeit in the context of an insurance contract.

[362] It is considered that, on a true construction of *ibid.* s.35(d), it is not necessary to show a practical impossibility of continuing the business under limb (a), although this view is, for example, advanced in *Miller's Partnership* (2nd ed), pp. 485, 486 (dealing with Scots law).

[363] See *Charlton v. Poulter* (1753) 19 Ves.Jr. 148, note; *Waters v. Taylor* (1813) 2 V. & B. 299; *Marshall v. Colman* (1820) 2 J. & W. 266; *Smith v. Jeyes* (1841) 4 Beav. 503; *Harrison v. Tennant* (1856) 21 Beav. 482, *infra*, para. 24-83. Note, however, that the test under limb (b) is whether it is "reasonably practicable" for the other partners to carry on the business with the partner whose conduct is in question, whereas Lord Lindley referred to the partners' mutual confidence being "utterly" destroyed: see *infra*, para. 24-81, n. 365.

[364] See *Goodman v. Whitcomb* (1820) 1 Jac. & W. 589; *Marshall v. Colman* (1820) 2 Jac. & W. 266; *Wray v. Hutchinson* (1834) 2 M. & K. 235; *Roberts v. Eberhardt* (1853) Kay 148. See also *Re Davis and Collett Ltd.* [1935] Ch. 693; *Re Lundie Brothers* [1965] 1 W.L.R. 1051.

[365] The original text in fact read "utterly to destroy"; however, the word "utterly" was expunged in the 6th ed. of this work.

the mutual confidence which must subsist between partners if they are to continue to carry on their business together."[366]

Although the discretion conferred on the court is now arguably wider than when Lord Lindley wrote the above passage,[367] the general reluctance to which he referred is still likely to persist, so that partners should be wary of over-exaggerating the consequences of a minor difference of opinion or breach of the agreement.[368] By way of example, in *Thakrar v. Vadera*,[369] Arden J., when considering a power of expulsion exercisable in a case falling within this ground, observed that "trivial breaches would not lead the court to exercise its powers . . . ". Equally, little sympathy is likely to be extended to a partner who is intent on flouting the terms of the agreement, even in relatively unimportant respects.

Nature and degree of misconduct

24–82   Lord Lindley, again writing prior to the Partnership Act 1890, pointed out that, where a dissolution is sought on the grounds of a partner's misconduct:

> " . . . it would seem that the misconduct must be such as to affect the business, not merely by shaking its credit in the eyes of the world, but by rendering it impossible for the partners to conduct their business together according to the agreement into which they have entered."[370]

The current editor considers that this passage may have become accidentally misplaced between the 5th and 6th editions of this work, since it is clearly more apposite to the previous ground.[371] Lord Lindley cannot properly be taken to have suggested that the court's discretion is limited to those cases in which a partner's conduct adversely affects the public image of the firm, thus penalising partners for their ability to mask internal strife from the public gaze. Indeed, he himself went on to observe:

> "It is not necessary, in order to induce the Court to interfere, to show personal rudeness on the part of one partner to the other, or even any gross misconduct as a partner. All that is necessary is to satisfy the Court that it is impossible for the partners to place that confidence in each other which each has a right to expect, and that such impossibility has not been caused by the person seeking to take advantage of it."[372]

24–83   A clear (but somewhat unusual) example of the type of misconduct required is to be found in *Harrison v. Tennant*.[373] There A, B and C carried on practice as

---

[366] See *Smith v. Jeyes* (1841) 4 Beav. 503; *Harrison v. Tennant* (1856) 21 Beav. 482, *infra*, para. 24–81. The remainder of this passage is reproduced *infra*, at the beginning of para. 24–82.

[367] See *supra*, n. 363.

[368] See *Goodman v. Whitcomb* (1820) 1 Jac. & W. 589, 592 *per* Lord Eldon; *Loscombe v. Russell* (1830) 4 Sim. 8, 11 *per* Shadwell V.-C.; *Anderson v. Anderson* (1857) 25 Beav. 190.

[369] March 31, 1999 (unreported).

[370] See *Anon.* (1856) 2 K. & J. 441: noted *supra*, para. 24–75.

[371] See *supra*, paras 24–73 *et seq*.

[372] See *Re Yenidje Tobacco Co. Ltd.* [1916] 2 Ch. 426, 430, where this passage was cited with approval by Cozens-Hardy M.R. See also *Re Davis and Collett Ltd.* [1935] Ch. 693; *Ebrahimi v. Westbourne Galleries Ltd.* [1973] A.C. 360; and note *Jesner v. Jarrad Properties Ltd.* 1994 S.L.T. 83. As to proving a loss of trust and confidence, see *Lauffer v. Barking, Havering and Redbridge University Hospitals NHS Trust* [2010] Med. L.R. 68 (an employment case).

[373] (1856) 21 Beav. 482.

solicitors in partnership, in succession to the practice formerly carried on by A and B. Proceedings were commenced against A and B in respect of the conduct of that former practice and involved allegations of gross misconduct and fraud against A. Against B and C's express wishes, A placed himself on the record instead of the firm and put in his own defence to the proceedings without consulting them.[374] B and C accordingly sought a dissolution, which A attempted to resist, arguing that he was not guilty of any misconduct towards his co-partners in relation to the partnership business nor of any breach of the partnership agreement. However, a dissolution was ordered, on the grounds that:

(1) mutual confidence had, not unreasonably, ceased;

(2) the business could no longer be carried on in the way the partners had originally contemplated; and

(3) although there had not as yet been any open conflict between the partners, continuation of the partnership would make this inevitable, to the detriment of them all.

What is in essence required is conduct which leads to a serious and irretrievable breakdown in the relationship between the partners.[375] A physical assault by one partner on another, even if provoked, would undoubtedly justify a dissolution,[376] as would the wrongful exclusion of a partner,[377] a groundless accusation of fraud,[378] use of partnership money for private purposes[379] or failure to account to the firm for sums received on its behalf.[380] Conduct which disrupts the running of the partnership business may be sufficient, *e.g.* a refusal to attend meetings with the other partners.[381] Moreover, even a relatively trifling argument precipitated by one partner may cause such hostility to develop between the partners that a continuation of the partnership is no longer possible; indeed, Lord Lindley specifically referred to the following as possible grounds for a dissolution[382]:

24–84

" . . . continued quarrelling, and such a state of animosity as precludes all reasonable hope of reconciliation and friendly co-operation . . . ".

It is the current editor's view that the service of an invalid expulsion or dissolution notice under an express power in the agreement may, in itself, give

[374] As to the extent of a partner's implied authority to defend actions brought against the firm, see *supra*, paras 12–35, 14–69.
[375] Note also, in this context, *Re Baumler (UK) Ltd.* [2005] 1 B.C.L.C. 92, albeit a decision concerning a quasi-partnership company on an application under what is now the Companies Act 2006, s.994; *cf. McKee v. O'Reilly* [2004] 2 B.C.L.C. 145, a similar case where relief was refused.
[376] See *Greenaway v. Greenaway* (1940) 84 S.J. 43, which in fact concerned an expulsion under an express power.
[377] See *Mullins v. Laughton* [2003] Ch. 250.
[378] *Leary v. Shout* (1864) 33 Beav. 582; *Re Yenidje Tobacco Co. Ltd.* [1916] 2 Ch. 426, 431 *per* Cozens-Hardy M.R. *cf. DB Rare Books Ltd. v. Antiqbooks* [1995] 2 B.C.L.C. 306 (CA), noted *supra*, para. 10–117, where a partner had wrongly suspected that his partners had underdeclared tax. This was, however, a case of expulsion.
[379] See *Smith v. Jeyes* (1841) 4 Beav. 502.
[380] *Cheeseman v. Price* (1865) 35 Beav. 142.
[381] *De Berenger v. Hammel* (1829) 7 Jar.Byth, 3rd ed., 83.
[382] *Baxter v. West* (1858) 1 Dr. & Sm. 173; *Watney v. Wells* (1861) 30 Beav. 56; *Pease v. Hewitt* (1862) 31 Beav. 22; *Leary v. Shout* (1864) 33 Beav. 582.

the recipient partner(s) grounds to seek a dissolution under this head, provided that their own behaviour has not invited the service of that notice.[383]

Misconduct with a view to dissolution

24–85   Lord Lindley pointed out that:

> " . . . the Court will never permit a partner, by misconducting himself and rendering it impossible for his partners to act in harmony with him, to obtain a dissolution on the ground of the impossibility so created by himself."[384]

This is still, in theory, the position.[385] However, if injunctive or other relief cannot, for whatever reason, be obtained,[386] the other partners may in practice have no option other than to apply for a dissolution, even though this is precisely what the miscreant partner had intended; the court clearly cannot authorise that partner's expulsion in the absence of an express power in the agreement.[387]

Who may seek dissolution

24–86   It follows from the previous paragraph that only the innocent partners may apply for a dissolution on this ground.[388]

(e) Partnership Business Carried on at a Loss

24–87   Partnership being "the relation which subsists between persons carrying on a business in common with a view of profit",[389] the expectation of profit must be implied in every partnership.[390] It is thus a natural consequence that the court may dissolve a partnership where that expectation no longer exists and the business can only be carried on at a loss.[391]

It was on this basis that a dissolution was ordered in *Jennings v. Baddeley*,[392] where the partnership capital had been exhausted and the business could only have continued to make a profit if the partners contributed further funds, which some of them were unable or unwilling to do. Lord Lindley observed of this case:

> "Under such circumstances as these it is unimportant whether the concern is already embarrassed or not. After everything has been done which was agreed to be done,

---

[383] Where the recipients' behaviour *has* invited expulsion, a dissolution could still, in theory, be sought under the Partnership Act 1890, s.35(f), *infra.* paras 24–89, 24–90.

[384] See *Harrison v. Tennant* (1856) 21 Beav. 482, 493–494 *per* Sir John Romilly M.R.; *Fairthorne v. Weston* (1844) 3 Hare 387.

[385] See the Partnership Act 1890, s.35(d), *supra*, para. 24–47.

[386] See *supra*, paras 23–135 *et seq.*

[387] See *infra*, paras 24–98 *et seq.* Note, however, the jurisdiction of the court to make a *Syers v. Syers* order: see *supra*, para. 23–187.

[388] Partnership Act 1890, s.35(d), *supra*, para. 24–47.

[389] *ibid.* s.1, *supra*, paras 2–01 *et seq.*

[390] See *Jennings v. Baddeley* (1856) 3 K. & J. 78, 83 *per* Page Wood V.-C.

[391] Partnership Act 1890, s.35(e), *supra*, para. 24–47. This principle was well established prior to the Act: *Baring v. Dix* (1786) 1 Cox 213; *Bailey v. Ford* (1843) 13 Sim. 495; *Jennings v. Baddeley*, *supra*. See also *Re Suburban Hotel Co.* (1867) 2 Ch.App. 732, 744–745 *per* Laing L.J.; *Wilson v. Church* (1879) 13 Ch.D. 1, 65 *per* Cotton L.J. As to the position where there is *no* business to be carried on (whether at a loss or otherwise), see *supra*, para. 24–46.

[392] (1856) 3 K. & J. 78, which concerned a mining partnership.

and certain loss is the only result of going on, any partner is entitled to have the concern dissolved . . . ".

The same theme was developed by Farwell J. in *Handyside v. Campbell*,[393] where he expressed the view that a dissolution on this ground would only be ordered where it could be proved that there was a practical *impossibility* of profit; such an impossibility would not be inferred where the losses could be attributed to special circumstances, rather than to an inherent defect in the business itself.

Insolvency

A dissolution on this ground is not dependent on proof of actual insolvency; indeed, the partners would risk disqualification orders by carrying on the business knowing it to be insolvent.[394] If a partner is not himself in a position to present a winding up petition against the firm,[395] the court may, in a clear case, be prepared to intervene on a summary[396] or interim basis,[397] as Lord Lindley explained:

> "If . . . the firm is already insolvent and becomes more and more so every day, the court will interfere on motion,[398] and appoint a person to sell the business and wind up the affairs of the partnership, although it is not usual to grant such relief until the hearing of the cause."[399]

24–88

(f) The Just and Equitable Ground

This represents the final "catch all" ground on which a court may order a dissolution.[400] It will not be construed *ejusdem generis* with the grounds which precede it in section 35 of the Partnership Act 1890,[401] nor will the court tie itself down to any rigid rules governing its application.[402] It is inevitable that, in the exercise of its discretion, the court will take into account all relevant factors,

24–89

---

[393] [1901] 17 T.L.R. 623, 624. See also *Janson v. McMullen* [1922] N.Z.L.R. 677; *Landford Greens Ltd. v. 746370 Ontario Inc.* (1994) 12 B.L.R. (2d) 196. *cf. Wilson v. Church* (1879) 13 Ch.D. 1, 65, where Cotton L.J. referred to the court's willingness to order a dissolution where "the purposes of the partnership cannot be carried into effect with any *reasonable prospect* of profit" (emphasis supplied). And note *Re A Company, ex p. Burr* [1992] B.C.L.C. 724 (a decision under what is now the Companies Act 2006, s.994).

[394] Insolvency Act 1986, s.214; Company Directors Disqualification Act 1986, s.10, as applied by the Insolvent Partnerships Order 1994, art. 16 (as itself amended by the Insolvency Partnerships (Amendment) Order 2001 (SI 2001/767), art. 2(2)). See further, *infra*, para. 27–64.

[395] See *infra*, paras 27–13, 27–14, 27–33.

[396] *i.e.* under CPR Pt 24: see *supra*, para. 24–60.

[397] *i.e.* under *ibid.* Pt 25: see *supra*, paras 23–205. Note that the court will be more reluctant to appoint a receiver, even where a dissolution is inevitable: see *supra*, para. 23–157; also *supra*, para. 23–170.

[398] This terminology is now outdated. All applications for relief of the type discussed in the text will be made by means of an application under CPR Pt 23.

[399] *Bailey v. Ford* (1843) 13 Sim. 495; and see *Heywood v. B.D.C. Properties* [1963] 1 W.L.R. 975. It is thought likely that the courts will still, in general, be reluctant to grant relief of this nature on an interim basis, notwithstanding the changes introduced by the CPR.

[400] Partnership Act, s.35(f), *supra*, para. 24–47.

[401] See *Re Yenidje Tobacco Co.* [1916] 2 Ch. 426, 432 *per* Cozens-Hardy M.R., 435 *per* Warrington L.J.; also *Re Amalgamated Syndicate* [1897] 2 Ch. 600; *Loch v. John Blackwood Ltd.* [1924] A.C. 783.

[402] See *Re Yenidje Tobacco Co., supra; Ebrahimi v. Westbourne Galleries Ltd.* [1973] A.C. 360 and the cases there cited.

including the terms of the partnership agreement and the availability of any alternative remedy thereunder.[403] It could also, in theory, take into account the partners' conduct *before* the formation of the partnership, if this has a bearing on the dissolution issue, *e.g.* as explaining a loss of trust and confidence,[404] and the potential impact which making an order or, conversely, not making an order would have on the partners.[405]

It is apprehended that, as was the position prior to the Act,[406] an order is likely to be made if, for whatever reason, the objects for which the partnership was formed can no longer be attained, either at all or in the manner originally contemplated by the partners, and a dissolution cannot be obtained on one of the other grounds.[407] Wrongful exclusion of a partner will clearly justify an immediate dissolution.[408] A complete breakdown in the relationship between the partners will, in general, justify a dissolution, as will circumstances in which the applicant partner(s) have lost trust and confidence in the other partners.[409] Where there is a loss of trust and confidence in only *some* of those other partners, *e.g.* a managing or senior partner or the members of a management committee, the

---

[403] See *supra*, para. 24–63. *Quaere* is there any scope under this ground for invoking the "last straw" test recognised in employment cases, such as *Omilaju v Waltham Forest London Borough Council (No. 2)* [2005] I.C.R. 481 (CA). Note also, in this connection, *Royle v. Greater Manchester Police Authority* [2007] I.R.L.R. 281 (EAT), as to the effect of affirmation in relation to a continuous course of conduct and the ability to look at such conduct in its totality. This may be of particular relevance in the current context.

[404] In *Bland v. Sparkes, The Times*, December 17, 1999, the defendants had engaged the claimant to supply consultancy services to their organisation on terms that they could terminate his engagement if he was guilty of conduct bringing that organisation into disrepute. The Court of Appeal held that the defendants were entitled to exercise that power of termination by reference to conduct which predated the agreement and expressly recognised that such conduct could have the effect of destroying the relationship of confidence between the contracting parties. *cf. Andrewes v. Garstin* (1861) 10 C.B.(N.S.) 444, noticed *supra*, para. 16–06, n. 26.

[405] *PWA Corp v. Gemini Group Automated Distribution Systems Inc.* [1993] 103 D.L.R. (4th) 609, 613 *per* Dublin C.J.O. (dissenting), 643 *per* Griffiths and Arbour JJ.A.

[406] See generally, *Harrison v. Tennant* (1856) 21 Beav. 482; *Baring v. Dix* (1786) 1 Cox 213. See also *supra*, para. 24–83.

[407] This is a new formulation of principle. Writing in his Supplement on the Partnership Act 1890, Lord Lindley put it in this way: "Any case . . . in which it is no longer reasonably practicable to carry out the partnership contract according to its terms will, it is apprehended, be within this section." In later editions (including the 15th), this was expanded to read " . . . any case in which it is no longer reasonably practicable to attain the object with a view to which the partnership was entered into or to carry out the partnership contract according to its terms will, it is apprehended, be within this section."

[408] *Mullins v. Laughton* [2003] Ch. 250, a fairly extreme case. Oddly the decision in *Thakrar v. Vadera, supra*, was not founded on the basis of the wrongful expulsion.

[409] In *Rowe v. Briant*, June 15, 1995 (unreported), H.H. Judge Weeks Q.C., sitting as a judge of the Chancery Division, ordered a dissolution of a partnership of chartered accountants on the basis that there had been a "simple breakdown in personal relationships" and that matters had reached the stage where "the parties to [*the*] action cannot reasonably be expected to carry on business together in partnership". *Thakrar v. Vadera*, March 31, 1999 (an unreported decision of Arden J.) was, in many ways, a similar case, although one partner has served an invalid expulsion notice on the other. Equally, in *Ruut v. Head* (1996) A.C.S.R. 160, Santow J. recognised that a partnership might "limp along" for a period, notwithstanding an irretrievable breakdown in trust and confidence, unless there was complete deadlock as between the partners; note also the *obiter* observation of Lord Hoffmann in *O'Neill v. Phillips* [1999] 1 W.L.R. 1092, 1104. And see *Landford Greens Ltd. v. 746370 Ontario Inc.* (1994) 12 B.L.R. (2d) 196, where it was held that, on the facts, there was no breakdown in the partners' relationship. A loss of trust and confidence must be proved, not merely asserted: *Lauffer v. Barking, Havering and Redbridge University Hospitals NHS Trust* [2010] Med. L.R. 68 (an employment case). Needless to say, it is no partner's duty to *continue* to place trust and confidence in his partners, irrespective of the circumstances: *Johnson v. Snaddon* [2001] V.S.C.A. 91.

attitude of the court will be less predictable.[410] Equally, the mental disorder of a single partner would, in all probability, suffice, in a case where the Court of Protection either cannot or declines to intervene.[411] Despite the views expressed by the Court of Appeal in *Harrison v. Povey*,[412] the current editor submits that it is not necessary to establish a breach "going to the root of the agreement" before a dissolution can be ordered on this ground.

If the applicant partner(s) have an extraneous motive for seeking a dissolution, *e.g.* a personal benefit to be derived therefrom,[413] this will be taken into account and may militate against an order being made.[414]

Conduct of the applicant(s)

Although there is no express bar on a partner who is guilty of misconduct **24–90** applying for a dissolution on this ground,[415] an order is unlikely to be made in his favour.[416] Thus, in *Thakrar v. Vadera*,[417] Arden J. having held that the conduct of the applicant did not *per se* exclude him from obtaining an order on this ground, went on to observe that:

"the court would be loath to exercise the jurisdiction at the request of a party who is responsible for the breakdown of mutual trust and confidence."

In applying this principle, H.H. Judge Weeks in *Rowe v. Briant*[418] analysed the causes of the breakdown in the relationship between the partners and, whilst finding that the defendant was more sinned against than sinning,[419] nevertheless concluded that the real cause was a genuine difference of view between the partners. On that basis, he ordered a dissolution of the partnership. On the other hand, in *Ruut v. Head*,[420] it was accepted that the breakdown had resulted from the claimant's improper exclusion of the defendant from the partnership. Santow J. emphasised that the court retained a general discretion, notwithstanding the

---

[410] In such a case, the issue may be whether the majority, when apprised of the conduct of the partner(s) in question, have unreasonably chosen to do nothing and thereby effectively adopted such conduct as their own.

[411] See *supra*, paras 24–64, 24–69.

[412] (1956) 168 E.G. 613.

[413] *i.e.* where a property owning partner wishes to dissolve his firm in order to recover vacant possession: see *J.E. Cade & Son Ltd.* [1991] B.C.C. 360 (a company case).

[414] Note that, in the case of dissolution by notice under the Partnership Act 1890, s.26(1) and/or 32(c) or under an express contractual power, the existence of such a collateral benefit may be regarded as immaterial: see *supra*, para. 24–21.

[415] *cf.* the Partnership Act 1890, s.35(b)–(d), *supra*, para. 24–47. For an interesting discussion of this issue, see *PWA Corp v. Gemini Group Automated Distribution Systems Inc.* [1993] 103 D.L.R. (4th) 609, where the members of the Ontario Court of Appeal had different perspectives.

[416] See *Harrison v. Tennant* (1856) 21 Beav. 482, 493–494 *per* Sir John Romilly M.R.; *cf. Fairthorne v. Weston* (1844) 3 Hare 387; *Re Yenidje Tobacco Co. Ltd.* [1916] 2 Ch. 426, 430 *per* Cozens-Hardy M.R.; *Ebrahimi v. Westbourne Galleries Ltd.* [1973] A.C. 360, 387 *per* Lord Cross; also *Landford Greens Ltd. v. 746370 Ontario Inc.* (1994) 12 B.L.R. (2d) 196. And see *supra*, para. 24–65.

[417] March 31, 1999 (unreported).

[418] June 15, 1995 (unreported). H.H. Judge Weeks Q.C. was sitting as a judge of the Chancery Division.

[419] Interestingly, one of the causes of the breakdown was the claimants' insistence that they had the right unilaterally to vary the profit shares under the partnership agreement, based on erroneous advice received. They had also threatened to serve a notice of expulsion on the defendant and, subsequently, a notice of dissolution, even though the partnership was not at will.

[420] (1996) 20 A.C.S.R. 160.

claimant's conduct[421] but, in the event, declined to order a dissolution on the grounds that it was premature. He gave the partners three months in which to try to resolve their differences by implementing their contractual options or by selling the partnership business voluntarily, but it seems likely that he would have made an order at the end of that period barring a relevant change of circumstances in the meantime.[422] The *obiter* view expressed by Santow J. that:

> "[t]here may even be a public interest in not allowing partnerships providing important services to the public to continue to trade, or practise a profession, where their partners are simply unable to work together"[423]

is, however, more questionable. *PWA Corp v. Gemini Group Automated Distribution Systems Inc.*[424] was another instance in which the court declined to order a dissolution in the face of allegations of deadlock and a loss of mutual trust and confidence between the members of a *limited* partnership.[425]

In practice, the very fact that a dissolution application is made, and the other partners' response to it, may lead, directly or indirectly, to an irresistible inference that mutual trust and confidence has been destroyed,[426] although H.H. Judge Weeks in *Rowe v. Briant*[427] rightly warned about the danger of such applications becoming self-fulfilling.

E.   DATE OF DISSOLUTION

24–91   Section 35 of the Partnership Act 1890 does not specify the date on which the partnership will stand dissolved; accordingly the old law still applies, as Lord Lindley noted in his Supplement on the Act:

> "The rule ... was, and still is,[428] that where the order of the Court is necessary for the dissolution of the partnership, the dissolution will, in the absence of special reasons, date from the judgment."[429]

The court can, of course, declare a partnership dissolved with effect from a date earlier than the date of judgment where the dissolution resulted from the service of a notice[430] or the occurrence of some other determining event specified

---

[421] *ibid.* p. 162.
[422] See *ibid.* p. 163.
[423] *ibid.*
[424] *supra.* Note that Dublin C.J.O. (dissenting) would have ordered a dissolution on the basis that the differences between the partners had become irreconcilable and a sufficient state of animosity and distrust existed between them (p. 624). Griffiths and Arbour JJ.A. were *inter alia* not convinced that, given the nature of the partnership, there was any real deadlock (p. 639).
[425] Note that there was also a breach of fiduciary duty which was attributable to the applicant partner in this case.
[426] See also *supra*, paras 24–80 *et seq.*
[427] *supra.*
[428] See *ibid.* s.46.
[429] *Lyon v. Tweddell* (1881) 17 Ch.D. 529; *Besch v. Frolich* (1842) 1 Ph. 172; but see *Essell v. Hayward* (1860) 30 Beav. 158 (which can, however, no longer be regarded as good law as regards the date of dissolution).
[430] See *supra*, paras 10–137 *et seq.*, 24–18 *et seq.* And see *supra*, para. 24–67, n. 333.

in the Act or in the agreement.[431] Although there is one New Zealand authority which *appears* to be authority for the proposition that the court can order a dissolution retrospectively,[432] the partnership was at will and was clearly dissolved by the service of the writ.[433] If the decision went any further than merely recognising this, it was, in the current editor's view, *per incuriam*.[434] Interestingly, in *Mullins v. Laughton*,[435] Neuberger J. recognised that the dissolution could only have effect as from the date of his judgment, but nevertheless allowed the claimant to elect as between that date and the date of his exclusion from the partnership for the purposes of taking certain accounts. The basis on which he did so is, however, open to doubt, even allowing for his expressed disapproval of the defendants' behaviour.

What is less clear is whether a dissolution can be ordered to have effect as from a *future* date. Such a possibility appears to be recognised in Australia,[436] but the current editor is not aware of any instance in which this course has been adopted by an English court. Equally, there is certainly nothing in section 35 of the Partnership Act 1890[437] which would preclude such an order, although the circumstances in which this would be appropriate will inevitable be rare.

4.   ASSIGNMENT OF SHARE

Although Lord Lindley was vexed by the question whether the assignment of a partner's share would work a dissolution,[438] the current editor submits that, since the Partnership Act 1890 itself recognises the validity of such an assignment[439] and does not specify it as a ground of dissolution,[440] the point is now virtually unarguable. Indeed, Buckley J. clearly did not countenance such a possibility in *Re Garwood's Trusts*.[441] Admittedly, an assignment might justify the other partners seeking a dissolution on the "just and equitable" or some other ground[442] but, unless it involved a deliberate breach of the agreement,[443] exceptional circumstances would need to be shown before the court would be prepared to make an order. On any footing, the assignee could not himself make the application.[444]

24–92

---

[431] See generally *supra*, paras 24–05 *et seq.*, 24–15 *et seq.*

[432] *Phillips v. Melville* [1921] N.Z.L.R. 571.

[433] *ibid.* pp. 573, 574 *per* Cooper J.

[434] Cooper J. purported to follow the decision in *Unsworth v. Jordan* [1896] W.N. 2(5), which was clearly a case involving a partnership at will.

[435] [2003] Ch. 250 at [124].

[436] See *Ruut v. Head* (1996) A.C.S.R. 160, 163 *per* Santow J.

[437] See *supra*, para. 24–47.

[438] For a summary of Lord Lindley's views, see the 15th ed. of this work at pp. 707, 708.

[439] *ibid.* s.31: see *supra*, paras 19–51 *et seq.*

[440] *ibid.* s.35, *supra*, para. 24–47; see also *ibid.* s.33(2), *supra*, para. 24–38. Reference might also be made in this context to the observations of Lord Millett in *Hurst v. Bryk* [2002] 1 A.C. 185, 195, as adopted in *Mullins v. Laughton*, *supra*.

[441] [1903] 1 Ch. 236, 239. See also *Campbell v. Campbell* (1893) 6 R. 137 (which concerned the construction of an express clause in the agreement). But note the terms of the Partnership Act 1890, s.46; see *Sturgeon v. Salmon* (1906) 22 T.L.R. 584; *Emanuel v. Symon* [1907] 1 K.B. 235, 241–242 *per* Channell J. (the actual decision being reversed at [1908] 1 K.B. 302).

[442] *e.g.* under the Partnership Act 1890, s.35(c) or (d), *supra*, paras 24–73 *et seq.*, 24–80 *et seq.* See also *Pollock on Partnership* (15th ed.), p. 77.

[443] *ibid.* s.35(d).

[444] *ibid.* ss.31, 35.

It will, however, be recalled that if a charging order is made on a partner's share, the other partners will normally have the option to dissolve the partnership without involving the court.[445]

5.   THE RIGHT TO RETIRE

Lord Lindley's rules on retirement

24–93   Writing prior to the Partnership Act 1890, Lord Lindley formulated the following three rules, which still accurately summarise the position under the Act:

1. " . . . it is competent for a partner to retire with the consent of his co-partners at any time and upon any terms."

2. " . . . it is competent for him to retire without their consent by dissolving the firm, if he is in a position to dissolve it."

3. " . . . it is not competent for a partner to retire from a partnership which he cannot dissolve, and from which his co-partners are not willing that he should retire."

To rule 1 must be added the obvious rider that such consent may be granted prospectively, by the inclusion of an express right to retire in the partnership agreement.[446] Equally, it has already been seen that retirement pursuant to an express power can, in certain circumstances, bring about a general dissolution of the firm.[447] Whether a partner who has agreed to retire under threat of being expelled could seek to argue that this is not a true retirement is questionable.[448]

Position where no power to retire

Partnership at will

24–94   If a partner decides to retire from a partnership at will,[449] his departure will cause a *general* dissolution of the firm,[450] unless by the act of retiring he can be taken to have forfeited his right to force a sale of the partnership assets, etc., in exchange for a right to be paid out the market value of his share as at the date of his "retirement".[451]

---

[445] *ibid.* s.33(2), *supra*, para. 24–38.

[446] See *supra*, paras 10–108 *et seq.*

[447] See *supra*, para. 24–25.

[448] It is considered that an analogy cannot properly be drawn with the employment cases, such as *Sandhu v. Jan de Rijk Transport Ltd.* [2007] I.C.R. 1137 (CA). There Pill L.J. observed at [37]: "Resignation . . . implies some form of negotiation and discussion; it predicates a result which is a genuine choice on the part of the employee".

[449] *i.e.* pursuant to the Partnership Act 1890, ss.26(1) and/or 32(c), *supra*, para. 24–18.

[450] See, as to the meaning of this expression, *supra*, para. 24–03.

[451] See *Sobell v. Boston* [1975] 1 W.L.R. 1587. See also *supra*, paras 19–11, 23–184.

Partnership for a term

On the other hand, if the partnership is for a fixed term, a partner who has no **24–95** right to retire[452] will be effectively "locked into" the firm and, if his co-partners are unwilling to negotiate terms for his departure, his only legitimate option may be to seek a dissolution from the court under section 35 of the Partnership Act 1890.[453] The consequences of any partner actively seeking grounds to dissolve are too obvious to require comment.[454]

If the frustrated partner chooses to ignore his legal obligations and merely walks out of the partnership, the other partners will have a number of courses open to them, *i.e.* they may:

(a) apply for a dissolution of the partnership[455];

(b) seek injunctive relief[456];

(c) continue to treat the recalcitrant partner as a member of the firm,[457] but force him to account for any profits he may make elsewhere[458] and/or seek damages for breach of the partnership agreement[459]; or

(d) attempt to negotiate terms.

Since course (a) will merely achieve the freedom which the recalcitrant partner **24–96** seeks and may, at the same time, penalise the innocent partners,[460] a combination of courses (b) and (c) should, in practice, be used as a prelude to a negotiated settlement. Theoretical remedies are of no real avail once a partner has determined to leave and the sooner that this is recognised by the other partners the better.

Although an express power of expulsion might be seen as the answer in cases of this sort,[461] particularly if its exercise will permit the other partners to acquire the recalcitrant partner's share on favourable terms, the firm will still be deprived of his services earlier than any partner had originally contemplated and, moreover, in circumstances which may even threaten the continued viability of its business.

---

[452] The position may be no different where the right to retire is restricted, *e.g.* where not more than a set number of partners may retire within a given time frame: see also *supra*, paras 10–108, 10–112.

[453] This will, of course, result in a general dissolution: see, as to the implications for the other partners, the Partnership Act 1890, ss.39, 44; and see further *supra*, paras 19–08 *et seq.*, 19–24 *et seq.*, 23–183 *et seq.* and *infra*, paras 25–44 *et seq. cf. Sobell v. Boston* [1975] 1 W.L.R. 1587.

[454] But see *supra*, paras 23–141, 24–85, 24–90 and *infra*, para. 24–100.

[455] *i.e.* under the Partnership Act 1890, s.35(c), (d) and/or (f): see *supra*, paras 24–73 *et seq.*, 24–89, 24–90. It is no longer possible to treat the conduct as repudiatory and, thus, on acceptance as bringing about an automatic dissolution: see *supra*, paras 24–05 *et seq.*

[456] See *England v. Curling* (1844) 8 Beav. 129 and *supra*, paras 23–46, 23–135 *et seq.* There should be no problem in obtaining so-called "springboard" relief in such a case: see *Dass Solicitors v. Southcott* (2009) (Lawtel 14/12/09), a decision concerning an employee leaving without notice.

[457] It follows that he will still be entitled to his profit share; but see *Airey v. Borham* (1861) 29 Beav. 620, *supra*, para. 20–48.

[458] See *supra*, paras 16–13 *et seq.*

[459] See *supra*, paras 23–208 *et seq.*

[460] *Per contra*, perhaps, if the firm is in a parlous financial state, since a dissolution will affix liability for the partnership debts and obligations on *all* the partners, including the recalcitrant partner. The remaining partners can, of course, reform as a "phoenix" firm straight away. See further *supra*, para. 10–199.

[461] See *supra*, paras 10–113 *et seq.* and *infra*, paras 24–98 *et seq.*

Retirement from insolvent firm

24–97   Lord Lindley observed:

> " . . . a partner desirous of retiring from an insolvent firm, is at perfect liberty to sell his interest in it for any sum the continuing partners think proper to give him; and a sale by him to them cannot be set aside or impeached as a fraud upon the creditors of the firm unless there be clear evidence *aliunde* of such fraud.[462] At the same time, the present share of a partner in an insolvent firm[463] is obviously less than nothing, whatever may be the amount of the capital brought in by him. Consequently a partner who retires from an insolvent firm, and withdraws from it a sum of money which he is pleased to call his share, is defrauding the creditors of the firm; and such a transaction cannot stand and may be impeached by the trustee in bankruptcy of the continuing firm."[464]

The current editor considers that the position will be no different under the current insolvency legislation, subject to the time limits within which transactions at an undervalue may be set aside[465]; since, however, the retired partner will in any event be liable as a contributory if the firm is wound up as an unregistered company,[466] the point is only likely to become critical if he is also insolvent, so that his own separate creditors are, in this respect, in direct competition with the joint creditors.[467]

Similar considerations will arise if a retiring partner relinquishes his share at an undervalue and *subsequently* becomes insolvent.[468]

6.   THE RIGHT TO EXPEL

The general principle

24–98   Prior to the Partnership Act 1890, Lord Lindley wrote:

> "In the absence of an express agreement to that effect, there is no right on the part of the members of a partnership to expel any other member. Nor, in the absence of express agreement, can any of the members of an ordinary partnership forfeit the

---

[462] See *Ex p. Birch* (1801) 2 Ves.Jr. 260, note; *Ex p. Peake* (1816) 1 Madd. 346; *Parker v. Ramsbottom* (1824) 3 B. & C. 257; *Ex p. Carpenter* (1826) Mont. & MacA. 1.

[463] Lord Lindley, referring to the definition of an insolvent firm in *Ex p. Carpenter* (1826) Mont. & MacA. 1, 5 *per* Sir John Leach M.R., stated that "An insolvent firm is one in which the joint assets are less than the joint liabilities. Such a firm is insolvent whatever the wealth of the individual partners composing it may be."

[464] See *Anderson v. Maltby* (1793) 2 Ves.Jr. 244; *Re Kemptner* (1869) L.R. 8 Eq. 286. It is immaterial that the agreement was binding as between the partners: *ibid.*; see also *Billiter v. Young* (1856) 6 E. & B. 1, 40 *per* Jervis C.J.

[465] See the Insolvency Act 1986, ss.238 *et seq.*, 339 *et seq.* and *infra*, para. 27–101. See also *ibid.* s.423. *Quaere* whether such a transaction could be set aside as a fraud on the insolvency laws: see further, *supra*, paras 10–152, 10–153 and *infra*, para. 27–71.

[466] See *infra*, paras 27–61 *et seq.*

[467] See *infra*, paras 27–106 *et seq.* As to the circumstances in which insolvency orders may be made against the firm and against one or more partners, see *infra*, paras 27–04 *et seq.*, 27–24 *et seq.*

[468] See the Insolvency Act 1986, ss.238 *et seq.*, 339 *et seq.*, 423. See also *supra*, paras 10–152, 10–153 and *infra*, paras 27–70, 27–71.

share of any other member, or compel him to quit the firm on taking what is due to him. As there is no method, except a dissolution, by which a partner can retire against the will of his co-partners, so there is no method except a dissolution by which one partner can be got rid of against his own will."[469]

Partnership Act 1890, section 25

This basic level of security is preserved by the Partnership Act 1890, which **24–99** provides as follows:

> "25. No majority of partners can expel any partner unless a power to do so has been conferred by express agreement between the partners."

Alternative remedies

It has already been seen that where a partner, by his own conduct, seeks to **24–100** force his co-partners into a dissolution, the court will readily interfere with injunctive or other relief, but clearly cannot authorise an expulsion in the absence of a specific power in the agreement.[470] Equally, what the court may be prepared to do is to order a dissolution *and* a compulsory sale of that partner's share to his former partners, thus avoiding the need for a full-scale winding up.[471]

Express powers of expulsion

A power of expulsion is now, as a matter of routine, included in most well **24–101** drawn agreements.[472] The exercise of such a power has already been considered earlier in this work.[473]

Expulsion and partnerships at will

Although a contrary view was voiced by Browne-Wilkinson V-C. in *Walters v.* **24–102** *Bingham*,[474] the current editor submits that a power of expulsion is *not* consistent with the existence of a partnership at will; accordingly, in the absence of an express agreement, it is by no means certain that such a power will survive the expiration of a fixed term partnership.[475]

---

[469] See *Clarke v. Hart* (1858) 6 H.L.C. 633; also *Crawshay v. Collins* (1808) 15 Ves.Jr. 218, 226 *per* Lord Eldon; *Featherstonhaugh v. Fenwick* (1810) 17 Ves.Jr. 298.

[470] See *Fairthorne v. Weston* (1844) 3 Hare 387 and *supra*, paras 23–141, 24–85.

[471] See *Syers v. Syers* (1876) 1 App.Cas. 174, considered *supra*, paras 23–187 *et seq.*

[472] See *supra*, paras 10–113 *et seq.* See further, as to drafting such a power, the *Encyclopedia of Professional Partnerships*, Precedent 1, cl. 21.

[473] See *supra*, paras 10–124 *et seq.*

[474] [1988] 1 F.T.L.R. 260, 268–269.

[475] Partnership Act 1890, s.27; *Clark v. Leach* (1863) 32 Beav. 14; *Campbell v. Campbell* (1893) 6 R. 137. See further, *supra*, paras 10–23 *et seq.*

CHAPTER 25

WINDING UP THE PARTNERSHIP AFFAIRS

1.   CONSEQUENCES OF DISSOLUTION

Effect on business

IT has already been seen that, when a partnership is dissolved, each partner's   **25–01**
authority will continue for the purposes of winding up its affairs.[1] However,
unless the dissolution is of a purely technical nature[2] or is otherwise legislated for
in the partnership agreement,[3] it will inevitably have an appreciable impact on
the partnership business. This will be felt most keenly in the case of a professional firm, since the partners will be obliged to complete any work then in
progress, but strictly ought not to take on any new work.[4] Such an ongoing
"limbo" state may render a sale of the business as a going concern a practical
impossibility, despite the theoretical need for such a sale. The impact will be less
severe in the case of many trading concerns, *e.g.* shops and restaurants, where a
continuation of the business does not involve undertaking anything other than
short term contractual commitments.[5] Indeed, there may be no appreciable
difference in such cases between the outward appearance of the business on the
day before the dissolution as compared with that on the day after.

Employees

Although it has been decided that a general dissolution will terminate the   **25–02**
contracts of employment of all the firm's employees, thus inevitably leading to
claims for unfair dismissal or redundancy payments,[6] much may ultimately
depend on the manner in which the dissolution was brought about. Thus, in an
obiter section of the judgment in *Rose v. Dodd*,[7] the Court of Appeal considered
the effect of an intervention in a solicitors' practice and appeared to accept that
there may be cases where employment can continue unaffected by a general
dissolution, citing *inter alia* the potential application of section 38 of the Partnership Act 1890.[8] The court's reasoning supports the view expressed in previous

---

[1] Partnership Act 1890, s.38, *supra*, paras 13–62 *et seq.*
[2] See *supra*, paras 24–02, 24–03.
[3] See *supra*, para. 10–266.
[4] See *supra*, paras 10–200, 13–63, 16–30.
[5] Equally, the appointment of a receiver and manager will be more feasible in the case of such a
business, although the courts are no longer willing to make such appointments as a matter of routine:
see *supra*, para. 23–157.
[6] *Tunstall v. Condon* [1980] I.C.R. 786; see also *Briggs v. Oates* [1990] I.C.R. 473; *Barnes v.
Leavesley* [2000] I.C.R. 38. It will, of course, be necessary to take into account the precise terms of
each contract of employment: see *Brace v. Calder* [1895] 2 Q.B. 253, *supra*, para. 3–41; *Philips v.
Alhambra Palace Co.* [1901] 1 Q.B. 59.
[7] [2005] I.C.R. 1776 at [49].
[8] See *supra*, paras 13–62 *et seq.*; also *infra*, para. 25–55.

editions of this work, namely that if the partnership continues for the purposes of the winding up, it is difficult to see why those contracts should not continue until the winding up is complete and the continuation partnership finally comes to an end.[9] On the other hand, a *technical* dissolution brought about by the death, retirement or expulsion of a partner is unlikely to bring about a termination of the employees' contracts, provided that the partnership continues in existence.[10] Equally, if one or more members of a dissolved firm continue to carry on its business following the dissolution and are treated as having re-engaged some or all of its staff, those employees will, in any event, enjoy continuity of employment by virtue of the Employment Rights Act 1996.[11]

Transfer of Undertakings (Protection of Employment) Regulations 2006

25–03   The received view[12] was (and to a large extent remains) that, where the business of a dissolved firm is sold or transferred to one or more of the former partners (or to a third party) following a dissolution, the Transfer of Undertakings (Protection of Employment) Regulations 2006[13] will apply, so that the employees will automatically become the employees of the purchasers.[14] However, the current editor has always doubted the correctness of this proposition on the basis that, if it is right that the employees' contracts have already been determined by the dissolution,[15] it cannot properly be said that they would "otherwise be terminated by the transfer" for the purposes of regulation 4(1),[16] whether or not that transfer was in contemplation at the time when the firm was dissolved.[17] This

---

[9] But see *Tunstall v. Condon, supra,* at pp. 793, 794 *per* Talbot J. *Semble,* the Tribunal was not asked to consider the effect of s.38.

[10] See *supra,* para. 3–15.

[11] *ibid.* s.218(5). See *Stevens v. Bower* [2004] I.R.L.R. 957 (CA), applying *obiter* views expressed in *Jeetle v. Elster* [1985] I.C.R. 389.

[12] The point was not even argued in *Hynd v. Armstrong* [2007] I.R.L.R. 338 (Ct. of Session), where a Scottish firm of solicitors was demerging to form two separate firms and the employee had been dismissed *prior* to the demerger. See also Blackett-Ord's *Partnership Law* (3rd ed.), para. 18.25. Note that the 1981 TUPE Regulations were held to apply following the "terminal insolvency" of a company (which is clearly analogous to a dissolution) in *Transport & General Workers Union v. Swissport (UK) Ltd.* [2007] I.C.R. 1593 (EAT).

[13] SI 2006/246. These regulations revoked and replaced the Transfer of Undertakings (Protection of Employment) Regulations 1981 (SI 1981/1794). Note that they may have extra-territorial effect, even outside the EU: *Holis Metal Industries Ltd. v. GMB* [2008] I.R.L.R. 187 (EAT).

[14] *ibid.* reg. 4(1) (so far as material) provides " . . . a relevant transfer shall not operate so as to terminate the contract of employment of any person employed by the transferor and assigned to the organised grouping of resources or employees that is subject to the relevant transfer, which would otherwise be terminated by the transfer, but any such contract shall have effect after the transfer as if originally made between the person so employed and the transferee." A person is "employed by the transferor and assigned to the organised grouping of resources or employees" if he is "so employed immediately before the transfer, or . . . would have been so employed if he had not been dismissed in the circumstances described in regulation 7(1) . . . ": reg. 4(3). Regulation 7(1) applies to treat an employee of the transferor or transferee as unfairly dismissed if the sole or principle reason for his dismissal is the transfer itself or a "reason connected with the transfer that is not an economic, technical or organisational reason entailing changes in the workforce".

[15] See *supra,* para. 25–02.

[16] See *Wilson v. St Helens Borough Council* [1999] 2 A.C. 52 (HL); also *Secretary of State for Employment v. Spence* [1987] Q.B. 179. *cf. Litster v. Forth Dry Dock & Engineering Co. Ltd.* [1990] 1 A.C. 546 (HL).

[17] The analysis in the text would seem to be borne out by the decision in *Barnes v. Leavesley* [2000] I.C.R. 38, where the Employment Appeal Tribunal distinguished between the effects of a dissolution and an intervention in a solicitors' practice by the Law Society.

analysis was accepted by the Court of Appeal in *Rose v. Dodd*[18] but, save in the case supposed, the court was not prepared to lay down any hard and fast rules as to whether the then 1981 TUPE Regulations would apply and emphasised that much would depend on the particular circumstances. The issue has clearly not been laid to rest by the 2006 Regulations themselves, despite a slight change of wording.

Subject to that technical point, there would seem to be little doubt that the Regulations will apply where a group of partners *de facto* take over part of the goodwill of the firm on dissolution, *otherwise* than by means of a formal purchase, either by virtue of being a transfer of part of an undertaking[19] or a "service provision change".[20] Where part of the goodwill is divided between several groups of partners, it will be necessary to determine to which group the relevant employees should be treated as transferred.[21] Moreover, if a client decides to transfer his work to another firm, on or following the dissolution, the TUPE Regulations are likely to apply to any "organised grouping of employees" who are principally (but not necessarily exclusively) dedicated to servicing that client, irrespective of whether any of the former partners have also moved to that firm.[22]

Occupation of premises

If, whilst the partnership was continuing, one partner permitted his co-partners **25–04** to use and occupy premises on a non-exclusive licence basis,[23] the current editor is of the view that he will be unable to terminate those licences immediately following the dissolution, if by so doing he would prevent an orderly winding up of the partnership affairs.[24] Somewhat anomalously, in *Latchman v. Pickard*[25] it appears to have been held that Dr. Latchman's implied licence over part of the partnership premises had been terminated, even though the firm's contract with the Primary Care Trust still had some time to run. Although she had a continuing licence to occupy the remainder of the premises, she was refused injunctive relief because of the state of her relationship with the other partners.

---

[18] [2005] I.C.R. 1776 at [57], [58]. The proposition was, of course, formulated by reference to the Transfer of Undertakings (Protection of Employment) Regulations 1981, reg. 5(1).

[19] See the Transfer of Undertakings (Protection of Employment) Regulations 2006, reg. 3(1)(a), (6); *Fairhurst Ward Abbotts Ltd. v. Botes Building Ltd.* [2004] I.C.R. 919 (CA); *Marra v. Express Gifts Ltd.* [2009] B.P.I.R. 508 (ET), neither of which involved partnerships. In *Jones v. Beardmore* (UKEAT/0392/09/DM (Lawtel 9/4/10) an employee of a dissolved partnership took a different job with a different business owned by one of the partners. It was held that the TUPE regulations did not apply.

[20] See *ibid.* reg. 3(1)(b)(ii), (3). See further, as to what the Tribunal will look for in assessing whether there has been such a change, *Metropolitan Resources Ltd. v. Churchill Dulwich Ltd.* [2009] I.R.L.R. 700 (EAT); *Ward Hadaway Solicitors v. Love* (UKEAT/0471/09/SM) (Lawtel 20/4/10).

[21] See, as to the correct approach, *Kimberley Group Housing Ltd. v. Hambley* [2008] I.C.R. 1030 (EAT). In essence, much is likely to depend on the comparative sizes of the goodwill shares taken over.

[22] *Hunt v. Storm Communications*, noted at (2007) L.S. Gaz., June 28; *Royden v. Barnetts Solicitors* (Case No. 2103451/07), February 4, 2009 (Lawtel 24/4/09) (ET).

[23] See *Harrison-Broadley v. Smith* [1964] 1 W.L.R. 456; and see *supra*, paras 10–45, 18–34.

[24] See *Harrison-Broadley v. Smith, supra*, p. 465 *per* Harman L.J.; also *I.R.C. v. Graham's Trustees* 1971 S.L.T. 46, 48 *per* Lord Reid. *cf. Doe v. Bluck* (1838) 8 C. & P. 464; *Benham v. Gray* (1847) 5 C.B. 138.

[25] [2005] EWHC 1011 (Ch) (Lawtel 12/5/05).

Agricultural floating charges

25–05   It should also be noted that an agricultural floating charge on partnership property under the provisions of the Agricultural Credits Act 1928 will crystallise into a fixed charge on a dissolution.[26]

25–06   Having noticed these incidental points, the remainder of this chapter is devoted to a consideration of the following topics:

1. The return of premiums;

2. The treatment of post-dissolution profits.

3. The distribution of assets.

At the very end of the chapter appears a brief recapitulation of the general principles applicable in winding up the partnership affairs, which are considered in greater detail elsewhere in this work.

2.   THE RETURN OF PREMIUMS

Nature of premium

25–07   Prior to the Partnership Act 1890, Lord Lindley wrote:

> "It frequently happens, when one person is admitted into partnership with another already established in business, that it is agreed that the incoming partner shall pay the other a premium, *i.e.* a sum of money for his own private benefit . . . The consideration for the premium is not only the creation of a partnership between the person who takes, and him who parts with, the money, but also the continuance of that partnership . . . ".

The premium is thus, in its true sense, the price of entry into partnership: it does *not* represent the purchase price for a share of goodwill or any other asset nor a contribution towards the capital of the firm.[27] In those circumstances, it will come as no surprise that the popularity of the premium has over the years seen a drastic decline, to such an extent that it is now rare to encounter a case in which an incoming partner is asked to make such a payment.[28]

Nevertheless, where an incoming partner *has* paid a premium in the expectation that the partnership will endure for a certain period, the question inevitably arises whether he is entitled to the return of the whole or any part of that sum if the partnership is determined prematurely.

---

[26] ss.5 (as amended), 7(1)(a)(iii).

[27] See *Re Bruges and Gow* [1926] N.Z.L.R. 893.

[28] For details of a recent instance in which partners had sought (unsuccessfully) to argue that a goodwill payment was, in reality, a disguised premium, see *Lee v. Jewitt* [2000] S.T.C. (S.C.D.) 517.

A.   PARTNERSHIP INDUCED BY FRAUD

Even before the Partnership Act 1890, there was no doubt that a return of **25–08**
premium could be obtained in cases of fraud. Lord Lindley explained the rights
of the incoming partner in these terms:

> "If a person has been deluded into becoming a partner by false and fraudulent
> representations, and has paid a premium, he may take one of two courses; *viz.* either
> abide by the contract and claim compensation for the loss occasioned by the fraud,
> which he may do in taking the partnership accounts; or he may disaffirm the contract,
> and thereby entitle himself to a return of the whole of the money he has paid."[29]

This is still the position: it was only those cases which were *not* tainted by
fraud where the authorities prior to the 1890 Act were, in Lord Lindley's own
words, "not easy to reconcile" and, thus, merited legislative attention.

If the fraudulent partner is insolvent, the incoming partner may prove against
his estate for the amount of the premium in competition with his separate
creditors.[30]

B.   PARTNERSHIP AT WILL

Just as it did not seek to regulate the return of premiums in cases of fraud, the **25–09**
Partnership Act 1890 did not deal with the position following the dissolution of
a partnership at will,[31] so that the law seemingly remains in the same state as
when Lord Lindley wrote the following passage:

> "Where a partnership is entered into for no specified time, and there is no agreement
> for a return or an apportionment of the premium in the event of an unexpected
> determination of the partnership, no part of the premium is returnable on the
> happening of such event. A case of fraud must be dealt with on its own demerits; and
> a person taking another into partnership for no definite time cannot, as soon as he has
> received the premium, dissolve the partnership and retain what has been paid as the
> consideration for it.[32] But laying aside fraud, and supposing there to be nothing
> except a partnership created for no specified time and determined soon after its
> creation, it is difficult to hold that it was in fact entered into for a longer time, and
> that the person who came in, paying a premium, has not got all for which he
> stipulated."[33]

---

[29] See further, as to rescission for fraud, *supra*, paras 23–52 *et seq*. And see *infra*, para. 25–13.

[30] *Ex p. Turquand* (1841) 2 M.D. & D. 339; also *Bury v. Allen* (1845) 1 Colly. 589. The decision
in *Ex p. Broome* (1811) 1 Rose 69 appears to be to the contrary: but see the footnote in *Bury v. Allen,*
supra, p. 598; also the observations of Knight Bruce V.-C. at *ibid.* p. 607.

[31] The Partnership Act 1890, s.40 applies only to partnerships for a fixed term: see *infra*, para.
25–10.

[32] *Featherstonhaugh v. Turner* (1858) 25 Beav. 382. See also *Hamil v. Stokes* (1817) 4 Price 161;
Burdon v. Barkus (1862) 4 De G.F. & J. 42, 52 *per* Turner L.J.

[33] See *Tattersall v. Groote* (1800) 2 Bos. & Pul. 131, 134 *per* Lord Eldon.

C.   PARTNERSHIP FOR A FIXED TERM

Partnership Act 1890, section 40

25–10   In an attempt to settle the uncertainties raised by the decided cases,[34] section 40 of the Partnership Act 1890 provided as follows:

> "40. Where one partner has paid a premium[35] to another on entering into a partnership for a fixed term, and the partnership is dissolved before the expiration of that term otherwise than by the death of a partner, the Court may order the repayment of the premium, or of such part thereof as it thinks just, having regard to the terms of the partnership contract and to the length of time during which the partnership has continued; unless
>
> > (a)   the dissolution is, in the judgment of the Court, wholly or chiefly due to the misconduct of the partner who paid the premium, or
> > (b)   the partnership has been dissolved by an agreement containing no provision for a return of any part of the premium."

Save in the event of a dissolution brought about by the death of a partner and in the cases specifically mentioned in paragraphs (a) and (b), the section confers an unfettered discretion on the court, which will, perhaps, be guided in the exercise of that discretion by the pre-1890 authorities.

Importance of agreement

25–11   It is largely self evident that, if the partners originally agreed terms for the return (or non-return) of the premium in the event of a dissolution, effect will, in the absence of fraud,[36] normally be given thereto[37]; *a fortiori*, if an agreement was entered into at the time of the dissolution.[38] Writing prior to the Partnership Act 1890, Lord Lindley explained that if a dissolution agreement:

> " . . . is silent with respect to the premium, the inference is that the parties did not intend to deal with it, nor to vary their rights to it under the original agreement for its payment."

This inference has now been given statutory force. It is, however, questionable whether a partner will be regarded as having entered into such an agreement merely by consenting to a dissolution sought by his co-partners.[39]

Cause of dissolution

25–12   Where there is no such agreement, the exercise of the court's discretion is likely to depend on the manner in which the dissolution was brought about.

---

[34] In his Supplement on the Partnership Act 1890, Lord Lindley pointed out that "This section, according to a statement in the memorandum to the original bill, is intended to adopt the law laid down in the case of *Atwood v. Maude* (1868) L.R. 3 Ch.App. 369."

[35] There is no definition of this word in the Act.

[36] See *supra*, para. 25–08.

[37] *Handyside v. Campbell* [1901] 17 T.L.R. 623, 624 *per* Farwell J. Note also that the Partnership Act 1890, s.40 expressly directs the court to have regard to the terms of the partnership contract, when determining the quantum of the premium to be returned.

[38] *ibid.* s.40(b); see also, prior to the Act, *Lee v. Page* (1861) 30 L.J.Ch. 857.

[39] See *Bury v. Allen* (1845) 1 Colly. 589; *Astle v. Wright* (1856) 23 Beav. 77; *Wilson v. Johnstone* (1873) L.R. 16 Eq. 606.

(1) *Death*[40]

Prior to the Partnership Act 1890, a return of premium could not normally be obtained where the partnership was dissolved by the death of a partner since, in Lord Lindley's own words:

"Death is a contingency which all persons entering into partnership know may unexpectedly put an end to it."

This exception is now embodied in the section 40 of the 1890 Act.[41]

Nevertheless, a return of premium may still conceivably be obtained if fraud can be proved. Lord Lindley cited the following example: **25–13**

" . . . if a person knows himself to be in a dangerous state of health, and conceals that fact, and induces another to enter into partnership with him, and to pay him a premium, and shortly afterwards dies, the fraud so practised will entitle the partner paying the premium to a return of part of it; and, if so, he can obtain such return in an action for a partnership account: he need not rescind the contract *in toto*."[42]

Whether a court would readily override the *express* provisions of the 1890 Act in such a case remains open to doubt.[43]

(2) *Insolvency of firm or partner*[44]

Lord Lindley apprehended that the insolvency of a firm or of a partner would not justify a court ordering the repayment of any part of a premium, again on the basis that this is: **25–14**

"a contingency which every one may fairly be taken as contemplating."[45]

The position is, if anything, *a fortiori* where a firm is wound up as an unregistered company under the current insolvency legislation.[46]

On the other hand, where the recipient of the premium was, unknown to the incoming partner, already in financial difficulties when the partnership commenced, a dissolution caused by his subsequent bankruptcy was, prior to the 1890 Act, treated as a sufficient ground for ordering a partial repayment[47]; *per contra*, if the incoming partner was aware of such difficulties before paying the premium.[48] There appears to be no reported case dealing with the position where the bankruptcy of the recipient was not anticipated, but the current editor tentatively submits that such an event should be regarded no differently from death or the insolvency of the firm or of any other partner, *i.e.* as a normal contingency.

---

[40] See the Partnership Act 1890, s.33(1), *supra*, paras 24–29 *et seq.*

[41] See *supra*, para. 25–10. And see, as to the position prior to the Act, *Whincup v. Hughes* (1871) L.R. 6 C.P. 78; *Ferns v. Carr* (1885) 28 Ch.D. 409.

[42] *Mackenna v. Parkes* (1867) 36 L.J.Ch. 366. See also *supra*, para. 25–08.

[43] Lord Lindley did, however, cite this as a continuing exception in his Supplement on the Partnership Act 1890; *ibid.* p. 105.

[44] See the Partnership Act 1890, s.33(1), *supra*, paras 24–28, 24–32 *et seq.* and *infra*, paras 27–02 *et seq.*

[45] See *Akhurst v. Jackson* (1818) 1 Swan. 85.

[46] See generally, *infra*, paras 27–04 *et seq.*

[47] *Freeland v. Stansfeld* (1854) 2 Sm. & G. 479.

[48] *Akhurst v. Jackson* (1818) 1 Swan. 85.

If the dissolution is brought about by the bankruptcy of the partner who *paid* the premium, an order for repayment will be unlikely, save (perhaps) where the petition was presented by the recipient partner.[49]

It has already been noticed that the insolvency of a corporate partner will not, of itself, bring about a dissolution,[50] so that no question of a return of premium will arise.

(3) *Disagreements and misconduct*

25–15   Prior to the Partnership Act 1890, Lord Lindley wrote:

> "Disagreements between the partners resulting in a dissolution[51] have given rise to much difficulty. The tendency . . . is to apportion the premium in these cases not only where neither partner is to blame[52]; but *a fortiori* where the partner receiving the premium has so misconducted himself as to give the partner paying it a right to have the partnership dissolved[53]; and it matters not that the latter may himself not be altogether free from blame[54]; nor is the rule altered by the fact that the partners have consented to dissolve since the institution of legal proceedings."[55]

It would seem likely that the court would now adopt a similar approach, although a return of premium cannot in any event be ordered where the court takes the view that dissolution was caused "wholly or chiefly" by the misconduct of the partner who paid it.[56] The existence of such misconduct will normally presuppose a dissolution obtained on the application of some other partner,[57] who might in fact be the recipient of the premium.[58]

Equally, a dissolution brought about by the misconduct of a partner will not relieve him of the liability to pay a premium which is due but unpaid.[59]

(4) *Lack of mental capacity*

25–16   It has already been seen that the Court of Protection seemingly may now have no power to dissolve a partnership on the grounds of a partner's lack of capacity,[60] but could certainly order that proceedings be commenced on behalf of that partner seeking a dissolution and, indeed, an order for the return of any

---

[49] See *Hamil v. Stokes* (1817) 4 Price 161. Lord Lindley took care to observe that, in this case, "the contract of partnership was not rescinded on the ground of fraud".

[50] See *supra*, para. 24–35.

[51] See now the Partnership Act 1890, s.35(c), (d) and (f), *supra*, paras 24–47, 24–73 *et seq.*, 24–80 *et seq.*, 24–89, 24–90.

[52] *Atwood v. Maude* (1868) L.R. 3 Ch.App. 369. And see *supra*, para. 25–10, n. 34.

[53] *Bullock v. Crockett* (1862) 3 Giff. 507. See also *Rooke v. Nisbet* (1881) 50 L.J.Ch. 588.

[54] See *Atwood v. Maude* (1868) L.R. 3 Ch.App. 369; also *Astle v. Wright* (1856) 23 Beav. 77; *Pease v. Hewitt* (1862) 31 Beav. 22. *cf. Airey v. Borham* (1861) 29 Beav. 620.

[55] *Bury v. Allen* (1845) 1 Colly. 589; *Astle v. Wright* (1856) 23 Beav. 77; *Wilson v. Johnstone* (1873) L.R. 16 Eq. 606. *cf. Lee v. Page* (1861) 30 L.J.Ch. 857.

[56] Partnership Act 1890, s.40(a), *supra*, para. 25–10. And see, as to the position prior to the Act, *Airey v. Borham* (1861) 29 Beav. 620; *Atwood v. Maude* (1868) L.R. 3 Ch.App. 369; *Wilson v. Johnstone* (1873) L.R. 16 Eq. 606; *Bluck v. Capstick* (1879) 12 Ch.D. 863.

[57] Alternatively, the dissolution might be brought about pursuant to an express power in the agreement: see further, *supra*, paras 10–137 *et seq.*

[58] A dissolution cannot be obtained under the Partnership Act 1890, s.35(c) or (d) (or, perhaps, (f)) at the instance of a partner guilty of misconduct: see *supra*, paras 24–47, 24–73 *et seq.*, 24–80 *et seq.*, 24–89, 24–90.

[59] *Akhurst v. Jackson* (1818) 1 Swan. 85; *Bluck v. Capstick* (1879) Ch.D. 863.

[60] See *supra*, paras 24–47, 24–60 *et seq.*

premium he may have paid on entry to the partnership. It is also doubtful whether that Court could itself make an order under section 41 of the 1890 Act.[61]

(5) *Illegality*[62]

Although a return of premium could theoretically be ordered where a partner- **25–17** ship is dissolved by reason of illegality, the current editor considers that, in general, the court would not be prepared to intervene[63]; much will, however, depend on the precise circumstances.[64] It is in any event clear that an action to enforce the *payment* of a premium in such a case will not succeed.[65]

D.   AMOUNT OF PREMIUM RETURNABLE

It has already been seen that a wide discretion is conferred on the court under **25–18** section 40 of the Partnership Act 1890.[66] Nevertheless, it is considered that the following observations made by Lord Lindley prior to the Act are still pertinent:

> "There is no definite rule for deciding in any particular case the amount which ought to be returned. The time for which the partnership was entered into, and the time for which it has in fact lasted, are the most important matters to be considered; but other circumstances must often been taken into account in order to decide what is fair between the parties.[67] At the same time, the rule generally adopted is to apportion the premium with reference to the agreed and actual duration of the partnership."[68]

In his Supplement on the Act, Lord Lindley qualified his view as follows: **25–19**

> "In the exercise of [*the Court's*] discretion attention must be paid to the terms of the partnership contract, and to the length of time during which the partnership has continued, and it would seem . . . that the Court is not to take other matters into consideration; if this be so the discretion of the Court will be more limited than has hitherto been the case."

Yet, if the court is to take all the circumstances into account when determining whether or not to order a return of premium,[69] it is somewhat surprising if those circumstances must be ignored when it comes to considering the *quantum* of any repayment.[70] Consistently therewith, in one New Zealand case[71] where the

---

[61] *Semble*, the position was different under the Mental Health Act 1983, ss.95, 96.

[62] Partnership Act 1890, s.34, *supra*, paras 24–43 *et seq*.

[63] See *supra*, paras 8–63 *et seq*.

[64] A previous editor suggested that relevant factors might include the foreseeability of the event making the business illegal: *quaere*, can this be correct?

[65] *Williams v. Jones* (1826) 5 B. & C. 108. See also *supra*, para. 8–60.

[66] See *supra*, para. 25–10.

[67] See *Lyon v. Tweddell* (1881) 17 Ch.D. 529.

[68] See *Bury v. Allen* (1845) 1 Colly. 589; *Astle v. Wright* (1856) 23 Beav. 77; *Pease v. Hewitt* (1862) 31 Beav. 22; *Atwood v. Maude* (1868) L.R. 3 Ch.App. 369; *Wilson v. Johnstone* (1873) L.R. 16 Eq. 606. *cf. Hamil v. Stokes* (1817) 4 Price 161; *Freeland v. Stansfeld* (1854) 1 Sm. & G. 479; *Bullock v. Crockett* (1862) 3 Giff. 507.

[69] See *supra*, paras 25–12 *et seq*.

[70] *Quaere* whether, even though the court must take into account the factors mentioned in the section, it retains a residual discretion as to other factors.

[71] *Janson v. McMullen* [1922] N.Z.L.R. 677.

recipient of the premium had lost the agencies which the partnership had been formed to work, the court ordered a dissolution of the partnership and the return of the *whole* premium.[72]

An exercise of the court's discretion will not normally be overturned on appeal.[73]

Time for application

25–20   Where a claimant issues proceedings seeking a dissolution and also wishes to claim a return of premium, he should plead that claim specifically and, in general, seek the order for its return as part of the substantive dissolution order; similar principles apply where such an order is sought to be obtained by way of counterclaim. A court[74] may well be reluctant to order an inquiry as to whether a return of premium is justified if this is raised for the first time *after* the dissolution order has been secured.[75]

Arbitration

25–21   An arbitrator may certainly order a return of premium if power to dissolve the firm is conferred on him by the partnership agreement,[76] but such power is probably exercisable in any event.[77]

3.   THE TREATMENT OF POST-DISSOLUTION PROFITS

25–22   It has already been seen that an account of partnership dealings and transactions must be kept open following the date of dissolution,[78] since each partner's authority continues for the purposes of winding up the firm's affairs.[79] In previous editions of this work it has been stated, consistently with the decision of the Court of Appeal in *Hopper v. Hopper*,[80] that where all the partners are actively involved in the winding up, profits realised following the dissolution will be shared in the normal profit sharing ratios,[81] unless some special allowance is given to a particular partner by the court.[82] In terms of the ultimate *entitlement* to those profits, that is certainly right, but the current editor questions whether those profits should, absent agreement or a court order, actually be distributed to the partners whilst the winding up is continuing and any debts remain unpaid.[83]

---

[72] *ibid.* pp. 681, 682 *per* Sim A.C.J.

[73] *Lyon v. Tweddell* (1881) 17 Ch.D. 529.

[74] An arbitrator is likely to adopt a similar attitude.

[75] *Edmunds v. Robinson* (1885) 29 Ch.D. 170.

[76] *Belfield v. Bourne* [1894] 1 Ch. 521, explaining *Tattersall v. Groote* (1800) 2 Bos. & Pul. 131.

[77] See, as to the powers of an arbitrator, the Arbitration Act 1996, s.48 and *supra*, paras 10–272, 10–279 *et seq.*

[78] See *supra*, para. 23–128.

[79] Partnership Act 1890, s.38, *supra*, paras 13–62 *et seq.*

[80] [2008] EWCA Civ. 1417 (Lawtel 12/12/08). See further *infra*, para. 25–25.

[81] See *Popat v. Shonchhatra* [1997] 1 W.L.R. 1367, 1374, as to the size of the partners' shares (albeit not in the context of s.38).

[82] As in *Emerson v. Estate of Emerson* [2004] 1 B.C.L.C. 575 (CA); see also *supra*, paras 20–46, 23–126.

[83] See *supra*, paras 10–84, 13–72; also *infra*, para. 25–25.

Different considerations will, however, arise where the winding up is delayed and, in the interim, the business is carried on by one or more of the former partners to the exclusion of the others or where the entitlement of a deceased or outgoing partner in respect of his share is not satisfied on the due date.[84]

As an introduction to the law as it stood prior to the Partnership Act 1890, Lord Lindley analysed the circumstances in which a person who has employed another person's property in his trade may be rendered liable to account for any profits made thereby. This analysis has not been retained.[85]

Position prior to the Partnership Act 1890

The right of a former partner to an account of profits where the business was carried on following a dissolution was well settled prior to the Partnership Act 1890. Thus, after citing the more important cases, which established the nature of that right following a dissolution brought about by the death[86] or bankruptcy[87] of a partner, Lord Lindley went on: **25–23**

> "The rule established in these cases has been applied in a variety of instances; *e.g.* where a managing partner had continued the business after the period fixed for the dissolution and winding up of the partnership[88]; where a partner had become lunatic and the firm had been dissolved, but the business had been continued by the other partners, and they had not paid out the capital of the lunatic partner[89]; where partners had agreed to dissolve and to have the partnership business wound up, and its assets got in and converted by a third person, and one of the partners nevertheless carried on the business in the meantime for his own benefit[90]; where a mining partnership had been dissolved, but one of the partners had obtained a renewed lease of the mine, and had continued to work it for his own benefit."[91]

Partnership Act 1890, section 42

The treatment of post-dissolution profits is now governed by section 42 of the Partnership Act 1890, which provides as follows: **25–24**

---

[84] In the latter case, there is no need to prove impropriety or fraud on the part of the partners who continue to carry on the business: *Oddy v. Fry* [1998] 1 V.A.R. 142. Equally, it would now seem that, in such a case, it is not possible to seek interest under the Senior Courts Act 1981, s.35A (formerly the Supreme Court Act 1981: Constitutional Reform Act 2005, Sched. 11, Pt 1, para. 1(1)): see *supra*, para. 20–41 and *infra*, para. 25–43.

[85] The relevant passage is to be found in 15th edition of this work, at pp. 719–723. Note that its omission from subsequent editions appears to have been regretted by the Court of Appeal in *Hopper v. Hopper, supra*, at [45].

[86] *Crawshay v. Collins* (1808) 15 Ves.Jr. 218; (1820) 1 J. & W. 267; (1826) 2 Russ. 325. Lord Eldon later pointed out that the decision reported at 15 Ves.Jr. 218 did not go as far was commonly supposed: see *Brown v. De Tastet* (1821) Jac. 284, 297; *Cook v. Collingridge* (1822) Jac. 607, 622; *Crawshay v. Collins* (1826) 2 Russ. 325, 330.

[87] *Yates v. Finn* (1880) 13 Ch.D. 839; see also *Brown v. De Tastet* (1821) Jac. 284 (the decision in which was apparently affirmed by the House of Lords, although the claimant later abandoned his claim, having found it impossible to implement the decree: see *Docker v. Somes* (1834) 2 M. & K. 655, 658). And see *Booth v. Parkes* (1829) Beatty 444; *Featherstonhaugh v. Turner* (1858) 25 Beav. 382; *Smith v. Everett* (1859) 27 Beav. 446.

[88] *Parsons v. Hayward* (1862) 4 De G.F. & J. 474.

[89] *Mellersh v. Keen* (1859) 27 Beav. 236.

[90] *Turner v. Major* (1862) 3 Giff. 442.

[91] *Featherstonhaugh v. Fenwick* (1810) 17 Ves.Jr. 298. See also *Clements v. Hall* (1858) 2 De.G. & J. 173.

"42.—(1) Where any member of a firm has died or otherwise ceased to be a partner, and the surviving or continuing partners carry on the business of the firm with its capital or assets without any final settlement of accounts as between the firm and the outgoing partner[92] or his estate, then, in the absence of any agreement to the contrary, the outgoing partner or his estate is entitled at the option of himself or his representatives to such share of the profits[93] made since the dissolution as the Court may find to be attributable to the use of his share of the partnership assets,[94] or to interest at the rate of five per cent. per annum[95] on the amount of his share of the partnership assets.

(2) Provided that where by the partnership contract an option is given to surviving or continuing partners to purchase the interest of a deceased or outgoing partner, and the option is duly exercised, the estate of the deceased partner, or the outgoing partner or his estate, as the case may be, is not entitled to any further or other share of profits; but if any partner assuming to act in exercise of the option does not in all material respects comply with the terms thereof, he is liable to account under the foregoing provisions of this section."

25–25   In *Hopper v. Hopper*,[96] Etherton L.J. sought to summarise the function of this section in the following terms:

"[*It*] governs what happens in relation to post-dissolution[97] profits if (1) the business of the former partnership is continued by one of more of the former partners, not for the purposes of winding up the former partnership, but for the personal benefit of those continuing to run the business, and (2) those persons do not include all the former partners and the personal representatives of the deceased partner, but (3) there are retained within the continuing business all or part of the shares of the assets of the former partnership to which those non-participants in the continuing business were entitled (in their personal capacity or as personal representatives) on dissolution of the former partnership."

If the partners carrying on the business were doing so pursuant to section 38 of the Partnership Act 1890,[98] there would be no doubt as to the entitlement of the

---

[92] This expression is capable of including any partner who does not participate in the carrying on of the business following the dissolution: *Hopper v. Hopper* [2008] EWCA Civ. 1417 (Lawtel 12/12/08) (CA) at [49].

[93] See, as to the meaning of "profits", *Barclays Bank Trust Co. Ltd. v. Bluff* [1982] Ch. 172, *infra*, para. 25–32; also *Chandroutie v. Gajadhar* [1987] A.C. 147, 154C (PC); *Popat v. Shonchhatra* [1997] 1 W.L.R. 1367, 1374H (CA).

[94] See, as to the meaning of the expression "his share in the partnership assets", *Sandhu v. Gill* [2006] Ch. 456 (CA) at [18] *et seq. per* Neuberger L.J. See further, *infra*, para. 25–29. The share clearly includes a share in any goodwill: *Manley v. Sartori* [1927] 1 Ch. 157.

[95] This rate has remained unchanged, despite judicial and Law Commission prompting: see *Sobell v. Boston* [1975] 1 W.L.R. 1587, 1593 *per* Goff J.; the Law Commission Report "Law of Contract: Report on Interest", Part VI, para. 245, reproduced at (1978) 122 S.J. 468 and its Report on Partnership Law of November 2003 (Law Com No. 283), paras 8–53, 8–74. And see *infra*, para. 25–30.

[96] [2008] EWCA Civ. 1417 (Lawtel 12/12/08) (CA) at [48].

[97] It goes without saying that there must be a general (and not merely technical) dissolution before the section is engaged, subject to the scenarios considered, *infra*, paras 25–37, 25–38. This was confirmed in *HLB Kidsons v. Lloyd's Underwriters* [2009] 1 All E.R. (Comm) 760, at [16] *per* Judge Mackie Q.C. (sitting as a judge of the Chancery Division), albeit that the point appears not to have been fully canvassed before him.

[98] See *supra*, paras 13–62 *et seq.*

other partners or the estate of a deceased partner to a share of any profits made, but whether such profits are distributable in the same way as prior to the dissolution is, in the current editor's view, more questionable.[99]

Nature of the option under section 42(1)

Although the partner whose entitlement has not been paid out[100] theoretically has an option to take a share of profits or interest at five per cent in all cases, that option will in fact be exercisable only where the continuing partners can be shown to have derived profits from the use of his share and where that partner does actually have a share in the assets in question.

Profits derived from use of the share

Save in the most obvious case, *i.e.* where the business has made no profits whatsoever,[101] this is not as straightforward a question as it might seem, as Lord Lindley explained prior to the Act, when considering the rights of the executors of a deceased partner[102]:

> "It is very easy to say [*the share of profits to which the executors are entitled*] can be calculated by the rule of three—as the whole capital is to the whole profits, so is the late partner's share in the capital to his share of the profits—but this assumes that the profits in question have been made by capital only. Profits, and very large profits, may be made by skill, and an extensive connection, with little or no capital; and even if there be capital, the profits may be attributable less to it than to other matters, and it may be impossible to determine with any precision the extent to which the capital has contributed to the realisation of the profits obtained.[103] Special inquiries on this subject, therefore, are almost always necessary,[104] and if it can be shown that, having regard to the nature of the business or other circumstances, the profits which have been made cannot be justly attributed to the use of the capital or assets of the late partner, his prima facie right to share such profits will be effectually rebutted."

In *Willet v. Blanford*,[105] Wigram V.-C., concluding that it was not possible to lay down any general rules in this area, observed that:

> " . . . the nature of the trade, the manner of carrying it on, the capital employed, the state of the account between the partnership and the deceased partner at the time of

25–26

25–27

25–28

---

[99] This was the assumption in *Hopper v. Hopper, supra,* at [47], presumably made by reference to the statement of principle *supra,* para. 25–22, but is this correct? See *supra,* paras 10–84, 13–72.

[100] By definition, such a partner has not been invited to participate in the carrying on of the business following the dissolution and is, thus, an "outgoing partner" within the meaning of s.42(1): *Hopper v. Hopper, supra,* at [49].

[101] As in *Re Arlidge* [1894] 2 Ch. 97, which concerned a claim for remuneration by the *surviving* partner.

[102] This passage in fact *preceded* Lord Lindley's consideration of the treatment of post-dissolution profits *stricto sensu.*

[103] See *Featherstonhaugh v. Turner* (1858) 25 Beav. 382, *infra,* para. 25–28, n. 108; also *Page v. Ratcliffe* (1897) 75 L.T. 371; *Oddy v. Fry* [1998] 1 V.R. 142.

[104] See, for example, *Manley v. Sartori* [1927] 1 Ch. 157.

[105] (1842) 1 Hare 253.

his death, and the conduct of the parties after his death, may materially affect the rights of the parties."[106]

Thus, in *Wedderburn v. Wedderburn*,[107] it was demonstrated that the greater part of the profits realised by successive firms following a partner's death were attributable not to the surplus assets of the original firm, in which he had an interest, but to the goodwill and business connection of that firm, in which he had *no* interest,[108] and to the reputation, skill and ability of the partners in each successive firm. On that basis, the deceased partner's estate was held not to be entitled to a share of such profits.[109] *Simpson v. Chapman*[110] was a somewhat similar case, although there it was shown that the deceased partner had no capital in the firm (in the ordinary sense of that word)[111] and, moreover, it appears merely to have been *assumed* that the goodwill belonged to the surviving partners.[112]

Equally, when dealing with the dissolution of a newsagents' business in *Popat v. Shonchhatra*,[113] Neuberger J. did not appear to be troubled by such concerns and accepted that, subject to an allowance to the defendant for his troubles in carrying on the business,[114] the balance of the profits should be shared between the former partners in their profit shares without further inquiry.[115] This decision no doubt reflected the largely mechanical nature of the business in question.

Quantum of the non-participating partner's share in the assets

25–29   In *Sandhu v. Gill*,[116] the Court of Appeal held that a partner cannot maintain a claim for a share of profits (or, for that matter, interest) under section 42(1) if his share in the partnership assets would, based on an account taken as at the date of dissolution, be nil. Although Neuberger L.J. was troubled by the apparent need to carry out a notional valuation exercise as at the date of dissolution, whenever

---

[106] Lord Lindley added that "This conclusion of the Vice-Chancellor was entirely in accordance with previous decisions" and referred, in particular, to Lord Eldon's observations on *Crawshay v. Collins* (1808) 15 Ves.Jr. 218 in *Brown v. De Tastet* (1821) Jac. 284, 297; *Cook v. Collingridge* (1822) Jac. 607, 622; *Crawshay v. Collins* (1826) 2 Russ. 325, 330.

[107] (1856) 22 Beav. 84; as to the original order, see (1836) 2 Keen 722; (1838) 4 Myl. & Cr. 41.

[108] This was the result of an express provision in the agreement. *cf. Featherstonhaugh v. Turner* (1858) 25 Beav. 382, where an inquiry was directed with a view to ascertaining whether any and, if so, what profits made since the date of death were attributable to persons who had become customers by reason of the deceased partner having been a member of the firm; also *Manley v. Sartori* [1927] 1 Ch. 157. And see *Gordon v. Gonda* [1955] 1 W.L.R. 885; *Pathirana v. Pathirana* [1967] 1 A.C. 233 (PC); *Oddy v. Fry, supra*.

[109] In fact, Sir John Romilly M.R. appears to have accepted the entitlement of the estate to a share of profits derived from *other* sources, but he effectively held that this would be covered by interest on the value of the deceased's share: see (1856) 22 Beav. 84, 121.

[110] (1853) 4 De G.M. & G. 154. Lord Lindley noted that "This case is the more important as the non-liability to account for subsequent profits was decided on the hearing of the cause."

[111] Although, at the time of the partner's death, the firm's assets exceeded its liabilities, one of those assets was in fact a debt due from the deceased partner; if no account had been taken of that debt, the firm would have been insolvent.

[112] Such an assumption will rarely be justified: see *supra*, para. 10–203.

[113] [1995] 1 W.L.R. 908.

[114] See further, as to such allowances, *supra*, paras 20–46, 23–126 and *infra*, para. 25–33.

[115] [1995] 1 W.L.R. 913H. The division of post-dissolution revenue profits was not challenged on the appeal: see [1997] 1 W.L.R. 1367, 1373H–1374A.

[116] [2006] Ch. 456 (CA). This decision in fact endorsed views expressed by H.H. Judge Behrens in *Taylor v. Grier (No. 3)*, May 12, 2003 (Lawtel 20/5/2003), although the court made no reference thereto. See also *Duncan v. MFV Marigold PD 145* 2006 S.L.T. 975 (OH).

the subsection is sought to be invoked,[117] the current editor submits that this is to ignore the fact that, in most cases, such a claim will be actively pursued, in terms of quantum, only when *finalising* the dissolution accounts. At that stage the net financial position of each former partner should be fairly clear. *A fortiori* in the case of a claim for interest.

Other problems associated with the option under section 42(1)

As is apparent from the preceding paragraphs, in many cases the right to opt for a share of profits may be more theoretical than real. To this must be added the practical difficulties associated with an exercise of that right, as expressed by Lord Lindley in the following passage written prior to the Act:

25–30

" . . . owing to the extreme difficulty of taking an account of subsequent profits, so far as they are attributable only to one particular source, the tendency of the courts . . . appears to be rather in favour of not exercising than of exercising the power alluded to, except in cases of gross fraud or breach of trust."

He then observed in a footnote:

"Judgments for an account of profits after dissolution are fearfully oppressive; and the writer is not aware of any instance in which such a judgment has been worked out and has resulted beneficially to the person in whose favour it was made."[118]

It was these practical difficulties which prompted Lord Lindley, in his Supplement on the Partnership Act 1890, to express regret that the court was not empowered to award interest at a rate greater than five per cent. An increase in that rate has been suggested over the years,[119] although fluctuations in interest rates tend to alter the perspective from time to time.

25–31

Equally, it would be wrong to infer from the views expressed by Lord Lindley that such problems will arise in all cases. Thus, in the case of a small retail-based business, it may be a straightforward matter to apply the section, as is demonstrated by the decision in *Popat v. Shonchhatra*.[120]

Any doubt which may have existed as to who would qualify as an "outgoing partner" for the purposes of the sub-section were resolved by the Court of Appeal in *Hopper v. Hopper*,[121] which held that it includes *any* partner[122] who does not participate in the carrying on of the former partnership business following the dissolution.

---

[117] [2006] Ch. 456, at [53].

[118] Unaccountably, this comment was relegated to a footnote. And see also *Hugh Stevenson and Sons v. Aktiengesellschaft fur Cartonnagen-Industrie* [1917] 1 K.B. 842, 849 *per* Swinfen Eady L.J.

[119] See *Sobell v. Boston* [1975] 1 W.L.R. 1587, 1593 *per* Goff J.; also the Law Commission Report "Law of Contract: Report on Interest", Part VI, para. 245, reproduced at (1978) 122 S.J. 468 and its Report on Partnership Law of November 2003 (Law Com No. 283), paras 8–53, 8–74. And see *infra*, para. 25–43.

[120] [1995] 1 W.L.R. 908, 913H–914D. This aspect of the case was not pursued in the Court of Appeal: see [1997] 1 W.L.R. 1367, 1373H–1374A. See also, *supra*, para. 25–28.

[121] [2008] EWCA Civ 1417 (Lawtel 12/12/08).

[122] Including the estate of a deceased partner.

Capital profits

25–32   Section 42(1) of the Partnership Act 1890 has no application where the profits realised by the continuing or surviving partners are of a *capital* nature. This was established in *Barclays Bank Trust Co. Ltd v. Bluff*.[123] There a father and son carried on a farming business in partnership. The father died, thus dissolving the firm. There was a substantial delay in winding up the partnership affairs, during which time the son continued to carry on the business and the value of the farm appreciated considerably. It was held that the father's executor was entitled, at its election, to interest at the rate of five per cent on the father's share of the partnership assets or to a share of the profits accruing in the ordinary course of carrying on the business since the date of death, *i.e.* profits arising from the use of the farm land and buildings, but that those profits did not include any capital profits which might be realised on a sale of the land and buildings, to a share of which the father's estate was entitled quite apart from the provisions of section 42.[124] It should, however, be noted that the position might have been different if the land and buildings had been trading stock.[125]

To the same effect was the decision in *Emerson v. Estate of Emerson*,[126] where it was held that compensation received for the slaughter of livestock following the outbreak of foot and mouth disease constituted capital profits, so that section 42 had no application.

Remuneration for services

25–33   Prior to the Partnership Act 1890, Lord Lindley pointed out that:

> " . . . in taking an account of subsequent profits, the partner by whose exertions they have been made is usually allowed compensation for his trouble,[127] unless he is, in the proper sense of the word, a trustee, and guilty of a breach of trust, when no such compensation is allowed."[128]

---

[123] [1982] Ch. 172, where the unsatisfactory Irish decision of *Meagher v. Meagher* [1961] I.R. 96 was distinguished. The facts in *Meagher v. Meagher* were similar to those in *Barclays Bank Trust Co. Ltd. v. Bluff*, save that the premises in question were part of the trading stock of the firm and had been sold prior to the action. The Supreme Court of Eire held that: (1) the value of the deceased partner's share at the date of dissolution should be based on the actual proceeds of sale with such deductions as the facts might justify; (2) the increased value of the assets should be treated as profits; and (3) any interest payable under the Partnership Act 1890, s.42(1) should be calculated on the value of the deceased partner's share as at the date of his death. However, the difficulties inherent in the decision were avoided when it came to the point of ascertaining the value of the deceased partner's share, since the court made no attempt to separate the capital and profit elements therein.

[124] See also *Chandroutie v. Gajadhar* [1987] A.C. 147 (PC); *Popat v. Shonchhatra* [1997] 1 W.L.R. 1367 (CA); *Sandhu v. Gill* [2005] 1 W.L.R. 1979 at [7] and [2006] Ch. 456 (CA) at [10] *per* Neuberger L.J. and [102] *per* Mummery L.J. *cf.* the position of a retired partner: see *Sobell v. Boston* [1975] 1 W.L.R. 1587.

[125] See [1982] Ch. 172, 183 *per* H.E. Francis Q.C. (sitting as a deputy judge of the Chancery Division).

[126] [2004] 1 B.C.L.C. 575 (CA).

[127] *Brown v. De Tastet* (1819) Jac. 284; *Yates v. Finn* (1880) 13 Ch.D. 839. See also *Cook v. Collingridge* (1822) Jac. 623; *Featherstonhaugh v. Turner* (1858) 25 Beav. 382; *Mellersh v. Keen* (1859) 27 Beav. 236.

[128] *Burden v. Burden* (1813) 1 Ves. & Bea. 170; *Stocken v. Dawson* (1843) 6 Beav. 371 and (1848) 17 L.J.Ch. 282. But see *Cook v. Collingridge* (1822) Jac. 607, 622–623 *per* Lord Eldon.

Such an allowance is still afforded where an order is made under section 42.[129]

Election to take interest in lieu of profits

If a claim to a share of profits is not sustainable[130] or the outgoing partner or his estate so elects, simple interest will be payable at the rate of five per cent, a rate which has remained unchanged over the years.[131]   **25–34**

An election for the payment of interest will not, of itself, deprive the outgoing partner or his estate of his rightful share of any increase in the value of the partnership assets (save, perhaps, for stock in trade) between the date of dissolution and the date of sale. This was clearly established in *Barclays Bank Trust Co. Ltd. v. Bluff.*[132]

Personal representatives unable to sue

Although the rights conferred by section 42(1) of the Partnership Act 1890 ought properly to be enforced by the deceased partner's personal representatives, if this is not, for whatever reason, possible, the persons interested in his estate may do so.[133]   **25–35**

Alien enemy

Where a partnership is dissolved by the outbreak of war,[134] any partner who is treated as an alien enemy will not be deprived of his rights under section 42(1) of the Partnership Act 1890, but will not be in a position to enforce those rights until the hostilities are over.[135]   **25–36**

Exclusion of right to profits

It is clear that the right of election under section 42(1) of the Partnership Act 1890 may be excluded by the partnership agreement.[136] Moreover, it is also provided that the right to a share of profits is not available where the continuing   **25–37**

---

[129] See the Partnership Act 1890, s.46; *Page v. Ratcliffe* (1897) 75 L.T. 371; *Manley v. Sartori* [1927] 1 Ch. 157; *Popat v. Shonchhatra* [1995] 1 W.L.R. 908, 913H *per* Neuberger J. (this was not challenged in the Court of Appeal: see [1997] 1 W.L.R. 1367, 1373H–1374A); *Ryder v. Frohlich* [2004] NSWCA 472 at [202]; *Sandhu v. Gill* [2005] 1 W.L.R. 1979 at [10] and [2006] Ch. 456 (CA) at [8], [102]. See also *Castle v. Castle* [1951] G.L.R. 541. Equally, if there are *no* profits, there will be no option to take a share of profits and no allowance can be made: see *supra*, paras 25–26, 25–27. See also *Castle v. Castle* [1951] G.L.R. 541. Note that, whilst in *Emerson v. Estate of Emerson*, *supra*, an allowance was made in the amount of the loss borne by the surviving partner in carrying on the business, this was *not* a case falling with s.42.

[130] See *supra*, paras 25–26 *et seq.*

[131] It has been suggested that the rate should be increased: see *supra*, para. 25–30, n. 119.

[132] [1982] Ch. 172. See further, *supra*, para. 25–32.

[133] See *Travis v. Milne* (1851) 9 Hare 141; *Beningfield v. Baxter* (1887) 12 App.Cas. 167, 178–179. And see *infra*, para. 26–34.

[134] See *supra*, paras 4–04 *et seq.*

[135] *Hugh Stevenson & Sons Ltd. v. Aktiengesellschaft für Cartonnagen-Industrie* [1918] A.C. 239; *Gordon v. Gonda* [1955] 1 W.L.R. 885.

[136] The subsection contains the words "in the absence of any agreement to the contrary": see *supra*, para. 25–24.

or surviving partners have an option to acquire the outgoing or deceased partner's share, provided that the option is duly exercised *and* its terms subsequently adhered to. In his Supplement on the Act, Lord Lindley explained that this rule:

> " ... is in accordance with the statement of the law by Lord Cairns in *Vyse v. Foster*.[137] [*Subsection (2)*] deals with the case of an option to purchase, as in *Willett v. Blanford*,[138] and not with an executed contract to purchase, which was the case in *Vyse v. Foster*. In the latter case the continuing partners will not in the absence of fraud be liable to account for profits, unless by neglecting to fulfil some condition, or not complying with some stipulation of the essence of the contract, or otherwise, they repudiate[139] or give the representatives of the deceased partner[140] a right to rescind the contract."

25–38   In *Vyse v. Foster*,[141] the agreement provided that, on the death of a partner, the value of his share should be ascertained and paid, with interest, by instalments over a two year period. One partner died leaving three executors, one of whom was a surviving partner. The deceased's share was ascertained but, instead of being paid out as contemplated by the agreement, was retained in the business, which was carried on for many years, first by one and then by two of the executors, with other persons. Interest was paid on the deceased's share and all the beneficiaries interested in his estate, except the claimant (who was minor), acquiesced in this arrangement. The claimant, having attained the vesting age specified in the will, demanded payment of her share of the estate and the profits made by its employment in the business. She was offered the principal sum due to her, together with compound interest at the rate of five per cent, but no share of profits. She commenced proceedings solely against the executors, seeking an account of the profits and succeeded at first instance, but the decision was overturned on appeal. Whilst recognising that there had been a technical breach of trust, the Court of Appeal held that the executors had at all times acted with perfect fairness and were not bound to account for any profits received by them. This decision was affirmed by the House of Lords, who went on to analyse the distinction between a contract and an option to purchase a deceased partner's share.[142]

---

[137] (1874) L.R. 7 H.L. 318, 329.

[138] (1842) 1 Hare 253.

[139] Note that the doctrine of repudiation would be capable of applying at this stage: see *supra*, para. 24–08.

[140] An outgoing partner will, of course, be in the same position.

[141] (1872) L.R. 8 Ch.App. 309, affirmed (1874) L.R. 7 H.L. 318. Lord Lindley pointed out that: "The decision in this case is extremely important, as it decided, 1, that the clause in the partnership articles was binding both on the executors of the deceased partner and on the surviving partners, although one of them was also an executor; 2, that the amount due to the estate of the deceased was in effect a loan to the survivors, and its non-payment at the time and in manner prescribed by the articles of partnership did not entitle the plaintiff to any profits, but only to interest; 3, that even if the plaintiff's claim to profits could have been sustained, the executor who was not a partner would not have been liable for such profits; and 4, that the executors who were partners would not have been liable for more profits than they respectively themselves received." Note also the subsequent proceedings reported at (1875) L.R. 10 Ch.App. 236.

[142] (1874) L.R. 7 H.L. 334–335 *per* Lord Cairns, 337–339 *per* Lord Hatherley; see also *Hordern v. Hordern* [1910] A.C. 465.

It follows that any provision for the automatic accruer of an outgoing partner's share[143] will necessarily exclude his rights under section 42(1).

Option to purchase

It would seem that the right to a share of profits or interest may be exercisable **25–39** in respect of the period between the date of dissolution and the date on which the option is exercised, although much will depend on the precise terms of the agreement.[144] Whilst section 42(2) also appears to preserve the outgoing partner's right to *interest* even where there is an option which is duly exercised,[145] the current editor considers that this right will normally be excluded by necessary implication.[146]

Position where surviving partners are also personal representatives

Where the executors or trustees of the deceased partner's will or the admin- **25–40** istrators of his estate[147] are surviving partners or are admitted to the partnership after the date of his death, it would seem that the rights of the legatees or next-of-kin are strictly analogous to those which exist under section 42 of the Partnership Act 1890. Writing prior to the Act, Lord Lindley summarised these rights as follows:

> "The right of the *cestui que trust* against his trustee in these cases is to an account of profits made by him by the use of the trust property, or at the option of the *cestui que trust* to simple interest at £5 per cent.[148]; or in special cases to compound interest."[149]

In his Supplement on the Act, he added:

> "If the partners are also trustees and bound to accumulate, compound interest may be charged against them, but the liability is a liability *qua* trustee and not *qua* partner and is therefore beyond the scope of this section."

Save in such cases, it is largely academic whether the proceedings against such partners are framed under section 42(1) or otherwise.

---

[143] See *supra*, para. 10–151.

[144] A similar point was canvassed in *Kelly v. Denman* (an unreported decision of Rimer J. in May 1996, discussed at [1996] 11 Comm. Lawyer 74), where the agreement provided that an outgoing partner's share would only accrue to the continuing partners if he or they so elected. Thus, in substance, it amounted to a put and call option. No election had been made within the time limit specified. Rimer J. declined to decide whether time was of the essence for such an election, but appeared to accept that a s.42 claim would, in principle, lie whether or not such an election was made.

[145] The subsection is quite specific: "the outgoing partner or his estate . . . is not entitled to any further or other share of profits": see *supra*, para. 25–24.

[146] *e.g.* an option which provides for the outgoing partner's share to be paid by instalments without interest would clearly be a contrary agreement excluding the operation of *ibid.* subs.(1).

[147] Lord Lindley dealt with this subject primarily in terms of executors and trustees but the administrators of a deceased partner will, of course, be in no different position.

[148] *Heathcote v. Hulme* (1819) 1 Jac. & W. 122.

[149] *Jones v. Foxall* (1852) 15 Beav. 388; *Williams v. Powell* (1852) 15 Beav. 461; *Vyse v. Foster* (1874) L.R. 7 H.L. 318, 346 *per* Lord Selborne. Note also, in this context, *Roxburgh Dinardo & Partners' Judicial Factor v. Dinardo* 1993 S.L.T. 16 (2nd Div.).

Extent of liability to account

25–41   In cases of this type, the personal representatives are not liable to account for any profits other than those which they have actually received. Although originally subject to some doubt,[150] this was decided in *Vyse v. Foster*.[151] It follows that, if they are not the only surviving partners, all such partners should be joined as parties to the proceedings.[152] However, the effective joinder of partners admitted *after* the date of death will be dependent on establishing that they are implicated in the breach of trust, as in *Flockton v. Bunning*.[153] The following account of this case was prepared by Lord Lindley from the shorthand writer's notes[154]:

> " . . . a partner died, leaving his wife his executrix, and having directed her to get in his estate and invest it for the benefit of herself and children. She wound up the partnership in which her husband was engaged, but continued to carry on the business with his capital, in partnership with other persons, who knew that in so doing she and they were committing a breach of trust.[155] A bill was filed by some of the children against her and her co-partners, seeking to make them jointly and severally liable for the trust estate employed in the business, and for the profits made by its use; and a decree to that effect was made and was affirmed on an appeal by the wife's partners. This case was decided on the principle that the wife's partners were clearly implicated in the breach of trust committed by her, and were jointly and severally responsible with her for the trust estate and all the profits made thereby. The widow's capital was trust property; there was no loan as in *Stroud v. Gwyer*,[156] but the widow's capital became part of the capital of the firm; and she and her co-partners wrongfully traded with it.[157] Both L.J. Wood and L.J. Selwyn agreed that a mere loan, although in breach of trust, would not involve liability to account for profits, but that trust property which was traded with by a trustee in partnership with others could not be regarded as a loan."[158]

25–42   *Cook v. Collingridge*[159] is a more extreme case. There the executors of a deceased partner sold his share to the surviving partners, who included one of the executors; those partners then proceeded to resell the share to another of the executors. A legatee succeeded in getting the sale set aside and the surviving partners were ordered to account for profits made since the date of death, even though the proceeds from the sale of the share were not retained in the business.

[150] See *Palmer v. Mitchell* (1809) 2 M. & K. 672, note; *Docker v. Somes* (1834) 2 M. & K. 655; *Macdonald v. Richardson* (1858) 1 Giff. 81; *Townend v. Townend* (1859) 1 Giff. 201.

[151] (1874) L.R. 7 H.L. 318, 333–334 *per* Lord Cairns.

[152] The claim against the non-executor/trustee partners will, of course, be brought under the Partnership Act 1890, s.42(1).

[153] (1868) L.R. 8 Ch.App. 323, note.

[154] Lord Lindley was, in fact, counsel for the appellants and his account of the case differs marginally from that in the report.

[155] In fact, she agreed to indemnify them against the consequences.

[156] (1860) 28 Beav. 130.

[157] *cf. Vyse v. Foster* (1874) L.R. 7 H.L. 318, *supra*, para. 25–38.

[158] See also *Travis v. Milne* (1851) 9 Hare 141, where no account of profits was sought: see *ibid.* pp. 147–148.

[159] (1822) Jac. 607; see also the decree in (1825) 27 Beav. 456. *Stocken v. Dawson* (1848) 17 L.J.Ch. 282 was a somewhat similar case.

Interest under the Senior Courts Act 1981[160]

It has already been seen[161] that it is doubtful to what extent section 43 of the **25-43** Partnership Act 1890 will apply in the case of a *general* dissolution. Although in earlier editions of this work the current editor expressed the view that, notwithstanding the more general application of section 42, in a case falling within section 43, the outgoing partner might be able to claim interest under section 35A of the Senior Courts 1981[162] in lieu of his entitlement under section 42, it appears that such a claim cannot be sustained.[163]

4. DISTRIBUTION OF ASSETS AND ADJUSTMENT OF ACCOUNTS

Importance of agreement

Before the winding up of the partnership affairs can be concluded, it is **25-44** necessary to complete the partnership accounts by incorporating any final adjustments which may be required to reflect the respective rights, entitlements and obligations of each partner.[164] At this point it will be necessary to pay close attention to the terms of the partnership agreement,[165] as well as to the partners' subsequent conduct, even though this is not always decisive. As Lord Lindley explained prior to the Partnership Act 1890:

" . . . an express agreement with reference to the taking of accounts may be, and frequently is, only applicable to the case of a continuing partnership, and may not be intended to be observed on a final dissolution of the firm, or even on the retirement of one of its members.[166] A similar observation applies to the mode in which the partners themselves have been in the habit of keeping their accounts: that which has been done for the purpose of sharing annual profits or losses is by no means

---

[160] Formerly the Supreme Court Act 1981: Constitutional Reform Act 2005, Sched. 11, Pt 1, para. 1(1).

[161] See *supra*, paras 19–35, 23–34; also *infra*, para. 26–03.

[162] Similarly in the case of the County Courts Act 1984, s.69, as amended by the Courts and Legal Services Act 1990, Sched. 18, para. 46.

[163] *Williams v. Williams* [1999] C.L.Y. 4095. See further *supra*, paras 19–12, 20–41.

[164] This represents an obligation of all the partners under the Partnership Act 1890, s.28: see *Winning v. Cunningham* 2009 GWD 01–19 (Sh.Ct.). For an example of a case in which such final adjustments were made, see *Stocking v. Montila* [2005] EWHC 2210 (Ch) (Lawtel 24/10/05). It goes without saying that account must be taken of any sums due *from* a partner to the firm: *ibid.* And see *supra*, paras 19–24 *et seq.*

[165] In *Faulks v. Faulks* [1992] 1 E.G.L.R. 9, the agreement provided for a tenancy of certain land (which enjoyed the benefit of a milk quota) to revert to the ownership of a particular partner in the event of a dissolution. It was held that because milk quota cannot exist independently of the land to which it relates, the quota could not be treated as a partnership asset and its value fell to be ignored on the dissolution. However, this decision must be read subject to the views expressed by Jacob J. in *Swift v. Dairywise Farms Ltd.* [2000] 1 W.L.R. 1177 (although an appeal from that decision ultimately went off on other grounds: see [2003] 1 W.L.R. 1606): see further, *supra*, para. 18–18. There can be no such doubts over the existence of work in progress: *Browell v. Goodyear*, October 24, 2000; *cf.* the unsatisfactory decision in *Robertson v. Brent* [1972] N.Z.L.R. 406, noted *supra*, para. 23–201.

[166] See *supra*, paras 10–76, 10–163 *et seq.*; also *Watson v. Haggitt* [1928] A.C. 127; and note *Re London India Rubber Co.* (1868) L.R. 5 Eq. 519; *Re Bridgewater Navigation Co.* [1891] 2 Ch. 317, varied *sub. nom. Birch v. Cropper* (1889) 14 App.Cas. 525. *cf. Re Barber* (1870) L.R. 5 Ch.App. 687.

necessarily a precedent to be followed when a partnership account has to be finally closed."[167]

Partnership Act 1890, section 44

25–45   Subject to any contrary agreement, the rules which govern the final settlement of a partnership account on dissolution are contained in section 44 of the Partnership Act 1890,[168] which provides as follows:

> "44. In settling accounts between the partners after a dissolution of partnership, the following rules shall, subject to any agreement, be observed:
>
> (a) Losses, including losses and deficiencies of capital,[169] shall be paid first out of profits, next out of capital, and lastly, if necessary, by the partners individually in the proportion in which they were entitled to share profits:
>
> (b) The assets of the firm including the sums, if any, contributed by the partners to make up losses or deficiencies of capital, shall be applied in the following manner and order:
>
>> 1. In paying the debts and liabilities of the firm to persons who are not partners therein:
>> 2. In paying to each partner rateably what is due from the firm to him for advances as distinguished from capital[170]:
>> 3. In paying to each partner rateably what is due from the firm to him in respect of capital:
>> 4. The ultimate residue,[171] if any, shall be divided among the partners in the proportion in which profits are divisible."[172]

Although it is traditionally said that only debts and advances have priority over the costs of dissolution proceedings,[173] it would seem that each partner's capital entitlement should also be taken into account before determining how any excess costs are to be borne.[174]

Application of the section

25–46   Section 44(b) requires the partners to proceed through each of the four stages in turn, and to identify whether there is a deficiency of assets at any of the first

---

[167] *e.g.* goodwill rarely, if ever, features in a firm's annual accounts but may, nevertheless, be one of its most valuable assets: see *Wade v. Jenkins* (1860) 2 Giff. 509; *Steuart v. Gladstone* (1878) 10 Ch.D. 626, 659 *per* Jessel M.R. See also *supra*, paras 10–76, 10–163 *et seq.* Where an asset has been realised, regard must naturally be had to its actual rather than its book value: *Re Bridgewater Navigation Co.* [1891] 2 Ch. 317, 329 *per* Lindley L.J.

[168] See generally, as to this section, *Duncan v. The MFV Marigold PD145* 2006 S.L.T. 975 (OH) at [19] *et seq. per* Lord Reed.

[169] There can be no such deficiency caused by a partner's own failure to contribute capital: *Re Ward* [1985] 2 N.Z.L.R. 352, 355.

[170] It follows that a partner will have no independent cause of action to recover an advance: *Green v. Hertzog* [1954] 1 W.L.R. 1309. See also *supra*, paras 19–06, 22–05.

[171] Before quantifying this ultimate residue, it may be necessary to ascertain whether a share of any post-dissolution income is carried by the partners' capital contributions: see *supra*, para. 20–35 and *infra*, para. 25–47.

[172] In his Supplement on the Partnership Act 1890, Lord Lindley rightly pointed out that the section follows "almost word for word" the statement of the law set out in the 5th ed. of this work at p. 402. See further, as to the position prior to the Act, *Crawshay v. Collins* (1826) 2 Russ. 325; *Richardson v. Bank of England* (1838) 4 Myl. & Cr. 165; *Binney v. Mutrie* (1886) 12 App.Cas. 160.

[173] See *Austin v. Jackson* (1879) 11 Ch.D. 942, note; *Potter v. Jackson* (1880) 13 Ch.D. 845.

[174] *Ross v. White* [1894] 3 Ch. 326. See also *supra*, para. 23–122.

three stages. If there is, that deficiency must be treated as a loss and borne by the partners as such. Writing prior to the Partnership Act 1890, Lord Lindley explained the process in this way:

"If the assets are not sufficient to pay the debts and liabilities to non-partners, the partners must treat the difference as a loss and make it up by contributions *inter se*. If the assets are more than sufficient to pay the debts and liabilities of the partnership to non-partners, but are not sufficient to repay the partners their respective advances, the amount of unpaid advances ought, it is conceived, to be treated as a loss, to be met like other losses. In such a case the advances ought to be treated as a debt of the firm, but payable to one of the partners instead of to a stranger.[175] If, after paying all the debts and liabilities of the firm and the advances of the partners, there is still a surplus, but not sufficient to pay each partner his capital, the balances of capitals remaining unpaid must be treated as so many losses to be met like other losses."[176]

If there is an insufficiency at stage 1, the overall loss borne by the partners will be that amount together with any sums which would otherwise be payable to them at stages 2 and 3 (which, by definition, cannot be returned to them); if the insufficiency occurs at stage 2, the loss will comprise that amount together with any sum otherwise payable at stage 3. In either of these cases, a global calculation of each partner's share of the loss may be possible.[177]

Income carried by capital contributions

It has already been seen[178] that where realisation of the surplus assets has produced a fund which is more than sufficient to repay all the partners' capital contributions, they may, at the end of stage 3, be entitled to claim such part of the income of that fund as was carried by those contributions.[179] It is only after those shares of the income have been accounted for that the ultimate residue will be established for the purposes of stage 4.   **25–47**

Division of ultimate residue

If there is an ultimate residue to be divided between the partners at stage 4,[180] the relevant profit shares will be those applied to residual or capital profits.[181]   **25–48**

---

[175] See *Wood v. Scoles* (1866) L.R. 1 Ch.App. 369.

[176] See now the Partnership Act 1890, s.24(1), *supra*, paras 20–03 *et seq. cf. Binney v. Mutrie* (1886) 12 App.Cas. 160. As to costs, see *supra*, paras 23–122, 25–45.

[177] Thus, suppose that partners A and B share profits and losses equally. A has made an advance of £1,000 and a capital contribution of £2,000, whilst B has made an advance of £2,000 and a capital contribution of £2,000. The surplus assets remaining after stage 1 are merely £1,500, so that £1,500 of the advances and the entirety of the capital has been lost. Technically, the £1,500 will at stage 2 be divided rateably between A and B, A receiving £500 and B £1,000. The lost balance of £1,500 will be shared equally between them, so that A must in fact refund £250 of the £500 notionally received. The lost capital will not require an adjustment. The same result could be achieved by taking the overall loss of £5,500, of which A and B each bear £2,750. B is thus entitled to the return of his advance and capital contribution (£2,000 + £2,000) less his share of the loss (£2,750) : £1,250. He should thus be paid that sum out of the available surplus, the remainder being paid to A. See also *infra*, para. 25–49.

[178] See *supra*, para. 20–35.

[179] This should not be confused with a partner's entitlement to a share of *profits* under the Partnership Act 1890, s.42(1), as to which see *supra*, paras 25–22 *et seq.*

[180] See, however, *supra*, para. 25–47.

[181] See *supra*, paras 10–79, 17–04.

Any form of preferential profit share which is only applicable to profits of an *income* nature, *e.g.* so-called "salaries", "bonus shares" or "incentive profit shares", must be left out of account.[182] In the case of a graduated profit sharing system, whether by reference to a partner's holding of "points" or his position on a "lockstep" system, the relevant profit sharing proportions will in general be those which applied at the date of dissolution.[183]

Of course, it may be that a partner, though entitled to a share of the firm's income profits, is excluded from participating in the division of capital profits.[184] The existence of such a partner will naturally be ignored for present purposes.[185]

Equality of loss and inequality of capital

25–49   Where the partners have contributed (and thereafter own)[186] capital in unequal proportions but share profits and losses equally, any loss of capital must in general be shared *equally*, in the same way as any other loss.[187] Accordingly, any surplus assets remaining after payment of the debts and advances must be distributed between the partners in such a way as to achieve that equality.[188] Thus, if partner A has contributed capital of £10,000 and partner B £5,000, but the surplus is only £10,000, the loss of £5,000 must be shared equally, so that A will receive £7,500 and B £2,500. If equality cannot be achieved in this way, then the necessary contributions must be made as between the partners.[189] Thus if, in the previous example, the surplus is only £3,000, in order to ensure that the loss of £12,000 is shared equally A must receive the entire surplus of £3,000, together with a contribution from B of a further £1,000. Although at first sight surprising, this result is, in fact, entirely logical, once it is appreciated that the benefit of the lost capital must have accrued to the partners in their profit sharing ratios, since it will either have been applied in the acquisition of additional assets[190] or in reducing the trading losses. The same principles will, of course, be applied where the partners share profits and losses otherwise than in equal proportions.

If, however, the partners' true intention is that, once the debts and advances have been paid, any surplus assets will be divided between them in their normal profit sharing ratios or in proportion to their original capital contributions or in some other manner, effect must be given to that agreement; in such a case, those partners with the largest capital contributions will bear the majority of the loss.[191]

---

[182] See *supra*, paras 10–80, 10–83.

[183] But see *supra*, para. 10–85.

[184] *e.g.* in the case of a salaried partner: see *supra*, para. 18–02.

[185] In *Stekel v. Ellice* [1973] 1 W.L.R. 191, 202, Megarry J. expressed doubts whether such a partner could properly seek an order for the winding up of the firm's affairs.

[186] See *supra*, paras 17–07, 17–08.

[187] Partnership Act 1890, s.24(1), *supra*, paras 20–03 *et seq. cf. Binney v. Mutrie* (1886) 12 App.Cas. 160.

[188] See *Ex p. Maude* (1867) L.R. 6 Ch.App. 51; *Re Weymouth Steam Packet Co.* [1891] 1 Ch. 66; *Re Wakefield Rolling Stock Co.* [1892] 3 Ch. 165.

[189] *Binney v. Mutrie* (1886) 12 App.Cas. 160; also *Nowell v. Nowell* (1869) L.R. 7 Eq. 538. And see *Re Anglesea Colliery Co.* (1866) L.R. 1 Ch.App. 555; *Re Crookhaven Mining Co.* (1866) L.R. 3 Eq. 69.

[190] Those additional assets (or their proceeds) will prima facie have been applied in liquidation of debts owed to third parties.

[191] See *Wood v. Scoles* (1866) L.R. 1 Ch.App. 369; also *Re Holyford Mining Co.* (1869) I.R. 3 Eq. 208; *Re Eclipse Gold Mining Co.* (1874) L.R. 17 Eq. 490; *Binney v. Mutrie* (1886) 12 App.Cas. 160.

The rule in *Garner v. Murray*

The position is more complex where one of the partners is insolvent and thus **25–50** unable to contribute his share of the lost capital. In *Garner v. Murray*[192] Joyce J. held that section 44 of the Partnership Act 1890 does not compel the solvent partners to make up any shortfall resulting from that inability, so that a deficiency in the capital available for distribution is inevitable. Since such capital as is available must be distributed rateably, the deficiency will ultimately be borne by the partners *pro rata* to their capital contributions and not equally. This is, with deceptive simplicity, styled "the rule in *Garner v. Murray*".

Thus, suppose that partner A has contributed capital of £10,000, partner B, £5,000 and partner C, £1,000, but that profits and losses are shared equally. C is insolvent and the surplus remaining after discharging the debts and advances is £10,000, *i.e.* a loss of £6,000. A, B and C each bear £2,000 of that loss, but C is unable to contribute his share. Accordingly, the total assets available for distribution consist of the surplus (£10,000) and the notional contributions of lost capital from A and B (£4,000), *i.e.* £14,000. That amount is shared rateably between A and B in the proportions 21 (reflecting the size of their original capital contributions),[193] *i.e.* A notionally receives £9,333 and B, £4,666. However, there must be deducted from each partner's entitlement his share of the loss, so that A ultimately receives £7,333 and B, £2,666.[194]

Where the insolvent partner's capital account is already overdrawn before **25–51** the loss of capital is deducted,[195] there appear to be two schools of thought as to the correct method of proceeding. Either that deficit is ignored when applying the rule or the deficit is itself treated as a loss *which must be shared between all the partners*. It has been submitted that the latter represents the true effect of the decision in *Garner v. Murray*,[196] but this cannot be elicited from the terms of the judgment reportedly delivered by Joyce J.[197]

The application of the rule would seem to presuppose that the insolvent partner's capital account is overdrawn either at the date of dissolution or when his share of the lost capital is debited thereto.[198]

It was submitted in earlier editions of this work that the rule works logically, since the insolvent partner must already have received his share of the lost capital

---

[192] [1904] 1 Ch. 57.

[193] If, in fact, any partner has withdrawn a part of his original contribution, regard will be had to the partners' respective capital entitlements as at the date of dissolution (as in *Garner v. Murray* itself).

[194] This appears to be the conventional method of calculation and reflects the requirements of the words "including the sums, if any, contributed by the partners to make up losses or deficiencies of capital" in the Partnership Act 1890, s.44(b), *supra*, para. 25–45. However, precisely the same result is in fact achieved if the partners' respective shares of the loss are deducted from their capital entitlements and the deficiency attributable to C's failure to contribute his share (*i.e.* £1,000–£2,000, a net deficiency of £1,000) is shared between A and B pro rata to their original contributions.

[195] This was in fact the position in *Garner v. Murray*.

[196] This view appears to be based on the actual terms of the order made by Joyce J., although this is not set out in the reports; *quaere* is it borne out by the statement of the facts at [1904] 52 W.R. 208? The whole question appears to have been subject to detailed analysis in Australia: the current editor expresses his gratitude to Professor K. A. Houghton for drawing his attention to various articles in the journal Abacus. See in particular, Vol. 17, No. 1, p. 41 and Vol. 18, No. 1, p. 91. The issue is also considered in Fletcher, *The Law of Partnership in Australia* (9th ed.) at para. 7–200.

[197] But see the terms of the Partnership Act 1890, s.44(a), *supra*, para. 25–45.

[198] If there were a positive balance *after* debiting the insolvent partner's share of the loss, there would in fact be no shortfall.

in one of the ways previously described[199] or by making excessive (and presumably unauthorised) drawings on his capital account, so that there is no justification for requiring the solvent partners to restore sums which they have not received prior to the return of their capital. However, in the current editor's view, this somewhat over-simplifies the position, particularly if it is right that the deficit on the insolvent partner's capital account must itself be treated as a loss.

Need for court order

25-52 There is no reason why the affairs of a partnership should not be wound up by the partners or their representatives without the intervention of the court,[200] save where disputes arise.[201]

Adjustments pursuant to court order

25-53 If the surplus assets are distributed amongst the partners pursuant to a court order which is later reversed, any partner who has received more than his true entitlement will be ordered to repay the excess.[202]

5. SUMMARY OF WINDING UP PRINCIPLES

25-54 Various consequences of a partnership dissolution which impinge directly on the winding up of its affairs have been considered in this work and may, for convenience, be summarised in the following general principles:

A. PRINCIPLES WHICH APPLY AS REGARDS CREDITORS

(1) A dissolution, whether general or technical,[203] will not, of itself, discharge any partner from a debt or liability incurred prior to the dissolution.[204]

(2) In order to secure a discharge from such a debt or liability a partner must, in general, show that the creditor has (a) been paid or otherwise satisfied; (b) released or discharged him; or (c) accepted a substitute debtor or security.[205]

---

[199] See *supra*, para. 25–49.

[200] See *Lyon v. Haynes* (1843) 5 Man. & G. 505.

[201] See the Partnership Act 1890, s.39, *supra*, paras 19–25 *et seq.* Lord Lindley, referring to the (then exclusive) jurisdiction of the Chancery Division, observed that, in the event of any dispute, "it is under [*that Division's*] superintendence only that the assets of the partnership can be properly sold and applied, that the partnership accounts can be satisfactorily taken, and that contribution can be enforced." To the same effect were Lord Millett's observations in *Hurst v. Bryk* [2002] 1 A.C. 185, 194.

[202] *Re Birkbeck Permanent Building Society* [1915] 1 Ch. 91.

[203] See *supra*, paras 24–02, 24–03.

[204] See *supra*, paras 13–78 *et seq.*

[205] See *supra*, paras 13–81 *et seq.*

(3) Notwithstanding the dissolution, the partners will be obliged to attend to any unfinished business and, in the course of so doing, must exercise a proper degree of care and skill.[206]

(4) Save in a few exceptional cases,[207] a partner will remain liable for the *future* acts of his former co-partners until such time as the dissolution is duly notified.[208]

(5) Notice of dissolution will, in general, be given by advertisement, but this is unlikely to be sufficient in the case of existing customers.[209]

(6) Even after the dissolution has been notified, a partner may be liable for the acts of his former co-partners in winding up the partnership affairs.[210]

(7) Furthermore, a partner will remain liable for the acts of his former co-partners if he allows them to hold him out as a continuing partner.[211]

B. PRINCIPLES WHICH APPLY AS BETWEEN THE PARTNERS

(1) Each partner is, in general, entitled to have dissolution accounts taken as between him and his co-partners.[212]   **25–55**

(2) Each partner is entitled to have the partnership property applied in liquidation of the partnership debts, and to have any surplus assets divided.[213]

(3) Each partner is, in general, entitled to force a sale of all partnership assets which are capable of being sold and to have the value of any unsaleable asset brought into account by the partner who retains it.[214]

(4) As a corollary of (3), save in special circumstances, no partner can insist on taking the share of any other partner at a valuation or to insist on a division of the partnership assets in specie.[215]

(5) No partner can retain the exclusive right to any increase in the value of the partnership assets between dissolution and sale,[216] but more

---

[206] See *supra*, paras 13–62 *et seq. Quaere* to what extent (if at all) they can take on *new* business: see *supra*, paras 10–199, 16–30.

[207] See *supra*, paras 13–46 *et seq.*

[208] See *supra*, paras 13–38 *et seq.*

[209] See *supra*, paras 13–74 *et seq.*

[210] See *supra*, paras 13–62 *et seq.*

[211] See *supra*, para. 13–58.

[212] See the Partnership Act 1890, s.28 *infra*, para. A1–29 and the decision in *Winning v. Cunningham* 2009 GWD 01–19 (Sh.Ct.). See also *supra*, paras 22–10, 23–75.

[213] See *supra*, paras 19–24 *et seq.*

[214] See *supra*, paras 10–150, 10–200, 19–05 *et seq.*, 23–183 *et seq.*

[215] See *supra*, paras 10–150, 19–10 *et seq.*, 23–184 *et seq.*

[216] See *supra*, para. 25–32.

difficult questions may arise in relation to trading profits realised during that period.[217]

25–56

(6) Both the authority of each partner and the duties which he owes to the other partners continue whilst the partnership affairs are being wound up.[218] As Lord Lindley put it:

> "For the purposes of winding up, the partnership is deemed to continue; the good faith and honourable conduct due from every partner to his co-partners during the continuance of the partnership being equally due so long as its affairs remain unsettled[219]; and that which was partnership property before, continuing to be so for the purpose of dissolution, as the rights of the partners require."[220]

Account must, however, be taken of any agreement between the partners.[221]

(7) Each partner can insist that no further business is transacted or acts done, otherwise than with a view to the winding up.[222]

(8) In the absence of some contrary agreement, the right to wind up the partnership affairs does not fall on any particular partner to the exclusion of the others. If any dispute arises, the winding up should proceed under the supervision of the court.[223]

(9) The right to wind up the partnership affairs is, however, personal to the partners, so that the representatives of a deceased, insolvent or mentally incapacitated partner will not normally be permitted to interfere.[224]

25–57

(10) A return of premium may be ordered if the partnership was dissolved prior to the expiration of a fixed term.[225]

(11) If, on settling the final account, the partnership assets are insufficient to pay the partnership debts, or to repay the sums due to each partner in respect of advances or capital, the deficiency must, subject to any contrary agreement, be made good by the partners in their profit sharing ratios.[226]

---

[217] See *supra*, paras 25–22 *et seq*. See also, as to whether such profits should be distributed to the partners , *supra*, paras 10–84, 13–72, 25–22.

[218] See *supra*, paras 13–62 *et seq*.

[219] See *supra*, paras 16–14 *et seq*.

[220] See *Ex p. Williams* (1805) 11 Ves.Jr. 3; *Crawshay v. Collins* (1826) 2 Russ. 325, 342–343 *per* Lord Eldon; *Nerot v. Burnand* (1827) 4 Russ. 247, affirmed at (1828) 2 Bli. (N.S.) 215; *Payne v. Hornby* (1858) 25 Beav. 280; also *Ex p. Trueman* (1832) 1 D. & Ch. 464. This passage was cited with approval in *Thompson's Trustee v. Heaton* [1974] 1 W.L.R. 605, 613 *per* Pennycuick V.-C.

[221] See, for example, *Souhrada v. Bank of New South Wales* [1976] 2 Lloyd's Rep. 444.

[222] See *Ex p. Williams* (1805) 11 Ves. Jr. 3; *Wilson v. Greenwood* (1818) 1 Swan. 471; *Crawshay v. Maule* (1818) 1 Swan. 495; also *supra*, paras 13–57 *et seq*. *Quaere*, what is the position where new business must be taken on to preserve the goodwill of the firm pending its realisation? See *supra*, paras 10–201, 13–71, 16–30.

[223] See *supra*, paras 23–69 *et seq*. Thus, the court will, where necessary, appoint a receiver, direct the sale of assets and the payment of debts and liabilities and restrain a partner from interfering with the conduct of the winding up.

[224] See *supra*, para. 23–147.

[225] See *supra*, paras 25–10 *et seq*. As to cases of fraud, see *supra*, para. 25–08.

[226] See *supra*, paras 25–45 *et seq*.

(12) Although interest on capital is not normally payable following a dissolution,[227] a partner's capital contribution may carry any income attributable thereto.[228]

(13) Unless that right is excluded by agreement, each partner is entitled to give notice of the dissolution[229] and, where appropriate, to prevent his former co-partners from continuing to hold him out as a partner by using the old firm name.[230]

(14) Once the winding up is complete, each partner will, in general, be entitled to start up a business of the same nature as that carried on by the dissolved firm, either alone or in partnership with others.[231] It may, however, be that a partner will have this right *before* the completion of the winding up.[232]

---

[227] See *supra*, para. 20–33.

[228] See *supra*, paras 20–35, 25–47.

[229] See *supra*, paras 13–37 *et seq.*

[230] Lord Lindley described each partner's right in these terms: "It seems that he has also a right to restrain [*the other partners*] from carrying on business under the old name, if such name is or includes his own; for even if their continued use of the old name, with his knowledge, is not of itself sufficient to render him liable, by virtue of the doctrine of holding out, such use undoubtedly exposes him to the risk of having actions brought against him as if he still belonged to the firm, and in the case supposed his co-partners have no right to expose him to that risk." See *supra*, paras 5–45 *et seq.*, 10–201, 10–202, 23–149. The position will, of course, be different where the other partners have acquired the right to use the old firm name, by purchase or otherwise.

[231] See *supra*, paras 10–201, 10–206 *et seq.* Lord Lindley put it thus: " . . . each partner has a right to commence a new business in the old line, and in the old neighbourhood; either alone, or in partnership with other people."

[232] See *supra*, para. 10–200.

CHAPTER 26

DEATH OF A PARTNER

It is convenient to analyse the consequences of a partner's death in terms of the **26–01** respective rights and, where relevant, duties of the three groups of persons actually or potentially affected thereby, namely:

1. The surviving partners and the personal representatives of the deceased partner.

2. The creditors of the partnership.

3. The separate creditors and legatees, etc., of the deceased partner.

Each group will be considered in turn.

1. THE SURVIVING PARTNERS AND PERSONAL REPRESENTATIVES OF THE DECEASED PARTNER

Dissolution and winding up

It has already been seen that, subject to any contrary agreement, the death of **26–02** a partner dissolves the partnership as regards *all* the partners.[1] Although the doctrine of survivorship will not in general apply to any part of the deceased partner's beneficial share,[2] the conduct of the winding up is vested exclusively in the surviving partners.[3] It follows that the rights of the personal representatives are limited, as Lord Lindley explained:

> "Unless all the partners have agreed to the contrary, when one of them dies, his executors have no right to become partners with the surviving partners[4]; nor to interfere with the partnership business[5]; but the executors of the deceased represent him for all purposes of account, and, unless restrained by special agreement, they have the power, by bringing an action, to have the affairs of the partnership wound up in a manner which is generally ruinous to the other partners."[6]

The reference to the "ruinous" effects of a winding up reflects the fact that a deceased partner's share will normally be ascertained and paid out by means of

---

[1] Partnership Act 1890, s.33(1), *supra*, paras 24–29 *et seq.*

[2] See *supra*, para. 19–13; also *supra*, para. 10–203. As to the devolution of *title* to the partnership assets, see *supra*, paras 18–61 *et seq.*

[3] Partnership Act 1890, s.38, *supra*, paras 13–62 *et seq.*

[4] *Pearce v. Chamberlain* (1750) 2 Ves.Sen. 33. See also *McClean v. Kennard* (1874) 9 L.R. Ch.App. 336.

[5] See *supra*, para. 23–147.

[6] Partnership Act 1890, s.39, *supra*, paras 19–25 *et seq.*

a sale of all the partnership assets, whether or not pursuant to a court order, since the surviving partners have no inherent right to acquire that share at a valuation.[7] Equally, the surviving partners will be obliged to complete any business left unfinished at the date of dissolution,[8] so that the court may defer a forced sale of those assets and the ultimate adjustment of accounts as between the partners until a particular subsisting contract has been fully performed.[9]

Deceased partner's share as a debt

26–03   Section 43 of the Partnership Act 1890 provides that the amount due to the personal representatives of a deceased partner in respect of his share is a debt accruing at the date of death.[10] Although the application of this section is not open to doubt where it is recognised, either expressly or by implication, that the partnership will continue notwithstanding a partner's death,[11] the position is less clear where the death brings about a *general* dissolution. If the share is indeed converted into a debt on such a dissolution, it is a debt of a most unusual nature, since the estate is clearly entitled to a full share of any increase in the value of the partnership assets accruing in the period between the date of death and the date of realisation[12] and, conversely, must bear a full share of any diminution in value during that period.[13] For this reason, the current editor shares Lord Lindley's view[14] that the section was not intended to apply in such a case.[15]

Sale of share and arrangements to avoid general dissolution

26–04   Because of the potential implications for the surviving partners, the personal representatives of a deceased partner will often wish to explore ways in which a general dissolution and winding up can be avoided.

There is, in general, no bar on the personal representatives selling the deceased's share to the surviving partners, unless one of those representatives is also a member of the firm.[16] If such a sale cannot, for whatever reason, be arranged, the only option may be to leave the deceased's share in the business. This course

---

[7] See *supra*, paras 19–05 *et seq.*, 23–183 *et seq.*

[8] See *supra*, paras 13–62 *et seq.*

[9] *McClean v. Kennard* (1874) 9 Ch.App. 336. See also *supra*, para. 23–204.

[10] See *supra*, para. 23–34. And see also the Partnership Act 1890, s.39, *supra*, paras 19–25 *et seq.*

[11] See *supra*, paras 10–39, 19–10, 19–11, 23–34. Nevertheless, *cf. HLB Kidsons v. Lloyd's Underwriters* [2009] 1 All E.R. (Comm) 760 at [16] *per* Judge Mackie Q.C. (sitting as a judge of the Chancery Division), noted *supra*, para. 23–34, n. 128. Clearly the section will apply if a *new* partnership comes into existence after the date of death: see *Patel v. Patel* [2008] EWCA Civ 1520 (Lawtel 7/4/08).

[12] See *Barclays Bank Trust Co. Ltd. v. Bluff* [1982] Ch. 172; *Chandroutie v. Gajadhar* [1987] A.C. 147 (PC); *Popat v. Shonchhatra* [1997] 1 W.L.R. 1367 (CA). And see also *supra*, para. 25–32.

[13] There does not appear to be any decision to this effect but it is in the natural corollary of the decision in *Barclays Bank Trust Co. Ltd. v. Bluff, supra*. This presupposes that the loss cannot be attributed to the misconduct of the surviving partners: see *supra*, paras 20–10 *et seq.*

[14] See *supra*, para. 23–34. Unaccountably, this view was only expressed in relation to the position under *Scots* law. See also *supra*, para. 19–35.

[15] *cf. HLB Kidsons v. Lloyd's Underwriters, supra.* Equally, it is undeniable that the Partnership Act 1890, s.42 will potentially apply in the case of a general dissolution: see *supra*, paras 25–24 *et seq.* and *infra*, para. 26–07. One of the options under this section is a claim for interest "on the amount of [*the deceased's*] share of the partnership assets". This refers to his share of the assets as at the date of dissolution (see *Sandhu v. Gill* [2006] Ch. 456 (CA)), so that s.43 *may* apply for this limited purpose.

[16] See *supra*, paras 23–61 *et seq.* and *infra*, paras 26–05, 26–36.

is not without risk, even if the consent of the beneficiaries is obtained,[17] since the representatives might inadvertently become (or be held out as) partners[18] and thereby incur personal liability for the continuing firm's debts and obligations, notwithstanding their trustee status.[19] Lord Lindley summarised the difficulty which executors[20] face in these terms:

> "The position of the executors of a deceased partner is, in fact, often one of considerable hardship and difficulty; if they insist on an immediate winding up of the firm, they may ruin those whom the deceased may have been most anxious to benefit; whilst if for their advantage the partnership is allowed to go on, the executors may run the risk of being ruined themselves."[21]

Accordingly, the representatives may in practice have no choice *but* to force a sale of all the assets and a winding up of the partnership affairs in the normal way.

Position where surviving partner is appointed executor

Needless to say, the foregoing difficulties are exacerbated rather than resolved where one of the surviving partners has been appointed an executor of the deceased partner's will, as Lord Lindley explained:

26–05

> " . . . his own personal interest as a surviving partner is brought into direct conflict with his duty as an executor. Everything therefore which he does is liable to question and misconstruction on the part of the persons beneficially entitled to the estate of the deceased; and he is practically much more fettered in the discharge of his duties, and in the exercise of his rights, than if he did not have to act in the double character imposed upon him."[22]

Debts paid to and by surviving partners

The surviving partners are clearly the proper persons to get in and pay the partnership debts.[23] It is, perhaps, self evident that any sums got in will reduce the debts owed to the former firm, whilst any sums paid out will reduce the debts owed by it,[24] but this may have important consequences as between the surviving partners and the personal representatives of the deceased partner. Thus, the representatives will, on the one hand, be entitled to treat payments received by the surviving partners from a debtor of the former firm as made in respect of a

26–06

[17] The representatives will not necessarily have power to adopt this course: see *infra*, paras 26–24, 26–25.

[18] See the Partnership Act 1890, ss.2(3), 14, *supra*, paras 5–18 *et seq.*, 5–35 *et seq.* As to the position prior to the Act, see *Holme v. Hammond* (1872) L.R. 7 Ex. 218 (where the personal representatives were not liable); *cf. Ex p. Garland* (1804) 10 Ves.Jr. 110; *Wightman v. Townroe* (1813) 1 M. & S. 412; *Ex p. Holdsworth* (1841) 1 M.D. & D. 475.

[19] A trustee partner's liability is normally no different from that of any other partner: see *Muir v. City of Glasgow Bank* (1879) 4 App.Cas. 337.

[20] Administrators are in no different position.

[21] See *infra*, paras 26–21 *et seq.*, 26–40 *et seq.*

[22] See, generally, *Hutton v. Rosseter* (1855) 7 De G.M. & G. 12; *Wright v. Morgan* [1926] A.C. 788, 796–798.

[23] See *supra*, paras 13–61 *et seq.*, 18–64.

[24] In book-keeping terms, the payment of debts owed to the former firm will result in a debit entry in the list of its debtors, and the payment of debts owed by it will result in a credit entry in the list of its creditors.

debt owed to it,[25] whilst the surviving partners will, on the other hand, be entitled to reimbursement out of the deceased partner's estate if they pay his share of the debts owed by the former firm.[26]

Post-dissolution profits

26–07   It has already been seen that, if the surviving partners have carried on the partnership business without any final settlement of accounts as between them and the personal representatives of the deceased partner, the latter are entitled, at their option, to the share of profits attributable to the use of the deceased's share of the partnership assets or to interest thereon at the rate of five per cent.[27] However, in such a case, the surviving partners will normally be made an allowance out of the profits in recognition of their efforts, unless they are also the deceased's personal representatives.[28]

Actions by surviving partners against deceased's estate

26–08   Surviving partners may commence proceedings against the estate of a deceased partner in two distinct capacities,[29] as identified by Lord Lindley in the following passage:

> "A surviving partner, if a creditor of the deceased, may sue either in that character for a common administration judgment, or, in the character of a partner, for a judgment for a partnership account and for payment of what is due on that account; and if assets are not admitted, then for a judgment for the administration of the estate of the deceased."

The surviving partners will, of course, be creditors of the estate for any sums found due to them on taking the partnership accounts and may seek an administration order in that capacity.[30]

The deceased partner's personal representatives must be joined as parties to any action for an account brought by one or more of the surviving partners[31] and, in such a case, it is permissible to commence proceedings against the estate where no grant of probate or letters of administration has been obtained.[32] However, an application must then be made to have someone appointed to represent the estate in the proceedings.[33] The persons so appointed might conceivably be the personal representatives named in the deceased partner's will (if any).

---

[25] *Lees v. Laforest* (1851) 14 Beav. 250.

[26] *Musson v. May* (1814) 3 V. & B. 194.

[27] Partnership Act 1890, s.42(1), *supra*, paras 25–24 *et seq.* Note also *ibid.* s.29, *supra*, paras 16–14, 16–27. It is generally not possible to seek interest under the Senior Courts Act 1981, s.35A (formerly the Supreme Court Act 1981: Constitutional Reform Act 2005, Sched. 11, Pt 1, para. 1(1)): see *supra*, paras 20–41, 25–43.

[28] See *supra*, para. 25–33.

[29] Proceedings may obviously be framed in the alternative, where appropriate: CPR r. 7.3.

[30] See *Addis v. Knight* (1817) 2 Mer. 117; *Robinson v. Alexander* (1834) 2 Cl. & F. 717.

[31] Lord Lindley noted that: "If there is no . . . representative, but the assets of the deceased or of the partnership are in danger, and the object of the plaintiff is to have them protected, he should confine his claim for relief accordingly, and not seek for an account: *Rawlings v. Lambert* (1860) 1 J. & H. 458." *Semble*, it would not be fatal if the relief claimed were *not* so confined.

[32] CPR r. 19.8(2)(b)(i). And see *Re Amirteymour* [1979] 1 W.L.R. 63 (a decision under the former RSC Ord. 15, r. 6A).

[33] CPR r. 19.8(2)(b)(ii).

Rights of representatives where administration order made

Where an administration order is made in respect of a deceased partner's **26–09** estate, his personal representatives will, in general, be free from all forms of personal liability. Lord Lindley summarised the rights of a deceased partner's executors in these terms:

" . . . his executors, if they act properly, are personally protected from all consequences, and no action can be sustained against them in respect of what they so do.[34]
If there are liabilities which will have to be met, the Court will order part of the assets
to be set aside to meet them when they arise.[35] But if the liabilities are remote and
contingent, and may possibly never arise at all, the utmost that the executors can
obtain in the shape of indemnity, in addition to that afforded by the orders of the
Court itself, is a covenant from the testator's legatees or next of kin."[36]

Surviving partners' right to carry on similar business

Unless the goodwill of the former firm has been or is to be sold in the course **26–10** of winding up its affairs,[37] the surviving partners will seemingly be free to start up a "new" business under the old firm name.[38]

2.   THE CREDITORS OF THE PARTNERSHIP

The rights of partnership creditors against the estate of a deceased partner will **26–11** vary according to whether their debts were incurred before or after the date of his death.

A.   DEBTS INCURRED PRIOR TO A PARTNER'S DEATH

General rules affecting liability of estate

Numerous decided cases illustrating the consequences of a partner's death on his liability to existing partnership creditors are noticed elsewhere in this work. It is accordingly sufficient, in the present context, to formulate a number of general rules and, where necessary, to classify the authorities by reference thereto.

---

[34] *Waller v. Barrett* (1857) 24 Beav. 413.
[35] *Fletcher v. Stevenson* (1844) 3 Hare 360; *Brewer v. Pocock* (1857) 23 Beav. 310.
[36] See *Dean v. Allen* (1855) 20 Beav. 1; *Waller v. Barrett* (1857) 24 Beav. 413; *Addams v. Ferick* (1859) 26 Beav. 384; *Bennett v. Lytton* (1860) 2 J. & H. 155; also *Re Nixon* [1904] 1 Ch. 638 and the cases there cited.
[37] See *supra*, paras 10–200 *et seq.*
[38] See *Hill v. Fearis* [1905] 1 Ch. 466; also *supra*, para. 10–201.

26–12   *Rule 1*:   The estate of a deceased partner will, in general, remain
                                liable not only for all partnership debts and obligations
                                incurred prior to the date of his death[39] but also for any
                                tort,[40] fraud or breach of trust committed prior to that date
                                which can be imputed to the firm.[41]

The authorities may be classified as follows:

Group A: Ordinary case (liability unaffected).

   Sub-group (i): contracts.[42]

   Sub-group (ii): torts, frauds and breaches of trust.[43]

Group B: Exceptional case (liability extinguished).[44]

26–13   *Rule 2*:   The liability of the estate will be unaffected by any arrange-
                                ment between the personal representatives and the surviving
                                partners.[45]

            Rule 3:   The liability of the estate will be unaffected by any sub-
                                sequent dealings between the creditors and the surviving
                                partners,[46] unless it can be established either that the credi-

---

[39] See generally, *supra*, paras 13–06 *et seq.* Lord Lindley also referred readers to the "celebrated judgment in *Devaynes v. Noble* (1839) 1 Mer. 529".

[40] Note that, with the sole exception of defamation, tortious claims by or against a partner are unaffected by his death: Law Reform (Miscellaneous Provisions) Act 1934, s.1(1) (as amended).

[41] See *supra*, paras 13–12, 13–13.

[42] See *Lane v. Williams* (1692) 2 Vern. 292; *Clavering v. Westley* (1735) 3 P.W. 402; *Simpson v. Vaughan* (1739) 2 Atk. 31; *Darwent v. Walton* (1742) 2 Atk. 510; *Jacomb v. Harwood* (1751) 2 Ves.Sen. 265; *Bishop v. Church* (1751) 2 Ves.Sen. 371 (*supra*, para. 13–08); *Thomas v. Frazer* (1797) 3 Ves.Jr. 399; *Burn v. Burn* (1798) 3 Ves.Jr. 573; *Orr v. Chase* (1812) 1 Mer. 729; *Devaynes v. Noble* (1816) 1 Mer. 529 and (1831) 2 R. & M. 495; *Cheetham v. Crook* (1825) McCle. & Yo. 307; *Wilkinson v. Henderson* (1833) 1 M. & K. 583; *Thorpe v. Jackson* (1837) 2 Y. & C.Ex. 553; *Harris v. Farwell* (1846) 13 Beav. 403; *Hills v. Mc'Rae* (1851) 9 Hare 297; *Brett v. Beckwith* (1856) 3 Jur. (N.S.) 31 (*infra*, para. 26–17); *Beresford v. Browning* (1875) L.R. 20 Eq. 564 (*supra*, para. 13–08).

[43] See *Clayton's case* (1816) 1 Mer. 576 (*supra*, paras 12–116, 13–85); *Warde's case* (1816) 1 Mer. 624; *Vulliamy v. Noble* (1817) 3 Mer. 619; *Sadler v. Lee* (1843) 6 Beav. 324 (*supra*, para. 12–118); *Blair v. Bromley* (1847) 2 Ph. 354 (*supra*, para. 12–119); *Sawyer v. Goodwin* (1867) 36 L.J.Ch. 578 (negligence); *New Sombrero Phosphate Co. v. Erlanger* (1877) 5 Ch.D. 73 (fraud); *Blyth v. Fladgate* [1891] 1 Ch. 337; *Smith v. Blyth* [1891] 1 Ch. 337, 366 *per* Stirling J. (negligence); *Moore v. Knight* [1891] 1 Ch. 547.

[44] See *Sumner v. Powell* (1823) Tur. & Rus. 423 (*supra*, para. 13–10); *Clarke v. Bickers* (1845) 14 Sim. 639 (*supra*, para. 13–11); *Wilmer v. Currey* (1848) 2 De G. & Sm. 347 (*supra*, para. 13–11); *Hill's case* (1875) L.R. 20 Eq. 585 (joint holders of shares).

[45] See *supra*, paras 13–101 *et seq.*

[46] See *Jacomb v. Harwood* (1751) 2 Ves.Sen. 265; *Daniel v. Cross* (1796) 3 Ves.Jr. 277; *Sleech's case* (1816) 1 Mer. 539; *Clayton's case* (1816) 1 Mer. 572 (*supra*, paras 12–116, 13–85); *Palmer's case* (1816) 1 Mer. 623; *Braithwaite v. Britain* (1836) 1 Keen 206; *Winter v. Innes* (1838) 4 Myl. & Cr. 101 (which Lord Lindley described as "very important"); *Harris v. Farwell* (1851) 15 Beav. 31 (*supra*, para. 13–123); *Re Hodgson* (1885) 31 Ch.D. 177; *Re Head* [1893] 3 Ch. 426 (*supra*, para. 13–122); *cf. Head v. Head (No. 2)* [1894] 2 Ch. 236. And see *supra*, paras 13–101 *et seq.*

tors have lost or abandoned their rights against the estate[47] or that the debts have been paid or discharged.[48]

Rule 4:   Although the estate may be discharged by the expiration of the relevant limitation period, it will, in general, be bound by an acknowledgement or part payment given by the surviving partners.[49]

Creditor's right to proceed first against the estate

Prior to the Partnership Act 1890, Lord Lindley wrote: **26–14**

" . . . whatever doubt there may formerly have been upon the subject,[50] it has been long settled that a creditor of the firm can proceed against the estate of a deceased partner, without first having recourse to the surviving partners, and without reference to the state of the accounts between them and the deceased.[51] But it is necessary to make the surviving partners parties to the action, for they are interested in the issues raised between him and the executors."[52]

This is still the position,[53] although a creditor's failure to join the surviving partners as parties to the action would not, in itself, be fatal.[54] In practice, a single action brought against the surviving partners and the deceased partner's personal representatives is generally to be preferred.[55]

Creditor's rights postponed to separate debts

A partnership creditor who seeks payment out of a deceased partner's estate   **26–15** will not rank equally with his separate creditors: this is clearly established by the

---

[47] See (i) as to the effect of general dealings, *Brown v. Gordon* (1852) 16 Beav. 302 (*supra*, para. 13–125); also *Wilson v. Lloyd* (1873) L.R. 16 Eq. 60 (which is, however, unreliable: see *supra*, para. 13–99, n. 324); (ii) as to the effect of opening a new account, *Head v. Head (No. 2)* [1894] 2 Ch. 236 *supra*, para. 13–122; *cf. Re Head* [1893] 3 Ch. 426; and (iii) as to the position where the deceased partner has become a surety for the surviving partner's obligations, *Oakeley v. Pasheller* (1836) 10 Bli. (N.S.) 548 and 4 Cl. & F. 207 (*supra*, para. 13–99).

[48] See *Clayton's case* (1816) 1 Mer. 572 (*supra*, paras 12–116, 13–85); *Merriman v. Ward* (1860) 1 J. & H. 371, of which Lord Lindley commented "This case is important as showing that where a debt of a deceased partner has been discharged by the application of the rule in *Clayton's case*, it is not competent for his executors to revive such a debt against his estate."

[49] See *supra*, para. 13–135.

[50] *cf. Braithwaite v. Britain* (1836) 1 Keen 206; *Winter v. Innes* (1838) 4 Myl. & Cr. 101; *Way v. Bassett* (1845) 5 Hare 55; *Brown v. Gordon* (1852) 16 Beav. 302.

[51] *Wilkinson v. Henderson* (1833) 1 M. & K. 582; *Thorpe v. Jackson* (1837) 2 Y. & C.Ex. 553; *Devaynes v. Noble* (1839) 2 R. & M. 495; *Re McRae* (1883) 25 Ch.D. 16; *Re Hodgson* (1885) 31 Ch.D. 177. Equally, the surviving partners cannot insist on the creditors proceeding first against the deceased partner's estate: *Ex p. Kendall* (1811) 17 Ves.Jr. 514.

[52] See, in addition to the cases in the last note, *Stephenson v. Chiswell* (1797) 3 Ves.Jr. 566; *Sleech's case* (1816) 1 Mer. 539; *Rice v. Gordon* (1848) 11 Beav. 265; *Hills v. M'Rae* (1851) 9 Hare 297.

[53] See *supra*, paras 13–07 *et seq.*

[54] Unlike the RSC Ord. 15, r. 6(1), the CPR do not contain a provision specifically dealing with non-joinder, but see *ibid.* r. 19.2(2)(a). Note also the terms of *ibid.* r. 3.10 (power to remedy an error of procedure) and the court's case management powers under *ibid.* rr. 1.4, 3.1, 26. See also *supra*, para. 14–58.

[55] See *infra*, para. 26–18.

Partnership Act 1890.[56] The creditor's rights are circumscribed in such a case, as Lord Lindley explained:

> "The right of the creditor . . . is to have the separate estate of the deceased ascertained and applied in payment of his separate debts and liabilities, and to have the surplus applied in payment of his joint liabilities."[57]

The corollary is, of course, that the separate creditors have no rights against the deceased's share in the firm until all the partnership debts have been paid.[58]

The same basic rule applies in the administration of an insolvent estate.[59]

Form of administration order

26–16   If there is, in fact, sufficient to meet the demands of all the deceased's creditors, both joint and separate, the estate can be administered as a single fund and the creditors paid out *pari passu*.[60] However, since the solvency of the estate cannot be assured, a partnership creditor will not, unless he is also a separate creditor of the deceased, be entitled to the usual form of administration order, but to an order designed to ensure the proper distribution of the estate between the two potentially competing classes of creditors.[61] Such an order should normally be sought by issuing a Part 7 claim form.[62]

---

[56] *ibid.* s.9, *supra*, para. 13–03. And see also, as to the effect of this section, *supra*, para. 13–07.

[57] *Hills v. M'Rae* (1851) 9 Hare 297; *Re McRae* (1883) 25 Ch.D. 16; *Re Hodgson* (1885) 31 Ch.D. 177; *Re Barnard* (1886) 32 Ch.D. 447; *Smith v. Blyth* [1891] 1 Ch. 337, 367 *per* Stirling J.; *Moore v. Knight* [1891] 1 Ch. 547; also *Kendall v. Hamilton* (1879) 4 App.Cas. 504. *cf. Burn v. Burn* (1798) 3 Ves.Jr. 573, where a joint and several bond had been given by the partners.

[58] See *Hills v. M'Rae, supra*; *Ridgway v. Clare* (1854) 19 Beav. 111; *Moore v. Knight* [1891] 1 Ch. 547; *Re Ritson* [1899] 1 Ch. 128.

[59] See *infra*, para. 26–19.

[60] See *Ridgway v. Clare* (1854) 19 Beav. 111, where there were four separate actions relating to the estates of two deceased partners.

[61] See *Hills v. M'Rae* (1851) 9 Hare 297, as followed in *Re Hodgson* (1885) 31 Ch.D. 177; *Smith v. Blyth* [1891] 1 Ch. 337; *Moore v. Knight* [1891] 1 Ch. 547. See also *Harris v. Farwell* (1846) 13 Beav. 403; *Rice v. Gordon* (1848) 11 Beav. 265. Lord Lindley summarised the substance of the judgment given as follows: "1. It is declared that all persons who are creditors of the deceased, are entitled to the benefit of the judgment. 2. It is declared that the surplus of the estate of the deceased, after satisfying his funeral and testamentary expenses and separate debts, was liable at the time of his death to the joint debts of the firm, but without prejudice to the liability of the surviving partner, as between himself and the estate of the deceased. 3. An account is directed to be taken of the funeral and testamentary expenses and separate debts of the deceased, and of the debts of the firm. If the surviving partner is not a party to the action, liberty is given him to attend in the prosecution of this last inquiry. 4. An account is directed to be taken of the *personal* estate of the deceased. 5. It is ordered that his *personal* estate be applied, in the first instance, in the payment of his separate debts and funeral expenses, in a due course of administration, and then in payment of the debts of the firm. 6. *And if the personal estate of the deceased is insufficient for the purposes of the action, inquiries are ordered to be made for the purpose of ascertaining the real estate to which the deceased was entitled.*" Those parts of the judgment which appear in italics do not accord with the order in which assets are now applied under the Administration of Estates Act 1925, Sched. 1, Pt II. As to the normal form of administration order, see *Atkin's Court Forms* (2nd ed., Vol. 2 (2008 issue), para. [89]; *Heward's Chancery Orders*, p. 66. But see also *infra*, para. 26–18, n. 71.

[62] CPR rr. 7.2, 16.2. PPrior to the advent of the CPR, the originating summons procedure would have been inappropriate (*Re Barnard* (1886) 32 Ch.D. 447), so *ibid.* 8PD, Section A, para. 3.3 will clearly not apply.

If an administration action is already proceeding, a partnership creditor should be able to obtain the requisite order without bringing an action of his own.[63]

Accounts, inquiries, etc.

Although it is correct to say that a partnership creditor is not directly con- **26–17** cerned with the state of the accounts as between the partners,[64] it is clear from the decision in *Brett v. Beckwith*[65] that this will not always be the case. There a firm comprised two partners, A and B. A was bankrupt and B had died. A creditor of the firm commenced proceedings against B's executors and A's assignees[66] seeking *inter alia* administration of B's estate and the taking of accounts as between A and B. The court held that he was entitled to have the estate fully administered and, for that purpose, to have such accounts taken in order to determine what was comprised in the joint estate.

The court will order any inquiry which appears necessary,[67] *e.g.* with a view to ascertaining whether the partnership creditors have continued to deal with the surviving partners and, thereby, released the deceased's estate from liability.[68]

Although directions could, in an appropriate case, be made for the joint and separate estates to be kept distinct, it seems that, historically at least, this was not usually done.[69]

Parties to actions

The creditor can issue one set of proceedings against the surviving partners **26–18** and the personal representatives of the deceased partner or he may proceed against them separately.[70] If he adopts the former course, priority will still be accorded to the deceased's separate creditors, so that in practice he may have to look for payment solely to the surviving partners.[71] It has already been seen that the surviving partners will in any event be necessary parties if accounts are to be taken pursuant to the administration order in respect of the estate.[72]

If more than one partner is dead, the creditor may seek an administration order against each estate in the same proceedings.[73]

---

[63] *Gray v. Chiswell* (1803) 9 Ves.Jr. 118; *Cowell v. Sikes* (1827) 2 Russ. 191. See also *Re McRae* (1883) 25 Ch.D. 16. It seem unlikely that the position has changed under the CPR.

[64] See *supra*, para. 26–14.

[65] (1856) 3 Jur.(N.S.) 31.

[66] The forerunners of the trustee in bankruptcy.

[67] See, for example, *Barber v. Mackrell* (1879) 12 Ch.D. 534, where one partner had fraudulently withdrawn money from the firm.

[68] *Devaynes v. Noble* (1839) 1 Mer. 530.

[69] See *Paynter v. Houston* (1817) 3 Mer. 297; *Woolley v. Gordon* (1829) Tam. 11; *Rice v. Gordon* (1848) 11 Beav. 271; *Ridgway v. Clare* (1854) 19 Beav. 111.

[70] Judgment against the surviving partners was not a bar to proceedings against the estate of a deceased partner (and vice versa) even prior to the Civil Liability (Contribution) Act 1978: see *supra*, para. 13–06. Note also that the feasibility of a single set of proceedings prior to the Judicature Acts appears to have been sufficiently uncertain to have required specific comment: for a summary of the position, see the 15th ed. of this work at p. 752.

[71] The order made against the estate will be in the form considered *supra*, para. 26–16, unless, in Lord Lindley's words "assets are admitted". This would seem to indicate that, in a clear case, a money judgment might be ordered; *sed quaere*.

[72] See *supra*, para. 26–14.

[73] See *Brown v. Douglas* (1840) 11 Sim. 283; *Brown v. Weatherby* (1841) 12 Sim. 6.

Insolvent estate

26–19   A basic principle of the old bankruptcy laws, and of the current insolvency legislation, is that partnership debts are primarily payable out of the joint estate and the separate debts of each partner are primarily payable out of his separate estate,[74] unless the joint estate is insufficient to pay the partnership debts,[75] when the shortfall may now, in certain circumstances, rank equally with the separate debts of any insolvent partners in the administration of their separate estates.[76] The same principle is applied in the administration of an insolvent estate,[77] although the priority accorded to the separate creditors is established by section 9 of the Partnership Act 1890[78] rather than by the Insolvency Act 1986.[79] It follows that the existence of a shortfall will never of itself be sufficient to qualify the partnership creditors to rank equally with the separate creditors and that some other exceptional circumstances will be required.[80]

Similarly, a surviving partner will not be permitted to prove against the separate estate of his deceased co-partner if, by so doing, he would compete with his own creditors, *i.e.* the partnership creditors.[81] If, however, the separate estate

---

[74] See *infra*, paras 27–78 *et seq.*

[75] See, as to such debts, *infra*, paras 27–88 *et seq.*

[76] Insolvency Act 1986, ss.175A(5), 175B(1)(b) (as added, where concurrent petitions have been presented, by the Insolvent Partnerships Order 1994, Sched. 4, Pt II, para. 23 and applied, as regards the firm, by *ibid.* s.221(5) (as itself amended by the Insolvent Partnerships Order 1994, art. 8(1) (as amended by the Insolvent Partnerships (Amendment) Order 2002 (SI 2002/1308), art. 4(2)), (2), Sched. 4, Pt I, para. 3 (creditor's petition) and *ibid.* art. 10(1)(a), Sched. 6, para. 4 (member's petition)) and, as regards the partners, by the Insolvent Partnerships Order 1994, arts 8(4)–(8) (creditor's petition), 10(2)–(6) (as amended by the Insolvent Partnerships (Amendment) Order 2005 (SI 2005/1516), art. 5(b)) (member's petition)), 328A(5), 328B(1)(b) (and applied, where all the partners have presented a joint bankruptcy petition without winding up the firm, by *ibid.* art. 11, Sched. 7, para. 21). In either case, the debt is provable by the responsible insolvency practitioner, rather than by the relevant creditor: *ibid.* In any other case, *e.g.* where the firm is wound up on a creditor's petition and one or more partners are bankrupted *otherwise* than on concurrent petitions, the above provisions will not apply and the shortfall will seemingly rank *after* the separate debts, unless those provisions are applied by an order under the Insolvent Partnerships Order 1994, art. 14(1). See further *infra*, paras 27–85, 27–86.

[77] See the Administration of Insolvent Estates of Deceased Persons Order 1986 (SI 1986/1999), art. 4, which obliges the personal representatives, where the estate is insolvent but is not being administered in bankruptcy, to apply the same rules as to the priority of and proof of debts, etc., as if an insolvency administration order had been made. As to when an estate is insolvent, see the Insolvency Act 1986, s.421(4); also the following pre-Act decisions: *Re Leng* [1895] 1 Ch. 652; *Re Whitaker* [1904] 1 Ch. 299; *Re Pink* [1927] 1 Ch. 237.

[78] See *supra*, paras 13–03 *et seq.*, 26–15. And see the following older cases: *Croft v. Pyke* (1733) 3 P.W. 180; *Gray v. Chiswell* (1803) 9 Ves.Jr. 118; *Addis v. Knight* (1817) 2 Mer. 117; *Lodge v. Prichard* (1863) 1 De G.J. & S. 610; *Whittingstall v. Grover* (1886) 10 W.R. 53.

[79] The Insolvency Act 1986, ss.175A(1), 328A(1), as respectively added and applied in the manner set out *supra*, n. 76, only apply in a case falling within the ambit of the Insolvent Partnerships Order 1994, arts 8, 10 or 11. *Semble*, the result will be the same in any other case.

[80] See the exceptions considered *infra*, paras 27–128 *et seq.* Lord Lindley appeared to consider that the only exception which clearly applied under the old bankruptcy laws was that where "there is not and never was, since the death of the deceased, any joint estate whatever, and no solvent partner": see *Cowell v. Sikes* (1827) 2 Russ. 191; *Lodge v. Prichard, supra*; also *infra*, para. 27–129. *Quaere*, why should the other exceptions not apply?

[81] *Lacey v. Hill* (1872) 8 Ch.App. 441; (1876) 4 Ch.D. 537; also *infra*, para. 27–136. The inability of a partner to prove in competition with his own joint creditors is expressly recognised by the Insolvency Act 1986, ss.175C(2), 328C(2), as respectively amended and applied in the manner set out *supra*, n. 76. Competition is permitted in only two cases, *i.e.* debts arising as a result of fraud or in the ordinary course of carrying on a separate business: *ibid. Semble*, these provisions may, where appropriate, apply by virtue of the Administration of Insolvent Estates of Deceased Persons Order 1986, art. 4.

is insufficient to pay the separate creditors, there will be nothing available for distribution to the partnership creditors and no question of the surviving partner competing with them will arise. Accordingly, in such a case his proof will be allowed.[82]

A creditor who holds a security on any part of the deceased's partner's estate may realise his security and prove for the balance of his debt or give up his security and prove for the whole debt.[83]

Administration in bankruptcy

Provided that no proceedings for the administration of the estate have been **26–20** commenced, a creditor, temporary administrator,[84] liquidator[85] or the supervisor of a voluntary arrangement in effect in relation to the deceased partner or any person bound thereby may petition for an insolvency administration order, with a view to the estate being administered under a modified version of the Insolvency Act 1986.[86] Where administration proceedings are already on foot, the court may, if satisfied that the estate is insolvent, transfer them to the relevant bankruptcy court.[87] It is presumed that, if insolvency petitions are subsequently presented against one or more of the surviving partners, the proceedings can be consolidated, although there appears to be no provision authorising this in the Act or the rules made thereunder.[88]

Although the Insolvency Act 1986, as modified, does not state that the deceased's separate creditors have priority over the partnership creditors, as under the general law,[89] it seems clear that this rule will still continue to apply.[90]

---

[82] *Ex p. Head* [1894] 1 Q.B. 638; *Ex p. Topping* (1865) 4 De G.J. & S. 551. See also the other exceptions considered *infra*, paras 27–137 *et seq.*

[83] See *infra*, para. 27–111.

[84] Within the meaning of Council Regulation (EC) No. 1346/2000 of May 29, 2000 on insolvency proceedings, Art. 38.

[85] Within the meaning of *ibid.* Art. 2(b) and appointed in proceedings by virtue of *ibid.* Art. 3(1).

[86] Insolvency Act 1986, ss.264, 271(2), 272, as respectively amended and/or substituted and applied by the Administration of Insolvent Estates of Deceased Persons Order 1986, art. 3(1), Sched. 1, Pt II, paras 1, 5, 6, as itself amended, in the case of para. 1, by the Adminstration of Insolvent Estates of Deceased Persons (Amendment) Order 2002 (SI 2002/1309), art. 3(1). Note that, where a criminal bankruptcy order is in force, a petition may also be presented by the Official Petitioner or other specified person (see *ibid.* s.264(1)(d)), but this category will be removed from a day to be appointed by virtue of the Criminal Justice Act 1988, Sched. 16. Note that the petition will be deemed to have been presented and the insolvency administration order made as at the date of death: Administration of Insolvent Estates of Deceased Persons Order 1986, art. 3(1), Sched. 1, Pt II, para. 12. As to when an estate is regarded as insolvent, see the Insolvency Act 1986, s.421(4).

[87] *ibid.* s.271(3), as substituted and applied by the Administration of Insolvent Estates of Deceased Persons Order 1986, Sched. 1, Pt II, para. 5. And see *Morley v. White* (1872) L.R. 8 Ch.App. 214; *Ex p. Gordon* (1873) L.R. 8 Ch.App. 555; *Hulme v. Rowbotham* [1907] W.N. 162 and 189.

[88] See the Insolvency Act 1998, ss.168(5A), 303(2A), (2B), as inserted by the Insolvent Partnerships Order 1994, art. 14 and reproduced *infra*, para. 27–21; also the Insolvency Rules 1986 (SI 1986/1925), r. 6.236, as amended by the Insolvency (Amendment) Rules 2010, (SI 2010/686), Sched.1, para. 1. Consolidation was possible under the old bankruptcy laws: see *Re C. Greaves* [1904] 2 K.B. 493.

[89] See *supra*, para. 26–15.

[90] As noted, *supra*, para. 26–19, certain provisions of the Insolvency Act 1986 (as amended and applied pursuant to the Insolvent Partnerships Order 1994) do expressly recognise the effect of the Partnership Act 1890, s.9. See also *infra*, para. 27–86.

B.   DEBTS INCURRED AFTER A PARTNER'S DEATH

The general rule: estate not directly liable

26–21   The general rule was summarised by Lord Lindley in these terms:

> " . . . it may be taken as a general proposition that the estate of a deceased partner is not liable to third parties for what may be done after his decease by the surviving partners[91]; and on that ground it has been held that they cannot be restrained at the suit of the executors of the deceased from continuing to carry on the business of the late firm in the old name."[92]

The rationale behind this rule seemingly lies in the limited control which the deceased partner's personal representatives are entitled to exercise over the conduct of the surviving partners.[93] However, whilst third parties may have no direct rights against it, the estate may be liable, *vis-à-vis* the surviving partners, to bear a share of any debts or liabilities properly incurred in winding up the partnership affairs.[94]

Liability of personal representatives

26–22   If the deceased partner's personal representatives are admitted as partners they will obviously incur personal liability for the debts and obligations of the new firm, on normal principles.[95] However, as Lord Lindley observed:

> " . . . the acts of an executor, to whatever extent they may render him personally liable, do not impose liability on the assets of the deceased, unless those acts have been properly performed by the executor in the execution of his duty as executor."

An administrator is, essentially, in the same position.

Liability of estate for acts of personal representatives

26–23   In order to determine whether the estate is liable for the acts of the personal representatives, regard must be had to the nature of those acts and to the terms

---

[91] See *Bagel v. Miller* [1903] 2 K.B. 212.

[92] *Webster v. Webster* (1791) 3 Swan. 490, note. The words "on that ground" are significant, since the court will, in general, intervene with a view to protecting the firm's goodwill pending sale: see *supra*, paras 10–199 *et seq.*

[93] See *Devaynes v. Noble, Houlton's case, Johnes's case*, and *Brice's case* (1816) 1 Mer. 529, 616 *et seq.*; and, in particular, pp. 622–623 *per* Sir William Grant M.R. See also *Vulliamy v. Noble* (1817) 3 Mer. 593 and *supra*, para. 26–02.

[94] See *supra*, paras 13–61 *et seq.*

[95] See *Wightman v. Townroe* (1813) 1 M. & S. 412; *Labouchere v. Tupper* (1857) 11 Moo. P.C. 198; *Ex p. Garland* (1804) 10 Ves.Jr. 110; *Ex p. Holdsworth* (1841) 1 M.D. & D. 475. But personal representatives will not necessarily render themselves liable as partners merely by sharing profits with the surviving partners: see the Partnership Act 1890, s.2(3), *supra*, paras 5–02, 5–17 *et seq.* and, prior to the Act, *Holme v. Hammond* (1872) L.R. 7 Ex. 218. See also, as to the liability of personal representatives on bills of exchange or promissory notes accepted or indorsed in the course of carrying on the deceased's business, *Liverpool Borough Bank v. Walker* (1859) 4 De G &. J. 24; *Lucas v. Williams* (1862) 3 Giff. 150.

of the deceased partner's will or, if he died intestate, the provisions of the Administration of Estates Act 1925.[96]

Authority of personal representatives to carry on business, etc.

Lord Lindley wrote: **26–24**

> "Executors, unless authorised by their testator so to do, ought not to leave his assets outstanding in the trade or business in which he was engaged when he died. It has been laid down as a rule without exception, that to authorise executors to carry on a trade, or to permit it to be carried on with the property of a testator held by them in trust, there ought to be the most distinct and positive authority, and direction given by the testator for that purpose."[97]

Thus, a bequest of a partnership share to one partner for life, and then to another, does not, without more, warrant the trustees of his will leaving the share unconverted.[98] Again a trust to sell a business may not be equivalent to a trust to carry it on until sale,[99] but a power to *postpone* sale will normally authorise the executors to carry the business on during any period of postponement,[100] but not indefinitely.[101]

A general direction to carry on a business in which the testator was engaged   **26–25**
at the time of his death has been held not to authorise the employment of any *additional* assets therein.[102] Moreover, a testator does not, merely by authorising his share to be left in the partnership business, necessarily contemplate that his executors or trustees should do anything more than leave it outstanding by way of loan.[103]

It should be noted that, even where this is not directly or indirectly authorised by the will, a personal representative will usually be entitled to carry on the deceased's business for a short period, purely with a view to realisation.[104]

Acts which impose liability on estate

There are certain acts which, if done by a personal representative, may   **26–26**
automatically impose liability on the estate.[105] Lord Lindley pointed out that:

> " . . . if a partner appoints a co-partner his executor, and dies, and the executor continues to carry on the business, it is possible that some of his acts, attributed to

---

[96] See, in particular, *ibid.* ss.33(1), 39 (as respectively amended by the Trusts of Land and Appointment of Trustees Act 1996, Sched. 2, para. 5(2) and Sched. 3, para. 6(2) and, in the case of s.39 only, by the Trustee Act 2000, Sched. 2, Pt II, para. 28).

[97] *Kirkman v. Booth* (1848) 11 Beav. 273; and see *Williams, Mortimer and Sunnucks on Executors, Administrators and Probate* (19th ed.), paras 55–85 *et seq.* An express power conferred on executors may not be available to an administrator: *Lambert v. Rendle* (1863) 3 New Rep. 247.

[98] See *Kirkman v. Booth, supra; Skirving v. Williams* (1857) 24 Beav. 275; *Re Chancellor* (1884) 26 Ch.D. 42.

[99] *Strickland v. Symons* (1884) 26 Ch.D. 245; *Re Rooke* [1953] Ch. 716.

[100] *Re Crowther* [1895] 2 Ch. 56. But *cf. Re Rooke, supra; Re Berry* [1962] Ch. 97.

[101] *Re Smith* [1896] 1 Ch. 171; *Re Berry, supra.*

[102] See *McNeillie v. Acton* (1853) 4 De G.M. & G. 744; *Re Cameron* (1884) 26 Ch.D. 19.

[103] See *Travis v. Milne* (1851) 9 Hare 141.

[104] *Marshall v. Broadhurst* (1831) 1 C. & J. 403; *Garrett v. Noble* (1834) 6 Sim. 504; also *Dowse v. Gorton* [1891] A.C. 190, 199 *per* Lord Herschell. And see *Williams, Mortimer and Sunnucks on Executors, Administrators and Probate* (19th ed.), para. 55–89.

[105] See *Williams, Mortimer and Sunnucks on Executors, Administrators and Probate* (19th ed.), para. 55–98.

him not as a partner but as executor, may render the assets of the deceased liable for what may have occurred since his death.[106] But this is quite an exceptional case."[107]

Assets actually employed in business

26–27   If any part of the deceased partner's estate is properly employed in carrying on the partnership business, it will obviously be available to meet partnership debts incurred since the date of death and cannot be proved for in the event of the firm's insolvency. However, such proof will be allowed to the extent that assets are employed in the business *without* authority. This is demonstrated by the decision in *Ex p. Garland*.[108]

Right to indemnity

26–28   If the deceased partner's personal representatives carry on the partnership business pursuant to a direction in his will or their statutory powers,[109] or with a view to realisation, or otherwise with the consent of the beneficiaries, they will be entitled to an indemnity out of the estate for any personal liability thereby incurred.[110] It is, however, clear that the liability of the estate will not, in general, exceed the amount (if any) expressly authorised by the deceased to be employed in the business.[111]

It does not follow from the existence of this right to indemnity that the personal representatives' trade creditors can necessarily stand in their place with a view to seeking payment out of the estate,[112] as Lord Lindley explained:

"Prima facie, a creditor must look for payment to his legal debtor, and the fact that the latter is entitled to be indemnified by some one else, or out of some estate, does not confer any additional right on the creditor. To avail the creditor something more

---

[106] See *Vulliamy v. Noble* (1817) 3 Mer. 593, 614. What was contemplated there was the executor having dealings with customers *in that capacity.*

[107] See *Farhall v. Farhall* (1871) L.R. 7 Ch.App. 123; *Owen v. Delamere* (1872) L.R. 15 Eq. 134; *Re Johnson* (1880) 15 Ch.D. 548; *Strickland v. Symons* (1884) 26 Ch.D. 245; *Re Evans* (1887) 34 Ch.D. 597.

[108] (1804) 10 Ves.Jr. 110. See also *Ex p. Richardson* (1818) Buck. 202; *Thompson v. Andrews* (1832) 1 M. & K. 116; *Cutbush v. Cutbush* (1839) 1 Beav. 184; *Ex p. Butterfield* (1847) De G. 570; *Scott v. Izon* (1865) 34 Beav. 434; and see *Hall v. Fennell* (1875) Ir.Rep. 9 Eq. 615. *cf. Ex p. Edmonds* (1862) 4 De G.F. & J. 488. See also, *infra,* para. 27–114.

[109] Administration of Estates Act 1925, ss.33(1), 39 (as respectively amended by the Trusts of Land and Appointment of Trustees Act 1996, Sched. 2, para. 5(2) and Sched. 3, para. 6(2) and, in the case of s.39 only, by the Trustee Act 2000, Sched. 2, Pt II, para. 28) and *supra,* para. 26–24. See also, in the case of land, the Trusts of Land and Appointment of Trustees Act 1996, ss.4, 6 (as amended by the Trustee Act 2000, Sched. 2, Pt II, para. 45 and the Charities Act 2006, Sched. 8, para. 182), 11.

[110] *Ex p. Garland* (1804) 10 Ves.Jr. 110; *Labouchere v. Tupper* (1857) 11 Moo. P.C. 198; *Re Johnson* (1880) 15 Ch.D. 548; *Dowse v. Gorton* [1891] A.C. 190; *Re Bracey* [1936] Ch. 690. The indemnity will be available even in respect of a tortious liability: *Benett v. Wyndham* (1862) 4 De G.F. & J. 259; *Re Raybould* [1900] 1 Ch. 199. *Semble* the duty of care imposed on personal representatives by the Trustee Act 2000, ss.1, 35(1) does not apply in cases of this type: see *ibid.* Sched. 1.

[111] *Cutbush v. Cutbush* (1839) 1 Beav. 184; *McNeillie v. Acton* (1853) 4 De G.M. & G. 744; *Owen v. Delamere* (1872) L.R. 15 Eq. 134; *Re Johnson* (1880) 15 Ch.D. 548; *Strickland v. Symons* (1884) 26 Ch.D. 245. Lord Kenyon's decision in *Hankey v. Hammock* (1786) Buck. 210 was formerly thought to justify the view that the liability extended to *all* the assets of the estate.

[112] A creditor of a personal representative is not a creditor of the deceased: see *Re Kitson* [1911] 2 K.B. 109. However, a right of subrogation will generally be available: see *Williams, Mortimer and Sunnucks on Executors, Administrators and Probate* (19th ed.), para. 55–99.

is necessary, namely the existence of a trust fund expressly devoted to carrying on the business in respect of which the debt to the creditor has been contracted."[113]

In cases of the latter type, the trade creditors are, ironically, placed in a better position than the creditors of an ordinary partnership, since they have a right of recourse both against the personal representatives and against the estate.[114] However, the normal priority accorded to the deceased's creditors[115] will not be affected unless those creditors have in fact consented to the business being carried on for their benefit.[116] **26–29**

Any default by the personal representative must, in general, be made good before his creditors can obtain anything out of the relevant fund.[117] Where there are two or more personal representatives, each will enjoy a separate right to indemnity, so that one will not be prejudiced by the default of the other.[118]

3.   THE SEPARATE CREDITORS, LEGATEES, ETC., OF THE DECEASED

The consequences of a partner's death as regards his separate creditors and the persons interested in his estate are, for the most part, entirely straightforward; complications only arise when the deceased's share is continued in the business or, on occasion, where that share is specifically bequeathed. **26–30**

A.   THE GENERAL RULE

As might be expected, a deceased partner's separate creditors and the persons beneficially interested in his estate will, as a general rule, only have a right of recourse against his personal representatives. Lord Lindley summarised the position in the following way: **26–31**

"Under ordinary circumstances, the separate creditors, legatees, and next-of-kin of a deceased partner, must look for payment of what is due to them out of his assets to

---

[113] See *Strickland v. Symons* (1884) 26 Ch.D. 245; *Re Evans* (1887) 34 Ch.D. 597.

[114] As Lord Lindley put it: "the creditors have not only the personal security of the executors and trustees who carry on the business, but also a right to stand in their place to the extent to which they are entitled to indemnity out of the assets of the deceased." See generally *Re Johnson* (1880) 15 Ch.D. 548.

[115] Lord Lindley's formulation of this general principle was in these terms: "The liability of the estate of a deceased partner to persons who become creditors after his decease, is subject to its liability to those who were his creditors at his decease."

[116] *Dowse v. Gorton* [1891] A.C. 190; *Re Oxley* [1914] 1 Ch. 604. It is not enough to show that the deceased's creditors knew that the business was being carried on and took no steps to prevent it: *Re Oxley, supra.* The decisions to the contrary in *Re Brooke* [1894] 2 Ch. 600 and in the Irish case, *Re Hodges* [1899] 1 I.R. 480, cannot be relied on.

[117] *Re Johnson* (1880) 15 Ch.D. 548 (where the previous authorities were reviewed by Jessel M.R.); *Dowse v. Gorton, supra.* See also *Re British Power Electric Traction Co. Ltd.* [1910] 2 Ch. 470.

[118] *Re Frith* [1902] 1 Ch. 342. As to the position in the event of the personal representative's insolvency, see *Jennings v. Mather* [1902] 1 K.B. 1. *cf. St. Thomas's Hospital v. Richardson* [1910] 1 K.B. 271; *Ex p. Governors of St. Thomas's Hospital* [1911] 2 K.B. 705.

his legal personal representative, and to him alone.[119] The executors[120] are, under ordinary circumstances, the only persons who have a right to call upon the surviving partners for an account; and of this right they do not divest themselves by a sale and assignment of the share of the deceased; for the effect of such sale and assignment is only to make the executors trustees for the purchaser."[121]

Account ordered against personal representatives

26–32   However, this does not mean that an account in respect of the deceased partner's share cannot be taken in proceedings brought against the personal representatives: in Lord Lindley's words, it is "the common course" to direct an inquiry as to the sum due to the estate in respect of that share.[122] Whilst the point is not entirely free from doubt, it even appears that such an inquiry ought to be pursued under a normal administration order, as Lord Lindley explained:

> "It seems that, under an ordinary judgment for the administration of the estate of a deceased partner, the partnership accounts will not be gone into, unless the Court specially directs some inquiry to be made with reference to the share of the deceased. But it is difficult to see how any account of his personal estate can be taken without such an inquiry; and it has been decided more than once, that if the surviving partners seek to obtain payment of a balance from the estate of the deceased on the partnership accounts, these accounts must be taken, although no special direction as to them may be contained in the judgment."[123]

Be that as it may, it is clear that the surviving partners cannot be ordered to pay any sum found due to the estate on completion of the inquiry: to obtain such payment, a Part 20 claim[124] or other proceedings by the personal representatives will be required.

Account on footing of wilful default

26–33   Subject to any provision contained in the deceased partner's will, his personal representatives will have power at their discretion to postpone the conversion of his estate without being liable for any consequential losses.[125] It follows that, unless they have effectively ignored the terms of the will or they are otherwise in breach of their overriding duty to administer the estate for the benefit of the persons interested therein, only in exceptional circumstances will the personal

---

[119] *Langley v. Earl of Oxford* (1748) 2 Amb. 795; *Alsager v. Rowley* (1802) 6 Ves.Jr. 748; *Seeley v. Boehm* (1817) 2 Madd. 176, 180 *per* Sir Thomas Plumer V.-C.; *Davies v. Davies* (1837) 2 Keen 534; *Travis v. Milne* (1851) 9 Hare 141; *Saunders v. Druce* (1855) 3 Drew. 140. As to the position where there is no personal representative, see *supra*, para. 26–08; also *Maclean v. Dawson* (1859) 5 Jur. (N.S.) 1091.

[120] Similarly in the case of an administrator.

[121] *Clegg v. Fishwick* (1849) 1 Mac & G. 294; *Stainton v. The Carron Company* (1853) 18 Beav. 146.

[122] As in *Macdonald v. Richardson* (1858) 1 Giff. 81. See also *Pointon v. Pointon* (1871) L.R. 12 Eq. 547, where the only surviving partner was an executor and trustee.

[123] See *Paynter v. Houston* (1817) 3 Mer. 297; *Woolley v. Gordon* (1829) Tam. 11; *Baker v. Martin* (1832) 5 Sim. 380.

[124] CPR r. 20.2(1)(b).

[125] Administration of Estates Act 1925, ss.33, 39 (as respectively amended by the Trusts of Land and Appointment of Trustees Act 1996, Sched. 2, para. 5 and Sched. 3, para. 6(2) and the Trustee Act 2000, Sched. 2, Pt II, paras 27, 28). As to the application of the former section (in its unamended form), see *Public Trustee v. Trollope* [1927] 1 Ch. 596; *Re McKee* [1931] 2 Ch. 145; *Re Plowman* [1943] Ch. 269.

representatives be liable to account for sums which they have not actually received during any period of postponement.[126]

Account ordered against surviving partners

The general rule which precludes a deceased partner's separate creditors and   **26–34** legatees, etc., from proceeding against the surviving partners is not absolute, although, historically, the extent of the exceptions was not clearly defined. Lord Lindley analysed the position in this way:

> " . . . there are cases to be met with, which apparently warrant the inference that surviving partners may always be sued along with the executor or administrator of the deceased.[127] But the authority of these cases has . . . been called in question, and the better opinion now is that some special circumstances are necessary to justify such a course."[128]

The "special circumstances" which have been held sufficient for this purpose have all involved a degree of actual or potential impropriety on the part of the personal representatives. Thus, proceedings against the personal representatives and the surviving partners will be permissible where they are in collusion,[129] where the personal representatives have refused to seek an account from the surviving partners[130] or have, by their dealings, precluded themselves from seeking such an account,[131] where they are themselves partners[132] or, in Lord Lindley's words, generally:

> " . . . where the relation between the executors[133] and the surviving partners is such as to present a substantial impediment to the prosecution, by the executors, of the rights of the persons interested in the estate of the deceased, against the surviving partners . . . ".[134]

Given the overriding objective which lies at the heart of the Civil Procedure Rules,[135] the court may be prepared to recognise other "special circumstances" if the interests of justice so require.

---

[126] As to charging the executor of a deceased partner with wilful default, see *Ward v. Ward* (1843) 2 H.L.C. 777; *Kirkman v. Booth* (1848) 11 Beav. 273; *Rowley v. Adams* (1849) 2 H.L.C. 726; *Grayburn v. Clarkson* (1868) L.R. 3 Ch.App. 605; *Sculthorpe v. Tipper* (1871) L.R. 13 Eq. 232.
[127] See *Newland v. Champion* (1748) 1 Ves.Sen. 106; *Bowsher v. Watkins* (1830) 1 R. & M. 277.
[128] See *Davies v. Davies* (1837) 2 Keen 534; *Law v. Law* (1847) 11 Jur. 463; *Travis v. Milne* (1851) 9 Hare 141; *Stainton v. The Carron Co.* (1853) 18 Beav. 146; *Yeatman v. Yeatman* (1877) 7 Ch.D. 210.
[129] *Doran v. Simpson* (1799) 4 Ves.Jr. 651; *Alsager v. Rowley* (1802) 6 Ves.Jr. 748; *Gedge v. Traill* (1823) 1 R. & M. 281, note.
[130] *Burroughs v. Elton* (1805) 11 Ves.Jr. 29; but *cf. Yeatman v. Yeatman* (1877) 7 Ch.D. 210, where a mere refusal was held *not* to be sufficient.
[131] *Braithwaite v. Britain* (1836) 1 Keen 206; *Law v. Law* (1847) 11 Jur. 463.
[132] *Cropper v. Knapman* (1836) 2 Y. & C. Ex. 338; *Travis v. Milne* (1851) 9 Hare 141; *Beningfield v. Baxter* (1886) 12 App.Cas. 167. And see, as to the position where the deceased's assets are continued in the business, *infra*, paras 26–40 *et seq.*
[133] Or administrators.
[134] *Travis v. Milne* (1851) 9 Hare 141.
[135] *ibid.* r. 1.1(2).

Account settled between personal representatives and surviving partners

26–35   A bona fide account settled between the personal representatives and the surviving partners, provided that they are not the same persons, will bind the deceased partner's separate creditors and all persons interested in his estate.[136]

Surviving partners as personal representatives

26–36   It is self evident that no such account can be settled when the personal representatives are also surviving partners; indeed, as Lord Lindley pointed out:

> "if the executors are themselves the surviving partners, or some of them, it becomes exceedingly difficult to make any arrangement which will be binding on the persons interested in the estate of the deceased; for even if any arrangement is assented to by such persons, it will be liable to be successfully disputed, on any of those numerous grounds which are held to invalidate arrangements between trustees and their *cestuis que trustent*, and by which trustees do, or may, obtain a benefit at the expense of the trust estate."

A graphic and, in many ways, extreme demonstration of this principle is to be found in *Wedderburn v. Wedderburn*,[137] where an account was directed, on the application of the persons beneficially interested in a deceased partner's estate, 30 years after the date of his death, notwithstanding subsequent changes in the firm and partial releases given to the executors by the beneficiaries.[138]

Costs

26–37   The costs of an administration action brought by a deceased partner's separate creditor are, where payable out of the estate, paid in priority to the claims of his joint creditors.[139]

B.   DECEASED PARTNER'S SHARE LEFT IN BUSINESS

26–38   It has already been seen that, subject to the terms of the deceased partner's will[140] and to their right to postpone the realisation of his estate with a view to sale, the personal representatives ought not properly to leave his share outstanding in the partnership business, whether or not they are themselves members of the firm.[141]

---

[136] *Davies v. Davies* (1837) 2 Keen 534; *Smith v. Everett* (1859) 27 Beav. 446. And see the Trustee Act 1925, s.15 (as amended by the Trustee Act 2000, Sched. 2, Pt II, para. 20); also *Re Houghton* [1904] 1 Ch. 622 (a decision under a predecessor section); *Re Hoyle* [1947] I.R. 61.

[137] (1836) 2 Keen 722 and (1838) 4 Myl. & Cr. 41. See further, as to this case, *supra*, para. 25–28.

[138] See *Beningfield v. Baxter* (1886) 12 App.Cas. 167 and the other cases cited *supra*, paras 25–40 *et seq.*

[139] *Re McRea* (1883) 32 Ch.D. 613.

[140] It is, for present purposes, assumed that there are no provisions in the partnership agreement which would entitle the continuing partners to retain the deceased's share in the business.

[141] See *supra*, paras 26–24, 26–25. *Semble*, the court could authorise trustees (but not personal representatives as such) to adopt such a course, pursuant to the Trustee Act 1925, s.57 or the Variation of Trusts Act 1958, s.1 (as amended). And see, generally, *Trustees of the British Museum v. Att.-Gen.* [1984] 1 W.L.R. 418.

If they nevertheless do so, it is necessary to ascertain the extent of their and the surviving partners' liability to account for any profits made by the employment of the share.

Loan of deceased's share

In the most simple case, *i.e.* where the personal representatives lend the deceased's share to the surviving partners at interest pursuant to an express power in his will, the surviving partners will obviously be bound to pay such interest, but will not otherwise be accountable for any profits made by the use of the share.[142] This will be the position even where the surviving partners do not pay off the loan on the due date.[143] At the same time, the personal representatives will not be liable for any loss resulting from the exercise of such a power, provided that they scrupulously adhere to its terms.[144]

26–39

It is apprehended that the separate creditors and legatees, etc., will enjoy no greater rights where the loan is made in breach of trust, save where the surviving partners are implicated therein.[145]

It goes without saying that, subject to the terms of the will, the position will be otherwise where the personal representatives are also surviving partners.

Share employed in business by personal representative

It has already been seen that where a personal representative who is also a surviving partner continues to employ the deceased partner's share in the partnership business, he will normally be liable to account for the value of the share together with interest at the rate of five per cent. or, at the option of the persons beneficially interested in the estate, any profits received by the personal representative which are attributable to the use of the share.[146] This obligation seemingly co-exists with the statutory obligation under section 42 of the Partnership Act 1890, since it derives from a simple breach of trust, as Lord Lindley explained prior to that Act:

26–40

" . . . the obligation of the executor[147] . . . to account is founded on a breach of trust committed by him, for which he is liable, at all events to the extent to which he has benefited by it, whether other persons are also liable or not; and being founded on a breach of trust, an action in respect of it may be sustained against the executor alone, though he may only be one of several, by whom the profits have been made."[148]

It is, perhaps, self evident that the potentially onerous nature of the obligation imposed on the personal representative in such a case is no justification for

26–41

---

[142] *Parker v. Bloxham* (1855) 20 Beav. 295; *Vyse v. Foster* (1872) L.R. 8 Ch. App. 309, affirmed at (1874) L.R. 7 H.L. 318. In the latter case, one of the executors was a surviving partner: see further, *supra*, para. 25–29.

[143] *Vyse v. Foster, supra.*

[144] *Paddon v. Richardson* (1855) 7 De G.M. & G. 563. See also, as to the construction of such powers, *supra*, para. 3–11. If the personal representatives are, during the continuance of the loan, authorised to examine the accounts of the firm with a view to satisfying themselves as to its solvency, the costs of so doing will be payable out of the capital of the estate: *Re Bennett* [1896] 1 Ch. 778.

[145] See *Stroud v. Gwyer* (1860) 28 Beav. 130; *Flockton v. Bunning* (1868) L.R. 8 Ch.App. 323, note. See also *supra*, para. 25–41.

[146] See *supra*, paras 25–40 *et seq.*

[147] The position of an administrator is no different.

[148] See also *supra*, para. 25–40.

depriving the separate creditors and legatees, etc., of their right to opt for profits in lieu of interest. Lord Lindley put it thus:

" . . . such persons are not deprived of this option by the circumstance that it will be difficult and expensive to ascertain what part of the profits has arisen from the employment of the assets of the deceased; for whatever difficulty may exist is attributable to the conduct of the executor himself, and cannot therefore be effectually urged by him as a reason why no account of profits should be taken."[149]

Where the option is exercised, it will usually be desirable to join the other surviving partners, so as to ensure that any profits attributable to the use of the deceased's share can be recovered, even though they have not been received by the personal representative.[150]

Compound interest will be awarded in certain cases,[151] but a mixed claim which is comprised of part interest and part profits will not be permitted, unless there has been an intermediate settlement of account[152] or other special circumstances.[153]

Liability of surviving partners who are not personal representatives

26–42   The extent of the liability attaching to the surviving partners who are *not* the deceased partner's personal representatives is less clear. Their obligation under section 42 of the Partnership Act 1890 is, of course, well defined.[154] However, writing prior to that Act, Lord Lindley expressed the following view:

"Upon the principle that everyone concerned in a breach of trust with notice of the trust is answerable for such breach, it follows that if a partner dies, and his surviving partners allow his assets to remain in their business, with the knowledge that to suffer them so to remain is a breach of trust on the part of the executors, the surviving partners will themselves be responsible to the separate creditors, legatees, or next-of-kin of the deceased, for any loss which may be thereby sustained."[155]

The current editor is, however, of the opinion that, as long as they are not also the deceased partner's personal representatives, the surviving partners will, in general, be entitled to assume that his share has been properly left in the business unless they either know, or ought to know, that a breach of trust is being committed. The burden of proof will, in such cases, lie on the persons who seek to hold the surviving partners liable.[156]

---

[149] *Docker v. Somes* (1834) 2 M. & K. 655; *Townend v. Townend* (1859) 1 Giff. 201; *Flockton v. Bunning* (1868) L.R. 8 Ch.App. 323, noted *supra*, para. 25–41.

[150] See *supra*, para. 25–41. Note, however, the problems associated with such claims: see *supra*, paras 25–30, 25–31.

[151] See *Jones v. Foxall* (1852) 15 Beav. 388; *Williams v. Powell* (1852) 15 Beav. 461; *Vyse v. Foster* (1874) L.R. 7 H.L. 318, 346 *per* Lord Selborne. See also *supra*, para. 25–40. And note the exceptional decision in *Roxburgh Dinardo & Partners' Judicial Factor v. Dinardo* 1993 S.L.T. 16 (2nd Div.).

[152] *Heathcote v. Hulme* (1819) 1 J. & W. 122.

[153] As in *Townend v. Townend* (1859) 1 Giff. 201.

[154] See *supra*, paras 25–24 *et seq*. It is now clear that interest cannot, in the alternative, be claimed under the Senior Courts Act 1981, s.35A (formerly the Supreme Court Act 1981: Constitutional Reform Act 2005, Sched. 11, Pt 1, para. 1(1)): see *supra*, paras 20–41, 25–43.

[155] See *Wilson v. Moore* (1834) 1 M. & K. 337; *Booth v. Booth* (1838) 1 Beav. 125; *Travis v. Milne* (1851) 9 Hare 141. *cf. Ex p. Barnewall* (1855) 6 De G.M. & G. 795. And see also *supra*, para. 12–134.

[156] See, for example, the approach adopted prior to 1926 in the case of sales of leasehold property: *Re Whistler* (1887) 35 Ch.D. 561; *Venn and Furze's Contract* [1894] 2 Ch. 101; *Verrell's Contract* [1903] 1 Ch. 65. And see also *supra*, para. 12–134.

Personal representative becoming partner

Where a personal representative is admitted to the partnership by the surviving   **26–43**
partners, the question arises whether any share of profits received by him *qua*
partner belongs to him personally or to the estate which he represents. The
answer will inevitably depend on the circumstances, as Lord Lindley made
clear:

> "If he became a partner in his representative character, or, as in *Cook v. Colling-*
> *ridge*,[157] under circumstances entitling the legatees to treat him still as their trustee,
> he must account for any profits which he may have obtained as a partner. On the other
> hand, if, as in *Simpson v. Chapman*,[158] he became a partner not in his representative
> character, nor under such circumstances as those above mentioned, the profits
> accruing to him as a partner will be his own, and not form part of the assets for which
> he must account as executor."

The decided cases

Those cases in which an account of profits has been sought following the death   **26–44**
of a partner, to which reference has been made elsewhere in this work,[159] may
conveniently be classified as follows:

Group 1: Account of profits decreed

    A. Personal representatives against surviving partners.[160]

    B. Legatees against personal representatives who were not partners.[161]

    C. Legatees against personal representatives who were, or who became,
       partners.[162]

Group 2: Account of profits refused

    A. Personal representatives against surviving partners.[163]

---

[157] (1822) Jac. 607. See *supra*, para. 25–42.

[158] (1853) 4 De G.M. & G. 154. And see *supra*, para. 25–28.

[159] See *supra*, paras 25–26 *et seq.*

[160] *Brown v. De Tastet* (1819) Jac. 284; *Booth v. Parks* (1829) Beatty 444; *Featherstonhaugh v. Turner* (1858) 25 Beav. 382; *Smith v. Everett* (1859) 27 Beav. 446; *Yates v. Finn* (1880) 13 Ch.D. 839; *Manley v. Sartori* [1927] 1 Ch. 157; *Pathirana v. Pathirana* [1967] A.C. 233; *Barclays Bank Trust Co. Ltd. v. Bluff* [1982] Ch. 172 (where it was held that the executor had not yet elected between interest and profits and there was a declaration accordingly: see *supra*, para. 25–32); *Chandroutie v. Gajadhar* [1987] A.C. 147 (PC).

[161] *Palmer v. Mitchell* (1809) 2 M. & K. 672, note; *Heathcote v. Hulme* (1819) 1 J. & W. 122; *Docker v. Somes* (1834) 2 M. & K. 654.

[162] *Cook v. Collingridge* (1822) Jac. 607 (*supra*, para. 25–42); *Wedderburn v. Wedderburn* (1836) 2 Keen 722, (1838) 4 Myl. & Cr. 41 and (1856) 22 Beav. 84 (*supra*, paras 25–28, 26–36); *Willett v. Blandford* (1842) 1 Hare 253; *Stocken v. Dawson* (1843) 6 Beav. 371 and (1848) 17 L.J. Ch. 282; *Macdonald v. Richardson* (1858) 1 Giff. 81; *Townend v. Townend* (1859) Giff. 201; *Flockton v. Bunning* (1868) L.R. 8 Ch.App. 323, note (*supra*, para. 25–41).

[163] *Knox v. Gye* (1872) L.R. 5 H.L. 656, *supra*, para. 23–34. In this case, the claim was statute barred.

B. Legatees against personal representatives who were, or who became, partners.[164]

C.   SPECIFIC BEQUESTS OF PARTNERSHIP SHARES

26–45   A partner will normally have complete freedom to dispose of his partnership share by will,[165] even though, as noticed hereafter, the subject matter of the bequest will, in practice, normally be represented by his financial entitlement under the agreement[166] or the Partnership Act 1890.[167]

Construction of particular bequests

26–46   The normal form of bequest will be of "all that the share and interest of the testator in the capital, assets and profits of the partnership." However, where a more limited form of words is used, questions of construction will inevitably arise.[168]

Bequest of capital

26–47   A bequest of a partner's capital has been held to include what was due to him in respect of advances.[169] Although it is probable that such a bequest would also include undrawn profits credited to the deceased partner's capital account, which are withdrawable at will and do not form part of the firm's fixed capital,[170] such a construction could not be guaranteed.

Bequest of goodwill

26–48   In *Robertson v. Quiddington*[171] it was held that a legatee of a deceased partner's share of goodwill could not sue the surviving partner for a sale of the goodwill and payment out of his share, even though an assent had been made in his favour by the deceased's executors. However, Lord Lindley commented:

> "This case was somewhat peculiar as in truth the surviving partner was entitled to everything which gave a saleable value to the goodwill."[172]

Bequest of net profits

26–49   A bequest of a partner's share of the net profits in his partnership business will entitle the legatee to the share of such profits receivable by his executors whilst

[164] *Simpson v. Chapman* (1853) 4 De G.M. & G. 154 (*supra*, para. 25–28); *Vyse v. Foster* (1872) L.R. 8 Ch.App. 309 and (1874) L.R. 7 H.L. 318 (*supra*, para. 25–38). See also *Wedderburn v. Wedderburn, supra*; *Willett v. Blandford, supra*; *Hordern v. Hordern* [1910] A.C. 465; *Re Mulholland's Will Trusts* [1949] W.N. 103.

[165] For a case in which this was held to be the position notwithstanding the inclusion in the agreement of what at first sight appeared to be a power of appointment in respect of the share: see *Ponton v. Dunn* (1830) 1 R. & M. 402.

[166] See generally, *supra*, paras 10–157 *et seq.*, 19–10 *et seq.*

[167] See *ibid.* s.44, *supra*, paras 25–45 *et seq.* But see also, *supra*, paras 19–10 *et seq.*

[168] See, generally, *Re Rhagg* [1938] Ch. 828 and the cases there cited.

[169] *Bevan v. Att.-Gen.* (1863) 4 Giff. 361. And see *Terry v. Terry* (1863) 33 Beav. 232.

[170] See further, as to the practice of dealing with profits in this way, *supra*, para. 17–06.

[171] (1860) 28 Beav. 529.

[172] See further *supra*, para. 10–203.

the partnership business is being carried on, but will not entitle him to any interest in the partnership assets.[173]

Bequest of specific partnership asset or a share therein

Given the nature of a partnership share,[174] it is obviously not competent for **26–50** one partner, *vis-à-vis* his co-partners, to dispose of a particular partnership asset by will,[175] although such a bequest may, if coupled with legacies in favour of the surviving partners, put the latter to their election whether to allow the asset to go to the legatee or to compensate him out of their own legacies.[176]

It does not, however, follow that such a bequest will be ineffective as between the beneficiaries claiming under the deceased partner's will: effect will, so far as possible, be given to a bequest of his share in the particular asset and, for this purpose, the partnership debts will be treated as primarily payable out of the other partnership assets.[177] If the partnership is insolvent, the legatee will, of course, receive nothing: in such a case, the solvency of the partners (including the deceased partner) is immaterial.[178]

Ademption

A specific bequest of a partnership share will be adeemed if the testator, after **26–51** making his will, leaves the firm and is paid out the value of that share. However, there will be no ademption so long as he remains a partner, even if the size or nature of his share is altered after the date of the will.[179] Indeed, such a bequest may even carry the entire business where the testator has acquired his co-partners' shares prior to the date of his death.[180]

Legacy to partner indebted to testator

A legatee is not entitled to receive any payment out of the testator's estate until **26–52** he has discharged any debts which he owes to that estate.[181] This principle does not, however, apply where the debt is due, not from the legatee personally, but only from a partnership of which he is a member.[182]

---

[173] *Re Lawes-Wittewronge* [1915] 1 Ch. 408.

[174] See generally, *supra*, paras 19–01 *et seq.*

[175] But see *supra*, para. 17–03. It is, of course, permissible for a partner to retain the right to all capital profits attributable to a particular asset, thus effectively preserving its value in his estate. See *infra*, para. 35–05.

[176] See generally, as to the doctrine of election, *Re Dicey* [1957] Ch. 145; *Re Gordon's Will Trusts* [1978] Ch. 145, and the cases there cited.

[177] *Re Holland* [1907] 2 Ch. 88. Note also the concession made in *Re Rhagg* [1938] Ch. 828.

[178] *Farquhar v. Hadden* (1871) L.R. 7 Ch.App. 1.

[179] *Backwell v. Child* (1755) Amb. 260; *Ellis v. Walker* (1756) Amb. 309; also *Re Rhagg* [1938] Ch. 828. *cf. Re Quibell's Will Trusts* [1956] 3 All E.R. 679. And see, as to the position where a legatee of a share is admitted to the partnership during the testator's lifetime, *Lacon v. Lacon* [1891] 2 Ch. 482.

[180] *Re Russell* (1882) L.R. 19 Ch.D. 432.

[181] See *Cherry v. Boultbee* (1839) 3 Keen 319, affirmed at 4 My. & Cr. 442. See also *Williams, Mortimer and Sunnucks on Executors, Administrators and Probate* (19th ed.), paras 51–10 *et seq.* See also, as to the application of this rule in the case of an insolvency, *Re SSSL Realisations (2002) Ltd.* [2006] Ch. 610 (CA); *Mills v. HSBC Trustee (CI) Ltd.* [2010] W.T.L.R. 235.

[182] *Turner v. Turner* [1911] 1 Ch. 716, explaining and distinguishing *Smith v. Smith* (1861) 3 Giff. 263. See also *Re Pennington and Owen Ltd.* [1925] Ch. 825.

Nomination of successor partner

26–53   It need hardly be observed that a specific bequest of a partnership share will not entitle the beneficiary to become a partner, unless there is an agreement to that effect which is binding on the surviving partners. In those (increasingly rare) cases where a partner is entitled to nominate a successor by will,[183] a mere bequest of residue is unlikely to be treated as a sufficient nomination.[184]

Effect of bequest

26–54   A specific bequest of a partnership share confers only limited rights on the legatee, as Lord Lindley explained:

> "The right of the legatee is simply to be paid the amount due to the testator at the time of his death in respect of his share[185]; and also, under the circumstances and subject to the qualifications already noticed,[186] to receive a proportion of the profits made since the testator's death. However, as between the legatee and the executor, the legatee is entitled to have the share kept in the business, if he so wishes, subject only to the superior right of the executor to sell the testator's estate for the payment of debts."[187]

The current editor does, however, consider that the beneficiary cannot force the executor to leave the share in the business if he will thereby risk incurring personal liability as a partner.[188]

Settled share

26–55   Where the testator has settled his share on life interest trusts, the question arises whether it must be converted into money and the proceeds invested pursuant to the rule in *Howe v. Lord Dartmouth*.[189] Since a share generally constitutes personal property,[190] the application of the rule will depend on the terms of the will.[191] Clear language is required if the life tenant is to be entitled to have the share kept unconverted[192]: neither an express power to postpone sale nor a provision directing the executors to treat any "dividends rents interest or moneys of the nature of income" as income will suffice.[193]

---

[183] See *supra*, paras 10–258 *et seq.*

[184] See *Beamish v. Beamish* (1869) I.R. 4 Eq. 120.

[185] *Re Ritson* [1699] 1 Ch. 128, noted, *supra*, para. 19–28; also *Farquhar v. Hadden* (1871) L.R. 7 Ch.App. 1 (where the bequest was of the deceased's share of a partnership lease). As to what is comprised in the share, see *supra*, paras 19–01 *et seq.*; also *Re Rhagg* [1938] Ch. 828; *Re White* [1958] Ch. 762. It should not, however, be assumed that the value of the share must be ascertained as at the date of death in all cases, notwithstanding the terms of the Partnership Act 1890, s.43: see *supra*, paras 19–10, 19–11, 23–34, 26–03.

[186] See *supra*, paras 26–38 *et seq.*

[187] See *Fryer v. Ward* (1862) 31 Beav. 602, where the legatees were entitled to elect whether or not to take over the business.

[188] See *supra*, paras 26–04, 26–22.

[189] (1802) 7 Ves.Jr. 137a; also *Dimes v. Scott* (1828) 4 Russ. 195.

[190] *Per contra* in a case where the partnership assets include land, since the repeal of the Partnership Act 1890, s.22: see *supra*, para. 19–14.

[191] See *Re Trollope* [1927] 1 Ch. 596.

[192] See *Re Chancellor* (1884) 26 Ch.D. 42; *Re Crowther* [1895] 2 Ch. 56.

[193] *Re Berry* [1962] Ch. 97; see also *Re Robbins* [1941] Ch. 434.

On the other hand, in the case of an intestacy, the deceased partner's personal representatives can distribute the income derived from the share as if the rule in *Howe v. Lord Dartmouth* did not exist.[194]

It should be noted that trading losses attributable to the share must not be thrown on capital so as to benefit a life tenant at the expense of the remaindermen.[195]

Legatee's or life tenant's right to profits

The legatee's or life tenant's entitlement in respect of profits may not, on normal principles, extend to profits declared prior to the testator's death[196] nor to profits which, though declared after his death, were earned and ought to have been declared before the death.[197] If so, the testator's share of such profits will prima facie form part of his general estate.[198]   **26–56**

Where a legatee is, under the terms of the will, entitled to receive profits earned and declared *before* the testator's death, *e.g.* where the legacy is expressed to include the testator's share of all moneys standing to the credit of the partnership bank account at the time of his death and those moneys include such profits, the legatee will be entitled to receive such share without any deduction on account of basic or higher rate income tax assessable by reference thereto.[199]

Apportionment of profits

Partnership profits are not within the Apportionment Act 1870.[200]   **26–57**

---

[194] *Re Trollope* [1927] 1 Ch. 596, 604 *per* Tomlin J.; *Re Fisher* [1943] Ch. 377; Administration of Estates Act 1925, ss.33(5), (7), 49 (as amended).

[195] See *Upton v. Brown* (1884) 26 Ch.D. 588; *cf. Gow v. Forster* (1884) 26 Ch.D. 672. As to the apportionment of profits and losses between the life tenant and the remainderman where the share ought to be realised, see *Re Earl of Chesterfield's Trusts* (1883) 24 Ch.D. 643; *Re Godden* [1893] 1 Ch. 292; *Re Hengler* [1893] 1 Ch. 586; *Re Elford* [1910] 1 Ch. 814; *Re Parry* [1947] Ch. 23; *Re Berry* [1962] Ch. 97. Note also, as to the position where the purchase price of the share is payable by instalments, *Re Hollebone* [1919] 2 Ch. 93.

[196] *Ibbotson v. Elam* (1865) L.R. 1 Eq. 188; *Browne v. Collins* (1871) L.R. 12 Eq. 586. See also *Jacques v. Chambers* (1846) 2 Colly. 435; *Wright v. Warren* (1851) 4 De G. & Sm. 367. Note, however, that if declared, but undrawn, profits have been treated as a form of circulating capital (see *supra*, para. 17–06), they may properly fall to be regarded as part of the *corpus* of the share.

[197] *Browne v. Collins* (1871) L.R. 12 Eq. 586. *cf. Ibbotson v. Elam, supra.*

[198] *Browne v. Collins, supra.*

[199] See *Re Betts* [1949] W.N. 91; *Re White* [1958] Ch. 762. Now, of course, income tax assessed by reference to partnership profits is no longer a partnership debt for which all the surviving partners are jointly liable (see *infra*, para. 34–19), so that the position is, if anything, *a fortiori*. Whilst the result could be different if there is a right of retention in respect of such tax in the agreement, provisions of that type have become more rare under the current tax regime: see *supra*, paras 10–90, 10–157.

[200] *Jones v. Ogle* (1872) L.R. 8 Ch.App. 192; *Re Cox's Trusts* (1878) 9 Ch.D. 159. As to the position prior to the Act, see *Johnston v. Moore* (1858) 27 L.J.Ch. 453; *Ibbotson v. Elam* (1865) L.R. 1 Eq. 188; *Browne v. Collins* (1871) L.R. 12 Eq. 586.

CHAPTER 27

INSOLVENCY

1. INTRODUCTION

THE law of bankruptcy, which had evolved through successive Bankruptcy Acts,[1]   **27–01**
was completely reformulated by the Insolvency Act 1985, which swept away
most of the previous legislation, including the Bankruptcy Acts 1914 and 1926.[2]
However, before the majority of the provisions contained in the 1985 Act came
into force, they were themselves repealed and replaced by the consolidating
Insolvency Act 1986.[3] The present insolvency legislation is now principally
contained in the latter Act and the Insolvency Rules 1986 (as amended), although
the regime governing insolvent partners and partnerships is contained in the
Insolvent Partnerships Order 1994.[4] This Order, like its predecessor,[5] seeks to
adapt the provisions of the 1986 Act piecemeal in order to accommodate the
procedures applicable on the winding up of an insolvent firm, whether in
conjunction with or independently of the insolvency of one or more of the
partners. The product of this approach is an indigestible patchwork of provisions,
some of which are in certain respects ill-suited to their task.

In earlier editions of this work, the present chapter contained a detailed
account of the law of bankruptcy as it affected partners and partnerships, much
of which will now be of only historic interest. Readers interested in such material
are referred to those earlier editions.[6] Equally, the rules governing the administration of what are conveniently styled the "joint" estate (*i.e.* the partnership
property) and the partners' "separate" estates (*i.e.* their own property) has been
preserved, so that a consideration thereof still remains essential.[7]

Given the scope of this work, a detailed review of general insolvency law or
the position under Council Regulation (EC) 1346/2000 on insolvency proceedings would be inappropriate and readers should refer to the standard works in
relation thereto.[8] What this chapter will, however, attempt to do is to identify
those areas which give rise to questions peculiar to partners and partnerships
under the current legislation.

---

[1] Bankruptcy Act 1883; Bankruptcy Act 1890; Bankruptcy and Deeds of Arrangement Act 1913,
Pt 1; Bankruptcy Act 1914; Bankruptcy (Amendment) Act 1926.

[2] Insolvency Act 1985, s.235(3), Sched. 10.

[3] Insolvency Act 1986, s.438, Sched. 12.

[4] SI 1994/2421, as amended. It should be noted that this Order did not apply where a winding up
or bankruptcy order had been made under the Insolvent Partnerships Order 1986 (SI 1986/2142) or
where proceedings under that Order were pending (*i.e.* if a written or statutory demand had been
served or a winding up/bankruptcy petition had been presented: Insolvent Partnerships Order 1994,
art. 19(3)) when the 1994 Order came into force (*i.e.* December 1, 1994: see *ibid.* art. 19(1), (2)). For
the position under the 1986 Order, readers are referred to the 17th edition of this work at paras 27–01
et seq.

[5] See the preceding footnote.

[6] See the 15th ed. of this work at pp. 774 *et seq.*

[7] See *infra* paras 27–78 *et seq.*

[8] *e.g. Muir Hunter On Personal Insolvency*; *Palmer's Company Law* (25th ed.).

The statutory approach to insolvent partners and partnerships

27–02   Under the Bankruptcy Act 1914, the same regime applied both to insolvent
partners and to insolvent partnerships, save in the case of a firm with eight or
more partners, which could formerly be wound up under the Companies Acts as
an unregistered company.[9] In its application to all insolvent partnerships,[10]
irrespective of size, the current legislation, as applied by the Insolvent Partnerships Order 1994, endeavours to assimilate firms into the general framework of
corporate insolvency.[11]

Apart from those cases involving a partnership voluntary arrangement[12] or an
administration order,[13] there are now, in essence, five ways in which the insolvency legislation may be applied to a partnership, namely:

> (a) where the firm itself is wound up as an unregistered company on the
> application of a creditor (or other third party)[14] or a partner, *no* con-
> current petitions being presented against the partners[15];

> (b) where the firm is wound up as an unregistered company on the applica-
> tion of a creditor (or other third party), but with concurrent petitions
> being presented against one or more partners or former partners[16];

> (c) where the firm is wound up as an unregistered company on the applica-
> tion of a partner, but with concurrent petitions being presented against
> *all* the partners[17];

> (d) where all the individual partners present a joint bankruptcy petition
> against themselves, but the firm itself is *not* wound up as an unregis-
> tered company[18]; and

---

[9] See the Companies Act 1985, ss.665(1)(c), 666 (repealed by the Insolvency Act 1986, s.438,
Sched. 12); Companies Act 1948, ss.398(1)(c), 399.

[10] As to when a partnership will be regarded as insolvent, see *Re Hough, The Independent*, April
23, 1990. Note, however, that this presupposes the existence of a partnership in law: *Re C. & M.
Ashberg, The Times*, July 17, 1990. The fact that a person held out as a partner is *deemed* to be a
member of the firm (see the definition of "member" in the Insolvent Partnerships Order 1994, art.
2(1)) does not alter this fundamental requirement.

[11] The position is otherwise in Scotland: see *Smith v. Smith* 1998 S.C.L.R. 818 (OH).

[12] Insolvent Partnerships Order 1994, art. 4, Sched. 1, as respectively amended/substituted by the
Insolvent Partnerships (Amendment) (No. 2) Order 2002 (SI 2002/2708), arts 4, 6, Sched. 1 and, in
the case of Sched. 1, further amended by the Insolvent Partnerships (Amendment) Order 2005 (SI
2005/1516), art. 6: see *infra*, paras 27–151 *et seq.*

[13] *ibid.* art. 6, Sched. 2, as respectively substituted by the Insolvent Partnerships (Amendment)
Order 2005, arts 3, 7, Sched. 1 and, in the case of Sched. 2, amended by the Insolvent Partnerships
(Amendment) Order 2006 (SI 2006/622), art. 5: see *infra*, paras 27–160 *et seq.*

[14] See *infra*, para. 27–13.

[15] *ibid.* art. 7 (as amended by the Insolvent Partnerships (Amendment) Order 1996 (SI 1996/1308),
art. 2 and the Insolvent Partnerships (Amendment) Order 2002 (SI 2002/1308), art. 3), Sched. 3 as
amended (creditor's, etc., petition), art. 9, Scheds 3 (as amended), 5 (member's petition). See further,
infra, paras 27–04 *et seq.*

[16] *ibid.* art. 8 (as amended by the Insolvent Partnerships (Amendment) Order 2002, art. 4), Sched.
4 as amended. See further, *infra*, paras 27–24 *et seq.* As to the position of an insolvent corporate
partner in such a case, see *ibid.* art. 8(4), (5) and *infra*, paras 27–27 *et seq.*

[17] *ibid.* art. 10 (as amended by the Insolvent Partnerships (Amendment) Order 2005, art. 5), Scheds
4, 6 (as respectively amended). See further, *infra*, paras 27–24 *et seq.* As to the position of an
insolvent corporate partner in such a case, see *ibid.* art. 10(2), (3) and *infra*, paras 27–27 *et seq.*

[18] *ibid.* art. 11, Sched. 7 (as amended). See further, *infra*, paras 27–44 *et seq.*

(e) where petitions for a bankruptcy order[19] are presented against one or more partners but not against others, no attempt being made to wind up the firm.[20]

The first three cases, more than either of the other two, typify the approach of the new legislation and will be considered together.

It should, however, be noted that in *Lancefield v. Lancefield*,[21] Neuberger J.   **27–03**
ordered the winding up of an insolvent partnership on the application of a partner *without* the prior service of a petition.[22] The circumstances were exceptional, *i.e.* following a dissolution it was clear that the business was not only insolvent but also unsaleable, so much so that a court appointed receiver had, in effect, been discharged.[23] A winding up order was perceived to be necessary to protect the position of third parties and, most significantly, there was no opposition to such an order. The decision, whilst attractive from a practical point of view, is difficult to reconcile with the regime outlined above.

2.   INSOLVENCY INVOLVING THE WINDING UP OF THE FIRM AS AN UNREGISTERED COMPANY

Winding up as an unregistered company under specific statutory jurisdiction

The court has jurisdiction to wind up a partnership as an unregistered company   **27–04**
where it is (or was) authorised under the Financial Services And Markets Act 2000,[24] or an appointed representative[25] or carrying on a regulated activity[26] in contravention of the Act,[27] on a petition presented by the Financial Services Authority on the just and equitable ground.[28] This jurisdiction is not affected by the Insolvent Partnerships Order 1994.[29]

---

[19] See generally, the Insolvency Act 1986, ss.264 *et seq.*

[20] Insolvent Partnerships Order 1994, art. 19(5), preserving the creditor's rights in this respect. See further, *infra*, paras 27–48 *et seq.*

[21] [2002] B.P.I.R. 1108.

[22] Note, however, that Neuberger J. was satisfied that one or more (if not all) of the circumstances set out in the Insolvency Act 1986, s.221(7), as amended and applied by the Insolvent Partnerships Order 1994, art. 7, Sched. 3, para. 3 (as then formulated), were satisfied: *ibid.* at p. 1112.

[23] Note that he made an application for directions as to his remuneration and expenses but Neuberger J. declined to make an order at that stage.

[24] See, as to authorisation, the Financial Services and Markets Act 2000, ss.31 *et seq.* See further *supra*, paras 8–45 *et seq.*

[25] See *ibid.* s.39.

[26] This expression is defined in *ibid.* s.22.

[27] *i.e.* when neither authorised nor exempt. See further, as to when a firm may be exempt, *ibid.* ss.38, 39, 327.

[28] *ibid.* s.367(1)–(3), (6)(a), (7). See further, as to orders on this basis, *Re Intertia Partnership LLP* [2007] Bus. L.R. 879. An order may, alternatively, be made on the ground that the partnership is unable to pay its debts, but in such a case it will *not* be wound up an unregistered company: *ibid.* s.367(3)(a), (4).

[29] Insolvent Partnerships Order 1994, art. 19(4), as substituted by the Financial Services and Markets Act 2000 (Consequential Amendments and Repeals) Order 2001 (SI 2001/3649), Pt 9, art. 467 and amended by the Insolvent Partnerships (Amendment) (No. 2) Order 2002, art. 5.

Provision is made in the Banking Act 2009 for the application of the modified insolvency regime contained in Part 2 to be applied to banking partnerships, but this power has not yet been exercised.[30]

Winding up as an unregistered company in other cases

27–05 It goes almost without saying that a firm can only be wound up as an unregistered company if, as a matter of law, a partnership actually exists. If two or more persons merely hold themselves out as partners,[31] there will be no partnership to be wound up.[32] The fact that, under the Insolvent Partnerships Order 1994, a person held out as a partner is *treated* as a member of the firm[33] cannot, in the current editor's view, eliminate this requirement.

Where a firm is wound up as an unregistered company, most of the normal legislation governing company insolvencies will apply subject only to the specific amendments introduced by the Insolvent Partnerships Order 1994,[34] and the Insolvency Rules 1986 and other subordinate legislation will apply with all such modifications as are required to give effect thereto.[35] As already noted, a winding up order may be obtained with or without concurrent petitions against one or more of the partners and the procedure and consequences will naturally differ according to the nature of the order sought.

A. WINDING UP ORDER AGAINST FIRM WITHOUT CONCURRENT PETITIONS

27–06 It has already been seen that a firm may be wound up as an unregistered company on the petition of a creditor, member or other permitted third party,[36] although in exceptional circumstances it may also be wound up on that basis without the service of any petition.[37] It is not clear whether, if a petition is presented against the firm and, only subsequently, petitions are presented against the partners, the case will be taken out of this class.[38]

Since there are clear similarities in the above petition procedures, they will, for convenience, be considered together.

---

[30] Banking Act 2009, s.132(1).

[31] As to holding out, see the Partnership Act 1890, s.14 and *supra*, paras 5–35 *et seq.*

[32] *Re C. & M. Ashberg, The Times*, July 17, 1990.

[33] See the definition of "member" in the Insolvent Partnerships Order 1994, art. 2(1), as inserted in the Insolvency Act 1986, s.436 by virtue of *ibid.* art. 2(2).

[34] Insolvent Partnerships Order 1994, art. 7, Sched. 3 (winding up on creditor's, etc., petition without concurrent petitions); art. 8, Sched. 4 (winding up on creditor's, etc., petition *with* concurrent petitions); art. 9, Scheds 3, 5 (winding up on member's petition without concurrent petitions); art. 10, Scheds 4, 6 (winding up on member's petition *with* concurrent petitions). The amendments to these provisions are not particularised in this footnote.

[35] *ibid.* art. 18(1), Sched. 10, as amended by the Insolvent Partnerships (Amendment) Order 2005, art. 13.

[36] The expression "creditor's petition" will hereafter be used for convenience, even though petitions may also be presented by the Secretary of State or other third parties pursuant to the same procedure: see *infra*, para. 27–13.

[37] *Lancefield v. Lancefield* [2002] B.P.I.R. 1108, noticed *supra*, para. 27–03.

[38] The point was raised but not, ultimately, answered in *HM Customs & Excise v. Jack Baars Wholesale* [2004] B.P.I.R. 543.

Jurisdiction

The Insolvent Partnerships Order 1994 deems an insolvent partnership to be an **27–07** unregistered company,[39] thus enabling it to be wound up under the Insolvency Act 1986.[40] However, a winding up will only be possible on a creditor's petition if the firm has (or has at any time had) a principal place of business in England and Wales or, in the case of a petition based on a debt,[41] if that debt arose in the course of carrying on the firm's business from premises in England and Wales.[42] Only the former condition applies in the case of a member's petition.[43] Moreover, the firm must also, in either case, have carried on business in England and Wales within the period of three years ending with the day on which the petition is presented.[44]

Grounds for petition

A petition to wind up an insolvent partnership may only be presented on a **27–08** limited number of grounds, namely:

    (a) if the firm has already been dissolved, whether or not its business is being carried on in the course of winding up its affairs[45];

    (b) if it has ceased to carry on business without being dissolved[46];

    (c) if it is unable to pay its debts[47];

    (d) on the "just and equitable" ground[48]; or

---

[39] Insolvency Act 1986, s.220, as amended and applied by the Insolvent Partnerships Order 1994, art. 7(1) (as itself amended by the Insolvent Partnerships (Amendment) Order 1996, art. 2 and the Insolvent Partnerships (Amendment) Order 2002, art. 3), (2), Sched. 3, Pt I, para. 2 (creditor's petition) and *ibid.* art. 9(b), Sched. 3, Pt I, para. 2 (member's petition).

[40] Note, however, the decision in *Lancefield v. Lancefield* [2002] B.P.I.R. 1108, noticed *supra*, para. 27–03, where the partnership was ordered to be wound up even though no petition had been presented.

[41] See *infra*, paras 27–08, 27–09.

[42] Insolvency Act 1986, s.221(1), as amended and applied by the Insolvent Partnerships Order 1994, art. 7(1) (as amended: see *supra*, para. 27–07, n. 39), (2), Sched. 3, Pt I, para. 3.

[43] *ibid.* s.221(1), as amended and applied by the Insolvent Partnerships Order 1994, art. 9(a), Sched. 5, para. 2.

[44] *ibid.* s.221(2), as amended and applied by the Insolvent Partnerships Order 1994, art. 7(1) (as amended: see *supra*, para. 27–07, n. 39), (2), Sched. 3, Pt I, para. 3 (creditor's petition) and *ibid.* art. 9(b), Sched. 3, Pt I, para. 2 (member's petition). As to when a firm will be treated as having carried on business in England and Wales within the requisite period, note *Re A Debtor (No. 784 of 1991)* [1992] Ch. 554 (a decision under *ibid.* s.265(1)(c)(ii), applying *Theophile v. Solicitor-General* [1950] A.C. 186).

[45] Insolvency Act 1986, s.221(7)(a), as amended and applied by the Insolvent Partnerships Order 1994, art. 7(1) (as amended: see *supra*, para. 27–07, n. 39), (2), Sched. 3, Pt I, para. 3 (creditor's, etc., petition) and *ibid.* art. 9(a), Sched. 5, para. 2 (member's petition). The current editor submits that the distinction between a partnership which has been dissolved and one which is "carrying on business only for the purpose of winding up its affairs" may be of little or no substance, save that the dissolved firm may not be able to take on any *new* business. See further, as to the authority and obligations of the members of a dissolved firm, the Partnership Act 1890, s.38, considered *supra*, paras 13–62 *et seq.*

[46] *ibid.* And see further, as to the possible effects of a firm ceasing to carry on any business whatsoever, *supra*, para. 24–46.

[47] *ibid.* s.221(7)(b) (as amended and applied by *ibid.*).

[48] *ibid.* s.221(7)(c) (as amended and applied by *ibid.*).

(e) (in the case of a creditor's petition only) where, on the coming to an end of a moratorium under section 1A of the Insolvency Act 1986, no voluntary arrangement approved under Part 1 of that Act is in effect.[49]

It should be noted that, in *Lancefield v. Lancefield*,[50] it was held that, in an exceptional case, a winding up could be ordered on one or more of the above grounds even in the *absence* of a petition.

27–09 *Firm's inability to pay its debts*: There are a number of circumstances in which a firm will be *deemed* unable to pay its debts, which are set out in the Act.[51] They may be summarised as follows:

(i) where a creditor, to whom the firm is then indebted in a sum exceeding £750,[52] has served[53] a written demand[54] on the firm and the sum due has not been paid, secured or compounded for within three weeks[55];

(ii) where proceedings have been instituted against any partner for any debt or demand due[56] or claimed to be due from the firm or from that partner (in his capacity as a member of the firm) of which notice in writing has been served on the firm[57] and the firm has not within three

---

[49] *ibid.* 221(7)(d), (7A), as amended and applied by the Insolvent Partnerships Order 1994, art. 7(1) (as amended: see *supra*, para. 27–07, n. 39), (2), Sched. 3, Pt I, para. 3, as itself amended by the Insolvent Partnerships (Amendment) (No. 2) Order 2002, art. 8).

[50] [2002] B.P.I.R. 1018, noted *supra*, para. 27–03.

[51] *ibid.* ss.222–224, as amended and applied by the Insolvent Partnerships Order 1994, art. 7(1) (as amended: see *supra*, para. 27–07, n. 39), (2), Sched. 3, Pt I, paras 4, 5 (creditor's petition) and *ibid.* art. 9(b), Sched. 3, Pt I, paras 4, 5 (member's petition).

[52] This sum may be increased: *ibid.* s.222(3), as amended and applied by the Insolvent Partnerships Order 1994, art. 7(1) (as amended: see *supra*, para. 27–07, n. 39), (2), Sched. 3, Pt I, para. 4 (creditor's petition) and *ibid.* art. 9(b), Sched. 3, Pt I, para. 4 (member's petition). There is, needless to say, no need to obtain a judgment against the firm before adopting this procedure: see *Schooler v. Customs & Excise* [1995] 2 B.C.L.C. 610 (CA).

[53] Service may be effected by leaving the demand at the firm's principal place of business in England and Wales or at the premises in England and Wales at which the business "in the course of which" the debt was incurred was carried on, or by delivering it to an "officer" of the partnership or in such other manner as the Court may approve or direct: *ibid.* s.222(2), as amended and applied by *ibid.*

[54] The demand must be in the prescribed form: Insolvent Partnerships Order 1994, art. 17(1), Sched. 9, Form 4 (as substituted by the Insolvent Partnerships (Amendment) Order 2005, art. 12(c), Sched. 2).

[55] Insolvency Act 1986, s.222(1), as amended and applied by the Insolvent Partnerships Order 1994, art. 7(1) (as amended: see *supra*, para. 27–07, n. 39), (2), Sched. 3, Pt I, para. 4 (creditor's petition) and *ibid.* art. 9(b), Sched. 3, Pt I, para. 4 (member's petition). As to the position where payment of the debt is tendered prior to the hearing of the petition, see *Smith v. Ian Simpson & Co.* [2001] Ch. 239 (CA), a decision under the Insolvency Act 1986, s.271(1). See also, as to when a debt has been compounded for, *Artman v. Artman* [1996] B.P.I.R. 511.

[56] The expression used is merely "due" not "then due": *cf. ibid.* s.222(1).

[57] *ibid.* s.223(1)(a), as amended and applied by the Insolvent Partnerships Order 1994, art. 7(1) (as amended: see *supra*, para. 27–07, n. 39), (2), Sched. 3, Pt I, para. 5 (creditor's petition) and *ibid.* art. 9(b), Sched. 3, Pt I, para. 5 (member's petition). Note that the subsection does not technically state *by whom* the notice is to be served. Service is effected in the same way as under *ibid.* s.222(2) (see *supra*, n. 53): *ibid.* s.223(2) (as amended and applied by *ibid.*).

weeks paid, secured or compounded for the debt or demand, had the proceedings stayed or indemnified the defendant partner "to his reasonable satisfaction against the action or proceeding, and against all costs, damages and expenses to be incurred by him because of it"[58];

(iii) where "execution or other process"[59] issued on a judgment[60] obtained against the firm or against any partner as such,[61] whatever the sum involved,[62] is returned unsatisfied[63];

(iv) where it is proved to the court's satisfaction that the firm is unable to pay its debts (whatever may be their amount) as and when they fall due[64];

(v) where it is proved to the court's satisfaction that the firm's liabilities, whether actual, contingent or prospective, exceed the value of its assets[65]; or

(vi) where the petition is presented by a partner's liquidator or trustee who is able to satisfy the court that an insolvency order has been made

---

[58] *ibid.* s.223(1)(b) (as amended and applied by *ibid.*). The current editor doubts whether, in the normal case, a full indemnity would be appropriate, since the partner against whom the proceedings are instituted will have to bear his share of the liability in any event; *cf. ibid.* s.221A(2)(c) (as added and applied by *ibid.* art. 9(a), Sched. 5, para. 2), where the expression used is "reimbursement". *Semble*, it would not be reasonable (in terms of the subsection) for a partner to decline an appropriate partial indemnity in such circumstances. The position may be otherwise in the case of a salaried partner who is entitled to an indemnity in any event: see further, *supra*, para. 20–06. *Quaere*, in any event, why a creditor would pursue a partner, when his ultimate aim is to wind up the firm. It is questionable whether this ground will in practice be relied on by petitioners.

[59] It should be noted that the service of a demand under *ibid.* s.222(1)(a) will not constitute execution or other process for these purposes.

[60] It would seem that the court may enquire into the validity of the contract, etc., on which the judgment was obtained, as under the old law: see *Re a Debtor (No. 169 of 1997)* [1998] C.L.Y. 3284 (where there was an application to annul a bankruptcy order); *Re Thorogood (No. 1)* [2003] B.P.I.R. 1468; *Lambeth London Borough Council v. Simon* [2007] B.P.I.R. 1629; also, under the old law, *Ex p. Troup* [1895] 1 Q.B. 404; *Ex p. Beauchamp* [1904] 1 K.B. 572; *Re A Debtor* [1927] 2 Ch. 367; *cf. Re A Debtor* [1929] 1 Ch. 125 (where the court refused to go behind the compromise); and see *Bowes v. Hope Life Insurance and Guarantee Company* (1865) 11 H.L.Cas. 389; *Railway Finance Co.* (1866) 14 W.R. 785; *Ex p. Kibble* (1875) 10 Ch. 373; *Re Ex p. Banner* (1881) 17 Ch.D. 480; *Ex p. Lennox* (1885) 16 Q.B.D. 315, explained in *Ex p. Scotch Whisky Distillers Ltd.* (1888) 22 Q.B.D. 83; *Ex p. Central Bank of London* [1892] 2 Q.B. 633; also *Ex p. Revell* (1884) 13 Q.B.D. 720; *Ex p. Edwards* (1884) 14 Q.B.D. 415; *Ex p. Anderson* (1885) 14 Q.B.D. 606. And see *Brandon v. McHenry* [1891] 1 Q.B. 538; *Ex p. Lancaster* [1911] 2 K.B. 981. *cf.* the position where an application is made to set aside a statutory demand based on a judgment debt: *Re A Debtor (No. 657/SD/91)* [1992] S.T.C. 751; also the CPR Practice Direction on Insolvency Proceedings, para. 12.3.

[61] Accordingly, the judgment against a partner must be obtained in respect of a partnership debt.

[62] In such a case, there is no prescribed minimum amount for the debt in question; *cf. ibid.* s.222(1)(a), noted *supra*.

[63] *ibid.* s.224(1)(a), as applied by the Insolvent Partnerships Order 1994, arts 7(1) (as amended: see *supra*, para. 27–07, n. 39) (creditor's petition), 9(b) (member's petition). As to the position in Scotland or Northern Ireland, see *ibid.* s.224(1)(b), (c).

[64] *ibid.* s.224(1)(d) (as applied by *ibid.*). And note the decision in *Taylors Industrial Flooring Ltd. v. M & H Plant Hire (Manchester) Ltd.* [1990] B.C.C. 44 (a decision under *ibid.* s.123(1)(e)); also *Re Clemence plc* (1992) 59 B.L.R. 56.

[65] *ibid.* s.224(2) (as applied by *ibid.*) (as amended by the Insolvent Partnerships (Amendment) Order 2002 (SI 2002/1308), art. 4(1)).

against that partner by reason of his inability to pay a joint debt, unless the firm is able to prove its ability to meet its debts.[66]

It is, of course, also possible to prove that the firm is unable to pay its debts in some other way.

27–10 *Just and equitable ground*: Although, on a member's petition, the court's approach may, broadly, track that adopted on an application for the dissolution of a solvent partnership under section 35(f) of the Partnership Act 1890,[67] the same cannot be said in the case of any other petition. What is clear is that the court will have a wide-ranging discretion in either case.

Group and sub-partnerships

27–11 The grounds will be the same where a petition is to be presented against an insolvent member firm of a group partnership,[68] unless the group partnership is itself insolvent and concurrent petitions are to be presented.[69]

In the case of a sub-partnership,[70] the solvency (or otherwise) of the head partnership will be irrelevant.[71]

Firm comprising minor or foreign partners

27–12 The current editor submits that, provided that the court has jurisdiction to wind up the firm,[72] there is no bar to a petition against a firm comprising minor or foreign partners.[73]

Who may present petition

27–13 A petition on the above grounds may be presented by:

(a) a creditor[74];

(b) the liquidator of a present or former corporate partner;

(c) a liquidator appointed in proceedings by virtue of Article 3(1) of Council Regulation (EC) No. 1346/2000 of May 29, 2000 on insolvency proceedings;

---

[66] *ibid.* s.221A(3), as added by the Insolvent Partnerships Order 1994, art. 7(2), Sched. 3, para. 3.

[67] See *supra*, paras 24–89, 24–90.

[68] See further, as to such partnerships, *supra*, paras 11–17 *et seq.*

[69] As to the position where the group partnership is insolvent, see *infra*, para. 27–29.

[70] See, as to such partnerships, *supra*, paras 5–67 *et seq.*

[71] See *infra*, para. 27–29.

[72] See *supra*, para. 27–07.

[73] This is not a possibility catered for under the legislation.

[74] There would seem to be no reason why a creditor, who is not a member of the firm but has been held out as such or who was formerly a member thereof, should not petition as such: see *Ex p. Notley* (1833) 1 Mont. & Ayr. 46; *Ex p. Richardson* (1833) 3 D. & Ch. 244. See also *infra*, para. 27–48.

(d) the administrator of the partnership[75] or a temporary administrator[76];

(e) the trustee of a present or former bankrupt partner's estate;

(f) the supervisor of a corporate or individual partner's voluntary arrangement[77];

(g) the Secretary of State;

(h) any other person who is *not* a partner[78]; or

(i) any partner.[79]

It should, however, be noted that a petition on the ground that there is no voluntary arrangement in place after a moratorium has come to an end[80] can only be presented by one or more creditors.[81]

A *partner's* freedom to petition for the winding up of his firm is restricted if the firm consists of less than eight partners.[82] In such a case, a petition can only be presented with the leave of the court following the service on the firm of a written demand[83] in respect of a joint debt (or debts) exceeding £750 which, although then due from the firm, has been paid by the petitioning partner otherwise than out of partnership property.[84] The court will only grant such leave if the partner concerned has obtained a judgment or order entitling him to be reimbursed by the firm[85] and taken all reasonable steps[86] to enforce that judgment or order.[87]

27–14

---

[75] See further, as to administration orders, *infra*, paras 27–160 *et seq*.

[76] Within the meaning of Council Regulation (EC) No. 1346/2000 of May 29, 2000 on insolvency proceedings, Art. 38.

[77] See further as to partners' voluntary arrangements, *infra*, paras 27–158, 27–159.

[78] This is the combined effect of the Insolvency Act 1986, s.221A(1), as added by the Insolvent Partnerships Order 1994, art. 7(2), Sched. 3, para. 3 and Insolvent Partnerships Order 1994, art. 7(1), as amended by the Insolvent Partnerships (Amendment) Order 1996, art. 2 and the Insolvent Partnerships (Amendment) Order 2002, art. 3. The final "catch-all" class (h) will authorise a petition to be served by, *inter alios*, the Financial Services Authority. Where the petition is presented by the liquidator, etc., of an insolvent corporate or individual partner, the petitioner's costs may, if the partnership assets ultimately prove to be insufficient, be paid out of that partner's assets: *ibid.* s.221A(6) (as added by *ibid.*).

[79] Insolvent Partnerships Order 1994, art. 9; also the Insolvency Act 1986, s.221A(1), as applied by *ibid.* and noted *infra*, para. 27–15.

[80] See *supra*, para. 27–08.

[81] Insolvency Act 1986, 221(7A), as amended and applied by the Insolvent Partnerships Order 1994, art. 7(1) (as amended: see *supra*, n. 78), (2), Sched. 3, Pt 1, para. 3, as itself amended by the Insolvent Partnerships (Amendment) (No. 2) Order 2002, art. 8.

[82] Insolvency Act 1986, s.221A(1), as added by the Insolvent Partnerships Order 1994, art. 9(a), Sched. 5, para. 2.

[83] For the form of the demand, see the Insolvent Partnerships Order 1994, Sched. 9, Form 10. Note that the form requires the demand to be dealt with within 21 days, even though there is no reference to such a period in the relevant section of the Act: see n. 84 *infra*.

[84] Insolvency Act 1986, s.221A(2)(a), as added by the Insolvent Partnerships Order 1994, art. 9(a), Sched. 5, para. 2. The amount of £750 may be increased under the Insolvency Act 1986, s.416: *ibid.* s.221A(3), as added by *ibid.*

[85] *Quaere*, can such an order ever be obtained without taking an account as between the partners. See further, *supra*, paras 23–74 *et seq.*; also the decision in *Hurst v. Bennett* [2001] B.P.I.R. 287 (CA), noted *infra*, para. 27–49.

[86] Other than insolvency proceedings.

[87] Once the partner has obtained permission, he can serve a petition on any of the grounds set out *supra*, para. 27–08, other than the last. However, given the written demand procedure outlined in the text, he will almost inevitably petition on the basis of the firm's inability to pay its debts.

Form and service of petition

27–15   Save where it is presented by an insolvency practitioner,[88] the petition will be in the normal form,[89] but must be verified by an affidavit in a specific form.[90] Service will in general be effected at the firm's principal place of business by handing the petition to a partner (including any person held out as such), employee or other person authorised to accept service.[91]

Presentation of the petition will be to the High Court[92] or to a county court within whose insolvency district the firm has (or has at any time had) "a" principal place of business[93] or, in the case of a creditor's petition based on a debt,[94] premises at which the firm's business was carried on when the debt was incurred.[95]

Consequences of presentation of petition

Avoidance of transactions

27–16   Since the winding up of a partnership is generally deemed to commence when the petition is presented,[96] any disposition of partnership property, transfer of shares or "alteration in the status of the [*partners*]" after that date is void unless sanctioned by the court.[97] This would clearly invalidate any agreement between the partners to treat a partnership asset as belonging to one or more of their

---

[88] Insolvency Act 1986, s.221A(1), as added by the Insolvent Partnerships Order 1994, art. 7(2), Sched. 3, Pt I, para. 3; Insolvent Partnerships Order 1994, Sched. 9, Form 3, as substituted by the Insolvent Partnerships (Amendment) Order 2002, art. 6, Sched.

[89] Insolvency Rules 1986, r. 4.7(1) (as amended by the Insolvency (Amendment) Rules 2010 (SI 2010/686), Sched. 1, para. 142(2)), Sched. 4, Form 4.2, as substituted by the Insolvency (Amendment) Rules 2002, Sched., Pt 2 and amended by the Insolvency (Amendment) Rules 2009 (SI 2009/642), r. 11(c) and the Insolvency Rules 2010, Sched. 1, para. 518.

[90] Insolvency Act 1986, s.221(8), as amended and applied by the Insolvent Partnerships Order 1994, art. 7(1) (as amended: see *supra*, para. 27–13, n. 78), (2), Sched. 3, Pt I, para. 3 (creditor's petition) and *ibid.* art. 9(a), Sched. 5, (member's petition); Insolvent Partnerships Order 1994, Sched. 9, Form 2.

[91] Insolvency Rules 1986, r. 4.8(2), (3)(a), (b), read subject to the Insolvent Partnerships Order 1994, art. 18(1).

[92] Insolvency Act 1986, s.117(1), as amended, in the case of a creditor's petition, by the Insolvent Partnerships Order 1994, Sched. 3, Pt II, para. 6 and applied by the Insolvency Act 1986, s.221(5) (as itself amended and applied by the Insolvent Partnerships Order 1994, art. 7(1) (as amended: see *supra*, para. 27–13, n. 78), (2), Sched. 3, Pt I, para. 3) and, in the case of a member's petition, as amended and applied by the Insolvent Partnerships Order 1994, art. 9(a), Sched. 5, para. 1.

[93] *ibid.* s.117(2)(a), as amended by the Insolvent Partnerships Order 1994, Sched. 3, Pt II, para. 6 and applied by the Insolvency Act 1986, s.221(5), as amended (creditor's petition); *ibid.* s.117(2), as amended and applied by *ibid.* art. 9(a), Sched. 5, para. 1 (member's petition). Note that the existence of more than one principal place of business is clearly contemplated.

[94] See *supra*, paras 27–08, 27–09.

[95] *ibid.* s.117(2)(b), as amended by the Insolvent Partnerships Order 1994, Sched. 3, Pt II, para. 6 and applied by the Insolvency Act 1986, s.221(5), as amended.

[96] *ibid.* s.129 (as amended by the Enterprise Act 2002, Sched. 17, para. 16), as applied by *ibid.* s.221(5) (as itself amended and applied by the Insolvent Partnerships Order 1994, art. 7(1) (as amended: see *supra*, para. 27–13, n. 78), (2), Sched. 3, Pt I, para. 3 (creditor's petition) and *ibid.* art. 9(a), Sched. 5, para. 2 (member's petition)).

[97] *ibid.* s.127 (as amended by the Enterprise Act 2002, Sched. 17, para. 15), as applied by *ibid.* The discretion under the section is a wide one: see *Denney v. John Hudson & Co. Ltd.* [1992] B.C.L.C. 901 (CA); *Re Dewrun Ltd.* See *Royal Bank of Scotland Plc v. Bhardwaj* [2002] B.C.C. 57. And see, generally, *Re Burton & Deakin Ltd.* [1977] 1 W.L.R. 390; *Re Gray's Inn Construction Co. Ltd.* [1980] 1 W.L.R. 711 (both decisions under the Companies Act 1948, s.227); also *cf. Hollicourt (Contracts) Ltd. v. Bank of Ireland* [2000] 1 W.L.R. 895 and *Coutts & Co. v. Stock* [2000] 1 W.L.R. 906.

number[98] and would also, seemingly, operate to freeze the membership of the firm so that no existing partner may retire or be expelled nor any new partner be admitted after the relevant date.[99] *A fortiori* in the case of an attempt to turn the firm into a limited partnership.[100]

Stay of proceedings

An application to the court to stay any proceedings pending against the firm or any member thereof may be made at any time after the presentation of the petition and prior to a winding up order being made, by the firm itself or by any partner or creditor.[101]

27–17

Appointment of provisional liquidator

A provisional liquidator may be appointed following the presentation of the petition,[102] and may, in the case of a petition presented by an insolvency practitioner,[103] be the petitioner himself.[104]

27–18

The winding up order and its consequences

When it hears the petition, the court will have a wide discretion when determining whether a winding up order against the firm should be made,[105] unless an administration order is already in force.[106] The order itself will follow the same form as an order made against a company.[107]

27–19

---

[98] See, as to such agreements, *supra*, paras 18–44 *et seq.* and *infra*, paras 27–100 *et seq.*

[99] Even if the incoming partner does not acquire any interest in the capital or assets of the firm, the creation of his profit share will almost inevitably involve a "transfer" of part of the existing partners' profit shares as well as a change in their status, *i.e.* when they become members of the "new" firm constituted following the incoming partner's admission.

[100] See generally, as to the formalities which would otherwise be required in order to effect such conversion, *infra*, paras 29–01 *et seq.* An attempt to form a limited liability partnership would be even more objectionable, since it would *necessarily* involve the dissolution of the existing firm: see further, as to such "partnerships", *supra*, paras 2–39 *et seq.*

[101] Insolvency Act 1986, ss.126, 227, as respectively applied by *ibid.* s.221(5) (as amended and applied: see *supra*, para. 27–15, n. 92). For these purposes a partner is clearly a "contributory": see *ibid.* s.226(1) and *infra*, paras 27–59, 27–61 *et seq.* Although *ibid.* s.227 refers to "actions or proceedings against any contributory", thus seemingly including actions in respect of a partner's separate debts, the current editor submits that it should not be so construed: *cf. ibid.* s.228 (as amended), where the position is clear.

[102] *ibid.* s.135(1), (2), as applied by *ibid.* s.221(5) (as amended and applied *supra*, para. 27–15, n. 92). As to the manner in which the application is made, see the Insolvency Rules 1986, r. 4.25, as amended by the Insolvency (Amendment) Rules 2002, r. 6(5) and the Insolvency (Amendment) Rules 2010, Sched. 1, paras 1, 156.

[103] *ibid.* s.221A(1), as added by the Insolvent Partnerships Order 1994, art. 7(1 (as amended: see *supra*, para. 27–13, n. 78), (2), Sched. 3, Pt I, para. 3. See further *supra*, para. 27–13.

[104] *ibid.* s.221A(4), as added by *ibid.*.

[105] *ibid.* s.125(1), as applied by *ibid.* s.221(5) (as amended and applied *supra*, para. 27–15, n. 92).

[106] See *infra*, para. 27–164.

[107] Insolvency Rules 1986, Sched. 4, Form 4.11, as substituted by the Insolvency (Amendment) Rules 2005, Sched., Pt B.

Stay of proceedings and executions

27–20   Once a winding up order has been made, proceedings may only be commenced or continued against the firm[108] or any partner[109] in respect of a partnership debt if the leave of the court is obtained. There is an express restriction on all forms of execution against the partnership assets[110] but seemingly not against the partners' separate estates. Nevertheless, on the footing that execution in respect of a partnership debt amounts to a "proceeding,"[111] leave would be required even in the latter case.[112]

Orders relating to subsequent insolvency proceedings against a partner

27–21   Although there is no restriction on insolvency proceedings brought against a partner in respect of his separate debts,[113] section 168(5A) of the Insolvency Act 1986[114] provides as follows:

> "(5A) Where at any time after a winding up petition has been presented to the court against any person (including an insolvent partnership or other body which may be wound up under Part V of the Act as an unregistered company), whether by virtue of the provisions of the Insolvent Partnerships Order 1994 or not, the attention of the court is drawn to the fact that the person in question is a member of an insolvent partnership,[115] the court may make an order as to the future conduct of the insolvency proceedings[116] and any such order may apply any provisions of that Order with any necessary modifications."

In parallel with this provision, section 303(2A) of the 1986 Act[117] provides:

---

[108] Insolvency Act 1986, s.130(2) (as amended), as applied by *ibid.* s.221(5) (as amended and applied *supra*, para. 27–15, n. 92). The discretion is a wide one: *Re Aro Ltd.* [1980] Ch. 196; as to the factors to be taken into account, see *Re Exchange Securities & Commodities Ltd.* [1983] B.C.L.C. 186; *New Cap Reinsurance Corp. Ltd. v. HIH Casualty & General Insurance Ltd.* [2002] B.C.L.C. 228; *Bourne v. Charit-Email Technology Partnership LLP* [2009] EWHC 1901 (Ch) (Lawtel 30/7/09).

[109] *ibid.* s.228 (as amended), as applied by the Insolvent Partnerships Order 1994, art. 7(1) (as amended: see *supra*, para. 27–13, n. 78) (creditor's petition) and *ibid.* art. 9(b) (member's petition). For these purposes a partner is clearly a "contributory": see *ibid.* s.226(1) (as applied by *ibid.*) and *infra*, paras 27–59, 27–61 *et seq. cf.* the terms of *ibid.* s.227: see *supra*, para. 27–17, n. 101.

[110] *ibid.* s.128, as applied by *ibid.* s.221(5) (as amended and applied *supra*, para. 27–15, n. 92). Although seemingly absolute in its terms, the section may be overridden by an order under *ibid.* s.130(2) (as applied by *ibid.*): see *The Constellation* [1966] 1 W.L.R. 272 (a decision under the Companies Act 1948, ss.228, 231).

[111] *Re Artistic Colour Printing Company* (1880) 14 Ch.D. 502, 505 *per* Jessel M.R.; *The Constellation, supra*. Note that it has been held that "proceedings" for the purposes of the Insolvency Act 1986, s.11(3)(d) must be of a legal or quasi-legal nature: *Bristol Airport plc v. Powdrill* [1990] Ch. 744.

[112] Insolvency Act 1986, s.228 (as amended), as applied by the Insolvent Partnerships Order 1994, art. 7(1) (as amended: see *supra*, para. 27–13, n. 78) (creditor's petition) and *ibid.* art. 9(b) (member's petition). It is submitted that proceedings by the liquidator in order to enforce a call on a partner *qua* contributory (see *infra*, para. 27–62) would also require permission: see *Williams v. Harding* (1866) L.R. 1 H.L. 9. *Sed quaere.*

[113] *ibid.* s.228 will not apply in such a case; *per contra* if the proceedings are brought in respect of a partnership debt.

[114] As added by the Insolvent Partnerships Order 1994, art. 14(1).

[115] This will include a person who is merely held out as a partner: see the definition of "member" in the Insolvent Partnerships Order 1994, art. 2(1), as added to the Insolvency Act 1986, s.436 by *ibid.* art. 2(2). *cf. Re C. & M. Ashberg, The Times*, July 17, 1990, noted *supra*, para. 27–05.

[116] See further, as to the directions which may be made, the Insolvency Act 1986, s.168(5B), as also added by the Insolvent Partnerships Order 1994, art. 14(1).

[117] As added by the Insolvent Partnerships Order 1994, art. 14(2).

"(2A) Where at any time after a bankruptcy petition has been presented to the court against any person, whether by virtue of the provisions of the Insolvent Partnerships Order 1994 or not, the attention of the court is drawn to the fact that the person in question is a member of an insolvent partnership,[118] the court may make an order as to the future conduct of the insolvency proceedings[119] and any such order may apply any provisions of that Order with any necessary modifications."

Although the application of the former subsection is not facilitated by the definitions imported into the Insolvency Act 1986 by the Insolvent Partnerships Order 1994,[120] the discretion under both subsections is a wide one and may be exercised on the application of the official receiver, a responsible insolvency practitioner[121] the trustee of the partnership or "any other interested person".[122] The width of the discretion is demonstrated by the decision in *Official Receiver v. Hollens*,[123] where an order was made for the winding up of an insolvent partnership even though the partners had presented individual bankruptcy petitions and had been discharged before the order was made.

It would seem to follow that, where an insolvency order is made against a partner in subsequent proceedings, directions may now, in an appropriate case, be given for the administration of his separate estate in conjunction with the joint partnership estate, rather than the two proceeding independently.[124]

27–22

Administration of the joint partnership estate

The mechanics of such administration will be considered hereafter.[125]

27–23

B.   WINDING UP ORDER AGAINST FIRM WITH CONCURRENT PETITIONS AGAINST THE PARTNERS

If an insolvent partnership[126] is to be wound up in this way, there must, in the case of a petition by a creditor or other permitted third party,[127] be concurrent

27–24

---

[118] See *supra*, n. 115.

[119] See further, as to the directions which may be made, the Insolvency Act 1986, s.303(2C), as also added by the Insolvent Partnerships Order 1994, art. 14(2).

[120] The definitions in the Insolvent Partnerships Order 1994, art. 2(1) are, by *ibid.* art. 2(2), added to the Insolvency Act 1986, s.436, which applies "except in so far as the context otherwise requires". The expression "insolvent member" is defined therein as a "member of an insolvent partnership, against whom an insolvency petition is being or has been presented", whilst "insolvency petition" is in turn defined in terms which include *only* a petition presented in conjunction with a petition for the winding up of the partnership. In the case presently supposed (*i.e.* a winding up order previously made against the firm) the presentation of such a petition would be an effective impossibility, so that the power would not be exercisable by the court. It is considered that that the context will require the latter definition to be ignored, particularly give the terms of the Insolvency Act 1986, s.303(2A), *supra*. It should be noted that this confusion is carried forward from the Insolvent Partnerships Order 1986, art. 14(1), which appeared in *ibid.* Pt 4, under the title "Insolvency Proceedings against members of Insolvent Partnership *not involving the Winding Up of the Partnership as an Unregistered Company*" (emphasis supplied). By way of contrast, art. 14(1) of the 1994 Order appears in Part VI under the title "Provisions applying in insolvency proceedings in relation to insolvent partnerships".

[121] This expression is again defined in the Insolvent Partnerships Order 1994, art. 2(1).

[122] See the Insolvency Act 1986, ss.168(5B), 303(2C).

[123] [2007] Bus. L.R. 1402, a decision under *ibid.* s.303(2A)–(2C).

[124] See *infra*, paras 27–48 *et seq.*, 27–86.

[125] See *infra*, paras 27–78 *et seq.*

[126] This procedure will not be possible if, in reality, no partnership exists: see *Re C. & M. Ashberg, The Times*, July 17, 1990, noted *supra*, para. 27–05.

[127] The expression "creditor's petition" will hereafter be used for convenience, even though petitions may also be presented by a liquidator or temporary administrator pursuant to the same procedure: see *infra*, para. 27–33.

petitions[128] against one or more (but not necessarily all) partners or former partners[129] whilst, in the case of a member's petition, concurrent petitions must be presented against *all* the partners.[130]

Jurisdiction

27-25   As in the case previously considered, the Insolvent Partnerships Order 1994 deems an insolvent partnership to be an unregistered company.[131] However, the court will only have jurisdiction where the firm has (or has at any time had) a principal place of business in England and Wales[132] or, in the case of a creditor's petition only, if the debt on which the petition is based arose in the course of carrying on the firm's business from premises in England and Wales.[133] In either case, the firm must also have carried on business in England and Wales within three years of the presentation of the petition.[134]

Grounds for petition against firm

27-26   In this instance, there are two possible grounds on which a petition may be presented against the firm, namely that it is unable to pay its debts,[135] and in the case of a creditor's petition, where, on the coming to an end of a moratorium under section 1A of the Insolvency Act 1986, no voluntary arrangement approved under Part 1 of the Act is in effect.[136] As regards the former ground, the circumstances in which a firm will be *deemed* unable to pay its debts are strictly limited.[137] Thus, on a creditor's petition, the creditor, to whom the firm must be indebted in a sum exceeding £750[138] then due, must have served[139] written/

---

[128] Such petitions may either consist of a petition for a winding up order against a corporate partner or a petition for a bankruptcy order against an individual partner: see the definition of "insolvency petition" in the Insolvent Partnerships Order 1994, art. 2(1).

[129] *ibid.* art. 8(1), as amended by the Insolvent Partnerships (Amendment) Order 2002, art. 4(1).

[130] *ibid.* art. 10(1).

[131] Insolvency Act 1986, s.220, as amended and applied by the Insolvent Partnerships Order 1994, art. 8(1) (as amended: see *supra*, n. 129), (2), Sched. 4, Pt I, para. 2 (creditor's petition) and *ibid.* art. 10(1)(b), Sched. 4, Pt I, para. 2 (member's petition).

[132] *ibid.* s.221(1)(a), as amended and applied by the Insolvent Partnerships Order 1994, art. 8(1) (as amended: see *supra*, n. 129), (2), Sched. 4, Pt I, para. 3 (creditor's petition); *ibid.* s.221(1), as amended and applied by *ibid.* art. 10(1)(a), Sched. 6, para. 4 (member's petition).

[133] *ibid.* s.221(1)(b), as amended and applied by *ibid.* art. 8(1) (as amended: see *supra*, n. 129), (2), Sched. 4, Pt I, para. 3.

[134] *ibid.* s.221(2), as amended and applied by *ibid.* art. 8(1) (as amended: see *supra*, n. 129), (2), Sched. 4, Pt I, para. 3 (creditor's petition) and *ibid.* art. 10(1)(a), Sched. 6, para. 4 (member's petition). As to when a firm will be treated as having carried on business in England and Wales within the requisite period, note *Re A Debtor (No. 784 of 1991)* [1992] Ch. 554 (a decision under *ibid.* s.265(1)(c)(ii), applying *Theophile v. Solicitor-General* [1950] A.C. 186).

[135] Insolvency Act 1986, s.221(8)(a), as amended and applied by the Insolvent Partnerships Order 1994, art. 8(1) (as amended: see *supra*, para. 27–24, n. 129), (2), Sched. 4, Pt I, para. 3, as itself amended by the Insolvent Partnerships (Amendment) (No. 2) Order 2002, art. 9(2) (creditor's petition) and *ibid.* s.221(8), as amended and applied by *ibid.* art. 10(1)(a), Sched. 6, para. 4 (member's petition). *ibid.* ss.223, 224 do not apply: Insolvent Partnerships Order 1994, arts 8(1) (creditor's petition), 10(1) (member's petition).

[136] *ibid.* 221(8)(b), as amended and applied in the manner set out in the preceding footnote.

[137] *cf.* the position where a petition is presented against the firm alone: see *supra*, para. 27–09.

[138] This sum may be increased: Insolvency Act 1986, s.222(3), as amended and applied by the Insolvent Partnerships Order 1994, art. 8(1) (as amended: see *supra*, para. 27–24, n. 129), (2), Sched. 4, Pt I, para. 4. As might be expected, there is no need to obtain a judgment against the firm in respect of the debt: see *Schooler v. Customs & Excise* [1995] 2 B.C.L.C. 610 (CA).

[139] Service on the firm may be effected by leaving the demand at the firm's principal place of business in England and Wales or at premises in England and Wales at which the business "in the

statutory demands on the firm and on one or more of the partners or former partners[140] (who need not be the partners/former partners against whom the concurrent petitions are presented) and the sum due must not have been paid, secured or compounded for to the creditor's satisfaction[141] within three weeks of the date on which the last demand was served.[142] There is no equivalent provision in the case of a member's petition, so that a petitioner must prove the firm's inability to pay its debts in some other way.

Grounds for petition against corporate partner

If the court has jurisdiction to wind up the firm, it also has jurisdiction to wind **27–27** up a current or former corporate member thereof.[143] As in the case of the firm, a petition against such a partner may only be presented on the ground that it is unable to pay its debts[144] or if there is a creditor[145] to whom the firm is indebted and to whom the corporate partner is liable in respect of the same debt and, on the coming to an end of a moratorium under section 1A of the Insolvency Act 1986 in favour of the firm, no voluntary arrangement approved under Part 1 of that Act is in effect.[146] The firm will be *deemed* to be unable to pay its debts for the purposes of a petition presented by a creditor where the relevant partnership debt is not paid, secured or compounded for to his satisfaction following completion of the written/statutory demand procedure described in the preceding paragraph.[147] Otherwise, the corporate partner's inability to pay its debts must be proved in some other way.

---

course of which" the debt was incurred was carried on, or by delivering it to an "officer" of the partnership or in such other manner as the court may approve or direct: *ibid.* s.222(2), as amended and applied by *ibid.* Service on a corporate partner must be at its registered office: *ibid.* s.222(1)(b), as amended and applied by *ibid.*; *cf. ibid.* s.123(2), as amended and applied by *ibid.* art. 8(3), Sched. 4, Pt II, para. 7(a). As regards service on an individual partner, although *ibid.* s.222(1)(b) refers to service "in accordance with the rules" (*i.e.* the Insolvency Rules 1986), this should be contrasted with the provisions of *ibid.* s.268(2), as amended and applied by *ibid.* art. 8(3), Sched. 4, Pt II, para. 7(b).

[140] The demands served on the firm and on the partners must be in Form 4 set out in the Insolvent Partnerships Order 1994, Sched. 9 (as substituted by the Insolvent Partnerships (Amendment) Order 2005, art. 12(c), Sched. 2).

[141] *cf.* the Insolvency Act 1986, s.223(1)(b), as amended and applied, in the case of a petition against the firm alone, by the Insolvent Partnerships Order 1994, art. 7(1) (as amended), (2), Sched. 3, Pt I, para. 5, which refers to the creditor's "reasonable satisfaction". See further *supra*, para. 27–09.

[142] *ibid.* s.222(1), as amended and applied by *ibid.* art. 8(1) (as amended: see *supra*, para. 27–24, n. 129), (2), Sched. 4, Pt I, para. 4. As to the position where payment of the debt is tendered prior to the hearing of the petition, see *Smith v. Ian Simpson & Co.* [2001] Ch. 239 (CA), a decision under the Insolvency Act 1986, s.271(1). And see, as to when a debt has been compounded for, *Artman v. Artman* [1996] B.P.I.R. 511.

[143] *ibid.* s.117(5), as amended and applied by the Insolvent Partnerships Order 1994, art. 8(4), (5), (8), Sched. 4, Pt II, para. 5 (creditor's petition) and *ibid.* art. 10(1)(a), Sched. 6, para. 1 (member's petition).

[144] *ibid.* s.122(a), as amended and applied by *ibid.* art. 8(4), (5), (8), Sched. 4, Pt II, para. 6(a) (creditor's petition) and *ibid.* art. 10(2), (3), (6) (as substituted by the Insolvent Partnerships (Amendment) Order 2005, art. 5(b)), Sched. 4, Pt II, para. 6(a) (member's petition).

[145] By assignment or otherwise.

[146] *ibid.* s.122(b), as amended and applied by *ibid.*

[147] *ibid.* s.123, as amended and applied by *ibid.* art. 8(4), (5), (8), Sched. 4, Pt II, para. 7(a).

Foreign corporate partner

27–28 A concurrent petition may be presented against a corporate partner or former corporate partner registered outside England and Wales, provided that the court has jurisdiction to wind up the partnership.[148]

Group and sub-partnerships[149]

27–29 Where a group partnership is insolvent, each constituent firm will be treated as a corporate member of the group for the above purposes.[150] If petitions are not to be presented against the partners, a winding up order may be sought against the group partnership in the normal way.[151]

It is the view of the current editor that a sub-partnership will not fall to be similarly treated in the event of the insolvency of the head partnership.[152]

Grounds for petition against individual partner

27–30 A creditor's petition for a bankruptcy order may only be presented against an individual partner (or former partner) in respect of one or more joint debts owed by the insolvent firm[153] if he appears unable to pay[154] those debts and they are liquidated, immediately due, unsecured[155] and total £750 or more[156] or if, on the coming to an end of a moratorium under section 1A of the Insolvency Act 1986 in favour of the firm, no voluntary arrangement approved under Part 1 of that Act is in effect.[157] A partner will display an apparent inability to pay such debt(s) where, within the three weeks following completion of the written/statutory

---

[148] *ibid.* s.117(5), as amended and applied by the Insolvent Partnerships Order 1994, art. 8(4), (5), (8), Sched. 4, Pt II, para. 5 (creditor's petition) and *ibid.* art. 10(2), (3), (6) (as substituted by the Insolvent Partnerships (Amendment) Order 2005, art. 5(b)), Sched. 4, Pt II, para. 5 (member's petition).

[149] See, as to such partnerships, *supra*, paras 5–67 *et seq.*, 11–17 *et seq.*

[150] Insolvent Partnerships Order 1994, art. 12. Note that a petition to wind up one of the constituent firms without winding up the group partnership will proceed in the normal way: see *supra*, para. 27–11.

[151] See *supra*, paras 27–08 *et seq.*

[152] To apply the Insolvent Partnerships Order 1994, art. 12 in such a case would involve ignoring the true nature of a sub-partnership: in a normal case, only one of the sub-partners will in fact be a member of the head partnership and it is only that sub-partner who will be liable to a creditor of the head partnership; *vis-à-vis* the sub-partnership, that creditor will be no more than a separate creditor of one of the sub-partners. There would seem to be little point in deeming that sub-partner to be a corporate partner (whether he be a company or an individual), unless the underlying intention is to render the sub-partnership itself as a member of the head partnership and liable to be wound up accordingly. *Semble* this cannot be the effect of art. 12. Note also that the same approach is, more logically, adopted in the case of any other body which can be wound up as an unregistered company under the Insolvency Act 1986, Pt V: *ibid.* art. 12. A petition to wind up a sub-partnership without winding up the head partnership will be no different from a petition against any other firm: see *supra*, para. 27–11.

[153] Insolvency Act 1986, s.267(1), as amended and applied by the Insolvent Partnerships Order 1994, art. 8(6)–(8), Sched. 4, Pt II, para. 6(b).

[154] *ibid.* s.267(2)(c), as amended and applied by *ibid.*

[155] *ibid.* s.267(2)(b), as amended and applied by *ibid.* It follows that future debts cannot found a petition: see *ibid.* s.267(2)(b) in its original form.

[156] *ibid.* s.267(2)(a), (3), as amended and applied by *ibid.* This sum may, of course, be increased: *ibid.*

[157] *ibid.* s.267(2), (2A), as amended and applied by the Insolvent Partnerships Order 1994, art. 8(6)–(8), Sched. 4, Pt II, para. 6(b), as itself amended by the Insolvent Partnerships (Amendment) (No. 2) Order 2002, art. 9(4)

demand procedure described above,[158] the relevant debts are not paid, secured or compounded for to the creditor's satisfaction and the demand against that partner has not been set aside.[159]

Minor or foreign partners

A court which has jurisdiction to wind up the partnership will also have jurisdiction to hear a bankruptcy petition presented against a minor or foreign partner.[160]

27–31

Personal representatives

Where personal representatives carry on the deceased's business in the old firm name and, in the course of so doing, incur joint debts, they cannot be treated as partners for insolvency purposes unless that is in fact the relationship between them.[161]

27–32

Who may present petitions

Petitions against the firm and against any current or former corporate or individual partners may be presented by a liquidator appointed in proceedings by virtue of Article 3(1) of Council Regulation (EC) No. 1346/2000 of May 29, 2000 on insolvency proceedings, a temporary administrator[162] or by one or more of the firm's joint creditors, provided that the firm and the member/former member in question are indebted to the petitioner(s) in respect of a liquidated sum payable immediately.[163] However, a corporate or individual partner may present its or his own petition on the ground that the firm is unable to pay its

27–33

---

[158] See *supra*, para. 27–26.

[159] Insolvency Act 1986, s.286(1), as amended and applied by the Insolvent Partnerships Order 1994, art. 8(6)–(8), Sched. 4, Pt II, para. 7(b). *Quaere* whether a petition may properly be presented if there is an outstanding application to set aside the statutory demand served on the partner concerned at the end of the three week period specified in that subsection. As to the procedure for setting aside a statutory demand, see the Insolvency Rules 1986, rr. 6.4, 6.5, as respectively amended by the Insolvency (Amendment) Rules 2009, rr. 5, 34 and the Insolvency (Amendment) Rules 2010, Sched. 1, paras 304, 305; *Re A Debtor (No. 415–50–1993)* [1994] 1 W.L.R. 917; *Re a Debtor (No. 544/SD/98)* [2000] B.C.L.C. 103 (CA); also the CPR Practice Direction on Insolvency Proceedings, Pt 3, para. 12. As to the position where payment of the debt is tendered prior to the hearing of the petition, see *Smith v. Ian Simpson & Co.* [2001] Ch. 239 (CA), a decision under the Insolvency Act 1986, s.271(1). As to when a debt has been compounded for, see *Artman v. Artman* [1996] B.P.I.R. 511.

[160] *ibid.* s.117(5), as amended and applied by the Insolvent Partnerships Order 1994, art. 8(4), (5), (8), Sched. 4, Pt II, para. 5 (creditor's petition) and *ibid.* art. 10(4)–(6) (the latter as substituted by the Insolvent Partnerships (Amendment) Order 2005, art. 5(b)), Sched. 6, para. 1 (member's petition). It is assumed that, as under the Bankruptcy Act 1914, for a valid petition to be presented against a minor, it would be necessary to establish his liability for the debts and obligations of the firm: see, generally, *Re A Debtor (No. 564 of 1949)* [1950] Ch. 282; also *Ex p. Jones* (1881) 18 Ch.D. 109; *Ex p. Magrett* [1891] 1 Q.B. 413; *Re Davenport* [1963] 1 W.L.R. 817. See also *supra*, paras 4–07 *et seq.* CPR Pt 21 will apply in such a case: Insolvency Rules 1986, r. 7.51A(2), as substituted by the Insolvency (Amendment) Rules 2010, Sched., para. 469.

[161] See *Re Fisher & Sons* [1912] 2 K.B. 491, noted *supra*, para. 5–07, n. 32.

[162] Within the meaning of Article 38 of Council Regulation (EC) No. 1346/2000.

[163] *ibid.* s.124(1), (2), as amended by the Insolvent Partnerships Order 1994, Sched. 4, Pt II, para. 8 (as itself amended by the Insolvent Partnerships (Amendment) Order 2002, art. 5(4)).and applied, as regards the firm, by the Insolvency Act 1986, s.221(5) (as itself amended by the Insolvent Partnerships Order 1994, art. 8(1) (as amended by the Insolvent Partnerships (Amendment) Order, art. 4(2)), (2), Sched. 4, Pt I, para. 3) and, as regards the partners (in lieu of *ibid.* s.264), by the Insolvent Partnerships Order 1994, art. 8(4)–(8).

debts, provided that petitions are at the same time presented against the firm and against all the other partners, individual or corporate, and those other partners are willing to have insolvency orders made against them.[164] However, the court may dispense with service on the partnership and/or specified partners in an appropriate case.[165]

Form and service of petitions

27–34   The form of all the petitions referred to in the foregoing paragraph is prescribed by the Insolvent Partnerships Order 1994[166] and they must contain particulars of the concurrent petitions which have been presented, identifying the firm and partners concerned.[167] Service on the firm will generally be effected at its principal place of business by handing the petition to a partner (including any person held out as such), employee or other person authorised to accept service.[168] Service on a corporate or individual partner is effected in the normal way.[169]

The petitions must all be presented at the same time and to the same court[170] and, save in the case of petitions against the individual partners, advertised in the appropriate form.[171] They can be presented to the High Court[172] or a county court

---

[164] *ibid.* s.124(1), (2), as amended and applied by the Insolvent Partnerships Order 1994, art. 10(1)(a), Sched. 6, para. 2.

[165] *ibid.* s.124(3), as amended and applied by *ibid.*

[166] See the Insolvent Partnerships Order 1994, Sched. 9, Forms 5, 6 and 7, as substituted by the Insolvent Partnerships (Amendment) (No. 2) Order 2002, Sched. (creditor's petition against the firm, a corporate partner and an individual partner respectively), Forms 11, 12, 13, as substituted by *ibid.* (member's petition against the firm, a corporate partner and an individual partner respectively). See also the Insolvency Act 1986, s.124(1), as amended and applied by virtue of *ibid.* art. 8(3)–(5), (8), Sched. 4, Pt II, para. 8 (creditor's petition) and *ibid.* art. 10(1)(a), Sched. 6, para. 2 (member's petition).

[167] Insolvency Act 1986, s.124(5), as amended and applied by *ibid.*

[168] Insolvency Rules 1986, r. 4.8(3)(a), (b), read subject to the Insolvent Partnerships Order 1994, art. 18(1).

[169] *ibid.* rr. 4.8, as amended (corporate partners), 6.14, as amended (individual partners).

[170] Insolvency Act 1986, s.124(3)(a), as amended by the Insolvent Partnerships Order 1994, Sched. 4, Pt II, para. 8 and applied, as regards the firm, by the Insolvency Act 1986, s.221(5) (as itself amended and applied by the Insolvent Partnerships Order 1994, art. 8(1)–(3) (as amended: see supra, n. 163), Sched. 4, Pt I, para. 3) and, as regards the partners, by the Insolvent Partnerships Order 1994, art. 8(4)–(8) (creditor's petition); *ibid.* s.124(4)(a), as amended and applied, as regards the firm, by *ibid.* art. 10(1)(a), Sched. 6, para. 2 and *ibid.* s.124(3)(a)) as amended the Insolvent Partnerships Order 1994, Sched. 4, Pt II, para. 8 and applied, as regards the corporate and individual partners, by the Insolvent Partnerships Order, art. 10(2)–(6), as amended by the Insolvent Partnerships (Amendment) Order 2005, art. 5(b) (member's petition).

[171] *ibid.* s.124(3)(b), as amended and applied by *ibid.* (creditor's petition); *ibid.* s.124(4)(b), as amended and applied by *ibid.* (member's petition). The advertisement must be in Form 8 in the Insolvent Partnerships Order 1994, Sched. 9: *ibid.*

[172] *ibid.* s.117(1), (5), as amended, in the case of a creditor's petition, by the Insolvent Partnerships Order 1994, Sched. 4, Pt II, para. 5 and applied, as regards the firm, by the Insolvency Act 1986, s.221(5) (as itself amended by the Insolvent Partnerships Order 1994, art. 8(1) (as amended: see *supra*, n. 163), (2), Sched. 4, Pt I, para. 3) and, as regards the partners, by the Insolvent Partnerships Order 1994, art. 8(4)–(8) and, in the case of a member's petition, as amended and applied, as regards the firm, by *ibid.* art. 10(1)(a), Sched. 6, para. 1 and applied, as regards the corporate and individual partners, by the Insolvent Partnerships Order, art. 10(2)–(6), as amended by the Insolvent Partnerships (Amendment) Order 2005, art. 5(b). Note that, where a petition is to be presented against an individual partner, the petitions may not be presented to a district registry: *ibid.* s.117(6), as amended and applied by *ibid.*

with winding up jurisdiction[173] within whose insolvency district the firm has (or has at any time had) "a" principal place of business[174] or, in the case of a creditor's petition, premises at which the firm's business was carried on when the relevant debt was incurred.[175]

Withdrawal of petitions and addition of parties

A petitioner may withdraw all the petitions which he has presented,[176] but the court can, in the case of a creditor's petition, permit another creditor of the firm to be substituted.[177] **27–35**

Additional partners can, with the leave of the court, be added to the proceedings at any time after the presentation of a creditor's petition.[178]

Consequences of presentation of petitions

Consequences for the firm and any corporate partner

The position where a petition is presented for the winding up of a partnership has already been noted.[179] A corporate partner against whom a petition is presented will be subject to the same regime.[180] **27–36**

Consequences for an individual partner

An *individual* partner against whom a bankruptcy petition is presented will be subject to a general restriction on his ability to dispose of property in his hands,[181] including any assets vested in him on trust for the firm.[182] An interim **27–37**

---

[173] *ibid.* s.117(7), as amended and applied by *ibid.* and further amended by the Lord Chancellor (Transfer of Functions and Supplementary Provisions) Order 2006 (SI 2006/680), Sched. 2, para. 7. Note that a county court may only be given winding up jurisdiction if it also has jurisdiction for the purposes of the bankruptcy provisions of the 1986 Act: *ibid.*

[174] *ibid.* s.117(2)(a), as amended and applied in the manner set out *supra*, n. 172 (creditor's petition); *ibid.* s.117(2), as amended and applied by *ibid.* art. 10(1)(a), Sched. 6, para. 1 (member's petition). Note that the existence of more than one principal place of business is clearly contemplated.

[175] *ibid.* s.117(2)(b), as amended and applied by *ibid.*

[176] *ibid.* s.124(9), (10), as amended by the Insolvent Partnerships Order 1994, Sched. 4, Pt II, para. 8 and applied in the manner set out *supra*, n. 172 (creditor's petition) and as amended and applied by *ibid.* art. 10(1)(a), Sched. 6, para. 2 (member's petition). As regards the petitions against the partners, the former version technically applies even in the latter case: see *supra*, para. 27–34, n. 170.

[177] *ibid.* s.124(11), as amended and applied by *ibid.*

[178] *ibid.* s.124(4), as amended and applied by *ibid.*

[179] See *supra*, paras 27–16 *et seq.* And see *ibid.* s.221(5), (6), as amended and applied by *ibid.* art. 8(1) (as amended: see *supra*, para. 27–33, n. 163), (2), Sched. 4, Pt I, para. 3, as itself amended by the Insolvent Partnerships (Amendment) Order 2006, art. 7 (creditor's petition) and *ibid.* art. 10(1)(a), Sched. 6, para. 4, as amended by *ibid.* art. 9 (member's petition).

[180] Insolvent Partnerships Order 1994, art. 8(4), (5), (8), Sched. 4, Pt II (creditor's petition) and art. 10(2), (3), (6) (as substituted by the Insolvent Partnerships (Amendment) Order 2005, art. 5(b)), Sched. 4, Pt II (member's petition).

[181] Insolvency Act 1986, s.284, as amended and applied by the Insolvent Partnerships Order 1994, art. 8(6)–(8), Sched. 4, Pt II, para. 29 (creditor's petition) and *ibid.* art. 10(4)–(6) (as amended by the Insolvent Partnerships (Amendment) Order 2005, art. 5(b)), Sched. 4, Pt II, para. 29 (member's petition). See further *Re Flint* [1993] Ch. 319. Note also the decisions under *ibid.* s.127, noted *supra*, para. 27–16, n. 97, although the two regimes are different: see *Pettit v. Novakovic* [2007] B.C.C. 462.

[182] *ibid.* s.284(6), as amended and applied by *ibid. Per contra* in the case of other forms of trust property.

receiver of his estate may be appointed if that is necessary for the protection of his property.[183]

The insolvency orders and their consequences

Order against the firm

27–38　　The court must hear the petition against the firm *before* the petitions against the partners[184] and will have a general discretion in deciding whether or not to make the order sought,[185] unless an administration order is already in force.[186] This will also extend to any directions which the court may make as to the future conduct of insolvency proceedings against partners who are already subject to an insolvency order.[187] The order will follow the normal form.[188]

Order against the corporate and individual partners

27–39　　On the hearing of the petitions against the members of the firm, the court's attention must be drawn to the result of the hearing of the petition against the firm.[189] If no order has yet been made on that petition, the hearing of the petitions against the members may be adjourned.[190]

If an order has been made against the firm, it is likely that orders will be made against both corporate and individual partners, provided that the requirements of the Insolvency Act 1986[191] have been met, but the court retains full discretion in the matter.[192] Equally, a petition against a partner may be dismissed if there has

---

[183] *ibid.* s.286, as applied by *ibid.* art. 8(6), (7) (creditor's petition) and *ibid.* art. 10(4), (5) (member's petition). As to the manner in which the application is made, see the Insolvency Rules 1986, r. 6.51, as amended by the Insolvency (Amendment) Rules 2002, r. 8(4) and the Insolvency (Amendment) Rules 2010, Sched. 1, paras 1, 326.

[184] *ibid.* s.124(6), as amended by the Insolvent Partnerships Order 1994, Sched. 4, Pt II, para. 8 and applied, as regards the firm, by the Insolvency Act 1986, s.221(5) (as itself amended by the Insolvent Partnerships Order 1994, art. 8(1) (as amended: see *supra*, para. 27–33, n. 163), (2), Sched. 4, Pt I, para. 3) and, as regards the partners, by the Insolvent Partnerships Order 1994, art. 8(4)–(8) (creditor's petition) and as amended and applied, as regards the firm, by the Insolvent Partnerships Order 1994, art. 10(1)(a), Sched. 6, para. 2 and, as regards the partners, by *ibid.* art. 10(2)–(6) (as amended by the Insolvent Partnerships (Amendment) Order 2005, art. 5(b)), Sched. 4, Pt II, para. 8 (member's petition). Note, however, that all the petitions will normally be heard on the same day: *Re Marr* [1990] Ch. 773, 784C (a decision under the equivalent provisions introduced by the Insolvent Partnerships Order 1984).

[185] *ibid.* s.125(1), as amended by the Insolvent Partnerships Order 1994, Sched. 4, Pt II, para. 9 and applied in the manner set out *supra*, n. 184 (creditor's petition) and amended and applied as regards the firm, by *ibid.* art. 10(1)(a), Sched. 6, para. 3 and, as regards the partners, by *ibid.* art. 10(2)–(6) (as amended by the Insolvent Partnerships (Amendment) Order 2005, art. 5(b)), Sched. 4, Pt II, para. 9 (member's petition).

[186] See *infra*, para. 27–164.

[187] *ibid.* s.125(2), as amended and applied by *ibid.*

[188] Insolvency Rules 1986, Sched. 4, Form 4.11, as substituted by the Insolvency (Amendment) Rules 2005, Sched., Pt B.

[189] Insolvency Act 1986, s.125A(1), as added by the Insolvent Partnerships Order 1994, Sched. 4, Pt II, para. 9 and applied, as regards the firm, by the Insolvency Act 1986, s.221(5) (as amended) and, as regards the partners, by the Insolvent Partnerships Order 1994, art. 8(4)–(8) (creditor's petition) and as added and applied, as regards the firm, by *ibid.* art. 10(1)(a), Sched. 6, para. 3 and, as regards the partners, by *ibid.* art. 10(2)–(6) (as amended by the Insolvent Partnerships (Amendment) Order 2005, art. 5(b)), Sched. 4, Pt II, para. 9 (member's petition).

[190] *ibid.* s.125A(2), as added and applied by *ibid.*

[191] See *supra*, paras 27–27, 27–30.

[192] Insolvency Act 1986, s.125A(3), as added and applied by *ibid.* Note also, in the case of limited partners, *ibid.* s.125A(7), as added and applied by *ibid.*; see also *infra*, para. 33–06.

been a change in circumstances since the order was made against the firm.[193] It follows that the type of situation which arose in *Re Marr*[194] is unlikely to recur under the 1994 Order. There the petitioner's debt was paid *after* a winding up order had been made against the firm but bankruptcy orders were, nevertheless, made against the partners, although these orders were, ultimately, annulled by the Court of Appeal.

If no order has been made on the petitions against the partners within 28 days after the order against the firm, the proceedings against the firm continue as if the petition had been presented against the firm alone.[195] If the petition against the firm has been dismissed, the court still has discretion to make orders against one or more of the partners[196] but is, perhaps, unlikely to do so unless the relevant debt is clearly due from the partner(s) in question.

The orders made will be in the appropriate forms.[197]

Stay of proceedings and executions

As in the case of an order made against a firm *without* concurrent petitions against the partners, a winding up order will operate to stay all existing and future proceedings, etc., against the firm[198] and its members, including those partners in respect of whom no concurrent petitions have been presented.[199] **27-40**

Orders relating to subsequent insolvency proceedings against a partner

The provisions of sections 168(5A) and 303(2A) of the Insolvency Act 1986[200] have already been noted.[201] They confer wide discretion on the court to make orders regarding the further conduct of insolvency proceedings against corporate **27-41**

---

[193] *ibid.* s.125A(6), as added and applied by *ibid.*

[194] [1990] Ch. 773 (CA). Although the orders had, with some diffidence, been confirmed by Mervyn Davies J. (*ibid.* p. 777), in allowing the partners' appeals the Court of Appeal adopted a purposive construction of the then legislation, *i.e.* the Insolvency Act 1986, s.271, as amended and applied by the Insolvent Partnerships Order 1986, art. 8(2), Sched. 2, Pt III, para. 7.

[195] *ibid.* s.125A(4), as added by and applied in the manner set out, *supra*, n. 189.

[196] *ibid.* s.125A(5), as added and applied by *ibid.* If such an order *is* made, the proceedings against the partner in question proceed without account being taken of most of the modifications to the Insolvency Act 1986 made by the Insolvent Partnerships Order 1994: *ibid.*

[197] See, in the case of a corporate partner, the Insolvency Rules 1986, Sched. 4, Form 4.11, as substituted by the Insolvency (Amendment) Rules 2005, Sched., Pt B and, in the case of an individual partner, *ibid.* Forms 6.25, as substituted by the Insolvency (Amendment) Rules 2003 (SI 2003/1730), Sched. 2, Pt C (creditor's petition), 6.30, as substituted by *ibid.* and amended by the Insolvency (Amendment) Rules 2010, Sched., para. 550 (member's petition).

[198] Insolvency Act 1986, s.130(2), as applied by *ibid.* s.221(5) (as itself amended and applied by the Insolvent Partnerships Order 1994, art. 8(1) (as amended by the Insolvent Partnerships (Amendment) Order 2002, art. 4(1)), (2), Sched. 4, Pt I, para. 3 (creditor's petition) and by *ibid.* art. 10(1)(a), Sched. 6, para. 2 (member's petition)).

[199] *ibid.* s.228, as applied by the Insolvent Partnerships Order 1994, art. 8(1) (as amended: see the preceding footnote) (creditor's petition) and *ibid.* art. 10(1)(b) (member's petition). For these purposes a partner is clearly a "contributory": see *ibid.* s.226(1) (as applied by *ibid.*) and *infra*, para. 27–59. And see *supra*, para. 27–20. See also, in the case of insolvent corporate partners, *ibid.* ss.130(2), 183, as applied by *ibid.* art. 8(4), (5) (creditor's petition) and *ibid.* art. 10(2), (3) (member's petition) and, in the case of insolvent individual partners, *ibid.* ss.285, 346 and 347, as applied by *ibid.* art. 8(6), (7) (creditor's petition) and *ibid.* art. 10(4), (5) (member's petition).

[200] As respectively added by the Insolvent Partnerships Order 1994, art. 14(1), (2).

[201] See *supra*, para. 27–21.

or individual partners, whether the petitions against them have been presented concurrently with or independently of the petition against the firm.

Administration of the joint estate and separate estates

27–42   This subject will be considered in a subsequent section of this chapter.[202]

3.   INSOLVENCY NOT INVOLVING WINDING UP THE FIRM AS AN UNREGISTERED COMPANY

27–43   In each of the following cases, insolvency proceedings will be initiated against one or more of the partners, either by a creditor or by the partners themselves and may lead to the firm being wound up, but *not* as an unregistered company.[203]

Joint bankruptcy petition presented by the partners

27–44   A joint bankruptcy petition may only be presented on the ground that the partnership is unable to pay its debts.[204] All the partners must be individuals[205] and must, in general, concur in such presentation,[206] and the firm must have carried on business in England and Wales within the period of three years ending with the date on which the joint petition is presented.[207] Once presented, it may not be withdrawn save with the leave of the court.[208]

If a winding up order has previously been made against the firm and this is drawn to the attention of the court at any time after the presentation of the joint

---

[202] See *infra*, para. 27–78 *et seq.*

[203] Even where the proceedings do not in themselves involve a winding up of the firm, *e.g.* where a petition is presented against a single partner in respect of a joint or separate debt (see *infra*, para. 27–48), they may still cause the firm to be dissolved: see the Partnership Act 1890, ss.33(1), 35, considered *supra*, paras 24–29, 24–47 *et seq.*

[204] Insolvency Act 1986, s.272(1), as amended and applied by the Insolvent Partnerships Order 1994, art. 11, Sched. 7, para. 5. There is no procedure for establishing a firm's *deemed* inability to pay its debts; *cf. supra*, paras 27–09 (firm wound up as an unregistered company with no concurrent petitions), 27–29 (firm wound up as an unregistered company *with* concurrent petitions). And see the decision in *Taylors Industrial Flooring Ltd. v. M & H Plant Hire (Manchester) Ltd.* [1990] B.C.C. 44 (a decision under the Insolvency Act 1986, s.123(1)(e)); also *Re Clemence plc* (1992) 59 B.L.R. 56. *Semble*, a joint bankruptcy petition may not be presented where two or more persons merely hold themselves out as partners: see *Re C. & M. Ashberg, The Times*, July 17, 1990, noted *supra*, para. 27–05. The current editor takes this view notwithstanding the fact that the definition of "member" in the Insolvent Partnerships Order 1994, art. 2(1) (as added to the Insolvency Act 1986, s.436 by *ibid.* art. 2(2)) *includes* a person held out as a partner.

[205] *ibid.* s.264(1), as amended and applied by the Insolvent Partnerships Order 1994, art. 11, Sched. 7, para. 2. This procedure is not available in the case of a limited partnership (*ibid.*) or a partnership which is authorised to accept deposits under the Financial Services and Markets Act 2000 (*ibid.* s.264(2)(a), as substituted by the Financial Services and Markets Act 2000 (Consequential Amendments and Repeals) Order 2001 (SI 2001/3649), Pt 9, art. 469(1)).

[206] *ibid.* s.264(4), as amended and applied by *ibid.* Note, however, that the court has power to dispense with the concurrence of some members where obtaining it would be impracticable: *ibid.* s.266(1), as amended and applied by *ibid.*

[207] *ibid.* s.265(2), as amended and applied by *ibid.*

[208] *ibid.* s.266(2), as amended and applied by *ibid.*

petition, the court will have a discretion as to the future conduct of the proceedings.[209] Equally, if an administration order against the firm is already in force, the joint petition must be dismissed.[210]

Minor or foreign partners

This procedure may seemingly be used in the case of a firm comprising a **27–45** minor[211] or foreign partner.[212]

Form and presentation of petition

The form of the petition is prescribed by the Insolvent Partnerships Order **27–46** 1994[213] and will request the partners' trustee to wind up the firm's business and administer its assets without the partnership being wound up as an unregistered company.[214] An order made on such a petition may include orders for the winding up of the partnership business and administration of its property, but not, technically, for its dissolution.[215]

The petition can be presented to the High Court if the firm has (or has at any time had) "a" principal place of business in England and Wales[216] or to a county court within whose insolvency district the firm has or had a principal place of business.[217]

Consequences of presentation of joint petition

A partner against whom the joint bankruptcy petition is presented will be **27–47** subject to a general restriction on his ability to dispose of property in his hands,[218] including any assets vested in him on trust for the firm.[219] An interim

---

[209] *ibid.* s.303(2A), as added by the Insolvent Partnerships Order 1994, art. 14(2). See also *supra*, para. 27–21. See, as to the width of the discretion under this section, *Official Receiver v. Hollens* [2007] Bus L.R. 1402. And see *infra*, para. 27–50.

[210] See *infra*, para. 27–164.

[211] The provisions of CPR Pt 21 will apply in such a case: Insolvency Rules 1986, r. 7.51A(2), as substituted by the Insolvency (Amendment) Rules 2010, Sched., para. 469. See also *supra*, para. 4–10.

[212] The foreign partner will, almost by definition, concur in the service of the petition. If he does not, the court is unlikely to dispense with his concurrence under the Insolvency Act 1986, s.266(1), as amended and applied by the Insolvent Partnerships Order 1994, art. 11, Sched. 7, para. 5.

[213] Form 9 in the Insolvent Partnerships Order 1994, Sched. 9: *ibid.* s.264(3)(a), as amended and applied by the Insolvent Partnerships Order 1994, art. 11, Sched. 7, para. 2.

[214] *ibid.* s.264(3)(b), as amended and applied by *ibid.*

[215] *ibid.* s.264(5), as amended and applied by *ibid.* Also the Insolvent Partnerships Order 1994, Sched. 9, Form 16, as substituted by the Insolvent Partnerships (Amendment) Order 2005, Sched. 2. The point is, however, academic, given the provisions of the Partnership Act 1890, s.33(1), as to which see *supra*, paras 24–29, 24–32 *et seq.* Even if there were some agreement purporting to negate the effects of a partner's bankruptcy (see *supra*, para. 10–39), the bankruptcy of all the partners must inevitably work a dissolution: *Official Receiver v. Hollens* [2007] Bus.L.R. 1402, noticed *supra*, para. 27–22.

[216] *ibid.* s.265(1)(a), as amended and applied by the Insolvent Partnerships Order 1994, art. 11, Sched. 7, para. 3. The existence of more than one principal place of business is clearly contemplated. Note that the petition may not be presented to a district registry: *ibid.*

[217] *ibid.* s.265(1)(b), as amended and applied by *ibid.*

[218] Insolvency Act 1986, s.284, as amended and applied by *ibid.* art. 11, Sched. 7, para. 8. See further *Re Flint* [1993] Ch. 319. Note also the decisions under *ibid.* s.127, noted *supra*, para. 27–16, n. 97, although the two regimes are different: see *Pettit v. Novakovic* [2007] B.C.C. 462.

[219] *ibid.* s.284(6), as amended and applied by *ibid.* Per contra in the case of other forms of trust property.

receiver of his estate may be appointed if that is necessary for the protection of his property.[220]

Creditor's petition against one or more partners

27–48   Where a partnership debt remains unpaid, the creditor retains the option of presenting a petition against some or all of the partners without seeking to wind up the firm as an unregistered company.[221] It is not necessary that, in such a case, a judgment should first have been obtained against the firm.[222] The court has a wide discretion to give directions as to the future conduct of the insolvency proceedings and may (*inter alia*) direct their consolidation or apply any provision of the Insolvent Partnerships Order 1994 "with any necessary modifications".[223] Otherwise, the 1994 Order will not apply and the petitioner's debt will, in effect, be treated as the debt of the partner against whom the petition is presented.[224] Where separate petitions are presented against two partners in respect of the same partnership debt, it *may* be possible for the petitioner to agree terms with one partner, whilst proceeding with the petition against the other.[225] The procedure in cases of this type will follow the normal course of insolvency proceedings against an individual or corporate partner and falls outside the scope of this work.[226]

Petition presented by one partner against another

27–49   In an appropriate case, a partner may present a petition against a co-partner, provided that he can do so in the capacity of creditor.[227] If his claim is dependent on the taking of a partnership account,[228] he will not be in a position to petition

---

[220] *ibid.* s.286, as applied by *ibid.* art. 11(2)(a). See, as to the manner in which the application is made, the Insolvency Rules 1986, r. 6.51, as amended by the Insolvency (Amendment) Rules 2002, r. 8(4) and the Insolvency (Amendment) Rules 2010, Sched. 1, paras 1, 326.

[221] Insolvent Partnerships Order 1994, art. 19(5).

[222] *Schooler v. Customs and Excise Commissioners* [1995] 2 B.C.L.C. 610 (CA), a decision under the equivalent provisions of the Insolvent Partnerships Order 1986.

[223] Insolvency Act 1986, s.303(2A), (2B), as added by the Insolvent Partnerships Order 1994, art. 14(2); Insolvent Partnerships Order 1994, art. 19(6).

[224] This is not expressly stated in the Insolvent Partnerships Order 1994; *cf.* the Insolvent Partnerships Order 1986, art. 15(3).

[225] *Artman v. Artman* [1996] B.P.I.R. 511. The position will, of course, be otherwise if the partnership debt has itself been paid in full or compounded for by reason of the arrangement with one of the partners.

[226] See the standard works dealing with insolvency, *e.g. Muir Hunter on Personal Insolvency, Palmer's Company Law* 25th ed.

[227] See, for example, *Ex p. Notley* (1833) 1 Mont. & Ayr. 46, where the petitioning creditor had lent the bankrupt a sum of money on terms that he would receive interest and a share in the net profits of the bankrupt's business as long as the principal remained unpaid; by reason of this agreement, the petitioning creditor was liable to third parties as if he were a partner of the bankrupt (see, further, *supra*, paras 5–28 *et seq.*) but was nevertheless able to petition on the basis of the principal sum outstanding together with certain arrears of interest. Similarly, in *Ex p. Richardson* (1833) 3 D. & Ch. 244 a member of a dissolved firm presented a petition against his former partner in respect of sums found due to him on the taking of an account together with other moneys borrowed from him after the dissolution. *cf. Ex p. Gray* (1835) 2 Mont. & Ayr. 283. See also *Ex p. Nokes* (1801) and *Ex p. Maberley* (1808) 1 Mont. on Part., Note N, p. 62; *Windham v. Paterson* (1815) 2 Rose 466; *Ex p. Page* (1821) 1 Gl. & J. 100; *Hope v. Meek* (1855) 10 Ex. 842.

[228] See *supra*, para. 23–76. And see *Ex p. Notley* and *Ex p. Richardson, supra*; also *Re a Debtor, Debtor v. Brown*, unreported, November 29, 1985 (C.A.T. No. 787), [1986] C.L.Y. 131, where an adjournment of bankruptcy proceedings was refused because the debtor's claim for an account would not be completed within the foreseeable future.

until such time as the account has been concluded and the sum due to him ordered to be paid. In the normal course, an account will not be taken without dissolving the firm, so that the older cases dealing with petitions presented with a view to obtaining a dissolution are now unlikely to be of relevance in this context.[229]

A striking and relatively recent example of circumstances in which the court applied the above principle is to be found in *Hurst v. Bennett*.[230] There the partnership agreement entitled certain partners, in whose names leasehold premises were vested as trustees, to an indemnity from the partnership and from the other partners in respect of liabilities under the lease. Following the dissolution of the partnership[231] and before its accounts had been taken, the trustee partners served a statutory demand on the appellant, Mr Hurst, in respect of the sum said to be owing by him under the indemnity. The Court of Appeal held that the demand was served by the trustee partners in their capacity as trustees and not as partners and was not dependent on the taking of the partnership accounts; it accordingly could not be set aside. However, the court went on to hold that Mr Hurst's potential cross-claim in respect of his interest in the dissolved firm *was* dependent on the taking of an account, and therefore, even if there had been mutuality,[232] could not be relied on by way of set-off until the account had been completed.[233]

Orders relating to subsequent insolvency proceedings against a partner

Reference has already been made to the provisions of section 303(2A) of the Insolvency Act 1986,[234] which will enable a court, once it is aware that a debtor is a member of an insolvent partnership, to apply any provisions of the Insolvent Partnerships Order 1994 with any necessary modifications and to consolidate bankruptcy proceedings against an individual partner with proceedings against another partner.[235]   **27–50**

Partners' individual bankruptcy petitions

Where all the partners present individual bankruptcy petitions and orders are made on those petitions, this is likely to result in a dissolution of the firm.[236] In such a case, if the court is satisfied that the partnership is insolvent, an order can   **27–51**

---

[229] These cases include *Ex p. Browne* (1810) 1 Rose 151; *Ex p. Christie* (1832) Mont. & Bl. 352; *Ex p. Johnson* (1842) 2 M.D. & D. 678; *Ex p. Phipps* (1844) 3 M.D. & D. 505; *Ex p. Upfill* (1866) 1 Ch. 439; *King v. Henderson* [1898] A.C. 720.

[230] [2001] B.P.I.R. 287 (CA).

[231] As to the circumstances in which the firm came to be dissolved, see *Hurst v. Bryk* [2001] 1 A.C. 185 (HL); also *supra*, paras 24–04 *et seq.*

[232] See further as to mutuality, *infra*, para. 27–73, n. 351.

[233] It appears that, on the facts, the claim may, in any event, have had little substance: see [2001] B.P.I.R. 287 at [41] *per* Arden L.J., [56] *per* Peter Gibson L.J. The decision is, however, unsatisfactory in some respects: see *supra*, para. 23–76.

[234] As added by the Insolvent Partnerships Order 1994, art. 14(2): see *supra*, para. 27–21.

[235] Insolvency Act 1986, s.303(2A), (2B), as added by *ibid.*; also the Insolvent Partnerships Order 1994, art. 19(6). See, as to the width of the discretion under this section, *Official Receiver v. Hollens* [2007] Bus L.R. 1402.

[236] See the Partnership Act 1890, s.33(1) and *Official Receiver v. Hollens, supra*, at [6] *per* Blackburne J.

be made for it to be wound up as an unregistered company,[237] even though the partners have already been discharged.[238]

4.   APPOINTMENT OF LIQUIDATORS AND TRUSTEES

Appointment of liquidator

Interim appointment

27–52   Where a firm is wound up as an unregistered company, whether or not on a petition presented concurrently with petitions against one or more of the partners,[239] the Official Receiver will normally act as liquidator until such time as another person is appointed in his place.[240] However, if the petition against the firm was presented by the liquidator or administrator of a present or former corporate partner, the trustee of a present or former bankrupt partner's estate or the supervisor of a corporate or individual partner's voluntary arrangement and there were *no* concurrent petitions, the court can appoint the petitioner as liquidator, thus relieving the Official Receiver of his duties.[241]

If a corporate partner is wound up on a separate or concurrent petition, the Official Receiver will initially act as liquidator in the normal way.[242] This ensures that, in the latter case, the same person will act as liquidator both of the firm and of any insolvent corporate partner.

Subsequent appointment

27–53   When no concurrent petitions have been presented against the partners, the Official Receiver has the normal discretion to call a joint meeting of the creditors and partners (*qua* contributories)[243] with a view to the appointment of another liquidator of the firm in his place.[244] Where concurrent petitions have been presented, the Official Receiver can call a joint meeting to be attended by the creditors of the firm and of any insolvent partner in respect of whom the Official

---

[237] Under the power conferred by the Insolvency Act 1986, s.303(2A).

[238] See *Official Receiver v. Hollens, supra*

[239] See *supra*, paras 27–08 *et seq.*, 27–24 *et seq.*

[240] Insolvency Act 1986, s.136(2), as applied by *ibid.* s.221(5) (as itself amended by the Insolvent Partnerships Order 1994, art. 7(1) (as amended by the Insolvent Partnerships (Amendment) Order 2002, art. 3), (2), Sched. 3, Pt I, para. 3 (creditor's petition with no concurrent petitions), *ibid.* art. 8(1) (as amended by the Insolvent Partnerships (Amendment) Order 2002, art. 4(1)), (2), Sched. 4, Pt I, para. 3 (creditor's petition *with* concurrent petitions), *ibid.* art. 9(a), Sched. 5, para. 2 (member's petition with no concurrent petitions) and *ibid.* art. 10(1)(a), Sched. 6, para. 4 (member's petition *with* concurrent petitions)).

[241] *ibid.* s.221A(5), as added by the Insolvent Partnerships Order 1994, art. 7(1) (as amended: see the preceding footnote), (2), Sched. 3, Pt I, para. 3.

[242] *ibid.* s.136(2). In the case of concurrent petitions, *ibid.* s.136(2) is amended by the Insolvent Partnerships Order 1994, Sched. 4, Pt II, para. 12 and applied by *ibid.* arts 8(4), (5), (8) (creditor's petition), 10(2), (3), (6) (as substituted by the Insolvent Partnerships (Amendment) Order 2005, art. 5(b)) (member's petition).

[243] See *infra*, para. 27–59.

[244] *ibid.* s.136(4), (5), as applied by *ibid.* s.221(5) (as itself amended by the Insolvent Partnerships Order 1994, art. 7(1) (as amended: see *supra*, para. 27–52, n. 240), (2), Sched. 3, Pt I, para. 3 (creditor's petition) and *ibid.* art. 9(a), Sched. 5, para. 2 (member's petition)).

Receiver is the responsible insolvency practitioner.[245] In every case, the Official Receiver must consider the exercise of this discretion within 12 weeks of the date on which the insolvency order was made against the firm and notify the court and the creditors of the firm and of any insolvent partner(s) accordingly.[246] He *must* call such a meeting if required to do so by one quarter in value of the firm's or an insolvent partner's creditors.[247] This option is naturally not available when the petition has been presented by an insolvency practitioner and he has been appointed as liquidator.[248]

If a liquidator is not appointed at such a meeting, the Official Receiver must consider whether to apply for an appointment by the Secretary of State.[249] Special provision is made for the consequences of such an application in a case where a firm is wound up on a petition with concurrent petitions against one or more of the partners.[250]

The same provisions apply in the case of an insolvent corporate partner, whether it is wound up on a separate or concurrent petition.[251]

Appointment of trustee

When a bankruptcy order is made against an individual partner otherwise than on a concurrent petition, the Official Receiver will act as his receiver and manager until such time as a trustee is appointed.[252] The trustee will then be appointed by a general meeting of the partner's creditors, unless the Official Receiver decides to act as trustee.[253] If there were concurrent petitions, the Official Receiver will act as his trustee in bankruptcy until such time as he is

27–54

[245] *ibid.* s.136(4), as amended by the Insolvent Partnerships Order 1994, Sched. 4, Pt II, para. 12 and applied by the Insolvency Act 1986, s.221(5) (as itself amended by the Insolvent Partnerships Order 1994, art. 8(1) (as amended: see *supra*, para. 27–52, n. 240), (2), Sched. 4, Pt I, para. 3 (creditor's petition) and *ibid.* art. 10(1)(a), Sched. 6, para. 4 (member's petition)). Note that the partners against whom insolvency orders have been made on concurrent petitions will not rank as contributories "unless the contrary intention appears": *ibid.* s.221(7), as amended and applied by *ibid.*

[246] See, in the case where no concurrent petitions are presented, *ibid.* s.136(5)(a), (b), as applied by *ibid.* s.221(5) (as itself amended by the Insolvent Partnerships Order 1994, art. 7(1) (as amended: see *supra*, para. 27–52, n. 240), (2), Sched. 3, Pt I, para. 3 (creditor's petition) and *ibid.* art. 9(a), Sched. 5, para. 2 (member's petition)); as to the position where there are concurrent petitions, see *ibid.* s.136A(a), (b), as added by the Insolvent Partnerships Order 1994, Sched. 4, Pt II, para. 12 and applied by the Insolvency Act 1986, s.221(5) (as itself amended by the Insolvent Partnerships Order 1994, art. 8(1) (as amended: see *supra*, para. 27–52, n. 240), (2), Sched. 4, Pt I, para. 3 (creditor's petition) and *ibid.* art. 10(1)(a), Sched. 6, para. 4 (member's petition)).

[247] *ibid.* ss.136(5)(c), 136A(1)(c), as respectively applied/added by *ibid.*

[248] See, *supra*, para. 27–52.

[249] See, in the case where no concurrent petitions are presented, *ibid.* s.137(1), (2), as applied by *ibid.* s.221(5) (as itself amended in the manner set out *supra*, n. 246); as to the position where there are concurrent petitions, see *ibid.* s.137(2), (3), as amended by the Insolvent Partnerships Order 1994, Sched. 4, Pt II, para. 13 and applied by *ibid.* s.221(5) (as itself amended in the manner set out *supra*, n. 246).

[250] *ibid.* s.137A, as added by the Insolvent Partnerships Order 1994, Sched. 4, Pt II, para. 13 and applied by the Insolvency Act 1986, s.221(5) (as itself amended by the Insolvent Partnerships Order 1994, art. 8(1) (as amended: see *supra*, para. 27–52, n. 240), (2), Sched. 4, Pt I, para. 3 (creditor's petition) and *ibid.* art. 10(1)(a), Sched. 6, para. 4 (member's petition)).

[251] See, as to the position where a concurrent petition is presented, the Insolvent Partnerships Order 1994, art. 8(4), (5), (8) (creditor's petition) and *ibid.* art. 10(2), (3), (6) (member's petition). In either case, the Insolvency Act 1986, ss.136 *et seq.* apply with the amendments set out in the Insolvent Partnerships Order 1994, Sched. 4, Pt II, paras 12, 13: *ibid.*

[252] *ibid.* s.287(1).

[253] *ibid.* s.293, as amended by the Enterprise Act 2002, Sched. 23, para. 7, Sched. 26.

replaced by a joint meeting of the creditors of the firm and of the bankrupt partner,[254] thereby ensuring that the assets of the firm and of the insolvent partners are administered by the same person. The position is broadly the same where an order is made on a joint bankruptcy petition presented by the partners,[255] even though the partnership is itself not ordered to be wound up.[256] This will again ensure that the joint and separate estates will be administered by the same trustee.

If a trustee is not appointed at the relevant meeting, the Official Receiver must consider whether to apply for an appointment by the Secretary of State.[257]

Subsequent order on concurrent petition

27–55   Where a firm has been wound up on a petition presented with concurrent petitions against one or more partners, the person appointed to act as the responsible insolvency practitioner in respect of the firm and any insolvent member by a joint creditors' meeting[258] will automatically be appointed as the liquidator/trustee of any partner against whom an order on a concurrent petition is subsequently made.[259]

Conflicts of interest

27–56   Where an insolvency practitioner appointed as liquidator of a firm and as liquidator/trustee of an insolvent partner pursuant to insolvency orders made on concurrent petitions encounters a conflict of interest as between his various functions, he can apply to the court for directions and may be replaced as

---

[254] *ibid.* s.136(2), as amended by the Insolvent Partnerships Order 1994, Sched. 4, Pt II, para. 12 and applied by *ibid.* arts 8(6)–(8) (creditor's petition), 10(4)–(6) (as amended by the Insolvent Partnerships (Amendment) Order 2005, art. 5(b)) (member's petition)). See further as to the calling of such a joint meeting, see *supra*, para. 27–53.

[255] See *supra*, para. 27–44.

[256] Insolvency Act 1986, ss.292, 293, as amended and applied by the Insolvent Partnerships Order 1994, art. 11, Sched. 7, paras 10, 11. Note that both sections contemplate that the official receiver or other appointee will act as "trustee" of the partnership. As to calling a joint creditors' meeting, see *ibid.* s.293(3), (4)

[257] *ibid.* s.295 (bankruptcy petition against an individual partner); *ibid.* s.137(2), (3), as amended by the Insolvent Partnerships Order 1994, Sched. 4, Pt II, para. 13 and applied by *ibid.* arts 8(6)–(8) (creditor's petition with concurrent petitions), 10(4)–(6) (as amended by the Insolvent Partnerships (Amendment) Order 2005, art. 5(b)) (member's petition with concurrent petitions)); *ibid.* s.295, as amended and applied by the Insolvent Partnerships Order 1994, art. 11, Sched. 7, para. 11 (joint bankruptcy petition).

[258] *i.e.* pursuant to *ibid.* s.136(4), as amended by the Insolvent Partnerships Order 1994, Sched. 4, Pt II, para. 12 and applied, as regards the firm, by the Insolvency Act 1986, s.221(5) (as itself amended by the Insolvent Partnerships Order 1994, art. 8(1) (as amended: see *supra*, para. 27–52, n. 240), (2), Sched. 4, Pt I, para. 3) and, as regards individual partners, by the Insolvent Partnerships Order 1994, art. 8(6)–(8) (creditor's petition with concurrent petitions) and as amended and applied, as regards the firm, by the Insolvent Partnerships Order 1994, art. 10(1)(a), Sched. 6, para. 2 and, as regards individual partners, by *ibid.* art. 10(4)–(6) (as amended by the Insolvent Partnerships (Amendment) Order 2005, art. 5(b)) (member's petition with concurrent petitions).

[259] *ibid.* s.136A(5), as added and applied by *ibid.* Similarly where the appointment has been made by the Secretary of State: *ibid.* s.137A(3), as added by *ibid.* Sched. 4, Pt II, para. 13 (creditor's petition) and applied by *ibid.* arts 8(6)–(8) (creditor's petition), 10(4)–(6) (as amended by the Insolvent Partnerships (Amendment) Order 2005, art. 5(b)) (member's petition).

liquidator of the firm or of any corporate partner and/or as trustee of any one or more of the bankrupt partners.[260]

Removal and resignation

Special provision is made for the removal and resignation of liquidators/ **27–57** trustees appointed pursuant to insolvency orders made on concurrent petitions.[261]

Meetings, etc.

The detailed provisions of the Insolvency Act 1986, as amended and applied **27–58** by the Insolvent Partnerships Order 1994, relating to meetings, the appointment of liquidation and creditors' committees and the release of liquidators and trustees are outside the scope of this work.[262]

5. STATUS AND DUTIES OF THE PARTNERS IN THE WINDING UP OF A FIRM

Firm wound up as an unregistered company

Where a firm is wound up as an unregistered company, each partner may be **27–59** treated as having a dual capacity, *i.e.* both as a "contributory"[263] and as an "officer" of the partnership.[264] Save in the case of orders made on concurrent

---

[260] *ibid.* s.230A, as added by the Insolvent Partnerships Order 1994, Sched. 4, Pt II, para. 26 and applied, as regards the firm, by the Insolvency Act 1986, s.221(5) (as itself amended by the Insolvent Partnerships Order 1994, art. 8(1) (as amended: see *supra*, para. 27–52, n. 240), (2), Sched. 4, Pt I, para. 3 (creditor's petition) and *ibid.* art. 10(1)(a), Sched. 6, para. 4 (member's petition)) and, as regards corporate or individual partners, by the Insolvent Partnerships Order 1994, arts 8(4)–(8) (creditor's petition), 10(2)–(6) (as amended by the Insolvent Partnerships (Amendment) Order 2005, art. 5(b)) (member's petition). Similarly, in the case of trustee appointed following an order made on a joint bankruptcy petition: *ibid.* s.292A, as added by the Insolvent Partnerships Order 1994, art. 11, Sched. 7, para. 10. For an example of a case in which a trustee in bankruptcy's duties as such conflicted with his duties as liquidator of an insolvent company, see *Re Corbenstoke (No. 2)* (1989) 5 B.C.C. 767.

[261] *ibid.* s.172, as amended by the Insolvent Partnerships Order 1994, Sched. 4, Pt II, para. 21 and applied in the manner set out in the preceding footnote. In the case of a joint bankruptcy petition, see *ibid.* s.298, as amended and applied by the Insolvent Partnerships Order 1994, art. 11, Sched. 7, para. 15.

[262] The main amendments are to be found in *ibid.* Sched. 4, Pt II, paras 14 (amending the Insolvency Act 1986, s.139), 16 (amending *ibid.* ss.141, 301, 302), 18 (amending *ibid.* ss.146, 331), 22 (amending *ibid.* ss.174, 299), which apply in the case of insolvency orders made on concurrent petitions: Insolvency Act 1986, s.221(5), as amended and applied in the manner set out *supra*, n. 260. In the case of a joint bankruptcy petition, see the Insolvent Partnerships Order 1994, Sched. 7, paras 16 (amending the Insolvency Act 1986, s.299), 18 (amending *ibid.* s.301), 22 (amending *ibid.* s.331).

[263] As applied to partnerships, the Insolvency Act 1986, s.79(1) provides that "the expression 'contributory' means every person liable to contribute to the assets of a [*firm*] in the event of it being wound up".

[264] See the Insolvent Partnerships Order 1994, arts 2(1) (definition of "officer"), 3(4).

petitions,[265] a partner's status as a contributory is not affected by the fact that he is insolvent.[266] However, it is not only the current partners (in the true sense of that word) who will be so treated. Section 226 of the Insolvency Act 1986[267] in effect provides as follows:

> "(1) In the event of [*a firm*] being wound up, every person is deemed a contributory who is liable to pay or contribute to the payment of any debt or liability of the [*firm*], or to pay or contribute to the payment of any sum for the adjustment of the rights of members amongst themselves, or to pay or contribute to the payment of the expenses of winding up the [*firm*].
>
> (2) Every contributory is liable to contribute to the [*firm's*] assets all sums due from him in respect of any such liability as is mentioned above."

The foregoing words are apt to include an outgoing partner who remains directly liable to creditors of the firm[268] or who has (exceptionally) agreed to bear a share of a particular ongoing liability *vis-à-vis* his former partners.[269] It should, however, be noted that section 226 does not apply in the case of a winding up on a *member's* concurrent petition.[270]

It is clear that a person who has merely been held out as a partner will be regarded as a member and, thus, as a contributory.[271]

Firm not wound up as an unregistered company

27–60   Neither of the foregoing provisions will have any application where an order is made on a joint bankruptcy petition or on a petition presented against one or

---

[265] In such a case, the partners against whom orders are made are not to be treated as contributories "unless the contrary intention appears": Insolvency Act 1986, s.221(7), as amended and applied by the Insolvent Partnerships Order 1994, art. 8(1) (as amended: see *supra*, para. 27–52, n. 240), (2), Sched. 4, Pt I, para. 3 (creditor's petition) and art. 10(1)(a), Sched. 6, para. 4 (member's petition). But see also, as to the position where orders are made on a member's concurrent petition, *infra*, n. 270.

[266] *Quaere*, how this is intended to work, consistently with the framework established under the Insolvent Partnerships Order 1994. Is the liquidator of the firm required to treat himself as a contributory *qua* liquidator/trustee of a corporate or bankrupt partner? No such difficulty will arise where a partner had previously been made subject to an insolvency order, when the relevant liquidator/trustee would presumably be treated as the contributory: see *infra*, para. 27–61.

[267] As applied by the Insolvent Partnerships Order 1994, arts 7(1), as amended: see *supra*, para. 27–52, n. 240 (creditor's petition with no concurrent petitions), 8(1), as amended: see *supra*, para. 27–52, n. 240 (creditor's petition *with* concurrent petitions), 9(b) (member's petition with no concurrent petitions), and read subject to *ibid.* art. 3.

[268] See, in particular, the Partnership Act 1890, ss.9, 17(2), 36, *supra*, paras 13–03 *et seq.*, 13–40 *et seq.* and 13–78 *et seq.*

[269] For example, a partner might, as a condition of being permitted to retire on a date earlier than that permitted by the agreement, undertake a continuing obligation to contribute towards the firm's liability in respect of a particularly onerous asset, *e.g.* a lease of premises or equipment, even though he is not directly liable as a signatory thereto.

[270] Since it is not listed in the Insolvent Partnerships Order 1994, art. 10(1). However, the Insolvency Act 1986, s.74(1) seemingly *does* apply in such a case (see *ibid.* s.221(5), (6), as amended by the Insolvent Partnerships Order 1994, art. 10(1)(a), Sched. 6, para. 4, as itself amended by the Insolvent Partnerships (Amendment) Order 2006, art. 9), but must be read subject to *ibid.* s.221(7), as so amended: see *supra*, n. 265.

[271] See the definition of "member" in the Insolvent Partnerships Order 1994, art. 2(1), which is added to the Insolvency Act 1986, s.436 by *ibid.* art. 2(2). And see, generally, as to holding out, the Partnership Act 1890, s.14, considered *supra*, paras 5–35 *et seq.* It should, however, be noted that where persons merely hold themselves out as partners but no partnership in law exists, there will be no firm to be wound up: see *Re C. & M. Ashberg*, *The Times*, July 17, 1990. If there is no firm, it can have no members.

more partners, even though the former will inevitably result in the firm being wound up.[272]

Liability of partners as contributories

The liability of a partner, as a contributory, to meet calls made by the liquidator of an insolvent firm represents a specialty debt accruing at the time that such liability commenced,[273] so that the limitation period is extended to 12 years.[274] If a partner dies or becomes bankrupt before or after his name has been placed on the list of contributories, his personal representatives or trustee[275] will be liable as contributories.[276] This will seemingly cover the case where a partner's death or bankruptcy precedes the order against the firm.

27–61

The measure of a partner's liability *qua* contributory will reflect his unlimited liability under the general law[277] and any adjustments necessary to ensure that an appropriate contribution is made by each partner.[278] This may, however raise particularly difficult issues where the liability of the partners in respect of a specific debt sought to be proved is limited to the assets of the partnership and excludes personal liability on their part.[279] Even if the contribution takes account of this limitation, the assets flowing into the joint estate will seemingly be available to all proving creditors. A former partner's liability will be limited only to those debts, etc., incurred whilst he remained (or was held out) as a partner,[280] subject to account being taken of any right which he may have to an indemnity from the continuing partners.[281] The provisions of the Insolvency Act 1986 which establish the liability of the former members of a company[282] are inapplicable to partners.[283]

A partner's (or former partner's) liability *qua* contributory cannot be increased by seeking to treat him as a "director . . . whose liability is under the Companies Act unlimited".[284]

[272] See *supra*, paras 27–43 *et seq.*

[273] Insolvency Act 1986, s.80, as applied by *ibid.* s.221(5) (as itself amended by the Insolvent Partnerships Order 1994, art. 7(1) (as amended: see *supra*, para. 27–52, n. 240), (2), Sched. 3, Pt I, para. 3 (creditor's petition with no concurrent petitions), *ibid.* art. 8(1) (as amended: see *supra*, para. 27–52, n. 240), (2), Sched. 4, Pt I, para. 3 (creditor's petition *with* concurrent petitions), *ibid.* art. 9(a), Sched. 5, para. 2 (member's petition with no concurrent petitions) and *ibid.* art. 10(1)(a), Sched. 6, para. 4 (member's petition *with* concurrent petitions)). Note, however, that, in the latter case, *ibid.* s.226(2) clearly does not apply: see *supra*, para. 27–59.

[274] Limitation Act 1980, s.8(1).

[275] It is assumed that this will include the liquidator of an insolvent corporate partner.

[276] Insolvency Act 1986, ss.81, 82, as applied in the manner set out *supra*, n. 273.

[277] See *supra*, paras 13–11, 13–12. But see *Investment and Advisory Service Ltd. v. Gray* [1990] B.C.L.C. 38, 42 *per* Morritt J.

[278] This is conceived to be the effect of the Insolvency Act 1986, s.226(1), (2), which states the primary liability of each partner under subs. (2) in terms of the qualifying liability identified under subs. (1). Both subsections are reproduced *supra*, para. 27–59.

[279] As in *Prudential Assurance Co. Ltd. v. Ayres* [2008] 1 All E.R. 1266 (CA), noted *supra*, para. 13–15.

[280] See *supra*, paras 13–32 *et seq.*

[281] See *supra*, para. 10–248.

[282] *i.e.* the Insolvency Act 1986, s.74(2)(a)–(c).

[283] *ibid.* s.221(6), as amended and applied by the Insolvent Partnerships Order 1994, art. 7(1) (as amended: see *supra*, para. 27–52, n. 240), (2), Sched. 3, Pt I, para. 3 (creditor's petition with no concurrent petitions), *ibid.* art. 8(1) (as amended: see *supra*, para. 27–52, n. 240), (2), Sched. 4, Pt I, para. 3 (creditor's petition *with* concurrent petitions), *ibid.* art. 9(a), Sched. 5, para. 2 (member's petition with no concurrent petitions) and *ibid.* art. 10(1)(a), Sched. 6, para. 4 (member's petition *with* concurrent petitions).

[284] *ibid.* s.75 is inapplicable: *ibid.* s.221(6), as amended and applied by *ibid.*

Calls on contributories

27–62   The liquidator is responsible, under powers delegated to him by the court,[285] for drawing up a list of the firm's contributories[286] and for making calls upon them in order to settle the firm's debts and liabilities.[287] He is also required to adjust the rights of the contributories *inter se* and may accordingly be obliged to return to a partner any sum which that partner has paid in excess of his due share, if the amount of that excess is in fact contributed by the other partners.[288] Enforcement of the payment required by a call is by order of the court[289] and will seemingly require permission.[290]

Partners as officers

27–63   Each partner is treated as an officer of a firm which is being wound up as an unregistered company, although that expression will also extend to any other person who has management and control of the partnership business.[291] Although this exposes a partner to a claim that he is guilty of fraudulent or wrongful trading,[292] it is not considered that this will result in any overall increase in his liability.[293]

Disqualification orders

27–64   Where a firm is wound up as an unregistered company or has entered administration, the court[294] has jurisdiction to make a disqualification order[295] against a

---

[285] *ibid.* s.160(1)(b), (d) (as amended), as applied by *ibid.* s.221(5) (as itself amended and applied by *ibid.*); Insolvency Rules 1986, rr. 4.195, 4.202.

[286] Insolvency Act 1986, s.148 (as amended), as applied by *ibid.*; Insolvency Rules 1986, rr. 4.196 *et seq.* See in particular *ibid.*, r. 4.198 (as amended by the Insolvency (Amendment) Rules 2009, r. 5), as to the procedure for notifying the contributories of their appearance in the list and for dealing with objections received in response thereto.

[287] Insolvency Act 1986, s.150, as applied by *ibid.*; Insolvency Rules 1986, rr. 4.202 *et seq.* Note that a call may only be made with the consent of the liquidation committee or the court: Insolvency Rules 1986, rr. 4.203, 4.204, as respectively amended by the Insolvency (Amendment) Rules 2010, Sched. 1, paras 1, 249, 250.

[288] Insolvency Act 1986, s.154, as applied by *ibid.*; Insolvency Rules 1986, rr. 4.221, 4.222.

[289] Insolvency Rules 1986, r. 4.205(2).

[290] Since any attempt at enforcement would involve a "proceeding . . . in respect of any debt of the [*firm*]" and, thus, fall within the Insolvency Act 1986, s.228; see further *supra*, para. 27–20; also *Williams v. Harding* (1866) L.R. 1 H.L. 9, as to the need for permission prior to commencing insolvency proceedings.

[291] See the Insolvent Partnerships Order 1994, arts. 2(1) (definition of "officer"), 3(4). See also *supra*, para. 27–59.

[292] In essence, fraudulent trading involves a business being carried on with intent to defraud creditors or for a fraudulent purpose (Insolvency Act 1986, s.213), whilst wrongful trading connotes a business being carried on in the knowledge (actual or constructive) that an insolvent liquidation is unavoidable (*ibid.* s.214). See generally, as to the application of these sections in the case of an insolvent company, *Palmer's Company Law* (25th ed.), paras 15.599.16 *et seq.*

[293] *Quaere* could a finding of either sort against some (but not all) of the partners alter their respective liabilities *qua* contributories, notwithstanding their primary obligations under the partnership agreement and/or the Partnership Act 1890? It is thought not.

[294] See the Company Directors Disqualification Act 1986, s.6(4)–(4C), as amended and applied by the Insolvent Partnerships Order 1994, art. 16, Sched. 8 (as respectively amended by the Insolvent Partnerships (Amendment) Order 2001 (SI 2001/767), arts 2(2), 3(2) and, in the case of Sched. 8 only, by the Insolvent Partnerships (Amendment) Order 2005, art. 11(2)(c)).

[295] See, as to the nature of such an order, *ibid.* s.1, as amended by the Insolvency Act 2000, s.5(1), (2), Sched. 4, Pt I, para. 2 and the Enterprise Act 2002, s.204(3) and applied by the Insolvent Partnerships Order 1994, art. 16 (as amended: see the preceding footnote). The minimum period of disqualification is 2 years and the maximum is 15 years: *ibid.* s.6(5), as amended and applied by *ibid.*

current or former partner under the Company Directors Disqualification Act 1986.[296] It should be noted that such an order can only be made where the court is satisfied that his conduct as a partner is of such a nature as, when taken with his conduct as a member of any other firm or as a director of any company, to render him "unfit to be concerned in the management of a *company*" (emphasis supplied).[297] It follows that his fitness to be a partner in that or any other firm is strictly irrelevant. Such an order can also be made on the application of the Secretary of State or (at his direction) the Official Receiver,[298] although a disqualification undertaking may be accepted from the partner in such a case.[299]

Where a partner is found guilty of wrongful or fraudulent trading,[300] a disqualification order can be made without further inquiry into his conduct or suitability.[301]

It should be noted that there is seemingly *no* power to order the disqualification of a partner from entering into another partnership, irrespective of the nature of his conduct.[302]

Delivery up of partnership property

Where a winding up order is made against a firm, whether or not there are concurrent petitions against one or more of the partners,[303] the authority of all the   **27–65**

---

[296] *ibid.* s.6(1), (2), as amended and applied by *ibid.* art. 16 (as amended: see *supra*, n. 294), Sched. 8, as amended by the Insolvent Partnerships (Amendment) Order 2005, art. 11(2)(a), (b).

[297] *ibid.* s.6(1)(b). His conduct in relation to any matter connected with or arising out of the insolvency of any firm or company will be take into account: *ibid.* s.6(3), as amended and applied by *ibid.* And see, generally, *ibid.* s.9, Sched. 1, as amended and applied by *ibid.* art. 16, Sched. 8 (as respectively amended by the Insolvent Partnerships (Amendment) Order 2001, arts 2(2), 3(5) and, in the case of Sched. 8 only, by the Insolvent Partnerships (Amendment) Order 2005, art. 11(4)). In the case of a general partner of a limited partnership, account will be taken of his failure to attend to any registration requirements under the Limited Partnerships Act 1907: Company Directors Disqualification Act 1986, Sched. 1, Pt I, para. 6 (as so amended and applied).

[298] Company Directors Disqualification Act 1986, s.7(1), as amended and applied by the Insolvent Partnerships Order 1994, art. 16, Sched. 8 (as respectively amended by the Insolvent Partnerships (Amendment) Order 2001, arts 2(2), 3(3)(a)). Such an application can only be made within 2 years of the insolvency: *ibid.* s.7(2). As to applications for a disqualification order following an investigation, see *ibid.* s.8, as applied by the Insolvent Partnerships Order 1994, art. 16 (as amended) and amended by *ibid.* Sched. 8 (as itself amended by the Insolvent Partnerships (Amendment) Order 2001, art. 3(4) and the Financial Services and Markets Act 2000 (Consequential Amendments and Repeals) Order 2001 (SI 2001/3649), Pt 9, art. 470).

[299] *ibid.* ss.1A (as added by the Insolvency Act 2000, s.6(2)), 7(2A), as applied by the Insolvent Partnerships Order 1994, art. 16 (as amended (see *supra*, n. 294) and, in the case of s.7(2A), amended by *ibid.* Sched. 8 (as itself amended by the Insolvent Partnerships (Amendment) Order 2001, art. 3(3)(b)).

[300] See *supra*, para. 27–63.

[301] Company Directors Disqualification Act 1986, s.10(1), as applied by the Insolvent Partnerships Order 1994, art. 16 (as amended: see *supra*, n. 294). In this case there is merely a maximum period of disqualification of 15 years: *ibid.* s.10(2).

[302] This appears to follow from the fact that a partnership can only be wound up under the Insolvency Act 1986, Pt V where it is insolvent: see the Insolvent Partnerships Order 1994, arts 7–10. If it is solvent, a partnership is not a company within the meaning of the Company Directors Disqualification Act 1986, s.22(2)(b) (as substituted by the Companies Act 2006 (Consequential Amendments, Transitional Provisions and Savings) Order 2009 (SI 2009/1941), Sched. 1, para. 85(11)(a)). See also *Re Chartmore Ltd.* [1990] B.C.L.C. 673, 675e *per* Harman J.; *Re Probe Data Systems (No. 3)* [1991] B.C.C. 428, 434D *per* Harman J. *Semble*, this view is shared by the Department of Trade and Industry. See also Davis, Steiner & Cohen, *Insolvent Partnerships* (1996), para. 9.2.

[303] See *supra*, paras 27–08 *et seq.*, 27–24 *et seq.*

partners (solvent and insolvent) to bind the firm or to dispose of its assets[304] is automatically terminated and each partner is obliged to deliver up to the liquidator any partnership property[305] in his hands.[306] A similar obligation is imposed on former partners. If such property is in the hands of a third party, *e.g.* a partner's spouse, the liquidator can apply to the court for an order for such delivery up.[307]

Where orders are made on a joint bankruptcy petition,[308] the partners will be subject to the same obligation as regards the trustee.[309]

Statement of affairs

27–66   Once a winding up order has been made against a firm or a provisional liquidator appointed,[310] the Official Receiver may require any of the partners or former partners to submit a statement of the firm's affairs, including particulars of its assets, debts and liabilities.[311] Where an insolvency order has been made against a corporate or individual partner on a concurrent petition,[312] the statement in relation to that partner must distinguish between the assets and liabilities of the firm and of the partner in question.[313] Where an individual partner is bankrupted on a joint bankruptcy petition,[314] the normal provisions regarding his statement of affairs apply.[315]

6.   SHARE OF AN INSOLVENT PARTNER WHEN FIRM NOT WOUND UP

Dissolution of firm and conduct of winding up

27–67   It has already been seen[316] that, in the absence of some other agreement, the bankruptcy of an individual partner or the winding up and ultimate dissolution of

---

[304] In such a case, the Partnership Act 1890, s.38 clearly has no application: see *supra*, paras 13–62 *et seq.*

[305] This expression is defined by reference to the Partnership Act 1890: Insolvent Partnerships Order 1994, art. 2(1). See further *supra*, paras 18–03 *et seq.*

[306] Insolvency Act 1986, s.234, as amended where there are no concurrent petitions, by the Insolvent Partnerships Order 1994, Sched. 3, Pt II, para. 9 and applied by the Insolvency Act 1986, s.221(5) (as itself amended by the Insolvent Partnerships Order 1994, art. 7(1) (as amended: see *supra*, para. 27–52, n. 240), (2), Sched. 3, Pt I, para. 3 (creditor's petition) and *ibid.* art. 9(a), Sched. 5, para. 2 (member's petition)) and as amended, where there *are* concurrent petitions, by *ibid.* Sched. 4, Pt II, para. 27 and applied by the Insolvency Act 1986, s.221(5) (as itself amended by the Insolvent Partnerships Order 1994, art. 8(1) (as amended: see *supra*, para. 27–52, n. 240), (2), Sched. 4, Pt I, para. 3 (creditor's petition) and *ibid.* art. 10(1)(a), Sched. 6, para. 4 (member's petition)).

[307] Insolvency Act 1986, s.234(3); also *ibid.* s.237, as applied by *ibid.*

[308] See *supra*, para. 27–44.

[309] *ibid.* s.312(2), as amended and applied by the Insolvent Partnerships Order 1994, art. 11, Sched. 7, para. 20.

[310] See, as to the appointment of provisional liquidators, *supra*, para. 27–18.

[311] Insolvency Act 1986, s.131, as amended by the Insolvent Partnerships Order 1994, Sched. 3, Pt II, para. 7 (no concurrent petitions) and Sched. 4, Pt II, para. 10 (concurrent petitions) and applied in the manner set out *supra*, para. 27–65, n. 306.

[312] See *supra*, para. 27–39.

[313] Insolvency Act 1986, s.131(1)(b), (c), (3)(a), as amended by the Insolvent Partnerships Order 1994, Sched. 4, Pt II, para. 10 and applied by *ibid.* art. 8(4)–(8) (creditor's petition) and *ibid.* art. 10(2)–(6) (member's petition).

[314] See *supra*, para. 27–44.

[315] Insolvency Act 1986, s.288, as applied by the Insolvent Partnerships Order 1994, art. 11(1), (2).

[316] Partnership Act 1890, s.33(1), *supra*, paras 10–39, 11–10 and 24–35 *et seq.*

a corporate partner will dissolve the firm. Thereafter the authority of the solvent partners to wind up the firm's affairs and to dispose of its assets will derive from the agreement or, more usually, from the Partnership Act 1890.[317] The insolvent partner will have no such authority, although his former partners may be liable for his acts on the basis of holding out.[318]

Since the insolvent partner's trustee or liquidator has no right to step into the shoes of the insolvent partner and to become a partner in his place, he will not be entitled to interfere in the winding up of the partnership affairs,[319] unless the solvent partners are guilty of misconduct or they are all either dead or abroad.[320] Moreover, although the trustee or liquidator cannot compel the solvent partners to deliver up possession of the partnership books,[321] they can be summoned before the court for examination and ordered to produce the books for that purpose.[322]

Solvent partner acting as receiver

It follows from the foregoing that, if there is a dispute between the trustee or liquidator and the solvent partners as to the winding up of the partnership affairs and there is no reason to impugn the conduct of the latter, the court may appoint one of them receiver of the partnership property.[323]   **27–68**

Dealings with partnership land

If land is vested in the partners as a partnership asset[324] and one of the partners becomes insolvent, it seems clear that the trustee or liquidator of that partner will not become a joint tenant of the legal estate in his place.[325] Even if he did, the solvent partners could prima facie compel the trustee or liquidator to give effect   **27–69**

---

[317] *ibid.* s.38, *supra*, paras 13–62 *et seq*. And see, in particular, the following cases decided before the Act: *Fox v. Hanbury* (1776) Cowp. 445; *Harvey v. Crickett* (1816) 5 M. & S. 336; *Morgan v. Marquis* (1853) 9 Ex. 145; *Ex p. Robinson* (1833) 3 D. & Ch. 376. Note the decision in *Ex p. McGae* (1816) 19 Ves.Jr. 607, regarding the position where bills are accepted and notes issued in the name of a firm after the bankruptcy of one or more partners.

[318] Partnership Act 1890, s.38, proviso; *Thomason v. Frere* (1809) 10 East 418; *Lacy v. Woolcott* (1823) 2 D. & R. 458; *Craven v. Edmondson* (1830) 6 Bing. 734. See also *ibid.* s.14, *supra*, paras 5–35 *et seq*.

[319] See *Francis v. Spittle* (1840) 9 L.J.Ch. 230.

[320] See, as to the latter eventualities, *Hankey v. Garratt* (1792) 1 Ves.Jr. 236; *Everett v. Backhouse* (1804) 10 Ves.Jr. 94; *Barker v. Goodair* (1805) 11 Ves.Jr. 78; *Dutton v. Morrison* (1810) 17 Ves.Jr. 193.

[321] *Ex p. Finch* (1832) 1 D. & Ch. 274. See also *Ex p. Good* (1882) 21 Ch.D. 868; *Re Burnand* [1904] 2 K.B. 68. And note the exceptional decision in *Davidson v. Napier* (1827) 1 Sim. 297.

[322] Insolvency Act 1986, ss.236, 366, as respectively amended by the Legislative Reform (Insolvency) (Miscellaneous Provisions) Order 2010 (SI 2010/18), arts. 5(6), (7); Insolvency Rules 1986, rr. 9.1 *et seq.*, as amended. See generally, *Cloverbay Ltd. v. Bank of Credit and Commerce International SA* [1991] Ch. 90 and *Re British & Commonwealth Holdings plc (Nos 1 and 2)* [1993] A.C. 426 (HL) (both cases under *ibid.* s.236). And see, under the old bankruptcy laws, *Ex p. Trueman* (1832) 1 D. & C. 464; also *Re Burnand, supra*.

[323] See *Ex p. Stoveld* (1823) 1 Gl. & J. 303; *Freeland v. Stansfield* (1854) 2 Sm. & G. 479; *Collins v. Barker* [1893] 1 Ch. 578. See further *supra*, para. 23–176.

[324] Of course, the legal estate can only be vested in up to four partners: Law of Property Act 1925, s.34(2), as amended by the Trusts of Land and Appointment of Trustees, Act 1996, Sched. 2, para. 3(2); Trustee Act 1925, s.34(2), as amended by *ibid.* Sched. 3, para. 3(9). Land held in this way will now be subject to a trust of land under the Trusts of Land and Appointment of Trustees, Act 1996, s.1(1): see further *supra*, para. 18–62.

[325] This was stated in emphatic (albeit *obiter*) terms in *Rooney v. Cardona* [1999] 1 W.L.R. 1388, 1397 (CA). The point was conceded in *Re Holliday* [1981] Ch. 405, 411. See also *Re Turner* [1974] 1 W.L.R. 1556.

to directions given pursuant to the authority conferred on them by the Partnership Act 1890,[326] or by means of an application under the Trusts of Land and Appointment of Trustees Act 1996,[327] although the position may be otherwise if the application is made by the trustee in bankruptcy under that Act[328] since, in that case, the creditors' interests will generally prevail, absent exceptional circumstances.[329]

Rights in relation to insolvent partner's share

27–70   All that vests in the liquidator or trustee is the insolvent partner's share in the partnership, subject to the liens and other rights of the solvent partners.[330] Accordingly, he can claim nothing until all the partnership debts have been paid and the accounts as between the partners duly settled.[331] However, unless the agreement so provides,[332] the solvent partners cannot insist on buying out the insolvent partner's share at a valuation[333]; that share can only be ascertained and paid out following a sale of the partnership assets and the application of the proceeds in the manner specified in section 44 of the Partnership Act 1890.[334] In settling the accounts between the solvent partners and the trustee or liquidator, the latter will, on normal principles, be entitled to share in any capital profits attributable to the partnership assets since the date of dissolution,[335] together with

---

[326] Partnership Act 1890, s.38, *supra*, paras 13–62 *et seq.*

[327] ss.14(1), (2)(a), 15. See further, *supra*, paras 18–62, 23–193. *Semble*, where the land is not a partnership asset, the court might, in the exercise of its discretion, decline to compel the other partners to sell where the partnership continues as between them: see, for example, *Mortgage Corp. v. Shaire* [2001] Ch. 743; *cf. Bank of Ireland Home Mortgages Ltd. v. Bell* [2001] 2 All E.R. (Comm) 920 (CA); also note *Barca v. Mears* [2005] B.P.I.R. 15. All these decisions related to residential premises occupied by a bankrupt and his family. It is clear that the discretion under s.14 of the 1996 Act is wider than under its predecessor, *i.e.* the Law of Property Act 1925, s.30. Cautious reference may, nevertheless, be made to the following decisions under the latter section: *Re Turner* [1974] 1 W.L.R. 1556; *Re McCarthy* [1975] 1 W.L.R. 807, 809; *Re Densham* [1975] 1 W.L.R. 1519, 1531 *per* Goff J.; *Re a Debtor (No. 24 of 1971)* [1976] 1 W.L.R. 952; *Re Bailey (No. 25 of 1975)* [1977] 1 W.L.R. 278; *Re Holliday* [1981] Ch. 405; *Re Lowrie* [1981] 3 All E.R. 353; *Re Citro* [1991] Ch. 142 (applied in *Barca v. Mears, supra*). As to the right of a trustee in bankruptcy of a co-owner to an occupation rent, see *French v. Barcham* [2009] 1 W.L.R. 1124, where the earlier authorities are reviewed.

[328] In such a case *ibid.* s.15 does not apply (*ibid.* s.15(4)) and the position is instead governed by the Insolvency Act 1986, s.335A, as added by *ibid.* Sched. 3, para. 23.

[329] *Barca v. Mears, supra; Avis v. Turner* [2008] Ch. 218 (CA) at [36] *per* Chadwick L.J.

[330] See the Partnership Act 1890, s.39, *supra*, paras 19–25 *et seq.* See also *Anon.* (1700) 3 Salk. 61 and 12 Mod. 446; *West v. Skip* (1749) 1 Ves.Sen. 239; *Fox v. Hanbury* (1776) Cowp. 445; *Bolton v. Puller* (1796) 1 Bos. & Pul. 539; 1 Mont. Part., note P., p. 66; *Re Ward* [1985] N.Z.L.R. 352. And see also, generally, as to the nature of a partnership share, *supra*, paras 19–01 *et seq.*

[331] *Richardson v. Gooding* (1693) 2 Vern. 293; *Gross v. Dufresnay* (1735) 2 Eq.Ca.Abr. 110, pl. 5; *West v. Skip* (1749) 1 Ves.Sen. 239 and (1750) 1 Ves.Sen. 456; *Taylor v. Fields* (1799) 4 Ves.Jr. 396; *Ex p. Terrell* (1819) Buck 345; *Holderness v. Shackels* (1828) 8 B. & C. 612; also *Re Ward, supra.* And see *supra*, para. 23–76.

[332] It is considered that such an agreement would be effective, unless it were construed as working a forfeiture of the share and, thus, contravening the anti-deprivation principle: see *Perpetual Trustee Co. Ltd. v. BNY Corporate Trustee Services Ltd.* [2010] 3 W.L.R. 87, where many of the earlier cases are reviewed; *Mayhew v. King* [2010] EWHC 1121 (Ch) (Lawtel 21/5/10). See also *Wilson v. Greenwood* (1818) 1 Swan. 471 (where the circumstances were exceptional); *Whitmore v. Mason* (1861) 2 J. & H. 204 (where no attempt was made to avoid the main valuation provisions); *Collins v. Barker* [1893] 1 Ch. 578; *Borland's Trustee v. Steel Bros & Co. Ltd.* [1901] 1 Ch. 279. And see *supra*, paras 10–152, 10–153.

[333] But see *supra*, paras 19–11, 23–187.

[334] See generally, *supra*, paras 19–09, 25–44 *et seq.* And see also *Crawshay v. Collins* (1808) 15 Ves.Jr. 218, 229 *per* Lord Eldon; *Wilson v. Greenwood* (1818) 1 Swan. 471.

[335] *Barclays Bank Trust Co. Ltd. v. Bluff* [1982] Ch. 172, noted *supra*, para. 25–32.

interest or the share of *income* profits attributable to the continued use of the insolvent partner's share.[336]

Expulsion prior to insolvency order

If the partnership agreement entitles the other partners to expel an insolvent   **27–71**
partner *before* a formal bankruptcy or winding up order can be made and thereupon to acquire his share, it must first be determined whether the provision offends against the anti-deprivation principle[337]; if it does, it will, seemingly, be struck down.[338] If it does not and the right is duly exercised but the share has not been paid out at the date of the order, what will vest in the trustee or liquidator is merely the right to the relevant payment. If the provision is framed as an automatic accruer, thus representing a limitation inherent in the share itself,[339] it is doubtful whether, in a case to which the anti-deprivation principle does *not*, for whatever reason, apply, its operation could be avoided under section 127[340] or 284[341] of the Insolvency Act 1986; *per contra* in the case of an option in favour of the continuing partners which is exercised after the presentation of the petition.[342]

Charging order on share

It has already been seen that a charging order obtained by a judgment creditor   **27–72**
pursuant to section 23 of the Partnership Act 1890 is a completed execution for the purposes of section 183 or 346 of the Insolvency Act 1986 only if it is made final prior to the bankruptcy order (in the case of an individual partner) or the presentation of the petition (in the case of a corporate partner).[343] Otherwise the order will not be enforceable against that partner's share in the trustee's or liquidator's hands.

7.   SET-OFF AND MUTUAL CREDIT

The equitable doctrine of set-off and mutual credit, which was applied even   **27–73**
before it was expressly recognised by the bankruptcy legislation,[344] has been

---

[336] Partnership Act 1890, s.42, *supra*, paras 25–24 *et seq.*

[337] See *Perpetual Trustee Co. Ltd. v. BNY Corporate Trustee Services Ltd.*, *supra*; *Mayhew v. King*, *supra*. See also the other cases cited *supra*, para. 27–70, n. 332. And see *supra*, paras 10–152, 10–153.

[338] *Quaere*, will the court strike down the right of expulsion itself or merely the terms on which the insolvent partner's share is to be acquired by the continuing partners? The current editor submits that the latter is more likely, although much will depend on the nature of the provision.

[339] See further, *supra*, para. 10–151 and *infra*, paras 35–16, 36–42.

[340] As amended by the Enterprise Act 2002, Sched. 17, para. 15. This section in general avoids any disposition of a corporate partner's property after the presentation of the winding up petition (see *ibid.* s.129(1A), (2), the former having been added by the Enterprise Act 2002, Sched. 17, para. 16), unless the court orders otherwise: see also *supra*, para. 27–16. Note also the court's jurisdiction under *ibid.* s.423 (transactions defrauding creditors).

[341] This section similarly avoids any disposition of a bankrupt partner's property after the presentation of the petition (see subs.(3)), except to the extent that it is approved or ratified by the court. Again, the court's jurisdiction under *ibid.* s.423 should be noted.

[342] See *supra*, paras 10–151 *et seq.*

[343] See *supra*, para. 19–44.

[344] See *Anon.* (1676) 1 Mod. 215; *Chapman v. Derby* (1689) 2 Vern. 117.

preserved under the Insolvency Act 1986 and the rules made thereunder. Accordingly, set-off will be applied not only on the bankruptcy of an individual partner[345] or the winding up of a corporate partner,[346] but also where a firm is wound up as an unregistered company, with or without concurrent petitions against one or more partners.[347]

Although a general consideration of the circumstances in which cross demands may be set off against each other is strictly outside the scope of this work,[348] the following summary of the rule (taken from a formulation appearing in earlier editions) may be useful:

1. Both demands must be money demands[349] and the sum sought to be set off against the trustee or liquidator must be provable in the bankruptcy or liquidation[350];

2. The demands must be mutual[351];

3. The demands must have arisen before the creditor had notice of the presentation of the petition or, where relevant, of an application for an administration order.[352]

Where those conditions are satisfied, set-off is mandatory.[353]

---

[345] Insolvency Act 1986, s.323.

[346] Insolvency Rules 1986, r. 4.90, as substituted by the Insolvency (Amendment) Rules 2005, r. 23. Somewhat surprisingly, the Insolvency Act 1986 itself contains no provision relating to set-off in the case of a liquidation.

[347] *ibid.* See generally, as to the circumstances in which a firm may be so wound up, *supra*, paras 27–04 *et seq.*

[348] See the notes to the Insolvency Act 1986, s.323 in *Muir Hunter on Personal Insolvency*; also (as to the old law) the 15th ed. of this work, at pp. 815 *et seq.*

[349] See *Rose v. Hart* (1818) 8 Taunt. 499; also *Palmer v. Day & Sons* [1895] 2 Q.B. 618; *Ellis & Co.'s Trustee v. Dixon Johnson* [1925] A.C. 489. And see *Ex p. Bolland* (1878) 8 Ch.D. 225; *Eberle's Hotels Co. v. Jonas* (1887) 18 Q.B.D. 459; *Great Eastern Ry. Co. v. Lord's Trustee* [1908] A.C. 109; *Re H.E. Thorne & Sons Ltd.* [1914] 2 Ch. 438. As to the position where part of a demand constitutes a preferential debt, see *Re Unit 2 Windows Ltd.* [1985] 1 W.L.R. 1383.

[350] Insolvency Act 1986, s.323(1), (4); Insolvency Rules 1986, r. 4.90(1), (8), as substituted by the Insolvency (Amendment) Rules 2005, r. 23. As to the extent to which contingent claims may be set off, see *Carreras Rothmans Ltd. v. Freeman Mathews Treasure Ltd.* [1985] Ch. 207; *Re Charge Card Services Ltd.* [1987] Ch. 150 (affirmed at [1989] Ch. 497); *Williams v. Bateman* [2009] B.P.I.R. 973. It follows that there can be no set-off in the case of a secured debt which is not sought to be proved: *Re Norman Holding Co. Ltd.* [1991] 1 W.L.R. 10; *cf. M.S. Fashions Ltd. v. Bank of Credit and Commerce International SA* [1993] Ch. 425, p. 446B. Similarly, where the creditor has agreed not to prove: *Kitchen's Trustee v. Madders* [1949] Ch. 588.

[351] See *National Westminster Bank Ltd. v. Halesowen Presswork & Assemblies Ltd.* [1972] A.C. 785 (HL), affirming the judgment of Buckley L.J. on the set-off point, reported at [1971] 1 Q.B. 1; *Secretary of State for Trade & Industry v. Frid* [2004] 2 A.C. 506 (HL). For an example of a case in which there was no mutuality, despite both debtor and petitioners being partners, see *Hurst v. Bennett* [2001] B.P.I.R. 287 (CA), noted *supra*, para. 27–49. See also *Forster v. Wilson* (1843) 12 M. & W. 191; *British Guiana Bank v. Official Receiver* (1911) 104 L.T. 754; *Rolls Razor v. Cox* [1967] 1 Q.B. 552; *Carreras Rothmans Ltd. v. Freeman Mathews Treasure Ltd.* [1985] Ch. 207; *Re Charge Card Services Ltd.*, *supra*; *M.S. Fashions Ltd. v. Bank of Credit and Commerce International SA*, *supra*; *Penwith District Council v. VP Developments Ltd.* [2005] B.C.C. 393.

[352] Insolvency Act 1986, s.323(3); Insolvency Rules 1986, r. 4.90(2)(a), (b)(ii), as substituted by the Insolvency (Amendment) Rules 2005, r. 23. *A fortiori* where a debt accrued after the bankruptcy or winding up order: see *Kitchen's Trustee v. Madders* [1949] Ch. 588; *Re A Debtor* [1956] 1 W.L.R. 1226; *cf. Ashurst v. Coe* [1999] B.P.I.R. 662. See also *Re Eros Films* [1963] Ch. 565. As to setting off future debts, see *Re Kaupthing Singer and Friedlander Ltd.* [2010] B.P.I.R. 839.

[353] *National Westminster Bank Ltd. v. Halesowen Presswork & Assemblies Ltd.* [1972] A.C. 785 (HL); *British Eagle International Air Lines Ltd. v. Compagnie Nationale Air France* [1975] 1 W.L.R. 758 (HL); *Willment Brothers v. North West Thames Regional Health Authority* (1984) 26 Build.L.R.

Joint debts cannot be set off against separate debts

It follows from the requirement for mutuality that a demand against a firm **27–74**
cannot in general be set off against a cross-demand by one or more of the partners
or vice versa.[354] Thus, in *Watts v. Christie*,[355] bankers were indebted to A on his
separate account but creditors of A & Co. on their joint account. Whilst the
bankers were in financial difficulties (but before they had committed an act of
bankruptcy, as the law then stood), A assigned to A & Co. the sum due to him
on his separate account and directed the bankers to transfer that sum to the credit
of A & Co., but this was not done. On the bankruptcy of the bankers, it was held
that A & Co. could not set off what was due from them to the bankers against
what was due from the bankers to A.

The position will be no different where a debt due to a firm is sought to be set
off against a debt incurred by a partner who has acquired the firm's business on
or following a dissolution.[356] Even if only one partner is insolvent and his
separate estate is more than sufficient to pay his separate debts, a debt due to the
firm cannot be set off against a debt due from him alone.[357]

The same principle will prevent a joint debt being split with a view to
permitting a set-off. Thus, if A, B and C are jointly indebted to D, and D is
separately indebted to them on several different accounts, the latter debts cannot
be met by setting them off against A's, B's and C's respective proportions of the
debt owing by them jointly to D.[358]

Insolvency of one or more partners

The Insolvent Partnerships Order 1994 expressly preserves the right of a **27–75**
creditor to petition for an insolvency order against an individual or corporate
partner on the basis of a partnership debt without at the same time petitioning for
the winding up of the firm.[359] The normal rules of set off considered above will
apply in such a case,[360] although where a partnership debt is both joint *and
separate*,[361] set-off against a sum due to the insolvent partner may be
possible.[362]

51; *Re Unit 2 Windows Ltd.* [1985] 1 W.L.R. 1383; *M.S. Fashions Ltd. v. Bank of Credit and
Commerce International SA* [1993] Ch. 425; *Stein v. Blake* [1996] A.C. 243 (HL); *Re Bank of Credit
and Commerce International SA (No. 8)* [1998] A.C. 214 (HL). The court has no power to disapply
the rule: *Re Bank of Credit and Commerce International SA (No. 10)* [1997] Ch. 796. See also *infra*,
para. 27–77.

[354] See *Re Pennington and Owen Ltd.* [1925] Ch. 825. The decision in *James v. Kynnier* (1799) 5
Ves.Jr. 108 is not inconsistent with this principle, being a case of payment rather than set-off. As to
the position between solvent partners, see *supra*, paras 14–75 *et seq.*

[355] (1849) 11 Beav. 546.

[356] *Ex p. Ross* (1817) Buck 125. The marginal note in this case is somewhat misleading.

[357] *Ex p. Twogood* (1805) 11 Ves.Jr. 517; and see *Re Jane* (1914) 110 L.T. 556, *supra*, para. 5–22,
n. 94. *cf. Ex p. Edwards* (1745) 1 Atk. 100 and *Ex p. Quintin* (1798) 3 Ves.Jr. 248, which Lord Lindley
regarded as unreliable authorities.

[358] *Ex p. Christie* (1804) 10 Ves.Jr. 105.

[359] Insolvent Partnerships Order 1994, art. 19(5): see *supra*, para. 27–48.

[360] *cf.* the position under the Insolvent Partnerships Order 1984, art. 15(3): see the 17th ed. of this
work at para. 27–71.

[361] For an example of debts falling within this category, see *infra*, para. 27–91.

[362] See, however, as to proof of debts by such a creditor, *infra*, paras 27–146 *et seq.*

Set-off as between firm and partner

27–76   If, following a winding up order being made against the firm,[363] the court were prepared to treat the firm as an unlimited company for the purposes of section 149(2)(a) of the Insolvency Act 1986,[364] a partner might be permitted to set off against sums due from him to the firm (otherwise than pursuant to a call by the liquidator) any sum due to him in respect of an "independent dealing or contract" with the firm[365]; *sed quaere.*

Agreements as to set-off

27–77   A bona fide agreement permitting a joint debt to be set off against a separate debt, or vice versa, will be perfectly valid and binding as between the parties but of no effect on their insolvency.[366]

8.   ADMINISTRATION OF THE ESTATES OF INSOLVENT FIRMS AND PARTNERS

The general principle: distinction between joint and separate debts and estates

27–78   Notwithstanding the introduction of a wholly new regime of insolvency, the old rule governing the priority of debts as between the respective estates of an insolvent firm and an insolvent partner remains broadly unchanged.[367] Indeed, the following statement of principle retains as much relevance today as when it was originally formulated by Lord Lindley:

> "In administering the estate of a bankrupt firm or of some or one only of its members, it is necessary to distinguish accurately, first, joint from separate estate; and, secondly, joint from separate debts: for the leading principle of administration is, if possible, to pay the debts of the firm (joint debts) out of the assets of the firm (joint estate), and the private debts of each partner (separate debts) out of his own private

---

[363] See *supra*, paras 27–04 *et seq.*

[364] Interestingly, *ibid.* s.149 is *not* one of the sections expressly disapplied by *ibid.* s.221(6), as itself amended and applied by the Insolvent Partnerships Order 1994, art. 7(1) (as amended by the Insolvent Partnerships (Amendment) Order 2002, art. 3), (2), Sched. 3, Pt I, para. 3, as itself amended by the Insolvent Partnerships (Amendment) Order 2006, art. 6 (creditor's petition with no concurrent petitions), *ibid.* art. 8(1) (as amended by the Insolvent Partnerships (Amendment) Order 2002, art. 4(1)), (2), Sched. 4, Pt I, para. 3, as itself amended by the Insolvent Partnerships (Amendment) Order 2006, art. 7 (creditor's petition *with* concurrent petitions), *ibid.* art. 9(a), Sched. 5, para. 2, as itself amended by the Insolvent Partnerships (Amendment) Order 2006, art. 8 (member's petition with no concurrent petitions) and *ibid.* art. 10(1)(a), Sched. 6, para. 4, as itself amended by the Insolvent Partnerships (Amendment) Order 2006, art. 9 (member's petition *with* concurrent petitions).

[365] Note that, even if a set-off were entertained, it would clearly not extend to sums due to a partner in that capacity, *e.g.* in respect of profits.

[366] *National Westminster Bank Ltd. v. Halesowen Presswork & Assemblies Ltd.* [1972] A.C. 785 (HL) and the other cases cited *supra*, para. 27–73, n. 353. The position was formerly otherwise: see *Kinnerley v. Hossack* (1809) 2 Taunt. 170; *Vulliamy v. Noble* (1817) 3 Mer. 593; *Ex p. Flint* (1818) 1 Swan. 30; *Young v. Bank of Bengal* (1836) 1 Deac. 622.

[367] Some inroads were made by the Insolvent Partnerships Order 1994: see *infra*, paras 27–82 *et seq.*

property (separate estate): in other words, to make each estate pay its own creditors."[368]

A clear and authoritative judicial recognition of this long established rule is to be found in *Ex p. Cook*,[369] where Lord King observed: **27–79**

"It is settled, and is a resolution of convenience, that the joint creditors shall be first paid out of the partnership or joint estate, and the separate creditors out of the separate estate of each partner; and if there be a surplus of the joint estate, besides what will pay the joint creditors, the same shall be applied to pay the separate creditors; and if there be, on the other hand, a surplus of the separate estate beyond what will satisfy the separate creditors, it shall go to supply any deficiency that may remain as to the joint creditors."

The rule appeared in successive Bankruptcy Acts[370] and is now largely preserved by the Insolvent Partnerships Order 1994.[371] However, one major change has been introduced: thus, it may now be possible, where the joint estate is insufficient, for the joint debts (and interest thereon) to be proved against the insolvent partners' separate estates *in competition* with their separate creditors.[372]

Cases falling within the scope of the Insolvent Partnerships Order 1994

The Insolvent Partnerships Order 1994 contains detailed rules relating to the priority of expenses and debts which are automatically applied in the case of certain types of insolvency order made thereunder. It should, however, be noted that the provision introduced into the Insolvency Act 1986[373] in order to secure a share of the assets for the unsecured creditors where property is subject to a floating charge, does *not* apply where an insolvent partnership is wound up as an unregistered company, with or without concurrent petitions.[374]   **27–80**

---

[368] *Ex p. Elton* (1796) 3 Ves.Jr. 238, and see 1 Mont.Part. 110, Note 2D.

[369] (1728) 2 P.W. 500, applied in *Re Rudd & Son Ltd.* [1984] Ch. 237. See also *Ex p. Crowder* (1715) 2 Vern. 706; *Twiss v. Massey* (1737) 1 Atk. 67.

[370] See for example, the Bankruptcy Act 1883, ss.40(3), 59; the Bankruptcy Act 1914, ss.33(6), 63. Note, however, that its existence, as a rule of convenience, was independent of those Acts: *Re Rudd & Son Ltd.* [1984] Ch. 237, 241, 242 *per* Nourse J.

[371] The relevant rules are, in fact to be found in sections of the Insolvency Act 1986, as amended and applied by the Insolvent Partnerships Order 1994: see *infra*, paras 27–82 *et seq. cf.* the provisions of the Insolvent Partnerships Order 1984, considered in the 17th ed. of this work at paras 27–74 *et seq.*

[372] See *infra*, paras 27–79, 27–106. As to the burden of expenses as between the estates, see *infra*, paras 27–81, 27–103.

[373] s.176A, as added by the Enterprise Act 2002, s.252.

[374] See *ibid.* s.221(6), as itself amended and applied by the Insolvent Partnerships Order 1994, art. 7(1) (as amended by the Insolvent Partnerships (Amendment) Order 2002, art. 3), (2), Sched. 3, Pt I, para. 3, as itself amended by the Insolvent Partnerships (Amendment) Order 2006, art. 6 (creditor's petition with no concurrent petitions), *ibid.* art. 8(1) (as amended by the Insolvent Partnerships (Amendment) Order 2002, art. 4(1)), (2), Sched. 4, Pt I, para. 3, as itself amended by the Insolvent Partnerships (Amendment) Order 2006, art. 7 (creditor's petition *with* concurrent petitions), *ibid.* art. 9(a), Sched. 5, para. 2, as itself amended by the Insolvent Partnerships (Amendment) Order 2006, art. 8 (member's petition with no concurrent petitions) and *ibid.* art. 10(1)(a), Sched. 6, para. 4, as itself amended by the Insolvent Partnerships (Amendment) Order 2006, art. 9 (member's petition *with* concurrent petitions). Note that the various amendments introduced by the Insolvent Partnerships (Amendment) Order 2005, arts. 4, 5(a) referring to s.176A were subsequently revoked by the Insolvent Partnerships (Amendment) Order 2006, arts. 3, 4.

Priority of expenses

27–81   Where an insolvency order is made against a firm and against one or more partners on concurrent petitions,[375] the priority of expenses is governed by the following section of the Insolvency Act 1986[376]:

> "*Priority of expenses*
>
> **175.**—(1) The provisions of this section shall apply in a case where article 8 of the Insolvent Partnerships Order 1994 applies,[377] as regards priority of expenses incurred by a responsible insolvency practitioner[378] of an insolvent partnership, and of any insolvent member of that partnership against whom an insolvency order has been made.
>
> (2) The joint estate of the partnership shall be applicable in the first instance in payment of the joint expenses and the separate estate of each insolvent member shall be applicable in the first instance in payment of the separate expenses relating to that member.
>
> (3) Where the joint estate is insufficient for the payment in full of the joint expenses, the unpaid balance shall be apportioned equally between the separate estates of the insolvent members against whom insolvency orders have been made and shall form part of the expenses to be paid out of those estates.
>
> (4) Where any separate estate of an insolvent member is insufficient for the payment in full of the separate expenses to be paid out of that estate, the unpaid balance shall form part of the expenses to be paid out of the joint estate.
>
> (5) Where after the transfer of any unpaid balance in accordance with subsection (3) or (4) any estate is insufficient for the payment in full of the expenses to be paid out of that estate, the balance then remaining unpaid shall be apportioned equally between the other estates.
>
> (6) Where after an apportionment under subsection (5) one or more estates are insufficient for the payment in full of the expenses to be paid out of those estates, the total of the unpaid balances of the expenses to be paid out of those estates shall continue to be apportioned equally between the other estates until provision is made for the payment in full of the expenses or there is no estate available for the payment of the balance finally remaining unpaid, in which case it abates in equal proportions between all the estates.
>
> (7) Without prejudice to subsections (3) to (6) above, the responsible insolvency practitioner may, with the sanction of any creditors' committee established under section 141 or with the leave of the court obtained on application—
>
> (a)   pay out of the joint estate as part of the expenses to be paid out of that estate any expenses incurred for any separate estate of an insolvent member; or
>
> (b)   pay out of any separate estate of an insolvent member any part of the expenses incurred for the joint estate which affects that separate estate."

[375] Such petitions may be presented by a creditor, etc., against the firm and one or more partners or by a member against the firm and *all* the partners: see *supra*, paras 27–24 *et seq.*

[376] As amended in the manner set out in the Insolvent Partnerships Order 1994, Sched. 4, Pt II, para. 23 and applied, as regards the firm, by *ibid.* s.221(5) (as itself amended by the Insolvent Partnerships Order 1994, art. 8(1) (as amended by the Insolvent Partnerships (Amendment) Order 2002, art. 4(1)), (2), Sched. 4, Pt I, para. 3 (creditor's petition *with* concurrent petitions) and *ibid.* art. 10(1)(a), Sched. 6, para. 4 (member's petition *with* concurrent petitions)) and, as regards insolvent corporate and individual partners, by the Insolvent Partnerships Order 1994, arts 8(4)–(8) (creditor's petition), 10(2)–(6) (as amended by the Insolvent Partnerships (Amendment) Order 2005, art. 5(b)) (member's petition).

[377] This reference is unhelpful in cases to which *ibid.* art. 10 applies.

[378] This expression is defined in the Insolvent Partnerships Order 1994, art. 2(1) and added to the Insolvency Act 1986, s.436 by *ibid.* art. 2(2).

Where orders are made on a joint bankruptcy petition presented by all the partners,[379] the position is governed by section 328 of the Insolvency Act 1986,[380] which is in virtually identical terms.[381]

Priority of debts in the joint and separate estates

In the case of orders on concurrent petitions,[382] the following sections of the Insolvency Act 1986[383] apply: **27–82**

"*Priority of debts in joint estate*

175A.—(1) The provisions of this section and the next (which are subject to the provisions of section 9 of the Partnership Act 1890[384] as respects the liability of the estate of a deceased member) shall apply as regards priority of debts in a case where article 8 of the Insolvent Partnerships Order 1994 applies.[385]

(2) After payment of expenses in accordance with section 175 and subject to section 175C(2), the joint debts of the partnership shall be paid out of its joint estate in the following order of priority—

  (a) the preferential debts[386];
  (b) the debts which are neither preferential debts nor postponed debts[387];
  (c) interest under section 189[388] on the joint debts (other than postponed debts);
  (d) the postponed debts;
  (e) interest under section 189 on the postponed debts.

---

[379] See *supra*, para. 27–44.

[380] As amended and applied by the Insolvent Partnerships Order 1994, art. 11, Sched. 7, para. 21.

[381] Needless to say, unlike *ibid.* s.175, it does not cross-refer to the Insolvent Partnerships Order 1994, art. 8.

[382] See *supra*, paras 27–24 *et seq.*

[383] As amended by the Insolvent Partnerships Order 1994, Sched. 4, Pt II, para. 23 and applied, as regards the firm, by the Insolvency Act 1986, s.221(5) (as itself amended by the Insolvent Partnerships Order 1994, art. 8(1) (as amended by the Insolvent Partnerships (Amendment) Order 2002, art. 4(2)), (2), Sched. 4, Pt I, para. 3 (creditor's petition *with* concurrent petitions) and *ibid.* art. 10(1)(a), Sched. 6, para. 4 (member's petition *with* concurrent petitions)) and, as regards insolvent corporate and individual partners, by the Insolvent Partnerships Order 1994, arts 8(4)–(8) (creditor's petition), 10(2)–(6), as amended by the Insolvent Partnerships (Amendment) Order 2005, art. 5(b) (member's petition).

[384] See *supra*, paras 12–87 *et seq.*

[385] Again the reference to art. 8 is unhelpful in a case where orders have been made under *ibid.* art. 10.

[386] See, as to such debts, the Insolvency Act 1986, s.386, Sched. 6, as respectively amended by the Enterprise Act 2002, s.251(1), (3), Sched. 26.

[387] This expression is defined as "a debt the payment of which is postponed by or under any provision of the Act or any other enactment": see the Insolvent Partnerships Order 1994, art. 2(1) (the definition being added to the Insolvency Act 1986, s.436 by *ibid.* art. 2(2)). One obvious example would be debt falling within the Partnership Act 1890, s.3: see *supra*, paras 5–33 *et seq.*

[388] As amended by the Insolvent Partnerships Order 1994, Sched. 4, Pt II, para. 24 and applied, as regards the firm, by the Insolvency Act 1986, s.221(5) (as itself amended by the Insolvent Partnerships Order 1994, art. 8(1) (as amended: see *supra*, n. 383), (2), Sched. 4, Pt I, para. 3 (creditor's petition *with* concurrent petitions) and *ibid.* art. 10(1)(a), Sched. 6, para. 4 (member's petition *with* concurrent petitions)) and, as regards insolvent corporate and individual partners, by the Insolvent Partnerships Order 1994, arts 8(4)–(8) (creditor's petition), 10(2)–(6), as amended by the Insolvent Partnerships (Amendment) Order 2005, art. 5(b) (member's petition).

(3) The responsible insolvency practitioner[389] shall adjust the rights among themselves of the members of the partnership as contributories[390] and shall distribute any surplus to the members or, where applicable, to the separate estates of the members, according to their respective rights and interests in it.

(4) The debts referred to in each of paragraphs (a) and (b) of subsection (2) rank equally between themselves, and in each case if the joint estate is insufficient for meeting them, they abate in equal proportions between themselves.[391]

(5) Where the joint estate is not sufficient for the payment of the joint debts in accordance with paragraphs (a) and (b) of subsection (2), the responsible insolvency practitioner shall aggregate the value of those debts to the extent that they have not been satisfied or are not capable of being satisfied, and that aggregate amount shall be a claim against the separate estate of each member of the partnership against whom an insolvency order has been made which—

(a) shall be a debt provable by the responsible insolvency practitioner in each such estate, and

(b) shall rank equally with the debts of the member referred to in section 175B(1)(b) below.

(6) Where the joint estate is sufficient for the payment of the joint debts in accordance with paragraphs (a) and (b) of subsection (2) but not for the payment of interest under paragraph (c) of that subsection, the responsible insolvency practitioner shall aggregate the value of that interest to the extent that it has not been satisfied or is not capable of being satisfied, and that aggregate amount shall be a claim against the separate estate of each member of the partnership against whom an insolvency order has been made which—

(a) shall be a debt provable by the responsible insolvency practitioner in each such estate, and

(b) shall rank equally with the interest on the separate debts referred to in section 175B(1)(c) below.

(7) Where the joint estate is not sufficient for the payment of the postponed joint debts in accordance with paragraph (d) of subsection (2), the responsible insolvency practitioner shall aggregate the value of those debts to the extent that they have not been satisfied or are not capable of being satisfied, and that aggregate amount shall be a claim against the separate estate of each member of the partnership against whom an insolvency order has been made which—

(a) shall be a debt provable by the responsible insolvency practitioner in each such estate, and

(b) shall rank equally with the postponed debts of the member referred to in section 175B(1)(d) below.

(8) Where the joint estate is sufficient for the payment of the postponed joint debts in accordance with paragraph (d) of subsection (2) but not for the payment of interest under paragraph (e) of that subsection, the responsible insolvency practitioner shall aggregate the value of that interest to the extent that it has not been satisfied or is not capable of being satisfied, and that aggregate amount shall be a claim against the separate estate of each member of the partnership against whom an insolvency order has been made which—

---

[389] This expression is defined in the Insolvent Partnerships Order 1994, art. 2(1) and added to the Insolvency Act 1986, s.436 by *ibid.* art. 2(2).

[390] See *supra*, paras 27–61 *et seq.*

[391] It would, however, seem that the rights of a creditor may be subordinated with his agreement: *Re Maxwell Communications Corporation Plc* [1993] 1 W.L.R. 1402, distinguishing *National Westminster Bank Ltd. v. Halesowen Presswork & Assemblies Ltd.* [1972] A.C. 785 (HL) and *British Eagle International Air Lines Ltd. v. Compagnie Nationale Air France* [1975] 1 W.L.R. 758 (HL).

(a) shall be a debt provable by the responsible insolvency practitioner in each such estate, and

(b) shall rank equally with the interest on the postponed debts referred to in section 175B(1)(e) below.

(9) Where the responsible insolvency practitioner receives any distribution from the separate estate of a member in respect of a debt referred to in paragraph (a) of subsection (5), (6), (7) or (8) above, that distribution shall become part of the joint estate and shall be distributed in accordance with the order of priority set out in subsection (2) above.

Priority of debts in separate estate

175B.—(1) The separate estate of each member of the partnership against whom **27–83** an insolvency order has been made shall be applicable, after payment of expenses in accordance with section 175 and subject to section 175C(2) below, in payment of the separate debts of that member in the following order of priority—

(a) the preferential debts;

(b) the debts which are neither preferential debts nor postponed debts (including any debt referred to in section 175A(5)(a));

(c) interest under section 189 on the separate debts and under section 175A(6);

(d) the postponed debts of the member (including any debt referred to in section 175A(7)(a));

(e) interest under section 189 on the postponed debts of the member and under section 175A(8).

(2) The debts referred to in each of paragraphs (a) and (b) of subsection (1) rank equally between themselves, and in each case if the separate estate is insufficient for meeting them, they abate in equal proportions between themselves.

(3) Where the responsible insolvency practitioner receives any distribution from the joint estate or from the separate estate of another member of the partnership against whom an insolvency order has been made, that distribution shall become part of the separate estate and shall be distributed in accordance with the order of priority set out in subsection (1) of this section.

Provisions generally applicable in distribution of joint and separate estates

175C.—(1) Distinct accounts shall be kept of the joint estate of the partnership and **27–84** of the separate estate of each member of that partnership against whom an insolvency order is made.

(2) No member of the partnership shall prove for a joint or separate debt in competition with the joint creditors, unless the debt has arisen—

(a) as a result of fraud, or

(b) in the ordinary course of a business carried on separately from the partnership business.

(3) For the purpose of establishing the value of any debt referred to in section 175A(5)(a) or (7)(a), that value may be estimated by the responsible insolvency practitioner in accordance with section 322 or (as the case may be) in accordance with the rules.

(4) Interest under section 189 on preferential debts ranks equally with interest on debts which are neither preferential debts nor postponed debts.

(5) Sections 175A and 175B are without prejudice to any provision of this Act or of any other enactment concerning the ranking between themselves of postponed debts and interest thereon, but in the absence of any such provision postponed debts and interest thereon rank equally between themselves.

(6) If any two or more members of an insolvent partnership constitute a separate partnership, the creditors of such separate partnership shall be deemed to be a

separate set of creditors and subject to the same statutory provisions as the separate creditors of any member of the insolvent partnership.

(7) Where any surplus remains after the administration of the estate of a separate partnership, the surplus shall be distributed to the members or, where applicable, to the separate estates of the members of that partnership according to their respective rights and interests in it.

(8) Neither the official receiver, the Secretary of State nor a responsible insolvency practitioner shall be entitled to remuneration or fees under the Insolvency Rules 1986, the Insolvency Regulations 1986 or the Insolvency Fees Order 1986 for his services in connection with—

    (a)   the transfer of a surplus from the joint estate to a separate estate under section 175A(3),

    (b)   a distribution from a separate estate to the joint estate in respect of a claim referred to in section 175A(5), (6), (7) or (8), or

a distribution from the estate of a separate partnership to the separate estates of the members of that partnership under subsection (7) above."

The provisions of sections 328A to 328C of the Insolvency Act 1986,[392] which apply in the case of orders made on a joint bankruptcy petition presented by all the partners,[393] are again in virtually identical terms.[394]

Cases brought within the scope of the Order

27–85   The court has power to apply any or all of the above provisions (with any necessary modifications) where, following the presentation of a petition against a corporate or individual partner, it appears that such a partner is "a member of an insolvent partnership".[395] This will include a case where bankruptcy petitions are successively presented against a number of partners.[396]

Cases falling outside scope of Order

27–86   It should not be assumed that, absent an order of the type described in the preceding paragraph, no question of priority as between the joint and separate estates will arise. Admittedly, there will be no question of apportioning the expenses of insolvency proceedings where the respective estates of an insolvent firm and of one or more insolvent partners are being separately administered, but the current editor considers that the rule of convenience that the joint debts should principally be paid out of the joint estate and the separate debts out of the relevant separate estate, which exists independently of the insolvency legislation,[397] must still be applied. Moreover, even when administering the assets of an

---

[392] As amended and applied by the Insolvent Partnerships Order 1994, art. 11, Sched. 7, para. 21. As to interest on debts, see the Insolvency Act 1986, s.328D, as amended and applied by *ibid.*

[393] See *supra*, para. 27–44.

[394] The main difference, predictably, is to be found in *ibid.* s.328A(1). Interestingly, whilst *ibid.* s.328 (as amended) refers throughout to "the trustee", *ibid.* ss.328A to 328C revert to the expression "the responsible insolvency practitioner", just as in the case of *ibid.* ss.175A–175C.

[395] Insolvency Act 1986, ss.168(5A) (winding up jurisdiction), 303(2A) (bankruptcy jurisdiction), as respectively added by the Insolvent Partnerships Order 1994, art. 14(1), (2). Similarly where the partner in question is itself a partnership capable of being wound up as an unregistered company: *ibid.* See also *supra*, para. 27–21.

[396] *i.e.* in the manner noted *supra*, para. 27–48.

[397] See *Re Rudd & Son Ltd.* [1984] Ch. 237, 242B *per* Nourse J.

insolvent partnership or an insolvent partner, it will still be necessary to distinguish between those assets which belong to the firm and those which belong to one or more of the partners and, at least to an extent, between joint and separate debts.[398]

Joint and separate debts and estates

Given that, in any insolvency involving a partnership or a partner, it is **27–87** necessary to distinguish between, on the one hand, the joint and separate debts and, on the other, the joint and separate estates, the current editor submits that the principles to be applied by the court will be the same as under the old bankruptcy laws. Accordingly, the following summary, adapted from material appearing in earlier editions of this work, will still be of relevance.

(a) Joint and separate debts

Creditors may be divided into three classes, *viz.*:   **27–88**

   (i) The joint creditors[399] of the firm, to whom all the partners are jointly liable.[400]

   (ii) The separate creditors of each partner, to whom only that partner is liable.

   (iii) The joint and separate creditors, to whom the partners are at one and the same time liable both jointly and separately in respect of the same debt.[401]

The circumstances in which a debt can properly be regarded as a debt of the firm were considered earlier in this work and reference should be made thereto.[402] However, the following brief recapitulation may be useful in the present context:

---

[398] This will be of particular relevance where any question of set-off arises: see *supra*, paras 27–73 *et seq*.

[399] Although this expression is conventionally used, it is in truth something of a misnomer: joint creditors, properly so called, are persons who are jointly entitled to the same debt, rather than, as here, persons who have no such joint entitlement but who merely happen to have the same joint debtors. A more accurate expression might perhaps be "joint estate creditors". Equally, the expression "joint creditors" *is* used in the Insolvency Act 1986 (as amended by the Insolvent Partnerships Order 1994): see *ibid*. ss.175C(2) (*supra*, para. 27–84), 328C(2) (as amended).

[400] Note that creditors may have a dual capacity as regards the firm and the partners. If four out of five members of a firm are jointly liable to a creditor, he will be a separate creditor as regards the firm, but may be a joint creditor as regards the four partners. See also *ibid*. ss.175C(6) (*supra*, para. 27–84), 328C(6) (as amended).

[401] A creditor who has obtained a judgment against several persons in respect of a joint debt can levy execution against any one or more of them but is not properly styled a joint and separate creditor; he remains a joint creditor: see *Ex p. Christie* (1832) Mont. & Bl. 352. Under the old bankruptcy law, no distinction was made between creditors to whom the partners were jointly indebted in connection with the partnership business and other creditors to whom they were also jointly indebted: see *Hoare v. Oriental Bank Corporation* (1877) 2 App.Cas. 589. It would seem that this is no longer the position, since the Insolvency Act 1986, s.175A(2) (as amended: see *supra*, para. 27–82) refers to the "joint debts of the partnership"; similarly, in the case of *ibid*. s.328A(2) (as amended); *sed quaere*.

[402] See *supra*, paras 12–01 *et seq*. and 13–16 *et seq*.

Original status of debt

27–89   Having regard to the joint nature of a partner's liability,[403] it can be said that, as a general rule, a debt of the firm will not also be the separate debt of any partner, unless he has agreed to be severally liable therefor.[404]

Dormant and apparent partners

27–90   Where a firm comprises two partners, one of whom actively participates in the business and the other of whom is dormant or merely held out to the world as a partner,[405] a creditor of the firm will seemingly have a choice: he may treat the debt as a joint debt of both "partners"[406] or as a separate debt of the partner who is the real or apparent proprietor of the business.[407]

Torts, frauds, etc., and breaches of trust

27–91   Where a tort, fraud or other wrong, misapplication of money or property or breach of trust can be imputed to a firm, the liability of the partners will be joint and several.[408]

Bills of exchange

27–92   Subject to questions of authority and notice,[409] bills drawn, indorsed or accepted in the name of a firm will give rise to a joint debt,[410] whilst those drawn, accepted or indorsed in the names of some, but not all, of the partners will not.[411] A separate creditor of one partner who takes the firm's bill in settlement of his debt must show that it was given with the authority of all the partners if it is to be treated as creating a joint debt.[412]

---

[403] Partnership Act 1890, s.9: see *supra* paras 13–03 *et seq.*

[404] See *Ex p. Dobinson* (1837) 2 Deac. 341; *Ex p. Carlisle Canal Co.* (1837) 2 Deac. 349; *Ex p. Appleby* (1837) 2 Deac. 482; *Ex p. Benson* (1842) 2 M.D. & D. 750. See also, as to bills of exchange, *Ex p. Wilson* (1842) 3 M.D. & D. 57; *Ex p. Flintoff* (1844) 3 M.D. & D. 726; *Re Clarke* (1845) De Gex 153; *Ex p. Buckley* (1845) 14 M. & W. 469.

[405] See, further, the Partnership Act 1890, s.14, *supra*, paras 5–35 *et seq.*

[406] Note that a person held out as a partner is regarded as a member of an insolvent firm: see the definition of "member" in the Insolvent Partnerships Order 1994, art. 2(1), as added to the Insolvency Act 1986, s.436 by *ibid.* art. 2(2). Equally, a firm cannot exist if there are not at least two partners in law: see *Re C. & M. Ashberg, The Times*, July 17, 1990, noted *supra*, para. 27–05.

[407] See *Ex p. Hodgkinson* (1815) 19 Ves.Jr. 291; *Ex p. Norfolk* (1815) 19 Ves.Jr. 455; *Ex p. Law* (1839) 3 Deac. 541; *Ex p. Arbouin* (1846) De Gex 359. See also *Scarf v. Jardine* (1882) 7 App.Cas. 345, *supra*, paras 5–52, 13–04. But see also the preceding footnote.

[408] See *supra*, paras 13–12, 13–13. As to frauds, see *Ex p. Unity Joint-Stock Mutual Banking Association* (1858) 3 De G. & J. 63; *Ex p. Adamson* (1878) 8 Ch.D. 807. As to breaches of trust, see *Ex p. Poulson* (1844) De Gex 79; *Ex p. Barnewall* (1855) 6 De G.M. & G. 795. *cf. Ex p. Geaves* (1856) 8 De G.M. & G. 291; *Ex p. White* (1871) L.R. 6 Ch. 397. And see also *Ex p. Burton* (1843) 3 M.D. & D. 364. See further, as to the right of proof in such cases, *infra*, paras 27–146 *et seq.*

[409] See *Ex p. Holdsworth* (1841) 1 M.D. & D. 475; also *Rooth v. Quin* (1819) 7 Price 193. And see further, *supra*, paras 12–137 *et seq.*

[410] *Ex p. Bushell* (1844) 3 M.D. & D. 615. And see *supra*, paras 12–161 *et seq.*

[411] Bills of Exchange Act 1882, s.23; *Ex p. Bolitho* (1817) Buck 100. As to the position where the firm and the acceptor share the same name, see *Ex p. Law* (1839) 3 Deac. 541.

[412] Partnership Act 1890, s.7, *supra*, para. 12–138. And see *Ex p. Agace* (1792) 2 Cox 312; *Ex p. Bonbonus* (1803) 8 Ves.Jr. 540; *Ex p. Goulding and Davies* (1829) 2 Gl. & J. 118; *Ex p. Thorpe* (1836) 3 M. & A. 716; *Ex p. Austen* (1840) 1 M.D. & D. 247.

Money of which firm has had the benefit

A separate creditor cannot be treated as a joint creditor merely because the firm   **27–93**
has had the benefit of the money in question, nor can a joint creditor be treated
as the separate creditor of a partner because the latter has had such benefit.[413]

Loss of right to prove and conversion of joint and separate debts

A joint creditor who releases one of his debtors cannot subsequently prove   **27–94**
against the estates of the others.[414] Moreover, if a higher security is taken or
judgment obtained in respect of a joint or separate debt, the right to prove against
the relevant estate may be lost by virtue of the doctrine of merger.[415] Alternatively, that right may be lost if there is a substitution of debtors.[416]

Merger

Thus, by taking a separate bond from one partner to secure a debt of the firm,   **27–95**
the creditor will become entitled to a separate debt in place of that joint debt,
which will prima facie be destroyed[417]; similarly, if a joint bond is taken to secure
a separate debt. Whilst a judgment no longer *per se* has the same effect,[418] a joint
judgment in respect of a joint and several debt will seemingly create a joint
debt,[419] although a separate judgment in respect thereof will not have a corresponding effect.[420]

Position where additional security taken

Where a creditor obtains an *additional* security for a pre-existing debt, in   **27–96**
circumstances which do not give rise to a merger, he may still prove for his
original debt if the additional security later becomes unavailable. Thus, a creditor
who takes a joint bill for a separate debt[421] or vice versa[422] becomes, as he
intended, a joint and separate creditor and may, if necessary, fall back on the
original debt, unless the bill was taken in satisfaction thereof[423] or there has been
a substitution of debtors.[424]

[413] *Ex p. Hunter* (1742) 1 Atk. 223; *Ex p. Wheatley* (1797) Cooke's *Bankruptcy Law* (8th ed.), p.
534; *Ex p. Peele* (1802) 6 Ves.Jr. 602; *Ex p. Hartop* (1806) 12 Ves.Jr. 349; *Ex p. Emly* (1811) 1 Rose
61: *Re Ferrar* (1859) 9 Ir.Ch. 289. See also *supra*, paras 12–175 *et seq.*
[414] *Ex p. Slater* (1801) 6 Ves.Jr. 146; *cf. Artman v. Artman* [1996] B.P.I.R. 511, where there was
clearly no release. As to the discharge of a surety, see *Ex p. Webster* (1847) De Gex 414; *Re Darwen
and Pearce* [1927] 1 Ch. 176. See also *supra*, paras 13–94 *et seq.*
[415] See further *supra*, paras 13–126 *et seq.*
[416] See further *supra*, paras 13–100 *et seq.*
[417] See *Ex p. Hernaman* (1848) 12 Jur. 643. See further, *supra*, para. 13–127.
[418] See the Civil Liability (Contribution) Act 1978, considered *supra*, paras 13–05, 13–130,
20–23.
[419] *Ex p. Christie* (1832) Mont. & Bl. 352. But this does not apply to breaches of trust in respect
of which there is a joint and several liability: see *Re Davison* (1884) 13 Q.B.D. 50.
[420] *Drake v. Mitchell* (1803) 3 East 251; *Re Clarkes* (1845) 2 Jo. & La T. 212; *Ex p. Bate* (1838)
3 Deac. 358. And see *Ex p. Waterfall* (1851) 4 De G. & Sm. 199. See also *supra*, para. 13–131.
[421] *Ex p. Seddon* (1788) 2 Cox 49; *Ex p. Lobb* (1802) 7 Ves.Jr. 592; *Ex p. Hay* (1808) 15 Ves.Jr.
4; *Ex p. Kedie* (1832) 2 D. & Ch. 321; *Ex p. Meinertzhagen* (1838) 3 Deac. 101.
[422] *Ex p. Hodgkinson* (1815) 19 Ves.Jr. 291; *Bottomley v. Nuttall* (1858) 5 C.B. (N.S.) 122; *Keay
v. Fenwick* (1876) 1 C.P.D. 745. See also *Ex p. Fairlie* (1830) Mont. 17; *Ex p. Raleigh* (1838) 3 M.
& A. 670.
[423] See, generally, *Wegg Prosser v. Evans* [1895] 1 Q.B. 108.
[424] See *Ex p. Whitmore* (1838) 3 Deac. 365; also *Ex p. Kirby* (1819) Buck 511; *Ex p. Jackson*
(1841) 2 M.D. & D. 146.

Substitution of debtors

27–97 A substitution of debtors can only be effected with the consent of the relevant creditor. Accordingly if, following the dissolution of a partnership, one partner agrees to carry on its business and to pay its debts, the creditors of the firm do not become the separate creditors of that partner unless they accede to the arrangements made between the former partners[425] or, knowing of those arrangements, deal with that partner in such a way as to prejudice the rights of the others, thereby discharging them.[426] On the same basis, a separate debt existing before the creation of a partnership is not converted into a joint debt merely because the partners have agreed, as between themselves, to treat it as such.[427]

It is, as a general rule, easier for a separate creditor to establish a right to prove against the joint estate than it is for a joint creditor to establish a right to prove against a separate estate. This is because, in the former case, it is merely necessary to prove that *additional* persons have become liable to the creditor[428] whilst, in the latter, it must be shown that one of several debtors has alone agreed to undertake liability for the debt. The practical difficulty of establishing that a joint debtor's conduct is referable to his intention to take over sole liability for the debt rather than to the continuation of his existing joint liability should be self evident; if more is required, it is merely necessary to refer to the numerous cases in which just such an argument has failed.[429]

(b) Joint and separate estates

27–98 Since the doctrine of reputed ownership no longer has any place in insolvency law,[430] identification of the assets comprised in the joint estate of the firm and the separate estates of the partners is dependent on the agreement of the partners, express or implied, and on the operation of the Partnership Act 1890.[431] Since

---

[425] Partnership Act 1890, s.17(2), (3): see *supra*, paras 13–79 *et seq.*, 13–102. See also *Ex p. Freeman* (1819) Buck 471; *Ex p. Fry* (1821) 1 Gl. & J. 96; *Ex p. Appleby* (1837) 2 Deac. 482; *Ex p. Gurney* (1842) 2 M.D. & D. 541.

[426] *Rouse v. Bradford Banking Co.* [1894] A.C. 586. And see *supra*, paras 13–98, 13–99.

[427] Partnership Act 1890, s.17(1): see *supra*, paras 13–23 *et seq.* See also *Ex p. Jackson* (1790) 1 Ves.Jr. 130; *Ex p. Peele* (1802) 6 Ves.Jr. 602; *Ex p. Williams* (1817) Buck 13; *Ex p. Hitchcock* (1839) 3 Deac. 507; *Ex p. Parker* (1842) 2 M.D. & D. 511; *Ex p. Graham* (1842) 2 M.D. & D. 781; *Re Littles* (1847) 10 Ir.Eq. 275. As to the evidence necessary to show the creditor's accession to the new arrangement, see *Rolfe v. Flower* (1865) L.R. 1 P.C. 27; *Bilborough v. Holmes* (1876) 5 Ch.D. 255; *Scarf v. Jardine* (1882) 7 App.Cas. 345, noted *supra*, paras 5–52, 13–04. Lord Lindley also observed: "Mr. Cooke, indeed, lays it down that if new partners come into a firm, and it is agreed that the stock and debts of the old firm shall become those of the new firm, and the latter becomes bankrupt, the creditors of the old firm may prove against the joint estate of the new firm; and he cites *Ex p. Bingham* and *Ex p. Clowes* (1789) 2 Bro.C.C. 595 (Cooke's *Bankruptcy Law*, 534, 8th ed.). The facts of the first of these two cases are not stated. *Ex p. Clowes* was a very peculiar case, and if it was ever an authority for the doctrine that a separate debt can, as between the partners and the creditor, become a joint debt, or *vice versa*, without the privity of the creditor, the case must be considered as no longer law. See 1 Mont. Part., note 2 F., p. 117, in notes. Perhaps Mr. Cooke rested the right of proof on the absence of joint estate, as in *Ex p. Taylor* (1842) 2 M.D. & D. 753."

[428] A written agreement is not necessary: *Ex p. Lane* (1846) De Ger 300.

[429] See *Ex p. Fairlie* (1830) Mont. 17; *Ex p. Raleigh* (1838) 3 M. & A. 670; *Ex p. Smith* (1840) 1 M.D. & D. 165. See also *Bilborough v. Holmes* (1876) 5 Ch.D. 255 and the cases cited *supra*, para. 27–97, n. 425. *cf. Ex p. Bradbury* (1839) Mont. & C. 625. As to the position where there is no joint estate, see *Ex p. Taylor* (1842) 2 M.D. & D. 753 and *infra*, para. 27–129.

[430] See, formerly, the Bankruptcy Act 1914, s.38(c) and the 15th ed. of this work at pp. 844 *et seq.*

[431] *ibid.* s.20, *supra*, para. 18–03.

this subject has already been considered in detail,[432] it is merely necessary to consider whether a notional joint estate can now be created by holding out and then to refer to the manner in which joint estate can be converted into separate estate and vice versa.

Joint estate created by holding out

Lord Lindley observed that: 27–99

" . . . if A allows B to carry on business with his, A's, goods and on his, A's, behalf, although not in his name, but credit is given to them both on the supposition that they are partners, the property with which the business is carried on will be treated as the joint estate of the two, and not as the separate estate of A."[433]

This view was expressed against a background of the doctrine of reputed ownership,[434] which has not been preserved under the Insolvency Act 1986, and was, in any event, confined within narrow parameters.[435] The current editor considers that a similar approach could not be justified under the 1986 Act, since it specifically refers to "the joint estate of the partnership"[436] and a partnership by holding out is not a true partnership in the eyes of the law.[437] Even if that were not the case, the circumstances in which credit could be said to have been given in the manner contemplated by Lord Lindley must now be severely reduced, assuming compliance with the requirements of Part 41 of the Companies Act 2006.[438]

Agreements converting joint into separate estate and vice versa

It has already been seen that a bona fide agreement between partners to convert   27–100
partnership property into the separate property of one of their number was, under the old bankruptcy laws, treated as binding on a trustee in bankruptcy, provided

---

[432] See *supra*, paras 18–06 *et seq.*

[433] See *Re Rowland and Crankshaw* (1866) L.R. 1 Ch. 421; *Ex p. Hayman* (1878) 8 Ch.D. 11. In any such case, the respective interests of the partners in the apparent joint estate were ignored: see *Ex p. Hunter* (1816) 2 Rose 382.

[434] See the then Bankruptcy Act 1883, s.44(iii).

[435] See, as to the position where there are dormant or apparent partners, *supra*, para. 27–90.

[436] See, for example, the Insolvency Act 1986, ss.175–175C (as amended), *supra*, paras 27–81 *et seq.* Note, however, that the liquidator of an insolvent firm has power to obtain an order for the delivery up of "any property . . . to which the partnership *appears* to be entitled" (emphasis supplied): *ibid.* s.234(3), as amended, where there are no concurrent petitions, by the Insolvent Partnerships Order 1994, Sched. 3, Pt II, para. 9 and applied by the Insolvency Act 1986, s.221(5) (as itself amended by the Insolvent Partnerships Order 1994, art. 7(1) (as amended by the Insolvent Partnerships (Amendment) Order 2002, art. 3), (2), Sched. 3, Pt I, para. 3 (creditor's petition)) and *ibid.* art. 9(a), Sched. 5, para. 2 (member's petition) and as amended, where there *are* concurrent petitions, by *ibid.* Sched. 4, Pt II, para. 27 and applied by the Insolvency Act 1986, s.221(5) (as itself amended by the Insolvent Partnerships Order 1994, art. 8(1) (as amended by the Insolvent Partnerships (Amendment) Order 2002, art. 4(1)), (2), Sched. 4, Pt I, para. 3 (creditor's petition) and *ibid.* art. 10(1)(a), Sched. 6, para. 4 (member's petition)). Clearly this does not determine the issue of whether that property is applicable as *part* of the joint estate.

[437] The Partnership Act 1890, s.14 (see *supra*, paras 5–35 *et seq.*) does not cause the person held out actually to be a partner but merely renders him *liable* as if he were: see *Hudgell Yeates & Co. v. Watson* [1978] Q.B. 451, 467 *per* Waller L.J.; also *Re C. & M. Ashberg, The Times*, July 17, 1990, noted *supra*, para. 27–05. Equally, such a person *is* regarded as a member of an insolvent firm: see the definition of "member" in the Insolvent Partnerships Order 1994, art. 2(1), as added to the Insolvency Act 1986, s.436 by *ibid.* art. 2(2).

[438] See generally, *supra*, paras 3–26 *et seq.*

that it preceded the commission of an act of bankruptcy.[439] The current editor suggests that the position will in general be the same under the current insolvency legislation, save that the relevant date will be the presentation of the petition.[440] Accordingly, the observations of Lord Lindley on the decision in *Ex p. Ruffin*[441] still hold good, *viz.*:

> "This case [*Ex p. Ruffin*] has been followed by many others, and it is therefore now beyond dispute that if a partnership is dissolved, and a *bona fide* agreement is come to between the partners, to the effect that what was the partnership property shall become the property of him who continues the business, and afterwards the firm or the continuing partner becomes bankrupt, that which was the partnership property cannot be distributed as the joint estate of the firm, but must be treated as the separate estate of the continuing partner.[442] The creditors of the firm have no lien on its property which can prevent the partners from bona fide changing its character, and converting it into the separate estate of one of them."[443]

This would even seem to be the position even where the partnership liabilities exceed its assets at the time of the agreement.[444]

It should be noted that the same principle will apply whenever there is a change in a firm, which results in the technical dissolution of the old firm and the formation of a new firm.[445] Thus assets which were applicable as the joint estate of the former will, following the change, only be applicable as the joint estate of the latter. This is a consequence which is often overlooked.

Exceptions to the general rule

27–101   However, there are three well established exceptions, in the face of which no such agreement can stand; they are as follows:

---

[439] See *supra*, paras 18–44 *et seq.*

[440] Insolvency Act 1986, ss.127(1) (as amended by the Enterprise Act 2002, Sched. 17, para. 15), 129(2), as applied, in the case of the firm, by *ibid.* s.221(5) (as itself amended by the Insolvent Partnerships Order 1994, art. 7(1) (as amended: see *supra*, n. 436), (2), Sched. 3, Pt I, para. 3 (creditor's petition with no concurrent petitions), *ibid.* art. 8(1) (as amended: see *supra*, n. 436), (2), Sched. 4, Pt I, para. 3 (creditor's petition *with* concurrent petitions), *ibid.* art. 9(a), Sched. 5, para. 2 (member's petition with no concurrent petitions) and *ibid.* art. 10(1)(a), Sched. 6, para. 4 (member's petition *with* concurrent petitions)) and, in the case of a corporate partner wound up on a concurrent petition, by the Insolvent Partnerships Order 1994, arts 8(4), (5) (creditor's petition), 10(2), (3) (member's petition). As regards an individual partner, see *ibid.* s.284, as amended, in the case of concurrent petitions, by the Insolvent Partnerships Order 1994, Sched. 4, Pt II, para. 29 and applied by *ibid.* arts 8(6), (8) (creditor's petition), 10(4)–(6), as amended by the Insolvent Partnerships (Amendment) Order 2005, art. 5(b) (member's petition) and, in the case of a joint bankruptcy petition, as amended and applied by *ibid.* art. 11(2), (3), Sched. 7, para. 8. In each case, the court could theoretically sanction the agreement, but it is difficult to imagine the circumstances where this would be appropriate. It should be noted that the regimes under the Insolvency Act 1986, s.127 and 284 are different: see *Pettit v. Novakovic* [2007] B.C.C. 462. Note, as to the exercise of the discretion conferred by s.127, *Royal Bank of Scotland v. Bhardwaj* [2002] B.C.C. 57.

[441] (1801) 6 Ves.Jr. 119. See also *supra*, para. 18–52.

[442] *Ex p. Timer* (1746) 1 Atk. 136; *Bolton v. Puller* (1796) 1 Bos. & P. 539; *Ex p. Fell* (1805) 10 Ves.Jr. 347; *Ex p. Williams* (1805) 11 Ves.Jr. 3; *Ex p. Clarkson* (1834) 4 D. & Ch. 56; *Ex p. Gurney* (1842) 2 M.D. & D. 541; *Ex p. Walker* (1862) 4 De G.F. & J. 509; *Re Simpson* (1874) L.R. 9 Ch. 572.

[443] *Ex p. Ruffin* (1801) 6 Ves.Jr. 119; *Ex p. Williams* (1805) 11 Ves.Jr. 3; *Stuart v. Ferguson* (1832) Hayes (Ir.Ex.) 452. *cf.* the cases cited *infra*, para. 27–101, n. 446. And see *supra*, para. 18–45.

[444] *Ex p. Peake* (1816) 1 Madd. 346; *Ex p. Clarkson* (1834) 4 D. & C. 56, 66 *per* Sir G. Rose; *Ex p. Walker* (1862) 4 De G.F. & J. 509; and see *Ex p. Carpenter* (1826) Mont. & MacA. 1. *cf. Re Kemptner* (1869) 8 Eq. 286, where *mala fides* was proved.

[445] See *supra*, paras 3–01 *et seq.*, 24–02.

1. Fraud, whether practised against a partner or against creditors[446];

2. Where the agreement remains executory[447];

3. Where the former partnership property is still subject to the liens of the other partners.[448]

To these exceptions must be added the power of the court under the Insolvency Act 1986 to set aside any transaction entered into by individual partners in the period of five years (in the case of the conversion of separate into joint property)[449] or two years (in the case of the conversion of joint into separate property)[450] ending with the presentation of the relevant petition, if it was unsupported by consideration or otherwise at an undervalue.[451] A similar power is exercisable in the case of preferences to creditors, etc.,[452] although it is

---

[446] See *Anderson v. Maltby* (1793) 2 Ves.Jr. 244; *Ex p. Rowlandson* (1813) 2 V. & B. 172; *Ex p. Mayor* (1865) 4 De G.J. & S. 664; *Re Kemptner* (1869) 8 Eq. 286. *cf. supra*, nn. 443, 444; also *Pearce v. Bulteel* [1916] 2 Ch. 544. See further *supra*, para. 18–46. And see the Insolvency Act 1986, ss.206, 207, as applied by *ibid.* s.221(5) (as itself amended by the Insolvent Partnerships Order 1994, art. 7(1) (as amended: see *supra*, para. 27–99, n. 436), (2), Sched. 3, Pt I, para. 3 (creditor's petition with no concurrent petitions), *ibid.* art. 8(1) (as amended: see *supra*, para. 27–99, n. 436), (2), Sched. 4, Pt I, para. 3 (creditor's petition *with* concurrent petitions), *ibid.* art. 9(a), Sched. 5, para. 2 (member's petition with no concurrent petitions) and *ibid.* art. 10(1)(a), Sched. 6, para. 4 (member's petition *with* concurrent petitions)). There may also be a contravention of the anti-deprivation principle, as explored in *Perpetual Trustee Co. Ltd. v. BNY Corporate Trustee Services Ltd.* [2010] 3 W.L.R. 87 (CA) (*i.e.* a fraud on the insolvency laws), as to which see *supra*, paras 10–152, 10–153.

[447] *Ex p. Wheeler* (1817) Buck 25; *Ex p. Cooper* (1840) 1 M.D. & D. 358; *Ex p. Gurney* (1842) 2 M.D. & D. 541; *Re Kemptner* (1869) 8 Eq. 286; *Ex p. Wood* (1879) 10 Ch.D. 554; *Pearce v. Bulteel* [1916] 2 Ch. 544; *cf. Ex p. Clarkson* (1834) 4 D. & Ch. 56, 64 *per* Erskine C.J., 67 *per* Sir G. Rose; also *Re Jane* (1914) 110 L.T. 556. See further, *supra*, para. 18–47.

[448] See *Ex p. Morley* (1873) L.R. 8 Ch. 1026; *Ex p. Dear* (1876) 1 Ch.D. 514; *Ex p. Manchester Bank* (1879) 12 Ch.D. 917 and, *sub nom. Ex p. Butcher* (1880) 13 Ch.D. 465. *cf. Re Simpson* (1874) L.R. 9 Ch. 572. As to partners' liens generally, see the Partnership Act 1890, s.39 and *supra*, paras 19–24 *et seq.*

[449] Insolvency Act 1986, s.341(1)(a). In a case where a bankruptcy order has been made against an individual partner on a concurrent petition, that subsection is applied by the Insolvent Partnerships Order 1994, art. 8(6), (7) (creditor's petition) and *ibid.* art. 10(4), (5) (member's petition). The period will be only two years in the case of a corporate partner: *ibid.* s.240(1)(a), as applied by *ibid.* art. 8(4), (5) (creditor's petition) and *ibid.* art. 10(2), (3) (member's petition).

[450] Insolvency Act 1986, s.240(1)(a), as applied by *ibid.* s.221(5) (as itself amended by the Insolvent Partnerships Order 1994, art. 7(1) (as amended: see *supra*, para. 27–99, n. 436), (2), Sched. 3, Pt I, para. 3 (creditor's petition with no concurrent petitions), *ibid.* art. 8(1) (as amended: see *supra*, para. 27–99 n. 436), (2), Sched. 4, Pt I, para. 3 (creditor's petition with concurrent petitions), *ibid.* art. 9(a), Sched. 5, para. 2 (member's petition with no concurrent petitions) and *ibid.* art. 10(1)(a), Sched. 6, para. 4 (member's petition with concurrent petitions)).

[451] *ibid.* ss.238(2), (4) (winding up), 339(1), (3)(a), (c) (bankruptcy), as respectively applied in the manner set out *supra* nn. 449, 450. As to what transactions will be treated as at an undervalue, see *Re M.C. Bacon Ltd.* [1990] B.C.L.C. 324, 340 *per* Millett J. (a decision under *ibid.* s.238); *Re Kumar* [1993] 1 W.L.R. 224; *Doyle v. Saville* [2002] B.P.I.R. 947; *Re Rich* [2008] B.P.I.R. 485 (all decisions under *ibid.* s.339); and, as to the nature of the court's discretion, see *Re Paramount Airways Ltd.* [1993] Ch. 223, 239 *et seq.* (CA); *Singla v. Brown* [2008] Ch. 357. See also, as to general assignments of book debts by individuals, the Insolvency Act 1986, s.344; *cf. Re Burfoot* [2000] B.P.I.R. 1038.

[452] *ibid.* ss.239 (winding up), 340 (bankruptcy), as applied by *ibid.* As to the relevant periods in this case, see *ibid.* ss.240(1)(a), (b) (winding up), 341(1)(a), (b) (bankruptcy). And see, generally, *Re M. C. Bacon Ltd., supra*; *Re Beacon Leisure Ltd.* [1992] B.C.L.C. 565 (both decisions under *ibid.* s.239); *Re Ledingham-Smith* [1993] B.C.L.C. 635; *Doyle v. Saville, supra* (both decisions under *ibid.* s.340).

doubtful whether the statutory presumption of a desire to prefer[453] is applicable where an apparent preference is given by a partner to the *joint* creditors of the firm.[454] Equally, the 1986 Act confers a general power on the court to set aside transactions at an undervalue independently of the existence of any insolvency proceedings.[455]

Evidence of such agreements

27–102   The mere fact that a partnership has been dissolved or that a partner has retired is not of itself sufficient evidence of an agreement to convert a partnership asset into the separate property of a continuing partner, since the asset might be in his hands simply for the purposes of winding up the affairs of the old firm.[456]

Priority of expenses

27–103   It has already been seen that, where insolvency orders have been made against the firm and against any one or more of the partners on concurrent petitions, the same person will in general act as liquidator of the partnership and of any corporate partner and as trustee of any bankrupt partner[457]; similarly in any case in which bankruptcy orders are made against all the partners on a joint bankruptcy petition[458] and in any other relevant case in which the provisions of the Insolvent Partnerships Order 1994 are applied by order of the court.[459] In each of the above cases, the expenses incurred by the liquidator/trustee of the firm and/or any insolvent member which are attributable to the joint and separate estates are paid out of those estates respectively.[460] If the expenses attributable to the joint estate cannot be met out of that estate, the balance is, as might be expected, apportioned between the separate estates of the insolvent partners, but in equal shares.[461] Equally, if the expenses attributable to a partner's separate estate cannot be met out of that estate, the balance is treated as an expense of the joint

---

[453] *ibid.* ss.239(6) (winding up), 340(5) (bankruptcy), as applied by *ibid.* Partners will be treated as "connected with" the firm for the purposes of the former subsection (*ibid.* s.249) and "associates" of each other for the purposes of the latter (*ibid.* s.435(3), as amended by the Civil Partnership Act 2004, Sched. 27, para. 122(3)). And see, generally, as to this statutory presumption, *Re Beacon Leisure Ltd.*, *supra*; *Re Ledingham-Smith*, *supra*.

[454] Note that an individual partner is not treated as an associate of his own *firm*: *ibid.* s.435(3), as amended.

[455] *ibid.* ss.423–425 (as amended), as applied by *ibid.* See, generally, *Arbuthnot Leasing International Ltd. v. Havelet Leasing Ltd. (No. 2)* [1990] B.C.C. 636; *Chohan v. Saggar* [1992] B.C.C. 306 and 750; *Agricultural Mortgage Corporation plc v. Woodward* [1995] 1 B.C.L.C. 1 (CA); *Moon v. Franklin* [1996] B.P.I.R. 196; *National Westminster Bank plc v. Jones*, *The Times*, November 19, 2001 (CA); *Law Society v. Southall* [2002] B.P.I.R. 336 (CA); *I.R.C. v. Hashmi* [2002] 2 B.C.L.C. 489 (CA); *Hill v. Spread Trustee Co. Ltd.* [2007] 1 W.L.R. 2404 (CA); *Department for the Environment, Food and Rural Affairs v. Feakins* [2007] B.C.C. 54 (CA); *Barnett v. Semenyuk* [2008] B.P.I.R. 1427; *4Eng Ltd. v. Harper*, *The Times*, November 6, 2009.

[456] *Ex p. Williams* (1805) 11 Ves.Jr. 3; *Ex p. Leaf* (1840) 4 Deac. 287; *Ex p. Cooper* (1840) 1 M.D. & D. 358.

[457] See *supra*, para. 27–53.

[458] See *supra*, para. 27–54.

[459] See *supra*, paras 27–21, 27–22, 27–40.

[460] Insolvency Act 1986, s.175(2), *supra*, para. 27–81 (creditor's and member's petitions); *ibid.* s.328(2), as amended and applied by the Insolvent Partnerships Order 1994, art. 11, Sched. 7, para. 21 (joint bankruptcy petition).

[461] *ibid.* ss.175(3), 328(3). Thus, the size of each such partner's share in the firm is ignored.

estate.[462] If, after a transfer of the unpaid expenses in either of the above ways, there is still an insufficiency of assets, the surplus is apportioned between the separate estates of the *other* insolvent partners, again in equal shares.[463] Any insufficiency produced by such an apportionment continues to be reapportioned until such time as the expenses are met.[464] In this way, the separate estate of one partner may be liable for expenses attributable to the separate estate of another. As an alternative to the above procedure, leave to discharge a partner's separate expenses directly out of the joint estate or vice versa may be obtained from the court.[465]

Where the joint and separate estates are administered independently, no question of apportionment of expenses will arise.

Distinct accounts to be kept

Where the joint and separate estates are being administered by the same   **27–104**
liquidator/trustee, he must keep distinct accounts of each estate.[466] This accords with the previous bankruptcy law.[467]

Correcting mistakes, etc.

Where debts or expenses are paid out of the wrong estate, the amount paid   **27–105**
must be refunded by the estate which ought properly to have borne them.[468]

Priority and proof of debts

The general rule

It has already been seen that, where joint and separate estates are being   **27–106**
administered together[469] or independently,[470] questions of priority of debts will inevitably arise.

In those cases in which insolvency orders are made against the firm and one or more partners on concurrent petitions[471] or against all the partners on a joint bankruptcy petition[472] or where the Insolvent Partnerships Order 1994 is applied by order of the court,[473] the Insolvency Act 1986 in the first instance requires the

---

[462] *ibid.* ss.175(4), 328(4).

[463] *ibid.* ss.175(5), 328(5).

[464] *ibid.* ss.175(6), 328(6).

[465] *ibid.* ss.175(7), 328(7).

[466] *ibid.* s.175C(1), *supra*, para. 27–84 (creditor's and member's petitions); *ibid.* s.328C(1), as amended and applied by the Insolvent Partnerships Order 1994, art. 11, Sched. 7, para. 21 (joint bankruptcy petition).

[467] See *Ex p. Voguel* (1743) 1 Atk. 132; *Dutton v. Morrison* (1810) 17 Ves.Jr. 193; *Re Wait* (1820) 1 J. & W. 610. Note also *Ex p. Marlin* (1785) 2 Bro. C.C. 15.

[468] See *Re Hind & Sons* (1889) L.R. (Ir.) 23 Ch.D. 217.

[469] See *supra*, paras 27–82, 27–85.

[470] See *supra*, para. 27–86.

[471] Insolvent Partnerships Order 1994, arts 8, 10: see *supra*, paras 27–24 *et seq.*

[472] *ibid.* art. 11: see *supra*, para. 27–44.

[473] Insolvency Act 1986, ss.168(5A), 303(2A), as added by the Insolvent Partnerships Order 1994, art. 14: see *supra*, para. 27–21, 27–41, 27–50.

joint estate to be applied in paying the joint debts[474] and the separate estate of each partner to be applied in paying his separate debts.[475] All the joint debts rank equally,[476] other than preferential debts,[477] those postponed under section 3 of the Partnership Act 1890[478] or under some other Act[479] and, seemingly, those postponed with the agreement of the creditor in question.[480] Interest on the non-postponed joint debts predictably ranks before the postponed joint debts.[481] A similar order of priority applies in the insolvent partners' separate estates.[482] Only the surplus joint estate remaining after payment of the joint debts will be available for transfer to the partners' respective separate estates.[483] Where however, the joint estate is insufficient to pay any class of joint debts and/or interest in order of priority, the responsible insolvency practitioner[484] (but not the joint creditors themselves) can prove for the aggregate amount of those debts/that

---

[474] *ibid.* s.175A(2), *supra*, para. 27–82 (creditor's and member's concurrent petitions); *ibid.* s.328A(2), as amended and applied by the Insolvent Partnerships Order 1994, art. 11, Sched. 7, para. 21 (joint bankruptcy petition).

[475] *ibid.* s.175B(1), *supra*, para. 27–83 (creditor's and member's concurrent petitions); *ibid.* s.328B(1), as amended and applied by the Insolvent Partnerships Order 1994, art. 11, Sched. 7, para. 21 (joint bankruptcy petition).

[476] *ibid.* s.175A(2)(b), (4), *supra*, para. 27–82 (creditor's and member's concurrent petitions); *ibid.* s.328A(2)(b), (4), as amended and applied by the Insolvent Partnerships Order 1994, art. 11, Sched. 7, para. 21 (joint bankruptcy petition).

[477] *ibid.* ss.175A(2)(a), (4) (creditor's and member's concurrent petitions), 328A(2)(a), (4), as amended and applied by the Insolvent Partnerships Order 1994, art. 11, Sched. 7, para. 21 (joint bankruptcy petition). As to what debts are treated as preferential, see the Insolvency Act 1986, s.386, Sched. 6, as respectively amended by the Enterprise Act 2002, s.251(1), (3), Sched. 26.

[478] See *supra*, para. 5–33.

[479] Insolvency Act 1986, ss.175A(2)(d) (creditor's and member's concurrent petitions), 328A(2)(d), as amended and applied by the Insolvent Partnerships Order 1994, art. 11, Sched. 7, para. 21 (joint bankruptcy petition). The expression "postponed debt" is defined in the Insolvent Partnerships Order 1994, art. 2(1), as "a debt the payment of which is postponed by or under any provision of the Act or any other enactment" and the definition is added to the Insolvency Act 1986, s.436 by *ibid.* art. 2(2). This clearly covers a debt falling within the Partnership Act 1890, s.3.

[480] See *Re Maxwell Communications Corporation Plc* [1993] 1 W.L.R. 1042, distinguishing *Halesowen Presswork Assemblies Ltd. v. National Westminster Bank Ltd.* [1972] A.C. 785 and *British Eagle International Airlines Ltd. v. Compagnie Nationale Air France* [1975] 1 W.L.R. 758 (HL). *Sed quaere*, given the definition of "postponed debt" noticed in the preceding footnote; also the Insolvency Act 1986, s.175C(5), *supra*, para. 27–84 (creditor's and member's concurrent petitions); *ibid.* s.328C(5), as amended and applied by the Insolvent Partnerships Order 1994, art. 11, Sched. 7, para. 21 (joint bankruptcy petition).

[481] *ibid.* ss.175A(2)(c) (creditor's and member's concurrent petitions), 328A(2)(c), as amended and applied by the Insolvent Partnerships Order 1994, art. 11, Sched. 7, para. 21 (joint bankruptcy petition). Note, however, that interest on preferential and other non-postponed debts ranks equally: *ibid.* s.175C(4), *supra*, para. 27–84 (creditor's and member's concurrent petitions); *ibid.* s.328C(4), as amended and applied by the Insolvent Partnerships Order 1994, art. 11, Sched. 7, para. 21 (joint bankruptcy petition).

[482] *ibid.* s.175B(1), (2), *supra*, para. 27–83 (creditor's and member's concurrent petitions); *ibid.* s.328B(1), (2), as amended and applied by the Insolvent Partnerships Order 1994, art. 11, Sched. 7, para. 21 (joint bankruptcy petition).

[483] *ibid.* s.175A(3), *supra*, para. 27–82 (creditor's and member's concurrent petitions); *ibid.* s.328A(3), as amended and applied by the Insolvent Partnerships Order 1994, art. 11, Sched. 7, para. 21 (joint bankruptcy petition).

[484] This expression is defined in the Insolvent Partnerships Order 1994, art. 2(1) and the definition is added to the Insolvency Act 1986, s.436 by *ibid.* art. 2(2). As might be expected, it means the liquidator of an insolvent firm or corporate partner or the trustee of an insolvent individual partner. Note, however, that in a case falling within *ibid.* art. 11 (joint bankruptcy petition), the responsible insolvency practitioner will, in fact, act as the *trustee* of the insolvent firm: see the Insolvency Act 1986, s.292(1), as amended and applied by the Insolvent Partnerships Order 1994, Sched. 7, para. 10.

interest in the separate estates of the insolvent partners and in *direct* competition with the equivalent class of separate creditors.[485] This was an innovation first introduced by the Insolvent Partnerships Order 1994.[486] Needless to say, there is no corresponding right for separate debts to be proved against the joint estate.

In any other case, the normal rigid distinction between the joint and separate debts and estates will be fully maintained.[487]

Group and sub-partnerships

The creditors of a constituent firm of a group partnership[488] are, *vis-à-vis* the group partnership, treated as *separate* creditors under the Insolvency Act 1986.[489] Accordingly, a share of any surplus arising in the joint estate of the group partnership will be transferred into the constituent firm's joint estate. Only if there is a surplus in the latter will there be a transfer into the separate estates of the members of that firm.[490]

The current editor considers that the same regime will not apply in the case of a sub-partnership between a partner and a third party.[491] Nevertheless, since a share of any surplus transferred to a sub-partner out of the joint estate of the head partnership will form part of the sub-partnership's joint estate rather than part of his separate estate, the ultimate result may be the same.

Relevance of old bankruptcy law

In those instances in which it addresses the priority of debts,[492] the Insolvent Partnerships Order 1994 purports to introduce a complete code and, unlike its predecessor,[493] does not expressly preserve any rule of law applicable thereto. A familiarity with the rules developed under the old bankruptcy laws is, nevertheless, helpful, not only in understanding the practical application of the above code,[494] but also to cater for those cases in which the relevant provisions of the Order do *not* apply. As in previous editions of this work, these rules will be considered first in relation to proof against the joint estate and then in relation to

27–107

27–108

---

[485] Insolvency Act 1986, s.175A(5)–(8), *supra*, para. 27–82 (creditor's and member's concurrent petitions); *ibid.* s.328A(5)–(8), as amended and applied by the Insolvent Partnerships Order 1994, art. 11, Sched. 7, para. 21 (joint bankruptcy petition). See also *ibid.* ss.175C(3), 328C(3), as to valuing debts.

[486] *cf.* the Insolvent Partnerships Order 1986, art. 10.

[487] See *supra*, paras 27–78, 27–79.

[488] See further, as to such partnerships, *supra*, paras 11–17 *et seq.*, 27–11 and 27–29.

[489] Insolvency Act 1986, s.175C(6), *supra*, para. 27–84 (creditor's and member's concurrent petitions); *ibid.* s.328C(6), as amended and applied by the Insolvent Partnerships Order 1994, art. 11, Sched. 7, para. 21 (joint bankruptcy petition).

[490] *ibid.* s.175C(7), *supra*, para. 27–84 (creditor's and member's concurrent petitions); *ibid.* s.328C(7), as amended and applied by the Insolvent Partnerships Order 1994, art. 11, Sched. 7, para. 21 (joint bankruptcy petition).

[491] See further, as to such partnerships, *supra*, paras 5–67 *et seq.*, 27–11, 27–29. *Quaere* whether, if two or more members of a single sub-partnership are (unusually) both members of the head partnership, it could be argued that, notwithstanding the interests of third parties, such members "constitute a separate partnership" for the purposes of *ibid.* s.175C(6) or 328C(6) (as the case may be). The current editor considers that such a construction would not be permissible.

[492] See *supra*, para. 27–106.

[493] Insolvent Partnerships Order 1986, art. 10(7).

[494] Note, however, that the courts have, in general, proved reluctant to follow rules developed under the old bankruptcy laws when applying the current insolvency legislation: see, for example, *Re A Debtor (No. 1 of 1987)* [1989] 1 W.L.R. 271; *Re Smith* [1990] 2 A.C. 215, 237–238; *Re M. C. Bacon* [1990] B.C.L.C. 324, 335 *per* Millett J.

proof against the separate estates. Where relevant, similarities to or a divergence from the statutory code will be noticed.

A.   PROOF AGAINST THE JOINT ESTATE

27–109   This subject can best be analysed in terms of:

(a) The rights of the joint creditors.

(b) The rights of the partners.

(c) The rights of their separate creditors.

(a) Rights of the joint creditors

27–110   The general right of such creditors to be paid the entirety of their debts out of the joint estate has already been noticed[495] and does not require further elaboration. Their debts will, in general, rank equally,[496] unless they are either preferential[497] or postponed.[498] Although debts due to a bankrupt partner's spouse or civil partner will be postponed in administering his or her separate estate,[499] it is submitted that this will not affect the priority of a *joint* debt due to that spouse/civil partner.[500]

Secured creditors

27–111   A secured creditor may in general realise his security and prove for the balance of his debt or surrender his security and prove for the whole debt[501]; what he cannot do is both retain the benefit of the security and prove for the *whole* debt. However, under the old bankruptcy laws, there was an established exception to

---

[495] See *supra*, paras 27–78, 27–79, 27–106.

[496] Insolvency Act 1986, s.328(3). The position is the same where insolvency orders are made on concurrent petitions (Insolvency Act 1986, s.175A(2), (4), *supra*, para. 27–82) and on joint bankruptcy petitions (*ibid.* s.328A(2), (4), as amended and applied by the Insolvent Partnerships Order 1994, art. 11, Sched. 7, para. 21). See further *supra*, para. 27–106. As to the position on a winding up of a firm as an unregistered company, see the Insolvency Rules 1986, r. 4.181(1), as amended.

[497] As to what debts are treated as preferential, see the Insolvency Act 1986, s.386, Sched. 6, as respectively amended by the Enterprise Act 2002, s.251(1), (3), Sched. 26.

[498] See the Insolvency Act 1986, s.328(6). This will include debts which are postponed: (i) under the Partnership Act 1890, s.3 (see *supra*, para. 5–33) or under some other Act or, seemingly, (ii) by agreement: see *Re Maxwell Communications Corporation plc* [1993] 1 W.L.R. 1042, distinguishing *Halesowen Presswork Assemblies Ltd. v. National Westminster Bank Ltd.* [1972] A.C. 785 and *British Eagle International Airlines Ltd. v. Compagnie Nationale Air France* [1975] 1 W.L.R. 758 (HL). But see also *supra*, para. 27–106, n. 480. Note also, where the firm is being wound up as an unregistered company, the provisions of the Insolvency Act 1986, s.74(2)(f), as considered in *Soden v. British & Commonwealth Holdings plc* [1998] A.C. 298 (HL), do apply. Otherwise there is no concept of "postponed debts" under the company insolvency regime: see the Insolvency Rules 1986, r. 4.181, as amended.

[499] Insolvency Act 1986, s.329, as amended by the Civil Partnership Act 2004, Sched. 27, para. 116.

[500] See *Ex p. Nottingham* (1887) 19 Q.B.D. 88 (a decision under the Married Women's Property Act 1882, s.3).

[501] Insolvency Rules 1986, rr. 4.88, 4.95 *et seq.* (winding up), 6.109, 6.115 *et seq.* (bankruptcy). See also the Insolvency Act 1986, ss.269(1), 383(2).

this rule, applicable only in the case of a partnership,[502] where the debt was payable out of one estate and the security derived from another.[503] Thus, a creditor of a bankrupt two partner firm, who held a security given by a larger firm of which those two partners were members, was entitled both to prove for the whole amount of the debt against the joint estate of the bankrupt firm and to retain the security given by the larger (solvent) firm.[504] The position was the same where a partner had mortgaged his own property to secure a joint debt.[505] However, that exception did not apply if, unbeknown to the creditor, the property over which the security was given in fact belonged to the estate out of which the secured debt was payable.[506] Numerous other examples may be imagined.[507] The current editor submits that the same exception continues to apply under the current insolvency legislation.[508]

The foregoing exception will naturally not apply in the case of a creditor who has advanced money to a partner and taken a security from him, merely because the money has subsequently been applied for the firm's benefit: in such a case, there is clearly no joint debt payable out of the joint estate and the creditor has no *locus standi* against the firm.[509]

---

[502] See *Re A Debtor (No. 5 of 1967)* [1972] Ch. 197.

[503] See *Ex p. West Riding Union Banking Co.* (1881) 19 Ch.D. 105; *Ex p. Cocks, Biddulph & Co.* [1894] 2 Q.B. 256; also *Ex p. Brett* (1871) L.R. 6 Ch. 838.

[504] *Ex p. Bloxham* (1801) 6 Ves.Jr. 449; *Ex p. Parr* (1811) 1 Rose 76; *Ex p. Goodman* (1818) 3 Madd. 373; *Ex p. Sammon* (1832) 1 D. & C. 564; also *Ex p. Wilson* (1838) 2 Jur. 67; *Ex p. English and American Bank* (1868) L.R. 4 Ch.App. 49 (both cases involving a creditor of two firms which had engaged in a joint transaction).

[505] *Ex p. Peacock* (1825) 2 Gl. & J. 27; *Ex p. Adams* (1837) 3 M. & Ayr. 157; *Ex p. Groom* (1837) 2 Deac. 265; *Ex p. Caldicott* (1884) 25 Ch.D. 716; *Re Hind & Sons* (1889) L.R. (Ir.) 23 Ch.D. 217. See also *Ex p. Manchester and Liverpool District Banking Co.* (1874) 18 Eq. 249 and the cases cited in the next note.

[506] *Ex p. Connell* (1838) 3 Deac. 201; *Ex p. Manchester and County Bank* (1876) 3 Ch.D. 481.

[507] The following passage (based on Lord Lindley's original formulation) appeared in earlier editions of this work: "Again, if A and B are partners, and A gives a separate security for a partnership debt and dies, and B becomes bankrupt, the creditor can prove against B's estate without giving up his security. [*Ex p. Bowden (1832) 1 D. & Ch. 135; Ex p. Smyth (1839) 3 Deac. 597.*] So, where a creditor of a firm has a security belonging to the firm and also a separate covenant for payment by each partner, such creditor may, on the bankruptcy of the firm, retain his security and prove against the separate estates of the covenantors. [*Re Plummer (1841) 1 Ph. 56.*] So, too, if a creditor holds a security on the separate property of one partner for the joint debt of his firm, and has also the separate guarantee of that partner for the joint debt, he may prove against the separate estate of that partner, for the amount due under his guarantee without realising or accounting for the security, because the security is not a security for the partner's separate debt under the guarantee, but for the joint debt of the firm. [*Ex p. Manchester and Liverpool District Banking Co. [1924] 2 Ch. 199.*] Again, where a firm has assigned its property in trust for its creditors, whose rights against the separate estates of the partners are expressly reserved, a creditor who is both a joint and a separate creditor may claim the benefit of the assignment, and yet prove as a separate creditor against one of the firm if he becomes bankrupt. [*Ex p. Thornton (1858) 5 Jur. (N.S.) 212; also Ex p. Greaves (1856) 8 De G.M. & G. 291.*] Where, however, one partner only is bankrupt, and a joint creditor is secured by a mortgage of the bankrupt's separate estate, that creditor cannot prove as a separate creditor without giving up his security [*Ex p. West Riding Union Banking Co. (1881) 19 Ch.D. 105*]; and if the mortgage is a mere equitable mortgage giving the creditor no *locus standi* as a separate creditor and nothing more than a lien, he will not be a separate creditor of the bankrupt, or be allowed to prove against his separate estate at all. [*Ex p. Leicestershire Banking Co. (1846) 1 De Gex 292; Ex p. Lloyd (1838) 3 M. & A. 601.*]" Note, however, that an equitable mortgage by deposit of title deeds may no longer be created: *United Bank of Kuwait plc v. Sahib* [1997] Ch. 107 (CA).

[508] The position would appear to be analogous to that in *Cleaver v. Delta American Reinsurance Co.* [2001] 2 A.C. 328, where the Privy Council decided that sums proved in a foreign liquidation did not have to be brought into hotchpot on an English liquidation: see, in particular, *ibid.* at [26].

[509] *Ex p. Hunter* (1742) 1 Atk. 223; *Ex p. Emly* (1811) 1 Rose 61; *Lloyd v. Freshfield* (1826) 9 D. & R. 19. See also, *supra*, paras 12–175 *et seq.*

(b) Rights of the partners

27–112   Lord Lindley stated that, subject to certain exceptions:

> " . . . it is an established rule that a partner in a bankrupt firm shall not prove in
> competition with the creditors of the firm. They are, in fact, his own creditors, and
> he cannot be permitted to diminish the partnership assets to the prejudice of those
> who are not only creditors of the firm, but also of himself.[510] If, therefore, a partner
> is a creditor of the firm, neither he nor his separate creditors (for they are in no better
> position than himself) can compete with the joint creditors as against the joint estate.
> Lord Hardwicke, it is true, in *Ex p. Hunter*,[511] allowed this to be done; but that case
> has not, in this respect, been followed, and has long been considered as
> overruled."[512]

It has already been seen that precisely the same rule is preserved by sections
175C(2) and 328C(2) of the Insolvency Act 1986, as amended by the Insolvent
Partnerships Order 1994.[513]

Holding out

27–113   A person who has rendered himself liable for joint debts on the basis of
holding out[514] will, as regards his ability to prove against the joint estate, be in
no better position than a true partner.[515]

Personal representatives of a deceased partner

27–114   Since a deceased partner's estate is liable for the debts of the firm,[516] it follows
from the general principle described above that, whilst such liability continues,
his personal representatives will not be permitted to prove against the joint estate
of the surviving partners for the amount due from them to his estate[517]; but, once
such debts are paid or the estate freed from liability therefor,[518] such proof will
be permitted.[519] Even then, the personal representatives may be prevented from
proving in respect of any sum which they have brought into or left in the business
as part of the deceased's capital. In such a case, their proof will in general only
be admissible once all the debts contracted both before and after the death have

---

[510] See *Ex p. Hargreaves* (1788) 1 Cox. 440; *Ex p. Reeve* (1804) 9 Ves.Jr. 588; *Ex p. Rawson* (1821)
Jac. 274; *Ex p. Sillitoe* (1824) 1 Gl. & J. 374; *Ex p. Williams* (1843) 3 M.D. & D. 433; *Nanson v.
Gordon* (1876) 1 App.Cas. 195 (HL); see also *Ex p. Mawde* (1867) L.R. 2 Ch. 550; *Ex p. Gliddon*
(1884) L.R. 13 Q.B.D. 43.

[511] (1742) 1 Atk. 223.

[512] *Ex p. Parker* (1780); *Ex p. Burrell* (1783); *Ex p. Pine* (1783), all cited in Cooke's *Bankruptcy
Law* (8th ed.), p. 528; and see *Ex p. Harris* (1813) 1 Rose 438.

[513] See *supra*, para. 27–84. See also, in the case of the winding up of a firm as an unregistered
company, the Insolvency Act 1986, s.74(2)(f), as considered in *Soden v. British & Commonwealth
Holdings plc* [1998] A.C. 298 (HL).

[514] See the Partnership Act 1890, s.14, *supra*, paras 5–35 *et seq.*

[515] In cases to which the Insolvent Partnerships Order 1994 applies, he will actually be regarded
as a member of the firm: see the definition of that expression in *ibid.* art. 2(1), as added to the
Insolvency Act 1986, s.436 by *ibid.* art. 2(2).

[516] Partnership Act 1890, s.9: see *supra*, paras 13–03, 13–06 *et seq.*

[517] *Nanson v. Gordon* (1876) 1 App.Cas. 195; *Ex p. Blythe* (1881) 16 Ch.D. 620.

[518] *Ex p. Moore* (1826) 2 Gl. & J. 166. It is clear from the decision in *Ex p. Andrews* (1884) 25
Ch.D. 505 that the outstanding joint liabilities need not be paid: it is enough that there is no proof in
respect of any of them. Note, however, that there was in that case no reason to suppose the debts ever
would be proved.

[519] *Ex p. Edmonds* (1862) 4 De G.F. & J. 488; *Ex p. Executors of James Douglas* [1930] 1 Ch.
342.

been paid.[520] However, if that sum was brought into the business in breach of trust, it will not form part of the joint estate and proof will be allowed, even in competition with the joint creditors whose debts accrued during the deceased partner's lifetime[521]; *per contra*, if it was merely improperly *left* in the business.[522]

It would seem that the same rule will apply under sections 175A and 328A of the Insolvency Act 1986, as amended by the Insolvent Partnerships Order 1994, since both sections are expressly stated to be subject to section 9 of the Partnership Act 1890.[523]

Two firms with common partner

The same principle may even be applied where a partner in one firm seeks to   **27–115**
prove against the joint estate of another which shares a common partner. In this connection, Lord Lindley referred to the decision in *Ex p. Brown*,[524] the effect of which he summarised thus:

> "There, in substance, there were two firms, with a common partner, *viz.* A and B, and A and C: C had made himself separately liable for a debt owing by A and B; both firms became bankrupt. The principal creditor proved against C's separate estate, and received a dividend. A claim was then made on behalf of C's separate estate, to prove for the amount thus paid out of it against the joint estate of A and B. But it was held that this proof could not be allowed, for the principal creditor not having been paid in full, he had a right of proof against the joint estate of A and B, and that, consequently, C could not diminish that estate to his prejudice."

When a partner may compete with his own creditors

There are three established circumstances in which the principle under con-   **27–116**
sideration will not apply, but only the first two are referred to in sections 175C(2) and 328C(2) of the Insolvency Act 1986, as amended by the Insolvent Partnerships Order 1994.[525] They are as follows:

(i) *Fraud*

Where the separate property of one partner has been converted to the use of the firm by a fraud practised by the other partners, proof on behalf of his separate

---

[520] *Ex p. Butterfield* (1847) De Gex 570; *Ex p. Corbridge* (1876) 4 Ch.D. 246; see also *Ex p. Garland* (1804) 10 Ves.Jr. 110, where proof in respect of assets improperly employed in the business was admitted but proof in respect of assets properly employed rejected; *Ex p. Thompson* (1842) 2 M.D. & D. 761; *Scott v. Izon* (1865) 34 Beav. 434. *cf. Ex p. Edmonds* (1862) 4 De G.F. & J. 488, where the money was continued in the business in the form of an interest bearing loan. Note that, in this case, the debts in respect of which the deceased's estate was liable had been paid, distinguishing it from *Nanson v. Gordon* (1876) 1 App.Cas. 195. See also *Ex p. Hill* (1837) 3 M. & A. 175; *Ex p. Crofts* (1837) 2 Deac. 102 (trust money lent to partners held to be provable as a joint debt); *Ex p. Executors of James Douglas* [1930] 1 Ch. 342. And note *Re Meade* [1951] Ch. 774, where an advance of money by the bankrupt's mistress to be employed in his business was held to be a contribution of capital and not a loan and so not provable.

[521] *Ex p. Garland* (1804) 10 Ves.Jr. 110; *Ex p. Westcott* (1874) L.R. 9 Ch. 626. See also *supra*, paras 26–19 *et seq.*

[522] The current editor submits that, in such a case, proof will not be allowed unless the debts of the firm contracted during the deceased partner's lifetime have been paid.

[523] *ibid.* ss.175A(1) (*supra*, para. 27–82), 328A(1), as amended and applied by the Insolvent Partnerships Order 1994, art. 11, Sched. 7, para. 21.

[524] (1842) 2 M.D. & D. 718; also *Ex p. Rawson* (1821) Jac. 274.

[525] See *supra*, para. 27–84.

estate in competition with the joint creditors will be allowed in respect of such property.[526]

(ii) *Distinct trades*

27–117 Lord Lindley summarised this exception in the following way:

> "If one of two firms, carrying on distinct trades, becomes creditor of the other in the ordinary way of their trade, the creditor firm may prove against the joint estate of the debtor firm, in competition with its other joint creditors, although one or more persons may be partners in both firms."[527]

The formulation in sections 175C(2)[528] and 328C(2)[529] of the Insolvency Act 1986 is simpler:

> " . . . the debt has arisen . . . in the ordinary course of a business carried on separately from the partnership business."

If the two firms merely have one or more partners in common, *e.g.* one firm comprising A and B and the other comprising B and C, either firm may in any event rank as a joint creditor of the other, because the creditors of the one are not creditors of the other.[530]

27–118 Where, however, all the partners of one firm are partners of the other, *e.g.* one firm comprising A, B and C ("the ABC Partnership") and the other comprising A and B ("the AB Partnership"), the ability to prove will vary according to which firm is the creditor. Whilst all the creditors of the ABC Partnership are inevitably creditors of the AB partnership, the converse proposition does not hold good. Consequently, although the ABC Partnership does not compete with its own creditors if it seeks to prove against the joint estate of the AB Partnership, the AB Partnership must necessarily do so if it seeks to prove against the joint

---

[526] *Ex p. Sillitoe* (1824) 1 Gl. & J. 374, 382 *per* Lord Eldon; also *Ex p. Harris* (1813) 1 Rose 437. *Quaere* whether, in such a case, it must be shown that there is an overall balance due to the defrauded partner on the taking of the partnership accounts before the proof will be allowed: see *Ex p. Maude* (1867) L.R. 2 Ch. 550 (a case of distinct trades: see *infra*, paras 27–117 *et seq.*). As to the position where a partner fraudulently converts partnership property into his own separate property, see *infra*, para. 27–133.

[527] *Ex p. Cook* (1831) Mont. 228; also *Ex p. Ring* (1796), *Ex p. Freeman* (1796), *Ex p. Johns* (1802), cited in Cooke's *Bankruptcy Law* (8th ed.), p. 534, *cf. Ex p. Gliddon* (1884) 13 Q.B.D. 43. It should be noted that Lord Lindley had earlier summarised this exception in these terms: "Where there are two distinct trades, carried on by the firm, and by one or more of the members of it, *with distinct capitals*" (emphasis supplied). The reference to distinct capitals is somewhat misleading: it relates to the existence of two separate joint estates against which debts can be proved, rather than to the manner in which each trade is financed.

[528] As amended by the Insolvent Partnerships Order 1994, Sched. 4, Pt II, para. 23 and applied, as regards the firm, by the Insolvency Act 1986, s.221(5) (as itself amended by the Insolvent Partnerships Order 1994, art. 8(1) (as amended by the Insolvent Partnerships (Amendment) Order 2005, art. 4(1)), (2), Sched. 4, Pt I, para. 3 (creditor's petition with concurrent petitions) and *ibid.* art. 10(1)(a), Sched. 6, para. 4 (member's petition with concurrent petitions)) and, as regards insolvent corporate and individual partners, by the Insolvent Partnerships Order 1994, arts 8(4)–(8) (creditor's petition), 10(2)–(6) (as amended by the Insolvent Partnerships (Amendment) Order 2005, art. 5(b)) (member's petition).

[529] As amended and applied by the Insolvent Partnerships Order 1994, art. 11, Sched. 7, para. 21.

[530] *Ex p. Thompson* (1834) 3 D. & Ch. 612.

estate of the ABC partnership. Although Lord Lindley pointed out that this had long been settled law,[531] he went on:

> "However, it seems now settled that if the two trades are distinct, and if the larger firm has become indebted to the smaller in the regular way of their trades,[532] the smaller firm may prove, like any other joint creditor, against the joint estate of the larger. This was decided in *Ex p. Cook*,[533] where one partner, who carried on a separate business, was allowed to rank as a joint creditor against the joint estate of the firm of which he was a member, and which had become indebted to him in the ordinary way of their and his respective trades."

If this exception is to apply, two fundamental conditions must be fulfilled. First, there must be two distinct trades: if the smaller firm is merely a branch of the larger and is in truth carrying on a part of the latter's business, the condition will not be satisfied and the proof will be disallowed.[534] Secondly, the debt sought to be proved must have arisen from dealings between the two firms in the ordinary way of business,[535] and must *not* have been converted into a mere personal debt.[536] The position is, needless to say, exactly the same under sections 175C(2) and 328C(2) of the Insolvency Act 1986.[537]

Lord Lindley then went on to add the following comment: **27–119**

> "Even in these excepted cases, however, proof by one partner is not allowed unless on taking the partnership accounts a balance still remains due to him."

He then cited *Ex p. Maude*[538] as authority. The current editor submits that Lord Lindley's additional condition cannot be justified in the context of distinct trades, which connote that the partner in his separate trade has been treated as a creditor of his firm. It is right that a proof was rejected in *Ex p. Maude* on the ground that no account had been taken, but the "debt" in question appears to have related to an obligation to contribute capital to the firm, so would never have been within the exception under consideration.[539]

(iii) *Discharge of bankrupt partner*

Where a partner has been discharged from bankruptcy[540] or has otherwise been   **27–120**
discharged from the joint debts,[541] and has subsequently become a creditor of the

---

[531] As to proof by the larger firm, see *Ex p. St. Barbe* (1805) 11 Ves.Jr. 413; *Ex p. Hesham* (1810) 1 Rose 146; *Ex p. Castell* (1826) 2 Gl. & J. 124; as to proof by the smaller firm, see *Ex p. Hargreaves* (1788) 1 Cox 440; *Ex p. Adams* (1812) 1 Rose 305; *Ex p. Sillitoe* (1824) 1 Gl. & J. 374.

[532] This is essential: see also *infra*, para. 27–134.

[533] (1831) Mont. 228.

[534] *Ex p. Hargreaves* (1788) 1 Cox 440.

[535] *Ex p. Sillitoe* (1824) 1 Gl. & J. 374; *Ex p. Williams* (1843) 3 M.D. & D. 433; also *Ex p. Maude* (1867) L.R. 2 Ch. 550.

[536] *Ex p. Kaye* (1892) 9 Morr. 269.

[537] See *supra*, paras 27–84, 27–117.

[538] (1867) L.R. 2 Ch. App. 550.

[539] *ibid.* p. 555 *per* Sir G.J. Turner L.J. See generally, as to the need to take an account as between partners, *supra*, para. 23–76.

[540] See, as to the effect of such a discharge, the Insolvency Act 1986, s.281 (as amended). And note also, as to the position between the partners, *Wood v. Dodgson* (1813) 2 M. & S. 195; and see *Wright v. Hunter* (1800) 1 East 20; *Ex p. Carpenter* (1826) Mont. & MacA. 1; *Aflalo v. Fourdrinier* (1829) 6 Bing. 306.

[541] *e.g.* by a compromise or by limitation. See *Ex p. Executors of James Douglas* [1930] 1 Ch. 342, 350 *per* Luxmoore J.; also *Ex p. Smith* (1884) 14 Q.B.D. 394.

firm,[542] he will no longer be a debtor *vis-à-vis* the joint creditors of the firm and will, accordingly, not be competing with his own creditors. There is no reason to suppose that the same exception will not apply in cases governed by sections 175C(2) or 328C(2) of the Insolvency Act 1986, as amended by the Insolvent Partnerships Order 1994,[543] even though not expressly mentioned therein.

Partnership not yet commenced

27–121   Although it does not, unlike the cases considered in the preceding paragraphs, strictly represent an exception to the general principle, it should be noted that there is no restriction on the right of proof in the case of a person who merely *intends* to enter into partnership, provided that he has not already been held out as a partner and thereby rendered himself liable for the joint debts.[544] This is illustrated by the decision in *Ex p. Turquand*[545] where, in substance, A had agreed to enter into partnership with B and C, who were already carrying on business in partnership under the names B and C. A was to bring in a certain sum of cash and the firm name was to be altered to B, C & Co. A advanced the cash to B and C and the firm name was duly altered, but no partnership agreement was signed; A refused to proceed any further until he was satisfied as to B and C's solvency. There was no evidence of holding out. On B and C's bankruptcy, A was allowed to prove for the advance he had made.

(c) Rights of separate creditors

27–122   Lord Lindley observed that:

> "The principle which prohibits a partner from competing with the joint creditors of the firm evidently has no application as between one partner and the separate creditors of his co-partners. Moreover, the lien which each partner has upon the assets of the firm[546] must be satisfied before any part of the joint estate can be divided amongst the members of the firm, or, which comes to the same thing, be carried to the account of their respective separate estates."[547]

The current editor submits that this still represents a correct statement of the position under the current insolvency legislation, albeit that a partner's lien will be unenforceable against the liquidator (and, in any event, largely irrelevant) where a firm is wound up as an unregistered company.[548] In those cases to which section 175A or 328A of the Insolvency Act 1986 apply,[549] the responsible insolvency practitioner is expressly directed to distribute the surplus in the joint

---

[542] *Ex p. Atkins* (1820) Buck 479; *Ex p. Smith* (1884) 14 Q.B.D. 394.

[543] See *supra*, para. 27–84.

[544] The position will be no different under the Insolvency Act 1986, s.175C(2) or 328C(2) (as amended and applied): see *supra*, paras 27–84, 27–117.

[545] (1841) 2 M.D. & D. 339. See also *Ex p. Hickin* (1850) 3 De G. & Sm. 662; *Ex p. Davis* (1863) 4 De G.J. & Sm. 523. Note that, where money is advanced for a particular purpose which fails, it may, in appropriate circumstances, be claimed that the money is held upon a resulting trust for the person making the advance: see *Barclays Bank v. Quistclose Investments* [1970] A.C. 567; *Carreras Rothmans Ltd. v. Freeman Mathews Treasure Ltd.* [1985] Ch. 207.

[546] See generally, as to this lien, *supra*, paras 19–24 *et seq.*

[547] See *Ex p. Reeve* (1804) 9 Ves.Jr. 588; *Ex p. King* (1810) 17 Ves.Jr. 115; *Ex p. Reid* (1814) 2 Rose 84; *Ex p. Terrell* (1819) Buck 345; *Holderness v. Shackels* (1828) 8 B. & C. 612; *Fereday v. Wightwick* (1829) Tam. 250.

[548] See *supra*, para. 19–36.

[549] See *supra*, para. 27–106.

estate "to the members or, where applicable, to the separate estates of the members, according to their respective rights and interests in it".[550]

Where a partner's lien is exercisable, it may effectively prefer his separate creditors over the separate creditors of any partner who cannot exercise such a lien.[551] If, in such a case, the joint estate is not sufficient to satisfy the lien, the deficiency will be provable against the separate estates of the other partners liable therefor.[552]

Surplus of joint estate

When the surplus joint estate is divided between the partners' separate estates, according to their respective entitlements,[553] it will effectively cease to form part of the joint estate and thereafter be comprised in those partners' separate estates.[554] However, it is submitted that, as under the old bankruptcy law,[555] joint estate which is prematurely divided must be restored by the recipients.[556]

27–123

B.   PROOF AGAINST THE SEPARATE ESTATES

As in the case of proof against the joint estate, it is most convenient to consider this subject under three headings, namely:

27–124

(a) The rights of the separate creditors.

(b) The rights of the joint creditors.

(c) The rights of the partners.

(a) Rights of separate creditors

It has already been seen that, where questions of priority arise, a partner's separate debts are primarily payable out of his separate estate,[557] although where the firm is insolvent and the joint estate is insufficient, the joint debts may be provable in competition with them.[558] In such a case, interest on the separate debts will only be payable once the non-postponed separate *and* joint debts have

27–125

---

[550] *ibid.* s.175A(3), *supra*, para. 27–82 (creditor's and member's concurrent petitions); *ibid.* s.328A(3), as amended and applied by the Insolvent Partnerships Order 1994, art. 11, Sched. 7, para. 21 (joint bankruptcy petition).

[551] *Ex p. King, supra*; *Ex p. Reid* (1814) 2 Rose 84. As to the circumstances in which a partner may lose his lien, see *supra*, paras 19–34, 19–35.

[552] *Ex p. King, supra*; *Ex p. Terrell* (1819) Buck 345; *Ex p. Watson* (1819) Buck 449; also *Ex p. Moore* (1826) 2 Gl. & J. 172.

[553] See, in particular, the Insolvency Act 1986, ss.175A(3), 328A(3), noted *supra*, para. 27–122.

[554] *ibid.* s.175B(3), *supra*, para. 27–83 (creditor's and member's concurrent petitions); *ibid.* s.328B(3), as amended and applied by the Insolvent Partnerships Order 1994, art. 11, Sched. 7, para. 21 (joint bankruptcy petition).

[555] See *Ex p. Lanfear* (1813) 1 Rose 442.

[556] In the case of a firm wound up as an unregistered company, the partners would in any event be liable to have calls made upon them in respect of any deficiency in the joint estate: see *supra*, paras 27–61 *et seq.*

[557] See *supra*, paras 27–78, 27–82 *et seq.*

[558] See *supra*, para. 27–106. As to the priority of interest on the separate debts, see the Insolvency Act 1986, s.175B(1)(c), (e), *supra*, para. 27–83 (creditor's and member's concurrent petitions); *ibid.* s.328B(1)(c), (e), as amended and applied by the Insolvent Partnerships Order 1994, art. 11, Sched. 7, para. 21 (joint bankruptcy petition).

been paid.[559] *Per contra* where the estates of the insolvent firm and its members are administered independently.[560]

A partner's separate debts will in general rank equally,[561] unless they are preferential[562] or postponed by statute[563] or, seemingly, with the agreement of the creditor concerned.[564] Joint debts provable against the separate estate rank equally with the equivalent class of separate debts.[565]

Secured creditors

27–126   The rights of a secured creditor have already been noticed in relation to the joint estate.[566]

(b) Rights of joint creditors

27–127   Lord Lindley observed that, save in certain exceptional cases:

" . . . the joint creditors of partners[567] are not entitled to payment out of their separate estates, in competition with their separate creditors."[568]

[559] Insolvency Act 1986, s.175B(1), *supra*, para. 27–83 (creditor's and member's concurrent petitions); *ibid.* s.328B(1), as amended and applied by the Insolvent Partnerships Order 1994, art. 11, Sched. 7, para. 21 (joint bankruptcy petition).

[560] See *supra*, para. 27–86.

[561] *ibid.* s.175B(1)(b), (2), *supra*, para. 27–83 (creditor's and member's concurrent petitions); *ibid.* s.328B(1)(b), (2), as amended and applied by the Insolvent Partnerships Order 1994, art. 11, Sched. 7, para. 21 (joint bankruptcy petition).

[562] *ibid.* ss.175B(1)(a), (2) (creditor's and member's concurrent petitions), 328B(1)(a), (2), as amended and applied by the Insolvent Partnerships Order 1994, art. 11, Sched. 7, para. 21 (joint bankruptcy petition). As to what debts are treated as preferential, see the Insolvency Act 1986, s.386, Sched. 6, as respectively amended by the Enterprise Act 2002, s.251(1), (3), Sched. 26.

[563] *ibid.* ss.175B(1)(d) (creditor's and member's concurrent petitions), 328A(1)(d), as amended and applied by the Insolvent Partnerships Order 1994, art. 11, Sched. 7, para. 21 (joint bankruptcy petition). The expression "postponed debt" is defined in the Insolvent Partnerships Order 1994, art. 2(1) as "a debt the payment of which is postponed by or under any provisions of the Act or any other enactment" and this definition is added to the Insolvency Act 1986, s.436 by *ibid.* art. 2(2), This will clearly include debts postponed under the Partnership Act 1890, s.3 (see *supra*, para. 5–33) and debts due to the partner's spouse or civil partner (Insolvency Act 1986, s.329, as amended by the Civil Partnership Act 2004, Sched. 27, para. 116). The latter restriction will seemingly *not* preclude a partner's spouse/civil partner from proving against the joint estate of the firm in respect of a loan to that partner and his/her co-partners jointly: see *Ex p. Nottingham* (1887) 19 Q.B.D. 88 (a decision under the Married Women's Property Act 1882, s.3).

[564] See *Re Maxwell Communications Corporation plc* [1993] 1 W.L.R. 1042, distinguishing *Halesowen Presswork Assemblies Ltd. v. National Westminster Bank Ltd.* [1972] A.C. 785 and *British Eagle International Airlines Ltd. v. Compagnie Nationale Air France* [1975] 1 W.L.R. 758 (HL). *Sed quaere*, given the definition of "postponed debt" noticed in the preceding footnote; also the Insolvency Act 1986, s.175C(5), *supra*, para. 27–84 (creditor's and member's concurrent petitions); *ibid.* s.328C(5), as amended and applied by the Insolvent Partnerships Order 1994, art. 11, Sched. 7, para. 21 (joint bankruptcy petition).

[565] *ibid.* s.175A(5)(b), (7)(b), *supra*, para. 27–82 (creditor's and member's concurrent petitions); *ibid.* s.328A(5)(b), (7)(b), as amended and applied by the Insolvent Partnerships Order 1994, art. 11, Sched. 7, para. 21 (joint bankruptcy petition).

[566] See *supra*, para. 27–111.

[567] As to joint debtors who are not partners, see *Ex p. Crosfield* (1836) 1 Deac. 405; *Ex p. Buckingham* (1840) 1 M.D. & D. 235; *Ex p. Field* (1842) 3 M.D. & D. 95.

[568] Lord Lindley went on: "The Bankruptcy Act 1883 mentions no exceptions, and it has not yet been decided that there are any; owing to the language of section 59(1) it is doubtful whether they exist in cases where one partner only is bankrupt. But it would be strange if the exceptions existed (and it is apprehended that the first three do exist) where a separate estate is administered under a joint adjudication against a firm, and not where the separate property of one partner is administered under an adjudication against himself alone." The equivalent provision under the Bankruptcy Act 1914 was s.63(1).

It has already been seen that, in certain instances, this general rule no longer holds good, albeit that the proof of the unpaid joint debts is by the responsible insolvency practitioner, rather than the joint creditors themselves.[569] Nevertheless, the principles established under the old bankruptcy laws will still be relevant in a case under which the above regime does *not* apply.[570]

Before considering the various established exceptions to the general rule, it should be noted that a joint *and separate* creditor may, in general, prove against either the joint or the separate estate, but not both.[571]

When joint creditors may compete with separate creditors

Under the old bankruptcy law, there were four cases[572] in which such competi-   **27–128**
tion was allowed, notwithstanding the general principle to which Lord Lindley referred. The current editor submits that these exceptions are equally applicable under the current insolvency legislation, save in those cases in which such proof is expressly regulated by the Insolvency Act 1986, as amended by the Insolvent Partnerships Order 1994.[573]

(i) *No joint estate*

Where there is no joint estate, the joint creditors are entitled to rank as separate   **27–129**
creditors against the separate estates of the individual partners[574]; *per contra* where there is a joint estate, however small.[575] This exception might entitle a joint creditor to rank as a separate creditor of a single bankrupt partner,[576] if there are no apparent partners who are solvent.[577] For this purpose, no account will seemingly be taken of the existence of a dormant[578] or deceased[579] partner, even though he, or his estate, may be solvent. The position will be the same where a number of firms enter into partnership together and one becomes insolvent, save only that it will be necessary for the joint creditors of the main partnership to

---

[569] See *supra*, paras 27–106, 27–125.

[570] See *supra*, para. 27–86.

[571] See *infra*, paras 27–146 *et seq.*

[572] To these should, perhaps, be added the theoretical possibility of a change of status by substitution: see *supra*, para. 27–97.

[573] See *supra*, paras 27–82 *et seq.*

[574] *Re Carpenter* (1890) 7 Morr. 270; *Re Budgett* [1894] 2 Ch. 557.

[575] *Ex p. Peake* (1814) 2 Rose 54; *Ex p. Harris* (1816) 1 Madd. 583; *Ex p. Kennedy* (1852) 2 De G.M. & G. 228. *cf. Ex p. Birley* (1841) 2 M.D. & D. 354; *Ex p. Burdekin* (1842) 2 M.D. & D. 704. It would seem that the existence of joint property which is pledged for more than its value or which cannot, for any reason, be made available for the benefit of creditors will be ignored: *Ex p. Hill* (1802) 2 Bos. & Pul.N.R. 191, note; *Ex p. Peake, supra*; *Ex p. Geller* (1817) 2 Madd. 262; but see *Ex p. Clay* (1808) 1 Mont.Part. 132, note; *Ex p. Kennedy, supra*. A joint creditor holding such a pledge must sell it or have it valued before he can claim to rank as a separate creditor; until he has done so, he cannot say that there is no joint estate: see *Ex p. Smith* (1813) 2 Rose 63; *Ex p. Barclay* (1822) 1 Gl. & J. 272. In *Ex p. Hill, supra*, the pledge had been sold, and the creditor proved for the difference.

[576] See *Ex p. Hayden* (1785) 1 Bro.C.C. 454; *Ex p. Sadler* (1808) 15 Ves.Jr. 52; *Ex p. Bradshaw* (1821) 1 Gl. & J. 99; *Ex p. Bauerman* (1838) 3 Deac. 476.

[577] See *Ex p. Kensington* (1813) 14 Ves.Jr. 447; *Ex p. Janson* (1818) 3 Madd. 229. The latter case demonstrates that, for this purpose, a person is solvent if he is not bankrupt. As to the position where the solvent partner is not in this country, see *Ex p. Pinkerton* (1801) 6 Ves.Jr. 814, note.

[578] See *Ex p. Hodgkinson* (1815) 19 Ves.Jr. 291; *Ex p. Norfolk* (1815) 19 Ves.Jr. 455; *Ex p. Chuck* (1832) 8 Bing. 469.

[579] See *Ex p. Bauerman* (1838) 3 Deac. 476. The surviving partner's separate creditors cannot insist on the joint creditors proceeding first against the deceased partner's estate: see *Ex p. Kendall* (1811) 17 Ves.Jr. 514.

show that all the partners in the solvent firms are abroad before they can prove against the insolvent firm's joint estate.[580]

If it is doubtful whether any joint estate exists, an inquiry will be directed.[581]

27–130 *Firm wound up as unregistered company.* In such a case, the liquidator has power to make calls on the partners *qua* contributories,[582] and may thereby himself constitute a joint estate where none previously existed.

27–131 *Subsequent realisation of joint estate.* If joint creditors prove against the separate estate of a partner on the footing that there is no joint estate, but such an estate is subsequently realised, they must repay any dividend received.[583]

27–132 *Joint creditors paying separate creditors.* Joint creditors can acquire a right to prove against the separate estate of any partner by paying his separate creditors the full amount of their provable debts.[584]

(ii) *Fraud*

27–133 If a partner fraudulently converts partnership property to his own use, such property cannot properly be treated as part of his separate estate. Consequently, in such a case, proof on behalf of the joint estate (and, thus, the joint creditors) is admitted against the separate estate in competition with the separate creditors,[585] even though the value of the latter estate may not have been increased by the fraud.[586]

The mere fact that one partner is indebted to the firm is naturally no proof of fraud; nor is a breach of the agreement, particularly if its provisions have habitually been ignored by the partners. What is required is an act tantamount to the theft of partnership property and a breach of good faith which has not been condoned by the other partners.[587] Any arrangement between the partners which results in the debt arising by reason of the fraud being treated as a mere matter of accounting between the partners will prevent any proof by the joint estate.[588]

(iii) *Distinct trades*

27–134 The circumstances in which a partner who carries on a distinct trade will be permitted to prove against the joint estate of his firm in competition with the joint

---

[580] *Ex p. Machel* (1813) 1 Rose 447; *Ex p. Nolte* (1826) 2 Gl. & J. 295.

[581] *Ex p. Birley* (1840) 1 M.D. & D. 387 and (1841) 2 M.D. & D. 354.

[582] See *supra*, paras 27–61 *et seq.*

[583] See *Ex p. Willock* (1816) 2 Rose 392.

[584] See *Ex p. Chandler* (1803) 9 Ves.Jr. 35; *Ex p. Taitt* (1809) 16 Ves.Jr. 193.

[585] *Ex p. Cust* (1774) Cooke's *Bankruptcy Law* (8th ed.), p. 531; *Ex p. Lodge and Fendal* (1790) 1 Ves.Jr. 166; *Ex p. Smith* (1821) 1 Gl. & J. 74; *Ex p. Watkins* (1828) Mont. & McA. 57. See also, as to the converse situation (*i.e.* where a partner's separate property is fraudulently converted to the use of the firm by his co-partners), *supra*, para. 27–116.

[586] *Lacey v. Hill* (1876) 4 Ch.D. 537, affirmed *sub nom. Read v. Bailey* (1877) 3 App.Cas. 94.

[587] See *Ex p. Yonge* (1814) 3 V. & B. 31; *Ex p. Smith* (1821) 1 Gl. & J. 74; *Ex p. Turner* (1833) 4 D. & Ch. 169; *Ex p. Crofts* (1837) 2 Deac. 102; *Ex p. Hinds* (1850) 3 De. G. & Sm. 613.

[588] See *Ex p. Turner* (1833) 4 D. & Ch. 169.

creditors have already been noticed.[589] On the same principle, the firm[590] or, if it is insolvent, the joint estate[591] will be permitted to prove against the separate estate of a partner in competition with his separate creditors, provided that he became indebted to the firm in the ordinary course of carrying on a similarly distinct trade.[592] Lord Eldon stated the principle thus: " . . . a joint trade may prove against a separate trade; but not a partner against a partner."[593]

An attempt to invoke this principle failed in *Ex p. Gliddon*,[594] where there appeared to be two wholly independent firms but, in fact, one was no more than the agent of a partner in the other and there was no such trading between the two supposed firms as was necessary to create a provable debt.[595]

(iv) *Petitioning creditor*

Where the petitioning creditor is a joint creditor, he will be permitted to prove in competition with the separate creditors.[596]   **27–135**

(c) **Rights of the partners**

One partner will not be permitted to prove against the separate estate of his co-partner if, by so doing, he will reduce the surplus available for transfer to the joint estate. Lord Lindley analysed the position in this way: **27–136**

> "The principle that a debtor shall not be allowed to compete with his own creditors, is as strictly carried out in administering the separate estates of individual partners, as in administering the joint estate of a firm. The separate estate of each partner is liable to the debts of the firm, subject only to the prior claims of his separate creditors; whence it is obvious that one partner cannot compete with the separate creditors of his co-partner, without diminishing the fund which, subject to their claims, is applicable to the payment of the joint debts, and therefore of his own creditors. In other words, the rights of the joint creditors preclude one partner from ranking as a separate creditor of his co-partner, until the joint creditors are paid in full."[597]

The same rule will in general prevent the insolvent partner's firm proving a debt against his separate estate, since this would involve a proof by that partner and his co-partners.[598]

---

[589] See *supra*, paras 27–117 *et seq.*

[590] *Ex p. Johns* (1802) Cooke's *Bankruptcy Law* (8th ed.), p. 534 and *Watson on Partnership*, p. 286; *Ex p. Hesham* (1810) 1 Rose 146; *Ex p. Castell* (1826) 2 Gl. & J. 124.

[591] *Ex p. St. Barbe* (1805) 11 Ves.Jr. 413.

[592] See *Ex p. Hargreaves* (1788) 1 Cox 440; *Ex p. Sillitoe* (1824) 1 Gl. & J. 382; *Ex p. Williams* (1843) 3 M.D. & D. 433; also *supra*, para. 27–117.

[593] *Ex p. St. Barbe* (1805) 11 Ves.Jr. 413, 414.

[594] (1884) 13 Q.B.D. 43.

[595] In fact, the real debt was owing by the principal behind the "agent" firm to himself and his co-partner.

[596] See *Ex p. Hall* (1804) 9 Ves.Jr. 349; *Ex p. Ackerman* (1808) 14 Ves.Jr. 604; *Ex p. De Tastet* (1810) 17 Ves.Jr. 247; *Ex p. Burnett* (1841) 2 M.D. & D. 357.

[597] See *Ex p. Collinge* (1863) 4 De G.J. & S. 533, where the result of such proof would have benefited the joint creditors; also *Ex p. Rawson* (1821) Jac. 274; *Ex p. Carter* (1827) 2 Gl. & J. 233; *Ex p. Ellis* (1827) 2 Gl. & J. 312; *Ex p. Robinson* (1834) 4 D. & Ch. 499; *Ex p. May* (1838) 3 Deac. 382.

[598] See *Ex p. Smith* (1821) 1 Gl. & J. 74; *Ex p. Turner* (1833) 4 D. & Ch. 169.

In those cases in which the unpaid joint debts are, in any event, provable against the separate estates of the partners,[599] the rule is now give statutory force.[600]

When co-partners can compete with separate creditors

27–137   Notwithstanding the rule described in the preceding paragraph, there are a number of circumstances in which a co-partner will be permitted to prove in competition with the separate creditors, albeit that only the second and third are recognised by sections 175C(2) and 328C(2) of the Insolvency Act 1986, as amended by the Insolvent Partnerships Order 1994.[601]

(i) *Joint creditors not prejudiced*

27–138   If it can be shown that proof by the co-partner will not involve competition with the joint creditors, there will be no reason to invoke the rule and competition with the separate creditors will be allowed. The fact that the latter will thereby be prejudiced is of no relevance, since the rule was not developed for their benefit. There will be no competition with the joint creditors in the following cases:

27–139   *No joint debts.* If there never were any joint debts or such joint debts as there were have ceased to exist,[602] because they have been paid or satisfied, statute-barred or converted into separate debts,[603] proof will be allowed.[604] It is not, however, sufficient for the co-partner merely to offer an indemnity against such debts.[605]

This exception would seem to be equally applicable in those cases in which proof is regulated by the Insolvency Act 1986, as amended by the Insolvent Partnerships Order 1994.[606]

27–140   *Separate estate insolvent.* If the separate estate is clearly insufficient to pay the separate debts, excluding that owed to the co-partner, there will be no possibility of any surplus being transferred to the joint estate for the benefit of the joint creditors and the co-partner's proof will be allowed.[607] No objection can be taken to such proof on the grounds that the dividends received will eventually go to swell the surplus of the co-partner's separate estate divisible among the joint creditors.[608]

---

[599] See *supra*, paras 27–106, 27–125.

[600] Insolvency Act 1986, s.175C(2), *supra*, para. 27–84 (creditor's and member's concurrent petitions); *ibid.* s.328C(2), as amended and applied by the Insolvent Partnerships Order 1994, art. 11, Sched. 7, para. 21 (joint bankruptcy petition).

[601] See *supra*, n. 600.

[602] It appears to be sufficient to show that the joint debts have not been, and are not likely to be, proved: see *Ex p. Andrews* (1884) 25 Ch.D. 505.

[603] See *Ex p. Grazebrook* (1832) 2 D. & Ch. 186.

[604] *Ex p. Grazebrook, supra*; *Ex p. Head* [1894] 1 Q.B. 638. See also *Ex p. Hall* (1838) 3 Deac. 125; *Ex p. Gill* (1863) 9 Jur.(N.S.) 1303. In *Ex p. Dodgson* (1830) Mont. & MacA. 445, there were no joint debts; similarly in *Ex p. Davis* (1863) 4 De G.J. & S. 523.

[605] *Ex p. Moore* (1826) 2 Gl. & J. 166. *cf.* the earlier cases: *Ex p. Taylor* (1814) 2 Rose 175; *Ex p. Ogilvy* (1814) 2 Rose 177.

[606] See *supra*, paras 27–82 *et seq.*

[607] *Ex p. Topping* (1865) 4 De G.J. & S. 551; *Ex p. Head* [1894] 1 Q.B. 638. See also *Ex p. Sheen* (1877) 6 Ch.D. 235, where the proof was by a person who had held himself out as a partner.

[608] *Ex p. Head, supra*.

This exception will clearly be inapplicable where, by virtue of the Insolvent Partnerships Order 1994, the joint debts can be proved against the separate estates of insolvent partners.[609]

Co-partner paying joint debts. If the co-partner has paid the joint debts, he will   **27–141** be entitled to prove as a separate creditor for the amount of the share which the insolvent partner ought to have paid.[610]

Where the right to prove is established, it will generally be necessary to take the partnership accounts before the proof is admitted, since the alleged debt may in fact not exist.[611]

There would seem to be no reason in principle why the same exception should not exist where proof is regulated by the Insolvency Act 1986, as amended by the Insolvent Partnerships Order 1994.[612]

(ii) *Fraud*

The right of proof in the case of the fraudulent conversion of partnership property   **27–142** has already been noted.[613]

In addition, where a person is fraudulently induced to enter into partnership, he may prove against the separate estate of the person who practised the fraud for any amount paid to him as consideration for admission to the partnership.[614]

---

[609] See *supra*, paras 27–106, 27–125.

[610] See *Wood v. Dodgson* (1813) 2 M. & S. 195; *Ex p. Watson* (1819) 4 Madd. 477; *Ex p. Carpenter* (1826) Mont. & MacA. 1. In the first two cases the partner who had paid the debts had retired and been indemnified against them by the bankrupt partner. It seemingly does not matter whether the debts were paid before or after the insolvency order: *ibid.* See also *Ex p. Young* (1814) 2 Rose 40; *Parker v. Ramsbottom* (1824) 3 B. & C. 257; *Moody v. King* (1825) 2 B. & C. 558. It should be noted that the amount provable is not calculated merely by reference to the partners' respective shares, with no account being taken of their ability to pay; rather, each partner is liable to contribute not only his own share of the debts but also a share of any amount due from the other partners, which they are unable to contribute, *i.e.* those who can pay must make up for those who cannot: see *Ex p. Hunter* (1820) Buck 552; *Ex p. Moore* (1826) 2 Gl. & J. 166; *Ex p. Plowden* (1837) 2 Deac. 456. *cf.* the position when settling accounts as between partners: see *supra*, paras 25–50 *et seq.*

[611] See *Ex p. Maude* (1867) L.R. 2 Ch.App. 550; and note *Ex p. Grazebrook* (1832) 2 D. & Ch. 186.

[612] Insolvency Act 1986, ss.175C(2) (*supra*, para. 27–84) or 328C(2) (as amended and applied by the Insolvent Partnerships Order 1994, art. 11, Sched. 7, para. 21) will clearly have no application in such a case.

[613] See further, *supra*, para. 27–133. And see *Ex p. Yonge* (1814) 3 V. & B. 31 and 2 Rose 40.

[614] Lord Lindley observed that: "At one time it was supposed that when a person had been induced by the fraud of another to join him in partnership, the former could not, on the bankruptcy of the latter, prove against his separate estate, for the amount paid to the bankrupt as a consideration for the partnership. This opinion was founded on the case of *Ex p. Broome* [(1811) 1 Rose 69]. There A was induced, by the false and fraudulent representations of B, to enter into partnership with him, and to pay him a considerable premium. Shortly afterwards B became bankrupt, and A sought to recover out of B's estate the amount of the premium paid as above mentioned. According to the report this was refused, upon the ground that, although A might be entitled to recover the money as between himself and B, yet he was liable with B to third persons, *viz.* the creditors of the firm. The report of this case, however, is not warranted by the order which was actually made in it. [*See the order in (1845) 1 Coll. 598.*] Indeed, the order expressly directed that A should be at liberty to prove against B's estate, and that A should be paid a dividend in respect of his proof, rateably with B's other creditors. This order is in conformity with the opinion expressed by Lord Thurlow in *Ex p. Lodge and Fendal* [(1790) 1 Ves.Jr. 166], and with the cases of *Hamil v. Stokes* [(1817) 4 Price 161] and *Bury v. Allen* [(1845) 1 Coll. 589]."

(iii) *Distinct Trades*

27–143 The circumstances in which proof for a debt contracted by a partner in the normal course of carrying on a distinct trade will be allowed have already been noted.[615]

Partnership not yet commenced

27–144 If a person intends to enter into partnership with another but does not ultimately do so, he may prove against the latter's separate estate for any advances he may have made in anticipation of such partnership, provided that he has not permitted himself to be held out as a partner.[616]

Surplus of separate estate

27–145 Once all his separate creditors have been paid, the surplus in a partner's separate estate will be transferred to the joint estate. If he was in fact a member of several insolvent firms, that surplus must be divided between the various joint estates in proportion to the amount of the debts proved against each such estate.[617]

  No such transfer will, obviously, fall to be made where the unpaid joint debts have been proved against the separate estate in competition with the separate creditors.[618]

C. PROOF AGAINST BOTH JOINT AND SEPARATE ESTATES

Rights of joint and separate creditors

27–146 It has already been seen that partners will only rarely be treated as having undertaken joint and several liability to creditors of the firm, thus giving the latter the option of suing all the partners jointly or one or more of them separately.[619] Nevertheless, under the old bankruptcy law, special considerations affected the right of proof of such joint and separate creditors and it is possible that such considerations may still be of relevance under the current insolvency legislation.

The general rule

27–147 The general rule was formulated by Lord Lindley in this way:

  " . . . a person to whom the members of a firm are bound jointly and severally is not allowed in bankruptcy to rank as a creditor both against the joint estate and also

---

[615] See *Ex p. Maude* (1867) L.R. 2 Ch. 550; also *supra*, paras 27–117 *et seq.*, 27–134.

[616] *Ex p. Turquand* (1841) 2 M.D. & D. 339, *supra*, para. 27–121. Note also *Ex p. Megarey* (1845) De Gex. 167. The position will be no different where proof is regulated by the Insolvency Act 1986, as amended and applied by the Insolvent Partnerships Order 1994 (see *supra*, paras 27–82 *et seq.*), since *ibid.* s.175C(2) (*supra*, para. 27–84, in the case of a creditor's or member's concurrent petition) or 328C(2) (as amended and applied by the Insolvent Partnerships Order 1994, art. 11, Sched. 7, para. 21 in the case of a joint bankruptcy petition) will clearly not apply.

[617] *Ex p. Franklyn* (1819) Buck 332.

[618] See *supra*, paras 27–106, 27–125. And note the terms of the Insolvency Act 1986, s.175A(9), *supra*, para. 27–82 (creditor's and member's concurrent petitions); *ibid.* 328A(9), as amended and applied by the Insolvent Partnerships Order 1994, art. 11, Sched. 7, para. 21 (joint bankruptcy petition).

[619] See *supra*, paras 13–02 *et seq.*

against the separate estates, or any of them; he is compelled to elect whether he will rank as a joint creditor or as a separate creditor.[620] If he elects to rank as a joint creditor he must, like other joint creditors, go in the first place against the joint estate, and he has no greater rights than they against the separate estates, or any of them; whilst, on the other hand, if he elects to rank as a separate creditor he must, like other separate creditors, confine himself in the first place to the separate estate, and he has no greater rights than they to the joint estate."[621]

An election was required even though the creditor became a joint creditor under one instrument and a separate creditor under another, provided that the debt was one and the same.[622] The position was, however, otherwise if the creditor could not properly be regarded as a joint and separate creditor. Thus, if, following a dissolution, one partner agreed to take over all the firm's debts, that arrangement would not affect a creditor of the firm unless he acceded to it: only when he had done so could he properly be treated as a separate creditor of that partner.[623]

Where an election was required to be made, the creditor was entitled to know how the joint and separate estates stood before being forced to make a binding election.[624]

Exceptions to the general rule

The general rule was originally subject to an exception in the case of separate trades[625] but was effectively abolished, as regards contracts, by the Bankruptcy Acts,[626] so much so that Lord Lindley observed: **27–148**

"The old rule against double proof still remains; but it is now subject to so large a class of exceptions as to render the rule itself practically of little consequence."

Accordingly, the application of the rule was in real terms confined to torts, frauds, etc., and breaches of trust.

Position under Insolvency Act 1986

In those cases in which the priority of debts if governed by the provisions of the Insolvency Act 1986, as amended by the Insolvent Partnerships Order   **27–149**

---

[620] See *Ex p. Rowlandson* (1735) 3 P.W. 405; *Ex p. Banks* (1740) 1 Atk. 106; *Ex p. Bond* (1742) 1 Atk. 98; *Ex p. Bevan* (1804) 10 Ves.Jr. 106; *Ex p. Hay* (1808) 15 Ves.Jr. 4.

[621] *Ex p. Bevan* (1804) 10 Ves.Jr. 106; *Bradley v. Millar* (1812) 1 Rose 273.

[622] *Ex p. Hill* (1837) 2 Deac. 249.

[623] *Ex p. Freeman* (1819) Buck 471; *Ex p. Fry* (1821) 1 Gl. & J. 96; see also *supra*, para. 27–97.

[624] Lord Lindley summarised the rights of the creditor thus: " . . . in order to make his election he must have a reasonable time to inquire into the state of the different funds. He is entitled to defer his election until a dividend is declared, or at least until the trustee is possessed of a fund to make a dividend": see Cooke's *Bankruptcy Law* (8th ed.), p. 275; *Ex p. Bond* (1742) 1 Atk. 98; *Ex p. Bentley* (1790) 2 Cox 218; *Ex p. Bolton* (1816) 2 Rose 389. It appears that the creditor ought properly to have proved against both estates, but elected before taking a dividend: *Ex p. Bentley* (1790) 2 Cox 218; and see also *Ex p. Bielby* (1806) 13 Ves.Jr. 70; *Ex p. Masson* (1811) 1 Rose 159; *Ex p. Dixon* (1841) 2 M.D. & D. 312. Presentation of a joint petition against a firm was regarded as a prima facie election to be treated as a joint creditor; *per contra* in the case of a separate petition against one of the partners: *Ex p. Bolton* (1816) 2 Rose 390, 391 *per* Lord Eldon; see also, as to withdrawing a joint proof, *Ex p. Chandler* (1884) 13 Q.B.D. 50.

[625] See *Ex p. Adam* (1813) 1 V. & B. 493; *Ex p. Bigg* (1814) 2 Rose 37.

[626] Bankruptcy Act 1861, s.152; Bankruptcy Act 1869, s.37; Bankruptcy Act 1883, Sched. II, r. 18; Bankruptcy Act 1914, Sched. 2, r. 19.

1994,[627] an unpaid joint creditor's debt will be provable against an insolvent partner's separate estate in competition with his separate creditors.[628] It follows that there would be no benefit in a creditor electing to be treated as a separate creditor, even assuming that such an election were required.

Secured joint and separate creditors

27–150   Even where the rule against double proof applied, a joint and separate creditor with a security for his debt had two options, summarised by Lord Lindley in the following terms:

> "1. He may prove for his whole debt against the estate to which the security does not belong, and retain and make what he can of his security[629]; or
>
> 2. He may give up his security; prove for the whole debt due on it (*i.e.*, the whole secured debt) against the estate to which the security belongs, and then prove for the residue of his debt against the other estate: thus in fact splitting his demand and proving for part against the joint estate, and for the residue against the separate estates of the partners, or *vice versa*."[630]

The considerations would be different if such options continued to be available in a case where the priority of debts is governed by the Insolvency Act 1986, as amended by the Insolvent Partnerships Order,[631] since the joint debts might be provable against the separate estates of the partners in any event.[632]

9.   VOLUNTARY ARRANGEMENTS WITH CREDITORS

Partnership voluntary arrangements

27–151   The Insolvent Partnerships Order 1994 for the first time extended the voluntary arrangement regime to partnerships as opposed to individual and corporate partners but its application was substantially amended in 2002.[633] Thus, where a partnership is insolvent it is now possible to propose a partnership voluntary arrangement[634] (PVA), under which a nominee qualified to act as an insolvency

---

[627] See *supra*, paras 27–82 *et seq.*

[628] See *supra*, paras 27–106, 27–125.

[629] As in *Ex p. Groom* (1837) 2 Deac. 265; *Ex p. Bate* (1838) 3 Deac. 358; *Ex p. Smyth* (1839) 3 Deac. 597. Lord Lindley observed in a footnote at this point that "He can now, it is apprehended, prove against the other estate for the difference between his debt and the value of the security."

[630] *Ex p. Ladbroke* (1826) 2 Gl. & J. 81; *Ex p. Hill* (1837) 2 Deac. 249.

[631] See *supra*, paras 27–82 *et seq.*

[632] See *supra*, paras 27–106, 27–125.

[633] Insolvent Partnerships Order 1994, art. 4, Sched. 1, as respectively amended/substituted by the Insolvent Partnerships (Amendment) (No. 2) Order 2002, arts 4, 6, Sched. 1 and further amended by the Insolvent Partnerships (Amendment) Order 2005, art. 6. Note, however, that the 1994 Order will only apply to a partnership which the court has jurisdiction to wind up: *ibid.* art. 1(2)(a).

[634] As to the type of arrangement which is capable of being approved, see *I.R.C. v. Adams, The Times*, August 2, 1999 (a decision concerning *company* voluntary arrangements); also generally, as to the nature of a voluntary arrangement, *Johnson v. Davies* [1999] Ch. 117 (CA). And see *infra*, paras 27–155, 27–156.

practitioner[635] will supervise the implementation of the proposed scheme of arrangement.[636]

It should, however, be noted that the take up rate for PVAs appears to have been low.[637]

Who may propose a PVA

Although a PVA can be proposed by the partners,[638] this option is not available where an administration order is in force,[639] where the firm is being wound up as an unregistered company[640] or where an order has been made on a joint bankruptcy petition.[641] In any such case, the proposal must be made by the administrator, liquidator or trustee of the firm.[642] **27–152**

In the absence of a provision in the partnership agreement authorising a PVA to be proposed on a majority vote, the unanimous agreement of the partners will seemingly be required.[643] It should be noted that a person who is merely held out as a partner, whilst not a partner in law,[644] will be regarded as a member of the firm for this purpose.[645] However, this does not, as such, confer any voting rights on him unless he is entitled to exercise such rights under the agreement, as will sometimes be the case.[646]

Moratorium

An insolvent partnership which satisfies two or more of the qualifying conditions during the year ending with the date on which the application documents are filed or in the tax year ended next before that date may apply for a moratorium with a view to putting a voluntary arrangement in place.[647] Those qualifying conditions are that the firm's turnover must not be more than £5.8 million, its assets must not be more than £2.8 million and it must have not more **27–153**

---

[635] See, as to such qualification, the Insolvency Act 1986, Pt XIII, as applied by the Insolvent Partnerships Order 1994, art. 4(2), (3) (as amended *supra*, n. 633).

[636] *ibid.* s.1(2), as amended and applied by the Insolvent Partnerships Order 1994, art. 4(1), Sched. 1, Pt 1 (as amended *supra*, n. 633).

[637] For a recent decision involving a PVA, see *Firth v. Everitt* [2007] EWHC 1979 (Ch) (Lawtel 25/9/07). However, no general principles can be derived therefrom.

[638] Insolvency Act 1986, s.1(1), as amended and applied by the Insolvent Partnerships Order 1994, art. 4(1), Sched. 1, Pt 1 (as amended *supra*, n. 633).

[639] See *infra*, paras 27–160 *et seq.*

[640] Whether or not with concurrent petitions presented against one or more partners: see *supra*, paras 27–08 *et seq.* (winding up without concurrent petitions), 27–27 *et seq.* (winding up with concurrent petitions).

[641] See *supra*, para. 27–44.

[642] Insolvency Act 1986, s.1(3), as amended and applied by the Insolvent Partnerships Order 1994, art. 4(1), Sched. 1, Pt 1 (as amended *supra*, para. 27–151, n. 633).

[643] It is not considered that such a decision could properly be described as an "ordinary matter connected with the partnership business", thus falling within the Partnership Act 1890, s.24(8): see further as to this subsection, *supra*, paras 15–04 *et seq.*

[644] See *supra*, paras 5–35 *et seq.*

[645] See the definition of "member" in the Insolvent Partnerships Order 1994, art. 2(1), as inserted in the Insolvency Act 1986, s.436 by *ibid.* art. 2(2).

[646] *e.g.* in the case of so-called "salaried" partners: see *supra*, para. 5–54.

[647] Insolvency Act 1986, s.1A(1)–(3), Sched. A1, para. 3(1), (2), as substituted and applied by the Insolvent Partnerships Order 1994, art. 4(1), Sched. 1, Pt II (as amended *supra*, para. 27–151, n. 633). As to the procedure, see the Insolvency Act 1986, Sched. A1, Pt II as applied by *ibid.* art. 4(1) (as amended) and read subject to the Insolvency Act 1986, s.1A(2)(b), (7), as substituted and applied by *ibid.* art. 4(1), Sched. 1, Pt I (as amended).

than 50 employees on average during the relevant period.[648] However, a partnership will not be eligible for a moratorium if, predictably, it is not in a position to propose a PVA in the first place[649] or in a number of other specified events.[650]

A moratorium will protect the firm, *inter alia*, against the presentation of a winding up or joint bankruptcy petition, the making of an administration application or a winding up or administration order, enforcement of any security over the partnership property, the commencement or continuation of proceedings (save with the permission of the court) or, more significantly, an application or order for a dissolution under section 35 of the Partnership Act 1890.[651]

Nominee's report

27–154 Where the partners are *not* proposing to apply for a moratorium[652] then, unless the PVA is proposed by the administrator/liquidator/trustee, the nominee must within 28 days[653] prepare and submit a report to the court, stating whether in his opinion the proposed PVA has a "reasonable prospect" of being approved and implemented and whether in his opinion meetings of the partners and of the firm's creditors[654] should be summoned to consider and, if appropriate, approve the PVA and, if so, when.[655] In preparing his report the nominee will take into account the statement of affairs and other information required to be supplied to him by the partners with the original proposal.[656] The nominee may be replaced if he fails to produce such a report or if it is either impracticable or inappropriate for him to continue to act as such.[657]

Approval of the PVA

27–155 A PVA will only have effect if it is approved by separate meetings of the partners and of the firm's creditors,[658] but may be modified before such approval is obtained.[659] However, it must not alter the priority of the preferential debts of

---

[648] *ibid.* Sched. A1, para. 3(3)–(7), as substituted and applied by *ibid.*

[649] See *supra*, para. 27–152.

[650] *ibid.* Sched. A1, para. 4(1), as substituted and applied by *ibid.* The other events are if: (a) an agricultural receiver has been appointed, (b) a voluntary arrangement is already in effect, (c) a provisional liquidator has been appointed, (d) a moratorium has already been in force during the preceding 12 months and either no PVA had effect when it came to an end or any PVA has come to an end prematurely, (e) a PVA was in effect but during the preceding 12 months has come to an end prematurely and a stay of insolvency proceedings has been ordered under *ibid.* s.5(3)(a) (as substituted and applied by *ibid.*), and (f) orders have been made on a joint bankruptcy petition presented by the individual partners.

[651] *ibid.* Sched. A1, para. 12(1), as substituted and applied by *ibid.* See further, as to applications under s.35 of the 1890 Act, *supra*, paras 24–47 *et seq.*

[652] See *supra*, para. 27–153.

[653] Or such longer period as the court allows.

[654] The creditors will only comprise those persons of whom the nominee is aware: Insolvency Act 1986, s.3(3), as amended and applied by the Insolvent Partnerships Order 1994, art. 4(1), Sched. 1, Pt 1 (as amended *supra*, para. 27–151, n. 633).

[655] *ibid.*, s.2(1), (2), as amended and applied by *ibid.* The nominee must also state whether there are any insolvency proceedings on foot against the firm or any of the partners: *ibid.* s.2(3), as amended and applied by *ibid.*

[656] *ibid.* s.2(4), as amended and applied by *ibid.*

[657] *ibid.* s.2(5), as amended and applied by *ibid.*

[658] *ibid.* ss.3, 4(1), as amended and applied by *ibid.*

[659] *ibid.* s.4(1), (2), as amended and applied by *ibid.* See also *supra*, para. 27–151, n. 634.

the partnership nor must it prefer one preferential creditor over another, without the express consent of the creditors affected.[660] Similarly, it must not affect the rights of a secured creditor without his concurrence.[661]

A PVA requires the approval of at least 75 per cent of the creditors by value.[662] If a creditor's debt is of an unliquidated or unascertained amount, it will, for voting purposes, now be valued at £1, unless the chairman of the meeting agrees to place a higher value on it.[663]

In addition, the PVA must also be approved by a simple majority of the partners, voting in accordance with the terms of the partnership agreement or, if the agreement is silent, in proportion to their interests in the partnership.[664] It has already been seen that a person who is merely held out as a partner will be treated as a member for certain purposes,[665] but will not have a vote on this issue.[666]

27–156

If decisions to approve the PVA are taken at both the partners' and creditors' meetings in the same terms, the approval will naturally have effect,[667] but if those decisions are taken in *different* terms, then the decision taken at the creditors' meeting will have effect,[668] unless a partner applies to the court within 28 days and the court thereupon orders that the decision at the partners' meeting will have effect or makes such other order as it sees fit.[669] If the firm is or has been authorised under the Financial Services and Markets Act 2000, an appointed representative thereunder or carrying on a regulated business in breach of that Act, the Financial Services Authority is entitled to be heard on such an application.[670] It is an offence to make false representations with a view to obtaining approval to a PVA.[671]

Effect of approval

Once the PVA has been approved, it becomes binding on all the partners and on any person who was entitled to vote at the creditors' meeting, whether or not he actually attended it, or who would have been entitled to such a vote if he had

27–157

---

[660] *ibid.* s.4(4), as amended and applied by *ibid.* As to what debts are preferential, see *ibid.* s.386, Sched. 6, as respectively amended by the Enterprise Act 2002, s.251(1), (3), Sched. 26.

[661] *ibid.* s.4(3), as amended and applied by *ibid.* See *Peck v. Craighead* [1995] B.C.L.C. 337 (a decision under *ibid.* s.258(4)); also *Hylands v. McClintock* [1999] N.I. 28 (a decision under equivalent provision of the Insolvency (Northern Ireland) Order 1989).

[662] Insolvency Rules 1986, rr. 1.17, 1.19 (as amended), as applied by the Insolvent Partnerships Order 1994, art. 18(1), Sched. 10 and read subject to *ibid.* art. 3. And see also, as to the procedure at the meeting, *ibid.* r.1.17A, as substituted by the Insolvency (Amendment) (No. 2) Rules 2002, Sched., Pt I, para. 8.

[663] Insolvency Rules 1986, r. 1.17(3), as substituted by *ibid.* Note that, in certain circumstances, it may be possible to split a debt, so that the creditor can, as to part, vote on (and be bound by) the arrangement, but not as to the balance: see *Re K.G. Hoare* [1997] B.P.I.R. 683.

[664] *ibid.* r. 1.18(1), 1.20(1), as amended by the Insolvency (Amendment) Rules 1987 (SI 1987/1919), Sched., Pt I, para. 5.

[665] See *supra*, para. 27–152.

[666] This is the result of the revocation of the Insolvency Rules 1986, rr. 1.18(2), 1.20(2) by the Insolvency (Amendment) (No. 2) Rules 2002, Sched., Pt I, para. 10.

[667] Insolvency Act 1986, s.4A(2)(a), as amended and applied by the Insolvent Partnerships Order 1994, Sched. 1, Pt I (as amended *supra*, para. 27–151, n. 633).

[668] *ibid.* s.4A(2)(b) as amended and applied by *ibid.*

[669] *ibid.* s.4A(3), (4), (6) as amended and applied by *ibid.*

[670] *ibid.* s.4A(5), (7), as amended and applied by *ibid.*

[671] *ibid.* s.6A, as amended and applied by *ibid.*

had notice of the meeting.[672] The court will then have power to discharge any administrator previously appointed or to stay further proceedings under any insolvency order made against the firm and/or the partners[673] or to give directions for the implementation of the arrangement with respect thereto.[674] It should, however, be noted that a person who was deprived of his right to vote by reason of not having had notice of the creditor's meeting will still be entitled to any sum due to him when the PVA ceases to have effect provided that it did not come to an end prematurely.[675]

The supervisor of the PVA[676] will be responsible for implementation of the arrangement and may seek directions from the court as and when it is appropriate to do so.[677] This will include, in an appropriate case, directions as to his remuneration.[678]

Company and individual voluntary arrangements

27–158   The Insolvency Act 1986 contains detailed provisions governing voluntary arrangements entered into by insolvent companies[679] and individuals,[680] whether before or after insolvency orders are made, and these provisions are, naturally, applicable to corporate and individual partners,[681] including those cases in which orders are made against the firm and one or more partners on concurrent petitions[682] or on all the partners on a joint bankruptcy petition.[683] In the former case, references in the Act to the creditors of the relevant corporate or individual partner will include references to the creditors of the partnership.[684]

The detailed procedure applicable to such voluntary arrangements is outside the scope of the present work. It should, however, be noted that it *may* be possible to bring partnership debts under a company or individual voluntary arrangement where no order is made for the winding up of the firm,[685] but this would not, in

---

[672] Insolvency Act 1986, s.5(1), (2), as amended and applied by the Insolvent Partnerships Order 1994, art. 4(1), Sched. 1, Pt 1 (as amended *supra*, para. 27–151, n. 633). Note, however, the decision in *K.G. Hoare, supra*. And see also, as to the rights of a creditor, partner or other specified person (including someone who was not give notice of the creditor's meeting and was thereby deprived of his right to vote) who feels that the arrangement unfairly prejudices the interests of a creditor, partner or contributory or that the meetings were conducted irregularly, *ibid.* s.6, as amended and applied by *ibid.*

[673] *ibid.* s.5(3)(a), as amended and applied by *ibid.* This will include a case where an order has been made against one or more partners on a concurrent petition (see *supra*, paras 27–24 *et seq.*) or on a joint bankruptcy petition (see *infra*, para. 27–44). Note that the orders against the partners must have been made in "related insolvency proceedings": *ibid.* s.5(3)(a)(i).

[674] *ibid.* s.5(3)(b), as amended and applied by *ibid.*

[675] *ibid.* s.5(2A), as amended and applied by *ibid.*

[676] *ibid.* s.7(2), as amended and applied by *ibid.*

[677] *ibid.* s.7(4), as amended and applied by *ibid.* A creditor or other person may apply to the court if dissatisfied with the supervisor's conduct of the arrangement: *ibid.* s.7(3).

[678] See *Re Pinson Wholesale Ltd.* [2008] B.C.C. 112. Note that the court reached its decision on the basis that the CVA in question could properly be regarded as including an implied term as to the supervisor's remuneration.

[679] Insolvency Act 1986, Pt I, ss.1 *et seq.*

[680] *ibid.* Pt VIII, ss.252 *et seq.*

[681] Insolvent Partnerships Order 1994, art. 5(2).

[682] See *supra*, paras 27–24 *et seq.*

[683] See *supra*, para. 27–44.

[684] Insolvent Partnerships Order 1994, art. 5(1).

[685] See the tentative views voiced by Sir Thomas Bingham M.R. in *Re Cupit* [1996] B.P.I.R. 560, 564. Note, however, that these views were expressed at a time when the Insolvent Partnerships Order 1986 was still in force.

general, prevent a creditor proceeding against the other partners in respect of a partnership debt for which they are jointly liable.[686]

Interlocking PVA and company/individual voluntary arrangements

It should be noted that, in many cases, a PVA will only be approved by the partnership creditors if the partners also enter into individual or company voluntary arrangements; otherwise, the separate estates of the partners will not be subject to the voluntary arrangement regime.[687]   **27–159**

10.   PARTNERSHIP ADMINISTRATION ORDERS

The ability of the court to make an administration order in respect of a partnership was again introduced for the first time by the Insolvent Partnerships Order 1994,[688] but, following the substantial reform of the company administration procedure by the Enterprise Act 2002,[689] the revised procedure[690] is applied to partnerships with appropriate modifications by that Order in an updated form.[691] Provision is contained in the Banking Act 2009 for the modified administration procedure under Part 3 of that Act (banking administration orders) to be applied to banking partnerships, but this power has not yet been exercised.[692]   **27–160**

Jurisdiction and power to appoint administrator

Under the new procedure, an administration order can only be made in relation to a partnership if the court is satisfied that the partnership is unable to pay its debts[693] and that the order is "reasonably likely to achieve the purpose of administration".[694] The purpose of administration is, in essence, to rescue the partnership, to achieve a better result for its creditors than a winding up or to   **27–161**

---

[686] *Johnson v. Davies* [1999] Ch. 117 (CA). *Per contra*, if the arrangement effects a release of the solvent partners: *ibid.* See also *Re Goldspan Ltd.* [2003] B.P.I.R. 93.

[687] It should be noted that no interlocking IVAs had been proposed in *Firth v. Everitt* [2007] EWHC 1979 (Ch) (Lawtel 25/9/07).

[688] Insolvent Partnerships Order 1994, art. 6.

[689] s.248, Sched. 16.

[690] As set out in the Insolvency Act 1986, Pt II, Sched. B1.

[691] Insolvent Partnerships Order 1994, art. 6, Sched. 2, as respectively substituted by the Insolvent Partnerships (Amendment) Order 2005 (SI 2005/1516), arts 3, 7, Sched. 1 and, in the case of Sched. 2 only, as further amended by the Insolvent Partnerships (Amendment) Order 2006 (SI 2006/622), art. 5.

[692] Banking Act 2009, s.163(1).

[693] Insolvency Act 1986, Sched. B1, para. 11(a), as substituted and applied by the Insolvent Partnerships Order 1994, art. 6(1), Sched. 2, para. 5 (as amended: see *supra*, n. 691). Note that this does not import *ibid.* ss.222 and 223, as amended and applied by the Insolvent Partnerships Order 1994, art. 7(1) (as amended), (2), Sched. 3, Pt I, paras 4, 5 or, for that matter, *ibid.* s.222 as applied by *ibid.* art. 8(1) (as amended), (2), Sched. 4, Pt I, para. 3. Note that, unlike the equivalent provision applicable to companies, a *likelihood* of an inability to pay debts is not sufficient: see, as to the distinction, *Re H.S. Smith, The Times*, January 6, 1999, noticed *infra*. And see, generally, *Ice Media International Ltd. (In Liquidation) v Q3 Media Ltd.* [2006] B.P.I.R. 1219 (albeit a company case). As to the position where there is a disputed debt or cross claim, see *Hammonds (a Firm) v. Pro-Fit USA Ltd.* [2008] 2 B.C.L.C. 159.

[694] Insolvency Act 1986, Sched. B1, para. 11(b), as substituted and applied by *ibid.* As to the effect of this test, see *Ice Media International Ltd. (In Liquidation) v Q3 Media Ltd.*, *supra*; *Auto Management Services Ltd. v. Oracle Fleet UK Ltd.* [2008] B.C.C. 761.

realise property with a view to making a distribution to one or more secured or preferential creditors.[695] The second of these purposes was successfully relied on in *DKLL Solicitors v. Her Majesty's Revenue and Customs*,[696] where an order was sought by two equity partners in order to facilitate a sale of the partnership business at a favourable price. Petitions against the partnership and the two partners were pending at the time the order was made. The court relied heavily on the evidence of one of the proposed administrators as to the benefits to be derived from the proposed sale. It goes without saying that an application which is made when there is no genuine belief that the above statutory purpose can be achieved will be struck out.[697]

In this context, a partnership will still be regarded as unable to pay its debts where one or more of the partners are solvent and could afford to pay those debts out of their separate estates.[698]

It should be noted that an administrator of a partnership may also be appointed outside court by the holder of an agricultural floating charge or by the partners.[699] In the latter case, the appointment cannot be made within 12 months of a previous appointment.[700]

However, no administrator can in general be appointed, by the court or otherwise, where the partnership is already in administration,[701] or after an order has been made on a joint bankruptcy petition or for the winding up of the partnership as an unregistered company.[702]

Application for administration order and appointment of an administrator outside court

27–162   The application must be made by a petition in the prescribed form[703] and may be presented by the partners, one or more partnership creditors or any combination of them.[704] In the case of the partners, the decision to present such a petition must be taken in accordance with the partnership agreement; otherwise, it would seem to require their unanimous agreement.[705]

---

[695] See *ibid*. Sched. B1, para. 3, as applied by *ibid*. art. 6(1) (as amended: see *supra*, n. 691).

[696] [2007] B.C.C. 908. This was a so-called "pre-pack" administration order, where the sale arrangements had already been agreed when the order was sought; see also *Re Halliwells LLP* (2010) L.S. Gaz., August 19, p.14. *cf. Clydesdale Financial Services v. Smailes* [2009] B.C.C. 810, where the circumstances caused the court to remove the administrator who had been appointed (this decision concerned an LLP).

[697] *Re West Park Golf & Country Club* [1997] 1 B.C.L.C. 20.

[698] *Re H.S. Smith, supra.*

[699] *ibid*. Sched. B1, paras 2(b), (c), 14, 22, as substituted and applied by *ibid*. art. 6(1), Sched. 2, paras 2, 7, 9 (as amended: see *supra*, para. 27–160, n. 691).

[700] *ibid*. Sched. B1, para. 23(2), as substituted and applied by *ibid*. art. 6(1), Sched. 2, para. 10 (as amended: see *supra*, para. 27–160, n. 691).

[701] *ibid*. Sched. B1, para. 7, as substituted and applied by *ibid*. art. 6(1), Sched. 2, para. 3 (as amended: see *supra*, para. 27–160, n. 691).

[702] *ibid*. Sched. B1, para. 8, as substituted and applied by *ibid*. art. 6(1), Sched. 2, para. 4 (as amended: see *supra*, para. 27–160, n. 691).

[703] The form of the petition is set out in the Insolvent Partnerships Order 1994, Sched. 9, Form 1, as substituted by the Insolvent Partnerships (Amendment) Order 2002, art. 6, Sched.

[704] Insolvency Act 1986, Sched. B1, para. 12(1), as substituted and applied by the Insolvent Partnerships Order 1994, art. 6(1), Sched. 2, para. 6 (as amended: see *supra*, para. 27–160, n. 691).

[705] As in the case of a partnership voluntary arrangement (see *supra*, para. 27–152), the current editor considers that the decision to apply for an administration order would not fall within the Partnership Act 1890, s.24(8) (ordinary matters connected with the partnership business). *Per contra*, perhaps, in the case of a limited partnership: *Re Kaupthing Capital Partners II Master LP Inc.* [2010] EWHC 836 (Ch), which concerned a Guernsey limited partnership.

Notice of the petition must be given to any person who has appointed or is entitled to appoint an agricultural receiver, to anyone else who is entitled to appoint an administrator as the holder of an qualifying agricultural floating charge and to any other prescribed person.[706] If such a receiver is already in place, the petition is likely to be dismissed unless his appointor contents to the administration order.[707]

Where a person is entitled to appoint an administrator *without* a court order, he can only exercise that power after giving notice to the holder of any prior agricultural floating charge.[708] Notice can be dispensed with in the former case if the holder of the prior charge consents.[709] Partners seeking to make an appointment must also file a copy of the notice with the court, accompanied by a statutory declaration containing the required information.[710] On making the appointment, partners must also file notice thereof together with a further statutory declaration and a statement by the administrator.[711]

Effect of application

There is now a moratorium on most forms of insolvency proceedings and other legal process both when a partnership is actually in administration and when the above procedures have been initiated in order to place a partnership into administration.[712] Although in either case it is still possible to *present* a petition for the winding up of the firm (whether with or without concurrent petitions against one or more partners)[713] or a joint bankruptcy petition,[714] no order can be made on such petitions.[715] The moratorium will also preclude any partner from obtaining an order for the dissolution of the partnership under section 35 of the Partnership Act 1890.[716] However, a winding up order against the firm may still be made on public interest grounds or on a petition presented by the Financial Services Authority.[717] Needless to say, it will not be possible to enforce any security or

27–163

---

[706] Insolvency Act 1986, Sched. B1, paras 12(2), 14, as substituted and applied by *ibid.* art. 6(1), Sched. 2, paras 6, 7 (as amended: see *supra*, para. 27–160, n. 691). An agricultural receiver is a receiver appointed under an agricultural charge within the meaning of the Agricultural Credits Act 1928: see the definitions in the Insolvent Partnerships Order 1994, art. 2(1), as inserted in the Insolvency Act 1986, s.436 by *ibid.* art. 2(2).

[707] *ibid.* Sched. B1, para. 39(1), as amended and applied by *ibid.* art. 6(1), Sched. 2, para. 15 (as amended: see *supra*, para. 27–160, n. 691).

[708] *ibid.* Sched. B1, paras 14, 15(1) (appointment by holder of agricultural floating charge), 22, 26(1) (appointment by partners), as respectively substituted and applied by *ibid.* art. 6(1), Sched. 2, paras 7–9, 11 (as amended: see *supra*, para. 27–160, n. 691).

[709] *ibid.* Sched. B1, para. 15(1)(b).

[710] *ibid.* Sched. B1, para. 27, as substituted and applied by *ibid.* art. 6(1), Sched. 2, para. 12 (as amended: see *supra*, para. 27–160, n. 691).

[711] *ibid.* Sched. B1, para. 29, as substituted and applied by *ibid.* art. 6(1), Sched. 2, para. 13 (as amended: see *supra*, para. 27–160, n. 691).

[712] Insolvency Act 1986, Sched. B1, paras 42–44, as applied and (where relevant) substituted by *ibid.* art. 6(1), Sched. 2, paras 17, 18 (as amended: see *supra*, para. 27–160, n. 691).

[713] See *supra*, paras 27–08 *et seq.* (winding up without concurrent petitions) and paras 27–24 *et seq.* (winding up with concurrent petitions).

[714] See *supra*, para. 27–44.

[715] Insolvency Act 1986, Sched. B1, para. 42(2), (3), 44(5), as applied and (in the case of para. 42) substituted by the Insolvent Partnerships Order 1994, art. 6(1), Sched. 2, para. 17 (as amended: see *supra*, para. 27–160, n. 691).

[716] *ibid.* Sched. B1, para. 42(4), 44(5), as applied and (in the case of para. 42) substituted by *ibid.* See further, as to orders under the Partnership Act 1890, s.35, *supra*, paras 24–47 *et seq.*

[717] *ibid.* Sched. B1, para. 42(5), 44(5). as applied and (in the case of para. 42) substituted by *ibid.* If the administrator has notice of such an application, he must apply for directions: *ibid.* para. 42(6).

initiate or continue proceedings or execution, etc., against the firm or its assets, save with the consent of the administrator or the permission of the court.[718]

The court will, on the above account, be reluctant to adjourn an application for an administration order once made.[719]

Effect of administration order

27–164   Once an administration order has been made, the position will be the same as set out in the previous paragraph.[720] Any agricultural receiver previously appointed will automatically be required to vacate his office and any other receiver of the partnership's assets may be required by the administrator to vacate his office.[721]

Powers and status of the administrator

27–165   The administrator of a partnership will have wide powers under the Insolvency Act 1986 to do anything "necessary or expedient for the management of the affairs, business and property of the [*partnership*]".[722] He may also, as and when required, summon meetings of the firm's creditors and of the partners[723] or to apply to the court for directions.[724] Save with the consent of the administrator, no partner can interfere with the exercise of his powers, irrespective of the terms of the partnership agreement.[725]

Whilst the administrator will act as the agent of the partners,[726] they will seemingly not be personally liable for partnership debts and obligations incurred during the administration.[727] The administrator will not owe a duty of care to the unsecured creditors of a partnership.[728]

---

[718] *ibid.* Sched. B1, para. 43, 44(5), as amended and (in the case of para. 43), substituted by *ibid.* art. 6(1), Sched. 2, para. 18 (as amended: see *supra*, para. 27–160, n. 691). Note, however, that the appointment of an agricultural receiver does not require such consent: *ibid.* paras 39(2), 44(7)(c), as respectively substituted/amended and applied by *ibid.* art. 6(1), (3)(a), Sched. 2, para. 15 (as amended: see *supra*, para. 27–160, n. 691).

[719] See *Re Kyrris (No. 1)* [1998] B.P.I.R. 103; also *Re West Park Golf & Country Club* [1997] B.C.L.C. 20. There is, of course, *power* to adjourn in an appropriate case, whether or not on conditions: *ibid.* Sched. B1, para. 13(1)(c), as applied by *ibid.* art. 6(1) (as amended: see *supra*, para. 27–160, n. 691).

[720] Insolvency Act 1986, Sched. B1, paras 42, 43, as substituted and applied by *ibid.* art. 6(1), Sched. 2, paras 17, 18 (as amended: see *supra*, para. 27–160, n. 691).

[721] *ibid.* Sched. B1, para. 41, as substituted and applied by *ibid.* art. 6(1), Sched. 2, para. 16 (as amended: see *supra*, para. 27–160, n. 691).

[722] *ibid.* Sched. B1, paras 59(1), 60, Sched. 1, as applied by *ibid.* art. 6(1) and, in the case of Sched. 1, as substituted by *ibid.* Sched. 2, para. 43 (as amended: see *supra*, para. 27–160, n. 691). See also *Re Kyrris (No. 2)* [1998] B.P.I.R. 111.

[723] *ibid.* Sched. B1, para. 62, as applied by *ibid.* art. 6(1) (as amended: see *supra*, para. 27–160, n. 691).

[724] *ibid.* Sched. B1, para. 63, as applied by *ibid.* See also *Re Kyrris (No. 2)*, *supra*.

[725] *ibid.* Sched. B1, paras 61(a), 64, as applied and (in the case of para. 61) substituted by *ibid.* art. 6(1), Sched. 2, para. 22 (as amended: see *supra*, para. 27–160, n. 691). The administrator could appoint a partner to act as manager: *ibid.* Sched. B1, para. 61(b).

[726] *ibid.* Sched. B1, para. 69(1), as substituted and applied by *ibid.* art. 6(1), Sched. 2, para. 24 (as amended: see *supra*, para. 27–160, n. 691).

[727] *ibid.* Sched. B1, para. 69(2), as substituted and applied by *ibid.* It should, however, be noted that the expression used in this paragraph is "officer of the partnership", as compared to "members of the partnership" in para. 69(1). *Semble*, this distinction is likely to make no difference in practice.

[728] See *Oldham v. Kyrris* [2004] 1 B.C.L.C. 305 (CA).

If the administrator believes that the partnership has no assets, he must file a notice to that effect and this will bring his appointment to an end and, three months later, the partnership will be deemed to be dissolved, unless the court otherwise orders.[729] Whether in adapting that provision the distinction between dissolution of a company and dissolution of a partnership was fully appreciated is open to doubt.

The detailed procedure under an administration order is outside the scope of this work and readers are referred to the standard works on insolvency in relation thereto.[730]

---

[729] *ibid.* para. 84, as substituted and applied by *ibid.* art. 6(1), Sched. 2, para. 28 (as amended: see *supra*, para. 27–160, n. 691). As to the operation of this provision, see *Re Ballast Plc* [2005] 1 W.L.R. 1928 (a decision in relation to *ibid.* para. 84 as applied to companies).

[730] See, as to the parts of the Insolvency Act 1986 which apply, the Insolvent Partnerships Order 1994, art. 6(1), (4), (5) (as amended) read subject to *ibid.* art. 3.

Part Six

LIMITED PARTNERSHIPS

CHAPTER 28

INTRODUCTION

Nature of limited partnership

THE essence of limited partnership is the combination in a firm of: (1) one or **28–01**
more partners whose liability for the debts and obligations of the firm is unlimited and who alone are entitled to manage the firm's affairs, and (2) one or more
partners whose liability for such debts and obligations is limited in amount and
who are *excluded* from all management functions.

Such partnerships were, however, unknown to the law of England prior to
January 1, 1908, when the Limited Partnerships Act 1907 came into force.[1]
Pollock went so far as to observe:

> "The institution of partnership *en commandite*, or limited partnership, as we may call
> it in English, is unknown in the United Kingdom, and in these kingdoms alone, or
> almost alone, among all the civilised countries of the world."[2]

Origins of limited partnership

Limited partnership or partnership *en commandite* is said to have had its **28–02**
origins in Italy during the Middle Ages, and to have developed from a practice
adopted by the nobility, for whom it was at the time disgraceful or unlawful to
engage directly in trade. They circumvented this inhibition by investing in
commercial enterprises indirectly, through trusted merchants, on the understanding that they, whilst not in name parties, would receive a share of any profits
without accepting any liability for losses beyond the amount of their
contributions.[3]

Introduction of limited partnership into England

The possible introduction of limited partnership into the laws of England was **28–03**
considered and discussed from time to time during the nineteenth century. In a
Departmental Report on the Law of Partnership made by Mr Bellenden Ker to the
President of the Board of Trade on March 1, 1837, it was stated that it would not
be expedient to recommend the introduction of partnership *en commandite* until
further information as to the operation of the law in other states had been
obtained. In 1851, a Select Committee of the House of Commons was
appointed:

---

[1] See *Coope v. Eyre* (1788) 1 H.Bl. 37, 48 *per* Lord Loughborough L.C.J.
[2] *Essays on Jurisprudence and Ethics* (1882), p. 100.
[3] *ibid.*; Troubat's *Law of Commandatory and Limited Partnership in the United States* (1853),
p. 34; Law Review, Vol. 17 (1852–53), p. 352. See also *Ames v. Downing* (1850) 1 Brad. (New York
Surrogates' Court), 321 and 329; *Jacquin v. Buisson* (1855) 11 How. (New York) Practice Reports
385.

"to consider the Law of Partnership and the expediency of facilitating the Limitation of Liability with a view to encourage useful enterprise and the additional Employment of Labour."

The committee made their report on July 8, 1851, and while expressing themselves in favour of an easier means of borrowing additional capital without risk to the lender beyond the amount of the sum advanced, did no more than recommend the appointment of a Royal Commission to consider the question of limited and unlimited liability of partners.[4]

Bovill's Act

28–04   The Companies Act 1862 probably eased some of the pressure in favour of the introduction of limited partnership and then, in 1865, the Act generally known as Bovill's Act[5] was passed. As has already been seen,[6] this Act provided that, in certain cases, the receipt of a share of profits would not of itself constitute the recipient a partner or render him liable as such, but did not go so far as to enable a person to become a partner and at the same time avoid unlimited liability. The Act was, of course, in substance only declaratory of the principle laid down by the House of Lords in *Cox v. Hickman*[7] but when it was first passed it was generally supposed to have had more far reaching effects[8] and was popularly known as the Limited Partnership Act.[9]

Partnership Act 1890

28–05   After Bovill's Act, further attempts were made to introduce limited partnership but without success.[10] The Partnership Act 1890, while it repealed and re-enacted Bovill's Act, albeit with some modifications,[11] did not touch on the question of limited partnership, which was only addressed in the Limited Partnerships Act 1907.[12]

Limited Partnerships Act 1907

28–06   The Limited Partnerships Act 1907 for the first time under English law enabled a partnership to be formed which did not display three of the normal characteristics of an ordinary or general partnership,[13] namely:

(1) the unlimited liability of every partner[14];

---

[4] Report of Select Committee H. of C. 1851, No. 509, p. viii.

[5] Partnership Act 1865 (28 & 29 Vict. c.86).

[6] See *supra*, para. 5–31.

[7] (1860) 8 H.L.Cas. 267. See *supra*, paras 5–30 *et seq*.

[8] See *Holme v. Hammond* (1872) L.R. 7 Ex. 218, 232 *per* Bramwell B.

[9] See *Syers v. Syers* (1876) 1 App.Cas. 174, in which the Act was so referred to both in the agreement under consideration and in the judgments.

[10] See Pollock, *Digest of the Law of Partnership* (10th ed.), Preface, pp. vii and viii.

[11] *ibid.* ss.2, 48.

[12] The introduction of limited liability was recommended in the Report of the Company Law Amendment Committee appointed in 1905. See 1906 Cd. 3052, para. 89.

[13] Although these characteristics are normally to be found in a general partnership, it should not be inferred that a partnership cannot exist if one or more of them is absent: see *supra*, paras 2–12 *et seq*.

[14] Partnership Act 1890, s.9: see *supra*, paras 13–03 *et seq*.

(2) the implied authority of each partner to bind the firm and his co-partners in all matters within the ordinary scope of the partnership business[15]; and

(3) the right of each partner, subject to any contrary agreement, to take part in the management of that business.[16]

The policy of the Act was originally to give any number of persons not **28–07** exceeding 20 the freedom, subject to certain registration requirements,[17] to enter into partnership on terms that the liability of some of them (who are styled "limited partners") would be limited to the amount contributed by them in cash or property when the partnership was originally created,[18] and this remains the position, save that all limitations on the size of limited partnerships were finally swept away in 2002.[19] However, it was and still is a fundamental and unalterable condition that the liability of at least one of the partners (styled a "general partner") should be unlimited. Moreover, during the continuance of the partnership, a limited partner has no implied authority to bind the firm[20] and may neither be repaid any part of his capital contribution nor take part in the management of the firm, potentially severe penalties being imposed in the case of contravention of the latter prohibitions.[21] As a result, the limited partner is forced to adopt an essentially passive role akin to that of the more traditional dormant partner, although it seems likely that this passive role will be marginally eased in a future Legislative Reform Order.[22]

Application of the Partnership Act 1890 and the general law

It is important to bear in mind that, subject to the provisions of the Limited **28–08** Partnerships Act 1907, limited partnerships are governed by the Partnership Act 1890 and the rules of law and equity applicable to ordinary partnerships.[23] As a result, a formal partnership agreement will usually be indispensable.[24]

---

[15] ibid. s.5: see supra, paras 12–02 et seq.

[16] ibid. s.24(5): supra, paras 15–04 et seq.

[17] See infra, paras 29–16 et seq.

[18] A limited partner could subsequently increase his contribution and would then be liable up to that increased amount: see infra, para. 30–07.

[19] See the Regulatory Reform (Reform of 20 Member Limit in Partnerships etc.) Order 2002 (SI 2002/3203), reg. 2

[20] See infra, paras 30–03, 30–04. Note, however, that there is seemingly no penalty attached if a limited partner is, by agreement, given such authority: see infra, para. 30–04.

[21] See infra, paras 30–08 et seq., 31–04 et seq.

[22] Although it seems unlikely that the main recommendations made by the Law Commission in 2003 for the reform of partnership law in its Report "Partnership Law" (CM 6015) will ever be implemented, there appears to be a determination to adopt its proposals in relation to limited partnership law, albeit over time and in a piecemeal fashion, by means of a series of Legislative Reform Orders. The first (The Legislative Reform (Limited Partnerships) Order 2009 (SI 2009//1940)) came into force on October 1, 2009 and the Explanatory Note thereto (at para. 8) explained that further consultations would take place as to the best way to proceed with the further proposed amendments. In the event, no further Orders have yet materialised and the process has been interrupted following the recent change in Government and the consequent financial cutbacks.

[23] Limited Partnerships Act 1907, s.7.

[24] See, for example, the Encyclopedia of Professional Partnerships, Precedent 4. And see also the 8th and 9th eds. of this work.

Popularity of limited partnership

28–09   The limited partnership has never been a vehicle that has attracted public attention or, for that matter, particular notoriety. Although they have sometimes been used for tax planning purposes[25] (most recently with the advent of the so-called family limited partnership[26]) or in order to circumvent the agricultural holdings legislation,[27] their popularity in the twin fields of venture capital[28] and property development is more well known. This seems set to continue, despite the introduction of the limited liability partnership, which tends to be used more as a member of than as a substitute for a limited partnership.[29] Nevertheless, the number of limited partnerships on the register remains relatively small.[30]

28–10   In earlier editions of this work, after referring to the relative simplicity with which business can be carried on through the medium of a limited liability company, an attempt was made to summarise the perceived advantages of limited partnership in the following terms:

> "It may, perhaps, therefore be urged that there is not now any useful purpose to be served by limited partnership, but the following points in favour of limited partnership may be noted. First, where use is made of the Limited Partnerships Act 1907 the attendant publicity will be much less than in the case of a private company formed under the Companies Acts[31]; secondly, a return of capital from a limited company is not in ordinary circumstances practicable,[32] but this can be effected in the case of a limited partnership[33]; thirdly, limited partnerships are taxed in the same way as ordinary partnerships[34] and are not subject to corporation tax; and fourthly, trustees can, if they have sufficiently wide powers of investment, safely participate in a limited partnership since they are not exposed to unlimited personal liability. A fifth factor used to be the not inconsiderable expense of forming a limited company as

---

[25] See *Reed v. Young* [1986] 1 W.L.R. 649 (HL) (although the device there under consideration was subsequently nullified by the then Income and Corporation Taxes Act 1988, s.117: see *infra*, para. 34–49).

[26] This device is used as an alternative to a trust arrangement in order to pass assets down from one generation to another with more favourable tax consequences.

[27] See, for example, *Dickson v. MacGregor* 1992 S.L.T. 83 (Land Ct.); *MacFarlane v. Falfield Investments Ltd.*, 1998 S.L.T. 145 (1st Div). *Tufnell v. Townhead of Greenock Farm* 2008 S.L.C.R. 167 (Land Ct.) would seem to be another example, albeit that the decision ultimately turned on the existence of a binding agreement to dissolve the firm.

[28] See [1987] S.T.I. 783.

[29] See generally, *supra*, paras 2–39 *et seq.* and *infra*, para. 28–11.

[30] The number of limited partnerships on the register has increased steadily and, in respect of England and Wales, more than doubled between 1994 and 2000. At the time of the last edition it stood at a figure significantly in excess of 8,000 but, by March 31, 2010 had increased to 11,139. with an equivalent figure for Scotland of 6,234. Equally, since there is in general no power for the registrar to deregister a limited partnership (see *infra*, para. 29–29), the number of partnerships on the register at any time will include many that have long since been dissolved and wound up or ceased to be limited partnerships, although it seems clear from the statistics maintained by the Department for Business, Innovation and Skills that, where a limited partnership is known to have been dissolved and its affairs wound up, its name will be removed from the register.

[31] But see, in the case of *corporate* limited partnerships, the Partnerships (Accounts) Regulations 2008 (SI 2008/569), noted *supra*, para. 22–08 and *infra*, para. 31–18.

[32] Note, however, that a company may now in certain circumstances purchase its own shares: see the Companies Act 2006, ss.690 *et seq.*

[33] *Quaere* to what extent this is so: see *infra*, paras 30–09, 31–08, 31–15, 31–16.

[34] Note, however, that stringent restrictions apply in the case of relief for loan interest and the set off of losses in the case of a limited partner: see *infra*, paras 34–27, 34–49.

compared with forming a limited partnership, but since the advent of ready-made companies this factor is no longer valid."[35]

The current editor suggests that few of the foregoing "advantages" can be regarded as having any current significance[36]; indeed, the form of limited partnership most commonly encountered today is likely to be composed almost exclusively of limited liability companies.

Limited liability partnerships

It might be thought that the limited liability partnership or LLP, which is a **28–11** creation of the Limited Liability Partnerships Act 2000, is a direct offshoot of the limited partnership but the reality is very different. Not only is such a "partnership" a body corporate[37] to which no part of partnership law applies[38] but, unlike a limited partnership, all the members of the LLP[39] will enjoy limited liability[40] and there are no restrictions on their withdrawal of capital[41] or participation in the management of the LLP's business.[42] However, such advantages come at a price, in terms of disclosure of the LLP's accounts[43] and other trappings imported from company law.[44]

Overseas limited partnerships

Numerous other jurisdictions, both in Europe and elsewhere, have adopted the **28–12** limited partnership concept. Some accord separate legal personality to the firm, whilst others do not. This gives rise to the question of whether a court will recognise any limitation on the liability of the limited partners in an overseas limited partnership which carries on business in this country. This is, regrettably, a question which does not admit of an easy answer and is, in the current editor's view, largely dependent on whether the firm is properly to be regarded, by the laws of its place of formation, as a separate legal person. If it is, it seems clear that the court will respect that and will give effect to the legal incidents which

---

[35] See the 15th ed. of this work at page 928.

[36] Note, however, that the tax "transparency" of a partnership is regarded as a significant advantage.

[37] Limited Liability Partnerships Act 2000, s.1(2).

[38] See *ibid.* s.1(5). Although there is power to apply partnership law by regulation (*ibid.* s.15(c)), this power seems unlikely to be exercised. The default provisions set out in the Limited Liability Partnerships Regulations 2001 (SI 2001/1090), Pt VI, although modelled on sections of the Partnership Act 1890, represents a stand-alone regime. See also *supra*, para. 2–41.

[39] Members of an LLP should not properly be described as "partners": that expression is used neither in the Act nor in the Regulations. See further *supra*, para. 2–39.

[40] See the Limited Liability Partnerships Act 2000, s.1(4) and *supra*, para. 2–39, n. 144.

[41] Note, however, that, in the event of an insolvent liquidation of the LLP, there may be a clawback of any sums withdrawn by members in the preceding two years: Insolvency Act 1986, s.214A, as added by the Limited Liability Partnerships Regulations 2001, reg. 5, Sched. 3.

[42] Limited Liability Partnerships Regulations 2001, reg. 7(3). The right of members to participate in management may, however, be excluded by agreement: *ibid.* reg. 7.

[43] See the Limited Liability Partnerships (Accounts and Audit) (Application of Companies Act 2006) Regulations 2008 (SI 2008/1911), Pts 6, 7. And see also the Small Limited Liability Partnerships (Accounts) Regulations 2008 (SI 2008/1912) and the Large and Medium-sized Limited Liability Partnerships (Accounts) Regulations 2008 (SI 2008/1913).

[44] See the Limited Liability Partnerships (Application of Companies Act 2006) Regulations 2009 (SI 2009/1804). In particular, the Companies Act 2006, s.994 (unfair prejudice) will apply, unless it is excluded by agreement: *ibid.* reg. 48.

attach to that entity under those laws.[45] This will include any limitation on the liability of the limited partners provided that such limitation can, on a true analysis, properly be characterised as a matter of substantive, rather than procedural, law.[46] If, on the other hand, the limitation is only procedural, it will be ignored.[47]

28–13   It is in other cases that the position becomes more obscure. If an overseas firm which does not have separate legal personality carries on business here and contracts as a firm, the court is likely to regard it as a partnership within the meaning of the Partnership Act 1890, and personal liability for all the partners will follow as a matter of course.[48] If one partner only has contracted in his own name, it may be that liability would be imposed on the other partners through the mutual agency principle embodied in section 5 of the 1890 Act,[49] unless it is only possible to establish the liability of the other partners by reliance on the law of the firm's country of formation. In a case of the latter class, it seems difficult to see how a court could allow reliance on the foreign law for some purposes but not others.[50] The most difficult question arises where the overseas firm has expressly contracted as a limited partnership governed by the laws of its country of formation: in those circumstances, it is the view of the current editor that the court ought properly to give effect to any available limitation of liability under that system of law, provided that all the conditions required to secure it have been complied with.

---

[45] Dicey and Morris, *The Conflict of Laws* (14th ed.), paras 30R–009 *et seq*. And see *Dreyfus v. C.I.R.* (1929) 14 T.C. 560; *J.H. Rayner (Mincing Lane) Ltd. v. Department of Trade and Industry* [1990] 2 A.C. 418 (HL); *Rowan Companies Inc. v. Lambert Egglink Offshore Transport Consultants VOF* [1997] 2 Lloyd's Rep. 218 (the findings on the attributes of a Dutch VOF were not challenged on the subsequent appeal); *Re Kaupthing Capital Partners II Master LP Inc.* [2010] EWHC 836 (Ch) (Lawtel 1/4/10), which concerned a Guernsey limited partnership with elective separate personality. *cf. Oxnard Financing SA v. Rahn* [1998] 1 W.L.R. 1465, where the Court of Appeal held that proceedings could be commenced here against the members of a Swiss general partnership, even though it was a separate entity under Swiss law; however, it is clear that the court did not thereby seek to undermine the status of the firm under Swiss law.

[46] *Johnson Matthey & Wallace Ltd. v. Ahmad Alloush* (1984) 135 N.L.J. 1012 (CA), which concerned a Jordanian ordinary limited company, which was similar in form to a partnership. It was held that, under Jordanian law, the limitation on the liability of the partners was procedural only. See also *J.H. Rayner (Mincing Lane) Ltd. v. Department of Trade and Industry, supra*; *Oxnard Financing SA v. Rahn, supra*.

[47] *Johnson Matthey & Wallace Ltd. v. Ahmad Alloush; supra.*; *cf. Oxnard Financing SA. v. Rahn, supra*, at p. 1470C. See also Dicey & Morris, *The Conflict of Laws* (14th ed.), para. 30–010.

[48] See the arguments advanced (ultimately unsuccessfully) in *J.H. Rayner (Mincing Lane) Ltd. v. Department of Trade and Industry, supra*; note also *Oxnard Financing SA v. Rahn, supra*. The view set out in the text appears to be supported by John McDonnell Q.C. in an article entitled "Know your Limit" in The Lawyer, June 27, 2005, p. 36. He refers to an example involving a Delaware limited partnership of which Ivan Boesky was the general partner, although there seems to have been no formal judicial decision on the liability issue. As to the liability imposed on partners, see the Partnership Act 1890, ss.9 *et seq.*; *ibid.* s.14 (holding out) is not in point. The position is, however, likely to be different for tax purposes: see, for example, *Memec Plc. v. I.R.C.* [1996] S.T.C. 1336 (which concerned a German silent partnership); *Major v. Brodie* [1998] S.T.C. 491 (which concerned a Scottish partnership which, in any event, enjoys separate legal personality).

[49] See *supra*, paras 12–02 *et seq*.

[50] See *SEB Trygg Liv Holding AB v Manches* [2006] 1 W.L.R. 2276 (CA) and the discussion of the law governing the actual authority of an agent in *Dicey & Morris on the Conflict of Laws* (14th ed.) at paras 33–434 *et seq*. Alternatively, could an analogy perhaps be drawn with the decision in *Base Metal Trading Ltd. v. Shamurin* [2005] 1 W.L.R. 1157 (CA), which concerned the proper law governing the equitable duty owed by a director to his company?

CHAPTER 29

NATURE, FORMATION, DURATION AND REGISTRATION OF LIMITED PARTNERSHIPS

A limited partnership is not a legal entity like a limited company[1] or a limited liability partnership[2] but a form of partnership with a number of special characteristics introduced by the Limited Partnerships Act 1907. Although it is necessary to ensure strict compliance with the statutory conditions if the benefit of limited liability is to be obtained for all the partners,[3] such a partnership is otherwise governed by the general law.[4]   **29–01**

1.   NATURE, FORMATION AND DURATION

Number of partners

There are now no restrictions on the number of partners who may be members of a limited partnership.[5]   **29–02**

General partners

A limited partnership must consist of one or more general partners and one or more limited partners.[6] Any partner who is not a limited partner must be a general partner[7] and will, like any member of an ordinary partnership, be personally liable for all the debts and obligations of the firm.[8]   **29–03**

Limited partners

A limited partner must make a contribution of capital[9] and will not, subject to certain exceptions,[10] be liable for the debts and obligations of the firm beyond the   **29–04**

---

[1] See *Re Barnard* [1932] 1 Ch. 272.

[2] Limited Liability Partnerships Act 2000, s.1(2).

[3] Limited Partnerships Act 1907, ss.4(1), 5 (as amended by the Legislative Reform (Limited Partnerships) Order 2009 (SI 2009/1940), art. 8, as regards limited partnerships registered after October 1, 2009), *infra*, paras A3–04, A3–05. See further *infra*, paras 29–23, 29–26.

[4] *ibid.* s.7, *infra*, para. A3–07.

[5] See the Regulatory Reform (Reform of 20 Member Limit in Partnerships etc.) Order 2002 (SI 2002/3203), regs. 2, 3.

[6] Limited Partnerships Act 1907, s.4(2), *infra*, para. A3–04.

[7] *ibid.* s.3, *infra*, para. A3–03.

[8] *ibid.* s.4(2), *infra*, para. A3–04.

[9] This is not as clearly expressed in the Act as it might be, *viz.* "limited partners ... shall contribute ... *a sum or sums of cash* as capital or property valued at a stated amount ... " (emphasis supplied): *ibid.* s.4(2). It is submitted that no logical distinction can be drawn between cash and other property, and that a contribution in either form will become part of the firm's fixed capital. It does not matter that the limited partner's contribution is of a nominal amount: see *Dickson v. MacGregor* 1992 S.L.T. 83 (Land Ct.) and *MacFarlane v. Falfield Investments Ltd.* 1998 S.L.T. 145 (1st Div.), in each of which the limited partners' contributions were set at a mere £10.

[10] See the Limited Partnerships Act 1907, ss.4(3), 5, 6(1), *infra*, paras A3–04 *et seq.*

amount so contributed.[11] An initial contribution must be made *immediately* upon entry into partnership[12] and may consist of cash[13] or property. Any contribution of property must be fairly and honestly valued, so that the requisite particulars can be submitted for registration purposes.[14] What is not possible is for two or more limited partners to make a *joint* capital contribution, unless it is clearly allocated between them and registered accordingly.[15]

Change in liability of partners

29–05   Provided that the partnership at all times comprises at least one general partner and one limited partner,[16] any partner is free to change his status from general to limited partner or vice versa.[17]

Capacity

29–06   Any person who has the capacity to become a partner in an ordinary firm[18] may enter into a limited partnership as either a general or a limited partner.

Although the Act of 1907 specifically provides that a body corporate may be a limited partner,[19] it does not extend the powers of such a body. However, even if a particular company's constitution does not, on its true construction, authorise it to become a limited partner, its *capacity* to do so will be unaffected.[20] There is no reason to suppose that a limited company cannot be a general partner[21]; indeed this is a common occurrence.[22]

Business of the partnership

29–07   Any lawful business[23] which could be carried on by the members of an ordinary partnership without infringing any statute or rule of law may properly be carried on by a limited partnership. If it would be illegal for an unqualified

---

[11] *ibid.* s.4(2).

[12] See *MacCartaigh v. D* [1985] I.R. 73, where the limited partners did not contribute capital until some time after the date of their admission and, as a result, fell to be treated as general partners during the intervening period. But see also, *infra*, para. 30–07.

[13] A bank guarantee is not cash: *Rayner & Co. v. Rhodes* (1926) 24 Ll.L. Rep. 25.

[14] Limited Partnerships Act 1907, s.8A(2)(d) (as substituted by the Legislative Reform (Limited Partnerships) Order 2009, art. 5, as regards limited partnerships registered after October 1, 2009), *infra*, para. A3–09. See also the Perjury Act 1911, s.5 and *infra*, para. 29–24.

[15] The Limited Partnerships Act 1907, s.8A(2)(d) is very specific in referring to the "amount of the capital contribution of each limited partner". In its original form, *ibid.* s.8(g) referred to the "sum contributed by each limited partner". Were an undivided share in a joint capital sum to be contributed by two partners, it would be impossible to allocate it between them in the absence of some specific agreement. See also *ibid.* s.9(1)(f), *infra*, para. A3–12 and the Limited Partnerships (Forms) Rules 2009, Sched., Pt 1, Form LP5, *infra*, para. A4–04; also *infra*, para. 29–19. Equally, there is no reason why a joint capital account should not be maintained internally, although even this is not without its problems: see *supra*, para. 7–09.

[16] Limited Partnerships Act 1907, s.4(2), *infra*, para. A3–04.

[17] *ibid.* ss.9(1)(g), 10; infra, paras A3–12, A3–13; and see *infra*, paras 29–26, 29–28, 30–13.

[18] See *supra*, paras 4–01 *et seq.*

[19] Limited Partnerships Act 1907, s.4(4), *infra*, para. A3–04.

[20] Companies Act 2006, s.39(1). See further *supra*, para. 4–20.

[21] See *supra*, para. 11–07. *Quaere*: could it be argued that, because the Limited Partnerships Act 1907, s.4(4) expressly authorises a body corporate to be a *limited* partner, there is an implication that such a body may not be a general partner? In the view of the current editor, such an argument would not be sustained.

[22] See, for example, *Blythe Limited Partnership v. Customs & Excise Commissioners* [1999] S.T.I. 1178 (where both general and limited partners were companies).

[23] As to the meaning of the word "business", see the Limited Partnerships Act 1907, s.3 (*infra*, para. A3–03), applying the Partnership Act 1890, s.45. As to what businesses are lawful, see *supra*, paras 8–01 *et seq.*

person without more to be a member of the firm,[24] that illegality is unlikely to be cured by ensuring that he only participates in the business *qua* limited partner.

The general nature of the partnership business and any change therein must be registered.[25] Provided that this requirement is satisfied, there is no reason why a number of different businesses should not be carried on by the same firm.

Commencement of business

It has already been seen that, for a partnership to exist, a business in common must be carried on, even though trading need not necessarily have commenced.[26] The question therefore arises whether a partnership must actually exist as such *before* it can seek registration under the 1907 Act. This is not entirely clear since the Act requires the application for registration to be signed or otherwise authenticated "by or on behalf of each partner"[27] and, as previously noted, to state the general nature of the partnership business,[28] which is certainly indicative of such a requirement, but also directs that the application be made to the registrar for the part of the UK "in which the principal place of business of the limited partnership is to be situated".[29] The latter reference is entirely logical as it is the principal place of business of the limited partnership, not any predecessor partnership which is in point.[30] Although prospective limited partners would doubtless be concerned if liabilities were to be incurred before registration (and their own limitation of liability) was in place, in practice, the issue is an academic one, since the registrar has not historically taken the point, even if it exists,[31] and seems unlikely to do so in future. Equally, it is the view of the current editor that, consistently with the approach adopted by the House of Lords in *Khan v. Miah*,[32] it could properly be said that the act of applying for registration is, in itself, a sufficient preparatory act to demonstrate that a business is being carried on and, thus, to satisfy the requirements of section 1(1) of the Partnership Act 1890.[33]

29–08

Firm name

A limited partnership must have a firm name and that name and any change in it must be registered.[34]

29–09

---

[24] *e.g.* a dentists' or solicitors' partnership: see *supra*, paras 8–42, 8–52.

[25] Limited Partnerships Act 1907, ss.8A(2)(a) (as added by the Legislative Reform (Limited Partnerships) Order 2009, art. 5, as regards limited partnerships registered on or after October 1, 2009), 9(b), *infra*, paras A3–09, A3–12: see also *infra*, paras 29–19, 29–25.

[26] See *supra*, paras 2–02 *et seq.*

[27] Limited Partnerships Act 1907, s.8A(1)(c) (as added by *ibid.*), *infra*, para. A3–09. The original wording was "a statement signed by the partners": *ibid.* s.8.

[28] See *supra*, para. 29–07.

[29] Limited Partnerships Act 1907, s.8A(1)(d). The original wording in *ibid.* s.8 referred to the part of the UK in which the principal place of business "is situated or proposed to be situated". See further *infra*, para. 30–18.

[30] Similarly in the case of *ibid.* s.8C(4) (as added by the Legislative Reform (Limited Partnerships) Order 2009, art. 7, as regards limited partnerships registered on or after October 1, 2009), *infra*, para. A3–11, which provides that a certificate is conclusive evidence of the *existence* of a limited partnership, not of any predecessor firm.

[31] See *Blythe Limited Partnership v. Customs & Excise Commissioners* [1999] S.T.I. 1178, where the firm had clearly been registered before a partnership came into existence.

[32] [2000] 1 W.L.R. 2123. See further *supra*, paras 2–03, 13–20.

[33] See generally, *supra*, paras 2–01 *et seq.*

[34] Limited Partnerships Act 1907, ss.3, 8A(1)(a) (as added by the Legislative Reform (Limited Partnerships) Order 2009, art. 5, as regards limited partnerships registered after October 1, 2009), 9(1)(a), *infra*, paras A3–03, A3–09, A3–12. See also *infra*, paras 29–25, 29–26.

If the partnership was registered on an application made on or after October 1, 2009,[35] the firm name must disclose the fact that the partnership is a limited partnership by ensuring that the name ends with those words or the initials "LP",[36] but that requirement does not apply to pre-existing limited partnerships.[37] Subject to the former requirement and the general requirements of Part 41 of the Companies Act 2006,[38] the members of such a partnership have the same right as the members of an ordinary partnership to trade under any name of their choosing.[39] However, they may not adopt a name in which "limited"[40] or any contraction or imitation thereof appears as the *last* word.[41]

Use of limited partner's name: holding out

29–10   It might be thought that, if the firm name consists of or includes the name of a limited partner, this is *per se* sufficient to render him liable as a general partner on the basis of holding out.[42] However, it is clear that, whilst the law recognises both ordinary and limited partnerships and requires the latter to be made up of two kinds of partner and now insists that the firm name must disclose its status,[43] it does not prohibit the inclusion of a limited partner's name therein. In that context, the current editor submits that there is no justification for suggesting that, as a general proposition of law, the mere use of a limited partner's name *must* involve a representation that he is a partner of one kind rather than another.

This conclusion is to a large extent confirmed by the provisions of Part 41 of the Companies Act 2006,[44] which applies equally to limited and ordinary partnerships. Thus, if a limited partnership has a place of business and carries on business in the UK under a name which does not consist of the surnames of *all* the partners (together with any permitted additions),[45] the name of each limited

---

[35] See the Legislative Reform (Limited Partnerships) Order 2009, art. 2

[36] Limited Partnerships Act 1907, s.8B(1), (2) (as added by the Legislative Reform (Limited Partnerships) Order 2009, art. 6). In the case of initials, upper or lower case may be used, with or without punctuation: *ibid.* s.8B(2)(b). A partnership with its principal place of business in Wales may use the Welsh equivalents "partneriaeth cyfyngedig" or "PC": *ibid.* s.8B(3). Accordingly, the current position in effect now replicates that in the Bill for the Limited Partnerships Act 1907, which originally contained a provision that the firm name should contain the words "limited firm" as the last words in the name, whereas the Bill introduced into the House of Lords in 1906 provided that the firm name should not include the name of a limited partner. See also the Company and Business Names (Miscellaneous Provisions) Regulations 2009 (SI 2009/1085), reg. 14, Sched. 2, para. 3(n).

[37] Such a firm should not be affected by the Company and Business Names (Miscellaneous Provisions) Regulations 2009, reg. 14: see *ibid.* reg. 15(1)

[38] See *supra*, paras 3–26 *et seq.*; also *infra*, paras 29–10 *et seq.*

[39] See the Limited Partnerships Act 1907, s.7, *infra*, para. A3–07 and *supra*, paras 3–19 *et seq.*, 8–27.

[40] Or the Welsh equivalent.

[41] Companies Act 2006, s.1197; the Company and Business Names (Miscellaneous Provisions) Regulations 2009, reg. 13, Sched. 2, paras 1(a), (b), (2).

[42] See, generally, the Partnership Act 1890, s.14 and *supra*, paras 5–35 *et seq.*

[43] *Per contra* if the partnership was registered prior to October 1, 2009: see the preceding paragraph.

[44] See generally, *supra*, paras 3–26 *et seq.*

[45] Companies Act 2006, s.1200.

partner may be included in the firm name but must inevitably appear on all the firm's business letters and other documents, as well as in a notice displayed in the partnership premises.[46] Significantly, Part 41 makes no provision for distinguishing between general and limited partners on such letters, etc.,[47] and it cannot, in the current editor's view, be right that compliance with these statutory requirements will, of itself, expose a limited partner to a liability more extensive than that prescribed by the Limited Partnerships Act 1907, so long as the partnership is registered under that Act.[48]

The position may, however, be different if the limited partner was formerly a general partner or, indeed, the sole owner of the business, at least as regards any person who knew of his former status but has had no express notice of any change therein.[49]   **29–11**

In the absence of any authority on this point, a degree of caution is to be commended. Thus, any limited partner, irrespective of his previous status, would be well advised not to allow his name to appear in the firm name or on its business letters, etc., without some clear indication that he is a limited partner. What he cannot do is to compel his co-partners to omit all references to his name, since this would involve an offence under Part 41 of the Companies Act 2006.[50]

Duration of limited partnership

The rules governing the duration of ordinary partnerships apply to limited partnerships.[51] Thus, if no fixed term is adopted, the partnership will be determinable by the general partners at any time on notice.[52] However, subject to any contrary agreement, such a notice may not be given by a limited partner[53] and, moreover, the death or bankruptcy of such a partner will not automatically dissolve the firm.[54]   **29–12**

Where a limited partnership is formed for a fixed term, that term, beginning with the date of registration, must be specified in the application for first

---

[46] *ibid.* ss.1201 (as substituted by the Companies Act 2006 (Substitution of Section 1201) Regulations 2009 (SI 2009/3182), reg. 2), 1202(1), 1204(1). A limited exemption is afforded to partnerships of 20 or more persons: *ibid.* s.1203. It should also be noted that any customer of the partnership is entitled to request, and must be supplied with, a notice containing the names and addresses of all the partners: *ibid.* s.1202(2).

[47] Note, however, that the Secretary of State could in theory require a distinction to be drawn between general and limited partners in any notice to be provided to anyone who is entitled to request it pursuant to *ibid.* s.1202(2) or in the notice to be displayed in the partnership premises pursuant to *ibid.* s.1204(1)(b), by means of regulations made under *ibid.* s.1202(3) or 1204(2). No such regulations have been made.

[48] See also *infra*, paras 29–16 *et seq.*

[49] See *infra*, para. 29–28.

[50] Companies Act 2006, s.1205(1).

[51] Limited Partnerships Act 1907, s.7, *infra*, para. A3–07; Partnership Act 1890, ss.32 *et seq.* See further *supra*, paras 9–01 *et seq.*, 24–15 *et seq.*

[52] Partnership Act 1890, ss.26(1), 32(*c*); and see *supra*, paras 9–01 *et seq.*, 24–18.

[53] Limited Partnerships Act 1907, s.6(5)(e), *infra*, para. A3–06. It is clear that the provisions of this paragraph can be overridden by agreement: see the opening words of *ibid.* s.6(5).

[54] *ibid.* s.6(2). *Semble*, there is no reason why the agreement should not contain some contrary agreement. But *cf.* the terms of *ibid.* s.6(5).

registration[55] and notice must be given of any subsequent change therein.[56]

Continuation of partnership after expiration of term

29–13   An ordinary fixed term partnership which is continued after the expiration of its term will be converted into a partnership at will; such a continuance will be presumed where the business is carried on by those partners who habitually acted therein without any settlement of the partnership affairs.[57] It would seem that this rule is equally applicable to limited partnerships[58] so that, in the case of a limited partnership registered prior to October 1, 2009, a limited partner could find that a continuance of the business by the general partner has inadvertently deprived him of the protection of the Limited Partnerships Act 1907 by turning him into a general partner, unless the change in the term or character of the partnership has been duly registered.[59] In the case of a firm registered an application made on or after that date, the change in the term must still seemingly be registered, but a failure so to do will no longer result in the loss of limited liability for all the limited partners.[60]

Agreement for limited partnership

29–14   Although an agreement for a limited partnership need not be in any particular form, a formal deed or agreement is generally desirable.[61] Moreover, even if the initial agreement is oral, certain of its terms will inevitably have to be reduced to writing for registration purposes.[62]

Discrimination

29–15   Whilst it is unlawful to discriminate against a general partner (or a proposed general partner) on the grounds of sex, race, disability, religion or belief, sexual orientation, age[63] or, with effect from a date to be appointed, marital or civil

---

[55] *ibid.* s.8A(2)(f) (as added by the Legislative Reform (Limited Partnerships) Order 2009, art. 5), *infra*, para. A3–09; see also the Limited Partnerships (Forms) Rules 2009, Sched., Pt 1, Form LP5, *infra*, para. A4–04. In the case of firms registered prior to October 1, 2009, there was a similar requirement in *ibid.* s.8(e), but any date of commencement could be specified. If no definite term had been fixed, the conditions of the existence of the partnership had to be stated: see Form LP5 in the Appendix to the Limited Partnerships Rules 1907 (now revoked by the Limited Partnerships (Forms) Rules 2009, r. 2).

[56] Limited Partnerships Act 1907, s.9(1)(e), *infra*, para. A3–012. Note that the reference to the "character of the partnership" has been left in here, which scarcely ties in with the terms of *ibid.* s.8A2(d). See also *infra*, para. 29–25.

[57] Partnership Act 1890, s.27: see *supra*, paras 9–10, 10–18 *et seq.* Only the general partners can, by definition, habitually act in the business: see, *infra*, para. 31–02.

[58] Limited Partnerships Act 1907, s.7, *infra*, para. A3–07.

[59] See *infra*, paras 29–25, 29–26.

[60] *ibid.*

[61] See further *infra*, para. 31–15.

[62] Limited Partnerships Act 1907, s.8A (as added by the Legislative Reform (Limited Partnerships) Order 2009, art. 5), *infra*, para. A3–09; also Limited Partnerships (Forms) Rules 2009, Sched., Pt 1, Form LP5, *infra*, para. A4–04.

[63] See *supra*, paras 8–09 *et seq.*

partner status,[64] no sanctions are imposed in the case of discrimination against a *limited* partner.[65]

2.   REGISTRATION

Limited partnerships must be registered as such in accordance with the provi- **29–16**
sions of the Limited Partnerships Act 1907,[66] and the registrar of companies is
required to keep an index of the names of such registered partnerships.[67] However, for limited partnerships registered an application made on or after October
1, 2009, it is no longer the case that any form of misregistration will result in the
partnership being deemed to be a general partnership.[68]

Time for registration

The Act does not state when a limited partnership must be registered; however, **29–17**
since a partnership will only constitute a limited partnership once registered
under the Act,[69] there will be little sense in commencing to trade before that
process is complete.[70]

Manner and place of registration

Registration is effected by making an application containing the prescribed **29–18**
particulars to the registrar of limited partnerships[71] in that part of the UK in
which the limited partnership's principal place of business is to be situated.[72]

---

[64] See the Equality Act 2010, ss.8, 13(4).

[65] Sex Discrimination Act 1975, s.11(5); Race Relations Act 1976, s.10(4); Disability Discrimination Act 1995, s.6C(3) (as added by the Disability Discrimination Act 1995 (Amendment) Regulations 2003 (SI 2003/1673), reg. 6); the Employment Equality (Religion or Belief) Regulations 2003
(SI 2003/1660), reg. 14(5); the Employment Equality (Sexual Orientation) Regulations 2003 (SI
2003/1661), reg. 14(5); the Employment Equality (Age) Regulations 2006 (SI 2006/1031), reg. 17(5).
All these provisions will be consolidated by the Equality Act 2010, s.44(8).

[66] Limited Partnerships Act 1907, s.5 (as amended by the Legislative Reform (Limited Partnership)
Order 2009, art. 8 in the case of partnerships registered on or after October 1, 2009), *infra*, para.
A3–05.

[67] Companies Act 2006, s.1099(1), (3)(a). As to the statutory requirements and other consideration
affecting the choice of a firm name, see *supra*, paras 29–09 *et seq.*

[68] See the Limited Partnerships Act 1907, s.5, as amended *supra*, n. 66. See also the Legislative
Reform (Limited Partnership) Order 2009, art. 2

[69] *ibid*. Note that, in the case of a limited partnership registered *prior* to October 1, 2009, any defect
in the registration would still potentially result in it being deemed to remain a general partnership:
ibid. s.5 in its original form: see *infra*, para. 29–23.

[70] See further, *supra*, para. 29–08.

[71] Actually the registrar of companies: Limited Partnerships Act 1907, s.15(1) (as substituted by
the Companies Act 2006 (Consequential Amendments, Transitional Provisions and Savings) Order
2009, art. 2(1), Sched. 1, para. 2(5)), *infra*, para. A3–17.

[72] *ibid*. ss.8A(1)(d) (as added by the Legislative Reform (Limited Partnership) Order 2009, art. 5),
15(1) (as amended: see the preceding footnote), *infra*, paras A3–09, A3–17. It would not seem to
matter that a *proposed* principal place of business has not yet been established when registration is
sought. There would also appear to be no objection to the principal place of business being relocated
within *or outside* the UK after registration has taken place: see *infra*, para. 29–25, n. 99.

It is considered that a firm's principal place of business will be the place where its administrative headquarters are situated,[73] which is a question of fact. Accordingly, whilst the partners may designate a particular location as the principal place of business, that will not be conclusive. Given the terms of section 8A(1)(d) of the 1907 Act,[74] it would no longer seem to be arguable that a firm may have more than one principal place of business located in different parts of the UK,[75] so that the theoretical possibility of multiple registrations in different parts of the UK would not now appear to be open.[76]

Application for registration

29–19   The application must be signed or authenticated by or on behalf of all the partners, both general and limited, specify the name under which the partnership is to be registered,[77] and contain the following details[78]:

(1) the general nature of the business[79];

(2) the name of each general and limited partner[80];

(3) the amount of each limited partner's capital contribution and whether paid in cash or how otherwise[81];

(4) the address of the proposed principal place of business[82]; and

---

[73] See *De Beers Consolidated Mines Ltd. v. Howe* [1906] A.C. 455; *Palmer v. Caledonian Railway* [1892] 1 Q.B. 823; *The Rewia* [1991] 2 Lloyd's Rep. 325; *King v. Crown Energy Trading AG, The Times*, March 14, 2003; *Ministry of Defence and Support of the Armed Forces for the Islamic Republic of Iran v. Faz Aviation Ltd.* [2008] 1 All E.R. (Comm) 372 (all decisions relating to the principal place of business of a company).

[74] See *infra*, para. A3–09.

[75] This possibility is, in fact, expressly contemplated by the insolvency regime as applied to partnerships: see the Insolvency Act 1986, s.221(3), as respectively modified by the Insolvent Partnerships Order 1994 (SI 1994/2421), Sched. 3, Pt 1, para. 3, Sched. 4, Pt 1, para. 3, Sched. 5, para. 2 and Sched. 6, para. 4.

[76] This possibility appeared to be contemplated by the original wording of the Limited Partnerships Act 1907, s.15. In any event, that construction was never accepted by the Department of Trade and Industry and its successors, notwithstanding decisions such as *Beaver v. Master in Equity of Victoria* [1895] A.C. 251 (PC).

[77] Limited Partnerships Act 1907, ss.8A(1)(a), 8B, *infra*, paras A3–09, A3–10 The name must comply with the requirements of *ibid.* s.8B, i.e. it must end with the words "limited partnership" or "LP" or, in a case where the firm's principal place of business will be in Wales, the Welsh equivalents "partneriaeth cyfyngedig" or "PC". See also *supra*, para. 29–09.

[78] *ibid.* s.8A(1)(b), (2), *infra*, para. A3–09; see also the Limited Partnerships (Forms) Rules 2009, Sched., Pt 1, Form LP5, *infra*, para. A4–04. As to the fee payable, see the Registrar of Companies (Fees) Limited Partnerships and Newspaper Proprietors) Regulations 2009 (SI 2009/2392), reg. 3, Sched. 1, Pt 2, para. 5.

[79] See further, *supra*, para. 29–08.

[80] This requirement would not be satisfied if an English law partnership (or any other partnership which does not enjoy separate legal personality) is purportedly registered in its firm name. Nevertheless, the current editor is aware of cases in which this has happened. It is not clear whether there was such a registration in *James Hay Pension Trustees Ltd. v. Hird* [2005] EWHC 1093 (Ch) (Lawtel 9/6/05), where a partnership was formed in order to become a special partner in a limited partnership.

[81] It follows that it is not possible to register a sum of joint capital as between two or more limited partners, even though the current editor is aware of this being done in practice, especially where a firm has been (wrongly) registered as a single limited partner. See further *supra*, para. 29–04.

[82] See *supra*, para. 29–18.

(5) the term, if any, of the partnership, which must begin on the date of its registration.[83]

Two firms with identical partners

There would seem to be no objection to the submission of separate applications for registration by two firms composed of the same partners, provided that the make-up of each firm is different, *i.e.* one or more of the general partners in the first firm are limited partners in the second or vice versa.[84] What is less clear is whether two identical firms are entitled to apply for separate registrations merely because their registered particulars will be different, *e.g.* where they each carry on distinct businesses or have a differing capital structure. Obviously any difficulties can be avoided by the simple expedient of introducing an additional general or limited partner into *one* of the firms.

29–20

Certificate of registration

The application submitted by the partners must be filed by the registrar, who must issue and post a registration certificate to the firm.[85] The certificate is admissible as evidence in all legal proceedings, both civil and criminal,[86] and is, in the case of a limited partnership registered on an application made on or after October 1, 2009, conclusive evidence that it came into existence on the date of registration[87] but not necessarily that every limited partner enjoys such status.[88] On the other hand, in the case of a partnership registered prior to that date, the certificate will not be conclusive evidence that the partnership is registered in accordance with the provisions of the Act.[89]

29–21

Completion of registration

It is submitted that registration is complete as soon as the prescribed application has reached the registrar[90]; the filing of the application and the issue of the certificate are ministerial acts, failure to perform which would not deprive a limited partnership of the benefit of the Act.

29–22

---

[83] See also note 2 in Form LP5 in the Limited Partnerships (Forms) Rules 2009, Sched. 1, Pt 1, *infra*, para. A4–04. Previously Form LP5 required the conditions of existence of the partnership to be stated where there was no fixed term: see the Limited Partnerships Rules 1907, Appendix. See also *supra*, para. 29–12.

[84] See, for example, *H. Saunders v. The Commissioners* (1980) V.A.T.T.R. 53, noted *infra*, para. 37–10.

[85] Limited Partnerships Act 1907, ss.8 (as substituted by the Legislative Reform (Limited Partnership) Order 2009, art. 4), 13, *infra*, paras A3–08, A3–15.

[86] *ibid.* s.16(2) (as amended), *infra*, para. A3–18. As to the form of the certificate, see *ibid.* s.8C(2), (3) (as added by the Legislative Reform (Limited Partnership) Order 2009, art. 7), *infra*, para. A3–11.

[87] *ibid.* s.8C(4) (as added by *ibid.*).

[88] Although in such a case *ibid.* s.5 (as amended by *ibid.* art. 8), *infra*, para. A3–05 will no longer deem the entire partnership to be a general partnership when the requirements of the Act are not satisfied, a limited partner who, for example, does not contribute capital on admission will not satisfy the requirements of *ibid.* s.4(2) and therefore will not enjoy limited liability: see the Explanatory Document accompanying the Legislative Reform (Limited Partnership) Order 2009, para. 39.

[89] In such a case *ibid.* s.5 in its original form (see *infra*, para. A3–05) will apply.

[90] See *ibid.* s.8 (as substituted by the Legislative Reform (Limited Partnership) Order 2009, art. 4), *infra*, para. A3–08.

Effect of non-registration

29–23   In the case of a limited partnership formed prior to October 1, 2009 but which is not registered as such in accordance with the provisions of the Act, it is deemed to be a general partnership and *every* limited partner is deemed to be a general partner.[91] It naturally follows that, in such a case, the benefits of limited liability will be lost.[92] A graphic example of such a case was to be found in *MacCarthaigh v. D*,[93] where the limited partners had not made their capital contributions until some time *after* the firm had been registered.

    The position in the case of a limited partnership registered on an application made on or after October 1, 2009 is potentially very different, Now any mis-registration, *e.g.* of a contribution of capital which has not in fact been made, will prima facie not affect the validity of the firm's registration[94] but may well impact on a supposed limited partner's right to claim that status and, thus, the benefit of limited liability.[95] It follows that the actual result in *MacCarthaigh v. D* would be exactly the same if the same facts were to recur under the new regime.

False statements

29–24   The current editor submits that, in the case of a limited partnership formed prior to October 1, 2009, there will only be registration in accordance with the provisions of the Act if the particulars given in the statement submitted on registration were in substance true and this view would seem to be borne out by the decision in *Rayner & Co. v. Rhodes*.[96] It is less clear whether the position is the same in the case of a partnership registered on an application made on or after October 1, 2009. Although, as had already been seen,[97] the certificate of registration is conclusive evidence that the limited partnership exists as such, it is not conclusive evidence of compliance with the requirements of the Act. Nevertheless, the current editor believes that the consequences of submitting an application containing false particulars must be considered on a partner by partner basis and that the registration of the *firm* should not be affected thereby; *sed quaere*.

    It is an offence to make or send for registration a statement which is *known* to be false.[98]

Registration of changes in limited partnerships

29–25   If, during the continuance of the partnership, there is any change in the particulars originally submitted on first registration, a statement specifying the

---

[91] *ibid.* s.5 (in its original form), *infra*, para. A3–05.

[92] *ibid.* s.4(2), *infra*, para. A3–04. This was the position in *Rayner & Co. v. Rhodes* (1926) 24 Ll.L.R. 25.

[93] [1985] I.R. 73.

[94] See the Limited Partnerships Act 1907, ss.5, 8C(4) (as respectively amended or added by the Legislative Reform (Limited Partnership) Order 2009, arts. 8, 7).

[95] Thus, if the requirements of *ibid.* s.4(2), *infra*, para. A3–04 are not satisfied, the partner in question will not qualify as a limited partner and must be a general partner. See also the Explanatory Document accompanying the Legislative Reform (Limited Partnership) Order 2009, para. 39.

[96] (1926) 24 Ll.L.R. 25.

[97] See the preceding paragraph.

[98] Perjury Act 1911, s.5, replacing (as to England) the Limited Partnerships Act 1907, s.12: see *infra*, para. A3–14. As to Scotland, see the False Oaths Act 1933, s.2 (as amended).

nature of the change must be posted or delivered to the registrar within seven days.[99]

The statement must be signed "by the firm"[100] and not by the partners: as a result, it is considered that a signature in the firm name by any person who has the requisite authority will be sufficient.[101] A limited partner seemingly does not possess such authority.[102]

Default in registration of changes

Failure to deliver such a statement will involve the commission of an offence by the general partners, the penalty for which is a daily fine.[103] However, it is submitted that, in the case of a limited partnership formed prior to October 1, 2009, such a failure may have more serious implications for the limited partners, since a limited partnership which is not registered in accordance with the provisions of the Act is deemed to be a general partnership.[104] There would seem no logical reason to distinguish between an unregistered firm and a firm which is registered with inaccurate particulars, at least so long as the default continues.[105] If the Act were construed in some other way, a limited partner would retain the benefit of limited liability notwithstanding major changes in the firm, of which there is no record on the register. These might (*inter alia*) include changes in the firm's name, duration or business[106] or in the nature and extent of one or more partners' liability.[107] On the other hand, the statutory penalty for non-registration is only sought to be imposed on the general partners and a limited partner seemingly has no power to sign the statement required to be submitted to the registrar.[108] If this is indeed the position, a limited partner in such a firm should (where he is able to do so)[109] refuse to agree to any such change, otherwise than on terms which will ensure that the change only takes effect, if at all, when particulars thereof have been registered.

29–26

---

[99] Limited Partnerships Act 1907, s.9 (as amended), *infra*, para. A3–12; see also Form LP 6 in the Limited Partnerships (Forms) Rules 2009, Sched., Pt 2, *infra*, para. A4–05. This statement must also be filed by the registrar and a registration certificate sent to the firm: *ibid.* s.13, infra, para. A3–15. Note that it is seemingly possible to move the firm's principal place of business within *or outside* the UK without affecting the firm's registration, provided that the change is itself duly registered. Equally, the current editor has heard of one instance in which the registrar in Scotland declined to register such a change. *Semble* this cannot be a proper exercise of his powers.

[100] Limited Partnerships Act 1907, s.9(1); also Form LP 6, *supra*.

[101] Partnership Act 1890, s.6, *infra*, para. A1–07; Limited Partnerships Act 1907, s.7, *infra*, para. A3–07. *cf. Rogers, Eungblut & Co. v. Martin* [1911] 1 K.B. 19.

[102] Limited Partnerships Act 1907, s.6(1), *infra*, para. A3–06.

[103] *ibid.* s.9(2), *infra*, para. A3–12. It is also an offence knowingly to make or send a false statement: Perjury Act 1911, s.5 and *supra*, para. 29–24, n. 98.

[104] Limited Partnerships Act 1907, s.5 (in its original form), *infra*, para. A3–05.

[105] This analysis was accepted (*obiter*) by Wright J. in *Rayner & Co. v. Rhodes* (1926) 24 Ll.L.R. 25, 28.

[106] Changes in the business may alter the general partners' implied authority to bind the firm: Partnership Act 1890, s.5. See also *supra*, paras 12–02 *et seq.* and, *infra*, para. 30–01.

[107] The Limited Partnerships Act 1907, s.10, *infra*, para. A3–13, requires the change of a general into a limited partner to be advertised in the *Gazette*, and renders the change inoperative until it is so advertised. Although registration is not mentioned in that section, it is framed in negative terms; the current editor submits that the change will not in fact be operative until all the other requirements of the Act, including registration (*ibid.* s.9(1)(g), *infra*, para. A3–12), have been satisfied. But see also *infra*, paras 29–28, 30–06.

[108] See *ibid.* s.6(1).

[109] See *ibid.* s.6(3) and *infra*, paras 31–02 *et seq.*, 31–14 *et seq.*

On the other hand, where the limited partnership has been registered on an application made on or after October 1, 2009, the position is very different. Following the amendment of section 5 of the 1907 Act,[110] a failure to register a change in the particulars submitted on first registration will no longer result in the firm being deemed to forfeit its status as a limited partnership, notwithstanding the considerations referred to above. Clearly any change in the firm which affects a partner's status may not have effect until registered and, where necessary, advertised,[111] but any other default is seemingly now only attended with the imposition of a fine.[112]

Right to inspect statements

29–27   Any person has a right to inspect the statements filed by the registrar and to require a certificate of the registration of any limited partnership or a certified copy of, or extract from, any registered statement on payment of the prescribed fee.[113] Such a certificate or certified copy or extract is admissible as evidence in all legal proceedings.[114] The right to inspect can now be exercised by subscribing to Companies House Direct, by personal inspection at a Companies House Information Centre or by having a hard copy sent by post or left for collection.[115]

How far registration constitutes notice

29–28   Notwithstanding this general right of inspection, it is questionable whether, and if so to what extent, registration under the Limited Partnerships Act 1907 constitutes notice to third parties of the nature of the partnership or of its registered particulars. The Act itself suggests that registration will not in every case be sufficient notice of matters which require to be registered. Thus, where a general partner becomes a limited partner, the change in his status must be registered *and* immediately advertised in the *Gazette*.[116] Even then, a *Gazette* notice is not always sufficient notice of a fact advertised therein.[117]

The current editor submits that, whilst registration may be sufficient notice of the registered particulars to any person who deals with the firm knowing it to be

---

[110] By the Legislative Reform (Limited Partnership) Order 2009, art. 8: see *infra*, para. A3–05.

[111] Thus, a change from general to limited partner status must be registered *and* advertised (see *supra*, n. 107), whereas a change from limited to general partner status merely requires to be registered. *Quaere*, in the latter case, will the new general partner not be liable as such as soon as he agrees to the change of status since he no longer purports to be a limited partner for the purposes of the Limited Partnerships Act 1907, s.4(2). Naturally the incidence of changes of the latter type are few in number.

[112] There is, as such, no requirement in the 1907 Act that each limited partner's registered particulars must be up to date as a condition of retention of that status.

[113] *ibid*. ss.16(1), 17 (as respectively amended by the Companies Act 2006, s.1063(7)), *infra*, paras A3–18, A3–19. As to the actual fees payable, see the Registrar of Companies (Fees) (Limited Partnerships and Newspaper Proprietors) Regulations 2009, reg. 4, Sched. 2, paras 4, 5.

[114] Limited Partnerships Act 1907, s.16(2) (as amended).

[115] See the Registrar of Companies (Fees) (Limited Partnerships and Newspaper Proprietors) Regulations 2009, reg. 4, Sched. 2, paras 1, 4, 5.

[116] Limited Partnerships Act 1907, s.10, *infra*, para. A3–13. See further *supra*, para. 29–26, n. 107 and *infra*, 30–06.

[117] See *supra*, paras 13–74 *et seq*.

a limited partnership,[118] it may not be sufficient where the nature of the partnership is not known to him. Suppose that an existing firm was, prior to October 1, 2009, converted into a limited partnership without changing its name and that one or more of the existing partners became limited partners therein. Suppose further that the firm was duly registered and the change advertised in the *Gazette*, but no notice was given to the customers of the "old" firm, who remained totally unaware of the change. It is considered that such customers could properly hold any limited partner known to be a general partner in the "old" firm liable beyond the amount of his capital contribution in respect of liabilities incurred *after* the change.[119] The position would be the same in a case where the conversion occurred on or after October 1, 2009, save that it would be obligatory to change the firm name to include the words "limited partnership" or "LP",[120] so that the situation is less likely to arise. Nevertheless, on this basis, a general partner who becomes a limited partner should prudently take care to ensure that specific notice of the change in his status is given to every existing customer of the firm.

Deregistration

The Limited Partnerships Act 1907 does not contain any express power to **29–29** *deregister* a limited partnership. It follows that such a partnership's entry in the register will, seemingly, be capable of continuing even though it is no longer trading, has been dissolved or, indeed, has ceased to satisfy the conditions for continued existence as a limited partnership.[121] Nevertheless, it appears from the statistics produced by the Department for Business, Innovation and Skills that, where the registrar is aware that a limited partnership has been dissolved and its affairs wound up, its name is *de facto* removed from the register.

3. LIMITED PARTNERSHIPS AND THE FINANCIAL SERVICES AND MARKETS ACT 2000

Definition of collective investment scheme

The Financial Services and Markets Act 2000 contains the following **29–30** section:

> "235.—(1) In this Part 'collective investment scheme' means any arrangements with respect to property of any description, including money, the purpose or effect of which is to enable persons taking part in the arrangements (whether by becoming owners of the property or any part of it or otherwise) to participate in or receive profits or income arising from the acquisition, holding, management or disposal of the property or sums paid out of such profits or income.

[118] An analogy may perhaps be drawn with the principles enunciated in *Royal British Bank v. Turquand* (1856) 6 E. & B. 327, and other cases of that class.
[119] See the Limited Partnerships Act 1907, s.7, *infra*, para. A3–07; Partnership Act 1890, s.36(1). See also *supra*, paras 13–41 *et seq*.
[120] See *supra*, para. 29–09.
[121] *e.g.* if there is no longer at least one general and one limited partner: see the Limited Partnerships Act 1907, s.4(2), *infra*, para. A3–04. See *supra*, para. 29–03.

(2) The arrangements must be such that the persons who are to participate ('participants') do not have day-to-day control over the management of the property, whether or not they have the right to be consulted or to give directions.[122]

(3) The arrangements must also have either or both of the following characteristics—

(a) the contributions of the participants and the profits or income out of which payments are to be made to them are pooled[123];

(b) the property is to be managed as a whole by or on behalf of the operator of the scheme.

(4) If arrangements provide for such pooling as is mentioned in subsection (3)(a) in relation to separate parts of the property, the arrangements are not to be regarded as constituting a single collective investment scheme unless the participants are entitled to exchange rights in one part for rights in another.

(5) The Treasury may by order provide that arrangements do not amount to a collective investment scheme—

(a) in specified circumstances; or

(b) if the arrangements fall within a specified category of arrangement."

29–31   It is provided by regulation[124] that a collective investment scheme will not exist where each of the participants is a "permitted participant",[125] *i.e.* carries on a business which does not involve certain specified activities[126] otherwise than as a participant in the arrangement or as a member, partner or beneficiary of such a participant and enters into the arrangements for "commercial purposes related to that business."[127] Subsequent changes in the participants are, in effect, ignored for this purpose, but an incoming participant must have permitted status.[128]

---

[122] As to the type of arrangements falling within s.235(2), see *Financial Services Authority v. Fradley* [2006] 2 B.C.L.C. 616 (CA).

[123] See also subs. (4).

[124] See the Financial Services and Markets Act 2000 (Collective Investment Schemes) Order 2001 (SI 2001/1062), as amended, made pursuant to the Financial Services and Markets Act 2000, s.235(5).

[125] This expression is defined in the Financial Services and Markets Act 2000 (Collective Investment Schemes) Order 2001, Sched., para. 9(5), as substituted by the Financial Services and Markets Act 2000 (Collective Investment Schemes) (Amendment) Order 2008 (SI 2008/1641), art. 2(2) and amended by the Financial Services and Markets Act 2000 (Collective Investment Schemes) (Amendment) (No. 2) Order 2008 (SI 2008/1813), art. 2(2)(c). It expressly contemplates that the permitted participant may be a partnership, seemingly ignoring the fact that, under English law, a partnership does not have entity status: see *supra*, para. 4–27.

[126] *i.e.* any activities specified in the Financial Services and Markets Act 2000 (Regulated Activities) Order 2001 (SI 2001/544), arts 14, 21, 25, 25D, 37, 40, 45, 51 to 53 and 64, even if they are technically excluded from those articles thereunder. It does not matter if some other business involving such activities is also carried on.

[127] Financial Services and Markets Act 2000 (Collective Investment Schemes) Order 2001, Sched., para. 9(2), as substituted by the Financial Services and Markets Act 2000 (Collective Investment Schemes) (Amendment) Order 2008, art. 2(2). This blanket exemption applies where the arrangements are first entered into on or after July 15, 2008: *ibid.* However, the participants can voluntarily opt in to the collective investment scheme regime: *ibid.* para. 9(3), as substituted by *ibid.* and amended by the Financial Services and Markets Act 2000 (Collective Investment Schemes) (Amendment) (No. 2) Order 2008, art. 2(2)(b). As to arrangements which existed before July 15, 2008, see *ibid.* para. 9(1), as substituted by *ibid.* and amended by the Financial Services and Markets Act 2000 (Collective Investment Schemes) (Amendment) (No. 2) Order 2008, art. 2(2)(a).

[128] *ibid.* para. 9(4), (6), (7), as substituted, in the case of subss.(4) and (6), by the Financial Services and Markets Act 2000 (Collective Investment Schemes) (Amendment) Order 2008, art. 2(2) and, in the case of subs.(7), by the Financial Services and Markets Act 2000 (Collective Investment Schemes) (Amendment) (No. 2) Order 2008, art. 2(2)(d).

Although this regime would, at first sight, appear to exempt any limited partnership provided that its business does not involve such activities,[129] the regulations clearly contemplate that each of the participants is *already* carrying on the relevant business. On that basis, a limited partnership formed to carry on an entirely new business of a permitted type might theoretically constitute a collective investment scheme unless each of the limited partners can individually satisfy the condition in relation to his own business.[130] Similarly, where a new limited partner is admitted to an existing limited partnership. Nevertheless, it is understood that the Financial Services Authority does not, in practice, take this point.

The regulations also contains a number of other exceptions.[131]

Limited partnership as a collective investment scheme

Given the essential characteristics of a limited partnership[132] and, in particular, **29–32** the exclusion of the limited partners from any participation in the management of its affairs,[133] there can be no doubt that such a partnership will constitute a collective investment scheme, unless advantage can be taken of one of the exceptions designated by Treasury order.[134] Indeed this was expressly recognised in *Rose v. Lynx Express Ltd*.[135] However, it would seem that, in general, only the limited partners will be the participants in the scheme.[136]

It follows that:

(1) the shares of the limited partners will constitute "units" in that scheme[137] and, thus, investments[138];

(2) the establishment, operation or winding up of the partnership will constitute a regulated activity,[139] as will any dealings, etc., in relation to those "units"[140]; and

---

[129] Thus, each limited partner would be regarded as carrying on the partnership business through the agency of the general partner: Partnership Act 1890, s.5, as applied by the Limited Partnerships Act 1907, s.7.

[130] In order to satisfy this condition, it would not, in the current editor's view, be necessary to establish that each of the limited partners is carrying on the *same* business, but merely that the commercial purposes relate to each of their businesses.

[131] See the Financial Services and Markets Act 2000 (Collective Investment Schemes) Order 2001, Sched. (as amended).

[132] See *supra*, para. 28–01 and *infra*, paras 30–01 *et seq.*, 31–02 *et seq.*

[133] Limited Partnerships Act 1907, s.6(1), *infra*, para. A3–06; also *infra*, para. 31–04.

[134] See *supra*, para. 29–31.

[135] [2004] 1 B.C.L.C. 397 at [5] *per* John Powell Q.C., sitting as a deputy judge of the Chancery Division. The point was not mentioned on the appeal at [2004] 1 B.C.L.C. 455.

[136] This is the critical issue: the current editor derives support for his conclusion from the Financial Services and Markets Act 2000, s.235(2), *supra*, para. 29–30. However, he recognises that others may hold a contrary view. *Quaere*, if the general partner appoints a manager (see *infra*, n. 144), might he fall to be treated as a participant? Much may depend on the rights/functions (if any) which he retains. Note that if, for whatever reason, a general partner *is* regarded as a participant, he will retain that status even if he does have day-to-day control over the management of the firm: see *Russell-Cooke Trust Co. v. Elliott* [2001] 1 All E.R. (D) 197, a decision under the predecessor of *ibid.* s.235 (albeit not concerning a partnership). Note also *Russell-Cooke Trust Co v. Prentis* [2003] 2 All E.R. 478, which was a similar case.

[137] *ibid.* s.237(2).

[138] *ibid.* Sched. 2, Pt II, para. 16.

[139] *ibid.* Sched. 2, Pt I, para. 8.

[140] *ibid.* Sched. 2, Pt I, paras 2, 3, 6, 7.

(3) invitations and inducements to participate in the partnership may not in general be communicated to third parties.[141]

Accordingly, the general partner(s) would apparently need to seek authorisation under the Act,[142] unless they are exempt[143] or the partnership is in fact managed by some other authorised person.[144] Although the current editor is aware of the suggestion that the limited partnership itself, rather than the general partner, should seek authorisation, this does not reflect the general practice.

Limited partnership as a unit trust scheme

29–33   Section 237(1) of the Financial Services and Markets Act 2000 defines a unit trust scheme as "a collective investment scheme under which the property is held on trust for the participants". It has already been seen[145] that a limited partnership must be regarded as a collective investment scheme, but it does not follow that it must also be regarded as a unit trust scheme. In the first place, it will be rare for the general partner not to have any interest in the partnership property, even if that interest is small; if that is, indeed, the case, it is difficult to see how it could properly be said that the partnership property is held on trust for "the participants", *i.e.* the limited partners,[146] when it is, at best, held on trust for them and the general partner(s). The current editor would also question whether, given the true nature of a partner's share,[147] the interest of *any* partner in partnership property could, in any event, properly be characterised as held under a trust.[148]

---

[141] *ibid.* s.238.

[142] As to authorisation, see *ibid.* s.31 *et seq.* And see *supra*, paras 8–44 *et seq.*

[143] *ibid.* ss.38, 39, 327.

[144] It is, in practice, not uncommon to find that the general partner(s) will delegate the management of the partnership to a third party. *Semble*, in such a case the general partner would still be the "operator of the scheme" within the meaning of *ibid.* s.235(3)(b) and not a participant for the purposes of *ibid.* s.235(2). *Sed quaere*: see *supra*, n. 136.

[145] See *supra*, para. 29–32.

[146] *ibid. Per contra* if the general partner were also a participant: see *supra*, para. 29–32, n. 136.

[147] See *supra*, paras 19–01 *et seq.*

[148] Equally, it must be recognised that the Partnership Act 1890, s.20 may be said to operate at a trust level: see *supra*, para. 7–10.

CHAPTER 30

THE RIGHTS AND OBLIGATIONS OF THE PARTNERS AS REGARDS THIRD PARTIES

1. THE AUTHORITY OF PARTNERS TO BIND THE FIRM

General partners

A general partner in a limited partnership has the same implied authority to **30–01** bind the firm as a member of an ordinary partnership: the limits of that authority will accordingly be determined by the nature of the business and the way in which it is usually carried on.[1] However, whilst such a partner has the exclusive right to manage the partnership business,[2] it is considered that he does not have power, without the consent of the limited partners, to *alter* the nature of that business in order to extend his authority.[3]

Provided that he does not become bankrupt, a general partner's authority will continue after the dissolution of the firm for so long as is necessary to wind up its affairs and to complete any unfinished business[4]; indeed, in the absence of a court order to the contrary, it is the duty of a general partner to attend to such winding up.[5]

Deeds

In earlier editions of this work it has been submitted that the Limited Partner- **30–02** ships Act 1907[6] so modified the general rule that a partner has no implied authority to bind his firm by deed[7] as to confer such authority on the general partner(s), provided that the deed in question is framed and executed in the appropriate manner.[8] However, the current editor ventures to suggest that, even if this proposition is right, it will only rarely have any practical significance. If a deed is binding on the general partner, any claim thereunder will be enforceable against him and, if it was executed in pursuance of his authority as such, he will have authority to apply the partnership assets in settlement of that claim or otherwise to comply with any order a court may make, *e.g.* an order for specific

---

[1] Partnership Act 1890, s.5, *infra*, para. A1–06: Limited Partnerships Act 1907, s.7, *infra*, para. A3–07. See also *supra*, paras 12–02 *et seq*. Needless to say, such authority will only arise when a partnership has come into existence: *Blythe Limited Partnership v. Customs & Excise Commissioners* [1999] S.T.I. 1178.

[2] Limited Partnerships Act 1907, s.6(1), *infra*, para. A3–06.

[3] See *infra*, paras 31–02, 31–03.

[4] Partnership Act 1890, s.38, *infra*, para. A1–39; Limited Partnerships Act 1907, s.7, *infra*, para. A3–07. See also *supra*, paras 13–62 *et seq*.

[5] Limited Partnerships Act 1907, s.6(3), *infra*, para. A3–06.

[6] *ibid.* s.6(1), *infra*, para. A3–06.

[7] See *supra*, paras 12–62 *et seq*., 12–157 *et seq*.

[8] See the Partnership Act 1890, s.6, *infra*, para. A1–07 and *supra*, paras 12–157, 12–158. *Quaere*, does it matter that the partnership was not itself created by deed: see *supra*, para. 12–62.

performance. This is entirely consistent with the views expressed by Farwell J. in *Re Barnard*,[9] to the effect that there is no question of joint liability where there is only one general partner, since he alone is, in a normal case, liable for the debts.[10]

Limited partners

The general rule

30–03   The Limited Partnerships Act 1907 provides that a limited partner has no power to bind the firm and may not take part in the management of the partnership business.[11] It follows from the inability of a limited partner to bind the firm that any admission or representation which he may make will not be evidence against the firm[12] and, moreover, the firm will not automatically have notice of any matter of which he has notice.[13] It is also submitted that such a partner does not have the authority to sign the statement required to be submitted to the registrar following a change in the firm.[14]

If a limited partner purports to act on behalf of the firm, the firm will obviously not be bound but he may be liable in damages for breach of warranty of authority.[15] Save in exceptional circumstances, a partner so acting will not incur any liability if the person with whom he dealt knew of his lack of authority[16]; but, for this purpose, knowledge that he is a limited partner[17] would in itself appear to be insufficient, since he might have express authority to bind the firm.

Express authority

30–04   Notwithstanding the general statutory rule, it is submitted that a limited partner may be *expressly* authorised to act on behalf of the firm, either generally or for a particular purpose. In such a case, the firm will be bound by his acts within the scope of that authority, in the same way and to the same extent as it would be bound by the acts of any other agent. However, such a course is not without danger: if the limited partner, in pursuance of the authority conferred on him, performs some act which amounts to taking part in the management of the partnership business, he will forfeit the benefit of his limited liability for so long as such participation continues.[18]

---

[9] [1932] 1 Ch. 269, 274. See further *infra*, paras 33–07, 33–08.

[10] *Per contra*, if a limited partner has forfeited his limited liability by participating in the management of the firm: Limited Partnerships Act 1907 s.6(1): see *infra*, para. 31–04.

[11] Limited Partnerships Act 1907, s.6(1), *infra*, para. A3–06.

[12] But note, in this context, *PWA Corp. v. Gemini Group Automated Distribution Systems Inc.* [1993] 16 O.R. (3rd) 239 (CA, Ontario), a decision under a procedural regime which is not replicated in the CPR. *cf.* the Partnership Act 1890, s.15, *infra*, para. A1–16; and see *supra*, paras 12–21 *et seq.*

[13] *cf. ibid.* s.16, *infra*, para. A1–17; see also *supra*, paras 12–24 *et seq.*

[14] Limited Partnerships Act 1907, ss.6(1), 9, *infra*, paras A3–06, A3–12; see *supra*, para. 29–25.

[15] See *Collen v. Wright* (1857) 8 E. & B. 647; *Starkey v. Bank of England* [1903] A.C. 114; *Yonge v. Toynbee* [1910] 1 K.B. 215.

[16] See *Halbot v. Lens* [1901] 1 Ch. 344.

[17] As to how far registration constitutes notice of the fact that a person is a limited partner, see *supra*, para. 29–28.

[18] Limited Partnerships Act 1907, s.6(1), *infra*, para. A3–06; see further *infra*, paras 31–02 *et seq.*

2.   THE LIABILITY OF PARTNERS FOR THE DEBTS AND
OBLIGATIONS OF THE FIRM

A.   GENERAL PARTNERS

As might be expected, the liability of a general partner for the debts and **30–05**
obligations of a limited partnership is precisely the same as that of a member of
an ordinary partnership.[19]

Retirement

In order to avoid the risk of continuing liability following the retirement of a
general partner or the dissolution of the firm, it is advisable to advertise that fact
and to notify all the firm's existing or "old" customers, as in the case of an
ordinary partnership.[20] It would not on any footing be safe to rely on the firm's
amended registration as sufficient notice to such customers.[21]

Change of liability

A general partner may become a limited partner at any time during the **30–06**
continuance of the partnership, provided that there will still be at least one
continuing general partner.[22] Such a change of status can be effected by a suitable
arrangement[23] between the partners, but will not prejudice the rights of third
parties in respect of the *past* debts and obligations of the firm, where the
unlimited liability of the former general partner will continue. Moreover, such an
arrangement will also not affect his liability for *future* debts and obligations until
it has been advertised in the *Gazette*[24] and duly registered.[25] The current editor
does not subscribe to the view that the Act contemplates advertisement of the
change of status *before* it is registered so that it cannot be registered until
advertised.[26] Even where the advertisement and registration have been completed, it may still be necessary to give express notice to the firm's existing
customers.[27] Only when all these steps have been completed can he be assured
of the benefits of limited liability.

Since Part 41 of the Companies Act 2006 contains no provision requiring a
distinction to be drawn between general and limited partners in a firm's business

[19] *ibid.* ss.4(2), 7, *infra*, paras A3–04, A3–07; and see *supra*, paras 13–01 *et seq.*
[20] See *supra*, paras 13–37 *et seq.*
[21] See *supra*, para. 29–28.
[22] See the Limited Partnerships Act 1907, ss.4(2), 9(1)(g), *infra*, paras A3–04, A3–12.
[23] This is the actual expression used in *ibid.* s.10(1).
[24] *ibid.* s.10, *infra*, para. A3–13. Note that the section does not state by whom the change of status
is to be advertised. It is submitted that this responsibility will, in general, fall on the general partner
(see *ibid.* s.6(1), *infra*, para. A3–06) and this is, to an extent borne out by the assumptions underlying
the Directors Disqualification Act 1986, Sched. 1, para. 6, as substituted by the Insolvent Partnerships
Order 1994 (SI 1994/2421), Sched. 8.
[25] *ibid.* s.9(1)(g), *infra*, para. A3–12; see also *supra*, para. 29–26. If the change of liability is
registered within the permitted 7 days but is preceded by the *Gazette* notice, it will seemingly be
effective from the date of the notice; *per contra*, perhaps, if a person dealing with the firm had not
seen the notice but had inspected and relied upon the old registered particulars.
[26] See *infra*, para. 31–13, where this issue is considered in relation to the other limb of *ibid.* s.10,
i.e. on the assignment of a limited partner's share.
[27] See *supra*, para. 29–28.

letters, etc., or in any notice or list required to be displayed or made available,[28] no steps need be taken as a result of a mere change of liability.

B.   LIMITED PARTNERS

(a) Extent and Duration of Liability

Extent of liability

30–07   Save in the cases noted hereafter,[29] the liability of a limited partner for the debts and obligations of the firm is limited to the amount of his contribution to the partnership,[30] however small,[31] but his liability for debts and obligations *vis-à-vis* third parties must be contrasted with the sharing of trading losses as between the partners themselves: as to the latter, there is no necessary limitation on his liability.[32]

A limited partner may increase the amount of his original contribution[33] which will inevitably entail a corresponding increase in his liability, even though this is not expressly stated in the Act. Equally, there does not appear to be any objection to a limited partner making an initial contribution on becoming a partner and at the same time binding himself to make a further contribution at a later date. It is submitted that, if the agreement is bona fide, such a partner's liability will be restricted to the amount of his *current* contribution, no account being taken of any further contribution which has not yet fallen due.[34] *Per contra*, perhaps, if the agreement amounts to a deliberate attempt to evade the Act by so limiting his

---

[28] Companies Act 2006, ss.1201 (as substituted by the Companies Act 2006 (Substitution of Section 1201) Regulations 2009 (SI 2009/3182), reg. 2), 1202, 1204. The Secretary of State does, however, have power to make regulations specifying the form of any such notice or list: *ibid.* ss.1202(3), 1204(2). See also *supra*, paras 29–10 *et seq.*

[29] See *infra*, para. 30–08. To these exceptions should perhaps be added the illegality of the partnership: see *supra*, para. 29–07.

[30] Limited Partnerships Act 1907, s.4(2), *infra*, para. A3–04; and see *supra*, para. 29–04.

[31] See *Dickson v. MacGregor* 1992 S.L.T. 83 (Land Ct.) and *MacFarlane v. Falfield Investments Ltd.* 1998 S.L.T. 145 (1st Div.), in each of which the limited partners' contributions were £10.

[32] *Reed v. Young* [1986] 1 W.L.R. 649. However, a limited partner is now restricted in the use he can make of such losses: see the Income Tax Act 2007, ss.103A, 104, 105 (as respectively added or amended by the Finance Act 2007, Sched. 4, paras 8, 10, 11, 21, Sched. 27, Pt 2(1)), 114. The Partnerships (Restrictions on Contributions to a Trade) Regulations 2005 (SI 2005/2017) continue to have effect as if made under *ibid.* s.114 but with modifications: *ibid.* Sched. 2, para. 35. These provisions also apply to a person who "in substance acts as a limited partner" within the meaning of *ibid.* s.103(1)(b), (2), but this is, of course, not a concept recognised in limited partnership law. A non-active *general* partner is now also subject to a similar regime in the year in which he first carries on the trade and the next three years: *ibid.* ss.110–112 (as respective amended by the Finance Act 2007, Sched. 4, paras 10–13, 21, Sched. 27, Pt 2(1)). Specific provisions govern the use of film-related and other losses. See further *infra*, paras 34–49 *et seq.*

[33] Limited Partnerships Act 1907, s.9(1)(f), *infra*, para. A3–12.

[34] In such a case, particulars of the sum actually contributed will be given when the firm is registered: see *ibid.* s.8A(2)(d) (as added by the Legislative Reform (Limited Partnerships) Order 2009 (SI 2009/1940), art. 5), *infra*, para. A3–09. Particulars of the subsequent contribution will be given when it is made: *ibid.* s.9(1)(f), *infra*, para. A3–12. *Quaere*, if the limited partner agrees to make a further contribution but fails to do so on the due date, should particulars be given to the registrar? It is thought that they should, and that the limit of his liability will be the amount of his agreed contribution, irrespective of whether it has in fact been contributed. It is, however, unclear how effect would be given to the increase in his liability in such a case: see *infra*, paras 30–19 *et seq.* Presumably, it would be treated as analogous to a case of withdrawal of capital.

liability, whilst at the same time securing to him all the benefits which he would have enjoyed if the entirety of his contribution had been brought in from the outset.[35]

A limited partner may not during the continuance of the partnership draw out or receive back any part of his contribution, although the penalty for a breach of this prohibition does not amount to a substantial deterrent.[36]

Forfeiture of limited liability

Notwithstanding the general limitation on his liability, there are four circum-   **30–08** stances in which a limited partner may face a liability for the debts and obliga- tions of the firm beyond the amount of the contribution which he has invested in the firm. They are as follows:

(1) If, in the case of a limited partnership formed prior to October 1, 2009, the firm does not continue to be registered in accordance with the provisions of the Act,[37] a limited partner is deemed to be a general partner and, as such, his liability will unlimited.

(2) If, in the case of a limited partnership registered on an application made on or after October 1, 2009, a person registered as a limited partner does not satisfy the requirements of section 4(2) of the Act,[38] he will be a general partner and again his liability will be unlimited.[39]

(3) If he takes part in the management of the partnership business, a limited partner becomes liable as though he were a general partner for as long as such participation continues.[40]

(4) If, during the continuance of the partnership, he either directly or indirectly draws out or receives back any part of his contribution, the limited partner becomes liable up to the amount so drawn out or received back.[41]

Withdrawal of contribution

It appears that breach of the statutory prohibition on the withdrawal of a   **30–09** limited partner's contribution during the continuation of the partnership is attended *only* by the sanction of liability for the debts and obligations of the firm up to the amount so drawn out or received back. If this is, indeed, the position, the Act provides no real deterrent to such withdrawals, since limited liability is,

---

[35] *e.g.* an enlarged profit share. There would naturally be substantial problems of proof in such a case but, given the latitude afforded to them by the Act, it is hard to see why prospective partners should organise their affairs in this unnecessarily circuitous way.

[36] Limited Partnerships Act 1907, s.4(3), *infra*, para. A3–04. See further, *infra*, paras 30–09 *et seq.*

[37] *ibid.* s.5 (in its original form), *infra*, para. A3–05; and see *supra*, paras 29–23, 29–26.

[38] *e.g.* if he has not contributed any capital on admission to the firm.

[39] See *supra*, paras 29–23, 29–26. In such a case, the issue of a certificate of registration is conclusive evidence that a limited partnership exists (Limited Partnerships Act 1907, s.8C(4) (as added by the Legislative Reform (Limited Partnerships) Order 2009, art. 7), *infra*, para. A3–11) and *ibid.* s.5 applies in a truncated form: see *infra*, para. A3–05.

[40] *ibid.* s.6(1), *infra*, para. A3–06. See further, *infra*, paras 31–02 *et seq.*

[41] *ibid.* s.4(3), *infra*, para. A3–04.

in effect, preserved at the original level. Although the current editor considers that the Act could, conceivably, be construed in such a way as to impose on the limited partner both a liability up to the amount of the original contribution[42] and an *additional* liability in respect of the amount withdrawn,[43] *i.e.* an effective double penalty and a real disincentive to the early withdrawal of capital,[44] this would imply that a limited partner is in all cases personally liable up to the amount of his contribution, which does not appear to have been the legislative intention.[45]

30–10   In the face of the above possibility, it is of importance to identify what types of payment received by a limited partner will fall to be treated as a return of contribution. In earlier editions of this work it was submitted that:

> "any payment to a limited partner which directly or indirectly comes out of his contribution, whether such payment takes the form of a payment of interest on his capital or of a share of profits or any other form, will be a receipt by him of a part of his contribution, and will render him liable for the debts of the firm up to the amount he has so received."

The current editor considers that, as a general proposition, this goes too far: it will be a question of fact in each case whether any particular payment must be treated as an effective repayment of capital. Payments out of profits, whether framed as interest on capital or otherwise, can rarely, if ever, be regarded as such; *per contra*, if there are no profits and interest on capital is (exceptionally) funded out of the capital itself. Even if the Act were interpreted in a less benign way, once a partner has received a share of profits equal to the amount of his contribution, the receipt of any further profit distributions would not *increase* his liability, *i.e.* he could not be regarded as having been repaid his capital several times over.

Lost capital

30–11   A limited partner will seemingly enjoy the full benefits of limited liability even where his original contribution has been lost in the course of carrying on the firm's business. Since the Act does not require the partners to replace any lost capital out of profits, the current editor submits that the subsequent receipt of a share of profits should not be regarded as a repayment of that lost capital.

A more cautious view was, however, expressed in the following passage taken from the original Supplement to this work on the Limited Partnerships Act 1907 but, unaccountably, omitted from later editions:

> "It is apprehended that under this sub-section a question may arise whether, when there have been capital losses, a limited partner who shares in a division of profits before the losses are made good will be drawing out or receiving back part of his contribution. The question would appear to be similar to that which arises under the Companies Acts where dividends have been paid without making good capital losses. The decided cases under the Companies Acts seem to show that, provided the

---

[42] *i.e.* under *ibid.* s.4(2), *infra*, para. A3–04.

[43] *i.e.* under *ibid.* s.4(3).

[44] If this *were* the correct construction, it is submitted that the additional liability would automatically cease once the improperly withdrawn contribution has been repaid to the firm.

[45] This was clearly the view of Wright J. in *Rayner & Co. v. Rhodes* (1926) 24 Ll.L.R. 25, 27, when he stated that, on a limited partner making a partial withdrawal of capital, "*pro tanto* his liability was to be reinstated". See further *infra*, paras 30–11, 30–19, 30–20.

business of the limited company is, having regard to all the circumstances, fairly conducted, there may be cases in which it is not improper for the company to pay dividends notwithstanding that there have been losses of capital which have not been made good.[46]

In connection with this question a distinction has been drawn between 'fixed' and 'circulating' capital, the former being treated as a form of capital which need not be replaced before ascertaining profits available for dividend.[47]

The distinction, however, does not appear to have been universally accepted, nor is it one which is always easy of application,[48] and in any event, as in many businesses of the kind which are usually made the subject of partnerships, a great part of the capital is in its nature clearly 'circulating' rather than 'fixed,' a limited partner will in many cases certainly run the risk of being called upon to refund if he shares in a division of so-called profits, or receives interest on capital before capital losses have been made good."

Position following dissolution

It is considered that, for present purposes, a partnership will be regarded as **30–12** continuing until its affairs have been fully wound up or, at any rate, until all its debts and liabilities have been discharged.[49] It follows that the prohibition on the withdrawal of a limited partner's contribution will continue even after the dissolution of the firm.

Change of liability

If a limited partner becomes a general partner, particulars of the change must **30–13** be registered,[50] but no other formalities need be observed.[51] The former limited partner's liability for the debts and obligations of the firm incurred before he became a general partner will, in the normal way, be limited to the amount of his contribution,[52] but he will naturally have unlimited liability for all debts and obligations incurred after he gave up that status.[53]

Termination of liability as to future debts

The sections of the Act which prohibit the withdrawal of a limited partner's **30–14** contribution during the continuance of the partnership[54] and provide that a limited partnership is not dissolved by the death or bankruptcy of such a partner[55] raise questions of considerable difficulty when considering the termination of liability. Neither section is expressed to be the subject of any contrary agreement

---

[46] The editors referred in particular to *Verner v. General and Commercial Investment Trust* [1894] 2 Ch. 239; *Barrow Haematite Steel Co.* [1900] 2 Ch. 846, affirmed at [1901] 2 Ch. 746; *Dovey v. Cory* [1901] A.C. 477.

[47] *Verner v. General and Commercial Investment Trust, supra,* p. 266 *per* Lindley L.J.; *Dovey v. Cory, supra,* pp. 493, 494 *per* Lord Davey.

[48] *Dovey v. Corey, supra,* p. 487 *per* Earl of Halsbury L.C. and p. 494 *per* Lord Davey.

[49] See the Partnership Act 1890, s.38, *infra,* para. A1–39; the Limited Partnerships Act 1907, s.7, *infra,* para. A3–07. And see *supra,* paras 13–62 *et seq.*

[50] Limited Partnerships Act 1907, s.9(1)(g), *infra,* para. A3–12.

[51] *cf.* the position of a general partner who becomes a limited partner: see *supra,* para. 30–06.

[52] What will be the position if, following the change in his liability, he withdraws the contribution which he originally made as a limited partner? Will the Limited Partnerships Act 1907, s.4(3) still apply? It is thought not, since he will be withdrawing it in his capacity as a general partner; *sed quaere.*

[53] *Quaere* precisely when this will occur: see *supra,* para. 29–26, n. 111.

[54] Limited Partnerships Act 1907, s.4(3), *infra,* para. A3–04.

[55] *ibid.* s.6(2), *infra,* para. A3–06.

between the partners; in this respect, the latter section differs from the corresponding provision in the Partnership Act 1890.[56] Nevertheless, the terms upon which a partner may retire or otherwise cease to be a member of the firm, and the rights conferred on the personal representatives or trustee of a deceased or bankrupt partner in respect of his share, are matters which primarily affect the partners themselves and, as such, are in general left to their determination.[57] On that footing, the current editor submits that the partners may quite properly agree to permit the retirement of a limited partner and to accept that the death or bankruptcy of such a partner will cause the firm to be dissolved, either as between all of them or solely as regards that partner.[58] It follows that, so long as any change in the firm is duly registered,[59] the liability of a limited partner can be terminated as regards future debts and obligations, notwithstanding the fact that the partnership continues as between the remaining partners and that the outgoing partner or his estate has drawn out or received back the value of his contribution. However, in the case of retirement,[60] registration of the change should also be supplemented by the usual *Gazette* and other notices.[61]

30–15   What is less clear is whether the former limited partner (or his personal representatives or trustee in bankruptcy) is, in the absence of agreement, *entitled* to withdraw his contribution until the partnership is terminated by effluxion of time or is otherwise dissolved. In earlier editions of this work, it was submitted that there is no such right and that such a partner's contribution will remain liable for the debts and obligations of the firm, whether incurred before or after his retirement, death or bankruptcy. The current editor questions the correctness of this proposition: if it is right that the Limited Partnerships Act 1907 does not prohibit the withdrawal of a *former* limited partner's contribution because, on his retirement, a new partnership comes into existence,[62] there can be no warrant for the continuing partners insisting on the retention of that contribution, save (perhaps) until the firm's registration has been duly amended.[63]

Assignment of share

30–16   The liability of a limited partner for future debts and obligations may also be terminated by the assignment of his share, which will, in the absence of some contrary agreement, require the consent of the general partners.[64] However, his liability will continue until the assignment has been advertised in the *Gazette*[65] and duly registered.[66]

---

[56] See the Partnership Act 1890, s.33(1), *supra* para. 24–29; *cf.* the Limited Partnerships Act 1907, s.6(5).

[57] Partnership Act 1890, s.19, *infra*, para. A1–20; Limited Partnerships Act 1907, s.7, *infra*, para. A3–07.

[58] In the current editor's view, there will, in either case, be a dissolution as a matter of law, irrespective of the terms of the agreement: see *infra*, paras 30–15, 31–16. However, in the latter case the dissolution will only be of a technical nature: see *supra*, para. 24–02.

[59] Limited Partnerships Act 1907, s.9(1)(d), *infra*, para. A3–12; Limited Partnerships (Forms) Rules 2009, Sched., Pt 2, Form LP 6, Note 1, *infra*, para. A4–06. See further, *supra*, para. 29–25.

[60] Similar considerations will apply if a limited partner is expelled from the firm.

[61] Partnership Act 1890, ss.36, 37, *supra*, paras 13–40 *et seq.*; see also *supra*, para. 29–28.

[62] See *infra*, para. 31–16.

[63] Limited Partnerships Act 1907, s.9(1)(d), *infra*, para. A3–12.

[64] *ibid.* s.6(5)(b), *infra*, para. A3–06.

[65] *ibid.* s.10(1), *infra*, para. A3–13.

[66] See *ibid.* s.9(1)(d), *infra*, para. A3–12; and see *supra*, para. 29–26 and, as to the interaction between *ibid*, ss.9 and 10, *infra*, para. 31–13. As to withdrawals of capital pre- and post the assignment, see *infra*, para. 30–18.

Termination of liability as to past debts

It has already been seen that the retirement, expulsion, death or bankruptcy of **30–17** a partner does not terminate his liability to creditors for the existing debts and obligations of the firm.[67] Therefore, if a former limited partner withdraws or receives back (or has previously withdrawn or received back) any part of his contribution, he or his estate will at the very least remain liable for such debts and obligations up to the original amount of that contribution.[68] The position is less clear where a limited partner assigns his share in such a way as to render the assignee a limited partner in his place.[69] Earlier editions of this work contained the following analysis:

> "In the case of assignment with the consent of the general partners, the limited partner will not, as a rule, withdraw any part of his contribution; he will receive the purchase-money (if any) for his share out of the pocket of the assignee and not from the partnership. In such case, therefore, he will not be responsible for the past debts and obligations of the firm unless before the assignment he has incurred liability beyond the amount of his contribution."

The current editor questions whether such an approach is warranted by the **30–18** terms of the Act itself: a limited partner's liability does not depend on withdrawal of his contribution[70] although it is, in general, limited to the amount thereof.[71] By assigning his share in this way, he will certainly cease to be a limited partner and the assignee will become a limited partner in his place, but does it necessarily follow that a creditor will have a direct right of action against that assignee in respect of a debt or obligation incurred *prior* to the advertisement and registration of the change in the firm?[72] This will be of particular importance if the assignee has withdrawn any part of the assignor's original contribution. It is submitted that a clear statutory provision would be required to displace the liability of a former limited partner to such a creditor, which is not necessarily to be found in the Act.[73] It goes almost without saying that a suitable indemnity should be obtained from the assignee against the possibility of such continuing liability being imposed.[74] If the *assignor* withdrew part of his capital, it is, perhaps, more logical that the assignee should assume liability, as he is clearly on notice as to the position.[74a]

---

[67] See *supra*, paras 13–78 *et seq.*, 26–11 *et seq.*

[68] It is considered that, in such a case, there will not even be the *theoretical* risk of additional liability noticed, *supra*, para. 30–09.

[69] Limited Partnerships Act 1907, s.6(5)(b), *infra*, para. A3–06. However, an assignment will not always have this result: see *infra*, para. 31–13.

[70] Note that, on one construction of the Limited Partnerships Act 1907, such withdrawal might result in *additional* liability: see *supra*, para. 30–09.

[71] *ibid.* ss.4(2), 5, 6(1), *infra*, paras A3–04 *et seq.*

[72] See generally, *supra*, paras 13–22 *et seq.*

[73] Could it perhaps be argued that, since the assignee becomes entitled to all the rights of the assignor (Limited Partnerships Act 1907, s.6(5)(b), *infra*, para. A3–06), he must also by implication assume all of his duties and obligations? Surely this represents an impermissible gloss on the Act. Equally, does *ibid.* s.4(2), *infra*, para. A3–04 impose potential liability for all debts and obligations, *whenever incurred*? Perhaps this reflects the fact that the limited partner's contribution is intended to be available to meet all debts, irrespective of when he was admitted.

[74] Note, however, that such an indemnity will normally be implied: see *supra*, para. 19–57.

[74a] The withdrawal will not have been notified under *ibid.* s.9(1)(f) as the *contribution* remains unchanged, but the accounts should show the withdrawal.

(b) Nature of Liability

30–19   The Limited Partnerships Act 1907 does, with certain exceptions, take care to limit the liability of a limited partner to the amount of his contribution.[75] Somewhat surprisingly it contains no provision regulating proceedings by creditors of the firm nor any protection for the limited partners against any execution which may be levied against them by such creditors. The Act does not even *expressly* seek to modify the general law under which every partner is personally liable for the debts and obligations of the firm.[76] This omission has now, to a large extent, been remedied by the Civil Procedure Rules, which prevent a judgment or order made against a limited partnership being enforced against a limited partner without permission[77] unless he has acknowledged service of the claim form as a partner, been served within the jurisdiction in that capacity or been served out of the jurisdiction with the permission of the court.[78] It is obviously incumbent on a limited partner to make his status known when pleading his case, since a partnership membership statement[79] will not disclose that status. It would seem that, save in one of the excepted cases, permission to enforce the judgment will still be required where a limited partner has taken part in the management of the firm contrary to the provisions of section 6(1) of the Limited Partnerships Act 1907,[80] since in such a case he will still remain a limited partner, even though liable "as though he were a general partner"; *sed quaere.*

30–20   Quite apart from the foregoing, it is with considerable diffidence submitted that a limited partner's position under the Act is analogous to that of a married woman who had, prior to the Law Reform (Married Women and Tortfeasors) Act 1935, contracted debts which could only be met out of her separate estate,[81] and that a creditor of the firm cannot obtain a personal judgment against such a partner or properly issue execution against him,[82] unless he has incurred liability beyond the amount of his contribution. Some support for this view is to be found in the observations of Farwell J. in *Re Barnard,*[83] to the effect that there was no joint liability in the case of a bankrupt limited partnership comprising a single general partner, since only he was liable for its debts. The position of a former limited partner who has assigned his share to a third party may, however, be anomalous.[84]

Form of judgment

30–21   If the foregoing analysis is correct, it is considered that any judgment against a firm ought properly to be framed in such a way as to ensure that each limited

---

[75] See *supra*, para. 30–08. However, subject to the prohibition against the withdrawal of a limited partner's contribution, it would seem that limited liability is *not* dependent on his contribution still being retained by or invested in the firm: see *supra*, para. 30–11 and *infra*, para. 31–08.

[76] Partnership Act 1890, ss.9, 10, *infra*, paras A1–10, A1–11; Limited Partnerships Act 1907, s.7, *infra*, para. A3–07. See also *supra*, paras 13–03 *et seq.*

[77] See CPR 70PD, para. 6A.4, *infra*, para. A2–09.

[78] *ibid.* para. 6A.3, *infra*, para. A2–09. See also *supra*, paras 14–22, 14–93. As to service on a partner, see *supra*, paras 14–14 *et seq.*

[79] See CPR 7APD, paras 5B.1 *et seq.*, *infra*, para. A2–05.

[80] See *supra*, para. 30–04 and *infra*, paras 31–02 *et seq.*

[81] For a summary of the position prior to the 1935 Act, see the 14th ed. of this work, at pp. 60 *et seq.*

[82] But see CPR 70PD, para. 6A.3, noted *supra*.

[83] [1932] 1 Ch. 269; see further *infra*, paras 33–07, 33–08.

[84] See *supra*, para. 30–18.

partner enjoys the benefit of the limited liability conferred on him by the Act, but this is not a possibility which is reflected in the Civil Procedure Rules, even following the recent revisions.[85] Similar considerations naturally apply where judgment is to be entered directly against a limited partner.

Limited partner liable beyond the amount of his contribution, etc.

The position of a limited partner who falls to be treated as a general partner, by reason of default in the registration of the partnership,[86] a failure to satisfy the requirements of the Act[87] or participation in the management of the partnership business,[88] or who becomes liable for the firm's debts and obligations by drawing out or receiving back any part of his contribution[89] will be very different from that of a normal limited partner.   **30–22**

In the second of the above cases, a creditor of the firm should have all the remedies against the supposed limited partner which would be open to him against a general partner since he is not, as a matter of law, a limited partner. In the first and third cases, the limited partner is liable as a *deemed* general partner but his status is technically unaffected, so that the provisions of the Civil Procedure Rules regarding execution against limited partners would still seem to apply.[90] Subject to that factor, any judgment against the firm or against the limited partner would in any event need to take no special form, save as regards debts and obligations incurred whilst the limited partner *did* continue to enjoy limited liability.

The rights of a creditor in the fourth case are less clear, although again the limited partner would have the protection of the Civil Procedure Rules on execution. It is nevertheless submitted that any judgment obtained against the firm, whether in the firm name or in the names of the individual partners,[91] should properly be framed so as to leave the creditor free (subject as above) to levy execution against the limited partner personally up to the amount of the contribution drawn out or received back and that such a judgment could found a petition for an insolvency order against the firm and/or against that partner.[92]

3.   ACTIONS BY AND AGAINST PARTNERS

Since the Limited Partnerships Act 1907 does not seek to regulate the form of an action by or against a limited partnership, such an action will not, in terms of the   **30–23**

---

[85] See, as to the execution of judgments against a firm, CPR 70PD, paras 6A.2 *et seq. infra*, para. A2–09; also *supra*, paras 14–22, 14–93, 30–19. And see, as to the form of judgment against a firm where one partner is a minor, *Lovell v. Beauchamp* [1894] A.C. 607; also *supra*, para. 14–20.

[86] Limited Partnerships Act 1907, s.5 (in its original form), *infra*, para. A3–05. Save in the case of complete non-registration, this is only relevant where the limited partnership was formed prior to October 1, 2009: see *supra*, para. 29–23.

[87] *ibid.* s.4(2), *infra*, para. A3–04. This is, in practice, only relevant in the case of a limited partnership registered on or after October 1, 2009: see *supra*, paras 29–23, 29–26. In any other case, *ibid.* s.5 (9n its original form) will apply: see the preceding footnote.

[88] *ibid.* s.6(1), *infra*, para. A3–06. See *infra*, paras 31–02 *et seq.*

[89] *ibid.* s.4(3), *infra*, para. A3–04. See *supra*, paras 30–09 *et seq.* and *infra* para. 31–08.

[90] CPR 70PD, paras 6A.3, 6A.4, *infra*, para. A2–09. *Semble*, there should be no difficulty obtaining permission to execute the judgment in such a case.

[91] As to when the firm name should be used, see *supra*, paras 14–04 *et seq.*

[92] See *supra*, paras 27–08 *et seq.*, 27–26 *et seq.*, 27–48, and *infra*, paras 33–05, 33–06.

necessary parties, differ from an action by and against an ordinary partnership.[93] However, difficulties may in practice arise, particularly given the fact that the Civil Procedure Rules[94] do not take account of the possibility that one or more of the partners may enjoy the benefit of limited liability, save as regards the execution of judgments.[95]

Actions by the firm

30–24   It has already been seen that, under the general law, each partner has authority to bring an action on behalf of the firm.[96] It is, however, apprehended that a limited partner will not have such authority.[97] Nevertheless, a civil or all proceedings order[98] against such a partner will prevent the firm from instituting proceedings without the leave of the court.[99]

Actions against the firm

30–25   Actions must now, generally, be brought against an ordinary partnership in the firm name but may, in an appropriate case, be brought in the names of the individual partners[100] and any partner has authority to sign an acknowledgment of service in the firm name on behalf of all the partners.[101] It is clear that a limited partnership may also be sued in the firm name or, where necessary, in the names of the partners, including the limited partners, but it must be questionable whether a limited partner will have authority to acknowledge service on behalf of his co-partners. Although the Civil Procedure Rules do appear to give *any* partner the requisite authority,[102] this ignores the default position under the Limited Partnerships Act 1907.[103]

Service of claim form on limited partner

30–26   If an action is brought against a partnership in the firm name, it has already been seen that the claim form may, in certain circumstances, be personally served on a partner.[104] However, it is again not entirely clear whether service on a *limited* partner will constitute good service for this purpose[105]: it is a matter of regret that the Civil Procedure Rules still do not address this issue directly.

---

[93] See *supra*, paras 14–01 *et seq.*
[94] See, generally, CPR rr.6.5, 6.9, *infra*, paras A2–01, A2–02 (service of claim form) and *ibid.* 7APD, para. 5A, *infra*, para. A2–04 (proceedings in firm name).
[95] *ibid.* 70PD, para. 6A.3, *infra*, para. A2–09. See *supra*, para. 30–19.
[96] See *supra*, paras 12–35, 14–66 *et seq.*; also the Limited Partnerships Act 1907, s.6(5)(a), *infra*, para. A3–06.
[97] *ibid.* s.6(1), *infra*, para. A3–06; see also *supra*, para. 30–03.
[98] See, as to such orders, the Senior Court Act 1981 (as renamed by the Constitutional Reform Act 2005, Sched. 11, Pt 1, para. 1(1)), s.42, as amended by the Prosecution of Offences Act 1985, s.24.
[99] *Mephistopheles Debt Collection Service v. Lotay* [1994] 1 W.L.R. 1064.
[100] See CPR 7APD, paras 5A.1, 5A.3, *infra*, para. A2–04. See also *supra*, paras 14–04 *et seq.*
[101] *ibid.* 10PD, para. 4.4(2), *infra*, para. A2–07. And see *supra*, paras 14–19, 14–69.
[102] *ibid.*
[103] s.6(1), *infra*, para. A3–06. See also *supra*, paras 30–03 *et seq.*
[104] See *supra*, para. 14–14.
[105] Note the terms of the Limited Partnerships Act 1907, s.6(1), *infra*, para. A3–06. As to the form of a judgment against a limited partnership, see *supra*, para. 30–21. As to execution of a judgment, see *supra*, para. 30–19.

CHAPTER 31

THE RIGHTS AND OBLIGATIONS OF THE PARTNERS BETWEEN THEMSELVES

It has already been seen that, in matters of internal regulation, the Partnership Act 1890 gives partners complete freedom to agree the terms of their partnership[1] and that freedom is, with certain exceptions, expressly preserved by the Limited Partnerships Act 1907.[2] However, if the members of a limited partnership do *not* reach agreement on all aspects of their relationship, their mutual rights and obligations will in general be governed by the provisions of the 1890 Act and the rules of law and equity applicable to ordinary partnerships.[3] This may have consequences which the partners neither intended nor foresaw, particularly as regards their profit shares,[4] the division of surplus assets on a winding up[5] and the ownership of goodwill.[6]

31–01

There can be no doubt that partners in a limited partnership owe each other the same duty of good faith as would apply in a general partnership.[6a]

1.   THE MANAGEMENT OF THE PARTNERSHIP BUSINESS

General partners

The right to manage the partnership business is conferred on the general partners alone: any limited partner who seeks to participate therein may do so only at the cost of forfeiting his limited liability.[7] Moreover, a majority of the general partners may, subject to any agreement between the partners (both general *and* limited), decide any question arising in relation to ordinary matters connected with the partnership business.[8] There can be little doubt that, in the absence of some other agreement, a decision so taken will bind all the partners, general and limited alike, even though the latter may not have been

31–02

---

[1] Partnership Act 1890, s.19, *infra*, para. A1–20: see *supra*, paras 10–12 *et seq.*

[2] Limited Partnerships Act 1907, s.7, *infra*, para. A3–07.

[3] *ibid.*

[4] See *infra*, para. 31–10.

[5] See the Partnership Act 1890, s.44, *infra*, para. A1–45; also *supra*, paras 25–45 *et seq.*

[6] See *supra*, paras 10–197 *et seq.*, 18–17.

[6a] *BBGP Managing General Partner Ltd. v. Babcock & Brown Global Partners* [2010] EWHC 2176 (Ch) at [11] *per* Norris J.

[7] Limited Partnerships Act 1907, s.6(1), *infra*, para. A3–06.

[8] *ibid.* s.6(5)(a), *infra*, para. A3–06. *cf.* the Partnership Act 1890, s.24(8), *infra*, para. A1–25 and *supra*, paras 15–04 *et seq.*

consulted or given an opportunity of expressing their views.[9] It is thus of particular importance that the general partners exercise this power with the utmost good faith,[10] since any attempt at consultation with the limited partners might result in their direct or indirect participation in the management of the firm.

31–03   However, the current editor considers that the general partners' powers neither extend beyond the management of the partnership business nor authorise them to change that business without the consent of the limited partners. In the latter case, not only might a change in the business materially affect the extent of the general partners' implied authority to bind the firm,[11] but the limited partners could also properly say that they did not contribute capital to be applied for that purpose.[12] Similarly, the general partners cannot unilaterally change the terms of the partnership and, given the peculiar nature of a limited partner's position, his agreement to such a change could not be inferred merely from the conduct of the general partners.[13]

It would also seem that a general partner, acting alone, will not have power to give a good receipt for the proceeds of sale of land which is partnership property so as automatically to override the interests of the limited partners.[14]

An incoming general partner will not, by virtue of that status, automatically have the right to pursue a right of action which accrued in favour of the partnership prior to his admission.[15]

Limited partners

31–04   As noted above, a limited partner may not take part in the management of the partnership business,[16] either directly or indirectly: if he does so, he will be liable for all the debts and obligations of the firm incurred whilst his

---

[9] In practice, any agreement overriding the provisions of the Limited Partnerships Act 1907, s.6(5)(a) is likely to specify the manner in which the general partners may take such decisions (*e.g.* by requiring something other than a simple majority), rather than giving the limited partners a right to participate in the decision-making process, with the attendant risk of unlimited liability under *ibid.* s.6(1).

[10] See *supra*, paras 16–01 *et seq.* And note also, as to the exercise of a discretion conferred on a general partner under the agreement, *Greck v. Henderson Asia Pacific Equity Partners (FP) LP* [2008] CSOH 2 (OH), especially at [76] *per* Lord Glennie. See also *supra*, para. 10–101.

[11] Partnership Act 1890, s.5, *infra*, para. A1–06: see *supra*, paras 12–12 *et seq.*

[12] See *supra*, para. 15–09.

[13] Partnership Act 1890, s.19, *infra*, para. A1–20; see also *supra*, paras 10–12 *et seq.*

[14] The general partner's rights under the 1907 Act do not displace the requirements of the Law of Property Act 1925, s.27 (as amended by the Law of Property (Amendment) Act 1926, Sched. and the Trusts of Land and Appointment of Trustees Act 1996, Sched. 3, para. 4(8)). Note, however that, in practice, the limited partners' interests may be overridden in any event: see *supra*, para. 18–62, n. 202. *Semble* it is unlikely that the limited partners will be in actual occupation of the land and so be entitled to overriding interests.

[15] *Global Partners Fund Ltd. v. Babcock & Brown Ltd.* [2010] NSWSC 270 at [91] *per* Hammer-schlag J. (the appeal went off on other grounds: [2010] NSWCA 196); see also *supra*, para. 14–50.

[16] This expression is not defined. It is considered that any decision which constitutes an "ordinary matter connected with the partnership business" (see the Partnership Act 1890, s.24(8), *infra*, para. A1–25; the Limited Partnerships Act 1907, s.6(5)(a), *infra*, para. A3–06) is likely to trespass into the field of management, whereas any decision relating to the terms or structure of the partnership (*e.g.* the nature of the business carried on, the admission of new partners, the profit sharing ratios) will not. Nevertheless, there is a substantial "grey" area in between.

participation continues.[17] It is questionable whether a limited partner will participate in management when he merely acts as a director of or shareholder in a corporate general partner,[18] but there will always be the risk of straying over the line.[19]

However, a limited partner does enjoy a statutory right, exercisable either personally or by means of an agent, to inspect the partnership books,[20] to "examine into" the state and prospects of its business and to "advise with" the partners thereon.[21] It goes without saying that such rights, as well as any special powers conferred upon the limited partner by the agreement, must be exercised with particular care so as to avoid any suggestion of involvement in the management of the business.

2.   THE CAPITAL OF LIMITED PARTNERSHIPS

Initial capital and change of liability

A limited partnership must, by definition, have a fixed capital when it is **31–05** established, since the Act requires each limited partner to contribute a sum of capital on entry, particulars of which must be delivered on first registration.[22] That capital must be represented by cash or other property which is actually brought into the common stock on admission[23]: there will be no contribution of capital if a limited partner merely provides a guarantee for the firm's liability to a third party.[24] This requirement is a strict and inflexible one. In *MacCarthaigh*

---

[17] Limited Partnerships Act 1907, s.6(1), *infra*, para. A3–06. The current editor is of the opinion that such liability will not necessarily cease as soon as the limited partner withdraws from participation in management, at least so far as concerns any of "his" decisions which require to be implemented thereafter. *Sed quaere.*

[18] Note that, in *Revenue and Customs Commissioners v. Holland* [2009] S.T.C. 1639, it was held that a director of a corporate director of a company was not, merely by fulfilling his duties as such, to be regarded as a *de facto* director of that company. *Semble* this is analogous to the situation described in the text. Note also that in *PWA Corp v. Gemini Group Automated Distribution Systems Inc.* [1993] 103 D.L.R. (4th) 609 (CA, Ontario) the limited partners each owned one third of the issued shares in the general partner, a not uncommon scenario but, as noted in the text, not without risk.

[19] It would seem likely that some amelioration of this position may, in due course, be introduced under a future Legislative Reform Order, following the Law Commission's 2003 recommendations: see *supra*, para. 28–07.

[20] See *supra*, paras 22–10 *et seq.*

[21] Limited Partnerships Act 1907, s.6(1), *infra*, para. A3–06. The current editor considers that the words "advise with" connote discussion and an interchange of views falling short of any attempt to *influence* management decisions. A similar view was expressed in the original Supplement to this work on the Limited Partnerships Act 1907, where the editors observed " . . . it will not be safe for a limited partner to take part in the actual determination of any question upon which he advises with his co-partners."

[22] *ibid.* ss.4(2), 8A(2)(d) (as added by the Legislative Reform (Limited Partnerships) Order 2009 (SI 2009/1940), art. 5), *infra*, paras A3–04, A3–09: see further *supra*, paras 29–04, 29–19. It does not appear to matter that the contribution is of a nominal amount: see *Dickson v. MacGregor* 1992 S.L.T. 83 (Land Ct.); *MacFarlane v. Falfield Investments Ltd.* 1998 S.L.T. 145 (1st Div.). In both cases the amount was £10.

[23] *ibid.* s.4(2). Needless to say, the cash or property does not have to be physically placed in the firm's hands, but it must be *available* to the firm, *e.g.* where property is vested in the limited partner or a third party on trust for the firm: see generally, *supra*, paras 18–02 *et seq.*

[24] *Rayner & Co. v. Rhodes* (1926) 24 Ll.L.R. 25.

v. D[25] the limited partners did not contribute their capital until some time *after* their date of entry. This meant that the firm's registration was defective and, as the law then stood, they forfeited their limited liability until such time as the contributions had been made.[26] In the case of a limited partnership registered on an application on or after October 1, 2009, a limited partner in that position would be no better off, since he would not satisfy the requirements of section 4(2) of the 1907 Act and could not in law be a limited partner.[27] Were a limited partnership to be registered as such but, in point of fact, no limited partner contributed any capital on admission, the conclusiveness of the registration certificate[28] would be of no avail against a creditor since all the partners would be general partners.

31–06   However, there appears to be nothing in the Act which requires a limited partner's capital contribution, once made, to be retained by him; thus, like any other capital contribution, it may seemingly be divided between some or all of the partners in such proportions as they may agree.[29] By the same token, it would not seem to affect the limited partners' rights if their contributions are all lost in the course of carrying on the partnership business.[30]

A corresponding statutory obligation to contribute capital is not imposed on the general partners, so long as they retain that status. Where, however, a general partner wishes to become a limited partner, he must at that stage make a capital contribution. If he has already made such a contribution *qua* general partner, then the amount thereof (or such part of it as still remains in the firm) may properly be treated as forming part (or the whole) of his contribution *qua* limited partner and registered as such.[31] If such a partner fails to contribute any capital at all, he will continue as a general partner,[32] but the limited liability of the other limited partners will not be affected.[33]

Alteration of capital

31–07   Subject to the restrictions on the withdrawal of capital by limited partners[34] and to compliance with the registration requirements,[35] the partners are free to alter the firm's capital at any time, whether by way of increase or decrease. The current editor does, however, submit that such a change would require the consent of all the partners,[36] save where it results from the admission of a new

---

[25] [1985] I.R. 73.

[26] By virtue of the Limited Partnerships Act 1907, s.5 (in its original form), *infra*, para. A3–05 or *ibid.* s.4(2) noted *infra*.

[27] See *supra*, paras 29–23, 29–26.

[28] Limited Partnerships Act 1907, s.8C(4) (as added by the Legislative Reform (Limited Partnerships) Order 2009, art. 7), *infra*, para. A3–11.

[29] See generally, *supra*, paras 17–07 *et seq*. Details of such division would seemingly not require to be registered under the Limited Partnerships Act 1907, s.9(1)(f), *infra*, para. A3–12, on the footing that there is no alteration in "the sum contributed by any limited partner"; *sed quaere*.

[30] See *supra*, para. 30–11.

[31] Limited Partnerships Act 1907, s.9(1)(f), *infra*, para. A3–12.

[32] Since he will not satisfy the requirements of *ibid.* s.4(2), *infra*, para. A3–04. See *supra*, para. 31–05.

[33] *cf.* the position in the case of a limited partnership formed prior to October 1, 2009, when *ibid.* s.5 (in its original form) applies: see *supra*, para. 29–26.

[34] *ibid.* s.4(3), *infra*, para. A3–04: see *infra*, para. 31–08.

[35] *ibid.* s.9(1)(f), *infra*, para. A3–12.

[36] *ibid.* s.7 *infra*, para. A3–07; see also *supra*, para. 17–10.

partner which, under the Act, does *not* require the limited partners' consent,[37] or where it is expressly authorised under the agreement.

As already noted,[38] there appears to be no objection to a limited partner making an initial capital contribution and at the same time agreeing to make a further contribution at a later date.

Withdrawal of capital

There is a strict statutory prohibition on the direct or indirect withdrawal of a **31–08** limited partner's capital contribution whilst the partnership is continuing,[39] although there is no related requirement that such contribution must continue to be owned by the limited partner once it has been made.[40] Moreover, the prohibition is framed solely in terms of the limited partners. It would appear to follow that if, by the terms of the agreement or the general law, the whole or any part of a limited partner's contribution is treated as belonging to a general partner, the latter would, subject to obtaining his co-partners' consent, be free to withdraw it at any time without penalty to himself or to the limited partner.[41] This highlights the fundamental difference between a limited partnership and a limited company, since the general partners will remain personally liable for all the debts and obligations of the firm irrespective of the presence (or absence) of the partners' respective capital contributions.[42] It should also be noted that there is no restriction whatsoever on the members of an ordinary or limited partnership agreeing to convert the joint property of the firm into the separate property of one of their number or vice versa.[43]

If a limited partner *does* seek to withdraw his contribution, the current editor considers that the creditors of the firm could neither object to nor prevent such withdrawal.[44] Their real protection lies in that partner's liability for the debts of the firm up to the amount so withdrawn.[45]

Interest on capital

In the absence of some specific agreement, a limited partner will not be **31–09** entitled to interest on his capital contribution.[46]

---

[37] *ibid.* s.6(5)(d) *infra*, para. A3–06. Of course, this restriction may be overridden by the agreement: see the opening words of *ibid.* s.6(5).

[38] See *supra*, para. 30–07.

[39] Limited Partnerships Act 1907, s.4(3), *infra*, para. A3–04; see also *supra*, paras 30–08 *et seq*.

[40] See *supra*, para. 31–06. As to the position where capital has been lost, see *supra*, para. 30–11.

[41] There is no legitimate warrant for an inference that the limited partners' contributions should at all times be available to the firm in the form of cash or assets, *e.g.* capital may quite properly be risked in the business or applied in meeting day to day expenses (including any payments due to the general partners).

[42] This will be the position whether those contributions have been withdrawn by the partners or lost in the course of carrying on the partnership business.

[43] See *supra*, paras 18–44 *et seq*. But see also, in the case of insolvency, *supra*, paras 27–100 *et seq*.

[44] See *supra*, para. 18–45.

[45] Limited Partnerships Act 1907, s.4(3), *infra*, para. A3–04. See further, *supra*, para. 30–09.

[46] Partnership Act 1890, s.24(4), *infra*, para. A1–25; Limited Partnerships Act 1907, s.7, *infra*, para. A3–07; see also *supra*, paras 17–12, 20–33 *et seq*.

3.   SHARES IN LIMITED PARTNERSHIPS

Quantum: profits and losses

31–10   The Limited Partnerships Act 1907 does not lay down how the profits and losses of a limited partnership are to be shared between the partners. Those provisions of the Act which establish the extent of a limited partner's liability refer only to the debts and obligations of the firm[47] and, on that footing, in earlier editions of this work it was submitted that:

> "the same limit of liability will apply in making good losses between the partners as in the payment of the creditors of the firm, for under the Partnership Act 1890 losses and deficiencies of capital are met in the same way as any other losses."[48]

However, in *Reed v. Young*[49] the House of Lords emphatically held that, so far as concerns *trading* losses, there is no warrant for this view.[50] It follows that a limited partner may be liable for losses over and above the amount of his capital contribution, and this must always be borne in mind, particularly since there are now strict rules governing the relief available in respect of such losses for tax purposes.[51]

31–11   Subject as aforesaid and in the absence of any express agreement between the partners, the presumption of equality will apply to a limited partnership just as it applies to an ordinary partnership,[52] even though this will rarely, if ever, be what the partners intend. Care should accordingly be taken to record the agreed profit and loss shares, the nature of which are in the discretion of the partners themselves. It is, in practice, common to find that one or more partners benefit from a so-called "carried interest", *i.e.* a share of profits which is dependent on a specified threshold of profitability having been achieved or rate of return received by other partners.[53]

Having regard to the liability imposed on a limited partner who withdraws or

---

[47] See the Limited Partnerships Act 1907, ss.4(2), (3), 6(1), *infra*, paras A3–04, A3–06. *ibid.* s.5 (in its original form) is expressed in more general terms, but no longer applies to partnerships registered on or after October 1, 2009: see *infra*, para. A3–05. Note, in any event, that *ibid.* s.4(2) defines the liability of a general partner solely by reference to the debts and obligations of the firm.

[48] See the Partnership Act 1890, s.44, *supra*, paras 25–45 *et seq.*

[49] [1986] 1 W.L.R. 649.

[50] *Quaere*, can a distinction be drawn between trading and other losses, with a view to distinguishing *Reed v. Young*? Although the *ratio decidendi* is strictly confined to the treatment of losses for tax purposes, the House of Lords took care to draw a distinction between accounting losses on the one hand and liabilities to third parties on the other. The current editor considers that all losses as between the partners must be treated as falling within the former category, so that any distinction would in real terms be illusory.

[51] See *infra*, para. 34–49.

[52] Partnership Act 1890, s.24(1), *infra*, para. A1–25; Limited Partnerships Act 1907, s.7, *infra*, para. A3–07; see also *supra*, paras 19–16 *et seq.*, 20–04 *et seq.*

[53] Examples of typical structures are set out in the Memorandum of Understanding between the BVCA and the Inland Revenue on the income tax treatment of Venture Capital and Private Equity Limited Partnerships and Carried Interest dated July 22, 2003, section 7, reproduced at [2003] S.T.I. 1371, 1373 *et seq.* See also *infra*, n. 60.

receives back any part of his capital contribution during the continuance of the partnership,[54] care must be taken to avoid an inadvertent return of capital in the form of a supposed share of profits, *e.g.* where partners' preferential "salaries" are payable irrespective of the firm's profitability.[55]

Assignment: general partners

The assignment of a general partner's share is governed by the law applicable **31–12** to ordinary partnerships,[56] save that the assignee may normally be admitted to the firm without the consent of the limited partners.[57] Any such change in the firm would, of course, have to be registered.[58]

There is no reason why a general partner should not assign part of his share, in the same way as a member of a general partnership.[59] Indeed, assignment of a general partner's so-called "carried interest" to a third party is commonly encountered in the venture capital and related fields.[60]

Assignment: limited partners

Subject to any agreement between the partners, a limited partner may, with the **31–13** consent of the general partners, assign his share to a third party.[61] The assignment must be registered[62] and notice thereof given in the *Gazette*.[63] Until those formalities have been completed, the assignment will be of no effect, at least as regards third parties.[64] Thereafter, the assignee will become a limited partner in the place of the assignor and enjoy all the rights which were available to him.[65] Although the view has been expressed that the Act contemplates advertisement of the assignment *before* it can be registered[66] and, indeed, that it will not be

---

[54] Limited Partnerships Act 1907, s.4(3), *infra*, para. A3–04; see *supra*, paras 30–08 *et seq.*

[55] See also *supra*, para. 30–10. As to what falls to be treated as profits, see *supra*, paras 10–86, 21–02 and *infra*, para. 34–25.

[56] Partnership Act 1890, s.31, *infra*, para. A1–32; Limited Partnerships Act 1907, s.7 *infra*, para. A3–07; see also *supra*, paras 19–51 *et seq.*

[57] Limited Partnerships Act 1907, s.6(5)(d), *infra*, para. A3–06. It is, of course, open to the partners to agree otherwise: see the opening words of *ibid.* s.6(5).

[58] *ibid.* s.9(1)(d), *infra*, para. A3–12. See *supra*, paras 29–25, 29–26.

[59] See, *supra*, paras 19–50, 19–52.

[60] The "carried interest" generally represents an additional share of profits which will arise after a specified threshold of profitability or rate of return has been reached and/or after any loans made by the limited partners alongside their capital contributions have been fully repaid. Under the terms of the agreement, such an interest will usually be stated to be freely assignable. Note as to this device, *Greck v. Henderson Asia Pacific Equity Partners (FP) LP* [2008] CSOH 2 (OH).

[61] Limited Partnerships Act 1907, s.6(5)(d), *infra*, para. A3–06. See also *supra*, para. 30–16.

[62] *ibid.* s.9(1)(d), *infra*, para. A3–12. See also *supra*, paras 29–25, 29–26.

[63] *ibid.* s.10, *infra*, para. A3–13. It is not entirely clear who is required to place the notice in the *Gazette. Semble*, primary responsibility falls on the general partner: *supra* see para. 30–06.

[64] *ibid.* Note, however, that the penalty for failure to advertise applies only "for the purposes of this Act": see *infra*.

[65] *ibid.* s.6(5)(b), *infra*, para. A3–06. See also, *supra*, paras 30–17, 30–18.

[66] This construction clearly derives support from the fact that *ibid.* s.10 is framed in the future tense and refers to an arrangement under which the share of a limited partner *will* be assigned to any person. A similar point can be taken in relation to the other limb of *ibid.* s.10, which applies where a person "*will* cease to be a general partner . . . and *will* become a limited partner" (emphasis supplied).

registrable until advertised,[67] the current editor submits that this does not prop-erly accord with the framework and rationale of the Act, since it would produce a situation in which the assignee partner would, as a matter of law, be a partner[68] but cannot be registered as such because notice of the assignment has not, for whatever reason, been advertised.[69] The better view is that the notice requirement and the consequences of non-advertisement are directed more to the protection of third parties[70] than to interfering with the mechanics of registration.

However, the current editor submits that a limited partner has another option if he does not wish to obtain (or cannot obtain) the general partners' consent, namely to assign his share in such a way as to confer on the assignee the more limited rights specified in section 31 of the Partnership Act 1890.[71] Since, in such a case, the limited partner's liability would be unaffected and there would be no change in the firm's constitution,[72] neither advertisement nor registration would seem to be required.[73]

4.   CHANGES IN LIMITED PARTNERSHIPS

Admission and retirement of partners

31–14   Subject to any agreement between the partners, one or more new general or limited partners may be introduced at any time without the consent of the limited partners,[74] even though the consent of all the general partners will normally be required.[75]

In those cases where the agreement does not permit a general or limited partner to retire, *all* the partners' consent to any such retirement must be obtained.[76]

---

[67] On the basis that, by virtue of *ibid.* s.10 it is deemed to be of no effect for the purposes of the 1907 Act.

[68] There can be no doubt, given the terms of *ibid.* s.10, that the assignment is effective (see the preceding footnote) but where does this leave the assignee partner? He is clearly not a limited partner within the meaning of the Act. Does this mean that he falls to be treated as a general partner under *ibid.* s.4(2), *infra*, para. A3–04? That cannot be right. Is he a limited partner with no liability as such who could freely ignore the strictures of *ibid.* ss.4(3) (withdrawal of contribution) and 6(1) (participa-tion in management), *infra*, paras A3–04, A3–06? This would be a somewhat bizarre result, which would severely undermine the operation of the Act.

[69] Similar considerations would arise under the other limb of *ibid* s.10, *i.e.* on a general partner becoming a limited partner, but the considerations would not be so stark, as the former general partner would unquestionably remain registered (and liable) as such until the notice and registration process was complete.

[70] See *supra*, para. 29–28.

[71] See *supra*, paras 19–51 *et seq.*

[72] See *supra*, paras 19–53 *et seq.*

[73] Limited Partnerships Act 1907, ss.9(1)(d), 10, *infra*, paras A3–12, A3–13. Note in particular the words "for the purposes of this Act" in the latter section.

[74] Limited Partnerships Act 1907, s.6(5)(d), *infra*, para. A3–06.

[75] Partnership Act 1890, s.24(7), *infra*, para. A1–25; Limited Partnerships Act 1907, s.7, *infra*, para. A3–07.

[76] See *supra*, paras 24–93 *et seq.* And see also, as to the retirement of limited partners, *supra*, para. 30–14.

Equally, a limited partner may, with the consent of the general partners, achieve the same result merely by assigning his share to a third party.[77]

Any change in the firm must be duly registered.[78]

Death or bankruptcy of a limited partner

In earlier editions of this work, successive editors advanced the following view: **31–15**

> "If a limited partner dies or becomes bankrupt during the continuance of the partnership, it is apprehended that, in the absence of any agreement to the contrary, the continuing partners will have the right to retain his contribution in the business until the partnership is terminated by effluxion of time or is otherwise dissolved,[79] for the limited partner has no right to withdraw his contribution[80] nor to determine the partnership,[81] nor is it determined by his death or bankruptcy.[82] If this be the true construction of the Act, his estate will doubtless be entitled until the partnership is determined to receive the share of profits or other pecuniary advantages to which he would have been entitled had he not died or become bankrupt,[83] but the position of his executor or administrator or his trustee in bankruptcy is far from clear. As his bankruptcy does not dissolve the partnership, it may be that the bankrupt will still continue to be a partner though his share will have passed to his trustee in bankruptcy.[84] In the case of his death the partnership, so far as he personally is concerned, must come to an end, and as the Act does not provide for his executor or administrator becoming a partner, and he may leave more executors than one, there is a difficulty in supposing that the Act intended them to become partners in his place; yet unless his legal personal representatives do become limited partners in his place it is difficult to see how the partnership could continue if, as might well be the case, the deceased was the only limited partner in the firm, for there cannot be a limited partnership without a limited partner,[85] and the partnership agreement *ex hypothesi* is for a limited partnership and not a general one. Until these difficulties have been removed by decisions of the court all that can be done is to insert such provisions in the partnership agreement to meet these events as will carry out the intention of the partners."

However, a reappraisal of the legal position produces a different and, in many ways, more attractive result. The fact that the death or bankruptcy of a limited partner will not dissolve the partnership is undeniable in the face of the specific terms of the 1907 Act.[86] It naturally follows that the estate of a deceased limited partner would not be entitled to force a sale of the partnership assets or a general winding up of its affairs,[87] but is it right to assume that the Act also intended to confer on a limited partnership what amounts to a legal personality separate and **31–16**

---

[77] Limited Partnerships Act 1907, s.6(5)(b), *infra*, para. A3–06: see *supra*, para. 31–13.

[78] *ibid.* s.9(1)(d), *infra*, para. A3–12: see *supra*, paras 29–25, 29–26.

[79] See *supra*, paras 30–14, 30–15.

[80] Limited Partnerships Act 1907, s.4(3), *infra*, para. A3–04.

[81] *ibid.* s.6(5)(e), *infra*, para. A3–06.

[82] *ibid.* s.6(2), *infra*, para. A3–06.

[83] See, as to a limited partner's liability for losses, *supra*, paras 31–10, 31–11.

[84] If this were the case, there would be little appreciable impact on the firm, since a limited partner is, in any event, prohibited from taking part in the management of its business and has no power to bind the firm: Limited Partnerships Act 1907, s.6(1), *infra*, para. A3–06.

[85] See *ibid.* s.4(2), *infra*, para. A3–04.

[86] *ibid.* s.6(2), *infra*, para. A3–06.

[87] See generally, as to the position of an outgoing or deceased partner, *supra*, paras 19–05 *et seq.*, 23–183 *et seq.*

distinct from the partners who from time to time compose it? Yet, it is only if the partnership before and after a limited partner's death or bankruptcy can properly be regarded as one and the same legal entity that it can be argued, as in the passage quoted above, that his capital contribution cannot be withdrawn.[88] The current editor ventures to suggest that such an analysis cannot be correct, given that the Act specifically adopts the Partnership Act definition of the word "firm" as meaning the partners for the time being.[89] Although the word "partnership" is not itself defined, it should surely be treated as synonymous with "firm," so that the prohibition on a limited partner withdrawing his capital contribution "during the continuance of the partnership" applies only to the partnership of which he is a member; when he dies or retires, a different partnership comes into existence and the prohibition ceases to apply.[90]

Change of partner's status

31–17 So long as there continue to be at least one general and one limited partner in the firm, a general partner may become a limited partner or vice versa.[91] However, the current editor considers that such a change of status may in general only be achieved with the consent of all the partners or pursuant to an express provision of the agreement.[92]

It has already been seen that, in certain circumstances, a limited partner may be *deemed* to be a general partner,[93] but this will not involve a true change of status.

---

[88] If this argument is correct, what rights does a creditor whose debt was incurred after the date of death have against the estate of the deceased partner if the contribution is withdrawn in breach of the statutory prohibition? Surely there can be no privity with the personal representatives such as to give him a direct right of action.

[89] In *Jardine-Paterson v. Fraser* 1974 S.L.T. 93 (OH), 97, Lord Maxwell (considering the position of a general partnership in Scotland) observed "I am not satisfied that, as a matter of strict construction of the Partnership Act [*1890*], it necessarily follows that, because a partnership is not dissolved within the meaning of s.33, there is one continuing legal person before and after the death [*of the partner*]." After quoting from the Partnership Act 1890, s.4(1) and (2), he continued "The legal person is, therefore, the group of individuals who have entered into the partnership and prima facie one would think that a differently constituted group would be a different legal person. It is not clear to me why that prima facie view should not apply, even though the partners have agreed that their relationship *inter se* as partners should not be 'dissolved' by the death of one of their number." *cf. William S. Gordon & Co. Ltd. v. Mrs Mary Thomson Partnership* 1985 S.L.T. 122, although the correctness the decision was called into question in *Knapdale (Nominees) Ltd. v. Donald* 2000 S.C.L.R. 1013 (OH), 1032–1033; also *James & George Collie v. Donald* 1999 S.C.L.R. 420 (OH), 424B–F, 425F–426A *per* Lord McCluskey. Note also *Balmer v. HM Advocate* 2008 S.L.T. 799 (HCJ), a criminal case, where the effect of a dissolution on the legal personality of the firm was considered. The position is *a fortiori* in the case of an English partnership which does not enjoy a separate legal personality: see further *supra*, paras 3–04 *et seq.*

[90] Note, however, the terms of the Limited Partnerships Act 1907, s.9(1), *infra*, para. A3–12), which requires any change in the partners "during the continuance of a limited partnership" to be duly registered. Undoubtedly, if that section is complied with, the firm's registration is unaffected by the change.

[91] *ibid.* ss.4(2), 9(1)(g), 10, *infra*, paras A3–04, A3–12, A3–13; see also *supra*, paras 30–06, 30–13.

[92] Note, however, the terms of *ibid.* s.6(5)(b), (d), *infra*, para. A3–06, which might in certain circumstances permit the general partners alone to consent to the change of status.

[93] *ibid.* ss.5 (in its original form), 6(1), *infra*, paras A3–05, A3–06: see *supra*, paras 29–23, 29–26, 30–08, 31–02, 31–04. And note also the terms of *ibid.* s.10, *infra*, para. A3–13, another deeming provision.

5.   PARTNERSHIP ACCOUNTS

Partnerships (Accounts) Regulations 2008

It should be noted that where, as is often the case, all the partners in a limited   **31–18**
partnership are limited companies or Scottish partnerships which in turn comprise only limited companies (or, in either case, comparable undertakings formed
outside the UK),[94] the accounts of the partnership, along with a directors' report
and an auditor's report, will unquestionably have to be drawn up in compliance
with the Partnerships (Accounts) Regulations 2008.[95] It is, however, provided by
regulation 2(2) of those Regulations that:

> "Any reference in these Regulations to the members of a qualifying partnership shall
> be construed, in relation to a limited partnership, as a reference to its general partner
> or partners."

In consequence, there has been speculation that a limited partnership comprising
a corporate general partner and *individual* limited partners may also be affected
by the Regulations. In the current editor's view, this is to misread the above
regulation which does not purport to amend the definition of "qualifying partnership"[96] but merely the subsequent references to its *members*.[97] However, this
point will soon be academic, as amending regulations are to be made which will
ensure that the above Regulations *do* apply in such a case.[98] The provision quoted
above will, however, ensure that the limited partners are not obliged to undertake
functions which would place them in breach of the prohibition on participation
in management contained in section 6(1) of the Limited Partnerships Act 1907
and, thus, lead to forfeiture of their limited liability.[99]

---

[94] See the definition of "qualifying partnership" in the Partnerships (Accounts) Regulations 2008
(SI 2008/569), reg. 3(1). Such a partnership may also comprise an unlimited company all the
members of which are limited companies, but this is rare.

[95] See further *supra*, para. 22–08.

[96] In *ibid*. regs 2(1), 3(1).

[97] See, for example, *ibid*. regs 4(1), 5(1) (preparation and delivery of accounts).

[98] As and when passed these will be styled the Partnerships (Accounts) (Amendment) Regulations
2011 and will amend *ibid*. reg. 3. They are likely to have effect as from April 6, 2011. The
clarification is said to be necessary to ensure compliance with EU Directive 90/605/EEC.

[99] See *supra*, para. 31–04.

CHAPTER 32

DISSOLUTION AND WINDING UP

1. DISSOLUTION OTHERWISE THAN BY THE COURT

Events giving rise to dissolution

A limited partnership will in general be dissolved by any event which would **32–01** dissolve an ordinary partnership,[1] subject to certain specific exceptions which only relate to the limited partners. Thus the death or bankruptcy of a general partner will normally dissolve the partnership as regards all the partners.[2] Although such a dissolution can be avoided by agreement,[3] the death or bankruptcy of a *sole* general partner will inevitably affect the firm's status as a limited partnership, unless a new general partner is simultaneously admitted to the firm.[4]

The exceptions to the general rule stated above are as follows.

(1) *Death or bankruptcy of a limited partner*

It is specifically provided by the Limited Partnerships Act 1907 that the death **32–02** or bankruptcy of a limited partner will not dissolve the firm[5] and this is not in terms stated to be subject to any contrary agreement between the partners. Nevertheless, the current editor considers that such a qualification must be implied, so that either event *can* be treated as terminating the partnership if the partners so desire.[6]

(2) *Dissolution notice served by limited partner*

Unless such a power is conferred on him by agreement,[7] a limited partner is **32–03** not entitled to dissolve the partnership by notice.[8]

---

[1] Limited Partnerships Act 1907, s.7, *infra*, para. A3–07; see generally, *supra*, paras 24–04 *et seq.*
[2] Partnership Act 1890, s.33(1), *infra*, para. A1–34; Limited Partnerships Act 1907, s.7. See *supra*, paras 24–29 *et seq.*
[3] See *supra*, para. 10–39.
[4] A limited partnership must at all times comprise at least one general partner; Limited Partnerships Act 1907, s.4(2), *infra*, para. A3–04. Note also *ibid.* s.6(3), *infra*, para. A3–06: see *infra*, para. 32–13.
[5] *ibid.* s.6(2), *infra*, para. A3–06. *cf.* the Partnership Act 1890, s.33(1), *supra*, paras 24–29 *et seq.*
[6] See further, *supra*, paras 30–14, 31–15, 31–16.
[7] For a case in which such a power was conferred on a limited partner, see *Smith v. Smith* 1998 S.C.L.R. 818 (Sh. Ct).
[8] Limited Partnerships Act 1907, s.6(5)(e), *infra*, para. A3–06; *cf.* the Partnership Act 1890, ss.26(1), 32(c), *supra*, paras 9–01 *et seq.*, 24–18 *et seq.*

(3) *Charging order on limited or general partner's share*

32–04   Subject to any contrary agreement, the other partners are not entitled to dissolve the partnership merely because a limited partner has allowed his share to be charged for his separate debts.[9]

This may be contrasted with the position where a general partner allows his share to be so charged: in such a case, the current editor submits that a limited partner may safely exercise (or join with the other partners in exercising) the option to dissolve the partnership which is conferred by the Partnership Act 1890,[10] without being treated as having taken part in the management of the partnership business[11] or as having attempted to serve a dissolution notice.[12]

Dissolution under the partnership agreement

32–05   It is, of course, open to the partners to include in their agreement an express right to dissolve the firm on any basis they may see fit. Such a right may even be conferred on the firm's investment manager, as in *Aymard v. SISU Capital Ltd.*[13] Where such a right is conferred on the limited partners they must take care to ensure that a threat to exercise it is not used as an indirect means of controlling the way in which the partnership is managed, thus potentially exposing them to the risk of unlimited liability.[14]

2.   DISSOLUTION BY THE COURT

A.   JURISDICTION TO DISSOLVE A LIMITED PARTNERSHIP

32–06 The court's jurisdiction to dissolve and wind up a limited partnership is in general no different from that exercisable in respect of an ordinary partnership.[15]

Winding up as an unregistered company

32–07   The Limited Partnerships Act 1907 originally appeared to preclude the court from ordering the dissolution and winding up of a limited partnership otherwise than pursuant to the Companies Acts 1862 to 1900,[16] but the relevant subsection was subsequently repealed.[17] Thereafter, a limited partnership could be wound up

---

[9] Limited Partnerships Act 1907, s.6(5)(c), *infra*, para. A3–06.
[10] s.33(2), *supra*, paras 24–38 *et seq.*
[11] Limited Partnerships Act 1907, s.6(1), *infra*, para. A3–06: see *supra*, para. 31–04. Even if this were not the case, it is difficult to see what debts could have been incurred whilst the limited partner was so taking part.
[12] *ibid.* s.6(5)(e): see *supra*, para. 32–03.
[13] [2009] EWHC 3214 (QB) (Lawtel 21/12/09).
[14] Limited Partnerships Act 1907, s.6(1), considered *supra*, paras 31–02, 31–04.
[15] See generally *supra*, paras 24–47 *et seq.*
[16] Limited Partnerships Act 1907, s.6(4).
[17] Companies (Consolidation) Act 1908, s.286.

in the same way as an ordinary partnership, *i.e.* in the exercise of the court's normal jurisdiction or pursuant to the Companies (Consolidation) Act 1908.[18] However, the latter option was removed with effect from January 1, 1914,[19] and this remained the position under the Companies Act 1948.[20]

The culmination of this troubled history is to be found in changes introduced under the current insolvency legislation.[21] Thus, a petition for the winding up of a limited partnership as an unregistered company may now be presented by a creditor or other authorised person with or without concurrent petitions against one or more of the partners.[22] The partners' ability to serve such petitions is, however, restricted.[23]

The former statutory provisions governing the winding up of limited partnerships carrying on insurance and banking businesses have long since been repealed.[24]

Firms providing financial services

A limited partnership which is or was an authorised person[25] or an appointed **32–08** representative[26] under the Financial Services and Markets Act 2000 or which is or was improperly carrying on a regulated activity[27] may be wound up as an unregistered company on a petition presented by the Financial Services Authority[28] on the "just and equitable" ground.[29] Alternatively, such a partnership may

---

[18] *ibid.* ss.267, 268.

[19] Bankruptcy Act 1913, s.24.

[20] s.398. A limited exception was, however, introduced in the case of banking partnerships by the Banking Act 1979, s.18(2)(a).

[21] See the Insolvency Act 1986, s.420 and the Insolvent Partnerships Order 1994 (SI 1994/2421), as amended.

[22] Insolvent Partnerships Order 1994, arts 7(1) (as amended by the Insolvent Partnerships (Amendment) Order 1996 (SI 1996/1308), art. 2 and the Insolvent Partnerships (Amendment) Order 2002 (SI 2002/1308), art. 3), 8(1) (as amended by the Insolvent Partnerships (Amendment) Order 2002, art. 4(1). See further, *supra*, paras 27–06 *et seq.*, 27–24 *et seq.* The expression "insolvent partnership" is not defined in the Order and is clearly apt to include a limited partnership. Note that the Order nevertheless contains five separate references to limited partners or limited partnerships: these are to be found in *ibid.* art. 2(1) (definition of "limited partner"), Sched. 4, Pt II, para. 9 and Sched. 6, para. 3 (respectively introducing into the Insolvency Act 1986 a new s.125A: see *ibid.* subs. (7)), Sched. 7, para. 2 (modifying the Insolvency Act 1986, s.264: see *ibid.* subss. (1), (4)(a)) and Sched. 8 (modifying the Company Directors Disqualification Act 1986, Sched. 1: see *ibid.* Pt I, para. 6). See further *infra*, paras 33–02, 33–06.

[23] Insolvent Partnerships Order 1994, arts 9, 10(1): see *supra*, paras 27–14, 27–33.

[24] See the Financial Services and Markets Act 2000 (Consequential Amendments and Repeals) Order 2001 (SI 2001/3649), art. 3(1)(b), (d), repealing the Insurance Companies Act 1982, ss.53, 54 and the Banking Act 1987, s.92(1), (2).

[25] As to the authorisation of firms, see the Financial Services and Markets Act 2000, ss.31 *et seq.* and *supra*, paras 8–45 *et seq.*

[26] See *ibid.* s.39.

[27] *i.e.* when it is neither authorised nor exempt. The expression "regulated activity" is defined in *ibid.* s.22. As to exemption, see *ibid.* ss.38, 39, 327.

[28] *ibid.* s.367(1), (2). For an example of the use of this power, albeit not in the case of a limited partnership, see *In the Matter of Whiteley Insurance Consultants* [2009] Bus. L.R. 418. Note also the Insolvent Partnerships Order 1994, art. 19(4), as substituted by the Financial Services and Markets Act 2000 (Consequential Amendments and Repeals) Order 2001, Pt 9, art. 467 and amended by the Insolvent Partnerships (Amendment) (No. 2) Order 2002 (SI 2002/2708), art. 5.

[29] *ibid.* s.367(3)(b), (6)(a), (7).

be wound up on the ground that it is unable to pay its debts but, in this case, will *not* be treated as an unregistered company.[30]

B.   GROUNDS FOR DISSOLUTION BY THE COURT

Mental incapacity of a general or limited partner

32–09   In the case of a general partner's lack of mental capacity, it would seem that the court will have power to dissolve the partnership in the normal way.[31] However, the Limited Partnerships Act 1907 provides that the mental disorder of a *limited* partner is not a ground for dissolution by the court unless his share "cannot be otherwise ascertained and realised."[32] The underlying assumption appears to be that such a partner will usually enjoy a right to have his share ascertained and realised without a dissolution, even though the Act does not expressly provide for this. In earlier editions of this work it was argued that such an assumption is inconsistent with section 4 of the Limited Partnerships Act 1907[33] but, in the current editor's view, this argument is at the very least questionable.[34] An explanation may be that the reference to the realisation of the limited partner's share is no more than an allusion to his power to assign his share with the consent of the general partners[35] or to those cases in which the agreement contains provision for the purchase of a mentally incapacitated partner's share.[36]

It would seem to follow from the foregoing that, if the other partners are to avoid a general dissolution resulting from the mental incapacity of a limited partner, they must themselves purchase his share or arrange for its assignment to a third party who is acceptable to them as a partner.

Other grounds affecting a limited partner

32–10   Where dissolution proceedings are brought by a limited partner or are framed by reference to the conduct of or some other matter directly affecting such a partner, the exercise of the court's discretion will inevitably be influenced by his special status under the Act.[37] However, it does not follow that the court will necessarily be unsympathetic to such an application, as is evidenced by the decision in *Re Hughes & Co.*,[38] where an order appears to have been made on the "just and equitable" ground.

---

[30] *ibid.* s.367(3)(a).

[31] i.e. under the Partnership Act 1890, s.35, *infra*, para. A1–36. It is, however, by no means clear whether the Court of Protection has a right to order a dissolution under the Mental Capacity Act 2005, s.18(1): see *supra*, paras 24–48, 24–64 *et seq.*

[32] Limited Partnerships Act 1907, s.6(2), *infra*, para. A3–06.

[33] See *supra*, para. 31–15.

[34] See *supra*, paras 30–15, 31–16.

[35] Limited Partnerships Act 1907, s.6(5)(b), *infra*, para. A3–06: see *supra*, para. 31–13.

[36] Such a construction would support the arguments advanced *supra*, paras 30–15, 31–21.

[37] See, generally, the Partnership Act 1890, s.35, *supra*, paras 24–47, 24–69 *et seq.* Note, however, that this did not appear to figure as a consideration in *PWA Corp v. Gemini Group Automated Distribution Systems Inc.* [1993] 103 D.L.R. (4th) 609 (CA, Ontario), noted *supra*, para. 24–90.

[38] [1911] 1 Ch. 342, where a petition had been brought by the limited partner under the Companies (Consolidation) Act 1908. See also *Muirhead v. Borland* 1925 S.C. 474 (Ct. of Session). And see, as to the current position in Scotland, *Smith v. Smith* 1998 S.C.L.R. 818 (Sh. Ct).

Winding up of corporate partner

The existence of a corporate partnership[39] is not expressly contemplated by the **32–11** Partnership Act 1890 or by the Limited Partnerships Act 1907, so that no statutory provision establishes the effect of a winding up order against a corporate partner. It is submitted that, in the event of a corporate *general* partner going into liquidation, the court would in all probability order a dissolution on the "just and equitable" ground[40]; *a fortiori* if it was the sole general partner.[41] Moreover, the dissolution of such a partner would almost inevitably bring about a dissolution of the firm, in the absence of some other agreement.[42] However, the same cannot be said of a corporate limited partner: in either of the above instances, there is perhaps little more than an arguable case for a dissolution on the "just and equitable" ground.[43]

It should be noted that various special provisions apply under the insolvency legislation in the case of a corporate partner which is sought to be wound up on a petition presented concurrently with a petition for the winding up of the firm.[44]

Insolvency

The grounds on which an insolvent partnership may be wound up as an **32–12** unregistered company under the Insolvency Act 1986 are considered elsewhere in this work.[45]

3. WINDING UP

When a limited partnership is dissolved, the task of winding up its affairs is **32–13** entrusted to the general partners (or such of them as are solvent), unless the court directs otherwise.[46] Whilst a limited partner retains the right to apply for an order that the affairs of the partnership be wound up under the supervision of the court,[47] the current editor considers that such an application might not be entertained unless misconduct by the general partners or some other special circumstances could be shown to exist.

[39] See, as to the meaning of this expression, *supra*, para. 11–02.

[40] Partnership Act 1890, s.35(f), *infra*, para. A1–36; and see *supra*, paras 24–35, 24–89, 24–90. The liquidation of a corporate partner by no means implies that it is insolvent; see *supra*, para. 11–10.

[41] A limited partnership must comprise at least one general partner: Limited Partnerships Act 1907, s.4(2), *infra*, para. A3–04.

[42] Partnership Act 1890, s.33(1), *infra*, para. A1–34; see also *supra*, para. 24–36.

[43] Since the dissolution of a company may be equated with the death of an individual, it might be argued that the Limited Partnerships Act 1907, s.6(2), *infra*, para. A3–06 (which prevents the death of a limited partner from automatically dissolving the firm) is effective to prevent such a dissolution being ordered; *sed quaere*.

[44] Insolvent Partnerships Order 1994, art. 8(4), (5), (8), (creditor's petition); *ibid.* art. 10(2), (3), (6), as amended by the Insolvent Partnerships (Amendment) Order 2005 (SI 2005/1516), art. 5(b) (members' petition). See further *supra*, paras 27–27 *et seq.*, 27–36 *et seq.*

[45] See *supra*, paras 27–04 *et seq.*

[46] Limited Partnerships Act 1907, s.6(3), *infra*, para. A3–06; see also the Partnership Act 1890, s.38, *supra*, paras 13–62 *et seq.* As to insolvency, see *supra*, paras 27–67 *et seq.*

[47] Partnership Act 1890, s.39, *supra*, paras 19–25 *et seq.*

It goes almost without saying that, if the partnership is dissolved by the death or bankruptcy of a sole general partner or if, following a dissolution, the only solvent general partner dies or becomes insolvent before the winding up is complete, the limited partners will have to make an immediate application to the court.[48]

---

[48] *Quaere*, could it be argued that, in such a case, the Limited Partnerships Act 1907, s.6(3) does not apply, so that the limited partners are free to undertake the winding up (albeit perhaps not in that capacity)?

CHAPTER 33

INSOLVENCY

1. APPLICATION OF INSOLVENCY LAWS TO LIMITED PARTNERSHIPS

THE Insolvency Act 1986, as applied to partnerships by the Insolvent Partner- **33–01** ships Order 1994,[1] does not in general distinguish between limited and ordinary partnerships, so that, as has already been seen,[2] an insolvent limited partnership may in appropriate circumstances be wound up as an unregistered company on the petition of the firm, one or more of the partners or a creditor or other authorised person.

Position of limited partners

It is consistent with the treatment of a partnership as an unregistered company **33–02** that the partners should be treated as its officers[3] and, in this respect, limited partners are treated no differently from any other partner, despite the fact that they are precluded from participation in the management of the partnership business as a condition of retaining their limited liability.[4] However, this is, in practice, unlikely to have particularly serious implications for such a partner. He will, naturally enough, be obliged to deliver up to the liquidator possession of any partnership property in his hands[5] and may, moreover, be required to submit a statement of affairs relating to the firm[6] and to undergo a public examination.[7] Although it remains a theoretical possibility that he might also be made the subject of a disqualification order under the Company Directors Disqualification

---

[1] SI 1994/2421. This Order has since been amended by numerous Amendment Orders.

[2] See *supra*, paras 27–04 *et seq.*, 32–07.

[3] See the definition of "officer" in the Insolvent Partnerships Order 1994, art. 2(1), as added to the Insolvency Act 1986, s.436 by *ibid.* art. 2(2). See further *supra*, paras 27–59, 27–63.

[4] Limited Partnerships Act 1907, s.6(1), *infra*, para. A3–06: see *supra*, paras 30–08, 31–04.

[5] Insolvency Act 1986, s.234(2), as amended, where there are no concurrent petitions, by the Insolvent Partnerships Order 1994, Sched. 3, Pt II, para. 9 and applied by the Insolvency Act 1986, s.221(5) (as itself amended by the Insolvent Partnerships Order 1994, art. 7(1) (as amended by the Insolvent Partnerships (Amendment) Order 1996 (SI 1996/1308), art. 2 and the Insolvent Partnerships (Amendment) Order 2002 (SI 2002/ 1308), art. 3), (2), Sched. 3, Pt I, para. 3 (creditor's petition) and *ibid.* art. 9(a), Sched. 5, para. 2 (member's petition)) and as amended, where there *are* concurrent petitions, by *ibid.* Sched. 4, Pt II, para. 27 and applied by the Insolvency Act 1986, s.221(5) (as itself amended by the Insolvent Partnerships Order 1994, art. 8(1) (as amended by the Insolvent Partnerships (Amendment) Order 2002, art. 4(1)), (2), Sched. 4, Pt I, para. 3 (creditor's petition) and *ibid.* art. 10(1)(a), Sched. 6, para. 4 (member's petition)).

[6] *ibid.* s.131, as amended by the Insolvent Partnerships Order 1994, Sched. 3, Pt II, para. 7 (no concurrent petitions) and Sched. 4, Pt II, para. 10 (concurrent petitions) and applied in the manner set out in the preceding footnote.

[7] *ibid.* s.133, as amended by the Insolvent Partnerships Order 1994, Sched. 3, Pt II, para. 8 (no concurrent petitions) and Sched. 4, Pt II, para. 11 (concurrent petitions) and applied in the manner set out *supra*, n. 5.

Act 1986,[8] it seems unlikely that, given his restricted rights under the 1907 Act, his conduct as a limited partner will, of itself, be sufficient to render him unfit to be concerned in the management of a company.[9] *Per contra*, if he has forfeited his limited liability by participating in the management of the partnership[10] or, perhaps, if he has acted as its agent in entering into transactions on its behalf.[11]

33–03   It is clear that a limited partner will also be liable *qua* contributory[12] to the extent that he has received back any part of his contribution[13] and, perhaps, even where his capital contribution continues to be held by the firm.[14] However, the current editor is of the opinion that this will not involve any alteration in the quantum of a current or former limited partner's liability, although the position is far from clear.[15]

Authority of limited partners

33–04   It is apprehended that, in the absence of express authority, a limited partner would have no power to act for the firm in insolvency proceedings.[16] Equally, if such authority were conferred on him, its exercise would prima facie not involve participation in the management of the firm, thus causing him to forfeit his limited liability.[17]

2.   PETITIONS BY AND AGAINST LIMITED PARTNERS

Petitions by limited partners

33–05   The members of a limited partnership may not present a joint bankruptcy petition unless the firm is itself wound up as an unregistered company.[18]

---

[8] As applied by the Insolvent Partnerships Order 1994, art. 16 (as amended by the Insolvent Partnerships (Amendment) Order 2001 (SI 2001/767), art. 2) and modified by *ibid.* Sched. 8 (as amended).

[9] Company Directors Disqualification Act 1986, ss.6(1)(b), (3), 9, Sched. 1 (as applied and modified by the Insolvent Partnerships Order 1994, art. 16, Sched. 8, as amended). See further *supra*, para. 27–64. The detailed operation of the 1986 Act is outside the scope of the present work: readers are referred to standard works on company law, *e.g. Palmer's Company Law* (25th ed), Pt 8.

[10] See *supra*, paras 31–02 *et seq.*

[11] See *supra*, paras 30–03 *et seq.*

[12] Insolvency Act 1986, s.226, as applied by the Insolvent Partnerships Order 1994, arts 7(1) (as amended: see *supra*, n. 5) (creditor's petition with no concurrent petitions), 8(1) (as amended: see *supra*, n. 5) (creditor's petition *with* concurrent petitions) and 9(b) (member's petitions with no concurrent petitions). The section does not apply where a *member* serves concurrent petitions, but *ibid.* s.74(1) does: see *supra*, para. 27–59, n. 270.

[13] See, as to the effect of such withdrawal, the Limited Partnerships Act 1907, s.4(3), *infra*, para. A3–04 and *supra*, paras 30–08 *et seq.*

[14] The Insolvency Act 1986, s.226(1) provides that "every person is deemed a contributory who is liable to pay or contribute to the payment of any debt or liability of the [*firm*]": see further *supra*, para. 27–59. A limited partner is so liable, but only to the extent of his contribution: Limited Partnerships Act 1907, s.4(2), *infra*, para. A3–04; see also *supra*, paras 29–04, 30–07. But see also *infra*, para. 33–06.

[15] See *supra*, para. 27–61. As to the ability of a limited partner to retire from the firm, see *supra*, paras 30–14, 30–15, 31–15, 31–16.

[16] See *supra*, paras 12–36, 30–03.

[17] Limited Partnerships Act 1907, s.6(1), *infra*, para. A3–06. See *supra*, para. 30–04.

[18] Insolvency Act 1986, s.264(1), as amended and applied by the Insolvent Partnerships Order 1994, art. 11, Sched. 7, para. 2.

Petitions against limited partners

Where concurrent petitions are presented against the firm and against one or more of the partners, a limited partner may secure a dismissal of the petition against him, even though an order is made against the firm,[19] if he either lodges in court for the benefit of the firm's creditors "sufficient money or security . . . to meet his liability for the debts and obligations of the partnership" or satisfies the court that he is no longer under any liability in respect of such debts and obligations.[20] The current editor submits that a limited partner should be able to satisfy the latter condition by demonstrating that he has neither withdrawn his capital contribution nor forfeited his limited liability.[21] If that is not, for whatever reason, possible, the limited partner will have to lodge in court the amount of capital withdrawn or, if he has participated in the management of the firm, he will have to show that no liabilities were incurred whilst his participation was continuing.[22] Needless to say, the latter may be difficult, if not impossible, to demonstrate to the court's satisfaction.

33–06

3.   ADMINISTRATION OF INSOLVENT PARTNERS' ESTATES

Joint and separate estates

As in the case of the old bankruptcy law, in the event of the insolvency of a partnership, the joint debts are principally payable out of the joint estate and the separate debts out of the partners' respective separate estates, although in cases where a firm is wound up with concurrent petitions being presented against one or more of the partners or where orders are made on a joint bankruptcy petition, the Insolvent Partnerships Order 1994 now allows unpaid debts in the joint estate to be proved against a partner's separate estate in competition with his separate creditors.[23]

33–07

It is in this context that attention must be drawn to the old decision in *Re Barnard*.[24] There, a bankrupt, Barnard, was the sole general partner in two

[19] As to the position in the case of an ordinary partnership, see *supra*, para. 27–39.

[20] Insolvency Act 1986, ss.125(1), s.125A(7), as respectively amended and added by the Insolvent Partnerships Order 1994, Sched. 4, Pt II, para. 9 and applied, as regards the partners, by *ibid*. art. 8(4)–(8) (creditor's petition) and *ibid*. art. 10(2)–(6), as amended by the Insolvent Partnerships (Amendment) Order 2005 (SI 2005,1516), art. 5(b) (member's petition).

[21] See the Limited Partnerships Act 1907, ss.4(3), 6(1), considered *supra*, paras 30–08 *et seq.*, 31–02 *et seq.*

[22] See *supra*, para. 31–04.

[23] See, in the case of orders on concurrent petitions, the Insolvency Act 1986, s.175A(5), (7), as amended by the Insolvent Partnerships Order 1994, Sched. 4, Pt II, para. 23 and applied, as regards the firm, by the Insolvency Act 1986, s.221(5) (as itself amended by the Insolvent Partnerships Order 1994, art. 8(1) (as amended: see *supra*, n. 5), (2), Sched. 4, Pt I, para. 3 (creditor's petition *with* concurrent petitions) and *ibid*. art. 10(1)(a), Sched. 6, para. 4 (member's petition *with* concurrent petitions)) and, as regards insolvent corporate and individual partners, by the Insolvent Partnerships Order 1994, arts 8(4)–(8) (creditor's petition), 10(2)–(6) (as amended : see *supra*, n. 20) (member's petition). The equivalent provision in the case of a joint bankruptcy petition is *ibid*. s.328A(5), (7), as amended and applied by the Insolvent Partnerships Order 1994, art. 11, Sched. 7, para. 21. See further *supra*, paras 27–82 *et seq.*, 27–106. And see, as to the priority of expenses in the joint and separate estates, *ibid*. ss.175, 328, as respectively amended and applied by *ibid*. and *supra*, paras 27–81, 27–103.

[24] [1932] 1 Ch. 269.

limited partnerships known respectively as W. H. Barnard and the Scrap Metal Co. There was only one limited partner in the former firm, but three in the latter. Bills of exchange amounting to £9,869 were drawn on the Scrap Metal Co. and accepted by Barnard as managing partner. These bills were held by Martins Bank. In June, a receiving order was made against the first firm, W. H. Barnard, and Barnard was adjudicated bankrupt. In July, a receiving order was made against the second firm, Scrap Metal Co., and Barnard was again adjudicated bankrupt. Martins Bank lodged a proof for £9,869 in the second bankruptcy but later withdrew it and sought to prove their debt in the first. The trustee rejected the proof on the ground that Barnard was not a party to the bills. Farwell J. held that, in these circumstances, the receiving order against the firm, W. H. Barnard, operated against Barnard alone, that the signature of the Scrap Metal Co. to the bills was equivalent to Barnard's signature,[25] and that the bank was therefore entitled to prove in the bankruptcy of W. H. Barnard. He went on to point out that, as Barnard was the sole general partner in both firms, there was technically no question of any joint liability but he nevertheless expressed the opinion that the assets of W. H. Barnard must first be applied in payment of that firm's debts and the surplus in repaying the limited partner's contribution; only the balance would form part of Barnard's separate estate applicable towards his own private debts and any other debts incurred by him on behalf of other limited partnerships. The assets of the Scrap Metal Co. fell to be applied in a similar way.

33–08   It is the view of the current editor that, in a case of this type, a broadly similar result is likely to be achieved under the Insolvent Partnerships Order 1994, even where both firms are wound up with concurrent petitions against the general partner.[26] The critical question is whether the debts of each firm should, for this purpose, be characterised as joint or separate. Since the estate of each firm should properly be regarded as a joint estate,[27] it seems logical that the debts principally payable out of that estate should be similarly regarded.[28] If that is right, and there is insufficient in the relevant joint estate to discharge the "joint" debts, the shortfall will, where concurrent petitions have been presented, clearly be provable against the general partner's separate estate and will rank equally with his separate debts.[29] However, there is nothing in the Order which permits the shortfall in one joint estate to be proved in competition with the joint debts in another.

[25] See the Bills of Exchange Act 1882, s.23(2). And see *supra*, para. 12–162.

[26] This is, perhaps, a likely scenario in the circumstances supposed.

[27] An analysis which results in a single partner having more than one separate estate seems difficult to justify. If that were, indeed, the position, there is nothing in the Insolvent Partnerships Order 1994 which permits those estates to be aggregated or to be treated as indistinguishable from the general partner's own personal separate estate nor, for that matter, which permits debts unpaid in one separate estate to be proved in another.

[28] Note, however, that in *Re Barnard*, *supra*, at p. 275 Farwell J. stated that: "The balance [*of the assets in The Scrap Metal Co.*] will be applied in the first instance in repaying the limited partners, and the surplus will be part of Barnard's separate estate available for payment of his private debts, and debts incurred by him on behalf of some other limited partnership, which *for that purpose must be treated as separate debts*" (emphasis supplied). This appears to ignore the analytical difficulties referred to in the preceding footnote.

[29] Insolvency Act 1986, s.175A(5), (7), as amended and applied in the manner set out *supra*, para. 33–07, n. 23. Similarly where orders are made on a joint bankruptcy petition: *ibid.* s.328A(5), (7), as amended and applied by the Insolvent Partnerships Order 1994, art. 11, Sched. 7, para. 21. The proof is submitted by the responsible insolvency practitioner not by the unpaid creditor(s). See further, *supra*, paras 27–82 *et seq.*, 27–106.

The position is clearer where an insolvency petition is presented solely against the general partner or where petitions are presented against both firms and the general partner *otherwise* than concurrently, since in either case the provisions of the 1994 Order currently under consideration do not apply unless the court, in the exercise of its discretion, directs otherwise.[30]

---

[30] Insolvency Act 1986, ss.168(5A), 303(2A), as added by the Insolvent Partnerships Order 1994, art. 14(1). See further *supra*, paras 27–21, 27–22, 27–41, 27–50, 27–85.

Part Seven

TAXATION

CHAPTER 34

INCOME TAX

1. INTRODUCTION

The development of partnership taxation

REFERENCE has already been made earlier in this work to the fact that, under **34–01** English law, a partnership generally has no legal status or existence independently of the individual partners of which it is composed; in fact the term "partnership" is nothing more than a convenient method of referring to the existence of two or more persons who are carrying on a business in common with a view of profit.[1] The rights and liabilities of a partnership are nothing more than the aggregate of the rights and liabilities of the individual partners. On that basis, there was no reason in principle why the ordinary rules as to the taxation of the income of individuals should not have been applied to the taxation of partnerships from the outset, so that each partner would have been assessed to tax separately from his co-partners. However, because such an approach was perceived to necessitate the dissection of the partnership accounts and an apportionment of the overall expenses and gross receipts amongst the individual partners in order to determine their respective net incomes,[2] the Income Tax Act 1918 provided that where a trade was carried on by two or more persons jointly, income tax was to be computed and stated jointly and in one sum, separate and distinct from any other tax chargeable on those persons, and that a joint assessment was to be made in the firm name. These provisions were subsequently re-enacted on three occasions without alteration and were most recently contained in section 111 of the Income and Corporation Taxes Act 1988 as originally enacted. It was only on the introduction of self-assessment by the Finance Act 1994, that this long-standing approach was finally abandoned in favour of the individual assessment of each partner by reference to his share of the partnership profits.[3]

Nevertheless, even under the new regime the taxation of partnership income, **34–02** *i.e.* the income of the individual partners which is derived from partnership activities, stands on a different footing from the taxation of income derived by them from other sources and thus requires special attention, albeit that the position is now much simplified. Firms comprising one or more corporate

---

[1] See *supra*, paras 3–01 *et seq.* For a reaffirmation of this principle in an income tax case, see *MacKinlay v. Arthur Young McClelland Moores & Co.* [1990] 2 A.C. 239.

[2] This is the approach adopted in New Zealand: see *Hadlee v. Commissioner of Inland Revenue* [1993] A.C. 524, 528 (PC).

[3] See the Income and Corporation Taxes Act 1988, s.111, as substituted by the Finance Act 1994, s.215(1) (as later amended by the Finance Act 1995, s.117) and then amended by the Finance Act 1998, s.46(3)(a), Sched. 7, para. 1. As to the current legislation, see *infra*, paras 34–03 *et seq.*

partners remain subject to special rules, but these now in large measure track the provisions applicable to individual partners.[4]

The present code of income tax law for partnerships, which is substantially contained in the Taxes Management Act 1970, the Capital Allowances Act 2001, the Income Tax (Trading and Other Income) Act 2005 and the Income Tax Act 2007, embodies a number of special rules and principles which are peculiar to partnerships.[5] It should, in this connection, be noted that the long standing schedular based approach to the taxation of income has been abandoned, even though still frequently referred to in practice.[6] The taxation of companies which enter into partnership is now governed by the Corporation Tax Acts 2009 and 2010.

Given that the Inland Revenue has now been redesignated as HM Revenue & Customs,[7] it will for convenience in this and subsequent chapters be referred as HMRC.

2.   TAX TREATMENT OF PARTNERSHIPS

Partnerships and the Income Tax (Trading and Other Income) Act 2005

34–03   The main statutory provisions governing the taxation of partnership income, apart from capital allowances, are those contained in Part 9 of the Income Tax (Trading and Other Income) Act 2005. The key sections[8] provide as follows:

"*General provisions*

847.— (1) In this Act persons carrying on a trade in partnership are referred to collectively as a "firm".

(2) The provisions of this Part [which are expressed to apply to trades also apply, unless otherwise indicated (whether expressly or by implication)][9]—

(a)   to professions, and
(b)   in the case of this section and sections 849, 850, 857 and 858 to businesses that are not trades or professions.

(3) In those sections as applied by subsection (2)(b)—

(a)   references to a trade are references to a business, and
(b)   references to the profits of a trade are references to the income arising from a business.

---

[4] See *infra*, paras 34–55 *et seq.*

[5] It is proposed to consider only those rules and principles which are of particular importance in relation to partnerships. For all other matters, the reader is referred to the standard works on income tax, *e.g. Whiteman & Sherry on Income Tax* (4th ed.).

[6] Thus, the charge to tax on employees (formerly Schedule E) is now imposed under the Income Tax (Earnings and Pensions) Act 2003.

[7] Commissioners for Revenue and Customs Act 2005, s.4.

[8] Note that these sections are broadly replicated in the Corporation Tax Act 2009, Pt 17: see *infra*, paras 34–55 *et seq.*

[9] As substituted by the Corporation Tax Act 2009, Sched. 1, Pt 2, para. 638.

Assessment of partnerships

848.—Unless otherwise indicated (whether expressly or by implication), a firm is **34–04** not to be regarded for income tax purposes as an entity separate and distinct from the partners.

Calculation of firm's profits or losses

849.—(1) If—   **34–05**

(a) a firm carries on a trade, and

(b) any partner in the firm is chargeable to income tax,

the profits or losses of the trade are calculated on the basis set out in subsection (2) or (3), as the case may require.

(2) For any period of account in which the partner is a UK resident individual, the profits or losses of the trade are calculated as if the firm were a UK resident individual.

(3) For any period of account in which the partner is non-UK resident, the profits or losses of the trade are calculated as if the firm were a non-UK resident individual.

[(4) In calculating under subsection (2) or (3) the profits of a trade for any period of account no account is taken of any losses for another period of account.][10]

[*Allocation of firm's profits or losses between partners*

850.—(1) For any period of account a partner's share of a profit or loss of a trade **34–06** carried on by a firm is determined for income tax purposes in accordance with the firm's profit-sharing arrangements during that period.

This is subject to sections 850A and 850B.

(2) In this section and sections 850A and 850B "profit-sharing arrangements" means the rights of the partners to share in the profits of the trade and the liabilities of the partners to share in the losses of the trade.][11]

. . .

Carrying on by partner of notional trade

852.—(1) For each tax year in which a firm carries on a trade (the "actual trade"), **34–07** each partner's share of the firm's trading profits or losses is treated, for the purposes of Chapter 15 of Part 2 (basis periods), as profits or losses of a trade carried on by the partner alone (the "notional trade").

(2) A partner starts to carry on a notional trade at the later of—

(a) when becoming a partner in the firm, and

(b) when the firm starts to carry on the actual trade.

This is subject to subsection (3).

(3) If the partner carries on the actual trade alone before the firm starts to carry it on, the partner starts to carry on the notional trade when the partner starts to carry on the actual trade.

(4) A partner permanently ceases to carry on a notional trade at the earlier of—

(a) when the partner ceases to be a partner in the firm, and

(b) when the firm permanently ceases to carry on the actual trade.

This is subject to subsections (5) and (6).

(5) If the partner carries on the actual trade alone after the firm permanently ceases to carry it on, the partner permanently ceases to carry on the notional trade when the partner permanently ceases to carry on the actual trade.

(6) If—

---

[10] As added by *ibid.* para. 639.
[11] As substituted by *ibid.*, Sched. 1, Pt 2, para. 640.

(a) the firm carries on the actual trade wholly or partly outside the United Kingdom, and

(b) the partner becomes or ceases to be UK resident,

the partner is treated as permanently ceasing to carry on one notional trade when the change of residence occurs and starting to carry on another immediately afterwards.

(7) Subsection (6) does not prevent a loss made before the change of residence from being [deducted under section 83 of ITA 2007 from][12] profits arising after the change.

. . .

Carrying on by partner of notional business

34–08   854.—(1) For each tax year in which a firm—

(a) carries on a trade, and

(b) has untaxed income or relievable losses from other sources,

each partner's share of the firm's untaxed income or relievable losses other than trading profits or losses is treated, for the purposes of Chapter 15 of Part 2, as profits or losses of a trade carried on by the partner alone (the "notional business").

(2) A partner starts to carry on a notional business at the later of—

(a) when becoming a partner in the firm, and

(b) when the firm starts to carry on a trade.

(3) A notional business continues even if either or both of the following occur—

(a) separate sources of income that comprise the business start and cease, and

(b) no income arises during a particular tax year.

This is subject to subsections (4) and (5).

(4) A partner permanently ceases to carry on a notional business at the earlier of—

(a) when the partner ceases to be a partner in the firm, and

(b) when the firm permanently ceases to carry on a trade.

(5) If—

(a) the firm carries on the trade wholly or partly outside the United Kingdom, and

(b) the partner becomes or ceases to be UK resident,

the partner is treated as permanently ceasing to carry on one notional business when the change of residence occurs and starting to carry on another immediately afterwards.

(6) In this section "untaxed income" means any income that is not—

(a) income from which income tax has been deducted,

(b) income from or on which income tax is treated as having been deducted or paid, or

(c) dividends or other distributions of a company chargeable under Chapter 3 of Part 4."

[12] As amended by the Income Tax Act 2007, Sched. 1, Pt 2, para. 579.

It will be noted that the concept of partnership, albeit not defined in the Act, **34–09** is central to the application of the section. It follows that any partnership within the meaning of the Partnership Act 1890 must necessarily be regarded as a partnership or firm for the purposes of these sections. Where, however, the firm comprises one or more corporate partners,[13] a different set of provisions will, at least in the first instance, apply.[14]

The essence of the approach adopted under the above sections is to treat the partnership as a separate individual, but *only* for the purposes of computing the partnership profits.[15] Once the computation is complete and the share of each partner is determined,[16] he will be assessed to tax thereon as if that share was derived from a separate notional trade treated as carried on by him alone.[17] If any part of the partnership profits consist of untaxed income[18] or unrelieved losses, each partner's share thereof will be regarded as derived from an entirely separate notional business, again treated as carried on by him alone.[19] The commencement and cessation rules will be applied to each of these notional trades and businesses.[20] It is because tax is now assessed on each partner individually by reference to his notional trade and business that tax on partnership profits is no longer a joint liability attaching to all the partners.[21]

Partnership agreements and HMRC

(a) *Existence of partnership.* It was originally thought that a determination as to **34–10** the existence of a partnership involved a pure question of fact from which there could be no appeal[22] but, in view of the decision in *Keith Spicer Ltd. v. Mansell*,[23] it must now be recognised as involving a mixed question of law and fact. Thus, where the Tribunal[24] has made a finding that a partnership does or does not exist, an appeal will lie.[25]

As already noted,[26] in order to determine whether a partnership exists regard must be had to the substance of the transaction or the nature of the activity, rather

---

[13] See *supra*, paras 11–01 *et seq.*
[14] The charge to tax on the corporate partners will be governed by the Corporation Taxes Act 2009, Pt 17. See further, *infra*, paras 34–55 *et seq.*
[15] Income Tax (Trading and Other Income) Act 2005, s.849(2), (3).
[16] *ibid.* s.850. Note also *ibid.* ss.850A and 850B, noted *infra*, para. 34–21.
[17] *ibid.* s.852(1). This was formerly denoted a "deemed trade".
[18] As defined in *ibid.* s.854(6).
[19] *ibid.* s.854(1). This was formerly, and somewhat confusingly, denoted a second "deemed trade".
[20] *ibid.* s.852(2)–(5), 854(2), (4).
[21] *cf.* the Income and Corporation Taxes Act 1988, s.111 in its original form. And see *infra*, para. 34–19.
[22] See *Wood v. Duke of Argyll* (1844) 6 Man. & G. 928; *Lake v. Duke of Argyll* (1844) 6 Q.B. 477. And see *supra*, paras 5–36, 7–11.
[23] [1970] 1 W.L.R. 333. See also *Morden Rigg & Co. and R.B. Eskrigge & Co. v. Monks* (1923) 8 T.C. 450, 464 *per* Lord Sterndale M.R.
[24] *i.e.* the Tax Chamber of the First-tier Tribunal. Formerly, the initial finding as to the existence (or non-existence) of a partnership was normally made by the general or special commissioners: see, for example, *Alexander Bulloch & Co. v. IRC* [1976] S.T.C. 514; *Kings v. King* [2004] S.T.C. (SCD) 186; also *Morden Rigg & Co. and R.B. Eskrigge & Co. v. Monks, supra.*
[25] Thus, on any appeal from a first instance decision, the question can be decided *de novo*: *Keith Spicer Ltd. v. Mansell* [1970] 1 W.L.R. 333. And see *CIR v. Williamson* (1928) 14 T.C. 335.
[26] See *supra*, paras 5–03 *et seq.*

than to its outward form.[27] If, on a true analysis, the relationship of partnership exists, an express agreement purporting to negate such existence will be of no effect. Thus, in *Weiner v. Harris*,[28] Cozens-Hardy M.R. observed:

> "It is quite plain that by the mere use of a well-known legal phrase you cannot constitute a transaction that which you attempt to describe by that phrase. Perhaps the commonest instance of all, which has come before the Courts in many phases, is this: Two parties enter into a transaction and say 'It is hereby declared that there is no partnership between us.' The Court pays no regard to that. The Court looks at the transaction and says 'Is this, in point of law, really a partnership? It is not in the least conclusive that the parties have used a term or language intended to indicate that the transaction is not that which in law it is.' "[29]

Conversely, an attempt to dress up a transaction or activity in the form of a partnership, where one or more of the essential characteristics of that relationship are lacking, will be rejected as a mere sham.[30] Thus, in one case[31] a father owning two farms executed a deed of partnership whereby he was expressed to enter into partnership with his three sons. The deed provided for the signing of cheques by any of the partners, the sharing of profits, and the payment of rent to the father. In fact, however, they carried on as before, ignoring the terms of the deed. It was held that no partnership existed.[32]

34–11   It should be remembered in this context that it is not an essential characteristic of the partnership relation that all the partners must take an active part in the firm's affairs. Thus, there is no reason why a valid partnership should not exist between A, B and C when A is given the sole powers of management, B and C being merely dormant partners.[33] Indeed, this situation is expressly provided for, in connection with limited partnerships, by sections 4 and 6 of the Limited Partnerships Act 1907, and there can be no doubt but that a limited partnership is a partnership for tax purposes.[34] Moreover, the concept of a "non-active" partner now in terms features in the tax legislation.[35]

---

[27] In *Pratt v. Strick* (1932) 17 T.C. 459, the vendor of a medical practice agreed to continue in the practice for a short period in order to introduce the purchaser to his patients. Notwithstanding the fact that the vendor and the purchaser had agreed to share both receipts and outgoings during that period, it was held that no partnership had been created. See also the decision of the Supreme Court of Canada in *Backman v. R*, 3 I.T.L. Rep. 647, regarding the requirements for the existence of a partnership for tax purposes. And note *Kings v. King, supra*.

[28] [1910] 1 K.B. 285, 290.

[29] See also *CIR v. Williamson* (1929) 14 T.C. 335, 340 *per* the Lord President; *Reeves v. Evans, Boyce and Northcott Syndicate* (1971) 32 T.R. 483, 487 *per* Megarry J.; *Stekel v. Ellice* [1973] 1 W.L.R. 191, 199–200 *per* Megarry J.; *Alexander Bulloch & Co. v. IRC* [1976] S.T.C. 514, 580 *per* the Lord President; *Newstead v. Frost* [1980] 1 W.L.R. 135; *Saywell v. Pope* [1979] S.T.C. 824; *Engineer v. IRC* [1997] S.T.C. (S.C.D.) 189. Note that, in borderline cases, a statement of the parties' intentions may be more relevant: *Dragonfly Consultancy Ltd. v. Revenue & Customs Commissioners* [2008] S.T.C. 3030 at [55] *per* Henderson J.

[30] See, for example, *Protectacoat Firthglow Ltd. v. Szilagyi* [2009] I.R.L.R. 365, where an employment contract had been dressed up as a partnership. However, the court will not readily infer that a transaction is a sham: see, for example, *Hitch v. Stone* [1999] S.T.C. 431. See also, generally, as to sham transactions, *Snook v. London and West Riding Investments Ltd.* [1967] 2 Q.B. 786, 802 *per* Diplock L.J.

[31] *Dickenson v. Gross* (1927) 11 T.C. 614.

[32] See also *Alexander Bulloch & Co. v. IRC* [1976] S.T.C. 514.

[33] See, for example, the exceptional decision in *Ward v. Newall Insulation Co. Ltd.* [1998] 1 W.L.R. 1722 (CA), which was not, however, a tax case. *cf. Saywell v. Pope* [1979] S.T.C. 824.

[34] See, for example, the Income Tax Act 2007, s.104 (as amended), noticed *infra*, para. 34–49; also *Reed v. Young* [1986] 1 W.L.R. 649.

[35] See *ibid.* s.110 and *infra*, para. 34–50.

The continuing development of the so-called *Ramsay* principle[36] has added a degree of uncertainty in this area. Nevertheless, if a *genuine* partnership is interposed as a pre-ordained step in an overall tax avoidance scheme, the current editor submits that a court could not properly ignore its existence, particularly if enduring rights and liabilities have been created as between the partners. *A fortiori* if liabilities to third parties have been incurred.[37]

Finally, in this context it should be noted that where an individual provides **34-12** services to a client through a service partnership[38] in circumstances where he would otherwise fall to be regarded as an employee of that client,[39] he may, if one of three conditions is fulfilled,[40] fall to be taxed as an employee, rather than as a partner in the firm.[41] Here it is accepted that the court will have regard to the stated intention of the parties, even if this may be of only minimal value.[42] However, it must be appreciated that this is a piece of specific anti-avoidance legislation, which does not *per se* call the existence or validity of the partnership into question.[43]

(b) *Date of commencement or dissolution of the partnership.* It is a general **34-13** principle that a partnership deed cannot alter the past; whilst it may have effect as between the partners, HMRC are quite entitled to ignore it and to look at the

[36] See *W. T. Ramsay v. IRC* [1982] A.C. 300; *Furniss v. Dawson* [1984] A.C. 474. However, a restrictive interpretation was placed upon these decisions by a majority of the House of Lords in *Craven v. White* [1989] A.C. 398; see also *Shepherd v. Lyntress Ltd.* [1989] S.T.C. 617; *Ensign Tankers (Leasing) Ltd. v. Stokes* [1992] 1 A.C. 655 (HL); *IRC v. McGuckian* [1997] 1 W.L.R. 991 (HL); *Griffin v. Citibank Investments Ltd.* [2000] S.T.C. 1010; *Macniven v. Westmoreland Investments Ltd.* [2003] 1 A.C. 311 (HL); *I.R.C. v. Scottish Provident Institution* [2004] 1 W.L.R. 3172 (HL); *Barclays Mercantile Business Finance Ltd. v. Mawson* [2005] 1 A.C. 684 (HL).

[37] See, for example, *Ensign Tankers (Leasing) Ltd. v. Stokes* [1989] 1 W.L.R. 1222, where Millett J. dismissed the Inspector's argument that the creation of two limited partnerships could be treated as a step in a larger transaction. He observed (at *ibid.* p. 1243) that "it logically is impossible at one and the same time to find that the partnerships were trading and that the transactions into which they entered had no commercial purpose." This part of the decision was not appealed from: see [1991] 1 W.L.R. 341, 357H. In such a case, it can clearly be said that the creation of the partnership serves a genuine business purpose *apart* from the avoidance of tax, so that one of the fundamental conditions laid down in both *Ramsay* and *Furniss, supra*, and confirmed by all members of the House of Lords in *Craven v. White, supra*, will inevitably not be satisfied. See also *New Angel Court Ltd. v. Adam* [2004] 1 W.L.R. 1988 (CA).

[38] This is not an expression used in the legislation, but denotes the type of arrangement under which services are provided to one or more "captive" clients.

[39] See the Income Tax (Earnings and Pensions) Act 2003, s.49(1)(c). And see *Usetech Ltd. v. Young* [2004] S.T.C. 1671; *Dragonfly Consultancy Ltd. v. Revenue & Customs Commissioners* [2008] S.T.C. 3030. Note also the Social Security Contributions (Intermediaries) Regulations 2000 (SI 2000/727), as amended, and *Synaptek Ltd. v. Young* [2003] S.T.C. 543; *Future Online Ltd. v. Foulds* [2005] S.T.C. 198.

[40] The conditions are that: (a) the individual is (alone or with relatives) entitled to 60% or more of the partnership profits; or (b) most of those profits are derived from a single client (and its associates, where relevant); or (c) any partner's profit share is directly linked to the income derived from the provision of his services to the client: Income Tax (Earnings and Pensions) Act 2003, s.52(2), as amended by the Tax and Civil Partnerships Regulations 2005 (SI 2005/3229), reg. 138. The expression "relative" is defined by *ibid.*

[41] *ibid.* ss.49(1) (as amended by the Finance Act 2003, s.136(2)), 50(1). See also "IR35—revised guidance" issued by HMRC on June 8, 2005 and reproduced at [2005] S.T.I. 1048.

[42] *Dragonfly Consultancy Ltd. v. Revenue & Customs Commissioners, supra.*

[43] Note also the managed service company regime under the Income Tax (Earnings and Pensions) Act 2003, Pt 2, Chap. 9 and the HMRC Guidance Note "Service Companies—update on the nature of intermediaries" issued on December 2, 2008 and reproduced in [2008] S.T.I. 2712. This regime applies just as much to service partnerships of which the individual does not have control as companies.

true position.[44] Thus, a recital in such a deed that the partnership existed prior to the date of its execution is not conclusive.[45] What must be considered whenever the date of commencement of a partnership is called into question is whether a *de facto* partnership existed independently of the deed prior to its execution. As noted above, that question will involve a mixture of fact and law; the facts to be considered will include the provision (or absence of provision) for the sharing of profits and losses and the powers of management, etc., exercisable by the alleged "partners"[46]; the questions of law will include the construction to be placed upon any written partnership agreement and the conclusions to be drawn from the facts as found.

In *Waddington v. O'Callaghan*,[47] a father had given instructions to his solicitors to draw up a deed taking his son into partnership in his own solicitor's practice as from the date of the instructions, subject to the terms of the partnership deed being agreed between himself and his son. It was held that no partnership existed prior to the date of execution of the deed. In arriving at this decision, the court had regard to the fact that no formal notice had been given to clients (although it appears to have been generally known that the partnership had been arranged), no alteration had been made in the name of the firm, and no joint banking account had been opened prior to the execution of the deed. In cases of this type it is immaterial that the profits have been divided as from the notional date of commencement.

34–14   Similar considerations may arise when the date of dissolution of a partnership is in issue. If, for example, some or all of the activities associated with a firm's business are seen to be continuing, it will be necessary to determine whether the firm has ceased to trade and is merely engaged in winding up its affairs following a dissolution or is, in reality, continuing to trade.[48] Given the requirements of section 38 of the Partnership Act 1890,[49] activities carried out in the course of winding up the affairs of a dissolved firm may well, for tax purposes, be sufficient to amount to active trading.

34–15   (c) *Other agreements reached between partners.* It follows from the foregoing that any agreement which seeks to alter a partner's status or entitlement ex post facto can quite properly be implemented as between the partners, whether for accounting purposes or otherwise, but will not bind HMRC. Thus, where partners agreed to re-allocate the firm's income between themselves several years after it

---

[44] Note, in this context, the decisions in *Mansell v. Revenue & Customs Commissioners* [2006] S.T.C. (S.C.D.) 605 and *Chappell v. Revenue & Customs Commissioners* [2009] S.T.C. (S.C.D.) 11 at [7], considering the potential application of the principles discussed in *Khan v. Miah* [2000] 1 W.L.R. 2123 (HL) (noticed *supra*, para. 2–03) to the issue of when a partnership or trade is commenced for tax purposes.

[45] *Ayrshire Pullman Motor Services and D. M. Ritchie v. CIR* (1929) 14 T.C. 754; *Reeves v. Evans, Boyce and Northcott Syndicate* (1971) 32 T.R. 483; also *Saywell v. Pope* [1979] S.T.C. 824.

[46] See also *supra*, para. 5–59.

[47] (1931) 16 T.C. 187. See also *Saywell v. Pope, supra*, where two partners attempted (unsuccessfully) to introduce their wives into the partnership with retrospective effect. In the course of his judgment in the latter case, Slade J. observed (at p. 835d): "Partnership accounts cannot operate to make persons partners retrospectively, any more than a written partnership agreement can so operate."

[48] *O'Kane (J. & R.) & Co. v. CIR* (1922) 12 T.C. 303; *Hillerns & Fowler v. Murray* (1932) 17 T.C. 77; *Watts v. Hart* [1984] S.T.C. 548; *C. Connelly & Co. v. Wilbey* [1992] S.T.C. 783.

[49] See *supra*, paras 10–199, 13–62 *et seq.*

arose, so as to obtain the maximum benefit from available tax reliefs, the re-allocation was held to be of no effect *vis-à-vis* HMRC.[50]

On the other hand, a bona fide agreement which governs the partners' present and future relationship and which does not seek to have any retrospective effect will be equally valid as between the partners themselves and as between them and HMRC, provided that its terms are adhered to. Thus, it is, for example, open to the partners to agree that the entirety of a capital allowance or balancing charge[51] accruing in respect of a particular partnership asset will be enjoyed or borne by one or more of their number; or even that one partner will indemnify the others against a particular partnership liability, without affecting the deductibility of that liability in computing the profits of the firm for tax purposes.[52] Significant tax advantages can often be obtained from careful planning, coupled with the use of such agreements.[53]

(d) *Partnership as a settlement.* It seems likely that, in the case of partnerships **34–16** between a husband and wife or civil partners,[54] HMRC may seek to apply the settlement legislation[55] for income tax purposes, unless both partners are active participants in the business or the outright gift exemption applies.[56] It should be noted that the corporate structure in *Jones v. Garnett*[57] was held to have involved the required "element of bounty" to constitute a settlement and was only excluded because it entailed an outright gift. It appears that HMRC *will* regard the outright transfer of a share in a ordinary partnership as qualifying for the above exemption, but the position may well be different in the case of the transfer of a more limited interest in such a share or, indeed, a share in a limited partnership.[58] Equally, as in the case of service partnerships,[59] even if the settlement legislation *does* apply, this would not mean that the partnership does not exist, but might result in the whole of the partnership profits being taxed in the hands of only one spouse/civil partner *qua* settlor.

[50] *Bucks v. Bowers* [1970] Ch. 431, 441 *per* Pennycuick J. If such an *ex post facto* re-allocation of profit is desired, particular care should be taken to provide for the incidence of the burden of tax, *i.e.* is the re-allocated profit to be paid over subject to deduction of tax at the rate of the partner who is for tax purposes treated as entitled to it, or at the rate of the recipient partner, or subject to no deduction at all? If no specific provision is included, it may well be difficult to determine what deduction, if any, is to be made.

[51] There is no reason why the partnership agreement should not specifically allocate a capital allowance or balancing charge between the partners; in the absence of any such provision, the allowance or charge will prima facie be shared by the partners in their profit sharing ratios. See further, *infra*, para. 34–44.

[52] See *Bolton v. Halpern & Woolf* [1981] S.T.C. 14, where the indemnity was given by a retired partner.

[53] In such a way, it may be possible to depress the share of profits of one partner, and increase the share of another. But note, in this context, the terms of the Income Tax (Trading and Other Income) Act 2005, ss.850A, 850B, noticed *infra*, para. 34–21.

[54] Similarly, perhaps, in the case of partnerships involving other family members.

[55] See *ibid.* ss.620, 624, 625 (as amended).

[56] *ibid.* s.626, as amended by the Tax And Civil Partnership Regulations 2005, reg. 189. See further IR Tax Bulletins 64 (April 2003) and 69 (February 2004, reproduced at [2004] S.T.I. 460) and the Guidance at [2004] S.T.I. 2369; and see also [2003] S.T.I. 1921, 2246; [2004] S.T.I. 2446; and the Chartered Institute of Taxation's guidance note "Settlement provisions and disclosure issues" dated January 1, 2006, reproduced at [2006] S.T.I. 212.

[57] [2007] 1 W.L.R. 2030.

[58] See, as to such partnerships, *supra*, Pt 6.

[59] See *supra*, para. 34–12.

3.   METHOD OF ASSESSMENT

Partnership returns, etc.

34–17   HMRC may require a partner[60] identified in accordance with rules accompanying a notice given to all the partners, or that partner's "successor",[61] to make and deliver a partnership return, together with such accounts, statements and documents as may reasonably be required.[62] In the case of a firm comprising one or more individuals the notice may specify different days for the partnership return to be filed according to whether or not the return is electronic.[63] In the case of an electronic return the date must not be earlier than January 31 in the year following the year of assessment in question,[64] but otherwise the date must not be earlier than October 31 in that year.[65] Where, however, notice is given between July 31 and October 31 in that year, a non electronic return must be filed within 3 months[66] and where the notice is given after October 31 in that year, the return must in all cases again be filed within 3 months.[67] Where the partnership comprises one or more companies, the periods again depend on whether the return is electronic or non-electronic.[68] A non-electronic return must be filed not earlier than 9 months after the end of the relevant period,[69] whilst an electronic return may be filed on the first anniversary of the end of that period.[70] If notice is given more than 9 months after the end of the relevant period, the return must in all cases be filed within 3 months.[71]

---

[60] Note, however, that the power in question is technically exercisable against a "person" rather than a partner as such. See also *ibid.* n. 62.

[61] This will, in general, be a partner nominated for the purpose by the other partners: see *ibid.* s.12AA(11)(a), (12) (as added by the Finance Act 1996, s.123(4) and amended by the Finance Act 2001, Sched. 29, Pt 5, para. 18(3)). If no partner is so nominated, the successor will be identified in accordance with the rules accompanying the notice or will be nominated by HMRC: *ibid.* s.12AA(11)(b).

[62] *ibid.* s.12AA(1) (as added by the Finance Act 1994, s.184 and amended by the Finance Act 1995, s.104(6) and the Finance Act 1996, s.121(6)), (2) (as added by *ibid.* and amended by the Finance Act 1995, s.115(4) and the Finance Act 1996, s.123(1)). There is also an independent power to require any partner or his successor to make and submit a return: *ibid.* s.12AA(3) (as added by *ibid.* and amended by the Finance Act 1996, s.123(2)). As to the penalties for failing to submit a return, see *ibid.* s.93A (as added by the Finance Act 1994, Sched. 19, Pt 1, paras 26, 28 and amended by the Finance Act 1996, s.123(8)–(13), the Finance Act 2007, s.91(8), (9), Sched. 27, Pt 5(3) and the Transfer of Tribunal Functions and Revenue and Customs Appeals Order 2009 (SI 2009/56), Sched. 1, para. 42). The penalties for submitting an incorrect return are contained in the Finance Act 2007, Sched. 24 (as amended). Where an inaccuracy in the return affects the liability of a partner, a penalty assessment can also be made against him: *ibid.* Sched. 24, para. 20.

[63] Taxes Management Act 1970, s.12AA(4), as substituted by the Finance Act 2007, s.90(1). And see the HMRC Technical Note "Partnership filing dates—individual and corporate partners" issued on January 14, 2009 and reproduced at [2009] S.T.I. 179.

[64] *ibid.* s.12AA(4B), as added by *ibid.*

[65] *ibid.* s.12AA(4A), as added by *ibid.*

[66] *ibid.* s.12AA(4D), as added by *ibid.*

[67] *ibid.* s.12AA(4E), as added by *ibid.*

[68] See the Taxes Management Act 1970, s.12AA(5), as substituted by the Finance Act 2007, s.90(2). See also the HMRC Technical Note on filing dates: see *supra*, n. 63.

[69] *ibid.* s.12AA(5A), as added by *ibid.*

[70] *ibid.* s.12AA(5B), as added by *ibid.*

[71] *ibid.* s.12AA(5C) as added by *ibid.*

The role of the so-called "nominated partner"[72] is an important one and the partner in question will seemingly retain that status even following a dissolution.[73] If an inquiry into the return is to be made, notice must be given to that partner,[74] even though such notice does not need to be given in a particular form.[75]

The return must, *inter alia*, include the names and residences of each of the **34–18** other partners,[76] as well as particulars of any disposals of partnership property during the period to which the return relates.[77] It must also be accompanied by a partnership statement giving details of the firm's income or losses from each source and its charges on income in respect of each accounting period ending during the period covered by the return and specifying each partner's share of that income, loss or charge.[78] Various claims for relief, etc., will also be made by means of the partnership return.[79] The fact that a particular payment to a partner is characterised in a certain way in the partnership return and accompanying statement does not mean that he cannot subsequently seek to maintain that such characterisation is wrong.[80]

Where a partnership return is amended by HMRC following an enquiry and this leads to a consequential amendment to a partner's return,[81] he can bring an appeal against the amendment even if he is not the nominated partner.[82]

Tax no longer a joint debt

Unlike the position under the old tax regime,[83] tax on trading income is no **34–19** longer treated as a debt of the partnership, so that each partner will only be liable in respect of the tax assessable on his share of the partnership profits, just as if he were carrying on a wholly separate trade.[84] HMRC have confirmed that there

[72] This expression, which is not used or defined in the Taxes Management Act 1970, denotes the partner who is obliged to submit the return or his successor: see *supra*, n. 62. For an example if its use, see the cases cited in nn. 73 and 75.

[73] *Phillips v. Revenue & Customs Commissioners* [2010] S.F.T.D. 332.

[74] *ibid.* s.12AC(1), as substituted by the Finance Act 2001, Sched. 29, Pt 1, para. 5(1).

[75] See *Flaxmode Ltd. v. Revenue & Customs Commissioners* [2008] S.T.C. (S.C.D.) 666.

[76] *ibid.* s.12AA(6)(a), as added by the Finance Act 1994, s.184. It appears that compliance with this requirement is not always insisted on: see Ray, *Partnership Taxation*, para. 11.3.

[77] *ibid.* s.12AA(7), as added by the Finance Act 1984, s.184 and amended by the Finance Act 1996, Sched. 41, Pt V(6) and the Finance Act 2009, Sched. 47 (Consequential Amendments) Order 2009 (SI 2009/2035), Sched., para. 3.

[78] *ibid.* s.12AB(1), as added by the Finance Act 1994, s.185 and amended by the Finance Act 1995, ss.104(7) and the Finance Act 1996, s.123(5).

[79] *ibid.* s.42(6), as substituted by the Finance Act 1994, Sched. 19, Pt 1, para. 13 and amended by the Finance Act 2001, Sched. 29, Pt 5, para. 26. The provisions in question are listed in *ibid.* s.42(7), as amended.

[80] See *Morgan v. Customs & Excise Commissioners* [2009] S.F.T.D. 160 at [73] *et seq.* (in a *obiter* part of the decision of Tribunal Judge Brice).

[81] Under *ibid.* s.28B(4), as substituted by the Finance Act 2001, Sched. 29, para. 9 and amended by the Transfer of Tribunal Functions and Revenue and Customs Appeals Order 2009, Sched. 1, para. 18.

[82] *ibid.* s.31(1)b), as substituted by the Finance Act 2001, Sched. 29, Pt 5, para. 11, as considered in *Phillips v. Revenue & Customs Commissioners* [2010] S.F.T.D. 332.

[83] See the Income and Corporation Taxes Act 1988, s.111 in its original form; also *Stevens v. Britten* [1954] 1 W.L.R. 1340; *Harrison v. Willis Bros.* [1966] Ch. 619. See further the 17th ed. of this work, at paras 34–19 *seq.*

[84] See the Income Tax (Trading and Other Income) Act 2005, s.852(1): see further *supra*, paras 34–07, 34–09. Note that, where untaxed income (as defined in *ibid.* s.854(6)) is payable to a partnership, each partner's share thereof will be treated as profits arising from a notional business carried on by him alone and assessed on him accordingly: *ibid.* s.854(1), *supra*, para. 34–08.

will be no joint liability even where there is a loss attributable to fraudulent or negligent conduct[85] in relation to a partnership return, although in such cases assessments are likely to be made on each partner individually.[86]

It follows that tax will no longer fall within the ambit of the normal form of outgoing partner's indemnity.[87]

Ascertainment and apportionment of profits

The current year basis

34–20   The Finance Act 1994 dispensed with the former preceding year basis of assessment, with all its attendant anomalies,[88] in favour of a *current* year basis. Thus, tax will now be assessed on each partner by reference to his share of profits in the relevant basis period, *i.e.* the accounting period ending in the current year of assessment.[89] Where there is no such period, the relevant profits will be those of the year of assessment in question.[90]

It was made clear in *Herbert Smith v. Honour*[91] that the profits of a firm for a basis period must, in general, be computed by reference to accounts prepared in accordance with generally accepted principles of commercial accounting, and this is now reflected directly in the Income Tax (Trading and Other Income Act 2005.[92]

Ascertainment of partners' profit shares

34–21   The Income Tax (Trading and Other Income) Act 2005,[93] specifically states that a partner's share of any profit or loss will be determined in accordance with the firm's "profit-sharing arrangements" during the relevant accounting period. This expression includes both profit sharing and loss sharing ratios, where they differ.[94] The applicable arrangements will be those agreed between the partners or, in default of any such agreement, as determined pursuant to the Partnership Act 1890.[95] Where their entitlement in the relevant accounting period is clear, and profits have been apportioned between them by reference thereto, it is not

---

[85] See the Taxes Management Act 1970, s.36(2), as substituted by the Finance Act 1994, Sched. 19, Pt 1, para. 11(2).

[86] See RI 155, issued in August 1996 and reproduced at [1996] S.T.I. 1373.

[87] See, as to such indemnities, *supra*, paras 10–248 *et seq.*; also, as to the former position, *Stevens v. Britten* [1954] 1 W.L.R. 1340.

[88] See, as to these anomalies, the 17th ed. of this work at paras 34–23 *et seq.*

[89] Income Tax (Trading and Other Income) Act 2005, s.853(1), applying *ibid.* s.198(1). As to the position in the first and second tax years, see *ibid.* ss.199, 200.

[90] *ibid.* ss.200(4), 201.

[91] [1999] S.T.C. 173. In this case, the taxpayer firm successfully sought to make a provision in its accounts for future rent in respect of premises which it no longer intended to occupy. It is understood that the Inland Revenue (as it then was) ultimately decided not to appeal the decision. See also *Willingale v. International Commercial Bank Ltd.* [1978] A.C. 834 (HL); *Symons v. Weeks* [1983] S.T.C. 195; *Gallagher v. Jones* [1994] Ch. 107 (CA); *Small v. Mars (UK) Ltd.* [2005] S.T.C. 958.

[92] *ibid.* s.25(1). See further, *infra*, para. 34–22.

[93] *ibid.* s.850(1), as substituted by the Corporation Tax Act 2009, Sched. 1, Pt 2, para. 640: see *supra*, para. 34–06.

[94] *ibid.* s.850(2), as substituted by *ibid.*

[95] See the Partnership Act 1890, s.24(1). See further *supra*, paras 10–78 *et seq.*, 19–15 *et seq.*

open to the partners, otherwise than by way of an agreement *inter se*, subsequently to reallocate those profits in a different manner, so as to obtain a greater benefit from any reliefs which may be available to any one or more of them.[96] Equally, in one exceptional case,[97] the application of an agreed profit sharing adjustment resulted in the "payment" of negative salaries to some of the partners as part of the overall profit allocation and this was accepted as a valid means of allocating the firm's profit.

However, provision is also made to avoid the creation of a notional loss for a partner during a period when the partnership as a whole makes a profit. If, in such a case, the partner's share would be a loss, then it will be deemed to be a nil share and the remaining partners' profit shares will be adjusted accordingly.[98] If one or more of the *other* partners' shares would be a loss, then the share of the partner in question will be adjusted by reference to a formula.[99] Similarly, where a notional profit is shared by one or more partners during a period when the partnership has made an overall loss.[100] In applying this rule, account can be taken of any partner even if he or it is not subject to income tax.[101]

Equally, if the partnership agreement specifically provides that the partners should not be entitled to a certain proportion of the profits, *e.g.* where they are expressed to be taken to a reserve in which no partner has a specific interest, it might, at least theoretically, be argued that no apportionment of those profits is possible.[102] *Sed quaere*.

Accounting basis: "generally accepted accounting practice"

By virtue of changes originally introduced in 2002,[103] the profits of a trade, **34–22** profession or vocation must now be calculated in accordance with generally accepted accounting practice.[104] This has resulted in all firms being required to compute profits on a full earnings basis, so that it is not possible to opt for the more favourable "cash" or "bills delivered" bases,[105] under which the value of all work in progress and, in the former case, debtors, could be ignored.[106] Following the introduction of Application Note G[107] to Financial Reporting

---

[96] *Bucks v. Bowers* [1970] Ch. 431, 441 *per* Pennycuick J. This was, of course, a decision under the old preceding year basis regime of partnership taxation.

[97] *Chartered Accountants' Firm v. Braisby* [2005] S.T.C. (S.C.D.) 389.

[98] *ibid.* s.850A(1), as substituted by the Corporation Tax Act 2009, Sched. 1, Pt 2, para. 640.

[99] *ibid* s.850A(2)–(4), as substituted by *ibid*.

[100] *ibid.* s.850B, as substituted by *ibid*.

[101] See the definition of "partner" in *ibid.* ss.850A(5), 850B(5).

[102] See, for example, *Stocker v. CIR* (1919) 7 T.C. 304; *Franklin v. CIR* (1930) 15 T.C. 464; *Latilla v. CIR* (1943) 25 T.C. 107, 116 *per* Lord Greene M.R. These were, of course, decided under a different tax regime.

[103] Finance Act 2002, s.103(5). Formerly the requirement was for "true and fair" accounts: see the Finance Act 1998, s.42.

[104] Income Tax (Trading and Other Income) Act 2005, s.25(1). Nevertheless, the need to compute trading profits for income tax purposes on a *true and fair* basis was recognised by the House of Lords in *Revenue & Customs Commissioners v. William Grant Ltd.* [2007] 1 W.L.R. 1448. As a result, costs musts be matched with related revenues in each accounting period.

[105] Often together styled the "conventional" basis of accounting.

[106] Note, however, that even prior to the Finance Act 1998, the adoption of the earnings basis was not always disadvantageous: see, for example, *Symons v. Weeks* [1983] S.T.C. 195, where progress payments were payable to a firm of architects under long-term contracts.

[107] Entitled "Revenue Recognition".

Standard 5,[108] which was issued by the Accounting Standards Board in November 2003, and the subsequent advice issued relating to the position of professional practices by the Urgent Issues Taskforce on March 10, 2005 (commonly known as UITF 40),[109] firms have not only been required to account for work in progress[110] but, in most instances, also to recognise income attributable to work in progress before it is actually billed.[111] As a result of this change, it is likely that most firms will not, as such, value work in progress but will merely bring the accruing income attributable thereto into account under FRS5/UITF40.

Although it is often said that there is nothing which requires a firm to prepare its annual accounts on a particular basis, provided that the necessary adjustments are made for tax purposes[112] and that it can, if the partners wish, continue to prepare its accounts on a pure cash basis, the current editor doubts the correctness of this proposition given the terms of Application Note G and UITF 40, which would seem to be of general application in the preparation of those accounts. That is, of course, not to say that management and other internal accounts cannot be prepared for internal use, including as a basis for sharing profits between the partners, on any basis the firm sees fit.

It is clear that the need to comply with generally accepted accounting practice does not impose an obligation to have a firm's accounts audited, unless the partners choose to do so.[113]

Directors' fees, etc.

34–23   Where the members of a professional partnership are in receipt of directors' fees, those fees should properly be assessed on the individual partners under the Income Tax (Earnings and Pensions) Act 2003.[114] However, HMRC are prepared, by concession, to accept the inclusion of such fees in the firm's profits for tax purposes,[115] provided that two conditions are satisfied. First, the directorships must be normal incidents of the profession in general as well as of the particular practice in question: secondly, the fees must be only a small part of the partnership profits and be pooled for division among the partners under the terms of the

---

[108] Entitled "Reporting the Substance of Transactions".

[109] *i.e.* Abstract 40, "Revenue recognition and service contracts".

[110] The valuation of work in progress will be a matter for the application of normal accounting principles: see the Guidance Note agreed between the Inland Revenue and the Tax Faculty of the Institute of Chartered Accountants in England & Wales reproduced in IR Tax Bulletin 38 in December 1998, para. 19; also Statement of Standard Accounting Practice 9 (SSAP 9) which, in essence, requires work in progress to be valued at the lower of cost and net realisable value.

[111] This will not necessarily be the case, *e.g.* in the case of fees which are genuinely contingent. Note that the application of FRS5/UITF40 inevitably led to an adjustment charge under the Income Tax (Trading and Other Income) Act 2005, ss.226 *et seq.*, although the burden was relieved by a form of spreading relief introduced by the Finance Act 2006, s.102, Sched. 15. Where it applied, the relief enabled the adjustment income to be brought into the charge to tax over a period of up to six years, depending on the level of the firm's profits: *ibid.* Sched. 15, para. 2. Each partner's share of the additional amount brought into charge was determined by reference to his share of profits in the preceding 12-month period: *ibid.* Sched. 15, paras 7(3), (5). The benefit of the relief was not lost in the event of a partner's retirement, etc., or the firm's dissolution, but the amount brought into charge was, obviously, based on that partner's historic profit share and was no longer affected by the level of the firm's profits: *ibid.* Sched. 15, paras 3, 7(4). This is now of only historic interest.

[112] See the Income Tax (Trading and Other Income) Act 2005, s.25(1).

[113] See *ibid.* s.25(2)(b).

[114] Formerly known as Schedule E taxation.

[115] *i.e.* for the purpose of the Income Tax (Trading and Other Income) Act 2005, s.849, *supra*, para. 34–05.

partnership agreement.[116] The firm must request such treatment and will be required to give an undertaking that the fees received in full will be included in the gross income or receipts of the basis period, whether or not the directorships are still held in the relevant year of assessment and whether or not the partners holding them are still members of the firm. There is an example of similar treatment being accorded to a partner holding the office of sub-post-master.[116a]

Other sources of income

The shares of partners in partnership income derived from sources other than its trade will be computed in the same way as their shares of its trading profits.[117] Their shares of *untaxed* income[118] will, helpfully, be computed by reference to receipts in the relevant basis period, but will be deemed to arise in a separate notional business treated to be carried on by each partner.[119] Taxed income,[120] on the other hand, will continue to be assessed by reference to receipts in the year of assessment in question. All of such shares will be taxed under the relevant provisions of the Income Tax (Trading and Other Income) Act 2005, according to their nature.

34–24

Treatment of payments to partners

Payments made to partners,[121] such as so-called preferential "salaries" or interest on capital (but not, it is thought, interest on advances[122]), are not allowed as a deduction from the partnership profits because they represent payments for services rendered to the firm by a partner *in that capacity*.[123] The same goes for payments made to an outgoing partner, *e.g.* by way of compensation on his compulsory retirement from the firm, provided that it is received by him in his capacity as a partner.[124] It follows that such payments must be added back to the partnership profits and apportioned as an additional profit share to the partner(s)

34–25

---

[116] Extra Statutory Concession A37 (albeit framed by reference to the old tax regime). It is, however, understood that HMRC do not in practice accept the availability of such concessionary treatment in the case of offices held by doctors. *Sed quaere* in the case of other professions.

[116a] *Uppal v. Revenue & Customs Commissioners* [2010] UKFTT 215 (TC) [2010] S.T.I. 2382. Note, however, that the compensation payment was taxed as *employment* income.

[117] Income Tax (Trading and Other Income) Act 2005, s.851. See also *supra*, para. 34–09, 34–21.

[118] As defined in *ibid.* s.854(6), *supra*, para. 34–08.

[119] *ibid.* ss.854, 855. This treatment even applies to income taxable under *ibid.* ss.263 *et seq.* (formerly Schedule A), provided that it is derived from the *same* partnership: see the former Inland Revenue Interpretation (RI 137) issued in December 1995 (reproduced at [1996] S.T.I. 26), which was superseded by Enquiry Manual EM7002.

[120] *i.e.* income from which tax is deducted or treated as having been deducted or income chargeable under *ibid.* ss.382 *et seq.* (formerly Schedule F, *i.e.* dividends, etc.).

[121] For this purpose, it is immaterial whether the payments are made pursuant to the terms of a partnership agreement or otherwise.

[122] Such interest is expressly allowed by the Partnership Act 1890, s.24(3) and should accordingly be regarded as part of the cost of earning the (net) trading profit. If, however, in the absence of sufficient income, the burden of the interest is thrown on capital, it will clearly not be deductible: *Fitzleet Estates Ltd. v. Cherry* [1977] 1 W.L.R. 1345 (HL).

[123] See *Lewis v. CIR* (1933) 18 T.C. 174; *MacKinlay v. Arthur Young McLelland Moores & Co.* [1990] 2 A.C. 239 (HL), 249A–C; also *PDC Copyprint v. George* [1997] S.T.C. (S.C.D.) 326.

[124] See *Morgan v. Revenue & Customs Commissioners* [2009] S.F.T.D. 160.

or former partner(s) in receipt thereof.[125] An extreme example of this principle was seen in *Chartered Accountants' Firm v. Braisby*,[126] where certain partners were treated as receiving negative salaries, as a result of the manner in which they implemented an agreed adjustment to one partner's profit share. In terms of the overall profit of the firm, however, this naturally made no difference.

However, the position may be different in the case of other payments to partners, provided that the "wholly and exclusively" test[127] can be satisfied. Much will depend on the capacity in which any payment is received: rent receivable by a partner *qua* landlord will be deductible,[128] but reimbursement of removal expenses, which can only be received *qua* partner, will not.[129] It was formerly the case that, when a firm paid interest on a loan taken out by a partner in order to acquire premises occupied by the firm, the payment of such interest was, by concession, regarded as rent and, thus, deductible in computing the partnership profits,[130] but this concession is no longer available.

Deductibility of expenses incurred by individual partners

34–26 If one partner incurs expenses which are wholly and exclusively referable to the performance of his partnership duties but which, under the partnership agreement, he is required to bear out of his own pocket, such expenses may, on general principles, be deducted by him from his share of the partnership profits.[131] Such a situation will be encountered frequently in the case of medical partnerships, where partners may be required to use their private cars in the course of practice. To be deductible, the expenses must obviously be referable to the relevant accounting year,[132] and should be reflected in the partnership return, rather than in the individual partner's personal tax returns.[133] By way of contrast,

[125] Such payments accordingly cannot be assessed under the Income Tax (Earnings and Pensions) Act 2003 (nor can PAYE be deducted) save, perhaps, in an exceptional case where a partner has performed services for a client of the firm and HMRC seek to assess any payment to him under that Act, either: (a) on the basis that *ibid.* ss.48 *et seq.* (as amended) apply (see further, *supra*, para. 34–12) or, conceivably, (b) on the basis that he is in truth a "worker" whose services have been supplied by an "agency" for the purposes of *ibid.* ss.44 *et seq.* Where a salary is expressed to be payable to a partner *irrespective* of the firm's profitability and is duly paid in a year in which no profits are realised, it cannot properly be treated as a share of profits but must constitute capital in the hands of the recipient partner; it, by definition, will not give rise to an additional loss: *PDC Copyprint v. George* [1997] S.T.C. (S.C.D.) 326. *Per contra* in the case of a salaried partner taxable under the Income Tax (Earnings and Pensions) Act 2003. See generally, as to salaried partners, *supra*, paras 5–54 *et seq.*
[126] [2005] S.T.C. (S.C.D.) 389.
[127] Income Tax (Trading and Other Income) Act 2005, s.34(1)(a).
[128] *Heastie v. Veitch & Co.* [1934] 1 K.B. 535. Care must, however, be taken to ensure that a tenancy does in fact exist: see, as to the possible difficulties, *supra*, para. 10–45.
[129] See *MacKinlay v. Arthur Young McLelland Moores & Co.* [1990] 2 A.C. 239 (HL); also *Watson and Everitt v. Blunden* (1933) 18 T.C. 402.
[130] See the obsolete Statement of Practice (SP4/85) "Income Tax: Relief for Interest on Land Used to Buy Land Occupied for Partnership Business Purposes", para. 5. Any possible rationale went when the right to relief in respect of interest on loans to acquire land was withdrawn.
[131] See the Income Tax (Trading and Other Income) Act 2005, s.34(1)(a). For the principles upon which such deductions will be allowed, see generally *Whiteman & Sherry on Income Tax* (4th ed.), Chap. 7. And note that an expense may still be deductible even where one or more of the partners are indemnified in respect of any liability associated therewith: *Bolton v. Halpern & Woolf* [1981] S.T.C. 14. As to the treatment of expenditure incurred by partners prior to the commencement of the partnership, see *infra*, para. 34–48.
[132] *See Stephenson v. Payne Stone, Fraser & Co.* [1968] 1 W.L.R. 858.
[133] See Ray, *Partnership Taxation*, para. 3.77.

in *AB v. Revenue & Customs Commissioners*,[134] a firm had incurred disbursements whilst litigating on behalf of its senior partner and had met a costs order made against him in other proceedings. It was held that neither amounted to a deductible expense since they were not made for the sole purpose of enabling the firm to earn profits.

Loans taken out by partners

A partner will also be able to deduct from his share of the profits interest **34–27** payable by him in respect of a loan obtained either:

(i) to purchase a share in the partnership; or

(ii) to contribute capital or a premium[135] or to advance money to the partnership, provided that it is used wholly for the purposes of its business, or

(iii) in paying off a loan originally taken out for either of those purposes.[136]

Where, however, capital is withdrawn from the firm and *immediately* replaced by means of such a loan, relief is likely to be denied.[137] Similarly, where the loan is, in effect, used to service a partner's own drawings,[138] since it cannot properly be said to be used wholly for the purposes of the firm's business.[139]

A limited partner is not eligible for this relief.[140] A return of capital[141] which is not applied in repayment of the loan will reduce the amount of interest eligible for relief.[142]

---

[134] [2007] S.T.C. (S.C.D.) 99.

[135] This is conceptually rather odd as a premium will normally be paid to one or more of the existing partners, rather than the firm: see the Partnership Act 1890, s.40, considered *supra*, paras 25–10 *et seq.*

[136] Income Tax Act 2007, ss.383, 385(1), 398. Full relief is only available if the partner has at all times been a member of the partnership and has not received a repayment of his capital: see *ibid.* s.399(1)–(3). As to what will be treated as a return of capital for this purpose, see *ibid.* ss.406, 407. HMRC may in certain circumstances seek to argue that such a repayment has been received where a partner is permitted to overdraw on his current account. Relief will, in any event, be withdrawn as soon as the partner ceases to be a member of the firm: see Revenue Interpretation (RI41) "Loans to buy into partnerships" reproduced at [1993] S.T.I. 298. However by concession, the relief is continued following the incorporation of the partnership or a merger or demerger: Extra-Statutory Concession A43. No relief will be available if the partnership business consists of the occupation of commercial woodlands: see *ibid.* s.411.

[137] *Lancaster v. IRC* [2000] S.T.C. (S.C.D.) 138. Relief was, in this case, also denied under avoidance provisions contained in the Income and Corporation Taxes Act 1988, s.787 (as amended). It should be noted that this was an extreme case, the loan being taken from the taxpayer's spouse on an undocumented basis and funded through a joint account. Moreover, it appears that the firm was not at any point deprived of any funds, since the withdrawal and payment in took place on the same day.

[138] *e.g.* where his capital and/or current accounts are overdrawn and his drawings exceed his profit share.

[139] For an analogous case, decided under what is now the Income Tax (Trading and Other Income) Act 2005, s.34(1), see *Silk v. Fletcher* [1999] S.T.C. (S.C.D.) 220; *Silk v. Fletcher (No. 2)* [2000] S.T.C. (S.C.D.) 565. In this instance the taxpayer was a sole trader.

[140] Income Tax Act 2007, s.399(2)(a). See, as to such partners, *supra*. Pt 6.

[141] It is assumed that the position will be the same in the case of the return of a premium or advance; *sed quaere.*

[142] *ibid.* ss.406, 407(2). See also *supra*, n. 136.

Charges on income

34–28   Annual charges on income payable by the firm under deduction of tax will be apportioned to the partners in their profit-sharing ratios, in the absence of any agreement to the contrary.[143] Each partner is treated as personally paying his apportioned part of the charge, and may use the entirety of his taxable income to frank that part.[144]

Pre-owned assets charge

34–29   This charge, which was introduced with effect from the 2005/06 year of assessment,[145] will have no impact on the *partnership* profits, but should nevertheless be noted in the present context. Thus, where an individual partner disposes of land or a chattel (or an interest therein) but seeks to retain the occupation or use of that asset through his membership of the partnership, he may be subject to a charge to income tax by reference to the assessed rental value of the land or an assumed rate of interest on the value of the chattel, less any amounts which he is legally obliged to pay in respect of that occupation or use.[146] Similarly, where he directly or indirectly funds the acquisition of the relevant land or chattel.[147]

However, the above regime will not apply where the original disposal was of the whole of a partner's interest in the relevant property (apart from any rights reserved) under an arm's length transaction or what would be such a transaction if he was not treated as connected with his co-partners[148] or of part of his interest under such a transaction, provided that the consideration is not in the form of money or readily convertible assets.[149] On the latter basis, HMRC accept that, where a partner receives full, albeit non-monetary, consideration for a disposal of a share in the partnership to an incoming partner (even if they are connected otherwise than as partners), the exclusion will apply.[150] The regime will also not apply where the transaction involves or would, but for some available exemption, involve a gift with a reservation for inheritance tax purposes.[151] It is also possible to avoid the charge by *voluntarily* electing to apply the gift with a reservation rules.[152] The other exceptions and exemptions are unlikely to have a significant impact in the present context.[153]

---

[143] There would seem to be no reason why a charge on income should not be borne in shares specifically set out in the partnership agreement.

[144] See the Income Tax Act 2007, s.448.

[145] By the Finance Act 2004, s.84.

[146] *ibid.* Sched. 15, paras 3(1), (2)(a)(i), 4 (land) and 6(1), (2)(a)(i), 7 (chattels); also the Charge to Income Tax by Reference to Enjoyment of Property Previously Owned Regulations 2005 (SI 2005/724), reg. 4.

[147] *ibid.* Sched. 15, paras 3(2)(a)(ii), (3), 6(2)(a)(ii), (3).

[148] *ibid.* Sched. 15, para. 10(1)(a).

[149] *ibid.* Sched. 15, para. 14; the Charge to Income Tax by Reference to Enjoyment of Property Previously Owned Regulations 2005, reg. 5.

[150] See the partnership example in the Inland Revenue Press Release "Pre-owned assets—technical guidance" dated March 17, 2005, Appendix 1 and reproduced at [2005] S.T.I. 630, 645.

[151] *ibid.* Sched. 15, para. 11(5); and see *infra*, para. 36–31 *et seq.*

[152] *ibid.* Sched. 15, para. 21. See further, as to such elections, HMRC Technical Note "Income tax and pre-owned assets guidance", s.3. This Note was issued on October 26, 2007 and is reproduced at [2007] S.T.I. 2446. An election, once made, may be withdrawn: *ibid.* para. 3.1.3. As to the form of the election, see the Income Tax (Benefits Received by Former Owner of Property) Election for Inheritance Tax Treatment) Regulations 2007 (SI 2007/3000).

[153] See the Finance Act 1984, Sched. 15, paras 10(1)(b)–(e) (as amended), (2), 13.

A similar regime applies in the case of intangible property comprised in a   **34–30**
settlement where the settlor retains an interest.[154] It has already been seen that,
in some circumstances, a partnership may be regarded as a settlement.[155] HMRC
have confirmed that the arrangement of mutual life insurance policies to fund the
payment out of a deceased partner's share is excluded, provided that the partner
is not a beneficiary of his own policy.[156]

4.   COMMENCEMENT, CESSATION AND CONTINUANCE

Pre-trading expenditure

In certain circumstances, relief in respect of expenditure incurred by pro-   **34–31**
spective partners prior to the commencement of their partnership can be
obtained; this relief is considered in more detail hereafter in connection with the
treatment of losses.[157]

Taxation of new partnership or incoming partner

It has already been seen that each partner is treated as carrying on a notional   **34–32**
trade separate from that carried on by each of his co-partners.[158] It follows that,
when a new partner joins an existing firm or where two or more persons enter
into partnership for the first time, each of them will be treated as having set up
a new notional trade and assessed to tax under the opening rules.[159] Thus, the first
assessment on a partner, in respect of the tax year in which he joined the firm,[160]
will be based on his share of the partnership profits for that year[161]; the second
assessment will be based on his share of profits for the accounting period ending
in the next tax year[162] or, if that period is of less than 12 months' duration, the
12 month period beginning on the date he became a partner.[163] Thereafter, the
basis period will be determined in the usual way.[164]

Complex rules govern the position where the firm's accounting date changes
in the two years following the commencement year.[165]

---

[154] *ibid.* Sched. 15, paras 8, 9, as amended.

[155] See *supra*, para. 34–16.

[156] See the Inland Revenue Press Release "Pre-owned assets guidance amended" dated April 1,
2005, reproduced at [2005] S.T.I. 724.

[157] See *infra*, para. 34–48.

[158] See *supra*, para. 34–09.

[159] Income Tax (Trading and Other Income) Act 2005, ss.199, 202(2), 852(2), (3). Note that special
rules may apply where the first (or later) accounting date chosen by the firm falls on March 31 or
between April 1 and April 4 (see *ibid.* ss.208, 209) or where a variable accounting date is adopted
(see *ibid.* ss.211–213). As to when a trade or business can be taken to have commenced, see *Mansell
v. Revenue & Customs Commissioners* [2006] S.T.C. (S.C.D.) 605; *Chappell v. Revenue & Customs
Commissioners* [2009] S.T.C. (S.C.D.) 11.

[160] This is styled the "first tax year" in the heading to *ibid.* s.199.

[161] *ibid.* s.199(1). Special rules apply where the notional trade is commenced before April 1 (*ibid.*
s.210(2)) or after March 31 (*ibid.* s.210(4)).

[162] *ibid.* ss.198(1), 200(1), (3). As to the position where there is no accounting date during that year,
see *ibid.* s.210(3).

[163] *ibid.* s.200(1), (2).

[164] *ibid.* s.198(1).

[165] *ibid.* ss.214, 215. As to subsequent changes, see *ibid.* ss.216 *et seq.* See further, as to these rules,
Ray, *Partnership Taxation*, Chap. 6.

Although each partner[166] will, in the case of a partnership which carries on a trade of farming or market gardening, have the right, within certain limits, to average the profits of two consecutive years of assessment,[167] this option is not available in respect of a year of assessment in which the trade is (or is treated as)[168] set up and commenced or permanently ceases to be carried on.[169] The same right is also extended to the intensive rearing of livestock or fish on a commercial basis for food production and to a trade the profits of which are derived wholly or mainly from "creative works".[170]

Overlap profits

34–33   If, as a result of the application of the above commencement rules, an amount of profits is included in the computation for two successive years of assessment,[171] relief is given in respect of these so-called "overlap profits"[172] by deducting them from the profits of the basis period for the year of assessment in which the trade permanently ceases to be carried on[173] or where, following a change of accounting date in any tax year, the basis period for that year is of more than 12 months' duration, by deducting a proportion from the profits of that basis period.[174]

Where overlap profits arise in relation to a partner's notional business,[175] any amount which cannot be deducted from the profits of the relevant basis period derived therefrom can be set against his income from other sources.[176]

Taxation of discontinued partnership or outgoing partner

Outgoing partners

34–34   When a partner leaves an existing firm,[177] whether with a view to setting up some other business, joining another firm or retiring completely, the notional trade which he is treated as carrying on[178] will be treated as permanently ceasing.[179] The one exception is where one (or, perhaps, two or more) partners leave an existing firm and set up a new firm[180] which, by reason of the fact that he (or they) have taken away substantially the whole of the existing firm's client/

---

[166] *ibid.* s.221(1).

[167] *ibid.* ss.222 *et seq.* Relief must be claimed not later than 12 months after January 31 next following the end of the second year of assessment to which the claim relates: *ibid.* ss.222(5), 225(4).

[168] By virtue of *ibid.* s.852(4)–(6).

[169] *ibid.* s.222(4)(a). Similarly, in case of the "creative works" category (see *infra*), the years in which the trade first qualifies or ceases to be qualified are excluded: *ibid.* s.222(4)(b).

[170] *ibid.* s.221(2)(b), (c), (3).

[171] *e.g.* where the accounting period ending in the year of assessment after that in which the trade was commenced is of less than 12 months' duration: see *ibid.* s.200(2).

[172] This expression is defined by *ibid.* s.204.

[173] *ibid.* s.205.

[174] *ibid.* s.220.

[175] See, as to the circumstances in which a notional business is treated as carried on, *supra*, paras 34–08, 34–09, 34–24.

[176] *ibid.* s.856(2), (3).

[177] Whether by reason of death, retirement or expulsion.

[178] *ibid.* s.852(1), *supra*, para. 34–07.

[179] *ibid.* s.852(4)(a), *supra*, para. 34–08.

[180] Alone or with others.

customer base,[181] can properly be regarded as continuing to carry on its trade: in that event, it would seem that his (or their) respective notional trade(s) will be regarded as continuing.[182]

Where there is a cessation of an outgoing partner's notional trade, then provided that he does not leave the firm in the same year that he joined it, the basis period for the year of the cessation will be the period which began immediately after the end of the previous basis period and ended on the date of the cessation.[183] If he joins and leaves the firm in the same year, the basis period will be the period whilst he remained a partner.[184]

Special rules no longer apply where the outgoing partner has died, but an assessment can only be made within the period of three years beginning with January 31 next following the year of assessment in which the death occurred.[185]

Continuing partners

A change in a partnership, whether caused by the departure of an existing **34–35** partner or the admission of a new partner, will technically involve the dissolution of the old firm and the creation of a new firm, even though the partners may have agreed between themselves that their partnership is to continue.[186] Nevertheless, the retirement[187] of one or more partners should not result in a cessation of the notional trades (or notional businesses) of the continuing partners,[188] even though this issue is no longer addressed specifically in the legislation.[189] The absence of any form of cessation would seem to follow from the provisions of the Income Tax (Trading and Other Income) Act 2005,[190] subject only to what meaning is ascribed to the expression "a firm" therein.[191] It should be noted that a firm is not regarded as an entity separate and distinct from the partners who for the time being make it up[192] and this would potentially to let in the traditional analysis set out at the beginning of this paragraph. Such an approach would,

---

[181] See, as to the circumstances in which an outgoing partner will be free to take away clients, *supra*, paras 10–206 *et seq.*, 10–218 *et seq.*

[182] See the Income Tax (Trading and Other Income) Act 2005, s.852(5), *supra*, para. 34–07, which is, inexplicably, framed in terms of one partner continuing to carry on the actual trade *alone. Semble*, it should not matter if he carries it on with another former partner or partners. Alternatively, such a scenario might be regarded as an effective demerger, as to which see *infra*, para. 34–38. In the case supposed, it would seem inevitable that the notional trades of the other partners who do not join the new firm will permanently cease.

[183] *ibid.* s.202(1).

[184] *ibid.* s.202(2).

[185] Taxes Management Act 1970, s.40(1) (as amended by the Finance Act 1994, Sched. 19, para. 12).

[186] See, generally, the decision of the House of Lords in *C.I.T. v. Gibbs* [1942] A.C. 402 (albeit decided under the old tax regime). See also *supra*, paras 3–38, 10–39.

[187] Similarly in the case of death or expulsion.

[188] See *supra*, paras 34–07 *et seq.*

[189] *cf.* the former Income and Corporation Taxes Act 1988, s.113(1), (2) (as amended by the Finance Act 1994, s.216(1), Sched. 26, Pt V(24) and the Finance Act 1998, s.46(3)(a), Sched. 7, para. 1). This section presupposed that the same trade was carried on before and after the change: see *Maidment v. Kibby* [1993] S.T.C. 494 (albeit decided under a former tax regime).

[190] ss.852(1), (4)(a) (notional trade) and 854(1), (4)(a) (notional business): see *supra*, paras 34–07, 34–08.

[191] See *ibid.* ss.852(1), 854(1). Will there be a different "firm" before and after the change? For these purposes it is thought not.

[192] *ibid.* s.848, *supra*, para. 34–04. "Firm" is defined in *ibid.* s.847(1) merely as "persons carrying on a trade in partnership", which begs the question.

however, undermine the obvious purpose of the Act but the drafting, in this respect, remains less than satisfactory. A possible exception to the general rule identified above has already been noticed.[193]

The existence of a partner's notional business is clearly not affected by changes in the source of its income or, indeed, by an absence of income from that source.[194]

There will also be a permanent cessation and commencement of a partner's notional trade and business if the firm's *actual* trade is carried on outside the UK and he becomes non-resident.[195]

Dissolution and cessation of trade

34–36   Where a partnership permanently ceases to trade,[196] *e.g.* on or following a dissolution,[197] then a cessation of each partner's notional trade and business will be almost inevitable, unless it can be shown that one or more of them are demonstrably still carrying on the same trade either alone or, perhaps, in partnership together.[198]

Mergers

34–37   Where two partnerships carrying on different trades merge, the new combined business will in all probability represent a synthesis of trades and may, as such, be unrecognisable as a continuation of either. If, on a true analysis, both of the former trades have ceased and a wholly new trade commenced, the cessation and commencement rules must be applied to the notional trades and businesses of the partners (both old and new) in the normal way.[199] Where, however, the merged trades are of the same general nature, it may be possible to identify both trades as continuing in the merged firm and, in such a case, it is the practice of HMRC, as under the old tax regime, to accept this, thus avoiding a cessation of *either* trade.[200] Whether this option will be available involves a question of fact, although HMRC have indicated that they do not regard the disparity between the size of the old and new firms as significant for this purpose.[201]

---

[193] See *supra*, para. 34–34.

[194] *ibid.* s.854(3).

[195] *ibid.* ss.852(6), 854(5). It should be noted that the former subsection does not prevent losses made before the change of residence from being deducted from profits arising thereafter under the Income Tax Act 2007, s.83 (see *infra*, para. 34–64): Income Tax (Trading and Other Income) Act 2005, s.852(7), as amended by the Income Tax Act 2007, Sched. 1, Pt 2, para. 579.

[196] This will be a pure question of fact: see *O'Kane (J. & R.) & Co. v. CIR* (1922) 12 T.C. 303; *Hillerns & Fowler v. Murray* (1932) 17 T.C. 77; *Laycock v. Freeman Hardy & Willis Ltd.* [1939] 2 K.B. 1; *Watts v. Hart* [1984] S.T.C. 548; *C. Connelly & Co. v. Wilbey* [1992] S.T.C. 783 (a decision under the Finance Act 1981, Sched. 9, para. 21); *Maidment v. Kibby* [1993] S.T.C. 494.

[197] See *supra*, para. 34–14.

[198] As in the case noted *supra*, para. 34–34, it is considered that the position will be covered by the Income Tax (Trading and Other Income) Act 2005, ss.852(4)(b), 854(4)(b), *supra*, paras 34–07, 34–08. And see *supra*, para. 34–34 and *infra*, para. 34–38.

[199] See *supra*, paras 34–32, 34–34.

[200] See HMRC Statement of Practice (SP9/86) "Income Tax: Partnership Mergers and Demergers", para. 3, reproduced *infra*, para. A6–02. Although SP9/86 has not been updated to reflect the demise of the Income and Corporation Taxes Act 1988, s.113 (as amended), the approach set out therein still remains current.

[201] *ibid.* para. 4, *infra*, para. A6–02.

Hiving-off operations and demergers

There is a fundamental distinction between the cessation of a trade and a mere **34–38** reduction in the quantum of the trade being carried on. The fact that some part, or even a major part, of a trade is hived off to another entity will not bring about a cessation in relation to the remainder of that trade or have any effect on the notional trades or businesses[202] of the partners, provided that the scale of the hiving-off operation is not such that there is in reality no part of the original trade remaining.[203] Of course, the partners in the firm which carries on the hived-off part of the trade, if newly created, will be separately taxed under the normal commencement rules.[204]

Where partners wish to dissolve their firm and to divide the business between them, it will be a question of fact whether any of the "demerged" firms has in truth succeeded to the business of the original firm. Only where there is such a succession will it be possible to take advantage of HMRC practice,[205] thus ensuring that the notional trades and businesses of the partners who have joined that demerged firm are not regarded as ceasing; otherwise, the cessation rules will apply to *all* the partners' notional trades and businesses. In a case where HMRC practice is otherwise unlikely to apply, the safer course might, perhaps, be to initiate a hiving-off operation prior to the dissolution, so as to ensure that what remains is demonstrably continued in a demerged firm. However, for the reasons discussed in the preceding paragraph, there will obviously be a limit to the amount of the business which can be successfully hived off without jeopardising the position. HMRC will naturally closely scrutinise any demerger which appears to have been engineered for fiscal reasons.[206]

Overlap profits

In the event of a cessation of his notional trade or business, a partner will be **34–39** entitled to deduct any unrelieved overlap profits[207] from his share of profits in the basis period for the year of assessment in which the cessation occurs.[208]

Post-cessation receipts

Following a cessation of his notional trade, each partner will be assessable on **34–40** his share of any post-cessation receipts, being profits which were not brought into account under the full earnings basis.[209] However, if the right to such receipts is assigned to the new firm, they must be included in the profits of that firm, and

---

[202] See *supra*, paras 34–09. The effect of a change in the scope of a partner's notional business has already been seen *supra*, para. 34–35.

[203] See, for example, *Seaman v. Tucketts Ltd.* (1963) 41 T.C. 422; also *Whiteman & Sherry on Income Tax* (4th ed.), paras 5–008 *et seq.*

[204] See *supra*, paras 34–32 *et seq.*

[205] Statement of Practice (SP9/86) "Income Tax: Partnership Mergers and Demergers", para. 5, *infra*, para. A6–03. See *supra*, para. 34–37, n. 200.

[206] *ibid.* para. 6, *infra*, para. A6–03.

[207] As to the meaning of this expression, see the Income Tax (Trading and Other Income) Act 2005, s.204. See also *supra*, para. 34–33.

[208] *ibid.* s.205. See also, as to the use of the overlap profts from the notional business, *supra*, para. 34–33.

[209] Income Tax (Trading and Other Income) Act 2005, ss.241–245. See also, as to the deductions which will be allowable, *ibid.* ss.254, 255.

assessments will not be made on the partners of the old firm.[210] Provision is no longer made for a deduction in computing the profits of the new firm for debts taken over by it which are subsequently proved to be bad, in so far as they have not already been allowed to the old firm,[211] but relief may in such a case be available in respect of bad or doubtful debts on normal principles.[212]

Trading stock

34-41   On a permanent cessation of a trade,[213] trading stock[214] is dealt with as follows: if it is sold to another UK trader who is able to deduct the purchase price as an expense in computing his profits, then the amount of the actual purchase price will be treated as part of the trading profits of the former partnership unless the purchaser is connected with the firm.[215] In the latter case[216] or, indeed, in any other case,[217] a sum equal to the open market value of the stock must be brought into account.[218] In the case of a sale to a connected person where the open market value of the stock exceeds both the acquisition value (as defined) and, if greater, the actual purchase price, it is now possible for both parties to elect to use the greater of those amounts.[219]

Work in progress

34-42   The work in progress[220] of a professional firm is treated in broadly the same way as trading stock in the event of a permanent cessation of trade,[221] save that market value does not have to be substituted where the firm and the purchaser are connected. Thus, the actual amount realised (if any) will form part of the profits of the old firm if the work in progress is transferred in such circumstances that

---

[210] *ibid.* s.98.

[211] *cf.* the former Income and Corporation Taxes Act 1988, s.89 (as amended by the Finance Act 1998, s.46(3)(a), Sched. 7, para. 1).

[212] Income Tax (Trading and Other Income) Act 2005, s.35(1).

[213] Note that, in this instance, *ibid,* s.173(3) provides specifically that no revaluation is required when there is a change in the persons carrying on the trade, provided that one person continues to carry it on both before and after the change.

[214] This expression is defined in *ibid.* s.174. See also *Reed v. Nova Securities Ltd.* [1985] 1 W.L.R. 193.

[215] *ibid.* ss.175(2), 176, as respectively amended by the Corporation Tax Act 2009, Sched. 1, Pt 2, paras 605, 606. As to when parties are connected for this purpose, see *ibid.* s.179, as amended by the Income Tax Act 2007, Sched. 1, Pt 2, para. 501, which, *inter alia,* applies the test set out in the Income Tax Act 2007, s.993. A partner will clearly be connected with a firm of which he is a member, as will two firms with a common partner: see the Income Tax (Trading and Other Income) Act 2005, s.179(b), (d); also the Income Tax Act 2007 s.993(4).

[216] Income Tax (Trading and Other Income) Act 2005, s.177, as amended by the Corporation Tax Act 2009, Sched. 1, Pt 2, para. 607.

[217] *ibid.* ss.173(1), 175(1), (4).

[218] Note, however, that *ibid.* s.175(4) refers to "the amount which the stock would have realised if sold in the open market", whilst *ibid.* 177(2) refers to "the amount which would have been realised if the sale had been between independent persons dealing at arm's length". *Semble,* whichever subsection applies will produce a figure which represents market value.

[219] See *ibid.* s.178.

[220] This expression is defined in *ibid.* s.183.

[221] As in the case of trading stock, a change in the firm is ignored, provided that one person continues to carry on the profession both before and after the change: *ibid.* s.182(2)

its value can be deducted as an allowable expense in the accounts of the purchaser; otherwise the open market value must be brought into account.[222]

However, all the members the old firm may elect that the actual cost of the work in progress be credited in the accounts up to the date of the cessation, and that any sums received from the new firm in excess of such actual cost be treated as a post-cessation receipt and taxed accordingly.[223]

Post-cessation expenditure, etc.

Relief is available in the period of seven years beginning with the date of a **34–43** permanent cessation of a trade in respect of debts which prove to be bad[224] and various items of expenditure which relate to the old trade, *e.g.* remedial work, damages, legal expenses associated with defending claims against the firm, run off insurance cover and the cost of collecting debts,[225] by way of a set-off against the taxpayer's other income.[226] A former partner will clearly be free to claim this relief, irrespective of what the other partners may do.

5.   CAPITAL ALLOWANCES AND LOSSES

Capital allowances

Expenditure on capital items will be incurred by the firm and capital allow-   **34–44** ances will be claimed and received by it,[227] notwithstanding the fact that each partner is now deemed to carry on a separate notional trade.[228] It follows that, in the absence of some specific provision in the agreement, the benefit of such

---

[222] *ibid.* s.184, as amended by the Corporation Tax Act 2009, Sched. 1, Pt 2, para. 610; and see *ibid.* s.252. Note also *Symons v. Weeks* [1983] S.T.C. 195; *Browell v. Goodyear, The Times,* October 24, 2000 (which concerned the value of the work in progress of a solicitors' firm on a dissolution). Equally, if the firm does not value work in progress and merely brings the accruing income into account under FRS5/UITF40 (see *supra,* para. 34–22), this section may have little relevance.

[223] *ibid.* s.185(1). The election must be submitted in the period ending with January 31 of the year of assessment next following the year in which the trade ceased: *ibid.* s.185(2). It would not be possible for one partner to submit an election on an individual basis, notwithstanding the existence of his notional trade under *ibid.* s.852(1): see the Taxes Management Act 1970, s.42(2), (6), (7)(e), as substituted by the Finance Act 1994, Sched. 19, Pt 1, para. 13 and amended by the Finance Act 1995, s.107(2), the Finance Act 1998, Sched. 19, para. 20, the Finance Act 2001, Sched. 29, Pt 5, para. 26 and the Income Tax (Trading and Other Income) Act 2005, Sched. 1, Pt 2. para. 372. Post-cessation receipts are now charged to tax under the Income Tax (Trading and Other Income) Act 2005, ss.241 *et seq.*: see *supra,* para. 34–40.

[224] Income Tax Act 2007, ss.96, 98(5)–(8). Note also *ibid.* s.98(2), (3), as to debts which are released following a cessation.

[225] For the full range of expenditure which qualifies for the relief, see *ibid.* s.97.

[226] *ibid.* s.96. The relief must be claimed on or before the first anniversary of the normal filing date for the tax year in which the deduction is to be made: *ibid.* s.96(4). Provision is made to avoid double relief (see *ibid.* s.100) and to bring certain connected receipts into the charge to tax: see the Income Tax (Trading and Other Income) Act 2005, s.250, as amended by the Income Tax Act 2007, Sched. 1, Pt 2, para. 504.

[227] Taxes Management Act 1970, s.42(2), (6)(a), (7)(c) (as substituted by the Finance Act 1994, Sched. 19, Pt 1, para. 13 and amended by the Finance Act 1995, s.107(2), the Finance Act 1998, Sched. 19, para. 20, the Finance Act 2001, Sched. 29, Pt 5, para. 26 and the Capital Allowances Act 2001, Sched. 2, para. 1).

[228] Income Tax (Trading and Other Income) Act 2005, s.852(1), *supra,* para. 34–07.

allowances will ultimately be shared between the partners in their normal profit sharing ratios.[229]

Changes in firm

34–45   A change in the firm which does *not* involve all of the partners permanently ceasing to carry on the qualifying activity will effectively be ignored and the benefit of most allowances will automatically be available to the current partners in the firm.[230] Where, on the other hand, there is a such a permanent cessation, there will be a deemed sale to the new firm of the property used by the old firm at its open market value, and a balancing charge may be incurred on the residual value of the relevant capital items.[231] However, in the case of machinery and plant, if the old and new firms are treated as connected,[232] this result can be avoided by submitting a suitable form of election[233]; in the case of other assets, the partners may be able to elect for them to be taken over by the new firm at a value equal to the residual qualifying expenditure attributable to those assets.[234]

Machinery and plant

34–46   Particular attention should be drawn to the provisions relating to machinery and plant contained in section 264 of the Capital Allowances Act 2001. The effect of that section is to permit a claim for capital allowances where capital expenditure on machinery or plant to be used for the purposes of the firm is incurred by one or more of the partners personally. In such circumstances, for the purposes of claiming capital allowances, the machinery or plant is treated as partnership property,[235] but the allowances, will only be claimable by and for the benefit of those partners who actually incurred the expenditure.[236] Such treatment will not, however, be available where those partners have leased the machinery or plant to the firm, or have otherwise received any consideration for its use, if

---

[229] *ibid.* s.850, *supra*, para. 34–06. If the capital and income profit sharing ratios differ, the former should normally be applied. Equally, there would seem to be no reason why the partners should not agree to share capital allowances in some other way. Indeed, such an agreement may be advantageous: see further, *supra*, para. 34–15. Note that anti-avoidance provisions may, in certain circumstances, apply where a corporate partner's profit share is decreased or eliminated: Capital Allowances Act 2001, ss.212B, 212C(5), as added by the Finance Act 2010, Sched. 4.

[230] Capital Allowances Act 2001, ss.263(1), (1A) (machinery and plant), 558(1), (1A) (most other allowances), as respectively amended by the Corporation Tax Act 2009, Sched. 1, Pt 2, paras 495, 518. As to the scope of the latter section, see *ibid.* s.557.

[231] *ibid.* s.265, as amended by the Finance Act 2008, Sched. 24, Pt 1, para. 14 and the Corporation Tax Act 2009, Sched. 1, Pt 2, para. 495 (machinery and plant), 559, as amended by the Corporation Tax Act 2009, Sched. 1, Pt 2, para. 519 (most other allowances). The new firm will not be afforded any annual investment, first year or initial allowance on the deemed purchase: *ibid.* ss.265(4) (as amended by the Finance Act 2008, Sched. 24, Pt 1, para. 14), 559(4).

[232] See *ibid.* s.266(1)(a), (5), as amended by the Income Tax Act 2007, Sched. 1, Pt 2, para. 405.

[233] *ibid.* ss.266(2), 267.

[234] *ibid.* ss.567(2)(d), (3), 569, 570, as amended by the Finance Act 2001, Sched. 19, Pt II, para. 6, the Finance Act 2005, Sched. 6, para. 8 and the Commissioners for Revenue and Customs Act 2005, Sched. 4, para. 83(1). Note that *ibid.* s.569 is prospectively amended by the Finance Act 2008, Sched. 27, para. 15.

[235] *ibid.* s.264(2).

[236] Nothing in *ibid.* s.264 alters the incidence of any allowance, but merely enables such allowance to be claimed by the firm.

that consideration can be deducted in computing the profits or gains of the firm.[237] Although this provision affords considerable assistance to partners, there still appear to be a number of anomalies which are not at present covered by the legislation.[238] Ironically, in deeming the machinery and plant to be partnership property, the section ignores the fact that, for income tax purposes, each partner is then deemed to carry on a separate notional trade.[239]

Where a sale or gift of machinery or plant[240] used for partnership purposes is made by one or more partners to other partners, there will be no balancing allowance or balancing charge provided that the machinery or plant continues to be used by the firm.[241] Thus, where an outgoing partner assigns his share in such machinery or plant to an incoming partner or to the continuing partners, no adverse consequences will result.[242]

Losses

Where losses are made in a basis period,[243] they will be allocated between the partners in accordance with the terms of the partnership's profit and loss sharing arrangements.[244] In ascertaining the amount of each partner's share of any loss, account must be taken of any preferential salary or other entitlement which will, in practice, shift the entire burden of that loss onto the other partners.[245] Each partner's share of the loss will be treated as derived from a separate notional trade treated as carried on by him alone,[246] whilst his apportioned share of any other relievable losses will be treated as derived from a notional business.[247] Each partner will be able to use his losses in the same way as any other trading loss, *i.e.* by setting it or against his income from other sources in the same year, in the

34–47

---

[237] *ibid.* s.264(4).

[238] Thus, where machinery or plant is owned by the firm, but not all of the partners are entitled to share in its capital assets, *ibid.* s.264 will prima facie not apply, and it might be difficult for the firm to claim the allowances. Arguments in favour of such a claim do, however, exist: see Lawton, Goldberg and Fraser, *The Law of Partnership Taxation* (2nd ed.), paras 2.048 *et seq.* Be that as it may, so long as each partner has some, albeit small, share in the firm's capital assets, the requirements of the section would appear to be satisfied.

[239] See the Income Tax (Trading and Other Income) Act 2005, s.852(1), *supra*, para. 34–07. See also *supra*, para. 34–09.

[240] Or of a share therein: Capital Allowances Act 2001, s.270(1).

[241] *ibid.* s.264(3).

[242] The position is the same for the purposes of capital gains tax: see *infra*, para. 35–12.

[243] See the Income Tax Act 2007, s.62(2), (3)(b); see also *supra*, para. 34–20. However, where the same loss would otherwise fall to be taken into account in two years of assessment, it will be ignored in the second: *ibid.* s.63.

[244] Income Tax (Trading and Other Income) Act 2005, s.850, *supra*, para. 34–06; Income Tax Act 2007, s.62(3)(c). Losses may, of course, be borne in different proportions to the profit sharing ratios: see, generally, *supra*, paras 20–05 *et seq.* Note, that adjustments may fall to be made where one or more partners are entitled to a profit share in a year in which the firm makes an overall loss: Income Tax (Trading and Other Income) Act 2005, s.850B, as added by the Corporation Tax Act 2009, Sched. 1, Pt 2, para. 640. See also, *supra* para. 34–21.

[245] Thus, where a partner is entitled to his salary irrespective of the firm's profitability, he will only have sustained a loss to the extent (if at all) that his apportioned share of the partnership loss exceeds the amount of his salary. For a general discussion of this problem, see Lawton, Goldberg and Fraser, *The Law of Partnership Taxation* (2nd ed.), para. 2.070.

[246] Income Tax (Trading and Other Income) Act 2005, s.852(1), *supra*, para. 34–07. See also the Income Tax Act 2007, s.62(4).

[247] Income Tax (Trading and Other Income) Act 2005, s.854(1), *supra*, para. 34–08.

previous year or in both of those years,[248] or against his capital gains[249] or by carrying it forward to set against his future shares of profit in the same trade.[250]

A partner has a further option in respect of losses sustained in the year of assessment in which a trade is first carried on[251] or in any of the following three years: he may claim to carry back his share to set against his income for the three years of assessment preceding the year in which the losses were sustained.[252]

Pre-trading expenditure

34–48   Where a partner has, within seven years of the commencement of the partnership, incurred expenditure for the purposes of its business, and that expenditure would have constituted an allowable deduction if incurred after that time, he can claim to have it treated as a loss sustained in the year of assessment in which the partnership and, thus, both his notional trade and his notional business[253] commenced.[254] Such a loss can then be relieved in the same way as any other loss which might have been sustained in that year.

---

[248] Income Tax Act 2007, s.64(1)–(3). In either case, the trade must have been carried on on a commercial basis and with a view to the realisation of profit in the year in which the loss was incurred: *ibid.* s.66; and see *Delian Enterprises v. Ellis* [1999] S.T.C. (S.C.D.) 103. The following additional restrictions on the availability of this relief should be noted: (1) limited and non-participating partners: see *ibid.* ss.103A–105, noted, *infra*, para. 34–49); (2) capital allowances on machinery and plant: *ibid.* ss.75–79 (as amended); (3) farming and market gardening losses in five successive years: *ibid.* s.67; (4) partnerships dealing in commodity futures: *ibid.* s.81; (5) non-active partners (including non-active general partners in a limited partnership) in respect of losses in the early years of trade: *ibid.* ss.110–112, noted *infra*, para. 34–50; (6) firms exploiting films: *ibid.* ss.115, 116 (as amended); and (7) tax generated losses: *ibid.* s.74ZA, as added by the Finance Act 2010, Sched. 3, para. 5). And see also the additional charges noted *infra*, paras 34–50 *et seq.* As to losses arising in a property business, see *ibid.* ss.117 *et seq.* As to losses arising from miscellaneous transactions (formerly Case VI losses), see *ibid.* ss.152, 153.

[249] Taxation of Chargeable Gains Act 1992, ss.261B, 261C, as added by the Income Tax Act 2007, Sched. 1, Pt 1, para. 329 and amended, in the case of s.261C, by the Finance Act 2008, Sched. 2, para. 39.

[250] Income Tax Act 2007, ss.83, 84. It is submitted that, where a partner is treated as carrying on a separate notional trade and business, by virtue of the Income Tax (Trading and Other Income) Act 2005, ss.852(1), 854(1), *supra*, paras 34–07, 34–08, he can still carry forward losses in the notional trade with a view to setting them off against profits derived from the notional busines, or vice versa, since those subsections only apply for the purposes of *ibid.* Pt 2, Chap. 15 (basis periods).

[251] Again, it should be noted that a partner may be treated as carrying on both a notional trade and a notional business, albeit with the same commencement dates: *ibid.* ss.852(2), 854(2), *supra*, paras 34–07, 34–08.

[252] Income Tax Act 2007, ss.72 (as amended by the Finance Act 2008, s.66(4)(l)(ii), Sched. 21, para. 5), 73. The relief must be claimed on or before the first anniversary of January 31 next following the year of assessment in which the loss is sustained and is only available if, during the relevant period, the trade was being carried on on a commercial basis (as to which, see *Delian Enterprises v. Ellis* [1999] S.T.C. (S.C.D.) 103; *Walsh v. Taylor* [2004] S.T.C. (S.C.D.) 48) and in such a way that profits could reasonably be expected to be realised in that period or within a reasonable time thereafter: *ibid.* ss.72(3), 74. It is not, however, possible to apportion a loss so that a part is relieved under this section, whilst the remainder is relieved under some other section, *e.g. ibid.* s.64(1)–(3): see *Butt v. Haxby* [1983] S.T.C. 239. Most of the restrictions listed *supra*, para. 34–47, n. 248 also apply to this relief. Note also, as to the operation of the relief, *Gamble v. Rose* [1998] S.T.C. 1247.

[253] Income Tax (Trading and Other Income) Act 2005, ss.852(1), 854(1), *supra*, paras 34–07, 34–08. See further *supra*, para. 34–09.

[254] *ibid.* s.57. This relief will naturally not be available if the expenditure is already allowable as a deduction: *ibid.* s.57(2)(a).

Limited and non-participating partners

A partner who is a limited partner within the meaning of the Limited Partner- **34–49** ships Act 1907,[255] who in substance acts as a limited partner in relation to any trade,[256] *i.e.* he has no right to participate in the management of the firm and is entitled to be wholly or partially indemnified or relieved from liability for its debts and obligations, even though he in other respects enjoys the attributes of a full partner,[257] or who, in effect, satisfies the same conditions as a result of the application of the law of a territory outside the UK,[258] may not set his share of any loss derived from the carrying on of that trade against income derived from non-partnership sources[259] or against his capital gains[260] to the extent that it exceeds the aggregate amount of his capital contribution[261] and any undrawn profits for the time being left in the firm.[262] There is, moreover, a fixed cap[263] on the amount of any loss that can be set against such other income or capital gains.[264]

For the purposes of the above provision, any contribution made with the main purpose of obtaining relief by means of a set off against other income or capital gains (styled a "prohibited purpose") will be disregarded.[265] Moreover, it is by regulation[266] provided that, in computing a partner's capital contribution, the financial costs of repaying any loan taken out in connection with the financing of the contribution or the outstanding capital liability thereunder will be ignored,

---

[255] See the Income Tax Act 2007, s.103A(1)(a), as added by the Finance Act 2007, Sched. 4, para. 8. And see generally, as to such partners, *supra*, paras 29–03 *et seq.*

[256] But not a profession or vocation: see *ibid.* s.102(1), as amended by the Finance Act 2007, Sched. 4, para. 7(2).

[257] See *ibid.* s.103A(1)(b), (2), as added by *ibid.*

[258] *ibid.* s.103A(1)(c), (3) as added by *ibid.*

[259] This is styled "sideways relief": *ibid.* s.103(1). It has already been seen that each partner will be treated as carrying on a "notional trade" and, where relevant, a separate "notional business": Income Tax (Trading and Other Income) Act 2005, ss.852(1), 854(1). See further, *supra*, para. 34–09. *Semble*, a loss in the notional trade can still be set off against a loss in the notional business, since those subsections only apply for the purposes of *ibid.* Pt 2, Chap. 15 (basis periods).

[260] This is styled "capital gains relief": *ibid.* s.103(2). See the Taxation of Chargeable Gains Act 1992, s.261B, as added by the Income Tax Act 2007, Sched. 1, Pt 2, para. 329 and amended by the Transfer of Tribunal Functions and Revenue and Customs Appeals Order 2009, Sched. 1, para. 182.

[261] See the Income Tax Act 2007, s.105, as amended by the Finance Act 2007, Sched. 4, para. 11(a). This will include profits which have been capitalised: *ibid.* s.105(3). Note that the contribution must not have been directly or indirectly withdrawn: *ibid.* s.105(2), (4). In fact, a limited partner is technically not entitled to withdraw any part of his capital: see the Limited Partnerships Act 1907, s.4(3), considered *supra*, paras 30–09 *et seq. Quaere*, will an advance be similarly treated? It would seem not. *cf. ibid.* ss.406, 407(2), noted *supra*, para. 34–27.

[262] *ibid.* ss.104, 105, as respectively amended by the Finance Act 2007, Sched. 4, paras 10(a), 11(a). These sections and their predecessors reversed the effects of the decision in *Reed v. Young* [1986] 1 W.L.R. 649, in which the House of Lords had held that the Limited Partnerships Act 1907, s.4(2) did not apply to trading losses, as distinct from ordinary debts and liabilities. See further, *supra*, para. 30–07. A similar restriction applies to corporate limited partner: Corporation Tax Act 2010, ss.56–58.

[263] Currently £25,000.

[264] Income Tax Act 2007, s.103C, as added by the Finance Act 2007, Sched. 4, para. 1.

[265] Unless it was made pursuant to an obligation assumed before March 2, 2007: *ibid.* s.113A, as added by the Finance Act 2007, Sched. 4, para. 2.

[266] *ibid.* ss.105(11) (as amended by the Finance Act 2007, Sched. 4, para. 11(a)), 114; the Partnerships (Restrictions on Contributions to a Trade) Regulations 2005 (SI 2005/2017), which were originally made under the Income and Corporation Taxes Act 1988, ss.117(5), 118ZN, continue to have effect, subject to a number of amendments set out in the Income Tax Act 2007, Sched. 2, Pt 5, para. 35.

provided that one of a number of conditions is satisfied.[267] A similar exclusion applies where the financial cost of making the contribution is to be (or is in fact) reimbursed by another person.[268] There are a number of limited exceptions[269] which would appear to include, *inter alia*, the situation where a loan is to be repaid out of the contributing partner's profit share.[270]

Where relief has been given to the extent of a partner's contribution and that contribution is subsequently reduced, the excess relief can now be recovered from him.[271]

It has already been seen that similar restrictions apply in respect of the relief for interest on loans taken out in order to acquire a partnership share or otherwise to fund a capital contribution or advance, save that they are not confined in their application merely to trades and no relief is, in any event, available to a limited partner.[272]

Non-active general partners

34–50   Where a partner who is either a general partner within the meaning of the Limited Partnerships Act 1907[273] or a partner in a *general* partnership does not devote a significant amount of time[274] to the partnership business[275] during the first year of assessment[276] in which he is treated as carrying on his notional trade[277] or in any of the following three years, he will be restricted in the amount of any losses he can set off against income derived from non-partnership sources and capital gains.[278] As in the case considered in the preceding paragraph, the restriction is framed by reference to the partner's contribution to the firm,[279] and any capital contributed for a "prohibited purpose" (*i.e.* with a view to obtaining relief) will be automatically ignored[280] as will any element of the contribution specified in the applicable regulations.[281] Moreover, a fixed cap on the amount eligible for relief is, in any event, imposed.[282]

Where a non-active partner's contribution is reduced after relief has been

---

[267] Partnerships (Restrictions on Contributions to a Trade) Regulations 2005, reg. 4 (as amended). Those conditions are, in essence, designed to catch any arrangement under which the loan is (or is likely to be) paid off, assumed or released by another person or where the loan is made otherwise than on arm's length terms viewed over a 5-year period.

[268] *ibid.* reg. 5 (as amended).

[269] Specified in *ibid.* reg. 6 (as amended).

[270] *ibid.* reg. 6(c) (as amended).

[271] By means of a charge under the Income Tax Act 2007, ss.791–794, as amended, in the case of s.792, by the Finance Act 2007, Sched. 4, para. 17.

[272] See *supra*, para. 34–27.

[273] *ibid.* s.4(2).

[274] See, as to the meaning of this expression, the Income Tax Act 2007, s.103B(2), as added by the Finance Act 2007, Sched. 4, para. 8 and amended by the Finance Act 2008, s.61; also the Inland Revenue Press Release "Income tax: manipulation of partnership losses—examples" dated February 10, 2004, reproduced at [2004] S.T.I. 332.

[275] But not in the case of a partnership carrying on a profession or vocation: see *ibid.* s.102(1), as amended by the Finance Act 2007, Sched. 4, para. 7(2).

[276] *ibid.* s.103B(3), (4), as added by the Finance Act 2007, Sched. 4, para. 80.

[277] See the Income Tax (Trading and Other Income) Act 2005, s.852(1), *supra*, para. 34–07

[278] Income Tax Act 2007, ss.110–113 (as amended by the Finance Act 2007, Sched. 4, paras 10(c), 11(c) and 13 respectively).

[279] Including undrawn profits which have been capitalised: see *ibid.* s.111.

[280] *ibid.* s.113A, as added by the Finance Act 2007, Sched. 4, para. 2, noted *supra*, para. 34–49.

[281] See the Partnerships (Restrictions on Contributions to a Trade) Regulations 2005, noticed *supra*, para. 34–49.

[282] Income Tax Act 2007, s.103C, as added by the Finance Act 2007, Sched. 4, para. 1. The fixed cap is £25,000.

given, any excess relief can be recovered from him by an additional charge to tax.[283]

Provision is, however, made for the carry forward of unrelieved losses that are not eligible to be set off against other income or capital gains and these may become eligible for set off in future years, even following a dissolution, provided that the partner in question contributes assets to the firm.[284]

Film partnerships

A similar restriction on the use of losses applies to partners in a firm involved in the exploitation of films who do not devote a significant amount of time to that trade and are entitled to a guaranteed income.[285]   **34–51**

An additional charge to tax may also be imposed where a limited or non-active partner[286] whose film-related losses[287] have been relieved in one of the ways previously considered[288] then reduces the amount of his contribution to the firm to such an extent that it is less than the amount of those losses.[289] In computing the amount of the contribution, certain costs are excluded by regulation.[290] Similarly, where *any* partner who has enjoyed such relief disposes of his entitlement to profits and either receives a non-taxable consideration for such disposal or the amount of his capital contribution[291] becomes less than the amount of the claimed losses.[292] In relation to the latter provision, it is provided by regulation[293] that, where a partner disposes of his right to profits arising from the firm's trade and, as a result, his share of those profits is reduced or extinguished or his share of losses is increased and, at the same time or subsequently, a new partner is admitted who contributes a sum of capital, the incoming partner's contribution will be treated as apportioned between the existing partners in their pre-admission profit shares but the part apportioned to the disposing partner will be excluded for certain computation purposes.

Exploitation of licences

Where relief in respect of "licence-related trading losses" has been in one of the ways previously considered,[294] an additional charge to tax may be imposed   **34–52**

---

[283] *ibid.* ss.791–794, as amended, in the case of s.792, by the Finance Act 2007, Sched. 4, para. 17.

[284] *ibid.* s.113.

[285] *ibid.* ss.103D (as added by the Finance Act 2007, Sched. 4, para. 9), 115 (as amended by *ibid.* Sched. 4, paras 10(d), 15).

[286] See, as to the meaning of these expressions, *supra*, paras 34–49, 34–50.

[287] See *ibid.* s.800.

[288] *i.e.* under *ibid.* ss.64 *et seq.*, 72 *et seq.*: see *ibid.* s.790(3). And see *supra*, para. 34–47. Similarly in the case of a set off against capital gains under the Taxation of Chargeable Gains Act 1992, s.261B, as added by the Income Tax Act 2007, Sched. 1, Pt 2, para. 329 and amended by the Transfer of Tribunal Functions and Revenue and Customs Appeals Order 2009, Sched. 1, para. 182: Income Tax Act 2007, s.790(4).

[289] *ibid.* ss.791 *et seq.*, as amended, in the case of s.792, by the Finance Act 2007, Sched. 4, para. 17. A charge is imposed each time such an event occurs: *ibid.* s.792(4).

[290] *ibid.* s.793(2), applying *ibid.* s.114 and the Partnerships (Restrictions on Contributions to a Trade) Regulations 2005 (as amended): see *supra*, para. 34–49.

[291] See *ibid.* ss.801, 802.

[292] *ibid.* ss.796 *et seq.*

[293] See the Partnerships (Restrictions on Contributions to a Trade) Regulations 2006 (SI 2006/1639), regs. 3, 4. These regulations were originally made under the Finance Act 2004, s.122A but continue to have effect subject to a number of amendments: see the Income Tax Act 2007, Sched. 2, Pt 14, para. 148.

[294] As to which see *supra*, para. 34–51, n. 288.

on a non-active partner[295] who disposes of a licence acquired in carrying on the firm's trade or any right to income thereunder in exchange for a non-taxable consideration.[296]

Terminal loss relief

34–53 Where a partner leaves a firm and his notional trade thereby permanently ceases,[297] he will be entitled, as an alternative to any other form of relief,[298] to claim carry-back terminal loss relief under section 89 of the Income Tax Act 2007, *i.e.* he can set his terminal loss against the share of partnership profits[299] on which he has been assessed in the year in which the cessation occurred and in the three preceding years.[300] Obviously, this relief will also be available where the partnership trade permanently ceases, *e.g.* on or following a dissolution.[301]

The terminal loss will in all cases comprise:

(i) any loss sustained by the partner in question in the basis period in which the cessation occurred[302]; and

(ii) any loss sustained by him in the part of the preceding basis period beginning 12 months before the date of the cessation.[303]

Partnership business transferred to a company

34–54 Where a partnership business is transferred to a company in consideration solely or mainly of the issue of shares in that company to the former partners, each of them may carry forward his unrelieved losses (excluding his share of any unrelieved capital allowances) with a view to setting them off against any income derived from the company to which the business was transferred.[304] The relief can be claimed for any year of assessment throughout which the claimant is the beneficial owner of the shares allotted to him and the company carries on trading.[305]

6.   PARTNERSHIPS WITH CORPORATE MEMBERS

34–55 Special rules for the taxation of partnerships with one or more corporate members are contained in Part 17 of the Corporation Tax Act 2009, which amended

---

[295] See, as to the meaning of this expression, *ibid.* s.103B, noted *supra*, para. 34–50: *ibid.* s.809(1), as amended by the Finance Act 2007, Sched. 4, para. 18(a).

[296] *ibid.* ss.804 *et seq.*

[297] Income Tax (Trading and Other Income) Act 2005, s.852(1), (4)(a). Note that, whilst a partner is treated as carrying on both a notional trade and a notional business (see *ibid.* ss.852(1), 854(2), *supra*, paras 34–07, 34–08), this is only for the purposes of *ibid.* Pt 2, Chap. 15 (basis periods).

[298] Income Tax Act 2007, s.63.

[299] The profits may be notionally increased by virtue of *ibid.* s.92.

[300] *ibid.* ss.89, 91. The relief will be given so far as possible against a later rather than an earlier year: *ibid.* s.91. This relief applies to trades, professions and vocations: *ibid.* 89(4).

[301] See *supra*, paras 34–14, 34–36.

[302] *ibid.* s.90(1)(a), read subject to *ibid.* subss.(2), (6).

[303] *ibid.* s.90(1)(b), read subject to *ibid.* subss.(2), (6).

[304] *ibid.* s.86, applying *ibid.* ss.83, 84.

[305] *ibid.* s.86(3).

and consolidated the provisions formerly contained in the Income and Corpora-tion Taxes Act 1988.[306] As in the case of a partnership of individuals,[307] the partnership is not regarded as an entity separate and distinct from the partners.[308]

Computation of partnership profits or losses

Stage 1—Partnership profits/losses

For HMRC accounting purposes, the profits (or losses) of the partnership must, if the corporate partner is UK resident, be computed, in the first instance, just as if the firm were a company resident in the UK,[309] except that at this stage:

34–56

(a) interest paid and other distributions to the partners are disregarded[310];

(b) losses incurred in other accounting periods are disregarded[311];

(c) credits or debits in respect of a money debt owed by or to the firm or any loan relationship treated as arising from that debt are disre-garded[312]; and

(d) any changes in the persons carrying on the trade are disregarded, save that where there is a change in the corporate partners, and after the change there is no corporate partner who was a member of both the old and the new firms, the assumed company is treated as having ceased to trade and immediately started a new trade.[313]

A similar computation is made if the corporate partner is not UK resident.[314]

HMRC may determine by whom the partnership return is to be submitted and the information to be contained therein.[315]

---

[306] Note that under the amended rules, it is contemplated that, whilst a company may technically not itself be able to carry on a profession or vocation, it is nevertheless carrying on a trade or other business when a partner in a professional partnership: see the Corporation Tax Act 2009, s.1257 and the Explanatory Notes thereto, Annex 1, Change 2.

[307] See *supra*, para. 34–09.

[308] Corporation Tax Act 2009, s.1258.

[309] *ibid.* s.1259(2), (3). And note that a special regime may apply where a partner is a tonnage tax company: Finance Act 2000, Sched. 22, Pt XIII, paras 130, 131.

[310] *ibid.* s.1260(2).

[311] *ibid.* s.1260(1). Even though no longer specifically mentioned (*cf.* the Income and Corporation Taxes Act 1988, s.114(1)), this will include pre-trading expenditure.

[312] *ibid.* s.380(1), (2). Note that this may include a money debt which the corporate partner owes to or is owed by the firm: *ibid.* s.383. This, of course, goes against the partnership law analysis set out *supra*, para. 3–04. As see generally, as to what will be treated as a loan relationship, *ibid.* s.302(1)–(4), applying *ibid.* Pt 6.

[313] *ibid.* s.1261(2)(d), (5). As to the position where a corporate partner joins a partnership of individuals or where a sole corporate partner retires, see *ibid.* s.1261(2)(b), (c), (3), (4).

[314] *ibid.* s.1259(2), (4).

[315] Taxes Management Act 1970, s.12AA(1)–(3), (5)–(6) (as amended): see further, *supra*, para. 34–17.

Stage 2—Corporate partner's profit share

34–57   Having ascertained the profits (or losses) of the partnership, the corporate partner's share of those profits (or losses) is determined in accordance with the firm's profit sharing arrangements during the relevant period.[316] As in the case of individual partners, provision is made to avoid the creation of a notional loss for one or more partners during a period when the partnership as a whole makes a profit. If, in such a case, the corporate partner's share is a loss, it will be deemed to be nil,[317] but if one or more of the other partners' shares are a loss, then that partner's share will be adjusted according to a formula.[318] Similarly, where a notional profit is shared by one or more partners during a period when the partnership has made an overall loss.[319] In applying this rule, account can be taken of any partner even if he or it is not subject to corporation tax.[320] It is at this stage that credits or debits in respect of a money debt owed by or to the firm or a loan relationship treated as arising from that debt, which were disregarded at stage 1, are brought into account.[321]

Corporation tax is then, subject to any available reliefs,[322] chargeable on the resulting share of profits as if those profits were derived from a trade carried on by the corporate partner alone and an assessment will be made on it accordingly.[323] Where the corporate partner's accounting period does not coincide with that of the partnership, that share of profits will have to be apportioned between the relevant accounting periods.[324]

Stage 3—Individual partner's profit share

34–58   An individual partner's share of profits or losses will be ascertained and taxed in the same way as any other partnership, on the current year basis.[325]

Relief for losses

34–59   The individual partners' shares of any partnership losses will, as might be expected, be relieved in the normal way.[326] The regime governing the relief of a corporate partner's share of any such loss is broadly the same,[327] so that terminal loss relief now enables such a partner to carry the loss back to be set against its profits in the period of 3 years immediately preceding the accounting period in which the loss was incurred.[328]

---

[316] Corporation Tax Act 2009, s.1262(1), (4). As noted, *supra*, para. 34–21, these arrangements will normally be set out in the partnership agreement. If they are not, the position will, in all probability, be governed by the Partnership Act 1890, s.24(1): see *supra*, paras 10–78 *et seq.*, 19–15 *et seq.*
[317] *ibid.* s.1263(1).
[318] *ibid.* s.1263(2)–(4).
[319] *ibid*, s.1264.
[320] *ibid.* ss.1263(5), 1264(5).
[321] *ibid.* ss.380(3), (4), 381 *et seq.* See also RI 248 ("Partnerships and loan relationships"), reproduced at [2003] S.T.I. 60.
[322] See, as to loss relief, *infra*, para. 34–47.
[323] *ibid.* s.8.
[324] *ibid.* s.1265.
[325] Income Tax (Trading and Other Income) Act 2005, ss.849 *et seq.*, *supra*, paras 34–05 *et seq.* See further *supra*, paras 34–09, 34–20, 34–32 *et seq.*
[326] See *supra*, paras 34–47 *et seq.*
[327] See, generally, the Corporation Tax Act 2010, Pt 4. Note also, as to the position of a corporate *limited* partner (as defined in *ibid.* s.58), the terms of *ibid.* ss.56, 57. See also, *supra*, para. 34–49.
[328] *ibid.* ss.37, 39.

Anti-avoidance provisions

Where any arrangement exists under which any partner or a connected person **34–60** will receive a payment[329] in respect of the value or cost of the whole or any part of a corporate partner's share of a partnership profit or loss,[330] comprehensive anti-avoidance provisions effectively prevent that corporate partner from setting any other trading losses or reliefs against its share of the profit or setting its share of the loss against any income other than its share of the partnership profits (as the case may be).[331] There are no corresponding provisions relating to individual partners.

7. NON-RESIDENT AND DEEMED NON-RESIDENT PARTNERS

A partner who is resident and domiciled in the UK[332] will be taxed on his share **34–61** of the firm's profits, irrespective of where the firm carries on its business: his share will be computed and assessed in the normal way, whether those profits are derived from within or outside the UK.[333]

Even though a double tax agreement between the UK and the firm's country of residence might, in an appropriate case,[334] exempt a resident partner's share from liability to UK tax, that agreement will be ignored when determining such a partner's tax liability.[335]

Firms controlled in the UK

Where a firm which is controlled and managed[336] in the UK comprises one or **34–62** more individual non-UK resident partners, the firm's profits and losses will, as

---

[329] Or any benefit in money or money's worth.

[330] See *ibid*. s.959.

[331] *ibid*. ss.960–962.

[332] See, generally, the Guidance Note HMRC6 "Residence, Domicile and the Remittance Basis".

[333] Income Tax (Trading and Other Income) Act 2005, s.849(1), (2), *supra*, para. 34–05: see further *supra*, para. 34–09. Similarly in the case of a corporate partner: Corporation Tax Act 2009, s.1259(1), (3): see *supra*, paras 34–55 *et seq*. Note, however, that it cannot be assumed that a *foreign* partnership will automatically be treated as a partnership for income tax purposes: see *Dreyfus v. CIR* (1929) 14 T.C. 560, a case concerning a French *société en nom collectif*, which, by reason of its corporate status was held not to be a partnership for tax purposes. The status of a Jersey limited liability partnership remains in doubt: *R. v. IRC, ex p. Bishopp* [1999] S.T.C. 531; *cf. Padmore v. IRC* [1989] S.T.C. 493 (CA), which concerned an ordinary partnership formed under Jersey law.

[334] *i.e.* where the partnership is non-resident or its trade or business is controlled and managed outside the UK.

[335] Income Tax (Trading and Other Income) Act 2005, s.858(1), (2). This section (and its predecessors) reversed the effects of the decision in *Padmore v. IRC, supra*. A subsequent attempt to challenge the validity of the predecessor of this statutory provision failed: *Padmore v. IRC (No. 2)* [2001] S.T.C. 280. Note that the same rule applies to corporate partners: Corporation Tax Act 2009, s.1266(1), (2).

[336] The question of where the control and management of a trade or business is situated is a pure question of fact: see *Padmore v. IRC, supra*; also *Colquhoun v. Brooks* (1889) 14 App.Cas. 493; *Ogilvie v. Kitton* (1905) 5 T.C. 338; *Mitchell v. Egyptian Hotels Ltd.* [1915] A.C. 1022; *Unit Construction Co. Ltd. v. Bullock* [1960] A.C. 351; *Laerstate BV v. Revenue & Customs Commissioners* [2009] S.F.T.D. 551. Note also *R. v. Holden* [2004] S.T.C. (S.C.D.) 416, as to the effect of passing resolutions and signing documents consequent thereon.

regards those partners, be calculated as if it was a non-UK resident individual.[337] Although it is no longer stated in terms that the non-UK resident partner's notional trade[338] is to be treated as if it were carried on in the UK, it is clear that he will only be taxed on such part of his profit share as is derived from UK trading activities.[339]

A similar rule is applied in the case of a non-UK resident corporate partner.[340]

Firms controlled outside the UK

34–63   Where a firm is controlled and managed[341] outside the UK and carries on a trade wholly or partly outside the UK, any UK-resident individual partner who is either resident but not domiciled in the UK or not ordinarily resident in the UK and who makes a claim to that effect will have his share of the profits of the firm's trade arising in the UK ascertained and taxed in the normal way, but his share of profits arising *outside* the UK will be treated as relevant foreign income[342] and will be charged on the remittance basis.[343]

Effect of a change in residence

34–64   A change in an individual partner's residence will result in a permanent cessation of his notional trade or notional business[344] if the whole or any part of the firm's actual trade is carried on outside the UK, but will not affect that partner's right to carry forward any losses which accrued prior to his change of residence.[345]

8.   PAYMENTS TO OUTGOING PARTNERS AND THEIR DEPENDANTS

Consultancy agreements

34–65   Where an outgoing partner enters into a consultancy agreement or similar arrangement with the continuing partners, under which he will continue to provide his services to the firm in return for a fee or other payment, the tax treatment of such remuneration will in large measure depend on whether the consultancy can in truth be said to represent, in whole or in part, consideration for the acquisition of his share. If it was entirely independent of such acquisition,

---

[337] Income Tax (Trading and Other Income) Act 2005, s.849(1), (3), *supra*, para. 34–05.

[338] See *ibid*. s.852(1), *supra*, para. 34–07.

[339] *ibid*. s.6(2)(b).

[340] Corporation Tax Act 2009, ss.1259(2), (4), 1261(6).

[341] See *supra*, para. 34–62, n. 336.

[342] For the purposes of the Income Tax (Trading and Other Income) Act 2005, Pt 8.

[343] *ibid*. s.857 (as amended by the Finance Act 2008, Sched. 7, Pt 1, para. 70), applying (*inter alia*) the conditions set out in the Income Tax Act 2007, s.803B (as added by the Finance Act 2008, Sched. 7, Pt 1, para. 1). (See also *ibid*. ss.809D, 809E (as added by *ibid*. for other cases in which the remittance basis can apply).

[344] See further as to the expressions "notional trade" and "notional business", *supra*, para. 34–09.

[345] *ibid*. ss.852(6), (7) (as amended by the Income Tax Act 2007, Sched. 1, Pt 2, para. 579), 854(5). As to carrying forward losses, see the Income Tax Act 2007, s.83 and *supra*, para. 34–47.

and the outgoing partner provides genuine services to the firm which are not rewarded by a grossly disproportionate payment, his remuneration will constitute income in his hands and will be deductible in computing the partnership prof-its.[346] Where, however, there is a direct or, possibly, indirect connection between the consultancy and the acquisition of the outgoing partner's share, the "remuneration" will not be wholly referable to the services he provides and will not be deductible by the continuing partners.[347]

Accordingly, with a view to ensuring that any such remuneration paid to an outgoing partner *cannot* be treated as consideration for the acquisition of his share, it may be desirable to keep the consultancy agreement wholly separate from any other agreement and, if necessary, incorporated in a separate document. As an alternative, a partner who wishes to render consultancy services might prefer to continue as an active partner, albeit on a part-time basis and with a reduced profit share.

Partnership annuities and other payments

In order to determine the tax treatment of any payments received by an outgoing partner, or by his widow or dependants, *otherwise* than pursuant to a consultancy agreement as described above, it is necessary to determine whether those payments are of an income or capital nature, since dissection may well not be possible.[348] In many cases, the true nature will appear from the terms of the contractual arrangement under which the payments are made, and this will normally bind HMRC.[349] If the payments have the nature of capital, no income tax considerations will arise[350]; if, on the other hand, they are of an income

34–66

---

[346] Provided that the continuing partners can show that the remuneration was wholly and exclusively laid out for the purposes of the partnership business: Income Tax (Trading and Other Income) Act 2005, s.34(1)(a). Whether the consultancy fee is taxable under *ibid.* Pt 2 (formerly Sched. D) or the Income Tax (Earnings and Pensions) Act 2003, Pt 2 (formerly Sched. E) will, of course, depend on the consultant's precise status, *i.e.* independent contractor or employee. And see also, *supra*, para. 34–12, as to the provisions which might apply in the case of the provision of the consultant's services through a service partnership.

[347] See *Hale v. Shea* [1965] 1 W.L.R. 290. See also *Bucks v. Bowers* [1970] 1 Ch. 431; *Pegler v. Abell* [1973] 1 W.L.R. 155; *Lawrance v. Hayman* [1976] S.T.C. 227. In these circumstances, the remuneration would clearly *not* satisfy the requirements of the Income Tax (Trading and Other Income) Act 2005, s.34(1)(a). The capitalised value of the right to the remuneration might also, conceivably, be subject to capital gains tax in the consultant's hands: see the Taxation of Chargeable Gains Act 1992, s.37(3).

[348] As to the possibility of dissecting a payment into its capital and income elements, see *IRC v. Church Commissioners for England* [1977] A.C. 329 (HL).

[349] See, generally, *IRC v. Church Commissioners for England, supra*; but *cf. CIR v. Ledgard* (1937) 21 T.C. 129; *CIR v. Mallaby-Deeley* (1938) 23 T.C. 153; *CIR v. Hogarth* (1940) 23 T.C. 491. Account must also be taken of the application of the *Ramsay* principle in this context: see, in particular, *IRC v. Moodie* [1993] 1 W.L.R. 266 (HL), declining to follow *IRC v. Plummer* [1980] A.C. 896 (HL); also, *supra*, para. 34–11.

[350] Thus, the outgoing partner may receive a lump sum and himself purchase an annuity or, alternatively, the continuing partners may agree to pay a lump sum by instalments with interest on the balance from time to time outstanding. The capital element in either case would not be income taxable in the hands of the outgoing partner, and if it is borrowed by the continuing partners personally, they may obtain relief in respect of any interest payments under the Income Tax Act 2007, s.398. Note, however, the exceptional charges to tax on a non-taxable payment which might be imposed in the situations considered *supra*, paras 34–49 *et seq.* Such a payment would attract a charge to capital gains tax, if made in consideration of the assignment by the retiring partner of his share in the partnership to the continuing partners: see further, *infra*, para. 35–13.

nature, it is necessary to consider their status in the outgoing partner's hands and, moreover, whether they are deductible by the continuing partners.

34–67   Normally, an annuity payable to an outgoing partner (or his widow, surviving civil partner or dependants) which is made in consideration of his past services or in return for the acquisition by the continuing partners of his share in the partnership, will be taxed by deduction under section 848 or 900 of the Income Tax Act 2007, and will constitute a charge on income which is deductible by the continuing partners,[351] provided that it is paid "for genuine commercial reasons in connection with [*their*] trade, profession or vocation."[352] If this test is not satisfied, the annual payments will not be deductible[353] and will be treated as the income of the continuing partners under the settlement provisions.[354] It should, in general, be possible to justify an annuity as paid for bona fide commercial reasons where it falls to be made under the terms of a partnership agreement entered into on an arm's length basis, whether the paying partners are the original signatories to the agreement or have been admitted to the partnership subsequently. It should even, in an appropriate case, be possible to justify an annuity payable to a deceased partner's spouse, surviving civil partner or dependants in this way.

Where an annuity is paid *otherwise* than for genuine commercial reasons but, nevertheless, under a liability incurred for a consideration in money or money's worth which is not brought into the charge to tax in the hands of the paying partners,[355] it may, if not treated as a settlement, still be caught by anti-avoidance provisions and disallowed as a deduction.[356]

Whilst the annuity will, in the above way, be deductible by the continuing partners, it will usually be treated as investment income in the hands of the retiring partner.[357]

Commutation of annuity rights

34–68   Where the partners commute a retired partner's annuity rights that should constitute a revenue expense. Where, however, a company takes on the liability as part of the acquisition of the former partnership's business and then commutes the annuity, the payment will be a capital expense and therefore not deductible.[358]

---

[351] The charge will normally be deducted first from partnership income, and then in the manner most favourable to each partner: *ibid.* ss.23, 447, 448. See further, as to charges on income, *supra*, para. 34–28.

[352] *ibid.* s.900(1)(c). In such a case, the arrangement will not constitute a settlement within the meaning of the Income Tax (Trading and Other Income) Act 2005, 624(1) (see *ibid.* s.627(2)(a)) and the anti-avoidance provisions contained in the Income Tax Act 2007, s.899(5)(f) are also automatically disapplied (see *ibid.* s.904(5)).

[353] As the requirements of the Income Tax Act 2007, s.447(1)(b) will not be satisfied.

[354] Income Tax (Trading and Other Income) Act 2005, ss.620(1), 624(1). And see *supra*, para. 34–16.

[355] Income Tax Act 2007, s.904(1), (3).

[356] *ibid.* s.843.

[357] *Hale v. Shea* [1965] 1 W.L.R. 290; *Pegler v. Abell* [1973] 1 W.L.R. 155; *Lawrance v. Hayman* [1976] S.T.C. 227. Moreover, where the annuity is paid as consideration for the disposal by the outgoing partner of his share in the partnership, the capital value of the annuity will be subject to capital gains tax: see the Taxation of Chargeable Gains Act 1992, s.37(3). A certain degree of relief is, however, afforded by para. 8 of HMRC Statement of Practice "Capital Gains Tax: Partnerships" (D12); see further, *infra*, paras 35–20 *et seq.*, A6–12, A6–17.

[358] *Parnalls Solicitors Ltd. v. Revenue & Customs Commissioners* [2010] S.F.T.D. 284.

Other arrangements

In lieu of partnership annuities, which are problematic not only in terms of **34-69** taxation[359] but also in terms of their long term effect on the firm,[360] partners will often make provision for death or retirement on an individual basis, whether by way of endowment or life assurance or contributions under a registered pension scheme,[361] although the attractions of the latter have been severely diminished now that restricted tax relief is available for high earners.[362] However, this is largely a matter of individual financial planning, the further consideration of which is out of place in a work of this nature.[363]

---

[359] Thus, where an annuity is payable in consideration of the disposal of an outgoing partner's share, it would seem that a charge to both income tax and capital gains tax (on the capitalised value of the annuity) could be incurred: see *supra*, para. 34–67, n. 357. It should be noted that HMRC Statement of Practice "Capital Gains Tax: Partnerships" (D12), para. 8 (*infra*, para. A6–12) assumes that a charge to capital gains tax will be imposed *whenever* an annuity is payable to a retiring partner, whether or not in consideration of a disposal of his share. As discussed *infra*, para. 35–21, the current editor does not consider this "blanket" approach to be justifiable and the practice should, where appropriate, be resisted. In any event, if a double charge to tax is to be avoided, it would seem desirable that any annuity should be kept wholly separate from the consideration given for the disposal of the outgoing partner's share.

[360] The payment of such annuities to retired partners can lead to a high degree of resentment on the part of the continuing partners, who may (justly or unjustly) feel that their efforts are merely serving to benefit persons who contribute nothing to the success of the business: see further the *Encyclopedia of Professional Partnerships*, Precedent 2, Art. 6–06, notes.

[361] See the Finance Act 2004, Pt 4.

[362] See the Finance Act 2009, Sched. 35, as amended (*inter alia*) by the Finance Act 2010, s.48.

[363] Note, however, that inheritance tax considerations may arise in relation to such arrangements: see further, *infra*, para. 36–29.

CHAPTER 35

CAPITAL GAINS TAX

1.   INTRODUCTION

No special code for disposals of partnership assets

THE considerations which originally led to the introduction of a special code **35–01** for the taxation of partnership income[1] were never regarded as significant when taxing capital gains realised on the disposal of a partnership asset. Accordingly, section 59 of the Taxation of Chargeable Gains Act 1992 provides as follows:

"59. [(1)][2] Where 2 or more persons carry on a trade or business in partnership—

(a)   tax in respect of chargeable gains accruing to them on the disposal of any partnership assets shall, in Scotland as well as elsewhere in the United Kingdom, be assessed and charged on them separately, and

(b)   any partnership dealings shall be treated as dealings by the partners and not by the firm as such, [. . .]

(c)   [. . .].[3]

[(2) Subsection (3) applies if—

(a)   a person resident in the United Kingdom ("the resident partner") is a member of a partnership which resides outside the United Kingdom or which carries on any trade, profession or business the control and management of which is situated outside the United Kingdom, and

(b)   by virtue of any arrangements [that have effect under section 2(1) of TIOPA 2010] ("the arrangements") any of the capital gains of the partnership are relieved from capital gains tax [or corporation tax] in the United Kingdom.

(3) The arrangements [(so far as providing for that relief)] do not affect any liability to capital gains tax [or corporation tax] in respect of the resident partner's share of any capital gains of the partnership.]"[4]

Thus, no attempt is made to treat a partnership as a separate entity for the purposes of capital gains tax, even in Scotland where, under the general law, a partnership is a legal person distinct from its members.[5]

---

[1] See *supra*, para. 34–01. Of course, the current income tax regime is more comparable to that considered in the present chapter: see *supra*, paras 34–03 *et seq*.

[2] As so numbered by the Income Tax (Trading and Other Income) Act 2005, Sched. 1, Pt 2, para. 431(2).

[3] The words omitted were repealed by the Finance Act 1995, Sched. 29, Pt VIII(16).

[4] These subsections were added by the Income Tax (Trading and Other Income) Act 2005, Sched. 1, Pt 2, para. 431(3) and amended by the Corporation Tax Act 2009, Sched. 1, Pt 2, para. 365 and the Taxation (International and Other Provisions) Act 2010, Sched. 8, para. 43.

[5] Partnership Act 1890, s.4(2).

35–02 However, it would not be right to class the above approach as a success in fiscal terms: indeed, so extensive have been the potential anomalies over the years[6] that the taxation of partnership gains has in large measure had to be regulated by extra-statutory means. Thus, on January 17, 1975, the Inland Revenue, following discussions with both the Law Society and the Allied Accountancy Bodies, issued a Statement of Practice (now numbered D12) entitled "Capital Gains Tax: Partnerships", which was subsequently extended on two separate occasions[7] and reissued in a revised form in October 2002. Although the published practice has not resolved all the potential problems and is, in some respects, open to objection, the clarification which it affords is to be welcomed. Whether a taxpayer may at some future date mount a successful challenge to that practice remains to be seen.[8]

The essence of the HMRC practice is to treat each partner as entitled to a fractional share of each partnership asset, thus ignoring his true entitlement, namely the right to a proportion of the surplus remaining after the realisation of all the partnership assets and the payment of all the partnership debts and liabilities.[9]

Although the remainder of this chapter is to a large extent written by reference to the Revenue practice, every effort has been made to indicate where that practice does not accord with the strict law or is otherwise less than satisfactory.

2.   DISPOSALS OF PARTNERSHIP ASSETS OR OF SHARES THEREIN

35–03 A clear distinction must be drawn between the following types of disposal:

   A. disposals on the contribution of assets to a partnership;

   B. disposals of partnership assets to third parties;

   C. disposals of partnership shares;

---

[6] The provision now to be found in the Taxation of Chargeable Gains Act 1992, s.59 was originally contained in the Finance Act 1965, s.45(7) and then in the consolidating Capital Gains Tax Act 1979, s.60.

[7] The full text of the current version of the Statement of Practice (D12) is reproduced *infra*, paras A6–04 *et seq.* and the first extension thereof (SP1/79), which was originally issued on January 12, 1979 is reproduced *infra*, para. A6–17. The second extension (SP1/89) issued on February 1, 1989 is not reproduced as it has ceased to have effect, save as regards companies: see HMRC Brief 9/2009 "Capital Gains Tax—Rebasing Rules FA 2008 and Partnerships" issued on March 20, 2009, reproduced *infra*, paras A6–19 *et seq.* And see also, generally, [1975] B.T.R. 87. HMRC have confirmed that Statement of Practice D12 will apply to limited partnerships in the venture capital field: see the Statement issued by the British Venture Capital Association on May 26, 1987. It also in terms applies to limited liability partnerships formed under the Limited Liability Partnerships Act 2000: see *infra*, para. A6–04.

[8] See in particular *infra*, para. 35–12.

[9] See Statement of Practice D12, para. 1, *infra*, para. A6–05. As to how the size of a partner's share is determined, see *infra*, para. 35–06. For this purpose, the market value of a partner's fractional share in any particular asset suffers no discount by reason of its size: *ibid.* Thus, where a firm owns all the issued shares in a company, the value of the holding of a partner with a one-tenth share would be one-tenth of the value of the partnership's 100% holding. As to the precise nature of a partner's share under the general law, see *supra*, paras 19–01 *et seq.*

D. distribution of partnership assets amongst the partners.

Each of these categories will now be considered in turn.

A.   DISPOSALS ON THE CONTRIBUTION OF ASSETS TO A PARTNERSHIP

HMRC practice in relation to this type of disposal was not announced until early **35–04** January 2008, when Brief 03/2008 "Capital gains tax and corporation tax on chargeable gains—contribution of assets to a partnership" was first issued.[10] Consistently with the approach adopted in the case of disposals of partnership assets to third parties,[11] when a partner contributes an asset to a partnership by way of a capital contribution he will be regarded as retaining ownership of that fraction of the asset which is represented by what will be his share in asset surpluses under the partnership agreement.[12] It follows that he will be regarded as having disposed of the remainder of his interest to the other partners. If they are connected persons *vis-à-vis* him[13] or the arrangement is otherwise than at arm's length, then market value of the part disposed of will be substituted in the normal way.[14] In any other case, the consideration for the disposal will be that part of the actual consideration paid which is not represented by the fraction of the assets which he is treated as retaining and such consideration will, in HMRC's view, normally be represented by the resulting credit to the contributing partner's capital account.[15] Any allowable costs will be apportioned on the normal fractional basis which will apply once the asset has been brought into the firm.[16]

Entrepreneurs' relief may be available on any such disposal, provided that the other conditions for its availability are satisfied,[17] as may hold over relief where the transaction is not at arm's length.[18]

Taking an example considered in a previous edition of this work, if a partner **35–05** contributes a particular asset and his capital account is credited with its full value but all capital profits thereon are expressed to belong to the other partners, it would seem that the contributing partner will be treated as having disposed of the entire asset which will thereafter, under the HMRC practice, be regarded as the

---

[10] Issued on January 25, 2008 and reproduced *infra*, para. A6–18.

[11] See *infra*, paras 35–06 *et seq.*

[12] Statement of Practice D12, para. 2, *infra*, para. A6–06. And see *infra*, para. 35–06, n. 24.

[13] For the meaning of "connected persons" see the Taxation of Chargeable Gains Act 1992, s.286, as amended by the Finance Act 1995, Sched. 17, para. 31, the Finance Act 2006, Sched. 12, Pt 3, paras 25, 43, Sched. 26, Pt 3(15) and the Tax and Civil Partnership Regulations 2005 (SI 2005/3229), reg. 121. And see *infra*, para. 35–10.

[14] *ibid.* ss.17(1), 18(1), (2).

[15] This is somewhat ironic given that the ownership of capital is ignored when determining the size of each partner's fractional share in the partnership assets: see Statement of Practice D12, para. 2, considered *infra*, para. 35–06, n. 24.

[16] HMRC are at pains to point out in Brief 03/2008 that the application of Statement of Practice D12, para. 4, *infra*, para. A6–08 in this way is by way of effective concession.

[17] See the Taxation of Chargeable Gains Act 1992, s.169I(8)(a), as added by the Finance Act 2008, Sched. 3. See further, as to this relief, *infra*, para. 35–19.

[18] See *ibid* s.165 (as amended), noted *infra*, para. 35–09. Note that if the consideration treated as received under HMRC's practice will exceed the allowable costs, this will reduce the amount of the gain eligible for relief: *ibid.* s.165(7).

property of those other partners. This is a somewhat surprising result. Moreover since the contributing partner will be treated as having received full consideration (i.e. the credit in his capital account), no hold-over relief under the Taxation of Chargeable Gains Act 1992, s.165 (as amended) would be available. To avoid such a consequence, it may be preferable to proceed in stages: on Day 1, the partner who owns the asset can introduce it into the partnership on terms that all capital profits attributable thereto will belong to him alone,[19] so that he will be treated as continuing to own the asset. Then, on Day 2, the capital profit sharing ratios can be altered so as to ensure that the other partners become entitled to all such capital profits: this step will not seemingly involve any disposal.[20]

B.   DISPOSALS OF PARTNERSHIP ASSETS TO THIRD PARTIES

35–06   For the purposes of capital gains tax, partnership property is treated in the same way as any other property jointly owned by two or more persons, *i.e.* regard is had to the effect of a disposal on the persons beneficially entitled.[21] It has already been seen that the essence the HMRC practice is to regard each partner as entitled to a fractional share of each partnership asset.[22] It follows that, when a firm disposes of one of its assets, each partner is treated as having disposed of the entirety of his fractional share therein.[23]

Given the above approach, it is obviously necessary to identify the size of each partner's fractional share of any given asset. In this respect, the Revenue practice does go some way towards recognising the true *legal* nature of a partnership share, by allocating the disposal proceeds between the partners in the ratio of their shares in asset surpluses at the time of the disposal.[24] If, as will usually be the case, those shares are laid down in the original partnership agreement or in some other supplementary agreement, that will be the end of the matter. However, in the absence of any such specific provision, the allocation of the proceeds will follow the actual destination of the surplus as shown in the partnership accounts.[25] The acquisition cost of an asset is allocated in the same way, although it may fall to be readjusted in the event of a subsequent alteration in the sharing ratios.[26]

A firm might, in consequence, seek to avoid any charge to tax on a disposal of its assets by establishing a capital profits account or reserve into which all capital

---

[19] Whether or not he receives a corresponding credit in his capital account.

[20] See Statement of Practice D12, para. 4, considered, *infra*, para. 35–12.

[21] There is thus a direct analogy with the Taxation of Chargeable Gains Act 1992, s.60 (as amended by the Finance Act 2006, Sched. 6, para. 10), which governs the position of nominees and bare trustees. The current editor submits that the settled property provisions of the Act cannot apply, since the partners are together absolutely entitled to each partnership asset: see *Kidson v. Macdonald* [1974] Ch. 339; also *Booth v. Ellard* [1980] 1 W.L.R. 1443; *Jenkins v. Brown* [1989] 1 W.L.R. 1163.

[22] See Statement of Practice D12, para. 1, *infra*, para. A6–05, noticed *supra*, para. 35–02.

[23] Similarly, where there is a part disposal of an asset, there will be a part disposal of each partner's fractional share.

[24] Statement of Practice D12, para. 2, *infra*, para. A6–06. Note that, at this stage, no account is taken of the manner in which *capital* is owned, even though the value of the partnership assets may, at least in part, be attributable thereto: see further *supra*, para. 35–04. Where, under the terms of the partnership agreement, all future capital profits attributable to a particular asset are expressed to belong to one partner, it would seem that he will be regarded as the owner of that asset. This is not without its complications: see the example considered *supra*, para. 34–05.

[25] Regard will, of course, be had to any agreements outside the accounts.

[26] See further *infra*, para. 35–12.

gains are to be paid, no provision being made as to the respective entitlements of the partners thereto. The adoption of such a device is, however, anticipated by the Revenue practice: in the absence of any specified asset-surplus sharing ratios, the proceeds will be allocated in accordance with the ordinary profit-sharing ratios.[27]

Reliefs available on disposal of partnership assets

(i) *"Roll-over" relief.* Where the proceeds from the disposal[28] of any assets **35–07** which were throughout the period of their ownership[29] used only for the purposes of a trade are applied in or towards the acquisition of other assets taken in and used only for the purposes of the trade,[30] then "roll-over" relief may be available under section 152 of the Taxation of Chargeable Gains Act 1992. Both the assets disposed of and the assets acquired[31] must fall within the specified classes (but not necessarily the same class),[32] and the new assets must be

[27] Statement of Practice D12, para. 2, *infra*, para. A6–06. This to an extent anticipates the treatment of such a capital fund in the event of a dissolution: see the Partnership Act 1890, s.44(b), para. 4. The practice is, however, questionable given that, until a dissolution or other distribution, no one is legally entitled to the present enjoyment of the fund. And see *Stocker v. C.I.R.* (1919) 7 T.C. 304; *Franklin v. C.I.R.* (1930) 15 T.C. 464; *Latilla v. C.I.R.* (1943) 25 T.C. 107, 116 *per* Lord Greene M.R.

[28] This will include the consideration deemed to be realised on a disposal of an asset by way of gift, but *not* on a deemed disposal and reacquisition of the same asset: see the Institute of Taxation paper dated October 31, 1991, para. 1.6, reproduced at [1991] S.T.I. 1098.

[29] This will not include any period of ownership prior to March 31, 1982: Taxation of Chargeable Gains Act 1992, s.152(9).

[30] The assets acquired must, in general, be taken into use in the trade immediately if the relief is to be available: *Campbell Connelly & Co. Ltd. v. Barnett* [1994] S.T.C. 50. Note, however, in the case of an asset which requires improvement before it can be taken into use, the terms of Extra-Statutory Concession D24, as considered in *Steibelt v. Paling* [1999] S.T.C. 594. As to the position where the asset is only partially used for the purposes of the trade, note *Tod v. Mudd* [1987] S.T.C. 141.

[31] The asset acquired may be a further interest in an asset which is already in use for the purposes of the trade: Extra-Statutory Concession D25. However, it is not possible for a taxpayer to roll over a gain on the part disposal of an asset into the remainder of that asset retained by him, since this will not, on any footing, constitute a "new" asset: *Watton v. Tippett* [1997] S.T.C. 893 (CA).

[32] The specified classes, as set out in the Taxation of Chargeable Gains Act 1992, s.155 (as amended), are as follows:

    1. *Head A.* Buildings or land used and occupied only for the purposes of the trade (save, in general, where the trade is one of land dealing or developing, or of providing services for the occupier of land in which the trader is interested: see *ibid.* s.156(2));*Head B.* Fixed plant or machinery;

    2. Ships, aircraft and hovercraft;

    3. Satellites, space stations and spacecraft;

    4. Goodwill;

    5. Milk and potato quotas;

    6. Ewe and suckler cow premium quotas (as introduced by the Finance Act 1993, s.86(1), (4));

    7. Fish quota (as introduced by the Finance Act 1993, Section 86(2), (Fish Quota) Order 1999 (SI 1999/564), art. 3);

    7A. Payments under the income support scheme for farmers (as introduced by the Finance Act 1993, Section 86(2), (Single Payment Scheme) Order 2005 (SI 2005/409), art. 2(2));

    8. Lloyd's syndicate rights, etc. (as introduced by the Finance Act 1999, s.84(1)).

In *Anderton v. Lamb* [1981] S.T.C. 43, the scope of Class 1, Head A above was considered when a taxpayer sought to roll over gains realised on the sale of part of a farm into houses constructed for the occupation of two of his partners (who were also his sons). Goulding J. rejected the claim to relief on the ground that the houses were not occupied for the purposes of the trade, since it was not essential to the management of the farm that the partners should live in the houses, nor were they expressly required to do so under the terms of the partnership agreement. An appeal against that judgment was apparently settled by agreement: *The Times*, April 28, 1982. See also, as to the scope

acquired[33] within the period beginning 12 months prior to the disposal of the old assets and ending three years after that disposal.[34] Where only part of the proceeds is so applied, partial relief will be available.[35] The relief operates by treating the consideration for the disposal of the old assets as of such an amount as will secure neither a gain nor a loss on the disposal, and reducing the acquisition cost of the new assets by such part of the actual consideration received on the disposal of the old assets as exceeds the deemed consideration substituted therefor.[36] In this way, the charge to capital gains tax can be deferred until such time as assets are finally disposed of and the proceeds are not reapplied for business purposes.

In the case of a disposal of partnership assets, the relief will only be available to the extent that each partner has an interest both in the assets disposed of and in the assets acquired. If, between disposal and acquisition, a partner's share in asset surpluses is reduced, e.g. on the introduction of a new partner, the relief will be restricted to his reduced share of the acquisition cost of the new assets,[37] and any excess will attract a charge to tax. The incoming partner will obviously not be in a position to claim the relief. Similarly, if a partner retires between disposal and acquisition, no relief will be available in respect of his share of the disposal proceeds.[38]

The relief is available to partners who carry on more than one trade, either successively or at the same time.[39]

35–08 (ii) *Entrepreneurs' relief.* This relief may, in certain circumstances, be available on the disposal of partnership assets and is considered later in this chapter.[40]

---

of Class 1, Head B, *Williams v. Evans* [1982] 1 W.L.R. 972. In *Balloon Promotions Ltd. v. Wilson* [2006] S.T.C. (S.C.D.) 167, HMRC sought (unsuccessfully) to deny the availability of relief on the basis that Class 4 goodwill did not exist in respect of certain restaurant businesses. See also, as to HMRC's approach to the valuation of premises related goodwill, the Guidance Note "Goodwill in trade related properties background note" issued on January 30, 2009 and reproduced at [2009] S.T.I. 400. Note that HMRC do not regard the decision in *Faulks v. Faulks* [1992] 1 E.G.L.R. 9 (noted, *supra*, paras 18–19, 18–59) as having called into question the existence of Class 5 independently of Class 1: see [1993] S.T.I. 294 and [1994] S.T.I. 664; also *Cottle v. Coldicott* [1995] S.T.C. (S.C.D.) 239; *Foxton v. Revenue & Customs Commissioners* [2005] S.T.C. (S.C.D.) 661. For the treatment of assets which have been only partially used for the purposes of the business, see the Taxation of Chargeable Gains Act 1992, s.152(6), (7). And as to gains rolled over into depreciating assets, see *ibid.* s.154; also [1993] S.T.I. 892 and Extra-Statutory Concession D45.

[33] This will include an unconditional contract for the acquisition.

[34] Taxation of Chargeable Gains Act 1992, s.152(3), (4), as amended by the Finance Act 1996, s.141(1). HMRC do, however, have discretion to allow the relief even when the strict time limits are not adhered to: see further the Institute of Taxation paper dated October 31, 1991, paras 1.2 *et seq.*, reproduced at [1991] S.T.I. 1097; also *R v. I.R.C.* [2004] S.T.C. 763. This discretion is *not* exercisable by the Tribunal on appeal: *Steibelt v. Paling* [1999] S.T.C. 594.

[35] Taxation of Chargeable Gains Act 1992, s.153(1).

[36] *ibid.* s.152(1).

[37] This appeared from the Inland Revenue Booklet C.G.T. 8 (1980), para. 295, although this booklet has now long since been withdrawn.

[38] Unless he is able to invest his share in assets to be used in some other trade carried on by him.

[39] Taxation of Chargeable Gains Act 1992, s.152(8), as considered in *Steibelt v. Paling* [1999] S.T.C. 594. And see the Statement of Practice "Roll-over relief for replacement of business assets: trades carried on successively" (SP8/81) dated September 18, 1981; also the Institute of Taxation papers dated May 11, 1990 (reproduced at [1990] S.T.I. 446) and October 31, 1991, para. 5 (reproduced at [1991] S.T.I. 1099).

[40] See *infra*, para. 35–19.

(iii) *"Hold-over" relief.* This relief may only be claimed where, otherwise than   **35–09**
under a bargain at arm's length,[41] an individual disposes of an asset (or an
interest in an asset) used for the purposes of his trade, profession or vocation or
of agricultural property eligible for inheritance tax relief.[42] The transferee must,
however, be a UK resident.[43] The relief operates in much the same way as "roll-
over" relief, in that the transferor's chargeable gain and the transferee's acquisition cost are both reduced by the amount of "held-over gain", which will in most
cases be the amount of the chargeable gain itself.[44] Both the transferor and the
transferee must claim the benefit of the relief.[45]

C.   DISPOSALS OF PARTNERSHIP SHARES

The general treatment of dealings between partners

Whilst capital gains tax is normally charged by reference to the actual pro-   **35–10**
ceeds realised on the disposal of an asset, there are two occasions on which
market value will be substituted, namely:

   (a)   where the asset was acquired or disposed of otherwise than by way of
         a bargain made at arm's length[46] or

---

[41] A transaction will be treated as otherwise than by way of a bargain at arm's length where there
is a disposal between connected persons: *ibid.* s.18(1), (2). Partners are treated as connected persons,
except in relation to disposals of partnership assets pursuant to bona fide commercial arrangements:
ibid. s.286(4), as amended by the Tax And Civil Partnership Regulations 2005, reg. 121. Note also,
as to the likely attitude of a court when considering whether there is a bargain at arm's length, *Berry
v. Warnett* [1980] S.T.C. 631, 647g–j *per* Buckley L.J., as seemingly adopted by the House of Lords
on appeal at [1982] S.T.C. 396; *Bullivant Holdings Ltd. v. IRC* [1998] S.T.C. 905. Of course, where
there is a disposal otherwise than by way of a bargain at arm's length which confers a gratuitous
benefit on another, that disposal, whilst attracting capital gains tax relief, will also be likely to
constitute a potentially exempt transfer for the purposes of inheritance tax, as to which see *infra*, para.
36–02. Such a transfer may, however, qualify for 100% agricultural property/business relief: see
infra, paras 36–10 *et seq.*
[42] Taxation of Chargeable Gains Act 1992, s.165(1), (2)(a)(i), (5), Sched. 7, para. 1; and see [1989]
S.T.I. 845. Relief is also available in the case of any disposal of assets (business or non-business) on
which an immediate charge to inheritance tax is imposed: *ibid.* s.260 (as amended).
[43] Taxation of Chargeable Gains Act 1992, s.166(1).
[44] *ibid.* s.165(4). Where, however, actual consideration is given and received, and that consideration exceeds the allowable deductions on the disposal, then the "held-over gain" will be reduced by
the amount of that excess: *ibid.* s.165(6) (as amended by the Finance Act 1998, Sched. 27, Pt III(31)),
(7). If the consideration is incapable of being valued, and market value is substituted pursuant to *ibid.*
s.17(1)(b), the current editor submits that relief will still be available.
[45] *ibid.* s.165(1)(b). It is therefore possible for a transferee, who does not wish to acquire the asset
at a low base cost, to frustrate the application of the relief by refusing to make the claim therefor. In
order to avoid such a situation, the transferor and the transferee should expressly agree whether or not
such a claim is to be submitted before the disposal takes place.
[46] See, generally, as to the likely attitude of the court when considering a bargain alleged not to be
at arm's length, *Berry v. Warnett* [1980] S.T.C. 631, 647g–j *per* Buckley L.J., as seemingly adopted
by the House of Lords on appeal at [1982] S.T.C. 396; *Bullivant Holdings Ltd. v. IRC* [1998] S.T.C.
905. And note also *Mansworth v. Jelley* [2003] S.T.C. 53 (CA), although the effect of this decision
was reversed by the Taxation of Chargeable Gains Act 1992, s.144ZA, as added by the Finance Act
2003, s.158(1) and amended by the Finance (No. 2) Act 2005, Sched. 5, para. 1.

(b) where the asset was acquired or disposed of wholly or partly for a consideration that cannot be valued.[47]

A disposal will be treated as a transaction otherwise than by way of a bargain at arm's length where the parties are "connected persons".[48] Partners are normally treated as connected,[49] except in relation to acquisitions or disposals of partnership assets pursuant to bona fide commercial arrangements.[50] The latter exception will, however, only apply where there is no other connection between the partners.[51]

35–11   On the admission of a new partner, the existing partners will often wish to ensure that he becomes entitled to a share of the partnership assets; they will achieve this by reducing their own shares in order to create the incoming partner's share. Equally, partners may merely wish to rearrange their asset sharing ratios as between themselves, without admitting a new partner. In either case, any partner whose share is decreased will be treated as having disposed of part of that share. The rules described in the previous paragraph will apply to that disposal in the following way. If the consideration for the rearrangement is capable of being valued, tax will be charged by reference thereto, unless the partners can be treated as connected persons.[52] If, on the other hand, the consideration *cannot* be valued, *e.g.* where it is represented by an incoming partner's agreement to devote his whole time to the partnership business, then market value will be substituted, irrespective of any connection between the partners.[53] Of course, where the disposal is otherwise than under a bargain at arm's length, "hold-over" relief[54] can normally be claimed, thus effectively deferring any charge to tax until a subsequent disposal of the share, in respect of which the relief is not available.[55] Alternatively, advantage can be taken of any available entrepreneurs' relief.[56]

Whilst the foregoing represents the strict legal position, it must be read subject to the Revenue practice, the application of which may lead to some surprising results.

---

[47] Taxation of Chargeable Gains Act 1992, s.17(1).

[48] *ibid.* s.18(1), (2).

[49] For the meaning of "connected persons" see, generally, *ibid.* s.286, as amended by the Finance Act 1995, Sched. 17, para. 31, the Finance Act 2006, Sched. 12, Pt 3, paras 25, 43, Sched. 26, Pt 3(15) and the Tax and Civil Partnership Regulations 2005, reg. 121.

[50] *ibid.* s.286(4), as amended by the Tax and Civil Partnership Regulations 2005, reg. 121. Although it will be a question of fact in each case, dealings between partners will usually involve such an arrangement: see, for example, the decisions in *Att.-Gen. v. Boden* [1912] 1 K.B. 539 and *Att.-Gen. v. Ralli* (1936) 15 A.T.C. 523, considered *infra*, paras 36–03 *et seq.*

[51] *i.e.* by virtue of *ibid.* s.286(2), (as amended by the Tax and Civil Partnership Regulations 2005, reg. 121), (8). Note that, in Statement of Practice D12, para. 7, *infra*, para. A6–11, HMRC assume that an uncle and nephew are connected persons, but this is not warranted by the terms of the Act. *cf.* the terms of the Inheritance Tax Act 1984, s.270 (as amended by the Taxation of Chargeable Gains Act 1992, Sched. 10, para. 8(12)).

[52] HMRC will in general be bound to accept the value of a consideration honestly agreed between the parties to a bargain at arm's length: see *Stanton v. Drayton Commercial Investment Co. Ltd* [1983] A.C. 501.

[53] Taxation of Chargeable Gains Act 1992, s.17(1)(b). The current editor is of the opinion that if, in such a case, no bona fide commercial arrangement were involved, "hold-over" relief could be claimed under *ibid.* s.165. And see *Mansworth v. Jelley* [2003] S.T.C. 53 (CA), noted *supra*, para. 35–10, n. 46.

[54] Under *ibid.* s.165 (as amended).

[55] See further, as to this relief, *supra*, para. 35–09. And see *supra*, n. 53.

[56] See *infra*, para. 35–19.

HMRC practice: rearrangement of shares without payment

Where no monetary consideration is given on a rearrangement of shares, the **35–12** practice is to treat the consideration as the appropriate fraction of the current balance sheet value of each chargeable asset owned by the firm.[57] Thus, assuming no previous revaluation of those assets to have been reflected in the partnership accounts, HMRC will regard the disposal as having been made for a consideration equal to the disposing partner's acquisition cost[58] and neither a chargeable gain nor an allowable loss will result. Any actual, non-monetary consideration, *e.g.* a covenant by the incoming partner to devote his whole time to the partnership business, will be ignored. Herein lies the danger of this extra-statutory form of "hold-over" relief: the incoming partner may well have given full consideration for the acquisition of the share, yet he will acquire it at a low base cost and thereby store up a potentially large chargeable gain for the future. In such a case, there would seem to be every incentive for the incoming partner to reject the practice and to contend that his acquisition cost should be the market value of the share as at the date of his admission to the firm. Although the practice is not stated to be optional, the current editor regards it as unlikely that the Revenue would object if the partners *invited* a charge to tax, so as to prevent the incoming partner's acquisition cost being maintained at an artificially low level.[59]

Where the practice does apply, a partner whose share is reduced will naturally suffer a like reduction in his acquisition cost, that reduction being taken over as the acquisition cost of the partner whose share is created or increased. The part disposal rules for apportionment of acquisition costs do not apply, and all calculations are made on a fractional basis.[60]

Although the operation of the practice in many respects parallels (and, to an extent, duplicates) the effect of "hold-over" relief,[61] its application is not restricted on that account.

HMRC practice: rearrangement of shares coupled with a payment

Where one partner makes a payment to another in consideration of a reduction **35–13** in the latter's share, that payment will be treated as consideration for the disposal

---

[57] Statement of Practice D12, para. 4, *infra*, para. A6–08. See further, *supra*, para. 35–06.

[58] Note that, where the partner held the share on March 31, 1982, his acquisition cost will now, without the need for any election, be determined by reference to its market value on that date: Taxation of Chargeable Gains Act 1992, s.35(2), as amended by the Finance Act 2008, Sched. 2, para. 58(2). If he acquired it after that date but before April 6, 2008 by virtue of a no gain/no loss disposal (or a series of such disposals) and no rebasing election was in force at the time of the acquisition, 1982 rebasing will apply and account will also be taken of any indexation allowance for the period from March 31, 1982 to whichever is the earlier of the date of acquisition and April 1998: *ibid.* s.35A, as added by the Finance Act 2008, Sched. 2, para. 59, applying *ibid.* s.56(2). It is confirmed by HMRC Brief 9/2009 "Capital Gains Tax—Rebasing Rules FA 2008 and Partnerships" issued on March 20, 2009 (*infra*, para. A6–25) that any disposal to which Statement of Practice D12, para. 4 applies qualifies as a no gain/no loss disposal for this purpose. In any other case, there will now be no indexation allowance, which was, in effect, abolished as regards individuals by the Finance Act 2008, Sched. 2, para. 78.

[59] This aspect should, where necessary, be explained to an incoming partner, so as to avoid later recriminations. There is a marked contrast in a case where hold-over relief is claimable under *ibid.* s.165, since there the incoming partner can refuse to join in a claim for the relief, if it is against his interests so to do: *ibid.* subs. (1)(b): see *supra*, para. 35–10.

[60] Statement of Practice D12, para. 4, *infra*, para. A6–08.

[61] Under *ibid.* s.165 (as amended): see further, *supra*, para. 35–09.

and charged to tax accordingly,[62] although entrepreneurs' relief[63] or "roll-over" relief[64] may be available. Where the payment represents consideration for an asset which appears in the firm's balance sheet, the appropriate fractional share of the acquisition cost can be deducted in order to arrive at the chargeable gain; where, however, the asset does not appear therein, as will usually be the case with goodwill, there may be no relevant acquisition cost,[65] unless the asset was held on March 31, 1982 and was thus subject to automatic rebasing.[66] The amount of the payment will, of course, form part of the acquisition cost of the share of the partner making the payment.

It has already been seen that, where partners fall to be treated as connected persons in relation to a disposal,[67] market value should strictly be substituted for any consideration actually given. However, in the case of a rearrangement of partnership shares between connected persons which is effected either gratuitously or for a consideration of less than market value, HMRC will not seek to substitute market value if similar terms would have been negotiated between parties at arm's length.[68] In any other case, it would seem that market value *must* be substituted since there can, by definition, have been no bona fide commercial arrangement and the partners will be connected in that capacity, if in no other.[69]

HMRC practice: revaluation of partnership assets

35–14   The seemingly innocuous process of revaluing partnership assets may, under the HMRC practice, throw up an unexpected charge to tax but only if the revaluation is reflected in the partnership accounts.[70] The revaluation and the consequent adjustments in the accounts will not themselves attract such a charge, but HMRC will regard any partner whose share in the revalued assets is subsequently reduced as having made a disposal of part of his fractional interest

---

[62] Statement of Practice D12, para. 6, *infra*, para. A6–10.

[63] There will be a disposal of part of a business in such a case: see *infra*, para. 35–19.

[64] *i.e.* where the consideration consists of a fractional share in an asset which is introduced into the firm, *e.g.* by an incoming partner: see *ibid.* s.152 (as amended). See further, *supra*, para. 35–07 and *infra*. para. 35–19.

[65] If the partners write off goodwill in the balance sheet, this will not of itself create either a chargeable gain or an allowable loss; however, if the partners then rearrange their shares, there will be a disposal of goodwill and an allowable loss will arise. Alternatively, it could be argued that the value of the goodwill becomes negligible as soon as it is written off, so as to permit a claim for an allowable loss under the Taxation of Chargeable Gains Act 1992, s.24(2), as substituted by the Finance Act 1996, Sched. 39, para. 4 and amended by the Enactment of Extra-Statutory Concessions Order 2009 (SI 2009/730), art. 4(3). The latter argument apparently did not find favour with the (then) General Commissioners: see (1980) 77 L.S.Gaz. 127 and (1982) 79 L.S.Gaz. 257; but see also the cases discussed in Eastaway and Gilligan, *Tax and Financial Planning for Professional Partnerships* (3rd ed., 1996) pp. 116–123.

[66] Taxation of Chargeable Gains Act 1992, s.35(2), as amended by the Finance Act 2008, Sched.2, para. 58(2).

[67] See *supra*, para. 35–10.

[68] Statement of Practice D12, para. 7, *infra*, para. A6–11. *Quaere*, is this practice of any real significance given the availability of hold-over relief under the Taxation of Chargeable Gains Act 1992, s.165?

[69] *ibid.* ss.17(1)(a), 18(1), (2), 286(4), as amended by the Tax and Civil Partnership Regulations 2005, reg. 121. Hold-over relief would be available in such a case: see *supra*, para. 35–09.

[70] It is a commonly held misconception that, having had partnership assets revalued, *e.g.* on the retirement of a partner, the partnership accounts must necessarily be adjusted so as to incorporate the revised figures. It will frequently be desirable merely to alter the capital profit sharing ratios in order to reflect the revaluation, rather than to court a charge to tax under the HMRC practice.

therein for a consideration equal to the like part of the increased value shown in the accounts and tax will be charged accordingly.[71] The justification for imposing a charge in these circumstances is, in words of Statement D12, that the reduction in such a partner's share would otherwise "reduce his potential liability to capital gains tax on the eventual disposal of the assets without an equivalent reduction of the credit he has received in the accounts". The current editor submits that this reasoning is essentially flawed, since there will in reality be no question of such a partner *avoiding* a chargeable gain on a subsequent disposal: he will deduct from his share of the consideration his fractional share of the acquisition cost, and no account will be taken of balance sheet values. Moreover, why should the partner whose share is increased have his acquisition cost artificially augmented? The net position may conceivably be the same, whether the tax is collected from one partner or the other.[72] In this respect, the practice should, perhaps, not be accepted.

It may be noted that this charge on "balance sheet gains" will be in addition to any charge on the *actual* consideration received on the rearrangement.[73]

Entire disposal of partnership share

Where a partner retires (or is expelled) from the firm and disposes of the **35–15** entirety of his share to the continuing partners, the tax treatment will broadly accord with the position on a rearrangement of partnership shares. Thus, if no payment is made to the outgoing partner and the HMRC practice is accepted[74] or, where appropriate, hold-over relief is claimed,[75] no chargeable gain will be realised on the disposal. If, on the other hand, such a payment is made, otherwise than by way of an annuity (within the limits specified by HMRC),[76] a charge to tax will be almost inevitable and HMRC will usually seek to treat it as a payment for goodwill.[77] It will not, however, generally be possible for HMRC to impose a charge to income tax by reference to the disposal proceeds if they genuinely relate to the share.[78]

The position is less straightforward when, under the terms of the partnership **35–16** agreement, the share of an outgoing or deceased partner is expressed to accrue to the continuing partners.[79] It is theoretically possible to argue that, quite apart

---

[71] Statement of Practice D12, para. 5, *infra*, para. A6–09. See the criticisms of this practice set out in [1975] B.T.R. 87. *Quaere* could a partner faced with such a charge not seek to hold over the gain under *ibid.* s.165? There is certainly no "actual" consideration for the purposes of *ibid.* s.165(7)(a), although the deemed consideration does not strictly fall within the parenthetical words "(as opposed to the consideration equal to the market value which is deemed to be given by virtue of section 17(1))". See further, as to hold-over relief, *supra*, para. 35–09.

[72] *Per contra* if capital gains tax is charged on some partners at the higher rate: see the Taxation of Chargeable Gains Act 1992, s.4, as substituted by the Finance (No.2) Act 2010, Sched. 1, para. 2.

[73] Statement of Practice D12, para. 6, *infra*, para. A6–10.

[74] There are, however objections to the practice: see *supra*, para. 35–12.

[75] Taxation of Chargeable Gains Act 1992, s.165 (as amended): see *supra*, para. 35–09.

[76] The treatment of such annuities (whether or not coupled with a cash payment) is governed by Statement of Practice D12, para. 8 (*infra*, para. A6–12), as extended by the Statement of Practice dated January 12, 1979 (SP1/79), *infra* para. A6–17: see further, *infra*, paras 35–20 , 35–21.

[77] As to the availability of hold-over relief where actual consideration is given, see *ibid.* s.165(7). And see *supra*, para. 35–09, n. 44.

[78] *Chappell v. Revenue & Customs Commissioners* [2009] S.T.C. (S.C.D.) 11.

[79] See, for example, *Att.-Gen. v. Boden* [1912] 1 K.B. 539; *Att.-Gen. v. Ralli* (1936) 15 A.T.C. 523, noted *infra*, paras 36–03 *et seq.*

from the HMRC practice (or, indeed, any available claim to hold-over relief[80]), there will be no charge to tax when an outgoing partner's share accrues pursuant to such a provision,[81] whether or not any payment falls to be made to him at that stage. The current editor submits that, on a true analysis, the bundle of rights comprised in such a partner's share either becomes valueless when he ceases to be a partner or, where a payment falls to be made on the accruer, effectively contracts into the right to that payment.[82] Similarly, the prospect of a corresponding increase in value is inherent in the bundles of rights which make up the shares of the continuing partners. Thus, when the outgoing partner leaves the firm, it can be contended that there is neither a disposal by him nor an acquisition by the continuing partners, so that tax cannot be charged, irrespective of any payment which falls to be made by the latter.[83] Equally, it would seem to follow from the fact that the share of the outgoing partner merely becomes valueless or, where a payment falls to be made, assumes a fixed value, that the accruer is not an "occasion of the entire loss, destruction, dissipation or extinction" of the share.[84] Perhaps the share should more properly be treated as a wasting asset,[85] thus precluding any claim to a capital loss when its value becomes negligible[86]; however, this analysis is not without difficulty.[87]

Retirement in anticipation of emigration

35–17   Tax is, in general, chargeable only in respect of gains accruing to a person in a year of assessment during any part of which he is resident or ordinarily resident in the UK.[88] Accordingly, if an outgoing partner is intending to take up permanent residence abroad, no tax will normally be chargeable on gains realised by

---

[80] *ibid.* s.165 (as amended). See *supra*, para. 35–09.

[81] There will, in any event, be no charge to tax if the share accrues on death: *ibid.* s.62(1).

[82] See further, *infra*, paras 36–16, 36–24, 36–40, 36–42, 36–48.

[83] The current editor submits that such a payment cannot properly be regarded as compensation for the loss or depreciation of the share, thus attracting a charge to tax under the Taxation of Chargeable Gains Act 1992, s.22(1)(a): since the right to the payment itself forms part of the share, it surely cannot at the same time constitute compensation for its loss or depreciation. It should also be noted that *ibid.* s.30 (value shifting and tax-free benefits) could in theory apply in the case of a tax avoidance scheme which incorporates an accruer provision; however, in most cases it should be possible to show that the main purpose of the arrangement was not the avoidance of tax: see *ibid.* s.30(4), as amended by the Finance Act 1996, Sched. 20, para. 46; also *Att.-Gen. v. Ralli* (1936) 15 A.T.C. 523, 526 *per* Lawrence J.: see *infra*, para. 36–04.

[84] See *ibid.* s.24(1), as amended. Even if this subsection did apply, the share could still arguably be treated as a wasting asset (see *infra*) in order to determine its value at the moment of extinction; if it were not so treated, a substantial allowable loss would prima facie be realised on the disposal.

[85] *ibid.* s.44; and see, generally, *Whiteman & Sherry on Capital Gains Tax* (5th ed.), paras 8–81 *et seq.*

[86] *i.e.* on a claim being made under *ibid.* s.24(2), as substituted by the Finance Act 1996, Sched. 39, para. 4 and amended by the Enactment of Extra-Statutory Concessions Order 2009 (SI 2009/730), art. 4(3).

[87] *e.g.* can it be established that the share has a predictable life not exceeding 50 years? This may be possible if the partnership agreement makes provision for the compulsory retirement of partners on the grounds of age (assuming that not to involve any unlawful discrimination: see supra, paras 8–22 *et seq.*) or if the partnership is for a fixed term, but may be extremely difficult in other cases. Perhaps the life of the share might be ascertained by reference to the predictable expectation of life interests in settled property: see *ibid.* s.44(1)(d).

[88] *ibid.* s.2(1). Note, however that a charge to tax may still be incurred if the non-resident is carrying on a trade in the UK through a branch or agency (*ibid.* s.10, as amended by the Finance Act 2003, Sched. 27, para. 2(2), Sched. 43, Pt 3(6)) or if the non-residence is only temporary (*ibid.* s.10A, as added by the Finance Act 1998, s.127(1) and subsequently amended in divers respects).

him on the disposal of his share if he defers that disposal until the financial year *following* that in which he retired and became non-resident.[89]

Resident partner in non-resident firm

Where a firm which is non-resident or the business of which is controlled and managed outside the UK realises a gain, a UK resident partner in that firm will not be able to avail himself of any double tax treaty relief which would otherwise apply to the firm's capital gains in order to frank his share of that gain.[90]   **35–18**

Entrepreneurs' relief[91]

This relief is in many respects similar to the old retirement relief which was finally phased out in 2002/2003.[92] It applies whenever there is a material disposal of business assets consisting of a business or part of a business[93] or a disposal of assets (or an interest in assets) which, when the business ceases to be carried on, are used for the purposes of the business.[94] For this purpose, each partner who disposes of the whole or part of his fractional share of the partnership assets will be treated as disposing of all or part of the partnership business[95] and that business will be treated as owned by him.[96] However, to be eligible the partner disposing of all or part of his share must have owned that share throughout[97] the period of one year ending with the date of the disposal[98] or, in the case of the disposal of a partnership asset, the date the business ceased to be carried on and, in the latter case only, not more than 3 years have elapsed since that date.[99] The amount of the relief, which must claimed,[100] currently stands at a lifetime figure of £5 million and the aggregate qualifying gains less losses on the relevant   **35–19**

---

[89] However, account must be taken of the effect of the Partnership Act 1890, s.43 in such a case, *i.e.* has a disposal actually taken place on the retirement? The dangers are illustrated by the decision in *Beckman v. IRC* [2000] S.T.C. (S.C.D.) 59 (a decision in relation to business property relief for inheritance tax). The right of a partner to retain his share *in specie* following his retirement will ultimately depend on the terms of the partnership agreement. See also *supra*, paras 19–10 *et seq.*, 19–35, 23–34, 26–03.

[90] Taxation of Chargeable Gains Act 1992, s.59(2), (3), reproduced *supra*, para. 35–01.

[91] See *ibid.* Pt V, Chap. 3, as added by the Finance Act 2008, Sched. 3.

[92] Under *ibid.* s.163, Sched. 6 (as amended), as phased out pursuant to the Finance Act 1998, s.140(1).

[93] See, as to the meaning of this expression, *ibid.* s.169S(1), as added by the Finance Act 2008, Sched. 3.

[94] *ibid.* s.169I(1), (2), as added by *ibid.* Note that, in the case of a disposal of *part* of a business, there is no need for the disposing partner to withdraw from that business completely.

[95] *ibid.* s.169I(8)(b), as added by *ibid.* It would seem to follow that, as in the case of the former retirement relief, a disposal of even a small part of a partner's fractional share in the partnership assets will be treated as a disposal of part of a business. *Per contra* in the case of the disposal of a specific partnership asset, unless this is on a cessation of the partnership business, when *ibid.* s.169I(2)(b) will apply: see generally, *McGregor v. Adcock* [1977] 1 W.L.R. 864; *Atkinson v. Dancer* [1988] S.T.C. 758; *Pepper v. Duffurn* [1993] S.T.C. 466; *Wase v. Bourke* [1996] S.T.C. 18; *Barrett v. Powell* [1998] S.T.C. 283; *Purves v. Harrison* [2001] S.T.C. 267; *cf. Jarmin v. Rawlings* [1996] S.T.C. 1005. These are all decisions in relation to retirement relief.

[96] *ibid.* s.169I(8)(c), as added by *ibid.*

[97] See *Davenport v. Hasslacher* [1977] 1 W.L.R. 869, a decision in relation to retirement relief.

[98] Taxation of Chargeable Gains Act 1992, *ibid.* s.169I(3), as added by the Finance Act 2008, Sched. 3.

[99] *ibid.* s.169I(4), as added by *ibid.*

[100] *ibid.* s.169M(1), as added by *ibid.* The claim must be made on or before the first anniversary of January 31 following the tax year in which the disposal was made: *ibid.* s.169M(2).

disposal will be charged to tax at the rate of 10%, with any ineligible gains, the remaining 5/9ths being chargeable at the normal rates.[101]

Relief is also afforded to a partner who, as part of his "withdrawal . . . from participation in the business carried on by the partnership",[102] disposes of the whole or part of his share of the partnership assets and, by what is styled an "associated" disposal,[103] also disposes of an asset[104] which is *not* partnership property, provided that the asset has been used for the purposes of the partnership business throughout[105] the period of one year ending with the date of the disposal of his share or the cessation of the partnership business.[106] The gains eligible for relief will, however, be appropriately restricted if the asset in question has been used by the partnership for only part of the partner's period of ownership or he has been a partner for only part of that period, if only part of the asset has been so used or if a rent or other consideration has been paid in respect of its use.[107]

Partnership annuities

35–20   Although reference has already been made to the tax treatment of a straightforward capital payment made to an outgoing partner, if financial provision is made for such a partner by means of an annuity (whether in lieu of, or in addition to, a capital payment), different questions will arise. Although there is no doubt that the capitalised value of an annuity given as consideration for the disposal of an outgoing partner's share *can* be taken into account in computing any gains,[108] if the annuity does not in fact represent such consideration and is to be paid independently of the disposal, it should, as a matter of strict law, be ignored.

It is in the above context that the Revenue practice must be considered. If the firm buys a purchased life annuity for the benefit of the outgoing partner, the actual cost of the annuity will be treated as the consideration for the disposal of his share. If, on the other hand, the firm itself agrees to pay the annuity, its capitalised value will be taken into account, but only if it can be regarded as more than a reasonable recognition of the outgoing partner's past contribution of work and effort to the firm.[109] It will not be so regarded if the outgoing partner has been a partner for at least 10 years[110] and the annuity does not represent more than

---

[101] *ibid.* s.169N, as added by *ibid.* and amended by the Finance (No. 2) Act 2010, Sched. 1, para. 5.

[102] *Semble*, a partial withdrawal will not be sufficient to qualify for the relief: *sed quaere*.

[103] As to what will amount to an associated disposal, see *Clarke v. Mayo* [1994] S.T.C. 570, a decision on a similarly worded provision relating to retirement relief.

[104] Or an interest therein.

[105] See *supra*, n. 97.

[106] *ibid.* s.169K, as added by *ibid.*

[107] *ibid.* ss.169P, 169S(5) (definition of "rent"), as added by *ibid.* and, in the case of s.169P, amended by the Finance (No.2) Act 2010, Sched. 1, para. 7. In such a case the eligible gain will be restricted to what is "just and reasonable": *ibid.* s.169P(2). *Semble*, if the rent paid is clearly less than a market rent, a larger fraction of the gain should qualify. This was the position in relation to retirement relief, as appeared from the Statement of Practice "Capital Gains Tax: Retirement Relief" (D5) dated January 4, 1973, which was, however, classified as obsolete in November 1996. *Quaere* why this approach has continued to be adopted: if the asset has been used for the purposes of the partnership business, why should the payment of a rent affect the partners' entitlement to the relief?

[108] *ibid.* s.37(3).

[109] Statement of Practice D12, para. 8, *infra*, para. A6–12.

[110] This may include any period during which the outgoing partner was a member of another firm which merged with the firm from which he retires.

two-thirds of his average share of profits[111] in the best three of the last seven years in which he was required to devote substantially the whole of his time to partnership activities. If he has been a partner for less than 10 years, the relevant fraction of his average share of profits is determined in accordance with a graduated scale, varying between 1/60th (after one to five years) and 32/60ths (after nine years).[112]

Although the application of the above practice was originally denied where the annuity was payable *in addition* to a lump sum, HMRC now accept that, even in such a case, the capitalised value of the annuity can be left out of account, so long as the aggregate of the annuity and one-ninth of the lump sum does not exceed the appropriate fraction of the outgoing partner's average share of profits during the relevant years.[113] The lump sum itself will naturally continue to be taxable in the outgoing partner's hands. **35–21**

Where, under the practice, the purchase cost or the capitalised value of the annuity is treated as consideration for the disposal of the outgoing partner's share, it will naturally constitute allowable expenditure on the acquisition of the share by the continuing partners.[114]

It will perhaps be apparent that there is an assumption underlying the whole of the HMRC practice, namely that any annuity paid to an outgoing partner is inevitably given by way of consideration for the disposal of his share. The current editor submits that such an assumption is wholly unwarranted since there is no *necessary* connection between the annuity and the disposal, even though in practice such a connection will frequently exist. In this respect, the practice is potentially misleading and should be approached with caution; in an appropriate case, where the independent nature of the annuity arrangements is clear, the application of the practice (and of the underlying assumption) should be resisted.

Mergers and "roll-over" relief

Where two firms merge, and their respective assets are combined in the new merged firm, the partners of each constituent firm will, on a true analysis, have disposed of a proportionate part of their shares in the assets of that firm in return for an appropriate share in the assets of the other firm, and tax will be charged by reference to the actual value of that consideration, although "roll-over" relief[115] may be available. HMRC's practice in relation to mergers involves an application of the same principles as are applied to changes in the partners' sharing ratios, *i.e.* where no actual consideration is paid outside the accounts (and where no "balance sheet gain" is treated as realised),[116] neither a chargeable gain nor an allowable loss will result.[117] Even if a chargeable gain is thrown up, "roll-over" relief will still be available to the extent that the consideration received is actually rolled over into assets brought into the merged firm. The practice would, in this respect, appear to be beneficial, since it is now possible to effect a merger without incurring a charge to tax and without any necessary reliance on a claim **35–22**

---

[111] In assessing such share, no account will be taken of capital allowances or charges.

[112] See the Table set out in Statement of Practice D12, para. 8, *infra*, para. A6–12.

[113] See the Statement of Practice (SP1/79) dated January 12, 1979, *infra*, para. A6–17.

[114] Statement of Practice D12, para. 8, *infra*, para. A6–12.

[115] Under the Taxation of Chargeable Gains Act 1992, s.152 (as amended): see *supra*, para. 35–07.

[116] See *supra*, para. 35–14.

[117] Statement of Practice D12, para. 9, *infra*, para. A6–13.

to "roll-over" relief. Nevertheless, objection may still be taken to the basis upon which the practice is formulated.[118]

D.   DISTRIBUTION OF PARTNERSHIP ASSETS AMONGST PARTNERS

35–23   Except in the case of a limited partnership,[119] there is nothing to prevent partners agreeing to distribute partnership assets between themselves whilst the partnership is continuing, although such a distribution will more commonly be encountered following a dissolution. In either case, each partner will exchange his fractional share in the entirety of the distributed assets for absolute ownership of such of those assets as are received by him. Equally, if specific assets are appropriated to an outgoing partner in satisfaction of his share in the remaining assets, each of the continuing partners will be treated as disposing of his fractional share in the specific assets in exchange for a disposal by the outgoing partner of his fractional share in the remaining assets. Although a partner to whom such a distribution is made may, in terms of value, receive no more than his existing entitlement, there is, save as regards exchanges of land and associated milk quota between co-owners,[120] nothing in the Taxation of Chargeable Gains Act 1992 which prevents tax being charged on an exchange of assets,[121] and this much is clearly recognised by the HMRC practice. However, under that practice, the recipient of a distribution will (correctly) not be treated as having disposed of his fractional share in the assets distributed to him, even though there can be no doubt that the other partners have disposed of their shares in those assets.[122]

35–24   The practice requires the chargeable gain on such a distribution to be calculated in the following way[123]: the gain attributable to each partner (including the partner receiving the asset) is first calculated on the basis of a disposal at current market value. The fractional share of the gain deemed to have been realised by those partners who give up their interests in the asset will be chargeable to tax in the normal way,[124] but no such charge will be imposed on the remainder of the gain, which will be attributed to the recipient partner. The corollary is, of course, that such part of the gain will be deducted from the market value of the asset in order to determine the latter's acquisition cost. The operation of the practice may be illustrated by the following simple example. A firm comprises four equal partners and owns an asset which was originally acquired for £8,000 but now has market value of £24,000. That asset is distributed *in specie* to one partner, A, in satisfaction of his share on a dissolution. The total gain on the deemed disposal

---

[118] See *supra*, para. 35–12.

[119] See the Limited Partnerships Act 1907, s.4(3); and see further *supra*, paras 30–08 *et seq.*, 31–08.

[120] See the Taxation of Chargeable Gains Act 1992, ss.248A *et seq.*, as added by the Enactment of Extra-Statutory Concessions Order 2010 (SI 2010/157), art. 8. These provisions gave statutory force to Extra-Statutory Concession D26 but, unlike that concession, do not apply to potato quota.

[121] But see also *infra*, para. 35–25.

[122] Statement of Practice D12, para. 3, *infra*, para. A6–07.

[123] *ibid.*

[124] Subject, of course, to the availability of any applicable reliefs, *e.g.* "roll-over" or entrepreneurs' relief: see *supra*, paras 35–07, 35–19.

is £16,000, of which £12,000 is apportioned to the other three partners and charged to tax accordingly. A's acquisition cost will be the market value (£24,000) less the amount of his gain (£6,000 − £2,000 = £4,000), *i.e.* £20,000. A similar computation will be made when a loss arises on the distribution.

The illogicality of the practice will be self evident: having properly accepted that the recipient partner is not to be regarded as having disposed of his fractional share in the asset, the entirety of the practice is dependent upon his being deemed to have made just such a disposal and to have realised a gain thereon. This is a further example of HMRC treating a gain as having been realised when no disposal has in fact taken place,[125] and again the practice must be open to challenge. It should also be noted that its application is not restricted to dissolutions: an attempt could in theory be made to apply it to the purchase of partnership assets by a partner pursuant to a bona fide commercial arrangement,[126] although this should be strenuously resisted.

Where partners are treated as having disposed of their shares in land or other **35–25** qualifying assets on such a distribution and the new "roll-over" relief for exchanges of joint interests[127] does not apply,[128] HMRC are prepared, by concession, to allow a claim for "roll-over" relief,[129] provided that the partnership is dissolved immediately thereafter.[130] It is, of course, questionable whether this condition can be justified, given that the partnership "trade" and any new trade carried on by an individual partner will be treated as one and the same for the purposes of the relief, whether or not the firm is dissolved.[131]

A more fundamental objection to the latter concession and, indeed, to the entirety of the HMRC practice in this area is the underlying assumption that a partition of land or other assets as between partners must *necessarily* involve capital gains tax disposals by them. In *Jenkins v. Brown*,[132] Knox J. held that a partition of land as between beneficial co-owners did *not* involve such a disposal and the same reasoning applies in the case of a partition of land or other assets as between partners, provided that each "pool" of like assets is divided strictly in accordance with their fractional shares therein.[133] The position will obviously be otherwise if shares in one type of asset are exchanged for shares in another.[134]

---

[125] The first example was discussed *supra*, para. 35–14, in relation to Statement of Practice D12, para. 5.

[126] See the Taxation of Chargeable Gains Act 1992, s.286(4), as amended by the Tax and Civil Partnership Regulations 2005, reg. 121; also *supra*, para. 35–10.

[127] See *ibid.* ss.248A *et seq.*, as added by the Enactment of Extra-Statutory Concessions Order 2010, art. 8, which, as already noted, relates only to land and any associated milk quota.

[128] Clearly the relief will not apply if, on a true analysis, there is no exchange of interests in land/quota between all the interested partners. *Quaere*, in any event, whether the relief applies whilst the partnership continues. Equally, if the land/quota were partitioned following the dissolution and winding up of the firm, there would seem to be no reason why it should not.

[129] Under *ibid.* s.152: see further, *supra*, para. 35–07. Note also that, in such a case, some measure of hold-over relief may also be available: see *supra*, para. 35–09.

[130] Extra-Statutory Concession D23 entitled "Relief for the replacement of business assets: partition of land on the dissolution of a partnership", *infra*, para. A6–26.

[131] See the Taxation of Chargeable Gains Act 1992, s.152(8).

[132] [1989] 1 W.L.R. 1163.

[133] This is the interpretation adopted in Ray, *Partnership Taxation*, at para. 14.15 and in Sumption, *Capital Gains Tax*, at para. A3–211.

[134] See *supra*, para. 35–23.

3.   ADMINISTRATION AND COMPUTATION

Information about chargeable gains

35–26   Section 12AA(7)(a) of the Taxes Management Act 1970[135] requires any partnership return[136] to contain the like particulars of "any disposal of partnership property" during any period covered by the return, as if the partnership were liable to tax on any chargeable gain accruing thereon.[137] The subsection appears to draw a distinction between a disposal of partnership property and a disposal of a share or shares therein, which somewhat ironically runs directly counter to the express provisions of section 59 of the Taxation of Chargeable Gains Act 1992,[138] whereby all "partnership dealings" (*i.e.* disposals of partnership property) are to be treated as dealings by the partners and not by the firm as such. Nevertheless, the duty is strictly defined: if anything less than the entirety of the partners' shares in a given partnership asset is disposed of, the responsibility for submitting the return will fall on the individual partners.[139]

Computation of gains

35–27   No particular difficulties of computation arise in relation to partnerships,[140] save in two specific cases where HMRC have seen fit to publish their practice. Those cases are as follows:

(a) Partnership shares acquired in stages

Where a partner has acquired his share in stages,[141] HMRC's approach will vary according to the nature of the underlying partnership asset.[142] In the case of land,[143] it would seem that each partner's share therein will be regarded as a single asset, irrespective of any intervening changes in the size of that share. It also appears that HMRC will be prepared to regard goodwill which is self-generated and which does not appear in the firm's balance sheet as a non-fungible asset which will not therefore constitute "securities" for the purposes of share

---

[135] As inserted by the Finance Act 1994, s.184 and amended by the Finance Act 1996, Sched. 41, Pt V(6) and the Finance Act 2009, Schedule 47 (Consequential Amendments) Order 2009 (SI 2009/2035), Sched., para. 3.

[136] As to the duty to make and deliver a partnership return, see *ibid.* s.12AA(2), as added by the Finance Act 1994, s.184 and amended by the Finance Act 1995, s.115(4) and the Finance Act 1996, s.123(1). Note also that a partnership return must contain a partnership statement which will, *inter alia*, identify "the amount of the consideration which . . . has accrued to the partnership in respect of each disposal of partnership property during [*the relevant*] period": *ibid.* s.12AB(1)(a)(ia), as added by the Finance Act 1994, s.185 and amended by the Finance Act 1996, s.123(5)(c). As to the new dates for submission of partnership returns under *ibid.* s.12AA, see *supra*, para. 34–17.

[137] Note that the return need no longer contain particulars of any acquisition of partnership property, following the repeal of *ibid.* s.12AA(7)(b). by the Finance Act 2009, Schedule 47 (Consequential Amendments) Order 2009, Sched., para. 3.

[138] See *supra*, para. 35–01.

[139] See the Taxes Management Act 1970, ss.7–9, as amended.

[140] See, generally, the Taxation of Chargeable Gains Act 1992, Pt II.

[141] *i.e.* in one or more of the manners considered *supra*, paras 35–12 *et seq.*

[142] Goodwill is considered *infra*.

[143] It appears from *ibid.* para. 14.105 that HMRC seek to distinguish between land as a non-fungible asset and other assets which are regarded as fungibles. *Quaere*, are there any assets other than land and goodwill (as to which see *infra*) which will be regarded as non-fungible for this purpose?

pooling.[144] Similarly in the case of *acquired* goodwill which is not reflected in its balance sheet at a value exceeding cost, although such goodwill will be treated as an asset separate and distinct from any self-generated goodwill.[145] However, in the case of any other asset, HMRC will apparently insist on applying the identification provisions contained in the Taxation of Chargeable Gains Act 1992.[146] Thus, on a disposal of a partnership asset, each partner's fractional share therein will be identified first with any *additional* fractional share in that asset acquired in the ensuing 30 days[147] and then with the general pool of previous acquisitions, on a "last in, first out" (L.I.F.O.) basis.[148]

It is not clear whether, consistently with the original published practice of HMRC,[149] a sympathetic attitude may be adopted where it can be shown that the application of the above rules will produce an unreasonable result.

(b) Shares held as partnership assets

Where a firm holds securities[150] and a partner also hold securities of the same **35–28** class in his own right, they will not be regarded as part of the same pool since they are not held by the same person *in the same capacity*.[151]

---

[144] *i.e.* under the Taxation of Chargeable Gains Act 1992, s.104(3), as amended: see Statement of Practice D12, para.12, *infra*, para. A6–16. Equally, this approach is stated to apply for the purposes of taper relief under *ibid.* s.2A, which has now been repealed.

[145] *ibid.*

[146] Taxation of Chargeable Gains Act 1992, ss.104 (as amended by the Finance Act 1998, ss.123, 125(3), the Finance Act 2006, Sched. 12, para. 17 and the Finance Act 2008, Sched. 2, para. 85), 106A (as added by the Finance Act 1998, s.124(1) and amended by the Finance Act 2006, s.74(2) and the Finance Act 2008, Sched. 2, para. 87). It is thought that the definition of "securities" in *ibid.* s.104(3) is prima facie apt to cover the fractional shares which go to make up a partnership share, albeit that its application is not without difficulty.

[147] *ibid.* s.106A(5), as added by the Finance Act 1998, s.124(1). As to securities acquired at a time when the partner was not resident or ordinarily resident in the UK, see *ibid.* s.106A(5A), as added by the Finance Act 2006, s.74(2). In the unlikely event that the additional share is acquired on the *same* day, see *ibid.* s.105(1), as amended by the Finance Act 1998, s.124(2).

[148] *ibid.* s.106A(2), (6), as added by *ibid.* s.124(1) and amended by the Finance Act 2008, Sched. 2, para. 87(3).

[149] Statement of Practice D12, para. 10, *infra*, para. A6–14. Under this paragraph "first in, first out" (F.I.F.O.) not L.I.F.O. applied.

[150] As to the meaning of this expression, see the Taxation of Chargeable Gains Act 1992, s.104(3); also *supra*, para. 35–27, n. 146.

[151] *ibid.* s.104(1), as amended by the Finance Act 2006, Sched. 12, para. 17. And see also *ibid.* ss.105(1) (as amended by the Finance Act 1998, s.124(2)), 106A(3) (as added by *ibid.* s.124(1)).

CHAPTER 36

INHERITANCE TAX

1.   INTRODUCTION

INHERITANCE tax[1] is primarily chargeable on death, since *inter vivos* transfers of   **36–01**
value[2] between individuals are treated as potentially exempt and may never be
charged to tax.[3] However, the reintroduction of the estate duty concept of a
"benefit reserved" (now styled a "gift with a reservation")[4] has complicated the
relative simplicity of the original regime and effectively removed a number of the
tax planning options formerly presented within the confines of a partnership.

Arm's length transactions

The essence of the charge to inheritance tax in respect of an *inter vivos*   **36–02**
disposition is a transfer of value conferring a gratuitous benefit on another. If, in
such a case, the transfer is made by an individual in favour of another individual[5]
or a disabled trust,[6] it will qualify for potentially exempt status[7] and will only
come into the charge to tax in the event of the transferor's death within seven
years[8]; in any other case, it will be chargeable to tax forthwith.[9]

Where, on the other hand, it can be shown that a particular disposition was *not*
accompanied by any donative intent and that the transferor and the transferee
were not "connected" or, even if they were, that the transaction was of a normal
commercial nature, there will be no transfer of value by reference to which a

---

[1] The tax was formerly known as capital transfer tax, but its structure was radically altered, and its
name changed to inheritance tax, by the Finance Act 1986. As a result, what was formerly the
consolidating Capital Transfer Tax Act 1984 is now conventionally referred to as the Inheritance Tax
Act 1984: see the Finance Act 1986, s.100(1)(a).

[2] See, as to the meaning of this expression, the Inheritance Tax Act 1984, s.3(1), (4).

[3] See *infra*, para. 36–02.

[4] Finance Act 1986, ss.102, 102A, 102B (the latter two sections having been added by the Finance
Act 1999, s.104), Sched. 20. See further *infra*, paras 36–31 *et seq*. And see, as to gifts with a
reservation where there are certain types of interest in possession trust, *ibid.* s.102ZA, as added by
the Finance Act 2006, Sched. 20, Pt 3, para. 33(2) and amended by the Finance Act 2010,
s.53(8).

[5] Including a transfer to a limited class of interest in possession trusts in his favour, where the trust
property is treated as comprised in his estate: Inheritance Tax Act 1984, ss.3A(2) (as amended by
Finance (No.2) Act 1987, s.96(2)(a), (b), Sched. 9, Pt III and the Finance Act 2006, Sched. 20, Pt 3,
para. 9(4)), 49(1A) (as added by the Finance Act 2006, Sched. 20, Pt 2, para. 4(1) and amended by
the Finance Act 2010, s.53(4)(a)).

[6] *i.e.* within the meaning of the Inheritance Tax Act 1984, s.89 (as amended).

[7] *ibid.* s.3A(1A), as added by the Finance Act 2006, Sched. 20, Pt 3, para. 9(3)). As to transfers
made prior to March 22, 2006, see *ibid.* s.3A(1), as added by the Finance Act 1986, Sched. 19, para.
1 and amended by the Finance Act 2006, Sched. 20, Pt 3, para. 9(2).

[8] *ibid.* ss.3A(4), (5) (as added by the Finance Act 1986, Sched. 19, para. 1), 4(1).

[9] *ibid.* s.2.

charge to tax can be imposed nor, indeed, any gift with a reservation.[10] This important principle is embodied in section 10(1) of the Inheritance Tax Act 1984,[11] which provides:

> "(1) A disposition is not a transfer of value if it is shown that it was not intended, and was not made in a transaction intended, to confer any gratuitous benefit on any person and either—
>
> (a) that it was made in a transaction at arm's length between persons not connected with each other, or
>
> (b) that it was such as might be expected to be made in a transaction at arm's length between persons not connected with each other".[12]

The connected persons provisions of the Taxation of Chargeable Gains Act 1992[13] are, with certain extensions, applied for this purpose.[14] Thus, partners will normally be treated as connected persons, except in relation to bona fide commercial arrangements[15]; even then, the exception will only apply if they are not otherwise connected.[16]

36–03 Provided that a substantial element of reciprocity can be shown, it should be possible to justify most transactions between partners both as bona fide commercial arrangements and as arm's length transactions. The reciprocity test can, in particular, be satisfied by establishing that full consideration has been given and received, even though not in a monetary form. In this connection, a number of estate duty cases decided under section 3 of the Finance Act 1894[17] are of direct relevance.

In *Att.-Gen. v. Boden*,[18] a father entered into partnership with his two sons and the partnership agreement provided that, on the death of the father, his share was to accrue to the other partners, subject to the payment by them of its full value, but ignoring goodwill. For their part, the sons agreed to devote as much time and attention to the partnership business as its proper conduct required and further

---

[10] See the Finance Act 1986, ss.102(1), 102A(1), 102B(1) (the latter two sections having been added by the Finance Act 1999, s.104); note also *ibid.* Sched. 20, para. 6, as amended by the Tax and Civil Partnership Regulations 2005 (SI 2005/3229), reg. 46. And see, as to gifts with a reservation where there is an interest in possession trust, *ibid.* s.102ZA, as added by the Finance Act 2006, Sched. 20, Pt 5, para. 33(2) and amended by the Finance Act 2010, s.53(8).

[11] Note, generally, as to application of this section, *Fryer v. Revenue & Customs Commissioners* [2010] S.F.T.D. 632.

[12] See further, as to this limb, *IRC v. Spencer-Nairn* [1991] S.T.C. 60. Note also, in this context, the decisions cited *supra*, para. 35–09, n. 41.

[13] s.286, as amended by the Finance Act 1995, Sched. 17, para. 31, the Finance Act 2006, Sched. 12, Pt 3, paras 25, 43, Sched. 26, Pt 3(15) and the Tax and Civil Partnership Regulations 2005, reg. 121; see further *supra*, para. 35–10.

[14] Inheritance Tax Act 1984, s.270, as amended by the Taxation of Chargeable Gains Act 1992, Sched. 10, para. 8(12). The definition of "relative" in the Taxation of Chargeable Gains Act 1992, s.286(8) is extended to include an uncle, aunt, nephew and niece.

[15] Taxation of Chargeable Gains Act 1992, s.286(4), as amended by the Tax and Civil Partnership Regulations 2005, reg. 121.

[16] *e.g.* pursuant to *ibid.* s.286(2), as amended by the Tax and Civil Partnership Regulations 2005, reg. 121. And note, in particular, the extended meaning of "relative" for inheritance tax purposes: see *supra*, n. 14.

[17] This section, so far as material, provided as follows: "Estate duty shall not be payable in respect of property passing on the death of the deceased by reason only of a bona fide purchase from the person under whose disposition the property passes . . . where such purchase was made . . . for full consideration in money or money's worth paid to the vendor . . . for his own use or benefit."

[18] [1912] 1 K.B. 539. But note the Irish case of *Re Clark* (1906) 40 I.L.T. 117, considered *infra*, para. 36–24, n. 120.

agreed not to engage in any other trade or business without the father's consent. The father, on the other hand, was bound to give only so much time and attention to the business as he thought fit. In deciding whether estate duty should be paid in respect of the goodwill which accrued to the sons on the father's death, Hamilton J. held that: (1) having regard to the sons' obligations under the agreement, the father's share in goodwill had passed to them by reason only of a bona fide purchase for full consideration in money's worth and was accordingly not dutiable; and (2) whilst the goodwill was of little real value, the covenant on the part of the sons to give their full time and attention to the partnership business was both capable of being, and was in fact, adequate consideration for the father's share therein. In the course of his judgment, Hamilton J. observed:

> "Furthermore, the question whether full consideration was given or not may no doubt be solved by putting a value on the property which passed on the one side, and weighing against it the money value of the obligations assumed on the other; but that is not the only method of solving the question. Another method is by looking at the nature of the transaction and considering whether what is given is a fair equivalent for what is received; and that is the way in which the question should be approached in this case."[19]

Whilst part of the decision in this case was disapproved by the Privy Council in *Perpetual Executors & Trustees Association of Australia Ltd. v. Commissioner of Taxes of Australia*,[20] no adverse comment was made as to that part of *Boden's* case which turned on the application of section 3 of the 1894 Act.

A further illustration of the reciprocity principle can be seen in *Att.-Gen. v. Ralli*,[21] where Sir Lucas Ralli (the father) had in 1920 entered into a partnership agreement with his son, Strati Ralli, and a third party for carrying on the old established family business of merchant bankers. The nature of the business made it necessary that large reserves should be maintained and it was provided in a collateral partnership agreement that, on the retirement or death of one of the partners, his interest in the partnership reserves should entirely cease and become vested in the continuing or surviving partner or partners without any payment or liability to account whatsoever. Sir Lucas retired in 1931 and in fact died 18 days later. The Crown claimed that the vesting of the reserves on Sir Lucas' retirement was a gift which, having occurred less than three years before his death, was dutiable; in fact, the reserves in question were stated to be "very substantial" but Lawrence J., in holding that Sir Lucas' share of the reserves was not chargeable to estate duty, concluded:

36–04

> "The substance of the matter here, in my opinion, is not a gift. I think that the transaction carried out by the collateral agreement in 1920 was an ordinary commercial arrangement entered into between the three partners for valuable consideration, it had none of the elements of a gift in it. All partners were treated equally. It was in the interests of the partnership in this great business that large reserves should be carried in the business. It was in the interests of the partnership that on the retirement or death of any of the partners these reserves should not be depleted by his being paid out his share of the reserves. It therefore appears to me that it was ordinary business wisdom to provide, as the collateral agreement does provide, that the interest of the partners in the reserves should pass to the surviving partners. That was not intended to be a gift. It was not a gift. It was an ordinary business arrangement, and it applied

[19] [1912] 1 K.B. 539, 561.
[20] [1954] A.C. 114.
[21] (1936) 15 A.T.C. 523.

equally to all the partners. The consideration moving from the one partner to the other was the undertaking of each partner to be a partner on those terms, one of which was that his interest in the reserves should pass to his partners if he retired or died."[22]

It should be noted that the decision of Lawrence J., to the effect that there had been no gift but merely a business arrangement, was quite apart from his (almost subsidiary) decision that the exemption contained in section 3 of the Finance Act 1894 applied.[23]

36–05   Whilst a *Boden* and *Ralli* argument will not be sustainable in all cases, it should be possible to establish that a disposition which forms part of a bona fide business arrangement falls within section 10(1) of the Inheritance Tax Act 1984 and thus does not constitute a transfer of value. The argument is equally applicable where the partners are connected otherwise than as partners, although it may be that much more difficult to prove bona fides in such a case. Practical applications of the argument will be considered later in this chapter.

By way of contrast, it should be noted that, if advantage is to be taken of the exemption from the reservation of benefit provisions involving the occupation of land or the possession of chattels,[24] it is necessary to show that full consideration *in money or money's worth* was received.[25]

2.   EXEMPTIONS AND RELIEFS

36–06   Before considering the various circumstances in which a partner may make a transfer of value for the purposes of inheritance tax, it will be convenient to outline the various exemptions and reliefs which are available.

Transfers between spouses and civil partners

Any transfer of value will be exempt if it consists of a direct transfer of property to the transferor's spouse or civil partner or if, as a result of the transfer, the value of the spouse's/civil partner's estate is increased, *e.g.* where the transfer is made in favour a third party on terms that the third party will secure a benefit of corresponding value for the spouse/civil partner.[26] In the latter case, the exemption will be limited to the amount of such increase. However, care must be taken to ensure that a subsequent disposal by the spouse or civil partner is not

---

[22] *ibid.* p. 526.

[23] *ibid.* pp. 527–528.

[24] Finance Act 1986, ss.102A(3), 102B(3)(b) (as respectively added by the Finance Act 1999, s.104), Sched. 20, para. 6(1)(a); and see [1993] S.T.I. 1410. See further, *infra*, paras 36–31 *et seq.*

[25] Of course, if property is transferred under an arm's length bargain and, pursuant thereto, possession or enjoyment is retained by the transferor, there will have been no gift, so that the presence or absence of a consideration in money or money's worth will be irrelevant.

[26] Inheritance Tax Act 1984, s.18(1), as amended by the Tax and Civil Partnership Regulations 2005, reg. 7(2). And see, as to the treatment of transfers of value arising out of loans, *ibid.* s.29(2).

treated as an associated operation, thus forfeiting the benefit of the initial exempt transfer.[27]

Annual exemptions

Transfers of value in any year are exempt to the extent that the values **36–07** transferred do not in the aggregate exceed £3,000.[28] Any unused part of the exemption may be carried forward to the next year, but no further.[29] Although the Inheritance Tax Act 1984 appears to provide that potentially exempt transfers are in the first instance left out of account for the purposes of this exemption and that, if they subsequently prove to be chargeable, such transfers are to be treated as made *after* any other transfers of value in the year in question,[30] this is inconsistent with an earlier section the Act.[31] The HMRC practice is in fact to apply the exemption to transfers in the order in which they are made, whether they are chargeable or potentially exempt.[32] It follows that, in some cases, the exemption will be lost if the transferor lives for seven years after making a potentially exempt transfer to which that exemption is allocated.

Exemption is also conferred on outright gifts in any one year to any one person, if the value of the gift(s) does not exceed £250.[33] This exemption is in addition to the £3,000 annual exemption.

These exemptions may be of some value when it is desired to alter the capital or asset sharing ratios in a firm without consideration and without incurring even a potential charge to tax, although the failure to increase the exempt amounts since 1984 have rendered them largely irrelevant.

Normal expenditure out of income

A transferor who wishes to take advantage of this exemption must show: **36–08**

(a) that the transfer of value was part of his normal expenditure,

(b) that it was actually made out of his income (if necessary taking one year with another)[34]; and

---

[27] See *ibid.* s.268. As to what will amount to an associated operation, see *Macpherson v. IRC* [1989] A.C. 159; also *Reynaud v. IRC* [1999] S.T.C. (S.C.D.) 185. And, generally, Foster, *Inheritance Tax*, para. C1.16. Note also that the principles developed in *W.T. Ramsay Ltd. v. IRC* [1982] A.C. 300 and subsequent cases (see *supra*, para. 34–11) may apply to an inheritance tax avoidance scheme: see *IRC v. Fitzwilliam* [1993] 1 W.L.R. 1189 (HL), where, on the facts, all the steps in the scheme could not be shown to be pre-ordained.

[28] *ibid.* s.19(1).

[29] *ibid.* s.19(2).

[30] *ibid.* s.19(3A), as added by the Finance Act 1986, Sched. 19, para. 5.

[31] *ibid.* s.3A(1)(b), as added by the Finance Act 1986, Sched. 19, para. 1.

[32] *Quaere* whether there is any legislative authority for this practice; *cf.* ss.3A(1)(b) and 19(3A), *supra*. See also Foster, *Inheritance Tax*, para. C3.22.

[33] Inheritance Tax Act 1984, s.20. The exemption will not apply in the case of a gift which forms part of a larger gift.

[34] It is thus possible to aggregate more than one year's income in order to show that a particular item of expenditure falls within the exemption: this might be of particular relevance where the transferor's income fluctuates from year to year.

(c) that, after allowing for all other items of normal expenditure, he had sufficient income remaining to maintain his usual standard of living.[35]

Where, however, the transfer of value consists of a loan of money or other property,[36] the transferor must show merely that the transfer is a normal one on his part and that requirement (c) above is satisfied.[37]

Whether any particular expenditure or transfer can be regarded as normal for the transferor will clearly involve a question of fact, although, as with the corresponding estate duty exemption, the test would appear to be qualitative rather than quantitative[38]; as a result, it cannot properly be said that any recurring item of expenditure will *necessarily* be treated as normal, or that any non-recurring item will not. However, it would seem that a settled pattern of expenditure must be established, whether by reference to a prior commitment or resolution on the part of the transferor or by reference to the payments themselves.[39]

This exemption may be of particular relevance where annuities are paid to outgoing partners or their dependants, otherwise than pursuant to the partnership agreement.[40]

Dispositions allowable for income tax

36–09   Any disposition which is allowable in computing the transferor's profits for the purposes of income tax,[41] or which would be so allowable if those profits were sufficient and fell to be so computed, will not be treated as a transfer of value.[42]

Agricultural property relief

36–10   Relief is afforded whenever the whole or part of the value transferred by a transfer of value is attributable to the agricultural value[43] of agricultural prop-

---

[35] Inheritance Tax Act 1984, s.21(1). For an example of a case where neither condition (b) nor (c) could be satisfied, see *Nadin v. IRC* [1997] S.T.C. (S.C.D.) 107. It should be noted that the exemption is available "to the extent that" the conditions can be satisfied, so that only part of an item of expenditure may qualify as exempt.

[36] Such transfers are taxable on normal principles: see *infra*, para. 36–30. Formerly, they were subject to their own specific regime: see the Finance Act 1976, s.115 (now repealed).

[37] Inheritance Tax Act 1984, s.29(4).

[38] See, generally, *Att.-Gen. for Northern Ireland v. Heron* [1959] T.R. 1 (CA, Northern Ireland).

[39] *Bennett v. IRC* [1995] S.T.C. 54; also *Nadin v. IRC* [1997] S.T.C. (S.C.D.) 107.

[40] But note the possible income tax implications attendant on the payment of an annuity in such circumstances: see *supra*, para. 34–67.

[41] If the disposition is only partly allowable, then the allowable part will be treated as a separate disposition: Inheritance Tax Act 1984, s.12(5).

[42] *ibid.* s.12(1). As to dispositions which represent contributions to a registered pension scheme, etc., see *ibid.* s.12(2)–(2G), as amended/added by the Finance Act 2004, s.203(2) and the Finance Act 2006, Sched. 22, para. 2.

[43] The "agricultural value" of agricultural property is the value which the property would have if it were subject to a perpetual covenant prohibiting its use otherwise than as agricultural property: *ibid.* s.115(3), as amended by the Finance Act 2009, s.122(3).

erty,[44] provided that one of two conditions is satisfied.[45] Thus, to qualify for the relief the agricultural property must either have been occupied[46] by the transferor for the purposes of agriculture throughout the period of two years ending with the date of the transfer, or owned by him throughout the period of seven years ending with that date and occupied (by him or another) for the purposes of agriculture throughout that period.[47] Where the property constitutes a replacement for other property, the former condition may still be satisfied if the transferor can show that he occupied the original property and the replacement property[48] for an aggregate period of at least two years within the five years ending with the date of the transfer.[49] Otherwise, he must show that the original property and the replacement property were owned and occupied (by him or another) for the purposes of agriculture, for an aggregate period of at least seven years within the 10 years ending with the date of the transfer.[50] In either case, the relief will not exceed what it would have been if the replacement had not been made and, for this purpose, changes resulting from the formation, alteration or dissolution of a partnership will be disregarded.[51]

Where either condition is satisfied, the relief is given by means of a percentage reduction in the value attributable to the agricultural value of the agricultural property.[52] The appropriate reduction is now 100% if the transferor's interest in the property immediately before the transfer carried the right to vacant possession or the right to obtain it within the next 12 months[53] or, in the case of tenanted

36–11

---

[44] The expression "agricultural property" is defined in *ibid.* s.115(2); note also *ibid.* s.115(4). See, generally, *Starke v. I.R.C.* [1995] 1 W.L.R. 1439 (CA); also *Harrold v. IRC* [1996] S.T.I. 706; *Rosser v. I.R.C.* [2003] S.T.C. (S.C.D.) 311. Any part of the value of the land attributable to milk quota will qualify for the relief: see [1993] S.T.I. 295. This approach is consistent with the views expressed as to the nature of such quota in *Faulks v. Faulks* [1992] 1 E.G.L.R. 9 and *Davies v. H. & R. Eckroyd* [1996] 2 E.G.L.R. 5. If such quota is transferred separately from the land (see *Swift v. Dairywise Farms Ltd.* [2000] 1 W.L.R. 1177; also the Dairy Produce Quotas Regulations 2005 (SI 2005/465), reg. 13, as amended by the Dairy Produce Quotas (Amendment) Regulations 2008 (SI 2008/439), reg. 2, Sched., para. 4), this should attract business relief under *ibid.* s.104(1): see *infra*, paras 36–13 *et seq.* It is understood that HMRC regard potato quota as an asset which does *not* form part of the land; it follows that a transfer of such quota should again be eligible for business relief.

[45] *ibid.* s.116(1). The relief is only available in respect of agricultural property situated in the UK, the Channel Islands or the Isle of Man or in an EEA state (*ibid.* s.115(5), as substituted by the Finance Act 2009, s.122(3)), but is denied where the property is subject to a binding contract for sale: *ibid.* s.124(1). See further *infra*, para. 36–16, n. 88.

[46] See, as to the meaning of "occupation", *Williams v. Revenue & Customs Commissioners* [2005] S.T.C. (S.C.D.) 782; *Atkinson v. Revenue & Customs Commissioners* [2010] W.T.L.R. 745 (FTT (Tax)) (occupation by partnership).

[47] *ibid.* s.117. And see *Rosser v. I.R.C.* [2003] S.T.C. (S.C.D.) 311. As to the position where the transferor became entitled to the property on the death of another person, see *ibid.* s.120, as amended by the Tax and Civil Partnership Regulations 2005, reg. 22.

[48] Any number of replacements, direct or indirect, may apparently be taken into account for these purposes.

[49] Inheritance Tax Act 1984, s.118(1).

[50] *ibid.* s.118(2).

[51] *ibid.* s.118(3), (4).

[52] The relief is given before the deduction of any exemptions; *cf.* the former position under the Finance Act 1975, Sched. 8, para. 1(1) (now repealed).

[53] Inheritance Tax Act 1984, s.116(2)(a), as amended by the Finance (No. 2) Act 1992. Sched. 14, para. 4. For this purpose, the interest of a joint tenant or tenant in common will carry the right to vacant possession (or the right to obtain it) if the interests of all the joint tenants/tenants in common together carry that right: *ibid.* s.116(6).

land, if the tenancy began on or after September 1, 1995,[54] as well as in certain transitional cases[55]; otherwise the reduction is 50%.[56] It follows that there is no longer any need for a partner who owns agricultural land which is *not* to become a partnership asset to grant his partners a non-exclusive, terminable licence to occupy the land,[57] rather than a lease, in order to ensure that the maximum rate of relief is available.

This relief is not dependent on a claim being made and will be applied in priority to business relief.[58]

Potentially exempt transfers

36–12   Where agricultural property is the subject of a potentially exempt transfer,[59] that property, or some other agricultural property which replaces it,[60] must be retained by the transferee and occupied (by him or by another) for the purposes of agriculture, if the continued availability of relief is to be secured against the possibility that the transferor will die within seven years of the original transfer.[61]

The availability of the relief is, however, ignored when determining whether a transfer is potentially exempt or chargeable.[62]

Business relief

36–13   This relief is available where the whole or part of the value transferred by a transfer of value is attributable to the value of "relevant business property", provided that certain conditions can be satisfied.[63] Relevant business property

---

[54] *ibid.* s.116(2)(c), as added by the Finance Act 1995, s.155(1). The relevance of September 1, 1995 is that this was the date on which the Agricultural Tenancies Act 1995 came into force. In certain cases of succession, 100% relief will be available if the tenancy was originally granted *before* that date: *ibid.* s.116(5A)–(5D), as added by the Finance Act 1996, s.185(2).

[55] See, as to these transitional cases, *ibid.* s.116(2)(b), (3)–(5), as amended.

[56] *ibid.* s.116(2), as amended by the Finance (No. 2) Act 1992, Sched. 14, para. 4.

[57] As to the effect of such a licence: see *supra*, para. 10–45.

[58] Inheritance Tax Act 1984, s.114(1). In the case of the deemed transfer on death, the relief is, in effect, applied *after* the deduction of any available exemptions: *ibid.* s.39A, as added by the Finance Act 1986, s.105.

[59] *ibid.* s.3A(1A), as added by the Finance Act 2006, Sched. 20, Pt 3, para. 9(3). As noted *supra*, para. 36–02, such a transfer can now only be made in favour of an individual or a "disabled trust" within the meaning of the Inheritance Tax Act 1984, s.89 (as amended).

[60] *ibid.* s.124B(1), (3), as added by the Finance Act 1986, Sched. 19, para. 22. The replacement property must normally be acquired within 3 years after the disposal of the original property: *ibid.* s.124B(2)(a), (8), as added by *ibid.* and amended by the Finance Act 1994, s.247(2).

[61] *ibid.* ss.124A(1), (3), 124B(3), as added by the Finance Act 1986, Sched. 19, para. 22. Similarly, in the case of a chargeable transfer made within seven years of the transferor's death: *ibid.* s.124A(2). If the transferee predeceases the transferor, the conditions must be satisfied on *his* death: *ibid.* ss.124A(4), 124B(4). Equally, note that, where land has been transferred from one partner to another, continued use of that land by the partnership may attract a charge to *income* tax on the transferor partner, under the pre-owned assets regime, unless it amounts to a gift with a reservation: see *supra*, para. 34–29 and *infra*, paras 36–31 *et seq.*

[62] *ibid.* s.124A(7A), as added by the Finance Act 1996, s.185(4).

[63] *ibid.* s.104(1), as amended by the Finance Act 1987, Sched. 8, para. 4 and the Finance (No. 2) Act 1992, Sched. 14, para. 1. See generally, as to the operation of this section, *Nelson Dance Family Settlement Trustees v. Revenue & Customs Commissioners* [2009] S.T.C. 802.

includes property consisting of a business[64] or an interest in a business,[65] and any land or building, machinery or plant which immediately before the transfer was used[66] wholly or mainly for the purposes of a business carried on by a partnership of which the transferor was a member,[67] but does not include a business which consists wholly or mainly of dealings in securities, stocks or shares, land or buildings or making or holding investments.[68]

For the relief to apply, it must be shown that the relevant business property was owned by the transferor throughout the two years immediately preceding the transfer[69] or that it replaced other property and both the original and the replacement property were so owned for periods together comprising at least two years out of the five years immediately preceding the transfer.[70] In the case of replaced property, the relief will not exceed what it would have been if the replacement had not been made and, for this purpose, changes resulting from the formation, alteration or dissolution of a partnership will be disregarded.[71]

Where the above conditions are satisfied, the relief is given by way of a **36–14** percentage reduction in the value attributable to the relevant business property.[72] The appropriate reduction is 100% in the case of a business or an interest in a business, and 50% in the case of any land or building, machinery or plant used for the purposes of a business.[73] The value attributable to a business or an interest in a business, is ascertained by valuing the assets used in the business (including goodwill[74] but excluding any excepted assets[75]) reduced by the aggregate amount

---

[64] See, generally, *McCall v. Revenue & Customs Commissioners* [2008] S.T.C. (S.C.D.) 752. However this will not include a business carried on *otherwise* than for gain: *ibid.* s.103(3); also *Grimwood-Taylor v. IRC* [2000] S.T.C. (S.C.D.) 39.

[65] An amount due to a retired partner under the Partnership Act 1890, s.43 will not constitute an interest in a business: see *Beckman v. IRC* [2000] S.T.C. (S.C.D.) 59.

[66] User under the terms of a lease would appear to qualify.

[67] Inheritance Tax Act 1984, s.105(1)(a), (d). It should be noted that where relief is claimed in respect of any land, building, machinery or plant, it is also necessary to show that the transferor's interest in the business is itself relevant business property: *ibid.* s.105(6). Where the value of milk quota is not reflected in the value of the land to which it is attached, it should normally qualify for business relief: see [1993] S.T.I. 295 and *supra*, para. 36–10, n. 44. *Semble*, potato quota will *only* be eligible for business relief. Any property subject to a binding contract for sale is, with two limited exceptions, incapable of constituting relevant business property: *ibid.* s.113. See also *infra*, para. 36–16.

[68] *ibid.* s.105(3). But see, as to the scope of this exception, *Weston v. Commissioners of Inland Revenue* [2000] S.T.C. 1064; also *Furness v. IRC* [1999] S.T.C. (S.C.D.) 232; *Farmer v. IRC* [1999] S.T.C. (S.C.D.) 321; *I.R.C. v. George* [2004] S.T.C. 147 (CA); *Clark v. Revenue & Customs Commissioners* [2005] S.T.C. (S.C.D.) 823; *Phillips v. Revenue & Customs Commissioners* [2006] S.T.C. (S.C.D.) 639; *Brander v. Revenue & Customs Commissioners* [2009] S.F.T.D. 374; *McCall v. Revenue & Customs Commissioners* [2009] S.T.C. 990 (CA, NI); *Revenue & Customs Commissioners v. Brander* [2010] UKUT 300 (TCC) [2010] S.T.I. 2427.

[69] *ibid.* s.106.

[70] *ibid.* s.107(1). Ownership may apparently be traced through any number of replacements. Note, in this connection, *Brander v. Revenue & Customs Commissioners, supra*.

[71] *ibid.* s.107(2), (3).

[72] Although the relief was formerly given, in the case of the deemed transfer on death, *before* the deduction of any available exemptions, this is no longer the position: *ibid.* s.39A, as added by the Finance Act 1986, s.105.

[73] *ibid.* s.104(1), as amended by the Finance Act 1987, Sched. 8, para. 4 and the Finance (No. 2) Act 1992, Sched. 14, para. 1.

[74] As to the valuation of goodwill, see *infra*, para. 36–58.

[75] Excepted assets, as defined in *ibid.* s.112(2), are those which have neither been used wholly or mainly for the purposes of the business throughout the whole or the last two years of the transferor's ownership nor been required for future use in the business.

of any liabilities incurred for the purposes of the business.[76] The relief is applied automatically, but only to the extent that agricultural property relief is not available.[77]

Potentially exempt transfers

36–15   Where relevant business property is the subject of a potentially exempt transfer,[78] that property, or some other property which replaces it,[79] must be retained by the transferee in the form of relevant business property, if the continued availability of the relief is to be secured against the possibility that the transferor will die within seven years of the original transfer.[80]

The availability of the relief is, however, ignored when determining whether a transfer is potentially exempt or chargeable.[81]

Scope of the relief

36–16   The relief should be available in the case of most dispositions of partnership shares,[82] provided that the investment side of the partnership business (if any) has not assumed too dominant a position. It has, however, been made clear that the relief will be denied on the death of a partner if, under the terms of the partnership agreement (or some other agreement), the surviving partners are *obliged* to purchase his share.[83] In HMRC's view, such an agreement amounts to a binding contract for the sale of the share, so that it is incapable of constituting relevant business property at the date of death.[84] An unexercised option in favour of the surviving partners is obviously not regarded in the same way,[85] but the status of automatic accruer provisions is less clear. Since the prospect of the accruer and the resulting right to any cash payment are at all times inherent in the share itself,[86] the current editor submits that such a provision cannot properly be treated as a contract for its sale, and thus business relief should be available.

---

[76] *ibid.* s.110. See further *Fetherstonaugh v. IRC* [1985] Ch. 1 (CA); *IRC v. Mallender* [2001] S.T.C. 514; also *Hardcastle v. IRC* [2000] S.T.C. (S.C.D.) 532. The latter cases both concerned underwriting members of Lloyd's.

[77] *ibid.* s.114(1).

[78] *ibid.* s.3A(1A), as added by the Finance Act 2006, Sched. 20, Pt 3, para. 9(3). As noted *supra*, para. 36–02, such a transfer can now only be made in favour of an individual or a "disabled trust" within the meaning of the Inheritance Tax Act 1984, s.89 (as amended).

[79] *ibid.* s.113B(1), (3), as added by the Finance Act 1986, Sched. 19, para. 21. The replacement property must normally be acquired within 3 years after the disposal of the original property: *ibid.* s.113B(2)(a), (8), as amended by the Finance Act 1994, s.247(1).

[80] *ibid.* ss.113A(1), (3), 113B(3), as added by the Finance Act 1986, Sched. 19, para. 21 and, in the case of s.113A(3), amended by the Finance Act 1987, Sched. 8, para. 8(1). Similarly, in the case of a chargeable transfer made within seven years of the transferor's death: *ibid.* s.113A(2). If the transferee predeceases the transferor, the conditions must be satisfied on *his* death: *ibid.* ss.113A(4), 113B(4). And note also, as to the potential application of the pre-owned assets regime, *supra*, para. 36–12, n. 61.

[81] *ibid.* s.113A(7A), as added by the Finance Act 1996, s.184(4).

[82] *Per contra* in the case of a partner who has *already* retired when the disposition takes place, subject to the terms of the partnership agreement: *Beckman v. IRC* [2000] S.T.C. (S.C.D.) 59.

[83] See the Inland Revenue Statement of Practice (SP12/80) dated October 13, 1980 and entitled "Business Relief from Capital Transfer Tax: 'Buy and Sell Agreements'", reproduced *infra*, para. A6–27.

[84] Inheritance Tax Act 1984, s.113.

[85] See, as to such provisions *infra*, para. 36–25.

[86] See further *infra*, paras 36–24, 36–42.

Although it appears that HMRC do, in general, accept this,[87] their attitude will inevitably depend on the construction of the particular accruer provision adopted.[88]

Other exemptions and reliefs

There are a number of other miscellaneous exemptions and reliefs which do not appear to be of any special interest in relation to partnerships and will thus not be further referred to.[89] **36–17**

3.   CHARGEABLE TRANSFERS

In considering the impact of inheritance tax on partnerships, it is necessary to identify the possible tax charges which may result at each of the following stages in the life of a firm: **36–18**

A. formation

B. continuation

C. the retirement of a partner

D. the death of a partner

E. dissolution.

A.   FORMATION OF A PARTNERSHIP

Where, as will usually be the case, the intending partners are not already connected persons,[90] the formation of a partnership will not attract an actual or **36–19**

---

[87] See (1981) 78 L.S. Gaz. 480. In 1996 the (then) Inland Revenue confirmed that this article can still be relied on: see (1996) 93 L.S. Gaz., September 4, p. 35.

[88] See the exchange of correspondence reproduced at [1984] S.T.I. 651 *et seq.*; also *McCutcheon on Inheritance Tax* (3rd. ed.), paras 14–31 *et seq.* and an article at (1992) 89 L.S. Gaz., November 4, p. 30. Even if the accruer provision *were* capable of amounting to a contract for the sale of the deceased partner's share, it might in theory be possible to argue that the contract does not become binding until the partner has actually died *i.e.* after the deemed disposal under the Inheritance Act 1984, s.4(1); however, such an argument will be resisted by HMRC, who will refer to the provisions of *ibid.* s.3(4): see [1984] S.T.I. 653, 654. And see also *infra*, para. 36–48. *Semble*, a similar point does not arise in relation to *ibid.* s.124, since relief is only denied by that section where there is a binding contract for the sale of the agricultural property itself.

[89] It should, however, be noted that woodlands relief under the Inheritance Tax Act 1984, s.125 (as amended by the Finance Act 2009, s.122(5), (6)) would appear not to be available in respect of a deceased partner's share, since he is never "beneficially entitled" to any asset owned by the firm: *ibid.* s.125(1)(b). For a discussion of this problem, see Lawton, Goldberg and Fraser, *The Law of Partnership Taxation* (2nd ed.), paras 15.024–15.026. But note also, in this context, *Gray v. IRC* [1994] S.T.C. 360, 377 (CA); also *Walton v. IRC* [1996] S.T.C. 68 (CA).

[90] An incoming partner will not normally be connected with the members of an existing firm: see *infra*, para. 36–38, n. 194.

potential tax charge unless, exceptionally, one of those partners intends to confer a gratuitous benefit on another.[91] It follows that there will, in such circumstances, be no scope for any partner later being treated as having made a gift with a reservation.[92] On the other hand, where one or more of the partners *are* already connected,[93] a disposition of assets as between them will only be ignored for tax purposes if the partnership agreement as a whole could properly be regarded as an arm's length transaction in the absence of that connection.[94] This test will be easier to satisfy if at least one of the partners has no existing connection with the others, since it will then be possible to demonstrate that the same terms have been offered to connected and non-connected partners alike.

Particular attention must be paid to the following aspects on the formation of a partnership.

Capital and capital profits

36–20   A partner who contributes capital on his entry into a partnership will only be treated as having made a transfer of value if, under the terms of the agreement, he is effectively deprived of the whole or part of that contribution and does not receive a corresponding benefit of sufficient value to satisfy the normal arm's length test.[95] A simple example of such a case would be where the agreement requires partners to contribute capital unequally but provides that it is to be *owned* by them in equal shares.[96] Such an arrangement might, perhaps, be justified commercially by adjusting the capital and/or income profit sharing ratios in favour of the partners who thereby give up part of their contributions. How far it would be possible to rely on a *non-monetary* benefit, such as a covenant on the part of the other partners to devote their whole time to the partnership business, will depend on the particular circumstances, but there would seem to be no reason in principle why a suitable analogy should not be drawn with the estate duty decisions in *Att.-Gen. v. Boden*[97] and *Att.-Gen. v. Ralli*[98] noticed above.[99]

---

[91] Inheritance Tax Act 1984, s.10(1)(a).

[92] There can by definition be no "gift" for the purposes of the Finance Tax Act 1986, ss.102, 102A, 102B and Sched. 20 if there is no donative intent. Note, however, that the word "gift" is not defined.

[93] Inheritance Tax Act 1984, s.270 (as amended by the Taxation of Chargeable Gains Act 1992, Sched. 10, para. 8(12)), applying and extending the Taxation of Chargeable Gains Act 1992, s.286 (as itself amended by the Finance Act 1995, Sched. 17, para. 31, the Finance Act 2006, Sched. 12, Pt 3, paras 25, 43, Sched. 26, Pt 3(15) and the Tax and Civil Partnership Regulations 2005, reg. 121); see also *supra*, para. 35–10.

[94] See the Inheritance Tax Act 1984, s.10(1)(b). See further *supra*, paras 36–02 *et seq.*

[95] See *supra*, paras 36–02 *et seq.*

[96] This may be the result if the partners have not agreed any capital sharing ratios: see the Partnership Act 1890, s.24(1), considered *supra*, paras 17–07, 17–08. It could, of course, be argued that, even though each partner's contribution is fully recognised and preserved under the agreement, his estate is nevertheless reduced because his right to call for the return of his capital is effectively deferred until his death or retirement or the ultimate dissolution of the firm; however, the current editor considers that any such reduction would clearly fall within the Inheritance Tax Act 1984, s.10(1), *supra*, para. 36–02.

[97] [1912] 1 K.B. 539.

[98] (1936) 15 A.T.C. 523.

[99] See *supra*, paras 36–03 *et seq.* Both were cases where the share of a deceased or retiring partner accrued to the continuing partners; see also the Irish decision of *Re Clark* (1906) 40 I.L.T. 177, considered *infra*, para. 36–24, n. 120.

Any transfer of value which does arise in this way will, of course, be treated as potentially exempt if the recipient is an individual or a disabled trust.[100] As a result, no tax will normally be payable unless the transferor dies within seven-years.[101] It should, however, be noted that it is HMRC practice to apply the annual exemption[102] so as to frank part of what would otherwise qualify as a potentially exempt transfer,[103] which may result in an effective loss of that exemption if the transferor survives for the full seven-year period. Where it is *not* possible to follow the "potentially exempt transfer" route, gradual transfers of capital utilising the annual and normal expenditure out of income exemptions[104] may still be advantageous.[105]

Where an intending partner wishes from the outset to make gifts of capital (and **36–21** in particular where his life expectancy is in doubt), he should almost as a matter of course ensure that, under the terms of the partnership agreement, he is excluded from any share in future *capital* profits; such a provision will not in itself involve a transfer of value, since there will be no present reduction in the value of his estate, other than a loss of the prospect of future profit.[106]

The current editor submits that HMRC could not, in any of the above instances, successfully argue that the transferee of the share of capital (or capital profits) has not bona fide assumed possession and enjoyment thereof or, for that matter, that he does not enjoy the share to the entire exclusion of the transferor.[107] On that footing, the share will not be deemed to form part of the transferor's estate in the event of his death.[108]

---

[100] Inheritance Tax Act 1984, s.3A(1A)(c)(i), (ii), as added by the Finance Act 2006, Sched. 20 Pt 3, para. 9(3). A transfer to an individual will include a transfer to a limited class of interest in possession trusts in his favour, under which the trust property will be treated as comprised in his estate: *ibid.* ss.3A(2) (as added by *ibid.* and amended by Finance (No. 2) Act 1987, s.96(2)(a), (b), Sched. 9, Pt III and the Finance Act 2006, Sched. 20, Pt 3, para. 9(4)), 49(1A) (as added by the Finance Act 2006, Sched. 20, Pt 2, para. 4(1) and amended by the Finance Act 2010, s.53(4)(a)). As to the meaning of "disabled trust", see *ibid.* s.89, as amended.

[101] *ibid.* s.3A(4), as added by the Finance Act 1986, Sched. 19, para. 1.

[102] *ibid.* s.19. See *supra*, para. 36–07.

[103] It is by no means clear whether this practice has any legislative authority: *cf. ibid.* ss.3A(1)(b) and 19(3A), as respectively added by the Finance Act 1986, Sched. 19, paras 1 and 5. See further *supra*, para. 36–07 and Foster, *Inheritance Tax*, para. C3.22.

[104] *ibid.* ss.19–21. See *supra*, paras 36–07, 36–08.

[105] In such a case, business or agricultural property relief (as to which see *supra*, paras 36–10 *et seq.*) may also be available and can be deducted *before* applying the annual exemptions.

[106] But see, as to the possible capital gains tax consequences of such a provision, *supra*, para. 35–05, 35–06, n. 24. *cf.* the position where there is an *existing* fund of capital profits: see *infra*, para. 36–39.

[107] Finance Act 1986, s.102(1). And see *Re Nichol* [1931] N.Z.L.R. 718; *Baron-Hay v. Commissioner of Probate Duties* [1968] W.A.L.R. 81. *Quaere* whether, in the case of capital profits, it might be argued that it is possible to "look through" to the underlying assets producing those profits: see, for example, *Burdett-Coutts v. IRC* [1960] 1 W.L.R. 1027 (an estate duty case). Just such an approach appears to have been endorsed by the Court of Appeal in *Gray v. IRC* [1994] S.T.C. 360, 377 in relation to the valuation of property on death; similarly in *Walton v. IRC* [1996] S.T.C. 68 (CA). If the argument were sustained, there would be a clear gift with a reservation: see *Chick v. Commissioner of Stamp Duties* [1958] A.C. 435. *cf. Ingram v. IRC* [2000] 1 A.C. 293 (HL) and *Munro v. Commissioner of Stamp Duties* [1934] A.C. 61 (PC), noted *infra*, para. 36–33. It would also follow that, at least in relation to land or a chattel, there would be no scope for a charge to income tax under the pre-owned assets regime noted *supra*, paras 34–29, 34–30. But note that the future profits have never formed part of the transferor's estate. See also an article at (1992) 89 L.S. Gaz., May 6, p. 27.

[108] Finance Act 1986, s.102(3).

Goodwill[109]

36–22 Given that goodwill may ultimately prove to be one of the firm's most valuable assets, care must be taken to ensure that its value is not further inflated for tax purposes by the imposition of an *unnecessary* restriction on competition by outgoing partners.[110] This may be of particular importance if it is not proposed to provide that goodwill will accrue (or be treated as valueless)[111] on the death of a partner, so that the full value of a deceased partner's share therein will form part of his estate.[112] *Per contra*, if such a provision is to be included; indeed the restriction may, in such a case, form an integral part of an arm's length transaction between the intending partners.[113] An unwanted restriction can, of course, subsequently be released or varied by agreement between the partners.

Accruers and options

36–23 A properly drawn partnership agreement will in general entitle the continuing partners to acquire an outgoing partner's share by means of an automatic accruer or the exercise of an option.[114] The inclusion of either type of provision may in certain circumstances give rise to an immediate transfer of value which will, however, normally be potentially exempt.

Accruer clauses

36–24 Where (exceptionally) the partnership agreement provides for the accruer of an outgoing partner's share without payment,[115] there would at first sight appear to be an immediate reduction in the estate of each partner who contributes capital, since he will effectively exchange his absolute entitlement to such capital for a partnership share which will automatically cease to have any value when he dies or leaves the firm.[116] However, so long as the provision is of general application, such reduction should be offset by the prospect of benefiting from the accruer of the other partners' shares, at least where all the partners contribute capital and enjoy broadly similar life expectancies.[117] On this footing, there would be no transfer of value, even if the agreement as a whole does not satisfy the arm's length test under section 10(1) of the Inheritance Tax Act 1984. If, on the other

---

[109] See generally, as to goodwill *supra*, paras 10–193 *et seq.*

[110] See *infra*, para. 36–58. And see generally, as to such restrictions, *supra*, paras 10–218 *et seq.*

[111] Provisions of the latter type are now common, particularly in the professions, but may, ultimately, have the same effect as an accruer.

[112] See further *infra*, para. 36–46.

[113] As in *Att.-Gen. v. Boden* [1912] 1 K.B. 539. However, it is at least arguable that the accruer provision should be left out of account in valuing the share of the deceased partner: see *infra*, para. 36–48.

[114] See, generally, as to such provisions, *supra*, paras 10–150 *et seq.*

[115] This assumes that the outgoing partner will not even be entitled to the return of his capital contribution, which would be very rare.

[116] Where it is provided that a nominal sum will be paid to the outgoing partner (or his estate) on the accruer, it would seem that, when the share accrues, its value must equal that nominal sum. Although the current editor does not consider that the accruer provision will constitute an exclusion or restriction of the partner's right to dispose of his share for the purposes of the Inheritance Tax Act 1984, s.163(1), the contrary view is tenable: see *infra*, para. 36–48. *Quaere*, could the existence of such a provision affect the availability of business relief on the death of a partner? See further *supra*, para. 36–16.

[117] Any shortfall might itself be justified under *ibid.* s.10(1).

hand, one of the partners is much older than the others or, by reason of ill health, has a shorter life expectancy, the existence of the accruer must reduce the value of his estate; similarly, perhaps, where all the partners are of a comparable age but some of them do *not* contribute capital. To avoid a transfer of value in such a case, it would be necessary to justify the accruer as an integral part of an arm's length transaction, by demonstrating that sufficient (but not necessarily monetary) consideration has been provided by the other partners.[118]

Where the agreement provides for a substantive payment to be made on the accruer, there will only be scope for an immediate transfer of value (albeit potentially exempt) if that payment does not equate to the amount of the relevant partner's capital contribution or, in the case of a pre-existing partnership, the then value of his share.[119] Any shortfall must be justified on an arm's length basis in the manner described above.

The current editor submits that precisely the same reasoning applies where the entirety of a partner's share, and not merely his share of goodwill, is expressed to accrue to the continuing partners.[120]

Option clauses

If the agreement gives the continuing partners an option to acquire an outgoing partner's share at full market value, there will prima facie be no decrease in the value of any partner's estate[121] nor any immediate transfer of value. Where, however, the option price represents anything less than the amount of a given partner's capital contribution (or, in the case of an existing firm, the market value of his share as at the date of the agreement),[122] there would appear to be an immediate reduction in the value of his estate and he will be treated as having made a potentially exempt or other transfer of value unless that reduction is fully compensated by the prospect of exercising similar options in respect of the other partners' shares or the agreement as a whole can be justified on the usual arm's

36–25

---

[118] See *Att.-Gen. v. Boden* [1912] 1 K.B. 539; *Att.-Gen. v. Ralli* (1936) 15 A.T.C. 523, noted *supra*, paras 36–03 *et seq.*

[119] Taking into account the terms of any existing agreement. Note that it is conventionally provided that an outgoing partner will be repaid his capital and current accounts, even though the partnership assets may not be revalued for the purpose; see further *supra*, paras 10–157 *et seq.*

[120] It should, however, be noted that attempts have been made to confine the decisions in *Att.-Gen. v. Boden* [1912] 1 K.B. 539 and *Att.-Gen. v. Ralli* (1936) 15 A.T.C. 523 solely to the accruer of goodwill. The Irish case of *Re Clark* (1906) 40 I.L.T. 117 is usually cited in support of such an argument. This case did in fact turn upon the application of the Finance Act 1894, s.3 and involved facts remarkably similar to those in *Att.-Gen. v. Boden* save that, on the death of the father, not only did his share in the goodwill of the partnership business pass to his two sons without payment, but also his share in its capital, stock-in-trade and other assets. The Irish Court (consisting of Palles L.C.B., Johnson and Keeny JJ.) held that there was no sufficient consideration provided by the sons to support the contention that they had given full consideration in money or money's worth for the father's share. It is, however, submitted that the findings of the court were unsatisfactory: in the course of his judgment (with which the other two judges merely concurred), Palles L.C.B. referred to the obligation of the sons to give their full time and attention to the partnership business (the father not being so bound) and observed that, while this might constitute consideration for the purposes of a contract, he did "not look upon that as coming within the intention of these Acts": see *ibid.* p. 120. The detailed and carefully reasoned judgment of Hamilton J. in *Att.-Gen. v. Boden* would appear to be more convincing: see *supra*, para. 36–03.

[121] Such modest reduction in value as there may be should be capable of being justified under the Inheritance Tax Act 1984, s.10(1). Otherwise it might be franked by one of the available exemptions: see further *supra*, paras 36–06 *et seq.* As to the application of the annual exemption to a transfer which would otherwise qualify as potentially exempt, see *supra*, paras 36–07, 36–20.

[122] Unless his entitlement thereto is already restricted under an existing agreement.

length basis.[123] The position is, in this respect, broadly comparable with that discussed above in relation to accruers.[124]

The existence of such an option will normally be reflected in any subsequent valuation of a partner's share for inheritance tax purposes.[125]

Annuities

36–26   Where the partnership agreement provides for the payment of annuities to outgoing partners or their widows, surviving civil partners or dependants, it is necessary to determine whether the inclusion of such provision, or the payment of an annuity pursuant thereto, will constitute a transfer of value, albeit potentially exempt. The relevant considerations in the case of annuities payable to outgoing partners are in fact very different to those applicable to annuities payable to widows/surviving civil partners or dependants.

Annuities payable to outgoing partners

36–27   If the annuity is payable under the terms of the partnership agreement and that agreement was itself a commercial transaction, neither the incorporation of the annuity provision nor the subsequent payment of the annuity will involve a potentially exempt transfer, since the requirements of section 10(1) of the Inheritance Tax Act 1984 will be satisfied.[126] This was confirmed by the Capital Taxes Office under the capital transfer tax regime and the same principles naturally apply to inheritance tax.[127] It follows that each partner will be free to dispose of his annuity as he sees fit, *e.g.* by assigning it to his spouse or civil partner,[128] without imposing the risk of liability on his co-partners.

Annuities payable to widows, surviving civil partners or dependants

36–28   The potential tax consequences of including provision in the partnership agreement for the payment of annuities to the widows, surviving civil partners or dependants of outgoing partners vary according to whether: (a) the annuity will be enforceable by the recipient(s) or by the deceased partner's personal representatives[129] and (b) consideration in money or money's worth[130] was given therefor.

---

[123] The amount of any potentially exempt transfer will be reduced by any available exemptions: see the preceding footnote.

[124] Thus, the principle underlying *Att.-Gen. v. Boden* [1912] 1 K.B. 539 and *Att.-Gen. v. Ralli* (1936) 15 A.T.C. 523 will apply; but note, however, the decision in *Re Clark* (1906) 40 I.L.T. 117, considered *supra*, para. 36–24, n. 120.

[125] The current editor suggests that, in valuing a partnership share which is subject to an accruer, all that falls to be valued is the bundle of rights which comprise that share: see *infra*, paras 36–42, 36–48. On the other hand, in valuing a share which is subject to an option, the provisions of the Inheritance Tax Act 1984, s.163(1) will need to be taken into account: see *infra*, paras 36–43, 36–49. Note, however, that HMRC appear to take the view that s.163(1) applies to both options *and* accruers.

[126] See generally *supra*, paras 36–02 *et seq.*

[127] See the letter published at (1975) 72 L.S.Gaz. 699.

[128] And thus taking advantage of the exemption under the Inheritance Tax Act 1984, s.18(1), as amended by the Tax and Civil Partnership Regulations 2005, reg. 7(2); see *supra*, para. 36–06.

[129] See generally, as to the enforceability of annuities, the Contracts (Rights of Third Parties) Act 1999; also *Re Miller's Agreement* [1947] Ch. 615; *Beswick v. Beswick* [1968] A.C. 58; and see *supra*, paras 10–187 *et seq.*

[130] For the purposes of the Inheritance Tax Act 1984, s.5(5).

If the annuity is enforceable and each partner receives full consideration for the inclusion of the provision in the agreement, no transfer of value will be involved when the agreement is entered into[131] or when the annuity is paid.[132] On the other hand, if the annuity is unenforceable[133] or there is a total absence of consideration, the agreement itself will not involve any adverse tax consequences,[134] but each partner will inevitably make a potentially exempt transfer as and when any annuity payment is made, unless that transfer is wholly or partially franked by one of the available exemptions.[135] Less straightforward is the case of the enforceable annuity provision in respect of which each partner has received only *partial* consideration.[136] As in the previous case, no partner will be regarded as having made a potentially exempt transfer on entering into the agreement,[137] but it is certainly arguable that, if no other exemptions are available,[138] there will be such a transfer when the annuity is paid, at least to the extent that consideration was not given at the time of the original agreement. Whilst it should be possible to defeat such an argument by contending that the agreement as a whole constituted an arm's length bargain between the partners for the purposes of section 10(1) of the Inheritance Tax Act 1984, that contention is not without difficulty.[139]

Where it is intended to provide annuities for outgoing partners and their widows, surviving civil partners and/or dependants, it will generally be desirable to have separate annuities payable to each potential recipient, so as to ensure that

[131] It is submitted that, in such a case, there will be no reduction in the value of any partner's estate. Although the existence of the prospective liability to pay the annuity will be taken into account in valuing each such estate, provided that the consideration is in money or money's worth (see *ibid.* s.5(5)) the reduction in value attributable thereto should be balanced by such consideration.

[132] Since the annuity will be paid pursuant to an enforceable obligation incurred for full consideration.

[133] It is generally undesirable to permit a partner's widow, etc., to enforce an annuity provision directly, since this will greatly restrict the continuing partners' freedom of action and may necessitate such person(s) being made parties to any subsequent variation of the partnership agreement. However, a wholly unenforceable annuity will be fairly rare in practice; it is more likely to be encountered when an annuity provision is introduced on an ad hoc basis after a partner has retired or died. Note also the income tax position, considered *supra*, paras 34–66, 34–67.

[134] If the annuity is unenforceable, then obviously there will be no liability and thus no reduction in the value of any partner's estate. If, on the other hand, no consideration is received for the inclusion of the annuity provision, then under the Inheritance Tax Act 1984, s.5(5), the existence of the liability will not be taken into account in valuing any such estate.

[135] *e.g.* the annual and normal expenditure out of income exemptions: *ibid.* ss.19 *et seq.* See further *supra*, paras 36–07, 36–08. As to the application of the annual exemption to transfers which would otherwise be potentially exempt, see *supra*, paras 36–07, 36–20.

[136] This will be the most common case, since part of the consideration received for the inclusion of the annuity provision will usually consist of the value of the right to the annuity which will become comprised in the estate of each partner's spouse, civil partner or dependants. *Quaere*: can such consideration received by a third party be taken into account under *ibid.* s.5(5)? It is thought not.

[137] Under *ibid.* s.5(5) a liability may only be taken into account "to the extent that it was incurred for a consideration in money or money's worth". To that extent only, there should be no effective reduction in the value of any partner's estate: see *supra*, n. 131. The balance of the liability, in respect of which no consideration is received, will be discounted.

[138] See *supra*, n. 135.

[139] There is no doubt that HMRC are prepared to accept that a partnership agreement as a whole does constitute a commercial transaction: see the letter printed at (1975) 72 L.S.Gaz. 699. However, an agreement to pay an annuity to a third party must necessarily involve an element of gratuity. In those circumstances, it might in theory be difficult to show that the inclusion of the annuity provision "was not intended, and was not made in a transaction intended, to confer any gratuitous benefit on any person": see the Inheritance Tax Act 1984, s.10(1) and, *supra*, para. 36–02. It is thought that HMRC may well in practice not take this point.

the value of such a person's annuity does not form part of the outgoing partner's estate in the event of his death.[140] It is also undesirable, in cases where no consideration is to be given for the annuity provision, for the annuity to be charged on any of the partnership assets, since otherwise the settlement provisions contained in the Inheritance Tax Act 1984 will apply.[141]

Partnership assurance schemes

36–29   Where the partnership agreement establishes an assurance scheme, with life assurance policies being effected by each partner on terms that the policy moneys will be held on trust for the other partners, then the payment of each premium will constitute a chargeable transfer,[142] unless the scheme as a whole can be justified as forming part of an arm's length commercial transaction between the partners.[143] Furthermore, the trusts of the policy moneys would prima facie constitute settlements for tax purposes, thus attracting the application of either the "interest in possession" trust or the discretionary trust regimes established under the Inheritance Tax Act 1984, according to the nature of those trusts.[144] It is doubtful whether the general principle that a bona fide commercial transaction does not constitute a settlement can be invoked in this context,[145] but HMRC is prepared by "concession" not to treat the trusts of such policy moneys as settlements provided that the policies were effected prior to September 15, 1976 and the trusts have not been varied since that date.[146] Whether a taxpayer will, by invoking the above principle, be able to establish that, as a matter of law, the same treatment can be accorded to trusts of policies *irrespective* of the date on which they were effected remains to be seen. It should also be noted that HMRC have confirmed that such a scheme will not, in general, fall within the pre-owned assets regime for income tax purposes, provided that a partner is not a beneficiary of his own policy.[147]

---

[140] Where a partner (or former partner) dies, the right to the annuity must be valued immediately prior to his death, and the value of a continuing annuity will clearly be higher than an annuity ceasing on death. Where, of course, the annuity is payable in favour of the deceased partner's widow or surviving civil partner, the exemption under the Inheritance Tax Act 1988, s.18 will apply.

[141] *ibid.* s.43(2)(c).

[142] The transfer would only qualify as potentially exempt if it is made in favour of an individual (or a limited class of interest in possession trusts in his favour) or a disabled trust: *ibid.* s.3A(1A)(c), (2) (as respectively added by the Finance Act 2006, Sched. 20, Pt 3, para. 9 and the Finance Act 1986, Sched. 19, para. 1 and, in the case of subs.(2), amended by the Finance (No. 2) Act 1987, s.96(2)(a), (b), Sched. 9, Pt III and the Finance Act 2006, Sched. 20, Pt 3, para. 9(4)), 49(1A) (as added by the Finance Act 2006, Sched. 20, Pt 2, para. 4(1) and amended by the Finance Act 2010, s.53(4)(a)).

[143] *i.e.* within *ibid.* s.10(1). Where that subsection does not apply, it may be possible to show that one of the available exemptions applies: see *supra*, paras 36–06 *et seq.*

[144] See *ibid.* Pt III, Chaps. II and III, as amended. Note that the previously favourable interest in possession trust regime is now of strictly limited scope, following the amendments introduced by the Finance Act 2006, s.156, Sched. 20.

[145] See, for example, the approach adopted in *Re A.E.G. Unit Trust* [1957] Ch. 415; also *Bulmer v. IRC* [1967] Ch. 145; *IRC v. Plummer* [1980] A.C. 896 (HL); *IRC v. Levy* [1982] S.T.C. 442; *cf. IRC v. Moodie* [1993] 1 W.L.R. 266 (HL). Note, however, that the view is expressed in Foster, *Inheritance Tax*, para. E1.11, n. 5 that the principles established in the income tax cases do not apply to inheritance tax.

[146] See Extra-Statutory Concession F10.

[147] See the Inland Revenue Press Release "Pre-owned assets guidance amended" dated April 1, 2005, reproduced at [2005] S.T.I. 724. As to the pre-owned assets regime, see generally, *supra*, paras 34–29, 34–30.

Other types of partnership assurance and pension schemes[148] do not appear to give rise to any particular issues peculiar to partnerships and thus do not merit further consideration here.[149]

Property of a partner used by the firm

There is no specific provision governing the treatment of free loans of money **36–30** or other property by one partner in favour of his co-partners and such loans accordingly fall to be taxed on normal principles.[150] Thus, where an intending partner owns property which is to be used or occupied by the firm, but which is not to form part of its assets, he will make a potentially exempt transfer (or, where appropriate, a chargeable transfer) to the extent that the value of the consideration received falls short of the diminution in the value of his estate which results from permitting such use, unless he can show that the arrangement forms part of an arm's length transaction,[151] or that one of the available exemptions applies.[152] However, so long as he ensures that he has power to terminate the arrangement at any time, there should be no significant diminution in his estate; *per contra*, perhaps, if he expressly or impliedly binds himself to permit the firm or his co-partners to enjoy continued use or occupation for a fixed period.[153] In the latter case, any transfer of value may well involve a gift with a reservation[154]; if so, the entire value of the property may in any event continue to form part of his estate.

Where premises used by the firm are owned by *all* the partners in their personal capacities, either as joint tenants or as tenants in common, a transfer of value may be involved if one or more of the co-owners would be entitled to claim compensation from the other co-owners who are in occupation of the jointly owned premises[155] but chooses not to. The position will, if anything, be *a fortiori* if one or more of the co-owners leaves the firm but retains his interest in the premises or in the event of a partner's (or ex-partner's) death or the admission of

---

[148] *e.g.* under the Finance Act 2004, Pt 4.

[149] See generally, Foster, *Inheritance Tax*, paras E6.36, E6.37.

[150] Early in the capital transfer tax regime, such loans were governed by the detailed provisions of the Finance Act 1976, ss.115, 116, but both sections were later repealed. However, by *ibid.* s.115(7), it was provided that such provisions should not apply to loans by a partner (including a recently retired partner) or his spouse to the firm.

[151] *i.e.* within the Inheritance Tax Act 1984, s.10(1).

[152] See generally *supra*, paras 36–06 *et seq.*

[153] As to the ways in which a firm can be permitted to use or occupy property owned by one of the partners, see *supra*, paras 10–45, 18–34. It should be noted that the grant of a tenancy of agricultural property at a rack rent will not be treated as a transfer of value: Inheritance Tax Act 1984, s.16.

[154] Finance Act 1986, ss.102 (as amended), 102A, 102B (as added by the Finance Act 1996, s.104 and, in the case of s.102A, amended by the Tax and Civil Partnership Regulations 2005, reg. 45), Sched. 20 (as amended). Note also *ibid.* Sched. 20, para. 6 (as amended by the Tax and Civil Partnership Regulations 2005, reg. 46) and the exchange of correspondence reproduced at (1988) 85 L.S.Gaz., June 1, pp. 49 *et seq. ibid.* para. 6(1)(b) also applies in the case of a potential reservation of benefit under *ibid.* s.102A or 102B: *ibid.* s.102C(3), as added by the Finance Act 1996, s.104. And see also *infra*, paras 36–31 *et seq.*

[155] See the Trusts of Land and Appointment of Trustees Act 1996, s.13(6) and, in cases not covered by that Act, *French v. Barcham* [2009] 1 W.L.R. 1124, where the earlier authorities on the right to an occupation rent are reviewed; also *Amin v. Amin* [2009] EWHC 3356 (Ch) (Lawtel 5/1/10). The position will, of course, be otherwise, where no compensation or occupation rent is properly payable. See also *supra*, para. 5–08, n. 49.

a new partner who does not immediately acquire some interest in the premises.[156] Different principles apply in the case of personalty.[157]

Reservation of benefit

36–31   Where property is to be used or occupied by the firm pursuant to an arrange-ment of the type discussed above and that property or an interest therein has been acquired by one partner from another by way of gift[158] at any time within the previous seven years, questions of reservation of benefit will inevitably arise. The relevant considerations will depend on whether the property in question is an interest in land, an *undivided share* of an interest in land or some other asset.

Interest in land

36–32   In this case, a two-stage process is involved. First it must be determined whether the arrangement falls within section 102 of the Finance Act 1986; if it does not, then the arrangement may still be caught by section 102A.[159] If no reservation of benefit arises in such a case, the transferor partner *may* be subject to an income tax charge under the pre-owned assets regime,[160] unless he actively opts in to the reservation of benefit regime.[161]

36–33   *Section 102.* Under this section, there will be a reservation of benefit unless it can be shown that the donee partner bona fide assumed possession and enjoyment of the interest[162] immediately after the gift and that, throughout the relevant

[156] Leaving aside the position between the continuing and outgoing partners, as soon as a third party is let into occupation, a free loan will potentially be made in his favour, which could result in a tax charge. Whilst the continuing partners could doubtless rely on the Inheritance Tax Act 1984, s.10(1) to negate even a potentially exempt transfer, that option will not generally be available to an outgoing partner. It would accordingly seem desirable in such circumstances for some form of payment to be made to the outgoing partner, either by the incoming partner or by the firm. Neither course is, however, likely to be entirely satisfactory: if the incoming partner makes the payment, it may well not be a deductible expense; on the other hand, if the payment is made by the firm, each of the co-owning partners will strictly make a potentially exempt transfer in favour of the outgoing partner if he would *not* be entitled to compensation or an occupation rent from them, albeit that this may be franked by their annual exemptions: see *supra*, para. 36–07. *Quaere* whether HMRC would seek to take such a point given the amounts likely to be involved.

[157] The principles explored on *French v. Barcham, supra*, do not apply to personalty. It may thus be necessary for the firm to make a payment to the outgoing partner, so as to avoid a charge to tax being imposed upon him. The problems discussed in the preceding footnote would not appear to arise. As between themselves and the incoming partner, the continuing partners should be able to rely on the Inheritance Tax Act 1984, s.10(1).

[158] Finance Act 1986, ss.102(1), 102A(1), 102B(1) (the latter two subsections having been added by the Finance Act 1996, s.104). The word "gift" is not defined, but note that a gift may be treated as made where certain types of interest in possession come to an end during the holder's lifetime: *ibid.* s.102ZA, Sched. 20, para. 4A, as respectively added by the Finance Act 2006, Sched. 20, Pt 5, para. 33(2), (3) and, in the case of s.102ZA, amended by the Finance Act 2010, s.53(8). *ibid.* s.102 applies only where the original gift was made after March 18, 1986, whereas *ibid.* ss.102A and 102B apply where the gift was made after March 9, 1999.

[159] As added by the Finance Act 1999, s.104. If the Finance Act 1986, s.102 applies, *ibid.* s.102A will not apply: *ibid.* s.102C(7), as added by the Finance Act 1999, s.104.

[160] See the Finance Act 2004, Sched. 15.

[161] *i.e.* under *ibid.* Sched. 15, para. 21. See further *supra*, para. 34–29.

[162] In *Ingram v. IRC* [2000] 1 A.C. 293, the House of Lords made it clear that, whilst *ibid.* s.102 refers to "the property", this means not the physical asset in question (*i.e.* the land), but a specific interest therein. Note, however, that if the interest is an *undivided share* in an interest in land and *ibid.* s.102B applies, ss.102 and 102A are excluded: *ibid.* s.102C(6), as added by the Finance Act 1999, s.104. See further *infra*, para. 36–35.

seven-year period, he enjoyed the interest to the entire exclusion of the donor partner or of any benefit to him by contract or otherwise[163] or that the donor partner's continuing rights of occupation are for full consideration in money or money's worth.[164]

If, on a true analysis, it can be shown that the donor partner merely gave away an interest in the land and his continuing rights of occupation, etc., are referable to the interest which he retained, section 102 will not apply. This was confirmed by the landmark decision of the House of Lords in *Ingram v. IRC*,[165] where the landowner was held to have disposed of land subject to a lease in her own favour.[166] This approach mirrored that previously adopted by the courts under the old estate duty regime, from which the present gift with a reservation concept was derived. The most pertinent of those decisions in the present context is *Munro v. Commissioner of Stamp Duties*,[167] where a father owned certain land from which he carried on business in partnership with his sons, the firm occupying the land as his tenant or licensee. He subsequently transferred the land to his sons by way of gift, subject to the firm's occupation rights, and the firm thereafter continued in occupation as before. The Privy Council held that there was no reservation of benefit but rather an absolute gift of a limited interest in the land, *i.e.* the freehold subject to the firm's subsisting rights of occupation. This decision was cited with apparent approval by Lord Hoffmann in *Ingram v. IRC*[168] and the principles underlying it and other estate duty cases have for some time been accepted by HMRC as applicable to inheritance tax.[169]

Section 102A.[170] The tax avoidance device adopted in *Ingram v. IRC*[171] was sought to be countered by this section, which treats there as having been a gift with a reservation where the donor partner continues to enjoy a "significant right or interest"[172] or is a party to a "significant arrangement"[173] in relation to the   **36–34**

---

[163] *ibid.* s.102(1)(a), (b); see also, generally, *I.R.C. v. Eversden* [2002] S.T.C. 1109, although the final part of the decision seemingly no longer applies in the face of the amendment to *ibid.* s.102 by the Finance Act 2003, s.185 (only the spouse exemption issue was pursued on the appeal at [2003] S.T.C. 822); *Personal Representatives of Lyon v. Revenue & Customs Commissioners* [2007] S.T.C. (S.C.D.) 675. And see further [1993] S.T.I. 1409 and an article at (1992) 89 L.S.Gaz., May 6, p. 27. Note the limited statutory exception set out in *ibid.* Sched. 20, para. 6(1)(b), as amended by the Tax and Civil Partnership Regulations 2005, reg. 46.

[164] *ibid.* Sched. 20, para. 6(1)(a). This provision mirrors the Finance Act 1959, s.35(2). See also the letter from the Inland Revenue reproduced in (1988) 85 L.S. Gaz., June 1, p. 50; and see [1993] S.T.I. 1410 and an article at (1992) 89 L.S. Gaz., May 6, p. 31. Equally, there will be no income tax charge under the pre-owned assets regime in such a case: see *supra*, para. 34–29.

[165] [2000] 1 A.C. 293.

[166] *cf.* the position in Scotland: *Kildrummy (Jersey) Ltd. v. IRC* [1990] S.T.C. 657. In *Ingram v. IRC, supra,* the notion that English and Scots law were the same in this respect was emphatically rejected: see [2000] 1 A.C. 305F *per* Lord Hoffmann.

[167] [1934] A.C. 61. *cf. Re Nichols* [1975] 1 W.L.R. 534, considered by the House of Lords in *Ingram v. IRC, supra*; also *Chick v. Commissioner of Stamp Duties* [1958] A.C. 435 (albeit that the same result could not be achieved under the Finance Act 1986, s.102). And see *Re Nichol* [1931] N.Z.L.R. 718; *Baron-Hay v. Commissioner of Probate Duties* [1968] W.A.L.R. 81.

[168] [2000] 1 A.C. 300D.

[169] See the letter reproduced in (1988) 85 L.S.Gaz., June 1, p. 50.

[170] This section was added by the Finance Act 1999, s.104 and amended by the Finance Act 1989, s.171(5), the Finance Act 1998, Sched. 27, Pt IV, the Finance Act 2003, s.185 and the Tax and Civil Partnership Regulations 2005, reg. 45.

[171] [2000] 1 A.C. 293 (HL): see *supra*, para. 36–33.

[172] As to when a right or interest is not regarded as significant, see the Finance Act 1986, s.102A(4), (5).

[173] As to when an arrangement is not regarded as significant, see *ibid.* s.102A(4).

land.[174] Where, however, full consideration in money or money's worth is given for a right of occupation, there will be *no* reservation of benefit.[175] It follows that the type of arrangement adopted in *Munro v. Commissioner of Stamp Duty*[176] will now only be effective if: (a) the lease or other occupation rights were granted more than seven years before the gift of the freehold,[177] (b) a market rent (or equivalent) is reserved or (c) full consideration is otherwise provided under the partnership agreement.[178]

Undivided share of an interest in land

36–35   Where the donor partner has merely disposed of an undivided share of an interest in land and continues to occupy the land in conjunction with the donee partner(s), section 102B of the Finance Act 1986[179] will treat this as being a reservation of benefit in his favour unless he does not receive anything other than a negligible benefit provided by or at the expense of the donee partner(s) for some reason connected with the gift.[180] It is submitted that where the donor partner merely continues to occupy the land in right of his interest as a tenant in common/joint tenant, there should, in general, be no reservation of benefit for this purpose.[181]

Assets other than land

36–36   In the case of such an asset, the position will be governed by section 102,[182] as analysed in *Ingram v. IRC*[183] and subject to the principles developed in the older estate duty authorities.[184] Accordingly, the carving out of a retained interest will still theoretically be possible. However, if, in the case of a chattel, there is *no* reservation of benefit, an income tax charge under the pre-owned assets

---

[174] *ibid.* s.102A(2), as amended by the Tax and Civil Partnership Regulation 2005, reg. 45. Note that the limited exception set out in *ibid.* Sched. 20, para. 6(1)(b) (as amended by *ibid.* reg. 46) also applies in this case: *ibid.* s.102C(3), as added by the Finance Act 1999, s.104.

[175] *ibid.* 102A(3). There will be no income tax charge under the pre-owned assets regime in this case: see *supra*, para. 34–29.

[176] [1934] A.C. 61 (PC), noted *supra*, para. 36–33.

[177] *ibid.* s.102A(5).

[178] *ibid.* s.102A(3).

[179] As added by the Finance Act 1999, s.104.

[180] Finance Act 1986, s.102B(4). Note that the limited exception set out in *ibid.* Sched. 20, para. 6(1)(b) (as amended by the Tax and Civil Partnership Regulations 2005, reg. 46) also applies in this case: *ibid.* s.102C(3), as added by the Finance Act 1999, s.104.

[181] There would seem to be a direct analogy with the estate duty case of *Oakes v. Commissioner of Stamp Duties of New South Wales* [1954] A.C. 57. There the owner of certain grazing land had executed a declaration of trust under which he held the land upon trust for himself and his four children as tenants in common in equal shares. The Privy Council held (*inter alia*) that the mere fact that he continued to be interested in the land *qua* tenant in common did not involve a reservation of benefit out of the beneficial interests in that land which he had given to his children. Note, however, that the position may be otherwise if the donor does not bear his due share of any outgoings attributable to the land. Note that there may, however, be an income tax charge under the pre-owned assets regime in this case: see *supra*, para. 34–29.

[182] However, the exception in *ibid.* Sched. 20, para. 6(1)(a) applies only where the asset is question is an interest in land or a chattel. Note also that *ibid.* s.102 applies in the case of any property substituted for an interest in land which was the original subject of the gift: *ibid.* s.102C(5) (as added by the Finance Act 1999, s.104), Sched. 20, para. 2.

[183] [2000] 1 A.C. 293 (HL): see *supra*, para. 36–33.

[184] See *supra*, paras 36–33, 36–35.

regime may arise[185]; similarly in the case of intangible property, but only if it is comprised in a settlement in which the settlor retains an interest.[186]

Termination of reserved benefit

Where there is a gift with a reservation and the reserved benefit subsequently terminates during the lifetime of the donor partner, *e.g.* on his retirement, there will be no tax consequences if he survives for more than 7 years.[187] Otherwise, he will be treated as having made a potentially exempt transfer at that stage.[188] If the benefit terminates by reason of his death, the property will be treated as forming part of his estate.[189] Where a charge is imposed, agricultural property or business relief should, in general, be available.[190]

36–37

B. CONTINUATION OF A PARTNERSHIP

When considering the tax position during the currency of a partnership, it is necessary to distinguish between a transfer of value made by all the partners in favour of a third party with whom they are not connected,[191] and a transfer of value made by one partner in favour of another.

36–38

Where a gratuitous transfer is effectively made by the firm (*i.e.* all the partners acting together), which reduces the value of each partner's share,[192] tax will be chargeable on normal principles, unless (as will usually be the case) each partner's transfer qualifies in the first instance as potentially exempt.[193] If an

---

[185] See *supra*, paras 34–29.

[186] See *supra*, para. 34–30.

[187] In such a case the Finance Act 1986, s.102(1) does not apply: see the definition of "relevant period" therein.

[188] *ibid.* s.102(4), as applied by *ibid.* ss.102A(2)(b), 102B(2)(b). And see [1993] S.T.I. 1410. This provision is mandatory and it does not seem to matter that the requirements of the Inheritance Tax Act s.3A(1A) are not satisfied (as to which see *supra*, para. 36–02). See further Foster, *Inheritance Tax*, para. C4.41

[189] Finance Act 1986, s.102(3), as applied by *ibid.*

[190] *ibid.* Sched. 20, para. 8 (as amended), as applied by *ibid.* s.102C(4) (as itself added by the Finance Act 1999, s.104).

[191] See, as to the meaning of "connected persons," the Inheritance Tax Act 1984, s.270 (as amended by the Taxation of Chargeable Gains Act 1992, Sched. 10, para. 8(12)) applying and extending the Taxation of Chargeable Gains Act 1992, s.286 (as itself amended by the Finance Act 1995, Sched. 17, para. 31, the Finance Act 2006, Sched. 12, Pt 3, paras 25, 43, Sched. 26, Pt 3(15) and the Tax and Civil Partnership Regulations 2005, reg. 121). See also *supra*, para. 36–02.

[192] On a true analysis, no partner has an immediate or ascertainable beneficial interest in any asset owned by the firm, but merely a right to a proportionate part of the surplus remaining after the realisation of all the partnership assets, and the payment of all the partnership debts and liabilities: see generally, *supra*, paras 19–01 *et seq.* Accordingly, when an asset owned by the firm is the subject of a gratuitous transfer, the value transferred by each partner will be the amount by which his share has been devalued, subject to the availability of agricultural property or business relief: see *supra*, paras 36–10 *et seq.* Note, however, that in *Gray v. IRC* [1994] S.T.C. 360, 377, the Court of Appeal held that partners must be treated as owning undivided shares in the partnership assets, at least for valuation purposes; and see *Walton v. IRC* [1996] S.T.C. 68 (CA).

[193] Inheritance Tax Act 1984, s.3A(1A), as added by the Finance Act 2006, Sched. 20, Pt 2, para. 9. And see as to the availability of agricultural property/business relief, *supra*, paras 36–12, 36–15.

incoming partner is not already connected with the existing partners,[194] the tax considerations on his admission to the firm will be broadly identical to those discussed in relation to the formation of a partnership.

On the other hand, when considering transfers between the partners, it must be borne in mind that they and their spouses, civil partners and relatives will be connected persons "except in relation to acquisitions or disposals of partnership assets pursuant to bona fide commercial arrangements".[195] Where, as will usually be the case,[196] the partners are treated as connected, if the requirements of section 10(1) of the Inheritance Tax Act 1984 are to be satisfied, it must be shown that the transfer was made without any gratuitous intent, and was "such as might be expected to be made in a transaction at arm's length between persons not connected with each other".[197]

36–39   The tax consequences of a rearrangement of the capital sharing ratios, and of the introduction into the partnership agreement of provision for the payment of annuities to outgoing partners and their widows, surviving civil partners or dependants have already been considered in relation to the formation of partnership, and reference should be made thereto.[198] However, one point which is frequently overlooked on the admission of a new partner to an existing firm is the ownership not of the firm's capital but of its capital *profits*. Such profits will in general be divisible in the ordinary profit sharing ratios,[199] so that an incoming partner who becomes entitled to a share of profits may at the same time automatically become entitled to a share of any existing unrealised capital profits. Therein lies the potential for a wholly inadvertent transfer of value (albeit normally potentially exempt): if the assets of the firm appear in its balance sheet at a historic, written down value, there may be a very substantial "hidden" fund of capital profits so that the acquisition of even a small share therein might result in a significant reduction in the value of the existing partners' shares.[200] To avoid

---

[194] This will generally be the position, unless he is related to one or more of the existing partners within the meaning of the Taxation of Chargeable Gains Act 1992, s.286(2) (as amended by the Tax and Civil Partnership Regulations 2005, reg. 121), (8), as extended by the Inheritance Tax Act 1984, s.270.

[195] Taxation of Chargeable Gains Act 1992, s.286(4), as amended by the Tax and Civil Partnership Regulations 2005, reg. 121. However, this exception will only apply where the partners themselves are *not* otherwise related.

[196] Since the transfers will rarely concern "partnership assets" (in which no partner has an immediate or ascertainable beneficial interest: see *supra*, para. 36–38, n. 192) but will rather concern partnership shares, which are by definition *not* partnership assets: see further Lawton, Goldberg and Fraser, *The Law of Partnership Taxation* (2nd. ed.), para. 14.074. *cf.* the capital gains tax position, where each partner is treated as having a direct interest in each partnership asset: see *supra*, paras 35–02, 35–06.

[197] Inheritance Tax Act 1984, s.10(1)(b). The test would appear to be an objective one and the burden of satisfying it is imposed on the taxpayer.

[198] See *supra*, paras 36–20 *et seq.*, 36–26 *et seq.*

[199] See *supra*, para. 17–04.

[200] Where the capital profit sharing ratios are *deliberately* varied without at the same time altering the income profit sharing ratios, it might be argued that a partner whose capital profit share is reduced has made a gift with a reservation for the purposes of the Finance Act 1986, s.102(1): see an article at (1992) 89 L.S. Gaz. 27. Such an argument presupposes a direct correlation between a partner's income and capital profit sharing entitlements in all cases which is, in the current editor's view, wholly unjustified. Nevertheless, there may be cases in which such a correlation does exist, *i.e.* where the majority of the profits are produced by the firm's capital assets without any expenditure of time or effort by the partners. *Quaere* whether there would be a gift with a reservation if the incoming partner were to take on liability for a share of the firm's existing debts as part of such an arrangement. The current editor believes that, in most cases, the Inheritance Tax Act 1984, s.10(1) would apply so as to negate any donative intent. Given the true nature of a partner's share in the assets of the firm

such a consequence, it will be necessary either to justify the partnership agreement as a whole as an arm's length transaction,[201] or to ensure that the existing partners reserve those capital profits to themselves.[202]

It has already been seen[203] that the inclusion in a partnership agreement of a provision for the automatic accruer of the share of an outgoing partner or an option in favour of the continuing partners to acquire such share may have possible tax implications. Similar considerations will arise where either type of provision is introduced by way of variation of an existing agreement: on the introduction of an automatic accruer, each partner will exchange the bundle of rights which comprise his share for a bundle of rights which will become valueless or assume a fixed value in the event of his departure from the firm,[204] whilst on the introduction of an option exercisable at anything less than market value, there will be an immediate reduction in the value of each partner's share.[205] In either case, a potentially exempt transfer (or, where appropriate, a chargeable transfer) will be made by each partner when the accruer or option is first introduced, unless it can be shown:

36–40

(a) that the reduction in the value of his estate is offset by corresponding benefits conferred on him as part of the variation, *e.g.* the prospect of benefiting from an accruer/option to acquire the other partners' shares or, perhaps, compensation in the form of a new annuity entitlement[206];

(b) that the variation can be brought within section 10(1) of the Inheritance Tax Act 1984[207]; or

(c) (where relevant) that one of the available exemptions applies.[208]

The effect of such a provision on a subsequent valuation of a partner's share is considered further below.[209]

(see *supra*, para. 36–38, n. 192), there should properly be no scope for a reservation of benefit under *ibid.* ss.102A, 102B (as added by the Finance Act 1999, s.104), even where the assets comprise land, but HMRC might well attempt to look through to the underlying assets, *i.e.* adopting the same approach as in *Gray v. IRC* [1994] S.T.C. 360, 377 (CA). Note also, in this context, the potential application of the pre-owned assets regime: see *supra*, paras 34–29, 34–30, 36–32, 36–36.

[201] And thus within *ibid.* s.10(1): see further *supra*, paras 36–02 *et seq.*

[202] This can be done in one of two ways: specific capital profit sharing ratios can be introduced with respect of certain assets or those assets can be revalued and the surplus on the revaluation credited to the capital/current accounts of the existing partners. However, the latter course may have adverse capital gains tax implications: see *supra*, para. 35–14. There is seemingly no objection to the incoming partner being given a share of *future* capital profits: see as to this, *supra*, para. 36–21.

[203] See *supra*, paras 36–23 *et seq.*

[204] Where a payment falls to be made in respect of the accruer, the bundle of rights comprised in the outgoing partner's share will seemingly assume the value of that payment. The current editor submits that the accruer provision will *not* constitute an exclusion or restriction of the partner's right to dispose of his share for the purposes of the Inheritance Tax Act 1984, s.163(1): see further *infra*, para. 36–48.

[205] See *supra*, para. 36–25.

[206] See *supra*, paras 36–24 *et seq.*

[207] See *supra*, para. 36–02.

[208] See *supra*, paras 36–06 *et seq.*

[209] See *infra*, paras 36–42, 36–43, 36–47 *et seq.*

C.   THE RETIREMENT OF A PARTNER

36–41   Where, as will often be the case, the agreement provides for the partnership to continue following a partner's retirement[210] and for his share to be acquired at market value by the continuing partners,[211] no tax considerations will arise, unless the outgoing partner forgoes some part of his accrued entitlement. Of course, if he chooses to make a gratuitous assignment of his share to the continuing partners, an actual or potential charge to tax will be imposed on normal principles.[212]

More complex is the situation where, under the terms of the agreement,[213] the continuing partners are entitled to acquire the outgoing partner's share, either by way of an automatic accruer or option, for a consideration which represents *less* than the market value of that share.[214]

Accruer clauses

36–42   The current editor submits that, on a true analysis, no tax consequences should arise in such a case, since the retirement is merely an occasion on which a decrease in the value of the outgoing partner's share and an increase in the value of the continuing partners' shares, which were at all times respectively inherent in those shares, take effect. Thus, whilst there is an admitted reduction in the value of the outgoing partner's estate on his retirement, he cannot be treated as having made a potentially exempt (or chargeable) transfer.[215] It is not considered that an accruer can properly be regarded as a restriction on a partner's freedom to dispose of his share in the same way as an option,[216] but it is understood that HMRC take a different view.[217]

Option clauses

36–43   If no consideration in money or money's worth was originally given for the grant of the option, its existence cannot be taken into account when valuing the

[210] Where there is no such provision, the partnership may be dissolved on the retirement, unless it is argued that the concept of retirement necessarily implies the continuation of the firm: see, further *supra*, paras 23–184, 24–22. As to the possible tax consequences of a dissolution, see *infra*, para. 36–53. Similar considerations may conceivably arise in the case of a partner's expulsion or compulsory retirement.

[211] See generally, as to such provisions, *supra*, paras 10–150 *et seq.* And see also *supra*, para. 36–23.

[212] In an appropriate case, the outgoing partner will be able to take advantage of any available exemptions or reliefs: see *supra*, paras 36–06 *et seq.* As to business relief, see the Inland Revenue Statement of Practice (SP12/80) dated October 13, 1980 reproduced *infra*, para. A6–27; also [1984] S.T.I. 651 *et seq.* See further *supra*, para. 36–16.

[213] This will include any collateral agreement, or subsequent deed of variation: see for example, *Att.-Gen. v. Ralli* (1936) 15 A.T.C. 523, where the provision for accruer was introduced by a collateral agreement.

[214] This is a fairly common scenario, particularly in professional partnerships where an outgoing partner tends to receive no more than the balance standing to the credit of his current and capital accounts at the date of his departure.

[215] Since there will be no "disposition" for the purpose of the Inheritance Tax Act 1984, s.3(1). As to the possible tax consequences of entering into an agreement containing an accruer provision, see *supra*, para. 36–24.

[216] And thus falling within *ibid.* s.163(1).

[217] See Foster, *Inheritance Tax*, para. F2.31; also *Dymond's Capital Taxes*, paras 9.215, 9.227–229; *McCutcheon on Inheritance Tax* (5th ed.), para. 25–72. As to the position if *ibid.* s.163(1) *does* apply, see *infra*, paras 36–43, 36–48, n. 243.

outgoing partner's share at the date of exercise.[218] As a result, where the option price remains pegged at a low figure but the market value of the share has increased significantly since the date of grant, an exercise of the option may involve the outgoing partner incurring a *further* actual or potential charge to tax, over and above that incurred when he originally entered into the agreement.[219] On the other hand, where, as will normally be the case,[220] consideration was given for the grant of the option, its existence will be reflected in any valuation of the outgoing partner's share[221]; as a result, the value of his share at the date of exercise is likely to approximate closely to the option price.[222]

Annuities

If an annuity is payable to the outgoing partner under the terms of an **36–44** agreement which constituted an arm's length transaction within section 10(1) of the Inheritance Tax Act 1984,[223] no actual or potential charge to tax will arise.[224] If, however, the continuing partners voluntarily decide to pay such an annuity following a partner's retirement, they will each be regarded as making a series of potentially exempt transfers, unless those payments are franked by any available exemptions[225] or they are supported by full consideration, *e.g.* where the outgoing partner takes an annuity in lieu of a part of his share.[226]

Continuing use of outgoing partner's property

Where the outgoing partner, either alone or jointly with his co-partners, owns **36–45** property which is used or occupied by the firm, continuance of that arrangement following his retirement may involve possible tax consequences, the nature of which have already been discussed.[227]

---

[218] *ibid.* s.163(1)(a). An allowance will, however, be made for any value transferred at the date of grant: *ibid.* s.163(1)(b). Moreover, the option will only be left out of account on the *first* chargeable transfer after that date: *ibid.* s.163(1), (3).

[219] Where the market value has remained approximately constant, no charge should be incurred, since the value transferred as a result of the exercise of the option will already have suffered tax: *ibid.* s.163(1)(b). See further, as to the original transfer, *supra*, para. 36–25.

[220] *i.e.* where the original agreement constituted an arm's length transaction with no gratuitous element, for the purposes of *ibid.* s.10(1).

[221] *ibid.* s.163(1)(a).

[222] The current editor submits that the value of the share will reduce progressively as the retirement date, and thus the potential date of exercise, approaches.

[223] See generally *supra*, paras 36–02 *et seq.*, 36–27.

[224] See the letter from what is now HMRC reproduced at (1975) 72 L.S. Gaz. 699.

[225] *e.g.* the annual or normal expenditure out of income exemption: see *supra*, paras 36–07, 36–08. As to the application of the annual exemption to transfers which are potentially exempt, see *supra*, paras 36–07, 36–20.

[226] See generally *supra*, para. 36–28. Such an annuity would not be deductible by the continuing partners for income tax purposes, and would be treated as investment income in the hands of the recipient: see *supra*, paras 34–66 *et seq.* Moreover, capital gains tax would be chargeable by reference to the value of the right to the annuity: see *supra*, paras 35–20, 35–21.

[227] See *supra*, para. 36–30.

D.   THE DEATH OF A PARTNER

36–46   On the death of a partner, his share will normally[228] form part of his estate, and tax will be charged on normal principles by reference to the transfer of value deemed to have been made immediately prior to his death.[229] His estate will also be treated as comprising any property which is subject to a reservation of benefit in his favour,[230] as well as the appropriate percentage of the value transferred by any potentially exempt transfers made within the previous seven years.[231] The usual exemptions and reliefs will be available, *i.e.* principally, in this context, business relief[232] and/or (if appropriate) agricultural property relief.[233]

Valuation of share

36–47   Although this subject is considered more fully elsewhere in this chapter,[234] it is of particular relevance in the present context to note the effect of an accruer or option provision contained in the partnership agreement.[235]

Accruer clauses

36–48   Consistently with the views already expressed,[236] the current editor considers that the share of a deceased partner which is expressed to accrue to the surviving partners without payment[237] will automatically cease to have any value on his death.[238] It follows that, when the share falls to be valued for tax purposes immediately *prior* to the date of death, account must be taken of the limited nature of the rights comprised therein: on that footing, given the imminence of death, the share can have no significant value.[239] This argument is in no way

---

[228] Unless, of course, the deceased partner had disposed of his share during his lifetime. The position where the share is subject to an automatic accruer is considered further below; but note the views expressed in Lawton Goldberg and Fraser, *The Law of Partnership Taxation* (2nd ed.), paras 14.084 *et seq.*

[229] Inheritance Tax Act 1984, s.4(1). Note, in this context, the decision in *Gray v. IRC* [1994] S.T.C. 360 (CA), noted *infra*, para. 36–60; also *Walton v. IRC* [1996] S.T.C. 68 (CA). In the case of spouses or civil partners, any unused nil rate band on the death of the first to die will generally be available on the death of the survivor (at the then applicable level) if a suitable claim is made: *ibid.* ss.8A *et seq.*, as added by the Finance Act 2008, Sched. 4.

[230] Finance Act 1986, s.102(3); see also *ibid.* ss.102A(2)(b), 102B(2)(b), as respectively added by the Finance Act 1999, s.104.

[231] Inheritance Tax Act 1984, s.3A(4), 7(4), as respectively added by the Finance Act 1986, Sched. 19, paras 1, 2.

[232] See *supra*, paras 36–13 *et seq.* But note, that HMRC may seek to deny the availability of the relief, depending on the terms of the agreement: see *supra*, para. 36–16.

[233] See *supra*, paras 36–10 *et seq.*

[234] See *infra*, paras 36–57 *et seq.*

[235] As to the position of a partner entering into an agreement containing such a provision, see *supra*, paras 36–23 *et seq.*

[236] See *supra*, paras 36–24, 36–42.

[237] It should make no difference whether the accruer provision is contained in the original agreement or introduced by way of subsequent variation; note, however, the views expressed in Lawton, Goldberg and Fraser, *The Law of Partnership Taxation* (2nd ed.), paras 14.084 *et seq.* *Quaere* will business relief be available in respect of the share? See *supra*, para. 36–16.

[238] The potential decrease in value on the death is inherent in the bundle of rights which comprise the share. It is submitted that the view adopted by some commentators, to the effect that an accruer provision introduces an element of survivorship into the partnership, is misconceived.

[239] Where a payment falls to be made to the deceased partner's estate on the accruer, the value of the share immediately prior to the death should closely approximate the value of the payment.

dependent on the provisions of section 171 of the Inheritance Tax Act 1984 (which permits account to be taken of changes in value occurring *by reason* of the death), but is framed solely by reference to limitations which are at all times inherent in the share itself.[240] However, it would seem that HMRC may seek to argue[241] that the accruer constitutes an exclusion or restriction of the deceased partner's right to dispose of his share, so that its existence can only be taken into account to the extent that consideration was given for its introduction.[242] Therein lies a possible danger in cases where it cannot be shown that the original agreement constituted an arm's length transaction between the partners.[243]

Option clauses

Where the surviving partners have an option to acquire a deceased partner's share, a valuation of that share immediately prior to the date of death will only reflect the existence of the option to the extent that consideration was given for it.[244] In the absence of any such consideration, the option will be disregarded but an allowance will be made for any value transferred when it was originally granted.[245]   **36–49**

Other valuation considerations

In accordance with the normal statutory rule,[246] when a deceased partner's share is valued immediately prior to his death, account will be taken of any increase or decrease in value resulting therefrom, other than a decrease attributable to the termination of an interest on his death or the passing of an interest by survivorship.[247] This may be of considerable importance where the death of a   **36–50**

---

[240] This is perhaps the mirror image of an argument advanced by HMRC as set out at [1984] S.T.I. 653, 654. As to the difficulties presented by s.171, see *infra*, n. 243.

[241] See Foster, *Inheritance Tax*, para. F2.31; also *Dymond's Capital Taxes*, paras 9.215, 9.227–229.

[242] Inheritance Tax Act 1984, s.163(1).

[243] This will be especially in point where the intending partners were already connected persons and thus had difficulty satisfying the conditions of *ibid.* s.10(1): see generally *supra*, paras 36–02, 36–38. Even if the accruer provision *is* treated as an exclusion or restriction of a partner's right to dispose of his share, so that its existence must be left out of account by virtue of *ibid.* s.163(1), it could still arguably be taken into account indirectly under *ibid.* s.171, on the basis that a decrease in the value of the share will occur on the death when the accruer operates. It should, however, be noted that a decrease in value cannot be taken into account under that section if it consists of "the termination on the death of any interest": *ibid.* s.171(2). Whether it can be said that a partner's interest in his share terminates as a result of an accruer is not clear. In *Att.-Gen. v. Boden* [1912] 1 K.B. 539, Hamilton J. held that the father's interest in goodwill, which was subject to such a provision, was an "interest ceasing on the death" for the purposes of the Finance Act 1894, s.2(1)(b): see *ibid.* p. 556. The decision in *Att.-Gen. v. Ralli* (1936) 15 A.T.C. 523 is not inconsistent therewith: see *ibid.* pp. 526–527. However, the judgment of Hamilton J. was criticised by the Privy Council in *Perpetual Executors & Trustees Association of Australia Ltd. v. Commissioner of Taxes of Australia* [1954] A.C. 114, 131. The current editor submits that the application of s.171 can be supported on one of two bases, namely: (a) that the deceased partner's interest does not terminate on death, but merely becomes valueless (or, where a payment falls to be made on the accruer merely assumes the value of that payment), or (b) that his interest in the share does not terminate but the share itself ceases to exist. It must, however, be appreciated that the *Boden* decision does present considerable difficulties with regard to either argument.

[244] Inheritance Tax Act 1984, s.163(1)(a). See also *supra*, para. 36–43.

[245] *ibid.* s.163(1)(b).

[246] *ibid.* s.171(1). And see *supra*, para. 36–48, n. 243.

[247] *ibid.* s.171(2).

partner will have an adverse impact on the firm's business, *e.g.* if its goodwill is largely dependent upon his continued involvement.[248]

Annuities

36–51   Where, on the death of a partner, an annuity becomes payable to his widow, surviving civil partner or dependants, there should be no adverse tax consequences so far as concerns the surviving partners, so long as they can show that the annuity is enforceable and that either: (1) full consideration was received by each partner when the annuity provision was originally introduced or (2) the agreement under which the annuity is to be paid constituted an arm's length transaction between the partners.[249] If those conditions cannot be satisfied,[250] each annuity payment will involve a potentially exempt transfer by the surviving partners.[251]

Partnership assurance schemes

36–52   Where the firm has established such a scheme, under which each partner insures his own life for the benefit of his co-partners,[252] it must be ascertained whether the trusts of the policy moneys constitute a settlement for tax purposes[253] and whether each of the other partners has an interest in possession therein.[254] If so, then the estate of a deceased partner will be treated as comprising that part of each policy in which his interest in possession subsisted.[255]

E.   DISSOLUTION OF A PARTNERSHIP

36–53   It is the current editor's view that substantial tax complications are unlikely to arise on the dissolution of a partnership, which will normally involve a realisation of its assets, the discharge of its liabilities, and the payment to each partner of his full entitlement by way of a distribution of surplus cash or, in an

---

[248] See further, as to the valuation of goodwill, *infra*, para. 36–58.

[249] See the letter from what is now HMRC reproduced in (1975) 72 L.S. Gaz. 699. But note the difficulties discussed *supra*, para. 36–28, n. 139.

[250] See *supra*, para. 36–28.

[251] A transfer will only be treated as potentially exempt to the extent that no other exemptions are available, *e.g.* the annual or normal expenditure out of income exemption: see *supra*, paras 36–07, 36–08. But note that the position is less clear so far as concerns the annual exemption: see *supra*, paras 36–07, 36–20.

[252] See *supra*, para. 36–29.

[253] Where the policies were effected as part of a commercial transaction prior to September 15, 1976, and the trusts thereof have not been varied since that date, such trusts will not be treated as creating a settlement: see Extra-Statutory Concession F10. And see, as to the meaning of "settlement" for these purposes, the Inheritance Tax Act 1984, s.43(2); also *supra*, para. 36–29.

[254] See *ibid.* ss.49 (as amended by the Finance Act 2006, Sched. 20, Pt 2, para. 4), 50. As to what qualify as "transitional serial interests" for this purpose (*i.e.* in effect, interests in possession which came into existence prior to the amendment of *ibid.* s.49), see *ibid.* ss.49A–49E, as added by the Finance Act 2006, Sched. 20, Pt 2, para. 5.

[255] *ibid.* ss.4(1), 5(1), (1A) (as respectively amended/added by the Finance Act 2006, Sched. 20, Pt 3, para. 10(2), (3)), 49(1), (1A) (as added by *ibid.* Sched. 20, Pt 2, para. 4(1)). *ibid.* s.167(1) does not apply on death: *ibid.* s.167(2)(a).

appropriate case, of assets *in specie*.[256] On that basis, no reduction in the value of a partner's estate should be anticipated. Of course, if one partner gratuitously transfers or forgoes some part of his entitlement in favour of another, tax will be chargeable on normal principles.

It might, however, usefully be observed that goodwill is often of little or no value on a dissolution.[257]

4. FOREIGN ELEMENT

Excluded property

Tax is actually or potentially chargeable in respect of all gratuitous transfers of assets made by persons who are domiciled in the UK,[258] wherever such assets are situated. Thus, where a member of a foreign firm is domiciled in the UK, he will be chargeable in respect of any disposition which has the effect of reducing the value of his share.[259] Where, however, a non-domiciled individual owns property situated outside the UK, that property will be treated as "excluded property",[260] and will be left out of account in computing the value transferred by an *inter vivos* disposition[261] or on the deemed transfer on death.[262] It is accordingly of considerable importance to ascertain whether a non-domiciled partner's share does indeed constitute excluded property.

36–54

Situs of a partnership share

The situs of a partnership share will largely depend on the nature of the individual partners' interests in its assets. It has already been seen[263] that, under English law, a partner does in one sense have a beneficial interest in the capital and assets of the firm but that it should, on a true analysis, be expressed in terms of his right to a proportion of the net surplus remaining after realisation of all the partnership assets and payment of all its debts and liabilities. As a result, if the proper law governing the partnership[264] is English law or, in this respect, is

36–55

---

[256] See the Partnership Act 1890, ss.39, 44; also generally *supra*, paras 19–25 *et seq.*, 25–44.

[257] *i.e.* where the valuation is on a "break up" basis: see *infra*, para. 36–57.

[258] Certain persons are deemed to have a UK domicile for the purposes of the tax: Inheritance Tax Act 1984, s.267, as amended by the Finance Act 1993, s.208(3), Sched. 23, Pt V. See generally *McCutcheon on Inheritance Tax* (5th ed.), paras 30–14 *et seq.*

[259] It does not for this purpose matter that the share is treated as situate outside the UK.

[260] Inheritance Tax Act 1984, s.6(1).

[261] *ibid.* s.3(2).

[262] *ibid.* s.5(1)(b), as amended by the Finance Act 2006, Sched. 20, Pt 3, para. 10(2) and the Enactment of Extra-Statutory Concessions Order 2009 (SI 2009/730), art. 13(1).

[263] See *supra*, paras 19–01 *et seq.* Note, however, that in *Gray v. IRC* [1994] S.T.C. 360, 377, the Court of Appeal rejected an analysis of a partnership share in these terms when valuing it for the purposes of capital transfer tax on death; and see also *Walton v. IRC* [1996] S.T.C. 68 (CA).

[264] As to the method of determining the proper law governing a partnership agreement, it seems that Regulation (EC) 593/2008 of the European Parliament and of the Council of June 17, 2008 on the laws applicable to contractual obligations will not apply: *ibid.* art. 1, paragraph 2(f). See further Dicey and Morris, *The Conflict of Laws* (14th ed.) Chap. 30. In the circumstances, the proper law will, in essence, be the system of law which the parties have chosen to govern their agreement or, where there is no such clear intention, the system of law with which the agreement is most closely connected: *ibid.* paras 32–003 *et seq.*

similar to English law, the share will be treated as situate in the country in which the firm's principal place of business is located.[265] However, it should be noted that a firm which carries on a number of distinct businesses in different countries may conceivably have more than one principal place of business.[266]

Where the proper law governing the partnership gives each partner a *direct* interest in the firm's assets, it will be necessary to consider each item of property separately, in order to ascertain the situs of a partner's share therein.[267] In the case of an interest in land, the situs will depend on where the land itself lies,[268] whereas the situs of an interest in a chattel will be determined according to its current location.[269] Goodwill is normally located in the same place as the firm's principal place of business.[270]

It obviously follows from the foregoing that a non-domiciled partner in a foreign partnership who nevertheless has an identifiable beneficial interest in land situate in the UK will be chargeable to tax in respect of any disposition affecting the value of that interest.

Gift by foreign firm of UK property

36–56 Where a foreign firm makes a gratuitous disposition of property situate in the UK, thereby reducing the value of each partner's share, a partner will seemingly be treated as having made a transfer of value to the extent of such reduction, notwithstanding the fact that his share is not, for the reasons discussed above, situated in the UK.[271]

5. VALUATION AND ADMINISTRATION

Valuation of partnership shares

36–57 The value of a partnership share, like any other asset, will be the price which that share might reasonably be expected to fetch if sold in the open market at the

---

[265] *Laidley v. Lord Advocate* (1890) 15 App. Cas. 468 (HL); *Beaver v. Master in Equity of Victoria* [1895] A.C. 251 (PC); *Commissioner of Stamp Duties v. Salting* [1907] A.C. 449 (PC). Note also the following decisions concerning the principal place of business of a *company: De Beers Consolidated Mines Ltd. v. Howe* [1906] A.C. 455; *Palmer v. Caledonian Railway* [1892] 1 Q.B. 823; *The Rewia* [1991] 2 Lloyd's Rep. 325; *King v. Crown Energy Trading AG, The Times*, March 14, 2003; *Ministry of Defence and Support of the Armed Forces for the Islamic Republic of Iran v. Faz Aviation Ltd.* [2008] 1 All E.R. (Comm) 372.

[266] *Beaver v. Master in Equity of Victoria, supra.* However, the mere fact that the firm carries on business in more than one country does not *ipso facto* mean that the business should be so treated: this will be a question of fact in each case.

[267] As to the situs of particular items of property, see generally, Dicey and Morris, *The Conflict of Laws* (14th ed.), Chap. 22, and especially paras 22R–023 *et seq.*

[268] *Re Hoyles* [1911] 1 Ch. 179; *Re Berchtold* [1923] 1 Ch. 192; *Philipson-Stow v. IRC* [1961] A.C. 727; *Haque v. Haque (No. 2)* (1965) 114 C.L.R. 98.

[269] *Gammell v. Sewell* (1860) 5 H. & N. 728; *Re Haig* (1922) 17 A.T.C. 635.

[270] *IRC v. Muller & Co.'s Margarine Ltd.* [1901] A.C. 217; *B.J. Reuter Co. Ltd. v. Mulhens* [1954] Ch. 50, 94–95 *per* Romer L.J.

[271] Since the property transferred will not be "excluded property" for the purposes of the Inheritance Tax Act 1984, s.6(1). For a discussion of this and another somewhat anomalous problem (*i.e.* a charge to tax imposed upon a non-domiciled partner whose share is situate outside the UK when the firm makes a gift of assets situate *outside* the UK) see Lawton, Goldberg and Fraser, *The Law of Partnership Taxation* (2nd ed.), paras 15.045, 15.046.

relevant time,[272] However, it has already been seen that there are a number of complications in and about the valuation process, other than those presented by the peculiar nature of the share itself.[273] Thus, an exclusion or restriction on the right to dispose of a share may only be taken into account to the extent that its introduction was supported by consideration, although due allowance will be made for any value transferred at that time.[274] Further, where the valuation falls to be made immediately prior to the death of a partner,[275] account must be taken of any increase or decrease in value which may result from the death.[276]

The actual valuation of a share will normally be by reference to the value of the underlying assets of the firm, which will in turn depend upon whether the valuation is made on a "going concern" or "break up" basis.[277] Whilst a detailed consideration of the principles governing such valuations lies outside the scope of this work, some reference should be made to the valuation of goodwill, which may be one of the firm's most important assets,[278] as well as to the value of agricultural tenancies.

Valuation of goodwill

The value of goodwill is dependent on a number of factors. First and foremost, **36–58** the goodwill itself may be of such a nature as to attract a high or a low value, *e.g.* the goodwill of a firm of medical practitioners providing various types of medical services under the National Health Service cannot lawfully be sold[279] and therefore has no disposable value.[280] Equally, whatever the type of business, a large proportion of the firm's goodwill may depend on the continued presence of a particular partner. A further factor may be the presence or absence of a

---

[272] *ibid.* s.160. The price will not, however, suffer any reduction on the ground that the whole property is to be placed on the market at the same time: *ibid.* The hypothetical sale does, however, take place in the real world and a class of potential purchasers must not be invented: *Bower v. Revenue & Customs Commissioners* [2009] S.T.C. 510. It is considered that all valuations must take place on this statutory basis, even where some other basis is established under the agreement: see *Gray v. IRC* [1994] S.T.C. 360 (CA), noted *infra*, para. 36–60; *Walton v. IRC* [1996] S.T.C. 68 (CA); also the estate duty cases of *IRC v. Crossman* [1937] A.C. 26 (HL) and *Lynall v. IRC* [1972] A.C. 680 (HL).

[273] It has, for example, been noted that a share may comprise a bundle of rights with inherent limitations, which must be reflected in any valuation: see *supra*, para. 36–48.

[274] Inheritance Tax Act 1984, s.163, considered *supra*, paras 36–43, 36–48 *et seq.*

[275] *i.e.* pursuant to *ibid.* s.4(1).

[276] Inheritance Tax Act 1984, s.171, considered *supra*, para. 36–50.

[277] Thus, on a "break up" basis, goodwill is unlikely to have any significant value (and may, indeed, be completely valueless) and certain assets used by the firm may fall to be ignored: see, for example, *Eardley v. Broad, The Times*, April 28, 1970 and (1970) 215 E.G. 823. And see, generally, *Dymond's Capital Taxes*, paras 23.430 *et seq.*

[278] See generally, as to goodwill, *supra*, paras 10–193 *et seq.*

[279] National Health Service Act 2006, s.259, Sched. 21. A further prohibition on the sale of goodwill by various types of contractors and certain medical practitioners providing "essential services" is also to be found in the Primary Medical Services (Sale of Goodwill and Restrictions on Sub-contracting) Regulations 2004 (SI 2004/906), reg. 3(1), which continue to have effect under the 2006 Act: National Health Service (Consequential Provisions) Act 2006, Sched. 2, para. 1(2). See also *supra*, paras 6–04 *et seq.*, 23–200.

[280] Although the statutory prohibitions do not extinguish the goodwill (see *Whitehill v. Bradford* [1952] Ch. 236 (CA); *Kerr v. Morris* [1987] Ch. 90 (CA)), it is clear that they remove all its economic value: *R v. Waltham Forest NHS Primary Care Trust* [2007] 1 W.L.R. 2092 (CA). *Semble* there can be no hypothetical sale in such a case: *Bower v. Revenue & Customs Commissioners* [2009] S.T.C. 510, noticed *supra*, para. 36–57, n. 272. *cf.* the position where there are merely *contractual* restrictions on sale, which must, to an extent, be ignored: see *Gray v. IRC* [1994] S.T.C. 360 (CA) and the other cases noted *supra*, para. 36–57, n. 272.

restriction on competition by outgoing partners: if such partners can immediately set up a similar business in the same area as the firm, this may significantly depress the value of its goodwill.[281]

Where goodwill has a value, the actual method of valuation will be determined by the size of the business and the type of goodwill involved. Certain trades and professions have particular customary methods of valuing goodwill,[282] whereas, in valuing the goodwill of a large firm, one of the two recognised methods, *i.e.* "total capitalisation"[283] and "super profits",[284] will normally be adopted. All the circumstances must be considered before it is possible to determine which method will be appropriate in a given case and reference should be made to the standard works in relation thereto.[285]

Valuation of agricultural tenancies

36–59   Although a tenancy protected by the Agricultural Holdings Act 1986[286] will rarely be freely assignable,[287] HMRC have attempted to insist that, consistently with the principles enunciated in *IRC v. Crossman*,[288] such a tenancy may have a substantial value. The high-water mark of this approach was, perhaps to be seen in *Baird's Executors v. IRC*,[289] albeit that the case concerned the status of such a tenancy in Scotland.[290] Since then the Court of Appeal in *Walton v. IRC*[291] have, in analysing the nature of the hypothetical sale which is treated as taking place,[292] imposed some limits on the theoretical value which can be attributed to a partner's interest in a tenancy held as a partnership asset. Equally, there must

---

[281] See generally, as to such restrictions and the protection of goodwill in the absence thereof, *supra*, paras 10–206 *et seq.*, 10–218 *et seq.*

[282] See Foster, *Inheritance Tax*, para. H3.51.

[283] *i.e.* the average maintainable profit over a given period multiplied by the appropriate number of years' purchase, less the net value of the tangible trading assets. See, generally, *Findlay's Trustees v. IRC* (1938) 22 A.T.C. 437.

[284] *i.e.* the average maintainable profit over a given period, less the average assumed yield attributable to the tangible assets and a sum representing reasonable remuneration for the partners, the "super profit" thus found being multiplied by the appropriate number of years' purchase. In *Findlay's Trustees v. IRC*, *supra*, the expert witnesses did not consider the super profits method appropriate for valuing a share in the goodwill of a partnership owning a newspaper.

[285] Foster, Inheritance Tax, paras H3.53 *et seq.*; *Dymond's Capital Taxes*, paras 23.400 *et seq.*; *McCutcheon on Inheritance Tax* (5th. ed.), para. 25–43. See also *supra*, paras 10–214 *et seq.*

[286] Such tenancies were, in general, only capable of creation prior to September 1, 1995, when the Agricultural Tenancies Act 1995 came into force.

[287] As to the position where there is no tenancy agreement or where the agreement contains no express restriction on assignment, see the Agricultural Holdings Act 1986, s.6(1), Sched. 1, para. 9. There is no equivalent provision in the Agricultural Tenancies Act 1995.

[288] [1937] A.C. 26 (HL). See further *Gray v. IRC* [1994] S.T.C. 360 (CA); *Walton v. IRC* [1996] S.T.C. 68 (CA); see also *Alexander v. IRC* [1991] S.T.C. 112, which concerned a residential lease.

[289] 1991 S.L.T. 9 (Lands Trib.). In this case the tenancy was treated as having a value equal to 25% of the vacant possession value of the land. Although there is no such thing as a *standard* percentage of the vacant possession premium or value to be taken in this context, it would seem that the District Valuer has tended to use such a percentage as a starting point for negotiation: see (1992) 89 L.S. Gaz., March 18, p. 15.

[290] Special considerations apply to such tenancies, as evidenced by the provisions of the Inheritance Tax Act 1984, s.177.

[291] [1996] S.T.C. 68. The same principles apply when valuing a tenancy *otherwise* than for tax purposes: *Greenbank v. Pickles* [2000] 09 E.G. 230.

[292] *i.e.* under the Inheritance Tax Act 1984, s.160.

inevitably be some doubt as to the value which can properly be attributed to such a tenancy on the death of a *sole* tenant.[293]

Aggregation of tenancy and freehold

Special account must also be taken of the position where one of the partners is both a co-tenant *and* the freeholder. In *Gray v. IRC*[294] Lady Fox was the freehold owner of a substantial farm as well as a member of a partnership which was the tenant of that farm. She had a 92.5% interest in the partnership at the date of her death and the Court of Appeal had regard to the fact that she could have exercised a contractual power under the partnership agreement to dissolve the firm on 6 months' notice and thereupon acquired the remaining partners' shares, with a view to selling the farm with vacant possession. Since it had to be assumed that her partnership share could be sold to a third party,[295] it followed that a combined sale of the share and the freehold reversion would produce a greater price than if each were sold separately. On that basis, it was held that, in valuing Lady Fox's estate,[296] the share and the freehold reversion could properly be aggregated so as to achieve a value which more closely approximated to the vacant possession value of the farm.

36–60

Reliefs

Once the value of the share has been ascertained, it may be reduced for the purposes of the tax by any available agricultural property or business relief,[297] or a combination of the two.[298]

36–61

Administration

The administration of the tax does not appear to give rise to any particular problems in relation to partnerships, since any charge is levied by reference to transfers of value made or deemed to have been made by the individual partners and any returns must be delivered by those partners personally.[299]

36–62

Payment of tax by instalments

Partnership share

Where any of the tax payable in respect of a transfer of value deemed to have been made on death[300] is attributable to the value of a business or an interest in

36–63

---

[293] In such a case, the prospect of the landlord being able to recover possession of the land (as to which see the Agricultural Holdings Act 1986, s.26(2), Sched. 3, Pt 1, Case G) must be taken into account pursuant to the Inheritance Tax Act 1984, s.171. *Semble*, any right to succession under the Agricultural Holdings Act 1986, Pt IV does not form part of the deceased tenant's estate. See also (1990) 87 L.S. Gaz., November 14, at p. 26.

[294] [1994] S.T.C. 360.

[295] *ibid.* p. 378.

[296] *i.e.* pursuant to what is now the Inheritance Tax Act 1984, ss.160, 171.

[297] See generally, *supra*, paras 36–10 *et seq.* But note, in particular, the effect of the Inheritance Tax Act 1984, s.39A, as added by the Finance Act 1986, s.105.

[298] See *ibid.* s.114(1).

[299] See *ibid.* ss.216 *et seq.*

[300] *i.e.* pursuant to *ibid.* s.4(1).

a business, (which will clearly include a share in a partnership), an election may be made to pay the tax by 10 yearly instalments.[301] A similar right of election is available where the transfer of value was made as a result of an *inter vivos* disposition, *provided that the tax is borne by the donee*.[302] For these purposes, the value of a business means its net value, which is to be ascertained by deducting the aggregate amount of any liabilities incurred for the purposes of the business from the value of the assets used in the business (including goodwill)[303]; an interest in a business will be valued in the same way, no account being taken of any assets or liabilities other than those which would be taken into account in ascertaining the net value of the business itself.[304]

Where an election is made, the first instalment is due (in the case of a chargeable transfer on death) six months after the end of the month in which the death occurred[305] or (in the case of an *inter vivos* transfer) at the time the tax would have been due if it were not payable by instalments.[306] Interest on each instalment is only payable from the date when that instalment falls due.[307]

Forfeiture of the right to elect

36–64   Notwithstanding such an election, the whole or an appropriate proportion of the tax outstanding which is attributable to a partnership share will become immediately payable on the occurrence of any one of the following events:

    (i) a subsequent sale of the share,[308] *e.g.* where the continuing partners exercise an option to acquire an outgoing partner's share[309];

    (ii) the payment of any sum, pursuant to the partnership agreement or otherwise, in satisfaction of the whole or any part of the share, otherwise than on sale, *e.g.* where the share automatically accrues to the continuing partners and a payment falls to be made by them to the outgoing partner or his estate[310];

---

[301] *ibid.* s.227(1)(a), (2)(c). Note, however, that the election will not always be available where tax becomes payable on the death in respect of an *inter vivos* transfer made within the previous seven years: *ibid.* s.227(1A), (1C), as added by the Finance Act 1987, Sched. 8, para. 15.

[302] *ibid.* s.227(1)(b), (2)(c). The availability of the right to elect cannot be guaranteed where a potentially exempt transfer proves to be chargeable: *ibid.* s.227(1A)(a), (1C), as added by the Finance Act 1987, Sched. 8, para. 15. In the case of a transfer into settlement, see *ibid.* s.227(1)(c).

[303] *ibid.* s.227(7)(a), (b).

[304] *ibid.* s.227(7)(c). Thus, a right to an annuity on retirement (which clearly forms part of the bundle of rights which comprise the share) would be ignored; on the other hand, the liability to pay an annuity to a former partner *will* be taken into account.

[305] *ibid.* s.227(3)(a).

[306] *ibid.* s.227(3)(b). This will generally be six months after the end of the month in which the chargeable transfer was made or, in the case of such a transfer made between April 5 and October 1, on April 30 in the next year: *ibid.* s.226(1). However, in the case of a potentially exempt transfer which proves to be chargeable, the due date will be six months after the end of the month in which the transferor's death occurs: *ibid.* s.226(3A), as added by the Finance Act 1986, Sched. 19, para. 30.

[307] *ibid.* s.234(1).

[308] *ibid.* s.227(4), (6)(a).

[309] See further, as to the implications of granting such an option, *supra*, paras 36–25, 36–43, 36–49.

[310] *ibid.* s.227(6)(b). This will cause a deemed sale at the time of payment.

(iii) a subsequent chargeable transfer in relation to the share (other than a deemed transfer on death), if the transfer giving rise to the instalment election was itself made otherwise than on death.[311]

It is, of course, questionable to what extent the statutory conversion of an outgoing partner's share into a debt will result in forfeiture of the instalment election.[312] However, there is no certain method of avoiding this consequence, save to provide that such a partner's share will accrue to the continuing partners without payment.

Land

A similar right to pay tax by instalments is available where any of the tax **36–65** payable is attributable to the value of land of any description, wherever situated.[313] However, save in the case of agricultural land, interest on the unpaid portion of the tax will be added to each instalment.[314]

A gratuitous transfer of land owned and used by a firm for the purposes of its business will naturally reduce the value of each partner's share[315] and that reduction in value, if chargeable, will itself qualify for an instalment election as a transfer of an interest in a business.[316] Since the latter election will avoid the payment of interest, otherwise than on overdue instalments,[317] it will rarely be beneficial to submit an election on the former basis, save in the case of agricultural land or land which is not used in the business.[318]

---

[311] *ibid.* s.227(5)(a), as amended by the Finance Act 1986, Sched. 19, para. 31(2). Note also that, in the case of a settled partnership share, any outstanding tax will become payable forthwith if the share ceases to be comprised in the settlement: *ibid.* s.227(5)(b).

[312] Partnership Act 1890, s.43: see *supra*, paras 19–35, 23–34, 26–03.

[313] Inheritance Tax Act 1984, s.227(1), (2)(a).

[314] *ibid.* ss.227(3), 233 (as amended); the exemption contained in *ibid.* s.234(1)(a) applies only to shares, securities, businesses, interests in businesses and property eligible for relief under *ibid.* Chap. II, Pt V (agricultural property relief). See further, as to the latter relief, *supra*, paras 36–10 *et seq.*

[315] As already noted, a partner has no immediate or ascertainable beneficial interest in the land, but merely a right to a proportion of the surplus remaining after the realisation of all the partnership assets and the payment of all its debts and liabilities: see further, *supra*, paras 19–01 *et seq.*, 36–38. But see *Gray v. IRC* [1994] S.T.C. 360, 377 (CA); also *Walton v. IRC* [1996] S.T.C. 68 (CA).

[316] See *supra*, para. 36–63.

[317] Inheritance Tax Act 1984, s.234(1).

[318] Land which is not so used will be ignored when ascertaining the net value of a business, and thus of a share therein: see *ibid.* s.227(7)(b); also *supra*, para. 36–63.

CHAPTER 37

VALUE ADDED TAX

1.   REGISTRATION

Value added tax is chargeable on any taxable supply[1] of goods or services in the   **37-01**
UK made by a taxable person "in the course or furtherance of any business[2]
carried on by him", on the acquisition in the UK of any goods from another
Member State of the EU and on the importation of goods from outside the EU.[3]

---

[1] A taxable supply is a supply of goods or services made in the UK, other than an exempt supply:
Value Added Tax Act 1994, s.4(2). As to exempt supplies, see *ibid.* s.31, Sched. 9 (as amended). If
the consideration for an apparent supply of services is a share of profits, it will be a question of fact
whether a partnership does in fact exist; the mere receipt of a profit share will not in itself be decisive:
see *Strathearn Gordon Associates v. Customs & Excise Commissioners* (1985) V.A.T.T.R. 79; *Keydon
Estates v. The Commissioners* (LON/88/125) [1990] S.T.I. 179; *Fivegrange Ltd. v. The Commissioners* (LON/89/1631) [1990] S.T.I. 966; *cf. Stephanie A. Manuel t/a Stage Coach Centre for the
Performing Arts v. The Commissioners* (LON/90/807) [1992] S.T.I. 47. Note also *Alberni String
Quartet v. Customs & Excise Commissioners* (1990) 3 V.A.T.T.R. 166. And see generally, as to the
possible implications of profit sharing arrangements, *supra,* paras 5–17 *et seq.*

[2] "Business" includes any trade, profession or vocation: *ibid.* s.94(1). The definition is a wide one,
but it has been held that a business carried on in partnership within the meaning of the Partnership
Act 1890, s.1(1) will not *necessarily* constitute a business for this purpose: see *Three H. Aircraft Hire
v. Customs & Excise Commissioners* [1982] S.T.C. 653, where a partnership which owned and,
through a company, hired out an aircraft was held not to be carrying on a business and thus could not
be registered for the tax. However, the decision was an exceptional one: in the vast majority of cases
there will be no question of a partnership business not being regarded as a business for value added
tax purposes: see *ibid.* p. 660 *per* Webster J. Nevertheless, there was a strikingly similar decision in
Berwick v. Customs & Excise Commissioners, May 31, 2002 (Lawtel 18/7/02), where the VAT
Tribunal ordered the compulsory deregistration of a partnership purporting to carry on the business
of yacht chartering on the grounds that it was not carrying on any economic activity within the
meaning of Art. 4 of the Sixth Directive (*i.e.* EC Council Directive 77/388); also *Davies v. Revenue
& Customs Commissioners* February 2, 2007 (V & DTr) (Lawtel 19/6/07), where few charters had
actually been arranged. *cf. Heath House Charter Ltd. v. Revenue & Customs Commissioners* [2010]
S.F.T.D. 245, where a yacht chartering business *did* amount to an economic activity. And see
generally, *Processed Vegetable Growers Association Ltd. v. Customs & Excise Commissioners* (1973)
1 V.A.T.T.R. 87; *Coleman v. The Commissioners* (1976) V.A.T.T.R. 24; *Border Flying Company v.
The Commissioners* (1976) V.A.T.T.R. 132; *Customs & Excise Commissioners v. Morrison's Academy
Boarding Houses Association* [1978] S.T.C. 1; *The National Water Council v. Customs & Excise
Commissioners* [1979] S.T.C. 157; *Customs & Excise Commissioners v. Lord Fisher* [1981] S.T.C.
238; *Customs & Excise Commissioners v. Apple and Pear Development Council* [1985] S.T.C. 383
(CA), [1986] S.T.C. 192 (HL) and [1988] S.T.C. 221 (ECJ); *Gubby v. Customs & Excise Commis-
sioners* [1987] 3 C.M.L.R. 742; *Neuvale Ltd. v. Customs & Excise Commissioners* [1989] S.T.C. 395;
Customs & Excise Commissioners v. Yarburgh Children's Trust [2002] S.T.C. 207; *Customs & Excise
Commissioners v. St. Paul's Community Project Ltd.* [2005] S.T.C. 95; *Finanzamt Offenbach am
Main-Land v. Faxworld Vorgründungsgesellschaft etc.* [2005] S.T.C. 1192 (ECJ); *Riverside Housing
Association Ltd. v. Revenue & Customs Commissioners, The Times,* November 1, 2006. And note
also, as to the status of dealings between a partner and his own partnership, *Staatsecretaris van
Financiën v. Heerma* [2001] S.T.C. 1437 (ECJ).

[3] Value Added Tax Act 1994, s.1(1). See further, as to the scope of the tax in such cases, *ibid.* ss.10,
15.

A taxable person is any person who is or is required to be registered under the Value Added Tax Act 1994.[4]

Taxable supplies in the UK

37–02   A liability to be registered will arise if, at the end of any month, the value of a person's taxable supplies during the period of one year ending on that date exceeds the prescribed amount[5] or if, at any time, there are reasonable grounds for believing that the value of such supplies during the ensuing 30 days will exceed that amount.[6] In the former case, it may, however, be possible to avoid registration by demonstrating that the value of such supplies in the *forthcoming year*[7] will not exceed a (lesser) prescribed amount.[8] In addition, where a person qualifies for the flat-rate scheme for farmers, certain supplies of goods and services will be disregarded for registration purposes.[9]

The option of voluntary registration is open to any person who is *not* liable to be registered, provided that he can satisfy HMRC that he makes, or intends to make, taxable supplies[10] or supplies which would be taxable supplies if made in the UK.[11]

Supplies from other EU states

37–03   A person who is not required to register on account of the value of his taxable supplies[12] will nevertheless be liable to be registered if:

    (a)   the value of his relevant supplies[13] since January 1 in any year exceed £70,000[14];

    (b)   he makes a relevant supply of any value after having exercised an option under the laws of any Member State of the EU in which he is taxable to treat relevant supplies made by him as made *outside* that

---

[4] *ibid.* s.3(1).

[5] *ibid.* Sched. 1, para. 1(1)(a), as amended by the Value Added Tax (Increase of Registration Limits) Order 2010 (SI 2010/920), art. 3(a). Currently, the limit stands at £70,000. As to the position of a transferee of a business as a going concern, see *ibid.* Sched. 1, para. 1(2), as amended by the Finance Act 2007, s.100(8) and *ibid.* art. 3(a); and note the decision in *Ludovico v. Customs & Excise Commissioners,* May 24, 2004 (Lawtel 28/6/04) (VAT Trib.).

[6] *ibid.* Sched. 1, para. 1(1)(b), as amended by the Value Added Tax (Increase of Registration Limits) Order 2010, art. 3(a). The prescribed amount is currently £70,000. As to the operation of this limb, see *Bennett v. Customs & Excise Commissioners* [1999] S.T.C. 248.

[7] This will be the year commencing at the time when registration would otherwise have been necessary.

[8] *ibid.* Sched. 1, para. 1(3), as amended by the Value Added Tax (Increase of Registration Limits) Order 2010, art. 3(b). The prescribed amount is currently £68,000. As to the information which may be taken into account for this purpose, see *Gray (t/a William Gray & Sons) v. Commissioners of Customs & Excise* [2000] S.T.C. 880.

[9] *ibid.* s.54. See also the Value Added Tax Regulations 1995 (SI 1995/2518), Pt XXIV; also the Value Added Tax (Flat-rate Scheme for Farmers) (Designated Activities) Order 1992 (SI 1992/3220); the Value Added Tax (Flat-rate Scheme for Farmers) (Percentage Addition) Order 1992 (SI 1992/3221).

[10] Value Added Tax 1994, Sched. 1, para. 9. Note that the option of voluntary registration is now open to doctors and dentists practising within the National Health Service: see [1993] S.T.I. 536.

[11] *ibid.* Sched. 1, para. 10, as amended by the Finance Act 1997, s.32.

[12] See *supra,* para. 37–02.

[13] As to the meaning of this expression, see *ibid.* Sched. 2, para. 10.

[14] *ibid.* Sched. 2, para. 1(1).

State and those supplies involve the removal of goods from that State[15]; or

(c) he makes a supply of goods which satisfies certain specified conditions.[16]

Voluntary registration is available to any person who can satisfy HMRC either that he intends to make relevant supplies to which an option of the type noticed in (b) above will relate, irrespective of whether it has already been exercised,[17] or that he intends to make supplies of goods which satisfy the specified conditions.[18]

Acquisitions from other EU states

In addition, a person who is not otherwise liable to be registered will become **37–04** so liable if at the end of any month the value of his relevant acquisitions[19] since January 1 of that year exceeds the prescribed amount[20] or there are reasonable grounds to believe that the value of such acquisitions during the ensuing 30 days will exceed that amount.[21]

A person who can satisfy HMRC that he makes or intends to make relevant acquisitions may at any time apply for voluntary registration.[22]

Disposals where repayment of VAT claimed

A person who is not otherwise liable to be registered will become so liable if, **37–05** in the course or furtherance of his business, he makes (or is likely within the next 30 days to make) a taxable supply of goods which are assets of that business and he[23] has received or claimed or intends to claim repayment of VAT on that supply.[24] Registration will be necessary even where that person is, at the time of the relevant supply, registered but that registration is subsequently cancelled.[25] Exemption may, however, be available where such supply would be zero rated.[26]

Electronic services provided from outside the EU

Finally, a person who is not registered[27] or subject to a similar requirement in **37–06** another Member State and who maintains neither a business establishment nor a

---

[15] *ibid.* Sched. 2, para. 1(2). Note that, in such a case, the liability to be registered will continue for so long as the option is in force: *ibid.* para. 2(2).

[16] *ibid.* Sched. 2, para. 1(3).

[17] *ibid.* Sched. 2, para. 4(1)(a)(i), (ii).

[18] *ibid.* Sched. 2, para. 4(1)(a)(iii).

[19] As to the meaning of this expression, see *ibid.* Sched. 3, para. 11.

[20] *ibid.* Sched. 3, para. 1(1), as amended by the Value Added Tax (Increase of Registration Limits) Order 2010, art. 4. The prescribed amount is currently £70,000.

[21] *ibid.* Sched. 3, para. 1(2), as amended by the Value Added Tax (Increase of Registration Limits) Order 2010, art. 4.

[22] *ibid.* Sched. 3, para. 4(1), (2).

[23] Or a predecessor of his: *ibid.* Sched. 3A, para. 9(1)(c), (2), as added by the Finance Act 2000, Sched. 36.

[24] *ibid.* Sched. 3A, paras 1(1), 9(1), (3), as added by *ibid.* Such a supply is defined as a "relevant supply".

[25] *ibid.* Sched. 3A, para. 1(2), as added by *ibid.*

[26] *ibid.* Sched. 3A, para. 7, as added by *ibid.*

[27] Where the person is already registered under *ibid.* Sched. 1, he may apply for that registration to be cancelled: *ibid.* Sched. 1, para. 13(8), Sched. 3B, para. 18, as respectively added by the Finance Act 2003, Sched. 2, paras 3, 4.

fixed establishment in the UK or another Member State and who provides or intends to provide services electronically to a person in the UK or another member State otherwise than for the purposes of that person's business[28] may, on his request, be registered in a register kept for the purpose.[29]

Notification and registration

37–07   A person who becomes liable to be registered must notify HMRC, although the time limit for such notification varies according to the circumstances which gave rise to that liability,[30] as does the date from which the registration will have effect.[31] Until registration has taken place, that person will be in the highly disadvantageous position of an unregistered taxable person.[32]

Registration of partnerships

37–08   The Value Added Tax Act 1994 makes specific provision for the registration of partnerships,[33] but the application of that provision, as in the case of its

---

[28] These are styled "qualifying supplies": *ibid.* Sched. 3B, para. 3, as added by the Finance Act 2003, Sched. 2, para. 4.

[29] *ibid.* s.3A, Sched. 3B, paras 2–4, as respectively added by the Finance Act 2003, Sched. 2, paras 2, 4.

[30] *ibid.* Sched. 1, paras 5(1), 6(1), 7(1), Sched. 2, para. 3(1), Sched. 3, para. 3(1), Sched. 3A, para. 3(1) (as added by the Finance Act 2000, Sched. 36). See further *infra*, para. 37–30, as to the form of notification.

[31] *ibid.* Sched. 1, paras 5(2), 6(2), 7(2), Sched. 2, para. 3(2), Sched. 3, para. 3(2), (3), Sched. 3A, para. 3(2) (as added by the Finance Act 2000, Sched. 36). As to registration under *ibid.* Sched. 3B, see *ibid.* para. 5, as added by the Finance Act 2003, Sched. 2, para. 4.

[32] Thus, the unregistered taxable person must account for tax on taxable supplies made by him, but cannot issue valid tax invoices in respect of those supplies: see the Value Added Tax Regulations 1995 (SI 1995/2518), regs. 13, 14 (as amended). He may also be liable for interest and penalties: Value Added Tax Act 1994, ss.67, 74 (as amended). Note, however, the decision in *Smith v. The Commissioners* (LON/90/1094) [1991] S.T.I. 149, which was an exceptional case.

[33] This presupposes the existence of a partnership in the true sense: see, for example, *Britton v. Customs & Excise Commissioners* (1986) V.A.T.T.R. 209, where it was held that a husband and wife were *not* partners in a shopfitting business. For other instances in which HMRC have sought, unsuccessfully, to argue that a partnership exists, see *Parker and Parker (t/a Sea Breeze Café) v. Customs & Excise Commissioners* [2000] S.T.I. 269; *Taste of Bangladesh v. Customs & Excise Commissioners* [2000] S.T.I. 554; *Hunter, Kiernan, Wigglesworth and Wright (t/a Blues Hairshop) v. Customs & Excise Commissioners* [2000] S.T.I. 936; *Robert Wallace (t/a Inn House) v. Customs & Excise Commissioners*, Unreported February 26, 2001 (V & DTr); *cf. David Ewart Jones* (MAN/ 94/722) [1996] S.T.I. 717; *R. Wilson and J. Wilson (t/a Mount View Hotel) v. Customs & Excise Commissioners* [2000] S.T.I. 552; *Leonidas v. Customs & Excise Commissioners* [2000] B.V.C. 2316; also *Ali v. Customs & Excise Commissioners* [2004] S.T.I. 1302, where the daughter was held to be a partner. See also *Townsend and Townsend v. Customs & Excise Commissioners* [2001] S.T.I. 952, where the appellants had previously carried on a business in partnership with their son and daughter in law; in both *Plummer v. Customs & Excise Commissioners* [2001] S.T.I. 653 and *Newton and Newton (t/a R.E. Newton) v. Customs & Excise Commissioners* [2001] S.T.I. 1231 it was sought to be argued that two separate partnerships with common partners should, in effect, be regarded as a single firm. The taxpayer's argument that a company could not be a member of a partnership predictably failed in *Wild v. Revenue & Customs Commissioners* [2009] S.T.C. 566. Equally, it is clear that the Tribunal, will have regard to the substance and reality of the relationship (*Burrell v. Commissioners of Customs & Excise* [1997] S.T.C. 1413) and will, on normal principles, reject any attempt at artificial labelling. Note that a joint venture may well *not* constitute a partnership: see *Thorstone Developments Ltd. v. Commissioners of Customs & Excise*, Unreported October 14, 2002 (V & DTr); also *supra*, para. 5–06.

predecessors,[34] is not without difficulty. Under the heading "Partnerships," section 45 of the Act[35] now provides:

"(1) The registration under this Act of persons—

(a) carrying on a business in partnership, or

(b) carrying on in partnership any other activities in the course or furtherance of which they acquire goods from other member States,

may be in the name of the firm; and no account shall be taken, in determining for any purpose of this Act whether goods or services are supplied to or by such persons or are acquired by such persons from another member State, of any change in the partnership.

(2) Without prejudice to section 36 of the Partnership Act 1890 (rights of persons dealing with firm against apparent members of firm), until the date on which a change in the partnership is notified to the Commissioners, a person who has ceased to be a member of a partnership shall be regarded as continuing to be a partner for the purposes of this Act and, in particular, for the purpose of any liability for VAT on the supply of goods or services by the partnership or on the acquisition of goods by the partnership from another member State.[36]

(3) Where a person ceases to be a member of a partnership during a prescribed accounting period (or is treated as so doing by virtue of subsection (2) above) any notice, whether of assessment or otherwise, which is served on the partnership and relates to, or to any matter arising in, that period or any earlier period during the whole or part of which he was a member of the partnership shall be treated as served also on him.

(4) Without prejudice to section 16 of the Partnership Act 1890 (notice to acting partner to be notice to the firm) any notice, whether of assessment or otherwise, which is addressed to a partnership by the name in which it is registered by virtue of subsection (1) above and is served in accordance with this Act shall be treated for the purposes of this Act as served on the partnership and, accordingly, where subsection (3) above applies, as served also on the former partner.

(5) Subsections (1) and (3) above shall not affect the extent to which, under section 9 of the Partnership Act 1890, a partner is liable for VAT owed by the firm; but where a person is a partner in a firm during part only of a prescribed accounting period, his liability for VAT on the supply by the firm of goods or services during that accounting period or on the acquisition during that period by the firm of any goods from another member State shall be such proportion of the firm's liability as may be just."

It is clear from the terms of the section that HMRC have a discretion as to whether or not to effect the registration in the name of the firm. It is thus technically open to them to require the firm to be registered under the names of the individual partners,[37] although it is thought that this discretion will rarely be exercised.

---

[34] Finance Act 1972, s.22 (as amended); Value Added Tax Act 1983, s.30 (as amended).

[35] See also, as to the effect of this section, HMRC's Business Brief 21/04 "VAT—VAT position of share issues and partnership contributions following the ECJ decision in *KapHag Renditefonds*" issued on August 10, 2004, *infra*, para. A6–38.

[36] See further, as to the effect of this subsection, *Customs & Excise Commissioners v. Jamieson* [2002] S.T.C. 1418.

[37] Where the firm is registered in the names of the individual partners, the latter part of s.45(1) (no account being taken of changes in the partnership) will still apply; but see further, *infra*, para. 37–11. An individual partner may, of course, still be separately registered in respect of any business carried on by him either alone or in partnership with others.

37–09   Certain implications of one of the predecessors to section 45 were considered by the Divisional Court in *Customs & Excise Commissioners v. Glassborow*.[38] In that case, a husband and wife, Mr and Mrs Glassborow, carried on an estate agent's business in partnership under the name "Bertram & Co.", and a wholly separate land developer's business in partnership under the name "Glassborow & Glassborow". Application was made to the Commissioners for registration in respect of each separate partnership, but the Commissioners, having registered Mr and Mrs Glassborow under the name "Glassborow & Glassborow", refused a second registration under the name "Bertram & Co". The Divisional Court upheld that refusal, holding that the section was a permissive and procedural section, and that the persons who were registered for value added tax purposes were Mr and Mrs Glassborow, and not the business carried on by them in partnership. In the course of his judgment (with which Lord Widgery C.J. and Boreham J. agreed) May J. made the following observations on the treatment of partnerships for registration purposes:

> "By virtue of section 19 of the Interpretation Act 1889[39] the word 'person' in Part I of the [*Finance*] Act of 1972 must, unless a contrary intention appears, be construed as including an unincorporated body of persons, which more often than not will be the persons trading in partnership ... However, although we frequently use the words 'a partnership' as a collective label for the individuals who trade together in partnership, this is in my view strictly erroneous, save as a convenient shorthand. One cannot equate the word 'partnership' with the word 'person' in section 4[40] of and Schedule 1[41] to the Act of 1972 by virtue of section 19 of the earlier Act of 1889. It will be noticed that in section 22(1)[42] of the Finance Act 1972 the draftsman has been careful and, as I think, accurate in the words he has used.
>
> With this concept in mind it was conceded ... on behalf of the commissioners, and I think rightly conceded, that A carrying on business on his own account is for the purposes of the Act a different 'person' from A and B carrying on business in partnership. Similarly the 'person' comprising A, B and C trading in partnership is different from that comprising A, B and D so trading, because the two bodies of persons are different: they consist of different individuals ...
>
> ... notwithstanding the provisions of the Interpretation Act 1889, I think that in the particular context of the opening words of section 22(1) which I have quoted it is impossible to read the word 'persons' other than in its ordinary and natural meaning, that is to say individuals in the plural, and that consequently, although Glassborow and Glassborow has been registered as a firm name the persons who have in truth registered under Part I of the Act are those carrying on business in partnership as such, namely, Mr and Mrs Glassborow. That being so, the registration is apt to cover the taxable activities of these two individuals trading alternatively as Bertram & Co. In my judgment section 22 is permissive and procedural only, and once a firm name has been registered, the effect of the registration is as though the names of all the individuals trading under that name from time to time were recorded."[43]

---

[38] [1975] Q.B. 465. See also *Miller v. The Commissioners* (1977) V.A.T.T.R. 241; *Customs & Excise Commissioners v. Evans* [1982] S.T.C. 342 (although the main part of this decision has now been statutorily overruled: see *infra*, para. 37–34); also *Michaelis v. The Commissioners* (LON/ 90/925) [1991] S.T.I. 427.

[39] See, now, the Interpretation Act 1978, Sched. 1.

[40] Now the Value Added Tax Act 1994, s.4(1).

[41] Now the Value Added Tax Act 1994, Sched. 1.

[42] Now the Value Added Tax Act 1994, s.45(1), *supra*, para. 37–08.

[43] [1975] Q.B. 465, 473E–H, 474C–E. The last part of the passage cited in the text was followed in *Hawthorn v. Smallcorn* [1998] S.T.C. 591, 595a–f *per* Laws J. See also *Glasse Brothers v. The Commissioners* (LON/88/917) [1989] S.T.I. 619.

On the other hand, in *H. Saunders v. The Commissioners*,[44] it was held that **37–10** separate registrations *were* appropriate in the case of two limited partnerships between a Mr Saunders and a Mr Sorrell, since in the first partnership Mr Saunders was the general partner and Mr Sorrell the limited partner, whilst in the second those roles were reversed. However, the current editor submits that this decision was exceptional and explicable only by reference to the particular attributes of limited partnership.[45]

The implications of the *Glassborow* decision must be considered whenever **37–11** questions of registration arise as regards persons carrying on business in partnership. There should be little difficulty where only one firm is involved, since it will be treated as a separate "person" in order to determine whether its taxable supplies, etc.,[46] exceed the prescribed limits.[47] If those limits are exceeded, registration is applied for, and will normally be granted, in the firm name.[48] Unexpected complications may, however, arise where a number of firms have one or more members in common. This may be illustrated by supposing the existence of two separate firms, the first comprising A, B and C (the ABC partnership) and the second comprising A, B, C and D (the ABCD partnership). So long as the constitution of each firm remains unchanged, they will, on the above principles, be treated as separate "persons" for registration purposes. If D retires from the ABCD partnership[49] at a time when neither the ABC partnership nor the ABCD partnership is registered, it will be necessary to aggregate the taxable supplies, etc., of the two firms in order to determine whether A, B and C (as persons carrying on business in partnership) are obliged to register.[50] If registration is necessary, it may either be in the name of ABC or ABCD.[51] On the other hand, if both the ABC partnership and the ABCD partnership are already registered and notification is given of D's retirement,[52] HMRC could cancel the registration of either firm, and require A, B and C to continue both businesses under a single registration.[53] If only the ABC partnership is registered, the business of the ABCD partnership will be covered by the ABC partnership's registration and tax must be charged on all taxable supplies made by it.[54]

---

[44] (1980) V.A.T.T.R. 53.

[45] Had Mr Saunders and Mr Sorrell retained the same roles in both partnerships, the decision would in all probability have been different. See generally, as to limited partnerships, *supra*, paras 29–01 *et seq.*

[46] See *supra*, paras 37–02 *et seq.*

[47] *Customs & Excise Commissioners v. Glassborow* [1975] Q.B. 465; *Border Flying Company v. The Commissioners* (1976) V.A.T.T.R. 132, 139; *J. Procter (Waddington) Ltd. v. The Commissioners* (1976) V.A.T.T.R. 184, 195; *Miller v. The Commissioners* (1977) V.A.T.T.R. 241.

[48] Nevertheless, the form VAT 2 (see the Value Added Tax Regulations 1995, Sched. 1, as substituted by the Value Added Tax (Amendment) (No. 3) Regulations 2001 (SI 2001/3828), reg. 3, Sched.), which must accompany the application, will contain the names, addresses, telephone numbers, National Insurance numbers and signatures of each partner: see further, *infra*, para. 37–30. It has already been noted that, in an appropriate case, HMRC could insist that the firm is registered in the name of the individual partners: see *supra*, para. 37–08.

[49] The same questions will inevitably arise if D dies or, indeed, if he, for whatever reason, joins the ABC partnership.

[50] *J. Procter (Waddington) Ltd. v. The Commissioners* (1976) V.A.T.T.R. 184, 195.

[51] But not in both: see *Customs & Excise Commissioners v. Glassborow* [1975] Q.B. 465. It would seem to be open to the partners to decide under which name to apply for registration.

[52] See *infra*, para. 37–14.

[53] It is understood that HMRC *will* in practice cancel one of the registrations. It should be noted that this is the position, notwithstanding the express terms of the Value Added Tax Act 1994, s.45(1), which directs that no account is to be taken of any changes in a partnership.

[54] *J.O.W. & E.M. Harris t/a Advanced Structural Maintenance & Repair Co. and Harris & Harris v. The Commissioners*, (CAR/76/220).

It naturally follows that the status of a firm's registration (or non-registration) may need to be reviewed following any change in its membership, depending on the nature of the partners' other business interests.[55] Equally, it may be incumbent on HMRC, when applying the above principles, to ensure that the identity of the true partners is ascertained, if necessary by making further enquiries: they could not properly insist on cancelling the registration of one firm because it *appears* to have the same composition as another firm, if there is evidence in their possession which indicates that the real position is otherwise.[56]

37–12   Since section 45(1) of the Value Added Tax Act 1994 is a permissive and procedural provision, a change in the name of a firm will not affect its registration (even though that change should be notified to HMRC)[57] nor the liability of the partners under an assessment made in the registered name. Thus, an assessment was upheld in *Scrace v. Revenue & Customs Commissioners*,[58] where the partners had been compulsorily registered in a name which was not in use during part of the period covered by the assessment.

Equally, it should be noted that registration of two or more persons as partners under the section does not, *per se*, mean that they are all to be treated as partners in law or render them liable as such. In *Revenue & Customs Commissioners v. Pal*,[59] four supposed partners had allowed their names to be entered on form VAT 2 and they had been registered on that basis. In the event, it was demonstrated that only two of them were actually partners in the business. It was held that, despite the registration, the two non-partners were not liable on an assessment issued against the four, whether on the basis of holding out[60] or otherwise. However, the assessment was held to be valid as against the two partners who had been properly registered as such. It follows that the dangers identified above could exist in a case where there appear to be two separate firms with different memberships but, on a true analysis, the actual partners in each firm are identical.

Attempts to avoid registration

37–13   Given the position set out above, it might be thought that registration could be avoided by fragmenting a business whose turnover is likely to exceed the registration limits into a number of "separate" partnership businesses, none of which have a complete identity of partners. However, if HMRC are satisfied that the fragmentation is artificial and that each firm is making taxable supplies whilst carrying on activities which should properly be regarded as a single business, they may direct that all the firms should henceforth be treated as a single taxable person for registration purposes,[61] thereby constituting a deemed global

---

[55] Where two firms have identical partners and thus a single registration, a change resulting from the departure of one partner from, or the admission of a new partner to, one of those firms will automatically cause them to become separate taxable persons and their respective taxable supplies, etc., will no longer fall to be aggregated.

[56] See *Yasin and Hussain v. Customs & Excise Commissioners* [1999] S.T.I. 239. See also *Revenue & Customs Commissioners v. Pal* [2008] S.T.C. 2442, noted *infra*.

[57] See *infra*, para. 37–14.

[58] [2007] S.T.C. 269.

[59] [2008] S.T.C. 2442.

[60] *i.e.* under the Partnership Act 1890, s.14: see paras 5–35 *et seq*.

[61] Value Added Tax Act 1994, Sched. 1, paras 1A(1) (as added by the Finance Act 1997, s.31(1)), 2(1). For this purpose, HMRC will look at the extent to which the persons carrying on the fragmented business are "closely bound to one another by financial, economic and organisational links": *ibid.* Sched. 1, para. 1A(2), as added by the Finance Act 1997, s.31(1); also *Venuebest Ltd. v. Customs & Excise Commissioners* [2005] V. & D.R. 92. However, it is no longer necessary for HMRC to be

partnership comprising all the members of the constituent firms.[62] If any of those firms is already registered, its registration will be cancelled.[63] Supplementary directions may be issued if the existence of other elements of the fragmented business come to the attention of HMRC at a later date.[64]

Such a direction can equally well be made where one or more parts of the fragmented business are carried on by individuals or companies, *e.g.* if a partnership is dissolved by agreement and its assets are distributed *in specie* between the former partners in such a way as to permit the various elements of the business to be carried on by them.

Changes in the firm

Once a firm has registered, no account is in general taken of any subsequent **37–14** change in its members.[65] This will apply equally whether registration is in the name of the firm or in the names of the individual partners, although in the latter case the current editor understands that an appropriate amendment will be made in the registration to delete or add the name of the outgoing/incoming partner.[66] It should, however, be noted that such a change may in certain circumstances cause a firm's registration to be cancelled,[67] as well as affecting the registrability of other businesses carried on by the partners.[68]

Even though changes in the firm are ignored for registration purposes, the partners must within 30 days notify HMRC of:

(i) any change in the name or trading name of the firm;

satisfied that the main reason for the fragmentation exercise is the avoidance of a liability to be registered. A direction under para. 2(1) cannot have retrospective effect: *Elder and Elder v. Customs & Excise Commissioners* (1999) VAT Decision 15881; also *Newton and Newton (t/a R.E. Newton) v. Customs & Excise Commissioners* [2001] S.T.I. 1231. An attempt to invoke the paragraph failed in *Trippitt v. Customs & Excise Commissioners* [2002] S.T.I. 214; also in *Turner v. HMRC* [2005] S.T.I. 1446, because the directions were incorrectly issued. And see, generally, *Lewis v. The Commissioners* (MAN/88/260) [1989] S.T.I. 271; *Jervis v. The Commissioners* (MAN/88/596) [1989] S.T.I. 784; *Chamberlain v. Customs & Excise Commissioners* [1989] S.T.C. 505; *West End Health and Fitness Club v. The Commissioners* (EDN/89/70) [1989] S.T.I. 869; *Horsman v. The Commissioners* (1990) V.A.T.T.R. 151; *Hundsdoerfer v. The Commissioners* (1990) V.A.T.T.R. 158. Interestingly, HMRC in practice seem more likely to argue that the substance of the relationship between the proprietors of the various constituent parts of the allegedly fragmented business is one of partnership, rather than making a direction under this paragraph: see, for example, *Burrell v. Commissioners of Customs & Excise* [1997] S.T.C. 1413; *Garton and Davies (t/a The Dolly Tub) v. Customs & Excise Commissioners* [2000] S.T.I. 41; *Newton and Newton (t/a R.E. Newton) v. Customs & Excise Commissioners*, *supra*; *Skelton Waste Disposal v. Customs & Excise Commissioners* [2002] S.T.I. 215; *Barton v. Customs & Excise Commissioners* [2003] S.T.I. 1583; *Wild v. Revenue & Customs Commissioners* [2009] S.T.C. 566. *Semble*, the same result could not be achieved by applying the principles enunciated in *W. T. Ramsay Ltd. v. I.R.C.* [1982] A.C. 300 and *Furniss v. Dawson* [1984] A.C. 474; see also *Customs & Excise Commissioners v. Faith Construction Ltd.* [1990] 1 Q.B. 905 and *supra*, para. 34–11

[62] *ibid.* para. 2(7)(f).

[63] Value Added Tax Act 1994, Sched. 1, para. 2(5).

[64] *ibid.* para. 2(4), as amended by the Finance Act 1997, s.31(2).

[65] *ibid.* s.45(1), *supra*, para. 37–07. As to the liability of partners in respect of tax following a change, see *ibid.* s.45(2), (3), considered *infra*, para. 37–34.

[66] HMRC will, as a matter of practice, require a fresh form VAT 2 to be completed.

[67] *Customs & Excise Commissioners v. Glassborow* [1975] Q.B. 465. See also *Weakley v. The Commissioners* (LON/2/73/14S); 93 Taxation 343. And see *supra*, para. 37–11.

[68] Particular care must be taken to ensure that the business of one firm has not been brought under the registration of another, thus requiring tax to be charged on all its supplies, etc.: see *J.O.W. & E.M. Harris t/a Advanced Structural Maintenance & Repair Co. and Harris & Harris v. The Commissioners* (CAR/76/220), *supra*, para. 37–11.

(ii) any change in the name and/or address of any of the partners;

(iii) any change in the composition[69] of the firm;

(iv) any change in the address of its principal place of business; and

(v) the dissolution of the firm.[70]

The notification procedure, and the possible consequences of failure to comply therewith, will be considered further below.[71]

Cancellation of registration

37–15   The registration of a firm may now only be cancelled in a limited number of circumstances.[72] The firm itself may request such cancellation, if it ceases to be liable to be registered and in other prescribed circumstances.[73] Alternatively,

[69] HMRC only require notification where the change in composition involves a change in the identity of the partners, as opposed to a mere change in their capital or asset-surplus sharing ratios. Where two firms merge but only one firm is registered, there will be a change in the composition of the registered firm which must be duly notified. Where, however, both firms are registered, the position is more complex, although much will depend on the precise manner in which the merger is effected. The current editor considers that a merger is likely to bring about a change in the composition of each firm, so that two separate notifications are required. Thereafter, the registration of one of the merged firms must be cancelled. There would seem to be no reason why representations should not be made to HMRC as to which registration should be cancelled and which preserved: if no representations are made, the decision will be left to the discretion of HMRC. *Quaere*, in the case of a limited partnership, whether HMRC should be notified when a general partner becomes a limited partner or vice versa, having regard to the decision in *H. Saunders v. The Commissioners* (1980) V.A.T.T.R. 53, noted *supra*, para. 37–10.

[70] Value Added Tax Regulations 1995, reg. 5(2), as substituted by the Value Added Tax (Amendment) (No. 3) Regulations 2000 (SI 2000/794), reg. 4; Customs & Excise Notice No. 700 (the VAT Guide), paras 26.2, 26.3. In view of the terms of the latter Notice it is, perhaps, arguable that notification does not need to be given immediately following the date of dissolution, but only when the business is discontinued at or prior to the conclusion of the winding up process. Written notification is, in any event, mandatory: *The Bengal Brasserie v. The Commissioners* (LON/90/604) [1991] S.T.I. 662.

[71] See *infra*, paras 37–30, 37–31.

[72] *cf.* the Value Added Tax Act 1983, Sched. 1, paras 7 *et seq.* in their original form.

[73] *Registration pursuant to the Value Added Tax Act 1994, Sched. 1*: see *ibid.* para. 13(1). A firm will cease to be liable to be registered if HMRC are satisfied that it is not otherwise registrable under the Act (*ibid.* para. 13(4)) and it has ceased to make taxable supplies or the value of its taxable supplies in the ensuing year will not exceed £68,000: *ibid.* paras 3, 4(1), as amended by the Value Added Tax (Increase of Registration Limits) Order 2010. art. 3(b)). The registration will be cancelled with effect from the date of the request or such later date as may be agreed: *ibid.* para. 13(1). Note also *ibid.* para. 18, as added by the Finance Act 2003, Sched. 2, para. 3, where cancellation is sought prior to registration under *ibid.* Sched. 3B. *Registration pursuant to ibid. Sched. 2*: see *ibid.* para. 6(1). The procedure is by no means clear in this instance. The only provision authorising the cancellation of a registration on request is contained in *ibid.* para. 6(1), which applies where a registered person is able to satisfy HMRC that "he is not liable to be so registered", not that he has ceased to be liable to register. Yet if this paragraph is intended to cover the case of a person who was not liable to register *ab initio*, the difference of wording between that paragraph and *ibid.* para. 6(2)(a) is inexplicable. Be that as it may, a firm will cease to be liable to be registered if the value of its relevant supplies in the year ending on the previous December 31 did not exceed £70,000 and did not include any supplies satisfying the conditions specified in *ibid.* para. 1(3) and HMRC are satisfied that both requirements will continue to be met in the current year: *ibid.* para. 2(1). *Per contra*, if an option of the type specified in *ibid.* para. 1(2) is in force: *ibid.* para. 2(2). See also *supra*, para. 37–03. If *ibid.* para. 6(1) applies, the registration will be cancelled with effect from the date of the request or such later date as may be agreed. *Registration pursuant to ibid. Sched. 3*: see *ibid.* para. 6(1). Again the procedure is uncertain. The wording of *ibid.* para. 6(1) follows that adopted in *ibid.* Sched. 2, para. 6(1), *supra; cf. ibid.* Sched. 3, para. 6(2), (3). A firm will cease to be liable to be registered if the value of its relevant acquisitions in the year ending on the previous December 31 did not exceed £70,000 and

HMRC may initiate the cancellation, if they are satisfied that the firm has ceased to be registrable[74] or that it was not registrable on the date when it was originally registered.[75] In addition, a firm's registration may be cancelled where there is

HMRC are satisfied that the value of such acquisitions in the current year will not exceed that amount, unless there are reasonable grounds for believing that the value of such acquisitions will exceed that figure in the ensuing period of 30 days: *ibid.* para. 2, as amended by the Value Added Tax (Increase of Registration Limits) Order 2010, art. 4. If *ibid.* para. 6(1) applies, the registration will be cancelled with effect from the date of the request or such later date as may be agreed. *Registration pursuant to ibid. Sched. 3A*: Cancellation may, in effect, be applied for where the firm ceases to make or to have the intention of making relevant supplies (as defined), unless the firm otherwise remains liable/ entitled to be registered: *ibid.* Sched. 3A, para. 5, as added by the Finance Act 2000, Sched. 36. However, the registration will only be cancelled where HMRC are satisfied that the firm has ceased to be liable to be registered under the Schedule and is not otherwise registrable under any other provision of the Act: *ibid.* Sched. 3A, para. 6(1), (3), (4), as added by *ibid. Registration pursuant to ibid. Sched. 3B*: see *ibid.* para. 8(1). Cancellation may be applied for (and must be granted) where the firm notifies HMRC that it has ceased to make or to have the intention of making qualifying supplies (as defined) or to satisfy any of the eligibility conditions: *ibid.* Sched. 3B, para. 8(1)(a), (c), as added by the Finance Act 2003, Sched. 2, para. 4. The registration will be cancelled as from the date of the notification or such earlier date as may be agreed: *ibid.* Sched. 3B, para. 8(2), as added by *ibid.*

[74] *Registration pursuant to the Value Added Tax Act 1994, Sched. 1*: see *ibid.* para. 13(2). As to when a firm will cease to be registrable, see *supra*, n. 73. The registration will be cancelled with effect from the date on which the firm ceased to be registrable or such later date as may be agreed: *ibid.* para. 13(1). *Registration pursuant to ibid. Sched. 2: ibid.* para. 6(3). As to when a firm will cease to be registrable see *supra*, n. 73. In this case, HMRC's power is only exercisable where the proposed supplies have not been made or the place of supply option has not been exercised by the date specified in the original request for registration or where there is a contravention of any condition attached to the registration. The registration will, in general, be cancelled with effect from that specified date or the date of the contravention, as the case may be: *ibid.* para. 6(3); but see also *ibid.* para. 7(3). *Registration pursuant to ibid. Sched. 3*: see *ibid.* para. 6(2). As to when a firm will cease to be registrable, see *supra*, n. 73. The registration will be cancelled with effect from the date on which the firm ceased to be registrable or such later date as may be agreed: *ibid.* The power is also exercisable where the proposed acquisitions have not been made by the date specified in the original request for registration or where there is a contravention of any condition attached to the registration: *ibid.* para. 6(4). In such a case, the registration will, in general, be cancelled with effect from that specified date or the date of the contravention (as the case may be): *ibid. Registration pursuant to ibid. Sched. 3A*: see *ibid.* para. 6(2), as added by the Finance Act 2000, Sched. 36. As to when a firm will cease to be registrable, see *supra*, n. 73. The registration will be cancelled with effect from the date on which relevant supplies (as defined) ceased to be made or from such later date as may be agreed: *ibid.* However, the registration will only be cancelled where HMRC are satisfied that the firm has ceased to be liable to be registered under the Schedule *and* that it is not otherwise registrable under any provision of the Act: *ibid.* Sched. 3A, para. 6(1), (3), (4), as added by *ibid. Registration pursuant to ibid. Sched. 3B*: see *ibid.* para. 8(1). In this case the registration will be cancelled only where HMRC determines that the firm has ceased to make or to have the intention of making qualifying supplies (as defined) or to satisfy any of the eligibility conditions or that it has failed to comply with its obligations under the Schedule: *ibid.* Sched. 3B, para. 8(1)((b), (d), (e), as added by the Finance Act 2003, Sched. 2, para. 4. The registration will be cancelled as from the date of the determination or such earlier date as HMRC may direct: *ibid.* Sched. 3B, para. 8(3), as added by *ibid. Notifications*: Note that, if the firm ceases to make or to have the intention to make taxable supplies, HMRC must be notified: *ibid.* Sched. 1, para. 11. A similar requirement applies in the case of registration under *ibid.* Scheds. 2, 3 and 3A: see *ibid.* Sched. 2, para. 5, Sched. 3, para. 5, Sched. 3A, para. 5(1) (as added by the Finance Act 2000, Sched. 36), Sched. 3B, para. 7 (as added by the Finance Act 2003, Sched. 2, para. 4).

[75] *Registration pursuant to ibid. Sched. 1*: see *ibid.* para. 13(3). *Registration pursuant to ibid. Sched. 2*: see *ibid.* para. 6(2). In the case of registration under *ibid.* para. 4, it must also be shown that the firm had no intention to make the supplies in question: *ibid. Registration pursuant to ibid. Sched. 3*: see *ibid.* para. 6(3). In the case of registration under *ibid.* para. 4(2), it must also be shown that the firm had no intention to make relevant acquisitions: *ibid. Registration pursuant to ibid. Sched. 3A*: see *ibid.* para. 6(2), as added by the Finance Act 2000, Sched. 36. There is no equivalent under *ibid.* Sched. 3B. Where HMRC proceed under any of the above provisions, the registration is cancelled retrospectively. *Berwick v. Customs & Excise Commissioners*, May 31, 2002 (Lawtel 18/7/02), noticed *supra*, para. 37–01, n. 2, is a recent example of a case within this class.

already a subsisting registration in respect of a firm comprising the same persons[76] or where a direction is made by HMRC which has the effect of treating a number of notionally separate firms or persons as a single taxable person.[77]

2. TAXABLE SUPPLIES

37–16 The general treatment of taxable supplies of goods and services made by a firm is no different to that applied to any other taxable person and accordingly falls outside the scope of this work. It should, however, be noted that prior to January 1, 1978, tax was only chargeable on taxable supplies made "in the course of a business" but, after that date, was chargeable on taxable supplies made "in the course or furtherance of a business".[78] The additional words are of a very general and imprecise nature, and the scope of the tax at that stage appears to have been considerably enlarged.[79] Thus, the tribunal has held that a firm of solicitors makes a taxable supply "in the course of a business" when paying moneys into a client's deposit account, but not when paying moneys into the firm's own deposit account, even if that account is treated as a reserve fund, which may be called on in the event of a cash flow problem.[80] The current editor considers that HMRC could now contend that payments into such an account, whilst not made "in the course of a business," are made "in the furtherance of a business," since the maintenance of such a reserve is clearly beneficial to the business. On that footing, the payments would constitute taxable supplies. However, the point is arguable, given the imprecision of the words "in the furtherance of a business".

It is nevertheless of importance to refer to a number of specific transactions to which a firm or its members may be party, in order to identify whether a taxable supply is involved and, if so, its potential effect on the firm's registrability.[81]

Capital and other contributions

37–17 Following the decision of the European Court of Justice in *KapHag Renditefonds v. Finanzamt Charlottenberg*,[82] HM Customs & Excise set out its views on the taxability of various forms of contributions to partnerships in a Business Brief

---

[76] *Customs & Excise Commissioners v. Glassborow* [1975] Q.B. 465. And see *supra*, para. 37–09.

[77] Value Added Tax Act 1994, Sched. 1, para. 2(5). See further, *supra*, para. 37–13.

[78] Finance Act 1972, s.2(1), as substituted by the Finance Act 1977. See now the Value Added Tax Act 1994, s.4(1).

[79] In *Re Ward* [1941] Ch. 308 the word "furtherance" was considered to be synonymous with "advancement": *ibid.* p. 311 *per* MacKinnon L.J. However, this case concerned a charitable bequest, and too much reliance cannot be placed thereon in the present context. Equally, in *Express Newspapers Ltd. v. McShane* [1980] A.C. 672 and *Duport Steels Ltd. v. Sirs* [1980] 1 W.L.R. 142 it was held that the expression "in . . . furtherance" in the Trade Union and Labour Relations Act 1974, s.13(1) contemplated a subjective test. See also *R.H.M. Bakeries (Northern) Ltd. v. Customs & Excise Commissioners* [1979] S.T.C. 72; *Birketts v. Customs & Excise Commissioners* [2002] S.T.I. 371; *Oglethorpe Sturton & Gillibrand v. Customs & Excise Commissioners* [2002] S.T.I. 834.

[80] *Hedges and Mercer v. The Commissioners* (1976) V.A.T.T.R. 146.

[81] For example, the value of the supplies made by a firm during the course of winding up its affairs may be sufficient to exceed the prescribed limits, and thus to render the firm a taxable person.

[82] (Case C-442/01) [2005] S.T.C. 1500.

issued in 2004.[83] As might be expected, it is accepted that the mere contribution of capital, whether in the form of cash or a specific asset, by an incoming partner[84] does not in general involve a taxable supply, since there is no reciprocal supply by the partnership.[85] The position may however, be more complex, where the incoming partner is a taxable person in his own right, unless the contribution is made in cash. If it takes the form of goods which are used in his existing business and on the acquisition of which he recovered input tax, then the contribution will involve a taxable supply, even though no consideration is received.[86] In the case of land, the contribution will only involve a taxable supply if the incoming partner was entitled to deduct input tax in relation thereto.[87] If, unusually, the contribution consists of the incoming partner's own services,[88] no issue should arise.[89] If he merely allows the partnership to use goods or land which form part of his business and on which input tax was recovered then there will be a deemed supply of services which will be taxable, even though again no consideration is received.[90] Similarly in the case of the onward supply of services provided to the partner's own business.[91]

In those cases where a taxable supply is treated as made, that supply may be eligible to be treated as a transfer of a going concern.[92] Otherwise, the firm should be able to recover the input tax paid on normal principles.[93]

---

[83] Business Brief 21/04 entitled "VAT—VAT position of share issues and partnership contributions following the ECJ decision in *KapHag Renditefonds*" and dated August 10, 2004, section 1, reproduced *infra*, paras A6–28 *et seq*, The views set out in the Brief are applicable to all partnerships of individuals, corporate partnerships and limited partnerships, as well as limited liability partnerships: *ibid*. para. 1.B, *infra*, para. A6–30.

[84] The same considerations should apply in the case of an existing partner who contributes additional capital.

[85] Business Brief 21/04, para. 1.B, *infra*, para. A6–30.

[86] Value Added Tax Act 1994, Sched. 4, para. 5(1), (5), as amended by the Finance Act 1995, s.33(3)(a); Business Brief 21/04, para. 1.B(ii), *infra*, para. A6–32. See also, *infra*, para. 37–25. Note that where the partner originally acquired the goods under a transfer as a going concern (see *infra*, para. 37–23), this treatment will still apply. As to the position where the contribution takes the form of a computer within the Capital Goods Scheme, see *ibid*. para. 1.B(vi), *infra*, para. A6–36.

[87] *i.e.* by reason of an exercise of the option under *ibid*. Sched. 10, para. 2 (as substituted by the Value Added Tax (Buildings and Land) Order 2008 (SI 2008/1146), art. 2) or by reason of the land not falling within the exemption in *ibid*. Sched. 9, Pt II, Group 1. See Business Brief 21/04, para. 1.B(iii), *infra*, para. A6–33. See further the Value Added Tax Act 1994, Sched. 4, para. 9, applying *ibid*. para. 5(1), (5), *supra*, with modifications but treating the supply as a supply of *services*. As to the position where the contribution takes the form of an interest in land within the Capital Goods Scheme, see Business Brief 21/04, para. 1.B(vi), *infra*, para. A6–36.

[88] Most incoming partners will agree to provide their services for the benefit of the partnership, but it would be exceptional to see this classified as a capital contribution, which ought, in any event, properly to be expressed as a cash sum: see *supra*, para. 10–59.

[89] In such a case, even if the partner were regarded as supplying his services in the course or furtherance of his own business (which is, in the circumstances, unlikely), there will be no consideration for the supply and no tax will be chargeable: Value Added Tax Act 1994, s.5(2).

[90] Value Added Tax Act 1994, Sched. 4, paras 5(4), (5) (as amended by the Finance Act 1995, s.33(3)(a)), 9(1); Business Brief 21/04, para. 1.B(i), *infra*, para. A6–31. Note, however, that land is, unaccountably, not specifically mentioned in that paragraph. This treatment will still apply if the partner originally acquired the land under a transfer as a going concern, as to which see *infra*, para. 37–23.

[91] See the Value Added Tax (Supply of Services) Order 1993 (SI 1993/1507) as amended; also Business Brief 21/04, para. 1.B(i), *infra*, para. A6–31.

[92] Under the Value Added Tax Act 1994, s.49 and the Value Added Tax (Special Provisions) Order 1995 (SI 1995/1268), art. 5, noted *infra*, para. 37–23: see Business Brief 21/04, para. 1.B(iv), *infra*, para. A6–34.

[93] Business Brief 21/04, para. 1.B(v), *infra*, para. A6–35.

Offices held by partners

37–18   Section 94(4) of the Value Added Tax Act 1994 provides as follows:

> "(4) Where a person, in the course or furtherance of a trade, profession or vocation, accepts any office,[94] services supplied by him as the holder of that office are treated as supplied in the course or furtherance of the trade, profession or vocation."

The subsection only applies to an office and *not* to a position which has the nature of employment. Thus, a partner in a firm of solicitors who also held a part-time appointment as a salaried solicitor to a borough council was held to be an employee and, thus, not supplying services to the council.[95]

37–19   Whether an office held by an individual partner will involve the firm, as opposed to that partner, making a taxable supply will be a question of fact in each case. However, it should be noted that HMRC formerly adopted a fairly generous approach in determining what offices were held "in the course of a trade, profession or vocation",[96] and did not regard the fact that the office-holding partner accounted to the firm for any fees received as in itself decisive.[97] Although it must be recognised that almost any benefit which accrues to a firm from an office held by one of the partners[98] will or may further the partnership business, thus supporting an argument that the firm has made a taxable supply,[99] it would seem that HMRC are unlikely to depart from their former practice in applying section 94(4). This is to a large extent borne out by the terms of the joint Statement issued by the Law Society and HM Customs and Excise in 1979,[100] wherein it is stated that an office will be regarded as held in the course of a profession if the professional skills of the office-holder are exercised in the performance of the duties of the office, whilst an office will be regarded as held in the *furtherance* of a profession if possession of professional skills was a factor in the appointment or acceptance of the office was likely to enhance the reputation of the individual or firm concerned. Moreover, HMRC are apparently prepared to accept that there is no taxable supply by the firm, even if the office-holder accounts to it for his fees, provided that three conditions are satisfied, namely that:

---

[94] There is no longer any exemption for public offices: *cf.* the original provision contained in the Finance Act 1972, s.45(3), as considered in *Hempsons v. The Commissioners* (1977) V.A.T.T.R. 73. It follows that the fees of a Commissioner for Oaths are subject to the tax: see the replies of the Customs & Excise to the comments of the Consultative Committee of Accountancy Bodies on the Finance Bill 1977, reproduced at [1977] S.T.I. 276, 278. See also (1979) 76 L.S.Gaz. 1151.

[95] *Lean and Rose v. The Commissioners* (1974) 1 V.A.T.T.R. 7. *cf. Bray Walker v. Customs & Excise Commissioners* [2004] S.T.I. 575, where the partner was a director and could not be shown to be acting as an employee.

[96] See the original terms of the Finance Act 1972, s.45(3).

[97] See [1976] S.T.I. 107. It is understood that the principles there set out did not constitute the then *official* view of the Commissioners. As to the effect of the office-holder making use of partnership facilities as a matter of convenience, see *Hempsons v. The Commissioners* (1977) V.A.T.T.R. 73, 92–93.

[98] The benefit may be tangible (*e.g.* fees) or intangible (*e.g.* general goodwill).

[99] It seems that there was no intention to introduce a substantial change of practice, otherwise than in relation to public offices: see the replies of the Customs & Excise to the comments of the C.C.A.B. on the Finance Bill 1977, reproduced at [1977] S.T.I. 276, 278.

[100] (1979) 76 L.S.Gaz. 1151. The Statement is entitled "V.A.T. and Public Offices", but deals only with the position of solicitors. It does, however, provide a clear indication of the approach likely to be adopted by HMRC where offices are held by partners in other spheres.

(a) the office-holding has been arranged with the individual partner concerned and there is no written agreement between the firm and the organisation in which the office is held;

(b) the office-holding arises from some personal, family or significant financial interest of the partner in that organisation, rather than from his professional qualifications or interest; and

(c) the duties of the office do not involve significant use of the skills which the partner currently employs in practising his profession (unless such services are separately charged for by the firm).[101]

There is, nevertheless, some evidence of a hardening of attitude on the part of HMRC regarding offices and appointments held by partners, albeit that their challenges have met with no great success.[102]

It should also be noted that there may be no taxable supply where an office is accepted by a prospective partner *before* the commencement of the partnership business.[103]

Use of partnership property by the partners

A supply of services will be treated as made by a firm whenever goods or land **37–20** held or used by it for the purposes of its business are used or made available to a partner for his own personal benefit, rather than for business purposes.[104] Such a supply will automatically be treated as made in the course or furtherance of the business, if it would not otherwise be so treated.[105] The tribunal analysed this type of supply in *Border Flying Co. v. The Commissioners*,[106] where a group of five businessmen had formed a consortium to acquire an aircraft both for their

---

[101] *ibid.* para. 8.

[102] See the following VAT Tribunal decisions (all of which concerned offices held by partners in firms of solicitors): *Birketts v. Customs & Excise Commissioners* [2002] S.T.I. 371; *Oglethorpe Sturton & Gillibrand v. Customs & Excise Commissioners* [2002] S.T.I. 834; *Bray Walker v. Customs & Excise Commissioners* [2004] S.T.I. 834.

[103] *Gardner v. Customs & Excise Commissioners* (1989) V.A.T.T.R. 132.

[104] *ibid.* Sched. 4, para. 5(4), as applied, in the case of land, by *ibid.* para. 9(1). However, no such supply will be treated as made where credit for the input tax on the goods/land in question could not be obtained under *ibid.* ss.25, 26: *ibid.* Sched. 4, para. 5(5)(a), as amended by the Finance Act 1993, s.33(3)(a), the Finance Act 1998, s.21(4) and the Finance Act 2000, s.136(9). In the case of land or goods which have an economic life, a special set of provisions apply with a view to ensuring that the real cost of the supply is brought into account: see the Value Added Tax Regulations 1995 (SI 1995/2518), regs. 116A *et seq.*, as added by the Value Added Tax (Amendment) (No. 7) Regulations 2007 (SI 2007/3099), reg. 4. As to when goods have an economic life, see *ibid.* reg. 116C and, as to land, see *ibid.* reg. 116D. Equally, where the land or goods do *not* have an economic life at the time they are made available, the Value Added Tax Act 1994, Sched. 4, para. 5(4) is disapplied in its entirety: see the Value Added Tax (Special Provisions) Order 1995 (SI 1995/1268), art. 10A, as added by the Value Added Tax (Special Provisions) (Amendment) Order 2007 (SI 2007/2923), art. 3. In any other case, the value of the supply would appear to be its open market value, unless it forms part of a bona fide commercial arrangement between the partners: see *ibid.* Sched. 6, para. 1, as amended by the Corporation Tax Act 2010, Sched. 1, Pt 2, para. 285(b); Corporation Tax Act 2010, s.1122(7), (8).

[105] Value Added Tax Act 1994, Sched. 4, para. 5(6)(b), as amended by the Finance Act 1995, s.33(3)(a).

[106] (1976) V.A.T.T.R. 132. This decision was, of course, reached before the introduction of the revised provisions which are now contained in the Value Added Tax Act 1994, Sched. 4, para. 5(4). *cf.* the decision in *Three H. Aircraft Hire v. Customs & Excise Commissioners* [1982] S.T.C. 653, noticed *supra*, para. 37–01, n. 2.

own use and for public hire. Having found them to be partners, the tribunal went on to hold that each partner had a direct beneficial interest in the aircraft.[107] On that basis, whenever one partner chose to use the aircraft for his own private purposes, the other partners were treated as temporarily releasing (and therefore supplying) their beneficial interests to him and, moreover, he was treated as having supplied his own beneficial interest to himself. In the circumstances, it was clear that those supplies were made in the course of the firm's business.[108]

The above decision is unsatisfactory, since the tribunal treated each partner as having a direct beneficial interest in the aircraft, without considering whether that conclusion was justifiable in law, given the true nature of a partnership share.[109] On that footing it is open to challenge, even though there is now no doubt that a taxable supply occurs whenever a partner uses a partnership asset for his own purposes.[110]

Sales of partnership assets

Goods and land

37–21   A supply of goods is made whenever goods or land forming part of the assets of a business are transferred or disposed of so as no longer to form part of those assets, whether or not for a consideration,[111] and that supply will automatically be treated as made in the course or furtherance of the business.[112] The only exceptions relate to small gifts and gifts of industrial samples.[113]

Accordingly, whenever a firm disposes of such an asset, a taxable supply will be made, unless the asset is exempt[114] or otherwise outside the scope of the tax. This will include the case where one or more partners, either alone or with others, acquire assets from the firm.[115]

---

[107] (1976) V.A.T.T.R. 132, 138.

[108] *ibid.* pp. 137–138. As has been noted, such a supply would now automatically be treated as made in the course or furtherance of the business: Value Added Tax Act 1994, Sched. 4, para. 5(6)(b), as amended.

[109] *i.e.* an entitlement to a share in the surplus remaining after the realisation of all the partnership assets and the payment of all partnership debts and liabilities: see further, *supra*, paras 19–05 *et seq.* It should be noted that the approach adopted by the tribunal mirrors HMRC's treatment of disposals by partners for the purposes of capital gains tax (see *supra*, paras 35–06 *et seq.*) and the approach adopted by the court in *Gray v. I.R.C.* [1994] S.T.C. 360, 377 (CA).

[110] Value Added Tax Act 1994, Sched. 4, para. 5(4).

[111] Value Added Tax Act 1994, Sched. 4, para. 5(1), as applied, in the case of land, by *ibid.* para. 9. This effectively enacted the decision in *H. B. Mattia Ltd. v. The Commissioners* (1976) V.A.T.T.R. 33. Note also that, where land or goods forming part of the assets of the business are sold by a third party under a power exercisable by him (*e.g.* as mortgagee), a taxable supply will be treated as made in the course or furtherance of that business: *ibid.* paras 7, 9. As to the position where the goods are merely *removed* to another Member State of the EC in the course or furtherance of the business, see *ibid.* para. 6.

[112] *ibid.* Sched. 4, para. 5(6), as amended.

[113] *ibid.* Sched. 4, para. 5(2), as amended by the Finance Act 2003, s.21(2) (superseding the Value Added Tax (Business Gifts of Small Value) Order 2001 (SI 2001/1735)); also *ibid.* paras 5(2ZA), 5(2A), as respectively added by the Finance Act 2003, s.21(3) and the Finance Act 1998, s.21(3).

[114] See, as to exempt supplies, *ibid.* s.31, Sched. 9 (as amended).

[115] See *Fengate Developments v. Customs & Excise Commissioners* [2005] S.T.C. 191 (CA), where land in respect of which the partnership had elected to waive exemption was sold to a partner and his ex-wife, who were partners in another firm. See further, as to withdrawals of assets by partners, *infra*, paras 37–25, 37–26.

Goodwill

It has been seen[116] that goodwill will usually be an asset of the firm, but it is **37–22** questionable whether it can properly be described as "goods".[117] Nevertheless, in 1982 HM Customs and Excise announced that they will treat all sales of goodwill as taxable supplies, whether the goodwill takes some tangible form, *e.g.* a list of customers, or not.[118]

Sale of partnership business as a going concern

The tax treatment of a sale of an entire business as a going concern gave rise **37–23** to considerable difficulties prior to the introduction of what is now section 94(6) of the Value Added Tax Act 1994,[119] which provides:

> "(6) The disposition of a business[, or part of a business,] as a going concern,[120] or of [the assets or liabilities of the business or part of the business] (whether or not in connection with its reorganisation or winding up), is a supply made in the course or furtherance of the business."

The subsection requires the disposition to be treated as a "supply", but not necessarily as a "taxable supply".[121] It would accordingly still seem necessary to dissect the business into its constituent elements in order to determine which of its assets are exempt or outside the scope of the tax[122] and whether there has been

---

[116] See *supra*, paras 10–49, 10–197 *et seq.*, 18–17.

[117] The expression "goods" is not defined in the Value Added Tax Act 1994, although several provisions expressly treat certain types of supply as a supply of goods, *e.g.* see *ibid.* Sched. 4, paras 3, 4. It is submitted that, where no such provision applies, "goods" should be given its usual meaning, *i.e.* tangible chattels or choses in possession (as opposed to choses in action).

[118] HM Customs & Excise Press Release dated December 10, 1982, reproduced at [1982] S.T.I. 554. Formerly, goodwill was treated as outside the scope of the tax unless it took some tangible form: see, for example, the decision in *J. Procter (Waddington) Ltd. v. The Commissioners* (1976) V.A.T.T.R. 184.

[119] As amended by the Finance Act 2007, s.100(7). The original predecessor of this subsection was the Finance Act 1972, s.45(6), as added by the Finance Act 1977. In *J. Procter (Waddington) Ltd. v. The Commissioners*, *supra*, the tribunal had previously held that the sale of a business as a going concern was a taxable supply in the course of the business, since the business of a taxable person falls to be treated as the management of all the businesses which he carries on: *ibid.* p. 195. The decision is an unsatisfactory one, but note also *infra*, para. 37–28, n. 164.

[120] As to when there can properly be said to be a transfer of a business "as a going concern", see *Kenmir Ltd. v. Frizzell* [1968] 1 W.L.R. 329 (DC); *Nicholas and Nicholas (t/a A & P Scaffolding) v. Customs & Excise Commissioners* [1999] S.T.I. 793; *Sawadee Restaurant v. Customs & Excise Commissioners* [1999] S.T.I. 934; *Zargari v. Commissioners of Customs & Excise*, Unreported March 15, 2001 (V & DTr); *Shorter (t/a Ideal Scaffolding) v. Customs & Excise Commissioners* [2001] S.T.I. 1392 (assets taken over following the dissolution of a partnership); *International Supplier Auditing Ltd. v. Customs & Excise Commissioners* [2003] S.T.I. 1512 (sale of assets at a time when no business was being carried on); *Ludovico v. Customs & Excise Commissioners*, May 24, 2004 (Lawtel 28/6/04).

[121] This expression is defined in the Value Added Tax Act 1994, s.4(2) as "a supply of goods or services made in the United Kingdom other than an exempt supply."

[122] For an example of the dissection which is required, see *J. Procter (Waddington) Ltd. v. The Commissioners* (1976) V.A.T.T.R. 184. It should, however, be noted that goodwill is no longer treated as outside the scope of the tax (see *supra*, para. 37–22) and that the general exemption in respect of land has been severely curtailed and it is now, in any event, possible to opt in to the tax: Value Added Tax Act 1994, Sched. 9, Pt II, Group 1 (as amended by the Value Added Tax (Land) Order 1995 (SI 1995/282) and prospectively further amended by the Value Added Tax (Buildings and Land) Order 2008 (SI 2008/1146, art. 4), Sched. 10, para. 2(1) (as substituted by the Value Added Tax (Buildings and Land) Order 2008, art. 2). It may well be desirable, when drawing up a contract for the sale of a business as a going concern, to apportion the purchase price between the various assets sold, so that, subject to the apportionment being shown to be genuine, the dissection process will be simplified.

a taxable supply of goods or services. Furthermore, a supply will, in any event, only be treated as made where the business assets are transferred by a taxable person to a purchaser who is not, and does not as a result of the transfer become, a taxable person and who could not, for whatever reason, use the assets in carrying on the same kind of business, whether as a new business or as part of an existing business.[123]

For registration purposes, the purchaser will be treated as having carried on the business before as well as after the transfer.[124] It will generally fall to the purchaser to preserve the records of the business.[125]

Partnership ceasing to be a taxable person

37–24   The circumstances in which HMRC may cancel the registration of a firm which ceases to be a taxable person have already been noticed.[126] In such a case, any goods forming part of its assets will, in general, be treated as supplied in the course or furtherance of its business immediately before the firm lost that status.[127] An exception is, however, made where the business is transferred as a

---

[123] Value Added Tax Act 1994, s.49(2), as amended by the Finance Act 2007, s.100(3); the Value Added Tax (Special Provisions) Order 1995 (SI 1995/1268), art. 5(1) (as amended by the Value Added Tax (Special Provisions) (Amendment) Order 1998 (SI 1998/760), art. 4) in general prevents a supply of goods or services being treated as made on the sale of a business as a going concern where the business assets are transferred by a taxable person to another taxable person (or a person who immediately becomes a taxable person as a result of the transfer); see also *Customs & Excise Commissioners v. Dearwood Ltd.* [1986] S.T.C. 327; *Rakshit v. The Commissioners* (LON/87/716) [1989] S.T.I. 114; *Conard Systems and Engineering Ltd. v. The Commissioners* (MAN/89/23) [1990] S.T.I. 49; *Chevenings Ltd. v. The Commissioners* (LON/89/733) [1990] S.T.I. 841; *ECSG Ltd. v. The Commissioners* (LON/88/580) [1990] S.T.I. 873 (transfer following cessation of trading by insolvent firm); *The Golden Oak Partnership v. The Commissioners* (LON/90/958) [1992] S.T.I. 491 (sale of partially developed land); *cf. McMichael v. The Commissioners* (LON/88/98) [1990] S.T.I. 128; *Shorter (t/a Ideal Scaffolding) v. Customs & Excise Commissioners, supra.* Note, however, the exception in the case of certain categories of land and buildings: *ibid.* arts. 5(2), 5(2A), (2B), as amended or added by the Value Added Tax (Special Provisions) (Amendment) Order 2004 (SI 2004/779), arts 3, 4. There is now no specific provision covering the sale of a business by any person (other than a taxable person) to another person: *cf.* the Value Added Tax (Special Provisions) Order 1977, art. 12, which was revoked by the Value Added Tax (Special Provisions) Order 1981 (SI 1981/1741), art. 3(1). However, it is thought that, by implication, such a sale would not involve a supply of goods or services for the purposes of the tax, provided that the transferee is going to carry on the same kind of business as that carried on by the transferor and thus should, in most cases, not have the effect of turning an otherwise non-taxable person into a taxable person.

[124] Value Added Tax Act 1994, s.49(1)(a), as amended by the Finance Act 2007, s.100(2), Sched. 27, Pt 6(2); see also *ibid.* Sched. 1, para. 1(2), (3), as respectively amended by the Value Added Tax (Increase of Registration Limits) Order 2010 (SI 2010/920), art. 3(a), (b). In addition HMRC may make provision, by regulation, for securing continuity in the application of the Act: *ibid.* s.49(2) and (3), as respectively amended by the Finance Act 2007, s.100(3), (5). The current regulations are to be found in the Value Added Tax Regulations 1995 (SI 1995/2518), reg. 6, as amended by the Value Added Tax (Amendment) Regulations 1997 (SI 1997/1086), reg. 3, the Value Added Tax (Amendment) (No. 3) Regulations 2004 (SI 2004/1675), reg. 3 and the Value Added Tax (Amendment) (No. 5) Regulations 2007 (SI 2007/2085), regs. 3–5. Note also the decision in *Ponsonby v. Customs & Excise Commissioners* [1988] S.T.C. 28.

[125] Value Added Tax Act 1994, s.49(2A), as added by the Finance Act 2007, s.100(4); the Value Added Tax Regulations 1995, reg. 6(3)(f), as added by the Value Added Tax (Amendment) (No. 5) Regulations 2007, reg. 4(d).

[126] See *supra*, para. 37–15.

[127] Value Added Tax Act 1994, Sched. 4, para. 8(1), as amended by the Value Added Tax (Deemed Supply of Goods) Order 2000 (SI 2000/266), art. 2. Note that certain goods may be excepted: *ibid.* para. 8(2), as amended by the Finance Act 2007, s.100(9). The value of the supply will be determined in accordance with *ibid.* Sched. 6, para. 6 and will normally be the equivalent of their market value: *ibid.* para. 6(2)(a).

going concern to another taxable person[128] or is temporarily carried on following the death, bankruptcy or incapacity of all the partners,[129] or where the tax on the deemed supply would not exceed £1000.[130]

Withdrawal of assets by partners, etc.

Prior to dissolution

It has already been seen that a purchase of a partnership asset by a partner may **37–25** give rise to a taxable supply.[131] Other scenarios are addressed by HMRC in Business Brief 21/04.[132] Thus, where tax was chargeable on the partner's contribution of the asset and was recovered by the partnership, there will be a supply if that partner subsequently withdraws the asset, unless it qualifies as a transfer of a going concern.[133] Similarly, if the only reason why tax was not payable on the contribution was because it qualified as a transfer of the latter type.[134] If the withdrawing partner receives more or less assets than he originally contributed, tax will be charged on normal principles,[135] unless the transfer qualifies as a transfer of a going concern.[136] If, on the other hand, the partnership did not recover the input tax on the original contribution, then there will be no supply.

On dissolution

A taxable supply of all the goods (and land within the charge to tax)[137] owned **37–26** by a partnership will be almost inevitable in the event of a general dissolution.[138] It has already been seen[139] that the sale of a partnership asset, or of the partnership business as a going concern, may be treated as a taxable supply. In addition, the Act specifically provides that anything done in connection with the termination or intended termination of a business is treated as done in the course or furtherance of that business[140]: there can accordingly be no doubt that all supplies of goods and services made whilst the firm's affairs are being wound up

---

[128] *ibid.* Sched. 4, para. 8(1)(a).

[129] *ibid.* Sched. 4, para. 8(1)(b); Value Added Tax Regulations 1995, reg. 9(1). Such treatment is, however, in the discretion of HMRC: *ibid. Semble,* the position will be the same in the event of the firm being wound up as an unregistered company (as to which see *supra,* paras 27–04 *et seq.*): but note the terms of *ibid.* reg. 9(3), as amended by the Enterprise Act 2002 (Insolvency) Order 2003 (SI 2003/2096), Sched., Pt II, para. 56.

[130] Value Added Tax Act 1994, Sched. 4, para. 8(1)(c), as amended by the Value Added Tax (Deemed Supply of Goods) Order 2000, art. 2.

[131] See *supra,* para. 37–21.

[132] Entitled "VAT—VAT position of share issues and partnership contributions following the ECJ decision in *KapHag Renditefonds*" and dated August 10, 2004, section 1, reproduced *infra,* paras A6–28 *et seq.* See also *supra,* para. 37–17.

[133] Business Brief 21/04, para. 1.B(vii)(a), *infra,* para. A6–37. As to the basis for the charge, see *supra,* para. 37–21.

[134] Business Brief 21/04, para. 1.B(vii)(b), *infra,* para. A6–37.

[135] See *supra,* para. 37–21.

[136] Business Brief 21/04, para. 1.B(vii)(c), (d), *infra,* para. A6–37.

[137] See *supra,* para. 37–23, n. 122.

[138] This will be so whether or not any *actual* supplies are made in the course of winding up the firm's affairs.

[139] See *supra,* paras 37–21 *et seq.*

[140] Value Added Tax Act 1994, s.94(5). It would seem that no change of practice was contemplated when the wording of the original section (Finance Act 1972, s.45(5)) was amended: see the replies of the Customs & Excise to the comments of the Consultative Committee of Accountancy Bodies on the Finance Bill 1977, reproduced at [1977] S.T.I. 276, 278.

will be taxable.[141] This will, where relevant, include a supply to one of the partners.[142] Any remaining goods owned by the firm will in any event be the subject of a deemed supply immediately before the firm ceases to be a taxable person,[143] even though it may only have become such a person by reason of supplies made in the course of the winding up.[144] Nevertheless, as noted above,[145] if input tax was not deducted by the partnership when the asset in question was originally contributed by a partner, its return to him by a distribution *in specie* should not involve a taxable supply.[146]

Once the final deemed supply of all the firm's goods has been made, any subsequent supply of those goods will not be taxable,[147] unless it is made in the course or furtherance of a *new* business carried on by the partners in respect of which they are required to be registered.

Transfers of partnership shares

37–27   It has already been seen that, following the decision of the European Court of Justice in *KapHag Renditefonds v. Finanzamt Charlottenberg*,[148] HM Customs & Excise issued a Business Brief dealing with the tax treatment of contributions and withdrawals of assets by partners.[149] This was subsequently followed up by a further Business Brief[150] entitled "VAT and partnership 'shares'". The following propositions regarding the taxability of the transfer of a partnership share[151] can be drawn from that Business Brief and are, where necessary, tested against the analysis contained in the previous edition of this work[152]:

---

[141] In the absence of a specific provision, it might have been argued that there can be no supply in the course or furtherance of a business when the supply is made purely with a view to winding that business up. As to the continuing authority of the partners to make supplies in the course of winding up the firm's affairs, see the Partnership Act 1890, s.38, considered *supra*, paras 13–62 *et seq.*

[142] See *Shorter (t/a Ideal Scaffolding) v. Customs & Excise Commissioners* [2001] S.T.I. 1392 where, following a dissolution, one of the partners gave up his share in exchange for certain equipment and vehicles owned by the firm. The Commissioners sought (unsuccessfully) to argue that he could not deduct the input tax thereon because he had taken over part of the business and no tax was chargeable by virtue of the Value Added Tax (Special Provisions) Order 1995, art. 5(1). Naturally, there will be instances in which that Order *will* apply. And note also the decision in *Fengate Developments v. Customs & Excise Commissioners* [2005] S.T.C. 191 (CA), noticed *supra*, para. 37–21, n. 115, albeit that there the supply was not made on dissolution.

[143] Value Added Tax Act 1994, Sched. 4, para. 8(1), as amended: see *supra*, para. 37–24.

[144] Save in certain cases where the partnership business is sold as a going concern (as to which see *supra*, para. 37–23, n. 120), the sale of any goods which it owns may itself cause the value of its supplies to exceed the prescribed limits: see *supra*, paras 37–21, 37–22.

[145] See *supra*, para. 37–25.

[146] Business Brief 21/04, para. 1.B(vii)(d), *infra*, para. A6–37.

[147] See *Marshall v. The Commissioners* (1975) V.A.T.T.R. 98.

[148] (Case C-442/01) [2005] S.T.C. 1500.

[149] See the Business Brief 21/04 "VAT—VAT position of share issues and partnership contributions following the ECJ decision in *KapHag Renditefonds*" dated August 10, 2004, section 1, noticed *supra*, paras 37–17, 37–25 and reproduced *infra*, paras A6–28 *et seq.*

[150] No. 30/04, issued on November 19, 2004 and reproduced *infra*, paras A6–39 *et seq.*

[151] *Semble*, there can be no supply if there is no transfer. On that basis, the current editor suggests that, irrespective of the contents of Business Brief 30/04 there can be no taxable supply where a partner retires and, under the terms of the partnership agreement, his share is expressed to accrue to the continuing partners. In such circumstances it is submitted that the share of the retiring partner merely becomes valueless, whilst the shares of the continuing partners enjoy an inbuilt increase in value; at no stage is there either a transfer or a supply. See further, *supra*, paras 35–16, 36–42, 36–48.

[152] See the 18th ed. at paras 37–25 to 37–29.

(i) *A partnership share comprises services not goods.*[153] Although the view was expressed in the last edition of this work that such a share is outwith the scope of the tax,[154] even then the current editor accepted that HMRC might seek to argue that each partner had a direct beneficial interest in each partnership asset[155] and recognised that a supply of an undivided share in goods would amount to a supply of services.[156]

(ii) *A disposal of a share for no consideration will not, in any event, constitute a supply.*[157] This accords with the view expressed in the last edition of this work.[158]

(iii) *A disposal of a share which was originally acquired by a partner for investment purposes (i.e. he was intending to be a sleeping or limited partner) will not constitute a supply, even if made for a consideration, because no economic activity on his part is involved on that disposal.*[159] This again accords with the view expressed in the last edition of this work.[160]

(iv) *Where, however, the share was originally acquired by a partner who was a taxable person in his own right and in the course or furtherance of his own existing economic activities, its disposal for a consideration is likely to involve a supply.*[161] *The position is a fortiori where that partner's business is actually trading in partnership shares.*[162] This accords with the view expressed in the last edition of this work,[163] albeit that the current editor questioned whether a partner can properly be said to carry on any business in relation to his share, unless the share itself is properly to be regarded as a business carried on by him.[164]

37–28

(v) *Equally, where the share was originally acquired by a partner who was a taxable person in his own right and with a view to undertaking an active role in the partnership, its disposal for a consideration may also involve a supply.*[165] This again to a large extent mirrors the analysis advanced in the previous edition.[166]

---

[153] Business Brief 30/04, *infra*, para. A6–40 (first case).

[154] On the basis that the share is, on a true analysis, represented by the partner's right to a proportion of the surplus remaining after all the partnership assets have been sold, and all the partnership debts and liabilities discharged: see *supra*, paras 19–05 *et seq.*

[155] See, for example, *Border Flying Co. v. The Commissioners* (1976) V.A.T.T.R. 132, 138. See also *supra*, para. 37–20.

[156] Value Added Tax Act 1994, Sched. 4, para. 1(1)(a). See further the 18th ed. of this work at para. 37–28.

[157] Business Brief 30/04, *infra*, para. A6–40 (first case); Value Added Tax Act 1994, s.5(2)(a).

[158] See the 18th ed. of this work at para. 27–28.

[159] Business Brief 30/04, *infra*, para. A6–40 (second case).

[160] See the 18th ed. of this work at para. 37–29.

[161] Business Brief 30/04, *infra*, para. A6–41 (case 1).

[162] *ibid.* (case 3)

[163] See the 18th ed. of this work at para. 37–29.

[164] The current editor nevertheless recognised that such an argument could derive support from the decision in *J. Procter (Waddington) Ltd. v. The Commissioners* (1976) V.A.T.T.R. 184. In that case, the Tribunal decided that the business of a taxable person may comprise the management of one or more different and diversified businesses: *ibid.* p. 195. Thus, it could be said that one of the businesses carried on by a partner is the business which he carries on in partnership with his fellow partners.

[165] Business Brief 30/04, *infra*, para. A6–41 (case 2).

[166] See the 18th ed. of this work at para. 37–29.

(vi) *Section 45(1) of the Value Added Tax Act 1994 does not apply in any such case so as to negate the existence of a supply as between the partners.*[167] This is said to be the position notwithstanding the fact that the section states that "no account shall be taken, in determining *for any purpose of this Act whether goods or services are supplied to or by such persons*[168] ... of any change in the partnership" (emphasis supplied). Although the purpose behind the section is by no means clear,[169] one effect of the quoted words would, in the current editor's view, appear to be that any change in a firm, whether resulting from the admission or retirement of a partner or from a mere change in capital or asset-surplus sharing ratios, cannot give rise to a supply of goods or services. Clearly this is not the view of HMRC so that the distinction formerly drawn in this work between transfers between partners and transfers to third parties no longer holds good.[170]

(vii) *Significantly, a supply which is treated as made in any of the above ways will be an exempt financial service,*[171] *so that no tax will be chargeable.*[172] *This will obviously have an impact on the deductibility of any input tax.*[173] Whether the supply could also be ignored as a transfer of a going concern[174] is, thus, largely academic.[175]

Advice taken by the partnership/partners

37–29   Where advice is taken in relation to the business of a partnership by one or more of the partners, value added tax thereon will in general be recoverable on normal principles. Where, however on a true analysis it is the individual partners who are taking advice on their own position, the input tax thereon will not be allowable.[176]

3.   ADMINISTRATION

37–30   Although the administration of value added tax gives rise to few specific problems in its application to partnerships, certain points do merit particular mention.

---

[167] Business Brief 30/04, *infra*, para. A6–41: see also Business Brief 21/04, *infra*, para. A6–38.

[168] *i.e.* persons carrying on business in partnership.

[169] The current editor does not agree with HMRC that the entire subsection deals only with the mechanics of registration and is not intended to contain a general exemption for supplies between partners. Surely this ignores the words "for any purpose of this Act"? *cf.* the Finance Act 1972, s.22(1) in its original unamended form. And see the 18th ed. of this work at para. 37–26.

[170] See the 18th ed. of this work at paras 37–26 *et seq.*

[171] *i.e.* within the Value Added Tax Act 1994, Sched. 9, Group 5.

[172] Business Brief 30/04, *infra*, para. A6–42.

[173] *ibid.*, *infra*, para. A6–43.

[174] And thus within the Value Added Tax Act 1994, s.49 and the Value Added Tax (Special Provisions) Order 1995, art 5 (as amended): see *supra*, para. 37–23.

[175] See, as to this issue, the 18th ed. of this work at para. 37–28, n. 30.

[176] See *Revenue & Customs Commissioners v. Langran* (No. 20969) [2009] S.T.I. 972 (VAT Trib.).

Notification by partners

Reference has already been made to the circumstances in which partners must give a notification to HMRC, *e.g.* of their liability to be registered or of a change in or affecting the firm.[177] HMRC have wide powers to specify: (a) the form of any notification to be given under Schedules 1 to 3B to the Value Added Tax Act 1994,[178] and (b) by what persons anything required to be done under that Act is to be done where a business is carried on in partnership.[179] Thus, regulations provide that the notification by a partnership of its liability to be registered must include, on the form VAT 2,[180] the name, address, telephone number,[181] National Insurance number[182] and signature of each partner.[183] Moreover, it is the joint and several liability of all the partners to give any notice required to be given for the purposes of the Act or the regulations, although there will be sufficient compliance if one of the partners gives such notice.[184] It should, however, be noted in this context that it is only true partners who can be registered under the Act. Inclusion of the names of other persons who are merely held out as partners on form VAT 2 will not require them to be treated as partners or render them liable as such, even on the basis of holding out.[185]

Failure to notify change in firm

An outgoing partner will continue to be treated as a partner, and will be liable **37–31** as such, until such time as HMRC have been duly notified of the change in the firm.[186] Self evidently, a mere change in the *name* of the firm will not affect the liability of the partners under an assessment made in the registered name.[187]

Signature on forms

HMRC will seemingly require that any return or form which falls to be signed **37–32** by the firm is signed by one of the partners in his own name, rather than in the

---

[177] See *supra*, para. 37–14.

[178] Value Added Tax Act 1994, Sched. 1, para. 17; also Sched. 2, para. 9, Sched. 3, para. 10, Sched. 3A, para. 8 (as added by the Finance Act 2000, Sched. 36), Sched. 3B, para. 7(3) (as added by the Finance Act 2003, Sched. 2, para. 4).

[179] *ibid.* s.46(2).

[180] See the Value Added Tax Regulations 1995 (SI 1995/2518), Sched. 1, Form No. 2, as substituted by the Value Added Tax (Amendment) (No. 3) Regulations 2001 (SI 2001/3828), reg. 3, Sched.

[181] Including a mobile number, where appropriate.

[182] Or tax identifier in the relevant country of origin.

[183] *ibid.* reg. 5(1), as substituted by the Value Added Tax (Amendment) (No. 3) Regulations 2000 (SI 2000/794), reg. 4 and amended by the Value Added Tax (Amendment) (No. 3) Regulations 2004 (SI 2004/1675), reg. 2(1).

[184] *ibid.* reg. 7(1).

[185] *Revenue & Customs Commissioners v. Pal* [2008] S.T.C. 2442. See also, *supra*, paras 5–58, 37–12.

[186] Value Added Tax Act 1994, s.45(2), *supra*, para. 37–08; and note *The Bengal Brasserie v. The Commissioners* (LON/90/604) [1991] V.A.T.T.R. 210; also *Jamieson v. Customs & Excise Commissioners* [2002] S.T.C. 1418; *Hussein v. Customs & Excise Commissioners* [2003] V. & D.R. 439; *Miah v Customs & Excise Commissioners* [2004] S.T.I. 449. In all of these cases the partnership had been dissolved. Since the subsection is expressed to be without prejudice to the Partnership Act 1890, s.36 (see *supra*, paras 13–40 *et seq.*), it seemingly can have no application to deceased partners: see subs. (3) of the latter section. *Sed quaere* in the case of bankrupt partners.

[187] *Scrace v. Revenue & Customs Commissioners* [2007] S.T.C. 269. See also *supra*, para. 37–12.

firm name.[188] The justification for this requirement appears to lie in the need to identify the actual individual who appended the signature. A claim for overpaid value added tax[189] can be made by any person who signed the form VAT 2, provided that he is not known to HMRC to have ceased to be a partner, but following a dissolution the claim can be made by any person in respect of the period that he remained a partner.[190] In the case of a limited partnership,[191] the claim may be made only by a general partner or, in the case of a dissolved partnership, by one of the former general partners.[192]

Notices to partners

37–33   Any notice, whether of assessment or otherwise, addressed to a firm by the name in which it is registered and served in accordance with the Value Added Tax Act 1994[193] will be treated as served not only on the firm but also on any former partner, if it relates to, or to any matter arising in, the prescribed accounting period[194] during which he ceased to be a member of the firm, or any earlier period during the whole or part of which he was such a member.[195] It will not, however, affect any person who was merely held out as a partner.[196]

Liability for tax

37–34   The liability of partners[197] for tax due in respect of taxable supplies made in the course or furtherance of the partnership business is expressly laid down by reference to section 9 of the Partnership Act 1890, and is not affected by the provisions of section 45(1) or (3) of the Value Added Tax Act 1994.[198] Thus, whilst he is alive, each partner will be liable jointly with his fellow partners for tax due in respect of any prescribed accounting period during which he remained a partner; after his death, his estate will be severally liable therefor.[199] Where a partner dies or leaves the firm in the middle of a prescribed accounting period, an appropriate apportionment will be made,[200] provided that, in the latter case

---

[188] See the reply of the Customs & Excise to item 10(b) of the Memorandum of Comments of the Allied Accountancy Bodies submitted in January 1974, reproduced at [1974] S.T.I. 133, 137. This requirement is in marked contrast to the express provisions of the Partnership Act 1890, s.6: see *supra*, paras 12–149 *et seq*.

[189] *i.e.* under the Value Added Tax Act 1994, s.80, as amended.

[190] See the Guidance Note "Guidance on dealing with historic VAT claims" dated August 12, 2009, para. 7.4, reproduced at [2009] S.T.I. 2394.

[191] i.e. formed under the Limited Partnerships Act 1907: see *supra*, Pt 6.

[192] See the above Guidance Note, at para. 7.6, reproduced at [2009] S.T.I. 2395.

[193] See, in particular, the Value Added Tax Act 1994, s.98.

[194] See, as to the meaning of this expression, *ibid.* s.25(1); Value Added Tax Regulations 1995, reg. 25(1) (as amended).

[195] Value Added Tax Act 1994, s.45(3), (4), *supra*, para. 37–08. However, it does not follow that an outgoing partner will necessarily fall to be treated as such: this will depend on whether the appropriate notification has been given to HMRC: see *ibid.* s.45(2) and *supra*, para. 37–31. As to the position prior to the introduction of the above subsections (and their predecessors), see *Customs & Excise Commissioners v. Evans* [1982] S.T.C. 342.

[196] *Revenue & Customs Commissioners v. Pal* [2008] S.T.C. 2442.

[197] Only persons who are truly partners in law will, however, be liable: *Revenue & Customs Commissioners v. Pal, supra.* This is entirely consistent with liability being imposed under the Partnership Act 1890, s.9.

[198] *ibid.* s.45(5): see *supra*, para. 37–08.

[199] Partnership Act 1890, s.9: see *supra*, paras 13–03, 13–07 *et seq*.

[200] Value Added Tax Act 1994, s.45(5). The apportionment will be on such a basis "as may be just".

only, HMRC have been duly notified of the change in the firm.[201] If the proper notification has not been given, the outgoing partner will remain liable jointly with his former partners for all tax subsequently due until such time as the default is remedied, at which point he will be deemed to have retired. An apportionment will only be appropriate in respect of the prescribed accounting period in which fell the date of such *deemed* retirement.

Penalty assessments

A penalty assessment can, in an appropriate case, be made against partners[202] for inaccuracies in a firm's VAT return[203] and, procedurally, will be treated in the same way as a VAT assessment.[204] Accordingly, it will still be possible to make the assessment against the partners in the firm name[205] and they will be jointly liable for the penalty so assessed on normal principles.[206]

37–35

---

[201] *ibid.* s.45(2): see *supra*, para. 37–31; *Customs & Excise Commissioners v. Jamieson* [2002] S.T.C. 1418; also *Hussein v. Customs & Excise Commissioners* [2003] V. & D.R. 439; *Miah v Customs & Excise Commissioners* [2004] S.T.I. 449. It is submitted that the subsection has no application to deceased partners; *sed quaere* in the case of bankrupt partners.

[202] But not partners by holding out: see *Revenue & Customs Commissioners v. Pal* [2008] S.T.C. 2442, noticed *supra*, para. 37–30. However, note the Finance Act 2007, Sched. 24, para. 1A (as added by the Finance Act 2008, Sched. 40, para. 3), in a case where the person held out has himself supplied false or inaccurate information to the firm.

[203] See the Finance Act 2007, Sched. 24, paras 1, 13 (as amended), replacing the Value Added Tax Act 1994, s.60.

[204] *ibid.* Sched. 24, para. 13(1), (3), as amended by the Finance Act 2008, Sched. 40, para. 12(2), (4).

[205] Value Added Tax Act 1994, s.45(1), (4), *supra*, para. 37–08. And see, as to the position under the former provisions dealing with penalty assessments, *Akbar (t/a Mumtaz Paan House) v. Customs & Excise Commissioners* [1998] B.V.C. 2157; *Standard Tandoori Nepalese Restaurant v. Customs & Excise Commissioners* [2000] S.T.I. 744; *Islam v. Customs & Excise Commissioners* (No. 17834), July 25, 2002. *cf. Segger v. Customs & Excise Commissioners*, June 29, 2004 (Lawtel 9/9/04), where the wife's involvement as a partner was not admitted.

[206] See the Partnership Act 1890, ss.10, 12, *supra*, paras 12–87 *et seq.*, 13–12.

CHAPTER 38

STAMP DUTY LAND TAX

1. INTRODUCTION

THE 1980s saw the abolition of capital duty[1] and the *ad valorem* charge on voluntary dispositions,[2] as well as the removal of a significant number of the fixed heads of duty.[3] Many of the charging provisions were subsequently amended in 1999,[4] but their application was confined to stock and marketable securities when stamp duty land tax (SDLT) was introduced by the Finance Act 2003.[5] However, special provision was made for the exclusion of certain partnership transactions from the ambit of SDLT and for the continued application of the stamp duty regime to those transactions.[6] Partnerships were finally brought within the ambit of SDLT by the Finance Act 2004, which substituted an entirely new Part 3 in Schedule 15 to the Finance Act 2003,[7] at which point the exclusion noted above predictably ceased to apply.[8] As will be seen hereafter,[9] the incidence of a charge in the case of the *transfer* of a partnership share was then substantially restricted by amendments introduced by the Finance Act 2006.

38–01

Basis for the charge to SDLT

SDLT is only chargeable on a land transaction,[10] being the acquisition of a "chargeable interest",[11] *i.e.* an estate, interest, right or power in or over land in the UK or the benefit of an obligation, restriction or condition affecting the value of any such estate, interest, right or power. This clearly includes a lease but not a tenancy at will or a *licence* to use or occupy land which is an exempt interest and thus outwith the scope of SDLT,[12] although there may ultimately be a charge even in the latter cases if the tenant/licensee is given a power to direct or request

38–02

---

[1] Capital duty, which was levied on certain transactions affecting "capital companies" under the Finance Act 1973, was abolished by the Finance Act 1988, s.141. The statutory definition of "capital company" specifically included limited (but not ordinary) partnerships: Finance Act 1973, s.29(1)(b).

[2] This head of charge, which was introduced by the Finance (1909–1910) Act 1910, s.74, was abolished by the Finance Act 1985, s.82.

[3] Finance Act 1985, s.85(1), Sched. 24, amending the Stamp Act 1891, Sched. 1.

[4] See the Finance Act 1999, which *inter alia* substituted *ibid.* Sched. 13 for the Stamp Act 1891, Sched. 1.

[5] Finance Act 2003, s.125(1).

[6] *ibid.* s.125(8), Sched. 15, Pt 3 and, in particular, paras 9(1), 13.

[7] See the Finance Act 2004, s.304, Sched. 41, para. 1.

[8] Finance Act 2003, s.125(8), as amended by the Finance Act 2004, Sched. 41, para. 2(b).

[9] See *infra*, paras 38–12 *et seq*.

[10] As defined in the Finance Act 2003, s.43, as amended by the Finance Act 2004, s.297(2), Sched. 39, para. 2.

[11] As defined in *ibid.* s.48(1).

[12] *ibid.* s.48(2)(b), (c)(i).

that the land be conveyed to a third party or to himself and that contract is substantially performed.[13]

It should be noted that, unlike stamp duty, a charge to SDLT is not dependent on the existence or otherwise of any document *evidencing* a land transaction.

Partnerships affected by SDLT

38–03   The SDLT regime applies to all partnerships within the meaning of the Partnership Act 1890, as well as limited partnerships registered under the Limited Partnerships Act 1907[14] and limited liability partnerships formed under the Limited Liability Partnerships Act 2000.[15] However, as will be seen hereafter,[16] the scope of the provisions governing the transfer of partnership shares has now been restricted to so-called "property-investment partnerships",[17] by which is meant a partnership whose sole or main activity is investing or dealing in chargeable interests (where or not involving construction operations on the land).[18] Partnerships or limited liability partnerships formed under the laws of another jurisdiction are also within the ambit of SDLT, irrespective of whether they enjoy separate legal personality.[19]

All partnerships are regarded as transparent for SDLT purposes,[20] even though it is provided that a partnership has continuity notwithstanding a change in its membership.[21]

Partnership property

38–04   For the purposes of SDLT, a chargeable asset will be regarded as partnership property where it is "held by or on behalf of a partnership, *or the members of a partnership*, for the purposes of the partnership business" (emphasis supplied).[22] This appears artificially to extend the scope of partnership property to include an asset held by one or more partners *outside* the partnership, if they nevertheless hold it for the purposes of its business; *sed quaere*. This may represent a trap for the unwary, particularly on the subsequent dissolution of the partnership.[23]

Partnership shares

38–05   Where the size of a partner's share falls to be determined, regard is had only to his share of *income* profits, even though profits attributable to the chargeable asset in question may fall to be divided in some other way, *i.e.* in specified capital profit or asset surplus shares.[24] This approach is both inexplicable and logically insupportable and, moreover, departs from the approach adopted for the purposes

---

[13] *ibid.* s.44A, as added by the Finance Act 2004, Sched. 39, para. 4(1)
[14] As to which see *supra*, Pt 6.
[15] Finance Act 2003, Sched. 15, para. 1.
[16] See *infra*, paras 38–12 *et seq.*
[17] Finance Act 2003, Sched. 15, paras 9(1)(b), 14, as substituted by the Finance Act 2004, Sched. 41, para. 1 and, in the case of para. 14, amended by the Finance Act 2006, Sched. 24, para. 9(1), (2), the Finance Act 2007, s.72(6), Sched. 27, Pt 4(1) and the Finance Act 2008, Sched. 31, para. 1.
[18] *ibid.* Sched. 15, para. 14(8), as added by the Finance Act 2006, Sched. 24, para. 9(3).
[19] *ibid.* Sched. 15, paras 1, 2(2).
[20] *ibid.* Sched. 15, para. 2(1).
[21] *ibid.* Sched. 15, para. 3.
[22] *ibid.* Sched. 15, para. 34(1), as substituted by the Finance Act 2004, Sched. 41, para. 3.
[23] See *infra*, para. 38–21.
[24] See *ibid.* Sched. 15, para. 34(2), as substituted by the Finance Act 2004, Sched. 41, para. 3.

of capital gains tax.[25] It also appears wholly to ignore the existence of "salaried" or "fixed share" partners, who may have no entitlement whatsoever to share in the capital assets or profits of the firm and whose share of income profits may be limited to a fixed sum, perhaps even payable irrespective of the firm's profitability.[26] The approach adopted in the legislation thus militates in favour of all profits being shared in the same way in order to avoid anomalous results in those cases where an SDLT charge is likely to be incurred, but it must be recognised that this will not be possible in all cases. Equally, it would seem to follow that a change in the partners' capital profit or asset sharing ratios will not *per se* have any impact for SDLT purposes.[27]

Partners as connected persons

It should be noted that, whilst the corporation tax definition of "connected persons"[28] is applied for SDLT purposes, partners will only be treated as connected *otherwise* than through their relationship as partners.[29] It follows that, in the vast majority of cases, the connected persons rules will not apply. **38–06**

Exemptions and reliefs

There are a limited number of exemptions and reliefs from SDLT[30] and save for the exemption in cases where there is no chargeable consideration,[31] which is excluded in most cases,[32] these apply to the various types of acquisition considered hereafter, albeit with a number of modifications.[33] It is considered that these exemptions and reliefs will be of limited relevance to most partnerships and are not further considered here. **38–07**

2. ACQUISITIONS OF PARTNERSHIP LAND OR OF SHARES THEREIN

Much as in the case of capital gains tax, a distinction must be drawn between the following types of acquisition[34]: **38–08**

---

[25] See, *supra*, para. 35–06.
[26] See *supra*, paras 5–54, 5–59. See further *infra*, para. 38–14.
[27] See also *infra*, para. 38–14.
[28] See the Corporation Tax Act 2010, s.1122.
[29] Finance Act 2003, Sched. 15, para. 39(1), (2), as substituted by the Finance Act 2004, Sched. 41, para. 1 and amended by the Finance Act 2007, s.72(11) and Corporation Tax Act 2010, Sched. 1, Pt 2, para. 418(4)(a), (b). Thus the Corporation Tax Act 2010, s.1122(7) is expressly disapplied.
[30] See the Finance Act 2003, Scheds. 3 (miscellaneous exemptions), 6 (disadvantaged areas), 6A, as added by the Finance Act 2004, Sched. 39, para. 17(2) (acquisitions of residential property), 7 (group relief) and 8 (charities relief).
[31] *ibid*. Sched. 3, para. 1.
[32] *ibid*. Sched. 15, para. 25(1) (as substituted by the Finance Act 2004, Sched. 41, para. 1), which disapplies the exemption as regards *ibid*. paras 10, 14, 17 and 18, considered *infra*, paras 38–09, 38–13, 38–16, 38–21.
[33] See *ibid*. Sched. 15, paras 25(2) (general), 26 (disadvantaged areas), 27, 27A (group relief) and 28 (charities relief), as substituted by the Finance Act 2004, Sched. 41, para. 1 and, in the case of para. 26, amended by the Finance Act 2008, Sched. 31, para. 9 and, in the case of para. 27A, added by the Finance Act 2007, s.72(9).
[34] Equally, unlike capital gains tax, the focus is on acquisitions not disposals.

    A. contribution of land to a partnership;

    B. acquisition of land from third parties;

    C. acquisitions of partnership shares;

    D. distribution of partnership land amongst the partners.

Each of these categories will now be considered in turn, although it should be borne in mind that there is a blanket exemption for all *acquisitions* of partnership shares which do not fall within one of three specified charging provisions.[35] Moreover, the provisions considered hereafter will not apply in the case of a notional land transaction treated as taking place to counter an SDLT avoidance scheme in relation to a property-investment partnership.[36]

A.   CONTRIBUTION OF LAND TO A PARTNERSHIP

38–09 Where an incoming partner transfers a chargeable interest to a partnership on or after its formation, SDLT will be charged by reference to a proportion of the market value of that interest.[37] The relevant proportion will, in essence, be that which is *not* retained by the incoming partner and any individual partner(s) with whom he is connected otherwise than in that capacity, but the computation is a complex one and is dependent on identifying "the sum of the lower proportions".[38] This five step process involves ascertaining the lower of:

    (a) the total of the interest held by the incoming partner *prior* to the transfer apportioned between himself and any partner(s) with whom he is connected; and

    (b) the partnership shares[39] of the incoming partner and any individual partner(s) with whom he is connected immediately *after* the transfer.

This sum is then deducted from 100 and what remains, when expressed as a percentage, is the proportion of the market value treated as disposed of and thus chargeable to SDLT. Thus, where an incoming partner, A, contributes land to an equal partnership between himself and B, with whom he is not connected, he will, predictably, be regarded as having disposed of the land for a consideration equal to one-half of its then market value. Were A and B connected persons *otherwise* than as partners, then the land would still, in effect, be regarded as within A's ownership and no consideration would be deemed to have been paid.

---

[35] Finance Act 2003, Sched. 15, para. 29, as substituted by the Finance Act 2004, Sched. 41, para. 1.

[36] *i.e.* under *ibid.* s.75A(4)(b), as added by the Finance Act 2007, s.71: see *ibid.* s.75C(8A), as added by the Finance Act 2010, s.55(1)(b). For this purpose, an interest in a property-investment partnership is a chargeable interest so far as concerns land owned by it: *ibid.* s.75C(8), as added by *ibid.* and amended by the Finance Act 2010, s.55(1)(a).

[37] *ibid.* Sched. 15, para. 10(1), (2), as originally substituted by the Finance Act 2004, Sched. 41, para. 1 but, in the case of subs.(2), further substituted by the Finance Act 2006, Sched. 24, para. 2(1).

[38] See, as to this computation, *ibid.* Sched. 15, para. 12(1), as substituted by the Finance Act 2004, Sched. 41, para. 1 and amended by the Finance Act 2007, s.72(3).

[39] See, as to how the size of a partner's share is ascertained, *supra*, para. 38–05.

The position would be the same if a third party, C, connected with both A and B transferred the land to the partnership. If both A and B contribute land to the partnership, the same computation will have to be carried out in respect of each transfer. Clearly, in the case of a larger partnership, the computation process will be more complex. Any joint tenancy which may exist in the land prior to the transfer is ignored and treated as if it were a tenancy in common in equal shares.[40]

It is no longer necessary to take account of any actual consideration for the transfer provided by the firm.[41] However, special rules apply where there is a chargeable consideration consisting of or including rent.[42]

Where the transfer is to a property-investment partnership,[43] it is possible to opt out of the above regime and have the charge to tax imposed by reference to the market value of the chargeable interest transferred.[44] In that event, it will be classified as an ordinary partnership transaction.[45]

It should be noted that the above regime appears to apply not only where land **38–10** is transferred *into* a partnership, but also where a chargeable interest, such as a right of occupation, becomes partnership property.[46] This presupposes that either the owner of the land is (or becomes) a partner or is connected to a partner, otherwise SDLT would be chargeable (if at all) on normal principles. If, however, the only interest acquired by the firm were a tenancy at will or a licence, no SDLT would be chargeable in any event.[47]

Special rules apply where such a transfer is, within 3 years, followed by a withdrawal of capital, etc., from the firm.[48] However, the rules which applied in the case of a transfer of land to a corporate partnership where *all* the partners were bodies corporate and "the sum of the lower proportions" was 75 or more[49] have now gone.[50]

B.   ACQUISITIONS OF PARTNERSHIP LAND FROM THIRD PARTIES

Where a partnership acquires a chargeable interest from a third party (*i.e.* what **38–11** is styled an "ordinary partnership transaction"),[51] SDLT will be chargeable on

---

[40] Finance Act 2003, Sched. 15, para. 12(2), as substituted by the Finance Act 2004, Sched. 41, para. 1.

[41] *cf.* the position under the provisions formerly contained in *ibid.* Sched. 15, para. 10(2), (4), as substituted by the Finance Act 2004, Sched. 41, para. 1, prior to the amendments introduced by the Finance Act 2006, Sched. 24, para. 2(1).

[42] See *ibid.* Sched. 15, paras 10(6), 11, as respectively substituted by the Finance Act 2004, Sched. 41, para. 1 and amended by the Finance Act 2006, Sched. 24, paras 2(2), 3, Sched. 26, Pt 7(2) and, in the case of s.11, as further amended by the Finance Act 2008, s.95(11)(a). The effect of these provisions is to apply *ibid.* Sched. 5 with modifications.

[43] See, as to the meaning of this expression, *supra*, para. 38–03.

[44] Finance Act 2003, Sched. 15, para. 12A(1), (2)(b), as added by the Finance Act 2008, Sched. 31, para. 6. In such a case *ibid.* para. 18 is also disapplied: see *ibid.* para. 12A(2)(a): see *infra*, para. 38–21. Such an election, once made, is irrevocable: *ibid.* para. 12A(4).

[45] *ibid.* Sched. 15, para. 12A(2)(c), as added by *ibid.* See *infra*, para. 38–11.

[46] See *supra*, para. 38–04.

[47] Since such a right is outwith the scope of SDLT: see *supra*, para. 38–02.

[48] See *infra*, para. 38–18.

[49] See *ibid.* Sched. 15, para. 13, as substituted by the Finance Act 2004, Sched. 41, para. 1.

[50] See the Finance Act 2007, s.72(5), Sched. 27, Pt 4(1).

[51] See *ibid.* Sched. 15, para. 5, as amended by the Finance Act 2004, Sched. 41, para. 2(c).

normal principles. The partners at the date of the relevant transaction and any partner who joins the firm thereafter will be responsible for submitting a land transaction return and complying with the other obligations imposed on a purchaser but only the former will be jointly and severally liable for any tax due.[52] However, a majority of the partners may appoint one or more representative partners to fulfil their obligations, on giving notice to HMRC.[53]

C.   ACQUISITIONS OF PARTNERSHIP SHARES

38–12   The Finance Act 1996 introduced a substantial change in approach to the SDLT treatment of partnerships by confining the potential for a charge on the transfer of a partnership share to cases involving "property-investment partnerships".[54] In any other case the potential for a charge can be ignored, save in the case of those instances noted later in this chapter.[55]

Property-investment partnerships

38–13   In those instances where a charge may apply,[56] the key issue is to determine whether there is a transfer of the whole or any part of a share in a partnership which holds a chargeable interest as "relevant partnership property"[57] and whether there has been either an acquisition of or an increase in the share of an existing or incoming partner.[58] Although the presence of consideration for the transfer is no longer a critical factor,[59] it will ultimately determine whether the transfer is classified as a "Type A" or a "Type B" transfer. Thus, a Type A transfer will occur where there is an arrangement under which an existing partner's share is acquired either by another partner or by a third party for a consideration in money or money's worth[60] or under which a new partner joins the firm and an existing partner either retires completely or reduces the size of his share *and*, in effect, withdraws money introduced by the incoming partner, whether by way of a capital contribution or otherwise.[61] Any other form of transfer will be classified as a Type B transfer.[62] This classification of the transfer

---

[52] Finance Act 2003, Sched. 15, paras 6, 7, as amended by the Finance Act 2004, s.305.

[53] *ibid.* Sched. 15, para. 8, as amended by the Finance Act 2008, Sched. 30, para. 12.

[54] See, as to the meaning of this expression, *supra*, para. 38–03.

[55] See *infra*, paras 38–17 *et seq.*

[56] Note also the potential application of the Finance Act 2003, s.75A, as added by the Finance Act 2007, s.71. Where that section applies, the provisions of *ibid.* Sched. 15, Pt 3 are supplanted: see *supra*, para. 38–08.

[57] See the Finance Act 2003, Sched. 15, paras 14(1), 36, as substituted by the Finance Act 2004, Sched. 41, para. 1 and respectively amended/further substituted by the Finance Act 2007, s.72(6)(a) and the Finance Act 2007, s.72(10).

[58] See *ibid.* Sched. 15, para. 14(3), as substituted by the Finance Act 2004, Sched. 41, para. 1. That partner will be treated as the purchaser.

[59] *cf. ibid.* Sched. 15, para. 14(1)(b), (4), as substituted by *ibid.*, in their original form. Note that *ibid.* Sched. 3, para. 1 (general exemption where no chargeable consideration) is expressly disapplied by *ibid.* Sched. 15, para. 25(1), as substituted by the Finance Act 2004, Sched. 41, para. 1.

[60] See *ibid.* Sched. 15, para. 14(3A), as added by the Finance Act 2008, Sched. 31, para. 1.

[61] *ibid.* Sched. 15, para. 14(3B), as added by *ibid.* Note that the transfer will not qualify if the money or money's worth withdrawn already formed part of the firm's resources, *i.e.* a withdrawal by a partner of his own capital or current account balances will be ignored.

[62] *ibid.* Sched. 15, para. 14(3C), as added by *ibid.*

will determine what is to be regarded as the relevant partnership property,[63] by reference to a proportion of which SDLT will be charged.[64] In both cases, land transferred to the partnership in connection with the transfer of the share, *e.g.* land introduced by the incoming partner,[65] is ignored.[66] Moreover, a lease at a market rent and granted otherwise than for a premium will also, in general, be ignored, provided that, if the term is for more than five years, the rent is reviewed to a market rent every five years.[67] It should, however, be noted that an upwards only rent review would appear not to qualify for this purpose, since it, by definition, cannot be guaranteed that, following the review, a market rent will be payable.

Given the wide statutory definition of "transfer",[68] it would seem clear that where a share is subject to an automatic accruer, *e.g.* on retirement, there will still be a Type A or Type B transfer when the accruer has effect, even though the prospect of the accruer was at all times inherent in the share of the partner(s) in favour of whom it operates.[69]

The fact that the share transferred does not carry any direct or indirect right to   **38–14**
share in the chargeable interest held by the firm does not appear to matter.[70] This is, perhaps, consistent with the fact that, as has already been noted,[71] for SDLT purposes regard is only had to the *income* profit sharing ratios. It would seem to follow that an increase (or reduction) in the fixed share of profits of a salaried or fixed share partner will potentially be regarded as a transfer of a share in the partnership for this purpose. Indeed, assuming that the firm's profits do not remain static, there will almost inevitably be a variation in such a partner's share, expressed as a proportion of the whole profits, year on year. However, this issue is, in practice, of only academic interest since such a scenario is unlikely to arise in the case of a property-investment partnership. The corollary is that a change in the partners' *capital* profit sharing ratios would not involve an SDLT charge, even though it would clearly alter their interests in land owned by the firm and in the proceeds of any sale.[72]

---

[63] In the case of a Type A transfer, *ibid.* Sched. 14, para. 14(5), as substituted by the Finance Act 2004, Sched. 41, para. 1 and amended by the Finance Act 2008, Sched. 31, para. 1(3), applies and all chargeable interests held by the firm will be relevant partnership property other than such interest as was transferred to the firm in connection with the transfer and certain leases (as to which see *infra*) and any such interest which is not "attributable economically" to the share transferred. In the case of a Type B transfer, *ibid.* Sched. 15, para. 14(5A), as added by the Finance Act 2008, Sched. 31, para. 1(4), applies and there will be additional exclusions, namely chargeable interests transferred to the firm prior to July 22, 2004 or in respect of which an election to disapply *ibid.* para. 10 is in force and any other such interest falling outwith *ibid.* para. 10(1).

[64] *ibid.* Sched. 15, para. 14(6), as substituted by the Finance Act 2004, Sched. 41, para. 1. The relevant proportion will be represented by the incoming partner's share or the increase in the existing partner's share (as the case may be): *ibid.* Sched. 15, para. 14(7), as substituted by *ibid.*

[65] In such a case, the contribution of the asset will be chargeable according to the regime outlined *supra*, para. 38–09.

[66] *ibid.* Sched. 15, para. 14(5)(a), (5A)(a).

[67] *ibid.* Sched. 15, paras 14(5)(b), (5A)(b), 15, as substituted by the Finance Act 2004, Sched. 41, para. 1 and amended by the Finance Act 2008, Sched. 31, para. 2.

[68] *ibid.* Sched. 15, para. 36, as originally substituted by the Finance Act 2004, Sched. 41, para. 1 and further substituted by the Finance Act 2007, s.72(10).

[69] *cf.* the analysis of the effect of an accruer for capital gains tax or inheritance tax purposes: see *supra*, paras 35–16, 36–42.

[70] See *ibid.* Sched. 15, para. 14(1)(c), (5), (5A).

[71] See, *supra*, para. 38–05.

[72] Note, however, the interaction with *ibid.* Sched. 15, para. 17A (as amended), noticed *infra*, para. 38–18.

Amount of charge

38–15   In cases where an alteration of the partners' shares does involve a chargeable transaction,[73] the SDLT charge will be by reference to a proportion of the market value of the relevant chargeable interest equal to the increase in the acquiring partner's share of the firm's income profits[74] or, if an incoming partner acquired the whole or part of an existing partner's share, the proportion represented by the share of income profits so acquired.[75]

A chargeable transfer[76] of a partnership share is, however, not notifiable if the chargeable consideration does not exceed the zero rate threshold, *i.e.* £150,000, assuming that the firm does not own residential land.[77]

Other exceptional cases

38–16   It should be noted that an alteration in partnership shares could, in the case of *any* partnership, involve an exchange and thus attract the application of the special rules governing the chargeable consideration on exchanges.[78] The partition rules[79] will, in such a case, be excluded.[80]

Anti-avoidance provisions apply where a partnership share is transferred pursuant to "arrangements"[81] put in place when the land in question was originally transferred to the partnership.[82] In such a case, the subsequent transfer will be chargeable whether or not any consideration is received therefor.[83] This will seemingly cover any arrangements under the partnership agreement, *e.g.* for pre-determined changes in the income profit sharing ratios pursuant to a "lock-step" or similar arrangement or, possibly, even for the pre-determined retirement of a partner and the payment out of his share,[84] provided that the subsequent transfer is made by the partner who originally transferred the land to the firm. Again, the transaction is not notifiable if the chargeable consideration does not exceed the zero rate threshold.[85]

38–17   This anti-avoidance provision has now been supplemented by an automatic charge imposed on the partners in a firm when a transfer of a chargeable interest to the firm[86] is followed within three years by the transferor partner withdrawing money or money's worth (otherwise than in the form of income profits) by way

---

[73] See the Finance Act 2003, Sched. 15, para. 14(2), as substituted by *ibid.*

[74] See *ibid.* Sched. 15, paras 14(6), (7)(b), 34(2), as respectively substituted by the Finance Act 2004, Sched. 41, para. 1. See also *supra*, para. 38–05.

[75] See *ibid.* Sched. 15, paras 14(6), (7)(a), 34(2), as substituted by *ibid.*

[76] *i.e.* chargeable under *ibid.* Sched. 15, para. 14, as substituted by *ibid.*

[77] *ibid.* s.55, Table B, Sched. 15, para. 30, as substituted by *ibid.*

[78] *i.e. ibid.* Sched. 4, para. 5 (as amended): see *ibid.* Sched. 15, para. 16(1), (2), as substituted by the Finance Act 2004, Sched. 14, para. 1 and amended by the Finance Act 2008, Sched. 31, para. 3.

[79] See *ibid* Sched. 4, para. 6.

[80] *ibid.* Sched. 15, para. 16(3), as substituted by the Finance Act 2004, Sched. 41, para. 1.

[81] This expression is defined in *ibid.* Sched. 14, para. 40, as substituted by *ibid.*, as including "any scheme, agreement or understanding, whether or not legally enforceable".

[82] *ibid.* Sched. 15, para. 17, as substituted by *ibid.*

[83] Note that *ibid.* Sched. 3, para. 1 (general exemption where no chargeable consideration) is expressly disapplied by *ibid.* Sched. 15, para. 25(1), as substituted by the Finance Act 2004, Sched. 41, para. 1.

[84] *Quaere*, will this apply if under the arrangements all partners merely have the right to retire at any time on the same terms. It is thought not. See also *infra*, para. 38–19.

[85] *ibid.* s.55, Table B, Sched. 15, para. 30, as substituted by *ibid.*

[86] Within *ibid.* Sched. 15, para. 10(1), as substituted by *ibid.*

of a return of capital, a reduction in his share, retirement terms or a direct or indirect repayment of the whole or any part of a loan previously made to the firm.[87] Save where the original transfer was to a property-investment partnership and an election was made to treat it as an ordinary partnership transaction,[88] such a "qualifying event" is treated as a land transaction which is chargeable[89] and the consideration is the amount withdrawn or repaid, but may not, in the case of a loan, exceed the amount of that loan or, in any case, the market value of the chargeable interest at the date of the original transfer to the firm reduced by any amount previously charged to tax.[90] It would seem that all the partners are deemed to be purchasers for this purpose.[91] Logically, a partner who has, as part of the relevant qualifying event, retired from the firm would not be included but his status is not entirely clear. However, where the transfer also comes into the charge to tax as a transfer of an interest in a property-investment partnership,[92] the charge under the anti-avoidance provision is reduced by the amount of the charge under the latter regime.[93] In this instance the transaction will be notifiable in all cases.[94]

Incoming partners

The admission of a partner is unlikely to involve a charge to SDLT save in the case of a property-investment partnership,[95] whether or not he gives consideration for the acquisition of his share, *e.g.* by way of a premium. However, where there is a reduction of an existing partner's share in favour of an incoming partner within three years of that partner transferring a chargeable interest to the firm, there will be a charge to SDLT if the reduction is accompanied by a withdrawal of capital, etc. by that partner.[96]   **38–18**

Outgoing partners

There will be a potential charge to SDLT where an outgoing member of a property-investment partnership transfers his share to the continuing partners or to an incoming partner[97] or where, in the case of any partnership, the outgoing partner transfers his share pursuant to arrangements put in place when he originally transferred land into the partnership[98] or where he has retired, etc., within three years of transferring land to the firm.[99] As previously noted, in the first and second cases the position is not affected by the presence or absence of   **38–19**

---

[87] See the Finance Act 2003, Sched. 15, para. 17A(1)–(3), (5), as added by the Finance (No. 2) Act 2005, Sched. 10, para. 10 and, in the case of subs.(1), amended by the Finance Act 2008, Sched. 31, para. 8.

[88] *i.e.* under *ibid.* Sched. 15, para. 12A, as added by the Finance Act 2008, Sched. 31, para. 6: see *ibid.* Sched. 15, para. 17A(1)(d). See further *supra*, para. 38–09.

[89] *ibid.* Sched. 15, para. 17A(4).

[90] *ibid.* Sched. 15, para. 17A(7).

[91] *ibid.* Sched. 15, para. 17A(5).

[92] *ibid.* Sched. 15, para. 14: see *supra*, para. 38–13.

[93] *ibid.* Sched. 15, para. 17A(8), as added by the Finance Act 2006, Sched. 24, para. 10.

[94] As *ibid.* Sched. 15, para. 30, as substituted by the Finance Act 2004, Sched. 41, para. 1, does not apply.

[95] See *supra*, para. 38–13.

[96] Under *ibid.* Sched. 15, para. 17A: see *supra*, para. 38–17.

[97] See *ibid.* Sched. 15, paras 14, 36, noted *supra*, para. 38–13.

[98] See *ibid.* Sched. 15, para. 17, noted *supra*, para. 38–17.

[99] See *ibid.* Sched. 15, para. 17A, noted *supra*, para. 38–18.

actual consideration, so it would seem that use of an automatic accruer provision will not assist.

It follows that, in most cases, no charge to SDLT will be incurred when a partner who has not contributed land to the firm retires. Even where he has made such a contribution, an *ad hoc* retirement once the three-year period has elapsed will, in most cases, not attract a charge, irrespective of the nature of the financial arrangements governing payment out of his entitlement; *per contra* if a pre-determined retirement was provided for in the partnership agreement at the time of the contribution.[100] Subject thereto, an outgoing partner could receive a payment by reference to a revaluation of land owned by the firm without a charge to tax being incurred. This is somewhat surprising.

Residual stamp duty charge

38–20 It has already been seen that the charge to stamp duty has been abolished save in relation to instruments relating to stock or marketable securities.[101] Where there is a transfer of a partnership share which holds stock or marketable securities as part of its assets, *ad valorem* duty will be payable on that part of the share.[102] Special provision is, however, made to avoid a double charge to duty in the case of the transfer of a share in a partnership which holds, *inter alia*, a chargeable interest *and* stock or other marketable securities.[103] It was originally not clear whether the pre-existing stamp duty regime still applied to transfers of shares in other cases,[104] but now the doubt would appear to have been resolved,[105] even though an adjudication stamp will seemingly now be required all cases.[106]

D. DISTRIBUTION OF PARTNERSHIP LAND AMONGST THE PARTNERS

38–21 Where land owned by a partnership is transferred *in specie* to a partner or to any person(s) to whom a partner is connected otherwise than in that capacity,[107] SDLT will be chargeable by reference to that proportion of the

---

[100] *Semble* the mere inclusion in the agreement of a right for all partners to retire on notice would not amount to an arrangement of the type contemplated by *ibid.* Sched. 15, para. 17.

[101] See *supra*, para. 38–01.

[102] This is, apparently, regarded as the effect of *ibid.* Sched. 15, para. 33(3) (as substituted by the Finance Act 2004, Sched. 41, para. 1 and amended by the Finance (No. 2) Act 2005, Sched. 10, para. 21(3)), notwithstanding the fact that a partner does not, absent a specific provisions such as *ibid.* Sched. 15, para. 2(1)(a), have a direct interest in any of the partnership assets: see, generally, *supra*, paras 19–05 *et seq.*

[103] *ibid.* Sched. 15, para. 33, as substituted by the Finance Act 2004, Sched. 41, para. 1 and amended by the Finance (No. 2) Act 2005, Sched. 10, para. 21, Sched. 11, Pt 3(1).

[104] Given the terms of the Finance Act 2003, Sched. 15, para. 31(1), (2), which appeared to preserve the old regime in *all* cases.

[105] By *ibid.* Sched. 15, para. 33(1), (1A), as substituted by the Finance Act 2004, Sched. 41, para. 1 and further substituted by the Finance (No. 2) Act 2005, Sched. 10, para. 21(2)). This provision is of general application.

[106] Under the Stamp Act 1891, s.12: see *ibid.* Sched. 15, para. 33(1A), (8), as substituted by the Finance Act 2004, Sched. 41, para. 1.

[107] And thus ceases to be partnership property: *ibid.* Sched. 15, para. 37(a), as substituted by the Finance Act 2004, Sched. 41, para. 1. The position will be the same where what is transferred to the partner, etc., is a chargeable interest created out of land which is partnership property: *ibid.* para. 37(b).

market value of the land as is equal to 100 minus "the sum of the lower proportions",[108] although in this instance the comparison is as between the interest held by the recipient partner and any connected partners who are individuals after the transfer and their partnership shares immediately prior thereto.[109] It should be noted that special rules apply when determining the recipient partner's partnership share, according to whether the land was originally transferred to the firm before or after October 20, 2003 and, if the latter, whether stamp duty or SDLT was paid on the original transfer into the partnership.[110] In certain circumstances, the recipient's share under these rules may be zero. Where actual consideration is given, an additional charge is no longer imposed by reference thereto.[111] Where, however, the consideration consists of or includes rent, different rules apply.[112] It should be noted that this regime will not apply where, in the case of a property-investment partnership, an election was made to treat the original transfer to the firm as an ordinary partnership transaction,[113] but seemingly may apply in the case of a distribution of a chargeable interest in land which is *deemed* to be partnership property by reason of its use for partnership purposes.[114]

It should be noted that land held by a firm on its dissolution retains its character as partnership property until such time as a distribution occurs, irrespective of what the partners may have agreed and, seemingly, without limit of time.[115]

If partners agree to distribute land owned by the firm, whether on a dissolution or otherwise, in the same proportions as their then income profit shares, it might be expected that no charge to SDLT would be imposed, but this is by no means clear since the legislation must seemingly be applied to each partner individually.[116] It is difficult to see how the imposition of a charge in such circumstances could logically be justified, even where the special rules described above produce a deemed partnership share of zero. Equally, it must be recognised that, if no charge were imposed on the distribution, the land would cease to retain the character of partnership property[117] and would thereafter fall outwith partnership charging regime; *sed quaere.*

38–22

---

[108] *i.e.* the same approach as described *supra*, para. 38–09.

[109] Finance Act 2003, Sched. 15, paras 18(1), (2), 20(1), as substituted by the Finance Act 2004, Sched. 41, para. 1 and further respectively substituted/amended by the Finance Act 2006, Sched. 24, para. 5(1), (5) and the Finance Act 2007, s.72(7).

[110] *ibid.* Sched. 15, paras 21, 22, as substituted by the Finance Act 2004, Sched. 41, para. 1.

[111] *cf. ibid.* Sched. 15, para. 18(4), as substituted by *ibid.*, prior to its repeal by the Finance Act 2006, Sched. 24, para. 5(1).

[112] *ibid.* Sched. 15, paras 18(6), 19, as substituted by the Finance Act 2004, Sched. 41, para. 1 and respectively further amended by the Finance Act 2006, Sched. 24, paras 5(2), 6 and the Finance Act 2008, s.95(11)(b).

[113] *i.e.* under *ibid.* Sched. 15, para. 12A, as added by the Finance Act 2008, Sched. 31, para. 6: see *ibid.* Sched. 15, para. 18(8), as added by the Finance Act 2008, Sched. 31, para. 7. And see further, as to such elections, *supra*, para. 38–09.

[114] *ibid.* Sched. 15, para. 34(1), as substituted by the Finance Act 2004, Sched. 24, para. 1; see also *supra*, para. 38–04.

[115] *ibid.* Sched. 15, para. 18(7), as substituted by the Finance Act 2004, Sched. 41, para. 1.

[116] See *ibid.* Sched. 15, para. 18(1)(a), as substituted by *ibid.*

[117] Such a cessation is itself a transfer of a chargeable interest: see *ibid.* Sched. 15, para. 37(a), as substituted by *ibid.*

Special rules apply where the land is transferred out of a partnership which consists only of bodies corporate and "the sum of the lower proportions" is 75 or more[118] and where the recipient of the transfer is another partnership and there is a potential chargeable transfer on the land being introduced into that other partnership.[119]

[118] See *ibid.* Sched. 15, para. 24, as substituted by *ibid.* and amended by the Finance Act 2006, Sched. 24, para. 7.

[119] *ibid.* Sched. 15, para. 23, as substituted by *ibid.* and amended by the Finance Act 2006, Sched. 24, para. 8 and the Finance Act 2008, s.95(11)(c).

APPENDICES

PARTNERSHIP ACT 1890

53 & 54 Vict. c. 39

ARRANGEMENT OF SECTIONS

Nature of Partnership

34. Dissolution by illegality of partnership.
35. Dissolution by the Court.
36. Rights of persons dealing with firm against apparent members of firm.
37. Right of partners to notify dissolution.
38. Continuing authority of partners for purposes of winding up.
39. Rights of partners as to application of partnership property.
40. Apportionment of premium where partnership is prematurely dissolved.
41. Rights where partnership is dissolved for fraud or misrepresentation.
42. Right of outgoing partner in certain cases to share profits made after dissolution.
43. Retiring or deceased partner's share to be a debt.
44. Rule for distribution of assets on final settlement of accounts.

Supplemental

45. Definitions of "court" and "business."
46. Saving for rules of equity and common law.
47. Provision as to bankruptcy in Scotland.
48. Repeal.
49. Commencement of Act.
50. Short title.

SCHEDULE

An Act to declare and amend the Law of Partnership

[August 14, 1890.]

Nature of Partnership

Definition of partnership

A1–02   1.—(1) Partnership is the relation which subsists between persons[1] carrying on a business[2] in common with a view of profit.[3]

(2) But the relation between members of any company or association which is—

(a) [registered under the Companies Act 2006, or][4]

(b) Formed or incorporated by or in pursuance of any other Act of Parliament or letters patent, or Royal Charter; [. . .][5]

is not a partnership within the meaning of this Act.[6]

Rules for determining existence of partnership

A1–03   2. In determining whether a partnership does or does not exist regard shall be had to the following rules[7];

---

[1] By the Interpretation Act 1978, Sched. 1, person includes a corporation.
[2] For the definition of business, see s.45, *infra*, para. A1–46.
[3] See *supra*, paras 2–01 *et seq.*
[4] This paragraph was substituted by the Companies Act 2006 (Consequential Amendments, Transitional Provisions and Savings) Order 2009 (SI 2009/1941), art. 2(1), Sched. 1, para. 2.
[5] The word "or" and the original para. (c), referring to companies working mines subject to the Stannaries jurisdiction, were repealed by the Statute Law (Repeals) Act 1998, Sched. 1, Pt X, Group 1.
[6] See *supra*, paras 2–32 *et seq.*
[7] See *supra*, paras 5–01 *et seq.*

(1) Joint tenancy, tenancy in common, joint property, common property or part ownership does not of itself create a partnership as to anything so held or owned, whether the tenants or owners do or do not share any profits made by the use thereof.[8]

(2) The sharing of gross returns does not of itself create a partnership, whether the persons sharing such returns have or have not a joint or common right or interest in any property from which or from the use of which the returns are derived.[9]

(3) The receipt by a person of a share of the profits of a business is prima facie evidence that he is a partner in the business, but the receipt of such a share, or of a payment contingent on or varying with the profits of a business does not of itself make him a partner in the business; and in particular—

(a) The receipt by a person of a debt or other liquidated amount by instalments or otherwise out of the accruing profits of a business does not of itself make him a partner in the business or liable as such:

(b) A contract for the remuneration of a servant or agent of a person engaged in a business by a share of the profits of the business does not of itself make the servant or agent a partner in the business or liable as such[10]:

(c) A person being the widow[, widower, surviving civil partner][11] or child of a deceased partner, and receiving by way of annuity a portion of the profits made in the business in which the deceased person was a partner, is not by reason only of such receipt a partner in the business or liable as such:

(d) The advance of money by way of loan to a person engaged or about to engage in any business on a contract with that person that the lender shall receive a rate of interest varying with the profits, or shall receive a share of the profits arising from carrying on the business, does not of itself make the lender a partner with the person or persons carrying on the business or liable as such. Provided that the contract is in writing, and signed by or on behalf of all the parties thereto:

(e) A person receiving by way of annuity or otherwise a portion of the profits of a business in consideration of the sale by him of the goodwill of the business is not by reason only of such receipt a partner in the business or liable as such.[12]

Postponement of rights of person lending or selling in consideration of share of profits in case of insolvency

3. In the event of any person to whom money has been advanced by way of loan upon such a contract as is mentioned in the last foregoing section,[13] or of any buyer of a goodwill in consideration of a share of the profits of the business, being adjudged a bankrupt, entering into an arrangement to pay his creditors less than [one hundred pence][14] in the pound, or dying in insolvent circumstances, the lender of the loan shall not be entitled to recover anything in respect of his loan, and the seller of the goodwill shall not

A1–04

---

[8] See *supra*, paras 5–07 *et seq.*; see also s.20(3), *infra*, para. A1–21.

[9] See *supra*, paras 5–09, 5–12 *et seq.*

[10] This paragraph and paras (c), (d) and (e) and s.3 are substantially re-enactments of ss.2, 3, 1 and 4 of Bovill's Act.

[11] The words in square brackets were added by the Civil Partnership Act 2004, Sch. 27, para. 2.

[12] See *supra*, paras 5–17 *et seq.*

[13] *Quaere*, does this only apply to a contract in writing signed by the parties? See *supra*, para. 5–34.

[14] Substituted by the Decimal Currency Act 1969, s.10(1).

be entitled to recover anything in respect of the share of profits contracted for, until the claims of the other creditors of the borrower or buyer for valuable consideration in money or money's worth have been satisfied.[15]

Meaning of firm

A1–05   **4.**—(1) Persons who have entered into partnership with one another are for the purposes of this Act called collectively a firm, and the name under which their business is carried on is called the firm-name.[16]

(2) In Scotland a firm is a legal person distinct from the partners of whom it is composed,[17] but an individual partner may be charged on a decree of diligence directed against the firm, and on payment of the debts is entitled to relief *pro rata* from the firm and its other members.

Relations of Partners to Persons dealing with them

Power of partner to bind the firm

A1–06   **5.** Every partner is an agent of the firm and his other partners for the purpose of the business of the partnership; and the acts of every partner who does any act for carrying on in the usual way business of the kind carried on by the firm of which he is a member, bind the firm and his partners, unless the partner so acting has in fact no authority to act for the firm in the particular matter, and the person with whom he is dealing either knows that he has no authority, or does not know or believe him to be a partner.[18]

Partners bound by acts on behalf of firm

A1–07   **6.** An act or instrument relating to the business of the firm and done or executed in the firm-name, or in any other manner showing an intention to bind the firm, by any person thereto authorised, whether a partner or not, is binding on the firm and all the partners.

Provided that this section shall not affect any general rule of law relating to the execution of deeds or negotiable instruments.[19]

Partner using credit of firm for private purposes

A1–08   **7.** Where one partner pledges the credit of the firm for a purpose apparently not connected with the firm's ordinary course of business, the firm is not bound, unless he is in fact specially authorised by the other partners; but this section does not affect any personal liability incurred by an individual partner.[20]

Effect of notice that firm will not be bound by acts of partner

A1–09   **8.** If it has been agreed between the partners that any restriction shall be placed on the power of any one or more of them to bind the firm, no act done in contravention of the

---

[15] See *supra*, paras 5–33 *et seq.*

[16] See *supra*, paras 3–01 *et seq.* For the rules governing actions by and against partners in the firm name, see *infra*, paras A2–03 *et seq.* And see, generally, *supra*, paras 14–04 *et seq.*

[17] For an analysis of the effects of this part of the subsection, see *Major v. Brodie* [1998] S.T.C. 491. Note also, as to the effect on the legal personality of the firm of a change in its composition or a dissolution, *Jardine-Paterson v. Fraser* 1974 S.L.T. 93 (OH), 97, *per* Lord Maxwell; *Balmer v. HM Advocate* 2008 S.L.T. 799 (HCJ), a criminal case. See further *supra*, para. 31–16, n. 89.

[18] See *supra*, paras 12–01 *et seq.*; see also s.8, *infra*, para. A1–09.

[19] See *supra*, paras 12–62 *et seq.*, 12–148 *et seq.*

[20] See *supra*, paras 12–137 *et seq.*

agreement is binding on the firm with respect to persons having notice of the agreement.[21]

Liability of partners

9. Every partner in a firm is liable jointly with the other partners, and in Scotland severally also, for all debts and obligations of the firm incurred while he is a partner and after his death, his estate is also severally liable in a due course of administration for such debts and obligations, so far as they remain unsatisfied but subject in England or Ireland to the prior payment of his separate debts.[22]   **A1–10**

Liability of the firm for wrongs

10. Where, by any wrongful act or omission of any partner acting in the ordinary course of the business of the firm, or with the authority of his co-partners, loss or injury is caused to any person not being a partner in the firm, or any penalty is incurred, the firm is liable therefor to the same extent as the partner so acting or omitting to act.[23]   **A1–11**

Misapplication of money or property received for or in custody of the firm

11. In the following cases; namely—   **A1–12**

(a) Where one partner acting within the scope of his apparent authority receives the money or property of a third person and misapplies it; and

(b) Where a firm in the course of its business receives money or property of a third person, and the money or property so received is misapplied by one or more of the partners while it is in the custody of the firm;

the firm is liable to make good the loss.[24]

Liability for wrongs joint and several

12. Every partner is liable jointly with his co-partners and also severally for everything for which the firm while he is a partner therein becomes liable under either of the two last preceding sections.[25]   **A1–13**

Improper employment of trust property for partnership purposes

13. If a partner, being a trustee, improperly employs trust property in the business or on the account of the partnership, no other partner is liable for the trust property to the persons beneficially interested therein: **A1–14**
Provided as follows:

(1) This section shall not affect any liability incurred by any partner by reason of his having notice of a breach of trust; and

(2) Nothing in this section shall prevent trust money from being followed and recovered from the firm if still in its possession or under its control.[26]

---

[21] *ibid.*
[22] See *supra*, paras 13–02 *et seq.*
[23] See *supra*, paras 12–87 *et seq.* The liability under this section is joint and several: see s.12, *infra.*
[24] See *supra*, paras 12–103 *et seq.*
[25] See *supra*, para. 13–12.
[26] See *supra*, paras 12–126 *et seq.*

Persons liable by "holding out"

A1–15   **14.**—(1) Every one who by words spoken or written or by conduct represents himself, or who knowingly suffers himself to be represented, as a partner in a particular firm, is liable as a partner to any one who has on the faith of any such representation given credit to the firm, whether the representation has or has not been made or communicated to the person so giving credit by or with the knowledge of the apparent partner making the representation or suffering it to be made.

(2) Provided that where after a partner's death the partnership business is continued in the old firm-name, the continued use of that name or of the deceased partner's name as part thereof shall not of itself make his executors or administrators estate or effects liable for any partnership debts contracted after his death.[27]

Admissions and representation of partners

A1–16   **15.** An admission or representation made by any partner concerning the partnership affairs, and in the ordinary course of its business, is evidence against the firm.[28]

Notice to acting partner to be notice to the firm

A1–17   **16.** Notice to any partner who habitually acts in the partnership business of any matter relating to partnership affairs operates as notice to the firm, except in the case of a fraud on the firm committed by or with the consent of that partner.[29]

Liabilities of incoming and outgoing partners

A1–18   **17.**—(1) A person who is admitted as a partner into an existing firm does not thereby become liable to the creditors of the firm for anything done before he became a partner.[30]

(2) A partner who retires from a firm does not thereby cease to be liable for partnership debts or obligations incurred before his retirement.[31]

(3) A retiring partner may be discharged from any existing liabilities, by an agreement to that effect between himself and the members of the firm as newly constituted and the creditors, and this agreement may be either express or inferred as a fact from the course of dealing between the creditors and the firm as newly constituted.[32]

Revocation of continuing guaranty by change in firm

A1–19   **18.** A continuing guaranty or cautionary obligation given either to a firm or to a third person in respect of the transactions of a firm is, in the absence of agreement to the contrary, revoked as to future transactions by any change in the constitution of the firm to which, or of the firm in respect of the transactions of which, the guaranty or obligation was given.[33]

---

[27] See *supra*, paras 5–35 *et seq.* See also ss.36, 38, *infra*, paras A1–37, A1–39.
[28] See *supra*, paras 12–21 *et seq.*
[29] See *supra*, paras 12–23 *et seq.*
[30] See *supra*, paras 13–23 *et seq.*
[31] See *supra*, paras 13–78 *et seq.*; see also s.38, *infra*, para. A1–39.
[32] See *supra*, paras 13–101 *et seq.*
[33] See *supra*, paras 3–46 *et seq.* This is a re-enactment of the Mercantile Law Amendment (Scotland) Act 1856, s.4 and the Mercantile Law Amendment Act 1856, s.7, as repealed by the Partnership Act 1890, s.48.

Relations of Partners to one another

Variation by consent of terms of partnership

19. The mutual rights and duties of partners whether ascertained by agreement or defined by this Act may be varied by the consent of all the partners and such consent may be either express or inferred from a course of dealing.[34]
   A1–20

Partnership property

20.—(1) All property and rights and interests in property originally brought into the partnership stock or acquired, whether by purchase or otherwise, on account of the firm, or for the purposes and in the course of the partnership business, are called in this Act partnership property, and must be held and applied by the partners exclusively for the purposes of the partnership and in accordance with the partnership agreement.[35]
   A1–21

(2) Provided that the legal estate or interest in any land, or in Scotland the title to and interest in any heritable estate, which belongs to the partnership shall devolve according to the nature and tenure thereof, and the general rules of law thereto applicable, but in trust, so far as necessary, for the persons beneficially interested in the land under this section.[36]

(3) Where co-owners of an estate or interest in any land, or in Scotland of any heritable estate, not being itself partnership property are partners as to profits made by the use of that land or estate, and purchase other land or estate out of the profits to be used in like manner, the land or estate so purchased belongs to them, in the absence of an agreement to the contrary, not as partners, but as co-owners for the same respective estates and interests as are held by them in the land or estate first mentioned at the date of the purchase.[37]

Property bought with partnership money

21. Unless the contrary intention appears, property bought with money belonging to the firm is deemed to have been bought on account of the firm.[38]
   A1–22

Conversion into personal estate of land held as partnership property

22. *[Repealed by the Trusts of Land and Appointment of Trustees Act 1996, Sched. 4.]*[39]
   A1–23

Procedure against partnership property for a partner's separate judgment debt

23.—(1) [. . .][40] a writ of execution[41] shall not issue against any partnership property[42] except on a judgment against the firm.[43]
   A1–24

---

[34] See *supra*, paras 10–12 *et seq.*

[35] See *supra*, paras 18–03 *et seq.*; see also ss.29, 30, *infra*, paras A1–30, A1–31.

[36] See *supra*, paras 18–61 *et seq.*

[37] See *supra*, paras 18–03 *et seq.*; see also s.2(1), *supra*, para. A1–03.

[38] See paras 18–07 *et seq.*

[39] See *supra*, paras 19–14.

[40] The words "After the commencement of this Act", which originally appeared at this point, were repealed by the Statute Law Revision Act 1908.

[41] As to the meaning of this expression, see RSC Ord. 46, r. 1, as applied by CPR r. 50.1, Sched. 1.

[42] See s.20, *supra*, para. A1–21.

[43] For execution when judgment is obtained against a firm in the firm-name, see CPR 70PD, paras. 6A.1 *et seq.*, *infra*, para. A2–09. And see further, *supra*, paras 14–21, 14–87 *et seq.*

(2) The High Court, or a judge thereof, [. . .][44] or a county court, may, on the application by summons of any judgment creditor of a partner, make an order charging[45] that partner's interest in the partnership property and profits with payment of the amount of the judgment debt and interest thereon, and may by the same or a subsequent order appoint a receiver of that partner's share of profits (whether already declared or accruing), and of any other money which may be coming to him in respect of the partnership, and direct all accounts and inquiries, and give all other orders and directions which might have been directed or given if the charge had been made in favour of the judgment creditor by the partner,[46] or which the circumstances of the case may require.

(3) The other partner or partners shall be at liberty at any time to redeem the interest charged, or in case of a sale being directed, to purchase the same.

(4) *[Repealed by the Statute Law Repeals Act 1998, Sched. 1, Pt. X, Group 1.]*[47]

(5) This section shall not apply to Scotland.[48]

Rules as to interest and duties of partners subject to special agreement

A1–25   **24.** The interests of partners in the partnership property and their rights and duties in relation to the partnership shall be determined, subject to any agreement express or implied between the partners, by the following rules:

(1) All the partners are entitled to share equally in the capital and profits of the business, and must contribute equally towards the losses whether of capital or otherwise sustained by the firm.[49]

(2) The firm must indemnify every partner in respect of payments made and personal liabilities incurred by him—

    (a) In the ordinary and proper conduct of the business of the firm; or

    (b) In or about anything necessarily done for the preservation of the business or property of the firm.[50]

(3) A partner making, for the purpose of the partnership, any actual payment or advance beyond the amount of capital which he has agreed to subscribe is entitled to interest at the rate of five per cent. per annum from the date of the payment or advance.[51]

(4) A partner is not entitled, before the ascertainment of profits, to interest on the capital subscribed by him.[52]

(5) Every partner may take part in the management of the partnership business.[53]

(6) No partner shall be entitled to remuneration for acting in the partnership business.[54]

---

[44] The reference to the Chancery Court of the County Palatine of Lancaster, which formerly appeared at this point, was repealed by the Courts Act 1971, Sched. 11, Pt II.

[45] Such an order gives the other partners an option to dissolve the firm, see s.33(2), *infra*, para. A1–34.

[46] See, as to the rights of a mortgagee, s.31, *infra*, para. A1–32.

[47] This subsection formerly directed that cost-book companies should be treated as if they were partnerships for the purposes of this section.

[48] See *supra*, paras 19–37 *et seq.*

[49] See *supra*, paras 17–07 *et seq.*, 19–15 *et seq.*; see also s.44, *infra*, para. A1–45.

[50] See *supra*, paras 20–03 *et seq.*

[51] See *supra*, para. 20–36.

[52] See *supra*, paras 17–12, 20–34.

[53] See *supra*, paras 15–01 *et seq.*

[54] See *supra*, paras 20–43 *et seq.*

(7) No person may be introduced as a partner without the consent of all existing partners.[55]

(8) Any difference arising as to ordinary matters connected with the partnership business may be decided by a majority of the partners, but no change may be made in the nature of the partnership business without the consent of all existing partners.[56]

(9) The partnership books[57] are to be kept at the place of business of the partnership (or the principal place, if there is more than one), and every partner may, when he thinks fit, have access to and inspect and copy any of them.[58]

Expulsion of partner

25. No majority of the partners can expel any partner unless a power to do so has been conferred by express agreement between the partners.[59]   **A1–26**

Retirement from partnership at will

26.—(1) Where no fixed term has been agreed upon for the duration of the partnership, any partner may determine the partnership[60] at any time on giving notice of his intention so to do to all the other partners.[61]   **A1–27**

(2) Where the partnership has originally been constituted by deed, a notice in writing, signed by the partner giving it, shall be sufficient for this purpose.[62]

Where partnership for term is continued over, continuance on old terms presumed

27.—(1) Where a partnership entered into for a fixed term is continued after the term has expired, and without any express new agreement, the rights and duties of the partners remain the same as they were at the expiration of the term, so far as is consistent with the incidents of a partnership at will.   **A1–28**

(2) A continuance of the business by the partners or such of them as habitually acted therein during the term, without any settlement or liquidation of the partnership affairs, is presumed to be a continuance of the partnership.[63]

Duty of partners to render accounts, etc.

28. Partners are bound to render true accounts and full information of all things affecting the partnership to any partner or his legal representatives.[64]   **A1–29**

Accountability of partners for private profits

29.—(1) Every partner must account to the firm for any benefit derived by him without the consent of the other partners from any transaction concerning the partnership, or from any use by him of the partnership property name or business connexion.   **A1–30**

---

[55] See *supra*, paras 15–09, 19–49.
[56] See *supra*, paras 15–04 *et seq.*
[57] For the duty to keep accounts, see s.28, *infra*, para. A1–29.
[58] See *supra*, paras 22–10 *et seq.*
[59] See *supra*, paras 24–99 *et seq.*
[60] The heading to this section is somewhat misleading, since the power is to *dissolve* the firm, not to retire from it.
[61] See *supra*, paras 9–01 *et seq.*, 24–18 *et seq.* See also s.32, *infra*, para. A1–33.
[62] See *supra*, para. 24–23.
[63] See *supra*, paras 10–18 *et seq.*
[64] See *supra*, paras 16–03 *et seq.*, 22–10 *et seq.* For custody of books and rights of inspection, see s.24(9), *supra*, para. A1–25.

(2) This section applies also to transactions undertaken after a partnership has been dissolved by the death of a partner, and before the affairs thereof have been completely wound up, either by any surviving partner or by the representatives of the deceased partner.[65]

Duty of partner not to compete with firm

A1–31   **30.** If a partner, without the consent of the other partners, carries on any business of the same nature as and competing with that of the firm, he must account for and pay over to the firm all profits made by him in that business.[66]

Rights of assignee of share in partnership

A1–32   **31.**—(1) An assignment by any partner of his share in the partnership, either absolute or by way of mortgage or redeemable charge, does not, as against the other partners, entitle the assignee, during the continuance of the partnership, to interfere in the management or administration of the partnership business or affairs, or to require any accounts of the partnership transactions, or to inspect the partnership books, but entitles the assignee only to receive the share of profits to which the assigning partner would otherwise be entitled, and the assignee must accept the account of profits agreed by the partners.

(2) In case of a dissolution of the partnership, whether as respects all the partners or as respects the assigning partner, the assignee is entitled to receive the share of the partnership assets to which the assigning partner is entitled as between himself and the other partners, and, for the purpose of ascertaining that share, to an account as from the date of the dissolution.[67]

Dissolution of Partnership, and its consequences

Dissolution by expiration of notice

A1–33   **32.** Subject to any agreement between the partners, a partnership is dissolved—

(a) If entered into for a fixed term, by the expiration of that term[68];

(b) If entered into for a single adventure or undertaking, by the termination of that adventure or undertaking;

(c) If entered into for an undefined time, by the partner giving notice to the other or others of his intention to dissolve the partnership.

In the last-mentioned case the partnership is dissolved as from the date mentioned in the notice as the date of dissolution, or, if no date is so mentioned, as from the date of the communication of the notice.[69]

Dissolution by bankruptcy, death, or charge

A1–34   **33.**—(1) Subject to any agreement between the partners, every partnership is dissolved as regards all the partners by the death or bankruptcy[70] of any partner.[71]

---

[65] See *supra*, paras 16–13 *et seq.*
[66] *ibid.*
[67] See *supra*, paras 19–51 *et seq.*
[68] See s.27, *supra*, para. A1–28, as to the position where the partnership is continued *after* the term.
[69] See *supra*, paras 24–15 *et seq.*
[70] For meaning of bankruptcy as applied to Scotland, see s.47, *infra*, para. A1–48.
[71] See *supra*, paras 10–39, 24–29 *et seq.*

(2) A partnership may, at the option of the other partners, be dissolved if any partner suffers his share of the partnership property to be charged under this Act for his separate debt.[72]

Dissolution by illegality of partnership

34. A partnership is in every case dissolved by the happening of any event which makes it unlawful for the business of the firm to be carried on or for the members of the firm to carry it on in partnership.[73]

A1–35

Dissolution by the court

35. On application by a partner the Court[74] may decree a dissolution of the partnership in any of the following cases:

A1–36

(a) [*Repealed by the Mental Health Act 1959, Sched. 8.*][75]

(b) When a partner, other than the partner suing, becomes in any other way permanently incapable of performing his part of the partnership contract[76]:

(c) When a partner, other than the partner suing, has been guilty of such conduct as, in the opinion of the Court, regard being had to the nature of the business, is calculated to prejudicially affect the carrying on of the business[77]:

(d) When a partner, other than the partner suing, wilfully or persistently commits a breach of the partnership agreement, or otherwise so conducts himself in matters relating to the partnership business that it is not reasonably practicable for the other partner or partners to carry on the business in partnership with him[78]:

(e) When the business of the partnership can only be carried on at a loss[79]:

(f) Whenever in any case circumstances have arisen which, in the opinion of the Court, render it just and equitable that the partnership be dissolved.[80]

Rights of persons dealing with firm against apparent members of firm

36.—(1) Where a person deals with a firm after a change in its constitution he is entitled to treat all apparent members of the old firm as still being members of the firm until he has notice of the change.

A1–37

(2) An advertisement in the *London Gazette* as to a firm whose principal place of business is in England and Wales, in the *Edinburgh Gazette* as to a firm whose principal place of business is in Scotland, and in the [*Belfast*][81] *Gazette* as to a firm whose principal place of business is in Ireland, shall be notice as to persons who had no dealings with the firm before the date of the dissolution or change so advertised.

(3) The estate of a partner who dies, or who becomes bankrupt, or of a partner who, not having been known to the person dealing with the firm to be a partner, retires from the

---

[72] See *supra*, paras 24–38 *et seq.*; and see s.23, *supra*, para. A1–24.
[73] See *supra*, paras 8–59, 24–42 *et seq.*
[74] For the definition of court, see s.45, *infra*, para. A1–46 and *supra*, para. 24–53.
[75] See *supra*, paras 24–64 *et seq.*
[76] See *supra*, paras 24–69 *et seq.*
[77] See *supra*, paras 24–73 *et seq.*
[78] See *supra*, paras 24–80 *et seq.*
[79] See *supra*, paras 24–87, 24–88.
[80] See *supra*, paras 24–89, 24–90.
[81] A reference to the *Belfast Gazette* is substituted for the *Dublin Gazette* by virtue of the General Adaptation of Enactments (Northern Ireland) Order 1921 (S.R. & O. 1921 No. 1804), art. 7(a).

firm, is not liable for partnership debts contracted after the date of the death, bankruptcy, or retirement respectively.[82]

Right of partners to notify dissolution

A1–38   **37.** On the dissolution of a partnership or retirement of a partner, any partner may publicly notify the same, and may require the other partner or partners to concur for that purpose in all necessary or proper acts, if any, which cannot be done without his or their concurrence.[83]

Continuing authority of partners for purposes of "winding up"

A1–39   **38.** After the dissolution of a partnership the authority of each partner to bind the firm, and the other rights and obligations of the partners, continue notwithstanding the dissolution as far as may be necessary to wind up the affairs of the partnership, and to complete transactions begun but unfinished at the time of the dissolution, but not otherwise.

Provided that the firm is in no case bound by the acts of a partner who has become bankrupt; but this proviso does not affect the liability of any person who has after the bankruptcy represented himself or knowingly suffered himself to be represented as a partner of the bankrupt.[84]

Rights of partners as to application of partnership property

A1–40   **39.** On the dissolution of a partnership every partner is entitled, as against the other partners in the firm, and all persons claiming through them in respect of their interests as partners, to have the property of the partnership[85] applied in payment of the debts and liabilities of the firm, and to have the surplus assets after such applied in payment of what may be due to the partners respectively after deducting what may be due from them as partners to the firm[86]; and for that purpose any partner or his representatives may on the termination of the partnership apply to the Court[87] to wind up the business and affairs of the firm.[88]

Apportionment of premium where partnership prematurely dissolved

A1–41   **40.** Where one partner has paid a premium to another on entering into a partnership for a fixed term, and the partnership is dissolved before the expiration of that term otherwise than by the death of a partner, the Court[89] may order the repayment of the premium,[90] or such part thereof as it thinks just, having regard to the terms of the partnership contract and to the length of time during which the partnership has continued; unless

  (a) the dissolution is, in the judgment of the Court, wholly or chiefly due to the misconduct of the partner who paid the premium or,

  (b) the partnership has been dissolved by an agreement containing no provision for a return of any part of the premium.[91]

---

[82] See *supra*, paras 13–39 *et seq.*; see also s.14, *supra*, para. A1–15, as to liability by holding out.

[83] See *supra*, paras 13–39 *et seq.*

[84] See *supra*, paras 10–199, 13–62 *et seq.*

[85] See ss.20, 21, 29 and 30, *supra*, paras A1–21, A1–22, A1–30, A1–31.

[86] As to the rules governing the distribution of assets, see s.44, *infra*, para. A1–45 and, as to the right of lien where the partnership contract is rescinded for fraud, see s.41, *infra*, para. A1–42.

[87] See s.45, *infra*, para. A1–46 and *supra*, para. 24–53.

[88] See *supra*, paras 19–24 *et seq.*

[89] See s.45, *infra*, para. A1–46 and *supra*, para. 24–53.

[90] In cases of fraud, see s.41, *infra*.

[91] See *supra*, paras 25–10 *et seq.*

Rights where partnership dissolved for fraud or misrepresentation

41. Where a partnership contract is rescinded on the ground of the fraud or mis- **A1–42**
representation of one of the parties thereto, the party entitled to rescind is, without
prejudice to any other right, entitled—

    (a) to a lien on, or right of retention of, the surplus of the partnership assets, after
          satisfying the partnership liabilities, for any sum of money paid by him for the
          purchase of a share in the partnership and for any capital contributed by him, and
          is

    (b) to stand in the place of the creditors of the firm for any payments made by him
          in respect of the partnership liabilities, and

    (c) to be indemnified by the person guilty of the fraud or making the representation
          against all the debts and liabilities of the firm.[92]

Right of outgoing partner in certain cases to share profits made after dissolution

42.—(1) Where any member of a firm has died or otherwise ceased to be a partner, and **A1–43**
the surviving or continuing partners carry on the business of the firm with its capital or
assets without any final settlement of accounts as between the firm and the outgoing
partner or his estate, then, in the absence of any agreement to the contrary, the outgoing
partner or his estate is entitled at the option of himself or his representatives to such share
of the profits made since the dissolution as the Court may find to be attributable to the use
of his share of the partnership assets, or to interest at the rate of five per cent. per annum
on the amount of his share of the partnership assets.

    (2) Provided that where by the partnership contract an option is given to surviving or
continuing partners to purchase the interest of a deceased or outgoing partner, and that
option is duly exercised, the estate of the deceased partner, or the outgoing partner or his
estate, as the case may be, is not entitled to any further or other share of the profits; but
if any partner assuming to act in exercise of the option does not in all material respects
comply with the terms thereof, he is liable to account under the foregoing provisions of
this section.[93]

Retiring or deceased partner's share to be a debt

43. Subject to any agreement between the partners, the amount due from surviving or **A1–44**
continuing partners to an outgoing partner or the representatives of a deceased partner in
respect of the outgoing or deceased partner's share is a debt accruing at the date of the
dissolution or death.[94]

Rule for distribution of assets on final settlement of accounts

44. In settling accounts between the partners after a dissolution of partnership the **A1–45**
following rules shall, subject to any agreement, be observed:

    (a) Losses, including losses and deficiencies of capital, shall be paid first out of
          profits, next out of capital and lastly, if necessary, by the partners individually in
          the proportion in which they were entitled to share profits:

    (b) The assets of the firm including the sums, if any, contributed by the partners to
          make up losses or deficiencies of capital, shall be applied in the following
          manner and order:

---

[92] See *supra*, paras 23–53 *et seq.*
[93] See *supra*, paras 25–24 *et seq.*
[94] See *supra*, paras 19–35, 23–34, 26–03. *Quaere*, does s.9, *supra*, para. A1–10 apply in such a
case?

1. In paying the debts and liabilities of the firm to persons who are not partners therein:
2. In paying to each partner rateably what is due from the firm to him for advances as distinguished from capital:
3. In paying to each partner rateably what is due from the firm to him in respect of capital:
4. The ultimate residue, if any, shall be divided among the partners in the proportion in which profits are divisible.[95]

Supplemental

Definitions of "court" and "business"

A1–46   **45.** In this Act, unless the contrary intention appears,
The expression "court" includes every court and judge having jurisdiction in the case[96];
The expression "business" includes every trade, occupation, or profession.[97]

Saving for rules of equity and common law

A1–47   **46.** The rules of equity and of common law applicable to partnership shall continue in force except so far as they are inconsistent with the express provisions of this Act.

Provision as to bankruptcy in Scotland

A1–48   **47.**—(1) In the application of this Act to Scotland the bankruptcy of a firm or of an individual shall mean sequestration under the Bankruptcy (Scotland) Acts, and also in the case of an individual the issue against him of a decree of *cessio bonorum.*
(2) Nothing in this Act shall alter the rules of the law of Scotland relating to the bankruptcy of a firm or of the individual partners thereof.

Repeal

A1–49   **48.** *[Repealed by the Statute Law Revision Act 1908.]*

Commencement of Act

49. *[Repealed by the Statute Law Revision Act 1908.]*

Short Title

50. This Act may be cited as the Partnership Act 1890.

SCHEDULE

[Repealed by the Statute Law Revision Act 1908.]

---

[95] See *supra*, paras 25–45 *et seq.* And see also s.24(1), (3), *supra*, para. A1–25. As to the right of a partner to have the assets applied in accordance with this section, see s.39, *supra*, para. A1–40.
[96] See *supra*, para. 24–53.
[97] See *supra*, para. 2–02.

CIVIL PROCEDURE RULES

[NOTE: The rules and practice directions reproduced in this Appendix reflect (inter alia) the important amendments to the CPR introduced by the Civil Procedure (Amendment) Rules 2006 (SI 2006/1689) and the Civil Procedure (Amendment) Rules 2008 (SI 2008/2178). Given the rapidly changing content of the CPR, the precise current contents of any rule or practice direction should always be confirmed.]

Part 6

SERVICE OF DOCUMENTS

I. Service of the Claim Form in the Jurisdiction

. . .

6.5 Personal Service   A2–01

. . .

(3) A claim form is served personally on—

. . .

    (c) a partnership (where partners are being sued in the name of their firm) by leaving it with—

        (i) a partner; or

        (ii) a person who, at the time of service, has the control or management of the partnership business at its principal place of business.

. . .

6.9 Service of the claim form where the defendant does not give an address at which the defendant may be served   A2–02

(1) This rule applies where—

    (a) rule 6.5(1) (personal service);

    (b) rule 6.7 (service of claim form on solicitor); and

    (c) rule 6.8 (defendant gives address at which the defendant may be served),

do not apply and the claimant does not wish to effect personal service under rule 6.5(2).

(2) Subject to paragraphs (3) to (6), the claim form must be served on the defendant at the place shown in the following table.

Nature of defendant to be served	Place of service
1. Individual	Usual or last known residence.
2. Individual being sued in the name of a business	Usual or last known residence of the individual; or principal or last known place of business.
3. Individual being sued in the business name of a partnership	Usual or last known residence of the individual; or principal or last known place of business of the partnership.
4. Limited liability partnership	Principal office of the partnership; or any place of business of the partnership within the jurisdiction which has a real connection with the claim.
5. Corporation (other than a company) incorporated in England and Wales	Principal office of the corporation; or any place within the jurisdiction where the corporation carries on its activities and which has a real connection with the claim.
6. Company registered in England and Wales	Principal office of the company; or any place of business of the company within the jurisdiction which has a real connection with the claim.
7. Any other company or corporation	Any place within the jurisdiction where the corporation carries on its activities; or any place of business of the company within the jurisdiction.

(3) Where a claimant has reason to believe that the address of the defendant referred to in entries 1, 2 or 3 in the table in paragraph (2) is an address at which the defendant no longer resides or carries on business, the claimant must take reasonable steps to ascertain the address of the defendant's current residence or place of business ('current address').

(4) Where, having taken the reasonable steps required by paragraph (3), the claimant—

    (a) ascertains the defendant's current address, the claim form must be served at that address; or

    (b) is unable to ascertain the defendant's current address, the claimant must consider whether there is—

        (i) an alternative place where; or
        (ii) an alternative method by which,

service may be effected.

(5) If, under paragraph (4)(b), there is such a place where or a method by which service may be effected, the claimant must make an application under rule 6.15.

(6) Where paragraph (3) applies, the claimant may serve on the defendant's usual or last known address in accordance with the table in paragraph (2) where the claimant—

(a) cannot ascertain the defendant's current residence or place of business; and

(b) cannot ascertain an alternative place or an alternative method under paragraph (4)(b).

Part 7

How to Start Proceedings—The Claim Form

. . .

7.2A Practice direction 7A makes provision for procedures to be followed when claims are brought by or against a partnership within the jurisdiction.   **A2–03**

. . .

Practice Direction 7A—How to Start Proceedings—The Claim Form

This Practice Direction supplements CPR Part 7

. . .

Claims by and against partnerships within the jurisdiction   **A2–04**

5A.1 Paragraphs 5A and 5B apply to claims that are brought by or against two or more persons who—

(1) were partners; and

(2) carried on that partnership business within the jurisdiction, at the time when the cause of action accrued.

5A.2 For the purposes of this paragraph, 'partners' includes persons claiming to be entitled as partners and persons alleged to be partners.

5A.3 Where that partnership has a name, unless it is inappropriate to do so, claims must be brought in or against the name under which that partnership carried on business at the time the cause of action accrued.

Partnership membership statements   **A2–05**

5B.1 In this paragraph a 'partnership membership statement' is a written statement of the names and last known places of residence of all the persons who were partners in the partnership at the time when the cause of action accrued, being the date specified for this purpose in accordance with paragraph 5B.3.

5B.2 If the partners are requested to provide a copy of a partnership membership statement by any party to a claim, the partners must do so within 14 days of receipt of the request.

5B.3 In that request the party seeking a copy of a partnership membership statement must specify the date when the relevant cause of action accrued.

(Signing of the acknowledgment of service in the case of a partnership is dealt with in Paragraph 4.4 of Practice Direction Part 10)

A2–06   **Persons carrying on business in another name**

> **5C.1** This paragraph applies where—
>
> > (1) a claim is brought against an individual;
> >
> > (2) that individual carries on a business within the jurisdiction (even if not personally within the jurisdiction); and
> >
> > (3) that business is carried on in a name other than his own name ("the business name").
>
> **5C.2** The claim may be brought against the business name as if it were the name of a partnership.
>
> . . .

Part 10

ACKNOWLEDGMENT OF SERVICE

PRACTICE DIRECTION 10—ACKNOWLEDGEMENT OF SERVICE

This Practice Direction supplements CPR Part 10

. . .

A2–07   **4.4** Where a claim is brought against a partnership—

> (1) service must be acknowledged in the name of the partnership on behalf of all persons who were partners at the time when the cause of action accrued; and
>
> (2) the acknowledgment of service may be signed by any of those partners, or by any person authorised by any of those partners to sign it.

. . .

Part 16

STATEMENTS OF CASE

PRACTICE DIRECTION 16—STATEMENTS OF CASE

This Practice Direction supplements CPR Part 16

. . .

The Claim form

. . .

A2–08   **2.6** The claim form must be headed with the title of the proceedings, including the full name of each party. The full name means, in each case where it is known:

> (a) in the case of an individual, his full unabbreviated name and title by which he is known;

(b) in the case of an individual carrying on business in a name other than his own name, the full unabbreviated name of the individual, together with the title by which he is known, and the full trading name (for example, John Smith 'trading as' or 'T/as' 'JS Autos');

(c) in the case of a partnership (other than a limited liability partnership (LLP))—

  (i) where partners are being sued in the name of the partnership, the full name by which the partnership is known, together with the words '(A Firm)'; or

  (ii) where partners are being sued as individuals, the full unabbreviated name of each partner and the title by which he is known;

(d) in the case of a company or limited liability partnership registered in England and Wales, the full registered name, including suffix (plc, limited, LLP, etc), if any;

(e) in the case of any other company or corporation, the full name by which it is known, including suffix where appropriate.

(For information about how and where a claim may be started see Part 7 and Practice Direction 7A.)

Part 70

GENERAL RULES ABOUT ENFORCEMENT OF JUDGMENTS AND ORDERS

PRACTICE DIRECTION 70—ENFORCEMENT OF JUDGMENTS AND ORDERS

This Practice Direction supplements CPR Part 70

. . .

Enforcing a judgment or order against a partnership   A2–09

6A.1 A judgment or order made against a partnership may be enforced against any property of the partnership within the jurisdiction.

6A.2 Subject to paragraph 6A.3, a judgment or order made against a partnership may be enforced against any person who is not a limited partner and who—

(1) acknowledged service of the claim form as a partner;

(2) having been served as a partner with the claim form, failed to acknowledge service of it;

(3) admitted in his statement of case that he is or was a partner at a material time; or

(4) was found by the court to have been a partner at a material time.

6A.3 A judgment or order made against a partnership may not be enforced against a limited partner or a member of the partnership who was ordinarily resident outside the jurisdiction when the claim form was issued unless that partner or member—

(1) acknowledged service of the claim form as a partner;

(2) was served within the jurisdiction with the claim form as a partner; or

(3) was served out of the jurisdiction with the claim form, as a partner, with the permission of the court given under Section IV of Part 6.

6A.4 A judgment creditor wishing to enforce a judgment or order against a person in circumstances not set out in paragraphs 6A.2 or 6A.3 must apply to the court for permission to enforce the judgment or order.

. . .

Part 72

THIRD PARTY DEBT ORDERS

PRACTICE DIRECTION 72—THIRD PARTY DEBT ORDERS

This Practice Direction supplements CPR Part 72

. . .

A2–10 **Attachment of debts owed by a partnership**

3A.1 This paragraph relates to debts due or accruing due to a judgment creditor from a partnership.

3A.2 An interim third party debt order under rule 72.4(2) relating to such debts must be served on—

(1) a member of the partnership within the jurisdiction;

(2) a person authorised by a partner; or

(3) some other person having the control or management of the partnership business.

3A.3 Where an order made under rule 72.4(2) requires a partnership to appear before the court, it will be sufficient for a partner to appear before the court.

Part 73

CHARGING ORDERS, STOP ORDERS AND STOP NOTICES

. . .

A2–11 **73.22** Practice Direction 73 makes provision for the procedure to be followed when applying for an order under section 23 of the Partnership Act 1890.

PRACTICE DIRECTION 73—CHARGING ORDERS, STOP ORDERS AND STOP NOTICES

This Practice Direction supplements CPR Part 73

Section I—Charging orders

. . .

A2–12 **4A.1** A charging order or interim charging order may be made against any property, within the jurisdiction, belonging to a judgment debtor that is a partnership.

4A.2 For the purposes of rule 73.5(1)(a) (service of the interim order), the specified documents must be served on—

(1) a member of the partnership within the jurisdiction;

(2) a person authorised by a partner; or

(3) some other person having the control or management of the partnership business.

4A.3 Where an order requires a partnership to appear before the court, it will be sufficient for a partner to appear before the court.

. . .

Section III—Applications for orders made under section 23 of the Partnership Act 1890

6.1 This paragraph relates to orders made under section 23 of the Partnership Act 1890   **A2–13** ("Section 23").
6.2 The following applications must be made in accordance with Part 23—

    (1) an application for an order under Section 23 of the 1890 Act made by a judgment creditor of a partner;

    (2) an application for any order by a partner of the judgment debtor in consequence of any application made by the judgment creditor under Section 23.

6.3 The powers conferred on a judge by Section 23 may be exercised by—

    (1) a Master;

    (2) the Admiralty Registrar; or

    (3) a district judge.

6.4 Every application notice filed under this paragraph by a judgment creditor, and every order made following such an application, must be served on the judgment debtor and on any of the other partners that are within the jurisdiction.
6.5 Every application notice filed under this paragraph by a partner of a judgment debtor, and every order made following such an application, must be served—

    (1) on the judgment creditor and the judgment debtor; and

    (2) on the other partners of the judgment debtor who are not joined in the application and who are within the jurisdiction.

6.6 An application notice or order served under this paragraph on one or more, but not all, of the partners of a partnership shall be deemed to have been served on all the partners of that partnership.

LIMITED PARTNERSHIPS ACT 1907

A3–01

7 Edw. 7, c. 24

ARRANGEMENT OF SECTIONS

An Act to establish Limited Partnerships.

[August 28, 1907.]

Short title

1. This Act may be cited for all purposes as the Limited Partnerships Act 1907.

A3–02

Commencement of Act

2. [. . .][1]

Interpretation of terms

3. In the construction of this Act the following words and expressions shall have the meanings respectively assigned to them in this section, unless there be something in the subject or context repugnant to such construction—

"Firm," "firm name," and "business" have the same meanings as in the Partnership Act 1890;

"General partner" shall mean any partner who is not a limited partner as defined by this Act.[2]

A3–03

---

[1] This section was repealed by the Statute Law Revision Act 1927.

[2] See *supra*, paras 29–03 *et seq.*

Definition and constitution of limited partnership

A3–04   **4.**—(1) [...][3] limited partnerships may be formed in the manner and subject to the conditions by this Act provided.

(2) A limited partnership [...][4] must consist of one or more persons called general partners, who shall be liable for all debts and obligations of the firm, and one or more persons to be called limited partners, who shall at the time of entering into such partnership contribute thereto a sum or sums as capital or property valued at a stated amount, and who shall not be liable for the debts and obligations of the firm beyond the amount so contributed.[5]

(3) A limited partner shall not during the continuance of the partnership, either directly or indirectly, draw out or receive back any part of his contribution, and if he does so draw out or receive back any such part shall be liable for the debts and obligations of the firm up to the amount so drawn out or received back.[6]

(4) A body corporate may be a limited partner.[7]

Registration of limited partnership required

A3–05   **5.** Every limited partnership must be registered as such in accordance with the provisions of this Act[, *or in default thereof it shall be deemed to be a general partnership, and every limited partner shall be deemed to be a general partner*].[8]

Modifications of general law in case of limited partnerships

A3–06   **6.**—(1) A limited partner shall not take part in the management of the partnership business, and shall not have power to bind the firm:

Provided that a limited partner may by himself or his agent at any time inspect the books of the firm and examine into the state and prospects of the partnership business, and may advise with the partners thereon.[9]

If a limited partner takes part in the management of the partnership business he shall be liable for all debts and obligations of the firm incurred while he so takes part in the management as though he were a general partner.[10]

(2) A limited partnership shall not be dissolved by the death or bankruptcy of a limited partner, and the lunacy of a limited partner shall not be a ground for dissolution of the partnership by the court unless the lunatic's share cannot be otherwise ascertained and realised.[11]

(3) In the event of the dissolution of a limited partnership its affairs shall be wound up by the general partners unless the court otherwise orders.[12]

(4) *[Repealed by the Companies (Consolidation) Act 1908, s.286, Sched. 6, Part I.]*

---

[3] The words "From and after the commencement of this Act", which originally appeared at this point, were repealed by the Statute Law Revision Act 1927.

[4] The words "and shall not consist, in the case of a partnership carrying on the business of banking, of more than ten persons, and, in the case of any other partnership, of more than twenty persons, and", which originally appeared at this point, were repealed (as regards the reference to banking partnerships) by the Banking Act 1979, s.51(2), Sched. 7 and (as regards all other partnerships) by the Regulatory Reform (Reform of 20 Member Limit in Partnerships etc.) Order 2002 (SI 2002/3203), reg.3.

[5] See *supra*, paras 29–02 *et seq.*, 30–07, 31–05, 31–06.

[6] See *supra*, paras 30–08 *et seq.*, 30–18, 31–08, 31–15, 31–16.

[7] See *supra*, para. 29–06.

[8] The italicised words do not apply in the case of limited partnership registered on an application made on or after October 1, 2009: the Legislative Reform (Limited Partnerships) Order 2009 (2009/1940), arts. 2, 8. See *supra*, paras 29–23, 29–26.

[9] See *supra*, para. 31–04.

[10] See *supra*, paras 30–08, 31–02, 31–04.

[11] See *supra*, paras 31–15, 31–16, 32–01 *et seq.*

[12] See *supra*, para. 32–13.

(5) Subject to any agreement expressed or implied between the partners—

(a) Any difference arising as to ordinary matters connected with the partnership business may be decided by a majority of the general partners[13];

(b) A limited partner, may with the consent of the general partners, assign his share in the partnership, and upon such an assignment the assignee shall become a limited partner with all the rights of the assignor[14];

(c) The other partners shall not be entitled to dissolve the partnership by reason of any limited partner suffering his share to be charged for his separate debt[15];

(d) Any person may be introduced as a partner without the consent of the existing limited partners[16];

(e) A limited partner shall not be entitled to dissolve the partnership by notice.[17]

Law as to private[18] partnerships to apply where not excluded by this Act

7. Subject to the provisions of this Act, the Partnership Act 1890, and the rules of equity and of common law applicable to partnerships, except so far as they are inconsistent with the express provisions of the last-mentioned Act, shall apply to limited partnerships.[19]   **A3–07**

[Duty to register

8. The registrar shall register a limited partnership if an application is made to the registrar in accordance with section 8A].[20]   **A3–08**

[Application for registration

8A. (1) An application for registration must—   **A3–09**

(a) specify the firm name, complying with section 8B, under which the limited partnership is to be registered,

(b) contain the details listed in subsection (2),

(c) be signed or otherwise authenticated by or on behalf of each partner, and

(d) be made to the registrar for the part of the United Kingdom in which the principal place of business of the limited partnership is to be situated.

(2) The required details are—

(a) the general nature of the partnership business,

(b) the name of each general partner,

(c) the name of each limited partner,

---

[13] See *supra*, paras 31–02, 31–03.
[14] See *supra*, paras 30–16, 31–13.
[15] See *supra*, para. 32–04.
[16] See *supra*, para. 31–14.
[17] See *supra*, para. 32–03.
[18] The word "private" is apparently used because ordinary partnerships need not be registered.
[19] See *supra*, para. 28–08.
[20] This section was, as regards registrations on applications made on or after October 1, 2009, substituted by the Legislative Reform (Limited Partnerships) Order 2009, art.4. See further *supra*, paras 29–16 *et seq.*

(d) the amount of the capital contribution of each limited partner (and whether the contribution is paid in cash or in another specified form),

(e) the address of the proposed principal place of business of the limited partnership, and

(f) the term (if any) for which the limited partnership is to be entered into (beginning with the date of registration).][21]

[Name of limited partnership

A3–10   **8B.** (1) This section sets out conditions which must be satisfied by the firm name of a limited partnership as specified in the application for registration.
    (2) The name must end with—

(a) the words "limited partnership" (upper or lower case, or any combination), or

(b) the abbreviation "LP" (upper or lower case, or any combination, with or without punctuation).

(3) But if the principal place of business of a limited partnership is to be in Wales, its firm name may end with—

(a) the words "partneriaeth cyfyngedig" (upper or lower case, or any combination), or

(b) the abbreviation "PC" (upper or lower case, or any combination, with or without punctuation).][22]

[Certificate of registration

A3–11   **8C.** (1) On registering a limited partnership the registrar shall issue a certificate of registration.
    (2) The certificate must be—

(a) signed by the registrar, or

(b) authenticated with the registrar's seal.

(3) The certificate must state—

(a) the firm name of the limited partnership given in the application for registration,

(b) the limited partnership's registration number,

(c) the date of registration, and

(d) that the limited partnership is registered as a limited partnership under this Act.

(4) The certificate is conclusive evidence that a limited partnership came into existence on the date of registration.][23]

---

[21] This section was in like manner added by *ibid.* art. 5.
[22] This section was in like manner added by *ibid.* art 6.
[23] This section was in like manner added by *ibid.* art. 7.

Registration of changes in partnerships

9.—(1) If during the continuance of a limited partnership any change is made or occurs in—   **A3–12**

    (a) the firm name,

    (b) the general nature of the business,

    (c) the principal place of business,

    (d) the partners or the name of any partner,

    (e) the term or character of the partnership,

    (f) the sum contributed by any limited partner,

    (g) the liability of any partner by reason of his becoming a limited instead of a general partner or a general instead of a limited partner,

a statement, signed by the firm, specifying the nature of the change shall within seven days be sent by post or delivered to the registrar [...].[24]

(2) If default is made in compliance with the requirements of this section each of the general partners shall, on conviction under [the Magistrates Courts Act 1980],[25] be liable to a fine not exceeding one pound for each day during which the default continues.[26]

Advertisement in *Gazette* of statement of general partner becoming a limited partner and of assignment of share of limited partner

10.—(1) Notice of any arrangement or transaction under which any person will cease to be a general partner in any firm, and will become a limited partner in that firm, or under which the share of a limited partner in a firm will be assigned to any person, shall be forthwith advertised in the *Gazette*, and until notice of the arrangement or transaction is so advertised the arrangement or transaction shall, for the purposes of this Act, be deemed to be of no effect.[27]   **A3–13**

(2) For the purposes of this section, the expression "the *Gazette*" means—
In the case of a limited partnership registered in England, the *London Gazette*;
In the case of a limited partnership registered in Scotland, the *Edinburgh Gazette*;
In the case of a limited partnership registered in [Northern Ireland], the [*Belfast*] *Gazette*.[28]

Ad valorem stamp duty on contributions by limited partners

11. *[Repealed by Finance Act 1973, Sched. 22.]*   **A3–14**

Making false returns to be misdemeanour

12. *[This section was repealed as to England[29] by the Perjury Act 1911, s.17, and replaced by s.5 of that Act which, so far as material, provides as follows:*

---

[24] The words "at the register office in that part of the United Kingdom in which the partnership is registered" were omitted by the Companies Act 2006 (Consequential Amendments, Transitional Provisions and Savings) Order 2009 (SI 2009/1941), art. 2(1), Sched. 1, para. 3(2).

[25] These words are substituted by virtue of the Interpretation Act 1978, s.17(2)(a).

[26] See *supra*, para. 29–26.

[27] See *supra*, paras 29–26, 29–28, 30–06.

[28] The words in square brackets were substituted by the Companies Act 2006 (Consequential Amendments, Transitional Provisions and Savings) Order 2009, art. 2(1), Sched. 1, para. 2(3). The draftsman of that Order appears to have overlooked the fact that a reference to the *Belfast Gazette* had already been substituted for the *Dublin Gazette* by virtue of the General Adaptation of Enactments (Northern Ireland) Order 1921 (S.R. & O. 1921 No. 1804), art. 7(a).

[29] As to Scotland, the section was repealed by the False Oaths (Scotland) Act 1933, s.8.

"5. If any person knowingly and wilfully makes (otherwise than on oath) a statement false in a material particular, and the statement is made

. . .

(b) in an abstract, account, balance sheet, book, certificate, declaration, entry, estimate, inventory, notice, report, return, or other document which he is authorised or required to make, attest, or verify, by any public general Act of Parliament for the time being in force;

. . .

he shall be . . . liable on conviction thereof on indictment to imprisonment . . . for any term not exceeding two years, or to a fine or to both such imprisonment and fine."]

Registrar to file statement and issue certificate of registration

A3–15   **13.** On receiving any statement made in pursuance of this Act the registrar shall cause the same to be filed, and he shall send by post to the firm from whom such statement shall have been received a certificate of the registration thereof.[30]

Register and index to be kept

A3–16   **14.** [. . .] the registrar shall keep [. . .] a register and an index of all the limited partnerships registered as aforesaid, and of all the statements registered in relation to such partnerships.[31]

[The registrar

A3–17   **15.**—(1) The registrar of companies is the registrar of limited partnerships.
(2) In this Act—

(a) references to the registrar in relation to the registration of a limited partnership are to the registrar to whom the application for registration is to be made (see section 8A(1)(d));

(b) references to registration in a particular part of the United Kingdom are to registration by the registrar for that part of the United Kingdom;

(c) references to the registrar in relation to any other matter relating to a limited partnership are to the registrar for the part of the United Kingdom in which the partnership is registered.][32]

---

[30] See *supra*, para. 29–21.

[31] The words "At each of the register offices hereinafter referred to" and "in proper books to be provided for the purpose" were omitted at the points shown by the Companies Act 2006 (Consequential Amendments, Transitional Provisions and Savings) Order 2009, art. 2(1), Sched. 1, para. 2(4).

[32] This section was substituted by the Companies Act 2006 (Consequential Amendments, Transitional Provisions and Savings) Order 2009, art. 2(1), Sched. 1, para. 2(5), but formerly read as follows: "The registrar of joint stock companies shall be the registrar of limited partnerships, and the several offices for the registration of joint stock companies in London, Edinburgh, and Dublin shall be the offices for the registration of limited partnerships carrying on business within those parts of the United Kingdom in which they are respectively situated.", but had effect subject to the Government of Ireland (Companies, Societies etc.) Order 1992 (S.R. & O. 1922 No. 184), art. 9(b). See *supra*, para. 29–18.

Inspection of statements registered

16.—(1) Any person may inspect the statements filed by the registrar [. . .][33] [. . .][34];   **A3–18**
and any person may require a certificate of the registration of any limited partnership, or
a copy of or extract from any registered statement, to be certified by the registrar
[. . .].[35]

(2) A certificate of registration, or a copy of or extract from any statement registered
under this Act, if duly certified to be a true copy under the hand of the registrar [. . .]
(whom it shall not be necessary to prove to be the registrar [. . .]) shall, in all legal
proceedings, civil or criminal, and in all cases whatsoever be received in evidence.[36]

Power to Board of Trade to make rules

17. The Board of Trade[37] may make rules [. . .][38] concerning any of the following   **A3–19**
matters:

(a) [. . .][39];

(b) The duties or additional duties to be performed by the registrar for the purposes
of this Act;

(c) The performance by assistant registrars and other officers of acts by this Act
required to be done by the registrar;

(d) The forms to be used for the purposes of this Act;

(e) Generally the conduct and regulation of registration under this Act and any
matters incidental thereto.[40]

---

[33] The words "in the register offices aforesaid", which appeared at this point were revoked by by
the Companies Act 2006 (Consequential Amendments, Transitional Provisions and Savings) Order
2009, art. 2(1), Sched. 1, para. 2(6)(a),

[34] The words "and there shall be paid for such inspection such fees as may be appointed by the
Board of Trade, not exceeding 5p for each inspection", which appeared at this point, were repealed
by the Companies Act 2006, s.1063(7)(a)(i).

[35] The words ", and there shall be paid for such certificate of registration, certified copy, or extract
such fees as the Board of Trade may appoint, not exceeding [ten pence] for the certificate of
registration, and not exceeding [two and a half pence] for each folio of seventy-two words, or in
Scotland for each sheet of two hundred words", which appeared at this point (reflecting amendments
introduced by the Decimal Currency Act 1969, s.10(1)), were repealed by *ibid.* s.1063(7)(a)(ii). As
to the fees currently payable, see the Registrar of Companies (Fees) (Limited Partnerships and
Newspaper Proprietors) Regulations 2009 (SI 2009/2392), reg.4, Sched. 2.

[36] The omitted words "or one of the assistant registrars" and "or assistant registrar" were revoked
by the Companies Act 2006 (Consequential Amendments, Transitional Provisions and Savings)
Order 2009, art. 2(1), Sched. 1, para. 2(6)(b). See *supra*, para. 29–27.

[37] Now the Department of Business, Innovation and Skills.

[38] The words "(but as to fees with the concurrence of the Treasury)", which appeared at this point,
were repealed by the Companies Act 2006, s.1063(7)(b)(i).

[39] This paragraph which, as amended by the Decimal Currency Act 1969, s.10(1), provided "The
fees to be paid to the registrar under this Act, so that they do not exceed in the case of the original
registration of a limited partnership the sum of two pounds, and in any other case the sum of [twenty
five pence]", was repealed by *ibid.* s.1063(7)(b)(ii).

[40] As to the regulations made under this section, see the Limited Partnerships (Forms) Regulations
2009 (SI 2009/2160), *infra*, paras A4–01 *et seq.*

THE LIMITED PARTNERSHIPS (FORMS) RULES 2009 A4–01

(2009/2160)

Made - - - 31st July 2009
Coming into force - - - 1st October 2009

The Secretary of State makes the following Rules in exercise of the powers conferred by section 17 of the Limited Partnerships Act 1907 and now vested in the Secretary of State.

Citation, commencement and interpretation

1.—(1) These Rules may be cited as the Limited Partnerships (Forms) Rules 2009 and come into force on 1st October 2009.

(2) In these Rules—

(a) "the 1907 Act" means the Limited Partnerships Act 1907; and

(b) "the 1907 Rules" means the Limited Partnerships Rules 1907.

Revocation of the Limited Partnerships Rules 1907

2. The 1907 Rules (except for rule 3)[1] are revoked. A4–02

Forms to be used for the purpose of the Limited Partnerships Act 1907

3.—(1) The form in Part 1 of the Schedule must be used for any application for the A4–03 registration of a limited partnership under the 1907 Act.

(2) The form in Part 2 of the Schedule must be used for any statement sent or delivered to the registrar under section 9 of the 1907 Act.

A4–04

SCHEDULE

Rule 3

FORMS TO BE USED FOR THE PURPOSES OF THE LIMITED PARTNERSHIPS ACT 1907

PART 1

FORM FOR REGISTRATION OF LIMITED PARTNERSHIPS

---

[1] The fees specified in *ibid.* reg. 3 were temporarily preserved by the Companies Act 2006 (Commencement No. 1, Transitional Provisions and Savings) Order 2006 (SI 2006/3428), Sched. 5, Pt. 3, para. 6 but, even though the regulation remains unrevoked, the preservation ceased to have effect by virtue of *ibid.* para. 6(b), now that the applicable fees are specified in the Registrar of Companies (Fees) (Limited Partnerships and Newspaper Proprietors) Regulations 2009 (SI 2009/2932), regs. 3, 4, Scheds. 1, 2.

A fee is a payable with this form.   Form No. LP5

LIMITED PARTNERSHIPS ACT 1907

Application for Registration of a Limited Partnership

(in accordance with section 8A of the Limited Partnerships Act 1907)

Name of firm or partnership[1]

_____

We, the undersigned, being the partners of the above-named firm, hereby apply for registration as a limited partnership and for that purpose supply the following particulars:

_____

The general nature of the business

_____

The principal place of business

_____

The term, if any, for which the limited partnership is to be entered into[2]

_____

Please give the name and signature of each general partner

Name   Signatures
_____
_____
_____
_____

Please give the name, amount contributed and signature of each limited partner

Name   Amount contributed[3]   Signatures
_____
_____
_____
_____

Please be aware that all information on this form will be available on the public record.

When you have completed the form, please send to the Registrar of Companies.

Presented by: Presenter's reference:

---

[1] This must include the appropriate name ending
[2] This begins with the date of registration
[3] State the amount contributed by each limited partner, and whether paid in cash, or how otherwise

FORM FOR REGISTERING CHANGES TO LIMITED PARTNERSHIPS

LIMITED PARTNERSHIPS ACT 1907   Form No. LP6

Statement specifying the nature of a change in the limited partnership and statement of increase in the amount contributed (in cash or otherwise) by limited partners.

(Pursuant to section 9 of the Limited Partnerships Act 1907)

Registration No.

Name of firm _____

    The changes specified below have been made or have occurred in this limited partnership:

(Please see notes overleaf)

a.	The firm name	Previous name
		New name
b.	General nature of the business	Business previously carried on
		Business now carried on
c.	Principal place of business	Previous place of business
		New place of business
d.	Change in the partners or the name of a partner (see Note 1)	
e.	Term or character of the partnership (see Note 2)	Previous term
		New term
f.	Change in the sum contributed by a limited partner (see Note 3) (particulars of any increase in capital contributions must be provided at (h))	
g.	Change in the liability of any partner by reason of his becoming a limited instead of a general partner or vice versa	

h.   Statement of increase in capital contributions

Names of Limited Partners	Increase or additional sum now contributed (if otherwise than in cash, that fact, with particulars, must be stated)	Total amount contributed (if otherwise than in cash, that fact, with particulars, must be stated)

Signature of firm _____

Presented by: Presenter's reference:

NOTES
1.   Changes brought about by death, by transfer of interests, by increase in the number of partners, or by change of name of any partner, must be notified here.
2.   If there is, or was, no definite term, then state against 'previous term' the conditions under which the partnership was constituted and against any 'new term' the conditions under which it is now constituted.
3.   Any variation in the sum contributed by any limited partner must be stated at f. A statement of any increase in the amount of the partnership capital, whether arising from increase of contributions, or from introduction of fresh partners must also be stated at h. above.
4.   Each change must be entered in the proper section a., b., c., d., e., f., g., or h., as the case may be. Provision is made in this form for notifying all the changes required by the Act to be notified, but it will frequently happen that only one item of change has to be notified. In any such case, the word 'Nil' should be inserted in the other sections.
5.   The statement must be signed at the end by the firm, and sent by post or delivered to the Registrar of Companies for registration within seven days of the changes taking place.

APPENDIX 5

EU COMPETITION LAW

I. TREATY ON THE FUNCTIONING OF THE EUROPEAN UNION

ARTICLE 101 (FORMERLY ARTICLE 81 EC)[1]

1. The following shall be prohibited as incompatible with the common market: all **A5–01**
agreements between undertakings, decisions by associations of undertakings and concerted practices which may affect trade between Member States and which have as their
object or effect the prevention, restriction or distortion of competition within the common
market, and in particular those which:

(a) directly or indirectly fix purchase or selling prices or any other trading
conditions;

(b) limit or control production, markets, technical development, or investment;

(c) share markets or sources of supply;

(d) apply dissimilar conditions to equivalent transactions with other trading parties,
thereby placing them at a competitive disadvantage;

(e) make the conclusion of contracts subject to acceptance by the other parties of
supplementary obligations which, by their nature or according to commercial
usage, have no connection with the subject of such contracts.

2. Any agreements or decisions prohibited pursuant to this Article shall be automat- **A5–02**
ically void.
3. The provisions of paragraph 1 may, however, be declared inapplicable in the case
of:

—any agreement or category of agreements between undertakings;

—any decision or category of decisions by associations of undertakings;

—any concerted practice or category of concerted practices;

which contributes to improving the production or distribution of goods or to promoting
technical or economic progress, while allowing consumers a fair share of the resulting
benefit, and which does not:

(a) impose on the undertakings concerned restrictions which are not indispensable
to the attainment of these objectives;

(b) afford such undertakings the possibility of eliminating competition in respect of
a substantial part of the products in question.

---

[1] The former Art. 85 of the EC Treaty was renumbered 81 by the Treaty of Amsterdam, Art. 12.
It was then renumbered Art. 101 of the Treaty on the Functioning of the European Union by the
Treaty of Lisbon.

II. COUNCIL REGULATION (EC) NO. 1/2003 OF 16 DECEMBER 2002 ON THE IMPLEMENTATION OF THE RULES ON COMPETITION LAID DOWN IN ARTICLES 81 AND 82 OF THE TREATY[2]

CHAPTER I

PRINCIPLES

ARTICLE 1

Application of Articles 81 and 82 of the Treaty[3]

A5–03   **1.** Agreements, decisions and concerted practices caught by Article 81(1) of the Treaty which do not satisfy the conditions of Article 81(3) of the Treaty shall be prohibited, no prior decision to that effect being required.

2. Agreements, decisions and concerted practices caught by Article 81(1) of the Treaty which satisfy the conditions of Article 81(3) of the Treaty shall not be prohibited, no prior decision to that effect being required.

3. The abuse of a dominant position referred to in Article 82 of the Treaty shall be prohibited, no prior decision to that effect being required.

ARTICLE 2

Burden of proof

A5–04   In any national or Community proceedings for the application of Articles 81 and 82 of the Treaty,[4] the burden of proving an infringement of Article 81(1) or of Article 82 of the Treaty shall rest on the party or the authority alleging the infringement. The undertaking or association of undertakings claiming the benefit of Article 81(3) of the Treaty shall bear the burden of proving that the conditions of that paragraph are fulfilled.

ARTICLE 3

Relationship between Articles 81 and 82 of the Treaty[5] *and national competition laws*

A5–05   **1.** Where the competition authorities of the Member States or national courts apply national competition law to agreements, decisions by associations of undertakings or concerted practices within the meaning of Article 81(1) of the Treaty which may affect trade between Member States within the meaning of that provision, they shall also apply Article 81 of the Treaty to such agreements, decisions or concerted practices. Where the competition authorities of the Member States or national courts apply national competition law to any abuse prohibited by Article 82 of the Treaty, they shall also apply Article 82 of the Treaty.

2. The application of national competition law may not lead to the prohibition of agreements, decisions by associations of undertakings or concerted practices which may affect trade between Member States but which do not restrict competition within the meaning of Article 81(1) of the Treaty, or which fulfil the conditions of Article 81(3) of the Treaty or which are covered by a Regulation for the application of Article 81(3) of the Treaty. Member States shall not under this Regulation be precluded from adopting and applying on their territory stricter national laws which prohibit or sanction unilateral conduct engaged in by undertakings.

[2] Now Arts. 101 and 102 TFEU: see *supra* n. 1.
[3] See n. 2.
[4] See n. 2.
[5] See n. 2.

3. Without prejudice to general principles and other provisions of Community law, paragraphs 1 and 2 do not apply when the competition authorities and the courts of the Member States apply national merger control laws nor do they preclude the application of provisions of national law that predominantly pursue an objective different from that pursued by Articles 81 and 82 of the Treaty.

CHAPTER II

POWERS

ARTICLE 4

Powers of the Commission

For the purpose of applying Articles 81 and 82 of the Treaty,[6] the Commission shall have the powers provided for by this Regulation.

A5–06

ARTICLE 5

Powers of the competition authorities of the Members States

The competition authorities of the Member States shall have the power to apply Articles 81 and 82 of the Treaty[7] in individual cases. For this purpose, acting on their own initiative or on a complaint, they may take the following decisions:

A5–07

— requiring that an infringement be brought to an end,

— ordering interim measures,

— accepting commitments,

— imposing fines, periodic penalty payments or any other penalty provided for in their national law.

Where on the basis of the information in their possession the conditions for prohibition are not met they may likewise decide that there are no grounds for action on their part.

ARTICLE 6

Powers of the national courts

National courts shall have the power to apply Articles 81 and 82 of the Treaty.[8]

A5–08

CHAPTER III

COMMISSION DECISIONS

ARTICLE 7

Finding and termination of infringement

1. Where the Commission, acting on a complaint or on its own initiative, finds that there is an infringement of Article 81 or of Article 82 of the Treaty,[9] it may by decision require

A5–09

---

[6] See n. 2.
[7] See n. 2.
[8] See n. 2.
[9] See n. 2.

the undertakings and associations of undertakings concerned to bring such infringement to an end. For this purpose, it may impose on them any behavioural or structural remedies which are proportionate to the infringement committed and necessary to bring the infringement effectively to an end. Structural remedies can only be imposed either where there is no equally effective behavioural remedy or where any equally effective behavioural remedy would be more burdensome for the undertaking concerned than the structural remedy. If the Commission has a legitimate interest in doing so, it may also find that an infringement has been committed in the past.

2. Those entitled to lodge a complaint for the purposes of paragraph 1 are natural or legal persons who can show a legitimate interest and Member States.

ARTICLE 8

Interim measures

A5–10   1. In cases of urgency due to the risk of serious and irreparable damage to competition, the Commission, acting on its own initiative may by decision, on the basis of a prima facie finding of infringement, order interim measures.

2. A decision under paragraph 1 shall apply for a specified period of time and may be renewed in so far this is necessary and appropriate.

ARTICLE 9

Commitments

A5–11   1. Where the Commission intends to adopt a decision requiring that an infringement be brought to an end and the undertakings concerned offer commitments to meet the concerns expressed to them by the Commission in its preliminary assessment, the Commission may by decision make those commitments binding on the undertakings. Such a decision may be adopted for a specified period and shall conclude that there are no longer grounds for action by the Commission.

2. The Commission may, upon request or on its own initiative, reopen the proceedings:

    (a) where there has been a material change in any of the facts on which the decision was based;

    (b) where the undertakings concerned act contrary to their commitments; or

    (c) where the decision was based on incomplete, incorrect or misleading information provided by the parties.

ARTICLE 10

Finding of inapplicability

A5–12   Where the Community public interest relating to the application of Articles 81 and 82 of the Treaty[10] so requires, the Commission, acting on its own initiative, may by decision find that Article 81 of the Treaty is not applicable to an agreement, a decision by an association of undertakings or a concerted practice, either because the conditions of Article 81(1) of the Treaty are not fulfilled, or because the conditions of Article 81(3) of the Treaty are satisfied.

The Commission may likewise make such a finding with reference to Article 82 of the Treaty.

---

[10] See n. 2.

CHAPTER IV

COOPERATION

ARTICLE 11

Cooperation between the Commission and the competition authorities of the Member States

1. The Commission and the competition authorities of the Member States shall apply **A5–13** the Community competition rules in close cooperation.

2. The Commission shall transmit to the competition authorities of the Member States copies of the most important documents it has collected with a view to applying Articles 7, 8, 9, 10 and Article 29(1). At the request of the competition authority of a Member State, the Commission shall provide it with a copy of other existing documents necessary for the assessment of the case.

3. The competition authorities of the Member States shall, when acting under Article 81 or Article 82 of the Treaty,[11] inform the Commission in writing before or without delay after commencing the first formal investigative measure. This information may also be made available to the competition authorities of the other Member States.

4. No later than 30 days before the adoption of a decision requiring that an infringement be brought to an end, accepting commitments or withdrawing the benefit of a block exemption Regulation, the competition authorities of the Member States shall inform the Commission. To that effect, they shall provide the Commission with a summary of the case, the envisaged decision or, in the absence thereof, any other document indicating the proposed course of action. This information may also be made available to the competition authorities of the other Member States. At the request of the Commission, the acting competition authority shall make available to the Commission other documents it holds which are necessary for the assessment of the case. The information supplied to the Commission may be made available to the competition authorities of the other Member States. National competition authorities may also exchange between themselves information necessary for the assessment of a case that they are dealing with under Article 81 or Article 82 of the Treaty.

5. The competition authorities of the Member States may consult the Commission on any case involving the application of Community law.

6. The initiation by the Commission of proceedings for the adoption of a decision under Chapter III shall relieve the competition authorities of the Member States of their competence to apply Articles 81 and 82 of the Treaty. If a competition authority of a Member State is already acting on a case, the Commission shall only initiate proceedings after consulting with that national competition authority.

. . .

CHAPTER V

POWERS OF INVESTIGATION

ARTICLE 17

Investigation into sectors of the economy and into types of agreements

1. Where the trend of trade between Member States, the rigidity of prices or other **A5–14** circumstances suggest that competition may be restricted or distorted within the common market, the Commission may conduct its inquiry into a particular sector of the economy or into a particular type of agreements across various sectors. In the course of that inquiry, the Commission may request the undertakings or associations of undertakings concerned

---

[11] See n. 2.

to supply the information necessary for giving effect to Articles 81 and 82 of the Treaty[12] and may carry out any inspections necessary for that purpose.

The Commission may in particular request the undertakings or associations of undertakings concerned to communicate to it all agreements, decisions and concerted practices.

The Commission may publish a report on the results of its inquiry into particular sectors of the economy or particular types of agreements across various sectors and invite comments from interested parties.

2. Articles 14, 18, 19, 20, 22, 23 and 24 shall apply mutatis mutandis.

Article 18

Requests for information

A5–15   **1.** In order to carry out the duties assigned to it by this Regulation, the Commission may, by simple request or by decision, require undertakings and associations of undertakings to provide all necessary information.

2. When sending a simple request for information to an undertaking or association of undertakings, the Commission shall state the legal basis and the purpose of the request, specify what information is required and fix the time-limit within which the information is to be provided, and the penalties provided for in Article 23 for supplying incorrect or misleading information.

3. Where the Commission requires undertakings and associations of undertakings to supply information by decision, it shall state the legal basis and the purpose of the request, specify what information is required and fix the time-limit within which it is to be provided. It shall also indicate the penalties provided for in Article 23 and indicate or impose the penalties provided for in Article 24. It shall further indicate the right to have the decision reviewed by the Court of Justice.

4. The owners of the undertakings or their representatives and, in the case of legal persons, companies or firms, or associations having no legal personality, the persons authorised to represent them by law or by their constitution shall supply the information requested on behalf of the undertaking or the association of undertakings concerned. Lawyers duly authorised to act may supply the information on behalf of their clients. The latter shall remain fully responsible if the information supplied is incomplete, incorrect or misleading.

5. The Commission shall without delay forward a copy of the simple request or of the decision to the competition authority of the Member State in whose territory the seat of the undertaking or association of undertakings is situated and the competition authority of the Member State whose territory is affected.

6. At the request of the Commission the governments and competition authorities of the Member States shall provide the Commission with all necessary information to carry out the duties assigned to it by this Regulation.

. . .

Chapter VI

Penalties

Article 23

Fines

A5–16   **1.** The Commission may by decision impose on undertakings or associations of undertakings fines not exceeding 1% of the total turnover in the preceding business year where, intentionally or negligently:

[12] See n. 2.

   (a) they supply incorrect or misleading information in response to a request pursu-
       ant to Article 17 or Article 18(2);

   (b) in response to a request made by a decision adopted pursuant to Article 17 or
       Article 18(3), they supply incorrect, incomplete or misleading information or do
       not supply information within the time-limit;

   (c) they produce the required books or other records related to the business in
       incomplete form during inspections under Article 20 or refuse to submit to
       inspections ordered by a decision adopted pursuant to Article 20(4);

   (d) in response to a question asked in accordance with Article 20(2)(e),

       —they give an incorrect or misleading answer,
       —they fail to rectify within a time-limit set by the Commission an incorrect,
       incomplete or misleading answer given by a member of staff, or
       —they fail or refuse to provide a complete answer on facts relating to the
       subject-matter and purpose of an inspection ordered by a decision adopted
       pursuant to Article 20(4);

   (e) seals affixed in accordance with Article 20(2)(d) by officials or other accom-
       panying persons authorised by the Commission have been broken.

2. The Commission may by decision impose fines on undertakings and associations of   **A5–17**
undertakings where, either intentionally or negligently:

   (a) they infringe Article 81 or Article 82 of the Treaty[13]; or

   (b) they contravene a decision ordering interim measures under Article 8; or

   (c) they fail to comply with a commitment made binding by a decision pursuant to
       Article 9.

For each undertaking and association of undertakings participating in the infringement,
the fine shall not exceed 10 % of its total turnover in the preceding business year.

    Where the infringement of an association relates to the activities of its members, the
fine shall not exceed 10 % of the sum of the total turnover of each member active on the
market affected by the infringement of the association.

    3. In fixing the amount of the fine, regard shall be had both to the gravity and to the
duration of the infringement.

    4. When a fine is imposed on an association of undertakings taking account of the
turnover of its members and the association is not solvent, the association is obliged to call
for contributions from its members to cover the amount of the fine.

    Where such contributions have not been made to the association within a time-limit
fixed by the Commission, the Commission may require payment of the fine directly by any
of the undertakings whose representatives were members of the decision-making bodies
concerned of the association.

    After the Commission has required payment under the second subparagraph, where
necessary to ensure full payment of the fine, the Commission may require payment of the
balance by any of the members of the association which were active on the market on
which the infringement occurred.

    However, the Commission shall not require payment under the second or the third
subparagraph from undertakings which show that they have not implemented the infringing decision of the association and either were not aware of its existence or have actively
distanced themselves from it before the Commission started investigating the case.

    The financial liability of each undertaking in respect of the payment of the fine shall not
exceed 10 % of its total turnover in the preceding business year.

---

[13] See n. 2.

5. Decisions taken pursuant to paragraphs 1 and 2 shall not be of a criminal law nature.

ARTICLE 24

Periodic Penalty Payments

A5–18   **1.** The Commission may, by decision, impose on undertakings or associations of undertakings periodic penalty payments not exceeding 5% of the average daily turnover in the preceding business year per day and calculated from the date appointed by the decision, in order to compel them:

  (a) to put an end to an infringement of Article 81 or Article 82 of the Treaty,[14] in accordance with a decision taken pursuant to Article 7;

  (b) to comply with a decision ordering interim measures take pursuant to Article 8;

  (c) to comply with a commitment made binding by decision taken pursuant to Article 9;

  (d) to supply complete and correct information which it has requested by decision taken pursuant to Article 17 or Article 18(3);

  (e) to submit to an inspection which it has ordered by decision taken pursuant to Article 20(4).

  2. Where the undertakings or associations of undertakings have satisfied the obligation which the periodic penalty payment was intended to to enforce, the Commission may fix the definitive amount of the periodic penalty payment at a figure lower than that which would arise under the original decision. Article 23(4) shall apply correspondingly.

CHAPTER VII

LIMITATION PERIODS

ARTICLE 25

Limitation periods for the imposition of penalties

A5–19   **1.** The powers conferred on the Commission by Articles 23 and 24 shall be subject to the following limitation periods:

  (a) three years in the case of infringements of provisions concerning requests for information or the conduct of inspections;

  (b) five years in the case of all other infringements.

  2. Time shall begin to run on the day on which the infringement is committed. However, in the case of continuing or repeated infringements, time shall begin to run on the day on which the infringement ceases.

  3. Any action taken by the Commission or by the competition authority of a Member State for the purpose of the investigation or proceedings in respect of an infringement shall interrupt the limitation period for the imposition of fines or periodic penalty payments. The limitation period shall be interrupted with effect from the date on which the action is notified to at least one undertaking or association of undertakings which has participated in the infringement. Actions which interrupt the running of the period shall include in particular the following:

---

[14] See n. 2.

(a) written requests for information by the Commission or by the competition authority of a Member State;

(b) written authorisations to conduct inspections issued to its officials by the Commission or by the competition authority of a Member State;

(c) the initiation of proceedings by the Commission or by the competition authority of a Member State;

(d) notification of the statement of objections of the Commission or of the competition authority of a Member State.

4. The interruption of the limitation period shall apply for all the undertakings or associations of undertakings which have participated in the infringement.

5. Each interruption shall start time running afresh. However, the limitation period shall expire at the latest on the day on which a period equal to twice the limitation period has elapsed without the Commission having imposed a fine or a periodic penalty payment. That period shall be extended by the time during which limitation is suspended pursuant to paragraph 6.

6. The limitation period for the imposition of fines or periodic penalty payments shall be suspended for as long as the decision of the Commission is the subject of proceedings pending before the Court of Justice.

Article 26

Limitation period for the enforcement of penalties

1. The power of the Commission to enforce decisions taken pursuant to Articles 23 and   **A5–20**
24 shall be subject to a limitation period of five years.

2. Time shall begin to run on the day on which the decision becomes final.

3. The limitation period for the enforcement of penalties shall be interrupted:

(a) by notification of a decision varying the original amount of the fine or periodic penalty payment or refusing an application for variation;

(b) by any action of the Commission or of a Member State, acting at the request of the Commission, designed to enforce payment of the fine or periodic penalty payment.

4. Each interruption shall start time running afresh.

5. The limitation period for the enforcement of penalties shall be suspended for so long as:

(a) time to pay is allowed;

(b) enforcement of payment is suspended pursuant to a decision of the Court of Justice.

. . .

Chapter IX

Exemption Regulations

Article 29

Withdrawal in individual cases

1. Where the Commission, empowered by a Council Regulation, such as Regulations   **A5–21**
19/65/EEC, (EEC) No 2821/71, (EEC) No 3976/87, (EEC) No 1534/91 or (EEC) No

479/92, to apply Article 81(3) of the Treaty[15] by regulation, has declared Article 81(1) of the Treaty inapplicable to certain categories of agreements, decisions by associations of undertakings or concerted practices, it may, acting on its own initiative or on a complaint, withdraw the benefit of such an exemption Regulation when it finds that in any particular case an agreement, decision or concerted practice to which the exemption Regulation applies has certain effects which are incompatible with Article 81(3) of the Treaty.

2. Where, in any particular case, agreements, decisions by associations of undertakings or concerted practices to which a Commission Regulation referred to in paragraph 1 applies have effects which are incompatible with Article 81(3) of the Treaty in the territory of a Member State, or in a part thereof, which has all the characteristics of a distinct geographic market, the competition authority of that Member State may withdraw the benefit of the Regulation in question in respect of that territory.

. . .

Chapter XI

Transitional, Amending and Final Provisions

. . .

Article 45

Entry into force

A5–22   This Regulation shall enter into force on the 20th day following that of its publication in the Official Journal of the European Communities.

It shall apply from 1 May 2004.

This Regulation shall be binding in its entirety and directly applicable in all Member States.

---

[15] See n. 2.

HMRC STATEMENTS OF PRACTICE AND OTHER MATERIALS

I. Income Tax

STATEMENT OF PRACTICE (SP9/86)[1]

INCOME TAX: PARTNERSHIP MERGERS AND DEMERGERS *(Originally issued December 10, 1986)*

1. This statement explains the basis on which the Revenue apply the provisions of s.113, ICTA 1988[2] (change in ownership of trade, profession or vocation) to mergers and demergers of partnership businesses. In the following paragraphs, the word "business" means trades, professions or vocations carried on in partnership.

A6–01

Mergers

2. When two businesses which are carried on in partnership and which are different in nature merge, it may be that the result of the merger is a new business, different in nature from either of the previous businesses. Whether this is so is a question of fact to be determined according to the circumstances of each case. Where it is the case, the old businesses will have been permanently discontinued, and a new business commenced; s.113, ICTA 1988 will therefore not apply and the normal commencement and cessation provisions will apply to each business respectively.

A6–02

3. However, where two partnership businesses in different ownership carrying on the same sort of activities are merged and then carried on by the joint owners in partnership, the total activities of both businesses may continue, even though in a merged form *i.e.* the new partnership may succeed to the businesses of the old partnerships. In that event s.113, ICTA 1988 applies to both successions, so that both businesses are deemed to have continued.

4. It will of course be a question of fact whether succession has occurred and in this connection disparity in size between the old partnerships will not of itself be a significant matter.

Demergers

5. When a business carried on in partnership is divided up, and several separate partnerships are formed, it will again be a question of fact, to be determined according to the circumstances in each case, whether any of the separate partnerships carries on the same business as was carried on previously by the original partnership. It might be that one of the businesses carried on after the division was so large in relation to the rest as to be recognisably "the business" as previously carried on; but that will frequently not be the case, and if it is not then the business will have ceased.

A6–03

6. The Revenue would want to look carefully at any case where it was claimed that a demerger of a partnership had occurred but it appeared that the demerger was more apparent than real, and that the demerger seemed to have taken place for fiscal reasons. The Revenue might wish to argue that in such a case the same trade was being carried on after the demerger as before.

[Note: Despite the reference to partnership businesses in the text, the Revenue regard the principles set out in SP 9/86 as applying equally where

---

[1] Reproduced as it appears in HMRC's list of Statements of Practice as at April 23, 2010.

[2] This section, as amended, was repealed by the Income Tax (Trading and Other Income) Act 2005, Sched. 1, Pt. 1, para. 94, Sched.

- businesses previously carried on by sole traders are merged and are subsequently carried on by a partnership; and

- a business carried on by a partnership is demerged and the businesses are subsequently carried on by sole traders.]

II. Capital Gains Tax

STATEMENT OF PRACTICE (D12)[3]

CAPITAL GAINS TAX: PARTNERSHIPS *(Originally issued January 17, 1975 and amended in October 2002)*

A6–04   This statement of practice was originally issued by The Commissioners of Her Majesty's Revenue and Customs on 17 January 1975 following discussions with the Law Society and the Allied Accountancy Bodies on the Capital Gains Tax treatment of partnerships. This statement sets out a number of points of general practice which have been agreed in respect of partnerships to which TCGA92/s.594[4] applies.

The enactment of the Limited Liability Partnership Act 2000, has created, from April 2001, the concept of limited liability partnerships (as bodies corporate) in UK law. In conjunction with this, new Capital Gains Tax provisions dealing with such partnerships have been introduced through TCGA92/s.59A. TCGA92/s.59A(1) mirrors TCGA92/s.59[5] in treating any dealings in chargeable assets by a limited liability partnership as dealings by the individual members, as partners, for Capital Gains Tax purposes. Each member of a limited liability partnership to which s.59A(1) applies has therefore to be regarded, like a partner in any other (non-corporate) partnership, as owning a fractional share of each of the partnership assets and not an interest in the partnership itself.

This statement of practice has therefore been extended to limited liability partnerships which meet the requirements of TCGA92/s.59A(1), such that capital gains of a partnership fall to be charged on its members as partners. Accordingly, in the text of the statement of practice, all references to a "partnership" or "firm" include reference to limited liability partnerships to which TCGA92/s.59A(1) applies, and all references to "partner" include reference to a member of a limited liability partnership to which TCGA92/s.59A(1) applies.

For the avoidance of doubt, this statement of practice does not apply to the members of a limited liability partnership which ceases to be "fiscally transparent" by reason of its not being, or its no longer being, within TCGA92/s.59A(1).

1. *Valuation of a partner's share in a partnership asset*

A6–05   Where it is necessary to ascertain the market value of a partner's share in a partnership asset for Capital Gains Tax purposes, it will be taken as a fraction of the value of the total partnership interest in the asset without any discount for the size of his share. If, for example, a partnership owned all the issued shares in a company, the value of the interest in that holding of a partner with a one-tenth share would be one-tenth of the value of the partnership's 100 per cent holding.

2. *Disposals of assets by a partnership*

A6–06   Where an asset is disposed of by a partnership to an outside party each of the partners will be treated as disposing of his fractional share of the asset. In computing gains or losses the proceeds of disposal will be allocated between the partners in the ratio of their

---

[3] Reproduced as it appears in HMRC's list of Statements of Practice as at April 23, 2010.
[4] See now the Taxation of Chargeable Gains Act 1992, s.59(1) (as renumbered): see *supra*, para.35–01.
[5] See n. 4.

share in asset surpluses at the time of disposal. Where this is not specifically laid down the allocation will follow the actual destination of the surplus as shown in the partnership accounts; regard will of course have to be paid to any agreement outside the accounts. If the surplus is not allocated among the partners but, for example, put to a common reserve, regard will be had to the ordinary profit sharing ratio in the absence of a specified asset-surplus-sharing ratio. Expenditure on the acquisition of assets by a partnership will be allocated between the partners in the same way at the time of the acquisition. This allocation may require adjustment, however, if there is a subsequent change in the partnership sharing ratios (see paragraph 4).

3. *Partnership assets divided in kind among the partners*

Where a partnership distributes an asset in kind to one or more of the partners, for example on dissolution, a partner who receives the asset will not be regarded as disposing of his fractional share in it. A computation will first be necessary of the gains which would be chargeable on the individual partners if the asset has been disposed of at its current market value. Where this results in a gain being attributed to a partner not receiving the asset the gain will be charged at the time of the distribution of the asset. Where, however, the gain is allocated to a partner receiving the asset concerned there will be no charge on distribution. Instead, his Capital Gains Tax cost to be carried forward will be the market value of the asset at the date of distribution as reduced by the amount of his gain. The same principles will be applied where the computation results in a loss. **A6–07**

4. *Changes in partnership sharing ratios*

An occasion of charge also arises when there is a change in partnership sharing ratios including changes arising from a partner joining or leaving the partnership. In these circumstances a partner who reduces or gives up his share in asset surpluses will be treated as disposing of part of the whole of his share in each of the partnership assets and a partner who increases his share will be treated as making a similar acquisition. Subject to the qualifications mentioned at 6 and 7 below the disposal consideration will be a fraction (equal to the fractional share changing hands) of the current balance sheet value of each chargeable asset provided there is no direct payment of consideration outside the partnership. Where no adjustment is made through the partnership accounts (for example, by revaluation of the assets coupled with a corresponding increase or decrease in the partner's current or capital account at some date between the partner's acquisition and the reduction in his share) the disposal is treated as made for a consideration equal to his Capital Gains Tax cost and thus there will be neither a chargeable gain nor an allowable loss at that point. A partner whose share reduces will carry forward a smaller proportion of cost to set against a subsequent disposal of the asset and a partner whose share increases will carry forward a larger proportion of cost. **A6–08**

The general rules in TCGA92/s.42 for apportioning the total acquisition cost on a part-disposal of an asset will not be applied in the case of a partner reducing his asset-surplus share. Instead, the cost of the part disposed of will be calculated on a fractional basis.

5. *Adjustments through the accounts*

Where a partnership asset is revalued a partner will be credited in his current or capital account with a sum equal to his fractional share of the increase in value. An upward revaluation of chargeable assets is not itself an occasion of charge. If, however, there were to be a subsequent reduction in the partner's asset-surplus share, the effect would be to reduce his potential liability to Capital Gains Tax on the eventual disposal of the assets without an equivalent reduction of the credit he has received in the accounts. Consequently at the time of the reduction in sharing ratio he will be regarded as disposing of the fractional share of the partnership asset represented by the difference between his old and his new share for a consideration equal to that fraction of the increased value at the revaluation. The partner whose share correspondingly increases will have his acquisition **A6–09** cost to be carried forward for the asset increased by the same amount. The same principles will be applied in the case of a downward revaluation.

6. *Payments outside the accounts*

A6–10   Where on a change of partnership sharing ratios payments are made directly between two or more partners outside the framework of the partnership accounts, the payments represent consideration for the disposal of the whole or part of a partner's share in partnership assets in addition to any consideration calculated on the basis described in 4 and 5 above. Often such payments will be for goodwill not included in the balance sheet. In such cases the partner receiving the payment will have no Capital Gains Tax cost to set against it unless he made a similar payment for his share in the asset (for example, on entering the partnership) or elects to have the market value at 6 April 1965 treated as his acquisition cost.[6] The partner making the payment will only be allowed to deduct the amount in computing gains or losses on a subsequent disposal of his share in the asset. He will be able to claim a loss when he finally leaves the partnership or when his share is reduced provided that he then receives either no consideration or a lesser consideration for his share of the asset. Where the payment clearly constitutes payment for a share in assets included in the partnership accounts, the partner receiving it will be able to deduct the amount of the partnership acquisition cost represented by the fraction he is disposing of. Special treatment, as outlined in 7 below, may be necessary for transfers between persons not at arm's length.

7. *Transfers between persons not at arm's length*

A6–11   Where no payment is made either through or outside the accounts in connection with a change in partnership sharing ratio, a Capital Gains Tax charge will only arise if the transaction is otherwise than by way of a bargain made at arm's length and falls therefore within TCGA92/s.17 extended by TCGA92/s.18 for transactions between connected persons. Under TCGA92/s.286(4)[7] transfers of partnership assets between partners are not regarded as transactions between connected persons if they are pursuant to genuine commercial arrangements. This treatment will also be given to transactions between an incoming partner and the existing partners.

Where the partners (including incoming partners) are connected other than by partnership (for example, father and son) or are otherwise not at arm's length (for example, uncle and nephew) the transfer of a share in the partnership assets may fall to be treated as having been made at market value. Market value will not be substituted, however, if nothing would have been paid had the parties been at arm's length. Similarly if consideration of less than market value passes between partners connected other than by partnership or otherwise not at arm's length, the transfer will only be regarded as having been made for full market value if the consideration actually paid was less than that which would have been paid by parties at arm's length. Where a transfer has to be treated as if it had taken place for market value, the deemed disposal will fall to be treated in the same way as payments outside the accounts.

8. *Annuities provided by partnerships*

A6–12   A lump sum which is paid to a partner on leaving the partnership or on a reduction of his share in the partnership represents consideration for the disposal by the partner concerned of the whole or part of his share in the partnership assets and will be subject to the rules in 6 above. The same treatment will apply when a partnership buys a

---

[6] Note that now all assets have been rebased to their 1982 value: Taxation of Chargeable Gains Act 1992, s.35(2), as amended.

[7] As amended by the Tax and Civil Partnership Regulations 2005 (SI 2005/3229), reg.121.

purchased life annuity for a partner, the measure of the consideration being the actual costs of the annuity.

Where a partnership makes annual payments to a retired partner (whether under covenant or not) the capitalised value of the annuity will only be treated as consideration for the disposal of his share in the partnership assets under TCGA92/s.37(3), if it is more than can be regarded as a reasonable recognition of the past contribution of work and effort by the partner to the partnership. Provided that the former partner had been in the partnership for at least ten years an annuity will be regarded as reasonable for this purpose if it is no more than two-thirds of his average share of the profits in the best three of the last seven years in which he was required to devote substantially the whole of this time to acting as a partner. In arriving at a partner's share of the profits regard will be had to the partnership profits assessed before deduction of any capital allowances or charges. The ten year period will include any period during which the partner was a member of another firm whose business has been merged with that of the present firm. For lesser periods the following fractions will be used instead of two-thirds:

Complete years in partnership	Fraction
1–5	1/60 for each year
6	8/60
7	16/60
8	24/60
9	32/60

Where the capitalised value of an annuity is treated as consideration received by the retired partner, it will also be regarded as allowable expenditure by the remaining partners on the acquisition of their fractional shares in partnership assets from him.

9. Mergers

Where the members of two or more existing partnerships come together to form a new one, the Capital Gains Tax treatment will follow the same lines as that for changes in partnership sharing ratios. If gains arise for reasons similar to those covered in 5 and 6 above, it may be possible for rollover relief under TCGA92/s.152 to be claimed by any partner continuing in the partnership insofar as he disposes of part of his share in the assets of the old firm and acquires a share in other assets put into the "merged" firm. Where, however, in such cases the consideration given for the shares in chargeable assets acquired is less than the consideration for those disposed of, relief will be restricted under TCGA92/s.153.

A6–13

10. Shares acquired in stages

Where a share in a partnership is acquired in stages wholly after 5 April 1965, the acquisition costs of the various chargeable assets will be calculated by pooling the expenditure relating to each asset. Where a share built up in stages was acquired wholly or partly before 6 April 1965 the rules in TCGA92/Sch.2/Para.18, will normally be followed to identify the acquisition cost of the share in each asset which is disposed of on the occasion of a reduction in the partnership's share; that is, the disposal will normally be identified with shares acquired on a "first in, first out" basis. Special consideration will be given, however, to any case in which this rule appears to produce an unreasonable result when applied to temporary changes in the shares in a partnership, for example those occurring when a partner's departure and a new partner's arrival are out of step by a few months.[8]

A6–14

[8] Note that this paragraph is now largely irrelevant: see *supra*, para. 35–27.

11. Elections under TCGA92/Sch. 2/Para.4[9]

A6–15   Where the assets disposed of are quoted securities eligible for a pooling election under paragraph 4 of TCGA92/Sch.2, partners will be allowed to make separate elections in respect of shares or fixed interest securities held by the partnership as distinct from shares and securities which they hold on a personal basis. Each partner will have a separate right of election for his proportion of the partnership securities and the time limit for the purposes of Schedule 2 will run from the earlier of—

    (a) the first relevant disposal of shares or securities by the partnership; and

    (b) the first reduction of the particular partner's share in the partnership assets after 19 March 1968.

12. Partnership goodwill and taper relief[10]

A6–16   This paragraph applies where the value of goodwill which a partnership generates in the conduct of its business is not recognised in its balance sheet and where, as a matter of consistent practice, no value is placed on that goodwill in dealings between the partners. In such circumstances, the partnership goodwill will not be regarded as a "fungible asset" (and, therefore, will not be within the definition of "securities" in section TCGA92/ s.104(3) for the purpose of Capital Gains Tax taper relief under TCGA92/s.2A). Accordingly, on a disposal for actual consideration of any particular partner's interest in the goodwill of such a partnership, that interest will be treated as the same asset (or, in the case of a part disposal, a part of the same asset) as was originally acquired by that partner when first becoming entitled to a share in the goodwill of that partnership.

    The treatment described in the preceding paragraph will also be applied to goodwill acquired for consideration by a partnership but which is not, at any time, recognised in the partnership balance sheet at a value exceeding its cost of acquisition nor otherwise taken into account in dealings between partners. However, such purchased goodwill will continue to be treated for the purpose of computing capital gains tax taper relief as assets separate from the partnership's self-generated goodwill. On a disposal or part disposal for actual consideration of an interest in such purchased goodwill by any particular partner, that interest shall be treated for taper relief purposes as acquired either on the date of purchase by the partnership or on the date on which the disposing partner first became entitled to a share in that goodwill, whichever is the later.

Extension of Statement of Practice D12 (SP1/79)[11]

Capital Gains Tax—Partnerships *(Originally issued January 12, 1979)*

A6–17   Paragraph 8 of SP/D12[12] explains the circumstances in which the capitalised value of an annuity paid by a partnership to a retired partner will not be treated as consideration for the disposal of his share in the partnership assets. The Commissioners of Her Majesty's Revenue and Customs have now agreed that this practice will be extended to certain cases in which a lump sum is paid in addition to an annuity. Where the aggregate of the annuity and one-ninth of the lump sum does not exceed the appropriate fraction (as indicated in the Statement) of the retired partner's average share of the profits, the capitalised value of

---

[9] Pooling elections are no long made, so that this paragraph is also no longer relevant: see *supra*, para. 35–28 for the current position.

[10] Taper relief under the Taxation of Chargeable Gains Act 1992, s.2A (as originally added by the Finance Act 1998, s.121(1)) was abolished by the Finance Act 2008, Sched. 2, para. 25.

[11] Reproduced as it appears in HMRC's list of Statements of Practice as at April 23, 2010.

[12] See *supra*, para. A6–12.

the annuity will not be treated as consideration in the hands of the retired partner. The lump sum, however, will continue to be so treated.

This extension of the practice will be applied to all cases in which the liability has not been finally determined at the date of this Notice.

See also SP1/89.[13]

HMRC Brief 03/2008

CAPITAL GAINS TAX AND CORPORATION TAX ON CHARGEABLE GAINS—CONTRIBUTION OF ASSETS TO A PARTNERSHIP *(Originally issued January 25, 2008)*

This Revenue and Customs Brief clarifies HMRC's practice in relation to the treatment for capital gains purposes of a contribution of an asset to a partnership. **A6–18**

Statement of Practice D12 (SoP D12)[14] was published on 17 January 1975 following discussions with the Law Society and the allied accountancy bodies and sets out our understanding of how the legislation concerning the tax treatment of partnerships works in practice. It has been updated since 1975. It does not, however, deal with the situation where a partner contributes an asset to a partnership by means of a capital contribution.

We consider that, where an asset is transferred to a partnership by means of a capital contribution, the correct application of the capital gains legislation is that the partner in question has made a part disposal of the asset equal to the fractional share that passes to the other partners.

The market value rule would apply, if the transfer is between connected persons or the transaction is other than by way of a bargain made at arm's length, Otherwise, the consideration to be taken into account in computing the chargeable gain or loss on the part disposal will be a proportion of the total consideration given by the partnership for the asset. That proportion will be equal to the fractional share of the asset passing to the other partners. We take the view that a sum credited to the partner's capital account represents consideration for the disposal of the asset to the partnership.

Although the situation is similar in some respects to a change in partnership sharing ratios, it is not possible to calculate the disposal consideration on a capital contribution by reference to paragraph 4 of SoP D12,[15] as the asset in question would not have a balance sheet value in the partnership accounts. It has been our practice, however, to accept the apportionment of allowable costs on a fractional basis as provided for in paragraph 4, rather than by reference to the statutory A/A-B formula.

A gain will arise on a contribution of an asset where the disposal consideration, calculated by reference to a fractional proportion of the total consideration or, in appropriate cases, a proportion of the market value of the asset, exceeds the allowable costs based on a fraction of the partner's capital gain base costs.

It has been brought to our attention that in the past individual HMRC (previously Inland Revenue) officers may have erroneously applied paragraph 4 of SoP D12 more widely than was justified where an asset was contributed to a partnership. We apologise if this has resulted in a misunderstanding of our practice in this area. In our view these previous applications of SoP D12 were incorrect and inconsistent with statements made by other HMRC officers. We will consider ourselves bound by statements made in individual cases. In cases where we are not bound, including all future cases, the correct treatment as described above will be applied.

---

[13] This Statement of Practice is now only applicable to corporate partners: see *infra*, para. A6–24.

[14] See *supra*, paras. A6–04 *et seq.*

[15] See *supra*, para. A6–08.

HMRC Brief 9/2009

Capital Gains Tax—Rebasing Rules FA 2008 and Partnerships *(Originally issued March 20, 2009)*

A6–19   This Brief explains the CGT rebasing rules for disposals of partnership assets or changes in share of partnership assets from 2008–09 onwards. It applies only to non-corporate partners subject to capital gains tax, rather than corporation tax. HMRC intends its practice to be consistent with the previous treatment under SP1/89[16] and appendices contain examples of the difference in treatment of disposals before and after 6 April 2008.[17]

Introduction

A6–20   This Revenue & Customs Brief is about assets held by a partnership on 31 March 1982. Assets held on that date are subject to special rules (the "rebasing" rules) when working out capital gains and losses.

The changes to Capital Gains Tax in Finance Act (FA) 2008 amended the rebasing rules. The changes apply to disposals of assets from the start of the 2008–09 tax year (6 April 2008). The Brief explains how the rebasing rules apply for people who dispose of partnership assets or who change their share of partnership assets from 2008–09 onwards.

The Brief applies only to partners whose capital gains are subject to Capital Gains Tax. The changes in FA 2008 do not apply to Corporation Tax and companies liable to Corporation Tax on their gains are not affected.

Background

A6–21   Partnerships, including Scottish partnerships, are treated as transparent for Capital Gains Tax purposes. This means that any gains or losses accruing on disposals of partnership assets are chargeable on the partners rather than on the partnership itself. Partners are treated for this purpose as owning fractional interests in each of the partnership's assets. Disposals occur when the partnership disposes of an asset or when a partner's interest in an asset is reduced.

Statement of Practice D12 (SP D12)[18] explains how gains or losses accruing on disposals of interests in partnership assets are to be computed.

Section 6 and Schedule 2 FA 2008 make rebasing of cost to 31 March 1982 compulsory for assets held at that date. The changes have effect only for the purposes of Capital Gains Tax. They do not apply for the purposes of Corporation Tax on chargeable gains.

Rebasing rules for disposals before 6 April 2008

A6–22   The rebasing provisions for disposals before 6 April 2008 applied in respect of disposals on or after 6 April 1988 of assets held on 31 March 1982.

Assets held at 31 March 1982 were treated as if they had been acquired at their market value on that date so that gains or losses relating to changes in value before that date were not taken into account for Capital Gains Tax purposes. This approach was modified by the kink test which allowed for a comparison of the gain or loss based on the market value of the asset on 31 March 1982 with the gain or loss based on the actual cost before 31 March 1982. The lower of the gains was chargeable to Capital Gains Tax or the lower of the losses was allowable. If one computation resulted in a gain and the other in a loss, the person making the disposal was treated as realising neither a gain nor a loss.

---

[16] Entitled "Capital Gains Tax—Partnerships" and first issued on February 1, 1989.
[17] These appendices, which are voluminous, are not reproduced. They are set out in [2009] S.T.I. 736 *et seq.*
[18] See *supra*, paras. A6–04 *et seq.*

A person could opt out of the kink test by electing under section 35(5) Taxation of Chargeable Gains Act (TCGA) 1992 to have gains or losses computed as if all of their assets held on 31 March 1982 had been acquired at their market value on that date.

Section 35(7) TCGA 1992 required separate rebasing elections to be made by a person who held assets in more than one capacity. For example, an election made by an individual in respect of personal assets would not cover interests in partnership assets held by that individual in his or her capacity as a partner.

There were special rules for arriving at the expenditure allowable in computing the gain on the disposal of an asset which had been acquired since 31 March 1982 by way of a statutory "no gain/no loss transfer" (a disposal which is treated for Capital Gains Tax purposes as resulting in neither a gain nor a loss for the person making the disposal) or an unbroken series of such transfers. The gain was computed as if the person making the disposal had owned the asset at 31 March 1982.

Examples of how these rules applied in relation to disposals of interests in partnership assets are included in Appendix A to this Revenue & Customs Brief.[19]

Rebasing rules for disposals on or after 6 April 2008

Section 6 and Schedule 2 FA 2008 apply in respect of disposals on or after 6 April 2008 **A6–23** of assets held at 31 March 1982.

Gains or losses arising on disposals on or after 6 April 2008 are computed as if the assets disposed of had been acquired at their market value on 31 March 1982. In effect, allowable expenditure is "rebased" to 31 March 1982 thus dispensing with the need for the kink test and rebasing elections.

The new section 35A TCGA 1992 applies where a person ("P") disposes of an asset on or after 6 April 2008 and—

—P acquired the asset after 31 March 1982 and before 6 April 2008 under a statutory no gain/no loss provision and

—any previous disposal and acquisition of the asset after 31 March 1982 was one to which a statutory no gain/no loss provision applied and

—rebasing under section 35(2) TCGA 1992 did not apply to the relevant disposal, that is, the disposal of the asset to P.

Where these conditions are satisfied section 35A(2) TCGA 1992 provides that the allowable expenditure taken into account in computing a gain or loss when P disposes of the asset on or after 6 April 2008 includes the value of the asset at 31 March 1982 and the indexation allowance due for the period from 31 March 1982 to the month in which P acquired the asset or, if earlier, to April 1998. The previous approach of treating P as having owned the asset at 31 March 1982 with the appropriate consequences for indexation allowance no longer applies.

Examples of how these rules apply in relation to disposals of interests in partnership assets are included in Appendix B to this Revenue & Customs Brief.[20]

Statement of Practice 1/89 (SP1/89)

SP1/89 explains HM Revenue & Customs (HMRC) practice in relation to rebasing and **A6–24** indexation allowance where a transfer between partners of an interest in an asset that was held by a partnership on 31 March 1982 results in neither a gain nor a loss.

It enables transfers between partners of interests in partnership assets that result in neither gains nor losses to be treated as statutory no gain/no loss transfers for the purposes of the rebasing rules in sections 35 and 36 and Schedule 4 TCGA 1992. Partners who

---

[19] Not reproduced: see *supra*, n. 17.
[20] Not reproduced: see *supra*, n. 17.

dispose of interests in assets that had been acquired by them as a result of such transfers are treated as having held them on 31 March 1982.

SP1/89 provides that the disposal consideration for a transfer between partners of an interest in a partnership asset that results in neither a gain nor a loss may be calculated on the assumption that an unindexed gain will accrue to the transferor equal to the indexation allowance so that, after accounting for indexation allowance, neither a gain nor a loss accrues. Such a disposal may be treated as a statutory no gain/no loss disposal for the purposes of section 55(5) TCGA 1992.

For Capital Gains Tax purposes indexation allowance was frozen as at April 1998 and has been abolished for disposals on or after 6 April 2008.

For disposals of interests in partnership assets that occur on or after 6 April 2008 SP1/89 will apply only in relation to corporate partners whose capital gains are chargeable to Corporation Tax.

Disposals on or after 6 April 2008

A6–25   HMRC's practice in relation to rebasing for disposals by non-corporate partners on or after 6 April 2008 will be consistent with the previous treatment under SP1/89. Transfers between partners of interests in partnership assets after 31 March 1982 and before 6 April 2008 that resulted in neither gains nor losses may be treated as statutory no gain/no loss transfers for the purposes of section 35A(1)(b) TCGA 1992.

Where section 35A(2) TCGA 1992 applies in relation to disposals on or after 6 April 2008 the allowable expenditure to be taken into consideration in the calculation of a gain or loss includes the value of the asset at 31 March 1982 and any indexation allowance for the period from 31 March 1982 to the month in which the person making the disposal acquired it or, if earlier, to April 1998.

The effect of SP1/89 in relation to disposals of interests in partnership assets before and on or after 6 April 2008 is considered in the examples in Appendices A and B.[21]

EXTRA-STATUTORY CONCESSION D23[22]

RELIEF FOR THE REPLACEMENT OF BUSINESS ASSETS: PARTITION OF LAND ON THE DISSOLUTION OF A PARTNERSHIP

A6–26   Where land used for the purposes of a trade carried on in partnership is partitioned by the partners, the land acquired is treated for the purposes of Sections 152–158, TCGA 1992 as a "new asset" provided that the partnership is dissolved immediately thereafter. This concession also applies to other qualifying assets which are acquired on the partition.

III. Inheritance Tax

STATEMENT OF PRACTICE (SP12/80)[23]

BUSINESS PROPERTY RELIEF: "BUY AND SELL" AGREEMENTS *(Originally issued October 13, 1980)*

A6–27   The Commissioners of Her Majesty's Revenue and Customs understand that it is sometimes the practice for partners or shareholder directors of companies to enter into an agreement (known as a "Buy & Sell" Agreement) whereby, in the event of the death before retirement of one of them, the deceased's personal representatives are obliged to sell and the survivors are obliged to purchase the deceased's business interest or shares,

---

[21] Not reproduced: see *supra*, n. 17.

[22] Reproduced as it appears in HMRC's list of Extra-Statutory Concessions as at August 10, 2009.

[23] Reproduced as it appears in HMRC's list of Statements of Practice as at April 23, 2010.

funds for the purchase being frequently provided by means of appropriate life assurance polices.

In the Commissioners of Her Majesty's Revenue and Customs' view such an agreement, requiring as it does a sale and purchase and not merely conferring an option to sell or buy, is a binding contract for sale within Section 113 IHTA 1984. As a result the inheritance tax business property relief will not be due on the business interest or shares. (Section 113 IHTA 1984 provides that where any property would be relevant business property for the purpose of business property relief in relation to a transfer of value but a binding contract for its sale has been entered into at the time of the transfer, it is not relevant business property in relation to that transfer).

IV. Value Added Tax

BUSINESS BRIEF 21/04 (*Originally issued August 10, 2004*)

1. VAT: VAT position of share issues and partnership contributions following the European Court of Justice decision in *KapHag Renditefonds*

This Business Brief clarifies Customs' position on two issues arising from the decision   **A6–28**
of the European Court of Justice in the German case of *KapHag Renditefonds v. Finanz-amt Charlottenburg* (Case C-442/01):

    A—Whether the issue of shares constitutes a supply for VAT purposes; and

    B—The VAT position of contributions to partnerships.

The case of *KapHag* concerned the admission of a new partner into a partnership on payment of a capital contribution. The European Court held that no supply was being made by either the individual partners or the partnership to the incoming partner in return for the capital contribution.

A—Whether the issue of shares constitutes a supply

The *KapHag* decision has been cited as authority for the view that an issue of shares by   **A6–29**
a company is similarly not a supply for VAT purposes. It is claimed that an issue of shares therefore falls outside the terms of Item 6 of Group 5 of Schedule 9 to the Value Added Tax Act 1994. That Item exempts from VAT:

> "The issue, transfer or receipt of, or any dealing with, any security or secondary security . . . "

It is Customs' view that the formation or variation of a partnership arrangement is wholly distinguishable from the position where a company issues shares in return for consideration. *KapHag* was concerned solely with the issues surrounding a partnership. The VAT treatment of share issues has been considered by the Court of Appeal in *Trinity Mirror plc* ([2001] S.T.C. 192) where it was held that an issue of shares by a company did constitute a supply of services for VAT purposes and these fall to be exempt under Item 6 of Group 5 of Schedule 9 to the Act. In most circumstances there will then be a restriction of input tax under the partial exemption rules. Further information is available from VAT Notice 706 Partial Exemption.

B—Contributions to partnerships

Partnerships to which this section applies include "normal" partnerships of individuals   **A6–30**
or corporate bodies, limited partnerships whose members are individuals or corporate bodies, overseas limited partnerships that are registered as "normal" partnerships or corporate bodies and limited liability partnerships.

Background

In *KapHag*, the incoming partner was contributing cash in return for admission into the partnership but it will often be the case that the contribution is in the form of other assets. For example, a new partner's contribution may comprise land or interests in land. The European Court's decision tacitly accepted the Advocate-General's Opinion that the same principles would apply whether the contribution consisted of cash or other assets. Whatever the nature of the assets comprising the contribution, there is no reciprocal supply from the partnership. However, where the assets are not cash, the making of the partnership contribution may have other VAT consequences.

The Advocate-General was satisfied that there was "no doubt that the new partner is effecting an act of disposal of his assets, for which the admission to the partnership is not the consideration" (Paragraph 33 of the Opinion). Such a disposal can therefore have VAT consequences when the partner contributing the assets is a VAT registered person. These consequences will vary depending on the nature of the assets being contributed.

KapHag establishes that nothing is provided by the partnership in return for the assets contributed, therefore any such disposal by the incoming partner is made for no consideration. The VAT Act provides that certain things are subject to VAT even when they are provided or done for no consideration. Customs' view is that all those provisions will still apply where there is no consideration when there is a contribution to partnership assets. A VAT registered person may therefore have to account for tax if he contributes assets to the partnership in the circumstances described in the Act. The VAT consequences can be considered under several main heads:

    (i) Contribution to partnership comprising services;

    (ii) Contribution to partnership comprising goods other than land;

    (iii) Contribution to partnership comprising land or interests in land;

    (iv) Whether contribution to partnership can constitute the transfer of a going concern;

    (v) How the partnership can reclaim the output tax accounted for by an incoming partner on his contribution as its input tax;

    (vi) Capital Goods Scheme consequences; and

    (vii) Transfer of assets out of a partnership.

(i) *Contribution to partnership comprising services*

A6–31   A partnership contribution may comprise services rather than goods—examples of this could be a trademark or trading logo or the use of an asset the ownership of which is retained by the incoming partner. Two legislative provisions set out the circumstances in which such a contribution may be regarded as a taxable supply, paragraph 5(4) of Schedule 4 to the VAT Act and the Value Added Tax (Supply of Services) Order 1993 (SI 1993/1507).

A supply can arise under paragraph 5(4) where a taxable person applies business goods to private use or makes them available for purposes other than those of his business. The taxable person or his predecessor must have been entitled to input tax under sections 25 and 26 of the VAT Act on the supply of those goods (or anything comprised in them) to him.

The Supply of Services Order similarly provides that a supply arises where a taxable person applies bought-in services to private or non-business use for no consideration where he has been entitled to input tax credit under sections 25 and 26. The value of such a supply cannot exceed the taxable person's input tax entitlement.

Where the above criteria are satisfied, a VAT registered incoming partner will have to account for tax on the supply of services that he is regarded as making in the disposal of the services from his existing business. The partnership may be able to recover this as its input tax where the contributed services are to be used for its business. The procedure for doing this is described at (v) below.

(ii) *Contribution to partnership comprising goods other than land*

If a partnership contribution comprises goods other than land that a taxable person (the transferor) held as assets, then a deemed supply will be generated as a result of Paragraph 5(1) of Schedule 4 to the VAT Act. This deemed supply does not require there to be consideration when the goods are transferred. It does however only apply where the taxable person disposing of the goods, or their predecessor, if for example they obtained the goods by way of a TOGC, was entitled to full or partial credit for the VAT charged when the goods were supplied to him. Where such a deemed supply arises, the incoming partner will have to account for VAT. The partnership may be able to recover this as its input tax where the contributed assets are to be used for its business. The procedure for doing this is described at (v) below.   **A6–32**

(iii) *Contribution to partnership comprising land or interests in land*

The VAT treatment of land or interests in land also depends upon whether the incoming partner or his predecessor was entitled to deduct input tax in relation to the property that he is contributing to the partnership. For example, if he had opted to tax the property, or it was inherently taxable like new freehold commercial property, there may be a deemed supply as described at (ii) above. The incoming partner will then have to account for VAT on this supply. As with other contributed goods, the partnership may be entitled to recover this as input tax where the property is to be used for the partnership's business. The procedure for doing this is described at (v) below.   **A6–33**

Please note all submitted notifications of an option to tax need to be signed by "an authorised signatory" as described in paragraph 7.1 of VAT Notice 742A Opting to tax Land & Buildings.

(iv) *Whether contribution to partnership can constitute the transfer of a going concern*

It is possible that when assets are transferred by way of a partnership contribution that this could qualify to be treated as a transfer of a going concern (Section 49 of the VAT Act and Article 5 of the VAT (Special Provisions) Order 1995 (SI 1995/1268)). If the contribution meets the conditions to be treated as a transfer of a going concern no VAT will be due from the transferor.   **A6–34**

(v) *How the partnership can reclaim the output tax accounted for by an incoming partner on his contribution as its input tax*

When an incoming partner contributes goods and/or services (on which VAT is due as described above) and the partnership uses them for its business purposes, the partnership can recover the VAT as input tax subject to the normal rules. The incoming partner cannot issue a tax invoice, but in order to provide the partnership with acceptable evidence to support a claim for recovery of input tax, he may use his normal invoicing documentation overwritten with the following statement: **A6–35**

> "*Certificate for Tax on Partnership Contribution*
> No payment is necessary for these goods/services. Output tax has been accounted for on the supply."

The incoming partner must show full details of the goods and/or services on the documentation and the amount of VAT shown must be the amount of output tax accounted for to Customs and Excise.

(vi) *Capital Goods Scheme consequences*

A6–36   Where the capital contribution is in the form of an interest in land or a computer, it may be an existing capital item of the incoming partner under the Capital Goods Scheme (CGS). If the transfer to the partnership constitutes a supply which is a disposal of an existing CGS item, then this will wind up the existing CGS item and a disposal adjustment may be due. If the transfer constitutes a TOGC then this will end the current interval for the incoming partner and the partnership will then be responsible for making adjustments for any remaining intervals.

As transfers of assets capital contributions will always constitute either a supply or a TOGC, any existing CGS items will always either be subject to a disposal adjustment or continuing CGS adjustments.

Even if the asset transferred as a capital contribution is not a CGS item in the hands of the incoming partner, it may create a new CGS item for the partnership when its transfer constitutes a supply. If this happens the partnership will need to make adjustments in subsequent intervals in the normal way.

The CGS is further explained in VAT Notice 706/2 Capital Goods Scheme.

(vii) *Transfer of assets out of a partnership*

A6–37   *KapHag* was only concerned with assets moving into a partnership in the form of a partnership contribution. It did not cover the reverse situation, where partnership assets are paid out to an outgoing partner or otherwise disposed of by the partnership for no consideration. Where a transfer of assets out of a partnership for no consideration occurs, one of the following sets of circumstances will apply.

(a)   If the incoming partner accounted for output tax when he contributed the assets to the partnership and the partnership was entitled to recover all or part of this as its input tax, there will be a subsequent supply by the partnership when the same assets are transferred out unless the transfer out now satisfies the TOGC criteria.

(b)   If no output tax was accounted for when the assets were contributed to the partnership because they constituted a TOGC, the transfer out of the same assets will be a deemed supply upon which the partnership will have to account for tax unless the TOGC criteria are again satisfied.

(c)   The partnership may be transferring out more assets than those originally contributed to it. Although the original contribution to the partnership may not have been a TOGC, the subsequent transfer out may now satisfy the TOGC criteria. If it does, no VAT will be due from the partnership.

(d)   The original contribution to the partnership may have been a TOGC but the partnership may now be transferring out less of the assets than were originally contributed. Unless the assets being transferred out still meet the TOGC criteria in their own right, there may be a deemed supply upon which the partnership will have to account for the appropriate tax. As explained at (ii) and (iii) above, the entitlement of the partnership or its predecessor to deduct input tax in relation to the items that are the subject of the transfer out will determine whether or not there is a supply.

Application of section 45 of the VAT Act 1994

A6–38   In the past, there was uncertainty as to whether it was section 45(1) of the VAT Act that led to there being no supply from a partnership to an incoming partner. That section provides for the registration of partnerships in the following terms:

"45(1) The registration under this Act of persons—

(a)   carrying on a business in partnership, or

(b)   carrying on in partnership any other activities in the course or furtherance of which they acquire goods from other member States,

may be in the name of the firm; and no account shall be taken, in determining for any purpose of this Act whether goods or services are supplied to or by such persons or are acquired by such persons from another member State, of any change in the partnership."

Partnerships in England and Wales have no legal identity. A new partner joining a partnership, or old one leaving it, would result in a new partnership rather than change the composition of the existing one. Without s.45(1), deregistration and registration would be necessary every time a partner joined or left. The purpose of s.45(1) is to ensure continuity by providing that a business carried on in a firm's name is treated as a continuing business irrespective of changes in its composition. The situation addressed by s.45(1) is therefore entirely different to that considered in *KapHag*.

Further information

Further information on this change is available from Customs' National Advice Service on 0845 010 9000. This number should also be used for general enquiries.

[*The remainder of this Business Brief is not reproduced.*]

BUSINESS BRIEF 30/04 (*Originally issued November* 19, 2004)

VAT AND PARTNERSHIP "SHARES"

Background

Business Brief 21/04 clarified Customs' policy on share issues and partnership con-   **A6–39**
tributions following the European Court of Justice (ECJ) decision in *KapHag Rendite-fonds* (C-442/01). That Business Brief did not deal with the VAT position of transfers of partnership interests ("shares"). This Business Brief explains the VAT treatment of transactions involving the transfer of a partner's "share".

Is the disposal of a "share" in a partnership a supply?

KapHag established that a partnership entity or the existing partners are making no supply when a new partner is admitted in return for making a capital contribution. The question arises whether the subsequent disposal by the partner of that "share" in the partnership is a supply for VAT purposes. It is important to bear in mind that this "share" is distinct from the assets that were contributed by the partner when they joined the partnership. Therefore, even though the selling price of the "share" may be determined by the value of those assets, they are not the subject of the later sale, which has its own liability for VAT purposes.

Although the ECJ has not considered this type of transaction with respect to partnership "shares", there have been a number of cases where it has given a decision in respect of transactions involving shares in companies. The cases of *Polysar* (C-60/90), *Harnas and Helm* (C-80/95), *Wellcome Trust* (C-155/94) and *Regie Dauphinoise* (C-306/94) have established that the mere acquisition and holding of shares in a company is not to be regarded as an economic activity. However, it has stated that transactions in shares or interests in companies and associations may constitute economic activity in three situations:

(a)   Where the transactions constitute the direct, permanent and necessary extension of an economic activity.

(b) Where the transactions are effected in order to secure a direct or indirect involvement in the management of a company in which the holding is acquired.

(c) Where the transactions are effected as part of a commercial share-dealing activity.

Customs considers that the same principles apply to transactions involving partnership "shares". This means that in some circumstances the disposal of a partnership "share" will not constitute a supply and in others it will.

Circumstances in which the disposal of a partnership "share" will not constitute a supply

A6–40   This list is not exhaustive. The most common situations in which the disposal of a partnership "share" by a partner will not be a supply are likely to be:

1. *The "share" is disposed of for no consideration*—A "share" in a partnership comprises services rather than goods. When services are transferred, assigned or otherwise disposed of for no consideration, they do not constitute any supply for VAT purposes.

2. *The "share" being sold was acquired simply as an investment*—Where a partner has acquired his "share" merely to secure a share in any future profits and has had no involvement in running the partnership, the subsequent sale or assignment of that "share" for consideration will not be an economic activity. This will not constitute any supply for VAT purposes.

Circumstances in which the disposal of a partnership "share" will constitute a supply

A6–41   Again, this list is not exhaustive. The most common situations in which the disposal of a partnership "share" by a partner will be a supply are likely to be:

1. *Where the partnership "share" was acquired and disposed of as a direct extension of the partner's economic activities*—Where a partner is a taxable person in their own right, the partnership "share" may have been acquired in the course or furtherance of their own economic activities. If that is the case, the subsequent transfer or assignment of that "share" for a consideration will also be economic activity of that taxable person. For example, the partner may have a business asset to be sold and, rather than selling the asset directly, may have contributed that asset into a partnership and sold the resultant partnership "share" instead. The sale of that partnership "share" will constitute a supply for VAT purposes.

2. *Where the partnership "share" was acquired in order to obtain an active role in the business of the partnership*—Where a partner is a taxable person in their own right and had acquired the partnership "share" in order to actively participate in, or control, the business of the partnership, then the sale of that "share" can be economic activity on the partner's part. The sale of the "share" will constitute a supply for VAT purposes.

3. *Where the partnership "share" was acquired as part of a commercial partnership "share-dealing" activity*—A partner who is a taxable person may have a business of dealing in partnership "shares". This will be economic activity on the partner's part. Sales or assignments of the partnership "shares" that were acquired in the course of this activity that are for a consideration will constitute supplies for VAT purposes.

For the avoidance of any doubt, you should note that supplies of partnership "shares" in the above circumstances cannot be disregarded by virtue of section 45(1) of the VAT Act 1994. As Business Brief 21/04 explained, the purpose of s.45 (1) is to ensure continuity by providing that changes in the composition of a partnership do not create the need for a partnership to deregister and re-register for VAT every time the partners change. It also makes it unnecessary to take account of any changes in the composition of the partnership when determining what supplies have been made or received by the partnership business. The section has no effect upon any supply that one of the partners may be making as a taxable person in their own right.

Liability of supplies of partnership shares

In those circumstances where the disposal of a partnership "share" is a supply, that   **A6–42**
supply will be an exempt financial service.

Treatment of VAT on associated purchases

Where the disposal of an existing partnership "share" is not a supply, the VAT incurred   **A6–43**
in connection with the disposal will normally not be input tax. Where the disposal is a supply, the related VAT will be input tax, but recovery will normally be fully restricted under the partial exemption rules as the supply is exempt. This is subject to the de minimis provisions (see VAT Notice 706 'Partial Exemption').

Application to past transactions

This Business Brief clarifies existing policy and the above principles will be applied to   **A6–44**
all future transactions. Where a past transaction has been treated differently from the above and resulted in an underdeclaration Customs will take no further action. If a past transaction has been treated differently and resulted in an overdeclaration, businesses may use the voluntary disclosure procedure to reclaim the VAT. Any such claims will be subject to the "three-year capping rules" and rules relating to the payment of statutory interest.

Further information

For further help and advice please contact Customs' National Advice Service on 0845 010 9000.

INDEX

[References preceded by the letter A are to the statutory and other materials contained in the Appendices.]